Florida Rules of Court: KeyRules

Volume IIIA - Local

2013

Mat #41258909

ISBN: 978-0-314-65378-9

PREFACE

Florida Rules of Court: KeyRules provides the practitioner with a comprehensive "single source" procedural guide for civil practice in state courts, combining applicable provisions of both statewide and local rules of civil procedure with relevant analytical materials.

This book consists of outlines of the applicable rules of practice, timing requirements, filing and service requirements, format requirements, hearing requirements, checklists and other pertinent documents related to pleadings, motions, requests, notices, and applications in selected Florida courts.

The selected Florida courts include the following: Second Judicial Circuit, Fourth Judicial Circuit, Sixth Judicial Circuit, Seventh Judicial Circuit, Ninth Judicial Circuit, Eleventh Judicial Circuit, Seventeenth Judicial Circuit, and Twentieth Judicial Circuit.

THE PUBLISHER

March 2013

ADDITIONAL INFORMATION OR RESEARCH ASSISTANCE

For additional information or research assistance call the West reference attorneys at 1-800-REF-ATTY (1-800-733-2889). Contact West's editorial department directly with your questions and suggestions by e-mail at west.editor@thomson.com.

ADDITIONAL KEYRULES COVERAGE ON WESTLAW

Additional KeyRules documents for Florida Rules of Court: KeyRules are available on Westlaw in the KEYRULES-FL database. Included on Westlaw are all the documents in this book, plus the following:

Pleadings

- Jury Demand

Motions, Oppositions and Replies

- Motion for Continuance/Extension of Time
- Opposition to Motion for Continuance/Extension of Time
- Motion for Costs and Attorneys' Fees
- Opposition to Motion for Costs and Attorneys' Fees
- Motion for Declaratory Judgment
- Opposition to Motion for Declaratory Judgment
- Motion for Discovery Sanctions
- Opposition to Motion for Discovery Sanctions
- Motion for Disqualification of Judge
- Opposition to Motion for Disqualification of Judge
- Motion to Dismiss for Failure to State a Cause of Action
- Opposition to Motion to Dismiss for Failure to State a Cause of Action
- Motion to Dismiss for Improper Venue
- Opposition to Motion to Dismiss for Improper Venue
- Motion to Dismiss for Insufficiency of Process
- Opposition to Dismiss for Insufficiency of Process
- Motion to Dismiss for Insufficiency of Service of Process
- Opposition to Motion to Dismiss for Insufficiency of Service of Process
- Motion to Dismiss for Failure to Join Indispensible Parties
- Opposition to Motion to Dismiss for Failure to Join Indispensible Parties
- Motion to Dismiss for Lack of Personal Jurisdiction
- Opposition to Motion to Dismiss for Lack of Personal Jurisdiction
- Motion to Dismiss for Lack of Subject Matter Jurisdiction
- Opposition to Motion to Dismiss for Lack of Subject Matter Jurisdiction
- Motion for JNOV
- Opposition to Motion for JNOV
- Motion for Leave to File Crossclaim
- Opposition to Motion for Leave to File Crossclaim
- Motion for Leave to File Counterclaim
- Opposition to Motion for Leave to File Counterclaim
- Motion for New Trial and Rehearing
- Opposition to Motion for New Trial and Rehearing
- Motion for Preliminary Injunction

- Opposition to Motion for Preliminary Injunction
- Motion for Relief from Judgment
- Opposition to Motion for Relief from Judgment
- Motion for Temporary Injunction
- Opposition to Motion for Temporary Injunction
- Opposition to Motion for Leave to Amend
- Opposition to Motion for Sanctions
- Opposition to Motion to Strike
- Opposition to Motion for Summary Judgment
- Opposition to Motion to Compel Discovery
- Opposition to Motion for Directed Verdict

Requests, Notices and Applications

- Pretrial Conferences, Scheduling, Management
- Interrogatories
- Response to Interrogatories
- Response to Request for Admissions
- Response to Request for Production of Documents

Courts Covered

Second Judicial Circuit 1
Fourth Judicial Circuit 199
Sixth Judicial Circuit 397
Seventh Judicial Circuit 611
Ninth Judicial Circuit 813
Eleventh Judicial Circuit 1031
Seventeenth Judicial Circuit 1236
Twentieth Judicial Circuit 1456

*

Table of Contents

SECOND JUDICIAL CIRCUIT

Pleadings
Complaint 1
Amended Complaint 20
Answer 36
Amended Answer 53

Motions, Oppositions and Replies
Motion to Strike 69
Motion for Leave to Amend 82
Motion for Summary Judgment 96
Motion for Sanctions 110
Motion to Compel Discovery 124
Motion for Directed Verdict 138

Requests, Notices and Applications
Request for Production of Documents 151
Request for Admissions 166
Notice of Deposition 180

FOURTH JUDICIAL CIRCUIT

Pleadings
Complaint 199
Amended Complaint 218
Answer 234
Amended Answer 251

Motions, Oppositions and Replies
Motion to Strike 267
Motion for Leave to Amend 280
Motion for Summary Judgment 293
Motion for Sanctions 308
Motion to Compel Discovery 321
Motion for Directed Verdict 335

Requests, Notices and Applications
Request for Production of Documents 348
Request for Admissions 363
Notice of Deposition 377

SIXTH JUDICIAL CIRCUIT

Pleadings
Complaint 397
Amended Complaint 417
Answer 433
Amended Answer 451

Motions, Oppositions and Replies
Motion to Strike 468
Motion for Leave to Amend 482
Motion for Summary Judgment 498

Motion for Sanctions 514
Motion to Compel Discovery 529
Motion for Directed Verdict 545

Requests, Notices and Applications
Request for Production of Documents 560
Request for Admissions 576
Notice of Deposition 591

SEVENTH JUDICIAL CIRCUIT

Pleadings
Complaint 611
Amended Complaint 631
Answer 646
Amended Answer 663

Motions, Oppositions and Replies
Motion to Strike 680
Motion for Leave to Amend 693
Motion for Summary Judgment 707
Motion for Sanctions 721
Motion to Compel Discovery 735
Motion for Directed Verdict 750

Requests, Notices and Applications
Request for Production of Documents 764
Request for Admissions 779
Notice of Deposition 793

NINTH JUDICIAL CIRCUIT

Pleadings
Complaint 813
Amended Complaint 833
Answer 848
Amended Answer 866

Motions, Oppositions and Replies
Motion to Strike 882
Motion for Leave to Amend 898
Motion for Summary Judgment 914
Motion for Sanctions 931
Motion to Compel Discovery 947
Motion for Directed Verdict 963

Requests, Notices and Applications
Request for Production of Documents 979
Request for Admissions 995
Notice of Deposition 1011

ELEVENTH JUDICIAL CIRCUIT

Pleadings
Complaint 1031
Amended Complaint 1050
Answer 1066
Amended Answer 1083

Motions, Oppositions and Replies
Motion to Strike 1099
Motion for Leave to Amend 1113
Motion for Summary Judgment 1128
Motion for Sanctions 1143
Motion to Compel Discovery 1158
Motion for Directed Verdict 1173

Requests, Notices and Applications
Request for Production of Documents 1187
Request for Admissions 1203
Notice of Deposition 1217

SEVENTEENTH JUDICIAL CIRCUIT

Pleadings
Complaint 1236
Amended Complaint 1256
Answer 1273
Amended Answer 1292

Motions, Oppositions and Replies
Motion to Strike 1309
Motion for Leave to Amend 1325
Motion for Summary Judgment 1340
Motion for Sanctions 1357
Motion to Compel Discovery 1373
Motion for Directed Verdict 1389

Requests, Notices and Applications
Request for Production of Documents 1404
Request for Admissions 1421
Notice of Deposition 1436

TWENTIETH JUDICIAL CIRCUIT

Pleadings
Complaint 1456
Amended Complaint 1476
Answer 1492
Amended Answer 1510

Motions, Oppositions and Replies
Motion to Strike 1527
Motion for Leave to Amend 1544
Motion for Summary Judgment 1561
Motion for Sanctions 1578
Motion to Compel Discovery 1595
Motion for Directed Verdict 1612

Requests, Notices and Applications
Request for Production of Documents 1628
Request for Admissions 1645
Notice of Deposition 1660

APPENDIX - RELATED COURT DOCUMENTS
Complaint 1682
Amended Complaint 1685

Answer 1688
Amended Answer 1692
Motion to Strike 1696
Motion for Leave to Amend 1698
Motion for Summary Judgment 1701
Motion for Sanctions 1703
Motion to Compel Discovery 1709
Motion for Directed Verdict 1712

Table of Laws and Rules 1715

Table of Cases 1747

Index 1749

SECOND JUDICIAL CIRCUIT

Pleadings
Complaint

Document Last Updated January 2013

A. Applicable Rules

1. *State rules*
   a. Nonverification of pleadings. FL ST RCP Rule 1.030.
   b. When action commenced. FL ST RCP Rule 1.050.
   c. Process. FL ST RCP Rule 1.070.
   d. Service and filing of pleadings, orders, and documents. FL ST RCP Rule 1.080.
   e. Time. FL ST RCP Rule 1.090.
   f. Pleadings and motions. FL ST RCP Rule 1.100; FL ST RCP Rule 1.110; FL ST RCP Rule 1.120; FL ST RCP Rule 1.130; FL ST RCP Rule 1.170; FL ST RCP Rule 1.430.
   g. Relief from judgment, decrees, or orders. FL ST RCP Rule 1.540.
   h. Forms. FL ST RCP Rule 1.900.
   i. Minimization of the filing of sensitive information. FL ST J ADMIN Rule 2.425.
   j. Retention of court records. FL ST J ADMIN Rule 2.430.
   k. Foreign attorneys. FL ST J ADMIN Rule 2.510.
   l. Signature of attorneys and parties. FL ST J ADMIN Rule 2.515.
   m. Paper. FL ST J ADMIN Rule 2.520.
   n. Electronic filing. FL ST J ADMIN Rule 2.525.
   o. Accessibility of information and technology. FL ST J ADMIN Rule 2.526.
   p. Requests for accommodations by persons with disabilities. FL ST J ADMIN Rule 2.540.
   q. Service. FL ST § 48.011; FL ST § 48.021; FL ST § 48.031; FL ST § 48.041; FL ST § 48.042; FL ST § 48.051; FL ST § 48.061; FL ST § 48.071; FL ST § 48.081; FL ST § 48.091; FL ST § 48.101; FL ST § 48.111; FL ST § 48.121; FL ST § 48.131; FL ST § 48.141; FL ST § 48.151; FL ST § 48.161; FL ST § 48.171; FL ST § 48.181; FL ST § 48.183; FL ST § 48.19; FL ST § 48.193; FL ST § 48.194; FL ST § 48.20; FL ST § 48.21; FL ST § 48.25; FL ST § 48.31; FL ST § 49.011; FL ST § 49.021; FL ST § 49.031; FL ST § 49.041; FL ST § 49.051; FL ST § 49.061; FL ST § 49.071; FL ST § 49.08; FL ST § 49.09; FL ST § 49.10; FL ST § 49.11; FL ST § 49.12; FL ST § 50.011; FL ST § 50.021; FL ST § 50.031; FL ST § 50.041; FL ST § 50.051; FL ST § 50.061.
   r. Fees. FL ST § 57.081; FL ST § 57.085; FL ST § 28.241; FL ST § 34.041.
2. *Local rules*
   a. Notice of change of contact information. FL ST 2 J CIR 2007-05.

B. Timing

1. *Commencement of an action.* Every action of a civil nature shall be deemed commenced when the complaint or petition is filed except that ancillary proceedings shall be deemed commenced when the writ is issued or the pleading setting forth the claim of the party initiating the action is filed. FL ST RCP Rule 1.050.
2. *Summons; Time limit.* If service of the initial process and initial pleading is not made upon a defendant within one hundred twenty (120) days after filing of the initial pleading directed to that defendant the

court, on its own initiative after notice or on motion, shall direct that service be effected within a specified time or shall dismiss the action without prejudice or drop that defendant as a party; provided that if the plaintiff shows good cause or excusable neglect for the failure, the court shall extend the time for service for an appropriate period. FL ST RCP Rule 1.070(j).

3. *Computation of time*
   a. *Generally.* Computation of time shall be governed by FL ST J ADMIN Rule 2.514. FL ST RCP Rule 1.090(a). The following rules apply in computing time periods specified in any rule of procedure, local rule, court order, or statute that does not specify a method of computing time. FL ST J ADMIN Rule 2.514(a).
      i. *Period stated in days or a longer unit.* When the period is stated in days or a longer unit of time (A) exclude the day of the event that triggers the period; (B) count every day, including intermediate Saturdays, Sundays, and legal holidays; and (C) include the last day of the period, but if the last day is a Saturday, Sunday, or legal holiday, or falls within any period of time extended through an order of the chief justice under FL ST J ADMIN Rule 2.205(a)(2)(B)(iv), the period continues to run until the end of the next day that is not a Saturday, Sunday, or legal holiday and does not fall within any period of time extended through an order of the chief justice. FL ST J ADMIN Rule 2.514(a)(1).
      ii. *Period stated in hours.* When the period is stated in hours (A) begin counting immediately on the occurrence of the event that triggers the period; (B) count every hour, including hours during intermediate Saturdays, Sundays, and legal holidays; and (C) if the period would end on a Saturday, Sunday, or legal holiday, or during any period of time extended through an order of the chief justice under FL ST J ADMIN Rule 2.205(a)(2)(B)(iv), the period continues to run until the same time on the next day that is not a Saturday, Sunday, or legal holiday and does not fall within any period of time extended through an order of the chief justice. FL ST J ADMIN Rule 2.514(a)(2).
      iii. *Period stated in days less than seven (7) days.* When the period stated in days is less than seven (7) days, intermediate Saturdays, Sundays, and legal holidays shall be excluded in the computation. FL ST J ADMIN Rule 2.514(a)(3).
      iv. *"Last day" defined.* Unless a different time is set by a statute, local rule, or court order, the last day ends (A) for electronic filing or for service by any means, at midnight; and (B) for filing by other means, when the clerk's office is scheduled to close. FL ST J ADMIN Rule 2.514(a)(4).
      v. *"Next day" defined.* The "next day" is determined by continuing to count forward when the period is measured after an event and backward when measured before an event. FL ST J ADMIN Rule 2.514(a)(5).
      vi. *"Legal holiday" defined.* "Legal holiday" means (A) the day set aside by FL ST § 110.117, for observing New Year's Day, Martin Luther King, Jr.'s Birthday, Memorial Day, Independence Day, Labor Day, Veterans' Day, Thanksgiving Day, the Friday after Thanksgiving Day, or Christmas Day, and (B) any day observed as a holiday by the clerk's office or as designated by the chief judge. FL ST J ADMIN Rule 2.514(a)(6).
   b. *Additional time after service by mail or e-mail.* When a party may or must act within a specified time after service and service is made by mail or e-mail, five (5) days are added after the period that would otherwise expire under FL ST J ADMIN Rule 2.514(a). FL ST J ADMIN Rule 2.514(b).
   c. *Enlargement.* When an act is required or allowed to be done at or within a specified time by order of court, by the Florida Rules of Civil Procedure, or by notice given thereunder, for cause shown the court at any time in its discretion (1) with or without notice, may order the period enlarged if request therefor is made before the expiration of the period originally prescribed or as extended by a previous order, or (2) upon motion made and notice after the expiration of the specified period, may permit the act to be done when failure to act was the result of excusable neglect, but it may not extend the time for making a motion for new trial, for rehearing, or to alter or amend a judgment; making a motion for relief from a judgment under FL ST RCP Rule 1.540(b); taking an appeal or filing a petition for certiorari; or making a motion for a directed verdict. FL ST RCP Rule 1.090(b).

d. *Unaffected by expiration of term.* The period of time provided for the doing of any act or the taking of any proceeding shall not be affected or limited by the continued existence or expiration of a term of court. The continued existence or expiration of a term of court in no way affects the power of a court to do any act or take any proceeding in any action which is or has been pending before it. FL ST RCP Rule 1.090(c).

C. General Requirements

1. *General rules of pleading*

a. *Claims for relief*

i. A pleading which sets forth a claim for relief, whether an original claim, counterclaim, crossclaim, or third-party claim, must state a cause of action and shall contain

- A short and plain statement of the grounds upon which the court's jurisdiction depends, unless the court already has jurisdiction and the claim needs no new grounds of jurisdiction to support it (For information regarding acts subjecting persons to jurisdiction, please see FL ST § 48.193),
- A short and plain statement of the ultimate facts showing that the pleader is entitled to relief, and
- A demand for judgment for the relief to which the pleader deems himself or herself entitled. FL ST RCP Rule 1.110(b).

ii. Relief in the alternative or of several different types may be demanded. Every complaint shall be considered to demand general relief. FL ST RCP Rule 1.110(b).

b. *Verification.* Except when otherwise specifically provided by these rules or an applicable statute, every pleading or other document of a party represented by an attorney need not be verified or accompanied by an affidavit. FL ST RCP Rule 1.030. When filing an action for foreclosure of a mortgage on residential real property the complaint shall be verified. When verification of a document is required, the document filed shall include an oath, affirmation, or the following statement: "Under penalty of perjury, I declare that I have read the foregoing, and the facts alleged therein are true and correct to the best of my knowledge and belief." FL ST RCP Rule 1.110(b).

c. *Separate statements.* All averments of claim or defense shall be made in consecutively numbered paragraphs, the contents of each of which shall be limited as far as practicable to a statement of a single set of circumstances, and a paragraph may be referred to by number in all subsequent pleadings. Each claim founded upon a separate transaction or occurrence and each defense other than denials shall be stated in a separate count or defense when a separation facilitates the clear presentation of the matter set forth. FL ST RCP Rule 1.110(f).

d. *Statements adopted by reference.* Statements in a pleading may be adopted by reference in a different part of the same pleading, in another pleading, or in any motion. FL ST RCP Rule 1.130(b).

e. *Joinder of causes of action; Consistency.* A pleader may set up in the same action as many claims or causes of action or defenses in the same right as the pleader has, and claims for relief may be stated in the alternative if separate items make up the cause of action, or if two (2) or more causes of action are joined. A party may also set forth two (2) or more statements of a claim or defense alternatively, either in one (1) count or defense or in separate counts or defenses. When two (2) or more statements are made in the alternative and one (1) of them, if made independently, would be sufficient, the pleading is not made insufficient by the insufficiency of one (1) or more of the alternative statements. A party may also state as many separate claims or defenses as that party has, regardless of consistency and whether based on legal or equitable grounds or both. All pleadings shall be construed so as to do substantial justice. FL ST RCP Rule 1.110(g).

f. *Subsequent pleadings.* When the nature of an action permits pleadings subsequent to final judgment and the jurisdiction of the court over the parties has not terminated, the initial pleading subsequent to final judgment shall be designated a supplemental complaint or petition. The action shall then proceed in the same manner and time as though the supplemental complaint or petition were the initial pleading in the action, including the issuance of any needed process. FL ST RCP Rule

1.110(h) shall not apply to proceedings that may be initiated by motion under the Florida Rules of Civil Procedure. FL ST RCP Rule 1.110(h).

g. *Pleading basis for service.* When service of process is to be made under statutes authorizing service on nonresidents of Florida, it is sufficient to plead the basis for service in the language of the statute without pleading the facts supporting service. FL ST RCP Rule 1.070(h).

h. *Forms of pleadings.* Forms of action and technical forms for seeking relief and of pleas, pleadings, or motions are abolished. FL ST RCP Rule 1.110(a).

2. *Complaint; Generally*

a. *Purpose.* The purpose of a complaint is to advise the court and the defendant of the nature of a cause of action asserted by the plaintiff. FL-PP § 2:12.

b. *Sufficiency of complaint.* A complaint will be found to be insufficient if it contains only general conclusory allegations unsupported by any facts. The test to determine whether a complaint is sufficient is whether, if the factual allegations of the complaint are established, the plaintiff will be legally or equitably entitled to the claimed relief. Pizzi v. Central Bank & Trust Co., 250 So.2d 895, 896 (Fla. 1971); Bowen v. G H C Properties, Limited, 251 So.2d 359, 361 (Fla. 1st DCA 1971); FL-PP § 2:12. In determining the sufficiency of the complaint to state a cause of action, all allegations of the complaint are taken as true, and possible affirmative defenses are not considered. Strickland v. Commerce Loan Co. of Jacksonville, 158 So.2d 814 (Fla. 1st DCA 1963); FL-PP § 2:12.

i. The issues for trial in Florida must be settled by the pleadings. The issues cannot be raised by discovery. FL-PRACPROC § 7:6.

ii. Causes of action may be pleaded alternatively in the same count or in different counts and against the same or different defendants as long as the joinder of parties is proper. FL-PRACPROC § 7:6.

iii. Each count must state a cause of action. Each independent cause of action should be pleaded in a separate count. FL-PRACPROC § 7:6.

iv. Incorporation by reference of all allegations from one count to another is not proper. Separate counts facilitate reference to the pleading in which they appear in other pleadings, motions or papers as well as the assertion of defenses against some, but not all, causes of action. Some defenses may not apply to the initial pleading as a whole. FL-PRACPROC § 7:6.

3. *Pleading special matters*

a. *Capacity.* It is not necessary to aver the capacity of a party to sue or be sued, the authority of a party to sue or be sued in a representative capacity, or the legal existence of an organized association of persons that is made a party, except to the extent required to show the jurisdiction of the court. The initial pleading served on behalf of a minor party shall specifically aver the age of the minor party. When a party desires to raise an issue as to the legal existence of any party, the capacity of any party to sue or be sued, or the authority of a party to sue or be sued in a representative capacity, that party shall do so by specific negative averment which shall include such supporting particulars as are peculiarly within the pleader's knowledge. FL ST RCP Rule 1.120(a).

b. *Fraud, mistake, condition of the mind.* In all averments of fraud or mistake, the circumstances constituting fraud or mistake shall be stated with such particularity as the circumstances may permit. Malice, intent, knowledge, mental attitude, and other condition of mind of a person may be averred generally. FL ST RCP Rule 1.120(b).

c. *Conditions precedent.* In pleading the performance or occurrence of conditions precedent, it is sufficient to aver generally that all conditions precedent have been performed or have occurred. A denial of performance or occurrence shall be made specifically and with particularity. FL ST RCP Rule 1.120(c).

d. *Official document or act.* In pleading an official document or official act it is sufficient to aver that the document was issued or the act done in compliance with law. FL ST RCP Rule 1.120(c).

e. *Judgment or decree.* In pleading a judgment or decree of a domestic or foreign court, a judicial or quasi-judicial tribunal, or a board or officer, it is sufficient to aver the judgment or decree without setting forth matter showing jurisdiction to render it. FL ST RCP Rule 1.120(e).

f. *Time and place.* For the purpose of testing the sufficiency of a pleading, averments of time and place are material and shall be considered like all other averments of material matter. FL ST RCP Rule 1.120(f).

g. *Special damage.* When items of special damage are claimed, they shall be specifically stated. FL ST RCP Rule 1.120(g).

4. *Parties*

a. *Parties generally.* Every action may be prosecuted in the name of the real party in interest, but a personal representative, administrator, guardian, trustee of an express trust, a party with whom or in whose name a contract has been made for the benefit of another, or a party expressly authorized by statute may sue in that person's own name without joining the party for whose benefit the action is brought. All persons having an interest in the subject of the action and in obtaining the relief demanded may join as plaintiffs and any person may be made a defendant who has or claims an interest adverse to the plaintiff. Any person may at any time be made a party if that person's presence is necessary or proper to a complete determination of the cause. Persons having a united interest may be joined on the same side as plaintiffs or defendants, and anyone who refuses to join may for such reason be made a defendant. FL ST RCP Rule 1.210(a).

b. *Minors or incompetent persons.* When a minor or incompetent person has a representative, such as a guardian or other like fiduciary, the representative may sue or defend on behalf of the minor or incompetent person. A minor or incompetent person who does not have a duly appointed representative may sue by next friend or by a guardian ad litem. The court shall appoint a guardian ad litem for a minor or incompetent person not otherwise represented in an action or shall make such other order as it deems proper for the protection of the minor or incompetent person. FL ST RCP Rule 1.210(b).

c. For survivor and substitution of parties information, please see FL ST RCP Rule 1.260.

5. *Counterclaims and crossclaims*

a. *Compulsory counterclaims.* A pleading shall state as a counterclaim any claim which at the time of serving the pleading the pleader has against any opposing party, provided it arises out of the transaction or occurrence that is the subject matter of the opposing party's claim and does not require for its adjudication the presence of third parties over whom the court cannot acquire jurisdiction. But the pleader need not state a claim if (1) at the time the action was commenced the claim was the subject of another pending action, or (2) the opposing party brought suit upon that party's claim by attachment or other process by which the court did not acquire jurisdiction to render a personal judgment on the claim and the pleader is not stating a counterclaim under this rule. FL ST RCP Rule 1.170(a).

b. *Permissive counterclaim.* A pleading may state as a counterclaim any claim against an opposing party not arising out of the transaction or occurrence that is the subject matter of the opposing party's claim. FL ST RCP Rule 1.170(b).

c. *Counterclaim exceeding opposing claim.* A counterclaim may or may not diminish or defeat the recovery sought by the opposing party. It may claim relief exceeding in amount or different in kind from that sought in the pleading of the opposing party. FL ST RCP Rule 1.170(c).

d. *Counterclaim against the State.* The Florida Rules of Civil Procedure shall not be construed to enlarge beyond the limits established by law the right to assert counterclaims or to claim credits against the state or any of its subdivisions or other governmental organizations thereof subject to suit or against a municipal corporation or against an officer, agency, or administrative board of the state. FL ST RCP Rule 1.170(d).

e. *Counterclaim maturing or acquired after pleading.* A claim which matured or was acquired by the pleader after serving the pleading may be presented as a counterclaim by supplemental pleading with the permission of the court. FL ST RCP Rule 1.170(e).

f. *Omitted counterclaim or crossclaim.* When a pleader fails to set up a counterclaim or crossclaim through oversight, inadvertence, or excusable neglect, or when justice requires, the pleader may set up the counterclaim or crossclaim by amendment with leave of the court. FL ST RCP Rule 1.170(f).

g. *Crossclaim against co-party.* A pleading may state as a crossclaim any claim by one party against a co-party arising out of the transaction or occurrence that is the subject matter of either the original action or a counterclaim therein, or relating to any property that is the subject matter of the original action. The crossclaim may include a claim that the party against whom it is asserted is or may be liable to the crossclaimant for all or part of a claim asserted in the action against the crossclaimant. Service of a crossclaim on a party who has appeared in the action shall be made pursuant to FL ST RCP Rule 1.080. Service of a crossclaim against a party who has not appeared in the action shall be made in the manner provided for service of summons. FL ST RCP Rule 1.170(g).

h. *Additional parties may be brought in.* When the presence of parties other than those to the original action is required to grant complete relief in the determination of a counterclaim or crossclaim, they shall be named in the counterclaim or crossclaim and be served with process and shall be parties to the action thereafter if jurisdiction of them can be obtained and their joinder will not deprive the court of jurisdiction of the action. FL ST RCP Rule 1.250(b) and FL ST RCP Rule 1.250(c) apply to parties brought in under FL ST RCP Rule 1.170(h). FL ST RCP Rule 1.170(h).

i. *Separate trials; Separate judgment.* If the court orders separate trials as provided in FL ST RCP Rule 1.270(b), judgment on a counterclaim or crossclaim may be rendered when the court has jurisdiction to do so even if a claim of the opposing party has been dismissed or otherwise disposed of. FL ST RCP Rule 1.170(i).

j. *Demand exceeding jurisdiction; Transfer of action.* If the demand of any counterclaim or crossclaim exceeds the jurisdiction of the court in which the action is pending, the action shall be transferred forthwith to the court of the same county having jurisdiction of the demand in the counterclaim or crossclaim with only such alterations in the pleadings as are essential. The court shall order the transfer of the action and the transmittal of all papers in it to the proper court if the party asserting the demand exceeding the jurisdiction deposits with the court having jurisdiction a sum sufficient to pay the clerk's service charge in the court to which the action is transferred at the time of filing the counterclaim or crossclaim. Thereupon the original papers and deposit shall be transmitted and filed with a certified copy of the order. The court to which the action is transferred shall have full power and jurisdiction over the demands of all parties. Failure to make the service charge deposit at the time the counterclaim or crossclaim is filed, or within such further time as the court may allow, shall reduce a claim for damages to an amount within the jurisdiction of the court where the action is pending and waive the claim in other cases. FL ST RCP Rule 1.170(j).

6. *Misjoinder and nonjoinder of parties*

a. *Misjoinder.* Misjoinder of parties is not a ground for dismissal of an action. Any claim against a party may be severed and proceeded with separately. FL ST RCP Rule 1.250(a).

b. *Dropping parties.* Parties may be dropped by an adverse party in the manner provided for voluntary dismissal in FL ST RCP Rule 1.420(a)(1) subject to the exception stated in FL ST RCP Rule 1.420. If notice of lis pendens has been filed in the action against a party so dropped, the notice of dismissal shall be recorded and cancels the notice of lis pendens without the necessity of a court order. Parties may be dropped by order of court on its own initiative or the motion of any party at any stage of the action on such terms as are just. FL ST RCP Rule 1.250(b).

c. *Adding parties.* Parties may be added once as a matter of course within the same time that pleadings can be so amended under FL ST RCP Rule 1.190(a). If amendment by leave of court or stipulation of the parties is permitted, parties may be added in the amended pleading without further order of court. Parties may be added by order of court on its own initiative or on motion of any party at any stage of the action and on such terms as are just. FL ST RCP Rule 1.250(c).

7. *Jury demand*

a. *Right preserved.* The right of trial by jury as declared by the Constitution or by statute shall be preserved to the parties inviolate. FL ST RCP Rule 1.430(a).

b. *Demand.* Any party may demand a trial by jury of any issue triable of right by a jury by serving upon the other party a demand therefor in writing at any time after commencement of the action and not later than ten (10) days after the service of the last pleading directed to such issue. The demand may be indorsed upon a pleading of the party. FL ST RCP Rule 1.430(b).

c. *Specification of issues.* In the demand a party may specify the issues that the party wishes so tried; otherwise, the party is deemed to demand trial by jury for all issues so triable. FL ST RCP Rule 1.430(c).

   i. If a party has demanded trial by jury for only some of the issues, any other party may serve a demand for trial by jury of any other or all of the issues triable by jury ten (10) days after service of the demand or such lesser time as the court may order. FL ST RCP Rule 1.430(c).

d. *Waiver.* A party who fails to serve a demand as required by FL ST RCP Rule 1.430 waives trial by jury. FL ST RCP Rule 1.430(d).

   i. If waived, a jury trial may not be granted without the consent of the parties, but the court may allow an amendment in the proceedings to demand a trial by jury or order a trial by jury on its own motion. FL ST RCP Rule 1.430(d).

   ii. A demand for trial by jury may not be withdrawn without the consent of the parties. FL ST RCP Rule 1.430(d).

8. *Arbitration and mediation*

a. *Referral to arbitration and mediation.* Except as hereinafter provided or as otherwise prohibited by law, the presiding judge may enter an order referring all or any part of a contested civil matter to mediation or arbitration. The parties to any contested civil matter may file a written stipulation to mediate or arbitrate any issue between them at any time. Such stipulation shall be incorporated into the order of referral. FL ST RCP Rule 1.700(a).

b. *Arbitration*

   i. *Exclusions.* A civil action shall be ordered to arbitration or arbitration in conjunction with mediation upon stipulation of the parties. A civil action may be ordered to arbitration or arbitration in conjunction with mediation upon motion of any party or by the court, if the judge determines the action to be of such a nature that arbitration could be of benefit to the litigants or the court. FL ST RCP Rule 1.800.

      - Under no circumstances may the following categories of actions be referred to arbitration: (1) bond estreatures; (2) habeas corpus or other extraordinary writs; (3) bond validations; (4) civil or criminal contempt; (5) such other matters as may be specified by order of the chief judge in the circuit. FL ST RCP Rule 1.800.

   ii. For more information regarding arbitration, please see FL ST RCP Rule 1.810; FL ST RCP Rule 1.820; FL ST RCP Rule 1.830.

c. *Mediation.* For more information regarding mediation, please see FL ST RCP Rule 1.710; FL ST RCP Rule 1.720; FL ST RCP Rule 1.730; and FL ST RCP Rule 1.750.

9. *Rules of court*

a. *Rules of civil procedure.* The Florida Rules of Civil Procedure apply to all actions of a civil nature and all special statutory proceedings in the circuit courts and county courts except those to which the Florida Probate Rules, the Florida Family Law Rules of Procedure, or the Small Claims Rules apply. FL ST RCP Rule 1.010.

   i. The form, content, procedure, and time for pleading in all special statutory proceedings shall be as prescribed by the statutes governing the proceeding unless the Florida Rules of Civil Procedure specifically provide to the contrary. FL ST RCP Rule 1.010.

   ii. The Florida Rules of Civil Procedure shall be construed to secure the just, speedy, and inexpensive determination of every action. FL ST RCP Rule 1.010.

b. *Rules of judicial administration.* The Florida Rules of Judicial Administration shall apply to administrative matters in all courts to which the Florida Rules of Judicial Administration are applicable by their terms. The Florida Rules of Judicial Administration shall be construed to secure the speedy and inexpensive determination of every proceeding to which they are applicable. The Florida Rules of Judicial Administration shall supersede all conflicting rules and statutes. FL ST J ADMIN Rule 2.110.

10. *Notice of change of contact information.* The Clerk shall provide a change of address and/or telephone number form for use by attorneys and pro se litigants. With any change of address and/or telephone number, attorneys and pro se litigants governed by FL ST J ADMIN Rule 2.515 will provide to the Clerk and all parties promptly the change of address and/or telephone number form. This form should be submitted only once to the Clerk, who will then make the address and/or telephone number change in all court divisions. FL ST 2 J CIR 2007-05.

D. Documents

1. *Required documents*
   a. *Summons.* Upon the commencement of the action, summons or other process authorized by law shall be issued forthwith by the clerk or judge under the clerk's or the judge's signature and the seal of the court and delivered for service without praecipe. FL ST RCP Rule 1.070(a).
   b. *Complaint.* See the General Requirements section for the contents of the complaint.
      i. *Notices to persons with disabilities.* See the Format section of this KeyRules document for further information.
   c. *Civil cover sheet.* A civil cover sheet (FL ST RCP Form 1.997) shall be completed and filed with the clerk at the time an initial complaint or petition is filed by the party initiating the action. If the cover sheet is not filed, the clerk shall accept the complaint or petition for filing; but all proceedings in the action shall be abated until a properly executed cover sheet is completed and filed. The clerk shall complete the civil cover sheet for a party appearing pro se. FL ST RCP Rule 1.100(c)(2).
   d. *Return of execution process by process server.* Each person who effects service of process shall note on a return-of-service form attached thereto, the date and time when it comes to hand, the date and time when it is served, the manner of service, the name of the person on whom it was served and, if the person is served in a representative capacity, the position occupied by the person. The return-of-service form must be signed by the person who effects the service of process. However, a person employed by a sheriff who effects the service of process may sign the return-of-service form using an electronic signature certified by the sheriff. FL ST § 48.21(1).
      i. A failure to state the facts or to include the signature required by FL ST § 48.21(1) invalidates the service, but the return is amendable to state the facts or to include the signature at any time on application to the court from which the process issued. On amendment, service is as effective as if the return had originally stated the omitted facts or included the signature. A failure to state all the facts in or to include the signature on the return shall subject the person effecting service to a fine not exceeding $10, in the court's discretion. FL ST § 48.21(2).
   e. *Filing fees.* Filing fees are due at the time a party files a pleading to initiate a proceeding or files a pleading for relief. FL ST § 28.241. For a fee schedule, see FL ST § 28.241.
2. *Supplemental documents*
   a. *Exhibits.* All bonds, notes, bills of exchange, contracts, accounts, or documents upon which action may be brought or defense made, or a copy thereof or a copy of the portions thereof material to the pleadings, shall be incorporated in or attached to the pleading. No papers shall be unnecessarily annexed as exhibits. The pleadings shall contain no unnecessary recitals of deeds, documents, contracts, or other instruments. Any exhibit attached to a pleading shall be considered a part of the pleadings for all purposes. FL ST RCP Rule 1.130(a).
   b. *Notice of constitutional question.* A party that files a pleading, written motion, or other paper drawing into question the constitutionality of a state statute or a county or municipal charter, ordinance, or franchise must promptly (1) file a notice of constitutional question stating the question and identifying the paper that raises it; and (2) serve the notice and the pleading, written motion, or other paper drawing into question the constitutionality of a state statute or a county or municipal charter, ordinance, or franchise on the Attorney General or the state attorney of the judicial circuit in which the action is pending, by either certified or registered mail. Service of the notice and pleading, written motion, or other paper does not require joinder of the Attorney General or the state attorney as a party to the action. FL ST RCP Rule 1.071.

E. Format

1. *Documents; Type and size.* Documents subject to the exceptions set forth in FL ST J ADMIN Rule 2.525(d) shall be filed on recycled paper measuring eight and one half by eleven (8 1/2 by 11) inches. For purposes of FL ST J ADMIN Rule 2.520, paper is recycled if it contains a minimum content of fifty (50) percent waste paper. Xerographic reduction of legal-size (eight and one half by fourteen (8 1/2 by 14) inches) documents to letter size (eight and one half by eleven (8 1/2 by 11) inches) is prohibited. All other documents filed by electronic transmission shall be filed in a format capable of being printed in a format consistent with the provisions of FL ST J ADMIN Rule 2.250. FL ST J ADMIN Rule 2.520(b).
   a. *Exhibits.* Any exhibit or attachment filed with pleadings or papers may be filed in its original size. FL ST J ADMIN Rule 2.520(c).
   b. *Recording space.* On all papers and documents prepared and filed by the court or by any party to a proceeding which are to be recorded in the public records of any county, including but not limited to final money judgments and notices of lis pendens, a three (3) inch by three (3) inch space at the top right-hand corner on the first page and a one (1) inch by three (3) inch space at the top right-hand corner on each subsequent page shall be left blank and reserved for use by the clerk of court. FL ST J ADMIN Rule 2.520(d).
      i. *Exceptions to recording space.* Any papers or documents created by persons or entities over which the filing party has no control, including but not limited to wills, codicils, trusts, or other testamentary documents; documents prepared or executed by any public officer; documents prepared, executed, acknowledged, or proved outside of the State of Florida; or documents created by State or Federal government agencies, may be filed without the space required by FL ST J ADMIN Rule 2.520. FL ST J ADMIN Rule 2.520(e).
   c. *Noncompliance.* No clerk of court is permitted to refuse to file any document or paper because of noncompliance with the Florida Rules of Judicial Administration. However, upon request of the clerk of court, noncomplying documents must be resubmitted in accordance with the formatting rules. FL ST J ADMIN Rule 2.520(f).
2. *Caption.* Every pleading, motion, order, judgment, or other paper shall have a caption containing the name of the court, the file number, and except for in rem proceedings, including forfeiture proceedings, the name of the first party on each side with an appropriate indication of other parties, and a designation identifying the party filing it and its nature or the nature of the order, as the case may be. In any in rem proceeding, every pleading, motion, order, judgment, or other paper shall have a caption containing the name of the court, the file number, the style "In re" (followed by the name or general description of the property), and a designation of the person or entity filing it and its nature or the nature of the order, as the case may be. In an in rem forfeiture proceeding, the style shall be "In re forfeiture of" (followed by the name of the general description of the property). All papers filed in the action shall be styled in such a manner as to indicate clearly the subject matter of the paper and the party requesting or obtaining relief. FL ST RCP Rule 1.100(c)(1).
3. *Writing and written defined.* Writing or written means a document containing information, an application, or a stipulation. FL ST RCP Rule 1.080(c).
4. *Rule abbreviations*
   a. The Florida Rules of Civil Procedure and shall be abbreviated as Fla.R.Civ.P. FL ST RCP Rule 1.010.
   b. The Florida Rules of Judicial Administration shall be abbreviated as Fla. R. Jud. Admin. FL ST J ADMIN Rule 2.110.
5. *Nonverification.* Except when otherwise specifically provided by the Florida Rules of Civil Procedure or an applicable statute, every pleading or other document of a party represented by an attorney need not be verified or accompanied by an affidavit. FL ST RCP Rule 1.030; FL ST J ADMIN Rule 2.515(a).
6. *Attorney signature*
   a. *Attorney signature.* Every pleading and other document of a party represented by an attorney shall be signed by at least one (1) attorney of record in that attorney's individual name whose current record

Florida Bar address, telephone number, including area code, primary e-mail address and secondary e-mail addresses, if any, and Florida Bar number shall be stated, and who shall be duly licensed to practice law in Florida or who shall have received permission to appear in the particular case as provided in FL ST J ADMIN Rule 2.510. FL ST J ADMIN Rule 2.515(a).

i. The attorney may be required by the court to give the address of, and to vouch for the attorney's authority to represent, the party. FL ST J ADMIN Rule 2.515(a).

ii. The signature of an attorney shall constitute a certificate by the attorney that the attorney has read the pleading or other document; that to the best of the attorney's knowledge, information, and belief there is good ground to support it; and that it is not interposed for delay. FL ST J ADMIN Rule 2.515(a).

iii. If a pleading is not signed or is signed with intent to defeat the purpose of FL ST J ADMIN Rule 2.515, it may be stricken and the action may proceed as though the pleading or other document had not been served. FL ST J ADMIN Rule 2.515(a).

b. *Pro se litigant signature.* A party who is not represented by an attorney shall sign any pleading or other paper and state the party's address and telephone number, including area code. FL ST J ADMIN Rule 2.515(b).

c. *Form of signature*

i. The signatures required on pleadings and documents by FL ST J ADMIN Rule 2.515(a) and FL ST J ADMIN Rule 2.515(b) may be:

- Original signatures;
- Original signatures that have been reproduced by electronic means, such as on electronically transmitted documents or photocopied documents;
- Electronic signatures using the "/s/," "s/," or "/s" formats by or at the direction of the person signing; or
- Any other signature format authorized by general law, so long as the clerk where the proceeding is pending has the capability of receiving and has obtained approval from the Supreme Court of Florida to accept pleadings and documents with that signature format. FL ST J ADMIN Rule 2.515(c)(1).

ii. An attorney, party, or other person who files a pleading or paper by electronic transmission that does not contain the original signature of that attorney, party, or other person shall file that identical pleading or paper in paper form containing an original signature of that attorney, party, or other person (hereinafter called the follow-up filing) immediately thereafter. The follow-up filing is not required if the Supreme Court of Florida has entered an order directing the clerk of court to discontinue accepting the follow-up filing. FL ST J ADMIN Rule 2.515(c)(2).

7. *Forms*

a. *Process.* The forms of process, notice of lis pendens, and notice of action provided in the Florida Rules of Civil Procedure are sufficient. Variations from the forms do not void process or notices that are otherwise sufficient. FL ST RCP Rule 1.900(a).

b. *Other forms.* The other forms provided in the Florida Rules of Civil Procedure are sufficient for the matters that are covered by them. So long as the substance is expressed without prolixity, the forms may be varied to meet the facts of a particular case. FL ST RCP Rule 1.900(b).

c. *Formal matters.* Captions, except for the designation of the paper, are omitted from the forms provided in the Florida Rules of Civil Procedure. A general form of caption is the first form provided. Signatures are omitted from pleadings and motions. FL ST RCP Rule 1.900(c).

8. *Notices to persons with disabilities.* All notices of court proceedings to be held in a public facility, and all process compelling appearance at such proceedings, shall include the following statement in bold face, fourteen (14) point Times New Roman or Courier font: "If you are a person with a disability who needs any accommodation in order to participate in this proceeding, you are entitled, at no cost to you, to the provision of certain assistance. Please contact [identify applicable court personnel by name, address, and

telephone number] at least seven (7) days before your scheduled court appearance, or immediately upon receiving this notification if the time before the scheduled appearance is less than seven (7) days; if you are hearing or voice impaired, call 711." FL ST J ADMIN Rule 2.540(c)(1).

9. *Minimization of the filing of sensitive information*
   a. *Limitations for court filings.* Unless authorized by FL ST J ADMIN Rule 2.425(b), statute, another rule of court, or the court orders otherwise, designated sensitive information filed with the court must be limited to the following format:
      i. The initials of a person known to be a minor;
      ii. The year of birth of a person's birth date;
      iii. No portion of any: Social security number, Bank account number, Credit card account number, Charge account number, or Debit account number;
      iv. The last four digits of any: Taxpayer identification number (TIN), Employee identification number, Driver's license number, Passport number, Telephone number, Financial account number, except as set forth in FL ST J ADMIN Rule 2.425(a)(3), Brokerage account number, Insurance policy account number, Loan account number, Customer account number, or Patient or health care number;
      v. A truncated version of any: Email address, Computer user name, Password, or Personal identification number (PIN); and
      vi. A truncated version of any other sensitive information as provided by court order. FL ST J ADMIN Rule 2.425(a).
   b. *Exceptions.* FL ST J ADMIN Rule 2.425(a) does not apply to the following:
      i. An account number which identifies the property alleged to be the subject of a proceeding;
      ii. The record of an administrative or agency proceeding;
      iii. The record in appellate or review proceedings;
      iv. The birth date of a minor whenever the birth date is necessary for the court to establish or maintain subject matter jurisdiction;
      v. The name of a minor in any order relating to parental responsibility, time-sharing, or child support;
      vi. The name of a minor in any document or order affecting the minor's ownership of real property;
      vii. The birth date of a party in a writ of attachment or notice to payor;
      viii. In traffic and criminal proceedings: a pro se filing; a court filing that is related to a criminal matter or investigation and that is prepared before the filing of a criminal charge or is not filed as part of any docketed criminal case; an arrest or search warrant or any information in support thereof; a charging document and an affidavit or other documents filed in support of any charging document, including any driving records; a statement of particulars; discovery material introduced into evidence or otherwise filed with the court; and all information necessary for the proper issuance and execution of a subpoena duces tecum;
      ix. Information used by the clerk for case maintenance purposes or the courts for case management purposes; and
      x. Information which is relevant and material to an issue before the court. FL ST J ADMIN Rule 2.425(b).
   c. *Remedies.* Upon motion by a party or interested person or sua sponte by the court, the court may order remedies, sanctions or both for a violation of FL ST J ADMIN Rule 2.425(a). Following notice and an opportunity to respond, the court may impose sanctions if such filing was not made in good faith. FL ST J ADMIN Rule 2.425(c).
   d. *Motions not restricted.* FL ST J ADMIN Rule 2.425 does not restrict a party's right to move for protective order, to move to file documents under seal, or to request a determination of the confidentiality of records. FL ST J ADMIN Rule 2.425(d).

e. *Application.* FL ST J ADMIN Rule 2.425 does not affect the application of constitutional provisions, statutes, or rules of court regarding confidential information or access to public information. FL ST J ADMIN Rule 2.425(e).

F. Filing and Service Requirements

1. *Filing requirements.* All documents filed in any court shall be filed by electronic transmission in accordance with FL ST J ADMIN Rule 2.525. "Documents" means pleadings, motions, petitions, memoranda, briefs, notices, exhibits, declarations, affidavits, orders, judgments, decrees, writs, opinions, and any other paper or writing submitted to a court. FL ST J ADMIN Rule 2.520(a). All documents that are court records, as defined in FL ST J ADMIN Rule 2.430(a)(1), must be filed by electronic transmission, provided that: (1) the clerk has the ability to accept and retain such documents; (2) the clerk or the chief judge of the circuit has requested permission to accept documents filed by electronic transmission; and (3) the supreme court has entered an order granting permission to the clerk to accept documents filed by electronic transmission. FL ST J ADMIN Rule 2.525(c)(1).

   a. *Definition.* "Electronic transmission of documents" means the sending of information by electronic signals to, by or from a court or clerk, which when received can be transformed and stored or transmitted on paper, microfilm, magnetic storage device, optical imaging system, CD-ROM, flash drive, other electronic data storage system, server, case maintenance system ("CM"), electronic court filing ("ECF") system, statewide or local electronic portal ("e-portal"), or other electronic record keeping system authorized by the supreme court in a format sufficient to communicate the information on the original document in a readable format. Electronic transmission of documents includes electronic mail ("e-mail") and any internet-based transmission procedure, and may include procedures allowing for documents to be signed or verified by electronic means. FL ST J ADMIN Rule 2.525(a).

   b. *Application.* Any court or clerk of the court may accept the electronic transmission of documents for filing after the clerk, together with input from the chief judge of the circuit, has obtained approval of the procedures and program for doing so from the Supreme Court of Florida. FL ST J ADMIN Rule 2.525(b).

   c. *Exceptions*

      i. Paper documents and other submissions may be manually submitted to the clerk or court:

         - When the clerk does not have the ability to accept and retain documents by electronic filing or has not had ECF Procedures approved by the supreme court;
         - For filing by any self-represented party or any self-represented nonparty unless specific ECF Procedures provide a means to file documents electronically. However, any self-represented nonparty that is a governmental or public agency and any other agency, partnership, corporation, or business entity acting on behalf of any governmental or public agency may file documents by electronic transmission if such entity has the capability of filing documents electronically;
         - For filing by attorneys excused from e-mail service in accordance with FL ST J ADMIN Rule 2.516(b);
         - When submitting evidentiary exhibits or filing non-documentary materials;
         - When the filing involves documents in excess of twenty-five (25) megabytes (25MB) in size. For such filings, documents may be transmitted using an electronic storage medium that the clerk has the ability to accept, which may include a CD-ROM, flash drive, or similar storage medium;
         - When filed in open court, as permitted by the court;
         - When paper filing is permitted by any approved statewide or local ECF procedures; and
         - If any court determines that justice so requires. FL ST J ADMIN Rule 2.525(d).

      ii. Any document in paper form submitted under FL ST J ADMIN Rule 2.525(d) is filed when it is received by the clerk or court and the clerk shall immediately thereafter convert any filed paper document to an electronic document. "Convert to an electronic document" means optically capturing an image of a paper document and using character recognition software to recover as much of the document's text as practicable and then indexing and storing the document in the official court file. FL ST J ADMIN Rule 2.525(c)(4).

iii. Any storage medium submitted under FL ST J ADMIN Rule 2.525(d)(5) is filed when received by the clerk or court and the clerk shall immediately thereafter transfer the electronic documents from the storage device to the official court file. FL ST J ADMIN Rule 2.525(c)(5).

iv. If the filer of any paper document authorized under FL ST J ADMIN Rule 2.525(d) provides a self-addressed, postage-paid envelope for return of the paper document after it is converted to electronic form by the clerk, the clerk shall place the paper document in the envelope and deposit it in the mail. Except when a paper document is required to be maintained, the clerk may recycle any filed paper document that is not to be returned to the filer. FL ST J ADMIN Rule 2.525(c)(6).

v. The clerk may convert any paper document filed before the effective date of FL ST J ADMIN Rule 2.525 to an electronic document. Unless the clerk is required to maintain the paper document, if the paper document has been converted to an electronic document by the clerk, the paper document is no longer part of the official court file and may be removed and recycled. FL ST J ADMIN Rule 2.525(c)(7).

d. *Official court file.* For information on what constitutes the official court file, please see FL ST J ADMIN Rule 2.525(c)(2), FL ST J ADMIN Rule 2.525(c)(3).

e. *Administration.* All attorneys, parties, or other persons using this rule to file documents are required to make arrangements with the court or clerk for the payment of any charges authorized by general law or the supreme court before filing any document by electronic transmission. FL ST J ADMIN Rule 2.525(f)(2).

f. *Filing date.* The filing date for an electronically transmitted document is the date and time that such filing is acknowledged by an electronic stamp or otherwise, pursuant to any procedure set forth in any ECF Procedures approved by the supreme court, or the date the last page of such filing is received by the court or clerk. FL ST J ADMIN Rule 2.525(f)(3).

g. *Accessibility.* All documents transmitted in any electronic form under FL ST J ADMIN Rule 2.525 must comply with the accessibility requirements of FL ST J ADMIN Rule 2.526. FL ST J ADMIN Rule 2.525(g).

2. *Service requirements*

a. *Papers to be served.* At the time of personal service of process a copy of the initial pleading shall be delivered to the party upon whom service is made. The date and hour of service shall be endorsed on the original process and all copies of it by the person making the service. The party seeking to effect personal service shall furnish the person making service with the necessary copies. When the service is made by publication, copies of the initial pleadings shall be furnished to the clerk and mailed by the clerk with the notice of action to all parties whose addresses are stated in the initial pleading or sworn statement. FL ST RCP Rule 1.070(e).

b. *Issuance of summons.* Upon the commencement of the action, summons or other process authorized by law shall be issued forthwith by the clerk or judge under the clerk's or the judge's signature and the seal of the court and delivered for service without praecipe. FL ST RCP Rule 1.070(a).

i. *How directed.* Summons, subpoenas, and other process in civil actions run throughout the state. All process except subpoenas shall be directed to all and singular the sheriffs of the state. FL ST § 48.011.

ii. *Service as to numerous defendants.* If there is more than one (1) defendant, the clerk or judge shall issue as many writs of process against the several defendants as may be directed by the plaintiff or the plaintiff's attorney. FL ST RCP Rule 1.070(c).

c. *Who may serve process.* Service of process may be made by an officer authorized by law to serve process, but the court may appoint any competent person not interested in the action to serve the process. When so appointed, the person serving process shall make proof of service by affidavit promptly and in any event within the time during which the person served must respond to the process. Failure to make proof of service shall not affect the validity of the service. When any process is returned not executed or returned improperly executed for any defendant, the party causing its issuance shall be entitled to such additional process against the unserved party as is required to effect service. FL ST RCP Rule 1.070(b).

i. All process shall be served by the sheriff of the county where the person to be served is found, except initial nonenforceable civil process may be served by a special process server appointed by the sheriff as provided for in FL ST § 48.021 or by a certified process server as provided for in FL ST § 48.25 through FL ST § 48.31. FL ST § 48.021(1).

ii. The sheriff of each county may, in his or her discretion, establish an approved list of natural persons designated as special process servers. FL ST § 48.021(2)(a). For more information regarding process servers, please see FL ST § 48.021(2).

iii. A person serving process shall place, on the copy served, the date and time of service and his or her identification number and initials for all service of process. FL ST § 48.031(5).

d. *Service of process on Sunday*

i. Service or execution on Sunday of any writ, process, warrant, order, or judgment is void and the person serving or executing, or causing it to be served or executed, is liable to the party aggrieved for damages for so doing as if he or she had done it without any process, writ, warrant, order, or judgment. FL ST § 48.20.

ii. If affidavit is made by the person requesting service or execution that he or she has good reason to believe that any person liable to have any such writ, process, warrant, order, or judgment served on him or her intends to escape from this state under protection of Sunday, any officer furnished with an order authorizing service or execution by the trial court judge may serve or execute such writ, process, warrant, order, or judgment on Sunday, and it is as valid as if it had been done on any other day. FL ST § 48.20.

e. *Methods of service*

i. *Service of process generally.* Service of original process is made by delivering a copy of it to the person to be served with a copy of the complaint, petition, or other initial pleading or paper or by leaving the copies at his or her usual place of abode with any person residing therein who is fifteen (15) years of age or older and informing the person of their contents. Minors who are or have been married shall be served as provided in FL ST § 48.031. FL ST § 48.031(1)(a).

- Employers, when contacted by an individual authorized to make service of process, shall permit the authorized individual to make service on employees in a private area designated by the employer. FL ST § 48.031(1)(b).
- Substitute service may be made on the spouse of the person to be served at any place in the county, if the cause of action is not an adversary proceeding between the spouse and the person to be served, if the spouse requests such service, and if the spouse and person to be served are residing together in the same dwelling. FL ST § 48.031(2)(a).
- Substitute service may be made on an individual doing business as a sole proprietorship at his or her place of business, during regular business hours, by serving the person in charge of the business at the time of service if two (2) or more attempts to serve the owner have been made at the place of business. FL ST § 48.031(2)(b).
- If the only address for a person to be served, which is discoverable through public records, is a private mailbox, substitute service may be made by leaving a copy of the process with the person in charge of the private mailbox, but only if the process server determines that the person to be served maintains a mailbox at that location. FL ST § 48.031(6).

ii. *Service by mail.* A defendant may accept service of process by mail. FL ST RCP Rule 1.070(i). A plaintiff may notify any defendant of the commencement of the action and request that the defendant waive service of a summons. FL ST RCP Rule 1.070(i)(2).

- *Notice and request for waiver.* The notice and request shall: (1) be in writing and be addressed directly to the defendant, if an individual, or to an officer or managing or general agent of the defendant or other agent authorized by appointment or law to receive service of process; (2) be dispatched by certified mail, return receipt requested; (3) be accompanied by a copy of the complaint and shall identify the court in which it has been filed; (4) inform the defendant of the consequences of compliance and of failure to comply with the request; (5) state the date on which the request is sent; (6) allow the defendant twenty (20) days from the date on which the request is received to return the waiver, or, if the address of the defendant is outside of the United States, thirty (30) days from the date on which it is received to return the waiver; and (7) provide the defendant with an extra copy of the notice and request, including the waiver, as well as a prepaid means of compliance in writing. FL ST RCP Rule 1.070(i)(2).

- *Consequences of accepting/rejecting service by mail.* Acceptance of service of a complaint by mail does not thereby waive any objection to the venue or to the jurisdiction of the court over the person of the defendant. FL ST RCP Rule 1.070(i)(1). If a defendant fails to comply with a request for waiver within the time provided, the court shall impose the costs subsequently incurred in effecting service on the defendant unless good cause for the failure is shown. FL ST RCP Rule 1.070(i)(3). A defendant who, before being served with process, timely returns a waiver so requested is not required to respond to the complaint until sixty (60) days after the date the defendant received the request for waiver of service. For purposes of computing any time prescribed or allowed by the Florida Rules of Civil Procedure, service of process shall be deemed effected twenty (20) days before the time required to respond to the complaint. FL ST RCP Rule 1.070(i)(4). When the plaintiff files a waiver of service with the court, the action shall proceed, except as provided in FL ST RCP Rule 1.070(i)(4), as if a summons and complaint had been served at the time of filing the waiver, and no further proof of service shall be required. FL ST RCP Rule 1.070(i)(5).

iii. *Service on partnerships and limited partnerships*

- Process against a partnership shall be served on any partner and is as valid as if served on each individual partner. If a partner is not available during regular business hours to accept service on behalf of the partnership, he or she may designate an employee to accept such service. After one (1) attempt to serve a partner or designated employee has been made, process may be served on the person in charge of the partnership during regular business hours. After service on any partner, plaintiff may proceed to judgment and execution against that partner and the assets of the partnership. After service on a designated employee or other person in charge, plaintiff may proceed to judgment and execution against the partnership assets but not against the individual assets of any partner. FL ST § 48.061(1).
- Process against a domestic limited partnership may be served on any general partner or on the agent for service of process specified in its certificate of limited partnership or in its certificate as amended or restated and is as valid as if served on each individual member of the partnership. After service on a general partner or the agent, the plaintiff may proceed to judgment and execution against the limited partnership and all of the general partners individually. If a general partner cannot be found in this state and service cannot be made on an agent because of failure to maintain such an agent or because the agent cannot be found or served with the exercise of reasonable diligence, service of process may be effected by service upon the Secretary of State as agent of the limited partnership as provided for in FL ST § 48.181. Service of process may be made under FL ST § 48.071 and FL ST § 48.21 on limited partnerships. FL ST § 48.061(2).
- Process against a foreign limited partnership may be served on any general partner found in the state or on any agent for service of process specified in its application for registration and is as valid as if served on each individual member of the partnership. If a general partner cannot be found in this state and an agent for service of process has not been appointed or, if appointed, the agent's authority has been revoked or the agent cannot be

found or served with the exercise of reasonable diligence, service of process may be effected by service upon the Secretary of State as agent of the limited partnership as provided for in FL ST § 48.181, or process may be served as provided in FL ST § 48.071 and FL ST § 48.21. FL ST § 48.061(3).

iv. *Service on corporation*

- Process against any private corporation, domestic or foreign, may be served: (1) on the president or vice president, or other head of the corporation; (2) in the absence of any person described in FL ST § 48.081(1)(a), on the cashier, treasurer, secretary, or general manager; (3) in the absence of any person described in FL ST § 48.081(1)(a) or FL ST § 48.081(1)(b), on any director; or (4) in the absence of any person described in FL ST § 48.081(1)(a), FL ST § 48.081(1)(b), or FL ST § 48.081(1)(c), on any officer or business agent residing in the state. FL ST § 48.081(1).
- If a foreign corporation has none of the foregoing officers or agents in this state, service may be made on any agent transacting business for it in this state. FL ST § 48.081(2).
- As an alternative to all of the foregoing, process may be served on the agent designated by the corporation under FL ST § 48.091. However, if service cannot be made on a registered agent because of failure to comply with FL ST § 48.091, service of process shall be permitted on any employee at the corporation's principal place of business or on any employee of the registered agent. FL ST § 48.081(3)(a). If the address provided for the registered agent, officer, director, or principal place of business is a residence or private mailbox, service on the corporation may be made by serving the registered agent, officer, or director in accordance with FL ST § 48.031. FL ST § 48.081(3)(b).
- FL ST § 48.081 does not apply to service of process on insurance companies. FL ST § 48.081(4).
- When a corporation engages in substantial and not isolated activities within this state, or has a business office within the state and is actually engaged in the transaction of business therefrom, service upon any officer or business agent while on corporate business within this state may personally be made, pursuant to FL ST § 48.081, and it is not necessary in such case that the action, suit, or proceeding against the corporation shall have arisen out of any transaction or operation connected with or incidental to the business being transacted within the state. FL ST § 48.081(5).
- For information regarding service on a dissolved corporation refer to FL ST § 48.101.

v. *Personal service outside state*

- Except as otherwise provided herein, service of process on persons outside of this state shall be made in the same manner as service within this state by any officer authorized to serve process in the state where the person is served. No order of court is required. An affidavit of the officer shall be filed, stating the time, manner, and place of service. The court may consider the affidavit, or any other competent evidence, in determining whether service has been properly made. Service of process on persons outside the United States may be required to conform to the provisions of the Hague Convention on the Service Abroad of Judicial and Extrajudicial Documents in Civil or Commercial Matters. FL ST § 48.194(1).
- For further information on service of process in an in rem or quasi in rem action refer to FL ST § 48.194(2); FL ST § 48.194(3); and FL ST § 48.194(4).

vi. *Method of substituted service on nonresident*

- When authorized by law, substituted service of process on a nonresident or a person who conceals his or her whereabouts by serving a public officer designated by law shall be made by leaving a copy of the process with a fee of eight dollars and seventy-five cents ($8.75) with the public officer or in his or her office or by mailing the copies by certified mail to the public officer with the fee. The service is sufficient service on a defendant who has appointed a public officer as his or her agent for the service of process. FL ST § 48.161(1).

- Notice of service and a copy of the process shall be sent forthwith by registered or certified mail by the plaintiff or his or her attorney to the defendant, and the defendant's return receipt and the affidavit of the plaintiff or his or her attorney of compliance shall be filed on or before the return day of the process or within such time as the court allows, or the notice and copy shall be served on the defendant, if found within the state, by an officer authorized to serve legal process, or if found without the state, by a sheriff or a deputy sheriff of any county of this state or any duly constituted public officer qualified to serve like process in the state or jurisdiction where the defendant is found. The officer's return showing service shall be filed on or before the return day of the process or within such time as the court allows. The public officer shall keep a record of all process served on him or her showing the day and hour of service. FL ST § 48.161(1).
- If any person on whom service of process is authorized under FL ST § 48.161(1) dies, service may be made on his or her administrator, executor, curator, or personal representative in the same manner. FL ST § 48.161(2).
- FL ST § 48.161 does not apply to persons on whom service is authorized under FL ST § 48.151. FL ST § 48.161(3).
- The public officer may designate some other person in his or her office to accept service. FL ST § 48.161(4).

vii. *Service by publication.* Service of process by publication may be made as provided by statute. FL ST RCP Rule 1.070(d). Service of process by publication is allowable in cases listed in FL ST § 49.011 and upon the parties listed in FL ST § 49.021.

- As a condition precedent to service by publication, a statement shall be filed in the action executed by the plaintiff, the plaintiff's agent or attorney, setting forth substantially the matters hereafter required, which statement may be contained in a verified pleading, or in an affidavit or other sworn statement. FL ST § 49.031(1). After the entry of a final judgment or decree in any action no sworn statement shall ever be held defective for failure to state a required fact if the fact otherwise appears from the record in the action. FL ST § 49.031(3).
- For the sworn statement requirements for service of process by publication refer to FL ST § 49.041; FL ST § 49.051; FL ST § 49.061; and FL ST § 49.071.
- On filing the sworn statement, and otherwise complying with the foregoing requirements, the plaintiff is entitled to have issued by the clerk or judge, not later than sixty (60) days after filing the sworn statement, a notice of action which notice shall set forth: (1) the names of the known natural defendants; the names, status and description of the corporate defendants; a description of the unknown defendants who claim by, through, under or against a known party which may be described as "all parties claiming interests by, through, under or against (name of known party)" and a description of all unknown defendants which may be described as "all parties having or claiming to have any right, title or interest in the property herein described"; (2) the nature of the action or proceeding in short and simple terms (but neglect to do so is not jurisdictional); (3) the name of the court in which the action or proceeding was instituted and an abbreviated title of the case; (4) the description of real property, if any, proceeded against. FL ST § 49.08.
- For further information on service of process by publication refer to FL ST § 49.09; FL ST § 49.10; FL ST § 49.11; FL ST § 49.12; FL ST § 50.011; FL ST § 50.021; FL ST § 50.031; FL ST § 50.041; FL ST § 50.051; and FL ST § 50.061.

viii. *Service on agents of nonresidents doing business in the state.* When any natural person or partnership not residing or having a principal place of business in this state engages in business in this state, process may be served on the person who is in charge of any business in which the defendant is engaged within this state at the time of service, including agents soliciting orders for goods, wares, merchandise or services. FL ST § 48.071.

- Any process so served is as valid as if served personally on the nonresident person or partnership engaging in business in this state in any action against the person or partnership arising out of such business. FL ST § 48.071.

- A copy of such process with a notice of service on the person in charge of such business shall be sent forthwith to the nonresident person or partnership by registered or certified mail, return receipt requested. FL ST § 48.071.
- An affidavit of compliance with FL ST § 48.071 shall be filed before the return day or within such further time as the court may allow. FL ST § 48.071.

ix. *Service on nonresident engaging in business in state.* The acceptance by any person or persons, individually or associated together as a copartnership or any other form or type of association, who are residents of any other state or country, and all foreign corporations, and any person who is a resident of the state and who subsequently becomes a nonresident of the state or conceals his or her whereabouts, of the privilege extended by law to nonresidents and others to operate, conduct, engage in, or carry on a business or business venture in the state, or to have an office or agency in the state, constitutes an appointment by the persons and foreign corporations of the Secretary of State of the state as their agent on whom all process in any action or proceeding against them, or any of them, arising out of any transaction or operation connected with or incidental to the business or business venture may be served. The acceptance of the privilege is signification of the agreement of the persons and foreign corporations that the process against them which is so served is of the same validity as if served personally on the persons or foreign corporations. FL ST § 48.181(1).

- If a foreign corporation has a resident agent or officer in the state, process shall be served on the resident agent or officer. FL ST § 48.181(2).
- Any person, firm, or corporation which sells, consigns, or leases by any means whatsoever tangible or intangible personal property, through brokers, jobbers, wholesalers, or distributors to any person, firm, or corporation in this state is conclusively presumed to be both engaged in substantial and not isolated activities within this state and operating, conducting, engaging in, or carrying on a business or business venture in this state. FL ST § 48.181(3).

x. *Other service provisions:*

- Service on alien property custodian. FL ST § 48.131.
- Service on an incompetent person. FL ST § 48.042.
- Service on minor. FL ST § 48.041.
- Service on public agencies and officers. FL ST § 48.111.
- Service on the state. FL ST § 48.121.
- Service on a state prisoner. FL ST § 48.051.
- Service on labor unions. FL ST § 48.141.
- Service on statutory agents for certain persons. FL ST § 48.151.
- Service on nonresident motor vehicle owners. FL ST § 48.171.
- Service of process in action for possession of premises. FL ST § 48.183.
- Service on nonresidents operating aircraft or watercraft in the state. FL ST § 48.19.

f. *Crossclaims.* Service of a crossclaim on a party who has appeared in the action shall be made pursuant to FL ST RCP Rule 1.080. Service of a crossclaim against a party who has not appeared in the action shall be made in the manner provided for service of summons. FL ST RCP Rule 1.170(g).

g. *Fees.* The statutory compensation for making service shall not be increased by the simultaneous delivery or mailing of the copy of the initial pleading in conformity with FL ST RCP Rule 1.070. FL ST RCP Rule 1.070(g).

G. Hearings

1. There is no hearing required or contemplated in the Florida Rules of Civil Procedure governing the complaint and service of summons.

H. Forms

1. Official Complaint Forms for Florida

a. Caption. FL ST RCP Form 1.901.
b. Summons. FL ST RCP Form 1.902.
c. Crossclaim summons. FL ST RCP Form 1.903.
d. Third-party summons. FL ST RCP Form 1.904.
e. Notice of action, constructive service, no property. FL ST RCP Form 1.919.
f. Notice of action, constructive service, property. FL ST RCP Form 1.920.
g. Third-party complaint. FL ST RCP Form 1.948.
h. Civil cover sheet. FL ST RCP Form 1.997.
i. Fall down negligence complaint. FL ST RCP Form 1.951.
j. Notice of compliance when constitutional challenge is brought. FL ST RCP Form 1.975.

2. Complaint Forms for Florida

a. Complaint for damages; General form. FL-PP § 2:17.
b. Complaint; Negligent infliction of personal injury. FL-PP § 2:19.
c. Complaint; Fall down negligence. FL-PP § 2:20.
d. Complaint; Professional negligence. FL-PP § 2:23.
e. Complaint; Breach of contract. FL-PP § 2:24.
f. Complaint; Breach of personal services contract. FL-PP § 2:25.
g. Summons; General form. FL-PRACFORM § 3:4.
h. Summons; Natural person. FL-PRACFORM § 3:5.
i. Complaint; Assault and battery. FL-PRACFORM § 4:9.
j. Complaint; Breach of contract, general form. FL-PRACFORM § 4:17.
k. Complaint; Civil rights. FL-PRACFORM § 4:23.
l. Complaint; Conversion. FL-PRACFORM § 4:30.
m. Complaint; Employment contract. FL-PRACFORM § 4:44.
n. Complaint; False imprisonment. FL-PRACFORM § 4:46.
o. Complaint; Fraud, misrepresentation. FL-PRACFORM § 4:62.
p. Complaint; Lease, by landlord. FL-PRACFORM § 4:86.
q. Complaint; Lease, by tenant. FL-PRACFORM § 4:87.
r. Complaint; Libel. FL-PRACFORM § 4:89.
s. Complaint; Life insurance policy. FL-PRACFORM § 4:90.
t. Complaint; Medical malpractice, negligence. FL-PRACFORM § 4:95.
u. Complaint; Negligence, automobile, driver. FL-PRACFORM § 4:101.
v. Complaint; Negligence, hospital. FL-PRACFORM § 4:104.

3. Official Forms for Florida Circuit Court, Second Judicial Circuit

a. Notice of change of contact information. FL ST 2 J CIR 2007-05.

I. Checklist

(I) ❑ Matters to be considered by plaintiff
  (a) ❑ Required documents
    (1) ❑ Summons

(2) ❑ Complaint

(3) ❑ Civil cover sheet

(4) ❑ Return of execution process by process server

(5) ❑ Filing fees

(b) ❑ Supplemental documents

(1) ❑ Exhibits

(2) ❑ Notice of constitutional question

(c) ❑ Time for filing and serving complaint

(1) ❑ Service of the initial process and initial pleading should be made upon a defendant within one hundred twenty (120) days after the filing of the complaint with the court

(II) ❑ Matters to be considered by defendant

(a) ❑ Required documents

(1) ❑ Answer

(2) ❑ Certificate of service

(b) ❑ Supplemental documents

(1) ❑ Exhibits

(2) ❑ Notice of constitutional question

(c) ❑ Time for answer

(1) ❑ Unless a different time is prescribed in a statute of Florida, a defendant shall serve an answer within twenty (20) days after service of original process and the initial pleading on the defendant, or not later than the date fixed in a notice by publication

(2) ❑ A party served with a pleading stating a crossclaim against that party shall serve an answer to it within twenty (20) days after service on that party

(3) ❑ The plaintiff shall serve an answer to a counterclaim within twenty (20) days after service of the counterclaim

(4) ❑ A defendant who, before being served with process, timely returns a waiver so requested is not required to respond to the complaint until sixty (60) days after the date the defendant received the request for waiver of service; for purposes of computing any time prescribed or allowed by the Florida Rules of Civil Procedure, service of process shall be deemed effected twenty (20) days before the time required to respond to the complaint

(5) ❑ For timing requirements related to service on the state, service of motion impact, and responding when no responsive pleading is required, please see the Timing section of this document

Pleadings
Amended Complaint

Document Last Updated January 2013

A. Applicable Rules

1. *State rules*

a. Nonverification of papers. FL ST RCP Rule 1.030.

b. Process. FL ST RCP Rule 1.070.

c. Service and filing of pleadings, orders, and documents. FL ST RCP Rule 1.080.

d. Pleadings and motions. FL ST RCP Rule 1.100; FL ST RCP Rule 1.110; FL ST RCP Rule 1.120; FL ST RCP Rule 1.130; FL ST RCP Rule 1.190; FL ST § 48.193.

e. Pretrial procedure. FL ST RCP Rule 1.200.
f. Relief from judgment, decrees, or orders. FL ST RCP Rule 1.540.
g. Forms. FL ST RCP Rule 1.900.
h. Minimization of the filing of sensitive information. FL ST J ADMIN Rule 2.425.
i. Retention of court records. FL ST J ADMIN Rule 2.430.
j. Foreign attorneys. FL ST J ADMIN Rule 2.510.
k. Signature of attorneys and parties. FL ST J ADMIN Rule 2.515.
l. Paper. FL ST J ADMIN Rule 2.520.
m. Electronic filing. FL ST J ADMIN Rule 2.525.
n. Accessibility of information and technology. FL ST J ADMIN Rule 2.526.
o. Requests for accommodations by persons with disabilities. FL ST J ADMIN Rule 2.540.

2. *Local rules*
   a. Notice of change of contact information. FL ST 2 J CIR 2007-05.

B. Timing

1. *Amendment as a matter of course.* A party may amend a pleading once as a matter of course at any time before a responsive pleading is served or, if the pleading is one to which no responsive pleading is permitted and the action has not been placed on the trial calendar, may so amend it at any time within twenty (20) days after it is served. FL ST RCP Rule 1.190(a).
2. *Amendment by leave of court.* Otherwise a party may amend a pleading only by leave of court or by written consent of the adverse party. Leave of court shall be given freely when justice so requires. FL ST RCP Rule 1.190(a).
3. *Amendments in furtherance of justice.* At any time in furtherance of justice, upon such terms as may be just, the court may permit any process, proceeding, pleading, or record to be amended or material supplemental matter to be set forth in an amended or supplemental pleading. At every stage of the action the court must disregard any error or defect in the proceedings which does not affect the substantial rights of the parties. FL ST RCP Rule 1.190(e).
4. *Response to amended pleading.* A party shall plead in response to an amended pleading within ten (10) days after service of the amended pleading unless the court otherwise orders. FL ST RCP Rule 1.190(a).
5. *Computation of time*
   a. *Generally.* Computation of time shall be governed by FL ST J ADMIN Rule 2.514. FL ST RCP Rule 1.090(a). The following rules apply in computing time periods specified in any rule of procedure, local rule, court order, or statute that does not specify a method of computing time. FL ST J ADMIN Rule 2.514(a).
      i. *Period stated in days or a longer unit.* When the period is stated in days or a longer unit of time (A) exclude the day of the event that triggers the period; (B) count every day, including intermediate Saturdays, Sundays, and legal holidays; and (C) include the last day of the period, but if the last day is a Saturday, Sunday, or legal holiday, or falls within any period of time extended through an order of the chief justice under FL ST J ADMIN Rule 2.205(a)(2)(B)(iv), the period continues to run until the end of the next day that is not a Saturday, Sunday, or legal holiday and does not fall within any period of time extended through an order of the chief justice. FL ST J ADMIN Rule 2.514(a)(1).
      ii. *Period stated in hours.* When the period is stated in hours (A) begin counting immediately on the occurrence of the event that triggers the period; (B) count every hour, including hours during intermediate Saturdays, Sundays, and legal holidays; and (C) if the period would end on a Saturday, Sunday, or legal holiday, or during any period of time extended through an order of the chief justice under FL ST J ADMIN Rule 2.205(a)(2)(B)(iv), the period continues to run until the same time on the next day that is not a Saturday, Sunday, or legal holiday and does not

fall within any period of time extended through an order of the chief justice. FL ST J ADMIN Rule 2.514(a)(2).

iii. *Period stated in days less than seven (7) days.* When the period stated in days is less than seven (7) days, intermediate Saturdays, Sundays, and legal holidays shall be excluded in the computation. FL ST J ADMIN Rule 2.514(a)(3).

iv. *"Last day" defined.* Unless a different time is set by a statute, local rule, or court order, the last day ends (A) for electronic filing or for service by any means, at midnight; and (B) for filing by other means, when the clerk's office is scheduled to close. FL ST J ADMIN Rule 2.514(a)(4).

v. *"Next day" defined.* The "next day" is determined by continuing to count forward when the period is measured after an event and backward when measured before an event. FL ST J ADMIN Rule 2.514(a)(5).

vi. *"Legal holiday" defined.* "Legal holiday" means (A) the day set aside by FL ST § 110.117, for observing New Year's Day, Martin Luther King, Jr.'s Birthday, Memorial Day, Independence Day, Labor Day, Veterans' Day, Thanksgiving Day, the Friday after Thanksgiving Day, or Christmas Day, and (B) any day observed as a holiday by the clerk's office or as designated by the chief judge. FL ST J ADMIN Rule 2.514(a)(6).

b. *Additional time after service by mail or e-mail.* When a party may or must act within a specified time after service and service is made by mail or e-mail, five (5) days are added after the period that would otherwise expire under FL ST J ADMIN Rule 2.514(a). FL ST J ADMIN Rule 2.514(b).

c. *Enlargement.* When an act is required or allowed to be done at or within a specified time by order of court, by the Florida Rules of Civil Procedure, or by notice given thereunder, for cause shown the court at any time in its discretion (1) with or without notice, may order the period enlarged if request therefor is made before the expiration of the period originally prescribed or as extended by a previous order, or (2) upon motion made and notice after the expiration of the specified period, may permit the act to be done when failure to act was the result of excusable neglect, but it may not extend the time for making a motion for new trial, for rehearing, or to alter or amend a judgment; making a motion for relief from a judgment under FL ST RCP Rule 1.540(b); taking an appeal or filing a petition for certiorari; or making a motion for a directed verdict. FL ST RCP Rule 1.090(b).

d. *Unaffected by expiration of term.* The period of time provided for the doing of any act or the taking of any proceeding shall not be affected or limited by the continued existence or expiration of a term of court. The continued existence or expiration of a term of court in no way affects the power of a court to do any act or take any proceeding in any action which is or has been pending before it. FL ST RCP Rule 1.090(c).

C. General Requirements

1. *Amendments.* A party may amend a pleading once as a matter of course at any time before a responsive pleading is served or, if the pleading is one to which no responsive pleading is permitted and the action has not been placed on the trial calendar, may so amend it at any time within twenty (20) days after it is served. Otherwise a party may amend a pleading only by leave of court or by written consent of the adverse party. Leave of court shall be freely given when justice so requires. FL ST RCP Rule 1.190(a).

a. *Purpose of amendments.* Amendments can relate to the correction of mistakes, the insertion of jurisdictional averments, the correction or addition of verifications, the addition or substitution or striking out of parties, and generally the rectification of all formal defects in the pleading. The court can also allow amendments setting up an omitted counterclaim or cross-claim if the defendant failed to raise the claim through oversight, inadvertence, or excusable neglect. FL-PP § 2:151.

b. *Amendment to a pleading/Amended pleading.* A significant difference exists between an amendment to a pleading and an amended pleading. An amendment to a pleading corrects, adds to or deletes from the pleading. An amended pleading is substituted for the former pleading and the former pleading ceases to have any effect. Dee v. Southern Brewing Company, 146 Fla. 588, 1 So.2d 562 (Fla. 1941); Shannon v. McBride, 105 So.2d 16 (Fla. 2d DCA 1958); Hughes v. Home Sav. of America, F.S.B., 675 So.2d 649 (Fla. 2d DCA 1996); FL-PRACPROC § 14:2.

c. *Relation back of amendments.* When the claim or defense asserted in the amended pleading arose out of the conduct, transaction, or occurrence set forth or attempted to be set forth in the original pleading, the amendment shall relate back to the date of the original pleading. FL ST RCP Rule 1.190(c).

2. *General rules of pleading*
   a. *Claims for relief*
      i. A pleading which sets forth a claim for relief, whether an original claim, counterclaim, crossclaim, or third-party claim, must state a cause of action and shall contain
         - A short and plain statement of the grounds upon which the court's jurisdiction depends, unless the court already has jurisdiction and the claim needs no new grounds of jurisdiction to support it (For information regarding acts subjecting persons to jurisdiction, please see FL ST § 48.193),
         - A short and plain statement of the ultimate facts showing that the pleader is entitled to relief, and
         - A demand for judgment for the relief to which the pleader deems himself or herself entitled. FL ST RCP Rule 1.110(b).
      ii. Relief in the alternative or of several different types may be demanded. Every complaint shall be considered to demand general relief. FL ST RCP Rule 1.110(b).
   b. *Verification.* Except when otherwise specifically provided by these rules or an applicable statute, every pleading or other document of a party represented by an attorney need not be verified or accompanied by an affidavit. FL ST RCP Rule 1.030. When filing an action for foreclosure of a mortgage on residential real property the complaint shall be verified. When verification of a document is required, the document filed shall include an oath, affirmation, or the following statement: "Under penalty of perjury, I declare that I have read the foregoing, and the facts alleged therein are true and correct to the best of my knowledge and belief." FL ST RCP Rule 1.110(b).
   c. *Separate statements.* All averments of claim or defense shall be made in consecutively numbered paragraphs, the contents of each of which shall be limited as far as practicable to a statement of a single set of circumstances, and a paragraph may be referred to by number in all subsequent pleadings. Each claim founded upon a separate transaction or occurrence and each defense other than denials shall be stated in a separate count or defense when a separation facilitates the clear presentation of the matter set forth. FL ST RCP Rule 1.110(f).
   d. *Statements adopted by reference.* Statements in a pleading may be adopted by reference in a different part of the same pleading, in another pleading, or in any motion. FL ST RCP Rule 1.130(b).
   e. *Joinder of causes of action; Consistency.* A pleader may set up in the same action as many claims or causes of action or defenses in the same right as the pleader has, and claims for relief may be stated in the alternative if separate items make up the cause of action, or if two (2) or more causes of action are joined. A party may also set forth two (2) or more statements of a claim or defense alternatively, either in one (1) count or defense or in separate counts or defenses. When two (2) or more statements are made in the alternative and one (1) of them, if made independently, would be sufficient, the pleading is not made insufficient by the insufficiency of one (1) or more of the alternative statements. A party may also state as many separate claims or defenses as that party has, regardless of consistency and whether based on legal or equitable grounds or both. All pleadings shall be construed so as to do substantial justice. FL ST RCP Rule 1.110(g).
   f. *Subsequent pleadings.* When the nature of an action permits pleadings subsequent to final judgment and the jurisdiction of the court over the parties has not terminated, the initial pleading subsequent to final judgment shall be designated a supplemental complaint or petition. The action shall then proceed in the same manner and time as though the supplemental complaint or petition were the initial pleading in the action, including the issuance of any needed process. FL ST RCP Rule 1.110(h) shall not apply to proceedings that may be initiated by motion under the Florida Rules of Civil Procedure. FL ST RCP Rule 1.110(h).
   g. *Pleading basis for service.* When service of process is to be made under statutes authorizing service

on nonresidents of Florida, it is sufficient to plead the basis for service in the language of the statute without pleading the facts supporting service. FL ST RCP Rule 1.070(h).

h. *Forms of pleadings.* Forms of action and technical forms for seeking relief and of pleas, pleadings, or motions are abolished. FL ST RCP Rule 1.110(a).

3. *Complaint; Generally*
   a. *Purpose.* The purpose of a complaint is to advise the court and the defendant of the nature of a cause of action asserted by the plaintiff. FL-PP § 2:12.
   b. *Sufficiency of complaint.* A complaint will be found to be insufficient if it contains only general conclusory allegations unsupported by any facts. The test to determine whether a complaint is sufficient is whether, if the factual allegations of the complaint are established, the plaintiff will be legally or equitably entitled to the claimed relief. Pizzi v. Central Bank & Trust Co., 250 So.2d 895, 896 (Fla. 1971); Bowen v. G H C Properties, Limited, 251 So.2d 359, 361 (Fla. 1st DCA 1971); FL-PP § 2:12. In determining the sufficiency of the complaint to state a cause of action, all allegations of the complaint are taken as true, and possible affirmative defenses are not considered. Strickland v. Commerce Loan Co. of Jacksonville, 158 So.2d 814 (Fla. 1st DCA 1963); FL-PP § 2:12.
      i. The issues for trial in Florida must be settled by the pleadings. The issues cannot be raised by discovery. FL-PRACPROC § 7:6.
      ii. Causes of action may be pleaded alternatively in the same count or in different counts and against the same or different defendants as long as the joinder of parties is proper. FL-PRACPROC § 7:6.
      iii. Each count must state a cause of action. Each independent cause of action should be pleaded in a separate count. FL-PRACPROC § 7:6.
      iv. Incorporation by reference of all allegations from one count to another is not proper. Separate counts facilitate reference to the pleading in which they appear in other pleadings, motions or papers as well as the assertion of defenses against some, but not all, causes of action. Some defenses may not apply to the initial pleading as a whole. FL-PRACPROC § 7:6.
4. *Pleading special matters*
   a. *Capacity.* It is not necessary to aver the capacity of a party to sue or be sued, the authority of a party to sue or be sued in a representative capacity, or the legal existence of an organized association of persons that is made a party, except to the extent required to show the jurisdiction of the court. The initial pleading served on behalf of a minor party shall specifically aver the age of the minor party. When a party desires to raise an issue as to the legal existence of any party, the capacity of any party to sue or be sued, or the authority of a party to sue or be sued in a representative capacity, that party shall do so by specific negative averment which shall include such supporting particulars as are peculiarly within the pleader's knowledge. FL ST RCP Rule 1.120(a).
   b. *Fraud, mistake, condition of the mind.* In all averments of fraud or mistake, the circumstances constituting fraud or mistake shall be stated with such particularity as the circumstances may permit. Malice, intent, knowledge, mental attitude, and other condition of mind of a person may be averred generally. FL ST RCP Rule 1.120(b).
   c. *Conditions precedent.* In pleading the performance or occurrence of conditions precedent, it is sufficient to aver generally that all conditions precedent have been performed or have occurred. A denial of performance or occurrence shall be made specifically and with particularity. FL ST RCP Rule 1.120(c).
   d. *Official document or act.* In pleading an official document or official act it is sufficient to aver that the document was issued or the act done in compliance with law. FL ST RCP Rule 1.120(c).
   e. *Judgment or decree.* In pleading a judgment or decree of a domestic or foreign court, a judicial or quasi-judicial tribunal, or a board or officer, it is sufficient to aver the judgment or decree without setting forth matter showing jurisdiction to render it. FL ST RCP Rule 1.120(e).
   f. *Time and place.* For the purpose of testing the sufficiency of a pleading, averments of time and place are material and shall be considered like all other averments of material matter. FL ST RCP Rule 1.120(f).

g. *Special damage.* When items of special damage are claimed, they shall be specifically stated. FL ST RCP Rule 1.120(g).

5. *Parties*

a. *Parties generally.* Every action may be prosecuted in the name of the real party in interest, but a personal representative, administrator, guardian, trustee of an express trust, a party with whom or in whose name a contract has been made for the benefit of another, or a party expressly authorized by statute may sue in that person's own name without joining the party for whose benefit the action is brought. All persons having an interest in the subject of the action and in obtaining the relief demanded may join as plaintiffs and any person may be made a defendant who has or claims an interest adverse to the plaintiff. Any person may at any time be made a party if that person's presence is necessary or proper to a complete determination of the cause. Persons having a united interest may be joined on the same side as plaintiffs or defendants, and anyone who refuses to join may for such reason be made a defendant. FL ST RCP Rule 1.210(a).

b. *Minors or incompetent persons.* When a minor or incompetent person has a representative, such as a guardian or other like fiduciary, the representative may sue or defend on behalf of the minor or incompetent person. A minor or incompetent person who does not have a duly appointed representative may sue by next friend or by a guardian ad litem. The court shall appoint a guardian ad litem for a minor or incompetent person not otherwise represented in an action or shall make such other order as it deems proper for the protection of the minor or incompetent person. FL ST RCP Rule 1.210(b).

c. For survivor and substitution of parties information, please see FL ST RCP Rule 1.260.

6. *Counterclaims and crossclaims*

a. *Compulsory counterclaims.* A pleading shall state as a counterclaim any claim which at the time of serving the pleading the pleader has against any opposing party, provided it arises out of the transaction or occurrence that is the subject matter of the opposing party's claim and does not require for its adjudication the presence of third parties over whom the court cannot acquire jurisdiction. But the pleader need not state a claim if (1) at the time the action was commenced the claim was the subject of another pending action, or (2) the opposing party brought suit upon that party's claim by attachment or other process by which the court did not acquire jurisdiction to render a personal judgment on the claim and the pleader is not stating a counterclaim under this rule. FL ST RCP Rule 1.170(a).

b. *Permissive counterclaim.* A pleading may state as a counterclaim any claim against an opposing party not arising out of the transaction or occurrence that is the subject matter of the opposing party's claim. FL ST RCP Rule 1.170(b).

c. *Counterclaim exceeding opposing claim.* A counterclaim may or may not diminish or defeat the recovery sought by the opposing party. It may claim relief exceeding in amount or different in kind from that sought in the pleading of the opposing party. FL ST RCP Rule 1.170(c).

d. *Counterclaim against the State.* The Florida Rules of Civil Procedure shall not be construed to enlarge beyond the limits established by law the right to assert counterclaims or to claim credits against the state or any of its subdivisions or other governmental organizations thereof subject to suit or against a municipal corporation or against an officer, agency, or administrative board of the state. FL ST RCP Rule 1.170(d).

e. *Counterclaim maturing or acquired after pleading.* A claim which matured or was acquired by the pleader after serving the pleading may be presented as a counterclaim by supplemental pleading with the permission of the court. FL ST RCP Rule 1.170(e).

f. *Omitted counterclaim or crossclaim.* When a pleader fails to set up a counterclaim or crossclaim through oversight, inadvertence, or excusable neglect, or when justice requires, the pleader may set up the counterclaim or crossclaim by amendment with leave of the court. FL ST RCP Rule 1.170(f).

g. *Crossclaim against co-party.* A pleading may state as a crossclaim any claim by one party against a co-party arising out of the transaction or occurrence that is the subject matter of either the original action or a counterclaim therein, or relating to any property that is the subject matter of the original action. The crossclaim may include a claim that the party against whom it is asserted is or may be liable to the crossclaimant for all or part of a claim asserted in the action against the crossclaimant. Service of a crossclaim on a party who has appeared in the action shall be made pursuant to FL ST RCP Rule 1.080. Service of a crossclaim against a party who has not appeared in the action shall be made in the manner provided for service of summons. FL ST RCP Rule 1.170(g).

h. *Additional parties may be brought in.* When the presence of parties other than those to the original action is required to grant complete relief in the determination of a counterclaim or crossclaim, they shall be named in the counterclaim or crossclaim and be served with process and shall be parties to the action thereafter if jurisdiction of them can be obtained and their joinder will not deprive the court of jurisdiction of the action. FL ST RCP Rule 1.250(b) and FL ST RCP Rule 1.250(c) apply to parties brought in under FL ST RCP Rule 1.170(h). FL ST RCP Rule 1.170(h).

i. *Separate trials; Separate judgment.* If the court orders separate trials as provided in FL ST RCP Rule 1.270(b), judgment on a counterclaim or crossclaim may be rendered when the court has jurisdiction to do so even if a claim of the opposing party has been dismissed or otherwise disposed of. FL ST RCP Rule 1.170(i).

j. *Demand exceeding jurisdiction; Transfer of action.* If the demand of any counterclaim or crossclaim exceeds the jurisdiction of the court in which the action is pending, the action shall be transferred forthwith to the court of the same county having jurisdiction of the demand in the counterclaim or crossclaim with only such alterations in the pleadings as are essential. The court shall order the transfer of the action and the transmittal of all papers in it to the proper court if the party asserting the demand exceeding the jurisdiction deposits with the court having jurisdiction a sum sufficient to pay the clerk's service charge in the court to which the action is transferred at the time of filing the counterclaim or crossclaim. Thereupon the original papers and deposit shall be transmitted and filed with a certified copy of the order. The court to which the action is transferred shall have full power and jurisdiction over the demands of all parties. Failure to make the service charge deposit at the time the counterclaim or crossclaim is filed, or within such further time as the court may allow, shall reduce a claim for damages to an amount within the jurisdiction of the court where the action is pending and waive the claim in other cases. FL ST RCP Rule 1.170(j).

7. *Misjoinder and nonjoinder of parties*

a. *Misjoinder.* Misjoinder of parties is not a ground for dismissal of an action. Any claim against a party may be severed and proceeded with separately. FL ST RCP Rule 1.250(a).

b. *Dropping parties.* Parties may be dropped by an adverse party in the manner provided for voluntary dismissal in FL ST RCP Rule 1.420(a)(1) subject to the exception stated in FL ST RCP Rule 1.420. If notice of lis pendens has been filed in the action against a party so dropped, the notice of dismissal shall be recorded and cancels the notice of lis pendens without the necessity of a court order. Parties may be dropped by order of court on its own initiative or the motion of any party at any stage of the action on such terms as are just. FL ST RCP Rule 1.250(b).

c. *Adding parties.* Parties may be added once as a matter of course within the same time that pleadings can be so amended under FL ST RCP Rule 1.190(a). If amendment by leave of court or stipulation of the parties is permitted, parties may be added in the amended pleading without further order of court. Parties may be added by order of court on its own initiative or on motion of any party at any stage of the action and on such terms as are just. FL ST RCP Rule 1.250(c).

8. *Jury demand*

a. *Right preserved.* The right of trial by jury as declared by the Constitution or by statute shall be preserved to the parties inviolate. FL ST RCP Rule 1.430(a).

b. *Demand.* Any party may demand a trial by jury of any issue triable of right by a jury by serving upon the other party a demand therefor in writing at any time after commencement of the action and not later than ten (10) days after the service of the last pleading directed to such issue. The demand may be indorsed upon a pleading of the party. FL ST RCP Rule 1.430(b).

c. *Specification of issues.* In the demand a party may specify the issues that the party wishes so tried;

otherwise, the party is deemed to demand trial by jury for all issues so triable. FL ST RCP Rule 1.430(c).

i. If a party has demanded trial by jury for only some of the issues, any other party may serve a demand for trial by jury of any other or all of the issues triable by jury ten (10) days after service of the demand or such lesser time as the court may order. FL ST RCP Rule 1.430(c).

d. *Waiver.* A party who fails to serve a demand as required by FL ST RCP Rule 1.430 waives trial by jury. FL ST RCP Rule 1.430(d).

i. If waived, a jury trial may not be granted without the consent of the parties, but the court may allow an amendment in the proceedings to demand a trial by jury or order a trial by jury on its own motion. FL ST RCP Rule 1.430(d).

ii. A demand for trial by jury may not be withdrawn without the consent of the parties. FL ST RCP Rule 1.430(d).

9. *Arbitration and mediation*

a. *Referral to arbitration and mediation.* Except as hereinafter provided or as otherwise prohibited by law, the presiding judge may enter an order referring all or any part of a contested civil matter to mediation or arbitration. The parties to any contested civil matter may file a written stipulation to mediate or arbitrate any issue between them at any time. Such stipulation shall be incorporated into the order of referral. FL ST RCP Rule 1.700(a).

b. *Arbitration*

i. *Exclusions.* A civil action shall be ordered to arbitration or arbitration in conjunction with mediation upon stipulation of the parties. A civil action may be ordered to arbitration or arbitration in conjunction with mediation upon motion of any party or by the court, if the judge determines the action to be of such a nature that arbitration could be of benefit to the litigants or the court. FL ST RCP Rule 1.800.

- Under no circumstances may the following categories of actions be referred to arbitration: (1) bond estreatures; (2) habeas corpus or other extraordinary writs; (3) bond validations; (4) civil or criminal contempt; (5) such other matters as may be specified by order of the chief judge in the circuit. FL ST RCP Rule 1.800.

ii. For more information regarding arbitration, please see FL ST RCP Rule 1.810; FL ST RCP Rule 1.820; FL ST RCP Rule 1.830.

c. *Mediation.* For more information regarding mediation, please see FL ST RCP Rule 1.710; FL ST RCP Rule 1.720; FL ST RCP Rule 1.730; and FL ST RCP Rule 1.750.

10. *Rules of court*

a. *Rules of civil procedure.* The Florida Rules of Civil Procedure apply to all actions of a civil nature and all special statutory proceedings in the circuit courts and county courts except those to which the Florida Probate Rules, the Florida Family Law Rules of Procedure, or the Small Claims Rules apply. FL ST RCP Rule 1.010.

i. The form, content, procedure, and time for pleading in all special statutory proceedings shall be as prescribed by the statutes governing the proceeding unless the Florida Rules of Civil Procedure specifically provide to the contrary. FL ST RCP Rule 1.010.

ii. The Florida Rules of Civil Procedure shall be construed to secure the just, speedy, and inexpensive determination of every action. FL ST RCP Rule 1.010.

b. *Rules of judicial administration.* The Florida Rules of Judicial Administration shall apply to administrative matters in all courts to which the Florida Rules of Judicial Administration are applicable by their terms. The Florida Rules of Judicial Administration shall be construed to secure the speedy and inexpensive determination of every proceeding to which they are applicable. The Florida Rules of Judicial Administration shall supersede all conflicting rules and statutes. FL ST J ADMIN Rule 2.110.

11. *Notice of change of contact information.* The Clerk shall provide a change of address and/or telephone

number form for use by attorneys and pro se litigants. With any change of address and/or telephone number, attorneys and pro se litigants governed by FL ST J ADMIN Rule 2.515 will provide to the Clerk and all parties promptly the change of address and/or telephone number form. This form should be submitted only once to the Clerk, who will then make the address and/or telephone number change in all court divisions. FL ST 2 J CIR 2007-05.

D. Documents

1. *Required documents*
   a. *Amended complaint.* See the General Requirements section of this document for the content of an amended complaint. If a party files a motion to amend a pleading, the party shall attach the proposed amended pleading to the motion. FL ST RCP Rule 1.190(a). See the KeyRules Florida Circuit Court Motion for Leave to Amend document for further information.
      i. *Notices to persons with disabilities.* See the Format section of this KeyRules document for further information.
   b. *Certificate of service.* When any attorney certifies in substance: "I certify that a copy hereof has been furnished to (here insert name or names and addresses used for service) by (e-mail) (delivery) (mail) (fax) on .... (date) ....________________ Attorney" the certificate is taken as prima facie proof of such service in compliance with FL ST J ADMIN Rule 2.516. FL ST J ADMIN Rule 2.516(f).
2. *Supplemental documents*
   a. *Exhibits.* All bonds, notes, bills of exchange, contracts, accounts, or documents upon which action may be brought or defense made, or a copy thereof or a copy of the portions thereof material to the pleadings, shall be incorporated in or attached to the pleading. No papers shall be unnecessarily annexed as exhibits. The pleadings shall contain no unnecessary recitals of deeds, documents, contracts, or other instruments. Any exhibit attached to a pleading shall be considered a part of the pleadings for all purposes. FL ST RCP Rule 1.130(a).
   b. *Notice of constitutional question.* A party that files a pleading, written motion, or other paper drawing into question the constitutionality of a state statute or a county or municipal charter, ordinance, or franchise must promptly (1) file a notice of constitutional question stating the question and identifying the paper that raises it; and (2) serve the notice and the pleading, written motion, or other paper drawing into question the constitutionality of a state statute or a county or municipal charter, ordinance, or franchise on the Attorney General or the state attorney of the judicial circuit in which the action is pending, by either certified or registered mail. Service of the notice and pleading, written motion, or other paper does not require joinder of the Attorney General or the state attorney as a party to the action. FL ST RCP Rule 1.071.

E. Format

1. *Documents; Type and size.* Documents subject to the exceptions set forth in FL ST J ADMIN Rule 2.525(d) shall be filed on recycled paper measuring eight and one half by eleven (8 1/2 by 11) inches. For purposes of FL ST J ADMIN Rule 2.520, paper is recycled if it contains a minimum content of fifty (50) percent waste paper. Xerographic reduction of legal-size (eight and one half by fourteen (8 1/2 by 14) inches) documents to letter size (eight and one half by eleven (8 1/2 by 11) inches) is prohibited. All other documents filed by electronic transmission shall be filed in a format capable of being printed in a format consistent with the provisions of FL ST J ADMIN Rule 2.250. FL ST J ADMIN Rule 2.520(b).
   a. *Exhibits.* Any exhibit or attachment filed with pleadings or papers may be filed in its original size. FL ST J ADMIN Rule 2.520(c).
   b. *Recording space.* On all papers and documents prepared and filed by the court or by any party to a proceeding which are to be recorded in the public records of any county, including but not limited to final money judgments and notices of lis pendens, a three (3) inch by three (3) inch space at the top right-hand corner on the first page and a one (1) inch by three (3) inch space at the top right-hand corner on each subsequent page shall be left blank and reserved for use by the clerk of court. FL ST J ADMIN Rule 2.520(d).
      i. *Exceptions to recording space.* Any papers or documents created by persons or entities over

which the filing party has no control, including but not limited to wills, codicils, trusts, or other testamentary documents; documents prepared or executed by any public officer; documents prepared, executed, acknowledged, or proved outside of the State of Florida; or documents created by State or Federal government agencies, may be filed without the space required by FL ST J ADMIN Rule 2.520. FL ST J ADMIN Rule 2.520(e).

c. *Noncompliance.* No clerk of court is permitted to refuse to file any document or paper because of noncompliance with the Florida Rules of Judicial Administration. However, upon request of the clerk of court, noncomplying documents must be resubmitted in accordance with the formatting rules. FL ST J ADMIN Rule 2.520(f).

2. *Caption.* Every pleading, motion, order, judgment, or other paper shall have a caption containing the name of the court, the file number, and except for in rem proceedings, including forfeiture proceedings, the name of the first party on each side with an appropriate indication of other parties, and a designation identifying the party filing it and its nature or the nature of the order, as the case may be. In any in rem proceeding, every pleading, motion, order, judgment, or other paper shall have a caption containing the name of the court, the file number, the style "In re" (followed by the name or general description of the property), and a designation of the person or entity filing it and its nature or the nature of the order, as the case may be. In an in rem forfeiture proceeding, the style shall be "In re forfeiture of" (followed by the name of the general description of the property). All papers filed in the action shall be styled in such a manner as to indicate clearly the subject matter of the paper and the party requesting or obtaining relief. FL ST RCP Rule 1.100(c)(1).

3. *Writing and written defined.* Writing or written means a document containing information, an application, or a stipulation. FL ST RCP Rule 1.080(c).

4. *Rule abbreviations*

   a. The Florida Rules of Civil Procedure and shall be abbreviated as Fla.R.Civ.P. FL ST RCP Rule 1.010.

   b. The Florida Rules of Judicial Administration shall be abbreviated as Fla. R. Jud. Admin. FL ST J ADMIN Rule 2.110.

5. *Nonverification.* Except when otherwise specifically provided by the Florida Rules of Civil Procedure or an applicable statute, every pleading or other document of a party represented by an attorney need not be verified or accompanied by an affidavit. FL ST RCP Rule 1.030; FL ST J ADMIN Rule 2.515(a).

6. *Attorney signature*

   a. *Attorney signature.* Every pleading and other document of a party represented by an attorney shall be signed by at least one (1) attorney of record in that attorney's individual name whose current record Florida Bar address, telephone number, including area code, primary e-mail address and secondary e-mail addresses, if any, and Florida Bar number shall be stated, and who shall be duly licensed to practice law in Florida or who shall have received permission to appear in the particular case as provided in FL ST J ADMIN Rule 2.510. FL ST J ADMIN Rule 2.515(a).

      i. The attorney may be required by the court to give the address of, and to vouch for the attorney's authority to represent, the party. FL ST J ADMIN Rule 2.515(a).

      ii. The signature of an attorney shall constitute a certificate by the attorney that the attorney has read the pleading or other document; that to the best of the attorney's knowledge, information, and belief there is good ground to support it; and that it is not interposed for delay. FL ST J ADMIN Rule 2.515(a).

      iii. If a pleading is not signed or is signed with intent to defeat the purpose of FL ST J ADMIN Rule 2.515, it may be stricken and the action may proceed as though the pleading or other document had not been served. FL ST J ADMIN Rule 2.515(a).

   b. *Pro se litigant signature.* A party who is not represented by an attorney shall sign any pleading or other paper and state the party's address and telephone number, including area code. FL ST J ADMIN Rule 2.515(b).

c. *Form of signature*

i. The signatures required on pleadings and documents by FL ST J ADMIN Rule 2.515(a) and FL ST J ADMIN Rule 2.515(b) may be:

- Original signatures;
- Original signatures that have been reproduced by electronic means, such as on electronically transmitted documents or photocopied documents;
- Electronic signatures using the "/s/," "s/," or "/s" formats by or at the direction of the person signing; or
- Any other signature format authorized by general law, so long as the clerk where the proceeding is pending has the capability of receiving and has obtained approval from the Supreme Court of Florida to accept pleadings and documents with that signature format. FL ST J ADMIN Rule 2.515(c)(1).

ii. An attorney, party, or other person who files a pleading or paper by electronic transmission that does not contain the original signature of that attorney, party, or other person shall file that identical pleading or paper in paper form containing an original signature of that attorney, party, or other person (hereinafter called the follow-up filing) immediately thereafter. The follow-up filing is not required if the Supreme Court of Florida has entered an order directing the clerk of court to discontinue accepting the follow-up filing. FL ST J ADMIN Rule 2.515(c)(2).

7. *Forms*

a. *Process.* The forms of process, notice of lis pendens, and notice of action provided in the Florida Rules of Civil Procedure are sufficient. Variations from the forms do not void process or notices that are otherwise sufficient. FL ST RCP Rule 1.900(a).

b. *Other forms.* The other forms provided in the Florida Rules of Civil Procedure are sufficient for the matters that are covered by them. So long as the substance is expressed without prolixity, the forms may be varied to meet the facts of a particular case. FL ST RCP Rule 1.900(b).

c. *Formal matters.* Captions, except for the designation of the paper, are omitted from the forms provided in the Florida Rules of Civil Procedure. A general form of caption is the first form provided. Signatures are omitted from pleadings and motions. FL ST RCP Rule 1.900(c).

8. *Notices to persons with disabilities.* All notices of court proceedings to be held in a public facility, and all process compelling appearance at such proceedings, shall include the following statement in bold face, fourteen (14) point Times New Roman or Courier font: "If you are a person with a disability who needs any accommodation in order to participate in this proceeding, you are entitled, at no cost to you, to the provision of certain assistance. Please contact [identify applicable court personnel by name, address, and telephone number] at least seven (7) days before your scheduled court appearance, or immediately upon receiving this notification if the time before the scheduled appearance is less than seven (7) days; if you are hearing or voice impaired, call 711." FL ST J ADMIN Rule 2.540(c)(1).

9. *Minimization of the filing of sensitive information*

a. *Limitations for court filings.* Unless authorized by FL ST J ADMIN Rule 2.425(b), statute, another rule of court, or the court orders otherwise, designated sensitive information filed with the court must be limited to the following format:

i. The initials of a person known to be a minor;

ii. The year of birth of a person's birth date;

iii. No portion of any: Social security number, Bank account number, Credit card account number, Charge account number, or Debit account number;

iv. The last four digits of any: Taxpayer identification number (TIN), Employee identification number, Driver's license number, Passport number, Telephone number, Financial account number, except as set forth in FL ST J ADMIN Rule 2.425(a)(3), Brokerage account number, Insurance policy account number, Loan account number, Customer account number, or Patient or health care number;

v. A truncated version of any: Email address, Computer user name, Password, or Personal identification number (PIN); and

vi. A truncated version of any other sensitive information as provided by court order. FL ST J ADMIN Rule 2.425(a).

b. *Exceptions.* FL ST J ADMIN Rule 2.425(a) does not apply to the following:

i. An account number which identifies the property alleged to be the subject of a proceeding;

ii. The record of an administrative or agency proceeding;

iii. The record in appellate or review proceedings;

iv. The birth date of a minor whenever the birth date is necessary for the court to establish or maintain subject matter jurisdiction;

v. The name of a minor in any order relating to parental responsibility, time-sharing, or child support;

vi. The name of a minor in any document or order affecting the minor's ownership of real property;

vii. The birth date of a party in a writ of attachment or notice to payor;

viii. In traffic and criminal proceedings: a pro se filing; a court filing that is related to a criminal matter or investigation and that is prepared before the filing of a criminal charge or is not filed as part of any docketed criminal case; an arrest or search warrant or any information in support thereof; a charging document and an affidavit or other documents filed in support of any charging document, including any driving records; a statement of particulars; discovery material introduced into evidence or otherwise filed with the court; and all information necessary for the proper issuance and execution of a subpoena duces tecum;

ix. Information used by the clerk for case maintenance purposes or the courts for case management purposes; and

x. Information which is relevant and material to an issue before the court. FL ST J ADMIN Rule 2.425(b).

c. *Remedies.* Upon motion by a party or interested person or sua sponte by the court, the court may order remedies, sanctions or both for a violation of FL ST J ADMIN Rule 2.425(a). Following notice and an opportunity to respond, the court may impose sanctions if such filing was not made in good faith. FL ST J ADMIN Rule 2.425(c).

d. *Motions not restricted.* FL ST J ADMIN Rule 2.425 does not restrict a party's right to move for protective order, to move to file documents under seal, or to request a determination of the confidentiality of records. FL ST J ADMIN Rule 2.425(d).

e. *Application.* FL ST J ADMIN Rule 2.425 does not affect the application of constitutional provisions, statutes, or rules of court regarding confidential information or access to public information. FL ST J ADMIN Rule 2.425(e).

F. Filing and Service Requirements

1. *Filing requirements.* All original documents must be filed with the court either before service or immediately thereafter, unless otherwise provided for by general law or other rules. If the original of any bond or other document is not placed in the court file, a certified copy must be so placed by the clerk. FL ST J ADMIN Rule 2.516(d). All documents shall be filed in conformity with the requirements of FL ST J ADMIN Rule 2.525. FL ST RCP Rule 1.080(b). All documents filed in any court shall be filed by electronic transmission in accordance with FL ST J ADMIN Rule 2.525. "Documents" means pleadings, motions, petitions, memoranda, briefs, notices, exhibits, declarations, affidavits, orders, judgments, decrees, writs, opinions, and any other paper or writing submitted to a court. FL ST J ADMIN Rule 2.520(a). All documents that are court records, as defined in FL ST J ADMIN Rule 2.430(a)(1), must be filed by electronic transmission, provided that: (1) the clerk has the ability to accept and retain such documents; (2) the clerk or the chief judge of the circuit has requested permission to accept documents filed by electronic transmission; and (3) the supreme court has entered an order granting permission to the clerk to accept documents filed by electronic transmission. FL ST J ADMIN Rule 2.525(c)(1).

a. *Definition.* "Electronic transmission of documents" means the sending of information by electronic

signals to, by or from a court or clerk, which when received can be transformed and stored or transmitted on paper, microfilm, magnetic storage device, optical imaging system, CD-ROM, flash drive, other electronic data storage system, server, case maintenance system ("CM"), electronic court filing ("ECF") system, statewide or local electronic portal ("e-portal"), or other electronic record keeping system authorized by the supreme court in a format sufficient to communicate the information on the original document in a readable format. Electronic transmission of documents includes electronic mail ("e-mail") and any internet-based transmission procedure, and may include procedures allowing for documents to be signed or verified by electronic means. FL ST J ADMIN Rule 2.525(a).

i. The filing of documents with the court as required by the Florida Rules of Judicial Administration must be made by filing them with the clerk in accordance with FL ST J ADMIN Rule 2.525, except that the judge may permit documents to be filed with the judge, in which event the judge must note the filing date before him or her on the documents and transmit them to the clerk. The date of filing is that shown on the face of the document by the judge's notation or the clerk's time stamp, whichever is earlier. FL ST J ADMIN Rule 2.516(e).

b. *Application.* Any court or clerk of the court may accept the electronic transmission of documents for filing after the clerk, together with input from the chief judge of the circuit, has obtained approval of the procedures and program for doing so from the Supreme Court of Florida. FL ST J ADMIN Rule 2.525(b).

c. *Exceptions*

i. Paper documents and other submissions may be manually submitted to the clerk or court:

- When the clerk does not have the ability to accept and retain documents by electronic filing or has not had ECF Procedures approved by the supreme court;
- For filing by any self-represented party or any self-represented nonparty unless specific ECF Procedures provide a means to file documents electronically. However, any self-represented nonparty that is a governmental or public agency and any other agency, partnership, corporation, or business entity acting on behalf of any governmental or public agency may file documents by electronic transmission if such entity has the capability of filing documents electronically;
- For filing by attorneys excused from e-mail service in accordance with FL ST J ADMIN Rule 2.516(b);
- When submitting evidentiary exhibits or filing non-documentary materials;
- When the filing involves documents in excess of twenty-five (25) megabytes (25MB) in size. For such filings, documents may be transmitted using an electronic storage medium that the clerk has the ability to accept, which may include a CD-ROM, flash drive, or similar storage medium;
- When filed in open court, as permitted by the court;
- When paper filing is permitted by any approved statewide or local ECF procedures; and
- If any court determines that justice so requires. FL ST J ADMIN Rule 2.525(d).

ii. Any document in paper form submitted under FL ST J ADMIN Rule 2.525(d) is filed when it is received by the clerk or court and the clerk shall immediately thereafter convert any filed paper document to an electronic document. "Convert to an electronic document" means optically capturing an image of a paper document and using character recognition software to recover as much of the document's text as practicable and then indexing and storing the document in the official court file. FL ST J ADMIN Rule 2.525(c)(4).

iii. Any storage medium submitted under FL ST J ADMIN Rule 2.525(d)(5) is filed when received by the clerk or court and the clerk shall immediately thereafter transfer the electronic documents from the storage device to the official court file. FL ST J ADMIN Rule 2.525(c)(5).

iv. If the filer of any paper document authorized under FL ST J ADMIN Rule 2.525(d) provides a self-addressed, postage-paid envelope for return of the paper document after it is converted to

electronic form by the clerk, the clerk shall place the paper document in the envelope and deposit it in the mail. Except when a paper document is required to be maintained, the clerk may recycle any filed paper document that is not to be returned to the filer. FL ST J ADMIN Rule 2.525(c)(6).

v. The clerk may convert any paper document filed before the effective date of FL ST J ADMIN Rule 2.525 to an electronic document. Unless the clerk is required to maintain the paper document, if the paper document has been converted to an electronic document by the clerk, the paper document is no longer part of the official court file and may be removed and recycled. FL ST J ADMIN Rule 2.525(c)(7).

d. *Official court file.* For information on what constitutes the official court file, please see FL ST J ADMIN Rule 2.525(c)(2), FL ST J ADMIN Rule 2.525(c)(3).

e. *Administration.* All attorneys, parties, or other persons using this rule to file documents are required to make arrangements with the court or clerk for the payment of any charges authorized by general law or the supreme court before filing any document by electronic transmission. FL ST J ADMIN Rule 2.525(f)(2).

f. *Filing date.* The filing date for an electronically transmitted document is the date and time that such filing is acknowledged by an electronic stamp or otherwise, pursuant to any procedure set forth in any ECF Procedures approved by the supreme court, or the date the last page of such filing is received by the court or clerk. FL ST J ADMIN Rule 2.525(f)(3).

g. *Accessibility.* All documents transmitted in any electronic form under FL ST J ADMIN Rule 2.525 must comply with the accessibility requirements of FL ST J ADMIN Rule 2.526. FL ST J ADMIN Rule 2.525(g).

2. *Service requirements.* Every pleading subsequent to the initial pleading, all orders, and every other document filed in the action must be served in conformity with the requirements of FL ST J ADMIN Rule 2.516. FL ST RCP Rule 1.080(a).

a. *Service; When required.* Unless the court otherwise orders, or a statute or supreme court administrative order specifies a different means of service, every pleading subsequent to the initial pleading and every other document filed in any court proceeding, except applications for witness subpoenas and documents served by formal notice or required to be served in the manner provided for service of formal notice, must be served in accordance with FL ST J ADMIN Rule 2.516 on each party. No service need be made on parties against whom a default has been entered, except that pleadings asserting new or additional claims against them must be served in the manner provided for service of summons. FL ST J ADMIN Rule 2.516(a).

b. *Service; How made.* When service is required or permitted to be made upon a party represented by an attorney, service must be made upon the attorney unless service upon the party is ordered by the court. FL ST J ADMIN Rule 2.516(b).

i. *Service by electronic mail ("e-mail").* All documents required or permitted to be served on another party must be served by e-mail, unless FL ST J ADMIN Rule 2.516 otherwise provides. When, in addition to service by e-mail, the sender also utilizes another means of service provided for in FL ST J ADMIN Rule 2.516(b)(2), any differing time limits and other provisions applicable to that other means of service control. FL ST J ADMIN Rule 2.516(b)(1). Any document electronically transmitted to a court or clerk must also be served on all parties and interested persons in accordance with the applicable rules of court. FL ST J ADMIN Rule 2.525(e)(2).

- *Service on attorneys.* Upon appearing in a proceeding, an attorney must serve a designation of a primary e-mail address and may designate no more than two (2) secondary e-mail addresses. Thereafter, service must be directed to all designated e-mail addresses in that proceeding. Every document filed by an attorney thereafter must include the primary e-mail address of that attorney and any secondary e-mail addresses. If an attorney does not designate any e-mail address for service, documents may be served on that attorney at the e-mail address on record with The Florida Bar. FL ST J ADMIN Rule 2.516(b)(1)(A).

- *Exception to e-mail service on attorneys.* Service by an attorney on another attorney must be made by e-mail unless excused by the court. Upon motion by an attorney demonstrating that the attorney has no e-mail account and lacks access to the Internet at the attorney's office, the court may excuse the attorney from the requirements of e-mail service. Service on and by an attorney excused by the court from e-mail service must be by the means provided in FL ST J ADMIN Rule 2.516(b)(2). FL ST J ADMIN Rule 2.516(b)(1)(B).
- *Service on and by parties not represented by an attorney.* Any party not represented by an attorney may serve a designation of a primary e-mail address and also may designate no more than two (2) secondary e-mail addresses to which service must be directed in that proceeding by the means provided in FL ST J ADMIN Rule 2.516(b)(1). If a party not represented by an attorney does not designate an e-mail address for service in a proceeding, service on and by that party must be by the means provided in FL ST J ADMIN Rule 2.516(b)(2). FL ST J ADMIN Rule 2.516(b)(1)(C).
- *Time of service.* Service by e-mail is complete when it is sent. FL ST J ADMIN Rule 2.516(b)(1)(D). An e-mail is deemed served on the date it is sent. FL ST J ADMIN Rule 2.516(b)(1)(D)(i). If the sender learns that the e-mail did not reach the address of the person to be served, the sender must immediately send another copy by e-mail, or by a means authorized by FL ST J ADMIN Rule 2.516(b)(2). FL ST J ADMIN Rule 2.516(b)(1)(D)(ii). E-mail service is treated as service by mail for the computation of time. FL ST J ADMIN Rule 2.516(b)(1)(D)(iii).

ii. *Format of e-mail for service.* Service of a document by e-mail is made by attaching a copy of the document in PDF format to an e-mail sent to all addresses designated by the attorney or party. FL ST J ADMIN Rule 2.516(b)(1)(E).

- All documents served by e-mail must be attached to an e-mail message containing a subject line beginning with the words "SERVICE OF COURT DOCUMENT" in all capital letters, followed by the case number of the proceeding in which the documents are being served. FL ST J ADMIN Rule 2.516(b)(1)(E)(i).
- The body of the e-mail must identify the court in which the proceeding is pending, the case number, the name of the initial party on each side, the title of each document served with that e-mail, and the sender's name and telephone number. FL ST J ADMIN Rule 2.516(b)(1)(E)(ii).
- Any document served by e-mail may be signed by the "/s/" format, as long as the filed original is signed in accordance with the applicable rule of procedure. FL ST J ADMIN Rule 2.516(b)(1)(E)(iii).
- Any e-mail which, together with its attached documents, exceeds five megabytes (5MB) in size, must be divided and sent as separate e-mails, no one of which may exceed five megabytes (5MB) in size and each of which must be sequentially numbered in the subject line. FL ST J ADMIN Rule 2.516(b)(1)(E)(iv).

iii. *Service by other means.* In addition to, and not in lieu of, service by e-mail, service may also be made upon attorneys by any of the means specified in FL ST J ADMIN Rule 2.516(b)(2). Service on and by all parties who are not represented by an attorney and who do not designate an e-mail address, and on and by all attorneys excused from e-mail service, must be made by delivering a copy of the document or by mailing it to the party or attorney at their last known address or, if no address is known, by leaving it with the clerk of the court. Service by mail is complete upon mailing. Delivery of a copy within FL ST J ADMIN Rule 2.516 is complete upon:

- Handing it to the attorney or to the party,
- Leaving it at the attorney's or party's office with a clerk or other person in charge thereof,
- If there is no one in charge, leaving it in a conspicuous place therein,
- If the office is closed or the person to be served has no office, leaving it at the person's usual place of abode with some person of his or her family above fifteen (15) years of age and informing such person of the contents, or

- Transmitting it by facsimile to the attorney's or party's office with a cover sheet containing the sender's name, firm, address, telephone number, and facsimile number, and the number of pages transmitted. When service is made by facsimile, a copy must also be served by any other method permitted by FL ST J ADMIN Rule 2.516. Facsimile service occurs when transmission is complete. FL ST J ADMIN Rule 2.516(b)(2)(A) through FL ST J ADMIN Rule 2.516(b)(2)(E).
- Service by delivery after 5:00 p.m. must be deemed to have been made by mailing on the date of delivery. FL ST J ADMIN Rule 2.516(b)(2)(F).

c. *Service; Numerous defendants.* In actions when the parties are unusually numerous, the court may regulate the service contemplated by the Florida Rules of Judicial Administration on motion or on its own initiative in such manner as may be found to be just and reasonable. FL ST J ADMIN Rule 2.516(c).

d. *Service by clerk.* Service of notices and other documents required to be made by the clerk must also be done as provided in FL ST J ADMIN Rule 2.516(b). FL ST J ADMIN Rule 2.516(g).

G. Hearings

1. The parties may be required to participate in pretrial proceedings to consider and determine the necessity or desirability of an amendment to a pleading. FL ST RCP Rule 1.200(b)(2); FL-PP § 2:151.

H. Forms

1. Official Amended Complaint Forms for Florida

a. Caption. FL ST RCP Form 1.901.

b. Notice of compliance when constitutional challenge is brought. FL ST RCP Form 1.975.

2. Amended Complaint Forms for Florida

a. Consent; Of party; To amendment of pleadings. FL-PP § 2:154.

b. Notice of amended complaint. 3 FLPRAC § 190.1.

c. Complaint for damages; General form. FL-PP § 2:17.

d. Complaint; Negligent infliction of personal injury. FL-PP § 2:19.

e. Complaint; Fall down negligence. FL-PP § 2:20.

f. Complaint; Mortgage foreclosure. FL-PP § 2:21.

g. Complaint; Implied warranty. FL-PP § 2:22.

h. Complaint; Professional negligence. FL-PP § 2:23.

i. Complaint; Breach of contract. FL-PP § 2:24.

j. Complaint; Breach of personal services contract. FL-PP § 2:25.

3. Official Forms for Florida Circuit Court, Second Judicial Circuit

a. Notice of change of contact information. FL ST 2 J CIR 2007-05.

I. Checklist

(I) ❑ Matters to be considered by plaintiff

(a) ❑ Required documents

(1) ❑ Amended complaint

(2) ❑ Certificate of service

(b) ❑ Supplemental documents

(1) ❑ Exhibits

(2) ❑ Notice of constitutional question

(c) ❑ Timing

(1) ❑ A party may amend a pleading once as a matter of course at any time before a responsive pleading is served

(2) ❑ If the pleading is one to which no responsive pleading is permitted and the action has not been placed on the trial calendar, may so amend it at any time within twenty (20) days after it is served

Pleadings
Answer

Document Last Updated January 2013

A. Applicable Rules

1. *State rules*
   a. Nonverification of pleadings. FL ST RCP Rule 1.030.
   b. Process. FL ST RCP Rule 1.070.
   c. Service and filing of pleadings, orders, and documents. FL ST RCP Rule 1.080.
   d. Time. FL ST RCP Rule 1.090.
   e. Pleadings and motions. FL ST RCP Rule 1.100; FL ST RCP Rule 1.110; FL ST RCP Rule 1.120; FL ST RCP Rule 1.130; FL ST RCP Rule 1.190; FL ST RCP Rule 1.430.
   f. Defenses. FL ST RCP Rule 1.140.
   g. Relief from judgment, decrees, or orders. FL ST RCP Rule 1.540.
   h. Forms. FL ST RCP Rule 1.900.
   i. Minimization of the filing of sensitive information. FL ST J ADMIN Rule 2.425.
   j. Retention of court records. FL ST J ADMIN Rule 2.430.
   k. Foreign attorneys. FL ST J ADMIN Rule 2.510.
   l. Signature of attorneys and parties. FL ST J ADMIN Rule 2.515.
   m. Paper. FL ST J ADMIN Rule 2.520.
   n. Electronic filing. FL ST J ADMIN Rule 2.525.
   o. Accessibility of information and technology. FL ST J ADMIN Rule 2.526.
   p. Court reporting. FL ST J ADMIN Rule 2.535.
   q. Requests for accommodations by persons with disabilities. FL ST J ADMIN Rule 2.540.
   r. Waiver of sovereign immunity in tort actions; Recovery limits; Limitation on attorney fees; Statute of limitations; Exclusions; Indemnification; Risk management programs. FL ST § 768.28.
2. *Local rules*
   a. Notice of change of contact information. FL ST 2 J CIR 2007-05.

B. Timing

1. *General answer timing.* Unless a different time is prescribed in a statute of Florida, a defendant shall serve an answer within twenty (20) days after service of original process and the initial pleading on the defendant, or not later than the date fixed in a notice by publication. A party served with a pleading stating a crossclaim against that party shall serve an answer to it within twenty (20) days after service on that party. The plaintiff shall serve an answer to a counterclaim within twenty (20) days after service of the counterclaim. FL ST RCP Rule 1.140(a)(1).
   a. *Waiver of service.* A defendant who, before being served with process, timely returns a waiver so requested is not required to respond to the complaint until sixty (60) days after the date the defendant received the request for waiver of service. For purposes of computing any time prescribed or allowed by the Florida Rules of Civil Procedure, service of process shall be deemed effected twenty (20) days before the time required to respond to the complaint. FL ST RCP Rule 1.070(i)(4).
   b. *Service on the state.* Except when sued pursuant to FL ST § 768.28, the state of Florida, an agency

of the state, or an officer or employee of the state sued in an official capacity shall serve an answer to the complaint or crossclaim, or a reply to a counterclaim, within forty (40) days after service. When sued pursuant to FL ST § 768.28, the Department of Financial Services or the defendant state agency shall have thirty (30) days from the date of service within which to serve an answer to the complaint or crossclaim or a reply to a counterclaim. FL ST RCP Rule 1.140(a)(2).

c. *Service of motion impact on time periods for service of answer.* The service of a motion under FL ST RCP Rule 1.140, except a motion for judgment on the pleadings or a motion to strike under FL ST RCP Rule 1.140(f), alters these periods of time so that if the court denies the motion or postpones its disposition until the trial on the merits, the responsive pleadings shall be served within ten (10) days after notice of the court's action or, if the court grants a motion for a more definite statement, the responsive pleadings shall be served within ten (10) days after service of the more definite statement unless a different time is fixed by the court in either case. FL ST RCP Rule 1.140(a)(3).

d. *Responding if pleading does not require a responsive pleading.* If a pleading sets forth a claim for relief to which the adverse party is not required to serve a responsive pleading, the adverse party may assert any defense in law or fact to that claim for relief at the trial, except that the objection of failure to state a legal defense in an answer or reply shall be asserted by motion to strike the defense within twenty (20) days after service of the answer or reply. FL ST RCP Rule 1.140(b).

2. *Computation of time*

a. *Generally.* Computation of time shall be governed by FL ST J ADMIN Rule 2.514. FL ST RCP Rule 1.090(a). The following rules apply in computing time periods specified in any rule of procedure, local rule, court order, or statute that does not specify a method of computing time. FL ST J ADMIN Rule 2.514(a).

i. *Period stated in days or a longer unit.* When the period is stated in days or a longer unit of time (A) exclude the day of the event that triggers the period; (B) count every day, including intermediate Saturdays, Sundays, and legal holidays; and (C) include the last day of the period, but if the last day is a Saturday, Sunday, or legal holiday, or falls within any period of time extended through an order of the chief justice under FL ST J ADMIN Rule 2.205(a)(2)(B)(iv), the period continues to run until the end of the next day that is not a Saturday, Sunday, or legal holiday and does not fall within any period of time extended through an order of the chief justice. FL ST J ADMIN Rule 2.514(a)(1).

ii. *Period stated in hours.* When the period is stated in hours (A) begin counting immediately on the occurrence of the event that triggers the period; (B) count every hour, including hours during intermediate Saturdays, Sundays, and legal holidays; and (C) if the period would end on a Saturday, Sunday, or legal holiday, or during any period of time extended through an order of the chief justice under FL ST J ADMIN Rule 2.205(a)(2)(B)(iv), the period continues to run until the same time on the next day that is not a Saturday, Sunday, or legal holiday and does not fall within any period of time extended through an order of the chief justice. FL ST J ADMIN Rule 2.514(a)(2).

iii. *Period stated in days less than seven (7) days.* When the period stated in days is less than seven (7) days, intermediate Saturdays, Sundays, and legal holidays shall be excluded in the computation. FL ST J ADMIN Rule 2.514(a)(3).

iv. *"Last day" defined.* Unless a different time is set by a statute, local rule, or court order, the last day ends (A) for electronic filing or for service by any means, at midnight; and (B) for filing by other means, when the clerk's office is scheduled to close. FL ST J ADMIN Rule 2.514(a)(4).

v. *"Next day" defined.* The "next day" is determined by continuing to count forward when the period is measured after an event and backward when measured before an event. FL ST J ADMIN Rule 2.514(a)(5).

vi. *"Legal holiday" defined.* "Legal holiday" means (A) the day set aside by FL ST § 110.117, for observing New Year's Day, Martin Luther King, Jr.'s Birthday, Memorial Day, Independence Day, Labor Day, Veterans' Day, Thanksgiving Day, the Friday after Thanksgiving Day, or Christmas Day, and (B) any day observed as a holiday by the clerk's office or as designated by the chief judge. FL ST J ADMIN Rule 2.514(a)(6).

b. *Additional time after service by mail or e-mail.* When a party may or must act within a specified time after service and service is made by mail or e-mail, five (5) days are added after the period that would otherwise expire under FL ST J ADMIN Rule 2.514(a). FL ST J ADMIN Rule 2.514(b).

c. *Enlargement.* When an act is required or allowed to be done at or within a specified time by order of court, by the Florida Rules of Civil Procedure, or by notice given thereunder, for cause shown the court at any time in its discretion (1) with or without notice, may order the period enlarged if request therefor is made before the expiration of the period originally prescribed or as extended by a previous order, or (2) upon motion made and notice after the expiration of the specified period, may permit the act to be done when failure to act was the result of excusable neglect, but it may not extend the time for making a motion for new trial, for rehearing, or to alter or amend a judgment; making a motion for relief from a judgment under FL ST RCP Rule 1.540(b); taking an appeal or filing a petition for certiorari; or making a motion for a directed verdict. FL ST RCP Rule 1.090(b).

d. *Unaffected by expiration of term.* The period of time provided for the doing of any act or the taking of any proceeding shall not be affected or limited by the continued existence or expiration of a term of court. The continued existence or expiration of a term of court in no way affects the power of a court to do any act or take any proceeding in any action which is or has been pending before it. FL ST RCP Rule 1.090(c).

C. General Requirements

1. *General rules of pleading*

a. *Claims for relief*

i. A pleading which sets forth a claim for relief, whether an original claim, counterclaim, crossclaim, or third-party claim, must state a cause of action and shall contain

- A short and plain statement of the grounds upon which the court's jurisdiction depends, unless the court already has jurisdiction and the claim needs no new grounds of jurisdiction to support it (For information regarding acts subjecting persons to jurisdiction, please see FL ST § 48.193),
- A short and plain statement of the ultimate facts showing that the pleader is entitled to relief, and
- A demand for judgment for the relief to which the pleader deems himself or herself entitled. FL ST RCP Rule 1.110(b).

ii. Relief in the alternative or of several different types may be demanded. Every complaint shall be considered to demand general relief. FL ST RCP Rule 1.110(b).

b. *Verification.* Except when otherwise specifically provided by these rules or an applicable statute, every pleading or other document of a party represented by an attorney need not be verified or accompanied by an affidavit. FL ST RCP Rule 1.030. When filing an action for foreclosure of a mortgage on residential real property the complaint shall be verified. When verification of a document is required, the document filed shall include an oath, affirmation, or the following statement: "Under penalty of perjury, I declare that I have read the foregoing, and the facts alleged therein are true and correct to the best of my knowledge and belief." FL ST RCP Rule 1.110(b).

c. *Separate statements.* All averments of claim or defense shall be made in consecutively numbered paragraphs, the contents of each of which shall be limited as far as practicable to a statement of a single set of circumstances, and a paragraph may be referred to by number in all subsequent pleadings. Each claim founded upon a separate transaction or occurrence and each defense other than denials shall be stated in a separate count or defense when a separation facilitates the clear presentation of the matter set forth. FL ST RCP Rule 1.110(f).

d. *Statements adopted by reference.* Statements in a pleading may be adopted by reference in a different part of the same pleading, in another pleading, or in any motion. FL ST RCP Rule 1.130(b).

e. *Joinder of causes of action; Consistency.* A pleader may set up in the same action as many claims or causes of action or defenses in the same right as the pleader has, and claims for relief may be stated in the alternative if separate items make up the cause of action, or if two (2) or more causes of action are joined. A party may also set forth two (2) or more statements of a claim or defense alternatively, either in one (1) count or defense or in separate counts or defenses. When two (2) or more statements are made in the alternative and one (1) of them, if made independently, would be sufficient, the pleading is not made insufficient by the insufficiency of one (1) or more of the alternative statements. A party may also state as many separate claims or defenses as that party has, regardless of consistency and whether based on legal or equitable grounds or both. All pleadings shall be construed so as to do substantial justice. FL ST RCP Rule 1.110(g).

f. *Subsequent pleadings.* When the nature of an action permits pleadings subsequent to final judgment and the jurisdiction of the court over the parties has not terminated, the initial pleading subsequent to final judgment shall be designated a supplemental complaint or petition. The action shall then proceed in the same manner and time as though the supplemental complaint or petition were the initial pleading in the action, including the issuance of any needed process. FL ST RCP Rule 1.110(h) shall not apply to proceedings that may be initiated by motion under the Florida Rules of Civil Procedure. FL ST RCP Rule 1.110(h).

g. *Pleading basis for service.* When service of process is to be made under statutes authorizing service on nonresidents of Florida, it is sufficient to plead the basis for service in the language of the statute without pleading the facts supporting service. FL ST RCP Rule 1.070(h).

h. *Forms of pleadings.* Forms of action and technical forms for seeking relief and of pleas, pleadings, or motions are abolished. FL ST RCP Rule 1.110(a).

2. *Answer; Generally.* An answer has three (3) functions. First, it must respond to each allegation of the preceding pleading by admitting, denying or alleging that the pleader is without knowledge of the allegation. Second, it must contain any affirmative defenses that the pleader is interposing to any cause of action alleged in the preceding pleading. Third, the answer may claim affirmative relief against the plaintiff or petitioner by a counterclaim or against a codefendant by a crossclaim. FL-PRACPROC § 11:1.

a. *Content.* In the answer a pleader shall state in short and plain terms the pleader's defenses to each claim asserted and shall admit or deny the averments on which the adverse party relies. If the defendant is without knowledge, the defendant shall so state and such statement shall operate as a denial. Denial shall fairly meet the substance of the averments denied. When a pleader intends in good faith to deny only a part of an averment, the pleader shall specify so much of it as is true and shall deny the remainder. Unless the pleader intends in good faith to controvert all of the averments of the preceding pleading, the pleader may make denials as specific denials of designated averments or may generally deny all of the averments except such designated averments as the pleader expressly admits, but when the pleader does so intend to controvert all of its averments, including averments of the grounds upon which the court's jurisdiction depends, the pleader may do so by general denial. FL ST RCP Rule 1.110(c).

b. *Form of answer.* An answer contains a caption, commencement, body, signature and certificate of service. The caption is the same as that of the initial pleading, except for the designation as one of the types of answer. The body of an answer should contain an admission, denial or plea of without knowledge to each allegation of the preceding pleading, except for the additional allegations in response to a general allegation of conditions precedent and the denial of capacity to sue. FL-PRACPROC § 11:3.

i. *Responding sequentially.* The best method of responding is to answer each paragraph sequentially, combining admissions, denials or pleas of without knowledge when the sequence permits. The admissions, denials and allegations of without knowledge should be stated first, followed separately by any affirmative defenses and then by any counterclaim or crossclaim. A third party complaint may be a part of the same paper, but it is not a part of the answer as is a counterclaim or crossclaim. Paragraphs are numbered consecutively throughout the pleading whether in the answer, counterclaim or crossclaim. Denials for the record only are improper. FL-PRACPROC § 11:3.

c. *Defenses*

i. *Generally.* Every defense in law or fact to a claim for relief in a pleading shall be asserted in the responsive pleading, if one is required, but the following defenses may be made by motion at the option of the pleader: (1) lack of jurisdiction over the subject matter, (2) lack of jurisdiction over the person, (3) improper venue, (4) insufficiency of process, (5) insufficiency of service of process, (6) failure to state a cause of action, and (7) failure to join indispensable parties. A motion making any of these defenses shall be made before pleading if a further pleading is permitted. FL ST RCP Rule 1.140(b).

- *Stated specifically.* The grounds on which any of the enumerated defenses are based and the substantial matters of law intended to be argued shall be stated specifically and with particularity in the responsive pleading or motion. FL ST RCP Rule 1.140(b).
- *Waiver.* Any ground not stated shall be deemed to be waived except any ground showing that the court lacks jurisdiction of the subject matter may be made at any time. No defense or objection is waived by being joined with other defenses or objections in a responsive pleading or motion. FL ST RCP Rule 1.140(b). A party waives all defenses and objections that the party does not present either by motion under FL ST RCP Rule 1.140(b), FL ST RCP Rule 1.140(e), or FL ST RCP Rule 1.140(f) or, if the party has made no motion, in a responsive pleading except as provided in FL ST RCP Rule 1.140(h)(2). FL ST RCP Rule 1.140(h)(1). The defenses of failure to state a cause of action or a legal defense or to join an indispensable party may be raised by motion for judgment on the pleadings or at the trial on the merits in addition to being raised either in a motion under FL ST RCP Rule 1.140(b) or in the answer or reply. The defense of lack of jurisdiction of the subject matter may be raised at any time. FL ST RCP Rule 1.140(h)(2).

ii. *Affirmative defenses.* In pleading to a preceding pleading a party shall set forth affirmatively accord and satisfaction, arbitration and award, assumption of risk, contributory negligence, discharge in bankruptcy, duress, estoppel, failure of consideration, fraud, illegality, injury by fellow servant, laches, license, payment, release, res judicata, statute of frauds, statute of limitations, waiver, and any other matter constituting an avoidance or affirmative defense. When a party has mistakenly designated a defense as a counterclaim or a counterclaim as a defense, the court, on terms if justice so requires, shall treat the pleading as if there had been a proper designation. Affirmative defenses appearing on the face of a prior pleading may be asserted as grounds for a motion or defense under FL ST RCP Rule 1.140(b); provided this shall not limit amendments under FL ST RCP Rule 1.190 even if such ground is sustained. FL ST RCP Rule 1.110(d).

- *Format of defenses.* Affirmative defenses should be placed after the admissions, denials and allegations of without knowledge in the answer. All paragraphs must be numbered consecutively throughout the answer. If a defense is directed to only a part of a cause of action or to one or more, but not all, of several causes of action in the preceding pleading, the part or cause of action to which it is directed should be identified in the defense. Defenses should be identified by consecutive ordinal numbers such as "First Defense" and "Second Defense." FL-PRACPROC § 11:4.

iii. *Effect of failure to deny.* Averments in a pleading to which a responsive pleading is required, other than those as to the amount of damages, are admitted when not denied in the responsive pleading. Averments in a pleading to which no responsive pleading is required or permitted shall be taken as denied or avoided. FL ST RCP Rule 1.110(e). An admission in an answer binds the party and no proof is required. An admission does not extend beyond the scope of the allegation in the preceding pleading. FL-PRACPROC § 11:3.

3. *Pleading special matters*

a. *Capacity.* It is not necessary to aver the capacity of a party to sue or be sued, the authority of a party to sue or be sued in a representative capacity, or the legal existence of an organized association of persons that is made a party, except to the extent required to show the jurisdiction of the court. The initial pleading served on behalf of a minor party shall specifically aver the age of the minor party. When a party desires to raise an issue as to the legal existence of any party, the capacity of any party to sue or be sued, or the authority of a party to sue or be sued in a representative capacity, that party shall do so by specific negative averment which shall include such supporting particulars as are peculiarly within the pleader's knowledge. FL ST RCP Rule 1.120(a).

b. *Fraud, mistake, condition of the mind.* In all averments of fraud or mistake, the circumstances constituting fraud or mistake shall be stated with such particularity as the circumstances may permit. Malice, intent, knowledge, mental attitude, and other condition of mind of a person may be averred generally. FL ST RCP Rule 1.120(b).

c. *Conditions precedent.* In pleading the performance or occurrence of conditions precedent, it is sufficient to aver generally that all conditions precedent have been performed or have occurred. A denial of performance or occurrence shall be made specifically and with particularity. FL ST RCP Rule 1.120(c).

d. *Official document or act.* In pleading an official document or official act it is sufficient to aver that the document was issued or the act done in compliance with law. FL ST RCP Rule 1.120(c).

e. *Judgment or decree.* In pleading a judgment or decree of a domestic or foreign court, a judicial or quasi-judicial tribunal, or a board or officer, it is sufficient to aver the judgment or decree without setting forth matter showing jurisdiction to render it. FL ST RCP Rule 1.120(e).

f. *Time and place.* For the purpose of testing the sufficiency of a pleading, averments of time and place are material and shall be considered like all other averments of material matter. FL ST RCP Rule 1.120(f).

g. *Special damage.* When items of special damage are claimed, they shall be specifically stated. FL ST RCP Rule 1.120(g).

4. *Parties*

a. *Parties generally.* Every action may be prosecuted in the name of the real party in interest, but a personal representative, administrator, guardian, trustee of an express trust, a party with whom or in whose name a contract has been made for the benefit of another, or a party expressly authorized by statute may sue in that person's own name without joining the party for whose benefit the action is brought. All persons having an interest in the subject of the action and in obtaining the relief demanded may join as plaintiffs and any person may be made a defendant who has or claims an interest adverse to the plaintiff. Any person may at any time be made a party if that person's presence is necessary or proper to a complete determination of the cause. Persons having a united interest may be joined on the same side as plaintiffs or defendants, and anyone who refuses to join may for such reason be made a defendant. FL ST RCP Rule 1.210(a).

b. *Minors or incompetent persons.* When a minor or incompetent person has a representative, such as a guardian or other like fiduciary, the representative may sue or defend on behalf of the minor or incompetent person. A minor or incompetent person who does not have a duly appointed representative may sue by next friend or by a guardian ad litem. The court shall appoint a guardian ad litem for a minor or incompetent person not otherwise represented in an action or shall make such other order as it deems proper for the protection of the minor or incompetent person. FL ST RCP Rule 1.210(b).

c. For survivor and substitution of parties information, please see FL ST RCP Rule 1.260.

5. *Counterclaims and crossclaims*

a. *Compulsory counterclaims.* A pleading shall state as a counterclaim any claim which at the time of serving the pleading the pleader has against any opposing party, provided it arises out of the transaction or occurrence that is the subject matter of the opposing party's claim and does not require for its adjudication the presence of third parties over whom the court cannot acquire jurisdiction. But the pleader need not state a claim if (1) at the time the action was commenced the claim was the subject of another pending action, or (2) the opposing party brought suit upon that party's claim by attachment or other process by which the court did not acquire jurisdiction to render a personal judgment on the claim and the pleader is not stating a counterclaim under this rule. FL ST RCP Rule 1.170(a).

b. *Permissive counterclaim.* A pleading may state as a counterclaim any claim against an opposing party not arising out of the transaction or occurrence that is the subject matter of the opposing party's claim. FL ST RCP Rule 1.170(b).

c. *Counterclaim exceeding opposing claim.* A counterclaim may or may not diminish or defeat the recovery sought by the opposing party. It may claim relief exceeding in amount or different in kind from that sought in the pleading of the opposing party. FL ST RCP Rule 1.170(c).

d. *Counterclaim against the State.* The Florida Rules of Civil Procedure shall not be construed to enlarge beyond the limits established by law the right to assert counterclaims or to claim credits against the state or any of its subdivisions or other governmental organizations thereof subject to suit or against a municipal corporation or against an officer, agency, or administrative board of the state. FL ST RCP Rule 1.170(d).

e. *Counterclaim maturing or acquired after pleading.* A claim which matured or was acquired by the pleader after serving the pleading may be presented as a counterclaim by supplemental pleading with the permission of the court. FL ST RCP Rule 1.170(e).

f. *Omitted counterclaim or crossclaim.* When a pleader fails to set up a counterclaim or crossclaim through oversight, inadvertence, or excusable neglect, or when justice requires, the pleader may set up the counterclaim or crossclaim by amendment with leave of the court. FL ST RCP Rule 1.170(f).

g. *Crossclaim against co-party.* A pleading may state as a crossclaim any claim by one party against a co-party arising out of the transaction or occurrence that is the subject matter of either the original action or a counterclaim therein, or relating to any property that is the subject matter of the original action. The crossclaim may include a claim that the party against whom it is asserted is or may be liable to the crossclaimant for all or part of a claim asserted in the action against the crossclaimant. Service of a crossclaim on a party who has appeared in the action shall be made pursuant to FL ST RCP Rule 1.080. Service of a crossclaim against a party who has not appeared in the action shall be made in the manner provided for service of summons. FL ST RCP Rule 1.170(g).

h. *Additional parties may be brought in.* When the presence of parties other than those to the original action is required to grant complete relief in the determination of a counterclaim or crossclaim, they shall be named in the counterclaim or crossclaim and be served with process and shall be parties to the action thereafter if jurisdiction of them can be obtained and their joinder will not deprive the court of jurisdiction of the action. FL ST RCP Rule 1.250(b) and FL ST RCP Rule 1.250(c) apply to parties brought in under FL ST RCP Rule 1.170(h). FL ST RCP Rule 1.170(h).

i. *Separate trials; Separate judgment.* If the court orders separate trials as provided in FL ST RCP Rule 1.270(b), judgment on a counterclaim or crossclaim may be rendered when the court has jurisdiction to do so even if a claim of the opposing party has been dismissed or otherwise disposed of. FL ST RCP Rule 1.170(i).

j. *Demand exceeding jurisdiction; Transfer of action.* If the demand of any counterclaim or crossclaim exceeds the jurisdiction of the court in which the action is pending, the action shall be transferred forthwith to the court of the same county having jurisdiction of the demand in the counterclaim or crossclaim with only such alterations in the pleadings as are essential. The court shall order the transfer of the action and the transmittal of all papers in it to the proper court if the party asserting the demand exceeding the jurisdiction deposits with the court having jurisdiction a sum sufficient to pay the clerk's service charge in the court to which the action is transferred at the time of filing the counterclaim or crossclaim. Thereupon the original papers and deposit shall be transmitted and filed with a certified copy of the order. The court to which the action is transferred shall have full power and jurisdiction over the demands of all parties. Failure to make the service charge deposit at the time the counterclaim or crossclaim is filed, or within such further time as the court may allow, shall reduce a claim for damages to an amount within the jurisdiction of the court where the action is pending and waive the claim in other cases. FL ST RCP Rule 1.170(j).

6. *Misjoinder and nonjoinder of parties*

a. *Misjoinder.* Misjoinder of parties is not a ground for dismissal of an action. Any claim against a party may be severed and proceeded with separately. FL ST RCP Rule 1.250(a).

b. *Dropping parties.* Parties may be dropped by an adverse party in the manner provided for voluntary dismissal in FL ST RCP Rule 1.420(a)(1) subject to the exception stated in FL ST RCP Rule 1.420. If notice of lis pendens has been filed in the action against a party so dropped, the notice of dismissal shall be recorded and cancels the notice of lis pendens without the necessity of a court order. Parties may be dropped by order of court on its own initiative or the motion of any party at any stage of the action on such terms as are just. FL ST RCP Rule 1.250(b).

c. *Adding parties.* Parties may be added once as a matter of course within the same time that pleadings can be so amended under FL ST RCP Rule 1.190(a). If amendment by leave of court or stipulation of the parties is permitted, parties may be added in the amended pleading without further order of court. Parties may be added by order of court on its own initiative or on motion of any party at any stage of the action and on such terms as are just. FL ST RCP Rule 1.250(c).

7. *Jury demand*

   a. *Right preserved.* The right of trial by jury as declared by the Constitution or by statute shall be preserved to the parties inviolate. FL ST RCP Rule 1.430(a).

   b. *Demand.* Any party may demand a trial by jury of any issue triable of right by a jury by serving upon the other party a demand therefor in writing at any time after commencement of the action and not later than ten (10) days after the service of the last pleading directed to such issue. The demand may be indorsed upon a pleading of the party. FL ST RCP Rule 1.430(b).

   c. *Specification of issues.* In the demand a party may specify the issues that the party wishes so tried; otherwise, the party is deemed to demand trial by jury for all issues so triable. FL ST RCP Rule 1.430(c).

      i. If a party has demanded trial by jury for only some of the issues, any other party may serve a demand for trial by jury of any other or all of the issues triable by jury ten (10) days after service of the demand or such lesser time as the court may order. FL ST RCP Rule 1.430(c).

   d. *Waiver.* A party who fails to serve a demand as required by FL ST RCP Rule 1.430 waives trial by jury. FL ST RCP Rule 1.430(d).

      i. If waived, a jury trial may not be granted without the consent of the parties, but the court may allow an amendment in the proceedings to demand a trial by jury or order a trial by jury on its own motion. FL ST RCP Rule 1.430(d).

      ii. A demand for trial by jury may not be withdrawn without the consent of the parties. FL ST RCP Rule 1.430(d).

8. *Arbitration and mediation*

   a. *Referral to arbitration and mediation.* Except as hereinafter provided or as otherwise prohibited by law, the presiding judge may enter an order referring all or any part of a contested civil matter to mediation or arbitration. The parties to any contested civil matter may file a written stipulation to mediate or arbitrate any issue between them at any time. Such stipulation shall be incorporated into the order of referral. FL ST RCP Rule 1.700(a).

   b. *Arbitration*

      i. *Exclusions.* A civil action shall be ordered to arbitration or arbitration in conjunction with mediation upon stipulation of the parties. A civil action may be ordered to arbitration or arbitration in conjunction with mediation upon motion of any party or by the court, if the judge determines the action to be of such a nature that arbitration could be of benefit to the litigants or the court. FL ST RCP Rule 1.800.

         - Under no circumstances may the following categories of actions be referred to arbitration: (1) bond estreatures; (2) habeas corpus or other extraordinary writs; (3) bond validations; (4) civil or criminal contempt; (5) such other matters as may be specified by order of the chief judge in the circuit. FL ST RCP Rule 1.800.

      ii. For more information regarding arbitration, please see FL ST RCP Rule 1.810; FL ST RCP Rule 1.820; FL ST RCP Rule 1.830.

   c. *Mediation.* For more information regarding mediation, please see FL ST RCP Rule 1.710; FL ST RCP Rule 1.720; FL ST RCP Rule 1.730; and FL ST RCP Rule 1.750.

9. *Rules of court*

   a. *Rules of civil procedure.* The Florida Rules of Civil Procedure apply to all actions of a civil nature

and all special statutory proceedings in the circuit courts and county courts except those to which the Florida Probate Rules, the Florida Family Law Rules of Procedure, or the Small Claims Rules apply. FL ST RCP Rule 1.010.

i. The form, content, procedure, and time for pleading in all special statutory proceedings shall be as prescribed by the statutes governing the proceeding unless the Florida Rules of Civil Procedure specifically provide to the contrary. FL ST RCP Rule 1.010.

ii. The Florida Rules of Civil Procedure shall be construed to secure the just, speedy, and inexpensive determination of every action. FL ST RCP Rule 1.010.

b. *Rules of judicial administration.* The Florida Rules of Judicial Administration shall apply to administrative matters in all courts to which the Florida Rules of Judicial Administration are applicable by their terms. The Florida Rules of Judicial Administration shall be construed to secure the speedy and inexpensive determination of every proceeding to which they are applicable. The Florida Rules of Judicial Administration shall supersede all conflicting rules and statutes. FL ST J ADMIN Rule 2.110.

10. *Notice of change of contact information.* The Clerk shall provide a change of address and/or telephone number form for use by attorneys and pro se litigants. With any change of address and/or telephone number, attorneys and pro se litigants governed by FL ST J ADMIN Rule 2.515 will provide to the Clerk and all parties promptly the change of address and/or telephone number form. This form should be submitted only once to the Clerk, who will then make the address and/or telephone number change in all court divisions. FL ST 2 J CIR 2007-05.

D. Documents

1. *Required documents*

a. *Answer.* See the General Requirements section of this document for further information about the content of an answer.

i. *Notices to persons with disabilities.* See the Format section of this KeyRules document for further information.

b. *Certificate of service.* When any attorney certifies in substance: "I certify that a copy hereof has been furnished to (here insert name or names and addresses used for service) by (e-mail) (delivery) (mail) (fax) on .... (date) ....______________ Attorney" the certificate is taken as prima facie proof of such service in compliance with FL ST J ADMIN Rule 2.516. FL ST J ADMIN Rule 2.516(f).

2. *Supplemental documents*

a. *Exhibits.* All bonds, notes, bills of exchange, contracts, accounts, or documents upon which action may be brought or defense made, or a copy thereof or a copy of the portions thereof material to the pleadings, shall be incorporated in or attached to the pleading. No papers shall be unnecessarily annexed as exhibits. The pleadings shall contain no unnecessary recitals of deeds, documents, contracts, or other instruments. Any exhibit attached to a pleading shall be considered a part of the pleadings for all purposes. FL ST RCP Rule 1.130(a).

b. *Notice of constitutional question.* A party that files a pleading, written motion, or other paper drawing into question the constitutionality of a state statute or a county or municipal charter, ordinance, or franchise must promptly (1) file a notice of constitutional question stating the question and identifying the paper that raises it; and (2) serve the notice and the pleading, written motion, or other paper drawing into question the constitutionality of a state statute or a county or municipal charter, ordinance, or franchise on the Attorney General or the state attorney of the judicial circuit in which the action is pending, by either certified or registered mail. Service of the notice and pleading, written motion, or other paper does not require joinder of the Attorney General or the state attorney as a party to the action. FL ST RCP Rule 1.071.

E. Format

1. *Documents; Type and size.* Documents subject to the exceptions set forth in FL ST J ADMIN Rule 2.525(d) shall be filed on recycled paper measuring eight and one half by eleven (8 1/2 by 11) inches. For purposes of FL ST J ADMIN Rule 2.520, paper is recycled if it contains a minimum content of fifty (50)

percent waste paper. Xerographic reduction of legal-size (eight and one half by fourteen (8 1/2 by 14) inches) documents to letter size (eight and one half by eleven (8 1/2 by 11) inches) is prohibited. All other documents filed by electronic transmission shall be filed in a format capable of being printed in a format consistent with the provisions of FL ST J ADMIN Rule 2.250. FL ST J ADMIN Rule 2.520(b).

a. *Exhibits.* Any exhibit or attachment filed with pleadings or papers may be filed in its original size. FL ST J ADMIN Rule 2.520(c).

b. *Recording space.* On all papers and documents prepared and filed by the court or by any party to a proceeding which are to be recorded in the public records of any county, including but not limited to final money judgments and notices of lis pendens, a three (3) inch by three (3) inch space at the top right-hand corner on the first page and a one (1) inch by three (3) inch space at the top right-hand corner on each subsequent page shall be left blank and reserved for use by the clerk of court. FL ST J ADMIN Rule 2.520(d).

   i. *Exceptions to recording space.* Any papers or documents created by persons or entities over which the filing party has no control, including but not limited to wills, codicils, trusts, or other testamentary documents; documents prepared or executed by any public officer; documents prepared, executed, acknowledged, or proved outside of the State of Florida; or documents created by State or Federal government agencies, may be filed without the space required by FL ST J ADMIN Rule 2.520. FL ST J ADMIN Rule 2.520(e).

c. *Noncompliance.* No clerk of court is permitted to refuse to file any document or paper because of noncompliance with the Florida Rules of Judicial Administration. However, upon request of the clerk of court, noncomplying documents must be resubmitted in accordance with the formatting rules. FL ST J ADMIN Rule 2.520(f).

2. *Caption.* Every pleading, motion, order, judgment, or other paper shall have a caption containing the name of the court, the file number, and except for in rem proceedings, including forfeiture proceedings, the name of the first party on each side with an appropriate indication of other parties, and a designation identifying the party filing it and its nature or the nature of the order, as the case may be. In any in rem proceeding, every pleading, motion, order, judgment, or other paper shall have a caption containing the name of the court, the file number, the style "In re" (followed by the name or general description of the property), and a designation of the person or entity filing it and its nature or the nature of the order, as the case may be. In an in rem forfeiture proceeding, the style shall be "In re forfeiture of" (followed by the name of the general description of the property). All papers filed in the action shall be styled in such a manner as to indicate clearly the subject matter of the paper and the party requesting or obtaining relief. FL ST RCP Rule 1.100(c)(1).

3. *Writing and written defined.* Writing or written means a document containing information, an application, or a stipulation. FL ST RCP Rule 1.080(c).

4. *Rule abbreviations*

   a. The Florida Rules of Civil Procedure and shall be abbreviated as Fla.R.Civ.P. FL ST RCP Rule 1.010.

   b. The Florida Rules of Judicial Administration shall be abbreviated as Fla. R. Jud. Admin. FL ST J ADMIN Rule 2.110.

5. *Nonverification.* Except when otherwise specifically provided by the Florida Rules of Civil Procedure or an applicable statute, every pleading or other document of a party represented by an attorney need not be verified or accompanied by an affidavit. FL ST RCP Rule 1.030; FL ST J ADMIN Rule 2.515(a).

6. *Attorney signature*

   a. *Attorney signature.* Every pleading and other document of a party represented by an attorney shall be signed by at least one (1) attorney of record in that attorney's individual name whose current record Florida Bar address, telephone number, including area code, primary e-mail address and secondary e-mail addresses, if any, and Florida Bar number shall be stated, and who shall be duly licensed to practice law in Florida or who shall have received permission to appear in the particular case as provided in FL ST J ADMIN Rule 2.510. FL ST J ADMIN Rule 2.515(a).

      i. The attorney may be required by the court to give the address of, and to vouch for the attorney's authority to represent, the party. FL ST J ADMIN Rule 2.515(a).

ii. The signature of an attorney shall constitute a certificate by the attorney that the attorney has read the pleading or other document; that to the best of the attorney's knowledge, information, and belief there is good ground to support it; and that it is not interposed for delay. FL ST J ADMIN Rule 2.515(a).

iii. If a pleading is not signed or is signed with intent to defeat the purpose of FL ST J ADMIN Rule 2.515, it may be stricken and the action may proceed as though the pleading or other document had not been served. FL ST J ADMIN Rule 2.515(a).

b. *Pro se litigant signature.* A party who is not represented by an attorney shall sign any pleading or other paper and state the party's address and telephone number, including area code. FL ST J ADMIN Rule 2.515(b).

c. *Form of signature*

i. The signatures required on pleadings and documents by FL ST J ADMIN Rule 2.515(a) and FL ST J ADMIN Rule 2.515(b) may be:

- Original signatures;
- Original signatures that have been reproduced by electronic means, such as on electronically transmitted documents or photocopied documents;
- Electronic signatures using the "/s/," "s/," or "/s" formats by or at the direction of the person signing; or
- Any other signature format authorized by general law, so long as the clerk where the proceeding is pending has the capability of receiving and has obtained approval from the Supreme Court of Florida to accept pleadings and documents with that signature format. FL ST J ADMIN Rule 2.515(c)(1).

ii. An attorney, party, or other person who files a pleading or paper by electronic transmission that does not contain the original signature of that attorney, party, or other person shall file that identical pleading or paper in paper form containing an original signature of that attorney, party, or other person (hereinafter called the follow-up filing) immediately thereafter. The follow-up filing is not required if the Supreme Court of Florida has entered an order directing the clerk of court to discontinue accepting the follow-up filing. FL ST J ADMIN Rule 2.515(c)(2).

7. *Forms*

a. *Process.* The forms of process, notice of lis pendens, and notice of action provided in the Florida Rules of Civil Procedure are sufficient. Variations from the forms do not void process or notices that are otherwise sufficient. FL ST RCP Rule 1.900(a).

b. *Other forms.* The other forms provided in the Florida Rules of Civil Procedure are sufficient for the matters that are covered by them. So long as the substance is expressed without prolixity, the forms may be varied to meet the facts of a particular case. FL ST RCP Rule 1.900(b).

c. *Formal matters.* Captions, except for the designation of the paper, are omitted from the forms provided in the Florida Rules of Civil Procedure. A general form of caption is the first form provided. Signatures are omitted from pleadings and motions. FL ST RCP Rule 1.900(c).

8. *Notices to persons with disabilities.* All notices of court proceedings to be held in a public facility, and all process compelling appearance at such proceedings, shall include the following statement in bold face, fourteen (14) point Times New Roman or Courier font: "If you are a person with a disability who needs any accommodation in order to participate in this proceeding, you are entitled, at no cost to you, to the provision of certain assistance. Please contact [identify applicable court personnel by name, address, and telephone number] at least seven (7) days before your scheduled court appearance, or immediately upon receiving this notification if the time before the scheduled appearance is less than seven (7) days; if you are hearing or voice impaired, call 711." FL ST J ADMIN Rule 2.540(c)(1).

9. *Minimization of the filing of sensitive information*

a. *Limitations for court filings.* Unless authorized by FL ST J ADMIN Rule 2.425(b), statute, another

rule of court, or the court orders otherwise, designated sensitive information filed with the court must be limited to the following format:

i. The initials of a person known to be a minor;
ii. The year of birth of a person's birth date;
iii. No portion of any: Social security number, Bank account number, Credit card account number, Charge account number, or Debit account number;
iv. The last four digits of any: Taxpayer identification number (TIN), Employee identification number, Driver's license number, Passport number, Telephone number, Financial account number, except as set forth in FL ST J ADMIN Rule 2.425(a)(3), Brokerage account number, Insurance policy account number, Loan account number, Customer account number, or Patient or health care number;
v. A truncated version of any: Email address, Computer user name, Password, or Personal identification number (PIN); and
vi. A truncated version of any other sensitive information as provided by court order. FL ST J ADMIN Rule 2.425(a).

b. *Exceptions.* FL ST J ADMIN Rule 2.425(a) does not apply to the following:
i. An account number which identifies the property alleged to be the subject of a proceeding;
ii. The record of an administrative or agency proceeding;
iii. The record in appellate or review proceedings;
iv. The birth date of a minor whenever the birth date is necessary for the court to establish or maintain subject matter jurisdiction;
v. The name of a minor in any order relating to parental responsibility, time-sharing, or child support;
vi. The name of a minor in any document or order affecting the minor's ownership of real property;
vii. The birth date of a party in a writ of attachment or notice to payor;
viii. In traffic and criminal proceedings: a pro se filing; a court filing that is related to a criminal matter or investigation and that is prepared before the filing of a criminal charge or is not filed as part of any docketed criminal case; an arrest or search warrant or any information in support thereof; a charging document and an affidavit or other documents filed in support of any charging document, including any driving records; a statement of particulars; discovery material introduced into evidence or otherwise filed with the court; and all information necessary for the proper issuance and execution of a subpoena duces tecum;
ix. Information used by the clerk for case maintenance purposes or the courts for case management purposes; and
x. Information which is relevant and material to an issue before the court. FL ST J ADMIN Rule 2.425(b).

c. *Remedies.* Upon motion by a party or interested person or sua sponte by the court, the court may order remedies, sanctions or both for a violation of FL ST J ADMIN Rule 2.425(a). Following notice and an opportunity to respond, the court may impose sanctions if such filing was not made in good faith. FL ST J ADMIN Rule 2.425(c).

d. *Motions not restricted.* FL ST J ADMIN Rule 2.425 does not restrict a party's right to move for protective order, to move to file documents under seal, or to request a determination of the confidentiality of records. FL ST J ADMIN Rule 2.425(d).

e. *Application.* FL ST J ADMIN Rule 2.425 does not affect the application of constitutional provisions, statutes, or rules of court regarding confidential information or access to public information. FL ST J ADMIN Rule 2.425(e).

F. Filing and Service Requirements

1. *Filing requirements.* All original documents must be filed with the court either before service or

immediately thereafter, unless otherwise provided for by general law or other rules. If the original of any bond or other document is not placed in the court file, a certified copy must be so placed by the clerk. FL ST J ADMIN Rule 2.516(d). All documents shall be filed in conformity with the requirements of FL ST J ADMIN Rule 2.525. FL ST RCP Rule 1.080(b). All documents filed in any court shall be filed by electronic transmission in accordance with FL ST J ADMIN Rule 2.525. "Documents" means pleadings, motions, petitions, memoranda, briefs, notices, exhibits, declarations, affidavits, orders, judgments, decrees, writs, opinions, and any other paper or writing submitted to a court. FL ST J ADMIN Rule 2.520(a). All documents that are court records, as defined in FL ST J ADMIN Rule 2.430(a)(1), must be filed by electronic transmission, provided that: (1) the clerk has the ability to accept and retain such documents; (2) the clerk or the chief judge of the circuit has requested permission to accept documents filed by electronic transmission; and (3) the supreme court has entered an order granting permission to the clerk to accept documents filed by electronic transmission. FL ST J ADMIN Rule 2.525(c)(1).

a. *Definition.* "Electronic transmission of documents" means the sending of information by electronic signals to, by or from a court or clerk, which when received can be transformed and stored or transmitted on paper, microfilm, magnetic storage device, optical imaging system, CD-ROM, flash drive, other electronic data storage system, server, case maintenance system ("CM"), electronic court filing ("ECF") system, statewide or local electronic portal ("e-portal"), or other electronic record keeping system authorized by the supreme court in a format sufficient to communicate the information on the original document in a readable format. Electronic transmission of documents includes electronic mail ("e-mail") and any internet-based transmission procedure, and may include procedures allowing for documents to be signed or verified by electronic means. FL ST J ADMIN Rule 2.525(a).
    i. The filing of documents with the court as required by the Florida Rules of Judicial Administration must be made by filing them with the clerk in accordance with FL ST J ADMIN Rule 2.525, except that the judge may permit documents to be filed with the judge, in which event the judge must note the filing date before him or her on the documents and transmit them to the clerk. The date of filing is that shown on the face of the document by the judge's notation or the clerk's time stamp, whichever is earlier. FL ST J ADMIN Rule 2.516(e).
b. *Application.* Any court or clerk of the court may accept the electronic transmission of documents for filing after the clerk, together with input from the chief judge of the circuit, has obtained approval of the procedures and program for doing so from the Supreme Court of Florida. FL ST J ADMIN Rule 2.525(b).
c. *Exceptions*
    i. Paper documents and other submissions may be manually submitted to the clerk or court:
        - When the clerk does not have the ability to accept and retain documents by electronic filing or has not had ECF Procedures approved by the supreme court;
        - For filing by any self-represented party or any self-represented nonparty unless specific ECF Procedures provide a means to file documents electronically. However, any self-represented nonparty that is a governmental or public agency and any other agency, partnership, corporation, or business entity acting on behalf of any governmental or public agency may file documents by electronic transmission if such entity has the capability of filing documents electronically;
        - For filing by attorneys excused from e-mail service in accordance with FL ST J ADMIN Rule 2.516(b);
        - When submitting evidentiary exhibits or filing non-documentary materials;
        - When the filing involves documents in excess of twenty-five (25) megabytes (25MB) in size. For such filings, documents may be transmitted using an electronic storage medium that the clerk has the ability to accept, which may include a CD-ROM, flash drive, or similar storage medium;
        - When filed in open court, as permitted by the court;
        - When paper filing is permitted by any approved statewide or local ECF procedures; and

- If any court determines that justice so requires. FL ST J ADMIN Rule 2.525(d).

ii. Any document in paper form submitted under FL ST J ADMIN Rule 2.525(d) is filed when it is received by the clerk or court and the clerk shall immediately thereafter convert any filed paper document to an electronic document. "Convert to an electronic document" means optically capturing an image of a paper document and using character recognition software to recover as much of the document's text as practicable and then indexing and storing the document in the official court file. FL ST J ADMIN Rule 2.525(c)(4).

iii. Any storage medium submitted under FL ST J ADMIN Rule 2.525(d)(5) is filed when received by the clerk or court and the clerk shall immediately thereafter transfer the electronic documents from the storage device to the official court file. FL ST J ADMIN Rule 2.525(c)(5).

iv. If the filer of any paper document authorized under FL ST J ADMIN Rule 2.525(d) provides a self-addressed, postage-paid envelope for return of the paper document after it is converted to electronic form by the clerk, the clerk shall place the paper document in the envelope and deposit it in the mail. Except when a paper document is required to be maintained, the clerk may recycle any filed paper document that is not to be returned to the filer. FL ST J ADMIN Rule 2.525(c)(6).

v. The clerk may convert any paper document filed before the effective date of FL ST J ADMIN Rule 2.525 to an electronic document. Unless the clerk is required to maintain the paper document, if the paper document has been converted to an electronic document by the clerk, the paper document is no longer part of the official court file and may be removed and recycled. FL ST J ADMIN Rule 2.525(c)(7).

d. *Official court file.* For information on what constitutes the official court file, please see FL ST J ADMIN Rule 2.525(c)(2), FL ST J ADMIN Rule 2.525(c)(3).

e. *Administration.* All attorneys, parties, or other persons using this rule to file documents are required to make arrangements with the court or clerk for the payment of any charges authorized by general law or the supreme court before filing any document by electronic transmission. FL ST J ADMIN Rule 2.525(f)(2).

f. *Filing date.* The filing date for an electronically transmitted document is the date and time that such filing is acknowledged by an electronic stamp or otherwise, pursuant to any procedure set forth in any ECF Procedures approved by the supreme court, or the date the last page of such filing is received by the court or clerk. FL ST J ADMIN Rule 2.525(f)(3).

g. *Accessibility.* All documents transmitted in any electronic form under FL ST J ADMIN Rule 2.525 must comply with the accessibility requirements of FL ST J ADMIN Rule 2.526. FL ST J ADMIN Rule 2.525(g).

2. *Service requirements.* Every pleading subsequent to the initial pleading, all orders, and every other document filed in the action must be served in conformity with the requirements of FL ST J ADMIN Rule 2.516. FL ST RCP Rule 1.080(a).

a. *Service; When required.* Unless the court otherwise orders, or a statute or supreme court administrative order specifies a different means of service, every pleading subsequent to the initial pleading and every other document filed in any court proceeding, except applications for witness subpoenas and documents served by formal notice or required to be served in the manner provided for service of formal notice, must be served in accordance with FL ST J ADMIN Rule 2.516 on each party. No service need be made on parties against whom a default has been entered, except that pleadings asserting new or additional claims against them must be served in the manner provided for service of summons. FL ST J ADMIN Rule 2.516(a).

b. *Service; How made.* When service is required or permitted to be made upon a party represented by an attorney, service must be made upon the attorney unless service upon the party is ordered by the court. FL ST J ADMIN Rule 2.516(b).

i. *Service by electronic mail ("e-mail").* All documents required or permitted to be served on another party must be served by e-mail, unless FL ST J ADMIN Rule 2.516 otherwise provides. When, in addition to service by e-mail, the sender also utilizes another means of service

provided for in FL ST J ADMIN Rule 2.516(b)(2), any differing time limits and other provisions applicable to that other means of service control. FL ST J ADMIN Rule 2.516(b)(1). Any document electronically transmitted to a court or clerk must also be served on all parties and interested persons in accordance with the applicable rules of court. FL ST J ADMIN Rule 2.525(e)(2).

- *Service on attorneys.* Upon appearing in a proceeding, an attorney must serve a designation of a primary e-mail address and may designate no more than two (2) secondary e-mail addresses. Thereafter, service must be directed to all designated e-mail addresses in that proceeding. Every document filed by an attorney thereafter must include the primary e-mail address of that attorney and any secondary e-mail addresses. If an attorney does not designate any e-mail address for service, documents may be served on that attorney at the e-mail address on record with The Florida Bar. FL ST J ADMIN Rule 2.516(b)(1)(A).
- *Exception to e-mail service on attorneys.* Service by an attorney on another attorney must be made by e-mail unless excused by the court. Upon motion by an attorney demonstrating that the attorney has no e-mail account and lacks access to the Internet at the attorney's office, the court may excuse the attorney from the requirements of e-mail service. Service on and by an attorney excused by the court from e-mail service must be by the means provided in FL ST J ADMIN Rule 2.516(b)(2). FL ST J ADMIN Rule 2.516(b)(1)(B).
- *Service on and by parties not represented by an attorney.* Any party not represented by an attorney may serve a designation of a primary e-mail address and also may designate no more than two (2) secondary e-mail addresses to which service must be directed in that proceeding by the means provided in FL ST J ADMIN Rule 2.516(b)(1). If a party not represented by an attorney does not designate an e-mail address for service in a proceeding, service on and by that party must be by the means provided in FL ST J ADMIN Rule 2.516(b)(2). FL ST J ADMIN Rule 2.516(b)(1)(C).
- *Time of service.* Service by e-mail is complete when it is sent. FL ST J ADMIN Rule 2.516(b)(1)(D). An e-mail is deemed served on the date it is sent. FL ST J ADMIN Rule 2.516(b)(1)(D)(i). If the sender learns that the e-mail did not reach the address of the person to be served, the sender must immediately send another copy by e-mail, or by a means authorized by FL ST J ADMIN Rule 2.516(b)(2). FL ST J ADMIN Rule 2.516(b)(1)(D)(ii). E-mail service is treated as service by mail for the computation of time. FL ST J ADMIN Rule 2.516(b)(1)(D)(iii).

ii. *Format of e-mail for service.* Service of a document by e-mail is made by attaching a copy of the document in PDF format to an e-mail sent to all addresses designated by the attorney or party. FL ST J ADMIN Rule 2.516(b)(1)(E).

- All documents served by e-mail must be attached to an e-mail message containing a subject line beginning with the words "SERVICE OF COURT DOCUMENT" in all capital letters, followed by the case number of the proceeding in which the documents are being served. FL ST J ADMIN Rule 2.516(b)(1)(E)(i).
- The body of the e-mail must identify the court in which the proceeding is pending, the case number, the name of the initial party on each side, the title of each document served with that e-mail, and the sender's name and telephone number. FL ST J ADMIN Rule 2.516(b)(1)(E)(ii).
- Any document served by e-mail may be signed by the "/s/" format, as long as the filed original is signed in accordance with the applicable rule of procedure. FL ST J ADMIN Rule 2.516(b)(1)(E)(iii).
- Any e-mail which, together with its attached documents, exceeds five megabytes (5MB) in size, must be divided and sent as separate e-mails, no one of which may exceed five megabytes (5MB) in size and each of which must be sequentially numbered in the subject line. FL ST J ADMIN Rule 2.516(b)(1)(E)(iv).

iii. *Service by other means.* In addition to, and not in lieu of, service by e-mail, service may also be

made upon attorneys by any of the means specified in FL ST J ADMIN Rule 2.516(b)(2). Service on and by all parties who are not represented by an attorney and who do not designate an e-mail address, and on and by all attorneys excused from e-mail service, must be made by delivering a copy of the document or by mailing it to the party or attorney at their last known address or, if no address is known, by leaving it with the clerk of the court. Service by mail is complete upon mailing. Delivery of a copy within FL ST J ADMIN Rule 2.516 is complete upon:

- Handing it to the attorney or to the party,
- Leaving it at the attorney's or party's office with a clerk or other person in charge thereof,
- If there is no one in charge, leaving it in a conspicuous place therein,
- If the office is closed or the person to be served has no office, leaving it at the person's usual place of abode with some person of his or her family above fifteen (15) years of age and informing such person of the contents, or
- Transmitting it by facsimile to the attorney's or party's office with a cover sheet containing the sender's name, firm, address, telephone number, and facsimile number, and the number of pages transmitted. When service is made by facsimile, a copy must also be served by any other method permitted by FL ST J ADMIN Rule 2.516. Facsimile service occurs when transmission is complete. FL ST J ADMIN Rule 2.516(b)(2)(A) through FL ST J ADMIN Rule 2.516(b)(2)(E).
- Service by delivery after 5:00 p.m. must be deemed to have been made by mailing on the date of delivery. FL ST J ADMIN Rule 2.516(b)(2)(F).

c. *Service; Numerous defendants.* In actions when the parties are unusually numerous, the court may regulate the service contemplated by the Florida Rules of Judicial Administration on motion or on its own initiative in such manner as may be found to be just and reasonable. FL ST J ADMIN Rule 2.516(c).

d. *Service by clerk.* Service of notices and other documents required to be made by the clerk must also be done as provided in FL ST J ADMIN Rule 2.516(b). FL ST J ADMIN Rule 2.516(g).

G. Hearings

1. *Preliminary hearings.* The defenses in FL ST RCP Rule 1.140(b)(1) through FL ST RCP Rule 1.140(b)(7), whether made in a pleading or by motion, and the motion for judgment in FL ST RCP Rule 1.140(c) shall be heard and determined before trial on application of any party unless the court orders that the hearing and determination shall be deferred until the trial. FL ST RCP Rule 1.140(d).

H. Forms

1. Official Answer Forms for Florida

a. Caption. FL ST RCP Form 1.901.
b. Crossclaim summons. FL ST RCP Form 1.903.
c. Third-party summons. FL ST RCP Form 1.904.
d. Defense; Statute of limitations. FL ST RCP Form 1.965.
e. Defense; Payment. FL ST RCP Form 1.966.
f. Defense; Accord and satisfaction. FL ST RCP Form 1.967.
g. Defense; Failure of consideration. FL ST RCP Form 1.968.
h. Defense; Statute of frauds. FL ST RCP Form 1.969.
i. Defense; Release. FL ST RCP Form 1.970.
j. Notice of compliance when constitutional challenge is brought. FL ST RCP Form 1.975.

2. Answer Forms for Florida

a. Answer; General form, traverses. FL-PRACFORM § 5:4.

b. Answer; General form, traverses and affirmative defenses. FL-PRACFORM § 5:6.

c. Answer; General form, traverses, affirmative defenses and counterclaim. FL-PRACFORM § 5:7.

d. Answer; General form, traverses, affirmative defenses, counterclaim and crossclaim. FL-PRACFORM § 5:8.

e. Answer; Affirmative defense, fraud. FL-PRACFORM § 5:43.

f. Answer; Affirmative defense, laches. FL-PRACFORM § 5:47.

g. Answer; Affirmative defense, misjoinder. FL-PRACFORM § 5:49.

h. Answer; Affirmative defense, misrepresentation. FL-PRACFORM § 5:50.

i. Answer; Affirmative defense, self defense. FL-PRACFORM § 5:64.

j. Answer; Denial of conditions precedent. FL-PRACFORM § 5:80.

k. General denial. FL-PP § 2:58.

l. General denial; With specified admissions. FL-PP § 2:59.

m. Admission with qualification. FL-PP § 2:60.

n. Conclusions of law not requiring denial. FL-PP § 2:61.

o. Defenses stated in the alternative. FL-PP § 2:62.

p. Denial as to part of allegation. FL-PP § 2:63.

q. Pleader as without knowledge as to truth of allegation. FL-PP § 2:64.

3. Official Forms for Florida Circuit Court, Second Judicial Circuit

a. Notice of change of contact information. FL ST 2 J CIR 2007-05.

I. Checklist

(I) ❑ Matters to be considered by plaintiff

(a) ❑ Required documents

(1) ❑ Summons

(2) ❑ Complaint

(3) ❑ Civil cover sheet

(4) ❑ Return of execution process by process server

(5) ❑ Filing fees

(b) ❑ Supplemental documents

(1) ❑ Exhibits

(2) ❑ Notice of constitutional question

(c) ❑ Time for filing and serving complaint

(1) ❑ Service of the initial process and initial pleading should be made upon a defendant within one hundred twenty (120) days after the filing of the complaint with the court

(II) ❑ Matters to be considered by defendant

(a) ❑ Required documents

(1) ❑ Answer

(2) ❑ Certificate of service

(b) ❑ Supplemental documents

(1) ❑ Exhibits

(2) ❑ Notice of constitutional question

(c) ❑ Time for answer

(1) ❑ Unless a different time is prescribed in a statute of Florida, a defendant shall serve an answer

within twenty (20) days after service of original process and the initial pleading on the defendant, or not later than the date fixed in a notice by publication

(2) ❑ A party served with a pleading stating a crossclaim against that party shall serve an answer to it within twenty (20) days after service on that party

(3) ❑ The plaintiff shall serve an answer to a counterclaim within twenty (20) days after service of the counterclaim

(4) ❑ A defendant who, before being served with process, timely returns a waiver so requested is not required to respond to the complaint until sixty (60) days after the date the defendant received the request for waiver of service; for purposes of computing any time prescribed or allowed by the Florida Rules of Civil Procedure, service of process shall be deemed effected twenty (20) days before the time required to respond to the complaint

(5) ❑ For timing requirements related to service on the state, service of motion impact, and responding when no responsive pleading is required, please see the Timing section of this document

Pleadings
Amended Answer

Document Last Updated January 2013

A. Applicable Rules

1. *State rules*
   a. Nonverification of papers. FL ST RCP Rule 1.030.
   b. Service and filing of pleadings, orders, and documents. FL ST RCP Rule 1.080.
   c. Time. FL ST RCP Rule 1.090.
   d. Pleadings and motions. FL ST RCP Rule 1.100; FL ST RCP Rule 1.110; FL ST RCP Rule 1.120; FL ST RCP Rule 1.130; FL ST RCP Rule 1.190.
   e. Defenses. FL ST RCP Rule 1.140.
   f. Pretrial procedure. FL ST RCP Rule 1.200.
   g. Relief from judgment, decrees, or orders. FL ST RCP Rule 1.540.
   h. Forms. FL ST RCP Rule 1.900.
   i. Minimization of the filing of sensitive information. FL ST J ADMIN Rule 2.425.
   j. Foreign attorneys. FL ST J ADMIN Rule 2.510.
   k. Signature of attorneys and parties. FL ST J ADMIN Rule 2.515.
   l. Paper. FL ST J ADMIN Rule 2.520.
   m. Electronic filing. FL ST J ADMIN Rule 2.525.
   n. Accessibility of information and technology. FL ST J ADMIN Rule 2.526.
   o. Court reporting. FL ST J ADMIN Rule 2.535.
   p. Requests for accommodations by persons with disabilities. FL ST J ADMIN Rule 2.540.
2. *Local rules*
   a. Notice of change of contact information. FL ST 2 J CIR 2007-05.

B. Timing

1. *Amendment as a matter of course.* A party may amend a pleading once as a matter of course at any time before a responsive pleading is served or, if the pleading is one to which no responsive pleading is permitted and the action has not been placed on the trial calendar, may so amend it at any time within twenty (20) days after it is served. FL ST RCP Rule 1.190(a).

2. *Amendment by leave of court.* Otherwise a party may amend a pleading only by leave of court or by written consent of the adverse party. Leave of court shall be given freely when justice so requires. FL ST RCP Rule 1.190(a).
3. *Amendments in furtherance of justice.* At any time in furtherance of justice, upon such terms as may be just, the court may permit any process, proceeding, pleading, or record to be amended or material supplemental matter to be set forth in an amended or supplemental pleading. At every stage of the action the court must disregard any error or defect in the proceedings which does not affect the substantial rights of the parties. FL ST RCP Rule 1.190(e).
4. *Response to amended pleading.* A party shall plead in response to an amended pleading within ten (10) days after service of the amended pleading unless the court otherwise orders. FL ST RCP Rule 1.190(a).
5. *Computation of time*
   a. *Generally.* Computation of time shall be governed by FL ST J ADMIN Rule 2.514. FL ST RCP Rule 1.090(a). The following rules apply in computing time periods specified in any rule of procedure, local rule, court order, or statute that does not specify a method of computing time. FL ST J ADMIN Rule 2.514(a).
      i. *Period stated in days or a longer unit.* When the period is stated in days or a longer unit of time (A) exclude the day of the event that triggers the period; (B) count every day, including intermediate Saturdays, Sundays, and legal holidays; and (C) include the last day of the period, but if the last day is a Saturday, Sunday, or legal holiday, or falls within any period of time extended through an order of the chief justice under FL ST J ADMIN Rule 2.205(a)(2)(B)(iv), the period continues to run until the end of the next day that is not a Saturday, Sunday, or legal holiday and does not fall within any period of time extended through an order of the chief justice. FL ST J ADMIN Rule 2.514(a)(1).
      ii. *Period stated in hours.* When the period is stated in hours (A) begin counting immediately on the occurrence of the event that triggers the period; (B) count every hour, including hours during intermediate Saturdays, Sundays, and legal holidays; and (C) if the period would end on a Saturday, Sunday, or legal holiday, or during any period of time extended through an order of the chief justice under FL ST J ADMIN Rule 2.205(a)(2)(B)(iv), the period continues to run until the same time on the next day that is not a Saturday, Sunday, or legal holiday and does not fall within any period of time extended through an order of the chief justice. FL ST J ADMIN Rule 2.514(a)(2).
      iii. *Period stated in days less than seven (7) days.* When the period stated in days is less than seven (7) days, intermediate Saturdays, Sundays, and legal holidays shall be excluded in the computation. FL ST J ADMIN Rule 2.514(a)(3).
      iv. *"Last day" defined.* Unless a different time is set by a statute, local rule, or court order, the last day ends (A) for electronic filing or for service by any means, at midnight; and (B) for filing by other means, when the clerk's office is scheduled to close. FL ST J ADMIN Rule 2.514(a)(4).
      v. *"Next day" defined.* The "next day" is determined by continuing to count forward when the period is measured after an event and backward when measured before an event. FL ST J ADMIN Rule 2.514(a)(5).
      vi. *"Legal holiday" defined.* "Legal holiday" means (A) the day set aside by FL ST § 110.117, for observing New Year's Day, Martin Luther King, Jr.'s Birthday, Memorial Day, Independence Day, Labor Day, Veterans' Day, Thanksgiving Day, the Friday after Thanksgiving Day, or Christmas Day, and (B) any day observed as a holiday by the clerk's office or as designated by the chief judge. FL ST J ADMIN Rule 2.514(a)(6).
   b. *Additional time after service by mail or e-mail.* When a party may or must act within a specified time after service and service is made by mail or e-mail, five (5) days are added after the period that would otherwise expire under FL ST J ADMIN Rule 2.514(a). FL ST J ADMIN Rule 2.514(b).
   c. *Enlargement.* When an act is required or allowed to be done at or within a specified time by order of court, by the Florida Rules of Civil Procedure, or by notice given thereunder, for cause shown the court at any time in its discretion (1) with or without notice, may order the period enlarged if request

therefor is made before the expiration of the period originally prescribed or as extended by a previous order, or (2) upon motion made and notice after the expiration of the specified period, may permit the act to be done when failure to act was the result of excusable neglect, but it may not extend the time for making a motion for new trial, for rehearing, or to alter or amend a judgment; making a motion for relief from a judgment under FL ST RCP Rule 1.540(b); taking an appeal or filing a petition for certiorari; or making a motion for a directed verdict. FL ST RCP Rule 1.090(b).

d. *Unaffected by expiration of term.* The period of time provided for the doing of any act or the taking of any proceeding shall not be affected or limited by the continued existence or expiration of a term of court. The continued existence or expiration of a term of court in no way affects the power of a court to do any act or take any proceeding in any action which is or has been pending before it. FL ST RCP Rule 1.090(c).

C. General Requirements

1. *Amendments.* A party may amend a pleading once as a matter of course at any time before a responsive pleading is served or, if the pleading is one to which no responsive pleading is permitted and the action has not been placed on the trial calendar, may so amend it at any time within twenty (20) days after it is served. Otherwise a party may amend a pleading only by leave of court or by written consent of the adverse party. Leave of court shall be freely given when justice so requires. FL ST RCP Rule 1.190(a).

   a. *Purpose of amendments.* Amendments can relate to the correction of mistakes, the insertion of jurisdictional averments, the correction or addition of verifications, the addition or substitution or striking out of parties, and generally the rectification of all formal defects in the pleading. The court can also allow amendments setting up an omitted counterclaim or cross-claim if the defendant failed to raise the claim through oversight, inadvertence, or excusable neglect. FL-PP § 2:151.

   b. *Amendment to a pleading/Amended pleading.* A significant difference exists between an amendment to a pleading and an amended pleading. An amendment to a pleading corrects, adds to or deletes from the pleading. An amended pleading is substituted for the former pleading and the former pleading ceases to have any effect. Dee v. Southern Brewing Company, 146 Fla. 588, 1 So.2d 562 (Fla. 1941); Shannon v. McBride, 105 So.2d 16 (Fla. 2d DCA 1958); Hughes v. Home Sav. of America, F.S.B., 675 So.2d 649 (Fla. 2d DCA 1996); FL-PRACPROC § 14:2.

   c. *Relation back of amendments.* When the claim or defense asserted in the amended pleading arose out of the conduct, transaction, or occurrence set forth or attempted to be set forth in the original pleading, the amendment shall relate back to the date of the original pleading. FL ST RCP Rule 1.190(c).

2. *General rules of pleading*

   a. *Claims for relief*

      i. A pleading which sets forth a claim for relief, whether an original claim, counterclaim, crossclaim, or third-party claim, must state a cause of action and shall contain

         - A short and plain statement of the grounds upon which the court's jurisdiction depends, unless the court already has jurisdiction and the claim needs no new grounds of jurisdiction to support it (For information regarding acts subjecting persons to jurisdiction, please see FL ST § 48.193),
         - A short and plain statement of the ultimate facts showing that the pleader is entitled to relief, and
         - A demand for judgment for the relief to which the pleader deems himself or herself entitled. FL ST RCP Rule 1.110(b).

      ii. Relief in the alternative or of several different types may be demanded. Every complaint shall be considered to demand general relief. FL ST RCP Rule 1.110(b).

   b. *Verification.* Except when otherwise specifically provided by these rules or an applicable statute, every pleading or other document of a party represented by an attorney need not be verified or accompanied by an affidavit. FL ST RCP Rule 1.030. When filing an action for foreclosure of a mortgage on residential real property the complaint shall be verified. When verification of a document is required, the document filed shall include an oath, affirmation, or the following statement: "Under penalty of perjury, I declare that I have read the foregoing, and the facts alleged therein are true and correct to the best of my knowledge and belief." FL ST RCP Rule 1.110(b).

c. *Separate statements.* All averments of claim or defense shall be made in consecutively numbered paragraphs, the contents of each of which shall be limited as far as practicable to a statement of a single set of circumstances, and a paragraph may be referred to by number in all subsequent pleadings. Each claim founded upon a separate transaction or occurrence and each defense other than denials shall be stated in a separate count or defense when a separation facilitates the clear presentation of the matter set forth. FL ST RCP Rule 1.110(f).

d. *Statements adopted by reference.* Statements in a pleading may be adopted by reference in a different part of the same pleading, in another pleading, or in any motion. FL ST RCP Rule 1.130(b).

e. *Joinder of causes of action; Consistency.* A pleader may set up in the same action as many claims or causes of action or defenses in the same right as the pleader has, and claims for relief may be stated in the alternative if separate items make up the cause of action, or if two (2) or more causes of action are joined. A party may also set forth two (2) or more statements of a claim or defense alternatively, either in one (1) count or defense or in separate counts or defenses. When two (2) or more statements are made in the alternative and one (1) of them, if made independently, would be sufficient, the pleading is not made insufficient by the insufficiency of one (1) or more of the alternative statements. A party may also state as many separate claims or defenses as that party has, regardless of consistency and whether based on legal or equitable grounds or both. All pleadings shall be construed so as to do substantial justice. FL ST RCP Rule 1.110(g).

f. *Subsequent pleadings.* When the nature of an action permits pleadings subsequent to final judgment and the jurisdiction of the court over the parties has not terminated, the initial pleading subsequent to final judgment shall be designated a supplemental complaint or petition. The action shall then proceed in the same manner and time as though the supplemental complaint or petition were the initial pleading in the action, including the issuance of any needed process. FL ST RCP Rule 1.110(h) shall not apply to proceedings that may be initiated by motion under the Florida Rules of Civil Procedure. FL ST RCP Rule 1.110(h).

g. *Pleading basis for service.* When service of process is to be made under statutes authorizing service on nonresidents of Florida, it is sufficient to plead the basis for service in the language of the statute without pleading the facts supporting service. FL ST RCP Rule 1.070(h).

h. *Forms of pleadings.* Forms of action and technical forms for seeking relief and of pleas, pleadings, or motions are abolished. FL ST RCP Rule 1.110(a).

3. *Answer; Generally.* An answer has three (3) functions. First, it must respond to each allegation of the preceding pleading by admitting, denying or alleging that the pleader is without knowledge of the allegation. Second, it must contain any affirmative defenses that the pleader is interposing to any cause of action alleged in the preceding pleading. Third, the answer may claim affirmative relief against the plaintiff or petitioner by a counterclaim or against a codefendant by a crossclaim. FL-PRACPROC § 11:1.

a. *Content.* In the answer a pleader shall state in short and plain terms the pleader's defenses to each claim asserted and shall admit or deny the averments on which the adverse party relies. If the defendant is without knowledge, the defendant shall so state and such statement shall operate as a denial. Denial shall fairly meet the substance of the averments denied. When a pleader intends in good faith to deny only a part of an averment, the pleader shall specify so much of it as is true and shall deny the remainder. Unless the pleader intends in good faith to controvert all of the averments of the preceding pleading, the pleader may make denials as specific denials of designated averments or may generally deny all of the averments except such designated averments as the pleader expressly admits, but when the pleader does so intend to controvert all of its averments, including averments of the grounds upon which the court's jurisdiction depends, the pleader may do so by general denial. FL ST RCP Rule 1.110(c).

b. *Form of answer.* An answer contains a caption, commencement, body, signature and certificate of service. The caption is the same as that of the initial pleading, except for the designation as one of the types of answer. The body of an answer should contain an admission, denial or plea of without knowledge to each allegation of the preceding pleading, except for the additional allegations in response to a general allegation of conditions precedent and the denial of capacity to sue. FL-PRACPROC § 11:3.

i. *Responding sequentially.* The best method of responding is to answer each paragraph sequentially, combining admissions, denials or pleas of without knowledge when the sequence permits. The admissions, denials and allegations of without knowledge should be stated first, followed separately by any affirmative defenses and then by any counterclaim or crossclaim. A third party complaint may be a part of the same paper, but it is not a part of the answer as is a counterclaim or crossclaim. Paragraphs are numbered consecutively throughout the pleading whether in the answer, counterclaim or crossclaim. Denials for the record only are improper. FL-PRACPROC § 11:3.

c. *Defenses*

i. *Generally.* Every defense in law or fact to a claim for relief in a pleading shall be asserted in the responsive pleading, if one is required, but the following defenses may be made by motion at the option of the pleader: (1) lack of jurisdiction over the subject matter, (2) lack of jurisdiction over the person, (3) improper venue, (4) insufficiency of process, (5) insufficiency of service of process, (6) failure to state a cause of action, and (7) failure to join indispensable parties. A motion making any of these defenses shall be made before pleading if a further pleading is permitted. FL ST RCP Rule 1.140(b).

- *Stated specifically.* The grounds on which any of the enumerated defenses are based and the substantial matters of law intended to be argued shall be stated specifically and with particularity in the responsive pleading or motion. FL ST RCP Rule 1.140(b).
- *Waiver.* Any ground not stated shall be deemed to be waived except any ground showing that the court lacks jurisdiction of the subject matter may be made at any time. No defense or objection is waived by being joined with other defenses or objections in a responsive pleading or motion. FL ST RCP Rule 1.140(b). A party waives all defenses and objections that the party does not present either by motion under FL ST RCP Rule 1.140(b), FL ST RCP Rule 1.140(e), or FL ST RCP Rule 1.140(f) or, if the party has made no motion, in a responsive pleading except as provided in FL ST RCP Rule 1.140(h)(2). FL ST RCP Rule 1.140(h)(1). The defenses of failure to state a cause of action or a legal defense or to join an indispensable party may be raised by motion for judgment on the pleadings or at the trial on the merits in addition to being raised either in a motion under FL ST RCP Rule 1.140(b) or in the answer or reply. The defense of lack of jurisdiction of the subject matter may be raised at any time. FL ST RCP Rule 1.140(h)(2).

ii. *Affirmative defenses.* In pleading to a preceding pleading a party shall set forth affirmatively accord and satisfaction, arbitration and award, assumption of risk, contributory negligence, discharge in bankruptcy, duress, estoppel, failure of consideration, fraud, illegality, injury by fellow servant, laches, license, payment, release, res judicata, statute of frauds, statute of limitations, waiver, and any other matter constituting an avoidance or affirmative defense. When a party has mistakenly designated a defense as a counterclaim or a counterclaim as a defense, the court, on terms if justice so requires, shall treat the pleading as if there had been a proper designation. Affirmative defenses appearing on the face of a prior pleading may be asserted as grounds for a motion or defense under FL ST RCP Rule 1.140(b); provided this shall not limit amendments under FL ST RCP Rule 1.190 even if such ground is sustained. FL ST RCP Rule 1.110(d).

- *Format of defenses.* Affirmative defenses should be placed after the admissions, denials and allegations of without knowledge in the answer. All paragraphs must be numbered consecutively throughout the answer. If a defense is directed to only a part of a cause of action or to one or more, but not all, of several causes of action in the preceding pleading, the part or cause of action to which it is directed should be identified in the defense. Defenses should be identified by consecutive ordinal numbers such as "First Defense" and "Second Defense." FL-PRACPROC § 11:4.

iii. *Effect of failure to deny.* Averments in a pleading to which a responsive pleading is required,

other than those as to the amount of damages, are admitted when not denied in the responsive pleading. Averments in a pleading to which no responsive pleading is required or permitted shall be taken as denied or avoided. FL ST RCP Rule 1.110(e). An admission in an answer binds the party and no proof is required. An admission does not extend beyond the scope of the allegation in the preceding pleading. FL-PRACPROC § 11:3.

4. *Pleading special matters*

   a. *Capacity.* It is not necessary to aver the capacity of a party to sue or be sued, the authority of a party to sue or be sued in a representative capacity, or the legal existence of an organized association of persons that is made a party, except to the extent required to show the jurisdiction of the court. The initial pleading served on behalf of a minor party shall specifically aver the age of the minor party. When a party desires to raise an issue as to the legal existence of any party, the capacity of any party to sue or be sued, or the authority of a party to sue or be sued in a representative capacity, that party shall do so by specific negative averment which shall include such supporting particulars as are peculiarly within the pleader's knowledge. FL ST RCP Rule 1.120(a).

   b. *Fraud, mistake, condition of the mind.* In all averments of fraud or mistake, the circumstances constituting fraud or mistake shall be stated with such particularity as the circumstances may permit. Malice, intent, knowledge, mental attitude, and other condition of mind of a person may be averred generally. FL ST RCP Rule 1.120(b).

   c. *Conditions precedent.* In pleading the performance or occurrence of conditions precedent, it is sufficient to aver generally that all conditions precedent have been performed or have occurred. A denial of performance or occurrence shall be made specifically and with particularity. FL ST RCP Rule 1.120(c).

   d. *Official document or act.* In pleading an official document or official act it is sufficient to aver that the document was issued or the act done in compliance with law. FL ST RCP Rule 1.120(c).

   e. *Judgment or decree.* In pleading a judgment or decree of a domestic or foreign court, a judicial or quasi-judicial tribunal, or a board or officer, it is sufficient to aver the judgment or decree without setting forth matter showing jurisdiction to render it. FL ST RCP Rule 1.120(e).

   f. *Time and place.* For the purpose of testing the sufficiency of a pleading, averments of time and place are material and shall be considered like all other averments of material matter. FL ST RCP Rule 1.120(f).

   g. *Special damage.* When items of special damage are claimed, they shall be specifically stated. FL ST RCP Rule 1.120(g).

5. *Parties*

   a. *Parties generally.* Every action may be prosecuted in the name of the real party in interest, but a personal representative, administrator, guardian, trustee of an express trust, a party with whom or in whose name a contract has been made for the benefit of another, or a party expressly authorized by statute may sue in that person's own name without joining the party for whose benefit the action is brought. All persons having an interest in the subject of the action and in obtaining the relief demanded may join as plaintiffs and any person may be made a defendant who has or claims an interest adverse to the plaintiff. Any person may at any time be made a party if that person's presence is necessary or proper to a complete determination of the cause. Persons having a united interest may be joined on the same side as plaintiffs or defendants, and anyone who refuses to join may for such reason be made a defendant. FL ST RCP Rule 1.210(a).

   b. *Minors or incompetent persons.* When a minor or incompetent person has a representative, such as a guardian or other like fiduciary, the representative may sue or defend on behalf of the minor or incompetent person. A minor or incompetent person who does not have a duly appointed representative may sue by next friend or by a guardian ad litem. The court shall appoint a guardian ad litem for a minor or incompetent person not otherwise represented in an action or shall make such other order as it deems proper for the protection of the minor or incompetent person. FL ST RCP Rule 1.210(b).

   c. For survivor and substitution of parties information, please see FL ST RCP Rule 1.260.

6. *Counterclaims and crossclaims*

   a. *Compulsory counterclaims.* A pleading shall state as a counterclaim any claim which at the time of serving the pleading the pleader has against any opposing party, provided it arises out of the transaction or occurrence that is the subject matter of the opposing party's claim and does not require for its adjudication the presence of third parties over whom the court cannot acquire jurisdiction. But the pleader need not state a claim if (1) at the time the action was commenced the claim was the subject of another pending action, or (2) the opposing party brought suit upon that party's claim by attachment or other process by which the court did not acquire jurisdiction to render a personal judgment on the claim and the pleader is not stating a counterclaim under this rule. FL ST RCP Rule 1.170(a).

   b. *Permissive counterclaim.* A pleading may state as a counterclaim any claim against an opposing party not arising out of the transaction or occurrence that is the subject matter of the opposing party's claim. FL ST RCP Rule 1.170(b).

   c. *Counterclaim exceeding opposing claim.* A counterclaim may or may not diminish or defeat the recovery sought by the opposing party. It may claim relief exceeding in amount or different in kind from that sought in the pleading of the opposing party. FL ST RCP Rule 1.170(c).

   d. *Counterclaim against the State.* The Florida Rules of Civil Procedure shall not be construed to enlarge beyond the limits established by law the right to assert counterclaims or to claim credits against the state or any of its subdivisions or other governmental organizations thereof subject to suit or against a municipal corporation or against an officer, agency, or administrative board of the state. FL ST RCP Rule 1.170(d).

   e. *Counterclaim maturing or acquired after pleading.* A claim which matured or was acquired by the pleader after serving the pleading may be presented as a counterclaim by supplemental pleading with the permission of the court. FL ST RCP Rule 1.170(e).

   f. *Omitted counterclaim or crossclaim.* When a pleader fails to set up a counterclaim or crossclaim through oversight, inadvertence, or excusable neglect, or when justice requires, the pleader may set up the counterclaim or crossclaim by amendment with leave of the court. FL ST RCP Rule 1.170(f).

   g. *Crossclaim against co-party.* A pleading may state as a crossclaim any claim by one party against a co-party arising out of the transaction or occurrence that is the subject matter of either the original action or a counterclaim therein, or relating to any property that is the subject matter of the original action. The crossclaim may include a claim that the party against whom it is asserted is or may be liable to the crossclaimant for all or part of a claim asserted in the action against the crossclaimant. Service of a crossclaim on a party who has appeared in the action shall be made pursuant to FL ST RCP Rule 1.080. Service of a crossclaim against a party who has not appeared in the action shall be made in the manner provided for service of summons. FL ST RCP Rule 1.170(g).

   h. *Additional parties may be brought in.* When the presence of parties other than those to the original action is required to grant complete relief in the determination of a counterclaim or crossclaim, they shall be named in the counterclaim or crossclaim and be served with process and shall be parties to the action thereafter if jurisdiction of them can be obtained and their joinder will not deprive the court of jurisdiction of the action. FL ST RCP Rule 1.250(b) and FL ST RCP Rule 1.250(c) apply to parties brought in under FL ST RCP Rule 1.170(h). FL ST RCP Rule 1.170(h).

   i. *Separate trials; Separate judgment.* If the court orders separate trials as provided in FL ST RCP Rule 1.270(b), judgment on a counterclaim or crossclaim may be rendered when the court has jurisdiction to do so even if a claim of the opposing party has been dismissed or otherwise disposed of. FL ST RCP Rule 1.170(i).

   j. *Demand exceeding jurisdiction; Transfer of action.* If the demand of any counterclaim or crossclaim exceeds the jurisdiction of the court in which the action is pending, the action shall be transferred forthwith to the court of the same county having jurisdiction of the demand in the counterclaim or crossclaim with only such alterations in the pleadings as are essential. The court shall order the transfer of the action and the transmittal of all papers in it to the proper court if the party asserting the demand exceeding the jurisdiction deposits with the court having jurisdiction a sum sufficient to pay

the clerk's service charge in the court to which the action is transferred at the time of filing the counterclaim or crossclaim. Thereupon the original papers and deposit shall be transmitted and filed with a certified copy of the order. The court to which the action is transferred shall have full power and jurisdiction over the demands of all parties. Failure to make the service charge deposit at the time the counterclaim or crossclaim is filed, or within such further time as the court may allow, shall reduce a claim for damages to an amount within the jurisdiction of the court where the action is pending and waive the claim in other cases. FL ST RCP Rule 1.170(j).

7. *Misjoinder and nonjoinder of parties*
   a. *Misjoinder.* Misjoinder of parties is not a ground for dismissal of an action. Any claim against a party may be severed and proceeded with separately. FL ST RCP Rule 1.250(a).
   b. *Dropping parties.* Parties may be dropped by an adverse party in the manner provided for voluntary dismissal in FL ST RCP Rule 1.420(a)(1) subject to the exception stated in FL ST RCP Rule 1.420. If notice of lis pendens has been filed in the action against a party so dropped, the notice of dismissal shall be recorded and cancels the notice of lis pendens without the necessity of a court order. Parties may be dropped by order of court on its own initiative or the motion of any party at any stage of the action on such terms as are just. FL ST RCP Rule 1.250(b).
   c. *Adding parties.* Parties may be added once as a matter of course within the same time that pleadings can be so amended under FL ST RCP Rule 1.190(a). If amendment by leave of court or stipulation of the parties is permitted, parties may be added in the amended pleading without further order of court. Parties may be added by order of court on its own initiative or on motion of any party at any stage of the action and on such terms as are just. FL ST RCP Rule 1.250(c).
8. *Jury demand*
   a. *Right preserved.* The right of trial by jury as declared by the Constitution or by statute shall be preserved to the parties inviolate. FL ST RCP Rule 1.430(a).
   b. *Demand.* Any party may demand a trial by jury of any issue triable of right by a jury by serving upon the other party a demand therefor in writing at any time after commencement of the action and not later than ten (10) days after the service of the last pleading directed to such issue. The demand may be indorsed upon a pleading of the party. FL ST RCP Rule 1.430(b).
   c. *Specification of issues.* In the demand a party may specify the issues that the party wishes so tried; otherwise, the party is deemed to demand trial by jury for all issues so triable. FL ST RCP Rule 1.430(c).
      i. If a party has demanded trial by jury for only some of the issues, any other party may serve a demand for trial by jury of any other or all of the issues triable by jury ten (10) days after service of the demand or such lesser time as the court may order. FL ST RCP Rule 1.430(c).
   d. *Waiver.* A party who fails to serve a demand as required by FL ST RCP Rule 1.430 waives trial by jury. FL ST RCP Rule 1.430(d).
      i. If waived, a jury trial may not be granted without the consent of the parties, but the court may allow an amendment in the proceedings to demand a trial by jury or order a trial by jury on its own motion. FL ST RCP Rule 1.430(d).
      ii. A demand for trial by jury may not be withdrawn without the consent of the parties. FL ST RCP Rule 1.430(d).
9. *Arbitration and mediation*
   a. *Referral to arbitration and mediation.* Except as hereinafter provided or as otherwise prohibited by law, the presiding judge may enter an order referring all or any part of a contested civil matter to mediation or arbitration. The parties to any contested civil matter may file a written stipulation to mediate or arbitrate any issue between them at any time. Such stipulation shall be incorporated into the order of referral. FL ST RCP Rule 1.700(a).
   b. *Arbitration*
      i. *Exclusions.* A civil action shall be ordered to arbitration or arbitration in conjunction with

mediation upon stipulation of the parties. A civil action may be ordered to arbitration or arbitration in conjunction with mediation upon motion of any party or by the court, if the judge determines the action to be of such a nature that arbitration could be of benefit to the litigants or the court. FL ST RCP Rule 1.800.

- Under no circumstances may the following categories of actions be referred to arbitration: (1) bond estreatures; (2) habeas corpus or other extraordinary writs; (3) bond validations; (4) civil or criminal contempt; (5) such other matters as may be specified by order of the chief judge in the circuit. FL ST RCP Rule 1.800.

ii. For more information regarding arbitration, please see FL ST RCP Rule 1.810; FL ST RCP Rule 1.820; FL ST RCP Rule 1.830.

c. *Mediation.* For more information regarding mediation, please see FL ST RCP Rule 1.710; FL ST RCP Rule 1.720; FL ST RCP Rule 1.730; and FL ST RCP Rule 1.750.

10. *Rules of court*

a. *Rules of civil procedure.* The Florida Rules of Civil Procedure apply to all actions of a civil nature and all special statutory proceedings in the circuit courts and county courts except those to which the Florida Probate Rules, the Florida Family Law Rules of Procedure, or the Small Claims Rules apply. FL ST RCP Rule 1.010.

i. The form, content, procedure, and time for pleading in all special statutory proceedings shall be as prescribed by the statutes governing the proceeding unless the Florida Rules of Civil Procedure specifically provide to the contrary. FL ST RCP Rule 1.010.

ii. The Florida Rules of Civil Procedure shall be construed to secure the just, speedy, and inexpensive determination of every action. FL ST RCP Rule 1.010.

b. *Rules of judicial administration.* The Florida Rules of Judicial Administration shall apply to administrative matters in all courts to which the Florida Rules of Judicial Administration are applicable by their terms. The Florida Rules of Judicial Administration shall be construed to secure the speedy and inexpensive determination of every proceeding to which they are applicable. The Florida Rules of Judicial Administration shall supersede all conflicting rules and statutes. FL ST J ADMIN Rule 2.110.

11. *Notice of change of contact information.* The Clerk shall provide a change of address and/or telephone number form for use by attorneys and pro se litigants. With any change of address and/or telephone number, attorneys and pro se litigants governed by FL ST J ADMIN Rule 2.515 will provide to the Clerk and all parties promptly the change of address and/or telephone number form. This form should be submitted only once to the Clerk, who will then make the address and/or telephone number change in all court divisions. FL ST 2 J CIR 2007-05.

D. Documents

1. *Required documents*

a. *Amended answer.* See the General Requirements section of this document for the content of an amended answer. If a party files a motion to amend a pleading, the party shall attach the proposed amended pleading to the motion. FL ST RCP Rule 1.190(a). See the KeyRules Florida Circuit Court Motion for Leave to Amend document for further information.

i. *Notices to persons with disabilities.* See the Format section of this KeyRules document for further information.

b. *Certificate of service.* When any attorney certifies in substance: "I certify that a copy hereof has been furnished to (here insert name or names and addresses used for service) by (e-mail) (delivery) (mail) (fax) on .... (date) ....________________ Attorney" the certificate is taken as prima facie proof of such service in compliance with FL ST J ADMIN Rule 2.516. FL ST J ADMIN Rule 2.516(f).

2. *Supplemental documents*

a. *Exhibits.* All bonds, notes, bills of exchange, contracts, accounts, or documents upon which action may be brought or defense made, or a copy thereof or a copy of the portions thereof material to the pleadings, shall be incorporated in or attached to the pleading. No papers shall be unnecessarily annexed as exhibits. The pleadings shall contain no unnecessary recitals of deeds, documents, contracts, or other instruments. Any exhibit attached to a pleading shall be considered a part of the pleadings for all purposes. FL ST RCP Rule 1.130(a).

b. *Notice of constitutional question.* A party that files a pleading, written motion, or other paper drawing into question the constitutionality of a state statute or a county or municipal charter, ordinance, or franchise must promptly (1) file a notice of constitutional question stating the question and identifying the paper that raises it; and (2) serve the notice and the pleading, written motion, or other paper drawing into question the constitutionality of a state statute or a county or municipal charter, ordinance, or franchise on the Attorney General or the state attorney of the judicial circuit in which the action is pending, by either certified or registered mail. Service of the notice and pleading, written motion, or other paper does not require joinder of the Attorney General or the state attorney as a party to the action. FL ST RCP Rule 1.071.

E. Format

1. *Documents; Type and size.* Documents subject to the exceptions set forth in FL ST J ADMIN Rule 2.525(d) shall be filed on recycled paper measuring eight and one half by eleven (8 1/2 by 11) inches. For purposes of FL ST J ADMIN Rule 2.520, paper is recycled if it contains a minimum content of fifty (50) percent waste paper. Xerographic reduction of legal-size (eight and one half by fourteen (8 1/2 by 14) inches) documents to letter size (eight and one half by eleven (8 1/2 by 11) inches) is prohibited. All other documents filed by electronic transmission shall be filed in a format capable of being printed in a format consistent with the provisions of FL ST J ADMIN Rule 2.250. FL ST J ADMIN Rule 2.520(b).

   a. *Exhibits.* Any exhibit or attachment filed with pleadings or papers may be filed in its original size. FL ST J ADMIN Rule 2.520(c).

   b. *Recording space.* On all papers and documents prepared and filed by the court or by any party to a proceeding which are to be recorded in the public records of any county, including but not limited to final money judgments and notices of lis pendens, a three (3) inch by three (3) inch space at the top right-hand corner on the first page and a one (1) inch by three (3) inch space at the top right-hand corner on each subsequent page shall be left blank and reserved for use by the clerk of court. FL ST J ADMIN Rule 2.520(d).

      i. *Exceptions to recording space.* Any papers or documents created by persons or entities over which the filing party has no control, including but not limited to wills, codicils, trusts, or other testamentary documents; documents prepared or executed by any public officer; documents prepared, executed, acknowledged, or proved outside of the State of Florida; or documents created by State or Federal government agencies, may be filed without the space required by FL ST J ADMIN Rule 2.520. FL ST J ADMIN Rule 2.520(e).

   c. *Noncompliance.* No clerk of court is permitted to refuse to file any document or paper because of noncompliance with the Florida Rules of Judicial Administration. However, upon request of the clerk of court, noncomplying documents must be resubmitted in accordance with the formatting rules. FL ST J ADMIN Rule 2.520(f).

2. *Caption.* Every pleading, motion, order, judgment, or other paper shall have a caption containing the name of the court, the file number, and except for in rem proceedings, including forfeiture proceedings, the name of the first party on each side with an appropriate indication of other parties, and a designation identifying the party filing it and its nature or the nature of the order, as the case may be. In any in rem proceeding, every pleading, motion, order, judgment, or other paper shall have a caption containing the name of the court, the file number, the style "In re" (followed by the name or general description of the property), and a designation of the person or entity filing it and its nature or the nature of the order, as the case may be. In an in rem forfeiture proceeding, the style shall be "In re forfeiture of" (followed by the name of the general description of the property). All papers filed in the action shall be styled in such a manner as to indicate clearly the subject matter of the paper and the party requesting or obtaining relief. FL ST RCP Rule 1.100(c)(1).

3. *Writing and written defined.* Writing or written means a document containing information, an application, or a stipulation. FL ST RCP Rule 1.080(c).

4. *Rule abbreviations*
   a. The Florida Rules of Civil Procedure and shall be abbreviated as Fla.R.Civ.P. FL ST RCP Rule 1.010.
   b. The Florida Rules of Judicial Administration shall be abbreviated as Fla. R. Jud. Admin. FL ST J ADMIN Rule 2.110.
5. *Nonverification.* Except when otherwise specifically provided by the Florida Rules of Civil Procedure or an applicable statute, every pleading or other document of a party represented by an attorney need not be verified or accompanied by an affidavit. FL ST RCP Rule 1.030; FL ST J ADMIN Rule 2.515(a).
6. *Attorney signature*
   a. *Attorney signature.* Every pleading and other document of a party represented by an attorney shall be signed by at least one (1) attorney of record in that attorney's individual name whose current record Florida Bar address, telephone number, including area code, primary e-mail address and secondary e-mail addresses, if any, and Florida Bar number shall be stated, and who shall be duly licensed to practice law in Florida or who shall have received permission to appear in the particular case as provided in FL ST J ADMIN Rule 2.510. FL ST J ADMIN Rule 2.515(a).
      i. The attorney may be required by the court to give the address of, and to vouch for the attorney's authority to represent, the party. FL ST J ADMIN Rule 2.515(a).
      ii. The signature of an attorney shall constitute a certificate by the attorney that the attorney has read the pleading or other document; that to the best of the attorney's knowledge, information, and belief there is good ground to support it; and that it is not interposed for delay. FL ST J ADMIN Rule 2.515(a).
      iii. If a pleading is not signed or is signed with intent to defeat the purpose of FL ST J ADMIN Rule 2.515, it may be stricken and the action may proceed as though the pleading or other document had not been served. FL ST J ADMIN Rule 2.515(a).
   b. *Pro se litigant signature.* A party who is not represented by an attorney shall sign any pleading or other paper and state the party's address and telephone number, including area code. FL ST J ADMIN Rule 2.515(b).
   c. *Form of signature*
      i. The signatures required on pleadings and documents by FL ST J ADMIN Rule 2.515(a) and FL ST J ADMIN Rule 2.515(b) may be:
         - Original signatures;
         - Original signatures that have been reproduced by electronic means, such as on electronically transmitted documents or photocopied documents;
         - Electronic signatures using the "/s/," "s/," or "/s" formats by or at the direction of the person signing; or
         - Any other signature format authorized by general law, so long as the clerk where the proceeding is pending has the capability of receiving and has obtained approval from the Supreme Court of Florida to accept pleadings and documents with that signature format. FL ST J ADMIN Rule 2.515(c)(1).
      ii. An attorney, party, or other person who files a pleading or paper by electronic transmission that does not contain the original signature of that attorney, party, or other person shall file that identical pleading or paper in paper form containing an original signature of that attorney, party, or other person (hereinafter called the follow-up filing) immediately thereafter. The follow-up filing is not required if the Supreme Court of Florida has entered an order directing the clerk of court to discontinue accepting the follow-up filing. FL ST J ADMIN Rule 2.515(c)(2).
7. *Forms*
   a. *Process.* The forms of process, notice of lis pendens, and notice of action provided in the Florida Rules of Civil Procedure are sufficient. Variations from the forms do not void process or notices that are otherwise sufficient. FL ST RCP Rule 1.900(a).

b. *Other forms.* The other forms provided in the Florida Rules of Civil Procedure are sufficient for the matters that are covered by them. So long as the substance is expressed without prolixity, the forms may be varied to meet the facts of a particular case. FL ST RCP Rule 1.900(b).

c. *Formal matters.* Captions, except for the designation of the paper, are omitted from the forms provided in the Florida Rules of Civil Procedure. A general form of caption is the first form provided. Signatures are omitted from pleadings and motions. FL ST RCP Rule 1.900(c).

8. *Notices to persons with disabilities.* All notices of court proceedings to be held in a public facility, and all process compelling appearance at such proceedings, shall include the following statement in bold face, fourteen (14) point Times New Roman or Courier font: "If you are a person with a disability who needs any accommodation in order to participate in this proceeding, you are entitled, at no cost to you, to the provision of certain assistance. Please contact [identify applicable court personnel by name, address, and telephone number] at least seven (7) days before your scheduled court appearance, or immediately upon receiving this notification if the time before the scheduled appearance is less than seven (7) days; if you are hearing or voice impaired, call 711." FL ST J ADMIN Rule 2.540(c)(1).

9. *Minimization of the filing of sensitive information*

a. *Limitations for court filings.* Unless authorized by FL ST J ADMIN Rule 2.425(b), statute, another rule of court, or the court orders otherwise, designated sensitive information filed with the court must be limited to the following format:

i. The initials of a person known to be a minor;

ii. The year of birth of a person's birth date;

iii. No portion of any: Social security number, Bank account number, Credit card account number, Charge account number, or Debit account number;

iv. The last four digits of any: Taxpayer identification number (TIN), Employee identification number, Driver's license number, Passport number, Telephone number, Financial account number, except as set forth in FL ST J ADMIN Rule 2.425(a)(3), Brokerage account number, Insurance policy account number, Loan account number, Customer account number, or Patient or health care number;

v. A truncated version of any: Email address, Computer user name, Password, or Personal identification number (PIN); and

vi. A truncated version of any other sensitive information as provided by court order. FL ST J ADMIN Rule 2.425(a).

b. *Exceptions.* FL ST J ADMIN Rule 2.425(a) does not apply to the following:

i. An account number which identifies the property alleged to be the subject of a proceeding;

ii. The record of an administrative or agency proceeding;

iii. The record in appellate or review proceedings;

iv. The birth date of a minor whenever the birth date is necessary for the court to establish or maintain subject matter jurisdiction;

v. The name of a minor in any order relating to parental responsibility, time-sharing, or child support;

vi. The name of a minor in any document or order affecting the minor's ownership of real property;

vii. The birth date of a party in a writ of attachment or notice to payor;

viii. In traffic and criminal proceedings: a pro se filing; a court filing that is related to a criminal matter or investigation and that is prepared before the filing of a criminal charge or is not filed as part of any docketed criminal case; an arrest or search warrant or any information in support thereof; a charging document and an affidavit or other documents filed in support of any charging document, including any driving records; a statement of particulars; discovery material introduced into evidence or otherwise filed with the court; and all information necessary for the proper issuance and execution of a subpoena duces tecum;

ix. Information used by the clerk for case maintenance purposes or the courts for case management purposes; and

x. Information which is relevant and material to an issue before the court. FL ST J ADMIN Rule 2.425(b).

c. *Remedies.* Upon motion by a party or interested person or sua sponte by the court, the court may order remedies, sanctions or both for a violation of FL ST J ADMIN Rule 2.425(a). Following notice and an opportunity to respond, the court may impose sanctions if such filing was not made in good faith. FL ST J ADMIN Rule 2.425(c).

d. *Motions not restricted.* FL ST J ADMIN Rule 2.425 does not restrict a party's right to move for protective order, to move to file documents under seal, or to request a determination of the confidentiality of records. FL ST J ADMIN Rule 2.425(d).

e. *Application.* FL ST J ADMIN Rule 2.425 does not affect the application of constitutional provisions, statutes, or rules of court regarding confidential information or access to public information. FL ST J ADMIN Rule 2.425(e).

F. Filing and Service Requirements

1. *Filing requirements.* All original documents must be filed with the court either before service or immediately thereafter, unless otherwise provided for by general law or other rules. If the original of any bond or other document is not placed in the court file, a certified copy must be so placed by the clerk. FL ST J ADMIN Rule 2.516(d). All documents shall be filed in conformity with the requirements of FL ST J ADMIN Rule 2.525. FL ST RCP Rule 1.080(b). All documents filed in any court shall be filed by electronic transmission in accordance with FL ST J ADMIN Rule 2.525. "Documents" means pleadings, motions, petitions, memoranda, briefs, notices, exhibits, declarations, affidavits, orders, judgments, decrees, writs, opinions, and any other paper or writing submitted to a court. FL ST J ADMIN Rule 2.520(a). All documents that are court records, as defined in FL ST J ADMIN Rule 2.430(a)(1), must be filed by electronic transmission, provided that: (1) the clerk has the ability to accept and retain such documents; (2) the clerk or the chief judge of the circuit has requested permission to accept documents filed by electronic transmission; and (3) the supreme court has entered an order granting permission to the clerk to accept documents filed by electronic transmission. FL ST J ADMIN Rule 2.525(c)(1).

a. *Definition.* "Electronic transmission of documents" means the sending of information by electronic signals to, by or from a court or clerk, which when received can be transformed and stored or transmitted on paper, microfilm, magnetic storage device, optical imaging system, CD-ROM, flash drive, other electronic data storage system, server, case maintenance system ("CM"), electronic court filing ("ECF") system, statewide or local electronic portal ("e-portal"), or other electronic record keeping system authorized by the supreme court in a format sufficient to communicate the information on the original document in a readable format. Electronic transmission of documents includes electronic mail ("e-mail") and any internet-based transmission procedure, and may include procedures allowing for documents to be signed or verified by electronic means. FL ST J ADMIN Rule 2.525(a).

i. The filing of documents with the court as required by the Florida Rules of Judicial Administration must be made by filing them with the clerk in accordance with FL ST J ADMIN Rule 2.525, except that the judge may permit documents to be filed with the judge, in which event the judge must note the filing date before him or her on the documents and transmit them to the clerk. The date of filing is that shown on the face of the document by the judge's notation or the clerk's time stamp, whichever is earlier. FL ST J ADMIN Rule 2.516(e).

b. *Application.* Any court or clerk of the court may accept the electronic transmission of documents for filing after the clerk, together with input from the chief judge of the circuit, has obtained approval of the procedures and program for doing so from the Supreme Court of Florida. FL ST J ADMIN Rule 2.525(b).

c. *Exceptions*

i. Paper documents and other submissions may be manually submitted to the clerk or court:

- When the clerk does not have the ability to accept and retain documents by electronic filing or has not had ECF Procedures approved by the supreme court;

- For filing by any self-represented party or any self-represented nonparty unless specific ECF Procedures provide a means to file documents electronically. However, any self-represented nonparty that is a governmental or public agency and any other agency, partnership, corporation, or business entity acting on behalf of any governmental or public agency may file documents by electronic transmission if such entity has the capability of filing documents electronically;
- For filing by attorneys excused from e-mail service in accordance with FL ST J ADMIN Rule 2.516(b);
- When submitting evidentiary exhibits or filing non-documentary materials;
- When the filing involves documents in excess of twenty-five (25) megabytes (25MB) in size. For such filings, documents may be transmitted using an electronic storage medium that the clerk has the ability to accept, which may include a CD-ROM, flash drive, or similar storage medium;
- When filed in open court, as permitted by the court;
- When paper filing is permitted by any approved statewide or local ECF procedures; and
- If any court determines that justice so requires. FL ST J ADMIN Rule 2.525(d).

ii. Any document in paper form submitted under FL ST J ADMIN Rule 2.525(d) is filed when it is received by the clerk or court and the clerk shall immediately thereafter convert any filed paper document to an electronic document. "Convert to an electronic document" means optically capturing an image of a paper document and using character recognition software to recover as much of the document’s text as practicable and then indexing and storing the document in the official court file. FL ST J ADMIN Rule 2.525(c)(4).

iii. Any storage medium submitted under FL ST J ADMIN Rule 2.525(d)(5) is filed when received by the clerk or court and the clerk shall immediately thereafter transfer the electronic documents from the storage device to the official court file. FL ST J ADMIN Rule 2.525(c)(5).

iv. If the filer of any paper document authorized under FL ST J ADMIN Rule 2.525(d) provides a self-addressed, postage-paid envelope for return of the paper document after it is converted to electronic form by the clerk, the clerk shall place the paper document in the envelope and deposit it in the mail. Except when a paper document is required to be maintained, the clerk may recycle any filed paper document that is not to be returned to the filer. FL ST J ADMIN Rule 2.525(c)(6).

v. The clerk may convert any paper document filed before the effective date of FL ST J ADMIN Rule 2.525 to an electronic document. Unless the clerk is required to maintain the paper document, if the paper document has been converted to an electronic document by the clerk, the paper document is no longer part of the official court file and may be removed and recycled. FL ST J ADMIN Rule 2.525(c)(7).

d. *Official court file.* For information on what constitutes the official court file, please see FL ST J ADMIN Rule 2.525(c)(2), FL ST J ADMIN Rule 2.525(c)(3).

e. *Administration.* All attorneys, parties, or other persons using this rule to file documents are required to make arrangements with the court or clerk for the payment of any charges authorized by general law or the supreme court before filing any document by electronic transmission. FL ST J ADMIN Rule 2.525(f)(2).

f. *Filing date.* The filing date for an electronically transmitted document is the date and time that such filing is acknowledged by an electronic stamp or otherwise, pursuant to any procedure set forth in any ECF Procedures approved by the supreme court, or the date the last page of such filing is received by the court or clerk. FL ST J ADMIN Rule 2.525(f)(3).

g. *Accessibility.* All documents transmitted in any electronic form under FL ST J ADMIN Rule 2.525 must comply with the accessibility requirements of FL ST J ADMIN Rule 2.526. FL ST J ADMIN Rule 2.525(g).

2. *Service requirements.* Every pleading subsequent to the initial pleading, all orders, and every other

document filed in the action must be served in conformity with the requirements of FL ST J ADMIN Rule 2.516. FL ST RCP Rule 1.080(a).

a. *Service; When required.* Unless the court otherwise orders, or a statute or supreme court administrative order specifies a different means of service, every pleading subsequent to the initial pleading and every other document filed in any court proceeding, except applications for witness subpoenas and documents served by formal notice or required to be served in the manner provided for service of formal notice, must be served in accordance with FL ST J ADMIN Rule 2.516 on each party. No service need be made on parties against whom a default has been entered, except that pleadings asserting new or additional claims against them must be served in the manner provided for service of summons. FL ST J ADMIN Rule 2.516(a).

b. *Service; How made.* When service is required or permitted to be made upon a party represented by an attorney, service must be made upon the attorney unless service upon the party is ordered by the court. FL ST J ADMIN Rule 2.516(b).

   i. *Service by electronic mail ("e-mail").* All documents required or permitted to be served on another party must be served by e-mail, unless FL ST J ADMIN Rule 2.516 otherwise provides. When, in addition to service by e-mail, the sender also utilizes another means of service provided for in FL ST J ADMIN Rule 2.516(b)(2), any differing time limits and other provisions applicable to that other means of service control. FL ST J ADMIN Rule 2.516(b)(1). Any document electronically transmitted to a court or clerk must also be served on all parties and interested persons in accordance with the applicable rules of court. FL ST J ADMIN Rule 2.525(e)(2).

      - *Service on attorneys.* Upon appearing in a proceeding, an attorney must serve a designation of a primary e-mail address and may designate no more than two (2) secondary e-mail addresses. Thereafter, service must be directed to all designated e-mail addresses in that proceeding. Every document filed by an attorney thereafter must include the primary e-mail address of that attorney and any secondary e-mail addresses. If an attorney does not designate any e-mail address for service, documents may be served on that attorney at the e-mail address on record with The Florida Bar. FL ST J ADMIN Rule 2.516(b)(1)(A).

      - *Exception to e-mail service on attorneys.* Service by an attorney on another attorney must be made by e-mail unless excused by the court. Upon motion by an attorney demonstrating that the attorney has no e-mail account and lacks access to the Internet at the attorney's office, the court may excuse the attorney from the requirements of e-mail service. Service on and by an attorney excused by the court from e-mail service must be by the means provided in FL ST J ADMIN Rule 2.516(b)(2). FL ST J ADMIN Rule 2.516(b)(1)(B).

      - *Service on and by parties not represented by an attorney.* Any party not represented by an attorney may serve a designation of a primary e-mail address and also may designate no more than two (2) secondary e-mail addresses to which service must be directed in that proceeding by the means provided in FL ST J ADMIN Rule 2.516(b)(1). If a party not represented by an attorney does not designate an e-mail address for service in a proceeding, service on and by that party must be by the means provided in FL ST J ADMIN Rule 2.516(b)(2). FL ST J ADMIN Rule 2.516(b)(1)(C).

      - *Time of service.* Service by e-mail is complete when it is sent. FL ST J ADMIN Rule 2.516(b)(1)(D). An e-mail is deemed served on the date it is sent. FL ST J ADMIN Rule 2.516(b)(1)(D)(i). If the sender learns that the e-mail did not reach the address of the person to be served, the sender must immediately send another copy by e-mail, or by a means authorized by FL ST J ADMIN Rule 2.516(b)(2). FL ST J ADMIN Rule 2.516(b)(1)(D)(ii). E-mail service is treated as service by mail for the computation of time. FL ST J ADMIN Rule 2.516(b)(1)(D)(iii).

   ii. *Format of e-mail for service.* Service of a document by e-mail is made by attaching a copy of the document in PDF format to an e-mail sent to all addresses designated by the attorney or party. FL ST J ADMIN Rule 2.516(b)(1)(E).

      - All documents served by e-mail must be attached to an e-mail message containing a

subject line beginning with the words "SERVICE OF COURT DOCUMENT" in all capital letters, followed by the case number of the proceeding in which the documents are being served. FL ST J ADMIN Rule 2.516(b)(1)(E)(i).

- The body of the e-mail must identify the court in which the proceeding is pending, the case number, the name of the initial party on each side, the title of each document served with that e-mail, and the sender's name and telephone number. FL ST J ADMIN Rule 2.516(b)(1)(E)(ii).
- Any document served by e-mail may be signed by the "/s/" format, as long as the filed original is signed in accordance with the applicable rule of procedure. FL ST J ADMIN Rule 2.516(b)(1)(E)(iii).
- Any e-mail which, together with its attached documents, exceeds five megabytes (5MB) in size, must be divided and sent as separate e-mails, no one of which may exceed five megabytes (5MB) in size and each of which must be sequentially numbered in the subject line. FL ST J ADMIN Rule 2.516(b)(1)(E)(iv).

iii. *Service by other means.* In addition to, and not in lieu of, service by e-mail, service may also be made upon attorneys by any of the means specified in FL ST J ADMIN Rule 2.516(b)(2). Service on and by all parties who are not represented by an attorney and who do not designate an e-mail address, and on and by all attorneys excused from e-mail service, must be made by delivering a copy of the document or by mailing it to the party or attorney at their last known address or, if no address is known, by leaving it with the clerk of the court. Service by mail is complete upon mailing. Delivery of a copy within FL ST J ADMIN Rule 2.516 is complete upon:

- Handing it to the attorney or to the party,
- Leaving it at the attorney's or party's office with a clerk or other person in charge thereof,
- If there is no one in charge, leaving it in a conspicuous place therein,
- If the office is closed or the person to be served has no office, leaving it at the person's usual place of abode with some person of his or her family above fifteen (15) years of age and informing such person of the contents, or
- Transmitting it by facsimile to the attorney's or party's office with a cover sheet containing the sender's name, firm, address, telephone number, and facsimile number, and the number of pages transmitted. When service is made by facsimile, a copy must also be served by any other method permitted by FL ST J ADMIN Rule 2.516. Facsimile service occurs when transmission is complete. FL ST J ADMIN Rule 2.516(b)(2)(A) through FL ST J ADMIN Rule 2.516(b)(2)(E).
- Service by delivery after 5:00 p.m. must be deemed to have been made by mailing on the date of delivery. FL ST J ADMIN Rule 2.516(b)(2)(F).

c. *Service; Numerous defendants.* In actions when the parties are unusually numerous, the court may regulate the service contemplated by the Florida Rules of Judicial Administration on motion or on its own initiative in such manner as may be found to be just and reasonable. FL ST J ADMIN Rule 2.516(c).

d. *Service by clerk.* Service of notices and other documents required to be made by the clerk must also be done as provided in FL ST J ADMIN Rule 2.516(b). FL ST J ADMIN Rule 2.516(g).

G. Hearings

1. The parties may be required to participate in pretrial proceedings to consider and determine the necessity or desirability of an amendment to a pleading. FL ST RCP Rule 1.200(b)(2); FL-PP § 2:151.

H. Forms

1. Official Amended Answer Forms for Florida

a. Caption. FL ST RCP Form 1.901.

b. Notice of compliance when constitutional challenge is brought. FL ST RCP Form 1.975.

2. Amended Answer Forms for Florida

a. Form for amendment to answer. FL-RCPF R 1.190(50).

b. Form for supplement to pleading. FL-RCPF R 1.190(102).

3. Official Forms for Florida Circuit Court, Second Judicial Circuit

a. Notice of change of contact information. FL ST 2 J CIR 2007-05.

I. Checklist

(I) ❑ Matters to be considered by plaintiff

(a) ❑ Required documents

(1) ❑ Amended answer

(2) ❑ Certificate of service

(b) ❑ Supplemental documents

(1) ❑ Exhibits

(2) ❑ Notice of constitutional question

(c) ❑ Timing

(1) ❑ A party may amend a pleading once as a matter of course at any time before a responsive pleading is served

(2) ❑ If the pleading is one to which no responsive pleading is permitted and the action has not been placed on the trial calendar, may so amend it at any time within twenty (20) days after it is served

Motions, Oppositions and Replies
Motion to Strike

Document Last Updated January 2013

A. Applicable Rules

1. *State rules*

a. Rules of court. FL ST RCP Rule 1.010; FL ST J ADMIN Rule 2.110.

b. Nonverification of pleadings. FL ST RCP Rule 1.030.

c. Service and filing of pleadings, orders, and documents. FL ST RCP Rule 1.080.

d. Time. FL ST RCP Rule 1.090.

e. Pleadings and motions. FL ST RCP Rule 1.100.

f. Defenses. FL ST RCP Rule 1.140.

g. Sham pleadings. FL ST RCP Rule 1.150.

h. Motions. FL ST RCP Rule 1.160.

i. Relief from judgment, decrees, or orders. FL ST RCP Rule 1.540.

j. Mediation and arbitration. FL ST RCP Rule 1.700; FL ST RCP Rule 1.710; FL ST RCP Rule 1.720; FL ST RCP Rule 1.730; FL ST RCP Rule 1.750; FL ST RCP Rule 1.800; FL ST RCP Rule 1.810; FL ST RCP Rule 1.820; FL ST RCP Rule 1.830.

k. Forms. FL ST RCP Rule 1.900.

l. Minimization of the filing of sensitive information. FL ST J ADMIN Rule 2.425.

m. Retention of court records. FL ST J ADMIN Rule 2.430.

n. Foreign attorneys. FL ST J ADMIN Rule 2.510.

o. Signature of attorneys and parties. FL ST J ADMIN Rule 2.515.

p. Paper. FL ST J ADMIN Rule 2.520.
q. Electronic filing. FL ST J ADMIN Rule 2.525.
r. Accessibility of information and technology. FL ST J ADMIN Rule 2.526.
s. Communication equipment. FL ST J ADMIN Rule 2.530.
t. Court reporting. FL ST J ADMIN Rule 2.535.
u. Requests for accommodations by persons with disabilities. FL ST J ADMIN Rule 2.540.

2. *Local rules*
   a. Notice of change of contact information. FL ST 2 J CIR 2007-05.

B. Timing

1. *Motion to strike.* A party may move to strike or the court may strike redundant, immaterial, impertinent, or scandalous matter from any pleading at any time. FL ST RCP Rule 1.140(f).
2. *Motion to strike; Failure to state a legal defense.* If a pleading sets forth a claim for relief to which the adverse party is not required to serve a responsive pleading, the adverse party may assert any defense in law or fact to that claim for relief at the trial, except that the objection of failure to state a legal defense in an answer or reply shall be asserted by motion to strike the defense within twenty (20) days after service of the answer or reply. FL ST RCP Rule 1.140(b).
3. *Motion to strike; Sham pleadings.* If a party deems any pleading or part thereof filed by another party to be a sham, that party may move to strike the pleading or part thereof before the cause is set for trial. FL ST RCP Rule 1.150(a).
4. *General motion timing.* A copy of any written motion which may not be heard ex parte and a copy of the notice of the hearing thereof shall be served a reasonable time before the time specified for the hearing. FL ST RCP Rule 1.090(d).
5. *Computation of time*
   a. *Generally.* Computation of time shall be governed by FL ST J ADMIN Rule 2.514. FL ST RCP Rule 1.090(a). The following rules apply in computing time periods specified in any rule of procedure, local rule, court order, or statute that does not specify a method of computing time. FL ST J ADMIN Rule 2.514(a).
      i. *Period stated in days or a longer unit.* When the period is stated in days or a longer unit of time (A) exclude the day of the event that triggers the period; (B) count every day, including intermediate Saturdays, Sundays, and legal holidays; and (C) include the last day of the period, but if the last day is a Saturday, Sunday, or legal holiday, or falls within any period of time extended through an order of the chief justice under FL ST J ADMIN Rule 2.205(a)(2)(B)(iv), the period continues to run until the end of the next day that is not a Saturday, Sunday, or legal holiday and does not fall within any period of time extended through an order of the chief justice. FL ST J ADMIN Rule 2.514(a)(1).
      ii. *Period stated in hours.* When the period is stated in hours (A) begin counting immediately on the occurrence of the event that triggers the period; (B) count every hour, including hours during intermediate Saturdays, Sundays, and legal holidays; and (C) if the period would end on a Saturday, Sunday, or legal holiday, or during any period of time extended through an order of the chief justice under FL ST J ADMIN Rule 2.205(a)(2)(B)(iv), the period continues to run until the same time on the next day that is not a Saturday, Sunday, or legal holiday and does not fall within any period of time extended through an order of the chief justice. FL ST J ADMIN Rule 2.514(a)(2).
      iii. *Period stated in days less than seven (7) days.* When the period stated in days is less than seven (7) days, intermediate Saturdays, Sundays, and legal holidays shall be excluded in the computation. FL ST J ADMIN Rule 2.514(a)(3).
      iv. *"Last day" defined.* Unless a different time is set by a statute, local rule, or court order, the last day ends (A) for electronic filing or for service by any means, at midnight; and (B) for filing by other means, when the clerk's office is scheduled to close. FL ST J ADMIN Rule 2.514(a)(4).

v. *"Next day" defined.* The "next day" is determined by continuing to count forward when the period is measured after an event and backward when measured before an event. FL ST J ADMIN Rule 2.514(a)(5).

vi. *"Legal holiday" defined.* "Legal holiday" means (A) the day set aside by FL ST § 110.117, for observing New Year's Day, Martin Luther King, Jr.'s Birthday, Memorial Day, Independence Day, Labor Day, Veterans' Day, Thanksgiving Day, the Friday after Thanksgiving Day, or Christmas Day, and (B) any day observed as a holiday by the clerk's office or as designated by the chief judge. FL ST J ADMIN Rule 2.514(a)(6).

b. *Additional time after service by mail or e-mail.* When a party may or must act within a specified time after service and service is made by mail or e-mail, five (5) days are added after the period that would otherwise expire under FL ST J ADMIN Rule 2.514(a). FL ST J ADMIN Rule 2.514(b).

c. *Enlargement.* When an act is required or allowed to be done at or within a specified time by order of court, by the Florida Rules of Civil Procedure, or by notice given thereunder, for cause shown the court at any time in its discretion (1) with or without notice, may order the period enlarged if request therefor is made before the expiration of the period originally prescribed or as extended by a previous order, or (2) upon motion made and notice after the expiration of the specified period, may permit the act to be done when failure to act was the result of excusable neglect, but it may not extend the time for making a motion for new trial, for rehearing, or to alter or amend a judgment; making a motion for relief from a judgment under FL ST RCP Rule 1.540(b); taking an appeal or filing a petition for certiorari; or making a motion for a directed verdict. FL ST RCP Rule 1.090(b).

d. *Unaffected by expiration of term.* The period of time provided for the doing of any act or the taking of any proceeding shall not be affected or limited by the continued existence or expiration of a term of court. The continued existence or expiration of a term of court in no way affects the power of a court to do any act or take any proceeding in any action which is or has been pending before it. FL ST RCP Rule 1.090(c).

C. General Requirements

1. *Motions generally*

a. *Contents.* An application to the court for an order shall be by motion which shall be made in writing unless made during a hearing or trial, shall state with particularity the grounds therefor, and shall set forth the relief or order sought. The requirement of writing is fulfilled if the motion is stated in a written notice of the hearing of the motion. All notices of hearing shall specify each motion or other matter to be heard. FL ST RCP Rule 1.100(b).

b. *Particularity requirement.* The court considers a motion in the light of the substantive law, rule or statute to make its determination. Some rules require a statement of the grounds for a motion under the rule. Failure to give the grounds will result in denial of the motion. This should be the result in all situations when the ground for the motion is not inherent in the rule. FL-PRACPROC § 9:3. The requirement is nevertheless an important one, first because of the due process notice rights of the respondent, as well as for the assistance it provides to the court in its preparation for the hearing or, absent a hearing, for disposition. 4 FLPRAC R 1.100.

2. *Motion to strike under FL ST RCP Rule 1.140.* Two (2) types of motion to strike are authorized by FL ST RCP Rule 1.140. One is used to eliminate immaterial, redundant, impertinent or scandalous allegations. The other is used to test the legal sufficiency of a defense. FL-PRACPROC § 10:6.

a. *Motion to strike to eliminate immaterial, redundant, impertinent or scandalous allegations*

i. As used in FL ST RCP Rule 1.140(f), redundant means allegations that are foreign to the issues or needless repetition of allegations. Immaterial means allegations having no essential or important relationship to the issues or unnecessary elaboration of material allegations. Impertinent means allegations that do not belong to the issue and are not necessary to it. Scandalous means unnecessary allegations censuring or accusing a party. FL-PRACPROC § 10:6.

ii. The motion can be made at any time and does not toll the time for pleading. FL-PRACPROC § 10:6.

iii. The motion reaches improper allegations of damages. When directed to an entire paragraph and any part of it is proper, the motion should be denied. Leave to amend should be granted after striking part of a pleading unless a proper amendment cannot be made. FL-PRACPROC § 10:6.

iv. The use of a motion to strike is not favored by the courts and the remedy is used sparingly. Florida courts have held that an allegation must be "wholly irrelevant" and that if there is some doubt it must be resolved in support of the pleading and against the party moving to strike. If any part of an allegation is relevant, then that part should not be stricken from the pleading. 5 FLPRAC § 7:30.

b. *Motion to strike the legal sufficiency of a defense*

i. The legal insufficiency of a defense alleged in an answer or reply is attacked by a motion to strike. It is the counterpart of a motion to dismiss for failure to state a cause of action directed to a pleading seeking affirmative relief. FL-PRACPROC § 10:7.

ii. A motion to strike a defense tests only the legal sufficiency of the defense, and it is reversible error for a trial court to strike the defense where evidence may be presented to support it. Burns v. Equilease Corp., 357 So.2d 786, 24, 24 U.C.C. Rep.Serv. 254 (Fla. 3d DCA 1978); 20 FLPRAC § 3:15.

3. *Sham pleadings.* If a party deems any pleading or part thereof filed by another party to be a sham, that party may move to strike the pleading or part thereof before the cause is set for trial and the court shall hear the motion, taking evidence of the respective parties, and if the motion is sustained, the pleading to which the motion is directed shall be stricken. Default and summary judgment on the merits may be entered in the discretion of the court or the court may permit additional pleadings to be filed for good cause shown. FL ST RCP Rule 1.150(a).

a. *Contents of motion.* The motion to strike shall be verified and shall set forth fully the facts on which the movant relies and may be supported by affidavit. No traverse of the motion shall be required. FL ST RCP Rule 1.150(b).

b. *Allegations supported by evidence.* The issue is not whether the allegations are material or proper, but whether the allegations are supported by evidence. 5 FLPRAC § 7:30.

4. *Arbitration and mediation*

a. *Referral to arbitration and mediation.* Except as hereinafter provided or as otherwise prohibited by law, the presiding judge may enter an order referring all or any part of a contested civil matter to mediation or arbitration. The parties to any contested civil matter may file a written stipulation to mediate or arbitrate any issue between them at any time. Such stipulation shall be incorporated into the order of referral. FL ST RCP Rule 1.700(a).

b. *Arbitration*

i. *Exclusions.* A civil action shall be ordered to arbitration or arbitration in conjunction with mediation upon stipulation of the parties. A civil action may be ordered to arbitration or arbitration in conjunction with mediation upon motion of any party or by the court, if the judge determines the action to be of such a nature that arbitration could be of benefit to the litigants or the court. FL ST RCP Rule 1.800.

- Under no circumstances may the following categories of actions be referred to arbitration: (1) bond estreatures; (2) habeas corpus or other extraordinary writs; (3) bond validations; (4) civil or criminal contempt; (5) such other matters as may be specified by order of the chief judge in the circuit. FL ST RCP Rule 1.800.

ii. For more information regarding arbitration, please see FL ST RCP Rule 1.810; FL ST RCP Rule 1.820; FL ST RCP Rule 1.830.

c. *Mediation.* For more information regarding mediation, please see FL ST RCP Rule 1.710; FL ST RCP Rule 1.720; FL ST RCP Rule 1.730; and FL ST RCP Rule 1.750.

5. *Rules of court*

a. *Rules of civil procedure.* The Florida Rules of Civil Procedure apply to all actions of a civil nature and all special statutory proceedings in the circuit courts and county courts except those to which the

Florida Probate Rules, the Florida Family Law Rules of Procedure, or the Small Claims Rules apply. FL ST RCP Rule 1.010.

i. The form, content, procedure, and time for pleading in all special statutory proceedings shall be as prescribed by the statutes governing the proceeding unless the Florida Rules of Civil Procedure specifically provide to the contrary. FL ST RCP Rule 1.010.

ii. The Florida Rules of Civil Procedure shall be construed to secure the just, speedy, and inexpensive determination of every action. FL ST RCP Rule 1.010.

b. *Rules of judicial administration.* The Florida Rules of Judicial Administration shall apply to administrative matters in all courts to which the Florida Rules of Judicial Administration are applicable by their terms. The Florida Rules of Judicial Administration shall be construed to secure the speedy and inexpensive determination of every proceeding to which they are applicable. The Florida Rules of Judicial Administration shall supersede all conflicting rules and statutes. FL ST J ADMIN Rule 2.110.

6. *Notice of change of contact information.* The Clerk shall provide a change of address and/or telephone number form for use by attorneys and pro se litigants. With any change of address and/or telephone number, attorneys and pro se litigants governed by FL ST J ADMIN Rule 2.515 will provide to the Clerk and all parties promptly the change of address and/or telephone number form. This form should be submitted only once to the Clerk, who will then make the address and/or telephone number change in all court divisions. FL ST 2 J CIR 2007-05.

D. Documents

1. *Required documents*

a. *Notice of hearing/Motion.* An application to the court for an order shall be by motion which shall be made in writing unless made during a hearing or trial, shall state with particularity the grounds therefor, and shall set forth the relief or order sought. The requirement of writing is fulfilled if the motion is stated in a written notice of the hearing of the motion. All notices of hearing shall specify each motion or other matter to be heard. FL ST RCP Rule 1.100(b).

i. *Notices to persons with disabilities.* See the Format section of this KeyRules document for further information.

b. *Certificate of service.* When any attorney certifies in substance: "I certify that a copy hereof has been furnished to (here insert name or names and addresses used for service) by (e-mail) (delivery) (mail) (fax) on .... (date) ....______________ Attorney" the certificate is taken as prima facie proof of such service in compliance with FL ST J ADMIN Rule 2.516. FL ST J ADMIN Rule 2.516(f).

2. *Supplemental documents*

a. *Proposed order.* The court may require that orders or judgments be prepared by a party, may require the party to furnish the court with stamped, addressed envelopes for service of the order or judgment, and may require that proposed orders and judgments be furnished to all parties before entry by the court of the order or judgment. FL ST J ADMIN Rule 2.516(h)(1).

b. *Notice of constitutional question.* A party that files a pleading, written motion, or other paper drawing into question the constitutionality of a state statute or a county or municipal charter, ordinance, or franchise must promptly (1) file a notice of constitutional question stating the question and identifying the paper that raises it; and (2) serve the notice and the pleading, written motion, or other paper drawing into question the constitutionality of a state statute or a county or municipal charter, ordinance, or franchise on the Attorney General or the state attorney of the judicial circuit in which the action is pending, by either certified or registered mail. Service of the notice and pleading, written motion, or other paper does not require joinder of the Attorney General or the state attorney as a party to the action. FL ST RCP Rule 1.071.

E. Format

1. *Documents; Type and size.* Documents subject to the exceptions set forth in FL ST J ADMIN Rule 2.525(d) shall be filed on recycled paper measuring eight and one half by eleven (8 1/2 by 11) inches. For purposes of FL ST J ADMIN Rule 2.520, paper is recycled if it contains a minimum content of fifty (50)

percent waste paper. Xerographic reduction of legal-size (eight and one half by fourteen (8 1/2 by 14) inches) documents to letter size (eight and one half by eleven (8 1/2 by 11) inches) is prohibited. All other documents filed by electronic transmission shall be filed in a format capable of being printed in a format consistent with the provisions of FL ST J ADMIN Rule 2.250. FL ST J ADMIN Rule 2.520(b).

a. *Exhibits.* Any exhibit or attachment filed with pleadings or papers may be filed in its original size. FL ST J ADMIN Rule 2.520(c).

b. *Recording space.* On all papers and documents prepared and filed by the court or by any party to a proceeding which are to be recorded in the public records of any county, including but not limited to final money judgments and notices of lis pendens, a three (3) inch by three (3) inch space at the top right-hand corner on the first page and a one (1) inch by three (3) inch space at the top right-hand corner on each subsequent page shall be left blank and reserved for use by the clerk of court. FL ST J ADMIN Rule 2.520(d).

    i. *Exceptions to recording space.* Any papers or documents created by persons or entities over which the filing party has no control, including but not limited to wills, codicils, trusts, or other testamentary documents; documents prepared or executed by any public officer; documents prepared, executed, acknowledged, or proved outside of the State of Florida; or documents created by State or Federal government agencies, may be filed without the space required by FL ST J ADMIN Rule 2.520. FL ST J ADMIN Rule 2.520(e).

c. *Noncompliance.* No clerk of court is permitted to refuse to file any document or paper because of noncompliance with the Florida Rules of Judicial Administration. However, upon request of the clerk of court, noncomplying documents must be resubmitted in accordance with the formatting rules. FL ST J ADMIN Rule 2.520(f).

2. *Caption.* Every pleading, motion, order, judgment, or other paper shall have a caption containing the name of the court, the file number, and except for in rem proceedings, including forfeiture proceedings, the name of the first party on each side with an appropriate indication of other parties, and a designation identifying the party filing it and its nature or the nature of the order, as the case may be. In any in rem proceeding, every pleading, motion, order, judgment, or other paper shall have a caption containing the name of the court, the file number, the style "In re" (followed by the name or general description of the property), and a designation of the person or entity filing it and its nature or the nature of the order, as the case may be. In an in rem forfeiture proceeding, the style shall be "In re forfeiture of" (followed by the name of the general description of the property). All papers filed in the action shall be styled in such a manner as to indicate clearly the subject matter of the paper and the party requesting or obtaining relief. FL ST RCP Rule 1.100(c)(1).

3. *Writing and written defined.* Writing or written means a document containing information, an application, or a stipulation. FL ST RCP Rule 1.080(c).

4. *Rule abbreviations*

    a. The Florida Rules of Civil Procedure and shall be abbreviated as Fla.R.Civ.P. FL ST RCP Rule 1.010.

    b. The Florida Rules of Judicial Administration shall be abbreviated as Fla. R. Jud. Admin. FL ST J ADMIN Rule 2.110.

5. *Nonverification.* Except when otherwise specifically provided by the Florida Rules of Civil Procedure or an applicable statute, every pleading or other document of a party represented by an attorney need not be verified or accompanied by an affidavit. FL ST RCP Rule 1.030; FL ST J ADMIN Rule 2.515(a).

6. *Attorney signature*

    a. *Attorney signature.* Every pleading and other document of a party represented by an attorney shall be signed by at least one (1) attorney of record in that attorney's individual name whose current record Florida Bar address, telephone number, including area code, primary e-mail address and secondary e-mail addresses, if any, and Florida Bar number shall be stated, and who shall be duly licensed to practice law in Florida or who shall have received permission to appear in the particular case as provided in FL ST J ADMIN Rule 2.510. FL ST J ADMIN Rule 2.515(a).

        i. The attorney may be required by the court to give the address of, and to vouch for the attorney's authority to represent, the party. FL ST J ADMIN Rule 2.515(a).

ii. The signature of an attorney shall constitute a certificate by the attorney that the attorney has read the pleading or other document; that to the best of the attorney's knowledge, information, and belief there is good ground to support it; and that it is not interposed for delay. FL ST J ADMIN Rule 2.515(a).

iii. If a pleading is not signed or is signed with intent to defeat the purpose of FL ST J ADMIN Rule 2.515, it may be stricken and the action may proceed as though the pleading or other document had not been served. FL ST J ADMIN Rule 2.515(a).

b. *Pro se litigant signature.* A party who is not represented by an attorney shall sign any pleading or other paper and state the party's address and telephone number, including area code. FL ST J ADMIN Rule 2.515(b).

c. *Form of signature*

i. The signatures required on pleadings and documents by FL ST J ADMIN Rule 2.515(a) and FL ST J ADMIN Rule 2.515(b) may be:

- Original signatures;
- Original signatures that have been reproduced by electronic means, such as on electronically transmitted documents or photocopied documents;
- Electronic signatures using the "/s/," "s/," or "/s" formats by or at the direction of the person signing; or
- Any other signature format authorized by general law, so long as the clerk where the proceeding is pending has the capability of receiving and has obtained approval from the Supreme Court of Florida to accept pleadings and documents with that signature format. FL ST J ADMIN Rule 2.515(c)(1).

ii. An attorney, party, or other person who files a pleading or paper by electronic transmission that does not contain the original signature of that attorney, party, or other person shall file that identical pleading or paper in paper form containing an original signature of that attorney, party, or other person (hereinafter called the follow-up filing) immediately thereafter. The follow-up filing is not required if the Supreme Court of Florida has entered an order directing the clerk of court to discontinue accepting the follow-up filing. FL ST J ADMIN Rule 2.515(c)(2).

7. *Forms*

a. *Process.* The forms of process, notice of lis pendens, and notice of action provided in the Florida Rules of Civil Procedure are sufficient. Variations from the forms do not void process or notices that are otherwise sufficient. FL ST RCP Rule 1.900(a).

b. *Other forms.* The other forms provided in the Florida Rules of Civil Procedure are sufficient for the matters that are covered by them. So long as the substance is expressed without prolixity, the forms may be varied to meet the facts of a particular case. FL ST RCP Rule 1.900(b).

c. *Formal matters.* Captions, except for the designation of the paper, are omitted from the forms provided in the Florida Rules of Civil Procedure. A general form of caption is the first form provided. Signatures are omitted from pleadings and motions. FL ST RCP Rule 1.900(c).

8. *Notices to persons with disabilities.* All notices of court proceedings to be held in a public facility, and all process compelling appearance at such proceedings, shall include the following statement in bold face, fourteen (14) point Times New Roman or Courier font: "If you are a person with a disability who needs any accommodation in order to participate in this proceeding, you are entitled, at no cost to you, to the provision of certain assistance. Please contact [identify applicable court personnel by name, address, and telephone number] at least seven (7) days before your scheduled court appearance, or immediately upon receiving this notification if the time before the scheduled appearance is less than seven (7) days; if you are hearing or voice impaired, call 711." FL ST J ADMIN Rule 2.540(c)(1).

9. *Minimization of the filing of sensitive information*

a. *Limitations for court filings.* Unless authorized by FL ST J ADMIN Rule 2.425(b), statute, another

rule of court, or the court orders otherwise, designated sensitive information filed with the court must be limited to the following format:

i. The initials of a person known to be a minor;

ii. The year of birth of a person's birth date;

iii. No portion of any: Social security number, Bank account number, Credit card account number, Charge account number, or Debit account number;

iv. The last four digits of any: Taxpayer identification number (TIN), Employee identification number, Driver's license number, Passport number, Telephone number, Financial account number, except as set forth in FL ST J ADMIN Rule 2.425(a)(3), Brokerage account number, Insurance policy account number, Loan account number, Customer account number, or Patient or health care number;

v. A truncated version of any: Email address, Computer user name, Password, or Personal identification number (PIN); and

vi. A truncated version of any other sensitive information as provided by court order. FL ST J ADMIN Rule 2.425(a).

b. *Exceptions.* FL ST J ADMIN Rule 2.425(a) does not apply to the following:

i. An account number which identifies the property alleged to be the subject of a proceeding;

ii. The record of an administrative or agency proceeding;

iii. The record in appellate or review proceedings;

iv. The birth date of a minor whenever the birth date is necessary for the court to establish or maintain subject matter jurisdiction;

v. The name of a minor in any order relating to parental responsibility, time-sharing, or child support;

vi. The name of a minor in any document or order affecting the minor's ownership of real property;

vii. The birth date of a party in a writ of attachment or notice to payor;

viii. In traffic and criminal proceedings: a pro se filing; a court filing that is related to a criminal matter or investigation and that is prepared before the filing of a criminal charge or is not filed as part of any docketed criminal case; an arrest or search warrant or any information in support thereof; a charging document and an affidavit or other documents filed in support of any charging document, including any driving records; a statement of particulars; discovery material introduced into evidence or otherwise filed with the court; and all information necessary for the proper issuance and execution of a subpoena duces tecum;

ix. Information used by the clerk for case maintenance purposes or the courts for case management purposes; and

x. Information which is relevant and material to an issue before the court. FL ST J ADMIN Rule 2.425(b).

c. *Remedies.* Upon motion by a party or interested person or sua sponte by the court, the court may order remedies, sanctions or both for a violation of FL ST J ADMIN Rule 2.425(a). Following notice and an opportunity to respond, the court may impose sanctions if such filing was not made in good faith. FL ST J ADMIN Rule 2.425(c).

d. *Motions not restricted.* FL ST J ADMIN Rule 2.425 does not restrict a party's right to move for protective order, to move to file documents under seal, or to request a determination of the confidentiality of records. FL ST J ADMIN Rule 2.425(d).

e. *Application.* FL ST J ADMIN Rule 2.425 does not affect the application of constitutional provisions, statutes, or rules of court regarding confidential information or access to public information. FL ST J ADMIN Rule 2.425(e).

F. Filing and Service Requirements

1. *Filing requirements.* All original documents must be filed with the court either before service or

immediately thereafter, unless otherwise provided for by general law or other rules. If the original of any bond or other document is not placed in the court file, a certified copy must be so placed by the clerk. FL ST J ADMIN Rule 2.516(d). All documents shall be filed in conformity with the requirements of FL ST J ADMIN Rule 2.525. FL ST RCP Rule 1.080(b). All documents filed in any court shall be filed by electronic transmission in accordance with FL ST J ADMIN Rule 2.525. "Documents" means pleadings, motions, petitions, memoranda, briefs, notices, exhibits, declarations, affidavits, orders, judgments, decrees, writs, opinions, and any other paper or writing submitted to a court. FL ST J ADMIN Rule 2.520(a). All documents that are court records, as defined in FL ST J ADMIN Rule 2.430(a)(1), must be filed by electronic transmission, provided that: (1) the clerk has the ability to accept and retain such documents; (2) the clerk or the chief judge of the circuit has requested permission to accept documents filed by electronic transmission; and (3) the supreme court has entered an order granting permission to the clerk to accept documents filed by electronic transmission. FL ST J ADMIN Rule 2.525(c)(1).

a. *Definition.* "Electronic transmission of documents" means the sending of information by electronic signals to, by or from a court or clerk, which when received can be transformed and stored or transmitted on paper, microfilm, magnetic storage device, optical imaging system, CD-ROM, flash drive, other electronic data storage system, server, case maintenance system ("CM"), electronic court filing ("ECF") system, statewide or local electronic portal ("e-portal"), or other electronic record keeping system authorized by the supreme court in a format sufficient to communicate the information on the original document in a readable format. Electronic transmission of documents includes electronic mail ("e-mail") and any internet-based transmission procedure, and may include procedures allowing for documents to be signed or verified by electronic means. FL ST J ADMIN Rule 2.525(a).

    i. The filing of documents with the court as required by the Florida Rules of Judicial Administration must be made by filing them with the clerk in accordance with FL ST J ADMIN Rule 2.525, except that the judge may permit documents to be filed with the judge, in which event the judge must note the filing date before him or her on the documents and transmit them to the clerk. The date of filing is that shown on the face of the document by the judge's notation or the clerk's time stamp, whichever is earlier. FL ST J ADMIN Rule 2.516(e).

b. *Application.* Any court or clerk of the court may accept the electronic transmission of documents for filing after the clerk, together with input from the chief judge of the circuit, has obtained approval of the procedures and program for doing so from the Supreme Court of Florida. FL ST J ADMIN Rule 2.525(b).

c. *Exceptions*

    i. Paper documents and other submissions may be manually submitted to the clerk or court:

        - When the clerk does not have the ability to accept and retain documents by electronic filing or has not had ECF Procedures approved by the supreme court;
        - For filing by any self-represented party or any self-represented nonparty unless specific ECF Procedures provide a means to file documents electronically. However, any self-represented nonparty that is a governmental or public agency and any other agency, partnership, corporation, or business entity acting on behalf of any governmental or public agency may file documents by electronic transmission if such entity has the capability of filing documents electronically;
        - For filing by attorneys excused from e-mail service in accordance with FL ST J ADMIN Rule 2.516(b);
        - When submitting evidentiary exhibits or filing non-documentary materials;
        - When the filing involves documents in excess of twenty-five (25) megabytes (25MB) in size. For such filings, documents may be transmitted using an electronic storage medium that the clerk has the ability to accept, which may include a CD-ROM, flash drive, or similar storage medium;
        - When filed in open court, as permitted by the court;
        - When paper filing is permitted by any approved statewide or local ECF procedures; and

- If any court determines that justice so requires. FL ST J ADMIN Rule 2.525(d).

ii. Any document in paper form submitted under FL ST J ADMIN Rule 2.525(d) is filed when it is received by the clerk or court and the clerk shall immediately thereafter convert any filed paper document to an electronic document. "Convert to an electronic document" means optically capturing an image of a paper document and using character recognition software to recover as much of the document's text as practicable and then indexing and storing the document in the official court file. FL ST J ADMIN Rule 2.525(c)(4).

iii. Any storage medium submitted under FL ST J ADMIN Rule 2.525(d)(5) is filed when received by the clerk or court and the clerk shall immediately thereafter transfer the electronic documents from the storage device to the official court file. FL ST J ADMIN Rule 2.525(c)(5).

iv. If the filer of any paper document authorized under FL ST J ADMIN Rule 2.525(d) provides a self-addressed, postage-paid envelope for return of the paper document after it is converted to electronic form by the clerk, the clerk shall place the paper document in the envelope and deposit it in the mail. Except when a paper document is required to be maintained, the clerk may recycle any filed paper document that is not to be returned to the filer. FL ST J ADMIN Rule 2.525(c)(6).

v. The clerk may convert any paper document filed before the effective date of FL ST J ADMIN Rule 2.525 to an electronic document. Unless the clerk is required to maintain the paper document, if the paper document has been converted to an electronic document by the clerk, the paper document is no longer part of the official court file and may be removed and recycled. FL ST J ADMIN Rule 2.525(c)(7).

d. *Official court file.* For information on what constitutes the official court file, please see FL ST J ADMIN Rule 2.525(c)(2), FL ST J ADMIN Rule 2.525(c)(3).

e. *Administration.* All attorneys, parties, or other persons using this rule to file documents are required to make arrangements with the court or clerk for the payment of any charges authorized by general law or the supreme court before filing any document by electronic transmission. FL ST J ADMIN Rule 2.525(f)(2).

f. *Filing date.* The filing date for an electronically transmitted document is the date and time that such filing is acknowledged by an electronic stamp or otherwise, pursuant to any procedure set forth in any ECF Procedures approved by the supreme court, or the date the last page of such filing is received by the court or clerk. FL ST J ADMIN Rule 2.525(f)(3).

g. *Accessibility.* All documents transmitted in any electronic form under FL ST J ADMIN Rule 2.525 must comply with the accessibility requirements of FL ST J ADMIN Rule 2.526. FL ST J ADMIN Rule 2.525(g).

2. *Service requirements.* Every pleading subsequent to the initial pleading, all orders, and every other document filed in the action must be served in conformity with the requirements of FL ST J ADMIN Rule 2.516. FL ST RCP Rule 1.080(a).

a. *Service; When required.* Unless the court otherwise orders, or a statute or supreme court administrative order specifies a different means of service, every pleading subsequent to the initial pleading and every other document filed in any court proceeding, except applications for witness subpoenas and documents served by formal notice or required to be served in the manner provided for service of formal notice, must be served in accordance with FL ST J ADMIN Rule 2.516 on each party. No service need be made on parties against whom a default has been entered, except that pleadings asserting new or additional claims against them must be served in the manner provided for service of summons. FL ST J ADMIN Rule 2.516(a).

b. *Service; How made.* When service is required or permitted to be made upon a party represented by an attorney, service must be made upon the attorney unless service upon the party is ordered by the court. FL ST J ADMIN Rule 2.516(b).

i. *Service by electronic mail ("e-mail").* All documents required or permitted to be served on another party must be served by e-mail, unless FL ST J ADMIN Rule 2.516 otherwise provides. When, in addition to service by e-mail, the sender also utilizes another means of service

provided for in FL ST J ADMIN Rule 2.516(b)(2), any differing time limits and other provisions applicable to that other means of service control. FL ST J ADMIN Rule 2.516(b)(1). Any document electronically transmitted to a court or clerk must also be served on all parties and interested persons in accordance with the applicable rules of court. FL ST J ADMIN Rule 2.525(e)(2).

- *Service on attorneys.* Upon appearing in a proceeding, an attorney must serve a designation of a primary e-mail address and may designate no more than two (2) secondary e-mail addresses. Thereafter, service must be directed to all designated e-mail addresses in that proceeding. Every document filed by an attorney thereafter must include the primary e-mail address of that attorney and any secondary e-mail addresses. If an attorney does not designate any e-mail address for service, documents may be served on that attorney at the e-mail address on record with The Florida Bar. FL ST J ADMIN Rule 2.516(b)(1)(A).
- *Exception to e-mail service on attorneys.* Service by an attorney on another attorney must be made by e-mail unless excused by the court. Upon motion by an attorney demonstrating that the attorney has no e-mail account and lacks access to the Internet at the attorney's office, the court may excuse the attorney from the requirements of e-mail service. Service on and by an attorney excused by the court from e-mail service must be by the means provided in FL ST J ADMIN Rule 2.516(b)(2). FL ST J ADMIN Rule 2.516(b)(1)(B).
- *Service on and by parties not represented by an attorney.* Any party not represented by an attorney may serve a designation of a primary e-mail address and also may designate no more than two (2) secondary e-mail addresses to which service must be directed in that proceeding by the means provided in FL ST J ADMIN Rule 2.516(b)(1). If a party not represented by an attorney does not designate an e-mail address for service in a proceeding, service on and by that party must be by the means provided in FL ST J ADMIN Rule 2.516(b)(2). FL ST J ADMIN Rule 2.516(b)(1)(C).
- *Time of service.* Service by e-mail is complete when it is sent. FL ST J ADMIN Rule 2.516(b)(1)(D). An e-mail is deemed served on the date it is sent. FL ST J ADMIN Rule 2.516(b)(1)(D)(i). If the sender learns that the e-mail did not reach the address of the person to be served, the sender must immediately send another copy by e-mail, or by a means authorized by FL ST J ADMIN Rule 2.516(b)(2). FL ST J ADMIN Rule 2.516(b)(1)(D)(ii). E-mail service is treated as service by mail for the computation of time. FL ST J ADMIN Rule 2.516(b)(1)(D)(iii).

ii. *Format of e-mail for service.* Service of a document by e-mail is made by attaching a copy of the document in PDF format to an e-mail sent to all addresses designated by the attorney or party. FL ST J ADMIN Rule 2.516(b)(1)(E).

- All documents served by e-mail must be attached to an e-mail message containing a subject line beginning with the words "SERVICE OF COURT DOCUMENT" in all capital letters, followed by the case number of the proceeding in which the documents are being served. FL ST J ADMIN Rule 2.516(b)(1)(E)(i).
- The body of the e-mail must identify the court in which the proceeding is pending, the case number, the name of the initial party on each side, the title of each document served with that e-mail, and the sender's name and telephone number. FL ST J ADMIN Rule 2.516(b)(1)(E)(ii).
- Any document served by e-mail may be signed by the "/s/" format, as long as the filed original is signed in accordance with the applicable rule of procedure. FL ST J ADMIN Rule 2.516(b)(1)(E)(iii).
- Any e-mail which, together with its attached documents, exceeds five megabytes (5MB) in size, must be divided and sent as separate e-mails, no one of which may exceed five megabytes (5MB) in size and each of which must be sequentially numbered in the subject line. FL ST J ADMIN Rule 2.516(b)(1)(E)(iv).

iii. *Service by other means.* In addition to, and not in lieu of, service by e-mail, service may also be

made upon attorneys by any of the means specified in FL ST J ADMIN Rule 2.516(b)(2). Service on and by all parties who are not represented by an attorney and who do not designate an e-mail address, and on and by all attorneys excused from e-mail service, must be made by delivering a copy of the document or by mailing it to the party or attorney at their last known address or, if no address is known, by leaving it with the clerk of the court. Service by mail is complete upon mailing. Delivery of a copy within FL ST J ADMIN Rule 2.516 is complete upon:

- Handing it to the attorney or to the party,
- Leaving it at the attorney's or party's office with a clerk or other person in charge thereof,
- If there is no one in charge, leaving it in a conspicuous place therein,
- If the office is closed or the person to be served has no office, leaving it at the person's usual place of abode with some person of his or her family above fifteen (15) years of age and informing such person of the contents, or
- Transmitting it by facsimile to the attorney's or party's office with a cover sheet containing the sender's name, firm, address, telephone number, and facsimile number, and the number of pages transmitted. When service is made by facsimile, a copy must also be served by any other method permitted by FL ST J ADMIN Rule 2.516. Facsimile service occurs when transmission is complete. FL ST J ADMIN Rule 2.516(b)(2)(A) through FL ST J ADMIN Rule 2.516(b)(2)(E).
- Service by delivery after 5:00 p.m. must be deemed to have been made by mailing on the date of delivery. FL ST J ADMIN Rule 2.516(b)(2)(F).

c. *Service; Numerous defendants.* In actions when the parties are unusually numerous, the court may regulate the service contemplated by the Florida Rules of Judicial Administration on motion or on its own initiative in such manner as may be found to be just and reasonable. FL ST J ADMIN Rule 2.516(c).

d. *Service by clerk.* Service of notices and other documents required to be made by the clerk must also be done as provided in FL ST J ADMIN Rule 2.516(b). FL ST J ADMIN Rule 2.516(g).

G. Hearings

1. *Communication equipment*

a. *Definition.* Communication equipment means a conference telephone or other electronic device that permits all those appearing or participating to hear and speak to each other, provided that all conversation of all parties is audible to all persons present. FL ST J ADMIN Rule 2.530(a).

b. *Use by all parties.* A county or circuit court judge may, upon the court's own motion or upon the written request of a party, direct that communication equipment be used for a motion hearing, pretrial conference, or a status conference. A judge must give notice to the parties and consider any objections they may have to the use of communication equipment before directing that communication equipment be used. The decision to use communication equipment over the objection of parties will be in the sound discretion of the trial court, except as noted below. FL ST J ADMIN Rule 2.530(b).

c. *Use only by requesting party.* A county or circuit court judge may, upon the written request of a party upon reasonable notice to all other parties, permit a requesting party to participate through communication equipment in a scheduled motion hearing; however, any such request (except in criminal, juvenile, and appellate proceedings) must be granted, absent a showing of good cause to deny the same, where the hearing is set for not longer than fifteen (15) minutes. FL ST J ADMIN Rule 2.530(c).

d. *Testimony*

i. *Generally.* A county or circuit court judge, general magistrate, special magistrate, or hearing officer may allow testimony to be taken through communication equipment if all parties consent or if permitted by another applicable rule of procedure. FL ST J ADMIN Rule 2.530(d)(1).

ii. *Procedure.* Any party desiring to present testimony through communication equipment shall, prior to the hearing or trial at which the testimony is to be presented, contact all parties to determine whether each party consents to this form of testimony. The party seeking to present the testimony shall move for permission to present testimony through communication equipment, which motion shall set forth good cause as to why the testimony should be allowed in this form. FL ST J ADMIN Rule 2.530(d)(2).

iii. *Oath.* Testimony may be taken through communication equipment only if a notary public or other person authorized to administer oaths in the witness's jurisdiction is present with the witness and administers the oath consistent with the laws of the jurisdiction. FL ST J ADMIN Rule 2.530(d)(3).

iv. *Confrontation rights.* In juvenile and criminal proceedings the defendant must make an informed waiver of any confrontation rights that may be abridged by the use of communication equipment. FL ST J ADMIN Rule 2.530(d)(4).

v. *Video testimony.* If the testimony to be presented utilizes video conferencing or comparable two-way visual capabilities, the court in its discretion may modify the procedures set forth in FL ST J ADMIN Rule 2.530 to accommodate the technology utilized. FL ST J ADMIN Rule 2.530(d)(5).

e. *Burden of expense.* The cost for the use of the communication equipment is the responsibility of the requesting party unless otherwise directed by the court. FL ST J ADMIN Rule 2.530(e).

H. Forms

1. Official Motion to Strike Forms for Florida

a. Caption. FL ST RCP Form 1.901.

b. Notice of compliance when constitutional challenge is brought. FL ST RCP Form 1.975.

2. Motion to Strike Forms for Florida

a. Motion to strike. FL-PP § 2:128.

b. Form for motion to strike. FL-RCPF R 1.140(802).

c. Form for motion to strike insufficient pleading. FL-RCPF R 1.140(803).

d. Form for motion to strike claim for business or financial losses. FL-RCPF R 1.140(804).

e. Motion; Strike, complaint signed by corporation. FL-PRACFORM § 7:176.

f. Motion; Strike, defenses. FL-PRACFORM § 7:177.

g. Motion; Strike, ejectment chain of title. FL-PRACFORM § 7:178.

h. Motion; Strike, pleading, departure. FL-PRACFORM § 7:180.

i. Motion; Strike, pleading, improper signature. FL-PRACFORM § 7:181.

j. Motion; Strike, sham pleading. FL-PRACFORM § 7:182.

k. Motion; Strike, sham, defenses, statute of limitations and failure of consideration. FL-PRACFORM § 7:183.

l. Motion; Strike, third party complaint. FL-PRACFORM § 7:184.

3. Official Forms for Florida Circuit Court, Second Judicial Circuit

a. Notice of change of contact information. FL ST 2 J CIR 2007-05.

I. Checklist

(I) ❑ Matters to be considered by moving party

(a) ❑ Required documents

(1) ❑ Notice of hearing/Motion

(2) ❑ Certificate of service

(b) ❑ Supplemental documents
  (1) ❑ Proposed order
  (2) ❑ Notice of constitutional question
(c) ❑ Time for making motion
  (1) ❑ A party may move to strike or the court may strike redundant, immaterial, impertinent, or scandalous matter from any pleading at any time
  (2) ❑ If a pleading sets forth a claim for relief to which the adverse party is not required to serve a responsive pleading, the adverse party may assert any defense in law or fact to that claim for relief at the trial, except that the objection of failure to state a legal defense in an answer or reply shall be asserted by motion to strike the defense within twenty (20) days after service of the answer or reply
  (3) ❑ If a party deems any pleading or part thereof filed by another party to be a sham, that party may move to strike the pleading or part thereof before the cause is set for trial
  (4) ❑ A copy of any written motion which may not be heard ex parte and a copy of the notice of the hearing thereof shall be served a reasonable time before the time specified for the hearing

(II) ❑ Matters to be considered by opposing party
(a) ❑ Required documents
  (1) ❑ Response to motion
  (2) ❑ Certificate of service
(b) ❑ Supplemental documents
  (1) ❑ Proposed order
  (2) ❑ Notice of constitutional question
(c) ❑ Time for service and filing of opposition
  (1) ❑ No time specified for responding to a motion

Motions, Oppositions and Replies
Motion for Leave to Amend

Document Last Updated January 2013

A. Applicable Rules

1. *State rules*
   a. Rules of court. FL ST RCP Rule 1.010; FL ST J ADMIN Rule 2.110.
   b. Nonverification of pleadings. FL ST RCP Rule 1.030.
   c. Process. FL ST RCP Rule 1.070.
   d. Service and filing of pleadings, orders, and documents. FL ST RCP Rule 1.080.
   e. Time. FL ST RCP Rule 1.090.
   f. Pleadings and motions. FL ST RCP Rule 1.100.
   g. Defenses. FL ST RCP Rule 1.140.
   h. Motions. FL ST RCP Rule 1.160.
   i. Amended and supplemental pleadings. FL ST RCP Rule 1.190.
   j. Relief from judgment, decrees, or orders. FL ST RCP Rule 1.540.
   k. Mediation and arbitration. FL ST RCP Rule 1.700; FL ST RCP Rule 1.710; FL ST RCP Rule 1.720; FL ST RCP Rule 1.730; FL ST RCP Rule 1.750; FL ST RCP Rule 1.800; FL ST RCP Rule 1.810; FL ST RCP Rule 1.820; FL ST RCP Rule 1.830.

l. Forms. FL ST RCP Rule 1.900.
m. Minimization of the filing of sensitive information. FL ST J ADMIN Rule 2.425.
n. Retention of court records. FL ST J ADMIN Rule 2.430.
o. Foreign attorneys. FL ST J ADMIN Rule 2.510.
p. Signature of attorneys and parties. FL ST J ADMIN Rule 2.515.
q. Paper. FL ST J ADMIN Rule 2.520.
r. Electronic filing. FL ST J ADMIN Rule 2.525.
s. Accessibility of information and technology. FL ST J ADMIN Rule 2.526.
t. Communication equipment. FL ST J ADMIN Rule 2.530.
u. Court reporting. FL ST J ADMIN Rule 2.535.
v. Requests for accommodations by persons with disabilities. FL ST J ADMIN Rule 2.540.

2. *Local rules*
   a. Notice of change of contact information. FL ST 2 J CIR 2007-05.

B. Timing

1. *Amended pleadings as a matter of course.* A party may amend a pleading once as a matter of course at any time before a responsive pleading is served or, if the pleading is one to which no responsive pleading is permitted and the action has not been placed on the trial calendar, may amend it at any time within twenty (20) days after it is served. Otherwise a party may amend a pleading only by leave of court or by written consent of the adverse party. FL ST RCP Rule 1.190(a).
2. *Amended pleadings with leave of court.* Leave of court shall be given freely when justice so requires. FL ST RCP Rule 1.190(a). Under the Florida Rules of Civil Procedure, there is no time limit as to when an amendment with leave of court may be sought. Amendments of the pleadings may be permitted, with the court's discretion, at any stage of the proceedings in furtherance of justice. McSwiggan v. Edson, 186 So.2d 13, 15 (Fla. 1966); FL-PP § 2:153. Nevertheless, the liberality in permitting amendment of pleadings diminishes as the case progresses to trial. Versen v. Versen, 347 So.2d 1047, 1050 (Fla. 4th DCA 1977); FL-PP § 2:153.
3. *Claims for punitive damages.* A motion for leave to amend a pleading to assert a claim for punitive damages can be filed separately and before the supporting evidence or proffer, but each shall be served on all parties at least twenty (20) days before the hearing. FL ST RCP Rule 1.190(f).
4. *Post motion for leave to amend*
   a. If the court permits or requires an amended or responsive pleading or a more definite statement, the pleading or statement shall be served within ten (10) days after notice of the court's action. FL ST RCP Rule 1.140(a)(4).
   b. When a motion for leave to amend with the attached proposed amended complaint is filed, the one hundred twenty (120) day period for service of amended complaints on the new party or parties shall begin upon the entry of an order granting leave to amend. FL ST RCP Rule 1.070(j).
5. *General motion timing.* A copy of any written motion which may not be heard ex parte and a copy of the notice of the hearing thereof shall be served a reasonable time before the time specified for the hearing. FL ST RCP Rule 1.090(d).
6. *Computation of time*
   a. *Generally.* Computation of time shall be governed by FL ST J ADMIN Rule 2.514. FL ST RCP Rule 1.090(a). The following rules apply in computing time periods specified in any rule of procedure, local rule, court order, or statute that does not specify a method of computing time. FL ST J ADMIN Rule 2.514(a).
      i. *Period stated in days or a longer unit.* When the period is stated in days or a longer unit of time (A) exclude the day of the event that triggers the period; (B) count every day, including intermediate Saturdays, Sundays, and legal holidays; and (C) include the last day of the period,

but if the last day is a Saturday, Sunday, or legal holiday, or falls within any period of time extended through an order of the chief justice under FL ST J ADMIN Rule 2.205(a)(2)(B)(iv), the period continues to run until the end of the next day that is not a Saturday, Sunday, or legal holiday and does not fall within any period of time extended through an order of the chief justice. FL ST J ADMIN Rule 2.514(a)(1).

ii. *Period stated in hours.* When the period is stated in hours (A) begin counting immediately on the occurrence of the event that triggers the period; (B) count every hour, including hours during intermediate Saturdays, Sundays, and legal holidays; and (C) if the period would end on a Saturday, Sunday, or legal holiday, or during any period of time extended through an order of the chief justice under FL ST J ADMIN Rule 2.205(a)(2)(B)(iv), the period continues to run until the same time on the next day that is not a Saturday, Sunday, or legal holiday and does not fall within any period of time extended through an order of the chief justice. FL ST J ADMIN Rule 2.514(a)(2).

iii. *Period stated in days less than seven (7) days.* When the period stated in days is less than seven (7) days, intermediate Saturdays, Sundays, and legal holidays shall be excluded in the computation. FL ST J ADMIN Rule 2.514(a)(3).

iv. *"Last day" defined.* Unless a different time is set by a statute, local rule, or court order, the last day ends (A) for electronic filing or for service by any means, at midnight; and (B) for filing by other means, when the clerk's office is scheduled to close. FL ST J ADMIN Rule 2.514(a)(4).

v. *"Next day" defined.* The "next day" is determined by continuing to count forward when the period is measured after an event and backward when measured before an event. FL ST J ADMIN Rule 2.514(a)(5).

vi. *"Legal holiday" defined.* "Legal holiday" means (A) the day set aside by FL ST § 110.117, for observing New Year's Day, Martin Luther King, Jr.'s Birthday, Memorial Day, Independence Day, Labor Day, Veterans' Day, Thanksgiving Day, the Friday after Thanksgiving Day, or Christmas Day, and (B) any day observed as a holiday by the clerk's office or as designated by the chief judge. FL ST J ADMIN Rule 2.514(a)(6).

b. *Additional time after service by mail or e-mail.* When a party may or must act within a specified time after service and service is made by mail or e-mail, five (5) days are added after the period that would otherwise expire under FL ST J ADMIN Rule 2.514(a). FL ST J ADMIN Rule 2.514(b).

c. *Enlargement.* When an act is required or allowed to be done at or within a specified time by order of court, by the Florida Rules of Civil Procedure, or by notice given thereunder, for cause shown the court at any time in its discretion (1) with or without notice, may order the period enlarged if request therefor is made before the expiration of the period originally prescribed or as extended by a previous order, or (2) upon motion made and notice after the expiration of the specified period, may permit the act to be done when failure to act was the result of excusable neglect, but it may not extend the time for making a motion for new trial, for rehearing, or to alter or amend a judgment; making a motion for relief from a judgment under FL ST RCP Rule 1.540(b); taking an appeal or filing a petition for certiorari; or making a motion for a directed verdict. FL ST RCP Rule 1.090(b).

d. *Unaffected by expiration of term.* The period of time provided for the doing of any act or the taking of any proceeding shall not be affected or limited by the continued existence or expiration of a term of court. The continued existence or expiration of a term of court in no way affects the power of a court to do any act or take any proceeding in any action which is or has been pending before it. FL ST RCP Rule 1.090(c).

C. General Requirements

1. *Motions generally*

a. *Contents.* An application to the court for an order shall be by motion which shall be made in writing unless made during a hearing or trial, shall state with particularity the grounds therefor, and shall set forth the relief or order sought. The requirement of writing is fulfilled if the motion is stated in a written notice of the hearing of the motion. All notices of hearing shall specify each motion or other matter to be heard. FL ST RCP Rule 1.100(b).

b. *Particularity requirement.* The court considers a motion in the light of the substantive law, rule or statute to make its determination. Some rules require a statement of the grounds for a motion under the rule. Failure to give the grounds will result in denial of the motion. This should be the result in all situations when the ground for the motion is not inherent in the rule. FL-PRACPROC § 9:3. The requirement is nevertheless an important one, first because of the due process notice rights of the respondent, as well as for the assistance it provides to the court in its preparation for the hearing or, absent a hearing, for disposition. 4 FLPRAC R 1.100.

2. *Motion for leave to amend.* Although the Florida Rules of Civil Procedure do not specify a procedure for obtaining leave to amend, it is usually accomplished by way of a motion. FL-PP § 2:153. At any time in furtherance of justice, upon such terms as may be just, the court may permit any process, proceeding, pleading, or record to be amended or material supplemental matter to be set forth in an amended or supplemental pleading. At every stage of the action the court must disregard any error or defect in the proceedings which does not affect the substantial rights of the parties. FL ST RCP Rule 1.190(e).

   a. *Permissible amendments.* Amendments can relate to the correction of mistakes, the insertion of jurisdictional averments, the correction or addition of verifications, the addition or substitution or striking out of parties, and generally the rectification of all formal defects in the pleading. The court can also allow amendments setting up an omitted counterclaim or cross-claim if the defendant failed to raise the claim through oversight, inadvertence, or excusable neglect. FL-PP § 2:151.

   b. *Amendments to conform with the evidence.* When issues not raised by the pleadings are tried by express or implied consent of the parties, they shall be treated in all respects as if they had been raised in the pleadings. Such amendment of the pleadings as may be necessary to cause them to conform to the evidence and to raise these issues may be made upon motion of any party at any time, even after judgment, but failure so to amend shall not affect the result of the trial of these issues. If the evidence is objected to at the trial on the ground that it is not within the issues made by the pleadings, the court may allow the pleadings to be amended to conform with the evidence and shall do so freely when the merits of the cause are more effectually presented thereby and the objecting party fails to satisfy the court that the admission of such evidence will prejudice the objecting party in maintaining an action or defense upon the merits. FL ST RCP Rule 1.190(b).

      i. The courts have been extremely liberal in permitting amendments after trial to conform pleadings to the evidence where the issues were tried by the express or implied consent of the parties. Turner v. Long, 225 So.2d 434 (Fla. 1st DCA 1969); FL-PP § 2:152.

   c. *Procedure for adding parties.* Parties may be added once as a matter of course within the same time that pleadings can be so amended. If amendment by leave of court or stipulation of the parties is permitted, parties may be added in the amended pleading without further order of court. Parties may be added by order of court on its own initiative or on motion of any party at any stage of the action and on such terms as are just. FL ST RCP Rule 1.250(c).

   d. *Claims for punitive damages.* A motion for leave to amend a pleading to assert a claim for punitive damages shall make a reasonable showing by evidence in the record or evidence to be proffered by the claimant that provides a reasonable basis for recovery of such damages. The motion to amend can be filed separately and before the supporting evidence or proffer, but each shall be served on all parties at least twenty (20) days before the hearing. FL ST RCP Rule 1.190(f). Leave of court to amend the complaint must be obtained before a plaintiff may assert a punitive damages claim in the complaint. Failure to do so will result in the claims being dismissed or stricken. FL-PP § 2:151.

   e. *Relation back of amendments.* When the claim or defense asserted in the amended pleading arose out of the conduct, transaction, or occurrence set forth or attempted to be set forth in the original pleading, the amendment shall relate back to the date of the original pleading. FL ST RCP Rule 1.190(c).

      i. The doctrine of relation back becomes critical in applying the statute of limitations. For example, it has been held that the doctrine of relation back may not be utilized to circumvent the statute of limitations to permit an amendment where a claim could have been filed as an independent action but was not timely asserted and would otherwise be barred under the statute of limitations. Cox v. Seaboard Coast Line R. Co., 360 So.2d 8 (Fla. 2d DCA 1978); FL-PP § 2:152.

3. *Arbitration and mediation*

   a. *Referral to arbitration and mediation.* Except as hereinafter provided or as otherwise prohibited by law, the presiding judge may enter an order referring all or any part of a contested civil matter to mediation or arbitration. The parties to any contested civil matter may file a written stipulation to mediate or arbitrate any issue between them at any time. Such stipulation shall be incorporated into the order of referral. FL ST RCP Rule 1.700(a).

   b. *Arbitration*

      i. *Exclusions.* A civil action shall be ordered to arbitration or arbitration in conjunction with mediation upon stipulation of the parties. A civil action may be ordered to arbitration or arbitration in conjunction with mediation upon motion of any party or by the court, if the judge determines the action to be of such a nature that arbitration could be of benefit to the litigants or the court. FL ST RCP Rule 1.800.

         - Under no circumstances may the following categories of actions be referred to arbitration: (1) bond estreatures; (2) habeas corpus or other extraordinary writs; (3) bond validations; (4) civil or criminal contempt; (5) such other matters as may be specified by order of the chief judge in the circuit. FL ST RCP Rule 1.800.

      ii. For more information regarding arbitration, please see FL ST RCP Rule 1.810; FL ST RCP Rule 1.820; FL ST RCP Rule 1.830.

   c. *Mediation.* For more information regarding mediation, please see FL ST RCP Rule 1.710; FL ST RCP Rule 1.720; FL ST RCP Rule 1.730; and FL ST RCP Rule 1.750.

4. *Rules of court*

   a. *Rules of civil procedure.* The Florida Rules of Civil Procedure apply to all actions of a civil nature and all special statutory proceedings in the circuit courts and county courts except those to which the Florida Probate Rules, the Florida Family Law Rules of Procedure, or the Small Claims Rules apply. FL ST RCP Rule 1.010.

      i. The form, content, procedure, and time for pleading in all special statutory proceedings shall be as prescribed by the statutes governing the proceeding unless the Florida Rules of Civil Procedure specifically provide to the contrary. FL ST RCP Rule 1.010.

      ii. The Florida Rules of Civil Procedure shall be construed to secure the just, speedy, and inexpensive determination of every action. FL ST RCP Rule 1.010.

   b. *Rules of judicial administration.* The Florida Rules of Judicial Administration shall apply to administrative matters in all courts to which the Florida Rules of Judicial Administration are applicable by their terms. The Florida Rules of Judicial Administration shall be construed to secure the speedy and inexpensive determination of every proceeding to which they are applicable. The Florida Rules of Judicial Administration shall supersede all conflicting rules and statutes. FL ST J ADMIN Rule 2.110.

5. *Notice of change of contact information.* The Clerk shall provide a change of address and/or telephone number form for use by attorneys and pro se litigants. With any change of address and/or telephone number, attorneys and pro se litigants governed by FL ST J ADMIN Rule 2.515 will provide to the Clerk and all parties promptly the change of address and/or telephone number form. This form should be submitted only once to the Clerk, who will then make the address and/or telephone number change in all court divisions. FL ST 2 J CIR 2007-05.

D. Documents

1. *Required documents*

   a. *Notice of hearing/Motion.* An application to the court for an order shall be by motion which shall be made in writing unless made during a hearing or trial, shall state with particularity the grounds therefor, and shall set forth the relief or order sought. The requirement of writing is fulfilled if the motion is stated in a written notice of the hearing of the motion. All notices of hearing shall specify each motion or other matter to be heard. FL ST RCP Rule 1.100(b).

      i. *Notices to persons with disabilities.* See the Format section of this KeyRules document for further information.

b. *Proposed amended pleading.* The moving party shall attach the proposed amended pleading to the motion. FL ST RCP Rule 1.190(a).

c. *Certificate of service.* When any attorney certifies in substance: "I certify that a copy hereof has been furnished to (here insert name or names and addresses used for service) by (e-mail) (delivery) (mail) (fax) on .... (date) ....______________ Attorney" the certificate is taken as prima facie proof of such service in compliance with FL ST J ADMIN Rule 2.516. FL ST J ADMIN Rule 2.516(f).

2. *Supplemental documents*

a. *Proposed order.* The court may require that orders or judgments be prepared by a party, may require the party to furnish the court with stamped, addressed envelopes for service of the order or judgment, and may require that proposed orders and judgments be furnished to all parties before entry by the court of the order or judgment. FL ST J ADMIN Rule 2.516(h)(1).

b. *Notice of constitutional question.* A party that files a pleading, written motion, or other paper drawing into question the constitutionality of a state statute or a county or municipal charter, ordinance, or franchise must promptly (1) file a notice of constitutional question stating the question and identifying the paper that raises it; and (2) serve the notice and the pleading, written motion, or other paper drawing into question the constitutionality of a state statute or a county or municipal charter, ordinance, or franchise on the Attorney General or the state attorney of the judicial circuit in which the action is pending, by either certified or registered mail. Service of the notice and pleading, written motion, or other paper does not require joinder of the Attorney General or the state attorney as a party to the action. FL ST RCP Rule 1.071.

E. Format

1. *Documents; Type and size.* Documents subject to the exceptions set forth in FL ST J ADMIN Rule 2.525(d) shall be filed on recycled paper measuring eight and one half by eleven (8 1/2 by 11) inches. For purposes of FL ST J ADMIN Rule 2.520, paper is recycled if it contains a minimum content of fifty (50) percent waste paper. Xerographic reduction of legal-size (eight and one half by fourteen (8 1/2 by 14) inches) documents to letter size (eight and one half by eleven (8 1/2 by 11) inches) is prohibited. All other documents filed by electronic transmission shall be filed in a format capable of being printed in a format consistent with the provisions of FL ST J ADMIN Rule 2.250. FL ST J ADMIN Rule 2.520(b).

a. *Exhibits.* Any exhibit or attachment filed with pleadings or papers may be filed in its original size. FL ST J ADMIN Rule 2.520(c).

b. *Recording space.* On all papers and documents prepared and filed by the court or by any party to a proceeding which are to be recorded in the public records of any county, including but not limited to final money judgments and notices of lis pendens, a three (3) inch by three (3) inch space at the top right-hand corner on the first page and a one (1) inch by three (3) inch space at the top right-hand corner on each subsequent page shall be left blank and reserved for use by the clerk of court. FL ST J ADMIN Rule 2.520(d).

i. *Exceptions to recording space.* Any papers or documents created by persons or entities over which the filing party has no control, including but not limited to wills, codicils, trusts, or other testamentary documents; documents prepared or executed by any public officer; documents prepared, executed, acknowledged, or proved outside of the State of Florida; or documents created by State or Federal government agencies, may be filed without the space required by FL ST J ADMIN Rule 2.520. FL ST J ADMIN Rule 2.520(e).

c. *Noncompliance.* No clerk of court is permitted to refuse to file any document or paper because of noncompliance with the Florida Rules of Judicial Administration. However, upon request of the clerk of court, noncomplying documents must be resubmitted in accordance with the formatting rules. FL ST J ADMIN Rule 2.520(f).

2. *Caption.* Every pleading, motion, order, judgment, or other paper shall have a caption containing the name of the court, the file number, and except for in rem proceedings, including forfeiture proceedings, the name of the first party on each side with an appropriate indication of other parties, and a designation identifying the party filing it and its nature or the nature of the order, as the case may be. In any in rem proceeding, every pleading, motion, order, judgment, or other paper shall have a caption containing the

name of the court, the file number, the style "In re" (followed by the name or general description of the property), and a designation of the person or entity filing it and its nature or the nature of the order, as the case may be. In an in rem forfeiture proceeding, the style shall be "In re forfeiture of" (followed by the name of the general description of the property). All papers filed in the action shall be styled in such a manner as to indicate clearly the subject matter of the paper and the party requesting or obtaining relief. FL ST RCP Rule 1.100(c)(1).

3. *Writing and written defined.* Writing or written means a document containing information, an application, or a stipulation. FL ST RCP Rule 1.080(c).
4. *Rule abbreviations*
   a. The Florida Rules of Civil Procedure and shall be abbreviated as Fla.R.Civ.P. FL ST RCP Rule 1.010.
   b. The Florida Rules of Judicial Administration shall be abbreviated as Fla. R. Jud. Admin. FL ST J ADMIN Rule 2.110.
5. *Nonverification.* Except when otherwise specifically provided by the Florida Rules of Civil Procedure or an applicable statute, every pleading or other document of a party represented by an attorney need not be verified or accompanied by an affidavit. FL ST RCP Rule 1.030; FL ST J ADMIN Rule 2.515(a).
6. *Attorney signature*
   a. *Attorney signature.* Every pleading and other document of a party represented by an attorney shall be signed by at least one (1) attorney of record in that attorney's individual name whose current record Florida Bar address, telephone number, including area code, primary e-mail address and secondary e-mail addresses, if any, and Florida Bar number shall be stated, and who shall be duly licensed to practice law in Florida or who shall have received permission to appear in the particular case as provided in FL ST J ADMIN Rule 2.510. FL ST J ADMIN Rule 2.515(a).
      i. The attorney may be required by the court to give the address of, and to vouch for the attorney's authority to represent, the party. FL ST J ADMIN Rule 2.515(a).
      ii. The signature of an attorney shall constitute a certificate by the attorney that the attorney has read the pleading or other document; that to the best of the attorney's knowledge, information, and belief there is good ground to support it; and that it is not interposed for delay. FL ST J ADMIN Rule 2.515(a).
      iii. If a pleading is not signed or is signed with intent to defeat the purpose of FL ST J ADMIN Rule 2.515, it may be stricken and the action may proceed as though the pleading or other document had not been served. FL ST J ADMIN Rule 2.515(a).
   b. *Pro se litigant signature.* A party who is not represented by an attorney shall sign any pleading or other paper and state the party's address and telephone number, including area code. FL ST J ADMIN Rule 2.515(b).
   c. *Form of signature*
      i. The signatures required on pleadings and documents by FL ST J ADMIN Rule 2.515(a) and FL ST J ADMIN Rule 2.515(b) may be:
         - Original signatures;
         - Original signatures that have been reproduced by electronic means, such as on electronically transmitted documents or photocopied documents;
         - Electronic signatures using the "/s/," "s/," or "/s" formats by or at the direction of the person signing; or
         - Any other signature format authorized by general law, so long as the clerk where the proceeding is pending has the capability of receiving and has obtained approval from the Supreme Court of Florida to accept pleadings and documents with that signature format. FL ST J ADMIN Rule 2.515(c)(1).
      ii. An attorney, party, or other person who files a pleading or paper by electronic transmission that does not contain the original signature of that attorney, party, or other person shall file that

identical pleading or paper in paper form containing an original signature of that attorney, party, or other person (hereinafter called the follow-up filing) immediately thereafter. The follow-up filing is not required if the Supreme Court of Florida has entered an order directing the clerk of court to discontinue accepting the follow-up filing. FL ST J ADMIN Rule 2.515(c)(2).

7. *Forms*
   a. *Process.* The forms of process, notice of lis pendens, and notice of action provided in the Florida Rules of Civil Procedure are sufficient. Variations from the forms do not void process or notices that are otherwise sufficient. FL ST RCP Rule 1.900(a).
   b. *Other forms.* The other forms provided in the Florida Rules of Civil Procedure are sufficient for the matters that are covered by them. So long as the substance is expressed without prolixity, the forms may be varied to meet the facts of a particular case. FL ST RCP Rule 1.900(b).
   c. *Formal matters.* Captions, except for the designation of the paper, are omitted from the forms provided in the Florida Rules of Civil Procedure. A general form of caption is the first form provided. Signatures are omitted from pleadings and motions. FL ST RCP Rule 1.900(c).
8. *Notices to persons with disabilities.* All notices of court proceedings to be held in a public facility, and all process compelling appearance at such proceedings, shall include the following statement in bold face, fourteen (14) point Times New Roman or Courier font: "If you are a person with a disability who needs any accommodation in order to participate in this proceeding, you are entitled, at no cost to you, to the provision of certain assistance. Please contact [identify applicable court personnel by name, address, and telephone number] at least seven (7) days before your scheduled court appearance, or immediately upon receiving this notification if the time before the scheduled appearance is less than seven (7) days; if you are hearing or voice impaired, call 711." FL ST J ADMIN Rule 2.540(c)(1).
9. *Minimization of the filing of sensitive information*
   a. *Limitations for court filings.* Unless authorized by FL ST J ADMIN Rule 2.425(b), statute, another rule of court, or the court orders otherwise, designated sensitive information filed with the court must be limited to the following format:
      i. The initials of a person known to be a minor;
      ii. The year of birth of a person's birth date;
      iii. No portion of any: Social security number, Bank account number, Credit card account number, Charge account number, or Debit account number;
      iv. The last four digits of any: Taxpayer identification number (TIN), Employee identification number, Driver's license number, Passport number, Telephone number, Financial account number, except as set forth in FL ST J ADMIN Rule 2.425(a)(3), Brokerage account number, Insurance policy account number, Loan account number, Customer account number, or Patient or health care number;
      v. A truncated version of any: Email address, Computer user name, Password, or Personal identification number (PIN); and
      vi. A truncated version of any other sensitive information as provided by court order. FL ST J ADMIN Rule 2.425(a).
   b. *Exceptions.* FL ST J ADMIN Rule 2.425(a) does not apply to the following:
      i. An account number which identifies the property alleged to be the subject of a proceeding;
      ii. The record of an administrative or agency proceeding;
      iii. The record in appellate or review proceedings;
      iv. The birth date of a minor whenever the birth date is necessary for the court to establish or maintain subject matter jurisdiction;
      v. The name of a minor in any order relating to parental responsibility, time-sharing, or child support;
      vi. The name of a minor in any document or order affecting the minor's ownership of real property;

vii. The birth date of a party in a writ of attachment or notice to payor;

viii. In traffic and criminal proceedings: a pro se filing; a court filing that is related to a criminal matter or investigation and that is prepared before the filing of a criminal charge or is not filed as part of any docketed criminal case; an arrest or search warrant or any information in support thereof; a charging document and an affidavit or other documents filed in support of any charging document, including any driving records; a statement of particulars; discovery material introduced into evidence or otherwise filed with the court; and all information necessary for the proper issuance and execution of a subpoena duces tecum;

ix. Information used by the clerk for case maintenance purposes or the courts for case management purposes; and

x. Information which is relevant and material to an issue before the court. FL ST J ADMIN Rule 2.425(b).

c. *Remedies.* Upon motion by a party or interested person or sua sponte by the court, the court may order remedies, sanctions or both for a violation of FL ST J ADMIN Rule 2.425(a). Following notice and an opportunity to respond, the court may impose sanctions if such filing was not made in good faith. FL ST J ADMIN Rule 2.425(c).

d. *Motions not restricted.* FL ST J ADMIN Rule 2.425 does not restrict a party's right to move for protective order, to move to file documents under seal, or to request a determination of the confidentiality of records. FL ST J ADMIN Rule 2.425(d).

e. *Application.* FL ST J ADMIN Rule 2.425 does not affect the application of constitutional provisions, statutes, or rules of court regarding confidential information or access to public information. FL ST J ADMIN Rule 2.425(e).

F. Filing and Service Requirements

1. *Filing requirements.* All original documents must be filed with the court either before service or immediately thereafter, unless otherwise provided for by general law or other rules. If the original of any bond or other document is not placed in the court file, a certified copy must be so placed by the clerk. FL ST J ADMIN Rule 2.516(d). All documents shall be filed in conformity with the requirements of FL ST J ADMIN Rule 2.525. FL ST RCP Rule 1.080(b). All documents filed in any court shall be filed by electronic transmission in accordance with FL ST J ADMIN Rule 2.525. "Documents" means pleadings, motions, petitions, memoranda, briefs, notices, exhibits, declarations, affidavits, orders, judgments, decrees, writs, opinions, and any other paper or writing submitted to a court. FL ST J ADMIN Rule 2.520(a). All documents that are court records, as defined in FL ST J ADMIN Rule 2.430(a)(1), must be filed by electronic transmission, provided that: (1) the clerk has the ability to accept and retain such documents; (2) the clerk or the chief judge of the circuit has requested permission to accept documents filed by electronic transmission; and (3) the supreme court has entered an order granting permission to the clerk to accept documents filed by electronic transmission. FL ST J ADMIN Rule 2.525(c)(1).

a. *Definition.* "Electronic transmission of documents" means the sending of information by electronic signals to, by or from a court or clerk, which when received can be transformed and stored or transmitted on paper, microfilm, magnetic storage device, optical imaging system, CD-ROM, flash drive, other electronic data storage system, server, case maintenance system ("CM"), electronic court filing ("ECF") system, statewide or local electronic portal ("e-portal"), or other electronic record keeping system authorized by the supreme court in a format sufficient to communicate the information on the original document in a readable format. Electronic transmission of documents includes electronic mail ("e-mail") and any internet-based transmission procedure, and may include procedures allowing for documents to be signed or verified by electronic means. FL ST J ADMIN Rule 2.525(a).

i. The filing of documents with the court as required by the Florida Rules of Judicial Administration must be made by filing them with the clerk in accordance with FL ST J ADMIN Rule 2.525, except that the judge may permit documents to be filed with the judge, in which event the judge must note the filing date before him or her on the documents and transmit them to the clerk. The date of filing is that shown on the face of the document by the judge's notation or the clerk's time stamp, whichever is earlier. FL ST J ADMIN Rule 2.516(e).

b. *Application.* Any court or clerk of the court may accept the electronic transmission of documents for filing after the clerk, together with input from the chief judge of the circuit, has obtained approval of the procedures and program for doing so from the Supreme Court of Florida. FL ST J ADMIN Rule 2.525(b).

c. *Exceptions*

   i. Paper documents and other submissions may be manually submitted to the clerk or court:

      - When the clerk does not have the ability to accept and retain documents by electronic filing or has not had ECF Procedures approved by the supreme court;
      - For filing by any self-represented party or any self-represented nonparty unless specific ECF Procedures provide a means to file documents electronically. However, any self-represented nonparty that is a governmental or public agency and any other agency, partnership, corporation, or business entity acting on behalf of any governmental or public agency may file documents by electronic transmission if such entity has the capability of filing documents electronically;
      - For filing by attorneys excused from e-mail service in accordance with FL ST J ADMIN Rule 2.516(b);
      - When submitting evidentiary exhibits or filing non-documentary materials;
      - When the filing involves documents in excess of twenty-five (25) megabytes (25MB) in size. For such filings, documents may be transmitted using an electronic storage medium that the clerk has the ability to accept, which may include a CD-ROM, flash drive, or similar storage medium;
      - When filed in open court, as permitted by the court;
      - When paper filing is permitted by any approved statewide or local ECF procedures; and
      - If any court determines that justice so requires. FL ST J ADMIN Rule 2.525(d).

   ii. Any document in paper form submitted under FL ST J ADMIN Rule 2.525(d) is filed when it is received by the clerk or court and the clerk shall immediately thereafter convert any filed paper document to an electronic document. "Convert to an electronic document" means optically capturing an image of a paper document and using character recognition software to recover as much of the document's text as practicable and then indexing and storing the document in the official court file. FL ST J ADMIN Rule 2.525(c)(4).

   iii. Any storage medium submitted under FL ST J ADMIN Rule 2.525(d)(5) is filed when received by the clerk or court and the clerk shall immediately thereafter transfer the electronic documents from the storage device to the official court file. FL ST J ADMIN Rule 2.525(c)(5).

   iv. If the filer of any paper document authorized under FL ST J ADMIN Rule 2.525(d) provides a self-addressed, postage-paid envelope for return of the paper document after it is converted to electronic form by the clerk, the clerk shall place the paper document in the envelope and deposit it in the mail. Except when a paper document is required to be maintained, the clerk may recycle any filed paper document that is not to be returned to the filer. FL ST J ADMIN Rule 2.525(c)(6).

   v. The clerk may convert any paper document filed before the effective date of FL ST J ADMIN Rule 2.525 to an electronic document. Unless the clerk is required to maintain the paper document, if the paper document has been converted to an electronic document by the clerk, the paper document is no longer part of the official court file and may be removed and recycled. FL ST J ADMIN Rule 2.525(c)(7).

d. *Official court file.* For information on what constitutes the official court file, please see FL ST J ADMIN Rule 2.525(c)(2), FL ST J ADMIN Rule 2.525(c)(3).

e. *Administration.* All attorneys, parties, or other persons using this rule to file documents are required to make arrangements with the court or clerk for the payment of any charges authorized by general law or the supreme court before filing any document by electronic transmission. FL ST J ADMIN Rule 2.525(f)(2).

f. *Filing date.* The filing date for an electronically transmitted document is the date and time that such filing is acknowledged by an electronic stamp or otherwise, pursuant to any procedure set forth in any ECF Procedures approved by the supreme court, or the date the last page of such filing is received by the court or clerk. FL ST J ADMIN Rule 2.525(f)(3).

g. *Accessibility.* All documents transmitted in any electronic form under FL ST J ADMIN Rule 2.525 must comply with the accessibility requirements of FL ST J ADMIN Rule 2.526. FL ST J ADMIN Rule 2.525(g).

2. *Service requirements.* Every pleading subsequent to the initial pleading, all orders, and every other document filed in the action must be served in conformity with the requirements of FL ST J ADMIN Rule 2.516. FL ST RCP Rule 1.080(a).

   a. *Service; When required.* Unless the court otherwise orders, or a statute or supreme court administrative order specifies a different means of service, every pleading subsequent to the initial pleading and every other document filed in any court proceeding, except applications for witness subpoenas and documents served by formal notice or required to be served in the manner provided for service of formal notice, must be served in accordance with FL ST J ADMIN Rule 2.516 on each party. No service need be made on parties against whom a default has been entered, except that pleadings asserting new or additional claims against them must be served in the manner provided for service of summons. FL ST J ADMIN Rule 2.516(a).

   b. *Service; How made.* When service is required or permitted to be made upon a party represented by an attorney, service must be made upon the attorney unless service upon the party is ordered by the court. FL ST J ADMIN Rule 2.516(b).

      i. *Service by electronic mail ("e-mail").* All documents required or permitted to be served on another party must be served by e-mail, unless FL ST J ADMIN Rule 2.516 otherwise provides. When, in addition to service by e-mail, the sender also utilizes another means of service provided for in FL ST J ADMIN Rule 2.516(b)(2), any differing time limits and other provisions applicable to that other means of service control. FL ST J ADMIN Rule 2.516(b)(1). Any document electronically transmitted to a court or clerk must also be served on all parties and interested persons in accordance with the applicable rules of court. FL ST J ADMIN Rule 2.525(e)(2).

         - *Service on attorneys.* Upon appearing in a proceeding, an attorney must serve a designation of a primary e-mail address and may designate no more than two (2) secondary e-mail addresses. Thereafter, service must be directed to all designated e-mail addresses in that proceeding. Every document filed by an attorney thereafter must include the primary e-mail address of that attorney and any secondary e-mail addresses. If an attorney does not designate any e-mail address for service, documents may be served on that attorney at the e-mail address on record with The Florida Bar. FL ST J ADMIN Rule 2.516(b)(1)(A).
         - *Exception to e-mail service on attorneys.* Service by an attorney on another attorney must be made by e-mail unless excused by the court. Upon motion by an attorney demonstrating that the attorney has no e-mail account and lacks access to the Internet at the attorney's office, the court may excuse the attorney from the requirements of e-mail service. Service on and by an attorney excused by the court from e-mail service must be by the means provided in FL ST J ADMIN Rule 2.516(b)(2). FL ST J ADMIN Rule 2.516(b)(1)(B).
         - *Service on and by parties not represented by an attorney.* Any party not represented by an attorney may serve a designation of a primary e-mail address and also may designate no more than two (2) secondary e-mail addresses to which service must be directed in that proceeding by the means provided in FL ST J ADMIN Rule 2.516(b)(1). If a party not represented by an attorney does not designate an e-mail address for service in a proceeding, service on and by that party must be by the means provided in FL ST J ADMIN Rule 2.516(b)(2). FL ST J ADMIN Rule 2.516(b)(1)(C).
         - *Time of service.* Service by e-mail is complete when it is sent. FL ST J ADMIN Rule 2.516(b)(1)(D). An e-mail is deemed served on the date it is sent. FL ST J ADMIN Rule 2.516(b)(1)(D)(i). If the sender learns that the e-mail did not reach the address of the

person to be served, the sender must immediately send another copy by e-mail, or by a means authorized by FL ST J ADMIN Rule 2.516(b)(2). FL ST J ADMIN Rule 2.516(b)(1)(D)(ii). E-mail service is treated as service by mail for the computation of time. FL ST J ADMIN Rule 2.516(b)(1)(D)(iii).

ii. *Format of e-mail for service.* Service of a document by e-mail is made by attaching a copy of the document in PDF format to an e-mail sent to all addresses designated by the attorney or party. FL ST J ADMIN Rule 2.516(b)(1)(E).

- All documents served by e-mail must be attached to an e-mail message containing a subject line beginning with the words "SERVICE OF COURT DOCUMENT" in all capital letters, followed by the case number of the proceeding in which the documents are being served. FL ST J ADMIN Rule 2.516(b)(1)(E)(i).
- The body of the e-mail must identify the court in which the proceeding is pending, the case number, the name of the initial party on each side, the title of each document served with that e-mail, and the sender's name and telephone number. FL ST J ADMIN Rule 2.516(b)(1)(E)(ii).
- Any document served by e-mail may be signed by the "/s/" format, as long as the filed original is signed in accordance with the applicable rule of procedure. FL ST J ADMIN Rule 2.516(b)(1)(E)(iii).
- Any e-mail which, together with its attached documents, exceeds five megabytes (5MB) in size, must be divided and sent as separate e-mails, no one of which may exceed five megabytes (5MB) in size and each of which must be sequentially numbered in the subject line. FL ST J ADMIN Rule 2.516(b)(1)(E)(iv).

iii. *Service by other means.* In addition to, and not in lieu of, service by e-mail, service may also be made upon attorneys by any of the means specified in FL ST J ADMIN Rule 2.516(b)(2). Service on and by all parties who are not represented by an attorney and who do not designate an e-mail address, and on and by all attorneys excused from e-mail service, must be made by delivering a copy of the document or by mailing it to the party or attorney at their last known address or, if no address is known, by leaving it with the clerk of the court. Service by mail is complete upon mailing. Delivery of a copy within FL ST J ADMIN Rule 2.516 is complete upon:

- Handing it to the attorney or to the party,
- Leaving it at the attorney's or party's office with a clerk or other person in charge thereof,
- If there is no one in charge, leaving it in a conspicuous place therein,
- If the office is closed or the person to be served has no office, leaving it at the person's usual place of abode with some person of his or her family above fifteen (15) years of age and informing such person of the contents, or
- Transmitting it by facsimile to the attorney's or party's office with a cover sheet containing the sender's name, firm, address, telephone number, and facsimile number, and the number of pages transmitted. When service is made by facsimile, a copy must also be served by any other method permitted by FL ST J ADMIN Rule 2.516. Facsimile service occurs when transmission is complete. FL ST J ADMIN Rule 2.516(b)(2)(A) through FL ST J ADMIN Rule 2.516(b)(2)(E).
- Service by delivery after 5:00 p.m. must be deemed to have been made by mailing on the date of delivery. FL ST J ADMIN Rule 2.516(b)(2)(F).

c. *Service; Numerous defendants.* In actions when the parties are unusually numerous, the court may regulate the service contemplated by the Florida Rules of Judicial Administration on motion or on its own initiative in such manner as may be found to be just and reasonable. FL ST J ADMIN Rule 2.516(c).

d. *Service by clerk.* Service of notices and other documents required to be made by the clerk must also be done as provided in FL ST J ADMIN Rule 2.516(b). FL ST J ADMIN Rule 2.516(g).

G. Hearings

1. *Communication equipment*

   a. *Definition.* Communication equipment means a conference telephone or other electronic device that permits all those appearing or participating to hear and speak to each other, provided that all conversation of all parties is audible to all persons present. FL ST J ADMIN Rule 2.530(a).

   b. *Use by all parties.* A county or circuit court judge may, upon the court's own motion or upon the written request of a party, direct that communication equipment be used for a motion hearing, pretrial conference, or a status conference. A judge must give notice to the parties and consider any objections they may have to the use of communication equipment before directing that communication equipment be used. The decision to use communication equipment over the objection of parties will be in the sound discretion of the trial court, except as noted below. FL ST J ADMIN Rule 2.530(b).

   c. *Use only by requesting party.* A county or circuit court judge may, upon the written request of a party upon reasonable notice to all other parties, permit a requesting party to participate through communication equipment in a scheduled motion hearing; however, any such request (except in criminal, juvenile, and appellate proceedings) must be granted, absent a showing of good cause to deny the same, where the hearing is set for not longer than fifteen (15) minutes. FL ST J ADMIN Rule 2.530(c).

   d. *Testimony*

      i. *Generally.* A county or circuit court judge, general magistrate, special magistrate, or hearing officer may allow testimony to be taken through communication equipment if all parties consent or if permitted by another applicable rule of procedure. FL ST J ADMIN Rule 2.530(d)(1).

      ii. *Procedure.* Any party desiring to present testimony through communication equipment shall, prior to the hearing or trial at which the testimony is to be presented, contact all parties to determine whether each party consents to this form of testimony. The party seeking to present the testimony shall move for permission to present testimony through communication equipment, which motion shall set forth good cause as to why the testimony should be allowed in this form. FL ST J ADMIN Rule 2.530(d)(2).

      iii. *Oath.* Testimony may be taken through communication equipment only if a notary public or other person authorized to administer oaths in the witness's jurisdiction is present with the witness and administers the oath consistent with the laws of the jurisdiction. FL ST J ADMIN Rule 2.530(d)(3).

      iv. *Confrontation rights.* In juvenile and criminal proceedings the defendant must make an informed waiver of any confrontation rights that may be abridged by the use of communication equipment. FL ST J ADMIN Rule 2.530(d)(4).

      v. *Video testimony.* If the testimony to be presented utilizes video conferencing or comparable two-way visual capabilities, the court in its discretion may modify the procedures set forth in FL ST J ADMIN Rule 2.530 to accommodate the technology utilized. FL ST J ADMIN Rule 2.530(d)(5).

   e. *Burden of expense.* The cost for the use of the communication equipment is the responsibility of the requesting party unless otherwise directed by the court. FL ST J ADMIN Rule 2.530(e).

H. Forms

1. Official Motion for Leave to Amend Forms for Florida

   a. Caption. FL ST RCP Form 1.901.

   b. Notice of compliance when constitutional challenge is brought. FL ST RCP Form 1.975.

2. Motion for Leave to Amend Forms for Florida

   a. Motion; For leave of court; To amend complaint. FL-PP § 2:155.

   b. Motion; For leave of court; To add claim for punitive damages. FL-PP § 2:156.

c. Motion; For leave of court; To amend complaint; To conform to evidence. FL-PP § 2:157.
d. Motion; For leave of court; To permit admission of evidence. FL-PP § 2:158.
e. Order; Granting leave to amend complaint. FL-PP § 2:163.
f. Order; Granting leave to amend complaint; To conform to evidence. FL-PP § 2:164.
g. Order; Granting leave to amend complaint; To permit admission of evidence. FL-PP § 2:165.
h. Form for motion for leave to amend complaint. FL-RCPF R 1.190(39).
i. Form for amendment to complaint with leave of court. FL-RCPF R 1.190(40).
j. Form for motion to amend amended complaint. FL-RCPF R 1.190(42).
k. Form for amendment to amended complaint (or second amended complaint). FL-RCPF R 1.190(43).
l. Form for motion to amend complaint to add count. FL-RCPF R 1.190(44).

3. Official Forms for Florida Circuit Court, Second Judicial Circuit

a. Notice of change of contact information. FL ST 2 J CIR 2007-05.

I. Checklist

(I) ❑ Matters to be considered by moving party
- (a) ❑ Required documents
  - (1) ❑ Notice of hearing/Motion
  - (2) ❑ Proposed amended pleading
  - (3) ❑ Certificate of service
- (b) ❑ Supplemental documents
  - (1) ❑ Proposed order
  - (2) ❑ Notice of constitutional question
- (c) ❑ Time for making motion
  - (1) ❑ A party may amend a pleading once as a matter of course at any time before a responsive pleading is served or, if the pleading is one to which no responsive pleading is permitted and the action has not been placed on the trial calendar, may amend it at any time within twenty (20) days after it is served
  - (2) ❑ Under the Florida Rules of Civil Procedure, there is no time limit as to when an amendment with leave of court may be sought; amendments of the pleadings may be permitted, with the court's discretion, at any stage of the proceedings in furtherance of justice
  - (3) ❑ A motion for leave to amend a pleading to assert a claim for punitive damages can be filed separately and before the supporting evidence or proffer, but each shall be served on all parties at least twenty (20) days before the hearing
  - (4) ❑ A copy of any written motion which may not be heard ex parte and a copy of the notice of the hearing thereof shall be served a reasonable time before the time specified for the hearing

(II) ❑ Matters to be considered by opposing party
- (a) ❑ Required documents
  - (1) ❑ Response to motion
  - (2) ❑ Certificate of service
- (b) ❑ Supplemental documents
  - (1) ❑ Proposed order
  - (2) ❑ Notice of constitutional question
- (c) ❑ Time for service and filing of opposition
  - (1) ❑ No time specified for responding to a motion

Motions, Oppositions and Replies
Motion for Summary Judgment

Document Last Updated January 2013

A. Applicable Rules

1. *State rules*
   a. Rules of court. FL ST RCP Rule 1.010; FL ST J ADMIN Rule 2.110.
   b. Nonverification of pleadings. FL ST RCP Rule 1.030.
   c. Service and filing of pleadings, orders, and documents. FL ST RCP Rule 1.080.
   d. Time. FL ST RCP Rule 1.090.
   e. Pleadings and motions. FL ST RCP Rule 1.100.
   f. Motions. FL ST RCP Rule 1.160.
   g. Summary judgment. FL ST RCP Rule 1.510.
   h. Relief from judgment, decrees, or orders. FL ST RCP Rule 1.540.
   i. Mediation and arbitration. FL ST RCP Rule 1.700; FL ST RCP Rule 1.710; FL ST RCP Rule 1.720; FL ST RCP Rule 1.730; FL ST RCP Rule 1.750; FL ST RCP Rule 1.800; FL ST RCP Rule 1.810; FL ST RCP Rule 1.820; FL ST RCP Rule 1.830.
   j. Forms. FL ST RCP Rule 1.900.
   k. Minimization of the filing of sensitive information. FL ST J ADMIN Rule 2.425.
   l. Retention of court records. FL ST J ADMIN Rule 2.430.
   m. Foreign attorneys. FL ST J ADMIN Rule 2.510.
   n. Signature of attorneys and parties. FL ST J ADMIN Rule 2.515.
   o. Paper. FL ST J ADMIN Rule 2.520.
   p. Electronic filing. FL ST J ADMIN Rule 2.525.
   q. Accessibility of information and technology. FL ST J ADMIN Rule 2.526.
   r. Communication equipment. FL ST J ADMIN Rule 2.530.
   s. Court reporting. FL ST J ADMIN Rule 2.535.
   t. Requests for accommodations by persons with disabilities. FL ST J ADMIN Rule 2.540.
2. *Local rules*
   a. Notice of change of contact information. FL ST 2 J CIR 2007-05.

B. Timing

1. *Motion for summary judgment*
   a. *For the claimant.* A party seeking to recover upon a claim, counterclaim, crossclaim or third-party claim or to obtain a declaratory judgment may move for a summary judgment in that party's favor at any time after the expiration of twenty (20) days from the commencement of the action or after service of a motion for summary judgment by the adverse party. FL ST RCP Rule 1.510(a).
   b. *For defending party.* A party against whom a claim, counterclaim, crossclaim, or third-party claim is asserted or a declaratory judgment is sought may move for a summary judgment in that party's favor as to all or any part thereof at any time with or without supporting affidavits. FL ST RCP Rule 1.510(b).
      i. A defending party is not required to serve his responsive pleading before moving for summary judgment. He may make the motion at any time, setting out his defenses by affidavit, and thus effect a speedy termination of the action if no genuine issue exists as to any fact or facts pertaining to a defense that would defeat the claim. FL ST RCP Rule 1.510, notes.

2. *Service of motion.* The movant shall serve the motion for summary judgment at least twenty (20) days before the time fixed for the hearing, and shall also serve at that time a copy of any summary judgment evidence on which the movant relies that has not already been filed with the court. FL ST RCP Rule 1.510(c).
3. *Computation of time*
   a. *Generally.* Computation of time shall be governed by FL ST J ADMIN Rule 2.514. FL ST RCP Rule 1.090(a). The following rules apply in computing time periods specified in any rule of procedure, local rule, court order, or statute that does not specify a method of computing time. FL ST J ADMIN Rule 2.514(a).
      i. *Period stated in days or a longer unit.* When the period is stated in days or a longer unit of time (A) exclude the day of the event that triggers the period; (B) count every day, including intermediate Saturdays, Sundays, and legal holidays; and (C) include the last day of the period, but if the last day is a Saturday, Sunday, or legal holiday, or falls within any period of time extended through an order of the chief justice under FL ST J ADMIN Rule 2.205(a)(2)(B)(iv), the period continues to run until the end of the next day that is not a Saturday, Sunday, or legal holiday and does not fall within any period of time extended through an order of the chief justice. FL ST J ADMIN Rule 2.514(a)(1).
      ii. *Period stated in hours.* When the period is stated in hours (A) begin counting immediately on the occurrence of the event that triggers the period; (B) count every hour, including hours during intermediate Saturdays, Sundays, and legal holidays; and (C) if the period would end on a Saturday, Sunday, or legal holiday, or during any period of time extended through an order of the chief justice under FL ST J ADMIN Rule 2.205(a)(2)(B)(iv), the period continues to run until the same time on the next day that is not a Saturday, Sunday, or legal holiday and does not fall within any period of time extended through an order of the chief justice. FL ST J ADMIN Rule 2.514(a)(2).
      iii. *Period stated in days less than seven (7) days.* When the period stated in days is less than seven (7) days, intermediate Saturdays, Sundays, and legal holidays shall be excluded in the computation. FL ST J ADMIN Rule 2.514(a)(3).
      iv. *"Last day" defined.* Unless a different time is set by a statute, local rule, or court order, the last day ends (A) for electronic filing or for service by any means, at midnight; and (B) for filing by other means, when the clerk's office is scheduled to close. FL ST J ADMIN Rule 2.514(a)(4).
      v. *"Next day" defined.* The "next day" is determined by continuing to count forward when the period is measured after an event and backward when measured before an event. FL ST J ADMIN Rule 2.514(a)(5).
      vi. *"Legal holiday" defined.* "Legal holiday" means (A) the day set aside by FL ST § 110.117, for observing New Year's Day, Martin Luther King, Jr.'s Birthday, Memorial Day, Independence Day, Labor Day, Veterans' Day, Thanksgiving Day, the Friday after Thanksgiving Day, or Christmas Day, and (B) any day observed as a holiday by the clerk's office or as designated by the chief judge. FL ST J ADMIN Rule 2.514(a)(6).
   b. *Additional time after service by mail or e-mail.* When a party may or must act within a specified time after service and service is made by mail or e-mail, five (5) days are added after the period that would otherwise expire under FL ST J ADMIN Rule 2.514(a). FL ST J ADMIN Rule 2.514(b).
   c. *Enlargement.* When an act is required or allowed to be done at or within a specified time by order of court, by the Florida Rules of Civil Procedure, or by notice given thereunder, for cause shown the court at any time in its discretion (1) with or without notice, may order the period enlarged if request therefor is made before the expiration of the period originally prescribed or as extended by a previous order, or (2) upon motion made and notice after the expiration of the specified period, may permit the act to be done when failure to act was the result of excusable neglect, but it may not extend the time for making a motion for new trial, for rehearing, or to alter or amend a judgment; making a motion for relief from a judgment under FL ST RCP Rule 1.540(b); taking an appeal or filing a petition for certiorari; or making a motion for a directed verdict. FL ST RCP Rule 1.090(b).

d. *Unaffected by expiration of term.* The period of time provided for the doing of any act or the taking of any proceeding shall not be affected or limited by the continued existence or expiration of a term of court. The continued existence or expiration of a term of court in no way affects the power of a court to do any act or take any proceeding in any action which is or has been pending before it. FL ST RCP Rule 1.090(c).

C. General Requirements

1. *Motions generally*

   a. *Contents.* An application to the court for an order shall be by motion which shall be made in writing unless made during a hearing or trial, shall state with particularity the grounds therefor, and shall set forth the relief or order sought. The requirement of writing is fulfilled if the motion is stated in a written notice of the hearing of the motion. All notices of hearing shall specify each motion or other matter to be heard. FL ST RCP Rule 1.100(b).

   b. *Particularity requirement.* The court considers a motion in the light of the substantive law, rule or statute to make its determination. Some rules require a statement of the grounds for a motion under the rule. Failure to give the grounds will result in denial of the motion. This should be the result in all situations when the ground for the motion is not inherent in the rule. FL-PRACPROC § 9:3. The requirement is nevertheless an important one, first because of the due process notice rights of the respondent, as well as for the assistance it provides to the court in its preparation for the hearing or, absent a hearing, for disposition. 4 FLPRAC R 1.100.

2. *Summary judgment.* A party seeking to recover upon or defend against a claim, counterclaim, crossclaim, or third-party claim or to obtain a declaratory judgment may move for a summary judgment. FL ST RCP Rule 1.510(a); FL ST RCP Rule 1.510(b).

   a. *General motion for summary judgment information*

      i. *Contents of motion.* The motion shall state with particularity the grounds upon which it is based and the substantial matters of law to be argued and shall specifically identify any affidavits, answers to interrogatories, admissions, depositions, and other materials as would be admissible in evidence ("summary judgment evidence") on which the movant relies. FL ST RCP Rule 1.510(c).

      ii. *Evidence relied upon.* The movant shall also serve at that time a copy of any summary judgment evidence on which the movant relies that has not already been filed with the court. FL ST RCP Rule 1.510(c).

      iii. *Judgment as a matter of law.* The judgment sought shall be rendered forthwith if the pleadings and summary judgment evidence on file show that there is no genuine issue as to any material fact and that the moving party is entitled to a judgment as a matter of law. A summary judgment, interlocutory in character, may be rendered on the issue of liability alone although there is a genuine issue as to the amount of damages. FL ST RCP Rule 1.510(c).

   b. *Sham pleadings.* If a party deems any pleading or part thereof filed by another party to be a sham, that party may move to strike the pleading or part thereof before the cause is set for trial and the court shall hear the motion, taking evidence of the respective parties, and if the motion is sustained, the pleading to which the motion is directed shall be stricken. Default and summary judgment on the merits may be entered in the discretion of the court or the court may permit additional pleadings to be filed for good cause shown. FL ST RCP Rule 1.150(a).

   c. *Burden of proof*

      i. The moving party in a motion for summary judgment has the initial burden of demonstrating the nonexistence of any genuine issue of fact. Landers v. Milton, 370 So.2d 368, 370 (Fla. 1979); Gardner v. Sabal Point Properties, Inc., 616 So.2d 1111, 1112 (Fla. 5th DCA 1993); FL-PP § 6:7.

      ii. If the record raises the slightest doubt that material issues could be present, that doubt must be resolved against the movant and the motion for summary judgment denied. Moore v. Morris, 475 So.2d 666, 668 (Fla. 1985); Henderson v. CSX Transportation, Inc., 617 So.2d 770 (Fla. 1st

DCA 1993); Jones v. Directors Guild of America, Inc., 584 So.2d 1057 (Fla. 1st DCA 1991); FL-PP § 6:7.

iii. Until the moving party meets the initial burden of showing there is no issue of material fact, the opposing party need do nothing. Holl v. Talcott, 191 So.2d 40, 43 (Fla. 1966); Spradley v. Stick, 622 So.2d 610 (Fla. 1st DCA 1993); FL-RCPF R 1.510(404).

iv. When the movant has tendered competent evidence in support of its motion, the burden shifts to the nonmoving party to come forward with opposing evidence to show that a question of material fact exists. Landers v. Milton, 370 So.2d 368, 370 (Fla. 1979); Holl v. Talcott, 191 So.2d 40, 43-44 (Fla. 1966); Lenhal Realty, Inc. v. Transamerica Commercial Finance Corp., 615 So.2d 207 (Fla. 4th DCA 1993); FL-PP § 6:7.

d. *Affidavits*

i. *Form of affidavits; Further testimony.* Supporting and opposing affidavits shall be made on personal knowledge, shall set forth such facts as would be admissible in evidence, and shall show affirmatively that the affiant is competent to testify to the matters stated. Sworn or certified copies of all papers or parts referred to in an affidavit shall be attached to or served with the affidavit. The court may permit affidavits to be supplemented or opposed by depositions, answers to interrogatories, or by further affidavits. FL ST RCP Rule 1.510(e).

ii. *When affidavits are unavailable.* If it appears from the affidavits of a party opposing the motion that the party cannot for reasons stated present by affidavit facts essential to justify opposition, the court may refuse the application for judgment or may order a continuance to permit affidavits to be obtained or depositions to be taken or discovery to be had or may make such other order as is just. FL ST RCP Rule 1.510(f).

iii. *Affidavits made in bad faith.* If it appears to the satisfaction of the court at any time that any of the affidavits presented pursuant to FL ST RCP Rule 1.510 are presented in bad faith or solely for the purpose of delay, the court shall forthwith order the party employing them to pay to the other party the amount of the reasonable expenses that the filing of the affidavits caused the other party to incur, including reasonable attorneys' fees, and any offending party or attorney may be adjudged guilty of contempt. FL ST RCP Rule 1.510(g).

e. *Case not fully adjudicated on motion.* On motion under FL ST RCP Rule 1.510 if judgment is not rendered upon the whole case or for all the relief asked and a trial or the taking of testimony and a final hearing is necessary, the court at the hearing of the motion, by examining the pleadings and the evidence before it and by interrogating counsel, shall ascertain, if practicable, what material facts exist without substantial controversy and what material facts are actually and in good faith controverted. FL ST RCP Rule 1.510(d).

i. It shall thereupon make an order specifying the facts that appear without substantial controversy, including the extent to which the amount of damages or other relief is not in controversy, and directing such further proceedings in the action as are just. FL ST RCP Rule 1.510(d).

ii. On the trial or final hearing of the action the facts so specified shall be deemed established, and the trial or final hearing shall be conducted accordingly. FL ST RCP Rule 1.510(d).

3. *Arbitration and mediation*

a. *Referral to arbitration and mediation.* Except as hereinafter provided or as otherwise prohibited by law, the presiding judge may enter an order referring all or any part of a contested civil matter to mediation or arbitration. The parties to any contested civil matter may file a written stipulation to mediate or arbitrate any issue between them at any time. Such stipulation shall be incorporated into the order of referral. FL ST RCP Rule 1.700(a).

b. *Arbitration*

i. *Exclusions.* A civil action shall be ordered to arbitration or arbitration in conjunction with mediation upon stipulation of the parties. A civil action may be ordered to arbitration or arbitration in conjunction with mediation upon motion of any party or by the court, if the judge determines the action to be of such a nature that arbitration could be of benefit to the litigants or the court. FL ST RCP Rule 1.800.

- Under no circumstances may the following categories of actions be referred to arbitration: (1) bond estreatures; (2) habeas corpus or other extraordinary writs; (3) bond validations; (4) civil or criminal contempt; (5) such other matters as may be specified by order of the chief judge in the circuit. FL ST RCP Rule 1.800.

ii. For more information regarding arbitration, please see FL ST RCP Rule 1.810; FL ST RCP Rule 1.820; FL ST RCP Rule 1.830.

c. *Mediation.* For more information regarding mediation, please see FL ST RCP Rule 1.710; FL ST RCP Rule 1.720; FL ST RCP Rule 1.730; and FL ST RCP Rule 1.750.

4. *Rules of court*

a. *Rules of civil procedure.* The Florida Rules of Civil Procedure apply to all actions of a civil nature and all special statutory proceedings in the circuit courts and county courts except those to which the Florida Probate Rules, the Florida Family Law Rules of Procedure, or the Small Claims Rules apply. FL ST RCP Rule 1.010.

i. The form, content, procedure, and time for pleading in all special statutory proceedings shall be as prescribed by the statutes governing the proceeding unless the Florida Rules of Civil Procedure specifically provide to the contrary. FL ST RCP Rule 1.010.

ii. The Florida Rules of Civil Procedure shall be construed to secure the just, speedy, and inexpensive determination of every action. FL ST RCP Rule 1.010.

b. *Rules of judicial administration.* The Florida Rules of Judicial Administration shall apply to administrative matters in all courts to which the Florida Rules of Judicial Administration are applicable by their terms. The Florida Rules of Judicial Administration shall be construed to secure the speedy and inexpensive determination of every proceeding to which they are applicable. The Florida Rules of Judicial Administration shall supersede all conflicting rules and statutes. FL ST J ADMIN Rule 2.110.

5. *Notice of change of contact information.* The Clerk shall provide a change of address and/or telephone number form for use by attorneys and pro se litigants. With any change of address and/or telephone number, attorneys and pro se litigants governed by FL ST J ADMIN Rule 2.515 will provide to the Clerk and all parties promptly the change of address and/or telephone number form. This form should be submitted only once to the Clerk, who will then make the address and/or telephone number change in all court divisions. FL ST 2 J CIR 2007-05.

D. Documents

1. *Required documents*

a. *Notice of hearing/Motion.* An application to the court for an order shall be by motion which shall be made in writing unless made during a hearing or trial, shall state with particularity the grounds therefor, and shall set forth the relief or order sought. The requirement of writing is fulfilled if the motion is stated in a written notice of the hearing of the motion. All notices of hearing shall specify each motion or other matter to be heard. FL ST RCP Rule 1.100(b).

i. *Notices to persons with disabilities.* See the Format section of this KeyRules document for further information.

b. *Certificate of service.* When any attorney certifies in substance: "I certify that a copy hereof has been furnished to (here insert name or names and addresses used for service) by (e-mail) (delivery) (mail) (fax) on .... (date) ....________________ Attorney" the certificate is taken as prima facie proof of such service in compliance with FL ST J ADMIN Rule 2.516. FL ST J ADMIN Rule 2.516(f).

2. *Supplemental documents*

a. *Affidavits.* Supporting and opposing affidavits shall be made on personal knowledge, shall set forth such facts as would be admissible in evidence, and shall show affirmatively that the affiant is competent to testify to the matters stated therein. Sworn or certified copies of all papers or parts thereof referred to in an affidavit shall be attached thereto or served therewith. FL ST RCP Rule 1.510(e). For further information regarding affidavits made in the context of a motion for summary judgment see FL ST RCP Rule 1.510(e) through FL ST RCP Rule 1.510(g).

b. *Other evidence.* The movant shall also serve at that time a copy of any summary judgment evidence on which the movant relies that has not already been filed with the court. FL ST RCP Rule 1.510(c).

c. *Proposed order.* The court may require that orders or judgments be prepared by a party, may require the party to furnish the court with stamped, addressed envelopes for service of the order or judgment, and may require that proposed orders and judgments be furnished to all parties before entry by the court of the order or judgment. FL ST J ADMIN Rule 2.516(h)(1).

d. *Notice of constitutional question.* A party that files a pleading, written motion, or other paper drawing into question the constitutionality of a state statute or a county or municipal charter, ordinance, or franchise must promptly (1) file a notice of constitutional question stating the question and identifying the paper that raises it; and (2) serve the notice and the pleading, written motion, or other paper drawing into question the constitutionality of a state statute or a county or municipal charter, ordinance, or franchise on the Attorney General or the state attorney of the judicial circuit in which the action is pending, by either certified or registered mail. Service of the notice and pleading, written motion, or other paper does not require joinder of the Attorney General or the state attorney as a party to the action. FL ST RCP Rule 1.071.

E. Format

1. *Documents; Type and size.* Documents subject to the exceptions set forth in FL ST J ADMIN Rule 2.525(d) shall be filed on recycled paper measuring eight and one half by eleven (8 1/2 by 11) inches. For purposes of FL ST J ADMIN Rule 2.520, paper is recycled if it contains a minimum content of fifty (50) percent waste paper. Xerographic reduction of legal-size (eight and one half by fourteen (8 1/2 by 14) inches) documents to letter size (eight and one half by eleven (8 1/2 by 11) inches) is prohibited. All other documents filed by electronic transmission shall be filed in a format capable of being printed in a format consistent with the provisions of FL ST J ADMIN Rule 2.250. FL ST J ADMIN Rule 2.520(b).

   a. *Exhibits.* Any exhibit or attachment filed with pleadings or papers may be filed in its original size. FL ST J ADMIN Rule 2.520(c).

   b. *Recording space.* On all papers and documents prepared and filed by the court or by any party to a proceeding which are to be recorded in the public records of any county, including but not limited to final money judgments and notices of lis pendens, a three (3) inch by three (3) inch space at the top right-hand corner on the first page and a one (1) inch by three (3) inch space at the top right-hand corner on each subsequent page shall be left blank and reserved for use by the clerk of court. FL ST J ADMIN Rule 2.520(d).

      i. *Exceptions to recording space.* Any papers or documents created by persons or entities over which the filing party has no control, including but not limited to wills, codicils, trusts, or other testamentary documents; documents prepared or executed by any public officer; documents prepared, executed, acknowledged, or proved outside of the State of Florida; or documents created by State or Federal government agencies, may be filed without the space required by FL ST J ADMIN Rule 2.520. FL ST J ADMIN Rule 2.520(e).

   c. *Noncompliance.* No clerk of court is permitted to refuse to file any document or paper because of noncompliance with the Florida Rules of Judicial Administration. However, upon request of the clerk of court, noncomplying documents must be resubmitted in accordance with the formatting rules. FL ST J ADMIN Rule 2.520(f).

2. *Caption.* Every pleading, motion, order, judgment, or other paper shall have a caption containing the name of the court, the file number, and except for in rem proceedings, including forfeiture proceedings, the name of the first party on each side with an appropriate indication of other parties, and a designation identifying the party filing it and its nature or the nature of the order, as the case may be. In any in rem proceeding, every pleading, motion, order, judgment, or other paper shall have a caption containing the name of the court, the file number, the style "In re" (followed by the name or general description of the property), and a designation of the person or entity filing it and its nature or the nature of the order, as the

case may be. In an in rem forfeiture proceeding, the style shall be "In re forfeiture of" (followed by the name of the general description of the property). All papers filed in the action shall be styled in such a manner as to indicate clearly the subject matter of the paper and the party requesting or obtaining relief. FL ST RCP Rule 1.100(c)(1).

3. *Writing and written defined.* Writing or written means a document containing information, an application, or a stipulation. FL ST RCP Rule 1.080(c).
4. *Rule abbreviations*
    a. The Florida Rules of Civil Procedure and shall be abbreviated as Fla.R.Civ.P. FL ST RCP Rule 1.010.
    b. The Florida Rules of Judicial Administration shall be abbreviated as Fla. R. Jud. Admin. FL ST J ADMIN Rule 2.110.
5. *Nonverification.* Except when otherwise specifically provided by the Florida Rules of Civil Procedure or an applicable statute, every pleading or other document of a party represented by an attorney need not be verified or accompanied by an affidavit. FL ST RCP Rule 1.030; FL ST J ADMIN Rule 2.515(a).
6. *Attorney signature*
    a. *Attorney signature.* Every pleading and other document of a party represented by an attorney shall be signed by at least one (1) attorney of record in that attorney's individual name whose current record Florida Bar address, telephone number, including area code, primary e-mail address and secondary e-mail addresses, if any, and Florida Bar number shall be stated, and who shall be duly licensed to practice law in Florida or who shall have received permission to appear in the particular case as provided in FL ST J ADMIN Rule 2.510. FL ST J ADMIN Rule 2.515(a).
        i. The attorney may be required by the court to give the address of, and to vouch for the attorney's authority to represent, the party. FL ST J ADMIN Rule 2.515(a).
        ii. The signature of an attorney shall constitute a certificate by the attorney that the attorney has read the pleading or other document; that to the best of the attorney's knowledge, information, and belief there is good ground to support it; and that it is not interposed for delay. FL ST J ADMIN Rule 2.515(a).
        iii. If a pleading is not signed or is signed with intent to defeat the purpose of FL ST J ADMIN Rule 2.515, it may be stricken and the action may proceed as though the pleading or other document had not been served. FL ST J ADMIN Rule 2.515(a).
    b. *Pro se litigant signature.* A party who is not represented by an attorney shall sign any pleading or other paper and state the party's address and telephone number, including area code. FL ST J ADMIN Rule 2.515(b).
    c. *Form of signature*
        i. The signatures required on pleadings and documents by FL ST J ADMIN Rule 2.515(a) and FL ST J ADMIN Rule 2.515(b) may be:
            - Original signatures;
            - Original signatures that have been reproduced by electronic means, such as on electronically transmitted documents or photocopied documents;
            - Electronic signatures using the "/s/," "s/," or "/s" formats by or at the direction of the person signing; or
            - Any other signature format authorized by general law, so long as the clerk where the proceeding is pending has the capability of receiving and has obtained approval from the Supreme Court of Florida to accept pleadings and documents with that signature format. FL ST J ADMIN Rule 2.515(c)(1).
        ii. An attorney, party, or other person who files a pleading or paper by electronic transmission that does not contain the original signature of that attorney, party, or other person shall file that identical pleading or paper in paper form containing an original signature of that attorney, party, or other person (hereinafter called the follow-up filing) immediately thereafter. The follow-up

filing is not required if the Supreme Court of Florida has entered an order directing the clerk of court to discontinue accepting the follow-up filing. FL ST J ADMIN Rule 2.515(c)(2).

7. *Forms*
   a. *Process.* The forms of process, notice of lis pendens, and notice of action provided in the Florida Rules of Civil Procedure are sufficient. Variations from the forms do not void process or notices that are otherwise sufficient. FL ST RCP Rule 1.900(a).
   b. *Other forms.* The other forms provided in the Florida Rules of Civil Procedure are sufficient for the matters that are covered by them. So long as the substance is expressed without prolixity, the forms may be varied to meet the facts of a particular case. FL ST RCP Rule 1.900(b).
   c. *Formal matters.* Captions, except for the designation of the paper, are omitted from the forms provided in the Florida Rules of Civil Procedure. A general form of caption is the first form provided. Signatures are omitted from pleadings and motions. FL ST RCP Rule 1.900(c).
8. *Notices to persons with disabilities.* All notices of court proceedings to be held in a public facility, and all process compelling appearance at such proceedings, shall include the following statement in bold face, fourteen (14) point Times New Roman or Courier font: "If you are a person with a disability who needs any accommodation in order to participate in this proceeding, you are entitled, at no cost to you, to the provision of certain assistance. Please contact [identify applicable court personnel by name, address, and telephone number] at least seven (7) days before your scheduled court appearance, or immediately upon receiving this notification if the time before the scheduled appearance is less than seven (7) days; if you are hearing or voice impaired, call 711." FL ST J ADMIN Rule 2.540(c)(1).
9. *Minimization of the filing of sensitive information*
   a. *Limitations for court filings.* Unless authorized by FL ST J ADMIN Rule 2.425(b), statute, another rule of court, or the court orders otherwise, designated sensitive information filed with the court must be limited to the following format:
      i. The initials of a person known to be a minor;
      ii. The year of birth of a person's birth date;
      iii. No portion of any: Social security number, Bank account number, Credit card account number, Charge account number, or Debit account number;
      iv. The last four digits of any: Taxpayer identification number (TIN), Employee identification number, Driver's license number, Passport number, Telephone number, Financial account number, except as set forth in FL ST J ADMIN Rule 2.425(a)(3), Brokerage account number, Insurance policy account number, Loan account number, Customer account number, or Patient or health care number;
      v. A truncated version of any: Email address, Computer user name, Password, or Personal identification number (PIN); and
      vi. A truncated version of any other sensitive information as provided by court order. FL ST J ADMIN Rule 2.425(a).
   b. *Exceptions.* FL ST J ADMIN Rule 2.425(a) does not apply to the following:
      i. An account number which identifies the property alleged to be the subject of a proceeding;
      ii. The record of an administrative or agency proceeding;
      iii. The record in appellate or review proceedings;
      iv. The birth date of a minor whenever the birth date is necessary for the court to establish or maintain subject matter jurisdiction;
      v. The name of a minor in any order relating to parental responsibility, time-sharing, or child support;
      vi. The name of a minor in any document or order affecting the minor's ownership of real property;
      vii. The birth date of a party in a writ of attachment or notice to payor;

viii. In traffic and criminal proceedings: a pro se filing; a court filing that is related to a criminal matter or investigation and that is prepared before the filing of a criminal charge or is not filed as part of any docketed criminal case; an arrest or search warrant or any information in support thereof; a charging document and an affidavit or other documents filed in support of any charging document, including any driving records; a statement of particulars; discovery material introduced into evidence or otherwise filed with the court; and all information necessary for the proper issuance and execution of a subpoena duces tecum;

ix. Information used by the clerk for case maintenance purposes or the courts for case management purposes; and

x. Information which is relevant and material to an issue before the court. FL ST J ADMIN Rule 2.425(b).

c. *Remedies.* Upon motion by a party or interested person or sua sponte by the court, the court may order remedies, sanctions or both for a violation of FL ST J ADMIN Rule 2.425(a). Following notice and an opportunity to respond, the court may impose sanctions if such filing was not made in good faith. FL ST J ADMIN Rule 2.425(c).

d. *Motions not restricted.* FL ST J ADMIN Rule 2.425 does not restrict a party's right to move for protective order, to move to file documents under seal, or to request a determination of the confidentiality of records. FL ST J ADMIN Rule 2.425(d).

e. *Application.* FL ST J ADMIN Rule 2.425 does not affect the application of constitutional provisions, statutes, or rules of court regarding confidential information or access to public information. FL ST J ADMIN Rule 2.425(e).

F. Filing and Service Requirements

1. *Filing requirements.* All original documents must be filed with the court either before service or immediately thereafter, unless otherwise provided for by general law or other rules. If the original of any bond or other document is not placed in the court file, a certified copy must be so placed by the clerk. FL ST J ADMIN Rule 2.516(d). All documents shall be filed in conformity with the requirements of FL ST J ADMIN Rule 2.525. FL ST RCP Rule 1.080(b). All documents filed in any court shall be filed by electronic transmission in accordance with FL ST J ADMIN Rule 2.525. "Documents" means pleadings, motions, petitions, memoranda, briefs, notices, exhibits, declarations, affidavits, orders, judgments, decrees, writs, opinions, and any other paper or writing submitted to a court. FL ST J ADMIN Rule 2.520(a). All documents that are court records, as defined in FL ST J ADMIN Rule 2.430(a)(1), must be filed by electronic transmission, provided that: (1) the clerk has the ability to accept and retain such documents; (2) the clerk or the chief judge of the circuit has requested permission to accept documents filed by electronic transmission; and (3) the supreme court has entered an order granting permission to the clerk to accept documents filed by electronic transmission. FL ST J ADMIN Rule 2.525(c)(1).

a. *Definition.* "Electronic transmission of documents" means the sending of information by electronic signals to, by or from a court or clerk, which when received can be transformed and stored or transmitted on paper, microfilm, magnetic storage device, optical imaging system, CD-ROM, flash drive, other electronic data storage system, server, case maintenance system ("CM"), electronic court filing ("ECF") system, statewide or local electronic portal ("e-portal"), or other electronic record keeping system authorized by the supreme court in a format sufficient to communicate the information on the original document in a readable format. Electronic transmission of documents includes electronic mail ("e-mail") and any internet-based transmission procedure, and may include procedures allowing for documents to be signed or verified by electronic means. FL ST J ADMIN Rule 2.525(a).

i. The filing of documents with the court as required by the Florida Rules of Judicial Administration must be made by filing them with the clerk in accordance with FL ST J ADMIN Rule 2.525, except that the judge may permit documents to be filed with the judge, in which event the judge must note the filing date before him or her on the documents and transmit them to the clerk. The date of filing is that shown on the face of the document by the judge's notation or the clerk's time stamp, whichever is earlier. FL ST J ADMIN Rule 2.516(e).

b. *Application.* Any court or clerk of the court may accept the electronic transmission of documents for

filing after the clerk, together with input from the chief judge of the circuit, has obtained approval of the procedures and program for doing so from the Supreme Court of Florida. FL ST J ADMIN Rule 2.525(b).

c. *Exceptions*
   i. Paper documents and other submissions may be manually submitted to the clerk or court:
      - When the clerk does not have the ability to accept and retain documents by electronic filing or has not had ECF Procedures approved by the supreme court;
      - For filing by any self-represented party or any self-represented nonparty unless specific ECF Procedures provide a means to file documents electronically. However, any self-represented nonparty that is a governmental or public agency and any other agency, partnership, corporation, or business entity acting on behalf of any governmental or public agency may file documents by electronic transmission if such entity has the capability of filing documents electronically;
      - For filing by attorneys excused from e-mail service in accordance with FL ST J ADMIN Rule 2.516(b);
      - When submitting evidentiary exhibits or filing non-documentary materials;
      - When the filing involves documents in excess of twenty-five (25) megabytes (25MB) in size. For such filings, documents may be transmitted using an electronic storage medium that the clerk has the ability to accept, which may include a CD-ROM, flash drive, or similar storage medium;
      - When filed in open court, as permitted by the court;
      - When paper filing is permitted by any approved statewide or local ECF procedures; and
      - If any court determines that justice so requires. FL ST J ADMIN Rule 2.525(d).
   ii. Any document in paper form submitted under FL ST J ADMIN Rule 2.525(d) is filed when it is received by the clerk or court and the clerk shall immediately thereafter convert any filed paper document to an electronic document. "Convert to an electronic document" means optically capturing an image of a paper document and using character recognition software to recover as much of the document's text as practicable and then indexing and storing the document in the official court file. FL ST J ADMIN Rule 2.525(c)(4).
   iii. Any storage medium submitted under FL ST J ADMIN Rule 2.525(d)(5) is filed when received by the clerk or court and the clerk shall immediately thereafter transfer the electronic documents from the storage device to the official court file. FL ST J ADMIN Rule 2.525(c)(5).
   iv. If the filer of any paper document authorized under FL ST J ADMIN Rule 2.525(d) provides a self-addressed, postage-paid envelope for return of the paper document after it is converted to electronic form by the clerk, the clerk shall place the paper document in the envelope and deposit it in the mail. Except when a paper document is required to be maintained, the clerk may recycle any filed paper document that is not to be returned to the filer. FL ST J ADMIN Rule 2.525(c)(6).
   v. The clerk may convert any paper document filed before the effective date of FL ST J ADMIN Rule 2.525 to an electronic document. Unless the clerk is required to maintain the paper document, if the paper document has been converted to an electronic document by the clerk, the paper document is no longer part of the official court file and may be removed and recycled. FL ST J ADMIN Rule 2.525(c)(7).

d. *Official court file.* For information on what constitutes the official court file, please see FL ST J ADMIN Rule 2.525(c)(2), FL ST J ADMIN Rule 2.525(c)(3).

e. *Administration.* All attorneys, parties, or other persons using this rule to file documents are required to make arrangements with the court or clerk for the payment of any charges authorized by general law or the supreme court before filing any document by electronic transmission. FL ST J ADMIN Rule 2.525(f)(2).

f. *Filing date.* The filing date for an electronically transmitted document is the date and time that such filing is acknowledged by an electronic stamp or otherwise, pursuant to any procedure set forth in any ECF Procedures approved by the supreme court, or the date the last page of such filing is received by the court or clerk. FL ST J ADMIN Rule 2.525(f)(3).

g. *Accessibility.* All documents transmitted in any electronic form under FL ST J ADMIN Rule 2.525 must comply with the accessibility requirements of FL ST J ADMIN Rule 2.526. FL ST J ADMIN Rule 2.525(g).

2. *Service requirements.* Every pleading subsequent to the initial pleading, all orders, and every other document filed in the action must be served in conformity with the requirements of FL ST J ADMIN Rule 2.516. FL ST RCP Rule 1.080(a).

   a. *Service; When required.* Unless the court otherwise orders, or a statute or supreme court administrative order specifies a different means of service, every pleading subsequent to the initial pleading and every other document filed in any court proceeding, except applications for witness subpoenas and documents served by formal notice or required to be served in the manner provided for service of formal notice, must be served in accordance with FL ST J ADMIN Rule 2.516 on each party. No service need be made on parties against whom a default has been entered, except that pleadings asserting new or additional claims against them must be served in the manner provided for service of summons. FL ST J ADMIN Rule 2.516(a).

   b. *Service; How made.* When service is required or permitted to be made upon a party represented by an attorney, service must be made upon the attorney unless service upon the party is ordered by the court. FL ST J ADMIN Rule 2.516(b).

      i. *Service by electronic mail ("e-mail").* All documents required or permitted to be served on another party must be served by e-mail, unless FL ST J ADMIN Rule 2.516 otherwise provides. When, in addition to service by e-mail, the sender also utilizes another means of service provided for in FL ST J ADMIN Rule 2.516(b)(2), any differing time limits and other provisions applicable to that other means of service control. FL ST J ADMIN Rule 2.516(b)(1). Any document electronically transmitted to a court or clerk must also be served on all parties and interested persons in accordance with the applicable rules of court. FL ST J ADMIN Rule 2.525(e)(2).

         - *Service on attorneys.* Upon appearing in a proceeding, an attorney must serve a designation of a primary e-mail address and may designate no more than two (2) secondary e-mail addresses. Thereafter, service must be directed to all designated e-mail addresses in that proceeding. Every document filed by an attorney thereafter must include the primary e-mail address of that attorney and any secondary e-mail addresses. If an attorney does not designate any e-mail address for service, documents may be served on that attorney at the e-mail address on record with The Florida Bar. FL ST J ADMIN Rule 2.516(b)(1)(A).

         - *Exception to e-mail service on attorneys.* Service by an attorney on another attorney must be made by e-mail unless excused by the court. Upon motion by an attorney demonstrating that the attorney has no e-mail account and lacks access to the Internet at the attorney's office, the court may excuse the attorney from the requirements of e-mail service. Service on and by an attorney excused by the court from e-mail service must be by the means provided in FL ST J ADMIN Rule 2.516(b)(2). FL ST J ADMIN Rule 2.516(b)(1)(B).

         - *Service on and by parties not represented by an attorney.* Any party not represented by an attorney may serve a designation of a primary e-mail address and also may designate no more than two (2) secondary e-mail addresses to which service must be directed in that proceeding by the means provided in FL ST J ADMIN Rule 2.516(b)(1). If a party not represented by an attorney does not designate an e-mail address for service in a proceeding, service on and by that party must be by the means provided in FL ST J ADMIN Rule 2.516(b)(2). FL ST J ADMIN Rule 2.516(b)(1)(C).

         - *Time of service.* Service by e-mail is complete when it is sent. FL ST J ADMIN Rule 2.516(b)(1)(D). An e-mail is deemed served on the date it is sent. FL ST J ADMIN Rule 2.516(b)(1)(D)(i). If the sender learns that the e-mail did not reach the address of the

person to be served, the sender must immediately send another copy by e-mail, or by a means authorized by FL ST J ADMIN Rule 2.516(b)(2). FL ST J ADMIN Rule 2.516(b)(1)(D)(ii). E-mail service is treated as service by mail for the computation of time. FL ST J ADMIN Rule 2.516(b)(1)(D)(iii).

ii. *Format of e-mail for service.* Service of a document by e-mail is made by attaching a copy of the document in PDF format to an e-mail sent to all addresses designated by the attorney or party. FL ST J ADMIN Rule 2.516(b)(1)(E).

- All documents served by e-mail must be attached to an e-mail message containing a subject line beginning with the words "SERVICE OF COURT DOCUMENT" in all capital letters, followed by the case number of the proceeding in which the documents are being served. FL ST J ADMIN Rule 2.516(b)(1)(E)(i).
- The body of the e-mail must identify the court in which the proceeding is pending, the case number, the name of the initial party on each side, the title of each document served with that e-mail, and the sender's name and telephone number. FL ST J ADMIN Rule 2.516(b)(1)(E)(ii).
- Any document served by e-mail may be signed by the "/s/" format, as long as the filed original is signed in accordance with the applicable rule of procedure. FL ST J ADMIN Rule 2.516(b)(1)(E)(iii).
- Any e-mail which, together with its attached documents, exceeds five megabytes (5MB) in size, must be divided and sent as separate e-mails, no one of which may exceed five megabytes (5MB) in size and each of which must be sequentially numbered in the subject line. FL ST J ADMIN Rule 2.516(b)(1)(E)(iv).

iii. *Service by other means.* In addition to, and not in lieu of, service by e-mail, service may also be made upon attorneys by any of the means specified in FL ST J ADMIN Rule 2.516(b)(2). Service on and by all parties who are not represented by an attorney and who do not designate an e-mail address, and on and by all attorneys excused from e-mail service, must be made by delivering a copy of the document or by mailing it to the party or attorney at their last known address or, if no address is known, by leaving it with the clerk of the court. Service by mail is complete upon mailing. Delivery of a copy within FL ST J ADMIN Rule 2.516 is complete upon:

- Handing it to the attorney or to the party,
- Leaving it at the attorney's or party's office with a clerk or other person in charge thereof,
- If there is no one in charge, leaving it in a conspicuous place therein,
- If the office is closed or the person to be served has no office, leaving it at the person's usual place of abode with some person of his or her family above fifteen (15) years of age and informing such person of the contents, or
- Transmitting it by facsimile to the attorney's or party's office with a cover sheet containing the sender's name, firm, address, telephone number, and facsimile number, and the number of pages transmitted. When service is made by facsimile, a copy must also be served by any other method permitted by FL ST J ADMIN Rule 2.516. Facsimile service occurs when transmission is complete. FL ST J ADMIN Rule 2.516(b)(2)(A) through FL ST J ADMIN Rule 2.516(b)(2)(E).
- Service by delivery after 5:00 p.m. must be deemed to have been made by mailing on the date of delivery. FL ST J ADMIN Rule 2.516(b)(2)(F).

c. *Service; Numerous defendants.* In actions when the parties are unusually numerous, the court may regulate the service contemplated by the Florida Rules of Judicial Administration on motion or on its own initiative in such manner as may be found to be just and reasonable. FL ST J ADMIN Rule 2.516(c).

d. *Service by clerk.* Service of notices and other documents required to be made by the clerk must also be done as provided in FL ST J ADMIN Rule 2.516(b). FL ST J ADMIN Rule 2.516(g).

G. Hearings

1. *Hearing on motion for summary judgment.* The summary judgment rule does not provide the trial court with discretion to decide whether a hearing is required. A failure to hold a hearing on a motion for summary judgment violates due process as well as rule of procedure governing summary judgment procedure. Kozich v. Hartford Ins. Co. of Midwest, 609 So.2d 147, 148 (Fla. 4th DCA 1992); FL-RCPF R 1.510(102).
2. *Summary judgment consideration at pretrial conference.* A summary judgment can be granted at the pretrial conference. The standard and procedure for granting summary judgment is the same at a pretrial conference as at other times. The notice time for a pretrial conference and for service of a motion for summary judgment is the same, so summary judgment can be entered at the conference if no genuine issue of material fact exists. FL-PRACPROC § 19:4.
3. *Communication equipment*
    a. *Definition.* Communication equipment means a conference telephone or other electronic device that permits all those appearing or participating to hear and speak to each other, provided that all conversation of all parties is audible to all persons present. FL ST J ADMIN Rule 2.530(a).
    b. *Use by all parties.* A county or circuit court judge may, upon the court's own motion or upon the written request of a party, direct that communication equipment be used for a motion hearing, pretrial conference, or a status conference. A judge must give notice to the parties and consider any objections they may have to the use of communication equipment before directing that communication equipment be used. The decision to use communication equipment over the objection of parties will be in the sound discretion of the trial court, except as noted below. FL ST J ADMIN Rule 2.530(b).
    c. *Use only by requesting party.* A county or circuit court judge may, upon the written request of a party upon reasonable notice to all other parties, permit a requesting party to participate through communication equipment in a scheduled motion hearing; however, any such request (except in criminal, juvenile, and appellate proceedings) must be granted, absent a showing of good cause to deny the same, where the hearing is set for not longer than fifteen (15) minutes. FL ST J ADMIN Rule 2.530(c).
    d. *Testimony*
        i. *Generally.* A county or circuit court judge, general magistrate, special magistrate, or hearing officer may allow testimony to be taken through communication equipment if all parties consent or if permitted by another applicable rule of procedure. FL ST J ADMIN Rule 2.530(d)(1).
        ii. *Procedure.* Any party desiring to present testimony through communication equipment shall, prior to the hearing or trial at which the testimony is to be presented, contact all parties to determine whether each party consents to this form of testimony. The party seeking to present the testimony shall move for permission to present testimony through communication equipment, which motion shall set forth good cause as to why the testimony should be allowed in this form. FL ST J ADMIN Rule 2.530(d)(2).
        iii. *Oath.* Testimony may be taken through communication equipment only if a notary public or other person authorized to administer oaths in the witness's jurisdiction is present with the witness and administers the oath consistent with the laws of the jurisdiction. FL ST J ADMIN Rule 2.530(d)(3).
        iv. *Confrontation rights.* In juvenile and criminal proceedings the defendant must make an informed waiver of any confrontation rights that may be abridged by the use of communication equipment. FL ST J ADMIN Rule 2.530(d)(4).
        v. *Video testimony.* If the testimony to be presented utilizes video conferencing or comparable two-way visual capabilities, the court in its discretion may modify the procedures set forth in FL ST J ADMIN Rule 2.530 to accommodate the technology utilized. FL ST J ADMIN Rule 2.530(d)(5).
    e. *Burden of expense.* The cost for the use of the communication equipment is the responsibility of the requesting party unless otherwise directed by the court. FL ST J ADMIN Rule 2.530(e).

H. Forms

1. Official Motion for Summary Judgment Forms for Florida

a. Caption. FL ST RCP Form 1.901.

b. Notice of compliance when constitutional challenge is brought. FL ST RCP Form 1.975.

2. Motion for Summary Judgment Forms for Florida

a. Motion for summary judgment; By plaintiff. FL-PP § 6:9.

b. Motion for summary judgment; By defendant. FL-PP § 6:10.

c. Affidavit; Supporting motion for summary judgment; By plaintiff's attorney. FL-PP § 6:11.

d. Affidavit; Opposing motion for summary judgment; By defendant's attorney. FL-PP § 6:12.

e. Affidavit; Opposing motion for summary judgment; By party; Inability to present facts. FL-PP § 6:13.

f. Order; Establishing uncontroverted facts and stating issues requiring further determination. FL-PP § 6:14.

g. Summary judgment. FL-PP § 6:15.

h. Motion; Summary judgment, by defendant. FL-PRACFORM § 7:190.

i. Motion; Summary judgment, by plaintiff. FL-PRACFORM § 7:191.

j. Motion; Summary judgment, partial, by defendant. FL-PRACFORM § 7:192.

k. Motion; Summary judgment, part of claim. FL-PRACFORM § 7:193.

l. Form for plaintiff's motion for summary judgment. FL-RCPF R 1.510(128).

m. Form for notice of motion for summary judgment by plaintiff. FL-RCPF R 1.510(129).

n. Form for notice of cross-motion for summary judgment by plaintiff. FL-RCPF R 1.510(130).

o. Form for order denying motion for summary judgment and specifying uncontroverted facts. FL-RCPF R 1.510(304).

p. Form for motion for partial summary judgment. FL-RCPF R 1.510(305).

q. Form for motion for partial summary judgment-affirmative defenses. FL-RCPF R 1.510(305.1).

3. Official Forms for Florida Circuit Court, Second Judicial Circuit

a. Notice of change of contact information. FL ST 2 J CIR 2007-05.

I. Checklist

(I) ❑ Matters to be considered by moving party

- (a) ❑ Required documents
  - (1) ❑ Notice of hearing/Motion
  - (2) ❑ Certificate of service
- (b) ❑ Supplemental documents
  - (1) ❑ Affidavits
  - (2) ❑ Other evidence
  - (3) ❑ Proposed order
  - (4) ❑ Notice of constitutional question
- (c) ❑ Time for making motion
  - (1) ❑ By the plaintiff, after the expiration of twenty (20) days from the commencement of the action (claimant), or after service of a motion for summary judgment by the adverse party
  - (2) ❑ By the defending party at any time
  - (3) ❑ The motion for summary judgment must be served at least twenty (20) days before the time fixed for the hearing

(II) ❑ Matters to be considered by opposing party
- (a) ❑ Required documents
  - (1) ❑ Response to motion
  - (2) ❑ Certificate of service
- (b) ❑ Supplemental documents
  - (1) ❑ Affidavits
  - (2) ❑ Notice of evidence relied upon
  - (3) ❑ Other evidence
  - (4) ❑ Proposed order
  - (5) ❑ Notice of constitutional question
- (c) ❑ Time for service and filing of opposition
  - (1) ❑ The adverse party shall identify, by notice mailed to the movant's attorney at least five (5) days prior to the day of the hearing, or delivered no later than 5:00 p.m. two (2) business days prior to the day of the hearing, any summary judgment evidence on which the adverse party relies
  - (2) ❑ To the extent that summary judgment evidence has not already been filed with the court, the adverse party shall serve a copy on the movant by mail at least five (5) days prior to the day of the hearing, or by delivery to the movant's attorney no later than 5:00 p.m. two (2) business days prior to the day of hearing

Motions, Oppositions and Replies
Motion for Sanctions

Document Last Updated January 2013

A. Applicable Rules

1. *State rules*
   - a. Attorney's fee; Sanctions for raising unsupported claims or defenses; Exceptions; Service of motions; Damages for delay of litigation. FL ST § 57.105.
   - b. Administrative Procedure Act. FL ST § 120.50; FL ST § 120.52; FL ST § 120.68; FL ST § 120.81.
   - c. Offer of judgment and demand for judgment. FL ST § 768.79.
   - d. Proposals for settlement. FL ST RCP Rule 1.442.
   - e. Motions for costs and attorneys' fees. FL ST RCP Rule 1.525.
   - f. Rules of court. FL ST RCP Rule 1.010; FL ST J ADMIN Rule 2.110.
   - g. Nonverification of pleadings. FL ST RCP Rule 1.030.
   - h. Service and filing of pleadings, orders, and documents. FL ST RCP Rule 1.080.
   - i. Time. FL ST RCP Rule 1.090.
   - j. Pleadings and motions. FL ST RCP Rule 1.100.
   - k. Motions. FL ST RCP Rule 1.160.
   - l. Relief from judgment, decrees, or orders. FL ST RCP Rule 1.540.
   - m. Mediation and arbitration. FL ST RCP Rule 1.700; FL ST RCP Rule 1.710; FL ST RCP Rule 1.720; FL ST RCP Rule 1.730; FL ST RCP Rule 1.750; FL ST RCP Rule 1.800; FL ST RCP Rule 1.810; FL ST RCP Rule 1.820; FL ST RCP Rule 1.830.
   - n. Forms. FL ST RCP Rule 1.900.
   - o. Minimization of the filing of sensitive information. FL ST J ADMIN Rule 2.425.

p. Retention of court records. FL ST J ADMIN Rule 2.430.
q. Foreign attorneys. FL ST J ADMIN Rule 2.510.
r. Signature of attorneys and parties. FL ST J ADMIN Rule 2.515.
s. Paper. FL ST J ADMIN Rule 2.520.
t. Electronic filing. FL ST J ADMIN Rule 2.525.
u. Accessibility of information and technology. FL ST J ADMIN Rule 2.526.
v. Communication equipment. FL ST J ADMIN Rule 2.530.
w. Court reporting. FL ST J ADMIN Rule 2.535.
x. Requests for accommodations by persons with disabilities. FL ST J ADMIN Rule 2.540.

2. *Local rules*
   a. Notice of change of contact information. FL ST 2 J CIR 2007-05.

B. Timing

1. *Motion for sanctions.* A motion by a party seeking sanctions under FL ST § 57.105 must be served but may not be filed with or presented to the court unless, within twenty one (21) days after service of the motion, the challenged paper, claim, defense, contention, allegation, or denial is not withdrawn or appropriately corrected. FL ST § 57.105(4).
2. *Sanctions in relation to proposals for settlement.* Any party seeking sanctions pursuant to applicable Florida law, based on the failure of the proposal's recipient to accept a proposal, shall do so by serving a motion in accordance with FL ST RCP Rule 1.525. FL ST RCP Rule 1.442(g). Any party seeking a judgment taxing costs, attorneys' fees, or both shall serve a motion no later than thirty (30) days after filing of the judgment, including a judgment of dismissal, or the service of a notice of voluntary dismissal, which judgment or notice concludes the action as to that party. FL ST RCP Rule 1.525.
3. *General motion timing.* A copy of any written motion which may not be heard ex parte and a copy of the notice of the hearing thereof shall be served a reasonable time before the time specified for the hearing. FL ST RCP Rule 1.090(d).
4. *Computation of time*
   a. *Generally.* Computation of time shall be governed by FL ST J ADMIN Rule 2.514. FL ST RCP Rule 1.090(a). The following rules apply in computing time periods specified in any rule of procedure, local rule, court order, or statute that does not specify a method of computing time. FL ST J ADMIN Rule 2.514(a).
      i. *Period stated in days or a longer unit.* When the period is stated in days or a longer unit of time (A) exclude the day of the event that triggers the period; (B) count every day, including intermediate Saturdays, Sundays, and legal holidays; and (C) include the last day of the period, but if the last day is a Saturday, Sunday, or legal holiday, or falls within any period of time extended through an order of the chief justice under FL ST J ADMIN Rule 2.205(a)(2)(B)(iv), the period continues to run until the end of the next day that is not a Saturday, Sunday, or legal holiday and does not fall within any period of time extended through an order of the chief justice. FL ST J ADMIN Rule 2.514(a)(1).
      ii. *Period stated in hours.* When the period is stated in hours (A) begin counting immediately on the occurrence of the event that triggers the period; (B) count every hour, including hours during intermediate Saturdays, Sundays, and legal holidays; and (C) if the period would end on a Saturday, Sunday, or legal holiday, or during any period of time extended through an order of the chief justice under FL ST J ADMIN Rule 2.205(a)(2)(B)(iv), the period continues to run until the same time on the next day that is not a Saturday, Sunday, or legal holiday and does not fall within any period of time extended through an order of the chief justice. FL ST J ADMIN Rule 2.514(a)(2).
      iii. *Period stated in days less than seven (7) days.* When the period stated in days is less than seven (7) days, intermediate Saturdays, Sundays, and legal holidays shall be excluded in the computation. FL ST J ADMIN Rule 2.514(a)(3).

iv. *"Last day" defined.* Unless a different time is set by a statute, local rule, or court order, the last day ends (A) for electronic filing or for service by any means, at midnight; and (B) for filing by other means, when the clerk's office is scheduled to close. FL ST J ADMIN Rule 2.514(a)(4).

v. *"Next day" defined.* The "next day" is determined by continuing to count forward when the period is measured after an event and backward when measured before an event. FL ST J ADMIN Rule 2.514(a)(5).

vi. *"Legal holiday" defined.* "Legal holiday" means (A) the day set aside by FL ST § 110.117, for observing New Year's Day, Martin Luther King, Jr.'s Birthday, Memorial Day, Independence Day, Labor Day, Veterans' Day, Thanksgiving Day, the Friday after Thanksgiving Day, or Christmas Day, and (B) any day observed as a holiday by the clerk's office or as designated by the chief judge. FL ST J ADMIN Rule 2.514(a)(6).

b. *Additional time after service by mail or e-mail.* When a party may or must act within a specified time after service and service is made by mail or e-mail, five (5) days are added after the period that would otherwise expire under FL ST J ADMIN Rule 2.514(a). FL ST J ADMIN Rule 2.514(b).

c. *Enlargement.* When an act is required or allowed to be done at or within a specified time by order of court, by the Florida Rules of Civil Procedure, or by notice given thereunder, for cause shown the court at any time in its discretion (1) with or without notice, may order the period enlarged if request therefor is made before the expiration of the period originally prescribed or as extended by a previous order, or (2) upon motion made and notice after the expiration of the specified period, may permit the act to be done when failure to act was the result of excusable neglect, but it may not extend the time for making a motion for new trial, for rehearing, or to alter or amend a judgment; making a motion for relief from a judgment under FL ST RCP Rule 1.540(b); taking an appeal or filing a petition for certiorari; or making a motion for a directed verdict. FL ST RCP Rule 1.090(b).

d. *Unaffected by expiration of term.* The period of time provided for the doing of any act or the taking of any proceeding shall not be affected or limited by the continued existence or expiration of a term of court. The continued existence or expiration of a term of court in no way affects the power of a court to do any act or take any proceeding in any action which is or has been pending before it. FL ST RCP Rule 1.090(c).

C. General Requirements

1. *Motions generally*

a. *Contents.* An application to the court for an order shall be by motion which shall be made in writing unless made during a hearing or trial, shall state with particularity the grounds therefor, and shall set forth the relief or order sought. The requirement of writing is fulfilled if the motion is stated in a written notice of the hearing of the motion. All notices of hearing shall specify each motion or other matter to be heard. FL ST RCP Rule 1.100(b).

b. *Particularity requirement.* The court considers a motion in the light of the substantive law, rule or statute to make its determination. Some rules require a statement of the grounds for a motion under the rule. Failure to give the grounds will result in denial of the motion. This should be the result in all situations when the ground for the motion is not inherent in the rule. FL-PRACPROC § 9:3. The requirement is nevertheless an important one, first because of the due process notice rights of the respondent, as well as for the assistance it provides to the court in its preparation for the hearing or, absent a hearing, for disposition. 4 FLPRAC R 1.100.

2. *Motion for sanctions*

a. *Sanctions for raising unsupported claims or defenses*

i. *No material facts; No law supporting material facts.* Upon the court's initiative or motion of any party, the court shall award a reasonable attorney's fee, including prejudgment interest, to be paid to the prevailing party in equal amounts by the losing party and the losing party's attorney on any claim or defense at any time during a civil proceeding or action in which the court finds that the losing party or the losing party's attorney knew or should have known that a claim or defense when initially presented to the court or at any time before trial was not supported by the material facts necessary to establish the claim or defense; or would not be supported by the application of then-existing law to those material facts. FL ST § 57.105(1).

ii. *Unreasonable delay.* At any time in any civil proceeding or action in which the moving party proves by a preponderance of the evidence that any action taken by the opposing party, including, but not limited to, the filing of any pleading or part thereof, the assertion of or response to any discovery demand, the assertion of any claim or defense, or the response to any request by any other party, was taken primarily for the purpose of unreasonable delay, the court shall award damages to the moving party for its reasonable expenses incurred in obtaining the order, which may include attorney's fees, and other loss resulting from the improper delay. FL ST § 57.105(2).

iii. *Limit on monetary sanctions.* Notwithstanding FL ST § 57.105(1) and FL ST § 57.105(2), monetary sanctions may not be awarded:

- Under FL ST § 57.105(1)(b) if the court determines that the claim or defense was initially presented to the court as a good faith argument for the extension, modification, or reversal of existing law or the establishment of new law, as it applied to the material facts, with a reasonable expectation of success. FL ST § 57.105(3)(a).
- Under FL ST § 57.105(1)(a) or FL ST § 57.105(1)(b) against the losing party's attorney if he or she has acted in good faith, based on the representations of his or her client as to the existence of those material facts. FL ST § 57.105(3)(b).
- Under FL ST § 57.105(1)(b) against a represented party. FL ST § 57.105(3)(c).
- On the court's initiative under FL ST § 57.105(1) and FL ST § 57.105(2) unless sanctions are awarded before a voluntary dismissal or settlement of the claims made by or against the party that is, or whose attorneys are, to be sanctioned. FL ST § 57.105(3)(d).

iv. *Other sanctions available.* The provisions of FL ST § 57.105 are supplemental to other sanctions or remedies available under law or under court rules. FL ST § 57.105(6).

v. *Fees provided for in contract.* If a contract contains a provision allowing attorney's fees to a party when he or she is required to take any action to enforce the contract, the court may also allow reasonable attorney's fees to the other party when that party prevails in any action, whether as plaintiff or defendant, with respect to the contract. FL ST § 57.105(7) applies to any contract entered into on or after October 1, 1988. FL ST § 57.105(7).

b. *Sanctions in relation to proposals for settlement*

i. *Generally.* Any party seeking sanctions pursuant to applicable Florida law, based on the failure of the proposal's recipient to accept a proposal, shall do so by serving a motion in accordance with FL ST RCP Rule 1.525. FL ST RCP Rule 1.442(g). Any party seeking a judgment taxing costs, attorneys' fees, or both shall serve a motion no later than thirty (30) days after filing of the judgment, including a judgment of dismissal, or the service of a notice of voluntary dismissal, which judgment or notice concludes the action as to that party. FL ST RCP Rule 1.525.

ii. *Motion after judgment, voluntary or involuntary dismissal.* Upon motion made by the offeror within thirty (30) days after the entry of judgment or after voluntary or involuntary dismissal, the court shall determine the following:

- If a defendant serves an offer which is not accepted by the plaintiff, and if the judgment obtained by the plaintiff is at least twenty-five (25%) percent less than the amount of the offer, the defendant shall be awarded reasonable costs, including investigative expenses, and attorney's fees, calculated in accordance with the guidelines promulgated by the Supreme Court, incurred from the date the offer was served, and the court shall set off such costs in attorney's fees against the award. When such costs and attorney's fees total more than the amount of the judgment, the court shall enter judgment for the defendant against the plaintiff for the amount of the costs and fees, less the amount of the award to the plaintiff. FL ST § 768.79(6)(a).
- If a plaintiff serves an offer which is not accepted by the defendant, and if the judgment obtained by the plaintiff is at least twenty-five (25%) percent more than the amount of the offer, the plaintiff shall be awarded reasonable costs, including investigative expenses, and attorney's fees, calculated in accordance with the guidelines promulgated by the Supreme Court, incurred from the date the offer was served. FL ST § 768.79(6)(b).

- For purposes of the determination required by FL ST § 768.79(6)(a), the term "judgment obtained" means the amount of the net judgment entered, plus any postoffer collateral source payments received or due as of the date of the judgment, plus any postoffer settlement amounts by which the verdict was reduced. For purposes of the determination required by FL ST § 768.79(6)(b), the term "judgment obtained" means the amount of the net judgment entered, plus any postoffer settlement amounts by which the verdict was reduced. FL ST § 768.79(6).

iii. For further information please see FL ST § 768.79 and FL ST RCP Rule 1.442.

3. *Arbitration and mediation*

a. *Referral to arbitration and mediation.* Except as hereinafter provided or as otherwise prohibited by law, the presiding judge may enter an order referring all or any part of a contested civil matter to mediation or arbitration. The parties to any contested civil matter may file a written stipulation to mediate or arbitrate any issue between them at any time. Such stipulation shall be incorporated into the order of referral. FL ST RCP Rule 1.700(a).

b. *Arbitration*

i. *Exclusions.* A civil action shall be ordered to arbitration or arbitration in conjunction with mediation upon stipulation of the parties. A civil action may be ordered to arbitration or arbitration in conjunction with mediation upon motion of any party or by the court, if the judge determines the action to be of such a nature that arbitration could be of benefit to the litigants or the court. FL ST RCP Rule 1.800.

- Under no circumstances may the following categories of actions be referred to arbitration: (1) bond estreatures; (2) habeas corpus or other extraordinary writs; (3) bond validations; (4) civil or criminal contempt; (5) such other matters as may be specified by order of the chief judge in the circuit. FL ST RCP Rule 1.800.

ii. For more information regarding arbitration, please see FL ST RCP Rule 1.810; FL ST RCP Rule 1.820; FL ST RCP Rule 1.830.

c. *Mediation.* For more information regarding mediation, please see FL ST RCP Rule 1.710; FL ST RCP Rule 1.720; FL ST RCP Rule 1.730; and FL ST RCP Rule 1.750.

4. *Rules of court*

a. *Rules of civil procedure.* The Florida Rules of Civil Procedure apply to all actions of a civil nature and all special statutory proceedings in the circuit courts and county courts except those to which the Florida Probate Rules, the Florida Family Law Rules of Procedure, or the Small Claims Rules apply. FL ST RCP Rule 1.010.

i. The form, content, procedure, and time for pleading in all special statutory proceedings shall be as prescribed by the statutes governing the proceeding unless the Florida Rules of Civil Procedure specifically provide to the contrary. FL ST RCP Rule 1.010.

ii. The Florida Rules of Civil Procedure shall be construed to secure the just, speedy, and inexpensive determination of every action. FL ST RCP Rule 1.010.

b. *Rules of judicial administration.* The Florida Rules of Judicial Administration shall apply to administrative matters in all courts to which the Florida Rules of Judicial Administration are applicable by their terms. The Florida Rules of Judicial Administration shall be construed to secure the speedy and inexpensive determination of every proceeding to which they are applicable. The Florida Rules of Judicial Administration shall supersede all conflicting rules and statutes. FL ST J ADMIN Rule 2.110.

5. *Notice of change of contact information.* The Clerk shall provide a change of address and/or telephone number form for use by attorneys and pro se litigants. With any change of address and/or telephone number, attorneys and pro se litigants governed by FL ST J ADMIN Rule 2.515 will provide to the Clerk and all parties promptly the change of address and/or telephone number form. This form should be submitted only once to the Clerk, who will then make the address and/or telephone number change in all court divisions. FL ST 2 J CIR 2007-05.

D. Documents

1. *Required documents*

   a. *Notice of hearing/Motion.* An application to the court for an order shall be by motion which shall be made in writing unless made during a hearing or trial, shall state with particularity the grounds therefor, and shall set forth the relief or order sought. The requirement of writing is fulfilled if the motion is stated in a written notice of the hearing of the motion. All notices of hearing shall specify each motion or other matter to be heard. FL ST RCP Rule 1.100(b).

      i. *Notices to persons with disabilities.* See the Format section of this KeyRules document for further information.

   b. *Certificate of service.* When any attorney certifies in substance: "I certify that a copy hereof has been furnished to (here insert name or names and addresses used for service) by (e-mail) (delivery) (mail) (fax) on .... (date) ....____________ Attorney" the certificate is taken as prima facie proof of such service in compliance with FL ST J ADMIN Rule 2.516. FL ST J ADMIN Rule 2.516(f).

2. *Supplemental documents*

   a. *Proposed order.* The court may require that orders or judgments be prepared by a party, may require the party to furnish the court with stamped, addressed envelopes for service of the order or judgment, and may require that proposed orders and judgments be furnished to all parties before entry by the court of the order or judgment. FL ST J ADMIN Rule 2.516(h)(1).

   b. *Notice of constitutional question.* A party that files a pleading, written motion, or other paper drawing into question the constitutionality of a state statute or a county or municipal charter, ordinance, or franchise must promptly (1) file a notice of constitutional question stating the question and identifying the paper that raises it; and (2) serve the notice and the pleading, written motion, or other paper drawing into question the constitutionality of a state statute or a county or municipal charter, ordinance, or franchise on the Attorney General or the state attorney of the judicial circuit in which the action is pending, by either certified or registered mail. Service of the notice and pleading, written motion, or other paper does not require joinder of the Attorney General or the state attorney as a party to the action. FL ST RCP Rule 1.071.

E. Format

1. *Documents; Type and size.* Documents subject to the exceptions set forth in FL ST J ADMIN Rule 2.525(d) shall be filed on recycled paper measuring eight and one half by eleven (8 1/2 by 11) inches. For purposes of FL ST J ADMIN Rule 2.520, paper is recycled if it contains a minimum content of fifty (50) percent waste paper. Xerographic reduction of legal-size (eight and one half by fourteen (8 1/2 by 14) inches) documents to letter size (eight and one half by eleven (8 1/2 by 11) inches) is prohibited. All other documents filed by electronic transmission shall be filed in a format capable of being printed in a format consistent with the provisions of FL ST J ADMIN Rule 2.250. FL ST J ADMIN Rule 2.520(b).

   a. *Exhibits.* Any exhibit or attachment filed with pleadings or papers may be filed in its original size. FL ST J ADMIN Rule 2.520(c).

   b. *Recording space.* On all papers and documents prepared and filed by the court or by any party to a proceeding which are to be recorded in the public records of any county, including but not limited to final money judgments and notices of lis pendens, a three (3) inch by three (3) inch space at the top right-hand corner on the first page and a one (1) inch by three (3) inch space at the top right-hand corner on each subsequent page shall be left blank and reserved for use by the clerk of court. FL ST J ADMIN Rule 2.520(d).

      i. *Exceptions to recording space.* Any papers or documents created by persons or entities over which the filing party has no control, including but not limited to wills, codicils, trusts, or other testamentary documents; documents prepared or executed by any public officer; documents prepared, executed, acknowledged, or proved outside of the State of Florida; or documents created by State or Federal government agencies, may be filed without the space required by FL ST J ADMIN Rule 2.520. FL ST J ADMIN Rule 2.520(e).

   c. *Noncompliance.* No clerk of court is permitted to refuse to file any document or paper because of noncompliance with the Florida Rules of Judicial Administration. However, upon request of the clerk of court, noncomplying documents must be resubmitted in accordance with the formatting rules. FL ST J ADMIN Rule 2.520(f).

2. *Caption.* Every pleading, motion, order, judgment, or other paper shall have a caption containing the name of the court, the file number, and except for in rem proceedings, including forfeiture proceedings, the name of the first party on each side with an appropriate indication of other parties, and a designation identifying the party filing it and its nature or the nature of the order, as the case may be. In any in rem proceeding, every pleading, motion, order, judgment, or other paper shall have a caption containing the name of the court, the file number, the style "In re" (followed by the name or general description of the property), and a designation of the person or entity filing it and its nature or the nature of the order, as the case may be. In an in rem forfeiture proceeding, the style shall be "In re forfeiture of" (followed by the name of the general description of the property). All papers filed in the action shall be styled in such a manner as to indicate clearly the subject matter of the paper and the party requesting or obtaining relief. FL ST RCP Rule 1.100(c)(1).
3. *Writing and written defined.* Writing or written means a document containing information, an application, or a stipulation. FL ST RCP Rule 1.080(c).
4. *Rule abbreviations*
   a. The Florida Rules of Civil Procedure and shall be abbreviated as Fla.R.Civ.P. FL ST RCP Rule 1.010.
   b. The Florida Rules of Judicial Administration shall be abbreviated as Fla. R. Jud. Admin. FL ST J ADMIN Rule 2.110.
5. *Nonverification.* Except when otherwise specifically provided by the Florida Rules of Civil Procedure or an applicable statute, every pleading or other document of a party represented by an attorney need not be verified or accompanied by an affidavit. FL ST RCP Rule 1.030; FL ST J ADMIN Rule 2.515(a).
6. *Attorney signature*
   a. *Attorney signature.* Every pleading and other document of a party represented by an attorney shall be signed by at least one (1) attorney of record in that attorney's individual name whose current record Florida Bar address, telephone number, including area code, primary e-mail address and secondary e-mail addresses, if any, and Florida Bar number shall be stated, and who shall be duly licensed to practice law in Florida or who shall have received permission to appear in the particular case as provided in FL ST J ADMIN Rule 2.510. FL ST J ADMIN Rule 2.515(a).
      i. The attorney may be required by the court to give the address of, and to vouch for the attorney's authority to represent, the party. FL ST J ADMIN Rule 2.515(a).
      ii. The signature of an attorney shall constitute a certificate by the attorney that the attorney has read the pleading or other document; that to the best of the attorney's knowledge, information, and belief there is good ground to support it; and that it is not interposed for delay. FL ST J ADMIN Rule 2.515(a).
      iii. If a pleading is not signed or is signed with intent to defeat the purpose of FL ST J ADMIN Rule 2.515, it may be stricken and the action may proceed as though the pleading or other document had not been served. FL ST J ADMIN Rule 2.515(a).
   b. *Pro se litigant signature.* A party who is not represented by an attorney shall sign any pleading or other paper and state the party's address and telephone number, including area code. FL ST J ADMIN Rule 2.515(b).
   c. *Form of signature*
      i. The signatures required on pleadings and documents by FL ST J ADMIN Rule 2.515(a) and FL ST J ADMIN Rule 2.515(b) may be:
         - Original signatures;
         - Original signatures that have been reproduced by electronic means, such as on electronically transmitted documents or photocopied documents;

- Electronic signatures using the "/s/," "s/," or "/s" formats by or at the direction of the person signing; or
- Any other signature format authorized by general law, so long as the clerk where the proceeding is pending has the capability of receiving and has obtained approval from the Supreme Court of Florida to accept pleadings and documents with that signature format. FL ST J ADMIN Rule 2.515(c)(1).

ii. An attorney, party, or other person who files a pleading or paper by electronic transmission that does not contain the original signature of that attorney, party, or other person shall file that identical pleading or paper in paper form containing an original signature of that attorney, party, or other person (hereinafter called the follow-up filing) immediately thereafter. The follow-up filing is not required if the Supreme Court of Florida has entered an order directing the clerk of court to discontinue accepting the follow-up filing. FL ST J ADMIN Rule 2.515(c)(2).

7. *Forms*

a. *Process.* The forms of process, notice of lis pendens, and notice of action provided in the Florida Rules of Civil Procedure are sufficient. Variations from the forms do not void process or notices that are otherwise sufficient. FL ST RCP Rule 1.900(a).

b. *Other forms.* The other forms provided in the Florida Rules of Civil Procedure are sufficient for the matters that are covered by them. So long as the substance is expressed without prolixity, the forms may be varied to meet the facts of a particular case. FL ST RCP Rule 1.900(b).

c. *Formal matters.* Captions, except for the designation of the paper, are omitted from the forms provided in the Florida Rules of Civil Procedure. A general form of caption is the first form provided. Signatures are omitted from pleadings and motions. FL ST RCP Rule 1.900(c).

8. *Notices to persons with disabilities.* All notices of court proceedings to be held in a public facility, and all process compelling appearance at such proceedings, shall include the following statement in bold face, fourteen (14) point Times New Roman or Courier font: "If you are a person with a disability who needs any accommodation in order to participate in this proceeding, you are entitled, at no cost to you, to the provision of certain assistance. Please contact [identify applicable court personnel by name, address, and telephone number] at least seven (7) days before your scheduled court appearance, or immediately upon receiving this notification if the time before the scheduled appearance is less than seven (7) days; if you are hearing or voice impaired, call 711." FL ST J ADMIN Rule 2.540(c)(1).

9. *Minimization of the filing of sensitive information*

a. *Limitations for court filings.* Unless authorized by FL ST J ADMIN Rule 2.425(b), statute, another rule of court, or the court orders otherwise, designated sensitive information filed with the court must be limited to the following format:

i. The initials of a person known to be a minor;

ii. The year of birth of a person's birth date;

iii. No portion of any: Social security number, Bank account number, Credit card account number, Charge account number, or Debit account number;

iv. The last four digits of any: Taxpayer identification number (TIN), Employee identification number, Driver's license number, Passport number, Telephone number, Financial account number, except as set forth in FL ST J ADMIN Rule 2.425(a)(3), Brokerage account number, Insurance policy account number, Loan account number, Customer account number, or Patient or health care number;

v. A truncated version of any: Email address, Computer user name, Password, or Personal identification number (PIN); and

vi. A truncated version of any other sensitive information as provided by court order. FL ST J ADMIN Rule 2.425(a).

b. *Exceptions.* FL ST J ADMIN Rule 2.425(a) does not apply to the following:

i. An account number which identifies the property alleged to be the subject of a proceeding;

ii. The record of an administrative or agency proceeding;

iii. The record in appellate or review proceedings;

iv. The birth date of a minor whenever the birth date is necessary for the court to establish or maintain subject matter jurisdiction;

v. The name of a minor in any order relating to parental responsibility, time-sharing, or child support;

vi. The name of a minor in any document or order affecting the minor's ownership of real property;

vii. The birth date of a party in a writ of attachment or notice to payor;

viii. In traffic and criminal proceedings: a pro se filing; a court filing that is related to a criminal matter or investigation and that is prepared before the filing of a criminal charge or is not filed as part of any docketed criminal case; an arrest or search warrant or any information in support thereof; a charging document and an affidavit or other documents filed in support of any charging document, including any driving records; a statement of particulars; discovery material introduced into evidence or otherwise filed with the court; and all information necessary for the proper issuance and execution of a subpoena duces tecum;

ix. Information used by the clerk for case maintenance purposes or the courts for case management purposes; and

x. Information which is relevant and material to an issue before the court. FL ST J ADMIN Rule 2.425(b).

c. *Remedies.* Upon motion by a party or interested person or sua sponte by the court, the court may order remedies, sanctions or both for a violation of FL ST J ADMIN Rule 2.425(a). Following notice and an opportunity to respond, the court may impose sanctions if such filing was not made in good faith. FL ST J ADMIN Rule 2.425(c).

d. *Motions not restricted.* FL ST J ADMIN Rule 2.425 does not restrict a party's right to move for protective order, to move to file documents under seal, or to request a determination of the confidentiality of records. FL ST J ADMIN Rule 2.425(d).

e. *Application.* FL ST J ADMIN Rule 2.425 does not affect the application of constitutional provisions, statutes, or rules of court regarding confidential information or access to public information. FL ST J ADMIN Rule 2.425(e).

F. Filing and Service Requirements

1. *Filing requirements.* All original documents must be filed with the court either before service or immediately thereafter, unless otherwise provided for by general law or other rules. If the original of any bond or other document is not placed in the court file, a certified copy must be so placed by the clerk. FL ST J ADMIN Rule 2.516(d). All documents shall be filed in conformity with the requirements of FL ST J ADMIN Rule 2.525. FL ST RCP Rule 1.080(b). All documents filed in any court shall be filed by electronic transmission in accordance with FL ST J ADMIN Rule 2.525. "Documents" means pleadings, motions, petitions, memoranda, briefs, notices, exhibits, declarations, affidavits, orders, judgments, decrees, writs, opinions, and any other paper or writing submitted to a court. FL ST J ADMIN Rule 2.520(a). All documents that are court records, as defined in FL ST J ADMIN Rule 2.430(a)(1), must be filed by electronic transmission, provided that: (1) the clerk has the ability to accept and retain such documents; (2) the clerk or the chief judge of the circuit has requested permission to accept documents filed by electronic transmission; and (3) the supreme court has entered an order granting permission to the clerk to accept documents filed by electronic transmission. FL ST J ADMIN Rule 2.525(c)(1).

a. *Definition.* "Electronic transmission of documents" means the sending of information by electronic signals to, by or from a court or clerk, which when received can be transformed and stored or transmitted on paper, microfilm, magnetic storage device, optical imaging system, CD-ROM, flash drive, other electronic data storage system, server, case maintenance system ("CM"), electronic court filing ("ECF") system, statewide or local electronic portal ("e-portal"), or other electronic record keeping system authorized by the supreme court in a format sufficient to communicate the information on the original document in a readable format. Electronic transmission of documents

includes electronic mail ("e-mail") and any internet-based transmission procedure, and may include procedures allowing for documents to be signed or verified by electronic means. FL ST J ADMIN Rule 2.525(a).

i. The filing of documents with the court as required by the Florida Rules of Judicial Administration must be made by filing them with the clerk in accordance with FL ST J ADMIN Rule 2.525, except that the judge may permit documents to be filed with the judge, in which event the judge must note the filing date before him or her on the documents and transmit them to the clerk. The date of filing is that shown on the face of the document by the judge's notation or the clerk's time stamp, whichever is earlier. FL ST J ADMIN Rule 2.516(e).

b. *Application.* Any court or clerk of the court may accept the electronic transmission of documents for filing after the clerk, together with input from the chief judge of the circuit, has obtained approval of the procedures and program for doing so from the Supreme Court of Florida. FL ST J ADMIN Rule 2.525(b).

c. *Exceptions*

i. Paper documents and other submissions may be manually submitted to the clerk or court:

- When the clerk does not have the ability to accept and retain documents by electronic filing or has not had ECF Procedures approved by the supreme court;
- For filing by any self-represented party or any self-represented nonparty unless specific ECF Procedures provide a means to file documents electronically. However, any self-represented nonparty that is a governmental or public agency and any other agency, partnership, corporation, or business entity acting on behalf of any governmental or public agency may file documents by electronic transmission if such entity has the capability of filing documents electronically;
- For filing by attorneys excused from e-mail service in accordance with FL ST J ADMIN Rule 2.516(b);
- When submitting evidentiary exhibits or filing non-documentary materials;
- When the filing involves documents in excess of twenty-five (25) megabytes (25MB) in size. For such filings, documents may be transmitted using an electronic storage medium that the clerk has the ability to accept, which may include a CD-ROM, flash drive, or similar storage medium;
- When filed in open court, as permitted by the court;
- When paper filing is permitted by any approved statewide or local ECF procedures; and
- If any court determines that justice so requires. FL ST J ADMIN Rule 2.525(d).

ii. Any document in paper form submitted under FL ST J ADMIN Rule 2.525(d) is filed when it is received by the clerk or court and the clerk shall immediately thereafter convert any filed paper document to an electronic document. "Convert to an electronic document" means optically capturing an image of a paper document and using character recognition software to recover as much of the document's text as practicable and then indexing and storing the document in the official court file. FL ST J ADMIN Rule 2.525(c)(4).

iii. Any storage medium submitted under FL ST J ADMIN Rule 2.525(d)(5) is filed when received by the clerk or court and the clerk shall immediately thereafter transfer the electronic documents from the storage device to the official court file. FL ST J ADMIN Rule 2.525(c)(5).

iv. If the filer of any paper document authorized under FL ST J ADMIN Rule 2.525(d) provides a self-addressed, postage-paid envelope for return of the paper document after it is converted to electronic form by the clerk, the clerk shall place the paper document in the envelope and deposit it in the mail. Except when a paper document is required to be maintained, the clerk may recycle any filed paper document that is not to be returned to the filer. FL ST J ADMIN Rule 2.525(c)(6).

v. The clerk may convert any paper document filed before the effective date of FL ST J ADMIN

Rule 2.525 to an electronic document. Unless the clerk is required to maintain the paper document, if the paper document has been converted to an electronic document by the clerk, the paper document is no longer part of the official court file and may be removed and recycled. FL ST J ADMIN Rule 2.525(c)(7).

d. *Official court file.* For information on what constitutes the official court file, please see FL ST J ADMIN Rule 2.525(c)(2), FL ST J ADMIN Rule 2.525(c)(3).

e. *Administration.* All attorneys, parties, or other persons using this rule to file documents are required to make arrangements with the court or clerk for the payment of any charges authorized by general law or the supreme court before filing any document by electronic transmission. FL ST J ADMIN Rule 2.525(f)(2).

f. *Filing date.* The filing date for an electronically transmitted document is the date and time that such filing is acknowledged by an electronic stamp or otherwise, pursuant to any procedure set forth in any ECF Procedures approved by the supreme court, or the date the last page of such filing is received by the court or clerk. FL ST J ADMIN Rule 2.525(f)(3).

g. *Accessibility.* All documents transmitted in any electronic form under FL ST J ADMIN Rule 2.525 must comply with the accessibility requirements of FL ST J ADMIN Rule 2.526. FL ST J ADMIN Rule 2.525(g).

2. *Service requirements.* Every pleading subsequent to the initial pleading, all orders, and every other document filed in the action must be served in conformity with the requirements of FL ST J ADMIN Rule 2.516. FL ST RCP Rule 1.080(a).

a. *Service; When required.* Unless the court otherwise orders, or a statute or supreme court administrative order specifies a different means of service, every pleading subsequent to the initial pleading and every other document filed in any court proceeding, except applications for witness subpoenas and documents served by formal notice or required to be served in the manner provided for service of formal notice, must be served in accordance with FL ST J ADMIN Rule 2.516 on each party. No service need be made on parties against whom a default has been entered, except that pleadings asserting new or additional claims against them must be served in the manner provided for service of summons. FL ST J ADMIN Rule 2.516(a).

b. *Service; How made.* When service is required or permitted to be made upon a party represented by an attorney, service must be made upon the attorney unless service upon the party is ordered by the court. FL ST J ADMIN Rule 2.516(b).

i. *Service by electronic mail ("e-mail").* All documents required or permitted to be served on another party must be served by e-mail, unless FL ST J ADMIN Rule 2.516 otherwise provides. When, in addition to service by e-mail, the sender also utilizes another means of service provided for in FL ST J ADMIN Rule 2.516(b)(2), any differing time limits and other provisions applicable to that other means of service control. FL ST J ADMIN Rule 2.516(b)(1). Any document electronically transmitted to a court or clerk must also be served on all parties and interested persons in accordance with the applicable rules of court. FL ST J ADMIN Rule 2.525(e)(2).

- *Service on attorneys.* Upon appearing in a proceeding, an attorney must serve a designation of a primary e-mail address and may designate no more than two (2) secondary e-mail addresses. Thereafter, service must be directed to all designated e-mail addresses in that proceeding. Every document filed by an attorney thereafter must include the primary e-mail address of that attorney and any secondary e-mail addresses. If an attorney does not designate any e-mail address for service, documents may be served on that attorney at the e-mail address on record with The Florida Bar. FL ST J ADMIN Rule 2.516(b)(1)(A).

- *Exception to e-mail service on attorneys.* Service by an attorney on another attorney must be made by e-mail unless excused by the court. Upon motion by an attorney demonstrating that the attorney has no e-mail account and lacks access to the Internet at the attorney's office, the court may excuse the attorney from the requirements of e-mail service. Service on and by an attorney excused by the court from e-mail service must be by the means provided in FL ST J ADMIN Rule 2.516(b)(2). FL ST J ADMIN Rule 2.516(b)(1)(B).

- *Service on and by parties not represented by an attorney.* Any party not represented by an attorney may serve a designation of a primary e-mail address and also may designate no more than two (2) secondary e-mail addresses to which service must be directed in that proceeding by the means provided in FL ST J ADMIN Rule 2.516(b)(1). If a party not represented by an attorney does not designate an e-mail address for service in a proceeding, service on and by that party must be by the means provided in FL ST J ADMIN Rule 2.516(b)(2). FL ST J ADMIN Rule 2.516(b)(1)(C).
- *Time of service.* Service by e-mail is complete when it is sent. FL ST J ADMIN Rule 2.516(b)(1)(D). An e-mail is deemed served on the date it is sent. FL ST J ADMIN Rule 2.516(b)(1)(D)(i). If the sender learns that the e-mail did not reach the address of the person to be served, the sender must immediately send another copy by e-mail, or by a means authorized by FL ST J ADMIN Rule 2.516(b)(2). FL ST J ADMIN Rule 2.516(b)(1)(D)(ii). E-mail service is treated as service by mail for the computation of time. FL ST J ADMIN Rule 2.516(b)(1)(D)(iii).

ii. *Format of e-mail for service.* Service of a document by e-mail is made by attaching a copy of the document in PDF format to an e-mail sent to all addresses designated by the attorney or party. FL ST J ADMIN Rule 2.516(b)(1)(E).

- All documents served by e-mail must be attached to an e-mail message containing a subject line beginning with the words "SERVICE OF COURT DOCUMENT" in all capital letters, followed by the case number of the proceeding in which the documents are being served. FL ST J ADMIN Rule 2.516(b)(1)(E)(i).
- The body of the e-mail must identify the court in which the proceeding is pending, the case number, the name of the initial party on each side, the title of each document served with that e-mail, and the sender's name and telephone number. FL ST J ADMIN Rule 2.516(b)(1)(E)(ii).
- Any document served by e-mail may be signed by the "/s/" format, as long as the filed original is signed in accordance with the applicable rule of procedure. FL ST J ADMIN Rule 2.516(b)(1)(E)(iii).
- Any e-mail which, together with its attached documents, exceeds five megabytes (5MB) in size, must be divided and sent as separate e-mails, no one of which may exceed five megabytes (5MB) in size and each of which must be sequentially numbered in the subject line. FL ST J ADMIN Rule 2.516(b)(1)(E)(iv).

iii. *Service by other means.* In addition to, and not in lieu of, service by e-mail, service may also be made upon attorneys by any of the means specified in FL ST J ADMIN Rule 2.516(b)(2). Service on and by all parties who are not represented by an attorney and who do not designate an e-mail address, and on and by all attorneys excused from e-mail service, must be made by delivering a copy of the document or by mailing it to the party or attorney at their last known address or, if no address is known, by leaving it with the clerk of the court. Service by mail is complete upon mailing. Delivery of a copy within FL ST J ADMIN Rule 2.516 is complete upon:

- Handing it to the attorney or to the party,
- Leaving it at the attorney's or party's office with a clerk or other person in charge thereof,
- If there is no one in charge, leaving it in a conspicuous place therein,
- If the office is closed or the person to be served has no office, leaving it at the person's usual place of abode with some person of his or her family above fifteen (15) years of age and informing such person of the contents, or
- Transmitting it by facsimile to the attorney's or party's office with a cover sheet containing the sender's name, firm, address, telephone number, and facsimile number, and the number of pages transmitted. When service is made by facsimile, a copy must also be served by any other method permitted by FL ST J ADMIN Rule 2.516. Facsimile service occurs when transmission is complete. FL ST J ADMIN Rule 2.516(b)(2)(A) through FL ST J ADMIN Rule 2.516(b)(2)(E).

- Service by delivery after 5:00 p.m. must be deemed to have been made by mailing on the date of delivery. FL ST J ADMIN Rule 2.516(b)(2)(F).

c. *Service; Numerous defendants.* In actions when the parties are unusually numerous, the court may regulate the service contemplated by the Florida Rules of Judicial Administration on motion or on its own initiative in such manner as may be found to be just and reasonable. FL ST J ADMIN Rule 2.516(c).

d. *Service by clerk.* Service of notices and other documents required to be made by the clerk must also be done as provided in FL ST J ADMIN Rule 2.516(b). FL ST J ADMIN Rule 2.516(g).

G. Hearings

1. *Communication equipment*

a. *Definition.* Communication equipment means a conference telephone or other electronic device that permits all those appearing or participating to hear and speak to each other, provided that all conversation of all parties is audible to all persons present. FL ST J ADMIN Rule 2.530(a).

b. *Use by all parties.* A county or circuit court judge may, upon the court's own motion or upon the written request of a party, direct that communication equipment be used for a motion hearing, pretrial conference, or a status conference. A judge must give notice to the parties and consider any objections they may have to the use of communication equipment before directing that communication equipment be used. The decision to use communication equipment over the objection of parties will be in the sound discretion of the trial court, except as noted below. FL ST J ADMIN Rule 2.530(b).

c. *Use only by requesting party.* A county or circuit court judge may, upon the written request of a party upon reasonable notice to all other parties, permit a requesting party to participate through communication equipment in a scheduled motion hearing; however, any such request (except in criminal, juvenile, and appellate proceedings) must be granted, absent a showing of good cause to deny the same, where the hearing is set for not longer than fifteen (15) minutes. FL ST J ADMIN Rule 2.530(c).

d. *Testimony*

i. *Generally.* A county or circuit court judge, general magistrate, special magistrate, or hearing officer may allow testimony to be taken through communication equipment if all parties consent or if permitted by another applicable rule of procedure. FL ST J ADMIN Rule 2.530(d)(1).

ii. *Procedure.* Any party desiring to present testimony through communication equipment shall, prior to the hearing or trial at which the testimony is to be presented, contact all parties to determine whether each party consents to this form of testimony. The party seeking to present the testimony shall move for permission to present testimony through communication equipment, which motion shall set forth good cause as to why the testimony should be allowed in this form. FL ST J ADMIN Rule 2.530(d)(2).

iii. *Oath.* Testimony may be taken through communication equipment only if a notary public or other person authorized to administer oaths in the witness's jurisdiction is present with the witness and administers the oath consistent with the laws of the jurisdiction. FL ST J ADMIN Rule 2.530(d)(3).

iv. *Confrontation rights.* In juvenile and criminal proceedings the defendant must make an informed waiver of any confrontation rights that may be abridged by the use of communication equipment. FL ST J ADMIN Rule 2.530(d)(4).

v. *Video testimony.* If the testimony to be presented utilizes video conferencing or comparable two-way visual capabilities, the court in its discretion may modify the procedures set forth in FL ST J ADMIN Rule 2.530 to accommodate the technology utilized. FL ST J ADMIN Rule 2.530(d)(5).

e. *Burden of expense.* The cost for the use of the communication equipment is the responsibility of the requesting party unless otherwise directed by the court. FL ST J ADMIN Rule 2.530(e).

H. Forms

1. Official Motion for Sanctions Forms for Florida

a. Caption. FL ST RCP Form 1.901.

b. Notice of compliance when constitutional challenge is brought. FL ST RCP Form 1.975.

2. Motion for Sanctions Forms for Florida

a. Motion; By defendant; For sanctions for refusal of offer of judgment. FL-PP § 61:22.

b. Motion; Sanctions, proposal for settlement. FL-PRACFORM § 7:165.

3. Official Forms for Florida Circuit Court, Second Judicial Circuit

a. Notice of change of contact information. FL ST 2 J CIR 2007-05.

I. Checklist

(I) ❑ Matters to be considered by moving party

- (a) ❑ Required documents
  - (1) ❑ Notice of hearing/Motion
  - (2) ❑ Certificate of service
- (b) ❑ Supplemental documents
  - (1) ❑ Proposed order
  - (2) ❑ Notice of constitutional question
- (c) ❑ Time for making motion
  - (1) ❑ A motion by a party seeking sanctions under FL ST § 57.105 must be served but may not be filed with or presented to the court unless, within twenty one (21) days after service of the motion, the challenged paper, claim, defense, contention, allegation, or denial is not withdrawn or appropriately corrected
  - (2) ❑ Any party seeking a judgment taxing costs, attorneys' fees, or both shall serve a motion no later than thirty (30) days after filing of the judgment, including a judgment of dismissal, or the service of a notice of voluntary dismissal
  - (3)) ❑ A copy of any written motion which may not be heard ex parte and a copy of the notice of the hearing thereof shall be served a reasonable time before the time specified for the hearing

(II) ❑ Matters to be considered by opposing party

- (a) ❑ Required documents
  - (1) ❑ Response to motion
  - (2) ❑ Certificate of service
- (b) ❑ Supplemental documents
  - (1) ❑ Proposed order
  - (2) ❑ Notice of constitutional question
- (c) ❑ Time for service and filing of opposition
  - (1) ❑ No time specified for responding to a motion

Motions, Oppositions and Replies
Motion to Compel Discovery

Document Last Updated January 2013

A. Applicable Rules

1. *State rules*
   a. Rules of court. FL ST RCP Rule 1.010; FL ST J ADMIN Rule 2.110.
   b. Nonverification of pleadings. FL ST RCP Rule 1.030.
   c. Service and filing of pleadings, orders, and documents. FL ST RCP Rule 1.080.
   d. Time. FL ST RCP Rule 1.090.
   e. Pleadings and motions. FL ST RCP Rule 1.100.
   f. Motions. FL ST RCP Rule 1.160.
   g. General provisions governing discovery. FL ST RCP Rule 1.280.
   h. Depositions. FL ST RCP Rule 1.310; FL ST RCP Rule 1.320; FL ST FAM LAW Rule 12.310.
   i. Interrogatories to parties. FL ST RCP Rule 1.340.
   j. Production of documents and things and entry upon land for inspection and other purposes. FL ST RCP Rule 1.350.
   k. Examination of persons. FL ST RCP Rule 1.360.
   l. Failure to make discovery; Sanctions. FL ST RCP Rule 1.380.
   m. Relief from judgment, decrees, or orders. FL ST RCP Rule 1.540.
   n. Mediation and arbitration. FL ST RCP Rule 1.700; FL ST RCP Rule 1.710; FL ST RCP Rule 1.720; FL ST RCP Rule 1.730; FL ST RCP Rule 1.750; FL ST RCP Rule 1.800; FL ST RCP Rule 1.810; FL ST RCP Rule 1.820; FL ST RCP Rule 1.830.
   o. Forms. FL ST RCP Rule 1.900.
   p. Minimization of the filing of sensitive information. FL ST J ADMIN Rule 2.425.
   q. Retention of court records. FL ST J ADMIN Rule 2.430.
   r. Foreign attorneys. FL ST J ADMIN Rule 2.510.
   s. Signature of attorneys and parties. FL ST J ADMIN Rule 2.515.
   t. Paper. FL ST J ADMIN Rule 2.520.
   u. Electronic filing. FL ST J ADMIN Rule 2.525.
   v. Accessibility of information and technology. FL ST J ADMIN Rule 2.526.
   w. Communication equipment. FL ST J ADMIN Rule 2.530.
   x. Court reporting. FL ST J ADMIN Rule 2.535.
   y. Requests for accommodations by persons with disabilities. FL ST J ADMIN Rule 2.540.
2. *Local rules*
   a. Notice of change of contact information. FL ST 2 J CIR 2007-05.

B. Timing

1. *Motion to compel discovery.* Upon reasonable notice to other parties and all persons affected, a party may apply for an order compelling discovery. FL ST RCP Rule 1.380(a).
2. *General motion timing.* A copy of any written motion which may not be heard ex parte and a copy of the notice of the hearing thereof shall be served a reasonable time before the time specified for the hearing. FL ST RCP Rule 1.090(d).

3. *Computation of time*

   a. *Generally.* Computation of time shall be governed by FL ST J ADMIN Rule 2.514. FL ST RCP Rule 1.090(a). The following rules apply in computing time periods specified in any rule of procedure, local rule, court order, or statute that does not specify a method of computing time. FL ST J ADMIN Rule 2.514(a).

      i. *Period stated in days or a longer unit.* When the period is stated in days or a longer unit of time (A) exclude the day of the event that triggers the period; (B) count every day, including intermediate Saturdays, Sundays, and legal holidays; and (C) include the last day of the period, but if the last day is a Saturday, Sunday, or legal holiday, or falls within any period of time extended through an order of the chief justice under FL ST J ADMIN Rule 2.205(a)(2)(B)(iv), the period continues to run until the end of the next day that is not a Saturday, Sunday, or legal holiday and does not fall within any period of time extended through an order of the chief justice. FL ST J ADMIN Rule 2.514(a)(1).

      ii. *Period stated in hours.* When the period is stated in hours (A) begin counting immediately on the occurrence of the event that triggers the period; (B) count every hour, including hours during intermediate Saturdays, Sundays, and legal holidays; and (C) if the period would end on a Saturday, Sunday, or legal holiday, or during any period of time extended through an order of the chief justice under FL ST J ADMIN Rule 2.205(a)(2)(B)(iv), the period continues to run until the same time on the next day that is not a Saturday, Sunday, or legal holiday and does not fall within any period of time extended through an order of the chief justice. FL ST J ADMIN Rule 2.514(a)(2).

      iii. *Period stated in days less than seven (7) days.* When the period stated in days is less than seven (7) days, intermediate Saturdays, Sundays, and legal holidays shall be excluded in the computation. FL ST J ADMIN Rule 2.514(a)(3).

      iv. *"Last day" defined.* Unless a different time is set by a statute, local rule, or court order, the last day ends (A) for electronic filing or for service by any means, at midnight; and (B) for filing by other means, when the clerk's office is scheduled to close. FL ST J ADMIN Rule 2.514(a)(4).

      v. *"Next day" defined.* The "next day" is determined by continuing to count forward when the period is measured after an event and backward when measured before an event. FL ST J ADMIN Rule 2.514(a)(5).

      vi. *"Legal holiday" defined.* "Legal holiday" means (A) the day set aside by FL ST § 110.117, for observing New Year's Day, Martin Luther King, Jr.'s Birthday, Memorial Day, Independence Day, Labor Day, Veterans' Day, Thanksgiving Day, the Friday after Thanksgiving Day, or Christmas Day, and (B) any day observed as a holiday by the clerk's office or as designated by the chief judge. FL ST J ADMIN Rule 2.514(a)(6).

   b. *Additional time after service by mail or e-mail.* When a party may or must act within a specified time after service and service is made by mail or e-mail, five (5) days are added after the period that would otherwise expire under FL ST J ADMIN Rule 2.514(a). FL ST J ADMIN Rule 2.514(b).

   c. *Enlargement.* When an act is required or allowed to be done at or within a specified time by order of court, by the Florida Rules of Civil Procedure, or by notice given thereunder, for cause shown the court at any time in its discretion (1) with or without notice, may order the period enlarged if request therefor is made before the expiration of the period originally prescribed or as extended by a previous order, or (2) upon motion made and notice after the expiration of the specified period, may permit the act to be done when failure to act was the result of excusable neglect, but it may not extend the time for making a motion for new trial, for rehearing, or to alter or amend a judgment; making a motion for relief from a judgment under FL ST RCP Rule 1.540(b); taking an appeal or filing a petition for certiorari; or making a motion for a directed verdict. FL ST RCP Rule 1.090(b).

   d. *Unaffected by expiration of term.* The period of time provided for the doing of any act or the taking of any proceeding shall not be affected or limited by the continued existence or expiration of a term of court. The continued existence or expiration of a term of court in no way affects the power of a court to do any act or take any proceeding in any action which is or has been pending before it. FL ST RCP Rule 1.090(c).

C. General Requirements

1. *Motions generally*

   a. *Contents.* An application to the court for an order shall be by motion which shall be made in writing unless made during a hearing or trial, shall state with particularity the grounds therefor, and shall set forth the relief or order sought. The requirement of writing is fulfilled if the motion is stated in a written notice of the hearing of the motion. All notices of hearing shall specify each motion or other matter to be heard. FL ST RCP Rule 1.100(b).

   b. *Particularity requirement.* The court considers a motion in the light of the substantive law, rule or statute to make its determination. Some rules require a statement of the grounds for a motion under the rule. Failure to give the grounds will result in denial of the motion. This should be the result in all situations when the ground for the motion is not inherent in the rule. FL-PRACPROC § 9:3. The requirement is nevertheless an important one, first because of the due process notice rights of the respondent, as well as for the assistance it provides to the court in its preparation for the hearing or, absent a hearing, for disposition. 4 FLPRAC R 1.100.

2. *Failure to make discovery; Types of available relief.* Three (3) categories of relief are available for failure to make discovery. FL-PRACPROC § 16:14.

   a. The first category is an order compelling discovery. This is obtained by a motion to compel discovery. The motion is made in the court in which the action is pending, except when a deposition is being taken out of the territorial jurisdiction of the court and protective relief is sought in accordance with FL ST RCP Rule 1.310(d) or when a deponent is not a party. When one of the exceptions occurs, the motion is made in the circuit court of the county where the deposition is being taken. FL-PRACPROC § 16:14.

   b. The second category results from a failure to comply with an order to make discovery. The sanctions should not be applied until a hearing on the merits of the failure is held, including an opportunity to present evidence of explanation or mitigation. FL-PRACPROC § 16:14.

   c. The third category is available: (1) if a party or a person designated by an organization to answer questions at a deposition fails to appear before the officer who is to take the deposition after being served with a proper notice; (2) fails to serve answers or objections to interrogatories after proper service of the interrogatories; or (3) a party fails to serve a response to a request for production, inspection and entry after proper service of the request. FL-PRACPROC § 16:14. For further information regarding discovery sanctions please see the KeyRules Motion for Discovery Sanctions documents.

3. *Motion for order compelling discovery*

   a. *Reasonable notice.* Upon reasonable notice to other parties and all persons affected, a party may apply for an order compelling discovery. FL ST RCP Rule 1.380(a).

   b. *Appropriate court.* An application for an order to a party may be made to the court in which the action is pending or in accordance with FL ST RCP Rule 1.310(d). An application for an order to a deponent who is not a party shall be made to the circuit court where the deposition is being taken. FL ST RCP Rule 1.380(a)(1).

   c. *Motion*

      i. *Grounds.* The discovering party may move for an order compelling an answer, or a designation or an order compelling inspection, or an order compelling an examination in accordance with the request:

         - If a deponent fails to answer a question propounded or submitted under FL ST RCP Rule 1.310 or FL ST RCP Rule 1.320;
         - Or a corporation or other entity fails to make a designation under FL ST RCP Rule 1.310(b)(6) or FL ST RCP Rule 1.320(a);
         - Or a party fails to answer an interrogatory submitted under FL ST RCP Rule 1.340;
         - Or if a party in response to a request for inspection submitted under FL ST RCP Rule 1.350

fails to respond that inspection will be permitted as requested or fails to permit inspection as requested;

- Or if a party in response to a request for examination of a person submitted under FL ST RCP Rule 1.360(a) objects to the examination, fails to respond that the examination will be permitted as requested, or fails to submit to or to produce a person in that party's custody or legal control for examination. FL ST RCP Rule 1.380(a)(2).

ii. *Certification.* The motion must include a certification that the movant, in good faith, has conferred or attempted to confer with the person or party failing to make the discovery in an effort to secure the information or material without court action. FL ST RCP Rule 1.380(a)(2).

iii. *During deposition.* When taking a deposition on oral examination, the proponent of the question may complete or adjourn the examination before applying for an order. FL ST RCP Rule 1.380(a)(2).

iv. *Protective order.* If the court denies the motion in whole or in part, it may make such protective order as it would have been empowered to make on a motion made pursuant to FL ST RCP Rule 1.280(c). FL ST RCP Rule 1.380(a)(2).

d. *Evasive or incomplete answer.* For purposes of FL ST RCP Rule 1.380(a) an evasive or incomplete answer shall be treated as a failure to answer. FL ST RCP Rule 1.380(a)(3).

e. *Award of expenses of motion*

i. *Motion granted.* If the motion is granted and after opportunity for hearing, the court shall require the party or deponent whose conduct necessitated the motion or the party or counsel advising the conduct to pay to the moving party the reasonable expenses incurred in obtaining the order that may include attorneys' fees, unless the court finds that the movant failed to certify in the motion that a good faith effort was made to obtain the discovery without court action, that the opposition to the motion was justified, or that other circumstances make an award of expenses unjust. FL ST RCP Rule 1.380(a)(4).

ii. *Motion denied.* If the motion is denied and after opportunity for hearing, the court shall require the moving party to pay to the party or deponent who opposed the motion the reasonable expenses incurred in opposing the motion that may include attorneys' fees, unless the court finds that the making of the motion was substantially justified or that other circumstances make an award of expenses unjust. FL ST RCP Rule 1.380(a)(4).

iii. *Motion granted in part and denied in part.* If the motion is granted in part and denied in part, the court may apportion the reasonable expenses incurred as a result of making the motion among the parties and persons. FL ST RCP Rule 1.380(a)(4).

iv. *Electronically stored information; Sanctions for failure to preserve.* Absent exceptional circumstances, a court may not impose sanctions under these rules on a party for failing to provide electronically stored information lost as a result of the routine, good faith operation of an electronic information system. FL ST RCP Rule 1.380(e).

4. *Limitations on discovery of electronically stored information*

a. A person may object to discovery of electronically stored information from sources that the person identifies as not reasonably accessible because of burden or cost. On motion to compel discovery or for a protective order, the person from whom discovery is sought must show that the information sought or the format requested is not reasonably accessible because of undue burden or cost. If that showing is made, the court may nonetheless order the discovery from such sources or in such formats if the requesting party shows good cause. The court may specify conditions of the discovery, including ordering that some or all of the expenses incurred by the person from whom discovery is sought be paid by the party seeking the discovery. FL ST RCP Rule 1.280(d)(1).

b. In determining any motion involving discovery of electronically stored information, the court must limit the frequency or extent of discovery otherwise allowed by the Florida Rules of Civil Procedure if it determines that (i) the discovery sought is unreasonably cumulative or duplicative, or can be obtained from another source or in another manner that is more convenient, less burdensome, or less expensive; or (ii) the burden or expense of the discovery outweighs its likely benefit, considering the needs of the case, the amount in controversy, the parties' resources, the importance of the issues at stake in the action, and the importance of the discovery in resolving the issues. FL ST RCP Rule 1.280(d)(2).

5. *Arbitration and mediation*
   a. *Referral to arbitration and mediation.* Except as hereinafter provided or as otherwise prohibited by law, the presiding judge may enter an order referring all or any part of a contested civil matter to mediation or arbitration. The parties to any contested civil matter may file a written stipulation to mediate or arbitrate any issue between them at any time. Such stipulation shall be incorporated into the order of referral. FL ST RCP Rule 1.700(a).
   b. *Arbitration*
      i. *Exclusions.* A civil action shall be ordered to arbitration or arbitration in conjunction with mediation upon stipulation of the parties. A civil action may be ordered to arbitration or arbitration in conjunction with mediation upon motion of any party or by the court, if the judge determines the action to be of such a nature that arbitration could be of benefit to the litigants or the court. FL ST RCP Rule 1.800.
         - Under no circumstances may the following categories of actions be referred to arbitration: (1) bond estreatures; (2) habeas corpus or other extraordinary writs; (3) bond validations; (4) civil or criminal contempt; (5) such other matters as may be specified by order of the chief judge in the circuit. FL ST RCP Rule 1.800.
      ii. For more information regarding arbitration, please see FL ST RCP Rule 1.810; FL ST RCP Rule 1.820; FL ST RCP Rule 1.830.
   c. *Mediation.* For more information regarding mediation, please see FL ST RCP Rule 1.710; FL ST RCP Rule 1.720; FL ST RCP Rule 1.730; and FL ST RCP Rule 1.750.
6. *Rules of court*
   a. *Rules of civil procedure.* The Florida Rules of Civil Procedure apply to all actions of a civil nature and all special statutory proceedings in the circuit courts and county courts except those to which the Florida Probate Rules, the Florida Family Law Rules of Procedure, or the Small Claims Rules apply. FL ST RCP Rule 1.010.
      i. The form, content, procedure, and time for pleading in all special statutory proceedings shall be as prescribed by the statutes governing the proceeding unless the Florida Rules of Civil Procedure specifically provide to the contrary. FL ST RCP Rule 1.010.
      ii. The Florida Rules of Civil Procedure shall be construed to secure the just, speedy, and inexpensive determination of every action. FL ST RCP Rule 1.010.
   b. *Rules of judicial administration.* The Florida Rules of Judicial Administration shall apply to administrative matters in all courts to which the Florida Rules of Judicial Administration are applicable by their terms. The Florida Rules of Judicial Administration shall be construed to secure the speedy and inexpensive determination of every proceeding to which they are applicable. The Florida Rules of Judicial Administration shall supersede all conflicting rules and statutes. FL ST J ADMIN Rule 2.110.
7. *Notice of change of contact information.* The Clerk shall provide a change of address and/or telephone number form for use by attorneys and pro se litigants. With any change of address and/or telephone number, attorneys and pro se litigants governed by FL ST J ADMIN Rule 2.515 will provide to the Clerk and all parties promptly the change of address and/or telephone number form. This form should be submitted only once to the Clerk, who will then make the address and/or telephone number change in all court divisions. FL ST 2 J CIR 2007-05.

D. Documents

1. *Required documents*
   a. *Notice of hearing/Motion.* An application to the court for an order shall be by motion which shall be

made in writing unless made during a hearing or trial, shall state with particularity the grounds therefor, and shall set forth the relief or order sought. The requirement of writing is fulfilled if the motion is stated in a written notice of the hearing of the motion. All notices of hearing shall specify each motion or other matter to be heard. FL ST RCP Rule 1.100(b).

i. *Certification.* The motion must include a certification that the movant, in good faith, has conferred or attempted to confer with the person or party failing to make the discovery in an effort to secure the information or material without court action. FL ST RCP Rule 1.380(a)(2).

ii. *Notices to persons with disabilities.* See the Format section of this KeyRules document for further information.

b. *Certificate of service.* When any attorney certifies in substance: "I certify that a copy hereof has been furnished to (here insert name or names and addresses used for service) by (e-mail) (delivery) (mail) (fax) on .... (date) ....______________ Attorney" the certificate is taken as prima facie proof of such service in compliance with FL ST J ADMIN Rule 2.516. FL ST J ADMIN Rule 2.516(f).

2. *Supplemental documents*

a. *Proposed order.* The court may require that orders or judgments be prepared by a party, may require the party to furnish the court with stamped, addressed envelopes for service of the order or judgment, and may require that proposed orders and judgments be furnished to all parties before entry by the court of the order or judgment. FL ST J ADMIN Rule 2.516(h)(1).

b. *Notice of constitutional question.* A party that files a pleading, written motion, or other paper drawing into question the constitutionality of a state statute or a county or municipal charter, ordinance, or franchise must promptly (1) file a notice of constitutional question stating the question and identifying the paper that raises it; and (2) serve the notice and the pleading, written motion, or other paper drawing into question the constitutionality of a state statute or a county or municipal charter, ordinance, or franchise on the Attorney General or the state attorney of the judicial circuit in which the action is pending, by either certified or registered mail. Service of the notice and pleading, written motion, or other paper does not require joinder of the Attorney General or the state attorney as a party to the action. FL ST RCP Rule 1.071.

E. Format

1. *Documents; Type and size.* Documents subject to the exceptions set forth in FL ST J ADMIN Rule 2.525(d) shall be filed on recycled paper measuring eight and one half by eleven (8 1/2 by 11) inches. For purposes of FL ST J ADMIN Rule 2.520, paper is recycled if it contains a minimum content of fifty (50) percent waste paper. Xerographic reduction of legal-size (eight and one half by fourteen (8 1/2 by 14) inches) documents to letter size (eight and one half by eleven (8 1/2 by 11) inches) is prohibited. All other documents filed by electronic transmission shall be filed in a format capable of being printed in a format consistent with the provisions of FL ST J ADMIN Rule 2.250. FL ST J ADMIN Rule 2.520(b).

a. *Exhibits.* Any exhibit or attachment filed with pleadings or papers may be filed in its original size. FL ST J ADMIN Rule 2.520(c).

b. *Recording space.* On all papers and documents prepared and filed by the court or by any party to a proceeding which are to be recorded in the public records of any county, including but not limited to final money judgments and notices of lis pendens, a three (3) inch by three (3) inch space at the top right-hand corner on the first page and a one (1) inch by three (3) inch space at the top right-hand corner on each subsequent page shall be left blank and reserved for use by the clerk of court. FL ST J ADMIN Rule 2.520(d).

i. *Exceptions to recording space.* Any papers or documents created by persons or entities over which the filing party has no control, including but not limited to wills, codicils, trusts, or other testamentary documents; documents prepared or executed by any public officer; documents prepared, executed, acknowledged, or proved outside of the State of Florida; or documents created by State or Federal government agencies, may be filed without the space required by FL ST J ADMIN Rule 2.520. FL ST J ADMIN Rule 2.520(e).

c. *Noncompliance.* No clerk of court is permitted to refuse to file any document or paper because of noncompliance with the Florida Rules of Judicial Administration. However, upon request of the

clerk of court, noncomplying documents must be resubmitted in accordance with the formatting rules. FL ST J ADMIN Rule 2.520(f).

2. *Caption.* Every pleading, motion, order, judgment, or other paper shall have a caption containing the name of the court, the file number, and except for in rem proceedings, including forfeiture proceedings, the name of the first party on each side with an appropriate indication of other parties, and a designation identifying the party filing it and its nature or the nature of the order, as the case may be. In any in rem proceeding, every pleading, motion, order, judgment, or other paper shall have a caption containing the name of the court, the file number, the style "In re" (followed by the name or general description of the property), and a designation of the person or entity filing it and its nature or the nature of the order, as the case may be. In an in rem forfeiture proceeding, the style shall be "In re forfeiture of" (followed by the name of the general description of the property). All papers filed in the action shall be styled in such a manner as to indicate clearly the subject matter of the paper and the party requesting or obtaining relief. FL ST RCP Rule 1.100(c)(1).
3. *Writing and written defined.* Writing or written means a document containing information, an application, or a stipulation. FL ST RCP Rule 1.080(c).
4. *Rule abbreviations*
    a. The Florida Rules of Civil Procedure and shall be abbreviated as Fla.R.Civ.P. FL ST RCP Rule 1.010.
    b. The Florida Rules of Judicial Administration shall be abbreviated as Fla. R. Jud. Admin. FL ST J ADMIN Rule 2.110.
5. *Nonverification.* Except when otherwise specifically provided by the Florida Rules of Civil Procedure or an applicable statute, every pleading or other document of a party represented by an attorney need not be verified or accompanied by an affidavit. FL ST RCP Rule 1.030; FL ST J ADMIN Rule 2.515(a).
6. *Attorney signature*
    a. *Attorney signature.* Every pleading and other document of a party represented by an attorney shall be signed by at least one (1) attorney of record in that attorney's individual name whose current record Florida Bar address, telephone number, including area code, primary e-mail address and secondary e-mail addresses, if any, and Florida Bar number shall be stated, and who shall be duly licensed to practice law in Florida or who shall have received permission to appear in the particular case as provided in FL ST J ADMIN Rule 2.510. FL ST J ADMIN Rule 2.515(a).
        i. The attorney may be required by the court to give the address of, and to vouch for the attorney's authority to represent, the party. FL ST J ADMIN Rule 2.515(a).
        ii. The signature of an attorney shall constitute a certificate by the attorney that the attorney has read the pleading or other document; that to the best of the attorney's knowledge, information, and belief there is good ground to support it; and that it is not interposed for delay. FL ST J ADMIN Rule 2.515(a).
        iii. If a pleading is not signed or is signed with intent to defeat the purpose of FL ST J ADMIN Rule 2.515, it may be stricken and the action may proceed as though the pleading or other document had not been served. FL ST J ADMIN Rule 2.515(a).
    b. *Pro se litigant signature.* A party who is not represented by an attorney shall sign any pleading or other paper and state the party's address and telephone number, including area code. FL ST J ADMIN Rule 2.515(b).
    c. *Form of signature*
        i. The signatures required on pleadings and documents by FL ST J ADMIN Rule 2.515(a) and FL ST J ADMIN Rule 2.515(b) may be:
            - Original signatures;
            - Original signatures that have been reproduced by electronic means, such as on electronically transmitted documents or photocopied documents;
            - Electronic signatures using the "/s/," "s/," or "/s" formats by or at the direction of the person signing; or

- Any other signature format authorized by general law, so long as the clerk where the proceeding is pending has the capability of receiving and has obtained approval from the Supreme Court of Florida to accept pleadings and documents with that signature format. FL ST J ADMIN Rule 2.515(c)(1).

ii. An attorney, party, or other person who files a pleading or paper by electronic transmission that does not contain the original signature of that attorney, party, or other person shall file that identical pleading or paper in paper form containing an original signature of that attorney, party, or other person (hereinafter called the follow-up filing) immediately thereafter. The follow-up filing is not required if the Supreme Court of Florida has entered an order directing the clerk of court to discontinue accepting the follow-up filing. FL ST J ADMIN Rule 2.515(c)(2).

7. *Forms*

a. *Process.* The forms of process, notice of lis pendens, and notice of action provided in the Florida Rules of Civil Procedure are sufficient. Variations from the forms do not void process or notices that are otherwise sufficient. FL ST RCP Rule 1.900(a).

b. *Other forms.* The other forms provided in the Florida Rules of Civil Procedure are sufficient for the matters that are covered by them. So long as the substance is expressed without prolixity, the forms may be varied to meet the facts of a particular case. FL ST RCP Rule 1.900(b).

c. *Formal matters.* Captions, except for the designation of the paper, are omitted from the forms provided in the Florida Rules of Civil Procedure. A general form of caption is the first form provided. Signatures are omitted from pleadings and motions. FL ST RCP Rule 1.900(c).

8. *Notices to persons with disabilities.* All notices of court proceedings to be held in a public facility, and all process compelling appearance at such proceedings, shall include the following statement in bold face, fourteen (14) point Times New Roman or Courier font: "If you are a person with a disability who needs any accommodation in order to participate in this proceeding, you are entitled, at no cost to you, to the provision of certain assistance. Please contact [identify applicable court personnel by name, address, and telephone number] at least seven (7) days before your scheduled court appearance, or immediately upon receiving this notification if the time before the scheduled appearance is less than seven (7) days; if you are hearing or voice impaired, call 711." FL ST J ADMIN Rule 2.540(c)(1).

9. *Minimization of the filing of sensitive information*

a. *Limitations for court filings.* Unless authorized by FL ST J ADMIN Rule 2.425(b), statute, another rule of court, or the court orders otherwise, designated sensitive information filed with the court must be limited to the following format:

i. The initials of a person known to be a minor;

ii. The year of birth of a person's birth date;

iii. No portion of any: Social security number, Bank account number, Credit card account number, Charge account number, or Debit account number;

iv. The last four digits of any: Taxpayer identification number (TIN), Employee identification number, Driver's license number, Passport number, Telephone number, Financial account number, except as set forth in FL ST J ADMIN Rule 2.425(a)(3), Brokerage account number, Insurance policy account number, Loan account number, Customer account number, or Patient or health care number;

v. A truncated version of any: Email address, Computer user name, Password, or Personal identification number (PIN); and

vi. A truncated version of any other sensitive information as provided by court order. FL ST J ADMIN Rule 2.425(a).

b. *Exceptions.* FL ST J ADMIN Rule 2.425(a) does not apply to the following:

i. An account number which identifies the property alleged to be the subject of a proceeding;

ii. The record of an administrative or agency proceeding;

iii. The record in appellate or review proceedings;

- iv. The birth date of a minor whenever the birth date is necessary for the court to establish or maintain subject matter jurisdiction;
- v. The name of a minor in any order relating to parental responsibility, time-sharing, or child support;
- vi. The name of a minor in any document or order affecting the minor's ownership of real property;
- vii. The birth date of a party in a writ of attachment or notice to payor;
- viii. In traffic and criminal proceedings: a pro se filing; a court filing that is related to a criminal matter or investigation and that is prepared before the filing of a criminal charge or is not filed as part of any docketed criminal case; an arrest or search warrant or any information in support thereof; a charging document and an affidavit or other documents filed in support of any charging document, including any driving records; a statement of particulars; discovery material introduced into evidence or otherwise filed with the court; and all information necessary for the proper issuance and execution of a subpoena duces tecum;
- ix. Information used by the clerk for case maintenance purposes or the courts for case management purposes; and
- x. Information which is relevant and material to an issue before the court. FL ST J ADMIN Rule 2.425(b).

c. *Remedies.* Upon motion by a party or interested person or sua sponte by the court, the court may order remedies, sanctions or both for a violation of FL ST J ADMIN Rule 2.425(a). Following notice and an opportunity to respond, the court may impose sanctions if such filing was not made in good faith. FL ST J ADMIN Rule 2.425(c).

d. *Motions not restricted.* FL ST J ADMIN Rule 2.425 does not restrict a party's right to move for protective order, to move to file documents under seal, or to request a determination of the confidentiality of records. FL ST J ADMIN Rule 2.425(d).

e. *Application.* FL ST J ADMIN Rule 2.425 does not affect the application of constitutional provisions, statutes, or rules of court regarding confidential information or access to public information. FL ST J ADMIN Rule 2.425(e).

F. Filing and Service Requirements

1. *Filing requirements.* All original documents must be filed with the court either before service or immediately thereafter, unless otherwise provided for by general law or other rules. If the original of any bond or other document is not placed in the court file, a certified copy must be so placed by the clerk. FL ST J ADMIN Rule 2.516(d). All documents shall be filed in conformity with the requirements of FL ST J ADMIN Rule 2.525. FL ST RCP Rule 1.080(b). All documents filed in any court shall be filed by electronic transmission in accordance with FL ST J ADMIN Rule 2.525. "Documents" means pleadings, motions, petitions, memoranda, briefs, notices, exhibits, declarations, affidavits, orders, judgments, decrees, writs, opinions, and any other paper or writing submitted to a court. FL ST J ADMIN Rule 2.520(a). All documents that are court records, as defined in FL ST J ADMIN Rule 2.430(a)(1), must be filed by electronic transmission, provided that: (1) the clerk has the ability to accept and retain such documents; (2) the clerk or the chief judge of the circuit has requested permission to accept documents filed by electronic transmission; and (3) the supreme court has entered an order granting permission to the clerk to accept documents filed by electronic transmission. FL ST J ADMIN Rule 2.525(c)(1).

   a. *Definition.* "Electronic transmission of documents" means the sending of information by electronic signals to, by or from a court or clerk, which when received can be transformed and stored or transmitted on paper, microfilm, magnetic storage device, optical imaging system, CD-ROM, flash drive, other electronic data storage system, server, case maintenance system ("CM"), electronic court filing ("ECF") system, statewide or local electronic portal ("e-portal"), or other electronic record keeping system authorized by the supreme court in a format sufficient to communicate the information on the original document in a readable format. Electronic transmission of documents includes electronic mail ("e-mail") and any internet-based transmission procedure, and may include procedures allowing for documents to be signed or verified by electronic means. FL ST J ADMIN Rule 2.525(a).

      i. The filing of documents with the court as required by the Florida Rules of Judicial Adminis-

tration must be made by filing them with the clerk in accordance with FL ST J ADMIN Rule 2.525, except that the judge may permit documents to be filed with the judge, in which event the judge must note the filing date before him or her on the documents and transmit them to the clerk. The date of filing is that shown on the face of the document by the judge's notation or the clerk's time stamp, whichever is earlier. FL ST J ADMIN Rule 2.516(e).

b. *Application.* Any court or clerk of the court may accept the electronic transmission of documents for filing after the clerk, together with input from the chief judge of the circuit, has obtained approval of the procedures and program for doing so from the Supreme Court of Florida. FL ST J ADMIN Rule 2.525(b).

c. *Exceptions*

   i. Paper documents and other submissions may be manually submitted to the clerk or court:

      - When the clerk does not have the ability to accept and retain documents by electronic filing or has not had ECF Procedures approved by the supreme court;
      - For filing by any self-represented party or any self-represented nonparty unless specific ECF Procedures provide a means to file documents electronically. However, any self-represented nonparty that is a governmental or public agency and any other agency, partnership, corporation, or business entity acting on behalf of any governmental or public agency may file documents by electronic transmission if such entity has the capability of filing documents electronically;
      - For filing by attorneys excused from e-mail service in accordance with FL ST J ADMIN Rule 2.516(b);
      - When submitting evidentiary exhibits or filing non-documentary materials;
      - When the filing involves documents in excess of twenty-five (25) megabytes (25MB) in size. For such filings, documents may be transmitted using an electronic storage medium that the clerk has the ability to accept, which may include a CD-ROM, flash drive, or similar storage medium;
      - When filed in open court, as permitted by the court;
      - When paper filing is permitted by any approved statewide or local ECF procedures; and
      - If any court determines that justice so requires. FL ST J ADMIN Rule 2.525(d).

   ii. Any document in paper form submitted under FL ST J ADMIN Rule 2.525(d) is filed when it is received by the clerk or court and the clerk shall immediately thereafter convert any filed paper document to an electronic document. "Convert to an electronic document" means optically capturing an image of a paper document and using character recognition software to recover as much of the document's text as practicable and then indexing and storing the document in the official court file. FL ST J ADMIN Rule 2.525(c)(4).

   iii. Any storage medium submitted under FL ST J ADMIN Rule 2.525(d)(5) is filed when received by the clerk or court and the clerk shall immediately thereafter transfer the electronic documents from the storage device to the official court file. FL ST J ADMIN Rule 2.525(c)(5).

   iv. If the filer of any paper document authorized under FL ST J ADMIN Rule 2.525(d) provides a self-addressed, postage-paid envelope for return of the paper document after it is converted to electronic form by the clerk, the clerk shall place the paper document in the envelope and deposit it in the mail. Except when a paper document is required to be maintained, the clerk may recycle any filed paper document that is not to be returned to the filer. FL ST J ADMIN Rule 2.525(c)(6).

   v. The clerk may convert any paper document filed before the effective date of FL ST J ADMIN Rule 2.525 to an electronic document. Unless the clerk is required to maintain the paper document, if the paper document has been converted to an electronic document by the clerk, the paper document is no longer part of the official court file and may be removed and recycled. FL ST J ADMIN Rule 2.525(c)(7).

d. *Official court file.* For information on what constitutes the official court file, please see FL ST J ADMIN Rule 2.525(c)(2), FL ST J ADMIN Rule 2.525(c)(3).

e. *Administration.* All attorneys, parties, or other persons using this rule to file documents are required to make arrangements with the court or clerk for the payment of any charges authorized by general law or the supreme court before filing any document by electronic transmission. FL ST J ADMIN Rule 2.525(f)(2).

f. *Filing date.* The filing date for an electronically transmitted document is the date and time that such filing is acknowledged by an electronic stamp or otherwise, pursuant to any procedure set forth in any ECF Procedures approved by the supreme court, or the date the last page of such filing is received by the court or clerk. FL ST J ADMIN Rule 2.525(f)(3).

g. *Accessibility.* All documents transmitted in any electronic form under FL ST J ADMIN Rule 2.525 must comply with the accessibility requirements of FL ST J ADMIN Rule 2.526. FL ST J ADMIN Rule 2.525(g).

2. *Service requirements.* Every pleading subsequent to the initial pleading, all orders, and every other document filed in the action must be served in conformity with the requirements of FL ST J ADMIN Rule 2.516. FL ST RCP Rule 1.080(a).

a. *Service; When required.* Unless the court otherwise orders, or a statute or supreme court administrative order specifies a different means of service, every pleading subsequent to the initial pleading and every other document filed in any court proceeding, except applications for witness subpoenas and documents served by formal notice or required to be served in the manner provided for service of formal notice, must be served in accordance with FL ST J ADMIN Rule 2.516 on each party. No service need be made on parties against whom a default has been entered, except that pleadings asserting new or additional claims against them must be served in the manner provided for service of summons. FL ST J ADMIN Rule 2.516(a).

b. *Service; How made.* When service is required or permitted to be made upon a party represented by an attorney, service must be made upon the attorney unless service upon the party is ordered by the court. FL ST J ADMIN Rule 2.516(b).

i. *Service by electronic mail ("e-mail").* All documents required or permitted to be served on another party must be served by e-mail, unless FL ST J ADMIN Rule 2.516 otherwise provides. When, in addition to service by e-mail, the sender also utilizes another means of service provided for in FL ST J ADMIN Rule 2.516(b)(2), any differing time limits and other provisions applicable to that other means of service control. FL ST J ADMIN Rule 2.516(b)(1). Any document electronically transmitted to a court or clerk must also be served on all parties and interested persons in accordance with the applicable rules of court. FL ST J ADMIN Rule 2.525(e)(2).

- *Service on attorneys.* Upon appearing in a proceeding, an attorney must serve a designation of a primary e-mail address and may designate no more than two (2) secondary e-mail addresses. Thereafter, service must be directed to all designated e-mail addresses in that proceeding. Every document filed by an attorney thereafter must include the primary e-mail address of that attorney and any secondary e-mail addresses. If an attorney does not designate any e-mail address for service, documents may be served on that attorney at the e-mail address on record with The Florida Bar. FL ST J ADMIN Rule 2.516(b)(1)(A).

- *Exception to e-mail service on attorneys.* Service by an attorney on another attorney must be made by e-mail unless excused by the court. Upon motion by an attorney demonstrating that the attorney has no e-mail account and lacks access to the Internet at the attorney's office, the court may excuse the attorney from the requirements of e-mail service. Service on and by an attorney excused by the court from e-mail service must be by the means provided in FL ST J ADMIN Rule 2.516(b)(2). FL ST J ADMIN Rule 2.516(b)(1)(B).

- *Service on and by parties not represented by an attorney.* Any party not represented by an attorney may serve a designation of a primary e-mail address and also may designate no more than two (2) secondary e-mail addresses to which service must be directed in that proceeding by the means provided in FL ST J ADMIN Rule 2.516(b)(1). If a party not represented by an attorney does not designate an e-mail address for service in a proceeding, service on and by that party must be by the means provided in FL ST J ADMIN Rule 2.516(b)(2). FL ST J ADMIN Rule 2.516(b)(1)(C).

- *Time of service.* Service by e-mail is complete when it is sent. FL ST J ADMIN Rule 2.516(b)(1)(D). An e-mail is deemed served on the date it is sent. FL ST J ADMIN Rule 2.516(b)(1)(D)(i). If the sender learns that the e-mail did not reach the address of the person to be served, the sender must immediately send another copy by e-mail, or by a means authorized by FL ST J ADMIN Rule 2.516(b)(2). FL ST J ADMIN Rule 2.516(b)(1)(D)(ii). E-mail service is treated as service by mail for the computation of time. FL ST J ADMIN Rule 2.516(b)(1)(D)(iii).

ii. *Format of e-mail for service.* Service of a document by e-mail is made by attaching a copy of the document in PDF format to an e-mail sent to all addresses designated by the attorney or party. FL ST J ADMIN Rule 2.516(b)(1)(E).

- All documents served by e-mail must be attached to an e-mail message containing a subject line beginning with the words "SERVICE OF COURT DOCUMENT" in all capital letters, followed by the case number of the proceeding in which the documents are being served. FL ST J ADMIN Rule 2.516(b)(1)(E)(i).
- The body of the e-mail must identify the court in which the proceeding is pending, the case number, the name of the initial party on each side, the title of each document served with that e-mail, and the sender's name and telephone number. FL ST J ADMIN Rule 2.516(b)(1)(E)(ii).
- Any document served by e-mail may be signed by the "/s/" format, as long as the filed original is signed in accordance with the applicable rule of procedure. FL ST J ADMIN Rule 2.516(b)(1)(E)(iii).
- Any e-mail which, together with its attached documents, exceeds five megabytes (5MB) in size, must be divided and sent as separate e-mails, no one of which may exceed five megabytes (5MB) in size and each of which must be sequentially numbered in the subject line. FL ST J ADMIN Rule 2.516(b)(1)(E)(iv).

iii. *Service by other means.* In addition to, and not in lieu of, service by e-mail, service may also be made upon attorneys by any of the means specified in FL ST J ADMIN Rule 2.516(b)(2). Service on and by all parties who are not represented by an attorney and who do not designate an e-mail address, and on and by all attorneys excused from e-mail service, must be made by delivering a copy of the document or by mailing it to the party or attorney at their last known address or, if no address is known, by leaving it with the clerk of the court. Service by mail is complete upon mailing. Delivery of a copy within FL ST J ADMIN Rule 2.516 is complete upon:

- Handing it to the attorney or to the party,
- Leaving it at the attorney's or party's office with a clerk or other person in charge thereof,
- If there is no one in charge, leaving it in a conspicuous place therein,
- If the office is closed or the person to be served has no office, leaving it at the person's usual place of abode with some person of his or her family above fifteen (15) years of age and informing such person of the contents, or
- Transmitting it by facsimile to the attorney's or party's office with a cover sheet containing the sender's name, firm, address, telephone number, and facsimile number, and the number of pages transmitted. When service is made by facsimile, a copy must also be served by any other method permitted by FL ST J ADMIN Rule 2.516. Facsimile service occurs when transmission is complete. FL ST J ADMIN Rule 2.516(b)(2)(A) through FL ST J ADMIN Rule 2.516(b)(2)(E).
- Service by delivery after 5:00 p.m. must be deemed to have been made by mailing on the date of delivery. FL ST J ADMIN Rule 2.516(b)(2)(F).

c. *Service; Numerous defendants.* In actions when the parties are unusually numerous, the court may regulate the service contemplated by the Florida Rules of Judicial Administration on motion or on its own initiative in such manner as may be found to be just and reasonable. FL ST J ADMIN Rule 2.516(c).

d. *Service by clerk.* Service of notices and other documents required to be made by the clerk must also be done as provided in FL ST J ADMIN Rule 2.516(b). FL ST J ADMIN Rule 2.516(g).

G. Hearings

1. *Communication equipment*

a. *Definition.* Communication equipment means a conference telephone or other electronic device that permits all those appearing or participating to hear and speak to each other, provided that all conversation of all parties is audible to all persons present. FL ST J ADMIN Rule 2.530(a).

b. *Use by all parties.* A county or circuit court judge may, upon the court's own motion or upon the written request of a party, direct that communication equipment be used for a motion hearing, pretrial conference, or a status conference. A judge must give notice to the parties and consider any objections they may have to the use of communication equipment before directing that communication equipment be used. The decision to use communication equipment over the objection of parties will be in the sound discretion of the trial court, except as noted below. FL ST J ADMIN Rule 2.530(b).

c. *Use only by requesting party.* A county or circuit court judge may, upon the written request of a party upon reasonable notice to all other parties, permit a requesting party to participate through communication equipment in a scheduled motion hearing; however, any such request (except in criminal, juvenile, and appellate proceedings) must be granted, absent a showing of good cause to deny the same, where the hearing is set for not longer than fifteen (15) minutes. FL ST J ADMIN Rule 2.530(c).

d. *Testimony*

i. *Generally.* A county or circuit court judge, general magistrate, special magistrate, or hearing officer may allow testimony to be taken through communication equipment if all parties consent or if permitted by another applicable rule of procedure. FL ST J ADMIN Rule 2.530(d)(1).

ii. *Procedure.* Any party desiring to present testimony through communication equipment shall, prior to the hearing or trial at which the testimony is to be presented, contact all parties to determine whether each party consents to this form of testimony. The party seeking to present the testimony shall move for permission to present testimony through communication equipment, which motion shall set forth good cause as to why the testimony should be allowed in this form. FL ST J ADMIN Rule 2.530(d)(2).

iii. *Oath.* Testimony may be taken through communication equipment only if a notary public or other person authorized to administer oaths in the witness's jurisdiction is present with the witness and administers the oath consistent with the laws of the jurisdiction. FL ST J ADMIN Rule 2.530(d)(3).

iv. *Confrontation rights.* In juvenile and criminal proceedings the defendant must make an informed waiver of any confrontation rights that may be abridged by the use of communication equipment. FL ST J ADMIN Rule 2.530(d)(4).

v. *Video testimony.* If the testimony to be presented utilizes video conferencing or comparable two-way visual capabilities, the court in its discretion may modify the procedures set forth in FL ST J ADMIN Rule 2.530 to accommodate the technology utilized. FL ST J ADMIN Rule 2.530(d)(5).

e. *Burden of expense.* The cost for the use of the communication equipment is the responsibility of the requesting party unless otherwise directed by the court. FL ST J ADMIN Rule 2.530(e).

H. Forms

1. Official Motion to Compel Discovery Forms for Florida

a. Caption. FL ST RCP Form 1.901.

b. Notice of compliance when constitutional challenge is brought. FL ST RCP Form 1.975.

2. Motion to Compel Discovery Forms for Florida

a. Motion to compel attendance and for sanctions. FL-PP § 3:160.

b. Motion; To compel answer to questions asked on oral examination or written questions. FL-PP § 3:161.

c. Order; Directing deponent to answer questions asked on oral examination; Costs and attorney fees to moving party. FL-PP § 3:162.

d. Order; Compelling answer to written questions. FL-PP § 3:163.

e. Motion; For order finding person in contempt of court; Refusal, after order, to answer question. FL-PP § 3:167.

f. Motion; For order compelling opposing party to pay expenses incurred in proving facts the party refused to admit. FL-PP § 3:168.

g. Motion; Compel discovery, deposition. FL-PRACFORM § 7:37.

h. Motion; Compel discovery, interrogatories. FL-PRACFORM § 7:38.

i. Form for motion to compel answer on deposition. FL-RCPF R 1.380(6).

j. Form for certificate of non-appearance at deposition. FL-RCPF R 1.380(7).

k. Form for notice of motion. FL-RCPF R 1.380(8).

l. Form for order on motion to compel answer. FL-RCPF R 1.380(9).

m. Form for notice and motion to compel. FL-RCPF R 1.380(10).

n. Form for order to compel discovery. FL-RCPF R 1.380(18).

o. Form for order to comply with discovery and answer interrogatories. FL-RCPF R 1.380(19).

3. Official Forms for Florida Circuit Court, Second Judicial Circuit

a. Notice of change of contact information. FL ST 2 J CIR 2007-05.

I. Checklist

(I) ❑ Matters to be considered by moving party

(a) ❑ Required documents

(1) ❑ Notice of hearing/Motion

(2) ❑ Certificate of service

(b) ❑ Supplemental documents

(1) ❑ Proposed order

(2) ❑ Notice of constitutional question

(c) ❑ Time for making motion

(1) ❑ Upon reasonable notice to other parties and all persons affected, a party may apply for an order compelling discovery

(2) ❑ A copy of any written motion which may not be heard ex parte and a copy of the notice of the hearing thereof shall be served a reasonable time before the time specified for the hearing

(II) ❑ Matters to be considered by opposing party

(a) ❑ Required documents

(1) ❑ Response to motion

(2) ❑ Certificate of service

(b) ❑ Supplemental documents

(1) ❑ Proposed order

(2) ❑ Notice of constitutional question

(c) ❑ Time for service and filing of opposition

(1) ❑ No time specified for responding to a motion

Motions, Oppositions and Replies
Motion for Directed Verdict

Document Last Updated January 2013

A. Applicable Rules

1. *State rules*
   a. Motion for a directed verdict. FL ST RCP Rule 1.480.
   b. Rules of court. FL ST RCP Rule 1.010; FL ST J ADMIN Rule 2.110.
   c. Nonverification of pleadings. FL ST RCP Rule 1.030.
   d. Service and filing of pleadings, orders, and documents. FL ST RCP Rule 1.080.
   e. Time. FL ST RCP Rule 1.090.
   f. Pleadings and motions. FL ST RCP Rule 1.100.
   g. Motions. FL ST RCP Rule 1.160.
   h. Relief from judgment, decrees, or orders. FL ST RCP Rule 1.540.
   i. Mediation and arbitration. FL ST RCP Rule 1.700; FL ST RCP Rule 1.710; FL ST RCP Rule 1.720; FL ST RCP Rule 1.730; FL ST RCP Rule 1.750; FL ST RCP Rule 1.800; FL ST RCP Rule 1.810; FL ST RCP Rule 1.820; FL ST RCP Rule 1.830.
   j. Forms. FL ST RCP Rule 1.900.
   k. Minimization of the filing of sensitive information. FL ST J ADMIN Rule 2.425.
   l. Retention of court records. FL ST J ADMIN Rule 2.430.
   m. Foreign attorneys. FL ST J ADMIN Rule 2.510.
   n. Signature of attorneys and parties. FL ST J ADMIN Rule 2.515.
   o. Paper. FL ST J ADMIN Rule 2.520.
   p. Electronic filing. FL ST J ADMIN Rule 2.525.
   q. Accessibility of information and technology. FL ST J ADMIN Rule 2.526.
   r. Communication equipment. FL ST J ADMIN Rule 2.530.
   s. Court reporting. FL ST J ADMIN Rule 2.535.
   t. Requests for accommodations by persons with disabilities. FL ST J ADMIN Rule 2.540.
2. *Local rules*
   a. Notice of change of contact information. FL ST 2 J CIR 2007-05.

B. Timing

1. *Before a verdict is returned.* A directed verdict is available to the defendant at the close of the plaintiff's evidence or to either party at the close of all of the evidence. A verdict may be directed either by the court on its own motion or on the motion of counsel. FL ST RCP Rule 1.480(a); FL-PP § 5:83. The movant should be prepared to argue the motion immediately. FL-PRACPROC § 22:14.
2. *After a verdict is returned.* Within ten (10) days after the return of a verdict, a party who has timely moved for a directed verdict may serve a motion to enter judgment in accordance with the motion for a directed verdict. FL ST RCP Rule 1.480(b).
3. *No verdict is returned.* If a verdict was not returned, a party who has timely moved for a directed verdict may serve a motion for judgment in accordance with the motion for a directed verdict within ten (10) days after discharge of the jury. FL ST RCP Rule 1.480(b).
4. *General motion timing.* A copy of any written motion which may not be heard ex parte and a copy of the notice of the hearing thereof shall be served a reasonable time before the time specified for the hearing. FL ST RCP Rule 1.090(d).

5. *Computation of time*

   a. *Generally.* Computation of time shall be governed by FL ST J ADMIN Rule 2.514. FL ST RCP Rule 1.090(a). The following rules apply in computing time periods specified in any rule of procedure, local rule, court order, or statute that does not specify a method of computing time. FL ST J ADMIN Rule 2.514(a).

      i. *Period stated in days or a longer unit.* When the period is stated in days or a longer unit of time (A) exclude the day of the event that triggers the period; (B) count every day, including intermediate Saturdays, Sundays, and legal holidays; and (C) include the last day of the period, but if the last day is a Saturday, Sunday, or legal holiday, or falls within any period of time extended through an order of the chief justice under FL ST J ADMIN Rule 2.205(a)(2)(B)(iv), the period continues to run until the end of the next day that is not a Saturday, Sunday, or legal holiday and does not fall within any period of time extended through an order of the chief justice. FL ST J ADMIN Rule 2.514(a)(1).

      ii. *Period stated in hours.* When the period is stated in hours (A) begin counting immediately on the occurrence of the event that triggers the period; (B) count every hour, including hours during intermediate Saturdays, Sundays, and legal holidays; and (C) if the period would end on a Saturday, Sunday, or legal holiday, or during any period of time extended through an order of the chief justice under FL ST J ADMIN Rule 2.205(a)(2)(B)(iv), the period continues to run until the same time on the next day that is not a Saturday, Sunday, or legal holiday and does not fall within any period of time extended through an order of the chief justice. FL ST J ADMIN Rule 2.514(a)(2).

      iii. *Period stated in days less than seven (7) days.* When the period stated in days is less than seven (7) days, intermediate Saturdays, Sundays, and legal holidays shall be excluded in the computation. FL ST J ADMIN Rule 2.514(a)(3).

      iv. *"Last day" defined.* Unless a different time is set by a statute, local rule, or court order, the last day ends (A) for electronic filing or for service by any means, at midnight; and (B) for filing by other means, when the clerk's office is scheduled to close. FL ST J ADMIN Rule 2.514(a)(4).

      v. *"Next day" defined.* The "next day" is determined by continuing to count forward when the period is measured after an event and backward when measured before an event. FL ST J ADMIN Rule 2.514(a)(5).

      vi. *"Legal holiday" defined.* "Legal holiday" means (A) the day set aside by FL ST § 110.117, for observing New Year's Day, Martin Luther King, Jr.'s Birthday, Memorial Day, Independence Day, Labor Day, Veterans' Day, Thanksgiving Day, the Friday after Thanksgiving Day, or Christmas Day, and (B) any day observed as a holiday by the clerk's office or as designated by the chief judge. FL ST J ADMIN Rule 2.514(a)(6).

   b. *Additional time after service by mail or e-mail.* When a party may or must act within a specified time after service and service is made by mail or e-mail, five (5) days are added after the period that would otherwise expire under FL ST J ADMIN Rule 2.514(a). FL ST J ADMIN Rule 2.514(b).

   c. *Enlargement.* When an act is required or allowed to be done at or within a specified time by order of court, by the Florida Rules of Civil Procedure, or by notice given thereunder, for cause shown the court at any time in its discretion (1) with or without notice, may order the period enlarged if request therefor is made before the expiration of the period originally prescribed or as extended by a previous order, or (2) upon motion made and notice after the expiration of the specified period, may permit the act to be done when failure to act was the result of excusable neglect, but it may not extend the time for making a motion for new trial, for rehearing, or to alter or amend a judgment; making a motion for relief from a judgment under FL ST RCP Rule 1.540(b); taking an appeal or filing a petition for certiorari; or making a motion for a directed verdict. FL ST RCP Rule 1.090(b).

   d. *Unaffected by expiration of term.* The period of time provided for the doing of any act or the taking of any proceeding shall not be affected or limited by the continued existence or expiration of a term of court. The continued existence or expiration of a term of court in no way affects the power of a court to do any act or take any proceeding in any action which is or has been pending before it. FL ST RCP Rule 1.090(c).

C. General Requirements

1. *Motions generally*

   a. *Contents.* An application to the court for an order shall be by motion which shall be made in writing unless made during a hearing or trial, shall state with particularity the grounds therefor, and shall set forth the relief or order sought. The requirement of writing is fulfilled if the motion is stated in a written notice of the hearing of the motion. All notices of hearing shall specify each motion or other matter to be heard. FL ST RCP Rule 1.100(b).

   b. *Particularity requirement.* The court considers a motion in the light of the substantive law, rule or statute to make its determination. Some rules require a statement of the grounds for a motion under the rule. Failure to give the grounds will result in denial of the motion. This should be the result in all situations when the ground for the motion is not inherent in the rule. FL-PRACPROC § 9:3. The requirement is nevertheless an important one, first because of the due process notice rights of the respondent, as well as for the assistance it provides to the court in its preparation for the hearing or, absent a hearing, for disposition. 4 FLPRAC R 1.100.

2. *Motion for directed verdict*

   a. *Effect of a motion for directed verdict.* A party who moves for a directed verdict at the close of the evidence offered by the adverse party may offer evidence in the event the motion is denied without having reserved the right to do so and to the same extent as if the motion had not been made. The denial of a motion for a directed verdict shall not operate to discharge the jury. A motion for a directed verdict shall state the specific grounds therefor. The order directing a verdict is effective without any assent of the jury. FL ST RCP Rule 1.480(a).

   b. *Reservation of decision on motion.* When a motion for a directed verdict is denied or for any reason is not granted, the court is deemed to have submitted the action to the jury subject to a later determination of the legal questions raised by the motion. Within ten (10) days after the return of a verdict, a party who has timely moved for a directed verdict may serve a motion to set aside the verdict and any judgment entered thereon and to enter judgment in accordance with the motion for a directed verdict. If a verdict was not returned, a party who has timely moved for a directed verdict may serve a motion for judgment in accordance with the motion for a directed verdict within ten (10) days after discharge of the jury. FL ST RCP Rule 1.480(b).

   c. *Joined with motion for new trial.* A motion for a new trial may be joined with a motion for directed verdict or a new trial may be requested in the alternative. If a verdict was returned, the court may allow the judgment to stand or may reopen the judgment and either order a new trial or direct the entry of judgment as if the requested verdict had been directed. If no verdict was returned, the court may direct the entry of judgment as if the requested verdict had been directed or may order a new trial. FL ST RCP Rule 1.480(c).

   d. *General procedures on a motion for directed verdict*

      i. *Proper method.* The proper method of advocating that a party is entitled to prevail on a claim or defense as a matter of law is to make a motion for a directed verdict at the close of the evidence offered by the opposing party. The trial judge has authority to direct a verdict in favor of one party and against another, without submitting the case to the jury, if there is no other verdict the jury could lawfully return. 5 FLPRAC § 22:5.

      ii. *Directed verdict only in a jury trial.* A motion for directed verdict is proper only in a jury trial. The equivalent motion in nonjury trial is called a motion for involuntary dismissal. 5 FLPRAC § 22:5.

      iii. *Test for the sufficiency of the evidence.* A motion for directed verdict is used primarily to test the sufficiency of the evidence offered in support of a claim or defense. It may also be used to raise legal issues other than the sufficiency of the evidence, but that is less common because most pure issues of law can be resolved on a motion to dismiss or a motion for summary judgment before the case is set for trial. If there is no evidence to support a claim or defense, the trial judge has a duty to direct a verdict for the opposing party on that claim or defense. 5 FLPRAC § 22:5.

         - The trial judge must view all of the facts and factual inferences in a light most favorable to the party opposing the motion. 5 FLPRAC § 22:5.

- The rule has often been stated by the Florida courts in the negative, that is, a motion for directed verdict should not be granted unless the court, after viewing the evidence and testimony in the light most favorable to the nonmoving party, determines that no reasonable jury could render a verdict for the nonmoving party. Under this rule, the trial judge may not direct a verdict against a party if there is any evidence upon which the jury could lawfully make a finding in favor of that party. 5 FLPRAC § 22:5.

3. *Arbitration and mediation*
   a. *Referral to arbitration and mediation.* Except as hereinafter provided or as otherwise prohibited by law, the presiding judge may enter an order referring all or any part of a contested civil matter to mediation or arbitration. The parties to any contested civil matter may file a written stipulation to mediate or arbitrate any issue between them at any time. Such stipulation shall be incorporated into the order of referral. FL ST RCP Rule 1.700(a).
   b. *Arbitration*
      i. *Exclusions.* A civil action shall be ordered to arbitration or arbitration in conjunction with mediation upon stipulation of the parties. A civil action may be ordered to arbitration or arbitration in conjunction with mediation upon motion of any party or by the court, if the judge determines the action to be of such a nature that arbitration could be of benefit to the litigants or the court. FL ST RCP Rule 1.800.
         - Under no circumstances may the following categories of actions be referred to arbitration: (1) bond estreatures; (2) habeas corpus or other extraordinary writs; (3) bond validations; (4) civil or criminal contempt; (5) such other matters as may be specified by order of the chief judge in the circuit. FL ST RCP Rule 1.800.
      ii. For more information regarding arbitration, please see FL ST RCP Rule 1.810; FL ST RCP Rule 1.820; FL ST RCP Rule 1.830.
   c. *Mediation.* For more information regarding mediation, please see FL ST RCP Rule 1.710; FL ST RCP Rule 1.720; FL ST RCP Rule 1.730; and FL ST RCP Rule 1.750.
4. *Rules of court*
   a. *Rules of civil procedure.* The Florida Rules of Civil Procedure apply to all actions of a civil nature and all special statutory proceedings in the circuit courts and county courts except those to which the Florida Probate Rules, the Florida Family Law Rules of Procedure, or the Small Claims Rules apply. FL ST RCP Rule 1.010.
      i. The form, content, procedure, and time for pleading in all special statutory proceedings shall be as prescribed by the statutes governing the proceeding unless the Florida Rules of Civil Procedure specifically provide to the contrary. FL ST RCP Rule 1.010.
      ii. The Florida Rules of Civil Procedure shall be construed to secure the just, speedy, and inexpensive determination of every action. FL ST RCP Rule 1.010.
   b. *Rules of judicial administration.* The Florida Rules of Judicial Administration shall apply to administrative matters in all courts to which the Florida Rules of Judicial Administration are applicable by their terms. The Florida Rules of Judicial Administration shall be construed to secure the speedy and inexpensive determination of every proceeding to which they are applicable. The Florida Rules of Judicial Administration shall supersede all conflicting rules and statutes. FL ST J ADMIN Rule 2.110.
5. *Notice of change of contact information.* The Clerk shall provide a change of address and/or telephone number form for use by attorneys and pro se litigants. With any change of address and/or telephone number, attorneys and pro se litigants governed by FL ST J ADMIN Rule 2.515 will provide to the Clerk and all parties promptly the change of address and/or telephone number form. This form should be submitted only once to the Clerk, who will then make the address and/or telephone number change in all court divisions. FL ST 2 J CIR 2007-05.

D. Documents

1. *Required documents*
   a. *Notice of hearing/Motion.* An application to the court for an order shall be by motion which shall be

made in writing unless made during a hearing or trial, shall state with particularity the grounds therefor, and shall set forth the relief or order sought. The requirement of writing is fulfilled if the motion is stated in a written notice of the hearing of the motion. All notices of hearing shall specify each motion or other matter to be heard. FL ST RCP Rule 1.100(b).

i. *Notices to persons with disabilities.* See the Format section of this KeyRules document for further information.

b. *Certificate of service.* When any attorney certifies in substance: "I certify that a copy hereof has been furnished to (here insert name or names and addresses used for service) by (e-mail) (delivery) (mail) (fax) on .... (date) ....________________ Attorney" the certificate is taken as prima facie proof of such service in compliance with FL ST J ADMIN Rule 2.516. FL ST J ADMIN Rule 2.516(f).

2. *Supplemental documents*

a. *Proposed order.* The court may require that orders or judgments be prepared by a party, may require the party to furnish the court with stamped, addressed envelopes for service of the order or judgment, and may require that proposed orders and judgments be furnished to all parties before entry by the court of the order or judgment. FL ST J ADMIN Rule 2.516(h)(1).

b. *Notice of constitutional question.* A party that files a pleading, written motion, or other paper drawing into question the constitutionality of a state statute or a county or municipal charter, ordinance, or franchise must promptly (1) file a notice of constitutional question stating the question and identifying the paper that raises it; and (2) serve the notice and the pleading, written motion, or other paper drawing into question the constitutionality of a state statute or a county or municipal charter, ordinance, or franchise on the Attorney General or the state attorney of the judicial circuit in which the action is pending, by either certified or registered mail. Service of the notice and pleading, written motion, or other paper does not require joinder of the Attorney General or the state attorney as a party to the action. FL ST RCP Rule 1.071.

E. Format

1. *Documents; Type and size.* Documents subject to the exceptions set forth in FL ST J ADMIN Rule 2.525(d) shall be filed on recycled paper measuring eight and one half by eleven (8 1/2 by 11) inches. For purposes of FL ST J ADMIN Rule 2.520, paper is recycled if it contains a minimum content of fifty (50) percent waste paper. Xerographic reduction of legal-size (eight and one half by fourteen (8 1/2 by 14) inches) documents to letter size (eight and one half by eleven (8 1/2 by 11) inches) is prohibited. All other documents filed by electronic transmission shall be filed in a format capable of being printed in a format consistent with the provisions of FL ST J ADMIN Rule 2.250. FL ST J ADMIN Rule 2.520(b).

a. *Exhibits.* Any exhibit or attachment filed with pleadings or papers may be filed in its original size. FL ST J ADMIN Rule 2.520(c).

b. *Recording space.* On all papers and documents prepared and filed by the court or by any party to a proceeding which are to be recorded in the public records of any county, including but not limited to final money judgments and notices of lis pendens, a three (3) inch by three (3) inch space at the top right-hand corner on the first page and a one (1) inch by three (3) inch space at the top right-hand corner on each subsequent page shall be left blank and reserved for use by the clerk of court. FL ST J ADMIN Rule 2.520(d).

i. *Exceptions to recording space.* Any papers or documents created by persons or entities over which the filing party has no control, including but not limited to wills, codicils, trusts, or other testamentary documents; documents prepared or executed by any public officer; documents prepared, executed, acknowledged, or proved outside of the State of Florida; or documents created by State or Federal government agencies, may be filed without the space required by FL ST J ADMIN Rule 2.520. FL ST J ADMIN Rule 2.520(e).

c. *Noncompliance.* No clerk of court is permitted to refuse to file any document or paper because of noncompliance with the Florida Rules of Judicial Administration. However, upon request of the clerk of court, noncomplying documents must be resubmitted in accordance with the formatting rules. FL ST J ADMIN Rule 2.520(f).

2. *Caption.* Every pleading, motion, order, judgment, or other paper shall have a caption containing the

name of the court, the file number, and except for in rem proceedings, including forfeiture proceedings, the name of the first party on each side with an appropriate indication of other parties, and a designation identifying the party filing it and its nature or the nature of the order, as the case may be. In any in rem proceeding, every pleading, motion, order, judgment, or other paper shall have a caption containing the name of the court, the file number, the style "In re" (followed by the name or general description of the property), and a designation of the person or entity filing it and its nature or the nature of the order, as the case may be. In an in rem forfeiture proceeding, the style shall be "In re forfeiture of" (followed by the name of the general description of the property). All papers filed in the action shall be styled in such a manner as to indicate clearly the subject matter of the paper and the party requesting or obtaining relief. FL ST RCP Rule 1.100(c)(1).

3. *Writing and written defined.* Writing or written means a document containing information, an application, or a stipulation. FL ST RCP Rule 1.080(c).
4. *Rule abbreviations*
   a. The Florida Rules of Civil Procedure and shall be abbreviated as Fla.R.Civ.P. FL ST RCP Rule 1.010.
   b. The Florida Rules of Judicial Administration shall be abbreviated as Fla. R. Jud. Admin. FL ST J ADMIN Rule 2.110.
5. *Nonverification.* Except when otherwise specifically provided by the Florida Rules of Civil Procedure or an applicable statute, every pleading or other document of a party represented by an attorney need not be verified or accompanied by an affidavit. FL ST RCP Rule 1.030; FL ST J ADMIN Rule 2.515(a).
6. *Attorney signature*
   a. *Attorney signature.* Every pleading and other document of a party represented by an attorney shall be signed by at least one (1) attorney of record in that attorney's individual name whose current record Florida Bar address, telephone number, including area code, primary e-mail address and secondary e-mail addresses, if any, and Florida Bar number shall be stated, and who shall be duly licensed to practice law in Florida or who shall have received permission to appear in the particular case as provided in FL ST J ADMIN Rule 2.510. FL ST J ADMIN Rule 2.515(a).
      i. The attorney may be required by the court to give the address of, and to vouch for the attorney's authority to represent, the party. FL ST J ADMIN Rule 2.515(a).
      ii. The signature of an attorney shall constitute a certificate by the attorney that the attorney has read the pleading or other document; that to the best of the attorney's knowledge, information, and belief there is good ground to support it; and that it is not interposed for delay. FL ST J ADMIN Rule 2.515(a).
      iii. If a pleading is not signed or is signed with intent to defeat the purpose of FL ST J ADMIN Rule 2.515, it may be stricken and the action may proceed as though the pleading or other document had not been served. FL ST J ADMIN Rule 2.515(a).
   b. *Pro se litigant signature.* A party who is not represented by an attorney shall sign any pleading or other paper and state the party's address and telephone number, including area code. FL ST J ADMIN Rule 2.515(b).
   c. *Form of signature*
      i. The signatures required on pleadings and documents by FL ST J ADMIN Rule 2.515(a) and FL ST J ADMIN Rule 2.515(b) may be:
         - Original signatures;
         - Original signatures that have been reproduced by electronic means, such as on electronically transmitted documents or photocopied documents;
         - Electronic signatures using the "/s/," "s/," or "/s" formats by or at the direction of the person signing; or
         - Any other signature format authorized by general law, so long as the clerk where the proceeding is pending has the capability of receiving and has obtained approval from the

Supreme Court of Florida to accept pleadings and documents with that signature format. FL ST J ADMIN Rule 2.515(c)(1).

ii. An attorney, party, or other person who files a pleading or paper by electronic transmission that does not contain the original signature of that attorney, party, or other person shall file that identical pleading or paper in paper form containing an original signature of that attorney, party, or other person (hereinafter called the follow-up filing) immediately thereafter. The follow-up filing is not required if the Supreme Court of Florida has entered an order directing the clerk of court to discontinue accepting the follow-up filing. FL ST J ADMIN Rule 2.515(c)(2).

7. *Forms*

a. *Process.* The forms of process, notice of lis pendens, and notice of action provided in the Florida Rules of Civil Procedure are sufficient. Variations from the forms do not void process or notices that are otherwise sufficient. FL ST RCP Rule 1.900(a).

b. *Other forms.* The other forms provided in the Florida Rules of Civil Procedure are sufficient for the matters that are covered by them. So long as the substance is expressed without prolixity, the forms may be varied to meet the facts of a particular case. FL ST RCP Rule 1.900(b).

c. *Formal matters.* Captions, except for the designation of the paper, are omitted from the forms provided in the Florida Rules of Civil Procedure. A general form of caption is the first form provided. Signatures are omitted from pleadings and motions. FL ST RCP Rule 1.900(c).

8. *Notices to persons with disabilities.* All notices of court proceedings to be held in a public facility, and all process compelling appearance at such proceedings, shall include the following statement in bold face, fourteen (14) point Times New Roman or Courier font: "If you are a person with a disability who needs any accommodation in order to participate in this proceeding, you are entitled, at no cost to you, to the provision of certain assistance. Please contact [identify applicable court personnel by name, address, and telephone number] at least seven (7) days before your scheduled court appearance, or immediately upon receiving this notification if the time before the scheduled appearance is less than seven (7) days; if you are hearing or voice impaired, call 711." FL ST J ADMIN Rule 2.540(c)(1).

9. *Minimization of the filing of sensitive information*

a. *Limitations for court filings.* Unless authorized by FL ST J ADMIN Rule 2.425(b), statute, another rule of court, or the court orders otherwise, designated sensitive information filed with the court must be limited to the following format:

i. The initials of a person known to be a minor;

ii. The year of birth of a person's birth date;

iii. No portion of any: Social security number, Bank account number, Credit card account number, Charge account number, or Debit account number;

iv. The last four digits of any: Taxpayer identification number (TIN), Employee identification number, Driver's license number, Passport number, Telephone number, Financial account number, except as set forth in FL ST J ADMIN Rule 2.425(a)(3), Brokerage account number, Insurance policy account number, Loan account number, Customer account number, or Patient or health care number;

v. A truncated version of any: Email address, Computer user name, Password, or Personal identification number (PIN); and

vi. A truncated version of any other sensitive information as provided by court order. FL ST J ADMIN Rule 2.425(a).

b. *Exceptions.* FL ST J ADMIN Rule 2.425(a) does not apply to the following:

i. An account number which identifies the property alleged to be the subject of a proceeding;

ii. The record of an administrative or agency proceeding;

iii. The record in appellate or review proceedings;

iv. The birth date of a minor whenever the birth date is necessary for the court to establish or maintain subject matter jurisdiction;

v. The name of a minor in any order relating to parental responsibility, time-sharing, or child support;

vi. The name of a minor in any document or order affecting the minor's ownership of real property;

vii. The birth date of a party in a writ of attachment or notice to payor;

viii. In traffic and criminal proceedings: a pro se filing; a court filing that is related to a criminal matter or investigation and that is prepared before the filing of a criminal charge or is not filed as part of any docketed criminal case; an arrest or search warrant or any information in support thereof; a charging document and an affidavit or other documents filed in support of any charging document, including any driving records; a statement of particulars; discovery material introduced into evidence or otherwise filed with the court; and all information necessary for the proper issuance and execution of a subpoena duces tecum;

ix. Information used by the clerk for case maintenance purposes or the courts for case management purposes; and

x. Information which is relevant and material to an issue before the court. FL ST J ADMIN Rule 2.425(b).

c. *Remedies.* Upon motion by a party or interested person or sua sponte by the court, the court may order remedies, sanctions or both for a violation of FL ST J ADMIN Rule 2.425(a). Following notice and an opportunity to respond, the court may impose sanctions if such filing was not made in good faith. FL ST J ADMIN Rule 2.425(c).

d. *Motions not restricted.* FL ST J ADMIN Rule 2.425 does not restrict a party's right to move for protective order, to move to file documents under seal, or to request a determination of the confidentiality of records. FL ST J ADMIN Rule 2.425(d).

e. *Application.* FL ST J ADMIN Rule 2.425 does not affect the application of constitutional provisions, statutes, or rules of court regarding confidential information or access to public information. FL ST J ADMIN Rule 2.425(e).

F. Filing and Service Requirements

1. *Filing requirements.* All original documents must be filed with the court either before service or immediately thereafter, unless otherwise provided for by general law or other rules. If the original of any bond or other document is not placed in the court file, a certified copy must be so placed by the clerk. FL ST J ADMIN Rule 2.516(d). All documents shall be filed in conformity with the requirements of FL ST J ADMIN Rule 2.525. FL ST RCP Rule 1.080(b). All documents filed in any court shall be filed by electronic transmission in accordance with FL ST J ADMIN Rule 2.525. "Documents" means pleadings, motions, petitions, memoranda, briefs, notices, exhibits, declarations, affidavits, orders, judgments, decrees, writs, opinions, and any other paper or writing submitted to a court. FL ST J ADMIN Rule 2.520(a). All documents that are court records, as defined in FL ST J ADMIN Rule 2.430(a)(1), must be filed by electronic transmission, provided that: (1) the clerk has the ability to accept and retain such documents; (2) the clerk or the chief judge of the circuit has requested permission to accept documents filed by electronic transmission; and (3) the supreme court has entered an order granting permission to the clerk to accept documents filed by electronic transmission. FL ST J ADMIN Rule 2.525(c)(1).

a. *Definition.* "Electronic transmission of documents" means the sending of information by electronic signals to, by or from a court or clerk, which when received can be transformed and stored or transmitted on paper, microfilm, magnetic storage device, optical imaging system, CD-ROM, flash drive, other electronic data storage system, server, case maintenance system ("CM"), electronic court filing ("ECF") system, statewide or local electronic portal ("e-portal"), or other electronic record keeping system authorized by the supreme court in a format sufficient to communicate the information on the original document in a readable format. Electronic transmission of documents includes electronic mail ("e-mail") and any internet-based transmission procedure, and may include procedures allowing for documents to be signed or verified by electronic means. FL ST J ADMIN Rule 2.525(a).

i. The filing of documents with the court as required by the Florida Rules of Judicial Administration must be made by filing them with the clerk in accordance with FL ST J ADMIN Rule

2.525, except that the judge may permit documents to be filed with the judge, in which event the judge must note the filing date before him or her on the documents and transmit them to the clerk. The date of filing is that shown on the face of the document by the judge's notation or the clerk's time stamp, whichever is earlier. FL ST J ADMIN Rule 2.516(e).

b. *Application.* Any court or clerk of the court may accept the electronic transmission of documents for filing after the clerk, together with input from the chief judge of the circuit, has obtained approval of the procedures and program for doing so from the Supreme Court of Florida. FL ST J ADMIN Rule 2.525(b).

c. *Exceptions*

i. Paper documents and other submissions may be manually submitted to the clerk or court:

- When the clerk does not have the ability to accept and retain documents by electronic filing or has not had ECF Procedures approved by the supreme court;
- For filing by any self-represented party or any self-represented nonparty unless specific ECF Procedures provide a means to file documents electronically. However, any self-represented nonparty that is a governmental or public agency and any other agency, partnership, corporation, or business entity acting on behalf of any governmental or public agency may file documents by electronic transmission if such entity has the capability of filing documents electronically;
- For filing by attorneys excused from e-mail service in accordance with FL ST J ADMIN Rule 2.516(b);
- When submitting evidentiary exhibits or filing non-documentary materials;
- When the filing involves documents in excess of twenty-five (25) megabytes (25MB) in size. For such filings, documents may be transmitted using an electronic storage medium that the clerk has the ability to accept, which may include a CD-ROM, flash drive, or similar storage medium;
- When filed in open court, as permitted by the court;
- When paper filing is permitted by any approved statewide or local ECF procedures; and
- If any court determines that justice so requires. FL ST J ADMIN Rule 2.525(d).

ii. Any document in paper form submitted under FL ST J ADMIN Rule 2.525(d) is filed when it is received by the clerk or court and the clerk shall immediately thereafter convert any filed paper document to an electronic document. "Convert to an electronic document" means optically capturing an image of a paper document and using character recognition software to recover as much of the document's text as practicable and then indexing and storing the document in the official court file. FL ST J ADMIN Rule 2.525(c)(4).

iii. Any storage medium submitted under FL ST J ADMIN Rule 2.525(d)(5) is filed when received by the clerk or court and the clerk shall immediately thereafter transfer the electronic documents from the storage device to the official court file. FL ST J ADMIN Rule 2.525(c)(5).

iv. If the filer of any paper document authorized under FL ST J ADMIN Rule 2.525(d) provides a self-addressed, postage-paid envelope for return of the paper document after it is converted to electronic form by the clerk, the clerk shall place the paper document in the envelope and deposit it in the mail. Except when a paper document is required to be maintained, the clerk may recycle any filed paper document that is not to be returned to the filer. FL ST J ADMIN Rule 2.525(c)(6).

v. The clerk may convert any paper document filed before the effective date of FL ST J ADMIN Rule 2.525 to an electronic document. Unless the clerk is required to maintain the paper document, if the paper document has been converted to an electronic document by the clerk, the paper document is no longer part of the official court file and may be removed and recycled. FL ST J ADMIN Rule 2.525(c)(7).

d. *Official court file.* For information on what constitutes the official court file, please see FL ST J ADMIN Rule 2.525(c)(2), FL ST J ADMIN Rule 2.525(c)(3).

e. *Administration.* All attorneys, parties, or other persons using this rule to file documents are required to make arrangements with the court or clerk for the payment of any charges authorized by general law or the supreme court before filing any document by electronic transmission. FL ST J ADMIN Rule 2.525(f)(2).

f. *Filing date.* The filing date for an electronically transmitted document is the date and time that such filing is acknowledged by an electronic stamp or otherwise, pursuant to any procedure set forth in any ECF Procedures approved by the supreme court, or the date the last page of such filing is received by the court or clerk. FL ST J ADMIN Rule 2.525(f)(3).

g. *Accessibility.* All documents transmitted in any electronic form under FL ST J ADMIN Rule 2.525 must comply with the accessibility requirements of FL ST J ADMIN Rule 2.526. FL ST J ADMIN Rule 2.525(g).

2. *Service requirements.* Every pleading subsequent to the initial pleading, all orders, and every other document filed in the action must be served in conformity with the requirements of FL ST J ADMIN Rule 2.516. FL ST RCP Rule 1.080(a).

a. *Service; When required.* Unless the court otherwise orders, or a statute or supreme court administrative order specifies a different means of service, every pleading subsequent to the initial pleading and every other document filed in any court proceeding, except applications for witness subpoenas and documents served by formal notice or required to be served in the manner provided for service of formal notice, must be served in accordance with FL ST J ADMIN Rule 2.516 on each party. No service need be made on parties against whom a default has been entered, except that pleadings asserting new or additional claims against them must be served in the manner provided for service of summons. FL ST J ADMIN Rule 2.516(a).

b. *Service; How made.* When service is required or permitted to be made upon a party represented by an attorney, service must be made upon the attorney unless service upon the party is ordered by the court. FL ST J ADMIN Rule 2.516(b).

i. *Service by electronic mail ("e-mail").* All documents required or permitted to be served on another party must be served by e-mail, unless FL ST J ADMIN Rule 2.516 otherwise provides. When, in addition to service by e-mail, the sender also utilizes another means of service provided for in FL ST J ADMIN Rule 2.516(b)(2), any differing time limits and other provisions applicable to that other means of service control. FL ST J ADMIN Rule 2.516(b)(1). Any document electronically transmitted to a court or clerk must also be served on all parties and interested persons in accordance with the applicable rules of court. FL ST J ADMIN Rule 2.525(e)(2).

- *Service on attorneys.* Upon appearing in a proceeding, an attorney must serve a designation of a primary e-mail address and may designate no more than two (2) secondary e-mail addresses. Thereafter, service must be directed to all designated e-mail addresses in that proceeding. Every document filed by an attorney thereafter must include the primary e-mail address of that attorney and any secondary e-mail addresses. If an attorney does not designate any e-mail address for service, documents may be served on that attorney at the e-mail address on record with The Florida Bar. FL ST J ADMIN Rule 2.516(b)(1)(A).

- *Exception to e-mail service on attorneys.* Service by an attorney on another attorney must be made by e-mail unless excused by the court. Upon motion by an attorney demonstrating that the attorney has no e-mail account and lacks access to the Internet at the attorney's office, the court may excuse the attorney from the requirements of e-mail service. Service on and by an attorney excused by the court from e-mail service must be by the means provided in FL ST J ADMIN Rule 2.516(b)(2). FL ST J ADMIN Rule 2.516(b)(1)(B).

- *Service on and by parties not represented by an attorney.* Any party not represented by an attorney may serve a designation of a primary e-mail address and also may designate no more than two (2) secondary e-mail addresses to which service must be directed in that proceeding by the means provided in FL ST J ADMIN Rule 2.516(b)(1). If a party not represented by an attorney does not designate an e-mail address for service in a proceeding, service on and by that party must be by the means provided in FL ST J ADMIN Rule 2.516(b)(2). FL ST J ADMIN Rule 2.516(b)(1)(C).

- *Time of service.* Service by e-mail is complete when it is sent. FL ST J ADMIN Rule 2.516(b)(1)(D). An e-mail is deemed served on the date it is sent. FL ST J ADMIN Rule 2.516(b)(1)(D)(i). If the sender learns that the e-mail did not reach the address of the person to be served, the sender must immediately send another copy by e-mail, or by a means authorized by FL ST J ADMIN Rule 2.516(b)(2). FL ST J ADMIN Rule 2.516(b)(1)(D)(ii). E-mail service is treated as service by mail for the computation of time. FL ST J ADMIN Rule 2.516(b)(1)(D)(iii).

ii. *Format of e-mail for service.* Service of a document by e-mail is made by attaching a copy of the document in PDF format to an e-mail sent to all addresses designated by the attorney or party. FL ST J ADMIN Rule 2.516(b)(1)(E).

- All documents served by e-mail must be attached to an e-mail message containing a subject line beginning with the words "SERVICE OF COURT DOCUMENT" in all capital letters, followed by the case number of the proceeding in which the documents are being served. FL ST J ADMIN Rule 2.516(b)(1)(E)(i).
- The body of the e-mail must identify the court in which the proceeding is pending, the case number, the name of the initial party on each side, the title of each document served with that e-mail, and the sender's name and telephone number. FL ST J ADMIN Rule 2.516(b)(1)(E)(ii).
- Any document served by e-mail may be signed by the "/s/" format, as long as the filed original is signed in accordance with the applicable rule of procedure. FL ST J ADMIN Rule 2.516(b)(1)(E)(iii).
- Any e-mail which, together with its attached documents, exceeds five megabytes (5MB) in size, must be divided and sent as separate e-mails, no one of which may exceed five megabytes (5MB) in size and each of which must be sequentially numbered in the subject line. FL ST J ADMIN Rule 2.516(b)(1)(E)(iv).

iii. *Service by other means.* In addition to, and not in lieu of, service by e-mail, service may also be made upon attorneys by any of the means specified in FL ST J ADMIN Rule 2.516(b)(2). Service on and by all parties who are not represented by an attorney and who do not designate an e-mail address, and on and by all attorneys excused from e-mail service, must be made by delivering a copy of the document or by mailing it to the party or attorney at their last known address or, if no address is known, by leaving it with the clerk of the court. Service by mail is complete upon mailing. Delivery of a copy within FL ST J ADMIN Rule 2.516 is complete upon:

- Handing it to the attorney or to the party,
- Leaving it at the attorney's or party's office with a clerk or other person in charge thereof,
- If there is no one in charge, leaving it in a conspicuous place therein,
- If the office is closed or the person to be served has no office, leaving it at the person's usual place of abode with some person of his or her family above fifteen (15) years of age and informing such person of the contents, or
- Transmitting it by facsimile to the attorney's or party's office with a cover sheet containing the sender's name, firm, address, telephone number, and facsimile number, and the number of pages transmitted. When service is made by facsimile, a copy must also be served by any other method permitted by FL ST J ADMIN Rule 2.516. Facsimile service occurs when transmission is complete. FL ST J ADMIN Rule 2.516(b)(2)(A) through FL ST J ADMIN Rule 2.516(b)(2)(E).
- Service by delivery after 5:00 p.m. must be deemed to have been made by mailing on the date of delivery. FL ST J ADMIN Rule 2.516(b)(2)(F).

c. *Service; Numerous defendants.* In actions when the parties are unusually numerous, the court may regulate the service contemplated by the Florida Rules of Judicial Administration on motion or on its own initiative in such manner as may be found to be just and reasonable. FL ST J ADMIN Rule 2.516(c).

d. *Service by clerk.* Service of notices and other documents required to be made by the clerk must also be done as provided in FL ST J ADMIN Rule 2.516(b). FL ST J ADMIN Rule 2.516(g).

G. Hearings

1. *Communication equipment*

a. *Definition.* Communication equipment means a conference telephone or other electronic device that permits all those appearing or participating to hear and speak to each other, provided that all conversation of all parties is audible to all persons present. FL ST J ADMIN Rule 2.530(a).

b. *Use by all parties.* A county or circuit court judge may, upon the court's own motion or upon the written request of a party, direct that communication equipment be used for a motion hearing, pretrial conference, or a status conference. A judge must give notice to the parties and consider any objections they may have to the use of communication equipment before directing that communication equipment be used. The decision to use communication equipment over the objection of parties will be in the sound discretion of the trial court, except as noted below. FL ST J ADMIN Rule 2.530(b).

c. *Use only by requesting party.* A county or circuit court judge may, upon the written request of a party upon reasonable notice to all other parties, permit a requesting party to participate through communication equipment in a scheduled motion hearing; however, any such request (except in criminal, juvenile, and appellate proceedings) must be granted, absent a showing of good cause to deny the same, where the hearing is set for not longer than fifteen (15) minutes. FL ST J ADMIN Rule 2.530(c).

d. *Testimony*

i. *Generally.* A county or circuit court judge, general magistrate, special magistrate, or hearing officer may allow testimony to be taken through communication equipment if all parties consent or if permitted by another applicable rule of procedure. FL ST J ADMIN Rule 2.530(d)(1).

ii. *Procedure.* Any party desiring to present testimony through communication equipment shall, prior to the hearing or trial at which the testimony is to be presented, contact all parties to determine whether each party consents to this form of testimony. The party seeking to present the testimony shall move for permission to present testimony through communication equipment, which motion shall set forth good cause as to why the testimony should be allowed in this form. FL ST J ADMIN Rule 2.530(d)(2).

iii. *Oath.* Testimony may be taken through communication equipment only if a notary public or other person authorized to administer oaths in the witness's jurisdiction is present with the witness and administers the oath consistent with the laws of the jurisdiction. FL ST J ADMIN Rule 2.530(d)(3).

iv. *Confrontation rights.* In juvenile and criminal proceedings the defendant must make an informed waiver of any confrontation rights that may be abridged by the use of communication equipment. FL ST J ADMIN Rule 2.530(d)(4).

v. *Video testimony.* If the testimony to be presented utilizes video conferencing or comparable two-way visual capabilities, the court in its discretion may modify the procedures set forth in FL ST J ADMIN Rule 2.530 to accommodate the technology utilized. FL ST J ADMIN Rule 2.530(d)(5).

e. *Burden of expense.* The cost for the use of the communication equipment is the responsibility of the requesting party unless otherwise directed by the court. FL ST J ADMIN Rule 2.530(e).

H. Forms

1. Official Motion for Directed Verdict Forms for Florida

a. Caption. FL ST RCP Form 1.901.

b. Notice of compliance when constitutional challenge is brought. FL ST RCP Form 1.975.

2. Motion for Directed Verdict Forms for Florida

a. Motion; For directed verdict; At close of adverse party's evidence. FL-PP § 5:86.

b. Motion; For directed verdict; At close of all of evidence. FL-PP § 5:87.

c. Motion; Request to go to jury if motions by both parties are denied. FL-PP § 5:88.

d. Order; Granting defendant's motion for directed verdict; Insufficiency of plaintiff's evidence. FL-PP § 5:89.

e. Motion; Directed verdict, renewed. FL-PRACFORM § 7:62.

f. Form for motion for directed verdict at close of plaintiff's case. FL-RCPF R 1.480(24).

g. Form for motion for directed verdict at close of defendant's case. FL-RCPF R 1.480(25).

h. Form for motion to set aside verdict and enter directed verdict. FL-RCPF R 1.480(26).

3. Official Forms for Florida Circuit Court, Second Judicial Circuit

a. Notice of change of contact information. FL ST 2 J CIR 2007-05.

I. Checklist

(I) ❑ Matters to be considered by moving party

(a) ❑ Required documents

(1) ❑ Notice of hearing/Motion

(2) ❑ Certificate of service

(b) ❑ Supplemental documents

(1) ❑ Proposed order

(2) ❑ Notice of constitutional question

(c) ❑ Time for making motion

(1) ❑ Before a verdict is returned - A directed verdict is available to the defendant at the close of the plaintiff's evidence or to either party at the close of all of the evidence

(2) ❑ After a verdict is returned - Within ten (10) days after the return of a verdict, a party who has timely moved for a directed verdict may serve a motion to enter judgment in accordance with the motion for a directed verdict

(3) ❑ No verdict is returned - If a verdict was not returned, a party who has timely moved for a directed verdict may serve a motion for judgment in accordance with the motion for a directed verdict within ten (10) days after discharge of the jury

(4) ❑ General motion timing - A copy of any written motion which may not be heard ex parte and a copy of the notice of the hearing thereof shall be served a reasonable time before the time specified for the hearing

(II) ❑ Matters to be considered by opposing party

(a) ❑ Required documents

(1) ❑ Response to motion

(2) ❑ Certificate of service

(b) ❑ Supplemental documents

(1) ❑ Proposed order

(2) ❑ Notice of constitutional question

(c) ❑ Time for service and filing of opposition

(1) ❑ No time specified for responding to a motion

Requests, Notices and Applications
Request for Production of Documents

Document Last Updated January 2013

A. Applicable Rules

1. *State rules*
   a. Nonverification of pleadings. FL ST RCP Rule 1.030.
   b. Service and filing of pleadings, orders, and documents. FL ST RCP Rule 1.080.
   c. Time. FL ST RCP Rule 1.090.
   d. Pleadings and motions. FL ST RCP Rule 1.100.
   e. Pretrial procedure. FL ST RCP Rule 1.200.
   f. General provisions governing discovery. FL ST RCP Rule 1.280.
   g. Depositions upon oral examination. FL ST RCP Rule 1.310.
   h. Interrogatories to parties. FL ST RCP Rule 1.340.
   i. Production of documents and things and entry upon land for inspection and other purposes. FL ST RCP Rule 1.350.
   j. Production of documents and things without deposition. FL ST RCP Rule 1.351.
   k. Examination of persons. FL ST RCP Rule 1.360.
   l. Requests for admission. FL ST RCP Rule 1.370.
   m. Failure to make discovery; Sanctions. FL ST RCP Rule 1.380.
   n. Depositions of expert witnesses. FL ST RCP Rule 1.390.
   o. Relief from judgment, decrees, or orders. FL ST RCP Rule 1.540.
   p. Forms. FL ST RCP Rule 1.900.
   q. Minimization of the filing of sensitive information. FL ST J ADMIN Rule 2.425.
   r. Retention of court records. FL ST J ADMIN Rule 2.430.
   s. Foreign attorneys. FL ST J ADMIN Rule 2.510.
   t. Signature of attorneys and parties. FL ST J ADMIN Rule 2.515.
   u. Paper. FL ST J ADMIN Rule 2.520.
   v. Electronic filing. FL ST J ADMIN Rule 2.525.
   w. Accessibility of information and technology. FL ST J ADMIN Rule 2.526.
   x. Requests for accommodations by persons with disabilities. FL ST J ADMIN Rule 2.540.
2. *Local rules*
   a. Notice of change of contact information. FL ST 2 J CIR 2007-05.

B. Timing

1. *Request for production of documents.* Without leave of court the request may be served on the plaintiff after commencement of the action and on any other party with or after service of the process and initial pleading on that party. FL ST RCP Rule 1.350(b).
2. *Notice of intent to serve subpoena.* A party desiring production under FL ST RCP Rule 1.351 shall serve notice as provided in FL ST RCP Rule 1.080 on every other party of the intent to serve a subpoena under FL ST RCP Rule 1.351 at least ten (10) days before the subpoena is issued if service is by delivery and fifteen (15) days before the subpoena is issued if the service is by mail or e-mail. FL ST RCP Rule 1.351(b).
3. *Sequence and timing of discovery.* Except as provided in FL ST RCP Rule 1.280(b)(5) or unless the court

upon motion for the convenience of parties and witnesses and in the interest of justice orders otherwise, methods of discovery may be used in any sequence, and the fact that a party is conducting discovery, whether by deposition or otherwise, shall not delay any other party's discovery. FL ST RCP Rule 1.280(e).

4. *Computation of time*
   a. *Generally.* Computation of time shall be governed by FL ST J ADMIN Rule 2.514. FL ST RCP Rule 1.090(a). The following rules apply in computing time periods specified in any rule of procedure, local rule, court order, or statute that does not specify a method of computing time. FL ST J ADMIN Rule 2.514(a).
      i. *Period stated in days or a longer unit.* When the period is stated in days or a longer unit of time (A) exclude the day of the event that triggers the period; (B) count every day, including intermediate Saturdays, Sundays, and legal holidays; and (C) include the last day of the period, but if the last day is a Saturday, Sunday, or legal holiday, or falls within any period of time extended through an order of the chief justice under FL ST J ADMIN Rule 2.205(a)(2)(B)(iv), the period continues to run until the end of the next day that is not a Saturday, Sunday, or legal holiday and does not fall within any period of time extended through an order of the chief justice. FL ST J ADMIN Rule 2.514(a)(1).
      ii. *Period stated in hours.* When the period is stated in hours (A) begin counting immediately on the occurrence of the event that triggers the period; (B) count every hour, including hours during intermediate Saturdays, Sundays, and legal holidays; and (C) if the period would end on a Saturday, Sunday, or legal holiday, or during any period of time extended through an order of the chief justice under FL ST J ADMIN Rule 2.205(a)(2)(B)(iv), the period continues to run until the same time on the next day that is not a Saturday, Sunday, or legal holiday and does not fall within any period of time extended through an order of the chief justice. FL ST J ADMIN Rule 2.514(a)(2).
      iii. *Period stated in days less than seven (7) days.* When the period stated in days is less than seven (7) days, intermediate Saturdays, Sundays, and legal holidays shall be excluded in the computation. FL ST J ADMIN Rule 2.514(a)(3).
      iv. *"Last day" defined.* Unless a different time is set by a statute, local rule, or court order, the last day ends (A) for electronic filing or for service by any means, at midnight; and (B) for filing by other means, when the clerk's office is scheduled to close. FL ST J ADMIN Rule 2.514(a)(4).
      v. *"Next day" defined.* The "next day" is determined by continuing to count forward when the period is measured after an event and backward when measured before an event. FL ST J ADMIN Rule 2.514(a)(5).
      vi. *"Legal holiday" defined.* "Legal holiday" means (A) the day set aside by FL ST § 110.117, for observing New Year's Day, Martin Luther King, Jr.'s Birthday, Memorial Day, Independence Day, Labor Day, Veterans' Day, Thanksgiving Day, the Friday after Thanksgiving Day, or Christmas Day, and (B) any day observed as a holiday by the clerk's office or as designated by the chief judge. FL ST J ADMIN Rule 2.514(a)(6).
   b. *Additional time after service by mail or e-mail.* When a party may or must act within a specified time after service and service is made by mail or e-mail, five (5) days are added after the period that would otherwise expire under FL ST J ADMIN Rule 2.514(a). FL ST J ADMIN Rule 2.514(b).
   c. *Enlargement.* When an act is required or allowed to be done at or within a specified time by order of court, by the Florida Rules of Civil Procedure, or by notice given thereunder, for cause shown the court at any time in its discretion (1) with or without notice, may order the period enlarged if request therefor is made before the expiration of the period originally prescribed or as extended by a previous order, or (2) upon motion made and notice after the expiration of the specified period, may permit the act to be done when failure to act was the result of excusable neglect, but it may not extend the time for making a motion for new trial, for rehearing, or to alter or amend a judgment; making a motion for relief from a judgment under FL ST RCP Rule 1.540(b); taking an appeal or filing a petition for certiorari; or making a motion for a directed verdict. FL ST RCP Rule 1.090(b).

d. *Unaffected by expiration of term.* The period of time provided for the doing of any act or the taking of any proceeding shall not be affected or limited by the continued existence or expiration of a term of court. The continued existence or expiration of a term of court in no way affects the power of a court to do any act or take any proceeding in any action which is or has been pending before it. FL ST RCP Rule 1.090(c).

C. General Requirements

1. *General provisions governing discovery*

a. *Discovery methods.* Parties may obtain discovery by one or more of the following methods: depositions upon oral examination or written questions; written interrogatories; production of documents or things or permission to enter upon land or other property for inspection and other purposes; physical and mental examinations; and requests for admission. Unless the court orders otherwise and under FL ST RCP Rule 1.280(c), the frequency of use of these methods is not limited, except as provided in FL ST RCP Rule 1.200, FL ST RCP Rule 1.340, and FL ST RCP Rule 1.370. FL ST RCP Rule 1.280(a).

b. *Scope of discovery.* Unless otherwise limited by order of the court in accordance with the Florida Rules of Civil Procedure, the scope of discovery is as follows:

i. *In general.* Parties may obtain discovery regarding any matter, not privileged, that is relevant to the subject matter of the pending action, whether it relates to the claim or defense of the party seeking discovery or the claim or defense of any other party, including the existence, description, nature, custody, condition, and location of any books, documents, or other tangible things and the identity and location of persons having knowledge of any discoverable matter. It is not ground for objection that the information sought will be inadmissible at the trial if the information sought appears reasonably calculated to lead to the discovery of admissible evidence. FL ST RCP Rule 1.280(b)(1).

ii. *Indemnity agreements.* A party may obtain discovery of the existence and contents of any agreement under which any person may be liable to satisfy part or all of a judgment that may be entered in the action or to indemnify or to reimburse a party for payments made to satisfy the judgment. Information concerning the agreement is not admissible in evidence at trial by reason of disclosure. FL ST RCP Rule 1.280(b)(2).

iii. *Electronically stored information.* A party may obtain discovery of electronically stored information in accordance with the Florida Rules of Civil Procedure. FL ST RCP Rule 1.280(b)(3).

iv. *Trial preparation; Materials.* Subject to the provisions of FL ST RCP Rule 1.280(b)(5), a party may obtain discovery of documents and tangible things otherwise discoverable under FL ST RCP Rule 1.280(b)(1) and prepared in anticipation of litigation or for trial by or for another party or by or for that party's representative, including that party's attorney, consultant, surety, indemnitor, insurer, or agent, only upon a showing that the party seeking discovery has need of the materials in the preparation of the case and is unable without undue hardship to obtain the substantial equivalent of the materials by other means. FL ST RCP Rule 1.280(b)(4).

- In ordering discovery of the materials when the required showing has been made, the court shall protect against disclosure of the mental impressions, conclusions, opinions, or legal theories of an attorney or other representative of a party concerning the litigation. FL ST RCP Rule 1.280(b)(4).
- Without the required showing a party may obtain a copy of a statement concerning the action or its subject matter previously made by that party. FL ST RCP Rule 1.280(b)(4).
- Upon request without the required showing a person not a party may obtain a copy of a statement concerning the action or its subject matter previously made by that person. If the request is refused, the person may move for an order to obtain a copy. The provisions of FL ST RCP Rule 1.380(a)(5) apply to the award of expenses incurred as a result of making the motion. FL ST RCP Rule 1.280(b)(4).
- For purposes of FL ST RCP Rule 1.280(b)(4), a statement previously made is a written

statement signed or otherwise adopted or approved by the person making it, or a stenographic, mechanical, electrical, or other recording or transcription of it that is a substantially verbatim recital of an oral statement by the person making it and contemporaneously recorded. FL ST RCP Rule 1.280(b)(4).

v. *Trial preparation; Experts.* Discovery of facts known and opinions held by experts, otherwise discoverable under the provisions of FL ST RCP Rule 1.280(b)(1) and acquired or developed in anticipation of litigation or for trial, may be obtained only as follows:

- By interrogatories a party may require any other party to identify each person whom the other party expects to call as an expert witness at trial and to state the subject matter on which the expert is expected to testify, and to state the substance of the facts and opinions to which the expert is expected to testify and a summary of the grounds for each opinion. FL ST RCP Rule 1.280(b)(5)(A)(i).
- Any person disclosed by interrogatories or otherwise as a person expected to be called as an expert witness at trial may be deposed in accordance with FL ST RCP Rule 1.390 without motion or order of court. FL ST RCP Rule 1.280(b)(5)(A)(ii).
- A party may obtain the following discovery regarding any person disclosed by interrogatories or otherwise as a person expected to be called as an expert witness at trial: The scope of employment in the pending case and the compensation for such service, FL ST RCP Rule 1.280(b)(5)(A)(iii)(1); The expert's general litigation experience, including the percentage of work performed for plaintiffs and defendants, FL ST RCP Rule 1.280(b)(5)(A)(iii)(2); The identity of other cases, within a reasonable time period, in which the expert has testified by deposition or at trial, FL ST RCP Rule 1.280(b)(5)(A)(iii)(3); An approximation of the portion of the expert's involvement as an expert witness, which may be based on the number of hours, percentage of hours, or percentage of earned income derived from serving as an expert witness; however, the expert shall not be required to disclose his or her earnings as an expert witness or income derived from other services. FL ST RCP Rule 1.280(b)(5)(A)(iii)(4).
- An expert may be required to produce financial and business records only under the most unusual or compelling circumstances and may not be compelled to compile or produce nonexistent documents. Upon motion, the court may order further discovery by other means, subject to such restrictions as to scope and other provisions pursuant to FL ST RCP Rule 1.280(b)(5)(C) concerning fees and expenses as the court may deem appropriate. FL ST RCP Rule 1.280(b)(5).
- A party may discover facts known or opinions held by an expert who has been retained or specially employed by another party in anticipation of litigation or preparation for trial and who is not expected to be called as a witness at trial, only as provided in FL ST RCP Rule 1.360(b) or upon a showing of exceptional circumstances under which it is impracticable for the party seeking discovery to obtain facts or opinions on the same subject by other means. FL ST RCP Rule 1.280(b)(5)(B).
- Unless manifest injustice would result, the court shall require that the party seeking discovery pay the expert a reasonable fee for time spent in responding to discovery under FL ST RCP Rule 1.280(b)(5)(A) and FL ST RCP Rule 1.280(b)(5)(B); and concerning discovery from an expert obtained under FL ST RCP Rule 1.280(b)(5)(A) the court may require, and concerning discovery obtained under FL ST RCP Rule 1.280(b)(5)(B) shall require, the party seeking discovery to pay the other party a fair part of the fees and expenses reasonably incurred by the latter party in obtaining facts and opinions from the expert. FL ST RCP Rule 1.280(b)(5)(C).
- As used in the Florida Rules of Civil Procedure an expert shall be an expert witness as defined in FL ST RCP Rule 1.390(a). FL ST RCP Rule 1.280(b)(5)(D).

vi. *Claims to privilege or protection.* When a party withholds information otherwise discoverable under the Florida Rules of Civil Procedure by claiming that it is privileged or subject to protection as trial preparation material, the party shall make the claim expressly and shall describe the nature of the documents, communications, or things not produced or disclosed in a manner that, without revealing information itself privileged or protected, will enable other parties to assess the applicability of the privilege or protection. FL ST RCP Rule 1.280(b)(6).

c. *Limitations on discovery of electronically stored information*

   i. A person may object to discovery of electronically stored information from sources that the person identifies as not reasonably accessible because of burden or cost. On motion to compel discovery or for a protective order, the person from whom discovery is sought must show that the information sought or the format requested is not reasonably accessible because of undue burden or cost. If that showing is made, the court may nonetheless order the discovery from such sources or in such formats if the requesting party shows good cause. The court may specify conditions of the discovery, including ordering that some or all of the expenses incurred by the person from whom discovery is sought be paid by the party seeking the discovery. FL ST RCP Rule 1.280(d)(1).

   ii. In determining any motion involving discovery of electronically stored information, the court must limit the frequency or extent of discovery otherwise allowed by the Florida Rules of Civil Procedure if it determines that (i) the discovery sought is unreasonably cumulative or duplicative, or can be obtained from another source or in another manner that is more convenient, less burdensome, or less expensive; or (ii) the burden or expense of the discovery outweighs its likely benefit, considering the needs of the case, the amount in controversy, the parties' resources, the importance of the issues at stake in the action, and the importance of the discovery in resolving the issues. FL ST RCP Rule 1.280(d)(2).

d. For information on inadvertent disclosure of privileged materials, see FL ST RCP Rule 1.285.

2. *Request for production of documents*

a. *Scope of request.* Any party may request any other party:

   i. To produce and permit the party making the request, or someone acting in the requesting party's behalf, to inspect and copy any designated documents, including electronically stored information, writings, drawings, graphs, charts, photographs, phono-records, and other data compilations from which information can be obtained, translated, if necessary, by the party to whom the request is directed through detection devices into reasonably usable form, that constitute or contain matters within the scope of FL ST RCP Rule 1.280(b) and that are in the possession, custody, or control of the party to whom the request is directed;

   ii. To inspect and copy, test, or sample any tangible things that constitute or contain matters within the scope of FL ST RCP Rule 1.280(b) and that are in the possession, custody, or control of the party to whom the request is directed; or

   iii. To permit entry upon designated land or other property in the possession or control of the party upon whom the request is served for the purpose of inspection and measuring, surveying, photographing, testing, or sampling the property or any designated object or operation on it within the scope of FL ST RCP Rule 1.280(b). FL ST RCP Rule 1.350(a).

b. *Contents of request*

   i. The request shall set forth the items to be inspected, either by individual item or category, and describe each item and category with reasonable particularity. The request shall specify a reasonable time, place, and manner of making the inspection or performing the related acts. FL ST RCP Rule 1.350(b).

   ii. A request for electronically stored information may specify the form or forms in which electronically stored information is to be produced. If the responding party objects to a requested form, or if no form is specified in the request, the responding party must state the form or forms it intends to use. If a request for electronically stored information does not specify the form of production, the producing party must produce the information in a form or forms in which it is ordinarily maintained or in a reasonably usable form or forms. FL ST RCP Rule 1.350(b).

c. *Failure to respond to requests.* The party submitting the request may move for an order under FL ST

RCP Rule 1.380 concerning any objection, failure to respond to the request, or any part of it, or failure to permit the inspection as requested. FL ST RCP Rule 1.350(b). Please see FL ST RCP Rule 1.380(d) and the KeyRules Motion to Compel Discovery documents for further information regarding compelling discovery and discovery sanctions.

i. *Response requirements.* For each item or category the response shall state that inspection and related activities will be permitted as requested unless the request is objected to, in which event the reasons for the objection shall be stated. If an objection is made to part of an item or category, the part shall be specified. When producing documents, the producing party shall either produce them as they are kept in the usual course of business or shall identify them to correspond with the categories in the request. If the responding party objects to a requested form (for electronic information), or if no form is specified in the request, the responding party must state the form or forms it intends to use. If a request for electronically stored information does not specify the form of production, the producing party must produce the information in a form or forms in which it is ordinarily maintained or in a reasonably usable form or forms. FL ST RCP Rule 1.350(b).

3. *Requests to a non-party*

a. *Independent action not prohibited.* FL ST RCP Rule 1.350 does not preclude an independent action against a person not a party for production of documents and things and permission to enter upon land. FL ST RCP Rule 1.350(c). FL ST RCP Rule 1.351 does not affect the right of any party to bring an independent action for production of documents and things or permission to enter upon land. FL ST RCP Rule 1.351(f).

b. *Scope.* A party may seek inspection and copying of any documents or things within the scope of FL ST RCP Rule 1.350(a) from a person who is not a party by issuance of a subpoena directing the production of the documents or things when the requesting party does not seek to depose the custodian or other person in possession of the documents or things. FL ST RCP Rule 1.351 provides the exclusive procedure for obtaining documents or things by subpoena from nonparties without deposing the custodian or other person in possession of the documents or things pursuant to FL ST RCP Rule 1.310. FL ST RCP Rule 1.351(a).

i. *Procedure.* The proposed subpoena shall be attached to the notice and shall state the time, place, and method for production of the documents or things, and the name and address of the person who is to produce the documents or things, if known, and if not known, a general description sufficient to identify the person or the particular class or group to which the person belongs; shall include a designation of the items to be produced; and shall state that the person who will be asked to produce the documents or things has the right to object to the production under FL ST RCP Rule 1.351 and that the person will not be required to surrender the documents or things. A copy of the notice and proposed subpoena shall not be furnished to the person upon whom the subpoena is to be served. If any party serves an objection to production under FL ST RCP Rule 1.351 within ten (10) days of service of the notice, the documents or things shall not be produced pending resolution of the objection in accordance with FL ST RCP Rule 1.351(d). FL ST RCP Rule 1.351(b).

ii. *Subpoena.* If no objection is made by a party under FL ST RCP Rule 1.351(b), an attorney of record in the action may issue a subpoena or the party desiring production shall deliver to the clerk for issuance a subpoena together with a certificate of counsel or pro se party that no timely objection has been received from any party, and the clerk shall issue the subpoena and deliver it to the party desiring production. FL ST RCP Rule 1.351(c).

- The subpoena shall be identical to the copy attached to the notice and shall specify that no testimony may be taken and shall require only production of the documents or things specified in it. FL ST RCP Rule 1.351(c).
- The subpoena may give the recipient an option to deliver or mail legible copies of the documents or things to the party serving the subpoena. FL ST RCP Rule 1.351(c).
- The person upon whom the subpoena is served may condition the preparation of copies on the payment in advance of the reasonable costs of preparing the copies. FL ST RCP Rule 1.351(c).

- The subpoena shall require production only in the county of the residence of the custodian or other person in possession of the documents or things or in the county where the documents or things are located or where the custodian or person in possession usually conducts business. FL ST RCP Rule 1.351(c).
- If the person upon whom the subpoena is served objects at any time before the production of the documents or things, the documents or things shall not be produced under FL ST RCP Rule 1.351, and relief may be obtained pursuant to FL ST RCP Rule 1.310. FL ST RCP Rule 1.351(c).

iii. *Ruling on objection.* If an objection is made by a party under FL ST RCP Rule 1.351(b), the party desiring production may file a motion with the court seeking a ruling on the objection or may proceed pursuant to FL ST RCP Rule 1.310. FL ST RCP Rule 1.351(d).

iv. *Copies furnished.* If the subpoena is complied with by delivery or mailing of copies as provided in FL ST RCP Rule 1.351(c), the party receiving the copies shall furnish a legible copy of each item furnished to any other party who requests it upon the payment of the reasonable cost of preparing the copies. FL ST RCP Rule 1.351(e).

4. *Arbitration and mediation*

a. *Referral to arbitration and mediation.* Except as hereinafter provided or as otherwise prohibited by law, the presiding judge may enter an order referring all or any part of a contested civil matter to mediation or arbitration. The parties to any contested civil matter may file a written stipulation to mediate or arbitrate any issue between them at any time. Such stipulation shall be incorporated into the order of referral. FL ST RCP Rule 1.700(a).

b. *Arbitration*

i. *Exclusions.* A civil action shall be ordered to arbitration or arbitration in conjunction with mediation upon stipulation of the parties. A civil action may be ordered to arbitration or arbitration in conjunction with mediation upon motion of any party or by the court, if the judge determines the action to be of such a nature that arbitration could be of benefit to the litigants or the court. FL ST RCP Rule 1.800.

- Under no circumstances may the following categories of actions be referred to arbitration: (1) bond estreatures; (2) habeas corpus or other extraordinary writs; (3) bond validations; (4) civil or criminal contempt; (5) such other matters as may be specified by order of the chief judge in the circuit. FL ST RCP Rule 1.800.

ii. For more information regarding arbitration, please see FL ST RCP Rule 1.810; FL ST RCP Rule 1.820; FL ST RCP Rule 1.830.

c. *Mediation.* For more information regarding mediation, please see FL ST RCP Rule 1.710; FL ST RCP Rule 1.720; FL ST RCP Rule 1.730; and FL ST RCP Rule 1.750.

5. *Rules of court*

a. *Rules of civil procedure.* The Florida Rules of Civil Procedure apply to all actions of a civil nature and all special statutory proceedings in the circuit courts and county courts except those to which the Florida Probate Rules, the Florida Family Law Rules of Procedure, or the Small Claims Rules apply. FL ST RCP Rule 1.010.

i. The form, content, procedure, and time for pleading in all special statutory proceedings shall be as prescribed by the statutes governing the proceeding unless the Florida Rules of Civil Procedure specifically provide to the contrary. FL ST RCP Rule 1.010.

ii. The Florida Rules of Civil Procedure shall be construed to secure the just, speedy, and inexpensive determination of every action. FL ST RCP Rule 1.010.

b. *Rules of judicial administration.* The Florida Rules of Judicial Administration shall apply to administrative matters in all courts to which the Florida Rules of Judicial Administration are applicable by their terms. The Florida Rules of Judicial Administration shall be construed to secure the speedy and inexpensive determination of every proceeding to which they are applicable. The Florida Rules of Judicial Administration shall supersede all conflicting rules and statutes. FL ST J ADMIN Rule 2.110.

6. *Notice of change of contact information.* The Clerk shall provide a change of address and/or telephone number form for use by attorneys and pro se litigants. With any change of address and/or telephone number, attorneys and pro se litigants governed by FL ST J ADMIN Rule 2.515 will provide to the Clerk and all parties promptly the change of address and/or telephone number form. This form should be submitted only once to the Clerk, who will then make the address and/or telephone number change in all court divisions. FL ST 2 J CIR 2007-05.

D. Documents

1. *Required documents*
   a. *Request for production.* Please see the General Requirements section of this document for more information on the contents of the request for production.
      i. *Notices to persons with disabilities.* See the Format section of this KeyRules document for further information.
   b. *Certificate of service.* A certificate of service of the interrogatories shall be filed, giving the date of service and the name of the party to whom they were directed. FL ST RCP Rule 1.340(e). When any attorney certifies in substance: "I certify that a copy hereof has been furnished to (here insert name or names and addresses used for service) by (e-mail) (delivery) (mail) (fax) on .... (date) ....______________ Attorney" the certificate is taken as prima facie proof of such service in compliance with FL ST J ADMIN Rule 2.516. FL ST J ADMIN Rule 2.516(f).
2. *Supplemental documents*
   a. *Notice of intent to serve subpoena/Subpoena.* Please see the General Requirements section of this document for more information.

E. Format

1. *Documents; Type and size.* Documents subject to the exceptions set forth in FL ST J ADMIN Rule 2.525(d) shall be filed on recycled paper measuring eight and one half by eleven (8 1/2 by 11) inches. For purposes of FL ST J ADMIN Rule 2.520, paper is recycled if it contains a minimum content of fifty (50) percent waste paper. Xerographic reduction of legal-size (eight and one half by fourteen (8 1/2 by 14) inches) documents to letter size (eight and one half by eleven (8 1/2 by 11) inches) is prohibited. All other documents filed by electronic transmission shall be filed in a format capable of being printed in a format consistent with the provisions of FL ST J ADMIN Rule 2.250. FL ST J ADMIN Rule 2.520(b).
   a. *Exhibits.* Any exhibit or attachment filed with pleadings or papers may be filed in its original size. FL ST J ADMIN Rule 2.520(c).
   b. *Recording space.* On all papers and documents prepared and filed by the court or by any party to a proceeding which are to be recorded in the public records of any county, including but not limited to final money judgments and notices of lis pendens, a three (3) inch by three (3) inch space at the top right-hand corner on the first page and a one (1) inch by three (3) inch space at the top right-hand corner on each subsequent page shall be left blank and reserved for use by the clerk of court. FL ST J ADMIN Rule 2.520(d).
      i. *Exceptions to recording space.* Any papers or documents created by persons or entities over which the filing party has no control, including but not limited to wills, codicils, trusts, or other testamentary documents; documents prepared or executed by any public officer; documents prepared, executed, acknowledged, or proved outside of the State of Florida; or documents created by State or Federal government agencies, may be filed without the space required by FL ST J ADMIN Rule 2.520. FL ST J ADMIN Rule 2.520(e).
   c. *Noncompliance.* No clerk of court is permitted to refuse to file any document or paper because of noncompliance with the Florida Rules of Judicial Administration. However, upon request of the clerk of court, noncomplying documents must be resubmitted in accordance with the formatting rules. FL ST J ADMIN Rule 2.520(f).
2. *Caption.* Every pleading, motion, order, judgment, or other paper shall have a caption containing the name of the court, the file number, and except for in rem proceedings, including forfeiture proceedings, the name of the first party on each side with an appropriate indication of other parties, and a designation

identifying the party filing it and its nature or the nature of the order, as the case may be. In any in rem proceeding, every pleading, motion, order, judgment, or other paper shall have a caption containing the name of the court, the file number, the style "In re" (followed by the name or general description of the property), and a designation of the person or entity filing it and its nature or the nature of the order, as the case may be. In an in rem forfeiture proceeding, the style shall be "In re forfeiture of" (followed by the name of the general description of the property). All papers filed in the action shall be styled in such a manner as to indicate clearly the subject matter of the paper and the party requesting or obtaining relief. FL ST RCP Rule 1.100(c)(1).

3. *Writing and written defined.* Writing or written means a document containing information, an application, or a stipulation. FL ST RCP Rule 1.080(c).
4. *Rule abbreviations*
   a. The Florida Rules of Civil Procedure and shall be abbreviated as Fla.R.Civ.P. FL ST RCP Rule 1.010.
   b. The Florida Rules of Judicial Administration shall be abbreviated as Fla. R. Jud. Admin. FL ST J ADMIN Rule 2.110.
5. *Nonverification.* Except when otherwise specifically provided by the Florida Rules of Civil Procedure or an applicable statute, every pleading or other document of a party represented by an attorney need not be verified or accompanied by an affidavit. FL ST RCP Rule 1.030; FL ST J ADMIN Rule 2.515(a).
6. *Attorney signature*
   a. *Attorney signature.* Every pleading and other document of a party represented by an attorney shall be signed by at least one (1) attorney of record in that attorney's individual name whose current record Florida Bar address, telephone number, including area code, primary e-mail address and secondary e-mail addresses, if any, and Florida Bar number shall be stated, and who shall be duly licensed to practice law in Florida or who shall have received permission to appear in the particular case as provided in FL ST J ADMIN Rule 2.510. FL ST J ADMIN Rule 2.515(a).
      i. The attorney may be required by the court to give the address of, and to vouch for the attorney's authority to represent, the party. FL ST J ADMIN Rule 2.515(a).
      ii. The signature of an attorney shall constitute a certificate by the attorney that the attorney has read the pleading or other document; that to the best of the attorney's knowledge, information, and belief there is good ground to support it; and that it is not interposed for delay. FL ST J ADMIN Rule 2.515(a).
      iii. If a pleading is not signed or is signed with intent to defeat the purpose of FL ST J ADMIN Rule 2.515, it may be stricken and the action may proceed as though the pleading or other document had not been served. FL ST J ADMIN Rule 2.515(a).
   b. *Pro se litigant signature.* A party who is not represented by an attorney shall sign any pleading or other paper and state the party's address and telephone number, including area code. FL ST J ADMIN Rule 2.515(b).
   c. *Form of signature*
      i. The signatures required on pleadings and documents by FL ST J ADMIN Rule 2.515(a) and FL ST J ADMIN Rule 2.515(b) may be:
         - Original signatures;
         - Original signatures that have been reproduced by electronic means, such as on electronically transmitted documents or photocopied documents;
         - Electronic signatures using the "/s/," "s/," or "/s" formats by or at the direction of the person signing; or
         - Any other signature format authorized by general law, so long as the clerk where the proceeding is pending has the capability of receiving and has obtained approval from the Supreme Court of Florida to accept pleadings and documents with that signature format. FL ST J ADMIN Rule 2.515(c)(1).

ii. An attorney, party, or other person who files a pleading or paper by electronic transmission that does not contain the original signature of that attorney, party, or other person shall file that identical pleading or paper in paper form containing an original signature of that attorney, party, or other person (hereinafter called the follow-up filing) immediately thereafter. The follow-up filing is not required if the Supreme Court of Florida has entered an order directing the clerk of court to discontinue accepting the follow-up filing. FL ST J ADMIN Rule 2.515(c)(2).

7. *Forms*
   a. *Process.* The forms of process, notice of lis pendens, and notice of action provided in the Florida Rules of Civil Procedure are sufficient. Variations from the forms do not void process or notices that are otherwise sufficient. FL ST RCP Rule 1.900(a).
   b. *Other forms.* The other forms provided in the Florida Rules of Civil Procedure are sufficient for the matters that are covered by them. So long as the substance is expressed without prolixity, the forms may be varied to meet the facts of a particular case. FL ST RCP Rule 1.900(b).
   c. *Formal matters.* Captions, except for the designation of the paper, are omitted from the forms provided in the Florida Rules of Civil Procedure. A general form of caption is the first form provided. Signatures are omitted from pleadings and motions. FL ST RCP Rule 1.900(c).
8. *Notices to persons with disabilities.* All notices of court proceedings to be held in a public facility, and all process compelling appearance at such proceedings, shall include the following statement in bold face, fourteen (14) point Times New Roman or Courier font: "If you are a person with a disability who needs any accommodation in order to participate in this proceeding, you are entitled, at no cost to you, to the provision of certain assistance. Please contact [identify applicable court personnel by name, address, and telephone number] at least seven (7) days before your scheduled court appearance, or immediately upon receiving this notification if the time before the scheduled appearance is less than seven (7) days; if you are hearing or voice impaired, call 711." FL ST J ADMIN Rule 2.540(c)(1).
9. *Minimization of the filing of sensitive information*
   a. *Limitations for court filings.* Unless authorized by FL ST J ADMIN Rule 2.425(b), statute, another rule of court, or the court orders otherwise, designated sensitive information filed with the court must be limited to the following format:
      i. The initials of a person known to be a minor;
      ii. The year of birth of a person's birth date;
      iii. No portion of any: Social security number, Bank account number, Credit card account number, Charge account number, or Debit account number;
      iv. The last four digits of any: Taxpayer identification number (TIN), Employee identification number, Driver's license number, Passport number, Telephone number, Financial account number, except as set forth in FL ST J ADMIN Rule 2.425(a)(3), Brokerage account number, Insurance policy account number, Loan account number, Customer account number, or Patient or health care number;
      v. A truncated version of any: Email address, Computer user name, Password, or Personal identification number (PIN); and
      vi. A truncated version of any other sensitive information as provided by court order. FL ST J ADMIN Rule 2.425(a).
   b. *Exceptions.* FL ST J ADMIN Rule 2.425(a) does not apply to the following:
      i. An account number which identifies the property alleged to be the subject of a proceeding;
      ii. The record of an administrative or agency proceeding;
      iii. The record in appellate or review proceedings;
      iv. The birth date of a minor whenever the birth date is necessary for the court to establish or maintain subject matter jurisdiction;
      v. The name of a minor in any order relating to parental responsibility, time-sharing, or child support;

vi. The name of a minor in any document or order affecting the minor's ownership of real property;

vii. The birth date of a party in a writ of attachment or notice to payor;

viii. In traffic and criminal proceedings: a pro se filing; a court filing that is related to a criminal matter or investigation and that is prepared before the filing of a criminal charge or is not filed as part of any docketed criminal case; an arrest or search warrant or any information in support thereof; a charging document and an affidavit or other documents filed in support of any charging document, including any driving records; a statement of particulars; discovery material introduced into evidence or otherwise filed with the court; and all information necessary for the proper issuance and execution of a subpoena duces tecum;

ix. Information used by the clerk for case maintenance purposes or the courts for case management purposes; and

x. Information which is relevant and material to an issue before the court. FL ST J ADMIN Rule 2.425(b).

c. *Remedies.* Upon motion by a party or interested person or sua sponte by the court, the court may order remedies, sanctions or both for a violation of FL ST J ADMIN Rule 2.425(a). Following notice and an opportunity to respond, the court may impose sanctions if such filing was not made in good faith. FL ST J ADMIN Rule 2.425(c).

d. *Motions not restricted.* FL ST J ADMIN Rule 2.425 does not restrict a party's right to move for protective order, to move to file documents under seal, or to request a determination of the confidentiality of records. FL ST J ADMIN Rule 2.425(d).

e. *Application.* FL ST J ADMIN Rule 2.425 does not affect the application of constitutional provisions, statutes, or rules of court regarding confidential information or access to public information. FL ST J ADMIN Rule 2.425(e).

F. Filing and Service Requirements

1. *Court filing of documents and discovery.* Information obtained during discovery shall not be filed with the court until such time as it is filed for good cause. The requirement of good cause is satisfied only where the filing of the information is allowed or required by another applicable rule of procedure or by court order. All filings of discovery documents shall comply with FL ST J ADMIN Rule 2.425. The court shall have the authority to impose sanctions for violation of FL ST RCP Rule 1.280. FL ST RCP Rule 1.280(g).

   a. Unless required by the court, a party shall not file any of the documents or things produced with the response. Documents or things may be filed in compliance with FL ST J ADMIN Rule 2.425 and FL ST RCP Rule 1.280(g) when they should be considered by the court in determining a matter pending before the court. FL ST RCP Rule 1.350(d).

2. *Filing requirements.* All original documents must be filed with the court either before service or immediately thereafter, unless otherwise provided for by general law or other rules. If the original of any bond or other document is not placed in the court file, a certified copy must be so placed by the clerk. FL ST J ADMIN Rule 2.516(d). All documents shall be filed in conformity with the requirements of FL ST J ADMIN Rule 2.525. FL ST RCP Rule 1.080(b). All documents filed in any court shall be filed by electronic transmission in accordance with FL ST J ADMIN Rule 2.525. "Documents" means pleadings, motions, petitions, memoranda, briefs, notices, exhibits, declarations, affidavits, orders, judgments, decrees, writs, opinions, and any other paper or writing submitted to a court. FL ST J ADMIN Rule 2.520(a). All documents that are court records, as defined in FL ST J ADMIN Rule 2.430(a)(1), must be filed by electronic transmission, provided that: (1) the clerk has the ability to accept and retain such documents; (2) the clerk or the chief judge of the circuit has requested permission to accept documents filed by electronic transmission; and (3) the supreme court has entered an order granting permission to the clerk to accept documents filed by electronic transmission. FL ST J ADMIN Rule 2.525(c)(1).

   a. *Definition.* "Electronic transmission of documents" means the sending of information by electronic signals to, by or from a court or clerk, which when received can be transformed and stored or transmitted on paper, microfilm, magnetic storage device, optical imaging system, CD-ROM, flash drive, other electronic data storage system, server, case maintenance system ("CM"), electronic court filing ("ECF") system, statewide or local electronic portal ("e-portal"), or other electronic record keeping system authorized by the supreme court in a format sufficient to communicate the information on the original document in a readable format. Electronic transmission of documents includes electronic mail ("e-mail") and any internet-based transmission procedure, and may include procedures allowing for documents to be signed or verified by electronic means. FL ST J ADMIN Rule 2.525(a).

i. The filing of documents with the court as required by the Florida Rules of Judicial Administration must be made by filing them with the clerk in accordance with FL ST J ADMIN Rule 2.525, except that the judge may permit documents to be filed with the judge, in which event the judge must note the filing date before him or her on the documents and transmit them to the clerk. The date of filing is that shown on the face of the document by the judge's notation or the clerk's time stamp, whichever is earlier. FL ST J ADMIN Rule 2.516(e).

b. *Application.* Any court or clerk of the court may accept the electronic transmission of documents for filing after the clerk, together with input from the chief judge of the circuit, has obtained approval of the procedures and program for doing so from the Supreme Court of Florida. FL ST J ADMIN Rule 2.525(b).

c. *Exceptions*

i. Paper documents and other submissions may be manually submitted to the clerk or court:

- When the clerk does not have the ability to accept and retain documents by electronic filing or has not had ECF Procedures approved by the supreme court;
- For filing by any self-represented party or any self-represented nonparty unless specific ECF Procedures provide a means to file documents electronically. However, any self-represented nonparty that is a governmental or public agency and any other agency, partnership, corporation, or business entity acting on behalf of any governmental or public agency may file documents by electronic transmission if such entity has the capability of filing documents electronically;
- For filing by attorneys excused from e-mail service in accordance with FL ST J ADMIN Rule 2.516(b);
- When submitting evidentiary exhibits or filing non-documentary materials;
- When the filing involves documents in excess of twenty-five (25) megabytes (25MB) in size. For such filings, documents may be transmitted using an electronic storage medium that the clerk has the ability to accept, which may include a CD-ROM, flash drive, or similar storage medium;
- When filed in open court, as permitted by the court;
- When paper filing is permitted by any approved statewide or local ECF procedures; and
- If any court determines that justice so requires. FL ST J ADMIN Rule 2.525(d).

ii. Any document in paper form submitted under FL ST J ADMIN Rule 2.525(d) is filed when it is received by the clerk or court and the clerk shall immediately thereafter convert any filed paper document to an electronic document. "Convert to an electronic document" means optically capturing an image of a paper document and using character recognition software to recover as much of the document's text as practicable and then indexing and storing the document in the official court file. FL ST J ADMIN Rule 2.525(c)(4).

iii. Any storage medium submitted under FL ST J ADMIN Rule 2.525(d)(5) is filed when received by the clerk or court and the clerk shall immediately thereafter transfer the electronic documents from the storage device to the official court file. FL ST J ADMIN Rule 2.525(c)(5).

iv. If the filer of any paper document authorized under FL ST J ADMIN Rule 2.525(d) provides a self-addressed, postage-paid envelope for return of the paper document after it is converted to electronic form by the clerk, the clerk shall place the paper document in the envelope and deposit it in the mail. Except when a paper document is required to be maintained, the clerk may recycle any filed paper document that is not to be returned to the filer. FL ST J ADMIN Rule 2.525(c)(6).

v. The clerk may convert any paper document filed before the effective date of FL ST J ADMIN Rule 2.525 to an electronic document. Unless the clerk is required to maintain the paper document, if the paper document has been converted to an electronic document by the clerk, the paper document is no longer part of the official court file and may be removed and recycled. FL ST J ADMIN Rule 2.525(c)(7).

d. *Official court file.* For information on what constitutes the official court file, please see FL ST J ADMIN Rule 2.525(c)(2), FL ST J ADMIN Rule 2.525(c)(3).

e. *Administration.* All attorneys, parties, or other persons using this rule to file documents are required to make arrangements with the court or clerk for the payment of any charges authorized by general law or the supreme court before filing any document by electronic transmission. FL ST J ADMIN Rule 2.525(f)(2).

f. *Filing date.* The filing date for an electronically transmitted document is the date and time that such filing is acknowledged by an electronic stamp or otherwise, pursuant to any procedure set forth in any ECF Procedures approved by the supreme court, or the date the last page of such filing is received by the court or clerk. FL ST J ADMIN Rule 2.525(f)(3).

g. *Accessibility.* All documents transmitted in any electronic form under FL ST J ADMIN Rule 2.525 must comply with the accessibility requirements of FL ST J ADMIN Rule 2.526. FL ST J ADMIN Rule 2.525(g).

3. *Service requirements.* Every pleading subsequent to the initial pleading, all orders, and every other document filed in the action must be served in conformity with the requirements of FL ST J ADMIN Rule 2.516. FL ST RCP Rule 1.080(a).

a. *Service; When required.* Unless the court otherwise orders, or a statute or supreme court administrative order specifies a different means of service, every pleading subsequent to the initial pleading and every other document filed in any court proceeding, except applications for witness subpoenas and documents served by formal notice or required to be served in the manner provided for service of formal notice, must be served in accordance with FL ST J ADMIN Rule 2.516 on each party. No service need be made on parties against whom a default has been entered, except that pleadings asserting new or additional claims against them must be served in the manner provided for service of summons. FL ST J ADMIN Rule 2.516(a).

b. *Service; How made.* When service is required or permitted to be made upon a party represented by an attorney, service must be made upon the attorney unless service upon the party is ordered by the court. FL ST J ADMIN Rule 2.516(b).

i. *Service by electronic mail ("e-mail").* All documents required or permitted to be served on another party must be served by e-mail, unless FL ST J ADMIN Rule 2.516 otherwise provides. When, in addition to service by e-mail, the sender also utilizes another means of service provided for in FL ST J ADMIN Rule 2.516(b)(2), any differing time limits and other provisions applicable to that other means of service control. FL ST J ADMIN Rule 2.516(b)(1). Any document electronically transmitted to a court or clerk must also be served on all parties and interested persons in accordance with the applicable rules of court. FL ST J ADMIN Rule 2.525(e)(2).

- *Service on attorneys.* Upon appearing in a proceeding, an attorney must serve a designation of a primary e-mail address and may designate no more than two (2) secondary e-mail addresses. Thereafter, service must be directed to all designated e-mail addresses in that proceeding. Every document filed by an attorney thereafter must include the primary e-mail address of that attorney and any secondary e-mail addresses. If an attorney does not designate any e-mail address for service, documents may be served on that attorney at the e-mail address on record with The Florida Bar. FL ST J ADMIN Rule 2.516(b)(1)(A).

- *Exception to e-mail service on attorneys.* Service by an attorney on another attorney must be made by e-mail unless excused by the court. Upon motion by an attorney demonstrating that the attorney has no e-mail account and lacks access to the Internet at the attorney's office, the court may excuse the attorney from the requirements of e-mail service. Service

on and by an attorney excused by the court from e-mail service must be by the means provided in FL ST J ADMIN Rule 2.516(b)(2). FL ST J ADMIN Rule 2.516(b)(1)(B).

- *Service on and by parties not represented by an attorney.* Any party not represented by an attorney may serve a designation of a primary e-mail address and also may designate no more than two (2) secondary e-mail addresses to which service must be directed in that proceeding by the means provided in FL ST J ADMIN Rule 2.516(b)(1). If a party not represented by an attorney does not designate an e-mail address for service in a proceeding, service on and by that party must be by the means provided in FL ST J ADMIN Rule 2.516(b)(2). FL ST J ADMIN Rule 2.516(b)(1)(C).
- *Time of service.* Service by e-mail is complete when it is sent. FL ST J ADMIN Rule 2.516(b)(1)(D). An e-mail is deemed served on the date it is sent. FL ST J ADMIN Rule 2.516(b)(1)(D)(i). If the sender learns that the e-mail did not reach the address of the person to be served, the sender must immediately send another copy by e-mail, or by a means authorized by FL ST J ADMIN Rule 2.516(b)(2). FL ST J ADMIN Rule 2.516(b)(1)(D)(ii). E-mail service is treated as service by mail for the computation of time. FL ST J ADMIN Rule 2.516(b)(1)(D)(iii).

ii. *Format of e-mail for service.* Service of a document by e-mail is made by attaching a copy of the document in PDF format to an e-mail sent to all addresses designated by the attorney or party. FL ST J ADMIN Rule 2.516(b)(1)(E).

- All documents served by e-mail must be attached to an e-mail message containing a subject line beginning with the words "SERVICE OF COURT DOCUMENT" in all capital letters, followed by the case number of the proceeding in which the documents are being served. FL ST J ADMIN Rule 2.516(b)(1)(E)(i).
- The body of the e-mail must identify the court in which the proceeding is pending, the case number, the name of the initial party on each side, the title of each document served with that e-mail, and the sender's name and telephone number. FL ST J ADMIN Rule 2.516(b)(1)(E)(ii).
- Any document served by e-mail may be signed by the "/s/" format, as long as the filed original is signed in accordance with the applicable rule of procedure. FL ST J ADMIN Rule 2.516(b)(1)(E)(iii).
- Any e-mail which, together with its attached documents, exceeds five megabytes (5MB) in size, must be divided and sent as separate e-mails, no one of which may exceed five megabytes (5MB) in size and each of which must be sequentially numbered in the subject line. FL ST J ADMIN Rule 2.516(b)(1)(E)(iv).

iii. *Service by other means.* In addition to, and not in lieu of, service by e-mail, service may also be made upon attorneys by any of the means specified in FL ST J ADMIN Rule 2.516(b)(2). Service on and by all parties who are not represented by an attorney and who do not designate an e-mail address, and on and by all attorneys excused from e-mail service, must be made by delivering a copy of the document or by mailing it to the party or attorney at their last known address or, if no address is known, by leaving it with the clerk of the court. Service by mail is complete upon mailing. Delivery of a copy within FL ST J ADMIN Rule 2.516 is complete upon:

- Handing it to the attorney or to the party,
- Leaving it at the attorney's or party's office with a clerk or other person in charge thereof,
- If there is no one in charge, leaving it in a conspicuous place therein,
- If the office is closed or the person to be served has no office, leaving it at the person's usual place of abode with some person of his or her family above fifteen (15) years of age and informing such person of the contents, or
- Transmitting it by facsimile to the attorney's or party's office with a cover sheet containing the sender's name, firm, address, telephone number, and facsimile number, and the

number of pages transmitted. When service is made by facsimile, a copy must also be served by any other method permitted by FL ST J ADMIN Rule 2.516. Facsimile service occurs when transmission is complete. FL ST J ADMIN Rule 2.516(b)(2)(A) through FL ST J ADMIN Rule 2.516(b)(2)(E).

- Service by delivery after 5:00 p.m. must be deemed to have been made by mailing on the date of delivery. FL ST J ADMIN Rule 2.516(b)(2)(F).

c. *Service; Numerous defendants.* In actions when the parties are unusually numerous, the court may regulate the service contemplated by the Florida Rules of Judicial Administration on motion or on its own initiative in such manner as may be found to be just and reasonable. FL ST J ADMIN Rule 2.516(c).

d. *Service by clerk.* Service of notices and other documents required to be made by the clerk must also be done as provided in FL ST J ADMIN Rule 2.516(b). FL ST J ADMIN Rule 2.516(g).

G. Hearings

1. There is no hearing required or contemplated with regard to requests for production of documents in the Florida Rules of Civil Procedure.

H. Forms

1. Official Request for Production of Documents Forms for Florida

a. Caption. FL ST RCP Form 1.901.

b. Subpoena duces tecum for trial. FL ST RCP Form 1.911.

c. Notice of production from nonparty. FL ST RCP Form 1.921.

d. Subpoena duces tecum without deposition. FL ST RCP Form 1.922.

2. Request for Production of Documents Forms for Florida

a. Request for production; Documents. FL-PRACFORM § 8:29.

b. Request for inspection; Documents, deposition. FL-PRACFORM § 8:30.

c. Request for inspection; Tangible things. FL-PRACFORM § 8:31.

d. Request for entry; Real property. FL-PRACFORM § 8:32.

e. Request for production; Documents, response. FL-PRACFORM § 8:33.

f. Request for inspection; Response, tangible things. FL-PRACFORM § 8:34.

g. Request for entry; Response, land and buildings. FL-PRACFORM § 8:35.

h. Production of documents; Nonparty, notice. FL-PRACFORM § 8:36.

i. Production of documents; Nonparty, objection. FL-PRACFORM § 8:37.

j. Request; Production of documents for inspection and copying. FL-PP § 3:115.

k. Notice of request for production from nonparty. FL-PP § 3:116.

l. Request; For permission to enter on land; To inspect and photograph. FL-PP § 3:127.

3. Official Forms for Florida Circuit Court, Second Judicial Circuit

a. Notice of change of contact information. FL ST 2 J CIR 2007-05.

I. Checklist

(I) ❑ Matters to be considered by requesting party

(a) ❑ Required documents

(1) ❑ Request

(2) ❑ Certificate of service

(b) ❑ Supplemental documents

(1) ❑ Notice of intent to serve subpoena/Subpoena

(c) ❑ Time for request

(1) ❑ Without leave of court the request may be served on the plaintiff after commencement of the action and on any other party with or after service of the process and initial pleading on that party

(2) ❑ A party desiring production under FL ST RCP Rule 1.351 shall serve notice as provided in FL ST RCP Rule 1.080 on every other party of the intent to serve a subpoena under FL ST RCP Rule 1.351 at least ten (10) days before the subpoena is issued if service is by delivery and fifteen (15) days before the subpoena is issued if the service is by mail or e-mail

(II) ❑ Matters to be considered by responding party

(a) ❑ Required documents

(1) ❑ Response to request

(2) ❑ Certificate of service

(b) ❑ Supplemental documents

(1) ❑ Objections

(c) ❑ Time for response

(1) ❑ The party to whom the request is directed shall serve a written response within thirty (30) days after service of the request, except that a defendant may serve a response within forty-five (45) days after service of the process and initial pleading on that defendant; the court may allow a shorter or longer time

Requests, Notices and Applications
Request for Admissions

Document Last Updated January 2013

A. Applicable Rules

1. *State rules*

a. Nonverification of pleadings. FL ST RCP Rule 1.030.

b. Service and filing of pleadings, orders, and documents. FL ST RCP Rule 1.080.

c. Time. FL ST RCP Rule 1.090.

d. Pleadings and motions. FL ST RCP Rule 1.100.

e. Pretrial procedure. FL ST RCP Rule 1.200.

f. General provisions governing discovery. FL ST RCP Rule 1.280.

g. Interrogatories to parties. FL ST RCP Rule 1.340.

h. Examination of persons. FL ST RCP Rule 1.360.

i. Requests for admission. FL ST RCP Rule 1.370.

j. Failure to make discovery; Sanctions. FL ST RCP Rule 1.380.

k. Depositions of expert witnesses. FL ST RCP Rule 1.390.

l. Relief from judgment, decrees, or orders. FL ST RCP Rule 1.540.

m. Forms. FL ST RCP Rule 1.900.

n. Minimization of the filing of sensitive information. FL ST J ADMIN Rule 2.425.

o. Retention of court records. FL ST J ADMIN Rule 2.430.

p. Foreign attorneys. FL ST J ADMIN Rule 2.510.

q. Signature of attorneys and parties. FL ST J ADMIN Rule 2.515.

r. Paper. FL ST J ADMIN Rule 2.520.

s. Electronic filing. FL ST J ADMIN Rule 2.525.

t. Accessibility of information and technology. FL ST J ADMIN Rule 2.526.

u. Requests for accommodations by persons with disabilities. FL ST J ADMIN Rule 2.540.

2. *Local rules*

a. Notice of change of contact information. FL ST 2 J CIR 2007-05.

B. Timing

1. *Request for admission.* Without leave of court the request may be served upon the plaintiff after commencement of the action and upon any other party with or after service of the process and initial pleading upon that party. FL ST RCP Rule 1.370(a).

2. *Sequence and timing of discovery.* Except as provided in FL ST RCP Rule 1.280(b)(5) or unless the court upon motion for the convenience of parties and witnesses and in the interest of justice orders otherwise, methods of discovery may be used in any sequence, and the fact that a party is conducting discovery, whether by deposition or otherwise, shall not delay any other party's discovery. FL ST RCP Rule 1.280(e).

3. *Computation of time*

a. *Generally.* Computation of time shall be governed by FL ST J ADMIN Rule 2.514. FL ST RCP Rule 1.090(a). The following rules apply in computing time periods specified in any rule of procedure, local rule, court order, or statute that does not specify a method of computing time. FL ST J ADMIN Rule 2.514(a).

i. *Period stated in days or a longer unit.* When the period is stated in days or a longer unit of time (A) exclude the day of the event that triggers the period; (B) count every day, including intermediate Saturdays, Sundays, and legal holidays; and (C) include the last day of the period, but if the last day is a Saturday, Sunday, or legal holiday, or falls within any period of time extended through an order of the chief justice under FL ST J ADMIN Rule 2.205(a)(2)(B)(iv), the period continues to run until the end of the next day that is not a Saturday, Sunday, or legal holiday and does not fall within any period of time extended through an order of the chief justice. FL ST J ADMIN Rule 2.514(a)(1).

ii. *Period stated in hours.* When the period is stated in hours (A) begin counting immediately on the occurrence of the event that triggers the period; (B) count every hour, including hours during intermediate Saturdays, Sundays, and legal holidays; and (C) if the period would end on a Saturday, Sunday, or legal holiday, or during any period of time extended through an order of the chief justice under FL ST J ADMIN Rule 2.205(a)(2)(B)(iv), the period continues to run until the same time on the next day that is not a Saturday, Sunday, or legal holiday and does not fall within any period of time extended through an order of the chief justice. FL ST J ADMIN Rule 2.514(a)(2).

iii. *Period stated in days less than seven (7) days.* When the period stated in days is less than seven (7) days, intermediate Saturdays, Sundays, and legal holidays shall be excluded in the computation. FL ST J ADMIN Rule 2.514(a)(3).

iv. *"Last day" defined.* Unless a different time is set by a statute, local rule, or court order, the last day ends (A) for electronic filing or for service by any means, at midnight; and (B) for filing by other means, when the clerk's office is scheduled to close. FL ST J ADMIN Rule 2.514(a)(4).

v. *"Next day" defined.* The "next day" is determined by continuing to count forward when the period is measured after an event and backward when measured before an event. FL ST J ADMIN Rule 2.514(a)(5).

vi. *"Legal holiday" defined.* "Legal holiday" means (A) the day set aside by FL ST § 110.117, for observing New Year's Day, Martin Luther King, Jr.'s Birthday, Memorial Day, Independence Day, Labor Day, Veterans' Day, Thanksgiving Day, the Friday after Thanksgiving Day, or Christmas Day, and (B) any day observed as a holiday by the clerk's office or as designated by the chief judge. FL ST J ADMIN Rule 2.514(a)(6).

b. *Additional time after service by mail or e-mail.* When a party may or must act within a specified time after service and service is made by mail or e-mail, five (5) days are added after the period that would otherwise expire under FL ST J ADMIN Rule 2.514(a). FL ST J ADMIN Rule 2.514(b).

c. *Enlargement.* When an act is required or allowed to be done at or within a specified time by order of court, by the Florida Rules of Civil Procedure, or by notice given thereunder, for cause shown the court at any time in its discretion (1) with or without notice, may order the period enlarged if request therefor is made before the expiration of the period originally prescribed or as extended by a previous order, or (2) upon motion made and notice after the expiration of the specified period, may permit the act to be done when failure to act was the result of excusable neglect, but it may not extend the time for making a motion for new trial, for rehearing, or to alter or amend a judgment; making a motion for relief from a judgment under FL ST RCP Rule 1.540(b); taking an appeal or filing a petition for certiorari; or making a motion for a directed verdict. FL ST RCP Rule 1.090(b).

d. *Unaffected by expiration of term.* The period of time provided for the doing of any act or the taking of any proceeding shall not be affected or limited by the continued existence or expiration of a term of court. The continued existence or expiration of a term of court in no way affects the power of a court to do any act or take any proceeding in any action which is or has been pending before it. FL ST RCP Rule 1.090(c).

C. General Requirements

1. *General provisions governing discovery*

   a. *Discovery methods.* Parties may obtain discovery by one or more of the following methods: depositions upon oral examination or written questions; written interrogatories; production of documents or things or permission to enter upon land or other property for inspection and other purposes; physical and mental examinations; and requests for admission. Unless the court orders otherwise and under FL ST RCP Rule 1.280(c), the frequency of use of these methods is not limited, except as provided in FL ST RCP Rule 1.200, FL ST RCP Rule 1.340, and FL ST RCP Rule 1.370. FL ST RCP Rule 1.280(a).

   b. *Scope of discovery.* Unless otherwise limited by order of the court in accordance with the Florida Rules of Civil Procedure, the scope of discovery is as follows:

      i. *In general.* Parties may obtain discovery regarding any matter, not privileged, that is relevant to the subject matter of the pending action, whether it relates to the claim or defense of the party seeking discovery or the claim or defense of any other party, including the existence, description, nature, custody, condition, and location of any books, documents, or other tangible things and the identity and location of persons having knowledge of any discoverable matter. It is not ground for objection that the information sought will be inadmissible at the trial if the information sought appears reasonably calculated to lead to the discovery of admissible evidence. FL ST RCP Rule 1.280(b)(1).

      ii. *Indemnity agreements.* A party may obtain discovery of the existence and contents of any agreement under which any person may be liable to satisfy part or all of a judgment that may be entered in the action or to indemnify or to reimburse a party for payments made to satisfy the judgment. Information concerning the agreement is not admissible in evidence at trial by reason of disclosure. FL ST RCP Rule 1.280(b)(2).

      iii. *Electronically stored information.* A party may obtain discovery of electronically stored information in accordance with the Florida Rules of Civil Procedure. FL ST RCP Rule 1.280(b)(3).

      iv. *Trial preparation; Materials.* Subject to the provisions of FL ST RCP Rule 1.280(b)(5), a party may obtain discovery of documents and tangible things otherwise discoverable under FL ST RCP Rule 1.280(b)(1) and prepared in anticipation of litigation or for trial by or for another party or by or for that party's representative, including that party's attorney, consultant, surety, indemnitor, insurer, or agent, only upon a showing that the party seeking discovery has need of the materials in the preparation of the case and is unable without undue hardship to obtain the substantial equivalent of the materials by other means. FL ST RCP Rule 1.280(b)(4).

         - In ordering discovery of the materials when the required showing has been made, the court shall protect against disclosure of the mental impressions, conclusions, opinions, or legal theories of an attorney or other representative of a party concerning the litigation. FL ST RCP Rule 1.280(b)(4).

- Without the required showing a party may obtain a copy of a statement concerning the action or its subject matter previously made by that party. FL ST RCP Rule 1.280(b)(4).
- Upon request without the required showing a person not a party may obtain a copy of a statement concerning the action or its subject matter previously made by that person. If the request is refused, the person may move for an order to obtain a copy. The provisions of FL ST RCP Rule 1.380(a)(5) apply to the award of expenses incurred as a result of making the motion. FL ST RCP Rule 1.280(b)(4).
- For purposes of FL ST RCP Rule 1.280(b)(4), a statement previously made is a written statement signed or otherwise adopted or approved by the person making it, or a stenographic, mechanical, electrical, or other recording or transcription of it that is a substantially verbatim recital of an oral statement by the person making it and contemporaneously recorded. FL ST RCP Rule 1.280(b)(4).

v. *Trial preparation; Experts.* Discovery of facts known and opinions held by experts, otherwise discoverable under the provisions of FL ST RCP Rule 1.280(b)(1) and acquired or developed in anticipation of litigation or for trial, may be obtained only as follows:

- By interrogatories a party may require any other party to identify each person whom the other party expects to call as an expert witness at trial and to state the subject matter on which the expert is expected to testify, and to state the substance of the facts and opinions to which the expert is expected to testify and a summary of the grounds for each opinion. FL ST RCP Rule 1.280(b)(5)(A)(i).
- Any person disclosed by interrogatories or otherwise as a person expected to be called as an expert witness at trial may be deposed in accordance with FL ST RCP Rule 1.390 without motion or order of court. FL ST RCP Rule 1.280(b)(5)(A)(ii).
- A party may obtain the following discovery regarding any person disclosed by interrogatories or otherwise as a person expected to be called as an expert witness at trial: The scope of employment in the pending case and the compensation for such service, FL ST RCP Rule 1.280(b)(5)(A)(iii)(1); The expert's general litigation experience, including the percentage of work performed for plaintiffs and defendants, FL ST RCP Rule 1.280(b)(5)(A)(iii)(2); The identity of other cases, within a reasonable time period, in which the expert has testified by deposition or at trial, FL ST RCP Rule 1.280(b)(5)(A)(iii)(3); An approximation of the portion of the expert's involvement as an expert witness, which may be based on the number of hours, percentage of hours, or percentage of earned income derived from serving as an expert witness; however, the expert shall not be required to disclose his or her earnings as an expert witness or income derived from other services. FL ST RCP Rule 1.280(b)(5)(A)(iii)(4).
- An expert may be required to produce financial and business records only under the most unusual or compelling circumstances and may not be compelled to compile or produce nonexistent documents. Upon motion, the court may order further discovery by other means, subject to such restrictions as to scope and other provisions pursuant to FL ST RCP Rule 1.280(b)(5)(C) concerning fees and expenses as the court may deem appropriate. FL ST RCP Rule 1.280(b)(5).
- A party may discover facts known or opinions held by an expert who has been retained or specially employed by another party in anticipation of litigation or preparation for trial and who is not expected to be called as a witness at trial, only as provided in FL ST RCP Rule 1.360(b) or upon a showing of exceptional circumstances under which it is impracticable for the party seeking discovery to obtain facts or opinions on the same subject by other means. FL ST RCP Rule 1.280(b)(5)(B).
- Unless manifest injustice would result, the court shall require that the party seeking

discovery pay the expert a reasonable fee for time spent in responding to discovery under FL ST RCP Rule 1.280(b)(5)(A) and FL ST RCP Rule 1.280(b)(5)(B); and concerning discovery from an expert obtained under FL ST RCP Rule 1.280(b)(5)(A) the court may require, and concerning discovery obtained under FL ST RCP Rule 1.280(b)(5)(B) shall require, the party seeking discovery to pay the other party a fair part of the fees and expenses reasonably incurred by the latter party in obtaining facts and opinions from the expert. FL ST RCP Rule 1.280(b)(5)(C).

- As used in the Florida Rules of Civil Procedure an expert shall be an expert witness as defined in FL ST RCP Rule 1.390(a). FL ST RCP Rule 1.280(b)(5)(D).

vi. *Claims to privilege or protection.* When a party withholds information otherwise discoverable under the Florida Rules of Civil Procedure by claiming that it is privileged or subject to protection as trial preparation material, the party shall make the claim expressly and shall describe the nature of the documents, communications, or things not produced or disclosed in a manner that, without revealing information itself privileged or protected, will enable other parties to assess the applicability of the privilege or protection. FL ST RCP Rule 1.280(b)(6).

c. *Limitations on discovery of electronically stored information*

i. A person may object to discovery of electronically stored information from sources that the person identifies as not reasonably accessible because of burden or cost. On motion to compel discovery or for a protective order, the person from whom discovery is sought must show that the information sought or the format requested is not reasonably accessible because of undue burden or cost. If that showing is made, the court may nonetheless order the discovery from such sources or in such formats if the requesting party shows good cause. The court may specify conditions of the discovery, including ordering that some or all of the expenses incurred by the person from whom discovery is sought be paid by the party seeking the discovery. FL ST RCP Rule 1.280(d)(1).

ii. In determining any motion involving discovery of electronically stored information, the court must limit the frequency or extent of discovery otherwise allowed by the Florida Rules of Civil Procedure if it determines that (i) the discovery sought is unreasonably cumulative or duplicative, or can be obtained from another source or in another manner that is more convenient, less burdensome, or less expensive; or (ii) the burden or expense of the discovery outweighs its likely benefit, considering the needs of the case, the amount in controversy, the parties' resources, the importance of the issues at stake in the action, and the importance of the discovery in resolving the issues. FL ST RCP Rule 1.280(d)(2).

d. For information on inadvertent disclosure of privileged materials, see FL ST RCP Rule 1.285.

2. *Requests for admission.* It is an advantage to use requests for admission. The biggest advantage is that if an adversary denies a request for an admission and the denied matter is later proven to be true, the adversary may have to pay the costs of proving the genuineness of the document or the truth of the matter requested to be admitted. FL-PP § 3:143.

a. *Scope.* A party may serve upon any other party a written request for the admission of the truth of any matters within the scope of FL ST RCP Rule 1.280(b) set forth in the request that relate to statements or opinions of fact or of the application of law to fact, including the genuineness of any documents described in the request. FL ST RCP Rule 1.370(a).

b. *Copies of documents.* Copies of documents shall be served with the request unless they have been or are otherwise furnished or made available for inspection and copying. FL ST RCP Rule 1.370(a).

c. *Number of requests.* The request for admission shall not exceed thirty (30) requests, including all subparts, unless the court permits a larger number on motion and notice and for good cause, or the parties propounding and responding to the requests stipulate to a larger number. Each matter of which an admission is requested shall be separately set forth. FL ST RCP Rule 1.370(a).

d. *Sufficiency of responses.* The party who has requested the admissions may move to determine the sufficiency of the answers or objections. Unless the court determines that an objection is justified, it shall order that an answer be served. If the court determines that an answer does not comply with the requirements of this rule, it may order either that the matter is admitted or that an amended answer be served. Instead of these orders the court may determine that final disposition of the request be made at a pretrial conference or at a designated time before trial. The provisions of FL ST RCP Rule 1.380(a)(4) apply to the award of expenses incurred in relation to the motion. FL ST RCP Rule 1.370(a).

e. *Effect of admission.* Any matter admitted under FL ST RCP Rule 1.370 is conclusively established unless the court on motion permits withdrawal or amendment of the admission. Subject to FL ST RCP Rule 1.200 governing amendment of a pretrial order, the court may permit withdrawal or amendment when the presentation of the merits of the action will be subserved by it and the party who obtained the admission fails to satisfy the court that withdrawal or amendment will prejudice that party in maintaining an action or defense on the merits. Any admission made by a party under this rule is for the purpose of the pending action only and is not an admission for any other purpose nor may it be used against that party in any other proceeding. FL ST RCP Rule 1.370(b).

f. *Answer requirements.* The matter is admitted unless the party to whom the request is directed serves upon the party requesting the admission a written answer or objection addressed to the matter within thirty (30) days after service of the request or such shorter or longer time as the court may allow but, unless the court shortens the time, a defendant shall not be required to serve answers or objections before the expiration of forty-five (45) days after service of the process and initial pleading upon the defendant. If objection is made, the reasons shall be stated. The answer shall specifically deny the matter or set forth in detail the reasons why the answering party cannot truthfully admit or deny the matter. A denial shall fairly meet the substance of the requested admission, and when good faith requires that a party qualify an answer or deny only a part of the matter of which an admission is requested, the party shall specify so much of it as is true and qualify or deny the remainder. An answering party may not give lack of information or knowledge as a reason for failure to admit or deny unless that party states that that party has made reasonable inquiry and that the information known or readily obtainable by that party is insufficient to enable that party to admit or deny. A party who considers that a matter of which an admission has been requested presents a genuine issue for trial may not object to the request on that ground alone; the party may deny the matter or set forth reasons why the party cannot admit or deny it, subject to FL ST RCP Rule 1.380(c). FL ST RCP Rule 1.370(a).

3. *Arbitration and mediation*

a. *Referral to arbitration and mediation.* Except as hereinafter provided or as otherwise prohibited by law, the presiding judge may enter an order referring all or any part of a contested civil matter to mediation or arbitration. The parties to any contested civil matter may file a written stipulation to mediate or arbitrate any issue between them at any time. Such stipulation shall be incorporated into the order of referral. FL ST RCP Rule 1.700(a).

b. *Arbitration*

i. *Exclusions.* A civil action shall be ordered to arbitration or arbitration in conjunction with mediation upon stipulation of the parties. A civil action may be ordered to arbitration or arbitration in conjunction with mediation upon motion of any party or by the court, if the judge determines the action to be of such a nature that arbitration could be of benefit to the litigants or the court. FL ST RCP Rule 1.800.

- Under no circumstances may the following categories of actions be referred to arbitration: (1) bond estreatures; (2) habeas corpus or other extraordinary writs; (3) bond validations; (4) civil or criminal contempt; (5) such other matters as may be specified by order of the chief judge in the circuit. FL ST RCP Rule 1.800.

ii. For more information regarding arbitration, please see FL ST RCP Rule 1.810; FL ST RCP Rule 1.820; FL ST RCP Rule 1.830.

c. *Mediation.* For more information regarding mediation, please see FL ST RCP Rule 1.710; FL ST RCP Rule 1.720; FL ST RCP Rule 1.730; and FL ST RCP Rule 1.750.

4. *Rules of court*

a. *Rules of civil procedure.* The Florida Rules of Civil Procedure apply to all actions of a civil nature

and all special statutory proceedings in the circuit courts and county courts except those to which the Florida Probate Rules, the Florida Family Law Rules of Procedure, or the Small Claims Rules apply. FL ST RCP Rule 1.010.

i. The form, content, procedure, and time for pleading in all special statutory proceedings shall be as prescribed by the statutes governing the proceeding unless the Florida Rules of Civil Procedure specifically provide to the contrary. FL ST RCP Rule 1.010.

ii. The Florida Rules of Civil Procedure shall be construed to secure the just, speedy, and inexpensive determination of every action. FL ST RCP Rule 1.010.

b. *Rules of judicial administration.* The Florida Rules of Judicial Administration shall apply to administrative matters in all courts to which the Florida Rules of Judicial Administration are applicable by their terms. The Florida Rules of Judicial Administration shall be construed to secure the speedy and inexpensive determination of every proceeding to which they are applicable. The Florida Rules of Judicial Administration shall supersede all conflicting rules and statutes. FL ST J ADMIN Rule 2.110.

5. *Notice of change of contact information.* The Clerk shall provide a change of address and/or telephone number form for use by attorneys and pro se litigants. With any change of address and/or telephone number, attorneys and pro se litigants governed by FL ST J ADMIN Rule 2.515 will provide to the Clerk and all parties promptly the change of address and/or telephone number form. This form should be submitted only once to the Clerk, who will then make the address and/or telephone number change in all court divisions. FL ST 2 J CIR 2007-05.

D. Documents

1. *Required documents*

a. *Request for admission.* Please see the General Requirements section of this document for more information on the contents of the request for admission.

i. *Notices to persons with disabilities.* See the Format section of this KeyRules document for further information.

b. *Copies of documents.* Copies of documents shall be served with the request unless they have been or are otherwise furnished or made available for inspection and copying. FL ST RCP Rule 1.370(a).

c. *Certificate of service.* A certificate of service of the interrogatories shall be filed, giving the date of service and the name of the party to whom they were directed. FL ST RCP Rule 1.340(e). When any attorney certifies in substance: "I certify that a copy hereof has been furnished to (here insert name or names and addresses used for service) by (e-mail) (delivery) (mail) (fax) on .... (date) ....________________ Attorney" the certificate is taken as prima facie proof of such service in compliance with FL ST J ADMIN Rule 2.516. FL ST J ADMIN Rule 2.516(f).

E. Format

1. *Documents; Type and size.* Documents subject to the exceptions set forth in FL ST J ADMIN Rule 2.525(d) shall be filed on recycled paper measuring eight and one half by eleven (8 1/2 by 11) inches. For purposes of FL ST J ADMIN Rule 2.520, paper is recycled if it contains a minimum content of fifty (50) percent waste paper. Xerographic reduction of legal-size (eight and one half by fourteen (8 1/2 by 14) inches) documents to letter size (eight and one half by eleven (8 1/2 by 11) inches) is prohibited. All other documents filed by electronic transmission shall be filed in a format capable of being printed in a format consistent with the provisions of FL ST J ADMIN Rule 2.250. FL ST J ADMIN Rule 2.520(b).

a. *Exhibits.* Any exhibit or attachment filed with pleadings or papers may be filed in its original size. FL ST J ADMIN Rule 2.520(c).

b. *Recording space.* On all papers and documents prepared and filed by the court or by any party to a proceeding which are to be recorded in the public records of any county, including but not limited to final money judgments and notices of lis pendens, a three (3) inch by three (3) inch space at the top right-hand corner on the first page and a one (1) inch by three (3) inch space at the top right-hand corner on each subsequent page shall be left blank and reserved for use by the clerk of court. FL ST J ADMIN Rule 2.520(d).

i. *Exceptions to recording space.* Any papers or documents created by persons or entities over

which the filing party has no control, including but not limited to wills, codicils, trusts, or other testamentary documents; documents prepared or executed by any public officer; documents prepared, executed, acknowledged, or proved outside of the State of Florida; or documents created by State or Federal government agencies, may be filed without the space required by FL ST J ADMIN Rule 2.520. FL ST J ADMIN Rule 2.520(e).

c. *Noncompliance.* No clerk of court is permitted to refuse to file any document or paper because of noncompliance with the Florida Rules of Judicial Administration. However, upon request of the clerk of court, noncomplying documents must be resubmitted in accordance with the formatting rules. FL ST J ADMIN Rule 2.520(f).

2. *Caption.* Every pleading, motion, order, judgment, or other paper shall have a caption containing the name of the court, the file number, and except for in rem proceedings, including forfeiture proceedings, the name of the first party on each side with an appropriate indication of other parties, and a designation identifying the party filing it and its nature or the nature of the order, as the case may be. In any in rem proceeding, every pleading, motion, order, judgment, or other paper shall have a caption containing the name of the court, the file number, the style "In re" (followed by the name or general description of the property), and a designation of the person or entity filing it and its nature or the nature of the order, as the case may be. In an in rem forfeiture proceeding, the style shall be "In re forfeiture of" (followed by the name of the general description of the property). All papers filed in the action shall be styled in such a manner as to indicate clearly the subject matter of the paper and the party requesting or obtaining relief. FL ST RCP Rule 1.100(c)(1).

3. *Writing and written defined.* Writing or written means a document containing information, an application, or a stipulation. FL ST RCP Rule 1.080(c).

4. *Rule abbreviations*

   a. The Florida Rules of Civil Procedure and shall be abbreviated as Fla.R.Civ.P. FL ST RCP Rule 1.010.

   b. The Florida Rules of Judicial Administration shall be abbreviated as Fla. R. Jud. Admin. FL ST J ADMIN Rule 2.110.

5. *Nonverification.* Except when otherwise specifically provided by the Florida Rules of Civil Procedure or an applicable statute, every pleading or other document of a party represented by an attorney need not be verified or accompanied by an affidavit. FL ST RCP Rule 1.030; FL ST J ADMIN Rule 2.515(a).

6. *Attorney signature*

   a. *Attorney signature.* Every pleading and other document of a party represented by an attorney shall be signed by at least one (1) attorney of record in that attorney's individual name whose current record Florida Bar address, telephone number, including area code, primary e-mail address and secondary e-mail addresses, if any, and Florida Bar number shall be stated, and who shall be duly licensed to practice law in Florida or who shall have received permission to appear in the particular case as provided in FL ST J ADMIN Rule 2.510. FL ST J ADMIN Rule 2.515(a).

      i. The attorney may be required by the court to give the address of, and to vouch for the attorney's authority to represent, the party. FL ST J ADMIN Rule 2.515(a).

      ii. The signature of an attorney shall constitute a certificate by the attorney that the attorney has read the pleading or other document; that to the best of the attorney's knowledge, information, and belief there is good ground to support it; and that it is not interposed for delay. FL ST J ADMIN Rule 2.515(a).

      iii. If a pleading is not signed or is signed with intent to defeat the purpose of FL ST J ADMIN Rule 2.515, it may be stricken and the action may proceed as though the pleading or other document had not been served. FL ST J ADMIN Rule 2.515(a).

   b. *Pro se litigant signature.* A party who is not represented by an attorney shall sign any pleading or other paper and state the party's address and telephone number, including area code. FL ST J ADMIN Rule 2.515(b).

c. *Form of signature*

i. The signatures required on pleadings and documents by FL ST J ADMIN Rule 2.515(a) and FL ST J ADMIN Rule 2.515(b) may be:

- Original signatures;
- Original signatures that have been reproduced by electronic means, such as on electronically transmitted documents or photocopied documents;
- Electronic signatures using the "/s/," "s/," or "/s" formats by or at the direction of the person signing; or
- Any other signature format authorized by general law, so long as the clerk where the proceeding is pending has the capability of receiving and has obtained approval from the Supreme Court of Florida to accept pleadings and documents with that signature format. FL ST J ADMIN Rule 2.515(c)(1).

ii. An attorney, party, or other person who files a pleading or paper by electronic transmission that does not contain the original signature of that attorney, party, or other person shall file that identical pleading or paper in paper form containing an original signature of that attorney, party, or other person (hereinafter called the follow-up filing) immediately thereafter. The follow-up filing is not required if the Supreme Court of Florida has entered an order directing the clerk of court to discontinue accepting the follow-up filing. FL ST J ADMIN Rule 2.515(c)(2).

7. *Forms*

a. *Process.* The forms of process, notice of lis pendens, and notice of action provided in the Florida Rules of Civil Procedure are sufficient. Variations from the forms do not void process or notices that are otherwise sufficient. FL ST RCP Rule 1.900(a).

b. *Other forms.* The other forms provided in the Florida Rules of Civil Procedure are sufficient for the matters that are covered by them. So long as the substance is expressed without prolixity, the forms may be varied to meet the facts of a particular case. FL ST RCP Rule 1.900(b).

c. *Formal matters.* Captions, except for the designation of the paper, are omitted from the forms provided in the Florida Rules of Civil Procedure. A general form of caption is the first form provided. Signatures are omitted from pleadings and motions. FL ST RCP Rule 1.900(c).

8. *Notices to persons with disabilities.* All notices of court proceedings to be held in a public facility, and all process compelling appearance at such proceedings, shall include the following statement in bold face, fourteen (14) point Times New Roman or Courier font: "If you are a person with a disability who needs any accommodation in order to participate in this proceeding, you are entitled, at no cost to you, to the provision of certain assistance. Please contact [identify applicable court personnel by name, address, and telephone number] at least seven (7) days before your scheduled court appearance, or immediately upon receiving this notification if the time before the scheduled appearance is less than seven (7) days; if you are hearing or voice impaired, call 711." FL ST J ADMIN Rule 2.540(c)(1).

9. *Minimization of the filing of sensitive information*

a. *Limitations for court filings.* Unless authorized by FL ST J ADMIN Rule 2.425(b), statute, another rule of court, or the court orders otherwise, designated sensitive information filed with the court must be limited to the following format:

i. The initials of a person known to be a minor;

ii. The year of birth of a person's birth date;

iii. No portion of any: Social security number, Bank account number, Credit card account number, Charge account number, or Debit account number;

iv. The last four digits of any: Taxpayer identification number (TIN), Employee identification number, Driver's license number, Passport number, Telephone number, Financial account number, except as set forth in FL ST J ADMIN Rule 2.425(a)(3), Brokerage account number, Insurance policy account number, Loan account number, Customer account number, or Patient or health care number;

v. A truncated version of any: Email address, Computer user name, Password, or Personal identification number (PIN); and

vi. A truncated version of any other sensitive information as provided by court order. FL ST J ADMIN Rule 2.425(a).

b. *Exceptions.* FL ST J ADMIN Rule 2.425(a) does not apply to the following:

i. An account number which identifies the property alleged to be the subject of a proceeding;

ii. The record of an administrative or agency proceeding;

iii. The record in appellate or review proceedings;

iv. The birth date of a minor whenever the birth date is necessary for the court to establish or maintain subject matter jurisdiction;

v. The name of a minor in any order relating to parental responsibility, time-sharing, or child support;

vi. The name of a minor in any document or order affecting the minor's ownership of real property;

vii. The birth date of a party in a writ of attachment or notice to payor;

viii. In traffic and criminal proceedings: a pro se filing; a court filing that is related to a criminal matter or investigation and that is prepared before the filing of a criminal charge or is not filed as part of any docketed criminal case; an arrest or search warrant or any information in support thereof; a charging document and an affidavit or other documents filed in support of any charging document, including any driving records; a statement of particulars; discovery material introduced into evidence or otherwise filed with the court; and all information necessary for the proper issuance and execution of a subpoena duces tecum;

ix. Information used by the clerk for case maintenance purposes or the courts for case management purposes; and

x. Information which is relevant and material to an issue before the court. FL ST J ADMIN Rule 2.425(b).

c. *Remedies.* Upon motion by a party or interested person or sua sponte by the court, the court may order remedies, sanctions or both for a violation of FL ST J ADMIN Rule 2.425(a). Following notice and an opportunity to respond, the court may impose sanctions if such filing was not made in good faith. FL ST J ADMIN Rule 2.425(c).

d. *Motions not restricted.* FL ST J ADMIN Rule 2.425 does not restrict a party's right to move for protective order, to move to file documents under seal, or to request a determination of the confidentiality of records. FL ST J ADMIN Rule 2.425(d).

e. *Application.* FL ST J ADMIN Rule 2.425 does not affect the application of constitutional provisions, statutes, or rules of court regarding confidential information or access to public information. FL ST J ADMIN Rule 2.425(e).

F. Filing and Service Requirements

1. *Court filing of documents and discovery.* Information obtained during discovery shall not be filed with the court until such time as it is filed for good cause. The requirement of good cause is satisfied only where the filing of the information is allowed or required by another applicable rule of procedure or by court order. All filings of discovery documents shall comply with FL ST J ADMIN Rule 2.425. The court shall have the authority to impose sanctions for violation of FL ST RCP Rule 1.280. FL ST RCP Rule 1.280(g).

2. *Filing requirements.* All original documents must be filed with the court either before service or immediately thereafter, unless otherwise provided for by general law or other rules. If the original of any bond or other document is not placed in the court file, a certified copy must be so placed by the clerk. FL ST J ADMIN Rule 2.516(d). All documents shall be filed in conformity with the requirements of FL ST J ADMIN Rule 2.525. FL ST RCP Rule 1.080(b). All documents filed in any court shall be filed by electronic transmission in accordance with FL ST J ADMIN Rule 2.525. "Documents" means pleadings, motions, petitions, memoranda, briefs, notices, exhibits, declarations, affidavits, orders, judgments, decrees, writs, opinions, and any other paper or writing submitted to a court. FL ST J ADMIN Rule

2.520(a). All documents that are court records, as defined in FL ST J ADMIN Rule 2.430(a)(1), must be filed by electronic transmission, provided that: (1) the clerk has the ability to accept and retain such documents; (2) the clerk or the chief judge of the circuit has requested permission to accept documents filed by electronic transmission; and (3) the supreme court has entered an order granting permission to the clerk to accept documents filed by electronic transmission. FL ST J ADMIN Rule 2.525(c)(1).

a. *Definition.* "Electronic transmission of documents" means the sending of information by electronic signals to, by or from a court or clerk, which when received can be transformed and stored or transmitted on paper, microfilm, magnetic storage device, optical imaging system, CD-ROM, flash drive, other electronic data storage system, server, case maintenance system ("CM"), electronic court filing ("ECF") system, statewide or local electronic portal ("e-portal"), or other electronic record keeping system authorized by the supreme court in a format sufficient to communicate the information on the original document in a readable format. Electronic transmission of documents includes electronic mail ("e-mail") and any internet-based transmission procedure, and may include procedures allowing for documents to be signed or verified by electronic means. FL ST J ADMIN Rule 2.525(a).

   i. The filing of documents with the court as required by the Florida Rules of Judicial Administration must be made by filing them with the clerk in accordance with FL ST J ADMIN Rule 2.525, except that the judge may permit documents to be filed with the judge, in which event the judge must note the filing date before him or her on the documents and transmit them to the clerk. The date of filing is that shown on the face of the document by the judge's notation or the clerk's time stamp, whichever is earlier. FL ST J ADMIN Rule 2.516(e).

b. *Application.* Any court or clerk of the court may accept the electronic transmission of documents for filing after the clerk, together with input from the chief judge of the circuit, has obtained approval of the procedures and program for doing so from the Supreme Court of Florida. FL ST J ADMIN Rule 2.525(b).

c. *Exceptions*

   i. Paper documents and other submissions may be manually submitted to the clerk or court:

      - When the clerk does not have the ability to accept and retain documents by electronic filing or has not had ECF Procedures approved by the supreme court;
      - For filing by any self-represented party or any self-represented nonparty unless specific ECF Procedures provide a means to file documents electronically. However, any self-represented nonparty that is a governmental or public agency and any other agency, partnership, corporation, or business entity acting on behalf of any governmental or public agency may file documents by electronic transmission if such entity has the capability of filing documents electronically;
      - For filing by attorneys excused from e-mail service in accordance with FL ST J ADMIN Rule 2.516(b);
      - When submitting evidentiary exhibits or filing non-documentary materials;
      - When the filing involves documents in excess of twenty-five (25) megabytes (25MB) in size. For such filings, documents may be transmitted using an electronic storage medium that the clerk has the ability to accept, which may include a CD-ROM, flash drive, or similar storage medium;
      - When filed in open court, as permitted by the court;
      - When paper filing is permitted by any approved statewide or local ECF procedures; and
      - If any court determines that justice so requires. FL ST J ADMIN Rule 2.525(d).

   ii. Any document in paper form submitted under FL ST J ADMIN Rule 2.525(d) is filed when it is received by the clerk or court and the clerk shall immediately thereafter convert any filed paper document to an electronic document. "Convert to an electronic document" means optically capturing an image of a paper document and using character recognition software to recover as much of the document's text as practicable and then indexing and storing the document in the official court file. FL ST J ADMIN Rule 2.525(c)(4).

iii. Any storage medium submitted under FL ST J ADMIN Rule 2.525(d)(5) is filed when received by the clerk or court and the clerk shall immediately thereafter transfer the electronic documents from the storage device to the official court file. FL ST J ADMIN Rule 2.525(c)(5).

iv. If the filer of any paper document authorized under FL ST J ADMIN Rule 2.525(d) provides a self-addressed, postage-paid envelope for return of the paper document after it is converted to electronic form by the clerk, the clerk shall place the paper document in the envelope and deposit it in the mail. Except when a paper document is required to be maintained, the clerk may recycle any filed paper document that is not to be returned to the filer. FL ST J ADMIN Rule 2.525(c)(6).

v. The clerk may convert any paper document filed before the effective date of FL ST J ADMIN Rule 2.525 to an electronic document. Unless the clerk is required to maintain the paper document, if the paper document has been converted to an electronic document by the clerk, the paper document is no longer part of the official court file and may be removed and recycled. FL ST J ADMIN Rule 2.525(c)(7).

d. *Official court file.* For information on what constitutes the official court file, please see FL ST J ADMIN Rule 2.525(c)(2), FL ST J ADMIN Rule 2.525(c)(3).

e. *Administration.* All attorneys, parties, or other persons using this rule to file documents are required to make arrangements with the court or clerk for the payment of any charges authorized by general law or the supreme court before filing any document by electronic transmission. FL ST J ADMIN Rule 2.525(f)(2).

f. *Filing date.* The filing date for an electronically transmitted document is the date and time that such filing is acknowledged by an electronic stamp or otherwise, pursuant to any procedure set forth in any ECF Procedures approved by the supreme court, or the date the last page of such filing is received by the court or clerk. FL ST J ADMIN Rule 2.525(f)(3).

g. *Accessibility.* All documents transmitted in any electronic form under FL ST J ADMIN Rule 2.525 must comply with the accessibility requirements of FL ST J ADMIN Rule 2.526. FL ST J ADMIN Rule 2.525(g).

3. *Service requirements.* Every pleading subsequent to the initial pleading, all orders, and every other document filed in the action must be served in conformity with the requirements of FL ST J ADMIN Rule 2.516. FL ST RCP Rule 1.080(a).

a. *Service; When required.* Unless the court otherwise orders, or a statute or supreme court administrative order specifies a different means of service, every pleading subsequent to the initial pleading and every other document filed in any court proceeding, except applications for witness subpoenas and documents served by formal notice or required to be served in the manner provided for service of formal notice, must be served in accordance with FL ST J ADMIN Rule 2.516 on each party. No service need be made on parties against whom a default has been entered, except that pleadings asserting new or additional claims against them must be served in the manner provided for service of summons. FL ST J ADMIN Rule 2.516(a).

b. *Service; How made.* When service is required or permitted to be made upon a party represented by an attorney, service must be made upon the attorney unless service upon the party is ordered by the court. FL ST J ADMIN Rule 2.516(b).

i. *Service by electronic mail ("e-mail").* All documents required or permitted to be served on another party must be served by e-mail, unless FL ST J ADMIN Rule 2.516 otherwise provides. When, in addition to service by e-mail, the sender also utilizes another means of service provided for in FL ST J ADMIN Rule 2.516(b)(2), any differing time limits and other provisions applicable to that other means of service control. FL ST J ADMIN Rule 2.516(b)(1). Any document electronically transmitted to a court or clerk must also be served on all parties and interested persons in accordance with the applicable rules of court. FL ST J ADMIN Rule 2.525(e)(2).

- *Service on attorneys.* Upon appearing in a proceeding, an attorney must serve a designation of a primary e-mail address and may designate no more than two (2) secondary e-mail

addresses. Thereafter, service must be directed to all designated e-mail addresses in that proceeding. Every document filed by an attorney thereafter must include the primary e-mail address of that attorney and any secondary e-mail addresses. If an attorney does not designate any e-mail address for service, documents may be served on that attorney at the e-mail address on record with The Florida Bar. FL ST J ADMIN Rule 2.516(b)(1)(A).

- *Exception to e-mail service on attorneys.* Service by an attorney on another attorney must be made by e-mail unless excused by the court. Upon motion by an attorney demonstrating that the attorney has no e-mail account and lacks access to the Internet at the attorney's office, the court may excuse the attorney from the requirements of e-mail service. Service on and by an attorney excused by the court from e-mail service must be by the means provided in FL ST J ADMIN Rule 2.516(b)(2). FL ST J ADMIN Rule 2.516(b)(1)(B).
- *Service on and by parties not represented by an attorney.* Any party not represented by an attorney may serve a designation of a primary e-mail address and also may designate no more than two (2) secondary e-mail addresses to which service must be directed in that proceeding by the means provided in FL ST J ADMIN Rule 2.516(b)(1). If a party not represented by an attorney does not designate an e-mail address for service in a proceeding, service on and by that party must be by the means provided in FL ST J ADMIN Rule 2.516(b)(2). FL ST J ADMIN Rule 2.516(b)(1)(C).
- *Time of service.* Service by e-mail is complete when it is sent. FL ST J ADMIN Rule 2.516(b)(1)(D). An e-mail is deemed served on the date it is sent. FL ST J ADMIN Rule 2.516(b)(1)(D)(i). If the sender learns that the e-mail did not reach the address of the person to be served, the sender must immediately send another copy by e-mail, or by a means authorized by FL ST J ADMIN Rule 2.516(b)(2). FL ST J ADMIN Rule 2.516(b)(1)(D)(ii). E-mail service is treated as service by mail for the computation of time. FL ST J ADMIN Rule 2.516(b)(1)(D)(iii).

ii. *Format of e-mail for service.* Service of a document by e-mail is made by attaching a copy of the document in PDF format to an e-mail sent to all addresses designated by the attorney or party. FL ST J ADMIN Rule 2.516(b)(1)(E).

- All documents served by e-mail must be attached to an e-mail message containing a subject line beginning with the words "SERVICE OF COURT DOCUMENT" in all capital letters, followed by the case number of the proceeding in which the documents are being served. FL ST J ADMIN Rule 2.516(b)(1)(E)(i).
- The body of the e-mail must identify the court in which the proceeding is pending, the case number, the name of the initial party on each side, the title of each document served with that e-mail, and the sender's name and telephone number. FL ST J ADMIN Rule 2.516(b)(1)(E)(ii).
- Any document served by e-mail may be signed by the "/s/" format, as long as the filed original is signed in accordance with the applicable rule of procedure. FL ST J ADMIN Rule 2.516(b)(1)(E)(iii).
- Any e-mail which, together with its attached documents, exceeds five megabytes (5MB) in size, must be divided and sent as separate e-mails, no one of which may exceed five megabytes (5MB) in size and each of which must be sequentially numbered in the subject line. FL ST J ADMIN Rule 2.516(b)(1)(E)(iv).

iii. *Service by other means.* In addition to, and not in lieu of, service by e-mail, service may also be made upon attorneys by any of the means specified in FL ST J ADMIN Rule 2.516(b)(2). Service on and by all parties who are not represented by an attorney and who do not designate an e-mail address, and on and by all attorneys excused from e-mail service, must be made by delivering a copy of the document or by mailing it to the party or attorney at their last known address or, if no address is known, by leaving it with the clerk of the court. Service by mail is complete upon mailing. Delivery of a copy within FL ST J ADMIN Rule 2.516 is complete upon:

- Handing it to the attorney or to the party,

- Leaving it at the attorney's or party's office with a clerk or other person in charge thereof,
- If there is no one in charge, leaving it in a conspicuous place therein,
- If the office is closed or the person to be served has no office, leaving it at the person's usual place of abode with some person of his or her family above fifteen (15) years of age and informing such person of the contents, or
- Transmitting it by facsimile to the attorney's or party's office with a cover sheet containing the sender's name, firm, address, telephone number, and facsimile number, and the number of pages transmitted. When service is made by facsimile, a copy must also be served by any other method permitted by FL ST J ADMIN Rule 2.516. Facsimile service occurs when transmission is complete. FL ST J ADMIN Rule 2.516(b)(2)(A) through FL ST J ADMIN Rule 2.516(b)(2)(E).
- Service by delivery after 5:00 p.m. must be deemed to have been made by mailing on the date of delivery. FL ST J ADMIN Rule 2.516(b)(2)(F).

c. *Service; Numerous defendants.* In actions when the parties are unusually numerous, the court may regulate the service contemplated by the Florida Rules of Judicial Administration on motion or on its own initiative in such manner as may be found to be just and reasonable. FL ST J ADMIN Rule 2.516(c).

d. *Service by clerk.* Service of notices and other documents required to be made by the clerk must also be done as provided in FL ST J ADMIN Rule 2.516(b). FL ST J ADMIN Rule 2.516(g).

G. Hearings

1. There is no hearing required or contemplated with regard to requests for admission in the Florida Rules of Civil Procedure.

H. Forms

1. Official Request for Admissions Forms for Florida

a. Caption. FL ST RCP Form 1.901.

2. Request for Admissions Forms for Florida

a. Requests for admissions; Negligence, fall down. FL-PRACFORM § 8:41.
b. Requests for admissions; Promissory note. FL-PRACFORM § 8:42.
c. Requests for admissions; Open account. FL-PRACFORM § 8:43.
d. Requests for admissions; Mortgage foreclosure. FL-PRACFORM § 8:44.
e. Request for admissions; General form. FL-PP § 3:146.
f. Request for admissions; Facts and genuineness of documents. FL-PP § 3:147.
g. Motion; To determine sufficiency of reply to request for admissions. FL-PP § 3:152.
h. Form for request for admissions. FL-RCPF R 1.370(5).
i. Form for request for admissions (another form). FL-RCPF R 1.370(6).
j. Form for request for admissions served concurrently with interrogatories. FL-RCPF R 1.370(7).
k. Form for request for admissions as to factual situation and refinement of issues. FL-RCPF R 1.370(9).
l. Form for request to admit party uses electronic data storage. FL-RCPF R 1.370(10).

3. Official Forms for Florida Circuit Court, Second Judicial Circuit

a. Notice of change of contact information. FL ST 2 J CIR 2007-05.

I. Checklist

(I) ❑ Matters to be considered by requesting party

(a) ❑ Required documents

(1) ❑ Request

(2) ❑ Copies of documents

(3) ❑ Certificate of service

(b) ❑ Time for request

(1) ❑ Without leave of court the request may be served upon the plaintiff after commencement of the action and upon any other party with or after service of the process and initial pleading upon that party

(II) ❑ Matters to be considered by responding party

(a) ❑ Required documents

(1) ❑ Response to request

(2) ❑ Certificate of service

(b) ❑ Time for response

(1) ❑ The party to whom the request is directed shall serve a written response within thirty (30) days after service of the request, except that a defendant may serve a response within forty-five (45) days after service of the process and initial pleading on that defendant

Requests, Notices and Applications
Notice of Deposition

Document Last Updated January 2013

A. Applicable Rules

1. *State rules*

a. Pleadings and motions. FL ST RCP Rule 1.100.

b. Nonverification of pleadings. FL ST RCP Rule 1.030.

c. Service and filing of pleadings, orders, and documents. FL ST RCP Rule 1.080.

d. Time. FL ST RCP Rule 1.090.

e. General provisions governing discovery. FL ST RCP Rule 1.280.

f. Depositions before action or pending appeal. FL ST RCP Rule 1.290.

g. Persons before whom depositions may be taken. FL ST RCP Rule 1.300.

h. Depositions upon oral examination. FL ST RCP Rule 1.310.

i. Depositions upon written questions. FL ST RCP Rule 1.320.

j. Use of depositions in court proceedings. FL ST RCP Rule 1.330.

k. Failure to make discovery; Sanctions. FL ST RCP Rule 1.380.

l. Depositions of expert witnesses. FL ST RCP Rule 1.390.

m. Relief from judgment, decrees, or orders. FL ST RCP Rule 1.540.

n. Forms. FL ST RCP Rule 1.900.

o. Minimization of the filing of sensitive information. FL ST J ADMIN Rule 2.425.

p. Retention of court records. FL ST J ADMIN Rule 2.430.

q. Foreign attorneys. FL ST J ADMIN Rule 2.510.

r. Signature of attorneys and parties. FL ST J ADMIN Rule 2.515.

s. Paper. FL ST J ADMIN Rule 2.520.

t. Electronic filing. FL ST J ADMIN Rule 2.525.

u. Accessibility of information and technology. FL ST J ADMIN Rule 2.526.

v. Requests for accommodations by persons with disabilities. FL ST J ADMIN Rule 2.540.

2. *Local rules*

a. Notice of change of contact information. FL ST 2 J CIR 2007-05.

B. Timing

1. *Depositions upon oral examination.* After commencement of the action any party may take the testimony of any person, including a party, by deposition upon oral examination. Leave of court, granted with or without notice, must be obtained only if the plaintiff seeks to take a deposition within thirty (30) days after service of the process and initial pleading upon any defendant, except that leave is not required (1) if a defendant has served a notice of taking deposition or otherwise sought discovery, or (2) if special notice is given as provided in FL ST RCP Rule 1.310(b)(2). The attendance of witnesses may be compelled by subpoena as provided in FL ST RCP Rule 1.410. The deposition of a person confined in prison may be taken only by leave of court on such terms as the court prescribes. FL ST RCP Rule 1.310(a). A party desiring to take the deposition of any person upon oral examination shall give reasonable notice in writing to every other party to the action. FL ST RCP Rule 1.310(b)(1).

2. *Depositions upon written questions.* After commencement of the action any party may take the testimony of any person, including a party, by deposition upon written questions. The attendance of witnesses may be compelled by the use of subpoena as provided in FL ST RCP Rule 1.410. The deposition of a person confined in prison may be taken only by leave of court on such terms as the court prescribes. Within thrity (30) days after the notice and written questions are served, a party may serve cross questions upon all other parties. Within ten (10) days after being served with cross questions, a party may serve redirect questions upon all other parties. Within ten (10) days after being served with redirect questions, a party may serve recross questions upon all other parties. The court may for cause shown enlarge or shorten the time. FL ST RCP Rule 1.320(a).

3. *Depositions before action or pending appeal.* For information on petitions and motions for depositions before an action or pending appeal, please see the General Requirements section below.

4. *Sequence and timing of discovery.* Except as provided in FL ST RCP Rule 1.280(b)(5) or unless the court upon motion for the convenience of parties and witnesses and in the interest of justice orders otherwise, methods of discovery may be used in any sequence, and the fact that a party is conducting discovery, whether by deposition or otherwise, shall not delay any other party's discovery. FL ST RCP Rule 1.280(e).

5. *Computation of time*

a. *Generally.* Computation of time shall be governed by FL ST J ADMIN Rule 2.514. FL ST RCP Rule 1.090(a). The following rules apply in computing time periods specified in any rule of procedure, local rule, court order, or statute that does not specify a method of computing time. FL ST J ADMIN Rule 2.514(a).

i. *Period stated in days or a longer unit.* When the period is stated in days or a longer unit of time (A) exclude the day of the event that triggers the period; (B) count every day, including intermediate Saturdays, Sundays, and legal holidays; and (C) include the last day of the period, but if the last day is a Saturday, Sunday, or legal holiday, or falls within any period of time extended through an order of the chief justice under FL ST J ADMIN Rule 2.205(a)(2)(B)(iv), the period continues to run until the end of the next day that is not a Saturday, Sunday, or legal holiday and does not fall within any period of time extended through an order of the chief justice. FL ST J ADMIN Rule 2.514(a)(1).

ii. *Period stated in hours.* When the period is stated in hours (A) begin counting immediately on the occurrence of the event that triggers the period; (B) count every hour, including hours during intermediate Saturdays, Sundays, and legal holidays; and (C) if the period would end on a Saturday, Sunday, or legal holiday, or during any period of time extended through an order of the chief justice under FL ST J ADMIN Rule 2.205(a)(2)(B)(iv), the period continues to run until the same time on the next day that is not a Saturday, Sunday, or legal holiday and does not fall within any period of time extended through an order of the chief justice. FL ST J ADMIN Rule 2.514(a)(2).

iii. *Period stated in days less than seven (7) days.* When the period stated in days is less than seven (7) days, intermediate Saturdays, Sundays, and legal holidays shall be excluded in the computation. FL ST J ADMIN Rule 2.514(a)(3).

iv. *"Last day" defined.* Unless a different time is set by a statute, local rule, or court order, the last day ends (A) for electronic filing or for service by any means, at midnight; and (B) for filing by other means, when the clerk's office is scheduled to close. FL ST J ADMIN Rule 2.514(a)(4).

v. *"Next day" defined.* The "next day" is determined by continuing to count forward when the period is measured after an event and backward when measured before an event. FL ST J ADMIN Rule 2.514(a)(5).

vi. *"Legal holiday" defined.* "Legal holiday" means (A) the day set aside by FL ST § 110.117, for observing New Year's Day, Martin Luther King, Jr.'s Birthday, Memorial Day, Independence Day, Labor Day, Veterans' Day, Thanksgiving Day, the Friday after Thanksgiving Day, or Christmas Day, and (B) any day observed as a holiday by the clerk's office or as designated by the chief judge. FL ST J ADMIN Rule 2.514(a)(6).

b. *Additional time after service by mail or e-mail.* When a party may or must act within a specified time after service and service is made by mail or e-mail, five (5) days are added after the period that would otherwise expire under FL ST J ADMIN Rule 2.514(a). FL ST J ADMIN Rule 2.514(b).

c. *Enlargement.* When an act is required or allowed to be done at or within a specified time by order of court, by the Florida Rules of Civil Procedure, or by notice given thereunder, for cause shown the court at any time in its discretion (1) with or without notice, may order the period enlarged if request therefor is made before the expiration of the period originally prescribed or as extended by a previous order, or (2) upon motion made and notice after the expiration of the specified period, may permit the act to be done when failure to act was the result of excusable neglect, but it may not extend the time for making a motion for new trial, for rehearing, or to alter or amend a judgment; making a motion for relief from a judgment under FL ST RCP Rule 1.540(b); taking an appeal or filing a petition for certiorari; or making a motion for a directed verdict. FL ST RCP Rule 1.090(b).

d. *Unaffected by expiration of term.* The period of time provided for the doing of any act or the taking of any proceeding shall not be affected or limited by the continued existence or expiration of a term of court. The continued existence or expiration of a term of court in no way affects the power of a court to do any act or take any proceeding in any action which is or has been pending before it. FL ST RCP Rule 1.090(c).

C. General Requirements

1. *General provisions governing discovery*

a. *Discovery methods.* Parties may obtain discovery by one or more of the following methods: depositions upon oral examination or written questions; written interrogatories; production of documents or things or permission to enter upon land or other property for inspection and other purposes; physical and mental examinations; and requests for admission. Unless the court orders otherwise and under FL ST RCP Rule 1.280(c), the frequency of use of these methods is not limited, except as provided in FL ST RCP Rule 1.200, FL ST RCP Rule 1.340, and FL ST RCP Rule 1.370. FL ST RCP Rule 1.280(a).

b. *Scope of discovery.* Unless otherwise limited by order of the court in accordance with the Florida Rules of Civil Procedure, the scope of discovery is as follows:

i. *In general.* Parties may obtain discovery regarding any matter, not privileged, that is relevant to the subject matter of the pending action, whether it relates to the claim or defense of the party seeking discovery or the claim or defense of any other party, including the existence, description, nature, custody, condition, and location of any books, documents, or other tangible things and the identity and location of persons having knowledge of any discoverable matter. It is not ground for objection that the information sought will be inadmissible at the trial if the information sought appears reasonably calculated to lead to the discovery of admissible evidence. FL ST RCP Rule 1.280(b)(1).

ii. *Indemnity agreements.* A party may obtain discovery of the existence and contents of any agreement under which any person may be liable to satisfy part or all of a judgment that may be entered in the action or to indemnify or to reimburse a party for payments made to satisfy the judgment. Information concerning the agreement is not admissible in evidence at trial by reason of disclosure. FL ST RCP Rule 1.280(b)(2).

iii. *Electronically stored information.* A party may obtain discovery of electronically stored information in accordance with the Florida Rules of Civil Procedure. FL ST RCP Rule 1.280(b)(3).

iv. *Trial preparation; Materials.* Subject to the provisions of FL ST RCP Rule 1.280(b)(5), a party may obtain discovery of documents and tangible things otherwise discoverable under FL ST RCP Rule 1.280(b)(1) and prepared in anticipation of litigation or for trial by or for another party or by or for that party's representative, including that party's attorney, consultant, surety, indemnitor, insurer, or agent, only upon a showing that the party seeking discovery has need of the materials in the preparation of the case and is unable without undue hardship to obtain the substantial equivalent of the materials by other means. FL ST RCP Rule 1.280(b)(4).

- In ordering discovery of the materials when the required showing has been made, the court shall protect against disclosure of the mental impressions, conclusions, opinions, or legal theories of an attorney or other representative of a party concerning the litigation. FL ST RCP Rule 1.280(b)(4).
- Without the required showing a party may obtain a copy of a statement concerning the action or its subject matter previously made by that party. FL ST RCP Rule 1.280(b)(4).
- Upon request without the required showing a person not a party may obtain a copy of a statement concerning the action or its subject matter previously made by that person. If the request is refused, the person may move for an order to obtain a copy. The provisions of FL ST RCP Rule 1.380(a)(5) apply to the award of expenses incurred as a result of making the motion. FL ST RCP Rule 1.280(b)(4).
- For purposes of FL ST RCP Rule 1.280(b)(4), a statement previously made is a written statement signed or otherwise adopted or approved by the person making it, or a stenographic, mechanical, electrical, or other recording or transcription of it that is a substantially verbatim recital of an oral statement by the person making it and contemporaneously recorded. FL ST RCP Rule 1.280(b)(4).

v. *Trial preparation; Experts.* Discovery of facts known and opinions held by experts, otherwise discoverable under the provisions of FL ST RCP Rule 1.280(b)(1) and acquired or developed in anticipation of litigation or for trial, may be obtained only as follows:

- By interrogatories a party may require any other party to identify each person whom the other party expects to call as an expert witness at trial and to state the subject matter on which the expert is expected to testify, and to state the substance of the facts and opinions to which the expert is expected to testify and a summary of the grounds for each opinion. FL ST RCP Rule 1.280(b)(5)(A)(i).
- Any person disclosed by interrogatories or otherwise as a person expected to be called as an expert witness at trial may be deposed in accordance with FL ST RCP Rule 1.390 without motion or order of court. FL ST RCP Rule 1.280(b)(5)(A)(ii).
- A party may obtain the following discovery regarding any person disclosed by interrogatories or otherwise as a person expected to be called as an expert witness at trial: The scope of employment in the pending case and the compensation for such service, FL ST RCP Rule 1.280(b)(5)(A)(iii)(1); The expert's general litigation experience, including the percentage of work performed for plaintiffs and defendants, FL ST RCP Rule 1.280(b)(5)(A)(iii)(2); The identity of other cases, within a reasonable time period, in which the expert has testified by deposition or at trial, FL ST RCP Rule 1.280(b)(5)(A)(iii)(3); An approximation of the portion of the expert's involvement as an expert witness, which may be based on the number of hours, percentage of hours, or percentage of earned income derived from serving as an expert witness; however, the

expert shall not be required to disclose his or her earnings as an expert witness or income derived from other services. FL ST RCP Rule 1.280(b)(5)(A)(iii)(4).

- An expert may be required to produce financial and business records only under the most unusual or compelling circumstances and may not be compelled to compile or produce nonexistent documents. Upon motion, the court may order further discovery by other means, subject to such restrictions as to scope and other provisions pursuant to FL ST RCP Rule 1.280(b)(5)(C) concerning fees and expenses as the court may deem appropriate. FL ST RCP Rule 1.280(b)(5).
- A party may discover facts known or opinions held by an expert who has been retained or specially employed by another party in anticipation of litigation or preparation for trial and who is not expected to be called as a witness at trial, only as provided in FL ST RCP Rule 1.360(b) or upon a showing of exceptional circumstances under which it is impracticable for the party seeking discovery to obtain facts or opinions on the same subject by other means. FL ST RCP Rule 1.280(b)(5)(B).
- Unless manifest injustice would result, the court shall require that the party seeking discovery pay the expert a reasonable fee for time spent in responding to discovery under FL ST RCP Rule 1.280(b)(5)(A) and FL ST RCP Rule 1.280(b)(5)(B); and concerning discovery from an expert obtained under FL ST RCP Rule 1.280(b)(5)(A) the court may require, and concerning discovery obtained under FL ST RCP Rule 1.280(b)(5)(B) shall require, the party seeking discovery to pay the other party a fair part of the fees and expenses reasonably incurred by the latter party in obtaining facts and opinions from the expert. FL ST RCP Rule 1.280(b)(5)(C).
- As used in the Florida Rules of Civil Procedure an expert shall be an expert witness as defined in FL ST RCP Rule 1.390(a). FL ST RCP Rule 1.280(b)(5)(D).

vi. *Claims to privilege or protection.* When a party withholds information otherwise discoverable under the Florida Rules of Civil Procedure by claiming that it is privileged or subject to protection as trial preparation material, the party shall make the claim expressly and shall describe the nature of the documents, communications, or things not produced or disclosed in a manner that, without revealing information itself privileged or protected, will enable other parties to assess the applicability of the privilege or protection. FL ST RCP Rule 1.280(b)(6).

c. *Limitations on discovery of electronically stored information*

i. A person may object to discovery of electronically stored information from sources that the person identifies as not reasonably accessible because of burden or cost. On motion to compel discovery or for a protective order, the person from whom discovery is sought must show that the information sought or the format requested is not reasonably accessible because of undue burden or cost. If that showing is made, the court may nonetheless order the discovery from such sources or in such formats if the requesting party shows good cause. The court may specify conditions of the discovery, including ordering that some or all of the expenses incurred by the person from whom discovery is sought be paid by the party seeking the discovery. FL ST RCP Rule 1.280(d)(1).

ii. In determining any motion involving discovery of electronically stored information, the court must limit the frequency or extent of discovery otherwise allowed by the Florida Rules of Civil Procedure if it determines that (i) the discovery sought is unreasonably cumulative or duplicative, or can be obtained from another source or in another manner that is more convenient, less burdensome, or less expensive; or (ii) the burden or expense of the discovery outweighs its likely benefit, considering the needs of the case, the amount in controversy, the parties' resources, the importance of the issues at stake in the action, and the importance of the discovery in resolving the issues. FL ST RCP Rule 1.280(d)(2).

d. For information on inadvertent disclosure of privileged materials, see FL ST RCP Rule 1.285.

2. *Notice of deposition*

a. *Upon oral examination.* A party desiring to take the deposition of any person upon oral examination shall give reasonable notice in writing to every other party to the action. The notice shall state the time and place for taking the deposition and the name and address of each person to be examined, if known, and, if the name is not known, a general description sufficient to identify the person or the particular class or group to which the person belongs. If a subpoena duces tecum is to be served on the person to be examined, the designation of the materials to be produced under the subpoena shall be attached to or included in the notice. FL ST RCP Rule 1.310(b)(1).

b. *Upon written examination.* A party desiring to take a deposition upon written questions shall serve a notice stating: (1) the name and address of the person who is to answer them, if known, and, if the name is not known, a general description sufficient to identify the person or the particular class or group to which that person belongs, and (2) the name or descriptive title and address of the officer before whom the deposition is to be taken. FL ST RCP Rule 1.320(a).

3. *When leave of court required.* Leave of court, granted with or without notice, must be obtained only if the plaintiff seeks to take a deposition within thirty (30) days after service of the process and initial pleading upon any defendant, except that leave is not required if a defendant has served a notice of taking deposition or otherwise sought discovery. FL ST RCP Rule 1.310(a).

   a. *Exceptions.* Leave of court is not required for the taking of a deposition by plaintiff if the notice states that the person to be examined is about to go out of the state and will be unavailable for examination unless a deposition is taken before expiration of the thirty (30) day period. If a party shows that when served with notice under FL ST RCP Rule 1.310(b) that party was unable through the exercise of diligence to obtain counsel to represent the party at the taking of the deposition, the deposition may not be used against that party. FL ST RCP Rule 1.310(b)(2).

   b. *Persons in prison.* The deposition of a person confined in prison may be taken only by leave of court on such terms as the court prescribes. FL ST RCP Rule 1.310(a); FL ST RCP Rule 1.320(a).

4. *Deposition procedure*

   a. *Who may take depositions.* Depositions may be taken before any notary public or judicial officer or before any officer authorized by the statutes of Florida to take acknowledgments or proof of executions of deeds or by any person appointed by the court in which the action is pending. FL ST RCP Rule 1.300(a).

      i. *In foreign countries.* In a foreign country depositions may be taken: on notice before a person authorized to administer oaths in the place in which the examination is held, either by the law thereof or by the law of Florida or of the United States; before a person commissioned by the court, and a person so commissioned shall have the power by virtue of the commission to administer any necessary oath and take testimony; or pursuant to a letter rogatory. FL ST RCP Rule 1.300(b).

      ii. *Selection by stipulation.* If the parties so stipulate in writing, depositions may be taken before any person at any time or place upon any notice and in any manner and when so taken may be used like other depositions. FL ST RCP Rule 1.300(c).

      iii. *Persons disqualified.* Unless so stipulated by the parties, no deposition shall be taken before a person who is a relative, employee, attorney, or counsel of any of the parties, is a relative or employee of any of the parties' attorney or counsel, or is financially interested in the action. FL ST RCP Rule 1.300(d).

   b. *Depositions before action*

      i. *Petition.* A person who desires to perpetuate that person's own testimony or that of another person regarding any matter that may be cognizable in any Florida court may file a verified petition in the circuit court in the county of the residence of any expected adverse party. The petition shall be entitled in the name of the petitioner and shall show:

         - That the petitioner expects to be a party to an action cognizable in a court of Florida, but is presently unable to bring the action;
         - The subject matter of the expected action and the petitioner's interest therein;
         - The facts which the petitioner desires to establish by the proposed testimony and the petitioner's reasons for desiring to perpetuate it;

- The names or a description of the persons the petitioner expects will be adverse parties and their addresses so far as known; and
- The names and addresses of the persons to be examined and the substance of the testimony which the petitioner expects to elicit from each; and shall ask for an order authorizing the petitioner to take the deposition of the persons to be examined named in the petition for the purpose of perpetuating their testimony. FL ST RCP Rule 1.290(a)(1).

ii. *Notice and service.* After submitting the petition, the petitioner must thereafter serve a notice upon each person named in the petition as an expected adverse party, together with a copy of the petition, stating that the petitioner will apply to the court at a time and place named therein for an order described in the petition. At least twenty (20) days before the date of hearing the notice shall be served either within or without the county in the manner provided by law for service of summons, but if such service cannot with due diligence be made upon any expected adverse party named in the petition, the court may make an order for service by publication or otherwise, and shall appoint an attorney for persons not served in the manner provided by law for service of summons who shall represent them, and if they are not otherwise represented, shall cross-examine the deponent. FL ST RCP Rule 1.290(a)(2).

iii. *Order and examination.* If the court is satisfied that the perpetuation of the testimony may prevent a failure or delay of justice, it shall make an order designating or describing the persons whose depositions may be taken and specifying the subject matter of the examination and whether the deposition shall be taken upon oral examination or written interrogatories. The deposition may then be taken in accordance with the rules governing depositions. FL ST RCP Rule 1.290(a)(3).

iv. *Use of deposition.* A deposition taken before an action and in accordance with the procedures above may be used in any action involving the same subject matter subsequently brought in any court. FL ST RCP Rule 1.290(a)(4).

c. *Depositions upon oral examination*

i. *Enlargement of time.* For cause shown the court may enlarge or shorten the time for taking the deposition. FL ST RCP Rule 1.310(b)(3).

ii. *Videotaped depositions.* Any deposition may be recorded by videotape without leave of the court or stipulation of the parties, provided the deposition is taken in accordance with the following:

- *Notice.* A party intending to videotape a deposition shall state in the notice that the deposition is to be videotaped and shall give the name and address of the operator. Any subpoena served on the person to be examined shall state the method or methods for recording the testimony. FL ST RCP Rule 1.310(b)(4)(A).
- *Stenographer.* Videotaped depositions shall also be recorded stenographically, unless all parties agree otherwise. FL ST RCP Rule 1.310(b)(4)(B).
- *Procedure.* At the beginning of the deposition, the officer before whom it is taken shall, on camera: (i) identify the style of the action, (ii) state the date, and (iii) swear the witness. FL ST RCP Rule 1.310(b)(4)(C).
- *Custody of tape and copies.* The attorney for the party requesting the videotaping of the deposition shall take custody of and be responsible for the safeguarding of the videotape, shall permit the viewing of it by the opposing party, and, if requested, shall provide a copy of the videotape at the expense of the party requesting the copy. FL ST RCP Rule 1.310(b)(4)(D).
- *Cost of videotaped depositions.* The party requesting the videotaping shall bear the initial cost of videotaping. FL ST RCP Rule 1.310(b)(4)(E).

iii. *Production of documents.* The notice to a party deponent may be accompanied by a request for the production of documents and tangible things at the taking of the deposition. The procedure of FL ST RCP Rule 1.350 shall apply to the request. FL ST RCP Rule 1.351 provides the

exclusive procedure for obtaining documents or things by subpoena from nonparties without deposing the custodian or other person in possession of the documents. FL ST RCP Rule 1.310(b)(5).

iv. *Deposing organizations.* In the notice a party may name as the deponent a public or private corporation, a partnership or association, or a governmental agency, and designate with reasonable particularity the matters on which examination is requested. The organization so named shall designate one or more officers, directors, or managing agents, or other persons who consent to do so, to testify on its behalf and may state the matters on which each person designated will testify. The persons so designated shall testify about matters known or reasonably available to the organization. FL ST RCP Rule 1.310(b)(6).

v. *Depositions by telephone.* On motion the court may order that the testimony at a deposition be taken by telephone. The order may prescribe the manner in which the deposition will be taken. A party may also arrange for a stenographic transcription at that party's own initial expense. FL ST RCP Rule 1.310(b)(7).

vi. *Deposing a minor.* Any minor subpoenaed for testimony shall have the right to be accompanied by a parent or guardian at all times during the taking of testimony notwithstanding the invocation of the rule of sequestration of section FL ST § 90.616, except upon a showing that the presence of a parent or guardian is likely to have a material, negative impact on the credibility or accuracy of the minor's testimony, or that the interests of the parent or guardian are in actual or potential conflict with the interests of the minor. FL ST RCP Rule 1.310(b)(8).

vii. *Examination and cross-examination.* Examination and cross-examination of witnesses may proceed as permitted at the trial. FL ST RCP Rule 1.310(c).

viii. *Oath.* The officer before whom the deposition is to be taken shall put the witness on oath and shall personally, or by someone acting under the officer's direction and in the officer's presence, record the testimony of the witness, except that when a deposition is being taken by telephone, the witness shall be sworn by a person present with the witness who is qualified to administer an oath in that location. FL ST RCP Rule 1.310(c).

ix. *Record of examination.* The deposition testimony must be taken stenographically or recorded by any other means ordered. If requested by one of the parties, the testimony shall be transcribed at the initial cost of the requesting party and prompt notice of the request shall be given to all other parties. FL ST RCP Rule 1.310(c).

x. *Objections.* All objections made at time of the examination to the qualifications of the officer taking the deposition, the manner of taking it, the evidence presented, or the conduct of any party, and any other objection to the proceedings shall be noted by the officer upon the deposition. Any objection during a deposition shall be stated concisely and in a nonargumentative and nonsuggestive manner. A party may instruct a deponent not to answer only when necessary to preserve a privilege, to enforce a limitation on evidence directed by the court, or to present a motion under FL ST RCP Rule 1.310(d). FL ST RCP Rule 1.310(c).

- Otherwise, evidence objected to shall be taken subject to the objections. Instead of participating in the oral examination, parties may serve written questions in a sealed envelope on the party taking the deposition and that party shall transmit them to the officer, who shall propound them to the witness and record the answers verbatim. FL ST RCP Rule 1.310(c).

xi. *Motion to terminate or limit examination.* At any time during the taking of the deposition, on motion of a party or of the deponent and upon a showing that the examination is being conducted in bad faith or in such manner as unreasonably to annoy, embarrass, or oppress the deponent or party, or that improper objections and instructions to a deponent not to answer are being made, the court in which the action is pending or the circuit court where the deposition is being taken may order the officer conducting the examination to cease forthwith from taking the deposition or may limit the scope and manner of the taking of the deposition under the scope of permissible discovery. FL ST RCP Rule 1.310(d).

- If the order terminates the examination, it shall be resumed thereafter only upon the order of the court in which the action is pending. Upon demand of any party or the deponent, the taking of the deposition shall be suspended for the time necessary to make a motion for an order. FL ST RCP Rule 1.310(d).

xii. *Deponent review.* If the testimony is transcribed, the transcript shall be furnished to the witness for examination and shall be read to or by the witness unless the examination and reading are waived by the witness and by the parties. Any changes in form or substance that the witness wants to make shall be listed in writing by the officer with a statement of the reasons given by the witness for making the changes. The changes shall be attached to the transcript. It shall then be signed by the witness unless the parties waived the signing or the witness is ill, cannot be found, or refuses to sign. If the transcript is not signed by the witness within a reasonable time after it is furnished to the witness, the officer shall sign the transcript and state on the transcript the waiver, illness, absence of the witness, or refusal to sign with any reasons given. The deposition may then be used as fully as though signed unless the court holds that the reasons given for the refusal to sign require rejection of the deposition wholly or partly, on motion under FL ST RCP Rule 1.330(d)(4). FL ST RCP Rule 1.310(e).

xiii. *Certification and inspection.* If the deposition is transcribed, the officer shall certify on each copy of the deposition that the witness was duly sworn by the officer and that the deposition is a true record of the testimony given by the witness. Documents and things produced for inspection during the examination of the witness shall be marked for identification and annexed to and returned with the deposition upon the request of a party, and may be inspected and copied by any party, except that the person producing the materials may substitute copies to be marked for identification if that person affords to all parties fair opportunity to verify the copies by comparison with the originals. If the person producing the materials requests their return, the officer shall mark them, give each party an opportunity to inspect and copy them, and return them to the person producing them and the materials may then be used in the same manner as if annexed to and returned with the deposition. FL ST RCP Rule 1.310(f)(1).

xiv. *Copies.* Upon payment of reasonable charges, the officer shall furnish a copy of the deposition to any party or to the deponent. FL ST RCP Rule 1.310(f)(2). A party or witness who does not have a copy of the deposition may obtain it from the officer taking the deposition unless the court orders otherwise. If the deposition is obtained from a person other than the officer, the reasonable cost of reproducing the copies shall be paid to the person by the requesting party or witness. FL ST RCP Rule 1.310(g).

d. *Depositions upon written examination*

i. *Deposing an organization upon written examination.* A deposition upon written questions may be taken of a public or private corporation, a partnership or association, or a governmental agency in accordance with FL ST RCP Rule 1.310(b)(6). FL ST RCP Rule 1.320(a).

ii. *Cross, redirect, and recross questions.* Within thirty (30) days after the notice and written questions are served, a party may serve cross questions upon all other parties. Within ten (10) days after being served with cross questions, a party may serve redirect questions upon all other parties. Within ten (10) days after being served with redirect questions, a party may serve recross questions upon all other parties. The court may for cause shown enlarge or shorten the time. FL ST RCP Rule 1.320(a).

iii. *Procedure.* A copy of the notice and copies of all questions served shall be delivered by the party taking the depositions to the officer designated in the notice, who shall proceed promptly to take the testimony of the witness in the manner provided by FL ST RCP Rule 1.310(c), FL ST RCP Rule 1.310(e), and FL ST RCP Rule 1.310(f) in response to the questions and to prepare the deposition, attaching the copy of the notice and the questions received by the officer. The questions shall not be filed separately from the deposition unless a party seeks to have the court consider the questions before the questions are submitted to the witness. FL ST RCP Rule 1.320(b).

5. *Arbitration and mediation*

a. *Referral to arbitration and mediation.* Except as hereinafter provided or as otherwise prohibited by

law, the presiding judge may enter an order referring all or any part of a contested civil matter to mediation or arbitration. The parties to any contested civil matter may file a written stipulation to mediate or arbitrate any issue between them at any time. Such stipulation shall be incorporated into the order of referral. FL ST RCP Rule 1.700(a).

b. *Arbitration*

   i. *Exclusions.* A civil action shall be ordered to arbitration or arbitration in conjunction with mediation upon stipulation of the parties. A civil action may be ordered to arbitration or arbitration in conjunction with mediation upon motion of any party or by the court, if the judge determines the action to be of such a nature that arbitration could be of benefit to the litigants or the court. FL ST RCP Rule 1.800.

      - Under no circumstances may the following categories of actions be referred to arbitration: (1) bond estreatures; (2) habeas corpus or other extraordinary writs; (3) bond validations; (4) civil or criminal contempt; (5) such other matters as may be specified by order of the chief judge in the circuit. FL ST RCP Rule 1.800.

   ii. For more information regarding arbitration, please see FL ST RCP Rule 1.810; FL ST RCP Rule 1.820; FL ST RCP Rule 1.830.

c. *Mediation.* For more information regarding mediation, please see FL ST RCP Rule 1.710; FL ST RCP Rule 1.720; FL ST RCP Rule 1.730; and FL ST RCP Rule 1.750.

6. *Rules of court*

   a. *Rules of civil procedure.* The Florida Rules of Civil Procedure apply to all actions of a civil nature and all special statutory proceedings in the circuit courts and county courts except those to which the Florida Probate Rules, the Florida Family Law Rules of Procedure, or the Small Claims Rules apply. FL ST RCP Rule 1.010.

      i. The form, content, procedure, and time for pleading in all special statutory proceedings shall be as prescribed by the statutes governing the proceeding unless the Florida Rules of Civil Procedure specifically provide to the contrary. FL ST RCP Rule 1.010.

      ii. The Florida Rules of Civil Procedure shall be construed to secure the just, speedy, and inexpensive determination of every action. FL ST RCP Rule 1.010.

   b. *Rules of judicial administration.* The Florida Rules of Judicial Administration shall apply to administrative matters in all courts to which the Florida Rules of Judicial Administration are applicable by their terms. The Florida Rules of Judicial Administration shall be construed to secure the speedy and inexpensive determination of every proceeding to which they are applicable. The Florida Rules of Judicial Administration shall supersede all conflicting rules and statutes. FL ST J ADMIN Rule 2.110.

7. *Notice of change of contact information.* The Clerk shall provide a change of address and/or telephone number form for use by attorneys and pro se litigants. With any change of address and/or telephone number, attorneys and pro se litigants governed by FL ST J ADMIN Rule 2.515 will provide to the Clerk and all parties promptly the change of address and/or telephone number form. This form should be submitted only once to the Clerk, who will then make the address and/or telephone number change in all court divisions. FL ST 2 J CIR 2007-05.

D. Documents

1. *Deposition upon oral or written examination*

   a. *Required documents*

      i. *Notice of deposition.* Please see the General Requirements section of this document for information on the content of a notice of deposition upon oral examination.

      ii. *Certificate of service.* A certificate of service of the interrogatories shall be filed, giving the date of service and the name of the party to whom they were directed. FL ST RCP Rule 1.340(e). When any attorney certifies in substance: "I certify that a copy hereof has been furnished to (here insert name or names and addresses used for service) by (e-mail) (delivery) (mail) (fax) on .... (date) ....________________ Attorney" the certificate is taken as prima facie proof of such service in compliance with FL ST J ADMIN Rule 2.516. FL ST J ADMIN Rule 2.516(f).

b. *Supplemental documents*

   i. *Motion for leave to take deposition.* See the Timing section for information on when leave is required.

   ii. *Subpoena.* See the Timing section for requirements of when a subpoena is required.

   iii. *Request for production of documents.* See the General Requirements section for further information.

E. Format

1. *Documents; Type and size.* Documents subject to the exceptions set forth in FL ST J ADMIN Rule 2.525(d) shall be filed on recycled paper measuring eight and one half by eleven (8 1/2 by 11) inches. For purposes of FL ST J ADMIN Rule 2.520, paper is recycled if it contains a minimum content of fifty (50) percent waste paper. Xerographic reduction of legal-size (eight and one half by fourteen (8 1/2 by 14) inches) documents to letter size (eight and one half by eleven (8 1/2 by 11) inches) is prohibited. All other documents filed by electronic transmission shall be filed in a format capable of being printed in a format consistent with the provisions of FL ST J ADMIN Rule 2.250. FL ST J ADMIN Rule 2.520(b).

   a. *Exhibits.* Any exhibit or attachment filed with pleadings or papers may be filed in its original size. FL ST J ADMIN Rule 2.520(c).

   b. *Recording space.* On all papers and documents prepared and filed by the court or by any party to a proceeding which are to be recorded in the public records of any county, including but not limited to final money judgments and notices of lis pendens, a three (3) inch by three (3) inch space at the top right-hand corner on the first page and a one (1) inch by three (3) inch space at the top right-hand corner on each subsequent page shall be left blank and reserved for use by the clerk of court. FL ST J ADMIN Rule 2.520(d).

      i. *Exceptions to recording space.* Any papers or documents created by persons or entities over which the filing party has no control, including but not limited to wills, codicils, trusts, or other testamentary documents; documents prepared or executed by any public officer; documents prepared, executed, acknowledged, or proved outside of the State of Florida; or documents created by State or Federal government agencies, may be filed without the space required by FL ST J ADMIN Rule 2.520. FL ST J ADMIN Rule 2.520(e).

   c. *Noncompliance.* No clerk of court is permitted to refuse to file any document or paper because of noncompliance with the Florida Rules of Judicial Administration. However, upon request of the clerk of court, noncomplying documents must be resubmitted in accordance with the formatting rules. FL ST J ADMIN Rule 2.520(f).

2. *Caption.* Every pleading, motion, order, judgment, or other paper shall have a caption containing the name of the court, the file number, and except for in rem proceedings, including forfeiture proceedings, the name of the first party on each side with an appropriate indication of other parties, and a designation identifying the party filing it and its nature or the nature of the order, as the case may be. In any in rem proceeding, every pleading, motion, order, judgment, or other paper shall have a caption containing the name of the court, the file number, the style "In re" (followed by the name or general description of the property), and a designation of the person or entity filing it and its nature or the nature of the order, as the case may be. In an in rem forfeiture proceeding, the style shall be "In re forfeiture of" (followed by the name of the general description of the property). All papers filed in the action shall be styled in such a manner as to indicate clearly the subject matter of the paper and the party requesting or obtaining relief. FL ST RCP Rule 1.100(c)(1).

3. *Writing and written defined.* Writing or written means a document containing information, an application, or a stipulation. FL ST RCP Rule 1.080(c).

4. *Rule abbreviations*

   a. The Florida Rules of Civil Procedure and shall be abbreviated as Fla.R.Civ.P. FL ST RCP Rule 1.010.

b. The Florida Rules of Judicial Administration shall be abbreviated as Fla. R. Jud. Admin. FL ST J ADMIN Rule 2.110.

5. *Nonverification.* Except when otherwise specifically provided by the Florida Rules of Civil Procedure or an applicable statute, every pleading or other document of a party represented by an attorney need not be verified or accompanied by an affidavit. FL ST RCP Rule 1.030; FL ST J ADMIN Rule 2.515(a).

6. *Attorney signature*

   a. *Attorney signature.* Every pleading and other document of a party represented by an attorney shall be signed by at least one (1) attorney of record in that attorney's individual name whose current record Florida Bar address, telephone number, including area code, primary e-mail address and secondary e-mail addresses, if any, and Florida Bar number shall be stated, and who shall be duly licensed to practice law in Florida or who shall have received permission to appear in the particular case as provided in FL ST J ADMIN Rule 2.510. FL ST J ADMIN Rule 2.515(a).

      i. The attorney may be required by the court to give the address of, and to vouch for the attorney's authority to represent, the party. FL ST J ADMIN Rule 2.515(a).

      ii. The signature of an attorney shall constitute a certificate by the attorney that the attorney has read the pleading or other document; that to the best of the attorney's knowledge, information, and belief there is good ground to support it; and that it is not interposed for delay. FL ST J ADMIN Rule 2.515(a).

      iii. If a pleading is not signed or is signed with intent to defeat the purpose of FL ST J ADMIN Rule 2.515, it may be stricken and the action may proceed as though the pleading or other document had not been served. FL ST J ADMIN Rule 2.515(a).

   b. *Pro se litigant signature.* A party who is not represented by an attorney shall sign any pleading or other paper and state the party's address and telephone number, including area code. FL ST J ADMIN Rule 2.515(b).

   c. *Form of signature*

      i. The signatures required on pleadings and documents by FL ST J ADMIN Rule 2.515(a) and FL ST J ADMIN Rule 2.515(b) may be:

         - Original signatures;
         - Original signatures that have been reproduced by electronic means, such as on electronically transmitted documents or photocopied documents;
         - Electronic signatures using the "/s/," "s/," or "/s" formats by or at the direction of the person signing; or
         - Any other signature format authorized by general law, so long as the clerk where the proceeding is pending has the capability of receiving and has obtained approval from the Supreme Court of Florida to accept pleadings and documents with that signature format. FL ST J ADMIN Rule 2.515(c)(1).

      ii. An attorney, party, or other person who files a pleading or paper by electronic transmission that does not contain the original signature of that attorney, party, or other person shall file that identical pleading or paper in paper form containing an original signature of that attorney, party, or other person (hereinafter called the follow-up filing) immediately thereafter. The follow-up filing is not required if the Supreme Court of Florida has entered an order directing the clerk of court to discontinue accepting the follow-up filing. FL ST J ADMIN Rule 2.515(c)(2).

7. *Forms*

   a. *Process.* The forms of process, notice of lis pendens, and notice of action provided in the Florida Rules of Civil Procedure are sufficient. Variations from the forms do not void process or notices that are otherwise sufficient. FL ST RCP Rule 1.900(a).

   b. *Other forms.* The other forms provided in the Florida Rules of Civil Procedure are sufficient for the matters that are covered by them. So long as the substance is expressed without prolixity, the forms may be varied to meet the facts of a particular case. FL ST RCP Rule 1.900(b).

c. *Formal matters.* Captions, except for the designation of the paper, are omitted from the forms provided in the Florida Rules of Civil Procedure. A general form of caption is the first form provided. Signatures are omitted from pleadings and motions. FL ST RCP Rule 1.900(c).

8. *Notices to persons with disabilities.* All notices of court proceedings to be held in a public facility, and all process compelling appearance at such proceedings, shall include the following statement in bold face, fourteen (14) point Times New Roman or Courier font: "If you are a person with a disability who needs any accommodation in order to participate in this proceeding, you are entitled, at no cost to you, to the provision of certain assistance. Please contact [identify applicable court personnel by name, address, and telephone number] at least seven (7) days before your scheduled court appearance, or immediately upon receiving this notification if the time before the scheduled appearance is less than seven (7) days; if you are hearing or voice impaired, call 711." FL ST J ADMIN Rule 2.540(c)(1).

9. *Minimization of the filing of sensitive information*

a. *Limitations for court filings.* Unless authorized by FL ST J ADMIN Rule 2.425(b), statute, another rule of court, or the court orders otherwise, designated sensitive information filed with the court must be limited to the following format:

i. The initials of a person known to be a minor;

ii. The year of birth of a person's birth date;

iii. No portion of any: Social security number, Bank account number, Credit card account number, Charge account number, or Debit account number;

iv. The last four digits of any: Taxpayer identification number (TIN), Employee identification number, Driver's license number, Passport number, Telephone number, Financial account number, except as set forth in FL ST J ADMIN Rule 2.425(a)(3), Brokerage account number, Insurance policy account number, Loan account number, Customer account number, or Patient or health care number;

v. A truncated version of any: Email address, Computer user name, Password, or Personal identification number (PIN); and

vi. A truncated version of any other sensitive information as provided by court order. FL ST J ADMIN Rule 2.425(a).

b. *Exceptions.* FL ST J ADMIN Rule 2.425(a) does not apply to the following:

i. An account number which identifies the property alleged to be the subject of a proceeding;

ii. The record of an administrative or agency proceeding;

iii. The record in appellate or review proceedings;

iv. The birth date of a minor whenever the birth date is necessary for the court to establish or maintain subject matter jurisdiction;

v. The name of a minor in any order relating to parental responsibility, time-sharing, or child support;

vi. The name of a minor in any document or order affecting the minor's ownership of real property;

vii. The birth date of a party in a writ of attachment or notice to payor;

viii. In traffic and criminal proceedings: a pro se filing; a court filing that is related to a criminal matter or investigation and that is prepared before the filing of a criminal charge or is not filed as part of any docketed criminal case; an arrest or search warrant or any information in support thereof; a charging document and an affidavit or other documents filed in support of any charging document, including any driving records; a statement of particulars; discovery material introduced into evidence or otherwise filed with the court; and all information necessary for the proper issuance and execution of a subpoena duces tecum;

ix. Information used by the clerk for case maintenance purposes or the courts for case management purposes; and

x. Information which is relevant and material to an issue before the court. FL ST J ADMIN Rule 2.425(b).

c. *Remedies.* Upon motion by a party or interested person or sua sponte by the court, the court may order remedies, sanctions or both for a violation of FL ST J ADMIN Rule 2.425(a). Following notice and an opportunity to respond, the court may impose sanctions if such filing was not made in good faith. FL ST J ADMIN Rule 2.425(c).

d. *Motions not restricted.* FL ST J ADMIN Rule 2.425 does not restrict a party's right to move for protective order, to move to file documents under seal, or to request a determination of the confidentiality of records. FL ST J ADMIN Rule 2.425(d).

e. *Application.* FL ST J ADMIN Rule 2.425 does not affect the application of constitutional provisions, statutes, or rules of court regarding confidential information or access to public information. FL ST J ADMIN Rule 2.425(e).

F. Filing and Service Requirements

1. *Court filing of documents and discovery.* Information obtained during discovery shall not be filed with the court until such time as it is filed for good cause. The requirement of good cause is satisfied only where the filing of the information is allowed or required by another applicable rule of procedure or by court order. All filings of discovery documents shall comply with FL ST J ADMIN Rule 2.425. The court shall have the authority to impose sanctions for violation of FL ST RCP Rule 1.280. FL ST RCP Rule 1.280(g).

   a. *Filing of copies.* A copy of a deposition may be filed only under the following circumstances:

      i. It may be filed in compliance with FL ST J ADMIN Rule 2.425 and FL ST RCP Rule 1.280(f) by a party or the witness when the contents of the deposition must be considered by the court on any matter pending before the court. Prompt notice of the filing of the deposition shall be given to all parties unless notice is waived. A party filing the deposition shall furnish a copy of the deposition or the part being filed to other parties unless the party already has a copy. FL ST RCP Rule 1.310(f)(3)(A).

      ii. If the court determines that a deposition previously taken is necessary for the decision of a matter pending before the court, the court may order that a copy be filed by any party at the initial cost of the party, and the filing party shall comply with FL ST J ADMIN Rule 2.425 and FL ST RCP Rule 1.280(f). FL ST RCP Rule 1.310(f)(3)(B).

2. *Filing requirements.* All original documents must be filed with the court either before service or immediately thereafter, unless otherwise provided for by general law or other rules. If the original of any bond or other document is not placed in the court file, a certified copy must be so placed by the clerk. FL ST J ADMIN Rule 2.516(d). All documents shall be filed in conformity with the requirements of FL ST J ADMIN Rule 2.525. FL ST RCP Rule 1.080(b). All documents filed in any court shall be filed by electronic transmission in accordance with FL ST J ADMIN Rule 2.525. "Documents" means pleadings, motions, petitions, memoranda, briefs, notices, exhibits, declarations, affidavits, orders, judgments, decrees, writs, opinions, and any other paper or writing submitted to a court. FL ST J ADMIN Rule 2.520(a). All documents that are court records, as defined in FL ST J ADMIN Rule 2.430(a)(1), must be filed by electronic transmission, provided that: (1) the clerk has the ability to accept and retain such documents; (2) the clerk or the chief judge of the circuit has requested permission to accept documents filed by electronic transmission; and (3) the supreme court has entered an order granting permission to the clerk to accept documents filed by electronic transmission. FL ST J ADMIN Rule 2.525(c)(1).

   a. *Definition.* "Electronic transmission of documents" means the sending of information by electronic signals to, by or from a court or clerk, which when received can be transformed and stored or transmitted on paper, microfilm, magnetic storage device, optical imaging system, CD-ROM, flash drive, other electronic data storage system, server, case maintenance system ("CM"), electronic court filing ("ECF") system, statewide or local electronic portal ("e-portal"), or other electronic record keeping system authorized by the supreme court in a format sufficient to communicate the information on the original document in a readable format. Electronic transmission of documents includes electronic mail ("e-mail") and any internet-based transmission procedure, and may include procedures allowing for documents to be signed or verified by electronic means. FL ST J ADMIN Rule 2.525(a).

      i. The filing of documents with the court as required by the Florida Rules of Judicial Adminis-

tration must be made by filing them with the clerk in accordance with FL ST J ADMIN Rule 2.525, except that the judge may permit documents to be filed with the judge, in which event the judge must note the filing date before him or her on the documents and transmit them to the clerk. The date of filing is that shown on the face of the document by the judge's notation or the clerk's time stamp, whichever is earlier. FL ST J ADMIN Rule 2.516(e).

b. *Application.* Any court or clerk of the court may accept the electronic transmission of documents for filing after the clerk, together with input from the chief judge of the circuit, has obtained approval of the procedures and program for doing so from the Supreme Court of Florida. FL ST J ADMIN Rule 2.525(b).

c. *Exeptions*

   i. Paper documents and other submissions may be manually submitted to the clerk or court:

      - When the clerk does not have the ability to accept and retain documents by electronic filing or has not had ECF Procedures approved by the supreme court;
      - For filing by any self-represented party or any self-represented nonparty unless specific ECF Procedures provide a means to file documents electronically. However, any self-represented nonparty that is a governmental or public agency and any other agency, partnership, corporation, or business entity acting on behalf of any governmental or public agency may file documents by electronic transmission if such entity has the capability of filing documents electronically;
      - For filing by attorneys excused from e-mail service in accordance with FL ST J ADMIN Rule 2.516(b);
      - When submitting evidentiary exhibits or filing non-documentary materials;
      - When the filing involves documents in excess of twenty-five (25) megabytes (25MB) in size. For such filings, documents may be transmitted using an electronic storage medium that the clerk has the ability to accept, which may include a CD-ROM, flash drive, or similar storage medium;
      - When filed in open court, as permitted by the court;
      - When paper filing is permitted by any approved statewide or local ECF procedures; and
      - If any court determines that justice so requires. FL ST J ADMIN Rule 2.525(d).

   ii. Any document in paper form submitted under FL ST J ADMIN Rule 2.525(d) is filed when it is received by the clerk or court and the clerk shall immediately thereafter convert any filed paper document to an electronic document. "Convert to an electronic document" means optically capturing an image of a paper document and using character recognition software to recover as much of the document's text as practicable and then indexing and storing the document in the official court file. FL ST J ADMIN Rule 2.525(c)(4).

   iii. Any storage medium submitted under FL ST J ADMIN Rule 2.525(d)(5) is filed when received by the clerk or court and the clerk shall immediately thereafter transfer the electronic documents from the storage device to the official court file. FL ST J ADMIN Rule 2.525(c)(5).

   iv. If the filer of any paper document authorized under FL ST J ADMIN Rule 2.525(d) provides a self-addressed, postage-paid envelope for return of the paper document after it is converted to electronic form by the clerk, the clerk shall place the paper document in the envelope and deposit it in the mail. Except when a paper document is required to be maintained, the clerk may recycle any filed paper document that is not to be returned to the filer. FL ST J ADMIN Rule 2.525(c)(6).

   v. The clerk may convert any paper document filed before the effective date of FL ST J ADMIN Rule 2.525 to an electronic document. Unless the clerk is required to maintain the paper document, if the paper document has been converted to an electronic document by the clerk, the paper document is no longer part of the official court file and may be removed and recycled. FL ST J ADMIN Rule 2.525(c)(7).

d. *Official court file.* For information on what constitutes the official court file, please see FL ST J ADMIN Rule 2.525(c)(2), FL ST J ADMIN Rule 2.525(c)(3).

e. *Administration.* All attorneys, parties, or other persons using this rule to file documents are required to make arrangements with the court or clerk for the payment of any charges authorized by general law or the supreme court before filing any document by electronic transmission. FL ST J ADMIN Rule 2.525(f)(2).

f. *Filing date.* The filing date for an electronically transmitted document is the date and time that such filing is acknowledged by an electronic stamp or otherwise, pursuant to any procedure set forth in any ECF Procedures approved by the supreme court, or the date the last page of such filing is received by the court or clerk. FL ST J ADMIN Rule 2.525(f)(3).

g. *Accessibility.* All documents transmitted in any electronic form under FL ST J ADMIN Rule 2.525 must comply with the accessibility requirements of FL ST J ADMIN Rule 2.526. FL ST J ADMIN Rule 2.525(g).

3. *Service requirements.* Every pleading subsequent to the initial pleading, all orders, and every other document filed in the action must be served in conformity with the requirements of FL ST J ADMIN Rule 2.516. FL ST RCP Rule 1.080(a).

   a. *Service; When required.* Unless the court otherwise orders, or a statute or supreme court administrative order specifies a different means of service, every pleading subsequent to the initial pleading and every other document filed in any court proceeding, except applications for witness subpoenas and documents served by formal notice or required to be served in the manner provided for service of formal notice, must be served in accordance with FL ST J ADMIN Rule 2.516 on each party. No service need be made on parties against whom a default has been entered, except that pleadings asserting new or additional claims against them must be served in the manner provided for service of summons. FL ST J ADMIN Rule 2.516(a).

   b. *Service; How made.* When service is required or permitted to be made upon a party represented by an attorney, service must be made upon the attorney unless service upon the party is ordered by the court. FL ST J ADMIN Rule 2.516(b).

      i. *Service by electronic mail ("e-mail").* All documents required or permitted to be served on another party must be served by e-mail, unless FL ST J ADMIN Rule 2.516 otherwise provides. When, in addition to service by e-mail, the sender also utilizes another means of service provided for in FL ST J ADMIN Rule 2.516(b)(2), any differing time limits and other provisions applicable to that other means of service control. FL ST J ADMIN Rule 2.516(b)(1). Any document electronically transmitted to a court or clerk must also be served on all parties and interested persons in accordance with the applicable rules of court. FL ST J ADMIN Rule 2.525(e)(2).

         - *Service on attorneys.* Upon appearing in a proceeding, an attorney must serve a designation of a primary e-mail address and may designate no more than two (2) secondary e-mail addresses. Thereafter, service must be directed to all designated e-mail addresses in that proceeding. Every document filed by an attorney thereafter must include the primary e-mail address of that attorney and any secondary e-mail addresses. If an attorney does not designate any e-mail address for service, documents may be served on that attorney at the e-mail address on record with The Florida Bar. FL ST J ADMIN Rule 2.516(b)(1)(A).

         - *Exception to e-mail service on attorneys.* Service by an attorney on another attorney must be made by e-mail unless excused by the court. Upon motion by an attorney demonstrating that the attorney has no e-mail account and lacks access to the Internet at the attorney's office, the court may excuse the attorney from the requirements of e-mail service. Service on and by an attorney excused by the court from e-mail service must be by the means provided in FL ST J ADMIN Rule 2.516(b)(2). FL ST J ADMIN Rule 2.516(b)(1)(B).

         - *Service on and by parties not represented by an attorney.* Any party not represented by an attorney may serve a designation of a primary e-mail address and also may designate no more than two (2) secondary e-mail addresses to which service must be directed in that proceeding by the means provided in FL ST J ADMIN Rule 2.516(b)(1). If a party not represented by an attorney does not designate an e-mail address for service in a proceeding, service on and by that party must be by the means provided in FL ST J ADMIN Rule 2.516(b)(2). FL ST J ADMIN Rule 2.516(b)(1)(C).

- *Time of service.* Service by e-mail is complete when it is sent. FL ST J ADMIN Rule 2.516(b)(1)(D). An e-mail is deemed served on the date it is sent. FL ST J ADMIN Rule 2.516(b)(1)(D)(i). If the sender learns that the e-mail did not reach the address of the person to be served, the sender must immediately send another copy by e-mail, or by a means authorized by FL ST J ADMIN Rule 2.516(b)(2). FL ST J ADMIN Rule 2.516(b)(1)(D)(ii). E-mail service is treated as service by mail for the computation of time. FL ST J ADMIN Rule 2.516(b)(1)(D)(iii).

ii. *Format of e-mail for service.* Service of a document by e-mail is made by attaching a copy of the document in PDF format to an e-mail sent to all addresses designated by the attorney or party. FL ST J ADMIN Rule 2.516(b)(1)(E).

- All documents served by e-mail must be attached to an e-mail message containing a subject line beginning with the words "SERVICE OF COURT DOCUMENT" in all capital letters, followed by the case number of the proceeding in which the documents are being served. FL ST J ADMIN Rule 2.516(b)(1)(E)(i).
- The body of the e-mail must identify the court in which the proceeding is pending, the case number, the name of the initial party on each side, the title of each document served with that e-mail, and the sender's name and telephone number. FL ST J ADMIN Rule 2.516(b)(1)(E)(ii).
- Any document served by e-mail may be signed by the "/s/" format, as long as the filed original is signed in accordance with the applicable rule of procedure. FL ST J ADMIN Rule 2.516(b)(1)(E)(iii).
- Any e-mail which, together with its attached documents, exceeds five megabytes (5MB) in size, must be divided and sent as separate e-mails, no one of which may exceed five megabytes (5MB) in size and each of which must be sequentially numbered in the subject line. FL ST J ADMIN Rule 2.516(b)(1)(E)(iv).

iii. *Service by other means.* In addition to, and not in lieu of, service by e-mail, service may also be made upon attorneys by any of the means specified in FL ST J ADMIN Rule 2.516(b)(2). Service on and by all parties who are not represented by an attorney and who do not designate an e-mail address, and on and by all attorneys excused from e-mail service, must be made by delivering a copy of the document or by mailing it to the party or attorney at their last known address or, if no address is known, by leaving it with the clerk of the court. Service by mail is complete upon mailing. Delivery of a copy within FL ST J ADMIN Rule 2.516 is complete upon:

- Handing it to the attorney or to the party,
- Leaving it at the attorney's or party's office with a clerk or other person in charge thereof,
- If there is no one in charge, leaving it in a conspicuous place therein,
- If the office is closed or the person to be served has no office, leaving it at the person's usual place of abode with some person of his or her family above fifteen (15) years of age and informing such person of the contents, or
- Transmitting it by facsimile to the attorney's or party's office with a cover sheet containing the sender's name, firm, address, telephone number, and facsimile number, and the number of pages transmitted. When service is made by facsimile, a copy must also be served by any other method permitted by FL ST J ADMIN Rule 2.516. Facsimile service occurs when transmission is complete. FL ST J ADMIN Rule 2.516(b)(2)(A) through FL ST J ADMIN Rule 2.516(b)(2)(E).
- Service by delivery after 5:00 p.m. must be deemed to have been made by mailing on the date of delivery. FL ST J ADMIN Rule 2.516(b)(2)(F).

c. *Service; Numerous defendants.* In actions when the parties are unusually numerous, the court may regulate the service contemplated by the Florida Rules of Judicial Administration on motion or on its own initiative in such manner as may be found to be just and reasonable. FL ST J ADMIN Rule 2.516(c).

d. *Service by clerk.* Service of notices and other documents required to be made by the clerk must also be done as provided in FL ST J ADMIN Rule 2.516(b). FL ST J ADMIN Rule 2.516(g).

G. Hearings

1. There is no hearing required or contemplated with regard to notices of deposition in the Florida Rules of Civil Procedure.

H. Forms

1. Official Notice of Deposition Forms for Florida

a. Caption. FL ST RCP Form 1.901.

2. Notice of Deposition Forms for Florida

a. Form for motion by plaintiff for leave to take deposition within 20-day period. FL-RCPF R 1.310(6).
b. Form for order on motion for leave to take deposition within 20-day period. FL-RCPF R 1.310(8).
c. Notice of examination; Time and place. FL-RCPF R 1.310(9).
d. Nonparty witness, subpoena required. FL-RCPF R 1.310(10).
e. Form for notice to take deposition on oral examination. FL-RCPF R 1.310(11).
f. Form for notice of taking multiple depositions. FL-RCPF R 1.310(11.1).
g. Form for notice of taking deposition and examination of documents. FL-RCPF R 1.310(12).
h. Form for notice of taking video deposition duces tecum. FL-RCPF R 1.310(13).
i. Form for motion to modify time for taking deposition. FL-RCPF R 1.310(14).
j. Form for motion to take deposition by telephone. FL-RCPF R 1.310(16).
k. Form for order permitting deposition by telephone. FL-RCPF R 1.310(17).
l. Form for notice of taking deposition by telephone. FL-RCPF R 1.310(18).
m. Form for notice of deposition upon written questions. FL-RCPF R 1.320(2).
n. Form of questions. FL-RCPF R 1.320(3).
o. Form of cross-questions. FL-RCPF R 1.320(4).
p. Form for objection to form of written questions. FL-RCPF R 1.320(6).

3. Official Forms for Florida Circuit Court, Second Judicial Circuit

a. Notice of change of contact information. FL ST 2 J CIR 2007-05.

I. Checklist

(I) ❑ Matters to be considered by deposing party (oral depositions)
- (a) ❑ Required documents
  - (1) ❑ Notice of deposition
  - (2) ❑ Certificate of service
- (b) ❑ Supplemental documents
  - (1) ❑ Motion for leave to request deposition
  - (2) ❑ Subpoena
  - (3) ❑ Request for production of documents
- (c) ❑ Time for service of notice of deposition
  - (1) ❑ After commencement of action
  - (2) ❑ Within thirty (30) days after service of initial pleadings by leave of court only

(II) ❑ Matters to be considered by deponent (oral depositions)
- (a) ❑ Required documents
  - (1) ❑ Production of documents (if subpoenaed)

(III) ❑ Matters to be considered by deposing party (depositions by written questions)

(a) ❑ Required documents

(1) ❑ Notice of deposition

(2) ❑ Written questions

(3) ❑ Certificate of service

(b) ❑ Supplemental documents

(1) ❑ Motion for leave to request deposition

(2) ❑ Subpoena

(3) ❑ Request for production of documents

(c) ❑ Time for service of direct and redirect questions

(1) ❑ Within ten (10) days after being served with cross questions, a party may serve redirect questions upon all other parties

(2) ❑ Objections to the form of the question must be served within the time for service of redirect questions or ten (10) days after service of recross questions

(IV) ❑ Matters to be considered by deponent (depositions by written questions)

(a) ❑ Required documents

(1) ❑ Cross questions, with certificate of service

(2) ❑ Recross questions with certificate of service

(b) ❑ Time for service of cross and recross questions

(1) ❑ Within thirty (30) days after the notice and written questions are served, a party may serve cross questions upon all other parties

(2) ❑ Within ten (10) days after being served with redirect questions, a party may serve recross questions upon all other parties

(3) ❑ Objections to the form of the questions must be served within the time for serving succeeding questions

FOURTH JUDICIAL CIRCUIT

Pleadings
Complaint

Document Last Updated January 2013

A. Applicable Rules

1. *State rules*
   a. Nonverification of pleadings. FL ST RCP Rule 1.030.
   b. When action commenced. FL ST RCP Rule 1.050.
   c. Process. FL ST RCP Rule 1.070.
   d. Constitutional challenge to state statute or county or municipal charter, ordinance, or franchise; Notice by party. FL ST RCP Rule 1.071.
   e. Service and filing of pleadings, orders, and documents. FL ST RCP Rule 1.080.
   f. Time. FL ST RCP Rule 1.090.
   g. Pleadings and motions. FL ST RCP Rule 1.100; FL ST RCP Rule 1.110; FL ST RCP Rule 1.120; FL ST RCP Rule 1.130; FL ST RCP Rule 1.170; FL ST RCP Rule 1.430.
   h. Relief from judgment, decrees, or orders. FL ST RCP Rule 1.540.
   i. Forms. FL ST RCP Rule 1.900.
   j. Retention of court records. FL ST J ADMIN Rule 2.430.
   k. Foreign attorneys. FL ST J ADMIN Rule 2.510.
   l. Signature of attorneys and parties. FL ST J ADMIN Rule 2.515.
   m. Paper. FL ST J ADMIN Rule 2.520.
   n. Electronic filing. FL ST J ADMIN Rule 2.525.
   o. Requests for accommodations by persons with disabilities. FL ST J ADMIN Rule 2.540.
   p. Service. FL ST § 48.011; FL ST § 48.021; FL ST § 48.031; FL ST § 48.041; FL ST § 48.042; FL ST § 48.051; FL ST § 48.061; FL ST § 48.071; FL ST § 48.081; FL ST § 48.091; FL ST § 48.101; FL ST § 48.111; FL ST § 48.121; FL ST § 48.131; FL ST § 48.141; FL ST § 48.151; FL ST § 48.161; FL ST § 48.171; FL ST § 48.181; FL ST § 48.183; FL ST § 48.19; FL ST § 48.193; FL ST § 48.194; FL ST § 48.20; FL ST § 48.21; FL ST § 48.25; FL ST § 48.31; FL ST § 49.011; FL ST § 49.021; FL ST § 49.031; FL ST § 49.041; FL ST § 49.051; FL ST § 49.061; FL ST § 49.071; FL ST § 49.08; FL ST § 49.09; FL ST § 49.10; FL ST § 49.11; FL ST § 49.12; FL ST § 50.011; FL ST § 50.021; FL ST § 50.031; FL ST § 50.041; FL ST § 50.051; FL ST § 50.061.
   q. Fees. FL ST § 57.081; FL ST § 57.085; FL ST § 28.241; FL ST § 34.041.
   r. Minimization of the filing of sensitive information. FL ST J ADMIN Rule 2.425.
   s. Accessibility of information and technology. FL ST J ADMIN Rule 2.526.
2. *Local rules*
   a. Procedures for certification of insolvency in civil divisions of the circuit court. FL ST 4 J CIR 95-5 (A1).
   b. Sealing court records. FL ST 4 J CIR 2006-05.

B. Timing

1. *Commencement of an action.* Every action of a civil nature shall be deemed commenced when the complaint or petition is filed except that ancillary proceedings shall be deemed commenced when the writ

is issued or the pleading setting forth the claim of the party initiating the action is filed. FL ST RCP Rule 1.050.

2. *Summons; Time limit.* If service of the initial process and initial pleading is not made upon a defendant within one hundred twenty (120) days after filing of the initial pleading directed to that defendant the court, on its own initiative after notice or on motion, shall direct that service be effected within a specified time or shall dismiss the action without prejudice or drop that defendant as a party; provided that if the plaintiff shows good cause or excusable neglect for the failure, the court shall extend the time for service for an appropriate period. FL ST RCP Rule 1.070(j).

3. *Computation of time*

   a. *Generally.* Computation of time shall be governed by FL ST J ADMIN Rule 2.514. FL ST RCP Rule 1.090(a). The following rules apply in computing time periods specified in any rule of procedure, local rule, court order, or statute that does not specify a method of computing time. FL ST J ADMIN Rule 2.514(a).

      i. *Period stated in days or a longer unit.* When the period is stated in days or a longer unit of time (A) exclude the day of the event that triggers the period; (B) count every day, including intermediate Saturdays, Sundays, and legal holidays; and (C) include the last day of the period, but if the last day is a Saturday, Sunday, or legal holiday, or falls within any period of time extended through an order of the chief justice under FL ST J ADMIN Rule 2.205(a)(2)(B)(iv), the period continues to run until the end of the next day that is not a Saturday, Sunday, or legal holiday and does not fall within any period of time extended through an order of the chief justice. FL ST J ADMIN Rule 2.514(a)(1).

      ii. *Period stated in hours.* When the period is stated in hours (A) begin counting immediately on the occurrence of the event that triggers the period; (B) count every hour, including hours during intermediate Saturdays, Sundays, and legal holidays; and (C) if the period would end on a Saturday, Sunday, or legal holiday, or during any period of time extended through an order of the chief justice under FL ST J ADMIN Rule 2.205(a)(2)(B)(iv), the period continues to run until the same time on the next day that is not a Saturday, Sunday, or legal holiday and does not fall within any period of time extended through an order of the chief justice. FL ST J ADMIN Rule 2.514(a)(2).

      iii. *Period stated in days less than seven (7) days.* When the period stated in days is less than seven (7) days, intermediate Saturdays, Sundays, and legal holidays shall be excluded in the computation. FL ST J ADMIN Rule 2.514(a)(3).

      iv. *"Last day" defined.* Unless a different time is set by a statute, local rule, or court order, the last day ends (A) for electronic filing or for service by any means, at midnight; and (B) for filing by other means, when the clerk's office is scheduled to close. FL ST J ADMIN Rule 2.514(a)(4).

      v. *"Next day" defined.* The "next day" is determined by continuing to count forward when the period is measured after an event and backward when measured before an event. FL ST J ADMIN Rule 2.514(a)(5).

      vi. *"Legal holiday" defined.* "Legal holiday" means (A) the day set aside by FL ST § 110.117, for observing New Year's Day, Martin Luther King, Jr.'s Birthday, Memorial Day, Independence Day, Labor Day, Veterans' Day, Thanksgiving Day, the Friday after Thanksgiving Day, or Christmas Day, and (B) any day observed as a holiday by the clerk's office or as designated by the chief judge. FL ST J ADMIN Rule 2.514(a)(6).

   b. *Additional time after service by mail or e-mail.* When a party may or must act within a specified time after service and service is made by mail or e-mail, five (5) days are added after the period that would otherwise expire under FL ST J ADMIN Rule 2.514(a). FL ST J ADMIN Rule 2.514(b).

   c. *Enlargement.* When an act is required or allowed to be done at or within a specified time by order of court, by the Florida Rules of Civil Procedure, or by notice given thereunder, for cause shown the court at any time in its discretion (1) with or without notice, may order the period enlarged if request therefor is made before the expiration of the period originally prescribed or as extended by a previous order, or (2) upon motion made and notice after the expiration of the specified period, may permit the act to be done when failure to act was the result of excusable neglect, but it may not extend the time for making a motion for new trial, for rehearing, or to alter or amend a judgment; making a motion for relief from a judgment under FL ST RCP Rule 1.540(b); taking an appeal or filing a petition for certiorari; or making a motion for a directed verdict. FL ST RCP Rule 1.090(b).

d. *Unaffected by expiration of term.* The period of time provided for the doing of any act or the taking of any proceeding shall not be affected or limited by the continued existence or expiration of a term of court. The continued existence or expiration of a term of court in no way affects the power of a court to do any act or take any proceeding in any action which is or has been pending before it. FL ST RCP Rule 1.090(c).

C. General Requirements

1. *General rules of pleading*

a. *Claims for relief*

i. A pleading which sets forth a claim for relief, whether an original claim, counterclaim, crossclaim, or third-party claim, must state a cause of action and shall contain

- A short and plain statement of the grounds upon which the court's jurisdiction depends, unless the court already has jurisdiction and the claim needs no new grounds of jurisdiction to support it (For information regarding acts subjecting persons to jurisdiction, please see FL ST § 48.193),
- A short and plain statement of the ultimate facts showing that the pleader is entitled to relief, and
- A demand for judgment for the relief to which the pleader deems himself or herself entitled. FL ST RCP Rule 1.110(b).

ii. Relief in the alternative or of several different types may be demanded. Every complaint shall be considered to demand general relief. FL ST RCP Rule 1.110(b).

b. *Verification.* Except when otherwise specifically provided by these rules or an applicable statute, every pleading or other document of a party represented by an attorney need not be verified or accompanied by an affidavit. FL ST RCP Rule 1.030. When filing an action for foreclosure of a mortgage on residential real property the complaint shall be verified. When verification of a document is required, the document filed shall include an oath, affirmation, or the following statement: "Under penalty of perjury, I declare that I have read the foregoing, and the facts alleged therein are true and correct to the best of my knowledge and belief." FL ST RCP Rule 1.110(b).

c. *Separate statements.* All averments of claim or defense shall be made in consecutively numbered paragraphs, the contents of each of which shall be limited as far as practicable to a statement of a single set of circumstances, and a paragraph may be referred to by number in all subsequent pleadings. Each claim founded upon a separate transaction or occurrence and each defense other than denials shall be stated in a separate count or defense when a separation facilitates the clear presentation of the matter set forth. FL ST RCP Rule 1.110(f).

d. *Statements adopted by reference.* Statements in a pleading may be adopted by reference in a different part of the same pleading, in another pleading, or in any motion. FL ST RCP Rule 1.130(b).

e. *Joinder of causes of action; Consistency.* A pleader may set up in the same action as many claims or causes of action or defenses in the same right as the pleader has, and claims for relief may be stated in the alternative if separate items make up the cause of action, or if two (2) or more causes of action are joined. A party may also set forth two (2) or more statements of a claim or defense alternatively, either in one (1) count or defense or in separate counts or defenses. When two (2) or more statements are made in the alternative and one (1) of them, if made independently, would be sufficient, the pleading is not made insufficient by the insufficiency of one (1) or more of the alternative statements. A party may also state as many separate claims or defenses as that party has, regardless of consistency and whether based on legal or equitable grounds or both. All pleadings shall be construed so as to do substantial justice. FL ST RCP Rule 1.110(g).

f. *Subsequent pleadings.* When the nature of an action permits pleadings subsequent to final judgment and the jurisdiction of the court over the parties has not terminated, the initial pleading subsequent to final judgment shall be designated a supplemental complaint or petition. The action shall then proceed in the same manner and time as though the supplemental complaint or petition were the initial pleading in the action, including the issuance of any needed process. FL ST RCP Rule 1.110(h) shall not apply to proceedings that may be initiated by motion under the Florida Rules of Civil Procedure. FL ST RCP Rule 1.110(h).

g. *Pleading basis for service.* When service of process is to be made under statutes authorizing service on nonresidents of Florida, it is sufficient to plead the basis for service in the language of the statute without pleading the facts supporting service. FL ST RCP Rule 1.070(h).

h. *Forms of pleadings.* Forms of action and technical forms for seeking relief and of pleas, pleadings, or motions are abolished. FL ST RCP Rule 1.110(a).

2. *Complaint; Generally*

a. *Purpose.* The purpose of a complaint is to advise the court and the defendant of the nature of a cause of action asserted by the plaintiff. FL-PP § 2:12.

b. *Sufficiency of complaint.* A complaint will be found to be insufficient if it contains only general conclusory allegations unsupported by any facts. The test to determine whether a complaint is sufficient is whether, if the factual allegations of the complaint are established, the plaintiff will be legally or equitably entitled to the claimed relief. Pizzi v. Central Bank & Trust Co., 250 So.2d 895, 896 (Fla. 1971); Bowen v. G H C Properties, Limited, 251 So.2d 359, 361 (Fla. 1st DCA 1971); FL-PP § 2:12. In determining the sufficiency of the complaint to state a cause of action, all allegations of the complaint are taken as true, and possible affirmative defenses are not considered. Strickland v. Commerce Loan Co. of Jacksonville, 158 So.2d 814 (Fla. 1st DCA 1963); FL-PP § 2:12.

i. The issues for trial in Florida must be settled by the pleadings. The issues cannot be raised by discovery. FL-PRACPROC § 7:6.

ii. Causes of action may be pleaded alternatively in the same count or in different counts and against the same or different defendants as long as the joinder of parties is proper. FL-PRACPROC § 7:6.

iii. Each count must state a cause of action. Each independent cause of action should be pleaded in a separate count. FL-PRACPROC § 7:6.

iv. Incorporation by reference of all allegations from one count to another is not proper. Separate counts facilitate reference to the pleading in which they appear in other pleadings, motions or papers as well as the assertion of defenses against some, but not all, causes of action. Some defenses may not apply to the initial pleading as a whole. FL-PRACPROC § 7:6.

3. *Pleading special matters*

a. *Capacity.* It is not necessary to aver the capacity of a party to sue or be sued, the authority of a party to sue or be sued in a representative capacity, or the legal existence of an organized association of persons that is made a party, except to the extent required to show the jurisdiction of the court. The initial pleading served on behalf of a minor party shall specifically aver the age of the minor party. When a party desires to raise an issue as to the legal existence of any party, the capacity of any party to sue or be sued, or the authority of a party to sue or be sued in a representative capacity, that party shall do so by specific negative averment which shall include such supporting particulars as are peculiarly within the pleader's knowledge. FL ST RCP Rule 1.120(a).

b. *Fraud, mistake, condition of the mind.* In all averments of fraud or mistake, the circumstances constituting fraud or mistake shall be stated with such particularity as the circumstances may permit. Malice, intent, knowledge, mental attitude, and other condition of mind of a person may be averred generally. FL ST RCP Rule 1.120(b).

c. *Conditions precedent.* In pleading the performance or occurrence of conditions precedent, it is sufficient to aver generally that all conditions precedent have been performed or have occurred. A denial of performance or occurrence shall be made specifically and with particularity. FL ST RCP Rule 1.120(c).

d. *Official document or act.* In pleading an official document or official act it is sufficient to aver that the document was issued or the act done in compliance with law. FL ST RCP Rule 1.120(c).

e. *Judgment or decree.* In pleading a judgment or decree of a domestic or foreign court, a judicial or quasi-judicial tribunal, or a board or officer, it is sufficient to aver the judgment or decree without setting forth matter showing jurisdiction to render it. FL ST RCP Rule 1.120(e).

f. *Time and place.* For the purpose of testing the sufficiency of a pleading, averments of time and place are material and shall be considered like all other averments of material matter. FL ST RCP Rule 1.120(f).

g. *Special damage.* When items of special damage are claimed, they shall be specifically stated. FL ST RCP Rule 1.120(g).

4. *Parties*

a. *Parties generally.* Every action may be prosecuted in the name of the real party in interest, but a personal representative, administrator, guardian, trustee of an express trust, a party with whom or in whose name a contract has been made for the benefit of another, or a party expressly authorized by statute may sue in that person's own name without joining the party for whose benefit the action is brought. All persons having an interest in the subject of the action and in obtaining the relief demanded may join as plaintiffs and any person may be made a defendant who has or claims an interest adverse to the plaintiff. Any person may at any time be made a party if that person's presence is necessary or proper to a complete determination of the cause. Persons having a united interest may be joined on the same side as plaintiffs or defendants, and anyone who refuses to join may for such reason be made a defendant. FL ST RCP Rule 1.210(a).

b. *Minors or incompetent persons.* When a minor or incompetent person has a representative, such as a guardian or other like fiduciary, the representative may sue or defend on behalf of the minor or incompetent person. A minor or incompetent person who does not have a duly appointed representative may sue by next friend or by a guardian ad litem. The court shall appoint a guardian ad litem for a minor or incompetent person not otherwise represented in an action or shall make such other order as it deems proper for the protection of the minor or incompetent person. FL ST RCP Rule 1.210(b).

c. For survivor and substitution of parties information, please see FL ST RCP Rule 1.260.

5. *Counterclaims and crossclaims*

a. *Compulsory counterclaims.* A pleading shall state as a counterclaim any claim which at the time of serving the pleading the pleader has against any opposing party, provided it arises out of the transaction or occurrence that is the subject matter of the opposing party's claim and does not require for its adjudication the presence of third parties over whom the court cannot acquire jurisdiction. But the pleader need not state a claim if (1) at the time the action was commenced the claim was the subject of another pending action, or (2) the opposing party brought suit upon that party's claim by attachment or other process by which the court did not acquire jurisdiction to render a personal judgment on the claim and the pleader is not stating a counterclaim under this rule. FL ST RCP Rule 1.170(a).

b. *Permissive counterclaim.* A pleading may state as a counterclaim any claim against an opposing party not arising out of the transaction or occurrence that is the subject matter of the opposing party's claim. FL ST RCP Rule 1.170(b).

c. *Counterclaim exceeding opposing claim.* A counterclaim may or may not diminish or defeat the recovery sought by the opposing party. It may claim relief exceeding in amount or different in kind from that sought in the pleading of the opposing party. FL ST RCP Rule 1.170(c).

d. *Counterclaim against the State.* The Florida Rules of Civil Procedure shall not be construed to enlarge beyond the limits established by law the right to assert counterclaims or to claim credits against the state or any of its subdivisions or other governmental organizations thereof subject to suit or against a municipal corporation or against an officer, agency, or administrative board of the state. FL ST RCP Rule 1.170(d).

e. *Counterclaim maturing or acquired after pleading.* A claim which matured or was acquired by the

pleader after serving the pleading may be presented as a counterclaim by supplemental pleading with the permission of the court. FL ST RCP Rule 1.170(e).

f. *Omitted counterclaim or crossclaim.* When a pleader fails to set up a counterclaim or crossclaim through oversight, inadvertence, or excusable neglect, or when justice requires, the pleader may set up the counterclaim or crossclaim by amendment with leave of the court. FL ST RCP Rule 1.170(f).

g. *Crossclaim against co-party.* A pleading may state as a crossclaim any claim by one party against a co-party arising out of the transaction or occurrence that is the subject matter of either the original action or a counterclaim therein, or relating to any property that is the subject matter of the original action. The crossclaim may include a claim that the party against whom it is asserted is or may be liable to the crossclaimant for all or part of a claim asserted in the action against the crossclaimant. Service of a crossclaim on a party who has appeared in the action shall be made pursuant to FL ST RCP Rule 1.080. Service of a crossclaim against a party who has not appeared in the action shall be made in the manner provided for service of summons. FL ST RCP Rule 1.170(g).

h. *Additional parties may be brought in.* When the presence of parties other than those to the original action is required to grant complete relief in the determination of a counterclaim or crossclaim, they shall be named in the counterclaim or crossclaim and be served with process and shall be parties to the action thereafter if jurisdiction of them can be obtained and their joinder will not deprive the court of jurisdiction of the action. FL ST RCP Rule 1.250(b) and FL ST RCP Rule 1.250(c) apply to parties brought in under FL ST RCP Rule 1.170(h). FL ST RCP Rule 1.170(h).

i. *Separate trials; Separate judgment.* If the court orders separate trials as provided in FL ST RCP Rule 1.270(b), judgment on a counterclaim or crossclaim may be rendered when the court has jurisdiction to do so even if a claim of the opposing party has been dismissed or otherwise disposed of. FL ST RCP Rule 1.170(i).

j. *Demand exceeding jurisdiction; Transfer of action.* If the demand of any counterclaim or crossclaim exceeds the jurisdiction of the court in which the action is pending, the action shall be transferred forthwith to the court of the same county having jurisdiction of the demand in the counterclaim or crossclaim with only such alterations in the pleadings as are essential. The court shall order the transfer of the action and the transmittal of all papers in it to the proper court if the party asserting the demand exceeding the jurisdiction deposits with the court having jurisdiction a sum sufficient to pay the clerk's service charge in the court to which the action is transferred at the time of filing the counterclaim or crossclaim. Thereupon the original papers and deposit shall be transmitted and filed with a certified copy of the order. The court to which the action is transferred shall have full power and jurisdiction over the demands of all parties. Failure to make the service charge deposit at the time the counterclaim or crossclaim is filed, or within such further time as the court may allow, shall reduce a claim for damages to an amount within the jurisdiction of the court where the action is pending and waive the claim in other cases. FL ST RCP Rule 1.170(j).

6. *Misjoinder and nonjoinder of parties*

a. *Misjoinder.* Misjoinder of parties is not a ground for dismissal of an action. Any claim against a party may be severed and proceeded with separately. FL ST RCP Rule 1.250(a).

b. *Dropping parties.* Parties may be dropped by an adverse party in the manner provided for voluntary dismissal in FL ST RCP Rule 1.420(a)(1) subject to the exception stated in FL ST RCP Rule 1.420. If notice of lis pendens has been filed in the action against a party so dropped, the notice of dismissal shall be recorded and cancels the notice of lis pendens without the necessity of a court order. Parties may be dropped by order of court on its own initiative or the motion of any party at any stage of the action on such terms as are just. FL ST RCP Rule 1.250(b).

c. *Adding parties.* Parties may be added once as a matter of course within the same time that pleadings can be so amended under FL ST RCP Rule 1.190(a). If amendment by leave of court or stipulation of the parties is permitted, parties may be added in the amended pleading without further order of court. Parties may be added by order of court on its own initiative or on motion of any party at any stage of the action and on such terms as are just. FL ST RCP Rule 1.250(c).

7. *Jury demand*

a. *Right preserved.* The right of trial by jury as declared by the Constitution or by statute shall be preserved to the parties inviolate. FL ST RCP Rule 1.430(a).

b. *Demand.* Any party may demand a trial by jury of any issue triable of right by a jury by serving upon the other party a demand therefor in writing at any time after commencement of the action and not later than ten (10) days after the service of the last pleading directed to such issue. The demand may be indorsed upon a pleading of the party. FL ST RCP Rule 1.430(b).

c. *Specification of issues.* In the demand a party may specify the issues that the party wishes so tried; otherwise, the party is deemed to demand trial by jury for all issues so triable. FL ST RCP Rule 1.430(c).

   i. If a party has demanded trial by jury for only some of the issues, any other party may serve a demand for trial by jury of any other or all of the issues triable by jury ten (10) days after service of the demand or such lesser time as the court may order. FL ST RCP Rule 1.430(c).

d. *Waiver.* A party who fails to serve a demand as required by FL ST RCP Rule 1.430 waives trial by jury. FL ST RCP Rule 1.430(d).

   i. If waived, a jury trial may not be granted without the consent of the parties, but the court may allow an amendment in the proceedings to demand a trial by jury or order a trial by jury on its own motion. FL ST RCP Rule 1.430(d).

   ii. A demand for trial by jury may not be withdrawn without the consent of the parties. FL ST RCP Rule 1.430(d).

8. *Arbitration and mediation*

   a. *Referral to arbitration and mediation.* Except as hereinafter provided or as otherwise prohibited by law, the presiding judge may enter an order referring all or any part of a contested civil matter to mediation or arbitration. The parties to any contested civil matter may file a written stipulation to mediate or arbitrate any issue between them at any time. Such stipulation shall be incorporated into the order of referral. FL ST RCP Rule 1.700(a).

   b. *Arbitration*

      i. *Exclusions.* A civil action shall be ordered to arbitration or arbitration in conjunction with mediation upon stipulation of the parties. A civil action may be ordered to arbitration or arbitration in conjunction with mediation upon motion of any party or by the court, if the judge determines the action to be of such a nature that arbitration could be of benefit to the litigants or the court. FL ST RCP Rule 1.800.

         - Under no circumstances may the following categories of actions be referred to arbitration: (1) bond estreatures; (2) habeas corpus or other extraordinary writs; (3) bond validations; (4) civil or criminal contempt; (5) such other matters as may be specified by order of the chief judge in the circuit. FL ST RCP Rule 1.800.

      ii. For more information regarding arbitration, please see FL ST RCP Rule 1.810; FL ST RCP Rule 1.820; FL ST RCP Rule 1.830.

   c. *Mediation.* For more information regarding mediation, please see FL ST RCP Rule 1.710; FL ST RCP Rule 1.720; FL ST RCP Rule 1.730; and FL ST RCP Rule 1.750.

9. *Rules of court*

   a. *Rules of civil procedure.* The Florida Rules of Civil Procedure apply to all actions of a civil nature and all special statutory proceedings in the circuit courts and county courts except those to which the Florida Probate Rules, the Florida Family Law Rules of Procedure, or the Small Claims Rules apply. FL ST RCP Rule 1.010.

      i. The form, content, procedure, and time for pleading in all special statutory proceedings shall be as prescribed by the statutes governing the proceeding unless the Florida Rules of Civil Procedure specifically provide to the contrary. FL ST RCP Rule 1.010.

      ii. The Florida Rules of Civil Procedure shall be construed to secure the just, speedy, and inexpensive determination of every action. FL ST RCP Rule 1.010.

   b. *Rules of judicial administration.* The Florida Rules of Judicial Administration shall apply to administrative matters in all courts to which the Florida Rules of Judicial Administration are applicable by their terms. The Florida Rules of Judicial Administration shall be construed to secure the speedy and inexpensive determination of every proceeding to which they are applicable. The Florida Rules of Judicial Administration shall supersede all conflicting rules and statutes. FL ST J ADMIN Rule 2.110.

D. Documents

1. *Required documents*

   a. *Summons.* Upon the commencement of the action, summons or other process authorized by law shall be issued forthwith by the clerk or judge under the clerk's or the judge's signature and the seal of the court and delivered for service without praecipe. FL ST RCP Rule 1.070(a).

   b. *Complaint.* See the General Requirements section for the contents of the complaint.

      i. *Notices to persons with disabilities.* See the Format section of this KeyRules document for further information.

   c. *Civil cover sheet.* A civil cover sheet (FL ST RCP Form 1.997) shall be completed and filed with the clerk at the time an initial complaint or petition is filed by the party initiating the action. If the cover sheet is not filed, the clerk shall accept the complaint or petition for filing; but all proceedings in the action shall be abated until a properly executed cover sheet is completed and filed. The clerk shall complete the civil cover sheet for a party appearing pro se. FL ST RCP Rule 1.100(c)(2).

   d. *Return of execution process by process server.* Each person who effects service of process shall note on a return-of-service form attached thereto, the date and time when it comes to hand, the date and time when it is served, the manner of service, the name of the person on whom it was served and, if the person is served in a representative capacity, the position occupied by the person. The return-of-service form must be signed by the person who effects the service of process. However, a person employed by a sheriff who effects the service of process may sign the return-of-service form using an electronic signature certified by the sheriff. FL ST § 48.21(1).

      i. A failure to state the facts or to include the signature required by FL ST § 48.21(1) invalidates the service, but the return is amendable to state the facts or to include the signature at any time on application to the court from which the process issued. On amendment, service is as effective as if the return had originally stated the omitted facts or included the signature. A failure to state all the facts in or to include the signature on the return shall subject the person effecting service to a fine not exceeding $10, in the court's discretion. FL ST § 48.21(2).

   e. *Filing fees.* Filing fees are due at the time a party files a pleading to initiate a proceeding or files a pleading for relief. FL ST § 28.241. For a fee schedule, see FL ST § 28.241.

      i. For more information regarding exemption from payment of filing costs, please see FL ST 4 J CIR 95-5 (A1).

2. *Supplemental documents*

   a. *Exhibits.* All bonds, notes, bills of exchange, contracts, accounts, or documents upon which action may be brought or defense made, or a copy thereof or a copy of the portions thereof material to the pleadings, shall be incorporated in or attached to the pleading. No papers shall be unnecessarily annexed as exhibits. The pleadings shall contain no unnecessary recitals of deeds, documents, contracts, or other instruments. Any exhibit attached to a pleading shall be considered a part of the pleadings for all purposes. FL ST RCP Rule 1.130(a).

   b. *Notice of constitutional question.* A party that files a pleading, written motion, or other paper drawing into question the constitutionality of a state statute or a county or municipal charter, ordinance, or franchise must promptly (1) file a notice of constitutional question stating the question and identifying the paper that raises it; and (2) serve the notice and the pleading, written motion, or other paper drawing into question the constitutionality of a state statute or a county or municipal charter, ordinance, or franchise on the Attorney General or the state attorney of the judicial circuit in which the action is pending, by either certified or registered mail. Service of the notice and pleading, written motion, or other paper does not require joinder of the Attorney General or the state attorney as a party to the action. FL ST RCP Rule 1.071.

E. Format

1. *Documents; Type and size.* Documents subject to the exceptions set forth in FL ST J ADMIN Rule 2.525(d) shall be filed on recycled paper measuring eight and one half by eleven (8 1/2 by 11) inches. For purposes of FL ST J ADMIN Rule 2.520, paper is recycled if it contains a minimum content of fifty (50) percent waste paper. Xerographic reduction of legal-size (eight and one half by fourteen (8 1/2 by 14) inches) documents to letter size (eight and one half by eleven (8 1/2 by 11) inches) is prohibited. All other documents filed by electronic transmission shall be filed in a format capable of being printed in a format consistent with the provisions of FL ST J ADMIN Rule 2.250. FL ST J ADMIN Rule 2.520(b).
   a. *Exhibits.* Any exhibit or attachment filed with pleadings or papers may be filed in its original size. FL ST J ADMIN Rule 2.520(c).
   b. *Recording space.* On all papers and documents prepared and filed by the court or by any party to a proceeding which are to be recorded in the public records of any county, including but not limited to final money judgments and notices of lis pendens, a three (3) inch by three (3) inch space at the top right-hand corner on the first page and a one (1) inch by three (3) inch space at the top right-hand corner on each subsequent page shall be left blank and reserved for use by the clerk of court. FL ST J ADMIN Rule 2.520(d).
      i. *Exceptions to recording space.* Any papers or documents created by persons or entities over which the filing party has no control, including but not limited to wills, codicils, trusts, or other testamentary documents; documents prepared or executed by any public officer; documents prepared, executed, acknowledged, or proved outside of the State of Florida; or documents created by State or Federal government agencies, may be filed without the space required by FL ST J ADMIN Rule 2.520. FL ST J ADMIN Rule 2.520(e).
   c. *Noncompliance.* No clerk of court is permitted to refuse to file any document or paper because of noncompliance with the Florida Rules of Judicial Administration. However, upon request of the clerk of court, noncomplying documents must be resubmitted in accordance with the formatting rules. FL ST J ADMIN Rule 2.520(f).
2. *Caption.* Every pleading, motion, order, judgment, or other paper shall have a caption containing the name of the court, the file number, and except for in rem proceedings, including forfeiture proceedings, the name of the first party on each side with an appropriate indication of other parties, and a designation identifying the party filing it and its nature or the nature of the order, as the case may be. In any in rem proceeding, every pleading, motion, order, judgment, or other paper shall have a caption containing the name of the court, the file number, the style "In re" (followed by the name or general description of the property), and a designation of the person or entity filing it and its nature or the nature of the order, as the case may be. In an in rem forfeiture proceeding, the style shall be "In re forfeiture of" (followed by the name of the general description of the property). All papers filed in the action shall be styled in such a manner as to indicate clearly the subject matter of the paper and the party requesting or obtaining relief. FL ST RCP Rule 1.100(c)(1).
3. *Writing and written defined.* Writing or written means a document containing information, an application, or a stipulation. FL ST RCP Rule 1.080(c).
4. *Rule abbreviations*
   a. The Florida Rules of Civil Procedure and shall be abbreviated as Fla.R.Civ.P. FL ST RCP Rule 1.010.
   b. The Florida Rules of Judicial Administration shall be abbreviated as Fla. R. Jud. Admin. FL ST J ADMIN Rule 2.110.
5. *Nonverification.* Except when otherwise specifically provided by the Florida Rules of Civil Procedure or an applicable statute, every pleading or other document of a party represented by an attorney need not be verified or accompanied by an affidavit. FL ST RCP Rule 1.030; FL ST J ADMIN Rule 2.515(a).
6. *Attorney signature*
   a. *Attorney signature.* Every pleading and other document of a party represented by an attorney shall be signed by at least one (1) attorney of record in that attorney's individual name whose current record

Florida Bar address, telephone number, including area code, primary e-mail address and secondary e-mail addresses, if any, and Florida Bar number shall be stated, and who shall be duly licensed to practice law in Florida or who shall have received permission to appear in the particular case as provided in FL ST J ADMIN Rule 2.510. FL ST J ADMIN Rule 2.515(a).

i. The attorney may be required by the court to give the address of, and to vouch for the attorney's authority to represent, the party. FL ST J ADMIN Rule 2.515(a).

ii. The signature of an attorney shall constitute a certificate by the attorney that the attorney has read the pleading or other document; that to the best of the attorney's knowledge, information, and belief there is good ground to support it; and that it is not interposed for delay. FL ST J ADMIN Rule 2.515(a).

iii. If a pleading is not signed or is signed with intent to defeat the purpose of FL ST J ADMIN Rule 2.515, it may be stricken and the action may proceed as though the pleading or other document had not been served. FL ST J ADMIN Rule 2.515(a).

b. *Pro se litigant signature.* A party who is not represented by an attorney shall sign any pleading or other paper and state the party's address and telephone number, including area code. FL ST J ADMIN Rule 2.515(b).

c. *Form of signature*

i. The signatures required on pleadings and documents by FL ST J ADMIN Rule 2.515(a) and FL ST J ADMIN Rule 2.515(b) may be:

- Original signatures;
- Original signatures that have been reproduced by electronic means, such as on electronically transmitted documents or photocopied documents;
- Electronic signatures using the "/s/," "s/," or "/s" formats by or at the direction of the person signing; or
- Any other signature format authorized by general law, so long as the clerk where the proceeding is pending has the capability of receiving and has obtained approval from the Supreme Court of Florida to accept pleadings and documents with that signature format. FL ST J ADMIN Rule 2.515(c)(1).

ii. An attorney, party, or other person who files a pleading or paper by electronic transmission that does not contain the original signature of that attorney, party, or other person shall file that identical pleading or paper in paper form containing an original signature of that attorney, party, or other person (hereinafter called the follow-up filing) immediately thereafter. The follow-up filing is not required if the Supreme Court of Florida has entered an order directing the clerk of court to discontinue accepting the follow-up filing. FL ST J ADMIN Rule 2.515(c)(2).

7. *Forms*

a. *Process.* The forms of process, notice of lis pendens, and notice of action provided in the Florida Rules of Civil Procedure are sufficient. Variations from the forms do not void process or notices that are otherwise sufficient. FL ST RCP Rule 1.900(a).

b. *Other forms.* The other forms provided in the Florida Rules of Civil Procedure are sufficient for the matters that are covered by them. So long as the substance is expressed without prolixity, the forms may be varied to meet the facts of a particular case. FL ST RCP Rule 1.900(b).

c. *Formal matters.* Captions, except for the designation of the paper, are omitted from the forms provided in the Florida Rules of Civil Procedure. A general form of caption is the first form provided. Signatures are omitted from pleadings and motions. FL ST RCP Rule 1.900(c).

8. *Notices to persons with disabilities.* All notices of court proceedings to be held in a public facility, and all process compelling appearance at such proceedings, shall include the following statement in bold face, fourteen (14) point Times New Roman or Courier font: "If you are a person with a disability who needs any accommodation in order to participate in this proceeding, you are entitled, at no cost to you, to the provision of certain assistance. Please contact [identify applicable court personnel by name, address, and

telephone number] at least seven (7) days before your scheduled court appearance, or immediately upon receiving this notification if the time before the scheduled appearance is less than seven (7) days; if you are hearing or voice impaired, call 711." FL ST J ADMIN Rule 2.540(c)(1).

9. *Minimization of the filing of sensitive information*
   a. *Limitations for court filings.* Unless authorized by FL ST J ADMIN Rule 2.425(b), statute, another rule of court, or the court orders otherwise, designated sensitive information filed with the court must be limited to the following format:
      i. The initials of a person known to be a minor;
      ii. The year of birth of a person's birth date;
      iii. No portion of any: Social security number, Bank account number, Credit card account number, Charge account number, or Debit account number;
      iv. The last four digits of any: Taxpayer identification number (TIN), Employee identification number, Driver's license number, Passport number, Telephone number, Financial account number, except as set forth in FL ST J ADMIN Rule 2.425(a)(3), Brokerage account number, Insurance policy account number, Loan account number, Customer account number, or Patient or health care number;
      v. A truncated version of any: Email address, Computer user name, Password, or Personal identification number (PIN); and
      vi. A truncated version of any other sensitive information as provided by court order. FL ST J ADMIN Rule 2.425(a).
   b. *Exceptions.* FL ST J ADMIN Rule 2.425(a) does not apply to the following:
      i. An account number which identifies the property alleged to be the subject of a proceeding;
      ii. The record of an administrative or agency proceeding;
      iii. The record in appellate or review proceedings;
      iv. The birth date of a minor whenever the birth date is necessary for the court to establish or maintain subject matter jurisdiction;
      v. The name of a minor in any order relating to parental responsibility, time-sharing, or child support;
      vi. The name of a minor in any document or order affecting the minor's ownership of real property;
      vii. The birth date of a party in a writ of attachment or notice to payor;
      viii. In traffic and criminal proceedings: a pro se filing; a court filing that is related to a criminal matter or investigation and that is prepared before the filing of a criminal charge or is not filed as part of any docketed criminal case; an arrest or search warrant or any information in support thereof; a charging document and an affidavit or other documents filed in support of any charging document, including any driving records; a statement of particulars; discovery material introduced into evidence or otherwise filed with the court; and all information necessary for the proper issuance and execution of a subpoena duces tecum;
      ix. Information used by the clerk for case maintenance purposes or the courts for case management purposes; and
      x. Information which is relevant and material to an issue before the court. FL ST J ADMIN Rule 2.425(b).
   c. *Remedies.* Upon motion by a party or interested person or sua sponte by the court, the court may order remedies, sanctions or both for a violation of FL ST J ADMIN Rule 2.425(a). Following notice and an opportunity to respond, the court may impose sanctions if such filing was not made in good faith. FL ST J ADMIN Rule 2.425(c).
   d. *Motions not restricted.* FL ST J ADMIN Rule 2.425 does not restrict a party's right to move for

protective order, to move to file documents under seal, or to request a determination of the confidentiality of records. FL ST J ADMIN Rule 2.425(d).

i. For more information regarding sealing court records, please see FL ST 4 J CIR 2006-05.

e. *Application.* FL ST J ADMIN Rule 2.425 does not affect the application of constitutional provisions, statutes, or rules of court regarding confidential information or access to public information. FL ST J ADMIN Rule 2.425(e).

F. Filing and Service Requirements

1. *Filing requirements.* All documents filed in any court shall be filed by electronic transmission in accordance with FL ST J ADMIN Rule 2.525. "Documents" means pleadings, motions, petitions, memoranda, briefs, notices, exhibits, declarations, affidavits, orders, judgments, decrees, writs, opinions, and any other paper or writing submitted to a court. FL ST J ADMIN Rule 2.520(a). All documents that are court records, as defined in FL ST J ADMIN Rule 2.430(a)(1), must be filed by electronic transmission, provided that: (1) the clerk has the ability to accept and retain such documents; (2) the clerk or the chief judge of the circuit has requested permission to accept documents filed by electronic transmission; and (3) the supreme court has entered an order granting permission to the clerk to accept documents filed by electronic transmission. FL ST J ADMIN Rule 2.525(c)(1).

a. *Definition.* "Electronic transmission of documents" means the sending of information by electronic signals to, by or from a court or clerk, which when received can be transformed and stored or transmitted on paper, microfilm, magnetic storage device, optical imaging system, CD-ROM, flash drive, other electronic data storage system, server, case maintenance system ("CM"), electronic court filing ("ECF") system, statewide or local electronic portal ("e-portal"), or other electronic record keeping system authorized by the supreme court in a format sufficient to communicate the information on the original document in a readable format. Electronic transmission of documents includes electronic mail ("e-mail") and any internet-based transmission procedure, and may include procedures allowing for documents to be signed or verified by electronic means. FL ST J ADMIN Rule 2.525(a).

b. *Application.* Any court or clerk of the court may accept the electronic transmission of documents for filing after the clerk, together with input from the chief judge of the circuit, has obtained approval of the procedures and program for doing so from the Supreme Court of Florida. FL ST J ADMIN Rule 2.525(b).

c. *Exceptions*

i. Paper documents and other submissions may be manually submitted to the clerk or court:

- When the clerk does not have the ability to accept and retain documents by electronic filing or has not had ECF Procedures approved by the supreme court;
- For filing by any self-represented party or any self-represented nonparty unless specific ECF Procedures provide a means to file documents electronically. However, any self-represented nonparty that is a governmental or public agency and any other agency, partnership, corporation, or business entity acting on behalf of any governmental or public agency may file documents by electronic transmission if such entity has the capability of filing documents electronically;
- For filing by attorneys excused from e-mail service in accordance with FL ST J ADMIN Rule 2.516(b);
- When submitting evidentiary exhibits or filing non-documentary materials;
- When the filing involves documents in excess of twenty-five (25) megabytes (25MB) in size. For such filings, documents may be transmitted using an electronic storage medium that the clerk has the ability to accept, which may include a CD-ROM, flash drive, or similar storage medium;
- When filed in open court, as permitted by the court;
- When paper filing is permitted by any approved statewide or local ECF procedures; and
- If any court determines that justice so requires. FL ST J ADMIN Rule 2.525(d).

ii. Any document in paper form submitted under FL ST J ADMIN Rule 2.525(d) is filed when it is received by the clerk or court and the clerk shall immediately thereafter convert any filed paper document to an electronic document. "Convert to an electronic document" means optically capturing an image of a paper document and using character recognition software to recover as much of the document's text as practicable and then indexing and storing the document in the official court file. FL ST J ADMIN Rule 2.525(c)(4).

iii. Any storage medium submitted under FL ST J ADMIN Rule 2.525(d)(5) is filed when received by the clerk or court and the clerk shall immediately thereafter transfer the electronic documents from the storage device to the official court file. FL ST J ADMIN Rule 2.525(c)(5).

iv. If the filer of any paper document authorized under FL ST J ADMIN Rule 2.525(d) provides a self-addressed, postage-paid envelope for return of the paper document after it is converted to electronic form by the clerk, the clerk shall place the paper document in the envelope and deposit it in the mail. Except when a paper document is required to be maintained, the clerk may recycle any filed paper document that is not to be returned to the filer. FL ST J ADMIN Rule 2.525(c)(6).

v. The clerk may convert any paper document filed before the effective date of FL ST J ADMIN Rule 2.525 to an electronic document. Unless the clerk is required to maintain the paper document, if the paper document has been converted to an electronic document by the clerk, the paper document is no longer part of the official court file and may be removed and recycled. FL ST J ADMIN Rule 2.525(c)(7).

d. *Official court file.* For information on what constitutes the official court file, please see FL ST J ADMIN Rule 2.525(c)(2), FL ST J ADMIN Rule 2.525(c)(3).

e. *Administration.* All attorneys, parties, or other persons using this rule to file documents are required to make arrangements with the court or clerk for the payment of any charges authorized by general law or the supreme court before filing any document by electronic transmission. FL ST J ADMIN Rule 2.525(f)(2).

f. *Filing date.* The filing date for an electronically transmitted document is the date and time that such filing is acknowledged by an electronic stamp or otherwise, pursuant to any procedure set forth in any ECF Procedures approved by the supreme court, or the date the last page of such filing is received by the court or clerk. FL ST J ADMIN Rule 2.525(f)(3).

g. *Accessibility.* All documents transmitted in any electronic form under FL ST J ADMIN Rule 2.525 must comply with the accessibility requirements of FL ST J ADMIN Rule 2.526. FL ST J ADMIN Rule 2.525(g).

2. *Service requirements*

a. *Papers to be served.* At the time of personal service of process a copy of the initial pleading shall be delivered to the party upon whom service is made. The date and hour of service shall be endorsed on the original process and all copies of it by the person making the service. The party seeking to effect personal service shall furnish the person making service with the necessary copies. When the service is made by publication, copies of the initial pleadings shall be furnished to the clerk and mailed by the clerk with the notice of action to all parties whose addresses are stated in the initial pleading or sworn statement. FL ST RCP Rule 1.070(e).

b. *Issuance of summons.* Upon the commencement of the action, summons or other process authorized by law shall be issued forthwith by the clerk or judge under the clerk's or the judge's signature and the seal of the court and delivered for service without praecipe. FL ST RCP Rule 1.070(a).

i. *How directed.* Summons, subpoenas, and other process in civil actions run throughout the state. All process except subpoenas shall be directed to all and singular the sheriffs of the state. FL ST § 48.011.

ii. *Service as to numerous defendants.* If there is more than one (1) defendant, the clerk or judge shall issue as many writs of process against the several defendants as may be directed by the plaintiff or the plaintiff's attorney. FL ST RCP Rule 1.070(c).

c. *Who may serve process.* Service of process may be made by an officer authorized by law to serve process, but the court may appoint any competent person not interested in the action to serve the process. When so appointed, the person serving process shall make proof of service by affidavit promptly and in any event within the time during which the person served must respond to the process. Failure to make proof of service shall not affect the validity of the service. When any process is returned not executed or returned improperly executed for any defendant, the party causing its issuance shall be entitled to such additional process against the unserved party as is required to effect service. FL ST RCP Rule 1.070(b).

i. All process shall be served by the sheriff of the county where the person to be served is found, except initial nonenforceable civil process may be served by a special process server appointed by the sheriff as provided for in FL ST § 48.021 or by a certified process server as provided for in FL ST § 48.25 through FL ST § 48.31. FL ST § 48.021(1).

ii. The sheriff of each county may, in his or her discretion, establish an approved list of natural persons designated as special process servers. FL ST § 48.021(2)(a). For more information regarding process servers, please see FL ST § 48.021(2).

iii. A person serving process shall place, on the copy served, the date and time of service and his or her identification number and initials for all service of process. FL ST § 48.031(5).

d. *Service of process on Sunday*

i. Service or execution on Sunday of any writ, process, warrant, order, or judgment is void and the person serving or executing, or causing it to be served or executed, is liable to the party aggrieved for damages for so doing as if he or she had done it without any process, writ, warrant, order, or judgment. FL ST § 48.20.

ii. If affidavit is made by the person requesting service or execution that he or she has good reason to believe that any person liable to have any such writ, process, warrant, order, or judgment served on him or her intends to escape from this state under protection of Sunday, any officer furnished with an order authorizing service or execution by the trial court judge may serve or execute such writ, process, warrant, order, or judgment on Sunday, and it is as valid as if it had been done on any other day. FL ST § 48.20.

e. *Methods of service*

i. *Service of process generally.* Service of original process is made by delivering a copy of it to the person to be served with a copy of the complaint, petition, or other initial pleading or paper or by leaving the copies at his or her usual place of abode with any person residing therein who is fifteen (15) years of age or older and informing the person of their contents. Minors who are or have been married shall be served as provided in FL ST § 48.031. FL ST § 48.031(1)(a).

- Employers, when contacted by an individual authorized to make service of process, shall permit the authorized individual to make service on employees in a private area designated by the employer. FL ST § 48.031(1)(b).
- Substitute service may be made on the spouse of the person to be served at any place in the county, if the cause of action is not an adversary proceeding between the spouse and the person to be served, if the spouse requests such service, and if the spouse and person to be served are residing together in the same dwelling. FL ST § 48.031(2)(a).
- Substitute service may be made on an individual doing business as a sole proprietorship at his or her place of business, during regular business hours, by serving the person in charge of the business at the time of service if two (2) or more attempts to serve the owner have been made at the place of business. FL ST § 48.031(2)(b).
- If the only address for a person to be served, which is discoverable through public records, is a private mailbox, substitute service may be made by leaving a copy of the process with the person in charge of the private mailbox, but only if the process server determines that the person to be served maintains a mailbox at that location. FL ST § 48.031(6).

ii. *Service by mail.* A defendant may accept service of process by mail. FL ST RCP Rule 1.070(i).

A plaintiff may notify any defendant of the commencement of the action and request that the defendant waive service of a summons. FL ST RCP Rule 1.070(i)(2).

- *Notice and request for waiver.* The notice and request shall: (1) be in writing and be addressed directly to the defendant, if an individual, or to an officer or managing or general agent of the defendant or other agent authorized by appointment or law to receive service of process; (2) be dispatched by certified mail, return receipt requested; (3) be accompanied by a copy of the complaint and shall identify the court in which it has been filed; (4) inform the defendant of the consequences of compliance and of failure to comply with the request; (5) state the date on which the request is sent; (6) allow the defendant twenty (20) days from the date on which the request is received to return the waiver, or, if the address of the defendant is outside of the United States, thirty (30) days from the date on which it is received to return the waiver; and (7) provide the defendant with an extra copy of the notice and request, including the waiver, as well as a prepaid means of compliance in writing. FL ST RCP Rule 1.070(i)(2).
- *Consequences of accepting/rejecting service by mail.* Acceptance of service of a complaint by mail does not thereby waive any objection to the venue or to the jurisdiction of the court over the person of the defendant. FL ST RCP Rule 1.070(i)(1). If a defendant fails to comply with a request for waiver within the time provided, the court shall impose the costs subsequently incurred in effecting service on the defendant unless good cause for the failure is shown. FL ST RCP Rule 1.070(i)(3). A defendant who, before being served with process, timely returns a waiver so requested is not required to respond to the complaint until sixty (60) days after the date the defendant received the request for waiver of service. For purposes of computing any time prescribed or allowed by the Florida Rules of Civil Procedure, service of process shall be deemed effected twenty (20) days before the time required to respond to the complaint. FL ST RCP Rule 1.070(i)(4). When the plaintiff files a waiver of service with the court, the action shall proceed, except as provided in FL ST RCP Rule 1.070(i)(4), as if a summons and complaint had been served at the time of filing the waiver, and no further proof of service shall be required. FL ST RCP Rule 1.070(i)(5).

iii. *Service on partnerships and limited partnerships*

- Process against a partnership shall be served on any partner and is as valid as if served on each individual partner. If a partner is not available during regular business hours to accept service on behalf of the partnership, he or she may designate an employee to accept such service. After one (1) attempt to serve a partner or designated employee has been made, process may be served on the person in charge of the partnership during regular business hours. After service on any partner, plaintiff may proceed to judgment and execution against that partner and the assets of the partnership. After service on a designated employee or other person in charge, plaintiff may proceed to judgment and execution against the partnership assets but not against the individual assets of any partner. FL ST § 48.061(1).
- Process against a domestic limited partnership may be served on any general partner or on the agent for service of process specified in its certificate of limited partnership or in its certificate as amended or restated and is as valid as if served on each individual member of the partnership. After service on a general partner or the agent, the plaintiff may proceed to judgment and execution against the limited partnership and all of the general partners individually. If a general partner cannot be found in this state and service cannot be made on an agent because of failure to maintain such an agent or because the agent cannot be found or served with the exercise of reasonable diligence, service of process may be effected by service upon the Secretary of State as agent of the limited partnership as provided for in FL ST § 48.181. Service of process may be made under FL ST § 48.071 and FL ST § 48.21 on limited partnerships. FL ST § 48.061(2).
- Process against a foreign limited partnership may be served on any general partner found in the state or on any agent for service of process specified in its application for registration

and is as valid as if served on each individual member of the partnership. If a general partner cannot be found in this state and an agent for service of process has not been appointed or, if appointed, the agent's authority has been revoked or the agent cannot be found or served with the exercise of reasonable diligence, service of process may be effected by service upon the Secretary of State as agent of the limited partnership as provided for in FL ST § 48.181, or process may be served as provided in FL ST § 48.071 and FL ST § 48.21. FL ST § 48.061(3).

iv. *Service on corporation*

- Process against any private corporation, domestic or foreign, may be served: (1) on the president or vice president, or other head of the corporation; (2) in the absence of any person described in FL ST § 48.081(1)(a), on the cashier, treasurer, secretary, or general manager; (3) in the absence of any person described in FL ST § 48.081(1)(a) or FL ST § 48.081(1)(b), on any director; or (4) in the absence of any person described in FL ST § 48.081(1)(a), FL ST § 48.081(1)(b), or FL ST § 48.081(1)(c), on any officer or business agent residing in the state. FL ST § 48.081(1).
- If a foreign corporation has none of the foregoing officers or agents in this state, service may be made on any agent transacting business for it in this state. FL ST § 48.081(2).
- As an alternative to all of the foregoing, process may be served on the agent designated by the corporation under FL ST § 48.091. However, if service cannot be made on a registered agent because of failure to comply with FL ST § 48.091, service of process shall be permitted on any employee at the corporation's principal place of business or on any employee of the registered agent. FL ST § 48.081(3)(a). If the address provided for the registered agent, officer, director, or principal place of business is a residence or private mailbox, service on the corporation may be made by serving the registered agent, officer, or director in accordance with FL ST § 48.031. FL ST § 48.081(3)(b).
- FL ST § 48.081 does not apply to service of process on insurance companies. FL ST § 48.081(4).
- When a corporation engages in substantial and not isolated activities within this state, or has a business office within the state and is actually engaged in the transaction of business therefrom, service upon any officer or business agent while on corporate business within this state may personally be made, pursuant to FL ST § 48.081, and it is not necessary in such case that the action, suit, or proceeding against the corporation shall have arisen out of any transaction or operation connected with or incidental to the business being transacted within the state. FL ST § 48.081(5).
- For information regarding service on a dissolved corporation refer to FL ST § 48.101.

v. *Personal service outside state*

- Except as otherwise provided herein, service of process on persons outside of this state shall be made in the same manner as service within this state by any officer authorized to serve process in the state where the person is served. No order of court is required. An affidavit of the officer shall be filed, stating the time, manner, and place of service. The court may consider the affidavit, or any other competent evidence, in determining whether service has been properly made. Service of process on persons outside the United States may be required to conform to the provisions of the Hague Convention on the Service Abroad of Judicial and Extrajudicial Documents in Civil or Commercial Matters. FL ST § 48.194(1).
- For further information on service of process in an in rem or quasi in rem action refer to FL ST § 48.194(2); FL ST § 48.194(3); and FL ST § 48.194(4).

vi. *Method of substituted service on nonresident*

- When authorized by law, substituted service of process on a nonresident or a person who conceals his or her whereabouts by serving a public officer designated by law shall be made by leaving a copy of the process with a fee of eight dollars and seventy-five cents

($8.75) with the public officer or in his or her office or by mailing the copies by certified mail to the public officer with the fee. The service is sufficient service on a defendant who has appointed a public officer as his or her agent for the service of process. FL ST § 48.161(1).

- Notice of service and a copy of the process shall be sent forthwith by registered or certified mail by the plaintiff or his or her attorney to the defendant, and the defendant's return receipt and the affidavit of the plaintiff or his or her attorney of compliance shall be filed on or before the return day of the process or within such time as the court allows, or the notice and copy shall be served on the defendant, if found within the state, by an officer authorized to serve legal process, or if found without the state, by a sheriff or a deputy sheriff of any county of this state or any duly constituted public officer qualified to serve like process in the state or jurisdiction where the defendant is found. The officer's return showing service shall be filed on or before the return day of the process or within such time as the court allows. The public officer shall keep a record of all process served on him or her showing the day and hour of service. FL ST § 48.161(1).
- If any person on whom service of process is authorized under FL ST § 48.161(1) dies, service may be made on his or her administrator, executor, curator, or personal representative in the same manner. FL ST § 48.161(2).
- FL ST § 48.161 does not apply to persons on whom service is authorized under FL ST § 48.151. FL ST § 48.161(3).
- The public officer may designate some other person in his or her office to accept service. FL ST § 48.161(4).

vii. *Service by publication.* Service of process by publication may be made as provided by statute. FL ST RCP Rule 1.070(d). Service of process by publication is allowable in cases listed in FL ST § 49.011 and upon the parties listed in FL ST § 49.021.

- As a condition precedent to service by publication, a statement shall be filed in the action executed by the plaintiff, the plaintiff's agent or attorney, setting forth substantially the matters hereafter required, which statement may be contained in a verified pleading, or in an affidavit or other sworn statement. FL ST § 49.031(1). After the entry of a final judgment or decree in any action no sworn statement shall ever be held defective for failure to state a required fact if the fact otherwise appears from the record in the action. FL ST § 49.031(3).
- For the sworn statement requirements for service of process by publication refer to FL ST § 49.041; FL ST § 49.051; FL ST § 49.061; and FL ST § 49.071.
- On filing the sworn statement, and otherwise complying with the foregoing requirements, the plaintiff is entitled to have issued by the clerk or judge, not later than sixty (60) days after filing the sworn statement, a notice of action which notice shall set forth: (1) the names of the known natural defendants; the names, status and description of the corporate defendants; a description of the unknown defendants who claim by, through, under or against a known party which may be described as "all parties claiming interests by, through, under or against (name of known party)" and a description of all unknown defendants which may be described as "all parties having or claiming to have any right, title or interest in the property herein described"; (2) the nature of the action or proceeding in short and simple terms (but neglect to do so is not jurisdictional); (3) the name of the court in which the action or proceeding was instituted and an abbreviated title of the case; (4) the description of real property, if any, proceeded against. FL ST § 49.08.
- For further information on service of process by publication refer to FL ST § 49.09; FL ST § 49.10; FL ST § 49.11; FL ST § 49.12; FL ST § 50.011; FL ST § 50.021; FL ST § 50.031; FL ST § 50.041; FL ST § 50.051; and FL ST § 50.061.

viii. *Service on agents of nonresidents doing business in the state.* When any natural person or partnership not residing or having a principal place of business in this state engages in business in this state, process may be served on the person who is in charge of any business in which the defendant is engaged within this state at the time of service, including agents soliciting orders for goods, wares, merchandise or services. FL ST § 48.071.

- Any process so served is as valid as if served personally on the nonresident person or partnership engaging in business in this state in any action against the person or partnership arising out of such business. FL ST § 48.071.
- A copy of such process with a notice of service on the person in charge of such business shall be sent forthwith to the nonresident person or partnership by registered or certified mail, return receipt requested. FL ST § 48.071.
- An affidavit of compliance with FL ST § 48.071 shall be filed before the return day or within such further time as the court may allow. FL ST § 48.071.

ix. *Service on nonresident engaging in business in state.* The acceptance by any person or persons, individually or associated together as a copartnership or any other form or type of association, who are residents of any other state or country, and all foreign corporations, and any person who is a resident of the state and who subsequently becomes a nonresident of the state or conceals his or her whereabouts, of the privilege extended by law to nonresidents and others to operate, conduct, engage in, or carry on a business or business venture in the state, or to have an office or agency in the state, constitutes an appointment by the persons and foreign corporations of the Secretary of State of the state as their agent on whom all process in any action or proceeding against them, or any of them, arising out of any transaction or operation connected with or incidental to the business or business venture may be served. The acceptance of the privilege is signification of the agreement of the persons and foreign corporations that the process against them which is so served is of the same validity as if served personally on the persons or foreign corporations. FL ST § 48.181(1).

- If a foreign corporation has a resident agent or officer in the state, process shall be served on the resident agent or officer. FL ST § 48.181(2).
- Any person, firm, or corporation which sells, consigns, or leases by any means whatsoever tangible or intangible personal property, through brokers, jobbers, wholesalers, or distributors to any person, firm, or corporation in this state is conclusively presumed to be both engaged in substantial and not isolated activities within this state and operating, conducting, engaging in, or carrying on a business or business venture in this state. FL ST § 48.181(3).

x. *Other service provisions:*

- Service on alien property custodian. FL ST § 48.131.
- Service on an incompetent person. FL ST § 48.042.
- Service on minor. FL ST § 48.041.
- Service on public agencies and officers. FL ST § 48.111.
- Service on the state. FL ST § 48.121.
- Service on a state prisoner. FL ST § 48.051.
- Service on labor unions. FL ST § 48.141.
- Service on statutory agents for certain persons. FL ST § 48.151.
- Service on nonresident motor vehicle owners. FL ST § 48.171.
- Service of process in action for possession of premises. FL ST § 48.183.
- Service on nonresidents operating aircraft or watercraft in the state. FL ST § 48.19.

f. *Crossclaims.* Service of a crossclaim on a party who has appeared in the action shall be made pursuant to FL ST RCP Rule 1.080. Service of a crossclaim against a party who has not appeared in the action shall be made in the manner provided for service of summons. FL ST RCP Rule 1.170(g).

g. *Fees.* The statutory compensation for making service shall not be increased by the simultaneous delivery or mailing of the copy of the initial pleading in conformity with FL ST RCP Rule 1.070. FL ST RCP Rule 1.070(g).

G. Hearings

1. There is no hearing required or contemplated in the Florida rules governing the complaint and service of summons.

H. Forms

1. Official Complaint and Summons Forms for Florida

a. Caption. FL ST RCP Form 1.901.

b. Summons. FL ST RCP Form 1.902.

c. Crossclaim summons. FL ST RCP Form 1.903.

d. Third-party summons. FL ST RCP Form 1.904.

e. Notice of action; Constructive service; No property. FL ST RCP Form 1.919.

f. Notice of action; Constructive service; Property. FL ST RCP Form 1.920.

g. Third-party complaint. FL ST RCP Form 1.948.

h. Civil cover sheet. FL ST RCP Form 1.997.

i. Fall-down negligence complaint. FL ST RCP Form 1.951.

j. Notice of compliance when constitutional challenge is brought. FL ST RCP Form 1.975.

2. Complaint Forms for Florida

a. Complaint for damages; General form. FL-PP § 2:17.

b. Complaint; Negligent infliction of personal injury. FL-PP § 2:19.

c. Complaint; Fall down negligence. FL-PP § 2:20.

d. Complaint; Professional negligence. FL-PP § 2:23.

e. Complaint; Breach of contract. FL-PP § 2:24.

f. Complaint; Breach of personal services contract. FL-PP § 2:25.

g. Summons; General form. FL-PRACFORM § 3:4.

h. Summons; Natural person. FL-PRACFORM § 3:5.

i. Complaint; Assault and battery. FL-PRACFORM § 4:9.

j. Complaint; Breach of contract, general form. FL-PRACFORM § 4:17.

k. Complaint; Civil rights. FL-PRACFORM § 4:23.

l. Complaint; Conversion. FL-PRACFORM § 4:30.

m. Complaint; Employment contract. FL-PRACFORM § 4:44.

n. Complaint; False imprisonment. FL-PRACFORM § 4:46.

o. Complaint; Fraud, misrepresentation. FL-PRACFORM § 4:62.

p. Complaint; Lease, by landlord. FL-PRACFORM § 4:86.

q. Complaint; Lease, by tenant. FL-PRACFORM § 4:87.

r. Complaint; Libel. FL-PRACFORM § 4:89.

s. Complaint; Life insurance policy. FL-PRACFORM § 4:90.

t. Complaint; Medical malpractice, negligence. FL-PRACFORM § 4:95.

u. Complaint; Negligence, automobile, driver. FL-PRACFORM § 4:101.

v. Complaint; Negligence, hospital. FL-PRACFORM § 4:104.

I. Checklist

(I) ❑ Matters to be considered by plaintiff

- (a) ❑ Required documents
  - (1) ❑ Summons
  - (2) ❑ Complaint
  - (3) ❑ Civil cover sheet
  - (4) ❑ Return of execution process by process server
  - (5) ❑ Filing fees
- (b) ❑ Supplemental documents
  - (1) ❑ Exhibits
  - (2) ❑ Notice of constitutional question
- (c) ❑ Time for filing and serving complaint
  - (1) ❑ Service of the initial process and initial pleading should be made upon a defendant within one hundred twenty (120) days after the filing of the complaint with the court

(II) ❑ Matters to be considered by defendant

- (a) ❑ Required documents
  - (1) ❑ Answer
  - (2) ❑ Certificate of service
- (b) ❑ Supplemental documents
  - (1) ❑ Exhibits
  - (2) ❑ Notice of constitutional question
- (c) ❑ Time for answer
  - (1) ❑ Unless a different time is prescribed in a statute of Florida, a defendant shall serve an answer within twenty (20) days after service of original process and the initial pleading on the defendant, or not later than the date fixed in a notice by publication
  - (2) ❑ A party served with a pleading stating a crossclaim against that party shall serve an answer to it within twenty (20) days after service on that party
  - (3) ❑ The plaintiff shall serve an answer to a counterclaim within twenty (20) days after service of the counterclaim
  - (4) ❑ A defendant who, before being served with process, timely returns a waiver so requested is not required to respond to the complaint until sixty (60) days after the date the defendant received the request for waiver of service; for purposes of computing any time prescribed or allowed by the Florida Rules of Civil Procedure, service of process shall be deemed effected twenty (20) days before the time required to respond to the complaint
  - (5) ❑ For timing requirements related to service on the state, service of motion impact, and responding when no responsive pleading is required, please see the Timing section of this document

Pleadings
Amended Complaint

Document Last Updated January 2013

A. Applicable Rules

1. *State rules*
   a. Nonverification of papers. FL ST RCP Rule 1.030.

b. Process. FL ST RCP Rule 1.070.
c. Constitutional challenge to state statute or county or municipal charter, ordinance, or franchise; Notice by party. FL ST RCP Rule 1.071.
d. Service and filing of pleadings, orders, and documents. FL ST RCP Rule 1.080.
e. Pleadings and motions. FL ST RCP Rule 1.100; FL ST RCP Rule 1.110; FL ST RCP Rule 1.120; FL ST RCP Rule 1.130; FL ST RCP Rule 1.190; FL ST § 48.193.
f. Pretrial procedure. FL ST RCP Rule 1.200.
g. Relief from judgment, decrees, or orders. FL ST RCP Rule 1.540.
h. Forms. FL ST RCP Rule 1.900.
i. Minimization of the filing of sensitive information. FL ST J ADMIN Rule 2.425.
j. Retention of court records. FL ST J ADMIN Rule 2.430.
k. Foreign attorneys. FL ST J ADMIN Rule 2.510.
l. Signature of attorneys and parties. FL ST J ADMIN Rule 2.515.
m. Paper. FL ST J ADMIN Rule 2.520.
n. Electronic filing. FL ST J ADMIN Rule 2.525.
o. Accessibility of information and technology. FL ST J ADMIN Rule 2.526.
p. Requests for accommodations by persons with disabilities. FL ST J ADMIN Rule 2.540.

2. *Local rules*
   a. Sealing court records. FL ST 4 J CIR 2006-05.

B. Timing

1. *Amendment as a matter of course.* A party may amend a pleading once as a matter of course at any time before a responsive pleading is served or, if the pleading is one to which no responsive pleading is permitted and the action has not been placed on the trial calendar, may so amend it at any time within twenty (20) days after it is served. FL ST RCP Rule 1.190(a).
2. *Amendment by leave of court.* Otherwise a party may amend a pleading only by leave of court or by written consent of the adverse party. Leave of court shall be given freely when justice so requires. FL ST RCP Rule 1.190(a).
3. *Amendments in furtherance of justice.* At any time in furtherance of justice, upon such terms as may be just, the court may permit any process, proceeding, pleading, or record to be amended or material supplemental matter to be set forth in an amended or supplemental pleading. At every stage of the action the court must disregard any error or defect in the proceedings which does not affect the substantial rights of the parties. FL ST RCP Rule 1.190(e).
4. *Response to amended pleading.* A party shall plead in response to an amended pleading within ten (10) days after service of the amended pleading unless the court otherwise orders. FL ST RCP Rule 1.190(a).
5. *Computation of time*
   a. *Generally.* Computation of time shall be governed by FL ST J ADMIN Rule 2.514. FL ST RCP Rule 1.090(a). The following rules apply in computing time periods specified in any rule of procedure, local rule, court order, or statute that does not specify a method of computing time. FL ST J ADMIN Rule 2.514(a).
      i. *Period stated in days or a longer unit.* When the period is stated in days or a longer unit of time (A) exclude the day of the event that triggers the period; (B) count every day, including intermediate Saturdays, Sundays, and legal holidays; and (C) include the last day of the period, but if the last day is a Saturday, Sunday, or legal holiday, or falls within any period of time extended through an order of the chief justice under FL ST J ADMIN Rule 2.205(a)(2)(B)(iv), the period continues to run until the end of the next day that is not a Saturday, Sunday, or legal holiday and does not fall within any period of time extended through an order of the chief justice. FL ST J ADMIN Rule 2.514(a)(1).

ii. *Period stated in hours.* When the period is stated in hours (A) begin counting immediately on the occurrence of the event that triggers the period; (B) count every hour, including hours during intermediate Saturdays, Sundays, and legal holidays; and (C) if the period would end on a Saturday, Sunday, or legal holiday, or during any period of time extended through an order of the chief justice under FL ST J ADMIN Rule 2.205(a)(2)(B)(iv), the period continues to run until the same time on the next day that is not a Saturday, Sunday, or legal holiday and does not fall within any period of time extended through an order of the chief justice. FL ST J ADMIN Rule 2.514(a)(2).

iii. *Period stated in days less than seven (7) days.* When the period stated in days is less than seven (7) days, intermediate Saturdays, Sundays, and legal holidays shall be excluded in the computation. FL ST J ADMIN Rule 2.514(a)(3).

iv. "Last day" defined. Unless a different time is set by a statute, local rule, or court order, the last day ends (A) for electronic filing or for service by any means, at midnight; and (B) for filing by other means, when the clerk's office is scheduled to close. FL ST J ADMIN Rule 2.514(a)(4).

v. *"Next day" defined.* The "next day" is determined by continuing to count forward when the period is measured after an event and backward when measured before an event. FL ST J ADMIN Rule 2.514(a)(5).

vi. *"Legal holiday" defined.* "Legal holiday" means (A) the day set aside by FL ST § 110.117, for observing New Year's Day, Martin Luther King, Jr.'s Birthday, Memorial Day, Independence Day, Labor Day, Veterans' Day, Thanksgiving Day, the Friday after Thanksgiving Day, or Christmas Day, and (B) any day observed as a holiday by the clerk's office or as designated by the chief judge. FL ST J ADMIN Rule 2.514(a)(6).

b. *Additional time after service by mail or e-mail.* When a party may or must act within a specified time after service and service is made by mail or e-mail, five (5) days are added after the period that would otherwise expire under FL ST J ADMIN Rule 2.514(a). FL ST J ADMIN Rule 2.514(b).

c. *Enlargement.* When an act is required or allowed to be done at or within a specified time by order of court, by the Florida Rules of Civil Procedure, or by notice given thereunder, for cause shown the court at any time in its discretion (1) with or without notice, may order the period enlarged if request therefor is made before the expiration of the period originally prescribed or as extended by a previous order, or (2) upon motion made and notice after the expiration of the specified period, may permit the act to be done when failure to act was the result of excusable neglect, but it may not extend the time for making a motion for new trial, for rehearing, or to alter or amend a judgment; making a motion for relief from a judgment under FL ST RCP Rule 1.540(b); taking an appeal or filing a petition for certiorari; or making a motion for a directed verdict. FL ST RCP Rule 1.090(b).

d. *Unaffected by expiration of term.* The period of time provided for the doing of any act or the taking of any proceeding shall not be affected or limited by the continued existence or expiration of a term of court. The continued existence or expiration of a term of court in no way affects the power of a court to do any act or take any proceeding in any action which is or has been pending before it. FL ST RCP Rule 1.090(c).

C. General Requirements

1. *Amendments.* A party may amend a pleading once as a matter of course at any time before a responsive pleading is served or, if the pleading is one to which no responsive pleading is permitted and the action has not been placed on the trial calendar, may so amend it at any time within twenty (20) days after it is served. Otherwise a party may amend a pleading only by leave of court or by written consent of the adverse party. Leave of court shall be freely given when justice so requires. FL ST RCP Rule 1.190(a).

a. *Purpose of amendments.* Amendments can relate to the correction of mistakes, the insertion of jurisdictional averments, the correction or addition of verifications, the addition or substitution or striking out of parties, and generally the rectification of all formal defects in the pleading. The court can also allow amendments setting up an omitted counterclaim or cross-claim if the defendant failed to raise the claim through oversight, inadvertence, or excusable neglect. FL-PP § 2:151.

b. *Amendment to a pleading/Amended pleading.* A significant difference exists between an amendment to a pleading and an amended pleading. An amendment to a pleading corrects, adds to or deletes from the pleading. An amended pleading is substituted for the former pleading and the former pleading ceases to have any effect. Dee v. Southern Brewing Company, 146 Fla. 588, 1 So.2d 562 (Fla. 1941); Shannon v. McBride, 105 So.2d 16 (Fla. 2d DCA 1958); Hughes v. Home Sav. of America, F.S.B., 675 So.2d 649 (Fla. 2d DCA 1996); FL-PRACPROC § 14:2.

c. *Relation back of amendments.* When the claim or defense asserted in the amended pleading arose out of the conduct, transaction, or occurrence set forth or attempted to be set forth in the original pleading, the amendment shall relate back to the date of the original pleading. FL ST RCP Rule 1.190(c).

2. *General rules of pleading*

a. *Claims for relief*

i. A pleading which sets forth a claim for relief, whether an original claim, counterclaim, crossclaim, or third-party claim, must state a cause of action and shall contain

- A short and plain statement of the grounds upon which the court's jurisdiction depends, unless the court already has jurisdiction and the claim needs no new grounds of jurisdiction to support it (For information regarding acts subjecting persons to jurisdiction, please see FL ST § 48.193),
- A short and plain statement of the ultimate facts showing that the pleader is entitled to relief, and
- A demand for judgment for the relief to which the pleader deems himself or herself entitled. FL ST RCP Rule 1.110(b).

ii. Relief in the alternative or of several different types may be demanded. Every complaint shall be considered to demand general relief. FL ST RCP Rule 1.110(b).

b. *Verification.* Except when otherwise specifically provided by these rules or an applicable statute, every pleading or other document of a party represented by an attorney need not be verified or accompanied by an affidavit. FL ST RCP Rule 1.030. When filing an action for foreclosure of a mortgage on residential real property the complaint shall be verified. When verification of a document is required, the document filed shall include an oath, affirmation, or the following statement: "Under penalty of perjury, I declare that I have read the foregoing, and the facts alleged therein are true and correct to the best of my knowledge and belief." FL ST RCP Rule 1.110(b).

c. *Separate statements.* All averments of claim or defense shall be made in consecutively numbered paragraphs, the contents of each of which shall be limited as far as practicable to a statement of a single set of circumstances, and a paragraph may be referred to by number in all subsequent pleadings. Each claim founded upon a separate transaction or occurrence and each defense other than denials shall be stated in a separate count or defense when a separation facilitates the clear presentation of the matter set forth. FL ST RCP Rule 1.110(f).

d. *Statements adopted by reference.* Statements in a pleading may be adopted by reference in a different part of the same pleading, in another pleading, or in any motion. FL ST RCP Rule 1.130(b).

e. *Joinder of causes of action; Consistency.* A pleader may set up in the same action as many claims or causes of action or defenses in the same right as the pleader has, and claims for relief may be stated in the alternative if separate items make up the cause of action, or if two (2) or more causes of action are joined. A party may also set forth two (2) or more statements of a claim or defense alternatively, either in one (1) count or defense or in separate counts or defenses. When two (2) or more statements are made in the alternative and one (1) of them, if made independently, would be sufficient, the pleading is not made insufficient by the insufficiency of one (1) or more of the alternative statements. A party may also state as many separate claims or defenses as that party has, regardless of consistency and whether based on legal or equitable grounds or both. All pleadings shall be construed so as to do substantial justice. FL ST RCP Rule 1.110(g).

f. *Subsequent pleadings.* When the nature of an action permits pleadings subsequent to final judgment and the jurisdiction of the court over the parties has not terminated, the initial pleading subsequent to final judgment shall be designated a supplemental complaint or petition. The action shall then proceed in the same manner and time as though the supplemental complaint or petition were the initial pleading in the action, including the issuance of any needed process. FL ST RCP Rule 1.110(h) shall not apply to proceedings that may be initiated by motion under the Florida Rules of Civil Procedure. FL ST RCP Rule 1.110(h).

g. *Pleading basis for service.* When service of process is to be made under statutes authorizing service on nonresidents of Florida, it is sufficient to plead the basis for service in the language of the statute without pleading the facts supporting service. FL ST RCP Rule 1.070(h).

h. *Forms of pleadings.* Forms of action and technical forms for seeking relief and of pleas, pleadings, or motions are abolished. FL ST RCP Rule 1.110(a).

3. *Complaint; Generally*

a. *Purpose.* The purpose of a complaint is to advise the court and the defendant of the nature of a cause of action asserted by the plaintiff. FL-PP § 2:12.

b. *Sufficiency of complaint.* A complaint will be found to be insufficient if it contains only general conclusory allegations unsupported by any facts. The test to determine whether a complaint is sufficient is whether, if the factual allegations of the complaint are established, the plaintiff will be legally or equitably entitled to the claimed relief. Pizzi v. Central Bank & Trust Co., 250 So.2d 895, 896 (Fla. 1971); Bowen v. G H C Properties, Limited, 251 So.2d 359, 361 (Fla. 1st DCA 1971); FL-PP § 2:12. In determining the sufficiency of the complaint to state a cause of action, all allegations of the complaint are taken as true, and possible affirmative defenses are not considered. Strickland v. Commerce Loan Co. of Jacksonville, 158 So.2d 814 (Fla. 1st DCA 1963); FL-PP § 2:12.

i. The issues for trial in Florida must be settled by the pleadings. The issues cannot be raised by discovery. FL-PRACPROC § 7:6.

ii. Causes of action may be pleaded alternatively in the same count or in different counts and against the same or different defendants as long as the joinder of parties is proper. FL-PRACPROC § 7:6.

iii. Each count must state a cause of action. Each independent cause of action should be pleaded in a separate count. FL-PRACPROC § 7:6.

iv. Incorporation by reference of all allegations from one count to another is not proper. Separate counts facilitate reference to the pleading in which they appear in other pleadings, motions or papers as well as the assertion of defenses against some, but not all, causes of action. Some defenses may not apply to the initial pleading as a whole. FL-PRACPROC § 7:6.

4. *Pleading special matters*

a. *Capacity.* It is not necessary to aver the capacity of a party to sue or be sued, the authority of a party to sue or be sued in a representative capacity, or the legal existence of an organized association of persons that is made a party, except to the extent required to show the jurisdiction of the court. The initial pleading served on behalf of a minor party shall specifically aver the age of the minor party. When a party desires to raise an issue as to the legal existence of any party, the capacity of any party to sue or be sued, or the authority of a party to sue or be sued in a representative capacity, that party shall do so by specific negative averment which shall include such supporting particulars as are peculiarly within the pleader's knowledge. FL ST RCP Rule 1.120(a).

b. *Fraud, mistake, condition of the mind.* In all averments of fraud or mistake, the circumstances constituting fraud or mistake shall be stated with such particularity as the circumstances may permit. Malice, intent, knowledge, mental attitude, and other condition of mind of a person may be averred generally. FL ST RCP Rule 1.120(b).

c. *Conditions precedent.* In pleading the performance or occurrence of conditions precedent, it is sufficient to aver generally that all conditions precedent have been performed or have occurred. A denial of performance or occurrence shall be made specifically and with particularity. FL ST RCP Rule 1.120(c).

d. *Official document or act.* In pleading an official document or official act it is sufficient to aver that the document was issued or the act done in compliance with law. FL ST RCP Rule 1.120(c).

e. *Judgment or decree.* In pleading a judgment or decree of a domestic or foreign court, a judicial or quasi-judicial tribunal, or a board or officer, it is sufficient to aver the judgment or decree without setting forth matter showing jurisdiction to render it. FL ST RCP Rule 1.120(e).

f. *Time and place.* For the purpose of testing the sufficiency of a pleading, averments of time and place are material and shall be considered like all other averments of material matter. FL ST RCP Rule 1.120(f).

g. *Special damage.* When items of special damage are claimed, they shall be specifically stated. FL ST RCP Rule 1.120(g).

5. *Parties*

a. *Parties generally.* Every action may be prosecuted in the name of the real party in interest, but a personal representative, administrator, guardian, trustee of an express trust, a party with whom or in whose name a contract has been made for the benefit of another, or a party expressly authorized by statute may sue in that person's own name without joining the party for whose benefit the action is brought. All persons having an interest in the subject of the action and in obtaining the relief demanded may join as plaintiffs and any person may be made a defendant who has or claims an interest adverse to the plaintiff. Any person may at any time be made a party if that person's presence is necessary or proper to a complete determination of the cause. Persons having a united interest may be joined on the same side as plaintiffs or defendants, and anyone who refuses to join may for such reason be made a defendant. FL ST RCP Rule 1.210(a).

b. *Minors or incompetent persons.* When a minor or incompetent person has a representative, such as a guardian or other like fiduciary, the representative may sue or defend on behalf of the minor or incompetent person. A minor or incompetent person who does not have a duly appointed representative may sue by next friend or by a guardian ad litem. The court shall appoint a guardian ad litem for a minor or incompetent person not otherwise represented in an action or shall make such other order as it deems proper for the protection of the minor or incompetent person. FL ST RCP Rule 1.210(b).

c. For survivor and substitution of parties information, please see FL ST RCP Rule 1.260.

6. *Counterclaims and crossclaims*

a. *Compulsory counterclaims.* A pleading shall state as a counterclaim any claim which at the time of serving the pleading the pleader has against any opposing party, provided it arises out of the transaction or occurrence that is the subject matter of the opposing party's claim and does not require for its adjudication the presence of third parties over whom the court cannot acquire jurisdiction. But the pleader need not state a claim if (1) at the time the action was commenced the claim was the subject of another pending action, or (2) the opposing party brought suit upon that party's claim by attachment or other process by which the court did not acquire jurisdiction to render a personal judgment on the claim and the pleader is not stating a counterclaim under this rule. FL ST RCP Rule 1.170(a).

b. *Permissive counterclaim.* A pleading may state as a counterclaim any claim against an opposing party not arising out of the transaction or occurrence that is the subject matter of the opposing party's claim. FL ST RCP Rule 1.170(b).

c. *Counterclaim exceeding opposing claim.* A counterclaim may or may not diminish or defeat the recovery sought by the opposing party. It may claim relief exceeding in amount or different in kind from that sought in the pleading of the opposing party. FL ST RCP Rule 1.170(c).

d. *Counterclaim against the State.* The Florida Rules of Civil Procedure shall not be construed to enlarge beyond the limits established by law the right to assert counterclaims or to claim credits against the state or any of its subdivisions or other governmental organizations thereof subject to suit or against a municipal corporation or against an officer, agency, or administrative board of the state. FL ST RCP Rule 1.170(d).

e. *Counterclaim maturing or acquired after pleading.* A claim which matured or was acquired by the pleader after serving the pleading may be presented as a counterclaim by supplemental pleading with the permission of the court. FL ST RCP Rule 1.170(e).

f. *Omitted counterclaim or crossclaim.* When a pleader fails to set up a counterclaim or crossclaim through oversight, inadvertence, or excusable neglect, or when justice requires, the pleader may set up the counterclaim or crossclaim by amendment with leave of the court. FL ST RCP Rule 1.170(f).

g. *Crossclaim against co-party.* A pleading may state as a crossclaim any claim by one party against a co-party arising out of the transaction or occurrence that is the subject matter of either the original action or a counterclaim therein, or relating to any property that is the subject matter of the original action. The crossclaim may include a claim that the party against whom it is asserted is or may be liable to the crossclaimant for all or part of a claim asserted in the action against the crossclaimant. Service of a crossclaim on a party who has appeared in the action shall be made pursuant to FL ST RCP Rule 1.080. Service of a crossclaim against a party who has not appeared in the action shall be made in the manner provided for service of summons. FL ST RCP Rule 1.170(g).

h. *Additional parties may be brought in.* When the presence of parties other than those to the original action is required to grant complete relief in the determination of a counterclaim or crossclaim, they shall be named in the counterclaim or crossclaim and be served with process and shall be parties to the action thereafter if jurisdiction of them can be obtained and their joinder will not deprive the court of jurisdiction of the action. FL ST RCP Rule 1.250(b) and FL ST RCP Rule 1.250(c) apply to parties brought in under FL ST RCP Rule 1.170(h). FL ST RCP Rule 1.170(h).

i. *Separate trials; Separate judgment.* If the court orders separate trials as provided in FL ST RCP Rule 1.270(b), judgment on a counterclaim or crossclaim may be rendered when the court has jurisdiction to do so even if a claim of the opposing party has been dismissed or otherwise disposed of. FL ST RCP Rule 1.170(i).

j. *Demand exceeding jurisdiction; Transfer of action.* If the demand of any counterclaim or crossclaim exceeds the jurisdiction of the court in which the action is pending, the action shall be transferred forthwith to the court of the same county having jurisdiction of the demand in the counterclaim or crossclaim with only such alterations in the pleadings as are essential. The court shall order the transfer of the action and the transmittal of all papers in it to the proper court if the party asserting the demand exceeding the jurisdiction deposits with the court having jurisdiction a sum sufficient to pay the clerk's service charge in the court to which the action is transferred at the time of filing the counterclaim or crossclaim. Thereupon the original papers and deposit shall be transmitted and filed with a certified copy of the order. The court to which the action is transferred shall have full power and jurisdiction over the demands of all parties. Failure to make the service charge deposit at the time the counterclaim or crossclaim is filed, or within such further time as the court may allow, shall reduce a claim for damages to an amount within the jurisdiction of the court where the action is pending and waive the claim in other cases. FL ST RCP Rule 1.170(j).

7. *Misjoinder and nonjoinder of parties*

a. *Misjoinder.* Misjoinder of parties is not a ground for dismissal of an action. Any claim against a party may be severed and proceeded with separately. FL ST RCP Rule 1.250(a).

b. *Dropping parties.* Parties may be dropped by an adverse party in the manner provided for voluntary dismissal in FL ST RCP Rule 1.420(a)(1) subject to the exception stated in FL ST RCP Rule 1.420. If notice of lis pendens has been filed in the action against a party so dropped, the notice of dismissal shall be recorded and cancels the notice of lis pendens without the necessity of a court order. Parties may be dropped by order of court on its own initiative or the motion of any party at any stage of the action on such terms as are just. FL ST RCP Rule 1.250(b).

c. *Adding parties.* Parties may be added once as a matter of course within the same time that pleadings can be so amended under FL ST RCP Rule 1.190(a). If amendment by leave of court or stipulation of the parties is permitted, parties may be added in the amended pleading without further order of court. Parties may be added by order of court on its own initiative or on motion of any party at any stage of the action and on such terms as are just. FL ST RCP Rule 1.250(c).

8. *Jury demand*

a. *Right preserved.* The right of trial by jury as declared by the Constitution or by statute shall be preserved to the parties inviolate. FL ST RCP Rule 1.430(a).

b. *Demand.* Any party may demand a trial by jury of any issue triable of right by a jury by serving upon the other party a demand therefor in writing at any time after commencement of the action and not later than ten (10) days after the service of the last pleading directed to such issue. The demand may be indorsed upon a pleading of the party. FL ST RCP Rule 1.430(b).

c. *Specification of issues.* In the demand a party may specify the issues that the party wishes so tried; otherwise, the party is deemed to demand trial by jury for all issues so triable. FL ST RCP Rule 1.430(c).

   i. If a party has demanded trial by jury for only some of the issues, any other party may serve a demand for trial by jury of any other or all of the issues triable by jury ten (10) days after service of the demand or such lesser time as the court may order. FL ST RCP Rule 1.430(c).

d. *Waiver.* A party who fails to serve a demand as required by FL ST RCP Rule 1.430 waives trial by jury. FL ST RCP Rule 1.430(d).

   i. If waived, a jury trial may not be granted without the consent of the parties, but the court may allow an amendment in the proceedings to demand a trial by jury or order a trial by jury on its own motion. FL ST RCP Rule 1.430(d).

   ii. A demand for trial by jury may not be withdrawn without the consent of the parties. FL ST RCP Rule 1.430(d).

9. *Arbitration and mediation*

   a. *Referral to arbitration and mediation.* Except as hereinafter provided or as otherwise prohibited by law, the presiding judge may enter an order referring all or any part of a contested civil matter to mediation or arbitration. The parties to any contested civil matter may file a written stipulation to mediate or arbitrate any issue between them at any time. Such stipulation shall be incorporated into the order of referral. FL ST RCP Rule 1.700(a).

   b. *Arbitration*

      i. *Exclusions.* A civil action shall be ordered to arbitration or arbitration in conjunction with mediation upon stipulation of the parties. A civil action may be ordered to arbitration or arbitration in conjunction with mediation upon motion of any party or by the court, if the judge determines the action to be of such a nature that arbitration could be of benefit to the litigants or the court. FL ST RCP Rule 1.800.

         - Under no circumstances may the following categories of actions be referred to arbitration: (1) bond estreatures; (2) habeas corpus or other extraordinary writs; (3) bond validations; (4) civil or criminal contempt; (5) such other matters as may be specified by order of the chief judge in the circuit. FL ST RCP Rule 1.800.

      ii. For more information regarding arbitration, please see FL ST RCP Rule 1.810; FL ST RCP Rule 1.820; FL ST RCP Rule 1.830.

   c. *Mediation.* For more information regarding mediation, please see FL ST RCP Rule 1.710; FL ST RCP Rule 1.720; FL ST RCP Rule 1.730; and FL ST RCP Rule 1.750.

10. *Rules of court*

   a. *Rules of civil procedure.* The Florida Rules of Civil Procedure apply to all actions of a civil nature and all special statutory proceedings in the circuit courts and county courts except those to which the Florida Probate Rules, the Florida Family Law Rules of Procedure, or the Small Claims Rules apply. FL ST RCP Rule 1.010.

      i. The form, content, procedure, and time for pleading in all special statutory proceedings shall be as prescribed by the statutes governing the proceeding unless the Florida Rules of Civil Procedure specifically provide to the contrary. FL ST RCP Rule 1.010.

      ii. The Florida Rules of Civil Procedure shall be construed to secure the just, speedy, and inexpensive determination of every action. FL ST RCP Rule 1.010.

   b. *Rules of judicial administration.* The Florida Rules of Judicial Administration shall apply to administrative matters in all courts to which the Florida Rules of Judicial Administration are applicable by their terms. The Florida Rules of Judicial Administration shall be construed to secure the speedy and inexpensive determination of every proceeding to which they are applicable. The Florida Rules of Judicial Administration shall supersede all conflicting rules and statutes. FL ST J ADMIN Rule 2.110.

D. Documents

1. *Required documents*
   a. *Amended complaint.* See the General Requirements section of this document for the content of an amended complaint. If a party files a motion to amend a pleading, the party shall attach the proposed amended pleading to the motion. FL ST RCP Rule 1.190(a). See the KeyRules Florida Circuit Court Motion for Leave to Amend document for further information.
      i. *Notices to persons with disabilities.* See the Format section of this KeyRules document for further information.
   b. *Certificate of service.* When any attorney certifies in substance: "I certify that a copy hereof has been furnished to (here insert name or names and addresses used for service) by (e-mail) (delivery) (mail) (fax) on .... (date) ....______________ Attorney" the certificate is taken as prima facie proof of such service in compliance with FL ST J ADMIN Rule 2.516. FL ST J ADMIN Rule 2.516(f).
2. *Supplemental documents*
   a. *Exhibits.* All bonds, notes, bills of exchange, contracts, accounts, or documents upon which action may be brought or defense made, or a copy thereof or a copy of the portions thereof material to the pleadings, shall be incorporated in or attached to the pleading. No papers shall be unnecessarily annexed as exhibits. The pleadings shall contain no unnecessary recitals of deeds, documents, contracts, or other instruments. Any exhibit attached to a pleading shall be considered a part of the pleadings for all purposes. FL ST RCP Rule 1.130(a).
   b. *Notice of constitutional question.* A party that files a pleading, written motion, or other paper drawing into question the constitutionality of a state statute or a county or municipal charter, ordinance, or franchise must promptly (1) file a notice of constitutional question stating the question and identifying the paper that raises it; and (2) serve the notice and the pleading, written motion, or other paper drawing into question the constitutionality of a state statute or a county or municipal charter, ordinance, or franchise on the Attorney General or the state attorney of the judicial circuit in which the action is pending, by either certified or registered mail. Service of the notice and pleading, written motion, or other paper does not require joinder of the Attorney General or the state attorney as a party to the action. FL ST RCP Rule 1.071.

E. Format

1. *Documents; Type and size.* Documents subject to the exceptions set forth in FL ST J ADMIN Rule 2.525(d) shall be filed on recycled paper measuring eight and one half by eleven (8 1/2 by 11) inches. For purposes of FL ST J ADMIN Rule 2.520, paper is recycled if it contains a minimum content of fifty (50) percent waste paper. Xerographic reduction of legal-size (eight and one half by fourteen (8 1/2 by 14) inches) documents to letter size (eight and one half by eleven (8 1/2 by 11) inches) is prohibited. All other documents filed by electronic transmission shall be filed in a format capable of being printed in a format consistent with the provisions of FL ST J ADMIN Rule 2.250. FL ST J ADMIN Rule 2.520(b).
   a. *Exhibits.* Any exhibit or attachment filed with pleadings or papers may be filed in its original size. FL ST J ADMIN Rule 2.520(c).
   b. *Recording space.* On all papers and documents prepared and filed by the court or by any party to a proceeding which are to be recorded in the public records of any county, including but not limited to final money judgments and notices of lis pendens, a three (3) inch by three (3) inch space at the top right-hand corner on the first page and a one (1) inch by three (3) inch space at the top right-hand corner on each subsequent page shall be left blank and reserved for use by the clerk of court. FL ST J ADMIN Rule 2.520(d).
      i. *Exceptions to recording space.* Any papers or documents created by persons or entities over which the filing party has no control, including but not limited to wills, codicils, trusts, or other

testamentary documents; documents prepared or executed by any public officer; documents prepared, executed, acknowledged, or proved outside of the State of Florida; or documents created by State or Federal government agencies, may be filed without the space required by FL ST J ADMIN Rule 2.520. FL ST J ADMIN Rule 2.520(e).

c. *Noncompliance.* No clerk of court is permitted to refuse to file any document or paper because of noncompliance with the Florida Rules of Judicial Administration. However, upon request of the clerk of court, noncomplying documents must be resubmitted in accordance with the formatting rules. FL ST J ADMIN Rule 2.520(f).

2. *Caption.* Every pleading, motion, order, judgment, or other paper shall have a caption containing the name of the court, the file number, and except for in rem proceedings, including forfeiture proceedings, the name of the first party on each side with an appropriate indication of other parties, and a designation identifying the party filing it and its nature or the nature of the order, as the case may be. In any in rem proceeding, every pleading, motion, order, judgment, or other paper shall have a caption containing the name of the court, the file number, the style "In re" (followed by the name or general description of the property), and a designation of the person or entity filing it and its nature or the nature of the order, as the case may be. In an in rem forfeiture proceeding, the style shall be "In re forfeiture of" (followed by the name of the general description of the property). All papers filed in the action shall be styled in such a manner as to indicate clearly the subject matter of the paper and the party requesting or obtaining relief. FL ST RCP Rule 1.100(c)(1).

3. *Writing and written defined.* Writing or written means a document containing information, an application, or a stipulation. FL ST RCP Rule 1.080(c).

4. *Rule abbreviations*

   a. The Florida Rules of Civil Procedure and shall be abbreviated as Fla.R.Civ.P. FL ST RCP Rule 1.010.

   b. The Florida Rules of Judicial Administration shall be abbreviated as Fla. R. Jud. Admin. FL ST J ADMIN Rule 2.110.

5. *Nonverification.* Except when otherwise specifically provided by the Florida Rules of Civil Procedure or an applicable statute, every pleading or other document of a party represented by an attorney need not be verified or accompanied by an affidavit. FL ST RCP Rule 1.030; FL ST J ADMIN Rule 2.515(a).

6. *Attorney signature*

   a. *Attorney signature.* Every pleading and other document of a party represented by an attorney shall be signed by at least one (1) attorney of record in that attorney's individual name whose current record Florida Bar address, telephone number, including area code, primary e-mail address and secondary e-mail addresses, if any, and Florida Bar number shall be stated, and who shall be duly licensed to practice law in Florida or who shall have received permission to appear in the particular case as provided in FL ST J ADMIN Rule 2.510. FL ST J ADMIN Rule 2.515(a).

      i. The attorney may be required by the court to give the address of, and to vouch for the attorney's authority to represent, the party. FL ST J ADMIN Rule 2.515(a).

      ii. The signature of an attorney shall constitute a certificate by the attorney that the attorney has read the pleading or other document; that to the best of the attorney's knowledge, information, and belief there is good ground to support it; and that it is not interposed for delay. FL ST J ADMIN Rule 2.515(a).

      iii. If a pleading is not signed or is signed with intent to defeat the purpose of FL ST J ADMIN Rule 2.515, it may be stricken and the action may proceed as though the pleading or other document had not been served. FL ST J ADMIN Rule 2.515(a).

   b. *Pro se litigant signature.* A party who is not represented by an attorney shall sign any pleading or other paper and state the party's address and telephone number, including area code. FL ST J ADMIN Rule 2.515(b).

c. *Form of signature*

i. The signatures required on pleadings and documents by FL ST J ADMIN Rule 2.515(a) and FL ST J ADMIN Rule 2.515(b) may be:

- Original signatures;
- Original signatures that have been reproduced by electronic means, such as on electronically transmitted documents or photocopied documents;
- Electronic signatures using the "/s/," "s/," or "/s" formats by or at the direction of the person signing; or
- Any other signature format authorized by general law, so long as the clerk where the proceeding is pending has the capability of receiving and has obtained approval from the Supreme Court of Florida to accept pleadings and documents with that signature format. FL ST J ADMIN Rule 2.515(c)(1).

ii. An attorney, party, or other person who files a pleading or paper by electronic transmission that does not contain the original signature of that attorney, party, or other person shall file that identical pleading or paper in paper form containing an original signature of that attorney, party, or other person (hereinafter called the follow-up filing) immediately thereafter. The follow-up filing is not required if the Supreme Court of Florida has entered an order directing the clerk of court to discontinue accepting the follow-up filing. FL ST J ADMIN Rule 2.515(c)(2).

7. *Forms*

a. *Process.* The forms of process, notice of lis pendens, and notice of action provided in the Florida Rules of Civil Procedure are sufficient. Variations from the forms do not void process or notices that are otherwise sufficient. FL ST RCP Rule 1.900(a).

b. *Other forms.* The other forms provided in the Florida Rules of Civil Procedure are sufficient for the matters that are covered by them. So long as the substance is expressed without prolixity, the forms may be varied to meet the facts of a particular case. FL ST RCP Rule 1.900(b).

c. *Formal matters.* Captions, except for the designation of the paper, are omitted from the forms provided in the Florida Rules of Civil Procedure. A general form of caption is the first form provided. Signatures are omitted from pleadings and motions. FL ST RCP Rule 1.900(c).

8. *Notices to persons with disabilities.* All notices of court proceedings to be held in a public facility, and all process compelling appearance at such proceedings, shall include the following statement in bold face, fourteen (14) point Times New Roman or Courier font: "If you are a person with a disability who needs any accommodation in order to participate in this proceeding, you are entitled, at no cost to you, to the provision of certain assistance. Please contact [identify applicable court personnel by name, address, and telephone number] at least seven (7) days before your scheduled court appearance, or immediately upon receiving this notification if the time before the scheduled appearance is less than seven (7) days; if you are hearing or voice impaired, call 711." FL ST J ADMIN Rule 2.540(c)(1).

9. *Minimization of the filing of sensitive information*

a. *Limitations for court filings.* Unless authorized by FL ST J ADMIN Rule 2.425(b), statute, another rule of court, or the court orders otherwise, designated sensitive information filed with the court must be limited to the following format:

i. The initials of a person known to be a minor;

ii. The year of birth of a person's birth date;

iii. No portion of any: Social security number, Bank account number, Credit card account number, Charge account number, or Debit account number;

iv. The last four digits of any: Taxpayer identification number (TIN), Employee identification number, Driver's license number, Passport number, Telephone number, Financial account number, except as set forth in FL ST J ADMIN Rule 2.425(a)(3), Brokerage account number, Insurance policy account number, Loan account number, Customer account number, or Patient or health care number;

v. A truncated version of any: Email address, Computer user name, Password, or Personal identification number (PIN); and

vi. A truncated version of any other sensitive information as provided by court order. FL ST J ADMIN Rule 2.425(a).

b. *Exceptions.* FL ST J ADMIN Rule 2.425(a) does not apply to the following:

i. An account number which identifies the property alleged to be the subject of a proceeding;

ii. The record of an administrative or agency proceeding;

iii. The record in appellate or review proceedings;

iv. The birth date of a minor whenever the birth date is necessary for the court to establish or maintain subject matter jurisdiction;

v. The name of a minor in any order relating to parental responsibility, time-sharing, or child support;

vi. The name of a minor in any document or order affecting the minor's ownership of real property;

vii. The birth date of a party in a writ of attachment or notice to payor;

viii. In traffic and criminal proceedings: a pro se filing; a court filing that is related to a criminal matter or investigation and that is prepared before the filing of a criminal charge or is not filed as part of any docketed criminal case; an arrest or search warrant or any information in support thereof; a charging document and an affidavit or other documents filed in support of any charging document, including any driving records; a statement of particulars; discovery material introduced into evidence or otherwise filed with the court; and all information necessary for the proper issuance and execution of a subpoena duces tecum;

ix. Information used by the clerk for case maintenance purposes or the courts for case management purposes; and

x. Information which is relevant and material to an issue before the court. FL ST J ADMIN Rule 2.425(b).

c. *Remedies.* Upon motion by a party or interested person or sua sponte by the court, the court may order remedies, sanctions or both for a violation of FL ST J ADMIN Rule 2.425(a). Following notice and an opportunity to respond, the court may impose sanctions if such filing was not made in good faith. FL ST J ADMIN Rule 2.425(c).

d. *Motions not restricted.* FL ST J ADMIN Rule 2.425 does not restrict a party's right to move for protective order, to move to file documents under seal, or to request a determination of the confidentiality of records. FL ST J ADMIN Rule 2.425(d).

i. For more information regarding sealing court records, please see FL ST 4 J CIR 2006-05.

e. *Application.* FL ST J ADMIN Rule 2.425 does not affect the application of constitutional provisions, statutes, or rules of court regarding confidential information or access to public information. FL ST J ADMIN Rule 2.425(e).

F. Filing and Service Requirements

1. *Filing requirements.* All original documents must be filed with the court either before service or immediately thereafter, unless otherwise provided for by general law or other rules. If the original of any bond or other document is not placed in the court file, a certified copy must be so placed by the clerk. FL ST J ADMIN Rule 2.516(d). All documents shall be filed in conformity with the requirements of FL ST J ADMIN Rule 2.525. FL ST RCP Rule 1.080(b). All documents filed in any court shall be filed by electronic transmission in accordance with FL ST J ADMIN Rule 2.525. "Documents" means pleadings, motions, petitions, memoranda, briefs, notices, exhibits, declarations, affidavits, orders, judgments, decrees, writs, opinions, and any other paper or writing submitted to a court. FL ST J ADMIN Rule 2.520(a). All documents that are court records, as defined in FL ST J ADMIN Rule 2.430(a)(1), must be filed by electronic transmission, provided that: (1) the clerk has the ability to accept and retain such documents; (2) the clerk or the chief judge of the circuit has requested permission to accept documents

filed by electronic transmission; and (3) the supreme court has entered an order granting permission to the clerk to accept documents filed by electronic transmission. FL ST J ADMIN Rule 2.525(c)(1).

a. *Definition.* "Electronic transmission of documents" means the sending of information by electronic signals to, by or from a court or clerk, which when received can be transformed and stored or transmitted on paper, microfilm, magnetic storage device, optical imaging system, CD-ROM, flash drive, other electronic data storage system, server, case maintenance system ("CM"), electronic court filing ("ECF") system, statewide or local electronic portal ("e-portal"), or other electronic record keeping system authorized by the supreme court in a format sufficient to communicate the information on the original document in a readable format. Electronic transmission of documents includes electronic mail ("e-mail") and any internet-based transmission procedure, and may include procedures allowing for documents to be signed or verified by electronic means. FL ST J ADMIN Rule 2.525(a).
   i. The filing of documents with the court as required by the Florida Rules of Judicial Administration must be made by filing them with the clerk in accordance with FL ST J ADMIN Rule 2.525, except that the judge may permit documents to be filed with the judge, in which event the judge must note the filing date before him or her on the documents and transmit them to the clerk. The date of filing is that shown on the face of the document by the judge's notation or the clerk's time stamp, whichever is earlier. FL ST J ADMIN Rule 2.516(e).

b. *Application.* Any court or clerk of the court may accept the electronic transmission of documents for filing after the clerk, together with input from the chief judge of the circuit, has obtained approval of the procedures and program for doing so from the Supreme Court of Florida. FL ST J ADMIN Rule 2.525(b).

c. *Exceptions*
   i. Paper documents and other submissions may be manually submitted to the clerk or court:
      - When the clerk does not have the ability to accept and retain documents by electronic filing or has not had ECF Procedures approved by the supreme court;
      - For filing by any self-represented party or any self-represented nonparty unless specific ECF Procedures provide a means to file documents electronically. However, any self-represented nonparty that is a governmental or public agency and any other agency, partnership, corporation, or business entity acting on behalf of any governmental or public agency may file documents by electronic transmission if such entity has the capability of filing documents electronically;
      - For filing by attorneys excused from e-mail service in accordance with FL ST J ADMIN Rule 2.516(b);
      - When submitting evidentiary exhibits or filing non-documentary materials;
      - When the filing involves documents in excess of twenty-five (25) megabytes (25MB) in size. For such filings, documents may be transmitted using an electronic storage medium that the clerk has the ability to accept, which may include a CD-ROM, flash drive, or similar storage medium;
      - When filed in open court, as permitted by the court;
      - When paper filing is permitted by any approved statewide or local ECF procedures; and
      - If any court determines that justice so requires. FL ST J ADMIN Rule 2.525(d).
   ii. Any document in paper form submitted under FL ST J ADMIN Rule 2.525(d) is filed when it is received by the clerk or court and the clerk shall immediately thereafter convert any filed paper document to an electronic document. "Convert to an electronic document" means optically capturing an image of a paper document and using character recognition software to recover as much of the document's text as practicable and then indexing and storing the document in the official court file. FL ST J ADMIN Rule 2.525(c)(4).
   iii. Any storage medium submitted under FL ST J ADMIN Rule 2.525(d)(5) is filed when received by the clerk or court and the clerk shall immediately thereafter transfer the electronic documents from the storage device to the official court file. FL ST J ADMIN Rule 2.525(c)(5).

iv. If the filer of any paper document authorized under FL ST J ADMIN Rule 2.525(d) provides a self-addressed, postage-paid envelope for return of the paper document after it is converted to electronic form by the clerk, the clerk shall place the paper document in the envelope and deposit it in the mail. Except when a paper document is required to be maintained, the clerk may recycle any filed paper document that is not to be returned to the filer. FL ST J ADMIN Rule 2.525(c)(6).

v. The clerk may convert any paper document filed before the effective date of FL ST J ADMIN Rule 2.525 to an electronic document. Unless the clerk is required to maintain the paper document, if the paper document has been converted to an electronic document by the clerk, the paper document is no longer part of the official court file and may be removed and recycled. FL ST J ADMIN Rule 2.525(c)(7).

d. *Official court file.* For information on what constitutes the official court file, please see FL ST J ADMIN Rule 2.525(c)(2), FL ST J ADMIN Rule 2.525(c)(3).

e. *Administration.* All attorneys, parties, or other persons using this rule to file documents are required to make arrangements with the court or clerk for the payment of any charges authorized by general law or the supreme court before filing any document by electronic transmission. FL ST J ADMIN Rule 2.525(f)(2).

f. *Filing date.* The filing date for an electronically transmitted document is the date and time that such filing is acknowledged by an electronic stamp or otherwise, pursuant to any procedure set forth in any ECF Procedures approved by the supreme court, or the date the last page of such filing is received by the court or clerk. FL ST J ADMIN Rule 2.525(f)(3).

g. *Accessibility.* All documents transmitted in any electronic form under FL ST J ADMIN Rule 2.525 must comply with the accessibility requirements of FL ST J ADMIN Rule 2.526. FL ST J ADMIN Rule 2.525(g).

2. *Service requirements.* Every pleading subsequent to the initial pleading, all orders, and every other document filed in the action must be served in conformity with the requirements of FL ST J ADMIN Rule 2.516. FL ST RCP Rule 1.080(a).

a. *Service; When required.* Unless the court otherwise orders, or a statute or supreme court administrative order specifies a different means of service, every pleading subsequent to the initial pleading and every other document filed in any court proceeding, except applications for witness subpoenas and documents served by formal notice or required to be served in the manner provided for service of formal notice, must be served in accordance with FL ST J ADMIN Rule 2.516 on each party. No service need be made on parties against whom a default has been entered, except that pleadings asserting new or additional claims against them must be served in the manner provided for service of summons. FL ST J ADMIN Rule 2.516(a).

b. *Service; How made.* When service is required or permitted to be made upon a party represented by an attorney, service must be made upon the attorney unless service upon the party is ordered by the court. FL ST J ADMIN Rule 2.516(b).

i. *Service by electronic mail ("e-mail").* All documents required or permitted to be served on another party must be served by e-mail, unless FL ST J ADMIN Rule 2.516 otherwise provides. When, in addition to service by e-mail, the sender also utilizes another means of service provided for in FL ST J ADMIN Rule 2.516(b)(2), any differing time limits and other provisions applicable to that other means of service control. FL ST J ADMIN Rule 2.516(b)(1). Any document electronically transmitted to a court or clerk must also be served on all parties and interested persons in accordance with the applicable rules of court. FL ST J ADMIN Rule 2.525(e)(2).

- *Service on attorneys.* Upon appearing in a proceeding, an attorney must serve a designation of a primary e-mail address and may designate no more than two (2) secondary e-mail addresses. Thereafter, service must be directed to all designated e-mail addresses in that proceeding. Every document filed by an attorney thereafter must include the primary e-mail address of that attorney and any secondary e-mail addresses. If an attorney does not designate any e-mail address for service, documents may be served on that attorney at the e-mail address on record with The Florida Bar. FL ST J ADMIN Rule 2.516(b)(1)(A).

- *Exception to e-mail service on attorneys.* Service by an attorney on another attorney must be made by e-mail unless excused by the court. Upon motion by an attorney demonstrating that the attorney has no e-mail account and lacks access to the Internet at the attorney's office, the court may excuse the attorney from the requirements of e-mail service. Service on and by an attorney excused by the court from e-mail service must be by the means provided in FL ST J ADMIN Rule 2.516(b)(2). FL ST J ADMIN Rule 2.516(b)(1)(B).
- *Service on and by parties not represented by an attorney.* Any party not represented by an attorney may serve a designation of a primary e-mail address and also may designate no more than two (2) secondary e-mail addresses to which service must be directed in that proceeding by the means provided in FL ST J ADMIN Rule 2.516(b)(1). If a party not represented by an attorney does not designate an e-mail address for service in a proceeding, service on and by that party must be by the means provided in FL ST J ADMIN Rule 2.516(b)(2). FL ST J ADMIN Rule 2.516(b)(1)(C).
- *Time of service.* Service by e-mail is complete when it is sent. FL ST J ADMIN Rule 2.516(b)(1)(D). An e-mail is deemed served on the date it is sent. FL ST J ADMIN Rule 2.516(b)(1)(D)(i). If the sender learns that the e-mail did not reach the address of the person to be served, the sender must immediately send another copy by e-mail, or by a means authorized by FL ST J ADMIN Rule 2.516(b)(2). FL ST J ADMIN Rule 2.516(b)(1)(D)(ii). E-mail service is treated as service by mail for the computation of time. FL ST J ADMIN Rule 2.516(b)(1)(D)(iii).

ii. *Format of e-mail for service.* Service of a document by e-mail is made by attaching a copy of the document in PDF format to an e-mail sent to all addresses designated by the attorney or party. FL ST J ADMIN Rule 2.516(b)(1)(E).

- All documents served by e-mail must be attached to an e-mail message containing a subject line beginning with the words "SERVICE OF COURT DOCUMENT" in all capital letters, followed by the case number of the proceeding in which the documents are being served. FL ST J ADMIN Rule 2.516(b)(1)(E)(i).
- The body of the e-mail must identify the court in which the proceeding is pending, the case number, the name of the initial party on each side, the title of each document served with that e-mail, and the sender's name and telephone number. FL ST J ADMIN Rule 2.516(b)(1)(E)(ii).
- Any document served by e-mail may be signed by the "/s/" format, as long as the filed original is signed in accordance with the applicable rule of procedure. FL ST J ADMIN Rule 2.516(b)(1)(E)(iii).
- Any e-mail which, together with its attached documents, exceeds five megabytes (5MB) in size, must be divided and sent as separate e-mails, no one of which may exceed five megabytes (5MB) in size and each of which must be sequentially numbered in the subject line. FL ST J ADMIN Rule 2.516(b)(1)(E)(iv).

iii. *Service by other means.* In addition to, and not in lieu of, service by e-mail, service may also be made upon attorneys by any of the means specified in FL ST J ADMIN Rule 2.516(b)(2). Service on and by all parties who are not represented by an attorney and who do not designate an e-mail address, and on and by all attorneys excused from e-mail service, must be made by delivering a copy of the document or by mailing it to the party or attorney at their last known address or, if no address is known, by leaving it with the clerk of the court. Service by mail is complete upon mailing. Delivery of a copy within FL ST J ADMIN Rule 2.516 is complete upon:

- Handing it to the attorney or to the party,
- Leaving it at the attorney's or party's office with a clerk or other person in charge thereof,
- If there is no one in charge, leaving it in a conspicuous place therein,

- If the office is closed or the person to be served has no office, leaving it at the person's usual place of abode with some person of his or her family above fifteen (15) years of age and informing such person of the contents, or
- Transmitting it by facsimile to the attorney's or party's office with a cover sheet containing the sender's name, firm, address, telephone number, and facsimile number, and the number of pages transmitted. When service is made by facsimile, a copy must also be served by any other method permitted by FL ST J ADMIN Rule 2.516. Facsimile service occurs when transmission is complete. FL ST J ADMIN Rule 2.516(b)(2)(A) through FL ST J ADMIN Rule 2.516(b)(2)(E).
- Service by delivery after 5:00 p.m. must be deemed to have been made by mailing on the date of delivery. FL ST J ADMIN Rule 2.516(b)(2)(F).

c. *Service; Numerous defendants.* In actions when the parties are unusually numerous, the court may regulate the service contemplated by the Florida Rules of Judicial Administration on motion or on its own initiative in such manner as may be found to be just and reasonable. FL ST J ADMIN Rule 2.516(c).

d. *Service by clerk.* Service of notices and other documents required to be made by the clerk must also be done as provided in FL ST J ADMIN Rule 2.516(b). FL ST J ADMIN Rule 2.516(g).

G. Hearings

1. The parties may be required to participate in pretrial proceedings to consider and determine the necessity or desirability of an amendment to a pleading. FL ST RCP Rule 1.200(b)(2); FL-PP § 2:151.

H. Forms

1. Official Amended Complaint Forms for Florida

a. Caption. FL ST RCP Form 1.901.

b. Notice of compliance when constitutional challenge is brought. FL ST RCP Form 1.975.

2. Amended Complaint Forms for Florida

a. Consent; Of party; To amendment of pleadings. FL-PP § 2:154.

b. Notice of amended complaint. 3 FLPRAC § 190.1.

c. Complaint for damages; General form. FL-PP § 2:17.

d. Complaint; Negligent infliction of personal injury. FL-PP § 2:19.

e. Complaint; Fall down negligence. FL-PP § 2:20.

f. Complaint; Mortgage foreclosure. FL-PP § 2:21.

g. Complaint; Implied warranty. FL-PP § 2:22.

h. Complaint; Professional negligence. FL-PP § 2:23.

i. Complaint; Breach of contract. FL-PP § 2:24.

j. Complaint; Breach of personal services contract. FL-PP § 2:25.

k. Notice of compliance when constitutional challenge is brought. FL ST RCP Form 1.975.

I. Checklist

(I) ❑ Matters to be considered by plaintiff

(a) ❑ Required documents

(1) ❑ Amended complaint

(2) ❑ Certificate of service

(b) ❑ Supplemental documents

(1) ❑ Exhibits

(2) ❑ Notice of constitutional question

(c) ❑ Timing

(1) ❑ A party may amend a pleading once as a matter of course at any time before a responsive pleading is served

(2) ❑ If the pleading is one to which no responsive pleading is permitted and the action has not been placed on the trial calendar, may so amend it at any time within twenty (20) days after it is served

Pleadings
Answer

Document Last Updated January 2013

A. Applicable Rules

1. *State rules*
   a. Nonverification of pleadings. FL ST RCP Rule 1.030.
   b. Process. FL ST RCP Rule 1.070.
   c. Service and filing of pleadings, orders, and documents. FL ST RCP Rule 1.080.
   d. Time. FL ST RCP Rule 1.090.
   e. Pleadings and motions. FL ST RCP Rule 1.100; FL ST RCP Rule 1.110; FL ST RCP Rule 1.120; FL ST RCP Rule 1.130; FL ST RCP Rule 1.190; FL ST RCP Rule 1.430.
   f. Defenses. FL ST RCP Rule 1.140.
   g. Relief from judgment, decrees, or orders. FL ST RCP Rule 1.540.
   h. Forms. FL ST RCP Rule 1.900.
   i. Minimization of the filing of sensitive information. FL ST J ADMIN Rule 2.425.
   j. Retention of court records. FL ST J ADMIN Rule 2.430.
   k. Foreign attorneys. FL ST J ADMIN Rule 2.510.
   l. Signature of attorneys and parties. FL ST J ADMIN Rule 2.515.
   m. Paper. FL ST J ADMIN Rule 2.520.
   n. Electronic filing. FL ST J ADMIN Rule 2.525.
   o. Accessibility of information and technology. FL ST J ADMIN Rule 2.526.
   p. Court reporting. FL ST J ADMIN Rule 2.535.
   q. Requests for accommodations by persons with disabilities. FL ST J ADMIN Rule 2.540.
   r. Waiver of sovereign immunity in tort actions; Recovery limits; Limitation on attorney fees; Statute of limitations; Exclusions; Indemnification; Risk management programs. FL ST § 768.28.
2. *Local rules*
   a. Sealing court records. FL ST 4 J CIR 2006-05.

B. Timing

1. *General answer timing.* Unless a different time is prescribed in a statute of Florida, a defendant shall serve an answer within twenty (20) days after service of original process and the initial pleading on the defendant, or not later than the date fixed in a notice by publication. A party served with a pleading stating a crossclaim against that party shall serve an answer to it within twenty (20) days after service on that party. The plaintiff shall serve an answer to a counterclaim within twenty (20) days after service of the counterclaim. FL ST RCP Rule 1.140(a)(1).
   a. *Waiver of service.* A defendant who, before being served with process, timely returns a waiver so requested is not required to respond to the complaint until sixty (60) days after the date the defendant

received the request for waiver of service. For purposes of computing any time prescribed or allowed by the Florida Rules of Civil Procedure, service of process shall be deemed effected twenty (20) days before the time required to respond to the complaint. FL ST RCP Rule 1.070(i)(4).

b. *Service on the state.* Except when sued pursuant to FL ST § 768.28, the state of Florida, an agency of the state, or an officer or employee of the state sued in an official capacity shall serve an answer to the complaint or crossclaim, or a reply to a counterclaim, within forty (40) days after service. When sued pursuant to FL ST § 768.28, the Department of Financial Services or the defendant state agency shall have thirty (30) days from the date of service within which to serve an answer to the complaint or crossclaim or a reply to a counterclaim. FL ST RCP Rule 1.140(a)(2).

c. *Service of motion impact on time periods for service of answer.* The service of a motion under FL ST RCP Rule 1.140, except a motion for judgment on the pleadings or a motion to strike under FL ST RCP Rule 1.140(f), alters these periods of time so that if the court denies the motion or postpones its disposition until the trial on the merits, the responsive pleadings shall be served within ten (10) days after notice of the court's action or, if the court grants a motion for a more definite statement, the responsive pleadings shall be served within ten (10) days after service of the more definite statement unless a different time is fixed by the court in either case. FL ST RCP Rule 1.140(a)(3).

d. *Responding if pleading does not require a responsive pleading.* If a pleading sets forth a claim for relief to which the adverse party is not required to serve a responsive pleading, the adverse party may assert any defense in law or fact to that claim for relief at the trial, except that the objection of failure to state a legal defense in an answer or reply shall be asserted by motion to strike the defense within twenty (20) days after service of the answer or reply. FL ST RCP Rule 1.140(b).

2. *Computation of time*

a. *Generally.* Computation of time shall be governed by FL ST J ADMIN Rule 2.514. FL ST RCP Rule 1.090(a). The following rules apply in computing time periods specified in any rule of procedure, local rule, court order, or statute that does not specify a method of computing time. FL ST J ADMIN Rule 2.514(a).

i. *Period stated in days or a longer unit.* When the period is stated in days or a longer unit of time (A) exclude the day of the event that triggers the period; (B) count every day, including intermediate Saturdays, Sundays, and legal holidays; and (C) include the last day of the period, but if the last day is a Saturday, Sunday, or legal holiday, or falls within any period of time extended through an order of the chief justice under FL ST J ADMIN Rule 2.205(a)(2)(B)(iv), the period continues to run until the end of the next day that is not a Saturday, Sunday, or legal holiday and does not fall within any period of time extended through an order of the chief justice. FL ST J ADMIN Rule 2.514(a)(1).

ii. *Period stated in hours.* When the period is stated in hours (A) begin counting immediately on the occurrence of the event that triggers the period; (B) count every hour, including hours during intermediate Saturdays, Sundays, and legal holidays; and (C) if the period would end on a Saturday, Sunday, or legal holiday, or during any period of time extended through an order of the chief justice under FL ST J ADMIN Rule 2.205(a)(2)(B)(iv), the period continues to run until the same time on the next day that is not a Saturday, Sunday, or legal holiday and does not fall within any period of time extended through an order of the chief justice. FL ST J ADMIN Rule 2.514(a)(2).

iii. *Period stated in days less than seven (7) days.* When the period stated in days is less than seven (7) days, intermediate Saturdays, Sundays, and legal holidays shall be excluded in the computation. FL ST J ADMIN Rule 2.514(a)(3).

iv. *"Last day" defined.* Unless a different time is set by a statute, local rule, or court order, the last day ends (A) for electronic filing or for service by any means, at midnight; and (B) for filing by other means, when the clerk's office is scheduled to close. FL ST J ADMIN Rule 2.514(a)(4).

v. *"Next day" defined.* The "next day" is determined by continuing to count forward when the period is measured after an event and backward when measured before an event. FL ST J ADMIN Rule 2.514(a)(5).

vi. *"Legal holiday" defined.* "Legal holiday" means (A) the day set aside by FL ST § 110.117, for observing New Year's Day, Martin Luther King, Jr.'s Birthday, Memorial Day, Independence Day, Labor Day, Veterans' Day, Thanksgiving Day, the Friday after Thanksgiving Day, or Christmas Day, and (B) any day observed as a holiday by the clerk's office or as designated by the chief judge. FL ST J ADMIN Rule 2.514(a)(6).

b. *Additional time after service by mail or e-mail.* When a party may or must act within a specified time after service and service is made by mail or e-mail, five (5) days are added after the period that would otherwise expire under FL ST J ADMIN Rule 2.514(a). FL ST J ADMIN Rule 2.514(b).

c. *Enlargement.* When an act is required or allowed to be done at or within a specified time by order of court, by the Florida Rules of Civil Procedure, or by notice given thereunder, for cause shown the court at any time in its discretion (1) with or without notice, may order the period enlarged if request therefor is made before the expiration of the period originally prescribed or as extended by a previous order, or (2) upon motion made and notice after the expiration of the specified period, may permit the act to be done when failure to act was the result of excusable neglect, but it may not extend the time for making a motion for new trial, for rehearing, or to alter or amend a judgment; making a motion for relief from a judgment under FL ST RCP Rule 1.540(b); taking an appeal or filing a petition for certiorari; or making a motion for a directed verdict. FL ST RCP Rule 1.090(b).

d. *Unaffected by expiration of term.* The period of time provided for the doing of any act or the taking of any proceeding shall not be affected or limited by the continued existence or expiration of a term of court. The continued existence or expiration of a term of court in no way affects the power of a court to do any act or take any proceeding in any action which is or has been pending before it. FL ST RCP Rule 1.090(c).

C. General Requirements

1. *General rules of pleading*

a. *Claims for relief*

i. A pleading which sets forth a claim for relief, whether an original claim, counterclaim, crossclaim, or third-party claim, must state a cause of action and shall contain

- A short and plain statement of the grounds upon which the court's jurisdiction depends, unless the court already has jurisdiction and the claim needs no new grounds of jurisdiction to support it (For information regarding acts subjecting persons to jurisdiction, please see FL ST § 48.193),
- A short and plain statement of the ultimate facts showing that the pleader is entitled to relief, and
- A demand for judgment for the relief to which the pleader deems himself or herself entitled. FL ST RCP Rule 1.110(b).

ii. Relief in the alternative or of several different types may be demanded. Every complaint shall be considered to demand general relief. FL ST RCP Rule 1.110(b).

b. *Verification.* Except when otherwise specifically provided by these rules or an applicable statute, every pleading or other document of a party represented by an attorney need not be verified or accompanied by an affidavit. FL ST RCP Rule 1.030. When filing an action for foreclosure of a mortgage on residential real property the complaint shall be verified. When verification of a document is required, the document filed shall include an oath, affirmation, or the following statement: "Under penalty of perjury, I declare that I have read the foregoing, and the facts alleged therein are true and correct to the best of my knowledge and belief." FL ST RCP Rule 1.110(b).

c. *Separate statements.* All averments of claim or defense shall be made in consecutively numbered paragraphs, the contents of each of which shall be limited as far as practicable to a statement of a single set of circumstances, and a paragraph may be referred to by number in all subsequent pleadings. Each claim founded upon a separate transaction or occurrence and each defense other than denials shall be stated in a separate count or defense when a separation facilitates the clear presentation of the matter set forth. FL ST RCP Rule 1.110(f).

d. *Statements adopted by reference.* Statements in a pleading may be adopted by reference in a different part of the same pleading, in another pleading, or in any motion. FL ST RCP Rule 1.130(b).

e. *Joinder of causes of action; Consistency.* A pleader may set up in the same action as many claims or causes of action or defenses in the same right as the pleader has, and claims for relief may be stated in the alternative if separate items make up the cause of action, or if two (2) or more causes of action are joined. A party may also set forth two (2) or more statements of a claim or defense alternatively, either in one (1) count or defense or in separate counts or defenses. When two (2) or more statements are made in the alternative and one (1) of them, if made independently, would be sufficient, the pleading is not made insufficient by the insufficiency of one (1) or more of the alternative statements. A party may also state as many separate claims or defenses as that party has, regardless of consistency and whether based on legal or equitable grounds or both. All pleadings shall be construed so as to do substantial justice. FL ST RCP Rule 1.110(g).

f. *Subsequent pleadings.* When the nature of an action permits pleadings subsequent to final judgment and the jurisdiction of the court over the parties has not terminated, the initial pleading subsequent to final judgment shall be designated a supplemental complaint or petition. The action shall then proceed in the same manner and time as though the supplemental complaint or petition were the initial pleading in the action, including the issuance of any needed process. FL ST RCP Rule 1.110(h) shall not apply to proceedings that may be initiated by motion under the Florida Rules of Civil Procedure. FL ST RCP Rule 1.110(h).

g. *Pleading basis for service.* When service of process is to be made under statutes authorizing service on nonresidents of Florida, it is sufficient to plead the basis for service in the language of the statute without pleading the facts supporting service. FL ST RCP Rule 1.070(h).

h. *Forms of pleadings.* Forms of action and technical forms for seeking relief and of pleas, pleadings, or motions are abolished. FL ST RCP Rule 1.110(a).

2. *Answer; Generally.* An answer has three (3) functions. First, it must respond to each allegation of the preceding pleading by admitting, denying or alleging that the pleader is without knowledge of the allegation. Second, it must contain any affirmative defenses that the pleader is interposing to any cause of action alleged in the preceding pleading. Third, the answer may claim affirmative relief against the plaintiff or petitioner by a counterclaim or against a codefendant by a crossclaim. FL-PRACPROC § 11:1.

   a. *Content.* In the answer a pleader shall state in short and plain terms the pleader's defenses to each claim asserted and shall admit or deny the averments on which the adverse party relies. If the defendant is without knowledge, the defendant shall so state and such statement shall operate as a denial. Denial shall fairly meet the substance of the averments denied. When a pleader intends in good faith to deny only a part of an averment, the pleader shall specify so much of it as is true and shall deny the remainder. Unless the pleader intends in good faith to controvert all of the averments of the preceding pleading, the pleader may make denials as specific denials of designated averments or may generally deny all of the averments except such designated averments as the pleader expressly admits, but when the pleader does so intend to controvert all of its averments, including averments of the grounds upon which the court's jurisdiction depends, the pleader may do so by general denial. FL ST RCP Rule 1.110(c).

   b. *Form of answer.* An answer contains a caption, commencement, body, signature and certificate of service. The caption is the same as that of the initial pleading, except for the designation as one of the types of answer. The body of an answer should contain an admission, denial or plea of without knowledge to each allegation of the preceding pleading, except for the additional allegations in response to a general allegation of conditions precedent and the denial of capacity to sue. FL-PRACPROC § 11:3.

      i. *Responding sequentially.* The best method of responding is to answer each paragraph sequentially, combining admissions, denials or pleas of without knowledge when the sequence permits. The admissions, denials and allegations of without knowledge should be stated first, followed separately by any affirmative defenses and then by any counterclaim or crossclaim. A third party complaint may be a part of the same paper, but it is not a part of the answer as is a counterclaim or crossclaim. Paragraphs are numbered consecutively throughout the pleading whether in the answer, counterclaim or crossclaim. Denials for the record only are improper. FL-PRACPROC § 11:3.

c. *Defenses*

i. *Generally.* Every defense in law or fact to a claim for relief in a pleading shall be asserted in the responsive pleading, if one is required, but the following defenses may be made by motion at the option of the pleader: (1) lack of jurisdiction over the subject matter, (2) lack of jurisdiction over the person, (3) improper venue, (4) insufficiency of process, (5) insufficiency of service of process, (6) failure to state a cause of action, and (7) failure to join indispensable parties. A motion making any of these defenses shall be made before pleading if a further pleading is permitted. FL ST RCP Rule 1.140(b).

- *Stated specifically.* The grounds on which any of the enumerated defenses are based and the substantial matters of law intended to be argued shall be stated specifically and with particularity in the responsive pleading or motion. FL ST RCP Rule 1.140(b).
- *Waiver.* Any ground not stated shall be deemed to be waived except any ground showing that the court lacks jurisdiction of the subject matter may be made at any time. No defense or objection is waived by being joined with other defenses or objections in a responsive pleading or motion. FL ST RCP Rule 1.140(b). A party waives all defenses and objections that the party does not present either by motion under FL ST RCP Rule 1.140(b), FL ST RCP Rule 1.140(e), or FL ST RCP Rule 1.140(f) or, if the party has made no motion, in a responsive pleading except as provided in FL ST RCP Rule 1.140(h)(2). FL ST RCP Rule 1.140(h)(1). The defenses of failure to state a cause of action or a legal defense or to join an indispensable party may be raised by motion for judgment on the pleadings or at the trial on the merits in addition to being raised either in a motion under FL ST RCP Rule 1.140(b) or in the answer or reply. The defense of lack of jurisdiction of the subject matter may be raised at any time. FL ST RCP Rule 1.140(h)(2).

ii. *Affirmative defenses.* In pleading to a preceding pleading a party shall set forth affirmatively accord and satisfaction, arbitration and award, assumption of risk, contributory negligence, discharge in bankruptcy, duress, estoppel, failure of consideration, fraud, illegality, injury by fellow servant, laches, license, payment, release, res judicata, statute of frauds, statute of limitations, waiver, and any other matter constituting an avoidance or affirmative defense. When a party has mistakenly designated a defense as a counterclaim or a counterclaim as a defense, the court, on terms if justice so requires, shall treat the pleading as if there had been a proper designation. Affirmative defenses appearing on the face of a prior pleading may be asserted as grounds for a motion or defense under FL ST RCP Rule 1.140(b); provided this shall not limit amendments under FL ST RCP Rule 1.190 even if such ground is sustained. FL ST RCP Rule 1.110(d).

- *Format of defenses.* Affirmative defenses should be placed after the admissions, denials and allegations of without knowledge in the answer. All paragraphs must be numbered consecutively throughout the answer. If a defense is directed to only a part of a cause of action or to one or more, but not all, of several causes of action in the preceding pleading, the part or cause of action to which it is directed should be identified in the defense. Defenses should be identified by consecutive ordinal numbers such as "First Defense" and "Second Defense." FL-PRACPROC § 11:4.

iii. *Effect of failure to deny.* Averments in a pleading to which a responsive pleading is required, other than those as to the amount of damages, are admitted when not denied in the responsive pleading. Averments in a pleading to which no responsive pleading is required or permitted shall be taken as denied or avoided. FL ST RCP Rule 1.110(e). An admission in an answer binds the party and no proof is required. An admission does not extend beyond the scope of the allegation in the preceding pleading. FL-PRACPROC § 11:3.

3. *Pleading special matters*

a. *Capacity.* It is not necessary to aver the capacity of a party to sue or be sued, the authority of a party to sue or be sued in a representative capacity, or the legal existence of an organized association of persons that is made a party, except to the extent required to show the jurisdiction of the court. The initial pleading served on behalf of a minor party shall specifically aver the age of the minor party. When a party desires to raise an issue as to the legal existence of any party, the capacity of any party to sue or be sued, or the authority of a party to sue or be sued in a representative capacity, that party shall do so by specific negative averment which shall include such supporting particulars as are peculiarly within the pleader's knowledge. FL ST RCP Rule 1.120(a).

b. *Fraud, mistake, condition of the mind.* In all averments of fraud or mistake, the circumstances constituting fraud or mistake shall be stated with such particularity as the circumstances may permit. Malice, intent, knowledge, mental attitude, and other condition of mind of a person may be averred generally. FL ST RCP Rule 1.120(b).

c. *Conditions precedent.* In pleading the performance or occurrence of conditions precedent, it is sufficient to aver generally that all conditions precedent have been performed or have occurred. A denial of performance or occurrence shall be made specifically and with particularity. FL ST RCP Rule 1.120(c).

d. *Official document or act.* In pleading an official document or official act it is sufficient to aver that the document was issued or the act done in compliance with law. FL ST RCP Rule 1.120(c).

e. *Judgment or decree.* In pleading a judgment or decree of a domestic or foreign court, a judicial or quasi-judicial tribunal, or a board or officer, it is sufficient to aver the judgment or decree without setting forth matter showing jurisdiction to render it. FL ST RCP Rule 1.120(e).

f. *Time and place.* For the purpose of testing the sufficiency of a pleading, averments of time and place are material and shall be considered like all other averments of material matter. FL ST RCP Rule 1.120(f).

g. *Special damage.* When items of special damage are claimed, they shall be specifically stated. FL ST RCP Rule 1.120(g).

4. *Parties*

a. *Parties generally.* Every action may be prosecuted in the name of the real party in interest, but a personal representative, administrator, guardian, trustee of an express trust, a party with whom or in whose name a contract has been made for the benefit of another, or a party expressly authorized by statute may sue in that person's own name without joining the party for whose benefit the action is brought. All persons having an interest in the subject of the action and in obtaining the relief demanded may join as plaintiffs and any person may be made a defendant who has or claims an interest adverse to the plaintiff. Any person may at any time be made a party if that person's presence is necessary or proper to a complete determination of the cause. Persons having a united interest may be joined on the same side as plaintiffs or defendants, and anyone who refuses to join may for such reason be made a defendant. FL ST RCP Rule 1.210(a).

b. *Minors or incompetent persons.* When a minor or incompetent person has a representative, such as a guardian or other like fiduciary, the representative may sue or defend on behalf of the minor or incompetent person. A minor or incompetent person who does not have a duly appointed representative may sue by next friend or by a guardian ad litem. The court shall appoint a guardian ad litem for a minor or incompetent person not otherwise represented in an action or shall make such other order as it deems proper for the protection of the minor or incompetent person. FL ST RCP Rule 1.210(b).

c. For survivor and substitution of parties information, please see FL ST RCP Rule 1.260.

5. *Counterclaims and crossclaims*

a. *Compulsory counterclaims.* A pleading shall state as a counterclaim any claim which at the time of serving the pleading the pleader has against any opposing party, provided it arises out of the transaction or occurrence that is the subject matter of the opposing party's claim and does not require for its adjudication the presence of third parties over whom the court cannot acquire jurisdiction. But the pleader need not state a claim if (1) at the time the action was commenced the claim was the subject of another pending action, or (2) the opposing party brought suit upon that party's claim by attachment or other process by which the court did not acquire jurisdiction to render a personal judgment on the claim and the pleader is not stating a counterclaim under this rule. FL ST RCP Rule 1.170(a).

b. *Permissive counterclaim.* A pleading may state as a counterclaim any claim against an opposing party not arising out of the transaction or occurrence that is the subject matter of the opposing party's claim. FL ST RCP Rule 1.170(b).

c. *Counterclaim exceeding opposing claim.* A counterclaim may or may not diminish or defeat the recovery sought by the opposing party. It may claim relief exceeding in amount or different in kind from that sought in the pleading of the opposing party. FL ST RCP Rule 1.170(c).

d. *Counterclaim against the State.* The Florida Rules of Civil Procedure shall not be construed to enlarge beyond the limits established by law the right to assert counterclaims or to claim credits against the state or any of its subdivisions or other governmental organizations thereof subject to suit or against a municipal corporation or against an officer, agency, or administrative board of the state. FL ST RCP Rule 1.170(d).

e. *Counterclaim maturing or acquired after pleading.* A claim which matured or was acquired by the pleader after serving the pleading may be presented as a counterclaim by supplemental pleading with the permission of the court. FL ST RCP Rule 1.170(e).

f. *Omitted counterclaim or crossclaim.* When a pleader fails to set up a counterclaim or crossclaim through oversight, inadvertence, or excusable neglect, or when justice requires, the pleader may set up the counterclaim or crossclaim by amendment with leave of the court. FL ST RCP Rule 1.170(f).

g. *Crossclaim against co-party.* A pleading may state as a crossclaim any claim by one party against a co-party arising out of the transaction or occurrence that is the subject matter of either the original action or a counterclaim therein, or relating to any property that is the subject matter of the original action. The crossclaim may include a claim that the party against whom it is asserted is or may be liable to the crossclaimant for all or part of a claim asserted in the action against the crossclaimant. Service of a crossclaim on a party who has appeared in the action shall be made pursuant to FL ST RCP Rule 1.080. Service of a crossclaim against a party who has not appeared in the action shall be made in the manner provided for service of summons. FL ST RCP Rule 1.170(g).

h. *Additional parties may be brought in.* When the presence of parties other than those to the original action is required to grant complete relief in the determination of a counterclaim or crossclaim, they shall be named in the counterclaim or crossclaim and be served with process and shall be parties to the action thereafter if jurisdiction of them can be obtained and their joinder will not deprive the court of jurisdiction of the action. FL ST RCP Rule 1.250(b) and FL ST RCP Rule 1.250(c) apply to parties brought in under FL ST RCP Rule 1.170(h). FL ST RCP Rule 1.170(h).

i. *Separate trials; Separate judgment.* If the court orders separate trials as provided in FL ST RCP Rule 1.270(b), judgment on a counterclaim or crossclaim may be rendered when the court has jurisdiction to do so even if a claim of the opposing party has been dismissed or otherwise disposed of. FL ST RCP Rule 1.170(i).

j. *Demand exceeding jurisdiction; Transfer of action.* If the demand of any counterclaim or crossclaim exceeds the jurisdiction of the court in which the action is pending, the action shall be transferred forthwith to the court of the same county having jurisdiction of the demand in the counterclaim or crossclaim with only such alterations in the pleadings as are essential. The court shall order the transfer of the action and the transmittal of all papers in it to the proper court if the party asserting the demand exceeding the jurisdiction deposits with the court having jurisdiction a sum sufficient to pay the clerk's service charge in the court to which the action is transferred at the time of filing the counterclaim or crossclaim. Thereupon the original papers and deposit shall be transmitted and filed with a certified copy of the order. The court to which the action is transferred shall have full power and jurisdiction over the demands of all parties. Failure to make the service charge deposit at the time the counterclaim or crossclaim is filed, or within such further time as the court may allow, shall reduce a claim for damages to an amount within the jurisdiction of the court where the action is pending and waive the claim in other cases. FL ST RCP Rule 1.170(j).

6. *Misjoinder and nonjoinder of parties*

   a. *Misjoinder.* Misjoinder of parties is not a ground for dismissal of an action. Any claim against a party may be severed and proceeded with separately. FL ST RCP Rule 1.250(a).

b. *Dropping parties.* Parties may be dropped by an adverse party in the manner provided for voluntary dismissal in FL ST RCP Rule 1.420(a)(1) subject to the exception stated in FL ST RCP Rule 1.420. If notice of lis pendens has been filed in the action against a party so dropped, the notice of dismissal shall be recorded and cancels the notice of lis pendens without the necessity of a court order. Parties may be dropped by order of court on its own initiative or the motion of any party at any stage of the action on such terms as are just. FL ST RCP Rule 1.250(b).

c. *Adding parties.* Parties may be added once as a matter of course within the same time that pleadings can be so amended under FL ST RCP Rule 1.190(a). If amendment by leave of court or stipulation of the parties is permitted, parties may be added in the amended pleading without further order of court. Parties may be added by order of court on its own initiative or on motion of any party at any stage of the action and on such terms as are just. FL ST RCP Rule 1.250(c).

7. *Jury demand*

a. *Right preserved.* The right of trial by jury as declared by the Constitution or by statute shall be preserved to the parties inviolate. FL ST RCP Rule 1.430(a).

b. *Demand.* Any party may demand a trial by jury of any issue triable of right by a jury by serving upon the other party a demand therefor in writing at any time after commencement of the action and not later than ten (10) days after the service of the last pleading directed to such issue. The demand may be indorsed upon a pleading of the party. FL ST RCP Rule 1.430(b).

c. *Specification of issues.* In the demand a party may specify the issues that the party wishes so tried; otherwise, the party is deemed to demand trial by jury for all issues so triable. FL ST RCP Rule 1.430(c).

i. If a party has demanded trial by jury for only some of the issues, any other party may serve a demand for trial by jury of any other or all of the issues triable by jury ten (10) days after service of the demand or such lesser time as the court may order. FL ST RCP Rule 1.430(c).

d. *Waiver.* A party who fails to serve a demand as required by FL ST RCP Rule 1.430 waives trial by jury. FL ST RCP Rule 1.430(d).

i. If waived, a jury trial may not be granted without the consent of the parties, but the court may allow an amendment in the proceedings to demand a trial by jury or order a trial by jury on its own motion. FL ST RCP Rule 1.430(d).

ii. A demand for trial by jury may not be withdrawn without the consent of the parties. FL ST RCP Rule 1.430(d).

8. *Arbitration and mediation*

a. *Referral to arbitration and mediation.* Except as hereinafter provided or as otherwise prohibited by law, the presiding judge may enter an order referring all or any part of a contested civil matter to mediation or arbitration. The parties to any contested civil matter may file a written stipulation to mediate or arbitrate any issue between them at any time. Such stipulation shall be incorporated into the order of referral. FL ST RCP Rule 1.700(a).

b. *Arbitration*

i. *Exclusions.* A civil action shall be ordered to arbitration or arbitration in conjunction with mediation upon stipulation of the parties. A civil action may be ordered to arbitration or arbitration in conjunction with mediation upon motion of any party or by the court, if the judge determines the action to be of such a nature that arbitration could be of benefit to the litigants or the court. FL ST RCP Rule 1.800.

- Under no circumstances may the following categories of actions be referred to arbitration: (1) bond estreatures; (2) habeas corpus or other extraordinary writs; (3) bond validations; (4) civil or criminal contempt; (5) such other matters as may be specified by order of the chief judge in the circuit. FL ST RCP Rule 1.800.

ii. For more information regarding arbitration, please see FL ST RCP Rule 1.810; FL ST RCP Rule 1.820; FL ST RCP Rule 1.830.

c. *Mediation.* For more information regarding mediation, please see FL ST RCP Rule 1.710; FL ST RCP Rule 1.720; FL ST RCP Rule 1.730; and FL ST RCP Rule 1.750.

9. *Rules of court*

   a. *Rules of civil procedure.* The Florida Rules of Civil Procedure apply to all actions of a civil nature and all special statutory proceedings in the circuit courts and county courts except those to which the Florida Probate Rules, the Florida Family Law Rules of Procedure, or the Small Claims Rules apply. FL ST RCP Rule 1.010.

      i. The form, content, procedure, and time for pleading in all special statutory proceedings shall be as prescribed by the statutes governing the proceeding unless the Florida Rules of Civil Procedure specifically provide to the contrary. FL ST RCP Rule 1.010.

      ii. The Florida Rules of Civil Procedure shall be construed to secure the just, speedy, and inexpensive determination of every action. FL ST RCP Rule 1.010.

   b. *Rules of judicial administration.* The Florida Rules of Judicial Administration shall apply to administrative matters in all courts to which the Florida Rules of Judicial Administration are applicable by their terms. The Florida Rules of Judicial Administration shall be construed to secure the speedy and inexpensive determination of every proceeding to which they are applicable. The Florida Rules of Judicial Administration shall supersede all conflicting rules and statutes. FL ST J ADMIN Rule 2.110.

D. Documents

1. *Required documents*

   a. *Answer.* See the General Requirements section of this document for further information about the content of an answer.

      i. *Notices to persons with disabilities.* See the Format section of this KeyRules document for further information.

   b. *Certificate of service.* When any attorney certifies in substance: "I certify that a copy hereof has been furnished to (here insert name or names and addresses used for service) by (e-mail) (delivery) (mail) (fax) on .... (date) ....________________ Attorney" the certificate is taken as prima facie proof of such service in compliance with FL ST J ADMIN Rule 2.516. FL ST J ADMIN Rule 2.516(f).

2. *Supplemental documents*

   a. *Exhibits.* All bonds, notes, bills of exchange, contracts, accounts, or documents upon which action may be brought or defense made, or a copy thereof or a copy of the portions thereof material to the pleadings, shall be incorporated in or attached to the pleading. No papers shall be unnecessarily annexed as exhibits. The pleadings shall contain no unnecessary recitals of deeds, documents, contracts, or other instruments. Any exhibit attached to a pleading shall be considered a part of the pleadings for all purposes. FL ST RCP Rule 1.130(a).

   b. *Notice of constitutional question.* A party that files a pleading, written motion, or other paper drawing into question the constitutionality of a state statute or a county or municipal charter, ordinance, or franchise must promptly (1) file a notice of constitutional question stating the question and identifying the paper that raises it; and (2) serve the notice and the pleading, written motion, or other paper drawing into question the constitutionality of a state statute or a county or municipal charter, ordinance, or franchise on the Attorney General or the state attorney of the judicial circuit in which the action is pending, by either certified or registered mail. Service of the notice and pleading, written motion, or other paper does not require joinder of the Attorney General or the state attorney as a party to the action. FL ST RCP Rule 1.071.

E. Format

1. *Documents; Type and size.* Documents subject to the exceptions set forth in FL ST J ADMIN Rule 2.525(d) shall be filed on recycled paper measuring eight and one half by eleven (8 1/2 by 11) inches. For purposes of FL ST J ADMIN Rule 2.520, paper is recycled if it contains a minimum content of fifty (50) percent waste paper. Xerographic reduction of legal-size (eight and one half by fourteen (8 1/2 by 14) inches) documents to letter size (eight and one half by eleven (8 1/2 by 11) inches) is prohibited. All other

documents filed by electronic transmission shall be filed in a format capable of being printed in a format consistent with the provisions of FL ST J ADMIN Rule 2.250. FL ST J ADMIN Rule 2.520(b).

a. *Exhibits.* Any exhibit or attachment filed with pleadings or papers may be filed in its original size. FL ST J ADMIN Rule 2.520(c).

b. *Recording space.* On all papers and documents prepared and filed by the court or by any party to a proceeding which are to be recorded in the public records of any county, including but not limited to final money judgments and notices of lis pendens, a three (3) inch by three (3) inch space at the top right-hand corner on the first page and a one (1) inch by three (3) inch space at the top right-hand corner on each subsequent page shall be left blank and reserved for use by the clerk of court. FL ST J ADMIN Rule 2.520(d).

   i. *Exceptions to recording space.* Any papers or documents created by persons or entities over which the filing party has no control, including but not limited to wills, codicils, trusts, or other testamentary documents; documents prepared or executed by any public officer; documents prepared, executed, acknowledged, or proved outside of the State of Florida; or documents created by State or Federal government agencies, may be filed without the space required by FL ST J ADMIN Rule 2.520. FL ST J ADMIN Rule 2.520(e).

c. *Noncompliance.* No clerk of court is permitted to refuse to file any document or paper because of noncompliance with the Florida Rules of Judicial Administration. However, upon request of the clerk of court, noncomplying documents must be resubmitted in accordance with the formatting rules. FL ST J ADMIN Rule 2.520(f).

2. *Caption.* Every pleading, motion, order, judgment, or other paper shall have a caption containing the name of the court, the file number, and except for in rem proceedings, including forfeiture proceedings, the name of the first party on each side with an appropriate indication of other parties, and a designation identifying the party filing it and its nature or the nature of the order, as the case may be. In any in rem proceeding, every pleading, motion, order, judgment, or other paper shall have a caption containing the name of the court, the file number, the style "In re" (followed by the name or general description of the property), and a designation of the person or entity filing it and its nature or the nature of the order, as the case may be. In an in rem forfeiture proceeding, the style shall be "In re forfeiture of" (followed by the name of the general description of the property). All papers filed in the action shall be styled in such a manner as to indicate clearly the subject matter of the paper and the party requesting or obtaining relief. FL ST RCP Rule 1.100(c)(1).

3. *Writing and written defined.* Writing or written means a document containing information, an application, or a stipulation. FL ST RCP Rule 1.080(c).

4. *Rule abbreviations*

   a. The Florida Rules of Civil Procedure and shall be abbreviated as Fla.R.Civ.P. FL ST RCP Rule 1.010.

   b. The Florida Rules of Judicial Administration shall be abbreviated as Fla. R. Jud. Admin. FL ST J ADMIN Rule 2.110.

5. *Nonverification.* Except when otherwise specifically provided by the Florida Rules of Civil Procedure or an applicable statute, every pleading or other document of a party represented by an attorney need not be verified or accompanied by an affidavit. FL ST RCP Rule 1.030; FL ST J ADMIN Rule 2.515(a).

6. *Attorney signature*

   a. *Attorney signature.* Every pleading and other document of a party represented by an attorney shall be signed by at least one (1) attorney of record in that attorney's individual name whose current record Florida Bar address, telephone number, including area code, primary e-mail address and secondary e-mail addresses, if any, and Florida Bar number shall be stated, and who shall be duly licensed to practice law in Florida or who shall have received permission to appear in the particular case as provided in FL ST J ADMIN Rule 2.510. FL ST J ADMIN Rule 2.515(a).

      i. The attorney may be required by the court to give the address of, and to vouch for the attorney's authority to represent, the party. FL ST J ADMIN Rule 2.515(a).

ii. The signature of an attorney shall constitute a certificate by the attorney that the attorney has read the pleading or other document; that to the best of the attorney's knowledge, information, and belief there is good ground to support it; and that it is not interposed for delay. FL ST J ADMIN Rule 2.515(a).

iii. If a pleading is not signed or is signed with intent to defeat the purpose of FL ST J ADMIN Rule 2.515, it may be stricken and the action may proceed as though the pleading or other document had not been served. FL ST J ADMIN Rule 2.515(a).

b. *Pro se litigant signature.* A party who is not represented by an attorney shall sign any pleading or other paper and state the party's address and telephone number, including area code. FL ST J ADMIN Rule 2.515(b).

c. *Form of signature*

i. The signatures required on pleadings and documents by FL ST J ADMIN Rule 2.515(a) and FL ST J ADMIN Rule 2.515(b) may be:

- Original signatures;
- Original signatures that have been reproduced by electronic means, such as on electronically transmitted documents or photocopied documents;
- Electronic signatures using the "/s/," "s/," or "/s" formats by or at the direction of the person signing; or
- Any other signature format authorized by general law, so long as the clerk where the proceeding is pending has the capability of receiving and has obtained approval from the Supreme Court of Florida to accept pleadings and documents with that signature format. FL ST J ADMIN Rule 2.515(c)(1).

ii. An attorney, party, or other person who files a pleading or paper by electronic transmission that does not contain the original signature of that attorney, party, or other person shall file that identical pleading or paper in paper form containing an original signature of that attorney, party, or other person (hereinafter called the follow-up filing) immediately thereafter. The follow-up filing is not required if the Supreme Court of Florida has entered an order directing the clerk of court to discontinue accepting the follow-up filing. FL ST J ADMIN Rule 2.515(c)(2).

7. *Forms*

a. *Process.* The forms of process, notice of lis pendens, and notice of action provided in the Florida Rules of Civil Procedure are sufficient. Variations from the forms do not void process or notices that are otherwise sufficient. FL ST RCP Rule 1.900(a).

b. *Other forms.* The other forms provided in the Florida Rules of Civil Procedure are sufficient for the matters that are covered by them. So long as the substance is expressed without prolixity, the forms may be varied to meet the facts of a particular case. FL ST RCP Rule 1.900(b).

c. *Formal matters.* Captions, except for the designation of the paper, are omitted from the forms provided in the Florida Rules of Civil Procedure. A general form of caption is the first form provided. Signatures are omitted from pleadings and motions. FL ST RCP Rule 1.900(c).

8. *Notices to persons with disabilities.* All notices of court proceedings to be held in a public facility, and all process compelling appearance at such proceedings, shall include the following statement in bold face, fourteen (14) point Times New Roman or Courier font: "If you are a person with a disability who needs any accommodation in order to participate in this proceeding, you are entitled, at no cost to you, to the provision of certain assistance. Please contact [identify applicable court personnel by name, address, and telephone number] at least seven (7) days before your scheduled court appearance, or immediately upon receiving this notification if the time before the scheduled appearance is less than seven (7) days; if you are hearing or voice impaired, call 711." FL ST J ADMIN Rule 2.540(c)(1).

9. *Minimization of the filing of sensitive information*

a. *Limitations for court filings.* Unless authorized by FL ST J ADMIN Rule 2.425(b), statute, another

rule of court, or the court orders otherwise, designated sensitive information filed with the court must be limited to the following format:

i. The initials of a person known to be a minor;
ii. The year of birth of a person's birth date;
iii. No portion of any: Social security number, Bank account number, Credit card account number, Charge account number, or Debit account number;
iv. The last four digits of any: Taxpayer identification number (TIN), Employee identification number, Driver's license number, Passport number, Telephone number, Financial account number, except as set forth in FL ST J ADMIN Rule 2.425(a)(3), Brokerage account number, Insurance policy account number, Loan account number, Customer account number, or Patient or health care number;
v. A truncated version of any: Email address, Computer user name, Password, or Personal identification number (PIN); and
vi. A truncated version of any other sensitive information as provided by court order. FL ST J ADMIN Rule 2.425(a).

b. *Exceptions.* FL ST J ADMIN Rule 2.425(a) does not apply to the following:
   i. An account number which identifies the property alleged to be the subject of a proceeding;
   ii. The record of an administrative or agency proceeding;
   iii. The record in appellate or review proceedings;
   iv. The birth date of a minor whenever the birth date is necessary for the court to establish or maintain subject matter jurisdiction;
   v. The name of a minor in any order relating to parental responsibility, time-sharing, or child support;
   vi. The name of a minor in any document or order affecting the minor's ownership of real property;
   vii. The birth date of a party in a writ of attachment or notice to payor;
   viii. In traffic and criminal proceedings: a pro se filing; a court filing that is related to a criminal matter or investigation and that is prepared before the filing of a criminal charge or is not filed as part of any docketed criminal case; an arrest or search warrant or any information in support thereof; a charging document and an affidavit or other documents filed in support of any charging document, including any driving records; a statement of particulars; discovery material introduced into evidence or otherwise filed with the court; and all information necessary for the proper issuance and execution of a subpoena duces tecum;
   ix. Information used by the clerk for case maintenance purposes or the courts for case management purposes; and
   x. Information which is relevant and material to an issue before the court. FL ST J ADMIN Rule 2.425(b).

c. *Remedies.* Upon motion by a party or interested person or sua sponte by the court, the court may order remedies, sanctions or both for a violation of FL ST J ADMIN Rule 2.425(a). Following notice and an opportunity to respond, the court may impose sanctions if such filing was not made in good faith. FL ST J ADMIN Rule 2.425(c).

d. *Motions not restricted.* FL ST J ADMIN Rule 2.425 does not restrict a party's right to move for protective order, to move to file documents under seal, or to request a determination of the confidentiality of records. FL ST J ADMIN Rule 2.425(d).
   i. For more information regarding sealing court records, please see FL ST 4 J CIR 2006-05.

e. *Application.* FL ST J ADMIN Rule 2.425 does not affect the application of constitutional provisions, statutes, or rules of court regarding confidential information or access to public information. FL ST J ADMIN Rule 2.425(e).

F. Filing and Service Requirements

1. *Filing requirements.* All original documents must be filed with the court either before service or immediately thereafter, unless otherwise provided for by general law or other rules. If the original of any bond or other document is not placed in the court file, a certified copy must be so placed by the clerk. FL ST J ADMIN Rule 2.516(d). All documents shall be filed in conformity with the requirements of FL ST J ADMIN Rule 2.525. FL ST RCP Rule 1.080(b). All documents filed in any court shall be filed by electronic transmission in accordance with FL ST J ADMIN Rule 2.525. "Documents" means pleadings, motions, petitions, memoranda, briefs, notices, exhibits, declarations, affidavits, orders, judgments, decrees, writs, opinions, and any other paper or writing submitted to a court. FL ST J ADMIN Rule 2.520(a). All documents that are court records, as defined in FL ST J ADMIN Rule 2.430(a)(1), must be filed by electronic transmission, provided that: (1) the clerk has the ability to accept and retain such documents; (2) the clerk or the chief judge of the circuit has requested permission to accept documents filed by electronic transmission; and (3) the supreme court has entered an order granting permission to the clerk to accept documents filed by electronic transmission. FL ST J ADMIN Rule 2.525(c)(1).
    a. *Definition.* "Electronic transmission of documents" means the sending of information by electronic signals to, by or from a court or clerk, which when received can be transformed and stored or transmitted on paper, microfilm, magnetic storage device, optical imaging system, CD-ROM, flash drive, other electronic data storage system, server, case maintenance system ("CM"), electronic court filing ("ECF") system, statewide or local electronic portal ("e-portal"), or other electronic record keeping system authorized by the supreme court in a format sufficient to communicate the information on the original document in a readable format. Electronic transmission of documents includes electronic mail ("e-mail") and any internet-based transmission procedure, and may include procedures allowing for documents to be signed or verified by electronic means. FL ST J ADMIN Rule 2.525(a).
        i. The filing of documents with the court as required by the Florida Rules of Judicial Administration must be made by filing them with the clerk in accordance with FL ST J ADMIN Rule 2.525, except that the judge may permit documents to be filed with the judge, in which event the judge must note the filing date before him or her on the documents and transmit them to the clerk. The date of filing is that shown on the face of the document by the judge's notation or the clerk's time stamp, whichever is earlier. FL ST J ADMIN Rule 2.516(e).
    b. *Application.* Any court or clerk of the court may accept the electronic transmission of documents for filing after the clerk, together with input from the chief judge of the circuit, has obtained approval of the procedures and program for doing so from the Supreme Court of Florida. FL ST J ADMIN Rule 2.525(b).
    c. *Exceptions*
        i. Paper documents and other submissions may be manually submitted to the clerk or court:
            - When the clerk does not have the ability to accept and retain documents by electronic filing or has not had ECF Procedures approved by the supreme court;
            - For filing by any self-represented party or any self-represented nonparty unless specific ECF Procedures provide a means to file documents electronically. However, any self-represented nonparty that is a governmental or public agency and any other agency, partnership, corporation, or business entity acting on behalf of any governmental or public agency may file documents by electronic transmission if such entity has the capability of filing documents electronically;
            - For filing by attorneys excused from e-mail service in accordance with FL ST J ADMIN Rule 2.516(b);
            - When submitting evidentiary exhibits or filing non-documentary materials;
            - When the filing involves documents in excess of twenty-five (25) megabytes (25MB) in size. For such filings, documents may be transmitted using an electronic storage medium that the clerk has the ability to accept, which may include a CD-ROM, flash drive, or similar storage medium;

- When filed in open court, as permitted by the court;
- When paper filing is permitted by any approved statewide or local ECF procedures; and
- If any court determines that justice so requires. FL ST J ADMIN Rule 2.525(d).

ii. Any document in paper form submitted under FL ST J ADMIN Rule 2.525(d) is filed when it is received by the clerk or court and the clerk shall immediately thereafter convert any filed paper document to an electronic document. "Convert to an electronic document" means optically capturing an image of a paper document and using character recognition software to recover as much of the document's text as practicable and then indexing and storing the document in the official court file. FL ST J ADMIN Rule 2.525(c)(4).

iii. Any storage medium submitted under FL ST J ADMIN Rule 2.525(d)(5) is filed when received by the clerk or court and the clerk shall immediately thereafter transfer the electronic documents from the storage device to the official court file. FL ST J ADMIN Rule 2.525(c)(5).

iv. If the filer of any paper document authorized under FL ST J ADMIN Rule 2.525(d) provides a self-addressed, postage-paid envelope for return of the paper document after it is converted to electronic form by the clerk, the clerk shall place the paper document in the envelope and deposit it in the mail. Except when a paper document is required to be maintained, the clerk may recycle any filed paper document that is not to be returned to the filer. FL ST J ADMIN Rule 2.525(c)(6).

v. The clerk may convert any paper document filed before the effective date of FL ST J ADMIN Rule 2.525 to an electronic document. Unless the clerk is required to maintain the paper document, if the paper document has been converted to an electronic document by the clerk, the paper document is no longer part of the official court file and may be removed and recycled. FL ST J ADMIN Rule 2.525(c)(7).

d. *Official court file.* For information on what constitutes the official court file, please see FL ST J ADMIN Rule 2.525(c)(2), FL ST J ADMIN Rule 2.525(c)(3).

e. *Administration.* All attorneys, parties, or other persons using this rule to file documents are required to make arrangements with the court or clerk for the payment of any charges authorized by general law or the supreme court before filing any document by electronic transmission. FL ST J ADMIN Rule 2.525(f)(2).

f. *Filing date.* The filing date for an electronically transmitted document is the date and time that such filing is acknowledged by an electronic stamp or otherwise, pursuant to any procedure set forth in any ECF Procedures approved by the supreme court, or the date the last page of such filing is received by the court or clerk. FL ST J ADMIN Rule 2.525(f)(3).

g. *Accessibility.* All documents transmitted in any electronic form under FL ST J ADMIN Rule 2.525 must comply with the accessibility requirements of FL ST J ADMIN Rule 2.526. FL ST J ADMIN Rule 2.525(g).

2. *Service requirements.* Every pleading subsequent to the initial pleading, all orders, and every other document filed in the action must be served in conformity with the requirements of FL ST J ADMIN Rule 2.516. FL ST RCP Rule 1.080(a).

a. *Service; When required.* Unless the court otherwise orders, or a statute or supreme court administrative order specifies a different means of service, every pleading subsequent to the initial pleading and every other document filed in any court proceeding, except applications for witness subpoenas and documents served by formal notice or required to be served in the manner provided for service of formal notice, must be served in accordance with FL ST J ADMIN Rule 2.516 on each party. No service need be made on parties against whom a default has been entered, except that pleadings asserting new or additional claims against them must be served in the manner provided for service of summons. FL ST J ADMIN Rule 2.516(a).

b. *Service; How made.* When service is required or permitted to be made upon a party represented by an attorney, service must be made upon the attorney unless service upon the party is ordered by the court. FL ST J ADMIN Rule 2.516(b).

i. *Service by electronic mail ("e-mail").* All documents required or permitted to be served on

another party must be served by e-mail, unless FL ST J ADMIN Rule 2.516 otherwise provides. When, in addition to service by e-mail, the sender also utilizes another means of service provided for in FL ST J ADMIN Rule 2.516(b)(2), any differing time limits and other provisions applicable to that other means of service control. FL ST J ADMIN Rule 2.516(b)(1). Any document electronically transmitted to a court or clerk must also be served on all parties and interested persons in accordance with the applicable rules of court. FL ST J ADMIN Rule 2.525(e)(2).

- *Service on attorneys.* Upon appearing in a proceeding, an attorney must serve a designation of a primary e-mail address and may designate no more than two (2) secondary e-mail addresses. Thereafter, service must be directed to all designated e-mail addresses in that proceeding. Every document filed by an attorney thereafter must include the primary e-mail address of that attorney and any secondary e-mail addresses. If an attorney does not designate any e-mail address for service, documents may be served on that attorney at the e-mail address on record with The Florida Bar. FL ST J ADMIN Rule 2.516(b)(1)(A).
- *Exception to e-mail service on attorneys.* Service by an attorney on another attorney must be made by e-mail unless excused by the court. Upon motion by an attorney demonstrating that the attorney has no e-mail account and lacks access to the Internet at the attorney's office, the court may excuse the attorney from the requirements of e-mail service. Service on and by an attorney excused by the court from e-mail service must be by the means provided in FL ST J ADMIN Rule 2.516(b)(2). FL ST J ADMIN Rule 2.516(b)(1)(B).
- *Service on and by parties not represented by an attorney.* Any party not represented by an attorney may serve a designation of a primary e-mail address and also may designate no more than two (2) secondary e-mail addresses to which service must be directed in that proceeding by the means provided in FL ST J ADMIN Rule 2.516(b)(1). If a party not represented by an attorney does not designate an e-mail address for service in a proceeding, service on and by that party must be by the means provided in FL ST J ADMIN Rule 2.516(b)(2). FL ST J ADMIN Rule 2.516(b)(1)(C).
- *Time of service.* Service by e-mail is complete when it is sent. FL ST J ADMIN Rule 2.516(b)(1)(D). An e-mail is deemed served on the date it is sent. FL ST J ADMIN Rule 2.516(b)(1)(D)(i). If the sender learns that the e-mail did not reach the address of the person to be served, the sender must immediately send another copy by e-mail, or by a means authorized by FL ST J ADMIN Rule 2.516(b)(2). FL ST J ADMIN Rule 2.516(b)(1)(D)(ii). E-mail service is treated as service by mail for the computation of time. FL ST J ADMIN Rule 2.516(b)(1)(D)(iii).

ii. *Format of e-mail for service.* Service of a document by e-mail is made by attaching a copy of the document in PDF format to an e-mail sent to all addresses designated by the attorney or party. FL ST J ADMIN Rule 2.516(b)(1)(E).

- All documents served by e-mail must be attached to an e-mail message containing a subject line beginning with the words "SERVICE OF COURT DOCUMENT" in all capital letters, followed by the case number of the proceeding in which the documents are being served. FL ST J ADMIN Rule 2.516(b)(1)(E)(i).
- The body of the e-mail must identify the court in which the proceeding is pending, the case number, the name of the initial party on each side, the title of each document served with that e-mail, and the sender's name and telephone number. FL ST J ADMIN Rule 2.516(b)(1)(E)(ii).
- Any document served by e-mail may be signed by the "/s/" format, as long as the filed original is signed in accordance with the applicable rule of procedure. FL ST J ADMIN Rule 2.516(b)(1)(E)(iii).
- Any e-mail which, together with its attached documents, exceeds five megabytes (5MB) in size, must be divided and sent as separate e-mails, no one of which may exceed five megabytes (5MB) in size and each of which must be sequentially numbered in the subject line. FL ST J ADMIN Rule 2.516(b)(1)(E)(iv).

iii. *Service by other means.* In addition to, and not in lieu of, service by e-mail, service may also be made upon attorneys by any of the means specified in FL ST J ADMIN Rule 2.516(b)(2). Service on and by all parties who are not represented by an attorney and who do not designate an e-mail address, and on and by all attorneys excused from e-mail service, must be made by delivering a copy of the document or by mailing it to the party or attorney at their last known address or, if no address is known, by leaving it with the clerk of the court. Service by mail is complete upon mailing. Delivery of a copy within FL ST J ADMIN Rule 2.516 is complete upon:

- Handing it to the attorney or to the party,
- Leaving it at the attorney's or party's office with a clerk or other person in charge thereof,
- If there is no one in charge, leaving it in a conspicuous place therein,
- If the office is closed or the person to be served has no office, leaving it at the person's usual place of abode with some person of his or her family above fifteen (15) years of age and informing such person of the contents, or
- Transmitting it by facsimile to the attorney's or party's office with a cover sheet containing the sender's name, firm, address, telephone number, and facsimile number, and the number of pages transmitted. When service is made by facsimile, a copy must also be served by any other method permitted by FL ST J ADMIN Rule 2.516. Facsimile service occurs when transmission is complete. FL ST J ADMIN Rule 2.516(b)(2)(A) through FL ST J ADMIN Rule 2.516(b)(2)(E).
- Service by delivery after 5:00 p.m. must be deemed to have been made by mailing on the date of delivery. FL ST J ADMIN Rule 2.516(b)(2)(F).

c. *Service; Numerous defendants.* In actions when the parties are unusually numerous, the court may regulate the service contemplated by the Florida Rules of Judicial Administration on motion or on its own initiative in such manner as may be found to be just and reasonable. FL ST J ADMIN Rule 2.516(c).

d. *Service by clerk.* Service of notices and other documents required to be made by the clerk must also be done as provided in FL ST J ADMIN Rule 2.516(b). FL ST J ADMIN Rule 2.516(g).

G. Hearings

1. *Preliminary hearings.* The defenses in FL ST RCP Rule 1.140(b)(1) through FL ST RCP Rule 1.140(b)(7), whether made in a pleading or by motion, and the motion for judgment in FL ST RCP Rule 1.140(c) shall be heard and determined before trial on application of any party unless the court orders that the hearing and determination shall be deferred until the trial. FL ST RCP Rule 1.140(d).

H. Forms

1. Official Answer Forms for Florida

a. Caption. FL ST RCP Form 1.901.

b. Crossclaim summons. FL ST RCP Form 1.903.

c. Third-party summons. FL ST RCP Form 1.904.

d. Defense; Statute of limitations. FL ST RCP Form 1.965.

e. Defense; Payment. FL ST RCP Form 1.966.

f. Defense; Accord and satisfaction. FL ST RCP Form 1.967.

g. Defense; Failure of consideration. FL ST RCP Form 1.968.

h. Defense; Statute of frauds. FL ST RCP Form 1.969.

i. Defense; Release. FL ST RCP Form 1.970.

j. Notice of compliance when constitutional challenge is brought. FL ST RCP Form 1.975.

2. Answer Forms for Florida

a. Answer; General form, traverses. FL-PRACFORM § 5:4.

b. Answer; General form, traverses and affirmative defenses. FL-PRACFORM § 5:6.
c. Answer; General form, traverses, affirmative defenses and counterclaim. FL-PRACFORM § 5:7.
d. Answer; General form, traverses, affirmative defenses, counterclaim and crossclaim. FL-PRACFORM § 5:8.
e. Answer; Affirmative defense, fraud. FL-PRACFORM § 5:43.
f. Answer; Affirmative defense, laches. FL-PRACFORM § 5:47.
g. Answer; Affirmative defense, misjoinder. FL-PRACFORM § 5:49.
h. Answer; Affirmative defense, misrepresentation. FL-PRACFORM § 5:50.
i. Answer; Affirmative defense, self defense. FL-PRACFORM § 5:64.
j. Answer; Denial of conditions precedent. FL-PRACFORM § 5:80.
k. General denial. FL-PP § 2:58.
l. General denial; With specified admissions. FL-PP § 2:59.
m. Admission with qualification. FL-PP § 2:60.
n. Conclusions of law not requiring denial. FL-PP § 2:61.
o. Defenses stated in the alternative. FL-PP § 2:62.
p. Denial as to part of allegation. FL-PP § 2:63.
q. Pleader as without knowledge as to truth of allegation. FL-PP § 2:64.

I. Checklist

(I) ❑ Matters to be considered by plaintiff
- (a) ❑ Required documents
  - (1) ❑ Summons
  - (2) ❑ Complaint
  - (3) ❑ Civil cover sheet
  - (4) ❑ Return of execution process by process server
  - (5) ❑ Filing fees
- (b) ❑ Supplemental documents
  - (1) ❑ Exhibits
  - (2) ❑ Notice of constitutional question
- (c) ❑ Time for filing and serving complaint
  - (1) ❑ Service of the initial process and initial pleading should be made upon a defendant within one hundred twenty (120) days after the filing of the complaint with the court

(II) ❑ Matters to be considered by defendant
- (a) ❑ Required documents
  - (1) ❑ Answer
  - (2) ❑ Certificate of service
- (b) ❑ Supplemental documents
  - (1) ❑ Exhibits
  - (2) ❑ Notice of constitutional question
- (c) ❑ Time for answer
  - (1) ❑ Unless a different time is prescribed in a statute of Florida, a defendant shall serve an answer within twenty (20) days after service of original process and the initial pleading on the defendant, or not later than the date fixed in a notice by publication

(2) ❑ A party served with a pleading stating a crossclaim against that party shall serve an answer to it within twenty (20) days after service on that party

(3) ❑ The plaintiff shall serve an answer to a counterclaim within twenty (20) days after service of the counterclaim

(4) ❑ A defendant who, before being served with process, timely returns a waiver so requested is not required to respond to the complaint until sixty (60) days after the date the defendant received the request for waiver of service; for purposes of computing any time prescribed or allowed by the Florida Rules of Civil Procedure, service of process shall be deemed effected twenty (20) days before the time required to respond to the complaint

(5) ❑ For timing requirements related to service on the state, service of motion impact, and responding when no responsive pleading is required, please see the Timing section of this document

Pleadings
Amended Answer

Document Last Updated January 2013

A. Applicable Rules

1. *State rules*
   a. Nonverification of papers. FL ST RCP Rule 1.030.
   b. Service and filing of pleadings, orders, and documents. FL ST RCP Rule 1.080.
   c. Constitutional challenge to state statute or county or municipal charter, ordinance, or franchise; Notice by party. FL ST RCP Rule 1.071.
   d. Time. FL ST RCP Rule 1.090.
   e. Pleadings and motions. FL ST RCP Rule 1.100; FL ST RCP Rule 1.110; FL ST RCP Rule 1.120; FL ST RCP Rule 1.130; FL ST RCP Rule 1.190.
   f. Defenses. FL ST RCP Rule 1.140.
   g. Pretrial procedure. FL ST RCP Rule 1.200.
   h. Relief from judgment, decrees, or orders. FL ST RCP Rule 1.540.
   i. Forms. FL ST RCP Rule 1.900.
   j. Minimization of the filing of sensitive information. FL ST J ADMIN Rule 2.425.
   k. Foreign attorneys. FL ST J ADMIN Rule 2.510.
   l. Signature of attorneys and parties. FL ST J ADMIN Rule 2.515.
   m. Paper. FL ST J ADMIN Rule 2.520.
   n. Electronic filing. FL ST J ADMIN Rule 2.525.
   o. Accessibility of information and technology. FL ST J ADMIN Rule 2.526.
   p. Court reporting. FL ST J ADMIN Rule 2.535.
   q. Requests for accommodations by persons with disabilities. FL ST J ADMIN Rule 2.540.
2. *Local rules*
   a. Sealing court records. FL ST 4 J CIR 2006-05.

B. Timing

1. *Amendment as a matter of course.* A party may amend a pleading once as a matter of course at any time before a responsive pleading is served or, if the pleading is one to which no responsive pleading is permitted and the action has not been placed on the trial calendar, may so amend it at any time within twenty (20) days after it is served. FL ST RCP Rule 1.190(a).

2. *Amendment by leave of court.* Otherwise a party may amend a pleading only by leave of court or by written consent of the adverse party. Leave of court shall be given freely when justice so requires. FL ST RCP Rule 1.190(a).
3. *Amendments in furtherance of justice.* At any time in furtherance of justice, upon such terms as may be just, the court may permit any process, proceeding, pleading, or record to be amended or material supplemental matter to be set forth in an amended or supplemental pleading. At every stage of the action the court must disregard any error or defect in the proceedings which does not affect the substantial rights of the parties. FL ST RCP Rule 1.190(e).
4. *Response to amended pleading.* A party shall plead in response to an amended pleading within ten (10) days after service of the amended pleading unless the court otherwise orders. FL ST RCP Rule 1.190(a).
5. *Computation of time*
    a. *Generally.* Computation of time shall be governed by FL ST J ADMIN Rule 2.514. FL ST RCP Rule 1.090(a). The following rules apply in computing time periods specified in any rule of procedure, local rule, court order, or statute that does not specify a method of computing time. FL ST J ADMIN Rule 2.514(a).
        i. *Period stated in days or a longer unit.* When the period is stated in days or a longer unit of time (A) exclude the day of the event that triggers the period; (B) count every day, including intermediate Saturdays, Sundays, and legal holidays; and (C) include the last day of the period, but if the last day is a Saturday, Sunday, or legal holiday, or falls within any period of time extended through an order of the chief justice under FL ST J ADMIN Rule 2.205(a)(2)(B)(iv), the period continues to run until the end of the next day that is not a Saturday, Sunday, or legal holiday and does not fall within any period of time extended through an order of the chief justice. FL ST J ADMIN Rule 2.514(a)(1).
        ii. *Period stated in hours.* When the period is stated in hours (A) begin counting immediately on the occurrence of the event that triggers the period; (B) count every hour, including hours during intermediate Saturdays, Sundays, and legal holidays; and (C) if the period would end on a Saturday, Sunday, or legal holiday, or during any period of time extended through an order of the chief justice under FL ST J ADMIN Rule 2.205(a)(2)(B)(iv), the period continues to run until the same time on the next day that is not a Saturday, Sunday, or legal holiday and does not fall within any period of time extended through an order of the chief justice. FL ST J ADMIN Rule 2.514(a)(2).
        iii. *Period stated in days less than seven (7) days.* When the period stated in days is less than seven (7) days, intermediate Saturdays, Sundays, and legal holidays shall be excluded in the computation. FL ST J ADMIN Rule 2.514(a)(3).
        iv. *"Last day" defined.* Unless a different time is set by a statute, local rule, or court order, the last day ends (A) for electronic filing or for service by any means, at midnight; and (B) for filing by other means, when the clerk's office is scheduled to close. FL ST J ADMIN Rule 2.514(a)(4).
        v. *"Next day" defined.* The "next day" is determined by continuing to count forward when the period is measured after an event and backward when measured before an event. FL ST J ADMIN Rule 2.514(a)(5).
        vi. *"Legal holiday" defined.* "Legal holiday" means (A) the day set aside by FL ST § 110.117, for observing New Year's Day, Martin Luther King, Jr.'s Birthday, Memorial Day, Independence Day, Labor Day, Veterans' Day, Thanksgiving Day, the Friday after Thanksgiving Day, or Christmas Day, and (B) any day observed as a holiday by the clerk's office or as designated by the chief judge. FL ST J ADMIN Rule 2.514(a)(6).
    b. *Additional time after service by mail or e-mail.* When a party may or must act within a specified time after service and service is made by mail or e-mail, five (5) days are added after the period that would otherwise expire under FL ST J ADMIN Rule 2.514(a). FL ST J ADMIN Rule 2.514(b).
    c. *Enlargement.* When an act is required or allowed to be done at or within a specified time by order of court, by the Florida Rules of Civil Procedure, or by notice given thereunder, for cause shown the court at any time in its discretion (1) with or without notice, may order the period enlarged if request

therefor is made before the expiration of the period originally prescribed or as extended by a previous order, or (2) upon motion made and notice after the expiration of the specified period, may permit the act to be done when failure to act was the result of excusable neglect, but it may not extend the time for making a motion for new trial, for rehearing, or to alter or amend a judgment; making a motion for relief from a judgment under FL ST RCP Rule 1.540(b); taking an appeal or filing a petition for certiorari; or making a motion for a directed verdict. FL ST RCP Rule 1.090(b).

d. *Unaffected by expiration of term.* The period of time provided for the doing of any act or the taking of any proceeding shall not be affected or limited by the continued existence or expiration of a term of court. The continued existence or expiration of a term of court in no way affects the power of a court to do any act or take any proceeding in any action which is or has been pending before it. FL ST RCP Rule 1.090(c).

C. General Requirements

1. *Amendments.* A party may amend a pleading once as a matter of course at any time before a responsive pleading is served or, if the pleading is one to which no responsive pleading is permitted and the action has not been placed on the trial calendar, may so amend it at any time within twenty (20) days after it is served. Otherwise a party may amend a pleading only by leave of court or by written consent of the adverse party. Leave of court shall be freely given when justice so requires. FL ST RCP Rule 1.190(a).

   a. *Purpose of amendments.* Amendments can relate to the correction of mistakes, the insertion of jurisdictional averments, the correction or addition of verifications, the addition or substitution or striking out of parties, and generally the rectification of all formal defects in the pleading. The court can also allow amendments setting up an omitted counterclaim or cross-claim if the defendant failed to raise the claim through oversight, inadvertence, or excusable neglect. FL-PP § 2:151.

   b. *Amendment to a pleading/Amended pleading.* A significant difference exists between an amendment to a pleading and an amended pleading. An amendment to a pleading corrects, adds to or deletes from the pleading. An amended pleading is substituted for the former pleading and the former pleading ceases to have any effect. Dee v. Southern Brewing Company, 146 Fla. 588, 1 So.2d 562 (Fla. 1941); Shannon v. McBride, 105 So.2d 16 (Fla. 2d DCA 1958); Hughes v. Home Sav. of America, F.S.B., 675 So.2d 649 (Fla. 2d DCA 1996); FL-PRACPROC § 14:2.

   c. *Relation back of amendments.* When the claim or defense asserted in the amended pleading arose out of the conduct, transaction, or occurrence set forth or attempted to be set forth in the original pleading, the amendment shall relate back to the date of the original pleading. FL ST RCP Rule 1.190(c).

2. *General rules of pleading*

   a. *Claims for relief*

      i. A pleading which sets forth a claim for relief, whether an original claim, counterclaim, crossclaim, or third-party claim, must state a cause of action and shall contain

         - A short and plain statement of the grounds upon which the court's jurisdiction depends, unless the court already has jurisdiction and the claim needs no new grounds of jurisdiction to support it (For information regarding acts subjecting persons to jurisdiction, please see FL ST § 48.193),
         - A short and plain statement of the ultimate facts showing that the pleader is entitled to relief, and
         - A demand for judgment for the relief to which the pleader deems himself or herself entitled. FL ST RCP Rule 1.110(b).

      ii. Relief in the alternative or of several different types may be demanded. Every complaint shall be considered to demand general relief. FL ST RCP Rule 1.110(b).

   b. *Verification.* Except when otherwise specifically provided by these rules or an applicable statute, every pleading or other document of a party represented by an attorney need not be verified or accompanied by an affidavit. FL ST RCP Rule 1.030. When filing an action for foreclosure of a mortgage on residential real property the complaint shall be verified. When verification of a document is required, the document filed shall include an oath, affirmation, or the following statement: "Under penalty of perjury, I declare that I have read the foregoing, and the facts alleged therein are true and correct to the best of my knowledge and belief." FL ST RCP Rule 1.110(b).

c. *Separate statements.* All averments of claim or defense shall be made in consecutively numbered paragraphs, the contents of each of which shall be limited as far as practicable to a statement of a single set of circumstances, and a paragraph may be referred to by number in all subsequent pleadings. Each claim founded upon a separate transaction or occurrence and each defense other than denials shall be stated in a separate count or defense when a separation facilitates the clear presentation of the matter set forth. FL ST RCP Rule 1.110(f).

d. *Statements adopted by reference.* Statements in a pleading may be adopted by reference in a different part of the same pleading, in another pleading, or in any motion. FL ST RCP Rule 1.130(b).

e. *Joinder of causes of action; Consistency.* A pleader may set up in the same action as many claims or causes of action or defenses in the same right as the pleader has, and claims for relief may be stated in the alternative if separate items make up the cause of action, or if two (2) or more causes of action are joined. A party may also set forth two (2) or more statements of a claim or defense alternatively, either in one (1) count or defense or in separate counts or defenses. When two (2) or more statements are made in the alternative and one (1) of them, if made independently, would be sufficient, the pleading is not made insufficient by the insufficiency of one (1) or more of the alternative statements. A party may also state as many separate claims or defenses as that party has, regardless of consistency and whether based on legal or equitable grounds or both. All pleadings shall be construed so as to do substantial justice. FL ST RCP Rule 1.110(g).

f. *Subsequent pleadings.* When the nature of an action permits pleadings subsequent to final judgment and the jurisdiction of the court over the parties has not terminated, the initial pleading subsequent to final judgment shall be designated a supplemental complaint or petition. The action shall then proceed in the same manner and time as though the supplemental complaint or petition were the initial pleading in the action, including the issuance of any needed process. FL ST RCP Rule 1.110(h) shall not apply to proceedings that may be initiated by motion under the Florida Rules of Civil Procedure. FL ST RCP Rule 1.110(h).

g. *Pleading basis for service.* When service of process is to be made under statutes authorizing service on nonresidents of Florida, it is sufficient to plead the basis for service in the language of the statute without pleading the facts supporting service. FL ST RCP Rule 1.070(h).

h. *Forms of pleadings.* Forms of action and technical forms for seeking relief and of pleas, pleadings, or motions are abolished. FL ST RCP Rule 1.110(a).

3. *Answer; Generally.* An answer has three (3) functions. First, it must respond to each allegation of the preceding pleading by admitting, denying or alleging that the pleader is without knowledge of the allegation. Second, it must contain any affirmative defenses that the pleader is interposing to any cause of action alleged in the preceding pleading. Third, the answer may claim affirmative relief against the plaintiff or petitioner by a counterclaim or against a codefendant by a crossclaim. FL-PRACPROC § 11:1.

   a. *Content.* In the answer a pleader shall state in short and plain terms the pleader's defenses to each claim asserted and shall admit or deny the averments on which the adverse party relies. If the defendant is without knowledge, the defendant shall so state and such statement shall operate as a denial. Denial shall fairly meet the substance of the averments denied. When a pleader intends in good faith to deny only a part of an averment, the pleader shall specify so much of it as is true and shall deny the remainder. Unless the pleader intends in good faith to controvert all of the averments of the preceding pleading, the pleader may make denials as specific denials of designated averments or may generally deny all of the averments except such designated averments as the pleader expressly admits, but when the pleader does so intend to controvert all of its averments, including averments of the grounds upon which the court's jurisdiction depends, the pleader may do so by general denial. FL ST RCP Rule 1.110(c).

   b. *Form of answer.* An answer contains a caption, commencement, body, signature and certificate of service. The caption is the same as that of the initial pleading, except for the designation as one of the types of answer. The body of an answer should contain an admission, denial or plea of without knowledge to each allegation of the preceding pleading, except for the additional allegations in response to a general allegation of conditions precedent and the denial of capacity to sue. FL-PRACPROC § 11:3.

i. *Responding sequentially.* The best method of responding is to answer each paragraph sequentially, combining admissions, denials or pleas of without knowledge when the sequence permits. The admissions, denials and allegations of without knowledge should be stated first, followed separately by any affirmative defenses and then by any counterclaim or crossclaim. A third party complaint may be a part of the same paper, but it is not a part of the answer as is a counterclaim or crossclaim. Paragraphs are numbered consecutively throughout the pleading whether in the answer, counterclaim or crossclaim. Denials for the record only are improper. FL-PRACPROC § 11:3.

c. *Defenses*

i. *Generally.* Every defense in law or fact to a claim for relief in a pleading shall be asserted in the responsive pleading, if one is required, but the following defenses may be made by motion at the option of the pleader: (1) lack of jurisdiction over the subject matter, (2) lack of jurisdiction over the person, (3) improper venue, (4) insufficiency of process, (5) insufficiency of service of process, (6) failure to state a cause of action, and (7) failure to join indispensable parties. A motion making any of these defenses shall be made before pleading if a further pleading is permitted. FL ST RCP Rule 1.140(b).

- *Stated specifically.* The grounds on which any of the enumerated defenses are based and the substantial matters of law intended to be argued shall be stated specifically and with particularity in the responsive pleading or motion. FL ST RCP Rule 1.140(b).
- *Waiver.* Any ground not stated shall be deemed to be waived except any ground showing that the court lacks jurisdiction of the subject matter may be made at any time. No defense or objection is waived by being joined with other defenses or objections in a responsive pleading or motion. FL ST RCP Rule 1.140(b). A party waives all defenses and objections that the party does not present either by motion under FL ST RCP Rule 1.140(b), FL ST RCP Rule 1.140(e), or FL ST RCP Rule 1.140(f) or, if the party has made no motion, in a responsive pleading except as provided in FL ST RCP Rule 1.140(h)(2). FL ST RCP Rule 1.140(h)(1). The defenses of failure to state a cause of action or a legal defense or to join an indispensable party may be raised by motion for judgment on the pleadings or at the trial on the merits in addition to being raised either in a motion under FL ST RCP Rule 1.140(b) or in the answer or reply. The defense of lack of jurisdiction of the subject matter may be raised at any time. FL ST RCP Rule 1.140(h)(2).

ii. *Affirmative defenses.* In pleading to a preceding pleading a party shall set forth affirmatively accord and satisfaction, arbitration and award, assumption of risk, contributory negligence, discharge in bankruptcy, duress, estoppel, failure of consideration, fraud, illegality, injury by fellow servant, laches, license, payment, release, res judicata, statute of frauds, statute of limitations, waiver, and any other matter constituting an avoidance or affirmative defense. When a party has mistakenly designated a defense as a counterclaim or a counterclaim as a defense, the court, on terms if justice so requires, shall treat the pleading as if there had been a proper designation. Affirmative defenses appearing on the face of a prior pleading may be asserted as grounds for a motion or defense under FL ST RCP Rule 1.140(b); provided this shall not limit amendments under FL ST RCP Rule 1.190 even if such ground is sustained. FL ST RCP Rule 1.110(d).

- *Format of defenses.* Affirmative defenses should be placed after the admissions, denials and allegations of without knowledge in the answer. All paragraphs must be numbered consecutively throughout the answer. If a defense is directed to only a part of a cause of action or to one or more, but not all, of several causes of action in the preceding pleading, the part or cause of action to which it is directed should be identified in the defense. Defenses should be identified by consecutive ordinal numbers such as "First Defense" and "Second Defense." FL-PRACPROC § 11:4.

iii. *Effect of failure to deny.* Averments in a pleading to which a responsive pleading is required,

other than those as to the amount of damages, are admitted when not denied in the responsive pleading. Averments in a pleading to which no responsive pleading is required or permitted shall be taken as denied or avoided. FL ST RCP Rule 1.110(e). An admission in an answer binds the party and no proof is required. An admission does not extend beyond the scope of the allegation in the preceding pleading. FL-PRACPROC § 11:3.

4. *Pleading special matters*

   a. *Capacity.* It is not necessary to aver the capacity of a party to sue or be sued, the authority of a party to sue or be sued in a representative capacity, or the legal existence of an organized association of persons that is made a party, except to the extent required to show the jurisdiction of the court. The initial pleading served on behalf of a minor party shall specifically aver the age of the minor party. When a party desires to raise an issue as to the legal existence of any party, the capacity of any party to sue or be sued, or the authority of a party to sue or be sued in a representative capacity, that party shall do so by specific negative averment which shall include such supporting particulars as are peculiarly within the pleader's knowledge. FL ST RCP Rule 1.120(a).

   b. *Fraud, mistake, condition of the mind.* In all averments of fraud or mistake, the circumstances constituting fraud or mistake shall be stated with such particularity as the circumstances may permit. Malice, intent, knowledge, mental attitude, and other condition of mind of a person may be averred generally. FL ST RCP Rule 1.120(b).

   c. *Conditions precedent.* In pleading the performance or occurrence of conditions precedent, it is sufficient to aver generally that all conditions precedent have been performed or have occurred. A denial of performance or occurrence shall be made specifically and with particularity. FL ST RCP Rule 1.120(c).

   d. *Official document or act.* In pleading an official document or official act it is sufficient to aver that the document was issued or the act done in compliance with law. FL ST RCP Rule 1.120(c).

   e. *Judgment or decree.* In pleading a judgment or decree of a domestic or foreign court, a judicial or quasi-judicial tribunal, or a board or officer, it is sufficient to aver the judgment or decree without setting forth matter showing jurisdiction to render it. FL ST RCP Rule 1.120(e).

   f. *Time and place.* For the purpose of testing the sufficiency of a pleading, averments of time and place are material and shall be considered like all other averments of material matter. FL ST RCP Rule 1.120(f).

   g. *Special damage.* When items of special damage are claimed, they shall be specifically stated. FL ST RCP Rule 1.120(g).

5. *Parties*

   a. *Parties generally.* Every action may be prosecuted in the name of the real party in interest, but a personal representative, administrator, guardian, trustee of an express trust, a party with whom or in whose name a contract has been made for the benefit of another, or a party expressly authorized by statute may sue in that person's own name without joining the party for whose benefit the action is brought. All persons having an interest in the subject of the action and in obtaining the relief demanded may join as plaintiffs and any person may be made a defendant who has or claims an interest adverse to the plaintiff. Any person may at any time be made a party if that person's presence is necessary or proper to a complete determination of the cause. Persons having a united interest may be joined on the same side as plaintiffs or defendants, and anyone who refuses to join may for such reason be made a defendant. FL ST RCP Rule 1.210(a).

   b. *Minors or incompetent persons.* When a minor or incompetent person has a representative, such as a guardian or other like fiduciary, the representative may sue or defend on behalf of the minor or incompetent person. A minor or incompetent person who does not have a duly appointed representative may sue by next friend or by a guardian ad litem. The court shall appoint a guardian ad litem for a minor or incompetent person not otherwise represented in an action or shall make such other order as it deems proper for the protection of the minor or incompetent person. FL ST RCP Rule 1.210(b).

   c. For survivor and substitution of parties information, please see FL ST RCP Rule 1.260.

6. *Counterclaims and crossclaims*

   a. *Compulsory counterclaims.* A pleading shall state as a counterclaim any claim which at the time of serving the pleading the pleader has against any opposing party, provided it arises out of the transaction or occurrence that is the subject matter of the opposing party's claim and does not require for its adjudication the presence of third parties over whom the court cannot acquire jurisdiction. But the pleader need not state a claim if (1) at the time the action was commenced the claim was the subject of another pending action, or (2) the opposing party brought suit upon that party's claim by attachment or other process by which the court did not acquire jurisdiction to render a personal judgment on the claim and the pleader is not stating a counterclaim under this rule. FL ST RCP Rule 1.170(a).

   b. *Permissive counterclaim.* A pleading may state as a counterclaim any claim against an opposing party not arising out of the transaction or occurrence that is the subject matter of the opposing party's claim. FL ST RCP Rule 1.170(b).

   c. *Counterclaim exceeding opposing claim.* A counterclaim may or may not diminish or defeat the recovery sought by the opposing party. It may claim relief exceeding in amount or different in kind from that sought in the pleading of the opposing party. FL ST RCP Rule 1.170(c).

   d. *Counterclaim against the State.* The Florida Rules of Civil Procedure shall not be construed to enlarge beyond the limits established by law the right to assert counterclaims or to claim credits against the state or any of its subdivisions or other governmental organizations thereof subject to suit or against a municipal corporation or against an officer, agency, or administrative board of the state. FL ST RCP Rule 1.170(d).

   e. *Counterclaim maturing or acquired after pleading.* A claim which matured or was acquired by the pleader after serving the pleading may be presented as a counterclaim by supplemental pleading with the permission of the court. FL ST RCP Rule 1.170(e).

   f. *Omitted counterclaim or crossclaim.* When a pleader fails to set up a counterclaim or crossclaim through oversight, inadvertence, or excusable neglect, or when justice requires, the pleader may set up the counterclaim or crossclaim by amendment with leave of the court. FL ST RCP Rule 1.170(f).

   g. *Crossclaim against co-party.* A pleading may state as a crossclaim any claim by one party against a co-party arising out of the transaction or occurrence that is the subject matter of either the original action or a counterclaim therein, or relating to any property that is the subject matter of the original action. The crossclaim may include a claim that the party against whom it is asserted is or may be liable to the crossclaimant for all or part of a claim asserted in the action against the crossclaimant. Service of a crossclaim on a party who has appeared in the action shall be made pursuant to FL ST RCP Rule 1.080. Service of a crossclaim against a party who has not appeared in the action shall be made in the manner provided for service of summons. FL ST RCP Rule 1.170(g).

   h. *Additional parties may be brought in.* When the presence of parties other than those to the original action is required to grant complete relief in the determination of a counterclaim or crossclaim, they shall be named in the counterclaim or crossclaim and be served with process and shall be parties to the action thereafter if jurisdiction of them can be obtained and their joinder will not deprive the court of jurisdiction of the action. FL ST RCP Rule 1.250(b) and FL ST RCP Rule 1.250(c) apply to parties brought in under FL ST RCP Rule 1.170(h). FL ST RCP Rule 1.170(h).

   i. *Separate trials; Separate judgment.* If the court orders separate trials as provided in FL ST RCP Rule 1.270(b), judgment on a counterclaim or crossclaim may be rendered when the court has jurisdiction to do so even if a claim of the opposing party has been dismissed or otherwise disposed of. FL ST RCP Rule 1.170(i).

   j. *Demand exceeding jurisdiction; Transfer of action.* If the demand of any counterclaim or crossclaim exceeds the jurisdiction of the court in which the action is pending, the action shall be transferred forthwith to the court of the same county having jurisdiction of the demand in the counterclaim or crossclaim with only such alterations in the pleadings as are essential. The court shall order the transfer of the action and the transmittal of all papers in it to the proper court if the party asserting the demand exceeding the jurisdiction deposits with the court having jurisdiction a sum sufficient to pay

the clerk's service charge in the court to which the action is transferred at the time of filing the counterclaim or crossclaim. Thereupon the original papers and deposit shall be transmitted and filed with a certified copy of the order. The court to which the action is transferred shall have full power and jurisdiction over the demands of all parties. Failure to make the service charge deposit at the time the counterclaim or crossclaim is filed, or within such further time as the court may allow, shall reduce a claim for damages to an amount within the jurisdiction of the court where the action is pending and waive the claim in other cases. FL ST RCP Rule 1.170(j).

7. *Misjoinder and nonjoinder of parties*
   a. *Misjoinder.* Misjoinder of parties is not a ground for dismissal of an action. Any claim against a party may be severed and proceeded with separately. FL ST RCP Rule 1.250(a).
   b. *Dropping parties.* Parties may be dropped by an adverse party in the manner provided for voluntary dismissal in FL ST RCP Rule 1.420(a)(1) subject to the exception stated in FL ST RCP Rule 1.420. If notice of lis pendens has been filed in the action against a party so dropped, the notice of dismissal shall be recorded and cancels the notice of lis pendens without the necessity of a court order. Parties may be dropped by order of court on its own initiative or the motion of any party at any stage of the action on such terms as are just. FL ST RCP Rule 1.250(b).
   c. *Adding parties.* Parties may be added once as a matter of course within the same time that pleadings can be so amended under FL ST RCP Rule 1.190(a). If amendment by leave of court or stipulation of the parties is permitted, parties may be added in the amended pleading without further order of court. Parties may be added by order of court on its own initiative or on motion of any party at any stage of the action and on such terms as are just. FL ST RCP Rule 1.250(c).
8. *Jury demand*
   a. *Right preserved.* The right of trial by jury as declared by the Constitution or by statute shall be preserved to the parties inviolate. FL ST RCP Rule 1.430(a).
   b. *Demand.* Any party may demand a trial by jury of any issue triable of right by a jury by serving upon the other party a demand therefor in writing at any time after commencement of the action and not later than ten (10) days after the service of the last pleading directed to such issue. The demand may be indorsed upon a pleading of the party. FL ST RCP Rule 1.430(b).
   c. *Specification of issues.* In the demand a party may specify the issues that the party wishes so tried; otherwise, the party is deemed to demand trial by jury for all issues so triable. FL ST RCP Rule 1.430(c).
      i. If a party has demanded trial by jury for only some of the issues, any other party may serve a demand for trial by jury of any other or all of the issues triable by jury ten (10) days after service of the demand or such lesser time as the court may order. FL ST RCP Rule 1.430(c).
   d. *Waiver.* A party who fails to serve a demand as required by FL ST RCP Rule 1.430 waives trial by jury. FL ST RCP Rule 1.430(d).
      i. If waived, a jury trial may not be granted without the consent of the parties, but the court may allow an amendment in the proceedings to demand a trial by jury or order a trial by jury on its own motion. FL ST RCP Rule 1.430(d).
      ii. A demand for trial by jury may not be withdrawn without the consent of the parties. FL ST RCP Rule 1.430(d).
9. *Arbitration and mediation*
   a. *Referral to arbitration and mediation.* Except as hereinafter provided or as otherwise prohibited by law, the presiding judge may enter an order referring all or any part of a contested civil matter to mediation or arbitration. The parties to any contested civil matter may file a written stipulation to mediate or arbitrate any issue between them at any time. Such stipulation shall be incorporated into the order of referral. FL ST RCP Rule 1.700(a).
   b. *Arbitration*
      i. *Exclusions.* A civil action shall be ordered to arbitration or arbitration in conjunction with

mediation upon stipulation of the parties. A civil action may be ordered to arbitration or arbitration in conjunction with mediation upon motion of any party or by the court, if the judge determines the action to be of such a nature that arbitration could be of benefit to the litigants or the court. FL ST RCP Rule 1.800.

- Under no circumstances may the following categories of actions be referred to arbitration: (1) bond estreatures; (2) habeas corpus or other extraordinary writs; (3) bond validations; (4) civil or criminal contempt; (5) such other matters as may be specified by order of the chief judge in the circuit. FL ST RCP Rule 1.800.

ii. For more information regarding arbitration, please see FL ST RCP Rule 1.810; FL ST RCP Rule 1.820; FL ST RCP Rule 1.830.

c. *Mediation.* For more information regarding mediation, please see FL ST RCP Rule 1.710; FL ST RCP Rule 1.720; FL ST RCP Rule 1.730; and FL ST RCP Rule 1.750.

10. *Rules of court*

a. *Rules of civil procedure.* The Florida Rules of Civil Procedure apply to all actions of a civil nature and all special statutory proceedings in the circuit courts and county courts except those to which the Florida Probate Rules, the Florida Family Law Rules of Procedure, or the Small Claims Rules apply. FL ST RCP Rule 1.010.

i. The form, content, procedure, and time for pleading in all special statutory proceedings shall be as prescribed by the statutes governing the proceeding unless the Florida Rules of Civil Procedure specifically provide to the contrary. FL ST RCP Rule 1.010.

ii. The Florida Rules of Civil Procedure shall be construed to secure the just, speedy, and inexpensive determination of every action. FL ST RCP Rule 1.010.

b. *Rules of judicial administration.* The Florida Rules of Judicial Administration shall apply to administrative matters in all courts to which the Florida Rules of Judicial Administration are applicable by their terms. The Florida Rules of Judicial Administration shall be construed to secure the speedy and inexpensive determination of every proceeding to which they are applicable. The Florida Rules of Judicial Administration shall supersede all conflicting rules and statutes. FL ST J ADMIN Rule 2.110.

D. Documents

1. *Required documents*

a. *Amended answer.* See the General Requirements section of this document for the content of an amended answer. If a party files a motion to amend a pleading, the party shall attach the proposed amended pleading to the motion. FL ST RCP Rule 1.190(a). See the KeyRules Florida Circuit Court Motion for Leave to Amend document for further information.

i. *Notices to persons with disabilities.* See the Format section of this KeyRules document for further information.

b. *Certificate of service.* When any attorney certifies in substance: "I certify that a copy hereof has been furnished to (here insert name or names and addresses used for service) by (e-mail) (delivery) (mail) (fax) on .... (date) ....______________ Attorney" the certificate is taken as prima facie proof of such service in compliance with FL ST J ADMIN Rule 2.516. FL ST J ADMIN Rule 2.516(f).

2. *Supplemental documents*

a. *Exhibits.* All bonds, notes, bills of exchange, contracts, accounts, or documents upon which action may be brought or defense made, or a copy thereof or a copy of the portions thereof material to the pleadings, shall be incorporated in or attached to the pleading. No papers shall be unnecessarily annexed as exhibits. The pleadings shall contain no unnecessary recitals of deeds, documents, contracts, or other instruments. Any exhibit attached to a pleading shall be considered a part of the pleadings for all purposes. FL ST RCP Rule 1.130(a).

b. *Notice of constitutional question.* A party that files a pleading, written motion, or other paper drawing into question the constitutionality of a state statute or a county or municipal charter,

ordinance, or franchise must promptly (1) file a notice of constitutional question stating the question and identifying the paper that raises it; and (2) serve the notice and the pleading, written motion, or other paper drawing into question the constitutionality of a state statute or a county or municipal charter, ordinance, or franchise on the Attorney General or the state attorney of the judicial circuit in which the action is pending, by either certified or registered mail. Service of the notice and pleading, written motion, or other paper does not require joinder of the Attorney General or the state attorney as a party to the action. FL ST RCP Rule 1.071.

E. Format

1. *Documents; Type and size.* Documents subject to the exceptions set forth in FL ST J ADMIN Rule 2.525(d) shall be filed on recycled paper measuring eight and one half by eleven (8 1/2 by 11) inches. For purposes of FL ST J ADMIN Rule 2.520, paper is recycled if it contains a minimum content of fifty (50) percent waste paper. Xerographic reduction of legal-size (eight and one half by fourteen (8 1/2 by 14) inches) documents to letter size (eight and one half by eleven (8 1/2 by 11) inches) is prohibited. All other documents filed by electronic transmission shall be filed in a format capable of being printed in a format consistent with the provisions of FL ST J ADMIN Rule 2.250. FL ST J ADMIN Rule 2.520(b).
   a. *Exhibits.* Any exhibit or attachment filed with pleadings or papers may be filed in its original size. FL ST J ADMIN Rule 2.520(c).
   b. *Recording space.* On all papers and documents prepared and filed by the court or by any party to a proceeding which are to be recorded in the public records of any county, including but not limited to final money judgments and notices of lis pendens, a three (3) inch by three (3) inch space at the top right-hand corner on the first page and a one (1) inch by three (3) inch space at the top right-hand corner on each subsequent page shall be left blank and reserved for use by the clerk of court. FL ST J ADMIN Rule 2.520(d).
      i. *Exceptions to recording space.* Any papers or documents created by persons or entities over which the filing party has no control, including but not limited to wills, codicils, trusts, or other testamentary documents; documents prepared or executed by any public officer; documents prepared, executed, acknowledged, or proved outside of the State of Florida; or documents created by State or Federal government agencies, may be filed without the space required by FL ST J ADMIN Rule 2.520. FL ST J ADMIN Rule 2.520(e).
   c. *Noncompliance.* No clerk of court is permitted to refuse to file any document or paper because of noncompliance with the Florida Rules of Judicial Administration. However, upon request of the clerk of court, noncomplying documents must be resubmitted in accordance with the formatting rules. FL ST J ADMIN Rule 2.520(f).
2. *Caption.* Every pleading, motion, order, judgment, or other paper shall have a caption containing the name of the court, the file number, and except for in rem proceedings, including forfeiture proceedings, the name of the first party on each side with an appropriate indication of other parties, and a designation identifying the party filing it and its nature or the nature of the order, as the case may be. In any in rem proceeding, every pleading, motion, order, judgment, or other paper shall have a caption containing the name of the court, the file number, the style "In re" (followed by the name or general description of the property), and a designation of the person or entity filing it and its nature or the nature of the order, as the case may be. In an in rem forfeiture proceeding, the style shall be "In re forfeiture of" (followed by the name of the general description of the property). All papers filed in the action shall be styled in such a manner as to indicate clearly the subject matter of the paper and the party requesting or obtaining relief. FL ST RCP Rule 1.100(c)(1).
3. *Writing and written defined.* Writing or written means a document containing information, an application, or a stipulation. FL ST RCP Rule 1.080(c).
4. *Rule abbreviations*
   a. The Florida Rules of Civil Procedure and shall be abbreviated as Fla.R.Civ.P. FL ST RCP Rule 1.010.
   b. The Florida Rules of Judicial Administration shall be abbreviated as Fla. R. Jud. Admin. FL ST J ADMIN Rule 2.110.

5. *Nonverification.* Except when otherwise specifically provided by the Florida Rules of Civil Procedure or an applicable statute, every pleading or other document of a party represented by an attorney need not be verified or accompanied by an affidavit. FL ST RCP Rule 1.030; FL ST J ADMIN Rule 2.515(a).
6. *Attorney signature*
    a. *Attorney signature.* Every pleading and other document of a party represented by an attorney shall be signed by at least one (1) attorney of record in that attorney's individual name whose current record Florida Bar address, telephone number, including area code, primary e-mail address and secondary e-mail addresses, if any, and Florida Bar number shall be stated, and who shall be duly licensed to practice law in Florida or who shall have received permission to appear in the particular case as provided in FL ST J ADMIN Rule 2.510. FL ST J ADMIN Rule 2.515(a).
        i. The attorney may be required by the court to give the address of, and to vouch for the attorney's authority to represent, the party. FL ST J ADMIN Rule 2.515(a).
        ii. The signature of an attorney shall constitute a certificate by the attorney that the attorney has read the pleading or other document; that to the best of the attorney's knowledge, information, and belief there is good ground to support it; and that it is not interposed for delay. FL ST J ADMIN Rule 2.515(a).
        iii. If a pleading is not signed or is signed with intent to defeat the purpose of FL ST J ADMIN Rule 2.515, it may be stricken and the action may proceed as though the pleading or other document had not been served. FL ST J ADMIN Rule 2.515(a).
    b. *Pro se litigant signature.* A party who is not represented by an attorney shall sign any pleading or other paper and state the party's address and telephone number, including area code. FL ST J ADMIN Rule 2.515(b).
    c. *Form of signature*
        i. The signatures required on pleadings and documents by FL ST J ADMIN Rule 2.515(a) and FL ST J ADMIN Rule 2.515(b) may be:
            - Original signatures;
            - Original signatures that have been reproduced by electronic means, such as on electronically transmitted documents or photocopied documents;
            - Electronic signatures using the "/s/," "s/," or "/s" formats by or at the direction of the person signing; or
            - Any other signature format authorized by general law, so long as the clerk where the proceeding is pending has the capability of receiving and has obtained approval from the Supreme Court of Florida to accept pleadings and documents with that signature format. FL ST J ADMIN Rule 2.515(c)(1).
        ii. An attorney, party, or other person who files a pleading or paper by electronic transmission that does not contain the original signature of that attorney, party, or other person shall file that identical pleading or paper in paper form containing an original signature of that attorney, party, or other person (hereinafter called the follow-up filing) immediately thereafter. The follow-up filing is not required if the Supreme Court of Florida has entered an order directing the clerk of court to discontinue accepting the follow-up filing. FL ST J ADMIN Rule 2.515(c)(2).
7. *Forms*
    a. *Process.* The forms of process, notice of lis pendens, and notice of action provided in the Florida Rules of Civil Procedure are sufficient. Variations from the forms do not void process or notices that are otherwise sufficient. FL ST RCP Rule 1.900(a).
    b. *Other forms.* The other forms provided in the Florida Rules of Civil Procedure are sufficient for the matters that are covered by them. So long as the substance is expressed without prolixity, the forms may be varied to meet the facts of a particular case. FL ST RCP Rule 1.900(b).
    c. *Formal matters.* Captions, except for the designation of the paper, are omitted from the forms provided in the Florida Rules of Civil Procedure. A general form of caption is the first form provided. Signatures are omitted from pleadings and motions. FL ST RCP Rule 1.900(c).

8. *Notices to persons with disabilities.* All notices of court proceedings to be held in a public facility, and all process compelling appearance at such proceedings, shall include the following statement in bold face, fourteen (14) point Times New Roman or Courier font: "If you are a person with a disability who needs any accommodation in order to participate in this proceeding, you are entitled, at no cost to you, to the provision of certain assistance. Please contact [identify applicable court personnel by name, address, and telephone number] at least seven (7) days before your scheduled court appearance, or immediately upon receiving this notification if the time before the scheduled appearance is less than seven (7) days; if you are hearing or voice impaired, call 711." FL ST J ADMIN Rule 2.540(c)(1).
9. *Minimization of the filing of sensitive information*
   a. *Limitations for court filings.* Unless authorized by FL ST J ADMIN Rule 2.425(b), statute, another rule of court, or the court orders otherwise, designated sensitive information filed with the court must be limited to the following format:
      i. The initials of a person known to be a minor;
      ii. The year of birth of a person's birth date;
      iii. No portion of any: Social security number, Bank account number, Credit card account number, Charge account number, or Debit account number;
      iv. The last four digits of any: Taxpayer identification number (TIN), Employee identification number, Driver's license number, Passport number, Telephone number, Financial account number, except as set forth in FL ST J ADMIN Rule 2.425(a)(3), Brokerage account number, Insurance policy account number, Loan account number, Customer account number, or Patient or health care number;
      v. A truncated version of any: Email address, Computer user name, Password, or Personal identification number (PIN); and
      vi. A truncated version of any other sensitive information as provided by court order. FL ST J ADMIN Rule 2.425(a).
   b. *Exceptions.* FL ST J ADMIN Rule 2.425(a) does not apply to the following:
      i. An account number which identifies the property alleged to be the subject of a proceeding;
      ii. The record of an administrative or agency proceeding;
      iii. The record in appellate or review proceedings;
      iv. The birth date of a minor whenever the birth date is necessary for the court to establish or maintain subject matter jurisdiction;
      v. The name of a minor in any order relating to parental responsibility, time-sharing, or child support;
      vi. The name of a minor in any document or order affecting the minor's ownership of real property;
      vii. The birth date of a party in a writ of attachment or notice to payor;
      viii. In traffic and criminal proceedings: a pro se filing; a court filing that is related to a criminal matter or investigation and that is prepared before the filing of a criminal charge or is not filed as part of any docketed criminal case; an arrest or search warrant or any information in support thereof; a charging document and an affidavit or other documents filed in support of any charging document, including any driving records; a statement of particulars; discovery material introduced into evidence or otherwise filed with the court; and all information necessary for the proper issuance and execution of a subpoena duces tecum;
      ix. Information used by the clerk for case maintenance purposes or the courts for case management purposes; and
      x. Information which is relevant and material to an issue before the court. FL ST J ADMIN Rule 2.425(b).
   c. *Remedies.* Upon motion by a party or interested person or sua sponte by the court, the court may order remedies, sanctions or both for a violation of FL ST J ADMIN Rule 2.425(a). Following notice

and an opportunity to respond, the court may impose sanctions if such filing was not made in good faith. FL ST J ADMIN Rule 2.425(c).

d. *Motions not restricted.* FL ST J ADMIN Rule 2.425 does not restrict a party's right to move for protective order, to move to file documents under seal, or to request a determination of the confidentiality of records. FL ST J ADMIN Rule 2.425(d).

   i. For more information regarding sealing court records, please see FL ST 4 J CIR 2006-05.

e. *Application.* FL ST J ADMIN Rule 2.425 does not affect the application of constitutional provisions, statutes, or rules of court regarding confidential information or access to public information. FL ST J ADMIN Rule 2.425(e).

F. Filing and Service Requirements

1. *Filing requirements.* All original documents must be filed with the court either before service or immediately thereafter, unless otherwise provided for by general law or other rules. If the original of any bond or other document is not placed in the court file, a certified copy must be so placed by the clerk. FL ST J ADMIN Rule 2.516(d). All documents shall be filed in conformity with the requirements of FL ST J ADMIN Rule 2.525. FL ST RCP Rule 1.080(b). All documents filed in any court shall be filed by electronic transmission in accordance with FL ST J ADMIN Rule 2.525. "Documents" means pleadings, motions, petitions, memoranda, briefs, notices, exhibits, declarations, affidavits, orders, judgments, decrees, writs, opinions, and any other paper or writing submitted to a court. FL ST J ADMIN Rule 2.520(a). All documents that are court records, as defined in FL ST J ADMIN Rule 2.430(a)(1), must be filed by electronic transmission, provided that: (1) the clerk has the ability to accept and retain such documents; (2) the clerk or the chief judge of the circuit has requested permission to accept documents filed by electronic transmission; and (3) the supreme court has entered an order granting permission to the clerk to accept documents filed by electronic transmission. FL ST J ADMIN Rule 2.525(c)(1).

   a. *Definition.* "Electronic transmission of documents" means the sending of information by electronic signals to, by or from a court or clerk, which when received can be transformed and stored or transmitted on paper, microfilm, magnetic storage device, optical imaging system, CD-ROM, flash drive, other electronic data storage system, server, case maintenance system ("CM"), electronic court filing ("ECF") system, statewide or local electronic portal ("e-portal"), or other electronic record keeping system authorized by the supreme court in a format sufficient to communicate the information on the original document in a readable format. Electronic transmission of documents includes electronic mail ("e-mail") and any internet-based transmission procedure, and may include procedures allowing for documents to be signed or verified by electronic means. FL ST J ADMIN Rule 2.525(a).

      i. The filing of documents with the court as required by the Florida Rules of Judicial Administration must be made by filing them with the clerk in accordance with FL ST J ADMIN Rule 2.525, except that the judge may permit documents to be filed with the judge, in which event the judge must note the filing date before him or her on the documents and transmit them to the clerk. The date of filing is that shown on the face of the document by the judge's notation or the clerk's time stamp, whichever is earlier. FL ST J ADMIN Rule 2.516(e).

   b. *Application.* Any court or clerk of the court may accept the electronic transmission of documents for filing after the clerk, together with input from the chief judge of the circuit, has obtained approval of the procedures and program for doing so from the Supreme Court of Florida. FL ST J ADMIN Rule 2.525(b).

   c. *Exceptions*

      i. Paper documents and other submissions may be manually submitted to the clerk or court:

         - When the clerk does not have the ability to accept and retain documents by electronic filing or has not had ECF Procedures approved by the supreme court;
         - For filing by any self-represented party or any self-represented nonparty unless specific ECF Procedures provide a means to file documents electronically. However, any self-represented nonparty that is a governmental or public agency and any other agency, partnership, corporation, or business entity acting on behalf of any governmental or public

agency may file documents by electronic transmission if such entity has the capability of filing documents electronically;

- For filing by attorneys excused from e-mail service in accordance with FL ST J ADMIN Rule 2.516(b);
- When submitting evidentiary exhibits or filing non-documentary materials;
- When the filing involves documents in excess of twenty-five (25) megabytes (25MB) in size. For such filings, documents may be transmitted using an electronic storage medium that the clerk has the ability to accept, which may include a CD-ROM, flash drive, or similar storage medium;
- When filed in open court, as permitted by the court;
- When paper filing is permitted by any approved statewide or local ECF procedures; and
- If any court determines that justice so requires. FL ST J ADMIN Rule 2.525(d).

ii. Any document in paper form submitted under FL ST J ADMIN Rule 2.525(d) is filed when it is received by the clerk or court and the clerk shall immediately thereafter convert any filed paper document to an electronic document. "Convert to an electronic document" means optically capturing an image of a paper document and using character recognition software to recover as much of the document's text as practicable and then indexing and storing the document in the official court file. FL ST J ADMIN Rule 2.525(c)(4).

iii. Any storage medium submitted under FL ST J ADMIN Rule 2.525(d)(5) is filed when received by the clerk or court and the clerk shall immediately thereafter transfer the electronic documents from the storage device to the official court file. FL ST J ADMIN Rule 2.525(c)(5).

iv. If the filer of any paper document authorized under FL ST J ADMIN Rule 2.525(d) provides a self-addressed, postage-paid envelope for return of the paper document after it is converted to electronic form by the clerk, the clerk shall place the paper document in the envelope and deposit it in the mail. Except when a paper document is required to be maintained, the clerk may recycle any filed paper document that is not to be returned to the filer. FL ST J ADMIN Rule 2.525(c)(6).

v. The clerk may convert any paper document filed before the effective date of FL ST J ADMIN Rule 2.525 to an electronic document. Unless the clerk is required to maintain the paper document, if the paper document has been converted to an electronic document by the clerk, the paper document is no longer part of the official court file and may be removed and recycled. FL ST J ADMIN Rule 2.525(c)(7).

d. *Official court file.* For information on what constitutes the official court file, please see FL ST J ADMIN Rule 2.525(c)(2), FL ST J ADMIN Rule 2.525(c)(3).

e. *Administration.* All attorneys, parties, or other persons using this rule to file documents are required to make arrangements with the court or clerk for the payment of any charges authorized by general law or the supreme court before filing any document by electronic transmission. FL ST J ADMIN Rule 2.525(f)(2).

f. *Filing date.* The filing date for an electronically transmitted document is the date and time that such filing is acknowledged by an electronic stamp or otherwise, pursuant to any procedure set forth in any ECF Procedures approved by the supreme court, or the date the last page of such filing is received by the court or clerk. FL ST J ADMIN Rule 2.525(f)(3).

g. *Accessibility.* All documents transmitted in any electronic form under FL ST J ADMIN Rule 2.525 must comply with the accessibility requirements of FL ST J ADMIN Rule 2.526. FL ST J ADMIN Rule 2.525(g).

2. *Service requirements.* Every pleading subsequent to the initial pleading, all orders, and every other document filed in the action must be served in conformity with the requirements of FL ST J ADMIN Rule 2.516. FL ST RCP Rule 1.080(a).

a. *Service; When required.* Unless the court otherwise orders, or a statute or supreme court adminis-

trative order specifies a different means of service, every pleading subsequent to the initial pleading and every other document filed in any court proceeding, except applications for witness subpoenas and documents served by formal notice or required to be served in the manner provided for service of formal notice, must be served in accordance with FL ST J ADMIN Rule 2.516 on each party. No service need be made on parties against whom a default has been entered, except that pleadings asserting new or additional claims against them must be served in the manner provided for service of summons. FL ST J ADMIN Rule 2.516(a).

b. *Service; How made.* When service is required or permitted to be made upon a party represented by an attorney, service must be made upon the attorney unless service upon the party is ordered by the court. FL ST J ADMIN Rule 2.516(b).

   i. *Service by electronic mail ("e-mail").* All documents required or permitted to be served on another party must be served by e-mail, unless FL ST J ADMIN Rule 2.516 otherwise provides. When, in addition to service by e-mail, the sender also utilizes another means of service provided for in FL ST J ADMIN Rule 2.516(b)(2), any differing time limits and other provisions applicable to that other means of service control. FL ST J ADMIN Rule 2.516(b)(1). Any document electronically transmitted to a court or clerk must also be served on all parties and interested persons in accordance with the applicable rules of court. FL ST J ADMIN Rule 2.525(e)(2).

      - *Service on attorneys.* Upon appearing in a proceeding, an attorney must serve a designation of a primary e-mail address and may designate no more than two (2) secondary e-mail addresses. Thereafter, service must be directed to all designated e-mail addresses in that proceeding. Every document filed by an attorney thereafter must include the primary e-mail address of that attorney and any secondary e-mail addresses. If an attorney does not designate any e-mail address for service, documents may be served on that attorney at the e-mail address on record with The Florida Bar. FL ST J ADMIN Rule 2.516(b)(1)(A).
      - *Exception to e-mail service on attorneys.* Service by an attorney on another attorney must be made by e-mail unless excused by the court. Upon motion by an attorney demonstrating that the attorney has no e-mail account and lacks access to the Internet at the attorney's office, the court may excuse the attorney from the requirements of e-mail service. Service on and by an attorney excused by the court from e-mail service must be by the means provided in FL ST J ADMIN Rule 2.516(b)(2). FL ST J ADMIN Rule 2.516(b)(1)(B).
      - *Service on and by parties not represented by an attorney.* Any party not represented by an attorney may serve a designation of a primary e-mail address and also may designate no more than two (2) secondary e-mail addresses to which service must be directed in that proceeding by the means provided in FL ST J ADMIN Rule 2.516(b)(1). If a party not represented by an attorney does not designate an e-mail address for service in a proceeding, service on and by that party must be by the means provided in FL ST J ADMIN Rule 2.516(b)(2). FL ST J ADMIN Rule 2.516(b)(1)(C).
      - *Time of service.* Service by e-mail is complete when it is sent. FL ST J ADMIN Rule 2.516(b)(1)(D). An e-mail is deemed served on the date it is sent. FL ST J ADMIN Rule 2.516(b)(1)(D)(i). If the sender learns that the e-mail did not reach the address of the person to be served, the sender must immediately send another copy by e-mail, or by a means authorized by FL ST J ADMIN Rule 2.516(b)(2). FL ST J ADMIN Rule 2.516(b)(1)(D)(ii). E-mail service is treated as service by mail for the computation of time. FL ST J ADMIN Rule 2.516(b)(1)(D)(iii).

   ii. *Format of e-mail for service.* Service of a document by e-mail is made by attaching a copy of the document in PDF format to an e-mail sent to all addresses designated by the attorney or party. FL ST J ADMIN Rule 2.516(b)(1)(E).

      - All documents served by e-mail must be attached to an e-mail message containing a subject line beginning with the words "SERVICE OF COURT DOCUMENT" in all capital letters, followed by the case number of the proceeding in which the documents are being served. FL ST J ADMIN Rule 2.516(b)(1)(E)(i).

- The body of the e-mail must identify the court in which the proceeding is pending, the case number, the name of the initial party on each side, the title of each document served with that e-mail, and the sender's name and telephone number. FL ST J ADMIN Rule 2.516(b)(1)(E)(ii).
- Any document served by e-mail may be signed by the "/s/" format, as long as the filed original is signed in accordance with the applicable rule of procedure. FL ST J ADMIN Rule 2.516(b)(1)(E)(iii).
- Any e-mail which, together with its attached documents, exceeds five megabytes (5MB) in size, must be divided and sent as separate e-mails, no one of which may exceed five megabytes (5MB) in size and each of which must be sequentially numbered in the subject line. FL ST J ADMIN Rule 2.516(b)(1)(E)(iv).

iii. *Service by other means.* In addition to, and not in lieu of, service by e-mail, service may also be made upon attorneys by any of the means specified in FL ST J ADMIN Rule 2.516(b)(2). Service on and by all parties who are not represented by an attorney and who do not designate an e-mail address, and on and by all attorneys excused from e-mail service, must be made by delivering a copy of the document or by mailing it to the party or attorney at their last known address or, if no address is known, by leaving it with the clerk of the court. Service by mail is complete upon mailing. Delivery of a copy within FL ST J ADMIN Rule 2.516 is complete upon:

- Handing it to the attorney or to the party,
- Leaving it at the attorney's or party's office with a clerk or other person in charge thereof,
- If there is no one in charge, leaving it in a conspicuous place therein,
- If the office is closed or the person to be served has no office, leaving it at the person's usual place of abode with some person of his or her family above fifteen (15) years of age and informing such person of the contents, or
- Transmitting it by facsimile to the attorney's or party's office with a cover sheet containing the sender's name, firm, address, telephone number, and facsimile number, and the number of pages transmitted. When service is made by facsimile, a copy must also be served by any other method permitted by FL ST J ADMIN Rule 2.516. Facsimile service occurs when transmission is complete. FL ST J ADMIN Rule 2.516(b)(2)(A) through FL ST J ADMIN Rule 2.516(b)(2)(E).
- Service by delivery after 5:00 p.m. must be deemed to have been made by mailing on the date of delivery. FL ST J ADMIN Rule 2.516(b)(2)(F).

c. *Service; Numerous defendants.* In actions when the parties are unusually numerous, the court may regulate the service contemplated by the Florida Rules of Judicial Administration on motion or on its own initiative in such manner as may be found to be just and reasonable. FL ST J ADMIN Rule 2.516(c).

d. *Service by clerk.* Service of notices and other documents required to be made by the clerk must also be done as provided in FL ST J ADMIN Rule 2.516(b). FL ST J ADMIN Rule 2.516(g).

G. Hearings

1. The parties may be required to participate in pretrial proceedings to consider and determine the necessity or desirability of an amendment to a pleading. FL ST RCP Rule 1.200(b)(2); FL-PP § 2:151.

H. Forms

1. Official Amended Answer Forms for Florida

a. Caption. FL ST RCP Form 1.901.

b. Notice of compliance when constitutional challenge is brought. FL ST RCP Form 1.975.

2. Amended Answer Forms for Florida

a. Form for amendment to answer. FL-RCPF R 1.190(50).

b. Form for supplement to pleading. FL-RCPF R 1.190(102).

I. Checklist

(I) ❑ Matters to be considered by plaintiff
- (a) ❑ Required documents
  - (1) ❑ Amended answer
  - (2) ❑ Certificate of service
- (b) ❑ Supplemental documents
  - (1) ❑ Exhibits
  - (2) ❑ Notice of constitutional question
- (c) ❑ Timing
  - (1) ❑ A party may amend a pleading once as a matter of course at any time before a responsive pleading is served
  - (2) ❑ If the pleading is one to which no responsive pleading is permitted and the action has not been placed on the trial calendar, may so amend it at any time within twenty (20) days after it is served

Motions, Oppositions and Replies
Motion to Strike

Document Last Updated January 2013

A. Applicable Rules

1. *State rules*
   - a. Rules of court. FL ST RCP Rule 1.010; FL ST J ADMIN Rule 2.110.
   - b. Nonverification of pleadings. FL ST RCP Rule 1.030.
   - c. Service and filing of pleadings, orders, and documents. FL ST RCP Rule 1.080.
   - d. Time. FL ST RCP Rule 1.090.
   - e. Pleadings and motions. FL ST RCP Rule 1.100.
   - f. Defenses. FL ST RCP Rule 1.140.
   - g. Sham pleadings. FL ST RCP Rule 1.150.
   - h. Motions. FL ST RCP Rule 1.160.
   - i. Relief from judgment, decrees, or orders. FL ST RCP Rule 1.540.
   - j. Mediation and arbitration. FL ST RCP Rule 1.700; FL ST RCP Rule 1.710; FL ST RCP Rule 1.720; FL ST RCP Rule 1.730; FL ST RCP Rule 1.750; FL ST RCP Rule 1.800; FL ST RCP Rule 1.810; FL ST RCP Rule 1.820; FL ST RCP Rule 1.830.
   - k. Forms. FL ST RCP Rule 1.900.
   - l. Minimization of the filing of sensitive information. FL ST J ADMIN Rule 2.425.
   - m. Retention of court records. FL ST J ADMIN Rule 2.430.
   - n. Foreign attorneys. FL ST J ADMIN Rule 2.510.
   - o. Signature of attorneys and parties. FL ST J ADMIN Rule 2.515.
   - p. Paper. FL ST J ADMIN Rule 2.520.
   - q. Electronic filing. FL ST J ADMIN Rule 2.525.
   - r. Accessibility of information and technology. FL ST J ADMIN Rule 2.526.
   - s. Communication equipment. FL ST J ADMIN Rule 2.530.

t. Court reporting. FL ST J ADMIN Rule 2.535.

u. Requests for accommodations by persons with disabilities. FL ST J ADMIN Rule 2.540.

2. *Local rules*

a. Sealing court records. FL ST 4 J CIR 2006-05.

B. Timing

1. *Motion to strike.* A party may move to strike or the court may strike redundant, immaterial, impertinent, or scandalous matter from any pleading at any time. FL ST RCP Rule 1.140(f).

2. *Motion to strike; Failure to state a legal defense.* If a pleading sets forth a claim for relief to which the adverse party is not required to serve a responsive pleading, the adverse party may assert any defense in law or fact to that claim for relief at the trial, except that the objection of failure to state a legal defense in an answer or reply shall be asserted by motion to strike the defense within twenty (20) days after service of the answer or reply. FL ST RCP Rule 1.140(b).

3. *Motion to strike; Sham pleadings.* If a party deems any pleading or part thereof filed by another party to be a sham, that party may move to strike the pleading or part thereof before the cause is set for trial. FL ST RCP Rule 1.150(a).

4. *General motion timing.* A copy of any written motion which may not be heard ex parte and a copy of the notice of the hearing thereof shall be served a reasonable time before the time specified for the hearing. FL ST RCP Rule 1.090(d).

5. *Computation of time*

a. *Generally.* Computation of time shall be governed by FL ST J ADMIN Rule 2.514. FL ST RCP Rule 1.090(a). The following rules apply in computing time periods specified in any rule of procedure, local rule, court order, or statute that does not specify a method of computing time. FL ST J ADMIN Rule 2.514(a).

i. *Period stated in days or a longer unit.* When the period is stated in days or a longer unit of time (A) exclude the day of the event that triggers the period; (B) count every day, including intermediate Saturdays, Sundays, and legal holidays; and (C) include the last day of the period, but if the last day is a Saturday, Sunday, or legal holiday, or falls within any period of time extended through an order of the chief justice under FL ST J ADMIN Rule 2.205(a)(2)(B)(iv), the period continues to run until the end of the next day that is not a Saturday, Sunday, or legal holiday and does not fall within any period of time extended through an order of the chief justice. FL ST J ADMIN Rule 2.514(a)(1).

ii. *Period stated in hours.* When the period is stated in hours (A) begin counting immediately on the occurrence of the event that triggers the period; (B) count every hour, including hours during intermediate Saturdays, Sundays, and legal holidays; and (C) if the period would end on a Saturday, Sunday, or legal holiday, or during any period of time extended through an order of the chief justice under FL ST J ADMIN Rule 2.205(a)(2)(B)(iv), the period continues to run until the same time on the next day that is not a Saturday, Sunday, or legal holiday and does not fall within any period of time extended through an order of the chief justice. FL ST J ADMIN Rule 2.514(a)(2).

iii. *Period stated in days less than seven (7) days.* When the period stated in days is less than seven (7) days, intermediate Saturdays, Sundays, and legal holidays shall be excluded in the computation. FL ST J ADMIN Rule 2.514(a)(3).

iv. *"Last day" defined.* Unless a different time is set by a statute, local rule, or court order, the last day ends (A) for electronic filing or for service by any means, at midnight; and (B) for filing by other means, when the clerk's office is scheduled to close. FL ST J ADMIN Rule 2.514(a)(4).

v. *"Next day" defined.* The "next day" is determined by continuing to count forward when the period is measured after an event and backward when measured before an event. FL ST J ADMIN Rule 2.514(a)(5).

vi. *"Legal holiday" defined.* "Legal holiday" means (A) the day set aside by FL ST § 110.117, for

observing New Year's Day, Martin Luther King, Jr.'s Birthday, Memorial Day, Independence Day, Labor Day, Veterans' Day, Thanksgiving Day, the Friday after Thanksgiving Day, or Christmas Day, and (B) any day observed as a holiday by the clerk's office or as designated by the chief judge. FL ST J ADMIN Rule 2.514(a)(6).

b. *Additional time after service by mail or e-mail.* When a party may or must act within a specified time after service and service is made by mail or e-mail, five (5) days are added after the period that would otherwise expire under FL ST J ADMIN Rule 2.514(a). FL ST J ADMIN Rule 2.514(b).

c. *Enlargement.* When an act is required or allowed to be done at or within a specified time by order of court, by the Florida Rules of Civil Procedure, or by notice given thereunder, for cause shown the court at any time in its discretion (1) with or without notice, may order the period enlarged if request therefor is made before the expiration of the period originally prescribed or as extended by a previous order, or (2) upon motion made and notice after the expiration of the specified period, may permit the act to be done when failure to act was the result of excusable neglect, but it may not extend the time for making a motion for new trial, for rehearing, or to alter or amend a judgment; making a motion for relief from a judgment under FL ST RCP Rule 1.540(b); taking an appeal or filing a petition for certiorari; or making a motion for a directed verdict. FL ST RCP Rule 1.090(b).

d. *Unaffected by expiration of term.* The period of time provided for the doing of any act or the taking of any proceeding shall not be affected or limited by the continued existence or expiration of a term of court. The continued existence or expiration of a term of court in no way affects the power of a court to do any act or take any proceeding in any action which is or has been pending before it. FL ST RCP Rule 1.090(c).

C. General Requirements

1. *Motions generally*

   a. *Contents.* An application to the court for an order shall be by motion which shall be made in writing unless made during a hearing or trial, shall state with particularity the grounds therefor, and shall set forth the relief or order sought. The requirement of writing is fulfilled if the motion is stated in a written notice of the hearing of the motion. All notices of hearing shall specify each motion or other matter to be heard. FL ST RCP Rule 1.100(b).

   b. *Particularity requirement.* The court considers a motion in the light of the substantive law, rule or statute to make its determination. Some rules require a statement of the grounds for a motion under the rule. Failure to give the grounds will result in denial of the motion. This should be the result in all situations when the ground for the motion is not inherent in the rule. FL-PRACPROC § 9:3. The requirement is nevertheless an important one, first because of the due process notice rights of the respondent, as well as for the assistance it provides to the court in its preparation for the hearing or, absent a hearing, for disposition. 4 FLPRAC R 1.100.

2. *Motion to strike under FL ST RCP Rule 1.140.* Two (2) types of motion to strike are authorized by FL ST RCP Rule 1.140. One is used to eliminate immaterial, redundant, impertinent or scandalous allegations. The other is used to test the legal sufficiency of a defense. FL-PRACPROC § 10:6.

   a. *Motion to strike to eliminate immaterial, redundant, impertinent or scandalous allegations*

      i. As used in FL ST RCP Rule 1.140(f), redundant means allegations that are foreign to the issues or needless repetition of allegations. Immaterial means allegations having no essential or important relationship to the issues or unnecessary elaboration of material allegations. Impertinent means allegations that do not belong to the issue and are not necessary to it. Scandalous means unnecessary allegations censuring or accusing a party. FL-PRACPROC § 10:6.

      ii. The motion can be made at any time and does not toll the time for pleading. FL-PRACPROC § 10:6.

      iii. The motion reaches improper allegations of damages. When directed to an entire paragraph and any part of it is proper, the motion should be denied. Leave to amend should be granted after striking part of a pleading unless a proper amendment cannot be made. FL-PRACPROC § 10:6.

      iv. The use of a motion to strike is not favored by the courts and the remedy is used sparingly.

Florida courts have held that an allegation must be "wholly irrelevant" and that if there is some doubt it must be resolved in support of the pleading and against the party moving to strike. If any part of an allegation is relevant, then that part should not be stricken from the pleading. 5 FLPRAC § 7:30.

b. *Motion to strike the legal sufficiency of a defense*

   i. The legal insufficiency of a defense alleged in an answer or reply is attacked by a motion to strike. It is the counterpart of a motion to dismiss for failure to state a cause of action directed to a pleading seeking affirmative relief. FL-PRACPROC § 10:7.

   ii. A motion to strike a defense tests only the legal sufficiency of the defense, and it is reversible error for a trial court to strike the defense where evidence may be presented to support it. Burns v. Equilease Corp., 357 So.2d 786, 24, 24 U.C.C. Rep.Serv. 254 (Fla. 3d DCA 1978); 20 FLPRAC § 3:15.

3. *Sham pleadings.* If a party deems any pleading or part thereof filed by another party to be a sham, that party may move to strike the pleading or part thereof before the cause is set for trial and the court shall hear the motion, taking evidence of the respective parties, and if the motion is sustained, the pleading to which the motion is directed shall be stricken. Default and summary judgment on the merits may be entered in the discretion of the court or the court may permit additional pleadings to be filed for good cause shown. FL ST RCP Rule 1.150(a).

   a. *Contents of motion.* The motion to strike shall be verified and shall set forth fully the facts on which the movant relies and may be supported by affidavit. No traverse of the motion shall be required. FL ST RCP Rule 1.150(b).

   b. *Allegations supported by evidence.* The issue is not whether the allegations are material or proper, but whether the allegations are supported by evidence. 5 FLPRAC § 7:30.

4. *Arbitration and mediation*

   a. *Referral to arbitration and mediation.* Except as hereinafter provided or as otherwise prohibited by law, the presiding judge may enter an order referring all or any part of a contested civil matter to mediation or arbitration. The parties to any contested civil matter may file a written stipulation to mediate or arbitrate any issue between them at any time. Such stipulation shall be incorporated into the order of referral. FL ST RCP Rule 1.700(a).

   b. *Arbitration*

      i. *Exclusions.* A civil action shall be ordered to arbitration or arbitration in conjunction with mediation upon stipulation of the parties. A civil action may be ordered to arbitration or arbitration in conjunction with mediation upon motion of any party or by the court, if the judge determines the action to be of such a nature that arbitration could be of benefit to the litigants or the court. FL ST RCP Rule 1.800.

         - Under no circumstances may the following categories of actions be referred to arbitration: (1) bond estreatures; (2) habeas corpus or other extraordinary writs; (3) bond validations; (4) civil or criminal contempt; (5) such other matters as may be specified by order of the chief judge in the circuit. FL ST RCP Rule 1.800.

      ii. For more information regarding arbitration, please see FL ST RCP Rule 1.810; FL ST RCP Rule 1.820; FL ST RCP Rule 1.830.

   c. *Mediation.* For more information regarding mediation, please see FL ST RCP Rule 1.710; FL ST RCP Rule 1.720; FL ST RCP Rule 1.730; and FL ST RCP Rule 1.750.

5. *Rules of court*

   a. *Rules of civil procedure.* The Florida Rules of Civil Procedure apply to all actions of a civil nature and all special statutory proceedings in the circuit courts and county courts except those to which the Florida Probate Rules, the Florida Family Law Rules of Procedure, or the Small Claims Rules apply. FL ST RCP Rule 1.010.

      i. The form, content, procedure, and time for pleading in all special statutory proceedings shall be

as prescribed by the statutes governing the proceeding unless the Florida Rules of Civil Procedure specifically provide to the contrary. FL ST RCP Rule 1.010.

ii. The Florida Rules of Civil Procedure shall be construed to secure the just, speedy, and inexpensive determination of every action. FL ST RCP Rule 1.010.

b. *Rules of judicial administration.* The Florida Rules of Judicial Administration shall apply to administrative matters in all courts to which the Florida Rules of Judicial Administration are applicable by their terms. The Florida Rules of Judicial Administration shall be construed to secure the speedy and inexpensive determination of every proceeding to which they are applicable. The Florida Rules of Judicial Administration shall supersede all conflicting rules and statutes. FL ST J ADMIN Rule 2.110.

D. Documents

1. *Required documents*

a. *Notice of hearing/Motion.* An application to the court for an order shall be by motion which shall be made in writing unless made during a hearing or trial, shall state with particularity the grounds therefor, and shall set forth the relief or order sought. The requirement of writing is fulfilled if the motion is stated in a written notice of the hearing of the motion. All notices of hearing shall specify each motion or other matter to be heard. FL ST RCP Rule 1.100(b).

i. *Notices to persons with disabilities.* See the Format section of this KeyRules document for further information.

b. *Certificate of service.* When any attorney certifies in substance: "I certify that a copy hereof has been furnished to (here insert name or names and addresses used for service) by (e-mail) (delivery) (mail) (fax) on .... (date) ....________________ Attorney" the certificate is taken as prima facie proof of such service in compliance with FL ST J ADMIN Rule 2.516. FL ST J ADMIN Rule 2.516(f).

2. *Supplemental documents*

a. *Proposed order.* The court may require that orders or judgments be prepared by a party, may require the party to furnish the court with stamped, addressed envelopes for service of the order or judgment, and may require that proposed orders and judgments be furnished to all parties before entry by the court of the order or judgment. FL ST J ADMIN Rule 2.516(h)(1).

b. *Notice of constitutional question.* A party that files a pleading, written motion, or other paper drawing into question the constitutionality of a state statute or a county or municipal charter, ordinance, or franchise must promptly (1) file a notice of constitutional question stating the question and identifying the paper that raises it; and (2) serve the notice and the pleading, written motion, or other paper drawing into question the constitutionality of a state statute or a county or municipal charter, ordinance, or franchise on the Attorney General or the state attorney of the judicial circuit in which the action is pending, by either certified or registered mail. Service of the notice and pleading, written motion, or other paper does not require joinder of the Attorney General or the state attorney as a party to the action. FL ST RCP Rule 1.071.

E. Format

1. *Documents; Type and size.* Documents subject to the exceptions set forth in FL ST J ADMIN Rule 2.525(d) shall be filed on recycled paper measuring eight and one half by eleven (8 1/2 by 11) inches. For purposes of FL ST J ADMIN Rule 2.520, paper is recycled if it contains a minimum content of fifty (50) percent waste paper. Xerographic reduction of legal-size (eight and one half by fourteen (8 1/2 by 14) inches) documents to letter size (eight and one half by eleven (8 1/2 by 11) inches) is prohibited. All other documents filed by electronic transmission shall be filed in a format capable of being printed in a format consistent with the provisions of FL ST J ADMIN Rule 2.250. FL ST J ADMIN Rule 2.520(b).

a. *Exhibits.* Any exhibit or attachment filed with pleadings or papers may be filed in its original size. FL ST J ADMIN Rule 2.520(c).

b. *Recording space.* On all papers and documents prepared and filed by the court or by any party to a proceeding which are to be recorded in the public records of any county, including but not limited to final money judgments and notices of lis pendens, a three (3) inch by three (3) inch space at the top right-hand corner on the first page and a one (1) inch by three (3) inch space at the top right-hand corner on each subsequent page shall be left blank and reserved for use by the clerk of court. FL ST J ADMIN Rule 2.520(d).

i. *Exceptions to recording space.* Any papers or documents created by persons or entities over which the filing party has no control, including but not limited to wills, codicils, trusts, or other testamentary documents; documents prepared or executed by any public officer; documents prepared, executed, acknowledged, or proved outside of the State of Florida; or documents created by State or Federal government agencies, may be filed without the space required by FL ST J ADMIN Rule 2.520. FL ST J ADMIN Rule 2.520(e).

c. *Noncompliance.* No clerk of court is permitted to refuse to file any document or paper because of noncompliance with the Florida Rules of Judicial Administration. However, upon request of the clerk of court, noncomplying documents must be resubmitted in accordance with the formatting rules. FL ST J ADMIN Rule 2.520(f).

2. *Caption.* Every pleading, motion, order, judgment, or other paper shall have a caption containing the name of the court, the file number, and except for in rem proceedings, including forfeiture proceedings, the name of the first party on each side with an appropriate indication of other parties, and a designation identifying the party filing it and its nature or the nature of the order, as the case may be. In any in rem proceeding, every pleading, motion, order, judgment, or other paper shall have a caption containing the name of the court, the file number, the style "In re" (followed by the name or general description of the property), and a designation of the person or entity filing it and its nature or the nature of the order, as the case may be. In an in rem forfeiture proceeding, the style shall be "In re forfeiture of" (followed by the name of the general description of the property). All papers filed in the action shall be styled in such a manner as to indicate clearly the subject matter of the paper and the party requesting or obtaining relief. FL ST RCP Rule 1.100(c)(1).

3. *Writing and written defined.* Writing or written means a document containing information, an application, or a stipulation. FL ST RCP Rule 1.080(c).

4. *Rule abbreviations*

   a. The Florida Rules of Civil Procedure and shall be abbreviated as Fla.R.Civ.P. FL ST RCP Rule 1.010.

   b. The Florida Rules of Judicial Administration shall be abbreviated as Fla. R. Jud. Admin. FL ST J ADMIN Rule 2.110.

5. *Nonverification.* Except when otherwise specifically provided by the Florida Rules of Civil Procedure or an applicable statute, every pleading or other document of a party represented by an attorney need not be verified or accompanied by an affidavit. FL ST RCP Rule 1.030; FL ST J ADMIN Rule 2.515(a).

6. *Attorney signature*

   a. *Attorney signature.* Every pleading and other document of a party represented by an attorney shall be signed by at least one (1) attorney of record in that attorney's individual name whose current record Florida Bar address, telephone number, including area code, primary e-mail address and secondary e-mail addresses, if any, and Florida Bar number shall be stated, and who shall be duly licensed to practice law in Florida or who shall have received permission to appear in the particular case as provided in FL ST J ADMIN Rule 2.510. FL ST J ADMIN Rule 2.515(a).

      i. The attorney may be required by the court to give the address of, and to vouch for the attorney's authority to represent, the party. FL ST J ADMIN Rule 2.515(a).

      ii. The signature of an attorney shall constitute a certificate by the attorney that the attorney has read the pleading or other document; that to the best of the attorney's knowledge, information, and belief there is good ground to support it; and that it is not interposed for delay. FL ST J ADMIN Rule 2.515(a).

      iii. If a pleading is not signed or is signed with intent to defeat the purpose of FL ST J ADMIN Rule 2.515, it may be stricken and the action may proceed as though the pleading or other document had not been served. FL ST J ADMIN Rule 2.515(a).

b. *Pro se litigant signature.* A party who is not represented by an attorney shall sign any pleading or other paper and state the party's address and telephone number, including area code. FL ST J ADMIN Rule 2.515(b).

c. *Form of signature*

i. The signatures required on pleadings and documents by FL ST J ADMIN Rule 2.515(a) and FL ST J ADMIN Rule 2.515(b) may be:

- Original signatures;
- Original signatures that have been reproduced by electronic means, such as on electronically transmitted documents or photocopied documents;
- Electronic signatures using the "/s/," "s/," or "/s" formats by or at the direction of the person signing; or
- Any other signature format authorized by general law, so long as the clerk where the proceeding is pending has the capability of receiving and has obtained approval from the Supreme Court of Florida to accept pleadings and documents with that signature format. FL ST J ADMIN Rule 2.515(c)(1).

ii. An attorney, party, or other person who files a pleading or paper by electronic transmission that does not contain the original signature of that attorney, party, or other person shall file that identical pleading or paper in paper form containing an original signature of that attorney, party, or other person (hereinafter called the follow-up filing) immediately thereafter. The follow-up filing is not required if the Supreme Court of Florida has entered an order directing the clerk of court to discontinue accepting the follow-up filing. FL ST J ADMIN Rule 2.515(c)(2).

7. *Forms*

a. *Process.* The forms of process, notice of lis pendens, and notice of action provided in the Florida Rules of Civil Procedure are sufficient. Variations from the forms do not void process or notices that are otherwise sufficient. FL ST RCP Rule 1.900(a).

b. *Other forms.* The other forms provided in the Florida Rules of Civil Procedure are sufficient for the matters that are covered by them. So long as the substance is expressed without prolixity, the forms may be varied to meet the facts of a particular case. FL ST RCP Rule 1.900(b).

c. *Formal matters.* Captions, except for the designation of the paper, are omitted from the forms provided in the Florida Rules of Civil Procedure. A general form of caption is the first form provided. Signatures are omitted from pleadings and motions. FL ST RCP Rule 1.900(c).

8. *Notices to persons with disabilities.* All notices of court proceedings to be held in a public facility, and all process compelling appearance at such proceedings, shall include the following statement in bold face, fourteen (14) point Times New Roman or Courier font: "If you are a person with a disability who needs any accommodation in order to participate in this proceeding, you are entitled, at no cost to you, to the provision of certain assistance. Please contact [identify applicable court personnel by name, address, and telephone number] at least seven (7) days before your scheduled court appearance, or immediately upon receiving this notification if the time before the scheduled appearance is less than seven (7) days; if you are hearing or voice impaired, call 711." FL ST J ADMIN Rule 2.540(c)(1).

9. *Minimization of the filing of sensitive information*

a. *Limitations for court filings.* Unless authorized by FL ST J ADMIN Rule 2.425(b), statute, another rule of court, or the court orders otherwise, designated sensitive information filed with the court must be limited to the following format:

i. The initials of a person known to be a minor;

ii. The year of birth of a person's birth date;

iii. No portion of any: Social security number, Bank account number, Credit card account number, Charge account number, or Debit account number;

iv. The last four digits of any: Taxpayer identification number (TIN), Employee identification number, Driver's license number, Passport number, Telephone number, Financial account

number, except as set forth in FL ST J ADMIN Rule 2.425(a)(3), Brokerage account number, Insurance policy account number, Loan account number, Customer account number, or Patient or health care number;

v. A truncated version of any: Email address, Computer user name, Password, or Personal identification number (PIN); and

vi. A truncated version of any other sensitive information as provided by court order. FL ST J ADMIN Rule 2.425(a).

b. *Exceptions.* FL ST J ADMIN Rule 2.425(a) does not apply to the following:

i. An account number which identifies the property alleged to be the subject of a proceeding;

ii. The record of an administrative or agency proceeding;

iii. The record in appellate or review proceedings;

iv. The birth date of a minor whenever the birth date is necessary for the court to establish or maintain subject matter jurisdiction;

v. The name of a minor in any order relating to parental responsibility, time-sharing, or child support;

vi. The name of a minor in any document or order affecting the minor's ownership of real property;

vii. The birth date of a party in a writ of attachment or notice to payor;

viii. In traffic and criminal proceedings: a pro se filing; a court filing that is related to a criminal matter or investigation and that is prepared before the filing of a criminal charge or is not filed as part of any docketed criminal case; an arrest or search warrant or any information in support thereof; a charging document and an affidavit or other documents filed in support of any charging document, including any driving records; a statement of particulars; discovery material introduced into evidence or otherwise filed with the court; and all information necessary for the proper issuance and execution of a subpoena duces tecum;

ix. Information used by the clerk for case maintenance purposes or the courts for case management purposes; and

x. Information which is relevant and material to an issue before the court. FL ST J ADMIN Rule 2.425(b).

c. *Remedies.* Upon motion by a party or interested person or sua sponte by the court, the court may order remedies, sanctions or both for a violation of FL ST J ADMIN Rule 2.425(a). Following notice and an opportunity to respond, the court may impose sanctions if such filing was not made in good faith. FL ST J ADMIN Rule 2.425(c).

d. *Motions not restricted.* FL ST J ADMIN Rule 2.425 does not restrict a party's right to move for protective order, to move to file documents under seal, or to request a determination of the confidentiality of records. FL ST J ADMIN Rule 2.425(d).

i. For more information regarding sealing court records, please see FL ST 4 J CIR 2006-05.

e. *Application.* FL ST J ADMIN Rule 2.425 does not affect the application of constitutional provisions, statutes, or rules of court regarding confidential information or access to public information. FL ST J ADMIN Rule 2.425(e).

F. Filing and Service Requirements

1. *Filing requirements.* All original documents must be filed with the court either before service or immediately thereafter, unless otherwise provided for by general law or other rules. If the original of any bond or other document is not placed in the court file, a certified copy must be so placed by the clerk. FL ST J ADMIN Rule 2.516(d). All documents shall be filed in conformity with the requirements of FL ST J ADMIN Rule 2.525. FL ST RCP Rule 1.080(b). All documents filed in any court shall be filed by electronic transmission in accordance with FL ST J ADMIN Rule 2.525. "Documents" means pleadings, motions, petitions, memoranda, briefs, notices, exhibits, declarations, affidavits, orders, judgments, decrees, writs, opinions, and any other paper or writing submitted to a court. FL ST J ADMIN Rule

2.520(a). All documents that are court records, as defined in FL ST J ADMIN Rule 2.430(a)(1), must be filed by electronic transmission, provided that: (1) the clerk has the ability to accept and retain such documents; (2) the clerk or the chief judge of the circuit has requested permission to accept documents filed by electronic transmission; and (3) the supreme court has entered an order granting permission to the clerk to accept documents filed by electronic transmission. FL ST J ADMIN Rule 2.525(c)(1).

a. *Definition.* "Electronic transmission of documents" means the sending of information by electronic signals to, by or from a court or clerk, which when received can be transformed and stored or transmitted on paper, microfilm, magnetic storage device, optical imaging system, CD-ROM, flash drive, other electronic data storage system, server, case maintenance system ("CM"), electronic court filing ("ECF") system, statewide or local electronic portal ("e-portal"), or other electronic record keeping system authorized by the supreme court in a format sufficient to communicate the information on the original document in a readable format. Electronic transmission of documents includes electronic mail ("e-mail") and any internet-based transmission procedure, and may include procedures allowing for documents to be signed or verified by electronic means. FL ST J ADMIN Rule 2.525(a).

   i. The filing of documents with the court as required by the Florida Rules of Judicial Administration must be made by filing them with the clerk in accordance with FL ST J ADMIN Rule 2.525, except that the judge may permit documents to be filed with the judge, in which event the judge must note the filing date before him or her on the documents and transmit them to the clerk. The date of filing is that shown on the face of the document by the judge's notation or the clerk's time stamp, whichever is earlier. FL ST J ADMIN Rule 2.516(e).

b. *Application.* Any court or clerk of the court may accept the electronic transmission of documents for filing after the clerk, together with input from the chief judge of the circuit, has obtained approval of the procedures and program for doing so from the Supreme Court of Florida. FL ST J ADMIN Rule 2.525(b).

c. *Exceptions*

   i. Paper documents and other submissions may be manually submitted to the clerk or court:

      - When the clerk does not have the ability to accept and retain documents by electronic filing or has not had ECF Procedures approved by the supreme court;
      - For filing by any self-represented party or any self-represented nonparty unless specific ECF Procedures provide a means to file documents electronically. However, any self-represented nonparty that is a governmental or public agency and any other agency, partnership, corporation, or business entity acting on behalf of any governmental or public agency may file documents by electronic transmission if such entity has the capability of filing documents electronically;
      - For filing by attorneys excused from e-mail service in accordance with FL ST J ADMIN Rule 2.516(b);
      - When submitting evidentiary exhibits or filing non-documentary materials;
      - When the filing involves documents in excess of twenty-five (25) megabytes (25MB) in size. For such filings, documents may be transmitted using an electronic storage medium that the clerk has the ability to accept, which may include a CD-ROM, flash drive, or similar storage medium;
      - When filed in open court, as permitted by the court;
      - When paper filing is permitted by any approved statewide or local ECF procedures; and
      - If any court determines that justice so requires. FL ST J ADMIN Rule 2.525(d).

   ii. Any document in paper form submitted under FL ST J ADMIN Rule 2.525(d) is filed when it is received by the clerk or court and the clerk shall immediately thereafter convert any filed paper document to an electronic document. "Convert to an electronic document" means optically capturing an image of a paper document and using character recognition software to recover as much of the document's text as practicable and then indexing and storing the document in the official court file. FL ST J ADMIN Rule 2.525(c)(4).

iii. Any storage medium submitted under FL ST J ADMIN Rule 2.525(d)(5) is filed when received by the clerk or court and the clerk shall immediately thereafter transfer the electronic documents from the storage device to the official court file. FL ST J ADMIN Rule 2.525(c)(5).

iv. If the filer of any paper document authorized under FL ST J ADMIN Rule 2.525(d) provides a self-addressed, postage-paid envelope for return of the paper document after it is converted to electronic form by the clerk, the clerk shall place the paper document in the envelope and deposit it in the mail. Except when a paper document is required to be maintained, the clerk may recycle any filed paper document that is not to be returned to the filer. FL ST J ADMIN Rule 2.525(c)(6).

v. The clerk may convert any paper document filed before the effective date of FL ST J ADMIN Rule 2.525 to an electronic document. Unless the clerk is required to maintain the paper document, if the paper document has been converted to an electronic document by the clerk, the paper document is no longer part of the official court file and may be removed and recycled. FL ST J ADMIN Rule 2.525(c)(7).

d. *Official court file.* For information on what constitutes the official court file, please see FL ST J ADMIN Rule 2.525(c)(2), FL ST J ADMIN Rule 2.525(c)(3).

e. *Administration.* All attorneys, parties, or other persons using this rule to file documents are required to make arrangements with the court or clerk for the payment of any charges authorized by general law or the supreme court before filing any document by electronic transmission. FL ST J ADMIN Rule 2.525(f)(2).

f. *Filing date.* The filing date for an electronically transmitted document is the date and time that such filing is acknowledged by an electronic stamp or otherwise, pursuant to any procedure set forth in any ECF Procedures approved by the supreme court, or the date the last page of such filing is received by the court or clerk. FL ST J ADMIN Rule 2.525(f)(3).

g. *Accessibility.* All documents transmitted in any electronic form under FL ST J ADMIN Rule 2.525 must comply with the accessibility requirements of FL ST J ADMIN Rule 2.526. FL ST J ADMIN Rule 2.525(g).

2. *Service requirements.* Every pleading subsequent to the initial pleading, all orders, and every other document filed in the action must be served in conformity with the requirements of FL ST J ADMIN Rule 2.516. FL ST RCP Rule 1.080(a).

a. *Service; When required.* Unless the court otherwise orders, or a statute or supreme court administrative order specifies a different means of service, every pleading subsequent to the initial pleading and every other document filed in any court proceeding, except applications for witness subpoenas and documents served by formal notice or required to be served in the manner provided for service of formal notice, must be served in accordance with FL ST J ADMIN Rule 2.516 on each party. No service need be made on parties against whom a default has been entered, except that pleadings asserting new or additional claims against them must be served in the manner provided for service of summons. FL ST J ADMIN Rule 2.516(a).

b. *Service; How made.* When service is required or permitted to be made upon a party represented by an attorney, service must be made upon the attorney unless service upon the party is ordered by the court. FL ST J ADMIN Rule 2.516(b).

i. *Service by electronic mail ("e-mail").* All documents required or permitted to be served on another party must be served by e-mail, unless FL ST J ADMIN Rule 2.516 otherwise provides. When, in addition to service by e-mail, the sender also utilizes another means of service provided for in FL ST J ADMIN Rule 2.516(b)(2), any differing time limits and other provisions applicable to that other means of service control. FL ST J ADMIN Rule 2.516(b)(1). Any document electronically transmitted to a court or clerk must also be served on all parties and interested persons in accordance with the applicable rules of court. FL ST J ADMIN Rule 2.525(e)(2).

- *Service on attorneys.* Upon appearing in a proceeding, an attorney must serve a designation of a primary e-mail address and may designate no more than two (2) secondary e-mail

addresses. Thereafter, service must be directed to all designated e-mail addresses in that proceeding. Every document filed by an attorney thereafter must include the primary e-mail address of that attorney and any secondary e-mail addresses. If an attorney does not designate any e-mail address for service, documents may be served on that attorney at the e-mail address on record with The Florida Bar. FL ST J ADMIN Rule 2.516(b)(1)(A).

- *Exception to e-mail service on attorneys.* Service by an attorney on another attorney must be made by e-mail unless excused by the court. Upon motion by an attorney demonstrating that the attorney has no e-mail account and lacks access to the Internet at the attorney's office, the court may excuse the attorney from the requirements of e-mail service. Service on and by an attorney excused by the court from e-mail service must be by the means provided in FL ST J ADMIN Rule 2.516(b)(2). FL ST J ADMIN Rule 2.516(b)(1)(B).
- *Service on and by parties not represented by an attorney.* Any party not represented by an attorney may serve a designation of a primary e-mail address and also may designate no more than two (2) secondary e-mail addresses to which service must be directed in that proceeding by the means provided in FL ST J ADMIN Rule 2.516(b)(1). If a party not represented by an attorney does not designate an e-mail address for service in a proceeding, service on and by that party must be by the means provided in FL ST J ADMIN Rule 2.516(b)(2). FL ST J ADMIN Rule 2.516(b)(1)(C).
- *Time of service.* Service by e-mail is complete when it is sent. FL ST J ADMIN Rule 2.516(b)(1)(D). An e-mail is deemed served on the date it is sent. FL ST J ADMIN Rule 2.516(b)(1)(D)(i). If the sender learns that the e-mail did not reach the address of the person to be served, the sender must immediately send another copy by e-mail, or by a means authorized by FL ST J ADMIN Rule 2.516(b)(2). FL ST J ADMIN Rule 2.516(b)(1)(D)(ii). E-mail service is treated as service by mail for the computation of time. FL ST J ADMIN Rule 2.516(b)(1)(D)(iii).

ii. *Format of e-mail for service.* Service of a document by e-mail is made by attaching a copy of the document in PDF format to an e-mail sent to all addresses designated by the attorney or party. FL ST J ADMIN Rule 2.516(b)(1)(E).

- All documents served by e-mail must be attached to an e-mail message containing a subject line beginning with the words "SERVICE OF COURT DOCUMENT" in all capital letters, followed by the case number of the proceeding in which the documents are being served. FL ST J ADMIN Rule 2.516(b)(1)(E)(i).
- The body of the e-mail must identify the court in which the proceeding is pending, the case number, the name of the initial party on each side, the title of each document served with that e-mail, and the sender's name and telephone number. FL ST J ADMIN Rule 2.516(b)(1)(E)(ii).
- Any document served by e-mail may be signed by the "/s/" format, as long as the filed original is signed in accordance with the applicable rule of procedure. FL ST J ADMIN Rule 2.516(b)(1)(E)(iii).
- Any e-mail which, together with its attached documents, exceeds five megabytes (5MB) in size, must be divided and sent as separate e-mails, no one of which may exceed five megabytes (5MB) in size and each of which must be sequentially numbered in the subject line. FL ST J ADMIN Rule 2.516(b)(1)(E)(iv).

iii. *Service by other means.* In addition to, and not in lieu of, service by e-mail, service may also be made upon attorneys by any of the means specified in FL ST J ADMIN Rule 2.516(b)(2). Service on and by all parties who are not represented by an attorney and who do not designate an e-mail address, and on and by all attorneys excused from e-mail service, must be made by delivering a copy of the document or by mailing it to the party or attorney at their last known address or, if no address is known, by leaving it with the clerk of the court. Service by mail is complete upon mailing. Delivery of a copy within FL ST J ADMIN Rule 2.516 is complete upon:

- Handing it to the attorney or to the party,

- Leaving it at the attorney's or party's office with a clerk or other person in charge thereof,
- If there is no one in charge, leaving it in a conspicuous place therein,
- If the office is closed or the person to be served has no office, leaving it at the person's usual place of abode with some person of his or her family above fifteen (15) years of age and informing such person of the contents, or
- Transmitting it by facsimile to the attorney's or party's office with a cover sheet containing the sender's name, firm, address, telephone number, and facsimile number, and the number of pages transmitted. When service is made by facsimile, a copy must also be served by any other method permitted by FL ST J ADMIN Rule 2.516. Facsimile service occurs when transmission is complete. FL ST J ADMIN Rule 2.516(b)(2)(A) through FL ST J ADMIN Rule 2.516(b)(2)(E).
- Service by delivery after 5:00 p.m. must be deemed to have been made by mailing on the date of delivery. FL ST J ADMIN Rule 2.516(b)(2)(F).

c. *Service; Numerous defendants.* In actions when the parties are unusually numerous, the court may regulate the service contemplated by the Florida Rules of Judicial Administration on motion or on its own initiative in such manner as may be found to be just and reasonable. FL ST J ADMIN Rule 2.516(c).

d. *Service by clerk.* Service of notices and other documents required to be made by the clerk must also be done as provided in FL ST J ADMIN Rule 2.516(b). FL ST J ADMIN Rule 2.516(g).

G. Hearings

1. *Communication equipment*

a. *Definition.* Communication equipment means a conference telephone or other electronic device that permits all those appearing or participating to hear and speak to each other, provided that all conversation of all parties is audible to all persons present. FL ST J ADMIN Rule 2.530(a).

b. *Use by all parties.* A county or circuit court judge may, upon the court's own motion or upon the written request of a party, direct that communication equipment be used for a motion hearing, pretrial conference, or a status conference. A judge must give notice to the parties and consider any objections they may have to the use of communication equipment before directing that communication equipment be used. The decision to use communication equipment over the objection of parties will be in the sound discretion of the trial court, except as noted below. FL ST J ADMIN Rule 2.530(b).

c. *Use only by requesting party.* A county or circuit court judge may, upon the written request of a party upon reasonable notice to all other parties, permit a requesting party to participate through communication equipment in a scheduled motion hearing; however, any such request (except in criminal, juvenile, and appellate proceedings) must be granted, absent a showing of good cause to deny the same, where the hearing is set for not longer than fifteen (15) minutes. FL ST J ADMIN Rule 2.530(c).

d. *Testimony*

i. *Generally.* A county or circuit court judge, general magistrate, special magistrate, or hearing officer may allow testimony to be taken through communication equipment if all parties consent or if permitted by another applicable rule of procedure. FL ST J ADMIN Rule 2.530(d)(1).

ii. *Procedure.* Any party desiring to present testimony through communication equipment shall, prior to the hearing or trial at which the testimony is to be presented, contact all parties to determine whether each party consents to this form of testimony. The party seeking to present the testimony shall move for permission to present testimony through communication equipment, which motion shall set forth good cause as to why the testimony should be allowed in this form. FL ST J ADMIN Rule 2.530(d)(2).

iii. *Oath.* Testimony may be taken through communication equipment only if a notary public or other person authorized to administer oaths in the witness's jurisdiction is present with the witness and administers the oath consistent with the laws of the jurisdiction. FL ST J ADMIN Rule 2.530(d)(3).

iv. *Confrontation rights.* In juvenile and criminal proceedings the defendant must make an informed waiver of any confrontation rights that may be abridged by the use of communication equipment. FL ST J ADMIN Rule 2.530(d)(4).

v. *Video testimony.* If the testimony to be presented utilizes video conferencing or comparable two-way visual capabilities, the court in its discretion may modify the procedures set forth in FL ST J ADMIN Rule 2.530 to accommodate the technology utilized. FL ST J ADMIN Rule 2.530(d)(5).

e. *Burden of expense.* The cost for the use of the communication equipment is the responsibility of the requesting party unless otherwise directed by the court. FL ST J ADMIN Rule 2.530(e).

H. Forms

1. Official Motion to Strike Forms for Florida

a. Caption. FL ST RCP Form 1.901.

b. Notice of compliance when constitutional challenge is brought. FL ST RCP Form 1.975.

2. Motion to Strike Forms for Florida

a. Motion to strike. FL-PP § 2:128.

b. Form for motion to strike. FL-RCPF R 1.140(802).

c. Form for motion to strike insufficient pleading. FL-RCPF R 1.140(803).

d. Form for motion to strike claim for business or financial losses. FL-RCPF R 1.140(804).

e. Motion; Strike, complaint signed by corporation. FL-PRACFORM § 7:176.

f. Motion; Strike, defenses. FL-PRACFORM § 7:177.

g. Motion; Strike, ejectment chain of title. FL-PRACFORM § 7:178.

h. Motion; Strike, pleading, departure. FL-PRACFORM § 7:180.

i. Motion; Strike, pleading, improper signature. FL-PRACFORM § 7:181.

j. Motion; Strike, sham pleading. FL-PRACFORM § 7:182.

k. Motion; Strike, sham, defenses, statute of limitations and failure of consideration. FL-PRACFORM § 7:183.

l. Motion; Strike, third party complaint. FL-PRACFORM § 7:184.

I. Checklist

(I) ❑ Matters to be considered by moving party

(a) ❑ Required documents

(1) ❑ Notice of hearing/Motion

(2) ❑ Certificate of service

(b) ❑ Supplemental documents

(1) ❑ Proposed order

(2) ❑ Notice of constitutional question

(c) ❑ Time for making motion

(1) ❑ A party may move to strike or the court may strike redundant, immaterial, impertinent, or scandalous matter from any pleading at any time

(2) ❑ If a pleading sets forth a claim for relief to which the adverse party is not required to serve a responsive pleading, the adverse party may assert any defense in law or fact to that claim for relief at the trial, except that the objection of failure to state a legal defense in an answer or reply shall be asserted by motion to strike the defense within twenty (20) days after service of the answer or reply

(3) ❑ If a party deems any pleading or part thereof filed by another party to be a sham, that party may move to strike the pleading or part thereof before the cause is set for trial

(4) ❑ A copy of any written motion which may not be heard ex parte and a copy of the notice of the hearing thereof shall be served a reasonable time before the time specified for the hearing

(II) ❑ Matters to be considered by opposing party

(a) ❑ Required documents

(1) ❑ Response to motion

(2) ❑ Certificate of service

(b) ❑ Supplemental documents

(1) ❑ Proposed order

(2) ❑ Notice of constitutional question

(c) ❑ Time for service and filing of opposition

(1) ❑ No time specified for responding to a motion

Motions, Oppositions and Replies
Motion for Leave to Amend

Document Last Updated January 2013

A. Applicable Rules

1. *State rules*

a. Rules of court. FL ST RCP Rule 1.010; FL ST J ADMIN Rule 2.110.

b. Nonverification of pleadings. FL ST RCP Rule 1.030.

c. Process. FL ST RCP Rule 1.070.

d. Service and filing of pleadings, orders, and documents. FL ST RCP Rule 1.080.

e. Time. FL ST RCP Rule 1.090.

f. Pleadings and motions. FL ST RCP Rule 1.100.

g. Defenses. FL ST RCP Rule 1.140.

h. Motions. FL ST RCP Rule 1.160.

i. Amended and supplemental pleadings. FL ST RCP Rule 1.190.

j. Relief from judgment, decrees, or orders. FL ST RCP Rule 1.540.

k. Mediation and arbitration. FL ST RCP Rule 1.700; FL ST RCP Rule 1.710; FL ST RCP Rule 1.720; FL ST RCP Rule 1.730; FL ST RCP Rule 1.750; FL ST RCP Rule 1.800; FL ST RCP Rule 1.810; FL ST RCP Rule 1.820; FL ST RCP Rule 1.830.

l. Forms. FL ST RCP Rule 1.900.

m. Minimization of the filing of sensitive information. FL ST J ADMIN Rule 2.425.

n. Retention of court records. FL ST J ADMIN Rule 2.430.

o. Foreign attorneys. FL ST J ADMIN Rule 2.510.

p. Signature of attorneys and parties. FL ST J ADMIN Rule 2.515.

q. Paper. FL ST J ADMIN Rule 2.520.

r. Electronic filing. FL ST J ADMIN Rule 2.525.

s. Accessibility of information and technology. FL ST J ADMIN Rule 2.526.

t. Communication equipment. FL ST J ADMIN Rule 2.530.

u. Court reporting. FL ST J ADMIN Rule 2.535.

v. Requests for accommodations by persons with disabilities. FL ST J ADMIN Rule 2.540.

2. *Local rules*

a. Sealing court records. FL ST 4 J CIR 2006-05.

B. Timing

1. *Amended pleadings as a matter of course.* A party may amend a pleading once as a matter of course at any time before a responsive pleading is served or, if the pleading is one to which no responsive pleading is permitted and the action has not been placed on the trial calendar, may amend it at any time within twenty (20) days after it is served. Otherwise a party may amend a pleading only by leave of court or by written consent of the adverse party. FL ST RCP Rule 1.190(a).

2. *Amended pleadings with leave of court.* Leave of court shall be given freely when justice so requires. FL ST RCP Rule 1.190(a). Under the Florida Rules of Civil Procedure, there is no time limit as to when an amendment with leave of court may be sought. Amendments of the pleadings may be permitted, with the court's discretion, at any stage of the proceedings in furtherance of justice. McSwiggan v. Edson, 186 So.2d 13, 15 (Fla. 1966); FL-PP § 2:153. Nevertheless, the liberality in permitting amendment of pleadings diminishes as the case progresses to trial. Versen v. Versen, 347 So.2d 1047, 1050 (Fla. 4th DCA 1977); FL-PP § 2:153.

3. *Claims for punitive damages.* A motion for leave to amend a pleading to assert a claim for punitive damages can be filed separately and before the supporting evidence or proffer, but each shall be served on all parties at least twenty (20) days before the hearing. FL ST RCP Rule 1.190(f).

4. *Post motion for leave to amend*

a. If the court permits or requires an amended or responsive pleading or a more definite statement, the pleading or statement shall be served within ten (10) days after notice of the court's action. FL ST RCP Rule 1.140(a)(4).

b. When a motion for leave to amend with the attached proposed amended complaint is filed, the one hundred twenty (120) day period for service of amended complaints on the new party or parties shall begin upon the entry of an order granting leave to amend. FL ST RCP Rule 1.070(j).

5. *General motion timing.* A copy of any written motion which may not be heard ex parte and a copy of the notice of the hearing thereof shall be served a reasonable time before the time specified for the hearing. FL ST RCP Rule 1.090(d).

6. *Computation of time*

a. *Generally.* Computation of time shall be governed by FL ST J ADMIN Rule 2.514. FL ST RCP Rule 1.090(a). The following rules apply in computing time periods specified in any rule of procedure, local rule, court order, or statute that does not specify a method of computing time. FL ST J ADMIN Rule 2.514(a).

i. *Period stated in days or a longer unit.* When the period is stated in days or a longer unit of time (A) exclude the day of the event that triggers the period; (B) count every day, including intermediate Saturdays, Sundays, and legal holidays; and (C) include the last day of the period, but if the last day is a Saturday, Sunday, or legal holiday, or falls within any period of time extended through an order of the chief justice under FL ST J ADMIN Rule 2.205(a)(2)(B)(iv), the period continues to run until the end of the next day that is not a Saturday, Sunday, or legal holiday and does not fall within any period of time extended through an order of the chief justice. FL ST J ADMIN Rule 2.514(a)(1).

ii. *Period stated in hours.* When the period is stated in hours (A) begin counting immediately on the occurrence of the event that triggers the period; (B) count every hour, including hours during intermediate Saturdays, Sundays, and legal holidays; and (C) if the period would end on a Saturday, Sunday, or legal holiday, or during any period of time extended through an order of the chief justice under FL ST J ADMIN Rule 2.205(a)(2)(B)(iv), the period continues to run until the same time on the next day that is not a Saturday, Sunday, or legal holiday and does not fall within any period of time extended through an order of the chief justice. FL ST J ADMIN Rule 2.514(a)(2).

iii. *Period stated in days less than seven (7) days.* When the period stated in days is less than seven (7) days, intermediate Saturdays, Sundays, and legal holidays shall be excluded in the computation. FL ST J ADMIN Rule 2.514(a)(3).

iv. *"Last day" defined.* Unless a different time is set by a statute, local rule, or court order, the last day ends (A) for electronic filing or for service by any means, at midnight; and (B) for filing by other means, when the clerk's office is scheduled to close. FL ST J ADMIN Rule 2.514(a)(4).

v. *"Next day" defined.* The "next day" is determined by continuing to count forward when the period is measured after an event and backward when measured before an event. FL ST J ADMIN Rule 2.514(a)(5).

vi. *"Legal holiday" defined.* "Legal holiday" means (A) the day set aside by FL ST § 110.117, for observing New Year's Day, Martin Luther King, Jr.'s Birthday, Memorial Day, Independence Day, Labor Day, Veterans' Day, Thanksgiving Day, the Friday after Thanksgiving Day, or Christmas Day, and (B) any day observed as a holiday by the clerk's office or as designated by the chief judge. FL ST J ADMIN Rule 2.514(a)(6).

b. *Additional time after service by mail or e-mail.* When a party may or must act within a specified time after service and service is made by mail or e-mail, five (5) days are added after the period that would otherwise expire under FL ST J ADMIN Rule 2.514(a). FL ST J ADMIN Rule 2.514(b).

c. *Enlargement.* When an act is required or allowed to be done at or within a specified time by order of court, by the Florida Rules of Civil Procedure, or by notice given thereunder, for cause shown the court at any time in its discretion (1) with or without notice, may order the period enlarged if request therefor is made before the expiration of the period originally prescribed or as extended by a previous order, or (2) upon motion made and notice after the expiration of the specified period, may permit the act to be done when failure to act was the result of excusable neglect, but it may not extend the time for making a motion for new trial, for rehearing, or to alter or amend a judgment; making a motion for relief from a judgment under FL ST RCP Rule 1.540(b); taking an appeal or filing a petition for certiorari; or making a motion for a directed verdict. FL ST RCP Rule 1.090(b).

d. *Unaffected by expiration of term.* The period of time provided for the doing of any act or the taking of any proceeding shall not be affected or limited by the continued existence or expiration of a term of court. The continued existence or expiration of a term of court in no way affects the power of a court to do any act or take any proceeding in any action which is or has been pending before it. FL ST RCP Rule 1.090(c).

C. General Requirements

1. *Motions generally*

a. *Contents.* An application to the court for an order shall be by motion which shall be made in writing unless made during a hearing or trial, shall state with particularity the grounds therefor, and shall set forth the relief or order sought. The requirement of writing is fulfilled if the motion is stated in a written notice of the hearing of the motion. All notices of hearing shall specify each motion or other matter to be heard. FL ST RCP Rule 1.100(b).

b. *Particularity requirement.* The court considers a motion in the light of the substantive law, rule or statute to make its determination. Some rules require a statement of the grounds for a motion under the rule. Failure to give the grounds will result in denial of the motion. This should be the result in all situations when the ground for the motion is not inherent in the rule. FL-PRACPROC § 9:3. The requirement is nevertheless an important one, first because of the due process notice rights of the respondent, as well as for the assistance it provides to the court in its preparation for the hearing or, absent a hearing, for disposition. 4 FLPRAC R 1.100.

2. *Motion for leave to amend.* Although the Florida Rules of Civil Procedure do not specify a procedure for obtaining leave to amend, it is usually accomplished by way of a motion. FL-PP § 2:153. At any time in furtherance of justice, upon such terms as may be just, the court may permit any process, proceeding, pleading, or record to be amended or material supplemental matter to be set forth in an amended or supplemental pleading. At every stage of the action the court must disregard any error or defect in the proceedings which does not affect the substantial rights of the parties. FL ST RCP Rule 1.190(e).

a. *Permissible amendments.* Amendments can relate to the correction of mistakes, the insertion of jurisdictional averments, the correction or addition of verifications, the addition or substitution or striking out of parties, and generally the rectification of all formal defects in the pleading. The court can also allow amendments setting up an omitted counterclaim or cross-claim if the defendant failed to raise the claim through oversight, inadvertence, or excusable neglect. FL-PP § 2:151.

b. *Amendments to conform with the evidence.* When issues not raised by the pleadings are tried by express or implied consent of the parties, they shall be treated in all respects as if they had been raised in the pleadings. Such amendment of the pleadings as may be necessary to cause them to conform to the evidence and to raise these issues may be made upon motion of any party at any time, even after judgment, but failure so to amend shall not affect the result of the trial of these issues. If the evidence is objected to at the trial on the ground that it is not within the issues made by the pleadings, the court may allow the pleadings to be amended to conform with the evidence and shall do so freely when the merits of the cause are more effectually presented thereby and the objecting party fails to satisfy the court that the admission of such evidence will prejudice the objecting party in maintaining an action or defense upon the merits. FL ST RCP Rule 1.190(b).

   i. The courts have been extremely liberal in permitting amendments after trial to conform pleadings to the evidence where the issues were tried by the express or implied consent of the parties. Turner v. Long, 225 So.2d 434 (Fla. 1st DCA 1969); FL-PP § 2:152.

c. *Procedure for adding parties.* Parties may be added once as a matter of course within the same time that pleadings can be so amended. If amendment by leave of court or stipulation of the parties is permitted, parties may be added in the amended pleading without further order of court. Parties may be added by order of court on its own initiative or on motion of any party at any stage of the action and on such terms as are just. FL ST RCP Rule 1.250(c).

d. *Claims for punitive damages.* A motion for leave to amend a pleading to assert a claim for punitive damages shall make a reasonable showing by evidence in the record or evidence to be proffered by the claimant that provides a reasonable basis for recovery of such damages. The motion to amend can be filed separately and before the supporting evidence or proffer, but each shall be served on all parties at least twenty (20) days before the hearing. FL ST RCP Rule 1.190(f). Leave of court to amend the complaint must be obtained before a plaintiff may assert a punitive damages claim in the complaint. Failure to do so will result in the claims being dismissed or stricken. FL-PP § 2:151.

e. *Relation back of amendments.* When the claim or defense asserted in the amended pleading arose out of the conduct, transaction, or occurrence set forth or attempted to be set forth in the original pleading, the amendment shall relate back to the date of the original pleading. FL ST RCP Rule 1.190(c).

   i. The doctrine of relation back becomes critical in applying the statute of limitations. For example, it has been held that the doctrine of relation back may not be utilized to circumvent the statute of limitations to permit an amendment where a claim could have been filed as an independent action but was not timely asserted and would otherwise be barred under the statute of limitations. Cox v. Seaboard Coast Line R. Co., 360 So.2d 8 (Fla. 2d DCA 1978); FL-PP § 2:152.

3. *Arbitration and mediation*

   a. *Referral to arbitration and mediation.* Except as hereinafter provided or as otherwise prohibited by law, the presiding judge may enter an order referring all or any part of a contested civil matter to mediation or arbitration. The parties to any contested civil matter may file a written stipulation to mediate or arbitrate any issue between them at any time. Such stipulation shall be incorporated into the order of referral. FL ST RCP Rule 1.700(a).

   b. *Arbitration*

      i. *Exclusions.* A civil action shall be ordered to arbitration or arbitration in conjunction with mediation upon stipulation of the parties. A civil action may be ordered to arbitration or arbitration in conjunction with mediation upon motion of any party or by the court, if the judge determines the action to be of such a nature that arbitration could be of benefit to the litigants or the court. FL ST RCP Rule 1.800.

         - Under no circumstances may the following categories of actions be referred to arbitration:

(1) bond estreatures; (2) habeas corpus or other extraordinary writs; (3) bond validations; (4) civil or criminal contempt; (5) such other matters as may be specified by order of the chief judge in the circuit. FL ST RCP Rule 1.800.

ii. For more information regarding arbitration, please see FL ST RCP Rule 1.810; FL ST RCP Rule 1.820; FL ST RCP Rule 1.830.

c. *Mediation.* For more information regarding mediation, please see FL ST RCP Rule 1.710; FL ST RCP Rule 1.720; FL ST RCP Rule 1.730; and FL ST RCP Rule 1.750.

4. *Rules of court*

a. *Rules of civil procedure.* The Florida Rules of Civil Procedure apply to all actions of a civil nature and all special statutory proceedings in the circuit courts and county courts except those to which the Florida Probate Rules, the Florida Family Law Rules of Procedure, or the Small Claims Rules apply. FL ST RCP Rule 1.010.

i. The form, content, procedure, and time for pleading in all special statutory proceedings shall be as prescribed by the statutes governing the proceeding unless the Florida Rules of Civil Procedure specifically provide to the contrary. FL ST RCP Rule 1.010.

ii. The Florida Rules of Civil Procedure shall be construed to secure the just, speedy, and inexpensive determination of every action. FL ST RCP Rule 1.010.

b. *Rules of judicial administration.* The Florida Rules of Judicial Administration shall apply to administrative matters in all courts to which the Florida Rules of Judicial Administration are applicable by their terms. The Florida Rules of Judicial Administration shall be construed to secure the speedy and inexpensive determination of every proceeding to which they are applicable. The Florida Rules of Judicial Administration shall supersede all conflicting rules and statutes. FL ST J ADMIN Rule 2.110.

D. Documents

1. *Required documents*

a. *Notice of hearing/Motion.* An application to the court for an order shall be by motion which shall be made in writing unless made during a hearing or trial, shall state with particularity the grounds therefor, and shall set forth the relief or order sought. The requirement of writing is fulfilled if the motion is stated in a written notice of the hearing of the motion. All notices of hearing shall specify each motion or other matter to be heard. FL ST RCP Rule 1.100(b).

i. *Notices to persons with disabilities.* See the Format section of this KeyRules document for further information.

b. *Proposed amended pleading.* The moving party shall attach the proposed amended pleading to the motion. FL ST RCP Rule 1.190(a).

c. *Certificate of service.* When any attorney certifies in substance: "I certify that a copy hereof has been furnished to (here insert name or names and addresses used for service) by (e-mail) (delivery) (mail) (fax) on .... (date) ....________________ Attorney" the certificate is taken as prima facie proof of such service in compliance with FL ST J ADMIN Rule 2.516. FL ST J ADMIN Rule 2.516(f).

2. *Supplemental documents*

a. *Proposed order.* The court may require that orders or judgments be prepared by a party, may require the party to furnish the court with stamped, addressed envelopes for service of the order or judgment, and may require that proposed orders and judgments be furnished to all parties before entry by the court of the order or judgment. FL ST J ADMIN Rule 2.516(h)(1).

b. *Notice of constitutional question.* A party that files a pleading, written motion, or other paper drawing into question the constitutionality of a state statute or a county or municipal charter, ordinance, or franchise must promptly (1) file a notice of constitutional question stating the question and identifying the paper that raises it; and (2) serve the notice and the pleading, written motion, or other paper drawing into question the constitutionality of a state statute or a county or municipal charter, ordinance, or franchise on the Attorney General or the state attorney of the judicial circuit in which the action is pending, by either certified or registered mail. Service of the notice and pleading, written motion, or other paper does not require joinder of the Attorney General or the state attorney as a party to the action. FL ST RCP Rule 1.071.

E. Format

1. *Documents; Type and size.* Documents subject to the exceptions set forth in FL ST J ADMIN Rule 2.525(d) shall be filed on recycled paper measuring eight and one half by eleven (8 1/2 by 11) inches. For purposes of FL ST J ADMIN Rule 2.520, paper is recycled if it contains a minimum content of fifty (50) percent waste paper. Xerographic reduction of legal-size (eight and one half by fourteen (8 1/2 by 14) inches) documents to letter size (eight and one half by eleven (8 1/2 by 11) inches) is prohibited. All other documents filed by electronic transmission shall be filed in a format capable of being printed in a format consistent with the provisions of FL ST J ADMIN Rule 2.250. FL ST J ADMIN Rule 2.520(b).
   a. *Exhibits.* Any exhibit or attachment filed with pleadings or papers may be filed in its original size. FL ST J ADMIN Rule 2.520(c).
   b. *Recording space.* On all papers and documents prepared and filed by the court or by any party to a proceeding which are to be recorded in the public records of any county, including but not limited to final money judgments and notices of lis pendens, a three (3) inch by three (3) inch space at the top right-hand corner on the first page and a one (1) inch by three (3) inch space at the top right-hand corner on each subsequent page shall be left blank and reserved for use by the clerk of court. FL ST J ADMIN Rule 2.520(d).
      i. *Exceptions to recording space.* Any papers or documents created by persons or entities over which the filing party has no control, including but not limited to wills, codicils, trusts, or other testamentary documents; documents prepared or executed by any public officer; documents prepared, executed, acknowledged, or proved outside of the State of Florida; or documents created by State or Federal government agencies, may be filed without the space required by FL ST J ADMIN Rule 2.520. FL ST J ADMIN Rule 2.520(e).
   c. *Noncompliance.* No clerk of court is permitted to refuse to file any document or paper because of noncompliance with the Florida Rules of Judicial Administration. However, upon request of the clerk of court, noncomplying documents must be resubmitted in accordance with the formatting rules. FL ST J ADMIN Rule 2.520(f).
2. *Caption.* Every pleading, motion, order, judgment, or other paper shall have a caption containing the name of the court, the file number, and except for in rem proceedings, including forfeiture proceedings, the name of the first party on each side with an appropriate indication of other parties, and a designation identifying the party filing it and its nature or the nature of the order, as the case may be. In any in rem proceeding, every pleading, motion, order, judgment, or other paper shall have a caption containing the name of the court, the file number, the style "In re" (followed by the name or general description of the property), and a designation of the person or entity filing it and its nature or the nature of the order, as the case may be. In an in rem forfeiture proceeding, the style shall be "In re forfeiture of" (followed by the name of the general description of the property). All papers filed in the action shall be styled in such a manner as to indicate clearly the subject matter of the paper and the party requesting or obtaining relief. FL ST RCP Rule 1.100(c)(1).
3. *Writing and written defined.* Writing or written means a document containing information, an application, or a stipulation. FL ST RCP Rule 1.080(c).
4. *Rule abbreviations*
   a. The Florida Rules of Civil Procedure and shall be abbreviated as Fla.R.Civ.P. FL ST RCP Rule 1.010.
   b. The Florida Rules of Judicial Administration shall be abbreviated as Fla. R. Jud. Admin. FL ST J ADMIN Rule 2.110.
5. *Nonverification.* Except when otherwise specifically provided by the Florida Rules of Civil Procedure or an applicable statute, every pleading or other document of a party represented by an attorney need not be verified or accompanied by an affidavit. FL ST RCP Rule 1.030; FL ST J ADMIN Rule 2.515(a).

6. *Attorney signature*
   a. *Attorney signature.* Every pleading and other document of a party represented by an attorney shall be signed by at least one (1) attorney of record in that attorney's individual name whose current record Florida Bar address, telephone number, including area code, primary e-mail address and secondary e-mail addresses, if any, and Florida Bar number shall be stated, and who shall be duly licensed to practice law in Florida or who shall have received permission to appear in the particular case as provided in FL ST J ADMIN Rule 2.510. FL ST J ADMIN Rule 2.515(a).
      i. The attorney may be required by the court to give the address of, and to vouch for the attorney's authority to represent, the party. FL ST J ADMIN Rule 2.515(a).
      ii. The signature of an attorney shall constitute a certificate by the attorney that the attorney has read the pleading or other document; that to the best of the attorney's knowledge, information, and belief there is good ground to support it; and that it is not interposed for delay. FL ST J ADMIN Rule 2.515(a).
      iii. If a pleading is not signed or is signed with intent to defeat the purpose of FL ST J ADMIN Rule 2.515, it may be stricken and the action may proceed as though the pleading or other document had not been served. FL ST J ADMIN Rule 2.515(a).
   b. *Pro se litigant signature.* A party who is not represented by an attorney shall sign any pleading or other paper and state the party's address and telephone number, including area code. FL ST J ADMIN Rule 2.515(b).
   c. *Form of signature*
      i. The signatures required on pleadings and documents by FL ST J ADMIN Rule 2.515(a) and FL ST J ADMIN Rule 2.515(b) may be:
         - Original signatures;
         - Original signatures that have been reproduced by electronic means, such as on electronically transmitted documents or photocopied documents;
         - Electronic signatures using the "/s/," "s/," or "/s" formats by or at the direction of the person signing; or
         - Any other signature format authorized by general law, so long as the clerk where the proceeding is pending has the capability of receiving and has obtained approval from the Supreme Court of Florida to accept pleadings and documents with that signature format. FL ST J ADMIN Rule 2.515(c)(1).
      ii. An attorney, party, or other person who files a pleading or paper by electronic transmission that does not contain the original signature of that attorney, party, or other person shall file that identical pleading or paper in paper form containing an original signature of that attorney, party, or other person (hereinafter called the follow-up filing) immediately thereafter. The follow-up filing is not required if the Supreme Court of Florida has entered an order directing the clerk of court to discontinue accepting the follow-up filing. FL ST J ADMIN Rule 2.515(c)(2).
7. *Forms*
   a. *Process.* The forms of process, notice of lis pendens, and notice of action provided in the Florida Rules of Civil Procedure are sufficient. Variations from the forms do not void process or notices that are otherwise sufficient. FL ST RCP Rule 1.900(a).
   b. *Other forms.* The other forms provided in the Florida Rules of Civil Procedure are sufficient for the matters that are covered by them. So long as the substance is expressed without prolixity, the forms may be varied to meet the facts of a particular case. FL ST RCP Rule 1.900(b).
   c. *Formal matters.* Captions, except for the designation of the paper, are omitted from the forms provided in the Florida Rules of Civil Procedure. A general form of caption is the first form provided. Signatures are omitted from pleadings and motions. FL ST RCP Rule 1.900(c).
8. *Notices to persons with disabilities.* All notices of court proceedings to be held in a public facility, and all process compelling appearance at such proceedings, shall include the following statement in bold face,

fourteen (14) point Times New Roman or Courier font: "If you are a person with a disability who needs any accommodation in order to participate in this proceeding, you are entitled, at no cost to you, to the provision of certain assistance. Please contact [identify applicable court personnel by name, address, and telephone number] at least seven (7) days before your scheduled court appearance, or immediately upon receiving this notification if the time before the scheduled appearance is less than seven (7) days; if you are hearing or voice impaired, call 711." FL ST J ADMIN Rule 2.540(c)(1).

9. *Minimization of the filing of sensitive information*
   a. *Limitations for court filings.* Unless authorized by FL ST J ADMIN Rule 2.425(b), statute, another rule of court, or the court orders otherwise, designated sensitive information filed with the court must be limited to the following format:
      i. The initials of a person known to be a minor;
      ii. The year of birth of a person's birth date;
      iii. No portion of any: Social security number, Bank account number, Credit card account number, Charge account number, or Debit account number;
      iv. The last four digits of any: Taxpayer identification number (TIN), Employee identification number, Driver's license number, Passport number, Telephone number, Financial account number, except as set forth in FL ST J ADMIN Rule 2.425(a)(3), Brokerage account number, Insurance policy account number, Loan account number, Customer account number, or Patient or health care number;
      v. A truncated version of any: Email address, Computer user name, Password, or Personal identification number (PIN); and
      vi. A truncated version of any other sensitive information as provided by court order. FL ST J ADMIN Rule 2.425(a).
   b. *Exceptions.* FL ST J ADMIN Rule 2.425(a) does not apply to the following:
      i. An account number which identifies the property alleged to be the subject of a proceeding;
      ii. The record of an administrative or agency proceeding;
      iii. The record in appellate or review proceedings;
      iv. The birth date of a minor whenever the birth date is necessary for the court to establish or maintain subject matter jurisdiction;
      v. The name of a minor in any order relating to parental responsibility, time-sharing, or child support;
      vi. The name of a minor in any document or order affecting the minor's ownership of real property;
      vii. The birth date of a party in a writ of attachment or notice to payor;
      viii. In traffic and criminal proceedings: a pro se filing; a court filing that is related to a criminal matter or investigation and that is prepared before the filing of a criminal charge or is not filed as part of any docketed criminal case; an arrest or search warrant or any information in support thereof; a charging document and an affidavit or other documents filed in support of any charging document, including any driving records; a statement of particulars; discovery material introduced into evidence or otherwise filed with the court; and all information necessary for the proper issuance and execution of a subpoena duces tecum;
      ix. Information used by the clerk for case maintenance purposes or the courts for case management purposes; and
      x. Information which is relevant and material to an issue before the court. FL ST J ADMIN Rule 2.425(b).
   c. *Remedies.* Upon motion by a party or interested person or sua sponte by the court, the court may order remedies, sanctions or both for a violation of FL ST J ADMIN Rule 2.425(a). Following notice and an opportunity to respond, the court may impose sanctions if such filing was not made in good faith. FL ST J ADMIN Rule 2.425(c).

d. *Motions not restricted.* FL ST J ADMIN Rule 2.425 does not restrict a party's right to move for protective order, to move to file documents under seal, or to request a determination of the confidentiality of records. FL ST J ADMIN Rule 2.425(d).

   i. For more information regarding sealing court records, please see FL ST 4 J CIR 2006-05.

e. *Application.* FL ST J ADMIN Rule 2.425 does not affect the application of constitutional provisions, statutes, or rules of court regarding confidential information or access to public information. FL ST J ADMIN Rule 2.425(e).

F. Filing and Service Requirements

1. *Filing requirements.* All original documents must be filed with the court either before service or immediately thereafter, unless otherwise provided for by general law or other rules. If the original of any bond or other document is not placed in the court file, a certified copy must be so placed by the clerk. FL ST J ADMIN Rule 2.516(d). All documents shall be filed in conformity with the requirements of FL ST J ADMIN Rule 2.525. FL ST RCP Rule 1.080(b). All documents filed in any court shall be filed by electronic transmission in accordance with FL ST J ADMIN Rule 2.525. "Documents" means pleadings, motions, petitions, memoranda, briefs, notices, exhibits, declarations, affidavits, orders, judgments, decrees, writs, opinions, and any other paper or writing submitted to a court. FL ST J ADMIN Rule 2.520(a). All documents that are court records, as defined in FL ST J ADMIN Rule 2.430(a)(1), must be filed by electronic transmission, provided that: (1) the clerk has the ability to accept and retain such documents; (2) the clerk or the chief judge of the circuit has requested permission to accept documents filed by electronic transmission; and (3) the supreme court has entered an order granting permission to the clerk to accept documents filed by electronic transmission. FL ST J ADMIN Rule 2.525(c)(1).

   a. *Definition.* "Electronic transmission of documents" means the sending of information by electronic signals to, by or from a court or clerk, which when received can be transformed and stored or transmitted on paper, microfilm, magnetic storage device, optical imaging system, CD-ROM, flash drive, other electronic data storage system, server, case maintenance system ("CM"), electronic court filing ("ECF") system, statewide or local electronic portal ("e-portal"), or other electronic record keeping system authorized by the supreme court in a format sufficient to communicate the information on the original document in a readable format. Electronic transmission of documents includes electronic mail ("e-mail") and any internet-based transmission procedure, and may include procedures allowing for documents to be signed or verified by electronic means. FL ST J ADMIN Rule 2.525(a).

      i. The filing of documents with the court as required by the Florida Rules of Judicial Administration must be made by filing them with the clerk in accordance with FL ST J ADMIN Rule 2.525, except that the judge may permit documents to be filed with the judge, in which event the judge must note the filing date before him or her on the documents and transmit them to the clerk. The date of filing is that shown on the face of the document by the judge's notation or the clerk's time stamp, whichever is earlier. FL ST J ADMIN Rule 2.516(e).

   b. *Application.* Any court or clerk of the court may accept the electronic transmission of documents for filing after the clerk, together with input from the chief judge of the circuit, has obtained approval of the procedures and program for doing so from the Supreme Court of Florida. FL ST J ADMIN Rule 2.525(b).

   c. *Exceptions*

      i. Paper documents and other submissions may be manually submitted to the clerk or court:

         - When the clerk does not have the ability to accept and retain documents by electronic filing or has not had ECF Procedures approved by the supreme court;
         - For filing by any self-represented party or any self-represented nonparty unless specific ECF Procedures provide a means to file documents electronically. However, any self-represented nonparty that is a governmental or public agency and any other agency, partnership, corporation, or business entity acting on behalf of any governmental or public agency may file documents by electronic transmission if such entity has the capability of filing documents electronically;

- For filing by attorneys excused from e-mail service in accordance with FL ST J ADMIN Rule 2.516(b);
- When submitting evidentiary exhibits or filing non-documentary materials;
- When the filing involves documents in excess of twenty-five (25) megabytes (25MB) in size. For such filings, documents may be transmitted using an electronic storage medium that the clerk has the ability to accept, which may include a CD-ROM, flash drive, or similar storage medium;
- When filed in open court, as permitted by the court;
- When paper filing is permitted by any approved statewide or local ECF procedures; and
- If any court determines that justice so requires. FL ST J ADMIN Rule 2.525(d).

ii. Any document in paper form submitted under FL ST J ADMIN Rule 2.525(d) is filed when it is received by the clerk or court and the clerk shall immediately thereafter convert any filed paper document to an electronic document. "Convert to an electronic document" means optically capturing an image of a paper document and using character recognition software to recover as much of the document's text as practicable and then indexing and storing the document in the official court file. FL ST J ADMIN Rule 2.525(c)(4).

iii. Any storage medium submitted under FL ST J ADMIN Rule 2.525(d)(5) is filed when received by the clerk or court and the clerk shall immediately thereafter transfer the electronic documents from the storage device to the official court file. FL ST J ADMIN Rule 2.525(c)(5).

iv. If the filer of any paper document authorized under FL ST J ADMIN Rule 2.525(d) provides a self-addressed, postage-paid envelope for return of the paper document after it is converted to electronic form by the clerk, the clerk shall place the paper document in the envelope and deposit it in the mail. Except when a paper document is required to be maintained, the clerk may recycle any filed paper document that is not to be returned to the filer. FL ST J ADMIN Rule 2.525(c)(6).

v. The clerk may convert any paper document filed before the effective date of FL ST J ADMIN Rule 2.525 to an electronic document. Unless the clerk is required to maintain the paper document, if the paper document has been converted to an electronic document by the clerk, the paper document is no longer part of the official court file and may be removed and recycled. FL ST J ADMIN Rule 2.525(c)(7).

d. *Official court file.* For information on what constitutes the official court file, please see FL ST J ADMIN Rule 2.525(c)(2), FL ST J ADMIN Rule 2.525(c)(3).

e. *Administration.* All attorneys, parties, or other persons using this rule to file documents are required to make arrangements with the court or clerk for the payment of any charges authorized by general law or the supreme court before filing any document by electronic transmission. FL ST J ADMIN Rule 2.525(f)(2).

f. *Filing date.* The filing date for an electronically transmitted document is the date and time that such filing is acknowledged by an electronic stamp or otherwise, pursuant to any procedure set forth in any ECF Procedures approved by the supreme court, or the date the last page of such filing is received by the court or clerk. FL ST J ADMIN Rule 2.525(f)(3).

g. *Accessibility.* All documents transmitted in any electronic form under FL ST J ADMIN Rule 2.525 must comply with the accessibility requirements of FL ST J ADMIN Rule 2.526. FL ST J ADMIN Rule 2.525(g).

2. *Service requirements.* Every pleading subsequent to the initial pleading, all orders, and every other document filed in the action must be served in conformity with the requirements of FL ST J ADMIN Rule 2.516. FL ST RCP Rule 1.080(a).

a. *Service; When required.* Unless the court otherwise orders, or a statute or supreme court administrative order specifies a different means of service, every pleading subsequent to the initial pleading and every other document filed in any court proceeding, except applications for witness subpoenas and documents served by formal notice or required to be served in the manner provided for service

of formal notice, must be served in accordance with FL ST J ADMIN Rule 2.516 on each party. No service need be made on parties against whom a default has been entered, except that pleadings asserting new or additional claims against them must be served in the manner provided for service of summons. FL ST J ADMIN Rule 2.516(a).

b. *Service; How made.* When service is required or permitted to be made upon a party represented by an attorney, service must be made upon the attorney unless service upon the party is ordered by the court. FL ST J ADMIN Rule 2.516(b).

   i. *Service by electronic mail ("e-mail").* All documents required or permitted to be served on another party must be served by e-mail, unless FL ST J ADMIN Rule 2.516 otherwise provides. When, in addition to service by e-mail, the sender also utilizes another means of service provided for in FL ST J ADMIN Rule 2.516(b)(2), any differing time limits and other provisions applicable to that other means of service control. FL ST J ADMIN Rule 2.516(b)(1). Any document electronically transmitted to a court or clerk must also be served on all parties and interested persons in accordance with the applicable rules of court. FL ST J ADMIN Rule 2.525(e)(2).

      - *Service on attorneys.* Upon appearing in a proceeding, an attorney must serve a designation of a primary e-mail address and may designate no more than two (2) secondary e-mail addresses. Thereafter, service must be directed to all designated e-mail addresses in that proceeding. Every document filed by an attorney thereafter must include the primary e-mail address of that attorney and any secondary e-mail addresses. If an attorney does not designate any e-mail address for service, documents may be served on that attorney at the e-mail address on record with The Florida Bar. FL ST J ADMIN Rule 2.516(b)(1)(A).

      - *Exception to e-mail service on attorneys.* Service by an attorney on another attorney must be made by e-mail unless excused by the court. Upon motion by an attorney demonstrating that the attorney has no e-mail account and lacks access to the Internet at the attorney's office, the court may excuse the attorney from the requirements of e-mail service. Service on and by an attorney excused by the court from e-mail service must be by the means provided in FL ST J ADMIN Rule 2.516(b)(2). FL ST J ADMIN Rule 2.516(b)(1)(B).

      - *Service on and by parties not represented by an attorney.* Any party not represented by an attorney may serve a designation of a primary e-mail address and also may designate no more than two (2) secondary e-mail addresses to which service must be directed in that proceeding by the means provided in FL ST J ADMIN Rule 2.516(b)(1). If a party not represented by an attorney does not designate an e-mail address for service in a proceeding, service on and by that party must be by the means provided in FL ST J ADMIN Rule 2.516(b)(2). FL ST J ADMIN Rule 2.516(b)(1)(C).

      - *Time of service.* Service by e-mail is complete when it is sent. FL ST J ADMIN Rule 2.516(b)(1)(D). An e-mail is deemed served on the date it is sent. FL ST J ADMIN Rule 2.516(b)(1)(D)(i). If the sender learns that the e-mail did not reach the address of the person to be served, the sender must immediately send another copy by e-mail, or by a means authorized by FL ST J ADMIN Rule 2.516(b)(2). FL ST J ADMIN Rule 2.516(b)(1)(D)(ii). E-mail service is treated as service by mail for the computation of time. FL ST J ADMIN Rule 2.516(b)(1)(D)(iii).

   ii. *Format of e-mail for service.* Service of a document by e-mail is made by attaching a copy of the document in PDF format to an e-mail sent to all addresses designated by the attorney or party. FL ST J ADMIN Rule 2.516(b)(1)(E).

      - All documents served by e-mail must be attached to an e-mail message containing a subject line beginning with the words "SERVICE OF COURT DOCUMENT" in all capital letters, followed by the case number of the proceeding in which the documents are being served. FL ST J ADMIN Rule 2.516(b)(1)(E)(i).

      - The body of the e-mail must identify the court in which the proceeding is pending, the case number, the name of the initial party on each side, the title of each document served with that e-mail, and the sender's name and telephone number. FL ST J ADMIN Rule 2.516(b)(1)(E)(ii).

- Any document served by e-mail may be signed by the "/s/" format, as long as the filed original is signed in accordance with the applicable rule of procedure. FL ST J ADMIN Rule 2.516(b)(1)(E)(iii).
- Any e-mail which, together with its attached documents, exceeds five megabytes (5MB) in size, must be divided and sent as separate e-mails, no one of which may exceed five megabytes (5MB) in size and each of which must be sequentially numbered in the subject line. FL ST J ADMIN Rule 2.516(b)(1)(E)(iv).

iii. *Service by other means.* In addition to, and not in lieu of, service by e-mail, service may also be made upon attorneys by any of the means specified in FL ST J ADMIN Rule 2.516(b)(2). Service on and by all parties who are not represented by an attorney and who do not designate an e-mail address, and on and by all attorneys excused from e-mail service, must be made by delivering a copy of the document or by mailing it to the party or attorney at their last known address or, if no address is known, by leaving it with the clerk of the court. Service by mail is complete upon mailing. Delivery of a copy within FL ST J ADMIN Rule 2.516 is complete upon:

- Handing it to the attorney or to the party,
- Leaving it at the attorney's or party's office with a clerk or other person in charge thereof,
- If there is no one in charge, leaving it in a conspicuous place therein,
- If the office is closed or the person to be served has no office, leaving it at the person's usual place of abode with some person of his or her family above fifteen (15) years of age and informing such person of the contents, or
- Transmitting it by facsimile to the attorney's or party's office with a cover sheet containing the sender's name, firm, address, telephone number, and facsimile number, and the number of pages transmitted. When service is made by facsimile, a copy must also be served by any other method permitted by FL ST J ADMIN Rule 2.516. Facsimile service occurs when transmission is complete. FL ST J ADMIN Rule 2.516(b)(2)(A) through FL ST J ADMIN Rule 2.516(b)(2)(E).
- Service by delivery after 5:00 p.m. must be deemed to have been made by mailing on the date of delivery. FL ST J ADMIN Rule 2.516(b)(2)(F).

c. *Service; Numerous defendants.* In actions when the parties are unusually numerous, the court may regulate the service contemplated by the Florida Rules of Judicial Administration on motion or on its own initiative in such manner as may be found to be just and reasonable. FL ST J ADMIN Rule 2.516(c).

d. *Service by clerk.* Service of notices and other documents required to be made by the clerk must also be done as provided in FL ST J ADMIN Rule 2.516(b). FL ST J ADMIN Rule 2.516(g).

G. Hearings

1. *Communication equipment*

a. *Definition.* Communication equipment means a conference telephone or other electronic device that permits all those appearing or participating to hear and speak to each other, provided that all conversation of all parties is audible to all persons present. FL ST J ADMIN Rule 2.530(a).

b. *Use by all parties.* A county or circuit court judge may, upon the court's own motion or upon the written request of a party, direct that communication equipment be used for a motion hearing, pretrial conference, or a status conference. A judge must give notice to the parties and consider any objections they may have to the use of communication equipment before directing that communication equipment be used. The decision to use communication equipment over the objection of parties will be in the sound discretion of the trial court, except as noted below. FL ST J ADMIN Rule 2.530(b).

c. *Use only by requesting party.* A county or circuit court judge may, upon the written request of a party upon reasonable notice to all other parties, permit a requesting party to participate through communication equipment in a scheduled motion hearing; however, any such request (except in criminal, juvenile, and appellate proceedings) must be granted, absent a showing of good cause to deny the same, where the hearing is set for not longer than fifteen (15) minutes. FL ST J ADMIN Rule 2.530(c).

d. *Testimony*

i. *Generally.* A county or circuit court judge, general magistrate, special magistrate, or hearing officer may allow testimony to be taken through communication equipment if all parties consent or if permitted by another applicable rule of procedure. FL ST J ADMIN Rule 2.530(d)(1).

ii. *Procedure.* Any party desiring to present testimony through communication equipment shall, prior to the hearing or trial at which the testimony is to be presented, contact all parties to determine whether each party consents to this form of testimony. The party seeking to present the testimony shall move for permission to present testimony through communication equipment, which motion shall set forth good cause as to why the testimony should be allowed in this form. FL ST J ADMIN Rule 2.530(d)(2).

iii. *Oath.* Testimony may be taken through communication equipment only if a notary public or other person authorized to administer oaths in the witness's jurisdiction is present with the witness and administers the oath consistent with the laws of the jurisdiction. FL ST J ADMIN Rule 2.530(d)(3).

iv. *Confrontation rights.* In juvenile and criminal proceedings the defendant must make an informed waiver of any confrontation rights that may be abridged by the use of communication equipment. FL ST J ADMIN Rule 2.530(d)(4).

v. *Video testimony.* If the testimony to be presented utilizes video conferencing or comparable two-way visual capabilities, the court in its discretion may modify the procedures set forth in FL ST J ADMIN Rule 2.530 to accommodate the technology utilized. FL ST J ADMIN Rule 2.530(d)(5).

e. *Burden of expense.* The cost for the use of the communication equipment is the responsibility of the requesting party unless otherwise directed by the court. FL ST J ADMIN Rule 2.530(e).

H. Forms

1. Official Motion for Leave to Amend Forms for Florida

a. Caption. FL ST RCP Form 1.901.

b. Notice of compliance when constitutional challenge is brought. FL ST RCP Form 1.975.

2. Motion for Leave to Amend Forms for Florida

a. Motion; For leave of court; To amend complaint. FL-PP § 2:155.

b. Motion; For leave of court; To add claim for punitive damages. FL-PP § 2:156.

c. Motion; For leave of court; To amend complaint; To conform to evidence. FL-PP § 2:157.

d. Motion; For leave of court; To permit admission of evidence. FL-PP § 2:158.

e. Order; Granting leave to amend complaint. FL-PP § 2:163.

f. Order; Granting leave to amend complaint; To conform to evidence. FL-PP § 2:164.

g. Order; Granting leave to amend complaint; To permit admission of evidence. FL-PP § 2:165.

h. Form for motion for leave to amend complaint. FL-RCPF R 1.190(39).

i. Form for amendment to complaint with leave of court. FL-RCPF R 1.190(40).

j. Form for motion to amend amended complaint. FL-RCPF R 1.190(42).

k. Form for amendment to amended complaint (or second amended complaint). FL-RCPF R 1.190(43).

l. Form for motion to amend complaint to add count. FL-RCPF R 1.190(44).

I. Checklist

- (I) ❑ Matters to be considered by moving party
  - (a) ❑ Required documents
    - (1) ❑ Notice of hearing/Motion
    - (2) ❑ Proposed amended pleading
    - (3) ❑ Certificate of service
  - (b) ❑ Supplemental documents
    - (1) ❑ Proposed order
    - (2) ❑ Notice of constitutional question
  - (c) ❑ Time for making motion
    - (1) ❑ A party may amend a pleading once as a matter of course at any time before a responsive pleading is served or, if the pleading is one to which no responsive pleading is permitted and the action has not been placed on the trial calendar, may amend it at any time within twenty (20) days after it is served
    - (2) ❑ Under the Florida Rules of Civil Procedure, there is no time limit as to when an amendment with leave of court may be sought; amendments of the pleadings may be permitted, with the court's discretion, at any stage of the proceedings in furtherance of justice
    - (3) ❑ A motion for leave to amend a pleading to assert a claim for punitive damages can be filed separately and before the supporting evidence or proffer, but each shall be served on all parties at least twenty (20) days before the hearing
    - (4) ❑ A copy of any written motion which may not be heard ex parte and a copy of the notice of the hearing thereof shall be served a reasonable time before the time specified for the hearing
- (II) ❑ Matters to be considered by opposing party
  - (a) ❑ Required documents
    - (1) ❑ Response to motion
    - (2) ❑ Certificate of service
  - (b) ❑ Supplemental documents
    - (1) ❑ Proposed order
    - (2) ❑ Notice of constitutional question
  - (c) ❑ Time for service and filing of opposition
    - (1) ❑ No time specified for responding to a motion

Motions, Oppositions and Replies
Motion for Summary Judgment

Document Last Updated January 2013

A. Applicable Rules

1. *State rules*
   a. Rules of court. FL ST RCP Rule 1.010; FL ST J ADMIN Rule 2.110.
   b. Nonverification of pleadings. FL ST RCP Rule 1.030.
   c. Service and filing of pleadings, orders, and documents. FL ST RCP Rule 1.080.
   d. Time. FL ST RCP Rule 1.090.
   e. Pleadings and motions. FL ST RCP Rule 1.100.

f. Motions. FL ST RCP Rule 1.160.

g. Summary judgment. FL ST RCP Rule 1.510.

h. Relief from judgment, decrees, or orders. FL ST RCP Rule 1.540.

i. Mediation and arbitration. FL ST RCP Rule 1.700; FL ST RCP Rule 1.710; FL ST RCP Rule 1.720; FL ST RCP Rule 1.730; FL ST RCP Rule 1.750; FL ST RCP Rule 1.800; FL ST RCP Rule 1.810; FL ST RCP Rule 1.820; FL ST RCP Rule 1.830.

j. Forms. FL ST RCP Rule 1.900.

k. Minimization of the filing of sensitive information. FL ST J ADMIN Rule 2.425.

l. Retention of court records. FL ST J ADMIN Rule 2.430.

m. Foreign attorneys. FL ST J ADMIN Rule 2.510.

n. Signature of attorneys and parties. FL ST J ADMIN Rule 2.515.

o. Paper. FL ST J ADMIN Rule 2.520.

p. Electronic filing. FL ST J ADMIN Rule 2.525.

q. Accessibility of information and technology. FL ST J ADMIN Rule 2.526.

r. Communication equipment. FL ST J ADMIN Rule 2.530.

s. Court reporting. FL ST J ADMIN Rule 2.535.

t. Requests for accommodations by persons with disabilities. FL ST J ADMIN Rule 2.540.

2. *Local rules*

a. Sealing court records. FL ST 4 J CIR 2006-05.

B. Timing

1. *Motion for summary judgment*

a. *For the claimant.* A party seeking to recover upon a claim, counterclaim, crossclaim or third-party claim or to obtain a declaratory judgment may move for a summary judgment in that party's favor at any time after the expiration of twenty (20) days from the commencement of the action or after service of a motion for summary judgment by the adverse party. FL ST RCP Rule 1.510(a).

b. *For defending party.* A party against whom a claim, counterclaim, crossclaim, or third-party claim is asserted or a declaratory judgment is sought may move for a summary judgment in that party's favor as to all or any part thereof at any time with or without supporting affidavits. FL ST RCP Rule 1.510(b).

i. A defending party is not required to serve his responsive pleading before moving for summary judgment. He may make the motion at any time, setting out his defenses by affidavit, and thus effect a speedy termination of the action if no genuine issue exists as to any fact or facts pertaining to a defense that would defeat the claim. FL ST RCP Rule 1.510, notes.

2. *Service of motion.* The movant shall serve the motion for summary judgment at least twenty (20) days before the time fixed for the hearing, and shall also serve at that time a copy of any summary judgment evidence on which the movant relies that has not already been filed with the court. FL ST RCP Rule 1.510(c).

3. *Computation of time*

a. *Generally.* Computation of time shall be governed by FL ST J ADMIN Rule 2.514. FL ST RCP Rule 1.090(a). The following rules apply in computing time periods specified in any rule of procedure, local rule, court order, or statute that does not specify a method of computing time. FL ST J ADMIN Rule 2.514(a).

i. *Period stated in days or a longer unit.* When the period is stated in days or a longer unit of time (A) exclude the day of the event that triggers the period; (B) count every day, including intermediate Saturdays, Sundays, and legal holidays; and (C) include the last day of the period, but if the last day is a Saturday, Sunday, or legal holiday, or falls within any period of time extended through an order of the chief justice under FL ST J ADMIN Rule 2.205(a)(2)(B)(iv), the period continues to run until the end of the next day that is not a Saturday, Sunday, or legal holiday and does not fall within any period of time extended through an order of the chief justice. FL ST J ADMIN Rule 2.514(a)(1).

ii. *Period stated in hours.* When the period is stated in hours (A) begin counting immediately on the occurrence of the event that triggers the period; (B) count every hour, including hours during intermediate Saturdays, Sundays, and legal holidays; and (C) if the period would end on a Saturday, Sunday, or legal holiday, or during any period of time extended through an order of the chief justice under FL ST J ADMIN Rule 2.205(a)(2)(B)(iv), the period continues to run until the same time on the next day that is not a Saturday, Sunday, or legal holiday and does not fall within any period of time extended through an order of the chief justice. FL ST J ADMIN Rule 2.514(a)(2).

iii. *Period stated in days less than seven (7) days.* When the period stated in days is less than seven (7) days, intermediate Saturdays, Sundays, and legal holidays shall be excluded in the computation. FL ST J ADMIN Rule 2.514(a)(3).

iv. *"Last day" defined.* Unless a different time is set by a statute, local rule, or court order, the last day ends (A) for electronic filing or for service by any means, at midnight; and (B) for filing by other means, when the clerk's office is scheduled to close. FL ST J ADMIN Rule 2.514(a)(4).

v. *"Next day" defined.* The "next day" is determined by continuing to count forward when the period is measured after an event and backward when measured before an event. FL ST J ADMIN Rule 2.514(a)(5).

vi. *"Legal holiday" defined.* "Legal holiday" means (A) the day set aside by FL ST § 110.117, for observing New Year's Day, Martin Luther King, Jr.'s Birthday, Memorial Day, Independence Day, Labor Day, Veterans' Day, Thanksgiving Day, the Friday after Thanksgiving Day, or Christmas Day, and (B) any day observed as a holiday by the clerk's office or as designated by the chief judge. FL ST J ADMIN Rule 2.514(a)(6).

b. *Additional time after service by mail or e-mail.* When a party may or must act within a specified time after service and service is made by mail or e-mail, five (5) days are added after the period that would otherwise expire under FL ST J ADMIN Rule 2.514(a). FL ST J ADMIN Rule 2.514(b).

c. *Enlargement.* When an act is required or allowed to be done at or within a specified time by order of court, by the Florida Rules of Civil Procedure, or by notice given thereunder, for cause shown the court at any time in its discretion (1) with or without notice, may order the period enlarged if request therefor is made before the expiration of the period originally prescribed or as extended by a previous order, or (2) upon motion made and notice after the expiration of the specified period, may permit the act to be done when failure to act was the result of excusable neglect, but it may not extend the time for making a motion for new trial, for rehearing, or to alter or amend a judgment; making a motion for relief from a judgment under FL ST RCP Rule 1.540(b); taking an appeal or filing a petition for certiorari; or making a motion for a directed verdict. FL ST RCP Rule 1.090(b).

d. *Unaffected by expiration of term.* The period of time provided for the doing of any act or the taking of any proceeding shall not be affected or limited by the continued existence or expiration of a term of court. The continued existence or expiration of a term of court in no way affects the power of a court to do any act or take any proceeding in any action which is or has been pending before it. FL ST RCP Rule 1.090(c).

C. General Requirements

1. *Motions generally*

a. *Contents.* An application to the court for an order shall be by motion which shall be made in writing unless made during a hearing or trial, shall state with particularity the grounds therefor, and shall set forth the relief or order sought. The requirement of writing is fulfilled if the motion is stated in a written notice of the hearing of the motion. All notices of hearing shall specify each motion or other matter to be heard. FL ST RCP Rule 1.100(b).

b. *Particularity requirement.* The court considers a motion in the light of the substantive law, rule or

statute to make its determination. Some rules require a statement of the grounds for a motion under the rule. Failure to give the grounds will result in denial of the motion. This should be the result in all situations when the ground for the motion is not inherent in the rule. FL-PRACPROC § 9:3. The requirement is nevertheless an important one, first because of the due process notice rights of the respondent, as well as for the assistance it provides to the court in its preparation for the hearing or, absent a hearing, for disposition. 4 FLPRAC R 1.100.

2. *Summary judgment.* A party seeking to recover upon or defend against a claim, counterclaim, crossclaim, or third-party claim or to obtain a declaratory judgment may move for a summary judgment. FL ST RCP Rule 1.510(a); FL ST RCP Rule 1.510(b).
   a. *General motion for summary judgment information*
      i. *Contents of motion.* The motion shall state with particularity the grounds upon which it is based and the substantial matters of law to be argued and shall specifically identify any affidavits, answers to interrogatories, admissions, depositions, and other materials as would be admissible in evidence ("summary judgment evidence") on which the movant relies. FL ST RCP Rule 1.510(c).
      ii. *Evidence relied upon.* The movant shall also serve at that time a copy of any summary judgment evidence on which the movant relies that has not already been filed with the court. FL ST RCP Rule 1.510(c).
      iii. *Judgment as a matter of law.* The judgment sought shall be rendered forthwith if the pleadings and summary judgment evidence on file show that there is no genuine issue as to any material fact and that the moving party is entitled to a judgment as a matter of law. A summary judgment, interlocutory in character, may be rendered on the issue of liability alone although there is a genuine issue as to the amount of damages. FL ST RCP Rule 1.510(c).
   b. *Sham pleadings.* If a party deems any pleading or part thereof filed by another party to be a sham, that party may move to strike the pleading or part thereof before the cause is set for trial and the court shall hear the motion, taking evidence of the respective parties, and if the motion is sustained, the pleading to which the motion is directed shall be stricken. Default and summary judgment on the merits may be entered in the discretion of the court or the court may permit additional pleadings to be filed for good cause shown. FL ST RCP Rule 1.150(a).
   c. *Burden of proof*
      i. The moving party in a motion for summary judgment has the initial burden of demonstrating the nonexistence of any genuine issue of fact. Landers v. Milton, 370 So.2d 368, 370 (Fla. 1979); Gardner v. Sabal Point Properties, Inc., 616 So.2d 1111, 1112 (Fla. 5th DCA 1993); FL-PP § 6:7.
      ii. If the record raises the slightest doubt that material issues could be present, that doubt must be resolved against the movant and the motion for summary judgment denied. Moore v. Morris, 475 So.2d 666, 668 (Fla. 1985); Henderson v. CSX Transportation, Inc., 617 So.2d 770 (Fla. 1st DCA 1993); Jones v. Directors Guild of America, Inc., 584 So.2d 1057 (Fla. 1st DCA 1991); FL-PP § 6:7.
      iii. Until the moving party meets the initial burden of showing there is no issue of material fact, the opposing party need do nothing. Holl v. Talcott, 191 So.2d 40, 43 (Fla. 1966); Spradley v. Stick, 622 So.2d 610 (Fla. 1st DCA 1993); FL-RCPF R 1.510(404).
      iv. When the movant has tendered competent evidence in support of its motion, the burden shifts to the nonmoving party to come forward with opposing evidence to show that a question of material fact exists. Landers v. Milton, 370 So.2d 368, 370 (Fla. 1979); Holl v. Talcott, 191 So.2d 40, 43-44 (Fla. 1966); Lenhal Realty, Inc. v. Transamerica Commercial Finance Corp., 615 So.2d 207 (Fla. 4th DCA 1993); FL-PP § 6:7.
   d. *Affidavits*
      i. *Form of affidavits; Further testimony.* Supporting and opposing affidavits shall be made on personal knowledge, shall set forth such facts as would be admissible in evidence, and shall

show affirmatively that the affiant is competent to testify to the matters stated. Sworn or certified copies of all papers or parts referred to in an affidavit shall be attached to or served with the affidavit. The court may permit affidavits to be supplemented or opposed by depositions, answers to interrogatories, or by further affidavits. FL ST RCP Rule 1.510(e).

ii. *When affidavits are unavailable.* If it appears from the affidavits of a party opposing the motion that the party cannot for reasons stated present by affidavit facts essential to justify opposition, the court may refuse the application for judgment or may order a continuance to permit affidavits to be obtained or depositions to be taken or discovery to be had or may make such other order as is just. FL ST RCP Rule 1.510(f).

iii. *Affidavits made in bad faith.* If it appears to the satisfaction of the court at any time that any of the affidavits presented pursuant to FL ST RCP Rule 1.510 are presented in bad faith or solely for the purpose of delay, the court shall forthwith order the party employing them to pay to the other party the amount of the reasonable expenses that the filing of the affidavits caused the other party to incur, including reasonable attorneys' fees, and any offending party or attorney may be adjudged guilty of contempt. FL ST RCP Rule 1.510(g).

e. *Case not fully adjudicated on motion.* On motion under FL ST RCP Rule 1.510 if judgment is not rendered upon the whole case or for all the relief asked and a trial or the taking of testimony and a final hearing is necessary, the court at the hearing of the motion, by examining the pleadings and the evidence before it and by interrogating counsel, shall ascertain, if practicable, what material facts exist without substantial controversy and what material facts are actually and in good faith controverted. FL ST RCP Rule 1.510(d).

i. It shall thereupon make an order specifying the facts that appear without substantial controversy, including the extent to which the amount of damages or other relief is not in controversy, and directing such further proceedings in the action as are just. FL ST RCP Rule 1.510(d).

ii. On the trial or final hearing of the action the facts so specified shall be deemed established, and the trial or final hearing shall be conducted accordingly. FL ST RCP Rule 1.510(d).

3. *Arbitration and mediation*

a. *Referral to arbitration and mediation.* Except as hereinafter provided or as otherwise prohibited by law, the presiding judge may enter an order referring all or any part of a contested civil matter to mediation or arbitration. The parties to any contested civil matter may file a written stipulation to mediate or arbitrate any issue between them at any time. Such stipulation shall be incorporated into the order of referral. FL ST RCP Rule 1.700(a).

b. *Arbitration*

i. *Exclusions.* A civil action shall be ordered to arbitration or arbitration in conjunction with mediation upon stipulation of the parties. A civil action may be ordered to arbitration or arbitration in conjunction with mediation upon motion of any party or by the court, if the judge determines the action to be of such a nature that arbitration could be of benefit to the litigants or the court. FL ST RCP Rule 1.800.

- Under no circumstances may the following categories of actions be referred to arbitration: (1) bond estreatures; (2) habeas corpus or other extraordinary writs; (3) bond validations; (4) civil or criminal contempt; (5) such other matters as may be specified by order of the chief judge in the circuit. FL ST RCP Rule 1.800.

ii. For more information regarding arbitration, please see FL ST RCP Rule 1.810; FL ST RCP Rule 1.820; FL ST RCP Rule 1.830.

c. *Mediation.* For more information regarding mediation, please see FL ST RCP Rule 1.710; FL ST RCP Rule 1.720; FL ST RCP Rule 1.730; and FL ST RCP Rule 1.750.

4. *Rules of court*

a. *Rules of civil procedure.* The Florida Rules of Civil Procedure apply to all actions of a civil nature and all special statutory proceedings in the circuit courts and county courts except those to which the

Florida Probate Rules, the Florida Family Law Rules of Procedure, or the Small Claims Rules apply. FL ST RCP Rule 1.010.

i. The form, content, procedure, and time for pleading in all special statutory proceedings shall be as prescribed by the statutes governing the proceeding unless the Florida Rules of Civil Procedure specifically provide to the contrary. FL ST RCP Rule 1.010.

ii. The Florida Rules of Civil Procedure shall be construed to secure the just, speedy, and inexpensive determination of every action. FL ST RCP Rule 1.010.

b. *Rules of judicial administration.* The Florida Rules of Judicial Administration shall apply to administrative matters in all courts to which the Florida Rules of Judicial Administration are applicable by their terms. The Florida Rules of Judicial Administration shall be construed to secure the speedy and inexpensive determination of every proceeding to which they are applicable. The Florida Rules of Judicial Administration shall supersede all conflicting rules and statutes. FL ST J ADMIN Rule 2.110.

D. Documents

1. *Required documents*

a. *Notice of hearing/Motion.* An application to the court for an order shall be by motion which shall be made in writing unless made during a hearing or trial, shall state with particularity the grounds therefor, and shall set forth the relief or order sought. The requirement of writing is fulfilled if the motion is stated in a written notice of the hearing of the motion. All notices of hearing shall specify each motion or other matter to be heard. FL ST RCP Rule 1.100(b).

i. *Notices to persons with disabilities.* See the Format section of this KeyRules document for further information.

b. *Certificate of service.* When any attorney certifies in substance: "I certify that a copy hereof has been furnished to (here insert name or names and addresses used for service) by (e-mail) (delivery) (mail) (fax) on .... (date) ....________________ Attorney" the certificate is taken as prima facie proof of such service in compliance with FL ST J ADMIN Rule 2.516. FL ST J ADMIN Rule 2.516(f).

2. *Supplemental documents*

a. *Affidavits.* Supporting and opposing affidavits shall be made on personal knowledge, shall set forth such facts as would be admissible in evidence, and shall show affirmatively that the affiant is competent to testify to the matters stated therein. Sworn or certified copies of all papers or parts thereof referred to in an affidavit shall be attached thereto or served therewith. FL ST RCP Rule 1.510(e). For further information regarding affidavits made in the context of a motion for summary judgment see FL ST RCP Rule 1.510(e) through FL ST RCP Rule 1.510(g).

b. *Other evidence.* The movant shall also serve at that time a copy of any summary judgment evidence on which the movant relies that has not already been filed with the court. FL ST RCP Rule 1.510(c).

c. *Proposed order.* The court may require that orders or judgments be prepared by a party, may require the party to furnish the court with stamped, addressed envelopes for service of the order or judgment, and may require that proposed orders and judgments be furnished to all parties before entry by the court of the order or judgment. FL ST J ADMIN Rule 2.516(h)(1).

d. *Notice of constitutional question.* A party that files a pleading, written motion, or other paper drawing into question the constitutionality of a state statute or a county or municipal charter, ordinance, or franchise must promptly (1) file a notice of constitutional question stating the question and identifying the paper that raises it; and (2) serve the notice and the pleading, written motion, or other paper drawing into question the constitutionality of a state statute or a county or municipal charter, ordinance, or franchise on the Attorney General or the state attorney of the judicial circuit in which the action is pending, by either certified or registered mail. Service of the notice and pleading, written motion, or other paper does not require joinder of the Attorney General or the state attorney as a party to the action. FL ST RCP Rule 1.071.

E. Format

1. *Documents; Type and size.* Documents subject to the exceptions set forth in FL ST J ADMIN Rule

2.525(d) shall be filed on recycled paper measuring eight and one half by eleven (8 1/2 by 11) inches. For purposes of FL ST J ADMIN Rule 2.520, paper is recycled if it contains a minimum content of fifty (50) percent waste paper. Xerographic reduction of legal-size (eight and one half by fourteen (8 1/2 by 14) inches) documents to letter size (eight and one half by eleven (8 1/2 by 11) inches) is prohibited. All other documents filed by electronic transmission shall be filed in a format capable of being printed in a format consistent with the provisions of FL ST J ADMIN Rule 2.250. FL ST J ADMIN Rule 2.520(b).

a. *Exhibits.* Any exhibit or attachment filed with pleadings or papers may be filed in its original size. FL ST J ADMIN Rule 2.520(c).

b. *Recording space.* On all papers and documents prepared and filed by the court or by any party to a proceeding which are to be recorded in the public records of any county, including but not limited to final money judgments and notices of lis pendens, a three (3) inch by three (3) inch space at the top right-hand corner on the first page and a one (1) inch by three (3) inch space at the top right-hand corner on each subsequent page shall be left blank and reserved for use by the clerk of court. FL ST J ADMIN Rule 2.520(d).

   i. *Exceptions to recording space.* Any papers or documents created by persons or entities over which the filing party has no control, including but not limited to wills, codicils, trusts, or other testamentary documents; documents prepared or executed by any public officer; documents prepared, executed, acknowledged, or proved outside of the State of Florida; or documents created by State or Federal government agencies, may be filed without the space required by FL ST J ADMIN Rule 2.520. FL ST J ADMIN Rule 2.520(e).

c. *Noncompliance.* No clerk of court is permitted to refuse to file any document or paper because of noncompliance with the Florida Rules of Judicial Administration. However, upon request of the clerk of court, noncomplying documents must be resubmitted in accordance with the formatting rules. FL ST J ADMIN Rule 2.520(f).

2. *Caption.* Every pleading, motion, order, judgment, or other paper shall have a caption containing the name of the court, the file number, and except for in rem proceedings, including forfeiture proceedings, the name of the first party on each side with an appropriate indication of other parties, and a designation identifying the party filing it and its nature or the nature of the order, as the case may be. In any in rem proceeding, every pleading, motion, order, judgment, or other paper shall have a caption containing the name of the court, the file number, the style "In re" (followed by the name or general description of the property), and a designation of the person or entity filing it and its nature or the nature of the order, as the case may be. In an in rem forfeiture proceeding, the style shall be "In re forfeiture of" (followed by the name of the general description of the property). All papers filed in the action shall be styled in such a manner as to indicate clearly the subject matter of the paper and the party requesting or obtaining relief. FL ST RCP Rule 1.100(c)(1).

3. *Writing and written defined.* Writing or written means a document containing information, an application, or a stipulation. FL ST RCP Rule 1.080(c).

4. *Rule abbreviations*

   a. The Florida Rules of Civil Procedure and shall be abbreviated as Fla.R.Civ.P. FL ST RCP Rule 1.010.

   b. The Florida Rules of Judicial Administration shall be abbreviated as Fla. R. Jud. Admin. FL ST J ADMIN Rule 2.110.

5. *Nonverification.* Except when otherwise specifically provided by the Florida Rules of Civil Procedure or an applicable statute, every pleading or other document of a party represented by an attorney need not be verified or accompanied by an affidavit. FL ST RCP Rule 1.030; FL ST J ADMIN Rule 2.515(a).

6. *Attorney signature*

   a. *Attorney signature.* Every pleading and other document of a party represented by an attorney shall be signed by at least one (1) attorney of record in that attorney's individual name whose current record Florida Bar address, telephone number, including area code, primary e-mail address and secondary e-mail addresses, if any, and Florida Bar number shall be stated, and who shall be duly licensed to

practice law in Florida or who shall have received permission to appear in the particular case as provided in FL ST J ADMIN Rule 2.510. FL ST J ADMIN Rule 2.515(a).

i. The attorney may be required by the court to give the address of, and to vouch for the attorney's authority to represent, the party. FL ST J ADMIN Rule 2.515(a).

ii. The signature of an attorney shall constitute a certificate by the attorney that the attorney has read the pleading or other document; that to the best of the attorney's knowledge, information, and belief there is good ground to support it; and that it is not interposed for delay. FL ST J ADMIN Rule 2.515(a).

iii. If a pleading is not signed or is signed with intent to defeat the purpose of FL ST J ADMIN Rule 2.515, it may be stricken and the action may proceed as though the pleading or other document had not been served. FL ST J ADMIN Rule 2.515(a).

b. *Pro se litigant signature.* A party who is not represented by an attorney shall sign any pleading or other paper and state the party's address and telephone number, including area code. FL ST J ADMIN Rule 2.515(b).

c. *Form of signature*

i. The signatures required on pleadings and documents by FL ST J ADMIN Rule 2.515(a) and FL ST J ADMIN Rule 2.515(b) may be:

- Original signatures;
- Original signatures that have been reproduced by electronic means, such as on electronically transmitted documents or photocopied documents;
- Electronic signatures using the "/s/," "s/," or "/s" formats by or at the direction of the person signing; or
- Any other signature format authorized by general law, so long as the clerk where the proceeding is pending has the capability of receiving and has obtained approval from the Supreme Court of Florida to accept pleadings and documents with that signature format. FL ST J ADMIN Rule 2.515(c)(1).

ii. An attorney, party, or other person who files a pleading or paper by electronic transmission that does not contain the original signature of that attorney, party, or other person shall file that identical pleading or paper in paper form containing an original signature of that attorney, party, or other person (hereinafter called the follow-up filing) immediately thereafter. The follow-up filing is not required if the Supreme Court of Florida has entered an order directing the clerk of court to discontinue accepting the follow-up filing. FL ST J ADMIN Rule 2.515(c)(2).

7. *Forms*

a. *Process.* The forms of process, notice of lis pendens, and notice of action provided in the Florida Rules of Civil Procedure are sufficient. Variations from the forms do not void process or notices that are otherwise sufficient. FL ST RCP Rule 1.900(a).

b. *Other forms.* The other forms provided in the Florida Rules of Civil Procedure are sufficient for the matters that are covered by them. So long as the substance is expressed without prolixity, the forms may be varied to meet the facts of a particular case. FL ST RCP Rule 1.900(b).

c. *Formal matters.* Captions, except for the designation of the paper, are omitted from the forms provided in the Florida Rules of Civil Procedure. A general form of caption is the first form provided. Signatures are omitted from pleadings and motions. FL ST RCP Rule 1.900(c).

8. *Notices to persons with disabilities.* All notices of court proceedings to be held in a public facility, and all process compelling appearance at such proceedings, shall include the following statement in bold face, fourteen (14) point Times New Roman or Courier font: "If you are a person with a disability who needs any accommodation in order to participate in this proceeding, you are entitled, at no cost to you, to the provision of certain assistance. Please contact [identify applicable court personnel by name, address, and telephone number] at least seven (7) days before your scheduled court appearance, or immediately upon receiving this notification if the time before the scheduled appearance is less than seven (7) days; if you are hearing or voice impaired, call 711." FL ST J ADMIN Rule 2.540(c)(1).

9. *Minimization of the filing of sensitive information*

   a. *Limitations for court filings.* Unless authorized by FL ST J ADMIN Rule 2.425(b), statute, another rule of court, or the court orders otherwise, designated sensitive information filed with the court must be limited to the following format:

      i. The initials of a person known to be a minor;

      ii. The year of birth of a person's birth date;

      iii. No portion of any: Social security number, Bank account number, Credit card account number, Charge account number, or Debit account number;

      iv. The last four digits of any: Taxpayer identification number (TIN), Employee identification number, Driver's license number, Passport number, Telephone number, Financial account number, except as set forth in FL ST J ADMIN Rule 2.425(a)(3), Brokerage account number, Insurance policy account number, Loan account number, Customer account number, or Patient or health care number;

      v. A truncated version of any: Email address, Computer user name, Password, or Personal identification number (PIN); and

      vi. A truncated version of any other sensitive information as provided by court order. FL ST J ADMIN Rule 2.425(a).

   b. *Exceptions.* FL ST J ADMIN Rule 2.425(a) does not apply to the following:

      i. An account number which identifies the property alleged to be the subject of a proceeding;

      ii. The record of an administrative or agency proceeding;

      iii. The record in appellate or review proceedings;

      iv. The birth date of a minor whenever the birth date is necessary for the court to establish or maintain subject matter jurisdiction;

      v. The name of a minor in any order relating to parental responsibility, time-sharing, or child support;

      vi. The name of a minor in any document or order affecting the minor's ownership of real property;

      vii. The birth date of a party in a writ of attachment or notice to payor;

      viii. In traffic and criminal proceedings: a pro se filing; a court filing that is related to a criminal matter or investigation and that is prepared before the filing of a criminal charge or is not filed as part of any docketed criminal case; an arrest or search warrant or any information in support thereof; a charging document and an affidavit or other documents filed in support of any charging document, including any driving records; a statement of particulars; discovery material introduced into evidence or otherwise filed with the court; and all information necessary for the proper issuance and execution of a subpoena duces tecum;

      ix. Information used by the clerk for case maintenance purposes or the courts for case management purposes; and

      x. Information which is relevant and material to an issue before the court. FL ST J ADMIN Rule 2.425(b).

   c. *Remedies.* Upon motion by a party or interested person or sua sponte by the court, the court may order remedies, sanctions or both for a violation of FL ST J ADMIN Rule 2.425(a). Following notice and an opportunity to respond, the court may impose sanctions if such filing was not made in good faith. FL ST J ADMIN Rule 2.425(c).

   d. *Motions not restricted.* FL ST J ADMIN Rule 2.425 does not restrict a party's right to move for protective order, to move to file documents under seal, or to request a determination of the confidentiality of records. FL ST J ADMIN Rule 2.425(d).

      i. For more information regarding sealing court records, please see FL ST 4 J CIR 2006-05.

   e. *Application.* FL ST J ADMIN Rule 2.425 does not affect the application of constitutional provisions, statutes, or rules of court regarding confidential information or access to public information. FL ST J ADMIN Rule 2.425(e).

F. Filing and Service Requirements

1. *Filing requirements.* All original documents must be filed with the court either before service or immediately thereafter, unless otherwise provided for by general law or other rules. If the original of any bond or other document is not placed in the court file, a certified copy must be so placed by the clerk. FL ST J ADMIN Rule 2.516(d). All documents shall be filed in conformity with the requirements of FL ST J ADMIN Rule 2.525. FL ST RCP Rule 1.080(b). All documents filed in any court shall be filed by electronic transmission in accordance with FL ST J ADMIN Rule 2.525. "Documents" means pleadings, motions, petitions, memoranda, briefs, notices, exhibits, declarations, affidavits, orders, judgments, decrees, writs, opinions, and any other paper or writing submitted to a court. FL ST J ADMIN Rule 2.520(a). All documents that are court records, as defined in FL ST J ADMIN Rule 2.430(a)(1), must be filed by electronic transmission, provided that: (1) the clerk has the ability to accept and retain such documents; (2) the clerk or the chief judge of the circuit has requested permission to accept documents filed by electronic transmission; and (3) the supreme court has entered an order granting permission to the clerk to accept documents filed by electronic transmission. FL ST J ADMIN Rule 2.525(c)(1).
   a. *Definition.* "Electronic transmission of documents" means the sending of information by electronic signals to, by or from a court or clerk, which when received can be transformed and stored or transmitted on paper, microfilm, magnetic storage device, optical imaging system, CD-ROM, flash drive, other electronic data storage system, server, case maintenance system ("CM"), electronic court filing ("ECF") system, statewide or local electronic portal ("e-portal"), or other electronic record keeping system authorized by the supreme court in a format sufficient to communicate the information on the original document in a readable format. Electronic transmission of documents includes electronic mail ("e-mail") and any internet-based transmission procedure, and may include procedures allowing for documents to be signed or verified by electronic means. FL ST J ADMIN Rule 2.525(a).
      i. The filing of documents with the court as required by the Florida Rules of Judicial Administration must be made by filing them with the clerk in accordance with FL ST J ADMIN Rule 2.525, except that the judge may permit documents to be filed with the judge, in which event the judge must note the filing date before him or her on the documents and transmit them to the clerk. The date of filing is that shown on the face of the document by the judge's notation or the clerk's time stamp, whichever is earlier. FL ST J ADMIN Rule 2.516(e).
   b. *Application.* Any court or clerk of the court may accept the electronic transmission of documents for filing after the clerk, together with input from the chief judge of the circuit, has obtained approval of the procedures and program for doing so from the Supreme Court of Florida. FL ST J ADMIN Rule 2.525(b).
   c. *Exceptions*
      i. Paper documents and other submissions may be manually submitted to the clerk or court:
         - When the clerk does not have the ability to accept and retain documents by electronic filing or has not had ECF Procedures approved by the supreme court;
         - For filing by any self-represented party or any self-represented nonparty unless specific ECF Procedures provide a means to file documents electronically. However, any self-represented nonparty that is a governmental or public agency and any other agency, partnership, corporation, or business entity acting on behalf of any governmental or public agency may file documents by electronic transmission if such entity has the capability of filing documents electronically;
         - For filing by attorneys excused from e-mail service in accordance with FL ST J ADMIN Rule 2.516(b);
         - When submitting evidentiary exhibits or filing non-documentary materials;
         - When the filing involves documents in excess of twenty-five (25) megabytes (25MB) in size. For such filings, documents may be transmitted using an electronic storage medium

that the clerk has the ability to accept, which may include a CD-ROM, flash drive, or similar storage medium;

- When filed in open court, as permitted by the court;
- When paper filing is permitted by any approved statewide or local ECF procedures; and
- If any court determines that justice so requires. FL ST J ADMIN Rule 2.525(d).

ii. Any document in paper form submitted under FL ST J ADMIN Rule 2.525(d) is filed when it is received by the clerk or court and the clerk shall immediately thereafter convert any filed paper document to an electronic document. "Convert to an electronic document" means optically capturing an image of a paper document and using character recognition software to recover as much of the document's text as practicable and then indexing and storing the document in the official court file. FL ST J ADMIN Rule 2.525(c)(4).

iii. Any storage medium submitted under FL ST J ADMIN Rule 2.525(d)(5) is filed when received by the clerk or court and the clerk shall immediately thereafter transfer the electronic documents from the storage device to the official court file. FL ST J ADMIN Rule 2.525(c)(5).

iv. If the filer of any paper document authorized under FL ST J ADMIN Rule 2.525(d) provides a self-addressed, postage-paid envelope for return of the paper document after it is converted to electronic form by the clerk, the clerk shall place the paper document in the envelope and deposit it in the mail. Except when a paper document is required to be maintained, the clerk may recycle any filed paper document that is not to be returned to the filer. FL ST J ADMIN Rule 2.525(c)(6).

v. The clerk may convert any paper document filed before the effective date of FL ST J ADMIN Rule 2.525 to an electronic document. Unless the clerk is required to maintain the paper document, if the paper document has been converted to an electronic document by the clerk, the paper document is no longer part of the official court file and may be removed and recycled. FL ST J ADMIN Rule 2.525(c)(7).

d. *Official court file.* For information on what constitutes the official court file, please see FL ST J ADMIN Rule 2.525(c)(2), FL ST J ADMIN Rule 2.525(c)(3).

e. *Administration.* All attorneys, parties, or other persons using this rule to file documents are required to make arrangements with the court or clerk for the payment of any charges authorized by general law or the supreme court before filing any document by electronic transmission. FL ST J ADMIN Rule 2.525(f)(2).

f. *Filing date.* The filing date for an electronically transmitted document is the date and time that such filing is acknowledged by an electronic stamp or otherwise, pursuant to any procedure set forth in any ECF Procedures approved by the supreme court, or the date the last page of such filing is received by the court or clerk. FL ST J ADMIN Rule 2.525(f)(3).

g. *Accessibility.* All documents transmitted in any electronic form under FL ST J ADMIN Rule 2.525 must comply with the accessibility requirements of FL ST J ADMIN Rule 2.526. FL ST J ADMIN Rule 2.525(g).

2. *Service requirements.* Every pleading subsequent to the initial pleading, all orders, and every other document filed in the action must be served in conformity with the requirements of FL ST J ADMIN Rule 2.516. FL ST RCP Rule 1.080(a).

a. *Service; When required.* Unless the court otherwise orders, or a statute or supreme court administrative order specifies a different means of service, every pleading subsequent to the initial pleading and every other document filed in any court proceeding, except applications for witness subpoenas and documents served by formal notice or required to be served in the manner provided for service of formal notice, must be served in accordance with FL ST J ADMIN Rule 2.516 on each party. No service need be made on parties against whom a default has been entered, except that pleadings asserting new or additional claims against them must be served in the manner provided for service of summons. FL ST J ADMIN Rule 2.516(a).

b. *Service; How made.* When service is required or permitted to be made upon a party represented by

an attorney, service must be made upon the attorney unless service upon the party is ordered by the court. FL ST J ADMIN Rule 2.516(b).

i. *Service by electronic mail ("e-mail").* All documents required or permitted to be served on another party must be served by e-mail, unless FL ST J ADMIN Rule 2.516 otherwise provides. When, in addition to service by e-mail, the sender also utilizes another means of service provided for in FL ST J ADMIN Rule 2.516(b)(2), any differing time limits and other provisions applicable to that other means of service control. FL ST J ADMIN Rule 2.516(b)(1). Any document electronically transmitted to a court or clerk must also be served on all parties and interested persons in accordance with the applicable rules of court. FL ST J ADMIN Rule 2.525(e)(2).

- *Service on attorneys.* Upon appearing in a proceeding, an attorney must serve a designation of a primary e-mail address and may designate no more than two (2) secondary e-mail addresses. Thereafter, service must be directed to all designated e-mail addresses in that proceeding. Every document filed by an attorney thereafter must include the primary e-mail address of that attorney and any secondary e-mail addresses. If an attorney does not designate any e-mail address for service, documents may be served on that attorney at the e-mail address on record with The Florida Bar. FL ST J ADMIN Rule 2.516(b)(1)(A).
- *Exception to e-mail service on attorneys.* Service by an attorney on another attorney must be made by e-mail unless excused by the court. Upon motion by an attorney demonstrating that the attorney has no e-mail account and lacks access to the Internet at the attorney's office, the court may excuse the attorney from the requirements of e-mail service. Service on and by an attorney excused by the court from e-mail service must be by the means provided in FL ST J ADMIN Rule 2.516(b)(2). FL ST J ADMIN Rule 2.516(b)(1)(B).
- *Service on and by parties not represented by an attorney.* Any party not represented by an attorney may serve a designation of a primary e-mail address and also may designate no more than two (2) secondary e-mail addresses to which service must be directed in that proceeding by the means provided in FL ST J ADMIN Rule 2.516(b)(1). If a party not represented by an attorney does not designate an e-mail address for service in a proceeding, service on and by that party must be by the means provided in FL ST J ADMIN Rule 2.516(b)(2). FL ST J ADMIN Rule 2.516(b)(1)(C).
- *Time of service.* Service by e-mail is complete when it is sent. FL ST J ADMIN Rule 2.516(b)(1)(D). An e-mail is deemed served on the date it is sent. FL ST J ADMIN Rule 2.516(b)(1)(D)(i). If the sender learns that the e-mail did not reach the address of the person to be served, the sender must immediately send another copy by e-mail, or by a means authorized by FL ST J ADMIN Rule 2.516(b)(2). FL ST J ADMIN Rule 2.516(b)(1)(D)(ii). E-mail service is treated as service by mail for the computation of time. FL ST J ADMIN Rule 2.516(b)(1)(D)(iii).

ii. *Format of e-mail for service.* Service of a document by e-mail is made by attaching a copy of the document in PDF format to an e-mail sent to all addresses designated by the attorney or party. FL ST J ADMIN Rule 2.516(b)(1)(E).

- All documents served by e-mail must be attached to an e-mail message containing a subject line beginning with the words "SERVICE OF COURT DOCUMENT" in all capital letters, followed by the case number of the proceeding in which the documents are being served. FL ST J ADMIN Rule 2.516(b)(1)(E)(i).
- The body of the e-mail must identify the court in which the proceeding is pending, the case number, the name of the initial party on each side, the title of each document served with that e-mail, and the sender's name and telephone number. FL ST J ADMIN Rule 2.516(b)(1)(E)(ii).
- Any document served by e-mail may be signed by the "/s/" format, as long as the filed original is signed in accordance with the applicable rule of procedure. FL ST J ADMIN Rule 2.516(b)(1)(E)(iii).
- Any e-mail which, together with its attached documents, exceeds five megabytes (5MB) in

size, must be divided and sent as separate e-mails, no one of which may exceed five megabytes (5MB) in size and each of which must be sequentially numbered in the subject line. FL ST J ADMIN Rule 2.516(b)(1)(E)(iv).

iii. *Service by other means.* In addition to, and not in lieu of, service by e-mail, service may also be made upon attorneys by any of the means specified in FL ST J ADMIN Rule 2.516(b)(2). Service on and by all parties who are not represented by an attorney and who do not designate an e-mail address, and on and by all attorneys excused from e-mail service, must be made by delivering a copy of the document or by mailing it to the party or attorney at their last known address or, if no address is known, by leaving it with the clerk of the court. Service by mail is complete upon mailing. Delivery of a copy within FL ST J ADMIN Rule 2.516 is complete upon:

- Handing it to the attorney or to the party,
- Leaving it at the attorney's or party's office with a clerk or other person in charge thereof,
- If there is no one in charge, leaving it in a conspicuous place therein,
- If the office is closed or the person to be served has no office, leaving it at the person's usual place of abode with some person of his or her family above fifteen (15) years of age and informing such person of the contents, or
- Transmitting it by facsimile to the attorney's or party's office with a cover sheet containing the sender's name, firm, address, telephone number, and facsimile number, and the number of pages transmitted. When service is made by facsimile, a copy must also be served by any other method permitted by FL ST J ADMIN Rule 2.516. Facsimile service occurs when transmission is complete. FL ST J ADMIN Rule 2.516(b)(2)(A) through FL ST J ADMIN Rule 2.516(b)(2)(E).
- Service by delivery after 5:00 p.m. must be deemed to have been made by mailing on the date of delivery. FL ST J ADMIN Rule 2.516(b)(2)(F).

c. *Service; Numerous defendants.* In actions when the parties are unusually numerous, the court may regulate the service contemplated by the Florida Rules of Judicial Administration on motion or on its own initiative in such manner as may be found to be just and reasonable. FL ST J ADMIN Rule 2.516(c).

d. *Service by clerk.* Service of notices and other documents required to be made by the clerk must also be done as provided in FL ST J ADMIN Rule 2.516(b). FL ST J ADMIN Rule 2.516(g).

G. Hearings

1. *Hearing on motion for summary judgment.* The summary judgment rule does not provide the trial court with discretion to decide whether a hearing is required. A failure to hold a hearing on a motion for summary judgment violates due process as well as rule of procedure governing summary judgment procedure. Kozich v. Hartford Ins. Co. of Midwest, 609 So.2d 147, 148 (Fla. 4th DCA 1992); FL-RCPF R 1.510(102).

2. *Summary judgment consideration at pretrial conference.* A summary judgment can be granted at the pretrial conference. The standard and procedure for granting summary judgment is the same at a pretrial conference as at other times. The notice time for a pretrial conference and for service of a motion for summary judgment is the same, so summary judgment can be entered at the conference if no genuine issue of material fact exists. FL-PRACPROC § 19:4.

3. *Communication equipment*

a. *Definition.* Communication equipment means a conference telephone or other electronic device that permits all those appearing or participating to hear and speak to each other, provided that all conversation of all parties is audible to all persons present. FL ST J ADMIN Rule 2.530(a).

b. *Use by all parties.* A county or circuit court judge may, upon the court's own motion or upon the written request of a party, direct that communication equipment be used for a motion hearing, pretrial conference, or a status conference. A judge must give notice to the parties and consider any objections they may have to the use of communication equipment before directing that communication equipment be used. The decision to use communication equipment over the objection of parties will be in the sound discretion of the trial court, except as noted below. FL ST J ADMIN Rule 2.530(b).

c. *Use only by requesting party.* A county or circuit court judge may, upon the written request of a party upon reasonable notice to all other parties, permit a requesting party to participate through communication equipment in a scheduled motion hearing; however, any such request (except in criminal, juvenile, and appellate proceedings) must be granted, absent a showing of good cause to deny the same, where the hearing is set for not longer than fifteen (15) minutes. FL ST J ADMIN Rule 2.530(c).

d. *Testimony*

   i. *Generally.* A county or circuit court judge, general magistrate, special magistrate, or hearing officer may allow testimony to be taken through communication equipment if all parties consent or if permitted by another applicable rule of procedure. FL ST J ADMIN Rule 2.530(d)(1).

   ii. *Procedure.* Any party desiring to present testimony through communication equipment shall, prior to the hearing or trial at which the testimony is to be presented, contact all parties to determine whether each party consents to this form of testimony. The party seeking to present the testimony shall move for permission to present testimony through communication equipment, which motion shall set forth good cause as to why the testimony should be allowed in this form. FL ST J ADMIN Rule 2.530(d)(2).

   iii. *Oath.* Testimony may be taken through communication equipment only if a notary public or other person authorized to administer oaths in the witness's jurisdiction is present with the witness and administers the oath consistent with the laws of the jurisdiction. FL ST J ADMIN Rule 2.530(d)(3).

   iv. *Confrontation rights.* In juvenile and criminal proceedings the defendant must make an informed waiver of any confrontation rights that may be abridged by the use of communication equipment. FL ST J ADMIN Rule 2.530(d)(4).

   v. *Video testimony.* If the testimony to be presented utilizes video conferencing or comparable two-way visual capabilities, the court in its discretion may modify the procedures set forth in FL ST J ADMIN Rule 2.530 to accommodate the technology utilized. FL ST J ADMIN Rule 2.530(d)(5).

e. *Burden of expense.* The cost for the use of the communication equipment is the responsibility of the requesting party unless otherwise directed by the court. FL ST J ADMIN Rule 2.530(e).

H. Forms

1. Official Motion for Summary Judgment Forms for Florida

a. Caption. FL ST RCP Form 1.901.

b. Notice of compliance when constitutional challenge is brought. FL ST RCP Form 1.975.

2. Motion for Summary Judgment Forms for Florida

a. Motion for summary judgment; By plaintiff. FL-PP § 6:9.

b. Motion for summary judgment; By defendant. FL-PP § 6:10.

c. Affidavit; Supporting motion for summary judgment; By plaintiff's attorney. FL-PP § 6:11.

d. Affidavit; Opposing motion for summary judgment; By defendant's attorney. FL-PP § 6:12.

e. Affidavit; Opposing motion for summary judgment; By party; Inability to present facts. FL-PP § 6:13.

f. Order; Establishing uncontroverted facts and stating issues requiring further determination. FL-PP § 6:14.

g. Summary judgment. FL-PP § 6:15.

h. Motion; Summary judgment, by defendant. FL-PRACFORM § 7:190.

i. Motion; Summary judgment, by plaintiff. FL-PRACFORM § 7:191.

j. Motion; Summary judgment, partial, by defendant. FL-PRACFORM § 7:192.

k. Motion; Summary judgment, part of claim. FL-PRACFORM § 7:193.

l. Form for plaintiff's motion for summary judgment. FL-RCPF R 1.510(128).

m. Form for notice of motion for summary judgment by plaintiff. FL-RCPF R 1.510(129).

n. Form for notice of cross-motion for summary judgment by plaintiff. FL-RCPF R 1.510(130).

o. Form for order denying motion for summary judgment and specifying uncontroverted facts. FL-RCPF R 1.510(304).

p. Form for motion for partial summary judgment. FL-RCPF R 1.510(305).

q. Form for motion for partial summary judgment; Affirmative defenses. FL-RCPF R 1.510(305.1).

I. Checklist

(I) ❑ Matters to be considered by moving party

(a) ❑ Required documents

(1) ❑ Notice of hearing/Motion

(2) ❑ Certificate of service

(b) ❑ Supplemental documents

(1) ❑ Affidavits

(2) ❑ Other evidence

(3) ❑ Proposed order

(4) ❑ Notice of constitutional question

(c) ❑ Time for making motion

(1) ❑ By the plaintiff, after the expiration of twenty (20) days from the commencement of the action (claimant), or after service of a motion for summary judgment by the adverse party

(2) ❑ By the defending party at any time

(3) ❑ The motion for summary judgment must be served at least twenty (20) days before the time fixed for the hearing

(II) ❑ Matters to be considered by opposing party

(a) ❑ Required documents

(1) ❑ Response to motion

(2) ❑ Certificate of service

(b) ❑ Supplemental documents

(1) ❑ Affidavits

(2) ❑ Notice of evidence relied upon

(3) ❑ Other evidence

(4) ❑ Proposed order

(5) ❑ Notice of constitutional question

(c) ❑ Time for service and filing of opposition

(1) ❑ The adverse party shall identify, by notice mailed to the movant's attorney at least five (5) days prior to the day of the hearing, or delivered no later than 5:00 p.m. two (2) business days prior to the day of the hearing, any summary judgment evidence on which the adverse party relies

(2) ❑ To the extent that summary judgment evidence has not already been filed with the court, the

adverse party shall serve a copy on the movant by mail at least five (5) days prior to the day of the hearing, or by delivery to the movant's attorney no later than 5:00 p.m. two (2) business days prior to the day of hearing

Motions, Oppositions and Replies
Motion for Sanctions

Document Last Updated January 2013

A. Applicable Rules

1. *State rules*
   a. Attorney's fee; Sanctions for raising unsupported claims or defenses; Exceptions; Service of motions; Damages for delay of litigation. FL ST § 57.105.
   b. Administrative Procedure Act. FL ST § 120.50; FL ST § 120.52; FL ST § 120.68; FL ST § 120.81.
   c. Offer of judgment and demand for judgment. FL ST § 768.79.
   d. Proposals for settlement. FL ST RCP Rule 1.442.
   e. Motions for costs and attorneys' fees. FL ST RCP Rule 1.525.
   f. Rules of court. FL ST RCP Rule 1.010; FL ST J ADMIN Rule 2.110.
   g. Nonverification of pleadings. FL ST RCP Rule 1.030.
   h. Service and filing of pleadings, orders, and documents. FL ST RCP Rule 1.080.
   i. Time. FL ST RCP Rule 1.090.
   j. Pleadings and motions. FL ST RCP Rule 1.100.
   k. Motions. FL ST RCP Rule 1.160.
   l. Relief from judgment, decrees, or orders. FL ST RCP Rule 1.540.
   m. Mediation and arbitration. FL ST RCP Rule 1.700; FL ST RCP Rule 1.710; FL ST RCP Rule 1.720; FL ST RCP Rule 1.730; FL ST RCP Rule 1.750; FL ST RCP Rule 1.800; FL ST RCP Rule 1.810; FL ST RCP Rule 1.820; FL ST RCP Rule 1.830.
   n. Forms. FL ST RCP Rule 1.900.
   o. Minimization of the filing of sensitive information. FL ST J ADMIN Rule 2.425.
   p. Retention of court records. FL ST J ADMIN Rule 2.430.
   q. Foreign attorneys. FL ST J ADMIN Rule 2.510.
   r. Signature of attorneys and parties. FL ST J ADMIN Rule 2.515.
   s. Paper. FL ST J ADMIN Rule 2.520.
   t. Electronic filing. FL ST J ADMIN Rule 2.525.
   u. Accessibility of information and technology. FL ST J ADMIN Rule 2.526.
   v. Communication equipment. FL ST J ADMIN Rule 2.530.
   w. Court reporting. FL ST J ADMIN Rule 2.535.
   x. Requests for accommodations by persons with disabilities. FL ST J ADMIN Rule 2.540.
2. *Local rules*
   a. Sealing court records. FL ST 4 J CIR 2006-05.

B. Timing

1. *Motion for sanctions.* A motion by a party seeking sanctions under FL ST § 57.105 must be served but may not be filed with or presented to the court unless, within twenty one (21) days after service of the motion, the challenged paper, claim, defense, contention, allegation, or denial is not withdrawn or appropriately corrected. FL ST § 57.105(4).

2. *Sanctions in relation to proposals for settlement.* Any party seeking sanctions pursuant to applicable Florida law, based on the failure of the proposal's recipient to accept a proposal, shall do so by serving a motion in accordance with FL ST RCP Rule 1.525. FL ST RCP Rule 1.442(g). Any party seeking a judgment taxing costs, attorneys' fees, or both shall serve a motion no later than thirty (30) days after filing of the judgment, including a judgment of dismissal, or the service of a notice of voluntary dismissal, which judgment or notice concludes the action as to that party. FL ST RCP Rule 1.525.
3. *General motion timing.* A copy of any written motion which may not be heard ex parte and a copy of the notice of the hearing thereof shall be served a reasonable time before the time specified for the hearing. FL ST RCP Rule 1.090(d).
4. *Computation of time*
    a. *Generally.* Computation of time shall be governed by FL ST J ADMIN Rule 2.514. FL ST RCP Rule 1.090(a). The following rules apply in computing time periods specified in any rule of procedure, local rule, court order, or statute that does not specify a method of computing time. FL ST J ADMIN Rule 2.514(a).
        i. *Period stated in days or a longer unit.* When the period is stated in days or a longer unit of time (A) exclude the day of the event that triggers the period; (B) count every day, including intermediate Saturdays, Sundays, and legal holidays; and (C) include the last day of the period, but if the last day is a Saturday, Sunday, or legal holiday, or falls within any period of time extended through an order of the chief justice under FL ST J ADMIN Rule 2.205(a)(2)(B)(iv), the period continues to run until the end of the next day that is not a Saturday, Sunday, or legal holiday and does not fall within any period of time extended through an order of the chief justice. FL ST J ADMIN Rule 2.514(a)(1).
        ii. *Period stated in hours.* When the period is stated in hours (A) begin counting immediately on the occurrence of the event that triggers the period; (B) count every hour, including hours during intermediate Saturdays, Sundays, and legal holidays; and (C) if the period would end on a Saturday, Sunday, or legal holiday, or during any period of time extended through an order of the chief justice under FL ST J ADMIN Rule 2.205(a)(2)(B)(iv), the period continues to run until the same time on the next day that is not a Saturday, Sunday, or legal holiday and does not fall within any period of time extended through an order of the chief justice. FL ST J ADMIN Rule 2.514(a)(2).
        iii. *Period stated in days less than seven (7) days.* When the period stated in days is less than seven (7) days, intermediate Saturdays, Sundays, and legal holidays shall be excluded in the computation. FL ST J ADMIN Rule 2.514(a)(3).
        iv. *"Last day" defined.* Unless a different time is set by a statute, local rule, or court order, the last day ends (A) for electronic filing or for service by any means, at midnight; and (B) for filing by other means, when the clerk's office is scheduled to close. FL ST J ADMIN Rule 2.514(a)(4).
        v. *"Next day" defined.* The "next day" is determined by continuing to count forward when the period is measured after an event and backward when measured before an event. FL ST J ADMIN Rule 2.514(a)(5).
        vi. *"Legal holiday" defined.* "Legal holiday" means (A) the day set aside by FL ST § 110.117, for observing New Year's Day, Martin Luther King, Jr.'s Birthday, Memorial Day, Independence Day, Labor Day, Veterans' Day, Thanksgiving Day, the Friday after Thanksgiving Day, or Christmas Day, and (B) any day observed as a holiday by the clerk's office or as designated by the chief judge. FL ST J ADMIN Rule 2.514(a)(6).
    b. *Additional time after service by mail or e-mail.* When a party may or must act within a specified time after service and service is made by mail or e-mail, five (5) days are added after the period that would otherwise expire under FL ST J ADMIN Rule 2.514(a). FL ST J ADMIN Rule 2.514(b).
    c. *Enlargement.* When an act is required or allowed to be done at or within a specified time by order of court, by the Florida Rules of Civil Procedure, or by notice given thereunder, for cause shown the court at any time in its discretion (1) with or without notice, may order the period enlarged if request therefor is made before the expiration of the period originally prescribed or as extended by a previous

order, or (2) upon motion made and notice after the expiration of the specified period, may permit the act to be done when failure to act was the result of excusable neglect, but it may not extend the time for making a motion for new trial, for rehearing, or to alter or amend a judgment; making a motion for relief from a judgment under FL ST RCP Rule 1.540(b); taking an appeal or filing a petition for certiorari; or making a motion for a directed verdict. FL ST RCP Rule 1.090(b).

d. *Unaffected by expiration of term.* The period of time provided for the doing of any act or the taking of any proceeding shall not be affected or limited by the continued existence or expiration of a term of court. The continued existence or expiration of a term of court in no way affects the power of a court to do any act or take any proceeding in any action which is or has been pending before it. FL ST RCP Rule 1.090(c).

C. General Requirements

1. *Motions generally*

a. *Contents.* An application to the court for an order shall be by motion which shall be made in writing unless made during a hearing or trial, shall state with particularity the grounds therefor, and shall set forth the relief or order sought. The requirement of writing is fulfilled if the motion is stated in a written notice of the hearing of the motion. All notices of hearing shall specify each motion or other matter to be heard. FL ST RCP Rule 1.100(b).

b. *Particularity requirement.* The court considers a motion in the light of the substantive law, rule or statute to make its determination. Some rules require a statement of the grounds for a motion under the rule. Failure to give the grounds will result in denial of the motion. This should be the result in all situations when the ground for the motion is not inherent in the rule. FL-PRACPROC § 9:3. The requirement is nevertheless an important one, first because of the due process notice rights of the respondent, as well as for the assistance it provides to the court in its preparation for the hearing or, absent a hearing, for disposition. 4 FLPRAC R 1.100.

2. *Motion for sanctions*

a. *Sanctions for raising unsupported claims or defenses*

i. *No material facts; No law supporting material facts.* Upon the court's initiative or motion of any party, the court shall award a reasonable attorney's fee, including prejudgment interest, to be paid to the prevailing party in equal amounts by the losing party and the losing party's attorney on any claim or defense at any time during a civil proceeding or action in which the court finds that the losing party or the losing party's attorney knew or should have known that a claim or defense when initially presented to the court or at any time before trial was not supported by the material facts necessary to establish the claim or defense; or would not be supported by the application of then-existing law to those material facts. FL ST § 57.105(1).

ii. *Unreasonable delay.* At any time in any civil proceeding or action in which the moving party proves by a preponderance of the evidence that any action taken by the opposing party, including, but not limited to, the filing of any pleading or part thereof, the assertion of or response to any discovery demand, the assertion of any claim or defense, or the response to any request by any other party, was taken primarily for the purpose of unreasonable delay, the court shall award damages to the moving party for its reasonable expenses incurred in obtaining the order, which may include attorney's fees, and other loss resulting from the improper delay. FL ST § 57.105(2).

iii. *Limit on monetary sanctions.* Notwithstanding FL ST § 57.105(1) and FL ST § 57.105(2), monetary sanctions may not be awarded:

- Under FL ST § 57.105(1)(b) if the court determines that the claim or defense was initially presented to the court as a good faith argument for the extension, modification, or reversal of existing law or the establishment of new law, as it applied to the material facts, with a reasonable expectation of success. FL ST § 57.105(3)(a).
- Under FL ST § 57.105(1)(a) or FL ST § 57.105(1)(b) against the losing party's attorney if he or she has acted in good faith, based on the representations of his or her client as to the existence of those material facts. FL ST § 57.105(3)(b).

- Under FL ST § 57.105(1)(b) against a represented party. FL ST § 57.105(3)(c).
- On the court's initiative under FL ST § 57.105(1) and FL ST § 57.105(2) unless sanctions are awarded before a voluntary dismissal or settlement of the claims made by or against the party that is, or whose attorneys are, to be sanctioned. FL ST § 57.105(3)(d).

iv. *Other sanctions available.* The provisions of FL ST § 57.105 are supplemental to other sanctions or remedies available under law or under court rules. FL ST § 57.105(6).

v. *Fees provided for in contract.* If a contract contains a provision allowing attorney's fees to a party when he or she is required to take any action to enforce the contract, the court may also allow reasonable attorney's fees to the other party when that party prevails in any action, whether as plaintiff or defendant, with respect to the contract. FL ST § 57.105(7) applies to any contract entered into on or after October 1, 1988. FL ST § 57.105(7).

b. *Sanctions in relation to proposals for settlement*

i. *Generally.* Any party seeking sanctions pursuant to applicable Florida law, based on the failure of the proposal's recipient to accept a proposal, shall do so by serving a motion in accordance with FL ST RCP Rule 1.525. FL ST RCP Rule 1.442(g). Any party seeking a judgment taxing costs, attorneys' fees, or both shall serve a motion no later than thirty (30) days after filing of the judgment, including a judgment of dismissal, or the service of a notice of voluntary dismissal, which judgment or notice concludes the action as to that party. FL ST RCP Rule 1.525.

ii. *Motion after judgment, voluntary or involuntary dismissal.* Upon motion made by the offeror within thirty (30) days after the entry of judgment or after voluntary or involuntary dismissal, the court shall determine the following:

- If a defendant serves an offer which is not accepted by the plaintiff, and if the judgment obtained by the plaintiff is at least twenty-five (25%) percent less than the amount of the offer, the defendant shall be awarded reasonable costs, including investigative expenses, and attorney's fees, calculated in accordance with the guidelines promulgated by the Supreme Court, incurred from the date the offer was served, and the court shall set off such costs in attorney's fees against the award. When such costs and attorney's fees total more than the amount of the judgment, the court shall enter judgment for the defendant against the plaintiff for the amount of the costs and fees, less the amount of the award to the plaintiff. FL ST § 768.79(6)(a).
- If a plaintiff serves an offer which is not accepted by the defendant, and if the judgment obtained by the plaintiff is at least twenty-five (25%) percent more than the amount of the offer, the plaintiff shall be awarded reasonable costs, including investigative expenses, and attorney's fees, calculated in accordance with the guidelines promulgated by the Supreme Court, incurred from the date the offer was served. FL ST § 768.79(6)(b).
- For purposes of the determination required by FL ST § 768.79(6)(a), the term "judgment obtained" means the amount of the net judgment entered, plus any postoffer collateral source payments received or due as of the date of the judgment, plus any postoffer settlement amounts by which the verdict was reduced. For purposes of the determination required by FL ST § 768.79(6)(b), the term "judgment obtained" means the amount of the net judgment entered, plus any postoffer settlement amounts by which the verdict was reduced. FL ST § 768.79(6).

iii. For further information please see FL ST § 768.79 and FL ST RCP Rule 1.442.

3. *Arbitration and mediation*

a. *Referral to arbitration and mediation.* Except as hereinafter provided or as otherwise prohibited by law, the presiding judge may enter an order referring all or any part of a contested civil matter to mediation or arbitration. The parties to any contested civil matter may file a written stipulation to mediate or arbitrate any issue between them at any time. Such stipulation shall be incorporated into the order of referral. FL ST RCP Rule 1.700(a).

b. *Arbitration*

i. *Exclusions.* A civil action shall be ordered to arbitration or arbitration in conjunction with

mediation upon stipulation of the parties. A civil action may be ordered to arbitration or arbitration in conjunction with mediation upon motion of any party or by the court, if the judge determines the action to be of such a nature that arbitration could be of benefit to the litigants or the court. FL ST RCP Rule 1.800.

- Under no circumstances may the following categories of actions be referred to arbitration: (1) bond estreatures; (2) habeas corpus or other extraordinary writs; (3) bond validations; (4) civil or criminal contempt; (5) such other matters as may be specified by order of the chief judge in the circuit. FL ST RCP Rule 1.800.

ii. For more information regarding arbitration, please see FL ST RCP Rule 1.810; FL ST RCP Rule 1.820; FL ST RCP Rule 1.830.

c. *Mediation.* For more information regarding mediation, please see FL ST RCP Rule 1.710; FL ST RCP Rule 1.720; FL ST RCP Rule 1.730; and FL ST RCP Rule 1.750.

4. *Rules of court*

a. *Rules of civil procedure.* The Florida Rules of Civil Procedure apply to all actions of a civil nature and all special statutory proceedings in the circuit courts and county courts except those to which the Florida Probate Rules, the Florida Family Law Rules of Procedure, or the Small Claims Rules apply. FL ST RCP Rule 1.010.

i. The form, content, procedure, and time for pleading in all special statutory proceedings shall be as prescribed by the statutes governing the proceeding unless the Florida Rules of Civil Procedure specifically provide to the contrary. FL ST RCP Rule 1.010.

ii. The Florida Rules of Civil Procedure shall be construed to secure the just, speedy, and inexpensive determination of every action. FL ST RCP Rule 1.010.

b. *Rules of judicial administration.* The Florida Rules of Judicial Administration shall apply to administrative matters in all courts to which the Florida Rules of Judicial Administration are applicable by their terms. The Florida Rules of Judicial Administration shall be construed to secure the speedy and inexpensive determination of every proceeding to which they are applicable. The Florida Rules of Judicial Administration shall supersede all conflicting rules and statutes. FL ST J ADMIN Rule 2.110.

D. Documents

1. *Required documents*

a. *Notice of hearing/Motion.* An application to the court for an order shall be by motion which shall be made in writing unless made during a hearing or trial, shall state with particularity the grounds therefor, and shall set forth the relief or order sought. The requirement of writing is fulfilled if the motion is stated in a written notice of the hearing of the motion. All notices of hearing shall specify each motion or other matter to be heard. FL ST RCP Rule 1.100(b).

i. *Notices to persons with disabilities.* See the Format section of this KeyRules document for further information.

b. *Certificate of service.* When any attorney certifies in substance: "I certify that a copy hereof has been furnished to (here insert name or names and addresses used for service) by (e-mail) (delivery) (mail) (fax) on .... (date) ....______________ Attorney" the certificate is taken as prima facie proof of such service in compliance with FL ST J ADMIN Rule 2.516. FL ST J ADMIN Rule 2.516(f).

2. *Supplemental documents*

a. *Proposed order.* The court may require that orders or judgments be prepared by a party, may require the party to furnish the court with stamped, addressed envelopes for service of the order or judgment, and may require that proposed orders and judgments be furnished to all parties before entry by the court of the order or judgment. FL ST J ADMIN Rule 2.516(h)(1).

b. *Notice of constitutional question.* A party that files a pleading, written motion, or other paper drawing into question the constitutionality of a state statute or a county or municipal charter, ordinance, or franchise must promptly (1) file a notice of constitutional question stating the question

and identifying the paper that raises it; and (2) serve the notice and the pleading, written motion, or other paper drawing into question the constitutionality of a state statute or a county or municipal charter, ordinance, or franchise on the Attorney General or the state attorney of the judicial circuit in which the action is pending, by either certified or registered mail. Service of the notice and pleading, written motion, or other paper does not require joinder of the Attorney General or the state attorney as a party to the action. FL ST RCP Rule 1.071.

E. Format

1. *Documents; Type and size.* Documents subject to the exceptions set forth in FL ST J ADMIN Rule 2.525(d) shall be filed on recycled paper measuring eight and one half by eleven (8 1/2 by 11) inches. For purposes of FL ST J ADMIN Rule 2.520, paper is recycled if it contains a minimum content of fifty (50) percent waste paper. Xerographic reduction of legal-size (eight and one half by fourteen (8 1/2 by 14) inches) documents to letter size (eight and one half by eleven (8 1/2 by 11) inches) is prohibited. All other documents filed by electronic transmission shall be filed in a format capable of being printed in a format consistent with the provisions of FL ST J ADMIN Rule 2.250. FL ST J ADMIN Rule 2.520(b).
   a. *Exhibits.* Any exhibit or attachment filed with pleadings or papers may be filed in its original size. FL ST J ADMIN Rule 2.520(c).
   b. *Recording space.* On all papers and documents prepared and filed by the court or by any party to a proceeding which are to be recorded in the public records of any county, including but not limited to final money judgments and notices of lis pendens, a three (3) inch by three (3) inch space at the top right-hand corner on the first page and a one (1) inch by three (3) inch space at the top right-hand corner on each subsequent page shall be left blank and reserved for use by the clerk of court. FL ST J ADMIN Rule 2.520(d).
      i. *Exceptions to recording space.* Any papers or documents created by persons or entities over which the filing party has no control, including but not limited to wills, codicils, trusts, or other testamentary documents; documents prepared or executed by any public officer; documents prepared, executed, acknowledged, or proved outside of the State of Florida; or documents created by State or Federal government agencies, may be filed without the space required by FL ST J ADMIN Rule 2.520. FL ST J ADMIN Rule 2.520(e).
   c. *Noncompliance.* No clerk of court is permitted to refuse to file any document or paper because of noncompliance with the Florida Rules of Judicial Administration. However, upon request of the clerk of court, noncomplying documents must be resubmitted in accordance with the formatting rules. FL ST J ADMIN Rule 2.520(f).
2. *Caption.* Every pleading, motion, order, judgment, or other paper shall have a caption containing the name of the court, the file number, and except for in rem proceedings, including forfeiture proceedings, the name of the first party on each side with an appropriate indication of other parties, and a designation identifying the party filing it and its nature or the nature of the order, as the case may be. In any in rem proceeding, every pleading, motion, order, judgment, or other paper shall have a caption containing the name of the court, the file number, the style "In re" (followed by the name or general description of the property), and a designation of the person or entity filing it and its nature or the nature of the order, as the case may be. In an in rem forfeiture proceeding, the style shall be "In re forfeiture of" (followed by the name of the general description of the property). All papers filed in the action shall be styled in such a manner as to indicate clearly the subject matter of the paper and the party requesting or obtaining relief. FL ST RCP Rule 1.100(c)(1).
3. *Writing and written defined.* Writing or written means a document containing information, an application, or a stipulation. FL ST RCP Rule 1.080(c).
4. *Rule abbreviations*
   a. The Florida Rules of Civil Procedure and shall be abbreviated as Fla.R.Civ.P. FL ST RCP Rule 1.010.
   b. The Florida Rules of Judicial Administration shall be abbreviated as Fla. R. Jud. Admin. FL ST J ADMIN Rule 2.110.
5. *Nonverification.* Except when otherwise specifically provided by the Florida Rules of Civil Procedure or

an applicable statute, every pleading or other document of a party represented by an attorney need not be verified or accompanied by an affidavit. FL ST RCP Rule 1.030; FL ST J ADMIN Rule 2.515(a).

6. *Attorney signature*
   a. *Attorney signature.* Every pleading and other document of a party represented by an attorney shall be signed by at least one (1) attorney of record in that attorney's individual name whose current record Florida Bar address, telephone number, including area code, primary e-mail address and secondary e-mail addresses, if any, and Florida Bar number shall be stated, and who shall be duly licensed to practice law in Florida or who shall have received permission to appear in the particular case as provided in FL ST J ADMIN Rule 2.510. FL ST J ADMIN Rule 2.515(a).
      i. The attorney may be required by the court to give the address of, and to vouch for the attorney's authority to represent, the party. FL ST J ADMIN Rule 2.515(a).
      ii. The signature of an attorney shall constitute a certificate by the attorney that the attorney has read the pleading or other document; that to the best of the attorney's knowledge, information, and belief there is good ground to support it; and that it is not interposed for delay. FL ST J ADMIN Rule 2.515(a).
      iii. If a pleading is not signed or is signed with intent to defeat the purpose of FL ST J ADMIN Rule 2.515, it may be stricken and the action may proceed as though the pleading or other document had not been served. FL ST J ADMIN Rule 2.515(a).
   b. *Pro se litigant signature.* A party who is not represented by an attorney shall sign any pleading or other paper and state the party's address and telephone number, including area code. FL ST J ADMIN Rule 2.515(b).
   c. *Form of signature*
      i. The signatures required on pleadings and documents by FL ST J ADMIN Rule 2.515(a) and FL ST J ADMIN Rule 2.515(b) may be:
         - Original signatures;
         - Original signatures that have been reproduced by electronic means, such as on electronically transmitted documents or photocopied documents;
         - Electronic signatures using the "/s/," "s/," or "/s" formats by or at the direction of the person signing; or
         - Any other signature format authorized by general law, so long as the clerk where the proceeding is pending has the capability of receiving and has obtained approval from the Supreme Court of Florida to accept pleadings and documents with that signature format. FL ST J ADMIN Rule 2.515(c)(1).
      ii. An attorney, party, or other person who files a pleading or paper by electronic transmission that does not contain the original signature of that attorney, party, or other person shall file that identical pleading or paper in paper form containing an original signature of that attorney, party, or other person (hereinafter called the follow-up filing) immediately thereafter. The follow-up filing is not required if the Supreme Court of Florida has entered an order directing the clerk of court to discontinue accepting the follow-up filing. FL ST J ADMIN Rule 2.515(c)(2).

7. *Forms*
   a. *Process.* The forms of process, notice of lis pendens, and notice of action provided in the Florida Rules of Civil Procedure are sufficient. Variations from the forms do not void process or notices that are otherwise sufficient. FL ST RCP Rule 1.900(a).
   b. *Other forms.* The other forms provided in the Florida Rules of Civil Procedure are sufficient for the matters that are covered by them. So long as the substance is expressed without prolixity, the forms may be varied to meet the facts of a particular case. FL ST RCP Rule 1.900(b).
   c. *Formal matters.* Captions, except for the designation of the paper, are omitted from the forms provided in the Florida Rules of Civil Procedure. A general form of caption is the first form provided. Signatures are omitted from pleadings and motions. FL ST RCP Rule 1.900(c).

8. *Notices to persons with disabilities.* All notices of court proceedings to be held in a public facility, and all process compelling appearance at such proceedings, shall include the following statement in bold face, fourteen (14) point Times New Roman or Courier font: "If you are a person with a disability who needs any accommodation in order to participate in this proceeding, you are entitled, at no cost to you, to the provision of certain assistance. Please contact [identify applicable court personnel by name, address, and telephone number] at least seven (7) days before your scheduled court appearance, or immediately upon receiving this notification if the time before the scheduled appearance is less than seven (7) days; if you are hearing or voice impaired, call 711." FL ST J ADMIN Rule 2.540(c)(1).
9. *Minimization of the filing of sensitive information*
   a. *Limitations for court filings.* Unless authorized by FL ST J ADMIN Rule 2.425(b), statute, another rule of court, or the court orders otherwise, designated sensitive information filed with the court must be limited to the following format:
      i. The initials of a person known to be a minor;
      ii. The year of birth of a person's birth date;
      iii. No portion of any: Social security number, Bank account number, Credit card account number, Charge account number, or Debit account number;
      iv. The last four digits of any: Taxpayer identification number (TIN), Employee identification number, Driver's license number, Passport number, Telephone number, Financial account number, except as set forth in FL ST J ADMIN Rule 2.425(a)(3), Brokerage account number, Insurance policy account number, Loan account number, Customer account number, or Patient or health care number;
      v. A truncated version of any: Email address, Computer user name, Password, or Personal identification number (PIN); and
      vi. A truncated version of any other sensitive information as provided by court order. FL ST J ADMIN Rule 2.425(a).
   b. *Exceptions.* FL ST J ADMIN Rule 2.425(a) does not apply to the following:
      i. An account number which identifies the property alleged to be the subject of a proceeding;
      ii. The record of an administrative or agency proceeding;
      iii. The record in appellate or review proceedings;
      iv. The birth date of a minor whenever the birth date is necessary for the court to establish or maintain subject matter jurisdiction;
      v. The name of a minor in any order relating to parental responsibility, time-sharing, or child support;
      vi. The name of a minor in any document or order affecting the minor's ownership of real property;
      vii. The birth date of a party in a writ of attachment or notice to payor;
      viii. In traffic and criminal proceedings: a pro se filing; a court filing that is related to a criminal matter or investigation and that is prepared before the filing of a criminal charge or is not filed as part of any docketed criminal case; an arrest or search warrant or any information in support thereof; a charging document and an affidavit or other documents filed in support of any charging document, including any driving records; a statement of particulars; discovery material introduced into evidence or otherwise filed with the court; and all information necessary for the proper issuance and execution of a subpoena duces tecum;
      ix. Information used by the clerk for case maintenance purposes or the courts for case management purposes; and
      x. Information which is relevant and material to an issue before the court. FL ST J ADMIN Rule 2.425(b).
   c. *Remedies.* Upon motion by a party or interested person or sua sponte by the court, the court may order remedies, sanctions or both for a violation of FL ST J ADMIN Rule 2.425(a). Following notice

and an opportunity to respond, the court may impose sanctions if such filing was not made in good faith. FL ST J ADMIN Rule 2.425(c).

d. *Motions not restricted.* FL ST J ADMIN Rule 2.425 does not restrict a party's right to move for protective order, to move to file documents under seal, or to request a determination of the confidentiality of records. FL ST J ADMIN Rule 2.425(d).

   i. For more information regarding sealing court records, please see FL ST 4 J CIR 2006-05.

e. *Application.* FL ST J ADMIN Rule 2.425 does not affect the application of constitutional provisions, statutes, or rules of court regarding confidential information or access to public information. FL ST J ADMIN Rule 2.425(e).

F. Filing and Service Requirements

1. *Filing requirements.* All original documents must be filed with the court either before service or immediately thereafter, unless otherwise provided for by general law or other rules. If the original of any bond or other document is not placed in the court file, a certified copy must be so placed by the clerk. FL ST J ADMIN Rule 2.516(d). All documents shall be filed in conformity with the requirements of FL ST J ADMIN Rule 2.525. FL ST RCP Rule 1.080(b). All documents filed in any court shall be filed by electronic transmission in accordance with FL ST J ADMIN Rule 2.525. "Documents" means pleadings, motions, petitions, memoranda, briefs, notices, exhibits, declarations, affidavits, orders, judgments, decrees, writs, opinions, and any other paper or writing submitted to a court. FL ST J ADMIN Rule 2.520(a). All documents that are court records, as defined in FL ST J ADMIN Rule 2.430(a)(1), must be filed by electronic transmission, provided that: (1) the clerk has the ability to accept and retain such documents; (2) the clerk or the chief judge of the circuit has requested permission to accept documents filed by electronic transmission; and (3) the supreme court has entered an order granting permission to the clerk to accept documents filed by electronic transmission. FL ST J ADMIN Rule 2.525(c)(1).

   a. *Definition.* "Electronic transmission of documents" means the sending of information by electronic signals to, by or from a court or clerk, which when received can be transformed and stored or transmitted on paper, microfilm, magnetic storage device, optical imaging system, CD-ROM, flash drive, other electronic data storage system, server, case maintenance system ("CM"), electronic court filing ("ECF") system, statewide or local electronic portal ("e-portal"), or other electronic record keeping system authorized by the supreme court in a format sufficient to communicate the information on the original document in a readable format. Electronic transmission of documents includes electronic mail ("e-mail") and any internet-based transmission procedure, and may include procedures allowing for documents to be signed or verified by electronic means. FL ST J ADMIN Rule 2.525(a).

      i. The filing of documents with the court as required by the Florida Rules of Judicial Administration must be made by filing them with the clerk in accordance with FL ST J ADMIN Rule 2.525, except that the judge may permit documents to be filed with the judge, in which event the judge must note the filing date before him or her on the documents and transmit them to the clerk. The date of filing is that shown on the face of the document by the judge's notation or the clerk's time stamp, whichever is earlier. FL ST J ADMIN Rule 2.516(e).

   b. *Application.* Any court or clerk of the court may accept the electronic transmission of documents for filing after the clerk, together with input from the chief judge of the circuit, has obtained approval of the procedures and program for doing so from the Supreme Court of Florida. FL ST J ADMIN Rule 2.525(b).

   c. *Exceptions*

      i. Paper documents and other submissions may be manually submitted to the clerk or court:

         - When the clerk does not have the ability to accept and retain documents by electronic filing or has not had ECF Procedures approved by the supreme court;
         - For filing by any self-represented party or any self-represented nonparty unless specific ECF Procedures provide a means to file documents electronically. However, any self-represented nonparty that is a governmental or public agency and any other agency, partnership, corporation, or business entity acting on behalf of any governmental or public

agency may file documents by electronic transmission if such entity has the capability of filing documents electronically;

- For filing by attorneys excused from e-mail service in accordance with FL ST J ADMIN Rule 2.516(b);
- When submitting evidentiary exhibits or filing non-documentary materials;
- When the filing involves documents in excess of twenty-five (25) megabytes (25MB) in size. For such filings, documents may be transmitted using an electronic storage medium that the clerk has the ability to accept, which may include a CD-ROM, flash drive, or similar storage medium;
- When filed in open court, as permitted by the court;
- When paper filing is permitted by any approved statewide or local ECF procedures; and
- If any court determines that justice so requires. FL ST J ADMIN Rule 2.525(d).

ii. Any document in paper form submitted under FL ST J ADMIN Rule 2.525(d) is filed when it is received by the clerk or court and the clerk shall immediately thereafter convert any filed paper document to an electronic document. "Convert to an electronic document" means optically capturing an image of a paper document and using character recognition software to recover as much of the document's text as practicable and then indexing and storing the document in the official court file. FL ST J ADMIN Rule 2.525(c)(4).

iii. Any storage medium submitted under FL ST J ADMIN Rule 2.525(d)(5) is filed when received by the clerk or court and the clerk shall immediately thereafter transfer the electronic documents from the storage device to the official court file. FL ST J ADMIN Rule 2.525(c)(5).

iv. If the filer of any paper document authorized under FL ST J ADMIN Rule 2.525(d) provides a self-addressed, postage-paid envelope for return of the paper document after it is converted to electronic form by the clerk, the clerk shall place the paper document in the envelope and deposit it in the mail. Except when a paper document is required to be maintained, the clerk may recycle any filed paper document that is not to be returned to the filer. FL ST J ADMIN Rule 2.525(c)(6).

v. The clerk may convert any paper document filed before the effective date of FL ST J ADMIN Rule 2.525 to an electronic document. Unless the clerk is required to maintain the paper document, if the paper document has been converted to an electronic document by the clerk, the paper document is no longer part of the official court file and may be removed and recycled. FL ST J ADMIN Rule 2.525(c)(7).

d. *Official court file.* For information on what constitutes the official court file, please see FL ST J ADMIN Rule 2.525(c)(2), FL ST J ADMIN Rule 2.525(c)(3).

e. *Administration.* All attorneys, parties, or other persons using this rule to file documents are required to make arrangements with the court or clerk for the payment of any charges authorized by general law or the supreme court before filing any document by electronic transmission. FL ST J ADMIN Rule 2.525(f)(2).

f. *Filing date.* The filing date for an electronically transmitted document is the date and time that such filing is acknowledged by an electronic stamp or otherwise, pursuant to any procedure set forth in any ECF Procedures approved by the supreme court, or the date the last page of such filing is received by the court or clerk. FL ST J ADMIN Rule 2.525(f)(3).

g. *Accessibility.* All documents transmitted in any electronic form under FL ST J ADMIN Rule 2.525 must comply with the accessibility requirements of FL ST J ADMIN Rule 2.526. FL ST J ADMIN Rule 2.525(g).

2. *Service requirements.* Every pleading subsequent to the initial pleading, all orders, and every other document filed in the action must be served in conformity with the requirements of FL ST J ADMIN Rule 2.516. FL ST RCP Rule 1.080(a).

a. *Service; When required.* Unless the court otherwise orders, or a statute or supreme court adminis-

trative order specifies a different means of service, every pleading subsequent to the initial pleading and every other document filed in any court proceeding, except applications for witness subpoenas and documents served by formal notice or required to be served in the manner provided for service of formal notice, must be served in accordance with FL ST J ADMIN Rule 2.516 on each party. No service need be made on parties against whom a default has been entered, except that pleadings asserting new or additional claims against them must be served in the manner provided for service of summons. FL ST J ADMIN Rule 2.516(a).

b. *Service; How made.* When service is required or permitted to be made upon a party represented by an attorney, service must be made upon the attorney unless service upon the party is ordered by the court. FL ST J ADMIN Rule 2.516(b).

   i. *Service by electronic mail ("e-mail").* All documents required or permitted to be served on another party must be served by e-mail, unless FL ST J ADMIN Rule 2.516 otherwise provides. When, in addition to service by e-mail, the sender also utilizes another means of service provided for in FL ST J ADMIN Rule 2.516(b)(2), any differing time limits and other provisions applicable to that other means of service control. FL ST J ADMIN Rule 2.516(b)(1). Any document electronically transmitted to a court or clerk must also be served on all parties and interested persons in accordance with the applicable rules of court. FL ST J ADMIN Rule 2.525(e)(2).

      - *Service on attorneys.* Upon appearing in a proceeding, an attorney must serve a designation of a primary e-mail address and may designate no more than two (2) secondary e-mail addresses. Thereafter, service must be directed to all designated e-mail addresses in that proceeding. Every document filed by an attorney thereafter must include the primary e-mail address of that attorney and any secondary e-mail addresses. If an attorney does not designate any e-mail address for service, documents may be served on that attorney at the e-mail address on record with The Florida Bar. FL ST J ADMIN Rule 2.516(b)(1)(A).
      - *Exception to e-mail service on attorneys.* Service by an attorney on another attorney must be made by e-mail unless excused by the court. Upon motion by an attorney demonstrating that the attorney has no e-mail account and lacks access to the Internet at the attorney's office, the court may excuse the attorney from the requirements of e-mail service. Service on and by an attorney excused by the court from e-mail service must be by the means provided in FL ST J ADMIN Rule 2.516(b)(2). FL ST J ADMIN Rule 2.516(b)(1)(B).
      - *Service on and by parties not represented by an attorney.* Any party not represented by an attorney may serve a designation of a primary e-mail address and also may designate no more than two (2) secondary e-mail addresses to which service must be directed in that proceeding by the means provided in FL ST J ADMIN Rule 2.516(b)(1). If a party not represented by an attorney does not designate an e-mail address for service in a proceeding, service on and by that party must be by the means provided in FL ST J ADMIN Rule 2.516(b)(2). FL ST J ADMIN Rule 2.516(b)(1)(C).
      - *Time of service.* Service by e-mail is complete when it is sent. FL ST J ADMIN Rule 2.516(b)(1)(D). An e-mail is deemed served on the date it is sent. FL ST J ADMIN Rule 2.516(b)(1)(D)(i). If the sender learns that the e-mail did not reach the address of the person to be served, the sender must immediately send another copy by e-mail, or by a means authorized by FL ST J ADMIN Rule 2.516(b)(2). FL ST J ADMIN Rule 2.516(b)(1)(D)(ii). E-mail service is treated as service by mail for the computation of time. FL ST J ADMIN Rule 2.516(b)(1)(D)(iii).

   ii. *Format of e-mail for service.* Service of a document by e-mail is made by attaching a copy of the document in PDF format to an e-mail sent to all addresses designated by the attorney or party. FL ST J ADMIN Rule 2.516(b)(1)(E).

      - All documents served by e-mail must be attached to an e-mail message containing a subject line beginning with the words "SERVICE OF COURT DOCUMENT" in all capital letters, followed by the case number of the proceeding in which the documents are being served. FL ST J ADMIN Rule 2.516(b)(1)(E)(i).

- The body of the e-mail must identify the court in which the proceeding is pending, the case number, the name of the initial party on each side, the title of each document served with that e-mail, and the sender's name and telephone number. FL ST J ADMIN Rule 2.516(b)(1)(E)(ii).
- Any document served by e-mail may be signed by the "/s/" format, as long as the filed original is signed in accordance with the applicable rule of procedure. FL ST J ADMIN Rule 2.516(b)(1)(E)(iii).
- Any e-mail which, together with its attached documents, exceeds five megabytes (5MB) in size, must be divided and sent as separate e-mails, no one of which may exceed five megabytes (5MB) in size and each of which must be sequentially numbered in the subject line. FL ST J ADMIN Rule 2.516(b)(1)(E)(iv).

iii. *Service by other means.* In addition to, and not in lieu of, service by e-mail, service may also be made upon attorneys by any of the means specified in FL ST J ADMIN Rule 2.516(b)(2). Service on and by all parties who are not represented by an attorney and who do not designate an e-mail address, and on and by all attorneys excused from e-mail service, must be made by delivering a copy of the document or by mailing it to the party or attorney at their last known address or, if no address is known, by leaving it with the clerk of the court. Service by mail is complete upon mailing. Delivery of a copy within FL ST J ADMIN Rule 2.516 is complete upon:

- Handing it to the attorney or to the party,
- Leaving it at the attorney's or party's office with a clerk or other person in charge thereof,
- If there is no one in charge, leaving it in a conspicuous place therein,
- If the office is closed or the person to be served has no office, leaving it at the person's usual place of abode with some person of his or her family above fifteen (15) years of age and informing such person of the contents, or
- Transmitting it by facsimile to the attorney's or party's office with a cover sheet containing the sender's name, firm, address, telephone number, and facsimile number, and the number of pages transmitted. When service is made by facsimile, a copy must also be served by any other method permitted by FL ST J ADMIN Rule 2.516. Facsimile service occurs when transmission is complete. FL ST J ADMIN Rule 2.516(b)(2)(A) through FL ST J ADMIN Rule 2.516(b)(2)(E).
- Service by delivery after 5:00 p.m. must be deemed to have been made by mailing on the date of delivery. FL ST J ADMIN Rule 2.516(b)(2)(F).

c. *Service; Numerous defendants.* In actions when the parties are unusually numerous, the court may regulate the service contemplated by the Florida Rules of Judicial Administration on motion or on its own initiative in such manner as may be found to be just and reasonable. FL ST J ADMIN Rule 2.516(c).

d. *Service by clerk.* Service of notices and other documents required to be made by the clerk must also be done as provided in FL ST J ADMIN Rule 2.516(b). FL ST J ADMIN Rule 2.516(g).

G. Hearings

1. *Communication equipment*

a. *Definition.* Communication equipment means a conference telephone or other electronic device that permits all those appearing or participating to hear and speak to each other, provided that all conversation of all parties is audible to all persons present. FL ST J ADMIN Rule 2.530(a).

b. *Use by all parties.* A county or circuit court judge may, upon the court's own motion or upon the written request of a party, direct that communication equipment be used for a motion hearing, pretrial conference, or a status conference. A judge must give notice to the parties and consider any objections they may have to the use of communication equipment before directing that communication equipment be used. The decision to use communication equipment over the objection of parties will be in the sound discretion of the trial court, except as noted below. FL ST J ADMIN Rule 2.530(b).

c. *Use only by requesting party.* A county or circuit court judge may, upon the written request of a party upon reasonable notice to all other parties, permit a requesting party to participate through communication equipment in a scheduled motion hearing; however, any such request (except in criminal, juvenile, and appellate proceedings) must be granted, absent a showing of good cause to deny the same, where the hearing is set for not longer than fifteen (15) minutes. FL ST J ADMIN Rule 2.530(c).

d. *Testimony*

i. *Generally.* A county or circuit court judge, general magistrate, special magistrate, or hearing officer may allow testimony to be taken through communication equipment if all parties consent or if permitted by another applicable rule of procedure. FL ST J ADMIN Rule 2.530(d)(1).

ii. *Procedure.* Any party desiring to present testimony through communication equipment shall, prior to the hearing or trial at which the testimony is to be presented, contact all parties to determine whether each party consents to this form of testimony. The party seeking to present the testimony shall move for permission to present testimony through communication equipment, which motion shall set forth good cause as to why the testimony should be allowed in this form. FL ST J ADMIN Rule 2.530(d)(2).

iii. *Oath.* Testimony may be taken through communication equipment only if a notary public or other person authorized to administer oaths in the witness's jurisdiction is present with the witness and administers the oath consistent with the laws of the jurisdiction. FL ST J ADMIN Rule 2.530(d)(3).

iv. *Confrontation rights.* In juvenile and criminal proceedings the defendant must make an informed waiver of any confrontation rights that may be abridged by the use of communication equipment. FL ST J ADMIN Rule 2.530(d)(4).

v. *Video testimony.* If the testimony to be presented utilizes video conferencing or comparable two-way visual capabilities, the court in its discretion may modify the procedures set forth in FL ST J ADMIN Rule 2.530 to accommodate the technology utilized. FL ST J ADMIN Rule 2.530(d)(5).

e. *Burden of expense.* The cost for the use of the communication equipment is the responsibility of the requesting party unless otherwise directed by the court. FL ST J ADMIN Rule 2.530(e).

H. Forms

1. Official Motion for Sanctions Forms for Florida

a. Caption. FL ST RCP Form 1.901.

b. Notice of compliance when constitutional challenge is brought. FL ST RCP Form 1.975.

2. Motion for Sanctions Forms for Florida

a. Motion; By defendant; For sanctions for refusal of offer of judgment. FL-PP § 61:22.

b. Motion; Sanctions, proposal for settlement. FL-PRACFORM § 7:165.

I. Checklist

(I) ❑ Matters to be considered by moving party

(a) ❑ Required documents

(1) ❑ Notice of hearing/Motion

(2) ❑ Certificate of service

(b) ❑ Supplemental documents

(1) ❑ Proposed order

(2) ❑ Notice of constitutional question

(c) ❑ Time for making motion

(1) ❑ A motion by a party seeking sanctions under FL ST § 57.105 must be served but may not be

filed with or presented to the court unless, within twenty one (21) days after service of the motion, the challenged paper, claim, defense, contention, allegation, or denial is not withdrawn or appropriately corrected

(2) ❑ Any party seeking a judgment taxing costs, attorneys' fees, or both shall serve a motion no later than thirty (30) days after filing of the judgment, including a judgment of dismissal, or the service of a notice of voluntary dismissal

(3) ❑ A copy of any written motion which may not be heard ex parte and a copy of the notice of the hearing thereof shall be served a reasonable time before the time specified for the hearing

(II) ❑ Matters to be considered by opposing party

(a) ❑ Required documents

(1) ❑ Response to motion

(2) ❑ Certificate of service

(b) ❑ Supplemental documents

(1) ❑ Proposed order

(2) ❑ Notice of constitutional question

(c) ❑ Time for service and filing of opposition

(1) ❑ No time specified for responding to a motion

Motions, Oppositions and Replies
Motion to Compel Discovery

Document Last Updated January 2013

A. Applicable Rules

1. *State rules*

a. Rules of court. FL ST RCP Rule 1.010; FL ST J ADMIN Rule 2.110.

b. Nonverification of pleadings. FL ST RCP Rule 1.030.

c. Service and filing of pleadings, orders, and documents. FL ST RCP Rule 1.080.

d. Time. FL ST RCP Rule 1.090.

e. Pleadings and motions. FL ST RCP Rule 1.100.

f. Motions. FL ST RCP Rule 1.160.

g. General provisions governing discovery. FL ST RCP Rule 1.280.

h. Depositions. FL ST RCP Rule 1.310; FL ST RCP Rule 1.320; FL ST FAM LAW Rule 12.310.

i. Interrogatories to parties. FL ST RCP Rule 1.340.

j. Production of documents and things and entry upon land for inspection and other purposes. FL ST RCP Rule 1.350.

k. Examination of persons. FL ST RCP Rule 1.360.

l. Failure to make discovery; Sanctions. FL ST RCP Rule 1.380.

m. Relief from judgment, decrees, or orders. FL ST RCP Rule 1.540.

n. Mediation and arbitration. FL ST RCP Rule 1.700; FL ST RCP Rule 1.710; FL ST RCP Rule 1.720; FL ST RCP Rule 1.730; FL ST RCP Rule 1.750; FL ST RCP Rule 1.800; FL ST RCP Rule 1.810; FL ST RCP Rule 1.820; FL ST RCP Rule 1.830.

o. Forms. FL ST RCP Rule 1.900.

p. Minimization of the filing of sensitive information. FL ST J ADMIN Rule 2.425.

q. Retention of court records. FL ST J ADMIN Rule 2.430.

r. Foreign attorneys. FL ST J ADMIN Rule 2.510.

s. Signature of attorneys and parties. FL ST J ADMIN Rule 2.515.

t. Paper. FL ST J ADMIN Rule 2.520.

u. Electronic filing. FL ST J ADMIN Rule 2.525.

v. Accessibility of information and technology. FL ST J ADMIN Rule 2.526.

w. Communication equipment. FL ST J ADMIN Rule 2.530.

x. Court reporting. FL ST J ADMIN Rule 2.535.

y. Requests for accommodations by persons with disabilities. FL ST J ADMIN Rule 2.540.

2. *Local rules*

a. Sealing court records. FL ST 4 J CIR 2006-05.

B. Timing

1. *Motion to compel discovery.* Upon reasonable notice to other parties and all persons affected, a party may apply for an order compelling discovery. FL ST RCP Rule 1.380(a).

2. *General motion timing.* A copy of any written motion which may not be heard ex parte and a copy of the notice of the hearing thereof shall be served a reasonable time before the time specified for the hearing. FL ST RCP Rule 1.090(d).

3. *Computation of time*

a. *Generally.* Computation of time shall be governed by FL ST J ADMIN Rule 2.514. FL ST RCP Rule 1.090(a). The following rules apply in computing time periods specified in any rule of procedure, local rule, court order, or statute that does not specify a method of computing time. FL ST J ADMIN Rule 2.514(a).

i. *Period stated in days or a longer unit.* When the period is stated in days or a longer unit of time (A) exclude the day of the event that triggers the period; (B) count every day, including intermediate Saturdays, Sundays, and legal holidays; and (C) include the last day of the period, but if the last day is a Saturday, Sunday, or legal holiday, or falls within any period of time extended through an order of the chief justice under FL ST J ADMIN Rule 2.205(a)(2)(B)(iv), the period continues to run until the end of the next day that is not a Saturday, Sunday, or legal holiday and does not fall within any period of time extended through an order of the chief justice. FL ST J ADMIN Rule 2.514(a)(1).

ii. *Period stated in hours.* When the period is stated in hours (A) begin counting immediately on the occurrence of the event that triggers the period; (B) count every hour, including hours during intermediate Saturdays, Sundays, and legal holidays; and (C) if the period would end on a Saturday, Sunday, or legal holiday, or during any period of time extended through an order of the chief justice under FL ST J ADMIN Rule 2.205(a)(2)(B)(iv), the period continues to run until the same time on the next day that is not a Saturday, Sunday, or legal holiday and does not fall within any period of time extended through an order of the chief justice. FL ST J ADMIN Rule 2.514(a)(2).

iii. *Period stated in days less than seven (7) days.* When the period stated in days is less than seven (7) days, intermediate Saturdays, Sundays, and legal holidays shall be excluded in the computation. FL ST J ADMIN Rule 2.514(a)(3).

iv. *"Last day" defined.* Unless a different time is set by a statute, local rule, or court order, the last day ends (A) for electronic filing or for service by any means, at midnight; and (B) for filing by other means, when the clerk's office is scheduled to close. FL ST J ADMIN Rule 2.514(a)(4).

v. *"Next day" defined.* The "next day" is determined by continuing to count forward when the period is measured after an event and backward when measured before an event. FL ST J ADMIN Rule 2.514(a)(5).

vi. *"Legal holiday" defined.* "Legal holiday" means (A) the day set aside by FL ST § 110.117, for

observing New Year's Day, Martin Luther King, Jr.'s Birthday, Memorial Day, Independence Day, Labor Day, Veterans' Day, Thanksgiving Day, the Friday after Thanksgiving Day, or Christmas Day, and (B) any day observed as a holiday by the clerk's office or as designated by the chief judge. FL ST J ADMIN Rule 2.514(a)(6).

b. *Additional time after service by mail or e-mail.* When a party may or must act within a specified time after service and service is made by mail or e-mail, five (5) days are added after the period that would otherwise expire under FL ST J ADMIN Rule 2.514(a). FL ST J ADMIN Rule 2.514(b).

c. *Enlargement.* When an act is required or allowed to be done at or within a specified time by order of court, by the Florida Rules of Civil Procedure, or by notice given thereunder, for cause shown the court at any time in its discretion (1) with or without notice, may order the period enlarged if request therefor is made before the expiration of the period originally prescribed or as extended by a previous order, or (2) upon motion made and notice after the expiration of the specified period, may permit the act to be done when failure to act was the result of excusable neglect, but it may not extend the time for making a motion for new trial, for rehearing, or to alter or amend a judgment; making a motion for relief from a judgment under FL ST RCP Rule 1.540(b); taking an appeal or filing a petition for certiorari; or making a motion for a directed verdict. FL ST RCP Rule 1.090(b).

d. *Unaffected by expiration of term.* The period of time provided for the doing of any act or the taking of any proceeding shall not be affected or limited by the continued existence or expiration of a term of court. The continued existence or expiration of a term of court in no way affects the power of a court to do any act or take any proceeding in any action which is or has been pending before it. FL ST RCP Rule 1.090(c).

C. General Requirements

1. *Motions generally*

a. *Contents.* An application to the court for an order shall be by motion which shall be made in writing unless made during a hearing or trial, shall state with particularity the grounds therefor, and shall set forth the relief or order sought. The requirement of writing is fulfilled if the motion is stated in a written notice of the hearing of the motion. All notices of hearing shall specify each motion or other matter to be heard. FL ST RCP Rule 1.100(b).

b. *Particularity requirement.* The court considers a motion in the light of the substantive law, rule or statute to make its determination. Some rules require a statement of the grounds for a motion under the rule. Failure to give the grounds will result in denial of the motion. This should be the result in all situations when the ground for the motion is not inherent in the rule. FL-PRACPROC § 9:3. The requirement is nevertheless an important one, first because of the due process notice rights of the respondent, as well as for the assistance it provides to the court in its preparation for the hearing or, absent a hearing, for disposition. 4 FLPRAC R 1.100.

2. *Failure to make discovery; Types of available relief.* Three (3) categories of relief are available for failure to make discovery. FL-PRACPROC § 16:14.

a. The first category is an order compelling discovery. This is obtained by a motion to compel discovery. The motion is made in the court in which the action is pending, except when a deposition is being taken out of the territorial jurisdiction of the court and protective relief is sought in accordance with FL ST RCP Rule 1.310(d) or when a deponent is not a party. When one of the exceptions occurs, the motion is made in the circuit court of the county where the deposition is being taken. FL-PRACPROC § 16:14.

b. The second category results from a failure to comply with an order to make discovery. The sanctions should not be applied until a hearing on the merits of the failure is held, including an opportunity to present evidence of explanation or mitigation. FL-PRACPROC § 16:14.

c. The third category is available: (1) if a party or a person designated by an organization to answer questions at a deposition fails to appear before the officer who is to take the deposition after being served with a proper notice; (2) fails to serve answers or objections to interrogatories after proper service of the interrogatories; or (3) a party fails to serve a response to a request for production, inspection and entry after proper service of the request. FL-PRACPROC § 16:14. For further information regarding discovery sanctions please see the KeyRules Motion for Discovery Sanctions documents.

3. *Motion for order compelling discovery*

   a. *Reasonable notice.* Upon reasonable notice to other parties and all persons affected, a party may apply for an order compelling discovery. FL ST RCP Rule 1.380(a).

   b. *Appropriate court.* An application for an order to a party may be made to the court in which the action is pending or in accordance with FL ST RCP Rule 1.310(d). An application for an order to a deponent who is not a party shall be made to the circuit court where the deposition is being taken. FL ST RCP Rule 1.380(a)(1).

   c. *Motion*

      i. *Grounds.* The discovering party may move for an order compelling an answer, or a designation or an order compelling inspection, or an order compelling an examination in accordance with the request:

         - If a deponent fails to answer a question propounded or submitted under FL ST RCP Rule 1.310 or FL ST RCP Rule 1.320;
         - Or a corporation or other entity fails to make a designation under FL ST RCP Rule 1.310(b)(6) or FL ST RCP Rule 1.320(a);
         - Or a party fails to answer an interrogatory submitted under FL ST RCP Rule 1.340;
         - Or if a party in response to a request for inspection submitted under FL ST RCP Rule 1.350 fails to respond that inspection will be permitted as requested or fails to permit inspection as requested;
         - Or if a party in response to a request for examination of a person submitted under FL ST RCP Rule 1.360(a) objects to the examination, fails to respond that the examination will be permitted as requested, or fails to submit to or to produce a person in that party's custody or legal control for examination. FL ST RCP Rule 1.380(a)(2).

      ii. *Certification.* The motion must include a certification that the movant, in good faith, has conferred or attempted to confer with the person or party failing to make the discovery in an effort to secure the information or material without court action. FL ST RCP Rule 1.380(a)(2).

      iii. *During deposition.* When taking a deposition on oral examination, the proponent of the question may complete or adjourn the examination before applying for an order. FL ST RCP Rule 1.380(a)(2).

      iv. *Protective order.* If the court denies the motion in whole or in part, it may make such protective order as it would have been empowered to make on a motion made pursuant to FL ST RCP Rule 1.280(c). FL ST RCP Rule 1.380(a)(2).

   d. *Evasive or incomplete answer.* For purposes of FL ST RCP Rule 1.380(a) an evasive or incomplete answer shall be treated as a failure to answer. FL ST RCP Rule 1.380(a)(3).

   e. *Award of expenses of motion*

      i. *Motion granted.* If the motion is granted and after opportunity for hearing, the court shall require the party or deponent whose conduct necessitated the motion or the party or counsel advising the conduct to pay to the moving party the reasonable expenses incurred in obtaining the order that may include attorneys' fees, unless the court finds that the movant failed to certify in the motion that a good faith effort was made to obtain the discovery without court action, that the opposition to the motion was justified, or that other circumstances make an award of expenses unjust. FL ST RCP Rule 1.380(a)(4).

      ii. *Motion denied.* If the motion is denied and after opportunity for hearing, the court shall require the moving party to pay to the party or deponent who opposed the motion the reasonable expenses incurred in opposing the motion that may include attorneys' fees, unless the court finds that the making of the motion was substantially justified or that other circumstances make an award of expenses unjust. FL ST RCP Rule 1.380(a)(4).

iii. *Motion granted in part and denied in part.* If the motion is granted in part and denied in part, the court may apportion the reasonable expenses incurred as a result of making the motion among the parties and persons. FL ST RCP Rule 1.380(a)(4).

iv. *Electronically stored information; Sanctions for failure to preserve.* Absent exceptional circumstances, a court may not impose sanctions under these rules on a party for failing to provide electronically stored information lost as a result of the routine, good faith operation of an electronic information system. FL ST RCP Rule 1.380(e).

4. *Limitations on discovery of electronically stored information*

a. A person may object to discovery of electronically stored information from sources that the person identifies as not reasonably accessible because of burden or cost. On motion to compel discovery or for a protective order, the person from whom discovery is sought must show that the information sought or the format requested is not reasonably accessible because of undue burden or cost. If that showing is made, the court may nonetheless order the discovery from such sources or in such formats if the requesting party shows good cause. The court may specify conditions of the discovery, including ordering that some or all of the expenses incurred by the person from whom discovery is sought be paid by the party seeking the discovery. FL ST RCP Rule 1.280(d)(1).

b. In determining any motion involving discovery of electronically stored information, the court must limit the frequency or extent of discovery otherwise allowed by the Florida Rules of Civil Procedure if it determines that (i) the discovery sought is unreasonably cumulative or duplicative, or can be obtained from another source or in another manner that is more convenient, less burdensome, or less expensive; or (ii) the burden or expense of the discovery outweighs its likely benefit, considering the needs of the case, the amount in controversy, the parties' resources, the importance of the issues at stake in the action, and the importance of the discovery in resolving the issues. FL ST RCP Rule 1.280(d)(2).

5. *Arbitration and mediation*

a. *Referral to arbitration and mediation.* Except as hereinafter provided or as otherwise prohibited by law, the presiding judge may enter an order referring all or any part of a contested civil matter to mediation or arbitration. The parties to any contested civil matter may file a written stipulation to mediate or arbitrate any issue between them at any time. Such stipulation shall be incorporated into the order of referral. FL ST RCP Rule 1.700(a).

b. *Arbitration*

i. *Exclusions.* A civil action shall be ordered to arbitration or arbitration in conjunction with mediation upon stipulation of the parties. A civil action may be ordered to arbitration or arbitration in conjunction with mediation upon motion of any party or by the court, if the judge determines the action to be of such a nature that arbitration could be of benefit to the litigants or the court. FL ST RCP Rule 1.800.

- Under no circumstances may the following categories of actions be referred to arbitration: (1) bond estreatures; (2) habeas corpus or other extraordinary writs; (3) bond validations; (4) civil or criminal contempt; (5) such other matters as may be specified by order of the chief judge in the circuit. FL ST RCP Rule 1.800.

ii. For more information regarding arbitration, please see FL ST RCP Rule 1.810; FL ST RCP Rule 1.820; FL ST RCP Rule 1.830.

c. *Mediation.* For more information regarding mediation, please see FL ST RCP Rule 1.710; FL ST RCP Rule 1.720; FL ST RCP Rule 1.730; and FL ST RCP Rule 1.750.

6. *Rules of court*

a. *Rules of civil procedure.* The Florida Rules of Civil Procedure apply to all actions of a civil nature and all special statutory proceedings in the circuit courts and county courts except those to which the Florida Probate Rules, the Florida Family Law Rules of Procedure, or the Small Claims Rules apply. FL ST RCP Rule 1.010.

i. The form, content, procedure, and time for pleading in all special statutory proceedings shall be

as prescribed by the statutes governing the proceeding unless the Florida Rules of Civil Procedure specifically provide to the contrary. FL ST RCP Rule 1.010.

ii. The Florida Rules of Civil Procedure shall be construed to secure the just, speedy, and inexpensive determination of every action. FL ST RCP Rule 1.010.

b. *Rules of judicial administration.* The Florida Rules of Judicial Administration shall apply to administrative matters in all courts to which the Florida Rules of Judicial Administration are applicable by their terms. The Florida Rules of Judicial Administration shall be construed to secure the speedy and inexpensive determination of every proceeding to which they are applicable. The Florida Rules of Judicial Administration shall supersede all conflicting rules and statutes. FL ST J ADMIN Rule 2.110.

D. Documents

1. *Required documents*

a. *Notice of hearing/Motion.* An application to the court for an order shall be by motion which shall be made in writing unless made during a hearing or trial, shall state with particularity the grounds therefor, and shall set forth the relief or order sought. The requirement of writing is fulfilled if the motion is stated in a written notice of the hearing of the motion. All notices of hearing shall specify each motion or other matter to be heard. FL ST RCP Rule 1.100(b).

i. *Certification.* The motion must include a certification that the movant, in good faith, has conferred or attempted to confer with the person or party failing to make the discovery in an effort to secure the information or material without court action. FL ST RCP Rule 1.380(a)(2).

ii. *Notices to persons with disabilities.* See the Format section of this KeyRules document for further information.

b. *Certificate of service.* When any attorney certifies in substance: "I certify that a copy hereof has been furnished to (here insert name or names and addresses used for service) by (e-mail) (delivery) (mail) (fax) on .... (date) ....________________ Attorney" the certificate is taken as prima facie proof of such service in compliance with FL ST J ADMIN Rule 2.516. FL ST J ADMIN Rule 2.516(f).

2. *Supplemental documents*

a. *Proposed order.* The court may require that orders or judgments be prepared by a party, may require the party to furnish the court with stamped, addressed envelopes for service of the order or judgment, and may require that proposed orders and judgments be furnished to all parties before entry by the court of the order or judgment. FL ST J ADMIN Rule 2.516(h)(1).

b. *Notice of constitutional question.* A party that files a pleading, written motion, or other paper drawing into question the constitutionality of a state statute or a county or municipal charter, ordinance, or franchise must promptly (1) file a notice of constitutional question stating the question and identifying the paper that raises it; and (2) serve the notice and the pleading, written motion, or other paper drawing into question the constitutionality of a state statute or a county or municipal charter, ordinance, or franchise on the Attorney General or the state attorney of the judicial circuit in which the action is pending, by either certified or registered mail. Service of the notice and pleading, written motion, or other paper does not require joinder of the Attorney General or the state attorney as a party to the action. FL ST RCP Rule 1.071.

E. Format

1. *Documents; Type and size.* Documents subject to the exceptions set forth in FL ST J ADMIN Rule 2.525(d) shall be filed on recycled paper measuring eight and one half by eleven (8 1/2 by 11) inches. For purposes of FL ST J ADMIN Rule 2.520, paper is recycled if it contains a minimum content of fifty (50) percent waste paper. Xerographic reduction of legal-size (eight and one half by fourteen (8 1/2 by 14) inches) documents to letter size (eight and one half by eleven (8 1/2 by 11) inches) is prohibited. All other documents filed by electronic transmission shall be filed in a format capable of being printed in a format consistent with the provisions of FL ST J ADMIN Rule 2.250. FL ST J ADMIN Rule 2.520(b).

a. *Exhibits.* Any exhibit or attachment filed with pleadings or papers may be filed in its original size. FL ST J ADMIN Rule 2.520(c).

b. *Recording space.* On all papers and documents prepared and filed by the court or by any party to a proceeding which are to be recorded in the public records of any county, including but not limited to final money judgments and notices of lis pendens, a three (3) inch by three (3) inch space at the top right-hand corner on the first page and a one (1) inch by three (3) inch space at the top right-hand corner on each subsequent page shall be left blank and reserved for use by the clerk of court. FL ST J ADMIN Rule 2.520(d).

i. *Exceptions to recording space.* Any papers or documents created by persons or entities over which the filing party has no control, including but not limited to wills, codicils, trusts, or other testamentary documents; documents prepared or executed by any public officer; documents prepared, executed, acknowledged, or proved outside of the State of Florida; or documents created by State or Federal government agencies, may be filed without the space required by FL ST J ADMIN Rule 2.520. FL ST J ADMIN Rule 2.520(e).

c. *Noncompliance.* No clerk of court is permitted to refuse to file any document or paper because of noncompliance with the Florida Rules of Judicial Administration. However, upon request of the clerk of court, noncomplying documents must be resubmitted in accordance with the formatting rules. FL ST J ADMIN Rule 2.520(f).

2. *Caption.* Every pleading, motion, order, judgment, or other paper shall have a caption containing the name of the court, the file number, and except for in rem proceedings, including forfeiture proceedings, the name of the first party on each side with an appropriate indication of other parties, and a designation identifying the party filing it and its nature or the nature of the order, as the case may be. In any in rem proceeding, every pleading, motion, order, judgment, or other paper shall have a caption containing the name of the court, the file number, the style "In re" (followed by the name or general description of the property), and a designation of the person or entity filing it and its nature or the nature of the order, as the case may be. In an in rem forfeiture proceeding, the style shall be "In re forfeiture of" (followed by the name of the general description of the property). All papers filed in the action shall be styled in such a manner as to indicate clearly the subject matter of the paper and the party requesting or obtaining relief. FL ST RCP Rule 1.100(c)(1).

3. *Writing and written defined.* Writing or written means a document containing information, an application, or a stipulation. FL ST RCP Rule 1.080(c).

4. *Rule abbreviations*

a. The Florida Rules of Civil Procedure and shall be abbreviated as Fla.R.Civ.P. FL ST RCP Rule 1.010.

b. The Florida Rules of Judicial Administration shall be abbreviated as Fla. R. Jud. Admin. FL ST J ADMIN Rule 2.110.

5. *Nonverification.* Except when otherwise specifically provided by the Florida Rules of Civil Procedure or an applicable statute, every pleading or other document of a party represented by an attorney need not be verified or accompanied by an affidavit. FL ST RCP Rule 1.030; FL ST J ADMIN Rule 2.515(a).

6. *Attorney signature*

a. *Attorney signature.* Every pleading and other document of a party represented by an attorney shall be signed by at least one (1) attorney of record in that attorney's individual name whose current record Florida Bar address, telephone number, including area code, primary e-mail address and secondary e-mail addresses, if any, and Florida Bar number shall be stated, and who shall be duly licensed to practice law in Florida or who shall have received permission to appear in the particular case as provided in FL ST J ADMIN Rule 2.510. FL ST J ADMIN Rule 2.515(a).

i. The attorney may be required by the court to give the address of, and to vouch for the attorney's authority to represent, the party. FL ST J ADMIN Rule 2.515(a).

ii. The signature of an attorney shall constitute a certificate by the attorney that the attorney has read the pleading or other document; that to the best of the attorney's knowledge, information, and belief there is good ground to support it; and that it is not interposed for delay. FL ST J ADMIN Rule 2.515(a).

iii. If a pleading is not signed or is signed with intent to defeat the purpose of FL ST J ADMIN Rule

2.515, it may be stricken and the action may proceed as though the pleading or other document had not been served. FL ST J ADMIN Rule 2.515(a).

b. *Pro se litigant signature.* A party who is not represented by an attorney shall sign any pleading or other paper and state the party's address and telephone number, including area code. FL ST J ADMIN Rule 2.515(b).

c. *Form of signature*

i. The signatures required on pleadings and documents by FL ST J ADMIN Rule 2.515(a) and FL ST J ADMIN Rule 2.515(b) may be:

- Original signatures;
- Original signatures that have been reproduced by electronic means, such as on electronically transmitted documents or photocopied documents;
- Electronic signatures using the "/s/," "s/," or "/s" formats by or at the direction of the person signing; or
- Any other signature format authorized by general law, so long as the clerk where the proceeding is pending has the capability of receiving and has obtained approval from the Supreme Court of Florida to accept pleadings and documents with that signature format. FL ST J ADMIN Rule 2.515(c)(1).

ii. An attorney, party, or other person who files a pleading or paper by electronic transmission that does not contain the original signature of that attorney, party, or other person shall file that identical pleading or paper in paper form containing an original signature of that attorney, party, or other person (hereinafter called the follow-up filing) immediately thereafter. The follow-up filing is not required if the Supreme Court of Florida has entered an order directing the clerk of court to discontinue accepting the follow-up filing. FL ST J ADMIN Rule 2.515(c)(2).

7. *Forms*

a. *Process.* The forms of process, notice of lis pendens, and notice of action provided in the Florida Rules of Civil Procedure are sufficient. Variations from the forms do not void process or notices that are otherwise sufficient. FL ST RCP Rule 1.900(a).

b. *Other forms.* The other forms provided in the Florida Rules of Civil Procedure are sufficient for the matters that are covered by them. So long as the substance is expressed without prolixity, the forms may be varied to meet the facts of a particular case. FL ST RCP Rule 1.900(b).

c. *Formal matters.* Captions, except for the designation of the paper, are omitted from the forms provided in the Florida Rules of Civil Procedure. A general form of caption is the first form provided. Signatures are omitted from pleadings and motions. FL ST RCP Rule 1.900(c).

8. *Notices to persons with disabilities.* All notices of court proceedings to be held in a public facility, and all process compelling appearance at such proceedings, shall include the following statement in bold face, fourteen (14) point Times New Roman or Courier font: "If you are a person with a disability who needs any accommodation in order to participate in this proceeding, you are entitled, at no cost to you, to the provision of certain assistance. Please contact [identify applicable court personnel by name, address, and telephone number] at least seven (7) days before your scheduled court appearance, or immediately upon receiving this notification if the time before the scheduled appearance is less than seven (7) days; if you are hearing or voice impaired, call 711." FL ST J ADMIN Rule 2.540(c)(1).

9. *Minimization of the filing of sensitive information*

a. *Limitations for court filings.* Unless authorized by FL ST J ADMIN Rule 2.425(b), statute, another rule of court, or the court orders otherwise, designated sensitive information filed with the court must be limited to the following format:

i. The initials of a person known to be a minor;

ii. The year of birth of a person's birth date;

iii. No portion of any: Social security number, Bank account number, Credit card account number, Charge account number, or Debit account number;

iv. The last four digits of any: Taxpayer identification number (TIN), Employee identification number, Driver's license number, Passport number, Telephone number, Financial account number, except as set forth in FL ST J ADMIN Rule 2.425(a)(3), Brokerage account number, Insurance policy account number, Loan account number, Customer account number, or Patient or health care number;

v. A truncated version of any: Email address, Computer user name, Password, or Personal identification number (PIN); and

vi. A truncated version of any other sensitive information as provided by court order. FL ST J ADMIN Rule 2.425(a).

b. *Exceptions.* FL ST J ADMIN Rule 2.425(a) does not apply to the following:

i. An account number which identifies the property alleged to be the subject of a proceeding;

ii. The record of an administrative or agency proceeding;

iii. The record in appellate or review proceedings;

iv. The birth date of a minor whenever the birth date is necessary for the court to establish or maintain subject matter jurisdiction;

v. The name of a minor in any order relating to parental responsibility, time-sharing, or child support;

vi. The name of a minor in any document or order affecting the minor's ownership of real property;

vii. The birth date of a party in a writ of attachment or notice to payor;

viii. In traffic and criminal proceedings: a pro se filing; a court filing that is related to a criminal matter or investigation and that is prepared before the filing of a criminal charge or is not filed as part of any docketed criminal case; an arrest or search warrant or any information in support thereof; a charging document and an affidavit or other documents filed in support of any charging document, including any driving records; a statement of particulars; discovery material introduced into evidence or otherwise filed with the court; and all information necessary for the proper issuance and execution of a subpoena duces tecum;

ix. Information used by the clerk for case maintenance purposes or the courts for case management purposes; and

x. Information which is relevant and material to an issue before the court. FL ST J ADMIN Rule 2.425(b).

c. *Remedies.* Upon motion by a party or interested person or sua sponte by the court, the court may order remedies, sanctions or both for a violation of FL ST J ADMIN Rule 2.425(a). Following notice and an opportunity to respond, the court may impose sanctions if such filing was not made in good faith. FL ST J ADMIN Rule 2.425(c).

d. *Motions not restricted.* FL ST J ADMIN Rule 2.425 does not restrict a party's right to move for protective order, to move to file documents under seal, or to request a determination of the confidentiality of records. FL ST J ADMIN Rule 2.425(d).

i. For more information regarding sealing court records, please see FL ST 4 J CIR 2006-05.

e. *Application.* FL ST J ADMIN Rule 2.425 does not affect the application of constitutional provisions, statutes, or rules of court regarding confidential information or access to public information. FL ST J ADMIN Rule 2.425(e).

F. Filing and Service Requirements

1. *Filing requirements.* All original documents must be filed with the court either before service or immediately thereafter, unless otherwise provided for by general law or other rules. If the original of any bond or other document is not placed in the court file, a certified copy must be so placed by the clerk. FL ST J ADMIN Rule 2.516(d). All documents shall be filed in conformity with the requirements of FL ST J ADMIN Rule 2.525. FL ST RCP Rule 1.080(b). All documents filed in any court shall be filed by electronic transmission in accordance with FL ST J ADMIN Rule 2.525. "Documents" means pleadings,

motions, petitions, memoranda, briefs, notices, exhibits, declarations, affidavits, orders, judgments, decrees, writs, opinions, and any other paper or writing submitted to a court. FL ST J ADMIN Rule 2.520(a). All documents that are court records, as defined in FL ST J ADMIN Rule 2.430(a)(1), must be filed by electronic transmission, provided that: (1) the clerk has the ability to accept and retain such documents; (2) the clerk or the chief judge of the circuit has requested permission to accept documents filed by electronic transmission; and (3) the supreme court has entered an order granting permission to the clerk to accept documents filed by electronic transmission. FL ST J ADMIN Rule 2.525(c)(1).

a. *Definition.* "Electronic transmission of documents" means the sending of information by electronic signals to, by or from a court or clerk, which when received can be transformed and stored or transmitted on paper, microfilm, magnetic storage device, optical imaging system, CD-ROM, flash drive, other electronic data storage system, server, case maintenance system ("CM"), electronic court filing ("ECF") system, statewide or local electronic portal ("e-portal"), or other electronic record keeping system authorized by the supreme court in a format sufficient to communicate the information on the original document in a readable format. Electronic transmission of documents includes electronic mail ("e-mail") and any internet-based transmission procedure, and may include procedures allowing for documents to be signed or verified by electronic means. FL ST J ADMIN Rule 2.525(a).

   i. The filing of documents with the court as required by the Florida Rules of Judicial Administration must be made by filing them with the clerk in accordance with FL ST J ADMIN Rule 2.525, except that the judge may permit documents to be filed with the judge, in which event the judge must note the filing date before him or her on the documents and transmit them to the clerk. The date of filing is that shown on the face of the document by the judge's notation or the clerk's time stamp, whichever is earlier. FL ST J ADMIN Rule 2.516(e).

b. *Application.* Any court or clerk of the court may accept the electronic transmission of documents for filing after the clerk, together with input from the chief judge of the circuit, has obtained approval of the procedures and program for doing so from the Supreme Court of Florida. FL ST J ADMIN Rule 2.525(b).

c. *Exceptions*

   i. Paper documents and other submissions may be manually submitted to the clerk or court:
      - When the clerk does not have the ability to accept and retain documents by electronic filing or has not had ECF Procedures approved by the supreme court;
      - For filing by any self-represented party or any self-represented nonparty unless specific ECF Procedures provide a means to file documents electronically. However, any self-represented nonparty that is a governmental or public agency and any other agency, partnership, corporation, or business entity acting on behalf of any governmental or public agency may file documents by electronic transmission if such entity has the capability of filing documents electronically;
      - For filing by attorneys excused from e-mail service in accordance with FL ST J ADMIN Rule 2.516(b);
      - When submitting evidentiary exhibits or filing non-documentary materials;
      - When the filing involves documents in excess of twenty-five (25) megabytes (25MB) in size. For such filings, documents may be transmitted using an electronic storage medium that the clerk has the ability to accept, which may include a CD-ROM, flash drive, or similar storage medium;
      - When filed in open court, as permitted by the court;
      - When paper filing is permitted by any approved statewide or local ECF procedures; and
      - If any court determines that justice so requires. FL ST J ADMIN Rule 2.525(d).

   ii. Any document in paper form submitted under FL ST J ADMIN Rule 2.525(d) is filed when it is received by the clerk or court and the clerk shall immediately thereafter convert any filed paper document to an electronic document. "Convert to an electronic document" means optically capturing an image of a paper document and using character recognition software to recover as much of the document's text as practicable and then indexing and storing the document in the official court file. FL ST J ADMIN Rule 2.525(c)(4).

iii. Any storage medium submitted under FL ST J ADMIN Rule 2.525(d)(5) is filed when received by the clerk or court and the clerk shall immediately thereafter transfer the electronic documents from the storage device to the official court file. FL ST J ADMIN Rule 2.525(c)(5).

iv. If the filer of any paper document authorized under FL ST J ADMIN Rule 2.525(d) provides a self-addressed, postage-paid envelope for return of the paper document after it is converted to electronic form by the clerk, the clerk shall place the paper document in the envelope and deposit it in the mail. Except when a paper document is required to be maintained, the clerk may recycle any filed paper document that is not to be returned to the filer. FL ST J ADMIN Rule 2.525(c)(6).

v. The clerk may convert any paper document filed before the effective date of FL ST J ADMIN Rule 2.525 to an electronic document. Unless the clerk is required to maintain the paper document, if the paper document has been converted to an electronic document by the clerk, the paper document is no longer part of the official court file and may be removed and recycled. FL ST J ADMIN Rule 2.525(c)(7).

d. *Official court file.* For information on what constitutes the official court file, please see FL ST J ADMIN Rule 2.525(c)(2), FL ST J ADMIN Rule 2.525(c)(3).

e. *Administration.* All attorneys, parties, or other persons using this rule to file documents are required to make arrangements with the court or clerk for the payment of any charges authorized by general law or the supreme court before filing any document by electronic transmission. FL ST J ADMIN Rule 2.525(f)(2).

f. *Filing date.* The filing date for an electronically transmitted document is the date and time that such filing is acknowledged by an electronic stamp or otherwise, pursuant to any procedure set forth in any ECF Procedures approved by the supreme court, or the date the last page of such filing is received by the court or clerk. FL ST J ADMIN Rule 2.525(f)(3).

g. *Accessibility.* All documents transmitted in any electronic form under FL ST J ADMIN Rule 2.525 must comply with the accessibility requirements of FL ST J ADMIN Rule 2.526. FL ST J ADMIN Rule 2.525(g).

2. *Service requirements.* Every pleading subsequent to the initial pleading, all orders, and every other document filed in the action must be served in conformity with the requirements of FL ST J ADMIN Rule 2.516. FL ST RCP Rule 1.080(a).

a. *Service; When required.* Unless the court otherwise orders, or a statute or supreme court administrative order specifies a different means of service, every pleading subsequent to the initial pleading and every other document filed in any court proceeding, except applications for witness subpoenas and documents served by formal notice or required to be served in the manner provided for service of formal notice, must be served in accordance with FL ST J ADMIN Rule 2.516 on each party. No service need be made on parties against whom a default has been entered, except that pleadings asserting new or additional claims against them must be served in the manner provided for service of summons. FL ST J ADMIN Rule 2.516(a).

b. *Service; How made.* When service is required or permitted to be made upon a party represented by an attorney, service must be made upon the attorney unless service upon the party is ordered by the court. FL ST J ADMIN Rule 2.516(b).

i. *Service by electronic mail ("e-mail").* All documents required or permitted to be served on another party must be served by e-mail, unless FL ST J ADMIN Rule 2.516 otherwise provides. When, in addition to service by e-mail, the sender also utilizes another means of service provided for in FL ST J ADMIN Rule 2.516(b)(2), any differing time limits and other provisions applicable to that other means of service control. FL ST J ADMIN Rule 2.516(b)(1). Any document electronically transmitted to a court or clerk must also be served on all parties and interested persons in accordance with the applicable rules of court. FL ST J ADMIN Rule 2.525(e)(2).

- *Service on attorneys.* Upon appearing in a proceeding, an attorney must serve a designation of a primary e-mail address and may designate no more than two (2) secondary e-mail addresses. Thereafter, service must be directed to all designated e-mail addresses in that proceeding. Every document filed by an attorney thereafter must include the primary e-mail address of that attorney and any secondary e-mail addresses. If an attorney does not designate any e-mail address for service, documents may be served on that attorney at the e-mail address on record with The Florida Bar. FL ST J ADMIN Rule 2.516(b)(1)(A).
- *Exception to e-mail service on attorneys.* Service by an attorney on another attorney must be made by e-mail unless excused by the court. Upon motion by an attorney demonstrating that the attorney has no e-mail account and lacks access to the Internet at the attorney's office, the court may excuse the attorney from the requirements of e-mail service. Service on and by an attorney excused by the court from e-mail service must be by the means provided in FL ST J ADMIN Rule 2.516(b)(2). FL ST J ADMIN Rule 2.516(b)(1)(B).
- *Service on and by parties not represented by an attorney.* Any party not represented by an attorney may serve a designation of a primary e-mail address and also may designate no more than two (2) secondary e-mail addresses to which service must be directed in that proceeding by the means provided in FL ST J ADMIN Rule 2.516(b)(1). If a party not represented by an attorney does not designate an e-mail address for service in a proceeding, service on and by that party must be by the means provided in FL ST J ADMIN Rule 2.516(b)(2). FL ST J ADMIN Rule 2.516(b)(1)(C).
- *Time of service.* Service by e-mail is complete when it is sent. FL ST J ADMIN Rule 2.516(b)(1)(D). An e-mail is deemed served on the date it is sent. FL ST J ADMIN Rule 2.516(b)(1)(D)(i). If the sender learns that the e-mail did not reach the address of the person to be served, the sender must immediately send another copy by e-mail, or by a means authorized by FL ST J ADMIN Rule 2.516(b)(2). FL ST J ADMIN Rule 2.516(b)(1)(D)(ii). E-mail service is treated as service by mail for the computation of time. FL ST J ADMIN Rule 2.516(b)(1)(D)(iii).

ii. *Format of e-mail for service.* Service of a document by e-mail is made by attaching a copy of the document in PDF format to an e-mail sent to all addresses designated by the attorney or party. FL ST J ADMIN Rule 2.516(b)(1)(E).

- All documents served by e-mail must be attached to an e-mail message containing a subject line beginning with the words "SERVICE OF COURT DOCUMENT" in all capital letters, followed by the case number of the proceeding in which the documents are being served. FL ST J ADMIN Rule 2.516(b)(1)(E)(i).
- The body of the e-mail must identify the court in which the proceeding is pending, the case number, the name of the initial party on each side, the title of each document served with that e-mail, and the sender's name and telephone number. FL ST J ADMIN Rule 2.516(b)(1)(E)(ii).
- Any document served by e-mail may be signed by the "/s/" format, as long as the filed original is signed in accordance with the applicable rule of procedure. FL ST J ADMIN Rule 2.516(b)(1)(E)(iii).
- Any e-mail which, together with its attached documents, exceeds five megabytes (5MB) in size, must be divided and sent as separate e-mails, no one of which may exceed five megabytes (5MB) in size and each of which must be sequentially numbered in the subject line. FL ST J ADMIN Rule 2.516(b)(1)(E)(iv).

iii. *Service by other means.* In addition to, and not in lieu of, service by e-mail, service may also be made upon attorneys by any of the means specified in FL ST J ADMIN Rule 2.516(b)(2). Service on and by all parties who are not represented by an attorney and who do not designate an e-mail address, and on and by all attorneys excused from e-mail service, must be made by delivering a copy of the document or by mailing it to the party or attorney at their last known address or, if no address is known, by leaving it with the clerk of the court. Service by mail is complete upon mailing. Delivery of a copy within FL ST J ADMIN Rule 2.516 is complete upon:

- Handing it to the attorney or to the party,
- Leaving it at the attorney's or party's office with a clerk or other person in charge thereof,
- If there is no one in charge, leaving it in a conspicuous place therein,
- If the office is closed or the person to be served has no office, leaving it at the person's usual place of abode with some person of his or her family above fifteen (15) years of age and informing such person of the contents, or
- Transmitting it by facsimile to the attorney's or party's office with a cover sheet containing the sender's name, firm, address, telephone number, and facsimile number, and the number of pages transmitted. When service is made by facsimile, a copy must also be served by any other method permitted by FL ST J ADMIN Rule 2.516. Facsimile service occurs when transmission is complete. FL ST J ADMIN Rule 2.516(b)(2)(A) through FL ST J ADMIN Rule 2.516(b)(2)(E).
- Service by delivery after 5:00 p.m. must be deemed to have been made by mailing on the date of delivery. FL ST J ADMIN Rule 2.516(b)(2)(F).

c. *Service; Numerous defendants.* In actions when the parties are unusually numerous, the court may regulate the service contemplated by the Florida Rules of Judicial Administration on motion or on its own initiative in such manner as may be found to be just and reasonable. FL ST J ADMIN Rule 2.516(c).

d. *Service by clerk.* Service of notices and other documents required to be made by the clerk must also be done as provided in FL ST J ADMIN Rule 2.516(b). FL ST J ADMIN Rule 2.516(g).

G. Hearings

1. *Communication equipment*

a. *Definition.* Communication equipment means a conference telephone or other electronic device that permits all those appearing or participating to hear and speak to each other, provided that all conversation of all parties is audible to all persons present. FL ST J ADMIN Rule 2.530(a).

b. *Use by all parties.* A county or circuit court judge may, upon the court's own motion or upon the written request of a party, direct that communication equipment be used for a motion hearing, pretrial conference, or a status conference. A judge must give notice to the parties and consider any objections they may have to the use of communication equipment before directing that communication equipment be used. The decision to use communication equipment over the objection of parties will be in the sound discretion of the trial court, except as noted below. FL ST J ADMIN Rule 2.530(b).

c. *Use only by requesting party.* A county or circuit court judge may, upon the written request of a party upon reasonable notice to all other parties, permit a requesting party to participate through communication equipment in a scheduled motion hearing; however, any such request (except in criminal, juvenile, and appellate proceedings) must be granted, absent a showing of good cause to deny the same, where the hearing is set for not longer than fifteen (15) minutes. FL ST J ADMIN Rule 2.530(c).

d. *Testimony*

i. *Generally.* A county or circuit court judge, general magistrate, special magistrate, or hearing officer may allow testimony to be taken through communication equipment if all parties consent or if permitted by another applicable rule of procedure. FL ST J ADMIN Rule 2.530(d)(1).

ii. *Procedure.* Any party desiring to present testimony through communication equipment shall, prior to the hearing or trial at which the testimony is to be presented, contact all parties to

determine whether each party consents to this form of testimony. The party seeking to present the testimony shall move for permission to present testimony through communication equipment, which motion shall set forth good cause as to why the testimony should be allowed in this form. FL ST J ADMIN Rule 2.530(d)(2).

iii. *Oath.* Testimony may be taken through communication equipment only if a notary public or other person authorized to administer oaths in the witness's jurisdiction is present with the witness and administers the oath consistent with the laws of the jurisdiction. FL ST J ADMIN Rule 2.530(d)(3).

iv. *Confrontation rights.* In juvenile and criminal proceedings the defendant must make an informed waiver of any confrontation rights that may be abridged by the use of communication equipment. FL ST J ADMIN Rule 2.530(d)(4).

v. *Video testimony.* If the testimony to be presented utilizes video conferencing or comparable two-way visual capabilities, the court in its discretion may modify the procedures set forth in FL ST J ADMIN Rule 2.530 to accommodate the technology utilized. FL ST J ADMIN Rule 2.530(d)(5).

e. *Burden of expense.* The cost for the use of the communication equipment is the responsibility of the requesting party unless otherwise directed by the court. FL ST J ADMIN Rule 2.530(e).

H. Forms

1. Official Motion to Compel Discovery Forms for Florida

a. Caption. FL ST RCP Form 1.901.

b. Notice of compliance when constitutional challenge is brought. FL ST RCP Form 1.975.

2. Motion to Compel Discovery Forms for Florida

a. Motion to compel attendance and for sanctions. FL-PP § 3:160.

b. Motion; To compel answer to questions asked on oral examination or written questions. FL-PP § 3:161.

c. Order; Directing deponent to answer questions asked on oral examination; Costs and attorney fees to moving party. FL-PP § 3:162.

d. Order; Compelling answer to written questions. FL-PP § 3:163.

e. Motion; For order finding person in contempt of court; Refusal, after order, to answer question. FL-PP § 3:167.

f. Motion; For order compelling opposing party to pay expenses incurred in proving facts the party refused to admit. FL-PP § 3:168.

g. Motion; Compel discovery, deposition. FL-PRACFORM § 7:37.

h. Motion; Compel discovery, interrogatories. FL-PRACFORM § 7:38.

i. Form for motion to compel answer on deposition. FL-RCPF R 1.380(6).

j. Form for certificate of non-appearance at deposition. FL-RCPF R 1.380(7).

k. Form for notice of motion. FL-RCPF R 1.380(8).

l. Form for order on motion to compel answer. FL-RCPF R 1.380(9).

m. Form for notice and motion to compel. FL-RCPF R 1.380(10).

n. Form for order to compel discovery. FL-RCPF R 1.380(18).

o. Form for order to comply with discovery and answer interrogatories. FL-RCPF R 1.380(19).

I. Checklist

(I) ❑ Matters to be considered by moving party

(a) ❑ Required documents

(1) ❑ Notice of hearing/Motion

(2) ❑ Certificate of service

(b) ❑ Supplemental documents

(1) ❑ Proposed order

(2) ❑ Notice of constitutional question

(c) ❑ Time for making motion

(1) ❑ Upon reasonable notice to other parties and all persons affected, a party may apply for an order compelling discovery

(2) ❑ A copy of any written motion which may not be heard ex parte and a copy of the notice of the hearing thereof shall be served a reasonable time before the time specified for the hearing

(II) ❑ Matters to be considered by opposing party

(a) ❑ Required documents

(1) ❑ Response to motion

(2) ❑ Certificate of service

(b) ❑ Supplemental documents

(1) ❑ Proposed order

(2) ❑ Notice of constitutional question

(c) ❑ Time for service and filing of opposition

(1) ❑ No time specified for responding to a motion

Motions, Oppositions and Replies
Motion for Directed Verdict

Document Last Updated January 2013

A. Applicable Rules

1. *State rules*

   a. Motion for a directed verdict. FL ST RCP Rule 1.480.

   b. Rules of court. FL ST RCP Rule 1.010; FL ST J ADMIN Rule 2.110.

   c. Nonverification of pleadings. FL ST RCP Rule 1.030.

   d. Service and filing of pleadings, orders, and documents. FL ST RCP Rule 1.080.

   e. Time. FL ST RCP Rule 1.090.

   f. Pleadings and motions. FL ST RCP Rule 1.100.

   g. Motions. FL ST RCP Rule 1.160.

   h. Relief from judgment, decrees, or orders. FL ST RCP Rule 1.540.

   i. Mediation and arbitration. FL ST RCP Rule 1.700; FL ST RCP Rule 1.710; FL ST RCP Rule 1.720; FL ST RCP Rule 1.730; FL ST RCP Rule 1.750; FL ST RCP Rule 1.800; FL ST RCP Rule 1.810; FL ST RCP Rule 1.820; FL ST RCP Rule 1.830.

   j. Forms. FL ST RCP Rule 1.900.

   k. Minimization of the filing of sensitive information. FL ST J ADMIN Rule 2.425.

   l. Retention of court records. FL ST J ADMIN Rule 2.430.

   m. Foreign attorneys. FL ST J ADMIN Rule 2.510.

   n. Signature of attorneys and parties. FL ST J ADMIN Rule 2.515.

   o. Paper. FL ST J ADMIN Rule 2.520.

p. Electronic filing. FL ST J ADMIN Rule 2.525.
q. Accessibility of information and technology. FL ST J ADMIN Rule 2.526.
r. Communication equipment. FL ST J ADMIN Rule 2.530.
s. Court reporting. FL ST J ADMIN Rule 2.535.
t. Requests for accommodations by persons with disabilities. FL ST J ADMIN Rule 2.540.

2. *Local rules*
   a. Sealing court records. FL ST 4 J CIR 2006-05.

B. Timing

1. *Before a verdict is returned.* A directed verdict is available to the defendant at the close of the plaintiff's evidence or to either party at the close of all of the evidence. A verdict may be directed either by the court on its own motion or on the motion of counsel. FL ST RCP Rule 1.480(a); FL-PP § 5:83. The movant should be prepared to argue the motion immediately. FL-PRACPROC § 22:14.
2. *After a verdict is returned.* Within ten (10) days after the return of a verdict, a party who has timely moved for a directed verdict may serve a motion to enter judgment in accordance with the motion for a directed verdict. FL ST RCP Rule 1.480(b).
3. *No verdict is returned.* If a verdict was not returned, a party who has timely moved for a directed verdict may serve a motion for judgment in accordance with the motion for a directed verdict within ten (10) days after discharge of the jury. FL ST RCP Rule 1.480(b).
4. *General motion timing.* A copy of any written motion which may not be heard ex parte and a copy of the notice of the hearing thereof shall be served a reasonable time before the time specified for the hearing. FL ST RCP Rule 1.090(d).
5. *Computation of time*
   a. *Generally.* Computation of time shall be governed by FL ST J ADMIN Rule 2.514. FL ST RCP Rule 1.090(a). The following rules apply in computing time periods specified in any rule of procedure, local rule, court order, or statute that does not specify a method of computing time. FL ST J ADMIN Rule 2.514(a).
      i. *Period stated in days or a longer unit.* When the period is stated in days or a longer unit of time (A) exclude the day of the event that triggers the period; (B) count every day, including intermediate Saturdays, Sundays, and legal holidays; and (C) include the last day of the period, but if the last day is a Saturday, Sunday, or legal holiday, or falls within any period of time extended through an order of the chief justice under FL ST J ADMIN Rule 2.205(a)(2)(B)(iv), the period continues to run until the end of the next day that is not a Saturday, Sunday, or legal holiday and does not fall within any period of time extended through an order of the chief justice. FL ST J ADMIN Rule 2.514(a)(1).
      ii. *Period stated in hours.* When the period is stated in hours (A) begin counting immediately on the occurrence of the event that triggers the period; (B) count every hour, including hours during intermediate Saturdays, Sundays, and legal holidays; and (C) if the period would end on a Saturday, Sunday, or legal holiday, or during any period of time extended through an order of the chief justice under FL ST J ADMIN Rule 2.205(a)(2)(B)(iv), the period continues to run until the same time on the next day that is not a Saturday, Sunday, or legal holiday and does not fall within any period of time extended through an order of the chief justice. FL ST J ADMIN Rule 2.514(a)(2).
      iii. *Period stated in days less than seven (7) days.* When the period stated in days is less than seven (7) days, intermediate Saturdays, Sundays, and legal holidays shall be excluded in the computation. FL ST J ADMIN Rule 2.514(a)(3).
      iv. *"Last day" defined.* Unless a different time is set by a statute, local rule, or court order, the last day ends (A) for electronic filing or for service by any means, at midnight; and (B) for filing by other means, when the clerk's office is scheduled to close. FL ST J ADMIN Rule 2.514(a)(4).
      v. *"Next day" defined.* The "next day" is determined by continuing to count forward when the

period is measured after an event and backward when measured before an event. FL ST J ADMIN Rule 2.514(a)(5).

vi. *"Legal holiday" defined.* "Legal holiday" means (A) the day set aside by FL ST § 110.117, for observing New Year's Day, Martin Luther King, Jr.'s Birthday, Memorial Day, Independence Day, Labor Day, Veterans' Day, Thanksgiving Day, the Friday after Thanksgiving Day, or Christmas Day, and (B) any day observed as a holiday by the clerk's office or as designated by the chief judge. FL ST J ADMIN Rule 2.514(a)(6).

b. *Additional time after service by mail or e-mail.* When a party may or must act within a specified time after service and service is made by mail or e-mail, five (5) days are added after the period that would otherwise expire under FL ST J ADMIN Rule 2.514(a). FL ST J ADMIN Rule 2.514(b).

c. *Enlargement.* When an act is required or allowed to be done at or within a specified time by order of court, by the Florida Rules of Civil Procedure, or by notice given thereunder, for cause shown the court at any time in its discretion (1) with or without notice, may order the period enlarged if request therefor is made before the expiration of the period originally prescribed or as extended by a previous order, or (2) upon motion made and notice after the expiration of the specified period, may permit the act to be done when failure to act was the result of excusable neglect, but it may not extend the time for making a motion for new trial, for rehearing, or to alter or amend a judgment; making a motion for relief from a judgment under FL ST RCP Rule 1.540(b); taking an appeal or filing a petition for certiorari; or making a motion for a directed verdict. FL ST RCP Rule 1.090(b).

d. *Unaffected by expiration of term.* The period of time provided for the doing of any act or the taking of any proceeding shall not be affected or limited by the continued existence or expiration of a term of court. The continued existence or expiration of a term of court in no way affects the power of a court to do any act or take any proceeding in any action which is or has been pending before it. FL ST RCP Rule 1.090(c).

C. General Requirements

1. *Motions generally*

a. *Contents.* An application to the court for an order shall be by motion which shall be made in writing unless made during a hearing or trial, shall state with particularity the grounds therefor, and shall set forth the relief or order sought. The requirement of writing is fulfilled if the motion is stated in a written notice of the hearing of the motion. All notices of hearing shall specify each motion or other matter to be heard. FL ST RCP Rule 1.100(b).

b. *Particularity requirement.* The court considers a motion in the light of the substantive law, rule or statute to make its determination. Some rules require a statement of the grounds for a motion under the rule. Failure to give the grounds will result in denial of the motion. This should be the result in all situations when the ground for the motion is not inherent in the rule. FL-PRACPROC § 9:3. The requirement is nevertheless an important one, first because of the due process notice rights of the respondent, as well as for the assistance it provides to the court in its preparation for the hearing or, absent a hearing, for disposition. 4 FLPRAC R 1.100.

2. *Motion for directed verdict*

a. *Effect of a motion for directed verdict.* A party who moves for a directed verdict at the close of the evidence offered by the adverse party may offer evidence in the event the motion is denied without having reserved the right to do so and to the same extent as if the motion had not been made. The denial of a motion for a directed verdict shall not operate to discharge the jury. A motion for a directed verdict shall state the specific grounds therefor. The order directing a verdict is effective without any assent of the jury. FL ST RCP Rule 1.480(a).

b. *Reservation of decision on motion.* When a motion for a directed verdict is denied or for any reason is not granted, the court is deemed to have submitted the action to the jury subject to a later determination of the legal questions raised by the motion. Within ten (10) days after the return of a verdict, a party who has timely moved for a directed verdict may serve a motion to set aside the verdict and any judgment entered thereon and to enter judgment in accordance with the motion for a directed verdict. If a verdict was not returned, a party who has timely moved for a directed verdict may serve a motion for judgment in accordance with the motion for a directed verdict within ten (10) days after discharge of the jury. FL ST RCP Rule 1.480(b).

c. *Joined with motion for new trial.* A motion for a new trial may be joined with a motion for directed verdict or a new trial may be requested in the alternative. If a verdict was returned, the court may allow the judgment to stand or may reopen the judgment and either order a new trial or direct the entry of judgment as if the requested verdict had been directed. If no verdict was returned, the court may direct the entry of judgment as if the requested verdict had been directed or may order a new trial. FL ST RCP Rule 1.480(c).

d. *General procedures on a motion for directed verdict*

   i. *Proper method.* The proper method of advocating that a party is entitled to prevail on a claim or defense as a matter of law is to make a motion for a directed verdict at the close of the evidence offered by the opposing party. The trial judge has authority to direct a verdict in favor of one party and against another, without submitting the case to the jury, if there is no other verdict the jury could lawfully return. 5 FLPRAC § 22:5.

   ii. *Directed verdict only in a jury trial.* A motion for directed verdict is proper only in a jury trial. The equivalent motion in nonjury trial is called a motion for involuntary dismissal. 5 FLPRAC § 22:5.

   iii. *Test for the sufficiency of the evidence.* A motion for directed verdict is used primarily to test the sufficiency of the evidence offered in support of a claim or defense. It may also be used to raise legal issues other than the sufficiency of the evidence, but that is less common because most pure issues of law can be resolved on a motion to dismiss or a motion for summary judgment before the case is set for trial. If there is no evidence to support a claim or defense, the trial judge has a duty to direct a verdict for the opposing party on that claim or defense. 5 FLPRAC § 22:5.

   - The trial judge must view all of the facts and factual inferences in a light most favorable to the party opposing the motion. 5 FLPRAC § 22:5.
   - The rule has often been stated by the Florida courts in the negative, that is, a motion for directed verdict should not be granted unless the court, after viewing the evidence and testimony in the light most favorable to the nonmoving party, determines that no reasonable jury could render a verdict for the nonmoving party. Under this rule, the trial judge may not direct a verdict against a party if there is any evidence upon which the jury could lawfully make a finding in favor of that party. 5 FLPRAC § 22:5.

3. *Arbitration and mediation*

a. *Referral to arbitration and mediation.* Except as hereinafter provided or as otherwise prohibited by law, the presiding judge may enter an order referring all or any part of a contested civil matter to mediation or arbitration. The parties to any contested civil matter may file a written stipulation to mediate or arbitrate any issue between them at any time. Such stipulation shall be incorporated into the order of referral. FL ST RCP Rule 1.700(a).

b. *Arbitration*

   i. *Exclusions.* A civil action shall be ordered to arbitration or arbitration in conjunction with mediation upon stipulation of the parties. A civil action may be ordered to arbitration or arbitration in conjunction with mediation upon motion of any party or by the court, if the judge determines the action to be of such a nature that arbitration could be of benefit to the litigants or the court. FL ST RCP Rule 1.800.

   - Under no circumstances may the following categories of actions be referred to arbitration: (1) bond estreatures; (2) habeas corpus or other extraordinary writs; (3) bond validations; (4) civil or criminal contempt; (5) such other matters as may be specified by order of the chief judge in the circuit. FL ST RCP Rule 1.800.

   ii. For more information regarding arbitration, please see FL ST RCP Rule 1.810; FL ST RCP Rule 1.820; FL ST RCP Rule 1.830.

c. *Mediation.* For more information regarding mediation, please see FL ST RCP Rule 1.710; FL ST RCP Rule 1.720; FL ST RCP Rule 1.730; and FL ST RCP Rule 1.750.

4. *Rules of court*

   a. *Rules of civil procedure.* The Florida Rules of Civil Procedure apply to all actions of a civil nature and all special statutory proceedings in the circuit courts and county courts except those to which the Florida Probate Rules, the Florida Family Law Rules of Procedure, or the Small Claims Rules apply. FL ST RCP Rule 1.010.

      i. The form, content, procedure, and time for pleading in all special statutory proceedings shall be as prescribed by the statutes governing the proceeding unless the Florida Rules of Civil Procedure specifically provide to the contrary. FL ST RCP Rule 1.010.

      ii. The Florida Rules of Civil Procedure shall be construed to secure the just, speedy, and inexpensive determination of every action. FL ST RCP Rule 1.010.

   b. *Rules of judicial administration.* The Florida Rules of Judicial Administration shall apply to administrative matters in all courts to which the Florida Rules of Judicial Administration are applicable by their terms. The Florida Rules of Judicial Administration shall be construed to secure the speedy and inexpensive determination of every proceeding to which they are applicable. The Florida Rules of Judicial Administration shall supersede all conflicting rules and statutes. FL ST J ADMIN Rule 2.110.

D. Documents

1. *Required documents*

   a. *Notice of hearing/Motion.* An application to the court for an order shall be by motion which shall be made in writing unless made during a hearing or trial, shall state with particularity the grounds therefor, and shall set forth the relief or order sought. The requirement of writing is fulfilled if the motion is stated in a written notice of the hearing of the motion. All notices of hearing shall specify each motion or other matter to be heard. FL ST RCP Rule 1.100(b).

      i. *Notices to persons with disabilities.* See the Format section of this KeyRules document for further information.

   b. *Certificate of service.* When any attorney certifies in substance: "I certify that a copy hereof has been furnished to (here insert name or names and addresses used for service) by (e-mail) (delivery) (mail) (fax) on .... (date) ....________________ Attorney" the certificate is taken as prima facie proof of such service in compliance with FL ST J ADMIN Rule 2.516. FL ST J ADMIN Rule 2.516(f).

2. *Supplemental documents*

   a. *Proposed order.* The court may require that orders or judgments be prepared by a party, may require the party to furnish the court with stamped, addressed envelopes for service of the order or judgment, and may require that proposed orders and judgments be furnished to all parties before entry by the court of the order or judgment. FL ST J ADMIN Rule 2.516(h)(1).

   b. *Notice of constitutional question.* A party that files a pleading, written motion, or other paper drawing into question the constitutionality of a state statute or a county or municipal charter, ordinance, or franchise must promptly (1) file a notice of constitutional question stating the question and identifying the paper that raises it; and (2) serve the notice and the pleading, written motion, or other paper drawing into question the constitutionality of a state statute or a county or municipal charter, ordinance, or franchise on the Attorney General or the state attorney of the judicial circuit in which the action is pending, by either certified or registered mail. Service of the notice and pleading, written motion, or other paper does not require joinder of the Attorney General or the state attorney as a party to the action. FL ST RCP Rule 1.071.

E. Format

1. *Documents; Type and size.* Documents subject to the exceptions set forth in FL ST J ADMIN Rule 2.525(d) shall be filed on recycled paper measuring eight and one half by eleven (8 1/2 by 11) inches. For purposes of FL ST J ADMIN Rule 2.520, paper is recycled if it contains a minimum content of fifty (50) percent waste paper. Xerographic reduction of legal-size (eight and one half by fourteen (8 1/2 by 14) inches) documents to letter size (eight and one half by eleven (8 1/2 by 11) inches) is prohibited. All other

documents filed by electronic transmission shall be filed in a format capable of being printed in a format consistent with the provisions of FL ST J ADMIN Rule 2.250. FL ST J ADMIN Rule 2.520(b).

a. *Exhibits.* Any exhibit or attachment filed with pleadings or papers may be filed in its original size. FL ST J ADMIN Rule 2.520(c).

b. *Recording space.* On all papers and documents prepared and filed by the court or by any party to a proceeding which are to be recorded in the public records of any county, including but not limited to final money judgments and notices of lis pendens, a three (3) inch by three (3) inch space at the top right-hand corner on the first page and a one (1) inch by three (3) inch space at the top right-hand corner on each subsequent page shall be left blank and reserved for use by the clerk of court. FL ST J ADMIN Rule 2.520(d).

   i. *Exceptions to recording space.* Any papers or documents created by persons or entities over which the filing party has no control, including but not limited to wills, codicils, trusts, or other testamentary documents; documents prepared or executed by any public officer; documents prepared, executed, acknowledged, or proved outside of the State of Florida; or documents created by State or Federal government agencies, may be filed without the space required by FL ST J ADMIN Rule 2.520. FL ST J ADMIN Rule 2.520(e).

c. *Noncompliance.* No clerk of court is permitted to refuse to file any document or paper because of noncompliance with the Florida Rules of Judicial Administration. However, upon request of the clerk of court, noncomplying documents must be resubmitted in accordance with the formatting rules. FL ST J ADMIN Rule 2.520(f).

2. *Caption.* Every pleading, motion, order, judgment, or other paper shall have a caption containing the name of the court, the file number, and except for in rem proceedings, including forfeiture proceedings, the name of the first party on each side with an appropriate indication of other parties, and a designation identifying the party filing it and its nature or the nature of the order, as the case may be. In any in rem proceeding, every pleading, motion, order, judgment, or other paper shall have a caption containing the name of the court, the file number, the style "In re" (followed by the name or general description of the property), and a designation of the person or entity filing it and its nature or the nature of the order, as the case may be. In an in rem forfeiture proceeding, the style shall be "In re forfeiture of" (followed by the name of the general description of the property). All papers filed in the action shall be styled in such a manner as to indicate clearly the subject matter of the paper and the party requesting or obtaining relief. FL ST RCP Rule 1.100(c)(1).

3. *Writing and written defined.* Writing or written means a document containing information, an application, or a stipulation. FL ST RCP Rule 1.080(c).

4. *Rule abbreviations*

   a. The Florida Rules of Civil Procedure and shall be abbreviated as Fla.R.Civ.P. FL ST RCP Rule 1.010.

   b. The Florida Rules of Judicial Administration shall be abbreviated as Fla. R. Jud. Admin. FL ST J ADMIN Rule 2.110.

5. *Nonverification.* Except when otherwise specifically provided by the Florida Rules of Civil Procedure or an applicable statute, every pleading or other document of a party represented by an attorney need not be verified or accompanied by an affidavit. FL ST RCP Rule 1.030; FL ST J ADMIN Rule 2.515(a).

6. *Attorney signature*

   a. *Attorney signature.* Every pleading and other document of a party represented by an attorney shall be signed by at least one (1) attorney of record in that attorney's individual name whose current record Florida Bar address, telephone number, including area code, primary e-mail address and secondary e-mail addresses, if any, and Florida Bar number shall be stated, and who shall be duly licensed to practice law in Florida or who shall have received permission to appear in the particular case as provided in FL ST J ADMIN Rule 2.510. FL ST J ADMIN Rule 2.515(a).

      i. The attorney may be required by the court to give the address of, and to vouch for the attorney's authority to represent, the party. FL ST J ADMIN Rule 2.515(a).

ii. The signature of an attorney shall constitute a certificate by the attorney that the attorney has read the pleading or other document; that to the best of the attorney's knowledge, information, and belief there is good ground to support it; and that it is not interposed for delay. FL ST J ADMIN Rule 2.515(a).

iii. If a pleading is not signed or is signed with intent to defeat the purpose of FL ST J ADMIN Rule 2.515, it may be stricken and the action may proceed as though the pleading or other document had not been served. FL ST J ADMIN Rule 2.515(a).

b. *Pro se litigant signature.* A party who is not represented by an attorney shall sign any pleading or other paper and state the party's address and telephone number, including area code. FL ST J ADMIN Rule 2.515(b).

c. *Form of signature*

i. The signatures required on pleadings and documents by FL ST J ADMIN Rule 2.515(a) and FL ST J ADMIN Rule 2.515(b) may be:

- Original signatures;
- Original signatures that have been reproduced by electronic means, such as on electronically transmitted documents or photocopied documents;
- Electronic signatures using the "/s/," "s/," or "/s" formats by or at the direction of the person signing; or
- Any other signature format authorized by general law, so long as the clerk where the proceeding is pending has the capability of receiving and has obtained approval from the Supreme Court of Florida to accept pleadings and documents with that signature format. FL ST J ADMIN Rule 2.515(c)(1).

ii. An attorney, party, or other person who files a pleading or paper by electronic transmission that does not contain the original signature of that attorney, party, or other person shall file that identical pleading or paper in paper form containing an original signature of that attorney, party, or other person (hereinafter called the follow-up filing) immediately thereafter. The follow-up filing is not required if the Supreme Court of Florida has entered an order directing the clerk of court to discontinue accepting the follow-up filing. FL ST J ADMIN Rule 2.515(c)(2).

7. *Forms*

a. *Process.* The forms of process, notice of lis pendens, and notice of action provided in the Florida Rules of Civil Procedure are sufficient. Variations from the forms do not void process or notices that are otherwise sufficient. FL ST RCP Rule 1.900(a).

b. *Other forms.* The other forms provided in the Florida Rules of Civil Procedure are sufficient for the matters that are covered by them. So long as the substance is expressed without prolixity, the forms may be varied to meet the facts of a particular case. FL ST RCP Rule 1.900(b).

c. *Formal matters.* Captions, except for the designation of the paper, are omitted from the forms provided in the Florida Rules of Civil Procedure. A general form of caption is the first form provided. Signatures are omitted from pleadings and motions. FL ST RCP Rule 1.900(c).

8. *Notices to persons with disabilities.* All notices of court proceedings to be held in a public facility, and all process compelling appearance at such proceedings, shall include the following statement in bold face, fourteen (14) point Times New Roman or Courier font: "If you are a person with a disability who needs any accommodation in order to participate in this proceeding, you are entitled, at no cost to you, to the provision of certain assistance. Please contact [identify applicable court personnel by name, address, and telephone number] at least seven (7) days before your scheduled court appearance, or immediately upon receiving this notification if the time before the scheduled appearance is less than seven (7) days; if you are hearing or voice impaired, call 711." FL ST J ADMIN Rule 2.540(c)(1).

9. *Minimization of the filing of sensitive information*

a. *Limitations for court filings.* Unless authorized by FL ST J ADMIN Rule 2.425(b), statute, another

rule of court, or the court orders otherwise, designated sensitive information filed with the court must be limited to the following format:

i. The initials of a person known to be a minor;

ii. The year of birth of a person's birth date;

iii. No portion of any: Social security number, Bank account number, Credit card account number, Charge account number, or Debit account number;

iv. The last four digits of any: Taxpayer identification number (TIN), Employee identification number, Driver's license number, Passport number, Telephone number, Financial account number, except as set forth in FL ST J ADMIN Rule 2.425(a)(3), Brokerage account number, Insurance policy account number, Loan account number, Customer account number, or Patient or health care number;

v. A truncated version of any: Email address, Computer user name, Password, or Personal identification number (PIN); and

vi. A truncated version of any other sensitive information as provided by court order. FL ST J ADMIN Rule 2.425(a).

b. *Exceptions.* FL ST J ADMIN Rule 2.425(a) does not apply to the following:

i. An account number which identifies the property alleged to be the subject of a proceeding;

ii. The record of an administrative or agency proceeding;

iii. The record in appellate or review proceedings;

iv. The birth date of a minor whenever the birth date is necessary for the court to establish or maintain subject matter jurisdiction;

v. The name of a minor in any order relating to parental responsibility, time-sharing, or child support;

vi. The name of a minor in any document or order affecting the minor's ownership of real property;

vii. The birth date of a party in a writ of attachment or notice to payor;

viii. In traffic and criminal proceedings: a pro se filing; a court filing that is related to a criminal matter or investigation and that is prepared before the filing of a criminal charge or is not filed as part of any docketed criminal case; an arrest or search warrant or any information in support thereof; a charging document and an affidavit or other documents filed in support of any charging document, including any driving records; a statement of particulars; discovery material introduced into evidence or otherwise filed with the court; and all information necessary for the proper issuance and execution of a subpoena duces tecum;

ix. Information used by the clerk for case maintenance purposes or the courts for case management purposes; and

x. Information which is relevant and material to an issue before the court. FL ST J ADMIN Rule 2.425(b).

c. *Remedies.* Upon motion by a party or interested person or sua sponte by the court, the court may order remedies, sanctions or both for a violation of FL ST J ADMIN Rule 2.425(a). Following notice and an opportunity to respond, the court may impose sanctions if such filing was not made in good faith. FL ST J ADMIN Rule 2.425(c).

d. *Motions not restricted.* FL ST J ADMIN Rule 2.425 does not restrict a party's right to move for protective order, to move to file documents under seal, or to request a determination of the confidentiality of records. FL ST J ADMIN Rule 2.425(d).

i. For more information regarding sealing court records, please see FL ST 4 J CIR 2006-05.

e. *Application.* FL ST J ADMIN Rule 2.425 does not affect the application of constitutional provisions, statutes, or rules of court regarding confidential information or access to public information. FL ST J ADMIN Rule 2.425(e).

F. Filing and Service Requirements

1. *Filing requirements.* All original documents must be filed with the court either before service or immediately thereafter, unless otherwise provided for by general law or other rules. If the original of any bond or other document is not placed in the court file, a certified copy must be so placed by the clerk. FL ST J ADMIN Rule 2.516(d). All documents shall be filed in conformity with the requirements of FL ST J ADMIN Rule 2.525. FL ST RCP Rule 1.080(b). All documents filed in any court shall be filed by electronic transmission in accordance with FL ST J ADMIN Rule 2.525. "Documents" means pleadings, motions, petitions, memoranda, briefs, notices, exhibits, declarations, affidavits, orders, judgments, decrees, writs, opinions, and any other paper or writing submitted to a court. FL ST J ADMIN Rule 2.520(a). All documents that are court records, as defined in FL ST J ADMIN Rule 2.430(a)(1), must be filed by electronic transmission, provided that: (1) the clerk has the ability to accept and retain such documents; (2) the clerk or the chief judge of the circuit has requested permission to accept documents filed by electronic transmission; and (3) the supreme court has entered an order granting permission to the clerk to accept documents filed by electronic transmission. FL ST J ADMIN Rule 2.525(c)(1).
    a. *Definition.* "Electronic transmission of documents" means the sending of information by electronic signals to, by or from a court or clerk, which when received can be transformed and stored or transmitted on paper, microfilm, magnetic storage device, optical imaging system, CD-ROM, flash drive, other electronic data storage system, server, case maintenance system ("CM"), electronic court filing ("ECF") system, statewide or local electronic portal ("e-portal"), or other electronic record keeping system authorized by the supreme court in a format sufficient to communicate the information on the original document in a readable format. Electronic transmission of documents includes electronic mail ("e-mail") and any internet-based transmission procedure, and may include procedures allowing for documents to be signed or verified by electronic means. FL ST J ADMIN Rule 2.525(a).
        i. The filing of documents with the court as required by the Florida Rules of Judicial Administration must be made by filing them with the clerk in accordance with FL ST J ADMIN Rule 2.525, except that the judge may permit documents to be filed with the judge, in which event the judge must note the filing date before him or her on the documents and transmit them to the clerk. The date of filing is that shown on the face of the document by the judge's notation or the clerk's time stamp, whichever is earlier. FL ST J ADMIN Rule 2.516(e).
    b. *Application.* Any court or clerk of the court may accept the electronic transmission of documents for filing after the clerk, together with input from the chief judge of the circuit, has obtained approval of the procedures and program for doing so from the Supreme Court of Florida. FL ST J ADMIN Rule 2.525(b).
    c. *Exceptions*
        i. Paper documents and other submissions may be manually submitted to the clerk or court:
            - When the clerk does not have the ability to accept and retain documents by electronic filing or has not had ECF Procedures approved by the supreme court;
            - For filing by any self-represented party or any self-represented nonparty unless specific ECF Procedures provide a means to file documents electronically. However, any self-represented nonparty that is a governmental or public agency and any other agency, partnership, corporation, or business entity acting on behalf of any governmental or public agency may file documents by electronic transmission if such entity has the capability of filing documents electronically;
            - For filing by attorneys excused from e-mail service in accordance with FL ST J ADMIN Rule 2.516(b);
            - When submitting evidentiary exhibits or filing non-documentary materials;
            - When the filing involves documents in excess of twenty-five (25) megabytes (25MB) in size. For such filings, documents may be transmitted using an electronic storage medium that the clerk has the ability to accept, which may include a CD-ROM, flash drive, or similar storage medium;

- When filed in open court, as permitted by the court;
- When paper filing is permitted by any approved statewide or local ECF procedures; and
- If any court determines that justice so requires. FL ST J ADMIN Rule 2.525(d).

ii. Any document in paper form submitted under FL ST J ADMIN Rule 2.525(d) is filed when it is received by the clerk or court and the clerk shall immediately thereafter convert any filed paper document to an electronic document. "Convert to an electronic document" means optically capturing an image of a paper document and using character recognition software to recover as much of the document's text as practicable and then indexing and storing the document in the official court file. FL ST J ADMIN Rule 2.525(c)(4).

iii. Any storage medium submitted under FL ST J ADMIN Rule 2.525(d)(5) is filed when received by the clerk or court and the clerk shall immediately thereafter transfer the electronic documents from the storage device to the official court file. FL ST J ADMIN Rule 2.525(c)(5).

iv. If the filer of any paper document authorized under FL ST J ADMIN Rule 2.525(d) provides a self-addressed, postage-paid envelope for return of the paper document after it is converted to electronic form by the clerk, the clerk shall place the paper document in the envelope and deposit it in the mail. Except when a paper document is required to be maintained, the clerk may recycle any filed paper document that is not to be returned to the filer. FL ST J ADMIN Rule 2.525(c)(6).

v. The clerk may convert any paper document filed before the effective date of FL ST J ADMIN Rule 2.525 to an electronic document. Unless the clerk is required to maintain the paper document, if the paper document has been converted to an electronic document by the clerk, the paper document is no longer part of the official court file and may be removed and recycled. FL ST J ADMIN Rule 2.525(c)(7).

d. *Official court file.* For information on what constitutes the official court file, please see FL ST J ADMIN Rule 2.525(c)(2), FL ST J ADMIN Rule 2.525(c)(3).

e. *Administration.* All attorneys, parties, or other persons using this rule to file documents are required to make arrangements with the court or clerk for the payment of any charges authorized by general law or the supreme court before filing any document by electronic transmission. FL ST J ADMIN Rule 2.525(f)(2).

f. *Filing date.* The filing date for an electronically transmitted document is the date and time that such filing is acknowledged by an electronic stamp or otherwise, pursuant to any procedure set forth in any ECF Procedures approved by the supreme court, or the date the last page of such filing is received by the court or clerk. FL ST J ADMIN Rule 2.525(f)(3).

g. *Accessibility.* All documents transmitted in any electronic form under FL ST J ADMIN Rule 2.525 must comply with the accessibility requirements of FL ST J ADMIN Rule 2.526. FL ST J ADMIN Rule 2.525(g).

2. *Service requirements.* Every pleading subsequent to the initial pleading, all orders, and every other document filed in the action must be served in conformity with the requirements of FL ST J ADMIN Rule 2.516. FL ST RCP Rule 1.080(a).

a. *Service; When required.* Unless the court otherwise orders, or a statute or supreme court administrative order specifies a different means of service, every pleading subsequent to the initial pleading and every other document filed in any court proceeding, except applications for witness subpoenas and documents served by formal notice or required to be served in the manner provided for service of formal notice, must be served in accordance with FL ST J ADMIN Rule 2.516 on each party. No service need be made on parties against whom a default has been entered, except that pleadings asserting new or additional claims against them must be served in the manner provided for service of summons. FL ST J ADMIN Rule 2.516(a).

b. *Service; How made.* When service is required or permitted to be made upon a party represented by an attorney, service must be made upon the attorney unless service upon the party is ordered by the court. FL ST J ADMIN Rule 2.516(b).

i. *Service by electronic mail ("e-mail").* All documents required or permitted to be served on

another party must be served by e-mail, unless FL ST J ADMIN Rule 2.516 otherwise provides. When, in addition to service by e-mail, the sender also utilizes another means of service provided for in FL ST J ADMIN Rule 2.516(b)(2), any differing time limits and other provisions applicable to that other means of service control. FL ST J ADMIN Rule 2.516(b)(1). Any document electronically transmitted to a court or clerk must also be served on all parties and interested persons in accordance with the applicable rules of court. FL ST J ADMIN Rule 2.525(e)(2).

- *Service on attorneys.* Upon appearing in a proceeding, an attorney must serve a designation of a primary e-mail address and may designate no more than two (2) secondary e-mail addresses. Thereafter, service must be directed to all designated e-mail addresses in that proceeding. Every document filed by an attorney thereafter must include the primary e-mail address of that attorney and any secondary e-mail addresses. If an attorney does not designate any e-mail address for service, documents may be served on that attorney at the e-mail address on record with The Florida Bar. FL ST J ADMIN Rule 2.516(b)(1)(A).
- *Exception to e-mail service on attorneys.* Service by an attorney on another attorney must be made by e-mail unless excused by the court. Upon motion by an attorney demonstrating that the attorney has no e-mail account and lacks access to the Internet at the attorney's office, the court may excuse the attorney from the requirements of e-mail service. Service on and by an attorney excused by the court from e-mail service must be by the means provided in FL ST J ADMIN Rule 2.516(b)(2). FL ST J ADMIN Rule 2.516(b)(1)(B).
- *Service on and by parties not represented by an attorney.* Any party not represented by an attorney may serve a designation of a primary e-mail address and also may designate no more than two (2) secondary e-mail addresses to which service must be directed in that proceeding by the means provided in FL ST J ADMIN Rule 2.516(b)(1). If a party not represented by an attorney does not designate an e-mail address for service in a proceeding, service on and by that party must be by the means provided in FL ST J ADMIN Rule 2.516(b)(2). FL ST J ADMIN Rule 2.516(b)(1)(C).
- *Time of service.* Service by e-mail is complete when it is sent. FL ST J ADMIN Rule 2.516(b)(1)(D). An e-mail is deemed served on the date it is sent. FL ST J ADMIN Rule 2.516(b)(1)(D)(i). If the sender learns that the e-mail did not reach the address of the person to be served, the sender must immediately send another copy by e-mail, or by a means authorized by FL ST J ADMIN Rule 2.516(b)(2). FL ST J ADMIN Rule 2.516(b)(1)(D)(ii). E-mail service is treated as service by mail for the computation of time. FL ST J ADMIN Rule 2.516(b)(1)(D)(iii).

ii. *Format of e-mail for service.* Service of a document by e-mail is made by attaching a copy of the document in PDF format to an e-mail sent to all addresses designated by the attorney or party. FL ST J ADMIN Rule 2.516(b)(1)(E).

- All documents served by e-mail must be attached to an e-mail message containing a subject line beginning with the words "SERVICE OF COURT DOCUMENT" in all capital letters, followed by the case number of the proceeding in which the documents are being served. FL ST J ADMIN Rule 2.516(b)(1)(E)(i).
- The body of the e-mail must identify the court in which the proceeding is pending, the case number, the name of the initial party on each side, the title of each document served with that e-mail, and the sender's name and telephone number. FL ST J ADMIN Rule 2.516(b)(1)(E)(ii).
- Any document served by e-mail may be signed by the "/s/" format, as long as the filed original is signed in accordance with the applicable rule of procedure. FL ST J ADMIN Rule 2.516(b)(1)(E)(iii).
- Any e-mail which, together with its attached documents, exceeds five megabytes (5MB) in size, must be divided and sent as separate e-mails, no one of which may exceed five megabytes (5MB) in size and each of which must be sequentially numbered in the subject line. FL ST J ADMIN Rule 2.516(b)(1)(E)(iv).

iii. *Service by other means.* In addition to, and not in lieu of, service by e-mail, service may also be made upon attorneys by any of the means specified in FL ST J ADMIN Rule 2.516(b)(2). Service on and by all parties who are not represented by an attorney and who do not designate an e-mail address, and on and by all attorneys excused from e-mail service, must be made by delivering a copy of the document or by mailing it to the party or attorney at their last known address or, if no address is known, by leaving it with the clerk of the court. Service by mail is complete upon mailing. Delivery of a copy within FL ST J ADMIN Rule 2.516 is complete upon:

- Handing it to the attorney or to the party,
- Leaving it at the attorney's or party's office with a clerk or other person in charge thereof,
- If there is no one in charge, leaving it in a conspicuous place therein,
- If the office is closed or the person to be served has no office, leaving it at the person's usual place of abode with some person of his or her family above fifteen (15) years of age and informing such person of the contents, or
- Transmitting it by facsimile to the attorney's or party's office with a cover sheet containing the sender's name, firm, address, telephone number, and facsimile number, and the number of pages transmitted. When service is made by facsimile, a copy must also be served by any other method permitted by FL ST J ADMIN Rule 2.516. Facsimile service occurs when transmission is complete. FL ST J ADMIN Rule 2.516(b)(2)(A) through FL ST J ADMIN Rule 2.516(b)(2)(E).
- Service by delivery after 5:00 p.m. must be deemed to have been made by mailing on the date of delivery. FL ST J ADMIN Rule 2.516(b)(2)(F).

c. *Service; Numerous defendants.* In actions when the parties are unusually numerous, the court may regulate the service contemplated by the Florida Rules of Judicial Administration on motion or on its own initiative in such manner as may be found to be just and reasonable. FL ST J ADMIN Rule 2.516(c).

d. *Service by clerk.* Service of notices and other documents required to be made by the clerk must also be done as provided in FL ST J ADMIN Rule 2.516(b). FL ST J ADMIN Rule 2.516(g).

G. Hearings

1. *Communication equipment*

a. *Definition.* Communication equipment means a conference telephone or other electronic device that permits all those appearing or participating to hear and speak to each other, provided that all conversation of all parties is audible to all persons present. FL ST J ADMIN Rule 2.530(a).

b. *Use by all parties.* A county or circuit court judge may, upon the court's own motion or upon the written request of a party, direct that communication equipment be used for a motion hearing, pretrial conference, or a status conference. A judge must give notice to the parties and consider any objections they may have to the use of communication equipment before directing that communication equipment be used. The decision to use communication equipment over the objection of parties will be in the sound discretion of the trial court, except as noted below. FL ST J ADMIN Rule 2.530(b).

c. *Use only by requesting party.* A county or circuit court judge may, upon the written request of a party upon reasonable notice to all other parties, permit a requesting party to participate through communication equipment in a scheduled motion hearing; however, any such request (except in criminal, juvenile, and appellate proceedings) must be granted, absent a showing of good cause to deny the same, where the hearing is set for not longer than fifteen (15) minutes. FL ST J ADMIN Rule 2.530(c).

d. *Testimony*

i. *Generally.* A county or circuit court judge, general magistrate, special magistrate, or hearing officer may allow testimony to be taken through communication equipment if all parties consent or if permitted by another applicable rule of procedure. FL ST J ADMIN Rule 2.530(d)(1).

ii. *Procedure.* Any party desiring to present testimony through communication equipment shall, prior to the hearing or trial at which the testimony is to be presented, contact all parties to determine whether each party consents to this form of testimony. The party seeking to present the testimony shall move for permission to present testimony through communication equipment, which motion shall set forth good cause as to why the testimony should be allowed in this form. FL ST J ADMIN Rule 2.530(d)(2).

iii. *Oath.* Testimony may be taken through communication equipment only if a notary public or other person authorized to administer oaths in the witness's jurisdiction is present with the witness and administers the oath consistent with the laws of the jurisdiction. FL ST J ADMIN Rule 2.530(d)(3).

iv. *Confrontation rights.* In juvenile and criminal proceedings the defendant must make an informed waiver of any confrontation rights that may be abridged by the use of communication equipment. FL ST J ADMIN Rule 2.530(d)(4).

v. *Video testimony.* If the testimony to be presented utilizes video conferencing or comparable two-way visual capabilities, the court in its discretion may modify the procedures set forth in FL ST J ADMIN Rule 2.530 to accommodate the technology utilized. FL ST J ADMIN Rule 2.530(d)(5).

e. *Burden of expense.* The cost for the use of the communication equipment is the responsibility of the requesting party unless otherwise directed by the court. FL ST J ADMIN Rule 2.530(e).

H. Forms

1. Official Motion for Directed Verdict Forms for Florida

a. Caption. FL ST RCP Form 1.901.

b. Notice of compliance when constitutional challenge is brought. FL ST RCP Form 1.975.

2. Motion for Directed Verdict Forms for Florida

a. Motion; For directed verdict; At close of adverse party's evidence. FL-PP § 5:86.

b. Motion; For directed verdict; At close of all of evidence. FL-PP § 5:87.

c. Motion; Request to go to jury if motions by both parties are denied. FL-PP § 5:88.

d. Order; Granting defendant's motion for directed verdict; Insufficiency of plaintiff's evidence. FL-PP § 5:89.

e. Motion; Directed verdict, renewed. FL-PRACFORM § 7:62.

f. Form for motion for directed verdict at close of plaintiff's case. FL-RCPF R 1.480(24).

g. Form for motion for directed verdict at close of defendant's case. FL-RCPF R 1.480(25).

h. Form for motion to set aside verdict and enter directed verdict. FL-RCPF R 1.480(26).

I. Checklist

(I) ❑ Matters to be considered by moving party

(a) ❑ Required documents

(1) ❑ Notice of hearing/Motion

(2) ❑ Certificate of service

(b) ❑ Supplemental documents

(1) ❑ Proposed order

(2) ❑ Notice of constitutional question

(c) ❑ Time for making motion

(1) ❑ Before a verdict is returned - A directed verdict is available to the defendant at the close of the plaintiff's evidence or to either party at the close of all of the evidence

(2) ❑ After a verdict is returned - Within ten (10) days after the return of a verdict, a party who has

timely moved for a directed verdict may serve a motion to enter judgment in accordance with the motion for a directed verdict

(3) ❑ No verdict is returned - If a verdict was not returned, a party who has timely moved for a directed verdict may serve a motion for judgment in accordance with the motion for a directed verdict within ten (10) days after discharge of the jury

(4) ❑ General motion timing - A copy of any written motion which may not be heard ex parte and a copy of the notice of the hearing thereof shall be served a reasonable time before the time specified for the hearing

(II) ❑ Matters to be considered by opposing party

(a) ❑ Required documents

(1) ❑ Response to motion

(2) ❑ Certificate of service

(b) ❑ Supplemental documents

(1) ❑ Proposed order

(2) ❑ Notice of constitutional question

(c) ❑ Time for service and filing of opposition

(1) ❑ No time specified for responding to a motion

Requests, Notices and Applications
Request for Production of Documents

Document Last Updated January 2013

A. Applicable Rules

1. *State rules*

a. Nonverification of pleadings. FL ST RCP Rule 1.030.

b. Service and filing of pleadings, orders, and documents. FL ST RCP Rule 1.080.

c. Time. FL ST RCP Rule 1.090.

d. Pleadings and motions. FL ST RCP Rule 1.100.

e. Pretrial procedure. FL ST RCP Rule 1.200.

f. General provisions governing discovery. FL ST RCP Rule 1.280.

g. Depositions upon oral examination. FL ST RCP Rule 1.310.

h. Interrogatories to parties. FL ST RCP Rule 1.340.

i. Production of documents and things and entry upon land for inspection and other purposes. FL ST RCP Rule 1.350.

j. Production of documents and things without deposition. FL ST RCP Rule 1.351.

k. Examination of persons. FL ST RCP Rule 1.360.

l. Requests for admission. FL ST RCP Rule 1.370.

m. Failure to make discovery; Sanctions. FL ST RCP Rule 1.380.

n. Depositions of expert witnesses. FL ST RCP Rule 1.390.

o. Relief from judgment, decrees, or orders. FL ST RCP Rule 1.540.

p. Forms. FL ST RCP Rule 1.900.

q. Minimization of the filing of sensitive information. FL ST J ADMIN Rule 2.425.

r. Retention of court records. FL ST J ADMIN Rule 2.430.

s. Foreign attorneys. FL ST J ADMIN Rule 2.510.

t. Signature of attorneys and parties. FL ST J ADMIN Rule 2.515.

u. Paper. FL ST J ADMIN Rule 2.520.

v. Electronic filing. FL ST J ADMIN Rule 2.525.

w. Accessibility of information and technology. FL ST J ADMIN Rule 2.526.

x. Requests for accommodations by persons with disabilities. FL ST J ADMIN Rule 2.540.

2. *Local rules*

a. Sealing court records. FL ST 4 J CIR 2006-05.

B. Timing

1. *Request for production of documents.* Without leave of court the request may be served on the plaintiff after commencement of the action and on any other party with or after service of the process and initial pleading on that party. FL ST RCP Rule 1.350(b).

2. *Notice of intent to serve subpoena.* A party desiring production under FL ST RCP Rule 1.351 shall serve notice as provided in FL ST RCP Rule 1.080 on every other party of the intent to serve a subpoena under FL ST RCP Rule 1.351 at least ten (10) days before the subpoena is issued if service is by delivery and fifteen (15) days before the subpoena is issued if the service is by mail or e-mail. FL ST RCP Rule 1.351(b).

3. *Sequence and timing of discovery.* Except as provided in FL ST RCP Rule 1.280(b)(5) or unless the court upon motion for the convenience of parties and witnesses and in the interest of justice orders otherwise, methods of discovery may be used in any sequence, and the fact that a party is conducting discovery, whether by deposition or otherwise, shall not delay any other party's discovery. FL ST RCP Rule 1.280(e).

4. *Computation of time*

a. *Generally.* Computation of time shall be governed by FL ST J ADMIN Rule 2.514. FL ST RCP Rule 1.090(a). The following rules apply in computing time periods specified in any rule of procedure, local rule, court order, or statute that does not specify a method of computing time. FL ST J ADMIN Rule 2.514(a).

i. *Period stated in days or a longer unit.* When the period is stated in days or a longer unit of time (A) exclude the day of the event that triggers the period; (B) count every day, including intermediate Saturdays, Sundays, and legal holidays; and (C) include the last day of the period, but if the last day is a Saturday, Sunday, or legal holiday, or falls within any period of time extended through an order of the chief justice under FL ST J ADMIN Rule 2.205(a)(2)(B)(iv), the period continues to run until the end of the next day that is not a Saturday, Sunday, or legal holiday and does not fall within any period of time extended through an order of the chief justice. FL ST J ADMIN Rule 2.514(a)(1).

ii. *Period stated in hours.* When the period is stated in hours (A) begin counting immediately on the occurrence of the event that triggers the period; (B) count every hour, including hours during intermediate Saturdays, Sundays, and legal holidays; and (C) if the period would end on a Saturday, Sunday, or legal holiday, or during any period of time extended through an order of the chief justice under FL ST J ADMIN Rule 2.205(a)(2)(B)(iv), the period continues to run until the same time on the next day that is not a Saturday, Sunday, or legal holiday and does not fall within any period of time extended through an order of the chief justice. FL ST J ADMIN Rule 2.514(a)(2).

iii. *Period stated in days less than seven (7) days.* When the period stated in days is less than seven (7) days, intermediate Saturdays, Sundays, and legal holidays shall be excluded in the computation. FL ST J ADMIN Rule 2.514(a)(3).

iv. *"Last day" defined.* Unless a different time is set by a statute, local rule, or court order, the last day ends (A) for electronic filing or for service by any means, at midnight; and (B) for filing by other means, when the clerk's office is scheduled to close. FL ST J ADMIN Rule 2.514(a)(4).

v. *"Next day" defined.* The "next day" is determined by continuing to count forward when the period is measured after an event and backward when measured before an event. FL ST J ADMIN Rule 2.514(a)(5).

vi. *"Legal holiday" defined.* "Legal holiday" means (A) the day set aside by FL ST § 110.117, for observing New Year's Day, Martin Luther King, Jr.'s Birthday, Memorial Day, Independence Day, Labor Day, Veterans' Day, Thanksgiving Day, the Friday after Thanksgiving Day, or Christmas Day, and (B) any day observed as a holiday by the clerk's office or as designated by the chief judge. FL ST J ADMIN Rule 2.514(a)(6).

b. *Additional time after service by mail or e-mail.* When a party may or must act within a specified time after service and service is made by mail or e-mail, five (5) days are added after the period that would otherwise expire under FL ST J ADMIN Rule 2.514(a). FL ST J ADMIN Rule 2.514(b).

c. *Enlargement.* When an act is required or allowed to be done at or within a specified time by order of court, by the Florida Rules of Civil Procedure, or by notice given thereunder, for cause shown the court at any time in its discretion (1) with or without notice, may order the period enlarged if request therefor is made before the expiration of the period originally prescribed or as extended by a previous order, or (2) upon motion made and notice after the expiration of the specified period, may permit the act to be done when failure to act was the result of excusable neglect, but it may not extend the time for making a motion for new trial, for rehearing, or to alter or amend a judgment; making a motion for relief from a judgment under FL ST RCP Rule 1.540(b); taking an appeal or filing a petition for certiorari; or making a motion for a directed verdict. FL ST RCP Rule 1.090(b).

d. *Unaffected by expiration of term.* The period of time provided for the doing of any act or the taking of any proceeding shall not be affected or limited by the continued existence or expiration of a term of court. The continued existence or expiration of a term of court in no way affects the power of a court to do any act or take any proceeding in any action which is or has been pending before it. FL ST RCP Rule 1.090(c).

C. General Requirements

1. *General provisions governing discovery*

a. *Discovery methods.* Parties may obtain discovery by one or more of the following methods: depositions upon oral examination or written questions; written interrogatories; production of documents or things or permission to enter upon land or other property for inspection and other purposes; physical and mental examinations; and requests for admission. Unless the court orders otherwise and under FL ST RCP Rule 1.280(c), the frequency of use of these methods is not limited, except as provided in FL ST RCP Rule 1.200, FL ST RCP Rule 1.340, and FL ST RCP Rule 1.370. FL ST RCP Rule 1.280(a).

b. *Scope of discovery.* Unless otherwise limited by order of the court in accordance with the Florida Rules of Civil Procedure, the scope of discovery is as follows:

i. *In general.* Parties may obtain discovery regarding any matter, not privileged, that is relevant to the subject matter of the pending action, whether it relates to the claim or defense of the party seeking discovery or the claim or defense of any other party, including the existence, description, nature, custody, condition, and location of any books, documents, or other tangible things and the identity and location of persons having knowledge of any discoverable matter. It is not ground for objection that the information sought will be inadmissible at the trial if the information sought appears reasonably calculated to lead to the discovery of admissible evidence. FL ST RCP Rule 1.280(b)(1).

ii. *Indemnity agreements.* A party may obtain discovery of the existence and contents of any agreement under which any person may be liable to satisfy part or all of a judgment that may be entered in the action or to indemnify or to reimburse a party for payments made to satisfy the judgment. Information concerning the agreement is not admissible in evidence at trial by reason of disclosure. FL ST RCP Rule 1.280(b)(2).

iii. *Electronically stored information.* A party may obtain discovery of electronically stored information in accordance with the Florida Rules of Civil Procedure. FL ST RCP Rule 1.280(b)(3).

iv. *Trial preparation; Materials.* Subject to the provisions of FL ST RCP Rule 1.280(b)(5), a party may obtain discovery of documents and tangible things otherwise discoverable under FL ST RCP Rule 1.280(b)(1) and prepared in anticipation of litigation or for trial by or for another party or by or for that party's representative, including that party's attorney, consultant, surety, indemnitor, insurer, or agent, only upon a showing that the party seeking discovery has need of the materials in the preparation of the case and is unable without undue hardship to obtain the substantial equivalent of the materials by other means. FL ST RCP Rule 1.280(b)(4).

- In ordering discovery of the materials when the required showing has been made, the court shall protect against disclosure of the mental impressions, conclusions, opinions, or legal theories of an attorney or other representative of a party concerning the litigation. FL ST RCP Rule 1.280(b)(4).
- Without the required showing a party may obtain a copy of a statement concerning the action or its subject matter previously made by that party. FL ST RCP Rule 1.280(b)(4).
- Upon request without the required showing a person not a party may obtain a copy of a statement concerning the action or its subject matter previously made by that person. If the request is refused, the person may move for an order to obtain a copy. The provisions of FL ST RCP Rule 1.380(a)(5) apply to the award of expenses incurred as a result of making the motion. FL ST RCP Rule 1.280(b)(4).
- For purposes of FL ST RCP Rule 1.280(b)(4), a statement previously made is a written statement signed or otherwise adopted or approved by the person making it, or a stenographic, mechanical, electrical, or other recording or transcription of it that is a substantially verbatim recital of an oral statement by the person making it and contemporaneously recorded. FL ST RCP Rule 1.280(b)(4).

v. *Trial preparation; Experts.* Discovery of facts known and opinions held by experts, otherwise discoverable under the provisions of FL ST RCP Rule 1.280(b)(1) and acquired or developed in anticipation of litigation or for trial, may be obtained only as follows:

- By interrogatories a party may require any other party to identify each person whom the other party expects to call as an expert witness at trial and to state the subject matter on which the expert is expected to testify, and to state the substance of the facts and opinions to which the expert is expected to testify and a summary of the grounds for each opinion. FL ST RCP Rule 1.280(b)(5)(A)(i).
- Any person disclosed by interrogatories or otherwise as a person expected to be called as an expert witness at trial may be deposed in accordance with FL ST RCP Rule 1.390 without motion or order of court. FL ST RCP Rule 1.280(b)(5)(A)(ii).
- A party may obtain the following discovery regarding any person disclosed by interrogatories or otherwise as a person expected to be called as an expert witness at trial: The scope of employment in the pending case and the compensation for such service, FL ST RCP Rule 1.280(b)(5)(A)(iii)(1); The expert's general litigation experience, including the percentage of work performed for plaintiffs and defendants, FL ST RCP Rule 1.280(b)(5)(A)(iii)(2); The identity of other cases, within a reasonable time period, in which the expert has testified by deposition or at trial, FL ST RCP Rule 1.280(b)(5)(A)(iii)(3); An approximation of the portion of the expert's involvement as an expert witness, which may be based on the number of hours, percentage of hours, or percentage of earned income derived from serving as an expert witness; however, the expert shall not be required to disclose his or her earnings as an expert witness or income derived from other services. FL ST RCP Rule 1.280(b)(5)(A)(iii)(4).
- An expert may be required to produce financial and business records only under the most unusual or compelling circumstances and may not be compelled to compile or produce nonexistent documents. Upon motion, the court may order further discovery by other means, subject to such restrictions as to scope and other provisions pursuant to FL ST RCP Rule 1.280(b)(5)(C) concerning fees and expenses as the court may deem appropriate. FL ST RCP Rule 1.280(b)(5).

- A party may discover facts known or opinions held by an expert who has been retained or specially employed by another party in anticipation of litigation or preparation for trial and who is not expected to be called as a witness at trial, only as provided in FL ST RCP Rule 1.360(b) or upon a showing of exceptional circumstances under which it is impracticable for the party seeking discovery to obtain facts or opinions on the same subject by other means. FL ST RCP Rule 1.280(b)(5)(B).
- Unless manifest injustice would result, the court shall require that the party seeking discovery pay the expert a reasonable fee for time spent in responding to discovery under FL ST RCP Rule 1.280(b)(5)(A) and FL ST RCP Rule 1.280(b)(5)(B); and concerning discovery from an expert obtained under FL ST RCP Rule 1.280(b)(5)(A) the court may require, and concerning discovery obtained under FL ST RCP Rule 1.280(b)(5)(B) shall require, the party seeking discovery to pay the other party a fair part of the fees and expenses reasonably incurred by the latter party in obtaining facts and opinions from the expert. FL ST RCP Rule 1.280(b)(5)(C).
- As used in the Florida Rules of Civil Procedure an expert shall be an expert witness as defined in FL ST RCP Rule 1.390(a). FL ST RCP Rule 1.280(b)(5)(D).

vi. *Claims to privilege or protection.* When a party withholds information otherwise discoverable under the Florida Rules of Civil Procedure by claiming that it is privileged or subject to protection as trial preparation material, the party shall make the claim expressly and shall describe the nature of the documents, communications, or things not produced or disclosed in a manner that, without revealing information itself privileged or protected, will enable other parties to assess the applicability of the privilege or protection. FL ST RCP Rule 1.280(b)(6).

c. *Limitations on discovery of electronically stored information*

i. A person may object to discovery of electronically stored information from sources that the person identifies as not reasonably accessible because of burden or cost. On motion to compel discovery or for a protective order, the person from whom discovery is sought must show that the information sought or the format requested is not reasonably accessible because of undue burden or cost. If that showing is made, the court may nonetheless order the discovery from such sources or in such formats if the requesting party shows good cause. The court may specify conditions of the discovery, including ordering that some or all of the expenses incurred by the person from whom discovery is sought be paid by the party seeking the discovery. FL ST RCP Rule 1.280(d)(1).

ii. In determining any motion involving discovery of electronically stored information, the court must limit the frequency or extent of discovery otherwise allowed by the Florida Rules of Civil Procedure if it determines that (i) the discovery sought is unreasonably cumulative or duplicative, or can be obtained from another source or in another manner that is more convenient, less burdensome, or less expensive; or (ii) the burden or expense of the discovery outweighs its likely benefit, considering the needs of the case, the amount in controversy, the parties' resources, the importance of the issues at stake in the action, and the importance of the discovery in resolving the issues. FL ST RCP Rule 1.280(d)(2).

d. For information on inadvertent disclosure of privileged materials, see FL ST RCP Rule 1.285.

2. *Request for production of documents*

a. *Scope of request.* Any party may request any other party:

i. To produce and permit the party making the request, or someone acting in the requesting party's behalf, to inspect and copy any designated documents, including electronically stored information, writings, drawings, graphs, charts, photographs, phono-records, and other data compilations from which information can be obtained, translated, if necessary, by the party to whom the request is directed through detection devices into reasonably usable form, that constitute or contain matters within the scope of FL ST RCP Rule 1.280(b) and that are in the possession, custody, or control of the party to whom the request is directed;

ii. To inspect and copy, test, or sample any tangible things that constitute or contain matters within the scope of FL ST RCP Rule 1.280(b) and that are in the possession, custody, or control of the party to whom the request is directed; or

iii. To permit entry upon designated land or other property in the possession or control of the party upon whom the request is served for the purpose of inspection and measuring, surveying, photographing, testing, or sampling the property or any designated object or operation on it within the scope of FL ST RCP Rule 1.280(b). FL ST RCP Rule 1.350(a).

b. *Contents of request*

i. The request shall set forth the items to be inspected, either by individual item or category, and describe each item and category with reasonable particularity. The request shall specify a reasonable time, place, and manner of making the inspection or performing the related acts. FL ST RCP Rule 1.350(b).

ii. A request for electronically stored information may specify the form or forms in which electronically stored information is to be produced. If the responding party objects to a requested form, or if no form is specified in the request, the responding party must state the form or forms it intends to use. If a request for electronically stored information does not specify the form of production, the producing party must produce the information in a form or forms in which it is ordinarily maintained or in a reasonably usable form or forms. FL ST RCP Rule 1.350(b).

c. *Failure to respond to requests.* The party submitting the request may move for an order under FL ST RCP Rule 1.380 concerning any objection, failure to respond to the request, or any part of it, or failure to permit the inspection as requested. FL ST RCP Rule 1.350(b). Please see FL ST RCP Rule 1.380(d) and the KeyRules Motion to Compel Discovery documents for further information regarding compelling discovery and discovery sanctions.

i. *Response requirements.* For each item or category the response shall state that inspection and related activities will be permitted as requested unless the request is objected to, in which event the reasons for the objection shall be stated. If an objection is made to part of an item or category, the part shall be specified. When producing documents, the producing party shall either produce them as they are kept in the usual course of business or shall identify them to correspond with the categories in the request. If the responding party objects to a requested form (for electronic information), or if no form is specified in the request, the responding party must state the form or forms it intends to use. If a request for electronically stored information does not specify the form of production, the producing party must produce the information in a form or forms in which it is ordinarily maintained or in a reasonably usable form or forms. FL ST RCP Rule 1.350(b).

3. *Requests to a non-party*

a. *Independent action not prohibited.* FL ST RCP Rule 1.350 does not preclude an independent action against a person not a party for production of documents and things and permission to enter upon land. FL ST RCP Rule 1.350(c). FL ST RCP Rule 1.351 does not affect the right of any party to bring an independent action for production of documents and things or permission to enter upon land. FL ST RCP Rule 1.351(f).

b. *Scope.* A party may seek inspection and copying of any documents or things within the scope of FL ST RCP Rule 1.350(a) from a person who is not a party by issuance of a subpoena directing the production of the documents or things when the requesting party does not seek to depose the custodian or other person in possession of the documents or things. FL ST RCP Rule 1.351 provides the exclusive procedure for obtaining documents or things by subpoena from nonparties without deposing the custodian or other person in possession of the documents or things pursuant to FL ST RCP Rule 1.310. FL ST RCP Rule 1.351(a).

i. *Procedure.* The proposed subpoena shall be attached to the notice and shall state the time, place, and method for production of the documents or things, and the name and address of the person who is to produce the documents or things, if known, and if not known, a general description sufficient to identify the person or the particular class or group to which the person belongs; shall include a designation of the items to be produced; and shall state that the person who will be asked to produce the documents or things has the right to object to the production under FL ST RCP Rule 1.351 and that the person will not be required to surrender the documents or things. A copy of the notice and proposed subpoena shall not be furnished to the person upon whom the subpoena is to be served. If any party serves an objection to production under FL ST RCP Rule 1.351 within ten (10) days of service of the notice, the documents or things shall not be produced pending resolution of the objection in accordance with FL ST RCP Rule 1.351(d). FL ST RCP Rule 1.351(b).

ii. *Subpoena.* If no objection is made by a party under FL ST RCP Rule 1.351(b), an attorney of record in the action may issue a subpoena or the party desiring production shall deliver to the clerk for issuance a subpoena together with a certificate of counsel or pro se party that no timely objection has been received from any party, and the clerk shall issue the subpoena and deliver it to the party desiring production. FL ST RCP Rule 1.351(c).

- The subpoena shall be identical to the copy attached to the notice and shall specify that no testimony may be taken and shall require only production of the documents or things specified in it. FL ST RCP Rule 1.351(c).
- The subpoena may give the recipient an option to deliver or mail legible copies of the documents or things to the party serving the subpoena. FL ST RCP Rule 1.351(c).
- The person upon whom the subpoena is served may condition the preparation of copies on the payment in advance of the reasonable costs of preparing the copies. FL ST RCP Rule 1.351(c).
- The subpoena shall require production only in the county of the residence of the custodian or other person in possession of the documents or things or in the county where the documents or things are located or where the custodian or person in possession usually conducts business. FL ST RCP Rule 1.351(c).
- If the person upon whom the subpoena is served objects at any time before the production of the documents or things, the documents or things shall not be produced under FL ST RCP Rule 1.351, and relief may be obtained pursuant to FL ST RCP Rule 1.310. FL ST RCP Rule 1.351(c).

iii. *Ruling on objection.* If an objection is made by a party under FL ST RCP Rule 1.351(b), the party desiring production may file a motion with the court seeking a ruling on the objection or may proceed pursuant to FL ST RCP Rule 1.310. FL ST RCP Rule 1.351(d).

iv. *Copies furnished.* If the subpoena is complied with by delivery or mailing of copies as provided in FL ST RCP Rule 1.351(c), the party receiving the copies shall furnish a legible copy of each item furnished to any other party who requests it upon the payment of the reasonable cost of preparing the copies. FL ST RCP Rule 1.351(e).

4. *Arbitration and mediation*

a. *Referral to arbitration and mediation.* Except as hereinafter provided or as otherwise prohibited by law, the presiding judge may enter an order referring all or any part of a contested civil matter to mediation or arbitration. The parties to any contested civil matter may file a written stipulation to mediate or arbitrate any issue between them at any time. Such stipulation shall be incorporated into the order of referral. FL ST RCP Rule 1.700(a).

b. *Arbitration*

i. *Exclusions.* A civil action shall be ordered to arbitration or arbitration in conjunction with mediation upon stipulation of the parties. A civil action may be ordered to arbitration or arbitration in conjunction with mediation upon motion of any party or by the court, if the judge determines the action to be of such a nature that arbitration could be of benefit to the litigants or the court. FL ST RCP Rule 1.800.

- Under no circumstances may the following categories of actions be referred to arbitration: (1) bond estreatures; (2) habeas corpus or other extraordinary writs; (3) bond validations;

(4) civil or criminal contempt; (5) such other matters as may be specified by order of the chief judge in the circuit. FL ST RCP Rule 1.800.

ii. For more information regarding arbitration, please see FL ST RCP Rule 1.810; FL ST RCP Rule 1.820; FL ST RCP Rule 1.830.

c. *Mediation.* For more information regarding mediation, please see FL ST RCP Rule 1.710; FL ST RCP Rule 1.720; FL ST RCP Rule 1.730; and FL ST RCP Rule 1.750.

5. *Rules of court*

a. *Rules of civil procedure.* The Florida Rules of Civil Procedure apply to all actions of a civil nature and all special statutory proceedings in the circuit courts and county courts except those to which the Florida Probate Rules, the Florida Family Law Rules of Procedure, or the Small Claims Rules apply. FL ST RCP Rule 1.010.

i. The form, content, procedure, and time for pleading in all special statutory proceedings shall be as prescribed by the statutes governing the proceeding unless the Florida Rules of Civil Procedure specifically provide to the contrary. FL ST RCP Rule 1.010.

ii. The Florida Rules of Civil Procedure shall be construed to secure the just, speedy, and inexpensive determination of every action. FL ST RCP Rule 1.010.

b. *Rules of judicial administration.* The Florida Rules of Judicial Administration shall apply to administrative matters in all courts to which the Florida Rules of Judicial Administration are applicable by their terms. The Florida Rules of Judicial Administration shall be construed to secure the speedy and inexpensive determination of every proceeding to which they are applicable. The Florida Rules of Judicial Administration shall supersede all conflicting rules and statutes. FL ST J ADMIN Rule 2.110.

D. Documents

1. *Required documents*

a. *Request for production.* Please see the General Requirements section of this document for more information on the contents of the request for production.

i. *Notices to persons with disabilities.* See the Format section of this KeyRules document for further information.

b. *Certificate of service.* A certificate of service of the interrogatories shall be filed, giving the date of service and the name of the party to whom they were directed. FL ST RCP Rule 1.340(e). When any attorney certifies in substance: "I certify that a copy hereof has been furnished to (here insert name or names and addresses used for service) by (e-mail) (delivery) (mail) (fax) on .... (date) ....________________ Attorney" the certificate is taken as prima facie proof of such service in compliance with FL ST J ADMIN Rule 2.516. FL ST J ADMIN Rule 2.516(f).

2. *Supplemental documents*

a. *Notice of intent to serve subpoena/Subpoena.* Please see the General Requirements section of this document for more information.

E. Format

1. *Documents; Type and size.* Documents subject to the exceptions set forth in FL ST J ADMIN Rule 2.525(d) shall be filed on recycled paper measuring eight and one half by eleven (8 1/2 by 11) inches. For purposes of FL ST J ADMIN Rule 2.520, paper is recycled if it contains a minimum content of fifty (50) percent waste paper. Xerographic reduction of legal-size (eight and one half by fourteen (8 1/2 by 14) inches) documents to letter size (eight and one half by eleven (8 1/2 by 11) inches) is prohibited. All other documents filed by electronic transmission shall be filed in a format capable of being printed in a format consistent with the provisions of FL ST J ADMIN Rule 2.250. FL ST J ADMIN Rule 2.520(b).

a. *Exhibits.* Any exhibit or attachment filed with pleadings or papers may be filed in its original size. FL ST J ADMIN Rule 2.520(c).

b. *Recording space.* On all papers and documents prepared and filed by the court or by any party to a proceeding which are to be recorded in the public records of any county, including but not limited to final money judgments and notices of lis pendens, a three (3) inch by three (3) inch space at the top right-hand corner on the first page and a one (1) inch by three (3) inch space at the top right-hand corner on each subsequent page shall be left blank and reserved for use by the clerk of court. FL ST J ADMIN Rule 2.520(d).

i. *Exceptions to recording space.* Any papers or documents created by persons or entities over which the filing party has no control, including but not limited to wills, codicils, trusts, or other testamentary documents; documents prepared or executed by any public officer; documents prepared, executed, acknowledged, or proved outside of the State of Florida; or documents created by State or Federal government agencies, may be filed without the space required by FL ST J ADMIN Rule 2.520. FL ST J ADMIN Rule 2.520(e).

c. *Noncompliance.* No clerk of court is permitted to refuse to file any document or paper because of noncompliance with the Florida Rules of Judicial Administration. However, upon request of the clerk of court, noncomplying documents must be resubmitted in accordance with the formatting rules. FL ST J ADMIN Rule 2.520(f).

2. *Caption.* Every pleading, motion, order, judgment, or other paper shall have a caption containing the name of the court, the file number, and except for in rem proceedings, including forfeiture proceedings, the name of the first party on each side with an appropriate indication of other parties, and a designation identifying the party filing it and its nature or the nature of the order, as the case may be. In any in rem proceeding, every pleading, motion, order, judgment, or other paper shall have a caption containing the name of the court, the file number, the style "In re" (followed by the name or general description of the property), and a designation of the person or entity filing it and its nature or the nature of the order, as the case may be. In an in rem forfeiture proceeding, the style shall be "In re forfeiture of" (followed by the name of the general description of the property). All papers filed in the action shall be styled in such a manner as to indicate clearly the subject matter of the paper and the party requesting or obtaining relief. FL ST RCP Rule 1.100(c)(1).

3. *Writing and written defined.* Writing or written means a document containing information, an application, or a stipulation. FL ST RCP Rule 1.080(c).

4. *Rule abbreviations*

a. The Florida Rules of Civil Procedure and shall be abbreviated as Fla.R.Civ.P. FL ST RCP Rule 1.010.

b. The Florida Rules of Judicial Administration shall be abbreviated as Fla. R. Jud. Admin. FL ST J ADMIN Rule 2.110.

5. *Nonverification.* Except when otherwise specifically provided by the Florida Rules of Civil Procedure or an applicable statute, every pleading or other document of a party represented by an attorney need not be verified or accompanied by an affidavit. FL ST RCP Rule 1.030; FL ST J ADMIN Rule 2.515(a).

6. *Attorney signature*

a. *Attorney signature.* Every pleading and other document of a party represented by an attorney shall be signed by at least one (1) attorney of record in that attorney's individual name whose current record Florida Bar address, telephone number, including area code, primary e-mail address and secondary e-mail addresses, if any, and Florida Bar number shall be stated, and who shall be duly licensed to practice law in Florida or who shall have received permission to appear in the particular case as provided in FL ST J ADMIN Rule 2.510. FL ST J ADMIN Rule 2.515(a).

i. The attorney may be required by the court to give the address of, and to vouch for the attorney's authority to represent, the party. FL ST J ADMIN Rule 2.515(a).

ii. The signature of an attorney shall constitute a certificate by the attorney that the attorney has read the pleading or other document; that to the best of the attorney's knowledge, information, and belief there is good ground to support it; and that it is not interposed for delay. FL ST J ADMIN Rule 2.515(a).

iii. If a pleading is not signed or is signed with intent to defeat the purpose of FL ST J ADMIN Rule 2.515, it may be stricken and the action may proceed as though the pleading or other document had not been served. FL ST J ADMIN Rule 2.515(a).

b. *Pro se litigant signature.* A party who is not represented by an attorney shall sign any pleading or other paper and state the party's address and telephone number, including area code. FL ST J ADMIN Rule 2.515(b).

c. *Form of signature*

i. The signatures required on pleadings and documents by FL ST J ADMIN Rule 2.515(a) and FL ST J ADMIN Rule 2.515(b) may be:

- Original signatures;
- Original signatures that have been reproduced by electronic means, such as on electronically transmitted documents or photocopied documents;
- Electronic signatures using the "/s/," "s/," or "/s" formats by or at the direction of the person signing; or
- Any other signature format authorized by general law, so long as the clerk where the proceeding is pending has the capability of receiving and has obtained approval from the Supreme Court of Florida to accept pleadings and documents with that signature format. FL ST J ADMIN Rule 2.515(c)(1).

ii. An attorney, party, or other person who files a pleading or paper by electronic transmission that does not contain the original signature of that attorney, party, or other person shall file that identical pleading or paper in paper form containing an original signature of that attorney, party, or other person (hereinafter called the follow-up filing) immediately thereafter. The follow-up filing is not required if the Supreme Court of Florida has entered an order directing the clerk of court to discontinue accepting the follow-up filing. FL ST J ADMIN Rule 2.515(c)(2).

7. *Forms*

a. *Process.* The forms of process, notice of lis pendens, and notice of action provided in the Florida Rules of Civil Procedure are sufficient. Variations from the forms do not void process or notices that are otherwise sufficient. FL ST RCP Rule 1.900(a).

b. *Other forms.* The other forms provided in the Florida Rules of Civil Procedure are sufficient for the matters that are covered by them. So long as the substance is expressed without prolixity, the forms may be varied to meet the facts of a particular case. FL ST RCP Rule 1.900(b).

c. *Formal matters.* Captions, except for the designation of the paper, are omitted from the forms provided in the Florida Rules of Civil Procedure. A general form of caption is the first form provided. Signatures are omitted from pleadings and motions. FL ST RCP Rule 1.900(c).

8. *Notices to persons with disabilities.* All notices of court proceedings to be held in a public facility, and all process compelling appearance at such proceedings, shall include the following statement in bold face, fourteen (14) point Times New Roman or Courier font: "If you are a person with a disability who needs any accommodation in order to participate in this proceeding, you are entitled, at no cost to you, to the provision of certain assistance. Please contact [identify applicable court personnel by name, address, and telephone number] at least seven (7) days before your scheduled court appearance, or immediately upon receiving this notification if the time before the scheduled appearance is less than seven (7) days; if you are hearing or voice impaired, call 711." FL ST J ADMIN Rule 2.540(c)(1).

9. *Minimization of the filing of sensitive information*

a. *Limitations for court filings.* Unless authorized by FL ST J ADMIN Rule 2.425(b), statute, another rule of court, or the court orders otherwise, designated sensitive information filed with the court must be limited to the following format:

i. The initials of a person known to be a minor;

ii. The year of birth of a person's birth date;

iii. No portion of any: Social security number, Bank account number, Credit card account number, Charge account number, or Debit account number;

iv. The last four digits of any: Taxpayer identification number (TIN), Employee identification number, Driver's license number, Passport number, Telephone number, Financial account

number, except as set forth in FL ST J ADMIN Rule 2.425(a)(3), Brokerage account number, Insurance policy account number, Loan account number, Customer account number, or Patient or health care number;

v. A truncated version of any: Email address, Computer user name, Password, or Personal identification number (PIN); and

vi. A truncated version of any other sensitive information as provided by court order. FL ST J ADMIN Rule 2.425(a).

b. *Exceptions.* FL ST J ADMIN Rule 2.425(a) does not apply to the following:

i. An account number which identifies the property alleged to be the subject of a proceeding;

ii. The record of an administrative or agency proceeding;

iii. The record in appellate or review proceedings;

iv. The birth date of a minor whenever the birth date is necessary for the court to establish or maintain subject matter jurisdiction;

v. The name of a minor in any order relating to parental responsibility, time-sharing, or child support;

vi. The name of a minor in any document or order affecting the minor's ownership of real property;

vii. The birth date of a party in a writ of attachment or notice to payor;

viii. In traffic and criminal proceedings: a pro se filing; a court filing that is related to a criminal matter or investigation and that is prepared before the filing of a criminal charge or is not filed as part of any docketed criminal case; an arrest or search warrant or any information in support thereof; a charging document and an affidavit or other documents filed in support of any charging document, including any driving records; a statement of particulars; discovery material introduced into evidence or otherwise filed with the court; and all information necessary for the proper issuance and execution of a subpoena duces tecum;

ix. Information used by the clerk for case maintenance purposes or the courts for case management purposes; and

x. Information which is relevant and material to an issue before the court. FL ST J ADMIN Rule 2.425(b).

c. *Remedies.* Upon motion by a party or interested person or sua sponte by the court, the court may order remedies, sanctions or both for a violation of FL ST J ADMIN Rule 2.425(a). Following notice and an opportunity to respond, the court may impose sanctions if such filing was not made in good faith. FL ST J ADMIN Rule 2.425(c).

d. *Motions not restricted.* FL ST J ADMIN Rule 2.425 does not restrict a party's right to move for protective order, to move to file documents under seal, or to request a determination of the confidentiality of records. FL ST J ADMIN Rule 2.425(d).

i. For more information regarding sealing court records, please see FL ST 4 J CIR 2006-05.

e. *Application.* FL ST J ADMIN Rule 2.425 does not affect the application of constitutional provisions, statutes, or rules of court regarding confidential information or access to public information. FL ST J ADMIN Rule 2.425(e).

F. Filing and Service Requirements

1. *Court filing of documents and discovery.* Information obtained during discovery shall not be filed with the court until such time as it is filed for good cause. The requirement of good cause is satisfied only where the filing of the information is allowed or required by another applicable rule of procedure or by court order. All filings of discovery documents shall comply with FL ST J ADMIN Rule 2.425. The court shall have the authority to impose sanctions for violation of FL ST RCP Rule 1.280. FL ST RCP Rule 1.280(g).

a. Unless required by the court, a party shall not file any of the documents or things produced with the response. Documents or things may be filed in compliance with FL ST J ADMIN Rule 2.425 and FL ST RCP Rule 1.280(g) when they should be considered by the court in determining a matter pending before the court. FL ST RCP Rule 1.350(d).

2. *Filing requirements.* All original documents must be filed with the court either before service or immediately thereafter, unless otherwise provided for by general law or other rules. If the original of any bond or other document is not placed in the court file, a certified copy must be so placed by the clerk. FL ST J ADMIN Rule 2.516(d). All documents shall be filed in conformity with the requirements of FL ST J ADMIN Rule 2.525. FL ST RCP Rule 1.080(b). All documents filed in any court shall be filed by electronic transmission in accordance with FL ST J ADMIN Rule 2.525. "Documents" means pleadings, motions, petitions, memoranda, briefs, notices, exhibits, declarations, affidavits, orders, judgments, decrees, writs, opinions, and any other paper or writing submitted to a court. FL ST J ADMIN Rule 2.520(a). All documents that are court records, as defined in FL ST J ADMIN Rule 2.430(a)(1), must be filed by electronic transmission, provided that: (1) the clerk has the ability to accept and retain such documents; (2) the clerk or the chief judge of the circuit has requested permission to accept documents filed by electronic transmission; and (3) the supreme court has entered an order granting permission to the clerk to accept documents filed by electronic transmission. FL ST J ADMIN Rule 2.525(c)(1).
   a. *Definition.* "Electronic transmission of documents" means the sending of information by electronic signals to, by or from a court or clerk, which when received can be transformed and stored or transmitted on paper, microfilm, magnetic storage device, optical imaging system, CD-ROM, flash drive, other electronic data storage system, server, case maintenance system ("CM"), electronic court filing ("ECF") system, statewide or local electronic portal ("e-portal"), or other electronic record keeping system authorized by the supreme court in a format sufficient to communicate the information on the original document in a readable format. Electronic transmission of documents includes electronic mail ("e-mail") and any internet-based transmission procedure, and may include procedures allowing for documents to be signed or verified by electronic means. FL ST J ADMIN Rule 2.525(a).
      i. The filing of documents with the court as required by the Florida Rules of Judicial Administration must be made by filing them with the clerk in accordance with FL ST J ADMIN Rule 2.525, except that the judge may permit documents to be filed with the judge, in which event the judge must note the filing date before him or her on the documents and transmit them to the clerk. The date of filing is that shown on the face of the document by the judge's notation or the clerk's time stamp, whichever is earlier. FL ST J ADMIN Rule 2.516(e).
   b. *Application.* Any court or clerk of the court may accept the electronic transmission of documents for filing after the clerk, together with input from the chief judge of the circuit, has obtained approval of the procedures and program for doing so from the Supreme Court of Florida. FL ST J ADMIN Rule 2.525(b).
   c. *Exceptions*
      i. Paper documents and other submissions may be manually submitted to the clerk or court:
         - When the clerk does not have the ability to accept and retain documents by electronic filing or has not had ECF Procedures approved by the supreme court;
         - For filing by any self-represented party or any self-represented nonparty unless specific ECF Procedures provide a means to file documents electronically. However, any self-represented nonparty that is a governmental or public agency and any other agency, partnership, corporation, or business entity acting on behalf of any governmental or public agency may file documents by electronic transmission if such entity has the capability of filing documents electronically;
         - For filing by attorneys excused from e-mail service in accordance with FL ST J ADMIN Rule 2.516(b);
         - When submitting evidentiary exhibits or filing non-documentary materials;
         - When the filing involves documents in excess of twenty-five (25) megabytes (25MB) in size. For such filings, documents may be transmitted using an electronic storage medium that the clerk has the ability to accept, which may include a CD-ROM, flash drive, or similar storage medium;
         - When filed in open court, as permitted by the court;

- When paper filing is permitted by any approved statewide or local ECF procedures; and
- If any court determines that justice so requires. FL ST J ADMIN Rule 2.525(d).

ii. Any document in paper form submitted under FL ST J ADMIN Rule 2.525(d) is filed when it is received by the clerk or court and the clerk shall immediately thereafter convert any filed paper document to an electronic document. "Convert to an electronic document" means optically capturing an image of a paper document and using character recognition software to recover as much of the document's text as practicable and then indexing and storing the document in the official court file. FL ST J ADMIN Rule 2.525(c)(4).

iii. Any storage medium submitted under FL ST J ADMIN Rule 2.525(d)(5) is filed when received by the clerk or court and the clerk shall immediately thereafter transfer the electronic documents from the storage device to the official court file. FL ST J ADMIN Rule 2.525(c)(5).

iv. If the filer of any paper document authorized under FL ST J ADMIN Rule 2.525(d) provides a self-addressed, postage-paid envelope for return of the paper document after it is converted to electronic form by the clerk, the clerk shall place the paper document in the envelope and deposit it in the mail. Except when a paper document is required to be maintained, the clerk may recycle any filed paper document that is not to be returned to the filer. FL ST J ADMIN Rule 2.525(c)(6).

v. The clerk may convert any paper document filed before the effective date of FL ST J ADMIN Rule 2.525 to an electronic document. Unless the clerk is required to maintain the paper document, if the paper document has been converted to an electronic document by the clerk, the paper document is no longer part of the official court file and may be removed and recycled. FL ST J ADMIN Rule 2.525(c)(7).

d. *Official court file.* For information on what constitutes the official court file, please see FL ST J ADMIN Rule 2.525(c)(2), FL ST J ADMIN Rule 2.525(c)(3).

e. *Administration.* All attorneys, parties, or other persons using this rule to file documents are required to make arrangements with the court or clerk for the payment of any charges authorized by general law or the supreme court before filing any document by electronic transmission. FL ST J ADMIN Rule 2.525(f)(2).

f. *Filing date.* The filing date for an electronically transmitted document is the date and time that such filing is acknowledged by an electronic stamp or otherwise, pursuant to any procedure set forth in any ECF Procedures approved by the supreme court, or the date the last page of such filing is received by the court or clerk. FL ST J ADMIN Rule 2.525(f)(3).

g. *Accessibility.* All documents transmitted in any electronic form under FL ST J ADMIN Rule 2.525 must comply with the accessibility requirements of FL ST J ADMIN Rule 2.526. FL ST J ADMIN Rule 2.525(g).

3. *Service requirements.* Every pleading subsequent to the initial pleading, all orders, and every other document filed in the action must be served in conformity with the requirements of FL ST J ADMIN Rule 2.516. FL ST RCP Rule 1.080(a).

a. *Service; When required.* Unless the court otherwise orders, or a statute or supreme court administrative order specifies a different means of service, every pleading subsequent to the initial pleading and every other document filed in any court proceeding, except applications for witness subpoenas and documents served by formal notice or required to be served in the manner provided for service of formal notice, must be served in accordance with FL ST J ADMIN Rule 2.516 on each party. No service need be made on parties against whom a default has been entered, except that pleadings asserting new or additional claims against them must be served in the manner provided for service of summons. FL ST J ADMIN Rule 2.516(a).

b. *Service; How made.* When service is required or permitted to be made upon a party represented by an attorney, service must be made upon the attorney unless service upon the party is ordered by the court. FL ST J ADMIN Rule 2.516(b).

i. *Service by electronic mail ("e-mail").* All documents required or permitted to be served on

another party must be served by e-mail, unless FL ST J ADMIN Rule 2.516 otherwise provides. When, in addition to service by e-mail, the sender also utilizes another means of service provided for in FL ST J ADMIN Rule 2.516(b)(2), any differing time limits and other provisions applicable to that other means of service control. FL ST J ADMIN Rule 2.516(b)(1). Any document electronically transmitted to a court or clerk must also be served on all parties and interested persons in accordance with the applicable rules of court. FL ST J ADMIN Rule 2.525(e)(2).

- *Service on attorneys.* Upon appearing in a proceeding, an attorney must serve a designation of a primary e-mail address and may designate no more than two (2) secondary e-mail addresses. Thereafter, service must be directed to all designated e-mail addresses in that proceeding. Every document filed by an attorney thereafter must include the primary e-mail address of that attorney and any secondary e-mail addresses. If an attorney does not designate any e-mail address for service, documents may be served on that attorney at the e-mail address on record with The Florida Bar. FL ST J ADMIN Rule 2.516(b)(1)(A).
- *Exception to e-mail service on attorneys.* Service by an attorney on another attorney must be made by e-mail unless excused by the court. Upon motion by an attorney demonstrating that the attorney has no e-mail account and lacks access to the Internet at the attorney's office, the court may excuse the attorney from the requirements of e-mail service. Service on and by an attorney excused by the court from e-mail service must be by the means provided in FL ST J ADMIN Rule 2.516(b)(2). FL ST J ADMIN Rule 2.516(b)(1)(B).
- *Service on and by parties not represented by an attorney.* Any party not represented by an attorney may serve a designation of a primary e-mail address and also may designate no more than two (2) secondary e-mail addresses to which service must be directed in that proceeding by the means provided in FL ST J ADMIN Rule 2.516(b)(1). If a party not represented by an attorney does not designate an e-mail address for service in a proceeding, service on and by that party must be by the means provided in FL ST J ADMIN Rule 2.516(b)(2). FL ST J ADMIN Rule 2.516(b)(1)(C).
- *Time of service.* Service by e-mail is complete when it is sent. FL ST J ADMIN Rule 2.516(b)(1)(D). An e-mail is deemed served on the date it is sent. FL ST J ADMIN Rule 2.516(b)(1)(D)(i). If the sender learns that the e-mail did not reach the address of the person to be served, the sender must immediately send another copy by e-mail, or by a means authorized by FL ST J ADMIN Rule 2.516(b)(2). FL ST J ADMIN Rule 2.516(b)(1)(D)(ii). E-mail service is treated as service by mail for the computation of time. FL ST J ADMIN Rule 2.516(b)(1)(D)(iii).

ii. *Format of e-mail for service.* Service of a document by e-mail is made by attaching a copy of the document in PDF format to an e-mail sent to all addresses designated by the attorney or party. FL ST J ADMIN Rule 2.516(b)(1)(E).

- All documents served by e-mail must be attached to an e-mail message containing a subject line beginning with the words "SERVICE OF COURT DOCUMENT" in all capital letters, followed by the case number of the proceeding in which the documents are being served. FL ST J ADMIN Rule 2.516(b)(1)(E)(i).
- The body of the e-mail must identify the court in which the proceeding is pending, the case number, the name of the initial party on each side, the title of each document served with that e-mail, and the sender's name and telephone number. FL ST J ADMIN Rule 2.516(b)(1)(E)(ii).
- Any document served by e-mail may be signed by the "/s/" format, as long as the filed original is signed in accordance with the applicable rule of procedure. FL ST J ADMIN Rule 2.516(b)(1)(E)(iii).
- Any e-mail which, together with its attached documents, exceeds five megabytes (5MB) in size, must be divided and sent as separate e-mails, no one of which may exceed five megabytes (5MB) in size and each of which must be sequentially numbered in the subject line. FL ST J ADMIN Rule 2.516(b)(1)(E)(iv).

iii. *Service by other means.* In addition to, and not in lieu of, service by e-mail, service may also be made upon attorneys by any of the means specified in FL ST J ADMIN Rule 2.516(b)(2). Service on and by all parties who are not represented by an attorney and who do not designate an e-mail address, and on and by all attorneys excused from e-mail service, must be made by delivering a copy of the document or by mailing it to the party or attorney at their last known address or, if no address is known, by leaving it with the clerk of the court. Service by mail is complete upon mailing. Delivery of a copy within FL ST J ADMIN Rule 2.516 is complete upon:

- Handing it to the attorney or to the party,
- Leaving it at the attorney's or party's office with a clerk or other person in charge thereof,
- If there is no one in charge, leaving it in a conspicuous place therein,
- If the office is closed or the person to be served has no office, leaving it at the person's usual place of abode with some person of his or her family above fifteen (15) years of age and informing such person of the contents, or
- Transmitting it by facsimile to the attorney's or party's office with a cover sheet containing the sender's name, firm, address, telephone number, and facsimile number, and the number of pages transmitted. When service is made by facsimile, a copy must also be served by any other method permitted by FL ST J ADMIN Rule 2.516. Facsimile service occurs when transmission is complete. FL ST J ADMIN Rule 2.516(b)(2)(A) through FL ST J ADMIN Rule 2.516(b)(2)(E).
- Service by delivery after 5:00 p.m. must be deemed to have been made by mailing on the date of delivery. FL ST J ADMIN Rule 2.516(b)(2)(F).

c. *Service; Numerous defendants.* In actions when the parties are unusually numerous, the court may regulate the service contemplated by the Florida Rules of Judicial Administration on motion or on its own initiative in such manner as may be found to be just and reasonable. FL ST J ADMIN Rule 2.516(c).

d. *Service by clerk.* Service of notices and other documents required to be made by the clerk must also be done as provided in FL ST J ADMIN Rule 2.516(b). FL ST J ADMIN Rule 2.516(g).

G. Hearings

1. There is no hearing required or contemplated with regard to requests for production of documents in the Florida Rules of Civil Procedure.

H. Forms

1. Official Request for Production of Documents Forms for Florida

a. Caption. FL ST RCP Form 1.901.

b. Subpoena duces tecum for trial. FL ST RCP Form 1.911.

c. Notice of production from nonparty. FL ST RCP Form 1.921.

d. Subpoena duces tecum without deposition. FL ST RCP Form 1.922.

2. Request for Production of Documents Forms for Florida

a. Request for production; Documents. FL-PRACFORM § 8:29.

b. Request for inspection; Documents, deposition. FL-PRACFORM § 8:30.

c. Request for inspection; Tangible things. FL-PRACFORM § 8:31.

d. Request for entry; Real property. FL-PRACFORM § 8:32.

e. Request for production; Documents, response. FL-PRACFORM § 8:33.

f. Request for inspection; Response, tangible things. FL-PRACFORM § 8:34.

g. Request for entry; Response, land and buildings. FL-PRACFORM § 8:35.

h. Production of documents; Nonparty, notice. FL-PRACFORM § 8:36.

i. Production of documents; Nonparty, objection. FL-PRACFORM § 8:37.

j. Request; Production of documents for inspection and copying. FL-PP § 3:115.

k. Notice of request for production from nonparty. FL-PP § 3:116.

l. Request; For permission to enter on land; To inspect and photograph. FL-PP § 3:127.

I. Checklist

(I) ❑ Matters to be considered by requesting party

(a) ❑ Required documents

(1) ❑ Request

(2) ❑ Certificate of service

(b) ❑ Supplemental documents

(1) ❑ Notice of intent to serve subpoena/Subpoena

(c) ❑ Time for request

(1) ❑ Without leave of court the request may be served on the plaintiff after commencement of the action and on any other party with or after service of the process and initial pleading on that party

(2) ❑ A party desiring production under FL ST RCP Rule 1.351 shall serve notice as provided in FL ST RCP Rule 1.080 on every other party of the intent to serve a subpoena under FL ST RCP Rule 1.351 at least ten (10) days before the subpoena is issued if service is by delivery and fifteen (15) days before the subpoena is issued if the service is by mail or e-mail

(II) ❑ Matters to be considered by responding party

(a) ❑ Required documents

(1) ❑ Response to request

(2) ❑ Certificate of service

(b) ❑ Supplemental documents

(1) ❑ Objections

(c) ❑ Time for response

(1) ❑ The party to whom the request is directed shall serve a written response within thirty (30) days after service of the request, except that a defendant may serve a response within forty-five (45) days after service of the process and initial pleading on that defendant; the court may allow a shorter or longer time

Requests, Notices and Applications
Request for Admissions

Document Last Updated January 2013

A. Applicable Rules

1. *State rules*

a. Nonverification of pleadings. FL ST RCP Rule 1.030.

b. Service and filing of pleadings, orders, and documents. FL ST RCP Rule 1.080.

c. Time. FL ST RCP Rule 1.090.

d. Pleadings and motions. FL ST RCP Rule 1.100.

e. Pretrial procedure. FL ST RCP Rule 1.200.

f. General provisions governing discovery. FL ST RCP Rule 1.280.

g. Interrogatories to parties. FL ST RCP Rule 1.340.
h. Examination of persons. FL ST RCP Rule 1.360.
i. Requests for admission. FL ST RCP Rule 1.370.
j. Failure to make discovery; Sanctions. FL ST RCP Rule 1.380.
k. Depositions of expert witnesses. FL ST RCP Rule 1.390.
l. Relief from judgment, decrees, or orders. FL ST RCP Rule 1.540.
m. Forms. FL ST RCP Rule 1.900.
n. Minimization of the filing of sensitive information. FL ST J ADMIN Rule 2.425.
o. Retention of court records. FL ST J ADMIN Rule 2.430.
p. Foreign attorneys. FL ST J ADMIN Rule 2.510.
q. Signature of attorneys and parties. FL ST J ADMIN Rule 2.515.
r. Paper. FL ST J ADMIN Rule 2.520.
s. Electronic filing. FL ST J ADMIN Rule 2.525.
t. Accessibility of information and technology. FL ST J ADMIN Rule 2.526.
u. Requests for accommodations by persons with disabilities. FL ST J ADMIN Rule 2.540.

2. *Local rules*
   a. Sealing court records. FL ST 4 J CIR 2006-05.

B. Timing

1. *Request for admission.* Without leave of court the request may be served upon the plaintiff after commencement of the action and upon any other party with or after service of the process and initial pleading upon that party. FL ST RCP Rule 1.370(a).
2. *Sequence and timing of discovery.* Except as provided in FL ST RCP Rule 1.280(b)(5) or unless the court upon motion for the convenience of parties and witnesses and in the interest of justice orders otherwise, methods of discovery may be used in any sequence, and the fact that a party is conducting discovery, whether by deposition or otherwise, shall not delay any other party's discovery. FL ST RCP Rule 1.280(e).
3. *Computation of time*
   a. *Generally.* Computation of time shall be governed by FL ST J ADMIN Rule 2.514. FL ST RCP Rule 1.090(a). The following rules apply in computing time periods specified in any rule of procedure, local rule, court order, or statute that does not specify a method of computing time. FL ST J ADMIN Rule 2.514(a).
      i. *Period stated in days or a longer unit.* When the period is stated in days or a longer unit of time (A) exclude the day of the event that triggers the period; (B) count every day, including intermediate Saturdays, Sundays, and legal holidays; and (C) include the last day of the period, but if the last day is a Saturday, Sunday, or legal holiday, or falls within any period of time extended through an order of the chief justice under FL ST J ADMIN Rule 2.205(a)(2)(B)(iv), the period continues to run until the end of the next day that is not a Saturday, Sunday, or legal holiday and does not fall within any period of time extended through an order of the chief justice. FL ST J ADMIN Rule 2.514(a)(1).
      ii. *Period stated in hours.* When the period is stated in hours (A) begin counting immediately on the occurrence of the event that triggers the period; (B) count every hour, including hours during intermediate Saturdays, Sundays, and legal holidays; and (C) if the period would end on a Saturday, Sunday, or legal holiday, or during any period of time extended through an order of the chief justice under FL ST J ADMIN Rule 2.205(a)(2)(B)(iv), the period continues to run until the same time on the next day that is not a Saturday, Sunday, or legal holiday and does not fall within any period of time extended through an order of the chief justice. FL ST J ADMIN Rule 2.514(a)(2).

iii. *Period stated in days less than seven (7) days.* When the period stated in days is less than seven (7) days, intermediate Saturdays, Sundays, and legal holidays shall be excluded in the computation. FL ST J ADMIN Rule 2.514(a)(3).

iv. *"Last day" defined.* Unless a different time is set by a statute, local rule, or court order, the last day ends (A) for electronic filing or for service by any means, at midnight; and (B) for filing by other means, when the clerk's office is scheduled to close. FL ST J ADMIN Rule 2.514(a)(4).

v. *"Next day" defined.* The "next day" is determined by continuing to count forward when the period is measured after an event and backward when measured before an event. FL ST J ADMIN Rule 2.514(a)(5).

vi. *"Legal holiday" defined.* "Legal holiday" means (A) the day set aside by FL ST § 110.117, for observing New Year's Day, Martin Luther King, Jr.'s Birthday, Memorial Day, Independence Day, Labor Day, Veterans' Day, Thanksgiving Day, the Friday after Thanksgiving Day, or Christmas Day, and (B) any day observed as a holiday by the clerk's office or as designated by the chief judge. FL ST J ADMIN Rule 2.514(a)(6).

b. *Additional time after service by mail or e-mail.* When a party may or must act within a specified time after service and service is made by mail or e-mail, five (5) days are added after the period that would otherwise expire under FL ST J ADMIN Rule 2.514(a). FL ST J ADMIN Rule 2.514(b).

c. *Enlargement.* When an act is required or allowed to be done at or within a specified time by order of court, by the Florida Rules of Civil Procedure, or by notice given thereunder, for cause shown the court at any time in its discretion (1) with or without notice, may order the period enlarged if request therefor is made before the expiration of the period originally prescribed or as extended by a previous order, or (2) upon motion made and notice after the expiration of the specified period, may permit the act to be done when failure to act was the result of excusable neglect, but it may not extend the time for making a motion for new trial, for rehearing, or to alter or amend a judgment; making a motion for relief from a judgment under FL ST RCP Rule 1.540(b); taking an appeal or filing a petition for certiorari; or making a motion for a directed verdict. FL ST RCP Rule 1.090(b).

d. *Unaffected by expiration of term.* The period of time provided for the doing of any act or the taking of any proceeding shall not be affected or limited by the continued existence or expiration of a term of court. The continued existence or expiration of a term of court in no way affects the power of a court to do any act or take any proceeding in any action which is or has been pending before it. FL ST RCP Rule 1.090(c).

C. General Requirements

1. *General provisions governing discovery*

a. *Discovery methods.* Parties may obtain discovery by one or more of the following methods: depositions upon oral examination or written questions; written interrogatories; production of documents or things or permission to enter upon land or other property for inspection and other purposes; physical and mental examinations; and requests for admission. Unless the court orders otherwise and under FL ST RCP Rule 1.280(c), the frequency of use of these methods is not limited, except as provided in FL ST RCP Rule 1.200, FL ST RCP Rule 1.340, and FL ST RCP Rule 1.370. FL ST RCP Rule 1.280(a).

b. *Scope of discovery.* Unless otherwise limited by order of the court in accordance with the Florida Rules of Civil Procedure, the scope of discovery is as follows:

i. *In general.* Parties may obtain discovery regarding any matter, not privileged, that is relevant to the subject matter of the pending action, whether it relates to the claim or defense of the party seeking discovery or the claim or defense of any other party, including the existence, description, nature, custody, condition, and location of any books, documents, or other tangible things and the identity and location of persons having knowledge of any discoverable matter. It is not ground for objection that the information sought will be inadmissible at the trial if the information sought appears reasonably calculated to lead to the discovery of admissible evidence. FL ST RCP Rule 1.280(b)(1).

ii. *Indemnity agreements.* A party may obtain discovery of the existence and contents of any agreement under which any person may be liable to satisfy part or all of a judgment that may be entered in the action or to indemnify or to reimburse a party for payments made to satisfy the judgment. Information concerning the agreement is not admissible in evidence at trial by reason of disclosure. FL ST RCP Rule 1.280(b)(2).

iii. *Electronically stored information.* A party may obtain discovery of electronically stored information in accordance with the Florida Rules of Civil Procedure. FL ST RCP Rule 1.280(b)(3).

iv. *Trial preparation; Materials.* Subject to the provisions of FL ST RCP Rule 1.280(b)(5), a party may obtain discovery of documents and tangible things otherwise discoverable under FL ST RCP Rule 1.280(b)(1) and prepared in anticipation of litigation or for trial by or for another party or by or for that party's representative, including that party's attorney, consultant, surety, indemnitor, insurer, or agent, only upon a showing that the party seeking discovery has need of the materials in the preparation of the case and is unable without undue hardship to obtain the substantial equivalent of the materials by other means. FL ST RCP Rule 1.280(b)(4).

- In ordering discovery of the materials when the required showing has been made, the court shall protect against disclosure of the mental impressions, conclusions, opinions, or legal theories of an attorney or other representative of a party concerning the litigation. FL ST RCP Rule 1.280(b)(4).
- Without the required showing a party may obtain a copy of a statement concerning the action or its subject matter previously made by that party. FL ST RCP Rule 1.280(b)(4).
- Upon request without the required showing a person not a party may obtain a copy of a statement concerning the action or its subject matter previously made by that person. If the request is refused, the person may move for an order to obtain a copy. The provisions of FL ST RCP Rule 1.380(a)(5) apply to the award of expenses incurred as a result of making the motion. FL ST RCP Rule 1.280(b)(4).
- For purposes of FL ST RCP Rule 1.280(b)(4), a statement previously made is a written statement signed or otherwise adopted or approved by the person making it, or a stenographic, mechanical, electrical, or other recording or transcription of it that is a substantially verbatim recital of an oral statement by the person making it and contemporaneously recorded. FL ST RCP Rule 1.280(b)(4).

v. *Trial preparation; Experts.* Discovery of facts known and opinions held by experts, otherwise discoverable under the provisions of FL ST RCP Rule 1.280(b)(1) and acquired or developed in anticipation of litigation or for trial, may be obtained only as follows:

- By interrogatories a party may require any other party to identify each person whom the other party expects to call as an expert witness at trial and to state the subject matter on which the expert is expected to testify, and to state the substance of the facts and opinions to which the expert is expected to testify and a summary of the grounds for each opinion. FL ST RCP Rule 1.280(b)(5)(A)(i).
- Any person disclosed by interrogatories or otherwise as a person expected to be called as an expert witness at trial may be deposed in accordance with FL ST RCP Rule 1.390 without motion or order of court. FL ST RCP Rule 1.280(b)(5)(A)(ii).
- A party may obtain the following discovery regarding any person disclosed by interrogatories or otherwise as a person expected to be called as an expert witness at trial: The scope of employment in the pending case and the compensation for such service, FL ST RCP Rule 1.280(b)(5)(A)(iii)(1); The expert's general litigation experience, including the percentage of work performed for plaintiffs and defendants, FL ST RCP Rule 1.280(b)(5)(A)(iii)(2); The identity of other cases, within a reasonable time period, in which the expert has testified by deposition or at trial, FL ST RCP Rule 1.280(b)(5)(A)(iii)(3); An approximation of the portion of the expert's involvement as an expert witness, which may be based on the number of hours, percentage of hours, or percentage of earned income derived from serving as an expert witness; however, the

expert shall not be required to disclose his or her earnings as an expert witness or income derived from other services. FL ST RCP Rule 1.280(b)(5)(A)(iii)(4).

- An expert may be required to produce financial and business records only under the most unusual or compelling circumstances and may not be compelled to compile or produce nonexistent documents. Upon motion, the court may order further discovery by other means, subject to such restrictions as to scope and other provisions pursuant to FL ST RCP Rule 1.280(b)(5)(C) concerning fees and expenses as the court may deem appropriate. FL ST RCP Rule 1.280(b)(5).
- A party may discover facts known or opinions held by an expert who has been retained or specially employed by another party in anticipation of litigation or preparation for trial and who is not expected to be called as a witness at trial, only as provided in FL ST RCP Rule 1.360(b) or upon a showing of exceptional circumstances under which it is impracticable for the party seeking discovery to obtain facts or opinions on the same subject by other means. FL ST RCP Rule 1.280(b)(5)(B).
- Unless manifest injustice would result, the court shall require that the party seeking discovery pay the expert a reasonable fee for time spent in responding to discovery under FL ST RCP Rule 1.280(b)(5)(A) and FL ST RCP Rule 1.280(b)(5)(B); and concerning discovery from an expert obtained under FL ST RCP Rule 1.280(b)(5)(A) the court may require, and concerning discovery obtained under FL ST RCP Rule 1.280(b)(5)(B) shall require, the party seeking discovery to pay the other party a fair part of the fees and expenses reasonably incurred by the latter party in obtaining facts and opinions from the expert. FL ST RCP Rule 1.280(b)(5)(C).
- As used in the Florida Rules of Civil Procedure an expert shall be an expert witness as defined in FL ST RCP Rule 1.390(a). FL ST RCP Rule 1.280(b)(5)(D).

vi. *Claims to privilege or protection.* When a party withholds information otherwise discoverable under the Florida Rules of Civil Procedure by claiming that it is privileged or subject to protection as trial preparation material, the party shall make the claim expressly and shall describe the nature of the documents, communications, or things not produced or disclosed in a manner that, without revealing information itself privileged or protected, will enable other parties to assess the applicability of the privilege or protection. FL ST RCP Rule 1.280(b)(6).

c. *Limitations on discovery of electronically stored information*

i. A person may object to discovery of electronically stored information from sources that the person identifies as not reasonably accessible because of burden or cost. On motion to compel discovery or for a protective order, the person from whom discovery is sought must show that the information sought or the format requested is not reasonably accessible because of undue burden or cost. If that showing is made, the court may nonetheless order the discovery from such sources or in such formats if the requesting party shows good cause. The court may specify conditions of the discovery, including ordering that some or all of the expenses incurred by the person from whom discovery is sought be paid by the party seeking the discovery. FL ST RCP Rule 1.280(d)(1).

ii. In determining any motion involving discovery of electronically stored information, the court must limit the frequency or extent of discovery otherwise allowed by the Florida Rules of Civil Procedure if it determines that (i) the discovery sought is unreasonably cumulative or duplicative, or can be obtained from another source or in another manner that is more convenient, less burdensome, or less expensive; or (ii) the burden or expense of the discovery outweighs its likely benefit, considering the needs of the case, the amount in controversy, the parties' resources, the importance of the issues at stake in the action, and the importance of the discovery in resolving the issues. FL ST RCP Rule 1.280(d)(2).

d. For information on inadvertent disclosure of privileged materials, see FL ST RCP Rule 1.285.

2. *Requests for admission.* It is an advantage to use requests for admission. The biggest advantage is that if an adversary denies a request for an admission and the denied matter is later proven to be true, the

adversary may have to pay the costs of proving the genuineness of the document or the truth of the matter requested to be admitted. FL-PP § 3:143.

a. *Scope.* A party may serve upon any other party a written request for the admission of the truth of any matters within the scope of FL ST RCP Rule 1.280(b) set forth in the request that relate to statements or opinions of fact or of the application of law to fact, including the genuineness of any documents described in the request. FL ST RCP Rule 1.370(a).

b. *Copies of documents.* Copies of documents shall be served with the request unless they have been or are otherwise furnished or made available for inspection and copying. FL ST RCP Rule 1.370(a).

c. *Number of requests.* The request for admission shall not exceed thirty (30) requests, including all subparts, unless the court permits a larger number on motion and notice and for good cause, or the parties propounding and responding to the requests stipulate to a larger number. Each matter of which an admission is requested shall be separately set forth. FL ST RCP Rule 1.370(a).

d. *Sufficiency of responses.* The party who has requested the admissions may move to determine the sufficiency of the answers or objections. Unless the court determines that an objection is justified, it shall order that an answer be served. If the court determines that an answer does not comply with the requirements of this rule, it may order either that the matter is admitted or that an amended answer be served. Instead of these orders the court may determine that final disposition of the request be made at a pretrial conference or at a designated time before trial. The provisions of FL ST RCP Rule 1.380(a)(4) apply to the award of expenses incurred in relation to the motion. FL ST RCP Rule 1.370(a).

e. *Effect of admission.* Any matter admitted under FL ST RCP Rule 1.370 is conclusively established unless the court on motion permits withdrawal or amendment of the admission. Subject to FL ST RCP Rule 1.200 governing amendment of a pretrial order, the court may permit withdrawal or amendment when the presentation of the merits of the action will be subserved by it and the party who obtained the admission fails to satisfy the court that withdrawal or amendment will prejudice that party in maintaining an action or defense on the merits. Any admission made by a party under this rule is for the purpose of the pending action only and is not an admission for any other purpose nor may it be used against that party in any other proceeding. FL ST RCP Rule 1.370(b).

f. *Answer requirements.* The matter is admitted unless the party to whom the request is directed serves upon the party requesting the admission a written answer or objection addressed to the matter within thirty (30) days after service of the request or such shorter or longer time as the court may allow but, unless the court shortens the time, a defendant shall not be required to serve answers or objections before the expiration of forty-five (45) days after service of the process and initial pleading upon the defendant. If objection is made, the reasons shall be stated. The answer shall specifically deny the matter or set forth in detail the reasons why the answering party cannot truthfully admit or deny the matter. A denial shall fairly meet the substance of the requested admission, and when good faith requires that a party qualify an answer or deny only a part of the matter of which an admission is requested, the party shall specify so much of it as is true and qualify or deny the remainder. An answering party may not give lack of information or knowledge as a reason for failure to admit or deny unless that party states that that party has made reasonable inquiry and that the information known or readily obtainable by that party is insufficient to enable that party to admit or deny. A party who considers that a matter of which an admission has been requested presents a genuine issue for trial may not object to the request on that ground alone; the party may deny the matter or set forth reasons why the party cannot admit or deny it, subject to FL ST RCP Rule 1.380(c). FL ST RCP Rule 1.370(a).

3. *Arbitration and mediation*

a. *Referral to arbitration and mediation.* Except as hereinafter provided or as otherwise prohibited by law, the presiding judge may enter an order referring all or any part of a contested civil matter to mediation or arbitration. The parties to any contested civil matter may file a written stipulation to mediate or arbitrate any issue between them at any time. Such stipulation shall be incorporated into the order of referral. FL ST RCP Rule 1.700(a).

b. *Arbitration*

i. *Exclusions.* A civil action shall be ordered to arbitration or arbitration in conjunction with

mediation upon stipulation of the parties. A civil action may be ordered to arbitration or arbitration in conjunction with mediation upon motion of any party or by the court, if the judge determines the action to be of such a nature that arbitration could be of benefit to the litigants or the court. FL ST RCP Rule 1.800.

- Under no circumstances may the following categories of actions be referred to arbitration: (1) bond estreatures; (2) habeas corpus or other extraordinary writs; (3) bond validations; (4) civil or criminal contempt; (5) such other matters as may be specified by order of the chief judge in the circuit. FL ST RCP Rule 1.800.

ii. For more information regarding arbitration, please see FL ST RCP Rule 1.810; FL ST RCP Rule 1.820; FL ST RCP Rule 1.830.

c. *Mediation.* For more information regarding mediation, please see FL ST RCP Rule 1.710; FL ST RCP Rule 1.720; FL ST RCP Rule 1.730; and FL ST RCP Rule 1.750.

4. *Rules of court*

a. *Rules of civil procedure.* The Florida Rules of Civil Procedure apply to all actions of a civil nature and all special statutory proceedings in the circuit courts and county courts except those to which the Florida Probate Rules, the Florida Family Law Rules of Procedure, or the Small Claims Rules apply. FL ST RCP Rule 1.010.

i. The form, content, procedure, and time for pleading in all special statutory proceedings shall be as prescribed by the statutes governing the proceeding unless the Florida Rules of Civil Procedure specifically provide to the contrary. FL ST RCP Rule 1.010.

ii. The Florida Rules of Civil Procedure shall be construed to secure the just, speedy, and inexpensive determination of every action. FL ST RCP Rule 1.010.

b. *Rules of judicial administration.* The Florida Rules of Judicial Administration shall apply to administrative matters in all courts to which the Florida Rules of Judicial Administration are applicable by their terms. The Florida Rules of Judicial Administration shall be construed to secure the speedy and inexpensive determination of every proceeding to which they are applicable. The Florida Rules of Judicial Administration shall supersede all conflicting rules and statutes. FL ST J ADMIN Rule 2.110.

D. Documents

1. *Required documents*

a. *Request for admission.* Please see the General Requirements section of this document for more information on the contents of the request for admission.

i. *Notices to persons with disabilities.* See the Format section of this KeyRules document for further information.

b. *Copies of documents.* Copies of documents shall be served with the request unless they have been or are otherwise furnished or made available for inspection and copying. FL ST RCP Rule 1.370(a).

c. *Certificate of service.* A certificate of service of the interrogatories shall be filed, giving the date of service and the name of the party to whom they were directed. FL ST RCP Rule 1.340(e). When any attorney certifies in substance: "I certify that a copy hereof has been furnished to (here insert name or names and addresses used for service) by (e-mail) (delivery) (mail) (fax) on .... (date) ....________________ Attorney" the certificate is taken as prima facie proof of such service in compliance with FL ST J ADMIN Rule 2.516. FL ST J ADMIN Rule 2.516(f).

E. Format

1. *Documents; Type and size.* Documents subject to the exceptions set forth in FL ST J ADMIN Rule 2.525(d) shall be filed on recycled paper measuring eight and one half by eleven (8 1/2 by 11) inches. For purposes of FL ST J ADMIN Rule 2.520, paper is recycled if it contains a minimum content of fifty (50) percent waste paper. Xerographic reduction of legal-size (eight and one half by fourteen (8 1/2 by 14) inches) documents to letter size (eight and one half by eleven (8 1/2 by 11) inches) is prohibited. All other

documents filed by electronic transmission shall be filed in a format capable of being printed in a format consistent with the provisions of FL ST J ADMIN Rule 2.250. FL ST J ADMIN Rule 2.520(b).

a. *Exhibits.* Any exhibit or attachment filed with pleadings or papers may be filed in its original size. FL ST J ADMIN Rule 2.520(c).

b. *Recording space.* On all papers and documents prepared and filed by the court or by any party to a proceeding which are to be recorded in the public records of any county, including but not limited to final money judgments and notices of lis pendens, a three (3) inch by three (3) inch space at the top right-hand corner on the first page and a one (1) inch by three (3) inch space at the top right-hand corner on each subsequent page shall be left blank and reserved for use by the clerk of court. FL ST J ADMIN Rule 2.520(d).

i. *Exceptions to recording space.* Any papers or documents created by persons or entities over which the filing party has no control, including but not limited to wills, codicils, trusts, or other testamentary documents; documents prepared or executed by any public officer; documents prepared, executed, acknowledged, or proved outside of the State of Florida; or documents created by State or Federal government agencies, may be filed without the space required by FL ST J ADMIN Rule 2.520. FL ST J ADMIN Rule 2.520(e).

c. *Noncompliance.* No clerk of court is permitted to refuse to file any document or paper because of noncompliance with the Florida Rules of Judicial Administration. However, upon request of the clerk of court, noncomplying documents must be resubmitted in accordance with the formatting rules. FL ST J ADMIN Rule 2.520(f).

2. *Caption.* Every pleading, motion, order, judgment, or other paper shall have a caption containing the name of the court, the file number, and except for in rem proceedings, including forfeiture proceedings, the name of the first party on each side with an appropriate indication of other parties, and a designation identifying the party filing it and its nature or the nature of the order, as the case may be. In any in rem proceeding, every pleading, motion, order, judgment, or other paper shall have a caption containing the name of the court, the file number, the style "In re" (followed by the name or general description of the property), and a designation of the person or entity filing it and its nature or the nature of the order, as the case may be. In an in rem forfeiture proceeding, the style shall be "In re forfeiture of" (followed by the name of the general description of the property). All papers filed in the action shall be styled in such a manner as to indicate clearly the subject matter of the paper and the party requesting or obtaining relief. FL ST RCP Rule 1.100(c)(1).

3. *Writing and written defined.* Writing or written means a document containing information, an application, or a stipulation. FL ST RCP Rule 1.080(c).

4. *Rule abbreviations*

a. The Florida Rules of Civil Procedure and shall be abbreviated as Fla.R.Civ.P. FL ST RCP Rule 1.010.

b. The Florida Rules of Judicial Administration shall be abbreviated as Fla. R. Jud. Admin. FL ST J ADMIN Rule 2.110.

5. *Nonverification.* Except when otherwise specifically provided by the Florida Rules of Civil Procedure or an applicable statute, every pleading or other document of a party represented by an attorney need not be verified or accompanied by an affidavit. FL ST RCP Rule 1.030; FL ST J ADMIN Rule 2.515(a).

6. *Attorney signature*

a. *Attorney signature.* Every pleading and other document of a party represented by an attorney shall be signed by at least one (1) attorney of record in that attorney's individual name whose current record Florida Bar address, telephone number, including area code, primary e-mail address and secondary e-mail addresses, if any, and Florida Bar number shall be stated, and who shall be duly licensed to practice law in Florida or who shall have received permission to appear in the particular case as provided in FL ST J ADMIN Rule 2.510. FL ST J ADMIN Rule 2.515(a).

i. The attorney may be required by the court to give the address of, and to vouch for the attorney's authority to represent, the party. FL ST J ADMIN Rule 2.515(a).

ii. The signature of an attorney shall constitute a certificate by the attorney that the attorney has read the pleading or other document; that to the best of the attorney's knowledge, information, and belief there is good ground to support it; and that it is not interposed for delay. FL ST J ADMIN Rule 2.515(a).

iii. If a pleading is not signed or is signed with intent to defeat the purpose of FL ST J ADMIN Rule 2.515, it may be stricken and the action may proceed as though the pleading or other document had not been served. FL ST J ADMIN Rule 2.515(a).

b. *Pro se litigant signature.* A party who is not represented by an attorney shall sign any pleading or other paper and state the party's address and telephone number, including area code. FL ST J ADMIN Rule 2.515(b).

c. *Form of signature*

i. The signatures required on pleadings and documents by FL ST J ADMIN Rule 2.515(a) and FL ST J ADMIN Rule 2.515(b) may be:

- Original signatures;
- Original signatures that have been reproduced by electronic means, such as on electronically transmitted documents or photocopied documents;
- Electronic signatures using the "/s/," "s/," or "/s" formats by or at the direction of the person signing; or
- Any other signature format authorized by general law, so long as the clerk where the proceeding is pending has the capability of receiving and has obtained approval from the Supreme Court of Florida to accept pleadings and documents with that signature format. FL ST J ADMIN Rule 2.515(c)(1).

ii. An attorney, party, or other person who files a pleading or paper by electronic transmission that does not contain the original signature of that attorney, party, or other person shall file that identical pleading or paper in paper form containing an original signature of that attorney, party, or other person (hereinafter called the follow-up filing) immediately thereafter. The follow-up filing is not required if the Supreme Court of Florida has entered an order directing the clerk of court to discontinue accepting the follow-up filing. FL ST J ADMIN Rule 2.515(c)(2).

7. *Forms*

a. *Process.* The forms of process, notice of lis pendens, and notice of action provided in the Florida Rules of Civil Procedure are sufficient. Variations from the forms do not void process or notices that are otherwise sufficient. FL ST RCP Rule 1.900(a).

b. *Other forms.* The other forms provided in the Florida Rules of Civil Procedure are sufficient for the matters that are covered by them. So long as the substance is expressed without prolixity, the forms may be varied to meet the facts of a particular case. FL ST RCP Rule 1.900(b).

c. *Formal matters.* Captions, except for the designation of the paper, are omitted from the forms provided in the Florida Rules of Civil Procedure. A general form of caption is the first form provided. Signatures are omitted from pleadings and motions. FL ST RCP Rule 1.900(c).

8. *Notices to persons with disabilities.* All notices of court proceedings to be held in a public facility, and all process compelling appearance at such proceedings, shall include the following statement in bold face, fourteen (14) point Times New Roman or Courier font: "If you are a person with a disability who needs any accommodation in order to participate in this proceeding, you are entitled, at no cost to you, to the provision of certain assistance. Please contact [identify applicable court personnel by name, address, and telephone number] at least seven (7) days before your scheduled court appearance, or immediately upon receiving this notification if the time before the scheduled appearance is less than seven (7) days; if you are hearing or voice impaired, call 711." FL ST J ADMIN Rule 2.540(c)(1).

9. *Minimization of the filing of sensitive information*

a. *Limitations for court filings.* Unless authorized by FL ST J ADMIN Rule 2.425(b), statute, another

rule of court, or the court orders otherwise, designated sensitive information filed with the court must be limited to the following format:

i. The initials of a person known to be a minor;

ii. The year of birth of a person's birth date;

iii. No portion of any: Social security number, Bank account number, Credit card account number, Charge account number, or Debit account number;

iv. The last four digits of any: Taxpayer identification number (TIN), Employee identification number, Driver's license number, Passport number, Telephone number, Financial account number, except as set forth in FL ST J ADMIN Rule 2.425(a)(3), Brokerage account number, Insurance policy account number, Loan account number, Customer account number, or Patient or health care number;

v. A truncated version of any: Email address, Computer user name, Password, or Personal identification number (PIN); and

vi. A truncated version of any other sensitive information as provided by court order. FL ST J ADMIN Rule 2.425(a).

b. *Exceptions.* FL ST J ADMIN Rule 2.425(a) does not apply to the following:

i. An account number which identifies the property alleged to be the subject of a proceeding;

ii. The record of an administrative or agency proceeding;

iii. The record in appellate or review proceedings;

iv. The birth date of a minor whenever the birth date is necessary for the court to establish or maintain subject matter jurisdiction;

v. The name of a minor in any order relating to parental responsibility, time-sharing, or child support;

vi. The name of a minor in any document or order affecting the minor's ownership of real property;

vii. The birth date of a party in a writ of attachment or notice to payor;

viii. In traffic and criminal proceedings: a pro se filing; a court filing that is related to a criminal matter or investigation and that is prepared before the filing of a criminal charge or is not filed as part of any docketed criminal case; an arrest or search warrant or any information in support thereof; a charging document and an affidavit or other documents filed in support of any charging document, including any driving records; a statement of particulars; discovery material introduced into evidence or otherwise filed with the court; and all information necessary for the proper issuance and execution of a subpoena duces tecum;

ix. Information used by the clerk for case maintenance purposes or the courts for case management purposes; and

x. Information which is relevant and material to an issue before the court. FL ST J ADMIN Rule 2.425(b).

c. *Remedies.* Upon motion by a party or interested person or sua sponte by the court, the court may order remedies, sanctions or both for a violation of FL ST J ADMIN Rule 2.425(a). Following notice and an opportunity to respond, the court may impose sanctions if such filing was not made in good faith. FL ST J ADMIN Rule 2.425(c).

d. *Motions not restricted.* FL ST J ADMIN Rule 2.425 does not restrict a party's right to move for protective order, to move to file documents under seal, or to request a determination of the confidentiality of records. FL ST J ADMIN Rule 2.425(d).

i. For more information regarding sealing court records, please see FL ST 4 J CIR 2006-05.

e. *Application.* FL ST J ADMIN Rule 2.425 does not affect the application of constitutional provisions, statutes, or rules of court regarding confidential information or access to public information. FL ST J ADMIN Rule 2.425(e).

F. Filing and Service Requirements

1. *Court filing of documents and discovery.* Information obtained during discovery shall not be filed with the court until such time as it is filed for good cause. The requirement of good cause is satisfied only where the filing of the information is allowed or required by another applicable rule of procedure or by court order. All filings of discovery documents shall comply with FL ST J ADMIN Rule 2.425. The court shall have the authority to impose sanctions for violation of FL ST RCP Rule 1.280. FL ST RCP Rule 1.280(g).

2. *Filing requirements.* All original documents must be filed with the court either before service or immediately thereafter, unless otherwise provided for by general law or other rules. If the original of any bond or other document is not placed in the court file, a certified copy must be so placed by the clerk. FL ST J ADMIN Rule 2.516(d). All documents shall be filed in conformity with the requirements of FL ST J ADMIN Rule 2.525. FL ST RCP Rule 1.080(b). All documents filed in any court shall be filed by electronic transmission in accordance with FL ST J ADMIN Rule 2.525. "Documents" means pleadings, motions, petitions, memoranda, briefs, notices, exhibits, declarations, affidavits, orders, judgments, decrees, writs, opinions, and any other paper or writing submitted to a court. FL ST J ADMIN Rule 2.520(a). All documents that are court records, as defined in FL ST J ADMIN Rule 2.430(a)(1), must be filed by electronic transmission, provided that: (1) the clerk has the ability to accept and retain such documents; (2) the clerk or the chief judge of the circuit has requested permission to accept documents filed by electronic transmission; and (3) the supreme court has entered an order granting permission to the clerk to accept documents filed by electronic transmission. FL ST J ADMIN Rule 2.525(c)(1).

   a. *Definition.* "Electronic transmission of documents" means the sending of information by electronic signals to, by or from a court or clerk, which when received can be transformed and stored or transmitted on paper, microfilm, magnetic storage device, optical imaging system, CD-ROM, flash drive, other electronic data storage system, server, case maintenance system ("CM"), electronic court filing ("ECF") system, statewide or local electronic portal ("e-portal"), or other electronic record keeping system authorized by the supreme court in a format sufficient to communicate the information on the original document in a readable format. Electronic transmission of documents includes electronic mail ("e-mail") and any internet-based transmission procedure, and may include procedures allowing for documents to be signed or verified by electronic means. FL ST J ADMIN Rule 2.525(a).

      i. The filing of documents with the court as required by the Florida Rules of Judicial Administration must be made by filing them with the clerk in accordance with FL ST J ADMIN Rule 2.525, except that the judge may permit documents to be filed with the judge, in which event the judge must note the filing date before him or her on the documents and transmit them to the clerk. The date of filing is that shown on the face of the document by the judge's notation or the clerk's time stamp, whichever is earlier. FL ST J ADMIN Rule 2.516(e).

   b. *Application.* Any court or clerk of the court may accept the electronic transmission of documents for filing after the clerk, together with input from the chief judge of the circuit, has obtained approval of the procedures and program for doing so from the Supreme Court of Florida. FL ST J ADMIN Rule 2.525(b).

   c. *Exceptions*

      i. Paper documents and other submissions may be manually submitted to the clerk or court:

         - When the clerk does not have the ability to accept and retain documents by electronic filing or has not had ECF Procedures approved by the supreme court;
         - For filing by any self-represented party or any self-represented nonparty unless specific ECF Procedures provide a means to file documents electronically. However, any self-represented nonparty that is a governmental or public agency and any other agency, partnership, corporation, or business entity acting on behalf of any governmental or public agency may file documents by electronic transmission if such entity has the capability of filing documents electronically;
         - For filing by attorneys excused from e-mail service in accordance with FL ST J ADMIN Rule 2.516(b);

- When submitting evidentiary exhibits or filing non-documentary materials;
- When the filing involves documents in excess of twenty-five (25) megabytes (25MB) in size. For such filings, documents may be transmitted using an electronic storage medium that the clerk has the ability to accept, which may include a CD-ROM, flash drive, or similar storage medium;
- When filed in open court, as permitted by the court;
- When paper filing is permitted by any approved statewide or local ECF procedures; and
- If any court determines that justice so requires. FL ST J ADMIN Rule 2.525(d).

ii. Any document in paper form submitted under FL ST J ADMIN Rule 2.525(d) is filed when it is received by the clerk or court and the clerk shall immediately thereafter convert any filed paper document to an electronic document. "Convert to an electronic document" means optically capturing an image of a paper document and using character recognition software to recover as much of the document's text as practicable and then indexing and storing the document in the official court file. FL ST J ADMIN Rule 2.525(c)(4).

iii. Any storage medium submitted under FL ST J ADMIN Rule 2.525(d)(5) is filed when received by the clerk or court and the clerk shall immediately thereafter transfer the electronic documents from the storage device to the official court file. FL ST J ADMIN Rule 2.525(c)(5).

iv. If the filer of any paper document authorized under FL ST J ADMIN Rule 2.525(d) provides a self-addressed, postage-paid envelope for return of the paper document after it is converted to electronic form by the clerk, the clerk shall place the paper document in the envelope and deposit it in the mail. Except when a paper document is required to be maintained, the clerk may recycle any filed paper document that is not to be returned to the filer. FL ST J ADMIN Rule 2.525(c)(6).

v. The clerk may convert any paper document filed before the effective date of FL ST J ADMIN Rule 2.525 to an electronic document. Unless the clerk is required to maintain the paper document, if the paper document has been converted to an electronic document by the clerk, the paper document is no longer part of the official court file and may be removed and recycled. FL ST J ADMIN Rule 2.525(c)(7).

d. *Official court file.* For information on what constitutes the official court file, please see FL ST J ADMIN Rule 2.525(c)(2), FL ST J ADMIN Rule 2.525(c)(3).

e. *Administration.* All attorneys, parties, or other persons using this rule to file documents are required to make arrangements with the court or clerk for the payment of any charges authorized by general law or the supreme court before filing any document by electronic transmission. FL ST J ADMIN Rule 2.525(f)(2).

f. *Filing date.* The filing date for an electronically transmitted document is the date and time that such filing is acknowledged by an electronic stamp or otherwise, pursuant to any procedure set forth in any ECF Procedures approved by the supreme court, or the date the last page of such filing is received by the court or clerk. FL ST J ADMIN Rule 2.525(f)(3).

g. *Accessibility.* All documents transmitted in any electronic form under FL ST J ADMIN Rule 2.525 must comply with the accessibility requirements of FL ST J ADMIN Rule 2.526. FL ST J ADMIN Rule 2.525(g).

3. *Service requirements.* Every pleading subsequent to the initial pleading, all orders, and every other document filed in the action must be served in conformity with the requirements of FL ST J ADMIN Rule 2.516. FL ST RCP Rule 1.080(a).

a. *Service; When required.* Unless the court otherwise orders, or a statute or supreme court administrative order specifies a different means of service, every pleading subsequent to the initial pleading and every other document filed in any court proceeding, except applications for witness subpoenas and documents served by formal notice or required to be served in the manner provided for service of formal notice, must be served in accordance with FL ST J ADMIN Rule 2.516 on each party. No service need be made on parties against whom a default has been entered, except that pleadings asserting new or additional claims against them must be served in the manner provided for service of summons. FL ST J ADMIN Rule 2.516(a).

b. *Service; How made.* When service is required or permitted to be made upon a party represented by an attorney, service must be made upon the attorney unless service upon the party is ordered by the court. FL ST J ADMIN Rule 2.516(b).

   i. *Service by electronic mail ("e-mail").* All documents required or permitted to be served on another party must be served by e-mail, unless FL ST J ADMIN Rule 2.516 otherwise provides. When, in addition to service by e-mail, the sender also utilizes another means of service provided for in FL ST J ADMIN Rule 2.516(b)(2), any differing time limits and other provisions applicable to that other means of service control. FL ST J ADMIN Rule 2.516(b)(1). Any document electronically transmitted to a court or clerk must also be served on all parties and interested persons in accordance with the applicable rules of court. FL ST J ADMIN Rule 2.525(e)(2).

      - *Service on attorneys.* Upon appearing in a proceeding, an attorney must serve a designation of a primary e-mail address and may designate no more than two (2) secondary e-mail addresses. Thereafter, service must be directed to all designated e-mail addresses in that proceeding. Every document filed by an attorney thereafter must include the primary e-mail address of that attorney and any secondary e-mail addresses. If an attorney does not designate any e-mail address for service, documents may be served on that attorney at the e-mail address on record with The Florida Bar. FL ST J ADMIN Rule 2.516(b)(1)(A).

      - *Exception to e-mail service on attorneys.* Service by an attorney on another attorney must be made by e-mail unless excused by the court. Upon motion by an attorney demonstrating that the attorney has no e-mail account and lacks access to the Internet at the attorney's office, the court may excuse the attorney from the requirements of e-mail service. Service on and by an attorney excused by the court from e-mail service must be by the means provided in FL ST J ADMIN Rule 2.516(b)(2). FL ST J ADMIN Rule 2.516(b)(1)(B).

      - *Service on and by parties not represented by an attorney.* Any party not represented by an attorney may serve a designation of a primary e-mail address and also may designate no more than two (2) secondary e-mail addresses to which service must be directed in that proceeding by the means provided in FL ST J ADMIN Rule 2.516(b)(1). If a party not represented by an attorney does not designate an e-mail address for service in a proceeding, service on and by that party must be by the means provided in FL ST J ADMIN Rule 2.516(b)(2). FL ST J ADMIN Rule 2.516(b)(1)(C).

      - *Time of service.* Service by e-mail is complete when it is sent. FL ST J ADMIN Rule 2.516(b)(1)(D). An e-mail is deemed served on the date it is sent. FL ST J ADMIN Rule 2.516(b)(1)(D)(i). If the sender learns that the e-mail did not reach the address of the person to be served, the sender must immediately send another copy by e-mail, or by a means authorized by FL ST J ADMIN Rule 2.516(b)(2). FL ST J ADMIN Rule 2.516(b)(1)(D)(ii). E-mail service is treated as service by mail for the computation of time. FL ST J ADMIN Rule 2.516(b)(1)(D)(iii).

   ii. *Format of e-mail for service.* Service of a document by e-mail is made by attaching a copy of the document in PDF format to an e-mail sent to all addresses designated by the attorney or party. FL ST J ADMIN Rule 2.516(b)(1)(E).

      - All documents served by e-mail must be attached to an e-mail message containing a subject line beginning with the words "SERVICE OF COURT DOCUMENT" in all capital letters, followed by the case number of the proceeding in which the documents are being served. FL ST J ADMIN Rule 2.516(b)(1)(E)(i).

      - The body of the e-mail must identify the court in which the proceeding is pending, the case number, the name of the initial party on each side, the title of each document served with that e-mail, and the sender's name and telephone number. FL ST J ADMIN Rule 2.516(b)(1)(E)(ii).

      - Any document served by e-mail may be signed by the "/s/" format, as long as the filed original is signed in accordance with the applicable rule of procedure. FL ST J ADMIN Rule 2.516(b)(1)(E)(iii).

- Any e-mail which, together with its attached documents, exceeds five megabytes (5MB) in size, must be divided and sent as separate e-mails, no one of which may exceed five megabytes (5MB) in size and each of which must be sequentially numbered in the subject line. FL ST J ADMIN Rule 2.516(b)(1)(E)(iv).

iii. *Service by other means.* In addition to, and not in lieu of, service by e-mail, service may also be made upon attorneys by any of the means specified in FL ST J ADMIN Rule 2.516(b)(2). Service on and by all parties who are not represented by an attorney and who do not designate an e-mail address, and on and by all attorneys excused from e-mail service, must be made by delivering a copy of the document or by mailing it to the party or attorney at their last known address or, if no address is known, by leaving it with the clerk of the court. Service by mail is complete upon mailing. Delivery of a copy within FL ST J ADMIN Rule 2.516 is complete upon:

- Handing it to the attorney or to the party,
- Leaving it at the attorney's or party's office with a clerk or other person in charge thereof,
- If there is no one in charge, leaving it in a conspicuous place therein,
- If the office is closed or the person to be served has no office, leaving it at the person's usual place of abode with some person of his or her family above fifteen (15) years of age and informing such person of the contents, or
- Transmitting it by facsimile to the attorney's or party's office with a cover sheet containing the sender's name, firm, address, telephone number, and facsimile number, and the number of pages transmitted. When service is made by facsimile, a copy must also be served by any other method permitted by FL ST J ADMIN Rule 2.516. Facsimile service occurs when transmission is complete. FL ST J ADMIN Rule 2.516(b)(2)(A) through FL ST J ADMIN Rule 2.516(b)(2)(E).
- Service by delivery after 5:00 p.m. must be deemed to have been made by mailing on the date of delivery. FL ST J ADMIN Rule 2.516(b)(2)(F).

c. *Service; Numerous defendants.* In actions when the parties are unusually numerous, the court may regulate the service contemplated by the Florida Rules of Judicial Administration on motion or on its own initiative in such manner as may be found to be just and reasonable. FL ST J ADMIN Rule 2.516(c).

d. *Service by clerk.* Service of notices and other documents required to be made by the clerk must also be done as provided in FL ST J ADMIN Rule 2.516(b). FL ST J ADMIN Rule 2.516(g).

G. Hearings

1. There is no hearing required or contemplated with regard to requests for admission in the Florida Rules of Civil Procedure.

H. Forms

1. Official Request for Admissions Forms for Florida

a. Caption. FL ST RCP Form 1.901.

2. Request for Admissions Forms for Florida

a. Requests for admissions; Negligence, fall down. FL-PRACFORM § 8:41.

b. Requests for admissions; Promissory note. FL-PRACFORM § 8:42.

c. Requests for admissions; Open account. FL-PRACFORM § 8:43.

d. Requests for admissions; Mortgage foreclosure. FL-PRACFORM § 8:44.

e. Request for admissions; General form. FL-PP § 3:146.

f. Request for admissions; Facts and genuineness of documents. FL-PP § 3:147.

g. Motion; To determine sufficiency of reply to request for admissions. FL-PP § 3:152.

h. Form for request for admissions. FL-RCPF R 1.370(5).

i. Form for request for admissions (another form). FL-RCPF R 1.370(6).

j. Form for request for admissions served concurrently with interrogatories. FL-RCPF R 1.370(7).

k. Form for request for admissions as to factual situation and refinement of issues. FL-RCPF R 1.370(9).

l. Form for request to admit party uses electronic data storage. FL-RCPF R 1.370(10).

I. Checklist

(I) ❑ Matters to be considered by requesting party

(a) ❑ Required documents

(1) ❑ Request

(2) ❑ Copies of documents

(3) ❑ Certificate of service

(b) ❑ Time for request

(1) ❑ Without leave of court the request may be served upon the plaintiff after commencement of the action and upon any other party with or after service of the process and initial pleading upon that party

(II) ❑ Matters to be considered by responding party

(a) ❑ Required documents

(1) ❑ Response to request

(2) ❑ Certificate of service

(b) ❑ Time for response

(1) ❑ The party to whom the request is directed shall serve a written response within thirty (30) days after service of the request, except that a defendant may serve a response within forty-five (45) days after service of the process and initial pleading on that defendant

Requests, Notices and Applications
Notice of Deposition

Document Last Updated January 2013

A. Applicable Rules

1. *State rules*

a. Pleadings and motions. FL ST RCP Rule 1.100.

b. Depositions before action or pending appeal. FL ST RCP Rule 1.290.

c. Persons before whom depositions may be taken. FL ST RCP Rule 1.300.

d. Depositions upon oral examination. FL ST RCP Rule 1.310.

e. Depositions upon written questions. FL ST RCP Rule 1.320.

f. Use of depositions in court proceedings. FL ST RCP Rule 1.330.

g. Nonverification of pleadings. FL ST RCP Rule 1.030.

h. Service and filing of pleadings, orders, and documents. FL ST RCP Rule 1.080.

i. Time. FL ST RCP Rule 1.090.

j. General provisions governing discovery. FL ST RCP Rule 1.280.

k. Failure to make discovery; Sanctions. FL ST RCP Rule 1.380.

l. Depositions of expert witnesses. FL ST RCP Rule 1.390.
m. Relief from judgment, decrees, or orders. FL ST RCP Rule 1.540.
n. Forms. FL ST RCP Rule 1.900.
o. Minimization of the filing of sensitive information. FL ST J ADMIN Rule 2.425.
p. Retention of court records. FL ST J ADMIN Rule 2.430.
q. Foreign attorneys. FL ST J ADMIN Rule 2.510.
r. Signature of attorneys and parties. FL ST J ADMIN Rule 2.515.
s. Paper. FL ST J ADMIN Rule 2.520.
t. Electronic filing. FL ST J ADMIN Rule 2.525.
u. Accessibility of information and technology. FL ST J ADMIN Rule 2.526.
v. Requests for accommodations by persons with disabilities. FL ST J ADMIN Rule 2.540.

2. *Local rules*
   a. Sealing court records. FL ST 4 J CIR 2006-05.
   b. Filing of depositions in Duval County. FL ST 4 J CIR 2012-03.

B. Timing

1. *Depositions upon oral examination.* After commencement of the action any party may take the testimony of any person, including a party, by deposition upon oral examination. Leave of court, granted with or without notice, must be obtained only if the plaintiff seeks to take a deposition within thirty (30) days after service of the process and initial pleading upon any defendant, except that leave is not required (1) if a defendant has served a notice of taking deposition or otherwise sought discovery, or (2) if special notice is given as provided in FL ST RCP Rule 1.310(b)(2). The attendance of witnesses may be compelled by subpoena as provided in FL ST RCP Rule 1.410. The deposition of a person confined in prison may be taken only by leave of court on such terms as the court prescribes. FL ST RCP Rule 1.310(a). A party desiring to take the deposition of any person upon oral examination shall give reasonable notice in writing to every other party to the action. FL ST RCP Rule 1.310(b)(1).
2. *Depositions upon written questions.* After commencement of the action any party may take the testimony of any person, including a party, by deposition upon written questions. The attendance of witnesses may be compelled by the use of subpoena as provided in FL ST RCP Rule 1.410. The deposition of a person confined in prison may be taken only by leave of court on such terms as the court prescribes. Within thrity (30) days after the notice and written questions are served, a party may serve cross questions upon all other parties. Within ten (10) days after being served with cross questions, a party may serve redirect questions upon all other parties. Within ten (10) days after being served with redirect questions, a party may serve recross questions upon all other parties. The court may for cause shown enlarge or shorten the time. FL ST RCP Rule 1.320(a).
3. *Depositions before action or pending appeal.* For information on petitions and motions for depositions before an action or pending appeal, please see the General Requirements section below.
4. *Sequence and timing of discovery.* Except as provided in FL ST RCP Rule 1.280(b)(5) or unless the court upon motion for the convenience of parties and witnesses and in the interest of justice orders otherwise, methods of discovery may be used in any sequence, and the fact that a party is conducting discovery, whether by deposition or otherwise, shall not delay any other party's discovery. FL ST RCP Rule 1.280(e).
5. *Computation of time*
   a. *Generally.* Computation of time shall be governed by FL ST J ADMIN Rule 2.514. FL ST RCP Rule 1.090(a). The following rules apply in computing time periods specified in any rule of procedure, local rule, court order, or statute that does not specify a method of computing time. FL ST J ADMIN Rule 2.514(a).
      i. *Period stated in days or a longer unit.* When the period is stated in days or a longer unit of time

(A) exclude the day of the event that triggers the period; (B) count every day, including intermediate Saturdays, Sundays, and legal holidays; and (C) include the last day of the period, but if the last day is a Saturday, Sunday, or legal holiday, or falls within any period of time extended through an order of the chief justice under FL ST J ADMIN Rule 2.205(a)(2)(B)(iv), the period continues to run until the end of the next day that is not a Saturday, Sunday, or legal holiday and does not fall within any period of time extended through an order of the chief justice. FL ST J ADMIN Rule 2.514(a)(1).

ii. *Period stated in hours.* When the period is stated in hours (A) begin counting immediately on the occurrence of the event that triggers the period; (B) count every hour, including hours during intermediate Saturdays, Sundays, and legal holidays; and (C) if the period would end on a Saturday, Sunday, or legal holiday, or during any period of time extended through an order of the chief justice under FL ST J ADMIN Rule 2.205(a)(2)(B)(iv), the period continues to run until the same time on the next day that is not a Saturday, Sunday, or legal holiday and does not fall within any period of time extended through an order of the chief justice. FL ST J ADMIN Rule 2.514(a)(2).

iii. *Period stated in days less than seven (7) days.* When the period stated in days is less than seven (7) days, intermediate Saturdays, Sundays, and legal holidays shall be excluded in the computation. FL ST J ADMIN Rule 2.514(a)(3).

iv. *"Last day" defined.* Unless a different time is set by a statute, local rule, or court order, the last day ends (A) for electronic filing or for service by any means, at midnight; and (B) for filing by other means, when the clerk's office is scheduled to close. FL ST J ADMIN Rule 2.514(a)(4).

v. *"Next day" defined.* The "next day" is determined by continuing to count forward when the period is measured after an event and backward when measured before an event. FL ST J ADMIN Rule 2.514(a)(5).

vi. *"Legal holiday" defined.* "Legal holiday" means (A) the day set aside by FL ST § 110.117, for observing New Year's Day, Martin Luther King, Jr.'s Birthday, Memorial Day, Independence Day, Labor Day, Veterans' Day, Thanksgiving Day, the Friday after Thanksgiving Day, or Christmas Day, and (B) any day observed as a holiday by the clerk's office or as designated by the chief judge. FL ST J ADMIN Rule 2.514(a)(6).

b. *Additional time after service by mail or e-mail.* When a party may or must act within a specified time after service and service is made by mail or e-mail, five (5) days are added after the period that would otherwise expire under FL ST J ADMIN Rule 2.514(a). FL ST J ADMIN Rule 2.514(b).

c. *Enlargement.* When an act is required or allowed to be done at or within a specified time by order of court, by the Florida Rules of Civil Procedure, or by notice given thereunder, for cause shown the court at any time in its discretion (1) with or without notice, may order the period enlarged if request therefor is made before the expiration of the period originally prescribed or as extended by a previous order, or (2) upon motion made and notice after the expiration of the specified period, may permit the act to be done when failure to act was the result of excusable neglect, but it may not extend the time for making a motion for new trial, for rehearing, or to alter or amend a judgment; making a motion for relief from a judgment under FL ST RCP Rule 1.540(b); taking an appeal or filing a petition for certiorari; or making a motion for a directed verdict. FL ST RCP Rule 1.090(b).

d. *Unaffected by expiration of term.* The period of time provided for the doing of any act or the taking of any proceeding shall not be affected or limited by the continued existence or expiration of a term of court. The continued existence or expiration of a term of court in no way affects the power of a court to do any act or take any proceeding in any action which is or has been pending before it. FL ST RCP Rule 1.090(c).

C. General Requirements

1. *General provisions governing discovery*

a. *Discovery methods.* Parties may obtain discovery by one or more of the following methods: depositions upon oral examination or written questions; written interrogatories; production of documents or things or permission to enter upon land or other property for inspection and other purposes; physical and mental examinations; and requests for admission. Unless the court orders otherwise and under FL ST RCP Rule 1.280(c), the frequency of use of these methods is not limited, except as provided in FL ST RCP Rule 1.200, FL ST RCP Rule 1.340, and FL ST RCP Rule 1.370. FL ST RCP Rule 1.280(a).

b. *Scope of discovery.* Unless otherwise limited by order of the court in accordance with the Florida Rules of Civil Procedure, the scope of discovery is as follows:

   i. *In general.* Parties may obtain discovery regarding any matter, not privileged, that is relevant to the subject matter of the pending action, whether it relates to the claim or defense of the party seeking discovery or the claim or defense of any other party, including the existence, description, nature, custody, condition, and location of any books, documents, or other tangible things and the identity and location of persons having knowledge of any discoverable matter. It is not ground for objection that the information sought will be inadmissible at the trial if the information sought appears reasonably calculated to lead to the discovery of admissible evidence. FL ST RCP Rule 1.280(b)(1).

   ii. *Indemnity agreements.* A party may obtain discovery of the existence and contents of any agreement under which any person may be liable to satisfy part or all of a judgment that may be entered in the action or to indemnify or to reimburse a party for payments made to satisfy the judgment. Information concerning the agreement is not admissible in evidence at trial by reason of disclosure. FL ST RCP Rule 1.280(b)(2).

   iii. *Electronically stored information.* A party may obtain discovery of electronically stored information in accordance with the Florida Rules of Civil Procedure. FL ST RCP Rule 1.280(b)(3).

   iv. *Trial preparation; Materials.* Subject to the provisions of FL ST RCP Rule 1.280(b)(5), a party may obtain discovery of documents and tangible things otherwise discoverable under FL ST RCP Rule 1.280(b)(1) and prepared in anticipation of litigation or for trial by or for another party or by or for that party's representative, including that party's attorney, consultant, surety, indemnitor, insurer, or agent, only upon a showing that the party seeking discovery has need of the materials in the preparation of the case and is unable without undue hardship to obtain the substantial equivalent of the materials by other means. FL ST RCP Rule 1.280(b)(4).

      - In ordering discovery of the materials when the required showing has been made, the court shall protect against disclosure of the mental impressions, conclusions, opinions, or legal theories of an attorney or other representative of a party concerning the litigation. FL ST RCP Rule 1.280(b)(4).
      - Without the required showing a party may obtain a copy of a statement concerning the action or its subject matter previously made by that party. FL ST RCP Rule 1.280(b)(4).
      - Upon request without the required showing a person not a party may obtain a copy of a statement concerning the action or its subject matter previously made by that person. If the request is refused, the person may move for an order to obtain a copy. The provisions of FL ST RCP Rule 1.380(a)(5) apply to the award of expenses incurred as a result of making the motion. FL ST RCP Rule 1.280(b)(4).
      - For purposes of FL ST RCP Rule 1.280(b)(4), a statement previously made is a written statement signed or otherwise adopted or approved by the person making it, or a stenographic, mechanical, electrical, or other recording or transcription of it that is a substantially verbatim recital of an oral statement by the person making it and contemporaneously recorded. FL ST RCP Rule 1.280(b)(4).

   v. *Trial preparation; Experts.* Discovery of facts known and opinions held by experts, otherwise discoverable under the provisions of FL ST RCP Rule 1.280(b)(1) and acquired or developed in anticipation of litigation or for trial, may be obtained only as follows:

      - By interrogatories a party may require any other party to identify each person whom the other party expects to call as an expert witness at trial and to state the subject matter on which the expert is expected to testify, and to state the substance of the facts and opinions

to which the expert is expected to testify and a summary of the grounds for each opinion. FL ST RCP Rule 1.280(b)(5)(A)(i).

- Any person disclosed by interrogatories or otherwise as a person expected to be called as an expert witness at trial may be deposed in accordance with FL ST RCP Rule 1.390 without motion or order of court. FL ST RCP Rule 1.280(b)(5)(A)(ii).
- A party may obtain the following discovery regarding any person disclosed by interrogatories or otherwise as a person expected to be called as an expert witness at trial: The scope of employment in the pending case and the compensation for such service, FL ST RCP Rule 1.280(b)(5)(A)(iii)(1); The expert's general litigation experience, including the percentage of work performed for plaintiffs and defendants, FL ST RCP Rule 1.280(b)(5)(A)(iii)(2); The identity of other cases, within a reasonable time period, in which the expert has testified by deposition or at trial, FL ST RCP Rule 1.280(b)(5)(A)(iii)(3); An approximation of the portion of the expert's involvement as an expert witness, which may be based on the number of hours, percentage of hours, or percentage of earned income derived from serving as an expert witness; however, the expert shall not be required to disclose his or her earnings as an expert witness or income derived from other services. FL ST RCP Rule 1.280(b)(5)(A)(iii)(4).
- An expert may be required to produce financial and business records only under the most unusual or compelling circumstances and may not be compelled to compile or produce nonexistent documents. Upon motion, the court may order further discovery by other means, subject to such restrictions as to scope and other provisions pursuant to FL ST RCP Rule 1.280(b)(5)(C) concerning fees and expenses as the court may deem appropriate. FL ST RCP Rule 1.280(b)(5).
- A party may discover facts known or opinions held by an expert who has been retained or specially employed by another party in anticipation of litigation or preparation for trial and who is not expected to be called as a witness at trial, only as provided in FL ST RCP Rule 1.360(b) or upon a showing of exceptional circumstances under which it is impracticable for the party seeking discovery to obtain facts or opinions on the same subject by other means. FL ST RCP Rule 1.280(b)(5)(B).
- Unless manifest injustice would result, the court shall require that the party seeking discovery pay the expert a reasonable fee for time spent in responding to discovery under FL ST RCP Rule 1.280(b)(5)(A) and FL ST RCP Rule 1.280(b)(5)(B); and concerning discovery from an expert obtained under FL ST RCP Rule 1.280(b)(5)(A) the court may require, and concerning discovery obtained under FL ST RCP Rule 1.280(b)(5)(B) shall require, the party seeking discovery to pay the other party a fair part of the fees and expenses reasonably incurred by the latter party in obtaining facts and opinions from the expert. FL ST RCP Rule 1.280(b)(5)(C).
- As used in the Florida Rules of Civil Procedure an expert shall be an expert witness as defined in FL ST RCP Rule 1.390(a). FL ST RCP Rule 1.280(b)(5)(D).

vi. *Claims to privilege or protection.* When a party withholds information otherwise discoverable under the Florida Rules of Civil Procedure by claiming that it is privileged or subject to protection as trial preparation material, the party shall make the claim expressly and shall describe the nature of the documents, communications, or things not produced or disclosed in a manner that, without revealing information itself privileged or protected, will enable other parties to assess the applicability of the privilege or protection. FL ST RCP Rule 1.280(b)(6).

c. *Limitations on discovery of electronically stored information*

i. A person may object to discovery of electronically stored information from sources that the person identifies as not reasonably accessible because of burden or cost. On motion to compel discovery or for a protective order, the person from whom discovery is sought must show that the information sought or the format requested is not reasonably accessible because of undue burden or cost. If that showing is made, the court may nonetheless order the discovery from such sources or in such formats if the requesting party shows good cause. The court may specify

conditions of the discovery, including ordering that some or all of the expenses incurred by the person from whom discovery is sought be paid by the party seeking the discovery. FL ST RCP Rule 1.280(d)(1).

ii. In determining any motion involving discovery of electronically stored information, the court must limit the frequency or extent of discovery otherwise allowed by the Florida Rules of Civil Procedure if it determines that (i) the discovery sought is unreasonably cumulative or duplicative, or can be obtained from another source or in another manner that is more convenient, less burdensome, or less expensive; or (ii) the burden or expense of the discovery outweighs its likely benefit, considering the needs of the case, the amount in controversy, the parties' resources, the importance of the issues at stake in the action, and the importance of the discovery in resolving the issues. FL ST RCP Rule 1.280(d)(2).

d. For information on inadvertent disclosure of privileged materials, see FL ST RCP Rule 1.285.

2. *Notice of deposition*

a. *Upon oral examination.* A party desiring to take the deposition of any person upon oral examination shall give reasonable notice in writing to every other party to the action. The notice shall state the time and place for taking the deposition and the name and address of each person to be examined, if known, and, if the name is not known, a general description sufficient to identify the person or the particular class or group to which the person belongs. If a subpoena duces tecum is to be served on the person to be examined, the designation of the materials to be produced under the subpoena shall be attached to or included in the notice. FL ST RCP Rule 1.310(b)(1).

b. *Upon written examination.* A party desiring to take a deposition upon written questions shall serve a notice stating: (1) the name and address of the person who is to answer them, if known, and, if the name is not known, a general description sufficient to identify the person or the particular class or group to which that person belongs, and (2) the name or descriptive title and address of the officer before whom the deposition is to be taken. FL ST RCP Rule 1.320(a).

3. *When leave of court required.* Leave of court, granted with or without notice, must be obtained only if the plaintiff seeks to take a deposition within thirty (30) days after service of the process and initial pleading upon any defendant, except that leave is not required if a defendant has served a notice of taking deposition or otherwise sought discovery. FL ST RCP Rule 1.310(a).

a. *Exceptions.* Leave of court is not required for the taking of a deposition by plaintiff if the notice states that the person to be examined is about to go out of the state and will be unavailable for examination unless a deposition is taken before expiration of the thirty (30) day period. If a party shows that when served with notice under FL ST RCP Rule 1.310(b) that party was unable through the exercise of diligence to obtain counsel to represent the party at the taking of the deposition, the deposition may not be used against that party. FL ST RCP Rule 1.310(b)(2).

b. *Persons in prison.* The deposition of a person confined in prison may be taken only by leave of court on such terms as the court prescribes. FL ST RCP Rule 1.310(a); FL ST RCP Rule 1.320(a).

4. *Deposition procedure*

a. *Who may take depositions.* Depositions may be taken before any notary public or judicial officer or before any officer authorized by the statutes of Florida to take acknowledgments or proof of executions of deeds or by any person appointed by the court in which the action is pending. FL ST RCP Rule 1.300(a).

i. *In foreign countries.* In a foreign country depositions may be taken: on notice before a person authorized to administer oaths in the place in which the examination is held, either by the law thereof or by the law of Florida or of the United States; before a person commissioned by the court, and a person so commissioned shall have the power by virtue of the commission to administer any necessary oath and take testimony; or pursuant to a letter rogatory. FL ST RCP Rule 1.300(b).

ii. *Selection by stipulation.* If the parties so stipulate in writing, depositions may be taken before any person at any time or place upon any notice and in any manner and when so taken may be used like other depositions. FL ST RCP Rule 1.300(c).

iii. *Persons disqualified.* Unless so stipulated by the parties, no deposition shall be taken before a person who is a relative, employee, attorney, or counsel of any of the parties, is a relative or employee of any of the parties' attorney or counsel, or is financially interested in the action. FL ST RCP Rule 1.300(d).

b. *Depositions before action*

i. *Petition.* A person who desires to perpetuate that person's own testimony or that of another person regarding any matter that may be cognizable in any Florida court may file a verified petition in the circuit court in the county of the residence of any expected adverse party. The petition shall be entitled in the name of the petitioner and shall show:

- That the petitioner expects to be a party to an action cognizable in a court of Florida, but is presently unable to bring the action;
- The subject matter of the expected action and the petitioner's interest therein;
- The facts which the petitioner desires to establish by the proposed testimony and the petitioner's reasons for desiring to perpetuate it;
- The names or a description of the persons the petitioner expects will be adverse parties and their addresses so far as known; and
- The names and addresses of the persons to be examined and the substance of the testimony which the petitioner expects to elicit from each; and shall ask for an order authorizing the petitioner to take the deposition of the persons to be examined named in the petition for the purpose of perpetuating their testimony. FL ST RCP Rule 1.290(a)(1).

ii. *Notice and service.* After submitting the petition, the petitioner must thereafter serve a notice upon each person named in the petition as an expected adverse party, together with a copy of the petition, stating that the petitioner will apply to the court at a time and place named therein for an order described in the petition. At least twenty (20) days before the date of hearing the notice shall be served either within or without the county in the manner provided by law for service of summons, but if such service cannot with due diligence be made upon any expected adverse party named in the petition, the court may make an order for service by publication or otherwise, and shall appoint an attorney for persons not served in the manner provided by law for service of summons who shall represent them, and if they are not otherwise represented, shall cross-examine the deponent. FL ST RCP Rule 1.290(a)(2).

iii. *Order and examination.* If the court is satisfied that the perpetuation of the testimony may prevent a failure or delay of justice, it shall make an order designating or describing the persons whose depositions may be taken and specifying the subject matter of the examination and whether the deposition shall be taken upon oral examination or written interrogatories. The deposition may then be taken in accordance with the rules governing depositions. FL ST RCP Rule 1.290(a)(3).

iv. *Use of deposition.* A deposition taken before an action and in accordance with the procedures above may be used in any action involving the same subject matter subsequently brought in any court. FL ST RCP Rule 1.290(a)(4).

c. *Depositions upon oral examination*

i. *Enlargement of time.* For cause shown the court may enlarge or shorten the time for taking the deposition. FL ST RCP Rule 1.310(b)(3).

ii. *Videotaped depositions.* Any deposition may be recorded by videotape without leave of the court or stipulation of the parties, provided the deposition is taken in accordance with the following:

- *Notice.* A party intending to videotape a deposition shall state in the notice that the deposition is to be videotaped and shall give the name and address of the operator. Any subpoena served on the person to be examined shall state the method or methods for recording the testimony. FL ST RCP Rule 1.310(b)(4)(A).
- *Stenographer.* Videotaped depositions shall also be recorded stenographically, unless all parties agree otherwise. FL ST RCP Rule 1.310(b)(4)(B).

- *Procedure.* At the beginning of the deposition, the officer before whom it is taken shall, on camera: (i) identify the style of the action, (ii) state the date, and (iii) swear the witness. FL ST RCP Rule 1.310(b)(4)(C).
- *Custody of tape and copies.* The attorney for the party requesting the videotaping of the deposition shall take custody of and be responsible for the safeguarding of the videotape, shall permit the viewing of it by the opposing party, and, if requested, shall provide a copy of the videotape at the expense of the party requesting the copy. FL ST RCP Rule 1.310(b)(4)(D).
- *Cost of videotaped depositions.* The party requesting the videotaping shall bear the initial cost of videotaping. FL ST RCP Rule 1.310(b)(4)(E).

iii. *Production of documents.* The notice to a party deponent may be accompanied by a request for the production of documents and tangible things at the taking of the deposition. The procedure of FL ST RCP Rule 1.350 shall apply to the request. FL ST RCP Rule 1.351 provides the exclusive procedure for obtaining documents or things by subpoena from nonparties without deposing the custodian or other person in possession of the documents. FL ST RCP Rule 1.310(b)(5).

iv. *Deposing organizations.* In the notice a party may name as the deponent a public or private corporation, a partnership or association, or a governmental agency, and designate with reasonable particularity the matters on which examination is requested. The organization so named shall designate one or more officers, directors, or managing agents, or other persons who consent to do so, to testify on its behalf and may state the matters on which each person designated will testify. The persons so designated shall testify about matters known or reasonably available to the organization. FL ST RCP Rule 1.310(b)(6).

v. *Depositions by telephone.* On motion the court may order that the testimony at a deposition be taken by telephone. The order may prescribe the manner in which the deposition will be taken. A party may also arrange for a stenographic transcription at that party's own initial expense. FL ST RCP Rule 1.310(b)(7).

vi. *Deposing a minor.* Any minor subpoenaed for testimony shall have the right to be accompanied by a parent or guardian at all times during the taking of testimony notwithstanding the invocation of the rule of sequestration of section FL ST § 90.616, except upon a showing that the presence of a parent or guardian is likely to have a material, negative impact on the credibility or accuracy of the minor's testimony, or that the interests of the parent or guardian are in actual or potential conflict with the interests of the minor. FL ST RCP Rule 1.310(b)(8).

vii. *Examination and cross-examination.* Examination and cross-examination of witnesses may proceed as permitted at the trial. FL ST RCP Rule 1.310(c).

viii. *Oath.* The officer before whom the deposition is to be taken shall put the witness on oath and shall personally, or by someone acting under the officer's direction and in the officer's presence, record the testimony of the witness, except that when a deposition is being taken by telephone, the witness shall be sworn by a person present with the witness who is qualified to administer an oath in that location. FL ST RCP Rule 1.310(c).

ix. *Record of examination.* The deposition testimony must be taken stenographically or recorded by any other means ordered. If requested by one of the parties, the testimony shall be transcribed at the initial cost of the requesting party and prompt notice of the request shall be given to all other parties. FL ST RCP Rule 1.310(c).

x. *Objections.* All objections made at time of the examination to the qualifications of the officer taking the deposition, the manner of taking it, the evidence presented, or the conduct of any party, and any other objection to the proceedings shall be noted by the officer upon the deposition. Any objection during a deposition shall be stated concisely and in a nonargumentative and nonsuggestive manner. A party may instruct a deponent not to answer only when necessary to preserve a privilege, to enforce a limitation on evidence directed by the court, or to present a motion under FL ST RCP Rule 1.310(d). FL ST RCP Rule 1.310(c).

- Otherwise, evidence objected to shall be taken subject to the objections. Instead of participating in the oral examination, parties may serve written questions in a sealed envelope on the party taking the deposition and that party shall transmit them to the officer, who shall propound them to the witness and record the answers verbatim. FL ST RCP Rule 1.310(c).

xi. *Motion to terminate or limit examination.* At any time during the taking of the deposition, on motion of a party or of the deponent and upon a showing that the examination is being conducted in bad faith or in such manner as unreasonably to annoy, embarrass, or oppress the deponent or party, or that improper objections and instructions to a deponent not to answer are being made, the court in which the action is pending or the circuit court where the deposition is being taken may order the officer conducting the examination to cease forthwith from taking the deposition or may limit the scope and manner of the taking of the deposition under the scope of permissible discovery. FL ST RCP Rule 1.310(d).

- If the order terminates the examination, it shall be resumed thereafter only upon the order of the court in which the action is pending. Upon demand of any party or the deponent, the taking of the deposition shall be suspended for the time necessary to make a motion for an order. FL ST RCP Rule 1.310(d).

xii. *Deponent review.* If the testimony is transcribed, the transcript shall be furnished to the witness for examination and shall be read to or by the witness unless the examination and reading are waived by the witness and by the parties. Any changes in form or substance that the witness wants to make shall be listed in writing by the officer with a statement of the reasons given by the witness for making the changes. The changes shall be attached to the transcript. It shall then be signed by the witness unless the parties waived the signing or the witness is ill, cannot be found, or refuses to sign. If the transcript is not signed by the witness within a reasonable time after it is furnished to the witness, the officer shall sign the transcript and state on the transcript the waiver, illness, absence of the witness, or refusal to sign with any reasons given. The deposition may then be used as fully as though signed unless the court holds that the reasons given for the refusal to sign require rejection of the deposition wholly or partly, on motion under FL ST RCP Rule 1.330(d)(4). FL ST RCP Rule 1.310(e).

xiii. *Certification and inspection.* If the deposition is transcribed, the officer shall certify on each copy of the deposition that the witness was duly sworn by the officer and that the deposition is a true record of the testimony given by the witness. Documents and things produced for inspection during the examination of the witness shall be marked for identification and annexed to and returned with the deposition upon the request of a party, and may be inspected and copied by any party, except that the person producing the materials may substitute copies to be marked for identification if that person affords to all parties fair opportunity to verify the copies by comparison with the originals. If the person producing the materials requests their return, the officer shall mark them, give each party an opportunity to inspect and copy them, and return them to the person producing them and the materials may then be used in the same manner as if annexed to and returned with the deposition. FL ST RCP Rule 1.310(f)(1).

xiv. *Copies.* Upon payment of reasonable charges, the officer shall furnish a copy of the deposition to any party or to the deponent. FL ST RCP Rule 1.310(f)(2). A party or witness who does not have a copy of the deposition may obtain it from the officer taking the deposition unless the court orders otherwise. If the deposition is obtained from a person other than the officer, the reasonable cost of reproducing the copies shall be paid to the person by the requesting party or witness. FL ST RCP Rule 1.310(g).

d. *Depositions upon written examination*

i. *Deposing an organization upon written examination.* A deposition upon written questions may be taken of a public or private corporation, a partnership or association, or a governmental agency in accordance with FL ST RCP Rule 1.310(b)(6). FL ST RCP Rule 1.320(a).

ii. *Cross, redirect, and recross questions.* Within thirty (30) days after the notice and written questions are served, a party may serve cross questions upon all other parties. Within ten (10) days after being served with cross questions, a party may serve redirect questions upon all other parties. Within ten (10) days after being served with redirect questions, a party may serve recross questions upon all other parties. The court may for cause shown enlarge or shorten the time. FL ST RCP Rule 1.320(a).

iii. *Procedure.* A copy of the notice and copies of all questions served shall be delivered by the party taking the depositions to the officer designated in the notice, who shall proceed promptly to take the testimony of the witness in the manner provided by FL ST RCP Rule 1.310(c), FL ST RCP Rule 1.310(e), and FL ST RCP Rule 1.310(f) in response to the questions and to prepare the deposition, attaching the copy of the notice and the questions received by the officer. The questions shall not be filed separately from the deposition unless a party seeks to have the court consider the questions before the questions are submitted to the witness. FL ST RCP Rule 1.320(b).

5. *Arbitration and mediation*

   a. *Referral to arbitration and mediation.* Except as hereinafter provided or as otherwise prohibited by law, the presiding judge may enter an order referring all or any part of a contested civil matter to mediation or arbitration. The parties to any contested civil matter may file a written stipulation to mediate or arbitrate any issue between them at any time. Such stipulation shall be incorporated into the order of referral. FL ST RCP Rule 1.700(a).

   b. *Arbitration*

      i. *Exclusions.* A civil action shall be ordered to arbitration or arbitration in conjunction with mediation upon stipulation of the parties. A civil action may be ordered to arbitration or arbitration in conjunction with mediation upon motion of any party or by the court, if the judge determines the action to be of such a nature that arbitration could be of benefit to the litigants or the court. FL ST RCP Rule 1.800.

         - Under no circumstances may the following categories of actions be referred to arbitration: (1) bond estreatures; (2) habeas corpus or other extraordinary writs; (3) bond validations; (4) civil or criminal contempt; (5) such other matters as may be specified by order of the chief judge in the circuit. FL ST RCP Rule 1.800.

      ii. For more information regarding arbitration, please see FL ST RCP Rule 1.810; FL ST RCP Rule 1.820; FL ST RCP Rule 1.830.

   c. *Mediation.* For more information regarding mediation, please see FL ST RCP Rule 1.710; FL ST RCP Rule 1.720; FL ST RCP Rule 1.730; and FL ST RCP Rule 1.750.

6. *Rules of court*

   a. *Rules of civil procedure.* The Florida Rules of Civil Procedure apply to all actions of a civil nature and all special statutory proceedings in the circuit courts and county courts except those to which the Florida Probate Rules, the Florida Family Law Rules of Procedure, or the Small Claims Rules apply. FL ST RCP Rule 1.010.

      i. The form, content, procedure, and time for pleading in all special statutory proceedings shall be as prescribed by the statutes governing the proceeding unless the Florida Rules of Civil Procedure specifically provide to the contrary. FL ST RCP Rule 1.010.

      ii. The Florida Rules of Civil Procedure shall be construed to secure the just, speedy, and inexpensive determination of every action. FL ST RCP Rule 1.010.

   b. *Rules of judicial administration.* The Florida Rules of Judicial Administration shall apply to administrative matters in all courts to which the Florida Rules of Judicial Administration are applicable by their terms. The Florida Rules of Judicial Administration shall be construed to secure the speedy and inexpensive determination of every proceeding to which they are applicable. The Florida Rules of Judicial Administration shall supersede all conflicting rules and statutes. FL ST J ADMIN Rule 2.110.

D. Documents

1. *Deposition upon oral or written examination*
   a. *Required documents*
      i. *Notice of deposition.* Please see the General Requirements section of this document for information on the content of a notice of deposition upon oral examination.
      ii. *Certificate of service.* A certificate of service of the interrogatories shall be filed, giving the date of service and the name of the party to whom they were directed. FL ST RCP Rule 1.340(e). When any attorney certifies in substance: "I certify that a copy hereof has been furnished to (here insert name or names and addresses used for service) by (e-mail) (delivery) (mail) (fax) on .... (date) ....______________ Attorney" the certificate is taken as prima facie proof of such service in compliance with FL ST J ADMIN Rule 2.516. FL ST J ADMIN Rule 2.516(f).
   b. *Supplemental documents*
      i. *Motion for leave to take deposition.* See the Timing section for information on when leave is required.
      ii. *Subpoena.* See the Timing section for requirements of when a subpoena is required.
      iii. *Request for production of documents.* See the General Requirements section for further information.

E. Format

1. *Documents; Type and size.* Documents subject to the exceptions set forth in FL ST J ADMIN Rule 2.525(d) shall be filed on recycled paper measuring eight and one half by eleven (8 1/2 by 11) inches. For purposes of FL ST J ADMIN Rule 2.520, paper is recycled if it contains a minimum content of fifty (50) percent waste paper. Xerographic reduction of legal-size (eight and one half by fourteen (8 1/2 by 14) inches) documents to letter size (eight and one half by eleven (8 1/2 by 11) inches) is prohibited. All other documents filed by electronic transmission shall be filed in a format capable of being printed in a format consistent with the provisions of FL ST J ADMIN Rule 2.250. FL ST J ADMIN Rule 2.520(b).
   a. *Exhibits.* Any exhibit or attachment filed with pleadings or papers may be filed in its original size. FL ST J ADMIN Rule 2.520(c).
   b. *Recording space.* On all papers and documents prepared and filed by the court or by any party to a proceeding which are to be recorded in the public records of any county, including but not limited to final money judgments and notices of lis pendens, a three (3) inch by three (3) inch space at the top right-hand corner on the first page and a one (1) inch by three (3) inch space at the top right-hand corner on each subsequent page shall be left blank and reserved for use by the clerk of court. FL ST J ADMIN Rule 2.520(d).
      i. *Exceptions to recording space.* Any papers or documents created by persons or entities over which the filing party has no control, including but not limited to wills, codicils, trusts, or other testamentary documents; documents prepared or executed by any public officer; documents prepared, executed, acknowledged, or proved outside of the State of Florida; or documents created by State or Federal government agencies, may be filed without the space required by FL ST J ADMIN Rule 2.520. FL ST J ADMIN Rule 2.520(e).
   c. *Noncompliance.* No clerk of court is permitted to refuse to file any document or paper because of noncompliance with the Florida Rules of Judicial Administration. However, upon request of the clerk of court, noncomplying documents must be resubmitted in accordance with the formatting rules. FL ST J ADMIN Rule 2.520(f).
2. *Caption.* Every pleading, motion, order, judgment, or other paper shall have a caption containing the name of the court, the file number, and except for in rem proceedings, including forfeiture proceedings, the name of the first party on each side with an appropriate indication of other parties, and a designation identifying the party filing it and its nature or the nature of the order, as the case may be. In any in rem proceeding, every pleading, motion, order, judgment, or other paper shall have a caption containing the name of the court, the file number, the style "In re" (followed by the name or general description of the

property), and a designation of the person or entity filing it and its nature or the nature of the order, as the case may be. In an in rem forfeiture proceeding, the style shall be "In re forfeiture of" (followed by the name of the general description of the property). All papers filed in the action shall be styled in such a manner as to indicate clearly the subject matter of the paper and the party requesting or obtaining relief. FL ST RCP Rule 1.100(c)(1).

3. *Writing and written defined.* Writing or written means a document containing information, an application, or a stipulation. FL ST RCP Rule 1.080(c).
4. *Rule abbreviations*
   a. The Florida Rules of Civil Procedure and shall be abbreviated as Fla.R.Civ.P. FL ST RCP Rule 1.010.
   b. The Florida Rules of Judicial Administration shall be abbreviated as Fla. R. Jud. Admin. FL ST J ADMIN Rule 2.110.
5. *Nonverification.* Except when otherwise specifically provided by the Florida Rules of Civil Procedure or an applicable statute, every pleading or other document of a party represented by an attorney need not be verified or accompanied by an affidavit. FL ST RCP Rule 1.030; FL ST J ADMIN Rule 2.515(a).
6. *Attorney signature*
   a. *Attorney signature.* Every pleading and other document of a party represented by an attorney shall be signed by at least one (1) attorney of record in that attorney's individual name whose current record Florida Bar address, telephone number, including area code, primary e-mail address and secondary e-mail addresses, if any, and Florida Bar number shall be stated, and who shall be duly licensed to practice law in Florida or who shall have received permission to appear in the particular case as provided in FL ST J ADMIN Rule 2.510. FL ST J ADMIN Rule 2.515(a).
      i. The attorney may be required by the court to give the address of, and to vouch for the attorney's authority to represent, the party. FL ST J ADMIN Rule 2.515(a).
      ii. The signature of an attorney shall constitute a certificate by the attorney that the attorney has read the pleading or other document; that to the best of the attorney's knowledge, information, and belief there is good ground to support it; and that it is not interposed for delay. FL ST J ADMIN Rule 2.515(a).
      iii. If a pleading is not signed or is signed with intent to defeat the purpose of FL ST J ADMIN Rule 2.515, it may be stricken and the action may proceed as though the pleading or other document had not been served. FL ST J ADMIN Rule 2.515(a).
   b. *Pro se litigant signature.* A party who is not represented by an attorney shall sign any pleading or other paper and state the party's address and telephone number, including area code. FL ST J ADMIN Rule 2.515(b).
   c. *Form of signature*
      i. The signatures required on pleadings and documents by FL ST J ADMIN Rule 2.515(a) and FL ST J ADMIN Rule 2.515(b) may be:
         - Original signatures;
         - Original signatures that have been reproduced by electronic means, such as on electronically transmitted documents or photocopied documents;
         - Electronic signatures using the "/s/," "s/," or "/s" formats by or at the direction of the person signing; or
         - Any other signature format authorized by general law, so long as the clerk where the proceeding is pending has the capability of receiving and has obtained approval from the Supreme Court of Florida to accept pleadings and documents with that signature format. FL ST J ADMIN Rule 2.515(c)(1).
      ii. An attorney, party, or other person who files a pleading or paper by electronic transmission that does not contain the original signature of that attorney, party, or other person shall file that identical pleading or paper in paper form containing an original signature of that attorney, party,

or other person (hereinafter called the follow-up filing) immediately thereafter. The follow-up filing is not required if the Supreme Court of Florida has entered an order directing the clerk of court to discontinue accepting the follow-up filing. FL ST J ADMIN Rule 2.515(c)(2).

7. *Forms*
   a. *Process.* The forms of process, notice of lis pendens, and notice of action provided in the Florida Rules of Civil Procedure are sufficient. Variations from the forms do not void process or notices that are otherwise sufficient. FL ST RCP Rule 1.900(a).
   b. *Other forms.* The other forms provided in the Florida Rules of Civil Procedure are sufficient for the matters that are covered by them. So long as the substance is expressed without prolixity, the forms may be varied to meet the facts of a particular case. FL ST RCP Rule 1.900(b).
   c. *Formal matters.* Captions, except for the designation of the paper, are omitted from the forms provided in the Florida Rules of Civil Procedure. A general form of caption is the first form provided. Signatures are omitted from pleadings and motions. FL ST RCP Rule 1.900(c).
8. *Notices to persons with disabilities.* All notices of court proceedings to be held in a public facility, and all process compelling appearance at such proceedings, shall include the following statement in bold face, fourteen (14) point Times New Roman or Courier font: "If you are a person with a disability who needs any accommodation in order to participate in this proceeding, you are entitled, at no cost to you, to the provision of certain assistance. Please contact [identify applicable court personnel by name, address, and telephone number] at least seven (7) days before your scheduled court appearance, or immediately upon receiving this notification if the time before the scheduled appearance is less than seven (7) days; if you are hearing or voice impaired, call 711." FL ST J ADMIN Rule 2.540(c)(1).
9. *Minimization of the filing of sensitive information*
   a. *Limitations for court filings.* Unless authorized by FL ST J ADMIN Rule 2.425(b), statute, another rule of court, or the court orders otherwise, designated sensitive information filed with the court must be limited to the following format:
      i. The initials of a person known to be a minor;
      ii. The year of birth of a person's birth date;
      iii. No portion of any: Social security number, Bank account number, Credit card account number, Charge account number, or Debit account number;
      iv. The last four digits of any: Taxpayer identification number (TIN), Employee identification number, Driver's license number, Passport number, Telephone number, Financial account number, except as set forth in FL ST J ADMIN Rule 2.425(a)(3), Brokerage account number, Insurance policy account number, Loan account number, Customer account number, or Patient or health care number;
      v. A truncated version of any: Email address, Computer user name, Password, or Personal identification number (PIN); and
      vi. A truncated version of any other sensitive information as provided by court order. FL ST J ADMIN Rule 2.425(a).
   b. *Exceptions.* FL ST J ADMIN Rule 2.425(a) does not apply to the following:
      i. An account number which identifies the property alleged to be the subject of a proceeding;
      ii. The record of an administrative or agency proceeding;
      iii. The record in appellate or review proceedings;
      iv. The birth date of a minor whenever the birth date is necessary for the court to establish or maintain subject matter jurisdiction;
      v. The name of a minor in any order relating to parental responsibility, time-sharing, or child support;
      vi. The name of a minor in any document or order affecting the minor's ownership of real property;
      vii. The birth date of a party in a writ of attachment or notice to payor;

viii. In traffic and criminal proceedings: a pro se filing; a court filing that is related to a criminal matter or investigation and that is prepared before the filing of a criminal charge or is not filed as part of any docketed criminal case; an arrest or search warrant or any information in support thereof; a charging document and an affidavit or other documents filed in support of any charging document, including any driving records; a statement of particulars; discovery material introduced into evidence or otherwise filed with the court; and all information necessary for the proper issuance and execution of a subpoena duces tecum;

ix. Information used by the clerk for case maintenance purposes or the courts for case management purposes; and

x. Information which is relevant and material to an issue before the court. FL ST J ADMIN Rule 2.425(b).

c. *Remedies.* Upon motion by a party or interested person or sua sponte by the court, the court may order remedies, sanctions or both for a violation of FL ST J ADMIN Rule 2.425(a). Following notice and an opportunity to respond, the court may impose sanctions if such filing was not made in good faith. FL ST J ADMIN Rule 2.425(c).

d. *Motions not restricted.* FL ST J ADMIN Rule 2.425 does not restrict a party's right to move for protective order, to move to file documents under seal, or to request a determination of the confidentiality of records. FL ST J ADMIN Rule 2.425(d).

i. For more information regarding sealing court records, please see FL ST 4 J CIR 2006-05.

e. *Application.* FL ST J ADMIN Rule 2.425 does not affect the application of constitutional provisions, statutes, or rules of court regarding confidential information or access to public information. FL ST J ADMIN Rule 2.425(e).

F. Filing and Service Requirements

1. *Court filing of documents and discovery.* Information obtained during discovery shall not be filed with the court until such time as it is filed for good cause. The requirement of good cause is satisfied only where the filing of the information is allowed or required by another applicable rule of procedure or by court order. All filings of discovery documents shall comply with FL ST J ADMIN Rule 2.425. The court shall have the authority to impose sanctions for violation of FL ST RCP Rule 1.280. FL ST RCP Rule 1.280(g).

a. *Filing of copies*

i. No depositions in any civil case shall be filed with the clerk of court except as hereafter permitted. FL ST 4 J CIR 2012-03.

ii. Parties who wish to present deposition evidence at any hearing or trial shall bring the original or certified copy to court for the judge's use and shall provide a copy to opposing counsel, if needed, and as required by the Florida Rules of Civil Procedure. FL ST 4 J CIR 2012-03.

iii. After completion of the hearing or trial at which deposition evidence has been presented, any party may file the original or certified copy of the deposition or any relevant and material pat thereof, with the clerk of court. FL ST 4 J CIR 2012-03.

iv. A copy of a deposition may be filed only under the following circumstances:

- It may be filed in compliance with FL ST J ADMIN Rule 2.425 and FL ST RCP Rule 1.280(f) by a party or the witness when the contents of the deposition must be considered by the court on any matter pending before the court. Prompt notice of the filing of the deposition shall be given to all parties unless notice is waived. A party filing the deposition shall furnish a copy of the deposition or the part being filed to other parties unless the party already has a copy. FL ST RCP Rule 1.310(f)(3)(A).
- If the court determines that a deposition previously taken is necessary for the decision of a matter pending before the court, the court may order that a copy be filed by any party at the initial cost of the party, and the filing party shall comply with FL ST J ADMIN Rule 2.425 and FL ST RCP Rule 1.280(f). FL ST RCP Rule 1.310(f)(3)(B).

2. *Filing requirements.* All original documents must be filed with the court either before service or

immediately thereafter, unless otherwise provided for by general law or other rules. If the original of any bond or other document is not placed in the court file, a certified copy must be so placed by the clerk. FL ST J ADMIN Rule 2.516(d). All documents shall be filed in conformity with the requirements of FL ST J ADMIN Rule 2.525. FL ST RCP Rule 1.080(b). All documents filed in any court shall be filed by electronic transmission in accordance with FL ST J ADMIN Rule 2.525. "Documents" means pleadings, motions, petitions, memoranda, briefs, notices, exhibits, declarations, affidavits, orders, judgments, decrees, writs, opinions, and any other paper or writing submitted to a court. FL ST J ADMIN Rule 2.520(a). All documents that are court records, as defined in FL ST J ADMIN Rule 2.430(a)(1), must be filed by electronic transmission, provided that: (1) the clerk has the ability to accept and retain such documents; (2) the clerk or the chief judge of the circuit has requested permission to accept documents filed by electronic transmission; and (3) the supreme court has entered an order granting permission to the clerk to accept documents filed by electronic transmission. FL ST J ADMIN Rule 2.525(c)(1).

a. *Definition.* "Electronic transmission of documents" means the sending of information by electronic signals to, by or from a court or clerk, which when received can be transformed and stored or transmitted on paper, microfilm, magnetic storage device, optical imaging system, CD-ROM, flash drive, other electronic data storage system, server, case maintenance system ("CM"), electronic court filing ("ECF") system, statewide or local electronic portal ("e-portal"), or other electronic record keeping system authorized by the supreme court in a format sufficient to communicate the information on the original document in a readable format. Electronic transmission of documents includes electronic mail ("e-mail") and any internet-based transmission procedure, and may include procedures allowing for documents to be signed or verified by electronic means. FL ST J ADMIN Rule 2.525(a).

   i. The filing of documents with the court as required by the Florida Rules of Judicial Administration must be made by filing them with the clerk in accordance with FL ST J ADMIN Rule 2.525, except that the judge may permit documents to be filed with the judge, in which event the judge must note the filing date before him or her on the documents and transmit them to the clerk. The date of filing is that shown on the face of the document by the judge's notation or the clerk's time stamp, whichever is earlier. FL ST J ADMIN Rule 2.516(e).

b. *Application.* Any court or clerk of the court may accept the electronic transmission of documents for filing after the clerk, together with input from the chief judge of the circuit, has obtained approval of the procedures and program for doing so from the Supreme Court of Florida. FL ST J ADMIN Rule 2.525(b).

c. *Exceptions*

   i. Paper documents and other submissions may be manually submitted to the clerk or court:

      - When the clerk does not have the ability to accept and retain documents by electronic filing or has not had ECF Procedures approved by the supreme court;
      - For filing by any self-represented party or any self-represented nonparty unless specific ECF Procedures provide a means to file documents electronically. However, any self-represented nonparty that is a governmental or public agency and any other agency, partnership, corporation, or business entity acting on behalf of any governmental or public agency may file documents by electronic transmission if such entity has the capability of filing documents electronically;
      - For filing by attorneys excused from e-mail service in accordance with FL ST J ADMIN Rule 2.516(b);
      - When submitting evidentiary exhibits or filing non-documentary materials;
      - When the filing involves documents in excess of twenty-five (25) megabytes (25MB) in size. For such filings, documents may be transmitted using an electronic storage medium that the clerk has the ability to accept, which may include a CD-ROM, flash drive, or similar storage medium;
      - When filed in open court, as permitted by the court;
      - When paper filing is permitted by any approved statewide or local ECF procedures; and

- If any court determines that justice so requires. FL ST J ADMIN Rule 2.525(d).

ii. Any document in paper form submitted under FL ST J ADMIN Rule 2.525(d) is filed when it is received by the clerk or court and the clerk shall immediately thereafter convert any filed paper document to an electronic document. "Convert to an electronic document" means optically capturing an image of a paper document and using character recognition software to recover as much of the document's text as practicable and then indexing and storing the document in the official court file. FL ST J ADMIN Rule 2.525(c)(4).

iii. Any storage medium submitted under FL ST J ADMIN Rule 2.525(d)(5) is filed when received by the clerk or court and the clerk shall immediately thereafter transfer the electronic documents from the storage device to the official court file. FL ST J ADMIN Rule 2.525(c)(5).

iv. If the filer of any paper document authorized under FL ST J ADMIN Rule 2.525(d) provides a self-addressed, postage-paid envelope for return of the paper document after it is converted to electronic form by the clerk, the clerk shall place the paper document in the envelope and deposit it in the mail. Except when a paper document is required to be maintained, the clerk may recycle any filed paper document that is not to be returned to the filer. FL ST J ADMIN Rule 2.525(c)(6).

v. The clerk may convert any paper document filed before the effective date of FL ST J ADMIN Rule 2.525 to an electronic document. Unless the clerk is required to maintain the paper document, if the paper document has been converted to an electronic document by the clerk, the paper document is no longer part of the official court file and may be removed and recycled. FL ST J ADMIN Rule 2.525(c)(7).

d. *Official court file.* For information on what constitutes the official court file, please see FL ST J ADMIN Rule 2.525(c)(2), FL ST J ADMIN Rule 2.525(c)(3).

e. *Administration.* All attorneys, parties, or other persons using this rule to file documents are required to make arrangements with the court or clerk for the payment of any charges authorized by general law or the supreme court before filing any document by electronic transmission. FL ST J ADMIN Rule 2.525(f)(2).

f. *Filing date.* The filing date for an electronically transmitted document is the date and time that such filing is acknowledged by an electronic stamp or otherwise, pursuant to any procedure set forth in any ECF Procedures approved by the supreme court, or the date the last page of such filing is received by the court or clerk. FL ST J ADMIN Rule 2.525(f)(3).

g. *Accessibility.* All documents transmitted in any electronic form under FL ST J ADMIN Rule 2.525 must comply with the accessibility requirements of FL ST J ADMIN Rule 2.526. FL ST J ADMIN Rule 2.525(g).

3. *Service requirements.* Every pleading subsequent to the initial pleading, all orders, and every other document filed in the action must be served in conformity with the requirements of FL ST J ADMIN Rule 2.516. FL ST RCP Rule 1.080(a).

a. *Service; When required.* Unless the court otherwise orders, or a statute or supreme court administrative order specifies a different means of service, every pleading subsequent to the initial pleading and every other document filed in any court proceeding, except applications for witness subpoenas and documents served by formal notice or required to be served in the manner provided for service of formal notice, must be served in accordance with FL ST J ADMIN Rule 2.516 on each party. No service need be made on parties against whom a default has been entered, except that pleadings asserting new or additional claims against them must be served in the manner provided for service of summons. FL ST J ADMIN Rule 2.516(a).

b. *Service; How made.* When service is required or permitted to be made upon a party represented by an attorney, service must be made upon the attorney unless service upon the party is ordered by the court. FL ST J ADMIN Rule 2.516(b).

i. *Service by electronic mail ("e-mail").* All documents required or permitted to be served on another party must be served by e-mail, unless FL ST J ADMIN Rule 2.516 otherwise provides. When, in addition to service by e-mail, the sender also utilizes another means of service

provided for in FL ST J ADMIN Rule 2.516(b)(2), any differing time limits and other provisions applicable to that other means of service control. FL ST J ADMIN Rule 2.516(b)(1). Any document electronically transmitted to a court or clerk must also be served on all parties and interested persons in accordance with the applicable rules of court. FL ST J ADMIN Rule 2.525(e)(2).

- *Service on attorneys.* Upon appearing in a proceeding, an attorney must serve a designation of a primary e-mail address and may designate no more than two (2) secondary e-mail addresses. Thereafter, service must be directed to all designated e-mail addresses in that proceeding. Every document filed by an attorney thereafter must include the primary e-mail address of that attorney and any secondary e-mail addresses. If an attorney does not designate any e-mail address for service, documents may be served on that attorney at the e-mail address on record with The Florida Bar. FL ST J ADMIN Rule 2.516(b)(1)(A).
- *Exception to e-mail service on attorneys.* Service by an attorney on another attorney must be made by e-mail unless excused by the court. Upon motion by an attorney demonstrating that the attorney has no e-mail account and lacks access to the Internet at the attorney's office, the court may excuse the attorney from the requirements of e-mail service. Service on and by an attorney excused by the court from e-mail service must be by the means provided in FL ST J ADMIN Rule 2.516(b)(2). FL ST J ADMIN Rule 2.516(b)(1)(B).
- *Service on and by parties not represented by an attorney.* Any party not represented by an attorney may serve a designation of a primary e-mail address and also may designate no more than two (2) secondary e-mail addresses to which service must be directed in that proceeding by the means provided in FL ST J ADMIN Rule 2.516(b)(1). If a party not represented by an attorney does not designate an e-mail address for service in a proceeding, service on and by that party must be by the means provided in FL ST J ADMIN Rule 2.516(b)(2). FL ST J ADMIN Rule 2.516(b)(1)(C).
- *Time of service.* Service by e-mail is complete when it is sent. FL ST J ADMIN Rule 2.516(b)(1)(D). An e-mail is deemed served on the date it is sent. FL ST J ADMIN Rule 2.516(b)(1)(D)(i). If the sender learns that the e-mail did not reach the address of the person to be served, the sender must immediately send another copy by e-mail, or by a means authorized by FL ST J ADMIN Rule 2.516(b)(2). FL ST J ADMIN Rule 2.516(b)(1)(D)(ii). E-mail service is treated as service by mail for the computation of time. FL ST J ADMIN Rule 2.516(b)(1)(D)(iii).

ii. *Format of e-mail for service.* Service of a document by e-mail is made by attaching a copy of the document in PDF format to an e-mail sent to all addresses designated by the attorney or party. FL ST J ADMIN Rule 2.516(b)(1)(E).

- All documents served by e-mail must be attached to an e-mail message containing a subject line beginning with the words "SERVICE OF COURT DOCUMENT" in all capital letters, followed by the case number of the proceeding in which the documents are being served. FL ST J ADMIN Rule 2.516(b)(1)(E)(i).
- The body of the e-mail must identify the court in which the proceeding is pending, the case number, the name of the initial party on each side, the title of each document served with that e-mail, and the sender's name and telephone number. FL ST J ADMIN Rule 2.516(b)(1)(E)(ii).
- Any document served by e-mail may be signed by the "/s/" format, as long as the filed original is signed in accordance with the applicable rule of procedure. FL ST J ADMIN Rule 2.516(b)(1)(E)(iii).
- Any e-mail which, together with its attached documents, exceeds five megabytes (5MB) in size, must be divided and sent as separate e-mails, no one of which may exceed five megabytes (5MB) in size and each of which must be sequentially numbered in the subject line. FL ST J ADMIN Rule 2.516(b)(1)(E)(iv).

iii. *Service by other means.* In addition to, and not in lieu of, service by e-mail, service may also be

made upon attorneys by any of the means specified in FL ST J ADMIN Rule 2.516(b)(2). Service on and by all parties who are not represented by an attorney and who do not designate an e-mail address, and on and by all attorneys excused from e-mail service, must be made by delivering a copy of the document or by mailing it to the party or attorney at their last known address or, if no address is known, by leaving it with the clerk of the court. Service by mail is complete upon mailing. Delivery of a copy within FL ST J ADMIN Rule 2.516 is complete upon:

- Handing it to the attorney or to the party,
- Leaving it at the attorney's or party's office with a clerk or other person in charge thereof,
- If there is no one in charge, leaving it in a conspicuous place therein,
- If the office is closed or the person to be served has no office, leaving it at the person's usual place of abode with some person of his or her family above fifteen (15) years of age and informing such person of the contents, or
- Transmitting it by facsimile to the attorney's or party's office with a cover sheet containing the sender's name, firm, address, telephone number, and facsimile number, and the number of pages transmitted. When service is made by facsimile, a copy must also be served by any other method permitted by FL ST J ADMIN Rule 2.516. Facsimile service occurs when transmission is complete. FL ST J ADMIN Rule 2.516(b)(2)(A) through FL ST J ADMIN Rule 2.516(b)(2)(E).
- Service by delivery after 5:00 p.m. must be deemed to have been made by mailing on the date of delivery. FL ST J ADMIN Rule 2.516(b)(2)(F).

c. *Service; Numerous defendants.* In actions when the parties are unusually numerous, the court may regulate the service contemplated by the Florida Rules of Judicial Administration on motion or on its own initiative in such manner as may be found to be just and reasonable. FL ST J ADMIN Rule 2.516(c).

d. *Service by clerk.* Service of notices and other documents required to be made by the clerk must also be done as provided in FL ST J ADMIN Rule 2.516(b). FL ST J ADMIN Rule 2.516(g).

G. Hearings

1. There is no hearing required or contemplated with regard to responses to requests for admission in the Florida Rules of Civil Procedure.

H. Forms

1. Official Notice of Deposition Forms for Florida

a. Caption. FL ST RCP Form 1.901.

2. Notice of Deposition Forms for Florida

a. Form for motion by plaintiff for leave to take deposition within 20-day period. FL-RCPF R 1.310(6).

b. Form for order on motion for leave to take deposition within 20-day period. FL-RCPF R 1.310(8).

c. Notice of examination; Time and place. FL-RCPF R 1.310(9).

d. Nonparty witness, subpoena required. FL-RCPF R 1.310(10).

e. Form for notice to take deposition on oral examination. FL-RCPF R 1.310(11).

f. Form for notice of taking multiple depositions. FL-RCPF R 1.310(11.1).

g. Form for notice of taking deposition and examination of documents. FL-RCPF R 1.310(12).

h. Form for notice of taking video deposition duces tecum. FL-RCPF R 1.310(13).

i. Form for motion to modify time for taking deposition. FL-RCPF R 1.310(14).

j. Form for motion to take deposition by telephone. FL-RCPF R 1.310(16).

k. Form for order permitting deposition by telephone. FL-RCPF R 1.310(17).

l. Form for notice of taking deposition by telephone. FL-RCPF R 1.310(18).

m. Form for notice of deposition upon written questions. FL-RCPF R 1.320(2).
n. Form of questions. FL-RCPF R 1.320(3).
o. Form of cross-questions. FL-RCPF R 1.320(4).
p. Form for objection to form of written questions. FL-RCPF R 1.320(6).

I. Checklist

(I) ❑ Matters to be considered by deposing party (oral depositions)
- (a) ❑ Required documents
  - (1) ❑ Notice of deposition
  - (2) ❑ Certificate of service
- (b) ❑ Supplemental documents
  - (1) ❑ Motion for leave to request deposition
  - (2) ❑ Subpoena
  - (3) ❑ Request for production of documents
- (c) ❑ Time for service of notice of deposition
  - (1) ❑ After commencement of action
  - (2) ❑ Within thirty (30) days after service of initial pleadings by leave of court only

(II) ❑ Matters to be considered by deponent (oral depositions)
- (a) ❑ Required documents
  - (1) ❑ Production of documents (if subpoenaed)

(III) ❑ Matters to be considered by deposing party (depositions by written questions)
- (a) ❑ Required documents
  - (1) ❑ Notice of deposition
  - (2) ❑ Written questions
  - (3) ❑ Certificate of service
- (b) ❑ Supplemental documents
  - (1) ❑ Motion for leave to request deposition
  - (2) ❑ Subpoena
  - (3) ❑ Request for production of documents
- (c) ❑ Time for service of direct and redirect questions
  - (1) ❑ Within ten (10) days after being served with cross questions, a party may serve redirect questions upon all other parties
  - (2) ❑ Objections to the form of the question must be served within the time for service of redirect questions or ten (10) days after service of recross questions

(IV) ❑ Matters to be considered by deponent (depositions by written questions)
- (a) ❑ Required documents
  - (1) ❑ Cross questions, with certificate of service
  - (2) ❑ Recross questions with certificate of service
- (b) ❑ Time for service of cross and recross questions
  - (1) ❑ Within thirty (30) days after the notice and written questions are served, a party may serve cross questions upon all other parties
  - (2) ❑ Within ten (10) days after being served with redirect questions, a party may serve recross questions upon all other parties

(3) ❑ Objections to the form of the questions must be served within the time for serving succeeding questions

SIXTH JUDICIAL CIRCUIT

Pleadings
Complaint

Document Last Updated January 2013

A. Applicable Rules

1. *State rules*
   a. Nonverification of pleadings. FL ST RCP Rule 1.030.
   b. When action commenced. FL ST RCP Rule 1.050.
   c. Process. FL ST RCP Rule 1.070.
   d. Service and filing of pleadings, orders, and documents. FL ST RCP Rule 1.080.
   e. Time. FL ST RCP Rule 1.090.
   f. Pleadings and motions. FL ST RCP Rule 1.100; FL ST RCP Rule 1.110; FL ST RCP Rule 1.120; FL ST RCP Rule 1.130; FL ST RCP Rule 1.170; FL ST RCP Rule 1.430.
   g. Relief from judgment, decrees, or orders. FL ST RCP Rule 1.540.
   h. Forms. FL ST RCP Rule 1.900.
   i. Minimization of the filing of sensitive information. FL ST J ADMIN Rule 2.425.
   j. Retention of court records. FL ST J ADMIN Rule 2.430.
   k. Foreign attorneys. FL ST J ADMIN Rule 2.510.
   l. Signature of attorneys and parties. FL ST J ADMIN Rule 2.515.
   m. Paper. FL ST J ADMIN Rule 2.520.
   n. Electronic filing. FL ST J ADMIN Rule 2.525.
   o. Accessibility of information and technology. FL ST J ADMIN Rule 2.526.
   p. Requests for accommodations by persons with disabilities. FL ST J ADMIN Rule 2.540.
   q. Service. FL ST § 48.011; FL ST § 48.021; FL ST § 48.031; FL ST § 48.041; FL ST § 48.042; FL ST § 48.051; FL ST § 48.061; FL ST § 48.071; FL ST § 48.081; FL ST § 48.091; FL ST § 48.101; FL ST § 48.111; FL ST § 48.121; FL ST § 48.131; FL ST § 48.141; FL ST § 48.151; FL ST § 48.161; FL ST § 48.171; FL ST § 48.181; FL ST § 48.183; FL ST § 48.19; FL ST § 48.193; FL ST § 48.194; FL ST § 48.20; FL ST § 48.21; FL ST § 48.25; FL ST § 48.31; FL ST § 49.011; FL ST § 49.021; FL ST § 49.031; FL ST § 49.041; FL ST § 49.051; FL ST § 49.061; FL ST § 49.071; FL ST § 49.08; FL ST § 49.09; FL ST § 49.10; FL ST § 49.11; FL ST § 49.12; FL ST § 50.011; FL ST § 50.021; FL ST § 50.031; FL ST § 50.041; FL ST § 50.051; FL ST § 50.061.
   r. Fees. FL ST § 57.081; FL ST § 57.085; FL ST § 28.241; FL ST § 34.041.
2. *Local rules*
   a. Assignment of cases. FL ST 6 J CIR LOCAL Rule 3.
   b. Pretrial conferences. FL ST 6 J CIR PA/PI-CIR-98-49.
   c. Standards of professional courtesy. FL ST 6 J CIR 2009-066 PA/PI-CIR.
   d. Arbitration and mediation program circuit civil and family cases. FL ST 6 J CIR PA/PI-CIR-96-63; FL ST 6 J CIR 2011-006 PA/PI-CIR.

B. Timing

1. *Commencement of an action.* Every action of a civil nature shall be deemed commenced when the

complaint or petition is filed except that ancillary proceedings shall be deemed commenced when the writ is issued or the pleading setting forth the claim of the party initiating the action is filed. FL ST RCP Rule 1.050.

2. *Summons; Time limit.* If service of the initial process and initial pleading is not made upon a defendant within one hundred twenty (120) days after filing of the initial pleading directed to that defendant the court, on its own initiative after notice or on motion, shall direct that service be effected within a specified time or shall dismiss the action without prejudice or drop that defendant as a party; provided that if the plaintiff shows good cause or excusable neglect for the failure, the court shall extend the time for service for an appropriate period. FL ST RCP Rule 1.070(j).
3. *Computation of time*
   a. *Generally.* Computation of time shall be governed by FL ST J ADMIN Rule 2.514. FL ST RCP Rule 1.090(a). The following rules apply in computing time periods specified in any rule of procedure, local rule, court order, or statute that does not specify a method of computing time. FL ST J ADMIN Rule 2.514(a).
      i. *Period stated in days or a longer unit.* When the period is stated in days or a longer unit of time (A) exclude the day of the event that triggers the period; (B) count every day, including intermediate Saturdays, Sundays, and legal holidays; and (C) include the last day of the period, but if the last day is a Saturday, Sunday, or legal holiday, or falls within any period of time extended through an order of the chief justice under FL ST J ADMIN Rule 2.205(a)(2)(B)(iv), the period continues to run until the end of the next day that is not a Saturday, Sunday, or legal holiday and does not fall within any period of time extended through an order of the chief justice. FL ST J ADMIN Rule 2.514(a)(1).
      ii. *Period stated in hours.* When the period is stated in hours (A) begin counting immediately on the occurrence of the event that triggers the period; (B) count every hour, including hours during intermediate Saturdays, Sundays, and legal holidays; and (C) if the period would end on a Saturday, Sunday, or legal holiday, or during any period of time extended through an order of the chief justice under FL ST J ADMIN Rule 2.205(a)(2)(B)(iv), the period continues to run until the same time on the next day that is not a Saturday, Sunday, or legal holiday and does not fall within any period of time extended through an order of the chief justice. FL ST J ADMIN Rule 2.514(a)(2).
      iii. *Period stated in days less than seven (7) days.* When the period stated in days is less than seven (7) days, intermediate Saturdays, Sundays, and legal holidays shall be excluded in the computation. FL ST J ADMIN Rule 2.514(a)(3).
      iv. *"Last day" defined.* Unless a different time is set by a statute, local rule, or court order, the last day ends (A) for electronic filing or for service by any means, at midnight; and (B) for filing by other means, when the clerk's office is scheduled to close. FL ST J ADMIN Rule 2.514(a)(4).
      v. *"Next day" defined.* The "next day" is determined by continuing to count forward when the period is measured after an event and backward when measured before an event. FL ST J ADMIN Rule 2.514(a)(5).
      vi. *"Legal holiday" defined.* "Legal holiday" means (A) the day set aside by FL ST § 110.117, for observing New Year's Day, Martin Luther King, Jr.'s Birthday, Memorial Day, Independence Day, Labor Day, Veterans' Day, Thanksgiving Day, the Friday after Thanksgiving Day, or Christmas Day, and (B) any day observed as a holiday by the clerk's office or as designated by the chief judge. FL ST J ADMIN Rule 2.514(a)(6).
   b. *Additional time after service by mail or e-mail.* When a party may or must act within a specified time after service and service is made by mail or e-mail, five (5) days are added after the period that would otherwise expire under FL ST J ADMIN Rule 2.514(a). FL ST J ADMIN Rule 2.514(b).
   c. *Enlargement.* When an act is required or allowed to be done at or within a specified time by order of court, by the Florida Rules of Civil Procedure, or by notice given thereunder, for cause shown the court at any time in its discretion (1) with or without notice, may order the period enlarged if request therefor is made before the expiration of the period originally prescribed or as extended by a previous

order, or (2) upon motion made and notice after the expiration of the specified period, may permit the act to be done when failure to act was the result of excusable neglect, but it may not extend the time for making a motion for new trial, for rehearing, or to alter or amend a judgment; making a motion for relief from a judgment under FL ST RCP Rule 1.540(b); taking an appeal or filing a petition for certiorari; or making a motion for a directed verdict. FL ST RCP Rule 1.090(b).

d. *Unaffected by expiration of term.* The period of time provided for the doing of any act or the taking of any proceeding shall not be affected or limited by the continued existence or expiration of a term of court. The continued existence or expiration of a term of court in no way affects the power of a court to do any act or take any proceeding in any action which is or has been pending before it. FL ST RCP Rule 1.090(c).

C. General Requirements

1. *General rules of pleading*

   a. *Claims for relief*

      i. A pleading which sets forth a claim for relief, whether an original claim, counterclaim, crossclaim, or third-party claim, must state a cause of action and shall contain

         - A short and plain statement of the grounds upon which the court's jurisdiction depends, unless the court already has jurisdiction and the claim needs no new grounds of jurisdiction to support it (For information regarding acts subjecting persons to jurisdiction, please see FL ST § 48.193),
         - A short and plain statement of the ultimate facts showing that the pleader is entitled to relief, and
         - A demand for judgment for the relief to which the pleader deems himself or herself entitled. FL ST RCP Rule 1.110(b).

      ii. Relief in the alternative or of several different types may be demanded. Every complaint shall be considered to demand general relief. FL ST RCP Rule 1.110(b).

   b. *Verification.* Except when otherwise specifically provided by these rules or an applicable statute, every pleading or other document of a party represented by an attorney need not be verified or accompanied by an affidavit. FL ST RCP Rule 1.030. When filing an action for foreclosure of a mortgage on residential real property the complaint shall be verified. When verification of a document is required, the document filed shall include an oath, affirmation, or the following statement: "Under penalty of perjury, I declare that I have read the foregoing, and the facts alleged therein are true and correct to the best of my knowledge and belief." FL ST RCP Rule 1.110(b).

   c. *Separate statements.* All averments of claim or defense shall be made in consecutively numbered paragraphs, the contents of each of which shall be limited as far as practicable to a statement of a single set of circumstances, and a paragraph may be referred to by number in all subsequent pleadings. Each claim founded upon a separate transaction or occurrence and each defense other than denials shall be stated in a separate count or defense when a separation facilitates the clear presentation of the matter set forth. FL ST RCP Rule 1.110(f).

   d. *Statements adopted by reference.* Statements in a pleading may be adopted by reference in a different part of the same pleading, in another pleading, or in any motion. FL ST RCP Rule 1.130(b).

   e. *Joinder of causes of action; Consistency.* A pleader may set up in the same action as many claims or causes of action or defenses in the same right as the pleader has, and claims for relief may be stated in the alternative if separate items make up the cause of action, or if two (2) or more causes of action are joined. A party may also set forth two (2) or more statements of a claim or defense alternatively, either in one (1) count or defense or in separate counts or defenses. When two (2) or more statements are made in the alternative and one (1) of them, if made independently, would be sufficient, the pleading is not made insufficient by the insufficiency of one (1) or more of the alternative statements. A party may also state as many separate claims or defenses as that party has, regardless of consistency and whether based on legal or equitable grounds or both. All pleadings shall be construed so as to do substantial justice. FL ST RCP Rule 1.110(g).

f. *Subsequent pleadings.* When the nature of an action permits pleadings subsequent to final judgment and the jurisdiction of the court over the parties has not terminated, the initial pleading subsequent to final judgment shall be designated a supplemental complaint or petition. The action shall then proceed in the same manner and time as though the supplemental complaint or petition were the initial pleading in the action, including the issuance of any needed process. FL ST RCP Rule 1.110(h) shall not apply to proceedings that may be initiated by motion under the Florida Rules of Civil Procedure. FL ST RCP Rule 1.110(h).

g. *Pleading basis for service.* When service of process is to be made under statutes authorizing service on nonresidents of Florida, it is sufficient to plead the basis for service in the language of the statute without pleading the facts supporting service. FL ST RCP Rule 1.070(h).

h. *Forms of pleadings.* Forms of action and technical forms for seeking relief and of pleas, pleadings, or motions are abolished. FL ST RCP Rule 1.110(a).

2. *Complaint; Generally*

a. *Purpose.* The purpose of a complaint is to advise the court and the defendant of the nature of a cause of action asserted by the plaintiff. FL-PP § 2:12.

b. *Sufficiency of complaint.* A complaint will be found to be insufficient if it contains only general conclusory allegations unsupported by any facts. The test to determine whether a complaint is sufficient is whether, if the factual allegations of the complaint are established, the plaintiff will be legally or equitably entitled to the claimed relief. Pizzi v. Central Bank & Trust Co., 250 So.2d 895, 896 (Fla. 1971); Bowen v. G H C Properties, Limited, 251 So.2d 359, 361 (Fla. 1st DCA 1971); FL-PP § 2:12. In determining the sufficiency of the complaint to state a cause of action, all allegations of the complaint are taken as true, and possible affirmative defenses are not considered. Strickland v. Commerce Loan Co. of Jacksonville, 158 So.2d 814 (Fla. 1st DCA 1963); FL-PP § 2:12.

i. The issues for trial in Florida must be settled by the pleadings. The issues cannot be raised by discovery. FL-PRACPROC § 7:6.

ii. Causes of action may be pleaded alternatively in the same count or in different counts and against the same or different defendants as long as the joinder of parties is proper. FL-PRACPROC § 7:6.

iii. Each count must state a cause of action. Each independent cause of action should be pleaded in a separate count. FL-PRACPROC § 7:6.

iv. Incorporation by reference of all allegations from one count to another is not proper. Separate counts facilitate reference to the pleading in which they appear in other pleadings, motions or papers as well as the assertion of defenses against some, but not all, causes of action. Some defenses may not apply to the initial pleading as a whole. FL-PRACPROC § 7:6.

3. *Pleading special matters*

a. *Capacity.* It is not necessary to aver the capacity of a party to sue or be sued, the authority of a party to sue or be sued in a representative capacity, or the legal existence of an organized association of persons that is made a party, except to the extent required to show the jurisdiction of the court. The initial pleading served on behalf of a minor party shall specifically aver the age of the minor party. When a party desires to raise an issue as to the legal existence of any party, the capacity of any party to sue or be sued, or the authority of a party to sue or be sued in a representative capacity, that party shall do so by specific negative averment which shall include such supporting particulars as are peculiarly within the pleader's knowledge. FL ST RCP Rule 1.120(a).

b. *Fraud, mistake, condition of the mind.* In all averments of fraud or mistake, the circumstances constituting fraud or mistake shall be stated with such particularity as the circumstances may permit. Malice, intent, knowledge, mental attitude, and other condition of mind of a person may be averred generally. FL ST RCP Rule 1.120(b).

c. *Conditions precedent.* In pleading the performance or occurrence of conditions precedent, it is sufficient to aver generally that all conditions precedent have been performed or have occurred. A denial of performance or occurrence shall be made specifically and with particularity. FL ST RCP Rule 1.120(c).

d. *Official document or act.* In pleading an official document or official act it is sufficient to aver that the document was issued or the act done in compliance with law. FL ST RCP Rule 1.120(c).

e. *Judgment or decree.* In pleading a judgment or decree of a domestic or foreign court, a judicial or quasi-judicial tribunal, or a board or officer, it is sufficient to aver the judgment or decree without setting forth matter showing jurisdiction to render it. FL ST RCP Rule 1.120(e).

f. *Time and place.* For the purpose of testing the sufficiency of a pleading, averments of time and place are material and shall be considered like all other averments of material matter. FL ST RCP Rule 1.120(f).

g. *Special damage.* When items of special damage are claimed, they shall be specifically stated. FL ST RCP Rule 1.120(g).

4. *Parties*

a. *Parties generally.* Every action may be prosecuted in the name of the real party in interest, but a personal representative, administrator, guardian, trustee of an express trust, a party with whom or in whose name a contract has been made for the benefit of another, or a party expressly authorized by statute may sue in that person's own name without joining the party for whose benefit the action is brought. All persons having an interest in the subject of the action and in obtaining the relief demanded may join as plaintiffs and any person may be made a defendant who has or claims an interest adverse to the plaintiff. Any person may at any time be made a party if that person's presence is necessary or proper to a complete determination of the cause. Persons having a united interest may be joined on the same side as plaintiffs or defendants, and anyone who refuses to join may for such reason be made a defendant. FL ST RCP Rule 1.210(a).

b. *Minors or incompetent persons.* When a minor or incompetent person has a representative, such as a guardian or other like fiduciary, the representative may sue or defend on behalf of the minor or incompetent person. A minor or incompetent person who does not have a duly appointed representative may sue by next friend or by a guardian ad litem. The court shall appoint a guardian ad litem for a minor or incompetent person not otherwise represented in an action or shall make such other order as it deems proper for the protection of the minor or incompetent person. FL ST RCP Rule 1.210(b).

c. For survivor and substitution of parties information, please see FL ST RCP Rule 1.260.

5. *Counterclaims and crossclaims*

a. *Compulsory counterclaims.* A pleading shall state as a counterclaim any claim which at the time of serving the pleading the pleader has against any opposing party, provided it arises out of the transaction or occurrence that is the subject matter of the opposing party's claim and does not require for its adjudication the presence of third parties over whom the court cannot acquire jurisdiction. But the pleader need not state a claim if (1) at the time the action was commenced the claim was the subject of another pending action, or (2) the opposing party brought suit upon that party's claim by attachment or other process by which the court did not acquire jurisdiction to render a personal judgment on the claim and the pleader is not stating a counterclaim under this rule. FL ST RCP Rule 1.170(a).

b. *Permissive counterclaim.* A pleading may state as a counterclaim any claim against an opposing party not arising out of the transaction or occurrence that is the subject matter of the opposing party's claim. FL ST RCP Rule 1.170(b).

c. *Counterclaim exceeding opposing claim.* A counterclaim may or may not diminish or defeat the recovery sought by the opposing party. It may claim relief exceeding in amount or different in kind from that sought in the pleading of the opposing party. FL ST RCP Rule 1.170(c).

d. *Counterclaim against the State.* The Florida Rules of Civil Procedure shall not be construed to enlarge beyond the limits established by law the right to assert counterclaims or to claim credits against the state or any of its subdivisions or other governmental organizations thereof subject to suit or against a municipal corporation or against an officer, agency, or administrative board of the state. FL ST RCP Rule 1.170(d).

e. *Counterclaim maturing or acquired after pleading.* A claim which matured or was acquired by the

pleader after serving the pleading may be presented as a counterclaim by supplemental pleading with the permission of the court. FL ST RCP Rule 1.170(e).

f. *Omitted counterclaim or crossclaim.* When a pleader fails to set up a counterclaim or crossclaim through oversight, inadvertence, or excusable neglect, or when justice requires, the pleader may set up the counterclaim or crossclaim by amendment with leave of the court. FL ST RCP Rule 1.170(f).

g. *Crossclaim against co-party.* A pleading may state as a crossclaim any claim by one party against a co-party arising out of the transaction or occurrence that is the subject matter of either the original action or a counterclaim therein, or relating to any property that is the subject matter of the original action. The crossclaim may include a claim that the party against whom it is asserted is or may be liable to the crossclaimant for all or part of a claim asserted in the action against the crossclaimant. Service of a crossclaim on a party who has appeared in the action shall be made pursuant to FL ST RCP Rule 1.080. Service of a crossclaim against a party who has not appeared in the action shall be made in the manner provided for service of summons. FL ST RCP Rule 1.170(g).

h. *Additional parties may be brought in.* When the presence of parties other than those to the original action is required to grant complete relief in the determination of a counterclaim or crossclaim, they shall be named in the counterclaim or crossclaim and be served with process and shall be parties to the action thereafter if jurisdiction of them can be obtained and their joinder will not deprive the court of jurisdiction of the action. FL ST RCP Rule 1.250(b) and FL ST RCP Rule 1.250(c) apply to parties brought in under FL ST RCP Rule 1.170(h). FL ST RCP Rule 1.170(h).

i. *Separate trials; Separate judgment.* If the court orders separate trials as provided in FL ST RCP Rule 1.270(b), judgment on a counterclaim or crossclaim may be rendered when the court has jurisdiction to do so even if a claim of the opposing party has been dismissed or otherwise disposed of. FL ST RCP Rule 1.170(i).

j. *Demand exceeding jurisdiction; Transfer of action.* If the demand of any counterclaim or crossclaim exceeds the jurisdiction of the court in which the action is pending, the action shall be transferred forthwith to the court of the same county having jurisdiction of the demand in the counterclaim or crossclaim with only such alterations in the pleadings as are essential. The court shall order the transfer of the action and the transmittal of all papers in it to the proper court if the party asserting the demand exceeding the jurisdiction deposits with the court having jurisdiction a sum sufficient to pay the clerk's service charge in the court to which the action is transferred at the time of filing the counterclaim or crossclaim. Thereupon the original papers and deposit shall be transmitted and filed with a certified copy of the order. The court to which the action is transferred shall have full power and jurisdiction over the demands of all parties. Failure to make the service charge deposit at the time the counterclaim or crossclaim is filed, or within such further time as the court may allow, shall reduce a claim for damages to an amount within the jurisdiction of the court where the action is pending and waive the claim in other cases. FL ST RCP Rule 1.170(j).

6. *Misjoinder and nonjoinder of parties*

a. *Misjoinder.* Misjoinder of parties is not a ground for dismissal of an action. Any claim against a party may be severed and proceeded with separately. FL ST RCP Rule 1.250(a).

b. *Dropping parties.* Parties may be dropped by an adverse party in the manner provided for voluntary dismissal in FL ST RCP Rule 1.420(a)(1) subject to the exception stated in FL ST RCP Rule 1.420. If notice of lis pendens has been filed in the action against a party so dropped, the notice of dismissal shall be recorded and cancels the notice of lis pendens without the necessity of a court order. Parties may be dropped by order of court on its own initiative or the motion of any party at any stage of the action on such terms as are just. FL ST RCP Rule 1.250(b).

c. *Adding parties.* Parties may be added once as a matter of course within the same time that pleadings can be so amended under FL ST RCP Rule 1.190(a). If amendment by leave of court or stipulation of the parties is permitted, parties may be added in the amended pleading without further order of court. Parties may be added by order of court on its own initiative or on motion of any party at any stage of the action and on such terms as are just. FL ST RCP Rule 1.250(c).

7. *Jury demand*

a. *Right preserved.* The right of trial by jury as declared by the Constitution or by statute shall be preserved to the parties inviolate. FL ST RCP Rule 1.430(a).

b. *Demand.* Any party may demand a trial by jury of any issue triable of right by a jury by serving upon the other party a demand therefor in writing at any time after commencement of the action and not later than ten (10) days after the service of the last pleading directed to such issue. The demand may be indorsed upon a pleading of the party. FL ST RCP Rule 1.430(b).

c. *Specification of issues.* In the demand a party may specify the issues that the party wishes so tried; otherwise, the party is deemed to demand trial by jury for all issues so triable. FL ST RCP Rule 1.430(c).

   i. If a party has demanded trial by jury for only some of the issues, any other party may serve a demand for trial by jury of any other or all of the issues triable by jury ten (10) days after service of the demand or such lesser time as the court may order. FL ST RCP Rule 1.430(c).

d. *Waiver.* A party who fails to serve a demand as required by FL ST RCP Rule 1.430 waives trial by jury. FL ST RCP Rule 1.430(d).

   i. If waived, a jury trial may not be granted without the consent of the parties, but the court may allow an amendment in the proceedings to demand a trial by jury or order a trial by jury on its own motion. FL ST RCP Rule 1.430(d).

   ii. A demand for trial by jury may not be withdrawn without the consent of the parties. FL ST RCP Rule 1.430(d).

8. *Companion cases in the Sixth Circuit*

   a. An attorney representing a party in a case to which there are companion cases shall file a notice of a companion case. FL ST 6 J CIR LOCAL Rule 3(B)(1).

   b. The original notice and sufficient copies for filing in each companion case shall be filed with the Clerk and a copy provided to the judge in the section which has been assigned the case bearing the lowest docket number. FL ST 6 J CIR LOCAL Rule 3(B)(1).

   c. Said judge may thereupon reassign all such companion cases to the section which has been assigned the case bearing the lowest docket number if the court finds that the companion cases involve common questions of law or fact or the reassignment would result in an efficient administration of justice. FL ST 6 J CIR LOCAL Rule 3(B)(1).

   d. The Clerk shall make appropriate notations on the file cover and the progress docket of such reassigned case or cases and thereafter all such companion cases shall be heard, tried, and determined by the judge assigned to the section having the companion case bearing the lowest docket number. FL ST 6 J CIR LOCAL Rule 3 (B)(1).

9. *Settlement and alternative dispute resolution*

   a. Unless there are strong and overriding issues of principle, attorneys will raise and explore the issue of settlement as soon as enough is known to make settlement discussions meaningful. FL ST 6 J CIR 2009-066 PA/PI-CIR(I)(1).

   b. Attorneys will not falsely hold out the possibility of settlement to adjourn discovery or delay trial. FL ST 6 J CIR 2009-066 PA/PI-CIR(I)(2).

   c. Attorneys will consider whether the client's interest could be adequately served and the controversy more expeditiously and economically disposed of by arbitration, mediation or other forms of alternative dispute resolution. FL ST 6 J CIR 2009-066 PA/PI-CIR(I)(3).

   d. Counsel and pro se litigants shall immediately notify the court in the event of settlement, and submit a stipulation for an order of dismissal and a final disposition form. FL ST 6 J CIR PA/PI-CIR-98-49(16).

10. *Arbitration and mediation*

    a. *Referral to arbitration and mediation.* Except as hereinafter provided or as otherwise prohibited by law, the presiding judge may enter an order referring all or any part of a contested civil matter to mediation or arbitration. The parties to any contested civil matter may file a written stipulation to mediate or arbitrate any issue between them at any time. Such stipulation shall be incorporated into the order of referral. FL ST RCP Rule 1.700(a).

b. *Arbitration*

i. *Exclusions.* A civil action shall be ordered to arbitration or arbitration in conjunction with mediation upon stipulation of the parties. A civil action may be ordered to arbitration or arbitration in conjunction with mediation upon motion of any party or by the court, if the judge determines the action to be of such a nature that arbitration could be of benefit to the litigants or the court. FL ST RCP Rule 1.800.

- Under no circumstances may the following categories of actions be referred to arbitration: (1) bond estreatures; (2) habeas corpus or other extraordinary writs; (3) bond validations; (4) civil or criminal contempt; (5) such other matters as may be specified by order of the chief judge in the circuit. FL ST RCP Rule 1.800.

ii. For more information regarding arbitration, please see FL ST RCP Rule 1.810; FL ST RCP Rule 1.820; FL ST RCP Rule 1.830.

c. *Mediation.* For more information regarding mediation, please see FL ST RCP Rule 1.710; FL ST RCP Rule 1.720; FL ST RCP Rule 1.730; and FL ST RCP Rule 1.750.

d. See FL ST 6 J CIR PA/PI-CIR-96-63 for more information about the Arbitration and Mediation Program for Florida's Sixth Judicial Circuit.

11. *Rules of court*

a. *Rules of civil procedure.* The Florida Rules of Civil Procedure apply to all actions of a civil nature and all special statutory proceedings in the circuit courts and county courts except those to which the Florida Probate Rules, the Florida Family Law Rules of Procedure, or the Small Claims Rules apply. FL ST RCP Rule 1.010.

i. The form, content, procedure, and time for pleading in all special statutory proceedings shall be as prescribed by the statutes governing the proceeding unless the Florida Rules of Civil Procedure specifically provide to the contrary. FL ST RCP Rule 1.010.

ii. The Florida Rules of Civil Procedure shall be construed to secure the just, speedy, and inexpensive determination of every action. FL ST RCP Rule 1.010.

b. *Rules of judicial administration.* The Florida Rules of Judicial Administration shall apply to administrative matters in all courts to which the Florida Rules of Judicial Administration are applicable by their terms. The Florida Rules of Judicial Administration shall be construed to secure the speedy and inexpensive determination of every proceeding to which they are applicable. The Florida Rules of Judicial Administration shall supersede all conflicting rules and statutes. FL ST J ADMIN Rule 2.110.

D. Documents

1. *Required documents*

a. *Summons.* Upon the commencement of the action, summons or other process authorized by law shall be issued forthwith by the clerk or judge under the clerk's or the judge's signature and the seal of the court and delivered for service without praecipe. FL ST RCP Rule 1.070(a).

b. *Complaint.* See the General Requirements section for the contents of the complaint.

i. *Notices to persons with disabilities.* See the Format section of this KeyRules document for further information.

c. *Civil cover sheet.* A civil cover sheet (FL ST RCP Form 1.997) shall be completed and filed with the clerk at the time an initial complaint or petition is filed by the party initiating the action. If the cover sheet is not filed, the clerk shall accept the complaint or petition for filing; but all proceedings in the action shall be abated until a properly executed cover sheet is completed and filed. The clerk shall complete the civil cover sheet for a party appearing pro se. FL ST RCP Rule 1.100(c)(2).

d. *Return of execution process by process server.* Each person who effects service of process shall note on a return-of-service form attached thereto, the date and time when it comes to hand, the date and time when it is served, the manner of service, the name of the person on whom it was served and, if the person is served in a representative capacity, the position occupied by the person. The return-of-service form must be signed by the person who effects the service of process. However, a person employed by a sheriff who effects the service of process may sign the return-of-service form using an electronic signature certified by the sheriff. FL ST § 48.21(1).

i. A failure to state the facts or to include the signature required by FL ST § 48.21(1) invalidates the service, but the return is amendable to state the facts or to include the signature at any time on application to the court from which the process issued. On amendment, service is as effective as if the return had originally stated the omitted facts or included the signature. A failure to state all the facts in or to include the signature on the return shall subject the person effecting service to a fine not exceeding $10, in the court's discretion. FL ST § 48.21(2).

e. *Filing fees.* Filing fees are due at the time a party files a pleading to initiate a proceeding or files a pleading for relief. FL ST § 28.241. For a fee schedule, see FL ST § 28.241.

2. *Supplemental documents*

a. *Exhibits.* All bonds, notes, bills of exchange, contracts, accounts, or documents upon which action may be brought or defense made, or a copy thereof or a copy of the portions thereof material to the pleadings, shall be incorporated in or attached to the pleading. No papers shall be unnecessarily annexed as exhibits. The pleadings shall contain no unnecessary recitals of deeds, documents, contracts, or other instruments. Any exhibit attached to a pleading shall be considered a part of the pleadings for all purposes. FL ST RCP Rule 1.130(a).

b. *Notice of constitutional question.* A party that files a pleading, written motion, or other paper drawing into question the constitutionality of a state statute or a county or municipal charter, ordinance, or franchise must promptly (1) file a notice of constitutional question stating the question and identifying the paper that raises it; and (2) serve the notice and the pleading, written motion, or other paper drawing into question the constitutionality of a state statute or a county or municipal charter, ordinance, or franchise on the Attorney General or the state attorney of the judicial circuit in which the action is pending, by either certified or registered mail. Service of the notice and pleading, written motion, or other paper does not require joinder of the Attorney General or the state attorney as a party to the action. FL ST RCP Rule 1.071.

c. *Notice of companion cases.* An attorney representing a party in a case to which there are companion cases shall file a notice of a companion case. FL ST 6 J CIR LOCAL Rule 3(B)(1).

E. Format

1. *Documents; Type and size.* Documents subject to the exceptions set forth in FL ST J ADMIN Rule 2.525(d) shall be filed on recycled paper measuring eight and one half by eleven (8 1/2 by 11) inches. For purposes of FL ST J ADMIN Rule 2.520, paper is recycled if it contains a minimum content of fifty (50) percent waste paper. Xerographic reduction of legal-size (eight and one half by fourteen (8 1/2 by 14) inches) documents to letter size (eight and one half by eleven (8 1/2 by 11) inches) is prohibited. All other documents filed by electronic transmission shall be filed in a format capable of being printed in a format consistent with the provisions of FL ST J ADMIN Rule 2.250. FL ST J ADMIN Rule 2.520(b).

a. *Exhibits.* Any exhibit or attachment filed with pleadings or papers may be filed in its original size. FL ST J ADMIN Rule 2.520(c).

b. *Recording space.* On all papers and documents prepared and filed by the court or by any party to a proceeding which are to be recorded in the public records of any county, including but not limited to final money judgments and notices of lis pendens, a three (3) inch by three (3) inch space at the top right-hand corner on the first page and a one (1) inch by three (3) inch space at the top right-hand corner on each subsequent page shall be left blank and reserved for use by the clerk of court. FL ST J ADMIN Rule 2.520(d).

i. *Exceptions to recording space.* Any papers or documents created by persons or entities over which the filing party has no control, including but not limited to wills, codicils, trusts, or other testamentary documents; documents prepared or executed by any public officer; documents prepared, executed, acknowledged, or proved outside of the State of Florida; or documents created by State or Federal government agencies, may be filed without the space required by FL ST J ADMIN Rule 2.520. FL ST J ADMIN Rule 2.520(e).

   c. *Noncompliance.* No clerk of court is permitted to refuse to file any document or paper because of noncompliance with the Florida Rules of Judicial Administration. However, upon request of the clerk of court, noncomplying documents must be resubmitted in accordance with the formatting rules. FL ST J ADMIN Rule 2.520(f).

2. *Caption.* Every pleading, motion, order, judgment, or other paper shall have a caption containing the name of the court, the file number, and except for in rem proceedings, including forfeiture proceedings, the name of the first party on each side with an appropriate indication of other parties, and a designation identifying the party filing it and its nature or the nature of the order, as the case may be. In any in rem proceeding, every pleading, motion, order, judgment, or other paper shall have a caption containing the name of the court, the file number, the style "In re" (followed by the name or general description of the property), and a designation of the person or entity filing it and its nature or the nature of the order, as the case may be. In an in rem forfeiture proceeding, the style shall be "In re forfeiture of" (followed by the name of the general description of the property). All papers filed in the action shall be styled in such a manner as to indicate clearly the subject matter of the paper and the party requesting or obtaining relief. FL ST RCP Rule 1.100(c)(1).

3. *Writing and written defined.* Writing or written means a document containing information, an application, or a stipulation. FL ST RCP Rule 1.080(c).

4. *Rule abbreviations*

   a. The Florida Rules of Civil Procedure and shall be abbreviated as Fla.R.Civ.P. FL ST RCP Rule 1.010.

   b. The Florida Rules of Judicial Administration shall be abbreviated as Fla. R. Jud. Admin. FL ST J ADMIN Rule 2.110.

5. *Nonverification.* Except when otherwise specifically provided by the Florida Rules of Civil Procedure or an applicable statute, every pleading or other document of a party represented by an attorney need not be verified or accompanied by an affidavit. FL ST RCP Rule 1.030; FL ST J ADMIN Rule 2.515(a).

6. *Attorney signature*

   a. *Attorney signature.* Every pleading and other document of a party represented by an attorney shall be signed by at least one (1) attorney of record in that attorney's individual name whose current record Florida Bar address, telephone number, including area code, primary e-mail address and secondary e-mail addresses, if any, and Florida Bar number shall be stated, and who shall be duly licensed to practice law in Florida or who shall have received permission to appear in the particular case as provided in FL ST J ADMIN Rule 2.510. FL ST J ADMIN Rule 2.515(a).

      i. The attorney may be required by the court to give the address of, and to vouch for the attorney's authority to represent, the party. FL ST J ADMIN Rule 2.515(a).

      ii. The signature of an attorney shall constitute a certificate by the attorney that the attorney has read the pleading or other document; that to the best of the attorney's knowledge, information, and belief there is good ground to support it; and that it is not interposed for delay. FL ST J ADMIN Rule 2.515(a).

      iii. If a pleading is not signed or is signed with intent to defeat the purpose of FL ST J ADMIN Rule 2.515, it may be stricken and the action may proceed as though the pleading or other document had not been served. FL ST J ADMIN Rule 2.515(a).

   b. *Pro se litigant signature.* A party who is not represented by an attorney shall sign any pleading or other paper and state the party's address and telephone number, including area code. FL ST J ADMIN Rule 2.515(b).

   c. *Form of signature*

      i. The signatures required on pleadings and documents by FL ST J ADMIN Rule 2.515(a) and FL ST J ADMIN Rule 2.515(b) may be:

         - Original signatures;
         - Original signatures that have been reproduced by electronic means, such as on electronically transmitted documents or photocopied documents;

- Electronic signatures using the "/s/," "s/," or "/s" formats by or at the direction of the person signing; or
- Any other signature format authorized by general law, so long as the clerk where the proceeding is pending has the capability of receiving and has obtained approval from the Supreme Court of Florida to accept pleadings and documents with that signature format. FL ST J ADMIN Rule 2.515(c)(1).

ii. An attorney, party, or other person who files a pleading or paper by electronic transmission that does not contain the original signature of that attorney, party, or other person shall file that identical pleading or paper in paper form containing an original signature of that attorney, party, or other person (hereinafter called the follow-up filing) immediately thereafter. The follow-up filing is not required if the Supreme Court of Florida has entered an order directing the clerk of court to discontinue accepting the follow-up filing. FL ST J ADMIN Rule 2.515(c)(2).

7. *Forms*

a. *Process.* The forms of process, notice of lis pendens, and notice of action provided in the Florida Rules of Civil Procedure are sufficient. Variations from the forms do not void process or notices that are otherwise sufficient. FL ST RCP Rule 1.900(a).

b. *Other forms.* The other forms provided in the Florida Rules of Civil Procedure are sufficient for the matters that are covered by them. So long as the substance is expressed without prolixity, the forms may be varied to meet the facts of a particular case. FL ST RCP Rule 1.900(b).

c. *Formal matters.* Captions, except for the designation of the paper, are omitted from the forms provided in the Florida Rules of Civil Procedure. A general form of caption is the first form provided. Signatures are omitted from pleadings and motions. FL ST RCP Rule 1.900(c).

8. *Notices to persons with disabilities.* All notices of court proceedings to be held in a public facility, and all process compelling appearance at such proceedings, shall include the following statement in bold face, fourteen (14) point Times New Roman or Courier font: "If you are a person with a disability who needs any accommodation in order to participate in this proceeding, you are entitled, at no cost to you, to the provision of certain assistance. Please contact [identify applicable court personnel by name, address, and telephone number] at least seven (7) days before your scheduled court appearance, or immediately upon receiving this notification if the time before the scheduled appearance is less than seven (7) days; if you are hearing or voice impaired, call 711." FL ST J ADMIN Rule 2.540(c)(1).

9. *Minimization of the filing of sensitive information*

a. *Limitations for court filings.* Unless authorized by FL ST J ADMIN Rule 2.425(b), statute, another rule of court, or the court orders otherwise, designated sensitive information filed with the court must be limited to the following format:

i. The initials of a person known to be a minor;

ii. The year of birth of a person's birth date;

iii. No portion of any: Social security number, Bank account number, Credit card account number, Charge account number, or Debit account number;

iv. The last four digits of any: Taxpayer identification number (TIN), Employee identification number, Driver's license number, Passport number, Telephone number, Financial account number, except as set forth in FL ST J ADMIN Rule 2.425(a)(3), Brokerage account number, Insurance policy account number, Loan account number, Customer account number, or Patient or health care number;

v. A truncated version of any: Email address, Computer user name, Password, or Personal identification number (PIN); and

vi. A truncated version of any other sensitive information as provided by court order. FL ST J ADMIN Rule 2.425(a).

b. *Exceptions.* FL ST J ADMIN Rule 2.425(a) does not apply to the following:

i. An account number which identifies the property alleged to be the subject of a proceeding;

ii. The record of an administrative or agency proceeding;

iii. The record in appellate or review proceedings;

iv. The birth date of a minor whenever the birth date is necessary for the court to establish or maintain subject matter jurisdiction;

v. The name of a minor in any order relating to parental responsibility, time-sharing, or child support;

vi. The name of a minor in any document or order affecting the minor's ownership of real property;

vii. The birth date of a party in a writ of attachment or notice to payor;

viii. In traffic and criminal proceedings: a pro se filing; a court filing that is related to a criminal matter or investigation and that is prepared before the filing of a criminal charge or is not filed as part of any docketed criminal case; an arrest or search warrant or any information in support thereof; a charging document and an affidavit or other documents filed in support of any charging document, including any driving records; a statement of particulars; discovery material introduced into evidence or otherwise filed with the court; and all information necessary for the proper issuance and execution of a subpoena duces tecum;

ix. Information used by the clerk for case maintenance purposes or the courts for case management purposes; and

x. Information which is relevant and material to an issue before the court. FL ST J ADMIN Rule 2.425(b).

c. *Remedies.* Upon motion by a party or interested person or sua sponte by the court, the court may order remedies, sanctions or both for a violation of FL ST J ADMIN Rule 2.425(a). Following notice and an opportunity to respond, the court may impose sanctions if such filing was not made in good faith. FL ST J ADMIN Rule 2.425(c).

d. *Motions not restricted.* FL ST J ADMIN Rule 2.425 does not restrict a party's right to move for protective order, to move to file documents under seal, or to request a determination of the confidentiality of records. FL ST J ADMIN Rule 2.425(d).

e. *Application.* FL ST J ADMIN Rule 2.425 does not affect the application of constitutional provisions, statutes, or rules of court regarding confidential information or access to public information. FL ST J ADMIN Rule 2.425(e).

F. Filing and Service Requirements

1. *Filing requirements.* All documents filed in any court shall be filed by electronic transmission in accordance with FL ST J ADMIN Rule 2.525. "Documents" means pleadings, motions, petitions, memoranda, briefs, notices, exhibits, declarations, affidavits, orders, judgments, decrees, writs, opinions, and any other paper or writing submitted to a court. FL ST J ADMIN Rule 2.520(a). All documents that are court records, as defined in FL ST J ADMIN Rule 2.430(a)(1), must be filed by electronic transmission, provided that: (1) the clerk has the ability to accept and retain such documents; (2) the clerk or the chief judge of the circuit has requested permission to accept documents filed by electronic transmission; and (3) the supreme court has entered an order granting permission to the clerk to accept documents filed by electronic transmission. FL ST J ADMIN Rule 2.525(c)(1).

a. *Definition.* "Electronic transmission of documents" means the sending of information by electronic signals to, by or from a court or clerk, which when received can be transformed and stored or transmitted on paper, microfilm, magnetic storage device, optical imaging system, CD-ROM, flash drive, other electronic data storage system, server, case maintenance system ("CM"), electronic court filing ("ECF") system, statewide or local electronic portal ("e-portal"), or other electronic record keeping system authorized by the supreme court in a format sufficient to communicate the information on the original document in a readable format. Electronic transmission of documents includes electronic mail ("e-mail") and any internet-based transmission procedure, and may include procedures allowing for documents to be signed or verified by electronic means. FL ST J ADMIN Rule 2.525(a).

b. *Application.* Any court or clerk of the court may accept the electronic transmission of documents for

filing after the clerk, together with input from the chief judge of the circuit, has obtained approval of the procedures and program for doing so from the Supreme Court of Florida. FL ST J ADMIN Rule 2.525(b).

c. *Exceptions*

   i. Paper documents and other submissions may be manually submitted to the clerk or court:

      - When the clerk does not have the ability to accept and retain documents by electronic filing or has not had ECF Procedures approved by the supreme court;
      - For filing by any self-represented party or any self-represented nonparty unless specific ECF Procedures provide a means to file documents electronically. However, any self-represented nonparty that is a governmental or public agency and any other agency, partnership, corporation, or business entity acting on behalf of any governmental or public agency may file documents by electronic transmission if such entity has the capability of filing documents electronically;
      - For filing by attorneys excused from e-mail service in accordance with FL ST J ADMIN Rule 2.516(b);
      - When submitting evidentiary exhibits or filing non-documentary materials;
      - When the filing involves documents in excess of twenty-five (25) megabytes (25MB) in size. For such filings, documents may be transmitted using an electronic storage medium that the clerk has the ability to accept, which may include a CD-ROM, flash drive, or similar storage medium;
      - When filed in open court, as permitted by the court;
      - When paper filing is permitted by any approved statewide or local ECF procedures; and
      - If any court determines that justice so requires. FL ST J ADMIN Rule 2.525(d).

   ii. Any document in paper form submitted under FL ST J ADMIN Rule 2.525(d) is filed when it is received by the clerk or court and the clerk shall immediately thereafter convert any filed paper document to an electronic document. "Convert to an electronic document" means optically capturing an image of a paper document and using character recognition software to recover as much of the document's text as practicable and then indexing and storing the document in the official court file. FL ST J ADMIN Rule 2.525(c)(4).

   iii. Any storage medium submitted under FL ST J ADMIN Rule 2.525(d)(5) is filed when received by the clerk or court and the clerk shall immediately thereafter transfer the electronic documents from the storage device to the official court file. FL ST J ADMIN Rule 2.525(c)(5).

   iv. If the filer of any paper document authorized under FL ST J ADMIN Rule 2.525(d) provides a self-addressed, postage-paid envelope for return of the paper document after it is converted to electronic form by the clerk, the clerk shall place the paper document in the envelope and deposit it in the mail. Except when a paper document is required to be maintained, the clerk may recycle any filed paper document that is not to be returned to the filer. FL ST J ADMIN Rule 2.525(c)(6).

   v. The clerk may convert any paper document filed before the effective date of FL ST J ADMIN Rule 2.525 to an electronic document. Unless the clerk is required to maintain the paper document, if the paper document has been converted to an electronic document by the clerk, the paper document is no longer part of the official court file and may be removed and recycled. FL ST J ADMIN Rule 2.525(c)(7).

d. *Official court file.* For information on what constitutes the official court file, please see FL ST J ADMIN Rule 2.525(c)(2), FL ST J ADMIN Rule 2.525(c)(3).

e. *Administration.* All attorneys, parties, or other persons using this rule to file documents are required to make arrangements with the court or clerk for the payment of any charges authorized by general law or the supreme court before filing any document by electronic transmission. FL ST J ADMIN Rule 2.525(f)(2).

f. *Filing date.* The filing date for an electronically transmitted document is the date and time that such filing is acknowledged by an electronic stamp or otherwise, pursuant to any procedure set forth in any ECF Procedures approved by the supreme court, or the date the last page of such filing is received by the court or clerk. FL ST J ADMIN Rule 2.525(f)(3).

g. *Accessibility.* All documents transmitted in any electronic form under FL ST J ADMIN Rule 2.525 must comply with the accessibility requirements of FL ST J ADMIN Rule 2.526. FL ST J ADMIN Rule 2.525(g).

2. *Service requirements*

a. *Papers to be served.* At the time of personal service of process a copy of the initial pleading shall be delivered to the party upon whom service is made. The date and hour of service shall be endorsed on the original process and all copies of it by the person making the service. The party seeking to effect personal service shall furnish the person making service with the necessary copies. When the service is made by publication, copies of the initial pleadings shall be furnished to the clerk and mailed by the clerk with the notice of action to all parties whose addresses are stated in the initial pleading or sworn statement. FL ST RCP Rule 1.070(e).

b. *Issuance of summons.* Upon the commencement of the action, summons or other process authorized by law shall be issued forthwith by the clerk or judge under the clerk's or the judge's signature and the seal of the court and delivered for service without praecipe. FL ST RCP Rule 1.070(a).

i. *How directed.* Summons, subpoenas, and other process in civil actions run throughout the state. All process except subpoenas shall be directed to all and singular the sheriffs of the state. FL ST § 48.011.

ii. *Service as to numerous defendants.* If there is more than one (1) defendant, the clerk or judge shall issue as many writs of process against the several defendants as may be directed by the plaintiff or the plaintiff's attorney. FL ST RCP Rule 1.070(c).

c. *Who may serve process.* Service of process may be made by an officer authorized by law to serve process, but the court may appoint any competent person not interested in the action to serve the process. When so appointed, the person serving process shall make proof of service by affidavit promptly and in any event within the time during which the person served must respond to the process. Failure to make proof of service shall not affect the validity of the service. When any process is returned not executed or returned improperly executed for any defendant, the party causing its issuance shall be entitled to such additional process against the unserved party as is required to effect service. FL ST RCP Rule 1.070(b).

i. All process shall be served by the sheriff of the county where the person to be served is found, except initial nonenforceable civil process may be served by a special process server appointed by the sheriff as provided for in FL ST § 48.021 or by a certified process server as provided for in FL ST § 48.25 through FL ST § 48.31. FL ST § 48.021(1).

ii. The sheriff of each county may, in his or her discretion, establish an approved list of natural persons designated as special process servers. FL ST § 48.021(2)(a). For more information regarding process servers, please see FL ST § 48.021(2).

iii. A person serving process shall place, on the copy served, the date and time of service and his or her identification number and initials for all service of process. FL ST § 48.031(5).

d. *Service of process on Sunday*

i. Service or execution on Sunday of any writ, process, warrant, order, or judgment is void and the person serving or executing, or causing it to be served or executed, is liable to the party aggrieved for damages for so doing as if he or she had done it without any process, writ, warrant, order, or judgment. FL ST § 48.20.

ii. If affidavit is made by the person requesting service or execution that he or she has good reason to believe that any person liable to have any such writ, process, warrant, order, or judgment served on him or her intends to escape from this state under protection of Sunday, any officer furnished with an order authorizing service or execution by the trial court judge may serve or execute such writ, process, warrant, order, or judgment on Sunday, and it is as valid as if it had been done on any other day. FL ST § 48.20.

e. *Methods of service*

i. *Service of process generally.* Service of original process is made by delivering a copy of it to the person to be served with a copy of the complaint, petition, or other initial pleading or paper or by leaving the copies at his or her usual place of abode with any person residing therein who is fifteen (15) years of age or older and informing the person of their contents. Minors who are or have been married shall be served as provided in FL ST § 48.031. FL ST § 48.031(1)(a).

- Employers, when contacted by an individual authorized to make service of process, shall permit the authorized individual to make service on employees in a private area designated by the employer. FL ST § 48.031(1)(b).
- Substitute service may be made on the spouse of the person to be served at any place in the county, if the cause of action is not an adversary proceeding between the spouse and the person to be served, if the spouse requests such service, and if the spouse and person to be served are residing together in the same dwelling. FL ST § 48.031(2)(a).
- Substitute service may be made on an individual doing business as a sole proprietorship at his or her place of business, during regular business hours, by serving the person in charge of the business at the time of service if two (2) or more attempts to serve the owner have been made at the place of business. FL ST § 48.031(2)(b).
- If the only address for a person to be served, which is discoverable through public records, is a private mailbox, substitute service may be made by leaving a copy of the process with the person in charge of the private mailbox, but only if the process server determines that the person to be served maintains a mailbox at that location. FL ST § 48.031(6).

ii. *Service by mail.* A defendant may accept service of process by mail. FL ST RCP Rule 1.070(i). A plaintiff may notify any defendant of the commencement of the action and request that the defendant waive service of a summons. FL ST RCP Rule 1.070(i)(2).

- *Notice and request for waiver.* The notice and request shall: (1) be in writing and be addressed directly to the defendant, if an individual, or to an officer or managing or general agent of the defendant or other agent authorized by appointment or law to receive service of process; (2) be dispatched by certified mail, return receipt requested; (3) be accompanied by a copy of the complaint and shall identify the court in which it has been filed; (4) inform the defendant of the consequences of compliance and of failure to comply with the request; (5) state the date on which the request is sent; (6) allow the defendant twenty (20) days from the date on which the request is received to return the waiver, or, if the address of the defendant is outside of the United States, thirty (30) days from the date on which it is received to return the waiver; and (7) provide the defendant with an extra copy of the notice and request, including the waiver, as well as a prepaid means of compliance in writing. FL ST RCP Rule 1.070(i)(2).
- *Consequences of accepting/rejecting service by mail.* Acceptance of service of a complaint by mail does not thereby waive any objection to the venue or to the jurisdiction of the court over the person of the defendant. FL ST RCP Rule 1.070(i)(1). If a defendant fails to comply with a request for waiver within the time provided, the court shall impose the costs subsequently incurred in effecting service on the defendant unless good cause for the failure is shown. FL ST RCP Rule 1.070(i)(3). A defendant who, before being served with process, timely returns a waiver so requested is not required to respond to the complaint until sixty (60) days after the date the defendant received the request for waiver of service. For purposes of computing any time prescribed or allowed by the Florida Rules of Civil Procedure, service of process shall be deemed effected twenty (20) days before the time required to respond to the complaint. FL ST RCP Rule 1.070(i)(4). When the plaintiff files a waiver of service with the court, the action shall proceed, except as provided in FL ST RCP Rule 1.070(i)(4), as if a summons and complaint had been served at the time of filing the waiver, and no further proof of service shall be required. FL ST RCP Rule 1.070(i)(5).

iii. *Service on partnerships and limited partnerships*

- Process against a partnership shall be served on any partner and is as valid as if served on each individual partner. If a partner is not available during regular business hours to accept service on behalf of the partnership, he or she may designate an employee to accept such service. After one (1) attempt to serve a partner or designated employee has been made, process may be served on the person in charge of the partnership during regular business hours. After service on any partner, plaintiff may proceed to judgment and execution against that partner and the assets of the partnership. After service on a designated employee or other person in charge, plaintiff may proceed to judgment and execution against the partnership assets but not against the individual assets of any partner. FL ST § 48.061(1).
- Process against a domestic limited partnership may be served on any general partner or on the agent for service of process specified in its certificate of limited partnership or in its certificate as amended or restated and is as valid as if served on each individual member of the partnership. After service on a general partner or the agent, the plaintiff may proceed to judgment and execution against the limited partnership and all of the general partners individually. If a general partner cannot be found in this state and service cannot be made on an agent because of failure to maintain such an agent or because the agent cannot be found or served with the exercise of reasonable diligence, service of process may be effected by service upon the Secretary of State as agent of the limited partnership as provided for in FL ST § 48.181. Service of process may be made under FL ST § 48.071 and FL ST § 48.21 on limited partnerships. FL ST § 48.061(2).
- Process against a foreign limited partnership may be served on any general partner found in the state or on any agent for service of process specified in its application for registration and is as valid as if served on each individual member of the partnership. If a general partner cannot be found in this state and an agent for service of process has not been appointed or, if appointed, the agent's authority has been revoked or the agent cannot be found or served with the exercise of reasonable diligence, service of process may be effected by service upon the Secretary of State as agent of the limited partnership as provided for in FL ST § 48.181, or process may be served as provided in FL ST § 48.071 and FL ST § 48.21. FL ST § 48.061(3).

iv. *Service on corporation*

- Process against any private corporation, domestic or foreign, may be served: (1) on the president or vice president, or other head of the corporation; (2) in the absence of any person described in FL ST § 48.081(1)(a), on the cashier, treasurer, secretary, or general manager; (3) in the absence of any person described in FL ST § 48.081(1)(a) or FL ST § 48.081(1)(b), on any director; or (4) in the absence of any person described in FL ST § 48.081(1)(a), FL ST § 48.081(1)(b), or FL ST § 48.081(1)(c), on any officer or business agent residing in the state. FL ST § 48.081(1).
- If a foreign corporation has none of the foregoing officers or agents in this state, service may be made on any agent transacting business for it in this state. FL ST § 48.081(2).
- As an alternative to all of the foregoing, process may be served on the agent designated by the corporation under FL ST § 48.091. However, if service cannot be made on a registered agent because of failure to comply with FL ST § 48.091, service of process shall be permitted on any employee at the corporation's principal place of business or on any employee of the registered agent. FL ST § 48.081(3)(a). If the address provided for the registered agent, officer, director, or principal place of business is a residence or private mailbox, service on the corporation may be made by serving the registered agent, officer, or director in accordance with FL ST § 48.031. FL ST § 48.081(3)(b).
- FL ST § 48.081 does not apply to service of process on insurance companies. FL ST § 48.081(4).
- When a corporation engages in substantial and not isolated activities within this state, or

has a business office within the state and is actually engaged in the transaction of business therefrom, service upon any officer or business agent while on corporate business within this state may personally be made, pursuant to FL ST § 48.081, and it is not necessary in such case that the action, suit, or proceeding against the corporation shall have arisen out of any transaction or operation connected with or incidental to the business being transacted within the state. FL ST § 48.081(5).

- For information regarding service on a dissolved corporation refer to FL ST § 48.101.

v. *Personal service outside state*

- Except as otherwise provided herein, service of process on persons outside of this state shall be made in the same manner as service within this state by any officer authorized to serve process in the state where the person is served. No order of court is required. An affidavit of the officer shall be filed, stating the time, manner, and place of service. The court may consider the affidavit, or any other competent evidence, in determining whether service has been properly made. Service of process on persons outside the United States may be required to conform to the provisions of the Hague Convention on the Service Abroad of Judicial and Extrajudicial Documents in Civil or Commercial Matters. FL ST § 48.194(1).
- For further information on service of process in an in rem or quasi in rem action refer to FL ST § 48.194(2); FL ST § 48.194(3); and FL ST § 48.194(4).

vi. *Method of substituted service on nonresident*

- When authorized by law, substituted service of process on a nonresident or a person who conceals his or her whereabouts by serving a public officer designated by law shall be made by leaving a copy of the process with a fee of eight dollars and seventy-five cents ($8.75) with the public officer or in his or her office or by mailing the copies by certified mail to the public officer with the fee. The service is sufficient service on a defendant who has appointed a public officer as his or her agent for the service of process. FL ST § 48.161(1).
- Notice of service and a copy of the process shall be sent forthwith by registered or certified mail by the plaintiff or his or her attorney to the defendant, and the defendant's return receipt and the affidavit of the plaintiff or his or her attorney of compliance shall be filed on or before the return day of the process or within such time as the court allows, or the notice and copy shall be served on the defendant, if found within the state, by an officer authorized to serve legal process, or if found without the state, by a sheriff or a deputy sheriff of any county of this state or any duly constituted public officer qualified to serve like process in the state or jurisdiction where the defendant is found. The officer's return showing service shall be filed on or before the return day of the process or within such time as the court allows. The public officer shall keep a record of all process served on him or her showing the day and hour of service. FL ST § 48.161(1).
- If any person on whom service of process is authorized under FL ST § 48.161(1) dies, service may be made on his or her administrator, executor, curator, or personal representative in the same manner. FL ST § 48.161(2).
- FL ST § 48.161 does not apply to persons on whom service is authorized under FL ST § 48.151. FL ST § 48.161(3).
- The public officer may designate some other person in his or her office to accept service. FL ST § 48.161(4).

vii. *Service by publication.* Service of process by publication may be made as provided by statute. FL ST RCP Rule 1.070(d). Service of process by publication is allowable in cases listed in FL ST § 49.011 and upon the parties listed in FL ST § 49.021.

- As a condition precedent to service by publication, a statement shall be filed in the action executed by the plaintiff, the plaintiff's agent or attorney, setting forth substantially the matters hereafter required, which statement may be contained in a verified pleading, or in an affidavit or other sworn statement. FL ST § 49.031(1). After the entry of a final judgment or decree in any action no sworn statement shall ever be held defective for failure to state a required fact if the fact otherwise appears from the record in the action. FL ST § 49.031(3).

- For the sworn statement requirements for service of process by publication refer to FL ST § 49.041; FL ST § 49.051; FL ST § 49.061; and FL ST § 49.071.
- On filing the sworn statement, and otherwise complying with the foregoing requirements, the plaintiff is entitled to have issued by the clerk or judge, not later than sixty (60) days after filing the sworn statement, a notice of action which notice shall set forth: (1) the names of the known natural defendants; the names, status and description of the corporate defendants; a description of the unknown defendants who claim by, through, under or against a known party which may be described as "all parties claiming interests by, through, under or against (name of known party)" and a description of all unknown defendants which may be described as "all parties having or claiming to have any right, title or interest in the property herein described"; (2) the nature of the action or proceeding in short and simple terms (but neglect to do so is not jurisdictional); (3) the name of the court in which the action or proceeding was instituted and an abbreviated title of the case; (4) the description of real property, if any, proceeded against. FL ST § 49.08.
- For further information on service of process by publication refer to FL ST § 49.09; FL ST § 49.10; FL ST § 49.11; FL ST § 49.12; FL ST § 50.011; FL ST § 50.021; FL ST § 50.031; FL ST § 50.041; FL ST § 50.051; and FL ST § 50.061.

viii. *Service on agents of nonresidents doing business in the state.* When any natural person or partnership not residing or having a principal place of business in this state engages in business in this state, process may be served on the person who is in charge of any business in which the defendant is engaged within this state at the time of service, including agents soliciting orders for goods, wares, merchandise or services. FL ST § 48.071.

- Any process so served is as valid as if served personally on the nonresident person or partnership engaging in business in this state in any action against the person or partnership arising out of such business. FL ST § 48.071.
- A copy of such process with a notice of service on the person in charge of such business shall be sent forthwith to the nonresident person or partnership by registered or certified mail, return receipt requested. FL ST § 48.071.
- An affidavit of compliance with FL ST § 48.071 shall be filed before the return day or within such further time as the court may allow. FL ST § 48.071.

ix. *Service on nonresident engaging in business in state.* The acceptance by any person or persons, individually or associated together as a copartnership or any other form or type of association, who are residents of any other state or country, and all foreign corporations, and any person who is a resident of the state and who subsequently becomes a nonresident of the state or conceals his or her whereabouts, of the privilege extended by law to nonresidents and others to operate, conduct, engage in, or carry on a business or business venture in the state, or to have an office or agency in the state, constitutes an appointment by the persons and foreign corporations of the Secretary of State of the state as their agent on whom all process in any action or proceeding against them, or any of them, arising out of any transaction or operation connected with or incidental to the business or business venture may be served. The acceptance of the privilege is signification of the agreement of the persons and foreign corporations that the process against them which is so served is of the same validity as if served personally on the persons or foreign corporations. FL ST § 48.181(1).

- If a foreign corporation has a resident agent or officer in the state, process shall be served on the resident agent or officer. FL ST § 48.181(2).
- Any person, firm, or corporation which sells, consigns, or leases by any means whatsoever tangible or intangible personal property, through brokers, jobbers, wholesalers, or dis-

tributors to any person, firm, or corporation in this state is conclusively presumed to be both engaged in substantial and not isolated activities within this state and operating, conducting, engaging in, or carrying on a business or business venture in this state. FL ST § 48.181(3).

x. *Other service provisions:*

- Service on alien property custodian. FL ST § 48.131.
- Service on an incompetent person. FL ST § 48.042.
- Service on minor. FL ST § 48.041.
- Service on public agencies and officers. FL ST § 48.111.
- Service on the state. FL ST § 48.121.
- Service on a state prisoner. FL ST § 48.051.
- Service on labor unions. FL ST § 48.141.
- Service on statutory agents for certain persons. FL ST § 48.151.
- Service on nonresident motor vehicle owners. FL ST § 48.171.
- Service of process in action for possession of premises. FL ST § 48.183.
- Service on nonresidents operating aircraft or watercraft in the state. FL ST § 48.19.

f. *Crossclaims.* Service of a crossclaim on a party who has appeared in the action shall be made pursuant to FL ST RCP Rule 1.080. Service of a crossclaim against a party who has not appeared in the action shall be made in the manner provided for service of summons. FL ST RCP Rule 1.170(g).

g. *Fees.* The statutory compensation for making service shall not be increased by the simultaneous delivery or mailing of the copy of the initial pleading in conformity with FL ST RCP Rule 1.070. FL ST RCP Rule 1.070(g).

h. *Standards of professional courtesy; Service*

i. The timing and manner of service should not be used to the disadvantage of the party receiving the papers. This includes the use of facsimile transmissions and any additional expedited means of communication approved by the court. FL ST 6 J CIR 2009-066 PA/PI-CIR(C)(1).

ii. Attorneys will not serve papers to take advantage of opposing counsel's known absence from the office or at a time or in a manner designed to inconvenience an opponent, such as late on Friday afternoon or the day preceding a secular or religious holiday. FL ST 6 J CIR 2009-066 PA/PI-CIR(C)(2).

iii. Attorneys will not serve papers, including briefs and memoranda, so close to a court appearance that the ability of opposing counsel to prepare for that appearance or, where permitted, to respond, is inhibited. FL ST 6 J CIR 2009-066 PA/PI-CIR(C)(3).

iv. Service should be made personally or by facsimile transmission when it is likely that service by mail, even when allowed, will prejudice the opposing party. FL ST 6 J CIR 2009-066 PA/PI-CIR(C)(4).

G. Hearings

1. There is no hearing required or contemplated in the Florida rules governing the complaint and service of summons.

H. Forms

1. Official Complaint Forms for Florida

a. Caption. FL ST RCP Form 1.901.

b. Summons. FL ST RCP Form 1.902.

c. Crossclaim summons. FL ST RCP Form 1.903.

d. Third-party summons. FL ST RCP Form 1.904.

e. Notice of action, constructive service, no property. FL ST RCP Form 1.919.
f. Notice of action, constructive service, property. FL ST RCP Form 1.920.
g. Third-party complaint. FL ST RCP Form 1.948.
h. Civil cover sheet. FL ST RCP Form 1.997.
i. Fall-down negligence complaint. FL ST RCP Form 1.951.
j. Notice of compliance when constitutional challenge is brought. FL ST RCP Form 1.975.

2. Complaint and Summons Forms for Florida

a. Complaint for damages; General form. FL-PP § 2:17.
b. Complaint; Negligent infliction of personal injury. FL-PP § 2:19.
c. Complaint; Fall down negligence. FL-PP § 2:20.
d. Complaint; Professional negligence. FL-PP § 2:23.
e. Complaint; Breach of contract. FL-PP § 2:24.
f. Complaint; Breach of personal services contract. FL-PP § 2:25.
g. Summons; General form. FL-PRACFORM § 3:4.
h. Summons; Natural person. FL-PRACFORM § 3:5.
i. Complaint; Assault and battery. FL-PRACFORM § 4:9.
j. Complaint; Breach of contract, general form. FL-PRACFORM § 4:17.
k. Complaint; Civil rights. FL-PRACFORM § 4:23.
l. Complaint; Conversion. FL-PRACFORM § 4:30.
m. Complaint; Employment contract. FL-PRACFORM § 4:44.
n. Complaint; False imprisonment. FL-PRACFORM § 4:46.
o. Complaint; Fraud, misrepresentation. FL-PRACFORM § 4:62.
p. Complaint; Lease, by landlord. FL-PRACFORM § 4:86.
q. Complaint; Lease, by tenant. FL-PRACFORM § 4:87.
r. Complaint; Libel. FL-PRACFORM § 4:89.
s. Complaint; Life insurance policy. FL-PRACFORM § 4:90.
t. Complaint; Medical malpractice, negligence. FL-PRACFORM § 4:95.
u. Complaint; Negligence, automobile, driver. FL-PRACFORM § 4:101.
v. Complaint; Negligence, hospital. FL-PRACFORM § 4:104.

I. Checklist

(I) ❑ Matters to be considered by plaintiff
- (a) ❑ Required documents
  - (1) ❑ Summons
  - (2) ❑ Complaint
  - (3) ❑ Civil cover sheet
  - (4) ❑ Return of execution process by process server
  - (5) ❑ Filing fees
- (b) ❑ Supplemental documents
  - (1) ❑ Exhibits
  - (2) ❑ Notice of constitutional question
  - (3) ❑ Notice of companion cases

(c) ❑ Time for filing and serving complaint
  (1) ❑ Service of the initial process and initial pleading should be made upon a defendant within one hundred twenty (120) days after the filing of the complaint with the court

(II) ❑ Matters to be considered by defendant
 (a) ❑ Required documents
  (1) ❑ Answer
  (2) ❑ Certificate of service
 (b) ❑ Supplemental documents
  (1) ❑ Exhibits
  (2) ❑ Notice of constitutional question
  (3) ❑ Notice of companion cases
 (c) ❑ Time for answer
  (1) ❑ Unless a different time is prescribed in a statute of Florida, a defendant shall serve an answer within twenty (20) days after service of original process and the initial pleading on the defendant, or not later than the date fixed in a notice by publication
  (2) ❑ A party served with a pleading stating a crossclaim against that party shall serve an answer to it within twenty (20) days after service on that party
  (3) ❑ The plaintiff shall serve an answer to a counterclaim within twenty (20) days after service of the counterclaim
  (4) ❑ A defendant who, before being served with process, timely returns a waiver so requested is not required to respond to the complaint until sixty (60) days after the date the defendant received the request for waiver of service; for purposes of computing any time prescribed or allowed by the Florida Rules of Civil Procedure, service of process shall be deemed effected twenty (20) days before the time required to respond to the complaint
  (5) ❑ For timing requirements related to service on the state, service of motion impact, and responding when no responsive pleading is required, please see the Timing section of this document

Pleadings
Amended Complaint

Document Last Updated January 2013

A. Applicable Rules

1. *State rules*
 a. Nonverification of papers. FL ST RCP Rule 1.030.
 b. Process. FL ST RCP Rule 1.070.
 c. Service and filing of pleadings, orders, and documents. FL ST RCP Rule 1.080.
 d. Pleadings and motions. FL ST RCP Rule 1.100; FL ST RCP Rule 1.110; FL ST RCP Rule 1.120; FL ST RCP Rule 1.130; FL ST RCP Rule 1.190; FL ST § 48.193.
 e. Pretrial procedure. FL ST RCP Rule 1.200.
 f. Relief from judgment, decrees, or orders. FL ST RCP Rule 1.540.
 g. Forms. FL ST RCP Rule 1.900.
 h. Minimization of the filing of sensitive information. FL ST J ADMIN Rule 2.425.
 i. Retention of court records. FL ST J ADMIN Rule 2.430.
 j. Foreign attorneys. FL ST J ADMIN Rule 2.510.

k. Signature of attorneys and parties. FL ST J ADMIN Rule 2.515.

l. Paper. FL ST J ADMIN Rule 2.520.

m. Electronic filing. FL ST J ADMIN Rule 2.525.

n. Accessibility of information and technology. FL ST J ADMIN Rule 2.526.

o. Requests for accommodations by persons with disabilities. FL ST J ADMIN Rule 2.540.

2. *Local rules*

a. Assignment of cases. FL ST 6 J CIR LOCAL Rule 3.

b. Standards of professional courtesy. FL ST 6 J CIR 2009-066 PA/PI-CIR.

c. Arbitration and mediation program circuit civil and family cases. FL ST 6 J CIR PA/PI-CIR-96-63; FL ST 6 J CIR 2011-006 PA/PI-CIR.

B. Timing

1. *Amendment as a matter of course.* A party may amend a pleading once as a matter of course at any time before a responsive pleading is served or, if the pleading is one to which no responsive pleading is permitted and the action has not been placed on the trial calendar, may so amend it at any time within twenty (20) days after it is served. FL ST RCP Rule 1.190(a).

2. *Amendment by leave of court.* Otherwise a party may amend a pleading only by leave of court or by written consent of the adverse party. Leave of court shall be given freely when justice so requires. FL ST RCP Rule 1.190(a).

3. *Amendments in furtherance of justice.* At any time in furtherance of justice, upon such terms as may be just, the court may permit any process, proceeding, pleading, or record to be amended or material supplemental matter to be set forth in an amended or supplemental pleading. At every stage of the action the court must disregard any error or defect in the proceedings which does not affect the substantial rights of the parties. FL ST RCP Rule 1.190(e).

4. *Response to amended pleading.* A party shall plead in response to an amended pleading within ten (10) days after service of the amended pleading unless the court otherwise orders. FL ST RCP Rule 1.190(a).

5. *Computation of time*

a. *Generally.* Computation of time shall be governed by FL ST J ADMIN Rule 2.514. FL ST RCP Rule 1.090(a). The following rules apply in computing time periods specified in any rule of procedure, local rule, court order, or statute that does not specify a method of computing time. FL ST J ADMIN Rule 2.514(a).

i. *Period stated in days or a longer unit.* When the period is stated in days or a longer unit of time (A) exclude the day of the event that triggers the period; (B) count every day, including intermediate Saturdays, Sundays, and legal holidays; and (C) include the last day of the period, but if the last day is a Saturday, Sunday, or legal holiday, or falls within any period of time extended through an order of the chief justice under FL ST J ADMIN Rule 2.205(a)(2)(B)(iv), the period continues to run until the end of the next day that is not a Saturday, Sunday, or legal holiday and does not fall within any period of time extended through an order of the chief justice. FL ST J ADMIN Rule 2.514(a)(1).

ii. *Period stated in hours.* When the period is stated in hours (A) begin counting immediately on the occurrence of the event that triggers the period; (B) count every hour, including hours during intermediate Saturdays, Sundays, and legal holidays; and (C) if the period would end on a Saturday, Sunday, or legal holiday, or during any period of time extended through an order of the chief justice under FL ST J ADMIN Rule 2.205(a)(2)(B)(iv), the period continues to run until the same time on the next day that is not a Saturday, Sunday, or legal holiday and does not fall within any period of time extended through an order of the chief justice. FL ST J ADMIN Rule 2.514(a)(2).

iii. *Period stated in days less than seven (7) days.* When the period stated in days is less than seven (7) days, intermediate Saturdays, Sundays, and legal holidays shall be excluded in the computation. FL ST J ADMIN Rule 2.514(a)(3).

iv. *"Last day" defined.* Unless a different time is set by a statute, local rule, or court order, the last day ends (A) for electronic filing or for service by any means, at midnight; and (B) for filing by other means, when the clerk's office is scheduled to close. FL ST J ADMIN Rule 2.514(a)(4).

v. *"Next day" defined.* The "next day" is determined by continuing to count forward when the period is measured after an event and backward when measured before an event. FL ST J ADMIN Rule 2.514(a)(5).

vi. *"Legal holiday" defined.* "Legal holiday" means (A) the day set aside by FL ST § 110.117, for observing New Year's Day, Martin Luther King, Jr.'s Birthday, Memorial Day, Independence Day, Labor Day, Veterans' Day, Thanksgiving Day, the Friday after Thanksgiving Day, or Christmas Day, and (B) any day observed as a holiday by the clerk's office or as designated by the chief judge. FL ST J ADMIN Rule 2.514(a)(6).

b. *Additional time after service by mail or e-mail.* When a party may or must act within a specified time after service and service is made by mail or e-mail, five (5) days are added after the period that would otherwise expire under FL ST J ADMIN Rule 2.514(a). FL ST J ADMIN Rule 2.514(b).

c. *Enlargement.* When an act is required or allowed to be done at or within a specified time by order of court, by the Florida Rules of Civil Procedure, or by notice given thereunder, for cause shown the court at any time in its discretion (1) with or without notice, may order the period enlarged if request therefor is made before the expiration of the period originally prescribed or as extended by a previous order, or (2) upon motion made and notice after the expiration of the specified period, may permit the act to be done when failure to act was the result of excusable neglect, but it may not extend the time for making a motion for new trial, for rehearing, or to alter or amend a judgment; making a motion for relief from a judgment under FL ST RCP Rule 1.540(b); taking an appeal or filing a petition for certiorari; or making a motion for a directed verdict. FL ST RCP Rule 1.090(b).

d. *Unaffected by expiration of term.* The period of time provided for the doing of any act or the taking of any proceeding shall not be affected or limited by the continued existence or expiration of a term of court. The continued existence or expiration of a term of court in no way affects the power of a court to do any act or take any proceeding in any action which is or has been pending before it. FL ST RCP Rule 1.090(c).

C. General Requirements

1. *Amendments.* A party may amend a pleading once as a matter of course at any time before a responsive pleading is served or, if the pleading is one to which no responsive pleading is permitted and the action has not been placed on the trial calendar, may so amend it at any time within twenty (20) days after it is served. Otherwise a party may amend a pleading only by leave of court or by written consent of the adverse party. Leave of court shall be freely given when justice so requires. FL ST RCP Rule 1.190(a).

a. *Purpose of amendments.* Amendments can relate to the correction of mistakes, the insertion of jurisdictional averments, the correction or addition of verifications, the addition or substitution or striking out of parties, and generally the rectification of all formal defects in the pleading. The court can also allow amendments setting up an omitted counterclaim or cross-claim if the defendant failed to raise the claim through oversight, inadvertence, or excusable neglect. FL-PP § 2:151.

b. *Amendment to a pleading/Amended pleading.* A significant difference exists between an amendment to a pleading and an amended pleading. An amendment to a pleading corrects, adds to or deletes from the pleading. An amended pleading is substituted for the former pleading and the former pleading ceases to have any effect. Dee v. Southern Brewing Company, 146 Fla. 588, 1 So.2d 562 (Fla. 1941); Shannon v. McBride, 105 So.2d 16 (Fla. 2d DCA 1958); Hughes v. Home Sav. of America, F.S.B., 675 So.2d 649 (Fla. 2d DCA 1996); FL-PRACPROC § 14:2.

c. *Relation back of amendments.* When the claim or defense asserted in the amended pleading arose out of the conduct, transaction, or occurrence set forth or attempted to be set forth in the original pleading, the amendment shall relate back to the date of the original pleading. FL ST RCP Rule 1.190(c).

2. *General rules of pleading*
   a. *Claims for relief*
      i. A pleading which sets forth a claim for relief, whether an original claim, counterclaim, crossclaim, or third-party claim, must state a cause of action and shall contain
         - A short and plain statement of the grounds upon which the court's jurisdiction depends, unless the court already has jurisdiction and the claim needs no new grounds of jurisdiction to support it (For information regarding acts subjecting persons to jurisdiction, please see FL ST § 48.193),
         - A short and plain statement of the ultimate facts showing that the pleader is entitled to relief, and
         - A demand for judgment for the relief to which the pleader deems himself or herself entitled. FL ST RCP Rule 1.110(b).
      ii. Relief in the alternative or of several different types may be demanded. Every complaint shall be considered to demand general relief. FL ST RCP Rule 1.110(b).
   b. *Verification.* Except when otherwise specifically provided by these rules or an applicable statute, every pleading or other document of a party represented by an attorney need not be verified or accompanied by an affidavit. FL ST RCP Rule 1.030. When filing an action for foreclosure of a mortgage on residential real property the complaint shall be verified. When verification of a document is required, the document filed shall include an oath, affirmation, or the following statement: "Under penalty of perjury, I declare that I have read the foregoing, and the facts alleged therein are true and correct to the best of my knowledge and belief." FL ST RCP Rule 1.110(b).
   c. *Separate statements.* All averments of claim or defense shall be made in consecutively numbered paragraphs, the contents of each of which shall be limited as far as practicable to a statement of a single set of circumstances, and a paragraph may be referred to by number in all subsequent pleadings. Each claim founded upon a separate transaction or occurrence and each defense other than denials shall be stated in a separate count or defense when a separation facilitates the clear presentation of the matter set forth. FL ST RCP Rule 1.110(f).
   d. *Statements adopted by reference.* Statements in a pleading may be adopted by reference in a different part of the same pleading, in another pleading, or in any motion. FL ST RCP Rule 1.130(b).
   e. *Joinder of causes of action; Consistency.* A pleader may set up in the same action as many claims or causes of action or defenses in the same right as the pleader has, and claims for relief may be stated in the alternative if separate items make up the cause of action, or if two (2) or more causes of action are joined. A party may also set forth two (2) or more statements of a claim or defense alternatively, either in one (1) count or defense or in separate counts or defenses. When two (2) or more statements are made in the alternative and one (1) of them, if made independently, would be sufficient, the pleading is not made insufficient by the insufficiency of one (1) or more of the alternative statements. A party may also state as many separate claims or defenses as that party has, regardless of consistency and whether based on legal or equitable grounds or both. All pleadings shall be construed so as to do substantial justice. FL ST RCP Rule 1.110(g).
   f. *Subsequent pleadings.* When the nature of an action permits pleadings subsequent to final judgment and the jurisdiction of the court over the parties has not terminated, the initial pleading subsequent to final judgment shall be designated a supplemental complaint or petition. The action shall then proceed in the same manner and time as though the supplemental complaint or petition were the initial pleading in the action, including the issuance of any needed process. FL ST RCP Rule 1.110(h) shall not apply to proceedings that may be initiated by motion under the Florida Rules of Civil Procedure. FL ST RCP Rule 1.110(h).
   g. *Pleading basis for service.* When service of process is to be made under statutes authorizing service on nonresidents of Florida, it is sufficient to plead the basis for service in the language of the statute without pleading the facts supporting service. FL ST RCP Rule 1.070(h).
   h. *Forms of pleadings.* Forms of action and technical forms for seeking relief and of pleas, pleadings, or motions are abolished. FL ST RCP Rule 1.110(a).

3. *Complaint; Generally*
    a. *Purpose.* The purpose of a complaint is to advise the court and the defendant of the nature of a cause of action asserted by the plaintiff. FL-PP § 2:12.
    b. *Sufficiency of complaint.* A complaint will be found to be insufficient if it contains only general conclusory allegations unsupported by any facts. The test to determine whether a complaint is sufficient is whether, if the factual allegations of the complaint are established, the plaintiff will be legally or equitably entitled to the claimed relief. Pizzi v. Central Bank & Trust Co., 250 So.2d 895, 896 (Fla. 1971); Bowen v. G H C Properties, Limited, 251 So.2d 359, 361 (Fla. 1st DCA 1971); FL-PP § 2:12. In determining the sufficiency of the complaint to state a cause of action, all allegations of the complaint are taken as true, and possible affirmative defenses are not considered. Strickland v. Commerce Loan Co. of Jacksonville, 158 So.2d 814 (Fla. 1st DCA 1963); FL-PP § 2:12.
        i. The issues for trial in Florida must be settled by the pleadings. The issues cannot be raised by discovery. FL-PRACPROC § 7:6.
        ii. Causes of action may be pleaded alternatively in the same count or in different counts and against the same or different defendants as long as the joinder of parties is proper. FL-PRACPROC § 7:6.
        iii. Each count must state a cause of action. Each independent cause of action should be pleaded in a separate count. FL-PRACPROC § 7:6.
        iv. Incorporation by reference of all allegations from one count to another is not proper. Separate counts facilitate reference to the pleading in which they appear in other pleadings, motions or papers as well as the assertion of defenses against some, but not all, causes of action. Some defenses may not apply to the initial pleading as a whole. FL-PRACPROC § 7:6.
4. *Pleading special matters*
    a. *Capacity.* It is not necessary to aver the capacity of a party to sue or be sued, the authority of a party to sue or be sued in a representative capacity, or the legal existence of an organized association of persons that is made a party, except to the extent required to show the jurisdiction of the court. The initial pleading served on behalf of a minor party shall specifically aver the age of the minor party. When a party desires to raise an issue as to the legal existence of any party, the capacity of any party to sue or be sued, or the authority of a party to sue or be sued in a representative capacity, that party shall do so by specific negative averment which shall include such supporting particulars as are peculiarly within the pleader's knowledge. FL ST RCP Rule 1.120(a).
    b. *Fraud, mistake, condition of the mind.* In all averments of fraud or mistake, the circumstances constituting fraud or mistake shall be stated with such particularity as the circumstances may permit. Malice, intent, knowledge, mental attitude, and other condition of mind of a person may be averred generally. FL ST RCP Rule 1.120(b).
    c. *Conditions precedent.* In pleading the performance or occurrence of conditions precedent, it is sufficient to aver generally that all conditions precedent have been performed or have occurred. A denial of performance or occurrence shall be made specifically and with particularity. FL ST RCP Rule 1.120(c).
    d. *Official document or act.* In pleading an official document or official act it is sufficient to aver that the document was issued or the act done in compliance with law. FL ST RCP Rule 1.120(c).
    e. *Judgment or decree.* In pleading a judgment or decree of a domestic or foreign court, a judicial or quasi-judicial tribunal, or a board or officer, it is sufficient to aver the judgment or decree without setting forth matter showing jurisdiction to render it. FL ST RCP Rule 1.120(e).
    f. *Time and place.* For the purpose of testing the sufficiency of a pleading, averments of time and place are material and shall be considered like all other averments of material matter. FL ST RCP Rule 1.120(f).
    g. *Special damage.* When items of special damage are claimed, they shall be specifically stated. FL ST RCP Rule 1.120(g).
5. *Parties*
    a. *Parties generally.* Every action may be prosecuted in the name of the real party in interest, but a

personal representative, administrator, guardian, trustee of an express trust, a party with whom or in whose name a contract has been made for the benefit of another, or a party expressly authorized by statute may sue in that person's own name without joining the party for whose benefit the action is brought. All persons having an interest in the subject of the action and in obtaining the relief demanded may join as plaintiffs and any person may be made a defendant who has or claims an interest adverse to the plaintiff. Any person may at any time be made a party if that person's presence is necessary or proper to a complete determination of the cause. Persons having a united interest may be joined on the same side as plaintiffs or defendants, and anyone who refuses to join may for such reason be made a defendant. FL ST RCP Rule 1.210(a).

b. *Minors or incompetent persons.* When a minor or incompetent person has a representative, such as a guardian or other like fiduciary, the representative may sue or defend on behalf of the minor or incompetent person. A minor or incompetent person who does not have a duly appointed representative may sue by next friend or by a guardian ad litem. The court shall appoint a guardian ad litem for a minor or incompetent person not otherwise represented in an action or shall make such other order as it deems proper for the protection of the minor or incompetent person. FL ST RCP Rule 1.210(b).

c. For survivor and substitution of parties information, please see FL ST RCP Rule 1.260.

6. *Counterclaims and crossclaims*

a. *Compulsory counterclaims.* A pleading shall state as a counterclaim any claim which at the time of serving the pleading the pleader has against any opposing party, provided it arises out of the transaction or occurrence that is the subject matter of the opposing party's claim and does not require for its adjudication the presence of third parties over whom the court cannot acquire jurisdiction. But the pleader need not state a claim if (1) at the time the action was commenced the claim was the subject of another pending action, or (2) the opposing party brought suit upon that party's claim by attachment or other process by which the court did not acquire jurisdiction to render a personal judgment on the claim and the pleader is not stating a counterclaim under this rule. FL ST RCP Rule 1.170(a).

b. *Permissive counterclaim.* A pleading may state as a counterclaim any claim against an opposing party not arising out of the transaction or occurrence that is the subject matter of the opposing party's claim. FL ST RCP Rule 1.170(b).

c. *Counterclaim exceeding opposing claim.* A counterclaim may or may not diminish or defeat the recovery sought by the opposing party. It may claim relief exceeding in amount or different in kind from that sought in the pleading of the opposing party. FL ST RCP Rule 1.170(c).

d. *Counterclaim against the State.* The Florida Rules of Civil Procedure shall not be construed to enlarge beyond the limits established by law the right to assert counterclaims or to claim credits against the state or any of its subdivisions or other governmental organizations thereof subject to suit or against a municipal corporation or against an officer, agency, or administrative board of the state. FL ST RCP Rule 1.170(d).

e. *Counterclaim maturing or acquired after pleading.* A claim which matured or was acquired by the pleader after serving the pleading may be presented as a counterclaim by supplemental pleading with the permission of the court. FL ST RCP Rule 1.170(e).

f. *Omitted counterclaim or crossclaim.* When a pleader fails to set up a counterclaim or crossclaim through oversight, inadvertence, or excusable neglect, or when justice requires, the pleader may set up the counterclaim or crossclaim by amendment with leave of the court. FL ST RCP Rule 1.170(f).

g. *Crossclaim against co-party.* A pleading may state as a crossclaim any claim by one party against a co-party arising out of the transaction or occurrence that is the subject matter of either the original action or a counterclaim therein, or relating to any property that is the subject matter of the original action. The crossclaim may include a claim that the party against whom it is asserted is or may be liable to the crossclaimant for all or part of a claim asserted in the action against the crossclaimant. Service of a crossclaim on a party who has appeared in the action shall be made pursuant to FL ST RCP Rule 1.080. Service of a crossclaim against a party who has not appeared in the action shall be made in the manner provided for service of summons. FL ST RCP Rule 1.170(g).

h. *Additional parties may be brought in.* When the presence of parties other than those to the original action is required to grant complete relief in the determination of a counterclaim or crossclaim, they shall be named in the counterclaim or crossclaim and be served with process and shall be parties to the action thereafter if jurisdiction of them can be obtained and their joinder will not deprive the court of jurisdiction of the action. FL ST RCP Rule 1.250(b) and FL ST RCP Rule 1.250(c) apply to parties brought in under FL ST RCP Rule 1.170(h). FL ST RCP Rule 1.170(h).

i. *Separate trials; Separate judgment.* If the court orders separate trials as provided in FL ST RCP Rule 1.270(b), judgment on a counterclaim or crossclaim may be rendered when the court has jurisdiction to do so even if a claim of the opposing party has been dismissed or otherwise disposed of. FL ST RCP Rule 1.170(i).

j. *Demand exceeding jurisdiction; Transfer of action.* If the demand of any counterclaim or crossclaim exceeds the jurisdiction of the court in which the action is pending, the action shall be transferred forthwith to the court of the same county having jurisdiction of the demand in the counterclaim or crossclaim with only such alterations in the pleadings as are essential. The court shall order the transfer of the action and the transmittal of all papers in it to the proper court if the party asserting the demand exceeding the jurisdiction deposits with the court having jurisdiction a sum sufficient to pay the clerk's service charge in the court to which the action is transferred at the time of filing the counterclaim or crossclaim. Thereupon the original papers and deposit shall be transmitted and filed with a certified copy of the order. The court to which the action is transferred shall have full power and jurisdiction over the demands of all parties. Failure to make the service charge deposit at the time the counterclaim or crossclaim is filed, or within such further time as the court may allow, shall reduce a claim for damages to an amount within the jurisdiction of the court where the action is pending and waive the claim in other cases. FL ST RCP Rule 1.170(j).

7. *Misjoinder and nonjoinder of parties*

a. *Misjoinder.* Misjoinder of parties is not a ground for dismissal of an action. Any claim against a party may be severed and proceeded with separately. FL ST RCP Rule 1.250(a).

b. *Dropping parties.* Parties may be dropped by an adverse party in the manner provided for voluntary dismissal in FL ST RCP Rule 1.420(a)(1) subject to the exception stated in FL ST RCP Rule 1.420. If notice of lis pendens has been filed in the action against a party so dropped, the notice of dismissal shall be recorded and cancels the notice of lis pendens without the necessity of a court order. Parties may be dropped by order of court on its own initiative or the motion of any party at any stage of the action on such terms as are just. FL ST RCP Rule 1.250(b).

c. *Adding parties.* Parties may be added once as a matter of course within the same time that pleadings can be so amended under FL ST RCP Rule 1.190(a). If amendment by leave of court or stipulation of the parties is permitted, parties may be added in the amended pleading without further order of court. Parties may be added by order of court on its own initiative or on motion of any party at any stage of the action and on such terms as are just. FL ST RCP Rule 1.250(c).

8. *Jury demand*

a. *Right preserved.* The right of trial by jury as declared by the Constitution or by statute shall be preserved to the parties inviolate. FL ST RCP Rule 1.430(a).

b. *Demand.* Any party may demand a trial by jury of any issue triable of right by a jury by serving upon the other party a demand therefor in writing at any time after commencement of the action and not later than ten (10) days after the service of the last pleading directed to such issue. The demand may be indorsed upon a pleading of the party. FL ST RCP Rule 1.430(b).

c. *Specification of issues.* In the demand a party may specify the issues that the party wishes so tried; otherwise, the party is deemed to demand trial by jury for all issues so triable. FL ST RCP Rule 1.430(c).

i. If a party has demanded trial by jury for only some of the issues, any other party may serve a demand for trial by jury of any other or all of the issues triable by jury ten (10) days after service of the demand or such lesser time as the court may order. FL ST RCP Rule 1.430(c).

d. *Waiver.* A party who fails to serve a demand as required by FL ST RCP Rule 1.430 waives trial by jury. FL ST RCP Rule 1.430(d).

   i. If waived, a jury trial may not be granted without the consent of the parties, but the court may allow an amendment in the proceedings to demand a trial by jury or order a trial by jury on its own motion. FL ST RCP Rule 1.430(d).

   ii. A demand for trial by jury may not be withdrawn without the consent of the parties. FL ST RCP Rule 1.430(d).

9. *Companion cases in the Sixth Circuit*

   a. An attorney representing a party in a case to which there are companion cases shall file a notice of a companion case. FL ST 6 J CIR LOCAL Rule 3(B)(1).

   b. The original notice and sufficient copies for filing in each companion case shall be filed with the Clerk and a copy provided to the judge in the section which has been assigned the case bearing the lowest docket number. FL ST 6 J CIR LOCAL Rule 3(B)(1).

   c. Said judge may thereupon reassign all such companion cases to the section which has been assigned the case bearing the lowest docket number if the court finds that the companion cases involve common questions of law or fact or the reassignment would result in an efficient administration of justice. FL ST 6 J CIR LOCAL Rule 3(B)(1).

   d. The Clerk shall make appropriate notations on the file cover and the progress docket of such reassigned case or cases and thereafter all such companion cases shall be heard, tried, and determined by the judge assigned to the section having the companion case bearing the lowest docket number. FL ST 6 J CIR LOCAL Rule 3 (B)(1).

10. *Arbitration and mediation*

   a. *Referral to arbitration and mediation.* Except as hereinafter provided or as otherwise prohibited by law, the presiding judge may enter an order referring all or any part of a contested civil matter to mediation or arbitration. The parties to any contested civil matter may file a written stipulation to mediate or arbitrate any issue between them at any time. Such stipulation shall be incorporated into the order of referral. FL ST RCP Rule 1.700(a).

   b. *Arbitration*

      i. *Exclusions.* A civil action shall be ordered to arbitration or arbitration in conjunction with mediation upon stipulation of the parties. A civil action may be ordered to arbitration or arbitration in conjunction with mediation upon motion of any party or by the court, if the judge determines the action to be of such a nature that arbitration could be of benefit to the litigants or the court. FL ST RCP Rule 1.800.

         - Under no circumstances may the following categories of actions be referred to arbitration: (1) bond estreatures; (2) habeas corpus or other extraordinary writs; (3) bond validations; (4) civil or criminal contempt; (5) such other matters as may be specified by order of the chief judge in the circuit. FL ST RCP Rule 1.800.

      ii. For more information regarding arbitration, please see FL ST RCP Rule 1.810; FL ST RCP Rule 1.820; FL ST RCP Rule 1.830.

   c. *Mediation.* For more information regarding mediation, please see FL ST RCP Rule 1.710; FL ST RCP Rule 1.720; FL ST RCP Rule 1.730; and FL ST RCP Rule 1.750.

   d. See FL ST 6 J CIR PA/PI-CIR-96-63 for more information about the Arbitration and Mediation Program for Florida's Sixth Judicial Circuit.

11. *Rules of court*

   a. *Rules of civil procedure.* The Florida Rules of Civil Procedure apply to all actions of a civil nature and all special statutory proceedings in the circuit courts and county courts except those to which the Florida Probate Rules, the Florida Family Law Rules of Procedure, or the Small Claims Rules apply. FL ST RCP Rule 1.010.

      i. The form, content, procedure, and time for pleading in all special statutory proceedings shall be

as prescribed by the statutes governing the proceeding unless the Florida Rules of Civil Procedure specifically provide to the contrary. FL ST RCP Rule 1.010.

ii. The Florida Rules of Civil Procedure shall be construed to secure the just, speedy, and inexpensive determination of every action. FL ST RCP Rule 1.010.

b. *Rules of judicial administration.* The Florida Rules of Judicial Administration shall apply to administrative matters in all courts to which the Florida Rules of Judicial Administration are applicable by their terms. The Florida Rules of Judicial Administration shall be construed to secure the speedy and inexpensive determination of every proceeding to which they are applicable. The Florida Rules of Judicial Administration shall supersede all conflicting rules and statutes. FL ST J ADMIN Rule 2.110.

D. Documents

1. *Required documents*

a. *Amended complaint.* See the General Requirements section of this document for the content of an amended complaint. If a party files a motion to amend a pleading, the party shall attach the proposed amended pleading to the motion. FL ST RCP Rule 1.190(a). See the KeyRules Florida Circuit Court Motion for Leave to Amend document for further information.

i. *Notices to persons with disabilities.* See the Format section of this KeyRules document for further information.

b. *Certificate of service.* When any attorney certifies in substance: "I certify that a copy hereof has been furnished to (here insert name or names and addresses used for service) by (e-mail) (delivery) (mail) (fax) on .... (date) ....________________ Attorney" the certificate is taken as prima facie proof of such service in compliance with FL ST J ADMIN Rule 2.516. FL ST J ADMIN Rule 2.516(f).

2. *Supplemental documents*

a. *Exhibits.* All bonds, notes, bills of exchange, contracts, accounts, or documents upon which action may be brought or defense made, or a copy thereof or a copy of the portions thereof material to the pleadings, shall be incorporated in or attached to the pleading. No papers shall be unnecessarily annexed as exhibits. The pleadings shall contain no unnecessary recitals of deeds, documents, contracts, or other instruments. Any exhibit attached to a pleading shall be considered a part of the pleadings for all purposes. FL ST RCP Rule 1.130(a).

b. *Notice of constitutional question.* A party that files a pleading, written motion, or other paper drawing into question the constitutionality of a state statute or a county or municipal charter, ordinance, or franchise must promptly (1) file a notice of constitutional question stating the question and identifying the paper that raises it; and (2) serve the notice and the pleading, written motion, or other paper drawing into question the constitutionality of a state statute or a county or municipal charter, ordinance, or franchise on the Attorney General or the state attorney of the judicial circuit in which the action is pending, by either certified or registered mail. Service of the notice and pleading, written motion, or other paper does not require joinder of the Attorney General or the state attorney as a party to the action. FL ST RCP Rule 1.071.

c. *Notice of companion cases.* An attorney representing a party in a case to which there are companion cases shall file a notice of a companion case. FL ST 6 J CIR LOCAL Rule 3(B)(1).

E. Format

1. *Documents; Type and size.* Documents subject to the exceptions set forth in FL ST J ADMIN Rule 2.525(d) shall be filed on recycled paper measuring eight and one half by eleven (8 1/2 by 11) inches. For purposes of FL ST J ADMIN Rule 2.520, paper is recycled if it contains a minimum content of fifty (50) percent waste paper. Xerographic reduction of legal-size (eight and one half by fourteen (8 1/2 by 14) inches) documents to letter size (eight and one half by eleven (8 1/2 by 11) inches) is prohibited. All other documents filed by electronic transmission shall be filed in a format capable of being printed in a format consistent with the provisions of FL ST J ADMIN Rule 2.250. FL ST J ADMIN Rule 2.520(b).

a. *Exhibits.* Any exhibit or attachment filed with pleadings or papers may be filed in its original size. FL ST J ADMIN Rule 2.520(c).

b. *Recording space.* On all papers and documents prepared and filed by the court or by any party to a proceeding which are to be recorded in the public records of any county, including but not limited to final money judgments and notices of lis pendens, a three (3) inch by three (3) inch space at the top right-hand corner on the first page and a one (1) inch by three (3) inch space at the top right-hand corner on each subsequent page shall be left blank and reserved for use by the clerk of court. FL ST J ADMIN Rule 2.520(d).

   i. *Exceptions to recording space.* Any papers or documents created by persons or entities over which the filing party has no control, including but not limited to wills, codicils, trusts, or other testamentary documents; documents prepared or executed by any public officer; documents prepared, executed, acknowledged, or proved outside of the State of Florida; or documents created by State or Federal government agencies, may be filed without the space required by FL ST J ADMIN Rule 2.520. FL ST J ADMIN Rule 2.520(e).

c. *Noncompliance.* No clerk of court is permitted to refuse to file any document or paper because of noncompliance with the Florida Rules of Judicial Administration. However, upon request of the clerk of court, noncomplying documents must be resubmitted in accordance with the formatting rules. FL ST J ADMIN Rule 2.520(f).

2. *Caption.* Every pleading, motion, order, judgment, or other paper shall have a caption containing the name of the court, the file number, and except for in rem proceedings, including forfeiture proceedings, the name of the first party on each side with an appropriate indication of other parties, and a designation identifying the party filing it and its nature or the nature of the order, as the case may be. In any in rem proceeding, every pleading, motion, order, judgment, or other paper shall have a caption containing the name of the court, the file number, the style "In re" (followed by the name or general description of the property), and a designation of the person or entity filing it and its nature or the nature of the order, as the case may be. In an in rem forfeiture proceeding, the style shall be "In re forfeiture of" (followed by the name of the general description of the property). All papers filed in the action shall be styled in such a manner as to indicate clearly the subject matter of the paper and the party requesting or obtaining relief. FL ST RCP Rule 1.100(c)(1).

3. *Writing and written defined.* Writing or written means a document containing information, an application, or a stipulation. FL ST RCP Rule 1.080(c).

4. *Rule abbreviations*

   a. The Florida Rules of Civil Procedure and shall be abbreviated as Fla.R.Civ.P. FL ST RCP Rule 1.010.

   b. The Florida Rules of Judicial Administration shall be abbreviated as Fla. R. Jud. Admin. FL ST J ADMIN Rule 2.110.

5. *Nonverification.* Except when otherwise specifically provided by the Florida Rules of Civil Procedure or an applicable statute, every pleading or other document of a party represented by an attorney need not be verified or accompanied by an affidavit. FL ST RCP Rule 1.030; FL ST J ADMIN Rule 2.515(a).

6. *Attorney signature*

   a. *Attorney signature.* Every pleading and other document of a party represented by an attorney shall be signed by at least one (1) attorney of record in that attorney's individual name whose current record Florida Bar address, telephone number, including area code, primary e-mail address and secondary e-mail addresses, if any, and Florida Bar number shall be stated, and who shall be duly licensed to practice law in Florida or who shall have received permission to appear in the particular case as provided in FL ST J ADMIN Rule 2.510. FL ST J ADMIN Rule 2.515(a).

      i. The attorney may be required by the court to give the address of, and to vouch for the attorney's authority to represent, the party. FL ST J ADMIN Rule 2.515(a).

      ii. The signature of an attorney shall constitute a certificate by the attorney that the attorney has read the pleading or other document; that to the best of the attorney's knowledge, information, and belief there is good ground to support it; and that it is not interposed for delay. FL ST J ADMIN Rule 2.515(a).

      iii. If a pleading is not signed or is signed with intent to defeat the purpose of FL ST J ADMIN Rule

2.515, it may be stricken and the action may proceed as though the pleading or other document had not been served. FL ST J ADMIN Rule 2.515(a).

b. *Pro se litigant signature.* A party who is not represented by an attorney shall sign any pleading or other paper and state the party's address and telephone number, including area code. FL ST J ADMIN Rule 2.515(b).

c. *Form of signature*

i. The signatures required on pleadings and documents by FL ST J ADMIN Rule 2.515(a) and FL ST J ADMIN Rule 2.515(b) may be:

- Original signatures;
- Original signatures that have been reproduced by electronic means, such as on electronically transmitted documents or photocopied documents;
- Electronic signatures using the "/s/," "s/," or "/s" formats by or at the direction of the person signing; or
- Any other signature format authorized by general law, so long as the clerk where the proceeding is pending has the capability of receiving and has obtained approval from the Supreme Court of Florida to accept pleadings and documents with that signature format. FL ST J ADMIN Rule 2.515(c)(1).

ii. An attorney, party, or other person who files a pleading or paper by electronic transmission that does not contain the original signature of that attorney, party, or other person shall file that identical pleading or paper in paper form containing an original signature of that attorney, party, or other person (hereinafter called the follow-up filing) immediately thereafter. The follow-up filing is not required if the Supreme Court of Florida has entered an order directing the clerk of court to discontinue accepting the follow-up filing. FL ST J ADMIN Rule 2.515(c)(2).

7. *Forms*

a. *Process.* The forms of process, notice of lis pendens, and notice of action provided in the Florida Rules of Civil Procedure are sufficient. Variations from the forms do not void process or notices that are otherwise sufficient. FL ST RCP Rule 1.900(a).

b. *Other forms.* The other forms provided in the Florida Rules of Civil Procedure are sufficient for the matters that are covered by them. So long as the substance is expressed without prolixity, the forms may be varied to meet the facts of a particular case. FL ST RCP Rule 1.900(b).

c. *Formal matters.* Captions, except for the designation of the paper, are omitted from the forms provided in the Florida Rules of Civil Procedure. A general form of caption is the first form provided. Signatures are omitted from pleadings and motions. FL ST RCP Rule 1.900(c).

8. *Notices to persons with disabilities.* All notices of court proceedings to be held in a public facility, and all process compelling appearance at such proceedings, shall include the following statement in bold face, fourteen (14) point Times New Roman or Courier font: "If you are a person with a disability who needs any accommodation in order to participate in this proceeding, you are entitled, at no cost to you, to the provision of certain assistance. Please contact [identify applicable court personnel by name, address, and telephone number] at least seven (7) days before your scheduled court appearance, or immediately upon receiving this notification if the time before the scheduled appearance is less than seven (7) days; if you are hearing or voice impaired, call 711." FL ST J ADMIN Rule 2.540(c)(1).

9. *Minimization of the filing of sensitive information*

a. *Limitations for court filings.* Unless authorized by FL ST J ADMIN Rule 2.425(b), statute, another rule of court, or the court orders otherwise, designated sensitive information filed with the court must be limited to the following format:

i. The initials of a person known to be a minor;

ii. The year of birth of a person's birth date;

iii. No portion of any: Social security number, Bank account number, Credit card account number, Charge account number, or Debit account number;

iv. The last four digits of any: Taxpayer identification number (TIN), Employee identification number, Driver's license number, Passport number, Telephone number, Financial account number, except as set forth in FL ST J ADMIN Rule 2.425(a)(3), Brokerage account number, Insurance policy account number, Loan account number, Customer account number, or Patient or health care number;

v. A truncated version of any: Email address, Computer user name, Password, or Personal identification number (PIN); and

vi. A truncated version of any other sensitive information as provided by court order. FL ST J ADMIN Rule 2.425(a).

b. *Exceptions.* FL ST J ADMIN Rule 2.425(a) does not apply to the following:

i. An account number which identifies the property alleged to be the subject of a proceeding;

ii. The record of an administrative or agency proceeding;

iii. The record in appellate or review proceedings;

iv. The birth date of a minor whenever the birth date is necessary for the court to establish or maintain subject matter jurisdiction;

v. The name of a minor in any order relating to parental responsibility, time-sharing, or child support;

vi. The name of a minor in any document or order affecting the minor's ownership of real property;

vii. The birth date of a party in a writ of attachment or notice to payor;

viii. In traffic and criminal proceedings: a pro se filing; a court filing that is related to a criminal matter or investigation and that is prepared before the filing of a criminal charge or is not filed as part of any docketed criminal case; an arrest or search warrant or any information in support thereof; a charging document and an affidavit or other documents filed in support of any charging document, including any driving records; a statement of particulars; discovery material introduced into evidence or otherwise filed with the court; and all information necessary for the proper issuance and execution of a subpoena duces tecum;

ix. Information used by the clerk for case maintenance purposes or the courts for case management purposes; and

x. Information which is relevant and material to an issue before the court. FL ST J ADMIN Rule 2.425(b).

c. *Remedies.* Upon motion by a party or interested person or sua sponte by the court, the court may order remedies, sanctions or both for a violation of FL ST J ADMIN Rule 2.425(a). Following notice and an opportunity to respond, the court may impose sanctions if such filing was not made in good faith. FL ST J ADMIN Rule 2.425(c).

d. *Motions not restricted.* FL ST J ADMIN Rule 2.425 does not restrict a party's right to move for protective order, to move to file documents under seal, or to request a determination of the confidentiality of records. FL ST J ADMIN Rule 2.425(d).

e. *Application.* FL ST J ADMIN Rule 2.425 does not affect the application of constitutional provisions, statutes, or rules of court regarding confidential information or access to public information. FL ST J ADMIN Rule 2.425(e).

F. Filing and Service Requirements

1. *Filing requirements.* All original documents must be filed with the court either before service or immediately thereafter, unless otherwise provided for by general law or other rules. If the original of any bond or other document is not placed in the court file, a certified copy must be so placed by the clerk. FL ST J ADMIN Rule 2.516(d). All documents shall be filed in conformity with the requirements of FL ST J ADMIN Rule 2.525. FL ST RCP Rule 1.080(b). All documents filed in any court shall be filed by electronic transmission in accordance with FL ST J ADMIN Rule 2.525. "Documents" means pleadings, motions, petitions, memoranda, briefs, notices, exhibits, declarations, affidavits, orders, judgments, decrees, writs, opinions, and any other paper or writing submitted to a court. FL ST J ADMIN Rule

2.520(a). All documents that are court records, as defined in FL ST J ADMIN Rule 2.430(a)(1), must be filed by electronic transmission, provided that: (1) the clerk has the ability to accept and retain such documents; (2) the clerk or the chief judge of the circuit has requested permission to accept documents filed by electronic transmission; and (3) the supreme court has entered an order granting permission to the clerk to accept documents filed by electronic transmission. FL ST J ADMIN Rule 2.525(c)(1).

a. *Definition.* "Electronic transmission of documents" means the sending of information by electronic signals to, by or from a court or clerk, which when received can be transformed and stored or transmitted on paper, microfilm, magnetic storage device, optical imaging system, CD-ROM, flash drive, other electronic data storage system, server, case maintenance system ("CM"), electronic court filing ("ECF") system, statewide or local electronic portal ("e-portal"), or other electronic record keeping system authorized by the supreme court in a format sufficient to communicate the information on the original document in a readable format. Electronic transmission of documents includes electronic mail ("e-mail") and any internet-based transmission procedure, and may include procedures allowing for documents to be signed or verified by electronic means. FL ST J ADMIN Rule 2.525(a).

   i. The filing of documents with the court as required by the Florida Rules of Judicial Administration must be made by filing them with the clerk in accordance with FL ST J ADMIN Rule 2.525, except that the judge may permit documents to be filed with the judge, in which event the judge must note the filing date before him or her on the documents and transmit them to the clerk. The date of filing is that shown on the face of the document by the judge's notation or the clerk's time stamp, whichever is earlier. FL ST J ADMIN Rule 2.516(e).

b. *Application.* Any court or clerk of the court may accept the electronic transmission of documents for filing after the clerk, together with input from the chief judge of the circuit, has obtained approval of the procedures and program for doing so from the Supreme Court of Florida. FL ST J ADMIN Rule 2.525(b).

c. *Exceptions*

   i. Paper documents and other submissions may be manually submitted to the clerk or court:

      - When the clerk does not have the ability to accept and retain documents by electronic filing or has not had ECF Procedures approved by the supreme court;
      - For filing by any self-represented party or any self-represented nonparty unless specific ECF Procedures provide a means to file documents electronically. However, any self-represented nonparty that is a governmental or public agency and any other agency, partnership, corporation, or business entity acting on behalf of any governmental or public agency may file documents by electronic transmission if such entity has the capability of filing documents electronically;
      - For filing by attorneys excused from e-mail service in accordance with FL ST J ADMIN Rule 2.516(b);
      - When submitting evidentiary exhibits or filing non-documentary materials;
      - When the filing involves documents in excess of twenty-five (25) megabytes (25MB) in size. For such filings, documents may be transmitted using an electronic storage medium that the clerk has the ability to accept, which may include a CD-ROM, flash drive, or similar storage medium;
      - When filed in open court, as permitted by the court;
      - When paper filing is permitted by any approved statewide or local ECF procedures; and
      - If any court determines that justice so requires. FL ST J ADMIN Rule 2.525(d).

   ii. Any document in paper form submitted under FL ST J ADMIN Rule 2.525(d) is filed when it is received by the clerk or court and the clerk shall immediately thereafter convert any filed paper document to an electronic document. "Convert to an electronic document" means optically capturing an image of a paper document and using character recognition software to recover as much of the document's text as practicable and then indexing and storing the document in the official court file. FL ST J ADMIN Rule 2.525(c)(4).

iii. Any storage medium submitted under FL ST J ADMIN Rule 2.525(d)(5) is filed when received by the clerk or court and the clerk shall immediately thereafter transfer the electronic documents from the storage device to the official court file. FL ST J ADMIN Rule 2.525(c)(5).

iv. If the filer of any paper document authorized under FL ST J ADMIN Rule 2.525(d) provides a self-addressed, postage-paid envelope for return of the paper document after it is converted to electronic form by the clerk, the clerk shall place the paper document in the envelope and deposit it in the mail. Except when a paper document is required to be maintained, the clerk may recycle any filed paper document that is not to be returned to the filer. FL ST J ADMIN Rule 2.525(c)(6).

v. The clerk may convert any paper document filed before the effective date of FL ST J ADMIN Rule 2.525 to an electronic document. Unless the clerk is required to maintain the paper document, if the paper document has been converted to an electronic document by the clerk, the paper document is no longer part of the official court file and may be removed and recycled. FL ST J ADMIN Rule 2.525(c)(7).

d. *Official court file.* For information on what constitutes the official court file, please see FL ST J ADMIN Rule 2.525(c)(2), FL ST J ADMIN Rule 2.525(c)(3).

e. *Administration.* All attorneys, parties, or other persons using this rule to file documents are required to make arrangements with the court or clerk for the payment of any charges authorized by general law or the supreme court before filing any document by electronic transmission. FL ST J ADMIN Rule 2.525(f)(2).

f. *Filing date.* The filing date for an electronically transmitted document is the date and time that such filing is acknowledged by an electronic stamp or otherwise, pursuant to any procedure set forth in any ECF Procedures approved by the supreme court, or the date the last page of such filing is received by the court or clerk. FL ST J ADMIN Rule 2.525(f)(3).

g. *Accessibility.* All documents transmitted in any electronic form under FL ST J ADMIN Rule 2.525 must comply with the accessibility requirements of FL ST J ADMIN Rule 2.526. FL ST J ADMIN Rule 2.525(g).

2. *Service requirements.* Every pleading subsequent to the initial pleading, all orders, and every other document filed in the action must be served in conformity with the requirements of FL ST J ADMIN Rule 2.516. FL ST RCP Rule 1.080(a).

a. *Service; When required.* Unless the court otherwise orders, or a statute or supreme court administrative order specifies a different means of service, every pleading subsequent to the initial pleading and every other document filed in any court proceeding, except applications for witness subpoenas and documents served by formal notice or required to be served in the manner provided for service of formal notice, must be served in accordance with FL ST J ADMIN Rule 2.516 on each party. No service need be made on parties against whom a default has been entered, except that pleadings asserting new or additional claims against them must be served in the manner provided for service of summons. FL ST J ADMIN Rule 2.516(a).

b. *Service; How made.* When service is required or permitted to be made upon a party represented by an attorney, service must be made upon the attorney unless service upon the party is ordered by the court. FL ST J ADMIN Rule 2.516(b).

i. *Service by electronic mail ("e-mail").* All documents required or permitted to be served on another party must be served by e-mail, unless FL ST J ADMIN Rule 2.516 otherwise provides. When, in addition to service by e-mail, the sender also utilizes another means of service provided for in FL ST J ADMIN Rule 2.516(b)(2), any differing time limits and other provisions applicable to that other means of service control. FL ST J ADMIN Rule 2.516(b)(1). Any document electronically transmitted to a court or clerk must also be served on all parties and interested persons in accordance with the applicable rules of court. FL ST J ADMIN Rule 2.525(e)(2).

- *Service on attorneys.* Upon appearing in a proceeding, an attorney must serve a designation of a primary e-mail address and may designate no more than two (2) secondary e-mail

addresses. Thereafter, service must be directed to all designated e-mail addresses in that proceeding. Every document filed by an attorney thereafter must include the primary e-mail address of that attorney and any secondary e-mail addresses. If an attorney does not designate any e-mail address for service, documents may be served on that attorney at the e-mail address on record with The Florida Bar. FL ST J ADMIN Rule 2.516(b)(1)(A).

- *Exception to e-mail service on attorneys.* Service by an attorney on another attorney must be made by e-mail unless excused by the court. Upon motion by an attorney demonstrating that the attorney has no e-mail account and lacks access to the Internet at the attorney's office, the court may excuse the attorney from the requirements of e-mail service. Service on and by an attorney excused by the court from e-mail service must be by the means provided in FL ST J ADMIN Rule 2.516(b)(2). FL ST J ADMIN Rule 2.516(b)(1)(B).
- *Service on and by parties not represented by an attorney.* Any party not represented by an attorney may serve a designation of a primary e-mail address and also may designate no more than two (2) secondary e-mail addresses to which service must be directed in that proceeding by the means provided in FL ST J ADMIN Rule 2.516(b)(1). If a party not represented by an attorney does not designate an e-mail address for service in a proceeding, service on and by that party must be by the means provided in FL ST J ADMIN Rule 2.516(b)(2). FL ST J ADMIN Rule 2.516(b)(1)(C).
- *Time of service.* Service by e-mail is complete when it is sent. FL ST J ADMIN Rule 2.516(b)(1)(D). An e-mail is deemed served on the date it is sent. FL ST J ADMIN Rule 2.516(b)(1)(D)(i). If the sender learns that the e-mail did not reach the address of the person to be served, the sender must immediately send another copy by e-mail, or by a means authorized by FL ST J ADMIN Rule 2.516(b)(2). FL ST J ADMIN Rule 2.516(b)(1)(D)(ii). E-mail service is treated as service by mail for the computation of time. FL ST J ADMIN Rule 2.516(b)(1)(D)(iii).

ii. *Format of e-mail for service.* Service of a document by e-mail is made by attaching a copy of the document in PDF format to an e-mail sent to all addresses designated by the attorney or party. FL ST J ADMIN Rule 2.516(b)(1)(E).

- All documents served by e-mail must be attached to an e-mail message containing a subject line beginning with the words "SERVICE OF COURT DOCUMENT" in all capital letters, followed by the case number of the proceeding in which the documents are being served. FL ST J ADMIN Rule 2.516(b)(1)(E)(i).
- The body of the e-mail must identify the court in which the proceeding is pending, the case number, the name of the initial party on each side, the title of each document served with that e-mail, and the sender's name and telephone number. FL ST J ADMIN Rule 2.516(b)(1)(E)(ii).
- Any document served by e-mail may be signed by the "/s/" format, as long as the filed original is signed in accordance with the applicable rule of procedure. FL ST J ADMIN Rule 2.516(b)(1)(E)(iii).
- Any e-mail which, together with its attached documents, exceeds five megabytes (5MB) in size, must be divided and sent as separate e-mails, no one of which may exceed five megabytes (5MB) in size and each of which must be sequentially numbered in the subject line. FL ST J ADMIN Rule 2.516(b)(1)(E)(iv).

iii. *Service by other means.* In addition to, and not in lieu of, service by e-mail, service may also be made upon attorneys by any of the means specified in FL ST J ADMIN Rule 2.516(b)(2). Service on and by all parties who are not represented by an attorney and who do not designate an e-mail address, and on and by all attorneys excused from e-mail service, must be made by delivering a copy of the document or by mailing it to the party or attorney at their last known address or, if no address is known, by leaving it with the clerk of the court. Service by mail is complete upon mailing. Delivery of a copy within FL ST J ADMIN Rule 2.516 is complete upon:

- Handing it to the attorney or to the party,

- Leaving it at the attorney's or party's office with a clerk or other person in charge thereof,
- If there is no one in charge, leaving it in a conspicuous place therein,
- If the office is closed or the person to be served has no office, leaving it at the person's usual place of abode with some person of his or her family above fifteen (15) years of age and informing such person of the contents, or
- Transmitting it by facsimile to the attorney's or party's office with a cover sheet containing the sender's name, firm, address, telephone number, and facsimile number, and the number of pages transmitted. When service is made by facsimile, a copy must also be served by any other method permitted by FL ST J ADMIN Rule 2.516. Facsimile service occurs when transmission is complete. FL ST J ADMIN Rule 2.516(b)(2)(A) through FL ST J ADMIN Rule 2.516(b)(2)(E).
- Service by delivery after 5:00 p.m. must be deemed to have been made by mailing on the date of delivery. FL ST J ADMIN Rule 2.516(b)(2)(F).

c. *Service; Numerous defendants.* In actions when the parties are unusually numerous, the court may regulate the service contemplated by the Florida Rules of Judicial Administration on motion or on its own initiative in such manner as may be found to be just and reasonable. FL ST J ADMIN Rule 2.516(c).

d. *Service by clerk.* Service of notices and other documents required to be made by the clerk must also be done as provided in FL ST J ADMIN Rule 2.516(b). FL ST J ADMIN Rule 2.516(g).

e. *Standards of professional courtesy; Service*

   i. The timing and manner of service should not be used to the disadvantage of the party receiving the papers. This includes the use of facsimile transmissions and any additional expedited means of communication approved by the court. FL ST 6 J CIR 2009-066 PA/PI-CIR(C)(1).

   ii. Attorneys will not serve papers to take advantage of opposing counsel's known absence from the office or at a time or in a manner designed to inconvenience an opponent, such as late on Friday afternoon or the day preceding a secular or religious holiday. FL ST 6 J CIR 2009-066 PA/PI-CIR(C)(2).

   iii. Attorneys will not serve papers, including briefs and memoranda, so close to a court appearance that the ability of opposing counsel to prepare for that appearance or, where permitted, to respond, is inhibited. FL ST 6 J CIR 2009-066 PA/PI-CIR(C)(3).

   iv. Service should be made personally or by facsimile transmission when it is likely that service by mail, even when allowed, will prejudice the opposing party. FL ST 6 J CIR 2009-066 PA/PI-CIR(C)(4).

G. Hearings

1. The parties may be required to participate in pretrial proceedings to consider and determine the necessity or desirability of an amendment to a pleading. FL ST RCP Rule 1.200(b)(2); FL-PP § 2:151.

H. Forms

1. Official Amended Complaint Forms for Florida

a. Caption. FL ST RCP Form 1.901.

2. Amended Complaint Forms for Florida

a. Consent; Of party; To amendment of pleadings. FL-PP § 2:154.

b. Notice of amended complaint. 3 FLPRAC § 190.1.

c. Complaint for damages; General form. FL-PP § 2:17.

d. Complaint; Negligent infliction of personal injury. FL-PP § 2:19.

e. Complaint; Fall down negligence. FL-PP § 2:20.

f. Complaint; Mortgage foreclosure. FL-PP § 2:21.

g. Complaint; Implied warranty. FL-PP § 2:22.

h. Complaint; Professional negligence. FL-PP § 2:23.
i. Complaint; Breach of contract. FL-PP § 2:24.
j. Complaint; Breach of personal services contract. FL-PP § 2:25.

I. Checklist

(I) ❑ Matters to be considered by plaintiff
- (a) ❑ Required documents
  - (1) ❑ Amended complaint
  - (2) ❑ Certificate of service
- (b) ❑ Supplemental documents
  - (1) ❑ Exhibits
  - (2) ❑ Notice of constitutional question
- (c) ❑ Timing
  - (1) ❑ A party may amend a pleading once as a matter of course at any time before a responsive pleading is served
  - (2) ❑ If the pleading is one to which no responsive pleading is permitted and the action has not been placed on the trial calendar, may so amend it at any time within twenty (20) days after it is served

Pleadings
Answer

Document Last Updated January 2013

A. Applicable Rules

1. *State rules*
   a. Nonverification of pleadings. FL ST RCP Rule 1.030.
   b. Process. FL ST RCP Rule 1.070.
   c. Service and filing of pleadings, orders, and documents. FL ST RCP Rule 1.080.
   d. Time. FL ST RCP Rule 1.090.
   e. Pleadings and motions. FL ST RCP Rule 1.100; FL ST RCP Rule 1.110; FL ST RCP Rule 1.120; FL ST RCP Rule 1.130; FL ST RCP Rule 1.190; FL ST RCP Rule 1.430.
   f. Defenses. FL ST RCP Rule 1.140.
   g. Relief from judgment, decrees, or orders. FL ST RCP Rule 1.540.
   h. Forms. FL ST RCP Rule 1.900.
   i. Minimization of the filing of sensitive information. FL ST J ADMIN Rule 2.425.
   j. Retention of court records. FL ST J ADMIN Rule 2.430.
   k. Foreign attorneys. FL ST J ADMIN Rule 2.510.
   l. Signature of attorneys and parties. FL ST J ADMIN Rule 2.515.
   m. Paper. FL ST J ADMIN Rule 2.520.
   n. Electronic filing. FL ST J ADMIN Rule 2.525.
   o. Accessibility of information and technology. FL ST J ADMIN Rule 2.526.
   p. Court reporting. FL ST J ADMIN Rule 2.535.
   q. Requests for accommodations by persons with disabilities. FL ST J ADMIN Rule 2.540.

r. Waiver of sovereign immunity in tort actions; Recovery limits; Limitation on attorney fees; Statute of limitations; Exclusions; Indemnification; Risk management programs. FL ST § 768.28.

2. *Local rules*

a. Assignment of cases. FL ST 6 J CIR LOCAL Rule 3.

b. Standards of professional courtesy. FL ST 6 J CIR 2009-066 PA/PI-CIR.

c. Arbitration and mediation program circuit civil and family cases. FL ST 6 J CIR PA/PI-CIR-96-63; FL ST 6 J CIR 2011-006 PA/PI-CIR.

B. Timing

1. *General answer timing.* Unless a different time is prescribed in a statute of Florida, a defendant shall serve an answer within twenty (20) days after service of original process and the initial pleading on the defendant, or not later than the date fixed in a notice by publication. A party served with a pleading stating a crossclaim against that party shall serve an answer to it within twenty (20) days after service on that party. The plaintiff shall serve an answer to a counterclaim within twenty (20) days after service of the counterclaim. FL ST RCP Rule 1.140(a)(1).

a. *Waiver of service.* A defendant who, before being served with process, timely returns a waiver so requested is not required to respond to the complaint until sixty (60) days after the date the defendant received the request for waiver of service. For purposes of computing any time prescribed or allowed by the Florida Rules of Civil Procedure, service of process shall be deemed effected twenty (20) days before the time required to respond to the complaint. FL ST RCP Rule 1.070(i)(4).

b. *Service on the state.* Except when sued pursuant to FL ST § 768.28, the state of Florida, an agency of the state, or an officer or employee of the state sued in an official capacity shall serve an answer to the complaint or crossclaim, or a reply to a counterclaim, within forty (40) days after service. When sued pursuant to FL ST § 768.28, the Department of Financial Services or the defendant state agency shall have thirty (30) days from the date of service within which to serve an answer to the complaint or crossclaim or a reply to a counterclaim. FL ST RCP Rule 1.140(a)(2).

c. *Service of motion impact on time periods for service of answer.* The service of a motion under FL ST RCP Rule 1.140, except a motion for judgment on the pleadings or a motion to strike under FL ST RCP Rule 1.140(f), alters these periods of time so that if the court denies the motion or postpones its disposition until the trial on the merits, the responsive pleadings shall be served within ten (10) days after notice of the court's action or, if the court grants a motion for a more definite statement, the responsive pleadings shall be served within ten (10) days after service of the more definite statement unless a different time is fixed by the court in either case. FL ST RCP Rule 1.140(a)(3).

d. *Responding if pleading does not require a responsive pleading.* If a pleading sets forth a claim for relief to which the adverse party is not required to serve a responsive pleading, the adverse party may assert any defense in law or fact to that claim for relief at the trial, except that the objection of failure to state a legal defense in an answer or reply shall be asserted by motion to strike the defense within twenty (20) days after service of the answer or reply. FL ST RCP Rule 1.140(b).

2. *Computation of time*

a. *Generally.* Computation of time shall be governed by FL ST J ADMIN Rule 2.514. FL ST RCP Rule 1.090(a). The following rules apply in computing time periods specified in any rule of procedure, local rule, court order, or statute that does not specify a method of computing time. FL ST J ADMIN Rule 2.514(a).

i. *Period stated in days or a longer unit.* When the period is stated in days or a longer unit of time (A) exclude the day of the event that triggers the period; (B) count every day, including intermediate Saturdays, Sundays, and legal holidays; and (C) include the last day of the period, but if the last day is a Saturday, Sunday, or legal holiday, or falls within any period of time extended through an order of the chief justice under FL ST J ADMIN Rule 2.205(a)(2)(B)(iv), the period continues to run until the end of the next day that is not a Saturday, Sunday, or legal holiday and does not fall within any period of time extended through an order of the chief justice. FL ST J ADMIN Rule 2.514(a)(1).

ii. *Period stated in hours.* When the period is stated in hours (A) begin counting immediately on the occurrence of the event that triggers the period; (B) count every hour, including hours during intermediate Saturdays, Sundays, and legal holidays; and (C) if the period would end on a Saturday, Sunday, or legal holiday, or during any period of time extended through an order of the chief justice under FL ST J ADMIN Rule 2.205(a)(2)(B)(iv), the period continues to run until the same time on the next day that is not a Saturday, Sunday, or legal holiday and does not fall within any period of time extended through an order of the chief justice. FL ST J ADMIN Rule 2.514(a)(2).

iii. *Period stated in days less than seven (7) days.* When the period stated in days is less than seven (7) days, intermediate Saturdays, Sundays, and legal holidays shall be excluded in the computation. FL ST J ADMIN Rule 2.514(a)(3).

iv. *"Last day" defined.* Unless a different time is set by a statute, local rule, or court order, the last day ends (A) for electronic filing or for service by any means, at midnight; and (B) for filing by other means, when the clerk's office is scheduled to close. FL ST J ADMIN Rule 2.514(a)(4).

v. *"Next day" defined.* The "next day" is determined by continuing to count forward when the period is measured after an event and backward when measured before an event. FL ST J ADMIN Rule 2.514(a)(5).

vi. *"Legal holiday" defined.* "Legal holiday" means (A) the day set aside by FL ST § 110.117, for observing New Year's Day, Martin Luther King, Jr.'s Birthday, Memorial Day, Independence Day, Labor Day, Veterans' Day, Thanksgiving Day, the Friday after Thanksgiving Day, or Christmas Day, and (B) any day observed as a holiday by the clerk's office or as designated by the chief judge. FL ST J ADMIN Rule 2.514(a)(6).

b. *Additional time after service by mail or e-mail.* When a party may or must act within a specified time after service and service is made by mail or e-mail, five (5) days are added after the period that would otherwise expire under FL ST J ADMIN Rule 2.514(a). FL ST J ADMIN Rule 2.514(b).

c. *Enlargement.* When an act is required or allowed to be done at or within a specified time by order of court, by the Florida Rules of Civil Procedure, or by notice given thereunder, for cause shown the court at any time in its discretion (1) with or without notice, may order the period enlarged if request therefor is made before the expiration of the period originally prescribed or as extended by a previous order, or (2) upon motion made and notice after the expiration of the specified period, may permit the act to be done when failure to act was the result of excusable neglect, but it may not extend the time for making a motion for new trial, for rehearing, or to alter or amend a judgment; making a motion for relief from a judgment under FL ST RCP Rule 1.540(b); taking an appeal or filing a petition for certiorari; or making a motion for a directed verdict. FL ST RCP Rule 1.090(b).

d. *Unaffected by expiration of term.* The period of time provided for the doing of any act or the taking of any proceeding shall not be affected or limited by the continued existence or expiration of a term of court. The continued existence or expiration of a term of court in no way affects the power of a court to do any act or take any proceeding in any action which is or has been pending before it. FL ST RCP Rule 1.090(c).

C. General Requirements

1. *General rules of pleading*

a. *Claims for relief*

i. A pleading which sets forth a claim for relief, whether an original claim, counterclaim, crossclaim, or third-party claim, must state a cause of action and shall contain

- A short and plain statement of the grounds upon which the court's jurisdiction depends, unless the court already has jurisdiction and the claim needs no new grounds of jurisdiction to support it (For information regarding acts subjecting persons to jurisdiction, please see FL ST § 48.193),
- A short and plain statement of the ultimate facts showing that the pleader is entitled to relief, and

- A demand for judgment for the relief to which the pleader deems himself or herself entitled. FL ST RCP Rule 1.110(b).

ii. Relief in the alternative or of several different types may be demanded. Every complaint shall be considered to demand general relief. FL ST RCP Rule 1.110(b).

b. *Verification.* Except when otherwise specifically provided by these rules or an applicable statute, every pleading or other document of a party represented by an attorney need not be verified or accompanied by an affidavit. FL ST RCP Rule 1.030. When filing an action for foreclosure of a mortgage on residential real property the complaint shall be verified. When verification of a document is required, the document filed shall include an oath, affirmation, or the following statement: "Under penalty of perjury, I declare that I have read the foregoing, and the facts alleged therein are true and correct to the best of my knowledge and belief." FL ST RCP Rule 1.110(b).

c. *Separate statements.* All averments of claim or defense shall be made in consecutively numbered paragraphs, the contents of each of which shall be limited as far as practicable to a statement of a single set of circumstances, and a paragraph may be referred to by number in all subsequent pleadings. Each claim founded upon a separate transaction or occurrence and each defense other than denials shall be stated in a separate count or defense when a separation facilitates the clear presentation of the matter set forth. FL ST RCP Rule 1.110(f).

d. *Statements adopted by reference.* Statements in a pleading may be adopted by reference in a different part of the same pleading, in another pleading, or in any motion. FL ST RCP Rule 1.130(b).

e. *Joinder of causes of action; Consistency.* A pleader may set up in the same action as many claims or causes of action or defenses in the same right as the pleader has, and claims for relief may be stated in the alternative if separate items make up the cause of action, or if two (2) or more causes of action are joined. A party may also set forth two (2) or more statements of a claim or defense alternatively, either in one (1) count or defense or in separate counts or defenses. When two (2) or more statements are made in the alternative and one (1) of them, if made independently, would be sufficient, the pleading is not made insufficient by the insufficiency of one (1) or more of the alternative statements. A party may also state as many separate claims or defenses as that party has, regardless of consistency and whether based on legal or equitable grounds or both. All pleadings shall be construed so as to do substantial justice. FL ST RCP Rule 1.110(g).

f. *Subsequent pleadings.* When the nature of an action permits pleadings subsequent to final judgment and the jurisdiction of the court over the parties has not terminated, the initial pleading subsequent to final judgment shall be designated a supplemental complaint or petition. The action shall then proceed in the same manner and time as though the supplemental complaint or petition were the initial pleading in the action, including the issuance of any needed process. FL ST RCP Rule 1.110(h) shall not apply to proceedings that may be initiated by motion under the Florida Rules of Civil Procedure. FL ST RCP Rule 1.110(h).

g. *Pleading basis for service.* When service of process is to be made under statutes authorizing service on nonresidents of Florida, it is sufficient to plead the basis for service in the language of the statute without pleading the facts supporting service. FL ST RCP Rule 1.070(h).

h. *Forms of pleadings.* Forms of action and technical forms for seeking relief and of pleas, pleadings, or motions are abolished. FL ST RCP Rule 1.110(a).

2. *Answer; Generally.* An answer has three (3) functions. First, it must respond to each allegation of the preceding pleading by admitting, denying or alleging that the pleader is without knowledge of the allegation. Second, it must contain any affirmative defenses that the pleader is interposing to any cause of action alleged in the preceding pleading. Third, the answer may claim affirmative relief against the plaintiff or petitioner by a counterclaim or against a codefendant by a crossclaim. FL-PRACPROC § 11:1.

a. *Content.* In the answer a pleader shall state in short and plain terms the pleader's defenses to each claim asserted and shall admit or deny the averments on which the adverse party relies. If the defendant is without knowledge, the defendant shall so state and such statement shall operate as a denial. Denial shall fairly meet the substance of the averments denied. When a pleader intends in good faith to deny only a part of an averment, the pleader shall specify so much of it as is true and

shall deny the remainder. Unless the pleader intends in good faith to controvert all of the averments of the preceding pleading, the pleader may make denials as specific denials of designated averments or may generally deny all of the averments except such designated averments as the pleader expressly admits, but when the pleader does so intend to controvert all of its averments, including averments of the grounds upon which the court's jurisdiction depends, the pleader may do so by general denial. FL ST RCP Rule 1.110(c).

b. *Form of answer.* An answer contains a caption, commencement, body, signature and certificate of service. The caption is the same as that of the initial pleading, except for the designation as one of the types of answer. The body of an answer should contain an admission, denial or plea of without knowledge to each allegation of the preceding pleading, except for the additional allegations in response to a general allegation of conditions precedent and the denial of capacity to sue. FL-PRACPROC § 11:3.

   i. *Responding sequentially.* The best method of responding is to answer each paragraph sequentially, combining admissions, denials or pleas of without knowledge when the sequence permits. The admissions, denials and allegations of without knowledge should be stated first, followed separately by any affirmative defenses and then by any counterclaim or crossclaim. A third party complaint may be a part of the same paper, but it is not a part of the answer as is a counterclaim or crossclaim. Paragraphs are numbered consecutively throughout the pleading whether in the answer, counterclaim or crossclaim. Denials for the record only are improper. FL-PRACPROC § 11:3.

c. *Defenses*

   i. *Generally.* Every defense in law or fact to a claim for relief in a pleading shall be asserted in the responsive pleading, if one is required, but the following defenses may be made by motion at the option of the pleader: (1) lack of jurisdiction over the subject matter, (2) lack of jurisdiction over the person, (3) improper venue, (4) insufficiency of process, (5) insufficiency of service of process, (6) failure to state a cause of action, and (7) failure to join indispensable parties. A motion making any of these defenses shall be made before pleading if a further pleading is permitted. FL ST RCP Rule 1.140(b).

      - *Stated specifically.* The grounds on which any of the enumerated defenses are based and the substantial matters of law intended to be argued shall be stated specifically and with particularity in the responsive pleading or motion. FL ST RCP Rule 1.140(b).
      - *Waiver.* Any ground not stated shall be deemed to be waived except any ground showing that the court lacks jurisdiction of the subject matter may be made at any time. No defense or objection is waived by being joined with other defenses or objections in a responsive pleading or motion. FL ST RCP Rule 1.140(b). A party waives all defenses and objections that the party does not present either by motion under FL ST RCP Rule 1.140(b), FL ST RCP Rule 1.140(e), or FL ST RCP Rule 1.140(f) or, if the party has made no motion, in a responsive pleading except as provided in FL ST RCP Rule 1.140(h)(2). FL ST RCP Rule 1.140(h)(1). The defenses of failure to state a cause of action or a legal defense or to join an indispensable party may be raised by motion for judgment on the pleadings or at the trial on the merits in addition to being raised either in a motion under FL ST RCP Rule 1.140(b) or in the answer or reply. The defense of lack of jurisdiction of the subject matter may be raised at any time. FL ST RCP Rule 1.140(h)(2).

   ii. *Affirmative defenses.* In pleading to a preceding pleading a party shall set forth affirmatively accord and satisfaction, arbitration and award, assumption of risk, contributory negligence, discharge in bankruptcy, duress, estoppel, failure of consideration, fraud, illegality, injury by fellow servant, laches, license, payment, release, res judicata, statute of frauds, statute of limitations, waiver, and any other matter constituting an avoidance or affirmative defense. When a party has mistakenly designated a defense as a counterclaim or a counterclaim as a defense, the court, on terms if justice so requires, shall treat the pleading as if there had been a proper designation. Affirmative defenses appearing on the face of a prior pleading may be asserted as grounds for a motion or defense under FL ST RCP Rule 1.140(b); provided this shall

not limit amendments under FL ST RCP Rule 1.190 even if such ground is sustained. FL ST RCP Rule 1.110(d).

- *Format of defenses.* Affirmative defenses should be placed after the admissions, denials and allegations of without knowledge in the answer. All paragraphs must be numbered consecutively throughout the answer. If a defense is directed to only a part of a cause of action or to one or more, but not all, of several causes of action in the preceding pleading, the part or cause of action to which it is directed should be identified in the defense. Defenses should be identified by consecutive ordinal numbers such as "First Defense" and "Second Defense." FL-PRACPROC § 11:4.

iii. *Effect of failure to deny.* Averments in a pleading to which a responsive pleading is required, other than those as to the amount of damages, are admitted when not denied in the responsive pleading. Averments in a pleading to which no responsive pleading is required or permitted shall be taken as denied or avoided. FL ST RCP Rule 1.110(e). An admission in an answer binds the party and no proof is required. An admission does not extend beyond the scope of the allegation in the preceding pleading. FL-PRACPROC § 11:3.

3. *Pleading special matters*

a. *Capacity.* It is not necessary to aver the capacity of a party to sue or be sued, the authority of a party to sue or be sued in a representative capacity, or the legal existence of an organized association of persons that is made a party, except to the extent required to show the jurisdiction of the court. The initial pleading served on behalf of a minor party shall specifically aver the age of the minor party. When a party desires to raise an issue as to the legal existence of any party, the capacity of any party to sue or be sued, or the authority of a party to sue or be sued in a representative capacity, that party shall do so by specific negative averment which shall include such supporting particulars as are peculiarly within the pleader's knowledge. FL ST RCP Rule 1.120(a).

b. *Fraud, mistake, condition of the mind.* In all averments of fraud or mistake, the circumstances constituting fraud or mistake shall be stated with such particularity as the circumstances may permit. Malice, intent, knowledge, mental attitude, and other condition of mind of a person may be averred generally. FL ST RCP Rule 1.120(b).

c. *Conditions precedent.* In pleading the performance or occurrence of conditions precedent, it is sufficient to aver generally that all conditions precedent have been performed or have occurred. A denial of performance or occurrence shall be made specifically and with particularity. FL ST RCP Rule 1.120(c).

d. *Official document or act.* In pleading an official document or official act it is sufficient to aver that the document was issued or the act done in compliance with law. FL ST RCP Rule 1.120(c).

e. *Judgment or decree.* In pleading a judgment or decree of a domestic or foreign court, a judicial or quasi-judicial tribunal, or a board or officer, it is sufficient to aver the judgment or decree without setting forth matter showing jurisdiction to render it. FL ST RCP Rule 1.120(e).

f. *Time and place.* For the purpose of testing the sufficiency of a pleading, averments of time and place are material and shall be considered like all other averments of material matter. FL ST RCP Rule 1.120(f).

g. *Special damage.* When items of special damage are claimed, they shall be specifically stated. FL ST RCP Rule 1.120(g).

4. *Parties*

a. *Parties generally.* Every action may be prosecuted in the name of the real party in interest, but a personal representative, administrator, guardian, trustee of an express trust, a party with whom or in whose name a contract has been made for the benefit of another, or a party expressly authorized by statute may sue in that person's own name without joining the party for whose benefit the action is brought. All persons having an interest in the subject of the action and in obtaining the relief demanded may join as plaintiffs and any person may be made a defendant who has or claims an interest adverse to the plaintiff. Any person may at any time be made a party if that person's presence is necessary or proper to a complete determination of the cause. Persons having a united interest may

be joined on the same side as plaintiffs or defendants, and anyone who refuses to join may for such reason be made a defendant. FL ST RCP Rule 1.210(a).

b. *Minors or incompetent persons.* When a minor or incompetent person has a representative, such as a guardian or other like fiduciary, the representative may sue or defend on behalf of the minor or incompetent person. A minor or incompetent person who does not have a duly appointed representative may sue by next friend or by a guardian ad litem. The court shall appoint a guardian ad litem for a minor or incompetent person not otherwise represented in an action or shall make such other order as it deems proper for the protection of the minor or incompetent person. FL ST RCP Rule 1.210(b).

c. For survivor and substitution of parties information, please see FL ST RCP Rule 1.260.

5. *Counterclaims and crossclaims*

a. *Compulsory counterclaims.* A pleading shall state as a counterclaim any claim which at the time of serving the pleading the pleader has against any opposing party, provided it arises out of the transaction or occurrence that is the subject matter of the opposing party's claim and does not require for its adjudication the presence of third parties over whom the court cannot acquire jurisdiction. But the pleader need not state a claim if (1) at the time the action was commenced the claim was the subject of another pending action, or (2) the opposing party brought suit upon that party's claim by attachment or other process by which the court did not acquire jurisdiction to render a personal judgment on the claim and the pleader is not stating a counterclaim under this rule. FL ST RCP Rule 1.170(a).

b. *Permissive counterclaim.* A pleading may state as a counterclaim any claim against an opposing party not arising out of the transaction or occurrence that is the subject matter of the opposing party's claim. FL ST RCP Rule 1.170(b).

c. *Counterclaim exceeding opposing claim.* A counterclaim may or may not diminish or defeat the recovery sought by the opposing party. It may claim relief exceeding in amount or different in kind from that sought in the pleading of the opposing party. FL ST RCP Rule 1.170(c).

d. *Counterclaim against the State.* The Florida Rules of Civil Procedure shall not be construed to enlarge beyond the limits established by law the right to assert counterclaims or to claim credits against the state or any of its subdivisions or other governmental organizations thereof subject to suit or against a municipal corporation or against an officer, agency, or administrative board of the state. FL ST RCP Rule 1.170(d).

e. *Counterclaim maturing or acquired after pleading.* A claim which matured or was acquired by the pleader after serving the pleading may be presented as a counterclaim by supplemental pleading with the permission of the court. FL ST RCP Rule 1.170(e).

f. *Omitted counterclaim or crossclaim.* When a pleader fails to set up a counterclaim or crossclaim through oversight, inadvertence, or excusable neglect, or when justice requires, the pleader may set up the counterclaim or crossclaim by amendment with leave of the court. FL ST RCP Rule 1.170(f).

g. *Crossclaim against co-party.* A pleading may state as a crossclaim any claim by one party against a co-party arising out of the transaction or occurrence that is the subject matter of either the original action or a counterclaim therein, or relating to any property that is the subject matter of the original action. The crossclaim may include a claim that the party against whom it is asserted is or may be liable to the crossclaimant for all or part of a claim asserted in the action against the crossclaimant. Service of a crossclaim on a party who has appeared in the action shall be made pursuant to FL ST RCP Rule 1.080. Service of a crossclaim against a party who has not appeared in the action shall be made in the manner provided for service of summons. FL ST RCP Rule 1.170(g).

h. *Additional parties may be brought in.* When the presence of parties other than those to the original action is required to grant complete relief in the determination of a counterclaim or crossclaim, they shall be named in the counterclaim or crossclaim and be served with process and shall be parties to the action thereafter if jurisdiction of them can be obtained and their joinder will not deprive the court of jurisdiction of the action. FL ST RCP Rule 1.250(b) and FL ST RCP Rule 1.250(c) apply to parties brought in under FL ST RCP Rule 1.170(h). FL ST RCP Rule 1.170(h).

i. *Separate trials; Separate judgment.* If the court orders separate trials as provided in FL ST RCP Rule 1.270(b), judgment on a counterclaim or crossclaim may be rendered when the court has jurisdiction to do so even if a claim of the opposing party has been dismissed or otherwise disposed of. FL ST RCP Rule 1.170(i).

j. *Demand exceeding jurisdiction; Transfer of action.* If the demand of any counterclaim or crossclaim exceeds the jurisdiction of the court in which the action is pending, the action shall be transferred forthwith to the court of the same county having jurisdiction of the demand in the counterclaim or crossclaim with only such alterations in the pleadings as are essential. The court shall order the transfer of the action and the transmittal of all papers in it to the proper court if the party asserting the demand exceeding the jurisdiction deposits with the court having jurisdiction a sum sufficient to pay the clerk's service charge in the court to which the action is transferred at the time of filing the counterclaim or crossclaim. Thereupon the original papers and deposit shall be transmitted and filed with a certified copy of the order. The court to which the action is transferred shall have full power and jurisdiction over the demands of all parties. Failure to make the service charge deposit at the time the counterclaim or crossclaim is filed, or within such further time as the court may allow, shall reduce a claim for damages to an amount within the jurisdiction of the court where the action is pending and waive the claim in other cases. FL ST RCP Rule 1.170(j).

6. *Misjoinder and nonjoinder of parties*

a. *Misjoinder.* Misjoinder of parties is not a ground for dismissal of an action. Any claim against a party may be severed and proceeded with separately. FL ST RCP Rule 1.250(a).

b. *Dropping parties.* Parties may be dropped by an adverse party in the manner provided for voluntary dismissal in FL ST RCP Rule 1.420(a)(1) subject to the exception stated in FL ST RCP Rule 1.420. If notice of lis pendens has been filed in the action against a party so dropped, the notice of dismissal shall be recorded and cancels the notice of lis pendens without the necessity of a court order. Parties may be dropped by order of court on its own initiative or the motion of any party at any stage of the action on such terms as are just. FL ST RCP Rule 1.250(b).

c. *Adding parties.* Parties may be added once as a matter of course within the same time that pleadings can be so amended under FL ST RCP Rule 1.190(a). If amendment by leave of court or stipulation of the parties is permitted, parties may be added in the amended pleading without further order of court. Parties may be added by order of court on its own initiative or on motion of any party at any stage of the action and on such terms as are just. FL ST RCP Rule 1.250(c).

7. *Jury demand*

a. *Right preserved.* The right of trial by jury as declared by the Constitution or by statute shall be preserved to the parties inviolate. FL ST RCP Rule 1.430(a).

b. *Demand.* Any party may demand a trial by jury of any issue triable of right by a jury by serving upon the other party a demand therefor in writing at any time after commencement of the action and not later than ten (10) days after the service of the last pleading directed to such issue. The demand may be indorsed upon a pleading of the party. FL ST RCP Rule 1.430(b).

c. *Specification of issues.* In the demand a party may specify the issues that the party wishes so tried; otherwise, the party is deemed to demand trial by jury for all issues so triable. FL ST RCP Rule 1.430(c).

i. If a party has demanded trial by jury for only some of the issues, any other party may serve a demand for trial by jury of any other or all of the issues triable by jury ten (10) days after service of the demand or such lesser time as the court may order. FL ST RCP Rule 1.430(c).

d. *Waiver.* A party who fails to serve a demand as required by FL ST RCP Rule 1.430 waives trial by jury. FL ST RCP Rule 1.430(d).

i. If waived, a jury trial may not be granted without the consent of the parties, but the court may allow an amendment in the proceedings to demand a trial by jury or order a trial by jury on its own motion. FL ST RCP Rule 1.430(d).

ii. A demand for trial by jury may not be withdrawn without the consent of the parties. FL ST RCP Rule 1.430(d).

8. *Companion cases in the Sixth Circuit*
   a. An attorney representing a party in a case to which there are companion cases shall file a notice of a companion case. FL ST 6 J CIR LOCAL Rule 3(B)(1).
   b. The original notice and sufficient copies for filing in each companion case shall be filed with the Clerk and a copy provided to the judge in the section which has been assigned the case bearing the lowest docket number. FL ST 6 J CIR LOCAL Rule 3(B)(1).
   c. Said judge may thereupon reassign all such companion cases to the section which has been assigned the case bearing the lowest docket number if the court finds that the companion cases involve common questions of law or fact or the reassignment would result in an efficient administration of justice. FL ST 6 J CIR LOCAL Rule 3(B)(1).
   d. The Clerk shall make appropriate notations on the file cover and the progress docket of such reassigned case or cases and thereafter all such companion cases shall be heard, tried, and determined by the judge assigned to the section having the companion case bearing the lowest docket number. FL ST 6 J CIR LOCAL Rule 3 (B)(1).
9. *Arbitration and mediation*
   a. *Referral to arbitration and mediation.* Except as hereinafter provided or as otherwise prohibited by law, the presiding judge may enter an order referring all or any part of a contested civil matter to mediation or arbitration. The parties to any contested civil matter may file a written stipulation to mediate or arbitrate any issue between them at any time. Such stipulation shall be incorporated into the order of referral. FL ST RCP Rule 1.700(a).
   b. *Arbitration*
      i. *Exclusions.* A civil action shall be ordered to arbitration or arbitration in conjunction with mediation upon stipulation of the parties. A civil action may be ordered to arbitration or arbitration in conjunction with mediation upon motion of any party or by the court, if the judge determines the action to be of such a nature that arbitration could be of benefit to the litigants or the court. FL ST RCP Rule 1.800.
         - Under no circumstances may the following categories of actions be referred to arbitration: (1) bond estreatures; (2) habeas corpus or other extraordinary writs; (3) bond validations; (4) civil or criminal contempt; (5) such other matters as may be specified by order of the chief judge in the circuit. FL ST RCP Rule 1.800.
      ii. For more information regarding arbitration, please see FL ST RCP Rule 1.810; FL ST RCP Rule 1.820; FL ST RCP Rule 1.830.
   c. *Mediation.* For more information regarding mediation, please see FL ST RCP Rule 1.710; FL ST RCP Rule 1.720; FL ST RCP Rule 1.730; and FL ST RCP Rule 1.750.
   d. See FL ST 6 J CIR PA/PI-CIR-96-63 for more information about the Arbitration and Mediation Program for Florida's Sixth Judicial Circuit.
10. *Rules of court*
   a. *Rules of civil procedure.* The Florida Rules of Civil Procedure apply to all actions of a civil nature and all special statutory proceedings in the circuit courts and county courts except those to which the Florida Probate Rules, the Florida Family Law Rules of Procedure, or the Small Claims Rules apply. FL ST RCP Rule 1.010.
      i. The form, content, procedure, and time for pleading in all special statutory proceedings shall be as prescribed by the statutes governing the proceeding unless the Florida Rules of Civil Procedure specifically provide to the contrary. FL ST RCP Rule 1.010.
      ii. The Florida Rules of Civil Procedure shall be construed to secure the just, speedy, and inexpensive determination of every action. FL ST RCP Rule 1.010.
   b. *Rules of judicial administration.* The Florida Rules of Judicial Administration shall apply to administrative matters in all courts to which the Florida Rules of Judicial Administration are applicable by their terms. The Florida Rules of Judicial Administration shall be construed to secure

the speedy and inexpensive determination of every proceeding to which they are applicable. The Florida Rules of Judicial Administration shall supersede all conflicting rules and statutes. FL ST J ADMIN Rule 2.110.

D. Documents

1. *Required documents*
   a. *Answer.* See the General Requirements section of this document for further information about the content of an answer.
      i. *Notices to persons with disabilities.* See the Format section of this KeyRules document for further information.
   b. *Certificate of service.* When any attorney certifies in substance: "I certify that a copy hereof has been furnished to (here insert name or names and addresses used for service) by (e-mail) (delivery) (mail) (fax) on .... (date) ....______________ Attorney" the certificate is taken as prima facie proof of such service in compliance with FL ST J ADMIN Rule 2.516. FL ST J ADMIN Rule 2.516(f).
2. *Supplemental documents*
   a. *Exhibits.* All bonds, notes, bills of exchange, contracts, accounts, or documents upon which action may be brought or defense made, or a copy thereof or a copy of the portions thereof material to the pleadings, shall be incorporated in or attached to the pleading. No papers shall be unnecessarily annexed as exhibits. The pleadings shall contain no unnecessary recitals of deeds, documents, contracts, or other instruments. Any exhibit attached to a pleading shall be considered a part of the pleadings for all purposes. FL ST RCP Rule 1.130(a).
   b. *Notice of constitutional question.* A party that files a pleading, written motion, or other paper drawing into question the constitutionality of a state statute or a county or municipal charter, ordinance, or franchise must promptly (1) file a notice of constitutional question stating the question and identifying the paper that raises it; and (2) serve the notice and the pleading, written motion, or other paper drawing into question the constitutionality of a state statute or a county or municipal charter, ordinance, or franchise on the Attorney General or the state attorney of the judicial circuit in which the action is pending, by either certified or registered mail. Service of the notice and pleading, written motion, or other paper does not require joinder of the Attorney General or the state attorney as a party to the action. FL ST RCP Rule 1.071.
   c. *Notice of companion cases.* An attorney representing a party in a case to which there are companion cases shall file a notice of a companion case. FL ST 6 J CIR LOCAL Rule 3(B)(1).

E. Format

1. *Documents; Type and size.* Documents subject to the exceptions set forth in FL ST J ADMIN Rule 2.525(d) shall be filed on recycled paper measuring eight and one half by eleven (8 1/2 by 11) inches. For purposes of FL ST J ADMIN Rule 2.520, paper is recycled if it contains a minimum content of fifty (50) percent waste paper. Xerographic reduction of legal-size (eight and one half by fourteen (8 1/2 by 14) inches) documents to letter size (eight and one half by eleven (8 1/2 by 11) inches) is prohibited. All other documents filed by electronic transmission shall be filed in a format capable of being printed in a format consistent with the provisions of FL ST J ADMIN Rule 2.250. FL ST J ADMIN Rule 2.520(b).
   a. *Exhibits.* Any exhibit or attachment filed with pleadings or papers may be filed in its original size. FL ST J ADMIN Rule 2.520(c).
   b. *Recording space.* On all papers and documents prepared and filed by the court or by any party to a proceeding which are to be recorded in the public records of any county, including but not limited to final money judgments and notices of lis pendens, a three (3) inch by three (3) inch space at the top right-hand corner on the first page and a one (1) inch by three (3) inch space at the top right-hand corner on each subsequent page shall be left blank and reserved for use by the clerk of court. FL ST J ADMIN Rule 2.520(d).
      i. *Exceptions to recording space.* Any papers or documents created by persons or entities over which the filing party has no control, including but not limited to wills, codicils, trusts, or other testamentary documents; documents prepared or executed by any public officer; documents

prepared, executed, acknowledged, or proved outside of the State of Florida; or documents created by State or Federal government agencies, may be filed without the space required by FL ST J ADMIN Rule 2.520. FL ST J ADMIN Rule 2.520(e).

c. *Noncompliance.* No clerk of court is permitted to refuse to file any document or paper because of noncompliance with the Florida Rules of Judicial Administration. However, upon request of the clerk of court, noncomplying documents must be resubmitted in accordance with the formatting rules. FL ST J ADMIN Rule 2.520(f).

2. *Caption.* Every pleading, motion, order, judgment, or other paper shall have a caption containing the name of the court, the file number, and except for in rem proceedings, including forfeiture proceedings, the name of the first party on each side with an appropriate indication of other parties, and a designation identifying the party filing it and its nature or the nature of the order, as the case may be. In any in rem proceeding, every pleading, motion, order, judgment, or other paper shall have a caption containing the name of the court, the file number, the style "In re" (followed by the name or general description of the property), and a designation of the person or entity filing it and its nature or the nature of the order, as the case may be. In an in rem forfeiture proceeding, the style shall be "In re forfeiture of" (followed by the name of the general description of the property). All papers filed in the action shall be styled in such a manner as to indicate clearly the subject matter of the paper and the party requesting or obtaining relief. FL ST RCP Rule 1.100(c)(1).

3. *Writing and written defined.* Writing or written means a document containing information, an application, or a stipulation. FL ST RCP Rule 1.080(c).

4. *Rule abbreviations*

   a. The Florida Rules of Civil Procedure and shall be abbreviated as Fla.R.Civ.P. FL ST RCP Rule 1.010.

   b. The Florida Rules of Judicial Administration shall be abbreviated as Fla. R. Jud. Admin. FL ST J ADMIN Rule 2.110.

5. *Nonverification.* Except when otherwise specifically provided by the Florida Rules of Civil Procedure or an applicable statute, every pleading or other document of a party represented by an attorney need not be verified or accompanied by an affidavit. FL ST RCP Rule 1.030; FL ST J ADMIN Rule 2.515(a).

6. *Attorney signature*

   a. *Attorney signature.* Every pleading and other document of a party represented by an attorney shall be signed by at least one (1) attorney of record in that attorney's individual name whose current record Florida Bar address, telephone number, including area code, primary e-mail address and secondary e-mail addresses, if any, and Florida Bar number shall be stated, and who shall be duly licensed to practice law in Florida or who shall have received permission to appear in the particular case as provided in FL ST J ADMIN Rule 2.510. FL ST J ADMIN Rule 2.515(a).

      i. The attorney may be required by the court to give the address of, and to vouch for the attorney's authority to represent, the party. FL ST J ADMIN Rule 2.515(a).

      ii. The signature of an attorney shall constitute a certificate by the attorney that the attorney has read the pleading or other document; that to the best of the attorney's knowledge, information, and belief there is good ground to support it; and that it is not interposed for delay. FL ST J ADMIN Rule 2.515(a).

      iii. If a pleading is not signed or is signed with intent to defeat the purpose of FL ST J ADMIN Rule 2.515, it may be stricken and the action may proceed as though the pleading or other document had not been served. FL ST J ADMIN Rule 2.515(a).

   b. *Pro se litigant signature.* A party who is not represented by an attorney shall sign any pleading or other paper and state the party's address and telephone number, including area code. FL ST J ADMIN Rule 2.515(b).

   c. *Form of signature*

      i. The signatures required on pleadings and documents by FL ST J ADMIN Rule 2.515(a) and FL ST J ADMIN Rule 2.515(b) may be:

         - Original signatures;

- Original signatures that have been reproduced by electronic means, such as on electronically transmitted documents or photocopied documents;
- Electronic signatures using the "/s/," "s/," or "/s" formats by or at the direction of the person signing; or
- Any other signature format authorized by general law, so long as the clerk where the proceeding is pending has the capability of receiving and has obtained approval from the Supreme Court of Florida to accept pleadings and documents with that signature format. FL ST J ADMIN Rule 2.515(c)(1).

ii. An attorney, party, or other person who files a pleading or paper by electronic transmission that does not contain the original signature of that attorney, party, or other person shall file that identical pleading or paper in paper form containing an original signature of that attorney, party, or other person (hereinafter called the follow-up filing) immediately thereafter. The follow-up filing is not required if the Supreme Court of Florida has entered an order directing the clerk of court to discontinue accepting the follow-up filing. FL ST J ADMIN Rule 2.515(c)(2).

7. *Forms*
   a. *Process.* The forms of process, notice of lis pendens, and notice of action provided in the Florida Rules of Civil Procedure are sufficient. Variations from the forms do not void process or notices that are otherwise sufficient. FL ST RCP Rule 1.900(a).
   b. *Other forms.* The other forms provided in the Florida Rules of Civil Procedure are sufficient for the matters that are covered by them. So long as the substance is expressed without prolixity, the forms may be varied to meet the facts of a particular case. FL ST RCP Rule 1.900(b).
   c. *Formal matters.* Captions, except for the designation of the paper, are omitted from the forms provided in the Florida Rules of Civil Procedure. A general form of caption is the first form provided. Signatures are omitted from pleadings and motions. FL ST RCP Rule 1.900(c).
8. *Notices to persons with disabilities.* All notices of court proceedings to be held in a public facility, and all process compelling appearance at such proceedings, shall include the following statement in bold face, fourteen (14) point Times New Roman or Courier font: "If you are a person with a disability who needs any accommodation in order to participate in this proceeding, you are entitled, at no cost to you, to the provision of certain assistance. Please contact [identify applicable court personnel by name, address, and telephone number] at least seven (7) days before your scheduled court appearance, or immediately upon receiving this notification if the time before the scheduled appearance is less than seven (7) days; if you are hearing or voice impaired, call 711." FL ST J ADMIN Rule 2.540(c)(1).
9. *Minimization of the filing of sensitive information*
   a. *Limitations for court filings.* Unless authorized by FL ST J ADMIN Rule 2.425(b), statute, another rule of court, or the court orders otherwise, designated sensitive information filed with the court must be limited to the following format:
      i. The initials of a person known to be a minor;
      ii. The year of birth of a person's birth date;
      iii. No portion of any: Social security number, Bank account number, Credit card account number, Charge account number, or Debit account number;
      iv. The last four digits of any: Taxpayer identification number (TIN), Employee identification number, Driver's license number, Passport number, Telephone number, Financial account number, except as set forth in FL ST J ADMIN Rule 2.425(a)(3), Brokerage account number, Insurance policy account number, Loan account number, Customer account number, or Patient or health care number;
      v. A truncated version of any: Email address, Computer user name, Password, or Personal identification number (PIN); and
      vi. A truncated version of any other sensitive information as provided by court order. FL ST J ADMIN Rule 2.425(a).

b. *Exceptions.* FL ST J ADMIN Rule 2.425(a) does not apply to the following:
   i. An account number which identifies the property alleged to be the subject of a proceeding;
   ii. The record of an administrative or agency proceeding;
   iii. The record in appellate or review proceedings;
   iv. The birth date of a minor whenever the birth date is necessary for the court to establish or maintain subject matter jurisdiction;
   v. The name of a minor in any order relating to parental responsibility, time-sharing, or child support;
   vi. The name of a minor in any document or order affecting the minor's ownership of real property;
   vii. The birth date of a party in a writ of attachment or notice to payor;
   viii. In traffic and criminal proceedings: a pro se filing; a court filing that is related to a criminal matter or investigation and that is prepared before the filing of a criminal charge or is not filed as part of any docketed criminal case; an arrest or search warrant or any information in support thereof; a charging document and an affidavit or other documents filed in support of any charging document, including any driving records; a statement of particulars; discovery material introduced into evidence or otherwise filed with the court; and all information necessary for the proper issuance and execution of a subpoena duces tecum;
   ix. Information used by the clerk for case maintenance purposes or the courts for case management purposes; and
   x. Information which is relevant and material to an issue before the court. FL ST J ADMIN Rule 2.425(b).

c. *Remedies.* Upon motion by a party or interested person or sua sponte by the court, the court may order remedies, sanctions or both for a violation of FL ST J ADMIN Rule 2.425(a). Following notice and an opportunity to respond, the court may impose sanctions if such filing was not made in good faith. FL ST J ADMIN Rule 2.425(c).

d. *Motions not restricted.* FL ST J ADMIN Rule 2.425 does not restrict a party's right to move for protective order, to move to file documents under seal, or to request a determination of the confidentiality of records. FL ST J ADMIN Rule 2.425(d).

e. *Application.* FL ST J ADMIN Rule 2.425 does not affect the application of constitutional provisions, statutes, or rules of court regarding confidential information or access to public information. FL ST J ADMIN Rule 2.425(e).

F. Filing and Service Requirements

1. *Filing requirements.* All original documents must be filed with the court either before service or immediately thereafter, unless otherwise provided for by general law or other rules. If the original of any bond or other document is not placed in the court file, a certified copy must be so placed by the clerk. FL ST J ADMIN Rule 2.516(d). All documents shall be filed in conformity with the requirements of FL ST J ADMIN Rule 2.525. FL ST RCP Rule 1.080(b). All documents filed in any court shall be filed by electronic transmission in accordance with FL ST J ADMIN Rule 2.525. "Documents" means pleadings, motions, petitions, memoranda, briefs, notices, exhibits, declarations, affidavits, orders, judgments, decrees, writs, opinions, and any other paper or writing submitted to a court. FL ST J ADMIN Rule 2.520(a). All documents that are court records, as defined in FL ST J ADMIN Rule 2.430(a)(1), must be filed by electronic transmission, provided that: (1) the clerk has the ability to accept and retain such documents; (2) the clerk or the chief judge of the circuit has requested permission to accept documents filed by electronic transmission; and (3) the supreme court has entered an order granting permission to the clerk to accept documents filed by electronic transmission. FL ST J ADMIN Rule 2.525(c)(1).

   a. *Definition.* "Electronic transmission of documents" means the sending of information by electronic signals to, by or from a court or clerk, which when received can be transformed and stored or transmitted on paper, microfilm, magnetic storage device, optical imaging system, CD-ROM, flash drive, other electronic data storage system, server, case maintenance system ("CM"), electronic

court filing ("ECF") system, statewide or local electronic portal ("e-portal"), or other electronic record keeping system authorized by the supreme court in a format sufficient to communicate the information on the original document in a readable format. Electronic transmission of documents includes electronic mail ("e-mail") and any internet-based transmission procedure, and may include procedures allowing for documents to be signed or verified by electronic means. FL ST J ADMIN Rule 2.525(a).

i. The filing of documents with the court as required by the Florida Rules of Judicial Administration must be made by filing them with the clerk in accordance with FL ST J ADMIN Rule 2.525, except that the judge may permit documents to be filed with the judge, in which event the judge must note the filing date before him or her on the documents and transmit them to the clerk. The date of filing is that shown on the face of the document by the judge's notation or the clerk's time stamp, whichever is earlier. FL ST J ADMIN Rule 2.516(e).

b. *Application.* Any court or clerk of the court may accept the electronic transmission of documents for filing after the clerk, together with input from the chief judge of the circuit, has obtained approval of the procedures and program for doing so from the Supreme Court of Florida. FL ST J ADMIN Rule 2.525(b).

c. *Exceptions*

i. Paper documents and other submissions may be manually submitted to the clerk or court:

- When the clerk does not have the ability to accept and retain documents by electronic filing or has not had ECF Procedures approved by the supreme court;
- For filing by any self-represented party or any self-represented nonparty unless specific ECF Procedures provide a means to file documents electronically. However, any self-represented nonparty that is a governmental or public agency and any other agency, partnership, corporation, or business entity acting on behalf of any governmental or public agency may file documents by electronic transmission if such entity has the capability of filing documents electronically;
- For filing by attorneys excused from e-mail service in accordance with FL ST J ADMIN Rule 2.516(b);
- When submitting evidentiary exhibits or filing non-documentary materials;
- When the filing involves documents in excess of twenty-five (25) megabytes (25MB) in size. For such filings, documents may be transmitted using an electronic storage medium that the clerk has the ability to accept, which may include a CD-ROM, flash drive, or similar storage medium;
- When filed in open court, as permitted by the court;
- When paper filing is permitted by any approved statewide or local ECF procedures; and
- If any court determines that justice so requires. FL ST J ADMIN Rule 2.525(d).

ii. Any document in paper form submitted under FL ST J ADMIN Rule 2.525(d) is filed when it is received by the clerk or court and the clerk shall immediately thereafter convert any filed paper document to an electronic document. "Convert to an electronic document" means optically capturing an image of a paper document and using character recognition software to recover as much of the document's text as practicable and then indexing and storing the document in the official court file. FL ST J ADMIN Rule 2.525(c)(4).

iii. Any storage medium submitted under FL ST J ADMIN Rule 2.525(d)(5) is filed when received by the clerk or court and the clerk shall immediately thereafter transfer the electronic documents from the storage device to the official court file. FL ST J ADMIN Rule 2.525(c)(5).

iv. If the filer of any paper document authorized under FL ST J ADMIN Rule 2.525(d) provides a self-addressed, postage-paid envelope for return of the paper document after it is converted to electronic form by the clerk, the clerk shall place the paper document in the envelope and deposit it in the mail. Except when a paper document is required to be maintained, the clerk may recycle any filed paper document that is not to be returned to the filer. FL ST J ADMIN Rule 2.525(c)(6).

v. The clerk may convert any paper document filed before the effective date of FL ST J ADMIN Rule 2.525 to an electronic document. Unless the clerk is required to maintain the paper document, if the paper document has been converted to an electronic document by the clerk, the paper document is no longer part of the official court file and may be removed and recycled. FL ST J ADMIN Rule 2.525(c)(7).

d. *Official court file.* For information on what constitutes the official court file, please see FL ST J ADMIN Rule 2.525(c)(2), FL ST J ADMIN Rule 2.525(c)(3).

e. *Administration.* All attorneys, parties, or other persons using this rule to file documents are required to make arrangements with the court or clerk for the payment of any charges authorized by general law or the supreme court before filing any document by electronic transmission. FL ST J ADMIN Rule 2.525(f)(2).

f. *Filing date.* The filing date for an electronically transmitted document is the date and time that such filing is acknowledged by an electronic stamp or otherwise, pursuant to any procedure set forth in any ECF Procedures approved by the supreme court, or the date the last page of such filing is received by the court or clerk. FL ST J ADMIN Rule 2.525(f)(3).

g. *Accessibility.* All documents transmitted in any electronic form under FL ST J ADMIN Rule 2.525 must comply with the accessibility requirements of FL ST J ADMIN Rule 2.526. FL ST J ADMIN Rule 2.525(g).

2. *Service requirements.* Every pleading subsequent to the initial pleading, all orders, and every other document filed in the action must be served in conformity with the requirements of FL ST J ADMIN Rule 2.516. FL ST RCP Rule 1.080(a).

a. *Service; When required.* Unless the court otherwise orders, or a statute or supreme court administrative order specifies a different means of service, every pleading subsequent to the initial pleading and every other document filed in any court proceeding, except applications for witness subpoenas and documents served by formal notice or required to be served in the manner provided for service of formal notice, must be served in accordance with FL ST J ADMIN Rule 2.516 on each party. No service need be made on parties against whom a default has been entered, except that pleadings asserting new or additional claims against them must be served in the manner provided for service of summons. FL ST J ADMIN Rule 2.516(a).

b. *Service; How made.* When service is required or permitted to be made upon a party represented by an attorney, service must be made upon the attorney unless service upon the party is ordered by the court. FL ST J ADMIN Rule 2.516(b).

i. *Service by electronic mail ("e-mail").* All documents required or permitted to be served on another party must be served by e-mail, unless FL ST J ADMIN Rule 2.516 otherwise provides. When, in addition to service by e-mail, the sender also utilizes another means of service provided for in FL ST J ADMIN Rule 2.516(b)(2), any differing time limits and other provisions applicable to that other means of service control. FL ST J ADMIN Rule 2.516(b)(1). Any document electronically transmitted to a court or clerk must also be served on all parties and interested persons in accordance with the applicable rules of court. FL ST J ADMIN Rule 2.525(e)(2).

- *Service on attorneys.* Upon appearing in a proceeding, an attorney must serve a designation of a primary e-mail address and may designate no more than two (2) secondary e-mail addresses. Thereafter, service must be directed to all designated e-mail addresses in that proceeding. Every document filed by an attorney thereafter must include the primary e-mail address of that attorney and any secondary e-mail addresses. If an attorney does not designate any e-mail address for service, documents may be served on that attorney at the e-mail address on record with The Florida Bar. FL ST J ADMIN Rule 2.516(b)(1)(A).

- *Exception to e-mail service on attorneys.* Service by an attorney on another attorney must be made by e-mail unless excused by the court. Upon motion by an attorney demonstrating that the attorney has no e-mail account and lacks access to the Internet at the attorney's office, the court may excuse the attorney from the requirements of e-mail service. Service

on and by an attorney excused by the court from e-mail service must be by the means provided in FL ST J ADMIN Rule 2.516(b)(2). FL ST J ADMIN Rule 2.516(b)(1)(B).

- *Service on and by parties not represented by an attorney.* Any party not represented by an attorney may serve a designation of a primary e-mail address and also may designate no more than two (2) secondary e-mail addresses to which service must be directed in that proceeding by the means provided in FL ST J ADMIN Rule 2.516(b)(1). If a party not represented by an attorney does not designate an e-mail address for service in a proceeding, service on and by that party must be by the means provided in FL ST J ADMIN Rule 2.516(b)(2). FL ST J ADMIN Rule 2.516(b)(1)(C).
- *Time of service.* Service by e-mail is complete when it is sent. FL ST J ADMIN Rule 2.516(b)(1)(D). An e-mail is deemed served on the date it is sent. FL ST J ADMIN Rule 2.516(b)(1)(D)(i). If the sender learns that the e-mail did not reach the address of the person to be served, the sender must immediately send another copy by e-mail, or by a means authorized by FL ST J ADMIN Rule 2.516(b)(2). FL ST J ADMIN Rule 2.516(b)(1)(D)(ii). E-mail service is treated as service by mail for the computation of time. FL ST J ADMIN Rule 2.516(b)(1)(D)(iii).

ii. *Format of e-mail for service.* Service of a document by e-mail is made by attaching a copy of the document in PDF format to an e-mail sent to all addresses designated by the attorney or party. FL ST J ADMIN Rule 2.516(b)(1)(E).

- All documents served by e-mail must be attached to an e-mail message containing a subject line beginning with the words "SERVICE OF COURT DOCUMENT" in all capital letters, followed by the case number of the proceeding in which the documents are being served. FL ST J ADMIN Rule 2.516(b)(1)(E)(i).
- The body of the e-mail must identify the court in which the proceeding is pending, the case number, the name of the initial party on each side, the title of each document served with that e-mail, and the sender's name and telephone number. FL ST J ADMIN Rule 2.516(b)(1)(E)(ii).
- Any document served by e-mail may be signed by the "/s/" format, as long as the filed original is signed in accordance with the applicable rule of procedure. FL ST J ADMIN Rule 2.516(b)(1)(E)(iii).
- Any e-mail which, together with its attached documents, exceeds five megabytes (5MB) in size, must be divided and sent as separate e-mails, no one of which may exceed five megabytes (5MB) in size and each of which must be sequentially numbered in the subject line. FL ST J ADMIN Rule 2.516(b)(1)(E)(iv).

iii. *Service by other means.* In addition to, and not in lieu of, service by e-mail, service may also be made upon attorneys by any of the means specified in FL ST J ADMIN Rule 2.516(b)(2). Service on and by all parties who are not represented by an attorney and who do not designate an e-mail address, and on and by all attorneys excused from e-mail service, must be made by delivering a copy of the document or by mailing it to the party or attorney at their last known address or, if no address is known, by leaving it with the clerk of the court. Service by mail is complete upon mailing. Delivery of a copy within FL ST J ADMIN Rule 2.516 is complete upon:

- Handing it to the attorney or to the party,
- Leaving it at the attorney's or party's office with a clerk or other person in charge thereof,
- If there is no one in charge, leaving it in a conspicuous place therein,
- If the office is closed or the person to be served has no office, leaving it at the person's usual place of abode with some person of his or her family above fifteen (15) years of age and informing such person of the contents, or
- Transmitting it by facsimile to the attorney's or party's office with a cover sheet containing the sender's name, firm, address, telephone number, and facsimile number, and the

number of pages transmitted. When service is made by facsimile, a copy must also be served by any other method permitted by FL ST J ADMIN Rule 2.516. Facsimile service occurs when transmission is complete. FL ST J ADMIN Rule 2.516(b)(2)(A) through FL ST J ADMIN Rule 2.516(b)(2)(E).

- Service by delivery after 5:00 p.m. must be deemed to have been made by mailing on the date of delivery. FL ST J ADMIN Rule 2.516(b)(2)(F).

c. *Service; Numerous defendants.* In actions when the parties are unusually numerous, the court may regulate the service contemplated by the Florida Rules of Judicial Administration on motion or on its own initiative in such manner as may be found to be just and reasonable. FL ST J ADMIN Rule 2.516(c).

d. *Service by clerk.* Service of notices and other documents required to be made by the clerk must also be done as provided in FL ST J ADMIN Rule 2.516(b). FL ST J ADMIN Rule 2.516(g).

e. *Standards of professional courtesy; Service*

i. The timing and manner of service should not be used to the disadvantage of the party receiving the papers. This includes the use of facsimile transmissions and any additional expedited means of communication approved by the court. FL ST 6 J CIR 2009-066 PA/PI-CIR(C)(1).

ii. Attorneys will not serve papers to take advantage of opposing counsel's known absence from the office or at a time or in a manner designed to inconvenience an opponent, such as late on Friday afternoon or the day preceding a secular or religious holiday. FL ST 6 J CIR 2009-066 PA/PI-CIR(C)(2).

iii. Attorneys will not serve papers, including briefs and memoranda, so close to a court appearance that the ability of opposing counsel to prepare for that appearance or, where permitted, to respond, is inhibited. FL ST 6 J CIR 2009-066 PA/PI-CIR(C)(3).

iv. Service should be made personally or by facsimile transmission when it is likely that service by mail, even when allowed, will prejudice the opposing party. FL ST 6 J CIR 2009-066 PA/PI-CIR(C)(4).

G. Hearings

1. *Preliminary hearings.* The defenses in FL ST RCP Rule 1.140(b)(1) through FL ST RCP Rule 1.140(b)(7), whether made in a pleading or by motion, and the motion for judgment in FL ST RCP Rule 1.140(c) shall be heard and determined before trial on application of any party unless the court orders that the hearing and determination shall be deferred until the trial. FL ST RCP Rule 1.140(d).

H. Forms

1. Official Answer Forms for Florida

a. Caption. FL ST RCP Form 1.901.

b. Crossclaim summons. FL ST RCP Form 1.903.

c. Third-party summons. FL ST RCP Form 1.904.

d. Defense; Statute of limitations. FL ST RCP Form 1.965.

e. Defense; Payment. FL ST RCP Form 1.966.

f. Defense; Accord and satisfaction. FL ST RCP Form 1.967.

g. Defense; Failure of consideration. FL ST RCP Form 1.968.

h. Defense; Statute of frauds. FL ST RCP Form 1.969.

i. Defense; Release. FL ST RCP Form 1.970.

j. Notice of compliance when constitutional challenge is brought. FL ST RCP Form 1.975.

2. Answer Forms for Florida

a. Answer; General form, traverses. FL-PRACFORM § 5:4.

b. Answer; General form, traverses and affirmative defenses. FL-PRACFORM § 5:6.

c. Answer; General form, traverses, affirmative defenses and counterclaim. FL-PRACFORM § 5:7.
d. Answer; General form, traverses, affirmative defenses, counterclaim and crossclaim. FL-PRACFORM § 5:8.
e. Answer; Affirmative defense, fraud. FL-PRACFORM § 5:43.
f. Answer; Affirmative defense, laches. FL-PRACFORM § 5:47.
g. Answer; Affirmative defense, misjoinder. FL-PRACFORM § 5:49.
h. Answer; Affirmative defense, misrepresentation. FL-PRACFORM § 5:50.
i. Answer; Affirmative defense, self defense. FL-PRACFORM § 5:64.
j. Answer; Denial of conditions precedent. FL-PRACFORM § 5:80.
k. General denial. FL-PP § 2:58.
l. General denial; With specified admissions. FL-PP § 2:59.
m. Admission with qualification. FL-PP § 2:60.
n. Conclusions of law not requiring denial. FL-PP § 2:61.
o. Defenses stated in the alternative. FL-PP § 2:62.
p. Denial as to part of allegation. FL-PP § 2:63.
q. Pleader as without knowledge as to truth of allegation. FL-PP § 2:64.

I. Checklist

(I) ❑ Matters to be considered by plaintiff
- (a) ❑ Required documents
  - (1) ❑ Summons
  - (2) ❑ Complaint
  - (3) ❑ Civil cover sheet
  - (4) ❑ Return of execution process by process server
  - (5) ❑ Filing fees
- (b) ❑ Supplemental documents
  - (1) ❑ Exhibits
  - (2) ❑ Notice of constitutional question
  - (3) ❑ Notice of companion cases
- (c) ❑ Time for filing and serving complaint
  - (1) ❑ Service of the initial process and initial pleading should be made upon a defendant within one hundred twenty (120) days after the filing of the complaint with the court

(II) ❑ Matters to be considered by defendant
- (a) ❑ Required documents
  - (1) ❑ Answer
  - (2) ❑ Certificate of service
- (b) ❑ Supplemental documents
  - (1) ❑ Exhibits
  - (2) ❑ Notice of constitutional question
  - (3) ❑ Notice of companion cases
- (c) ❑ Time for answer
  - (1) ❑ Unless a different time is prescribed in a statute of Florida, a defendant shall serve an answer

within twenty (20) days after service of original process and the initial pleading on the defendant, or not later than the date fixed in a notice by publication

(2) ❑ A party served with a pleading stating a crossclaim against that party shall serve an answer to it within twenty (20) days after service on that party

(3) ❑ The plaintiff shall serve an answer to a counterclaim within twenty (20) days after service of the counterclaim

(4) ❑ A defendant who, before being served with process, timely returns a waiver so requested is not required to respond to the complaint until sixty (60) days after the date the defendant received the request for waiver of service; for purposes of computing any time prescribed or allowed by the Florida Rules of Civil Procedure, service of process shall be deemed effected twenty (20) days before the time required to respond to the complaint

(5) ❑ For timing requirements related to service on the state, service of motion impact, and responding when no responsive pleading is required, please see the Timing section of this document

Pleadings
Amended Answer

Document Last Updated January 2013

A. Applicable Rules

1. *State rules*

   a. Nonverification of papers. FL ST RCP Rule 1.030.

   b. Service and filing of pleadings, orders, and documents. FL ST RCP Rule 1.080.

   c. Time. FL ST RCP Rule 1.090.

   d. Pleadings and motions. FL ST RCP Rule 1.100; FL ST RCP Rule 1.110; FL ST RCP Rule 1.120; FL ST RCP Rule 1.130; FL ST RCP Rule 1.190.

   e. Defenses. FL ST RCP Rule 1.140.

   f. Pretrial procedure. FL ST RCP Rule 1.200.

   g. Relief from judgment, decrees, or orders. FL ST RCP Rule 1.540.

   h. Forms. FL ST RCP Rule 1.900.

   i. Minimization of the filing of sensitive information. FL ST J ADMIN Rule 2.425.

   j. Signature of attorneys and parties. FL ST J ADMIN Rule 2.515.

   k. Paper. FL ST J ADMIN Rule 2.520.

   l. Electronic filing. FL ST J ADMIN Rule 2.525.

   m. Accessibility of information and technology. FL ST J ADMIN Rule 2.526.

   n. Court reporting. FL ST J ADMIN Rule 2.535.

   o. Requests for accommodations by persons with disabilities. FL ST J ADMIN Rule 2.540.

2. *Local rules*

   a. Assignment of cases. FL ST 6 J CIR LOCAL Rule 3.

   b. Standards of professional courtesy. FL ST 6 J CIR 2009-066 PA/PI-CIR.

   c. Arbitration and mediation program circuit civil and family cases. FL ST 6 J CIR PA/PI-CIR-96-63; FL ST 6 J CIR 2011-006 PA/PI-CIR.

B. Timing

1. *Amendment as a matter of course.* A party may amend a pleading once as a matter of course at any time

before a responsive pleading is served or, if the pleading is one to which no responsive pleading is permitted and the action has not been placed on the trial calendar, may so amend it at any time within twenty (20) days after it is served. FL ST RCP Rule 1.190(a).

2. *Amendment by leave of court.* Otherwise a party may amend a pleading only by leave of court or by written consent of the adverse party. Leave of court shall be given freely when justice so requires. FL ST RCP Rule 1.190(a).
3. *Amendments in furtherance of justice.* At any time in furtherance of justice, upon such terms as may be just, the court may permit any process, proceeding, pleading, or record to be amended or material supplemental matter to be set forth in an amended or supplemental pleading. At every stage of the action the court must disregard any error or defect in the proceedings which does not affect the substantial rights of the parties. FL ST RCP Rule 1.190(e).
4. *Response to amended pleading.* A party shall plead in response to an amended pleading within ten (10) days after service of the amended pleading unless the court otherwise orders. FL ST RCP Rule 1.190(a).
5. *Computation of time*
   a. *Generally.* Computation of time shall be governed by FL ST J ADMIN Rule 2.514. FL ST RCP Rule 1.090(a). The following rules apply in computing time periods specified in any rule of procedure, local rule, court order, or statute that does not specify a method of computing time. FL ST J ADMIN Rule 2.514(a).
      i. *Period stated in days or a longer unit.* When the period is stated in days or a longer unit of time (A) exclude the day of the event that triggers the period; (B) count every day, including intermediate Saturdays, Sundays, and legal holidays; and (C) include the last day of the period, but if the last day is a Saturday, Sunday, or legal holiday, or falls within any period of time extended through an order of the chief justice under FL ST J ADMIN Rule 2.205(a)(2)(B)(iv), the period continues to run until the end of the next day that is not a Saturday, Sunday, or legal holiday and does not fall within any period of time extended through an order of the chief justice. FL ST J ADMIN Rule 2.514(a)(1).
      ii. *Period stated in hours.* When the period is stated in hours (A) begin counting immediately on the occurrence of the event that triggers the period; (B) count every hour, including hours during intermediate Saturdays, Sundays, and legal holidays; and (C) if the period would end on a Saturday, Sunday, or legal holiday, or during any period of time extended through an order of the chief justice under FL ST J ADMIN Rule 2.205(a)(2)(B)(iv), the period continues to run until the same time on the next day that is not a Saturday, Sunday, or legal holiday and does not fall within any period of time extended through an order of the chief justice. FL ST J ADMIN Rule 2.514(a)(2).
      iii. *Period stated in days less than seven (7) days.* When the period stated in days is less than seven (7) days, intermediate Saturdays, Sundays, and legal holidays shall be excluded in the computation. FL ST J ADMIN Rule 2.514(a)(3).
      iv. *"Last day" defined.* Unless a different time is set by a statute, local rule, or court order, the last day ends (A) for electronic filing or for service by any means, at midnight; and (B) for filing by other means, when the clerk's office is scheduled to close. FL ST J ADMIN Rule 2.514(a)(4).
      v. *"Next day" defined.* The "next day" is determined by continuing to count forward when the period is measured after an event and backward when measured before an event. FL ST J ADMIN Rule 2.514(a)(5).
      vi. *"Legal holiday" defined.* "Legal holiday" means (A) the day set aside by FL ST § 110.117, for observing New Year's Day, Martin Luther King, Jr.'s Birthday, Memorial Day, Independence Day, Labor Day, Veterans' Day, Thanksgiving Day, the Friday after Thanksgiving Day, or Christmas Day, and (B) any day observed as a holiday by the clerk's office or as designated by the chief judge. FL ST J ADMIN Rule 2.514(a)(6).

   b. *Additional time after service by mail or e-mail.* When a party may or must act within a specified time after service and service is made by mail or e-mail, five (5) days are added after the period that would otherwise expire under FL ST J ADMIN Rule 2.514(a). FL ST J ADMIN Rule 2.514(b).

c. *Enlargement.* When an act is required or allowed to be done at or within a specified time by order of court, by the Florida Rules of Civil Procedure, or by notice given thereunder, for cause shown the court at any time in its discretion (1) with or without notice, may order the period enlarged if request therefor is made before the expiration of the period originally prescribed or as extended by a previous order, or (2) upon motion made and notice after the expiration of the specified period, may permit the act to be done when failure to act was the result of excusable neglect, but it may not extend the time for making a motion for new trial, for rehearing, or to alter or amend a judgment; making a motion for relief from a judgment under FL ST RCP Rule 1.540(b); taking an appeal or filing a petition for certiorari; or making a motion for a directed verdict. FL ST RCP Rule 1.090(b).

d. *Unaffected by expiration of term.* The period of time provided for the doing of any act or the taking of any proceeding shall not be affected or limited by the continued existence or expiration of a term of court. The continued existence or expiration of a term of court in no way affects the power of a court to do any act or take any proceeding in any action which is or has been pending before it. FL ST RCP Rule 1.090(c).

C. General Requirements

1. *Amendments.* A party may amend a pleading once as a matter of course at any time before a responsive pleading is served or, if the pleading is one to which no responsive pleading is permitted and the action has not been placed on the trial calendar, may so amend it at any time within twenty (20) days after it is served. Otherwise a party may amend a pleading only by leave of court or by written consent of the adverse party. Leave of court shall be freely given when justice so requires. FL ST RCP Rule 1.190(a).

a. *Purpose of amendments.* Amendments can relate to the correction of mistakes, the insertion of jurisdictional averments, the correction or addition of verifications, the addition or substitution or striking out of parties, and generally the rectification of all formal defects in the pleading. The court can also allow amendments setting up an omitted counterclaim or cross-claim if the defendant failed to raise the claim through oversight, inadvertence, or excusable neglect. FL-PP § 2:151.

b. *Amendment to a pleading/Amended pleading.* A significant difference exists between an amendment to a pleading and an amended pleading. An amendment to a pleading corrects, adds to or deletes from the pleading. An amended pleading is substituted for the former pleading and the former pleading ceases to have any effect. Dee v. Southern Brewing Company, 146 Fla. 588, 1 So.2d 562 (Fla. 1941); Shannon v. McBride, 105 So.2d 16 (Fla. 2d DCA 1958); Hughes v. Home Sav. of America, F.S.B., 675 So.2d 649 (Fla. 2d DCA 1996); FL-PRACPROC § 14:2.

c. *Relation back of amendments.* When the claim or defense asserted in the amended pleading arose out of the conduct, transaction, or occurrence set forth or attempted to be set forth in the original pleading, the amendment shall relate back to the date of the original pleading. FL ST RCP Rule 1.190(c).

2. *General rules of pleading*

a. *Claims for relief*

i. A pleading which sets forth a claim for relief, whether an original claim, counterclaim, crossclaim, or third-party claim, must state a cause of action and shall contain

- A short and plain statement of the grounds upon which the court's jurisdiction depends, unless the court already has jurisdiction and the claim needs no new grounds of jurisdiction to support it (For information regarding acts subjecting persons to jurisdiction, please see FL ST § 48.193),
- A short and plain statement of the ultimate facts showing that the pleader is entitled to relief, and
- A demand for judgment for the relief to which the pleader deems himself or herself entitled. FL ST RCP Rule 1.110(b).

ii. Relief in the alternative or of several different types may be demanded. Every complaint shall be considered to demand general relief. FL ST RCP Rule 1.110(b).

b. *Verification.* Except when otherwise specifically provided by these rules or an applicable statute, every pleading or other document of a party represented by an attorney need not be verified or accompanied by an affidavit. FL ST RCP Rule 1.030. When filing an action for foreclosure of a mortgage on residential real property the complaint shall be verified. When verification of a document is required, the document filed shall include an oath, affirmation, or the following statement: "Under penalty of perjury, I declare that I have read the foregoing, and the facts alleged therein are true and correct to the best of my knowledge and belief." FL ST RCP Rule 1.110(b).

c. *Separate statements.* All averments of claim or defense shall be made in consecutively numbered paragraphs, the contents of each of which shall be limited as far as practicable to a statement of a single set of circumstances, and a paragraph may be referred to by number in all subsequent pleadings. Each claim founded upon a separate transaction or occurrence and each defense other than denials shall be stated in a separate count or defense when a separation facilitates the clear presentation of the matter set forth. FL ST RCP Rule 1.110(f).

d. *Statements adopted by reference.* Statements in a pleading may be adopted by reference in a different part of the same pleading, in another pleading, or in any motion. FL ST RCP Rule 1.130(b).

e. *Joinder of causes of action; Consistency.* A pleader may set up in the same action as many claims or causes of action or defenses in the same right as the pleader has, and claims for relief may be stated in the alternative if separate items make up the cause of action, or if two (2) or more causes of action are joined. A party may also set forth two (2) or more statements of a claim or defense alternatively, either in one (1) count or defense or in separate counts or defenses. When two (2) or more statements are made in the alternative and one (1) of them, if made independently, would be sufficient, the pleading is not made insufficient by the insufficiency of one (1) or more of the alternative statements. A party may also state as many separate claims or defenses as that party has, regardless of consistency and whether based on legal or equitable grounds or both. All pleadings shall be construed so as to do substantial justice. FL ST RCP Rule 1.110(g).

f. *Subsequent pleadings.* When the nature of an action permits pleadings subsequent to final judgment and the jurisdiction of the court over the parties has not terminated, the initial pleading subsequent to final judgment shall be designated a supplemental complaint or petition. The action shall then proceed in the same manner and time as though the supplemental complaint or petition were the initial pleading in the action, including the issuance of any needed process. FL ST RCP Rule 1.110(h) shall not apply to proceedings that may be initiated by motion under the Florida Rules of Civil Procedure. FL ST RCP Rule 1.110(h).

g. *Pleading basis for service.* When service of process is to be made under statutes authorizing service on nonresidents of Florida, it is sufficient to plead the basis for service in the language of the statute without pleading the facts supporting service. FL ST RCP Rule 1.070(h).

h. *Forms of pleadings.* Forms of action and technical forms for seeking relief and of pleas, pleadings, or motions are abolished. FL ST RCP Rule 1.110(a).

3. *Answer; Generally.* An answer has three (3) functions. First, it must respond to each allegation of the preceding pleading by admitting, denying or alleging that the pleader is without knowledge of the allegation. Second, it must contain any affirmative defenses that the pleader is interposing to any cause of action alleged in the preceding pleading. Third, the answer may claim affirmative relief against the plaintiff or petitioner by a counterclaim or against a codefendant by a crossclaim. FL-PRACPROC § 11:1.

a. *Content.* In the answer a pleader shall state in short and plain terms the pleader's defenses to each claim asserted and shall admit or deny the averments on which the adverse party relies. If the defendant is without knowledge, the defendant shall so state and such statement shall operate as a denial. Denial shall fairly meet the substance of the averments denied. When a pleader intends in good faith to deny only a part of an averment, the pleader shall specify so much of it as is true and shall deny the remainder. Unless the pleader intends in good faith to controvert all of the averments of the preceding pleading, the pleader may make denials as specific denials of designated averments or may generally deny all of the averments except such designated averments as the pleader expressly admits, but when the pleader does so intend to controvert all of its averments, including averments of the grounds upon which the court's jurisdiction depends, the pleader may do so by general denial. FL ST RCP Rule 1.110(c).

b. *Form of answer.* An answer contains a caption, commencement, body, signature and certificate of service. The caption is the same as that of the initial pleading, except for the designation as one of the types of answer. The body of an answer should contain an admission, denial or plea of without knowledge to each allegation of the preceding pleading, except for the additional allegations in response to a general allegation of conditions precedent and the denial of capacity to sue. FL-PRACPROC § 11:3.

  i. *Responding sequentially.* The best method of responding is to answer each paragraph sequentially, combining admissions, denials or pleas of without knowledge when the sequence permits. The admissions, denials and allegations of without knowledge should be stated first, followed separately by any affirmative defenses and then by any counterclaim or crossclaim. A third party complaint may be a part of the same paper, but it is not a part of the answer as is a counterclaim or crossclaim. Paragraphs are numbered consecutively throughout the pleading whether in the answer, counterclaim or crossclaim. Denials for the record only are improper. FL-PRACPROC § 11:3.

c. *Defenses*

  i. *Generally.* Every defense in law or fact to a claim for relief in a pleading shall be asserted in the responsive pleading, if one is required, but the following defenses may be made by motion at the option of the pleader: (1) lack of jurisdiction over the subject matter, (2) lack of jurisdiction over the person, (3) improper venue, (4) insufficiency of process, (5) insufficiency of service of process, (6) failure to state a cause of action, and (7) failure to join indispensable parties. A motion making any of these defenses shall be made before pleading if a further pleading is permitted. FL ST RCP Rule 1.140(b).

    - *Stated specifically.* The grounds on which any of the enumerated defenses are based and the substantial matters of law intended to be argued shall be stated specifically and with particularity in the responsive pleading or motion. FL ST RCP Rule 1.140(b).

    - *Waiver.* Any ground not stated shall be deemed to be waived except any ground showing that the court lacks jurisdiction of the subject matter may be made at any time. No defense or objection is waived by being joined with other defenses or objections in a responsive pleading or motion. FL ST RCP Rule 1.140(b). A party waives all defenses and objections that the party does not present either by motion under FL ST RCP Rule 1.140(b), FL ST RCP Rule 1.140(e), or FL ST RCP Rule 1.140(f) or, if the party has made no motion, in a responsive pleading except as provided in FL ST RCP Rule 1.140(h)(2). FL ST RCP Rule 1.140(h)(1). The defenses of failure to state a cause of action or a legal defense or to join an indispensable party may be raised by motion for judgment on the pleadings or at the trial on the merits in addition to being raised either in a motion under FL ST RCP Rule 1.140(b) or in the answer or reply. The defense of lack of jurisdiction of the subject matter may be raised at any time. FL ST RCP Rule 1.140(h)(2).

  ii. *Affirmative defenses.* In pleading to a preceding pleading a party shall set forth affirmatively accord and satisfaction, arbitration and award, assumption of risk, contributory negligence, discharge in bankruptcy, duress, estoppel, failure of consideration, fraud, illegality, injury by fellow servant, laches, license, payment, release, res judicata, statute of frauds, statute of limitations, waiver, and any other matter constituting an avoidance or affirmative defense. When a party has mistakenly designated a defense as a counterclaim or a counterclaim as a defense, the court, on terms if justice so requires, shall treat the pleading as if there had been a proper designation. Affirmative defenses appearing on the face of a prior pleading may be asserted as grounds for a motion or defense under FL ST RCP Rule 1.140(b); provided this shall not limit amendments under FL ST RCP Rule 1.190 even if such ground is sustained. FL ST RCP Rule 1.110(d).

    - *Format of defenses.* Affirmative defenses should be placed after the admissions, denials and allegations of without knowledge in the answer. All paragraphs must be numbered consecutively throughout the answer. If a defense is directed to only a part of a cause of action or to one or more, but not all, of several causes of action in the preceding pleading, the part or cause of action to which it is directed should be identified in the defense.

Defenses should be identified by consecutive ordinal numbers such as "First Defense" and "Second Defense." FL-PRACPROC § 11:4.

iii. *Effect of failure to deny.* Averments in a pleading to which a responsive pleading is required, other than those as to the amount of damages, are admitted when not denied in the responsive pleading. Averments in a pleading to which no responsive pleading is required or permitted shall be taken as denied or avoided. FL ST RCP Rule 1.110(e). An admission in an answer binds the party and no proof is required. An admission does not extend beyond the scope of the allegation in the preceding pleading. FL-PRACPROC § 11:3.

4. *Pleading special matters*

a. *Capacity.* It is not necessary to aver the capacity of a party to sue or be sued, the authority of a party to sue or be sued in a representative capacity, or the legal existence of an organized association of persons that is made a party, except to the extent required to show the jurisdiction of the court. The initial pleading served on behalf of a minor party shall specifically aver the age of the minor party. When a party desires to raise an issue as to the legal existence of any party, the capacity of any party to sue or be sued, or the authority of a party to sue or be sued in a representative capacity, that party shall do so by specific negative averment which shall include such supporting particulars as are peculiarly within the pleader's knowledge. FL ST RCP Rule 1.120(a).

b. *Fraud, mistake, condition of the mind.* In all averments of fraud or mistake, the circumstances constituting fraud or mistake shall be stated with such particularity as the circumstances may permit. Malice, intent, knowledge, mental attitude, and other condition of mind of a person may be averred generally. FL ST RCP Rule 1.120(b).

c. *Conditions precedent.* In pleading the performance or occurrence of conditions precedent, it is sufficient to aver generally that all conditions precedent have been performed or have occurred. A denial of performance or occurrence shall be made specifically and with particularity. FL ST RCP Rule 1.120(c).

d. *Official document or act.* In pleading an official document or official act it is sufficient to aver that the document was issued or the act done in compliance with law. FL ST RCP Rule 1.120(c).

e. *Judgment or decree.* In pleading a judgment or decree of a domestic or foreign court, a judicial or quasi-judicial tribunal, or a board or officer, it is sufficient to aver the judgment or decree without setting forth matter showing jurisdiction to render it. FL ST RCP Rule 1.120(e).

f. *Time and place.* For the purpose of testing the sufficiency of a pleading, averments of time and place are material and shall be considered like all other averments of material matter. FL ST RCP Rule 1.120(f).

g. *Special damage.* When items of special damage are claimed, they shall be specifically stated. FL ST RCP Rule 1.120(g).

5. *Parties*

a. *Parties generally.* Every action may be prosecuted in the name of the real party in interest, but a personal representative, administrator, guardian, trustee of an express trust, a party with whom or in whose name a contract has been made for the benefit of another, or a party expressly authorized by statute may sue in that person's own name without joining the party for whose benefit the action is brought. All persons having an interest in the subject of the action and in obtaining the relief demanded may join as plaintiffs and any person may be made a defendant who has or claims an interest adverse to the plaintiff. Any person may at any time be made a party if that person's presence is necessary or proper to a complete determination of the cause. Persons having a united interest may be joined on the same side as plaintiffs or defendants, and anyone who refuses to join may for such reason be made a defendant. FL ST RCP Rule 1.210(a).

b. *Minors or incompetent persons.* When a minor or incompetent person has a representative, such as a guardian or other like fiduciary, the representative may sue or defend on behalf of the minor or incompetent person. A minor or incompetent person who does not have a duly appointed representative may sue by next friend or by a guardian ad litem. The court shall appoint a guardian ad litem for a minor or incompetent person not otherwise represented in an action or shall make such other order as it deems proper for the protection of the minor or incompetent person. FL ST RCP Rule 1.210(b).

c. For survivor and substitution of parties information, please see FL ST RCP Rule 1.260.

6. *Counterclaims and crossclaims*

a. *Compulsory counterclaims.* A pleading shall state as a counterclaim any claim which at the time of serving the pleading the pleader has against any opposing party, provided it arises out of the transaction or occurrence that is the subject matter of the opposing party's claim and does not require for its adjudication the presence of third parties over whom the court cannot acquire jurisdiction. But the pleader need not state a claim if (1) at the time the action was commenced the claim was the subject of another pending action, or (2) the opposing party brought suit upon that party's claim by attachment or other process by which the court did not acquire jurisdiction to render a personal judgment on the claim and the pleader is not stating a counterclaim under this rule. FL ST RCP Rule 1.170(a).

b. *Permissive counterclaim.* A pleading may state as a counterclaim any claim against an opposing party not arising out of the transaction or occurrence that is the subject matter of the opposing party's claim. FL ST RCP Rule 1.170(b).

c. *Counterclaim exceeding opposing claim.* A counterclaim may or may not diminish or defeat the recovery sought by the opposing party. It may claim relief exceeding in amount or different in kind from that sought in the pleading of the opposing party. FL ST RCP Rule 1.170(c).

d. *Counterclaim against the State.* The Florida Rules of Civil Procedure shall not be construed to enlarge beyond the limits established by law the right to assert counterclaims or to claim credits against the state or any of its subdivisions or other governmental organizations thereof subject to suit or against a municipal corporation or against an officer, agency, or administrative board of the state. FL ST RCP Rule 1.170(d).

e. *Counterclaim maturing or acquired after pleading.* A claim which matured or was acquired by the pleader after serving the pleading may be presented as a counterclaim by supplemental pleading with the permission of the court. FL ST RCP Rule 1.170(e).

f. *Omitted counterclaim or crossclaim.* When a pleader fails to set up a counterclaim or crossclaim through oversight, inadvertence, or excusable neglect, or when justice requires, the pleader may set up the counterclaim or crossclaim by amendment with leave of the court. FL ST RCP Rule 1.170(f).

g. *Crossclaim against co-party.* A pleading may state as a crossclaim any claim by one party against a co-party arising out of the transaction or occurrence that is the subject matter of either the original action or a counterclaim therein, or relating to any property that is the subject matter of the original action. The crossclaim may include a claim that the party against whom it is asserted is or may be liable to the crossclaimant for all or part of a claim asserted in the action against the crossclaimant. Service of a crossclaim on a party who has appeared in the action shall be made pursuant to FL ST RCP Rule 1.080. Service of a crossclaim against a party who has not appeared in the action shall be made in the manner provided for service of summons. FL ST RCP Rule 1.170(g).

h. *Additional parties may be brought in.* When the presence of parties other than those to the original action is required to grant complete relief in the determination of a counterclaim or crossclaim, they shall be named in the counterclaim or crossclaim and be served with process and shall be parties to the action thereafter if jurisdiction of them can be obtained and their joinder will not deprive the court of jurisdiction of the action. FL ST RCP Rule 1.250(b) and FL ST RCP Rule 1.250(c) apply to parties brought in under FL ST RCP Rule 1.170(h). FL ST RCP Rule 1.170(h).

i. *Separate trials; Separate judgment.* If the court orders separate trials as provided in FL ST RCP Rule 1.270(b), judgment on a counterclaim or crossclaim may be rendered when the court has jurisdiction to do so even if a claim of the opposing party has been dismissed or otherwise disposed of. FL ST RCP Rule 1.170(i).

j. *Demand exceeding jurisdiction; Transfer of action.* If the demand of any counterclaim or crossclaim exceeds the jurisdiction of the court in which the action is pending, the action shall be transferred forthwith to the court of the same county having jurisdiction of the demand in the counterclaim or crossclaim with only such alterations in the pleadings as are essential. The court shall order the transfer of the action and the transmittal of all papers in it to the proper court if the party asserting the demand exceeding the jurisdiction deposits with the court having jurisdiction a sum sufficient to pay the clerk's service charge in the court to which the action is transferred at the time of filing the counterclaim or crossclaim. Thereupon the original papers and deposit shall be transmitted and filed with a certified copy of the order. The court to which the action is transferred shall have full power and jurisdiction over the demands of all parties. Failure to make the service charge deposit at the time the counterclaim or crossclaim is filed, or within such further time as the court may allow, shall reduce a claim for damages to an amount within the jurisdiction of the court where the action is pending and waive the claim in other cases. FL ST RCP Rule 1.170(j).

7. *Misjoinder and nonjoinder of parties*
    a. *Misjoinder.* Misjoinder of parties is not a ground for dismissal of an action. Any claim against a party may be severed and proceeded with separately. FL ST RCP Rule 1.250(a).
    b. *Dropping parties.* Parties may be dropped by an adverse party in the manner provided for voluntary dismissal in FL ST RCP Rule 1.420(a)(1) subject to the exception stated in FL ST RCP Rule 1.420. If notice of lis pendens has been filed in the action against a party so dropped, the notice of dismissal shall be recorded and cancels the notice of lis pendens without the necessity of a court order. Parties may be dropped by order of court on its own initiative or the motion of any party at any stage of the action on such terms as are just. FL ST RCP Rule 1.250(b).
    c. *Adding parties.* Parties may be added once as a matter of course within the same time that pleadings can be so amended under FL ST RCP Rule 1.190(a). If amendment by leave of court or stipulation of the parties is permitted, parties may be added in the amended pleading without further order of court. Parties may be added by order of court on its own initiative or on motion of any party at any stage of the action and on such terms as are just. FL ST RCP Rule 1.250(c).
8. *Jury demand*
    a. *Right preserved.* The right of trial by jury as declared by the Constitution or by statute shall be preserved to the parties inviolate. FL ST RCP Rule 1.430(a).
    b. *Demand.* Any party may demand a trial by jury of any issue triable of right by a jury by serving upon the other party a demand therefor in writing at any time after commencement of the action and not later than ten (10) days after the service of the last pleading directed to such issue. The demand may be indorsed upon a pleading of the party. FL ST RCP Rule 1.430(b).
    c. *Specification of issues.* In the demand a party may specify the issues that the party wishes so tried; otherwise, the party is deemed to demand trial by jury for all issues so triable. FL ST RCP Rule 1.430(c).
        i. If a party has demanded trial by jury for only some of the issues, any other party may serve a demand for trial by jury of any other or all of the issues triable by jury ten (10) days after service of the demand or such lesser time as the court may order. FL ST RCP Rule 1.430(c).
    d. *Waiver.* A party who fails to serve a demand as required by FL ST RCP Rule 1.430 waives trial by jury. FL ST RCP Rule 1.430(d).
        i. If waived, a jury trial may not be granted without the consent of the parties, but the court may allow an amendment in the proceedings to demand a trial by jury or order a trial by jury on its own motion. FL ST RCP Rule 1.430(d).
        ii. A demand for trial by jury may not be withdrawn without the consent of the parties. FL ST RCP Rule 1.430(d).
9. *Companion cases in the Sixth Circuit*
    a. An attorney representing a party in a case to which there are companion cases shall file a notice of a companion case. FL ST 6 J CIR LOCAL Rule 3(B)(1).
    b. The original notice and sufficient copies for filing in each companion case shall be filed with the Clerk and a copy provided to the judge in the section which has been assigned the case bearing the lowest docket number. FL ST 6 J CIR LOCAL Rule 3(B)(1).

c. Said judge may thereupon reassign all such companion cases to the section which has been assigned the case bearing the lowest docket number if the court finds that the companion cases involve common questions of law or fact or the reassignment would result in an efficient administration of justice. FL ST 6 J CIR LOCAL Rule 3(B)(1).

d. The Clerk shall make appropriate notations on the file cover and the progress docket of such reassigned case or cases and thereafter all such companion cases shall be heard, tried, and determined by the judge assigned to the section having the companion case bearing the lowest docket number. FL ST 6 J CIR LOCAL Rule 3(B)(1).

10. *Arbitration and mediation*

a. *Referral to arbitration and mediation.* Except as hereinafter provided or as otherwise prohibited by law, the presiding judge may enter an order referring all or any part of a contested civil matter to mediation or arbitration. The parties to any contested civil matter may file a written stipulation to mediate or arbitrate any issue between them at any time. Such stipulation shall be incorporated into the order of referral. FL ST RCP Rule 1.700(a).

b. *Arbitration*

i. *Exclusions.* A civil action shall be ordered to arbitration or arbitration in conjunction with mediation upon stipulation of the parties. A civil action may be ordered to arbitration or arbitration in conjunction with mediation upon motion of any party or by the court, if the judge determines the action to be of such a nature that arbitration could be of benefit to the litigants or the court. FL ST RCP Rule 1.800.

- Under no circumstances may the following categories of actions be referred to arbitration: (1) bond estreatures; (2) habeas corpus or other extraordinary writs; (3) bond validations; (4) civil or criminal contempt; (5) such other matters as may be specified by order of the chief judge in the circuit. FL ST RCP Rule 1.800.

ii. For more information regarding arbitration, please see FL ST RCP Rule 1.810; FL ST RCP Rule 1.820; FL ST RCP Rule 1.830.

c. *Mediation.* For more information regarding mediation, please see FL ST RCP Rule 1.710; FL ST RCP Rule 1.720; FL ST RCP Rule 1.730; and FL ST RCP Rule 1.750.

d. See FL ST 6 J CIR PA/PI-CIR-96-63 for more information about the Arbitration and Mediation Program for Florida's Sixth Judicial Circuit.

11. *Rules of court*

a. *Rules of civil procedure.* The Florida Rules of Civil Procedure apply to all actions of a civil nature and all special statutory proceedings in the circuit courts and county courts except those to which the Florida Probate Rules, the Florida Family Law Rules of Procedure, or the Small Claims Rules apply. FL ST RCP Rule 1.010.

i. The form, content, procedure, and time for pleading in all special statutory proceedings shall be as prescribed by the statutes governing the proceeding unless the Florida Rules of Civil Procedure specifically provide to the contrary. FL ST RCP Rule 1.010.

ii. The Florida Rules of Civil Procedure shall be construed to secure the just, speedy, and inexpensive determination of every action. FL ST RCP Rule 1.010.

b. *Rules of judicial administration.* The Florida Rules of Judicial Administration shall apply to administrative matters in all courts to which the Florida Rules of Judicial Administration are applicable by their terms. The Florida Rules of Judicial Administration shall be construed to secure the speedy and inexpensive determination of every proceeding to which they are applicable. The Florida Rules of Judicial Administration shall supersede all conflicting rules and statutes. FL ST J ADMIN Rule 2.110.

D. Documents

1. *Required documents*

a. *Amended answer.* See the General Requirements section of this document for the content of an amended answer. If a party files a motion to amend a pleading, the party shall attach the proposed amended pleading to the motion. FL ST RCP Rule 1.190(a). See the KeyRules Florida Circuit Court Motion for Leave to Amend document for further information.

i. *Notices to persons with disabilities.* See the Format section of this KeyRules document for further information.

b. *Certificate of service.* When any attorney certifies in substance: "I certify that a copy hereof has been furnished to (here insert name or names and addresses used for service) by (e-mail) (delivery) (mail) (fax) on .... (date) ...._______________ Attorney" the certificate is taken as prima facie proof of such service in compliance with FL ST J ADMIN Rule 2.516. FL ST J ADMIN Rule 2.516(f).

2. *Supplemental documents*

a. *Exhibits.* All bonds, notes, bills of exchange, contracts, accounts, or documents upon which action may be brought or defense made, or a copy thereof or a copy of the portions thereof material to the pleadings, shall be incorporated in or attached to the pleading. No papers shall be unnecessarily annexed as exhibits. The pleadings shall contain no unnecessary recitals of deeds, documents, contracts, or other instruments. Any exhibit attached to a pleading shall be considered a part of the pleadings for all purposes. FL ST RCP Rule 1.130(a).

b. *Notice of constitutional question.* A party that files a pleading, written motion, or other paper drawing into question the constitutionality of a state statute or a county or municipal charter, ordinance, or franchise must promptly (1) file a notice of constitutional question stating the question and identifying the paper that raises it; and (2) serve the notice and the pleading, written motion, or other paper drawing into question the constitutionality of a state statute or a county or municipal charter, ordinance, or franchise on the Attorney General or the state attorney of the judicial circuit in which the action is pending, by either certified or registered mail. Service of the notice and pleading, written motion, or other paper does not require joinder of the Attorney General or the state attorney as a party to the action. FL ST RCP Rule 1.071.

c. *Notice of companion cases.* An attorney representing a party in a case to which there are companion cases shall file a notice of a companion case. FL ST 6 J CIR LOCAL Rule 3(B)(1).

E. Format

1. *Documents; Type and size.* Documents subject to the exceptions set forth in FL ST J ADMIN Rule 2.525(d) shall be filed on recycled paper measuring eight and one half by eleven (8 1/2 by 11) inches. For purposes of FL ST J ADMIN Rule 2.520, paper is recycled if it contains a minimum content of fifty (50) percent waste paper. Xerographic reduction of legal-size (eight and one half by fourteen (8 1/2 by 14) inches) documents to letter size (eight and one half by eleven (8 1/2 by 11) inches) is prohibited. All other documents filed by electronic transmission shall be filed in a format capable of being printed in a format consistent with the provisions of FL ST J ADMIN Rule 2.250. FL ST J ADMIN Rule 2.520(b).

a. *Exhibits.* Any exhibit or attachment filed with pleadings or papers may be filed in its original size. FL ST J ADMIN Rule 2.520(c).

b. *Recording space.* On all papers and documents prepared and filed by the court or by any party to a proceeding which are to be recorded in the public records of any county, including but not limited to final money judgments and notices of lis pendens, a three (3) inch by three (3) inch space at the top right-hand corner on the first page and a one (1) inch by three (3) inch space at the top right-hand corner on each subsequent page shall be left blank and reserved for use by the clerk of court. FL ST J ADMIN Rule 2.520(d).

i. *Exceptions to recording space.* Any papers or documents created by persons or entities over which the filing party has no control, including but not limited to wills, codicils, trusts, or other testamentary documents; documents prepared or executed by any public officer; documents prepared, executed, acknowledged, or proved outside of the State of Florida; or documents created by State or Federal government agencies, may be filed without the space required by FL ST J ADMIN Rule 2.520. FL ST J ADMIN Rule 2.520(e).

c. *Noncompliance.* No clerk of court is permitted to refuse to file any document or paper because of noncompliance with the Florida Rules of Judicial Administration. However, upon request of the

clerk of court, noncomplying documents must be resubmitted in accordance with the formatting rules. FL ST J ADMIN Rule 2.520(f).

2. *Caption.* Every pleading, motion, order, judgment, or other paper shall have a caption containing the name of the court, the file number, and except for in rem proceedings, including forfeiture proceedings, the name of the first party on each side with an appropriate indication of other parties, and a designation identifying the party filing it and its nature or the nature of the order, as the case may be. In any in rem proceeding, every pleading, motion, order, judgment, or other paper shall have a caption containing the name of the court, the file number, the style "In re" (followed by the name or general description of the property), and a designation of the person or entity filing it and its nature or the nature of the order, as the case may be. In an in rem forfeiture proceeding, the style shall be "In re forfeiture of" (followed by the name of the general description of the property). All papers filed in the action shall be styled in such a manner as to indicate clearly the subject matter of the paper and the party requesting or obtaining relief. FL ST RCP Rule 1.100(c)(1).
3. *Writing and written defined.* Writing or written means a document containing information, an application, or a stipulation. FL ST RCP Rule 1.080(c).
4. *Rule abbreviations*
    a. The Florida Rules of Civil Procedure and shall be abbreviated as Fla.R.Civ.P. FL ST RCP Rule 1.010.
    b. The Florida Rules of Judicial Administration shall be abbreviated as Fla. R. Jud. Admin. FL ST J ADMIN Rule 2.110.
5. *Nonverification.* Except when otherwise specifically provided by the Florida Rules of Civil Procedure or an applicable statute, every pleading or other document of a party represented by an attorney need not be verified or accompanied by an affidavit. FL ST RCP Rule 1.030; FL ST J ADMIN Rule 2.515(a).
6. *Attorney signature*
    a. *Attorney signature.* Every pleading and other document of a party represented by an attorney shall be signed by at least one (1) attorney of record in that attorney's individual name whose current record Florida Bar address, telephone number, including area code, primary e-mail address and secondary e-mail addresses, if any, and Florida Bar number shall be stated, and who shall be duly licensed to practice law in Florida or who shall have received permission to appear in the particular case as provided in FL ST J ADMIN Rule 2.510. FL ST J ADMIN Rule 2.515(a).
        i. The attorney may be required by the court to give the address of, and to vouch for the attorney's authority to represent, the party. FL ST J ADMIN Rule 2.515(a).
        ii. The signature of an attorney shall constitute a certificate by the attorney that the attorney has read the pleading or other document; that to the best of the attorney's knowledge, information, and belief there is good ground to support it; and that it is not interposed for delay. FL ST J ADMIN Rule 2.515(a).
        iii. If a pleading is not signed or is signed with intent to defeat the purpose of FL ST J ADMIN Rule 2.515, it may be stricken and the action may proceed as though the pleading or other document had not been served. FL ST J ADMIN Rule 2.515(a).
    b. *Pro se litigant signature.* A party who is not represented by an attorney shall sign any pleading or other paper and state the party's address and telephone number, including area code. FL ST J ADMIN Rule 2.515(b).
    c. *Form of signature*
        i. The signatures required on pleadings and documents by FL ST J ADMIN Rule 2.515(a) and FL ST J ADMIN Rule 2.515(b) may be:
            - Original signatures;
            - Original signatures that have been reproduced by electronic means, such as on electronically transmitted documents or photocopied documents;
            - Electronic signatures using the "/s/," "s/," or "/s" formats by or at the direction of the person signing; or

- Any other signature format authorized by general law, so long as the clerk where the proceeding is pending has the capability of receiving and has obtained approval from the Supreme Court of Florida to accept pleadings and documents with that signature format. FL ST J ADMIN Rule 2.515(c)(1).

ii. An attorney, party, or other person who files a pleading or paper by electronic transmission that does not contain the original signature of that attorney, party, or other person shall file that identical pleading or paper in paper form containing an original signature of that attorney, party, or other person (hereinafter called the follow-up filing) immediately thereafter. The follow-up filing is not required if the Supreme Court of Florida has entered an order directing the clerk of court to discontinue accepting the follow-up filing. FL ST J ADMIN Rule 2.515(c)(2).

7. *Forms*

a. *Process.* The forms of process, notice of lis pendens, and notice of action provided in the Florida Rules of Civil Procedure are sufficient. Variations from the forms do not void process or notices that are otherwise sufficient. FL ST RCP Rule 1.900(a).

b. *Other forms.* The other forms provided in the Florida Rules of Civil Procedure are sufficient for the matters that are covered by them. So long as the substance is expressed without prolixity, the forms may be varied to meet the facts of a particular case. FL ST RCP Rule 1.900(b).

c. *Formal matters.* Captions, except for the designation of the paper, are omitted from the forms provided in the Florida Rules of Civil Procedure. A general form of caption is the first form provided. Signatures are omitted from pleadings and motions. FL ST RCP Rule 1.900(c).

8. *Notices to persons with disabilities.* All notices of court proceedings to be held in a public facility, and all process compelling appearance at such proceedings, shall include the following statement in bold face, fourteen (14) point Times New Roman or Courier font: "If you are a person with a disability who needs any accommodation in order to participate in this proceeding, you are entitled, at no cost to you, to the provision of certain assistance. Please contact [identify applicable court personnel by name, address, and telephone number] at least seven (7) days before your scheduled court appearance, or immediately upon receiving this notification if the time before the scheduled appearance is less than seven (7) days; if you are hearing or voice impaired, call 711." FL ST J ADMIN Rule 2.540(c)(1).

9. *Minimization of the filing of sensitive information*

a. *Limitations for court filings.* Unless authorized by FL ST J ADMIN Rule 2.425(b), statute, another rule of court, or the court orders otherwise, designated sensitive information filed with the court must be limited to the following format:

i. The initials of a person known to be a minor;

ii. The year of birth of a person's birth date;

iii. No portion of any: Social security number, Bank account number, Credit card account number, Charge account number, or Debit account number;

iv. The last four digits of any: Taxpayer identification number (TIN), Employee identification number, Driver's license number, Passport number, Telephone number, Financial account number, except as set forth in FL ST J ADMIN Rule 2.425(a)(3), Brokerage account number, Insurance policy account number, Loan account number, Customer account number, or Patient or health care number;

v. A truncated version of any: Email address, Computer user name, Password, or Personal identification number (PIN); and

vi. A truncated version of any other sensitive information as provided by court order. FL ST J ADMIN Rule 2.425(a).

b. *Exceptions.* FL ST J ADMIN Rule 2.425(a) does not apply to the following:

i. An account number which identifies the property alleged to be the subject of a proceeding;

ii. The record of an administrative or agency proceeding;

iii. The record in appellate or review proceedings;

iv. The birth date of a minor whenever the birth date is necessary for the court to establish or maintain subject matter jurisdiction;

v. The name of a minor in any order relating to parental responsibility, time-sharing, or child support;

vi. The name of a minor in any document or order affecting the minor's ownership of real property;

vii. The birth date of a party in a writ of attachment or notice to payor;

viii. In traffic and criminal proceedings: a pro se filing; a court filing that is related to a criminal matter or investigation and that is prepared before the filing of a criminal charge or is not filed as part of any docketed criminal case; an arrest or search warrant or any information in support thereof; a charging document and an affidavit or other documents filed in support of any charging document, including any driving records; a statement of particulars; discovery material introduced into evidence or otherwise filed with the court; and all information necessary for the proper issuance and execution of a subpoena duces tecum;

ix. Information used by the clerk for case maintenance purposes or the courts for case management purposes; and

x. Information which is relevant and material to an issue before the court. FL ST J ADMIN Rule 2.425(b).

c. *Remedies.* Upon motion by a party or interested person or sua sponte by the court, the court may order remedies, sanctions or both for a violation of FL ST J ADMIN Rule 2.425(a). Following notice and an opportunity to respond, the court may impose sanctions if such filing was not made in good faith. FL ST J ADMIN Rule 2.425(c).

d. *Motions not restricted.* FL ST J ADMIN Rule 2.425 does not restrict a party's right to move for protective order, to move to file documents under seal, or to request a determination of the confidentiality of records. FL ST J ADMIN Rule 2.425(d).

e. *Application.* FL ST J ADMIN Rule 2.425 does not affect the application of constitutional provisions, statutes, or rules of court regarding confidential information or access to public information. FL ST J ADMIN Rule 2.425(e).

F. Filing and Service Requirements

1. *Filing requirements.* All original documents must be filed with the court either before service or immediately thereafter, unless otherwise provided for by general law or other rules. If the original of any bond or other document is not placed in the court file, a certified copy must be so placed by the clerk. FL ST J ADMIN Rule 2.516(d). All documents shall be filed in conformity with the requirements of FL ST J ADMIN Rule 2.525. FL ST RCP Rule 1.080(b). All documents filed in any court shall be filed by electronic transmission in accordance with FL ST J ADMIN Rule 2.525. "Documents" means pleadings, motions, petitions, memoranda, briefs, notices, exhibits, declarations, affidavits, orders, judgments, decrees, writs, opinions, and any other paper or writing submitted to a court. FL ST J ADMIN Rule 2.520(a). All documents that are court records, as defined in FL ST J ADMIN Rule 2.430(a)(1), must be filed by electronic transmission, provided that: (1) the clerk has the ability to accept and retain such documents; (2) the clerk or the chief judge of the circuit has requested permission to accept documents filed by electronic transmission; and (3) the supreme court has entered an order granting permission to the clerk to accept documents filed by electronic transmission. FL ST J ADMIN Rule 2.525(c)(1).

a. *Definition.* "Electronic transmission of documents" means the sending of information by electronic signals to, by or from a court or clerk, which when received can be transformed and stored or transmitted on paper, microfilm, magnetic storage device, optical imaging system, CD-ROM, flash drive, other electronic data storage system, server, case maintenance system ("CM"), electronic court filing ("ECF") system, statewide or local electronic portal ("e-portal"), or other electronic record keeping system authorized by the supreme court in a format sufficient to communicate the information on the original document in a readable format. Electronic transmission of documents includes electronic mail ("e-mail") and any internet-based transmission procedure, and may include procedures allowing for documents to be signed or verified by electronic means. FL ST J ADMIN Rule 2.525(a).

i. The filing of documents with the court as required by the Florida Rules of Judicial Adminis-

tration must be made by filing them with the clerk in accordance with FL ST J ADMIN Rule 2.525, except that the judge may permit documents to be filed with the judge, in which event the judge must note the filing date before him or her on the documents and transmit them to the clerk. The date of filing is that shown on the face of the document by the judge's notation or the clerk's time stamp, whichever is earlier. FL ST J ADMIN Rule 2.516(e).

b. *Application.* Any court or clerk of the court may accept the electronic transmission of documents for filing after the clerk, together with input from the chief judge of the circuit, has obtained approval of the procedures and program for doing so from the Supreme Court of Florida. FL ST J ADMIN Rule 2.525(b).

c. *Exceptions*

   i. Paper documents and other submissions may be manually submitted to the clerk or court:
      - When the clerk does not have the ability to accept and retain documents by electronic filing or has not had ECF Procedures approved by the supreme court;
      - For filing by any self-represented party or any self-represented nonparty unless specific ECF Procedures provide a means to file documents electronically. However, any self-represented nonparty that is a governmental or public agency and any other agency, partnership, corporation, or business entity acting on behalf of any governmental or public agency may file documents by electronic transmission if such entity has the capability of filing documents electronically;
      - For filing by attorneys excused from e-mail service in accordance with FL ST J ADMIN Rule 2.516(b);
      - When submitting evidentiary exhibits or filing non-documentary materials;
      - When the filing involves documents in excess of twenty-five (25) megabytes (25MB) in size. For such filings, documents may be transmitted using an electronic storage medium that the clerk has the ability to accept, which may include a CD-ROM, flash drive, or similar storage medium;
      - When filed in open court, as permitted by the court;
      - When paper filing is permitted by any approved statewide or local ECF procedures; and
      - If any court determines that justice so requires. FL ST J ADMIN Rule 2.525(d).

   ii. Any document in paper form submitted under FL ST J ADMIN Rule 2.525(d) is filed when it is received by the clerk or court and the clerk shall immediately thereafter convert any filed paper document to an electronic document. "Convert to an electronic document" means optically capturing an image of a paper document and using character recognition software to recover as much of the document's text as practicable and then indexing and storing the document in the official court file. FL ST J ADMIN Rule 2.525(c)(4).

   iii. Any storage medium submitted under FL ST J ADMIN Rule 2.525(d)(5) is filed when received by the clerk or court and the clerk shall immediately thereafter transfer the electronic documents from the storage device to the official court file. FL ST J ADMIN Rule 2.525(c)(5).

   iv. If the filer of any paper document authorized under FL ST J ADMIN Rule 2.525(d) provides a self-addressed, postage-paid envelope for return of the paper document after it is converted to electronic form by the clerk, the clerk shall place the paper document in the envelope and deposit it in the mail. Except when a paper document is required to be maintained, the clerk may recycle any filed paper document that is not to be returned to the filer. FL ST J ADMIN Rule 2.525(c)(6).

   v. The clerk may convert any paper document filed before the effective date of FL ST J ADMIN Rule 2.525 to an electronic document. Unless the clerk is required to maintain the paper document, if the paper document has been converted to an electronic document by the clerk, the paper document is no longer part of the official court file and may be removed and recycled. FL ST J ADMIN Rule 2.525(c)(7).

d. *Official court file.* For information on what constitutes the official court file, please see FL ST J ADMIN Rule 2.525(c)(2), FL ST J ADMIN Rule 2.525(c)(3).

e. *Administration.* All attorneys, parties, or other persons using this rule to file documents are required to make arrangements with the court or clerk for the payment of any charges authorized by general law or the supreme court before filing any document by electronic transmission. FL ST J ADMIN Rule 2.525(f)(2).

f. *Filing date.* The filing date for an electronically transmitted document is the date and time that such filing is acknowledged by an electronic stamp or otherwise, pursuant to any procedure set forth in any ECF Procedures approved by the supreme court, or the date the last page of such filing is received by the court or clerk. FL ST J ADMIN Rule 2.525(f)(3).

g. *Accessibility.* All documents transmitted in any electronic form under FL ST J ADMIN Rule 2.525 must comply with the accessibility requirements of FL ST J ADMIN Rule 2.526. FL ST J ADMIN Rule 2.525(g).

2. *Service requirements.* Every pleading subsequent to the initial pleading, all orders, and every other document filed in the action must be served in conformity with the requirements of FL ST J ADMIN Rule 2.516. FL ST RCP Rule 1.080(a).

a. *Service; When required.* Unless the court otherwise orders, or a statute or supreme court administrative order specifies a different means of service, every pleading subsequent to the initial pleading and every other document filed in any court proceeding, except applications for witness subpoenas and documents served by formal notice or required to be served in the manner provided for service of formal notice, must be served in accordance with FL ST J ADMIN Rule 2.516 on each party. No service need be made on parties against whom a default has been entered, except that pleadings asserting new or additional claims against them must be served in the manner provided for service of summons. FL ST J ADMIN Rule 2.516(a).

b. *Service; How made.* When service is required or permitted to be made upon a party represented by an attorney, service must be made upon the attorney unless service upon the party is ordered by the court. FL ST J ADMIN Rule 2.516(b).

i. *Service by electronic mail ("e-mail").* All documents required or permitted to be served on another party must be served by e-mail, unless FL ST J ADMIN Rule 2.516 otherwise provides. When, in addition to service by e-mail, the sender also utilizes another means of service provided for in FL ST J ADMIN Rule 2.516(b)(2), any differing time limits and other provisions applicable to that other means of service control. FL ST J ADMIN Rule 2.516(b)(1). Any document electronically transmitted to a court or clerk must also be served on all parties and interested persons in accordance with the applicable rules of court. FL ST J ADMIN Rule 2.525(e)(2).

- *Service on attorneys.* Upon appearing in a proceeding, an attorney must serve a designation of a primary e-mail address and may designate no more than two (2) secondary e-mail addresses. Thereafter, service must be directed to all designated e-mail addresses in that proceeding. Every document filed by an attorney thereafter must include the primary e-mail address of that attorney and any secondary e-mail addresses. If an attorney does not designate any e-mail address for service, documents may be served on that attorney at the e-mail address on record with The Florida Bar. FL ST J ADMIN Rule 2.516(b)(1)(A).

- *Exception to e-mail service on attorneys.* Service by an attorney on another attorney must be made by e-mail unless excused by the court. Upon motion by an attorney demonstrating that the attorney has no e-mail account and lacks access to the Internet at the attorney's office, the court may excuse the attorney from the requirements of e-mail service. Service on and by an attorney excused by the court from e-mail service must be by the means provided in FL ST J ADMIN Rule 2.516(b)(2). FL ST J ADMIN Rule 2.516(b)(1)(B).

- *Service on and by parties not represented by an attorney.* Any party not represented by an attorney may serve a designation of a primary e-mail address and also may designate no more than two (2) secondary e-mail addresses to which service must be directed in that proceeding by the means provided in FL ST J ADMIN Rule 2.516(b)(1). If a party not represented by an attorney does not designate an e-mail address for service in a proceeding, service on and by that party must be by the means provided in FL ST J ADMIN Rule 2.516(b)(2). FL ST J ADMIN Rule 2.516(b)(1)(C).

- *Time of service.* Service by e-mail is complete when it is sent. FL ST J ADMIN Rule 2.516(b)(1)(D). An e-mail is deemed served on the date it is sent. FL ST J ADMIN Rule 2.516(b)(1)(D)(i). If the sender learns that the e-mail did not reach the address of the person to be served, the sender must immediately send another copy by e-mail, or by a means authorized by FL ST J ADMIN Rule 2.516(b)(2). FL ST J ADMIN Rule 2.516(b)(1)(D)(ii). E-mail service is treated as service by mail for the computation of time. FL ST J ADMIN Rule 2.516(b)(1)(D)(iii).

ii. *Format of e-mail for service.* Service of a document by e-mail is made by attaching a copy of the document in PDF format to an e-mail sent to all addresses designated by the attorney or party. FL ST J ADMIN Rule 2.516(b)(1)(E).

- All documents served by e-mail must be attached to an e-mail message containing a subject line beginning with the words "SERVICE OF COURT DOCUMENT" in all capital letters, followed by the case number of the proceeding in which the documents are being served. FL ST J ADMIN Rule 2.516(b)(1)(E)(i).
- The body of the e-mail must identify the court in which the proceeding is pending, the case number, the name of the initial party on each side, the title of each document served with that e-mail, and the sender's name and telephone number. FL ST J ADMIN Rule 2.516(b)(1)(E)(ii).
- Any document served by e-mail may be signed by the "/s/" format, as long as the filed original is signed in accordance with the applicable rule of procedure. FL ST J ADMIN Rule 2.516(b)(1)(E)(iii).
- Any e-mail which, together with its attached documents, exceeds five megabytes (5MB) in size, must be divided and sent as separate e-mails, no one of which may exceed five megabytes (5MB) in size and each of which must be sequentially numbered in the subject line. FL ST J ADMIN Rule 2.516(b)(1)(E)(iv).

iii. *Service by other means.* In addition to, and not in lieu of, service by e-mail, service may also be made upon attorneys by any of the means specified in FL ST J ADMIN Rule 2.516(b)(2). Service on and by all parties who are not represented by an attorney and who do not designate an e-mail address, and on and by all attorneys excused from e-mail service, must be made by delivering a copy of the document or by mailing it to the party or attorney at their last known address or, if no address is known, by leaving it with the clerk of the court. Service by mail is complete upon mailing. Delivery of a copy within FL ST J ADMIN Rule 2.516 is complete upon:

- Handing it to the attorney or to the party,
- Leaving it at the attorney's or party's office with a clerk or other person in charge thereof,
- If there is no one in charge, leaving it in a conspicuous place therein,
- If the office is closed or the person to be served has no office, leaving it at the person's usual place of abode with some person of his or her family above fifteen (15) years of age and informing such person of the contents, or
- Transmitting it by facsimile to the attorney's or party's office with a cover sheet containing the sender's name, firm, address, telephone number, and facsimile number, and the number of pages transmitted. When service is made by facsimile, a copy must also be served by any other method permitted by FL ST J ADMIN Rule 2.516. Facsimile service occurs when transmission is complete. FL ST J ADMIN Rule 2.516(b)(2)(A) through FL ST J ADMIN Rule 2.516(b)(2)(E).
- Service by delivery after 5:00 p.m. must be deemed to have been made by mailing on the date of delivery. FL ST J ADMIN Rule 2.516(b)(2)(F).

c. *Service; Numerous defendants.* In actions when the parties are unusually numerous, the court may regulate the service contemplated by the Florida Rules of Judicial Administration on motion or on its own initiative in such manner as may be found to be just and reasonable. FL ST J ADMIN Rule 2.516(c).

d. *Service by clerk.* Service of notices and other documents required to be made by the clerk must also be done as provided in FL ST J ADMIN Rule 2.516(b). FL ST J ADMIN Rule 2.516(g).

e. *Standards of professional courtesy; Service*

i. The timing and manner of service should not be used to the disadvantage of the party receiving the papers. This includes the use of facsimile transmissions and any additional expedited means of communication approved by the court. FL ST 6 J CIR 2009-066 PA/PI-CIR(C)(1).

ii. Attorneys will not serve papers to take advantage of opposing counsel's known absence from the office or at a time or in a manner designed to inconvenience an opponent, such as late on Friday afternoon or the day preceding a secular or religious holiday. FL ST 6 J CIR 2009-066 PA/PI-CIR(C)(2).

iii. Attorneys will not serve papers, including briefs and memoranda, so close to a court appearance that the ability of opposing counsel to prepare for that appearance or, where permitted, to respond, is inhibited. FL ST 6 J CIR 2009-066 PA/PI-CIR(C)(3).

iv. Service should be made personally or by facsimile transmission when it is likely that service by mail, even when allowed, will prejudice the opposing party. FL ST 6 J CIR 2009-066 PA/PI-CIR(C)(4).

G. Hearings

1. The parties may be required to participate in pretrial proceedings to consider and determine the necessity or desirability of an amendment to a pleading. FL ST RCP Rule 1.200(b)(2); FL-PP § 2:151.

H. Forms

1. Official Amended Answer Forms for Florida

a. Caption. FL ST RCP Form 1.901.

b. Notice of compliance when constitutional challenge is brought. FL ST RCP Form 1.975.

2. Amended Answer Forms for Florida

a. Form for amendment to answer. FL-RCPF R 1.190(50).

b. Form for supplement to pleading. FL-RCPF R 1.190(102).

I. Checklist

(I) ❑ Matters to be considered by plaintiff

(a) ❑ Required documents

(1) ❑ Amended answer

(2) ❑ Certificate of service

(b) ❑ Supplemental documents

(1) ❑ Exhibits

(2) ❑ Notice of constitutional question

(3) ❑ Notice of companion cases

(c) ❑ Timing

(1) ❑ A party may amend a pleading once as a matter of course at any time before a responsive pleading is served

(2) ❑ If the pleading is one to which no responsive pleading is permitted and the action has not been placed on the trial calendar, may so amend it at any time within twenty (20) days after it is served

Motions, Oppositions and Replies
Motion to Strike

Document Last Updated January 2013

A. Applicable Rules

1. *State rules*
   a. Rules of court. FL ST RCP Rule 1.010; FL ST J ADMIN Rule 2.110.
   b. Nonverification of pleadings. FL ST RCP Rule 1.030.
   c. Service and filing of pleadings, orders, and documents. FL ST RCP Rule 1.080.
   d. Time. FL ST RCP Rule 1.090.
   e. Pleadings and motions. FL ST RCP Rule 1.100.
   f. Defenses. FL ST RCP Rule 1.140.
   g. Sham pleadings. FL ST RCP Rule 1.150.
   h. Motions. FL ST RCP Rule 1.160.
   i. Relief from judgment, decrees, or orders. FL ST RCP Rule 1.540.
   j. Mediation and arbitration. FL ST RCP Rule 1.700; FL ST RCP Rule 1.710; FL ST RCP Rule 1.720; FL ST RCP Rule 1.730; FL ST RCP Rule 1.750; FL ST RCP Rule 1.800; FL ST RCP Rule 1.810; FL ST RCP Rule 1.820; FL ST RCP Rule 1.830.
   k. Forms. FL ST RCP Rule 1.900.
   l. Minimization of the filing of sensitive information. FL ST J ADMIN Rule 2.425.
   m. Retention of court records. FL ST J ADMIN Rule 2.430.
   n. Foreign attorneys. FL ST J ADMIN Rule 2.510.
   o. Signature of attorneys and parties. FL ST J ADMIN Rule 2.515.
   p. Paper. FL ST J ADMIN Rule 2.520.
   q. Electronic filing. FL ST J ADMIN Rule 2.525.
   r. Accessibility of information and technology. FL ST J ADMIN Rule 2.526.
   s. Communication equipment. FL ST J ADMIN Rule 2.530.
   t. Court reporting. FL ST J ADMIN Rule 2.535.
   u. Requests for accommodations by persons with disabilities. FL ST J ADMIN Rule 2.540.
2. *Local rules*
   a. General motion rule. FL ST 6 J CIR LOCAL Rule 5.
   b. Telephonic hearings in circuit civil, county civil and small claims cases. FL ST 6 J CIR PA/PI-CIR-88-48.
   c. Arbitration and mediation program circuit civil and family cases. FL ST 6 J CIR PA/PI-CIR-96-63; FL ST 6 J CIR 2011-006 PA/PI-CIR.
   d. Pre-trial conferences. FL ST 6 J CIR PA/PI-CIR-98-49.
   e. Uniform motion calendar civil division. FL ST 6 J CIR PINELLAS CIR CT PI-CIR-98-30.
   f. Standards of professional courtesy. FL ST 6 J CIR 2009-066 PA/PI-CIR.

B. Timing

1. *Motion to strike.* A party may move to strike or the court may strike redundant, immaterial, impertinent, or scandalous matter from any pleading at any time. FL ST RCP Rule 1.140(f).
2. *Motion to strike; Failure to state a legal defense.* If a pleading sets forth a claim for relief to which the

adverse party is not required to serve a responsive pleading, the adverse party may assert any defense in law or fact to that claim for relief at the trial, except that the objection of failure to state a legal defense in an answer or reply shall be asserted by motion to strike the defense within twenty (20) days after service of the answer or reply. FL ST RCP Rule 1.140(b).

3. *Motion to strike; Sham pleadings.* If a party deems any pleading or part thereof filed by another party to be a sham, that party may move to strike the pleading or part thereof before the cause is set for trial. FL ST RCP Rule 1.150(a).

4. *General motion timing.* A copy of any written motion which may not be heard ex parte and a copy of the notice of the hearing thereof shall be served a reasonable time before the time specified for the hearing. FL ST RCP Rule 1.090(d).
   a. All motions, except motions in limine, shall be filed and heard prior to the pre-trial conference unless good cause exists why the motions were not heard prior to the pre-trial conference, including the inability to obtain hearing time prior to the pre-trial conference. FL ST 6 J CIR PA/PI-CIR-98-49(6).
   b. If such good cause exists, the court will hear such motions at the pre-trial conference or at a separate hearing following the pre-trial conference. FL ST 6 J CIR PA/PI-CIR-98-49(6).

5. *Computation of time*
   a. *Generally.* Computation of time shall be governed by FL ST J ADMIN Rule 2.514. FL ST RCP Rule 1.090(a). The following rules apply in computing time periods specified in any rule of procedure, local rule, court order, or statute that does not specify a method of computing time. FL ST J ADMIN Rule 2.514(a).
      i. *Period stated in days or a longer unit.* When the period is stated in days or a longer unit of time (A) exclude the day of the event that triggers the period; (B) count every day, including intermediate Saturdays, Sundays, and legal holidays; and (C) include the last day of the period, but if the last day is a Saturday, Sunday, or legal holiday, or falls within any period of time extended through an order of the chief justice under FL ST J ADMIN Rule 2.205(a)(2)(B)(iv), the period continues to run until the end of the next day that is not a Saturday, Sunday, or legal holiday and does not fall within any period of time extended through an order of the chief justice. FL ST J ADMIN Rule 2.514(a)(1).
      ii. *Period stated in hours.* When the period is stated in hours (A) begin counting immediately on the occurrence of the event that triggers the period; (B) count every hour, including hours during intermediate Saturdays, Sundays, and legal holidays; and (C) if the period would end on a Saturday, Sunday, or legal holiday, or during any period of time extended through an order of the chief justice under FL ST J ADMIN Rule 2.205(a)(2)(B)(iv), the period continues to run until the same time on the next day that is not a Saturday, Sunday, or legal holiday and does not fall within any period of time extended through an order of the chief justice. FL ST J ADMIN Rule 2.514(a)(2).
      iii. *Period stated in days less than seven (7) days.* When the period stated in days is less than seven (7) days, intermediate Saturdays, Sundays, and legal holidays shall be excluded in the computation. FL ST J ADMIN Rule 2.514(a)(3).
      iv. *"Last day" defined.* Unless a different time is set by a statute, local rule, or court order, the last day ends (A) for electronic filing or for service by any means, at midnight; and (B) for filing by other means, when the clerk's office is scheduled to close. FL ST J ADMIN Rule 2.514(a)(4).
      v. *"Next day" defined.* The "next day" is determined by continuing to count forward when the period is measured after an event and backward when measured before an event. FL ST J ADMIN Rule 2.514(a)(5).
      vi. *"Legal holiday" defined.* "Legal holiday" means (A) the day set aside by FL ST § 110.117, for observing New Year's Day, Martin Luther King, Jr.'s Birthday, Memorial Day, Independence Day, Labor Day, Veterans' Day, Thanksgiving Day, the Friday after Thanksgiving Day, or Christmas Day, and (B) any day observed as a holiday by the clerk's office or as designated by the chief judge. FL ST J ADMIN Rule 2.514(a)(6).
   b. *Additional time after service by mail or e-mail.* When a party may or must act within a specified time

after service and service is made by mail or e-mail, five (5) days are added after the period that would otherwise expire under FL ST J ADMIN Rule 2.514(a). FL ST J ADMIN Rule 2.514(b).

c. *Enlargement.* When an act is required or allowed to be done at or within a specified time by order of court, by the Florida Rules of Civil Procedure, or by notice given thereunder, for cause shown the court at any time in its discretion (1) with or without notice, may order the period enlarged if request therefor is made before the expiration of the period originally prescribed or as extended by a previous order, or (2) upon motion made and notice after the expiration of the specified period, may permit the act to be done when failure to act was the result of excusable neglect, but it may not extend the time for making a motion for new trial, for rehearing, or to alter or amend a judgment; making a motion for relief from a judgment under FL ST RCP Rule 1.540(b); taking an appeal or filing a petition for certiorari; or making a motion for a directed verdict. FL ST RCP Rule 1.090(b).

d. *Unaffected by expiration of term.* The period of time provided for the doing of any act or the taking of any proceeding shall not be affected or limited by the continued existence or expiration of a term of court. The continued existence or expiration of a term of court in no way affects the power of a court to do any act or take any proceeding in any action which is or has been pending before it. FL ST RCP Rule 1.090(c).

C. General Requirements

1. *Motions generally*

a. *Contents.* An application to the court for an order shall be by motion which shall be made in writing unless made during a hearing or trial, shall state with particularity the grounds therefor, and shall set forth the relief or order sought. The requirement of writing is fulfilled if the motion is stated in a written notice of the hearing of the motion. All notices of hearing shall specify each motion or other matter to be heard. FL ST RCP Rule 1.100(b).

b. *Particularity requirement.* The court considers a motion in the light of the substantive law, rule or statute to make its determination. Some rules require a statement of the grounds for a motion under the rule. Failure to give the grounds will result in denial of the motion. This should be the result in all situations when the ground for the motion is not inherent in the rule. FL-PRACPROC § 9:3. The requirement is nevertheless an important one, first because of the due process notice rights of the respondent, as well as for the assistance it provides to the court in its preparation for the hearing or, absent a hearing, for disposition. 4 FLPRAC R 1.100.

c. *Standards of professional courtesy; Motion practice*

i. Attorneys will make every reasonable effort to resolve the issue before setting a motion for hearing. FL ST 6 J CIR 2009-066 PA/PI-CIR(G)(1).

ii. Attorneys will not force opposing counsel to make motions attorneys do not intend to oppose unless circumstances require or the client requires. FL ST 6 J CIR 2009-066 PA/PI-CIR(G)(2).

2. *Motion to strike under FL ST RCP Rule 1.140.* Two (2) types of motion to strike are authorized by FL ST RCP Rule 1.140. One is used to eliminate immaterial, redundant, impertinent or scandalous allegations. The other is used to test the legal sufficiency of a defense. FL-PRACPROC § 10:6.

a. *Motion to strike to eliminate immaterial, redundant, impertinent or scandalous allegations*

i. As used in FL ST RCP Rule 1.140(f), redundant means allegations that are foreign to the issues or needless repetition of allegations. Immaterial means allegations having no essential or important relationship to the issues or unnecessary elaboration of material allegations. Impertinent means allegations that do not belong to the issue and are not necessary to it. Scandalous means unnecessary allegations censuring or accusing a party. FL-PRACPROC § 10:6.

ii. The motion can be made at any time and does not toll the time for pleading. FL-PRACPROC § 10:6.

iii. The motion reaches improper allegations of damages. When directed to an entire paragraph and any part of it is proper, the motion should be denied. Leave to amend should be granted after striking part of a pleading unless a proper amendment cannot be made. FL-PRACPROC § 10:6.

iv. The use of a motion to strike is not favored by the courts and the remedy is used sparingly.

Florida courts have held that an allegation must be "wholly irrelevant" and that if there is some doubt it must be resolved in support of the pleading and against the party moving to strike. If any part of an allegation is relevant, then that part should not be stricken from the pleading. 5 FLPRAC § 7:30.

b. *Motion to strike the legal sufficiency of a defense*

i. The legal insufficiency of a defense alleged in an answer or reply is attacked by a motion to strike. It is the counterpart of a motion to dismiss for failure to state a cause of action directed to a pleading seeking affirmative relief. FL-PRACPROC § 10:7.

ii. A motion to strike a defense tests only the legal sufficiency of the defense, and it is reversible error for a trial court to strike the defense where evidence may be presented to support it. Burns v. Equilease Corp., 357 So.2d 786, 24, 24 U.C.C. Rep.Serv. 254 (Fla. 3d DCA 1978); 20 FLPRAC § 3:15.

3. *Sham pleadings.* If a party deems any pleading or part thereof filed by another party to be a sham, that party may move to strike the pleading or part thereof before the cause is set for trial and the court shall hear the motion, taking evidence of the respective parties, and if the motion is sustained, the pleading to which the motion is directed shall be stricken. Default and summary judgment on the merits may be entered in the discretion of the court or the court may permit additional pleadings to be filed for good cause shown. FL ST RCP Rule 1.150(a).

a. *Contents of motion.* The motion to strike shall be verified and shall set forth fully the facts on which the movant relies and may be supported by affidavit. No traverse of the motion shall be required. FL ST RCP Rule 1.150(b).

b. *Allegations supported by evidence.* The issue is not whether the allegations are material or proper, but whether the allegations are supported by evidence. 5 FLPRAC § 7:30.

4. *Arbitration and mediation*

a. *Referral to arbitration and mediation.* Except as hereinafter provided or as otherwise prohibited by law, the presiding judge may enter an order referring all or any part of a contested civil matter to mediation or arbitration. The parties to any contested civil matter may file a written stipulation to mediate or arbitrate any issue between them at any time. Such stipulation shall be incorporated into the order of referral. FL ST RCP Rule 1.700(a).

b. *Arbitration*

i. *Exclusions.* A civil action shall be ordered to arbitration or arbitration in conjunction with mediation upon stipulation of the parties. A civil action may be ordered to arbitration or arbitration in conjunction with mediation upon motion of any party or by the court, if the judge determines the action to be of such a nature that arbitration could be of benefit to the litigants or the court. FL ST RCP Rule 1.800.

- Under no circumstances may the following categories of actions be referred to arbitration: (1) bond estreatures; (2) habeas corpus or other extraordinary writs; (3) bond validations; (4) civil or criminal contempt; (5) such other matters as may be specified by order of the chief judge in the circuit. FL ST RCP Rule 1.800.

ii. For more information regarding arbitration, please see FL ST RCP Rule 1.810; FL ST RCP Rule 1.820; FL ST RCP Rule 1.830.

c. *Mediation.* For more information regarding mediation, please see FL ST RCP Rule 1.710; FL ST RCP Rule 1.720; FL ST RCP Rule 1.730; and FL ST RCP Rule 1.750.

d. See FL ST 6 J CIR PA/PI-CIR-96-63 for more information about the Arbitration and Mediation Program for Florida's Sixth Judicial Circuit.

5. *Rules of court*

a. *Rules of civil procedure.* The Florida Rules of Civil Procedure apply to all actions of a civil nature and all special statutory proceedings in the circuit courts and county courts except those to which the

Florida Probate Rules, the Florida Family Law Rules of Procedure, or the Small Claims Rules apply. FL ST RCP Rule 1.010.

i. The form, content, procedure, and time for pleading in all special statutory proceedings shall be as prescribed by the statutes governing the proceeding unless the Florida Rules of Civil Procedure specifically provide to the contrary. FL ST RCP Rule 1.010.

ii. The Florida Rules of Civil Procedure shall be construed to secure the just, speedy, and inexpensive determination of every action. FL ST RCP Rule 1.010.

b. *Rules of judicial administration.* The Florida Rules of Judicial Administration shall apply to administrative matters in all courts to which the Florida Rules of Judicial Administration are applicable by their terms. The Florida Rules of Judicial Administration shall be construed to secure the speedy and inexpensive determination of every proceeding to which they are applicable. The Florida Rules of Judicial Administration shall supersede all conflicting rules and statutes. FL ST J ADMIN Rule 2.110.

6. *Settlement and alternative dispute resolution.* When a matter is scheduled for hearing and the matter is resolved by agreement or settlement, the party setting the matter for hearing shall notify the court. When a matter is scheduled for trial and the case settles, the plaintiff shall notify the court. Permission of the court must be obtained in order to cancel a trial. FL ST 6 J CIR LOCAL Rule 5(A).

a. Unless there are strong and overriding issues of principle, attorneys will raise and explore the issue of settlement as soon as enough is known to make settlement discussions meaningful. FL ST 6 J CIR 2009-066 PA/PI-CIR(I)(1).

b. Attorneys will not falsely hold out the possibility of settlement to adjourn discovery or delay trial. FL ST 6 J CIR 2009-066 PA/PI-CIR(I)(2).

c. Attorneys will consider whether the client's interest could be adequately served and the controversy more expeditiously and economically disposed of by arbitration, mediation or other forms of alternative dispute resolution. FL ST 6 J CIR 2009-066 PA/PI-CIR(I)(3).

D. Documents

1. *Required documents*

a. *Notice of hearing/Motion.* An application to the court for an order shall be by motion which shall be made in writing unless made during a hearing or trial, shall state with particularity the grounds therefor, and shall set forth the relief or order sought. The requirement of writing is fulfilled if the motion is stated in a written notice of the hearing of the motion. All notices of hearing shall specify each motion or other matter to be heard. FL ST RCP Rule 1.100(b).

i. *Notices to persons with disabilities.* See the Format section of this KeyRules document for further information.

b. *Certificate of service.* When any attorney certifies in substance: "I certify that a copy hereof has been furnished to (here insert name or names and addresses used for service) by (e-mail) (delivery) (mail) (fax) on .... (date) ....______________ Attorney" the certificate is taken as prima facie proof of such service in compliance with FL ST J ADMIN Rule 2.516. FL ST J ADMIN Rule 2.516(f).

2. *Supplemental documents*

a. *Proposed order.* The court may require that orders or judgments be prepared by a party, may require the party to furnish the court with stamped, addressed envelopes for service of the order or judgment, and may require that proposed orders and judgments be furnished to all parties before entry by the court of the order or judgment. FL ST J ADMIN Rule 2.516(h)(1).

i. After a hearing, attorneys will make a good faith effort to quickly agree or disagree upon a proposed order and submit the result to the court. Unless otherwise instructed by the court, or agreed to by counsel, all proposed orders shall be provided to other counsel for approval or comment prior to submission to the court. Attorneys will not submit controverted orders to the court with a copy to opposing counsel for "objections within ______ days". Courts prefer to know that the order is either agreed upon or opposed. FL ST 6 J CIR 2009-066 PA/PI-CIR(G)(3).

ii. Attorneys will not use post-hearing submissions of proposed orders as a guise to reargue the merits of the matter. FL ST 6 J CIR 2009-066 PA/PI-CIR(G)(4).

b. *Notice of constitutional question.* A party that files a pleading, written motion, or other paper drawing into question the constitutionality of a state statute or a county or municipal charter, ordinance, or franchise must promptly (1) file a notice of constitutional question stating the question and identifying the paper that raises it; and (2) serve the notice and the pleading, written motion, or other paper drawing into question the constitutionality of a state statute or a county or municipal charter, ordinance, or franchise on the Attorney General or the state attorney of the judicial circuit in which the action is pending, by either certified or registered mail. Service of the notice and pleading, written motion, or other paper does not require joinder of the Attorney General or the state attorney as a party to the action. FL ST RCP Rule 1.071.

E. Format

1. *Documents; Type and size.* Documents subject to the exceptions set forth in FL ST J ADMIN Rule 2.525(d) shall be filed on recycled paper measuring eight and one half by eleven (8 1/2 by 11) inches. For purposes of FL ST J ADMIN Rule 2.520, paper is recycled if it contains a minimum content of fifty (50) percent waste paper. Xerographic reduction of legal-size (eight and one half by fourteen (8 1/2 by 14) inches) documents to letter size (eight and one half by eleven (8 1/2 by 11) inches) is prohibited. All other documents filed by electronic transmission shall be filed in a format capable of being printed in a format consistent with the provisions of FL ST J ADMIN Rule 2.250. FL ST J ADMIN Rule 2.520(b).

   a. *Exhibits.* Any exhibit or attachment filed with pleadings or papers may be filed in its original size. FL ST J ADMIN Rule 2.520(c).

   b. *Recording space.* On all papers and documents prepared and filed by the court or by any party to a proceeding which are to be recorded in the public records of any county, including but not limited to final money judgments and notices of lis pendens, a three (3) inch by three (3) inch space at the top right-hand corner on the first page and a one (1) inch by three (3) inch space at the top right-hand corner on each subsequent page shall be left blank and reserved for use by the clerk of court. FL ST J ADMIN Rule 2.520(d).

      i. *Exceptions to recording space.* Any papers or documents created by persons or entities over which the filing party has no control, including but not limited to wills, codicils, trusts, or other testamentary documents; documents prepared or executed by any public officer; documents prepared, executed, acknowledged, or proved outside of the State of Florida; or documents created by State or Federal government agencies, may be filed without the space required by FL ST J ADMIN Rule 2.520. FL ST J ADMIN Rule 2.520(e).

   c. *Noncompliance.* No clerk of court is permitted to refuse to file any document or paper because of noncompliance with the Florida Rules of Judicial Administration. However, upon request of the clerk of court, noncomplying documents must be resubmitted in accordance with the formatting rules. FL ST J ADMIN Rule 2.520(f).

2. *Caption.* Every pleading, motion, order, judgment, or other paper shall have a caption containing the name of the court, the file number, and except for in rem proceedings, including forfeiture proceedings, the name of the first party on each side with an appropriate indication of other parties, and a designation identifying the party filing it and its nature or the nature of the order, as the case may be. In any in rem proceeding, every pleading, motion, order, judgment, or other paper shall have a caption containing the name of the court, the file number, the style "In re" (followed by the name or general description of the property), and a designation of the person or entity filing it and its nature or the nature of the order, as the case may be. In an in rem forfeiture proceeding, the style shall be "In re forfeiture of" (followed by the name of the general description of the property). All papers filed in the action shall be styled in such a manner as to indicate clearly the subject matter of the paper and the party requesting or obtaining relief. FL ST RCP Rule 1.100(c)(1).

3. *Writing and written defined.* Writing or written means a document containing information, an application, or a stipulation. FL ST RCP Rule 1.080(c).

4. *Rule abbreviations*

   a. The Florida Rules of Civil Procedure and shall be abbreviated as Fla.R.Civ.P. FL ST RCP Rule 1.010.

b. The Florida Rules of Judicial Administration shall be abbreviated as Fla. R. Jud. Admin. FL ST J ADMIN Rule 2.110.

5. *Nonverification.* Except when otherwise specifically provided by the Florida Rules of Civil Procedure or an applicable statute, every pleading or other document of a party represented by an attorney need not be verified or accompanied by an affidavit. FL ST RCP Rule 1.030; FL ST J ADMIN Rule 2.515(a).

6. *Attorney signature*

a. *Attorney signature.* Every pleading and other document of a party represented by an attorney shall be signed by at least one (1) attorney of record in that attorney's individual name whose current record Florida Bar address, telephone number, including area code, primary e-mail address and secondary e-mail addresses, if any, and Florida Bar number shall be stated, and who shall be duly licensed to practice law in Florida or who shall have received permission to appear in the particular case as provided in FL ST J ADMIN Rule 2.510. FL ST J ADMIN Rule 2.515(a).

i. The attorney may be required by the court to give the address of, and to vouch for the attorney's authority to represent, the party. FL ST J ADMIN Rule 2.515(a).

ii. The signature of an attorney shall constitute a certificate by the attorney that the attorney has read the pleading or other document; that to the best of the attorney's knowledge, information, and belief there is good ground to support it; and that it is not interposed for delay. FL ST J ADMIN Rule 2.515(a).

iii. If a pleading is not signed or is signed with intent to defeat the purpose of FL ST J ADMIN Rule 2.515, it may be stricken and the action may proceed as though the pleading or other document had not been served. FL ST J ADMIN Rule 2.515(a).

b. *Pro se litigant signature.* A party who is not represented by an attorney shall sign any pleading or other paper and state the party's address and telephone number, including area code. FL ST J ADMIN Rule 2.515(b).

c. *Form of signature*

i. The signatures required on pleadings and documents by FL ST J ADMIN Rule 2.515(a) and FL ST J ADMIN Rule 2.515(b) may be:

- Original signatures;
- Original signatures that have been reproduced by electronic means, such as on electronically transmitted documents or photocopied documents;
- Electronic signatures using the "/s/," "s/," or "/s" formats by or at the direction of the person signing; or
- Any other signature format authorized by general law, so long as the clerk where the proceeding is pending has the capability of receiving and has obtained approval from the Supreme Court of Florida to accept pleadings and documents with that signature format. FL ST J ADMIN Rule 2.515(c)(1).

ii. An attorney, party, or other person who files a pleading or paper by electronic transmission that does not contain the original signature of that attorney, party, or other person shall file that identical pleading or paper in paper form containing an original signature of that attorney, party, or other person (hereinafter called the follow-up filing) immediately thereafter. The follow-up filing is not required if the Supreme Court of Florida has entered an order directing the clerk of court to discontinue accepting the follow-up filing. FL ST J ADMIN Rule 2.515(c)(2).

7. *Forms*

a. *Process.* The forms of process, notice of lis pendens, and notice of action provided in the Florida Rules of Civil Procedure are sufficient. Variations from the forms do not void process or notices that are otherwise sufficient. FL ST RCP Rule 1.900(a).

b. *Other forms.* The other forms provided in the Florida Rules of Civil Procedure are sufficient for the matters that are covered by them. So long as the substance is expressed without prolixity, the forms may be varied to meet the facts of a particular case. FL ST RCP Rule 1.900(b).

c. *Formal matters.* Captions, except for the designation of the paper, are omitted from the forms provided in the Florida Rules of Civil Procedure. A general form of caption is the first form provided. Signatures are omitted from pleadings and motions. FL ST RCP Rule 1.900(c).

8. *Notices to persons with disabilities.* All notices of court proceedings to be held in a public facility, and all process compelling appearance at such proceedings, shall include the following statement in bold face, fourteen (14) point Times New Roman or Courier font: "If you are a person with a disability who needs any accommodation in order to participate in this proceeding, you are entitled, at no cost to you, to the provision of certain assistance. Please contact [identify applicable court personnel by name, address, and telephone number] at least seven (7) days before your scheduled court appearance, or immediately upon receiving this notification if the time before the scheduled appearance is less than seven (7) days; if you are hearing or voice impaired, call 711." FL ST J ADMIN Rule 2.540(c)(1).

9. *Minimization of the filing of sensitive information*

a. *Limitations for court filings.* Unless authorized by FL ST J ADMIN Rule 2.425(b), statute, another rule of court, or the court orders otherwise, designated sensitive information filed with the court must be limited to the following format:

i. The initials of a person known to be a minor;

ii. The year of birth of a person's birth date;

iii. No portion of any: Social security number, Bank account number, Credit card account number, Charge account number, or Debit account number;

iv. The last four digits of any: Taxpayer identification number (TIN), Employee identification number, Driver's license number, Passport number, Telephone number, Financial account number, except as set forth in FL ST J ADMIN Rule 2.425(a)(3), Brokerage account number, Insurance policy account number, Loan account number, Customer account number, or Patient or health care number;

v. A truncated version of any: Email address, Computer user name, Password, or Personal identification number (PIN); and

vi. A truncated version of any other sensitive information as provided by court order. FL ST J ADMIN Rule 2.425(a).

b. *Exceptions.* FL ST J ADMIN Rule 2.425(a) does not apply to the following:

i. An account number which identifies the property alleged to be the subject of a proceeding;

ii. The record of an administrative or agency proceeding;

iii. The record in appellate or review proceedings;

iv. The birth date of a minor whenever the birth date is necessary for the court to establish or maintain subject matter jurisdiction;

v. The name of a minor in any order relating to parental responsibility, time-sharing, or child support;

vi. The name of a minor in any document or order affecting the minor's ownership of real property;

vii. The birth date of a party in a writ of attachment or notice to payor;

viii. In traffic and criminal proceedings: a pro se filing; a court filing that is related to a criminal matter or investigation and that is prepared before the filing of a criminal charge or is not filed as part of any docketed criminal case; an arrest or search warrant or any information in support thereof; a charging document and an affidavit or other documents filed in support of any charging document, including any driving records; a statement of particulars; discovery material introduced into evidence or otherwise filed with the court; and all information necessary for the proper issuance and execution of a subpoena duces tecum;

ix. Information used by the clerk for case maintenance purposes or the courts for case management purposes; and

x. Information which is relevant and material to an issue before the court. FL ST J ADMIN Rule 2.425(b).

c. *Remedies.* Upon motion by a party or interested person or sua sponte by the court, the court may order remedies, sanctions or both for a violation of FL ST J ADMIN Rule 2.425(a). Following notice and an opportunity to respond, the court may impose sanctions if such filing was not made in good faith. FL ST J ADMIN Rule 2.425(c).

d. *Motions not restricted.* FL ST J ADMIN Rule 2.425 does not restrict a party's right to move for protective order, to move to file documents under seal, or to request a determination of the confidentiality of records. FL ST J ADMIN Rule 2.425(d).

e. *Application.* FL ST J ADMIN Rule 2.425 does not affect the application of constitutional provisions, statutes, or rules of court regarding confidential information or access to public information. FL ST J ADMIN Rule 2.425(e).

F. Filing and Service Requirements

1. *Filing requirements.* All original documents must be filed with the court either before service or immediately thereafter, unless otherwise provided for by general law or other rules. If the original of any bond or other document is not placed in the court file, a certified copy must be so placed by the clerk. FL ST J ADMIN Rule 2.516(d). All documents shall be filed in conformity with the requirements of FL ST J ADMIN Rule 2.525. FL ST RCP Rule 1.080(b). All documents filed in any court shall be filed by electronic transmission in accordance with FL ST J ADMIN Rule 2.525. "Documents" means pleadings, motions, petitions, memoranda, briefs, notices, exhibits, declarations, affidavits, orders, judgments, decrees, writs, opinions, and any other paper or writing submitted to a court. FL ST J ADMIN Rule 2.520(a). All documents that are court records, as defined in FL ST J ADMIN Rule 2.430(a)(1), must be filed by electronic transmission, provided that: (1) the clerk has the ability to accept and retain such documents; (2) the clerk or the chief judge of the circuit has requested permission to accept documents filed by electronic transmission; and (3) the supreme court has entered an order granting permission to the clerk to accept documents filed by electronic transmission. FL ST J ADMIN Rule 2.525(c)(1).

   a. *Definition.* "Electronic transmission of documents" means the sending of information by electronic signals to, by or from a court or clerk, which when received can be transformed and stored or transmitted on paper, microfilm, magnetic storage device, optical imaging system, CD-ROM, flash drive, other electronic data storage system, server, case maintenance system ("CM"), electronic court filing ("ECF") system, statewide or local electronic portal ("e-portal"), or other electronic record keeping system authorized by the supreme court in a format sufficient to communicate the information on the original document in a readable format. Electronic transmission of documents includes electronic mail ("e-mail") and any internet-based transmission procedure, and may include procedures allowing for documents to be signed or verified by electronic means. FL ST J ADMIN Rule 2.525(a).

      i. The filing of documents with the court as required by the Florida Rules of Judicial Administration must be made by filing them with the clerk in accordance with FL ST J ADMIN Rule 2.525, except that the judge may permit documents to be filed with the judge, in which event the judge must note the filing date before him or her on the documents and transmit them to the clerk. The date of filing is that shown on the face of the document by the judge's notation or the clerk's time stamp, whichever is earlier. FL ST J ADMIN Rule 2.516(e).

   b. *Application.* Any court or clerk of the court may accept the electronic transmission of documents for filing after the clerk, together with input from the chief judge of the circuit, has obtained approval of the procedures and program for doing so from the Supreme Court of Florida. FL ST J ADMIN Rule 2.525(b).

   c. *Exceptions*

      i. Paper documents and other submissions may be manually submitted to the clerk or court:

         - When the clerk does not have the ability to accept and retain documents by electronic filing or has not had ECF Procedures approved by the supreme court;
         - For filing by any self-represented party or any self-represented nonparty unless specific ECF Procedures provide a means to file documents electronically. However, any self-represented nonparty that is a governmental or public agency and any other agency,

partnership, corporation, or business entity acting on behalf of any governmental or public agency may file documents by electronic transmission if such entity has the capability of filing documents electronically;

- For filing by attorneys excused from e-mail service in accordance with FL ST J ADMIN Rule 2.516(b);
- When submitting evidentiary exhibits or filing non-documentary materials;
- When the filing involves documents in excess of twenty-five (25) megabytes (25MB) in size. For such filings, documents may be transmitted using an electronic storage medium that the clerk has the ability to accept, which may include a CD-ROM, flash drive, or similar storage medium;
- When filed in open court, as permitted by the court;
- When paper filing is permitted by any approved statewide or local ECF procedures; and
- If any court determines that justice so requires. FL ST J ADMIN Rule 2.525(d).

ii. Any document in paper form submitted under FL ST J ADMIN Rule 2.525(d) is filed when it is received by the clerk or court and the clerk shall immediately thereafter convert any filed paper document to an electronic document. "Convert to an electronic document" means optically capturing an image of a paper document and using character recognition software to recover as much of the document's text as practicable and then indexing and storing the document in the official court file. FL ST J ADMIN Rule 2.525(c)(4).

iii. Any storage medium submitted under FL ST J ADMIN Rule 2.525(d)(5) is filed when received by the clerk or court and the clerk shall immediately thereafter transfer the electronic documents from the storage device to the official court file. FL ST J ADMIN Rule 2.525(c)(5).

iv. If the filer of any paper document authorized under FL ST J ADMIN Rule 2.525(d) provides a self-addressed, postage-paid envelope for return of the paper document after it is converted to electronic form by the clerk, the clerk shall place the paper document in the envelope and deposit it in the mail. Except when a paper document is required to be maintained, the clerk may recycle any filed paper document that is not to be returned to the filer. FL ST J ADMIN Rule 2.525(c)(6).

v. The clerk may convert any paper document filed before the effective date of FL ST J ADMIN Rule 2.525 to an electronic document. Unless the clerk is required to maintain the paper document, if the paper document has been converted to an electronic document by the clerk, the paper document is no longer part of the official court file and may be removed and recycled. FL ST J ADMIN Rule 2.525(c)(7).

d. *Official court file.* For information on what constitutes the official court file, please see FL ST J ADMIN Rule 2.525(c)(2), FL ST J ADMIN Rule 2.525(c)(3).

e. *Administration.* All attorneys, parties, or other persons using this rule to file documents are required to make arrangements with the court or clerk for the payment of any charges authorized by general law or the supreme court before filing any document by electronic transmission. FL ST J ADMIN Rule 2.525(f)(2).

f. *Filing date.* The filing date for an electronically transmitted document is the date and time that such filing is acknowledged by an electronic stamp or otherwise, pursuant to any procedure set forth in any ECF Procedures approved by the supreme court, or the date the last page of such filing is received by the court or clerk. FL ST J ADMIN Rule 2.525(f)(3).

g. *Accessibility.* All documents transmitted in any electronic form under FL ST J ADMIN Rule 2.525 must comply with the accessibility requirements of FL ST J ADMIN Rule 2.526. FL ST J ADMIN Rule 2.525(g).

2. *Service requirements.* Every pleading subsequent to the initial pleading, all orders, and every other document filed in the action must be served in conformity with the requirements of FL ST J ADMIN Rule 2.516. FL ST RCP Rule 1.080(a).

a. *Service; When required.* Unless the court otherwise orders, or a statute or supreme court adminis-

trative order specifies a different means of service, every pleading subsequent to the initial pleading and every other document filed in any court proceeding, except applications for witness subpoenas and documents served by formal notice or required to be served in the manner provided for service of formal notice, must be served in accordance with FL ST J ADMIN Rule 2.516 on each party. No service need be made on parties against whom a default has been entered, except that pleadings asserting new or additional claims against them must be served in the manner provided for service of summons. FL ST J ADMIN Rule 2.516(a).

b. *Service; How made.* When service is required or permitted to be made upon a party represented by an attorney, service must be made upon the attorney unless service upon the party is ordered by the court. FL ST J ADMIN Rule 2.516(b).

   i. *Service by electronic mail ("e-mail").* All documents required or permitted to be served on another party must be served by e-mail, unless FL ST J ADMIN Rule 2.516 otherwise provides. When, in addition to service by e-mail, the sender also utilizes another means of service provided for in FL ST J ADMIN Rule 2.516(b)(2), any differing time limits and other provisions applicable to that other means of service control. FL ST J ADMIN Rule 2.516(b)(1). Any document electronically transmitted to a court or clerk must also be served on all parties and interested persons in accordance with the applicable rules of court. FL ST J ADMIN Rule 2.525(e)(2).

      - *Service on attorneys.* Upon appearing in a proceeding, an attorney must serve a designation of a primary e-mail address and may designate no more than two (2) secondary e-mail addresses. Thereafter, service must be directed to all designated e-mail addresses in that proceeding. Every document filed by an attorney thereafter must include the primary e-mail address of that attorney and any secondary e-mail addresses. If an attorney does not designate any e-mail address for service, documents may be served on that attorney at the e-mail address on record with The Florida Bar. FL ST J ADMIN Rule 2.516(b)(1)(A).
      - *Exception to e-mail service on attorneys.* Service by an attorney on another attorney must be made by e-mail unless excused by the court. Upon motion by an attorney demonstrating that the attorney has no e-mail account and lacks access to the Internet at the attorney's office, the court may excuse the attorney from the requirements of e-mail service. Service on and by an attorney excused by the court from e-mail service must be by the means provided in FL ST J ADMIN Rule 2.516(b)(2). FL ST J ADMIN Rule 2.516(b)(1)(B).
      - *Service on and by parties not represented by an attorney.* Any party not represented by an attorney may serve a designation of a primary e-mail address and also may designate no more than two (2) secondary e-mail addresses to which service must be directed in that proceeding by the means provided in FL ST J ADMIN Rule 2.516(b)(1). If a party not represented by an attorney does not designate an e-mail address for service in a proceeding, service on and by that party must be by the means provided in FL ST J ADMIN Rule 2.516(b)(2). FL ST J ADMIN Rule 2.516(b)(1)(C).
      - *Time of service.* Service by e-mail is complete when it is sent. FL ST J ADMIN Rule 2.516(b)(1)(D). An e-mail is deemed served on the date it is sent. FL ST J ADMIN Rule 2.516(b)(1)(D)(i). If the sender learns that the e-mail did not reach the address of the person to be served, the sender must immediately send another copy by e-mail, or by a means authorized by FL ST J ADMIN Rule 2.516(b)(2). FL ST J ADMIN Rule 2.516(b)(1)(D)(ii). E-mail service is treated as service by mail for the computation of time. FL ST J ADMIN Rule 2.516(b)(1)(D)(iii).

   ii. *Format of e-mail for service.* Service of a document by e-mail is made by attaching a copy of the document in PDF format to an e-mail sent to all addresses designated by the attorney or party. FL ST J ADMIN Rule 2.516(b)(1)(E).

      - All documents served by e-mail must be attached to an e-mail message containing a subject line beginning with the words "SERVICE OF COURT DOCUMENT" in all capital letters, followed by the case number of the proceeding in which the documents are being served. FL ST J ADMIN Rule 2.516(b)(1)(E)(i).

- The body of the e-mail must identify the court in which the proceeding is pending, the case number, the name of the initial party on each side, the title of each document served with that e-mail, and the sender's name and telephone number. FL ST J ADMIN Rule 2.516(b)(1)(E)(ii).
- Any document served by e-mail may be signed by the "/s/" format, as long as the filed original is signed in accordance with the applicable rule of procedure. FL ST J ADMIN Rule 2.516(b)(1)(E)(iii).
- Any e-mail which, together with its attached documents, exceeds five megabytes (5MB) in size, must be divided and sent as separate e-mails, no one of which may exceed five megabytes (5MB) in size and each of which must be sequentially numbered in the subject line. FL ST J ADMIN Rule 2.516(b)(1)(E)(iv).

iii. *Service by other means.* In addition to, and not in lieu of, service by e-mail, service may also be made upon attorneys by any of the means specified in FL ST J ADMIN Rule 2.516(b)(2). Service on and by all parties who are not represented by an attorney and who do not designate an e-mail address, and on and by all attorneys excused from e-mail service, must be made by delivering a copy of the document or by mailing it to the party or attorney at their last known address or, if no address is known, by leaving it with the clerk of the court. Service by mail is complete upon mailing. Delivery of a copy within FL ST J ADMIN Rule 2.516 is complete upon:

- Handing it to the attorney or to the party,
- Leaving it at the attorney's or party's office with a clerk or other person in charge thereof,
- If there is no one in charge, leaving it in a conspicuous place therein,
- If the office is closed or the person to be served has no office, leaving it at the person's usual place of abode with some person of his or her family above fifteen (15) years of age and informing such person of the contents, or
- Transmitting it by facsimile to the attorney's or party's office with a cover sheet containing the sender's name, firm, address, telephone number, and facsimile number, and the number of pages transmitted. When service is made by facsimile, a copy must also be served by any other method permitted by FL ST J ADMIN Rule 2.516. Facsimile service occurs when transmission is complete. FL ST J ADMIN Rule 2.516(b)(2)(A) through FL ST J ADMIN Rule 2.516(b)(2)(E).
- Service by delivery after 5:00 p.m. must be deemed to have been made by mailing on the date of delivery. FL ST J ADMIN Rule 2.516(b)(2)(F).

c. *Service; Numerous defendants.* In actions when the parties are unusually numerous, the court may regulate the service contemplated by the Florida Rules of Judicial Administration on motion or on its own initiative in such manner as may be found to be just and reasonable. FL ST J ADMIN Rule 2.516(c).

d. *Service by clerk.* Service of notices and other documents required to be made by the clerk must also be done as provided in FL ST J ADMIN Rule 2.516(b). FL ST J ADMIN Rule 2.516(g).

e. *Standards of professional courtesy; Service*

i. The timing and manner of service should not be used to the disadvantage of the party receiving the papers. This includes the use of facsimile transmissions and any additional expedited means of communication approved by the court. FL ST 6 J CIR 2009-066 PA/PI-CIR(C)(1).

ii. Attorneys will not serve papers to take advantage of opposing counsel's known absence from the office or at a time or in a manner designed to inconvenience an opponent, such as late on Friday afternoon or the day preceding a secular or religious holiday. FL ST 6 J CIR 2009-066 PA/PI-CIR(C)(2).

iii. Attorneys will not serve papers, including briefs and memoranda, so close to a court appearance that the ability of opposing counsel to prepare for that appearance or, where permitted, to respond, is inhibited. FL ST 6 J CIR 2009-066 PA/PI-CIR(C)(3).

iv. Service should be made personally or by facsimile transmission when it is likely that service by mail, even when allowed, will prejudice the opposing party. FL ST 6 J CIR 2009-066 PA/PI-CIR(C)(4).

G. Hearings

1. *Communication equipment*

a. *Definition.* Communication equipment means a conference telephone or other electronic device that permits all those appearing or participating to hear and speak to each other, provided that all conversation of all parties is audible to all persons present. FL ST J ADMIN Rule 2.530(a).

b. *Use by all parties.* A county or circuit court judge may, upon the court's own motion or upon the written request of a party, direct that communication equipment be used for a motion hearing, pretrial conference, or a status conference. A judge must give notice to the parties and consider any objections they may have to the use of communication equipment before directing that communication equipment be used. The decision to use communication equipment over the objection of parties will be in the sound discretion of the trial court, except as noted below. FL ST J ADMIN Rule 2.530(b).

c. *Use only by requesting party.* A county or circuit court judge may, upon the written request of a party upon reasonable notice to all other parties, permit a requesting party to participate through communication equipment in a scheduled motion hearing; however, any such request (except in criminal, juvenile, and appellate proceedings) must be granted, absent a showing of good cause to deny the same, where the hearing is set for not longer than fifteen (15) minutes. FL ST J ADMIN Rule 2.530(c).

d. *Testimony*

i. *Generally.* A county or circuit court judge, general magistrate, special magistrate, or hearing officer may allow testimony to be taken through communication equipment if all parties consent or if permitted by another applicable rule of procedure. FL ST J ADMIN Rule 2.530(d)(1).

ii. *Procedure.* Any party desiring to present testimony through communication equipment shall, prior to the hearing or trial at which the testimony is to be presented, contact all parties to determine whether each party consents to this form of testimony. The party seeking to present the testimony shall move for permission to present testimony through communication equipment, which motion shall set forth good cause as to why the testimony should be allowed in this form. FL ST J ADMIN Rule 2.530(d)(2).

iii. *Oath.* Testimony may be taken through communication equipment only if a notary public or other person authorized to administer oaths in the witness's jurisdiction is present with the witness and administers the oath consistent with the laws of the jurisdiction. FL ST J ADMIN Rule 2.530(d)(3).

iv. *Confrontation rights.* In juvenile and criminal proceedings the defendant must make an informed waiver of any confrontation rights that may be abridged by the use of communication equipment. FL ST J ADMIN Rule 2.530(d)(4).

v. *Video testimony.* If the testimony to be presented utilizes video conferencing or comparable two-way visual capabilities, the court in its discretion may modify the procedures set forth in FL ST J ADMIN Rule 2.530 to accommodate the technology utilized. FL ST J ADMIN Rule 2.530(d)(5).

e. *Burden of expense.* The cost for the use of the communication equipment is the responsibility of the requesting party unless otherwise directed by the court. FL ST J ADMIN Rule 2.530(e).

2. *Standards of professional courtesy; Scheduling*

a. Attorneys will communicate with opposing counsel to schedule depositions, hearings, and other proceedings, at times mutually convenient for all interested persons. FL ST 6 J CIR 2009-066 PA/PI-CIR(B)(1).

b. Attorneys will provide opposing counsel and other affected persons reasonable notice of all proceedings except upon agreement of counsel when expedited scheduling is necessary. Attorneys will immediately notify opposing counsel of any hearing time reserved. FL ST 6 J CIR 2009-066 PA/PI-CIR(B)(2).

c. Attorneys will request enough time for hearings and adjudicative proceedings to permit full and fair presentation of the matter and to permit response by opposing counsel. When scheduling depositions, Attorneys will schedule enough time to permit the conclusion of the deposition, including examination by all parties, without adjournment. FL ST 6 J CIR 2009-066 PA/PI-CIR(B)(3).

d. Attorneys will call potential scheduling problems to the attention of those affected, including the court, as soon as they become apparent. Attorneys will avoid last minute cancellations. FL ST 6 J CIR 2009-066 PA/PI-CIR(B)(4).

e. Attorneys will make request for changes only when necessary. Attorneys will not request rescheduling, cancellations, extension or postponements solely for the purpose of delay or obtaining unfair advantage. FL ST 6 J CIR 2009-066 PA/PI-CIR(B)(5).

f. Attorneys will cooperate with opposing counsel when conflicts and calendar changes are necessary and requested. FL ST 6 J CIR 2009-066 PA/PI-CIR(B)(6).

g. Attorneys will grant reasonable requests for scheduling, rescheduling, cancellations, extensions, and postponements that do not prejudice our client's opportunity for full, fair and prompt consideration and adjudication of the client's claim or defense. FL ST 6 J CIR 2009-066 PA/PI-CIR(B)(7).

h. First requests for reasonable extensions of time to respond to litigation deadlines relating to pleadings, discovery, or motions, should be granted as a matter of courtesy unless time is of the essence or other circumstances require otherwise. FL ST 6 J CIR 2009-066 PA/PI-CIR(B)(8).

i. Attorneys will resolve subsequent requests by balancing the need for expedition against the deference we should give to opposing counsel's schedule of professional and personal engagements, the reasonableness of the length of extension requested, opposing counsel's willingness to grant reciprocal extensions, the time needed for the task, and whether it is likely a court would grant the extension. FL ST 6 J CIR 2009-066 PA/PI-CIR(B)(9).

j. Attorneys will not attach unfair or extraneous conditions to extensions. Attorneys will impose conditions required to preserve rights that an extension might jeopardize. Attorneys may seek reciprocal scheduling concessions. When granting an extension, we will not try to preclude an opponent's substantive rights. FL ST 6 J CIR 2009-066 PA/PI-CIR(B)(10).

3. *Timing*

a. Hearings are limited to five (5) minutes per case. FL ST 6 J CIR PINELLAS CIR CT PI-CIR-98-30.

b. For more information regarding the timing of hearings, please see FL ST 6 J CIR PINELLAS CIR CT PI-CIR-98-30.

4. *Telephonic hearings.* For information regarding telephonic hearings, please see FL ST 6 J CIR PA/PI-CIR-88-48.

H. Forms

1. Official Motion to Strike Forms for Florida

a. Caption. FL ST RCP Form 1.901.

b. Notice of compliance when constitutional challenge is brought. FL ST RCP Form 1.975.

2. Motion to Strike Forms for Florida

a. Motion to strike. FL-PP § 2:128.

b. Form for motion to strike. FL-RCPF R 1.140(802).

c. Form for motion to strike insufficient pleading. FL-RCPF R 1.140(803).

d. Form for motion to strike claim for business or financial losses. FL-RCPF R 1.140(804).

e. Motion; Strike, complaint signed by corporation. FL-PRACFORM § 7:176.

f. Motion; Strike, defenses. FL-PRACFORM § 7:177.

g. Motion; Strike, ejectment chain of title. FL-PRACFORM § 7:178.

h. Motion; Strike, pleading, departure. FL-PRACFORM § 7:180.

i. Motion; Strike, pleading, improper signature. FL-PRACFORM § 7:181.

j. Motion; Strike, sham pleading. FL-PRACFORM § 7:182.

k. Motion; Strike, sham, defenses, statute of limitations and failure of consideration. FL-PRACFORM § 7:183.

l. Motion; Strike, third party complaint. FL-PRACFORM § 7:184.

I. Checklist

(I) ❑ Matters to be considered by moving party

(a) ❑ Required documents

(1) ❑ Notice of hearing/Motion

(2) ❑ Certificate of service

(b) ❑ Supplemental documents

(1) ❑ Proposed order

(2) ❑ Notice of constitutional question

(c) ❑ Time for making motion

(1) ❑ A party may move to strike or the court may strike redundant, immaterial, impertinent, or scandalous matter from any pleading at any time

(2) ❑ If a pleading sets forth a claim for relief to which the adverse party is not required to serve a responsive pleading, the adverse party may assert any defense in law or fact to that claim for relief at the trial, except that the objection of failure to state a legal defense in an answer or reply shall be asserted by motion to strike the defense within twenty (20) days after service of the answer or reply

(3) ❑ If a party deems any pleading or part thereof filed by another party to be a sham, that party may move to strike the pleading or part thereof before the cause is set for trial

(4) ❑ A copy of any written motion which may not be heard ex parte and a copy of the notice of the hearing thereof shall be served a reasonable time before the time specified for the hearing

(II) ❑ Matters to be considered by opposing party

(a) ❑ Required documents

(1) ❑ Response to motion

(2) ❑ Certificate of service

(b) ❑ Supplemental documents

(1) ❑ Proposed order

(2) ❑ Notice of constitutional question

(c) ❑ Time for service and filing of opposition

(1) ❑ No time specified for responding to a motion

Motions, Oppositions and Replies
Motion for Leave to Amend

Document Last Updated January 2013

A. Applicable Rules

1. *State rules*

a. Rules of court. FL ST RCP Rule 1.010; FL ST J ADMIN Rule 2.110.

b. Nonverification of pleadings. FL ST RCP Rule 1.030.
c. Process. FL ST RCP Rule 1.070.
d. Service and filing of pleadings, orders, and documents. FL ST RCP Rule 1.080.
e. Time. FL ST RCP Rule 1.090.
f. Pleadings and motions. FL ST RCP Rule 1.100.
g. Defenses. FL ST RCP Rule 1.140.
h. Motions. FL ST RCP Rule 1.160.
i. Amended and supplemental pleadings. FL ST RCP Rule 1.190.
j. Relief from judgment, decrees, or orders. FL ST RCP Rule 1.540.
k. Mediation and arbitration. FL ST RCP Rule 1.700; FL ST RCP Rule 1.710; FL ST RCP Rule 1.720; FL ST RCP Rule 1.730; FL ST RCP Rule 1.750; FL ST RCP Rule 1.800; FL ST RCP Rule 1.810; FL ST RCP Rule 1.820; FL ST RCP Rule 1.830.
l. Forms. FL ST RCP Rule 1.900.
m. Minimization of the filing of sensitive information. FL ST J ADMIN Rule 2.425.
n. Retention of court records. FL ST J ADMIN Rule 2.430.
o. Foreign attorneys. FL ST J ADMIN Rule 2.510.
p. Signature of attorneys and parties. FL ST J ADMIN Rule 2.515.
q. Paper. FL ST J ADMIN Rule 2.520.
r. Electronic filing. FL ST J ADMIN Rule 2.525.
s. Accessibility of information and technology. FL ST J ADMIN Rule 2.526.
t. Communication equipment. FL ST J ADMIN Rule 2.530.
u. Court reporting. FL ST J ADMIN Rule 2.535.
v. Requests for accommodations by persons with disabilities. FL ST J ADMIN Rule 2.540.

2. *Local rules*
   a. General motion rule. FL ST 6 J CIR LOCAL Rule 5.
   b. Telephonic hearings in circuit civil, county civil and small claims cases. FL ST 6 J CIR PA/PI-CIR-88-48.
   c. Standards of professional courtesy. FL ST 6 J CIR 2009-066 PA/PI-CIR.
   d. Arbitration and mediation program circuit civil and family cases. FL ST 6 J CIR PA/PI-CIR-96-63; FL ST 6 J CIR 2011-006 PA/PI-CIR.
   e. Pre-trial conferences. FL ST 6 J CIR PA/PI-CIR-98-49.
   f. Uniform motion calendar civil division. FL ST 6 J CIR PINELLAS CIR CT PI-CIR-98-30.

B. Timing

1. *Amended pleadings as a matter of course.* A party may amend a pleading once as a matter of course at any time before a responsive pleading is served or, if the pleading is one to which no responsive pleading is permitted and the action has not been placed on the trial calendar, may amend it at any time within twenty (20) days after it is served. Otherwise a party may amend a pleading only by leave of court or by written consent of the adverse party. FL ST RCP Rule 1.190(a).
2. *Amended pleadings with leave of court.* Leave of court shall be given freely when justice so requires. FL ST RCP Rule 1.190(a). Under the Florida Rules of Civil Procedure, there is no time limit as to when an amendment with leave of court may be sought. Amendments of the pleadings may be permitted, with the court's discretion, at any stage of the proceedings in furtherance of justice. McSwiggan v. Edson, 186 So.2d 13, 15 (Fla. 1966); FL-PP § 2:153. Nevertheless, the liberality in permitting amendment of pleadings diminishes as the case progresses to trial. Versen v. Versen, 347 So.2d 1047, 1050 (Fla. 4th DCA 1977); FL-PP § 2:153.

3. *Claims for punitive damages.* A motion for leave to amend a pleading to assert a claim for punitive damages can be filed separately and before the supporting evidence or proffer, but each shall be served on all parties at least twenty (20) days before the hearing. FL ST RCP Rule 1.190(f).
4. *Post motion for leave to amend*
   a. If the court permits or requires an amended or responsive pleading or a more definite statement, the pleading or statement shall be served within ten (10) days after notice of the court's action. FL ST RCP Rule 1.140(a)(4).
   b. When a motion for leave to amend with the attached proposed amended complaint is filed, the one hundred twenty (120) day period for service of amended complaints on the new party or parties shall begin upon the entry of an order granting leave to amend. FL ST RCP Rule 1.070(j).
5. *General motion timing.* A copy of any written motion which may not be heard ex parte and a copy of the notice of the hearing thereof shall be served a reasonable time before the time specified for the hearing. FL ST RCP Rule 1.090(d).
   a. All motions, except motions in limine, shall be filed and heard prior to the pre-trial conference unless good cause exists why the motions were not heard prior to the pre-trial conference, including the inability to obtain hearing time prior to the pre-trial conference. FL ST 6 J CIR PA/PI-CIR-98-49(6).
   b. If such good cause exists, the court will hear such motions at the pre-trial conference or at a separate hearing following the pre-trial conference. FL ST 6 J CIR PA/PI-CIR-98-49(6).
6. *Computation of time*
   a. *Generally.* Computation of time shall be governed by FL ST J ADMIN Rule 2.514. FL ST RCP Rule 1.090(a). The following rules apply in computing time periods specified in any rule of procedure, local rule, court order, or statute that does not specify a method of computing time. FL ST J ADMIN Rule 2.514(a).
      i. *Period stated in days or a longer unit.* When the period is stated in days or a longer unit of time (A) exclude the day of the event that triggers the period; (B) count every day, including intermediate Saturdays, Sundays, and legal holidays; and (C) include the last day of the period, but if the last day is a Saturday, Sunday, or legal holiday, or falls within any period of time extended through an order of the chief justice under FL ST J ADMIN Rule 2.205(a)(2)(B)(iv), the period continues to run until the end of the next day that is not a Saturday, Sunday, or legal holiday and does not fall within any period of time extended through an order of the chief justice. FL ST J ADMIN Rule 2.514(a)(1).
      ii. *Period stated in hours.* When the period is stated in hours (A) begin counting immediately on the occurrence of the event that triggers the period; (B) count every hour, including hours during intermediate Saturdays, Sundays, and legal holidays; and (C) if the period would end on a Saturday, Sunday, or legal holiday, or during any period of time extended through an order of the chief justice under FL ST J ADMIN Rule 2.205(a)(2)(B)(iv), the period continues to run until the same time on the next day that is not a Saturday, Sunday, or legal holiday and does not fall within any period of time extended through an order of the chief justice. FL ST J ADMIN Rule 2.514(a)(2).
      iii. *Period stated in days less than seven (7) days.* When the period stated in days is less than seven (7) days, intermediate Saturdays, Sundays, and legal holidays shall be excluded in the computation. FL ST J ADMIN Rule 2.514(a)(3).
      iv. *"Last day" defined.* Unless a different time is set by a statute, local rule, or court order, the last day ends (A) for electronic filing or for service by any means, at midnight; and (B) for filing by other means, when the clerk's office is scheduled to close. FL ST J ADMIN Rule 2.514(a)(4).
      v. *"Next day" defined.* The "next day" is determined by continuing to count forward when the period is measured after an event and backward when measured before an event. FL ST J ADMIN Rule 2.514(a)(5).
      vi. *"Legal holiday" defined.* "Legal holiday" means (A) the day set aside by FL ST § 110.117, for observing New Year's Day, Martin Luther King, Jr.'s Birthday, Memorial Day, Independence

Day, Labor Day, Veterans' Day, Thanksgiving Day, the Friday after Thanksgiving Day, or Christmas Day, and (B) any day observed as a holiday by the clerk's office or as designated by the chief judge. FL ST J ADMIN Rule 2.514(a)(6).

b. *Additional time after service by mail or e-mail.* When a party may or must act within a specified time after service and service is made by mail or e-mail, five (5) days are added after the period that would otherwise expire under FL ST J ADMIN Rule 2.514(a). FL ST J ADMIN Rule 2.514(b).

c. *Enlargement.* When an act is required or allowed to be done at or within a specified time by order of court, by the Florida Rules of Civil Procedure, or by notice given thereunder, for cause shown the court at any time in its discretion (1) with or without notice, may order the period enlarged if request therefor is made before the expiration of the period originally prescribed or as extended by a previous order, or (2) upon motion made and notice after the expiration of the specified period, may permit the act to be done when failure to act was the result of excusable neglect, but it may not extend the time for making a motion for new trial, for rehearing, or to alter or amend a judgment; making a motion for relief from a judgment under FL ST RCP Rule 1.540(b); taking an appeal or filing a petition for certiorari; or making a motion for a directed verdict. FL ST RCP Rule 1.090(b).

d. *Unaffected by expiration of term.* The period of time provided for the doing of any act or the taking of any proceeding shall not be affected or limited by the continued existence or expiration of a term of court. The continued existence or expiration of a term of court in no way affects the power of a court to do any act or take any proceeding in any action which is or has been pending before it. FL ST RCP Rule 1.090(c).

C. General Requirements

1. *Motions generally*

a. *Contents.* An application to the court for an order shall be by motion which shall be made in writing unless made during a hearing or trial, shall state with particularity the grounds therefor, and shall set forth the relief or order sought. The requirement of writing is fulfilled if the motion is stated in a written notice of the hearing of the motion. All notices of hearing shall specify each motion or other matter to be heard. FL ST RCP Rule 1.100(b).

b. *Particularity requirement.* The court considers a motion in the light of the substantive law, rule or statute to make its determination. Some rules require a statement of the grounds for a motion under the rule. Failure to give the grounds will result in denial of the motion. This should be the result in all situations when the ground for the motion is not inherent in the rule. FL-PRACPROC § 9:3. The requirement is nevertheless an important one, first because of the due process notice rights of the respondent, as well as for the assistance it provides to the court in its preparation for the hearing or, absent a hearing, for disposition. 4 FLPRAC R 1.100.

c. *Standards of professional courtesy; Motion practice*

i. Attorneys will make every reasonable effort to resolve the issue before setting a motion for hearing. FL ST 6 J CIR 2009-066 PA/PI-CIR(G)(1).

ii. Attorneys will not force opposing counsel to make motions attorneys do not intend to oppose unless circumstances require or the client requires. FL ST 6 J CIR 2009-066 PA/PI-CIR(G)(2).

2. *Motion for leave to amend.* Although the Florida Rules of Civil Procedure do not specify a procedure for obtaining leave to amend, it is usually accomplished by way of a motion. FL-PP § 2:153. At any time in furtherance of justice, upon such terms as may be just, the court may permit any process, proceeding, pleading, or record to be amended or material supplemental matter to be set forth in an amended or supplemental pleading. At every stage of the action the court must disregard any error or defect in the proceedings which does not affect the substantial rights of the parties. FL ST RCP Rule 1.190(e).

a. *Permissible amendments.* Amendments can relate to the correction of mistakes, the insertion of jurisdictional averments, the correction or addition of verifications, the addition or substitution or striking out of parties, and generally the rectification of all formal defects in the pleading. The court can also allow amendments setting up an omitted counterclaim or cross-claim if the defendant failed to raise the claim through oversight, inadvertence, or excusable neglect. FL-PP § 2:151.

b. *Amendments to conform with the evidence.* When issues not raised by the pleadings are tried by express or implied consent of the parties, they shall be treated in all respects as if they had been raised in the pleadings. Such amendment of the pleadings as may be necessary to cause them to conform to the evidence and to raise these issues may be made upon motion of any party at any time, even after judgment, but failure so to amend shall not affect the result of the trial of these issues. If the evidence is objected to at the trial on the ground that it is not within the issues made by the pleadings, the court may allow the pleadings to be amended to conform with the evidence and shall do so freely when the merits of the cause are more effectually presented thereby and the objecting party fails to satisfy the court that the admission of such evidence will prejudice the objecting party in maintaining an action or defense upon the merits. FL ST RCP Rule 1.190(b).

i. The courts have been extremely liberal in permitting amendments after trial to conform pleadings to the evidence where the issues were tried by the express or implied consent of the parties. Turner v. Long, 225 So.2d 434 (Fla. 1st DCA 1969); FL-PP § 2:152.

c. *Procedure for adding parties.* Parties may be added once as a matter of course within the same time that pleadings can be so amended. If amendment by leave of court or stipulation of the parties is permitted, parties may be added in the amended pleading without further order of court. Parties may be added by order of court on its own initiative or on motion of any party at any stage of the action and on such terms as are just. FL ST RCP Rule 1.250(c).

d. *Claims for punitive damages.* A motion for leave to amend a pleading to assert a claim for punitive damages shall make a reasonable showing by evidence in the record or evidence to be proffered by the claimant that provides a reasonable basis for recovery of such damages. The motion to amend can be filed separately and before the supporting evidence or proffer, but each shall be served on all parties at least twenty (20) days before the hearing. FL ST RCP Rule 1.190(f). Leave of court to amend the complaint must be obtained before a plaintiff may assert a punitive damages claim in the complaint. Failure to do so will result in the claims being dismissed or stricken. FL-PP § 2:151.

e. *Relation back of amendments.* When the claim or defense asserted in the amended pleading arose out of the conduct, transaction, or occurrence set forth or attempted to be set forth in the original pleading, the amendment shall relate back to the date of the original pleading. FL ST RCP Rule 1.190(c).

i. The doctrine of relation back becomes critical in applying the statute of limitations. For example, it has been held that the doctrine of relation back may not be utilized to circumvent the statute of limitations to permit an amendment where a claim could have been filed as an independent action but was not timely asserted and would otherwise be barred under the statute of limitations. Cox v. Seaboard Coast Line R. Co., 360 So.2d 8 (Fla. 2d DCA 1978); FL-PP § 2:152.

3. *Arbitration and mediation*

a. *Referral to arbitration and mediation.* Except as hereinafter provided or as otherwise prohibited by law, the presiding judge may enter an order referring all or any part of a contested civil matter to mediation or arbitration. The parties to any contested civil matter may file a written stipulation to mediate or arbitrate any issue between them at any time. Such stipulation shall be incorporated into the order of referral. FL ST RCP Rule 1.700(a).

b. *Arbitration*

i. *Exclusions.* A civil action shall be ordered to arbitration or arbitration in conjunction with mediation upon stipulation of the parties. A civil action may be ordered to arbitration or arbitration in conjunction with mediation upon motion of any party or by the court, if the judge determines the action to be of such a nature that arbitration could be of benefit to the litigants or the court. FL ST RCP Rule 1.800.

- Under no circumstances may the following categories of actions be referred to arbitration: (1) bond estreatures; (2) habeas corpus or other extraordinary writs; (3) bond validations; (4) civil or criminal contempt; (5) such other matters as may be specified by order of the chief judge in the circuit. FL ST RCP Rule 1.800.

ii. For more information regarding arbitration, please see FL ST RCP Rule 1.810; FL ST RCP Rule 1.820; FL ST RCP Rule 1.830.

c. *Mediation.* For more information regarding mediation, please see FL ST RCP Rule 1.710; FL ST RCP Rule 1.720; FL ST RCP Rule 1.730; and FL ST RCP Rule 1.750.

d. See FL ST 6 J CIR PA/PI-CIR-96-63 for more information about the Arbitration and Mediation Program for Florida's Sixth Judicial Circuit.

4. *Rules of court*

a. *Rules of civil procedure.* The Florida Rules of Civil Procedure apply to all actions of a civil nature and all special statutory proceedings in the circuit courts and county courts except those to which the Florida Probate Rules, the Florida Family Law Rules of Procedure, or the Small Claims Rules apply. FL ST RCP Rule 1.010.

i. The form, content, procedure, and time for pleading in all special statutory proceedings shall be as prescribed by the statutes governing the proceeding unless the Florida Rules of Civil Procedure specifically provide to the contrary. FL ST RCP Rule 1.010.

ii. The Florida Rules of Civil Procedure shall be construed to secure the just, speedy, and inexpensive determination of every action. FL ST RCP Rule 1.010.

b. *Rules of judicial administration.* The Florida Rules of Judicial Administration shall apply to administrative matters in all courts to which the Florida Rules of Judicial Administration are applicable by their terms. The Florida Rules of Judicial Administration shall be construed to secure the speedy and inexpensive determination of every proceeding to which they are applicable. The Florida Rules of Judicial Administration shall supersede all conflicting rules and statutes. FL ST J ADMIN Rule 2.110.

5. *Settlement and alternative dispute resolution.* When a matter is scheduled for hearing and the matter is resolved by agreement or settlement, the party setting the matter for hearing shall notify the court. When a matter is scheduled for trial and the case settles, the plaintiff shall notify the court. Permission of the court must be obtained in order to cancel a trial. FL ST 6 J CIR LOCAL Rule 5(A).

a. Unless there are strong and overriding issues of principle, attorneys will raise and explore the issue of settlement as soon as enough is known to make settlement discussions meaningful. FL ST 6 J CIR 2009-066 PA/PI-CIR(I)(1).

b. Attorneys will not falsely hold out the possibility of settlement to adjourn discovery or delay trial. FL ST 6 J CIR 2009-066 PA/PI-CIR(I)(2).

c. Attorneys will consider whether the client's interest could be adequately served and the controversy more expeditiously and economically disposed of by arbitration, mediation or other forms of alternative dispute resolution. FL ST 6 J CIR 2009-066 PA/PI-CIR(I)(3).

D. Documents

1. *Required documents*

a. *Notice of hearing/Motion.* An application to the court for an order shall be by motion which shall be made in writing unless made during a hearing or trial, shall state with particularity the grounds therefor, and shall set forth the relief or order sought. The requirement of writing is fulfilled if the motion is stated in a written notice of the hearing of the motion. All notices of hearing shall specify each motion or other matter to be heard. FL ST RCP Rule 1.100(b).

i. *Notices to persons with disabilities.* See the Format section of this KeyRules document for further information.

b. *Proposed amended pleading.* The moving party shall attach the proposed amended pleading to the motion. FL ST RCP Rule 1.190(a).

c. *Certificate of service.* When any attorney certifies in substance: "I certify that a copy hereof has been furnished to (here insert name or names and addresses used for service) by (e-mail) (delivery) (mail) (fax) on .... (date) ....________________ Attorney" the certificate is taken as prima facie proof of such service in compliance with FL ST J ADMIN Rule 2.516. FL ST J ADMIN Rule 2.516(f).

2. *Supplemental documents*

a. *Proposed order.* The court may require that orders or judgments be prepared by a party, may require

the party to furnish the court with stamped, addressed envelopes for service of the order or judgment, and may require that proposed orders and judgments be furnished to all parties before entry by the court of the order or judgment. FL ST J ADMIN Rule 2.516(h)(1).

i. After a hearing, attorneys will make a good faith effort to quickly agree or disagree upon a proposed order and submit the result to the court. Unless otherwise instructed by the court, or agreed to by counsel, all proposed orders shall be provided to other counsel for approval or comment prior to submission to the court. Attorneys will not submit controverted orders to the court with a copy to opposing counsel for "objections within ______ days". Courts prefer to know that the order is either agreed upon or opposed. FL ST 6 J CIR 2009-066 PA/PI-CIR(G)(3).

ii. Attorneys will not use post-hearing submissions of proposed orders as a guise to reargue the merits of the matter. FL ST 6 J CIR 2009-066 PA/PI-CIR(G)(4).

b. *Notice of constitutional question.* A party that files a pleading, written motion, or other paper drawing into question the constitutionality of a state statute or a county or municipal charter, ordinance, or franchise must promptly (1) file a notice of constitutional question stating the question and identifying the paper that raises it; and (2) serve the notice and the pleading, written motion, or other paper drawing into question the constitutionality of a state statute or a county or municipal charter, ordinance, or franchise on the Attorney General or the state attorney of the judicial circuit in which the action is pending, by either certified or registered mail. Service of the notice and pleading, written motion, or other paper does not require joinder of the Attorney General or the state attorney as a party to the action. FL ST RCP Rule 1.071.

E. Format

1. *Documents; Type and size.* Documents subject to the exceptions set forth in FL ST J ADMIN Rule 2.525(d) shall be filed on recycled paper measuring eight and one half by eleven (8 1/2 by 11) inches. For purposes of FL ST J ADMIN Rule 2.520, paper is recycled if it contains a minimum content of fifty (50) percent waste paper. Xerographic reduction of legal-size (eight and one half by fourteen (8 1/2 by 14) inches) documents to letter size (eight and one half by eleven (8 1/2 by 11) inches) is prohibited. All other documents filed by electronic transmission shall be filed in a format capable of being printed in a format consistent with the provisions of FL ST J ADMIN Rule 2.250. FL ST J ADMIN Rule 2.520(b).

a. *Exhibits.* Any exhibit or attachment filed with pleadings or papers may be filed in its original size. FL ST J ADMIN Rule 2.520(c).

b. *Recording space.* On all papers and documents prepared and filed by the court or by any party to a proceeding which are to be recorded in the public records of any county, including but not limited to final money judgments and notices of lis pendens, a three (3) inch by three (3) inch space at the top right-hand corner on the first page and a one (1) inch by three (3) inch space at the top right-hand corner on each subsequent page shall be left blank and reserved for use by the clerk of court. FL ST J ADMIN Rule 2.520(d).

i. *Exceptions to recording space.* Any papers or documents created by persons or entities over which the filing party has no control, including but not limited to wills, codicils, trusts, or other testamentary documents; documents prepared or executed by any public officer; documents prepared, executed, acknowledged, or proved outside of the State of Florida; or documents created by State or Federal government agencies, may be filed without the space required by FL ST J ADMIN Rule 2.520. FL ST J ADMIN Rule 2.520(e).

c. *Noncompliance.* No clerk of court is permitted to refuse to file any document or paper because of noncompliance with the Florida Rules of Judicial Administration. However, upon request of the clerk of court, noncomplying documents must be resubmitted in accordance with the formatting rules. FL ST J ADMIN Rule 2.520(f).

2. *Caption.* Every pleading, motion, order, judgment, or other paper shall have a caption containing the name of the court, the file number, and except for in rem proceedings, including forfeiture proceedings, the name of the first party on each side with an appropriate indication of other parties, and a designation identifying the party filing it and its nature or the nature of the order, as the case may be. In any in rem

proceeding, every pleading, motion, order, judgment, or other paper shall have a caption containing the name of the court, the file number, the style "In re" (followed by the name or general description of the property), and a designation of the person or entity filing it and its nature or the nature of the order, as the case may be. In an in rem forfeiture proceeding, the style shall be "In re forfeiture of" (followed by the name of the general description of the property). All papers filed in the action shall be styled in such a manner as to indicate clearly the subject matter of the paper and the party requesting or obtaining relief. FL ST RCP Rule 1.100(c)(1).

3. *Writing and written defined.* Writing or written means a document containing information, an application, or a stipulation. FL ST RCP Rule 1.080(c).
4. *Rule abbreviations*
   a. The Florida Rules of Civil Procedure and shall be abbreviated as Fla.R.Civ.P. FL ST RCP Rule 1.010.
   b. The Florida Rules of Judicial Administration shall be abbreviated as Fla. R. Jud. Admin. FL ST J ADMIN Rule 2.110.
5. *Nonverification.* Except when otherwise specifically provided by the Florida Rules of Civil Procedure or an applicable statute, every pleading or other document of a party represented by an attorney need not be verified or accompanied by an affidavit. FL ST RCP Rule 1.030; FL ST J ADMIN Rule 2.515(a).
6. *Attorney signature*
   a. *Attorney signature.* Every pleading and other document of a party represented by an attorney shall be signed by at least one (1) attorney of record in that attorney's individual name whose current record Florida Bar address, telephone number, including area code, primary e-mail address and secondary e-mail addresses, if any, and Florida Bar number shall be stated, and who shall be duly licensed to practice law in Florida or who shall have received permission to appear in the particular case as provided in FL ST J ADMIN Rule 2.510. FL ST J ADMIN Rule 2.515(a).
      i. The attorney may be required by the court to give the address of, and to vouch for the attorney's authority to represent, the party. FL ST J ADMIN Rule 2.515(a).
      ii. The signature of an attorney shall constitute a certificate by the attorney that the attorney has read the pleading or other document; that to the best of the attorney's knowledge, information, and belief there is good ground to support it; and that it is not interposed for delay. FL ST J ADMIN Rule 2.515(a).
      iii. If a pleading is not signed or is signed with intent to defeat the purpose of FL ST J ADMIN Rule 2.515, it may be stricken and the action may proceed as though the pleading or other document had not been served. FL ST J ADMIN Rule 2.515(a).
   b. *Pro se litigant signature.* A party who is not represented by an attorney shall sign any pleading or other paper and state the party's address and telephone number, including area code. FL ST J ADMIN Rule 2.515(b).
   c. *Form of signature*
      i. The signatures required on pleadings and documents by FL ST J ADMIN Rule 2.515(a) and FL ST J ADMIN Rule 2.515(b) may be:
         - Original signatures;
         - Original signatures that have been reproduced by electronic means, such as on electronically transmitted documents or photocopied documents;
         - Electronic signatures using the "/s/," "s/," or "/s" formats by or at the direction of the person signing; or
         - Any other signature format authorized by general law, so long as the clerk where the proceeding is pending has the capability of receiving and has obtained approval from the Supreme Court of Florida to accept pleadings and documents with that signature format. FL ST J ADMIN Rule 2.515(c)(1).
      ii. An attorney, party, or other person who files a pleading or paper by electronic transmission that

does not contain the original signature of that attorney, party, or other person shall file that identical pleading or paper in paper form containing an original signature of that attorney, party, or other person (hereinafter called the follow-up filing) immediately thereafter. The follow-up filing is not required if the Supreme Court of Florida has entered an order directing the clerk of court to discontinue accepting the follow-up filing. FL ST J ADMIN Rule 2.515(c)(2).

7. *Forms*
   a. *Process.* The forms of process, notice of lis pendens, and notice of action provided in the Florida Rules of Civil Procedure are sufficient. Variations from the forms do not void process or notices that are otherwise sufficient. FL ST RCP Rule 1.900(a).
   b. *Other forms.* The other forms provided in the Florida Rules of Civil Procedure are sufficient for the matters that are covered by them. So long as the substance is expressed without prolixity, the forms may be varied to meet the facts of a particular case. FL ST RCP Rule 1.900(b).
   c. *Formal matters.* Captions, except for the designation of the paper, are omitted from the forms provided in the Florida Rules of Civil Procedure. A general form of caption is the first form provided. Signatures are omitted from pleadings and motions. FL ST RCP Rule 1.900(c).
8. *Notices to persons with disabilities.* All notices of court proceedings to be held in a public facility, and all process compelling appearance at such proceedings, shall include the following statement in bold face, fourteen (14) point Times New Roman or Courier font: "If you are a person with a disability who needs any accommodation in order to participate in this proceeding, you are entitled, at no cost to you, to the provision of certain assistance. Please contact [identify applicable court personnel by name, address, and telephone number] at least seven (7) days before your scheduled court appearance, or immediately upon receiving this notification if the time before the scheduled appearance is less than seven (7) days; if you are hearing or voice impaired, call 711." FL ST J ADMIN Rule 2.540(c)(1).
9. *Minimization of the filing of sensitive information*
   a. *Limitations for court filings.* Unless authorized by FL ST J ADMIN Rule 2.425(b), statute, another rule of court, or the court orders otherwise, designated sensitive information filed with the court must be limited to the following format:
      i. The initials of a person known to be a minor;
      ii. The year of birth of a person's birth date;
      iii. No portion of any: Social security number, Bank account number, Credit card account number, Charge account number, or Debit account number;
      iv. The last four digits of any: Taxpayer identification number (TIN), Employee identification number, Driver's license number, Passport number, Telephone number, Financial account number, except as set forth in FL ST J ADMIN Rule 2.425(a)(3), Brokerage account number, Insurance policy account number, Loan account number, Customer account number, or Patient or health care number;
      v. A truncated version of any: Email address, Computer user name, Password, or Personal identification number (PIN); and
      vi. A truncated version of any other sensitive information as provided by court order. FL ST J ADMIN Rule 2.425(a).
   b. *Exceptions.* FL ST J ADMIN Rule 2.425(a) does not apply to the following:
      i. An account number which identifies the property alleged to be the subject of a proceeding;
      ii. The record of an administrative or agency proceeding;
      iii. The record in appellate or review proceedings;
      iv. The birth date of a minor whenever the birth date is necessary for the court to establish or maintain subject matter jurisdiction;
      v. The name of a minor in any order relating to parental responsibility, time-sharing, or child support;

vi. The name of a minor in any document or order affecting the minor's ownership of real property;

vii. The birth date of a party in a writ of attachment or notice to payor;

viii. In traffic and criminal proceedings: a pro se filing; a court filing that is related to a criminal matter or investigation and that is prepared before the filing of a criminal charge or is not filed as part of any docketed criminal case; an arrest or search warrant or any information in support thereof; a charging document and an affidavit or other documents filed in support of any charging document, including any driving records; a statement of particulars; discovery material introduced into evidence or otherwise filed with the court; and all information necessary for the proper issuance and execution of a subpoena duces tecum;

ix. Information used by the clerk for case maintenance purposes or the courts for case management purposes; and

x. Information which is relevant and material to an issue before the court. FL ST J ADMIN Rule 2.425(b).

c. *Remedies.* Upon motion by a party or interested person or sua sponte by the court, the court may order remedies, sanctions or both for a violation of FL ST J ADMIN Rule 2.425(a). Following notice and an opportunity to respond, the court may impose sanctions if such filing was not made in good faith. FL ST J ADMIN Rule 2.425(c).

d. *Motions not restricted.* FL ST J ADMIN Rule 2.425 does not restrict a party's right to move for protective order, to move to file documents under seal, or to request a determination of the confidentiality of records. FL ST J ADMIN Rule 2.425(d).

e. *Application.* FL ST J ADMIN Rule 2.425 does not affect the application of constitutional provisions, statutes, or rules of court regarding confidential information or access to public information. FL ST J ADMIN Rule 2.425(e).

F. Filing and Service Requirements

1. *Filing requirements.* All original documents must be filed with the court either before service or immediately thereafter, unless otherwise provided for by general law or other rules. If the original of any bond or other document is not placed in the court file, a certified copy must be so placed by the clerk. FL ST J ADMIN Rule 2.516(d). All documents shall be filed in conformity with the requirements of FL ST J ADMIN Rule 2.525. FL ST RCP Rule 1.080(b). All documents filed in any court shall be filed by electronic transmission in accordance with FL ST J ADMIN Rule 2.525. "Documents" means pleadings, motions, petitions, memoranda, briefs, notices, exhibits, declarations, affidavits, orders, judgments, decrees, writs, opinions, and any other paper or writing submitted to a court. FL ST J ADMIN Rule 2.520(a). All documents that are court records, as defined in FL ST J ADMIN Rule 2.430(a)(1), must be filed by electronic transmission, provided that: (1) the clerk has the ability to accept and retain such documents; (2) the clerk or the chief judge of the circuit has requested permission to accept documents filed by electronic transmission; and (3) the supreme court has entered an order granting permission to the clerk to accept documents filed by electronic transmission. FL ST J ADMIN Rule 2.525(c)(1).

a. *Definition.* "Electronic transmission of documents" means the sending of information by electronic signals to, by or from a court or clerk, which when received can be transformed and stored or transmitted on paper, microfilm, magnetic storage device, optical imaging system, CD-ROM, flash drive, other electronic data storage system, server, case maintenance system ("CM"), electronic court filing ("ECF") system, statewide or local electronic portal ("e-portal"), or other electronic record keeping system authorized by the supreme court in a format sufficient to communicate the information on the original document in a readable format. Electronic transmission of documents includes electronic mail ("e-mail") and any internet-based transmission procedure, and may include procedures allowing for documents to be signed or verified by electronic means. FL ST J ADMIN Rule 2.525(a).

i. The filing of documents with the court as required by the Florida Rules of Judicial Administration must be made by filing them with the clerk in accordance with FL ST J ADMIN Rule 2.525, except that the judge may permit documents to be filed with the judge, in which event the judge must note the filing date before him or her on the documents and transmit them to the

clerk. The date of filing is that shown on the face of the document by the judge's notation or the clerk's time stamp, whichever is earlier. FL ST J ADMIN Rule 2.516(e).

b. *Application.* Any court or clerk of the court may accept the electronic transmission of documents for filing after the clerk, together with input from the chief judge of the circuit, has obtained approval of the procedures and program for doing so from the Supreme Court of Florida. FL ST J ADMIN Rule 2.525(b).

c. *Exceptions*

   i. Paper documents and other submissions may be manually submitted to the clerk or court:

      - When the clerk does not have the ability to accept and retain documents by electronic filing or has not had ECF Procedures approved by the supreme court;
      - For filing by any self-represented party or any self-represented nonparty unless specific ECF Procedures provide a means to file documents electronically. However, any self-represented nonparty that is a governmental or public agency and any other agency, partnership, corporation, or business entity acting on behalf of any governmental or public agency may file documents by electronic transmission if such entity has the capability of filing documents electronically;
      - For filing by attorneys excused from e-mail service in accordance with FL ST J ADMIN Rule 2.516(b);
      - When submitting evidentiary exhibits or filing non-documentary materials;
      - When the filing involves documents in excess of twenty-five (25) megabytes (25MB) in size. For such filings, documents may be transmitted using an electronic storage medium that the clerk has the ability to accept, which may include a CD-ROM, flash drive, or similar storage medium;
      - When filed in open court, as permitted by the court;
      - When paper filing is permitted by any approved statewide or local ECF procedures; and
      - If any court determines that justice so requires. FL ST J ADMIN Rule 2.525(d).

   ii. Any document in paper form submitted under FL ST J ADMIN Rule 2.525(d) is filed when it is received by the clerk or court and the clerk shall immediately thereafter convert any filed paper document to an electronic document. "Convert to an electronic document" means optically capturing an image of a paper document and using character recognition software to recover as much of the document's text as practicable and then indexing and storing the document in the official court file. FL ST J ADMIN Rule 2.525(c)(4).

   iii. Any storage medium submitted under FL ST J ADMIN Rule 2.525(d)(5) is filed when received by the clerk or court and the clerk shall immediately thereafter transfer the electronic documents from the storage device to the official court file. FL ST J ADMIN Rule 2.525(c)(5).

   iv. If the filer of any paper document authorized under FL ST J ADMIN Rule 2.525(d) provides a self-addressed, postage-paid envelope for return of the paper document after it is converted to electronic form by the clerk, the clerk shall place the paper document in the envelope and deposit it in the mail. Except when a paper document is required to be maintained, the clerk may recycle any filed paper document that is not to be returned to the filer. FL ST J ADMIN Rule 2.525(c)(6).

   v. The clerk may convert any paper document filed before the effective date of FL ST J ADMIN Rule 2.525 to an electronic document. Unless the clerk is required to maintain the paper document, if the paper document has been converted to an electronic document by the clerk, the paper document is no longer part of the official court file and may be removed and recycled. FL ST J ADMIN Rule 2.525(c)(7).

d. *Official court file.* For information on what constitutes the official court file, please see FL ST J ADMIN Rule 2.525(c)(2), FL ST J ADMIN Rule 2.525(c)(3).

e. *Administration.* All attorneys, parties, or other persons using this rule to file documents are required to make arrangements with the court or clerk for the payment of any charges authorized by general law or the supreme court before filing any document by electronic transmission. FL ST J ADMIN Rule 2.525(f)(2).

f. *Filing date.* The filing date for an electronically transmitted document is the date and time that such filing is acknowledged by an electronic stamp or otherwise, pursuant to any procedure set forth in any ECF Procedures approved by the supreme court, or the date the last page of such filing is received by the court or clerk. FL ST J ADMIN Rule 2.525(f)(3).

g. *Accessibility.* All documents transmitted in any electronic form under FL ST J ADMIN Rule 2.525 must comply with the accessibility requirements of FL ST J ADMIN Rule 2.526. FL ST J ADMIN Rule 2.525(g).

2. *Service requirements.* Every pleading subsequent to the initial pleading, all orders, and every other document filed in the action must be served in conformity with the requirements of FL ST J ADMIN Rule 2.516. FL ST RCP Rule 1.080(a).

a. *Service; When required.* Unless the court otherwise orders, or a statute or supreme court administrative order specifies a different means of service, every pleading subsequent to the initial pleading and every other document filed in any court proceeding, except applications for witness subpoenas and documents served by formal notice or required to be served in the manner provided for service of formal notice, must be served in accordance with FL ST J ADMIN Rule 2.516 on each party. No service need be made on parties against whom a default has been entered, except that pleadings asserting new or additional claims against them must be served in the manner provided for service of summons. FL ST J ADMIN Rule 2.516(a).

b. *Service; How made.* When service is required or permitted to be made upon a party represented by an attorney, service must be made upon the attorney unless service upon the party is ordered by the court. FL ST J ADMIN Rule 2.516(b).

i. *Service by electronic mail ("e-mail").* All documents required or permitted to be served on another party must be served by e-mail, unless FL ST J ADMIN Rule 2.516 otherwise provides. When, in addition to service by e-mail, the sender also utilizes another means of service provided for in FL ST J ADMIN Rule 2.516(b)(2), any differing time limits and other provisions applicable to that other means of service control. FL ST J ADMIN Rule 2.516(b)(1). Any document electronically transmitted to a court or clerk must also be served on all parties and interested persons in accordance with the applicable rules of court. FL ST J ADMIN Rule 2.525(e)(2).

- *Service on attorneys.* Upon appearing in a proceeding, an attorney must serve a designation of a primary e-mail address and may designate no more than two (2) secondary e-mail addresses. Thereafter, service must be directed to all designated e-mail addresses in that proceeding. Every document filed by an attorney thereafter must include the primary e-mail address of that attorney and any secondary e-mail addresses. If an attorney does not designate any e-mail address for service, documents may be served on that attorney at the e-mail address on record with The Florida Bar. FL ST J ADMIN Rule 2.516(b)(1)(A).

- *Exception to e-mail service on attorneys.* Service by an attorney on another attorney must be made by e-mail unless excused by the court. Upon motion by an attorney demonstrating that the attorney has no e-mail account and lacks access to the Internet at the attorney's office, the court may excuse the attorney from the requirements of e-mail service. Service on and by an attorney excused by the court from e-mail service must be by the means provided in FL ST J ADMIN Rule 2.516(b)(2). FL ST J ADMIN Rule 2.516(b)(1)(B).

- *Service on and by parties not represented by an attorney.* Any party not represented by an attorney may serve a designation of a primary e-mail address and also may designate no more than two (2) secondary e-mail addresses to which service must be directed in that proceeding by the means provided in FL ST J ADMIN Rule 2.516(b)(1). If a party not represented by an attorney does not designate an e-mail address for service in a proceeding, service on and by that party must be by the means provided in FL ST J ADMIN Rule 2.516(b)(2). FL ST J ADMIN Rule 2.516(b)(1)(C).

- *Time of service.* Service by e-mail is complete when it is sent. FL ST J ADMIN Rule 2.516(b)(1)(D). An e-mail is deemed served on the date it is sent. FL ST J ADMIN Rule 2.516(b)(1)(D)(i). If the sender learns that the e-mail did not reach the address of the person to be served, the sender must immediately send another copy by e-mail, or by a means authorized by FL ST J ADMIN Rule 2.516(b)(2). FL ST J ADMIN Rule 2.516(b)(1)(D)(ii). E-mail service is treated as service by mail for the computation of time. FL ST J ADMIN Rule 2.516(b)(1)(D)(iii).

ii. *Format of e-mail for service.* Service of a document by e-mail is made by attaching a copy of the document in PDF format to an e-mail sent to all addresses designated by the attorney or party. FL ST J ADMIN Rule 2.516(b)(1)(E).

- All documents served by e-mail must be attached to an e-mail message containing a subject line beginning with the words "SERVICE OF COURT DOCUMENT" in all capital letters, followed by the case number of the proceeding in which the documents are being served. FL ST J ADMIN Rule 2.516(b)(1)(E)(i).
- The body of the e-mail must identify the court in which the proceeding is pending, the case number, the name of the initial party on each side, the title of each document served with that e-mail, and the sender's name and telephone number. FL ST J ADMIN Rule 2.516(b)(1)(E)(ii).
- Any document served by e-mail may be signed by the "/s/" format, as long as the filed original is signed in accordance with the applicable rule of procedure. FL ST J ADMIN Rule 2.516(b)(1)(E)(iii).
- Any e-mail which, together with its attached documents, exceeds five megabytes (5MB) in size, must be divided and sent as separate e-mails, no one of which may exceed five megabytes (5MB) in size and each of which must be sequentially numbered in the subject line. FL ST J ADMIN Rule 2.516(b)(1)(E)(iv).

iii. *Service by other means.* In addition to, and not in lieu of, service by e-mail, service may also be made upon attorneys by any of the means specified in FL ST J ADMIN Rule 2.516(b)(2). Service on and by all parties who are not represented by an attorney and who do not designate an e-mail address, and on and by all attorneys excused from e-mail service, must be made by delivering a copy of the document or by mailing it to the party or attorney at their last known address or, if no address is known, by leaving it with the clerk of the court. Service by mail is complete upon mailing. Delivery of a copy within FL ST J ADMIN Rule 2.516 is complete upon:

- Handing it to the attorney or to the party,
- Leaving it at the attorney's or party's office with a clerk or other person in charge thereof,
- If there is no one in charge, leaving it in a conspicuous place therein,
- If the office is closed or the person to be served has no office, leaving it at the person's usual place of abode with some person of his or her family above fifteen (15) years of age and informing such person of the contents, or
- Transmitting it by facsimile to the attorney's or party's office with a cover sheet containing the sender's name, firm, address, telephone number, and facsimile number, and the number of pages transmitted. When service is made by facsimile, a copy must also be served by any other method permitted by FL ST J ADMIN Rule 2.516. Facsimile service occurs when transmission is complete. FL ST J ADMIN Rule 2.516(b)(2)(A) through FL ST J ADMIN Rule 2.516(b)(2)(E).
- Service by delivery after 5:00 p.m. must be deemed to have been made by mailing on the date of delivery. FL ST J ADMIN Rule 2.516(b)(2)(F).

c. *Service; Numerous defendants.* In actions when the parties are unusually numerous, the court may regulate the service contemplated by the Florida Rules of Judicial Administration on motion or on its own initiative in such manner as may be found to be just and reasonable. FL ST J ADMIN Rule 2.516(c).

d. *Service by clerk.* Service of notices and other documents required to be made by the clerk must also be done as provided in FL ST J ADMIN Rule 2.516(b). FL ST J ADMIN Rule 2.516(g).

e. *Standards of professional courtesy; Service*

i. The timing and manner of service should not be used to the disadvantage of the party receiving the papers. This includes the use of facsimile transmissions and any additional expedited means of communication approved by the court. FL ST 6 J CIR 2009-066 PA/PI-CIR(C)(1).

ii. Attorneys will not serve papers to take advantage of opposing counsel's known absence from the office or at a time or in a manner designed to inconvenience an opponent, such as late on Friday afternoon or the day preceding a secular or religious holiday. FL ST 6 J CIR 2009-066 PA/PI-CIR(C)(2).

iii. Attorneys will not serve papers, including briefs and memoranda, so close to a court appearance that the ability of opposing counsel to prepare for that appearance or, where permitted, to respond, is inhibited. FL ST 6 J CIR 2009-066 PA/PI-CIR(C)(3).

iv. Service should be made personally or by facsimile transmission when it is likely that service by mail, even when allowed, will prejudice the opposing party. FL ST 6 J CIR 2009-066 PA/PI-CIR(C)(4).

G. Hearings

1. *Communication equipment*

a. *Definition.* Communication equipment means a conference telephone or other electronic device that permits all those appearing or participating to hear and speak to each other, provided that all conversation of all parties is audible to all persons present. FL ST J ADMIN Rule 2.530(a).

b. *Use by all parties.* A county or circuit court judge may, upon the court's own motion or upon the written request of a party, direct that communication equipment be used for a motion hearing, pretrial conference, or a status conference. A judge must give notice to the parties and consider any objections they may have to the use of communication equipment before directing that communication equipment be used. The decision to use communication equipment over the objection of parties will be in the sound discretion of the trial court, except as noted below. FL ST J ADMIN Rule 2.530(b).

c. *Use only by requesting party.* A county or circuit court judge may, upon the written request of a party upon reasonable notice to all other parties, permit a requesting party to participate through communication equipment in a scheduled motion hearing; however, any such request (except in criminal, juvenile, and appellate proceedings) must be granted, absent a showing of good cause to deny the same, where the hearing is set for not longer than fifteen (15) minutes. FL ST J ADMIN Rule 2.530(c).

d. *Testimony*

i. *Generally.* A county or circuit court judge, general magistrate, special magistrate, or hearing officer may allow testimony to be taken through communication equipment if all parties consent or if permitted by another applicable rule of procedure. FL ST J ADMIN Rule 2.530(d)(1).

ii. *Procedure.* Any party desiring to present testimony through communication equipment shall, prior to the hearing or trial at which the testimony is to be presented, contact all parties to determine whether each party consents to this form of testimony. The party seeking to present the testimony shall move for permission to present testimony through communication equipment, which motion shall set forth good cause as to why the testimony should be allowed in this form. FL ST J ADMIN Rule 2.530(d)(2).

iii. *Oath.* Testimony may be taken through communication equipment only if a notary public or other person authorized to administer oaths in the witness's jurisdiction is present with the witness and administers the oath consistent with the laws of the jurisdiction. FL ST J ADMIN Rule 2.530(d)(3).

iv. *Confrontation rights.* In juvenile and criminal proceedings the defendant must make an informed waiver of any confrontation rights that may be abridged by the use of communication equipment. FL ST J ADMIN Rule 2.530(d)(4).

v. *Video testimony.* If the testimony to be presented utilizes video conferencing or comparable two-way visual capabilities, the court in its discretion may modify the procedures set forth in FL ST J ADMIN Rule 2.530 to accommodate the technology utilized. FL ST J ADMIN Rule 2.530(d)(5).

e. *Burden of expense.* The cost for the use of the communication equipment is the responsibility of the requesting party unless otherwise directed by the court. FL ST J ADMIN Rule 2.530(e).

2. *Standards of professional courtesy; Scheduling*

a. Attorneys will communicate with opposing counsel to schedule depositions, hearings, and other proceedings, at times mutually convenient for all interested persons. FL ST 6 J CIR 2009-066 PA/PI-CIR(B)(1).

b. Attorneys will provide opposing counsel and other affected persons reasonable notice of all proceedings except upon agreement of counsel when expedited scheduling is necessary. Attorneys will immediately notify opposing counsel of any hearing time reserved. FL ST 6 J CIR 2009-066 PA/PI-CIR(B)(2).

c. Attorneys will request enough time for hearings and adjudicative proceedings to permit full and fair presentation of the matter and to permit response by opposing counsel. When scheduling depositions, Attorneys will schedule enough time to permit the conclusion of the deposition, including examination by all parties, without adjournment. FL ST 6 J CIR 2009-066 PA/PI-CIR(B)(3).

d. Attorneys will call potential scheduling problems to the attention of those affected, including the court, as soon as they become apparent. Attorneys will avoid last minute cancellations. FL ST 6 J CIR 2009-066 PA/PI-CIR(B)(4).

e. Attorneys will make request for changes only when necessary. Attorneys will not request rescheduling, cancellations, extension or postponements solely for the purpose of delay or obtaining unfair advantage. FL ST 6 J CIR 2009-066 PA/PI-CIR(B)(5).

f. Attorneys will cooperate with opposing counsel when conflicts and calendar changes are necessary and requested. FL ST 6 J CIR 2009-066 PA/PI-CIR(B)(6).

g. Attorneys will grant reasonable requests for scheduling, rescheduling, cancellations, extensions, and postponements that do not prejudice our client's opportunity for full, fair and prompt consideration and adjudication of the client's claim or defense. FL ST 6 J CIR 2009-066 PA/PI-CIR(B)(7).

h. First requests for reasonable extensions of time to respond to litigation deadlines relating to pleadings, discovery, or motions, should be granted as a matter of courtesy unless time is of the essence or other circumstances require otherwise. FL ST 6 J CIR 2009-066 PA/PI-CIR(B)(8).

i. Attorneys will resolve subsequent requests by balancing the need for expedition against the deference we should give to opposing counsel's schedule of professional and personal engagements, the reasonableness of the length of extension requested, opposing counsel's willingness to grant reciprocal extensions, the time needed for the task, and whether it is likely a court would grant the extension. FL ST 6 J CIR 2009-066 PA/PI-CIR(B)(9).

j. Attorneys will not attach unfair or extraneous conditions to extensions. Attorneys will impose conditions required to preserve rights that an extension might jeopardize. Attorneys may seek reciprocal scheduling concessions. When granting an extension, we will not try to preclude an opponent's substantive rights. FL ST 6 J CIR 2009-066 PA/PI-CIR(B)(10).

3. *Timing*

a. Hearings are limited to five (5) minutes per case. FL ST 6 J CIR PINELLAS CIR CT PI-CIR-98-30.

b. For more information regarding the timing of hearings, please see FL ST 6 J CIR PINELLAS CIR CT PI-CIR-98-30.

4. *Telephonic hearings.* For information regarding telephonic hearings, please see FL ST 6 J CIR PA/PI-CIR-88-48.

H. Forms

1. Official Motion for Leave to Amend Forms for Florida

a. Caption. FL ST RCP Form 1.901.

b. Notice of compliance when constitutional challenge is brought. FL ST RCP Form 1.975.

2. Motion for Leave to Amend Forms for Florida

a. Motion; For leave of court; To amend complaint. FL-PP § 2:155.

b. Motion; For leave of court; To add claim for punitive damages. FL-PP § 2:156.

c. Motion; For leave of court; To amend complaint; To conform to evidence. FL-PP § 2:157.

d. Motion; For leave of court; To permit admission of evidence. FL-PP § 2:158.

e. Order; Granting leave to amend complaint. FL-PP § 2:163.

f. Order; Granting leave to amend complaint; To conform to evidence. FL-PP § 2:164.

g. Order; Granting leave to amend complaint; To permit admission of evidence. FL-PP § 2:165.

h. Form for motion for leave to amend complaint. FL-RCPF R 1.190(39).

i. Form for amendment to complaint with leave of court. FL-RCPF R 1.190(40).

j. Form for motion to amend amended complaint. FL-RCPF R 1.190(42).

k. Form for amendment to amended complaint (or second amended complaint). FL-RCPF R 1.190(43).

l. Form for motion to amend complaint to add count. FL-RCPF R 1.190(44).

I. Checklist

(I) ❑ Matters to be considered by moving party

(a) ❑ Required documents

(1) ❑ Notice of hearing/Motion

(2) ❑ Proposed amended pleading

(3) ❑ Certificate of service

(b) ❑ Supplemental documents

(1) ❑ Proposed order

(2) ❑ Notice of constitutional question

(c) ❑ Time for making motion

(1) ❑ A party may amend a pleading once as a matter of course at any time before a responsive pleading is served or, if the pleading is one to which no responsive pleading is permitted and the action has not been placed on the trial calendar, may amend it at any time within twenty (20) days after it is served

(2) ❑ Under the Florida Rules of Civil Procedure, there is no time limit as to when an amendment with leave of court may be sought; amendments of the pleadings may be permitted, with the court's discretion, at any stage of the proceedings in furtherance of justice

(3) ❑ A motion for leave to amend a pleading to assert a claim for punitive damages can be filed separately and before the supporting evidence or proffer, but each shall be served on all parties at least twenty (20) days before the hearing

(4) ❑ A copy of any written motion which may not be heard ex parte and a copy of the notice of the hearing thereof shall be served a reasonable time before the time specified for the hearing

(II) ❑ Matters to be considered by opposing party

(a) ❑ Required documents

(1) ❑ Response to motion

(2) ❑ Certificate of service

(b) ❑ Supplemental documents
  (1) ❑ Proposed order
  (2) ❑ Notice of constitutional question
(c) ❑ Time for service and filing of opposition
  (1) ❑ No time specified for responding to a motion

Motions, Oppositions and Replies
Motion for Summary Judgment

Document Last Updated January 2013

A. Applicable Rules

1. *State rules*
   a. Rules of court. FL ST RCP Rule 1.010; FL ST J ADMIN Rule 2.110.
   b. Nonverification of pleadings. FL ST RCP Rule 1.030.
   c. Service and filing of pleadings, orders, and documents. FL ST RCP Rule 1.080.
   d. Time. FL ST RCP Rule 1.090.
   e. Pleadings and motions. FL ST RCP Rule 1.100.
   f. Motions. FL ST RCP Rule 1.160.
   g. Summary judgment. FL ST RCP Rule 1.510.
   h. Relief from judgment, decrees, or orders. FL ST RCP Rule 1.540.
   i. Mediation and arbitration. FL ST RCP Rule 1.700; FL ST RCP Rule 1.710; FL ST RCP Rule 1.720; FL ST RCP Rule 1.730; FL ST RCP Rule 1.750; FL ST RCP Rule 1.800; FL ST RCP Rule 1.810; FL ST RCP Rule 1.820; FL ST RCP Rule 1.830.
   j. Forms. FL ST RCP Rule 1.900.
   k. Minimization of the filing of sensitive information. FL ST J ADMIN Rule 2.425.
   l. Retention of court records. FL ST J ADMIN Rule 2.430.
   m. Foreign attorneys. FL ST J ADMIN Rule 2.510.
   n. Signature of attorneys and parties. FL ST J ADMIN Rule 2.515.
   o. Paper. FL ST J ADMIN Rule 2.520.
   p. Electronic filing. FL ST J ADMIN Rule 2.525.
   q. Accessibility of information and technology. FL ST J ADMIN Rule 2.526.
   r. Communication equipment. FL ST J ADMIN Rule 2.530.
   s. Court reporting. FL ST J ADMIN Rule 2.535.
   t. Requests for accommodations by persons with disabilities. FL ST J ADMIN Rule 2.540.
2. *Local rules*
   a. General motion rule. FL ST 6 J CIR LOCAL Rule 5.
   b. Telephonic hearings in circuit civil, county civil and small claims cases. FL ST 6 J CIR PA/PI-CIR-88-48.
   c. Pre-trial conferences. FL ST 6 J CIR PA/PI-CIR-98-49.
   d. Uniform motion calendar civil division. FL ST 6 J CIR PINELLAS CIR CT PI-CIR-98-30.
   e. Standards of professional courtesy. FL ST 6 J CIR 2009-066 PA/PI-CIR.
   f. Arbitration and mediation program circuit civil and family cases. FL ST 6 J CIR PA/PI-CIR-96-63; FL ST 6 J CIR 2011-006 PA/PI-CIR.

B. Timing

1. *Motion for summary judgment*
   a. *For the claimant.* A party seeking to recover upon a claim, counterclaim, crossclaim or third-party claim or to obtain a declaratory judgment may move for a summary judgment in that party's favor at any time after the expiration of twenty (20) days from the commencement of the action or after service of a motion for summary judgment by the adverse party. FL ST RCP Rule 1.510(a).
   b. *For defending party.* A party against whom a claim, counterclaim, crossclaim, or third-party claim is asserted or a declaratory judgment is sought may move for a summary judgment in that party's favor as to all or any part thereof at any time with or without supporting affidavits. FL ST RCP Rule 1.510(b).
      i. A defending party is not required to serve his responsive pleading before moving for summary judgment. He may make the motion at any time, setting out his defenses by affidavit, and thus effect a speedy termination of the action if no genuine issue exists as to any fact or facts pertaining to a defense that would defeat the claim. FL ST RCP Rule 1.510, notes.
2. *Service of motion.* The movant shall serve the motion for summary judgment at least twenty (20) days before the time fixed for the hearing, and shall also serve at that time a copy of any summary judgment evidence on which the movant relies that has not already been filed with the court. FL ST RCP Rule 1.510(c).
   a. All motions, except motions in limine, shall be filed and heard prior to the pre-trial conference unless good cause exists why the motions were not heard prior to the pre-trial conference, including the inability to obtain hearing time prior to the pre-trial conference. FL ST 6 J CIR PA/PI-CIR-98-49(6).
   b. If such good cause exists, the court will hear such motions at the pre-trial conference or at a separate hearing following the pre-trial conference. FL ST 6 J CIR PA/PI-CIR-98-49(6).
3. *Computation of time*
   a. *Generally.* Computation of time shall be governed by FL ST J ADMIN Rule 2.514. FL ST RCP Rule 1.090(a). The following rules apply in computing time periods specified in any rule of procedure, local rule, court order, or statute that does not specify a method of computing time. FL ST J ADMIN Rule 2.514(a).
      i. *Period stated in days or a longer unit.* When the period is stated in days or a longer unit of time (A) exclude the day of the event that triggers the period; (B) count every day, including intermediate Saturdays, Sundays, and legal holidays; and (C) include the last day of the period, but if the last day is a Saturday, Sunday, or legal holiday, or falls within any period of time extended through an order of the chief justice under FL ST J ADMIN Rule 2.205(a)(2)(B)(iv), the period continues to run until the end of the next day that is not a Saturday, Sunday, or legal holiday and does not fall within any period of time extended through an order of the chief justice. FL ST J ADMIN Rule 2.514(a)(1).
      ii. *Period stated in hours.* When the period is stated in hours (A) begin counting immediately on the occurrence of the event that triggers the period; (B) count every hour, including hours during intermediate Saturdays, Sundays, and legal holidays; and (C) if the period would end on a Saturday, Sunday, or legal holiday, or during any period of time extended through an order of the chief justice under FL ST J ADMIN Rule 2.205(a)(2)(B)(iv), the period continues to run until the same time on the next day that is not a Saturday, Sunday, or legal holiday and does not fall within any period of time extended through an order of the chief justice. FL ST J ADMIN Rule 2.514(a)(2).
      iii. *Period stated in days less than seven (7) days.* When the period stated in days is less than seven (7) days, intermediate Saturdays, Sundays, and legal holidays shall be excluded in the computation. FL ST J ADMIN Rule 2.514(a)(3).
      iv. *"Last day" defined.* Unless a different time is set by a statute, local rule, or court order, the last day ends (A) for electronic filing or for service by any means, at midnight; and (B) for filing by other means, when the clerk's office is scheduled to close. FL ST J ADMIN Rule 2.514(a)(4).

v. *"Next day" defined.* The "next day" is determined by continuing to count forward when the period is measured after an event and backward when measured before an event. FL ST J ADMIN Rule 2.514(a)(5).

vi. *"Legal holiday" defined.* "Legal holiday" means (A) the day set aside by FL ST § 110.117, for observing New Year's Day, Martin Luther King, Jr.'s Birthday, Memorial Day, Independence Day, Labor Day, Veterans' Day, Thanksgiving Day, the Friday after Thanksgiving Day, or Christmas Day, and (B) any day observed as a holiday by the clerk's office or as designated by the chief judge. FL ST J ADMIN Rule 2.514(a)(6).

b. *Additional time after service by mail or e-mail.* When a party may or must act within a specified time after service and service is made by mail or e-mail, five (5) days are added after the period that would otherwise expire under FL ST J ADMIN Rule 2.514(a). FL ST J ADMIN Rule 2.514(b).

c. *Enlargement.* When an act is required or allowed to be done at or within a specified time by order of court, by the Florida Rules of Civil Procedure, or by notice given thereunder, for cause shown the court at any time in its discretion (1) with or without notice, may order the period enlarged if request therefor is made before the expiration of the period originally prescribed or as extended by a previous order, or (2) upon motion made and notice after the expiration of the specified period, may permit the act to be done when failure to act was the result of excusable neglect, but it may not extend the time for making a motion for new trial, for rehearing, or to alter or amend a judgment; making a motion for relief from a judgment under FL ST RCP Rule 1.540(b); taking an appeal or filing a petition for certiorari; or making a motion for a directed verdict. FL ST RCP Rule 1.090(b).

d. *Unaffected by expiration of term.* The period of time provided for the doing of any act or the taking of any proceeding shall not be affected or limited by the continued existence or expiration of a term of court. The continued existence or expiration of a term of court in no way affects the power of a court to do any act or take any proceeding in any action which is or has been pending before it. FL ST RCP Rule 1.090(c).

C. General Requirements

1. *Motions generally*

a. *Contents.* An application to the court for an order shall be by motion which shall be made in writing unless made during a hearing or trial, shall state with particularity the grounds therefor, and shall set forth the relief or order sought. The requirement of writing is fulfilled if the motion is stated in a written notice of the hearing of the motion. All notices of hearing shall specify each motion or other matter to be heard. FL ST RCP Rule 1.100(b).

b. *Particularity requirement.* The court considers a motion in the light of the substantive law, rule or statute to make its determination. Some rules require a statement of the grounds for a motion under the rule. Failure to give the grounds will result in denial of the motion. This should be the result in all situations when the ground for the motion is not inherent in the rule. FL-PRACPROC § 9:3. The requirement is nevertheless an important one, first because of the due process notice rights of the respondent, as well as for the assistance it provides to the court in its preparation for the hearing or, absent a hearing, for disposition. 4 FLPRAC R 1.100.

c. *Standards of professional courtesy; Motion practice*

i. Attorneys will make every reasonable effort to resolve the issue before setting a motion for hearing. FL ST 6 J CIR 2009-066 PA/PI-CIR(G)(1).

ii. Attorneys will not force opposing counsel to make motions attorneys do not intend to oppose unless circumstances require or the client requires. FL ST 6 J CIR 2009-066 PA/PI-CIR(G)(2).

2. *Summary judgment.* A party seeking to recover upon or defend against a claim, counterclaim, crossclaim, or third-party claim or to obtain a declaratory judgment may move for a summary judgment. FL ST RCP Rule 1.510(a); FL ST RCP Rule 1.510(b).

a. *General motion for summary judgment information*

i. *Contents of motion.* The motion shall state with particularity the grounds upon which it is based and the substantial matters of law to be argued and shall specifically identify any affidavits, answers to interrogatories, admissions, depositions, and other materials as would be admissible in evidence ("summary judgment evidence") on which the movant relies. FL ST RCP Rule 1.510(c).

ii. *Evidence relied upon.* The movant shall also serve at that time a copy of any summary judgment evidence on which the movant relies that has not already been filed with the court. FL ST RCP Rule 1.510(c).

iii. *Judgment as a matter of law.* The judgment sought shall be rendered forthwith if the pleadings and summary judgment evidence on file show that there is no genuine issue as to any material fact and that the moving party is entitled to a judgment as a matter of law. A summary judgment, interlocutory in character, may be rendered on the issue of liability alone although there is a genuine issue as to the amount of damages. FL ST RCP Rule 1.510(c).

b. *Sham pleadings.* If a party deems any pleading or part thereof filed by another party to be a sham, that party may move to strike the pleading or part thereof before the cause is set for trial and the court shall hear the motion, taking evidence of the respective parties, and if the motion is sustained, the pleading to which the motion is directed shall be stricken. Default and summary judgment on the merits may be entered in the discretion of the court or the court may permit additional pleadings to be filed for good cause shown. FL ST RCP Rule 1.150(a).

c. *Burden of proof*

i. The moving party in a motion for summary judgment has the initial burden of demonstrating the nonexistence of any genuine issue of fact. Landers v. Milton, 370 So.2d 368, 370 (Fla. 1979); Gardner v. Sabal Point Properties, Inc., 616 So.2d 1111, 1112 (Fla. 5th DCA 1993); FL-PP § 6:7.

ii. If the record raises the slightest doubt that material issues could be present, that doubt must be resolved against the movant and the motion for summary judgment denied. Moore v. Morris, 475 So.2d 666, 668 (Fla. 1985); Henderson v. CSX Transportation, Inc., 617 So.2d 770 (Fla. 1st DCA 1993); Jones v. Directors Guild of America, Inc., 584 So.2d 1057 (Fla. 1st DCA 1991); FL-PP § 6:7.

iii. Until the moving party meets the initial burden of showing there is no issue of material fact, the opposing party need do nothing. Holl v. Talcott, 191 So.2d 40, 43 (Fla. 1966); Spradley v. Stick, 622 So.2d 610 (Fla. 1st DCA 1993); FL-RCPF R 1.510(404).

iv. When the movant has tendered competent evidence in support of its motion, the burden shifts to the nonmoving party to come forward with opposing evidence to show that a question of material fact exists. Landers v. Milton, 370 So.2d 368, 370 (Fla. 1979); Holl v. Talcott, 191 So.2d 40, 43-44 (Fla. 1966); Lenhal Realty, Inc. v. Transamerica Commercial Finance Corp., 615 So.2d 207 (Fla. 4th DCA 1993); FL-PP § 6:7.

d. *Affidavits*

i. *Form of affidavits; Further testimony.* Supporting and opposing affidavits shall be made on personal knowledge, shall set forth such facts as would be admissible in evidence, and shall show affirmatively that the affiant is competent to testify to the matters stated. Sworn or certified copies of all papers or parts referred to in an affidavit shall be attached to or served with the affidavit. The court may permit affidavits to be supplemented or opposed by depositions, answers to interrogatories, or by further affidavits. FL ST RCP Rule 1.510(e).

ii. *When affidavits are unavailable.* If it appears from the affidavits of a party opposing the motion that the party cannot for reasons stated present by affidavit facts essential to justify opposition, the court may refuse the application for judgment or may order a continuance to permit affidavits to be obtained or depositions to be taken or discovery to be had or may make such other order as is just. FL ST RCP Rule 1.510(f).

iii. *Affidavits made in bad faith.* If it appears to the satisfaction of the court at any time that any of the affidavits presented pursuant to FL ST RCP Rule 1.510 are presented in bad faith or solely for the purpose of delay, the court shall forthwith order the party employing them to pay to the other party the amount of the reasonable expenses that the filing of the affidavits caused the other party to incur, including reasonable attorneys' fees, and any offending party or attorney may be adjudged guilty of contempt. FL ST RCP Rule 1.510(g).

e. *Case not fully adjudicated on motion.* On motion under FL ST RCP Rule 1.510 if judgment is not rendered upon the whole case or for all the relief asked and a trial or the taking of testimony and a final hearing is necessary, the court at the hearing of the motion, by examining the pleadings and the evidence before it and by interrogating counsel, shall ascertain, if practicable, what material facts exist without substantial controversy and what material facts are actually and in good faith controverted. FL ST RCP Rule 1.510(d).

   i. It shall thereupon make an order specifying the facts that appear without substantial controversy, including the extent to which the amount of damages or other relief is not in controversy, and directing such further proceedings in the action as are just. FL ST RCP Rule 1.510(d).

   ii. On the trial or final hearing of the action the facts so specified shall be deemed established, and the trial or final hearing shall be conducted accordingly. FL ST RCP Rule 1.510(d).

3. *Arbitration and mediation*

   a. *Referral to arbitration and mediation.* Except as hereinafter provided or as otherwise prohibited by law, the presiding judge may enter an order referring all or any part of a contested civil matter to mediation or arbitration. The parties to any contested civil matter may file a written stipulation to mediate or arbitrate any issue between them at any time. Such stipulation shall be incorporated into the order of referral. FL ST RCP Rule 1.700(a).

   b. *Arbitration*

      i. *Exclusions.* A civil action shall be ordered to arbitration or arbitration in conjunction with mediation upon stipulation of the parties. A civil action may be ordered to arbitration or arbitration in conjunction with mediation upon motion of any party or by the court, if the judge determines the action to be of such a nature that arbitration could be of benefit to the litigants or the court. FL ST RCP Rule 1.800.

         - Under no circumstances may the following categories of actions be referred to arbitration: (1) bond estreatures; (2) habeas corpus or other extraordinary writs; (3) bond validations; (4) civil or criminal contempt; (5) such other matters as may be specified by order of the chief judge in the circuit. FL ST RCP Rule 1.800.

      ii. For more information regarding arbitration, please see FL ST RCP Rule 1.810; FL ST RCP Rule 1.820; FL ST RCP Rule 1.830.

   c. *Mediation.* For more information regarding mediation, please see FL ST RCP Rule 1.710; FL ST RCP Rule 1.720; FL ST RCP Rule 1.730; and FL ST RCP Rule 1.750.

   d. See FL ST 6 J CIR PA/PI-CIR-96-63 for more information about the Arbitration and Mediation Program for Florida's Sixth Judicial Circuit.

4. *Rules of court*

   a. *Rules of civil procedure.* The Florida Rules of Civil Procedure apply to all actions of a civil nature and all special statutory proceedings in the circuit courts and county courts except those to which the Florida Probate Rules, the Florida Family Law Rules of Procedure, or the Small Claims Rules apply. FL ST RCP Rule 1.010.

      i. The form, content, procedure, and time for pleading in all special statutory proceedings shall be as prescribed by the statutes governing the proceeding unless the Florida Rules of Civil Procedure specifically provide to the contrary. FL ST RCP Rule 1.010.

      ii. The Florida Rules of Civil Procedure shall be construed to secure the just, speedy, and inexpensive determination of every action. FL ST RCP Rule 1.010.

   b. *Rules of judicial administration.* The Florida Rules of Judicial Administration shall apply to administrative matters in all courts to which the Florida Rules of Judicial Administration are applicable by their terms. The Florida Rules of Judicial Administration shall be construed to secure the speedy and inexpensive determination of every proceeding to which they are applicable. The

Florida Rules of Judicial Administration shall supersede all conflicting rules and statutes. FL ST J ADMIN Rule 2.110.

5. *Settlement and alternative dispute resolution.* When a matter is scheduled for hearing and the matter is resolved by agreement or settlement, the party setting the matter for hearing shall notify the court. When a matter is scheduled for trial and the case settles, the plaintiff shall notify the court. Permission of the court must be obtained in order to cancel a trial. FL ST 6 J CIR LOCAL Rule 5(A).
   a. Unless there are strong and overriding issues of principle, attorneys will raise and explore the issue of settlement as soon as enough is known to make settlement discussions meaningful. FL ST 6 J CIR 2009-066 PA/PI-CIR(I)(1).
   b. Attorneys will not falsely hold out the possibility of settlement to adjourn discovery or delay trial. FL ST 6 J CIR 2009-066 PA/PI-CIR(I)(2).
   c. Attorneys will consider whether the client's interest could be adequately served and the controversy more expeditiously and economically disposed of by arbitration, mediation or other forms of alternative dispute resolution. FL ST 6 J CIR 2009-066 PA/PI-CIR(I)(3).

D. Documents

1. *Required documents*
   a. *Notice of hearing/Motion.* An application to the court for an order shall be by motion which shall be made in writing unless made during a hearing or trial, shall state with particularity the grounds therefor, and shall set forth the relief or order sought. The requirement of writing is fulfilled if the motion is stated in a written notice of the hearing of the motion. All notices of hearing shall specify each motion or other matter to be heard. FL ST RCP Rule 1.100(b).
      i. *Notices to persons with disabilities.* See the Format section of this KeyRules document for further information.
   b. *Certificate of service.* When any attorney certifies in substance: "I certify that a copy hereof has been furnished to (here insert name or names and addresses used for service) by (e-mail) (delivery) (mail) (fax) on .... (date) ....________________ Attorney" the certificate is taken as prima facie proof of such service in compliance with FL ST J ADMIN Rule 2.516. FL ST J ADMIN Rule 2.516(f).
2. *Supplemental documents*
   a. *Affidavits.* Supporting and opposing affidavits shall be made on personal knowledge, shall set forth such facts as would be admissible in evidence, and shall show affirmatively that the affiant is competent to testify to the matters stated therein. Sworn or certified copies of all papers or parts thereof referred to in an affidavit shall be attached thereto or served therewith. FL ST RCP Rule 1.510(e). For further information regarding affidavits made in the context of a motion for summary judgment see FL ST RCP Rule 1.510(e) through FL ST RCP Rule 1.510(g).
   b. *Other evidence.* The movant shall also serve at that time a copy of any summary judgment evidence on which the movant relies that has not already been filed with the court. FL ST RCP Rule 1.510(c).
   c. *Proposed order.* The court may require that orders or judgments be prepared by a party, may require the party to furnish the court with stamped, addressed envelopes for service of the order or judgment, and may require that proposed orders and judgments be furnished to all parties before entry by the court of the order or judgment. FL ST J ADMIN Rule 2.516(h)(1).
      i. After a hearing, attorneys will make a good faith effort to quickly agree or disagree upon a proposed order and submit the result to the court. Unless otherwise instructed by the court, or agreed to by counsel, all proposed orders shall be provided to other counsel for approval or comment prior to submission to the court. Attorneys will not submit controverted orders to the court with a copy to opposing counsel for "objections within ______ days". Courts prefer to know that the order is either agreed upon or opposed. FL ST 6 J CIR 2009-066 PA/PI-CIR(G)(3).
      ii. Attorneys will not use post-hearing submissions of proposed orders as a guise to reargue the merits of the matter. FL ST 6 J CIR 2009-066 PA/PI-CIR(G)(4).
   d. *Notice of constitutional question.* A party that files a pleading, written motion, or other paper

drawing into question the constitutionality of a state statute or a county or municipal charter, ordinance, or franchise must promptly (1) file a notice of constitutional question stating the question and identifying the paper that raises it; and (2) serve the notice and the pleading, written motion, or other paper drawing into question the constitutionality of a state statute or a county or municipal charter, ordinance, or franchise on the Attorney General or the state attorney of the judicial circuit in which the action is pending, by either certified or registered mail. Service of the notice and pleading, written motion, or other paper does not require joinder of the Attorney General or the state attorney as a party to the action. FL ST RCP Rule 1.071.

E. Format

1. *Documents; Type and size.* Documents subject to the exceptions set forth in FL ST J ADMIN Rule 2.525(d) shall be filed on recycled paper measuring eight and one half by eleven (8 1/2 by 11) inches. For purposes of FL ST J ADMIN Rule 2.520, paper is recycled if it contains a minimum content of fifty (50) percent waste paper. Xerographic reduction of legal-size (eight and one half by fourteen (8 1/2 by 14) inches) documents to letter size (eight and one half by eleven (8 1/2 by 11) inches) is prohibited. All other documents filed by electronic transmission shall be filed in a format capable of being printed in a format consistent with the provisions of FL ST J ADMIN Rule 2.250. FL ST J ADMIN Rule 2.520(b).
    a. *Exhibits.* Any exhibit or attachment filed with pleadings or papers may be filed in its original size. FL ST J ADMIN Rule 2.520(c).
    b. *Recording space.* On all papers and documents prepared and filed by the court or by any party to a proceeding which are to be recorded in the public records of any county, including but not limited to final money judgments and notices of lis pendens, a three (3) inch by three (3) inch space at the top right-hand corner on the first page and a one (1) inch by three (3) inch space at the top right-hand corner on each subsequent page shall be left blank and reserved for use by the clerk of court. FL ST J ADMIN Rule 2.520(d).
        i. *Exceptions to recording space.* Any papers or documents created by persons or entities over which the filing party has no control, including but not limited to wills, codicils, trusts, or other testamentary documents; documents prepared or executed by any public officer; documents prepared, executed, acknowledged, or proved outside of the State of Florida; or documents created by State or Federal government agencies, may be filed without the space required by FL ST J ADMIN Rule 2.520. FL ST J ADMIN Rule 2.520(e).
    c. *Noncompliance.* No clerk of court is permitted to refuse to file any document or paper because of noncompliance with the Florida Rules of Judicial Administration. However, upon request of the clerk of court, noncomplying documents must be resubmitted in accordance with the formatting rules. FL ST J ADMIN Rule 2.520(f).
2. *Caption.* Every pleading, motion, order, judgment, or other paper shall have a caption containing the name of the court, the file number, and except for in rem proceedings, including forfeiture proceedings, the name of the first party on each side with an appropriate indication of other parties, and a designation identifying the party filing it and its nature or the nature of the order, as the case may be. In any in rem proceeding, every pleading, motion, order, judgment, or other paper shall have a caption containing the name of the court, the file number, the style "In re" (followed by the name or general description of the property), and a designation of the person or entity filing it and its nature or the nature of the order, as the case may be. In an in rem forfeiture proceeding, the style shall be "In re forfeiture of" (followed by the name of the general description of the property). All papers filed in the action shall be styled in such a manner as to indicate clearly the subject matter of the paper and the party requesting or obtaining relief. FL ST RCP Rule 1.100(c)(1).
3. *Writing and written defined.* Writing or written means a document containing information, an application, or a stipulation. FL ST RCP Rule 1.080(c).
4. *Rule abbreviations*
    a. The Florida Rules of Civil Procedure and shall be abbreviated as Fla.R.Civ.P. FL ST RCP Rule 1.010.
    b. The Florida Rules of Judicial Administration shall be abbreviated as Fla. R. Jud. Admin. FL ST J ADMIN Rule 2.110.

5. *Nonverification.* Except when otherwise specifically provided by the Florida Rules of Civil Procedure or an applicable statute, every pleading or other document of a party represented by an attorney need not be verified or accompanied by an affidavit. FL ST RCP Rule 1.030; FL ST J ADMIN Rule 2.515(a).
6. *Attorney signature*
   a. *Attorney signature.* Every pleading and other document of a party represented by an attorney shall be signed by at least one (1) attorney of record in that attorney's individual name whose current record Florida Bar address, telephone number, including area code, primary e-mail address and secondary e-mail addresses, if any, and Florida Bar number shall be stated, and who shall be duly licensed to practice law in Florida or who shall have received permission to appear in the particular case as provided in FL ST J ADMIN Rule 2.510. FL ST J ADMIN Rule 2.515(a).
      i. The attorney may be required by the court to give the address of, and to vouch for the attorney's authority to represent, the party. FL ST J ADMIN Rule 2.515(a).
      ii. The signature of an attorney shall constitute a certificate by the attorney that the attorney has read the pleading or other document; that to the best of the attorney's knowledge, information, and belief there is good ground to support it; and that it is not interposed for delay. FL ST J ADMIN Rule 2.515(a).
      iii. If a pleading is not signed or is signed with intent to defeat the purpose of FL ST J ADMIN Rule 2.515, it may be stricken and the action may proceed as though the pleading or other document had not been served. FL ST J ADMIN Rule 2.515(a).
   b. *Pro se litigant signature.* A party who is not represented by an attorney shall sign any pleading or other paper and state the party's address and telephone number, including area code. FL ST J ADMIN Rule 2.515(b).
   c. *Form of signature*
      i. The signatures required on pleadings and documents by FL ST J ADMIN Rule 2.515(a) and FL ST J ADMIN Rule 2.515(b) may be:
         - Original signatures;
         - Original signatures that have been reproduced by electronic means, such as on electronically transmitted documents or photocopied documents;
         - Electronic signatures using the "/s/," "s/," or "/s" formats by or at the direction of the person signing; or
         - Any other signature format authorized by general law, so long as the clerk where the proceeding is pending has the capability of receiving and has obtained approval from the Supreme Court of Florida to accept pleadings and documents with that signature format. FL ST J ADMIN Rule 2.515(c)(1).
      ii. An attorney, party, or other person who files a pleading or paper by electronic transmission that does not contain the original signature of that attorney, party, or other person shall file that identical pleading or paper in paper form containing an original signature of that attorney, party, or other person (hereinafter called the follow-up filing) immediately thereafter. The follow-up filing is not required if the Supreme Court of Florida has entered an order directing the clerk of court to discontinue accepting the follow-up filing. FL ST J ADMIN Rule 2.515(c)(2).
7. *Forms*
   a. *Process.* The forms of process, notice of lis pendens, and notice of action provided in the Florida Rules of Civil Procedure are sufficient. Variations from the forms do not void process or notices that are otherwise sufficient. FL ST RCP Rule 1.900(a).
   b. *Other forms.* The other forms provided in the Florida Rules of Civil Procedure are sufficient for the matters that are covered by them. So long as the substance is expressed without prolixity, the forms may be varied to meet the facts of a particular case. FL ST RCP Rule 1.900(b).
   c. *Formal matters.* Captions, except for the designation of the paper, are omitted from the forms provided in the Florida Rules of Civil Procedure. A general form of caption is the first form provided. Signatures are omitted from pleadings and motions. FL ST RCP Rule 1.900(c).

8. *Notices to persons with disabilities.* All notices of court proceedings to be held in a public facility, and all process compelling appearance at such proceedings, shall include the following statement in bold face, fourteen (14) point Times New Roman or Courier font: "If you are a person with a disability who needs any accommodation in order to participate in this proceeding, you are entitled, at no cost to you, to the provision of certain assistance. Please contact [identify applicable court personnel by name, address, and telephone number] at least seven (7) days before your scheduled court appearance, or immediately upon receiving this notification if the time before the scheduled appearance is less than seven (7) days; if you are hearing or voice impaired, call 711." FL ST J ADMIN Rule 2.540(c)(1).
9. *Minimization of the filing of sensitive information*
    a. *Limitations for court filings.* Unless authorized by FL ST J ADMIN Rule 2.425(b), statute, another rule of court, or the court orders otherwise, designated sensitive information filed with the court must be limited to the following format:
        i. The initials of a person known to be a minor;
        ii. The year of birth of a person's birth date;
        iii. No portion of any: Social security number, Bank account number, Credit card account number, Charge account number, or Debit account number;
        iv. The last four digits of any: Taxpayer identification number (TIN), Employee identification number, Driver's license number, Passport number, Telephone number, Financial account number, except as set forth in FL ST J ADMIN Rule 2.425(a)(3), Brokerage account number, Insurance policy account number, Loan account number, Customer account number, or Patient or health care number;
        v. A truncated version of any: Email address, Computer user name, Password, or Personal identification number (PIN); and
        vi. A truncated version of any other sensitive information as provided by court order. FL ST J ADMIN Rule 2.425(a).
    b. *Exceptions.* FL ST J ADMIN Rule 2.425(a) does not apply to the following:
        i. An account number which identifies the property alleged to be the subject of a proceeding;
        ii. The record of an administrative or agency proceeding;
        iii. The record in appellate or review proceedings;
        iv. The birth date of a minor whenever the birth date is necessary for the court to establish or maintain subject matter jurisdiction;
        v. The name of a minor in any order relating to parental responsibility, time-sharing, or child support;
        vi. The name of a minor in any document or order affecting the minor's ownership of real property;
        vii. The birth date of a party in a writ of attachment or notice to payor;
        viii. In traffic and criminal proceedings: a pro se filing; a court filing that is related to a criminal matter or investigation and that is prepared before the filing of a criminal charge or is not filed as part of any docketed criminal case; an arrest or search warrant or any information in support thereof; a charging document and an affidavit or other documents filed in support of any charging document, including any driving records; a statement of particulars; discovery material introduced into evidence or otherwise filed with the court; and all information necessary for the proper issuance and execution of a subpoena duces tecum;
        ix. Information used by the clerk for case maintenance purposes or the courts for case management purposes; and
        x. Information which is relevant and material to an issue before the court. FL ST J ADMIN Rule 2.425(b).
    c. *Remedies.* Upon motion by a party or interested person or sua sponte by the court, the court may order remedies, sanctions or both for a violation of FL ST J ADMIN Rule 2.425(a). Following notice

and an opportunity to respond, the court may impose sanctions if such filing was not made in good faith. FL ST J ADMIN Rule 2.425(c).

d. *Motions not restricted.* FL ST J ADMIN Rule 2.425 does not restrict a party's right to move for protective order, to move to file documents under seal, or to request a determination of the confidentiality of records. FL ST J ADMIN Rule 2.425(d).

e. *Application.* FL ST J ADMIN Rule 2.425 does not affect the application of constitutional provisions, statutes, or rules of court regarding confidential information or access to public information. FL ST J ADMIN Rule 2.425(e).

F. Filing and Service Requirements

1. *Filing requirements.* All original documents must be filed with the court either before service or immediately thereafter, unless otherwise provided for by general law or other rules. If the original of any bond or other document is not placed in the court file, a certified copy must be so placed by the clerk. FL ST J ADMIN Rule 2.516(d). All documents shall be filed in conformity with the requirements of FL ST J ADMIN Rule 2.525. FL ST RCP Rule 1.080(b). All documents filed in any court shall be filed by electronic transmission in accordance with FL ST J ADMIN Rule 2.525. "Documents" means pleadings, motions, petitions, memoranda, briefs, notices, exhibits, declarations, affidavits, orders, judgments, decrees, writs, opinions, and any other paper or writing submitted to a court. FL ST J ADMIN Rule 2.520(a). All documents that are court records, as defined in FL ST J ADMIN Rule 2.430(a)(1), must be filed by electronic transmission, provided that: (1) the clerk has the ability to accept and retain such documents; (2) the clerk or the chief judge of the circuit has requested permission to accept documents filed by electronic transmission; and (3) the supreme court has entered an order granting permission to the clerk to accept documents filed by electronic transmission. FL ST J ADMIN Rule 2.525(c)(1).

a. *Definition.* "Electronic transmission of documents" means the sending of information by electronic signals to, by or from a court or clerk, which when received can be transformed and stored or transmitted on paper, microfilm, magnetic storage device, optical imaging system, CD-ROM, flash drive, other electronic data storage system, server, case maintenance system ("CM"), electronic court filing ("ECF") system, statewide or local electronic portal ("e-portal"), or other electronic record keeping system authorized by the supreme court in a format sufficient to communicate the information on the original document in a readable format. Electronic transmission of documents includes electronic mail ("e-mail") and any internet-based transmission procedure, and may include procedures allowing for documents to be signed or verified by electronic means. FL ST J ADMIN Rule 2.525(a).

i. The filing of documents with the court as required by the Florida Rules of Judicial Administration must be made by filing them with the clerk in accordance with FL ST J ADMIN Rule 2.525, except that the judge may permit documents to be filed with the judge, in which event the judge must note the filing date before him or her on the documents and transmit them to the clerk. The date of filing is that shown on the face of the document by the judge's notation or the clerk's time stamp, whichever is earlier. FL ST J ADMIN Rule 2.516(e).

b. *Application.* Any court or clerk of the court may accept the electronic transmission of documents for filing after the clerk, together with input from the chief judge of the circuit, has obtained approval of the procedures and program for doing so from the Supreme Court of Florida. FL ST J ADMIN Rule 2.525(b).

c. *Exceptions*

i. Paper documents and other submissions may be manually submitted to the clerk or court:

- When the clerk does not have the ability to accept and retain documents by electronic filing or has not had ECF Procedures approved by the supreme court;
- For filing by any self-represented party or any self-represented nonparty unless specific ECF Procedures provide a means to file documents electronically. However, any self-represented nonparty that is a governmental or public agency and any other agency, partnership, corporation, or business entity acting on behalf of any governmental or public agency may file documents by electronic transmission if such entity has the capability of filing documents electronically;

- For filing by attorneys excused from e-mail service in accordance with FL ST J ADMIN Rule 2.516(b);
- When submitting evidentiary exhibits or filing non-documentary materials;
- When the filing involves documents in excess of twenty-five (25) megabytes (25MB) in size. For such filings, documents may be transmitted using an electronic storage medium that the clerk has the ability to accept, which may include a CD-ROM, flash drive, or similar storage medium;
- When filed in open court, as permitted by the court;
- When paper filing is permitted by any approved statewide or local ECF procedures; and
- If any court determines that justice so requires. FL ST J ADMIN Rule 2.525(d).

ii. Any document in paper form submitted under FL ST J ADMIN Rule 2.525(d) is filed when it is received by the clerk or court and the clerk shall immediately thereafter convert any filed paper document to an electronic document. "Convert to an electronic document" means optically capturing an image of a paper document and using character recognition software to recover as much of the document's text as practicable and then indexing and storing the document in the official court file. FL ST J ADMIN Rule 2.525(c)(4).

iii. Any storage medium submitted under FL ST J ADMIN Rule 2.525(d)(5) is filed when received by the clerk or court and the clerk shall immediately thereafter transfer the electronic documents from the storage device to the official court file. FL ST J ADMIN Rule 2.525(c)(5).

iv. If the filer of any paper document authorized under FL ST J ADMIN Rule 2.525(d) provides a self-addressed, postage-paid envelope for return of the paper document after it is converted to electronic form by the clerk, the clerk shall place the paper document in the envelope and deposit it in the mail. Except when a paper document is required to be maintained, the clerk may recycle any filed paper document that is not to be returned to the filer. FL ST J ADMIN Rule 2.525(c)(6).

v. The clerk may convert any paper document filed before the effective date of FL ST J ADMIN Rule 2.525 to an electronic document. Unless the clerk is required to maintain the paper document, if the paper document has been converted to an electronic document by the clerk, the paper document is no longer part of the official court file and may be removed and recycled. FL ST J ADMIN Rule 2.525(c)(7).

d. *Official court file.* For information on what constitutes the official court file, please see FL ST J ADMIN Rule 2.525(c)(2), FL ST J ADMIN Rule 2.525(c)(3).

e. *Administration.* All attorneys, parties, or other persons using this rule to file documents are required to make arrangements with the court or clerk for the payment of any charges authorized by general law or the supreme court before filing any document by electronic transmission. FL ST J ADMIN Rule 2.525(f)(2).

f. *Filing date.* The filing date for an electronically transmitted document is the date and time that such filing is acknowledged by an electronic stamp or otherwise, pursuant to any procedure set forth in any ECF Procedures approved by the supreme court, or the date the last page of such filing is received by the court or clerk. FL ST J ADMIN Rule 2.525(f)(3).

g. *Accessibility.* All documents transmitted in any electronic form under FL ST J ADMIN Rule 2.525 must comply with the accessibility requirements of FL ST J ADMIN Rule 2.526. FL ST J ADMIN Rule 2.525(g).

2. *Service requirements.* Every pleading subsequent to the initial pleading, all orders, and every other document filed in the action must be served in conformity with the requirements of FL ST J ADMIN Rule 2.516. FL ST RCP Rule 1.080(a).

a. *Service; When required.* Unless the court otherwise orders, or a statute or supreme court administrative order specifies a different means of service, every pleading subsequent to the initial pleading and every other document filed in any court proceeding, except applications for witness subpoenas and documents served by formal notice or required to be served in the manner provided for service

of formal notice, must be served in accordance with FL ST J ADMIN Rule 2.516 on each party. No service need be made on parties against whom a default has been entered, except that pleadings asserting new or additional claims against them must be served in the manner provided for service of summons. FL ST J ADMIN Rule 2.516(a).

b. *Service; How made.* When service is required or permitted to be made upon a party represented by an attorney, service must be made upon the attorney unless service upon the party is ordered by the court. FL ST J ADMIN Rule 2.516(b).

   i. *Service by electronic mail ("e-mail").* All documents required or permitted to be served on another party must be served by e-mail, unless FL ST J ADMIN Rule 2.516 otherwise provides. When, in addition to service by e-mail, the sender also utilizes another means of service provided for in FL ST J ADMIN Rule 2.516(b)(2), any differing time limits and other provisions applicable to that other means of service control. FL ST J ADMIN Rule 2.516(b)(1). Any document electronically transmitted to a court or clerk must also be served on all parties and interested persons in accordance with the applicable rules of court. FL ST J ADMIN Rule 2.525(e)(2).

      - *Service on attorneys.* Upon appearing in a proceeding, an attorney must serve a designation of a primary e-mail address and may designate no more than two (2) secondary e-mail addresses. Thereafter, service must be directed to all designated e-mail addresses in that proceeding. Every document filed by an attorney thereafter must include the primary e-mail address of that attorney and any secondary e-mail addresses. If an attorney does not designate any e-mail address for service, documents may be served on that attorney at the e-mail address on record with The Florida Bar. FL ST J ADMIN Rule 2.516(b)(1)(A).

      - *Exception to e-mail service on attorneys.* Service by an attorney on another attorney must be made by e-mail unless excused by the court. Upon motion by an attorney demonstrating that the attorney has no e-mail account and lacks access to the Internet at the attorney's office, the court may excuse the attorney from the requirements of e-mail service. Service on and by an attorney excused by the court from e-mail service must be by the means provided in FL ST J ADMIN Rule 2.516(b)(2). FL ST J ADMIN Rule 2.516(b)(1)(B).

      - *Service on and by parties not represented by an attorney.* Any party not represented by an attorney may serve a designation of a primary e-mail address and also may designate no more than two (2) secondary e-mail addresses to which service must be directed in that proceeding by the means provided in FL ST J ADMIN Rule 2.516(b)(1). If a party not represented by an attorney does not designate an e-mail address for service in a proceeding, service on and by that party must be by the means provided in FL ST J ADMIN Rule 2.516(b)(2). FL ST J ADMIN Rule 2.516(b)(1)(C).

      - *Time of service.* Service by e-mail is complete when it is sent. FL ST J ADMIN Rule 2.516(b)(1)(D). An e-mail is deemed served on the date it is sent. FL ST J ADMIN Rule 2.516(b)(1)(D)(i). If the sender learns that the e-mail did not reach the address of the person to be served, the sender must immediately send another copy by e-mail, or by a means authorized by FL ST J ADMIN Rule 2.516(b)(2). FL ST J ADMIN Rule 2.516(b)(1)(D)(ii). E-mail service is treated as service by mail for the computation of time. FL ST J ADMIN Rule 2.516(b)(1)(D)(iii).

   ii. *Format of e-mail for service.* Service of a document by e-mail is made by attaching a copy of the document in PDF format to an e-mail sent to all addresses designated by the attorney or party. FL ST J ADMIN Rule 2.516(b)(1)(E).

      - All documents served by e-mail must be attached to an e-mail message containing a subject line beginning with the words "SERVICE OF COURT DOCUMENT" in all capital letters, followed by the case number of the proceeding in which the documents are being served. FL ST J ADMIN Rule 2.516(b)(1)(E)(i).

      - The body of the e-mail must identify the court in which the proceeding is pending, the case number, the name of the initial party on each side, the title of each document served with that e-mail, and the sender's name and telephone number. FL ST J ADMIN Rule 2.516(b)(1)(E)(ii).

- Any document served by e-mail may be signed by the "/s/" format, as long as the filed original is signed in accordance with the applicable rule of procedure. FL ST J ADMIN Rule 2.516(b)(1)(E)(iii).
- Any e-mail which, together with its attached documents, exceeds five megabytes (5MB) in size, must be divided and sent as separate e-mails, no one of which may exceed five megabytes (5MB) in size and each of which must be sequentially numbered in the subject line. FL ST J ADMIN Rule 2.516(b)(1)(E)(iv).

iii. *Service by other means.* In addition to, and not in lieu of, service by e-mail, service may also be made upon attorneys by any of the means specified in FL ST J ADMIN Rule 2.516(b)(2). Service on and by all parties who are not represented by an attorney and who do not designate an e-mail address, and on and by all attorneys excused from e-mail service, must be made by delivering a copy of the document or by mailing it to the party or attorney at their last known address or, if no address is known, by leaving it with the clerk of the court. Service by mail is complete upon mailing. Delivery of a copy within FL ST J ADMIN Rule 2.516 is complete upon:

- Handing it to the attorney or to the party,
- Leaving it at the attorney's or party's office with a clerk or other person in charge thereof,
- If there is no one in charge, leaving it in a conspicuous place therein,
- If the office is closed or the person to be served has no office, leaving it at the person's usual place of abode with some person of his or her family above fifteen (15) years of age and informing such person of the contents, or
- Transmitting it by facsimile to the attorney's or party's office with a cover sheet containing the sender's name, firm, address, telephone number, and facsimile number, and the number of pages transmitted. When service is made by facsimile, a copy must also be served by any other method permitted by FL ST J ADMIN Rule 2.516. Facsimile service occurs when transmission is complete. FL ST J ADMIN Rule 2.516(b)(2)(A) through FL ST J ADMIN Rule 2.516(b)(2)(E).
- Service by delivery after 5:00 p.m. must be deemed to have been made by mailing on the date of delivery. FL ST J ADMIN Rule 2.516(b)(2)(F).

c. *Service; Numerous defendants.* In actions when the parties are unusually numerous, the court may regulate the service contemplated by the Florida Rules of Judicial Administration on motion or on its own initiative in such manner as may be found to be just and reasonable. FL ST J ADMIN Rule 2.516(c).

d. *Service by clerk.* Service of notices and other documents required to be made by the clerk must also be done as provided in FL ST J ADMIN Rule 2.516(b). FL ST J ADMIN Rule 2.516(g).

e. *Standards of professional courtesy; Service*

i. The timing and manner of service should not be used to the disadvantage of the party receiving the papers. This includes the use of facsimile transmissions and any additional expedited means of communication approved by the court. FL ST 6 J CIR 2009-066 PA/PI-CIR(C)(1).

ii. Attorneys will not serve papers to take advantage of opposing counsel's known absence from the office or at a time or in a manner designed to inconvenience an opponent, such as late on Friday afternoon or the day preceding a secular or religious holiday. FL ST 6 J CIR 2009-066 PA/PI-CIR(C)(2).

iii. Attorneys will not serve papers, including briefs and memoranda, so close to a court appearance that the ability of opposing counsel to prepare for that appearance or, where permitted, to respond, is inhibited. FL ST 6 J CIR 2009-066 PA/PI-CIR(C)(3).

iv. Service should be made personally or by facsimile transmission when it is likely that service by mail, even when allowed, will prejudice the opposing party. FL ST 6 J CIR 2009-066 PA/PI-CIR(C)(4).

G. Hearings

1. *Hearing on motion for summary judgment.* The summary judgment rule does not provide the trial court with discretion to decide whether a hearing is required. A failure to hold a hearing on a motion for summary judgment violates due process as well as rule of procedure governing summary judgment procedure. Kozich v. Hartford Ins. Co. of Midwest, 609 So.2d 147, 148 (Fla. 4th DCA 1992); FL-RCPF R 1.510(102).
2. *Summary judgment consideration at pretrial conference.* A summary judgment can be granted at the pretrial conference. The standard and procedure for granting summary judgment is the same at a pretrial conference as at other times. The notice time for a pretrial conference and for service of a motion for summary judgment is the same, so summary judgment can be entered at the conference if no genuine issue of material fact exists. FL-PRACPROC § 19:4.
3. *Communication equipment*
   a. *Definition.* Communication equipment means a conference telephone or other electronic device that permits all those appearing or participating to hear and speak to each other, provided that all conversation of all parties is audible to all persons present. FL ST J ADMIN Rule 2.530(a).
   b. *Use by all parties.* A county or circuit court judge may, upon the court's own motion or upon the written request of a party, direct that communication equipment be used for a motion hearing, pretrial conference, or a status conference. A judge must give notice to the parties and consider any objections they may have to the use of communication equipment before directing that communication equipment be used. The decision to use communication equipment over the objection of parties will be in the sound discretion of the trial court, except as noted below. FL ST J ADMIN Rule 2.530(b).
   c. *Use only by requesting party.* A county or circuit court judge may, upon the written request of a party upon reasonable notice to all other parties, permit a requesting party to participate through communication equipment in a scheduled motion hearing; however, any such request (except in criminal, juvenile, and appellate proceedings) must be granted, absent a showing of good cause to deny the same, where the hearing is set for not longer than fifteen (15) minutes. FL ST J ADMIN Rule 2.530(c).
   d. *Testimony*
      i. *Generally.* A county or circuit court judge, general magistrate, special magistrate, or hearing officer may allow testimony to be taken through communication equipment if all parties consent or if permitted by another applicable rule of procedure. FL ST J ADMIN Rule 2.530(d)(1).
      ii. *Procedure.* Any party desiring to present testimony through communication equipment shall, prior to the hearing or trial at which the testimony is to be presented, contact all parties to determine whether each party consents to this form of testimony. The party seeking to present the testimony shall move for permission to present testimony through communication equipment, which motion shall set forth good cause as to why the testimony should be allowed in this form. FL ST J ADMIN Rule 2.530(d)(2).
      iii. *Oath.* Testimony may be taken through communication equipment only if a notary public or other person authorized to administer oaths in the witness's jurisdiction is present with the witness and administers the oath consistent with the laws of the jurisdiction. FL ST J ADMIN Rule 2.530(d)(3).
      iv. *Confrontation rights.* In juvenile and criminal proceedings the defendant must make an informed waiver of any confrontation rights that may be abridged by the use of communication equipment. FL ST J ADMIN Rule 2.530(d)(4).
      v. *Video testimony.* If the testimony to be presented utilizes video conferencing or comparable two-way visual capabilities, the court in its discretion may modify the procedures set forth in FL ST J ADMIN Rule 2.530 to accommodate the technology utilized. FL ST J ADMIN Rule 2.530(d)(5).
   e. *Burden of expense.* The cost for the use of the communication equipment is the responsibility of the requesting party unless otherwise directed by the court. FL ST J ADMIN Rule 2.530(e).

4. *Standards of professional courtesy; Scheduling*

   a. Attorneys will communicate with opposing counsel to schedule depositions, hearings, and other proceedings, at times mutually convenient for all interested persons. FL ST 6 J CIR 2009-066 PA/PI-CIR(B)(1).

   b. Attorneys will provide opposing counsel and other affected persons reasonable notice of all proceedings except upon agreement of counsel when expedited scheduling is necessary. Attorneys will immediately notify opposing counsel of any hearing time reserved. FL ST 6 J CIR 2009-066 PA/PI-CIR(B)(2).

   c. Attorneys will request enough time for hearings and adjudicative proceedings to permit full and fair presentation of the matter and to permit response by opposing counsel. When scheduling depositions, Attorneys will schedule enough time to permit the conclusion of the deposition, including examination by all parties, without adjournment. FL ST 6 J CIR 2009-066 PA/PI-CIR(B)(3).

   d. Attorneys will call potential scheduling problems to the attention of those affected, including the court, as soon as they become apparent. Attorneys will avoid last minute cancellations. FL ST 6 J CIR 2009-066 PA/PI-CIR(B)(4).

   e. Attorneys will make request for changes only when necessary. Attorneys will not request rescheduling, cancellations, extension or postponements solely for the purpose of delay or obtaining unfair advantage. FL ST 6 J CIR 2009-066 PA/PI-CIR(B)(5).

   f. Attorneys will cooperate with opposing counsel when conflicts and calendar changes are necessary and requested. FL ST 6 J CIR 2009-066 PA/PI-CIR(B)(6).

   g. Attorneys will grant reasonable requests for scheduling, rescheduling, cancellations, extensions, and postponements that do not prejudice our client's opportunity for full, fair and prompt consideration and adjudication of the client's claim or defense. FL ST 6 J CIR 2009-066 PA/PI-CIR(B)(7).

   h. First requests for reasonable extensions of time to respond to litigation deadlines relating to pleadings, discovery, or motions, should be granted as a matter of courtesy unless time is of the essence or other circumstances require otherwise. FL ST 6 J CIR 2009-066 PA/PI-CIR(B)(8).

   i. Attorneys will resolve subsequent requests by balancing the need for expedition against the deference we should give to opposing counsel's schedule of professional and personal engagements, the reasonableness of the length of extension requested, opposing counsel's willingness to grant reciprocal extensions, the time needed for the task, and whether it is likely a court would grant the extension. FL ST 6 J CIR 2009-066 PA/PI-CIR(B)(9).

   j. Attorneys will not attach unfair or extraneous conditions to extensions. Attorneys will impose conditions required to preserve rights that an extension might jeopardize. Attorneys may seek reciprocal scheduling concessions. When granting an extension, we will not try to preclude an opponent's substantive rights. FL ST 6 J CIR 2009-066 PA/PI-CIR(B)(10).

5. *Timing*

   a. Hearings are limited to five (5) minutes per case. FL ST 6 J CIR PINELLAS CIR CT PI-CIR-98-30.

   b. For more information regarding the timing of hearings, please see FL ST 6 J CIR PINELLAS CIR CT PI-CIR-98-30.

6. *Telephonic hearings.* For information regarding telephonic hearings, please see FL ST 6 J CIR PA/PI-CIR-88-48.

H. Forms

1. Official Motion for Summary Judgment Forms for Florida

   a. Caption. FL ST RCP Form 1.901.

   b. Notice of compliance when constitutional challenge is brought. FL ST RCP Form 1.975.

2. Motion for Summary Judgment Forms for Florida

   a. Motion for summary judgment; By plaintiff. FL-PP § 6:9.

   b. Motion for summary judgment; By defendant. FL-PP § 6:10.

c. Affidavit; Supporting motion for summary judgment; By plaintiff's attorney. FL-PP § 6:11.

d. Affidavit; Opposing motion for summary judgment; By defendant's attorney. FL-PP § 6:12.

e. Affidavit; Opposing motion for summary judgment; By party; Inability to present facts. FL-PP § 6:13.

f. Order; Establishing uncontroverted facts and stating issues requiring further determination. FL-PP § 6:14.

g. Summary judgment. FL-PP § 6:15.

h. Motion; Summary judgment, by defendant. FL-PRACFORM § 7:190.

i. Motion; Summary judgment, by plaintiff. FL-PRACFORM § 7:191.

j. Motion; Summary judgment, partial, by defendant. FL-PRACFORM § 7:192.

k. Motion; Summary judgment, part of claim. FL-PRACFORM § 7:193.

l. Form for plaintiff's motion for summary judgment. FL-RCPF R 1.510(128).

m. Form for notice of motion for summary judgment by plaintiff. FL-RCPF R 1.510(129).

n. Form for notice of cross-motion for summary judgment by plaintiff. FL-RCPF R 1.510(130).

o. Form for order denying motion for summary judgment and specifying uncontroverted facts. FL-RCPF R 1.510(304).

p. Form for motion for partial summary judgment. FL-RCPF R 1.510(305).

q. Form for motion for partial summary judgment; Affirmative defenses. FL-RCPF R 1.510(305.1).

I. Checklist

(I) ❑ Matters to be considered by moving party

- (a) ❑ Required documents
  - (1) ❑ Notice of hearing/Motion
  - (2) ❑ Certificate of service
- (b) ❑ Supplemental documents
  - (1) ❑ Affidavits
  - (2) ❑ Other evidence
  - (3) ❑ Proposed order
  - (4) ❑ Notice of constitutional question
- (c) ❑ Time for making motion
  - (1) ❑ By the plaintiff, after the expiration of twenty (20) days from the commencement of the action (claimant), or after service of a motion for summary judgment by the adverse party
  - (2) ❑ By the defending party at any time
  - (3) ❑ The motion for summary judgment must be served at least twenty (20) days before the time fixed for the hearing

(II) ❑ Matters to be considered by opposing party

- (a) ❑ Required documents
  - (1) ❑ Response to motion
  - (2) ❑ Certificate of service
- (b) ❑ Supplemental documents
  - (1) ❑ Affidavits
  - (2) ❑ Notice of evidence relied upon
  - (3) ❑ Other evidence

(4) ❑ Proposed order

(5) ❑ Notice of constitutional question

(c) ❑ Time for service and filing of opposition

(1) ❑ The adverse party shall identify, by notice mailed to the movant's attorney at least five (5) days prior to the day of the hearing, or delivered no later than 5:00 p.m. two (2) business days prior to the day of the hearing, any summary judgment evidence on which the adverse party relies

(2) ❑ To the extent that summary judgment evidence has not already been filed with the court, the adverse party shall serve a copy on the movant by mail at least five (5) days prior to the day of the hearing, or by delivery to the movant's attorney no later than 5:00 p.m. two (2) business days prior to the day of hearing

Motions, Oppositions and Replies
Motion for Sanctions

Document Last Updated January 2013

A. Applicable Rules

1. *State rules*

a. Attorney's fee; Sanctions for raising unsupported claims or defenses; Exceptions; Service of motions; Damages for delay of litigation. FL ST § 57.105.

b. Administrative Procedure Act. FL ST § 120.50; FL ST § 120.52; FL ST § 120.68; FL ST § 120.81.

c. Offer of judgment and demand for judgment. FL ST § 768.79.

d. Proposals for settlement. FL ST RCP Rule 1.442.

e. Motions for costs and attorneys' fees. FL ST RCP Rule 1.525.

f. Rules of court. FL ST RCP Rule 1.010; FL ST J ADMIN Rule 2.110.

g. Nonverification of pleadings. FL ST RCP Rule 1.030.

h. Service and filing of pleadings, orders, and documents. FL ST RCP Rule 1.080.

i. Time. FL ST RCP Rule 1.090.

j. Pleadings and motions. FL ST RCP Rule 1.100.

k. Motions. FL ST RCP Rule 1.160.

l. Relief from judgment, decrees, or orders. FL ST RCP Rule 1.540.

m. Mediation and arbitration. FL ST RCP Rule 1.700; FL ST RCP Rule 1.710; FL ST RCP Rule 1.720; FL ST RCP Rule 1.730; FL ST RCP Rule 1.750; FL ST RCP Rule 1.800; FL ST RCP Rule 1.810; FL ST RCP Rule 1.820; FL ST RCP Rule 1.830.

n. Forms. FL ST RCP Rule 1.900.

o. Minimization of the filing of sensitive information. FL ST J ADMIN Rule 2.425.

p. Retention of court records. FL ST J ADMIN Rule 2.430.

q. Foreign attorneys. FL ST J ADMIN Rule 2.510.

r. Signature of attorneys and parties. FL ST J ADMIN Rule 2.515.

s. Paper. FL ST J ADMIN Rule 2.520.

t. Electronic filing. FL ST J ADMIN Rule 2.525.

u. Accessibility of information and technology. FL ST J ADMIN Rule 2.526.

v. Communication equipment. FL ST J ADMIN Rule 2.530.

w. Court reporting. FL ST J ADMIN Rule 2.535.

x. Requests for accommodations by persons with disabilities. FL ST J ADMIN Rule 2.540.

2. *Local rules*
   a. General motion rule. FL ST 6 J CIR LOCAL Rule 5.
   b. Telephonic hearings in circuit civil, county civil and small claims cases. FL ST 6 J CIR PA/PI-CIR-88-48.
   c. Pre-trial conferences. FL ST 6 J CIR PA/PI-CIR-98-49.
   d. Uniform motion calendar civil division. FL ST 6 J CIR PINELLAS CIR CT PI-CIR-98-30.
   e. Standards of professional courtesy. FL ST 6 J CIR 2009-066 PA/PI-CIR.
   f. Arbitration and mediation program circuit civil and family cases. FL ST 6 J CIR PA/PI-CIR-96-63; FL ST 6 J CIR 2011-006 PA/PI-CIR.

B. Timing

1. *Motion for sanctions.* A motion by a party seeking sanctions under FL ST § 57.105 must be served but may not be filed with or presented to the court unless, within twenty one (21) days after service of the motion, the challenged paper, claim, defense, contention, allegation, or denial is not withdrawn or appropriately corrected. FL ST § 57.105(4).
2. *Sanctions in relation to proposals for settlement.* Any party seeking sanctions pursuant to applicable Florida law, based on the failure of the proposal's recipient to accept a proposal, shall do so by serving a motion in accordance with FL ST RCP Rule 1.525. FL ST RCP Rule 1.442(g). Any party seeking a judgment taxing costs, attorneys' fees, or both shall serve a motion no later than thirty (30) days after filing of the judgment, including a judgment of dismissal, or the service of a notice of voluntary dismissal, which judgment or notice concludes the action as to that party. FL ST RCP Rule 1.525.
3. *General motion timing.* A copy of any written motion which may not be heard ex parte and a copy of the notice of the hearing thereof shall be served a reasonable time before the time specified for the hearing. FL ST RCP Rule 1.090(d).
   a. All motions, except motions in limine, shall be filed and heard prior to the pre-trial conference unless good cause exists why the motions were not heard prior to the pre-trial conference, including the inability to obtain hearing time prior to the pre-trial conference. FL ST 6 J CIR PA/PI-CIR-98-49(6).
   b. If such good cause exists, the court will hear such motions at the pre-trial conference or at a separate hearing following the pre-trial conference. FL ST 6 J CIR PA/PI-CIR-98-49(6).
4. *Computation of time*
   a. *Generally.* Computation of time shall be governed by FL ST J ADMIN Rule 2.514. FL ST RCP Rule 1.090(a). The following rules apply in computing time periods specified in any rule of procedure, local rule, court order, or statute that does not specify a method of computing time. FL ST J ADMIN Rule 2.514(a).
      i. *Period stated in days or a longer unit.* When the period is stated in days or a longer unit of time (A) exclude the day of the event that triggers the period; (B) count every day, including intermediate Saturdays, Sundays, and legal holidays; and (C) include the last day of the period, but if the last day is a Saturday, Sunday, or legal holiday, or falls within any period of time extended through an order of the chief justice under FL ST J ADMIN Rule 2.205(a)(2)(B)(iv), the period continues to run until the end of the next day that is not a Saturday, Sunday, or legal holiday and does not fall within any period of time extended through an order of the chief justice. FL ST J ADMIN Rule 2.514(a)(1).
      ii. *Period stated in hours.* When the period is stated in hours (A) begin counting immediately on the occurrence of the event that triggers the period; (B) count every hour, including hours during intermediate Saturdays, Sundays, and legal holidays; and (C) if the period would end on a Saturday, Sunday, or legal holiday, or during any period of time extended through an order of the chief justice under FL ST J ADMIN Rule 2.205(a)(2)(B)(iv), the period continues to run until the same time on the next day that is not a Saturday, Sunday, or legal holiday and does not fall within any period of time extended through an order of the chief justice. FL ST J ADMIN Rule 2.514(a)(2).

iii. *Period stated in days less than seven (7) days.* When the period stated in days is less than seven (7) days, intermediate Saturdays, Sundays, and legal holidays shall be excluded in the computation. FL ST J ADMIN Rule 2.514(a)(3).

iv. *"Last day" defined.* Unless a different time is set by a statute, local rule, or court order, the last day ends (A) for electronic filing or for service by any means, at midnight; and (B) for filing by other means, when the clerk's office is scheduled to close. FL ST J ADMIN Rule 2.514(a)(4).

v. *"Next day" defined.* The "next day" is determined by continuing to count forward when the period is measured after an event and backward when measured before an event. FL ST J ADMIN Rule 2.514(a)(5).

vi. *"Legal holiday" defined.* "Legal holiday" means (A) the day set aside by FL ST § 110.117, for observing New Year's Day, Martin Luther King, Jr.'s Birthday, Memorial Day, Independence Day, Labor Day, Veterans' Day, Thanksgiving Day, the Friday after Thanksgiving Day, or Christmas Day, and (B) any day observed as a holiday by the clerk's office or as designated by the chief judge. FL ST J ADMIN Rule 2.514(a)(6).

b. *Additional time after service by mail or e-mail.* When a party may or must act within a specified time after service and service is made by mail or e-mail, five (5) days are added after the period that would otherwise expire under FL ST J ADMIN Rule 2.514(a). FL ST J ADMIN Rule 2.514(b).

c. *Enlargement.* When an act is required or allowed to be done at or within a specified time by order of court, by the Florida Rules of Civil Procedure, or by notice given thereunder, for cause shown the court at any time in its discretion (1) with or without notice, may order the period enlarged if request therefor is made before the expiration of the period originally prescribed or as extended by a previous order, or (2) upon motion made and notice after the expiration of the specified period, may permit the act to be done when failure to act was the result of excusable neglect, but it may not extend the time for making a motion for new trial, for rehearing, or to alter or amend a judgment; making a motion for relief from a judgment under FL ST RCP Rule 1.540(b); taking an appeal or filing a petition for certiorari; or making a motion for a directed verdict. FL ST RCP Rule 1.090(b).

d. *Unaffected by expiration of term.* The period of time provided for the doing of any act or the taking of any proceeding shall not be affected or limited by the continued existence or expiration of a term of court. The continued existence or expiration of a term of court in no way affects the power of a court to do any act or take any proceeding in any action which is or has been pending before it. FL ST RCP Rule 1.090(c).

C. General Requirements

1. *Motions generally*

a. *Contents.* An application to the court for an order shall be by motion which shall be made in writing unless made during a hearing or trial, shall state with particularity the grounds therefor, and shall set forth the relief or order sought. The requirement of writing is fulfilled if the motion is stated in a written notice of the hearing of the motion. All notices of hearing shall specify each motion or other matter to be heard. FL ST RCP Rule 1.100(b).

b. *Particularity requirement.* The court considers a motion in the light of the substantive law, rule or statute to make its determination. Some rules require a statement of the grounds for a motion under the rule. Failure to give the grounds will result in denial of the motion. This should be the result in all situations when the ground for the motion is not inherent in the rule. FL-PRACPROC § 9:3. The requirement is nevertheless an important one, first because of the due process notice rights of the respondent, as well as for the assistance it provides to the court in its preparation for the hearing or, absent a hearing, for disposition. 4 FLPRAC R 1.100.

c. *Standards of professional courtesy; Motion practice*

i. Attorneys will make every reasonable effort to resolve the issue before setting a motion for hearing. FL ST 6 J CIR 2009-066 PA/PI-CIR(G)(1).

ii. Attorneys will not force opposing counsel to make motions attorneys do not intend to oppose unless circumstances require or the client requires. FL ST 6 J CIR 2009-066 PA/PI-CIR(G)(2).

2. *Motion for sanctions*
   a. *Sanctions for raising unsupported claims or defenses*
      i. *No material facts; No law supporting material facts.* Upon the court's initiative or motion of any party, the court shall award a reasonable attorney's fee, including prejudgment interest, to be paid to the prevailing party in equal amounts by the losing party and the losing party's attorney on any claim or defense at any time during a civil proceeding or action in which the court finds that the losing party or the losing party's attorney knew or should have known that a claim or defense when initially presented to the court or at any time before trial was not supported by the material facts necessary to establish the claim or defense; or would not be supported by the application of then-existing law to those material facts. FL ST § 57.105(1).
      ii. *Unreasonable delay.* At any time in any civil proceeding or action in which the moving party proves by a preponderance of the evidence that any action taken by the opposing party, including, but not limited to, the filing of any pleading or part thereof, the assertion of or response to any discovery demand, the assertion of any claim or defense, or the response to any request by any other party, was taken primarily for the purpose of unreasonable delay, the court shall award damages to the moving party for its reasonable expenses incurred in obtaining the order, which may include attorney's fees, and other loss resulting from the improper delay. FL ST § 57.105(2).
      iii. *Limit on monetary sanctions.* Notwithstanding FL ST § 57.105(1) and FL ST § 57.105(2), monetary sanctions may not be awarded:
         - Under FL ST § 57.105(1)(b) if the court determines that the claim or defense was initially presented to the court as a good faith argument for the extension, modification, or reversal of existing law or the establishment of new law, as it applied to the material facts, with a reasonable expectation of success. FL ST § 57.105(3)(a).
         - Under FL ST § 57.105(1)(a) or FL ST § 57.105(1)(b) against the losing party's attorney if he or she has acted in good faith, based on the representations of his or her client as to the existence of those material facts. FL ST § 57.105(3)(b).
         - Under FL ST § 57.105(1)(b) against a represented party. FL ST § 57.105(3)(c).
         - On the court's initiative under FL ST § 57.105(1) and FL ST § 57.105(2) unless sanctions are awarded before a voluntary dismissal or settlement of the claims made by or against the party that is, or whose attorneys are, to be sanctioned. FL ST § 57.105(3)(d).
      iv. *Other sanctions available.* The provisions of FL ST § 57.105 are supplemental to other sanctions or remedies available under law or under court rules. FL ST § 57.105(6).
      v. *Fees provided for in contract.* If a contract contains a provision allowing attorney's fees to a party when he or she is required to take any action to enforce the contract, the court may also allow reasonable attorney's fees to the other party when that party prevails in any action, whether as plaintiff or defendant, with respect to the contract. FL ST § 57.105(7) applies to any contract entered into on or after October 1, 1988. FL ST § 57.105(7).
   b. *Sanctions in relation to proposals for settlement*
      i. *Generally.* Any party seeking sanctions pursuant to applicable Florida law, based on the failure of the proposal's recipient to accept a proposal, shall do so by serving a motion in accordance with FL ST RCP Rule 1.525. FL ST RCP Rule 1.442(g). Any party seeking a judgment taxing costs, attorneys' fees, or both shall serve a motion no later than thirty (30) days after filing of the judgment, including a judgment of dismissal, or the service of a notice of voluntary dismissal, which judgment or notice concludes the action as to that party. FL ST RCP Rule 1.525.
      ii. *Motion after judgment, voluntary or involuntary dismissal.* Upon motion made by the offeror within thirty (30) days after the entry of judgment or after voluntary or involuntary dismissal, the court shall determine the following:
         - If a defendant serves an offer which is not accepted by the plaintiff, and if the judgment obtained by the plaintiff is at least twenty-five (25%) percent less than the amount of the

offer, the defendant shall be awarded reasonable costs, including investigative expenses, and attorney's fees, calculated in accordance with the guidelines promulgated by the Supreme Court, incurred from the date the offer was served, and the court shall set off such costs in attorney's fees against the award. When such costs and attorney's fees total more than the amount of the judgment, the court shall enter judgment for the defendant against the plaintiff for the amount of the costs and fees, less the amount of the award to the plaintiff. FL ST § 768.79(6)(a).

- If a plaintiff serves an offer which is not accepted by the defendant, and if the judgment obtained by the plaintiff is at least twenty-five (25%) percent more than the amount of the offer, the plaintiff shall be awarded reasonable costs, including investigative expenses, and attorney's fees, calculated in accordance with the guidelines promulgated by the Supreme Court, incurred from the date the offer was served. FL ST § 768.79(6)(b).
- For purposes of the determination required by FL ST § 768.79(6)(a), the term "judgment obtained" means the amount of the net judgment entered, plus any postoffer collateral source payments received or due as of the date of the judgment, plus any postoffer settlement amounts by which the verdict was reduced. For purposes of the determination required by FL ST § 768.79(6)(b), the term "judgment obtained" means the amount of the net judgment entered, plus any postoffer settlement amounts by which the verdict was reduced. FL ST § 768.79(6).

iii. For further information please see FL ST § 768.79 and FL ST RCP Rule 1.442.

3. *Arbitration and mediation*

a. *Referral to arbitration and mediation.* Except as hereinafter provided or as otherwise prohibited by law, the presiding judge may enter an order referring all or any part of a contested civil matter to mediation or arbitration. The parties to any contested civil matter may file a written stipulation to mediate or arbitrate any issue between them at any time. Such stipulation shall be incorporated into the order of referral. FL ST RCP Rule 1.700(a).

b. *Arbitration*

i. *Exclusions.* A civil action shall be ordered to arbitration or arbitration in conjunction with mediation upon stipulation of the parties. A civil action may be ordered to arbitration or arbitration in conjunction with mediation upon motion of any party or by the court, if the judge determines the action to be of such a nature that arbitration could be of benefit to the litigants or the court. FL ST RCP Rule 1.800.

- Under no circumstances may the following categories of actions be referred to arbitration: (1) bond estreatures; (2) habeas corpus or other extraordinary writs; (3) bond validations; (4) civil or criminal contempt; (5) such other matters as may be specified by order of the chief judge in the circuit. FL ST RCP Rule 1.800.

ii. For more information regarding arbitration, please see FL ST RCP Rule 1.810; FL ST RCP Rule 1.820; FL ST RCP Rule 1.830.

c. *Mediation.* For more information regarding mediation, please see FL ST RCP Rule 1.710; FL ST RCP Rule 1.720; FL ST RCP Rule 1.730; and FL ST RCP Rule 1.750.

d. See FL ST 6 J CIR PA/PI-CIR-96-63 for more information about the Arbitration and Mediation Program for Florida's Sixth Judicial Circuit.

4. *Rules of court*

a. *Rules of civil procedure.* The Florida Rules of Civil Procedure apply to all actions of a civil nature and all special statutory proceedings in the circuit courts and county courts except those to which the Florida Probate Rules, the Florida Family Law Rules of Procedure, or the Small Claims Rules apply. FL ST RCP Rule 1.010.

i. The form, content, procedure, and time for pleading in all special statutory proceedings shall be as prescribed by the statutes governing the proceeding unless the Florida Rules of Civil Procedure specifically provide to the contrary. FL ST RCP Rule 1.010.

ii. The Florida Rules of Civil Procedure shall be construed to secure the just, speedy, and inexpensive determination of every action. FL ST RCP Rule 1.010.

b. *Rules of judicial administration.* The Florida Rules of Judicial Administration shall apply to administrative matters in all courts to which the Florida Rules of Judicial Administration are applicable by their terms. The Florida Rules of Judicial Administration shall be construed to secure the speedy and inexpensive determination of every proceeding to which they are applicable. The Florida Rules of Judicial Administration shall supersede all conflicting rules and statutes. FL ST J ADMIN Rule 2.110.

5. *Settlement and alternative dispute resolution.* When a matter is scheduled for hearing and the matter is resolved by agreement or settlement, the party setting the matter for hearing shall notify the court. When a matter is scheduled for trial and the case settles, the plaintiff shall notify the court. Permission of the court must be obtained in order to cancel a trial. FL ST 6 J CIR LOCAL Rule 5(A).

a. Unless there are strong and overriding issues of principle, attorneys will raise and explore the issue of settlement as soon as enough is known to make settlement discussions meaningful. FL ST 6 J CIR 2009-066 PA/PI-CIR(I)(1).

b. Attorneys will not falsely hold out the possibility of settlement to adjourn discovery or delay trial. FL ST 6 J CIR 2009-066 PA/PI-CIR(I)(2).

c. Attorneys will consider whether the client's interest could be adequately served and the controversy more expeditiously and economically disposed of by arbitration, mediation or other forms of alternative dispute resolution. FL ST 6 J CIR 2009-066 PA/PI-CIR(I)(3).

D. Documents

1. *Required documents*

a. *Notice of hearing/Motion.* An application to the court for an order shall be by motion which shall be made in writing unless made during a hearing or trial, shall state with particularity the grounds therefor, and shall set forth the relief or order sought. The requirement of writing is fulfilled if the motion is stated in a written notice of the hearing of the motion. All notices of hearing shall specify each motion or other matter to be heard. FL ST RCP Rule 1.100(b).

i. *Notices to persons with disabilities.* See the Format section of this KeyRules document for further information.

b. *Certificate of service.* When any attorney certifies in substance: "I certify that a copy hereof has been furnished to (here insert name or names and addresses used for service) by (e-mail) (delivery) (mail) (fax) on .... (date) ....________________ Attorney" the certificate is taken as prima facie proof of such service in compliance with FL ST J ADMIN Rule 2.516. FL ST J ADMIN Rule 2.516(f).

2. *Supplemental documents*

a. *Proposed order.* The court may require that orders or judgments be prepared by a party, may require the party to furnish the court with stamped, addressed envelopes for service of the order or judgment, and may require that proposed orders and judgments be furnished to all parties before entry by the court of the order or judgment. FL ST J ADMIN Rule 2.516(h)(1).

i. After a hearing, attorneys will make a good faith effort to quickly agree or disagree upon a proposed order and submit the result to the court. Unless otherwise instructed by the court, or agreed to by counsel, all proposed orders shall be provided to other counsel for approval or comment prior to submission to the court. Attorneys will not submit controverted orders to the court with a copy to opposing counsel for "objections within ______ days". Courts prefer to know that the order is either agreed upon or opposed. FL ST 6 J CIR 2009-066 PA/PI-CIR(G)(3).

ii. Attorneys will not use post-hearing submissions of proposed orders as a guise to reargue the merits of the matter. FL ST 6 J CIR 2009-066 PA/PI-CIR(G)(4).

b. *Notice of constitutional question.* A party that files a pleading, written motion, or other paper drawing into question the constitutionality of a state statute or a county or municipal charter, ordinance, or franchise must promptly (1) file a notice of constitutional question stating the question

and identifying the paper that raises it; and (2) serve the notice and the pleading, written motion, or other paper drawing into question the constitutionality of a state statute or a county or municipal charter, ordinance, or franchise on the Attorney General or the state attorney of the judicial circuit in which the action is pending, by either certified or registered mail. Service of the notice and pleading, written motion, or other paper does not require joinder of the Attorney General or the state attorney as a party to the action. FL ST RCP Rule 1.071.

E. Format

1. *Documents; Type and size.* Documents subject to the exceptions set forth in FL ST J ADMIN Rule 2.525(d) shall be filed on recycled paper measuring eight and one half by eleven (8 1/2 by 11) inches. For purposes of FL ST J ADMIN Rule 2.520, paper is recycled if it contains a minimum content of fifty (50) percent waste paper. Xerographic reduction of legal-size (eight and one half by fourteen (8 1/2 by 14) inches) documents to letter size (eight and one half by eleven (8 1/2 by 11) inches) is prohibited. All other documents filed by electronic transmission shall be filed in a format capable of being printed in a format consistent with the provisions of FL ST J ADMIN Rule 2.250. FL ST J ADMIN Rule 2.520(b).
   a. *Exhibits.* Any exhibit or attachment filed with pleadings or papers may be filed in its original size. FL ST J ADMIN Rule 2.520(c).
   b. *Recording space.* On all papers and documents prepared and filed by the court or by any party to a proceeding which are to be recorded in the public records of any county, including but not limited to final money judgments and notices of lis pendens, a three (3) inch by three (3) inch space at the top right-hand corner on the first page and a one (1) inch by three (3) inch space at the top right-hand corner on each subsequent page shall be left blank and reserved for use by the clerk of court. FL ST J ADMIN Rule 2.520(d).
      i. *Exceptions to recording space.* Any papers or documents created by persons or entities over which the filing party has no control, including but not limited to wills, codicils, trusts, or other testamentary documents; documents prepared or executed by any public officer; documents prepared, executed, acknowledged, or proved outside of the State of Florida; or documents created by State or Federal government agencies, may be filed without the space required by FL ST J ADMIN Rule 2.520. FL ST J ADMIN Rule 2.520(e).
   c. *Noncompliance.* No clerk of court is permitted to refuse to file any document or paper because of noncompliance with the Florida Rules of Judicial Administration. However, upon request of the clerk of court, noncomplying documents must be resubmitted in accordance with the formatting rules. FL ST J ADMIN Rule 2.520(f).
2. *Caption.* Every pleading, motion, order, judgment, or other paper shall have a caption containing the name of the court, the file number, and except for in rem proceedings, including forfeiture proceedings, the name of the first party on each side with an appropriate indication of other parties, and a designation identifying the party filing it and its nature or the nature of the order, as the case may be. In any in rem proceeding, every pleading, motion, order, judgment, or other paper shall have a caption containing the name of the court, the file number, the style "In re" (followed by the name or general description of the property), and a designation of the person or entity filing it and its nature or the nature of the order, as the case may be. In an in rem forfeiture proceeding, the style shall be "In re forfeiture of" (followed by the name of the general description of the property). All papers filed in the action shall be styled in such a manner as to indicate clearly the subject matter of the paper and the party requesting or obtaining relief. FL ST RCP Rule 1.100(c)(1).
3. *Writing and written defined.* Writing or written means a document containing information, an application, or a stipulation. FL ST RCP Rule 1.080(c).
4. *Rule abbreviations*
   a. The Florida Rules of Civil Procedure and shall be abbreviated as Fla.R.Civ.P. FL ST RCP Rule 1.010.
   b. The Florida Rules of Judicial Administration shall be abbreviated as Fla. R. Jud. Admin. FL ST J ADMIN Rule 2.110.
5. *Nonverification.* Except when otherwise specifically provided by the Florida Rules of Civil Procedure or

an applicable statute, every pleading or other document of a party represented by an attorney need not be verified or accompanied by an affidavit. FL ST RCP Rule 1.030; FL ST J ADMIN Rule 2.515(a).

6. *Attorney signature*
   a. *Attorney signature.* Every pleading and other document of a party represented by an attorney shall be signed by at least one (1) attorney of record in that attorney's individual name whose current record Florida Bar address, telephone number, including area code, primary e-mail address and secondary e-mail addresses, if any, and Florida Bar number shall be stated, and who shall be duly licensed to practice law in Florida or who shall have received permission to appear in the particular case as provided in FL ST J ADMIN Rule 2.510. FL ST J ADMIN Rule 2.515(a).
      i. The attorney may be required by the court to give the address of, and to vouch for the attorney's authority to represent, the party. FL ST J ADMIN Rule 2.515(a).
      ii. The signature of an attorney shall constitute a certificate by the attorney that the attorney has read the pleading or other document; that to the best of the attorney's knowledge, information, and belief there is good ground to support it; and that it is not interposed for delay. FL ST J ADMIN Rule 2.515(a).
      iii. If a pleading is not signed or is signed with intent to defeat the purpose of FL ST J ADMIN Rule 2.515, it may be stricken and the action may proceed as though the pleading or other document had not been served. FL ST J ADMIN Rule 2.515(a).
   b. *Pro se litigant signature.* A party who is not represented by an attorney shall sign any pleading or other paper and state the party's address and telephone number, including area code. FL ST J ADMIN Rule 2.515(b).
   c. *Form of signature*
      i. The signatures required on pleadings and documents by FL ST J ADMIN Rule 2.515(a) and FL ST J ADMIN Rule 2.515(b) may be:
         - Original signatures;
         - Original signatures that have been reproduced by electronic means, such as on electronically transmitted documents or photocopied documents;
         - Electronic signatures using the "/s/," "s/," or "/s" formats by or at the direction of the person signing; or
         - Any other signature format authorized by general law, so long as the clerk where the proceeding is pending has the capability of receiving and has obtained approval from the Supreme Court of Florida to accept pleadings and documents with that signature format. FL ST J ADMIN Rule 2.515(c)(1).
      ii. An attorney, party, or other person who files a pleading or paper by electronic transmission that does not contain the original signature of that attorney, party, or other person shall file that identical pleading or paper in paper form containing an original signature of that attorney, party, or other person (hereinafter called the follow-up filing) immediately thereafter. The follow-up filing is not required if the Supreme Court of Florida has entered an order directing the clerk of court to discontinue accepting the follow-up filing. FL ST J ADMIN Rule 2.515(c)(2).

7. *Forms*
   a. *Process.* The forms of process, notice of lis pendens, and notice of action provided in the Florida Rules of Civil Procedure are sufficient. Variations from the forms do not void process or notices that are otherwise sufficient. FL ST RCP Rule 1.900(a).
   b. *Other forms.* The other forms provided in the Florida Rules of Civil Procedure are sufficient for the matters that are covered by them. So long as the substance is expressed without prolixity, the forms may be varied to meet the facts of a particular case. FL ST RCP Rule 1.900(b).
   c. *Formal matters.* Captions, except for the designation of the paper, are omitted from the forms provided in the Florida Rules of Civil Procedure. A general form of caption is the first form provided. Signatures are omitted from pleadings and motions. FL ST RCP Rule 1.900(c).

8. *Notices to persons with disabilities.* All notices of court proceedings to be held in a public facility, and all process compelling appearance at such proceedings, shall include the following statement in bold face, fourteen (14) point Times New Roman or Courier font: "If you are a person with a disability who needs any accommodation in order to participate in this proceeding, you are entitled, at no cost to you, to the provision of certain assistance. Please contact [identify applicable court personnel by name, address, and telephone number] at least seven (7) days before your scheduled court appearance, or immediately upon receiving this notification if the time before the scheduled appearance is less than seven (7) days; if you are hearing or voice impaired, call 711." FL ST J ADMIN Rule 2.540(c)(1).
9. *Minimization of the filing of sensitive information*
   a. *Limitations for court filings.* Unless authorized by FL ST J ADMIN Rule 2.425(b), statute, another rule of court, or the court orders otherwise, designated sensitive information filed with the court must be limited to the following format:
      i. The initials of a person known to be a minor;
      ii. The year of birth of a person's birth date;
      iii. No portion of any: Social security number, Bank account number, Credit card account number, Charge account number, or Debit account number;
      iv. The last four digits of any: Taxpayer identification number (TIN), Employee identification number, Driver's license number, Passport number, Telephone number, Financial account number, except as set forth in FL ST J ADMIN Rule 2.425(a)(3), Brokerage account number, Insurance policy account number, Loan account number, Customer account number, or Patient or health care number;
      v. A truncated version of any: Email address, Computer user name, Password, or Personal identification number (PIN); and
      vi. A truncated version of any other sensitive information as provided by court order. FL ST J ADMIN Rule 2.425(a).
   b. *Exceptions.* FL ST J ADMIN Rule 2.425(a) does not apply to the following:
      i. An account number which identifies the property alleged to be the subject of a proceeding;
      ii. The record of an administrative or agency proceeding;
      iii. The record in appellate or review proceedings;
      iv. The birth date of a minor whenever the birth date is necessary for the court to establish or maintain subject matter jurisdiction;
      v. The name of a minor in any order relating to parental responsibility, time-sharing, or child support;
      vi. The name of a minor in any document or order affecting the minor's ownership of real property;
      vii. The birth date of a party in a writ of attachment or notice to payor;
      viii. In traffic and criminal proceedings: a pro se filing; a court filing that is related to a criminal matter or investigation and that is prepared before the filing of a criminal charge or is not filed as part of any docketed criminal case; an arrest or search warrant or any information in support thereof; a charging document and an affidavit or other documents filed in support of any charging document, including any driving records; a statement of particulars; discovery material introduced into evidence or otherwise filed with the court; and all information necessary for the proper issuance and execution of a subpoena duces tecum;
      ix. Information used by the clerk for case maintenance purposes or the courts for case management purposes; and
      x. Information which is relevant and material to an issue before the court. FL ST J ADMIN Rule 2.425(b).
   c. *Remedies.* Upon motion by a party or interested person or sua sponte by the court, the court may order remedies, sanctions or both for a violation of FL ST J ADMIN Rule 2.425(a). Following notice

and an opportunity to respond, the court may impose sanctions if such filing was not made in good faith. FL ST J ADMIN Rule 2.425(c).

d. *Motions not restricted.* FL ST J ADMIN Rule 2.425 does not restrict a party's right to move for protective order, to move to file documents under seal, or to request a determination of the confidentiality of records. FL ST J ADMIN Rule 2.425(d).

e. *Application.* FL ST J ADMIN Rule 2.425 does not affect the application of constitutional provisions, statutes, or rules of court regarding confidential information or access to public information. FL ST J ADMIN Rule 2.425(e).

F. Filing and Service Requirements

1. *Filing requirements.* All original documents must be filed with the court either before service or immediately thereafter, unless otherwise provided for by general law or other rules. If the original of any bond or other document is not placed in the court file, a certified copy must be so placed by the clerk. FL ST J ADMIN Rule 2.516(d). All documents shall be filed in conformity with the requirements of FL ST J ADMIN Rule 2.525. FL ST RCP Rule 1.080(b). All documents filed in any court shall be filed by electronic transmission in accordance with FL ST J ADMIN Rule 2.525. "Documents" means pleadings, motions, petitions, memoranda, briefs, notices, exhibits, declarations, affidavits, orders, judgments, decrees, writs, opinions, and any other paper or writing submitted to a court. FL ST J ADMIN Rule 2.520(a). All documents that are court records, as defined in FL ST J ADMIN Rule 2.430(a)(1), must be filed by electronic transmission, provided that: (1) the clerk has the ability to accept and retain such documents; (2) the clerk or the chief judge of the circuit has requested permission to accept documents filed by electronic transmission; and (3) the supreme court has entered an order granting permission to the clerk to accept documents filed by electronic transmission. FL ST J ADMIN Rule 2.525(c)(1).

a. *Definition.* "Electronic transmission of documents" means the sending of information by electronic signals to, by or from a court or clerk, which when received can be transformed and stored or transmitted on paper, microfilm, magnetic storage device, optical imaging system, CD-ROM, flash drive, other electronic data storage system, server, case maintenance system ("CM"), electronic court filing ("ECF") system, statewide or local electronic portal ("e-portal"), or other electronic record keeping system authorized by the supreme court in a format sufficient to communicate the information on the original document in a readable format. Electronic transmission of documents includes electronic mail ("e-mail") and any internet-based transmission procedure, and may include procedures allowing for documents to be signed or verified by electronic means. FL ST J ADMIN Rule 2.525(a).

i. The filing of documents with the court as required by the Florida Rules of Judicial Administration must be made by filing them with the clerk in accordance with FL ST J ADMIN Rule 2.525, except that the judge may permit documents to be filed with the judge, in which event the judge must note the filing date before him or her on the documents and transmit them to the clerk. The date of filing is that shown on the face of the document by the judge's notation or the clerk's time stamp, whichever is earlier. FL ST J ADMIN Rule 2.516(e).

b. *Application.* Any court or clerk of the court may accept the electronic transmission of documents for filing after the clerk, together with input from the chief judge of the circuit, has obtained approval of the procedures and program for doing so from the Supreme Court of Florida. FL ST J ADMIN Rule 2.525(b).

c. *Exceptions*

i. Paper documents and other submissions may be manually submitted to the clerk or court:

- When the clerk does not have the ability to accept and retain documents by electronic filing or has not had ECF Procedures approved by the supreme court;
- For filing by any self-represented party or any self-represented nonparty unless specific ECF Procedures provide a means to file documents electronically. However, any self-represented nonparty that is a governmental or public agency and any other agency, partnership, corporation, or business entity acting on behalf of any governmental or public agency may file documents by electronic transmission if such entity has the capability of filing documents electronically;

- For filing by attorneys excused from e-mail service in accordance with FL ST J ADMIN Rule 2.516(b);
- When submitting evidentiary exhibits or filing non-documentary materials;
- When the filing involves documents in excess of twenty-five (25) megabytes (25MB) in size. For such filings, documents may be transmitted using an electronic storage medium that the clerk has the ability to accept, which may include a CD-ROM, flash drive, or similar storage medium;
- When filed in open court, as permitted by the court;
- When paper filing is permitted by any approved statewide or local ECF procedures; and
- If any court determines that justice so requires. FL ST J ADMIN Rule 2.525(d).

ii. Any document in paper form submitted under FL ST J ADMIN Rule 2.525(d) is filed when it is received by the clerk or court and the clerk shall immediately thereafter convert any filed paper document to an electronic document. "Convert to an electronic document" means optically capturing an image of a paper document and using character recognition software to recover as much of the document's text as practicable and then indexing and storing the document in the official court file. FL ST J ADMIN Rule 2.525(c)(4).

iii. Any storage medium submitted under FL ST J ADMIN Rule 2.525(d)(5) is filed when received by the clerk or court and the clerk shall immediately thereafter transfer the electronic documents from the storage device to the official court file. FL ST J ADMIN Rule 2.525(c)(5).

iv. If the filer of any paper document authorized under FL ST J ADMIN Rule 2.525(d) provides a self-addressed, postage-paid envelope for return of the paper document after it is converted to electronic form by the clerk, the clerk shall place the paper document in the envelope and deposit it in the mail. Except when a paper document is required to be maintained, the clerk may recycle any filed paper document that is not to be returned to the filer. FL ST J ADMIN Rule 2.525(c)(6).

v. The clerk may convert any paper document filed before the effective date of FL ST J ADMIN Rule 2.525 to an electronic document. Unless the clerk is required to maintain the paper document, if the paper document has been converted to an electronic document by the clerk, the paper document is no longer part of the official court file and may be removed and recycled. FL ST J ADMIN Rule 2.525(c)(7).

d. *Official court file.* For information on what constitutes the official court file, please see FL ST J ADMIN Rule 2.525(c)(2), FL ST J ADMIN Rule 2.525(c)(3).

e. *Administration.* All attorneys, parties, or other persons using this rule to file documents are required to make arrangements with the court or clerk for the payment of any charges authorized by general law or the supreme court before filing any document by electronic transmission. FL ST J ADMIN Rule 2.525(f)(2).

f. *Filing date.* The filing date for an electronically transmitted document is the date and time that such filing is acknowledged by an electronic stamp or otherwise, pursuant to any procedure set forth in any ECF Procedures approved by the supreme court, or the date the last page of such filing is received by the court or clerk. FL ST J ADMIN Rule 2.525(f)(3).

g. *Accessibility.* All documents transmitted in any electronic form under FL ST J ADMIN Rule 2.525 must comply with the accessibility requirements of FL ST J ADMIN Rule 2.526. FL ST J ADMIN Rule 2.525(g).

2. *Service requirements.* Every pleading subsequent to the initial pleading, all orders, and every other document filed in the action must be served in conformity with the requirements of FL ST J ADMIN Rule 2.516. FL ST RCP Rule 1.080(a).

a. *Service; When required.* Unless the court otherwise orders, or a statute or supreme court administrative order specifies a different means of service, every pleading subsequent to the initial pleading and every other document filed in any court proceeding, except applications for witness subpoenas and documents served by formal notice or required to be served in the manner provided for service

of formal notice, must be served in accordance with FL ST J ADMIN Rule 2.516 on each party. No service need be made on parties against whom a default has been entered, except that pleadings asserting new or additional claims against them must be served in the manner provided for service of summons. FL ST J ADMIN Rule 2.516(a).

b. *Service; How made.* When service is required or permitted to be made upon a party represented by an attorney, service must be made upon the attorney unless service upon the party is ordered by the court. FL ST J ADMIN Rule 2.516(b).

   i. *Service by electronic mail ("e-mail").* All documents required or permitted to be served on another party must be served by e-mail, unless FL ST J ADMIN Rule 2.516 otherwise provides. When, in addition to service by e-mail, the sender also utilizes another means of service provided for in FL ST J ADMIN Rule 2.516(b)(2), any differing time limits and other provisions applicable to that other means of service control. FL ST J ADMIN Rule 2.516(b)(1). Any document electronically transmitted to a court or clerk must also be served on all parties and interested persons in accordance with the applicable rules of court. FL ST J ADMIN Rule 2.525(e)(2).

      - *Service on attorneys.* Upon appearing in a proceeding, an attorney must serve a designation of a primary e-mail address and may designate no more than two (2) secondary e-mail addresses. Thereafter, service must be directed to all designated e-mail addresses in that proceeding. Every document filed by an attorney thereafter must include the primary e-mail address of that attorney and any secondary e-mail addresses. If an attorney does not designate any e-mail address for service, documents may be served on that attorney at the e-mail address on record with The Florida Bar. FL ST J ADMIN Rule 2.516(b)(1)(A).

      - *Exception to e-mail service on attorneys.* Service by an attorney on another attorney must be made by e-mail unless excused by the court. Upon motion by an attorney demonstrating that the attorney has no e-mail account and lacks access to the Internet at the attorney's office, the court may excuse the attorney from the requirements of e-mail service. Service on and by an attorney excused by the court from e-mail service must be by the means provided in FL ST J ADMIN Rule 2.516(b)(2). FL ST J ADMIN Rule 2.516(b)(1)(B).

      - *Service on and by parties not represented by an attorney.* Any party not represented by an attorney may serve a designation of a primary e-mail address and also may designate no more than two (2) secondary e-mail addresses to which service must be directed in that proceeding by the means provided in FL ST J ADMIN Rule 2.516(b)(1). If a party not represented by an attorney does not designate an e-mail address for service in a proceeding, service on and by that party must be by the means provided in FL ST J ADMIN Rule 2.516(b)(2). FL ST J ADMIN Rule 2.516(b)(1)(C).

      - *Time of service.* Service by e-mail is complete when it is sent. FL ST J ADMIN Rule 2.516(b)(1)(D). An e-mail is deemed served on the date it is sent. FL ST J ADMIN Rule 2.516(b)(1)(D)(i). If the sender learns that the e-mail did not reach the address of the person to be served, the sender must immediately send another copy by e-mail, or by a means authorized by FL ST J ADMIN Rule 2.516(b)(2). FL ST J ADMIN Rule 2.516(b)(1)(D)(ii). E-mail service is treated as service by mail for the computation of time. FL ST J ADMIN Rule 2.516(b)(1)(D)(iii).

   ii. *Format of e-mail for service.* Service of a document by e-mail is made by attaching a copy of the document in PDF format to an e-mail sent to all addresses designated by the attorney or party. FL ST J ADMIN Rule 2.516(b)(1)(E).

      - All documents served by e-mail must be attached to an e-mail message containing a subject line beginning with the words "SERVICE OF COURT DOCUMENT" in all capital letters, followed by the case number of the proceeding in which the documents are being served. FL ST J ADMIN Rule 2.516(b)(1)(E)(i).

      - The body of the e-mail must identify the court in which the proceeding is pending, the case number, the name of the initial party on each side, the title of each document served with that e-mail, and the sender's name and telephone number. FL ST J ADMIN Rule 2.516(b)(1)(E)(ii).

- Any document served by e-mail may be signed by the "/s/" format, as long as the filed original is signed in accordance with the applicable rule of procedure. FL ST J ADMIN Rule 2.516(b)(1)(E)(iii).
- Any e-mail which, together with its attached documents, exceeds five megabytes (5MB) in size, must be divided and sent as separate e-mails, no one of which may exceed five megabytes (5MB) in size and each of which must be sequentially numbered in the subject line. FL ST J ADMIN Rule 2.516(b)(1)(E)(iv).

iii. *Service by other means.* In addition to, and not in lieu of, service by e-mail, service may also be made upon attorneys by any of the means specified in FL ST J ADMIN Rule 2.516(b)(2). Service on and by all parties who are not represented by an attorney and who do not designate an e-mail address, and on and by all attorneys excused from e-mail service, must be made by delivering a copy of the document or by mailing it to the party or attorney at their last known address or, if no address is known, by leaving it with the clerk of the court. Service by mail is complete upon mailing. Delivery of a copy within FL ST J ADMIN Rule 2.516 is complete upon:

- Handing it to the attorney or to the party,
- Leaving it at the attorney's or party's office with a clerk or other person in charge thereof,
- If there is no one in charge, leaving it in a conspicuous place therein,
- If the office is closed or the person to be served has no office, leaving it at the person's usual place of abode with some person of his or her family above fifteen (15) years of age and informing such person of the contents, or
- Transmitting it by facsimile to the attorney's or party's office with a cover sheet containing the sender's name, firm, address, telephone number, and facsimile number, and the number of pages transmitted. When service is made by facsimile, a copy must also be served by any other method permitted by FL ST J ADMIN Rule 2.516. Facsimile service occurs when transmission is complete. FL ST J ADMIN Rule 2.516(b)(2)(A) through FL ST J ADMIN Rule 2.516(b)(2)(E).
- Service by delivery after 5:00 p.m. must be deemed to have been made by mailing on the date of delivery. FL ST J ADMIN Rule 2.516(b)(2)(F).

c. *Service; Numerous defendants.* In actions when the parties are unusually numerous, the court may regulate the service contemplated by the Florida Rules of Judicial Administration on motion or on its own initiative in such manner as may be found to be just and reasonable. FL ST J ADMIN Rule 2.516(c).

d. *Service by clerk.* Service of notices and other documents required to be made by the clerk must also be done as provided in FL ST J ADMIN Rule 2.516(b). FL ST J ADMIN Rule 2.516(g).

e. *Standards of professional courtesy; Service*

i. The timing and manner of service should not be used to the disadvantage of the party receiving the papers. This includes the use of facsimile transmissions and any additional expedited means of communication approved by the court. FL ST 6 J CIR 2009-066 PA/PI-CIR(C)(1).

ii. Attorneys will not serve papers to take advantage of opposing counsel's known absence from the office or at a time or in a manner designed to inconvenience an opponent, such as late on Friday afternoon or the day preceding a secular or religious holiday. FL ST 6 J CIR 2009-066 PA/PI-CIR(C)(2).

iii. Attorneys will not serve papers, including briefs and memoranda, so close to a court appearance that the ability of opposing counsel to prepare for that appearance or, where permitted, to respond, is inhibited. FL ST 6 J CIR 2009-066 PA/PI-CIR(C)(3).

iv. Service should be made personally or by facsimile transmission when it is likely that service by mail, even when allowed, will prejudice the opposing party. FL ST 6 J CIR 2009-066 PA/PI-CIR(C)(4).

G. Hearings

1. *Communication equipment*
   a. *Definition.* Communication equipment means a conference telephone or other electronic device that permits all those appearing or participating to hear and speak to each other, provided that all conversation of all parties is audible to all persons present. FL ST J ADMIN Rule 2.530(a).
   b. *Use by all parties.* A county or circuit court judge may, upon the court's own motion or upon the written request of a party, direct that communication equipment be used for a motion hearing, pretrial conference, or a status conference. A judge must give notice to the parties and consider any objections they may have to the use of communication equipment before directing that communication equipment be used. The decision to use communication equipment over the objection of parties will be in the sound discretion of the trial court, except as noted below. FL ST J ADMIN Rule 2.530(b).
   c. *Use only by requesting party.* A county or circuit court judge may, upon the written request of a party upon reasonable notice to all other parties, permit a requesting party to participate through communication equipment in a scheduled motion hearing; however, any such request (except in criminal, juvenile, and appellate proceedings) must be granted, absent a showing of good cause to deny the same, where the hearing is set for not longer than fifteen (15) minutes. FL ST J ADMIN Rule 2.530(c).
   d. *Testimony*
      i. *Generally.* A county or circuit court judge, general magistrate, special magistrate, or hearing officer may allow testimony to be taken through communication equipment if all parties consent or if permitted by another applicable rule of procedure. FL ST J ADMIN Rule 2.530(d)(1).
      ii. *Procedure.* Any party desiring to present testimony through communication equipment shall, prior to the hearing or trial at which the testimony is to be presented, contact all parties to determine whether each party consents to this form of testimony. The party seeking to present the testimony shall move for permission to present testimony through communication equipment, which motion shall set forth good cause as to why the testimony should be allowed in this form. FL ST J ADMIN Rule 2.530(d)(2).
      iii. *Oath.* Testimony may be taken through communication equipment only if a notary public or other person authorized to administer oaths in the witness's jurisdiction is present with the witness and administers the oath consistent with the laws of the jurisdiction. FL ST J ADMIN Rule 2.530(d)(3).
      iv. *Confrontation rights.* In juvenile and criminal proceedings the defendant must make an informed waiver of any confrontation rights that may be abridged by the use of communication equipment. FL ST J ADMIN Rule 2.530(d)(4).
      v. *Video testimony.* If the testimony to be presented utilizes video conferencing or comparable two-way visual capabilities, the court in its discretion may modify the procedures set forth in FL ST J ADMIN Rule 2.530 to accommodate the technology utilized. FL ST J ADMIN Rule 2.530(d)(5).
   e. *Burden of expense.* The cost for the use of the communication equipment is the responsibility of the requesting party unless otherwise directed by the court. FL ST J ADMIN Rule 2.530(e).
2. *Standards of professional courtesy; Scheduling*
   a. Attorneys will communicate with opposing counsel to schedule depositions, hearings, and other proceedings, at times mutually convenient for all interested persons. FL ST 6 J CIR 2009-066 PA/PI-CIR(B)(1).
   b. Attorneys will provide opposing counsel and other affected persons reasonable notice of all proceedings except upon agreement of counsel when expedited scheduling is necessary. Attorneys will immediately notify opposing counsel of any hearing time reserved. FL ST 6 J CIR 2009-066 PA/PI-CIR(B)(2).

c. Attorneys will request enough time for hearings and adjudicative proceedings to permit full and fair presentation of the matter and to permit response by opposing counsel. When scheduling depositions, Attorneys will schedule enough time to permit the conclusion of the deposition, including examination by all parties, without adjournment. FL ST 6 J CIR 2009-066 PA/PI-CIR(B)(3).

d. Attorneys will call potential scheduling problems to the attention of those affected, including the court, as soon as they become apparent. Attorneys will avoid last minute cancellations. FL ST 6 J CIR 2009-066 PA/PI-CIR(B)(4).

e. Attorneys will make request for changes only when necessary. Attorneys will not request rescheduling, cancellations, extension or postponements solely for the purpose of delay or obtaining unfair advantage. FL ST 6 J CIR 2009-066 PA/PI-CIR(B)(5).

f. Attorneys will cooperate with opposing counsel when conflicts and calendar changes are necessary and requested. FL ST 6 J CIR 2009-066 PA/PI-CIR(B)(6).

g. Attorneys will grant reasonable requests for scheduling, rescheduling, cancellations, extensions, and postponements that do not prejudice our client's opportunity for full, fair and prompt consideration and adjudication of the client's claim or defense. FL ST 6 J CIR 2009-066 PA/PI-CIR(B)(7).

h. First requests for reasonable extensions of time to respond to litigation deadlines relating to pleadings, discovery, or motions, should be granted as a matter of courtesy unless time is of the essence or other circumstances require otherwise. FL ST 6 J CIR 2009-066 PA/PI-CIR(B)(8).

i. Attorneys will resolve subsequent requests by balancing the need for expedition against the deference we should give to opposing counsel's schedule of professional and personal engagements, the reasonableness of the length of extension requested, opposing counsel's willingness to grant reciprocal extensions, the time needed for the task, and whether it is likely a court would grant the extension. FL ST 6 J CIR 2009-066 PA/PI-CIR(B)(9).

j. Attorneys will not attach unfair or extraneous conditions to extensions. Attorneys will impose conditions required to preserve rights that an extension might jeopardize. Attorneys may seek reciprocal scheduling concessions. When granting an extension, we will not try to preclude an opponent's substantive rights. FL ST 6 J CIR 2009-066 PA/PI-CIR(B)(10).

3. *Timing*

   a. Hearings are limited to five (5) minutes per case. FL ST 6 J CIR PINELLAS CIR CT PI-CIR-98-30.

   b. For more information regarding the timing of hearings, please see FL ST 6 J CIR PINELLAS CIR CT PI-CIR-98-30.

4. *Telephonic hearings.* For information regarding telephonic hearings, please see FL ST 6 J CIR PA/PI-CIR-88-48.

H. Forms

1. Official Motion for Sanctions Forms for Florida

a. Caption. FL ST RCP Form 1.901.

b. Notice of compliance when constitutional challenge is brought. FL ST RCP Form 1.975.

2. Motion for Sanctions Forms for Florida

a. Motion; By defendant; For sanctions for refusal of offer of judgment. FL-PP § 61:22.

b. Motion; Sanctions, proposal for settlement. FL-PRACFORM § 7:165.

I. Checklist

(I) ❑ Matters to be considered by moving party

- (a) ❑ Required documents
  - (1) ❑ Notice of hearing/Motion
  - (2) ❑ Certificate of service
- (b) ❑ Supplemental documents
  - (1) ❑ Proposed order

(2) ❑ Notice of constitutional question

(c) ❑ Time for making motion

(1) ❑ A motion by a party seeking sanctions under FL ST § 57.105 must be served but may not be filed with or presented to the court unless, within twenty one (21) days after service of the motion, the challenged paper, claim, defense, contention, allegation, or denial is not withdrawn or appropriately corrected

(2) ❑ Any party seeking a judgment taxing costs, attorneys' fees, or both shall serve a motion no later than thirty (30) days after filing of the judgment, including a judgment of dismissal, or the service of a notice of voluntary dismissal

(3) ❑ A copy of any written motion which may not be heard ex parte and a copy of the notice of the hearing thereof shall be served a reasonable time before the time specified for the hearing

(II) ❑ Matters to be considered by opposing party

(a) ❑ Required documents

(1) ❑ Response to motion

(2) ❑ Certificate of service

(b) ❑ Supplemental documents

(1) ❑ Proposed order

(2) ❑ Notice of constitutional question

(c) ❑ Time for service and filing of opposition

(1) ❑ No time specified for responding to a motion

Motions, Oppositions and Replies
Motion to Compel Discovery

Document Last Updated January 2013

A. Applicable Rules

1. *State rules*

a. Rules of court. FL ST RCP Rule 1.010; FL ST J ADMIN Rule 2.110.

b. Nonverification of pleadings. FL ST RCP Rule 1.030.

c. Service and filing of pleadings, orders, and documents. FL ST RCP Rule 1.080.

d. Time. FL ST RCP Rule 1.090.

e. Pleadings and motions. FL ST RCP Rule 1.100.

f. Motions. FL ST RCP Rule 1.160.

g. General provisions governing discovery. FL ST RCP Rule 1.280.

h. Depositions. FL ST RCP Rule 1.310; FL ST RCP Rule 1.320; FL ST FAM LAW Rule 12.310.

i. Interrogatories to parties. FL ST RCP Rule 1.340.

j. Production of documents and things and entry upon land for inspection and other purposes. FL ST RCP Rule 1.350.

k. Examination of persons. FL ST RCP Rule 1.360.

l. Failure to make discovery; Sanctions. FL ST RCP Rule 1.380.

m. Relief from judgment, decrees, or orders. FL ST RCP Rule 1.540.

n. Mediation and arbitration. FL ST RCP Rule 1.700; FL ST RCP Rule 1.710; FL ST RCP Rule 1.720; FL ST RCP Rule.1.730; FL ST RCP Rule 1.750; FL ST RCP Rule 1.800; FL ST RCP Rule 1.810; FL ST RCP Rule 1.820; FL ST RCP Rule 1.830.

o. Forms. FL ST RCP Rule 1.900.

p. Minimization of the filing of sensitive information. FL ST J ADMIN Rule 2.425.

q. Retention of court records. FL ST J ADMIN Rule 2.430.

r. Foreign attorneys. FL ST J ADMIN Rule 2.510.

s. Signature of attorneys and parties. FL ST J ADMIN Rule 2.515.

t. Paper. FL ST J ADMIN Rule 2.520.

u. Electronic filing. FL ST J ADMIN Rule 2.525.

v. Accessibility of information and technology. FL ST J ADMIN Rule 2.526.

w. Communication equipment. FL ST J ADMIN Rule 2.530.

x. Court reporting. FL ST J ADMIN Rule 2.535.

y. Requests for accommodations by persons with disabilities. FL ST J ADMIN Rule 2.540.

2. *Local rules*

a. General. FL ST 6 J CIR LOCAL Rule 5.

b. Telephonic hearings in circuit civil, county civil and small claims cases. FL ST 6 J CIR PA/PI-CIR-88-48.

c. Pre-trial conferences. FL ST 6 J CIR PA/PI-CIR-98-49.

d. Uniform motion calendar civil division. FL ST 6 J CIR PINELLAS CIR CT PI-CIR-98-30.

e. Standards of professional courtesy. FL ST 6 J CIR 2009-066 PA/PI-CIR.

f. Arbitration and mediation program circuit civil and family cases. FL ST 6 J CIR PA/PI-CIR-96-63; FL ST 6 J CIR 2011-006 PA/PI-CIR.

g. Motions to compel discovery. FL ST 6 J CIR 2013-005 PA/PI-CIR.

B. Timing

1. *Motion to compel discovery.* Upon reasonable notice to other parties and all persons affected, a party may apply for an order compelling discovery. FL ST RCP Rule 1.380(a).

2. *General motion timing.* A copy of any written motion which may not be heard ex parte and a copy of the notice of the hearing thereof shall be served a reasonable time before the time specified for the hearing. FL ST RCP Rule 1.090(d).

a. All motions, except motions in limine, shall be filed and heard prior to the pre-trial conference unless good cause exists why the motions were not heard prior to the pre-trial conference, including the inability to obtain hearing time prior to the pre-trial conference. FL ST 6 J CIR PA/PI-CIR-98-49(6).

b. If such good cause exists, the court will hear such motions at the pre-trial conference or at a separate hearing following the pre-trial conference. FL ST 6 J CIR PA/PI-CIR-98-49(6).

3. *Computation of time*

a. *Generally.* Computation of time shall be governed by FL ST J ADMIN Rule 2.514. FL ST RCP Rule 1.090(a). The following rules apply in computing time periods specified in any rule of procedure, local rule, court order, or statute that does not specify a method of computing time. FL ST J ADMIN Rule 2.514(a).

i. *Period stated in days or a longer unit.* When the period is stated in days or a longer unit of time (A) exclude the day of the event that triggers the period; (B) count every day, including intermediate Saturdays, Sundays, and legal holidays; and (C) include the last day of the period, but if the last day is a Saturday, Sunday, or legal holiday, or falls within any period of time extended through an order of the chief justice under FL ST J ADMIN Rule 2.205(a)(2)(B)(iv), the period continues to run until the end of the next day that is not a Saturday, Sunday, or legal holiday and does not fall within any period of time extended through an order of the chief justice. FL ST J ADMIN Rule 2.514(a)(1).

ii. *Period stated in hours.* When the period is stated in hours (A) begin counting immediately on the occurrence of the event that triggers the period; (B) count every hour, including hours during intermediate Saturdays, Sundays, and legal holidays; and (C) if the period would end on a Saturday, Sunday, or legal holiday, or during any period of time extended through an order of the chief justice under FL ST J ADMIN Rule 2.205(a)(2)(B)(iv), the period continues to run until the same time on the next day that is not a Saturday, Sunday, or legal holiday and does not fall within any period of time extended through an order of the chief justice. FL ST J ADMIN Rule 2.514(a)(2).

iii. *Period stated in days less than seven (7) days.* When the period stated in days is less than seven (7) days, intermediate Saturdays, Sundays, and legal holidays shall be excluded in the computation. FL ST J ADMIN Rule 2.514(a)(3).

iv. *"Last day" defined.* Unless a different time is set by a statute, local rule, or court order, the last day ends (A) for electronic filing or for service by any means, at midnight; and (B) for filing by other means, when the clerk's office is scheduled to close. FL ST J ADMIN Rule 2.514(a)(4).

v. *"Next day" defined.* The "next day" is determined by continuing to count forward when the period is measured after an event and backward when measured before an event. FL ST J ADMIN Rule 2.514(a)(5).

vi. *"Legal holiday" defined.* "Legal holiday" means (A) the day set aside by FL ST § 110.117, for observing New Year's Day, Martin Luther King, Jr.'s Birthday, Memorial Day, Independence Day, Labor Day, Veterans' Day, Thanksgiving Day, the Friday after Thanksgiving Day, or Christmas Day, and (B) any day observed as a holiday by the clerk's office or as designated by the chief judge. FL ST J ADMIN Rule 2.514(a)(6).

b. *Additional time after service by mail or e-mail.* When a party may or must act within a specified time after service and service is made by mail or e-mail, five (5) days are added after the period that would otherwise expire under FL ST J ADMIN Rule 2.514(a). FL ST J ADMIN Rule 2.514(b).

c. *Enlargement.* When an act is required or allowed to be done at or within a specified time by order of court, by the Florida Rules of Civil Procedure, or by notice given thereunder, for cause shown the court at any time in its discretion (1) with or without notice, may order the period enlarged if request therefor is made before the expiration of the period originally prescribed or as extended by a previous order, or (2) upon motion made and notice after the expiration of the specified period, may permit the act to be done when failure to act was the result of excusable neglect, but it may not extend the time for making a motion for new trial, for rehearing, or to alter or amend a judgment; making a motion for relief from a judgment under FL ST RCP Rule 1.540(b); taking an appeal or filing a petition for certiorari; or making a motion for a directed verdict. FL ST RCP Rule 1.090(b).

d. *Unaffected by expiration of term.* The period of time provided for the doing of any act or the taking of any proceeding shall not be affected or limited by the continued existence or expiration of a term of court. The continued existence or expiration of a term of court in no way affects the power of a court to do any act or take any proceeding in any action which is or has been pending before it. FL ST RCP Rule 1.090(c).

C. General Requirements

1. *Motions generally*

a. *Contents.* An application to the court for an order shall be by motion which shall be made in writing unless made during a hearing or trial, shall state with particularity the grounds therefor, and shall set forth the relief or order sought. The requirement of writing is fulfilled if the motion is stated in a written notice of the hearing of the motion. All notices of hearing shall specify each motion or other matter to be heard. FL ST RCP Rule 1.100(b).

b. *Particularity requirement.* The court considers a motion in the light of the substantive law, rule or statute to make its determination. Some rules require a statement of the grounds for a motion under the rule. Failure to give the grounds will result in denial of the motion. This should be the result in all situations when the ground for the motion is not inherent in the rule. FL-PRACPROC § 9:3. The requirement is nevertheless an important one, first because of the due process notice rights of the respondent, as well as for the assistance it provides to the court in its preparation for the hearing or, absent a hearing, for disposition. 4 FLPRAC R 1.100.

c. *Standards of professional courtesy; Motion practice*

   i. Attorneys will make every reasonable effort to resolve the issue before setting a motion for hearing. FL ST 6 J CIR 2009-066 PA/PI-CIR(G)(1).

   ii. Attorneys will not force opposing counsel to make motions attorneys do not intend to oppose unless circumstances require or the client requires. FL ST 6 J CIR 2009-066 PA/PI-CIR(G)(2).

2. *Failure to make discovery; Types of available relief.* Three (3) categories of relief are available for failure to make discovery. FL-PRACPROC § 16:14.

   a. The first category is an order compelling discovery. This is obtained by a motion to compel discovery. The motion is made in the court in which the action is pending, except when a deposition is being taken out of the territorial jurisdiction of the court and protective relief is sought in accordance with FL ST RCP Rule 1.310(d) or when a deponent is not a party. When one of the exceptions occurs, the motion is made in the circuit court of the county where the deposition is being taken. FL-PRACPROC § 16:14.

   b. The second category results from a failure to comply with an order to make discovery. The sanctions should not be applied until a hearing on the merits of the failure is held, including an opportunity to present evidence of explanation or mitigation. FL-PRACPROC § 16:14.

   c. The third category is available: (1) if a party or a person designated by an organization to answer questions at a deposition fails to appear before the officer who is to take the deposition after being served with a proper notice; (2) fails to serve answers or objections to interrogatories after proper service of the interrogatories; or (3) a party fails to serve a response to a request for production, inspection and entry after proper service of the request. FL-PRACPROC § 16:14. For further information regarding discovery sanctions please see the KeyRules Motion for Discovery Sanctions documents.

3. *Motion for order compelling discovery*

   a. *Reasonable notice.* Upon reasonable notice to other parties and all persons affected, a party may apply for an order compelling discovery. FL ST RCP Rule 1.380(a).

   b. *Appropriate court.* An application for an order to a party may be made to the court in which the action is pending or in accordance with FL ST RCP Rule 1.310(d). An application for an order to a deponent who is not a party shall be made to the circuit court where the deposition is being taken. FL ST RCP Rule 1.380(a)(1).

   c. *Motion*

      i. *Grounds.* The discovering party may move for an order compelling an answer, or a designation or an order compelling inspection, or an order compelling an examination in accordance with the request:

         - If a deponent fails to answer a question propounded or submitted under FL ST RCP Rule 1.310 or FL ST RCP Rule 1.320;
         - Or a corporation or other entity fails to make a designation under FL ST RCP Rule 1.310(b)(6) or FL ST RCP Rule 1.320(a);
         - Or a party fails to answer an interrogatory submitted under FL ST RCP Rule 1.340;
         - Or if a party in response to a request for inspection submitted under FL ST RCP Rule 1.350 fails to respond that inspection will be permitted as requested or fails to permit inspection as requested;
         - Or if a party in response to a request for examination of a person submitted under FL ST RCP Rule 1.360(a) objects to the examination, fails to respond that the examination will be permitted as requested, or fails to submit to or to produce a person in that party's custody or legal control for examination. FL ST RCP Rule 1.380(a)(2).

      ii. *Certification.* The motion must include a certification that the movant, in good faith, has conferred or attempted to confer with the person or party failing to make the discovery in an effort to secure the information or material without court action. FL ST RCP Rule 1.380(a)(2).

         - Before filing a motion to compel or a motion for protective order, counsel for the moving party shall confer with counsel for the opposing party in a good faith effort to resolve by agreement the issues raised, and shall file with the court at the time of the filing of the motion a statement certifying that he or she has so conferred with opposing counsel and that counsel have been unable to resolve the dispute. FL ST 6 J CIR LOCAL Rule 5(C)(1).

iii. *During deposition.* When taking a deposition on oral examination, the proponent of the question may complete or adjourn the examination before applying for an order. FL ST RCP Rule 1.380(a)(2).

iv. *Protective order.* If the court denies the motion in whole or in part, it may make such protective order as it would have been empowered to make on a motion made pursuant to FL ST RCP Rule 1.280(c). FL ST RCP Rule 1.380(a)(2).

v. *Content.* Motions to compel discovery shall quote in full each interrogatory, question on deposition, request for admission or request for production to which the motion is addressed and the objection and grounds therefor as stated by the opposing party. FL ST 6 J CIR LOCAL Rule 5(C)(2).

d. *Evasive or incomplete answer.* For purposes of FL ST RCP Rule 1.380(a) an evasive or incomplete answer shall be treated as a failure to answer. FL ST RCP Rule 1.380(a)(3).

e. *Award of expenses of motion*

i. *Motion granted.* If the motion is granted and after opportunity for hearing, the court shall require the party or deponent whose conduct necessitated the motion or the party or counsel advising the conduct to pay to the moving party the reasonable expenses incurred in obtaining the order that may include attorneys' fees, unless the court finds that the movant failed to certify in the motion that a good faith effort was made to obtain the discovery without court action, that the opposition to the motion was justified, or that other circumstances make an award of expenses unjust. FL ST RCP Rule 1.380(a)(4).

ii. *Motion denied.* If the motion is denied and after opportunity for hearing, the court shall require the moving party to pay to the party or deponent who opposed the motion the reasonable expenses incurred in opposing the motion that may include attorneys' fees, unless the court finds that the making of the motion was substantially justified or that other circumstances make an award of expenses unjust. FL ST RCP Rule 1.380(a)(4).

iii. *Motion granted in part and denied in part.* If the motion is granted in part and denied in part, the court may apportion the reasonable expenses incurred as a result of making the motion among the parties and persons. FL ST RCP Rule 1.380(a)(4).

iv. *Electronically stored information; Sanctions for failure to preserve.* Absent exceptional circumstances, a court may not impose sanctions under these rules on a party for failing to provide electronically stored information lost as a result of the routine, good faith operation of an electronic information system. FL ST RCP Rule 1.380(e).

f. *Ex parte order.* When a motion to compel discovery is filed in accordance with FL ST RCP Rule 1.380(a)(2) and the motion alleges:

i. a complete failure to respond to or object to discovery, and

ii. a request for extension has not been filed, and

iii. the motion alleges that counsel has conferred with opposing counsel and has been unable to resolve the dispute, as provided for in the Standards of Professional Courtesy, FL ST 6 J CIR 2009-066 PA/PI-CIR, the court, without hearing, may enter an ex parte order requiring compliance with the original discovery demand. The movant must file the original motion with the Clerk and submit a copy of the motion to compel, a proposed order, and copies of the proposed order along with stamped, addressed envelopes to the Court. FL ST 6 J CIR 2013-005 PA/PI-CIR.

iv. The Court may impose sanctions in accordance with FL ST RCP Rule 1.380(b) if discovery is not completed within ten (10) days from the date of entry of the ex parte order and the proposed order should so provide. FL ST 6 J CIR 2013-005 PA/PI-CIR.

4. *Limitations on discovery of electronically stored information*

   a. A person may object to discovery of electronically stored information from sources that the person identifies as not reasonably accessible because of burden or cost. On motion to compel discovery or for a protective order, the person from whom discovery is sought must show that the information sought or the format requested is not reasonably accessible because of undue burden or cost. If that showing is made, the court may nonetheless order the discovery from such sources or in such formats if the requesting party shows good cause. The court may specify conditions of the discovery, including ordering that some or all of the expenses incurred by the person from whom discovery is sought be paid by the party seeking the discovery. FL ST RCP Rule 1.280(d)(1).

   b. In determining any motion involving discovery of electronically stored information, the court must limit the frequency or extent of discovery otherwise allowed by the Florida Rules of Civil Procedure if it determines that (i) the discovery sought is unreasonably cumulative or duplicative, or can be obtained from another source or in another manner that is more convenient, less burdensome, or less expensive; or (ii) the burden or expense of the discovery outweighs its likely benefit, considering the needs of the case, the amount in controversy, the parties' resources, the importance of the issues at stake in the action, and the importance of the discovery in resolving the issues. FL ST RCP Rule 1.280(d)(2).

5. *Arbitration and mediation*

   a. *Referral to arbitration and mediation.* Except as hereinafter provided or as otherwise prohibited by law, the presiding judge may enter an order referring all or any part of a contested civil matter to mediation or arbitration. The parties to any contested civil matter may file a written stipulation to mediate or arbitrate any issue between them at any time. Such stipulation shall be incorporated into the order of referral. FL ST RCP Rule 1.700(a).

   b. *Arbitration*

      i. *Exclusions.* A civil action shall be ordered to arbitration or arbitration in conjunction with mediation upon stipulation of the parties. A civil action may be ordered to arbitration or arbitration in conjunction with mediation upon motion of any party or by the court, if the judge determines the action to be of such a nature that arbitration could be of benefit to the litigants or the court. FL ST RCP Rule 1.800.

         - Under no circumstances may the following categories of actions be referred to arbitration: (1) bond estreatures; (2) habeas corpus or other extraordinary writs; (3) bond validations; (4) civil or criminal contempt; (5) such other matters as may be specified by order of the chief judge in the circuit. FL ST RCP Rule 1.800.

      ii. For more information regarding arbitration, please see FL ST RCP Rule 1.810; FL ST RCP Rule 1.820; FL ST RCP Rule 1.830.

   c. *Mediation.* For more information regarding mediation, please see FL ST RCP Rule 1.710; FL ST RCP Rule 1.720; FL ST RCP Rule 1.730; and FL ST RCP Rule 1.750.

   d. See FL ST 6 J CIR PA/PI-CIR-96-63 for more information about the Arbitration and Mediation Program for Florida's Sixth Judicial Circuit.

6. *Rules of court*

   a. *Rules of civil procedure.* The Florida Rules of Civil Procedure apply to all actions of a civil nature and all special statutory proceedings in the circuit courts and county courts except those to which the Florida Probate Rules, the Florida Family Law Rules of Procedure, or the Small Claims Rules apply. FL ST RCP Rule 1.010.

      i. The form, content, procedure, and time for pleading in all special statutory proceedings shall be as prescribed by the statutes governing the proceeding unless the Florida Rules of Civil Procedure specifically provide to the contrary. FL ST RCP Rule 1.010.

      ii. The Florida Rules of Civil Procedure shall be construed to secure the just, speedy, and inexpensive determination of every action. FL ST RCP Rule 1.010.

   b. *Rules of judicial administration.* The Florida Rules of Judicial Administration shall apply to

administrative matters in all courts to which the Florida Rules of Judicial Administration are applicable by their terms. The Florida Rules of Judicial Administration shall be construed to secure the speedy and inexpensive determination of every proceeding to which they are applicable. The Florida Rules of Judicial Administration shall supersede all conflicting rules and statutes. FL ST J ADMIN Rule 2.110.

7. *Settlement and alternative dispute resolution.* When a matter is scheduled for hearing and the matter is resolved by agreement or settlement, the party setting the matter for hearing shall notify the court. When a matter is scheduled for trial and the case settles, the plaintiff shall notify the court. Permission of the court must be obtained in order to cancel a trial. FL ST 6 J CIR LOCAL Rule 5(A).
   a. Unless there are strong and overriding issues of principle, attorneys will raise and explore the issue of settlement as soon as enough is known to make settlement discussions meaningful. FL ST 6 J CIR 2009-066 PA/PI-CIR(I)(1).
   b. Attorneys will not falsely hold out the possibility of settlement to adjourn discovery or delay trial. FL ST 6 J CIR 2009-066 PA/PI-CIR(I)(2).
   c. Attorneys will consider whether the client's interest could be adequately served and the controversy more expeditiously and economically disposed of by arbitration, mediation or other forms of alternative dispute resolution. FL ST 6 J CIR 2009-066 PA/PI-CIR(I)(3).

D. Documents

1. *Required documents*
   a. *Notice of hearing/Motion.* An application to the court for an order shall be by motion which shall be made in writing unless made during a hearing or trial, shall state with particularity the grounds therefor, and shall set forth the relief or order sought. The requirement of writing is fulfilled if the motion is stated in a written notice of the hearing of the motion. All notices of hearing shall specify each motion or other matter to be heard. FL ST RCP Rule 1.100(b).
      i. *Certification.* The motion must include a certification that the movant, in good faith, has conferred or attempted to confer with the person or party failing to make the discovery in an effort to secure the information or material without court action. FL ST RCP Rule 1.380(a)(2); FL ST 6 J CIR LOCAL Rule 5(C)(1).
      ii. *Notices to persons with disabilities.* See the Format section of this KeyRules document for further information.
   b. *Certificate of service.* When any attorney certifies in substance: "I certify that a copy hereof has been furnished to (here insert name or names and addresses used for service) by (e-mail) (delivery) (mail) (fax) on .... (date) ....________________ Attorney" the certificate is taken as prima facie proof of such service in compliance with FL ST J ADMIN Rule 2.516. FL ST J ADMIN Rule 2.516(f).
2. *Supplemental documents*
   a. *Proposed order.* The court may require that orders or judgments be prepared by a party, may require the party to furnish the court with stamped, addressed envelopes for service of the order or judgment, and may require that proposed orders and judgments be furnished to all parties before entry by the court of the order or judgment. FL ST J ADMIN Rule 2.516(h)(1).
      i. After a hearing, attorneys will make a good faith effort to quickly agree or disagree upon a proposed order and submit the result to the court. Unless otherwise instructed by the court, or agreed to by counsel, all proposed orders shall be provided to other counsel for approval or comment prior to submission to the court. Attorneys will not submit controverted orders to the court with a copy to opposing counsel for "objections within ______ days". Courts prefer to know that the order is either agreed upon or opposed. FL ST 6 J CIR 2009-066 PA/PI-CIR(G)(3).
      ii. Attorneys will not use post-hearing submissions of proposed orders as a guise to reargue the merits of the matter. FL ST 6 J CIR 2009-066 PA/PI-CIR(G)(4).
   b. *Notice of constitutional question.* A party that files a pleading, written motion, or other paper drawing into question the constitutionality of a state statute or a county or municipal charter,

ordinance, or franchise must promptly (1) file a notice of constitutional question stating the question and identifying the paper that raises it; and (2) serve the notice and the pleading, written motion, or other paper drawing into question the constitutionality of a state statute or a county or municipal charter, ordinance, or franchise on the Attorney General or the state attorney of the judicial circuit in which the action is pending, by either certified or registered mail. Service of the notice and pleading, written motion, or other paper does not require joinder of the Attorney General or the state attorney as a party to the action. FL ST RCP Rule 1.071.

E. Format

1. *Documents; Type and size.* Documents subject to the exceptions set forth in FL ST J ADMIN Rule 2.525(d) shall be filed on recycled paper measuring eight and one half by eleven (8 1/2 by 11) inches. For purposes of FL ST J ADMIN Rule 2.520, paper is recycled if it contains a minimum content of fifty (50) percent waste paper. Xerographic reduction of legal-size (eight and one half by fourteen (8 1/2 by 14) inches) documents to letter size (eight and one half by eleven (8 1/2 by 11) inches) is prohibited. All other documents filed by electronic transmission shall be filed in a format capable of being printed in a format consistent with the provisions of FL ST J ADMIN Rule 2.250. FL ST J ADMIN Rule 2.520(b).
    a. *Exhibits.* Any exhibit or attachment filed with pleadings or papers may be filed in its original size. FL ST J ADMIN Rule 2.520(c).
    b. *Recording space.* On all papers and documents prepared and filed by the court or by any party to a proceeding which are to be recorded in the public records of any county, including but not limited to final money judgments and notices of lis pendens, a three (3) inch by three (3) inch space at the top right-hand corner on the first page and a one (1) inch by three (3) inch space at the top right-hand corner on each subsequent page shall be left blank and reserved for use by the clerk of court. FL ST J ADMIN Rule 2.520(d).
        i. *Exceptions to recording space.* Any papers or documents created by persons or entities over which the filing party has no control, including but not limited to wills, codicils, trusts, or other testamentary documents; documents prepared or executed by any public officer; documents prepared, executed, acknowledged, or proved outside of the State of Florida; or documents created by State or Federal government agencies, may be filed without the space required by FL ST J ADMIN Rule 2.520. FL ST J ADMIN Rule 2.520(e).
    c. *Noncompliance.* No clerk of court is permitted to refuse to file any document or paper because of noncompliance with the Florida Rules of Judicial Administration. However, upon request of the clerk of court, noncomplying documents must be resubmitted in accordance with the formatting rules. FL ST J ADMIN Rule 2.520(f).
2. *Caption.* Every pleading, motion, order, judgment, or other paper shall have a caption containing the name of the court, the file number, and except for in rem proceedings, including forfeiture proceedings, the name of the first party on each side with an appropriate indication of other parties, and a designation identifying the party filing it and its nature or the nature of the order, as the case may be. In any in rem proceeding, every pleading, motion, order, judgment, or other paper shall have a caption containing the name of the court, the file number, the style "In re" (followed by the name or general description of the property), and a designation of the person or entity filing it and its nature or the nature of the order, as the case may be. In an in rem forfeiture proceeding, the style shall be "In re forfeiture of" (followed by the name of the general description of the property). All papers filed in the action shall be styled in such a manner as to indicate clearly the subject matter of the paper and the party requesting or obtaining relief. FL ST RCP Rule 1.100(c)(1).
3. *Writing and written defined.* Writing or written means a document containing information, an application, or a stipulation. FL ST RCP Rule 1.080(c).
4. *Rule abbreviations*
    a. The Florida Rules of Civil Procedure and shall be abbreviated as Fla.R.Civ.P. FL ST RCP Rule 1.010.
    b. The Florida Rules of Judicial Administration shall be abbreviated as Fla. R. Jud. Admin. FL ST J ADMIN Rule 2.110.

5. *Nonverification.* Except when otherwise specifically provided by the Florida Rules of Civil Procedure or an applicable statute, every pleading or other document of a party represented by an attorney need not be verified or accompanied by an affidavit. FL ST RCP Rule 1.030; FL ST J ADMIN Rule 2.515(a).
6. *Attorney signature*
   a. *Attorney signature.* Every pleading and other document of a party represented by an attorney shall be signed by at least one (1) attorney of record in that attorney's individual name whose current record Florida Bar address, telephone number, including area code, primary e-mail address and secondary e-mail addresses, if any, and Florida Bar number shall be stated, and who shall be duly licensed to practice law in Florida or who shall have received permission to appear in the particular case as provided in FL ST J ADMIN Rule 2.510. FL ST J ADMIN Rule 2.515(a).
      i. The attorney may be required by the court to give the address of, and to vouch for the attorney's authority to represent, the party. FL ST J ADMIN Rule 2.515(a).
      ii. The signature of an attorney shall constitute a certificate by the attorney that the attorney has read the pleading or other document; that to the best of the attorney's knowledge, information, and belief there is good ground to support it; and that it is not interposed for delay. FL ST J ADMIN Rule 2.515(a).
      iii. If a pleading is not signed or is signed with intent to defeat the purpose of FL ST J ADMIN Rule 2.515, it may be stricken and the action may proceed as though the pleading or other document had not been served. FL ST J ADMIN Rule 2.515(a).
   b. *Pro se litigant signature.* A party who is not represented by an attorney shall sign any pleading or other paper and state the party's address and telephone number, including area code. FL ST J ADMIN Rule 2.515(b).
   c. *Form of signature*
      i. The signatures required on pleadings and documents by FL ST J ADMIN Rule 2.515(a) and FL ST J ADMIN Rule 2.515(b) may be:
         - Original signatures;
         - Original signatures that have been reproduced by electronic means, such as on electronically transmitted documents or photocopied documents;
         - Electronic signatures using the "/s/," "s/," or "/s" formats by or at the direction of the person signing; or
         - Any other signature format authorized by general law, so long as the clerk where the proceeding is pending has the capability of receiving and has obtained approval from the Supreme Court of Florida to accept pleadings and documents with that signature format. FL ST J ADMIN Rule 2.515(c)(1).
      ii. An attorney, party, or other person who files a pleading or paper by electronic transmission that does not contain the original signature of that attorney, party, or other person shall file that identical pleading or paper in paper form containing an original signature of that attorney, party, or other person (hereinafter called the follow-up filing) immediately thereafter. The follow-up filing is not required if the Supreme Court of Florida has entered an order directing the clerk of court to discontinue accepting the follow-up filing. FL ST J ADMIN Rule 2.515(c)(2).
7. *Forms*
   a. *Process.* The forms of process, notice of lis pendens, and notice of action provided in the Florida Rules of Civil Procedure are sufficient. Variations from the forms do not void process or notices that are otherwise sufficient. FL ST RCP Rule 1.900(a).
   b. *Other forms.* The other forms provided in the Florida Rules of Civil Procedure are sufficient for the matters that are covered by them. So long as the substance is expressed without prolixity, the forms may be varied to meet the facts of a particular case. FL ST RCP Rule 1.900(b).
   c. *Formal matters.* Captions, except for the designation of the paper, are omitted from the forms provided in the Florida Rules of Civil Procedure. A general form of caption is the first form provided. Signatures are omitted from pleadings and motions. FL ST RCP Rule 1.900(c).

8. *Notices to persons with disabilities.* All notices of court proceedings to be held in a public facility, and all process compelling appearance at such proceedings, shall include the following statement in bold face, fourteen (14) point Times New Roman or Courier font: "If you are a person with a disability who needs any accommodation in order to participate in this proceeding, you are entitled, at no cost to you, to the provision of certain assistance. Please contact [identify applicable court personnel by name, address, and telephone number] at least seven (7) days before your scheduled court appearance, or immediately upon receiving this notification if the time before the scheduled appearance is less than seven (7) days; if you are hearing or voice impaired, call 711." FL ST J ADMIN Rule 2.540(c)(1).

9. *Minimization of the filing of sensitive information*

   a. *Limitations for court filings.* Unless authorized by FL ST J ADMIN Rule 2.425(b), statute, another rule of court, or the court orders otherwise, designated sensitive information filed with the court must be limited to the following format:

      i. The initials of a person known to be a minor;

      ii. The year of birth of a person's birth date;

      iii. No portion of any: Social security number, Bank account number, Credit card account number, Charge account number, or Debit account number;

      iv. The last four digits of any: Taxpayer identification number (TIN), Employee identification number, Driver's license number, Passport number, Telephone number, Financial account number, except as set forth in FL ST J ADMIN Rule 2.425(a)(3), Brokerage account number, Insurance policy account number, Loan account number, Customer account number, or Patient or health care number;

      v. A truncated version of any: Email address, Computer user name, Password, or Personal identification number (PIN); and

      vi. A truncated version of any other sensitive information as provided by court order. FL ST J ADMIN Rule 2.425(a).

   b. *Exceptions.* FL ST J ADMIN Rule 2.425(a) does not apply to the following:

      i. An account number which identifies the property alleged to be the subject of a proceeding;

      ii. The record of an administrative or agency proceeding;

      iii. The record in appellate or review proceedings;

      iv. The birth date of a minor whenever the birth date is necessary for the court to establish or maintain subject matter jurisdiction;

      v. The name of a minor in any order relating to parental responsibility, time-sharing, or child support;

      vi. The name of a minor in any document or order affecting the minor's ownership of real property;

      vii. The birth date of a party in a writ of attachment or notice to payor;

      viii. In traffic and criminal proceedings: a pro se filing; a court filing that is related to a criminal matter or investigation and that is prepared before the filing of a criminal charge or is not filed as part of any docketed criminal case; an arrest or search warrant or any information in support thereof; a charging document and an affidavit or other documents filed in support of any charging document, including any driving records; a statement of particulars; discovery material introduced into evidence or otherwise filed with the court; and all information necessary for the proper issuance and execution of a subpoena duces tecum;

      ix. Information used by the clerk for case maintenance purposes or the courts for case management purposes; and

      x. Information which is relevant and material to an issue before the court. FL ST J ADMIN Rule 2.425(b).

   c. *Remedies.* Upon motion by a party or interested person or sua sponte by the court, the court may order remedies, sanctions or both for a violation of FL ST J ADMIN Rule 2.425(a). Following notice

and an opportunity to respond, the court may impose sanctions if such filing was not made in good faith. FL ST J ADMIN Rule 2.425(c).

d. *Motions not restricted.* FL ST J ADMIN Rule 2.425 does not restrict a party's right to move for protective order, to move to file documents under seal, or to request a determination of the confidentiality of records. FL ST J ADMIN Rule 2.425(d).

e. *Application.* FL ST J ADMIN Rule 2.425 does not affect the application of constitutional provisions, statutes, or rules of court regarding confidential information or access to public information. FL ST J ADMIN Rule 2.425(e).

F. Filing and Service Requirements

1. *Filing requirements.* All original documents must be filed with the court either before service or immediately thereafter, unless otherwise provided for by general law or other rules. If the original of any bond or other document is not placed in the court file, a certified copy must be so placed by the clerk. FL ST J ADMIN Rule 2.516(d). All documents shall be filed in conformity with the requirements of FL ST J ADMIN Rule 2.525. FL ST RCP Rule 1.080(b). All documents filed in any court shall be filed by electronic transmission in accordance with FL ST J ADMIN Rule 2.525. "Documents" means pleadings, motions, petitions, memoranda, briefs, notices, exhibits, declarations, affidavits, orders, judgments, decrees, writs, opinions, and any other paper or writing submitted to a court. FL ST J ADMIN Rule 2.520(a). All documents that are court records, as defined in FL ST J ADMIN Rule 2.430(a)(1), must be filed by electronic transmission, provided that: (1) the clerk has the ability to accept and retain such documents; (2) the clerk or the chief judge of the circuit has requested permission to accept documents filed by electronic transmission; and (3) the supreme court has entered an order granting permission to the clerk to accept documents filed by electronic transmission. FL ST J ADMIN Rule 2.525(c)(1).

a. *Definition.* "Electronic transmission of documents" means the sending of information by electronic signals to, by or from a court or clerk, which when received can be transformed and stored or transmitted on paper, microfilm, magnetic storage device, optical imaging system, CD-ROM, flash drive, other electronic data storage system, server, case maintenance system ("CM"), electronic court filing ("ECF") system, statewide or local electronic portal ("e-portal"), or other electronic record keeping system authorized by the supreme court in a format sufficient to communicate the information on the original document in a readable format. Electronic transmission of documents includes electronic mail ("e-mail") and any internet-based transmission procedure, and may include procedures allowing for documents to be signed or verified by electronic means. FL ST J ADMIN Rule 2.525(a).

i. The filing of documents with the court as required by the Florida Rules of Judicial Administration must be made by filing them with the clerk in accordance with FL ST J ADMIN Rule 2.525, except that the judge may permit documents to be filed with the judge, in which event the judge must note the filing date before him or her on the documents and transmit them to the clerk. The date of filing is that shown on the face of the document by the judge's notation or the clerk's time stamp, whichever is earlier. FL ST J ADMIN Rule 2.516(e).

b. *Application.* Any court or clerk of the court may accept the electronic transmission of documents for filing after the clerk, together with input from the chief judge of the circuit, has obtained approval of the procedures and program for doing so from the Supreme Court of Florida. FL ST J ADMIN Rule 2.525(b).

c. *Exceptions*

i. Paper documents and other submissions may be manually submitted to the clerk or court:

- When the clerk does not have the ability to accept and retain documents by electronic filing or has not had ECF Procedures approved by the supreme court;
- For filing by any self-represented party or any self-represented nonparty unless specific ECF Procedures provide a means to file documents electronically. However, any self-represented nonparty that is a governmental or public agency and any other agency, partnership, corporation, or business entity acting on behalf of any governmental or public agency may file documents by electronic transmission if such entity has the capability of filing documents electronically;

- For filing by attorneys excused from e-mail service in accordance with FL ST J ADMIN Rule 2.516(b);
- When submitting evidentiary exhibits or filing non-documentary materials;
- When the filing involves documents in excess of twenty-five (25) megabytes (25MB) in size. For such filings, documents may be transmitted using an electronic storage medium that the clerk has the ability to accept, which may include a CD-ROM, flash drive, or similar storage medium;
- When filed in open court, as permitted by the court;
- When paper filing is permitted by any approved statewide or local ECF procedures; and
- If any court determines that justice so requires. FL ST J ADMIN Rule 2.525(d).

ii. Any document in paper form submitted under FL ST J ADMIN Rule 2.525(d) is filed when it is received by the clerk or court and the clerk shall immediately thereafter convert any filed paper document to an electronic document. "Convert to an electronic document" means optically capturing an image of a paper document and using character recognition software to recover as much of the document's text as practicable and then indexing and storing the document in the official court file. FL ST J ADMIN Rule 2.525(c)(4).

iii. Any storage medium submitted under FL ST J ADMIN Rule 2.525(d)(5) is filed when received by the clerk or court and the clerk shall immediately thereafter transfer the electronic documents from the storage device to the official court file. FL ST J ADMIN Rule 2.525(c)(5).

iv. If the filer of any paper document authorized under FL ST J ADMIN Rule 2.525(d) provides a self-addressed, postage-paid envelope for return of the paper document after it is converted to electronic form by the clerk, the clerk shall place the paper document in the envelope and deposit it in the mail. Except when a paper document is required to be maintained, the clerk may recycle any filed paper document that is not to be returned to the filer. FL ST J ADMIN Rule 2.525(c)(6).

v. The clerk may convert any paper document filed before the effective date of FL ST J ADMIN Rule 2.525 to an electronic document. Unless the clerk is required to maintain the paper document, if the paper document has been converted to an electronic document by the clerk, the paper document is no longer part of the official court file and may be removed and recycled. FL ST J ADMIN Rule 2.525(c)(7).

d. *Official court file.* For information on what constitutes the official court file, please see FL ST J ADMIN Rule 2.525(c)(2), FL ST J ADMIN Rule 2.525(c)(3).

e. *Administration.* All attorneys, parties, or other persons using this rule to file documents are required to make arrangements with the court or clerk for the payment of any charges authorized by general law or the supreme court before filing any document by electronic transmission. FL ST J ADMIN Rule 2.525(f)(2).

f. *Filing date.* The filing date for an electronically transmitted document is the date and time that such filing is acknowledged by an electronic stamp or otherwise, pursuant to any procedure set forth in any ECF Procedures approved by the supreme court, or the date the last page of such filing is received by the court or clerk. FL ST J ADMIN Rule 2.525(f)(3).

g. *Accessibility.* All documents transmitted in any electronic form under FL ST J ADMIN Rule 2.525 must comply with the accessibility requirements of FL ST J ADMIN Rule 2.526. FL ST J ADMIN Rule 2.525(g).

2. *Service requirements.* Every pleading subsequent to the initial pleading, all orders, and every other document filed in the action must be served in conformity with the requirements of FL ST J ADMIN Rule 2.516. FL ST RCP Rule 1.080(a).

a. *Service; When required.* Unless the court otherwise orders, or a statute or supreme court administrative order specifies a different means of service, every pleading subsequent to the initial pleading and every other document filed in any court proceeding, except applications for witness subpoenas and documents served by formal notice or required to be served in the manner provided for service

of formal notice, must be served in accordance with FL ST J ADMIN Rule 2.516 on each party. No service need be made on parties against whom a default has been entered, except that pleadings asserting new or additional claims against them must be served in the manner provided for service of summons. FL ST J ADMIN Rule 2.516(a).

b. *Service; How made.* When service is required or permitted to be made upon a party represented by an attorney, service must be made upon the attorney unless service upon the party is ordered by the court. FL ST J ADMIN Rule 2.516(b).

   i. *Service by electronic mail ("e-mail").* All documents required or permitted to be served on another party must be served by e-mail, unless FL ST J ADMIN Rule 2.516 otherwise provides. When, in addition to service by e-mail, the sender also utilizes another means of service provided for in FL ST J ADMIN Rule 2.516(b)(2), any differing time limits and other provisions applicable to that other means of service control. FL ST J ADMIN Rule 2.516(b)(1). Any document electronically transmitted to a court or clerk must also be served on all parties and interested persons in accordance with the applicable rules of court. FL ST J ADMIN Rule 2.525(e)(2).

      - *Service on attorneys.* Upon appearing in a proceeding, an attorney must serve a designation of a primary e-mail address and may designate no more than two (2) secondary e-mail addresses. Thereafter, service must be directed to all designated e-mail addresses in that proceeding. Every document filed by an attorney thereafter must include the primary e-mail address of that attorney and any secondary e-mail addresses. If an attorney does not designate any e-mail address for service, documents may be served on that attorney at the e-mail address on record with The Florida Bar. FL ST J ADMIN Rule 2.516(b)(1)(A).
      - *Exception to e-mail service on attorneys.* Service by an attorney on another attorney must be made by e-mail unless excused by the court. Upon motion by an attorney demonstrating that the attorney has no e-mail account and lacks access to the Internet at the attorney's office, the court may excuse the attorney from the requirements of e-mail service. Service on and by an attorney excused by the court from e-mail service must be by the means provided in FL ST J ADMIN Rule 2.516(b)(2). FL ST J ADMIN Rule 2.516(b)(1)(B).
      - *Service on and by parties not represented by an attorney.* Any party not represented by an attorney may serve a designation of a primary e-mail address and also may designate no more than two (2) secondary e-mail addresses to which service must be directed in that proceeding by the means provided in FL ST J ADMIN Rule 2.516(b)(1). If a party not represented by an attorney does not designate an e-mail address for service in a proceeding, service on and by that party must be by the means provided in FL ST J ADMIN Rule 2.516(b)(2). FL ST J ADMIN Rule 2.516(b)(1)(C).
      - *Time of service.* Service by e-mail is complete when it is sent. FL ST J ADMIN Rule 2.516(b)(1)(D). An e-mail is deemed served on the date it is sent. FL ST J ADMIN Rule 2.516(b)(1)(D)(i). If the sender learns that the e-mail did not reach the address of the person to be served, the sender must immediately send another copy by e-mail, or by a means authorized by FL ST J ADMIN Rule 2.516(b)(2). FL ST J ADMIN Rule 2.516(b)(1)(D)(ii). E-mail service is treated as service by mail for the computation of time. FL ST J ADMIN Rule 2.516(b)(1)(D)(iii).

   ii. *Format of e-mail for service.* Service of a document by e-mail is made by attaching a copy of the document in PDF format to an e-mail sent to all addresses designated by the attorney or party. FL ST J ADMIN Rule 2.516(b)(1)(E).

      - All documents served by e-mail must be attached to an e-mail message containing a subject line beginning with the words "SERVICE OF COURT DOCUMENT" in all capital letters, followed by the case number of the proceeding in which the documents are being served. FL ST J ADMIN Rule 2.516(b)(1)(E)(i).
      - The body of the e-mail must identify the court in which the proceeding is pending, the case number, the name of the initial party on each side, the title of each document served with that e-mail, and the sender's name and telephone number. FL ST J ADMIN Rule 2.516(b)(1)(E)(ii).

- Any document served by e-mail may be signed by the "/s/" format, as long as the filed original is signed in accordance with the applicable rule of procedure. FL ST J ADMIN Rule 2.516(b)(1)(E)(iii).
- Any e-mail which, together with its attached documents, exceeds five megabytes (5MB) in size, must be divided and sent as separate e-mails, no one of which may exceed five megabytes (5MB) in size and each of which must be sequentially numbered in the subject line. FL ST J ADMIN Rule 2.516(b)(1)(E)(iv).

iii. *Service by other means.* In addition to, and not in lieu of, service by e-mail, service may also be made upon attorneys by any of the means specified in FL ST J ADMIN Rule 2.516(b)(2). Service on and by all parties who are not represented by an attorney and who do not designate an e-mail address, and on and by all attorneys excused from e-mail service, must be made by delivering a copy of the document or by mailing it to the party or attorney at their last known address or, if no address is known, by leaving it with the clerk of the court. Service by mail is complete upon mailing. Delivery of a copy within FL ST J ADMIN Rule 2.516 is complete upon:

- Handing it to the attorney or to the party,
- Leaving it at the attorney's or party's office with a clerk or other person in charge thereof,
- If there is no one in charge, leaving it in a conspicuous place therein,
- If the office is closed or the person to be served has no office, leaving it at the person's usual place of abode with some person of his or her family above fifteen (15) years of age and informing such person of the contents, or
- Transmitting it by facsimile to the attorney's or party's office with a cover sheet containing the sender's name, firm, address, telephone number, and facsimile number, and the number of pages transmitted. When service is made by facsimile, a copy must also be served by any other method permitted by FL ST J ADMIN Rule 2.516. Facsimile service occurs when transmission is complete. FL ST J ADMIN Rule 2.516(b)(2)(A) through FL ST J ADMIN Rule 2.516(b)(2)(E).
- Service by delivery after 5:00 p.m. must be deemed to have been made by mailing on the date of delivery. FL ST J ADMIN Rule 2.516(b)(2)(F).

c. *Service; Numerous defendants.* In actions when the parties are unusually numerous, the court may regulate the service contemplated by the Florida Rules of Judicial Administration on motion or on its own initiative in such manner as may be found to be just and reasonable. FL ST J ADMIN Rule 2.516(c).

d. *Service by clerk.* Service of notices and other documents required to be made by the clerk must also be done as provided in FL ST J ADMIN Rule 2.516(b). FL ST J ADMIN Rule 2.516(g).

e. *Standards of professional courtesy; Service*

i. The timing and manner of service should not be used to the disadvantage of the party receiving the papers. This includes the use of facsimile transmissions and any additional expedited means of communication approved by the court. FL ST 6 J CIR 2009-066 PA/PI-CIR(C)(1).

ii. Attorneys will not serve papers to take advantage of opposing counsel's known absence from the office or at a time or in a manner designed to inconvenience an opponent, such as late on Friday afternoon or the day preceding a secular or religious holiday. FL ST 6 J CIR 2009-066 PA/PI-CIR(C)(2).

iii. Attorneys will not serve papers, including briefs and memoranda, so close to a court appearance that the ability of opposing counsel to prepare for that appearance or, where permitted, to respond, is inhibited. FL ST 6 J CIR 2009-066 PA/PI-CIR(C)(3).

iv. Service should be made personally or by facsimile transmission when it is likely that service by mail, even when allowed, will prejudice the opposing party. FL ST 6 J CIR 2009-066 PA/PI-CIR(C)(4).

G. Hearings

1. *Communication equipment*
   a. *Definition.* Communication equipment means a conference telephone or other electronic device that permits all those appearing or participating to hear and speak to each other, provided that all conversation of all parties is audible to all persons present. FL ST J ADMIN Rule 2.530(a).
   b. *Use by all parties.* A county or circuit court judge may, upon the court's own motion or upon the written request of a party, direct that communication equipment be used for a motion hearing, pretrial conference, or a status conference. A judge must give notice to the parties and consider any objections they may have to the use of communication equipment before directing that communication equipment be used. The decision to use communication equipment over the objection of parties will be in the sound discretion of the trial court, except as noted below. FL ST J ADMIN Rule 2.530(b).
   c. *Use only by requesting party.* A county or circuit court judge may, upon the written request of a party upon reasonable notice to all other parties, permit a requesting party to participate through communication equipment in a scheduled motion hearing; however, any such request (except in criminal, juvenile, and appellate proceedings) must be granted, absent a showing of good cause to deny the same, where the hearing is set for not longer than fifteen (15) minutes. FL ST J ADMIN Rule 2.530(c).
   d. *Testimony*
      i. *Generally.* A county or circuit court judge, general magistrate, special magistrate, or hearing officer may allow testimony to be taken through communication equipment if all parties consent or if permitted by another applicable rule of procedure. FL ST J ADMIN Rule 2.530(d)(1).
      ii. *Procedure.* Any party desiring to present testimony through communication equipment shall, prior to the hearing or trial at which the testimony is to be presented, contact all parties to determine whether each party consents to this form of testimony. The party seeking to present the testimony shall move for permission to present testimony through communication equipment, which motion shall set forth good cause as to why the testimony should be allowed in this form. FL ST J ADMIN Rule 2.530(d)(2).
      iii. *Oath.* Testimony may be taken through communication equipment only if a notary public or other person authorized to administer oaths in the witness's jurisdiction is present with the witness and administers the oath consistent with the laws of the jurisdiction. FL ST J ADMIN Rule 2.530(d)(3).
      iv. *Confrontation rights.* In juvenile and criminal proceedings the defendant must make an informed waiver of any confrontation rights that may be abridged by the use of communication equipment. FL ST J ADMIN Rule 2.530(d)(4).
      v. *Video testimony.* If the testimony to be presented utilizes video conferencing or comparable two-way visual capabilities, the court in its discretion may modify the procedures set forth in FL ST J ADMIN Rule 2.530 to accommodate the technology utilized. FL ST J ADMIN Rule 2.530(d)(5).
   e. *Burden of expense.* The cost for the use of the communication equipment is the responsibility of the requesting party unless otherwise directed by the court. FL ST J ADMIN Rule 2.530(e).
2. *Standards of professional courtesy; Scheduling*
   a. Attorneys will communicate with opposing counsel to schedule depositions, hearings, and other proceedings, at times mutually convenient for all interested persons. FL ST 6 J CIR 2009-066 PA/PI-CIR(B)(1).
   b. Attorneys will provide opposing counsel and other affected persons reasonable notice of all proceedings except upon agreement of counsel when expedited scheduling is necessary. Attorneys will immediately notify opposing counsel of any hearing time reserved. FL ST 6 J CIR 2009-066 PA/PI-CIR(B)(2).

c. Attorneys will request enough time for hearings and adjudicative proceedings to permit full and fair presentation of the matter and to permit response by opposing counsel. When scheduling depositions, Attorneys will schedule enough time to permit the conclusion of the deposition, including examination by all parties, without adjournment. FL ST 6 J CIR 2009-066 PA/PI-CIR(B)(3).

d. Attorneys will call potential scheduling problems to the attention of those affected, including the court, as soon as they become apparent. Attorneys will avoid last minute cancellations. FL ST 6 J CIR 2009-066 PA/PI-CIR(B)(4).

e. Attorneys will make request for changes only when necessary. Attorneys will not request rescheduling, cancellations, extension or postponements solely for the purpose of delay or obtaining unfair advantage. FL ST 6 J CIR 2009-066 PA/PI-CIR(B)(5).

f. Attorneys will cooperate with opposing counsel when conflicts and calendar changes are necessary and requested. FL ST 6 J CIR 2009-066 PA/PI-CIR(B)(6).

g. Attorneys will grant reasonable requests for scheduling, rescheduling, cancellations, extensions, and postponements that do not prejudice our client's opportunity for full, fair and prompt consideration and adjudication of the client's claim or defense. FL ST 6 J CIR 2009-066 PA/PI-CIR(B)(7).

h. First requests for reasonable extensions of time to respond to litigation deadlines relating to pleadings, discovery, or motions, should be granted as a matter of courtesy unless time is of the essence or other circumstances require otherwise. FL ST 6 J CIR 2009-066 PA/PI-CIR(B)(8).

i. Attorneys will resolve subsequent requests by balancing the need for expedition against the deference we should give to opposing counsel's schedule of professional and personal engagements, the reasonableness of the length of extension requested, opposing counsel's willingness to grant reciprocal extensions, the time needed for the task, and whether it is likely a court would grant the extension. FL ST 6 J CIR 2009-066 PA/PI-CIR(B)(9).

j. Attorneys will not attach unfair or extraneous conditions to extensions. Attorneys will impose conditions required to preserve rights that an extension might jeopardize. Attorneys may seek reciprocal scheduling concessions. When granting an extension, we will not try to preclude an opponent's substantive rights. FL ST 6 J CIR 2009-066 PA/PI-CIR(B)(10).

3. *Timing*

a. Hearings are limited to five (5) minutes per case. FL ST 6 J CIR PINELLAS CIR CT PI-CIR-98-30.

b. For more information regarding the timing of hearings, please see FL ST 6 J CIR PINELLAS CIR CT PI-CIR-98-30.

4. *Telephonic hearings.* For information regarding telephonic hearings, please see FL ST 6 J CIR PA/PI-CIR-88-48.

H. Forms

1. Official Motion to Compel Discovery Forms for Florida

a. Caption. FL ST RCP Form 1.901.

b. Notice of compliance when constitutional challenge is brought. FL ST RCP Form 1.975.

2. Motion to Compel Discovery Forms for Florida

a. Motion to compel attendance and for sanctions. FL-PP § 3:160.

b. Motion; To compel answer to questions asked on oral examination or written questions. FL-PP § 3:161.

c. Order; Directing deponent to answer questions asked on oral examination; Costs and attorney fees to moving party. FL-PP § 3:162.

d. Order; Compelling answer to written questions. FL-PP § 3:163.

e. Motion; For order finding person in contempt of court; Refusal, after order, to answer question. FL-PP § 3:167.

f. Motion; For order compelling opposing party to pay expenses incurred in proving facts the party refused to admit. FL-PP § 3:168.

g. Motion; Compel discovery, deposition. FL-PRACFORM § 7:37.
h. Motion; Compel discovery, interrogatories. FL-PRACFORM § 7:38.
i. Form for motion to compel answer on deposition. FL-RCPF R 1.380(6).
j. Form for certificate of non-appearance at deposition. FL-RCPF R 1.380(7).
k. Form for notice of motion. FL-RCPF R 1.380(8).
l. Form for order on motion to compel answer. FL-RCPF R 1.380(9).
m. Form for notice and motion to compel. FL-RCPF R 1.380(10).
n. Form for order to compel discovery. FL-RCPF R 1.380(18).
o. Form for order to comply with discovery and answer interrogatories. FL-RCPF R 1.380(19).

I. Checklist

- (I) ❑ Matters to be considered by moving party
  - (a) ❑ Required documents
    - (1) ❑ Notice of hearing/Motion
    - (2) ❑ Certificate of service
  - (b) ❑ Supplemental documents
    - (1) ❑ Proposed order
    - (2) ❑ Notice of constitutional question
  - (c) ❑ Time for making motion
    - (1) ❑ Upon reasonable notice to other parties and all persons affected, a party may apply for an order compelling discovery
    - (2) ❑ A copy of any written motion which may not be heard ex parte and a copy of the notice of the hearing thereof shall be served a reasonable time before the time specified for the hearing
- (II) ❑ Matters to be considered by opposing party
  - (a) ❑ Required documents
    - (1) ❑ Response to motion
    - (2) ❑ Certificate of service
  - (b) ❑ Supplemental documents
    - (1) ❑ Proposed order
    - (2) ❑ Notice of constitutional question
  - (c) ❑ Time for service and filing of opposition
    - (1) ❑ No time specified for responding to a motion

Motions, Oppositions and Replies
Motion for Directed Verdict

Document Last Updated January 2013

A. Applicable Rules

1. *State rules*

a. Motion for a directed verdict. FL ST RCP Rule 1.480.
b. Rules of court. FL ST RCP Rule 1.010; FL ST J ADMIN Rule 2.110.
c. Nonverification of pleadings. FL ST RCP Rule 1.030.
d. Service and filing of pleadings, orders, and documents. FL ST RCP Rule 1.080.

e. Time. FL ST RCP Rule 1.090.
f. Pleadings and motions. FL ST RCP Rule 1.100.
g. Motions. FL ST RCP Rule 1.160.
h. Relief from judgment, decrees, or orders. FL ST RCP Rule 1.540.
i. Mediation and arbitration. FL ST RCP Rule 1.700; FL ST RCP Rule 1.710; FL ST RCP Rule 1.720; FL ST RCP Rule 1.730; FL ST RCP Rule 1.750; FL ST RCP Rule 1.800; FL ST RCP Rule 1.810; FL ST RCP Rule 1.820; FL ST RCP Rule 1.830.
j. Forms. FL ST RCP Rule 1.900.
k. Minimization of the filing of sensitive information. FL ST J ADMIN Rule 2.425.
l. Retention of court records. FL ST J ADMIN Rule 2.430.
m. Foreign attorneys. FL ST J ADMIN Rule 2.510.
n. Signature of attorneys and parties. FL ST J ADMIN Rule 2.515.
o. Paper. FL ST J ADMIN Rule 2.520.
p. Electronic filing. FL ST J ADMIN Rule 2.525.
q. Accessibility of information and technology. FL ST J ADMIN Rule 2.526.
r. Communication equipment. FL ST J ADMIN Rule 2.530.
s. Court reporting. FL ST J ADMIN Rule 2.535.
t. Requests for accommodations by persons with disabilities. FL ST J ADMIN Rule 2.540.

2. *Local rules*
   a. General motion rule. FL ST 6 J CIR LOCAL Rule 5.
   b. Telephonic hearings in circuit civil, county civil and small claims cases. FL ST 6 J CIR PA/PI-CIR-88-48.
   c. Pre-trial conferences. FL ST 6 J CIR PA/PI-CIR-98-49.
   d. Uniform motion calendar civil division. FL ST 6 J CIR PINELLAS CIR CT PI-CIR-98-30.
   e. Standards of professional courtesy. FL ST 6 J CIR 2009-066 PA/PI-CIR.
   f. Arbitration and mediation program circuit civil and family cases. FL ST 6 J CIR PA/PI-CIR-96-63; FL ST 6 J CIR 2011-006 PA/PI-CIR.

B. Timing

1. *Before a verdict is returned.* A directed verdict is available to the defendant at the close of the plaintiff's evidence or to either party at the close of all of the evidence. A verdict may be directed either by the court on its own motion or on the motion of counsel. FL ST RCP Rule 1.480(a); FL-PP § 5:83. The movant should be prepared to argue the motion immediately. FL-PRACPROC § 22:14.
2. *After a verdict is returned.* Within ten (10) days after the return of a verdict, a party who has timely moved for a directed verdict may serve a motion to enter judgment in accordance with the motion for a directed verdict. FL ST RCP Rule 1.480(b).
3. *No verdict is returned.* If a verdict was not returned, a party who has timely moved for a directed verdict may serve a motion for judgment in accordance with the motion for a directed verdict within ten (10) days after discharge of the jury. FL ST RCP Rule 1.480(b).
4. *General motion timing.* A copy of any written motion which may not be heard ex parte and a copy of the notice of the hearing thereof shall be served a reasonable time before the time specified for the hearing. FL ST RCP Rule 1.090(d).
   a. All motions, except motions in limine, shall be filed and heard prior to the pre-trial conference unless good cause exists why the motions were not heard prior to the pre-trial conference, including the inability to obtain hearing time prior to the pre-trial conference. FL ST 6 J CIR PA/PI-CIR-98-49(6).
   b. If such good cause exists, the court will hear such motions at the pre-trial conference or at a separate hearing following the pre-trial conference. FL ST 6 J CIR PA/PI-CIR-98-49(6).

5. *Computation of time*

   a. *Generally.* Computation of time shall be governed by FL ST J ADMIN Rule 2.514. FL ST RCP Rule 1.090(a). The following rules apply in computing time periods specified in any rule of procedure, local rule, court order, or statute that does not specify a method of computing time. FL ST J ADMIN Rule 2.514(a).

      i. *Period stated in days or a longer unit.* When the period is stated in days or a longer unit of time (A) exclude the day of the event that triggers the period; (B) count every day, including intermediate Saturdays, Sundays, and legal holidays; and (C) include the last day of the period, but if the last day is a Saturday, Sunday, or legal holiday, or falls within any period of time extended through an order of the chief justice under FL ST J ADMIN Rule 2.205(a)(2)(B)(iv), the period continues to run until the end of the next day that is not a Saturday, Sunday, or legal holiday and does not fall within any period of time extended through an order of the chief justice. FL ST J ADMIN Rule 2.514(a)(1).

      ii. *Period stated in hours.* When the period is stated in hours (A) begin counting immediately on the occurrence of the event that triggers the period; (B) count every hour, including hours during intermediate Saturdays, Sundays, and legal holidays; and (C) if the period would end on a Saturday, Sunday, or legal holiday, or during any period of time extended through an order of the chief justice under FL ST J ADMIN Rule 2.205(a)(2)(B)(iv), the period continues to run until the same time on the next day that is not a Saturday, Sunday, or legal holiday and does not fall within any period of time extended through an order of the chief justice. FL ST J ADMIN Rule 2.514(a)(2).

      iii. *Period stated in days less than seven (7) days.* When the period stated in days is less than seven (7) days, intermediate Saturdays, Sundays, and legal holidays shall be excluded in the computation. FL ST J ADMIN Rule 2.514(a)(3).

      iv. *"Last day" defined.* Unless a different time is set by a statute, local rule, or court order, the last day ends (A) for electronic filing or for service by any means, at midnight; and (B) for filing by other means, when the clerk's office is scheduled to close. FL ST J ADMIN Rule 2.514(a)(4).

      v. *"Next day" defined.* The "next day" is determined by continuing to count forward when the period is measured after an event and backward when measured before an event. FL ST J ADMIN Rule 2.514(a)(5).

      vi. *"Legal holiday" defined.* "Legal holiday" means (A) the day set aside by FL ST § 110.117, for observing New Year's Day, Martin Luther King, Jr.'s Birthday, Memorial Day, Independence Day, Labor Day, Veterans' Day, Thanksgiving Day, the Friday after Thanksgiving Day, or Christmas Day, and (B) any day observed as a holiday by the clerk's office or as designated by the chief judge. FL ST J ADMIN Rule 2.514(a)(6).

   b. *Additional time after service by mail or e-mail.* When a party may or must act within a specified time after service and service is made by mail or e-mail, five (5) days are added after the period that would otherwise expire under FL ST J ADMIN Rule 2.514(a). FL ST J ADMIN Rule 2.514(b).

   c. *Enlargement.* When an act is required or allowed to be done at or within a specified time by order of court, by the Florida Rules of Civil Procedure, or by notice given thereunder, for cause shown the court at any time in its discretion (1) with or without notice, may order the period enlarged if request therefor is made before the expiration of the period originally prescribed or as extended by a previous order, or (2) upon motion made and notice after the expiration of the specified period, may permit the act to be done when failure to act was the result of excusable neglect, but it may not extend the time for making a motion for new trial, for rehearing, or to alter or amend a judgment; making a motion for relief from a judgment under FL ST RCP Rule 1.540(b); taking an appeal or filing a petition for certiorari; or making a motion for a directed verdict. FL ST RCP Rule 1.090(b).

   d. *Unaffected by expiration of term.* The period of time provided for the doing of any act or the taking of any proceeding shall not be affected or limited by the continued existence or expiration of a term of court. The continued existence or expiration of a term of court in no way affects the power of a court to do any act or take any proceeding in any action which is or has been pending before it. FL ST RCP Rule 1.090(c).

C. General Requirements

1. *Motions generally*
   a. *Contents.* An application to the court for an order shall be by motion which shall be made in writing unless made during a hearing or trial, shall state with particularity the grounds therefor, and shall set forth the relief or order sought. The requirement of writing is fulfilled if the motion is stated in a written notice of the hearing of the motion. All notices of hearing shall specify each motion or other matter to be heard. FL ST RCP Rule 1.100(b).
   b. *Particularity requirement.* The court considers a motion in the light of the substantive law, rule or statute to make its determination. Some rules require a statement of the grounds for a motion under the rule. Failure to give the grounds will result in denial of the motion. This should be the result in all situations when the ground for the motion is not inherent in the rule. FL-PRACPROC § 9:3. The requirement is nevertheless an important one, first because of the due process notice rights of the respondent, as well as for the assistance it provides to the court in its preparation for the hearing or, absent a hearing, for disposition. 4 FLPRAC R 1.100.
   c. *Standards of professional courtesy; Motion practice*
      i. Attorneys will make every reasonable effort to resolve the issue before setting a motion for hearing. FL ST 6 J CIR 2009-066 PA/PI-CIR(G)(1).
      ii. Attorneys will not force opposing counsel to make motions attorneys do not intend to oppose unless circumstances require or the client requires. FL ST 6 J CIR 2009-066 PA/PI-CIR(G)(2).
2. *Motion for directed verdict*
   a. *Effect of a motion for directed verdict.* A party who moves for a directed verdict at the close of the evidence offered by the adverse party may offer evidence in the event the motion is denied without having reserved the right to do so and to the same extent as if the motion had not been made. The denial of a motion for a directed verdict shall not operate to discharge the jury. A motion for a directed verdict shall state the specific grounds therefor. The order directing a verdict is effective without any assent of the jury. FL ST RCP Rule 1.480(a).
   b. *Reservation of decision on motion.* When a motion for a directed verdict is denied or for any reason is not granted, the court is deemed to have submitted the action to the jury subject to a later determination of the legal questions raised by the motion. Within ten (10) days after the return of a verdict, a party who has timely moved for a directed verdict may serve a motion to set aside the verdict and any judgment entered thereon and to enter judgment in accordance with the motion for a directed verdict. If a verdict was not returned, a party who has timely moved for a directed verdict may serve a motion for judgment in accordance with the motion for a directed verdict within ten (10) days after discharge of the jury. FL ST RCP Rule 1.480(b).
   c. *Joined with motion for new trial.* A motion for a new trial may be joined with a motion for directed verdict or a new trial may be requested in the alternative. If a verdict was returned, the court may allow the judgment to stand or may reopen the judgment and either order a new trial or direct the entry of judgment as if the requested verdict had been directed. If no verdict was returned, the court may direct the entry of judgment as if the requested verdict had been directed or may order a new trial. FL ST RCP Rule 1.480(c).
   d. *General procedures on a motion for directed verdict*
      i. *Proper method.* The proper method of advocating that a party is entitled to prevail on a claim or defense as a matter of law is to make a motion for a directed verdict at the close of the evidence offered by the opposing party. The trial judge has authority to direct a verdict in favor of one party and against another, without submitting the case to the jury, if there is no other verdict the jury could lawfully return. 5 FLPRAC § 22:5.
      ii. *Directed verdict only in a jury trial.* A motion for directed verdict is proper only in a jury trial. The equivalent motion in nonjury trial is called a motion for involuntary dismissal. 5 FLPRAC § 22:5.
      iii. *Test for the sufficiency of the evidence.* A motion for directed verdict is used primarily to test the

sufficiency of the evidence offered in support of a claim or defense. It may also be used to raise legal issues other than the sufficiency of the evidence, but that is less common because most pure issues of law can be resolved on a motion to dismiss or a motion for summary judgment before the case is set for trial. If there is no evidence to support a claim or defense, the trial judge has a duty to direct a verdict for the opposing party on that claim or defense. 5 FLPRAC § 22:5.

- The trial judge must view all of the facts and factual inferences in a light most favorable to the party opposing the motion. 5 FLPRAC § 22:5.
- The rule has often been stated by the Florida courts in the negative, that is, a motion for directed verdict should not be granted unless the court, after viewing the evidence and testimony in the light most favorable to the nonmoving party, determines that no reasonable jury could render a verdict for the nonmoving party. Under this rule, the trial judge may not direct a verdict against a party if there is any evidence upon which the jury could lawfully make a finding in favor of that party. 5 FLPRAC § 22:5.

3. *Arbitration and mediation*

    a. *Referral to arbitration and mediation.* Except as hereinafter provided or as otherwise prohibited by law, the presiding judge may enter an order referring all or any part of a contested civil matter to mediation or arbitration. The parties to any contested civil matter may file a written stipulation to mediate or arbitrate any issue between them at any time. Such stipulation shall be incorporated into the order of referral. FL ST RCP Rule 1.700(a).

    b. *Arbitration*

        i. *Exclusions.* A civil action shall be ordered to arbitration or arbitration in conjunction with mediation upon stipulation of the parties. A civil action may be ordered to arbitration or arbitration in conjunction with mediation upon motion of any party or by the court, if the judge determines the action to be of such a nature that arbitration could be of benefit to the litigants or the court. FL ST RCP Rule 1.800.

            - Under no circumstances may the following categories of actions be referred to arbitration: (1) bond estreatures; (2) habeas corpus or other extraordinary writs; (3) bond validations; (4) civil or criminal contempt; (5) such other matters as may be specified by order of the chief judge in the circuit. FL ST RCP Rule 1.800.

        ii. For more information regarding arbitration, please see FL ST RCP Rule 1.810; FL ST RCP Rule 1.820; FL ST RCP Rule 1.830.

    c. *Mediation.* For more information regarding mediation, please see FL ST RCP Rule 1.710; FL ST RCP Rule 1.720; FL ST RCP Rule 1.730; and FL ST RCP Rule 1.750.

    d. See FL ST 6 J CIR PA/PI-CIR-96-63 for more information about the Arbitration and Mediation Program for Florida's Sixth Judicial Circuit.

4. *Rules of court*

    a. *Rules of civil procedure.* The Florida Rules of Civil Procedure apply to all actions of a civil nature and all special statutory proceedings in the circuit courts and county courts except those to which the Florida Probate Rules, the Florida Family Law Rules of Procedure, or the Small Claims Rules apply. FL ST RCP Rule 1.010.

        i. The form, content, procedure, and time for pleading in all special statutory proceedings shall be as prescribed by the statutes governing the proceeding unless the Florida Rules of Civil Procedure specifically provide to the contrary. FL ST RCP Rule 1.010.

        ii. The Florida Rules of Civil Procedure shall be construed to secure the just, speedy, and inexpensive determination of every action. FL ST RCP Rule 1.010.

    b. *Rules of judicial administration.* The Florida Rules of Judicial Administration shall apply to administrative matters in all courts to which the Florida Rules of Judicial Administration are applicable by their terms. The Florida Rules of Judicial Administration shall be construed to secure the speedy and inexpensive determination of every proceeding to which they are applicable. The Florida Rules of Judicial Administration shall supersede all conflicting rules and statutes. FL ST J ADMIN Rule 2.110.

5. *Settlement and alternative dispute resolution.* When a matter is scheduled for hearing and the matter is resolved by agreement or settlement, the party setting the matter for hearing shall notify the court. When a matter is scheduled for trial and the case settles, the plaintiff shall notify the court. Permission of the court must be obtained in order to cancel a trial. FL ST 6 J CIR LOCAL Rule 5(A).

   a. Unless there are strong and overriding issues of principle, attorneys will raise and explore the issue of settlement as soon as enough is known to make settlement discussions meaningful. FL ST 6 J CIR 2009-066 PA/PI-CIR(I)(1).

   b. Attorneys will not falsely hold out the possibility of settlement to adjourn discovery or delay trial. FL ST 6 J CIR 2009-066 PA/PI-CIR(I)(2).

   c. Attorneys will consider whether the client's interest could be adequately served and the controversy more expeditiously and economically disposed of by arbitration, mediation or other forms of alternative dispute resolution. FL ST 6 J CIR 2009-066 PA/PI-CIR(I)(3).

D. Documents

1. *Required documents*

   a. *Notice of hearing/Motion.* An application to the court for an order shall be by motion which shall be made in writing unless made during a hearing or trial, shall state with particularity the grounds therefor, and shall set forth the relief or order sought. The requirement of writing is fulfilled if the motion is stated in a written notice of the hearing of the motion. All notices of hearing shall specify each motion or other matter to be heard. FL ST RCP Rule 1.100(b).

      i. *Notices to persons with disabilities.* See the Format section of this KeyRules document for further information.

   b. *Certificate of service.* When any attorney certifies in substance: "I certify that a copy hereof has been furnished to (here insert name or names and addresses used for service) by (e-mail) (delivery) (mail) (fax) on .... (date) ....________________ Attorney" the certificate is taken as prima facie proof of such service in compliance with FL ST J ADMIN Rule 2.516. FL ST J ADMIN Rule 2.516(f).

2. *Supplemental documents*

   a. *Proposed order.* The court may require that orders or judgments be prepared by a party, may require the party to furnish the court with stamped, addressed envelopes for service of the order or judgment, and may require that proposed orders and judgments be furnished to all parties before entry by the court of the order or judgment. FL ST J ADMIN Rule 2.516(h)(1).

      i. After a hearing, attorneys will make a good faith effort to quickly agree or disagree upon a proposed order and submit the result to the court. Unless otherwise instructed by the court, or agreed to by counsel, all proposed orders shall be provided to other counsel for approval or comment prior to submission to the court. Attorneys will not submit controverted orders to the court with a copy to opposing counsel for "objections within ______ days". Courts prefer to know that the order is either agreed upon or opposed. FL ST 6 J CIR 2009-066 PA/PI-CIR(G)(3).

      ii. Attorneys will not use post-hearing submissions of proposed orders as a guise to reargue the merits of the matter. FL ST 6 J CIR 2009-066 PA/PI-CIR(G)(4).

   b. *Notice of constitutional question.* A party that files a pleading, written motion, or other paper drawing into question the constitutionality of a state statute or a county or municipal charter, ordinance, or franchise must promptly (1) file a notice of constitutional question stating the question and identifying the paper that raises it; and (2) serve the notice and the pleading, written motion, or other paper drawing into question the constitutionality of a state statute or a county or municipal charter, ordinance, or franchise on the Attorney General or the state attorney of the judicial circuit in which the action is pending, by either certified or registered mail. Service of the notice and pleading, written motion, or other paper does not require joinder of the Attorney General or the state attorney as a party to the action. FL ST RCP Rule 1.071.

E. Format

1. *Documents; Type and size.* Documents subject to the exceptions set forth in FL ST J ADMIN Rule

2.525(d) shall be filed on recycled paper measuring eight and one half by eleven (8 1/2 by 11) inches. For purposes of FL ST J ADMIN Rule 2.520, paper is recycled if it contains a minimum content of fifty (50) percent waste paper. Xerographic reduction of legal-size (eight and one half by fourteen (8 1/2 by 14) inches) documents to letter size (eight and one half by eleven (8 1/2 by 11) inches) is prohibited. All other documents filed by electronic transmission shall be filed in a format capable of being printed in a format consistent with the provisions of FL ST J ADMIN Rule 2.250. FL ST J ADMIN Rule 2.520(b).

a. *Exhibits.* Any exhibit or attachment filed with pleadings or papers may be filed in its original size. FL ST J ADMIN Rule 2.520(c).

b. *Recording space.* On all papers and documents prepared and filed by the court or by any party to a proceeding which are to be recorded in the public records of any county, including but not limited to final money judgments and notices of lis pendens, a three (3) inch by three (3) inch space at the top right-hand corner on the first page and a one (1) inch by three (3) inch space at the top right-hand corner on each subsequent page shall be left blank and reserved for use by the clerk of court. FL ST J ADMIN Rule 2.520(d).

   i. *Exceptions to recording space.* Any papers or documents created by persons or entities over which the filing party has no control, including but not limited to wills, codicils, trusts, or other testamentary documents; documents prepared or executed by any public officer; documents prepared, executed, acknowledged, or proved outside of the State of Florida; or documents created by State or Federal government agencies, may be filed without the space required by FL ST J ADMIN Rule 2.520. FL ST J ADMIN Rule 2.520(e).

c. *Noncompliance.* No clerk of court is permitted to refuse to file any document or paper because of noncompliance with the Florida Rules of Judicial Administration. However, upon request of the clerk of court, noncomplying documents must be resubmitted in accordance with the formatting rules. FL ST J ADMIN Rule 2.520(f).

2. *Caption.* Every pleading, motion, order, judgment, or other paper shall have a caption containing the name of the court, the file number, and except for in rem proceedings, including forfeiture proceedings, the name of the first party on each side with an appropriate indication of other parties, and a designation identifying the party filing it and its nature or the nature of the order, as the case may be. In any in rem proceeding, every pleading, motion, order, judgment, or other paper shall have a caption containing the name of the court, the file number, the style "In re" (followed by the name or general description of the property), and a designation of the person or entity filing it and its nature or the nature of the order, as the case may be. In an in rem forfeiture proceeding, the style shall be "In re forfeiture of" (followed by the name of the general description of the property). All papers filed in the action shall be styled in such a manner as to indicate clearly the subject matter of the paper and the party requesting or obtaining relief. FL ST RCP Rule 1.100(c)(1).

3. *Writing and written defined.* Writing or written means a document containing information, an application, or a stipulation. FL ST RCP Rule 1.080(c).

4. *Rule abbreviations*

   a. The Florida Rules of Civil Procedure and shall be abbreviated as Fla.R.Civ.P. FL ST RCP Rule 1.010.

   b. The Florida Rules of Judicial Administration shall be abbreviated as Fla. R. Jud. Admin. FL ST J ADMIN Rule 2.110.

5. *Nonverification.* Except when otherwise specifically provided by the Florida Rules of Civil Procedure or an applicable statute, every pleading or other document of a party represented by an attorney need not be verified or accompanied by an affidavit. FL ST RCP Rule 1.030; FL ST J ADMIN Rule 2.515(a).

6. *Attorney signature*

   a. *Attorney signature.* Every pleading and other document of a party represented by an attorney shall be signed by at least one (1) attorney of record in that attorney's individual name whose current record Florida Bar address, telephone number, including area code, primary e-mail address and secondary e-mail addresses, if any, and Florida Bar number shall be stated, and who shall be duly licensed to

practice law in Florida or who shall have received permission to appear in the particular case as provided in FL ST J ADMIN Rule 2.510. FL ST J ADMIN Rule 2.515(a).

i. The attorney may be required by the court to give the address of, and to vouch for the attorney's authority to represent, the party. FL ST J ADMIN Rule 2.515(a).

ii. The signature of an attorney shall constitute a certificate by the attorney that the attorney has read the pleading or other document; that to the best of the attorney's knowledge, information, and belief there is good ground to support it; and that it is not interposed for delay. FL ST J ADMIN Rule 2.515(a).

iii. If a pleading is not signed or is signed with intent to defeat the purpose of FL ST J ADMIN Rule 2.515, it may be stricken and the action may proceed as though the pleading or other document had not been served. FL ST J ADMIN Rule 2.515(a).

b. *Pro se litigant signature.* A party who is not represented by an attorney shall sign any pleading or other paper and state the party's address and telephone number, including area code. FL ST J ADMIN Rule 2.515(b).

c. *Form of signature*

i. The signatures required on pleadings and documents by FL ST J ADMIN Rule 2.515(a) and FL ST J ADMIN Rule 2.515(b) may be:

- Original signatures;
- Original signatures that have been reproduced by electronic means, such as on electronically transmitted documents or photocopied documents;
- Electronic signatures using the "/s/," "s/," or "/s" formats by or at the direction of the person signing; or
- Any other signature format authorized by general law, so long as the clerk where the proceeding is pending has the capability of receiving and has obtained approval from the Supreme Court of Florida to accept pleadings and documents with that signature format. FL ST J ADMIN Rule 2.515(c)(1).

ii. An attorney, party, or other person who files a pleading or paper by electronic transmission that does not contain the original signature of that attorney, party, or other person shall file that identical pleading or paper in paper form containing an original signature of that attorney, party, or other person (hereinafter called the follow-up filing) immediately thereafter. The follow-up filing is not required if the Supreme Court of Florida has entered an order directing the clerk of court to discontinue accepting the follow-up filing. FL ST J ADMIN Rule 2.515(c)(2).

7. *Forms*

a. *Process.* The forms of process, notice of lis pendens, and notice of action provided in the Florida Rules of Civil Procedure are sufficient. Variations from the forms do not void process or notices that are otherwise sufficient. FL ST RCP Rule 1.900(a).

b. *Other forms.* The other forms provided in the Florida Rules of Civil Procedure are sufficient for the matters that are covered by them. So long as the substance is expressed without prolixity, the forms may be varied to meet the facts of a particular case. FL ST RCP Rule 1.900(b).

c. *Formal matters.* Captions, except for the designation of the paper, are omitted from the forms provided in the Florida Rules of Civil Procedure. A general form of caption is the first form provided. Signatures are omitted from pleadings and motions. FL ST RCP Rule 1.900(c).

8. *Notices to persons with disabilities.* All notices of court proceedings to be held in a public facility, and all process compelling appearance at such proceedings, shall include the following statement in bold face, fourteen (14) point Times New Roman or Courier font: "If you are a person with a disability who needs any accommodation in order to participate in this proceeding, you are entitled, at no cost to you, to the provision of certain assistance. Please contact [identify applicable court personnel by name, address, and telephone number] at least seven (7) days before your scheduled court appearance, or immediately upon receiving this notification if the time before the scheduled appearance is less than seven (7) days; if you are hearing or voice impaired, call 711." FL ST J ADMIN Rule 2.540(c)(1).

9. *Minimization of the filing of sensitive information*
   a. *Limitations for court filings.* Unless authorized by FL ST J ADMIN Rule 2.425(b), statute, another rule of court, or the court orders otherwise, designated sensitive information filed with the court must be limited to the following format:
      i. The initials of a person known to be a minor;
      ii. The year of birth of a person's birth date;
      iii. No portion of any: Social security number, Bank account number, Credit card account number, Charge account number, or Debit account number;
      iv. The last four digits of any: Taxpayer identification number (TIN), Employee identification number, Driver's license number, Passport number, Telephone number, Financial account number, except as set forth in FL ST J ADMIN Rule 2.425(a)(3), Brokerage account number, Insurance policy account number, Loan account number, Customer account number, or Patient or health care number;
      v. A truncated version of any: Email address, Computer user name, Password, or Personal identification number (PIN); and
      vi. A truncated version of any other sensitive information as provided by court order. FL ST J ADMIN Rule 2.425(a).
   b. *Exceptions.* FL ST J ADMIN Rule 2.425(a) does not apply to the following:
      i. An account number which identifies the property alleged to be the subject of a proceeding;
      ii. The record of an administrative or agency proceeding;
      iii. The record in appellate or review proceedings;
      iv. The birth date of a minor whenever the birth date is necessary for the court to establish or maintain subject matter jurisdiction;
      v. The name of a minor in any order relating to parental responsibility, time-sharing, or child support;
      vi. The name of a minor in any document or order affecting the minor's ownership of real property;
      vii. The birth date of a party in a writ of attachment or notice to payor;
      viii. In traffic and criminal proceedings: a pro se filing; a court filing that is related to a criminal matter or investigation and that is prepared before the filing of a criminal charge or is not filed as part of any docketed criminal case; an arrest or search warrant or any information in support thereof; a charging document and an affidavit or other documents filed in support of any charging document, including any driving records; a statement of particulars; discovery material introduced into evidence or otherwise filed with the court; and all information necessary for the proper issuance and execution of a subpoena duces tecum;
      ix. Information used by the clerk for case maintenance purposes or the courts for case management purposes; and
      x. Information which is relevant and material to an issue before the court. FL ST J ADMIN Rule 2.425(b).
   c. *Remedies.* Upon motion by a party or interested person or sua sponte by the court, the court may order remedies, sanctions or both for a violation of FL ST J ADMIN Rule 2.425(a). Following notice and an opportunity to respond, the court may impose sanctions if such filing was not made in good faith. FL ST J ADMIN Rule 2.425(c).
   d. *Motions not restricted.* FL ST J ADMIN Rule 2.425 does not restrict a party's right to move for protective order, to move to file documents under seal, or to request a determination of the confidentiality of records. FL ST J ADMIN Rule 2.425(d).
   e. *Application.* FL ST J ADMIN Rule 2.425 does not affect the application of constitutional provisions, statutes, or rules of court regarding confidential information or access to public information. FL ST J ADMIN Rule 2.425(e).

F. Filing and Service Requirements

1. *Filing requirements.* All original documents must be filed with the court either before service or immediately thereafter, unless otherwise provided for by general law or other rules. If the original of any bond or other document is not placed in the court file, a certified copy must be so placed by the clerk. FL ST J ADMIN Rule 2.516(d). All documents shall be filed in conformity with the requirements of FL ST J ADMIN Rule 2.525. FL ST RCP Rule 1.080(b). All documents filed in any court shall be filed by electronic transmission in accordance with FL ST J ADMIN Rule 2.525. "Documents" means pleadings, motions, petitions, memoranda, briefs, notices, exhibits, declarations, affidavits, orders, judgments, decrees, writs, opinions, and any other paper or writing submitted to a court. FL ST J ADMIN Rule 2.520(a). All documents that are court records, as defined in FL ST J ADMIN Rule 2.430(a)(1), must be filed by electronic transmission, provided that: (1) the clerk has the ability to accept and retain such documents; (2) the clerk or the chief judge of the circuit has requested permission to accept documents filed by electronic transmission; and (3) the supreme court has entered an order granting permission to the clerk to accept documents filed by electronic transmission. FL ST J ADMIN Rule 2.525(c)(1).
   a. *Definition.* "Electronic transmission of documents" means the sending of information by electronic signals to, by or from a court or clerk, which when received can be transformed and stored or transmitted on paper, microfilm, magnetic storage device, optical imaging system, CD-ROM, flash drive, other electronic data storage system, server, case maintenance system ("CM"), electronic court filing ("ECF") system, statewide or local electronic portal ("e-portal"), or other electronic record keeping system authorized by the supreme court in a format sufficient to communicate the information on the original document in a readable format. Electronic transmission of documents includes electronic mail ("e-mail") and any internet-based transmission procedure, and may include procedures allowing for documents to be signed or verified by electronic means. FL ST J ADMIN Rule 2.525(a).
      i. The filing of documents with the court as required by the Florida Rules of Judicial Administration must be made by filing them with the clerk in accordance with FL ST J ADMIN Rule 2.525, except that the judge may permit documents to be filed with the judge, in which event the judge must note the filing date before him or her on the documents and transmit them to the clerk. The date of filing is that shown on the face of the document by the judge's notation or the clerk's time stamp, whichever is earlier. FL ST J ADMIN Rule 2.516(e).
   b. *Application.* Any court or clerk of the court may accept the electronic transmission of documents for filing after the clerk, together with input from the chief judge of the circuit, has obtained approval of the procedures and program for doing so from the Supreme Court of Florida. FL ST J ADMIN Rule 2.525(b).
   c. *Exceptions*
      i. Paper documents and other submissions may be manually submitted to the clerk or court:
         - When the clerk does not have the ability to accept and retain documents by electronic filing or has not had ECF Procedures approved by the supreme court;
         - For filing by any self-represented party or any self-represented nonparty unless specific ECF Procedures provide a means to file documents electronically. However, any self-represented nonparty that is a governmental or public agency and any other agency, partnership, corporation, or business entity acting on behalf of any governmental or public agency may file documents by electronic transmission if such entity has the capability of filing documents electronically;
         - For filing by attorneys excused from e-mail service in accordance with FL ST J ADMIN Rule 2.516(b);
         - When submitting evidentiary exhibits or filing non-documentary materials;
         - When the filing involves documents in excess of twenty-five (25) megabytes (25MB) in size. For such filings, documents may be transmitted using an electronic storage medium that the clerk has the ability to accept, which may include a CD-ROM, flash drive, or similar storage medium;

- When filed in open court, as permitted by the court;
- When paper filing is permitted by any approved statewide or local ECF procedures; and
- If any court determines that justice so requires. FL ST J ADMIN Rule 2.525(d).

ii. Any document in paper form submitted under FL ST J ADMIN Rule 2.525(d) is filed when it is received by the clerk or court and the clerk shall immediately thereafter convert any filed paper document to an electronic document. "Convert to an electronic document" means optically capturing an image of a paper document and using character recognition software to recover as much of the document's text as practicable and then indexing and storing the document in the official court file. FL ST J ADMIN Rule 2.525(c)(4).

iii. Any storage medium submitted under FL ST J ADMIN Rule 2.525(d)(5) is filed when received by the clerk or court and the clerk shall immediately thereafter transfer the electronic documents from the storage device to the official court file. FL ST J ADMIN Rule 2.525(c)(5).

iv. If the filer of any paper document authorized under FL ST J ADMIN Rule 2.525(d) provides a self-addressed, postage-paid envelope for return of the paper document after it is converted to electronic form by the clerk, the clerk shall place the paper document in the envelope and deposit it in the mail. Except when a paper document is required to be maintained, the clerk may recycle any filed paper document that is not to be returned to the filer. FL ST J ADMIN Rule 2.525(c)(6).

v. The clerk may convert any paper document filed before the effective date of FL ST J ADMIN Rule 2.525 to an electronic document. Unless the clerk is required to maintain the paper document, if the paper document has been converted to an electronic document by the clerk, the paper document is no longer part of the official court file and may be removed and recycled. FL ST J ADMIN Rule 2.525(c)(7).

d. *Official court file.* For information on what constitutes the official court file, please see FL ST J ADMIN Rule 2.525(c)(2), FL ST J ADMIN Rule 2.525(c)(3).

e. *Administration.* All attorneys, parties, or other persons using this rule to file documents are required to make arrangements with the court or clerk for the payment of any charges authorized by general law or the supreme court before filing any document by electronic transmission. FL ST J ADMIN Rule 2.525(f)(2).

f. *Filing date.* The filing date for an electronically transmitted document is the date and time that such filing is acknowledged by an electronic stamp or otherwise, pursuant to any procedure set forth in any ECF Procedures approved by the supreme court, or the date the last page of such filing is received by the court or clerk. FL ST J ADMIN Rule 2.525(f)(3).

g. *Accessibility.* All documents transmitted in any electronic form under FL ST J ADMIN Rule 2.525 must comply with the accessibility requirements of FL ST J ADMIN Rule 2.526. FL ST J ADMIN Rule 2.525(g).

2. *Service requirements.* Every pleading subsequent to the initial pleading, all orders, and every other document filed in the action must be served in conformity with the requirements of FL ST J ADMIN Rule 2.516. FL ST RCP Rule 1.080(a).

a. *Service; When required.* Unless the court otherwise orders, or a statute or supreme court administrative order specifies a different means of service, every pleading subsequent to the initial pleading and every other document filed in any court proceeding, except applications for witness subpoenas and documents served by formal notice or required to be served in the manner provided for service of formal notice, must be served in accordance with FL ST J ADMIN Rule 2.516 on each party. No service need be made on parties against whom a default has been entered, except that pleadings asserting new or additional claims against them must be served in the manner provided for service of summons. FL ST J ADMIN Rule 2.516(a).

b. *Service; How made.* When service is required or permitted to be made upon a party represented by an attorney, service must be made upon the attorney unless service upon the party is ordered by the court. FL ST J ADMIN Rule 2.516(b).

i. *Service by electronic mail ("e-mail").* All documents required or permitted to be served on

another party must be served by e-mail, unless FL ST J ADMIN Rule 2.516 otherwise provides. When, in addition to service by e-mail, the sender also utilizes another means of service provided for in FL ST J ADMIN Rule 2.516(b)(2), any differing time limits and other provisions applicable to that other means of service control. FL ST J ADMIN Rule 2.516(b)(1). Any document electronically transmitted to a court or clerk must also be served on all parties and interested persons in accordance with the applicable rules of court. FL ST J ADMIN Rule 2.525(e)(2).

- *Service on attorneys.* Upon appearing in a proceeding, an attorney must serve a designation of a primary e-mail address and may designate no more than two (2) secondary e-mail addresses. Thereafter, service must be directed to all designated e-mail addresses in that proceeding. Every document filed by an attorney thereafter must include the primary e-mail address of that attorney and any secondary e-mail addresses. If an attorney does not designate any e-mail address for service, documents may be served on that attorney at the e-mail address on record with The Florida Bar. FL ST J ADMIN Rule 2.516(b)(1)(A).
- *Exception to e-mail service on attorneys.* Service by an attorney on another attorney must be made by e-mail unless excused by the court. Upon motion by an attorney demonstrating that the attorney has no e-mail account and lacks access to the Internet at the attorney's office, the court may excuse the attorney from the requirements of e-mail service. Service on and by an attorney excused by the court from e-mail service must be by the means provided in FL ST J ADMIN Rule 2.516(b)(2). FL ST J ADMIN Rule 2.516(b)(1)(B).
- *Service on and by parties not represented by an attorney.* Any party not represented by an attorney may serve a designation of a primary e-mail address and also may designate no more than two (2) secondary e-mail addresses to which service must be directed in that proceeding by the means provided in FL ST J ADMIN Rule 2.516(b)(1). If a party not represented by an attorney does not designate an e-mail address for service in a proceeding, service on and by that party must be by the means provided in FL ST J ADMIN Rule 2.516(b)(2). FL ST J ADMIN Rule 2.516(b)(1)(C).
- *Time of service.* Service by e-mail is complete when it is sent. FL ST J ADMIN Rule 2.516(b)(1)(D). An e-mail is deemed served on the date it is sent. FL ST J ADMIN Rule 2.516(b)(1)(D)(i). If the sender learns that the e-mail did not reach the address of the person to be served, the sender must immediately send another copy by e-mail, or by a means authorized by FL ST J ADMIN Rule 2.516(b)(2). FL ST J ADMIN Rule 2.516(b)(1)(D)(ii). E-mail service is treated as service by mail for the computation of time. FL ST J ADMIN Rule 2.516(b)(1)(D)(iii).

ii. *Format of e-mail for service.* Service of a document by e-mail is made by attaching a copy of the document in PDF format to an e-mail sent to all addresses designated by the attorney or party. FL ST J ADMIN Rule 2.516(b)(1)(E).

- All documents served by e-mail must be attached to an e-mail message containing a subject line beginning with the words "SERVICE OF COURT DOCUMENT" in all capital letters, followed by the case number of the proceeding in which the documents are being served. FL ST J ADMIN Rule 2.516(b)(1)(E)(i).
- The body of the e-mail must identify the court in which the proceeding is pending, the case number, the name of the initial party on each side, the title of each document served with that e-mail, and the sender's name and telephone number. FL ST J ADMIN Rule 2.516(b)(1)(E)(ii).
- Any document served by e-mail may be signed by the "/s/" format, as long as the filed original is signed in accordance with the applicable rule of procedure. FL ST J ADMIN Rule 2.516(b)(1)(E)(iii).
- Any e-mail which, together with its attached documents, exceeds five megabytes (5MB) in size, must be divided and sent as separate e-mails, no one of which may exceed five megabytes (5MB) in size and each of which must be sequentially numbered in the subject line. FL ST J ADMIN Rule 2.516(b)(1)(E)(iv).

iii. *Service by other means.* In addition to, and not in lieu of, service by e-mail, service may also be made upon attorneys by any of the means specified in FL ST J ADMIN Rule 2.516(b)(2). Service on and by all parties who are not represented by an attorney and who do not designate an e-mail address, and on and by all attorneys excused from e-mail service, must be made by delivering a copy of the document or by mailing it to the party or attorney at their last known address or, if no address is known, by leaving it with the clerk of the court. Service by mail is complete upon mailing. Delivery of a copy within FL ST J ADMIN Rule 2.516 is complete upon:

- Handing it to the attorney or to the party,
- Leaving it at the attorney's or party's office with a clerk or other person in charge thereof,
- If there is no one in charge, leaving it in a conspicuous place therein,
- If the office is closed or the person to be served has no office, leaving it at the person's usual place of abode with some person of his or her family above fifteen (15) years of age and informing such person of the contents, or
- Transmitting it by facsimile to the attorney's or party's office with a cover sheet containing the sender's name, firm, address, telephone number, and facsimile number, and the number of pages transmitted. When service is made by facsimile, a copy must also be served by any other method permitted by FL ST J ADMIN Rule 2.516. Facsimile service occurs when transmission is complete. FL ST J ADMIN Rule 2.516(b)(2)(A) through FL ST J ADMIN Rule 2.516(b)(2)(E).
- Service by delivery after 5:00 p.m. must be deemed to have been made by mailing on the date of delivery. FL ST J ADMIN Rule 2.516(b)(2)(F).

c. *Service; Numerous defendants.* In actions when the parties are unusually numerous, the court may regulate the service contemplated by the Florida Rules of Judicial Administration on motion or on its own initiative in such manner as may be found to be just and reasonable. FL ST J ADMIN Rule 2.516(c).

d. *Service by clerk.* Service of notices and other documents required to be made by the clerk must also be done as provided in FL ST J ADMIN Rule 2.516(b). FL ST J ADMIN Rule 2.516(g).

e. *Standards of professional courtesy; Service*

i. The timing and manner of service should not be used to the disadvantage of the party receiving the papers. This includes the use of facsimile transmissions and any additional expedited means of communication approved by the court. FL ST 6 J CIR 2009-066 PA/PI-CIR(C)(1).

ii. Attorneys will not serve papers to take advantage of opposing counsel's known absence from the office or at a time or in a manner designed to inconvenience an opponent, such as late on Friday afternoon or the day preceding a secular or religious holiday. FL ST 6 J CIR 2009-066 PA/PI-CIR(C)(2).

iii. Attorneys will not serve papers, including briefs and memoranda, so close to a court appearance that the ability of opposing counsel to prepare for that appearance or, where permitted, to respond, is inhibited. FL ST 6 J CIR 2009-066 PA/PI-CIR(C)(3).

iv. Service should be made personally or by facsimile transmission when it is likely that service by mail, even when allowed, will prejudice the opposing party. FL ST 6 J CIR 2009-066 PA/PI-CIR(C)(4).

G. Hearings

1. *Communication equipment*

a. *Definition.* Communication equipment means a conference telephone or other electronic device that permits all those appearing or participating to hear and speak to each other, provided that all conversation of all parties is audible to all persons present. FL ST J ADMIN Rule 2.530(a).

b. *Use by all parties.* A county or circuit court judge may, upon the court's own motion or upon the written request of a party, direct that communication equipment be used for a motion hearing, pretrial conference, or a status conference. A judge must give notice to the parties and consider any objections they may have to the use of communication equipment before directing that communication equipment be used. The decision to use communication equipment over the objection of parties will be in the sound discretion of the trial court, except as noted below. FL ST J ADMIN Rule 2.530(b).

c. *Use only by requesting party.* A county or circuit court judge may, upon the written request of a party upon reasonable notice to all other parties, permit a requesting party to participate through communication equipment in a scheduled motion hearing; however, any such request (except in criminal, juvenile, and appellate proceedings) must be granted, absent a showing of good cause to deny the same, where the hearing is set for not longer than fifteen (15) minutes. FL ST J ADMIN Rule 2.530(c).

d. *Testimony*

   i. *Generally.* A county or circuit court judge, general magistrate, special magistrate, or hearing officer may allow testimony to be taken through communication equipment if all parties consent or if permitted by another applicable rule of procedure. FL ST J ADMIN Rule 2.530(d)(1).

   ii. *Procedure.* Any party desiring to present testimony through communication equipment shall, prior to the hearing or trial at which the testimony is to be presented, contact all parties to determine whether each party consents to this form of testimony. The party seeking to present the testimony shall move for permission to present testimony through communication equipment, which motion shall set forth good cause as to why the testimony should be allowed in this form. FL ST J ADMIN Rule 2.530(d)(2).

   iii. *Oath.* Testimony may be taken through communication equipment only if a notary public or other person authorized to administer oaths in the witness's jurisdiction is present with the witness and administers the oath consistent with the laws of the jurisdiction. FL ST J ADMIN Rule 2.530(d)(3).

   iv. *Confrontation rights.* In juvenile and criminal proceedings the defendant must make an informed waiver of any confrontation rights that may be abridged by the use of communication equipment. FL ST J ADMIN Rule 2.530(d)(4).

   v. *Video testimony.* If the testimony to be presented utilizes video conferencing or comparable two-way visual capabilities, the court in its discretion may modify the procedures set forth in FL ST J ADMIN Rule 2.530 to accommodate the technology utilized. FL ST J ADMIN Rule 2.530(d)(5).

e. *Burden of expense.* The cost for the use of the communication equipment is the responsibility of the requesting party unless otherwise directed by the court. FL ST J ADMIN Rule 2.530(e).

2. *Standards of professional courtesy; Scheduling*

   a. Attorneys will communicate with opposing counsel to schedule depositions, hearings, and other proceedings, at times mutually convenient for all interested persons. FL ST 6 J CIR 2009-066 PA/PI-CIR(B)(1).

   b. Attorneys will provide opposing counsel and other affected persons reasonable notice of all proceedings except upon agreement of counsel when expedited scheduling is necessary. Attorneys will immediately notify opposing counsel of any hearing time reserved. FL ST 6 J CIR 2009-066 PA/PI-CIR(B)(2).

   c. Attorneys will request enough time for hearings and adjudicative proceedings to permit full and fair presentation of the matter and to permit response by opposing counsel. When scheduling depositions, Attorneys will schedule enough time to permit the conclusion of the deposition, including examination by all parties, without adjournment. FL ST 6 J CIR 2009-066 PA/PI-CIR(B)(3).

   d. Attorneys will call potential scheduling problems to the attention of those affected, including the court, as soon as they become apparent. Attorneys will avoid last minute cancellations. FL ST 6 J CIR 2009-066 PA/PI-CIR(B)(4).

e. Attorneys will make request for changes only when necessary. Attorneys will not request rescheduling, cancellations, extension or postponements solely for the purpose of delay or obtaining unfair advantage. FL ST 6 J CIR 2009-066 PA/PI-CIR(B)(5).

f. Attorneys will cooperate with opposing counsel when conflicts and calendar changes are necessary and requested. FL ST 6 J CIR 2009-066 PA/PI-CIR(B)(6).

g. Attorneys will grant reasonable requests for scheduling, rescheduling, cancellations, extensions, and postponements that do not prejudice our client's opportunity for full, fair and prompt consideration and adjudication of the client's claim or defense. FL ST 6 J CIR 2009-066 PA/PI-CIR(B)(7).

h. First requests for reasonable extensions of time to respond to litigation deadlines relating to pleadings, discovery, or motions, should be granted as a matter of courtesy unless time is of the essence or other circumstances require otherwise. FL ST 6 J CIR 2009-066 PA/PI-CIR(B)(8).

i. Attorneys will resolve subsequent requests by balancing the need for expedition against the deference we should give to opposing counsel's schedule of professional and personal engagements, the reasonableness of the length of extension requested, opposing counsel's willingness to grant reciprocal extensions, the time needed for the task, and whether it is likely a court would grant the extension. FL ST 6 J CIR 2009-066 PA/PI-CIR(B)(9).

j. Attorneys will not attach unfair or extraneous conditions to extensions. Attorneys will impose conditions required to preserve rights that an extension might jeopardize. Attorneys may seek reciprocal scheduling concessions. When granting an extension, we will not try to preclude an opponent's substantive rights. FL ST 6 J CIR 2009-066 PA/PI-CIR(B)(10).

3. *Timing*

a. Hearings are limited to five (5) minutes per case. FL ST 6 J CIR PINELLAS CIR CT PI-CIR-98-30.

b. For more information regarding the timing of hearings, please see FL ST 6 J CIR PINELLAS CIR CT PI-CIR-98-30.

4. *Telephonic hearings.* For information regarding telephonic hearings, please see FL ST 6 J CIR PA/PI-CIR-88-48.

H. Forms

1. Official Motion for Directed Verdict Forms for Florida

a. Caption. FL ST RCP Form 1.901.

b. Notice of compliance when constitutional challenge is brought. FL ST RCP Form 1.975.

2. Motion for Directed Verdict Forms for Florida

a. Motion; For directed verdict; At close of adverse party's evidence. FL-PP § 5:86.

b. Motion; For directed verdict; At close of all of evidence. FL-PP § 5:87.

c. Motion; Request to go to jury if motions by both parties are denied. FL-PP § 5:88.

d. Order; Granting defendant's motion for directed verdict; Insufficiency of plaintiff's evidence. FL-PP § 5:89.

e. Motion; Directed verdict, renewed. FL-PRACFORM § 7:62.

f. Form for motion for directed verdict at close of plaintiff's case. FL-RCPF R 1.480(24).

g. Form for motion for directed verdict at close of defendant's case. FL-RCPF R 1.480(25).

h. Form for motion to set aside verdict and enter directed verdict. FL-RCPF R 1.480(26).

I. Checklist

(I) ❑ Matters to be considered by moving party

(a) ❑ Required documents

(1) ❑ Notice of hearing/Motion

(2) ❑ Certificate of service

(b) ❑ Supplemental documents

(1) ❑ Proposed order

(2) ❑ Notice of constitutional question

(c) ❑ Time for making motion

(1) ❑ Before a verdict is returned - A directed verdict is available to the defendant at the close of the plaintiff's evidence or to either party at the close of all of the evidence

(2) ❑ After a verdict is returned - Within ten (10) days after the return of a verdict, a party who has timely moved for a directed verdict may serve a motion to enter judgment in accordance with the motion for a directed verdict

(3) ❑ No verdict is returned - If a verdict was not returned, a party who has timely moved for a directed verdict may serve a motion for judgment in accordance with the motion for a directed verdict within ten (10) days after discharge of the jury

(4) ❑ General motion timing - A copy of any written motion which may not be heard ex parte and a copy of the notice of the hearing thereof shall be served a reasonable time before the time specified for the hearing

(II) ❑ Matters to be considered by opposing party

(a) ❑ Required documents

(1) ❑ Response to motion

(2) ❑ Certificate of service

(b) ❑ Supplemental documents

(1) ❑ Proposed order

(2) ❑ Notice of constitutional question

(c) ❑ Time for service and filing of opposition

(1) ❑ No time specified for responding to a motion

Requests, Notices and Applications
Request for Production of Documents

Document Last Updated January 2013

A. Applicable Rules

1. *State rules*

a. Nonverification of pleadings. FL ST RCP Rule 1.030.

b. Service and filing of pleadings, orders, and documents. FL ST RCP Rule 1.080.

c. Time. FL ST RCP Rule 1.090.

d. Pleadings and motions. FL ST RCP Rule 1.100.

e. Pretrial procedure. FL ST RCP Rule 1.200.

f. General provisions governing discovery. FL ST RCP Rule 1.280.

g. Depositions upon oral examination. FL ST RCP Rule 1.310.

h. Interrogatories to parties. FL ST RCP Rule 1.340.

i. Production of documents and things and entry upon land for inspection and other purposes. FL ST RCP Rule 1.350.

j. Production of documents and things without deposition. FL ST RCP Rule 1.351.

k. Examination of persons. FL ST RCP Rule 1.360.

l. Requests for admission. FL ST RCP Rule 1.370.
m. Failure to make discovery; Sanctions. FL ST RCP Rule 1.380.
n. Depositions of expert witnesses. FL ST RCP Rule 1.390.
o. Relief from judgment, decrees, or orders. FL ST RCP Rule 1.540.
p. Forms. FL ST RCP Rule 1.900.
q. Minimization of the filing of sensitive information. FL ST J ADMIN Rule 2.425.
r. Retention of court records. FL ST J ADMIN Rule 2.430.
s. Foreign attorneys. FL ST J ADMIN Rule 2.510.
t. Signature of attorneys and parties. FL ST J ADMIN Rule 2.515.
u. Paper. FL ST J ADMIN Rule 2.520.
v. Electronic filing. FL ST J ADMIN Rule 2.525.
w. Accessibility of information and technology. FL ST J ADMIN Rule 2.526.
x. Requests for accommodations by persons with disabilities. FL ST J ADMIN Rule 2.540.

2. *Local rules*
   a. General motion rule. FL ST 6 J CIR LOCAL Rule 5.
   b. Standards of professional courtesy. FL ST 6 J CIR 2009-066 PA/PI-CIR.
   c. Arbitration and mediation program circuit civil and family cases. FL ST 6 J CIR PA/PI-CIR-96-63; FL ST 6 J CIR 2011-006 PA/PI-CIR.

B. Timing

1. *Request for production of documents.* Without leave of court the request may be served on the plaintiff after commencement of the action and on any other party with or after service of the process and initial pleading on that party. FL ST RCP Rule 1.350(b).
2. *Notice of intent to serve subpoena.* A party desiring production under FL ST RCP Rule 1.351 shall serve notice as provided in FL ST RCP Rule 1.080 on every other party of the intent to serve a subpoena under FL ST RCP Rule 1.351 at least ten (10) days before the subpoena is issued if service is by delivery and fifteen (15) days before the subpoena is issued if the service is by mail or e-mail. FL ST RCP Rule 1.351(b).
3. *Sequence and timing of discovery.* Except as provided in FL ST RCP Rule 1.280(b)(5) or unless the court upon motion for the convenience of parties and witnesses and in the interest of justice orders otherwise, methods of discovery may be used in any sequence, and the fact that a party is conducting discovery, whether by deposition or otherwise, shall not delay any other party's discovery. FL ST RCP Rule 1.280(e).
4. *Computation of time*
   a. *Generally.* Computation of time shall be governed by FL ST J ADMIN Rule 2.514. FL ST RCP Rule 1.090(a). The following rules apply in computing time periods specified in any rule of procedure, local rule, court order, or statute that does not specify a method of computing time. FL ST J ADMIN Rule 2.514(a).
      i. *Period stated in days or a longer unit.* When the period is stated in days or a longer unit of time (A) exclude the day of the event that triggers the period; (B) count every day, including intermediate Saturdays, Sundays, and legal holidays; and (C) include the last day of the period, but if the last day is a Saturday, Sunday, or legal holiday, or falls within any period of time extended through an order of the chief justice under FL ST J ADMIN Rule 2.205(a)(2)(B)(iv), the period continues to run until the end of the next day that is not a Saturday, Sunday, or legal holiday and does not fall within any period of time extended through an order of the chief justice. FL ST J ADMIN Rule 2.514(a)(1).
      ii. *Period stated in hours.* When the period is stated in hours (A) begin counting immediately on

the occurrence of the event that triggers the period; (B) count every hour, including hours during intermediate Saturdays, Sundays, and legal holidays; and (C) if the period would end on a Saturday, Sunday, or legal holiday, or during any period of time extended through an order of the chief justice under FL ST J ADMIN Rule 2.205(a)(2)(B)(iv), the period continues to run until the same time on the next day that is not a Saturday, Sunday, or legal holiday and does not fall within any period of time extended through an order of the chief justice. FL ST J ADMIN Rule 2.514(a)(2).

iii. *Period stated in days less than seven (7) days.* When the period stated in days is less than seven (7) days, intermediate Saturdays, Sundays, and legal holidays shall be excluded in the computation. FL ST J ADMIN Rule 2.514(a)(3).

iv. *"Last day" defined.* Unless a different time is set by a statute, local rule, or court order, the last day ends (A) for electronic filing or for service by any means, at midnight; and (B) for filing by other means, when the clerk's office is scheduled to close. FL ST J ADMIN Rule 2.514(a)(4).

v. *"Next day" defined.* The "next day" is determined by continuing to count forward when the period is measured after an event and backward when measured before an event. FL ST J ADMIN Rule 2.514(a)(5).

vi. *"Legal holiday" defined.* "Legal holiday" means (A) the day set aside by FL ST § 110.117, for observing New Year's Day, Martin Luther King, Jr.'s Birthday, Memorial Day, Independence Day, Labor Day, Veterans' Day, Thanksgiving Day, the Friday after Thanksgiving Day, or Christmas Day, and (B) any day observed as a holiday by the clerk's office or as designated by the chief judge. FL ST J ADMIN Rule 2.514(a)(6).

b. *Additional time after service by mail or e-mail.* When a party may or must act within a specified time after service and service is made by mail or e-mail, five (5) days are added after the period that would otherwise expire under FL ST J ADMIN Rule 2.514(a). FL ST J ADMIN Rule 2.514(b).

c. *Enlargement.* When an act is required or allowed to be done at or within a specified time by order of court, by the Florida Rules of Civil Procedure, or by notice given thereunder, for cause shown the court at any time in its discretion (1) with or without notice, may order the period enlarged if request therefor is made before the expiration of the period originally prescribed or as extended by a previous order, or (2) upon motion made and notice after the expiration of the specified period, may permit the act to be done when failure to act was the result of excusable neglect, but it may not extend the time for making a motion for new trial, for rehearing, or to alter or amend a judgment; making a motion for relief from a judgment under FL ST RCP Rule 1.540(b); taking an appeal or filing a petition for certiorari; or making a motion for a directed verdict. FL ST RCP Rule 1.090(b).

d. *Unaffected by expiration of term.* The period of time provided for the doing of any act or the taking of any proceeding shall not be affected or limited by the continued existence or expiration of a term of court. The continued existence or expiration of a term of court in no way affects the power of a court to do any act or take any proceeding in any action which is or has been pending before it. FL ST RCP Rule 1.090(c).

C. General Requirements

1. *General provisions governing discovery*

a. *Discovery methods.* Parties may obtain discovery by one or more of the following methods: depositions upon oral examination or written questions; written interrogatories; production of documents or things or permission to enter upon land or other property for inspection and other purposes; physical and mental examinations; and requests for admission. Unless the court orders otherwise and under FL ST RCP Rule 1.280(c), the frequency of use of these methods is not limited, except as provided in FL ST RCP Rule 1.200, FL ST RCP Rule 1.340, and FL ST RCP Rule 1.370. FL ST RCP Rule 1.280(a).

b. *Scope of discovery.* Unless otherwise limited by order of the court in accordance with the Florida Rules of Civil Procedure, the scope of discovery is as follows:

i. *In general.* Parties may obtain discovery regarding any matter, not privileged, that is relevant to the subject matter of the pending action, whether it relates to the claim or defense of the party seeking discovery or the claim or defense of any other party, including the existence, description, nature, custody, condition, and location of any books, documents, or other tangible things and the identity and location of persons having knowledge of any discoverable matter. It is not ground for objection that the information sought will be inadmissible at the trial if the information sought appears reasonably calculated to lead to the discovery of admissible evidence. FL ST RCP Rule 1.280(b)(1).

ii. *Indemnity agreements.* A party may obtain discovery of the existence and contents of any agreement under which any person may be liable to satisfy part or all of a judgment that may be entered in the action or to indemnify or to reimburse a party for payments made to satisfy the judgment. Information concerning the agreement is not admissible in evidence at trial by reason of disclosure. FL ST RCP Rule 1.280(b)(2).

iii. *Electronically stored information.* A party may obtain discovery of electronically stored information in accordance with the Florida Rules of Civil Procedure. FL ST RCP Rule 1.280(b)(3).

iv. *Trial preparation; Materials.* Subject to the provisions of FL ST RCP Rule 1.280(b)(5), a party may obtain discovery of documents and tangible things otherwise discoverable under FL ST RCP Rule 1.280(b)(1) and prepared in anticipation of litigation or for trial by or for another party or by or for that party's representative, including that party's attorney, consultant, surety, indemnitor, insurer, or agent, only upon a showing that the party seeking discovery has need of the materials in the preparation of the case and is unable without undue hardship to obtain the substantial equivalent of the materials by other means. FL ST RCP Rule 1.280(b)(4).

- In ordering discovery of the materials when the required showing has been made, the court shall protect against disclosure of the mental impressions, conclusions, opinions, or legal theories of an attorney or other representative of a party concerning the litigation. FL ST RCP Rule 1.280(b)(4).
- Without the required showing a party may obtain a copy of a statement concerning the action or its subject matter previously made by that party. FL ST RCP Rule 1.280(b)(4).
- Upon request without the required showing a person not a party may obtain a copy of a statement concerning the action or its subject matter previously made by that person. If the request is refused, the person may move for an order to obtain a copy. The provisions of FL ST RCP Rule 1.380(a)(5) apply to the award of expenses incurred as a result of making the motion. FL ST RCP Rule 1.280(b)(4).
- For purposes of FL ST RCP Rule 1.280(b)(4), a statement previously made is a written statement signed or otherwise adopted or approved by the person making it, or a stenographic, mechanical, electrical, or other recording or transcription of it that is a substantially verbatim recital of an oral statement by the person making it and contemporaneously recorded. FL ST RCP Rule 1.280(b)(4).

v. *Trial preparation; Experts.* Discovery of facts known and opinions held by experts, otherwise discoverable under the provisions of FL ST RCP Rule 1.280(b)(1) and acquired or developed in anticipation of litigation or for trial, may be obtained only as follows:

- By interrogatories a party may require any other party to identify each person whom the other party expects to call as an expert witness at trial and to state the subject matter on which the expert is expected to testify, and to state the substance of the facts and opinions to which the expert is expected to testify and a summary of the grounds for each opinion. FL ST RCP Rule 1.280(b)(5)(A)(i).
- Any person disclosed by interrogatories or otherwise as a person expected to be called as an expert witness at trial may be deposed in accordance with FL ST RCP Rule 1.390 without motion or order of court. FL ST RCP Rule 1.280(b)(5)(A)(ii).
- A party may obtain the following discovery regarding any person disclosed by interrogatories or otherwise as a person expected to be called as an expert witness at trial: The scope of employment in the pending case and the compensation for such service, FL ST RCP

Rule 1.280(b)(5)(A)(iii)(1); The expert's general litigation experience, including the percentage of work performed for plaintiffs and defendants, FL ST RCP Rule 1.280(b)(5)(A)(iii)(2); The identity of other cases, within a reasonable time period, in which the expert has testified by deposition or at trial, FL ST RCP Rule 1.280(b)(5)(A)(iii)(3); An approximation of the portion of the expert's involvement as an expert witness, which may be based on the number of hours, percentage of hours, or percentage of earned income derived from serving as an expert witness; however, the expert shall not be required to disclose his or her earnings as an expert witness or income derived from other services. FL ST RCP Rule 1.280(b)(5)(A)(iii)(4).

- An expert may be required to produce financial and business records only under the most unusual or compelling circumstances and may not be compelled to compile or produce nonexistent documents. Upon motion, the court may order further discovery by other means, subject to such restrictions as to scope and other provisions pursuant to FL ST RCP Rule 1.280(b)(5)(C) concerning fees and expenses as the court may deem appropriate. FL ST RCP Rule 1.280(b)(5).
- A party may discover facts known or opinions held by an expert who has been retained or specially employed by another party in anticipation of litigation or preparation for trial and who is not expected to be called as a witness at trial, only as provided in FL ST RCP Rule 1.360(b) or upon a showing of exceptional circumstances under which it is impracticable for the party seeking discovery to obtain facts or opinions on the same subject by other means. FL ST RCP Rule 1.280(b)(5)(B).
- Unless manifest injustice would result, the court shall require that the party seeking discovery pay the expert a reasonable fee for time spent in responding to discovery under FL ST RCP Rule 1.280(b)(5)(A) and FL ST RCP Rule 1.280(b)(5)(B); and concerning discovery from an expert obtained under FL ST RCP Rule 1.280(b)(5)(A) the court may require, and concerning discovery obtained under FL ST RCP Rule 1.280(b)(5)(B) shall require, the party seeking discovery to pay the other party a fair part of the fees and expenses reasonably incurred by the latter party in obtaining facts and opinions from the expert. FL ST RCP Rule 1.280(b)(5)(C).
- As used in the Florida Rules of Civil Procedure an expert shall be an expert witness as defined in FL ST RCP Rule 1.390(a). FL ST RCP Rule 1.280(b)(5)(D).

vi. *Claims to privilege or protection.* When a party withholds information otherwise discoverable under the Florida Rules of Civil Procedure by claiming that it is privileged or subject to protection as trial preparation material, the party shall make the claim expressly and shall describe the nature of the documents, communications, or things not produced or disclosed in a manner that, without revealing information itself privileged or protected, will enable other parties to assess the applicability of the privilege or protection. FL ST RCP Rule 1.280(b)(6).

c. *Limitations on discovery of electronically stored information*

i. A person may object to discovery of electronically stored information from sources that the person identifies as not reasonably accessible because of burden or cost. On motion to compel discovery or for a protective order, the person from whom discovery is sought must show that the information sought or the format requested is not reasonably accessible because of undue burden or cost. If that showing is made, the court may nonetheless order the discovery from such sources or in such formats if the requesting party shows good cause. The court may specify conditions of the discovery, including ordering that some or all of the expenses incurred by the person from whom discovery is sought be paid by the party seeking the discovery. FL ST RCP Rule 1.280(d)(1).

ii. In determining any motion involving discovery of electronically stored information, the court must limit the frequency or extent of discovery otherwise allowed by the Florida Rules of Civil Procedure if it determines that (i) the discovery sought is unreasonably cumulative or duplicative, or can be obtained from another source or in another manner that is more convenient, less burdensome, or less expensive; or (ii) the burden or expense of the discovery outweighs its likely benefit, considering the needs of the case, the amount in controversy, the parties' resources, the importance of the issues at stake in the action, and the importance of the discovery in resolving the issues. FL ST RCP Rule 1.280(d)(2).

d. For information on inadvertent disclosure of privileged materials, see FL ST RCP Rule 1.285.

e. *Standards of professional courtesy; Discovery*

   i. Attorneys will use discovery only when necessary to ascertain information, to perpetuate testimony, or to obtain documents or things necessary for the prosecution or defense of an action. Attorneys will never use discovery as a means of harassment or to impose an inordinate burden or expense. FL ST 6 J CIR 2009-066 PA/PI-CIR(F)(1).

   ii. Attorneys will file motions for protective orders as soon as possible and notice them for hearing as soon as practicable. Absent an agreement or court order a deposition may not be properly canceled due to a pending motion. FL ST 6 J CIR 2009-066 PA/PI-CIR(F)(2).

   iii. Prior to filing a motion to compel or for protective order, attorneys will confer with opposing counsel in a good faith effort to resolve the issues raised. Attorneys will file with the motion a statement certifying that attorneys have complied and been unable to resolve the dispute. FL ST 6 J CIR 2009-066 PA/PI-CIR(F)(3).

   iv. Motions to compel shall quote in full each interrogatory, question on deposition, request for admission or request for production to which the motion is addressed and the objection and grounds stated by opposing counsel. FL ST 6 J CIR 2009-066 PA/PI-CIR(F)(4).

2. *Request for production of documents*

   a. *Scope of request.* Any party may request any other party:

      i. To produce and permit the party making the request, or someone acting in the requesting party's behalf, to inspect and copy any designated documents, including electronically stored information, writings, drawings, graphs, charts, photographs, phono-records, and other data compilations from which information can be obtained, translated, if necessary, by the party to whom the request is directed through detection devices into reasonably usable form, that constitute or contain matters within the scope of FL ST RCP Rule 1.280(b) and that are in the possession, custody, or control of the party to whom the request is directed;

      ii. To inspect and copy, test, or sample any tangible things that constitute or contain matters within the scope of FL ST RCP Rule 1.280(b) and that are in the possession, custody, or control of the party to whom the request is directed; or

      iii. To permit entry upon designated land or other property in the possession or control of the party upon whom the request is served for the purpose of inspection and measuring, surveying, photographing, testing, or sampling the property or any designated object or operation on it within the scope of FL ST RCP Rule 1.280(b). FL ST RCP Rule 1.350(a).

   b. *Contents of request*

      i. The request shall set forth the items to be inspected, either by individual item or category, and describe each item and category with reasonable particularity. The request shall specify a reasonable time, place, and manner of making the inspection or performing the related acts. FL ST RCP Rule 1.350(b).

      ii. A request for electronically stored information may specify the form or forms in which electronically stored information is to be produced. If the responding party objects to a requested form, or if no form is specified in the request, the responding party must state the form or forms it intends to use. If a request for electronically stored information does not specify the form of production, the producing party must produce the information in a form or forms in which it is ordinarily maintained or in a reasonably usable form or forms. FL ST RCP Rule 1.350(b).

   c. *Failure to respond to requests.* The party submitting the request may move for an order under FL ST RCP Rule 1.380 concerning any objection, failure to respond to the request, or any part of it, or failure to permit the inspection as requested. FL ST RCP Rule 1.350(b). Please see FL ST RCP Rule

1.380(d) and the KeyRules Motion to Compel Discovery documents for further information regarding compelling discovery and discovery sanctions.

i. *Response requirements.* For each item or category the response shall state that inspection and related activities will be permitted as requested unless the request is objected to, in which event the reasons for the objection shall be stated. If an objection is made to part of an item or category, the part shall be specified. When producing documents, the producing party shall either produce them as they are kept in the usual course of business or shall identify them to correspond with the categories in the request. If the responding party objects to a requested form (for electronic information), or if no form is specified in the request, the responding party must state the form or forms it intends to use. If a request for electronically stored information does not specify the form of production, the producing party must produce the information in a form or forms in which it is ordinarily maintained or in a reasonably usable form or forms. FL ST RCP Rule 1.350(b).

3. *Requests to a non-party*

a. *Independent action not prohibited.* FL ST RCP Rule 1.350 does not preclude an independent action against a person not a party for production of documents and things and permission to enter upon land. FL ST RCP Rule 1.350(c). FL ST RCP Rule 1.351 does not affect the right of any party to bring an independent action for production of documents and things or permission to enter upon land. FL ST RCP Rule 1.351(f).

b. *Scope.* A party may seek inspection and copying of any documents or things within the scope of FL ST RCP Rule 1.350(a) from a person who is not a party by issuance of a subpoena directing the production of the documents or things when the requesting party does not seek to depose the custodian or other person in possession of the documents or things. FL ST RCP Rule 1.351 provides the exclusive procedure for obtaining documents or things by subpoena from nonparties without deposing the custodian or other person in possession of the documents or things pursuant to FL ST RCP Rule 1.310. FL ST RCP Rule 1.351(a).

i. *Procedure.* The proposed subpoena shall be attached to the notice and shall state the time, place, and method for production of the documents or things, and the name and address of the person who is to produce the documents or things, if known, and if not known, a general description sufficient to identify the person or the particular class or group to which the person belongs; shall include a designation of the items to be produced; and shall state that the person who will be asked to produce the documents or things has the right to object to the production under FL ST RCP Rule 1.351 and that the person will not be required to surrender the documents or things. A copy of the notice and proposed subpoena shall not be furnished to the person upon whom the subpoena is to be served. If any party serves an objection to production under FL ST RCP Rule 1.351 within ten (10) days of service of the notice, the documents or things shall not be produced pending resolution of the objection in accordance with FL ST RCP Rule 1.351(d). FL ST RCP Rule 1.351(b).

ii. *Subpoena.* If no objection is made by a party under FL ST RCP Rule 1.351(b), an attorney of record in the action may issue a subpoena or the party desiring production shall deliver to the clerk for issuance a subpoena together with a certificate of counsel or pro se party that no timely objection has been received from any party, and the clerk shall issue the subpoena and deliver it to the party desiring production. FL ST RCP Rule 1.351(c).

- The subpoena shall be identical to the copy attached to the notice and shall specify that no testimony may be taken and shall require only production of the documents or things specified in it. FL ST RCP Rule 1.351(c).
- The subpoena may give the recipient an option to deliver or mail legible copies of the documents or things to the party serving the subpoena. FL ST RCP Rule 1.351(c).
- The person upon whom the subpoena is served may condition the preparation of copies on the payment in advance of the reasonable costs of preparing the copies. FL ST RCP Rule 1.351(c).
- The subpoena shall require production only in the county of the residence of the custodian

or other person in possession of the documents or things or in the county where the documents or things are located or where the custodian or person in possession usually conducts business. FL ST RCP Rule 1.351(c).

- If the person upon whom the subpoena is served objects at any time before the production of the documents or things, the documents or things shall not be produced under FL ST RCP Rule 1.351, and relief may be obtained pursuant to FL ST RCP Rule 1.310. FL ST RCP Rule 1.351(c).

iii. *Ruling on objection.* If an objection is made by a party under FL ST RCP Rule 1.351(b), the party desiring production may file a motion with the court seeking a ruling on the objection or may proceed pursuant to FL ST RCP Rule 1.310. FL ST RCP Rule 1.351(d).

iv. *Copies furnished.* If the subpoena is complied with by delivery or mailing of copies as provided in FL ST RCP Rule 1.351(c), the party receiving the copies shall furnish a legible copy of each item furnished to any other party who requests it upon the payment of the reasonable cost of preparing the copies. FL ST RCP Rule 1.351(e).

4. *Arbitration and mediation*

a. *Referral to arbitration and mediation.* Except as hereinafter provided or as otherwise prohibited by law, the presiding judge may enter an order referring all or any part of a contested civil matter to mediation or arbitration. The parties to any contested civil matter may file a written stipulation to mediate or arbitrate any issue between them at any time. Such stipulation shall be incorporated into the order of referral. FL ST RCP Rule 1.700(a).

b. *Arbitration*

i. *Exclusions.* A civil action shall be ordered to arbitration or arbitration in conjunction with mediation upon stipulation of the parties. A civil action may be ordered to arbitration or arbitration in conjunction with mediation upon motion of any party or by the court, if the judge determines the action to be of such a nature that arbitration could be of benefit to the litigants or the court. FL ST RCP Rule 1.800.

- Under no circumstances may the following categories of actions be referred to arbitration: (1) bond estreatures; (2) habeas corpus or other extraordinary writs; (3) bond validations; (4) civil or criminal contempt; (5) such other matters as may be specified by order of the chief judge in the circuit. FL ST RCP Rule 1.800.

ii. For more information regarding arbitration, please see FL ST RCP Rule 1.810; FL ST RCP Rule 1.820; FL ST RCP Rule 1.830.

c. *Mediation.* For more information regarding mediation, please see FL ST RCP Rule 1.710; FL ST RCP Rule 1.720; FL ST RCP Rule 1.730; and FL ST RCP Rule 1.750.

d. See FL ST 6 J CIR PA/PI-CIR-96-63 for more information about the Arbitration and Mediation Program for Florida's Sixth Judicial Circuit.

5. *Rules of court*

a. *Rules of civil procedure.* The Florida Rules of Civil Procedure apply to all actions of a civil nature and all special statutory proceedings in the circuit courts and county courts except those to which the Florida Probate Rules, the Florida Family Law Rules of Procedure, or the Small Claims Rules apply. FL ST RCP Rule 1.010.

i. The form, content, procedure, and time for pleading in all special statutory proceedings shall be as prescribed by the statutes governing the proceeding unless the Florida Rules of Civil Procedure specifically provide to the contrary. FL ST RCP Rule 1.010.

ii. The Florida Rules of Civil Procedure shall be construed to secure the just, speedy, and inexpensive determination of every action. FL ST RCP Rule 1.010.

b. *Rules of judicial administration.* The Florida Rules of Judicial Administration shall apply to administrative matters in all courts to which the Florida Rules of Judicial Administration are applicable by their terms. The Florida Rules of Judicial Administration shall be construed to secure

the speedy and inexpensive determination of every proceeding to which they are applicable. The Florida Rules of Judicial Administration shall supersede all conflicting rules and statutes. FL ST J ADMIN Rule 2.110.

6. *Settlement and alternative dispute resolution.* When a matter is scheduled for hearing and the matter is resolved by agreement or settlement, the party setting the matter for hearing shall notify the court. When a matter is scheduled for trial and the case settles, the plaintiff shall notify the court. Permission of the court must be obtained in order to cancel a trial. FL ST 6 J CIR LOCAL Rule 5(A).
   a. Unless there are strong and overriding issues of principle, attorneys will raise and explore the issue of settlement as soon as enough is known to make settlement discussions meaningful. FL ST 6 J CIR 2009-066 PA/PI-CIR(I)(1).
   b. Attorneys will not falsely hold out the possibility of settlement to adjourn discovery or delay trial. FL ST 6 J CIR 2009-066 PA/PI-CIR(I)(2).
   c. Attorneys will consider whether the client's interest could be adequately served and the controversy more expeditiously and economically disposed of by arbitration, mediation or other forms of alternative dispute resolution. FL ST 6 J CIR 2009-066 PA/PI-CIR(I)(3).

D. Documents

1. *Required documents*
   a. *Request for production.* Please see the General Requirements section of this document for more information on the contents of the request for production.
      i. *Notices to persons with disabilities.* See the Format section of this KeyRules document for further information.
   b. *Certificate of service.* A certificate of service of the interrogatories shall be filed, giving the date of service and the name of the party to whom they were directed. FL ST RCP Rule 1.340(e). When any attorney certifies in substance: "I certify that a copy hereof has been furnished to (here insert name or names and addresses used for service) by (e-mail) (delivery) (mail) (fax) on .... (date) ....______________ Attorney" the certificate is taken as prima facie proof of such service in compliance with FL ST J ADMIN Rule 2.516. FL ST J ADMIN Rule 2.516(f).
2. *Supplemental documents*
   a. *Notice of intent to serve subpoena/Subpoena.* Please see the General Requirements section of this document for more information.

E. Format

1. *Documents; Type and size.* Documents subject to the exceptions set forth in FL ST J ADMIN Rule 2.525(d) shall be filed on recycled paper measuring eight and one half by eleven (8 1/2 by 11) inches. For purposes of FL ST J ADMIN Rule 2.520, paper is recycled if it contains a minimum content of fifty (50) percent waste paper. Xerographic reduction of legal-size (eight and one half by fourteen (8 1/2 by 14) inches) documents to letter size (eight and one half by eleven (8 1/2 by 11) inches) is prohibited. All other documents filed by electronic transmission shall be filed in a format capable of being printed in a format consistent with the provisions of FL ST J ADMIN Rule 2.250. FL ST J ADMIN Rule 2.520(b).
   a. *Exhibits.* Any exhibit or attachment filed with pleadings or papers may be filed in its original size. FL ST J ADMIN Rule 2.520(c).
   b. *Recording space.* On all papers and documents prepared and filed by the court or by any party to a proceeding which are to be recorded in the public records of any county, including but not limited to final money judgments and notices of lis pendens, a three (3) inch by three (3) inch space at the top right-hand corner on the first page and a one (1) inch by three (3) inch space at the top right-hand corner on each subsequent page shall be left blank and reserved for use by the clerk of court. FL ST J ADMIN Rule 2.520(d).
      i. *Exceptions to recording space.* Any papers or documents created by persons or entities over which the filing party has no control, including but not limited to wills, codicils, trusts, or other testamentary documents; documents prepared or executed by any public officer; documents

prepared, executed, acknowledged, or proved outside of the State of Florida; or documents created by State or Federal government agencies, may be filed without the space required by FL ST J ADMIN Rule 2.520. FL ST J ADMIN Rule 2.520(e).

c. *Noncompliance.* No clerk of court is permitted to refuse to file any document or paper because of noncompliance with the Florida Rules of Judicial Administration. However, upon request of the clerk of court, noncomplying documents must be resubmitted in accordance with the formatting rules. FL ST J ADMIN Rule 2.520(f).

2. *Caption.* Every pleading, motion, order, judgment, or other paper shall have a caption containing the name of the court, the file number, and except for in rem proceedings, including forfeiture proceedings, the name of the first party on each side with an appropriate indication of other parties, and a designation identifying the party filing it and its nature or the nature of the order, as the case may be. In any in rem proceeding, every pleading, motion, order, judgment, or other paper shall have a caption containing the name of the court, the file number, the style "In re" (followed by the name or general description of the property), and a designation of the person or entity filing it and its nature or the nature of the order, as the case may be. In an in rem forfeiture proceeding, the style shall be "In re forfeiture of" (followed by the name of the general description of the property). All papers filed in the action shall be styled in such a manner as to indicate clearly the subject matter of the paper and the party requesting or obtaining relief. FL ST RCP Rule 1.100(c)(1).

3. *Writing and written defined.* Writing or written means a document containing information, an application, or a stipulation. FL ST RCP Rule 1.080(c).

4. *Rule abbreviations*

a. The Florida Rules of Civil Procedure and shall be abbreviated as Fla.R.Civ.P. FL ST RCP Rule 1.010.

b. The Florida Rules of Judicial Administration shall be abbreviated as Fla. R. Jud. Admin. FL ST J ADMIN Rule 2.110.

5. *Nonverification.* Except when otherwise specifically provided by the Florida Rules of Civil Procedure or an applicable statute, every pleading or other document of a party represented by an attorney need not be verified or accompanied by an affidavit. FL ST RCP Rule 1.030; FL ST J ADMIN Rule 2.515(a).

6. *Attorney signature*

a. *Attorney signature.* Every pleading and other document of a party represented by an attorney shall be signed by at least one (1) attorney of record in that attorney's individual name whose current record Florida Bar address, telephone number, including area code, primary e-mail address and secondary e-mail addresses, if any, and Florida Bar number shall be stated, and who shall be duly licensed to practice law in Florida or who shall have received permission to appear in the particular case as provided in FL ST J ADMIN Rule 2.510. FL ST J ADMIN Rule 2.515(a).

i. The attorney may be required by the court to give the address of, and to vouch for the attorney's authority to represent, the party. FL ST J ADMIN Rule 2.515(a).

ii. The signature of an attorney shall constitute a certificate by the attorney that the attorney has read the pleading or other document; that to the best of the attorney's knowledge, information, and belief there is good ground to support it; and that it is not interposed for delay. FL ST J ADMIN Rule 2.515(a).

iii. If a pleading is not signed or is signed with intent to defeat the purpose of FL ST J ADMIN Rule 2.515, it may be stricken and the action may proceed as though the pleading or other document had not been served. FL ST J ADMIN Rule 2.515(a).

b. *Pro se litigant signature.* A party who is not represented by an attorney shall sign any pleading or other paper and state the party's address and telephone number, including area code. FL ST J ADMIN Rule 2.515(b).

c. *Form of signature*

i. The signatures required on pleadings and documents by FL ST J ADMIN Rule 2.515(a) and FL ST J ADMIN Rule 2.515(b) may be:

- Original signatures;

- Original signatures that have been reproduced by electronic means, such as on electronically transmitted documents or photocopied documents;
- Electronic signatures using the "/s/," "s/," or "/s" formats by or at the direction of the person signing; or
- Any other signature format authorized by general law, so long as the clerk where the proceeding is pending has the capability of receiving and has obtained approval from the Supreme Court of Florida to accept pleadings and documents with that signature format. FL ST J ADMIN Rule 2.515(c)(1).

ii. An attorney, party, or other person who files a pleading or paper by electronic transmission that does not contain the original signature of that attorney, party, or other person shall file that identical pleading or paper in paper form containing an original signature of that attorney, party, or other person (hereinafter called the follow-up filing) immediately thereafter. The follow-up filing is not required if the Supreme Court of Florida has entered an order directing the clerk of court to discontinue accepting the follow-up filing. FL ST J ADMIN Rule 2.515(c)(2).

7. *Forms*

a. *Process.* The forms of process, notice of lis pendens, and notice of action provided in the Florida Rules of Civil Procedure are sufficient. Variations from the forms do not void process or notices that are otherwise sufficient. FL ST RCP Rule 1.900(a).

b. *Other forms.* The other forms provided in the Florida Rules of Civil Procedure are sufficient for the matters that are covered by them. So long as the substance is expressed without prolixity, the forms may be varied to meet the facts of a particular case. FL ST RCP Rule 1.900(b).

c. *Formal matters.* Captions, except for the designation of the paper, are omitted from the forms provided in the Florida Rules of Civil Procedure. A general form of caption is the first form provided. Signatures are omitted from pleadings and motions. FL ST RCP Rule 1.900(c).

8. *Notices to persons with disabilities.* All notices of court proceedings to be held in a public facility, and all process compelling appearance at such proceedings, shall include the following statement in bold face, fourteen (14) point Times New Roman or Courier font: "If you are a person with a disability who needs any accommodation in order to participate in this proceeding, you are entitled, at no cost to you, to the provision of certain assistance. Please contact [identify applicable court personnel by name, address, and telephone number] at least seven (7) days before your scheduled court appearance, or immediately upon receiving this notification if the time before the scheduled appearance is less than seven (7) days; if you are hearing or voice impaired, call 711." FL ST J ADMIN Rule 2.540(c)(1).

9. *Minimization of the filing of sensitive information*

a. *Limitations for court filings.* Unless authorized by FL ST J ADMIN Rule 2.425(b), statute, another rule of court, or the court orders otherwise, designated sensitive information filed with the court must be limited to the following format:

i. The initials of a person known to be a minor;

ii. The year of birth of a person's birth date;

iii. No portion of any: Social security number, Bank account number, Credit card account number, Charge account number, or Debit account number;

iv. The last four digits of any: Taxpayer identification number (TIN), Employee identification number, Driver's license number, Passport number, Telephone number, Financial account number, except as set forth in FL ST J ADMIN Rule 2.425(a)(3), Brokerage account number, Insurance policy account number, Loan account number, Customer account number, or Patient or health care number;

v. A truncated version of any: Email address, Computer user name, Password, or Personal identification number (PIN); and

vi. A truncated version of any other sensitive information as provided by court order. FL ST J ADMIN Rule 2.425(a).

b. *Exceptions.* FL ST J ADMIN Rule 2.425(a) does not apply to the following:
   i. An account number which identifies the property alleged to be the subject of a proceeding;
   ii. The record of an administrative or agency proceeding;
   iii. The record in appellate or review proceedings;
   iv. The birth date of a minor whenever the birth date is necessary for the court to establish or maintain subject matter jurisdiction;
   v. The name of a minor in any order relating to parental responsibility, time-sharing, or child support;
   vi. The name of a minor in any document or order affecting the minor's ownership of real property;
   vii. The birth date of a party in a writ of attachment or notice to payor;
   viii. In traffic and criminal proceedings: a pro se filing; a court filing that is related to a criminal matter or investigation and that is prepared before the filing of a criminal charge or is not filed as part of any docketed criminal case; an arrest or search warrant or any information in support thereof; a charging document and an affidavit or other documents filed in support of any charging document, including any driving records; a statement of particulars; discovery material introduced into evidence or otherwise filed with the court; and all information necessary for the proper issuance and execution of a subpoena duces tecum;
   ix. Information used by the clerk for case maintenance purposes or the courts for case management purposes; and
   x. Information which is relevant and material to an issue before the court. FL ST J ADMIN Rule 2.425(b).

c. *Remedies.* Upon motion by a party or interested person or sua sponte by the court, the court may order remedies, sanctions or both for a violation of FL ST J ADMIN Rule 2.425(a). Following notice and an opportunity to respond, the court may impose sanctions if such filing was not made in good faith. FL ST J ADMIN Rule 2.425(c).

d. *Motions not restricted.* FL ST J ADMIN Rule 2.425 does not restrict a party's right to move for protective order, to move to file documents under seal, or to request a determination of the confidentiality of records. FL ST J ADMIN Rule 2.425(d).

e. *Application.* FL ST J ADMIN Rule 2.425 does not affect the application of constitutional provisions, statutes, or rules of court regarding confidential information or access to public information. FL ST J ADMIN Rule 2.425(e).

F. Filing and Service Requirements

1. *Court filing of documents and discovery.* Information obtained during discovery shall not be filed with the court until such time as it is filed for good cause. The requirement of good cause is satisfied only where the filing of the information is allowed or required by another applicable rule of procedure or by court order. All filings of discovery documents shall comply with FL ST J ADMIN Rule 2.425. The court shall have the authority to impose sanctions for violation of FL ST RCP Rule 1.280. FL ST RCP Rule 1.280(g).
   a. Unless required by the court, a party shall not file any of the documents or things produced with the response. Documents or things may be filed in compliance with FL ST J ADMIN Rule 2.425 and FL ST RCP Rule 1.280(g) when they should be considered by the court in determining a matter pending before the court. FL ST RCP Rule 1.350(d).

2. *Filing requirements.* All original documents must be filed with the court either before service or immediately thereafter, unless otherwise provided for by general law or other rules. If the original of any bond or other document is not placed in the court file, a certified copy must be so placed by the clerk. FL ST J ADMIN Rule 2.516(d). All documents shall be filed in conformity with the requirements of FL ST J ADMIN Rule 2.525. FL ST RCP Rule 1.080(b). All documents filed in any court shall be filed by electronic transmission in accordance with FL ST J ADMIN Rule 2.525. "Documents" means pleadings, motions, petitions, memoranda, briefs, notices, exhibits, declarations, affidavits, orders, judgments, decrees, writs, opinions, and any other paper or writing submitted to a court. FL ST J ADMIN Rule

2.520(a). All documents that are court records, as defined in FL ST J ADMIN Rule 2.430(a)(1), must be filed by electronic transmission, provided that: (1) the clerk has the ability to accept and retain such documents; (2) the clerk or the chief judge of the circuit has requested permission to accept documents filed by electronic transmission; and (3) the supreme court has entered an order granting permission to the clerk to accept documents filed by electronic transmission. FL ST J ADMIN Rule 2.525(c)(1).

a. *Definition.* "Electronic transmission of documents" means the sending of information by electronic signals to, by or from a court or clerk, which when received can be transformed and stored or transmitted on paper, microfilm, magnetic storage device, optical imaging system, CD-ROM, flash drive, other electronic data storage system, server, case maintenance system ("CM"), electronic court filing ("ECF") system, statewide or local electronic portal ("e-portal"), or other electronic record keeping system authorized by the supreme court in a format sufficient to communicate the information on the original document in a readable format. Electronic transmission of documents includes electronic mail ("e-mail") and any internet-based transmission procedure, and may include procedures allowing for documents to be signed or verified by electronic means. FL ST J ADMIN Rule 2.525(a).

   i. The filing of documents with the court as required by the Florida Rules of Judicial Administration must be made by filing them with the clerk in accordance with FL ST J ADMIN Rule 2.525, except that the judge may permit documents to be filed with the judge, in which event the judge must note the filing date before him or her on the documents and transmit them to the clerk. The date of filing is that shown on the face of the document by the judge's notation or the clerk's time stamp, whichever is earlier. FL ST J ADMIN Rule 2.516(e).

b. *Application.* Any court or clerk of the court may accept the electronic transmission of documents for filing after the clerk, together with input from the chief judge of the circuit, has obtained approval of the procedures and program for doing so from the Supreme Court of Florida. FL ST J ADMIN Rule 2.525(b).

c. *Exceptions*

   i. Paper documents and other submissions may be manually submitted to the clerk or court:

      - When the clerk does not have the ability to accept and retain documents by electronic filing or has not had ECF Procedures approved by the supreme court;
      - For filing by any self-represented party or any self-represented nonparty unless specific ECF Procedures provide a means to file documents electronically. However, any self-represented nonparty that is a governmental or public agency and any other agency, partnership, corporation, or business entity acting on behalf of any governmental or public agency may file documents by electronic transmission if such entity has the capability of filing documents electronically;
      - For filing by attorneys excused from e-mail service in accordance with FL ST J ADMIN Rule 2.516(b);
      - When submitting evidentiary exhibits or filing non-documentary materials;
      - When the filing involves documents in excess of twenty-five (25) megabytes (25MB) in size. For such filings, documents may be transmitted using an electronic storage medium that the clerk has the ability to accept, which may include a CD-ROM, flash drive, or similar storage medium;
      - When filed in open court, as permitted by the court;
      - When paper filing is permitted by any approved statewide or local ECF procedures; and
      - If any court determines that justice so requires. FL ST J ADMIN Rule 2.525(d).

   ii. Any document in paper form submitted under FL ST J ADMIN Rule 2.525(d) is filed when it is received by the clerk or court and the clerk shall immediately thereafter convert any filed paper document to an electronic document. "Convert to an electronic document" means optically capturing an image of a paper document and using character recognition software to recover as much of the document's text as practicable and then indexing and storing the document in the official court file. FL ST J ADMIN Rule 2.525(c)(4).

iii. Any storage medium submitted under FL ST J ADMIN Rule 2.525(d)(5) is filed when received by the clerk or court and the clerk shall immediately thereafter transfer the electronic documents from the storage device to the official court file. FL ST J ADMIN Rule 2.525(c)(5).

iv. If the filer of any paper document authorized under FL ST J ADMIN Rule 2.525(d) provides a self-addressed, postage-paid envelope for return of the paper document after it is converted to electronic form by the clerk, the clerk shall place the paper document in the envelope and deposit it in the mail. Except when a paper document is required to be maintained, the clerk may recycle any filed paper document that is not to be returned to the filer. FL ST J ADMIN Rule 2.525(c)(6).

v. The clerk may convert any paper document filed before the effective date of FL ST J ADMIN Rule 2.525 to an electronic document. Unless the clerk is required to maintain the paper document, if the paper document has been converted to an electronic document by the clerk, the paper document is no longer part of the official court file and may be removed and recycled. FL ST J ADMIN Rule 2.525(c)(7).

d. *Official court file.* For information on what constitutes the official court file, please see FL ST J ADMIN Rule 2.525(c)(2), FL ST J ADMIN Rule 2.525(c)(3).

e. *Administration.* All attorneys, parties, or other persons using this rule to file documents are required to make arrangements with the court or clerk for the payment of any charges authorized by general law or the supreme court before filing any document by electronic transmission. FL ST J ADMIN Rule 2.525(f)(2).

f. *Filing date.* The filing date for an electronically transmitted document is the date and time that such filing is acknowledged by an electronic stamp or otherwise, pursuant to any procedure set forth in any ECF Procedures approved by the supreme court, or the date the last page of such filing is received by the court or clerk. FL ST J ADMIN Rule 2.525(f)(3).

g. *Accessibility.* All documents transmitted in any electronic form under FL ST J ADMIN Rule 2.525 must comply with the accessibility requirements of FL ST J ADMIN Rule 2.526. FL ST J ADMIN Rule 2.525(g).

3. *Service requirements.* Every pleading subsequent to the initial pleading, all orders, and every other document filed in the action must be served in conformity with the requirements of FL ST J ADMIN Rule 2.516. FL ST RCP Rule 1.080(a).

a. *Service; When required.* Unless the court otherwise orders, or a statute or supreme court administrative order specifies a different means of service, every pleading subsequent to the initial pleading and every other document filed in any court proceeding, except applications for witness subpoenas and documents served by formal notice or required to be served in the manner provided for service of formal notice, must be served in accordance with FL ST J ADMIN Rule 2.516 on each party. No service need be made on parties against whom a default has been entered, except that pleadings asserting new or additional claims against them must be served in the manner provided for service of summons. FL ST J ADMIN Rule 2.516(a).

b. *Service; How made.* When service is required or permitted to be made upon a party represented by an attorney, service must be made upon the attorney unless service upon the party is ordered by the court. FL ST J ADMIN Rule 2.516(b).

i. *Service by electronic mail ("e-mail").* All documents required or permitted to be served on another party must be served by e-mail, unless FL ST J ADMIN Rule 2.516 otherwise provides. When, in addition to service by e-mail, the sender also utilizes another means of service provided for in FL ST J ADMIN Rule 2.516(b)(2), any differing time limits and other provisions applicable to that other means of service control. FL ST J ADMIN Rule 2.516(b)(1). Any document electronically transmitted to a court or clerk must also be served on all parties and interested persons in accordance with the applicable rules of court. FL ST J ADMIN Rule 2.525(e)(2).

- *Service on attorneys.* Upon appearing in a proceeding, an attorney must serve a designation of a primary e-mail address and may designate no more than two (2) secondary e-mail

addresses. Thereafter, service must be directed to all designated e-mail addresses in that proceeding. Every document filed by an attorney thereafter must include the primary e-mail address of that attorney and any secondary e-mail addresses. If an attorney does not designate any e-mail address for service, documents may be served on that attorney at the e-mail address on record with The Florida Bar. FL ST J ADMIN Rule 2.516(b)(1)(A).

- *Exception to e-mail service on attorneys.* Service by an attorney on another attorney must be made by e-mail unless excused by the court. Upon motion by an attorney demonstrating that the attorney has no e-mail account and lacks access to the Internet at the attorney's office, the court may excuse the attorney from the requirements of e-mail service. Service on and by an attorney excused by the court from e-mail service must be by the means provided in FL ST J ADMIN Rule 2.516(b)(2). FL ST J ADMIN Rule 2.516(b)(1)(B).
- *Service on and by parties not represented by an attorney.* Any party not represented by an attorney may serve a designation of a primary e-mail address and also may designate no more than two (2) secondary e-mail addresses to which service must be directed in that proceeding by the means provided in FL ST J ADMIN Rule 2.516(b)(1). If a party not represented by an attorney does not designate an e-mail address for service in a proceeding, service on and by that party must be by the means provided in FL ST J ADMIN Rule 2.516(b)(2). FL ST J ADMIN Rule 2.516(b)(1)(C).
- *Time of service.* Service by e-mail is complete when it is sent. FL ST J ADMIN Rule 2.516(b)(1)(D). An e-mail is deemed served on the date it is sent. FL ST J ADMIN Rule 2.516(b)(1)(D)(i). If the sender learns that the e-mail did not reach the address of the person to be served, the sender must immediately send another copy by e-mail, or by a means authorized by FL ST J ADMIN Rule 2.516(b)(2). FL ST J ADMIN Rule 2.516(b)(1)(D)(ii). E-mail service is treated as service by mail for the computation of time. FL ST J ADMIN Rule 2.516(b)(1)(D)(iii).

ii. *Format of e-mail for service.* Service of a document by e-mail is made by attaching a copy of the document in PDF format to an e-mail sent to all addresses designated by the attorney or party. FL ST J ADMIN Rule 2.516(b)(1)(E).

- All documents served by e-mail must be attached to an e-mail message containing a subject line beginning with the words "SERVICE OF COURT DOCUMENT" in all capital letters, followed by the case number of the proceeding in which the documents are being served. FL ST J ADMIN Rule 2.516(b)(1)(E)(i).
- The body of the e-mail must identify the court in which the proceeding is pending, the case number, the name of the initial party on each side, the title of each document served with that e-mail, and the sender's name and telephone number. FL ST J ADMIN Rule 2.516(b)(1)(E)(ii).
- Any document served by e-mail may be signed by the "/s/" format, as long as the filed original is signed in accordance with the applicable rule of procedure. FL ST J ADMIN Rule 2.516(b)(1)(E)(iii).
- Any e-mail which, together with its attached documents, exceeds five megabytes (5MB) in size, must be divided and sent as separate e-mails, no one of which may exceed five megabytes (5MB) in size and each of which must be sequentially numbered in the subject line. FL ST J ADMIN Rule 2.516(b)(1)(E)(iv).

iii. *Service by other means.* In addition to, and not in lieu of, service by e-mail, service may also be made upon attorneys by any of the means specified in FL ST J ADMIN Rule 2.516(b)(2). Service on and by all parties who are not represented by an attorney and who do not designate an e-mail address, and on and by all attorneys excused from e-mail service, must be made by delivering a copy of the document or by mailing it to the party or attorney at their last known address or, if no address is known, by leaving it with the clerk of the court. Service by mail is complete upon mailing. Delivery of a copy within FL ST J ADMIN Rule 2.516 is complete upon:

- Handing it to the attorney or to the party,

- Leaving it at the attorney's or party's office with a clerk or other person in charge thereof,
- If there is no one in charge, leaving it in a conspicuous place therein,
- If the office is closed or the person to be served has no office, leaving it at the person's usual place of abode with some person of his or her family above fifteen (15) years of age and informing such person of the contents, or
- Transmitting it by facsimile to the attorney's or party's office with a cover sheet containing the sender's name, firm, address, telephone number, and facsimile number, and the number of pages transmitted. When service is made by facsimile, a copy must also be served by any other method permitted by FL ST J ADMIN Rule 2.516. Facsimile service occurs when transmission is complete. FL ST J ADMIN Rule 2.516(b)(2)(A) through FL ST J ADMIN Rule 2.516(b)(2)(E).
- Service by delivery after 5:00 p.m. must be deemed to have been made by mailing on the date of delivery. FL ST J ADMIN Rule 2.516(b)(2)(F).

c. *Service; Numerous defendants.* In actions when the parties are unusually numerous, the court may regulate the service contemplated by the Florida Rules of Judicial Administration on motion or on its own initiative in such manner as may be found to be just and reasonable. FL ST J ADMIN Rule 2.516(c).

d. *Service by clerk.* Service of notices and other documents required to be made by the clerk must also be done as provided in FL ST J ADMIN Rule 2.516(b). FL ST J ADMIN Rule 2.516(g).

e. *Standards of professional courtesy; Service*

i. The timing and manner of service should not be used to the disadvantage of the party receiving the papers. This includes the use of facsimile transmissions and any additional expedited means of communication approved by the court. FL ST 6 J CIR 2009-066 PA/PI-CIR(C)(1).

ii. Attorneys will not serve papers to take advantage of opposing counsel's known absence from the office or at a time or in a manner designed to inconvenience an opponent, such as late on Friday afternoon or the day preceding a secular or religious holiday. FL ST 6 J CIR 2009-066 PA/PI-CIR(C)(2).

iii. Attorneys will not serve papers, including briefs and memoranda, so close to a court appearance that the ability of opposing counsel to prepare for that appearance or, where permitted, to respond, is inhibited. FL ST 6 J CIR 2009-066 PA/PI-CIR(C)(3).

iv. Service should be made personally or by facsimile transmission when it is likely that service by mail, even when allowed, will prejudice the opposing party. FL ST 6 J CIR 2009-066 PA/PI-CIR(C)(4).

G. Hearings

1. There is no hearing required or contemplated with regard to requests for production of documents in the Florida Rules of Civil Procedure.

H. Forms

1. Official Request for Production of Documents Forms for Florida

a. Caption. FL ST RCP Form 1.901.

b. Subpoena duces tecum for trial. FL ST RCP Form 1.911.

c. Notice of production from nonparty. FL ST RCP Form 1.921.

d. Subpoena duces tecum without deposition. FL ST RCP Form 1.922.

2. Florida Request for Production of Documents Forms

a. Request for production; Documents. FL-PRACFORM § 8:29.

b. Request for inspection; Documents, deposition. FL-PRACFORM § 8:30.

c. Request for inspection; Tangible things. FL-PRACFORM § 8:31.

d. Request for entry; Real property. FL-PRACFORM § 8:32.

e. Request for production; Documents, response. FL-PRACFORM § 8:33.

f. Request for inspection; Response, tangible things. FL-PRACFORM § 8:34.

g. Request for entry; Response, land and buildings. FL-PRACFORM § 8:35.

h. Production of documents; Nonparty, notice. FL-PRACFORM § 8:36.

i. Production of documents; Nonparty, objection. FL-PRACFORM § 8:37.

j. Request; Production of documents for inspection and copying. FL-PP § 3:115.

k. Notice of request for production from nonparty. FL-PP § 3:116.

l. Request; For permission to enter on land; To inspect and photograph. FL-PP § 3:127.

I. Checklist

(I) ❑ Matters to be considered by requesting party

(a) ❑ Required documents

(1) ❑ Request

(2) ❑ Certificate of service

(b) ❑ Supplemental documents

(1) ❑ Notice of intent to serve subpoena/Subpoena

(c) ❑ Time for request

(1) ❑ Without leave of court the request may be served on the plaintiff after commencement of the action and on any other party with or after service of the process and initial pleading on that party

(2) ❑ A party desiring production under FL ST RCP Rule 1.351 shall serve notice as provided in FL ST RCP Rule 1.080 on every other party of the intent to serve a subpoena under FL ST RCP Rule 1.351 at least ten (10) days before the subpoena is issued if service is by delivery and fifteen (15) days before the subpoena is issued if the service is by mail or e-mail

(II) ❑ Matters to be considered by responding party

(a) ❑ Required documents

(1) ❑ Response to request

(2) ❑ Certificate of service

(b) ❑ Supplemental documents

(1) ❑ Objections

(c) ❑ Time for response

(1) ❑ The party to whom the request is directed shall serve a written response within thirty (30) days after service of the request, except that a defendant may serve a response within forty-five (45) days after service of the process and initial pleading on that defendant; the court may allow a shorter or longer time

Requests, Notices and Applications
Request for Admissions

Document Last Updated January 2013

A. Applicable Rules

1. *State rules*

a. Nonverification of pleadings. FL ST RCP Rule 1.030.

b. Service and filing of pleadings, orders, and documents. FL ST RCP Rule 1.080.

c. Time. FL ST RCP Rule 1.090.
d. Pleadings and motions. FL ST RCP Rule 1.100.
e. Pretrial procedure. FL ST RCP Rule 1.200.
f. General provisions governing discovery. FL ST RCP Rule 1.280.
g. Interrogatories to parties. FL ST RCP Rule 1.340.
h. Examination of persons. FL ST RCP Rule 1.360.
i. Requests for admission. FL ST RCP Rule 1.370.
j. Failure to make discovery; Sanctions. FL ST RCP Rule 1.380.
k. Depositions of expert witnesses. FL ST RCP Rule 1.390.
l. Relief from judgment, decrees, or orders. FL ST RCP Rule 1.540.
m. Forms. FL ST RCP Rule 1.900.
n. Minimization of the filing of sensitive information. FL ST J ADMIN Rule 2.425.
o. Retention of court records. FL ST J ADMIN Rule 2.430.
p. Foreign attorneys. FL ST J ADMIN Rule 2.510.
q. Signature of attorneys and parties. FL ST J ADMIN Rule 2.515.
r. Paper. FL ST J ADMIN Rule 2.520.
s. Electronic filing. FL ST J ADMIN Rule 2.525.
t. Accessibility of information and technology. FL ST J ADMIN Rule 2.526.
u. Requests for accommodations by persons with disabilities. FL ST J ADMIN Rule 2.540.

2. *Local rules*
a. General motion rule. FL ST 6 J CIR LOCAL Rule 5.
b. Standards of professional courtesy. FL ST 6 J CIR 2009-066 PA/PI-CIR.
c. Arbitration and mediation program circuit civil and family cases. FL ST 6 J CIR PA/PI-CIR-96-63; FL ST 6 J CIR 2011-006 PA/PI-CIR.

B. Timing

1. *Request for admission.* Without leave of court the request may be served upon the plaintiff after commencement of the action and upon any other party with or after service of the process and initial pleading upon that party. FL ST RCP Rule 1.370(a).
2. *Sequence and timing of discovery.* Except as provided in FL ST RCP Rule 1.280(b)(5) or unless the court upon motion for the convenience of parties and witnesses and in the interest of justice orders otherwise, methods of discovery may be used in any sequence, and the fact that a party is conducting discovery, whether by deposition or otherwise, shall not delay any other party's discovery. FL ST RCP Rule 1.280(e).
3. *Computation of time*
a. *Generally.* Computation of time shall be governed by FL ST J ADMIN Rule 2.514. FL ST RCP Rule 1.090(a). The following rules apply in computing time periods specified in any rule of procedure, local rule, court order, or statute that does not specify a method of computing time. FL ST J ADMIN Rule 2.514(a).
i. *Period stated in days or a longer unit.* When the period is stated in days or a longer unit of time (A) exclude the day of the event that triggers the period; (B) count every day, including intermediate Saturdays, Sundays, and legal holidays; and (C) include the last day of the period, but if the last day is a Saturday, Sunday, or legal holiday, or falls within any period of time extended through an order of the chief justice under FL ST J ADMIN Rule 2.205(a)(2)(B)(iv), the period continues to run until the end of the next day that is not a Saturday, Sunday, or legal holiday and does not fall within any period of time extended through an order of the chief justice. FL ST J ADMIN Rule 2.514(a)(1).

ii. *Period stated in hours.* When the period is stated in hours (A) begin counting immediately on the occurrence of the event that triggers the period; (B) count every hour, including hours during intermediate Saturdays, Sundays, and legal holidays; and (C) if the period would end on a Saturday, Sunday, or legal holiday, or during any period of time extended through an order of the chief justice under FL ST J ADMIN Rule 2.205(a)(2)(B)(iv), the period continues to run until the same time on the next day that is not a Saturday, Sunday, or legal holiday and does not fall within any period of time extended through an order of the chief justice. FL ST J ADMIN Rule 2.514(a)(2).

iii. *Period stated in days less than seven (7) days.* When the period stated in days is less than seven (7) days, intermediate Saturdays, Sundays, and legal holidays shall be excluded in the computation. FL ST J ADMIN Rule 2.514(a)(3).

iv. *"Last day" defined.* Unless a different time is set by a statute, local rule, or court order, the last day ends (A) for electronic filing or for service by any means, at midnight; and (B) for filing by other means, when the clerk's office is scheduled to close. FL ST J ADMIN Rule 2.514(a)(4).

v. *"Next day" defined.* The "next day" is determined by continuing to count forward when the period is measured after an event and backward when measured before an event. FL ST J ADMIN Rule 2.514(a)(5).

vi. *"Legal holiday" defined.* "Legal holiday" means (A) the day set aside by FL ST § 110.117, for observing New Year's Day, Martin Luther King, Jr.'s Birthday, Memorial Day, Independence Day, Labor Day, Veterans' Day, Thanksgiving Day, the Friday after Thanksgiving Day, or Christmas Day, and (B) any day observed as a holiday by the clerk's office or as designated by the chief judge. FL ST J ADMIN Rule 2.514(a)(6).

b. *Additional time after service by mail or e-mail.* When a party may or must act within a specified time after service and service is made by mail or e-mail, five (5) days are added after the period that would otherwise expire under FL ST J ADMIN Rule 2.514(a). FL ST J ADMIN Rule 2.514(b).

c. *Enlargement.* When an act is required or allowed to be done at or within a specified time by order of court, by the Florida Rules of Civil Procedure, or by notice given thereunder, for cause shown the court at any time in its discretion (1) with or without notice, may order the period enlarged if request therefor is made before the expiration of the period originally prescribed or as extended by a previous order, or (2) upon motion made and notice after the expiration of the specified period, may permit the act to be done when failure to act was the result of excusable neglect, but it may not extend the time for making a motion for new trial, for rehearing, or to alter or amend a judgment; making a motion for relief from a judgment under FL ST RCP Rule 1.540(b); taking an appeal or filing a petition for certiorari; or making a motion for a directed verdict. FL ST RCP Rule 1.090(b).

d. *Unaffected by expiration of term.* The period of time provided for the doing of any act or the taking of any proceeding shall not be affected or limited by the continued existence or expiration of a term of court. The continued existence or expiration of a term of court in no way affects the power of a court to do any act or take any proceeding in any action which is or has been pending before it. FL ST RCP Rule 1.090(c).

C. General Requirements

1. *General provisions governing discovery*

a. *Discovery methods.* Parties may obtain discovery by one or more of the following methods: depositions upon oral examination or written questions; written interrogatories; production of documents or things or permission to enter upon land or other property for inspection and other purposes; physical and mental examinations; and requests for admission. Unless the court orders otherwise and under FL ST RCP Rule 1.280(c), the frequency of use of these methods is not limited, except as provided in FL ST RCP Rule 1.200, FL ST RCP Rule 1.340, and FL ST RCP Rule 1.370. FL ST RCP Rule 1.280(a).

b. *Scope of discovery.* Unless otherwise limited by order of the court in accordance with the Florida Rules of Civil Procedure, the scope of discovery is as follows:

i. *In general.* Parties may obtain discovery regarding any matter, not privileged, that is relevant to the subject matter of the pending action, whether it relates to the claim or defense of the party seeking discovery or the claim or defense of any other party, including the existence, description, nature, custody, condition, and location of any books, documents, or other tangible things and the identity and location of persons having knowledge of any discoverable matter. It is not ground for objection that the information sought will be inadmissible at the trial if the information sought appears reasonably calculated to lead to the discovery of admissible evidence. FL ST RCP Rule 1.280(b)(1).

ii. *Indemnity agreements.* A party may obtain discovery of the existence and contents of any agreement under which any person may be liable to satisfy part or all of a judgment that may be entered in the action or to indemnify or to reimburse a party for payments made to satisfy the judgment. Information concerning the agreement is not admissible in evidence at trial by reason of disclosure. FL ST RCP Rule 1.280(b)(2).

iii. *Electronically stored information.* A party may obtain discovery of electronically stored information in accordance with the Florida Rules of Civil Procedure. FL ST RCP Rule 1.280(b)(3).

iv. *Trial preparation; Materials.* Subject to the provisions of FL ST RCP Rule 1.280(b)(5), a party may obtain discovery of documents and tangible things otherwise discoverable under FL ST RCP Rule 1.280(b)(1) and prepared in anticipation of litigation or for trial by or for another party or by or for that party's representative, including that party's attorney, consultant, surety, indemnitor, insurer, or agent, only upon a showing that the party seeking discovery has need of the materials in the preparation of the case and is unable without undue hardship to obtain the substantial equivalent of the materials by other means. FL ST RCP Rule 1.280(b)(4).

- In ordering discovery of the materials when the required showing has been made, the court shall protect against disclosure of the mental impressions, conclusions, opinions, or legal theories of an attorney or other representative of a party concerning the litigation. FL ST RCP Rule 1.280(b)(4).
- Without the required showing a party may obtain a copy of a statement concerning the action or its subject matter previously made by that party. FL ST RCP Rule 1.280(b)(4).
- Upon request without the required showing a person not a party may obtain a copy of a statement concerning the action or its subject matter previously made by that person. If the request is refused, the person may move for an order to obtain a copy. The provisions of FL ST RCP Rule 1.380(a)(5) apply to the award of expenses incurred as a result of making the motion. FL ST RCP Rule 1.280(b)(4).
- For purposes of FL ST RCP Rule 1.280(b)(4), a statement previously made is a written statement signed or otherwise adopted or approved by the person making it, or a stenographic, mechanical, electrical, or other recording or transcription of it that is a substantially verbatim recital of an oral statement by the person making it and contemporaneously recorded. FL ST RCP Rule 1.280(b)(4).

v. *Trial preparation; Experts.* Discovery of facts known and opinions held by experts, otherwise discoverable under the provisions of FL ST RCP Rule 1.280(b)(1) and acquired or developed in anticipation of litigation or for trial, may be obtained only as follows:

- By interrogatories a party may require any other party to identify each person whom the other party expects to call as an expert witness at trial and to state the subject matter on which the expert is expected to testify, and to state the substance of the facts and opinions to which the expert is expected to testify and a summary of the grounds for each opinion. FL ST RCP Rule 1.280(b)(5)(A)(i).
- Any person disclosed by interrogatories or otherwise as a person expected to be called as an expert witness at trial may be deposed in accordance with FL ST RCP Rule 1.390 without motion or order of court. FL ST RCP Rule 1.280(b)(5)(A)(ii).
- A party may obtain the following discovery regarding any person disclosed by interrogatories or otherwise as a person expected to be called as an expert witness at trial: The scope

of employment in the pending case and the compensation for such service, FL ST RCP Rule 1.280(b)(5)(A)(iii)(1); The expert's general litigation experience, including the percentage of work performed for plaintiffs and defendants, FL ST RCP Rule 1.280(b)(5)(A)(iii)(2); The identity of other cases, within a reasonable time period, in which the expert has testified by deposition or at trial, FL ST RCP Rule 1.280(b)(5)(A)(iii)(3); An approximation of the portion of the expert's involvement as an expert witness, which may be based on the number of hours, percentage of hours, or percentage of earned income derived from serving as an expert witness; however, the expert shall not be required to disclose his or her earnings as an expert witness or income derived from other services. FL ST RCP Rule 1.280(b)(5)(A)(iii)(4).

- An expert may be required to produce financial and business records only under the most unusual or compelling circumstances and may not be compelled to compile or produce nonexistent documents. Upon motion, the court may order further discovery by other means, subject to such restrictions as to scope and other provisions pursuant to FL ST RCP Rule 1.280(b)(5)(C) concerning fees and expenses as the court may deem appropriate. FL ST RCP Rule 1.280(b)(5).
- A party may discover facts known or opinions held by an expert who has been retained or specially employed by another party in anticipation of litigation or preparation for trial and who is not expected to be called as a witness at trial, only as provided in FL ST RCP Rule 1.360(b) or upon a showing of exceptional circumstances under which it is impracticable for the party seeking discovery to obtain facts or opinions on the same subject by other means. FL ST RCP Rule 1.280(b)(5)(B).
- Unless manifest injustice would result, the court shall require that the party seeking discovery pay the expert a reasonable fee for time spent in responding to discovery under FL ST RCP Rule 1.280(b)(5)(A) and FL ST RCP Rule 1.280(b)(5)(B); and concerning discovery from an expert obtained under FL ST RCP Rule 1.280(b)(5)(A) the court may require, and concerning discovery obtained under FL ST RCP Rule 1.280(b)(5)(B) shall require, the party seeking discovery to pay the other party a fair part of the fees and expenses reasonably incurred by the latter party in obtaining facts and opinions from the expert. FL ST RCP Rule 1.280(b)(5)(C).
- As used in the Florida Rules of Civil Procedure an expert shall be an expert witness as defined in FL ST RCP Rule 1.390(a). FL ST RCP Rule 1.280(b)(5)(D).

vi. *Claims to privilege or protection.* When a party withholds information otherwise discoverable under the Florida Rules of Civil Procedure by claiming that it is privileged or subject to protection as trial preparation material, the party shall make the claim expressly and shall describe the nature of the documents, communications, or things not produced or disclosed in a manner that, without revealing information itself privileged or protected, will enable other parties to assess the applicability of the privilege or protection. FL ST RCP Rule 1.280(b)(6).

c. *Limitations on discovery of electronically stored information*

i. A person may object to discovery of electronically stored information from sources that the person identifies as not reasonably accessible because of burden or cost. On motion to compel discovery or for a protective order, the person from whom discovery is sought must show that the information sought or the format requested is not reasonably accessible because of undue burden or cost. If that showing is made, the court may nonetheless order the discovery from such sources or in such formats if the requesting party shows good cause. The court may specify conditions of the discovery, including ordering that some or all of the expenses incurred by the person from whom discovery is sought be paid by the party seeking the discovery. FL ST RCP Rule 1.280(d)(1).

ii. In determining any motion involving discovery of electronically stored information, the court must limit the frequency or extent of discovery otherwise allowed by the Florida Rules of Civil Procedure if it determines that (i) the discovery sought is unreasonably cumulative or duplicative, or can be obtained from another source or in another manner that is more convenient, less burdensome, or less expensive; or (ii) the burden or expense of the discovery outweighs its likely benefit, considering the needs of the case, the amount in controversy, the parties' resources, the importance of the issues at stake in the action, and the importance of the discovery in resolving the issues. FL ST RCP Rule 1.280(d)(2).

d. For information on inadvertent disclosure of privileged materials, see FL ST RCP Rule 1.285.

e. *Standards of professional courtesy; Discovery*

   i. Attorneys will use discovery only when necessary to ascertain information, to perpetuate testimony, or to obtain documents or things necessary for the prosecution or defense of an action. Attorneys will never use discovery as a means of harassment or to impose an inordinate burden or expense. FL ST 6 J CIR 2009-066 PA/PI-CIR(F)(1).

   ii. Attorneys will file motions for protective orders as soon as possible and notice them for hearing as soon as practicable. Absent an agreement or court order a deposition may not be properly canceled due to a pending motion. FL ST 6 J CIR 2009-066 PA/PI-CIR(F)(2).

   iii. Prior to filing a motion to compel or for protective order, attorneys will confer with opposing counsel in a good faith effort to resolve the issues raised. Attorneys will file with the motion a statement certifying that attorneys have complied and been unable to resolve the dispute. FL ST 6 J CIR 2009-066 PA/PI-CIR(F)(3).

   iv. Motions to compel shall quote in full each interrogatory, question on deposition, request for admission or request for production to which the motion is addressed and the objection and grounds stated by opposing counsel. FL ST 6 J CIR 2009-066 PA/PI-CIR(F)(4).

2. *Requests for admission.* It is an advantage to use requests for admission. The biggest advantage is that if an adversary denies a request for an admission and the denied matter is later proven to be true, the adversary may have to pay the costs of proving the genuineness of the document or the truth of the matter requested to be admitted. FL-PP § 3:143.

   a. *Scope.* A party may serve upon any other party a written request for the admission of the truth of any matters within the scope of FL ST RCP Rule 1.280(b) set forth in the request that relate to statements or opinions of fact or of the application of law to fact, including the genuineness of any documents described in the request. FL ST RCP Rule 1.370(a).

   b. *Copies of documents.* Copies of documents shall be served with the request unless they have been or are otherwise furnished or made available for inspection and copying. FL ST RCP Rule 1.370(a).

   c. *Number of requests.* The request for admission shall not exceed thirty (30) requests, including all subparts, unless the court permits a larger number on motion and notice and for good cause, or the parties propounding and responding to the requests stipulate to a larger number. Each matter of which an admission is requested shall be separately set forth. FL ST RCP Rule 1.370(a).

   d. *Sufficiency of responses.* The party who has requested the admissions may move to determine the sufficiency of the answers or objections. Unless the court determines that an objection is justified, it shall order that an answer be served. If the court determines that an answer does not comply with the requirements of this rule, it may order either that the matter is admitted or that an amended answer be served. Instead of these orders the court may determine that final disposition of the request be made at a pretrial conference or at a designated time before trial. The provisions of FL ST RCP Rule 1.380(a)(4) apply to the award of expenses incurred in relation to the motion. FL ST RCP Rule 1.370(a).

   e. *Effect of admission.* Any matter admitted under FL ST RCP Rule 1.370 is conclusively established unless the court on motion permits withdrawal or amendment of the admission. Subject to FL ST RCP Rule 1.200 governing amendment of a pretrial order, the court may permit withdrawal or amendment when the presentation of the merits of the action will be subserved by it and the party who obtained the admission fails to satisfy the court that withdrawal or amendment will prejudice that party in maintaining an action or defense on the merits. Any admission made by a party under this rule is for the purpose of the pending action only and is not an admission for any other purpose nor may it be used against that party in any other proceeding. FL ST RCP Rule 1.370(b).

   f. *Answer requirements.* The matter is admitted unless the party to whom the request is directed serves upon the party requesting the admission a written answer or objection addressed to the matter within thirty (30) days after service of the request or such shorter or longer time as the court may allow but, unless the court shortens the time, a defendant shall not be required to serve answers or objections before the expiration of forty-five (45) days after service of the process and initial pleading upon the defendant. If objection is made, the reasons shall be stated. The answer shall specifically deny the matter or set forth in detail the reasons why the answering party cannot truthfully admit or deny the matter. A denial shall fairly meet the substance of the requested admission, and when good faith requires that a party qualify an answer or deny only a part of the matter of which an admission is requested, the party shall specify so much of it as is true and qualify or deny the remainder. An answering party may not give lack of information or knowledge as a reason for failure to admit or deny unless that party states that that party has made reasonable inquiry and that the information known or readily obtainable by that party is insufficient to enable that party to admit or deny. A party who considers that a matter of which an admission has been requested presents a genuine issue for trial may not object to the request on that ground alone; the party may deny the matter or set forth reasons why the party cannot admit or deny it, subject to FL ST RCP Rule 1.380(c). FL ST RCP Rule 1.370(a).

3. *Arbitration and mediation*
   a. *Referral to arbitration and mediation.* Except as hereinafter provided or as otherwise prohibited by law, the presiding judge may enter an order referring all or any part of a contested civil matter to mediation or arbitration. The parties to any contested civil matter may file a written stipulation to mediate or arbitrate any issue between them at any time. Such stipulation shall be incorporated into the order of referral. FL ST RCP Rule 1.700(a).
   b. *Arbitration*
      i. *Exclusions.* A civil action shall be ordered to arbitration or arbitration in conjunction with mediation upon stipulation of the parties. A civil action may be ordered to arbitration or arbitration in conjunction with mediation upon motion of any party or by the court, if the judge determines the action to be of such a nature that arbitration could be of benefit to the litigants or the court. FL ST RCP Rule 1.800.
         - Under no circumstances may the following categories of actions be referred to arbitration: (1) bond estreatures; (2) habeas corpus or other extraordinary writs; (3) bond validations; (4) civil or criminal contempt; (5) such other matters as may be specified by order of the chief judge in the circuit. FL ST RCP Rule 1.800.
      ii. For more information regarding arbitration, please see FL ST RCP Rule 1.810; FL ST RCP Rule 1.820; FL ST RCP Rule 1.830.
   c. *Mediation.* For more information regarding mediation, please see FL ST RCP Rule 1.710; FL ST RCP Rule 1.720; FL ST RCP Rule 1.730; and FL ST RCP Rule 1.750.
4. *Rules of court*
   a. *Rules of civil procedure.* The Florida Rules of Civil Procedure apply to all actions of a civil nature and all special statutory proceedings in the circuit courts and county courts except those to which the Florida Probate Rules, the Florida Family Law Rules of Procedure, or the Small Claims Rules apply. FL ST RCP Rule 1.010.
      i. The form, content, procedure, and time for pleading in all special statutory proceedings shall be as prescribed by the statutes governing the proceeding unless the Florida Rules of Civil Procedure specifically provide to the contrary. FL ST RCP Rule 1.010.
      ii. The Florida Rules of Civil Procedure shall be construed to secure the just, speedy, and inexpensive determination of every action. FL ST RCP Rule 1.010.
   b. *Rules of judicial administration.* The Florida Rules of Judicial Administration shall apply to administrative matters in all courts to which the Florida Rules of Judicial Administration are applicable by their terms. The Florida Rules of Judicial Administration shall be construed to secure the speedy and inexpensive determination of every proceeding to which they are applicable. The Florida Rules of Judicial Administration shall supersede all conflicting rules and statutes. FL ST J ADMIN Rule 2.110.

D. Documents

1. *Required documents*

   a. *Request for admission.* Please see the General Requirements section of this document for more information on the contents of the request for admission.

      i. *Notices to persons with disabilities.* See the Format section of this KeyRules document for further information.

   b. *Copies of documents.* Copies of documents shall be served with the request unless they have been or are otherwise furnished or made available for inspection and copying. FL ST RCP Rule 1.370(a).

   c. *Certificate of service.* A certificate of service of the interrogatories shall be filed, giving the date of service and the name of the party to whom they were directed. FL ST RCP Rule 1.340(e). When any attorney certifies in substance: "I certify that a copy hereof has been furnished to (here insert name or names and addresses used for service) by (e-mail) (delivery) (mail) (fax) on .... (date) ....________________ Attorney" the certificate is taken as prima facie proof of such service in compliance with FL ST J ADMIN Rule 2.516. FL ST J ADMIN Rule 2.516(f).

E. Format

1. *Documents; Type and size.* Documents subject to the exceptions set forth in FL ST J ADMIN Rule 2.525(d) shall be filed on recycled paper measuring eight and one half by eleven (8 1/2 by 11) inches. For purposes of FL ST J ADMIN Rule 2.520, paper is recycled if it contains a minimum content of fifty (50) percent waste paper. Xerographic reduction of legal-size (eight and one half by fourteen (8 1/2 by 14) inches) documents to letter size (eight and one half by eleven (8 1/2 by 11) inches) is prohibited. All other documents filed by electronic transmission shall be filed in a format capable of being printed in a format consistent with the provisions of FL ST J ADMIN Rule 2.250. FL ST J ADMIN Rule 2.520(b).

   a. *Exhibits.* Any exhibit or attachment filed with pleadings or papers may be filed in its original size. FL ST J ADMIN Rule 2.520(c).

   b. *Recording space.* On all papers and documents prepared and filed by the court or by any party to a proceeding which are to be recorded in the public records of any county, including but not limited to final money judgments and notices of lis pendens, a three (3) inch by three (3) inch space at the top right-hand corner on the first page and a one (1) inch by three (3) inch space at the top right-hand corner on each subsequent page shall be left blank and reserved for use by the clerk of court. FL ST J ADMIN Rule 2.520(d).

      i. *Exceptions to recording space.* Any papers or documents created by persons or entities over which the filing party has no control, including but not limited to wills, codicils, trusts, or other testamentary documents; documents prepared or executed by any public officer; documents prepared, executed, acknowledged, or proved outside of the State of Florida; or documents created by State or Federal government agencies, may be filed without the space required by FL ST J ADMIN Rule 2.520. FL ST J ADMIN Rule 2.520(e).

   c. *Noncompliance.* No clerk of court is permitted to refuse to file any document or paper because of noncompliance with the Florida Rules of Judicial Administration. However, upon request of the clerk of court, noncomplying documents must be resubmitted in accordance with the formatting rules. FL ST J ADMIN Rule 2.520(f).

2. *Caption.* Every pleading, motion, order, judgment, or other paper shall have a caption containing the name of the court, the file number, and except for in rem proceedings, including forfeiture proceedings, the name of the first party on each side with an appropriate indication of other parties, and a designation identifying the party filing it and its nature or the nature of the order, as the case may be. In any in rem proceeding, every pleading, motion, order, judgment, or other paper shall have a caption containing the name of the court, the file number, the style "In re" (followed by the name or general description of the property), and a designation of the person or entity filing it and its nature or the nature of the order, as the case may be. In an in rem forfeiture proceeding, the style shall be "In re forfeiture of" (followed by the name of the general description of the property). All papers filed in the action shall be styled in such a manner as to indicate clearly the subject matter of the paper and the party requesting or obtaining relief. FL ST RCP Rule 1.100(c)(1).

3. *Writing and written defined.* Writing or written means a document containing information, an application, or a stipulation. FL ST RCP Rule 1.080(c).
4. *Rule abbreviations*
    a. The Florida Rules of Civil Procedure and shall be abbreviated as Fla.R.Civ.P. FL ST RCP Rule 1.010.
    b. The Florida Rules of Judicial Administration shall be abbreviated as Fla. R. Jud. Admin. FL ST J ADMIN Rule 2.110.
5. *Nonverification.* Except when otherwise specifically provided by the Florida Rules of Civil Procedure or an applicable statute, every pleading or other document of a party represented by an attorney need not be verified or accompanied by an affidavit. FL ST RCP Rule 1.030; FL ST J ADMIN Rule 2.515(a).
6. *Attorney signature*
    a. *Attorney signature.* Every pleading and other document of a party represented by an attorney shall be signed by at least one (1) attorney of record in that attorney's individual name whose current record Florida Bar address, telephone number, including area code, primary e-mail address and secondary e-mail addresses, if any, and Florida Bar number shall be stated, and who shall be duly licensed to practice law in Florida or who shall have received permission to appear in the particular case as provided in FL ST J ADMIN Rule 2.510. FL ST J ADMIN Rule 2.515(a).
        i. The attorney may be required by the court to give the address of, and to vouch for the attorney's authority to represent, the party. FL ST J ADMIN Rule 2.515(a).
        ii. The signature of an attorney shall constitute a certificate by the attorney that the attorney has read the pleading or other document; that to the best of the attorney's knowledge, information, and belief there is good ground to support it; and that it is not interposed for delay. FL ST J ADMIN Rule 2.515(a).
        iii. If a pleading is not signed or is signed with intent to defeat the purpose of FL ST J ADMIN Rule 2.515, it may be stricken and the action may proceed as though the pleading or other document had not been served. FL ST J ADMIN Rule 2.515(a).
    b. *Pro se litigant signature.* A party who is not represented by an attorney shall sign any pleading or other paper and state the party's address and telephone number, including area code. FL ST J ADMIN Rule 2.515(b).
    c. *Form of signature*
        i. The signatures required on pleadings and documents by FL ST J ADMIN Rule 2.515(a) and FL ST J ADMIN Rule 2.515(b) may be:
            - Original signatures;
            - Original signatures that have been reproduced by electronic means, such as on electronically transmitted documents or photocopied documents;
            - Electronic signatures using the "/s/," "s/," or "/s" formats by or at the direction of the person signing; or
            - Any other signature format authorized by general law, so long as the clerk where the proceeding is pending has the capability of receiving and has obtained approval from the Supreme Court of Florida to accept pleadings and documents with that signature format. FL ST J ADMIN Rule 2.515(c)(1).
        ii. An attorney, party, or other person who files a pleading or paper by electronic transmission that does not contain the original signature of that attorney, party, or other person shall file that identical pleading or paper in paper form containing an original signature of that attorney, party, or other person (hereinafter called the follow-up filing) immediately thereafter. The follow-up filing is not required if the Supreme Court of Florida has entered an order directing the clerk of court to discontinue accepting the follow-up filing. FL ST J ADMIN Rule 2.515(c)(2).
7. *Forms*
    a. *Process.* The forms of process, notice of lis pendens, and notice of action provided in the Florida

Rules of Civil Procedure are sufficient. Variations from the forms do not void process or notices that are otherwise sufficient. FL ST RCP Rule 1.900(a).

b. *Other forms.* The other forms provided in the Florida Rules of Civil Procedure are sufficient for the matters that are covered by them. So long as the substance is expressed without prolixity, the forms may be varied to meet the facts of a particular case. FL ST RCP Rule 1.900(b).

c. *Formal matters.* Captions, except for the designation of the paper, are omitted from the forms provided in the Florida Rules of Civil Procedure. A general form of caption is the first form provided. Signatures are omitted from pleadings and motions. FL ST RCP Rule 1.900(c).

8. *Notices to persons with disabilities.* All notices of court proceedings to be held in a public facility, and all process compelling appearance at such proceedings, shall include the following statement in bold face, fourteen (14) point Times New Roman or Courier font: "If you are a person with a disability who needs any accommodation in order to participate in this proceeding, you are entitled, at no cost to you, to the provision of certain assistance. Please contact [identify applicable court personnel by name, address, and telephone number] at least seven (7) days before your scheduled court appearance, or immediately upon receiving this notification if the time before the scheduled appearance is less than seven (7) days; if you are hearing or voice impaired, call 711." FL ST J ADMIN Rule 2.540(c)(1).

9. *Minimization of the filing of sensitive information*

a. *Limitations for court filings.* Unless authorized by FL ST J ADMIN Rule 2.425(b), statute, another rule of court, or the court orders otherwise, designated sensitive information filed with the court must be limited to the following format:

i. The initials of a person known to be a minor;

ii. The year of birth of a person's birth date;

iii. No portion of any: Social security number, Bank account number, Credit card account number, Charge account number, or Debit account number;

iv. The last four digits of any: Taxpayer identification number (TIN), Employee identification number, Driver's license number, Passport number, Telephone number, Financial account number, except as set forth in FL ST J ADMIN Rule 2.425(a)(3), Brokerage account number, Insurance policy account number, Loan account number, Customer account number, or Patient or health care number;

v. A truncated version of any: Email address, Computer user name, Password, or Personal identification number (PIN); and

vi. A truncated version of any other sensitive information as provided by court order. FL ST J ADMIN Rule 2.425(a).

b. *Exceptions.* FL ST J ADMIN Rule 2.425(a) does not apply to the following:

i. An account number which identifies the property alleged to be the subject of a proceeding;

ii. The record of an administrative or agency proceeding;

iii. The record in appellate or review proceedings;

iv. The birth date of a minor whenever the birth date is necessary for the court to establish or maintain subject matter jurisdiction;

v. The name of a minor in any order relating to parental responsibility, time-sharing, or child support;

vi. The name of a minor in any document or order affecting the minor's ownership of real property;

vii. The birth date of a party in a writ of attachment or notice to payor;

viii. In traffic and criminal proceedings: a pro se filing; a court filing that is related to a criminal matter or investigation and that is prepared before the filing of a criminal charge or is not filed as part of any docketed criminal case; an arrest or search warrant or any information in support thereof; a charging document and an affidavit or other documents filed in support of any charging document, including any driving records; a statement of particulars; discovery material introduced into evidence or otherwise filed with the court; and all information necessary for the proper issuance and execution of a subpoena duces tecum;

ix. Information used by the clerk for case maintenance purposes or the courts for case management purposes; and

x. Information which is relevant and material to an issue before the court. FL ST J ADMIN Rule 2.425(b).

c. *Remedies.* Upon motion by a party or interested person or sua sponte by the court, the court may order remedies, sanctions or both for a violation of FL ST J ADMIN Rule 2.425(a). Following notice and an opportunity to respond, the court may impose sanctions if such filing was not made in good faith. FL ST J ADMIN Rule 2.425(c).

d. *Motions not restricted.* FL ST J ADMIN Rule 2.425 does not restrict a party's right to move for protective order, to move to file documents under seal, or to request a determination of the confidentiality of records. FL ST J ADMIN Rule 2.425(d).

e. *Application.* FL ST J ADMIN Rule 2.425 does not affect the application of constitutional provisions, statutes, or rules of court regarding confidential information or access to public information. FL ST J ADMIN Rule 2.425(e).

F. Filing and Service Requirements

1. *Court filing of documents and discovery.* Information obtained during discovery shall not be filed with the court until such time as it is filed for good cause. The requirement of good cause is satisfied only where the filing of the information is allowed or required by another applicable rule of procedure or by court order. All filings of discovery documents shall comply with FL ST J ADMIN Rule 2.425. The court shall have the authority to impose sanctions for violation of FL ST RCP Rule 1.280. FL ST RCP Rule 1.280(g).

2. *Filing requirements.* All original documents must be filed with the court either before service or immediately thereafter, unless otherwise provided for by general law or other rules. If the original of any bond or other document is not placed in the court file, a certified copy must be so placed by the clerk. FL ST J ADMIN Rule 2.516(d). All documents shall be filed in conformity with the requirements of FL ST J ADMIN Rule 2.525. FL ST RCP Rule 1.080(b). All documents filed in any court shall be filed by electronic transmission in accordance with FL ST J ADMIN Rule 2.525. "Documents" means pleadings, motions, petitions, memoranda, briefs, notices, exhibits, declarations, affidavits, orders, judgments, decrees, writs, opinions, and any other paper or writing submitted to a court. FL ST J ADMIN Rule 2.520(a). All documents that are court records, as defined in FL ST J ADMIN Rule 2.430(a)(1), must be filed by electronic transmission, provided that: (1) the clerk has the ability to accept and retain such documents; (2) the clerk or the chief judge of the circuit has requested permission to accept documents filed by electronic transmission; and (3) the supreme court has entered an order granting permission to the clerk to accept documents filed by electronic transmission. FL ST J ADMIN Rule 2.525(c)(1).

a. *Definition.* "Electronic transmission of documents" means the sending of information by electronic signals to, by or from a court or clerk, which when received can be transformed and stored or transmitted on paper, microfilm, magnetic storage device, optical imaging system, CD-ROM, flash drive, other electronic data storage system, server, case maintenance system ("CM"), electronic court filing ("ECF") system, statewide or local electronic portal ("e-portal"), or other electronic record keeping system authorized by the supreme court in a format sufficient to communicate the information on the original document in a readable format. Electronic transmission of documents includes electronic mail ("e-mail") and any internet-based transmission procedure, and may include procedures allowing for documents to be signed or verified by electronic means. FL ST J ADMIN Rule 2.525(a).

i. The filing of documents with the court as required by the Florida Rules of Judicial Administration must be made by filing them with the clerk in accordance with FL ST J ADMIN Rule 2.525, except that the judge may permit documents to be filed with the judge, in which event the judge must note the filing date before him or her on the documents and transmit them to the clerk. The date of filing is that shown on the face of the document by the judge's notation or the clerk's time stamp, whichever is earlier. FL ST J ADMIN Rule 2.516(e).

b. *Application.* Any court or clerk of the court may accept the electronic transmission of documents for filing after the clerk, together with input from the chief judge of the circuit, has obtained approval of the procedures and program for doing so from the Supreme Court of Florida. FL ST J ADMIN Rule 2.525(b).

c. *Exceptions*

  i. Paper documents and other submissions may be manually submitted to the clerk or court:

  - When the clerk does not have the ability to accept and retain documents by electronic filing or has not had ECF Procedures approved by the supreme court;
  - For filing by any self-represented party or any self-represented nonparty unless specific ECF Procedures provide a means to file documents electronically. However, any self-represented nonparty that is a governmental or public agency and any other agency, partnership, corporation, or business entity acting on behalf of any governmental or public agency may file documents by electronic transmission if such entity has the capability of filing documents electronically;
  - For filing by attorneys excused from e-mail service in accordance with FL ST J ADMIN Rule 2.516(b);
  - When submitting evidentiary exhibits or filing non-documentary materials;
  - When the filing involves documents in excess of twenty-five (25) megabytes (25MB) in size. For such filings, documents may be transmitted using an electronic storage medium that the clerk has the ability to accept, which may include a CD-ROM, flash drive, or similar storage medium;
  - When filed in open court, as permitted by the court;
  - When paper filing is permitted by any approved statewide or local ECF procedures; and
  - If any court determines that justice so requires. FL ST J ADMIN Rule 2.525(d).

  ii. Any document in paper form submitted under FL ST J ADMIN Rule 2.525(d) is filed when it is received by the clerk or court and the clerk shall immediately thereafter convert any filed paper document to an electronic document. "Convert to an electronic document" means optically capturing an image of a paper document and using character recognition software to recover as much of the document's text as practicable and then indexing and storing the document in the official court file. FL ST J ADMIN Rule 2.525(c)(4).

  iii. Any storage medium submitted under FL ST J ADMIN Rule 2.525(d)(5) is filed when received by the clerk or court and the clerk shall immediately thereafter transfer the electronic documents from the storage device to the official court file. FL ST J ADMIN Rule 2.525(c)(5).

  iv. If the filer of any paper document authorized under FL ST J ADMIN Rule 2.525(d) provides a self-addressed, postage-paid envelope for return of the paper document after it is converted to electronic form by the clerk, the clerk shall place the paper document in the envelope and deposit it in the mail. Except when a paper document is required to be maintained, the clerk may recycle any filed paper document that is not to be returned to the filer. FL ST J ADMIN Rule 2.525(c)(6).

  v. The clerk may convert any paper document filed before the effective date of FL ST J ADMIN Rule 2.525 to an electronic document. Unless the clerk is required to maintain the paper document, if the paper document has been converted to an electronic document by the clerk, the paper document is no longer part of the official court file and may be removed and recycled. FL ST J ADMIN Rule 2.525(c)(7).

d. *Official court file.* For information on what constitutes the official court file, please see FL ST J ADMIN Rule 2.525(c)(2), FL ST J ADMIN Rule 2.525(c)(3).

e. *Administration.* All attorneys, parties, or other persons using this rule to file documents are required to make arrangements with the court or clerk for the payment of any charges authorized by general law or the supreme court before filing any document by electronic transmission. FL ST J ADMIN Rule 2.525(f)(2).

f. *Filing date.* The filing date for an electronically transmitted document is the date and time that such filing is acknowledged by an electronic stamp or otherwise, pursuant to any procedure set forth in any ECF Procedures approved by the supreme court, or the date the last page of such filing is received by the court or clerk. FL ST J ADMIN Rule 2.525(f)(3).

g. *Accessibility.* All documents transmitted in any electronic form under FL ST J ADMIN Rule 2.525 must comply with the accessibility requirements of FL ST J ADMIN Rule 2.526. FL ST J ADMIN Rule 2.525(g).

3. *Service requirements.* Every pleading subsequent to the initial pleading, all orders, and every other document filed in the action must be served in conformity with the requirements of FL ST J ADMIN Rule 2.516. FL ST RCP Rule 1.080(a).

a. *Service; When required.* Unless the court otherwise orders, or a statute or supreme court administrative order specifies a different means of service, every pleading subsequent to the initial pleading and every other document filed in any court proceeding, except applications for witness subpoenas and documents served by formal notice or required to be served in the manner provided for service of formal notice, must be served in accordance with FL ST J ADMIN Rule 2.516 on each party. No service need be made on parties against whom a default has been entered, except that pleadings asserting new or additional claims against them must be served in the manner provided for service of summons. FL ST J ADMIN Rule 2.516(a).

b. *Service; How made.* When service is required or permitted to be made upon a party represented by an attorney, service must be made upon the attorney unless service upon the party is ordered by the court. FL ST J ADMIN Rule 2.516(b).

i. *Service by electronic mail ("e-mail").* All documents required or permitted to be served on another party must be served by e-mail, unless FL ST J ADMIN Rule 2.516 otherwise provides. When, in addition to service by e-mail, the sender also utilizes another means of service provided for in FL ST J ADMIN Rule 2.516(b)(2), any differing time limits and other provisions applicable to that other means of service control. FL ST J ADMIN Rule 2.516(b)(1). Any document electronically transmitted to a court or clerk must also be served on all parties and interested persons in accordance with the applicable rules of court. FL ST J ADMIN Rule 2.525(e)(2).

- *Service on attorneys.* Upon appearing in a proceeding, an attorney must serve a designation of a primary e-mail address and may designate no more than two (2) secondary e-mail addresses. Thereafter, service must be directed to all designated e-mail addresses in that proceeding. Every document filed by an attorney thereafter must include the primary e-mail address of that attorney and any secondary e-mail addresses. If an attorney does not designate any e-mail address for service, documents may be served on that attorney at the e-mail address on record with The Florida Bar. FL ST J ADMIN Rule 2.516(b)(1)(A).
- *Exception to e-mail service on attorneys.* Service by an attorney on another attorney must be made by e-mail unless excused by the court. Upon motion by an attorney demonstrating that the attorney has no e-mail account and lacks access to the Internet at the attorney's office, the court may excuse the attorney from the requirements of e-mail service. Service on and by an attorney excused by the court from e-mail service must be by the means provided in FL ST J ADMIN Rule 2.516(b)(2). FL ST J ADMIN Rule 2.516(b)(1)(B).
- *Service on and by parties not represented by an attorney.* Any party not represented by an attorney may serve a designation of a primary e-mail address and also may designate no more than two (2) secondary e-mail addresses to which service must be directed in that proceeding by the means provided in FL ST J ADMIN Rule 2.516(b)(1). If a party not represented by an attorney does not designate an e-mail address for service in a proceeding, service on and by that party must be by the means provided in FL ST J ADMIN Rule 2.516(b)(2). FL ST J ADMIN Rule 2.516(b)(1)(C).
- *Time of service.* Service by e-mail is complete when it is sent. FL ST J ADMIN Rule 2.516(b)(1)(D). An e-mail is deemed served on the date it is sent. FL ST J ADMIN Rule 2.516(b)(1)(D)(i). If the sender learns that the e-mail did not reach the address of the

person to be served, the sender must immediately send another copy by e-mail, or by a means authorized by FL ST J ADMIN Rule 2.516(b)(2). FL ST J ADMIN Rule 2.516(b)(1)(D)(ii). E-mail service is treated as service by mail for the computation of time. FL ST J ADMIN Rule 2.516(b)(1)(D)(iii).

ii. *Format of e-mail for service.* Service of a document by e-mail is made by attaching a copy of the document in PDF format to an e-mail sent to all addresses designated by the attorney or party. FL ST J ADMIN Rule 2.516(b)(1)(E).

- All documents served by e-mail must be attached to an e-mail message containing a subject line beginning with the words "SERVICE OF COURT DOCUMENT" in all capital letters, followed by the case number of the proceeding in which the documents are being served. FL ST J ADMIN Rule 2.516(b)(1)(E)(i).
- The body of the e-mail must identify the court in which the proceeding is pending, the case number, the name of the initial party on each side, the title of each document served with that e-mail, and the sender's name and telephone number. FL ST J ADMIN Rule 2.516(b)(1)(E)(ii).
- Any document served by e-mail may be signed by the "/s/" format, as long as the filed original is signed in accordance with the applicable rule of procedure. FL ST J ADMIN Rule 2.516(b)(1)(E)(iii).
- Any e-mail which, together with its attached documents, exceeds five megabytes (5MB) in size, must be divided and sent as separate e-mails, no one of which may exceed five megabytes (5MB) in size and each of which must be sequentially numbered in the subject line. FL ST J ADMIN Rule 2.516(b)(1)(E)(iv).

iii. *Service by other means.* In addition to, and not in lieu of, service by e-mail, service may also be made upon attorneys by any of the means specified in FL ST J ADMIN Rule 2.516(b)(2). Service on and by all parties who are not represented by an attorney and who do not designate an e-mail address, and on and by all attorneys excused from e-mail service, must be made by delivering a copy of the document or by mailing it to the party or attorney at their last known address or, if no address is known, by leaving it with the clerk of the court. Service by mail is complete upon mailing. Delivery of a copy within FL ST J ADMIN Rule 2.516 is complete upon:

- Handing it to the attorney or to the party,
- Leaving it at the attorney's or party's office with a clerk or other person in charge thereof,
- If there is no one in charge, leaving it in a conspicuous place therein,
- If the office is closed or the person to be served has no office, leaving it at the person's usual place of abode with some person of his or her family above fifteen (15) years of age and informing such person of the contents, or
- Transmitting it by facsimile to the attorney's or party's office with a cover sheet containing the sender's name, firm, address, telephone number, and facsimile number, and the number of pages transmitted. When service is made by facsimile, a copy must also be served by any other method permitted by FL ST J ADMIN Rule 2.516. Facsimile service occurs when transmission is complete. FL ST J ADMIN Rule 2.516(b)(2)(A) through FL ST J ADMIN Rule 2.516(b)(2)(E).
- Service by delivery after 5:00 p.m. must be deemed to have been made by mailing on the date of delivery. FL ST J ADMIN Rule 2.516(b)(2)(F).

c. *Service; Numerous defendants.* In actions when the parties are unusually numerous, the court may regulate the service contemplated by the Florida Rules of Judicial Administration on motion or on its own initiative in such manner as may be found to be just and reasonable. FL ST J ADMIN Rule 2.516(c).

d. *Service by clerk.* Service of notices and other documents required to be made by the clerk must also be done as provided in FL ST J ADMIN Rule 2.516(b). FL ST J ADMIN Rule 2.516(g).

e. *Standards of professional courtesy; Service*

i. The timing and manner of service should not be used to the disadvantage of the party receiving the papers. This includes the use of facsimile transmissions and any additional expedited means of communication approved by the court. FL ST 6 J CIR 2009-066 PA/PI-CIR(C)(1).

ii. Attorneys will not serve papers to take advantage of opposing counsel's known absence from the office or at a time or in a manner designed to inconvenience an opponent, such as late on Friday afternoon or the day preceding a secular or religious holiday. FL ST 6 J CIR 2009-066 PA/PI-CIR(C)(2).

iii. Attorneys will not serve papers, including briefs and memoranda, so close to a court appearance that the ability of opposing counsel to prepare for that appearance or, where permitted, to respond, is inhibited. FL ST 6 J CIR 2009-066 PA/PI-CIR(C)(3).

iv. Service should be made personally or by facsimile transmission when it is likely that service by mail, even when allowed, will prejudice the opposing party. FL ST 6 J CIR 2009-066 PA/PI-CIR(C)(4).

G. Hearings

1. There is no hearing required or contemplated with regard to requests for admission in the Florida Rules of Civil Procedure.

H. Forms

1. Official Request for Admissions Forms for Florida

a. Caption. FL ST RCP Form 1.901.

2. Request for Admissions Forms for Florida

a. Requests for admissions; Negligence, fall down. FL-PRACFORM § 8:41.

b. Requests for admissions; Promissory note. FL-PRACFORM § 8:42.

c. Requests for admissions; Open account. FL-PRACFORM § 8:43.

d. Requests for admissions; Mortgage foreclosure. FL-PRACFORM § 8:44.

e. Request for admissions; General form. FL-PP § 3:146.

f. Request for admissions; Facts and genuineness of documents. FL-PP § 3:147.

g. Motion; To determine sufficiency of reply to request for admissions. FL-PP § 3:152.

h. Form for request for admissions. FL-RCPF R 1.370(5).

i. Form for request for admissions (another form). FL-RCPF R 1.370(6).

j. Form for request for admissions served concurrently with interrogatories. FL-RCPF R 1.370(7).

k. Form for request for admissions as to factual situation and refinement of issues. FL-RCPF R 1.370(9).

l. Form for request to admit party uses electronic data storage. FL-RCPF R 1.370(10).

I. Checklist

(I) ❑ Matters to be considered by requesting party

(a) ❑ Required documents

(1) ❑ Request

(2) ❑ Copies of documents

(3) ❑ Certificate of service

(b) ❑ Time for request

(1) ❑ Without leave of court the request may be served upon the plaintiff after commencement of the action and upon any other party with or after service of the process and initial pleading upon that party

(II) ❑ Matters to be considered by responding party

(a) ❑ Required documents

(1) ❑ Response to request

(2) ❑ Certificate of service

(b) ❑ Time for response

(1) ❑ The party to whom the request is directed shall serve a written response within thirty (30) days after service of the request, except that a defendant may serve a response within forty-five (45) days after service of the process and initial pleading on that defendant

Requests, Notices and Applications
Notice of Deposition

Document Last Updated January 2013

A. Applicable Rules

1. *State rules*
   a. Pleadings and motions. FL ST RCP Rule 1.100.
   b. Depositions before action or pending appeal. FL ST RCP Rule 1.290.
   c. Persons before whom depositions may be taken. FL ST RCP Rule 1.300.
   d. Depositions upon oral examination. FL ST RCP Rule 1.310.
   e. Depositions upon written questions. FL ST RCP Rule 1.320.
   f. Use of depositions in court proceedings. FL ST RCP Rule 1.330.
   g. Nonverification of pleadings. FL ST RCP Rule 1.030.
   h. Service and filing of pleadings, orders, and documents. FL ST RCP Rule 1.080.
   i. Time. FL ST RCP Rule 1.090.
   j. General provisions governing discovery. FL ST RCP Rule 1.280.
   k. Failure to make discovery; Sanctions. FL ST RCP Rule 1.380.
   l. Depositions of expert witnesses. FL ST RCP Rule 1.390.
   m. Relief from judgment, decrees, or orders. FL ST RCP Rule 1.540.
   n. Forms. FL ST RCP Rule 1.900.
   o. Minimization of the filing of sensitive information. FL ST J ADMIN Rule 2.425.
   p. Retention of court records. FL ST J ADMIN Rule 2.430.
   q. Foreign attorneys. FL ST J ADMIN Rule 2.510.
   r. Signature of attorneys and parties. FL ST J ADMIN Rule 2.515.
   s. Paper. FL ST J ADMIN Rule 2.520.
   t. Electronic filing. FL ST J ADMIN Rule 2.525.
   u. Accessibility of information and technology. FL ST J ADMIN Rule 2.526.
   v. Requests for accommodations by persons with disabilities. FL ST J ADMIN Rule 2.540.
2. *Local rules*
   a. General motion rule. FL ST 6 J CIR LOCAL Rule 5.
   b. Standards of professional courtesy. FL ST 6 J CIR 2009-066 PA/PI-CIR.
   c. Arbitration and mediation program circuit civil and family cases. FL ST 6 J CIR PA/PI-CIR-96-63; FL ST 6 J CIR 2011-006 PA/PI-CIR.

B. Timing

1. *Depositions upon oral examination.* After commencement of the action any party may take the testimony of any person, including a party, by deposition upon oral examination. Leave of court, granted with or without notice, must be obtained only if the plaintiff seeks to take a deposition within thirty (30) days after service of the process and initial pleading upon any defendant, except that leave is not required (1) if a defendant has served a notice of taking deposition or otherwise sought discovery, or (2) if special notice is given as provided in FL ST RCP Rule 1.310(b)(2). The attendance of witnesses may be compelled by subpoena as provided in FL ST RCP Rule 1.410. The deposition of a person confined in prison may be taken only by leave of court on such terms as the court prescribes. FL ST RCP Rule 1.310(a). A party desiring to take the deposition of any person upon oral examination shall give reasonable notice in writing to every other party to the action. FL ST RCP Rule 1.310(b)(1).
2. *Depositions upon written questions.* After commencement of the action any party may take the testimony of any person, including a party, by deposition upon written questions. The attendance of witnesses may be compelled by the use of subpoena as provided in FL ST RCP Rule 1.410. The deposition of a person confined in prison may be taken only by leave of court on such terms as the court prescribes. Within thrity (30) days after the notice and written questions are served, a party may serve cross questions upon all other parties. Within ten (10) days after being served with cross questions, a party may serve redirect questions upon all other parties. Within ten (10) days after being served with redirect questions, a party may serve recross questions upon all other parties. The court may for cause shown enlarge or shorten the time. FL ST RCP Rule 1.320(a).
3. *Depositions before action or pending appeal.* For information on petitions and motions for depositions before an action or pending appeal, please see the General Requirements section below.
4. *Sequence and timing of discovery.* Except as provided in FL ST RCP Rule 1.280(b)(5) or unless the court upon motion for the convenience of parties and witnesses and in the interest of justice orders otherwise, methods of discovery may be used in any sequence, and the fact that a party is conducting discovery, whether by deposition or otherwise, shall not delay any other party's discovery. FL ST RCP Rule 1.280(e).
5. *Computation of time*
    a. *Generally.* Computation of time shall be governed by FL ST J ADMIN Rule 2.514. FL ST RCP Rule 1.090(a). The following rules apply in computing time periods specified in any rule of procedure, local rule, court order, or statute that does not specify a method of computing time. FL ST J ADMIN Rule 2.514(a).
        i. *Period stated in days or a longer unit.* When the period is stated in days or a longer unit of time (A) exclude the day of the event that triggers the period; (B) count every day, including intermediate Saturdays, Sundays, and legal holidays; and (C) include the last day of the period, but if the last day is a Saturday, Sunday, or legal holiday, or falls within any period of time extended through an order of the chief justice under FL ST J ADMIN Rule 2.205(a)(2)(B)(iv), the period continues to run until the end of the next day that is not a Saturday, Sunday, or legal holiday and does not fall within any period of time extended through an order of the chief justice. FL ST J ADMIN Rule 2.514(a)(1).
        ii. *Period stated in hours.* When the period is stated in hours (A) begin counting immediately on the occurrence of the event that triggers the period; (B) count every hour, including hours during intermediate Saturdays, Sundays, and legal holidays; and (C) if the period would end on a Saturday, Sunday, or legal holiday, or during any period of time extended through an order of the chief justice under FL ST J ADMIN Rule 2.205(a)(2)(B)(iv), the period continues to run until the same time on the next day that is not a Saturday, Sunday, or legal holiday and does not fall within any period of time extended through an order of the chief justice. FL ST J ADMIN Rule 2.514(a)(2).
        iii. *Period stated in days less than seven (7) days.* When the period stated in days is less than seven (7) days, intermediate Saturdays, Sundays, and legal holidays shall be excluded in the computation. FL ST J ADMIN Rule 2.514(a)(3).
        iv. *"Last day" defined.* Unless a different time is set by a statute, local rule, or court order, the last

day ends (A) for electronic filing or for service by any means, at midnight; and (B) for filing by other means, when the clerk's office is scheduled to close. FL ST J ADMIN Rule 2.514(a)(4).

v. *"Next day" defined.* The "next day" is determined by continuing to count forward when the period is measured after an event and backward when measured before an event. FL ST J ADMIN Rule 2.514(a)(5).

vi. *"Legal holiday" defined.* "Legal holiday" means (A) the day set aside by FL ST § 110.117, for observing New Year's Day, Martin Luther King, Jr.'s Birthday, Memorial Day, Independence Day, Labor Day, Veterans' Day, Thanksgiving Day, the Friday after Thanksgiving Day, or Christmas Day, and (B) any day observed as a holiday by the clerk's office or as designated by the chief judge. FL ST J ADMIN Rule 2.514(a)(6).

b. *Additional time after service by mail or e-mail.* When a party may or must act within a specified time after service and service is made by mail or e-mail, five (5) days are added after the period that would otherwise expire under FL ST J ADMIN Rule 2.514(a). FL ST J ADMIN Rule 2.514(b).

c. *Enlargement.* When an act is required or allowed to be done at or within a specified time by order of court, by the Florida Rules of Civil Procedure, or by notice given thereunder, for cause shown the court at any time in its discretion (1) with or without notice, may order the period enlarged if request therefor is made before the expiration of the period originally prescribed or as extended by a previous order, or (2) upon motion made and notice after the expiration of the specified period, may permit the act to be done when failure to act was the result of excusable neglect, but it may not extend the time for making a motion for new trial, for rehearing, or to alter or amend a judgment; making a motion for relief from a judgment under FL ST RCP Rule 1.540(b); taking an appeal or filing a petition for certiorari; or making a motion for a directed verdict. FL ST RCP Rule 1.090(b).

d. *Unaffected by expiration of term.* The period of time provided for the doing of any act or the taking of any proceeding shall not be affected or limited by the continued existence or expiration of a term of court. The continued existence or expiration of a term of court in no way affects the power of a court to do any act or take any proceeding in any action which is or has been pending before it. FL ST RCP Rule 1.090(c).

C. General Requirements

1. *General provisions governing discovery*

a. *Discovery methods.* Parties may obtain discovery by one or more of the following methods: depositions upon oral examination or written questions; written interrogatories; production of documents or things or permission to enter upon land or other property for inspection and other purposes; physical and mental examinations; and requests for admission. Unless the court orders otherwise and under FL ST RCP Rule 1.280(c), the frequency of use of these methods is not limited, except as provided in FL ST RCP Rule 1.200, FL ST RCP Rule 1.340, and FL ST RCP Rule 1.370. FL ST RCP Rule 1.280(a).

b. *Scope of discovery.* Unless otherwise limited by order of the court in accordance with the Florida Rules of Civil Procedure, the scope of discovery is as follows:

i. *In general.* Parties may obtain discovery regarding any matter, not privileged, that is relevant to the subject matter of the pending action, whether it relates to the claim or defense of the party seeking discovery or the claim or defense of any other party, including the existence, description, nature, custody, condition, and location of any books, documents, or other tangible things and the identity and location of persons having knowledge of any discoverable matter. It is not ground for objection that the information sought will be inadmissible at the trial if the information sought appears reasonably calculated to lead to the discovery of admissible evidence. FL ST RCP Rule 1.280(b)(1).

ii. *Indemnity agreements.* A party may obtain discovery of the existence and contents of any agreement under which any person may be liable to satisfy part or all of a judgment that may be entered in the action or to indemnify or to reimburse a party for payments made to satisfy the judgment. Information concerning the agreement is not admissible in evidence at trial by reason of disclosure. FL ST RCP Rule 1.280(b)(2).

iii. *Electronically stored information.* A party may obtain discovery of electronically stored information in accordance with the Florida Rules of Civil Procedure. FL ST RCP Rule 1.280(b)(3).

iv. *Trial preparation; Materials.* Subject to the provisions of FL ST RCP Rule 1.280(b)(5), a party may obtain discovery of documents and tangible things otherwise discoverable under FL ST RCP Rule 1.280(b)(1) and prepared in anticipation of litigation or for trial by or for another party or by or for that party's representative, including that party's attorney, consultant, surety, indemnitor, insurer, or agent, only upon a showing that the party seeking discovery has need of the materials in the preparation of the case and is unable without undue hardship to obtain the substantial equivalent of the materials by other means. FL ST RCP Rule 1.280(b)(4).

- In ordering discovery of the materials when the required showing has been made, the court shall protect against disclosure of the mental impressions, conclusions, opinions, or legal theories of an attorney or other representative of a party concerning the litigation. FL ST RCP Rule 1.280(b)(4).
- Without the required showing a party may obtain a copy of a statement concerning the action or its subject matter previously made by that party. FL ST RCP Rule 1.280(b)(4).
- Upon request without the required showing a person not a party may obtain a copy of a statement concerning the action or its subject matter previously made by that person. If the request is refused, the person may move for an order to obtain a copy. The provisions of FL ST RCP Rule 1.380(a)(5) apply to the award of expenses incurred as a result of making the motion. FL ST RCP Rule 1.280(b)(4).
- For purposes of FL ST RCP Rule 1.280(b)(4), a statement previously made is a written statement signed or otherwise adopted or approved by the person making it, or a stenographic, mechanical, electrical, or other recording or transcription of it that is a substantially verbatim recital of an oral statement by the person making it and contemporaneously recorded. FL ST RCP Rule 1.280(b)(4).

v. *Trial preparation; Experts.* Discovery of facts known and opinions held by experts, otherwise discoverable under the provisions of FL ST RCP Rule 1.280(b)(1) and acquired or developed in anticipation of litigation or for trial, may be obtained only as follows:

- By interrogatories a party may require any other party to identify each person whom the other party expects to call as an expert witness at trial and to state the subject matter on which the expert is expected to testify, and to state the substance of the facts and opinions to which the expert is expected to testify and a summary of the grounds for each opinion. FL ST RCP Rule 1.280(b)(5)(A)(i).
- Any person disclosed by interrogatories or otherwise as a person expected to be called as an expert witness at trial may be deposed in accordance with FL ST RCP Rule 1.390 without motion or order of court. FL ST RCP Rule 1.280(b)(5)(A)(ii).
- A party may obtain the following discovery regarding any person disclosed by interrogatories or otherwise as a person expected to be called as an expert witness at trial: The scope of employment in the pending case and the compensation for such service, FL ST RCP Rule 1.280(b)(5)(A)(iii)(1); The expert's general litigation experience, including the percentage of work performed for plaintiffs and defendants, FL ST RCP Rule 1.280(b)(5)(A)(iii)(2); The identity of other cases, within a reasonable time period, in which the expert has testified by deposition or at trial, FL ST RCP Rule 1.280(b)(5)(A)(iii)(3); An approximation of the portion of the expert's involvement as an expert witness, which may be based on the number of hours, percentage of hours, or percentage of earned income derived from serving as an expert witness; however, the expert shall not be required to disclose his or her earnings as an expert witness or income derived from other services. FL ST RCP Rule 1.280(b)(5)(A)(iii)(4).
- An expert may be required to produce financial and business records only under the most unusual or compelling circumstances and may not be compelled to compile or produce

nonexistent documents. Upon motion, the court may order further discovery by other means, subject to such restrictions as to scope and other provisions pursuant to FL ST RCP Rule 1.280(b)(5)(C) concerning fees and expenses as the court may deem appropriate. FL ST RCP Rule 1.280(b)(5).

- A party may discover facts known or opinions held by an expert who has been retained or specially employed by another party in anticipation of litigation or preparation for trial and who is not expected to be called as a witness at trial, only as provided in FL ST RCP Rule 1.360(b) or upon a showing of exceptional circumstances under which it is impracticable for the party seeking discovery to obtain facts or opinions on the same subject by other means. FL ST RCP Rule 1.280(b)(5)(B).
- Unless manifest injustice would result, the court shall require that the party seeking discovery pay the expert a reasonable fee for time spent in responding to discovery under FL ST RCP Rule 1.280(b)(5)(A) and FL ST RCP Rule 1.280(b)(5)(B); and concerning discovery from an expert obtained under FL ST RCP Rule 1.280(b)(5)(A) the court may require, and concerning discovery obtained under FL ST RCP Rule 1.280(b)(5)(B) shall require, the party seeking discovery to pay the other party a fair part of the fees and expenses reasonably incurred by the latter party in obtaining facts and opinions from the expert. FL ST RCP Rule 1.280(b)(5)(C).
- As used in the Florida Rules of Civil Procedure an expert shall be an expert witness as defined in FL ST RCP Rule 1.390(a). FL ST RCP Rule 1.280(b)(5)(D).

vi. *Claims to privilege or protection.* When a party withholds information otherwise discoverable under the Florida Rules of Civil Procedure by claiming that it is privileged or subject to protection as trial preparation material, the party shall make the claim expressly and shall describe the nature of the documents, communications, or things not produced or disclosed in a manner that, without revealing information itself privileged or protected, will enable other parties to assess the applicability of the privilege or protection. FL ST RCP Rule 1.280(b)(6).

c. *Limitations on discovery of electronically stored information*

i. A person may object to discovery of electronically stored information from sources that the person identifies as not reasonably accessible because of burden or cost. On motion to compel discovery or for a protective order, the person from whom discovery is sought must show that the information sought or the format requested is not reasonably accessible because of undue burden or cost. If that showing is made, the court may nonetheless order the discovery from such sources or in such formats if the requesting party shows good cause. The court may specify conditions of the discovery, including ordering that some or all of the expenses incurred by the person from whom discovery is sought be paid by the party seeking the discovery. FL ST RCP Rule 1.280(d)(1).

ii. In determining any motion involving discovery of electronically stored information, the court must limit the frequency or extent of discovery otherwise allowed by the Florida Rules of Civil Procedure if it determines that (i) the discovery sought is unreasonably cumulative or duplicative, or can be obtained from another source or in another manner that is more convenient, less burdensome, or less expensive; or (ii) the burden or expense of the discovery outweighs its likely benefit, considering the needs of the case, the amount in controversy, the parties' resources, the importance of the issues at stake in the action, and the importance of the discovery in resolving the issues. FL ST RCP Rule 1.280(d)(2).

d. For information on inadvertent disclosure of privileged materials, see FL ST RCP Rule 1.285.

e. *Standards of professional courtesy; Discovery*

i. Attorneys will use discovery only when necessary to ascertain information, to perpetuate testimony, or to obtain documents or things necessary for the prosecution or defense of an action. Attorneys will never use discovery as a means of harassment or to impose an inordinate burden or expense. FL ST 6 J CIR 2009-066 PA/PI-CIR(F)(1).

ii. Attorneys will file motions for protective orders as soon as possible and notice them for hearing as soon as practicable. Absent an agreement or court order a deposition may not be properly canceled due to a pending motion. FL ST 6 J CIR 2009-066 PA/PI-CIR(F)(2).

iii. Prior to filing a motion to compel or for protective order, attorneys will confer with opposing counsel in a good faith effort to resolve the issues raised. Attorneys will file with the motion a statement certifying that attorneys have complied and been unable to resolve the dispute. FL ST 6 J CIR 2009-066 PA/PI-CIR(F)(3).

iv. Motions to compel shall quote in full each interrogatory, question on deposition, request for admission or request for production to which the motion is addressed and the objection and grounds stated by opposing counsel. FL ST 6 J CIR 2009-066 PA/PI-CIR(F)(4).

2. *Notice of deposition*

   a. *Upon oral examination.* A party desiring to take the deposition of any person upon oral examination shall give reasonable notice in writing to every other party to the action. The notice shall state the time and place for taking the deposition and the name and address of each person to be examined, if known, and, if the name is not known, a general description sufficient to identify the person or the particular class or group to which the person belongs. If a subpoena duces tecum is to be served on the person to be examined, the designation of the materials to be produced under the subpoena shall be attached to or included in the notice. FL ST RCP Rule 1.310(b)(1).

   b. *Upon written examination.* A party desiring to take a deposition upon written questions shall serve a notice stating: (1) the name and address of the person who is to answer them, if known, and, if the name is not known, a general description sufficient to identify the person or the particular class or group to which that person belongs, and (2) the name or descriptive title and address of the officer before whom the deposition is to be taken. FL ST RCP Rule 1.320(a).

3. *When leave of court required.* Leave of court, granted with or without notice, must be obtained only if the plaintiff seeks to take a deposition within thirty (30) days after service of the process and initial pleading upon any defendant, except that leave is not required if a defendant has served a notice of taking deposition or otherwise sought discovery. FL ST RCP Rule 1.310(a).

   a. *Exceptions.* Leave of court is not required for the taking of a deposition by plaintiff if the notice states that the person to be examined is about to go out of the state and will be unavailable for examination unless a deposition is taken before expiration of the thirty (30) day period. If a party shows that when served with notice under FL ST RCP Rule 1.310(b) that party was unable through the exercise of diligence to obtain counsel to represent the party at the taking of the deposition, the deposition may not be used against that party. FL ST RCP Rule 1.310(b)(2).

   b. *Persons in prison.* The deposition of a person confined in prison may be taken only by leave of court on such terms as the court prescribes. FL ST RCP Rule 1.310(a); FL ST RCP Rule 1.320(a).

4. *Deposition procedure*

   a. *Who may take depositions.* Depositions may be taken before any notary public or judicial officer or before any officer authorized by the statutes of Florida to take acknowledgments or proof of executions of deeds or by any person appointed by the court in which the action is pending. FL ST RCP Rule 1.300(a).

      i. *In foreign countries.* In a foreign country depositions may be taken: on notice before a person authorized to administer oaths in the place in which the examination is held, either by the law thereof or by the law of Florida or of the United States; before a person commissioned by the court, and a person so commissioned shall have the power by virtue of the commission to administer any necessary oath and take testimony; or pursuant to a letter rogatory. FL ST RCP Rule 1.300(b).

      ii. *Selection by stipulation.* If the parties so stipulate in writing, depositions may be taken before any person at any time or place upon any notice and in any manner and when so taken may be used like other depositions. FL ST RCP Rule 1.300(c).

      iii. *Persons disqualified.* Unless so stipulated by the parties, no deposition shall be taken before a person who is a relative, employee, attorney, or counsel of any of the parties, is a relative or employee of any of the parties' attorney or counsel, or is financially interested in the action. FL ST RCP Rule 1.300(d).

b. *Depositions before action*

i. *Petition.* A person who desires to perpetuate that person's own testimony or that of another person regarding any matter that may be cognizable in any Florida court may file a verified petition in the circuit court in the county of the residence of any expected adverse party. The petition shall be entitled in the name of the petitioner and shall show:

- That the petitioner expects to be a party to an action cognizable in a court of Florida, but is presently unable to bring the action;
- The subject matter of the expected action and the petitioner's interest therein;
- The facts which the petitioner desires to establish by the proposed testimony and the petitioner's reasons for desiring to perpetuate it;
- The names or a description of the persons the petitioner expects will be adverse parties and their addresses so far as known; and
- The names and addresses of the persons to be examined and the substance of the testimony which the petitioner expects to elicit from each; and shall ask for an order authorizing the petitioner to take the deposition of the persons to be examined named in the petition for the purpose of perpetuating their testimony. FL ST RCP Rule 1.290(a)(1).

ii. *Notice and service.* After submitting the petition, the petitioner must thereafter serve a notice upon each person named in the petition as an expected adverse party, together with a copy of the petition, stating that the petitioner will apply to the court at a time and place named therein for an order described in the petition. At least twenty (20) days before the date of hearing the notice shall be served either within or without the county in the manner provided by law for service of summons, but if such service cannot with due diligence be made upon any expected adverse party named in the petition, the court may make an order for service by publication or otherwise, and shall appoint an attorney for persons not served in the manner provided by law for service of summons who shall represent them, and if they are not otherwise represented, shall cross-examine the deponent. FL ST RCP Rule 1.290(a)(2).

iii. *Order and examination.* If the court is satisfied that the perpetuation of the testimony may prevent a failure or delay of justice, it shall make an order designating or describing the persons whose depositions may be taken and specifying the subject matter of the examination and whether the deposition shall be taken upon oral examination or written interrogatories. The deposition may then be taken in accordance with the rules governing depositions. FL ST RCP Rule 1.290(a)(3).

iv. *Use of deposition.* A deposition taken before an action and in accordance with the procedures above may be used in any action involving the same subject matter subsequently brought in any court. FL ST RCP Rule 1.290(a)(4).

c. *Depositions upon oral examination*

i. *Enlargement of time.* For cause shown the court may enlarge or shorten the time for taking the deposition. FL ST RCP Rule 1.310(b)(3).

ii. *Videotaped depositions.* Any deposition may be recorded by videotape without leave of the court or stipulation of the parties, provided the deposition is taken in accordance with the following:

- *Notice.* A party intending to videotape a deposition shall state in the notice that the deposition is to be videotaped and shall give the name and address of the operator. Any subpoena served on the person to be examined shall state the method or methods for recording the testimony. FL ST RCP Rule 1.310(b)(4)(A).
- *Stenographer.* Videotaped depositions shall also be recorded stenographically, unless all parties agree otherwise. FL ST RCP Rule 1.310(b)(4)(B).
- *Procedure.* At the beginning of the deposition, the officer before whom it is taken shall, on

camera: (i) identify the style of the action, (ii) state the date, and (iii) swear the witness. FL ST RCP Rule 1.310(b)(4)(C).

- *Custody of tape and copies.* The attorney for the party requesting the videotaping of the deposition shall take custody of and be responsible for the safeguarding of the videotape, shall permit the viewing of it by the opposing party, and, if requested, shall provide a copy of the videotape at the expense of the party requesting the copy. FL ST RCP Rule 1.310(b)(4)(D).
- *Cost of videotaped depositions.* The party requesting the videotaping shall bear the initial cost of videotaping. FL ST RCP Rule 1.310(b)(4)(E).

iii. *Production of documents.* The notice to a party deponent may be accompanied by a request for the production of documents and tangible things at the taking of the deposition. The procedure of FL ST RCP Rule 1.350 shall apply to the request. FL ST RCP Rule 1.351 provides the exclusive procedure for obtaining documents or things by subpoena from nonparties without deposing the custodian or other person in possession of the documents. FL ST RCP Rule 1.310(b)(5).

iv. *Deposing organizations.* In the notice a party may name as the deponent a public or private corporation, a partnership or association, or a governmental agency, and designate with reasonable particularity the matters on which examination is requested. The organization so named shall designate one or more officers, directors, or managing agents, or other persons who consent to do so, to testify on its behalf and may state the matters on which each person designated will testify. The persons so designated shall testify about matters known or reasonably available to the organization. FL ST RCP Rule 1.310(b)(6).

v. *Depositions by telephone.* On motion the court may order that the testimony at a deposition be taken by telephone. The order may prescribe the manner in which the deposition will be taken. A party may also arrange for a stenographic transcription at that party's own initial expense. FL ST RCP Rule 1.310(b)(7).

vi. *Deposing a minor.* Any minor subpoenaed for testimony shall have the right to be accompanied by a parent or guardian at all times during the taking of testimony notwithstanding the invocation of the rule of sequestration of section FL ST § 90.616, except upon a showing that the presence of a parent or guardian is likely to have a material, negative impact on the credibility or accuracy of the minor's testimony, or that the interests of the parent or guardian are in actual or potential conflict with the interests of the minor. FL ST RCP Rule 1.310(b)(8).

vii. *Examination and cross-examination.* Examination and cross-examination of witnesses may proceed as permitted at the trial. FL ST RCP Rule 1.310(c).

viii. *Oath.* The officer before whom the deposition is to be taken shall put the witness on oath and shall personally, or by someone acting under the officer's direction and in the officer's presence, record the testimony of the witness, except that when a deposition is being taken by telephone, the witness shall be sworn by a person present with the witness who is qualified to administer an oath in that location. FL ST RCP Rule 1.310(c).

ix. *Record of examination.* The deposition testimony must be taken stenographically or recorded by any other means ordered. If requested by one of the parties, the testimony shall be transcribed at the initial cost of the requesting party and prompt notice of the request shall be given to all other parties. FL ST RCP Rule 1.310(c).

x. *Objections.* All objections made at time of the examination to the qualifications of the officer taking the deposition, the manner of taking it, the evidence presented, or the conduct of any party, and any other objection to the proceedings shall be noted by the officer upon the deposition. Any objection during a deposition shall be stated concisely and in a nonargumentative and nonsuggestive manner. A party may instruct a deponent not to answer only when necessary to preserve a privilege, to enforce a limitation on evidence directed by the court, or to present a motion under FL ST RCP Rule 1.310(d). FL ST RCP Rule 1.310(c).

- Otherwise, evidence objected to shall be taken subject to the objections. Instead of participating in the oral examination, parties may serve written questions in a sealed envelope on the party taking the deposition and that party shall transmit them to the officer, who shall propound them to the witness and record the answers verbatim. FL ST RCP Rule 1.310(c).

xi. *Motion to terminate or limit examination.* At any time during the taking of the deposition, on motion of a party or of the deponent and upon a showing that the examination is being conducted in bad faith or in such manner as unreasonably to annoy, embarrass, or oppress the deponent or party, or that improper objections and instructions to a deponent not to answer are being made, the court in which the action is pending or the circuit court where the deposition is being taken may order the officer conducting the examination to cease forthwith from taking the deposition or may limit the scope and manner of the taking of the deposition under the scope of permissible discovery. FL ST RCP Rule 1.310(d).

- If the order terminates the examination, it shall be resumed thereafter only upon the order of the court in which the action is pending. Upon demand of any party or the deponent, the taking of the deposition shall be suspended for the time necessary to make a motion for an order. FL ST RCP Rule 1.310(d).

xii. *Deponent review.* If the testimony is transcribed, the transcript shall be furnished to the witness for examination and shall be read to or by the witness unless the examination and reading are waived by the witness and by the parties. Any changes in form or substance that the witness wants to make shall be listed in writing by the officer with a statement of the reasons given by the witness for making the changes. The changes shall be attached to the transcript. It shall then be signed by the witness unless the parties waived the signing or the witness is ill, cannot be found, or refuses to sign. If the transcript is not signed by the witness within a reasonable time after it is furnished to the witness, the officer shall sign the transcript and state on the transcript the waiver, illness, absence of the witness, or refusal to sign with any reasons given. The deposition may then be used as fully as though signed unless the court holds that the reasons given for the refusal to sign require rejection of the deposition wholly or partly, on motion under FL ST RCP Rule 1.330(d)(4). FL ST RCP Rule 1.310(e).

xiii. *Certification and inspection.* If the deposition is transcribed, the officer shall certify on each copy of the deposition that the witness was duly sworn by the officer and that the deposition is a true record of the testimony given by the witness. Documents and things produced for inspection during the examination of the witness shall be marked for identification and annexed to and returned with the deposition upon the request of a party, and may be inspected and copied by any party, except that the person producing the materials may substitute copies to be marked for identification if that person affords to all parties fair opportunity to verify the copies by comparison with the originals. If the person producing the materials requests their return, the officer shall mark them, give each party an opportunity to inspect and copy them, and return them to the person producing them and the materials may then be used in the same manner as if annexed to and returned with the deposition. FL ST RCP Rule 1.310(f)(1).

xiv. *Copies.* Upon payment of reasonable charges, the officer shall furnish a copy of the deposition to any party or to the deponent. FL ST RCP Rule 1.310(f)(2). A party or witness who does not have a copy of the deposition may obtain it from the officer taking the deposition unless the court orders otherwise. If the deposition is obtained from a person other than the officer, the reasonable cost of reproducing the copies shall be paid to the person by the requesting party or witness. FL ST RCP Rule 1.310(g).

d. *Depositions upon written examination*

i. *Deposing an organization upon written examination.* A deposition upon written questions may be taken of a public or private corporation, a partnership or association, or a governmental agency in accordance with FL ST RCP Rule 1.310(b)(6). FL ST RCP Rule 1.320(a).

ii. *Cross, redirect, and recross questions.* Within thirty (30) days after the notice and written questions are served, a party may serve cross questions upon all other parties. Within ten (10) days after being served with cross questions, a party may serve redirect questions upon all other parties. Within ten (10) days after being served with redirect questions, a party may serve recross questions upon all other parties. The court may for cause shown enlarge or shorten the time. FL ST RCP Rule 1.320(a).

iii. *Procedure.* A copy of the notice and copies of all questions served shall be delivered by the party taking the depositions to the officer designated in the notice, who shall proceed promptly to take the testimony of the witness in the manner provided by FL ST RCP Rule 1.310(c), FL ST RCP Rule 1.310(e), and FL ST RCP Rule 1.310(f) in response to the questions and to prepare the deposition, attaching the copy of the notice and the questions received by the officer. The questions shall not be filed separately from the deposition unless a party seeks to have the court consider the questions before the questions are submitted to the witness. FL ST RCP Rule 1.320(b).

5. *Standards of professional courtesy; Depositions*

a. In scheduling depositions, attorneys will make reasonable attempts to accommodate the schedule of the deponent, but not at the expense of their client's rights. FL ST 6 J CIR 2009-066 PA/PI-CIR(F)(5).

b. Attorneys will not inquire into a deponent's personal affairs or question a deponent's integrity unless the inquiry is relevant to the subject matter of the deposition. FL ST 6 J CIR 2009-066 PA/PI-CIR(F)(6).

c. Attorneys will refrain from repetitive and argumentative questions and those asked solely for purposes of harassment. FL ST 6 J CIR 2009-066 PA/PI-CIR(F)(7).

d. Attorneys will limit objections to those that are well founded and necessary to protect a client's interest. Most objections are preserved and must be interposed only when the form of a question is defective or privileged information is sought. FL ST 6 J CIR 2009-066 PA/PI-CIR(F)(8).

e. While a question is pending, attorneys will not, through objections or otherwise, coach the deponent or suggest answers. FL ST 6 J CIR 2009-066 PA/PI-CIR(F)(9).

f. Attorneys will not direct a deponent to refuse to answer questions unless they seek privileged information, are manifestly irrelevant, are calculated to harass, or are not calculated to lead to admissible evidence. FL ST 6 J CIR 2009-066 PA/PI-CIR(F)(10)

g. Attorneys will not make self-serving speeches during depositions. FL ST 6 J CIR 2009-066 PA/PI-CIR(F)(11).

h. Attorneys will not engage in any conduct during a deposition that would not be allowed in the presence of a judicial officer. FL ST 6 J CIR 2009-066 PA/PI-CIR(F)(12).

6. *Arbitration and mediation*

a. *Referral to arbitration and mediation.* Except as hereinafter provided or as otherwise prohibited by law, the presiding judge may enter an order referring all or any part of a contested civil matter to mediation or arbitration. The parties to any contested civil matter may file a written stipulation to mediate or arbitrate any issue between them at any time. Such stipulation shall be incorporated into the order of referral. FL ST RCP Rule 1.700(a).

b. *Arbitration*

i. *Exclusions.* A civil action shall be ordered to arbitration or arbitration in conjunction with mediation upon stipulation of the parties. A civil action may be ordered to arbitration or arbitration in conjunction with mediation upon motion of any party or by the court, if the judge determines the action to be of such a nature that arbitration could be of benefit to the litigants or the court. FL ST RCP Rule 1.800.

- Under no circumstances may the following categories of actions be referred to arbitration: (1) bond estreatures; (2) habeas corpus or other extraordinary writs; (3) bond validations; (4) civil or criminal contempt; (5) such other matters as may be specified by order of the chief judge in the circuit. FL ST RCP Rule 1.800.

ii. For more information regarding arbitration, please see FL ST RCP Rule 1.810; FL ST RCP Rule 1.820; FL ST RCP Rule 1.830.

c. *Mediation.* For more information regarding mediation, please see FL ST RCP Rule 1.710; FL ST RCP Rule 1.720; FL ST RCP Rule 1.730; and FL ST RCP Rule 1.750.

d. See FL ST 6 J CIR PA/PI-CIR-96-63 for more information about the Arbitration and Mediation Program for Florida's Sixth Judicial Circuit.

7. *Rules of court*

a. *Rules of civil procedure.* The Florida Rules of Civil Procedure apply to all actions of a civil nature and all special statutory proceedings in the circuit courts and county courts except those to which the Florida Probate Rules, the Florida Family Law Rules of Procedure, or the Small Claims Rules apply. FL ST RCP Rule 1.010.

i. The form, content, procedure, and time for pleading in all special statutory proceedings shall be as prescribed by the statutes governing the proceeding unless the Florida Rules of Civil Procedure specifically provide to the contrary. FL ST RCP Rule 1.010.

ii. The Florida Rules of Civil Procedure shall be construed to secure the just, speedy, and inexpensive determination of every action. FL ST RCP Rule 1.010.

b. *Rules of judicial administration.* The Florida Rules of Judicial Administration shall apply to administrative matters in all courts to which the Florida Rules of Judicial Administration are applicable by their terms. The Florida Rules of Judicial Administration shall be construed to secure the speedy and inexpensive determination of every proceeding to which they are applicable. The Florida Rules of Judicial Administration shall supersede all conflicting rules and statutes. FL ST J ADMIN Rule 2.110.

8. *Settlement and alternative dispute resolution.* When a matter is scheduled for hearing and the matter is resolved by agreement or settlement, the party setting the matter for hearing shall notify the court. When a matter is scheduled for trial and the case settles, the plaintiff shall notify the court. Permission of the court must be obtained in order to cancel a trial. FL ST 6 J CIR LOCAL Rule 5(A).

a. Unless there are strong and overriding issues of principle, attorneys will raise and explore the issue of settlement as soon as enough is known to make settlement discussions meaningful. FL ST 6 J CIR 2009-066 PA/PI-CIR(I)(1).

b. Attorneys will not falsely hold out the possibility of settlement to adjourn discovery or delay trial. FL ST 6 J CIR 2009-066 PA/PI-CIR(I)(2).

c. Attorneys will consider whether the client's interest could be adequately served and the controversy more expeditiously and economically disposed of by arbitration, mediation or other forms of alternative dispute resolution. FL ST 6 J CIR 2009-066 PA/PI-CIR(I)(3).

D. Documents

1. *Deposition upon oral or written examination*

a. *Required documents*

i. *Notice of deposition.* Please see the General Requirements section of this document for information on the content of a notice of deposition upon oral examination.

ii. *Certificate of service.* A certificate of service of the interrogatories shall be filed, giving the date of service and the name of the party to whom they were directed. FL ST RCP Rule 1.340(e). When any attorney certifies in substance: "I certify that a copy hereof has been furnished to (here insert name or names and addresses used for service) by (e-mail) (delivery) (mail) (fax) on .... (date) ....________________ Attorney" the certificate is taken as prima facie proof of such service in compliance with FL ST J ADMIN Rule 2.516. FL ST J ADMIN Rule 2.516(f).

b. *Supplemental documents*

i. *Motion for leave to take deposition.* See the Timing section for information on when leave is required.

ii. *Subpoena.* See the Timing section for requirements of when a subpoena is required.

iii. *Request for production of documents.* See the General Requirements section for further information.

E. Format

1. *Documents; Type and size.* Documents subject to the exceptions set forth in FL ST J ADMIN Rule 2.525(d) shall be filed on recycled paper measuring eight and one half by eleven (8 1/2 by 11) inches. For purposes of FL ST J ADMIN Rule 2.520, paper is recycled if it contains a minimum content of fifty (50) percent waste paper. Xerographic reduction of legal-size (eight and one half by fourteen (8 1/2 by 14) inches) documents to letter size (eight and one half by eleven (8 1/2 by 11) inches) is prohibited. All other documents filed by electronic transmission shall be filed in a format capable of being printed in a format consistent with the provisions of FL ST J ADMIN Rule 2.250. FL ST J ADMIN Rule 2.520(b).
   a. *Exhibits.* Any exhibit or attachment filed with pleadings or papers may be filed in its original size. FL ST J ADMIN Rule 2.520(c).
   b. *Recording space.* On all papers and documents prepared and filed by the court or by any party to a proceeding which are to be recorded in the public records of any county, including but not limited to final money judgments and notices of lis pendens, a three (3) inch by three (3) inch space at the top right-hand corner on the first page and a one (1) inch by three (3) inch space at the top right-hand corner on each subsequent page shall be left blank and reserved for use by the clerk of court. FL ST J ADMIN Rule 2.520(d).
      i. *Exceptions to recording space.* Any papers or documents created by persons or entities over which the filing party has no control, including but not limited to wills, codicils, trusts, or other testamentary documents; documents prepared or executed by any public officer; documents prepared, executed, acknowledged, or proved outside of the State of Florida; or documents created by State or Federal government agencies, may be filed without the space required by FL ST J ADMIN Rule 2.520. FL ST J ADMIN Rule 2.520(e).
   c. *Noncompliance.* No clerk of court is permitted to refuse to file any document or paper because of noncompliance with the Florida Rules of Judicial Administration. However, upon request of the clerk of court, noncomplying documents must be resubmitted in accordance with the formatting rules. FL ST J ADMIN Rule 2.520(f).
2. *Caption.* Every pleading, motion, order, judgment, or other paper shall have a caption containing the name of the court, the file number, and except for in rem proceedings, including forfeiture proceedings, the name of the first party on each side with an appropriate indication of other parties, and a designation identifying the party filing it and its nature or the nature of the order, as the case may be. In any in rem proceeding, every pleading, motion, order, judgment, or other paper shall have a caption containing the name of the court, the file number, the style "In re" (followed by the name or general description of the property), and a designation of the person or entity filing it and its nature or the nature of the order, as the case may be. In an in rem forfeiture proceeding, the style shall be "In re forfeiture of" (followed by the name of the general description of the property). All papers filed in the action shall be styled in such a manner as to indicate clearly the subject matter of the paper and the party requesting or obtaining relief. FL ST RCP Rule 1.100(c)(1).
3. *Writing and written defined.* Writing or written means a document containing information, an application, or a stipulation. FL ST RCP Rule 1.080(c).
4. *Rule abbreviations*
   a. The Florida Rules of Civil Procedure and shall be abbreviated as Fla.R.Civ.P. FL ST RCP Rule 1.010.
   b. The Florida Rules of Judicial Administration shall be abbreviated as Fla. R. Jud. Admin. FL ST J ADMIN Rule 2.110.
5. *Nonverification.* Except when otherwise specifically provided by the Florida Rules of Civil Procedure or an applicable statute, every pleading or other document of a party represented by an attorney need not be verified or accompanied by an affidavit. FL ST RCP Rule 1.030; FL ST J ADMIN Rule 2.515(a).
6. *Attorney signature*
   a. *Attorney signature.* Every pleading and other document of a party represented by an attorney shall be signed by at least one (1) attorney of record in that attorney's individual name whose current record

Florida Bar address, telephone number, including area code, primary e-mail address and secondary e-mail addresses, if any, and Florida Bar number shall be stated, and who shall be duly licensed to practice law in Florida or who shall have received permission to appear in the particular case as provided in FL ST J ADMIN Rule 2.510. FL ST J ADMIN Rule 2.515(a).

i. The attorney may be required by the court to give the address of, and to vouch for the attorney's authority to represent, the party. FL ST J ADMIN Rule 2.515(a).

ii. The signature of an attorney shall constitute a certificate by the attorney that the attorney has read the pleading or other document; that to the best of the attorney's knowledge, information, and belief there is good ground to support it; and that it is not interposed for delay. FL ST J ADMIN Rule 2.515(a).

iii. If a pleading is not signed or is signed with intent to defeat the purpose of FL ST J ADMIN Rule 2.515, it may be stricken and the action may proceed as though the pleading or other document had not been served. FL ST J ADMIN Rule 2.515(a).

b. *Pro se litigant signature.* A party who is not represented by an attorney shall sign any pleading or other paper and state the party's address and telephone number, including area code. FL ST J ADMIN Rule 2.515(b).

c. *Form of signature*

i. The signatures required on pleadings and documents by FL ST J ADMIN Rule 2.515(a) and FL ST J ADMIN Rule 2.515(b) may be:

- Original signatures;
- Original signatures that have been reproduced by electronic means, such as on electronically transmitted documents or photocopied documents;
- Electronic signatures using the "/s/," "s/," or "/s" formats by or at the direction of the person signing; or
- Any other signature format authorized by general law, so long as the clerk where the proceeding is pending has the capability of receiving and has obtained approval from the Supreme Court of Florida to accept pleadings and documents with that signature format. FL ST J ADMIN Rule 2.515(c)(1).

ii. An attorney, party, or other person who files a pleading or paper by electronic transmission that does not contain the original signature of that attorney, party, or other person shall file that identical pleading or paper in paper form containing an original signature of that attorney, party, or other person (hereinafter called the follow-up filing) immediately thereafter. The follow-up filing is not required if the Supreme Court of Florida has entered an order directing the clerk of court to discontinue accepting the follow-up filing. FL ST J ADMIN Rule 2.515(c)(2).

7. *Forms*

a. *Process.* The forms of process, notice of lis pendens, and notice of action provided in the Florida Rules of Civil Procedure are sufficient. Variations from the forms do not void process or notices that are otherwise sufficient. FL ST RCP Rule 1.900(a).

b. *Other forms.* The other forms provided in the Florida Rules of Civil Procedure are sufficient for the matters that are covered by them. So long as the substance is expressed without prolixity, the forms may be varied to meet the facts of a particular case. FL ST RCP Rule 1.900(b).

c. *Formal matters.* Captions, except for the designation of the paper, are omitted from the forms provided in the Florida Rules of Civil Procedure. A general form of caption is the first form provided. Signatures are omitted from pleadings and motions. FL ST RCP Rule 1.900(c).

8. *Notices to persons with disabilities.* All notices of court proceedings to be held in a public facility, and all process compelling appearance at such proceedings, shall include the following statement in bold face, fourteen (14) point Times New Roman or Courier font: "If you are a person with a disability who needs any accommodation in order to participate in this proceeding, you are entitled, at no cost to you, to the provision of certain assistance. Please contact [identify applicable court personnel by name, address, and

telephone number] at least seven (7) days before your scheduled court appearance, or immediately upon receiving this notification if the time before the scheduled appearance is less than seven (7) days; if you are hearing or voice impaired, call 711." FL ST J ADMIN Rule 2.540(c)(1).

9. *Minimization of the filing of sensitive information*
   a. *Limitations for court filings.* Unless authorized by FL ST J ADMIN Rule 2.425(b), statute, another rule of court, or the court orders otherwise, designated sensitive information filed with the court must be limited to the following format:
      i. The initials of a person known to be a minor;
      ii. The year of birth of a person's birth date;
      iii. No portion of any: Social security number, Bank account number, Credit card account number, Charge account number, or Debit account number;
      iv. The last four digits of any: Taxpayer identification number (TIN), Employee identification number, Driver's license number, Passport number, Telephone number, Financial account number, except as set forth in FL ST J ADMIN Rule 2.425(a)(3), Brokerage account number, Insurance policy account number, Loan account number, Customer account number, or Patient or health care number;
      v. A truncated version of any: Email address, Computer user name, Password, or Personal identification number (PIN); and
      vi. A truncated version of any other sensitive information as provided by court order. FL ST J ADMIN Rule 2.425(a).
   b. *Exceptions.* FL ST J ADMIN Rule 2.425(a) does not apply to the following:
      i. An account number which identifies the property alleged to be the subject of a proceeding;
      ii. The record of an administrative or agency proceeding;
      iii. The record in appellate or review proceedings;
      iv. The birth date of a minor whenever the birth date is necessary for the court to establish or maintain subject matter jurisdiction;
      v. The name of a minor in any order relating to parental responsibility, time-sharing, or child support;
      vi. The name of a minor in any document or order affecting the minor's ownership of real property;
      vii. The birth date of a party in a writ of attachment or notice to payor;
      viii. In traffic and criminal proceedings: a pro se filing; a court filing that is related to a criminal matter or investigation and that is prepared before the filing of a criminal charge or is not filed as part of any docketed criminal case; an arrest or search warrant or any information in support thereof; a charging document and an affidavit or other documents filed in support of any charging document, including any driving records; a statement of particulars; discovery material introduced into evidence or otherwise filed with the court; and all information necessary for the proper issuance and execution of a subpoena duces tecum;
      ix. Information used by the clerk for case maintenance purposes or the courts for case management purposes; and
      x. Information which is relevant and material to an issue before the court. FL ST J ADMIN Rule 2.425(b).
   c. *Remedies.* Upon motion by a party or interested person or sua sponte by the court, the court may order remedies, sanctions or both for a violation of FL ST J ADMIN Rule 2.425(a). Following notice and an opportunity to respond, the court may impose sanctions if such filing was not made in good faith. FL ST J ADMIN Rule 2.425(c).
   d. *Motions not restricted.* FL ST J ADMIN Rule 2.425 does not restrict a party's right to move for protective order, to move to file documents under seal, or to request a determination of the confidentiality of records. FL ST J ADMIN Rule 2.425(d).

e. *Application.* FL ST J ADMIN Rule 2.425 does not affect the application of constitutional provisions, statutes, or rules of court regarding confidential information or access to public information. FL ST J ADMIN Rule 2.425(e).

F. Filing and Service Requirements

1. *Court filing of documents and discovery.* Information obtained during discovery shall not be filed with the court until such time as it is filed for good cause. The requirement of good cause is satisfied only where the filing of the information is allowed or required by another applicable rule of procedure or by court order. All filings of discovery documents shall comply with FL ST J ADMIN Rule 2.425. The court shall have the authority to impose sanctions for violation of FL ST RCP Rule 1.280. FL ST RCP Rule 1.280(g).

   a. *Filing of copies.* A copy of a deposition may be filed only under the following circumstances:

      i. It may be filed in compliance with FL ST J ADMIN Rule 2.425 and FL ST RCP Rule 1.280(f) by a party or the witness when the contents of the deposition must be considered by the court on any matter pending before the court. Prompt notice of the filing of the deposition shall be given to all parties unless notice is waived. A party filing the deposition shall furnish a copy of the deposition or the part being filed to other parties unless the party already has a copy. FL ST RCP Rule 1.310(f)(3)(A).

      ii. If the court determines that a deposition previously taken is necessary for the decision of a matter pending before the court, the court may order that a copy be filed by any party at the initial cost of the party, and the filing party shall comply with FL ST J ADMIN Rule 2.425 and FL ST RCP Rule 1.280(f). FL ST RCP Rule 1.310(f)(3)(B).

2. *Filing requirements.* All original documents must be filed with the court either before service or immediately thereafter, unless otherwise provided for by general law or other rules. If the original of any bond or other document is not placed in the court file, a certified copy must be so placed by the clerk. FL ST J ADMIN Rule 2.516(d). All documents shall be filed in conformity with the requirements of FL ST J ADMIN Rule 2.525. FL ST RCP Rule 1.080(b). All documents filed in any court shall be filed by electronic transmission in accordance with FL ST J ADMIN Rule 2.525. "Documents" means pleadings, motions, petitions, memoranda, briefs, notices, exhibits, declarations, affidavits, orders, judgments, decrees, writs, opinions, and any other paper or writing submitted to a court. FL ST J ADMIN Rule 2.520(a). All documents that are court records, as defined in FL ST J ADMIN Rule 2.430(a)(1), must be filed by electronic transmission, provided that: (1) the clerk has the ability to accept and retain such documents; (2) the clerk or the chief judge of the circuit has requested permission to accept documents filed by electronic transmission; and (3) the supreme court has entered an order granting permission to the clerk to accept documents filed by electronic transmission. FL ST J ADMIN Rule 2.525(c)(1).

   a. *Definition.* "Electronic transmission of documents" means the sending of information by electronic signals to, by or from a court or clerk, which when received can be transformed and stored or transmitted on paper, microfilm, magnetic storage device, optical imaging system, CD-ROM, flash drive, other electronic data storage system, server, case maintenance system ("CM"), electronic court filing ("ECF") system, statewide or local electronic portal ("e-portal"), or other electronic record keeping system authorized by the supreme court in a format sufficient to communicate the information on the original document in a readable format. Electronic transmission of documents includes electronic mail ("e-mail") and any internet-based transmission procedure, and may include procedures allowing for documents to be signed or verified by electronic means. FL ST J ADMIN Rule 2.525(a).

      i. The filing of documents with the court as required by the Florida Rules of Judicial Administration must be made by filing them with the clerk in accordance with FL ST J ADMIN Rule 2.525, except that the judge may permit documents to be filed with the judge, in which event the judge must note the filing date before him or her on the documents and transmit them to the clerk. The date of filing is that shown on the face of the document by the judge's notation or the clerk's time stamp, whichever is earlier. FL ST J ADMIN Rule 2.516(e).

   b. *Application.* Any court or clerk of the court may accept the electronic transmission of documents for filing after the clerk, together with input from the chief judge of the circuit, has obtained approval of the procedures and program for doing so from the Supreme Court of Florida. FL ST J ADMIN Rule 2.525(b).

c. *Exceptions*

i. Paper documents and other submissions may be manually submitted to the clerk or court:

- When the clerk does not have the ability to accept and retain documents by electronic filing or has not had ECF Procedures approved by the supreme court;
- For filing by any self-represented party or any self-represented nonparty unless specific ECF Procedures provide a means to file documents electronically. However, any self-represented nonparty that is a governmental or public agency and any other agency, partnership, corporation, or business entity acting on behalf of any governmental or public agency may file documents by electronic transmission if such entity has the capability of filing documents electronically;
- For filing by attorneys excused from e-mail service in accordance with FL ST J ADMIN Rule 2.516(b);
- When submitting evidentiary exhibits or filing non-documentary materials;
- When the filing involves documents in excess of twenty-five (25) megabytes (25MB) in size. For such filings, documents may be transmitted using an electronic storage medium that the clerk has the ability to accept, which may include a CD-ROM, flash drive, or similar storage medium;
- When filed in open court, as permitted by the court;
- When paper filing is permitted by any approved statewide or local ECF procedures; and
- If any court determines that justice so requires. FL ST J ADMIN Rule 2.525(d).

ii. Any document in paper form submitted under FL ST J ADMIN Rule 2.525(d) is filed when it is received by the clerk or court and the clerk shall immediately thereafter convert any filed paper document to an electronic document. "Convert to an electronic document" means optically capturing an image of a paper document and using character recognition software to recover as much of the document's text as practicable and then indexing and storing the document in the official court file. FL ST J ADMIN Rule 2.525(c)(4).

iii. Any storage medium submitted under FL ST J ADMIN Rule 2.525(d)(5) is filed when received by the clerk or court and the clerk shall immediately thereafter transfer the electronic documents from the storage device to the official court file. FL ST J ADMIN Rule 2.525(c)(5).

iv. If the filer of any paper document authorized under FL ST J ADMIN Rule 2.525(d) provides a self-addressed, postage-paid envelope for return of the paper document after it is converted to electronic form by the clerk, the clerk shall place the paper document in the envelope and deposit it in the mail. Except when a paper document is required to be maintained, the clerk may recycle any filed paper document that is not to be returned to the filer. FL ST J ADMIN Rule 2.525(c)(6).

v. The clerk may convert any paper document filed before the effective date of FL ST J ADMIN Rule 2.525 to an electronic document. Unless the clerk is required to maintain the paper document, if the paper document has been converted to an electronic document by the clerk, the paper document is no longer part of the official court file and may be removed and recycled. FL ST J ADMIN Rule 2.525(c)(7).

d. *Official court file.* For information on what constitutes the official court file, please see FL ST J ADMIN Rule 2.525(c)(2), FL ST J ADMIN Rule 2.525(c)(3).

e. *Administration.* All attorneys, parties, or other persons using this rule to file documents are required to make arrangements with the court or clerk for the payment of any charges authorized by general law or the supreme court before filing any document by electronic transmission. FL ST J ADMIN Rule 2.525(f)(2).

f. *Filing date.* The filing date for an electronically transmitted document is the date and time that such filing is acknowledged by an electronic stamp or otherwise, pursuant to any procedure set forth in any ECF Procedures approved by the supreme court, or the date the last page of such filing is received by the court or clerk. FL ST J ADMIN Rule 2.525(f)(3).

g. *Accessibility.* All documents transmitted in any electronic form under FL ST J ADMIN Rule 2.525 must comply with the accessibility requirements of FL ST J ADMIN Rule 2.526. FL ST J ADMIN Rule 2.525(g).

3. *Service requirements.* Every pleading subsequent to the initial pleading, all orders, and every other document filed in the action must be served in conformity with the requirements of FL ST J ADMIN Rule 2.516. FL ST RCP Rule 1.080(a).

   a. *Service; When required.* Unless the court otherwise orders, or a statute or supreme court administrative order specifies a different means of service, every pleading subsequent to the initial pleading and every other document filed in any court proceeding, except applications for witness subpoenas and documents served by formal notice or required to be served in the manner provided for service of formal notice, must be served in accordance with FL ST J ADMIN Rule 2.516 on each party. No service need be made on parties against whom a default has been entered, except that pleadings asserting new or additional claims against them must be served in the manner provided for service of summons. FL ST J ADMIN Rule 2.516(a).

   b. *Service; How made.* When service is required or permitted to be made upon a party represented by an attorney, service must be made upon the attorney unless service upon the party is ordered by the court. FL ST J ADMIN Rule 2.516(b).

      i. *Service by electronic mail ("e-mail").* All documents required or permitted to be served on another party must be served by e-mail, unless FL ST J ADMIN Rule 2.516 otherwise provides. When, in addition to service by e-mail, the sender also utilizes another means of service provided for in FL ST J ADMIN Rule 2.516(b)(2), any differing time limits and other provisions applicable to that other means of service control. FL ST J ADMIN Rule 2.516(b)(1). Any document electronically transmitted to a court or clerk must also be served on all parties and interested persons in accordance with the applicable rules of court. FL ST J ADMIN Rule 2.525(e)(2).

         - *Service on attorneys.* Upon appearing in a proceeding, an attorney must serve a designation of a primary e-mail address and may designate no more than two (2) secondary e-mail addresses. Thereafter, service must be directed to all designated e-mail addresses in that proceeding. Every document filed by an attorney thereafter must include the primary e-mail address of that attorney and any secondary e-mail addresses. If an attorney does not designate any e-mail address for service, documents may be served on that attorney at the e-mail address on record with The Florida Bar. FL ST J ADMIN Rule 2.516(b)(1)(A).
         - *Exception to e-mail service on attorneys.* Service by an attorney on another attorney must be made by e-mail unless excused by the court. Upon motion by an attorney demonstrating that the attorney has no e-mail account and lacks access to the Internet at the attorney's office, the court may excuse the attorney from the requirements of e-mail service. Service on and by an attorney excused by the court from e-mail service must be by the means provided in FL ST J ADMIN Rule 2.516(b)(2). FL ST J ADMIN Rule 2.516(b)(1)(B).
         - *Service on and by parties not represented by an attorney.* Any party not represented by an attorney may serve a designation of a primary e-mail address and also may designate no more than two (2) secondary e-mail addresses to which service must be directed in that proceeding by the means provided in FL ST J ADMIN Rule 2.516(b)(1). If a party not represented by an attorney does not designate an e-mail address for service in a proceeding, service on and by that party must be by the means provided in FL ST J ADMIN Rule 2.516(b)(2). FL ST J ADMIN Rule 2.516(b)(1)(C).
         - *Time of service.* Service by e-mail is complete when it is sent. FL ST J ADMIN Rule 2.516(b)(1)(D). An e-mail is deemed served on the date it is sent. FL ST J ADMIN Rule 2.516(b)(1)(D)(i). If the sender learns that the e-mail did not reach the address of the person to be served, the sender must immediately send another copy by e-mail, or by a means authorized by FL ST J ADMIN Rule 2.516(b)(2). FL ST J ADMIN Rule 2.516(b)(1)(D)(ii). E-mail service is treated as service by mail for the computation of time. FL ST J ADMIN Rule 2.516(b)(1)(D)(iii).

ii. *Format of e-mail for service.* Service of a document by e-mail is made by attaching a copy of the document in PDF format to an e-mail sent to all addresses designated by the attorney or party. FL ST J ADMIN Rule 2.516(b)(1)(E).

- All documents served by e-mail must be attached to an e-mail message containing a subject line beginning with the words "SERVICE OF COURT DOCUMENT" in all capital letters, followed by the case number of the proceeding in which the documents are being served. FL ST J ADMIN Rule 2.516(b)(1)(E)(i).
- The body of the e-mail must identify the court in which the proceeding is pending, the case number, the name of the initial party on each side, the title of each document served with that e-mail, and the sender's name and telephone number. FL ST J ADMIN Rule 2.516(b)(1)(E)(ii).
- Any document served by e-mail may be signed by the "/s/" format, as long as the filed original is signed in accordance with the applicable rule of procedure. FL ST J ADMIN Rule 2.516(b)(1)(E)(iii).
- Any e-mail which, together with its attached documents, exceeds five megabytes (5MB) in size, must be divided and sent as separate e-mails, no one of which may exceed five megabytes (5MB) in size and each of which must be sequentially numbered in the subject line. FL ST J ADMIN Rule 2.516(b)(1)(E)(iv).

iii. *Service by other means.* In addition to, and not in lieu of, service by e-mail, service may also be made upon attorneys by any of the means specified in FL ST J ADMIN Rule 2.516(b)(2). Service on and by all parties who are not represented by an attorney and who do not designate an e-mail address, and on and by all attorneys excused from e-mail service, must be made by delivering a copy of the document or by mailing it to the party or attorney at their last known address or, if no address is known, by leaving it with the clerk of the court. Service by mail is complete upon mailing. Delivery of a copy within FL ST J ADMIN Rule 2.516 is complete upon:

- Handing it to the attorney or to the party,
- Leaving it at the attorney's or party's office with a clerk or other person in charge thereof,
- If there is no one in charge, leaving it in a conspicuous place therein,
- If the office is closed or the person to be served has no office, leaving it at the person's usual place of abode with some person of his or her family above fifteen (15) years of age and informing such person of the contents, or
- Transmitting it by facsimile to the attorney's or party's office with a cover sheet containing the sender's name, firm, address, telephone number, and facsimile number, and the number of pages transmitted. When service is made by facsimile, a copy must also be served by any other method permitted by FL ST J ADMIN Rule 2.516. Facsimile service occurs when transmission is complete. FL ST J ADMIN Rule 2.516(b)(2)(A) through FL ST J ADMIN Rule 2.516(b)(2)(E).
- Service by delivery after 5:00 p.m. must be deemed to have been made by mailing on the date of delivery. FL ST J ADMIN Rule 2.516(b)(2)(F).

c. *Service; Numerous defendants.* In actions when the parties are unusually numerous, the court may regulate the service contemplated by the Florida Rules of Judicial Administration on motion or on its own initiative in such manner as may be found to be just and reasonable. FL ST J ADMIN Rule 2.516(c).

d. *Service by clerk.* Service of notices and other documents required to be made by the clerk must also be done as provided in FL ST J ADMIN Rule 2.516(b). FL ST J ADMIN Rule 2.516(g).

e. *Standards of professional courtesy; Service*

i. The timing and manner of service should not be used to the disadvantage of the party receiving the papers. This includes the use of facsimile transmissions and any additional expedited means of communication approved by the court. FL ST 6 J CIR 2009-066 PA/PI-CIR(C)(1).

ii. Attorneys will not serve papers to take advantage of opposing counsel's known absence from the office or at a time or in a manner designed to inconvenience an opponent, such as late on Friday afternoon or the day preceding a secular or religious holiday. FL ST 6 J CIR 2009-066 PA/PI-CIR(C)(2).

iii. Attorneys will not serve papers, including briefs and memoranda, so close to a court appearance that the ability of opposing counsel to prepare for that appearance or, where permitted, to respond, is inhibited. FL ST 6 J CIR 2009-066 PA/PI-CIR(C)(3).

iv. Service should be made personally or by facsimile transmission when it is likely that service by mail, even when allowed, will prejudice the opposing party. FL ST 6 J CIR 2009-066 PA/PI-CIR(C)(4).

G. Hearings

1. There is no hearing required or contemplated with regard to responses to requests for admission in the Florida Rules of Civil Procedure.

H. Forms

1. Official Notice of Deposition Forms for Florida

a. Caption. FL ST RCP Form 1.901.

2. Notice of Deposition Forms for Florida

a. Form for motion by plaintiff for leave to take deposition within 20-day period. FL-RCPF R 1.310(6).
b. Form for order on motion for leave to take deposition within 20-day period. FL-RCPF R 1.310(8).
c. Notice of examination; Time and place. FL-RCPF R 1.310(9).
d. Nonparty witness, subpoena required. FL-RCPF R 1.310(10).
e. Form for notice to take deposition on oral examination. FL-RCPF R 1.310(11).
f. Form for notice of taking multiple depositions. FL-RCPF R 1.310(11.1).
g. Form for notice of taking deposition and examination of documents. FL-RCPF R 1.310(12).
h. Form for notice of taking video deposition duces tecum. FL-RCPF R 1.310(13).
i. Form for motion to modify time for taking deposition. FL-RCPF R 1.310(14).
j. Form for motion to take deposition by telephone. FL-RCPF R 1.310(16).
k. Form for order permitting deposition by telephone. FL-RCPF R 1.310(17).
l. Form for notice of taking deposition by telephone. FL-RCPF R 1.310(18).
m. Form for notice of deposition upon written questions. FL-RCPF R 1.320(2).
n. Form of questions. FL-RCPF R 1.320(3).
o. Form of cross-questions. FL-RCPF R 1.320(4).
p. Form for objection to form of written questions. FL-RCPF R 1.320(6).

I. Checklist

(I) ❑ Matters to be considered by deposing party (oral depositions)
- (a) ❑ Required documents
  - (1) ❑ Notice of deposition
  - (2) ❑ Certificate of service
- (b) ❑ Supplemental documents
  - (1) ❑ Motion for leave to request deposition
  - (2) ❑ Subpoena
  - (3) ❑ Request for production of documents

(c) ❑ Time for service of notice of deposition

(1) ❑ After commencement of action

(2) ❑ Within thirty (30) days after service of initial pleadings by leave of court only

(II) ❑ Matters to be considered by deponent (oral depositions)

(a) ❑ Required documents

(1) ❑ Production of documents (if subpoenaed)

(III) ❑ Matters to be considered by deposing party (depositions by written questions)

(a) ❑ Required documents

(1) ❑ Notice of deposition

(2) ❑ Written questions

(3) ❑ Certificate of service

(b) ❑ Supplemental documents

(1) ❑ Motion for leave to request deposition

(2) ❑ Subpoena

(3) ❑ Request for production of documents

(c) ❑ Time for service of direct and redirect questions

(1) ❑ Within ten (10) days after being served with cross questions, a party may serve redirect questions upon all other parties

(2) ❑ Objections to the form of the question must be served within the time for service of redirect questions or ten (10) days after service of recross questions

(IV) ❑ Matters to be considered by deponent (depositions by written questions)

(a) ❑ Required documents

(1) ❑ Cross questions, with certificate of service

(2) ❑ Recross questions with certificate of service

(b) ❑ Time for service of cross and recross questions

(1) ❑ Within thirty (30) days after the notice and written questions are served, a party may serve cross questions upon all other parties

(2) ❑ Within ten (10) days after being served with redirect questions, a party may serve recross questions upon all other parties

(3) ❑ Objections to the form of the questions must be served within the time for serving succeeding questions

SEVENTH JUDICIAL CIRCUIT

Pleadings
Complaint

Document Last Updated January 2013

A. Applicable Rules

1. *State rules*
   a. Nonverification of pleadings. FL ST RCP Rule 1.030.
   b. When action commenced. FL ST RCP Rule 1.050.
   c. Process. FL ST RCP Rule 1.070.
   d. Constitutional challenge to state statute or county or municipal charter, ordinance, or franchise; Notice by party. FL ST RCP Rule 1.071.
   e. Service and filing of pleadings, orders, and documents. FL ST RCP Rule 1.080.
   f. Time. FL ST RCP Rule 1.090.
   g. Pleadings and motions. FL ST RCP Rule 1.100; FL ST RCP Rule 1.110; FL ST RCP Rule 1.120; FL ST RCP Rule 1.130; FL ST RCP Rule 1.170; FL ST RCP Rule 1.430.
   h. Relief from judgment, decrees, or orders. FL ST RCP Rule 1.540.
   i. Forms. FL ST RCP Rule 1.900.
   j. Minimization of the filing of sensitive information. FL ST J ADMIN Rule 2.425.
   k. Retention of court records. FL ST J ADMIN Rule 2.430.
   l. Foreign attorneys. FL ST J ADMIN Rule 2.510.
   m. Signature of attorneys and parties. FL ST J ADMIN Rule 2.515.
   n. Paper. FL ST J ADMIN Rule 2.520.
   o. Electronic filing. FL ST J ADMIN Rule 2.525.
   p. Accessibility of information and technology. FL ST J ADMIN Rule 2.526.
   q. Requests for accommodations by persons with disabilities. FL ST J ADMIN Rule 2.540.
   r. Service. FL ST § 48.011; FL ST § 48.021; FL ST § 48.031; FL ST § 48.041; FL ST § 48.042; FL ST § 48.051; FL ST § 48.061; FL ST § 48.071; FL ST § 48.081; FL ST § 48.091; FL ST § 48.101; FL ST § 48.111; FL ST § 48.121; FL ST § 48.131; FL ST § 48.141; FL ST § 48.151; FL ST § 48.161; FL ST § 48.171; FL ST § 48.181; FL ST § 48.183; FL ST § 48.19; FL ST § 48.193; FL ST § 48.194; FL ST § 48.20; FL ST § 48.21; FL ST § 48.25; FL ST § 48.31; FL ST § 49.011; FL ST § 49.021; FL ST § 49.031; FL ST § 49.041; FL ST § 49.051; FL ST § 49.061; FL ST § 49.071; FL ST § 49.08; FL ST § 49.09; FL ST § 49.10; FL ST § 49.11; FL ST § 49.12; FL ST § 50.011; FL ST § 50.021; FL ST § 50.031; FL ST § 50.041; FL ST § 50.051; FL ST § 50.061.
   s. Fees. FL ST § 57.081; FL ST § 57.085; FL ST § 28.241; FL ST § 34.041.
2. *Local rules*
   a. Eminent domain cases. FL ST 7 J CIR CV-2000-011-VL.
   b. Civil pretrial procedures. FL ST 7 J CIR CV-2003-002-SC.
   c. Arbitration and mediation. FL ST 7 J CIR CV-2008-018-SC; FL ST 7 J CIR CV-2009-019-SC.
   d. Indigent status. FL ST 7 J CIR CV-2009-006-SC.
   e. Filing fee for petitions for 90-day extension in actions for personal injury or wrongful death arising out of medical negligence. FL ST 7 J CIR CV-2006-005-SC.

f. Assignment to judge or division Volusia County. FL ST 7 J CIR CV-2008-010-VL.

g. Service of civil process, St. Johns County. FL ST 7 J CIR CV-2009-021-SJ.

B. Timing

1. *Commencement of an action.* Every action of a civil nature shall be deemed commenced when the complaint or petition is filed except that ancillary proceedings shall be deemed commenced when the writ is issued or the pleading setting forth the claim of the party initiating the action is filed. FL ST RCP Rule 1.050.

2. *Summons; Time limit.* If service of the initial process and initial pleading is not made upon a defendant within one hundred twenty (120) days after filing of the initial pleading directed to that defendant the court, on its own initiative after notice or on motion, shall direct that service be effected within a specified time or shall dismiss the action without prejudice or drop that defendant as a party; provided that if the plaintiff shows good cause or excusable neglect for the failure, the court shall extend the time for service for an appropriate period. FL ST RCP Rule 1.070(j).

3. *Computation of time*

   a. *Generally.* Computation of time shall be governed by FL ST J ADMIN Rule 2.514. FL ST RCP Rule 1.090(a). The following rules apply in computing time periods specified in any rule of procedure, local rule, court order, or statute that does not specify a method of computing time. FL ST J ADMIN Rule 2.514(a).

      i. *Period stated in days or a longer unit.* When the period is stated in days or a longer unit of time (A) exclude the day of the event that triggers the period; (B) count every day, including intermediate Saturdays, Sundays, and legal holidays; and (C) include the last day of the period, but if the last day is a Saturday, Sunday, or legal holiday, or falls within any period of time extended through an order of the chief justice under FL ST J ADMIN Rule 2.205(a)(2)(B)(iv), the period continues to run until the end of the next day that is not a Saturday, Sunday, or legal holiday and does not fall within any period of time extended through an order of the chief justice. FL ST J ADMIN Rule 2.514(a)(1).

      ii. *Period stated in hours.* When the period is stated in hours (A) begin counting immediately on the occurrence of the event that triggers the period; (B) count every hour, including hours during intermediate Saturdays, Sundays, and legal holidays; and (C) if the period would end on a Saturday, Sunday, or legal holiday, or during any period of time extended through an order of the chief justice under FL ST J ADMIN Rule 2.205(a)(2)(B)(iv), the period continues to run until the same time on the next day that is not a Saturday, Sunday, or legal holiday and does not fall within any period of time extended through an order of the chief justice. FL ST J ADMIN Rule 2.514(a)(2).

      iii. *Period stated in days less than seven (7) days.* When the period stated in days is less than seven (7) days, intermediate Saturdays, Sundays, and legal holidays shall be excluded in the computation. FL ST J ADMIN Rule 2.514(a)(3).

      iv. *"Last day" defined.* Unless a different time is set by a statute, local rule, or court order, the last day ends (A) for electronic filing or for service by any means, at midnight; and (B) for filing by other means, when the clerk's office is scheduled to close. FL ST J ADMIN Rule 2.514(a)(4).

      v. *"Next day" defined.* The "next day" is determined by continuing to count forward when the period is measured after an event and backward when measured before an event. FL ST J ADMIN Rule 2.514(a)(5).

      vi. *"Legal holiday" defined.* "Legal holiday" means (A) the day set aside by FL ST § 110.117, for observing New Year's Day, Martin Luther King, Jr.'s Birthday, Memorial Day, Independence Day, Labor Day, Veterans' Day, Thanksgiving Day, the Friday after Thanksgiving Day, or Christmas Day, and (B) any day observed as a holiday by the clerk's office or as designated by the chief judge. FL ST J ADMIN Rule 2.514(a)(6).

   b. *Additional time after service by mail or e-mail.* When a party may or must act within a specified time after service and service is made by mail or e-mail, five (5) days are added after the period that would otherwise expire under FL ST J ADMIN Rule 2.514(a). FL ST J ADMIN Rule 2.514(b).

c. *Enlargement.* When an act is required or allowed to be done at or within a specified time by order of court, by the Florida Rules of Civil Procedure, or by notice given thereunder, for cause shown the court at any time in its discretion (1) with or without notice, may order the period enlarged if request therefor is made before the expiration of the period originally prescribed or as extended by a previous order, or (2) upon motion made and notice after the expiration of the specified period, may permit the act to be done when failure to act was the result of excusable neglect, but it may not extend the time for making a motion for new trial, for rehearing, or to alter or amend a judgment; making a motion for relief from a judgment under FL ST RCP Rule 1.540(b); taking an appeal or filing a petition for certiorari; or making a motion for a directed verdict. FL ST RCP Rule 1.090(b).

d. *Unaffected by expiration of term.* The period of time provided for the doing of any act or the taking of any proceeding shall not be affected or limited by the continued existence or expiration of a term of court. The continued existence or expiration of a term of court in no way affects the power of a court to do any act or take any proceeding in any action which is or has been pending before it. FL ST RCP Rule 1.090(c).

C. General Requirements

1. *General rules of pleading*

a. *Claims for relief*

i. A pleading which sets forth a claim for relief, whether an original claim, counterclaim, crossclaim, or third-party claim, must state a cause of action and shall contain

- A short and plain statement of the grounds upon which the court's jurisdiction depends, unless the court already has jurisdiction and the claim needs no new grounds of jurisdiction to support it (For information regarding acts subjecting persons to jurisdiction, please see FL ST § 48.193),
- A short and plain statement of the ultimate facts showing that the pleader is entitled to relief, and
- A demand for judgment for the relief to which the pleader deems himself or herself entitled. FL ST RCP Rule 1.110(b).

ii. Relief in the alternative or of several different types may be demanded. Every complaint shall be considered to demand general relief. FL ST RCP Rule 1.110(b).

b. *Verification.* Except when otherwise specifically provided by these rules or an applicable statute, every pleading or other document of a party represented by an attorney need not be verified or accompanied by an affidavit. FL ST RCP Rule 1.030. When filing an action for foreclosure of a mortgage on residential real property the complaint shall be verified. When verification of a document is required, the document filed shall include an oath, affirmation, or the following statement: "Under penalty of perjury, I declare that I have read the foregoing, and the facts alleged therein are true and correct to the best of my knowledge and belief." FL ST RCP Rule 1.110(b).

c. *Separate statements.* All averments of claim or defense shall be made in consecutively numbered paragraphs, the contents of each of which shall be limited as far as practicable to a statement of a single set of circumstances, and a paragraph may be referred to by number in all subsequent pleadings. Each claim founded upon a separate transaction or occurrence and each defense other than denials shall be stated in a separate count or defense when a separation facilitates the clear presentation of the matter set forth. FL ST RCP Rule 1.110(f).

d. *Statements adopted by reference.* Statements in a pleading may be adopted by reference in a different part of the same pleading, in another pleading, or in any motion. FL ST RCP Rule 1.130(b).

e. *Joinder of causes of action; Consistency.* A pleader may set up in the same action as many claims or causes of action or defenses in the same right as the pleader has, and claims for relief may be stated in the alternative if separate items make up the cause of action, or if two (2) or more causes of action are joined. A party may also set forth two (2) or more statements of a claim or defense alternatively, either in one (1) count or defense or in separate counts or defenses. When two (2) or more statements are made in the alternative and one (1) of them, if made independently, would be sufficient, the pleading is not made insufficient by the insufficiency of one (1) or more of the alternative statements. A party may also state as many separate claims or defenses as that party has, regardless of consistency and whether based on legal or equitable grounds or both. All pleadings shall be construed so as to do substantial justice. FL ST RCP Rule 1.110(g).

f. *Subsequent pleadings.* When the nature of an action permits pleadings subsequent to final judgment and the jurisdiction of the court over the parties has not terminated, the initial pleading subsequent to final judgment shall be designated a supplemental complaint or petition. The action shall then proceed in the same manner and time as though the supplemental complaint or petition were the initial pleading in the action, including the issuance of any needed process. FL ST RCP Rule 1.110(h) shall not apply to proceedings that may be initiated by motion under the Florida Rules of Civil Procedure. FL ST RCP Rule 1.110(h).

g. *Pleading basis for service.* When service of process is to be made under statutes authorizing service on nonresidents of Florida, it is sufficient to plead the basis for service in the language of the statute without pleading the facts supporting service. FL ST RCP Rule 1.070(h).

h. *Forms of pleadings.* Forms of action and technical forms for seeking relief and of pleas, pleadings, or motions are abolished. FL ST RCP Rule 1.110(a).

2. *Complaint; Generally*

   a. *Purpose.* The purpose of a complaint is to advise the court and the defendant of the nature of a cause of action asserted by the plaintiff. FL-PP § 2:12.

   b. *Sufficiency of complaint.* A complaint will be found to be insufficient if it contains only general conclusory allegations unsupported by any facts. The test to determine whether a complaint is sufficient is whether, if the factual allegations of the complaint are established, the plaintiff will be legally or equitably entitled to the claimed relief. Pizzi v. Central Bank & Trust Co., 250 So.2d 895, 896 (Fla. 1971); Bowen v. G H C Properties, Limited, 251 So.2d 359, 361 (Fla. 1st DCA 1971); FL-PP § 2:12. In determining the sufficiency of the complaint to state a cause of action, all allegations of the complaint are taken as true, and possible affirmative defenses are not considered. Strickland v. Commerce Loan Co. of Jacksonville, 158 So.2d 814 (Fla. 1st DCA 1963); FL-PP § 2:12.

      i. The issues for trial in Florida must be settled by the pleadings. The issues cannot be raised by discovery. FL-PRACPROC § 7:6.

      ii. Causes of action may be pleaded alternatively in the same count or in different counts and against the same or different defendants as long as the joinder of parties is proper. FL-PRACPROC § 7:6.

      iii. Each count must state a cause of action. Each independent cause of action should be pleaded in a separate count. FL-PRACPROC § 7:6.

      iv. Incorporation by reference of all allegations from one count to another is not proper. Separate counts facilitate reference to the pleading in which they appear in other pleadings, motions or papers as well as the assertion of defenses against some, but not all, causes of action. Some defenses may not apply to the initial pleading as a whole. FL-PRACPROC § 7:6.

3. *Pleading special matters*

   a. *Capacity.* It is not necessary to aver the capacity of a party to sue or be sued, the authority of a party to sue or be sued in a representative capacity, or the legal existence of an organized association of persons that is made a party, except to the extent required to show the jurisdiction of the court. The initial pleading served on behalf of a minor party shall specifically aver the age of the minor party. When a party desires to raise an issue as to the legal existence of any party, the capacity of any party to sue or be sued, or the authority of a party to sue or be sued in a representative capacity, that party shall do so by specific negative averment which shall include such supporting particulars as are peculiarly within the pleader's knowledge. FL ST RCP Rule 1.120(a).

   b. *Fraud, mistake, condition of the mind.* In all averments of fraud or mistake, the circumstances constituting fraud or mistake shall be stated with such particularity as the circumstances may permit. Malice, intent, knowledge, mental attitude, and other condition of mind of a person may be averred generally. FL ST RCP Rule 1.120(b).

c. *Conditions precedent.* In pleading the performance or occurrence of conditions precedent, it is sufficient to aver generally that all conditions precedent have been performed or have occurred. A denial of performance or occurrence shall be made specifically and with particularity. FL ST RCP Rule 1.120(c).

d. *Official document or act.* In pleading an official document or official act it is sufficient to aver that the document was issued or the act done in compliance with law. FL ST RCP Rule 1.120(c).

e. *Judgment or decree.* In pleading a judgment or decree of a domestic or foreign court, a judicial or quasi-judicial tribunal, or a board or officer, it is sufficient to aver the judgment or decree without setting forth matter showing jurisdiction to render it. FL ST RCP Rule 1.120(e).

f. *Time and place.* For the purpose of testing the sufficiency of a pleading, averments of time and place are material and shall be considered like all other averments of material matter. FL ST RCP Rule 1.120(f).

g. *Special damage.* When items of special damage are claimed, they shall be specifically stated. FL ST RCP Rule 1.120(g).

4. *Parties*

a. *Parties generally.* Every action may be prosecuted in the name of the real party in interest, but a personal representative, administrator, guardian, trustee of an express trust, a party with whom or in whose name a contract has been made for the benefit of another, or a party expressly authorized by statute may sue in that person's own name without joining the party for whose benefit the action is brought. All persons having an interest in the subject of the action and in obtaining the relief demanded may join as plaintiffs and any person may be made a defendant who has or claims an interest adverse to the plaintiff. Any person may at any time be made a party if that person's presence is necessary or proper to a complete determination of the cause. Persons having a united interest may be joined on the same side as plaintiffs or defendants, and anyone who refuses to join may for such reason be made a defendant. FL ST RCP Rule 1.210(a).

b. *Minors or incompetent persons.* When a minor or incompetent person has a representative, such as a guardian or other like fiduciary, the representative may sue or defend on behalf of the minor or incompetent person. A minor or incompetent person who does not have a duly appointed representative may sue by next friend or by a guardian ad litem. The court shall appoint a guardian ad litem for a minor or incompetent person not otherwise represented in an action or shall make such other order as it deems proper for the protection of the minor or incompetent person. FL ST RCP Rule 1.210(b).

c. For survivor and substitution of parties information, please see FL ST RCP Rule 1.260.

d. *Indigent party.* See FL ST 7 J CIR CV-2009-006-SC for procedures to apply for a determination of indigent status.

5. *Counterclaims and crossclaims*

a. *Compulsory counterclaims.* A pleading shall state as a counterclaim any claim which at the time of serving the pleading the pleader has against any opposing party, provided it arises out of the transaction or occurrence that is the subject matter of the opposing party's claim and does not require for its adjudication the presence of third parties over whom the court cannot acquire jurisdiction. But the pleader need not state a claim if (1) at the time the action was commenced the claim was the subject of another pending action, or (2) the opposing party brought suit upon that party's claim by attachment or other process by which the court did not acquire jurisdiction to render a personal judgment on the claim and the pleader is not stating a counterclaim under this rule. FL ST RCP Rule 1.170(a).

b. *Permissive counterclaim.* A pleading may state as a counterclaim any claim against an opposing party not arising out of the transaction or occurrence that is the subject matter of the opposing party's claim. FL ST RCP Rule 1.170(b).

c. *Counterclaim exceeding opposing claim.* A counterclaim may or may not diminish or defeat the recovery sought by the opposing party. It may claim relief exceeding in amount or different in kind from that sought in the pleading of the opposing party. FL ST RCP Rule 1.170(c).

d. *Counterclaim against the State.* The Florida Rules of Civil Procedure shall not be construed to enlarge beyond the limits established by law the right to assert counterclaims or to claim credits against the state or any of its subdivisions or other governmental organizations thereof subject to suit or against a municipal corporation or against an officer, agency, or administrative board of the state. FL ST RCP Rule 1.170(d).

e. *Counterclaim maturing or acquired after pleading.* A claim which matured or was acquired by the pleader after serving the pleading may be presented as a counterclaim by supplemental pleading with the permission of the court. FL ST RCP Rule 1.170(e).

f. *Omitted counterclaim or crossclaim.* When a pleader fails to set up a counterclaim or crossclaim through oversight, inadvertence, or excusable neglect, or when justice requires, the pleader may set up the counterclaim or crossclaim by amendment with leave of the court. FL ST RCP Rule 1.170(f).

g. *Crossclaim against co-party.* A pleading may state as a crossclaim any claim by one party against a co-party arising out of the transaction or occurrence that is the subject matter of either the original action or a counterclaim therein, or relating to any property that is the subject matter of the original action. The crossclaim may include a claim that the party against whom it is asserted is or may be liable to the crossclaimant for all or part of a claim asserted in the action against the crossclaimant. Service of a crossclaim on a party who has appeared in the action shall be made pursuant to FL ST RCP Rule 1.080. Service of a crossclaim against a party who has not appeared in the action shall be made in the manner provided for service of summons. FL ST RCP Rule 1.170(g).

h. *Additional parties may be brought in.* When the presence of parties other than those to the original action is required to grant complete relief in the determination of a counterclaim or crossclaim, they shall be named in the counterclaim or crossclaim and be served with process and shall be parties to the action thereafter if jurisdiction of them can be obtained and their joinder will not deprive the court of jurisdiction of the action. FL ST RCP Rule 1.250(b) and FL ST RCP Rule 1.250(c) apply to parties brought in under FL ST RCP Rule 1.170(h). FL ST RCP Rule 1.170(h).

i. *Separate trials; Separate judgment.* If the court orders separate trials as provided in FL ST RCP Rule 1.270(b), judgment on a counterclaim or crossclaim may be rendered when the court has jurisdiction to do so even if a claim of the opposing party has been dismissed or otherwise disposed of. FL ST RCP Rule 1.170(i).

j. *Demand exceeding jurisdiction; Transfer of action.* If the demand of any counterclaim or crossclaim exceeds the jurisdiction of the court in which the action is pending, the action shall be transferred forthwith to the court of the same county having jurisdiction of the demand in the counterclaim or crossclaim with only such alterations in the pleadings as are essential. The court shall order the transfer of the action and the transmittal of all papers in it to the proper court if the party asserting the demand exceeding the jurisdiction deposits with the court having jurisdiction a sum sufficient to pay the clerk's service charge in the court to which the action is transferred at the time of filing the counterclaim or crossclaim. Thereupon the original papers and deposit shall be transmitted and filed with a certified copy of the order. The court to which the action is transferred shall have full power and jurisdiction over the demands of all parties. Failure to make the service charge deposit at the time the counterclaim or crossclaim is filed, or within such further time as the court may allow, shall reduce a claim for damages to an amount within the jurisdiction of the court where the action is pending and waive the claim in other cases. FL ST RCP Rule 1.170(j).

6. *Misjoinder and nonjoinder of parties*

a. *Misjoinder.* Misjoinder of parties is not a ground for dismissal of an action. Any claim against a party may be severed and proceeded with separately. FL ST RCP Rule 1.250(a).

b. *Dropping parties.* Parties may be dropped by an adverse party in the manner provided for voluntary dismissal in FL ST RCP Rule 1.420(a)(1) subject to the exception stated in FL ST RCP Rule 1.420. If notice of lis pendens has been filed in the action against a party so dropped, the notice of dismissal shall be recorded and cancels the notice of lis pendens without the necessity of a court order. Parties may be dropped by order of court on its own initiative or the motion of any party at any stage of the action on such terms as are just. FL ST RCP Rule 1.250(b).

c. *Adding parties.* Parties may be added once as a matter of course within the same time that pleadings can be so amended under FL ST RCP Rule 1.190(a). If amendment by leave of court or stipulation of the parties is permitted, parties may be added in the amended pleading without further order of court. Parties may be added by order of court on its own initiative or on motion of any party at any stage of the action and on such terms as are just. FL ST RCP Rule 1.250(c).

7. *Jury demand*
    a. *Right preserved.* The right of trial by jury as declared by the Constitution or by statute shall be preserved to the parties inviolate. FL ST RCP Rule 1.430(a).
    b. *Demand.* Any party may demand a trial by jury of any issue triable of right by a jury by serving upon the other party a demand therefor in writing at any time after commencement of the action and not later than ten (10) days after the service of the last pleading directed to such issue. The demand may be indorsed upon a pleading of the party. FL ST RCP Rule 1.430(b).
    c. *Specification of issues.* In the demand a party may specify the issues that the party wishes so tried; otherwise, the party is deemed to demand trial by jury for all issues so triable. FL ST RCP Rule 1.430(c).
        i. If a party has demanded trial by jury for only some of the issues, any other party may serve a demand for trial by jury of any other or all of the issues triable by jury ten (10) days after service of the demand or such lesser time as the court may order. FL ST RCP Rule 1.430(c).
    d. *Waiver.* A party who fails to serve a demand as required by FL ST RCP Rule 1.430 waives trial by jury. FL ST RCP Rule 1.430(d).
        i. If waived, a jury trial may not be granted without the consent of the parties, but the court may allow an amendment in the proceedings to demand a trial by jury or order a trial by jury on its own motion. FL ST RCP Rule 1.430(d).
        ii. A demand for trial by jury may not be withdrawn without the consent of the parties. FL ST RCP Rule 1.430(d).
8. *Assignment to judge or division, Volusia County*
    a. See FL ST 7 J CIR CV-2008-010-VL for civil divisions in the Circuit and County courts of Volusia County.
    b. Upon the filing of a tobacco related lawsuit, the Clerk of the Circuit Court, in and for Volusia County, Florida, shall assign said case to Division 32.
9. *Arbitration and mediation*
    a. *Referral to arbitration and mediation.* Except as hereinafter provided or as otherwise prohibited by law, the presiding judge may enter an order referring all or any part of a contested civil matter to mediation or arbitration. The parties to any contested civil matter may file a written stipulation to mediate or arbitrate any issue between them at any time. Such stipulation shall be incorporated into the order of referral. FL ST RCP Rule 1.700(a).
    b. *Arbitration*
        i. *Exclusions.* A civil action shall be ordered to arbitration or arbitration in conjunction with mediation upon stipulation of the parties. A civil action may be ordered to arbitration or arbitration in conjunction with mediation upon motion of any party or by the court, if the judge determines the action to be of such a nature that arbitration could be of benefit to the litigants or the court. FL ST RCP Rule 1.800.
            - Under no circumstances may the following categories of actions be referred to arbitration: (1) bond estreatures; (2) habeas corpus or other extraordinary writs; (3) bond validations; (4) civil or criminal contempt; (5) such other matters as may be specified by order of the chief judge in the circuit. FL ST RCP Rule 1.800.
        ii. For more information regarding arbitration, please see FL ST RCP Rule 1.810; FL ST RCP Rule 1.820; FL ST RCP Rule 1.830; FL ST 7 J CIR CV-2009-019-SC; and FL ST 7 J CIR CV-2003-002-SC(1)(c).
    c. *Mediation.* For more information regarding mediation, please see FL ST RCP Rule 1.710; FL ST

RCP Rule 1.720; FL ST RCP Rule 1.730; FL ST RCP Rule 1.750; FL ST 7 J CIR CV-2008-018-SC; and FL ST 7 J CIR CV-2003-002-SC(1).

10. *Rules of court*

   a. *Rules of civil procedure.* The Florida Rules of Civil Procedure apply to all actions of a civil nature and all special statutory proceedings in the circuit courts and county courts except those to which the Florida Probate Rules, the Florida Family Law Rules of Procedure, or the Small Claims Rules apply. FL ST RCP Rule 1.010.

      i. The form, content, procedure, and time for pleading in all special statutory proceedings shall be as prescribed by the statutes governing the proceeding unless the Florida Rules of Civil Procedure specifically provide to the contrary. FL ST RCP Rule 1.010.

      ii. The Florida Rules of Civil Procedure shall be construed to secure the just, speedy, and inexpensive determination of every action. FL ST RCP Rule 1.010.

   b. *Rules of judicial administration.* The Florida Rules of Judicial Administration shall apply to administrative matters in all courts to which the Florida Rules of Judicial Administration are applicable by their terms. The Florida Rules of Judicial Administration shall be construed to secure the speedy and inexpensive determination of every proceeding to which they are applicable. The Florida Rules of Judicial Administration shall supersede all conflicting rules and statutes. FL ST J ADMIN Rule 2.110.

D. Documents

1. *Required documents*

   a. *Summons.* Upon the commencement of the action, summons or other process authorized by law shall be issued forthwith by the clerk or judge under the clerk's or the judge's signature and the seal of the court and delivered for service without praecipe. FL ST RCP Rule 1.070(a).

   b. *Complaint.* See the General Requirements section for the contents of the complaint.

      i. *Notices to persons with disabilities.* See the Format section of this KeyRules document for further information.

   c. *Civil cover sheet.* A civil cover sheet (FL ST RCP Form 1.997) shall be completed and filed with the clerk at the time an initial complaint or petition is filed by the party initiating the action. If the cover sheet is not filed, the clerk shall accept the complaint or petition for filing; but all proceedings in the action shall be abated until a properly executed cover sheet is completed and filed. The clerk shall complete the civil cover sheet for a party appearing pro se. FL ST RCP Rule 1.100(c)(2).

   d. *Return of execution process by process server.* Each person who effects service of process shall note on a return-of-service form attached thereto, the date and time when it comes to hand, the date and time when it is served, the manner of service, the name of the person on whom it was served and, if the person is served in a representative capacity, the position occupied by the person. The return-of-service form must be signed by the person who effects the service of process. However, a person employed by a sheriff who effects the service of process may sign the return-of-service form using an electronic signature certified by the sheriff. FL ST § 48.21(1).

      i. A failure to state the facts or to include the signature required by FL ST § 48.21(1) invalidates the service, but the return is amendable to state the facts or to include the signature at any time on application to the court from which the process issued. On amendment, service is as effective as if the return had originally stated the omitted facts or included the signature. A failure to state all the facts in or to include the signature on the return shall subject the person effecting service to a fine not exceeding $10, in the court's discretion. FL ST § 48.21(2).

   e. *Filing fees.* Filing fees are due at the time a party files a pleading to initiate a proceeding or files a pleading for relief. FL ST § 28.241. For a fee schedule, see FL ST § 28.241.

      i. The Seventh Circuit has established a filing fee for petitions for ninety (90) day extension in actions for personal injury or wrongful death arising out of medical negligence. See FL ST 7 J CIR CV-2006-005-SC.

2. *Supplemental documents*
   a. *Exhibits.* All bonds, notes, bills of exchange, contracts, accounts, or documents upon which action may be brought or defense made, or a copy thereof or a copy of the portions thereof material to the pleadings, shall be incorporated in or attached to the pleading. No papers shall be unnecessarily annexed as exhibits. The pleadings shall contain no unnecessary recitals of deeds, documents, contracts, or other instruments. Any exhibit attached to a pleading shall be considered a part of the pleadings for all purposes. FL ST RCP Rule 1.130(a).
   b. *Notice of constitutional question.* A party that files a pleading, written motion, or other paper drawing into question the constitutionality of a state statute or a county or municipal charter, ordinance, or franchise must promptly (1) file a notice of constitutional question stating the question and identifying the paper that raises it; and (2) serve the notice and the pleading, written motion, or other paper drawing into question the constitutionality of a state statute or a county or municipal charter, ordinance, or franchise on the Attorney General or the state attorney of the judicial circuit in which the action is pending, by either certified or registered mail. Service of the notice and pleading, written motion, or other paper does not require joinder of the Attorney General or the state attorney as a party to the action. FL ST RCP Rule 1.071.

E. Format

1. *Documents; Type and size.* Documents subject to the exceptions set forth in FL ST J ADMIN Rule 2.525(d) shall be filed on recycled paper measuring eight and one half by eleven (8 1/2 by 11) inches. For purposes of FL ST J ADMIN Rule 2.520, paper is recycled if it contains a minimum content of fifty (50) percent waste paper. Xerographic reduction of legal-size (eight and one half by fourteen (8 1/2 by 14) inches) documents to letter size (eight and one half by eleven (8 1/2 by 11) inches) is prohibited. All other documents filed by electronic transmission shall be filed in a format capable of being printed in a format consistent with the provisions of FL ST J ADMIN Rule 2.250. FL ST J ADMIN Rule 2.520(b).
   a. *Exhibits.* Any exhibit or attachment filed with pleadings or papers may be filed in its original size. FL ST J ADMIN Rule 2.520(c).
   b. *Recording space.* On all papers and documents prepared and filed by the court or by any party to a proceeding which are to be recorded in the public records of any county, including but not limited to final money judgments and notices of lis pendens, a three (3) inch by three (3) inch space at the top right-hand corner on the first page and a one (1) inch by three (3) inch space at the top right-hand corner on each subsequent page shall be left blank and reserved for use by the clerk of court. FL ST J ADMIN Rule 2.520(d).
      i. *Exceptions to recording space.* Any papers or documents created by persons or entities over which the filing party has no control, including but not limited to wills, codicils, trusts, or other testamentary documents; documents prepared or executed by any public officer; documents prepared, executed, acknowledged, or proved outside of the State of Florida; or documents created by State or Federal government agencies, may be filed without the space required by FL ST J ADMIN Rule 2.520. FL ST J ADMIN Rule 2.520(e).
   c. *Noncompliance.* No clerk of court is permitted to refuse to file any document or paper because of noncompliance with the Florida Rules of Judicial Administration. However, upon request of the clerk of court, noncomplying documents must be resubmitted in accordance with the formatting rules. FL ST J ADMIN Rule 2.520(f).
2. *Caption.* Every pleading, motion, order, judgment, or other paper shall have a caption containing the name of the court, the file number, and except for in rem proceedings, including forfeiture proceedings, the name of the first party on each side with an appropriate indication of other parties, and a designation identifying the party filing it and its nature or the nature of the order, as the case may be. In any in rem proceeding, every pleading, motion, order, judgment, or other paper shall have a caption containing the name of the court, the file number, the style "In re" (followed by the name or general description of the property), and a designation of the person or entity filing it and its nature or the nature of the order, as the case may be. In an in rem forfeiture proceeding, the style shall be "In re forfeiture of" (followed by the name of the general description of the property). All papers filed in the action shall be styled in such a manner as to indicate clearly the subject matter of the paper and the party requesting or obtaining relief. FL ST RCP Rule 1.100(c)(1).

3. *Writing and written defined.* Writing or written means a document containing information, an application, or a stipulation. FL ST RCP Rule 1.080(c).
4. *Rule abbreviations*
   a. The Florida Rules of Civil Procedure and shall be abbreviated as Fla.R.Civ.P. FL ST RCP Rule 1.010.
   b. The Florida Rules of Judicial Administration shall be abbreviated as Fla. R. Jud. Admin. FL ST J ADMIN Rule 2.110.
5. *Nonverification.* Except when otherwise specifically provided by the Florida Rules of Civil Procedure or an applicable statute, every pleading or other document of a party represented by an attorney need not be verified or accompanied by an affidavit. FL ST RCP Rule 1.030; FL ST J ADMIN Rule 2.515(a).
6. *Attorney signature*
   a. *Attorney signature.* Every pleading and other document of a party represented by an attorney shall be signed by at least one (1) attorney of record in that attorney's individual name whose current record Florida Bar address, telephone number, including area code, primary e-mail address and secondary e-mail addresses, if any, and Florida Bar number shall be stated, and who shall be duly licensed to practice law in Florida or who shall have received permission to appear in the particular case as provided in FL ST J ADMIN Rule 2.510. FL ST J ADMIN Rule 2.515(a).
      i. The attorney may be required by the court to give the address of, and to vouch for the attorney's authority to represent, the party. FL ST J ADMIN Rule 2.515(a).
      ii. The signature of an attorney shall constitute a certificate by the attorney that the attorney has read the pleading or other document; that to the best of the attorney's knowledge, information, and belief there is good ground to support it; and that it is not interposed for delay. FL ST J ADMIN Rule 2.515(a).
      iii. If a pleading is not signed or is signed with intent to defeat the purpose of FL ST J ADMIN Rule 2.515, it may be stricken and the action may proceed as though the pleading or other document had not been served. FL ST J ADMIN Rule 2.515(a).
   b. *Pro se litigant signature.* A party who is not represented by an attorney shall sign any pleading or other paper and state the party's address and telephone number, including area code. FL ST J ADMIN Rule 2.515(b).
   c. *Form of signature*
      i. The signatures required on pleadings and documents by FL ST J ADMIN Rule 2.515(a) and FL ST J ADMIN Rule 2.515(b) may be:
         - Original signatures;
         - Original signatures that have been reproduced by electronic means, such as on electronically transmitted documents or photocopied documents;
         - Electronic signatures using the "/s/," "s/," or "/s" formats by or at the direction of the person signing; or
         - Any other signature format authorized by general law, so long as the clerk where the proceeding is pending has the capability of receiving and has obtained approval from the Supreme Court of Florida to accept pleadings and documents with that signature format. FL ST J ADMIN Rule 2.515(c)(1).
      ii. An attorney, party, or other person who files a pleading or paper by electronic transmission that does not contain the original signature of that attorney, party, or other person shall file that identical pleading or paper in paper form containing an original signature of that attorney, party, or other person (hereinafter called the follow-up filing) immediately thereafter. The follow-up filing is not required if the Supreme Court of Florida has entered an order directing the clerk of court to discontinue accepting the follow-up filing. FL ST J ADMIN Rule 2.515(c)(2).
7. *Forms*
   a. *Process.* The forms of process, notice of lis pendens, and notice of action provided in the Florida

Rules of Civil Procedure are sufficient. Variations from the forms do not void process or notices that are otherwise sufficient. FL ST RCP Rule 1.900(a).

b. *Other forms.* The other forms provided in the Florida Rules of Civil Procedure are sufficient for the matters that are covered by them. So long as the substance is expressed without prolixity, the forms may be varied to meet the facts of a particular case. FL ST RCP Rule 1.900(b).

c. *Formal matters.* Captions, except for the designation of the paper, are omitted from the forms provided in the Florida Rules of Civil Procedure. A general form of caption is the first form provided. Signatures are omitted from pleadings and motions. FL ST RCP Rule 1.900(c).

8. *Notices to persons with disabilities.* All notices of court proceedings to be held in a public facility, and all process compelling appearance at such proceedings, shall include the following statement in bold face, fourteen (14) point Times New Roman or Courier font: "If you are a person with a disability who needs any accommodation in order to participate in this proceeding, you are entitled, at no cost to you, to the provision of certain assistance. Please contact [identify applicable court personnel by name, address, and telephone number] at least seven (7) days before your scheduled court appearance, or immediately upon receiving this notification if the time before the scheduled appearance is less than seven (7) days; if you are hearing or voice impaired, call 711." FL ST J ADMIN Rule 2.540(c)(1).

9. *Minimization of the filing of sensitive information*

a. *Limitations for court filings.* Unless authorized by FL ST J ADMIN Rule 2.425(b), statute, another rule of court, or the court orders otherwise, designated sensitive information filed with the court must be limited to the following format:

i. The initials of a person known to be a minor;

ii. The year of birth of a person's birth date;

iii. No portion of any: Social security number, Bank account number, Credit card account number, Charge account number, or Debit account number;

iv. The last four digits of any: Taxpayer identification number (TIN), Employee identification number, Driver's license number, Passport number, Telephone number, Financial account number, except as set forth in FL ST J ADMIN Rule 2.425(a)(3), Brokerage account number, Insurance policy account number, Loan account number, Customer account number, or Patient or health care number;

v. A truncated version of any: Email address, Computer user name, Password, or Personal identification number (PIN); and

vi. A truncated version of any other sensitive information as provided by court order. FL ST J ADMIN Rule 2.425(a).

b. *Exceptions.* FL ST J ADMIN Rule 2.425(a) does not apply to the following:

i. An account number which identifies the property alleged to be the subject of a proceeding;

ii. The record of an administrative or agency proceeding;

iii. The record in appellate or review proceedings;

iv. The birth date of a minor whenever the birth date is necessary for the court to establish or maintain subject matter jurisdiction;

v. The name of a minor in any order relating to parental responsibility, time-sharing, or child support;

vi. The name of a minor in any document or order affecting the minor's ownership of real property;

vii. The birth date of a party in a writ of attachment or notice to payor;

viii. In traffic and criminal proceedings: a pro se filing; a court filing that is related to a criminal matter or investigation and that is prepared before the filing of a criminal charge or is not filed as part of any docketed criminal case; an arrest or search warrant or any information in support thereof; a charging document and an affidavit or other documents filed in support of any charging document, including any driving records; a statement of particulars; discovery material introduced into evidence or otherwise filed with the court; and all information necessary for the proper issuance and execution of a subpoena duces tecum;

ix. Information used by the clerk for case maintenance purposes or the courts for case management purposes; and

x. Information which is relevant and material to an issue before the court. FL ST J ADMIN Rule 2.425(b).

c. *Remedies.* Upon motion by a party or interested person or sua sponte by the court, the court may order remedies, sanctions or both for a violation of FL ST J ADMIN Rule 2.425(a). Following notice and an opportunity to respond, the court may impose sanctions if such filing was not made in good faith. FL ST J ADMIN Rule 2.425(c).

d. *Motions not restricted.* FL ST J ADMIN Rule 2.425 does not restrict a party's right to move for protective order, to move to file documents under seal, or to request a determination of the confidentiality of records. FL ST J ADMIN Rule 2.425(d).

e. *Application.* FL ST J ADMIN Rule 2.425 does not affect the application of constitutional provisions, statutes, or rules of court regarding confidential information or access to public information. FL ST J ADMIN Rule 2.425(e).

F. Filing and Service Requirements

1. *Filing requirements.* All documents filed in any court shall be filed by electronic transmission in accordance with FL ST J ADMIN Rule 2.525. "Documents" means pleadings, motions, petitions, memoranda, briefs, notices, exhibits, declarations, affidavits, orders, judgments, decrees, writs, opinions, and any other paper or writing submitted to a court. FL ST J ADMIN Rule 2.520(a). All documents that are court records, as defined in FL ST J ADMIN Rule 2.430(a)(1), must be filed by electronic transmission, provided that: (1) the clerk has the ability to accept and retain such documents; (2) the clerk or the chief judge of the circuit has requested permission to accept documents filed by electronic transmission; and (3) the supreme court has entered an order granting permission to the clerk to accept documents filed by electronic transmission. FL ST J ADMIN Rule 2.525(c)(1).

a. *Definition.* "Electronic transmission of documents" means the sending of information by electronic signals to, by or from a court or clerk, which when received can be transformed and stored or transmitted on paper, microfilm, magnetic storage device, optical imaging system, CD-ROM, flash drive, other electronic data storage system, server, case maintenance system ("CM"), electronic court filing ("ECF") system, statewide or local electronic portal ("e-portal"), or other electronic record keeping system authorized by the supreme court in a format sufficient to communicate the information on the original document in a readable format. Electronic transmission of documents includes electronic mail ("e-mail") and any internet-based transmission procedure, and may include procedures allowing for documents to be signed or verified by electronic means. FL ST J ADMIN Rule 2.525(a).

b. *Application.* Any court or clerk of the court may accept the electronic transmission of documents for filing after the clerk, together with input from the chief judge of the circuit, has obtained approval of the procedures and program for doing so from the Supreme Court of Florida. FL ST J ADMIN Rule 2.525(b).

c. *Exceptions*

i. Paper documents and other submissions may be manually submitted to the clerk or court:

- When the clerk does not have the ability to accept and retain documents by electronic filing or has not had ECF Procedures approved by the supreme court;
- For filing by any self-represented party or any self-represented nonparty unless specific ECF Procedures provide a means to file documents electronically. However, any self-represented nonparty that is a governmental or public agency and any other agency, partnership, corporation, or business entity acting on behalf of any governmental or public agency may file documents by electronic transmission if such entity has the capability of filing documents electronically;

- For filing by attorneys excused from e-mail service in accordance with FL ST J ADMIN Rule 2.516(b);
- When submitting evidentiary exhibits or filing non-documentary materials;
- When the filing involves documents in excess of twenty-five (25) megabytes (25MB) in size. For such filings, documents may be transmitted using an electronic storage medium that the clerk has the ability to accept, which may include a CD-ROM, flash drive, or similar storage medium;
- When filed in open court, as permitted by the court;
- When paper filing is permitted by any approved statewide or local ECF procedures; and
- If any court determines that justice so requires. FL ST J ADMIN Rule 2.525(d).

ii. Any document in paper form submitted under FL ST J ADMIN Rule 2.525(d) is filed when it is received by the clerk or court and the clerk shall immediately thereafter convert any filed paper document to an electronic document. "Convert to an electronic document" means optically capturing an image of a paper document and using character recognition software to recover as much of the document's text as practicable and then indexing and storing the document in the official court file. FL ST J ADMIN Rule 2.525(c)(4).

iii. Any storage medium submitted under FL ST J ADMIN Rule 2.525(d)(5) is filed when received by the clerk or court and the clerk shall immediately thereafter transfer the electronic documents from the storage device to the official court file. FL ST J ADMIN Rule 2.525(c)(5).

iv. If the filer of any paper document authorized under FL ST J ADMIN Rule 2.525(d) provides a self-addressed, postage-paid envelope for return of the paper document after it is converted to electronic form by the clerk, the clerk shall place the paper document in the envelope and deposit it in the mail. Except when a paper document is required to be maintained, the clerk may recycle any filed paper document that is not to be returned to the filer. FL ST J ADMIN Rule 2.525(c)(6).

v. The clerk may convert any paper document filed before the effective date of FL ST J ADMIN Rule 2.525 to an electronic document. Unless the clerk is required to maintain the paper document, if the paper document has been converted to an electronic document by the clerk, the paper document is no longer part of the official court file and may be removed and recycled. FL ST J ADMIN Rule 2.525(c)(7).

d. *Official court file.* For information on what constitutes the official court file, please see FL ST J ADMIN Rule 2.525(c)(2), FL ST J ADMIN Rule 2.525(c)(3).

e. *Administration.* All attorneys, parties, or other persons using this rule to file documents are required to make arrangements with the court or clerk for the payment of any charges authorized by general law or the supreme court before filing any document by electronic transmission. FL ST J ADMIN Rule 2.525(f)(2).

f. *Filing date.* The filing date for an electronically transmitted document is the date and time that such filing is acknowledged by an electronic stamp or otherwise, pursuant to any procedure set forth in any ECF Procedures approved by the supreme court, or the date the last page of such filing is received by the court or clerk. FL ST J ADMIN Rule 2.525(f)(3).

g. *Accessibility.* All documents transmitted in any electronic form under FL ST J ADMIN Rule 2.525 must comply with the accessibility requirements of FL ST J ADMIN Rule 2.526. FL ST J ADMIN Rule 2.525(g).

2. *Service requirements*

a. *Papers to be served.* At the time of personal service of process a copy of the initial pleading shall be delivered to the party upon whom service is made. The date and hour of service shall be endorsed on the original process and all copies of it by the person making the service. The party seeking to effect personal service shall furnish the person making service with the necessary copies. When the service is made by publication, copies of the initial pleadings shall be furnished to the clerk and mailed by the clerk with the notice of action to all parties whose addresses are stated in the initial pleading or sworn statement. FL ST RCP Rule 1.070(e).

b. *Issuance of summons.* Upon the commencement of the action, summons or other process authorized by law shall be issued forthwith by the clerk or judge under the clerk's or the judge's signature and the seal of the court and delivered for service without praecipe. FL ST RCP Rule 1.070(a).

   i. *How directed.* Summons, subpoenas, and other process in civil actions run throughout the state. All process except subpoenas shall be directed to all and singular the sheriffs of the state. FL ST § 48.011.

   ii. *Service as to numerous defendants.* If there is more than one (1) defendant, the clerk or judge shall issue as many writs of process against the several defendants as may be directed by the plaintiff or the plaintiff's attorney. FL ST RCP Rule 1.070(c).

c. *Who may serve process.* Service of process may be made by an officer authorized by law to serve process, but the court may appoint any competent person not interested in the action to serve the process. When so appointed, the person serving process shall make proof of service by affidavit promptly and in any event within the time during which the person served must respond to the process. Failure to make proof of service shall not affect the validity of the service. When any process is returned not executed or returned improperly executed for any defendant, the party causing its issuance shall be entitled to such additional process against the unserved party as is required to effect service. FL ST RCP Rule 1.070(b).

   i. All process shall be served by the sheriff of the county where the person to be served is found, except initial nonenforceable civil process may be served by a special process server appointed by the sheriff as provided for in FL ST § 48.021 or by a certified process server as provided for in FL ST § 48.25 through FL ST § 48.31. FL ST § 48.021(1).

   ii. The sheriff of each county may, in his or her discretion, establish an approved list of natural persons designated as special process servers. FL ST § 48.021(2)(a). For more information regarding process servers, please see FL ST § 48.021(2).

      - See FL ST 7 J CIR CV-2009-021-SJ regarding special process servers in St. Johns County.

   iii. A person serving process shall place, on the copy served, the date and time of service and his or her identification number and initials for all service of process. FL ST § 48.031(5).

d. *Service of process on Sunday*

   i. Service or execution on Sunday of any writ, process, warrant, order, or judgment is void and the person serving or executing, or causing it to be served or executed, is liable to the party aggrieved for damages for so doing as if he or she had done it without any process, writ, warrant, order, or judgment. FL ST § 48.20.

   ii. If affidavit is made by the person requesting service or execution that he or she has good reason to believe that any person liable to have any such writ, process, warrant, order, or judgment served on him or her intends to escape from this state under protection of Sunday, any officer furnished with an order authorizing service or execution by the trial court judge may serve or execute such writ, process, warrant, order, or judgment on Sunday, and it is as valid as if it had been done on any other day. FL ST § 48.20.

e. *Methods of service*

   i. *Service of process generally.* Service of original process is made by delivering a copy of it to the person to be served with a copy of the complaint, petition, or other initial pleading or paper or by leaving the copies at his or her usual place of abode with any person residing therein who is fifteen (15) years of age or older and informing the person of their contents. Minors who are or have been married shall be served as provided in FL ST § 48.031. FL ST § 48.031(1)(a).

      - Employers, when contacted by an individual authorized to make service of process, shall permit the authorized individual to make service on employees in a private area designated by the employer. FL ST § 48.031(1)(b).
      - Substitute service may be made on the spouse of the person to be served at any place in the county, if the cause of action is not an adversary proceeding between the spouse and the person to be served, if the spouse requests such service, and if the spouse and person to be served are residing together in the same dwelling. FL ST § 48.031(2)(a).

- Substitute service may be made on an individual doing business as a sole proprietorship at his or her place of business, during regular business hours, by serving the person in charge of the business at the time of service if two (2) or more attempts to serve the owner have been made at the place of business. FL ST § 48.031(2)(b).
- If the only address for a person to be served, which is discoverable through public records, is a private mailbox, substitute service may be made by leaving a copy of the process with the person in charge of the private mailbox, but only if the process server determines that the person to be served maintains a mailbox at that location. FL ST § 48.031(6).

ii. *Service by mail.* A defendant may accept service of process by mail. FL ST RCP Rule 1.070(i). A plaintiff may notify any defendant of the commencement of the action and request that the defendant waive service of a summons. FL ST RCP Rule 1.070(i)(2).

- *Notice and request for waiver.* The notice and request shall: (1) be in writing and be addressed directly to the defendant, if an individual, or to an officer or managing or general agent of the defendant or other agent authorized by appointment or law to receive service of process; (2) be dispatched by certified mail, return receipt requested; (3) be accompanied by a copy of the complaint and shall identify the court in which it has been filed; (4) inform the defendant of the consequences of compliance and of failure to comply with the request; (5) state the date on which the request is sent; (6) allow the defendant twenty (20) days from the date on which the request is received to return the waiver, or, if the address of the defendant is outside of the United States, thirty (30) days from the date on which it is received to return the waiver; and (7) provide the defendant with an extra copy of the notice and request, including the waiver, as well as a prepaid means of compliance in writing. FL ST RCP Rule 1.070(i)(2).
- *Consequences of accepting/rejecting service by mail.* Acceptance of service of a complaint by mail does not thereby waive any objection to the venue or to the jurisdiction of the court over the person of the defendant. FL ST RCP Rule 1.070(i)(1). If a defendant fails to comply with a request for waiver within the time provided, the court shall impose the costs subsequently incurred in effecting service on the defendant unless good cause for the failure is shown. FL ST RCP Rule 1.070(i)(3). A defendant who, before being served with process, timely returns a waiver so requested is not required to respond to the complaint until sixty (60) days after the date the defendant received the request for waiver of service. For purposes of computing any time prescribed or allowed by the Florida Rules of Civil Procedure, service of process shall be deemed effected twenty (20) days before the time required to respond to the complaint. FL ST RCP Rule 1.070(i)(4). When the plaintiff files a waiver of service with the court, the action shall proceed, except as provided in FL ST RCP Rule 1.070(i)(4), as if a summons and complaint had been served at the time of filing the waiver, and no further proof of service shall be required. FL ST RCP Rule 1.070(i)(5).

iii. *Service on partnerships and limited partnerships*

- Process against a partnership shall be served on any partner and is as valid as if served on each individual partner. If a partner is not available during regular business hours to accept service on behalf of the partnership, he or she may designate an employee to accept such service. After one (1) attempt to serve a partner or designated employee has been made, process may be served on the person in charge of the partnership during regular business hours. After service on any partner, plaintiff may proceed to judgment and execution against that partner and the assets of the partnership. After service on a designated employee or other person in charge, plaintiff may proceed to judgment and execution against the partnership assets but not against the individual assets of any partner. FL ST § 48.061(1).
- Process against a domestic limited partnership may be served on any general partner or on the agent for service of process specified in its certificate of limited partnership or in its certificate as amended or restated and is as valid as if served on each individual member of the partnership. After service on a general partner or the agent, the plaintiff may proceed

to judgment and execution against the limited partnership and all of the general partners individually. If a general partner cannot be found in this state and service cannot be made on an agent because of failure to maintain such an agent or because the agent cannot be found or served with the exercise of reasonable diligence, service of process may be effected by service upon the Secretary of State as agent of the limited partnership as provided for in FL ST § 48.181. Service of process may be made under FL ST § 48.071 and FL ST § 48.21 on limited partnerships. FL ST § 48.061(2).

- Process against a foreign limited partnership may be served on any general partner found in the state or on any agent for service of process specified in its application for registration and is as valid as if served on each individual member of the partnership. If a general partner cannot be found in this state and an agent for service of process has not been appointed or, if appointed, the agent's authority has been revoked or the agent cannot be found or served with the exercise of reasonable diligence, service of process may be effected by service upon the Secretary of State as agent of the limited partnership as provided for in FL ST § 48.181, or process may be served as provided in FL ST § 48.071 and FL ST § 48.21. FL ST § 48.061(3).

iv. *Service on corporation*

- Process against any private corporation, domestic or foreign, may be served: (1) on the president or vice president, or other head of the corporation; (2) in the absence of any person described in FL ST § 48.081(1)(a), on the cashier, treasurer, secretary, or general manager; (3) in the absence of any person described in FL ST § 48.081(1)(a) or FL ST § 48.081(1)(b), on any director; or (4) in the absence of any person described in FL ST § 48.081(1)(a), FL ST § 48.081(1)(b), or FL ST § 48.081(1)(c), on any officer or business agent residing in the state. FL ST § 48.081(1).
- If a foreign corporation has none of the foregoing officers or agents in this state, service may be made on any agent transacting business for it in this state. FL ST § 48.081(2).
- As an alternative to all of the foregoing, process may be served on the agent designated by the corporation under FL ST § 48.091. However, if service cannot be made on a registered agent because of failure to comply with FL ST § 48.091, service of process shall be permitted on any employee at the corporation's principal place of business or on any employee of the registered agent. FL ST § 48.081(3)(a). If the address provided for the registered agent, officer, director, or principal place of business is a residence or private mailbox, service on the corporation may be made by serving the registered agent, officer, or director in accordance with FL ST § 48.031. FL ST § 48.081(3)(b).
- FL ST § 48.081 does not apply to service of process on insurance companies. FL ST § 48.081(4).
- When a corporation engages in substantial and not isolated activities within this state, or has a business office within the state and is actually engaged in the transaction of business therefrom, service upon any officer or business agent while on corporate business within this state may personally be made, pursuant to FL ST § 48.081, and it is not necessary in such case that the action, suit, or proceeding against the corporation shall have arisen out of any transaction or operation connected with or incidental to the business being transacted within the state. FL ST § 48.081(5).
- For information regarding service on a dissolved corporation refer to FL ST § 48.101.

v. *Personal service outside state*

- Except as otherwise provided herein, service of process on persons outside of this state shall be made in the same manner as service within this state by any officer authorized to serve process in the state where the person is served. No order of court is required. An affidavit of the officer shall be filed, stating the time, manner, and place of service. The court may consider the affidavit, or any other competent evidence, in determining whether service has been properly made. Service of process on persons outside the United States may be required to conform to the provisions of the Hague Convention on the Service Abroad of Judicial and Extrajudicial Documents in Civil or Commercial Matters. FL ST § 48.194(1).

- For further information on service of process in an in rem or quasi in rem action refer to FL ST § 48.194(2); FL ST § 48.194(3); and FL ST § 48.194(4).

vi. *Method of substituted service on nonresident*

- When authorized by law, substituted service of process on a nonresident or a person who conceals his or her whereabouts by serving a public officer designated by law shall be made by leaving a copy of the process with a fee of eight dollars and seventy-five cents ($8.75) with the public officer or in his or her office or by mailing the copies by certified mail to the public officer with the fee. The service is sufficient service on a defendant who has appointed a public officer as his or her agent for the service of process. FL ST § 48.161(1).
- Notice of service and a copy of the process shall be sent forthwith by registered or certified mail by the plaintiff or his or her attorney to the defendant, and the defendant's return receipt and the affidavit of the plaintiff or his or her attorney of compliance shall be filed on or before the return day of the process or within such time as the court allows, or the notice and copy shall be served on the defendant, if found within the state, by an officer authorized to serve legal process, or if found without the state, by a sheriff or a deputy sheriff of any county of this state or any duly constituted public officer qualified to serve like process in the state or jurisdiction where the defendant is found. The officer's return showing service shall be filed on or before the return day of the process or within such time as the court allows. The public officer shall keep a record of all process served on him or her showing the day and hour of service. FL ST § 48.161(1).
- If any person on whom service of process is authorized under FL ST § 48.161(1) dies, service may be made on his or her administrator, executor, curator, or personal representative in the same manner. FL ST § 48.161(2).
- FL ST § 48.161 does not apply to persons on whom service is authorized under FL ST § 48.151. FL ST § 48.161(3).
- The public officer may designate some other person in his or her office to accept service. FL ST § 48.161(4).

vii. *Service by publication.* Service of process by publication may be made as provided by statute. FL ST RCP Rule 1.070(d). Service of process by publication is allowable in cases listed in FL ST § 49.011 and upon the parties listed in FL ST § 49.021.

- As a condition precedent to service by publication, a statement shall be filed in the action executed by the plaintiff, the plaintiff's agent or attorney, setting forth substantially the matters hereafter required, which statement may be contained in a verified pleading, or in an affidavit or other sworn statement. FL ST § 49.031(1). After the entry of a final judgment or decree in any action no sworn statement shall ever be held defective for failure to state a required fact if the fact otherwise appears from the record in the action. FL ST § 49.031(3).
- For the sworn statement requirements for service of process by publication refer to FL ST § 49.041; FL ST § 49.051; FL ST § 49.061; and FL ST § 49.071.
- On filing the sworn statement, and otherwise complying with the foregoing requirements, the plaintiff is entitled to have issued by the clerk or judge, not later than sixty (60) days after filing the sworn statement, a notice of action which notice shall set forth: (1) the names of the known natural defendants; the names, status and description of the corporate defendants; a description of the unknown defendants who claim by, through, under or against a known party which may be described as "all parties claiming interests by, through, under or against (name of known party)" and a description of all unknown defendants which may be described as "all parties having or claiming to have any right,

title or interest in the property herein described"; (2) the nature of the action or proceeding in short and simple terms (but neglect to do so is not jurisdictional); (3) the name of the court in which the action or proceeding was instituted and an abbreviated title of the case; (4) the description of real property, if any, proceeded against. FL ST § 49.08.

- For further information on service of process by publication refer to FL ST § 49.09; FL ST § 49.10; FL ST § 49.11; FL ST § 49.12; FL ST § 50.011; FL ST § 50.021; FL ST § 50.031; FL ST § 50.041; FL ST § 50.051; and FL ST § 50.061.

viii. *Service on agents of nonresidents doing business in the state.* When any natural person or partnership not residing or having a principal place of business in this state engages in business in this state, process may be served on the person who is in charge of any business in which the defendant is engaged within this state at the time of service, including agents soliciting orders for goods, wares, merchandise or services. FL ST § 48.071.

- Any process so served is as valid as if served personally on the nonresident person or partnership engaging in business in this state in any action against the person or partnership arising out of such business. FL ST § 48.071.
- A copy of such process with a notice of service on the person in charge of such business shall be sent forthwith to the nonresident person or partnership by registered or certified mail, return receipt requested. FL ST § 48.071.
- An affidavit of compliance with FL ST § 48.071 shall be filed before the return day or within such further time as the court may allow. FL ST § 48.071.

ix. *Service on nonresident engaging in business in state.* The acceptance by any person or persons, individually or associated together as a copartnership or any other form or type of association, who are residents of any other state or country, and all foreign corporations, and any person who is a resident of the state and who subsequently becomes a nonresident of the state or conceals his or her whereabouts, of the privilege extended by law to nonresidents and others to operate, conduct, engage in, or carry on a business or business venture in the state, or to have an office or agency in the state, constitutes an appointment by the persons and foreign corporations of the Secretary of State of the state as their agent on whom all process in any action or proceeding against them, or any of them, arising out of any transaction or operation connected with or incidental to the business or business venture may be served. The acceptance of the privilege is signification of the agreement of the persons and foreign corporations that the process against them which is so served is of the same validity as if served personally on the persons or foreign corporations. FL ST § 48.181(1).

- If a foreign corporation has a resident agent or officer in the state, process shall be served on the resident agent or officer. FL ST § 48.181(2).
- Any person, firm, or corporation which sells, consigns, or leases by any means whatsoever tangible or intangible personal property, through brokers, jobbers, wholesalers, or distributors to any person, firm, or corporation in this state is conclusively presumed to be both engaged in substantial and not isolated activities within this state and operating, conducting, engaging in, or carrying on a business or business venture in this state. FL ST § 48.181(3).

x. *Other service provisions:*

- Service on alien property custodian. FL ST § 48.131.
- Service on an incompetent person. FL ST § 48.042.
- Service on minor. FL ST § 48.041.
- Service on public agencies and officers. FL ST § 48.111.
- Service on the state. FL ST § 48.121.
- Service on a state prisoner. FL ST § 48.051.
- Service on labor unions. FL ST § 48.141.

- Service on statutory agents for certain persons. FL ST § 48.151.
- Service on nonresident motor vehicle owners. FL ST § 48.171.
- Service of process in action for possession of premises. FL ST § 48.183.
- Service on nonresidents operating aircraft or watercraft in the state. FL ST § 48.19.

f. *Crossclaims.* Service of a crossclaim on a party who has appeared in the action shall be made pursuant to FL ST RCP Rule 1.080. Service of a crossclaim against a party who has not appeared in the action shall be made in the manner provided for service of summons. FL ST RCP Rule 1.170(g).

g. *Fees.* The statutory compensation for making service shall not be increased by the simultaneous delivery or mailing of the copy of the initial pleading in conformity with FL ST RCP Rule 1.070. FL ST RCP Rule 1.070(g).

G. Hearings

1. There is no hearing required or contemplated in the Florida rules governing the complaint and service of summons.

H. Forms

1. Official Complaint Forms for Florida

a. Caption. FL ST RCP Form 1.901.
b. Summons. FL ST RCP Form 1.902.
c. Crossclaim summons. FL ST RCP Form 1.903.
d. Third-party summons. FL ST RCP Form 1.904.
e. Notice of action, constructive service, no property. FL ST RCP Form 1.919.
f. Notice of action, constructive service, property. FL ST RCP Form 1.920.
g. Third-party complaint. FL ST RCP Form 1.948.
h. Civil cover sheet. FL ST RCP Form 1.997.
i. Fall-down negligence complaint. FL ST RCP Form 1.951.
j. Notice of compliance when constitutional challenge is brought. FL ST RCP Form 1.975.

2. Complaint Forms for Florida

a. Complaint for damages; General form. FL-PP § 2:17.
b. Complaint; Negligent infliction of personal injury. FL-PP § 2:19.
c. Complaint; Fall down negligence. FL-PP § 2:20.
d. Complaint; Professional negligence. FL-PP § 2:23.
e. Complaint; Breach of contract. FL-PP § 2:24.
f. Complaint; Breach of personal services contract. FL-PP § 2:25.
g. Summons; General form. FL-PRACFORM § 3:4.
h. Summons; Natural person. FL-PRACFORM § 3:5.
i. Complaint; Assault and battery. FL-PRACFORM § 4:9.
j. Complaint; Breach of contract, general form. FL-PRACFORM § 4:17.
k. Complaint; Civil rights. FL-PRACFORM § 4:23.
l. Complaint; Conversion. FL-PRACFORM § 4:30.
m. Complaint; Employment contract. FL-PRACFORM § 4:44.
n. Complaint; False imprisonment. FL-PRACFORM § 4:46.
o. Complaint; Fraud, misrepresentation. FL-PRACFORM § 4:62.
p. Complaint; Lease, by landlord. FL-PRACFORM § 4:86.

q. Complaint; Lease, by tenant. FL-PRACFORM § 4:87.

r. Complaint; Libel. FL-PRACFORM § 4:89.

s. Complaint; Life insurance policy. FL-PRACFORM § 4:90.

t. Complaint; Medical malpractice, negligence. FL-PRACFORM § 4:95.

u. Complaint; Negligence, automobile, driver. FL-PRACFORM § 4:101.

v. Complaint; Negligence, hospital. FL-PRACFORM § 4:104.

I. Checklist

(I) ❑ Matters to be considered by plaintiff

- (a) ❑ Required documents
  - (1) ❑ Summons
  - (2) ❑ Complaint
  - (3) ❑ Civil cover sheet
  - (4) ❑ Return of execution process by process server
  - (5) ❑ Filing fees
- (b) ❑ Supplemental documents
  - (1) ❑ Exhibits
  - (2) ❑ Notice of constitutional question
- (c) ❑ Time for filing and serving complaint
  - (1) ❑ Service of the initial process and initial pleading should be made upon a defendant within one hundred twenty (120) days after the filing of the complaint with the court

(II) ❑ Matters to be considered by defendant

- (a) ❑ Required documents
  - (1) ❑ Answer
  - (2) ❑ Certificate of service
- (b) ❑ Supplemental documents
  - (1) ❑ Exhibits
  - (2) ❑ Notice of constitutional question
- (c) ❑ Time for answer
  - (1) ❑ Unless a different time is prescribed in a statute of Florida, a defendant shall serve an answer within twenty (20) days after service of original process and the initial pleading on the defendant, or not later than the date fixed in a notice by publication
  - (2) ❑ A party served with a pleading stating a crossclaim against that party shall serve an answer to it within twenty (20) days after service on that party
  - (3) ❑ The plaintiff shall serve an answer to a counterclaim within twenty (20) days after service of the counterclaim
  - (4) ❑ A defendant who, before being served with process, timely returns a waiver so requested is not required to respond to the complaint until sixty (60) days after the date the defendant received the request for waiver of service; for purposes of computing any time prescribed or allowed by the Florida Rules of Civil Procedure, service of process shall be deemed effected twenty (20) days before the time required to respond to the complaint
  - (5) ❑ For timing requirements related to service on the state, service of motion impact, and responding when no responsive pleading is required, please see the Timing section of this document

Pleadings
Amended Complaint

Document Last Updated January 2013

A. Applicable Rules

1. *State rules*
   a. Nonverification of papers. FL ST RCP Rule 1.030.
   b. Process. FL ST RCP Rule 1.070.
   c. Constitutional challenge to state statute or county or municipal charter, ordinance, or franchise; Notice by party. FL ST RCP Rule 1.071.
   d. Service and filing of pleadings, orders, and documents. FL ST RCP Rule 1.080.
   e. Pleadings and motions. FL ST RCP Rule 1.100; FL ST RCP Rule 1.110; FL ST RCP Rule 1.120; FL ST RCP Rule 1.130; FL ST RCP Rule 1.190; FL ST § 48.193.
   f. Pretrial procedure. FL ST RCP Rule 1.200.
   g. Relief from judgment, decrees, or orders. FL ST RCP Rule 1.540.
   h. Forms. FL ST RCP Rule 1.900.
   i. Minimization of the filing of sensitive information. FL ST J ADMIN Rule 2.425.
   j. Retention of court records. FL ST J ADMIN Rule 2.430.
   k. Foreign attorneys. FL ST J ADMIN Rule 2.510.
   l. Signature of attorneys and parties. FL ST J ADMIN Rule 2.515.
   m. Paper. FL ST J ADMIN Rule 2.520.
   n. Electronic filing. FL ST J ADMIN Rule 2.525.
   o. Accessibility of information and technology. FL ST J ADMIN Rule 2.526.
   p. Requests for accommodations by persons with disabilities. FL ST J ADMIN Rule 2.540.
2. *Local rules*
   a. Eminent domain cases. FL ST 7 J CIR CV-2000-011-VL.
   b. Civil pretrial procedures. FL ST 7 J CIR CV-2003-002-SC.
   c. Arbitration and mediation. FL ST 7 J CIR CV-2008-018-SC; FL ST 7 J CIR CV-2009-019-SC.

B. Timing

1. *Amendment as a matter of course.* A party may amend a pleading once as a matter of course at any time before a responsive pleading is served or, if the pleading is one to which no responsive pleading is permitted and the action has not been placed on the trial calendar, may so amend it at any time within twenty (20) days after it is served. FL ST RCP Rule 1.190(a).
2. *Amendment by leave of court.* Otherwise a party may amend a pleading only by leave of court or by written consent of the adverse party. Leave of court shall be given freely when justice so requires. FL ST RCP Rule 1.190(a).
3. *Amendments in furtherance of justice.* At any time in furtherance of justice, upon such terms as may be just, the court may permit any process, proceeding, pleading, or record to be amended or material supplemental matter to be set forth in an amended or supplemental pleading. At every stage of the action the court must disregard any error or defect in the proceedings which does not affect the substantial rights of the parties. FL ST RCP Rule 1.190(e).
4. *Response to amended pleading.* A party shall plead in response to an amended pleading within ten (10) days after service of the amended pleading unless the court otherwise orders. FL ST RCP Rule 1.190(a).
5. *Computation of time*
   a. *Generally.* Computation of time shall be governed by FL ST J ADMIN Rule 2.514. FL ST RCP Rule

1.090(a). The following rules apply in computing time periods specified in any rule of procedure, local rule, court order, or statute that does not specify a method of computing time. FL ST J ADMIN Rule 2.514(a).

i. *Period stated in days or a longer unit.* When the period is stated in days or a longer unit of time (A) exclude the day of the event that triggers the period; (B) count every day, including intermediate Saturdays, Sundays, and legal holidays; and (C) include the last day of the period, but if the last day is a Saturday, Sunday, or legal holiday, or falls within any period of time extended through an order of the chief justice under FL ST J ADMIN Rule 2.205(a)(2)(B)(iv), the period continues to run until the end of the next day that is not a Saturday, Sunday, or legal holiday and does not fall within any period of time extended through an order of the chief justice. FL ST J ADMIN Rule 2.514(a)(1).

ii. *Period stated in hours.* When the period is stated in hours (A) begin counting immediately on the occurrence of the event that triggers the period; (B) count every hour, including hours during intermediate Saturdays, Sundays, and legal holidays; and (C) if the period would end on a Saturday, Sunday, or legal holiday, or during any period of time extended through an order of the chief justice under FL ST J ADMIN Rule 2.205(a)(2)(B)(iv), the period continues to run until the same time on the next day that is not a Saturday, Sunday, or legal holiday and does not fall within any period of time extended through an order of the chief justice. FL ST J ADMIN Rule 2.514(a)(2).

iii. *Period stated in days less than seven (7) days.* When the period stated in days is less than seven (7) days, intermediate Saturdays, Sundays, and legal holidays shall be excluded in the computation. FL ST J ADMIN Rule 2.514(a)(3).

iv. *"Last day" defined.* Unless a different time is set by a statute, local rule, or court order, the last day ends (A) for electronic filing or for service by any means, at midnight; and (B) for filing by other means, when the clerk's office is scheduled to close. FL ST J ADMIN Rule 2.514(a)(4).

v. *"Next day" defined.* The "next day" is determined by continuing to count forward when the period is measured after an event and backward when measured before an event. FL ST J ADMIN Rule 2.514(a)(5).

vi. *"Legal holiday" defined.* "Legal holiday" means (A) the day set aside by FL ST § 110.117, for observing New Year's Day, Martin Luther King, Jr.'s Birthday, Memorial Day, Independence Day, Labor Day, Veterans' Day, Thanksgiving Day, the Friday after Thanksgiving Day, or Christmas Day, and (B) any day observed as a holiday by the clerk's office or as designated by the chief judge. FL ST J ADMIN Rule 2.514(a)(6).

b. *Additional time after service by mail or e-mail.* When a party may or must act within a specified time after service and service is made by mail or e-mail, five (5) days are added after the period that would otherwise expire under FL ST J ADMIN Rule 2.514(a). FL ST J ADMIN Rule 2.514(b).

c. *Enlargement.* When an act is required or allowed to be done at or within a specified time by order of court, by the Florida Rules of Civil Procedure, or by notice given thereunder, for cause shown the court at any time in its discretion (1) with or without notice, may order the period enlarged if request therefor is made before the expiration of the period originally prescribed or as extended by a previous order, or (2) upon motion made and notice after the expiration of the specified period, may permit the act to be done when failure to act was the result of excusable neglect, but it may not extend the time for making a motion for new trial, for rehearing, or to alter or amend a judgment; making a motion for relief from a judgment under FL ST RCP Rule 1.540(b); taking an appeal or filing a petition for certiorari; or making a motion for a directed verdict. FL ST RCP Rule 1.090(b).

d. *Unaffected by expiration of term.* The period of time provided for the doing of any act or the taking of any proceeding shall not be affected or limited by the continued existence or expiration of a term of court. The continued existence or expiration of a term of court in no way affects the power of a court to do any act or take any proceeding in any action which is or has been pending before it. FL ST RCP Rule 1.090(c).

C. General Requirements

1. *Amendments.* A party may amend a pleading once as a matter of course at any time before a responsive

pleading is served or, if the pleading is one to which no responsive pleading is permitted and the action has not been placed on the trial calendar, may so amend it at any time within twenty (20) days after it is served. Otherwise a party may amend a pleading only by leave of court or by written consent of the adverse party. Leave of court shall be freely given when justice so requires. FL ST RCP Rule 1.190(a).

a. *Purpose of amendments.* Amendments can relate to the correction of mistakes, the insertion of jurisdictional averments, the correction or addition of verifications, the addition or substitution or striking out of parties, and generally the rectification of all formal defects in the pleading. The court can also allow amendments setting up an omitted counterclaim or cross-claim if the defendant failed to raise the claim through oversight, inadvertence, or excusable neglect. FL-PP § 2:151.

b. *Amendment to a pleading/Amended pleading.* A significant difference exists between an amendment to a pleading and an amended pleading. An amendment to a pleading corrects, adds to or deletes from the pleading. An amended pleading is substituted for the former pleading and the former pleading ceases to have any effect. Dee v. Southern Brewing Company, 146 Fla. 588, 1 So.2d 562 (Fla. 1941); Shannon v. McBride, 105 So.2d 16 (Fla. 2d DCA 1958); Hughes v. Home Sav. of America, F.S.B., 675 So.2d 649 (Fla. 2d DCA 1996); FL-PRACPROC § 14:2.

c. *Relation back of amendments.* When the claim or defense asserted in the amended pleading arose out of the conduct, transaction, or occurrence set forth or attempted to be set forth in the original pleading, the amendment shall relate back to the date of the original pleading. FL ST RCP Rule 1.190(c).

2. *General rules of pleading*

a. *Claims for relief*

i. A pleading which sets forth a claim for relief, whether an original claim, counterclaim, crossclaim, or third-party claim, must state a cause of action and shall contain

- A short and plain statement of the grounds upon which the court's jurisdiction depends, unless the court already has jurisdiction and the claim needs no new grounds of jurisdiction to support it (For information regarding acts subjecting persons to jurisdiction, please see FL ST § 48.193),
- A short and plain statement of the ultimate facts showing that the pleader is entitled to relief, and
- A demand for judgment for the relief to which the pleader deems himself or herself entitled. FL ST RCP Rule 1.110(b).

ii. Relief in the alternative or of several different types may be demanded. Every complaint shall be considered to demand general relief. FL ST RCP Rule 1.110(b).

b. *Verification.* Except when otherwise specifically provided by these rules or an applicable statute, every pleading or other document of a party represented by an attorney need not be verified or accompanied by an affidavit. FL ST RCP Rule 1.030. When filing an action for foreclosure of a mortgage on residential real property the complaint shall be verified. When verification of a document is required, the document filed shall include an oath, affirmation, or the following statement: "Under penalty of perjury, I declare that I have read the foregoing, and the facts alleged therein are true and correct to the best of my knowledge and belief." FL ST RCP Rule 1.110(b).

c. *Separate statements.* All averments of claim or defense shall be made in consecutively numbered paragraphs, the contents of each of which shall be limited as far as practicable to a statement of a single set of circumstances, and a paragraph may be referred to by number in all subsequent pleadings. Each claim founded upon a separate transaction or occurrence and each defense other than denials shall be stated in a separate count or defense when a separation facilitates the clear presentation of the matter set forth. FL ST RCP Rule 1.110(f).

d. *Statements adopted by reference.* Statements in a pleading may be adopted by reference in a different part of the same pleading, in another pleading, or in any motion. FL ST RCP Rule 1.130(b).

e. *Joinder of causes of action; Consistency.* A pleader may set up in the same action as many claims or causes of action or defenses in the same right as the pleader has, and claims for relief may be stated in the alternative if separate items make up the cause of action, or if two (2) or more causes of action are joined. A party may also set forth two (2) or more statements of a claim or defense alternatively, either in one (1) count or defense or in separate counts or defenses. When two (2) or more statements are made in the alternative and one (1) of them, if made independently, would be sufficient, the pleading is not made insufficient by the insufficiency of one (1) or more of the alternative statements. A party may also state as many separate claims or defenses as that party has, regardless of consistency and whether based on legal or equitable grounds or both. All pleadings shall be construed so as to do substantial justice. FL ST RCP Rule 1.110(g).

f. *Subsequent pleadings.* When the nature of an action permits pleadings subsequent to final judgment and the jurisdiction of the court over the parties has not terminated, the initial pleading subsequent to final judgment shall be designated a supplemental complaint or petition. The action shall then proceed in the same manner and time as though the supplemental complaint or petition were the initial pleading in the action, including the issuance of any needed process. FL ST RCP Rule 1.110(h) shall not apply to proceedings that may be initiated by motion under the Florida Rules of Civil Procedure. FL ST RCP Rule 1.110(h).

g. *Pleading basis for service.* When service of process is to be made under statutes authorizing service on nonresidents of Florida, it is sufficient to plead the basis for service in the language of the statute without pleading the facts supporting service. FL ST RCP Rule 1.070(h).

h. *Forms of pleadings.* Forms of action and technical forms for seeking relief and of pleas, pleadings, or motions are abolished. FL ST RCP Rule 1.110(a).

3. *Complaint; Generally*

a. *Purpose.* The purpose of a complaint is to advise the court and the defendant of the nature of a cause of action asserted by the plaintiff. FL-PP § 2:12.

b. *Sufficiency of complaint.* A complaint will be found to be insufficient if it contains only general conclusory allegations unsupported by any facts. The test to determine whether a complaint is sufficient is whether, if the factual allegations of the complaint are established, the plaintiff will be legally or equitably entitled to the claimed relief. Pizzi v. Central Bank & Trust Co., 250 So.2d 895, 896 (Fla. 1971); Bowen v. G H C Properties, Limited, 251 So.2d 359, 361 (Fla. 1st DCA 1971); FL-PP § 2:12. In determining the sufficiency of the complaint to state a cause of action, all allegations of the complaint are taken as true, and possible affirmative defenses are not considered. Strickland v. Commerce Loan Co. of Jacksonville, 158 So.2d 814 (Fla. 1st DCA 1963); FL-PP § 2:12.

i. The issues for trial in Florida must be settled by the pleadings. The issues cannot be raised by discovery. FL-PRACPROC § 7:6.

ii. Causes of action may be pleaded alternatively in the same count or in different counts and against the same or different defendants as long as the joinder of parties is proper. FL-PRACPROC § 7:6.

iii. Each count must state a cause of action. Each independent cause of action should be pleaded in a separate count. FL-PRACPROC § 7:6.

iv. Incorporation by reference of all allegations from one count to another is not proper. Separate counts facilitate reference to the pleading in which they appear in other pleadings, motions or papers as well as the assertion of defenses against some, but not all, causes of action. Some defenses may not apply to the initial pleading as a whole. FL-PRACPROC § 7:6.

4. *Pleading special matters*

a. *Capacity.* It is not necessary to aver the capacity of a party to sue or be sued, the authority of a party to sue or be sued in a representative capacity, or the legal existence of an organized association of persons that is made a party, except to the extent required to show the jurisdiction of the court. The initial pleading served on behalf of a minor party shall specifically aver the age of the minor party. When a party desires to raise an issue as to the legal existence of any party, the capacity of any party to sue or be sued, or the authority of a party to sue or be sued in a representative capacity, that party shall do so by specific negative averment which shall include such supporting particulars as are peculiarly within the pleader's knowledge. FL ST RCP Rule 1.120(a).

b. *Fraud, mistake, condition of the mind.* In all averments of fraud or mistake, the circumstances constituting fraud or mistake shall be stated with such particularity as the circumstances may permit. Malice, intent, knowledge, mental attitude, and other condition of mind of a person may be averred generally. FL ST RCP Rule 1.120(b).

c. *Conditions precedent.* In pleading the performance or occurrence of conditions precedent, it is sufficient to aver generally that all conditions precedent have been performed or have occurred. A denial of performance or occurrence shall be made specifically and with particularity. FL ST RCP Rule 1.120(c).

d. *Official document or act.* In pleading an official document or official act it is sufficient to aver that the document was issued or the act done in compliance with law. FL ST RCP Rule 1.120(c).

e. *Judgment or decree.* In pleading a judgment or decree of a domestic or foreign court, a judicial or quasi-judicial tribunal, or a board or officer, it is sufficient to aver the judgment or decree without setting forth matter showing jurisdiction to render it. FL ST RCP Rule 1.120(e).

f. *Time and place.* For the purpose of testing the sufficiency of a pleading, averments of time and place are material and shall be considered like all other averments of material matter. FL ST RCP Rule 1.120(f).

g. *Special damage.* When items of special damage are claimed, they shall be specifically stated. FL ST RCP Rule 1.120(g).

5. *Parties*

a. *Parties generally.* Every action may be prosecuted in the name of the real party in interest, but a personal representative, administrator, guardian, trustee of an express trust, a party with whom or in whose name a contract has been made for the benefit of another, or a party expressly authorized by statute may sue in that person's own name without joining the party for whose benefit the action is brought. All persons having an interest in the subject of the action and in obtaining the relief demanded may join as plaintiffs and any person may be made a defendant who has or claims an interest adverse to the plaintiff. Any person may at any time be made a party if that person's presence is necessary or proper to a complete determination of the cause. Persons having a united interest may be joined on the same side as plaintiffs or defendants, and anyone who refuses to join may for such reason be made a defendant. FL ST RCP Rule 1.210(a).

b. *Minors or incompetent persons.* When a minor or incompetent person has a representative, such as a guardian or other like fiduciary, the representative may sue or defend on behalf of the minor or incompetent person. A minor or incompetent person who does not have a duly appointed representative may sue by next friend or by a guardian ad litem. The court shall appoint a guardian ad litem for a minor or incompetent person not otherwise represented in an action or shall make such other order as it deems proper for the protection of the minor or incompetent person. FL ST RCP Rule 1.210(b).

c. For survivor and substitution of parties information, please see FL ST RCP Rule 1.260.

6. *Counterclaims and crossclaims*

a. *Compulsory counterclaims.* A pleading shall state as a counterclaim any claim which at the time of serving the pleading the pleader has against any opposing party, provided it arises out of the transaction or occurrence that is the subject matter of the opposing party's claim and does not require for its adjudication the presence of third parties over whom the court cannot acquire jurisdiction. But the pleader need not state a claim if (1) at the time the action was commenced the claim was the subject of another pending action, or (2) the opposing party brought suit upon that party's claim by attachment or other process by which the court did not acquire jurisdiction to render a personal judgment on the claim and the pleader is not stating a counterclaim under this rule. FL ST RCP Rule 1.170(a).

b. *Permissive counterclaim.* A pleading may state as a counterclaim any claim against an opposing party not arising out of the transaction or occurrence that is the subject matter of the opposing party's claim. FL ST RCP Rule 1.170(b).

c. *Counterclaim exceeding opposing claim.* A counterclaim may or may not diminish or defeat the recovery sought by the opposing party. It may claim relief exceeding in amount or different in kind from that sought in the pleading of the opposing party. FL ST RCP Rule 1.170(c).

d. *Counterclaim against the State.* The Florida Rules of Civil Procedure shall not be construed to enlarge beyond the limits established by law the right to assert counterclaims or to claim credits against the state or any of its subdivisions or other governmental organizations thereof subject to suit or against a municipal corporation or against an officer, agency, or administrative board of the state. FL ST RCP Rule 1.170(d).

e. *Counterclaim maturing or acquired after pleading.* A claim which matured or was acquired by the pleader after serving the pleading may be presented as a counterclaim by supplemental pleading with the permission of the court. FL ST RCP Rule 1.170(e).

f. *Omitted counterclaim or crossclaim.* When a pleader fails to set up a counterclaim or crossclaim through oversight, inadvertence, or excusable neglect, or when justice requires, the pleader may set up the counterclaim or crossclaim by amendment with leave of the court. FL ST RCP Rule 1.170(f).

g. *Crossclaim against co-party.* A pleading may state as a crossclaim any claim by one party against a co-party arising out of the transaction or occurrence that is the subject matter of either the original action or a counterclaim therein, or relating to any property that is the subject matter of the original action. The crossclaim may include a claim that the party against whom it is asserted is or may be liable to the crossclaimant for all or part of a claim asserted in the action against the crossclaimant. Service of a crossclaim on a party who has appeared in the action shall be made pursuant to FL ST RCP Rule 1.080. Service of a crossclaim against a party who has not appeared in the action shall be made in the manner provided for service of summons. FL ST RCP Rule 1.170(g).

h. *Additional parties may be brought in.* When the presence of parties other than those to the original action is required to grant complete relief in the determination of a counterclaim or crossclaim, they shall be named in the counterclaim or crossclaim and be served with process and shall be parties to the action thereafter if jurisdiction of them can be obtained and their joinder will not deprive the court of jurisdiction of the action. FL ST RCP Rule 1.250(b) and FL ST RCP Rule 1.250(c) apply to parties brought in under FL ST RCP Rule 1.170(h). FL ST RCP Rule 1.170(h).

i. *Separate trials; Separate judgment.* If the court orders separate trials as provided in FL ST RCP Rule 1.270(b), judgment on a counterclaim or crossclaim may be rendered when the court has jurisdiction to do so even if a claim of the opposing party has been dismissed or otherwise disposed of. FL ST RCP Rule 1.170(i).

j. *Demand exceeding jurisdiction; Transfer of action.* If the demand of any counterclaim or crossclaim exceeds the jurisdiction of the court in which the action is pending, the action shall be transferred forthwith to the court of the same county having jurisdiction of the demand in the counterclaim or crossclaim with only such alterations in the pleadings as are essential. The court shall order the transfer of the action and the transmittal of all papers in it to the proper court if the party asserting the demand exceeding the jurisdiction deposits with the court having jurisdiction a sum sufficient to pay the clerk's service charge in the court to which the action is transferred at the time of filing the counterclaim or crossclaim. Thereupon the original papers and deposit shall be transmitted and filed with a certified copy of the order. The court to which the action is transferred shall have full power and jurisdiction over the demands of all parties. Failure to make the service charge deposit at the time the counterclaim or crossclaim is filed, or within such further time as the court may allow, shall reduce a claim for damages to an amount within the jurisdiction of the court where the action is pending and waive the claim in other cases. FL ST RCP Rule 1.170(j).

7. *Misjoinder and nonjoinder of parties*

a. *Misjoinder.* Misjoinder of parties is not a ground for dismissal of an action. Any claim against a party may be severed and proceeded with separately. FL ST RCP Rule 1.250(a).

b. *Dropping parties.* Parties may be dropped by an adverse party in the manner provided for voluntary dismissal in FL ST RCP Rule 1.420(a)(1) subject to the exception stated in FL ST RCP Rule 1.420. If notice of lis pendens has been filed in the action against a party so dropped, the notice of dismissal shall be recorded and cancels the notice of lis pendens without the necessity of a court order. Parties may be dropped by order of court on its own initiative or the motion of any party at any stage of the action on such terms as are just. FL ST RCP Rule 1.250(b).

c. *Adding parties.* Parties may be added once as a matter of course within the same time that pleadings can be so amended under FL ST RCP Rule 1.190(a). If amendment by leave of court or stipulation of the parties is permitted, parties may be added in the amended pleading without further order of court. Parties may be added by order of court on its own initiative or on motion of any party at any stage of the action and on such terms as are just. FL ST RCP Rule 1.250(c).

8. *Jury demand*

a. *Right preserved.* The right of trial by jury as declared by the Constitution or by statute shall be preserved to the parties inviolate. FL ST RCP Rule 1.430(a).

b. *Demand.* Any party may demand a trial by jury of any issue triable of right by a jury by serving upon the other party a demand therefor in writing at any time after commencement of the action and not later than ten (10) days after the service of the last pleading directed to such issue. The demand may be indorsed upon a pleading of the party. FL ST RCP Rule 1.430(b).

c. *Specification of issues.* In the demand a party may specify the issues that the party wishes so tried; otherwise, the party is deemed to demand trial by jury for all issues so triable. FL ST RCP Rule 1.430(c).

i. If a party has demanded trial by jury for only some of the issues, any other party may serve a demand for trial by jury of any other or all of the issues triable by jury ten (10) days after service of the demand or such lesser time as the court may order. FL ST RCP Rule 1.430(c).

d. *Waiver.* A party who fails to serve a demand as required by FL ST RCP Rule 1.430 waives trial by jury. FL ST RCP Rule 1.430(d).

i. If waived, a jury trial may not be granted without the consent of the parties, but the court may allow an amendment in the proceedings to demand a trial by jury or order a trial by jury on its own motion. FL ST RCP Rule 1.430(d).

ii. A demand for trial by jury may not be withdrawn without the consent of the parties. FL ST RCP Rule 1.430(d).

9. *Arbitration and mediation*

a. *Referral to arbitration and mediation.* Except as hereinafter provided or as otherwise prohibited by law, the presiding judge may enter an order referring all or any part of a contested civil matter to mediation or arbitration. The parties to any contested civil matter may file a written stipulation to mediate or arbitrate any issue between them at any time. Such stipulation shall be incorporated into the order of referral. FL ST RCP Rule 1.700(a).

b. *Arbitration*

i. *Exclusions.* A civil action shall be ordered to arbitration or arbitration in conjunction with mediation upon stipulation of the parties. A civil action may be ordered to arbitration or arbitration in conjunction with mediation upon motion of any party or by the court, if the judge determines the action to be of such a nature that arbitration could be of benefit to the litigants or the court. FL ST RCP Rule 1.800.

- Under no circumstances may the following categories of actions be referred to arbitration: (1) bond estreatures; (2) habeas corpus or other extraordinary writs; (3) bond validations; (4) civil or criminal contempt; (5) such other matters as may be specified by order of the chief judge in the circuit. FL ST RCP Rule 1.800.

ii. For more information regarding arbitration, please see FL ST RCP Rule 1.810; FL ST RCP Rule 1.820; FL ST RCP Rule 1.830; FL ST 7 J CIR CV-2009-019-SC; and FL ST 7 J CIR CV-2003-002-SC(1)(c).

c. *Mediation.* For more information regarding mediation, please see FL ST RCP Rule 1.710; FL ST RCP Rule 1.720; FL ST RCP Rule 1.730; FL ST RCP Rule 1.750; FL ST 7 J CIR CV-2008-018-SC; and FL ST 7 J CIR CV-2003-002-SC(1).

10. *Rules of court*

   a. *Rules of civil procedure.* The Florida Rules of Civil Procedure apply to all actions of a civil nature and all special statutory proceedings in the circuit courts and county courts except those to which the Florida Probate Rules, the Florida Family Law Rules of Procedure, or the Small Claims Rules apply. FL ST RCP Rule 1.010.

      i. The form, content, procedure, and time for pleading in all special statutory proceedings shall be as prescribed by the statutes governing the proceeding unless the Florida Rules of Civil Procedure specifically provide to the contrary. FL ST RCP Rule 1.010.

      ii. The Florida Rules of Civil Procedure shall be construed to secure the just, speedy, and inexpensive determination of every action. FL ST RCP Rule 1.010.

   b. *Rules of judicial administration.* The Florida Rules of Judicial Administration shall apply to administrative matters in all courts to which the Florida Rules of Judicial Administration are applicable by their terms. The Florida Rules of Judicial Administration shall be construed to secure the speedy and inexpensive determination of every proceeding to which they are applicable. The Florida Rules of Judicial Administration shall supersede all conflicting rules and statutes. FL ST J ADMIN Rule 2.110.

D. Documents

1. *Required documents*

   a. *Amended complaint.* See the General Requirements section of this document for the content of an amended complaint. If a party files a motion to amend a pleading, the party shall attach the proposed amended pleading to the motion. FL ST RCP Rule 1.190(a). See the KeyRules Florida Circuit Court Motion for Leave to Amend document for further information.

      i. *Notices to persons with disabilities.* See the Format section of this KeyRules document for further information.

   b. *Certificate of service.* When any attorney certifies in substance: "I certify that a copy hereof has been furnished to (here insert name or names and addresses used for service) by (e-mail) (delivery) (mail) (fax) on .... (date) ....________________ Attorney" the certificate is taken as prima facie proof of such service in compliance with FL ST J ADMIN Rule 2.516. FL ST J ADMIN Rule 2.516(f).

2. *Supplemental documents*

   a. *Exhibits.* All bonds, notes, bills of exchange, contracts, accounts, or documents upon which action may be brought or defense made, or a copy thereof or a copy of the portions thereof material to the pleadings, shall be incorporated in or attached to the pleading. No papers shall be unnecessarily annexed as exhibits. The pleadings shall contain no unnecessary recitals of deeds, documents, contracts, or other instruments. Any exhibit attached to a pleading shall be considered a part of the pleadings for all purposes. FL ST RCP Rule 1.130(a).

   b. *Notice of constitutional question.* A party that files a pleading, written motion, or other paper drawing into question the constitutionality of a state statute or a county or municipal charter, ordinance, or franchise must promptly (1) file a notice of constitutional question stating the question and identifying the paper that raises it; and (2) serve the notice and the pleading, written motion, or other paper drawing into question the constitutionality of a state statute or a county or municipal charter, ordinance, or franchise on the Attorney General or the state attorney of the judicial circuit in which the action is pending, by either certified or registered mail. Service of the notice and pleading, written motion, or other paper does not require joinder of the Attorney General or the state attorney as a party to the action. FL ST RCP Rule 1.071.

E. Format

1. *Documents; Type and size.* Documents subject to the exceptions set forth in FL ST J ADMIN Rule 2.525(d) shall be filed on recycled paper measuring eight and one half by eleven (8 1/2 by 11) inches. For purposes of FL ST J ADMIN Rule 2.520, paper is recycled if it contains a minimum content of fifty (50) percent waste paper. Xerographic reduction of legal-size (eight and one half by fourteen (8 1/2 by 14) inches) documents to letter size (eight and one half by eleven (8 1/2 by 11) inches) is prohibited. All other

documents filed by electronic transmission shall be filed in a format capable of being printed in a format consistent with the provisions of FL ST J ADMIN Rule 2.250. FL ST J ADMIN Rule 2.520(b).

a. *Exhibits.* Any exhibit or attachment filed with pleadings or papers may be filed in its original size. FL ST J ADMIN Rule 2.520(c).

b. *Recording space.* On all papers and documents prepared and filed by the court or by any party to a proceeding which are to be recorded in the public records of any county, including but not limited to final money judgments and notices of lis pendens, a three (3) inch by three (3) inch space at the top right-hand corner on the first page and a one (1) inch by three (3) inch space at the top right-hand corner on each subsequent page shall be left blank and reserved for use by the clerk of court. FL ST J ADMIN Rule 2.520(d).

   i. *Exceptions to recording space.* Any papers or documents created by persons or entities over which the filing party has no control, including but not limited to wills, codicils, trusts, or other testamentary documents; documents prepared or executed by any public officer; documents prepared, executed, acknowledged, or proved outside of the State of Florida; or documents created by State or Federal government agencies, may be filed without the space required by FL ST J ADMIN Rule 2.520. FL ST J ADMIN Rule 2.520(e).

c. *Noncompliance.* No clerk of court is permitted to refuse to file any document or paper because of noncompliance with the Florida Rules of Judicial Administration. However, upon request of the clerk of court, noncomplying documents must be resubmitted in accordance with the formatting rules. FL ST J ADMIN Rule 2.520(f).

2. *Caption.* Every pleading, motion, order, judgment, or other paper shall have a caption containing the name of the court, the file number, and except for in rem proceedings, including forfeiture proceedings, the name of the first party on each side with an appropriate indication of other parties, and a designation identifying the party filing it and its nature or the nature of the order, as the case may be. In any in rem proceeding, every pleading, motion, order, judgment, or other paper shall have a caption containing the name of the court, the file number, the style "In re" (followed by the name or general description of the property), and a designation of the person or entity filing it and its nature or the nature of the order, as the case may be. In an in rem forfeiture proceeding, the style shall be "In re forfeiture of" (followed by the name of the general description of the property). All papers filed in the action shall be styled in such a manner as to indicate clearly the subject matter of the paper and the party requesting or obtaining relief. FL ST RCP Rule 1.100(c)(1).

   a. *Volusia County eminent domain cases.* All orders, pleadings, motions and other papers will bear the initial case style. Documents intended to apply only to particular parcel(s) will indicate in their caption the parcel number(s) to which they apply and sufficient copies shall be provided to the Clerk of Court to allow the filing and docketing of each relevant paper in each parcel file. FL ST 7 J CIR CV-2000-011-VL(b).

3. *Writing and written defined.* Writing or written means a document containing information, an application, or a stipulation. FL ST RCP Rule 1.080(c).

4. *Rule abbreviations*

   a. The Florida Rules of Civil Procedure and shall be abbreviated as Fla.R.Civ.P. FL ST RCP Rule 1.010.

   b. The Florida Rules of Judicial Administration shall be abbreviated as Fla. R. Jud. Admin. FL ST J ADMIN Rule 2.110.

5. *Nonverification.* Except when otherwise specifically provided by the Florida Rules of Civil Procedure or an applicable statute, every pleading or other document of a party represented by an attorney need not be verified or accompanied by an affidavit. FL ST RCP Rule 1.030; FL ST J ADMIN Rule 2.515(a).

6. *Attorney signature*

   a. *Attorney signature.* Every pleading and other document of a party represented by an attorney shall be signed by at least one (1) attorney of record in that attorney's individual name whose current record Florida Bar address, telephone number, including area code, primary e-mail address and secondary

e-mail addresses, if any, and Florida Bar number shall be stated, and who shall be duly licensed to practice law in Florida or who shall have received permission to appear in the particular case as provided in FL ST J ADMIN Rule 2.510. FL ST J ADMIN Rule 2.515(a).

i. The attorney may be required by the court to give the address of, and to vouch for the attorney's authority to represent, the party. FL ST J ADMIN Rule 2.515(a).

ii. The signature of an attorney shall constitute a certificate by the attorney that the attorney has read the pleading or other document; that to the best of the attorney's knowledge, information, and belief there is good ground to support it; and that it is not interposed for delay. FL ST J ADMIN Rule 2.515(a).

iii. If a pleading is not signed or is signed with intent to defeat the purpose of FL ST J ADMIN Rule 2.515, it may be stricken and the action may proceed as though the pleading or other document had not been served. FL ST J ADMIN Rule 2.515(a).

b. *Pro se litigant signature.* A party who is not represented by an attorney shall sign any pleading or other paper and state the party's address and telephone number, including area code. FL ST J ADMIN Rule 2.515(b).

c. *Form of signature*

i. The signatures required on pleadings and documents by FL ST J ADMIN Rule 2.515(a) and FL ST J ADMIN Rule 2.515(b) may be:

- Original signatures;
- Original signatures that have been reproduced by electronic means, such as on electronically transmitted documents or photocopied documents;
- Electronic signatures using the "/s/," "s/," or "/s" formats by or at the direction of the person signing; or
- Any other signature format authorized by general law, so long as the clerk where the proceeding is pending has the capability of receiving and has obtained approval from the Supreme Court of Florida to accept pleadings and documents with that signature format. FL ST J ADMIN Rule 2.515(c)(1).

ii. An attorney, party, or other person who files a pleading or paper by electronic transmission that does not contain the original signature of that attorney, party, or other person shall file that identical pleading or paper in paper form containing an original signature of that attorney, party, or other person (hereinafter called the follow-up filing) immediately thereafter. The follow-up filing is not required if the Supreme Court of Florida has entered an order directing the clerk of court to discontinue accepting the follow-up filing. FL ST J ADMIN Rule 2.515(c)(2).

7. *Forms*

a. *Process.* The forms of process, notice of lis pendens, and notice of action provided in the Florida Rules of Civil Procedure are sufficient. Variations from the forms do not void process or notices that are otherwise sufficient. FL ST RCP Rule 1.900(a).

b. *Other forms.* The other forms provided in the Florida Rules of Civil Procedure are sufficient for the matters that are covered by them. So long as the substance is expressed without prolixity, the forms may be varied to meet the facts of a particular case. FL ST RCP Rule 1.900(b).

c. *Formal matters.* Captions, except for the designation of the paper, are omitted from the forms provided in the Florida Rules of Civil Procedure. A general form of caption is the first form provided. Signatures are omitted from pleadings and motions. FL ST RCP Rule 1.900(c).

8. *Notices to persons with disabilities.* All notices of court proceedings to be held in a public facility, and all process compelling appearance at such proceedings, shall include the following statement in bold face, fourteen (14) point Times New Roman or Courier font: "If you are a person with a disability who needs any accommodation in order to participate in this proceeding, you are entitled, at no cost to you, to the provision of certain assistance. Please contact [identify applicable court personnel by name, address, and telephone number] at least seven (7) days before your scheduled court appearance, or immediately upon

receiving this notification if the time before the scheduled appearance is less than seven (7) days; if you are hearing or voice impaired, call 711." FL ST J ADMIN Rule 2.540(c)(1).

9. *Minimization of the filing of sensitive information*

   a. *Limitations for court filings.* Unless authorized by FL ST J ADMIN Rule 2.425(b), statute, another rule of court, or the court orders otherwise, designated sensitive information filed with the court must be limited to the following format:

      i. The initials of a person known to be a minor;

      ii. The year of birth of a person's birth date;

      iii. No portion of any: Social security number, Bank account number, Credit card account number, Charge account number, or Debit account number;

      iv. The last four digits of any: Taxpayer identification number (TIN), Employee identification number, Driver's license number, Passport number, Telephone number, Financial account number, except as set forth in FL ST J ADMIN Rule 2.425(a)(3), Brokerage account number, Insurance policy account number, Loan account number, Customer account number, or Patient or health care number;

      v. A truncated version of any: Email address, Computer user name, Password, or Personal identification number (PIN); and

      vi. A truncated version of any other sensitive information as provided by court order. FL ST J ADMIN Rule 2.425(a).

   b. *Exceptions.* FL ST J ADMIN Rule 2.425(a) does not apply to the following:

      i. An account number which identifies the property alleged to be the subject of a proceeding;

      ii. The record of an administrative or agency proceeding;

      iii. The record in appellate or review proceedings;

      iv. The birth date of a minor whenever the birth date is necessary for the court to establish or maintain subject matter jurisdiction;

      v. The name of a minor in any order relating to parental responsibility, time-sharing, or child support;

      vi. The name of a minor in any document or order affecting the minor's ownership of real property;

      vii. The birth date of a party in a writ of attachment or notice to payor;

      viii. In traffic and criminal proceedings: a pro se filing; a court filing that is related to a criminal matter or investigation and that is prepared before the filing of a criminal charge or is not filed as part of any docketed criminal case; an arrest or search warrant or any information in support thereof; a charging document and an affidavit or other documents filed in support of any charging document, including any driving records; a statement of particulars; discovery material introduced into evidence or otherwise filed with the court; and all information necessary for the proper issuance and execution of a subpoena duces tecum;

      ix. Information used by the clerk for case maintenance purposes or the courts for case management purposes; and

      x. Information which is relevant and material to an issue before the court. FL ST J ADMIN Rule 2.425(b).

   c. *Remedies.* Upon motion by a party or interested person or sua sponte by the court, the court may order remedies, sanctions or both for a violation of FL ST J ADMIN Rule 2.425(a). Following notice and an opportunity to respond, the court may impose sanctions if such filing was not made in good faith. FL ST J ADMIN Rule 2.425(c).

   d. *Motions not restricted.* FL ST J ADMIN Rule 2.425 does not restrict a party's right to move for protective order, to move to file documents under seal, or to request a determination of the confidentiality of records. FL ST J ADMIN Rule 2.425(d).

e. *Application.* FL ST J ADMIN Rule 2.425 does not affect the application of constitutional provisions, statutes, or rules of court regarding confidential information or access to public information. FL ST J ADMIN Rule 2.425(e).

F. Filing and Service Requirements

1. *Filing requirements.* All original documents must be filed with the court either before service or immediately thereafter, unless otherwise provided for by general law or other rules. If the original of any bond or other document is not placed in the court file, a certified copy must be so placed by the clerk. FL ST J ADMIN Rule 2.516(d). All documents shall be filed in conformity with the requirements of FL ST J ADMIN Rule 2.525. FL ST RCP Rule 1.080(b). All documents filed in any court shall be filed by electronic transmission in accordance with FL ST J ADMIN Rule 2.525. "Documents" means pleadings, motions, petitions, memoranda, briefs, notices, exhibits, declarations, affidavits, orders, judgments, decrees, writs, opinions, and any other paper or writing submitted to a court. FL ST J ADMIN Rule 2.520(a). All documents that are court records, as defined in FL ST J ADMIN Rule 2.430(a)(1), must be filed by electronic transmission, provided that: (1) the clerk has the ability to accept and retain such documents; (2) the clerk or the chief judge of the circuit has requested permission to accept documents filed by electronic transmission; and (3) the supreme court has entered an order granting permission to the clerk to accept documents filed by electronic transmission. FL ST J ADMIN Rule 2.525(c)(1).

   a. *Definition.* "Electronic transmission of documents" means the sending of information by electronic signals to, by or from a court or clerk, which when received can be transformed and stored or transmitted on paper, microfilm, magnetic storage device, optical imaging system, CD-ROM, flash drive, other electronic data storage system, server, case maintenance system ("CM"), electronic court filing ("ECF") system, statewide or local electronic portal ("e-portal"), or other electronic record keeping system authorized by the supreme court in a format sufficient to communicate the information on the original document in a readable format. Electronic transmission of documents includes electronic mail ("e-mail") and any internet-based transmission procedure, and may include procedures allowing for documents to be signed or verified by electronic means. FL ST J ADMIN Rule 2.525(a).

      i. The filing of documents with the court as required by the Florida Rules of Judicial Administration must be made by filing them with the clerk in accordance with FL ST J ADMIN Rule 2.525, except that the judge may permit documents to be filed with the judge, in which event the judge must note the filing date before him or her on the documents and transmit them to the clerk. The date of filing is that shown on the face of the document by the judge's notation or the clerk's time stamp, whichever is earlier. FL ST J ADMIN Rule 2.516(e).

   b. *Application.* Any court or clerk of the court may accept the electronic transmission of documents for filing after the clerk, together with input from the chief judge of the circuit, has obtained approval of the procedures and program for doing so from the Supreme Court of Florida. FL ST J ADMIN Rule 2.525(b).

   c. *Exceptions*

      i. Paper documents and other submissions may be manually submitted to the clerk or court:

         - When the clerk does not have the ability to accept and retain documents by electronic filing or has not had ECF Procedures approved by the supreme court;
         - For filing by any self-represented party or any self-represented nonparty unless specific ECF Procedures provide a means to file documents electronically. However, any self-represented nonparty that is a governmental or public agency and any other agency, partnership, corporation, or business entity acting on behalf of any governmental or public agency may file documents by electronic transmission if such entity has the capability of filing documents electronically;
         - For filing by attorneys excused from e-mail service in accordance with FL ST J ADMIN Rule 2.516(b);
         - When submitting evidentiary exhibits or filing non-documentary materials;
         - When the filing involves documents in excess of twenty-five (25) megabytes (25MB) in

size. For such filings, documents may be transmitted using an electronic storage medium that the clerk has the ability to accept, which may include a CD-ROM, flash drive, or similar storage medium;

- When filed in open court, as permitted by the court;
- When paper filing is permitted by any approved statewide or local ECF procedures; and
- If any court determines that justice so requires. FL ST J ADMIN Rule 2.525(d).

ii. Any document in paper form submitted under FL ST J ADMIN Rule 2.525(d) is filed when it is received by the clerk or court and the clerk shall immediately thereafter convert any filed paper document to an electronic document. "Convert to an electronic document" means optically capturing an image of a paper document and using character recognition software to recover as much of the document's text as practicable and then indexing and storing the document in the official court file. FL ST J ADMIN Rule 2.525(c)(4).

iii. Any storage medium submitted under FL ST J ADMIN Rule 2.525(d)(5) is filed when received by the clerk or court and the clerk shall immediately thereafter transfer the electronic documents from the storage device to the official court file. FL ST J ADMIN Rule 2.525(c)(5).

iv. If the filer of any paper document authorized under FL ST J ADMIN Rule 2.525(d) provides a self-addressed, postage-paid envelope for return of the paper document after it is converted to electronic form by the clerk, the clerk shall place the paper document in the envelope and deposit it in the mail. Except when a paper document is required to be maintained, the clerk may recycle any filed paper document that is not to be returned to the filer. FL ST J ADMIN Rule 2.525(c)(6).

v. The clerk may convert any paper document filed before the effective date of FL ST J ADMIN Rule 2.525 to an electronic document. Unless the clerk is required to maintain the paper document, if the paper document has been converted to an electronic document by the clerk, the paper document is no longer part of the official court file and may be removed and recycled. FL ST J ADMIN Rule 2.525(c)(7).

d. *Official court file.* For information on what constitutes the official court file, please see FL ST J ADMIN Rule 2.525(c)(2), FL ST J ADMIN Rule 2.525(c)(3).

e. *Administration.* All attorneys, parties, or other persons using this rule to file documents are required to make arrangements with the court or clerk for the payment of any charges authorized by general law or the supreme court before filing any document by electronic transmission. FL ST J ADMIN Rule 2.525(f)(2).

f. *Filing date.* The filing date for an electronically transmitted document is the date and time that such filing is acknowledged by an electronic stamp or otherwise, pursuant to any procedure set forth in any ECF Procedures approved by the supreme court, or the date the last page of such filing is received by the court or clerk. FL ST J ADMIN Rule 2.525(f)(3).

g. *Accessibility.* All documents transmitted in any electronic form under FL ST J ADMIN Rule 2.525 must comply with the accessibility requirements of FL ST J ADMIN Rule 2.526. FL ST J ADMIN Rule 2.525(g).

2. *Service requirements.* Every pleading subsequent to the initial pleading, all orders, and every other document filed in the action must be served in conformity with the requirements of FL ST J ADMIN Rule 2.516. FL ST RCP Rule 1.080(a).

a. *Service; When required.* Unless the court otherwise orders, or a statute or supreme court administrative order specifies a different means of service, every pleading subsequent to the initial pleading and every other document filed in any court proceeding, except applications for witness subpoenas and documents served by formal notice or required to be served in the manner provided for service of formal notice, must be served in accordance with FL ST J ADMIN Rule 2.516 on each party. No service need be made on parties against whom a default has been entered, except that pleadings asserting new or additional claims against them must be served in the manner provided for service of summons. FL ST J ADMIN Rule 2.516(a).

b. *Service; How made.* When service is required or permitted to be made upon a party represented by an attorney, service must be made upon the attorney unless service upon the party is ordered by the court. FL ST J ADMIN Rule 2.516(b).

i. *Service by electronic mail ("e-mail").* All documents required or permitted to be served on another party must be served by e-mail, unless FL ST J ADMIN Rule 2.516 otherwise provides. When, in addition to service by e-mail, the sender also utilizes another means of service provided for in FL ST J ADMIN Rule 2.516(b)(2), any differing time limits and other provisions applicable to that other means of service control. FL ST J ADMIN Rule 2.516(b)(1). Any document electronically transmitted to a court or clerk must also be served on all parties and interested persons in accordance with the applicable rules of court. FL ST J ADMIN Rule 2.525(e)(2).

- *Service on attorneys.* Upon appearing in a proceeding, an attorney must serve a designation of a primary e-mail address and may designate no more than two (2) secondary e-mail addresses. Thereafter, service must be directed to all designated e-mail addresses in that proceeding. Every document filed by an attorney thereafter must include the primary e-mail address of that attorney and any secondary e-mail addresses. If an attorney does not designate any e-mail address for service, documents may be served on that attorney at the e-mail address on record with The Florida Bar. FL ST J ADMIN Rule 2.516(b)(1)(A).
- *Exception to e-mail service on attorneys.* Service by an attorney on another attorney must be made by e-mail unless excused by the court. Upon motion by an attorney demonstrating that the attorney has no e-mail account and lacks access to the Internet at the attorney's office, the court may excuse the attorney from the requirements of e-mail service. Service on and by an attorney excused by the court from e-mail service must be by the means provided in FL ST J ADMIN Rule 2.516(b)(2). FL ST J ADMIN Rule 2.516(b)(1)(B).
- *Service on and by parties not represented by an attorney.* Any party not represented by an attorney may serve a designation of a primary e-mail address and also may designate no more than two (2) secondary e-mail addresses to which service must be directed in that proceeding by the means provided in FL ST J ADMIN Rule 2.516(b)(1). If a party not represented by an attorney does not designate an e-mail address for service in a proceeding, service on and by that party must be by the means provided in FL ST J ADMIN Rule 2.516(b)(2). FL ST J ADMIN Rule 2.516(b)(1)(C).
- *Time of service.* Service by e-mail is complete when it is sent. FL ST J ADMIN Rule 2.516(b)(1)(D). An e-mail is deemed served on the date it is sent. FL ST J ADMIN Rule 2.516(b)(1)(D)(i). If the sender learns that the e-mail did not reach the address of the person to be served, the sender must immediately send another copy by e-mail, or by a means authorized by FL ST J ADMIN Rule 2.516(b)(2). FL ST J ADMIN Rule 2.516(b)(1)(D)(ii). E-mail service is treated as service by mail for the computation of time. FL ST J ADMIN Rule 2.516(b)(1)(D)(iii).

ii. *Format of e-mail for service.* Service of a document by e-mail is made by attaching a copy of the document in PDF format to an e-mail sent to all addresses designated by the attorney or party. FL ST J ADMIN Rule 2.516(b)(1)(E).

- All documents served by e-mail must be attached to an e-mail message containing a subject line beginning with the words "SERVICE OF COURT DOCUMENT" in all capital letters, followed by the case number of the proceeding in which the documents are being served. FL ST J ADMIN Rule 2.516(b)(1)(E)(i).
- The body of the e-mail must identify the court in which the proceeding is pending, the case number, the name of the initial party on each side, the title of each document served with that e-mail, and the sender's name and telephone number. FL ST J ADMIN Rule 2.516(b)(1)(E)(ii).
- Any document served by e-mail may be signed by the "/s/" format, as long as the filed original is signed in accordance with the applicable rule of procedure. FL ST J ADMIN Rule 2.516(b)(1)(E)(iii).

- Any e-mail which, together with its attached documents, exceeds five megabytes (5MB) in size, must be divided and sent as separate e-mails, no one of which may exceed five megabytes (5MB) in size and each of which must be sequentially numbered in the subject line. FL ST J ADMIN Rule 2.516(b)(1)(E)(iv).

iii. *Service by other means.* In addition to, and not in lieu of, service by e-mail, service may also be made upon attorneys by any of the means specified in FL ST J ADMIN Rule 2.516(b)(2). Service on and by all parties who are not represented by an attorney and who do not designate an e-mail address, and on and by all attorneys excused from e-mail service, must be made by delivering a copy of the document or by mailing it to the party or attorney at their last known address or, if no address is known, by leaving it with the clerk of the court. Service by mail is complete upon mailing. Delivery of a copy within FL ST J ADMIN Rule 2.516 is complete upon:

- Handing it to the attorney or to the party,
- Leaving it at the attorney's or party's office with a clerk or other person in charge thereof,
- If there is no one in charge, leaving it in a conspicuous place therein,
- If the office is closed or the person to be served has no office, leaving it at the person's usual place of abode with some person of his or her family above fifteen (15) years of age and informing such person of the contents, or
- Transmitting it by facsimile to the attorney's or party's office with a cover sheet containing the sender's name, firm, address, telephone number, and facsimile number, and the number of pages transmitted. When service is made by facsimile, a copy must also be served by any other method permitted by FL ST J ADMIN Rule 2.516. Facsimile service occurs when transmission is complete. FL ST J ADMIN Rule 2.516(b)(2)(A) through FL ST J ADMIN Rule 2.516(b)(2)(E).
- Service by delivery after 5:00 p.m. must be deemed to have been made by mailing on the date of delivery. FL ST J ADMIN Rule 2.516(b)(2)(F).

c. *Service; Numerous defendants.* In actions when the parties are unusually numerous, the court may regulate the service contemplated by the Florida Rules of Judicial Administration on motion or on its own initiative in such manner as may be found to be just and reasonable. FL ST J ADMIN Rule 2.516(c).

d. *Service by clerk.* Service of notices and other documents required to be made by the clerk must also be done as provided in FL ST J ADMIN Rule 2.516(b). FL ST J ADMIN Rule 2.516(g).

G. Hearings

1. The parties may be required to participate in pretrial proceedings to consider and determine the necessity or desirability of an amendment to a pleading. FL ST RCP Rule 1.200(b)(2); FL-PP § 2:151.

H. Forms

1. Official Amended Complaint Forms for Florida

a. Caption. FL ST RCP Form 1.901.

b. Notice of compliance when constitutional challenge is brought. FL ST RCP Form 1.975.

2. Amended Complaint Forms for Florida

a. Consent; Of party; To amendment of pleadings. FL-PP § 2:154.

b. Notice of amended complaint. 3 FLPRAC § 190.1.

c. Complaint for damages; General form. FL-PP § 2:17.

d. Complaint; Negligent infliction of personal injury. FL-PP § 2:19.

e. Complaint; Fall down negligence. FL-PP § 2:20.

f. Complaint; Mortgage foreclosure. FL-PP § 2:21.

g. Complaint; Implied warranty. FL-PP § 2:22.

h. Complaint; Professional negligence. FL-PP § 2:23.
i. Complaint; Breach of contract. FL-PP § 2:24.
j. Complaint; Breach of personal services contract. FL-PP § 2:25.

I. Checklist

(I) ❑ Matters to be considered by plaintiff
  (a) ❑ Required documents
    (1) ❑ Amended complaint
    (2) ❑ Certificate of service
  (b) ❑ Supplemental documents
    (1) ❑ Exhibits
    (2) ❑ Notice of constitutional question
  (c) ❑ Timing
    (1) ❑ A party may amend a pleading once as a matter of course at any time before a responsive pleading is served
    (2) ❑ If the pleading is one to which no responsive pleading is permitted and the action has not been placed on the trial calendar, may so amend it at any time within twenty (20) days after it is served

Pleadings
Answer

Document Last Updated January 2013

A. Applicable Rules

1. *State rules*
  a. Nonverification of pleadings. FL ST RCP Rule 1.030.
  b. Process. FL ST RCP Rule 1.070.
  c. Constitutional challenge to state statute or county or municipal charter, ordinance, or franchise; Notice by party. FL ST RCP Rule 1.071.
  d. Service and filing of pleadings, orders, and documents. FL ST RCP Rule 1.080.
  e. Time. FL ST RCP Rule 1.090.
  f. Pleadings and motions. FL ST RCP Rule 1.100; FL ST RCP Rule 1.110; FL ST RCP Rule 1.120; FL ST RCP Rule 1.130; FL ST RCP Rule 1.190; FL ST RCP Rule 1.430.
  g. Defenses. FL ST RCP Rule 1.140.
  h. Relief from judgment, decrees, or orders. FL ST RCP Rule 1.540.
  i. Forms. FL ST RCP Rule 1.900.
  j. Minimization of the filing of sensitive information. FL ST J ADMIN Rule 2.425.
  k. Retention of court records. FL ST J ADMIN Rule 2.430.
  l. Foreign attorneys. FL ST J ADMIN Rule 2.510.
  m. Signature of attorneys and parties. FL ST J ADMIN Rule 2.515.
  n. Paper. FL ST J ADMIN Rule 2.520.
  o. Electronic filing. FL ST J ADMIN Rule 2.525.
  p. Accessibility of information and technology. FL ST J ADMIN Rule 2.526.
  q. Court reporting. FL ST J ADMIN Rule 2.535.

r. Requests for accommodations by persons with disabilities. FL ST J ADMIN Rule 2.540.

s. Waiver of sovereign immunity in tort actions; Recovery limits; Limitation on attorney fees; Statute of limitations; Exclusions; Indemnification; Risk management programs. FL ST § 768.28.

2. *Local rules*

a. Eminent domain cases. FL ST 7 J CIR CV-2000-011-VL.

b. Civil pretrial procedures. FL ST 7 J CIR CV-2003-002-SC.

c. Arbitration and mediation. FL ST 7 J CIR CV-2008-018-SC; FL ST 7 J CIR CV-2009-019-SC.

B. Timing

1. *General answer timing.* Unless a different time is prescribed in a statute of Florida, a defendant shall serve an answer within twenty (20) days after service of original process and the initial pleading on the defendant, or not later than the date fixed in a notice by publication. A party served with a pleading stating a crossclaim against that party shall serve an answer to it within twenty (20) days after service on that party. The plaintiff shall serve an answer to a counterclaim within twenty (20) days after service of the counterclaim. FL ST RCP Rule 1.140(a)(1).

a. *Waiver of service.* A defendant who, before being served with process, timely returns a waiver so requested is not required to respond to the complaint until sixty (60) days after the date the defendant received the request for waiver of service. For purposes of computing any time prescribed or allowed by the Florida Rules of Civil Procedure, service of process shall be deemed effected twenty (20) days before the time required to respond to the complaint. FL ST RCP Rule 1.070(i)(4).

b. *Service on the state.* Except when sued pursuant to FL ST § 768.28, the state of Florida, an agency of the state, or an officer or employee of the state sued in an official capacity shall serve an answer to the complaint or crossclaim, or a reply to a counterclaim, within forty (40) days after service. When sued pursuant to FL ST § 768.28, the Department of Financial Services or the defendant state agency shall have thirty (30) days from the date of service within which to serve an answer to the complaint or crossclaim or a reply to a counterclaim. FL ST RCP Rule 1.140(a)(2).

c. *Service of motion impact on time periods for service of answer.* The service of a motion under FL ST RCP Rule 1.140, except a motion for judgment on the pleadings or a motion to strike under FL ST RCP Rule 1.140(f), alters these periods of time so that if the court denies the motion or postpones its disposition until the trial on the merits, the responsive pleadings shall be served within ten (10) days after notice of the court's action or, if the court grants a motion for a more definite statement, the responsive pleadings shall be served within ten (10) days after service of the more definite statement unless a different time is fixed by the court in either case. FL ST RCP Rule 1.140(a)(3).

d. *Responding if pleading does not require a responsive pleading.* If a pleading sets forth a claim for relief to which the adverse party is not required to serve a responsive pleading, the adverse party may assert any defense in law or fact to that claim for relief at the trial, except that the objection of failure to state a legal defense in an answer or reply shall be asserted by motion to strike the defense within twenty (20) days after service of the answer or reply. FL ST RCP Rule 1.140(b).

2. *Computation of time*

a. *Generally.* Computation of time shall be governed by FL ST J ADMIN Rule 2.514. FL ST RCP Rule 1.090(a). The following rules apply in computing time periods specified in any rule of procedure, local rule, court order, or statute that does not specify a method of computing time. FL ST J ADMIN Rule 2.514(a).

i. *Period stated in days or a longer unit.* When the period is stated in days or a longer unit of time (A) exclude the day of the event that triggers the period; (B) count every day, including intermediate Saturdays, Sundays, and legal holidays; and (C) include the last day of the period, but if the last day is a Saturday, Sunday, or legal holiday, or falls within any period of time extended through an order of the chief justice under FL ST J ADMIN Rule 2.205(a)(2)(B)(iv), the period continues to run until the end of the next day that is not a Saturday, Sunday, or legal holiday and does not fall within any period of time extended through an order of the chief justice. FL ST J ADMIN Rule 2.514(a)(1).

ii. *Period stated in hours.* When the period is stated in hours (A) begin counting immediately on the occurrence of the event that triggers the period; (B) count every hour, including hours during intermediate Saturdays, Sundays, and legal holidays; and (C) if the period would end on a Saturday, Sunday, or legal holiday, or during any period of time extended through an order of the chief justice under FL ST J ADMIN Rule 2.205(a)(2)(B)(iv), the period continues to run until the same time on the next day that is not a Saturday, Sunday, or legal holiday and does not fall within any period of time extended through an order of the chief justice. FL ST J ADMIN Rule 2.514(a)(2).

iii. *Period stated in days less than seven (7) days.* When the period stated in days is less than seven (7) days, intermediate Saturdays, Sundays, and legal holidays shall be excluded in the computation. FL ST J ADMIN Rule 2.514(a)(3).

iv. *"Last day" defined.* Unless a different time is set by a statute, local rule, or court order, the last day ends (A) for electronic filing or for service by any means, at midnight; and (B) for filing by other means, when the clerk's office is scheduled to close. FL ST J ADMIN Rule 2.514(a)(4).

v. *"Next day" defined.* The "next day" is determined by continuing to count forward when the period is measured after an event and backward when measured before an event. FL ST J ADMIN Rule 2.514(a)(5).

vi. *"Legal holiday" defined.* "Legal holiday" means (A) the day set aside by FL ST § 110.117, for observing New Year's Day, Martin Luther King, Jr.'s Birthday, Memorial Day, Independence Day, Labor Day, Veterans' Day, Thanksgiving Day, the Friday after Thanksgiving Day, or Christmas Day, and (B) any day observed as a holiday by the clerk's office or as designated by the chief judge. FL ST J ADMIN Rule 2.514(a)(6).

b. *Additional time after service by mail or e-mail.* When a party may or must act within a specified time after service and service is made by mail or e-mail, five (5) days are added after the period that would otherwise expire under FL ST J ADMIN Rule 2.514(a). FL ST J ADMIN Rule 2.514(b).

c. *Enlargement.* When an act is required or allowed to be done at or within a specified time by order of court, by the Florida Rules of Civil Procedure, or by notice given thereunder, for cause shown the court at any time in its discretion (1) with or without notice, may order the period enlarged if request therefor is made before the expiration of the period originally prescribed or as extended by a previous order, or (2) upon motion made and notice after the expiration of the specified period, may permit the act to be done when failure to act was the result of excusable neglect, but it may not extend the time for making a motion for new trial, for rehearing, or to alter or amend a judgment; making a motion for relief from a judgment under FL ST RCP Rule 1.540(b); taking an appeal or filing a petition for certiorari; or making a motion for a directed verdict. FL ST RCP Rule 1.090(b).

d. *Unaffected by expiration of term.* The period of time provided for the doing of any act or the taking of any proceeding shall not be affected or limited by the continued existence or expiration of a term of court. The continued existence or expiration of a term of court in no way affects the power of a court to do any act or take any proceeding in any action which is or has been pending before it. FL ST RCP Rule 1.090(c).

C. General Requirements

1. *General rules of pleading*

a. *Claims for relief*

i. A pleading which sets forth a claim for relief, whether an original claim, counterclaim, crossclaim, or third-party claim, must state a cause of action and shall contain

- A short and plain statement of the grounds upon which the court's jurisdiction depends, unless the court already has jurisdiction and the claim needs no new grounds of jurisdiction to support it (For information regarding acts subjecting persons to jurisdiction, please see FL ST § 48.193),
- A short and plain statement of the ultimate facts showing that the pleader is entitled to relief, and

- A demand for judgment for the relief to which the pleader deems himself or herself entitled. FL ST RCP Rule 1.110(b).

ii. Relief in the alternative or of several different types may be demanded. Every complaint shall be considered to demand general relief. FL ST RCP Rule 1.110(b).

b. *Verification.* Except when otherwise specifically provided by these rules or an applicable statute, every pleading or other document of a party represented by an attorney need not be verified or accompanied by an affidavit. FL ST RCP Rule 1.030. When filing an action for foreclosure of a mortgage on residential real property the complaint shall be verified. When verification of a document is required, the document filed shall include an oath, affirmation, or the following statement: "Under penalty of perjury, I declare that I have read the foregoing, and the facts alleged therein are true and correct to the best of my knowledge and belief." FL ST RCP Rule 1.110(b).

c. *Separate statements.* All averments of claim or defense shall be made in consecutively numbered paragraphs, the contents of each of which shall be limited as far as practicable to a statement of a single set of circumstances, and a paragraph may be referred to by number in all subsequent pleadings. Each claim founded upon a separate transaction or occurrence and each defense other than denials shall be stated in a separate count or defense when a separation facilitates the clear presentation of the matter set forth. FL ST RCP Rule 1.110(f).

d. *Statements adopted by reference.* Statements in a pleading may be adopted by reference in a different part of the same pleading, in another pleading, or in any motion. FL ST RCP Rule 1.130(b).

e. *Joinder of causes of action; Consistency.* A pleader may set up in the same action as many claims or causes of action or defenses in the same right as the pleader has, and claims for relief may be stated in the alternative if separate items make up the cause of action, or if two (2) or more causes of action are joined. A party may also set forth two (2) or more statements of a claim or defense alternatively, either in one (1) count or defense or in separate counts or defenses. When two (2) or more statements are made in the alternative and one (1) of them, if made independently, would be sufficient, the pleading is not made insufficient by the insufficiency of one (1) or more of the alternative statements. A party may also state as many separate claims or defenses as that party has, regardless of consistency and whether based on legal or equitable grounds or both. All pleadings shall be construed so as to do substantial justice. FL ST RCP Rule 1.110(g).

f. *Subsequent pleadings.* When the nature of an action permits pleadings subsequent to final judgment and the jurisdiction of the court over the parties has not terminated, the initial pleading subsequent to final judgment shall be designated a supplemental complaint or petition. The action shall then proceed in the same manner and time as though the supplemental complaint or petition were the initial pleading in the action, including the issuance of any needed process. FL ST RCP Rule 1.110(h) shall not apply to proceedings that may be initiated by motion under the Florida Rules of Civil Procedure. FL ST RCP Rule 1.110(h).

g. *Pleading basis for service.* When service of process is to be made under statutes authorizing service on nonresidents of Florida, it is sufficient to plead the basis for service in the language of the statute without pleading the facts supporting service. FL ST RCP Rule 1.070(h).

h. *Forms of pleadings.* Forms of action and technical forms for seeking relief and of pleas, pleadings, or motions are abolished. FL ST RCP Rule 1.110(a).

2. *Answer; Generally.* An answer has three (3) functions. First, it must respond to each allegation of the preceding pleading by admitting, denying or alleging that the pleader is without knowledge of the allegation. Second, it must contain any affirmative defenses that the pleader is interposing to any cause of action alleged in the preceding pleading. Third, the answer may claim affirmative relief against the plaintiff or petitioner by a counterclaim or against a codefendant by a crossclaim. FL-PRACPROC § 11:1.

a. *Content.* In the answer a pleader shall state in short and plain terms the pleader's defenses to each claim asserted and shall admit or deny the averments on which the adverse party relies. If the defendant is without knowledge, the defendant shall so state and such statement shall operate as a denial. Denial shall fairly meet the substance of the averments denied. When a pleader intends in good faith to deny only a part of an averment, the pleader shall specify so much of it as is true and

shall deny the remainder. Unless the pleader intends in good faith to controvert all of the averments of the preceding pleading, the pleader may make denials as specific denials of designated averments or may generally deny all of the averments except such designated averments as the pleader expressly admits, but when the pleader does so intend to controvert all of its averments, including averments of the grounds upon which the court's jurisdiction depends, the pleader may do so by general denial. FL ST RCP Rule 1.110(c).

b. *Form of answer.* An answer contains a caption, commencement, body, signature and certificate of service. The caption is the same as that of the initial pleading, except for the designation as one of the types of answer. The body of an answer should contain an admission, denial or plea of without knowledge to each allegation of the preceding pleading, except for the additional allegations in response to a general allegation of conditions precedent and the denial of capacity to sue. FL-PRACPROC § 11:3.

   i. *Responding sequentially.* The best method of responding is to answer each paragraph sequentially, combining admissions, denials or pleas of without knowledge when the sequence permits. The admissions, denials and allegations of without knowledge should be stated first, followed separately by any affirmative defenses and then by any counterclaim or crossclaim. A third party complaint may be a part of the same paper, but it is not a part of the answer as is a counterclaim or crossclaim. Paragraphs are numbered consecutively throughout the pleading whether in the answer, counterclaim or crossclaim. Denials for the record only are improper. FL-PRACPROC § 11:3.

c. *Defenses*

   i. *Generally.* Every defense in law or fact to a claim for relief in a pleading shall be asserted in the responsive pleading, if one is required, but the following defenses may be made by motion at the option of the pleader: (1) lack of jurisdiction over the subject matter, (2) lack of jurisdiction over the person, (3) improper venue, (4) insufficiency of process, (5) insufficiency of service of process, (6) failure to state a cause of action, and (7) failure to join indispensable parties. A motion making any of these defenses shall be made before pleading if a further pleading is permitted. FL ST RCP Rule 1.140(b).

      - *Stated specifically.* The grounds on which any of the enumerated defenses are based and the substantial matters of law intended to be argued shall be stated specifically and with particularity in the responsive pleading or motion. FL ST RCP Rule 1.140(b).
      - *Waiver.* Any ground not stated shall be deemed to be waived except any ground showing that the court lacks jurisdiction of the subject matter may be made at any time. No defense or objection is waived by being joined with other defenses or objections in a responsive pleading or motion. FL ST RCP Rule 1.140(b). A party waives all defenses and objections that the party does not present either by motion under FL ST RCP Rule 1.140(b), FL ST RCP Rule 1.140(e), or FL ST RCP Rule 1.140(f) or, if the party has made no motion, in a responsive pleading except as provided in FL ST RCP Rule 1.140(h)(2). FL ST RCP Rule 1.140(h)(1). The defenses of failure to state a cause of action or a legal defense or to join an indispensable party may be raised by motion for judgment on the pleadings or at the trial on the merits in addition to being raised either in a motion under FL ST RCP Rule 1.140(b) or in the answer or reply. The defense of lack of jurisdiction of the subject matter may be raised at any time. FL ST RCP Rule 1.140(h)(2).

   ii. *Affirmative defenses.* In pleading to a preceding pleading a party shall set forth affirmatively accord and satisfaction, arbitration and award, assumption of risk, contributory negligence, discharge in bankruptcy, duress, estoppel, failure of consideration, fraud, illegality, injury by fellow servant, laches, license, payment, release, res judicata, statute of frauds, statute of limitations, waiver, and any other matter constituting an avoidance or affirmative defense. When a party has mistakenly designated a defense as a counterclaim or a counterclaim as a defense, the court, on terms if justice so requires, shall treat the pleading as if there had been a proper designation. Affirmative defenses appearing on the face of a prior pleading may be asserted as grounds for a motion or defense under FL ST RCP Rule 1.140(b); provided this shall

not limit amendments under FL ST RCP Rule 1.190 even if such ground is sustained. FL ST RCP Rule 1.110(d).

- *Format of defenses.* Affirmative defenses should be placed after the admissions, denials and allegations of without knowledge in the answer. All paragraphs must be numbered consecutively throughout the answer. If a defense is directed to only a part of a cause of action or to one or more, but not all, of several causes of action in the preceding pleading, the part or cause of action to which it is directed should be identified in the defense. Defenses should be identified by consecutive ordinal numbers such as "First Defense" and "Second Defense." FL-PRACPROC § 11:4.

iii. *Effect of failure to deny.* Averments in a pleading to which a responsive pleading is required, other than those as to the amount of damages, are admitted when not denied in the responsive pleading. Averments in a pleading to which no responsive pleading is required or permitted shall be taken as denied or avoided. FL ST RCP Rule 1.110(e). An admission in an answer binds the party and no proof is required. An admission does not extend beyond the scope of the allegation in the preceding pleading. FL-PRACPROC § 11:3.

3. *Pleading special matters*

a. *Capacity.* It is not necessary to aver the capacity of a party to sue or be sued, the authority of a party to sue or be sued in a representative capacity, or the legal existence of an organized association of persons that is made a party, except to the extent required to show the jurisdiction of the court. The initial pleading served on behalf of a minor party shall specifically aver the age of the minor party. When a party desires to raise an issue as to the legal existence of any party, the capacity of any party to sue or be sued, or the authority of a party to sue or be sued in a representative capacity, that party shall do so by specific negative averment which shall include such supporting particulars as are peculiarly within the pleader's knowledge. FL ST RCP Rule 1.120(a).

b. *Fraud, mistake, condition of the mind.* In all averments of fraud or mistake, the circumstances constituting fraud or mistake shall be stated with such particularity as the circumstances may permit. Malice, intent, knowledge, mental attitude, and other condition of mind of a person may be averred generally. FL ST RCP Rule 1.120(b).

c. *Conditions precedent.* In pleading the performance or occurrence of conditions precedent, it is sufficient to aver generally that all conditions precedent have been performed or have occurred. A denial of performance or occurrence shall be made specifically and with particularity. FL ST RCP Rule 1.120(c).

d. *Official document or act.* In pleading an official document or official act it is sufficient to aver that the document was issued or the act done in compliance with law. FL ST RCP Rule 1.120(c).

e. *Judgment or decree.* In pleading a judgment or decree of a domestic or foreign court, a judicial or quasi-judicial tribunal, or a board or officer, it is sufficient to aver the judgment or decree without setting forth matter showing jurisdiction to render it. FL ST RCP Rule 1.120(e).

f. *Time and place.* For the purpose of testing the sufficiency of a pleading, averments of time and place are material and shall be considered like all other averments of material matter. FL ST RCP Rule 1.120(f).

g. *Special damage.* When items of special damage are claimed, they shall be specifically stated. FL ST RCP Rule 1.120(g).

4. *Parties*

a. *Parties generally.* Every action may be prosecuted in the name of the real party in interest, but a personal representative, administrator, guardian, trustee of an express trust, a party with whom or in whose name a contract has been made for the benefit of another, or a party expressly authorized by statute may sue in that person's own name without joining the party for whose benefit the action is brought. All persons having an interest in the subject of the action and in obtaining the relief demanded may join as plaintiffs and any person may be made a defendant who has or claims an interest adverse to the plaintiff. Any person may at any time be made a party if that person's presence is necessary or proper to a complete determination of the cause. Persons having a united interest may

be joined on the same side as plaintiffs or defendants, and anyone who refuses to join may for such reason be made a defendant. FL ST RCP Rule 1.210(a).

b. *Minors or incompetent persons.* When a minor or incompetent person has a representative, such as a guardian or other like fiduciary, the representative may sue or defend on behalf of the minor or incompetent person. A minor or incompetent person who does not have a duly appointed representative may sue by next friend or by a guardian ad litem. The court shall appoint a guardian ad litem for a minor or incompetent person not otherwise represented in an action or shall make such other order as it deems proper for the protection of the minor or incompetent person. FL ST RCP Rule 1.210(b).

c. For survivor and substitution of parties information, please see FL ST RCP Rule 1.260.

5. *Counterclaims and crossclaims*

a. *Compulsory counterclaims.* A pleading shall state as a counterclaim any claim which at the time of serving the pleading the pleader has against any opposing party, provided it arises out of the transaction or occurrence that is the subject matter of the opposing party's claim and does not require for its adjudication the presence of third parties over whom the court cannot acquire jurisdiction. But the pleader need not state a claim if (1) at the time the action was commenced the claim was the subject of another pending action, or (2) the opposing party brought suit upon that party's claim by attachment or other process by which the court did not acquire jurisdiction to render a personal judgment on the claim and the pleader is not stating a counterclaim under this rule. FL ST RCP Rule 1.170(a).

b. *Permissive counterclaim.* A pleading may state as a counterclaim any claim against an opposing party not arising out of the transaction or occurrence that is the subject matter of the opposing party's claim. FL ST RCP Rule 1.170(b).

c. *Counterclaim exceeding opposing claim.* A counterclaim may or may not diminish or defeat the recovery sought by the opposing party. It may claim relief exceeding in amount or different in kind from that sought in the pleading of the opposing party. FL ST RCP Rule 1.170(c).

d. *Counterclaim against the State.* The Florida Rules of Civil Procedure shall not be construed to enlarge beyond the limits established by law the right to assert counterclaims or to claim credits against the state or any of its subdivisions or other governmental organizations thereof subject to suit or against a municipal corporation or against an officer, agency, or administrative board of the state. FL ST RCP Rule 1.170(d).

e. *Counterclaim maturing or acquired after pleading.* A claim which matured or was acquired by the pleader after serving the pleading may be presented as a counterclaim by supplemental pleading with the permission of the court. FL ST RCP Rule 1.170(e).

f. *Omitted counterclaim or crossclaim.* When a pleader fails to set up a counterclaim or crossclaim through oversight, inadvertence, or excusable neglect, or when justice requires, the pleader may set up the counterclaim or crossclaim by amendment with leave of the court. FL ST RCP Rule 1.170(f).

g. *Crossclaim against co-party.* A pleading may state as a crossclaim any claim by one party against a co-party arising out of the transaction or occurrence that is the subject matter of either the original action or a counterclaim therein, or relating to any property that is the subject matter of the original action. The crossclaim may include a claim that the party against whom it is asserted is or may be liable to the crossclaimant for all or part of a claim asserted in the action against the crossclaimant. Service of a crossclaim on a party who has appeared in the action shall be made pursuant to FL ST RCP Rule 1.080. Service of a crossclaim against a party who has not appeared in the action shall be made in the manner provided for service of summons. FL ST RCP Rule 1.170(g).

h. *Additional parties may be brought in.* When the presence of parties other than those to the original action is required to grant complete relief in the determination of a counterclaim or crossclaim, they shall be named in the counterclaim or crossclaim and be served with process and shall be parties to the action thereafter if jurisdiction of them can be obtained and their joinder will not deprive the court of jurisdiction of the action. FL ST RCP Rule 1.250(b) and FL ST RCP Rule 1.250(c) apply to parties brought in under FL ST RCP Rule 1.170(h). FL ST RCP Rule 1.170(h).

i. *Separate trials; Separate judgment.* If the court orders separate trials as provided in FL ST RCP Rule 1.270(b), judgment on a counterclaim or crossclaim may be rendered when the court has jurisdiction to do so even if a claim of the opposing party has been dismissed or otherwise disposed of. FL ST RCP Rule 1.170(i).

j. *Demand exceeding jurisdiction; Transfer of action.* If the demand of any counterclaim or crossclaim exceeds the jurisdiction of the court in which the action is pending, the action shall be transferred forthwith to the court of the same county having jurisdiction of the demand in the counterclaim or crossclaim with only such alterations in the pleadings as are essential. The court shall order the transfer of the action and the transmittal of all papers in it to the proper court if the party asserting the demand exceeding the jurisdiction deposits with the court having jurisdiction a sum sufficient to pay the clerk's service charge in the court to which the action is transferred at the time of filing the counterclaim or crossclaim. Thereupon the original papers and deposit shall be transmitted and filed with a certified copy of the order. The court to which the action is transferred shall have full power and jurisdiction over the demands of all parties. Failure to make the service charge deposit at the time the counterclaim or crossclaim is filed, or within such further time as the court may allow, shall reduce a claim for damages to an amount within the jurisdiction of the court where the action is pending and waive the claim in other cases. FL ST RCP Rule 1.170(j).

6. *Misjoinder and nonjoinder of parties*

a. *Misjoinder.* Misjoinder of parties is not a ground for dismissal of an action. Any claim against a party may be severed and proceeded with separately. FL ST RCP Rule 1.250(a).

b. *Dropping parties.* Parties may be dropped by an adverse party in the manner provided for voluntary dismissal in FL ST RCP Rule 1.420(a)(1) subject to the exception stated in FL ST RCP Rule 1.420. If notice of lis pendens has been filed in the action against a party so dropped, the notice of dismissal shall be recorded and cancels the notice of lis pendens without the necessity of a court order. Parties may be dropped by order of court on its own initiative or the motion of any party at any stage of the action on such terms as are just. FL ST RCP Rule 1.250(b).

c. *Adding parties.* Parties may be added once as a matter of course within the same time that pleadings can be so amended under FL ST RCP Rule 1.190(a). If amendment by leave of court or stipulation of the parties is permitted, parties may be added in the amended pleading without further order of court. Parties may be added by order of court on its own initiative or on motion of any party at any stage of the action and on such terms as are just. FL ST RCP Rule 1.250(c).

7. *Jury demand*

a. *Right preserved.* The right of trial by jury as declared by the Constitution or by statute shall be preserved to the parties inviolate. FL ST RCP Rule 1.430(a).

b. *Demand.* Any party may demand a trial by jury of any issue triable of right by a jury by serving upon the other party a demand therefor in writing at any time after commencement of the action and not later than ten (10) days after the service of the last pleading directed to such issue. The demand may be indorsed upon a pleading of the party. FL ST RCP Rule 1.430(b).

c. *Specification of issues.* In the demand a party may specify the issues that the party wishes so tried; otherwise, the party is deemed to demand trial by jury for all issues so triable. FL ST RCP Rule 1.430(c).

i. If a party has demanded trial by jury for only some of the issues, any other party may serve a demand for trial by jury of any other or all of the issues triable by jury ten (10) days after service of the demand or such lesser time as the court may order. FL ST RCP Rule 1.430(c).

d. *Waiver.* A party who fails to serve a demand as required by FL ST RCP Rule 1.430 waives trial by jury. FL ST RCP Rule 1.430(d).

i. If waived, a jury trial may not be granted without the consent of the parties, but the court may allow an amendment in the proceedings to demand a trial by jury or order a trial by jury on its own motion. FL ST RCP Rule 1.430(d).

ii. A demand for trial by jury may not be withdrawn without the consent of the parties. FL ST RCP Rule 1.430(d).

8. *Arbitration and mediation*

   a. *Referral to arbitration and mediation.* Except as hereinafter provided or as otherwise prohibited by law, the presiding judge may enter an order referring all or any part of a contested civil matter to mediation or arbitration. The parties to any contested civil matter may file a written stipulation to mediate or arbitrate any issue between them at any time. Such stipulation shall be incorporated into the order of referral. FL ST RCP Rule 1.700(a).

   b. *Arbitration*

      i. *Exclusions.* A civil action shall be ordered to arbitration or arbitration in conjunction with mediation upon stipulation of the parties. A civil action may be ordered to arbitration or arbitration in conjunction with mediation upon motion of any party or by the court, if the judge determines the action to be of such a nature that arbitration could be of benefit to the litigants or the court. FL ST RCP Rule 1.800.

         - Under no circumstances may the following categories of actions be referred to arbitration: (1) bond estreatures; (2) habeas corpus or other extraordinary writs; (3) bond validations; (4) civil or criminal contempt; (5) such other matters as may be specified by order of the chief judge in the circuit. FL ST RCP Rule 1.800.

      ii. For more information regarding arbitration, please see FL ST RCP Rule 1.810; FL ST RCP Rule 1.820; FL ST RCP Rule 1.830; FL ST 7 J CIR CV-2009-019-SC; and FL ST 7 J CIR CV-2003-002-SC(1)(c).

   c. *Mediation.* For more information regarding mediation, please see FL ST RCP Rule 1.710; FL ST RCP Rule 1.720; FL ST RCP Rule 1.730; FL ST RCP Rule 1.750; FL ST 7 J CIR CV-2008-018-SC; and FL ST 7 J CIR CV-2003-002-SC(1).

9. *Rules of court*

   a. *Rules of civil procedure.* The Florida Rules of Civil Procedure apply to all actions of a civil nature and all special statutory proceedings in the circuit courts and county courts except those to which the Florida Probate Rules, the Florida Family Law Rules of Procedure, or the Small Claims Rules apply. FL ST RCP Rule 1.010.

      i. The form, content, procedure, and time for pleading in all special statutory proceedings shall be as prescribed by the statutes governing the proceeding unless the Florida Rules of Civil Procedure specifically provide to the contrary. FL ST RCP Rule 1.010.

      ii. The Florida Rules of Civil Procedure shall be construed to secure the just, speedy, and inexpensive determination of every action. FL ST RCP Rule 1.010.

   b. *Rules of judicial administration.* The Florida Rules of Judicial Administration shall apply to administrative matters in all courts to which the Florida Rules of Judicial Administration are applicable by their terms. The Florida Rules of Judicial Administration shall be construed to secure the speedy and inexpensive determination of every proceeding to which they are applicable. The Florida Rules of Judicial Administration shall supersede all conflicting rules and statutes. FL ST J ADMIN Rule 2.110.

D. Documents

1. *Required documents*

   a. *Answer.* See the General Requirements section of this document for further information about the content of an answer.

      i. *Notices to persons with disabilities.* See the Format section of this KeyRules document for further information.

   b. *Certificate of service.* When any attorney certifies in substance: "I certify that a copy hereof has been furnished to (here insert name or names and addresses used for service) by (e-mail) (delivery) (mail) (fax) on .... (date) ....______________ Attorney" the certificate is taken as prima facie proof of such service in compliance with FL ST J ADMIN Rule 2.516. FL ST J ADMIN Rule 2.516(f).

2. *Supplemental documents*

   a. *Exhibits.* All bonds, notes, bills of exchange, contracts, accounts, or documents upon which action may be brought or defense made, or a copy thereof or a copy of the portions thereof material to the pleadings, shall be incorporated in or attached to the pleading. No papers shall be unnecessarily annexed as exhibits. The pleadings shall contain no unnecessary recitals of deeds, documents, contracts, or other instruments. Any exhibit attached to a pleading shall be considered a part of the pleadings for all purposes. FL ST RCP Rule 1.130(a).

b. *Notice of constitutional question.* A party that files a pleading, written motion, or other paper drawing into question the constitutionality of a state statute or a county or municipal charter, ordinance, or franchise must promptly (1) file a notice of constitutional question stating the question and identifying the paper that raises it; and (2) serve the notice and the pleading, written motion, or other paper drawing into question the constitutionality of a state statute or a county or municipal charter, ordinance, or franchise on the Attorney General or the state attorney of the judicial circuit in which the action is pending, by either certified or registered mail. Service of the notice and pleading, written motion, or other paper does not require joinder of the Attorney General or the state attorney as a party to the action. FL ST RCP Rule 1.071.

E. Format

1. *Documents; Type and size.* Documents subject to the exceptions set forth in FL ST J ADMIN Rule 2.525(d) shall be filed on recycled paper measuring eight and one half by eleven (8 1/2 by 11) inches. For purposes of FL ST J ADMIN Rule 2.520, paper is recycled if it contains a minimum content of fifty (50) percent waste paper. Xerographic reduction of legal-size (eight and one half by fourteen (8 1/2 by 14) inches) documents to letter size (eight and one half by eleven (8 1/2 by 11) inches) is prohibited. All other documents filed by electronic transmission shall be filed in a format capable of being printed in a format consistent with the provisions of FL ST J ADMIN Rule 2.250. FL ST J ADMIN Rule 2.520(b).

   a. *Exhibits.* Any exhibit or attachment filed with pleadings or papers may be filed in its original size. FL ST J ADMIN Rule 2.520(c).

   b. *Recording space.* On all papers and documents prepared and filed by the court or by any party to a proceeding which are to be recorded in the public records of any county, including but not limited to final money judgments and notices of lis pendens, a three (3) inch by three (3) inch space at the top right-hand corner on the first page and a one (1) inch by three (3) inch space at the top right-hand corner on each subsequent page shall be left blank and reserved for use by the clerk of court. FL ST J ADMIN Rule 2.520(d).

      i. *Exceptions to recording space.* Any papers or documents created by persons or entities over which the filing party has no control, including but not limited to wills, codicils, trusts, or other testamentary documents; documents prepared or executed by any public officer; documents prepared, executed, acknowledged, or proved outside of the State of Florida; or documents created by State or Federal government agencies, may be filed without the space required by FL ST J ADMIN Rule 2.520. FL ST J ADMIN Rule 2.520(e).

   c. *Noncompliance.* No clerk of court is permitted to refuse to file any document or paper because of noncompliance with the Florida Rules of Judicial Administration. However, upon request of the clerk of court, noncomplying documents must be resubmitted in accordance with the formatting rules. FL ST J ADMIN Rule 2.520(f).

2. *Caption.* Every pleading, motion, order, judgment, or other paper shall have a caption containing the name of the court, the file number, and except for in rem proceedings, including forfeiture proceedings, the name of the first party on each side with an appropriate indication of other parties, and a designation identifying the party filing it and its nature or the nature of the order, as the case may be. In any in rem proceeding, every pleading, motion, order, judgment, or other paper shall have a caption containing the name of the court, the file number, the style "In re" (followed by the name or general description of the property), and a designation of the person or entity filing it and its nature or the nature of the order, as the case may be. In an in rem forfeiture proceeding, the style shall be "In re forfeiture of" (followed by the name of the general description of the property). All papers filed in the action shall be styled in such a manner as to indicate clearly the subject matter of the paper and the party requesting or obtaining relief. FL ST RCP Rule 1.100(c)(1).

   a. *Volusia County eminent domain cases.* All orders, pleadings, motions and other papers will bear the initial case style. Documents intended to apply only to particular parcel(s) will indicate in their caption the parcel number(s) to which they apply and sufficient copies shall be provided to the Clerk of Court to allow the filing and docketing of each relevant paper in each parcel file. FL ST 7 J CIR CV-2000-011-VL(b).

3. *Writing and written defined.* Writing or written means a document containing information, an application, or a stipulation. FL ST RCP Rule 1.080(c).

4. *Rule abbreviations*

   a. The Florida Rules of Civil Procedure and shall be abbreviated as Fla.R.Civ.P. FL ST RCP Rule 1.010.

   b. The Florida Rules of Judicial Administration shall be abbreviated as Fla. R. Jud. Admin. FL ST J ADMIN Rule 2.110.

5. *Nonverification.* Except when otherwise specifically provided by the Florida Rules of Civil Procedure or an applicable statute, every pleading or other document of a party represented by an attorney need not be verified or accompanied by an affidavit. FL ST RCP Rule 1.030; FL ST J ADMIN Rule 2.515(a).

6. *Attorney signature*

   a. *Attorney signature.* Every pleading and other document of a party represented by an attorney shall be signed by at least one (1) attorney of record in that attorney's individual name whose current record Florida Bar address, telephone number, including area code, primary e-mail address and secondary e-mail addresses, if any, and Florida Bar number shall be stated, and who shall be duly licensed to practice law in Florida or who shall have received permission to appear in the particular case as provided in FL ST J ADMIN Rule 2.510. FL ST J ADMIN Rule 2.515(a).

      i. The attorney may be required by the court to give the address of, and to vouch for the attorney's authority to represent, the party. FL ST J ADMIN Rule 2.515(a).

      ii. The signature of an attorney shall constitute a certificate by the attorney that the attorney has read the pleading or other document; that to the best of the attorney's knowledge, information, and belief there is good ground to support it; and that it is not interposed for delay. FL ST J ADMIN Rule 2.515(a).

      iii. If a pleading is not signed or is signed with intent to defeat the purpose of FL ST J ADMIN Rule 2.515, it may be stricken and the action may proceed as though the pleading or other document had not been served. FL ST J ADMIN Rule 2.515(a).

   b. *Pro se litigant signature.* A party who is not represented by an attorney shall sign any pleading or other paper and state the party's address and telephone number, including area code. FL ST J ADMIN Rule 2.515(b).

   c. *Form of signature*

      i. The signatures required on pleadings and documents by FL ST J ADMIN Rule 2.515(a) and FL ST J ADMIN Rule 2.515(b) may be:

         - Original signatures;
         - Original signatures that have been reproduced by electronic means, such as on electronically transmitted documents or photocopied documents;
         - Electronic signatures using the "/s/," "s/," or "/s" formats by or at the direction of the person signing; or
         - Any other signature format authorized by general law, so long as the clerk where the proceeding is pending has the capability of receiving and has obtained approval from the Supreme Court of Florida to accept pleadings and documents with that signature format. FL ST J ADMIN Rule 2.515(c)(1).

      ii. An attorney, party, or other person who files a pleading or paper by electronic transmission that does not contain the original signature of that attorney, party, or other person shall file that identical pleading or paper in paper form containing an original signature of that attorney, party, or other person (hereinafter called the follow-up filing) immediately thereafter. The follow-up filing is not required if the Supreme Court of Florida has entered an order directing the clerk of court to discontinue accepting the follow-up filing. FL ST J ADMIN Rule 2.515(c)(2).

7. *Forms*
    a. *Process.* The forms of process, notice of lis pendens, and notice of action provided in the Florida Rules of Civil Procedure are sufficient. Variations from the forms do not void process or notices that are otherwise sufficient. FL ST RCP Rule 1.900(a).
    b. *Other forms.* The other forms provided in the Florida Rules of Civil Procedure are sufficient for the matters that are covered by them. So long as the substance is expressed without prolixity, the forms may be varied to meet the facts of a particular case. FL ST RCP Rule 1.900(b).
    c. *Formal matters.* Captions, except for the designation of the paper, are omitted from the forms provided in the Florida Rules of Civil Procedure. A general form of caption is the first form provided. Signatures are omitted from pleadings and motions. FL ST RCP Rule 1.900(c).
8. *Notices to persons with disabilities.* All notices of court proceedings to be held in a public facility, and all process compelling appearance at such proceedings, shall include the following statement in bold face, fourteen (14) point Times New Roman or Courier font: "If you are a person with a disability who needs any accommodation in order to participate in this proceeding, you are entitled, at no cost to you, to the provision of certain assistance. Please contact [identify applicable court personnel by name, address, and telephone number] at least seven (7) days before your scheduled court appearance, or immediately upon receiving this notification if the time before the scheduled appearance is less than seven (7) days; if you are hearing or voice impaired, call 711." FL ST J ADMIN Rule 2.540(c)(1).
9. *Minimization of the filing of sensitive information*
    a. *Limitations for court filings.* Unless authorized by FL ST J ADMIN Rule 2.425(b), statute, another rule of court, or the court orders otherwise, designated sensitive information filed with the court must be limited to the following format:
        i. The initials of a person known to be a minor;
        ii. The year of birth of a person's birth date;
        iii. No portion of any: Social security number, Bank account number, Credit card account number, Charge account number, or Debit account number;
        iv. The last four digits of any: Taxpayer identification number (TIN), Employee identification number, Driver's license number, Passport number, Telephone number, Financial account number, except as set forth in FL ST J ADMIN Rule 2.425(a)(3), Brokerage account number, Insurance policy account number, Loan account number, Customer account number, or Patient or health care number;
        v. A truncated version of any: Email address, Computer user name, Password, or Personal identification number (PIN); and
        vi. A truncated version of any other sensitive information as provided by court order. FL ST J ADMIN Rule 2.425(a).
    b. *Exceptions.* FL ST J ADMIN Rule 2.425(a) does not apply to the following:
        i. An account number which identifies the property alleged to be the subject of a proceeding;
        ii. The record of an administrative or agency proceeding;
        iii. The record in appellate or review proceedings;
        iv. The birth date of a minor whenever the birth date is necessary for the court to establish or maintain subject matter jurisdiction;
        v. The name of a minor in any order relating to parental responsibility, time-sharing, or child support;
        vi. The name of a minor in any document or order affecting the minor's ownership of real property;
        vii. The birth date of a party in a writ of attachment or notice to payor;

viii. In traffic and criminal proceedings: a pro se filing; a court filing that is related to a criminal matter or investigation and that is prepared before the filing of a criminal charge or is not filed as part of any docketed criminal case; an arrest or search warrant or any information in support thereof; a charging document and an affidavit or other documents filed in support of any charging document, including any driving records; a statement of particulars; discovery material introduced into evidence or otherwise filed with the court; and all information necessary for the proper issuance and execution of a subpoena duces tecum;

ix. Information used by the clerk for case maintenance purposes or the courts for case management purposes; and

x. Information which is relevant and material to an issue before the court. FL ST J ADMIN Rule 2.425(b).

c. *Remedies.* Upon motion by a party or interested person or sua sponte by the court, the court may order remedies, sanctions or both for a violation of FL ST J ADMIN Rule 2.425(a). Following notice and an opportunity to respond, the court may impose sanctions if such filing was not made in good faith. FL ST J ADMIN Rule 2.425(c).

d. *Motions not restricted.* FL ST J ADMIN Rule 2.425 does not restrict a party's right to move for protective order, to move to file documents under seal, or to request a determination of the confidentiality of records. FL ST J ADMIN Rule 2.425(d).

e. *Application.* FL ST J ADMIN Rule 2.425 does not affect the application of constitutional provisions, statutes, or rules of court regarding confidential information or access to public information. FL ST J ADMIN Rule 2.425(e).

F. Filing and Service Requirements

1. *Filing requirements.* All original documents must be filed with the court either before service or immediately thereafter, unless otherwise provided for by general law or other rules. If the original of any bond or other document is not placed in the court file, a certified copy must be so placed by the clerk. FL ST J ADMIN Rule 2.516(d). All documents shall be filed in conformity with the requirements of FL ST J ADMIN Rule 2.525. FL ST RCP Rule 1.080(b). All documents filed in any court shall be filed by electronic transmission in accordance with FL ST J ADMIN Rule 2.525. "Documents" means pleadings, motions, petitions, memoranda, briefs, notices, exhibits, declarations, affidavits, orders, judgments, decrees, writs, opinions, and any other paper or writing submitted to a court. FL ST J ADMIN Rule 2.520(a). All documents that are court records, as defined in FL ST J ADMIN Rule 2.430(a)(1), must be filed by electronic transmission, provided that: (1) the clerk has the ability to accept and retain such documents; (2) the clerk or the chief judge of the circuit has requested permission to accept documents filed by electronic transmission; and (3) the supreme court has entered an order granting permission to the clerk to accept documents filed by electronic transmission. FL ST J ADMIN Rule 2.525(c)(1).

a. *Definition.* "Electronic transmission of documents" means the sending of information by electronic signals to, by or from a court or clerk, which when received can be transformed and stored or transmitted on paper, microfilm, magnetic storage device, optical imaging system, CD-ROM, flash drive, other electronic data storage system, server, case maintenance system ("CM"), electronic court filing ("ECF") system, statewide or local electronic portal ("e-portal"), or other electronic record keeping system authorized by the supreme court in a format sufficient to communicate the information on the original document in a readable format. Electronic transmission of documents includes electronic mail ("e-mail") and any internet-based transmission procedure, and may include procedures allowing for documents to be signed or verified by electronic means. FL ST J ADMIN Rule 2.525(a).

i. The filing of documents with the court as required by the Florida Rules of Judicial Administration must be made by filing them with the clerk in accordance with FL ST J ADMIN Rule 2.525, except that the judge may permit documents to be filed with the judge, in which event the judge must note the filing date before him or her on the documents and transmit them to the clerk. The date of filing is that shown on the face of the document by the judge's notation or the clerk's time stamp, whichever is earlier. FL ST J ADMIN Rule 2.516(e).

b. *Application.* Any court or clerk of the court may accept the electronic transmission of documents for

filing after the clerk, together with input from the chief judge of the circuit, has obtained approval of the procedures and program for doing so from the Supreme Court of Florida. FL ST J ADMIN Rule 2.525(b).

c. *Exceptions*

   i. Paper documents and other submissions may be manually submitted to the clerk or court:

      - When the clerk does not have the ability to accept and retain documents by electronic filing or has not had ECF Procedures approved by the supreme court;
      - For filing by any self-represented party or any self-represented nonparty unless specific ECF Procedures provide a means to file documents electronically. However, any self-represented nonparty that is a governmental or public agency and any other agency, partnership, corporation, or business entity acting on behalf of any governmental or public agency may file documents by electronic transmission if such entity has the capability of filing documents electronically;
      - For filing by attorneys excused from e-mail service in accordance with FL ST J ADMIN Rule 2.516(b);
      - When submitting evidentiary exhibits or filing non-documentary materials;
      - When the filing involves documents in excess of twenty-five (25) megabytes (25MB) in size. For such filings, documents may be transmitted using an electronic storage medium that the clerk has the ability to accept, which may include a CD-ROM, flash drive, or similar storage medium;
      - When filed in open court, as permitted by the court;
      - When paper filing is permitted by any approved statewide or local ECF procedures; and
      - If any court determines that justice so requires. FL ST J ADMIN Rule 2.525(d).

   ii. Any document in paper form submitted under FL ST J ADMIN Rule 2.525(d) is filed when it is received by the clerk or court and the clerk shall immediately thereafter convert any filed paper document to an electronic document. "Convert to an electronic document" means optically capturing an image of a paper document and using character recognition software to recover as much of the document's text as practicable and then indexing and storing the document in the official court file. FL ST J ADMIN Rule 2.525(c)(4).

   iii. Any storage medium submitted under FL ST J ADMIN Rule 2.525(d)(5) is filed when received by the clerk or court and the clerk shall immediately thereafter transfer the electronic documents from the storage device to the official court file. FL ST J ADMIN Rule 2.525(c)(5).

   iv. If the filer of any paper document authorized under FL ST J ADMIN Rule 2.525(d) provides a self-addressed, postage-paid envelope for return of the paper document after it is converted to electronic form by the clerk, the clerk shall place the paper document in the envelope and deposit it in the mail. Except when a paper document is required to be maintained, the clerk may recycle any filed paper document that is not to be returned to the filer. FL ST J ADMIN Rule 2.525(c)(6).

   v. The clerk may convert any paper document filed before the effective date of FL ST J ADMIN Rule 2.525 to an electronic document. Unless the clerk is required to maintain the paper document, if the paper document has been converted to an electronic document by the clerk, the paper document is no longer part of the official court file and may be removed and recycled. FL ST J ADMIN Rule 2.525(c)(7).

d. *Official court file.* For information on what constitutes the official court file, please see FL ST J ADMIN Rule 2.525(c)(2), FL ST J ADMIN Rule 2.525(c)(3).

e. *Administration.* All attorneys, parties, or other persons using this rule to file documents are required to make arrangements with the court or clerk for the payment of any charges authorized by general law or the supreme court before filing any document by electronic transmission. FL ST J ADMIN Rule 2.525(f)(2).

f. *Filing date.* The filing date for an electronically transmitted document is the date and time that such filing is acknowledged by an electronic stamp or otherwise, pursuant to any procedure set forth in any ECF Procedures approved by the supreme court, or the date the last page of such filing is received by the court or clerk. FL ST J ADMIN Rule 2.525(f)(3).

g. *Accessibility.* All documents transmitted in any electronic form under FL ST J ADMIN Rule 2.525 must comply with the accessibility requirements of FL ST J ADMIN Rule 2.526. FL ST J ADMIN Rule 2.525(g).

2. *Service requirements.* Every pleading subsequent to the initial pleading, all orders, and every other document filed in the action must be served in conformity with the requirements of FL ST J ADMIN Rule 2.516. FL ST RCP Rule 1.080(a).

   a. *Service; When required.* Unless the court otherwise orders, or a statute or supreme court administrative order specifies a different means of service, every pleading subsequent to the initial pleading and every other document filed in any court proceeding, except applications for witness subpoenas and documents served by formal notice or required to be served in the manner provided for service of formal notice, must be served in accordance with FL ST J ADMIN Rule 2.516 on each party. No service need be made on parties against whom a default has been entered, except that pleadings asserting new or additional claims against them must be served in the manner provided for service of summons. FL ST J ADMIN Rule 2.516(a).

   b. *Service; How made.* When service is required or permitted to be made upon a party represented by an attorney, service must be made upon the attorney unless service upon the party is ordered by the court. FL ST J ADMIN Rule 2.516(b).

      i. *Service by electronic mail ("e-mail").* All documents required or permitted to be served on another party must be served by e-mail, unless FL ST J ADMIN Rule 2.516 otherwise provides. When, in addition to service by e-mail, the sender also utilizes another means of service provided for in FL ST J ADMIN Rule 2.516(b)(2), any differing time limits and other provisions applicable to that other means of service control. FL ST J ADMIN Rule 2.516(b)(1). Any document electronically transmitted to a court or clerk must also be served on all parties and interested persons in accordance with the applicable rules of court. FL ST J ADMIN Rule 2.525(e)(2).

         - *Service on attorneys.* Upon appearing in a proceeding, an attorney must serve a designation of a primary e-mail address and may designate no more than two (2) secondary e-mail addresses. Thereafter, service must be directed to all designated e-mail addresses in that proceeding. Every document filed by an attorney thereafter must include the primary e-mail address of that attorney and any secondary e-mail addresses. If an attorney does not designate any e-mail address for service, documents may be served on that attorney at the e-mail address on record with The Florida Bar. FL ST J ADMIN Rule 2.516(b)(1)(A).

         - *Exception to e-mail service on attorneys.* Service by an attorney on another attorney must be made by e-mail unless excused by the court. Upon motion by an attorney demonstrating that the attorney has no e-mail account and lacks access to the Internet at the attorney's office, the court may excuse the attorney from the requirements of e-mail service. Service on and by an attorney excused by the court from e-mail service must be by the means provided in FL ST J ADMIN Rule 2.516(b)(2). FL ST J ADMIN Rule 2.516(b)(1)(B).

         - *Service on and by parties not represented by an attorney.* Any party not represented by an attorney may serve a designation of a primary e-mail address and also may designate no more than two (2) secondary e-mail addresses to which service must be directed in that proceeding by the means provided in FL ST J ADMIN Rule 2.516(b)(1). If a party not represented by an attorney does not designate an e-mail address for service in a proceeding, service on and by that party must be by the means provided in FL ST J ADMIN Rule 2.516(b)(2). FL ST J ADMIN Rule 2.516(b)(1)(C).

         - *Time of service.* Service by e-mail is complete when it is sent. FL ST J ADMIN Rule 2.516(b)(1)(D). An e-mail is deemed served on the date it is sent. FL ST J ADMIN Rule 2.516(b)(1)(D)(i). If the sender learns that the e-mail did not reach the address of the

person to be served, the sender must immediately send another copy by e-mail, or by a means authorized by FL ST J ADMIN Rule 2.516(b)(2). FL ST J ADMIN Rule 2.516(b)(1)(D)(ii). E-mail service is treated as service by mail for the computation of time. FL ST J ADMIN Rule 2.516(b)(1)(D)(iii).

ii. *Format of e-mail for service.* Service of a document by e-mail is made by attaching a copy of the document in PDF format to an e-mail sent to all addresses designated by the attorney or party. FL ST J ADMIN Rule 2.516(b)(1)(E).

- All documents served by e-mail must be attached to an e-mail message containing a subject line beginning with the words "SERVICE OF COURT DOCUMENT" in all capital letters, followed by the case number of the proceeding in which the documents are being served. FL ST J ADMIN Rule 2.516(b)(1)(E)(i).
- The body of the e-mail must identify the court in which the proceeding is pending, the case number, the name of the initial party on each side, the title of each document served with that e-mail, and the sender's name and telephone number. FL ST J ADMIN Rule 2.516(b)(1)(E)(ii).
- Any document served by e-mail may be signed by the "/s/" format, as long as the filed original is signed in accordance with the applicable rule of procedure. FL ST J ADMIN Rule 2.516(b)(1)(E)(iii).
- Any e-mail which, together with its attached documents, exceeds five megabytes (5MB) in size, must be divided and sent as separate e-mails, no one of which may exceed five megabytes (5MB) in size and each of which must be sequentially numbered in the subject line. FL ST J ADMIN Rule 2.516(b)(1)(E)(iv).

iii. *Service by other means.* In addition to, and not in lieu of, service by e-mail, service may also be made upon attorneys by any of the means specified in FL ST J ADMIN Rule 2.516(b)(2). Service on and by all parties who are not represented by an attorney and who do not designate an e-mail address, and on and by all attorneys excused from e-mail service, must be made by delivering a copy of the document or by mailing it to the party or attorney at their last known address or, if no address is known, by leaving it with the clerk of the court. Service by mail is complete upon mailing. Delivery of a copy within FL ST J ADMIN Rule 2.516 is complete upon:

- Handing it to the attorney or to the party,
- Leaving it at the attorney's or party's office with a clerk or other person in charge thereof,
- If there is no one in charge, leaving it in a conspicuous place therein,
- If the office is closed or the person to be served has no office, leaving it at the person's usual place of abode with some person of his or her family above fifteen (15) years of age and informing such person of the contents, or
- Transmitting it by facsimile to the attorney's or party's office with a cover sheet containing the sender's name, firm, address, telephone number, and facsimile number, and the number of pages transmitted. When service is made by facsimile, a copy must also be served by any other method permitted by FL ST J ADMIN Rule 2.516. Facsimile service occurs when transmission is complete. FL ST J ADMIN Rule 2.516(b)(2)(A) through FL ST J ADMIN Rule 2.516(b)(2)(E).
- Service by delivery after 5:00 p.m. must be deemed to have been made by mailing on the date of delivery. FL ST J ADMIN Rule 2.516(b)(2)(F).

c. *Service; Numerous defendants.* In actions when the parties are unusually numerous, the court may regulate the service contemplated by the Florida Rules of Judicial Administration on motion or on its own initiative in such manner as may be found to be just and reasonable. FL ST J ADMIN Rule 2.516(c).

d. *Service by clerk.* Service of notices and other documents required to be made by the clerk must also be done as provided in FL ST J ADMIN Rule 2.516(b). FL ST J ADMIN Rule 2.516(g).

G. Hearings

1. *Preliminary hearings.* The defenses in FL ST RCP Rule 1.140(b)(1) through FL ST RCP Rule 1.140(b)(7), whether made in a pleading or by motion, and the motion for judgment in FL ST RCP Rule 1.140(c) shall be heard and determined before trial on application of any party unless the court orders that the hearing and determination shall be deferred until the trial. FL ST RCP Rule 1.140(d).

H. Forms

1. Official Answer Forms for Florida

a. Caption. FL ST RCP Form 1.901.

b. Crossclaim summons. FL ST RCP Form 1.903.

c. Third-party summons. FL ST RCP Form 1.904.

d. Defense; Statute of limitations. FL ST RCP Form 1.965.

e. Defense; Payment. FL ST RCP Form 1.966.

f. Defense; Accord and satisfaction. FL ST RCP Form 1.967.

g. Defense; Failure of consideration. FL ST RCP Form 1.968.

h. Defense; Statute of frauds. FL ST RCP Form 1.969.

i. Defense; Release. FL ST RCP Form 1.970.

j. Notice of compliance when constitutional challenge is brought. FL ST RCP Form 1.975.

2. Answer Forms for Florida

a. Answer; General form, traverses. FL-PRACFORM § 5:4.

b. Answer; General form, traverses and affirmative defenses. FL-PRACFORM § 5:6.

c. Answer; General form, traverses, affirmative defenses and counterclaim. FL-PRACFORM § 5:7.

d. Answer; General form, traverses, affirmative defenses, counterclaim and crossclaim. FL-PRACFORM § 5:8.

e. Answer; Affirmative defense, fraud. FL-PRACFORM § 5:43.

f. Answer; Affirmative defense, laches. FL-PRACFORM § 5:47.

g. Answer; Affirmative defense, misjoinder. FL-PRACFORM § 5:49.

h. Answer; Affirmative defense, misrepresentation. FL-PRACFORM § 5:50.

i. Answer; Affirmative defense, self defense. FL-PRACFORM § 5:64.

j. Answer; Denial of conditions precedent. FL-PRACFORM § 5:80.

k. General denial. FL-PP § 2:58.

l. General denial; With specified admissions. FL-PP § 2:59.

m. Admission with qualification. FL-PP § 2:60.

n. Conclusions of law not requiring denial. FL-PP § 2:61.

o. Defenses stated in the alternative. FL-PP § 2:62.

p. Denial as to part of allegation. FL-PP § 2:63.

q. Pleader as without knowledge as to truth of allegation. FL-PP § 2:64.

I. Checklist

(I) ❑ Matters to be considered by plaintiff

(a) ❑ Required documents

(1) ❑ Summons

(2) ❑ Complaint

(3) ❑ Civil cover sheet

(4) ❑ Return of execution process by process server

(5) ❑ Filing fees

(b) ❑ Supplemental documents

(1) ❑ Exhibits

(2) ❑ Notice of constitutional question

(c) ❑ Time for filing and serving complaint

(1) ❑ Service of the initial process and initial pleading should be made upon a defendant within one hundred twenty (120) days after the filing of the complaint with the court

(II) ❑ Matters to be considered by defendant

(a) ❑ Required documents

(1) ❑ Answer

(2) ❑ Certificate of service

(b) ❑ Supplemental documents

(1) ❑ Exhibits

(2) ❑ Notice of constitutional question

(c) ❑ Time for answer

(1) ❑ Unless a different time is prescribed in a statute of Florida, a defendant shall serve an answer within twenty (20) days after service of original process and the initial pleading on the defendant, or not later than the date fixed in a notice by publication

(2) ❑ A party served with a pleading stating a crossclaim against that party shall serve an answer to it within twenty (20) days after service on that party

(3) ❑ The plaintiff shall serve an answer to a counterclaim within twenty (20) days after service of the counterclaim

(4) ❑ A defendant who, before being served with process, timely returns a waiver so requested is not required to respond to the complaint until sixty (60) days after the date the defendant received the request for waiver of service; for purposes of computing any time prescribed or allowed by the Florida Rules of Civil Procedure, service of process shall be deemed effected twenty (20) days before the time required to respond to the complaint

(5) ❑ For timing requirements related to service on the state, service of motion impact, and responding when no responsive pleading is required, please see the Timing section of this document

Pleadings
Amended Answer

Document Last Updated January 2013

A. Applicable Rules

1. *State rules*

   a. Nonverification of papers. FL ST RCP Rule 1.030.

   b. Constitutional challenge to state statute or county or municipal charter, ordinance, or franchise; Notice by party. FL ST RCP Rule 1.071.

   c. Service and filing of pleadings, orders, and documents. FL ST RCP Rule 1.080.

   d. Time. FL ST RCP Rule 1.090.

   e. Pleadings and motions. FL ST RCP Rule 1.100; FL ST RCP Rule 1.110; FL ST RCP Rule 1.120; FL ST RCP Rule 1.130; FL ST RCP Rule 1.190.

f. Defenses. FL ST RCP Rule 1.140.

g. Pretrial procedure. FL ST RCP Rule 1.200.

h. Relief from judgment, decrees, or orders. FL ST RCP Rule 1.540.

i. Forms. FL ST RCP Rule 1.900.

j. Minimization of the filing of sensitive information. FL ST J ADMIN Rule 2.425.

k. Foreign attorneys. FL ST J ADMIN Rule 2.510.

l. Signature of attorneys and parties. FL ST J ADMIN Rule 2.515.

m. Paper. FL ST J ADMIN Rule 2.520.

n. Electronic filing. FL ST J ADMIN Rule 2.525.

o. Accessibility of information and technology. FL ST J ADMIN Rule 2.526.

p. Court reporting. FL ST J ADMIN Rule 2.535.

q. Requests for accommodations by persons with disabilities. FL ST J ADMIN Rule 2.540.

2. *Local rules*

a. Eminent domain cases. FL ST 7 J CIR CV-2000-011-VL.

b. Civil pretrial procedures. FL ST 7 J CIR CV-2003-002-SC.

c. Arbitration and mediation. FL ST 7 J CIR CV-2008-018-SC; FL ST 7 J CIR CV-2009-019-SC.

B. Timing

1. *Amendment as a matter of course.* A party may amend a pleading once as a matter of course at any time before a responsive pleading is served or, if the pleading is one to which no responsive pleading is permitted and the action has not been placed on the trial calendar, may so amend it at any time within twenty (20) days after it is served. FL ST RCP Rule 1.190(a).

2. *Amendment by leave of court.* Otherwise a party may amend a pleading only by leave of court or by written consent of the adverse party. Leave of court shall be given freely when justice so requires. FL ST RCP Rule 1.190(a).

3. *Amendments in furtherance of justice.* At any time in furtherance of justice, upon such terms as may be just, the court may permit any process, proceeding, pleading, or record to be amended or material supplemental matter to be set forth in an amended or supplemental pleading. At every stage of the action the court must disregard any error or defect in the proceedings which does not affect the substantial rights of the parties. FL ST RCP Rule 1.190(e).

4. *Response to amended pleading.* A party shall plead in response to an amended pleading within ten (10) days after service of the amended pleading unless the court otherwise orders. FL ST RCP Rule 1.190(a).

5. *Computation of time*

a. *Generally.* Computation of time shall be governed by FL ST J ADMIN Rule 2.514. FL ST RCP Rule 1.090(a). The following rules apply in computing time periods specified in any rule of procedure, local rule, court order, or statute that does not specify a method of computing time. FL ST J ADMIN Rule 2.514(a).

i. *Period stated in days or a longer unit.* When the period is stated in days or a longer unit of time (A) exclude the day of the event that triggers the period; (B) count every day, including intermediate Saturdays, Sundays, and legal holidays; and (C) include the last day of the period, but if the last day is a Saturday, Sunday, or legal holiday, or falls within any period of time extended through an order of the chief justice under FL ST J ADMIN Rule 2.205(a)(2)(B)(iv), the period continues to run until the end of the next day that is not a Saturday, Sunday, or legal holiday and does not fall within any period of time extended through an order of the chief justice. FL ST J ADMIN Rule 2.514(a)(1).

ii. *Period stated in hours.* When the period is stated in hours (A) begin counting immediately on the occurrence of the event that triggers the period; (B) count every hour, including hours during intermediate Saturdays, Sundays, and legal holidays; and (C) if the period would end on a Saturday, Sunday, or legal holiday, or during any period of time extended through an order of the chief justice under FL ST J ADMIN Rule 2.205(a)(2)(B)(iv), the period continues to run until the same time on the next day that is not a Saturday, Sunday, or legal holiday and does not fall within any period of time extended through an order of the chief justice. FL ST J ADMIN Rule 2.514(a)(2).

iii. *Period stated in days less than seven (7) days.* When the period stated in days is less than seven (7) days, intermediate Saturdays, Sundays, and legal holidays shall be excluded in the computation. FL ST J ADMIN Rule 2.514(a)(3).

iv. *"Last day" defined.* Unless a different time is set by a statute, local rule, or court order, the last day ends (A) for electronic filing or for service by any means, at midnight; and (B) for filing by other means, when the clerk's office is scheduled to close. FL ST J ADMIN Rule 2.514(a)(4).

v. *"Next day" defined.* The "next day" is determined by continuing to count forward when the period is measured after an event and backward when measured before an event. FL ST J ADMIN Rule 2.514(a)(5).

vi. *"Legal holiday" defined.* "Legal holiday" means (A) the day set aside by FL ST § 110.117, for observing New Year's Day, Martin Luther King, Jr.'s Birthday, Memorial Day, Independence Day, Labor Day, Veterans' Day, Thanksgiving Day, the Friday after Thanksgiving Day, or Christmas Day, and (B) any day observed as a holiday by the clerk's office or as designated by the chief judge. FL ST J ADMIN Rule 2.514(a)(6).

b. *Additional time after service by mail or e-mail.* When a party may or must act within a specified time after service and service is made by mail or e-mail, five (5) days are added after the period that would otherwise expire under FL ST J ADMIN Rule 2.514(a). FL ST J ADMIN Rule 2.514(b).

c. *Enlargement.* When an act is required or allowed to be done at or within a specified time by order of court, by the Florida Rules of Civil Procedure, or by notice given thereunder, for cause shown the court at any time in its discretion (1) with or without notice, may order the period enlarged if request therefor is made before the expiration of the period originally prescribed or as extended by a previous order, or (2) upon motion made and notice after the expiration of the specified period, may permit the act to be done when failure to act was the result of excusable neglect, but it may not extend the time for making a motion for new trial, for rehearing, or to alter or amend a judgment; making a motion for relief from a judgment under FL ST RCP Rule 1.540(b); taking an appeal or filing a petition for certiorari; or making a motion for a directed verdict. FL ST RCP Rule 1.090(b).

d. *Unaffected by expiration of term.* The period of time provided for the doing of any act or the taking of any proceeding shall not be affected or limited by the continued existence or expiration of a term of court. The continued existence or expiration of a term of court in no way affects the power of a court to do any act or take any proceeding in any action which is or has been pending before it. FL ST RCP Rule 1.090(c).

C. General Requirements

1. *Amendments.* A party may amend a pleading once as a matter of course at any time before a responsive pleading is served or, if the pleading is one to which no responsive pleading is permitted and the action has not been placed on the trial calendar, may so amend it at any time within twenty (20) days after it is served. Otherwise a party may amend a pleading only by leave of court or by written consent of the adverse party. Leave of court shall be freely given when justice so requires. FL ST RCP Rule 1.190(a).

   a. *Purpose of amendments.* Amendments can relate to the correction of mistakes, the insertion of jurisdictional averments, the correction or addition of verifications, the addition or substitution or striking out of parties, and generally the rectification of all formal defects in the pleading. The court can also allow amendments setting up an omitted counterclaim or cross-claim if the defendant failed to raise the claim through oversight, inadvertence, or excusable neglect. FL-PP § 2:151.

   b. *Amendment to a pleading/Amended pleading.* A significant difference exists between an amendment to a pleading and an amended pleading. An amendment to a pleading corrects, adds to or deletes from the pleading. An amended pleading is substituted for the former pleading and the former pleading ceases to have any effect. Dee v. Southern Brewing Company, 146 Fla. 588, 1 So.2d 562 (Fla. 1941); Shannon v. McBride, 105 So.2d 16 (Fla. 2d DCA 1958); Hughes v. Home Sav. of America, F.S.B., 675 So.2d 649 (Fla. 2d DCA 1996); FL-PRACPROC § 14:2.

c. *Relation back of amendments.* When the claim or defense asserted in the amended pleading arose out of the conduct, transaction, or occurrence set forth or attempted to be set forth in the original pleading, the amendment shall relate back to the date of the original pleading. FL ST RCP Rule 1.190(c).

2. *General rules of pleading*

a. *Claims for relief*

i. A pleading which sets forth a claim for relief, whether an original claim, counterclaim, crossclaim, or third-party claim, must state a cause of action and shall contain

- A short and plain statement of the grounds upon which the court's jurisdiction depends, unless the court already has jurisdiction and the claim needs no new grounds of jurisdiction to support it (For information regarding acts subjecting persons to jurisdiction, please see FL ST § 48.193),
- A short and plain statement of the ultimate facts showing that the pleader is entitled to relief, and
- A demand for judgment for the relief to which the pleader deems himself or herself entitled. FL ST RCP Rule 1.110(b).

ii. Relief in the alternative or of several different types may be demanded. Every complaint shall be considered to demand general relief. FL ST RCP Rule 1.110(b).

b. *Verification.* Except when otherwise specifically provided by these rules or an applicable statute, every pleading or other document of a party represented by an attorney need not be verified or accompanied by an affidavit. FL ST RCP Rule 1.030. When filing an action for foreclosure of a mortgage on residential real property the complaint shall be verified. When verification of a document is required, the document filed shall include an oath, affirmation, or the following statement: "Under penalty of perjury, I declare that I have read the foregoing, and the facts alleged therein are true and correct to the best of my knowledge and belief." FL ST RCP Rule 1.110(b).

c. *Separate statements.* All averments of claim or defense shall be made in consecutively numbered paragraphs, the contents of each of which shall be limited as far as practicable to a statement of a single set of circumstances, and a paragraph may be referred to by number in all subsequent pleadings. Each claim founded upon a separate transaction or occurrence and each defense other than denials shall be stated in a separate count or defense when a separation facilitates the clear presentation of the matter set forth. FL ST RCP Rule 1.110(f).

d. *Statements adopted by reference.* Statements in a pleading may be adopted by reference in a different part of the same pleading, in another pleading, or in any motion. FL ST RCP Rule 1.130(b).

e. *Joinder of causes of action; Consistency.* A pleader may set up in the same action as many claims or causes of action or defenses in the same right as the pleader has, and claims for relief may be stated in the alternative if separate items make up the cause of action, or if two (2) or more causes of action are joined. A party may also set forth two (2) or more statements of a claim or defense alternatively, either in one (1) count or defense or in separate counts or defenses. When two (2) or more statements are made in the alternative and one (1) of them, if made independently, would be sufficient, the pleading is not made insufficient by the insufficiency of one (1) or more of the alternative statements. A party may also state as many separate claims or defenses as that party has, regardless of consistency and whether based on legal or equitable grounds or both. All pleadings shall be construed so as to do substantial justice. FL ST RCP Rule 1.110(g).

f. *Subsequent pleadings.* When the nature of an action permits pleadings subsequent to final judgment and the jurisdiction of the court over the parties has not terminated, the initial pleading subsequent to final judgment shall be designated a supplemental complaint or petition. The action shall then proceed in the same manner and time as though the supplemental complaint or petition were the initial pleading in the action, including the issuance of any needed process. FL ST RCP Rule 1.110(h) shall not apply to proceedings that may be initiated by motion under the Florida Rules of Civil Procedure. FL ST RCP Rule 1.110(h).

g. *Pleading basis for service.* When service of process is to be made under statutes authorizing service on nonresidents of Florida, it is sufficient to plead the basis for service in the language of the statute without pleading the facts supporting service. FL ST RCP Rule 1.070(h).

h. *Forms of pleadings.* Forms of action and technical forms for seeking relief and of pleas, pleadings, or motions are abolished. FL ST RCP Rule 1.110(a).

3. *Answer; Generally.* An answer has three (3) functions. First, it must respond to each allegation of the preceding pleading by admitting, denying or alleging that the pleader is without knowledge of the allegation. Second, it must contain any affirmative defenses that the pleader is interposing to any cause of action alleged in the preceding pleading. Third, the answer may claim affirmative relief against the plaintiff or petitioner by a counterclaim or against a codefendant by a crossclaim. FL-PRACPROC § 11:1.

a. *Content.* In the answer a pleader shall state in short and plain terms the pleader's defenses to each claim asserted and shall admit or deny the averments on which the adverse party relies. If the defendant is without knowledge, the defendant shall so state and such statement shall operate as a denial. Denial shall fairly meet the substance of the averments denied. When a pleader intends in good faith to deny only a part of an averment, the pleader shall specify so much of it as is true and shall deny the remainder. Unless the pleader intends in good faith to controvert all of the averments of the preceding pleading, the pleader may make denials as specific denials of designated averments or may generally deny all of the averments except such designated averments as the pleader expressly admits, but when the pleader does so intend to controvert all of its averments, including averments of the grounds upon which the court's jurisdiction depends, the pleader may do so by general denial. FL ST RCP Rule 1.110(c).

b. *Form of answer.* An answer contains a caption, commencement, body, signature and certificate of service. The caption is the same as that of the initial pleading, except for the designation as one of the types of answer. The body of an answer should contain an admission, denial or plea of without knowledge to each allegation of the preceding pleading, except for the additional allegations in response to a general allegation of conditions precedent and the denial of capacity to sue. FL-PRACPROC § 11:3.

i. *Responding sequentially.* The best method of responding is to answer each paragraph sequentially, combining admissions, denials or pleas of without knowledge when the sequence permits. The admissions, denials and allegations of without knowledge should be stated first, followed separately by any affirmative defenses and then by any counterclaim or crossclaim. A third party complaint may be a part of the same paper, but it is not a part of the answer as is a counterclaim or crossclaim. Paragraphs are numbered consecutively throughout the pleading whether in the answer, counterclaim or crossclaim. Denials for the record only are improper. FL-PRACPROC § 11:3.

c. *Defenses*

i. *Generally.* Every defense in law or fact to a claim for relief in a pleading shall be asserted in the responsive pleading, if one is required, but the following defenses may be made by motion at the option of the pleader: (1) lack of jurisdiction over the subject matter, (2) lack of jurisdiction over the person, (3) improper venue, (4) insufficiency of process, (5) insufficiency of service of process, (6) failure to state a cause of action, and (7) failure to join indispensable parties. A motion making any of these defenses shall be made before pleading if a further pleading is permitted. FL ST RCP Rule 1.140(b).

- *Stated specifically.* The grounds on which any of the enumerated defenses are based and the substantial matters of law intended to be argued shall be stated specifically and with particularity in the responsive pleading or motion. FL ST RCP Rule 1.140(b).
- *Waiver.* Any ground not stated shall be deemed to be waived except any ground showing that the court lacks jurisdiction of the subject matter may be made at any time. No defense

or objection is waived by being joined with other defenses or objections in a responsive pleading or motion. FL ST RCP Rule 1.140(b). A party waives all defenses and objections that the party does not present either by motion under FL ST RCP Rule 1.140(b), FL ST RCP Rule 1.140(e), or FL ST RCP Rule 1.140(f) or, if the party has made no motion, in a responsive pleading except as provided in FL ST RCP Rule 1.140(h)(2). FL ST RCP Rule 1.140(h)(1). The defenses of failure to state a cause of action or a legal defense or to join an indispensable party may be raised by motion for judgment on the pleadings or at the trial on the merits in addition to being raised either in a motion under FL ST RCP Rule 1.140(b) or in the answer or reply. The defense of lack of jurisdiction of the subject matter may be raised at any time. FL ST RCP Rule 1.140(h)(2).

ii. *Affirmative defenses.* In pleading to a preceding pleading a party shall set forth affirmatively accord and satisfaction, arbitration and award, assumption of risk, contributory negligence, discharge in bankruptcy, duress, estoppel, failure of consideration, fraud, illegality, injury by fellow servant, laches, license, payment, release, res judicata, statute of frauds, statute of limitations, waiver, and any other matter constituting an avoidance or affirmative defense. When a party has mistakenly designated a defense as a counterclaim or a counterclaim as a defense, the court, on terms if justice so requires, shall treat the pleading as if there had been a proper designation. Affirmative defenses appearing on the face of a prior pleading may be asserted as grounds for a motion or defense under FL ST RCP Rule 1.140(b); provided this shall not limit amendments under FL ST RCP Rule 1.190 even if such ground is sustained. FL ST RCP Rule 1.110(d).

- *Format of defenses.* Affirmative defenses should be placed after the admissions, denials and allegations of without knowledge in the answer. All paragraphs must be numbered consecutively throughout the answer. If a defense is directed to only a part of a cause of action or to one or more, but not all, of several causes of action in the preceding pleading, the part or cause of action to which it is directed should be identified in the defense. Defenses should be identified by consecutive ordinal numbers such as "First Defense" and "Second Defense." FL-PRACPROC § 11:4.

iii. *Effect of failure to deny.* Averments in a pleading to which a responsive pleading is required, other than those as to the amount of damages, are admitted when not denied in the responsive pleading. Averments in a pleading to which no responsive pleading is required or permitted shall be taken as denied or avoided. FL ST RCP Rule 1.110(e). An admission in an answer binds the party and no proof is required. An admission does not extend beyond the scope of the allegation in the preceding pleading. FL-PRACPROC § 11:3.

4. *Pleading special matters*

a. *Capacity.* It is not necessary to aver the capacity of a party to sue or be sued, the authority of a party to sue or be sued in a representative capacity, or the legal existence of an organized association of persons that is made a party, except to the extent required to show the jurisdiction of the court. The initial pleading served on behalf of a minor party shall specifically aver the age of the minor party. When a party desires to raise an issue as to the legal existence of any party, the capacity of any party to sue or be sued, or the authority of a party to sue or be sued in a representative capacity, that party shall do so by specific negative averment which shall include such supporting particulars as are peculiarly within the pleader's knowledge. FL ST RCP Rule 1.120(a).

b. *Fraud, mistake, condition of the mind.* In all averments of fraud or mistake, the circumstances constituting fraud or mistake shall be stated with such particularity as the circumstances may permit. Malice, intent, knowledge, mental attitude, and other condition of mind of a person may be averred generally. FL ST RCP Rule 1.120(b).

c. *Conditions precedent.* In pleading the performance or occurrence of conditions precedent, it is sufficient to aver generally that all conditions precedent have been performed or have occurred. A denial of performance or occurrence shall be made specifically and with particularity. FL ST RCP Rule 1.120(c).

d. *Official document or act.* In pleading an official document or official act it is sufficient to aver that the document was issued or the act done in compliance with law. FL ST RCP Rule 1.120(c).

e. *Judgment or decree.* In pleading a judgment or decree of a domestic or foreign court, a judicial or quasi-judicial tribunal, or a board or officer, it is sufficient to aver the judgment or decree without setting forth matter showing jurisdiction to render it. FL ST RCP Rule 1.120(e).

f. *Time and place.* For the purpose of testing the sufficiency of a pleading, averments of time and place are material and shall be considered like all other averments of material matter. FL ST RCP Rule 1.120(f).

g. *Special damage.* When items of special damage are claimed, they shall be specifically stated. FL ST RCP Rule 1.120(g).

5. *Parties*

a. *Parties generally.* Every action may be prosecuted in the name of the real party in interest, but a personal representative, administrator, guardian, trustee of an express trust, a party with whom or in whose name a contract has been made for the benefit of another, or a party expressly authorized by statute may sue in that person's own name without joining the party for whose benefit the action is brought. All persons having an interest in the subject of the action and in obtaining the relief demanded may join as plaintiffs and any person may be made a defendant who has or claims an interest adverse to the plaintiff. Any person may at any time be made a party if that person's presence is necessary or proper to a complete determination of the cause. Persons having a united interest may be joined on the same side as plaintiffs or defendants, and anyone who refuses to join may for such reason be made a defendant. FL ST RCP Rule 1.210(a).

b. *Minors or incompetent persons.* When a minor or incompetent person has a representative, such as a guardian or other like fiduciary, the representative may sue or defend on behalf of the minor or incompetent person. A minor or incompetent person who does not have a duly appointed representative may sue by next friend or by a guardian ad litem. The court shall appoint a guardian ad litem for a minor or incompetent person not otherwise represented in an action or shall make such other order as it deems proper for the protection of the minor or incompetent person. FL ST RCP Rule 1.210(b).

c. For survivor and substitution of parties information, please see FL ST RCP Rule 1.260.

6. *Counterclaims and crossclaims*

a. *Compulsory counterclaims.* A pleading shall state as a counterclaim any claim which at the time of serving the pleading the pleader has against any opposing party, provided it arises out of the transaction or occurrence that is the subject matter of the opposing party's claim and does not require for its adjudication the presence of third parties over whom the court cannot acquire jurisdiction. But the pleader need not state a claim if (1) at the time the action was commenced the claim was the subject of another pending action, or (2) the opposing party brought suit upon that party's claim by attachment or other process by which the court did not acquire jurisdiction to render a personal judgment on the claim and the pleader is not stating a counterclaim under this rule. FL ST RCP Rule 1.170(a).

b. *Permissive counterclaim.* A pleading may state as a counterclaim any claim against an opposing party not arising out of the transaction or occurrence that is the subject matter of the opposing party's claim. FL ST RCP Rule 1.170(b).

c. *Counterclaim exceeding opposing claim.* A counterclaim may or may not diminish or defeat the recovery sought by the opposing party. It may claim relief exceeding in amount or different in kind from that sought in the pleading of the opposing party. FL ST RCP Rule 1.170(c).

d. *Counterclaim against the State.* The Florida Rules of Civil Procedure shall not be construed to enlarge beyond the limits established by law the right to assert counterclaims or to claim credits against the state or any of its subdivisions or other governmental organizations thereof subject to suit or against a municipal corporation or against an officer, agency, or administrative board of the state. FL ST RCP Rule 1.170(d).

e. *Counterclaim maturing or acquired after pleading.* A claim which matured or was acquired by the pleader after serving the pleading may be presented as a counterclaim by supplemental pleading with the permission of the court. FL ST RCP Rule 1.170(e).

f. *Omitted counterclaim or crossclaim.* When a pleader fails to set up a counterclaim or crossclaim through oversight, inadvertence, or excusable neglect, or when justice requires, the pleader may set up the counterclaim or crossclaim by amendment with leave of the court. FL ST RCP Rule 1.170(f).

g. *Crossclaim against co-party.* A pleading may state as a crossclaim any claim by one party against a co-party arising out of the transaction or occurrence that is the subject matter of either the original action or a counterclaim therein, or relating to any property that is the subject matter of the original action. The crossclaim may include a claim that the party against whom it is asserted is or may be liable to the crossclaimant for all or part of a claim asserted in the action against the crossclaimant. Service of a crossclaim on a party who has appeared in the action shall be made pursuant to FL ST RCP Rule 1.080. Service of a crossclaim against a party who has not appeared in the action shall be made in the manner provided for service of summons. FL ST RCP Rule 1.170(g).

h. *Additional parties may be brought in.* When the presence of parties other than those to the original action is required to grant complete relief in the determination of a counterclaim or crossclaim, they shall be named in the counterclaim or crossclaim and be served with process and shall be parties to the action thereafter if jurisdiction of them can be obtained and their joinder will not deprive the court of jurisdiction of the action. FL ST RCP Rule 1.250(b) and FL ST RCP Rule 1.250(c) apply to parties brought in under FL ST RCP Rule 1.170(h). FL ST RCP Rule 1.170(h).

i. *Separate trials; Separate judgment.* If the court orders separate trials as provided in FL ST RCP Rule 1.270(b), judgment on a counterclaim or crossclaim may be rendered when the court has jurisdiction to do so even if a claim of the opposing party has been dismissed or otherwise disposed of. FL ST RCP Rule 1.170(i).

j. *Demand exceeding jurisdiction; Transfer of action.* If the demand of any counterclaim or crossclaim exceeds the jurisdiction of the court in which the action is pending, the action shall be transferred forthwith to the court of the same county having jurisdiction of the demand in the counterclaim or crossclaim with only such alterations in the pleadings as are essential. The court shall order the transfer of the action and the transmittal of all papers in it to the proper court if the party asserting the demand exceeding the jurisdiction deposits with the court having jurisdiction a sum sufficient to pay the clerk's service charge in the court to which the action is transferred at the time of filing the counterclaim or crossclaim. Thereupon the original papers and deposit shall be transmitted and filed with a certified copy of the order. The court to which the action is transferred shall have full power and jurisdiction over the demands of all parties. Failure to make the service charge deposit at the time the counterclaim or crossclaim is filed, or within such further time as the court may allow, shall reduce a claim for damages to an amount within the jurisdiction of the court where the action is pending and waive the claim in other cases. FL ST RCP Rule 1.170(j).

7. *Misjoinder and nonjoinder of parties*

a. *Misjoinder.* Misjoinder of parties is not a ground for dismissal of an action. Any claim against a party may be severed and proceeded with separately. FL ST RCP Rule 1.250(a).

b. *Dropping parties.* Parties may be dropped by an adverse party in the manner provided for voluntary dismissal in FL ST RCP Rule 1.420(a)(1) subject to the exception stated in FL ST RCP Rule 1.420. If notice of lis pendens has been filed in the action against a party so dropped, the notice of dismissal shall be recorded and cancels the notice of lis pendens without the necessity of a court order. Parties may be dropped by order of court on its own initiative or the motion of any party at any stage of the action on such terms as are just. FL ST RCP Rule 1.250(b).

c. *Adding parties.* Parties may be added once as a matter of course within the same time that pleadings can be so amended under FL ST RCP Rule 1.190(a). If amendment by leave of court or stipulation of the parties is permitted, parties may be added in the amended pleading without further order of court. Parties may be added by order of court on its own initiative or on motion of any party at any stage of the action and on such terms as are just. FL ST RCP Rule 1.250(c).

8. *Jury demand*

a. *Right preserved.* The right of trial by jury as declared by the Constitution or by statute shall be preserved to the parties inviolate. FL ST RCP Rule 1.430(a).

b. *Demand.* Any party may demand a trial by jury of any issue triable of right by a jury by serving upon the other party a demand therefor in writing at any time after commencement of the action and not later than ten (10) days after the service of the last pleading directed to such issue. The demand may be indorsed upon a pleading of the party. FL ST RCP Rule 1.430(b).

c. *Specification of issues.* In the demand a party may specify the issues that the party wishes so tried; otherwise, the party is deemed to demand trial by jury for all issues so triable. FL ST RCP Rule 1.430(c).

   i. If a party has demanded trial by jury for only some of the issues, any other party may serve a demand for trial by jury of any other or all of the issues triable by jury ten (10) days after service of the demand or such lesser time as the court may order. FL ST RCP Rule 1.430(c).

d. *Waiver.* A party who fails to serve a demand as required by FL ST RCP Rule 1.430 waives trial by jury. FL ST RCP Rule 1.430(d).

   i. If waived, a jury trial may not be granted without the consent of the parties, but the court may allow an amendment in the proceedings to demand a trial by jury or order a trial by jury on its own motion. FL ST RCP Rule 1.430(d).

   ii. A demand for trial by jury may not be withdrawn without the consent of the parties. FL ST RCP Rule 1.430(d).

9. *Arbitration and mediation*

a. *Referral to arbitration and mediation.* Except as hereinafter provided or as otherwise prohibited by law, the presiding judge may enter an order referring all or any part of a contested civil matter to mediation or arbitration. The parties to any contested civil matter may file a written stipulation to mediate or arbitrate any issue between them at any time. Such stipulation shall be incorporated into the order of referral. FL ST RCP Rule 1.700(a).

b. *Arbitration*

   i. *Exclusions.* A civil action shall be ordered to arbitration or arbitration in conjunction with mediation upon stipulation of the parties. A civil action may be ordered to arbitration or arbitration in conjunction with mediation upon motion of any party or by the court, if the judge determines the action to be of such a nature that arbitration could be of benefit to the litigants or the court. FL ST RCP Rule 1.800.

      - Under no circumstances may the following categories of actions be referred to arbitration: (1) bond estreatures; (2) habeas corpus or other extraordinary writs; (3) bond validations; (4) civil or criminal contempt; (5) such other matters as may be specified by order of the chief judge in the circuit. FL ST RCP Rule 1.800.

   ii. For more information regarding arbitration, please see FL ST RCP Rule 1.810; FL ST RCP Rule 1.820; FL ST RCP Rule 1.830; FL ST 7 J CIR CV-2009-019-SC; and FL ST 7 J CIR CV-2003-002-SC(1)(c).

c. *Mediation.* For more information regarding mediation, please see FL ST RCP Rule 1.710; FL ST RCP Rule 1.720; FL ST RCP Rule 1.730; FL ST RCP Rule 1.750; FL ST 7 J CIR CV-2008-018-SC; and FL ST 7 J CIR CV-2003-002-SC(1).

10. *Rules of court*

a. *Rules of civil procedure.* The Florida Rules of Civil Procedure apply to all actions of a civil nature and all special statutory proceedings in the circuit courts and county courts except those to which the Florida Probate Rules, the Florida Family Law Rules of Procedure, or the Small Claims Rules apply. FL ST RCP Rule 1.010.

   i. The form, content, procedure, and time for pleading in all special statutory proceedings shall be as prescribed by the statutes governing the proceeding unless the Florida Rules of Civil Procedure specifically provide to the contrary. FL ST RCP Rule 1.010.

   ii. The Florida Rules of Civil Procedure shall be construed to secure the just, speedy, and inexpensive determination of every action. FL ST RCP Rule 1.010.

b. *Rules of judicial administration.* The Florida Rules of Judicial Administration shall apply to administrative matters in all courts to which the Florida Rules of Judicial Administration are applicable by their terms. The Florida Rules of Judicial Administration shall be construed to secure the speedy and inexpensive determination of every proceeding to which they are applicable. The Florida Rules of Judicial Administration shall supersede all conflicting rules and statutes. FL ST J ADMIN Rule 2.110.

D. Documents

1. *Required documents*

   a. *Amended answer.* See the General Requirements section of this document for the content of an amended answer. If a party files a motion to amend a pleading, the party shall attach the proposed amended pleading to the motion. FL ST RCP Rule 1.190(a). See the KeyRules Florida Circuit Court Motion for Leave to Amend document for further information.

      i. *Notices to persons with disabilities.* See the Format section of this KeyRules document for further information.

   b. *Certificate of service.* When any attorney certifies in substance: "I certify that a copy hereof has been furnished to (here insert name or names and addresses used for service) by (e-mail) (delivery) (mail) (fax) on .... (date) ...._________________ Attorney" the certificate is taken as prima facie proof of such service in compliance with FL ST J ADMIN Rule 2.516. FL ST J ADMIN Rule 2.516(f).

2. *Supplemental documents*

   a. *Exhibits.* All bonds, notes, bills of exchange, contracts, accounts, or documents upon which action may be brought or defense made, or a copy thereof or a copy of the portions thereof material to the pleadings, shall be incorporated in or attached to the pleading. No papers shall be unnecessarily annexed as exhibits. The pleadings shall contain no unnecessary recitals of deeds, documents, contracts, or other instruments. Any exhibit attached to a pleading shall be considered a part of the pleadings for all purposes. FL ST RCP Rule 1.130(a).

   b. *Notice of constitutional question.* A party that files a pleading, written motion, or other paper drawing into question the constitutionality of a state statute or a county or municipal charter, ordinance, or franchise must promptly (1) file a notice of constitutional question stating the question and identifying the paper that raises it; and (2) serve the notice and the pleading, written motion, or other paper drawing into question the constitutionality of a state statute or a county or municipal charter, ordinance, or franchise on the Attorney General or the state attorney of the judicial circuit in which the action is pending, by either certified or registered mail. Service of the notice and pleading, written motion, or other paper does not require joinder of the Attorney General or the state attorney as a party to the action. FL ST RCP Rule 1.071.

E. Format

1. *Documents; Type and size.* Documents subject to the exceptions set forth in FL ST J ADMIN Rule 2.525(d) shall be filed on recycled paper measuring eight and one half by eleven (8 1/2 by 11) inches. For purposes of FL ST J ADMIN Rule 2.520, paper is recycled if it contains a minimum content of fifty (50) percent waste paper. Xerographic reduction of legal-size (eight and one half by fourteen (8 1/2 by 14) inches) documents to letter size (eight and one half by eleven (8 1/2 by 11) inches) is prohibited. All other documents filed by electronic transmission shall be filed in a format capable of being printed in a format consistent with the provisions of FL ST J ADMIN Rule 2.250. FL ST J ADMIN Rule 2.520(b).

   a. *Exhibits.* Any exhibit or attachment filed with pleadings or papers may be filed in its original size. FL ST J ADMIN Rule 2.520(c).

   b. *Recording space.* On all papers and documents prepared and filed by the court or by any party to a proceeding which are to be recorded in the public records of any county, including but not limited to final money judgments and notices of lis pendens, a three (3) inch by three (3) inch space at the top right-hand corner on the first page and a one (1) inch by three (3) inch space at the top right-hand corner on each subsequent page shall be left blank and reserved for use by the clerk of court. FL ST J ADMIN Rule 2.520(d).

      i. *Exceptions to recording space.* Any papers or documents created by persons or entities over

which the filing party has no control, including but not limited to wills, codicils, trusts, or other testamentary documents; documents prepared or executed by any public officer; documents prepared, executed, acknowledged, or proved outside of the State of Florida; or documents created by State or Federal government agencies, may be filed without the space required by FL ST J ADMIN Rule 2.520. FL ST J ADMIN Rule 2.520(e).

c. *Noncompliance.* No clerk of court is permitted to refuse to file any document or paper because of noncompliance with the Florida Rules of Judicial Administration. However, upon request of the clerk of court, noncomplying documents must be resubmitted in accordance with the formatting rules. FL ST J ADMIN Rule 2.520(f).

2. *Caption.* Every pleading, motion, order, judgment, or other paper shall have a caption containing the name of the court, the file number, and except for in rem proceedings, including forfeiture proceedings, the name of the first party on each side with an appropriate indication of other parties, and a designation identifying the party filing it and its nature or the nature of the order, as the case may be. In any in rem proceeding, every pleading, motion, order, judgment, or other paper shall have a caption containing the name of the court, the file number, the style "In re" (followed by the name or general description of the property), and a designation of the person or entity filing it and its nature or the nature of the order, as the case may be. In an in rem forfeiture proceeding, the style shall be "In re forfeiture of" (followed by the name of the general description of the property). All papers filed in the action shall be styled in such a manner as to indicate clearly the subject matter of the paper and the party requesting or obtaining relief. FL ST RCP Rule 1.100(c)(1).

   a. *Volusia County eminent domain cases.* All orders, pleadings, motions and other papers will bear the initial case style. Documents intended to apply only to particular parcel(s) will indicate in their caption the parcel number(s) to which they apply and sufficient copies shall be provided to the Clerk of Court to allow the filing and docketing of each relevant paper in each parcel file. FL ST 7 J CIR CV-2000-011-VL(b).

3. *Writing and written defined.* Writing or written means a document containing information, an application, or a stipulation. FL ST RCP Rule 1.080(c).

4. *Rule abbreviations*

   a. The Florida Rules of Civil Procedure and shall be abbreviated as Fla.R.Civ.P. FL ST RCP Rule 1.010.

   b. The Florida Rules of Judicial Administration shall be abbreviated as Fla. R. Jud. Admin. FL ST J ADMIN Rule 2.110.

5. *Nonverification.* Except when otherwise specifically provided by the Florida Rules of Civil Procedure or an applicable statute, every pleading or other document of a party represented by an attorney need not be verified or accompanied by an affidavit. FL ST RCP Rule 1.030; FL ST J ADMIN Rule 2.515(a).

6. *Attorney signature*

   a. *Attorney signature.* Every pleading and other document of a party represented by an attorney shall be signed by at least one (1) attorney of record in that attorney's individual name whose current record Florida Bar address, telephone number, including area code, primary e-mail address and secondary e-mail addresses, if any, and Florida Bar number shall be stated, and who shall be duly licensed to practice law in Florida or who shall have received permission to appear in the particular case as provided in FL ST J ADMIN Rule 2.510. FL ST J ADMIN Rule 2.515(a).

      i. The attorney may be required by the court to give the address of, and to vouch for the attorney's authority to represent, the party. FL ST J ADMIN Rule 2.515(a).

      ii. The signature of an attorney shall constitute a certificate by the attorney that the attorney has read the pleading or other document; that to the best of the attorney's knowledge, information, and belief there is good ground to support it; and that it is not interposed for delay. FL ST J ADMIN Rule 2.515(a).

      iii. If a pleading is not signed or is signed with intent to defeat the purpose of FL ST J ADMIN Rule 2.515, it may be stricken and the action may proceed as though the pleading or other document had not been served. FL ST J ADMIN Rule 2.515(a).

b. *Pro se litigant signature.* A party who is not represented by an attorney shall sign any pleading or other paper and state the party's address and telephone number, including area code. FL ST J ADMIN Rule 2.515(b).

c. *Form of signature*

i. The signatures required on pleadings and documents by FL ST J ADMIN Rule 2.515(a) and FL ST J ADMIN Rule 2.515(b) may be:

- Original signatures;
- Original signatures that have been reproduced by electronic means, such as on electronically transmitted documents or photocopied documents;
- Electronic signatures using the "/s/," "s/," or "/s" formats by or at the direction of the person signing; or
- Any other signature format authorized by general law, so long as the clerk where the proceeding is pending has the capability of receiving and has obtained approval from the Supreme Court of Florida to accept pleadings and documents with that signature format. FL ST J ADMIN Rule 2.515(c)(1).

ii. An attorney, party, or other person who files a pleading or paper by electronic transmission that does not contain the original signature of that attorney, party, or other person shall file that identical pleading or paper in paper form containing an original signature of that attorney, party, or other person (hereinafter called the follow-up filing) immediately thereafter. The follow-up filing is not required if the Supreme Court of Florida has entered an order directing the clerk of court to discontinue accepting the follow-up filing. FL ST J ADMIN Rule 2.515(c)(2).

7. *Forms*

a. *Process.* The forms of process, notice of lis pendens, and notice of action provided in the Florida Rules of Civil Procedure are sufficient. Variations from the forms do not void process or notices that are otherwise sufficient. FL ST RCP Rule 1.900(a).

b. *Other forms.* The other forms provided in the Florida Rules of Civil Procedure are sufficient for the matters that are covered by them. So long as the substance is expressed without prolixity, the forms may be varied to meet the facts of a particular case. FL ST RCP Rule 1.900(b).

c. *Formal matters.* Captions, except for the designation of the paper, are omitted from the forms provided in the Florida Rules of Civil Procedure. A general form of caption is the first form provided. Signatures are omitted from pleadings and motions. FL ST RCP Rule 1.900(c).

8. *Notices to persons with disabilities.* All notices of court proceedings to be held in a public facility, and all process compelling appearance at such proceedings, shall include the following statement in bold face, fourteen (14) point Times New Roman or Courier font: "If you are a person with a disability who needs any accommodation in order to participate in this proceeding, you are entitled, at no cost to you, to the provision of certain assistance. Please contact [identify applicable court personnel by name, address, and telephone number] at least seven (7) days before your scheduled court appearance, or immediately upon receiving this notification if the time before the scheduled appearance is less than seven (7) days; if you are hearing or voice impaired, call 711." FL ST J ADMIN Rule 2.540(c)(1).

9. *Minimization of the filing of sensitive information*

a. *Limitations for court filings.* Unless authorized by FL ST J ADMIN Rule 2.425(b), statute, another rule of court, or the court orders otherwise, designated sensitive information filed with the court must be limited to the following format:

i. The initials of a person known to be a minor;

ii. The year of birth of a person's birth date;

iii. No portion of any: Social security number, Bank account number, Credit card account number, Charge account number, or Debit account number;

iv. The last four digits of any: Taxpayer identification number (TIN), Employee identification number, Driver's license number, Passport number, Telephone number, Financial account

number, except as set forth in FL ST J ADMIN Rule 2.425(a)(3), Brokerage account number, Insurance policy account number, Loan account number, Customer account number, or Patient or health care number;

v. A truncated version of any: Email address, Computer user name, Password, or Personal identification number (PIN); and

vi. A truncated version of any other sensitive information as provided by court order. FL ST J ADMIN Rule 2.425(a).

b. *Exceptions.* FL ST J ADMIN Rule 2.425(a) does not apply to the following:

i. An account number which identifies the property alleged to be the subject of a proceeding;

ii. The record of an administrative or agency proceeding;

iii. The record in appellate or review proceedings;

iv. The birth date of a minor whenever the birth date is necessary for the court to establish or maintain subject matter jurisdiction;

v. The name of a minor in any order relating to parental responsibility, time-sharing, or child support;

vi. The name of a minor in any document or order affecting the minor's ownership of real property;

vii. The birth date of a party in a writ of attachment or notice to payor;

viii. In traffic and criminal proceedings: a pro se filing; a court filing that is related to a criminal matter or investigation and that is prepared before the filing of a criminal charge or is not filed as part of any docketed criminal case; an arrest or search warrant or any information in support thereof; a charging document and an affidavit or other documents filed in support of any charging document, including any driving records; a statement of particulars; discovery material introduced into evidence or otherwise filed with the court; and all information necessary for the proper issuance and execution of a subpoena duces tecum;

ix. Information used by the clerk for case maintenance purposes or the courts for case management purposes; and

x. Information which is relevant and material to an issue before the court. FL ST J ADMIN Rule 2.425(b).

c. *Remedies.* Upon motion by a party or interested person or sua sponte by the court, the court may order remedies, sanctions or both for a violation of FL ST J ADMIN Rule 2.425(a). Following notice and an opportunity to respond, the court may impose sanctions if such filing was not made in good faith. FL ST J ADMIN Rule 2.425(c).

d. *Motions not restricted.* FL ST J ADMIN Rule 2.425 does not restrict a party's right to move for protective order, to move to file documents under seal, or to request a determination of the confidentiality of records. FL ST J ADMIN Rule 2.425(d).

e. *Application.* FL ST J ADMIN Rule 2.425 does not affect the application of constitutional provisions, statutes, or rules of court regarding confidential information or access to public information. FL ST J ADMIN Rule 2.425(e).

F. Filing and Service Requirements

1. *Filing requirements.* All original documents must be filed with the court either before service or immediately thereafter, unless otherwise provided for by general law or other rules. If the original of any bond or other document is not placed in the court file, a certified copy must be so placed by the clerk. FL ST J ADMIN Rule 2.516(d). All documents shall be filed in conformity with the requirements of FL ST J ADMIN Rule 2.525. FL ST RCP Rule 1.080(b). All documents filed in any court shall be filed by electronic transmission in accordance with FL ST J ADMIN Rule 2.525. "Documents" means pleadings, motions, petitions, memoranda, briefs, notices, exhibits, declarations, affidavits, orders, judgments, decrees, writs, opinions, and any other paper or writing submitted to a court. FL ST J ADMIN Rule 2.520(a). All documents that are court records, as defined in FL ST J ADMIN Rule 2.430(a)(1), must be filed by electronic transmission, provided that: (1) the clerk has the ability to accept and retain such

documents; (2) the clerk or the chief judge of the circuit has requested permission to accept documents filed by electronic transmission; and (3) the supreme court has entered an order granting permission to the clerk to accept documents filed by electronic transmission. FL ST J ADMIN Rule 2.525(c)(1).

a. *Definition.* "Electronic transmission of documents" means the sending of information by electronic signals to, by or from a court or clerk, which when received can be transformed and stored or transmitted on paper, microfilm, magnetic storage device, optical imaging system, CD-ROM, flash drive, other electronic data storage system, server, case maintenance system ("CM"), electronic court filing ("ECF") system, statewide or local electronic portal ("e-portal"), or other electronic record keeping system authorized by the supreme court in a format sufficient to communicate the information on the original document in a readable format. Electronic transmission of documents includes electronic mail ("e-mail") and any internet-based transmission procedure, and may include procedures allowing for documents to be signed or verified by electronic means. FL ST J ADMIN Rule 2.525(a).

   i. The filing of documents with the court as required by the Florida Rules of Judicial Administration must be made by filing them with the clerk in accordance with FL ST J ADMIN Rule 2.525, except that the judge may permit documents to be filed with the judge, in which event the judge must note the filing date before him or her on the documents and transmit them to the clerk. The date of filing is that shown on the face of the document by the judge's notation or the clerk's time stamp, whichever is earlier. FL ST J ADMIN Rule 2.516(e).

b. *Application.* Any court or clerk of the court may accept the electronic transmission of documents for filing after the clerk, together with input from the chief judge of the circuit, has obtained approval of the procedures and program for doing so from the Supreme Court of Florida. FL ST J ADMIN Rule 2.525(b).

c. *Exceptions*

   i. Paper documents and other submissions may be manually submitted to the clerk or court:

      - When the clerk does not have the ability to accept and retain documents by electronic filing or has not had ECF Procedures approved by the supreme court;
      - For filing by any self-represented party or any self-represented nonparty unless specific ECF Procedures provide a means to file documents electronically. However, any self-represented nonparty that is a governmental or public agency and any other agency, partnership, corporation, or business entity acting on behalf of any governmental or public agency may file documents by electronic transmission if such entity has the capability of filing documents electronically;
      - For filing by attorneys excused from e-mail service in accordance with FL ST J ADMIN Rule 2.516(b);
      - When submitting evidentiary exhibits or filing non-documentary materials;
      - When the filing involves documents in excess of twenty-five (25) megabytes (25MB) in size. For such filings, documents may be transmitted using an electronic storage medium that the clerk has the ability to accept, which may include a CD-ROM, flash drive, or similar storage medium;
      - When filed in open court, as permitted by the court;
      - When paper filing is permitted by any approved statewide or local ECF procedures; and
      - If any court determines that justice so requires. FL ST J ADMIN Rule 2.525(d).

   ii. Any document in paper form submitted under FL ST J ADMIN Rule 2.525(d) is filed when it is received by the clerk or court and the clerk shall immediately thereafter convert any filed paper document to an electronic document. "Convert to an electronic document" means optically capturing an image of a paper document and using character recognition software to recover as much of the document's text as practicable and then indexing and storing the document in the official court file. FL ST J ADMIN Rule 2.525(c)(4).

   iii. Any storage medium submitted under FL ST J ADMIN Rule 2.525(d)(5) is filed when received

by the clerk or court and the clerk shall immediately thereafter transfer the electronic documents from the storage device to the official court file. FL ST J ADMIN Rule 2.525(c)(5).

iv. If the filer of any paper document authorized under FL ST J ADMIN Rule 2.525(d) provides a self-addressed, postage-paid envelope for return of the paper document after it is converted to electronic form by the clerk, the clerk shall place the paper document in the envelope and deposit it in the mail. Except when a paper document is required to be maintained, the clerk may recycle any filed paper document that is not to be returned to the filer. FL ST J ADMIN Rule 2.525(c)(6).

v. The clerk may convert any paper document filed before the effective date of FL ST J ADMIN Rule 2.525 to an electronic document. Unless the clerk is required to maintain the paper document, if the paper document has been converted to an electronic document by the clerk, the paper document is no longer part of the official court file and may be removed and recycled. FL ST J ADMIN Rule 2.525(c)(7).

d. *Official court file.* For information on what constitutes the official court file, please see FL ST J ADMIN Rule 2.525(c)(2), FL ST J ADMIN Rule 2.525(c)(3).

e. *Administration.* All attorneys, parties, or other persons using this rule to file documents are required to make arrangements with the court or clerk for the payment of any charges authorized by general law or the supreme court before filing any document by electronic transmission. FL ST J ADMIN Rule 2.525(f)(2).

f. *Filing date.* The filing date for an electronically transmitted document is the date and time that such filing is acknowledged by an electronic stamp or otherwise, pursuant to any procedure set forth in any ECF Procedures approved by the supreme court, or the date the last page of such filing is received by the court or clerk. FL ST J ADMIN Rule 2.525(f)(3).

g. *Accessibility.* All documents transmitted in any electronic form under FL ST J ADMIN Rule 2.525 must comply with the accessibility requirements of FL ST J ADMIN Rule 2.526. FL ST J ADMIN Rule 2.525(g).

2. *Service requirements.* Every pleading subsequent to the initial pleading, all orders, and every other document filed in the action must be served in conformity with the requirements of FL ST J ADMIN Rule 2.516. FL ST RCP Rule 1.080(a).

a. *Service; When required.* Unless the court otherwise orders, or a statute or supreme court administrative order specifies a different means of service, every pleading subsequent to the initial pleading and every other document filed in any court proceeding, except applications for witness subpoenas and documents served by formal notice or required to be served in the manner provided for service of formal notice, must be served in accordance with FL ST J ADMIN Rule 2.516 on each party. No service need be made on parties against whom a default has been entered, except that pleadings asserting new or additional claims against them must be served in the manner provided for service of summons. FL ST J ADMIN Rule 2.516(a).

b. *Service; How made.* When service is required or permitted to be made upon a party represented by an attorney, service must be made upon the attorney unless service upon the party is ordered by the court. FL ST J ADMIN Rule 2.516(b).

i. *Service by electronic mail ("e-mail").* All documents required or permitted to be served on another party must be served by e-mail, unless FL ST J ADMIN Rule 2.516 otherwise provides. When, in addition to service by e-mail, the sender also utilizes another means of service provided for in FL ST J ADMIN Rule 2.516(b)(2), any differing time limits and other provisions applicable to that other means of service control. FL ST J ADMIN Rule 2.516(b)(1). Any document electronically transmitted to a court or clerk must also be served on all parties and interested persons in accordance with the applicable rules of court. FL ST J ADMIN Rule 2.525(e)(2).

- *Service on attorneys.* Upon appearing in a proceeding, an attorney must serve a designation of a primary e-mail address and may designate no more than two (2) secondary e-mail addresses. Thereafter, service must be directed to all designated e-mail addresses in that proceeding. Every document filed by an attorney thereafter must include the primary e-mail address of that attorney and any secondary e-mail addresses. If an attorney does not designate any e-mail address for service, documents may be served on that attorney at the e-mail address on record with The Florida Bar. FL ST J ADMIN Rule 2.516(b)(1)(A).

- *Exception to e-mail service on attorneys.* Service by an attorney on another attorney must be made by e-mail unless excused by the court. Upon motion by an attorney demonstrating that the attorney has no e-mail account and lacks access to the Internet at the attorney's office, the court may excuse the attorney from the requirements of e-mail service. Service on and by an attorney excused by the court from e-mail service must be by the means provided in FL ST J ADMIN Rule 2.516(b)(2). FL ST J ADMIN Rule 2.516(b)(1)(B).
- *Service on and by parties not represented by an attorney.* Any party not represented by an attorney may serve a designation of a primary e-mail address and also may designate no more than two (2) secondary e-mail addresses to which service must be directed in that proceeding by the means provided in FL ST J ADMIN Rule 2.516(b)(1). If a party not represented by an attorney does not designate an e-mail address for service in a proceeding, service on and by that party must be by the means provided in FL ST J ADMIN Rule 2.516(b)(2). FL ST J ADMIN Rule 2.516(b)(1)(C).
- *Time of service.* Service by e-mail is complete when it is sent. FL ST J ADMIN Rule 2.516(b)(1)(D). An e-mail is deemed served on the date it is sent. FL ST J ADMIN Rule 2.516(b)(1)(D)(i). If the sender learns that the e-mail did not reach the address of the person to be served, the sender must immediately send another copy by e-mail, or by a means authorized by FL ST J ADMIN Rule 2.516(b)(2). FL ST J ADMIN Rule 2.516(b)(1)(D)(ii). E-mail service is treated as service by mail for the computation of time. FL ST J ADMIN Rule 2.516(b)(1)(D)(iii).

ii. *Format of e-mail for service.* Service of a document by e-mail is made by attaching a copy of the document in PDF format to an e-mail sent to all addresses designated by the attorney or party. FL ST J ADMIN Rule 2.516(b)(1)(E).

- All documents served by e-mail must be attached to an e-mail message containing a subject line beginning with the words "SERVICE OF COURT DOCUMENT" in all capital letters, followed by the case number of the proceeding in which the documents are being served. FL ST J ADMIN Rule 2.516(b)(1)(E)(i).
- The body of the e-mail must identify the court in which the proceeding is pending, the case number, the name of the initial party on each side, the title of each document served with that e-mail, and the sender's name and telephone number. FL ST J ADMIN Rule 2.516(b)(1)(E)(ii).
- Any document served by e-mail may be signed by the "/s/" format, as long as the filed original is signed in accordance with the applicable rule of procedure. FL ST J ADMIN Rule 2.516(b)(1)(E)(iii).
- Any e-mail which, together with its attached documents, exceeds five megabytes (5MB) in size, must be divided and sent as separate e-mails, no one of which may exceed five megabytes (5MB) in size and each of which must be sequentially numbered in the subject line. FL ST J ADMIN Rule 2.516(b)(1)(E)(iv).

iii. *Service by other means.* In addition to, and not in lieu of, service by e-mail, service may also be made upon attorneys by any of the means specified in FL ST J ADMIN Rule 2.516(b)(2). Service on and by all parties who are not represented by an attorney and who do not designate an e-mail address, and on and by all attorneys excused from e-mail service, must be made by delivering a copy of the document or by mailing it to the party or attorney at their last known address or, if no address is known, by leaving it with the clerk of the court. Service by mail is complete upon mailing. Delivery of a copy within FL ST J ADMIN Rule 2.516 is complete upon:

- Handing it to the attorney or to the party,

- Leaving it at the attorney's or party's office with a clerk or other person in charge thereof,
- If there is no one in charge, leaving it in a conspicuous place therein,
- If the office is closed or the person to be served has no office, leaving it at the person's usual place of abode with some person of his or her family above fifteen (15) years of age and informing such person of the contents, or
- Transmitting it by facsimile to the attorney's or party's office with a cover sheet containing the sender's name, firm, address, telephone number, and facsimile number, and the number of pages transmitted. When service is made by facsimile, a copy must also be served by any other method permitted by FL ST J ADMIN Rule 2.516. Facsimile service occurs when transmission is complete. FL ST J ADMIN Rule 2.516(b)(2)(A) through FL ST J ADMIN Rule 2.516(b)(2)(E).
- Service by delivery after 5:00 p.m. must be deemed to have been made by mailing on the date of delivery. FL ST J ADMIN Rule 2.516(b)(2)(F).

c. *Service; Numerous defendants.* In actions when the parties are unusually numerous, the court may regulate the service contemplated by the Florida Rules of Judicial Administration on motion or on its own initiative in such manner as may be found to be just and reasonable. FL ST J ADMIN Rule 2.516(c).

d. *Service by clerk.* Service of notices and other documents required to be made by the clerk must also be done as provided in FL ST J ADMIN Rule 2.516(b). FL ST J ADMIN Rule 2.516(g).

G. Hearings

1. The parties may be required to participate in pretrial proceedings to consider and determine the necessity or desirability of an amendment to a pleading. FL ST RCP Rule 1.200(b)(2); FL-PP § 2:151.

H. Forms

1. Official Amended Answer Forms for Florida

a. Caption. FL ST RCP Form 1.901.

b. Notice of compliance when constitutional challenge is brought. FL ST RCP Form 1.975.

2. Amended Answer Forms for Florida

a. Form for amendment to answer. FL-RCPF R 1.190(50).

b. Form for supplement to pleading. FL-RCPF R 1.190(102).

I. Checklist

(I) ❑ Matters to be considered by plaintiff

(a) ❑ Required documents

(1) ❑ Amended answer

(2) ❑ Certificate of service

(b) ❑ Supplemental documents

(1) ❑ Exhibits

(2) ❑ Notice of constitutional question

(c) ❑ Timing

(1) ❑ A party may amend a pleading once as a matter of course at any time before a responsive pleading is served

(2) ❑ If the pleading is one to which no responsive pleading is permitted and the action has not been placed on the trial calendar, may so amend it at any time within twenty (20) days after it is served

Motions, Oppositions and Replies
Motion to Strike

Document Last Updated January 2013

A. Applicable Rules

1. *State rules*
   a. Rules of court. FL ST RCP Rule 1.010; FL ST J ADMIN Rule 2.110.
   b. Nonverification of pleadings. FL ST RCP Rule 1.030.
   c. Service and filing of pleadings, orders, and documents. FL ST RCP Rule 1.080.
   d. Time. FL ST RCP Rule 1.090.
   e. Pleadings and motions. FL ST RCP Rule 1.100.
   f. Defenses. FL ST RCP Rule 1.140.
   g. Sham pleadings. FL ST RCP Rule 1.150.
   h. Motions. FL ST RCP Rule 1.160.
   i. Relief from judgment, decrees, or orders. FL ST RCP Rule 1.540.
   j. Mediation and arbitration. FL ST RCP Rule 1.700; FL ST RCP Rule 1.710; FL ST RCP Rule 1.720; FL ST RCP Rule 1.730; FL ST RCP Rule 1.750; FL ST RCP Rule 1.800; FL ST RCP Rule 1.810; FL ST RCP Rule 1.820; FL ST RCP Rule 1.830.
   k. Forms. FL ST RCP Rule 1.900.
   l. Minimization of the filing of sensitive information. FL ST J ADMIN Rule 2.425.
   m. Retention of court records. FL ST J ADMIN Rule 2.430.
   n. Foreign attorneys. FL ST J ADMIN Rule 2.510.
   o. Signature of attorneys and parties. FL ST J ADMIN Rule 2.515.
   p. Paper. FL ST J ADMIN Rule 2.520.
   q. Electronic filing. FL ST J ADMIN Rule 2.525.
   r. Communication equipment. FL ST J ADMIN Rule 2.530.
   s. Court reporting. FL ST J ADMIN Rule 2.535.
   t. Accessibility of information and technology. FL ST J ADMIN Rule 2.526.
   u. Requests for accommodations by persons with disabilities. FL ST J ADMIN Rule 2.540.
2. *Local rules*
   a. Eminent domain cases. FL ST 7 J CIR CV-2000-011-VL.
   b. Civil pretrial procedures. FL ST 7 J CIR CV-2003-002-SC.
   c. Arbitration and mediation. FL ST 7 J CIR CV-2008-018-SC; FL ST 7 J CIR CV-2009-019-SC.

B. Timing

1. *Motion to strike.* A party may move to strike or the court may strike redundant, immaterial, impertinent, or scandalous matter from any pleading at any time. FL ST RCP Rule 1.140(f).
2. *Motion to strike; Failure to state a legal defense.* If a pleading sets forth a claim for relief to which the adverse party is not required to serve a responsive pleading, the adverse party may assert any defense in law or fact to that claim for relief at the trial, except that the objection of failure to state a legal defense in an answer or reply shall be asserted by motion to strike the defense within twenty (20) days after service of the answer or reply. FL ST RCP Rule 1.140(b).
3. *Motion to strike; Sham pleadings.* If a party deems any pleading or part thereof filed by another party to be a sham, that party may move to strike the pleading or part thereof before the cause is set for trial. FL ST RCP Rule 1.150(a).

4. *General motion timing.* A copy of any written motion which may not be heard ex parte and a copy of the notice of the hearing thereof shall be served a reasonable time before the time specified for the hearing. FL ST RCP Rule 1.090(d).
   a. Motions filed within thirty (30) days of the trial date will not be considered if predicated on matters the movant knew or should have known with the exercise of reasonable diligence at least thirty (30) days prior to the trial date. Because of busy court calendars, hearing time may not be available to consider motions filed close to the deadline. The inability of a party to obtain time will generally not constitute grounds for a continuance of the trial. FL ST 7 J CIR CV-2003-002-SC(6)(a).
   b. The failure of a party to call up for hearing any timely filed motion at least ten (10) days prior to the trial date may constitute a waiver thereof unless the grounds therefor did not exist or the party was not aware of the grounds for the motion(s) prior to the filing of such motion(s) after the exercise of reasonable diligence. FL ST 7 J CIR CV-2003-002-SC(6)(b).
5. *Computation of time*
   a. *Generally.* Computation of time shall be governed by FL ST J ADMIN Rule 2.514. FL ST RCP Rule 1.090(a). The following rules apply in computing time periods specified in any rule of procedure, local rule, court order, or statute that does not specify a method of computing time. FL ST J ADMIN Rule 2.514(a).
      i. *Period stated in days or a longer unit.* When the period is stated in days or a longer unit of time (A) exclude the day of the event that triggers the period; (B) count every day, including intermediate Saturdays, Sundays, and legal holidays; and (C) include the last day of the period, but if the last day is a Saturday, Sunday, or legal holiday, or falls within any period of time extended through an order of the chief justice under FL ST J ADMIN Rule 2.205(a)(2)(B)(iv), the period continues to run until the end of the next day that is not a Saturday, Sunday, or legal holiday and does not fall within any period of time extended through an order of the chief justice. FL ST J ADMIN Rule 2.514(a)(1).
      ii. *Period stated in hours.* When the period is stated in hours (A) begin counting immediately on the occurrence of the event that triggers the period; (B) count every hour, including hours during intermediate Saturdays, Sundays, and legal holidays; and (C) if the period would end on a Saturday, Sunday, or legal holiday, or during any period of time extended through an order of the chief justice under FL ST J ADMIN Rule 2.205(a)(2)(B)(iv), the period continues to run until the same time on the next day that is not a Saturday, Sunday, or legal holiday and does not fall within any period of time extended through an order of the chief justice. FL ST J ADMIN Rule 2.514(a)(2).
      iii. *Period stated in days less than seven (7) days.* When the period stated in days is less than seven (7) days, intermediate Saturdays, Sundays, and legal holidays shall be excluded in the computation. FL ST J ADMIN Rule 2.514(a)(3).
      iv. *"Last day" defined.* Unless a different time is set by a statute, local rule, or court order, the last day ends (A) for electronic filing or for service by any means, at midnight; and (B) for filing by other means, when the clerk's office is scheduled to close. FL ST J ADMIN Rule 2.514(a)(4).
      v. *"Next day" defined.* The "next day" is determined by continuing to count forward when the period is measured after an event and backward when measured before an event. FL ST J ADMIN Rule 2.514(a)(5).
      vi. *"Legal holiday" defined.* "Legal holiday" means (A) the day set aside by FL ST § 110.117, for observing New Year's Day, Martin Luther King, Jr.'s Birthday, Memorial Day, Independence Day, Labor Day, Veterans' Day, Thanksgiving Day, the Friday after Thanksgiving Day, or Christmas Day, and (B) any day observed as a holiday by the clerk's office or as designated by the chief judge. FL ST J ADMIN Rule 2.514(a)(6).
   b. *Additional time after service by mail or e-mail.* When a party may or must act within a specified time after service and service is made by mail or e-mail, five (5) days are added after the period that would otherwise expire under FL ST J ADMIN Rule 2.514(a). FL ST J ADMIN Rule 2.514(b).
   c. *Enlargement.* When an act is required or allowed to be done at or within a specified time by order of

court, by the Florida Rules of Civil Procedure, or by notice given thereunder, for cause shown the court at any time in its discretion (1) with or without notice, may order the period enlarged if request therefor is made before the expiration of the period originally prescribed or as extended by a previous order, or (2) upon motion made and notice after the expiration of the specified period, may permit the act to be done when failure to act was the result of excusable neglect, but it may not extend the time for making a motion for new trial, for rehearing, or to alter or amend a judgment; making a motion for relief from a judgment under FL ST RCP Rule 1.540(b); taking an appeal or filing a petition for certiorari; or making a motion for a directed verdict. FL ST RCP Rule 1.090(b).

d. *Unaffected by expiration of term.* The period of time provided for the doing of any act or the taking of any proceeding shall not be affected or limited by the continued existence or expiration of a term of court. The continued existence or expiration of a term of court in no way affects the power of a court to do any act or take any proceeding in any action which is or has been pending before it. FL ST RCP Rule 1.090(c).

C. General Requirements

1. *Motions generally*

a. *Contents.* An application to the court for an order shall be by motion which shall be made in writing unless made during a hearing or trial, shall state with particularity the grounds therefor, and shall set forth the relief or order sought. The requirement of writing is fulfilled if the motion is stated in a written notice of the hearing of the motion. All notices of hearing shall specify each motion or other matter to be heard. FL ST RCP Rule 1.100(b).

b. *Particularity requirement.* The court considers a motion in the light of the substantive law, rule or statute to make its determination. Some rules require a statement of the grounds for a motion under the rule. Failure to give the grounds will result in denial of the motion. This should be the result in all situations when the ground for the motion is not inherent in the rule. FL-PRACPROC § 9:3. The requirement is nevertheless an important one, first because of the due process notice rights of the respondent, as well as for the assistance it provides to the court in its preparation for the hearing or, absent a hearing, for disposition. 4 FLPRAC R 1.100.

2. *Motion to strike under FL ST RCP Rule 1.140.* Two (2) types of motion to strike are authorized by FL ST RCP Rule 1.140. One is used to eliminate immaterial, redundant, impertinent or scandalous allegations. The other is used to test the legal sufficiency of a defense. FL-PRACPROC § 10:6.

a. *Motion to strike to eliminate immaterial, redundant, impertinent or scandalous allegations*

i. As used in FL ST RCP Rule 1.140(f), redundant means allegations that are foreign to the issues or needless repetition of allegations. Immaterial means allegations having no essential or important relationship to the issues or unnecessary elaboration of material allegations. Impertinent means allegations that do not belong to the issue and are not necessary to it. Scandalous means unnecessary allegations censuring or accusing a party. FL-PRACPROC § 10:6.

ii. The motion can be made at any time and does not toll the time for pleading. FL-PRACPROC § 10:6.

iii. The motion reaches improper allegations of damages. When directed to an entire paragraph and any part of it is proper, the motion should be denied. Leave to amend should be granted after striking part of a pleading unless a proper amendment cannot be made. FL-PRACPROC § 10:6.

iv. The use of a motion to strike is not favored by the courts and the remedy is used sparingly. Florida courts have held that an allegation must be "wholly irrelevant" and that if there is some doubt it must be resolved in support of the pleading and against the party moving to strike. If any part of an allegation is relevant, then that part should not be stricken from the pleading. 5 FLPRAC § 7:30.

b. *Motion to strike the legal sufficiency of a defense*

i. The legal insufficiency of a defense alleged in an answer or reply is attacked by a motion to strike. It is the counterpart of a motion to dismiss for failure to state a cause of action directed to a pleading seeking affirmative relief. FL-PRACPROC § 10:7.

ii. A motion to strike a defense tests only the legal sufficiency of the defense, and it is reversible error for a trial court to strike the defense where evidence may be presented to support it. Burns v. Equilease Corp., 357 So.2d 786, 24, 24 U.C.C. Rep.Serv. 254 (Fla. 3d DCA 1978); 20 FLPRAC § 3:15.

3. *Sham pleadings.* If a party deems any pleading or part thereof filed by another party to be a sham, that party may move to strike the pleading or part thereof before the cause is set for trial and the court shall hear the motion, taking evidence of the respective parties, and if the motion is sustained, the pleading to which the motion is directed shall be stricken. Default and summary judgment on the merits may be entered in the discretion of the court or the court may permit additional pleadings to be filed for good cause shown. FL ST RCP Rule 1.150(a).

   a. *Contents of motion.* The motion to strike shall be verified and shall set forth fully the facts on which the movant relies and may be supported by affidavit. No traverse of the motion shall be required. FL ST RCP Rule 1.150(b).

   b. *Allegations supported by evidence.* The issue is not whether the allegations are material or proper, but whether the allegations are supported by evidence. 5 FLPRAC § 7:30.

4. *Arbitration and mediation*

   a. *Referral to arbitration and mediation.* Except as hereinafter provided or as otherwise prohibited by law, the presiding judge may enter an order referring all or any part of a contested civil matter to mediation or arbitration. The parties to any contested civil matter may file a written stipulation to mediate or arbitrate any issue between them at any time. Such stipulation shall be incorporated into the order of referral. FL ST RCP Rule 1.700(a).

   b. *Arbitration*

      i. *Exclusions.* A civil action shall be ordered to arbitration or arbitration in conjunction with mediation upon stipulation of the parties. A civil action may be ordered to arbitration or arbitration in conjunction with mediation upon motion of any party or by the court, if the judge determines the action to be of such a nature that arbitration could be of benefit to the litigants or the court. FL ST RCP Rule 1.800.

         - Under no circumstances may the following categories of actions be referred to arbitration: (1) bond estreatures; (2) habeas corpus or other extraordinary writs; (3) bond validations; (4) civil or criminal contempt; (5) such other matters as may be specified by order of the chief judge in the circuit. FL ST RCP Rule 1.800.

      ii. For more information regarding arbitration, please see FL ST RCP Rule 1.810; FL ST RCP Rule 1.820; FL ST RCP Rule 1.830; FL ST 7 J CIR CV-2009-019-SC; and FL ST 7 J CIR CV-2003-002-SC(1)(c).

   c. *Mediation.* For more information regarding mediation, please see FL ST RCP Rule 1.710; FL ST RCP Rule 1.720; FL ST RCP Rule 1.730; FL ST RCP Rule 1.750; FL ST 7 J CIR CV-2008-018-SC; and FL ST 7 J CIR CV-2003-002-SC(1).

5. *Rules of court*

   a. *Rules of civil procedure.* The Florida Rules of Civil Procedure apply to all actions of a civil nature and all special statutory proceedings in the circuit courts and county courts except those to which the Florida Probate Rules, the Florida Family Law Rules of Procedure, or the Small Claims Rules apply. FL ST RCP Rule 1.010.

      i. The form, content, procedure, and time for pleading in all special statutory proceedings shall be as prescribed by the statutes governing the proceeding unless the Florida Rules of Civil Procedure specifically provide to the contrary. FL ST RCP Rule 1.010.

      ii. The Florida Rules of Civil Procedure shall be construed to secure the just, speedy, and inexpensive determination of every action. FL ST RCP Rule 1.010.

   b. *Rules of judicial administration.* The Florida Rules of Judicial Administration shall apply to administrative matters in all courts to which the Florida Rules of Judicial Administration are applicable by their terms. The Florida Rules of Judicial Administration shall be construed to secure

the speedy and inexpensive determination of every proceeding to which they are applicable. The Florida Rules of Judicial Administration shall supersede all conflicting rules and statutes. FL ST J ADMIN Rule 2.110.

D. Documents

1. *Required documents*

a. *Notice of hearing/Motion.* An application to the court for an order shall be by motion which shall be made in writing unless made during a hearing or trial, shall state with particularity the grounds therefor, and shall set forth the relief or order sought. The requirement of writing is fulfilled if the motion is stated in a written notice of the hearing of the motion. All notices of hearing shall specify each motion or other matter to be heard. FL ST RCP Rule 1.100(b).

i. *Notices to persons with disabilities.* See the Format section of this KeyRules document for further information.

b. *Certificate of good faith.* Before any motion is filed, the moving party shall contact the opposing party and attempt, in good faith, to amicably resolve the issues raised by the motion(s), which shall contain a certificate of the movant's attorney if represented (or the moving party if unrepresented) certifying his/her compliance with this requirement. This does not apply to motions for summary judgment or other case dispositive motions. FL ST 7 J CIR CV-2003-002-SC(5)(c).

c. *Certificate of service.* When any attorney certifies in substance: "I certify that a copy hereof has been furnished to (here insert name or names and addresses used for service) by (e-mail) (delivery) (mail) (fax) on .... (date) ....______________ Attorney" the certificate is taken as prima facie proof of such service in compliance with FL ST J ADMIN Rule 2.516. FL ST J ADMIN Rule 2.516(f).

2. *Supplemental documents*

a. *Proposed order.* The court may require that orders or judgments be prepared by a party, may require the party to furnish the court with stamped, addressed envelopes for service of the order or judgment, and may require that proposed orders and judgments be furnished to all parties before entry by the court of the order or judgment. FL ST J ADMIN Rule 2.516(h)(1).

b. *Notice of constitutional question.* A party that files a pleading, written motion, or other paper drawing into question the constitutionality of a state statute or a county or municipal charter, ordinance, or franchise must promptly (1) file a notice of constitutional question stating the question and identifying the paper that raises it; and (2) serve the notice and the pleading, written motion, or other paper drawing into question the constitutionality of a state statute or a county or municipal charter, ordinance, or franchise on the Attorney General or the state attorney of the judicial circuit in which the action is pending, by either certified or registered mail. Service of the notice and pleading, written motion, or other paper does not require joinder of the Attorney General or the state attorney as a party to the action. FL ST RCP Rule 1.071.

E. Format

1. *Documents; Type and size.* Documents subject to the exceptions set forth in FL ST J ADMIN Rule 2.525(d) shall be filed on recycled paper measuring eight and one half by eleven (8 1/2 by 11) inches. For purposes of FL ST J ADMIN Rule 2.520, paper is recycled if it contains a minimum content of fifty (50) percent waste paper. Xerographic reduction of legal-size (eight and one half by fourteen (8 1/2 by 14) inches) documents to letter size (eight and one half by eleven (8 1/2 by 11) inches) is prohibited. All other documents filed by electronic transmission shall be filed in a format capable of being printed in a format consistent with the provisions of FL ST J ADMIN Rule 2.250. FL ST J ADMIN Rule 2.520(b).

a. *Exhibits.* Any exhibit or attachment filed with pleadings or papers may be filed in its original size. FL ST J ADMIN Rule 2.520(c).

b. *Recording space.* On all papers and documents prepared and filed by the court or by any party to a proceeding which are to be recorded in the public records of any county, including but not limited to final money judgments and notices of lis pendens, a three (3) inch by three (3) inch space at the top right-hand corner on the first page and a one (1) inch by three (3) inch space at the top right-hand

corner on each subsequent page shall be left blank and reserved for use by the clerk of court. FL ST J ADMIN Rule 2.520(d).

i. *Exceptions to recording space.* Any papers or documents created by persons or entities over which the filing party has no control, including but not limited to wills, codicils, trusts, or other testamentary documents; documents prepared or executed by any public officer; documents prepared, executed, acknowledged, or proved outside of the State of Florida; or documents created by State or Federal government agencies, may be filed without the space required by FL ST J ADMIN Rule 2.520. FL ST J ADMIN Rule 2.520(e).

c. *Noncompliance.* No clerk of court is permitted to refuse to file any document or paper because of noncompliance with the Florida Rules of Judicial Administration. However, upon request of the clerk of court, noncomplying documents must be resubmitted in accordance with the formatting rules. FL ST J ADMIN Rule 2.520(f).

2. *Caption.* Every pleading, motion, order, judgment, or other paper shall have a caption containing the name of the court, the file number, and except for in rem proceedings, including forfeiture proceedings, the name of the first party on each side with an appropriate indication of other parties, and a designation identifying the party filing it and its nature or the nature of the order, as the case may be. In any in rem proceeding, every pleading, motion, order, judgment, or other paper shall have a caption containing the name of the court, the file number, the style "In re" (followed by the name or general description of the property), and a designation of the person or entity filing it and its nature or the nature of the order, as the case may be. In an in rem forfeiture proceeding, the style shall be "In re forfeiture of" (followed by the name of the general description of the property). All papers filed in the action shall be styled in such a manner as to indicate clearly the subject matter of the paper and the party requesting or obtaining relief. FL ST RCP Rule 1.100(c)(1).

a. *Volusia County eminent domain cases.* All orders, pleadings, motions and other papers will bear the initial case style. Documents intended to apply only to particular parcel(s) will indicate in their caption the parcel number(s) to which they apply and sufficient copies shall be provided to the Clerk of Court to allow the filing and docketing of each relevant paper in each parcel file. FL ST 7 J CIR CV-2000-011-VL(b).

3. *Writing and written defined.* Writing or written means a document containing information, an application, or a stipulation. FL ST RCP Rule 1.080(c).

4. *Rule abbreviations*

a. The Florida Rules of Civil Procedure and shall be abbreviated as Fla.R.Civ.P. FL ST RCP Rule 1.010.

b. The Florida Rules of Judicial Administration shall be abbreviated as Fla. R. Jud. Admin. FL ST J ADMIN Rule 2.110.

5. *Nonverification.* Except when otherwise specifically provided by the Florida Rules of Civil Procedure or an applicable statute, every pleading or other document of a party represented by an attorney need not be verified or accompanied by an affidavit. FL ST RCP Rule 1.030; FL ST J ADMIN Rule 2.515(a).

6. *Attorney signature*

a. *Attorney signature.* Every pleading and other document of a party represented by an attorney shall be signed by at least one (1) attorney of record in that attorney's individual name whose current record Florida Bar address, telephone number, including area code, primary e-mail address and secondary e-mail addresses, if any, and Florida Bar number shall be stated, and who shall be duly licensed to practice law in Florida or who shall have received permission to appear in the particular case as provided in FL ST J ADMIN Rule 2.510. FL ST J ADMIN Rule 2.515(a).

i. The attorney may be required by the court to give the address of, and to vouch for the attorney's authority to represent, the party. FL ST J ADMIN Rule 2.515(a).

ii. The signature of an attorney shall constitute a certificate by the attorney that the attorney has read the pleading or other document; that to the best of the attorney's knowledge, information, and belief there is good ground to support it; and that it is not interposed for delay. FL ST J ADMIN Rule 2.515(a).

iii. If a pleading is not signed or is signed with intent to defeat the purpose of FL ST J ADMIN Rule 2.515, it may be stricken and the action may proceed as though the pleading or other document had not been served. FL ST J ADMIN Rule 2.515(a).

b. *Pro se litigant signature.* A party who is not represented by an attorney shall sign any pleading or other paper and state the party's address and telephone number, including area code. FL ST J ADMIN Rule 2.515(b).

c. *Form of signature*

i. The signatures required on pleadings and documents by FL ST J ADMIN Rule 2.515(a) and FL ST J ADMIN Rule 2.515(b) may be:

- Original signatures;
- Original signatures that have been reproduced by electronic means, such as on electronically transmitted documents or photocopied documents;
- Electronic signatures using the "/s/," "s/," or "/s" formats by or at the direction of the person signing; or
- Any other signature format authorized by general law, so long as the clerk where the proceeding is pending has the capability of receiving and has obtained approval from the Supreme Court of Florida to accept pleadings and documents with that signature format. FL ST J ADMIN Rule 2.515(c)(1).

ii. An attorney, party, or other person who files a pleading or paper by electronic transmission that does not contain the original signature of that attorney, party, or other person shall file that identical pleading or paper in paper form containing an original signature of that attorney, party, or other person (hereinafter called the follow-up filing) immediately thereafter. The follow-up filing is not required if the Supreme Court of Florida has entered an order directing the clerk of court to discontinue accepting the follow-up filing. FL ST J ADMIN Rule 2.515(c)(2).

7. *Forms*

a. *Process.* The forms of process, notice of lis pendens, and notice of action provided in the Florida Rules of Civil Procedure are sufficient. Variations from the forms do not void process or notices that are otherwise sufficient. FL ST RCP Rule 1.900(a).

b. *Other forms.* The other forms provided in the Florida Rules of Civil Procedure are sufficient for the matters that are covered by them. So long as the substance is expressed without prolixity, the forms may be varied to meet the facts of a particular case. FL ST RCP Rule 1.900(b).

c. *Formal matters.* Captions, except for the designation of the paper, are omitted from the forms provided in the Florida Rules of Civil Procedure. A general form of caption is the first form provided. Signatures are omitted from pleadings and motions. FL ST RCP Rule 1.900(c).

8. *Notices to persons with disabilities.* All notices of court proceedings to be held in a public facility, and all process compelling appearance at such proceedings, shall include the following statement in bold face, fourteen (14) point Times New Roman or Courier font: "If you are a person with a disability who needs any accommodation in order to participate in this proceeding, you are entitled, at no cost to you, to the provision of certain assistance. Please contact [identify applicable court personnel by name, address, and telephone number] at least seven (7) days before your scheduled court appearance, or immediately upon receiving this notification if the time before the scheduled appearance is less than seven (7) days; if you are hearing or voice impaired, call 711." FL ST J ADMIN Rule 2.540(c)(1).

9. *Minimization of the filing of sensitive information*

a. *Limitations for court filings.* Unless authorized by FL ST J ADMIN Rule 2.425(b), statute, another rule of court, or the court orders otherwise, designated sensitive information filed with the court must be limited to the following format:

i. The initials of a person known to be a minor;

ii. The year of birth of a person's birth date;

iii. No portion of any: Social security number, Bank account number, Credit card account number, Charge account number, or Debit account number;

iv. The last four digits of any: Taxpayer identification number (TIN), Employee identification number, Driver's license number, Passport number, Telephone number, Financial account number, except as set forth in FL ST J ADMIN Rule 2.425(a)(3), Brokerage account number, Insurance policy account number, Loan account number, Customer account number, or Patient or health care number;

v. A truncated version of any: Email address, Computer user name, Password, or Personal identification number (PIN); and

vi. A truncated version of any other sensitive information as provided by court order. FL ST J ADMIN Rule 2.425(a).

b. *Exceptions.* FL ST J ADMIN Rule 2.425(a) does not apply to the following:

i. An account number which identifies the property alleged to be the subject of a proceeding;

ii. The record of an administrative or agency proceeding;

iii. The record in appellate or review proceedings;

iv. The birth date of a minor whenever the birth date is necessary for the court to establish or maintain subject matter jurisdiction;

v. The name of a minor in any order relating to parental responsibility, time-sharing, or child support;

vi. The name of a minor in any document or order affecting the minor's ownership of real property;

vii. The birth date of a party in a writ of attachment or notice to payor;

viii. In traffic and criminal proceedings: a pro se filing; a court filing that is related to a criminal matter or investigation and that is prepared before the filing of a criminal charge or is not filed as part of any docketed criminal case; an arrest or search warrant or any information in support thereof; a charging document and an affidavit or other documents filed in support of any charging document, including any driving records; a statement of particulars; discovery material introduced into evidence or otherwise filed with the court; and all information necessary for the proper issuance and execution of a subpoena duces tecum;

ix. Information used by the clerk for case maintenance purposes or the courts for case management purposes; and

x. Information which is relevant and material to an issue before the court. FL ST J ADMIN Rule 2.425(b).

c. *Remedies.* Upon motion by a party or interested person or sua sponte by the court, the court may order remedies, sanctions or both for a violation of FL ST J ADMIN Rule 2.425(a). Following notice and an opportunity to respond, the court may impose sanctions if such filing was not made in good faith. FL ST J ADMIN Rule 2.425(c).

d. *Motions not restricted.* FL ST J ADMIN Rule 2.425 does not restrict a party's right to move for protective order, to move to file documents under seal, or to request a determination of the confidentiality of records. FL ST J ADMIN Rule 2.425(d).

e. *Application.* FL ST J ADMIN Rule 2.425 does not affect the application of constitutional provisions, statutes, or rules of court regarding confidential information or access to public information. FL ST J ADMIN Rule 2.425(e).

F. Filing and Service Requirements

1. *Filing requirements.* All original documents must be filed with the court either before service or immediately thereafter, unless otherwise provided for by general law or other rules. If the original of any bond or other document is not placed in the court file, a certified copy must be so placed by the clerk. FL ST J ADMIN Rule 2.516(d). All documents shall be filed in conformity with the requirements of FL ST J ADMIN Rule 2.525. FL ST RCP Rule 1.080(b). All documents filed in any court shall be filed by electronic transmission in accordance with FL ST J ADMIN Rule 2.525. "Documents" means pleadings, motions, petitions, memoranda, briefs, notices, exhibits, declarations, affidavits, orders, judgments, decrees, writs, opinions, and any other paper or writing submitted to a court. FL ST J ADMIN Rule

2.520(a). All documents that are court records, as defined in FL ST J ADMIN Rule 2.430(a)(1), must be filed by electronic transmission, provided that: (1) the clerk has the ability to accept and retain such documents; (2) the clerk or the chief judge of the circuit has requested permission to accept documents filed by electronic transmission; and (3) the supreme court has entered an order granting permission to the clerk to accept documents filed by electronic transmission. FL ST J ADMIN Rule 2.525(c)(1).

a. *Definition.* "Electronic transmission of documents" means the sending of information by electronic signals to, by or from a court or clerk, which when received can be transformed and stored or transmitted on paper, microfilm, magnetic storage device, optical imaging system, CD-ROM, flash drive, other electronic data storage system, server, case maintenance system ("CM"), electronic court filing ("ECF") system, statewide or local electronic portal ("e-portal"), or other electronic record keeping system authorized by the supreme court in a format sufficient to communicate the information on the original document in a readable format. Electronic transmission of documents includes electronic mail ("e-mail") and any internet-based transmission procedure, and may include procedures allowing for documents to be signed or verified by electronic means. FL ST J ADMIN Rule 2.525(a).

   i. The filing of documents with the court as required by the Florida Rules of Judicial Administration must be made by filing them with the clerk in accordance with FL ST J ADMIN Rule 2.525, except that the judge may permit documents to be filed with the judge, in which event the judge must note the filing date before him or her on the documents and transmit them to the clerk. The date of filing is that shown on the face of the document by the judge's notation or the clerk's time stamp, whichever is earlier. FL ST J ADMIN Rule 2.516(e).

b. *Application.* Any court or clerk of the court may accept the electronic transmission of documents for filing after the clerk, together with input from the chief judge of the circuit, has obtained approval of the procedures and program for doing so from the Supreme Court of Florida. FL ST J ADMIN Rule 2.525(b).

c. *Exceptions*

   i. Paper documents and other submissions may be manually submitted to the clerk or court:

      - When the clerk does not have the ability to accept and retain documents by electronic filing or has not had ECF Procedures approved by the supreme court;
      - For filing by any self-represented party or any self-represented nonparty unless specific ECF Procedures provide a means to file documents electronically. However, any self-represented nonparty that is a governmental or public agency and any other agency, partnership, corporation, or business entity acting on behalf of any governmental or public agency may file documents by electronic transmission if such entity has the capability of filing documents electronically;
      - For filing by attorneys excused from e-mail service in accordance with FL ST J ADMIN Rule 2.516(b);
      - When submitting evidentiary exhibits or filing non-documentary materials;
      - When the filing involves documents in excess of twenty-five (25) megabytes (25MB) in size. For such filings, documents may be transmitted using an electronic storage medium that the clerk has the ability to accept, which may include a CD-ROM, flash drive, or similar storage medium;
      - When filed in open court, as permitted by the court;
      - When paper filing is permitted by any approved statewide or local ECF procedures; and
      - If any court determines that justice so requires. FL ST J ADMIN Rule 2.525(d).

   ii. Any document in paper form submitted under FL ST J ADMIN Rule 2.525(d) is filed when it is received by the clerk or court and the clerk shall immediately thereafter convert any filed paper document to an electronic document. "Convert to an electronic document" means optically capturing an image of a paper document and using character recognition software to recover as much of the document's text as practicable and then indexing and storing the document in the official court file. FL ST J ADMIN Rule 2.525(c)(4).

iii. Any storage medium submitted under FL ST J ADMIN Rule 2.525(d)(5) is filed when received by the clerk or court and the clerk shall immediately thereafter transfer the electronic documents from the storage device to the official court file. FL ST J ADMIN Rule 2.525(c)(5).

iv. If the filer of any paper document authorized under FL ST J ADMIN Rule 2.525(d) provides a self-addressed, postage-paid envelope for return of the paper document after it is converted to electronic form by the clerk, the clerk shall place the paper document in the envelope and deposit it in the mail. Except when a paper document is required to be maintained, the clerk may recycle any filed paper document that is not to be returned to the filer. FL ST J ADMIN Rule 2.525(c)(6).

v. The clerk may convert any paper document filed before the effective date of FL ST J ADMIN Rule 2.525 to an electronic document. Unless the clerk is required to maintain the paper document, if the paper document has been converted to an electronic document by the clerk, the paper document is no longer part of the official court file and may be removed and recycled. FL ST J ADMIN Rule 2.525(c)(7).

d. *Official court file.* For information on what constitutes the official court file, please see FL ST J ADMIN Rule 2.525(c)(2), FL ST J ADMIN Rule 2.525(c)(3).

e. *Administration.* All attorneys, parties, or other persons using this rule to file documents are required to make arrangements with the court or clerk for the payment of any charges authorized by general law or the supreme court before filing any document by electronic transmission. FL ST J ADMIN Rule 2.525(f)(2).

f. *Filing date.* The filing date for an electronically transmitted document is the date and time that such filing is acknowledged by an electronic stamp or otherwise, pursuant to any procedure set forth in any ECF Procedures approved by the supreme court, or the date the last page of such filing is received by the court or clerk. FL ST J ADMIN Rule 2.525(f)(3).

g. *Accessibility.* All documents transmitted in any electronic form under FL ST J ADMIN Rule 2.525 must comply with the accessibility requirements of FL ST J ADMIN Rule 2.526. FL ST J ADMIN Rule 2.525(g).

2. *Service requirements.* Every pleading subsequent to the initial pleading, all orders, and every other document filed in the action must be served in conformity with the requirements of FL ST J ADMIN Rule 2.516. FL ST RCP Rule 1.080(a).

a. *Service; When required.* Unless the court otherwise orders, or a statute or supreme court administrative order specifies a different means of service, every pleading subsequent to the initial pleading and every other document filed in any court proceeding, except applications for witness subpoenas and documents served by formal notice or required to be served in the manner provided for service of formal notice, must be served in accordance with FL ST J ADMIN Rule 2.516 on each party. No service need be made on parties against whom a default has been entered, except that pleadings asserting new or additional claims against them must be served in the manner provided for service of summons. FL ST J ADMIN Rule 2.516(a).

b. *Service; How made.* When service is required or permitted to be made upon a party represented by an attorney, service must be made upon the attorney unless service upon the party is ordered by the court. FL ST J ADMIN Rule 2.516(b).

i. *Service by electronic mail ("e-mail").* All documents required or permitted to be served on another party must be served by e-mail, unless FL ST J ADMIN Rule 2.516 otherwise provides. When, in addition to service by e-mail, the sender also utilizes another means of service provided for in FL ST J ADMIN Rule 2.516(b)(2), any differing time limits and other provisions applicable to that other means of service control. FL ST J ADMIN Rule 2.516(b)(1). Any document electronically transmitted to a court or clerk must also be served on all parties and interested persons in accordance with the applicable rules of court. FL ST J ADMIN Rule 2.525(e)(2).

- *Service on attorneys.* Upon appearing in a proceeding, an attorney must serve a designation of a primary e-mail address and may designate no more than two (2) secondary e-mail

addresses. Thereafter, service must be directed to all designated e-mail addresses in that proceeding. Every document filed by an attorney thereafter must include the primary e-mail address of that attorney and any secondary e-mail addresses. If an attorney does not designate any e-mail address for service, documents may be served on that attorney at the e-mail address on record with The Florida Bar. FL ST J ADMIN Rule 2.516(b)(1)(A).

- *Exception to e-mail service on attorneys.* Service by an attorney on another attorney must be made by e-mail unless excused by the court. Upon motion by an attorney demonstrating that the attorney has no e-mail account and lacks access to the Internet at the attorney's office, the court may excuse the attorney from the requirements of e-mail service. Service on and by an attorney excused by the court from e-mail service must be by the means provided in FL ST J ADMIN Rule 2.516(b)(2). FL ST J ADMIN Rule 2.516(b)(1)(B).
- *Service on and by parties not represented by an attorney.* Any party not represented by an attorney may serve a designation of a primary e-mail address and also may designate no more than two (2) secondary e-mail addresses to which service must be directed in that proceeding by the means provided in FL ST J ADMIN Rule 2.516(b)(1). If a party not represented by an attorney does not designate an e-mail address for service in a proceeding, service on and by that party must be by the means provided in FL ST J ADMIN Rule 2.516(b)(2). FL ST J ADMIN Rule 2.516(b)(1)(C).
- *Time of service.* Service by e-mail is complete when it is sent. FL ST J ADMIN Rule 2.516(b)(1)(D). An e-mail is deemed served on the date it is sent. FL ST J ADMIN Rule 2.516(b)(1)(D)(i). If the sender learns that the e-mail did not reach the address of the person to be served, the sender must immediately send another copy by e-mail, or by a means authorized by FL ST J ADMIN Rule 2.516(b)(2). FL ST J ADMIN Rule 2.516(b)(1)(D)(ii). E-mail service is treated as service by mail for the computation of time. FL ST J ADMIN Rule 2.516(b)(1)(D)(iii).

ii. *Format of e-mail for service.* Service of a document by e-mail is made by attaching a copy of the document in PDF format to an e-mail sent to all addresses designated by the attorney or party. FL ST J ADMIN Rule 2.516(b)(1)(E).

- All documents served by e-mail must be attached to an e-mail message containing a subject line beginning with the words "SERVICE OF COURT DOCUMENT" in all capital letters, followed by the case number of the proceeding in which the documents are being served. FL ST J ADMIN Rule 2.516(b)(1)(E)(i).
- The body of the e-mail must identify the court in which the proceeding is pending, the case number, the name of the initial party on each side, the title of each document served with that e-mail, and the sender's name and telephone number. FL ST J ADMIN Rule 2.516(b)(1)(E)(ii).
- Any document served by e-mail may be signed by the "/s/" format, as long as the filed original is signed in accordance with the applicable rule of procedure. FL ST J ADMIN Rule 2.516(b)(1)(E)(iii).
- Any e-mail which, together with its attached documents, exceeds five megabytes (5MB) in size, must be divided and sent as separate e-mails, no one of which may exceed five megabytes (5MB) in size and each of which must be sequentially numbered in the subject line. FL ST J ADMIN Rule 2.516(b)(1)(E)(iv).

iii. *Service by other means.* In addition to, and not in lieu of, service by e-mail, service may also be made upon attorneys by any of the means specified in FL ST J ADMIN Rule 2.516(b)(2). Service on and by all parties who are not represented by an attorney and who do not designate an e-mail address, and on and by all attorneys excused from e-mail service, must be made by delivering a copy of the document or by mailing it to the party or attorney at their last known address or, if no address is known, by leaving it with the clerk of the court. Service by mail is complete upon mailing. Delivery of a copy within FL ST J ADMIN Rule 2.516 is complete upon:

- Handing it to the attorney or to the party,

- Leaving it at the attorney's or party's office with a clerk or other person in charge thereof,
- If there is no one in charge, leaving it in a conspicuous place therein,
- If the office is closed or the person to be served has no office, leaving it at the person's usual place of abode with some person of his or her family above fifteen (15) years of age and informing such person of the contents, or
- Transmitting it by facsimile to the attorney's or party's office with a cover sheet containing the sender's name, firm, address, telephone number, and facsimile number, and the number of pages transmitted. When service is made by facsimile, a copy must also be served by any other method permitted by FL ST J ADMIN Rule 2.516. Facsimile service occurs when transmission is complete. FL ST J ADMIN Rule 2.516(b)(2)(A) through FL ST J ADMIN Rule 2.516(b)(2)(E).
- Service by delivery after 5:00 p.m. must be deemed to have been made by mailing on the date of delivery. FL ST J ADMIN Rule 2.516(b)(2)(F).

c. *Service; Numerous defendants.* In actions when the parties are unusually numerous, the court may regulate the service contemplated by the Florida Rules of Judicial Administration on motion or on its own initiative in such manner as may be found to be just and reasonable. FL ST J ADMIN Rule 2.516(c).

d. *Service by clerk.* Service of notices and other documents required to be made by the clerk must also be done as provided in FL ST J ADMIN Rule 2.516(b). FL ST J ADMIN Rule 2.516(g).

G. Hearings

1. *Communication equipment*

a. *Definition.* Communication equipment means a conference telephone or other electronic device that permits all those appearing or participating to hear and speak to each other, provided that all conversation of all parties is audible to all persons present. FL ST J ADMIN Rule 2.530(a).

b. *Use by all parties.* A county or circuit court judge may, upon the court's own motion or upon the written request of a party, direct that communication equipment be used for a motion hearing, pretrial conference, or a status conference. A judge must give notice to the parties and consider any objections they may have to the use of communication equipment before directing that communication equipment be used. The decision to use communication equipment over the objection of parties will be in the sound discretion of the trial court, except as noted below. FL ST J ADMIN Rule 2.530(b).

c. *Use only by requesting party.* A county or circuit court judge may, upon the written request of a party upon reasonable notice to all other parties, permit a requesting party to participate through communication equipment in a scheduled motion hearing; however, any such request (except in criminal, juvenile, and appellate proceedings) must be granted, absent a showing of good cause to deny the same, where the hearing is set for not longer than fifteen (15) minutes. FL ST J ADMIN Rule 2.530(c).

d. *Testimony*

i. *Generally.* A county or circuit court judge, general magistrate, special magistrate, or hearing officer may allow testimony to be taken through communication equipment if all parties consent or if permitted by another applicable rule of procedure. FL ST J ADMIN Rule 2.530(d)(1).

ii. *Procedure.* Any party desiring to present testimony through communication equipment shall, prior to the hearing or trial at which the testimony is to be presented, contact all parties to determine whether each party consents to this form of testimony. The party seeking to present the testimony shall move for permission to present testimony through communication equipment, which motion shall set forth good cause as to why the testimony should be allowed in this form. FL ST J ADMIN Rule 2.530(d)(2).

iii. *Oath.* Testimony may be taken through communication equipment only if a notary public or other person authorized to administer oaths in the witness's jurisdiction is present with the witness and administers the oath consistent with the laws of the jurisdiction. FL ST J ADMIN Rule 2.530(d)(3).

iv. *Confrontation rights.* In juvenile and criminal proceedings the defendant must make an informed waiver of any confrontation rights that may be abridged by the use of communication equipment. FL ST J ADMIN Rule 2.530(d)(4).

v. *Video testimony.* If the testimony to be presented utilizes video conferencing or comparable two-way visual capabilities, the court in its discretion may modify the procedures set forth in FL ST J ADMIN Rule 2.530 to accommodate the technology utilized. FL ST J ADMIN Rule 2.530(d)(5).

e. *Burden of expense.* The cost for the use of the communication equipment is the responsibility of the requesting party unless otherwise directed by the court. FL ST J ADMIN Rule 2.530(e).

H. Forms

1. Official Motion to Strike Forms for Florida

a. Caption. FL ST RCP Form 1.901.

b. Notice of compliance when constitutional challenge is brought. FL ST RCP Form 1.975.

2. Motion to Strike Forms for Florida

a. Motion to strike. FL-PP § 2:128.

b. Form for motion to strike. FL-RCPF R 1.140(802).

c. Form for motion to strike insufficient pleading. FL-RCPF R 1.140(803).

d. Form for motion to strike claim for business or financial losses. FL-RCPF R 1.140(804).

e. Motion; Strike, complaint signed by corporation. FL-PRACFORM § 7:176.

f. Motion; Strike, defenses. FL-PRACFORM § 7:177.

g. Motion; Strike, ejectment chain of title. FL-PRACFORM § 7:178.

h. Motion; Strike, interrogatories, excess number. FL-PRACFORM § 7:179.

i. Motion; Strike, pleading, departure. FL-PRACFORM § 7:180.

j. Motion; Strike, pleading, improper signature. FL-PRACFORM § 7:181.

k. Motion; Strike, sham pleading. FL-PRACFORM § 7:182.

l. Motion; Strike, sham, defenses, statute of limitations and failure of consideration. FL-PRACFORM § 7:183.

m. Motion; Strike, third party complaint. FL-PRACFORM § 7:184.

I. Checklist

(I) ❑ Matters to be considered by moving party

(a) ❑ Required documents

(1) ❑ Notice of hearing/Motion

(2) ❑ Certificate of good faith

(3) ❑ Certificate of service

(b) ❑ Supplemental documents

(1) ❑ Proposed order

(2) ❑ Notice of constitutional question

(c) ❑ Time for making motion

(1) ❑ A party may move to strike or the court may strike redundant, immaterial, impertinent, or scandalous matter from any pleading at any time

(2) ❑ If a pleading sets forth a claim for relief to which the adverse party is not required to serve

a responsive pleading, the adverse party may assert any defense in law or fact to that claim for relief at the trial, except that the objection of failure to state a legal defense in an answer or reply shall be asserted by motion to strike the defense within twenty (20) days after service of the answer or reply

(3) ❑ If a party deems any pleading or part thereof filed by another party to be a sham, that party may move to strike the pleading or part thereof before the cause is set for trial

(4) ❑ A copy of any written motion which may not be heard ex parte and a copy of the notice of the hearing thereof shall be served a reasonable time before the time specified for the hearing

(II) ❑ Matters to be considered by opposing party

(a) ❑ Required documents

(1) ❑ Response to motion

(2) ❑ Certificate of service

(b) ❑ Supplemental documents

(1) ❑ Proposed order

(2) ❑ Notice of constitutional question

(c) ❑ Time for service and filing of opposition

(1) ❑ No time specified for responding to a motion

Motions, Oppositions and Replies
Motion for Leave to Amend

Document Last Updated January 2013

A. Applicable Rules

1. *State rules*

a. Rules of court. FL ST RCP Rule 1.010; FL ST J ADMIN Rule 2.110.

b. Nonverification of pleadings. FL ST RCP Rule 1.030.

c. Process. FL ST RCP Rule 1.070.

d. Service and filing of pleadings, orders, and documents. FL ST RCP Rule 1.080.

e. Time. FL ST RCP Rule 1.090.

f. Pleadings and motions. FL ST RCP Rule 1.100.

g. Defenses. FL ST RCP Rule 1.140.

h. Motions. FL ST RCP Rule 1.160.

i. Amended and supplemental pleadings. FL ST RCP Rule 1.190.

j. Relief from judgment, decrees, or orders. FL ST RCP Rule 1.540.

k. Mediation and arbitration. FL ST RCP Rule 1.700; FL ST RCP Rule 1.710; FL ST RCP Rule 1.720; FL ST RCP Rule 1.730; FL ST RCP Rule 1.750; FL ST RCP Rule 1.800; FL ST RCP Rule 1.810; FL ST RCP Rule 1.820; FL ST RCP Rule 1.830.

l. Forms. FL ST RCP Rule 1.900.

m. Minimization of the filing of sensitive information. FL ST J ADMIN Rule 2.425.

n. Retention of court records. FL ST J ADMIN Rule 2.430.

o. Foreign attorneys. FL ST J ADMIN Rule 2.510.

p. Signature of attorneys and parties. FL ST J ADMIN Rule 2.515.

q. Paper. FL ST J ADMIN Rule 2.520.

r. Electronic filing. FL ST J ADMIN Rule 2.525.

s. Accessibility of information and technology. FL ST J ADMIN Rule 2.526.

t. Communication equipment. FL ST J ADMIN Rule 2.530.

u. Court reporting. FL ST J ADMIN Rule 2.535.

v. Requests for accommodations by persons with disabilities. FL ST J ADMIN Rule 2.540.

2. *Local rules*

a. Eminent domain cases. FL ST 7 J CIR CV-2000-011-VL.

b. Civil pretrial procedures. FL ST 7 J CIR CV-2003-002-SC.

c. Arbitration and mediation. FL ST 7 J CIR CV-2008-018-SC; FL ST 7 J CIR CV-2009-019-SC.

B. Timing

1. *Amended pleadings as a matter of course.* A party may amend a pleading once as a matter of course at any time before a responsive pleading is served or, if the pleading is one to which no responsive pleading is permitted and the action has not been placed on the trial calendar, may amend it at any time within twenty (20) days after it is served. Otherwise a party may amend a pleading only by leave of court or by written consent of the adverse party. FL ST RCP Rule 1.190(a).

2. *Amended pleadings with leave of court.* Leave of court shall be given freely when justice so requires. FL ST RCP Rule 1.190(a). Under the Florida Rules of Civil Procedure, there is no time limit as to when an amendment with leave of court may be sought. Amendments of the pleadings may be permitted, with the court's discretion, at any stage of the proceedings in furtherance of justice. McSwiggan v. Edson, 186 So.2d 13, 15 (Fla. 1966); FL-PP § 2:153. Nevertheless, the liberality in permitting amendment of pleadings diminishes as the case progresses to trial. Versen v. Versen, 347 So.2d 1047, 1050 (Fla. 4th DCA 1977); FL-PP § 2:153.

3. *Claims for punitive damages.* A motion for leave to amend a pleading to assert a claim for punitive damages can be filed separately and before the supporting evidence or proffer, but each shall be served on all parties at least twenty (20) days before the hearing. FL ST RCP Rule 1.190(f).

4. *Post motion for leave to amend*

a. If the court permits or requires an amended or responsive pleading or a more definite statement, the pleading or statement shall be served within ten (10) days after notice of the court's action. FL ST RCP Rule 1.140(a)(4).

b. When a motion for leave to amend with the attached proposed amended complaint is filed, the one hundred twenty (120) day period for service of amended complaints on the new party or parties shall begin upon the entry of an order granting leave to amend. FL ST RCP Rule 1.070(j).

5. *General motion timing.* A copy of any written motion which may not be heard ex parte and a copy of the notice of the hearing thereof shall be served a reasonable time before the time specified for the hearing. FL ST RCP Rule 1.090(d).

a. Motions filed within thirty (30) days of the trial date will not be considered if predicated on matters the movant knew or should have known with the exercise of reasonable diligence at least thirty (30) days prior to the trial date. Because of busy court calendars, hearing time may not be available to consider motions filed close to the deadline. The inability of a party to obtain time will generally not constitute grounds for a continuance of the trial. FL ST 7 J CIR CV-2003-002-SC(6)(a).

b. The failure of a party to call up for hearing any timely filed motion at least ten (10) days prior to the trial date may constitute a waiver thereof unless the grounds therefor did not exist or the party was not aware of the grounds for the motion(s) prior to the filing of such motion(s) after the exercise of reasonable diligence. FL ST 7 J CIR CV-2003-002-SC(6)(b).

6. *Computation of time*

a. *Generally.* Computation of time shall be governed by FL ST J ADMIN Rule 2.514. FL ST RCP Rule 1.090(a). The following rules apply in computing time periods specified in any rule of procedure, local rule, court order, or statute that does not specify a method of computing time. FL ST J ADMIN Rule 2.514(a).

i. *Period stated in days or a longer unit.* When the period is stated in days or a longer unit of time (A) exclude the day of the event that triggers the period; (B) count every day, including intermediate Saturdays, Sundays, and legal holidays; and (C) include the last day of the period, but if the last day is a Saturday, Sunday, or legal holiday, or falls within any period of time extended through an order of the chief justice under FL ST J ADMIN Rule 2.205(a)(2)(B)(iv), the period continues to run until the end of the next day that is not a Saturday, Sunday, or legal holiday and does not fall within any period of time extended through an order of the chief justice. FL ST J ADMIN Rule 2.514(a)(1).

ii. *Period stated in hours.* When the period is stated in hours (A) begin counting immediately on the occurrence of the event that triggers the period; (B) count every hour, including hours during intermediate Saturdays, Sundays, and legal holidays; and (C) if the period would end on a Saturday, Sunday, or legal holiday, or during any period of time extended through an order of the chief justice under FL ST J ADMIN Rule 2.205(a)(2)(B)(iv), the period continues to run until the same time on the next day that is not a Saturday, Sunday, or legal holiday and does not fall within any period of time extended through an order of the chief justice. FL ST J ADMIN Rule 2.514(a)(2).

iii. *Period stated in days less than seven (7) days.* When the period stated in days is less than seven (7) days, intermediate Saturdays, Sundays, and legal holidays shall be excluded in the computation. FL ST J ADMIN Rule 2.514(a)(3).

iv. *"Last day" defined.* Unless a different time is set by a statute, local rule, or court order, the last day ends (A) for electronic filing or for service by any means, at midnight; and (B) for filing by other means, when the clerk's office is scheduled to close. FL ST J ADMIN Rule 2.514(a)(4).

v. *"Next day" defined.* The "next day" is determined by continuing to count forward when the period is measured after an event and backward when measured before an event. FL ST J ADMIN Rule 2.514(a)(5).

vi. *"Legal holiday" defined.* "Legal holiday" means (A) the day set aside by FL ST § 110.117, for observing New Year's Day, Martin Luther King, Jr.'s Birthday, Memorial Day, Independence Day, Labor Day, Veterans' Day, Thanksgiving Day, the Friday after Thanksgiving Day, or Christmas Day, and (B) any day observed as a holiday by the clerk's office or as designated by the chief judge. FL ST J ADMIN Rule 2.514(a)(6).

b. *Additional time after service by mail or e-mail.* When a party may or must act within a specified time after service and service is made by mail or e-mail, five (5) days are added after the period that would otherwise expire under FL ST J ADMIN Rule 2.514(a). FL ST J ADMIN Rule 2.514(b).

c. *Enlargement.* When an act is required or allowed to be done at or within a specified time by order of court, by the Florida Rules of Civil Procedure, or by notice given thereunder, for cause shown the court at any time in its discretion (1) with or without notice, may order the period enlarged if request therefor is made before the expiration of the period originally prescribed or as extended by a previous order, or (2) upon motion made and notice after the expiration of the specified period, may permit the act to be done when failure to act was the result of excusable neglect, but it may not extend the time for making a motion for new trial, for rehearing, or to alter or amend a judgment; making a motion for relief from a judgment under FL ST RCP Rule 1.540(b); taking an appeal or filing a petition for certiorari; or making a motion for a directed verdict. FL ST RCP Rule 1.090(b).

d. *Unaffected by expiration of term.* The period of time provided for the doing of any act or the taking of any proceeding shall not be affected or limited by the continued existence or expiration of a term of court. The continued existence or expiration of a term of court in no way affects the power of a court to do any act or take any proceeding in any action which is or has been pending before it. FL ST RCP Rule 1.090(c).

C. General Requirements

1. *Motions generally*

a. *Contents.* An application to the court for an order shall be by motion which shall be made in writing unless made during a hearing or trial, shall state with particularity the grounds therefor, and shall set forth the relief or order sought. The requirement of writing is fulfilled if the motion is stated in a written notice of the hearing of the motion. All notices of hearing shall specify each motion or other matter to be heard. FL ST RCP Rule 1.100(b).

b. *Particularity requirement.* The court considers a motion in the light of the substantive law, rule or statute to make its determination. Some rules require a statement of the grounds for a motion under the rule. Failure to give the grounds will result in denial of the motion. This should be the result in all situations when the ground for the motion is not inherent in the rule. FL-PRACPROC § 9:3. The requirement is nevertheless an important one, first because of the due process notice rights of the respondent, as well as for the assistance it provides to the court in its preparation for the hearing or, absent a hearing, for disposition. 4 FLPRAC R 1.100.

2. *Motion for leave to amend.* Although the Florida Rules of Civil Procedure do not specify a procedure for obtaining leave to amend, it is usually accomplished by way of a motion. FL-PP § 2:153. At any time in furtherance of justice, upon such terms as may be just, the court may permit any process, proceeding, pleading, or record to be amended or material supplemental matter to be set forth in an amended or supplemental pleading. At every stage of the action the court must disregard any error or defect in the proceedings which does not affect the substantial rights of the parties. FL ST RCP Rule 1.190(e).

   a. *Permissible amendments.* Amendments can relate to the correction of mistakes, the insertion of jurisdictional averments, the correction or addition of verifications, the addition or substitution or striking out of parties, and generally the rectification of all formal defects in the pleading. The court can also allow amendments setting up an omitted counterclaim or cross-claim if the defendant failed to raise the claim through oversight, inadvertence, or excusable neglect. FL-PP § 2:151.

   b. *Amendments to conform with the evidence.* When issues not raised by the pleadings are tried by express or implied consent of the parties, they shall be treated in all respects as if they had been raised in the pleadings. Such amendment of the pleadings as may be necessary to cause them to conform to the evidence and to raise these issues may be made upon motion of any party at any time, even after judgment, but failure so to amend shall not affect the result of the trial of these issues. If the evidence is objected to at the trial on the ground that it is not within the issues made by the pleadings, the court may allow the pleadings to be amended to conform with the evidence and shall do so freely when the merits of the cause are more effectually presented thereby and the objecting party fails to satisfy the court that the admission of such evidence will prejudice the objecting party in maintaining an action or defense upon the merits. FL ST RCP Rule 1.190(b).

      i. The courts have been extremely liberal in permitting amendments after trial to conform pleadings to the evidence where the issues were tried by the express or implied consent of the parties. Turner v. Long, 225 So.2d 434 (Fla. 1st DCA 1969); FL-PP § 2:152.

   c. *Procedure for adding parties.* Parties may be added once as a matter of course within the same time that pleadings can be so amended. If amendment by leave of court or stipulation of the parties is permitted, parties may be added in the amended pleading without further order of court. Parties may be added by order of court on its own initiative or on motion of any party at any stage of the action and on such terms as are just. FL ST RCP Rule 1.250(c).

   d. *Claims for punitive damages.* A motion for leave to amend a pleading to assert a claim for punitive damages shall make a reasonable showing by evidence in the record or evidence to be proffered by the claimant that provides a reasonable basis for recovery of such damages. The motion to amend can be filed separately and before the supporting evidence or proffer, but each shall be served on all parties at least twenty (20) days before the hearing. FL ST RCP Rule 1.190(f). Leave of court to amend the complaint must be obtained before a plaintiff may assert a punitive damages claim in the complaint. Failure to do so will result in the claims being dismissed or stricken. FL-PP § 2:151.

   e. *Relation back of amendments.* When the claim or defense asserted in the amended pleading arose out of the conduct, transaction, or occurrence set forth or attempted to be set forth in the original pleading, the amendment shall relate back to the date of the original pleading. FL ST RCP Rule 1.190(c).

      i. The doctrine of relation back becomes critical in applying the statute of limitations. For example, it has been held that the doctrine of relation back may not be utilized to circumvent the statute of limitations to permit an amendment where a claim could have been filed as an independent action but was not timely asserted and would otherwise be barred under the statute of limitations. Cox v. Seaboard Coast Line R. Co., 360 So.2d 8 (Fla. 2d DCA 1978); FL-PP § 2:152.

3. *Arbitration and mediation*
   a. *Referral to arbitration and mediation.* Except as hereinafter provided or as otherwise prohibited by law, the presiding judge may enter an order referring all or any part of a contested civil matter to mediation or arbitration. The parties to any contested civil matter may file a written stipulation to mediate or arbitrate any issue between them at any time. Such stipulation shall be incorporated into the order of referral. FL ST RCP Rule 1.700(a).
   b. *Arbitration*
      i. *Exclusions.* A civil action shall be ordered to arbitration or arbitration in conjunction with mediation upon stipulation of the parties. A civil action may be ordered to arbitration or arbitration in conjunction with mediation upon motion of any party or by the court, if the judge determines the action to be of such a nature that arbitration could be of benefit to the litigants or the court. FL ST RCP Rule 1.800.
         - Under no circumstances may the following categories of actions be referred to arbitration: (1) bond estreatures; (2) habeas corpus or other extraordinary writs; (3) bond validations; (4) civil or criminal contempt; (5) such other matters as may be specified by order of the chief judge in the circuit. FL ST RCP Rule 1.800.
      ii. For more information regarding arbitration, please see FL ST RCP Rule 1.810; FL ST RCP Rule 1.820; FL ST RCP Rule 1.830; FL ST 7 J CIR CV-2009-019-SC; and FL ST 7 J CIR CV-2003-002-SC(1)(c).
   c. *Mediation.* For more information regarding mediation, please see FL ST RCP Rule 1.710; FL ST RCP Rule 1.720; FL ST RCP Rule 1.730; FL ST RCP Rule 1.750; FL ST 7 J CIR CV-2008-018-SC; and FL ST 7 J CIR CV-2003-002-SC(1).
4. *Rules of court*
   a. *Rules of civil procedure.* The Florida Rules of Civil Procedure apply to all actions of a civil nature and all special statutory proceedings in the circuit courts and county courts except those to which the Florida Probate Rules, the Florida Family Law Rules of Procedure, or the Small Claims Rules apply. FL ST RCP Rule 1.010.
      i. The form, content, procedure, and time for pleading in all special statutory proceedings shall be as prescribed by the statutes governing the proceeding unless the Florida Rules of Civil Procedure specifically provide to the contrary. FL ST RCP Rule 1.010.
      ii. The Florida Rules of Civil Procedure shall be construed to secure the just, speedy, and inexpensive determination of every action. FL ST RCP Rule 1.010.
   b. *Rules of judicial administration.* The Florida Rules of Judicial Administration shall apply to administrative matters in all courts to which the Florida Rules of Judicial Administration are applicable by their terms. The Florida Rules of Judicial Administration shall be construed to secure the speedy and inexpensive determination of every proceeding to which they are applicable. The Florida Rules of Judicial Administration shall supersede all conflicting rules and statutes. FL ST J ADMIN Rule 2.110.

D. Documents

1. *Required documents*
   a. *Notice of hearing/Motion.* An application to the court for an order shall be by motion which shall be made in writing unless made during a hearing or trial, shall state with particularity the grounds therefor, and shall set forth the relief or order sought. The requirement of writing is fulfilled if the

motion is stated in a written notice of the hearing of the motion. All notices of hearing shall specify each motion or other matter to be heard. FL ST RCP Rule 1.100(b).

i. *Notices to persons with disabilities.* See the Format section of this KeyRules document for further information.

b. *Proposed amended pleading.* The moving party shall attach the proposed amended pleading to the motion. FL ST RCP Rule 1.190(a).

c. *Certificate of good faith.* Before any motion is filed, the moving party shall contact the opposing party and attempt, in good faith, to amicably resolve the issues raised by the motion(s), which shall contain a certificate of the movant's attorney if represented (or the moving party if unrepresented) certifying his/her compliance with this requirement. This does not apply to motions for summary judgment or other case dispositive motions. FL ST 7 J CIR CV-2003-002-SC(5)(c).

d. *Certificate of service.* When any attorney certifies in substance: "I certify that a copy hereof has been furnished to (here insert name or names and addresses used for service) by (e-mail) (delivery) (mail) (fax) on .... (date) ....________________ Attorney" the certificate is taken as prima facie proof of such service in compliance with FL ST J ADMIN Rule 2.516. FL ST J ADMIN Rule 2.516(f).

2. *Supplemental documents*

a. *Proposed order.* The court may require that orders or judgments be prepared by a party, may require the party to furnish the court with stamped, addressed envelopes for service of the order or judgment, and may require that proposed orders and judgments be furnished to all parties before entry by the court of the order or judgment. FL ST J ADMIN Rule 2.516(h)(1).

b. *Notice of constitutional question.* A party that files a pleading, written motion, or other paper drawing into question the constitutionality of a state statute or a county or municipal charter, ordinance, or franchise must promptly (1) file a notice of constitutional question stating the question and identifying the paper that raises it; and (2) serve the notice and the pleading, written motion, or other paper drawing into question the constitutionality of a state statute or a county or municipal charter, ordinance, or franchise on the Attorney General or the state attorney of the judicial circuit in which the action is pending, by either certified or registered mail. Service of the notice and pleading, written motion, or other paper does not require joinder of the Attorney General or the state attorney as a party to the action. FL ST RCP Rule 1.071.

E. Format

1. *Documents; Type and size.* Documents subject to the exceptions set forth in FL ST J ADMIN Rule 2.525(d) shall be filed on recycled paper measuring eight and one half by eleven (8 1/2 by 11) inches. For purposes of FL ST J ADMIN Rule 2.520, paper is recycled if it contains a minimum content of fifty (50) percent waste paper. Xerographic reduction of legal-size (eight and one half by fourteen (8 1/2 by 14) inches) documents to letter size (eight and one half by eleven (8 1/2 by 11) inches) is prohibited. All other documents filed by electronic transmission shall be filed in a format capable of being printed in a format consistent with the provisions of FL ST J ADMIN Rule 2.250. FL ST J ADMIN Rule 2.520(b).

a. *Exhibits.* Any exhibit or attachment filed with pleadings or papers may be filed in its original size. FL ST J ADMIN Rule 2.520(c).

b. *Recording space.* On all papers and documents prepared and filed by the court or by any party to a proceeding which are to be recorded in the public records of any county, including but not limited to final money judgments and notices of lis pendens, a three (3) inch by three (3) inch space at the top right-hand corner on the first page and a one (1) inch by three (3) inch space at the top right-hand corner on each subsequent page shall be left blank and reserved for use by the clerk of court. FL ST J ADMIN Rule 2.520(d).

i. *Exceptions to recording space.* Any papers or documents created by persons or entities over which the filing party has no control, including but not limited to wills, codicils, trusts, or other testamentary documents; documents prepared or executed by any public officer; documents prepared, executed, acknowledged, or proved outside of the State of Florida; or documents created by State or Federal government agencies, may be filed without the space required by FL ST J ADMIN Rule 2.520. FL ST J ADMIN Rule 2.520(e).

c. *Noncompliance.* No clerk of court is permitted to refuse to file any document or paper because of noncompliance with the Florida Rules of Judicial Administration. However, upon request of the clerk of court, noncomplying documents must be resubmitted in accordance with the formatting rules. FL ST J ADMIN Rule 2.520(f).

2. *Caption.* Every pleading, motion, order, judgment, or other paper shall have a caption containing the name of the court, the file number, and except for in rem proceedings, including forfeiture proceedings, the name of the first party on each side with an appropriate indication of other parties, and a designation identifying the party filing it and its nature or the nature of the order, as the case may be. In any in rem proceeding, every pleading, motion, order, judgment, or other paper shall have a caption containing the name of the court, the file number, the style "In re" (followed by the name or general description of the property), and a designation of the person or entity filing it and its nature or the nature of the order, as the case may be. In an in rem forfeiture proceeding, the style shall be "In re forfeiture of" (followed by the name of the general description of the property). All papers filed in the action shall be styled in such a manner as to indicate clearly the subject matter of the paper and the party requesting or obtaining relief. FL ST RCP Rule 1.100(c)(1).
   a. *Volusia County eminent domain cases.* All orders, pleadings, motions and other papers will bear the initial case style. Documents intended to apply only to particular parcel(s) will indicate in their caption the parcel number(s) to which they apply and sufficient copies shall be provided to the Clerk of Court to allow the filing and docketing of each relevant paper in each parcel file. FL ST 7 J CIR CV-2000-011-VL(b).

3. *Writing and written defined.* Writing or written means a document containing information, an application, or a stipulation. FL ST RCP Rule 1.080(c).

4. *Rule abbreviations*
   a. The Florida Rules of Civil Procedure and shall be abbreviated as Fla.R.Civ.P. FL ST RCP Rule 1.010.
   b. The Florida Rules of Judicial Administration shall be abbreviated as Fla. R. Jud. Admin. FL ST J ADMIN Rule 2.110.

5. *Nonverification.* Except when otherwise specifically provided by the Florida Rules of Civil Procedure or an applicable statute, every pleading or other document of a party represented by an attorney need not be verified or accompanied by an affidavit. FL ST RCP Rule 1.030; FL ST J ADMIN Rule 2.515(a).

6. *Attorney signature*
   a. *Attorney signature.* Every pleading and other document of a party represented by an attorney shall be signed by at least one (1) attorney of record in that attorney's individual name whose current record Florida Bar address, telephone number, including area code, primary e-mail address and secondary e-mail addresses, if any, and Florida Bar number shall be stated, and who shall be duly licensed to practice law in Florida or who shall have received permission to appear in the particular case as provided in FL ST J ADMIN Rule 2.510. FL ST J ADMIN Rule 2.515(a).
      i. The attorney may be required by the court to give the address of, and to vouch for the attorney's authority to represent, the party. FL ST J ADMIN Rule 2.515(a).
      ii. The signature of an attorney shall constitute a certificate by the attorney that the attorney has read the pleading or other document; that to the best of the attorney's knowledge, information, and belief there is good ground to support it; and that it is not interposed for delay. FL ST J ADMIN Rule 2.515(a).
      iii. If a pleading is not signed or is signed with intent to defeat the purpose of FL ST J ADMIN Rule 2.515, it may be stricken and the action may proceed as though the pleading or other document had not been served. FL ST J ADMIN Rule 2.515(a).
   b. *Pro se litigant signature.* A party who is not represented by an attorney shall sign any pleading or other paper and state the party's address and telephone number, including area code. FL ST J ADMIN Rule 2.515(b).

c. *Form of signature*

i. The signatures required on pleadings and documents by FL ST J ADMIN Rule 2.515(a) and FL ST J ADMIN Rule 2.515(b) may be:

- Original signatures;
- Original signatures that have been reproduced by electronic means, such as on electronically transmitted documents or photocopied documents;
- Electronic signatures using the "/s/," "s/," or "/s" formats by or at the direction of the person signing; or
- Any other signature format authorized by general law, so long as the clerk where the proceeding is pending has the capability of receiving and has obtained approval from the Supreme Court of Florida to accept pleadings and documents with that signature format. FL ST J ADMIN Rule 2.515(c)(1).

ii. An attorney, party, or other person who files a pleading or paper by electronic transmission that does not contain the original signature of that attorney, party, or other person shall file that identical pleading or paper in paper form containing an original signature of that attorney, party, or other person (hereinafter called the follow-up filing) immediately thereafter. The follow-up filing is not required if the Supreme Court of Florida has entered an order directing the clerk of court to discontinue accepting the follow-up filing. FL ST J ADMIN Rule 2.515(c)(2).

7. *Forms*

a. *Process.* The forms of process, notice of lis pendens, and notice of action provided in the Florida Rules of Civil Procedure are sufficient. Variations from the forms do not void process or notices that are otherwise sufficient. FL ST RCP Rule 1.900(a).

b. *Other forms.* The other forms provided in the Florida Rules of Civil Procedure are sufficient for the matters that are covered by them. So long as the substance is expressed without prolixity, the forms may be varied to meet the facts of a particular case. FL ST RCP Rule 1.900(b).

c. *Formal matters.* Captions, except for the designation of the paper, are omitted from the forms provided in the Florida Rules of Civil Procedure. A general form of caption is the first form provided. Signatures are omitted from pleadings and motions. FL ST RCP Rule 1.900(c).

8. *Notices to persons with disabilities.* All notices of court proceedings to be held in a public facility, and all process compelling appearance at such proceedings, shall include the following statement in bold face, fourteen (14) point Times New Roman or Courier font: "If you are a person with a disability who needs any accommodation in order to participate in this proceeding, you are entitled, at no cost to you, to the provision of certain assistance. Please contact [identify applicable court personnel by name, address, and telephone number] at least seven (7) days before your scheduled court appearance, or immediately upon receiving this notification if the time before the scheduled appearance is less than seven (7) days; if you are hearing or voice impaired, call 711." FL ST J ADMIN Rule 2.540(c)(1).

9. *Minimization of the filing of sensitive information*

a. *Limitations for court filings.* Unless authorized by FL ST J ADMIN Rule 2.425(b), statute, another rule of court, or the court orders otherwise, designated sensitive information filed with the court must be limited to the following format:

i. The initials of a person known to be a minor;

ii. The year of birth of a person's birth date;

iii. No portion of any: Social security number, Bank account number, Credit card account number, Charge account number, or Debit account number;

iv. The last four digits of any: Taxpayer identification number (TIN), Employee identification number, Driver's license number, Passport number, Telephone number, Financial account number, except as set forth in FL ST J ADMIN Rule 2.425(a)(3), Brokerage account number, Insurance policy account number, Loan account number, Customer account number, or Patient or health care number;

v. A truncated version of any: Email address, Computer user name, Password, or Personal identification number (PIN); and

vi. A truncated version of any other sensitive information as provided by court order. FL ST J ADMIN Rule 2.425(a).

b. *Exceptions.* FL ST J ADMIN Rule 2.425(a) does not apply to the following:

i. An account number which identifies the property alleged to be the subject of a proceeding;

ii. The record of an administrative or agency proceeding;

iii. The record in appellate or review proceedings;

iv. The birth date of a minor whenever the birth date is necessary for the court to establish or maintain subject matter jurisdiction;

v. The name of a minor in any order relating to parental responsibility, time-sharing, or child support;

vi. The name of a minor in any document or order affecting the minor's ownership of real property;

vii. The birth date of a party in a writ of attachment or notice to payor;

viii. In traffic and criminal proceedings: a pro se filing; a court filing that is related to a criminal matter or investigation and that is prepared before the filing of a criminal charge or is not filed as part of any docketed criminal case; an arrest or search warrant or any information in support thereof; a charging document and an affidavit or other documents filed in support of any charging document, including any driving records; a statement of particulars; discovery material introduced into evidence or otherwise filed with the court; and all information necessary for the proper issuance and execution of a subpoena duces tecum;

ix. Information used by the clerk for case maintenance purposes or the courts for case management purposes; and

x. Information which is relevant and material to an issue before the court. FL ST J ADMIN Rule 2.425(b).

c. *Remedies.* Upon motion by a party or interested person or sua sponte by the court, the court may order remedies, sanctions or both for a violation of FL ST J ADMIN Rule 2.425(a). Following notice and an opportunity to respond, the court may impose sanctions if such filing was not made in good faith. FL ST J ADMIN Rule 2.425(c).

d. *Motions not restricted.* FL ST J ADMIN Rule 2.425 does not restrict a party's right to move for protective order, to move to file documents under seal, or to request a determination of the confidentiality of records. FL ST J ADMIN Rule 2.425(d).

e. *Application.* FL ST J ADMIN Rule 2.425 does not affect the application of constitutional provisions, statutes, or rules of court regarding confidential information or access to public information. FL ST J ADMIN Rule 2.425(e).

F. Filing and Service Requirements

1. *Filing requirements.* All original documents must be filed with the court either before service or immediately thereafter, unless otherwise provided for by general law or other rules. If the original of any bond or other document is not placed in the court file, a certified copy must be so placed by the clerk. FL ST J ADMIN Rule 2.516(d). All documents shall be filed in conformity with the requirements of FL ST J ADMIN Rule 2.525. FL ST RCP Rule 1.080(b). All documents filed in any court shall be filed by electronic transmission in accordance with FL ST J ADMIN Rule 2.525. "Documents" means pleadings, motions, petitions, memoranda, briefs, notices, exhibits, declarations, affidavits, orders, judgments, decrees, writs, opinions, and any other paper or writing submitted to a court. FL ST J ADMIN Rule 2.520(a). All documents that are court records, as defined in FL ST J ADMIN Rule 2.430(a)(1), must be filed by electronic transmission, provided that: (1) the clerk has the ability to accept and retain such documents; (2) the clerk or the chief judge of the circuit has requested permission to accept documents filed by electronic transmission; and (3) the supreme court has entered an order granting permission to the clerk to accept documents filed by electronic transmission. FL ST J ADMIN Rule 2.525(c)(1).

a. *Definition.* "Electronic transmission of documents" means the sending of information by electronic

signals to, by or from a court or clerk, which when received can be transformed and stored or transmitted on paper, microfilm, magnetic storage device, optical imaging system, CD-ROM, flash drive, other electronic data storage system, server, case maintenance system ("CM"), electronic court filing ("ECF") system, statewide or local electronic portal ("e-portal"), or other electronic record keeping system authorized by the supreme court in a format sufficient to communicate the information on the original document in a readable format. Electronic transmission of documents includes electronic mail ("e-mail") and any internet-based transmission procedure, and may include procedures allowing for documents to be signed or verified by electronic means. FL ST J ADMIN Rule 2.525(a).

i. The filing of documents with the court as required by the Florida Rules of Judicial Administration must be made by filing them with the clerk in accordance with FL ST J ADMIN Rule 2.525, except that the judge may permit documents to be filed with the judge, in which event the judge must note the filing date before him or her on the documents and transmit them to the clerk. The date of filing is that shown on the face of the document by the judge's notation or the clerk's time stamp, whichever is earlier. FL ST J ADMIN Rule 2.516(e).

b. *Application.* Any court or clerk of the court may accept the electronic transmission of documents for filing after the clerk, together with input from the chief judge of the circuit, has obtained approval of the procedures and program for doing so from the Supreme Court of Florida. FL ST J ADMIN Rule 2.525(b).

c. *Exceptions*

i. Paper documents and other submissions may be manually submitted to the clerk or court:

- When the clerk does not have the ability to accept and retain documents by electronic filing or has not had ECF Procedures approved by the supreme court;
- For filing by any self-represented party or any self-represented nonparty unless specific ECF Procedures provide a means to file documents electronically. However, any self-represented nonparty that is a governmental or public agency and any other agency, partnership, corporation, or business entity acting on behalf of any governmental or public agency may file documents by electronic transmission if such entity has the capability of filing documents electronically;
- For filing by attorneys excused from e-mail service in accordance with FL ST J ADMIN Rule 2.516(b);
- When submitting evidentiary exhibits or filing non-documentary materials;
- When the filing involves documents in excess of twenty-five (25) megabytes (25MB) in size. For such filings, documents may be transmitted using an electronic storage medium that the clerk has the ability to accept, which may include a CD-ROM, flash drive, or similar storage medium;
- When filed in open court, as permitted by the court;
- When paper filing is permitted by any approved statewide or local ECF procedures; and
- If any court determines that justice so requires. FL ST J ADMIN Rule 2.525(d).

ii. Any document in paper form submitted under FL ST J ADMIN Rule 2.525(d) is filed when it is received by the clerk or court and the clerk shall immediately thereafter convert any filed paper document to an electronic document. "Convert to an electronic document" means optically capturing an image of a paper document and using character recognition software to recover as much of the document's text as practicable and then indexing and storing the document in the official court file. FL ST J ADMIN Rule 2.525(c)(4).

iii. Any storage medium submitted under FL ST J ADMIN Rule 2.525(d)(5) is filed when received by the clerk or court and the clerk shall immediately thereafter transfer the electronic documents from the storage device to the official court file. FL ST J ADMIN Rule 2.525(c)(5).

iv. If the filer of any paper document authorized under FL ST J ADMIN Rule 2.525(d) provides a self-addressed, postage-paid envelope for return of the paper document after it is converted to

electronic form by the clerk, the clerk shall place the paper document in the envelope and deposit it in the mail. Except when a paper document is required to be maintained, the clerk may recycle any filed paper document that is not to be returned to the filer. FL ST J ADMIN Rule 2.525(c)(6).

v. The clerk may convert any paper document filed before the effective date of FL ST J ADMIN Rule 2.525 to an electronic document. Unless the clerk is required to maintain the paper document, if the paper document has been converted to an electronic document by the clerk, the paper document is no longer part of the official court file and may be removed and recycled. FL ST J ADMIN Rule 2.525(c)(7).

d. *Official court file.* For information on what constitutes the official court file, please see FL ST J ADMIN Rule 2.525(c)(2), FL ST J ADMIN Rule 2.525(c)(3).

e. *Administration.* All attorneys, parties, or other persons using this rule to file documents are required to make arrangements with the court or clerk for the payment of any charges authorized by general law or the supreme court before filing any document by electronic transmission. FL ST J ADMIN Rule 2.525(f)(2).

f. *Filing date.* The filing date for an electronically transmitted document is the date and time that such filing is acknowledged by an electronic stamp or otherwise, pursuant to any procedure set forth in any ECF Procedures approved by the supreme court, or the date the last page of such filing is received by the court or clerk. FL ST J ADMIN Rule 2.525(f)(3).

g. *Accessibility.* All documents transmitted in any electronic form under FL ST J ADMIN Rule 2.525 must comply with the accessibility requirements of FL ST J ADMIN Rule 2.526. FL ST J ADMIN Rule 2.525(g).

2. *Service requirements.* Every pleading subsequent to the initial pleading, all orders, and every other document filed in the action must be served in conformity with the requirements of FL ST J ADMIN Rule 2.516. FL ST RCP Rule 1.080(a).

a. *Service; When required.* Unless the court otherwise orders, or a statute or supreme court administrative order specifies a different means of service, every pleading subsequent to the initial pleading and every other document filed in any court proceeding, except applications for witness subpoenas and documents served by formal notice or required to be served in the manner provided for service of formal notice, must be served in accordance with FL ST J ADMIN Rule 2.516 on each party. No service need be made on parties against whom a default has been entered, except that pleadings asserting new or additional claims against them must be served in the manner provided for service of summons. FL ST J ADMIN Rule 2.516(a).

b. *Service; How made.* When service is required or permitted to be made upon a party represented by an attorney, service must be made upon the attorney unless service upon the party is ordered by the court. FL ST J ADMIN Rule 2.516(b).

i. *Service by electronic mail ("e-mail").* All documents required or permitted to be served on another party must be served by e-mail, unless FL ST J ADMIN Rule 2.516 otherwise provides. When, in addition to service by e-mail, the sender also utilizes another means of service provided for in FL ST J ADMIN Rule 2.516(b)(2), any differing time limits and other provisions applicable to that other means of service control. FL ST J ADMIN Rule 2.516(b)(1). Any document electronically transmitted to a court or clerk must also be served on all parties and interested persons in accordance with the applicable rules of court. FL ST J ADMIN Rule 2.525(e)(2).

- *Service on attorneys.* Upon appearing in a proceeding, an attorney must serve a designation of a primary e-mail address and may designate no more than two (2) secondary e-mail addresses. Thereafter, service must be directed to all designated e-mail addresses in that proceeding. Every document filed by an attorney thereafter must include the primary e-mail address of that attorney and any secondary e-mail addresses. If an attorney does not designate any e-mail address for service, documents may be served on that attorney at the e-mail address on record with The Florida Bar. FL ST J ADMIN Rule 2.516(b)(1)(A).

- *Exception to e-mail service on attorneys.* Service by an attorney on another attorney must be made by e-mail unless excused by the court. Upon motion by an attorney demonstrating that the attorney has no e-mail account and lacks access to the Internet at the attorney's office, the court may excuse the attorney from the requirements of e-mail service. Service on and by an attorney excused by the court from e-mail service must be by the means provided in FL ST J ADMIN Rule 2.516(b)(2). FL ST J ADMIN Rule 2.516(b)(1)(B).
- *Service on and by parties not represented by an attorney.* Any party not represented by an attorney may serve a designation of a primary e-mail address and also may designate no more than two (2) secondary e-mail addresses to which service must be directed in that proceeding by the means provided in FL ST J ADMIN Rule 2.516(b)(1). If a party not represented by an attorney does not designate an e-mail address for service in a proceeding, service on and by that party must be by the means provided in FL ST J ADMIN Rule 2.516(b)(2). FL ST J ADMIN Rule 2.516(b)(1)(C).
- *Time of service.* Service by e-mail is complete when it is sent. FL ST J ADMIN Rule 2.516(b)(1)(D). An e-mail is deemed served on the date it is sent. FL ST J ADMIN Rule 2.516(b)(1)(D)(i). If the sender learns that the e-mail did not reach the address of the person to be served, the sender must immediately send another copy by e-mail, or by a means authorized by FL ST J ADMIN Rule 2.516(b)(2). FL ST J ADMIN Rule 2.516(b)(1)(D)(ii). E-mail service is treated as service by mail for the computation of time. FL ST J ADMIN Rule 2.516(b)(1)(D)(iii).

ii. *Format of e-mail for service.* Service of a document by e-mail is made by attaching a copy of the document in PDF format to an e-mail sent to all addresses designated by the attorney or party. FL ST J ADMIN Rule 2.516(b)(1)(E).

- All documents served by e-mail must be attached to an e-mail message containing a subject line beginning with the words "SERVICE OF COURT DOCUMENT" in all capital letters, followed by the case number of the proceeding in which the documents are being served. FL ST J ADMIN Rule 2.516(b)(1)(E)(i).
- The body of the e-mail must identify the court in which the proceeding is pending, the case number, the name of the initial party on each side, the title of each document served with that e-mail, and the sender's name and telephone number. FL ST J ADMIN Rule 2.516(b)(1)(E)(ii).
- Any document served by e-mail may be signed by the "/s/" format, as long as the filed original is signed in accordance with the applicable rule of procedure. FL ST J ADMIN Rule 2.516(b)(1)(E)(iii).
- Any e-mail which, together with its attached documents, exceeds five megabytes (5MB) in size, must be divided and sent as separate e-mails, no one of which may exceed five megabytes (5MB) in size and each of which must be sequentially numbered in the subject line. FL ST J ADMIN Rule 2.516(b)(1)(E)(iv).

iii. *Service by other means.* In addition to, and not in lieu of, service by e-mail, service may also be made upon attorneys by any of the means specified in FL ST J ADMIN Rule 2.516(b)(2). Service on and by all parties who are not represented by an attorney and who do not designate an e-mail address, and on and by all attorneys excused from e-mail service, must be made by delivering a copy of the document or by mailing it to the party or attorney at their last known address or, if no address is known, by leaving it with the clerk of the court. Service by mail is complete upon mailing. Delivery of a copy within FL ST J ADMIN Rule 2.516 is complete upon:

- Handing it to the attorney or to the party,
- Leaving it at the attorney's or party's office with a clerk or other person in charge thereof,
- If there is no one in charge, leaving it in a conspicuous place therein,
- If the office is closed or the person to be served has no office, leaving it at the person's usual place of abode with some person of his or her family above fifteen (15) years of age and informing such person of the contents, or

- Transmitting it by facsimile to the attorney's or party's office with a cover sheet containing the sender's name, firm, address, telephone number, and facsimile number, and the number of pages transmitted. When service is made by facsimile, a copy must also be served by any other method permitted by FL ST J ADMIN Rule 2.516. Facsimile service occurs when transmission is complete. FL ST J ADMIN Rule 2.516(b)(2)(A) through FL ST J ADMIN Rule 2.516(b)(2)(E).
- Service by delivery after 5:00 p.m. must be deemed to have been made by mailing on the date of delivery. FL ST J ADMIN Rule 2.516(b)(2)(F).

c. *Service; Numerous defendants.* In actions when the parties are unusually numerous, the court may regulate the service contemplated by the Florida Rules of Judicial Administration on motion or on its own initiative in such manner as may be found to be just and reasonable. FL ST J ADMIN Rule 2.516(c).

d. *Service by clerk.* Service of notices and other documents required to be made by the clerk must also be done as provided in FL ST J ADMIN Rule 2.516(b). FL ST J ADMIN Rule 2.516(g).

G. Hearings

1. *Communication equipment*

a. *Definition.* Communication equipment means a conference telephone or other electronic device that permits all those appearing or participating to hear and speak to each other, provided that all conversation of all parties is audible to all persons present. FL ST J ADMIN Rule 2.530(a).

b. *Use by all parties.* A county or circuit court judge may, upon the court's own motion or upon the written request of a party, direct that communication equipment be used for a motion hearing, pretrial conference, or a status conference. A judge must give notice to the parties and consider any objections they may have to the use of communication equipment before directing that communication equipment be used. The decision to use communication equipment over the objection of parties will be in the sound discretion of the trial court, except as noted below. FL ST J ADMIN Rule 2.530(b).

c. *Use only by requesting party.* A county or circuit court judge may, upon the written request of a party upon reasonable notice to all other parties, permit a requesting party to participate through communication equipment in a scheduled motion hearing; however, any such request (except in criminal, juvenile, and appellate proceedings) must be granted, absent a showing of good cause to deny the same, where the hearing is set for not longer than fifteen (15) minutes. FL ST J ADMIN Rule 2.530(c).

d. *Testimony*

i. *Generally.* A county or circuit court judge, general magistrate, special magistrate, or hearing officer may allow testimony to be taken through communication equipment if all parties consent or if permitted by another applicable rule of procedure. FL ST J ADMIN Rule 2.530(d)(1).

ii. *Procedure.* Any party desiring to present testimony through communication equipment shall, prior to the hearing or trial at which the testimony is to be presented, contact all parties to determine whether each party consents to this form of testimony. The party seeking to present the testimony shall move for permission to present testimony through communication equipment, which motion shall set forth good cause as to why the testimony should be allowed in this form. FL ST J ADMIN Rule 2.530(d)(2).

iii. *Oath.* Testimony may be taken through communication equipment only if a notary public or other person authorized to administer oaths in the witness's jurisdiction is present with the witness and administers the oath consistent with the laws of the jurisdiction. FL ST J ADMIN Rule 2.530(d)(3).

iv. *Confrontation rights.* In juvenile and criminal proceedings the defendant must make an informed waiver of any confrontation rights that may be abridged by the use of communication equipment. FL ST J ADMIN Rule 2.530(d)(4).

v. *Video testimony.* If the testimony to be presented utilizes video conferencing or comparable two-way visual capabilities, the court in its discretion may modify the procedures set forth in FL ST J ADMIN Rule 2.530 to accommodate the technology utilized. FL ST J ADMIN Rule 2.530(d)(5).

e. *Burden of expense.* The cost for the use of the communication equipment is the responsibility of the requesting party unless otherwise directed by the court. FL ST J ADMIN Rule 2.530(e).

H. Forms

1. Official Motion for Leave to Amend Forms for Florida

a. Caption. FL ST RCP Form 1.901.

b. Notice of compliance when constitutional challenge is brought. FL ST RCP Form 1.975.

2. Motion for Leave to Amend Forms for Florida

a. Motion; For leave of court; To amend complaint. FL-PP § 2:155.

b. Motion; For leave of court; To add claim for punitive damages. FL-PP § 2:156.

c. Motion; For leave of court; To amend complaint; To conform to evidence. FL-PP § 2:157.

d. Motion; For leave of court; To permit admission of evidence. FL-PP § 2:158.

e. Order; Granting leave to amend complaint. FL-PP § 2:163.

f. Order; Granting leave to amend complaint; To conform to evidence. FL-PP § 2:164.

g. Order; Granting leave to amend complaint; To permit admission of evidence. FL-PP § 2:165.

h. Form for motion for leave to amend complaint. FL-RCPF R 1.190(39).

i. Form for amendment to complaint with leave of court. FL-RCPF R 1.190(40).

j. Form for motion to amend amended complaint. FL-RCPF R 1.190(42).

k. Form for amendment to amended complaint (or second amended complaint). FL-RCPF R 1.190(43).

l. Form for motion to amend complaint to add count. FL-RCPF R 1.190(44).

I. Checklist

(I) ❑ Matters to be considered by moving party

(a) ❑ Required documents

(1) ❑ Notice of hearing/Motion

(2) ❑ Proposed amended pleading

(3) ❑ Certificate of good faith

(4) ❑ Certificate of service

(b) ❑ Supplemental documents

(1) ❑ Proposed order

(2) ❑ Notice of constitutional question

(c) ❑ Time for making motion

(1) ❑ A party may amend a pleading once as a matter of course at any time before a responsive pleading is served or, if the pleading is one to which no responsive pleading is permitted and the action has not been placed on the trial calendar, may amend it at any time within twenty (20) days after it is served

(2) ❑ Under the Florida Rules of Civil Procedure, there is no time limit as to when an amendment with leave of court may be sought; amendments of the pleadings may be permitted, with the court's discretion, at any stage of the proceedings in furtherance of justice

(3) ❑ A motion for leave to amend a pleading to assert a claim for punitive damages can be filed separately and before the supporting evidence or proffer, but each shall be served on all parties at least twenty (20) days before the hearing

(4) ❑ A copy of any written motion which may not be heard ex parte and a copy of the notice of the hearing thereof shall be served a reasonable time before the time specified for the hearing

(II) ❑ Matters to be considered by opposing party

(a) ❑ Required documents

(1) ❑ Response to motion

(2) ❑ Certificate of service

(b) ❑ Supplemental documents

(1) ❑ Proposed order

(2) ❑ Notice of constitutional question

(c) ❑ Time for service and filing of opposition

(1) ❑ No time specified for responding to a motion

Motions, Oppositions and Replies
Motion for Summary Judgment

Document Last Updated January 2013

A. Applicable Rules

1. *State rules*
   a. Rules of court. FL ST RCP Rule 1.010; FL ST J ADMIN Rule 2.110.
   b. Nonverification of pleadings. FL ST RCP Rule 1.030.
   c. Service and filing of pleadings, orders, and documents. FL ST RCP Rule 1.080.
   d. Time. FL ST RCP Rule 1.090.
   e. Pleadings and motions. FL ST RCP Rule 1.100.
   f. Motions. FL ST RCP Rule 1.160.
   g. Summary judgment. FL ST RCP Rule 1.510.
   h. Relief from judgment, decrees, or orders. FL ST RCP Rule 1.540.
   i. Mediation and arbitration. FL ST RCP Rule 1.700; FL ST RCP Rule 1.710; FL ST RCP Rule 1.720; FL ST RCP Rule 1.730; FL ST RCP Rule 1.750; FL ST RCP Rule 1.800; FL ST RCP Rule 1.810; FL ST RCP Rule 1.820; FL ST RCP Rule 1.830.
   j. Forms. FL ST RCP Rule 1.900.
   k. Minimization of the filing of sensitive information. FL ST J ADMIN Rule 2.425.
   l. Retention of court records. FL ST J ADMIN Rule 2.430.
   m. Foreign attorneys. FL ST J ADMIN Rule 2.510.
   n. Signature of attorneys and parties. FL ST J ADMIN Rule 2.515.
   o. Paper. FL ST J ADMIN Rule 2.520.
   p. Electronic filing. FL ST J ADMIN Rule 2.525.
   q. Accessibility of information and technology. FL ST J ADMIN Rule 2.526.
   r. Communication equipment. FL ST J ADMIN Rule 2.530.
   s. Court reporting. FL ST J ADMIN Rule 2.535.
   t. Requests for accommodations by persons with disabilities. FL ST J ADMIN Rule 2.540.
2. *Local rules*
   a. Addresses and social security numbers of parties on final judgments. FL ST 7 J CIR CV-2000-007-SC.

b. Eminent domain cases. FL ST 7 J CIR CV-2000-011-VL.

c. Civil pretrial procedures. FL ST 7 J CIR CV-2003-002-SC.

d. Arbitration and mediation. FL ST 7 J CIR CV-2008-018-SC; FL ST 7 J CIR CV-2009-019-SC.

B. Timing

1. *Motion for summary judgment*

a. *For the claimant.* A party seeking to recover upon a claim, counterclaim, crossclaim or third-party claim or to obtain a declaratory judgment may move for a summary judgment in that party's favor at any time after the expiration of twenty (20) days from the commencement of the action or after service of a motion for summary judgment by the adverse party. FL ST RCP Rule 1.510(a).

b. *For defending party.* A party against whom a claim, counterclaim, crossclaim, or third-party claim is asserted or a declaratory judgment is sought may move for a summary judgment in that party's favor as to all or any part thereof at any time with or without supporting affidavits. FL ST RCP Rule 1.510(b).

i. A defending party is not required to serve his responsive pleading before moving for summary judgment. He may make the motion at any time, setting out his defenses by affidavit, and thus effect a speedy termination of the action if no genuine issue exists as to any fact or facts pertaining to a defense that would defeat the claim. FL ST RCP Rule 1.510, notes.

2. *Service of motion.* The movant shall serve the motion for summary judgment at least twenty (20) days before the time fixed for the hearing, and shall also serve at that time a copy of any summary judgment evidence on which the movant relies that has not already been filed with the court. FL ST RCP Rule 1.510(c).

3. *Computation of time*

a. *Generally.* Computation of time shall be governed by FL ST J ADMIN Rule 2.514. FL ST RCP Rule 1.090(a). The following rules apply in computing time periods specified in any rule of procedure, local rule, court order, or statute that does not specify a method of computing time. FL ST J ADMIN Rule 2.514(a).

i. *Period stated in days or a longer unit.* When the period is stated in days or a longer unit of time (A) exclude the day of the event that triggers the period; (B) count every day, including intermediate Saturdays, Sundays, and legal holidays; and (C) include the last day of the period, but if the last day is a Saturday, Sunday, or legal holiday, or falls within any period of time extended through an order of the chief justice under FL ST J ADMIN Rule 2.205(a)(2)(B)(iv), the period continues to run until the end of the next day that is not a Saturday, Sunday, or legal holiday and does not fall within any period of time extended through an order of the chief justice. FL ST J ADMIN Rule 2.514(a)(1).

ii. *Period stated in hours.* When the period is stated in hours (A) begin counting immediately on the occurrence of the event that triggers the period; (B) count every hour, including hours during intermediate Saturdays, Sundays, and legal holidays; and (C) if the period would end on a Saturday, Sunday, or legal holiday, or during any period of time extended through an order of the chief justice under FL ST J ADMIN Rule 2.205(a)(2)(B)(iv), the period continues to run until the same time on the next day that is not a Saturday, Sunday, or legal holiday and does not fall within any period of time extended through an order of the chief justice. FL ST J ADMIN Rule 2.514(a)(2).

iii. *Period stated in days less than seven (7) days.* When the period stated in days is less than seven (7) days, intermediate Saturdays, Sundays, and legal holidays shall be excluded in the computation. FL ST J ADMIN Rule 2.514(a)(3).

iv. *"Last day" defined.* Unless a different time is set by a statute, local rule, or court order, the last day ends (A) for electronic filing or for service by any means, at midnight; and (B) for filing by other means, when the clerk's office is scheduled to close. FL ST J ADMIN Rule 2.514(a)(4).

v. *"Next day" defined.* The "next day" is determined by continuing to count forward when the period is measured after an event and backward when measured before an event. FL ST J ADMIN Rule 2.514(a)(5).

vi. *"Legal holiday" defined.* "Legal holiday" means (A) the day set aside by FL ST § 110.117, for observing New Year's Day, Martin Luther King, Jr.'s Birthday, Memorial Day, Independence Day, Labor Day, Veterans' Day, Thanksgiving Day, the Friday after Thanksgiving Day, or Christmas Day, and (B) any day observed as a holiday by the clerk's office or as designated by the chief judge. FL ST J ADMIN Rule 2.514(a)(6).

b. *Additional time after service by mail or e-mail.* When a party may or must act within a specified time after service and service is made by mail or e-mail, five (5) days are added after the period that would otherwise expire under FL ST J ADMIN Rule 2.514(a). FL ST J ADMIN Rule 2.514(b).

c. *Enlargement.* When an act is required or allowed to be done at or within a specified time by order of court, by the Florida Rules of Civil Procedure, or by notice given thereunder, for cause shown the court at any time in its discretion (1) with or without notice, may order the period enlarged if request therefor is made before the expiration of the period originally prescribed or as extended by a previous order, or (2) upon motion made and notice after the expiration of the specified period, may permit the act to be done when failure to act was the result of excusable neglect, but it may not extend the time for making a motion for new trial, for rehearing, or to alter or amend a judgment; making a motion for relief from a judgment under FL ST RCP Rule 1.540(b); taking an appeal or filing a petition for certiorari; or making a motion for a directed verdict. FL ST RCP Rule 1.090(b).

d. *Unaffected by expiration of term.* The period of time provided for the doing of any act or the taking of any proceeding shall not be affected or limited by the continued existence or expiration of a term of court. The continued existence or expiration of a term of court in no way affects the power of a court to do any act or take any proceeding in any action which is or has been pending before it. FL ST RCP Rule 1.090(c).

C. General Requirements

1. *Motions generally*

a. *Contents.* An application to the court for an order shall be by motion which shall be made in writing unless made during a hearing or trial, shall state with particularity the grounds therefor, and shall set forth the relief or order sought. The requirement of writing is fulfilled if the motion is stated in a written notice of the hearing of the motion. All notices of hearing shall specify each motion or other matter to be heard. FL ST RCP Rule 1.100(b).

b. *Particularity requirement.* The court considers a motion in the light of the substantive law, rule or statute to make its determination. Some rules require a statement of the grounds for a motion under the rule. Failure to give the grounds will result in denial of the motion. This should be the result in all situations when the ground for the motion is not inherent in the rule. FL-PRACPROC § 9:3. The requirement is nevertheless an important one, first because of the due process notice rights of the respondent, as well as for the assistance it provides to the court in its preparation for the hearing or, absent a hearing, for disposition. 4 FLPRAC R 1.100.

2. *Summary judgment.* A party seeking to recover upon or defend against a claim, counterclaim, crossclaim, or third-party claim or to obtain a declaratory judgment may move for a summary judgment. FL ST RCP Rule 1.510(a); FL ST RCP Rule 1.510(b).

a. *General motion for summary judgment information*

i. *Contents of motion.* The motion shall state with particularity the grounds upon which it is based and the substantial matters of law to be argued and shall specifically identify any affidavits, answers to interrogatories, admissions, depositions, and other materials as would be admissible in evidence ("summary judgment evidence") on which the movant relies. FL ST RCP Rule 1.510(c).

ii. *Evidence relied upon.* The movant shall also serve at that time a copy of any summary judgment evidence on which the movant relies that has not already been filed with the court. FL ST RCP Rule 1.510(c).

iii. *Judgment as a matter of law.* The judgment sought shall be rendered forthwith if the pleadings and summary judgment evidence on file show that there is no genuine issue as to any material fact and that the moving party is entitled to a judgment as a matter of law. A summary judgment,

interlocutory in character, may be rendered on the issue of liability alone although there is a genuine issue as to the amount of damages. FL ST RCP Rule 1.510(c).

b. *Sham pleadings.* If a party deems any pleading or part thereof filed by another party to be a sham, that party may move to strike the pleading or part thereof before the cause is set for trial and the court shall hear the motion, taking evidence of the respective parties, and if the motion is sustained, the pleading to which the motion is directed shall be stricken. Default and summary judgment on the merits may be entered in the discretion of the court or the court may permit additional pleadings to be filed for good cause shown. FL ST RCP Rule 1.150(a).

c. *Burden of proof*

   i. The moving party in a motion for summary judgment has the initial burden of demonstrating the nonexistence of any genuine issue of fact. Landers v. Milton, 370 So.2d 368, 370 (Fla. 1979); Gardner v. Sabal Point Properties, Inc., 616 So.2d 1111, 1112 (Fla. 5th DCA 1993); FL-PP § 6:7.

   ii. If the record raises the slightest doubt that material issues could be present, that doubt must be resolved against the movant and the motion for summary judgment denied. Moore v. Morris, 475 So.2d 666, 668 (Fla. 1985); Henderson v. CSX Transportation, Inc., 617 So.2d 770 (Fla. 1st DCA 1993); Jones v. Directors Guild of America, Inc., 584 So.2d 1057 (Fla. 1st DCA 1991); FL-PP § 6:7.

   iii. Until the moving party meets the initial burden of showing there is no issue of material fact, the opposing party need do nothing. Holl v. Talcott, 191 So.2d 40, 43 (Fla. 1966); Spradley v. Stick, 622 So.2d 610 (Fla. 1st DCA 1993); FL-RCPF R 1.510(404).

   iv. When the movant has tendered competent evidence in support of its motion, the burden shifts to the nonmoving party to come forward with opposing evidence to show that a question of material fact exists. Landers v. Milton, 370 So.2d 368, 370 (Fla. 1979); Holl v. Talcott, 191 So.2d 40, 43-44 (Fla. 1966); Lenhal Realty, Inc. v. Transamerica Commercial Finance Corp., 615 So.2d 207 (Fla. 4th DCA 1993); FL-PP § 6:7.

d. *Affidavits*

   i. *Form of affidavits; Further testimony.* Supporting and opposing affidavits shall be made on personal knowledge, shall set forth such facts as would be admissible in evidence, and shall show affirmatively that the affiant is competent to testify to the matters stated. Sworn or certified copies of all papers or parts referred to in an affidavit shall be attached to or served with the affidavit. The court may permit affidavits to be supplemented or opposed by depositions, answers to interrogatories, or by further affidavits. FL ST RCP Rule 1.510(e).

   ii. *When affidavits are unavailable.* If it appears from the affidavits of a party opposing the motion that the party cannot for reasons stated present by affidavit facts essential to justify opposition, the court may refuse the application for judgment or may order a continuance to permit affidavits to be obtained or depositions to be taken or discovery to be had or may make such other order as is just. FL ST RCP Rule 1.510(f).

   iii. *Affidavits made in bad faith.* If it appears to the satisfaction of the court at any time that any of the affidavits presented pursuant to FL ST RCP Rule 1.510 are presented in bad faith or solely for the purpose of delay, the court shall forthwith order the party employing them to pay to the other party the amount of the reasonable expenses that the filing of the affidavits caused the other party to incur, including reasonable attorneys' fees, and any offending party or attorney may be adjudged guilty of contempt. FL ST RCP Rule 1.510(g).

e. *Case not fully adjudicated on motion.* On motion under FL ST RCP Rule 1.510 if judgment is not rendered upon the whole case or for all the relief asked and a trial or the taking of testimony and a final hearing is necessary, the court at the hearing of the motion, by examining the pleadings and the evidence before it and by interrogating counsel, shall ascertain, if practicable, what material facts exist without substantial controversy and what material facts are actually and in good faith controverted. FL ST RCP Rule 1.510(d).

   i. It shall thereupon make an order specifying the facts that appear without substantial contro-

versy, including the extent to which the amount of damages or other relief is not in controversy, and directing such further proceedings in the action as are just. FL ST RCP Rule 1.510(d).

ii. On the trial or final hearing of the action the facts so specified shall be deemed established, and the trial or final hearing shall be conducted accordingly. FL ST RCP Rule 1.510(d).

3. *Arbitration and mediation*

a. *Referral to arbitration and mediation.* Except as hereinafter provided or as otherwise prohibited by law, the presiding judge may enter an order referring all or any part of a contested civil matter to mediation or arbitration. The parties to any contested civil matter may file a written stipulation to mediate or arbitrate any issue between them at any time. Such stipulation shall be incorporated into the order of referral. FL ST RCP Rule 1.700(a).

b. *Arbitration*

i. *Exclusions.* A civil action shall be ordered to arbitration or arbitration in conjunction with mediation upon stipulation of the parties. A civil action may be ordered to arbitration or arbitration in conjunction with mediation upon motion of any party or by the court, if the judge determines the action to be of such a nature that arbitration could be of benefit to the litigants or the court. FL ST RCP Rule 1.800.

- Under no circumstances may the following categories of actions be referred to arbitration: (1) bond estreatures; (2) habeas corpus or other extraordinary writs; (3) bond validations; (4) civil or criminal contempt; (5) such other matters as may be specified by order of the chief judge in the circuit. FL ST RCP Rule 1.800.

ii. For more information regarding arbitration, please see FL ST RCP Rule 1.810; FL ST RCP Rule 1.820; FL ST RCP Rule 1.830; FL ST 7 J CIR CV-2009-019-SC; and FL ST 7 J CIR CV-2003-002-SC(1)(c).

c. *Mediation.* For more information regarding mediation, please see FL ST RCP Rule 1.710; FL ST RCP Rule 1.720; FL ST RCP Rule 1.730; FL ST RCP Rule 1.750; FL ST 7 J CIR CV-2008-018-SC; and FL ST 7 J CIR CV-2003-002-SC(1).

4. *Rules of court*

a. *Rules of civil procedure.* The Florida Rules of Civil Procedure apply to all actions of a civil nature and all special statutory proceedings in the circuit courts and county courts except those to which the Florida Probate Rules, the Florida Family Law Rules of Procedure, or the Small Claims Rules apply. FL ST RCP Rule 1.010.

i. The form, content, procedure, and time for pleading in all special statutory proceedings shall be as prescribed by the statutes governing the proceeding unless the Florida Rules of Civil Procedure specifically provide to the contrary. FL ST RCP Rule 1.010.

ii. The Florida Rules of Civil Procedure shall be construed to secure the just, speedy, and inexpensive determination of every action. FL ST RCP Rule 1.010.

b. *Rules of judicial administration.* The Florida Rules of Judicial Administration shall apply to administrative matters in all courts to which the Florida Rules of Judicial Administration are applicable by their terms. The Florida Rules of Judicial Administration shall be construed to secure the speedy and inexpensive determination of every proceeding to which they are applicable. The Florida Rules of Judicial Administration shall supersede all conflicting rules and statutes. FL ST J ADMIN Rule 2.110.

D. Documents

1. *Required documents*

a. *Notice of hearing/Motion.* An application to the court for an order shall be by motion which shall be made in writing unless made during a hearing or trial, shall state with particularity the grounds therefor, and shall set forth the relief or order sought. The requirement of writing is fulfilled if the motion is stated in a written notice of the hearing of the motion. All notices of hearing shall specify each motion or other matter to be heard. FL ST RCP Rule 1.100(b).

i. *Notices to persons with disabilities.* See the Format section of this KeyRules document for further information.

b. *Certificate of service.* When any attorney certifies in substance: "I certify that a copy hereof has been furnished to (here insert name or names and addresses used for service) by (e-mail) (delivery) (mail) (fax) on .... (date) ....______________ Attorney" the certificate is taken as prima facie proof of such service in compliance with FL ST J ADMIN Rule 2.516. FL ST J ADMIN Rule 2.516(f).

2. *Supplemental documents*

a. *Affidavits.* Supporting and opposing affidavits shall be made on personal knowledge, shall set forth such facts as would be admissible in evidence, and shall show affirmatively that the affiant is competent to testify to the matters stated therein. Sworn or certified copies of all papers or parts thereof referred to in an affidavit shall be attached thereto or served therewith. FL ST RCP Rule 1.510(e). For further information regarding affidavits made in the context of a motion for summary judgment see FL ST RCP Rule 1.510(e) through FL ST RCP Rule 1.510(g).

b. *Other evidence.* The movant shall also serve at that time a copy of any summary judgment evidence on which the movant relies that has not already been filed with the court. FL ST RCP Rule 1.510(c).

c. *Proposed order.* The court may require that orders or judgments be prepared by a party, may require the party to furnish the court with stamped, addressed envelopes for service of the order or judgment, and may require that proposed orders and judgments be furnished to all parties before entry by the court of the order or judgment. FL ST J ADMIN Rule 2.516(h)(1).

i. When a party submits a proposed Final Judgment to the Clerk of the Court or to the Judge for signature, the Final Judgment shall contain the address and the social security number, if known to the prevailing party, of each person against whom judgment is rendered. FL ST 7 J CIR CV-2000-007-SC.

d. *Notice of constitutional question.* A party that files a pleading, written motion, or other paper drawing into question the constitutionality of a state statute or a county or municipal charter, ordinance, or franchise must promptly (1) file a notice of constitutional question stating the question and identifying the paper that raises it; and (2) serve the notice and the pleading, written motion, or other paper drawing into question the constitutionality of a state statute or a county or municipal charter, ordinance, or franchise on the Attorney General or the state attorney of the judicial circuit in which the action is pending, by either certified or registered mail. Service of the notice and pleading, written motion, or other paper does not require joinder of the Attorney General or the state attorney as a party to the action. FL ST RCP Rule 1.071.

E. Format

1. *Documents; Type and size.* Documents subject to the exceptions set forth in FL ST J ADMIN Rule 2.525(d) shall be filed on recycled paper measuring eight and one half by eleven (8 1/2 by 11) inches. For purposes of FL ST J ADMIN Rule 2.520, paper is recycled if it contains a minimum content of fifty (50) percent waste paper. Xerographic reduction of legal-size (eight and one half by fourteen (8 1/2 by 14) inches) documents to letter size (eight and one half by eleven (8 1/2 by 11) inches) is prohibited. All other documents filed by electronic transmission shall be filed in a format capable of being printed in a format consistent with the provisions of FL ST J ADMIN Rule 2.250. FL ST J ADMIN Rule 2.520(b).

a. *Exhibits.* Any exhibit or attachment filed with pleadings or papers may be filed in its original size. FL ST J ADMIN Rule 2.520(c).

b. *Recording space.* On all papers and documents prepared and filed by the court or by any party to a proceeding which are to be recorded in the public records of any county, including but not limited to final money judgments and notices of lis pendens, a three (3) inch by three (3) inch space at the top right-hand corner on the first page and a one (1) inch by three (3) inch space at the top right-hand corner on each subsequent page shall be left blank and reserved for use by the clerk of court. FL ST J ADMIN Rule 2.520(d).

i. *Exceptions to recording space.* Any papers or documents created by persons or entities over

which the filing party has no control, including but not limited to wills, codicils, trusts, or other testamentary documents; documents prepared or executed by any public officer; documents prepared, executed, acknowledged, or proved outside of the State of Florida; or documents created by State or Federal government agencies, may be filed without the space required by FL ST J ADMIN Rule 2.520. FL ST J ADMIN Rule 2.520(e).

c. *Noncompliance.* No clerk of court is permitted to refuse to file any document or paper because of noncompliance with the Florida Rules of Judicial Administration. However, upon request of the clerk of court, noncomplying documents must be resubmitted in accordance with the formatting rules. FL ST J ADMIN Rule 2.520(f).

2. *Caption.* Every pleading, motion, order, judgment, or other paper shall have a caption containing the name of the court, the file number, and except for in rem proceedings, including forfeiture proceedings, the name of the first party on each side with an appropriate indication of other parties, and a designation identifying the party filing it and its nature or the nature of the order, as the case may be. In any in rem proceeding, every pleading, motion, order, judgment, or other paper shall have a caption containing the name of the court, the file number, the style "In re" (followed by the name or general description of the property), and a designation of the person or entity filing it and its nature or the nature of the order, as the case may be. In an in rem forfeiture proceeding, the style shall be "In re forfeiture of" (followed by the name of the general description of the property). All papers filed in the action shall be styled in such a manner as to indicate clearly the subject matter of the paper and the party requesting or obtaining relief. FL ST RCP Rule 1.100(c)(1).

   a. *Volusia County eminent domain cases.* All orders, pleadings, motions and other papers will bear the initial case style. Documents intended to apply only to particular parcel(s) will indicate in their caption the parcel number(s) to which they apply and sufficient copies shall be provided to the Clerk of Court to allow the filing and docketing of each relevant paper in each parcel file. FL ST 7 J CIR CV-2000-011-VL(b).

3. *Writing and written defined.* Writing or written means a document containing information, an application, or a stipulation. FL ST RCP Rule 1.080(c).

4. *Rule abbreviations*

   a. The Florida Rules of Civil Procedure and shall be abbreviated as Fla.R.Civ.P. FL ST RCP Rule 1.010.

   b. The Florida Rules of Judicial Administration shall be abbreviated as Fla. R. Jud. Admin. FL ST J ADMIN Rule 2.110.

5. *Nonverification.* Except when otherwise specifically provided by the Florida Rules of Civil Procedure or an applicable statute, every pleading or other document of a party represented by an attorney need not be verified or accompanied by an affidavit. FL ST RCP Rule 1.030; FL ST J ADMIN Rule 2.515(a).

6. *Attorney signature*

   a. *Attorney signature.* Every pleading and other document of a party represented by an attorney shall be signed by at least one (1) attorney of record in that attorney's individual name whose current record Florida Bar address, telephone number, including area code, primary e-mail address and secondary e-mail addresses, if any, and Florida Bar number shall be stated, and who shall be duly licensed to practice law in Florida or who shall have received permission to appear in the particular case as provided in FL ST J ADMIN Rule 2.510. FL ST J ADMIN Rule 2.515(a).

      i. The attorney may be required by the court to give the address of, and to vouch for the attorney's authority to represent, the party. FL ST J ADMIN Rule 2.515(a).

      ii. The signature of an attorney shall constitute a certificate by the attorney that the attorney has read the pleading or other document; that to the best of the attorney's knowledge, information, and belief there is good ground to support it; and that it is not interposed for delay. FL ST J ADMIN Rule 2.515(a).

      iii. If a pleading is not signed or is signed with intent to defeat the purpose of FL ST J ADMIN Rule 2.515, it may be stricken and the action may proceed as though the pleading or other document had not been served. FL ST J ADMIN Rule 2.515(a).

b. *Pro se litigant signature.* A party who is not represented by an attorney shall sign any pleading or other paper and state the party's address and telephone number, including area code. FL ST J ADMIN Rule 2.515(b).

c. *Form of signature*

i. The signatures required on pleadings and documents by FL ST J ADMIN Rule 2.515(a) and FL ST J ADMIN Rule 2.515(b) may be:

- Original signatures;
- Original signatures that have been reproduced by electronic means, such as on electronically transmitted documents or photocopied documents;
- Electronic signatures using the "/s/," "s/," or "/s" formats by or at the direction of the person signing; or
- Any other signature format authorized by general law, so long as the clerk where the proceeding is pending has the capability of receiving and has obtained approval from the Supreme Court of Florida to accept pleadings and documents with that signature format. FL ST J ADMIN Rule 2.515(c)(1).

ii. An attorney, party, or other person who files a pleading or paper by electronic transmission that does not contain the original signature of that attorney, party, or other person shall file that identical pleading or paper in paper form containing an original signature of that attorney, party, or other person (hereinafter called the follow-up filing) immediately thereafter. The follow-up filing is not required if the Supreme Court of Florida has entered an order directing the clerk of court to discontinue accepting the follow-up filing. FL ST J ADMIN Rule 2.515(c)(2).

7. *Forms*

a. *Process.* The forms of process, notice of lis pendens, and notice of action provided in the Florida Rules of Civil Procedure are sufficient. Variations from the forms do not void process or notices that are otherwise sufficient. FL ST RCP Rule 1.900(a).

b. *Other forms.* The other forms provided in the Florida Rules of Civil Procedure are sufficient for the matters that are covered by them. So long as the substance is expressed without prolixity, the forms may be varied to meet the facts of a particular case. FL ST RCP Rule 1.900(b).

c. *Formal matters.* Captions, except for the designation of the paper, are omitted from the forms provided in the Florida Rules of Civil Procedure. A general form of caption is the first form provided. Signatures are omitted from pleadings and motions. FL ST RCP Rule 1.900(c).

8. *Notices to persons with disabilities.* All notices of court proceedings to be held in a public facility, and all process compelling appearance at such proceedings, shall include the following statement in bold face, fourteen (14) point Times New Roman or Courier font: "If you are a person with a disability who needs any accommodation in order to participate in this proceeding, you are entitled, at no cost to you, to the provision of certain assistance. Please contact [identify applicable court personnel by name, address, and telephone number] at least seven (7) days before your scheduled court appearance, or immediately upon receiving this notification if the time before the scheduled appearance is less than seven (7) days; if you are hearing or voice impaired, call 711." FL ST J ADMIN Rule 2.540(c)(1).

9. *Minimization of the filing of sensitive information*

a. *Limitations for court filings.* Unless authorized by FL ST J ADMIN Rule 2.425(b), statute, another rule of court, or the court orders otherwise, designated sensitive information filed with the court must be limited to the following format:

i. The initials of a person known to be a minor;

ii. The year of birth of a person's birth date;

iii. No portion of any: Social security number, Bank account number, Credit card account number, Charge account number, or Debit account number;

iv. The last four digits of any: Taxpayer identification number (TIN), Employee identification number, Driver's license number, Passport number, Telephone number, Financial account

number, except as set forth in FL ST J ADMIN Rule 2.425(a)(3), Brokerage account number, Insurance policy account number, Loan account number, Customer account number, or Patient or health care number;

v. A truncated version of any: Email address, Computer user name, Password, or Personal identification number (PIN); and

vi. A truncated version of any other sensitive information as provided by court order. FL ST J ADMIN Rule 2.425(a).

b. *Exceptions.* FL ST J ADMIN Rule 2.425(a) does not apply to the following:

i. An account number which identifies the property alleged to be the subject of a proceeding;

ii. The record of an administrative or agency proceeding;

iii. The record in appellate or review proceedings;

iv. The birth date of a minor whenever the birth date is necessary for the court to establish or maintain subject matter jurisdiction;

v. The name of a minor in any order relating to parental responsibility, time-sharing, or child support;

vi. The name of a minor in any document or order affecting the minor's ownership of real property;

vii. The birth date of a party in a writ of attachment or notice to payor;

viii. In traffic and criminal proceedings: a pro se filing; a court filing that is related to a criminal matter or investigation and that is prepared before the filing of a criminal charge or is not filed as part of any docketed criminal case; an arrest or search warrant or any information in support thereof; a charging document and an affidavit or other documents filed in support of any charging document, including any driving records; a statement of particulars; discovery material introduced into evidence or otherwise filed with the court; and all information necessary for the proper issuance and execution of a subpoena duces tecum;

ix. Information used by the clerk for case maintenance purposes or the courts for case management purposes; and

x. Information which is relevant and material to an issue before the court. FL ST J ADMIN Rule 2.425(b).

c. *Remedies.* Upon motion by a party or interested person or sua sponte by the court, the court may order remedies, sanctions or both for a violation of FL ST J ADMIN Rule 2.425(a). Following notice and an opportunity to respond, the court may impose sanctions if such filing was not made in good faith. FL ST J ADMIN Rule 2.425(c).

d. *Motions not restricted.* FL ST J ADMIN Rule 2.425 does not restrict a party's right to move for protective order, to move to file documents under seal, or to request a determination of the confidentiality of records. FL ST J ADMIN Rule 2.425(d).

e. *Application.* FL ST J ADMIN Rule 2.425 does not affect the application of constitutional provisions, statutes, or rules of court regarding confidential information or access to public information. FL ST J ADMIN Rule 2.425(e).

F. Filing and Service Requirements

1. *Filing requirements.* All original documents must be filed with the court either before service or immediately thereafter, unless otherwise provided for by general law or other rules. If the original of any bond or other document is not placed in the court file, a certified copy must be so placed by the clerk. FL ST J ADMIN Rule 2.516(d). All documents shall be filed in conformity with the requirements of FL ST J ADMIN Rule 2.525. FL ST RCP Rule 1.080(b). All documents filed in any court shall be filed by electronic transmission in accordance with FL ST J ADMIN Rule 2.525. "Documents" means pleadings, motions, petitions, memoranda, briefs, notices, exhibits, declarations, affidavits, orders, judgments, decrees, writs, opinions, and any other paper or writing submitted to a court. FL ST J ADMIN Rule 2.520(a). All documents that are court records, as defined in FL ST J ADMIN Rule 2.430(a)(1), must be filed by electronic transmission, provided that: (1) the clerk has the ability to accept and retain such

documents; (2) the clerk or the chief judge of the circuit has requested permission to accept documents filed by electronic transmission; and (3) the supreme court has entered an order granting permission to the clerk to accept documents filed by electronic transmission. FL ST J ADMIN Rule 2.525(c)(1).

a. *Definition.* "Electronic transmission of documents" means the sending of information by electronic signals to, by or from a court or clerk, which when received can be transformed and stored or transmitted on paper, microfilm, magnetic storage device, optical imaging system, CD-ROM, flash drive, other electronic data storage system, server, case maintenance system ("CM"), electronic court filing ("ECF") system, statewide or local electronic portal ("e-portal"), or other electronic record keeping system authorized by the supreme court in a format sufficient to communicate the information on the original document in a readable format. Electronic transmission of documents includes electronic mail ("e-mail") and any internet-based transmission procedure, and may include procedures allowing for documents to be signed or verified by electronic means. FL ST J ADMIN Rule 2.525(a).
   i. The filing of documents with the court as required by the Florida Rules of Judicial Administration must be made by filing them with the clerk in accordance with FL ST J ADMIN Rule 2.525, except that the judge may permit documents to be filed with the judge, in which event the judge must note the filing date before him or her on the documents and transmit them to the clerk. The date of filing is that shown on the face of the document by the judge's notation or the clerk's time stamp, whichever is earlier. FL ST J ADMIN Rule 2.516(e).

b. *Application.* Any court or clerk of the court may accept the electronic transmission of documents for filing after the clerk, together with input from the chief judge of the circuit, has obtained approval of the procedures and program for doing so from the Supreme Court of Florida. FL ST J ADMIN Rule 2.525(b).

c. *Exceptions*
   i. Paper documents and other submissions may be manually submitted to the clerk or court:
      - When the clerk does not have the ability to accept and retain documents by electronic filing or has not had ECF Procedures approved by the supreme court;
      - For filing by any self-represented party or any self-represented nonparty unless specific ECF Procedures provide a means to file documents electronically. However, any self-represented nonparty that is a governmental or public agency and any other agency, partnership, corporation, or business entity acting on behalf of any governmental or public agency may file documents by electronic transmission if such entity has the capability of filing documents electronically;
      - For filing by attorneys excused from e-mail service in accordance with FL ST J ADMIN Rule 2.516(b);
      - When submitting evidentiary exhibits or filing non-documentary materials;
      - When the filing involves documents in excess of twenty-five (25) megabytes (25MB) in size. For such filings, documents may be transmitted using an electronic storage medium that the clerk has the ability to accept, which may include a CD-ROM, flash drive, or similar storage medium;
      - When filed in open court, as permitted by the court;
      - When paper filing is permitted by any approved statewide or local ECF procedures; and
      - If any court determines that justice so requires. FL ST J ADMIN Rule 2.525(d).
   ii. Any document in paper form submitted under FL ST J ADMIN Rule 2.525(d) is filed when it is received by the clerk or court and the clerk shall immediately thereafter convert any filed paper document to an electronic document. "Convert to an electronic document" means optically capturing an image of a paper document and using character recognition software to recover as much of the document's text as practicable and then indexing and storing the document in the official court file. FL ST J ADMIN Rule 2.525(c)(4).
   iii. Any storage medium submitted under FL ST J ADMIN Rule 2.525(d)(5) is filed when received

by the clerk or court and the clerk shall immediately thereafter transfer the electronic documents from the storage device to the official court file. FL ST J ADMIN Rule 2.525(c)(5).

iv. If the filer of any paper document authorized under FL ST J ADMIN Rule 2.525(d) provides a self-addressed, postage-paid envelope for return of the paper document after it is converted to electronic form by the clerk, the clerk shall place the paper document in the envelope and deposit it in the mail. Except when a paper document is required to be maintained, the clerk may recycle any filed paper document that is not to be returned to the filer. FL ST J ADMIN Rule 2.525(c)(6).

v. The clerk may convert any paper document filed before the effective date of FL ST J ADMIN Rule 2.525 to an electronic document. Unless the clerk is required to maintain the paper document, if the paper document has been converted to an electronic document by the clerk, the paper document is no longer part of the official court file and may be removed and recycled. FL ST J ADMIN Rule 2.525(c)(7).

d. *Official court file.* For information on what constitutes the official court file, please see FL ST J ADMIN Rule 2.525(c)(2), FL ST J ADMIN Rule 2.525(c)(3).

e. *Administration.* All attorneys, parties, or other persons using this rule to file documents are required to make arrangements with the court or clerk for the payment of any charges authorized by general law or the supreme court before filing any document by electronic transmission. FL ST J ADMIN Rule 2.525(f)(2).

f. *Filing date.* The filing date for an electronically transmitted document is the date and time that such filing is acknowledged by an electronic stamp or otherwise, pursuant to any procedure set forth in any ECF Procedures approved by the supreme court, or the date the last page of such filing is received by the court or clerk. FL ST J ADMIN Rule 2.525(f)(3).

g. *Accessibility.* All documents transmitted in any electronic form under FL ST J ADMIN Rule 2.525 must comply with the accessibility requirements of FL ST J ADMIN Rule 2.526. FL ST J ADMIN Rule 2.525(g).

2. *Service requirements.* Every pleading subsequent to the initial pleading, all orders, and every other document filed in the action must be served in conformity with the requirements of FL ST J ADMIN Rule 2.516. FL ST RCP Rule 1.080(a).

a. *Service; When required.* Unless the court otherwise orders, or a statute or supreme court administrative order specifies a different means of service, every pleading subsequent to the initial pleading and every other document filed in any court proceeding, except applications for witness subpoenas and documents served by formal notice or required to be served in the manner provided for service of formal notice, must be served in accordance with FL ST J ADMIN Rule 2.516 on each party. No service need be made on parties against whom a default has been entered, except that pleadings asserting new or additional claims against them must be served in the manner provided for service of summons. FL ST J ADMIN Rule 2.516(a).

b. *Service; How made.* When service is required or permitted to be made upon a party represented by an attorney, service must be made upon the attorney unless service upon the party is ordered by the court. FL ST J ADMIN Rule 2.516(b).

i. *Service by electronic mail ("e-mail").* All documents required or permitted to be served on another party must be served by e-mail, unless FL ST J ADMIN Rule 2.516 otherwise provides. When, in addition to service by e-mail, the sender also utilizes another means of service provided for in FL ST J ADMIN Rule 2.516(b)(2), any differing time limits and other provisions applicable to that other means of service control. FL ST J ADMIN Rule 2.516(b)(1). Any document electronically transmitted to a court or clerk must also be served on all parties and interested persons in accordance with the applicable rules of court. FL ST J ADMIN Rule 2.525(e)(2).

- *Service on attorneys.* Upon appearing in a proceeding, an attorney must serve a designation of a primary e-mail address and may designate no more than two (2) secondary e-mail addresses. Thereafter, service must be directed to all designated e-mail addresses in that proceeding. Every document filed by an attorney thereafter must include the primary e-mail address of that attorney and any secondary e-mail addresses. If an attorney does not designate any e-mail address for service, documents may be served on that attorney at the e-mail address on record with The Florida Bar. FL ST J ADMIN Rule 2.516(b)(1)(A).

- *Exception to e-mail service on attorneys.* Service by an attorney on another attorney must be made by e-mail unless excused by the court. Upon motion by an attorney demonstrating that the attorney has no e-mail account and lacks access to the Internet at the attorney's office, the court may excuse the attorney from the requirements of e-mail service. Service on and by an attorney excused by the court from e-mail service must be by the means provided in FL ST J ADMIN Rule 2.516(b)(2). FL ST J ADMIN Rule 2.516(b)(1)(B).
- *Service on and by parties not represented by an attorney.* Any party not represented by an attorney may serve a designation of a primary e-mail address and also may designate no more than two (2) secondary e-mail addresses to which service must be directed in that proceeding by the means provided in FL ST J ADMIN Rule 2.516(b)(1). If a party not represented by an attorney does not designate an e-mail address for service in a proceeding, service on and by that party must be by the means provided in FL ST J ADMIN Rule 2.516(b)(2). FL ST J ADMIN Rule 2.516(b)(1)(C).
- *Time of service.* Service by e-mail is complete when it is sent. FL ST J ADMIN Rule 2.516(b)(1)(D). An e-mail is deemed served on the date it is sent. FL ST J ADMIN Rule 2.516(b)(1)(D)(i). If the sender learns that the e-mail did not reach the address of the person to be served, the sender must immediately send another copy by e-mail, or by a means authorized by FL ST J ADMIN Rule 2.516(b)(2). FL ST J ADMIN Rule 2.516(b)(1)(D)(ii). E-mail service is treated as service by mail for the computation of time. FL ST J ADMIN Rule 2.516(b)(1)(D)(iii).

ii. *Format of e-mail for service.* Service of a document by e-mail is made by attaching a copy of the document in PDF format to an e-mail sent to all addresses designated by the attorney or party. FL ST J ADMIN Rule 2.516(b)(1)(E).

- All documents served by e-mail must be attached to an e-mail message containing a subject line beginning with the words "SERVICE OF COURT DOCUMENT" in all capital letters, followed by the case number of the proceeding in which the documents are being served. FL ST J ADMIN Rule 2.516(b)(1)(E)(i).
- The body of the e-mail must identify the court in which the proceeding is pending, the case number, the name of the initial party on each side, the title of each document served with that e-mail, and the sender's name and telephone number. FL ST J ADMIN Rule 2.516(b)(1)(E)(ii).
- Any document served by e-mail may be signed by the "/s/" format, as long as the filed original is signed in accordance with the applicable rule of procedure. FL ST J ADMIN Rule 2.516(b)(1)(E)(iii).
- Any e-mail which, together with its attached documents, exceeds five megabytes (5MB) in size, must be divided and sent as separate e-mails, no one of which may exceed five megabytes (5MB) in size and each of which must be sequentially numbered in the subject line. FL ST J ADMIN Rule 2.516(b)(1)(E)(iv).

iii. *Service by other means.* In addition to, and not in lieu of, service by e-mail, service may also be made upon attorneys by any of the means specified in FL ST J ADMIN Rule 2.516(b)(2). Service on and by all parties who are not represented by an attorney and who do not designate an e-mail address, and on and by all attorneys excused from e-mail service, must be made by delivering a copy of the document or by mailing it to the party or attorney at their last known address or, if no address is known, by leaving it with the clerk of the court. Service by mail is complete upon mailing. Delivery of a copy within FL ST J ADMIN Rule 2.516 is complete upon:

- Handing it to the attorney or to the party,

- Leaving it at the attorney's or party's office with a clerk or other person in charge thereof,
- If there is no one in charge, leaving it in a conspicuous place therein,
- If the office is closed or the person to be served has no office, leaving it at the person's usual place of abode with some person of his or her family above fifteen (15) years of age and informing such person of the contents, or
- Transmitting it by facsimile to the attorney's or party's office with a cover sheet containing the sender's name, firm, address, telephone number, and facsimile number, and the number of pages transmitted. When service is made by facsimile, a copy must also be served by any other method permitted by FL ST J ADMIN Rule 2.516. Facsimile service occurs when transmission is complete. FL ST J ADMIN Rule 2.516(b)(2)(A) through FL ST J ADMIN Rule 2.516(b)(2)(E).
- Service by delivery after 5:00 p.m. must be deemed to have been made by mailing on the date of delivery. FL ST J ADMIN Rule 2.516(b)(2)(F).

c. *Service; Numerous defendants.* In actions when the parties are unusually numerous, the court may regulate the service contemplated by the Florida Rules of Judicial Administration on motion or on its own initiative in such manner as may be found to be just and reasonable. FL ST J ADMIN Rule 2.516(c).

d. *Service by clerk.* Service of notices and other documents required to be made by the clerk must also be done as provided in FL ST J ADMIN Rule 2.516(b). FL ST J ADMIN Rule 2.516(g).

G. Hearings

1. *Hearing on motion for summary judgment.* The summary judgment rule does not provide the trial court with discretion to decide whether a hearing is required. A failure to hold a hearing on a motion for summary judgment violates due process as well as rule of procedure governing summary judgment procedure. Kozich v. Hartford Ins. Co. of Midwest, 609 So.2d 147, 148 (Fla. 4th DCA 1992); FL-RCPF R 1.510(102).

2. *Summary judgment consideration at pretrial conference.* A summary judgment can be granted at the pretrial conference. The standard and procedure for granting summary judgment is the same at a pretrial conference as at other times. The notice time for a pretrial conference and for service of a motion for summary judgment is the same, so summary judgment can be entered at the conference if no genuine issue of material fact exists. FL-PRACPROC § 19:4.

3. *Communication equipment*

a. *Definition.* Communication equipment means a conference telephone or other electronic device that permits all those appearing or participating to hear and speak to each other, provided that all conversation of all parties is audible to all persons present. FL ST J ADMIN Rule 2.530(a).

b. *Use by all parties.* A county or circuit court judge may, upon the court's own motion or upon the written request of a party, direct that communication equipment be used for a motion hearing, pretrial conference, or a status conference. A judge must give notice to the parties and consider any objections they may have to the use of communication equipment before directing that communication equipment be used. The decision to use communication equipment over the objection of parties will be in the sound discretion of the trial court, except as noted below. FL ST J ADMIN Rule 2.530(b).

c. *Use only by requesting party.* A county or circuit court judge may, upon the written request of a party upon reasonable notice to all other parties, permit a requesting party to participate through communication equipment in a scheduled motion hearing; however, any such request (except in criminal, juvenile, and appellate proceedings) must be granted, absent a showing of good cause to deny the same, where the hearing is set for not longer than fifteen (15) minutes. FL ST J ADMIN Rule 2.530(c).

d. *Testimony*

i. *Generally.* A county or circuit court judge, general magistrate, special magistrate, or hearing officer may allow testimony to be taken through communication equipment if all parties consent or if permitted by another applicable rule of procedure. FL ST J ADMIN Rule 2.530(d)(1).

ii. *Procedure.* Any party desiring to present testimony through communication equipment shall, prior to the hearing or trial at which the testimony is to be presented, contact all parties to determine whether each party consents to this form of testimony. The party seeking to present the testimony shall move for permission to present testimony through communication equipment, which motion shall set forth good cause as to why the testimony should be allowed in this form. FL ST J ADMIN Rule 2.530(d)(2).

iii. *Oath.* Testimony may be taken through communication equipment only if a notary public or other person authorized to administer oaths in the witness's jurisdiction is present with the witness and administers the oath consistent with the laws of the jurisdiction. FL ST J ADMIN Rule 2.530(d)(3).

iv. *Confrontation rights.* In juvenile and criminal proceedings the defendant must make an informed waiver of any confrontation rights that may be abridged by the use of communication equipment. FL ST J ADMIN Rule 2.530(d)(4).

v. *Video testimony.* If the testimony to be presented utilizes video conferencing or comparable two-way visual capabilities, the court in its discretion may modify the procedures set forth in FL ST J ADMIN Rule 2.530 to accommodate the technology utilized. FL ST J ADMIN Rule 2.530(d)(5).

e. *Burden of expense.* The cost for the use of the communication equipment is the responsibility of the requesting party unless otherwise directed by the court. FL ST J ADMIN Rule 2.530(e).

H. Forms

1. Official Motion for Summary Judgment Forms for Florida

a. Caption. FL ST RCP Form 1.901.

b. Notice of compliance when constitutional challenge is brought. FL ST RCP Form 1.975.

2. Motion for Summary Judgment Forms for Florida

a. Motion for summary judgment; By plaintiff. FL-PP § 6:9.

b. Motion for summary judgment; By defendant. FL-PP § 6:10.

c. Affidavit; Supporting motion for summary judgment; By plaintiff's attorney. FL-PP § 6:11.

d. Affidavit; Opposing motion for summary judgment; By defendant's attorney. FL-PP § 6:12.

e. Affidavit; Opposing motion for summary judgment; By party; Inability to present facts. FL-PP § 6:13.

f. Order; Establishing uncontroverted facts and stating issues requiring further determination. FL-PP § 6:14.

g. Summary judgment. FL-PP § 6:15.

h. Motion; Summary judgment, by defendant. FL-PRACFORM § 7:190.

i. Motion; Summary judgment, by plaintiff. FL-PRACFORM § 7:191.

j. Motion; Summary judgment, partial, by defendant. FL-PRACFORM § 7:192.

k. Motion; Summary judgment, part of claim. FL-PRACFORM § 7:193.

l. Form for plaintiff's motion for summary judgment. FL-RCPF R 1.510(128).

m. Form for notice of motion for summary judgment by plaintiff. FL-RCPF R 1.510(129).

n. Form for notice of cross-motion for summary judgment by plaintiff. FL-RCPF R 1.510(130).

o. Form for order denying motion for summary judgment and specifying uncontroverted facts. FL-RCPF R 1.510(304).

p. Form for motion for partial summary judgment. FL-RCPF R 1.510(305).

q. Form for motion for partial summary judgment; Affirmative defenses. FL-RCPF R 1.510(305.1).

I. Checklist

(I) ❑ Matters to be considered by moving party

(a) ❑ Required documents

(1) ❑ Notice of hearing/Motion

(2) ❑ Certificate of service

(b) ❑ Supplemental documents

(1) ❑ Affidavits

(2) ❑ Other evidence

(3) ❑ Proposed order

(4) ❑ Notice of constitutional question

(c) ❑ Time for making motion

(1) ❑ By the plaintiff, after the expiration of twenty (20) days from the commencement of the action (claimant), or after service of a motion for summary judgment by the adverse party

(2) ❑ By the defending party at any time

(3) ❑ The motion for summary judgment must be served at least twenty (20) days before the time fixed for the hearing

(II) ❑ Matters to be considered by opposing party

(a) ❑ Required documents

(1) ❑ Response to motion

(2) ❑ Certificate of service

(b) ❑ Supplemental documents

(1) ❑ Affidavits

(2) ❑ Notice of evidence relied upon

(3) ❑ Other evidence

(4) ❑ Proposed order

(5) ❑ Notice of constitutional question

(c) ❑ Time for service and filing of opposition

(1) ❑ The adverse party shall identify, by notice mailed to the movant's attorney at least five (5) days prior to the day of the hearing, or delivered no later than 5:00 p.m. two (2) business days prior to the day of the hearing, any summary judgment evidence on which the adverse party relies

(2) ❑ To the extent that summary judgment evidence has not already been filed with the court, the adverse party shall serve a copy on the movant by mail at least five (5) days prior to the day of the hearing, or by delivery to the movant's attorney no later than 5:00 p.m. two (2) business days prior to the day of hearing

Motions, Oppositions and Replies
Motion for Sanctions

Document Last Updated January 2013

A. Applicable Rules

1. *State rules*

a. Attorney's fee; Sanctions for raising unsupported claims or defenses; Exceptions; Service of motions; Damages for delay of litigation. FL ST § 57.105.

b. Administrative Procedure Act. FL ST § 120.50; FL ST § 120.52; FL ST § 120.68; FL ST § 120.81
c. Offer of judgment and demand for judgment. FL ST § 768.79.
d. Proposals for settlement. FL ST RCP Rule 1.442.
e. Motions for costs and attorneys' fees. FL ST RCP Rule 1.525.
f. Rules of court. FL ST RCP Rule 1.010; FL ST J ADMIN Rule 2.110.
g. Nonverification of pleadings. FL ST RCP Rule 1.030.
h. Service and filing of pleadings, orders, and documents. FL ST RCP Rule 1.080.
i. Time. FL ST RCP Rule 1.090.
j. Pleadings and motions. FL ST RCP Rule 1.100.
k. Motions. FL ST RCP Rule 1.160.
l. Relief from judgment, decrees, or orders. FL ST RCP Rule 1.540.
m. Mediation and arbitration. FL ST RCP Rule 1.700; FL ST RCP Rule 1.710; FL ST RCP Rule 1.720; FL ST RCP Rule 1.730; FL ST RCP Rule 1.750; FL ST RCP Rule 1.800; FL ST RCP Rule 1.810; FL ST RCP Rule 1.820; FL ST RCP Rule 1.830.
n. Forms. FL ST RCP Rule 1.900.
o. Minimization of the filing of sensitive information. FL ST J ADMIN Rule 2.425.
p. Retention of court records. FL ST J ADMIN Rule 2.430.
q. Foreign attorneys. FL ST J ADMIN Rule 2.510.
r. Signature of attorneys and parties. FL ST J ADMIN Rule 2.515.
s. Paper. FL ST J ADMIN Rule 2.520.
t. Electronic filing. FL ST J ADMIN Rule 2.525.
u. Accessibility of information and technology. FL ST J ADMIN Rule 2.526.
v. Communication equipment. FL ST J ADMIN Rule 2.530.
w. Court reporting. FL ST J ADMIN Rule 2.535.
x. Requests for accommodations by persons with disabilities. FL ST J ADMIN Rule 2.540.

2. *Local rules*
   a. Eminent domain cases. FL ST 7 J CIR CV-2000-011-VL.
   b. Civil pretrial procedures. FL ST 7 J CIR CV-2003-002-SC.
   c. Arbitration and mediation. FL ST 7 J CIR CV-2008-018-SC; FL ST 7 J CIR CV-2009-019-SC.

B. Timing

1. *Motion for sanctions.* A motion by a party seeking sanctions under FL ST § 57.105 must be served but may not be filed with or presented to the court unless, within twenty one (21) days after service of the motion, the challenged paper, claim, defense, contention, allegation, or denial is not withdrawn or appropriately corrected. FL ST § 57.105(4).
2. *Sanctions in relation to proposals for settlement.* Any party seeking sanctions pursuant to applicable Florida law, based on the failure of the proposal's recipient to accept a proposal, shall do so by serving a motion in accordance with FL ST RCP Rule 1.525. FL ST RCP Rule 1.442(g). Any party seeking a judgment taxing costs, attorneys' fees, or both shall serve a motion no later than thirty (30) days after filing of the judgment, including a judgment of dismissal, or the service of a notice of voluntary dismissal, which judgment or notice concludes the action as to that party. FL ST RCP Rule 1.525.
3. *General motion timing.* A copy of any written motion which may not be heard ex parte and a copy of the notice of the hearing thereof shall be served a reasonable time before the time specified for the hearing. FL ST RCP Rule 1.090(d).
   a. Motions filed within thirty (30) days of the trial date will not be considered if predicated on matters

the movant knew or should have known with the exercise of reasonable diligence at least thirty (30) days prior to the trial date. Because of busy court calendars, hearing time may not be available to consider motions filed close to the deadline. The inability of a party to obtain time will generally not constitute grounds for a continuance of the trial. FL ST 7 J CIR CV-2003-002-SC(6)(a).

b. The failure of a party to call up for hearing any timely filed motion at least ten (10) days prior to the trial date may constitute a waiver thereof unless the grounds therefor did not exist or the party was not aware of the grounds for the motion(s) prior to the filing of such motion(s) after the exercise of reasonable diligence. FL ST 7 J CIR CV-2003-002-SC(6)(b).

4. *Computation of time*

a. *Generally.* Computation of time shall be governed by FL ST J ADMIN Rule 2.514. FL ST RCP Rule 1.090(a). The following rules apply in computing time periods specified in any rule of procedure, local rule, court order, or statute that does not specify a method of computing time. FL ST J ADMIN Rule 2.514(a).

i. *Period stated in days or a longer unit.* When the period is stated in days or a longer unit of time (A) exclude the day of the event that triggers the period; (B) count every day, including intermediate Saturdays, Sundays, and legal holidays; and (C) include the last day of the period, but if the last day is a Saturday, Sunday, or legal holiday, or falls within any period of time extended through an order of the chief justice under FL ST J ADMIN Rule 2.205(a)(2)(B)(iv), the period continues to run until the end of the next day that is not a Saturday, Sunday, or legal holiday and does not fall within any period of time extended through an order of the chief justice. FL ST J ADMIN Rule 2.514(a)(1).

ii. *Period stated in hours.* When the period is stated in hours (A) begin counting immediately on the occurrence of the event that triggers the period; (B) count every hour, including hours during intermediate Saturdays, Sundays, and legal holidays; and (C) if the period would end on a Saturday, Sunday, or legal holiday, or during any period of time extended through an order of the chief justice under FL ST J ADMIN Rule 2.205(a)(2)(B)(iv), the period continues to run until the same time on the next day that is not a Saturday, Sunday, or legal holiday and does not fall within any period of time extended through an order of the chief justice. FL ST J ADMIN Rule 2.514(a)(2).

iii. *Period stated in days less than seven (7) days.* When the period stated in days is less than seven (7) days, intermediate Saturdays, Sundays, and legal holidays shall be excluded in the computation. FL ST J ADMIN Rule 2.514(a)(3).

iv. *"Last day" defined.* Unless a different time is set by a statute, local rule, or court order, the last day ends (A) for electronic filing or for service by any means, at midnight; and (B) for filing by other means, when the clerk's office is scheduled to close. FL ST J ADMIN Rule 2.514(a)(4).

v. *"Next day" defined.* The "next day" is determined by continuing to count forward when the period is measured after an event and backward when measured before an event. FL ST J ADMIN Rule 2.514(a)(5).

vi. *"Legal holiday" defined.* "Legal holiday" means (A) the day set aside by FL ST § 110.117, for observing New Year's Day, Martin Luther King, Jr.'s Birthday, Memorial Day, Independence Day, Labor Day, Veterans' Day, Thanksgiving Day, the Friday after Thanksgiving Day, or Christmas Day, and (B) any day observed as a holiday by the clerk's office or as designated by the chief judge. FL ST J ADMIN Rule 2.514(a)(6).

b. *Additional time after service by mail or e-mail.* When a party may or must act within a specified time after service and service is made by mail or e-mail, five (5) days are added after the period that would otherwise expire under FL ST J ADMIN Rule 2.514(a). FL ST J ADMIN Rule 2.514(b).

c. *Enlargement.* When an act is required or allowed to be done at or within a specified time by order of court, by the Florida Rules of Civil Procedure, or by notice given thereunder, for cause shown the court at any time in its discretion (1) with or without notice, may order the period enlarged if request therefor is made before the expiration of the period originally prescribed or as extended by a previous order, or (2) upon motion made and notice after the expiration of the specified period, may permit the act to be done when failure to act was the result of excusable neglect, but it may not extend the time for making a motion for new trial, for rehearing, or to alter or amend a judgment; making a motion for relief from a judgment under FL ST RCP Rule 1.540(b); taking an appeal or filing a petition for certiorari; or making a motion for a directed verdict. FL ST RCP Rule 1.090(b).

d. *Unaffected by expiration of term.* The period of time provided for the doing of any act or the taking of any proceeding shall not be affected or limited by the continued existence or expiration of a term of court. The continued existence or expiration of a term of court in no way affects the power of a court to do any act or take any proceeding in any action which is or has been pending before it. FL ST RCP Rule 1.090(c).

C. General Requirements

1. *Motions generally*

a. *Contents.* An application to the court for an order shall be by motion which shall be made in writing unless made during a hearing or trial, shall state with particularity the grounds therefor, and shall set forth the relief or order sought. The requirement of writing is fulfilled if the motion is stated in a written notice of the hearing of the motion. All notices of hearing shall specify each motion or other matter to be heard. FL ST RCP Rule 1.100(b).

b. *Particularity requirement.* The court considers a motion in the light of the substantive law, rule or statute to make its determination. Some rules require a statement of the grounds for a motion under the rule. Failure to give the grounds will result in denial of the motion. This should be the result in all situations when the ground for the motion is not inherent in the rule. FL-PRACPROC § 9:3. The requirement is nevertheless an important one, first because of the due process notice rights of the respondent, as well as for the assistance it provides to the court in its preparation for the hearing or, absent a hearing, for disposition. 4 FLPRAC R 1.100.

2. *Motion for sanctions*

a. *Sanctions for raising unsupported claims or defenses*

i. *No material facts; No law supporting material facts.* Upon the court's initiative or motion of any party, the court shall award a reasonable attorney's fee, including prejudgment interest, to be paid to the prevailing party in equal amounts by the losing party and the losing party's attorney on any claim or defense at any time during a civil proceeding or action in which the court finds that the losing party or the losing party's attorney knew or should have known that a claim or defense when initially presented to the court or at any time before trial was not supported by the material facts necessary to establish the claim or defense; or would not be supported by the application of then-existing law to those material facts. FL ST § 57.105(1).

ii. *Unreasonable delay.* At any time in any civil proceeding or action in which the moving party proves by a preponderance of the evidence that any action taken by the opposing party, including, but not limited to, the filing of any pleading or part thereof, the assertion of or response to any discovery demand, the assertion of any claim or defense, or the response to any request by any other party, was taken primarily for the purpose of unreasonable delay, the court shall award damages to the moving party for its reasonable expenses incurred in obtaining the order, which may include attorney's fees, and other loss resulting from the improper delay. FL ST § 57.105(2).

iii. *Limit on monetary sanctions.* Notwithstanding FL ST § 57.105(1) and FL ST § 57.105(2), monetary sanctions may not be awarded:

- Under FL ST § 57.105(1)(b) if the court determines that the claim or defense was initially presented to the court as a good faith argument for the extension, modification, or reversal of existing law or the establishment of new law, as it applied to the material facts, with a reasonable expectation of success. FL ST § 57.105(3)(a).
- Under FL ST § 57.105(1)(a) or FL ST § 57.105(1)(b) against the losing party's attorney if he or she has acted in good faith, based on the representations of his or her client as to the existence of those material facts. FL ST § 57.105(3)(b).
- Under FL ST § 57.105(1)(b) against a represented party. FL ST § 57.105(3)(c).

- On the court's initiative under FL ST § 57.105(1) and FL ST § 57.105(2) unless sanctions are awarded before a voluntary dismissal or settlement of the claims made by or against the party that is, or whose attorneys are, to be sanctioned. FL ST § 57.105(3)(d).

iv. *Other sanctions available.* The provisions of FL ST § 57.105 are supplemental to other sanctions or remedies available under law or under court rules. FL ST § 57.105(6).

v. *Fees provided for in contract.* If a contract contains a provision allowing attorney's fees to a party when he or she is required to take any action to enforce the contract, the court may also allow reasonable attorney's fees to the other party when that party prevails in any action, whether as plaintiff or defendant, with respect to the contract. FL ST § 57.105(7) applies to any contract entered into on or after October 1, 1988. FL ST § 57.105(7).

b. *Sanctions in relation to proposals for settlement*

i. *Generally.* Any party seeking sanctions pursuant to applicable Florida law, based on the failure of the proposal's recipient to accept a proposal, shall do so by serving a motion in accordance with FL ST RCP Rule 1.525. FL ST RCP Rule 1.442(g). Any party seeking a judgment taxing costs, attorneys' fees, or both shall serve a motion no later than thirty (30) days after filing of the judgment, including a judgment of dismissal, or the service of a notice of voluntary dismissal, which judgment or notice concludes the action as to that party. FL ST RCP Rule 1.525.

ii. *Motion after judgment, voluntary or involuntary dismissal.* Upon motion made by the offeror within thirty (30) days after the entry of judgment or after voluntary or involuntary dismissal, the court shall determine the following:

- If a defendant serves an offer which is not accepted by the plaintiff, and if the judgment obtained by the plaintiff is at least twenty-five (25%) percent less than the amount of the offer, the defendant shall be awarded reasonable costs, including investigative expenses, and attorney's fees, calculated in accordance with the guidelines promulgated by the Supreme Court, incurred from the date the offer was served, and the court shall set off such costs in attorney's fees against the award. When such costs and attorney's fees total more than the amount of the judgment, the court shall enter judgment for the defendant against the plaintiff for the amount of the costs and fees, less the amount of the award to the plaintiff. FL ST § 768.79(6)(a).
- If a plaintiff serves an offer which is not accepted by the defendant, and if the judgment obtained by the plaintiff is at least twenty-five (25%) percent more than the amount of the offer, the plaintiff shall be awarded reasonable costs, including investigative expenses, and attorney's fees, calculated in accordance with the guidelines promulgated by the Supreme Court, incurred from the date the offer was served. FL ST § 768.79(6)(b).
- For purposes of the determination required by FL ST § 768.79(6)(a), the term "judgment obtained" means the amount of the net judgment entered, plus any postoffer collateral source payments received or due as of the date of the judgment, plus any postoffer settlement amounts by which the verdict was reduced. For purposes of the determination required by FL ST § 768.79(6)(b), the term "judgment obtained" means the amount of the net judgment entered, plus any postoffer settlement amounts by which the verdict was reduced. FL ST § 768.79(6).

iii. For further information please see FL ST § 768.79 and FL ST RCP Rule 1.442.

c. *Sanctions for failure to comply with local pretrial procedures.* The unexcused failure of counsel or any party to comply with the requirements of Seventh Circuit's Civil Pretrial Procedures (FL ST 7 J CIR CV-2003-002-SC) will subject the offending counsel or party to appropriate sanctions which may include, but are not limited to contempt, dismissal, default, the striking of pleadings, claims or defenses, the exclusion of evidence or witnesses, the assessment of fees or costs, or such other sanctions as may be appropriate. FL ST 7 J CIR CV-2003-002-SC(15).

3. *Arbitration and mediation*

a. *Referral to arbitration and mediation.* Except as hereinafter provided or as otherwise prohibited by law, the presiding judge may enter an order referring all or any part of a contested civil matter to mediation or arbitration. The parties to any contested civil matter may file a written stipulation to mediate or arbitrate any issue between them at any time. Such stipulation shall be incorporated into the order of referral. FL ST RCP Rule 1.700(a).

b. *Arbitration*

i. *Exclusions.* A civil action shall be ordered to arbitration or arbitration in conjunction with mediation upon stipulation of the parties. A civil action may be ordered to arbitration or arbitration in conjunction with mediation upon motion of any party or by the court, if the judge determines the action to be of such a nature that arbitration could be of benefit to the litigants or the court. FL ST RCP Rule 1.800.

- Under no circumstances may the following categories of actions be referred to arbitration: (1) bond estreatures; (2) habeas corpus or other extraordinary writs; (3) bond validations; (4) civil or criminal contempt; (5) such other matters as may be specified by order of the chief judge in the circuit. FL ST RCP Rule 1.800.

ii. For more information regarding arbitration, please see FL ST RCP Rule 1.810; FL ST RCP Rule 1.820; FL ST RCP Rule 1.830; FL ST 7 J CIR CV-2009-019-SC; and FL ST 7 J CIR CV-2003-002-SC(1)(c).

c. *Mediation.* For more information regarding mediation, please see FL ST RCP Rule 1.710; FL ST RCP Rule 1.720; FL ST RCP Rule 1.730; FL ST RCP Rule 1.750; FL ST 7 J CIR CV-2008-018-SC; and FL ST 7 J CIR CV-2003-002-SC(1).

4. *Rules of court*

a. *Rules of civil procedure.* The Florida Rules of Civil Procedure apply to all actions of a civil nature and all special statutory proceedings in the circuit courts and county courts except those to which the Florida Probate Rules, the Florida Family Law Rules of Procedure, or the Small Claims Rules apply. FL ST RCP Rule 1.010.

i. The form, content, procedure, and time for pleading in all special statutory proceedings shall be as prescribed by the statutes governing the proceeding unless the Florida Rules of Civil Procedure specifically provide to the contrary. FL ST RCP Rule 1.010.

ii. The Florida Rules of Civil Procedure shall be construed to secure the just, speedy, and inexpensive determination of every action. FL ST RCP Rule 1.010.

b. *Rules of judicial administration.* The Florida Rules of Judicial Administration shall apply to administrative matters in all courts to which the Florida Rules of Judicial Administration are applicable by their terms. The Florida Rules of Judicial Administration shall be construed to secure the speedy and inexpensive determination of every proceeding to which they are applicable. The Florida Rules of Judicial Administration shall supersede all conflicting rules and statutes. FL ST J ADMIN Rule 2.110.

D. Documents

1. *Required documents*

a. *Notice of hearing/Motion.* An application to the court for an order shall be by motion which shall be made in writing unless made during a hearing or trial, shall state with particularity the grounds therefor, and shall set forth the relief or order sought. The requirement of writing is fulfilled if the motion is stated in a written notice of the hearing of the motion. All notices of hearing shall specify each motion or other matter to be heard. FL ST RCP Rule 1.100(b).

i. *Notices to persons with disabilities.* See the Format section of this KeyRules document for further information.

b. *Certificate of good faith.* Before any motion is filed, the moving party shall contact the opposing party and attempt, in good faith, to amicably resolve the issues raised by the motion(s), which shall contain a certificate of the movant's attorney if represented (or the moving party if unrepresented) certifying his/her compliance with this requirement. This does not apply to motions for summary judgment or other case dispositive motions. FL ST 7 J CIR CV-2003-002-SC(5)(c).

c. *Certificate of service.* When any attorney certifies in substance: "I certify that a copy hereof has been furnished to (here insert name or names and addresses used for service) by (e-mail) (delivery) (mail) (fax) on .... (date) ....________________ Attorney" the certificate is taken as prima facie proof of such service in compliance with FL ST J ADMIN Rule 2.516. FL ST J ADMIN Rule 2.516(f).

2. *Supplemental documents*

   a. *Proposed order.* The court may require that orders or judgments be prepared by a party, may require the party to furnish the court with stamped, addressed envelopes for service of the order or judgment, and may require that proposed orders and judgments be furnished to all parties before entry by the court of the order or judgment. FL ST J ADMIN Rule 2.516(h)(1).

   b. *Notice of constitutional question.* A party that files a pleading, written motion, or other paper drawing into question the constitutionality of a state statute or a county or municipal charter, ordinance, or franchise must promptly (1) file a notice of constitutional question stating the question and identifying the paper that raises it; and (2) serve the notice and the pleading, written motion, or other paper drawing into question the constitutionality of a state statute or a county or municipal charter, ordinance, or franchise on the Attorney General or the state attorney of the judicial circuit in which the action is pending, by either certified or registered mail. Service of the notice and pleading, written motion, or other paper does not require joinder of the Attorney General or the state attorney as a party to the action. FL ST RCP Rule 1.071.

E. Format

1. *Documents; Type and size.* Documents subject to the exceptions set forth in FL ST J ADMIN Rule 2.525(d) shall be filed on recycled paper measuring eight and one half by eleven (8 1/2 by 11) inches. For purposes of FL ST J ADMIN Rule 2.520, paper is recycled if it contains a minimum content of fifty (50) percent waste paper. Xerographic reduction of legal-size (eight and one half by fourteen (8 1/2 by 14) inches) documents to letter size (eight and one half by eleven (8 1/2 by 11) inches) is prohibited. All other documents filed by electronic transmission shall be filed in a format capable of being printed in a format consistent with the provisions of FL ST J ADMIN Rule 2.250. FL ST J ADMIN Rule 2.520(b).

   a. *Exhibits.* Any exhibit or attachment filed with pleadings or papers may be filed in its original size. FL ST J ADMIN Rule 2.520(c).

   b. *Recording space.* On all papers and documents prepared and filed by the court or by any party to a proceeding which are to be recorded in the public records of any county, including but not limited to final money judgments and notices of lis pendens, a three (3) inch by three (3) inch space at the top right-hand corner on the first page and a one (1) inch by three (3) inch space at the top right-hand corner on each subsequent page shall be left blank and reserved for use by the clerk of court. FL ST J ADMIN Rule 2.520(d).

      i. *Exceptions to recording space.* Any papers or documents created by persons or entities over which the filing party has no control, including but not limited to wills, codicils, trusts, or other testamentary documents; documents prepared or executed by any public officer; documents prepared, executed, acknowledged, or proved outside of the State of Florida; or documents created by State or Federal government agencies, may be filed without the space required by FL ST J ADMIN Rule 2.520. FL ST J ADMIN Rule 2.520(e).

   c. *Noncompliance.* No clerk of court is permitted to refuse to file any document or paper because of noncompliance with the Florida Rules of Judicial Administration. However, upon request of the clerk of court, noncomplying documents must be resubmitted in accordance with the formatting rules. FL ST J ADMIN Rule 2.520(f).

2. *Caption.* Every pleading, motion, order, judgment, or other paper shall have a caption containing the name of the court, the file number, and except for in rem proceedings, including forfeiture proceedings, the name of the first party on each side with an appropriate indication of other parties, and a designation identifying the party filing it and its nature or the nature of the order, as the case may be. In any in rem proceeding, every pleading, motion, order, judgment, or other paper shall have a caption containing the name of the court, the file number, the style "In re" (followed by the name or general description of the property), and a designation of the person or entity filing it and its nature or the nature of the order, as the case may be. In an in rem forfeiture proceeding, the style shall be "In re forfeiture of" (followed by the

name of the general description of the property). All papers filed in the action shall be styled in such a manner as to indicate clearly the subject matter of the paper and the party requesting or obtaining relief. FL ST RCP Rule 1.100(c)(1).

a. *Volusia County eminent domain cases.* All orders, pleadings, motions and other papers will bear the initial case style. Documents intended to apply only to particular parcel(s) will indicate in their caption the parcel number(s) to which they apply and sufficient copies shall be provided to the Clerk of Court to allow the filing and docketing of each relevant paper in each parcel file. FL ST 7 J CIR CV-2000-011-VL(b).

3. *Writing and written defined.* Writing or written means a document containing information, an application, or a stipulation. FL ST RCP Rule 1.080(c).

4. *Rule abbreviations*

   a. The Florida Rules of Civil Procedure and shall be abbreviated as Fla.R.Civ.P. FL ST RCP Rule 1.010.

   b. The Florida Rules of Judicial Administration shall be abbreviated as Fla. R. Jud. Admin. FL ST J ADMIN Rule 2.110.

5. *Nonverification.* Except when otherwise specifically provided by the Florida Rules of Civil Procedure or an applicable statute, every pleading or other document of a party represented by an attorney need not be verified or accompanied by an affidavit. FL ST RCP Rule 1.030; FL ST J ADMIN Rule 2.515(a).

6. *Attorney signature*

   a. *Attorney signature.* Every pleading and other document of a party represented by an attorney shall be signed by at least one (1) attorney of record in that attorney's individual name whose current record Florida Bar address, telephone number, including area code, primary e-mail address and secondary e-mail addresses, if any, and Florida Bar number shall be stated, and who shall be duly licensed to practice law in Florida or who shall have received permission to appear in the particular case as provided in FL ST J ADMIN Rule 2.510. FL ST J ADMIN Rule 2.515(a).

      i. The attorney may be required by the court to give the address of, and to vouch for the attorney's authority to represent, the party. FL ST J ADMIN Rule 2.515(a).

      ii. The signature of an attorney shall constitute a certificate by the attorney that the attorney has read the pleading or other document; that to the best of the attorney's knowledge, information, and belief there is good ground to support it; and that it is not interposed for delay. FL ST J ADMIN Rule 2.515(a).

      iii. If a pleading is not signed or is signed with intent to defeat the purpose of FL ST J ADMIN Rule 2.515, it may be stricken and the action may proceed as though the pleading or other document had not been served. FL ST J ADMIN Rule 2.515(a).

   b. *Pro se litigant signature.* A party who is not represented by an attorney shall sign any pleading or other paper and state the party's address and telephone number, including area code. FL ST J ADMIN Rule 2.515(b).

   c. *Form of signature*

      i. The signatures required on pleadings and documents by FL ST J ADMIN Rule 2.515(a) and FL ST J ADMIN Rule 2.515(b) may be:

         - Original signatures;
         - Original signatures that have been reproduced by electronic means, such as on electronically transmitted documents or photocopied documents;
         - Electronic signatures using the "/s/," "s/," or "/s" formats by or at the direction of the person signing; or
         - Any other signature format authorized by general law, so long as the clerk where the proceeding is pending has the capability of receiving and has obtained approval from the Supreme Court of Florida to accept pleadings and documents with that signature format. FL ST J ADMIN Rule 2.515(c)(1).

ii. An attorney, party, or other person who files a pleading or paper by electronic transmission that does not contain the original signature of that attorney, party, or other person shall file that identical pleading or paper in paper form containing an original signature of that attorney, party, or other person (hereinafter called the follow-up filing) immediately thereafter. The follow-up filing is not required if the Supreme Court of Florida has entered an order directing the clerk of court to discontinue accepting the follow-up filing. FL ST J ADMIN Rule 2.515(c)(2).

7. *Forms*

a. *Process.* The forms of process, notice of lis pendens, and notice of action provided in the Florida Rules of Civil Procedure are sufficient. Variations from the forms do not void process or notices that are otherwise sufficient. FL ST RCP Rule 1.900(a).

b. *Other forms.* The other forms provided in the Florida Rules of Civil Procedure are sufficient for the matters that are covered by them. So long as the substance is expressed without prolixity, the forms may be varied to meet the facts of a particular case. FL ST RCP Rule 1.900(b).

c. *Formal matters.* Captions, except for the designation of the paper, are omitted from the forms provided in the Florida Rules of Civil Procedure. A general form of caption is the first form provided. Signatures are omitted from pleadings and motions. FL ST RCP Rule 1.900(c).

8. *Notices to persons with disabilities.* All notices of court proceedings to be held in a public facility, and all process compelling appearance at such proceedings, shall include the following statement in bold face, fourteen (14) point Times New Roman or Courier font: "If you are a person with a disability who needs any accommodation in order to participate in this proceeding, you are entitled, at no cost to you, to the provision of certain assistance. Please contact [identify applicable court personnel by name, address, and telephone number] at least seven (7) days before your scheduled court appearance, or immediately upon receiving this notification if the time before the scheduled appearance is less than seven (7) days; if you are hearing or voice impaired, call 711." FL ST J ADMIN Rule 2.540(c)(1).

9. *Minimization of the filing of sensitive information*

a. *Limitations for court filings.* Unless authorized by FL ST J ADMIN Rule 2.425(b), statute, another rule of court, or the court orders otherwise, designated sensitive information filed with the court must be limited to the following format:

i. The initials of a person known to be a minor;

ii. The year of birth of a person's birth date;

iii. No portion of any: Social security number, Bank account number, Credit card account number, Charge account number, or Debit account number;

iv. The last four (4) digits of any: Taxpayer identification number (TIN), Employee identification number, Driver's license number, Passport number, Telephone number, Financial account number, except as set forth in FL ST J ADMIN Rule 2.425(a)(3), Brokerage account number, Insurance policy account number, Loan account number, Customer account number, or Patient or health care number;

v. A truncated version of any: Email address, Computer user name, Password, or Personal identification number (PIN); and

vi. A truncated version of any other sensitive information as provided by court order. FL ST J ADMIN Rule 2.425(a).

b. *Exceptions.* FL ST J ADMIN Rule 2.425(a) does not apply to the following:

i. An account number which identifies the property alleged to be the subject of a proceeding;

ii. The record of an administrative or agency proceeding;

iii. The record in appellate or review proceedings;

iv. The birth date of a minor whenever the birth date is necessary for the court to establish or maintain subject matter jurisdiction;

v. The name of a minor in any order relating to parental responsibility, time-sharing, or child support;

vi. The name of a minor in any document or order affecting the minor's ownership of real property;

vii. The birth date of a party in a writ of attachment or notice to payor;

viii. In traffic and criminal proceedings: a pro se filing; a court filing that is related to a criminal matter or investigation and that is prepared before the filing of a criminal charge or is not filed as part of any docketed criminal case; an arrest or search warrant or any information in support thereof; a charging document and an affidavit or other documents filed in support of any charging document, including any driving records; a statement of particulars; discovery material introduced into evidence or otherwise filed with the court; and all information necessary for the proper issuance and execution of a subpoena duces tecum;

ix. Information used by the clerk for case maintenance purposes or the courts for case management purposes; and

x. Information which is relevant and material to an issue before the court. FL ST J ADMIN Rule 2.425(b).

c. *Remedies.* Upon motion by a party or interested person or sua sponte by the court, the court may order remedies, sanctions or both for a violation of FL ST J ADMIN Rule 2.425(a). Following notice and an opportunity to respond, the court may impose sanctions if such filing was not made in good faith. FL ST J ADMIN Rule 2.425(c).

d. *Motions not restricted.* FL ST J ADMIN Rule 2.425 does not restrict a party's right to move for protective order, to move to file documents under seal, or to request a determination of the confidentiality of records. FL ST J ADMIN Rule 2.425(d).

e. *Application.* FL ST J ADMIN Rule 2.425 does not affect the application of constitutional provisions, statutes, or rules of court regarding confidential information or access to public information. FL ST J ADMIN Rule 2.425(e).

F. Filing and Service Requirements

1. *Filing requirements.* All original documents must be filed with the court either before service or immediately thereafter, unless otherwise provided for by general law or other rules. If the original of any bond or other document is not placed in the court file, a certified copy must be so placed by the clerk. FL ST J ADMIN Rule 2.516(d). All documents shall be filed in conformity with the requirements of FL ST J ADMIN Rule 2.525. FL ST RCP Rule 1.080(b). All documents filed in any court shall be filed by electronic transmission in accordance with FL ST J ADMIN Rule 2.525. "Documents" means pleadings, motions, petitions, memoranda, briefs, notices, exhibits, declarations, affidavits, orders, judgments, decrees, writs, opinions, and any other paper or writing submitted to a court. FL ST J ADMIN Rule 2.520(a). All documents that are court records, as defined in FL ST J ADMIN Rule 2.430(a)(1), must be filed by electronic transmission, provided that: (1) the clerk has the ability to accept and retain such documents; (2) the clerk or the chief judge of the circuit has requested permission to accept documents filed by electronic transmission; and (3) the supreme court has entered an order granting permission to the clerk to accept documents filed by electronic transmission. FL ST J ADMIN Rule 2.525(c)(1).

a. *Definition.* "Electronic transmission of documents" means the sending of information by electronic signals to, by or from a court or clerk, which when received can be transformed and stored or transmitted on paper, microfilm, magnetic storage device, optical imaging system, CD-ROM, flash drive, other electronic data storage system, server, case maintenance system ("CM"), electronic court filing ("ECF") system, statewide or local electronic portal ("e-portal"), or other electronic record keeping system authorized by the supreme court in a format sufficient to communicate the information on the original document in a readable format. Electronic transmission of documents includes electronic mail ("e-mail") and any internet-based transmission procedure, and may include procedures allowing for documents to be signed or verified by electronic means. FL ST J ADMIN Rule 2.525(a).

i. The filing of documents with the court as required by the Florida Rules of Judicial Administration must be made by filing them with the clerk in accordance with FL ST J ADMIN Rule 2.525, except that the judge may permit documents to be filed with the judge, in which event the judge must note the filing date before him or her on the documents and transmit them to the

clerk. The date of filing is that shown on the face of the document by the judge's notation or the clerk's time stamp, whichever is earlier. FL ST J ADMIN Rule 2.516(e).

b. *Application.* Any court or clerk of the court may accept the electronic transmission of documents for filing after the clerk, together with input from the chief judge of the circuit, has obtained approval of the procedures and program for doing so from the Supreme Court of Florida. FL ST J ADMIN Rule 2.525(b).

c. *Exceptions*

   i. Paper documents and other submissions may be manually submitted to the clerk or court:

      - When the clerk does not have the ability to accept and retain documents by electronic filing or has not had ECF Procedures approved by the supreme court;
      - For filing by any self-represented party or any self-represented nonparty unless specific ECF Procedures provide a means to file documents electronically. However, any self-represented nonparty that is a governmental or public agency and any other agency, partnership, corporation, or business entity acting on behalf of any governmental or public agency may file documents by electronic transmission if such entity has the capability of filing documents electronically;
      - For filing by attorneys excused from e-mail service in accordance with FL ST J ADMIN Rule 2.516(b);
      - When submitting evidentiary exhibits or filing non-documentary materials;
      - When the filing involves documents in excess of twenty-five (25) megabytes (25MB) in size. For such filings, documents may be transmitted using an electronic storage medium that the clerk has the ability to accept, which may include a CD-ROM, flash drive, or similar storage medium;
      - When filed in open court, as permitted by the court;
      - When paper filing is permitted by any approved statewide or local ECF procedures; and
      - If any court determines that justice so requires. FL ST J ADMIN Rule 2.525(d).

   ii. Any document in paper form submitted under FL ST J ADMIN Rule 2.525(d) is filed when it is received by the clerk or court and the clerk shall immediately thereafter convert any filed paper document to an electronic document. "Convert to an electronic document" means optically capturing an image of a paper document and using character recognition software to recover as much of the document's text as practicable and then indexing and storing the document in the official court file. FL ST J ADMIN Rule 2.525(c)(4).

   iii. Any storage medium submitted under FL ST J ADMIN Rule 2.525(d)(5) is filed when received by the clerk or court and the clerk shall immediately thereafter transfer the electronic documents from the storage device to the official court file. FL ST J ADMIN Rule 2.525(c)(5).

   iv. If the filer of any paper document authorized under FL ST J ADMIN Rule 2.525(d) provides a self-addressed, postage-paid envelope for return of the paper document after it is converted to electronic form by the clerk, the clerk shall place the paper document in the envelope and deposit it in the mail. Except when a paper document is required to be maintained, the clerk may recycle any filed paper document that is not to be returned to the filer. FL ST J ADMIN Rule 2.525(c)(6).

   v. The clerk may convert any paper document filed before the effective date of FL ST J ADMIN Rule 2.525 to an electronic document. Unless the clerk is required to maintain the paper document, if the paper document has been converted to an electronic document by the clerk, the paper document is no longer part of the official court file and may be removed and recycled. FL ST J ADMIN Rule 2.525(c)(7).

d. *Official court file.* For information on what constitutes the official court file, please see FL ST J ADMIN Rule 2.525(c)(2), FL ST J ADMIN Rule 2.525(c)(3).

e. *Administration.* All attorneys, parties, or other persons using this rule to file documents are required to make arrangements with the court or clerk for the payment of any charges authorized by general law or the supreme court before filing any document by electronic transmission. FL ST J ADMIN Rule 2.525(f)(2).

f. *Filing date.* The filing date for an electronically transmitted document is the date and time that such filing is acknowledged by an electronic stamp or otherwise, pursuant to any procedure set forth in any ECF Procedures approved by the supreme court, or the date the last page of such filing is received by the court or clerk. FL ST J ADMIN Rule 2.525(f)(3).

g. *Accessibility.* All documents transmitted in any electronic form under FL ST J ADMIN Rule 2.525 must comply with the accessibility requirements of FL ST J ADMIN Rule 2.526. FL ST J ADMIN Rule 2.525(g).

2. *Service requirements.* Every pleading subsequent to the initial pleading, all orders, and every other document filed in the action must be served in conformity with the requirements of FL ST J ADMIN Rule 2.516. FL ST RCP Rule 1.080(a).

a. *Service; When required.* Unless the court otherwise orders, or a statute or supreme court administrative order specifies a different means of service, every pleading subsequent to the initial pleading and every other document filed in any court proceeding, except applications for witness subpoenas and documents served by formal notice or required to be served in the manner provided for service of formal notice, must be served in accordance with FL ST J ADMIN Rule 2.516 on each party. No service need be made on parties against whom a default has been entered, except that pleadings asserting new or additional claims against them must be served in the manner provided for service of summons. FL ST J ADMIN Rule 2.516(a).

b. *Service; How made.* When service is required or permitted to be made upon a party represented by an attorney, service must be made upon the attorney unless service upon the party is ordered by the court. FL ST J ADMIN Rule 2.516(b).

i. *Service by electronic mail ("e-mail").* All documents required or permitted to be served on another party must be served by e-mail, unless FL ST J ADMIN Rule 2.516 otherwise provides. When, in addition to service by e-mail, the sender also utilizes another means of service provided for in FL ST J ADMIN Rule 2.516(b)(2), any differing time limits and other provisions applicable to that other means of service control. FL ST J ADMIN Rule 2.516(b)(1). Any document electronically transmitted to a court or clerk must also be served on all parties and interested persons in accordance with the applicable rules of court. FL ST J ADMIN Rule 2.525(e)(2).

- *Service on attorneys.* Upon appearing in a proceeding, an attorney must serve a designation of a primary e-mail address and may designate no more than two (2) secondary e-mail addresses. Thereafter, service must be directed to all designated e-mail addresses in that proceeding. Every document filed by an attorney thereafter must include the primary e-mail address of that attorney and any secondary e-mail addresses. If an attorney does not designate any e-mail address for service, documents may be served on that attorney at the e-mail address on record with The Florida Bar. FL ST J ADMIN Rule 2.516(b)(1)(A).
- *Exception to e-mail service on attorneys.* Service by an attorney on another attorney must be made by e-mail unless excused by the court. Upon motion by an attorney demonstrating that the attorney has no e-mail account and lacks access to the Internet at the attorney's office, the court may excuse the attorney from the requirements of e-mail service. Service on and by an attorney excused by the court from e-mail service must be by the means provided in FL ST J ADMIN Rule 2.516(b)(2). FL ST J ADMIN Rule 2.516(b)(1)(B).
- *Service on and by parties not represented by an attorney.* Any party not represented by an attorney may serve a designation of a primary e-mail address and also may designate no more than two (2) secondary e-mail addresses to which service must be directed in that proceeding by the means provided in FL ST J ADMIN Rule 2.516(b)(1). If a party not represented by an attorney does not designate an e-mail address for service in a proceeding, service on and by that party must be by the means provided in FL ST J ADMIN Rule 2.516(b)(2). FL ST J ADMIN Rule 2.516(b)(1)(C).

- *Time of service.* Service by e-mail is complete when it is sent. FL ST J ADMIN Rule 2.516(b)(1)(D). An e-mail is deemed served on the date it is sent. FL ST J ADMIN Rule 2.516(b)(1)(D)(i). If the sender learns that the e-mail did not reach the address of the person to be served, the sender must immediately send another copy by e-mail, or by a means authorized by FL ST J ADMIN Rule 2.516(b)(2). FL ST J ADMIN Rule 2.516(b)(1)(D)(ii). E-mail service is treated as service by mail for the computation of time. FL ST J ADMIN Rule 2.516(b)(1)(D)(iii).

ii. *Format of e-mail for service.* Service of a document by e-mail is made by attaching a copy of the document in PDF format to an e-mail sent to all addresses designated by the attorney or party. FL ST J ADMIN Rule 2.516(b)(1)(E).

- All documents served by e-mail must be attached to an e-mail message containing a subject line beginning with the words "SERVICE OF COURT DOCUMENT" in all capital letters, followed by the case number of the proceeding in which the documents are being served. FL ST J ADMIN Rule 2.516(b)(1)(E)(i).
- The body of the e-mail must identify the court in which the proceeding is pending, the case number, the name of the initial party on each side, the title of each document served with that e-mail, and the sender's name and telephone number. FL ST J ADMIN Rule 2.516(b)(1)(E)(ii).
- Any document served by e-mail may be signed by the "/s/" format, as long as the filed original is signed in accordance with the applicable rule of procedure. FL ST J ADMIN Rule 2.516(b)(1)(E)(iii).
- Any e-mail which, together with its attached documents, exceeds five megabytes (5MB) in size, must be divided and sent as separate e-mails, no one of which may exceed five megabytes (5MB) in size and each of which must be sequentially numbered in the subject line. FL ST J ADMIN Rule 2.516(b)(1)(E)(iv).

iii. *Service by other means.* In addition to, and not in lieu of, service by e-mail, service may also be made upon attorneys by any of the means specified in FL ST J ADMIN Rule 2.516(b)(2). Service on and by all parties who are not represented by an attorney and who do not designate an e-mail address, and on and by all attorneys excused from e-mail service, must be made by delivering a copy of the document or by mailing it to the party or attorney at their last known address or, if no address is known, by leaving it with the clerk of the court. Service by mail is complete upon mailing. Delivery of a copy within FL ST J ADMIN Rule 2.516 is complete upon:

- Handing it to the attorney or to the party,
- Leaving it at the attorney's or party's office with a clerk or other person in charge thereof,
- If there is no one in charge, leaving it in a conspicuous place therein,
- If the office is closed or the person to be served has no office, leaving it at the person's usual place of abode with some person of his or her family above fifteen (15) years of age and informing such person of the contents, or
- Transmitting it by facsimile to the attorney's or party's office with a cover sheet containing the sender's name, firm, address, telephone number, and facsimile number, and the number of pages transmitted. When service is made by facsimile, a copy must also be served by any other method permitted by FL ST J ADMIN Rule 2.516. Facsimile service occurs when transmission is complete. FL ST J ADMIN Rule 2.516(b)(2)(A) through FL ST J ADMIN Rule 2.516(b)(2)(E).
- Service by delivery after 5:00 p.m. must be deemed to have been made by mailing on the date of delivery. FL ST J ADMIN Rule 2.516(b)(2)(F).

c. *Service; Numerous defendants.* In actions when the parties are unusually numerous, the court may regulate the service contemplated by the Florida Rules of Judicial Administration on motion or on its own initiative in such manner as may be found to be just and reasonable. FL ST J ADMIN Rule 2.516(c).

d. *Service by clerk.* Service of notices and other documents required to be made by the clerk must also be done as provided in FL ST J ADMIN Rule 2.516(b). FL ST J ADMIN Rule 2.516(g).

G. Hearings

1. *Communication equipment*

a. *Definition.* Communication equipment means a conference telephone or other electronic device that permits all those appearing or participating to hear and speak to each other, provided that all conversation of all parties is audible to all persons present. FL ST J ADMIN Rule 2.530(a).

b. *Use by all parties.* A county or circuit court judge may, upon the court's own motion or upon the written request of a party, direct that communication equipment be used for a motion hearing, pretrial conference, or a status conference. A judge must give notice to the parties and consider any objections they may have to the use of communication equipment before directing that communication equipment be used. The decision to use communication equipment over the objection of parties will be in the sound discretion of the trial court, except as noted below. FL ST J ADMIN Rule 2.530(b).

c. *Use only by requesting party.* A county or circuit court judge may, upon the written request of a party upon reasonable notice to all other parties, permit a requesting party to participate through communication equipment in a scheduled motion hearing; however, any such request (except in criminal, juvenile, and appellate proceedings) must be granted, absent a showing of good cause to deny the same, where the hearing is set for not longer than fifteen (15) minutes. FL ST J ADMIN Rule 2.530(c).

d. *Testimony*

i. *Generally.* A county or circuit court judge, general magistrate, special magistrate, or hearing officer may allow testimony to be taken through communication equipment if all parties consent or if permitted by another applicable rule of procedure. FL ST J ADMIN Rule 2.530(d)(1).

ii. *Procedure.* Any party desiring to present testimony through communication equipment shall, prior to the hearing or trial at which the testimony is to be presented, contact all parties to determine whether each party consents to this form of testimony. The party seeking to present the testimony shall move for permission to present testimony through communication equipment, which motion shall set forth good cause as to why the testimony should be allowed in this form. FL ST J ADMIN Rule 2.530(d)(2).

iii. *Oath.* Testimony may be taken through communication equipment only if a notary public or other person authorized to administer oaths in the witness's jurisdiction is present with the witness and administers the oath consistent with the laws of the jurisdiction. FL ST J ADMIN Rule 2.530(d)(3).

iv. *Confrontation rights.* In juvenile and criminal proceedings the defendant must make an informed waiver of any confrontation rights that may be abridged by the use of communication equipment. FL ST J ADMIN Rule 2.530(d)(4).

v. *Video testimony.* If the testimony to be presented utilizes video conferencing or comparable two-way visual capabilities, the court in its discretion may modify the procedures set forth in FL ST J ADMIN Rule 2.530 to accommodate the technology utilized. FL ST J ADMIN Rule 2.530(d)(5).

e. *Burden of expense.* The cost for the use of the communication equipment is the responsibility of the requesting party unless otherwise directed by the court. FL ST J ADMIN Rule 2.530(e).

H. Forms

1. Official Motion for Sanctions Forms for Florida

a. Caption. FL ST RCP Form 1.901.

b. Notice of compliance when constitutional challenge is brought. FL ST RCP Form 1.975.

2. Motion for Sanctions Forms for Florida

a. Motion; By defendant; For sanctions for refusal of offer of judgment. FL-PP § 61:22.

b. Motion; Sanctions, proposal for settlement. FL-PRACFORM § 7:165.

I. Checklist

(I) ❑ Matters to be considered by moving party

(a) ❑ Required documents

(1) ❑ Notice of hearing/Motion

(2) ❑ Certificate of good faith

(3) ❑ Certificate of service

(b) ❑ Supplemental documents

(1) ❑ Proposed order

(2) ❑ Notice of constitutional question

(c) ❑ Time for making motion

(1) ❑ A motion by a party seeking sanctions under FL ST § 57.105 must be served but may not be filed with or presented to the court unless, within twenty one (21) days after service of the motion, the challenged paper, claim, defense, contention, allegation, or denial is not withdrawn or appropriately corrected

(2) ❑ Any party seeking a judgment taxing costs, attorneys' fees, or both shall serve a motion no later than thirty (30) days after filing of the judgment, including a judgment of dismissal, or the service of a notice of voluntary dismissal

(3) ❑ A copy of any written motion which may not be heard ex parte and a copy of the notice of the hearing thereof shall be served a reasonable time before the time specified for the hearing

(II) ❑ Matters to be considered by opposing party

(a) ❑ Required documents

(1) ❑ Response to motion

(2) ❑ Certificate of service

(b) ❑ Supplemental documents

(1) ❑ Proposed order

(2) ❑ Notice of constitutional question

(c) ❑ Time for service and filing of opposition

(1) ❑ No time specified for responding to a motion

Motions, Oppositions and Replies
Motion to Compel Discovery

Document Last Updated January 2013

A. Applicable Rules

1. *State rules*

a. Rules of court. FL ST RCP Rule 1.010; FL ST J ADMIN Rule 2.110.

b. Nonverification of pleadings. FL ST RCP Rule 1.030.

c. Service and filing of pleadings, orders, and documents. FL ST RCP Rule 1.080.

d. Time. FL ST RCP Rule 1.090.

e. Pleadings and motions. FL ST RCP Rule 1.100.

f. Motions. FL ST RCP Rule 1.160.

g. General provisions governing discovery. FL ST RCP Rule 1.280.

h. Depositions. FL ST RCP Rule 1.310; FL ST RCP Rule 1.320; FL ST FAM LAW Rule 12.310.
i. Interrogatories to parties. FL ST RCP Rule 1.340.
j. Production of documents and things and entry upon land for inspection and other purposes. FL ST RCP Rule 1.350.
k. Examination of persons. FL ST RCP Rule 1.360.
l. Failure to make discovery; Sanctions. FL ST RCP Rule 1.380.
m. Relief from judgment, decrees, or orders. FL ST RCP Rule 1.540.
n. Mediation and arbitration. FL ST RCP Rule 1.700; FL ST RCP Rule 1.710; FL ST RCP Rule 1.720; FL ST RCP Rule 1.730; FL ST RCP Rule 1.750; FL ST RCP Rule 1.800; FL ST RCP Rule 1.810; FL ST RCP Rule 1.820; FL ST RCP Rule 1.830.
o. Forms. FL ST RCP Rule 1.900.
p. Minimization of the filing of sensitive information. FL ST J ADMIN Rule 2.425.
q. Retention of court records. FL ST J ADMIN Rule 2.430.
r. Foreign attorneys. FL ST J ADMIN Rule 2.510.
s. Signature of attorneys and parties. FL ST J ADMIN Rule 2.515.
t. Paper. FL ST J ADMIN Rule 2.520.
u. Electronic filing. FL ST J ADMIN Rule 2.525.
v. Accessibility of information and technology. FL ST J ADMIN Rule 2.526.
w. Communication equipment. FL ST J ADMIN Rule 2.530.
x. Court reporting. FL ST J ADMIN Rule 2.535.
y. Requests for accommodations by persons with disabilities. FL ST J ADMIN Rule 2.540.

2. *Local rules*
   a. Eminent domain cases. FL ST 7 J CIR CV-2000-011-VL.
   b. Civil pretrial procedures. FL ST 7 J CIR CV-2003-002-SC.
   c. Motions to compel discovery in civil actions. FL ST 7 J CIR CV-2004-004-SC (A).
   d. Arbitration and mediation. FL ST 7 J CIR CV-2008-018-SC; FL ST 7 J CIR CV-2009-019-SC.

B. Timing

1. *Motion to compel discovery.* Upon reasonable notice to other parties and all persons affected, a party may apply for an order compelling discovery. FL ST RCP Rule 1.380(a).
   a. *Pre-motion requirement.* The moving party must notify the opposing party, in writing, of the specific nature of the deficiencies of his/her discovery response and the specific actions necessary to cure said asserted deficiencies. Said written notice must provide ten (10) days, plus mailing time, for the opposing party to cure said asserted deficiencies, or such shorter time as may be required by the Court. FL ST 7 J CIR CV-2004-004-SC (A)(1).
   b. Upon failure to resolve the issue within the time mentioned in FL ST 7 J CIR CV-2004-004-SC (A)(1), the moving party may then file a motion to compel discovery and request that a hearing be set. FL ST 7 J CIR CV-2004-004-SC (A)(2).
2. *General motion timing.* A copy of any written motion which may not be heard ex parte and a copy of the notice of the hearing thereof shall be served a reasonable time before the time specified for the hearing. FL ST RCP Rule 1.090(d).
   a. Motions filed within thirty (30) days of the trial date will not be considered if predicated on matters the movant knew or should have known with the exercise of reasonable diligence at least thirty (30) days prior to the trial date. Because of busy court calendars, hearing time may not be available to consider motions filed close to the deadline. The inability of a party to obtain time will generally not constitute grounds for a continuance of the trial. FL ST 7 J CIR CV-2003-002-SC(6)(a).

b. The failure of a party to call up for hearing any timely filed motion at least ten (10) days prior to the trial date may constitute a waiver thereof unless the grounds therefor did not exist or the party was not aware of the grounds for the motion(s) prior to the filing of such motion(s) after the exercise of reasonable diligence. FL ST 7 J CIR CV-2003-002-SC(6)(b).

3. *Computation of time*

a. *Generally.* Computation of time shall be governed by FL ST J ADMIN Rule 2.514. FL ST RCP Rule 1.090(a). The following rules apply in computing time periods specified in any rule of procedure, local rule, court order, or statute that does not specify a method of computing time. FL ST J ADMIN Rule 2.514(a).

i. *Period stated in days or a longer unit.* When the period is stated in days or a longer unit of time (A) exclude the day of the event that triggers the period; (B) count every day, including intermediate Saturdays, Sundays, and legal holidays; and (C) include the last day of the period, but if the last day is a Saturday, Sunday, or legal holiday, or falls within any period of time extended through an order of the chief justice under FL ST J ADMIN Rule 2.205(a)(2)(B)(iv), the period continues to run until the end of the next day that is not a Saturday, Sunday, or legal holiday and does not fall within any period of time extended through an order of the chief justice. FL ST J ADMIN Rule 2.514(a)(1).

ii. *Period stated in hours.* When the period is stated in hours (A) begin counting immediately on the occurrence of the event that triggers the period; (B) count every hour, including hours during intermediate Saturdays, Sundays, and legal holidays; and (C) if the period would end on a Saturday, Sunday, or legal holiday, or during any period of time extended through an order of the chief justice under FL ST J ADMIN Rule 2.205(a)(2)(B)(iv), the period continues to run until the same time on the next day that is not a Saturday, Sunday, or legal holiday and does not fall within any period of time extended through an order of the chief justice. FL ST J ADMIN Rule 2.514(a)(2).

iii. *Period stated in days less than seven (7) days.* When the period stated in days is less than seven (7) days, intermediate Saturdays, Sundays, and legal holidays shall be excluded in the computation. FL ST J ADMIN Rule 2.514(a)(3).

iv. *"Last day" defined.* Unless a different time is set by a statute, local rule, or court order, the last day ends (A) for electronic filing or for service by any means, at midnight; and (B) for filing by other means, when the clerk's office is scheduled to close. FL ST J ADMIN Rule 2.514(a)(4).

v. *"Next day" defined.* The "next day" is determined by continuing to count forward when the period is measured after an event and backward when measured before an event. FL ST J ADMIN Rule 2.514(a)(5).

vi. *"Legal holiday" defined.* "Legal holiday" means (A) the day set aside by FL ST § 110.117, for observing New Year's Day, Martin Luther King, Jr.'s Birthday, Memorial Day, Independence Day, Labor Day, Veterans' Day, Thanksgiving Day, the Friday after Thanksgiving Day, or Christmas Day, and (B) any day observed as a holiday by the clerk's office or as designated by the chief judge. FL ST J ADMIN Rule 2.514(a)(6).

b. *Additional time after service by mail or e-mail.* When a party may or must act within a specified time after service and service is made by mail or e-mail, five (5) days are added after the period that would otherwise expire under FL ST J ADMIN Rule 2.514(a). FL ST J ADMIN Rule 2.514(b).

c. *Enlargement.* When an act is required or allowed to be done at or within a specified time by order of court, by the Florida Rules of Civil Procedure, or by notice given thereunder, for cause shown the court at any time in its discretion (1) with or without notice, may order the period enlarged if request therefor is made before the expiration of the period originally prescribed or as extended by a previous order, or (2) upon motion made and notice after the expiration of the specified period, may permit the act to be done when failure to act was the result of excusable neglect, but it may not extend the time for making a motion for new trial, for rehearing, or to alter or amend a judgment; making a motion for relief from a judgment under FL ST RCP Rule 1.540(b); taking an appeal or filing a petition for certiorari; or making a motion for a directed verdict. FL ST RCP Rule 1.090(b).

d. *Unaffected by expiration of term.* The period of time provided for the doing of any act or the taking of any proceeding shall not be affected or limited by the continued existence or expiration of a term of court. The continued existence or expiration of a term of court in no way affects the power of a court to do any act or take any proceeding in any action which is or has been pending before it. FL ST RCP Rule 1.090(c).

C. General Requirements

1. *Motions generally*

   a. *Contents.* An application to the court for an order shall be by motion which shall be made in writing unless made during a hearing or trial, shall state with particularity the grounds therefor, and shall set forth the relief or order sought. The requirement of writing is fulfilled if the motion is stated in a written notice of the hearing of the motion. All notices of hearing shall specify each motion or other matter to be heard. FL ST RCP Rule 1.100(b).

   b. *Particularity requirement.* The court considers a motion in the light of the substantive law, rule or statute to make its determination. Some rules require a statement of the grounds for a motion under the rule. Failure to give the grounds will result in denial of the motion. This should be the result in all situations when the ground for the motion is not inherent in the rule. FL-PRACPROC § 9:3. The requirement is nevertheless an important one, first because of the due process notice rights of the respondent, as well as for the assistance it provides to the court in its preparation for the hearing or, absent a hearing, for disposition. 4 FLPRAC R 1.100.

2. *Failure to make discovery; Types of available relief.* Three (3) categories of relief are available for failure to make discovery. FL-PRACPROC § 16:14.

   a. The first category is an order compelling discovery. This is obtained by a motion to compel discovery. The motion is made in the court in which the action is pending, except when a deposition is being taken out of the territorial jurisdiction of the court and protective relief is sought in accordance with FL ST RCP Rule 1.310(d) or when a deponent is not a party. When one of the exceptions occurs, the motion is made in the circuit court of the county where the deposition is being taken. FL-PRACPROC § 16:14.

   b. The second category results from a failure to comply with an order to make discovery. The sanctions should not be applied until a hearing on the merits of the failure is held, including an opportunity to present evidence of explanation or mitigation. FL-PRACPROC § 16:14.

      i. If the opposing party fails to respond to a proper discovery request, or responds in a manner deemed by the Court to be in bad faith, a presumption in favor of sanctions against the offending party shall arise. Said sanctions may include, but are not limited to, attorneys' fees and costs. Bad faith in propounding improper or unreasonable discovery requests may be sanctioned in a like manner. FL ST 7 J CIR CV-2004-004-SC (A)(4).

   c. The third category is available: (1) if a party or a person designated by an organization to answer questions at a deposition fails to appear before the officer who is to take the deposition after being served with a proper notice; (2) fails to serve answers or objections to interrogatories after proper service of the interrogatories; or (3) a party fails to serve a response to a request for production, inspection and entry after proper service of the request. FL-PRACPROC § 16:14. For further information regarding discovery sanctions please see the KeyRules Motion for Discovery Sanctions documents.

3. *Motion for order compelling discovery*

   a. *Reasonable notice.* Upon reasonable notice to other parties and all persons affected, a party may apply for an order compelling discovery. FL ST RCP Rule 1.380(a).

   b. *Appropriate court.* An application for an order to a party may be made to the court in which the action is pending or in accordance with FL ST RCP Rule 1.310(d). An application for an order to a deponent who is not a party shall be made to the circuit court where the deposition is being taken. FL ST RCP Rule 1.380(a)(1).

   c. *Motion*

      i. *Grounds.* The discovering party may move for an order compelling an answer, or a designation or an order compelling inspection, or an order compelling an examination in accordance with the request:

- If a deponent fails to answer a question propounded or submitted under FL ST RCP Rule 1.310 or FL ST RCP Rule 1.320;
- Or a corporation or other entity fails to make a designation under FL ST RCP Rule 1.310(b)(6) or FL ST RCP Rule 1.320(a);
- Or a party fails to answer an interrogatory submitted under FL ST RCP Rule 1.340;
- Or if a party in response to a request for inspection submitted under FL ST RCP Rule 1.350 fails to respond that inspection will be permitted as requested or fails to permit inspection as requested;
- Or if a party in response to a request for examination of a person submitted under FL ST RCP Rule 1.360(a) objects to the examination, fails to respond that the examination will be permitted as requested, or fails to submit to or to produce a person in that party's custody or legal control for examination. FL ST RCP Rule 1.380(a)(2).

ii. *Certification.* The motion must include a certification that the movant, in good faith, has conferred or attempted to confer with the person or party failing to make the discovery in an effort to secure the information or material without court action. FL ST RCP Rule 1.380(a)(2).

iii. *During deposition.* When taking a deposition on oral examination, the proponent of the question may complete or adjourn the examination before applying for an order. FL ST RCP Rule 1.380(a)(2).

iv. *Protective order.* If the court denies the motion in whole or in part, it may make such protective order as it would have been empowered to make on a motion made pursuant to FL ST RCP Rule 1.280(c). FL ST RCP Rule 1.380(a)(2).

d. *Evasive or incomplete answer.* For purposes of FL ST RCP Rule 1.380(a) an evasive or incomplete answer shall be treated as a failure to answer. FL ST RCP Rule 1.380(a)(3).

e. *Award of expenses of motion*

i. *Motion granted.* If the motion is granted and after opportunity for hearing, the court shall require the party or deponent whose conduct necessitated the motion or the party or counsel advising the conduct to pay to the moving party the reasonable expenses incurred in obtaining the order that may include attorneys' fees, unless the court finds that the movant failed to certify in the motion that a good faith effort was made to obtain the discovery without court action, that the opposition to the motion was justified, or that other circumstances make an award of expenses unjust. FL ST RCP Rule 1.380(a)(4).

ii. *Motion denied.* If the motion is denied and after opportunity for hearing, the court shall require the moving party to pay to the party or deponent who opposed the motion the reasonable expenses incurred in opposing the motion that may include attorneys' fees, unless the court finds that the making of the motion was substantially justified or that other circumstances make an award of expenses unjust. FL ST RCP Rule 1.380(a)(4).

iii. *Motion granted in part and denied in part.* If the motion is granted in part and denied in part, the court may apportion the reasonable expenses incurred as a result of making the motion among the parties and persons. FL ST RCP Rule 1.380(a)(4).

iv. *Electronically stored information; Sanctions for failure to preserve.* Absent exceptional circumstances, a court may not impose sanctions under these rules on a party for failing to provide electronically stored information lost as a result of the routine, good faith operation of an electronic information system. FL ST RCP Rule 1.380(e).

4. *Limitations on discovery of electronically stored information*

a. A person may object to discovery of electronically stored information from sources that the person identifies as not reasonably accessible because of burden or cost. On motion to compel discovery or for a protective order, the person from whom discovery is sought must show that the information sought or the format requested is not reasonably accessible because of undue burden or cost. If that showing is made, the court may nonetheless order the discovery from such sources or in such formats if the requesting party shows good cause. The court may specify conditions of the discovery, including ordering that some or all of the expenses incurred by the person from whom discovery is sought be paid by the party seeking the discovery. FL ST RCP Rule 1.280(d)(1).

b. In determining any motion involving discovery of electronically stored information, the court must limit the frequency or extent of discovery otherwise allowed by the Florida Rules of Civil Procedure if it determines that (i) the discovery sought is unreasonably cumulative or duplicative, or can be obtained from another source or in another manner that is more convenient, less burdensome, or less expensive; or (ii) the burden or expense of the discovery outweighs its likely benefit, considering the needs of the case, the amount in controversy, the parties' resources, the importance of the issues at stake in the action, and the importance of the discovery in resolving the issues. FL ST RCP Rule 1.280(d)(2).

5. *Arbitration and mediation*

a. *Referral to arbitration and mediation.* Except as hereinafter provided or as otherwise prohibited by law, the presiding judge may enter an order referring all or any part of a contested civil matter to mediation or arbitration. The parties to any contested civil matter may file a written stipulation to mediate or arbitrate any issue between them at any time. Such stipulation shall be incorporated into the order of referral. FL ST RCP Rule 1.700(a).

b. *Arbitration*

i. *Exclusions.* A civil action shall be ordered to arbitration or arbitration in conjunction with mediation upon stipulation of the parties. A civil action may be ordered to arbitration or arbitration in conjunction with mediation upon motion of any party or by the court, if the judge determines the action to be of such a nature that arbitration could be of benefit to the litigants or the court. FL ST RCP Rule 1.800.

- Under no circumstances may the following categories of actions be referred to arbitration: (1) bond estreatures; (2) habeas corpus or other extraordinary writs; (3) bond validations; (4) civil or criminal contempt; (5) such other matters as may be specified by order of the chief judge in the circuit. FL ST RCP Rule 1.800.

ii. For more information regarding arbitration, please see FL ST RCP Rule 1.810; FL ST RCP Rule 1.820; FL ST RCP Rule 1.830; FL ST 7 J CIR CV-2009-019-SC; and FL ST 7 J CIR CV-2003-002-SC(1)(c).

c. *Mediation.* For more information regarding mediation, please see FL ST RCP Rule 1.710; FL ST RCP Rule 1.720; FL ST RCP Rule 1.730; FL ST RCP Rule 1.750; FL ST 7 J CIR CV-2008-018-SC; and FL ST 7 J CIR CV-2003-002-SC(1).

6. *Rules of court*

a. *Rules of civil procedure.* The Florida Rules of Civil Procedure apply to all actions of a civil nature and all special statutory proceedings in the circuit courts and county courts except those to which the Florida Probate Rules, the Florida Family Law Rules of Procedure, or the Small Claims Rules apply. FL ST RCP Rule 1.010.

i. The form, content, procedure, and time for pleading in all special statutory proceedings shall be as prescribed by the statutes governing the proceeding unless the Florida Rules of Civil Procedure specifically provide to the contrary. FL ST RCP Rule 1.010.

ii. The Florida Rules of Civil Procedure shall be construed to secure the just, speedy, and inexpensive determination of every action. FL ST RCP Rule 1.010.

b. *Rules of judicial administration.* The Florida Rules of Judicial Administration shall apply to administrative matters in all courts to which the Florida Rules of Judicial Administration are applicable by their terms. The Florida Rules of Judicial Administration shall be construed to secure the speedy and inexpensive determination of every proceeding to which they are applicable. The Florida Rules of Judicial Administration shall supersede all conflicting rules and statutes. FL ST J ADMIN Rule 2.110.

D. Documents

1. *Required documents*

   a. *Notice of deficiency and response.* The moving party must notify the opposing party, in writing, of the specific nature of the deficiencies of his/her discovery response and the specific actions necessary to cure said asserted deficiencies. Said written notice must provide ten (10) days, plus mailing time, for the opposing party to cure said asserted deficiencies, or such shorter time as may be required by the Court. FL ST 7 J CIR CV-2004-004-SC (A)(1).

      i. A copy of the written notice of deficiency, and any response thereto, must be attached to the motion. FL ST 7 J CIR CV-2004-004-SC (A)(2).

   b. *Notice of hearing/Motion.* An application to the court for an order shall be by motion which shall be made in writing unless made during a hearing or trial, shall state with particularity the grounds therefor, and shall set forth the relief or order sought. The requirement of writing is fulfilled if the motion is stated in a written notice of the hearing of the motion. All notices of hearing shall specify each motion or other matter to be heard. FL ST RCP Rule 1.100(b).

      i. *Certification.* The motion must include a certification that the movant, in good faith, has conferred or attempted to confer with the person or party failing to make the discovery in an effort to secure the information or material without court action. FL ST RCP Rule 1.380(a)(2).

         - Before any motion is filed, the moving party shall contact the opposing party and attempt, in good faith, to amicably resolve the issues raised by the motion(s), which shall contain a certificate of the movant's attorney if represented (or the moving party if unrepresented) certifying his/her compliance with this requirement. This does not apply to motions for summary judgment or other case dispositive motions. FL ST 7 J CIR CV-2003-002-SC(5)(c).

      ii. *Notices to persons with disabilities.* See the Format section of this KeyRules document for further information.

   c. *Certificate of service.* When any attorney certifies in substance: "I certify that a copy hereof has been furnished to (here insert name or names and addresses used for service) by (e-mail) (delivery) (mail) (fax) on .... (date) ....________________ Attorney" the certificate is taken as prima facie proof of such service in compliance with FL ST J ADMIN Rule 2.516. FL ST J ADMIN Rule 2.516(f).

2. *Supplemental documents*

   a. *Proposed order.* The court may require that orders or judgments be prepared by a party, may require the party to furnish the court with stamped, addressed envelopes for service of the order or judgment, and may require that proposed orders and judgments be furnished to all parties before entry by the court of the order or judgment. FL ST J ADMIN Rule 2.516(h)(1).

   b. *Notice of constitutional question.* A party that files a pleading, written motion, or other paper drawing into question the constitutionality of a state statute or a county or municipal charter, ordinance, or franchise must promptly (1) file a notice of constitutional question stating the question and identifying the paper that raises it; and (2) serve the notice and the pleading, written motion, or other paper drawing into question the constitutionality of a state statute or a county or municipal charter, ordinance, or franchise on the Attorney General or the state attorney of the judicial circuit in which the action is pending, by either certified or registered mail. Service of the notice and pleading, written motion, or other paper does not require joinder of the Attorney General or the state attorney as a party to the action. FL ST RCP Rule 1.071.

E. Format

1. *Documents; Type and size.* Documents subject to the exceptions set forth in FL ST J ADMIN Rule 2.525(d) shall be filed on recycled paper measuring eight and one half by eleven (8 1/2 by 11) inches. For purposes of FL ST J ADMIN Rule 2.520, paper is recycled if it contains a minimum content of fifty (50) percent waste paper. Xerographic reduction of legal-size (eight and one half by fourteen (8 1/2 by 14) inches) documents to letter size (eight and one half by eleven (8 1/2 by 11) inches) is prohibited. All other

documents filed by electronic transmission shall be filed in a format capable of being printed in a format consistent with the provisions of FL ST J ADMIN Rule 2.250. FL ST J ADMIN Rule 2.520(b).

a. *Exhibits.* Any exhibit or attachment filed with pleadings or papers may be filed in its original size. FL ST J ADMIN Rule 2.520(c).

b. *Recording space.* On all papers and documents prepared and filed by the court or by any party to a proceeding which are to be recorded in the public records of any county, including but not limited to final money judgments and notices of lis pendens, a three (3) inch by three (3) inch space at the top right-hand corner on the first page and a one (1) inch by three (3) inch space at the top right-hand corner on each subsequent page shall be left blank and reserved for use by the clerk of court. FL ST J ADMIN Rule 2.520(d).

   i. *Exceptions to recording space.* Any papers or documents created by persons or entities over which the filing party has no control, including but not limited to wills, codicils, trusts, or other testamentary documents; documents prepared or executed by any public officer; documents prepared, executed, acknowledged, or proved outside of the State of Florida; or documents created by State or Federal government agencies, may be filed without the space required by FL ST J ADMIN Rule 2.520. FL ST J ADMIN Rule 2.520(e).

c. *Noncompliance.* No clerk of court is permitted to refuse to file any document or paper because of noncompliance with the Florida Rules of Judicial Administration. However, upon request of the clerk of court, noncomplying documents must be resubmitted in accordance with the formatting rules. FL ST J ADMIN Rule 2.520(f).

2. *Caption.* Every pleading, motion, order, judgment, or other paper shall have a caption containing the name of the court, the file number, and except for in rem proceedings, including forfeiture proceedings, the name of the first party on each side with an appropriate indication of other parties, and a designation identifying the party filing it and its nature or the nature of the order, as the case may be. In any in rem proceeding, every pleading, motion, order, judgment, or other paper shall have a caption containing the name of the court, the file number, the style "In re" (followed by the name or general description of the property), and a designation of the person or entity filing it and its nature or the nature of the order, as the case may be. In an in rem forfeiture proceeding, the style shall be "In re forfeiture of" (followed by the name of the general description of the property). All papers filed in the action shall be styled in such a manner as to indicate clearly the subject matter of the paper and the party requesting or obtaining relief. FL ST RCP Rule 1.100(c)(1).

   a. *Volusia County eminent domain cases.* All orders, pleadings, motions and other papers will bear the initial case style. Documents intended to apply only to particular parcel(s) will indicate in their caption the parcel number(s) to which they apply and sufficient copies shall be provided to the Clerk of Court to allow the filing and docketing of each relevant paper in each parcel file. FL ST 7 J CIR CV-2000-011-VL(b).

3. *Writing and written defined.* Writing or written means a document containing information, an application, or a stipulation. FL ST RCP Rule 1.080(c).

4. *Rule abbreviations*

   a. The Florida Rules of Civil Procedure and shall be abbreviated as Fla.R.Civ.P. FL ST RCP Rule 1.010.

   b. The Florida Rules of Judicial Administration shall be abbreviated as Fla. R. Jud. Admin. FL ST J ADMIN Rule 2.110.

5. *Nonverification.* Except when otherwise specifically provided by the Florida Rules of Civil Procedure or an applicable statute, every pleading or other document of a party represented by an attorney need not be verified or accompanied by an affidavit. FL ST RCP Rule 1.030; FL ST J ADMIN Rule 2.515(a).

6. *Attorney signature*

   a. *Attorney signature.* Every pleading and other document of a party represented by an attorney shall be signed by at least one (1) attorney of record in that attorney's individual name whose current record Florida Bar address, telephone number, including area code, primary e-mail address and secondary

e-mail addresses, if any, and Florida Bar number shall be stated, and who shall be duly licensed to practice law in Florida or who shall have received permission to appear in the particular case as provided in FL ST J ADMIN Rule 2.510. FL ST J ADMIN Rule 2.515(a).

i. The attorney may be required by the court to give the address of, and to vouch for the attorney's authority to represent, the party. FL ST J ADMIN Rule 2.515(a).

ii. The signature of an attorney shall constitute a certificate by the attorney that the attorney has read the pleading or other document; that to the best of the attorney's knowledge, information, and belief there is good ground to support it; and that it is not interposed for delay. FL ST J ADMIN Rule 2.515(a).

iii. If a pleading is not signed or is signed with intent to defeat the purpose of FL ST J ADMIN Rule 2.515, it may be stricken and the action may proceed as though the pleading or other document had not been served. FL ST J ADMIN Rule 2.515(a).

b. *Pro se litigant signature.* A party who is not represented by an attorney shall sign any pleading or other paper and state the party's address and telephone number, including area code. FL ST J ADMIN Rule 2.515(b).

c. *Form of signature*

i. The signatures required on pleadings and documents by FL ST J ADMIN Rule 2.515(a) and FL ST J ADMIN Rule 2.515(b) may be:

- Original signatures;
- Original signatures that have been reproduced by electronic means, such as on electronically transmitted documents or photocopied documents;
- Electronic signatures using the "/s/," "s/," or "/s" formats by or at the direction of the person signing; or
- Any other signature format authorized by general law, so long as the clerk where the proceeding is pending has the capability of receiving and has obtained approval from the Supreme Court of Florida to accept pleadings and documents with that signature format. FL ST J ADMIN Rule 2.515(c)(1).

ii. An attorney, party, or other person who files a pleading or paper by electronic transmission that does not contain the original signature of that attorney, party, or other person shall file that identical pleading or paper in paper form containing an original signature of that attorney, party, or other person (hereinafter called the follow-up filing) immediately thereafter. The follow-up filing is not required if the Supreme Court of Florida has entered an order directing the clerk of court to discontinue accepting the follow-up filing. FL ST J ADMIN Rule 2.515(c)(2).

7. *Forms*

a. *Process.* The forms of process, notice of lis pendens, and notice of action provided in the Florida Rules of Civil Procedure are sufficient. Variations from the forms do not void process or notices that are otherwise sufficient. FL ST RCP Rule 1.900(a).

b. *Other forms.* The other forms provided in the Florida Rules of Civil Procedure are sufficient for the matters that are covered by them. So long as the substance is expressed without prolixity, the forms may be varied to meet the facts of a particular case. FL ST RCP Rule 1.900(b).

c. *Formal matters.* Captions, except for the designation of the paper, are omitted from the forms provided in the Florida Rules of Civil Procedure. A general form of caption is the first form provided. Signatures are omitted from pleadings and motions. FL ST RCP Rule 1.900(c).

8. *Notices to persons with disabilities.* All notices of court proceedings to be held in a public facility, and all process compelling appearance at such proceedings, shall include the following statement in bold face, fourteen (14) point Times New Roman or Courier font: "If you are a person with a disability who needs any accommodation in order to participate in this proceeding, you are entitled, at no cost to you, to the provision of certain assistance. Please contact [identify applicable court personnel by name, address, and telephone number] at least seven (7) days before your scheduled court appearance, or immediately upon

receiving this notification if the time before the scheduled appearance is less than seven (7) days; if you are hearing or voice impaired, call 711." FL ST J ADMIN Rule 2.540(c)(1).

9. *Minimization of the filing of sensitive information*
   a. *Limitations for court filings.* Unless authorized by FL ST J ADMIN Rule 2.425(b), statute, another rule of court, or the court orders otherwise, designated sensitive information filed with the court must be limited to the following format:
      i. The initials of a person known to be a minor;
      ii. The year of birth of a person's birth date;
      iii. No portion of any: Social security number, Bank account number, Credit card account number, Charge account number, or Debit account number;
      iv. The last four (4) digits of any: Taxpayer identification number (TIN), Employee identification number, Driver's license number, Passport number, Telephone number, Financial account number, except as set forth in FL ST J ADMIN Rule 2.425(a)(3), Brokerage account number, Insurance policy account number, Loan account number, Customer account number, or Patient or health care number;
      v. A truncated version of any: Email address, Computer user name, Password, or Personal identification number (PIN); and
      vi. A truncated version of any other sensitive information as provided by court order. FL ST J ADMIN Rule 2.425(a).
   b. *Exceptions.* FL ST J ADMIN Rule 2.425(a) does not apply to the following:
      i. An account number which identifies the property alleged to be the subject of a proceeding;
      ii. The record of an administrative or agency proceeding;
      iii. The record in appellate or review proceedings;
      iv. The birth date of a minor whenever the birth date is necessary for the court to establish or maintain subject matter jurisdiction;
      v. The name of a minor in any order relating to parental responsibility, time-sharing, or child support;
      vi. The name of a minor in any document or order affecting the minor's ownership of real property;
      vii. The birth date of a party in a writ of attachment or notice to payor;
      viii. In traffic and criminal proceedings: a pro se filing; a court filing that is related to a criminal matter or investigation and that is prepared before the filing of a criminal charge or is not filed as part of any docketed criminal case; an arrest or search warrant or any information in support thereof; a charging document and an affidavit or other documents filed in support of any charging document, including any driving records; a statement of particulars; discovery material introduced into evidence or otherwise filed with the court; and all information necessary for the proper issuance and execution of a subpoena duces tecum;
      ix. Information used by the clerk for case maintenance purposes or the courts for case management purposes; and
      x. Information which is relevant and material to an issue before the court. FL ST J ADMIN Rule 2.425(b).
   c. *Remedies.* Upon motion by a party or interested person or sua sponte by the court, the court may order remedies, sanctions or both for a violation of FL ST J ADMIN Rule 2.425(a). Following notice and an opportunity to respond, the court may impose sanctions if such filing was not made in good faith. FL ST J ADMIN Rule 2.425(c).
   d. *Motions not restricted.* FL ST J ADMIN Rule 2.425 does not restrict a party's right to move for protective order, to move to file documents under seal, or to request a determination of the confidentiality of records. FL ST J ADMIN Rule 2.425(d).

e. *Application.* FL ST J ADMIN Rule 2.425 does not affect the application of constitutional provisions, statutes, or rules of court regarding confidential information or access to public information. FL ST J ADMIN Rule 2.425(e).

F. Filing and Service Requirements

1. *Filing requirements.* All original documents must be filed with the court either before service or immediately thereafter, unless otherwise provided for by general law or other rules. If the original of any bond or other document is not placed in the court file, a certified copy must be so placed by the clerk. FL ST J ADMIN Rule 2.516(d). All documents shall be filed in conformity with the requirements of FL ST J ADMIN Rule 2.525. FL ST RCP Rule 1.080(b). All documents filed in any court shall be filed by electronic transmission in accordance with FL ST J ADMIN Rule 2.525. "Documents" means pleadings, motions, petitions, memoranda, briefs, notices, exhibits, declarations, affidavits, orders, judgments, decrees, writs, opinions, and any other paper or writing submitted to a court. FL ST J ADMIN Rule 2.520(a). All documents that are court records, as defined in FL ST J ADMIN Rule 2.430(a)(1), must be filed by electronic transmission, provided that: (1) the clerk has the ability to accept and retain such documents; (2) the clerk or the chief judge of the circuit has requested permission to accept documents filed by electronic transmission; and (3) the supreme court has entered an order granting permission to the clerk to accept documents filed by electronic transmission. FL ST J ADMIN Rule 2.525(c)(1).

   a. *Definition.* "Electronic transmission of documents" means the sending of information by electronic signals to, by or from a court or clerk, which when received can be transformed and stored or transmitted on paper, microfilm, magnetic storage device, optical imaging system, CD-ROM, flash drive, other electronic data storage system, server, case maintenance system ("CM"), electronic court filing ("ECF") system, statewide or local electronic portal ("e-portal"), or other electronic record keeping system authorized by the supreme court in a format sufficient to communicate the information on the original document in a readable format. Electronic transmission of documents includes electronic mail ("e-mail") and any internet-based transmission procedure, and may include procedures allowing for documents to be signed or verified by electronic means. FL ST J ADMIN Rule 2.525(a).

      i. The filing of documents with the court as required by the Florida Rules of Judicial Administration must be made by filing them with the clerk in accordance with FL ST J ADMIN Rule 2.525, except that the judge may permit documents to be filed with the judge, in which event the judge must note the filing date before him or her on the documents and transmit them to the clerk. The date of filing is that shown on the face of the document by the judge's notation or the clerk's time stamp, whichever is earlier. FL ST J ADMIN Rule 2.516(e).

   b. *Application.* Any court or clerk of the court may accept the electronic transmission of documents for filing after the clerk, together with input from the chief judge of the circuit, has obtained approval of the procedures and program for doing so from the Supreme Court of Florida. FL ST J ADMIN Rule 2.525(b).

   c. *Exceptions*

      i. Paper documents and other submissions may be manually submitted to the clerk or court:

         - When the clerk does not have the ability to accept and retain documents by electronic filing or has not had ECF Procedures approved by the supreme court;
         - For filing by any self-represented party or any self-represented nonparty unless specific ECF Procedures provide a means to file documents electronically. However, any self-represented nonparty that is a governmental or public agency and any other agency, partnership, corporation, or business entity acting on behalf of any governmental or public agency may file documents by electronic transmission if such entity has the capability of filing documents electronically;
         - For filing by attorneys excused from e-mail service in accordance with FL ST J ADMIN Rule 2.516(b);
         - When submitting evidentiary exhibits or filing non-documentary materials;
         - When the filing involves documents in excess of twenty-five (25) megabytes (25MB) in

size. For such filings, documents may be transmitted using an electronic storage medium that the clerk has the ability to accept, which may include a CD-ROM, flash drive, or similar storage medium;

- When filed in open court, as permitted by the court;
- When paper filing is permitted by any approved statewide or local ECF procedures; and
- If any court determines that justice so requires. FL ST J ADMIN Rule 2.525(d).

ii. Any document in paper form submitted under FL ST J ADMIN Rule 2.525(d) is filed when it is received by the clerk or court and the clerk shall immediately thereafter convert any filed paper document to an electronic document. "Convert to an electronic document" means optically capturing an image of a paper document and using character recognition software to recover as much of the document's text as practicable and then indexing and storing the document in the official court file. FL ST J ADMIN Rule 2.525(c)(4).

iii. Any storage medium submitted under FL ST J ADMIN Rule 2.525(d)(5) is filed when received by the clerk or court and the clerk shall immediately thereafter transfer the electronic documents from the storage device to the official court file. FL ST J ADMIN Rule 2.525(c)(5).

iv. If the filer of any paper document authorized under FL ST J ADMIN Rule 2.525(d) provides a self-addressed, postage-paid envelope for return of the paper document after it is converted to electronic form by the clerk, the clerk shall place the paper document in the envelope and deposit it in the mail. Except when a paper document is required to be maintained, the clerk may recycle any filed paper document that is not to be returned to the filer. FL ST J ADMIN Rule 2.525(c)(6).

v. The clerk may convert any paper document filed before the effective date of FL ST J ADMIN Rule 2.525 to an electronic document. Unless the clerk is required to maintain the paper document, if the paper document has been converted to an electronic document by the clerk, the paper document is no longer part of the official court file and may be removed and recycled. FL ST J ADMIN Rule 2.525(c)(7).

d. *Official court file.* For information on what constitutes the official court file, please see FL ST J ADMIN Rule 2.525(c)(2), FL ST J ADMIN Rule 2.525(c)(3).

e. *Administration.* All attorneys, parties, or other persons using this rule to file documents are required to make arrangements with the court or clerk for the payment of any charges authorized by general law or the supreme court before filing any document by electronic transmission. FL ST J ADMIN Rule 2.525(f)(2).

f. *Filing date.* The filing date for an electronically transmitted document is the date and time that such filing is acknowledged by an electronic stamp or otherwise, pursuant to any procedure set forth in any ECF Procedures approved by the supreme court, or the date the last page of such filing is received by the court or clerk. FL ST J ADMIN Rule 2.525(f)(3).

g. *Accessibility.* All documents transmitted in any electronic form under FL ST J ADMIN Rule 2.525 must comply with the accessibility requirements of FL ST J ADMIN Rule 2.526. FL ST J ADMIN Rule 2.525(g).

2. *Service requirements.* Every pleading subsequent to the initial pleading, all orders, and every other document filed in the action must be served in conformity with the requirements of FL ST J ADMIN Rule 2.516. FL ST RCP Rule 1.080(a).

a. *Service; When required.* Unless the court otherwise orders, or a statute or supreme court administrative order specifies a different means of service, every pleading subsequent to the initial pleading and every other document filed in any court proceeding, except applications for witness subpoenas and documents served by formal notice or required to be served in the manner provided for service of formal notice, must be served in accordance with FL ST J ADMIN Rule 2.516 on each party. No service need be made on parties against whom a default has been entered, except that pleadings asserting new or additional claims against them must be served in the manner provided for service of summons. FL ST J ADMIN Rule 2.516(a).

b. *Service; How made.* When service is required or permitted to be made upon a party represented by an attorney, service must be made upon the attorney unless service upon the party is ordered by the court. FL ST J ADMIN Rule 2.516(b).

   i. *Service by electronic mail ("e-mail").* All documents required or permitted to be served on another party must be served by e-mail, unless FL ST J ADMIN Rule 2.516 otherwise provides. When, in addition to service by e-mail, the sender also utilizes another means of service provided for in FL ST J ADMIN Rule 2.516(b)(2), any differing time limits and other provisions applicable to that other means of service control. FL ST J ADMIN Rule 2.516(b)(1). Any document electronically transmitted to a court or clerk must also be served on all parties and interested persons in accordance with the applicable rules of court. FL ST J ADMIN Rule 2.525(e)(2).

      - *Service on attorneys.* Upon appearing in a proceeding, an attorney must serve a designation of a primary e-mail address and may designate no more than two (2) secondary e-mail addresses. Thereafter, service must be directed to all designated e-mail addresses in that proceeding. Every document filed by an attorney thereafter must include the primary e-mail address of that attorney and any secondary e-mail addresses. If an attorney does not designate any e-mail address for service, documents may be served on that attorney at the e-mail address on record with The Florida Bar. FL ST J ADMIN Rule 2.516(b)(1)(A).
      - *Exception to e-mail service on attorneys.* Service by an attorney on another attorney must be made by e-mail unless excused by the court. Upon motion by an attorney demonstrating that the attorney has no e-mail account and lacks access to the Internet at the attorney's office, the court may excuse the attorney from the requirements of e-mail service. Service on and by an attorney excused by the court from e-mail service must be by the means provided in FL ST J ADMIN Rule 2.516(b)(2). FL ST J ADMIN Rule 2.516(b)(1)(B).
      - *Service on and by parties not represented by an attorney.* Any party not represented by an attorney may serve a designation of a primary e-mail address and also may designate no more than two (2) secondary e-mail addresses to which service must be directed in that proceeding by the means provided in FL ST J ADMIN Rule 2.516(b)(1). If a party not represented by an attorney does not designate an e-mail address for service in a proceeding, service on and by that party must be by the means provided in FL ST J ADMIN Rule 2.516(b)(2). FL ST J ADMIN Rule 2.516(b)(1)(C).
      - *Time of service.* Service by e-mail is complete when it is sent. FL ST J ADMIN Rule 2.516(b)(1)(D). An e-mail is deemed served on the date it is sent. FL ST J ADMIN Rule 2.516(b)(1)(D)(i). If the sender learns that the e-mail did not reach the address of the person to be served, the sender must immediately send another copy by e-mail, or by a means authorized by FL ST J ADMIN Rule 2.516(b)(2). FL ST J ADMIN Rule 2.516(b)(1)(D)(ii). E-mail service is treated as service by mail for the computation of time. FL ST J ADMIN Rule 2.516(b)(1)(D)(iii).

   ii. *Format of e-mail for service.* Service of a document by e-mail is made by attaching a copy of the document in PDF format to an e-mail sent to all addresses designated by the attorney or party. FL ST J ADMIN Rule 2.516(b)(1)(E).

      - All documents served by e-mail must be attached to an e-mail message containing a subject line beginning with the words "SERVICE OF COURT DOCUMENT" in all capital letters, followed by the case number of the proceeding in which the documents are being served. FL ST J ADMIN Rule 2.516(b)(1)(E)(i).
      - The body of the e-mail must identify the court in which the proceeding is pending, the case number, the name of the initial party on each side, the title of each document served with that e-mail, and the sender's name and telephone number. FL ST J ADMIN Rule 2.516(b)(1)(E)(ii).
      - Any document served by e-mail may be signed by the "/s/" format, as long as the filed original is signed in accordance with the applicable rule of procedure. FL ST J ADMIN Rule 2.516(b)(1)(E)(iii).

- Any e-mail which, together with its attached documents, exceeds five megabytes (5MB) in size, must be divided and sent as separate e-mails, no one of which may exceed five megabytes (5MB) in size and each of which must be sequentially numbered in the subject line. FL ST J ADMIN Rule 2.516(b)(1)(E)(iv).

iii. *Service by other means.* In addition to, and not in lieu of, service by e-mail, service may also be made upon attorneys by any of the means specified in FL ST J ADMIN Rule 2.516(b)(2). Service on and by all parties who are not represented by an attorney and who do not designate an e-mail address, and on and by all attorneys excused from e-mail service, must be made by delivering a copy of the document or by mailing it to the party or attorney at their last known address or, if no address is known, by leaving it with the clerk of the court. Service by mail is complete upon mailing. Delivery of a copy within FL ST J ADMIN Rule 2.516 is complete upon:

- Handing it to the attorney or to the party,
- Leaving it at the attorney's or party's office with a clerk or other person in charge thereof,
- If there is no one in charge, leaving it in a conspicuous place therein,
- If the office is closed or the person to be served has no office, leaving it at the person's usual place of abode with some person of his or her family above fifteen (15) years of age and informing such person of the contents, or
- Transmitting it by facsimile to the attorney's or party's office with a cover sheet containing the sender's name, firm, address, telephone number, and facsimile number, and the number of pages transmitted. When service is made by facsimile, a copy must also be served by any other method permitted by FL ST J ADMIN Rule 2.516. Facsimile service occurs when transmission is complete. FL ST J ADMIN Rule 2.516(b)(2)(A) through FL ST J ADMIN Rule 2.516(b)(2)(E).
- Service by delivery after 5:00 p.m. must be deemed to have been made by mailing on the date of delivery. FL ST J ADMIN Rule 2.516(b)(2)(F).

c. *Service; Numerous defendants.* In actions when the parties are unusually numerous, the court may regulate the service contemplated by the Florida Rules of Judicial Administration on motion or on its own initiative in such manner as may be found to be just and reasonable. FL ST J ADMIN Rule 2.516(c).

d. *Service by clerk.* Service of notices and other documents required to be made by the clerk must also be done as provided in FL ST J ADMIN Rule 2.516(b). FL ST J ADMIN Rule 2.516(g).

G. Hearings

1. *Communication equipment*

a. *Definition.* Communication equipment means a conference telephone or other electronic device that permits all those appearing or participating to hear and speak to each other, provided that all conversation of all parties is audible to all persons present. FL ST J ADMIN Rule 2.530(a).

b. *Use by all parties.* A county or circuit court judge may, upon the court's own motion or upon the written request of a party, direct that communication equipment be used for a motion hearing, pretrial conference, or a status conference. A judge must give notice to the parties and consider any objections they may have to the use of communication equipment before directing that communication be used. The decision to use communication equipment over the objection of parties will be in the sound discretion of the trial court, except as noted below. FL ST J ADMIN Rule 2.530(b).

c. *Use only by requesting party.* A county or circuit court judge may, upon the written request of a party upon reasonable notice to all other parties, permit a requesting party to participate through communication equipment in a scheduled motion hearing; however, any such request (except in criminal, juvenile, and appellate proceedings) must be granted, absent a showing of good cause to deny the same, where the hearing is set for not longer than fifteen (15) minutes. FL ST J ADMIN Rule 2.530(c).

d. *Testimony*

i. *Generally.* A county or circuit court judge, general magistrate, special magistrate, or hearing officer may allow testimony to be taken through communication equipment if all parties consent or if permitted by another applicable rule of procedure. FL ST J ADMIN Rule 2.530(d)(1).

ii. *Procedure.* Any party desiring to present testimony through communication equipment shall, prior to the hearing or trial at which the testimony is to be presented, contact all parties to determine whether each party consents to this form of testimony. The party seeking to present the testimony shall move for permission to present testimony through communication equipment, which motion shall set forth good cause as to why the testimony should be allowed in this form. FL ST J ADMIN Rule 2.530(d)(2).

iii. *Oath.* Testimony may be taken through communication equipment only if a notary public or other person authorized to administer oaths in the witness's jurisdiction is present with the witness and administers the oath consistent with the laws of the jurisdiction. FL ST J ADMIN Rule 2.530(d)(3).

iv. *Confrontation rights.* In juvenile and criminal proceedings the defendant must make an informed waiver of any confrontation rights that may be abridged by the use of communication equipment. FL ST J ADMIN Rule 2.530(d)(4).

v. *Video testimony.* If the testimony to be presented utilizes video conferencing or comparable two-way visual capabilities, the court in its discretion may modify the procedures set forth in FL ST J ADMIN Rule 2.530 to accommodate the technology utilized. FL ST J ADMIN Rule 2.530(d)(5).

e. *Burden of expense.* The cost for the use of the communication equipment is the responsibility of the requesting party unless otherwise directed by the court. FL ST J ADMIN Rule 2.530(e).

2. *Cancellations.* Once set, the hearing [on a motion to compel discovery] may not be cancelled by either party without the Court's consent. FL ST 7 J CIR CV-2004-004-SC (A)(2).

H. Forms

1. Official Motion to Compel Discovery Forms for Florida

a. Caption. FL ST RCP Form 1.901.

b. Notice of compliance when constitutional challenge is brought. FL ST RCP Form 1.975.

2. Motion to Compel Discovery Forms for Florida

a. Motion to compel attendance and for sanctions. FL-PP § 3:160.

b. Motion; To compel answer to questions asked on oral examination or written questions. FL-PP § 3:161.

c. Order; Directing deponent to answer questions asked on oral examination; Costs and attorney fees to moving party. FL-PP § 3:162.

d. Order; Compelling answer to written questions. FL-PP § 3:163.

e. Motion; For order finding person in contempt of court; Refusal, after order, to answer question. FL-PP § 3:167.

f. Motion; For order compelling opposing party to pay expenses incurred in proving facts the party refused to admit. FL-PP § 3:168.

g. Motion; Compel discovery, deposition. FL-PRACFORM § 7:37.

h. Motion; Compel discovery, interrogatories. FL-PRACFORM § 7:38.

i. Form for motion to compel answer on deposition. FL-RCPF R 1.380(6).

j. Form for certificate of non-appearance at deposition. FL-RCPF R 1.380(7).

k. Form for notice of motion. FL-RCPF R 1.380(8).

l. Form for order on motion to compel answer. FL-RCPF R 1.380(9).

m. Form for notice and motion to compel. FL-RCPF R 1.380(10).

n. Form for order to compel discovery. FL-RCPF R 1.380(18).

o. Form for order to comply with discovery and answer interrogatories. FL-RCPF R 1.380(19).

I. Checklist

(I) ❑ Matters to be considered by moving party

(a) ❑ Required documents

(1) ❑ Notice of deficiency and response

(2) ❑ Notice of hearing/Motion

(3) ❑ Certificate of service

(b) ❑ Supplemental documents

(1) ❑ Proposed order

(2) ❑ Notice of constitutional question

(c) ❑ Time for making motion

(1) ❑ Moving party must provide ten (10) days' notice for opposing party to cure asserted deficiencies before filing motion

(2) ❑ Upon reasonable notice to other parties and all persons affected, a party may apply for an order compelling discovery

(3) ❑ A copy of any written motion which may not be heard ex parte and a copy of the notice of the hearing thereof shall be served a reasonable time before the time specified for the hearing

(II) ❑ Matters to be considered by opposing party

(a) ❑ Required documents

(1) ❑ Response to motion

(2) ❑ Certificate of service

(b) ❑ Supplemental documents

(1) ❑ Proposed order

(2) ❑ Notice of constitutional question

(c) ❑ Time for service and filing of opposition

(1) ❑ No time specified for responding to a motion

Motions, Oppositions and Replies
Motion for Directed Verdict

Document Last Updated January 2013

A. Applicable Rules

1. *State rules*

a. Motion for a directed verdict. FL ST RCP Rule 1.480.

b. Rules of court. FL ST RCP Rule 1.010; FL ST J ADMIN Rule 2.110.

c. Nonverification of pleadings. FL ST RCP Rule 1.030.

d. Service and filing of pleadings, orders, and documents. FL ST RCP Rule 1.080.

e. Time. FL ST RCP Rule 1.090.

f. Pleadings and motions. FL ST RCP Rule 1.100.

g. Motions. FL ST RCP Rule 1.160.

h. Relief from judgment, decrees, or orders. FL ST RCP Rule 1.540.

i. Mediation and arbitration. FL ST RCP Rule 1.700; FL ST RCP Rule 1.710; FL ST RCP Rule 1.720; FL ST RCP Rule 1.730; FL ST RCP Rule 1.750; FL ST RCP Rule 1.800; FL ST RCP Rule 1.810; FL ST RCP Rule 1.820; FL ST RCP Rule 1.830.

j. Forms. FL ST RCP Rule 1.900.

k. Retention of court records. FL ST J ADMIN Rule 2.430.

l. Foreign attorneys. FL ST J ADMIN Rule 2.510.

m. Signature of attorneys and parties. FL ST J ADMIN Rule 2.515.

n. Paper. FL ST J ADMIN Rule 2.520.

o. Electronic filing. FL ST J ADMIN Rule 2.525.

p. Communication equipment. FL ST J ADMIN Rule 2.530.

q. Court reporting. FL ST J ADMIN Rule 2.535.

r. Requests for accommodations by persons with disabilities. FL ST J ADMIN Rule 2.540.

2. *Local rules*

a. Addresses and social security numbers of parties on final judgments. FL ST 7 J CIR CV-2000-007-SC.

b. Eminent domain cases. FL ST 7 J CIR CV-2000-011-VL.

c. Civil pretrial procedures. FL ST 7 J CIR CV-2003-002-SC.

d. Arbitration and mediation. FL ST 7 J CIR CV-2008-018-SC; FL ST 7 J CIR CV-2009-019-SC.

B. Timing

1. *Before a verdict is returned.* A directed verdict is available to the defendant at the close of the plaintiff's evidence or to either party at the close of all of the evidence. A verdict may be directed either by the court on its own motion or on the motion of counsel. FL ST RCP Rule 1.480(a); FL-PP § 5:83. The movant should be prepared to argue the motion immediately. FL-PRACPROC § 22:14.

2. *After a verdict is returned.* Within ten (10) days after the return of a verdict, a party who has timely moved for a directed verdict may serve a motion to enter judgment in accordance with the motion for a directed verdict. FL ST RCP Rule 1.480(b).

3. *No verdict is returned.* If a verdict was not returned, a party who has timely moved for a directed verdict may serve a motion for judgment in accordance with the motion for a directed verdict within ten (10) days after discharge of the jury. FL ST RCP Rule 1.480(b).

4. *General motion timing.* A copy of any written motion which may not be heard ex parte and a copy of the notice of the hearing thereof shall be served a reasonable time before the time specified for the hearing. FL ST RCP Rule 1.090(d).

a. Motions filed within thirty (30) days of the trial date will not be considered if predicated on matters the movant knew or should have known with the exercise of reasonable diligence at least thirty (30) days prior to the trial date. Because of busy court calendars, hearing time may not be available to consider motions filed close to the deadline. The inability of a party to obtain time will generally not constitute grounds for a continuance of the trial. FL ST 7 J CIR CV-2003-002-SC(6)(a).

b. The failure of a party to call up for hearing any timely filed motion at least ten (10) days prior to the trial date may constitute a waiver thereof unless the grounds therefor did not exist or the party was not aware of the grounds for the motion(s) prior to the filing of such motion(s) after the exercise of reasonable diligence. FL ST 7 J CIR CV-2003-002-SC(6)(b).

5. *Computation of time*

a. *Generally.* Computation of time shall be governed by FL ST J ADMIN Rule 2.514. FL ST RCP Rule 1.090(a). The following rules apply in computing time periods specified in any rule of procedure, local rule, court order, or statute that does not specify a method of computing time. FL ST J ADMIN Rule 2.514(a).

i. *Period stated in days or a longer unit.* When the period is stated in days or a longer unit of time (A) exclude the day of the event that triggers the period; (B) count every day, including intermediate Saturdays, Sundays, and legal holidays; and (C) include the last day of the period, but if the last day is a Saturday, Sunday, or legal holiday, or falls within any period of time extended through an order of the chief justice under FL ST J ADMIN Rule 2.205(a)(2)(B)(iv), the period continues to run until the end of the next day that is not a Saturday, Sunday, or legal holiday and does not fall within any period of time extended through an order of the chief justice. FL ST J ADMIN Rule 2.514(a)(1).

ii. *Period stated in hours.* When the period is stated in hours (A) begin counting immediately on the occurrence of the event that triggers the period; (B) count every hour, including hours during intermediate Saturdays, Sundays, and legal holidays; and (C) if the period would end on a Saturday, Sunday, or legal holiday, or during any period of time extended through an order of the chief justice under FL ST J ADMIN Rule 2.205(a)(2)(B)(iv), the period continues to run until the same time on the next day that is not a Saturday, Sunday, or legal holiday and does not fall within any period of time extended through an order of the chief justice. FL ST J ADMIN Rule 2.514(a)(2).

iii. *Period stated in days less than seven (7) days.* When the period stated in days is less than seven (7) days, intermediate Saturdays, Sundays, and legal holidays shall be excluded in the computation. FL ST J ADMIN Rule 2.514(a)(3).

iv. *"Last day" defined.* Unless a different time is set by a statute, local rule, or court order, the last day ends (A) for electronic filing or for service by any means, at midnight; and (B) for filing by other means, when the clerk's office is scheduled to close. FL ST J ADMIN Rule 2.514(a)(4).

v. *"Next day" defined.* The "next day" is determined by continuing to count forward when the period is measured after an event and backward when measured before an event. FL ST J ADMIN Rule 2.514(a)(5).

vi. *"Legal holiday" defined.* "Legal holiday" means (A) the day set aside by FL ST § 110.117, for observing New Year's Day, Martin Luther King, Jr.'s Birthday, Memorial Day, Independence Day, Labor Day, Veterans' Day, Thanksgiving Day, the Friday after Thanksgiving Day, or Christmas Day, and (B) any day observed as a holiday by the clerk's office or as designated by the chief judge. FL ST J ADMIN Rule 2.514(a)(6).

b. *Additional time after service by mail or e-mail.* When a party may or must act within a specified time after service and service is made by mail or e-mail, five (5) days are added after the period that would otherwise expire under FL ST J ADMIN Rule 2.514(a). FL ST J ADMIN Rule 2.514(b).

c. *Enlargement.* When an act is required or allowed to be done at or within a specified time by order of court, by the Florida Rules of Civil Procedure, or by notice given thereunder, for cause shown the court at any time in its discretion (1) with or without notice, may order the period enlarged if request therefor is made before the expiration of the period originally prescribed or as extended by a previous order, or (2) upon motion made and notice after the expiration of the specified period, may permit the act to be done when failure to act was the result of excusable neglect, but it may not extend the time for making a motion for new trial, for rehearing, or to alter or amend a judgment; making a motion for relief from a judgment under FL ST RCP Rule 1.540(b); taking an appeal or filing a petition for certiorari; or making a motion for a directed verdict. FL ST RCP Rule 1.090(b).

d. *Unaffected by expiration of term.* The period of time provided for the doing of any act or the taking of any proceeding shall not be affected or limited by the continued existence or expiration of a term of court. The continued existence or expiration of a term of court in no way affects the power of a court to do any act or take any proceeding in any action which is or has been pending before it. FL ST RCP Rule 1.090(c).

C. General Requirements

1. *Motions generally*

a. *Contents.* An application to the court for an order shall be by motion which shall be made in writing unless made during a hearing or trial, shall state with particularity the grounds therefor, and shall set forth the relief or order sought. The requirement of writing is fulfilled if the motion is stated in a written notice of the hearing of the motion. All notices of hearing shall specify each motion or other matter to be heard. FL ST RCP Rule 1.100(b).

b. *Particularity requirement.* The court considers a motion in the light of the substantive law, rule or statute to make its determination. Some rules require a statement of the grounds for a motion under the rule. Failure to give the grounds will result in denial of the motion. This should be the result in all situations when the ground for the motion is not inherent in the rule. FL-PRACPROC § 9:3. The requirement is nevertheless an important one, first because of the due process notice rights of the respondent, as well as for the assistance it provides to the court in its preparation for the hearing or, absent a hearing, for disposition. 4 FLPRAC R 1.100.

2. *Motion for directed verdict*
   a. *Effect of a motion for directed verdict.* A party who moves for a directed verdict at the close of the evidence offered by the adverse party may offer evidence in the event the motion is denied without having reserved the right to do so and to the same extent as if the motion had not been made. The denial of a motion for a directed verdict shall not operate to discharge the jury. A motion for a directed verdict shall state the specific grounds therefor. The order directing a verdict is effective without any assent of the jury. FL ST RCP Rule 1.480(a).
   b. *Reservation of decision on motion.* When a motion for a directed verdict is denied or for any reason is not granted, the court is deemed to have submitted the action to the jury subject to a later determination of the legal questions raised by the motion. Within ten (10) days after the return of a verdict, a party who has timely moved for a directed verdict may serve a motion to set aside the verdict and any judgment entered thereon and to enter judgment in accordance with the motion for a directed verdict. If a verdict was not returned, a party who has timely moved for a directed verdict may serve a motion for judgment in accordance with the motion for a directed verdict within ten (10) days after discharge of the jury. FL ST RCP Rule 1.480(b).
   c. *Joined with motion for new trial.* A motion for a new trial may be joined with a motion for directed verdict or a new trial may be requested in the alternative. If a verdict was returned, the court may allow the judgment to stand or may reopen the judgment and either order a new trial or direct the entry of judgment as if the requested verdict had been directed. If no verdict was returned, the court may direct the entry of judgment as if the requested verdict had been directed or may order a new trial. FL ST RCP Rule 1.480(c).
   d. *General procedures on a motion for directed verdict*
      i. *Proper method.* The proper method of advocating that a party is entitled to prevail on a claim or defense as a matter of law is to make a motion for a directed verdict at the close of the evidence offered by the opposing party. The trial judge has authority to direct a verdict in favor of one party and against another, without submitting the case to the jury, if there is no other verdict the jury could lawfully return. 5 FLPRAC § 22:5.
      ii. *Directed verdict only in a jury trial.* A motion for directed verdict is proper only in a jury trial. The equivalent motion in nonjury trial is called a motion for involuntary dismissal. 5 FLPRAC § 22:5.
      iii. *Test for the sufficiency of the evidence.* A motion for directed verdict is used primarily to test the sufficiency of the evidence offered in support of a claim or defense. It may also be used to raise legal issues other than the sufficiency of the evidence, but that is less common because most pure issues of law can be resolved on a motion to dismiss or a motion for summary judgment before the case is set for trial. If there is no evidence to support a claim or defense, the trial judge has a duty to direct a verdict for the opposing party on that claim or defense. 5 FLPRAC § 22:5.
         - The trial judge must view all of the facts and factual inferences in a light most favorable to the party opposing the motion. 5 FLPRAC § 22:5.
         - The rule has often been stated by the Florida courts in the negative, that is, a motion for directed verdict should not be granted unless the court, after viewing the evidence and

testimony in the light most favorable to the nonmoving party, determines that no reasonable jury could render a verdict for the nonmoving party. Under this rule, the trial judge may not direct a verdict against a party if there is any evidence upon which the jury could lawfully make a finding in favor of that party. 5 FLPRAC § 22:5.

3. *Arbitration and mediation*

   a. *Referral to arbitration and mediation.* Except as hereinafter provided or as otherwise prohibited by law, the presiding judge may enter an order referring all or any part of a contested civil matter to mediation or arbitration. The parties to any contested civil matter may file a written stipulation to mediate or arbitrate any issue between them at any time. Such stipulation shall be incorporated into the order of referral. FL ST RCP Rule 1.700(a).

   b. *Arbitration*

      i. *Exclusions.* A civil action shall be ordered to arbitration or arbitration in conjunction with mediation upon stipulation of the parties. A civil action may be ordered to arbitration or arbitration in conjunction with mediation upon motion of any party or by the court, if the judge determines the action to be of such a nature that arbitration could be of benefit to the litigants or the court. FL ST RCP Rule 1.800.

         - Under no circumstances may the following categories of actions be referred to arbitration: (1) bond estreatures; (2) habeas corpus or other extraordinary writs; (3) bond validations; (4) civil or criminal contempt; (5) such other matters as may be specified by order of the chief judge in the circuit. FL ST RCP Rule 1.800.

      ii. For more information regarding arbitration, please see FL ST RCP Rule 1.810; FL ST RCP Rule 1.820; FL ST RCP Rule 1.830; FL ST 7 J CIR CV-2009-019-SC; and FL ST 7 J CIR CV-2003-002-SC(1)(c).

   c. *Mediation.* For more information regarding mediation, please see FL ST RCP Rule 1.710; FL ST RCP Rule 1.720; FL ST RCP Rule 1.730; FL ST RCP Rule 1.750; FL ST 7 J CIR CV-2008-018-SC; and FL ST 7 J CIR CV-2003-002-SC(1).

4. *Rules of court*

   a. *Rules of civil procedure.* The Florida Rules of Civil Procedure apply to all actions of a civil nature and all special statutory proceedings in the circuit courts and county courts except those to which the Florida Probate Rules, the Florida Family Law Rules of Procedure, or the Small Claims Rules apply. FL ST RCP Rule 1.010.

      i. The form, content, procedure, and time for pleading in all special statutory proceedings shall be as prescribed by the statutes governing the proceeding unless the Florida Rules of Civil Procedure specifically provide to the contrary. FL ST RCP Rule 1.010.

      ii. The Florida Rules of Civil Procedure shall be construed to secure the just, speedy, and inexpensive determination of every action. FL ST RCP Rule 1.010.

   b. *Rules of judicial administration.* The Florida Rules of Judicial Administration shall apply to administrative matters in all courts to which the Florida Rules of Judicial Administration are applicable by their terms. The Florida Rules of Judicial Administration shall be construed to secure the speedy and inexpensive determination of every proceeding to which they are applicable. The Florida Rules of Judicial Administration shall supersede all conflicting rules and statutes. FL ST J ADMIN Rule 2.110.

D. Documents

1. *Required documents*

   a. *Notice of hearing/Motion.* An application to the court for an order shall be by motion which shall be made in writing unless made during a hearing or trial, shall state with particularity the grounds therefor, and shall set forth the relief or order sought. The requirement of writing is fulfilled if the motion is stated in a written notice of the hearing of the motion. All notices of hearing shall specify each motion or other matter to be heard. FL ST RCP Rule 1.100(b).

      i. *Notices to persons with disabilities.* See the Format section of this KeyRules document for further information.

b. *Certificate of service.* When any attorney certifies in substance: "I certify that a copy hereof has been furnished to (here insert name or names and addresses used for service) by (e-mail) (delivery) (mail) (fax) on .... (date) ....________________ Attorney" the certificate is taken as prima facie proof of such service in compliance with FL ST J ADMIN Rule 2.516. FL ST J ADMIN Rule 2.516(f).

2. *Supplemental documents*

a. *Proposed order.* The court may require that orders or judgments be prepared by a party, may require the party to furnish the court with stamped, addressed envelopes for service of the order or judgment, and may require that proposed orders and judgments be furnished to all parties before entry by the court of the order or judgment. FL ST J ADMIN Rule 2.516(h)(1).

i. When a party submits a proposed Final Judgment to the Clerk of the Court or to the Judge for signature, the Final Judgment shall contain the address and the social security number, if known to the prevailing party, of each person against whom judgment is rendered. FL ST 7 J CIR CV-2000-007-SC.

b. *Notice of constitutional question.* A party that files a pleading, written motion, or other paper drawing into question the constitutionality of a state statute or a county or municipal charter, ordinance, or franchise must promptly (1) file a notice of constitutional question stating the question and identifying the paper that raises it; and (2) serve the notice and the pleading, written motion, or other paper drawing into question the constitutionality of a state statute or a county or municipal charter, ordinance, or franchise on the Attorney General or the state attorney of the judicial circuit in which the action is pending, by either certified or registered mail. Service of the notice and pleading, written motion, or other paper does not require joinder of the Attorney General or the state attorney as a party to the action. FL ST RCP Rule 1.071.

E. Format

1. *Documents; Type and size.* Documents subject to the exceptions set forth in FL ST J ADMIN Rule 2.525(d) shall be filed on recycled paper measuring eight and one half by eleven (8 1/2 by 11) inches. For purposes of FL ST J ADMIN Rule 2.520, paper is recycled if it contains a minimum content of fifty (50) percent waste paper. Xerographic reduction of legal-size (eight and one half by fourteen (8 1/2 by 14) inches) documents to letter size (eight and one half by eleven (8 1/2 by 11) inches) is prohibited. All other documents filed by electronic transmission shall be filed in a format capable of being printed in a format consistent with the provisions of FL ST J ADMIN Rule 2.250. FL ST J ADMIN Rule 2.520(b).

a. *Exhibits.* Any exhibit or attachment filed with pleadings or papers may be filed in its original size. FL ST J ADMIN Rule 2.520(c).

b. *Recording space.* On all papers and documents prepared and filed by the court or by any party to a proceeding which are to be recorded in the public records of any county, including but not limited to final money judgments and notices of lis pendens, a three (3) inch by three (3) inch space at the top right-hand corner on the first page and a one (1) inch by three (3) inch space at the top right-hand corner on each subsequent page shall be left blank and reserved for use by the clerk of court. FL ST J ADMIN Rule 2.520(d).

i. *Exceptions to recording space.* Any papers or documents created by persons or entities over which the filing party has no control, including but not limited to wills, codicils, trusts, or other testamentary documents; documents prepared or executed by any public officer; documents prepared, executed, acknowledged, or proved outside of the State of Florida; or documents created by State or Federal government agencies, may be filed without the space required by FL ST J ADMIN Rule 2.520. FL ST J ADMIN Rule 2.520(e).

c. *Noncompliance.* No clerk of court is permitted to refuse to file any document or paper because of noncompliance with the Florida Rules of Judicial Administration. However, upon request of the clerk of court, noncomplying documents must be resubmitted in accordance with the formatting rules. FL ST J ADMIN Rule 2.520(f).

2. *Caption.* Every pleading, motion, order, judgment, or other paper shall have a caption containing the name of the court, the file number, and except for in rem proceedings, including forfeiture proceedings, the name of the first party on each side with an appropriate indication of other parties, and a designation

identifying the party filing it and its nature or the nature of the order, as the case may be. In any in rem proceeding, every pleading, motion, order, judgment, or other paper shall have a caption containing the name of the court, the file number, the style "In re" (followed by the name or general description of the property), and a designation of the person or entity filing it and its nature or the nature of the order, as the case may be. In an in rem forfeiture proceeding, the style shall be "In re forfeiture of" (followed by the name of the general description of the property). All papers filed in the action shall be styled in such a manner as to indicate clearly the subject matter of the paper and the party requesting or obtaining relief. FL ST RCP Rule 1.100(c)(1).

a. *Volusia County eminent domain cases.* All orders, pleadings, motions and other papers will bear the initial case style. Documents intended to apply only to particular parcel(s) will indicate in their caption the parcel number(s) to which they apply and sufficient copies shall be provided to the Clerk of Court to allow the filing and docketing of each relevant paper in each parcel file. FL ST 7 J CIR CV-2000-011-VL(b).

3. *Writing and written defined.* Writing or written means a document containing information, an application, or a stipulation. FL ST RCP Rule 1.080(c).

4. *Rule abbreviations*

   a. The Florida Rules of Civil Procedure and shall be abbreviated as Fla.R.Civ.P. FL ST RCP Rule 1.010.

   b. The Florida Rules of Judicial Administration shall be abbreviated as Fla. R. Jud. Admin. FL ST J ADMIN Rule 2.110.

5. *Nonverification.* Except when otherwise specifically provided by the Florida Rules of Civil Procedure or an applicable statute, every pleading or other document of a party represented by an attorney need not be verified or accompanied by an affidavit. FL ST RCP Rule 1.030; FL ST J ADMIN Rule 2.515(a).

6. *Attorney signature*

   a. *Attorney signature.* Every pleading and other document of a party represented by an attorney shall be signed by at least one (1) attorney of record in that attorney's individual name whose current record Florida Bar address, telephone number, including area code, primary e-mail address and secondary e-mail addresses, if any, and Florida Bar number shall be stated, and who shall be duly licensed to practice law in Florida or who shall have received permission to appear in the particular case as provided in FL ST J ADMIN Rule 2.510. FL ST J ADMIN Rule 2.515(a).

      i. The attorney may be required by the court to give the address of, and to vouch for the attorney's authority to represent, the party. FL ST J ADMIN Rule 2.515(a).

      ii. The signature of an attorney shall constitute a certificate by the attorney that the attorney has read the pleading or other document; that to the best of the attorney's knowledge, information, and belief there is good ground to support it; and that it is not interposed for delay. FL ST J ADMIN Rule 2.515(a).

      iii. If a pleading is not signed or is signed with intent to defeat the purpose of FL ST J ADMIN Rule 2.515, it may be stricken and the action may proceed as though the pleading or other document had not been served. FL ST J ADMIN Rule 2.515(a).

   b. *Pro se litigant signature.* A party who is not represented by an attorney shall sign any pleading or other paper and state the party's address and telephone number, including area code. FL ST J ADMIN Rule 2.515(b).

   c. *Form of signature*

      i. The signatures required on pleadings and documents by FL ST J ADMIN Rule 2.515(a) and FL ST J ADMIN Rule 2.515(b) may be:

         - Original signatures;
         - Original signatures that have been reproduced by electronic means, such as on electronically transmitted documents or photocopied documents;
         - Electronic signatures using the "/s/," "s/," or "/s" formats by or at the direction of the person signing; or

- Any other signature format authorized by general law, so long as the clerk where the proceeding is pending has the capability of receiving and has obtained approval from the Supreme Court of Florida to accept pleadings and documents with that signature format. FL ST J ADMIN Rule 2.515(c)(1).

ii. An attorney, party, or other person who files a pleading or paper by electronic transmission that does not contain the original signature of that attorney, party, or other person shall file that identical pleading or paper in paper form containing an original signature of that attorney, party, or other person (hereinafter called the follow-up filing) immediately thereafter. The follow-up filing is not required if the Supreme Court of Florida has entered an order directing the clerk of court to discontinue accepting the follow-up filing. FL ST J ADMIN Rule 2.515(c)(2).

7. *Forms*

a. *Process.* The forms of process, notice of lis pendens, and notice of action provided in the Florida Rules of Civil Procedure are sufficient. Variations from the forms do not void process or notices that are otherwise sufficient. FL ST RCP Rule 1.900(a).

b. *Other forms.* The other forms provided in the Florida Rules of Civil Procedure are sufficient for the matters that are covered by them. So long as the substance is expressed without prolixity, the forms may be varied to meet the facts of a particular case. FL ST RCP Rule 1.900(b).

c. *Formal matters.* Captions, except for the designation of the paper, are omitted from the forms provided in the Florida Rules of Civil Procedure. A general form of caption is the first form provided. Signatures are omitted from pleadings and motions. FL ST RCP Rule 1.900(c).

8. *Notices to persons with disabilities.* All notices of court proceedings to be held in a public facility, and all process compelling appearance at such proceedings, shall include the following statement in bold face, fourteen (14) point Times New Roman or Courier font: "If you are a person with a disability who needs any accommodation in order to participate in this proceeding, you are entitled, at no cost to you, to the provision of certain assistance. Please contact [identify applicable court personnel by name, address, and telephone number] at least seven (7) days before your scheduled court appearance, or immediately upon receiving this notification if the time before the scheduled appearance is less than seven (7) days; if you are hearing or voice impaired, call 711." FL ST J ADMIN Rule 2.540(c)(1).

9. *Minimization of the filing of sensitive information*

a. *Limitations for court filings.* Unless authorized by FL ST J ADMIN Rule 2.425(b), statute, another rule of court, or the court orders otherwise, designated sensitive information filed with the court must be limited to the following format:

i. The initials of a person known to be a minor;

ii. The year of birth of a person's birth date;

iii. No portion of any: Social security number, Bank account number, Credit card account number, Charge account number, or Debit account number;

iv. The last four (4) digits of any: Taxpayer identification number (TIN), Employee identification number, Driver's license number, Passport number, Telephone number, Financial account number, except as set forth in FL ST J ADMIN Rule 2.425(a)(3), Brokerage account number, Insurance policy account number, Loan account number, Customer account number, or Patient or health care number;

v. A truncated version of any: Email address, Computer user name, Password, or Personal identification number (PIN); and

vi. A truncated version of any other sensitive information as provided by court order. FL ST J ADMIN Rule 2.425(a).

b. *Exceptions.* FL ST J ADMIN Rule 2.425(a) does not apply to the following:

i. An account number which identifies the property alleged to be the subject of a proceeding;

ii. The record of an administrative or agency proceeding;

iii. The record in appellate or review proceedings;

iv. The birth date of a minor whenever the birth date is necessary for the court to establish or maintain subject matter jurisdiction;

v. The name of a minor in any order relating to parental responsibility, time-sharing, or child support;

vi. The name of a minor in any document or order affecting the minor's ownership of real property;

vii. The birth date of a party in a writ of attachment or notice to payor;

viii. In traffic and criminal proceedings: a pro se filing; a court filing that is related to a criminal matter or investigation and that is prepared before the filing of a criminal charge or is not filed as part of any docketed criminal case; an arrest or search warrant or any information in support thereof; a charging document and an affidavit or other documents filed in support of any charging document, including any driving records; a statement of particulars; discovery material introduced into evidence or otherwise filed with the court; and all information necessary for the proper issuance and execution of a subpoena duces tecum;

ix. Information used by the clerk for case maintenance purposes or the courts for case management purposes; and

x. Information which is relevant and material to an issue before the court. FL ST J ADMIN Rule 2.425(b).

c. *Remedies.* Upon motion by a party or interested person or sua sponte by the court, the court may order remedies, sanctions or both for a violation of FL ST J ADMIN Rule 2.425(a). Following notice and an opportunity to respond, the court may impose sanctions if such filing was not made in good faith. FL ST J ADMIN Rule 2.425(c).

d. *Motions not restricted.* FL ST J ADMIN Rule 2.425 does not restrict a party's right to move for protective order, to move to file documents under seal, or to request a determination of the confidentiality of records. FL ST J ADMIN Rule 2.425(d).

e. *Application.* FL ST J ADMIN Rule 2.425 does not affect the application of constitutional provisions, statutes, or rules of court regarding confidential information or access to public information. FL ST J ADMIN Rule 2.425(e).

F. Filing and Service Requirements

1. *Filing requirements.* All original documents must be filed with the court either before service or immediately thereafter, unless otherwise provided for by general law or other rules. If the original of any bond or other document is not placed in the court file, a certified copy must be so placed by the clerk. FL ST J ADMIN Rule 2.516(d). All documents shall be filed in conformity with the requirements of FL ST J ADMIN Rule 2.525. FL ST RCP Rule 1.080(b). All documents filed in any court shall be filed by electronic transmission in accordance with FL ST J ADMIN Rule 2.525. "Documents" means pleadings, motions, petitions, memoranda, briefs, notices, exhibits, declarations, affidavits, orders, judgments, decrees, writs, opinions, and any other paper or writing submitted to a court. FL ST J ADMIN Rule 2.520(a). All documents that are court records, as defined in FL ST J ADMIN Rule 2.430(a)(1), must be filed by electronic transmission, provided that: (1) the clerk has the ability to accept and retain such documents; (2) the clerk or the chief judge of the circuit has requested permission to accept documents filed by electronic transmission; and (3) the supreme court has entered an order granting permission to the clerk to accept documents filed by electronic transmission. FL ST J ADMIN Rule 2.525(c)(1).

a. *Definition.* "Electronic transmission of documents" means the sending of information by electronic signals to, by or from a court or clerk, which when received can be transformed and stored or transmitted on paper, microfilm, magnetic storage device, optical imaging system, CD-ROM, flash drive, other electronic data storage system, server, case maintenance system ("CM"), electronic court filing ("ECF") system, statewide or local electronic portal ("e-portal"), or other electronic record keeping system authorized by the supreme court in a format sufficient to communicate the information on the original document in a readable format. Electronic transmission of documents includes electronic mail ("e-mail") and any internet-based transmission procedure, and may include procedures allowing for documents to be signed or verified by electronic means. FL ST J ADMIN Rule 2.525(a).

i. The filing of documents with the court as required by the Florida Rules of Judicial Adminis-

tration must be made by filing them with the clerk in accordance with FL ST J ADMIN Rule 2.525, except that the judge may permit documents to be filed with the judge, in which event the judge must note the filing date before him or her on the documents and transmit them to the clerk. The date of filing is that shown on the face of the document by the judge's notation or the clerk's time stamp, whichever is earlier. FL ST J ADMIN Rule 2.516(e).

b. *Application.* Any court or clerk of the court may accept the electronic transmission of documents for filing after the clerk, together with input from the chief judge of the circuit, has obtained approval of the procedures and program for doing so from the Supreme Court of Florida. FL ST J ADMIN Rule 2.525(b).

c. *Exceptions*

   i. Paper documents and other submissions may be manually submitted to the clerk or court:
      - When the clerk does not have the ability to accept and retain documents by electronic filing or has not had ECF Procedures approved by the supreme court;
      - For filing by any self-represented party or any self-represented nonparty unless specific ECF Procedures provide a means to file documents electronically. However, any self-represented nonparty that is a governmental or public agency and any other agency, partnership, corporation, or business entity acting on behalf of any governmental or public agency may file documents by electronic transmission if such entity has the capability of filing documents electronically;
      - For filing by attorneys excused from e-mail service in accordance with FL ST J ADMIN Rule 2.516(b);
      - When submitting evidentiary exhibits or filing non-documentary materials;
      - When the filing involves documents in excess of twenty-five (25) megabytes (25MB) in size. For such filings, documents may be transmitted using an electronic storage medium that the clerk has the ability to accept, which may include a CD-ROM, flash drive, or similar storage medium;
      - When filed in open court, as permitted by the court;
      - When paper filing is permitted by any approved statewide or local ECF procedures; and
      - If any court determines that justice so requires. FL ST J ADMIN Rule 2.525(d).

   ii. Any document in paper form submitted under FL ST J ADMIN Rule 2.525(d) is filed when it is received by the clerk or court and the clerk shall immediately thereafter convert any filed paper document to an electronic document. "Convert to an electronic document" means optically capturing an image of a paper document and using character recognition software to recover as much of the document's text as practicable and then indexing and storing the document in the official court file. FL ST J ADMIN Rule 2.525(c)(4).

   iii. Any storage medium submitted under FL ST J ADMIN Rule 2.525(d)(5) is filed when received by the clerk or court and the clerk shall immediately thereafter transfer the electronic documents from the storage device to the official court file. FL ST J ADMIN Rule 2.525(c)(5).

   iv. If the filer of any paper document authorized under FL ST J ADMIN Rule 2.525(d) provides a self-addressed, postage-paid envelope for return of the paper document after it is converted to electronic form by the clerk, the clerk shall place the paper document in the envelope and deposit it in the mail. Except when a paper document is required to be maintained, the clerk may recycle any filed paper document that is not to be returned to the filer. FL ST J ADMIN Rule 2.525(c)(6).

   v. The clerk may convert any paper document filed before the effective date of FL ST J ADMIN Rule 2.525 to an electronic document. Unless the clerk is required to maintain the paper document, if the paper document has been converted to an electronic document by the clerk, the paper document is no longer part of the official court file and may be removed and recycled. FL ST J ADMIN Rule 2.525(c)(7).

d. *Official court file.* For information on what constitutes the official court file, please see FL ST J ADMIN Rule 2.525(c)(2), FL ST J ADMIN Rule 2.525(c)(3).

e. *Administration.* All attorneys, parties, or other persons using this rule to file documents are required to make arrangements with the court or clerk for the payment of any charges authorized by general law or the supreme court before filing any document by electronic transmission. FL ST J ADMIN Rule 2.525(f)(2).

f. *Filing date.* The filing date for an electronically transmitted document is the date and time that such filing is acknowledged by an electronic stamp or otherwise, pursuant to any procedure set forth in any ECF Procedures approved by the supreme court, or the date the last page of such filing is received by the court or clerk. FL ST J ADMIN Rule 2.525(f)(3).

g. *Accessibility.* All documents transmitted in any electronic form under FL ST J ADMIN Rule 2.525 must comply with the accessibility requirements of FL ST J ADMIN Rule 2.526. FL ST J ADMIN Rule 2.525(g).

2. *Service requirements.* Every pleading subsequent to the initial pleading, all orders, and every other document filed in the action must be served in conformity with the requirements of FL ST J ADMIN Rule 2.516. FL ST RCP Rule 1.080(a).

   a. *Service; When required.* Unless the court otherwise orders, or a statute or supreme court administrative order specifies a different means of service, every pleading subsequent to the initial pleading and every other document filed in any court proceeding, except applications for witness subpoenas and documents served by formal notice or required to be served in the manner provided for service of formal notice, must be served in accordance with FL ST J ADMIN Rule 2.516 on each party. No service need be made on parties against whom a default has been entered, except that pleadings asserting new or additional claims against them must be served in the manner provided for service of summons. FL ST J ADMIN Rule 2.516(a).

   b. *Service; How made.* When service is required or permitted to be made upon a party represented by an attorney, service must be made upon the attorney unless service upon the party is ordered by the court. FL ST J ADMIN Rule 2.516(b).

      i. *Service by electronic mail ("e-mail").* All documents required or permitted to be served on another party must be served by e-mail, unless FL ST J ADMIN Rule 2.516 otherwise provides. When, in addition to service by e-mail, the sender also utilizes another means of service provided for in FL ST J ADMIN Rule 2.516(b)(2), any differing time limits and other provisions applicable to that other means of service control. FL ST J ADMIN Rule 2.516(b)(1). Any document electronically transmitted to a court or clerk must also be served on all parties and interested persons in accordance with the applicable rules of court. FL ST J ADMIN Rule 2.525(e)(2).

         - *Service on attorneys.* Upon appearing in a proceeding, an attorney must serve a designation of a primary e-mail address and may designate no more than two (2) secondary e-mail addresses. Thereafter, service must be directed to all designated e-mail addresses in that proceeding. Every document filed by an attorney thereafter must include the primary e-mail address of that attorney and any secondary e-mail addresses. If an attorney does not designate any e-mail address for service, documents may be served on that attorney at the e-mail address on record with The Florida Bar. FL ST J ADMIN Rule 2.516(b)(1)(A).

         - *Exception to e-mail service on attorneys.* Service by an attorney on another attorney must be made by e-mail unless excused by the court. Upon motion by an attorney demonstrating that the attorney has no e-mail account and lacks access to the Internet at the attorney's office, the court may excuse the attorney from the requirements of e-mail service. Service on and by an attorney excused by the court from e-mail service must be by the means provided in FL ST J ADMIN Rule 2.516(b)(2). FL ST J ADMIN Rule 2.516(b)(1)(B).

         - *Service on and by parties not represented by an attorney.* Any party not represented by an attorney may serve a designation of a primary e-mail address and also may designate no more than two (2) secondary e-mail addresses to which service must be directed in that proceeding by the means provided in FL ST J ADMIN Rule 2.516(b)(1). If a party not represented by an attorney does not designate an e-mail address for service in a proceeding, service on and by that party must be by the means provided in FL ST J ADMIN Rule 2.516(b)(2). FL ST J ADMIN Rule 2.516(b)(1)(C).

- *Time of service.* Service by e-mail is complete when it is sent. FL ST J ADMIN Rule 2.516(b)(1)(D). An e-mail is deemed served on the date it is sent. FL ST J ADMIN Rule 2.516(b)(1)(D)(i). If the sender learns that the e-mail did not reach the address of the person to be served, the sender must immediately send another copy by e-mail, or by a means authorized by FL ST J ADMIN Rule 2.516(b)(2). FL ST J ADMIN Rule 2.516(b)(1)(D)(ii). E-mail service is treated as service by mail for the computation of time. FL ST J ADMIN Rule 2.516(b)(1)(D)(iii).

ii. *Format of e-mail for service.* Service of a document by e-mail is made by attaching a copy of the document in PDF format to an e-mail sent to all addresses designated by the attorney or party. FL ST J ADMIN Rule 2.516(b)(1)(E).

- All documents served by e-mail must be attached to an e-mail message containing a subject line beginning with the words "SERVICE OF COURT DOCUMENT" in all capital letters, followed by the case number of the proceeding in which the documents are being served. FL ST J ADMIN Rule 2.516(b)(1)(E)(i).
- The body of the e-mail must identify the court in which the proceeding is pending, the case number, the name of the initial party on each side, the title of each document served with that e-mail, and the sender's name and telephone number. FL ST J ADMIN Rule 2.516(b)(1)(E)(ii).
- Any document served by e-mail may be signed by the "/s/" format, as long as the filed original is signed in accordance with the applicable rule of procedure. FL ST J ADMIN Rule 2.516(b)(1)(E)(iii).
- Any e-mail which, together with its attached documents, exceeds five megabytes (5MB) in size, must be divided and sent as separate e-mails, no one of which may exceed five megabytes (5MB) in size and each of which must be sequentially numbered in the subject line. FL ST J ADMIN Rule 2.516(b)(1)(E)(iv).

iii. *Service by other means.* In addition to, and not in lieu of, service by e-mail, service may also be made upon attorneys by any of the means specified in FL ST J ADMIN Rule 2.516(b)(2). Service on and by all parties who are not represented by an attorney and who do not designate an e-mail address, and on and by all attorneys excused from e-mail service, must be made by delivering a copy of the document or by mailing it to the party or attorney at their last known address or, if no address is known, by leaving it with the clerk of the court. Service by mail is complete upon mailing. Delivery of a copy within FL ST J ADMIN Rule 2.516 is complete upon:

- Handing it to the attorney or to the party,
- Leaving it at the attorney's or party's office with a clerk or other person in charge thereof,
- If there is no one in charge, leaving it in a conspicuous place therein,
- If the office is closed or the person to be served has no office, leaving it at the person's usual place of abode with some person of his or her family above fifteen (15) years of age and informing such person of the contents, or
- Transmitting it by facsimile to the attorney's or party's office with a cover sheet containing the sender's name, firm, address, telephone number, and facsimile number, and the number of pages transmitted. When service is made by facsimile, a copy must also be served by any other method permitted by FL ST J ADMIN Rule 2.516. Facsimile service occurs when transmission is complete. FL ST J ADMIN Rule 2.516(b)(2)(A) through FL ST J ADMIN Rule 2.516(b)(2)(E).
- Service by delivery after 5:00 p.m. must be deemed to have been made by mailing on the date of delivery. FL ST J ADMIN Rule 2.516(b)(2)(F).

c. *Service; Numerous defendants.* In actions when the parties are unusually numerous, the court may regulate the service contemplated by the Florida Rules of Judicial Administration on motion or on its own initiative in such manner as may be found to be just and reasonable. FL ST J ADMIN Rule 2.516(c).

d. *Service by clerk.* Service of notices and other documents required to be made by the clerk must also be done as provided in FL ST J ADMIN Rule 2.516(b). FL ST J ADMIN Rule 2.516(g).

G. Hearings

1. *Communication equipment*

a. *Definition.* Communication equipment means a conference telephone or other electronic device that permits all those appearing or participating to hear and speak to each other, provided that all conversation of all parties is audible to all persons present. FL ST J ADMIN Rule 2.530(a).

b. *Use by all parties.* A county or circuit court judge may, upon the court's own motion or upon the written request of a party, direct that communication equipment be used for a motion hearing, pretrial conference, or a status conference. A judge must give notice to the parties and consider any objections they may have to the use of communication equipment before directing that communication equipment be used. The decision to use communication equipment over the objection of parties will be in the sound discretion of the trial court, except as noted below. FL ST J ADMIN Rule 2.530(b).

c. *Use only by requesting party.* A county or circuit court judge may, upon the written request of a party upon reasonable notice to all other parties, permit a requesting party to participate through communication equipment in a scheduled motion hearing; however, any such request (except in criminal, juvenile, and appellate proceedings) must be granted, absent a showing of good cause to deny the same, where the hearing is set for not longer than fifteen (15) minutes. FL ST J ADMIN Rule 2.530(c).

d. *Testimony*

i. *Generally.* A county or circuit court judge, general magistrate, special magistrate, or hearing officer may allow testimony to be taken through communication equipment if all parties consent or if permitted by another applicable rule of procedure. FL ST J ADMIN Rule 2.530(d)(1).

ii. *Procedure.* Any party desiring to present testimony through communication equipment shall, prior to the hearing or trial at which the testimony is to be presented, contact all parties to determine whether each party consents to this form of testimony. The party seeking to present the testimony shall move for permission to present testimony through communication equipment, which motion shall set forth good cause as to why the testimony should be allowed in this form. FL ST J ADMIN Rule 2.530(d)(2).

iii. *Oath.* Testimony may be taken through communication equipment only if a notary public or other person authorized to administer oaths in the witness's jurisdiction is present with the witness and administers the oath consistent with the laws of the jurisdiction. FL ST J ADMIN Rule 2.530(d)(3).

iv. *Confrontation rights.* In juvenile and criminal proceedings the defendant must make an informed waiver of any confrontation rights that may be abridged by the use of communication equipment. FL ST J ADMIN Rule 2.530(d)(4).

v. *Video testimony.* If the testimony to be presented utilizes video conferencing or comparable two-way visual capabilities, the court in its discretion may modify the procedures set forth in FL ST J ADMIN Rule 2.530 to accommodate the technology utilized. FL ST J ADMIN Rule 2.530(d)(5).

e. *Burden of expense.* The cost for the use of the communication equipment is the responsibility of the requesting party unless otherwise directed by the court. FL ST J ADMIN Rule 2.530(e).

H. Forms

1. Official Motion for Directed Verdict Forms for Florida

a. Caption. FL ST RCP Form 1.901.

b. Notice of compliance when constitutional challenge is brought. FL ST RCP Form 1.975.

2. Motion for Directed Verdict Forms for Florida

a. Motion; For directed verdict; At close of adverse party's evidence. FL-PP § 5:86.

b. Motion; For directed verdict; At close of all of evidence. FL-PP § 5:87.

c. Motion; Request to go to jury if motions by both parties are denied. FL-PP § 5:88.

d. Order; Granting defendant's motion for directed verdict; Insufficiency of plaintiff's evidence. FL-PP § 5:89.

e. Motion; Directed verdict, renewed. FL-PRACFORM § 7:62.

f. Form for motion for directed verdict at close of plaintiff's case. FL-RCPF R 1.480(24).

g. Form for motion for directed verdict at close of defendant's case. FL-RCPF R 1.480(25).

h. Form for motion to set aside verdict and enter directed verdict. FL-RCPF R 1.480(26).

I. Checklist

(I) ❑ Matters to be considered by moving party

(a) ❑ Required documents

(1) ❑ Notice of hearing/Motion

(2) ❑ Certificate of service

(b) ❑ Supplemental documents

(1) ❑ Proposed order

(2) ❑ Notice of constitutional question

(c) ❑ Time for making motion

(1) ❑ Before a verdict is returned - A directed verdict is available to the defendant at the close of the plaintiff's evidence or to either party at the close of all of the evidence

(2) ❑ After a verdict is returned - Within ten (10) days after the return of a verdict, a party who has timely moved for a directed verdict may serve a motion to enter judgment in accordance with the motion for a directed verdict

(3) ❑ No verdict is returned - If a verdict was not returned, a party who has timely moved for a directed verdict may serve a motion for judgment in accordance with the motion for a directed verdict within ten (10) days after discharge of the jury

(4) ❑ General motion timing - A copy of any written motion which may not be heard ex parte and a copy of the notice of the hearing thereof shall be served a reasonable time before the time specified for the hearing

(II) ❑ Matters to be considered by opposing party

(a) ❑ Required documents

(1) ❑ Response to motion

(2) ❑ Certificate of service

(b) ❑ Supplemental documents

(1) ❑ Proposed order

(2) ❑ Notice of constitutional question

(c) ❑ Time for service and filing of opposition

(1) ❑ No time specified for responding to a motion

Requests, Notices and Applications
Request for Production of Documents

Document Last Updated January 2013

A. Applicable Rules

1. *State rules*
   a. Nonverification of pleadings. FL ST RCP Rule 1.030.
   b. Service and filing of pleadings, orders, and documents. FL ST RCP Rule 1.080.
   c. Time. FL ST RCP Rule 1.090.
   d. Pleadings and motions. FL ST RCP Rule 1.100.
   e. Pretrial procedure. FL ST RCP Rule 1.200.
   f. General provisions governing discovery. FL ST RCP Rule 1.280.
   g. Depositions upon oral examination. FL ST RCP Rule 1.310.
   h. Interrogatories to parties. FL ST RCP Rule 1.340.
   i. Production of documents and things and entry upon land for inspection and other purposes. FL ST RCP Rule 1.350.
   j. Production of documents and things without deposition. FL ST RCP Rule 1.351.
   k. Examination of persons. FL ST RCP Rule 1.360.
   l. Requests for admission. FL ST RCP Rule 1.370.
   m. Failure to make discovery; Sanctions. FL ST RCP Rule 1.380.
   n. Depositions of expert witnesses. FL ST RCP Rule 1.390.
   o. Relief from judgment, decrees, or orders. FL ST RCP Rule 1.540.
   p. Forms. FL ST RCP Rule 1.900.
   q. Minimization of the filing of sensitive information. FL ST J ADMIN Rule 2.425.
   r. Retention of court records. FL ST J ADMIN Rule 2.430.
   s. Foreign attorneys. FL ST J ADMIN Rule 2.510.
   t. Signature of attorneys and parties. FL ST J ADMIN Rule 2.515.
   u. Paper. FL ST J ADMIN Rule 2.520.
   v. Electronic filing. FL ST J ADMIN Rule 2.525.
   w. Accessibility of information and technology. FL ST J ADMIN Rule 2.526.
   x. Requests for accommodations by persons with disabilities. FL ST J ADMIN Rule 2.540.
2. *Local rules*
   a. Eminent domain cases. FL ST 7 J CIR CV-2000-011-VL.
   b. Arbitration and mediation. FL ST 7 J CIR CV-2009-019-SC; FL ST 7 J CIR CV-2008-018-SC.
   c. Civil pretrial procedures. FL ST 7 J CIR CV-2003-002-SC.

B. Timing

1. *Request for production of documents.* Without leave of court the request may be served on the plaintiff after commencement of the action and on any other party with or after service of the process and initial pleading on that party. FL ST RCP Rule 1.350(b).
   a. *Local requirement.* No interrogatories, requests to produce or requests for admissions shall be served later than forty-five (45) days prior to docket sounding. Exceptions shall be permitted only by written stipulation of the parties or by Court order. FL ST 7 J CIR CV-2003-002-SC.

2. *Notice of intent to serve subpoena.* A party desiring production under FL ST RCP Rule 1.351 shall serve notice as provided in FL ST RCP Rule 1.080 on every other party of the intent to serve a subpoena under FL ST RCP Rule 1.351 at least ten (10) days before the subpoena is issued if service is by delivery and fifteen (15) days before the subpoena is issued if the service is by mail or e-mail. FL ST RCP Rule 1.351(b).
3. *Sequence and timing of discovery.* Except as provided in FL ST RCP Rule 1.280(b)(5) or unless the court upon motion for the convenience of parties and witnesses and in the interest of justice orders otherwise, methods of discovery may be used in any sequence, and the fact that a party is conducting discovery, whether by deposition or otherwise, shall not delay any other party's discovery. FL ST RCP Rule 1.280(e).
   a. *Close of discovery.* Except as otherwise provided by FL ST 7 J CIR CV-2003-002-SC or agreed to by the parties in writing, discovery shall remain open until ten (10) days prior to docket sounding. FL ST 7 J CIR CV-2003-002-SC.
4. *Computation of time*
   a. *Generally.* Computation of time shall be governed by FL ST J ADMIN Rule 2.514. FL ST RCP Rule 1.090(a). The following rules apply in computing time periods specified in any rule of procedure, local rule, court order, or statute that does not specify a method of computing time. FL ST J ADMIN Rule 2.514(a).
      i. *Period stated in days or a longer unit.* When the period is stated in days or a longer unit of time (A) exclude the day of the event that triggers the period; (B) count every day, including intermediate Saturdays, Sundays, and legal holidays; and (C) include the last day of the period, but if the last day is a Saturday, Sunday, or legal holiday, or falls within any period of time extended through an order of the chief justice under FL ST J ADMIN Rule 2.205(a)(2)(B)(iv), the period continues to run until the end of the next day that is not a Saturday, Sunday, or legal holiday and does not fall within any period of time extended through an order of the chief justice. FL ST J ADMIN Rule 2.514(a)(1).
      ii. *Period stated in hours.* When the period is stated in hours (A) begin counting immediately on the occurrence of the event that triggers the period; (B) count every hour, including hours during intermediate Saturdays, Sundays, and legal holidays; and (C) if the period would end on a Saturday, Sunday, or legal holiday, or during any period of time extended through an order of the chief justice under FL ST J ADMIN Rule 2.205(a)(2)(B)(iv), the period continues to run until the same time on the next day that is not a Saturday, Sunday, or legal holiday and does not fall within any period of time extended through an order of the chief justice. FL ST J ADMIN Rule 2.514(a)(2).
      iii. *Period stated in days less than seven (7) days.* When the period stated in days is less than seven (7) days, intermediate Saturdays, Sundays, and legal holidays shall be excluded in the computation. FL ST J ADMIN Rule 2.514(a)(3).
      iv. *"Last day" defined.* Unless a different time is set by a statute, local rule, or court order, the last day ends (A) for electronic filing or for service by any means, at midnight; and (B) for filing by other means, when the clerk's office is scheduled to close. FL ST J ADMIN Rule 2.514(a)(4).
      v. *"Next day" defined.* The "next day" is determined by continuing to count forward when the period is measured after an event and backward when measured before an event. FL ST J ADMIN Rule 2.514(a)(5).
      vi. *"Legal holiday" defined.* "Legal holiday" means (A) the day set aside by FL ST § 110.117, for observing New Year's Day, Martin Luther King, Jr.'s Birthday, Memorial Day, Independence Day, Labor Day, Veterans' Day, Thanksgiving Day, the Friday after Thanksgiving Day, or Christmas Day, and (B) any day observed as a holiday by the clerk's office or as designated by the chief judge. FL ST J ADMIN Rule 2.514(a)(6).
   b. *Additional time after service by mail or e-mail.* When a party may or must act within a specified time after service and service is made by mail or e-mail, five (5) days are added after the period that would otherwise expire under FL ST J ADMIN Rule 2.514(a). FL ST J ADMIN Rule 2.514(b).

c. *Enlargement.* When an act is required or allowed to be done at or within a specified time by order of court, by the Florida Rules of Civil Procedure, or by notice given thereunder, for cause shown the court at any time in its discretion (1) with or without notice, may order the period enlarged if request therefor is made before the expiration of the period originally prescribed or as extended by a previous order, or (2) upon motion made and notice after the expiration of the specified period, may permit the act to be done when failure to act was the result of excusable neglect, but it may not extend the time for making a motion for new trial; for rehearing, or to alter or amend a judgment; making a motion for relief from a judgment under FL ST RCP Rule 1.540(b); taking an appeal or filing a petition for certiorari; or making a motion for a directed verdict. FL ST RCP Rule 1.090(b).

d. *Unaffected by expiration of term.* The period of time provided for the doing of any act or the taking of any proceeding shall not be affected or limited by the continued existence or expiration of a term of court. The continued existence or expiration of a term of court in no way affects the power of a court to do any act or take any proceeding in any action which is or has been pending before it. FL ST RCP Rule 1.090(c).

C. General Requirements

1. *General provisions governing discovery*

a. *Discovery methods.* Parties may obtain discovery by one or more of the following methods: depositions upon oral examination or written questions; written interrogatories; production of documents or things or permission to enter upon land or other property for inspection and other purposes; physical and mental examinations; and requests for admission. Unless the court orders otherwise and under FL ST RCP Rule 1.280(c), the frequency of use of these methods is not limited, except as provided in FL ST RCP Rule 1.200, FL ST RCP Rule 1.340, and FL ST RCP Rule 1.370. FL ST RCP Rule 1.280(a).

b. *Scope of discovery.* Unless otherwise limited by order of the court in accordance with the Florida Rules of Civil Procedure, the scope of discovery is as follows:

i. *In general.* Parties may obtain discovery regarding any matter, not privileged, that is relevant to the subject matter of the pending action, whether it relates to the claim or defense of the party seeking discovery or the claim or defense of any other party, including the existence, description, nature, custody, condition, and location of any books, documents, or other tangible things and the identity and location of persons having knowledge of any discoverable matter. It is not ground for objection that the information sought will be inadmissible at the trial if the information sought appears reasonably calculated to lead to the discovery of admissible evidence. FL ST RCP Rule 1.280(b)(1).

ii. *Indemnity agreements.* A party may obtain discovery of the existence and contents of any agreement under which any person may be liable to satisfy part or all of a judgment that may be entered in the action or to indemnify or to reimburse a party for payments made to satisfy the judgment. Information concerning the agreement is not admissible in evidence at trial by reason of disclosure. FL ST RCP Rule 1.280(b)(2).

iii. *Electronically stored information.* A party may obtain discovery of electronically stored information in accordance with the Florida Rules of Civil Procedure. FL ST RCP Rule 1.280(b)(3).

iv. *Trial preparation; Materials.* Subject to the provisions of FL ST RCP Rule 1.280(b)(5), a party may obtain discovery of documents and tangible things otherwise discoverable under FL ST RCP Rule 1.280(b)(1) and prepared in anticipation of litigation or for trial by or for another party or by or for that party's representative, including that party's attorney, consultant, surety, indemnitor, insurer, or agent, only upon a showing that the party seeking discovery has need of the materials in the preparation of the case and is unable without undue hardship to obtain the substantial equivalent of the materials by other means. FL ST RCP Rule 1.280(b)(4).

- In ordering discovery of the materials when the required showing has been made, the court shall protect against disclosure of the mental impressions, conclusions, opinions, or legal theories of an attorney or other representative of a party concerning the litigation. FL ST RCP Rule 1.280(b)(4).

- Without the required showing a party may obtain a copy of a statement concerning the action or its subject matter previously made by that party. FL ST RCP Rule 1.280(b)(4).
- Upon request without the required showing a person not a party may obtain a copy of a statement concerning the action or its subject matter previously made by that person. If the request is refused, the person may move for an order to obtain a copy. The provisions of FL ST RCP Rule 1.380(a)(5) apply to the award of expenses incurred as a result of making the motion. FL ST RCP Rule 1.280(b)(4).
- For purposes of FL ST RCP Rule 1.280(b)(4), a statement previously made is a written statement signed or otherwise adopted or approved by the person making it, or a stenographic, mechanical, electrical, or other recording or transcription of it that is a substantially verbatim recital of an oral statement by the person making it and contemporaneously recorded. FL ST RCP Rule 1.280(b)(4).

v. *Trial preparation; Experts.* Discovery of facts known and opinions held by experts, otherwise discoverable under the provisions of FL ST RCP Rule 1.280(b)(1) and acquired or developed in anticipation of litigation or for trial, may be obtained only as follows:

- By interrogatories a party may require any other party to identify each person whom the other party expects to call as an expert witness at trial and to state the subject matter on which the expert is expected to testify, and to state the substance of the facts and opinions to which the expert is expected to testify and a summary of the grounds for each opinion. FL ST RCP Rule 1.280(b)(5)(A)(i).
- Any person disclosed by interrogatories or otherwise as a person expected to be called as an expert witness at trial may be deposed in accordance with FL ST RCP Rule 1.390 without motion or order of court. FL ST RCP Rule 1.280(b)(5)(A)(ii).
- A party may obtain the following discovery regarding any person disclosed by interrogatories or otherwise as a person expected to be called as an expert witness at trial: The scope of employment in the pending case and the compensation for such service, FL ST RCP Rule 1.280(b)(5)(A)(iii)(1); The expert's general litigation experience, including the percentage of work performed for plaintiffs and defendants, FL ST RCP Rule 1.280(b)(5)(A)(iii)(2); The identity of other cases, within a reasonable time period, in which the expert has testified by deposition or at trial, FL ST RCP Rule 1.280(b)(5)(A)(iii)(3); An approximation of the portion of the expert's involvement as an expert witness, which may be based on the number of hours, percentage of hours, or percentage of earned income derived from serving as an expert witness; however, the expert shall not be required to disclose his or her earnings as an expert witness or income derived from other services. FL ST RCP Rule 1.280(b)(5)(A)(iii)(4).
- An expert may be required to produce financial and business records only under the most unusual or compelling circumstances and may not be compelled to compile or produce nonexistent documents. Upon motion, the court may order further discovery by other means, subject to such restrictions as to scope and other provisions pursuant to FL ST RCP Rule 1.280(b)(5)(C) concerning fees and expenses as the court may deem appropriate. FL ST RCP Rule 1.280(b)(5).
- A party may discover facts known or opinions held by an expert who has been retained or specially employed by another party in anticipation of litigation or preparation for trial and who is not expected to be called as a witness at trial, only as provided in FL ST RCP Rule 1.360(b) or upon a showing of exceptional circumstances under which it is impracticable for the party seeking discovery to obtain facts or opinions on the same subject by other means. FL ST RCP Rule 1.280(b)(5)(B).
- Unless manifest injustice would result, the court shall require that the party seeking discovery pay the expert a reasonable fee for time spent in responding to discovery under FL ST RCP Rule 1.280(b)(5)(A) and FL ST RCP Rule 1.280(b)(5)(B); and concerning discovery from an expert obtained under FL ST RCP Rule 1.280(b)(5)(A) the court may require, and concerning discovery obtained under FL ST RCP Rule 1.280(b)(5)(B) shall

require, the party seeking discovery to pay the other party a fair part of the fees and expenses reasonably incurred by the latter party in obtaining facts and opinions from the expert. FL ST RCP Rule 1.280(b)(5)(C).

- As used in the Florida Rules of Civil Procedure an expert shall be an expert witness as defined in FL ST RCP Rule 1.390(a). FL ST RCP Rule 1.280(b)(5)(D).

vi. *Claims to privilege or protection.* When a party withholds information otherwise discoverable under the Florida Rules of Civil Procedure by claiming that it is privileged or subject to protection as trial preparation material, the party shall make the claim expressly and shall describe the nature of the documents, communications, or things not produced or disclosed in a manner that, without revealing information itself privileged or protected, will enable other parties to assess the applicability of the privilege or protection. FL ST RCP Rule 1.280(b)(6).

c. *Limitations on discovery of electronically stored information*

i. A person may object to discovery of electronically stored information from sources that the person identifies as not reasonably accessible because of burden or cost. On motion to compel discovery or for a protective order, the person from whom discovery is sought must show that the information sought or the format requested is not reasonably accessible because of undue burden or cost. If that showing is made, the court may nonetheless order the discovery from such sources or in such formats if the requesting party shows good cause. The court may specify conditions of the discovery, including ordering that some or all of the expenses incurred by the person from whom discovery is sought be paid by the party seeking the discovery. FL ST RCP Rule 1.280(d)(1).

ii. In determining any motion involving discovery of electronically stored information, the court must limit the frequency or extent of discovery otherwise allowed by the Florida Rules of Civil Procedure if it determines that (i) the discovery sought is unreasonably cumulative or duplicative, or can be obtained from another source or in another manner that is more convenient, less burdensome, or less expensive; or (ii) the burden or expense of the discovery outweighs its likely benefit, considering the needs of the case, the amount in controversy, the parties' resources, the importance of the issues at stake in the action, and the importance of the discovery in resolving the issues. FL ST RCP Rule 1.280(d)(2).

d. For information on inadvertent disclosure of privileged materials, see FL ST RCP Rule 1.285.

2. *Request for production of documents*

a. *Scope of request.* Any party may request any other party:

i. To produce and permit the party making the request, or someone acting in the requesting party's behalf, to inspect and copy any designated documents, including electronically stored information, writings, drawings, graphs, charts, photographs, phono-records, and other data compilations from which information can be obtained, translated, if necessary, by the party to whom the request is directed through detection devices into reasonably usable form, that constitute or contain matters within the scope of FL ST RCP Rule 1.280(b) and that are in the possession, custody, or control of the party to whom the request is directed;

ii. To inspect and copy, test, or sample any tangible things that constitute or contain matters within the scope of FL ST RCP Rule 1.280(b) and that are in the possession, custody, or control of the party to whom the request is directed; or

iii. To permit entry upon designated land or other property in the possession or control of the party upon whom the request is served for the purpose of inspection and measuring, surveying, photographing, testing, or sampling the property or any designated object or operation on it within the scope of FL ST RCP Rule 1.280(b). FL ST RCP Rule 1.350(a).

b. *Contents of request*

i. The request shall set forth the items to be inspected, either by individual item or category, and describe each item and category with reasonable particularity. The request shall specify a reasonable time, place, and manner of making the inspection or performing the related acts. FL ST RCP Rule 1.350(b).

ii. A request for electronically stored information may specify the form or forms in which electronically stored information is to be produced. If the responding party objects to a requested form, or if no form is specified in the request, the responding party must state the form or forms it intends to use. If a request for electronically stored information does not specify the form of production, the producing party must produce the information in a form or forms in which it is ordinarily maintained or in a reasonably usable form or forms. FL ST RCP Rule 1.350(b).

c. *Failure to respond to requests.* The party submitting the request may move for an order under FL ST RCP Rule 1.380 concerning any objection, failure to respond to the request, or any part of it, or failure to permit the inspection as requested. FL ST RCP Rule 1.350(b). Please see FL ST RCP Rule 1.380(d) and the KeyRules Motion to Compel Discovery documents for further information regarding compelling discovery and discovery sanctions.

i. *Response requirements.* For each item or category the response shall state that inspection and related activities will be permitted as requested unless the request is objected to, in which event the reasons for the objection shall be stated. If an objection is made to part of an item or category, the part shall be specified. When producing documents, the producing party shall either produce them as they are kept in the usual course of business or shall identify them to correspond with the categories in the request. If the responding party objects to a requested form (for electronic information), or if no form is specified in the request, the responding party must state the form or forms it intends to use. If a request for electronically stored information does not specify the form of production, the producing party must produce the information in a form or forms in which it is ordinarily maintained or in a reasonably usable form or forms. FL ST RCP Rule 1.350(b).

3. *Requests to a non-party*

a. *Independent action not prohibited.* FL ST RCP Rule 1.350 does not preclude an independent action against a person not a party for production of documents and things and permission to enter upon land. FL ST RCP Rule 1.350(c). FL ST RCP Rule 1.351 does not affect the right of any party to bring an independent action for production of documents and things or permission to enter upon land. FL ST RCP Rule 1.351(f).

b. *Scope.* A party may seek inspection and copying of any documents or things within the scope of FL ST RCP Rule 1.350(a) from a person who is not a party by issuance of a subpoena directing the production of the documents or things when the requesting party does not seek to depose the custodian or other person in possession of the documents or things. FL ST RCP Rule 1.351 provides the exclusive procedure for obtaining documents or things by subpoena from nonparties without deposing the custodian or other person in possession of the documents or things pursuant to FL ST RCP Rule 1.310. FL ST RCP Rule 1.351(a).

i. *Procedure.* The proposed subpoena shall be attached to the notice and shall state the time, place, and method for production of the documents or things, and the name and address of the person who is to produce the documents or things, if known, and if not known, a general description sufficient to identify the person or the particular class or group to which the person belongs; shall include a designation of the items to be produced; and shall state that the person who will be asked to produce the documents or things has the right to object to the production under FL ST RCP Rule 1.351 and that the person will not be required to surrender the documents or things. A copy of the notice and proposed subpoena shall not be furnished to the person upon whom the subpoena is to be served. If any party serves an objection to production under FL ST RCP Rule 1.351 within ten (10) days of service of the notice, the documents or things shall not be produced pending resolution of the objection in accordance with FL ST RCP Rule 1.351(d). FL ST RCP Rule 1.351(b).

ii. *Subpoena.* If no objection is made by a party under FL ST RCP Rule 1.351(b), an attorney of record in the action may issue a subpoena or the party desiring production shall deliver to the clerk for issuance a subpoena together with a certificate of counsel or pro se party that no timely objection has been received from any party, and the clerk shall issue the subpoena and deliver it to the party desiring production. FL ST RCP Rule 1.351(c).

- The subpoena shall be identical to the copy attached to the notice and shall specify that no testimony may be taken and shall require only production of the documents or things specified in it. FL ST RCP Rule 1.351(c).

- The subpoena may give the recipient an option to deliver or mail legible copies of the documents or things to the party serving the subpoena. FL ST RCP Rule 1.351(c).
- The person upon whom the subpoena is served may condition the preparation of copies on the payment in advance of the reasonable costs of preparing the copies. FL ST RCP Rule 1.351(c).
- The subpoena shall require production only in the county of the residence of the custodian or other person in possession of the documents or things or in the county where the documents or things are located or where the custodian or person in possession usually conducts business. FL ST RCP Rule 1.351(c).
- If the person upon whom the subpoena is served objects at any time before the production of the documents or things, the documents or things shall not be produced under FL ST RCP Rule 1.351, and relief may be obtained pursuant to FL ST RCP Rule 1.310. FL ST RCP Rule 1.351(c).

iii. *Ruling on objection.* If an objection is made by a party under FL ST RCP Rule 1.351(b), the party desiring production may file a motion with the court seeking a ruling on the objection or may proceed pursuant to FL ST RCP Rule 1.310. FL ST RCP Rule 1.351(d).

iv. *Copies furnished.* If the subpoena is complied with by delivery or mailing of copies as provided in FL ST RCP Rule 1.351(c), the party receiving the copies shall furnish a legible copy of each item furnished to any other party who requests it upon the payment of the reasonable cost of preparing the copies. FL ST RCP Rule 1.351(e).

4. *Arbitration and mediation*

a. *Referral to arbitration and mediation.* Except as hereinafter provided or as otherwise prohibited by law, the presiding judge may enter an order referring all or any part of a contested civil matter to mediation or arbitration. The parties to any contested civil matter may file a written stipulation to mediate or arbitrate any issue between them at any time. Such stipulation shall be incorporated into the order of referral. FL ST RCP Rule 1.700(a).

b. *Arbitration*

i. *Exclusions.* A civil action shall be ordered to arbitration or arbitration in conjunction with mediation upon stipulation of the parties. A civil action may be ordered to arbitration or arbitration in conjunction with mediation upon motion of any party or by the court, if the judge determines the action to be of such a nature that arbitration could be of benefit to the litigants or the court. FL ST RCP Rule 1.800.

- Under no circumstances may the following categories of actions be referred to arbitration: (1) bond estreatures; (2) habeas corpus or other extraordinary writs; (3) bond validations; (4) civil or criminal contempt; (5) such other matters as may be specified by order of the chief judge in the circuit. FL ST RCP Rule 1.800.

ii. For more information regarding arbitration, please see FL ST RCP Rule 1.810; FL ST RCP Rule 1.820; FL ST RCP Rule 1.830; and FL ST 7 J CIR CV-2009-019-SC; and FL ST 7 J CIR CV-2003-002-SC(1)(c).

c. *Mediation.* For more information regarding mediation, please see FL ST RCP Rule 1.710; FL ST RCP Rule 1.720; FL ST RCP Rule 1.730; FL ST RCP Rule 1.750; FL ST 7 J CIR CV-2008-018-SC; and FL ST 7 J CIR CV-2003-002-SC(1).

5. *Rules of court*

a. *Rules of civil procedure.* The Florida Rules of Civil Procedure apply to all actions of a civil nature and all special statutory proceedings in the circuit courts and county courts except those to which the Florida Probate Rules, the Florida Family Law Rules of Procedure, or the Small Claims Rules apply. FL ST RCP Rule 1.010.

i. The form, content, procedure, and time for pleading in all special statutory proceedings shall be

as prescribed by the statutes governing the proceeding unless the Florida Rules of Civil Procedure specifically provide to the contrary. FL ST RCP Rule 1.010.

ii. The Florida Rules of Civil Procedure shall be construed to secure the just, speedy, and inexpensive determination of every action. FL ST RCP Rule 1.010.

b. *Rules of judicial administration.* The Florida Rules of Judicial Administration shall apply to administrative matters in all courts to which the Florida Rules of Judicial Administration are applicable by their terms. The Florida Rules of Judicial Administration shall be construed to secure the speedy and inexpensive determination of every proceeding to which they are applicable. The Florida Rules of Judicial Administration shall supersede all conflicting rules and statutes. FL ST J ADMIN Rule 2.110.

D. Documents

1. *Required documents*

a. *Request for production.* Please see the General Requirements section of this document for more information on the contents of the request for production.

i. *Notices to persons with disabilities.* See the Format section of this KeyRules document for further information.

b. *Certificate of service.* A certificate of service of the interrogatories shall be filed, giving the date of service and the name of the party to whom they were directed. FL ST RCP Rule 1.340(e). When any attorney certifies in substance: "I certify that a copy hereof has been furnished to (here insert name or names and addresses used for service) by (e-mail) (delivery) (mail) (fax) on .... (date) ....______________ Attorney" the certificate is taken as prima facie proof of such service in compliance with FL ST J ADMIN Rule 2.516. FL ST J ADMIN Rule 2.516(f).

2. *Supplemental documents*

a. *Notice of intent to serve subpoena/Subpoena.* Please see the General Requirements section of this document for more information.

E. Format

1. *Documents; Type and size.* Documents subject to the exceptions set forth in FL ST J ADMIN Rule 2.525(d) shall be filed on recycled paper measuring eight and one half by eleven (8 1/2 by 11) inches. For purposes of FL ST J ADMIN Rule 2.520, paper is recycled if it contains a minimum content of fifty (50) percent waste paper. Xerographic reduction of legal-size (eight and one half by fourteen (8 1/2 by 14) inches) documents to letter size (eight and one half by eleven (8 1/2 by 11) inches) is prohibited. All other documents filed by electronic transmission shall be filed in a format capable of being printed in a format consistent with the provisions of FL ST J ADMIN Rule 2.250. FL ST J ADMIN Rule 2.520(b).

a. *Exhibits.* Any exhibit or attachment filed with pleadings or papers may be filed in its original size. FL ST J ADMIN Rule 2.520(c).

b. *Recording space.* On all papers and documents prepared and filed by the court or by any party to a proceeding which are to be recorded in the public records of any county, including but not limited to final money judgments and notices of lis pendens, a three (3) inch by three (3) inch space at the top right-hand corner on the first page and a one (1) inch by three (3) inch space at the top right-hand corner on each subsequent page shall be left blank and reserved for use by the clerk of court. FL ST J ADMIN Rule 2.520(d).

i. *Exceptions to recording space.* Any papers or documents created by persons or entities over which the filing party has no control, including but not limited to wills, codicils, trusts, or other testamentary documents; documents prepared or executed by any public officer; documents prepared, executed, acknowledged, or proved outside of the State of Florida; or documents created by State or Federal government agencies, may be filed without the space required by FL ST J ADMIN Rule 2.520. FL ST J ADMIN Rule 2.520(e).

c. *Noncompliance.* No clerk of court is permitted to refuse to file any document or paper because of noncompliance with the Florida Rules of Judicial Administration. However, upon request of the clerk of court, noncomplying documents must be resubmitted in accordance with the formatting rules. FL ST J ADMIN Rule 2.520(f).

2. *Caption.* Every pleading, motion, order, judgment, or other paper shall have a caption containing the name of the court, the file number, and except for in rem proceedings, including forfeiture proceedings, the name of the first party on each side with an appropriate indication of other parties, and a designation identifying the party filing it and its nature or the nature of the order, as the case may be. In any in rem proceeding, every pleading, motion, order, judgment, or other paper shall have a caption containing the name of the court, the file number, the style "In re" (followed by the name or general description of the property), and a designation of the person or entity filing it and its nature or the nature of the order, as the case may be. In an in rem forfeiture proceeding, the style shall be "In re forfeiture of" (followed by the name of the general description of the property). All papers filed in the action shall be styled in such a manner as to indicate clearly the subject matter of the paper and the party requesting or obtaining relief. FL ST RCP Rule 1.100(c)(1).
    a. *Volusia County eminent domain cases.* All orders, pleadings, motions and other papers will bear the initial case style. Documents intended to apply only to particular parcel(s) will indicate in their caption the parcel number(s) to which they apply and sufficient copies shall be provided to the Clerk of Court to allow the filing and docketing of each relevant paper in each parcel file. FL ST 7 J CIR CV-2000-011-VL(b).
3. *Writing and written defined.* Writing or written means a document containing information, an application, or a stipulation. FL ST RCP Rule 1.080(c).
4. *Rule abbreviations*
    a. The Florida Rules of Civil Procedure and shall be abbreviated as Fla.R.Civ.P. FL ST RCP Rule 1.010.
    b. The Florida Rules of Judicial Administration shall be abbreviated as Fla. R. Jud. Admin. FL ST J ADMIN Rule 2.110.
5. *Nonverification.* Except when otherwise specifically provided by the Florida Rules of Civil Procedure or an applicable statute, every pleading or other document of a party represented by an attorney need not be verified or accompanied by an affidavit. FL ST RCP Rule 1.030; FL ST J ADMIN Rule 2.515(a).
6. *Attorney signature*
    a. *Attorney signature.* Every pleading and other document of a party represented by an attorney shall be signed by at least one (1) attorney of record in that attorney's individual name whose current record Florida Bar address, telephone number, including area code, primary e-mail address and secondary e-mail addresses, if any, and Florida Bar number shall be stated, and who shall be duly licensed to practice law in Florida or who shall have received permission to appear in the particular case as provided in FL ST J ADMIN Rule 2.510. FL ST J ADMIN Rule 2.515(a).
        i. The attorney may be required by the court to give the address of, and to vouch for the attorney's authority to represent, the party. FL ST J ADMIN Rule 2.515(a).
        ii. The signature of an attorney shall constitute a certificate by the attorney that the attorney has read the pleading or other document; that to the best of the attorney's knowledge, information, and belief there is good ground to support it; and that it is not interposed for delay. FL ST J ADMIN Rule 2.515(a).
        iii. If a pleading is not signed or is signed with intent to defeat the purpose of FL ST J ADMIN Rule 2.515, it may be stricken and the action may proceed as though the pleading or other document had not been served. FL ST J ADMIN Rule 2.515(a).
    b. *Pro se litigant signature.* A party who is not represented by an attorney shall sign any pleading or other paper and state the party's address and telephone number, including area code. FL ST J ADMIN Rule 2.515(b).
    c. *Form of signature*
        i. The signatures required on pleadings and documents by FL ST J ADMIN Rule 2.515(a) and FL ST J ADMIN Rule 2.515(b) may be:
            - Original signatures;
            - Original signatures that have been reproduced by electronic means, such as on electronically transmitted documents or photocopied documents;

- Electronic signatures using the "/s/," "s/," or "/s" formats by or at the direction of the person signing; or
- Any other signature format authorized by general law, so long as the clerk where the proceeding is pending has the capability of receiving and has obtained approval from the Supreme Court of Florida to accept pleadings and documents with that signature format. FL ST J ADMIN Rule 2.515(c)(1).

ii. An attorney, party, or other person who files a pleading or paper by electronic transmission that does not contain the original signature of that attorney, party, or other person shall file that identical pleading or paper in paper form containing an original signature of that attorney, party, or other person (hereinafter called the follow-up filing) immediately thereafter. The follow-up filing is not required if the Supreme Court of Florida has entered an order directing the clerk of court to discontinue accepting the follow-up filing. FL ST J ADMIN Rule 2.515(c)(2).

7. *Forms*

a. *Process.* The forms of process, notice of lis pendens, and notice of action provided in the Florida Rules of Civil Procedure are sufficient. Variations from the forms do not void process or notices that are otherwise sufficient. FL ST RCP Rule 1.900(a).

b. *Other forms.* The other forms provided in the Florida Rules of Civil Procedure are sufficient for the matters that are covered by them. So long as the substance is expressed without prolixity, the forms may be varied to meet the facts of a particular case. FL ST RCP Rule 1.900(b).

c. *Formal matters.* Captions, except for the designation of the paper, are omitted from the forms provided in the Florida Rules of Civil Procedure. A general form of caption is the first form provided. Signatures are omitted from pleadings and motions. FL ST RCP Rule 1.900(c).

8. *Notices to persons with disabilities.* All notices of court proceedings to be held in a public facility, and all process compelling appearance at such proceedings, shall include the following statement in bold face, fourteen (14) point Times New Roman or Courier font: "If you are a person with a disability who needs any accommodation in order to participate in this proceeding, you are entitled, at no cost to you, to the provision of certain assistance. Please contact [identify applicable court personnel by name, address, and telephone number] at least seven (7) days before your scheduled court appearance, or immediately upon receiving this notification if the time before the scheduled appearance is less than seven (7) days; if you are hearing or voice impaired, call 711." FL ST J ADMIN Rule 2.540(c)(1).

9. *Minimization of the filing of sensitive information*

a. *Limitations for court filings.* Unless authorized by FL ST J ADMIN Rule 2.425(b), statute, another rule of court, or the court orders otherwise, designated sensitive information filed with the court must be limited to the following format:

i. The initials of a person known to be a minor;

ii. The year of birth of a person's birth date;

iii. No portion of any: Social security number, Bank account number, Credit card account number, Charge account number, or Debit account number;

iv. The last four digits of any: Taxpayer identification number (TIN), Employee identification number, Driver's license number, Passport number, Telephone number, Financial account number, except as set forth in FL ST J ADMIN Rule 2.425(a)(3), Brokerage account number, Insurance policy account number, Loan account number, Customer account number, or Patient or health care number;

v. A truncated version of any: Email address, Computer user name, Password, or Personal identification number (PIN); and

vi. A truncated version of any other sensitive information as provided by court order. FL ST J ADMIN Rule 2.425(a).

b. *Exceptions.* FL ST J ADMIN Rule 2.425(a) does not apply to the following:

i. An account number which identifies the property alleged to be the subject of a proceeding;

ii. The record of an administrative or agency proceeding;

iii. The record in appellate or review proceedings;

iv. The birth date of a minor whenever the birth date is necessary for the court to establish or maintain subject matter jurisdiction;

v. The name of a minor in any order relating to parental responsibility, time-sharing, or child support;

vi. The name of a minor in any document or order affecting the minor's ownership of real property;

vii. The birth date of a party in a writ of attachment or notice to payor;

viii. In traffic and criminal proceedings: a pro se filing; a court filing that is related to a criminal matter or investigation and that is prepared before the filing of a criminal charge or is not filed as part of any docketed criminal case; an arrest or search warrant or any information in support thereof; a charging document and an affidavit or other documents filed in support of any charging document, including any driving records; a statement of particulars; discovery material introduced into evidence or otherwise filed with the court; and all information necessary for the proper issuance and execution of a subpoena duces tecum;

ix. Information used by the clerk for case maintenance purposes or the courts for case management purposes; and

x. Information which is relevant and material to an issue before the court. FL ST J ADMIN Rule 2.425(b).

c. *Remedies.* Upon motion by a party or interested person or sua sponte by the court, the court may order remedies, sanctions or both for a violation of FL ST J ADMIN Rule 2.425(a). Following notice and an opportunity to respond, the court may impose sanctions if such filing was not made in good faith. FL ST J ADMIN Rule 2.425(c).

d. *Motions not restricted.* FL ST J ADMIN Rule 2.425 does not restrict a party's right to move for protective order, to move to file documents under seal, or to request a determination of the confidentiality of records. FL ST J ADMIN Rule 2.425(d).

e. *Application.* FL ST J ADMIN Rule 2.425 does not affect the application of constitutional provisions, statutes, or rules of court regarding confidential information or access to public information. FL ST J ADMIN Rule 2.425(e).

F. Filing and Service Requirements

1. *Court filing of documents and discovery.* Information obtained during discovery shall not be filed with the court until such time as it is filed for good cause. The requirement of good cause is satisfied only where the filing of the information is allowed or required by another applicable rule of procedure or by court order. All filings of discovery documents shall comply with FL ST J ADMIN Rule 2.425. The court shall have the authority to impose sanctions for violation of FL ST RCP Rule 1.280. FL ST RCP Rule 1.280(g).

   a. Unless required by the court, a party shall not file any of the documents or things produced with the response. Documents or things may be filed in compliance with FL ST J ADMIN Rule 2.425 and FL ST RCP Rule 1.280(g) when they should be considered by the court in determining a matter pending before the court. FL ST RCP Rule 1.350(d).

2. *Filing requirements.* All original documents must be filed with the court either before service or immediately thereafter, unless otherwise provided for by general law or other rules. If the original of any bond or other document is not placed in the court file, a certified copy must be so placed by the clerk. FL ST J ADMIN Rule 2.516(d). All documents shall be filed in conformity with the requirements of FL ST J ADMIN Rule 2.525. FL ST RCP Rule 1.080(b). All documents filed in any court shall be filed by electronic transmission in accordance with FL ST J ADMIN Rule 2.525. "Documents" means pleadings, motions, petitions, memoranda, briefs, notices, exhibits, declarations, affidavits, orders, judgments, decrees, writs, opinions, and any other paper or writing submitted to a court. FL ST J ADMIN Rule 2.520(a). All documents that are court records, as defined in FL ST J ADMIN Rule 2.430(a)(1), must be filed by electronic transmission, provided that: (1) the clerk has the ability to accept and retain such documents; (2) the clerk or the chief judge of the circuit has requested permission to accept documents

filed by electronic transmission; and (3) the supreme court has entered an order granting permission to the clerk to accept documents filed by electronic transmission. FL ST J ADMIN Rule 2.525(c)(1).

a. *Definition.* "Electronic transmission of documents" means the sending of information by electronic signals to, by or from a court or clerk, which when received can be transformed and stored or transmitted on paper, microfilm, magnetic storage device, optical imaging system, CD-ROM, flash drive, other electronic data storage system, server, case maintenance system ("CM"), electronic court filing ("ECF") system, statewide or local electronic portal ("e-portal"), or other electronic record keeping system authorized by the supreme court in a format sufficient to communicate the information on the original document in a readable format. Electronic transmission of documents includes electronic mail ("e-mail") and any internet-based transmission procedure, and may include procedures allowing for documents to be signed or verified by electronic means. FL ST J ADMIN Rule 2.525(a).

   i. The filing of documents with the court as required by the Florida Rules of Judicial Administration must be made by filing them with the clerk in accordance with FL ST J ADMIN Rule 2.525, except that the judge may permit documents to be filed with the judge, in which event the judge must note the filing date before him or her on the documents and transmit them to the clerk. The date of filing is that shown on the face of the document by the judge's notation or the clerk's time stamp, whichever is earlier. FL ST J ADMIN Rule 2.516(e).

b. *Application.* Any court or clerk of the court may accept the electronic transmission of documents for filing after the clerk, together with input from the chief judge of the circuit, has obtained approval of the procedures and program for doing so from the Supreme Court of Florida. FL ST J ADMIN Rule 2.525(b).

c. *Exceptions*

   i. Paper documents and other submissions may be manually submitted to the clerk or court:

      - When the clerk does not have the ability to accept and retain documents by electronic filing or has not had ECF Procedures approved by the supreme court;
      - For filing by any self-represented party or any self-represented nonparty unless specific ECF Procedures provide a means to file documents electronically. However, any self-represented nonparty that is a governmental or public agency and any other agency, partnership, corporation, or business entity acting on behalf of any governmental or public agency may file documents by electronic transmission if such entity has the capability of filing documents electronically;
      - For filing by attorneys excused from e-mail service in accordance with FL ST J ADMIN Rule 2.516(b);
      - When submitting evidentiary exhibits or filing non-documentary materials;
      - When the filing involves documents in excess of twenty-five (25) megabytes (25MB) in size. For such filings, documents may be transmitted using an electronic storage medium that the clerk has the ability to accept, which may include a CD-ROM, flash drive, or similar storage medium;
      - When filed in open court, as permitted by the court;
      - When paper filing is permitted by any approved statewide or local ECF procedures; and
      - If any court determines that justice so requires. FL ST J ADMIN Rule 2.525(d).

   ii. Any document in paper form submitted under FL ST J ADMIN Rule 2.525(d) is filed when it is received by the clerk or court and the clerk shall immediately thereafter convert any filed paper document to an electronic document. "Convert to an electronic document" means optically capturing an image of a paper document and using character recognition software to recover as much of the document's text as practicable and then indexing and storing the document in the official court file. FL ST J ADMIN Rule 2.525(c)(4).

   iii. Any storage medium submitted under FL ST J ADMIN Rule 2.525(d)(5) is filed when received by the clerk or court and the clerk shall immediately thereafter transfer the electronic documents from the storage device to the official court file. FL ST J ADMIN Rule 2.525(c)(5).

iv. If the filer of any paper document authorized under FL ST J ADMIN Rule 2.525(d) provides a self-addressed, postage-paid envelope for return of the paper document after it is converted to electronic form by the clerk, the clerk shall place the paper document in the envelope and deposit it in the mail. Except when a paper document is required to be maintained, the clerk may recycle any filed paper document that is not to be returned to the filer. FL ST J ADMIN Rule 2.525(c)(6).

v. The clerk may convert any paper document filed before the effective date of FL ST J ADMIN Rule 2.525 to an electronic document. Unless the clerk is required to maintain the paper document, if the paper document has been converted to an electronic document by the clerk, the paper document is no longer part of the official court file and may be removed and recycled. FL ST J ADMIN Rule 2.525(c)(7).

d. *Official court file.* For information on what constitutes the official court file, please see FL ST J ADMIN Rule 2.525(c)(2), FL ST J ADMIN Rule 2.525(c)(3).

e. *Administration.* All attorneys, parties, or other persons using this rule to file documents are required to make arrangements with the court or clerk for the payment of any charges authorized by general law or the supreme court before filing any document by electronic transmission. FL ST J ADMIN Rule 2.525(f)(2).

f. *Filing date.* The filing date for an electronically transmitted document is the date and time that such filing is acknowledged by an electronic stamp or otherwise, pursuant to any procedure set forth in any ECF Procedures approved by the supreme court, or the date the last page of such filing is received by the court or clerk. FL ST J ADMIN Rule 2.525(f)(3).

g. *Accessibility.* All documents transmitted in any electronic form under FL ST J ADMIN Rule 2.525 must comply with the accessibility requirements of FL ST J ADMIN Rule 2.526. FL ST J ADMIN Rule 2.525(g).

3. *Service requirements.* Every pleading subsequent to the initial pleading, all orders, and every other document filed in the action must be served in conformity with the requirements of FL ST J ADMIN Rule 2.516. FL ST RCP Rule 1.080(a).

a. *Service; When required.* Unless the court otherwise orders, or a statute or supreme court administrative order specifies a different means of service, every pleading subsequent to the initial pleading and every other document filed in any court proceeding, except applications for witness subpoenas and documents served by formal notice or required to be served in the manner provided for service of formal notice, must be served in accordance with FL ST J ADMIN Rule 2.516 on each party. No service need be made on parties against whom a default has been entered, except that pleadings asserting new or additional claims against them must be served in the manner provided for service of summons. FL ST J ADMIN Rule 2.516(a).

b. *Service; How made.* When service is required or permitted to be made upon a party represented by an attorney, service must be made upon the attorney unless service upon the party is ordered by the court. FL ST J ADMIN Rule 2.516(b).

i. *Service by electronic mail ("e-mail").* All documents required or permitted to be served on another party must be served by e-mail, unless FL ST J ADMIN Rule 2.516 otherwise provides. When, in addition to service by e-mail, the sender also utilizes another means of service provided for in FL ST J ADMIN Rule 2.516(b)(2), any differing time limits and other provisions applicable to that other means of service control. FL ST J ADMIN Rule 2.516(b)(1). Any document electronically transmitted to a court or clerk must also be served on all parties and interested persons in accordance with the applicable rules of court. FL ST J ADMIN Rule 2.525(e)(2).

- *Service on attorneys.* Upon appearing in a proceeding, an attorney must serve a designation of a primary e-mail address and may designate no more than two (2) secondary e-mail addresses. Thereafter, service must be directed to all designated e-mail addresses in that proceeding. Every document filed by an attorney thereafter must include the primary e-mail address of that attorney and any secondary e-mail addresses. If an attorney does not designate any e-mail address for service, documents may be served on that attorney at the e-mail address on record with The Florida Bar. FL ST J ADMIN Rule 2.516(b)(1)(A).

- *Exception to e-mail service on attorneys.* Service by an attorney on another attorney must be made by e-mail unless excused by the court. Upon motion by an attorney demonstrating that the attorney has no e-mail account and lacks access to the Internet at the attorney's office, the court may excuse the attorney from the requirements of e-mail service. Service on and by an attorney excused by the court from e-mail service must be by the means provided in FL ST J ADMIN Rule 2.516(b)(2). FL ST J ADMIN Rule 2.516(b)(1)(B).
- *Service on and by parties not represented by an attorney.* Any party not represented by an attorney may serve a designation of a primary e-mail address and also may designate no more than two (2) secondary e-mail addresses to which service must be directed in that proceeding by the means provided in FL ST J ADMIN Rule 2.516(b)(1). If a party not represented by an attorney does not designate an e-mail address for service in a proceeding, service on and by that party must be by the means provided in FL ST J ADMIN Rule 2.516(b)(2). FL ST J ADMIN Rule 2.516(b)(1)(C).
- *Time of service.* Service by e-mail is complete when it is sent. FL ST J ADMIN Rule 2.516(b)(1)(D). An e-mail is deemed served on the date it is sent. FL ST J ADMIN Rule 2.516(b)(1)(D)(i). If the sender learns that the e-mail did not reach the address of the person to be served, the sender must immediately send another copy by e-mail, or by a means authorized by FL ST J ADMIN Rule 2.516(b)(2). FL ST J ADMIN Rule 2.516(b)(1)(D)(ii). E-mail service is treated as service by mail for the computation of time. FL ST J ADMIN Rule 2.516(b)(1)(D)(iii).

ii. *Format of e-mail for service.* Service of a document by e-mail is made by attaching a copy of the document in PDF format to an e-mail sent to all addresses designated by the attorney or party. FL ST J ADMIN Rule 2.516(b)(1)(E).

- All documents served by e-mail must be attached to an e-mail message containing a subject line beginning with the words "SERVICE OF COURT DOCUMENT" in all capital letters, followed by the case number of the proceeding in which the documents are being served. FL ST J ADMIN Rule 2.516(b)(1)(E)(i).
- The body of the e-mail must identify the court in which the proceeding is pending, the case number, the name of the initial party on each side, the title of each document served with that e-mail, and the sender's name and telephone number. FL ST J ADMIN Rule 2.516(b)(1)(E)(ii).
- Any document served by e-mail may be signed by the "/s/" format, as long as the filed original is signed in accordance with the applicable rule of procedure. FL ST J ADMIN Rule 2.516(b)(1)(E)(iii).
- Any e-mail which, together with its attached documents, exceeds five megabytes (5MB) in size, must be divided and sent as separate e-mails, no one of which may exceed five megabytes (5MB) in size and each of which must be sequentially numbered in the subject line. FL ST J ADMIN Rule 2.516(b)(1)(E)(iv).

iii. *Service by other means.* In addition to, and not in lieu of, service by e-mail, service may also be made upon attorneys by any of the means specified in FL ST J ADMIN Rule 2.516(b)(2). Service on and by all parties who are not represented by an attorney and who do not designate an e-mail address, and on and by all attorneys excused from e-mail service, must be made by delivering a copy of the document or by mailing it to the party or attorney at their last known address or, if no address is known, by leaving it with the clerk of the court. Service by mail is complete upon mailing. Delivery of a copy within FL ST J ADMIN Rule 2.516 is complete upon:

- Handing it to the attorney or to the party,
- Leaving it at the attorney's or party's office with a clerk or other person in charge thereof,
- If there is no one in charge, leaving it in a conspicuous place therein,

- If the office is closed or the person to be served has no office, leaving it at the person's usual place of abode with some person of his or her family above fifteen (15) years of age and informing such person of the contents, or
- Transmitting it by facsimile to the attorney's or party's office with a cover sheet containing the sender's name, firm, address, telephone number, and facsimile number, and the number of pages transmitted. When service is made by facsimile, a copy must also be served by any other method permitted by FL ST J ADMIN Rule 2.516. Facsimile service occurs when transmission is complete. FL ST J ADMIN Rule 2.516(b)(2)(A) through FL ST J ADMIN Rule 2.516(b)(2)(E).
- Service by delivery after 5:00 p.m. must be deemed to have been made by mailing on the date of delivery. FL ST J ADMIN Rule 2.516(b)(2)(F).

c. *Service; Numerous defendants.* In actions when the parties are unusually numerous, the court may regulate the service contemplated by the Florida Rules of Judicial Administration on motion or on its own initiative in such manner as may be found to be just and reasonable. FL ST J ADMIN Rule 2.516(c).

d. *Service by clerk.* Service of notices and other documents required to be made by the clerk must also be done as provided in FL ST J ADMIN Rule 2.516(b). FL ST J ADMIN Rule 2.516(g).

G. Hearings

1. There is no hearing required or contemplated with regard to requests for production of documents in the Florida Rules of Civil Procedure.

H. Forms

1. Official Request for Production Forms for Florida

a. Caption. FL ST RCP Form 1.901.

b. Subpoena duces tecum for trial. FL ST RCP Form 1.911.

c. Notice of production from nonparty. FL ST RCP Form 1.921.

d. Subpoena duces tecum without deposition. FL ST RCP Form 1.922.

2. Requests for Production Forms for Florida

a. Request for production; Documents. FL-PRACFORM § 8:29.

b. Request for inspection; Documents, deposition. FL-PRACFORM § 8:30.

c. Request for inspection; Tangible things. FL-PRACFORM § 8:31.

d. Request for entry; Real property. FL-PRACFORM § 8:32.

e. Request for production; Documents, response. FL-PRACFORM § 8:33.

f. Request for inspection; Response, tangible things. FL-PRACFORM § 8:34.

g. Request for entry; Response, land and buildings. FL-PRACFORM § 8:35.

h. Production of documents; Nonparty, notice. FL-PRACFORM § 8:36.

i. Production of documents; Nonparty, objection. FL-PRACFORM § 8:37.

j. Request; Production of documents for inspection and copying. FL-PP § 3:115.

k. Notice of request for production from nonparty. FL-PP § 3:116.

l. Request; For permission to enter on land; To inspect and photograph. FL-PP § 3:127.

I. Checklist

(I) ❑ Matters to be considered by requesting party

(a) ❑ Required documents

(1) ❑ Request

(2) ❑ Certificate of service

- (b) ❑ Supplemental documents
  - (1) ❑ Notice of intent to serve subpoena
- (c) ❑ Time for request
  - (1) ❑ Without leave of court the request may be served on the plaintiff after commencement of the action and on any other party with or after service of the process and initial pleading on that party
  - (2) ❑ A party desiring production under FL ST RCP Rule 1.351 shall serve notice as provided in FL ST RCP Rule 1.080 on every other party of the intent to serve a subpoena under FL ST RCP Rule 1.351 at least ten (10) days before the subpoena is issued if service is by delivery and fifteen (15) days before the subpoena is issued if the service is by mail or e-mail
  - (3) ❑ No requests to produce shall be served later than forty-five (45) days prior to docket sounding

(II) ❑ Matters to be considered by responding party

- (a) ❑ Required documents
  - (1) ❑ Response to request
  - (2) ❑ Certificate of service
- (b) ❑ Supplemental documents
  - (1) ❑ Objections
- (c) ❑ Time for response
  - (1) ❑ The party to whom the request is directed shall serve a written response within thirty (30) days after service of the request, except that a defendant may serve a response within forty-five (45) days after service of the process and initial pleading on that defendant; the court may allow a shorter or longer time

Requests, Notices and Applications
Request for Admissions

Document Last Updated January 2013

A. Applicable Rules

1. *State rules*
   - a. Nonverification of pleadings. FL ST RCP Rule 1.030.
   - b. Service and filing of pleadings, orders, and documents. FL ST RCP Rule 1.080.
   - c. Time. FL ST RCP Rule 1.090.
   - d. Pleadings and motions. FL ST RCP Rule 1.100.
   - e. Pretrial procedure. FL ST RCP Rule 1.200.
   - f. General provisions governing discovery. FL ST RCP Rule 1.280.
   - g. Interrogatories to parties. FL ST RCP Rule 1.340.
   - h. Examination of persons. FL ST RCP Rule 1.360.
   - i. Requests for admission. FL ST RCP Rule 1.370.
   - j. Failure to make discovery; Sanctions. FL ST RCP Rule 1.380.
   - k. Depositions of expert witnesses. FL ST RCP Rule 1.390.
   - l. Relief from judgment, decrees, or orders. FL ST RCP Rule 1.540.
   - m. Forms. FL ST RCP Rule 1.900.
   - n. Minimization of the filing of sensitive information. FL ST J ADMIN Rule 2.425.

o. Retention of court records. FL ST J ADMIN Rule 2.430.
p. Foreign attorneys. FL ST J ADMIN Rule 2.510.
q. Signature of attorneys and parties. FL ST J ADMIN Rule 2.515.
r. Paper. FL ST J ADMIN Rule 2.520.
s. Electronic filing. FL ST J ADMIN Rule 2.525.
t. Accessibility of information and technology. FL ST J ADMIN Rule 2.526.
u. Requests for accommodations by persons with disabilities. FL ST J ADMIN Rule 2.540.

2. *Local rules*
   a. Eminent domain cases. FL ST 7 J CIR CV-2000-011-VL.
   b. Arbitration and mediation. FL ST 7 J CIR CV-2009-019-SC; FL ST 7 J CIR CV-2008-018-SC.
   c. Civil pretrial procedures. FL ST 7 J CIR CV-2003-002-SC.

B. Timing

1. *Request for admission.* Without leave of court the request may be served upon the plaintiff after commencement of the action and upon any other party with or after service of the process and initial pleading upon that party. FL ST RCP Rule 1.370(a).
   a. *Local requirement.* No interrogatories, requests to produce or requests for admissions shall be served later than forty-five (45) days prior to docket sounding. Exceptions shall be permitted only by written stipulation of the parties or by Court order. FL ST 7 J CIR CV-2003-002-SC.
2. *Sequence and timing of discovery.* Except as provided in FL ST RCP Rule 1.280(b)(5) or unless the court upon motion for the convenience of parties and witnesses and in the interest of justice orders otherwise, methods of discovery may be used in any sequence, and the fact that a party is conducting discovery, whether by deposition or otherwise, shall not delay any other party's discovery. FL ST RCP Rule 1.280(e).
   a. *Close of discovery.* Except as otherwise provided by FL ST 7 J CIR CV-2003-002-SC or agreed to by the parties in writing, discovery shall remain open until ten (10) days prior to docket sounding. FL ST 7 J CIR CV-2003-002-SC.
3. *Computation of time*
   a. *Generally.* Computation of time shall be governed by FL ST J ADMIN Rule 2.514. FL ST RCP Rule 1.090(a). The following rules apply in computing time periods specified in any rule of procedure, local rule, court order, or statute that does not specify a method of computing time. FL ST J ADMIN Rule 2.514(a).
      i. *Period stated in days or a longer unit.* When the period is stated in days or a longer unit of time (A) exclude the day of the event that triggers the period; (B) count every day, including intermediate Saturdays, Sundays, and legal holidays; and (C) include the last day of the period, but if the last day is a Saturday, Sunday, or legal holiday, or falls within any period of time extended through an order of the chief justice under FL ST J ADMIN Rule 2.205(a)(2)(B)(iv), the period continues to run until the end of the next day that is not a Saturday, Sunday, or legal holiday and does not fall within any period of time extended through an order of the chief justice. FL ST J ADMIN Rule 2.514(a)(1).
      ii. *Period stated in hours.* When the period is stated in hours (A) begin counting immediately on the occurrence of the event that triggers the period; (B) count every hour, including hours during intermediate Saturdays, Sundays, and legal holidays; and (C) if the period would end on a Saturday, Sunday, or legal holiday, or during any period of time extended through an order of the chief justice under FL ST J ADMIN Rule 2.205(a)(2)(B)(iv), the period continues to run until the same time on the next day that is not a Saturday, Sunday, or legal holiday and does not fall within any period of time extended through an order of the chief justice. FL ST J ADMIN Rule 2.514(a)(2).
      iii. *Period stated in days less than seven (7) days.* When the period stated in days is less than seven

(7) days, intermediate Saturdays, Sundays, and legal holidays shall be excluded in the computation. FL ST J ADMIN Rule 2.514(a)(3).

iv. *"Last day" defined.* Unless a different time is set by a statute, local rule, or court order, the last day ends (A) for electronic filing or for service by any means, at midnight; and (B) for filing by other means, when the clerk's office is scheduled to close. FL ST J ADMIN Rule 2.514(a)(4).

v. *"Next day" defined.* The "next day" is determined by continuing to count forward when the period is measured after an event and backward when measured before an event. FL ST J ADMIN Rule 2.514(a)(5).

vi. *"Legal holiday" defined.* "Legal holiday" means (A) the day set aside by FL ST § 110.117, for observing New Year's Day, Martin Luther King, Jr.'s Birthday, Memorial Day, Independence Day, Labor Day, Veterans' Day, Thanksgiving Day, the Friday after Thanksgiving Day, or Christmas Day, and (B) any day observed as a holiday by the clerk's office or as designated by the chief judge. FL ST J ADMIN Rule 2.514(a)(6).

b. *Additional time after service by mail or e-mail.* When a party may or must act within a specified time after service and service is made by mail or e-mail, five (5) days are added after the period that would otherwise expire under FL ST J ADMIN Rule 2.514(a). FL ST J ADMIN Rule 2.514(b).

c. *Enlargement.* When an act is required or allowed to be done at or within a specified time by order of court, by the Florida Rules of Civil Procedure, or by notice given thereunder, for cause shown the court at any time in its discretion (1) with or without notice, may order the period enlarged if request therefor is made before the expiration of the period originally prescribed or as extended by a previous order, or (2) upon motion made and notice after the expiration of the specified period, may permit the act to be done when failure to act was the result of excusable neglect, but it may not extend the time for making a motion for new trial, for rehearing, or to alter or amend a judgment; making a motion for relief from a judgment under FL ST RCP Rule 1.540(b); taking an appeal or filing a petition for certiorari; or making a motion for a directed verdict. FL ST RCP Rule 1.090(b).

d. *Unaffected by expiration of term.* The period of time provided for the doing of any act or the taking of any proceeding shall not be affected or limited by the continued existence or expiration of a term of court. The continued existence or expiration of a term of court in no way affects the power of a court to do any act or take any proceeding in any action which is or has been pending before it. FL ST RCP Rule 1.090(c).

C. General Requirements

1. *General provisions governing discovery*

a. *Discovery methods.* Parties may obtain discovery by one or more of the following methods: depositions upon oral examination or written questions; written interrogatories; production of documents or things or permission to enter upon land or other property for inspection and other purposes; physical and mental examinations; and requests for admission. Unless the court orders otherwise and under FL ST RCP Rule 1.280(c), the frequency of use of these methods is not limited, except as provided in FL ST RCP Rule 1.200, FL ST RCP Rule 1.340, and FL ST RCP Rule 1.370. FL ST RCP Rule 1.280(a).

b. *Scope of discovery.* Unless otherwise limited by order of the court in accordance with the Florida Rules of Civil Procedure, the scope of discovery is as follows:

i. *In general.* Parties may obtain discovery regarding any matter, not privileged, that is relevant to the subject matter of the pending action, whether it relates to the claim or defense of the party seeking discovery or the claim or defense of any other party, including the existence, description, nature, custody, condition, and location of any books, documents, or other tangible things and the identity and location of persons having knowledge of any discoverable matter. It is not ground for objection that the information sought will be inadmissible at the trial if the information sought appears reasonably calculated to lead to the discovery of admissible evidence. FL ST RCP Rule 1.280(b)(1).

ii. *Indemnity agreements.* A party may obtain discovery of the existence and contents of any agreement under which any person may be liable to satisfy part or all of a judgment that may be entered in the action or to indemnify or to reimburse a party for payments made to satisfy the judgment. Information concerning the agreement is not admissible in evidence at trial by reason of disclosure. FL ST RCP Rule 1.280(b)(2).

iii. *Electronically stored information.* A party may obtain discovery of electronically stored information in accordance with the Florida Rules of Civil Procedure. FL ST RCP Rule 1.280(b)(3).

iv. *Trial preparation; Materials.* Subject to the provisions of FL ST RCP Rule 1.280(b)(5), a party may obtain discovery of documents and tangible things otherwise discoverable under FL ST RCP Rule 1.280(b)(1) and prepared in anticipation of litigation or for trial by or for another party or by or for that party's representative, including that party's attorney, consultant, surety, indemnitor, insurer, or agent, only upon a showing that the party seeking discovery has need of the materials in the preparation of the case and is unable without undue hardship to obtain the substantial equivalent of the materials by other means. FL ST RCP Rule 1.280(b)(4).

- In ordering discovery of the materials when the required showing has been made, the court shall protect against disclosure of the mental impressions, conclusions, opinions, or legal theories of an attorney or other representative of a party concerning the litigation. FL ST RCP Rule 1.280(b)(4).
- Without the required showing a party may obtain a copy of a statement concerning the action or its subject matter previously made by that party. FL ST RCP Rule 1.280(b)(4).
- Upon request without the required showing a person not a party may obtain a copy of a statement concerning the action or its subject matter previously made by that person. If the request is refused, the person may move for an order to obtain a copy. The provisions of FL ST RCP Rule 1.380(a)(5) apply to the award of expenses incurred as a result of making the motion. FL ST RCP Rule 1.280(b)(4).
- For purposes of FL ST RCP Rule 1.280(b)(4), a statement previously made is a written statement signed or otherwise adopted or approved by the person making it, or a stenographic, mechanical, electrical, or other recording or transcription of it that is a substantially verbatim recital of an oral statement by the person making it and contemporaneously recorded. FL ST RCP Rule 1.280(b)(4).

v. *Trial preparation; Experts.* Discovery of facts known and opinions held by experts, otherwise discoverable under the provisions of FL ST RCP Rule 1.280(b)(1) and acquired or developed in anticipation of litigation or for trial, may be obtained only as follows:

- By interrogatories a party may require any other party to identify each person whom the other party expects to call as an expert witness at trial and to state the subject matter on which the expert is expected to testify, and to state the substance of the facts and opinions to which the expert is expected to testify and a summary of the grounds for each opinion. FL ST RCP Rule 1.280(b)(5)(A)(i).
- Any person disclosed by interrogatories or otherwise as a person expected to be called as an expert witness at trial may be deposed in accordance with FL ST RCP Rule 1.390 without motion or order of court. FL ST RCP Rule 1.280(b)(5)(A)(ii).
- A party may obtain the following discovery regarding any person disclosed by interrogatories or otherwise as a person expected to be called as an expert witness at trial: The scope of employment in the pending case and the compensation for such service, FL ST RCP Rule 1.280(b)(5)(A)(iii)(1); The expert's general litigation experience, including the percentage of work performed for plaintiffs and defendants, FL ST RCP Rule 1.280(b)(5)(A)(iii)(2); The identity of other cases, within a reasonable time period, in which the expert has testified by deposition or at trial, FL ST RCP Rule 1.280(b)(5)(A)(iii)(3); An approximation of the portion of the expert's involvement as an expert witness, which may be based on the number of hours, percentage of hours, or percentage of earned income derived from serving as an expert witness; however, the expert shall not be required to disclose his or her earnings as an expert witness or income derived from other services. FL ST RCP Rule 1.280(b)(5)(A)(iii)(4).

- An expert may be required to produce financial and business records only under the most unusual or compelling circumstances and may not be compelled to compile or produce nonexistent documents. Upon motion, the court may order further discovery by other means, subject to such restrictions as to scope and other provisions pursuant to FL ST RCP Rule 1.280(b)(5)(C) concerning fees and expenses as the court may deem appropriate. FL ST RCP Rule 1.280(b)(5).
- A party may discover facts known or opinions held by an expert who has been retained or specially employed by another party in anticipation of litigation or preparation for trial and who is not expected to be called as a witness at trial, only as provided in FL ST RCP Rule 1.360(b) or upon a showing of exceptional circumstances under which it is impracticable for the party seeking discovery to obtain facts or opinions on the same subject by other means. FL ST RCP Rule 1.280(b)(5)(B).
- Unless manifest injustice would result, the court shall require that the party seeking discovery pay the expert a reasonable fee for time spent in responding to discovery under FL ST RCP Rule 1.280(b)(5)(A) and FL ST RCP Rule 1.280(b)(5)(B); and concerning discovery from an expert obtained under FL ST RCP Rule 1.280(b)(5)(A) the court may require, and concerning discovery obtained under FL ST RCP Rule 1.280(b)(5)(B) shall require, the party seeking discovery to pay the other party a fair part of the fees and expenses reasonably incurred by the latter party in obtaining facts and opinions from the expert. FL ST RCP Rule 1.280(b)(5)(C).
- As used in the Florida Rules of Civil Procedure an expert shall be an expert witness as defined in FL ST RCP Rule 1.390(a). FL ST RCP Rule 1.280(b)(5)(D).

vi. *Claims to privilege or protection.* When a party withholds information otherwise discoverable under the Florida Rules of Civil Procedure by claiming that it is privileged or subject to protection as trial preparation material, the party shall make the claim expressly and shall describe the nature of the documents, communications, or things not produced or disclosed in a manner that, without revealing information itself privileged or protected, will enable other parties to assess the applicability of the privilege or protection. FL ST RCP Rule 1.280(b)(6).

c. *Limitations on discovery of electronically stored information*

i. A person may object to discovery of electronically stored information from sources that the person identifies as not reasonably accessible because of burden or cost. On motion to compel discovery or for a protective order, the person from whom discovery is sought must show that the information sought or the format requested is not reasonably accessible because of undue burden or cost. If that showing is made, the court may nonetheless order the discovery from such sources or in such formats if the requesting party shows good cause. The court may specify conditions of the discovery, including ordering that some or all of the expenses incurred by the person from whom discovery is sought be paid by the party seeking the discovery. FL ST RCP Rule 1.280(d)(1).

ii. In determining any motion involving discovery of electronically stored information, the court must limit the frequency or extent of discovery otherwise allowed by the Florida Rules of Civil Procedure if it determines that (i) the discovery sought is unreasonably cumulative or duplicative, or can be obtained from another source or in another manner that is more convenient, less burdensome, or less expensive; or (ii) the burden or expense of the discovery outweighs its likely benefit, considering the needs of the case, the amount in controversy, the parties' resources, the importance of the issues at stake in the action, and the importance of the discovery in resolving the issues. FL ST RCP Rule 1.280(d)(2).

d. For information on inadvertent disclosure of privileged materials, see FL ST RCP Rule 1.285.

2. *Requests for admission.* It is an advantage to use requests for admission. The biggest advantage is that if an adversary denies a request for an admission and the denied matter is later proven to be true, the adversary may have to pay the costs of proving the genuineness of the document or the truth of the matter requested to be admitted. FL-PP § 3:143.

a. *Scope.* A party may serve upon any other party a written request for the admission of the truth of any matters within the scope of FL ST RCP Rule 1.280(b) set forth in the request that relate to statements or opinions of fact or of the application of law to fact, including the genuineness of any documents described in the request. FL ST RCP Rule 1.370(a).

b. *Copies of documents.* Copies of documents shall be served with the request unless they have been or are otherwise furnished or made available for inspection and copying. FL ST RCP Rule 1.370(a).

c. *Number of requests.* The request for admission shall not exceed thirty (30) requests, including all subparts, unless the court permits a larger number on motion and notice and for good cause, or the parties propounding and responding to the requests stipulate to a larger number. Each matter of which an admission is requested shall be separately set forth. FL ST RCP Rule 1.370(a).

d. *Sufficiency of responses.* The party who has requested the admissions may move to determine the sufficiency of the answers or objections. Unless the court determines that an objection is justified, it shall order that an answer be served. If the court determines that an answer does not comply with the requirements of this rule, it may order either that the matter is admitted or that an amended answer be served. Instead of these orders the court may determine that final disposition of the request be made at a pretrial conference or at a designated time before trial. The provisions of FL ST RCP Rule 1.380(a)(4) apply to the award of expenses incurred in relation to the motion. FL ST RCP Rule 1.370(a).

e. *Effect of admission.* Any matter admitted under FL ST RCP Rule 1.370 is conclusively established unless the court on motion permits withdrawal or amendment of the admission. Subject to FL ST RCP Rule 1.200 governing amendment of a pretrial order, the court may permit withdrawal or amendment when the presentation of the merits of the action will be subserved by it and the party who obtained the admission fails to satisfy the court that withdrawal or amendment will prejudice that party in maintaining an action or defense on the merits. Any admission made by a party under this rule is for the purpose of the pending action only and is not an admission for any other purpose nor may it be used against that party in any other proceeding. FL ST RCP Rule 1.370(b).

f. *Answer requirements.* The matter is admitted unless the party to whom the request is directed serves upon the party requesting the admission a written answer or objection addressed to the matter within thirty (30) days after service of the request or such shorter or longer time as the court may allow but, unless the court shortens the time, a defendant shall not be required to serve answers or objections before the expiration of forty-five (45) days after service of the process and initial pleading upon the defendant. If objection is made, the reasons shall be stated. The answer shall specifically deny the matter or set forth in detail the reasons why the answering party cannot truthfully admit or deny the matter. A denial shall fairly meet the substance of the requested admission, and when good faith requires that a party qualify an answer or deny only a part of the matter of which an admission is requested, the party shall specify so much of it as is true and qualify or deny the remainder. An answering party may not give lack of information or knowledge as a reason for failure to admit or deny unless that party states that that party has made reasonable inquiry and that the information known or readily obtainable by that party is insufficient to enable that party to admit or deny. A party who considers that a matter of which an admission has been requested presents a genuine issue for trial may not object to the request on that ground alone; the party may deny the matter or set forth reasons why the party cannot admit or deny it, subject to FL ST RCP Rule 1.380(c). FL ST RCP Rule 1.370(a).

3. *Arbitration and mediation*

a. *Referral to arbitration and mediation.* Except as hereinafter provided or as otherwise prohibited by law, the presiding judge may enter an order referring all or any part of a contested civil matter to mediation or arbitration. The parties to any contested civil matter may file a written stipulation to mediate or arbitrate any issue between them at any time. Such stipulation shall be incorporated into the order of referral. FL ST RCP Rule 1.700(a).

b. *Arbitration*

i. *Exclusions.* A civil action shall be ordered to arbitration or arbitration in conjunction with mediation upon stipulation of the parties. A civil action may be ordered to arbitration or arbitration in conjunction with mediation upon motion of any party or by the court, if the judge determines the action to be of such a nature that arbitration could be of benefit to the litigants or the court. FL ST RCP Rule 1.800.

- Under no circumstances may the following categories of actions be referred to arbitration: (1) bond estreatures; (2) habeas corpus or other extraordinary writs; (3) bond validations; (4) civil or criminal contempt; (5) such other matters as may be specified by order of the chief judge in the circuit. FL ST RCP Rule 1.800.

ii. For more information regarding arbitration, please see FL ST RCP Rule 1.810; FL ST RCP Rule 1.820; FL ST RCP Rule 1.830; and FL ST 7 J CIR CV-2009-019-SC; and FL ST 7 J CIR CV-2003-002-SC(1)(c).

c. *Mediation.* For more information regarding mediation, please see FL ST RCP Rule 1.710; FL ST RCP Rule 1.720; FL ST RCP Rule 1.730; FL ST RCP Rule 1.750; FL ST 7 J CIR CV-2008-018-SC; and FL ST 7 J CIR CV-2003-002-SC(1).

4. *Rules of court*

a. *Rules of civil procedure.* The Florida Rules of Civil Procedure apply to all actions of a civil nature and all special statutory proceedings in the circuit courts and county courts except those to which the Florida Probate Rules, the Florida Family Law Rules of Procedure, or the Small Claims Rules apply. FL ST RCP Rule 1.010.

i. The form, content, procedure, and time for pleading in all special statutory proceedings shall be as prescribed by the statutes governing the proceeding unless the Florida Rules of Civil Procedure specifically provide to the contrary. FL ST RCP Rule 1.010.

ii. The Florida Rules of Civil Procedure shall be construed to secure the just, speedy, and inexpensive determination of every action. FL ST RCP Rule 1.010.

b. *Rules of judicial administration.* The Florida Rules of Judicial Administration shall apply to administrative matters in all courts to which the Florida Rules of Judicial Administration are applicable by their terms. The Florida Rules of Judicial Administration shall be construed to secure the speedy and inexpensive determination of every proceeding to which they are applicable. The Florida Rules of Judicial Administration shall supersede all conflicting rules and statutes. FL ST J ADMIN Rule 2.110.

D. Documents

1. *Required documents*

a. *Request for admission.* Please see the General Requirements section of this document for more information on the contents of the request for admission.

i. *Notices to persons with disabilities.* See the Format section of this KeyRules document for further information.

b. *Copies of documents.* Copies of documents shall be served with the request unless they have been or are otherwise furnished or made available for inspection and copying. FL ST RCP Rule 1.370(a).

c. *Certificate of service.* A certificate of service of the interrogatories shall be filed, giving the date of service and the name of the party to whom they were directed. FL ST RCP Rule 1.340(e). When any attorney certifies in substance: "I certify that a copy hereof has been furnished to (here insert name or names and addresses used for service) by (e-mail) (delivery) (mail) (fax) on .... (date) ....________________ Attorney" the certificate is taken as prima facie proof of such service in compliance with FL ST J ADMIN Rule 2.516. FL ST J ADMIN Rule 2.516(f).

E. Format

1. *Documents; Type and size.* Documents subject to the exceptions set forth in FL ST J ADMIN Rule 2.525(d) shall be filed on recycled paper measuring eight and one half by eleven (8 1/2 by 11) inches. For purposes of FL ST J ADMIN Rule 2.520, paper is recycled if it contains a minimum content of fifty (50) percent waste paper. Xerographic reduction of legal-size (eight and one half by fourteen (8 1/2 by 14) inches) documents to letter size (eight and one half by eleven (8 1/2 by 11) inches) is prohibited. All other

documents filed by electronic transmission shall be filed in a format capable of being printed in a format consistent with the provisions of FL ST J ADMIN Rule 2.250. FL ST J ADMIN Rule 2.520(b).

a. *Exhibits.* Any exhibit or attachment filed with pleadings or papers may be filed in its original size. FL ST J ADMIN Rule 2.520(c).

b. *Recording space.* On all papers and documents prepared and filed by the court or by any party to a proceeding which are to be recorded in the public records of any county, including but not limited to final money judgments and notices of lis pendens, a three (3) inch by three (3) inch space at the top right-hand corner on the first page and a one (1) inch by three (3) inch space at the top right-hand corner on each subsequent page shall be left blank and reserved for use by the clerk of court. FL ST J ADMIN Rule 2.520(d).

i. *Exceptions to recording space.* Any papers or documents created by persons or entities over which the filing party has no control, including but not limited to wills, codicils, trusts, or other testamentary documents; documents prepared or executed by any public officer; documents prepared, executed, acknowledged, or proved outside of the State of Florida; or documents created by State or Federal government agencies, may be filed without the space required by FL ST J ADMIN Rule 2.520. FL ST J ADMIN Rule 2.520(e).

c. *Noncompliance.* No clerk of court is permitted to refuse to file any document or paper because of noncompliance with the Florida Rules of Judicial Administration. However, upon request of the clerk of court, noncomplying documents must be resubmitted in accordance with the formatting rules. FL ST J ADMIN Rule 2.520(f).

2. *Caption.* Every pleading, motion, order, judgment, or other paper shall have a caption containing the name of the court, the file number, and except for in rem proceedings, including forfeiture proceedings, the name of the first party on each side with an appropriate indication of other parties, and a designation identifying the party filing it and its nature or the nature of the order, as the case may be. In any in rem proceeding, every pleading, motion, order, judgment, or other paper shall have a caption containing the name of the court, the file number, the style "In re" (followed by the name or general description of the property), and a designation of the person or entity filing it and its nature or the nature of the order, as the case may be. In an in rem forfeiture proceeding, the style shall be "In re forfeiture of" (followed by the name of the general description of the property). All papers filed in the action shall be styled in such a manner as to indicate clearly the subject matter of the paper and the party requesting or obtaining relief. FL ST RCP Rule 1.100(c)(1).

a. *Volusia County eminent domain cases.* All orders, pleadings, motions and other papers will bear the initial case style. Documents intended to apply only to particular parcel(s) will indicate in their caption the parcel number(s) to which they apply and sufficient copies shall be provided to the Clerk of Court to allow the filing and docketing of each relevant paper in each parcel file. FL ST 7 J CIR CV-2000-011-VL(b).

3. *Writing and written defined.* Writing or written means a document containing information, an application, or a stipulation. FL ST RCP Rule 1.080(c).

4. *Rule abbreviations*

a. The Florida Rules of Civil Procedure and shall be abbreviated as Fla.R.Civ.P. FL ST RCP Rule 1.010.

b. The Florida Rules of Judicial Administration shall be abbreviated as Fla. R. Jud. Admin. FL ST J ADMIN Rule 2.110.

5. *Nonverification.* Except when otherwise specifically provided by the Florida Rules of Civil Procedure or an applicable statute, every pleading or other document of a party represented by an attorney need not be verified or accompanied by an affidavit. FL ST RCP Rule 1.030; FL ST J ADMIN Rule 2.515(a).

6. *Attorney signature*

a. *Attorney signature.* Every pleading and other document of a party represented by an attorney shall be signed by at least one (1) attorney of record in that attorney's individual name whose current record Florida Bar address, telephone number, including area code, primary e-mail address and secondary

e-mail addresses, if any, and Florida Bar number shall be stated, and who shall be duly licensed to practice law in Florida or who shall have received permission to appear in the particular case as provided in FL ST J ADMIN Rule 2.510. FL ST J ADMIN Rule 2.515(a).

i. The attorney may be required by the court to give the address of, and to vouch for the attorney's authority to represent, the party. FL ST J ADMIN Rule 2.515(a).

ii. The signature of an attorney shall constitute a certificate by the attorney that the attorney has read the pleading or other document; that to the best of the attorney's knowledge, information, and belief there is good ground to support it; and that it is not interposed for delay. FL ST J ADMIN Rule 2.515(a).

iii. If a pleading is not signed or is signed with intent to defeat the purpose of FL ST J ADMIN Rule 2.515, it may be stricken and the action may proceed as though the pleading or other document had not been served. FL ST J ADMIN Rule 2.515(a).

b. *Pro se litigant signature.* A party who is not represented by an attorney shall sign any pleading or other paper and state the party's address and telephone number, including area code. FL ST J ADMIN Rule 2.515(b).

c. *Form of signature*

i. The signatures required on pleadings and documents by FL ST J ADMIN Rule 2.515(a) and FL ST J ADMIN Rule 2.515(b) may be:

- Original signatures;
- Original signatures that have been reproduced by electronic means, such as on electronically transmitted documents or photocopied documents;
- Electronic signatures using the "/s/," "s/," or "/s" formats by or at the direction of the person signing; or
- Any other signature format authorized by general law, so long as the clerk where the proceeding is pending has the capability of receiving and has obtained approval from the Supreme Court of Florida to accept pleadings and documents with that signature format. FL ST J ADMIN Rule 2.515(c)(1).

ii. An attorney, party, or other person who files a pleading or paper by electronic transmission that does not contain the original signature of that attorney, party, or other person shall file that identical pleading or paper in paper form containing an original signature of that attorney, party, or other person (hereinafter called the follow-up filing) immediately thereafter. The follow-up filing is not required if the Supreme Court of Florida has entered an order directing the clerk of court to discontinue accepting the follow-up filing. FL ST J ADMIN Rule 2.515(c)(2).

7. *Forms*

a. *Process.* The forms of process, notice of lis pendens, and notice of action provided in the Florida Rules of Civil Procedure are sufficient. Variations from the forms do not void process or notices that are otherwise sufficient. FL ST RCP Rule 1.900(a).

b. *Other forms.* The other forms provided in the Florida Rules of Civil Procedure are sufficient for the matters that are covered by them. So long as the substance is expressed without prolixity, the forms may be varied to meet the facts of a particular case. FL ST RCP Rule 1.900(b).

c. *Formal matters.* Captions, except for the designation of the paper, are omitted from the forms provided in the Florida Rules of Civil Procedure. A general form of caption is the first form provided. Signatures are omitted from pleadings and motions. FL ST RCP Rule 1.900(c).

8. *Notices to persons with disabilities.* All notices of court proceedings to be held in a public facility, and all process compelling appearance at such proceedings, shall include the following statement in bold face, fourteen (14) point Times New Roman or Courier font: "If you are a person with a disability who needs any accommodation in order to participate in this proceeding, you are entitled, at no cost to you, to the provision of certain assistance. Please contact [identify applicable court personnel by name, address, and telephone number] at least seven (7) days before your scheduled court appearance, or immediately upon

receiving this notification if the time before the scheduled appearance is less than seven (7) days; if you are hearing or voice impaired, call 711." FL ST J ADMIN Rule 2.540(c)(1).

9. *Minimization of the filing of sensitive information*
   a. *Limitations for court filings.* Unless authorized by FL ST J ADMIN Rule 2.425(b), statute, another rule of court, or the court orders otherwise, designated sensitive information filed with the court must be limited to the following format:
      i. The initials of a person known to be a minor;
      ii. The year of birth of a person's birth date;
      iii. No portion of any: Social security number, Bank account number, Credit card account number, Charge account number, or Debit account number;
      iv. The last four digits of any: Taxpayer identification number (TIN), Employee identification number, Driver's license number, Passport number, Telephone number, Financial account number, except as set forth in FL ST J ADMIN Rule 2.425(a)(3), Brokerage account number, Insurance policy account number, Loan account number, Customer account number, or Patient or health care number;
      v. A truncated version of any: Email address, Computer user name, Password, or Personal identification number (PIN); and
      vi. A truncated version of any other sensitive information as provided by court order. FL ST J ADMIN Rule 2.425(a).
   b. *Exceptions.* FL ST J ADMIN Rule 2.425(a) does not apply to the following:
      i. An account number which identifies the property alleged to be the subject of a proceeding;
      ii. The record of an administrative or agency proceeding;
      iii. The record in appellate or review proceedings;
      iv. The birth date of a minor whenever the birth date is necessary for the court to establish or maintain subject matter jurisdiction;
      v. The name of a minor in any order relating to parental responsibility, time-sharing, or child support;
      vi. The name of a minor in any document or order affecting the minor's ownership of real property;
      vii. The birth date of a party in a writ of attachment or notice to payor;
      viii. In traffic and criminal proceedings: a pro se filing; a court filing that is related to a criminal matter or investigation and that is prepared before the filing of a criminal charge or is not filed as part of any docketed criminal case; an arrest or search warrant or any information in support thereof; a charging document and an affidavit or other documents filed in support of any charging document, including any driving records; a statement of particulars; discovery material introduced into evidence or otherwise filed with the court; and all information necessary for the proper issuance and execution of a subpoena duces tecum;
      ix. Information used by the clerk for case maintenance purposes or the courts for case management purposes; and
      x. Information which is relevant and material to an issue before the court. FL ST J ADMIN Rule 2.425(b).
   c. *Remedies.* Upon motion by a party or interested person or sua sponte by the court, the court may order remedies, sanctions or both for a violation of FL ST J ADMIN Rule 2.425(a). Following notice and an opportunity to respond, the court may impose sanctions if such filing was not made in good faith. FL ST J ADMIN Rule 2.425(c).
   d. *Motions not restricted.* FL ST J ADMIN Rule 2.425 does not restrict a party's right to move for protective order, to move to file documents under seal, or to request a determination of the confidentiality of records. FL ST J ADMIN Rule 2.425(d).

e. *Application.* FL ST J ADMIN Rule 2.425 does not affect the application of constitutional provisions, statutes, or rules of court regarding confidential information or access to public information. FL ST J ADMIN Rule 2.425(e).

F. Filing and Service Requirements

1. *Court filing of documents and discovery.* Information obtained during discovery shall not be filed with the court until such time as it is filed for good cause. The requirement of good cause is satisfied only where the filing of the information is allowed or required by another applicable rule of procedure or by court order. All filings of discovery documents shall comply with FL ST J ADMIN Rule 2.425. The court shall have the authority to impose sanctions for violation of FL ST RCP Rule 1.280. FL ST RCP Rule 1.280(g).
2. *Filing requirements.* All original documents must be filed with the court either before service or immediately thereafter, unless otherwise provided for by general law or other rules. If the original of any bond or other document is not placed in the court file, a certified copy must be so placed by the clerk. FL ST J ADMIN Rule 2.516(d). All documents shall be filed in conformity with the requirements of FL ST J ADMIN Rule 2.525. FL ST RCP Rule 1.080(b). All documents filed in any court shall be filed by electronic transmission in accordance with FL ST J ADMIN Rule 2.525. "Documents" means pleadings, motions, petitions, memoranda, briefs, notices, exhibits, declarations, affidavits, orders, judgments, decrees, writs, opinions, and any other paper or writing submitted to a court. FL ST J ADMIN Rule 2.520(a). All documents that are court records, as defined in FL ST J ADMIN Rule 2.430(a)(1), must be filed by electronic transmission, provided that: (1) the clerk has the ability to accept and retain such documents; (2) the clerk or the chief judge of the circuit has requested permission to accept documents filed by electronic transmission; and (3) the supreme court has entered an order granting permission to the clerk to accept documents filed by electronic transmission. FL ST J ADMIN Rule 2.525(c)(1).

   a. *Definition.* "Electronic transmission of documents" means the sending of information by electronic signals to, by or from a court or clerk, which when received can be transformed and stored or transmitted on paper, microfilm, magnetic storage device, optical imaging system, CD-ROM, flash drive, other electronic data storage system, server, case maintenance system ("CM"), electronic court filing ("ECF") system, statewide or local electronic portal ("e-portal"), or other electronic record keeping system authorized by the supreme court in a format sufficient to communicate the information on the original document in a readable format. Electronic transmission of documents includes electronic mail ("e-mail") and any internet-based transmission procedure, and may include procedures allowing for documents to be signed or verified by electronic means. FL ST J ADMIN Rule 2.525(a).

      i. The filing of documents with the court as required by the Florida Rules of Judicial Administration must be made by filing them with the clerk in accordance with FL ST J ADMIN Rule 2.525, except that the judge may permit documents to be filed with the judge, in which event the judge must note the filing date before him or her on the documents and transmit them to the clerk. The date of filing is that shown on the face of the document by the judge's notation or the clerk's time stamp, whichever is earlier. FL ST J ADMIN Rule 2.516(e).

   b. *Application.* Any court or clerk of the court may accept the electronic transmission of documents for filing after the clerk, together with input from the chief judge of the circuit, has obtained approval of the procedures and program for doing so from the Supreme Court of Florida. FL ST J ADMIN Rule 2.525(b).

   c. *Exceptions*

      i. Paper documents and other submissions may be manually submitted to the clerk or court:

         - When the clerk does not have the ability to accept and retain documents by electronic filing or has not had ECF Procedures approved by the supreme court;
         - For filing by any self-represented party or any self-represented nonparty unless specific ECF Procedures provide a means to file documents electronically. However, any self-represented nonparty that is a governmental or public agency and any other agency, partnership, corporation, or business entity acting on behalf of any governmental or public agency may file documents by electronic transmission if such entity has the capability of filing documents electronically;

- For filing by attorneys excused from e-mail service in accordance with FL ST J ADMIN Rule 2.516(b);
- When submitting evidentiary exhibits or filing non-documentary materials;
- When the filing involves documents in excess of twenty-five (25) megabytes (25MB) in size. For such filings, documents may be transmitted using an electronic storage medium that the clerk has the ability to accept, which may include a CD-ROM, flash drive, or similar storage medium;
- When filed in open court, as permitted by the court;
- When paper filing is permitted by any approved statewide or local ECF procedures; and
- If any court determines that justice so requires. FL ST J ADMIN Rule 2.525(d).

ii. Any document in paper form submitted under FL ST J ADMIN Rule 2.525(d) is filed when it is received by the clerk or court and the clerk shall immediately thereafter convert any filed paper document to an electronic document. "Convert to an electronic document" means optically capturing an image of a paper document and using character recognition software to recover as much of the document's text as practicable and then indexing and storing the document in the official court file. FL ST J ADMIN Rule 2.525(c)(4).

iii. Any storage medium submitted under FL ST J ADMIN Rule 2.525(d)(5) is filed when received by the clerk or court and the clerk shall immediately thereafter transfer the electronic documents from the storage device to the official court file. FL ST J ADMIN Rule 2.525(c)(5).

iv. If the filer of any paper document authorized under FL ST J ADMIN Rule 2.525(d) provides a self-addressed, postage-paid envelope for return of the paper document after it is converted to electronic form by the clerk, the clerk shall place the paper document in the envelope and deposit it in the mail. Except when a paper document is required to be maintained, the clerk may recycle any filed paper document that is not to be returned to the filer. FL ST J ADMIN Rule 2.525(c)(6).

v. The clerk may convert any paper document filed before the effective date of FL ST J ADMIN Rule 2.525 to an electronic document. Unless the clerk is required to maintain the paper document, if the paper document has been converted to an electronic document by the clerk, the paper document is no longer part of the official court file and may be removed and recycled. FL ST J ADMIN Rule 2.525(c)(7).

d. *Official court file.* For information on what constitutes the official court file, please see FL ST J ADMIN Rule 2.525(c)(2), FL ST J ADMIN Rule 2.525(c)(3).

e. *Administration.* All attorneys, parties, or other persons using this rule to file documents are required to make arrangements with the court or clerk for the payment of any charges authorized by general law or the supreme court before filing any document by electronic transmission. FL ST J ADMIN Rule 2.525(f)(2).

f. *Filing date.* The filing date for an electronically transmitted document is the date and time that such filing is acknowledged by an electronic stamp or otherwise, pursuant to any procedure set forth in any ECF Procedures approved by the supreme court, or the date the last page of such filing is received by the court or clerk. FL ST J ADMIN Rule 2.525(f)(3).

g. *Accessibility.* All documents transmitted in any electronic form under FL ST J ADMIN Rule 2.525 must comply with the accessibility requirements of FL ST J ADMIN Rule 2.526. FL ST J ADMIN Rule 2.525(g).

3. *Service requirements.* Every pleading subsequent to the initial pleading, all orders, and every other document filed in the action must be served in conformity with the requirements of FL ST J ADMIN Rule 2.516. FL ST RCP Rule 1.080(a).

   a. *Service; When required.* Unless the court otherwise orders, or a statute or supreme court administrative order specifies a different means of service, every pleading subsequent to the initial pleading and every other document filed in any court proceeding, except applications for witness subpoenas and documents served by formal notice or required to be served in the manner provided for service

of formal notice, must be served in accordance with FL ST J ADMIN Rule 2.516 on each party. No service need be made on parties against whom a default has been entered, except that pleadings asserting new or additional claims against them must be served in the manner provided for service of summons. FL ST J ADMIN Rule 2.516(a).

b. *Service; How made.* When service is required or permitted to be made upon a party represented by an attorney, service must be made upon the attorney unless service upon the party is ordered by the court. FL ST J ADMIN Rule 2.516(b).

   i. *Service by electronic mail ("e-mail").* All documents required or permitted to be served on another party must be served by e-mail, unless FL ST J ADMIN Rule 2.516 otherwise provides. When, in addition to service by e-mail, the sender also utilizes another means of service provided for in FL ST J ADMIN Rule 2.516(b)(2), any differing time limits and other provisions applicable to that other means of service control. FL ST J ADMIN Rule 2.516(b)(1). Any document electronically transmitted to a court or clerk must also be served on all parties and interested persons in accordance with the applicable rules of court. FL ST J ADMIN Rule 2.525(e)(2).

      - *Service on attorneys.* Upon appearing in a proceeding, an attorney must serve a designation of a primary e-mail address and may designate no more than two (2) secondary e-mail addresses. Thereafter, service must be directed to all designated e-mail addresses in that proceeding. Every document filed by an attorney thereafter must include the primary e-mail address of that attorney and any secondary e-mail addresses. If an attorney does not designate any e-mail address for service, documents may be served on that attorney at the e-mail address on record with The Florida Bar. FL ST J ADMIN Rule 2.516(b)(1)(A).
      - *Exception to e-mail service on attorneys.* Service by an attorney on another attorney must be made by e-mail unless excused by the court. Upon motion by an attorney demonstrating that the attorney has no e-mail account and lacks access to the Internet at the attorney's office, the court may excuse the attorney from the requirements of e-mail service. Service on and by an attorney excused by the court from e-mail service must be by the means provided in FL ST J ADMIN Rule 2.516(b)(2). FL ST J ADMIN Rule 2.516(b)(1)(B).
      - *Service on and by parties not represented by an attorney.* Any party not represented by an attorney may serve a designation of a primary e-mail address and also may designate no more than two (2) secondary e-mail addresses to which service must be directed in that proceeding by the means provided in FL ST J ADMIN Rule 2.516(b)(1). If a party not represented by an attorney does not designate an e-mail address for service in a proceeding, service on and by that party must be by the means provided in FL ST J ADMIN Rule 2.516(b)(2). FL ST J ADMIN Rule 2.516(b)(1)(C).
      - *Time of service.* Service by e-mail is complete when it is sent. FL ST J ADMIN Rule 2.516(b)(1)(D). An e-mail is deemed served on the date it is sent. FL ST J ADMIN Rule 2.516(b)(1)(D)(i). If the sender learns that the e-mail did not reach the address of the person to be served, the sender must immediately send another copy by e-mail, or by a means authorized by FL ST J ADMIN Rule 2.516(b)(2). FL ST J ADMIN Rule 2.516(b)(1)(D)(ii). E-mail service is treated as service by mail for the computation of time. FL ST J ADMIN Rule 2.516(b)(1)(D)(iii).

   ii. *Format of e-mail for service.* Service of a document by e-mail is made by attaching a copy of the document in PDF format to an e-mail sent to all addresses designated by the attorney or party. FL ST J ADMIN Rule 2.516(b)(1)(E).

      - All documents served by e-mail must be attached to an e-mail message containing a subject line beginning with the words "SERVICE OF COURT DOCUMENT" in all capital letters, followed by the case number of the proceeding in which the documents are being served. FL ST J ADMIN Rule 2.516(b)(1)(E)(i).
      - The body of the e-mail must identify the court in which the proceeding is pending, the case number, the name of the initial party on each side, the title of each document served with that e-mail, and the sender's name and telephone number. FL ST J ADMIN Rule 2.516(b)(1)(E)(ii).

- Any document served by e-mail may be signed by the "/s/" format, as long as the filed original is signed in accordance with the applicable rule of procedure. FL ST J ADMIN Rule 2.516(b)(1)(E)(iii).
- Any e-mail which, together with its attached documents, exceeds five megabytes (5MB) in size, must be divided and sent as separate e-mails, no one of which may exceed five megabytes (5MB) in size and each of which must be sequentially numbered in the subject line. FL ST J ADMIN Rule 2.516(b)(1)(E)(iv).

iii. *Service by other means.* In addition to, and not in lieu of, service by e-mail, service may also be made upon attorneys by any of the means specified in FL ST J ADMIN Rule 2.516(b)(2). Service on and by all parties who are not represented by an attorney and who do not designate an e-mail address, and on and by all attorneys excused from e-mail service, must be made by delivering a copy of the document or by mailing it to the party or attorney at their last known address or, if no address is known, by leaving it with the clerk of the court. Service by mail is complete upon mailing. Delivery of a copy within FL ST J ADMIN Rule 2.516 is complete upon:

- Handing it to the attorney or to the party,
- Leaving it at the attorney's or party's office with a clerk or other person in charge thereof,
- If there is no one in charge, leaving it in a conspicuous place therein,
- If the office is closed or the person to be served has no office, leaving it at the person's usual place of abode with some person of his or her family above fifteen (15) years of age and informing such person of the contents, or
- Transmitting it by facsimile to the attorney's or party's office with a cover sheet containing the sender's name, firm, address, telephone number, and facsimile number, and the number of pages transmitted. When service is made by facsimile, a copy must also be served by any other method permitted by FL ST J ADMIN Rule 2.516. Facsimile service occurs when transmission is complete. FL ST J ADMIN Rule 2.516(b)(2)(A) through FL ST J ADMIN Rule 2.516(b)(2)(E).
- Service by delivery after 5:00 p.m. must be deemed to have been made by mailing on the date of delivery. FL ST J ADMIN Rule 2.516(b)(2)(F).

c. *Service; Numerous defendants.* In actions when the parties are unusually numerous, the court may regulate the service contemplated by the Florida Rules of Judicial Administration on motion or on its own initiative in such manner as may be found to be just and reasonable. FL ST J ADMIN Rule 2.516(c).

d. *Service by clerk.* Service of notices and other documents required to be made by the clerk must also be done as provided in FL ST J ADMIN Rule 2.516(b). FL ST J ADMIN Rule 2.516(g).

G. Hearings

1. There is no hearing required or contemplated with regard to requests for admission in the Florida Rules of Civil Procedure.

H. Forms

1. Official Request for Admissions Forms for Florida

a. Caption. FL ST RCP Form 1.901.

2. Request for Admissions Forms for Florida

a. Requests for admissions; Negligence, fall down. FL-PRACFORM § 8:41.

b. Requests for admissions; Promissory note. FL-PRACFORM § 8:42.

c. Requests for admissions; Open account. FL-PRACFORM § 8:43.

d. Requests for admissions; Mortgage foreclosure. FL-PRACFORM § 8:44.

e. Request for admissions; General form. FL-PP § 3:146.

f. Request for admissions; Facts and genuineness of documents. FL-PP § 3:147.

g. Motion; To determine sufficiency of reply to request for admissions. FL-PP § 3:152.

h. Form for request for admissions. FL-RCPF R 1.370(5).

i. Form for request for admissions (another form). FL-RCPF R 1.370(6).

j. Form for request for admissions served concurrently with interrogatories. FL-RCPF R 1.370(7).

k. Form for request for admissions as to factual situation and refinement of issues. FL-RCPF R 1.370(9).

l. Form for request to admit party uses electronic data storage. FL-RCPF R 1.370(10).

I. Checklist

(I) ❑ Matters to be considered by requesting party

(a) ❑ Required documents

(1) ❑ Request

(2) ❑ Copies of documents

(3) ❑ Certificate of service

(b) ❑ Time for request

(1) ❑ Without leave of court the request may be served upon the plaintiff after commencement of the action and upon any other party with or after service of the process and initial pleading upon that party

(2) ❑ No requests for admissions shall be served later than forty-five (45) days prior to docket sounding

(II) ❑ Matters to be considered by responding party

(a) ❑ Required documents

(1) ❑ Response to request

(2) ❑ Certificate of service

(b) ❑ Time for response

(1) ❑ The party to whom the request is directed shall serve a written response within thirty (30) days after service of the request, except that a defendant may serve a response within forty-five (45) days after service of the process and initial pleading on that defendant

Requests, Notices and Applications
Notice of Deposition

Document Last Updated January 2013

A. Applicable Rules

1. *State rules*

a. Pleadings and motions. FL ST RCP Rule 1.100.

b. Depositions before action or pending appeal. FL ST RCP Rule 1.290.

c. Persons before whom depositions may be taken. FL ST RCP Rule 1.300.

d. Depositions upon oral examination. FL ST RCP Rule 1.310.

e. Depositions upon written questions. FL ST RCP Rule 1.320.

f. Use of depositions in court proceedings. FL ST RCP Rule 1.330.

g. Nonverification of pleadings. FL ST RCP Rule 1.030.

h. Service and filing of pleadings, orders, and documents. FL ST RCP Rule 1.080.

i. Time. FL ST RCP Rule 1.090.
j. General provisions governing discovery. FL ST RCP Rule 1.280.
k. Failure to make discovery; Sanctions. FL ST RCP Rule 1.380.
l. Depositions of expert witnesses. FL ST RCP Rule 1.390.
m. Relief from judgment, decrees, or orders. FL ST RCP Rule 1.540.
n. Forms. FL ST RCP Rule 1.900.
o. Minimization of the filing of sensitive information. FL ST J ADMIN Rule 2.425.
p. Retention of court records. FL ST J ADMIN Rule 2.430.
q. Foreign attorneys. FL ST J ADMIN Rule 2.510.
r. Signature of attorneys and parties. FL ST J ADMIN Rule 2.515.
s. Paper. FL ST J ADMIN Rule 2.520.
t. Electronic filing. FL ST J ADMIN Rule 2.525.
u. Accessibility of information and technology. FL ST J ADMIN Rule 2.526.
v. Requests for accommodations by persons with disabilities. FL ST J ADMIN Rule 2.540.

2. *Local rules*
   a. Eminent domain cases. FL ST 7 J CIR CV-2000-011-VL.
   b. Filing of deposition transcripts. FL ST 7 J CIR CV-2003-009-SC.
   c. Arbitration and mediation. FL ST 7 J CIR CV-2009-019-SC; FL ST 7 J CIR CV-2008-018-SC.
   d. Civil pretrial procedures. FL ST 7 J CIR CV-2003-002-SC.

B. Timing

1. *Depositions upon oral examination.* After commencement of the action any party may take the testimony of any person, including a party, by deposition upon oral examination. Leave of court, granted with or without notice, must be obtained only if the plaintiff seeks to take a deposition within thirty (30) days after service of the process and initial pleading upon any defendant, except that leave is not required (1) if a defendant has served a notice of taking deposition or otherwise sought discovery, or (2) if special notice is given as provided in FL ST RCP Rule 1.310(b)(2). The attendance of witnesses may be compelled by subpoena as provided in FL ST RCP Rule 1.410. The deposition of a person confined in prison may be taken only by leave of court on such terms as the court prescribes. FL ST RCP Rule 1.310(a). A party desiring to take the deposition of any person upon oral examination shall give reasonable notice in writing to every other party to the action. FL ST RCP Rule 1.310(b)(1).
2. *Depositions upon written questions.* After commencement of the action any party may take the testimony of any person, including a party, by deposition upon written questions. The attendance of witnesses may be compelled by the use of subpoena as provided in FL ST RCP Rule 1.410. The deposition of a person confined in prison may be taken only by leave of court on such terms as the court prescribes. Within thrity (30) days after the notice and written questions are served, a party may serve cross questions upon all other parties. Within ten (10) days after being served with cross questions, a party may serve redirect questions upon all other parties. Within ten (10) days after being served with redirect questions, a party may serve recross questions upon all other parties. The court may for cause shown enlarge or shorten the time. FL ST RCP Rule 1.320(a).
3. *Depositions before action or pending appeal.* For information on petitions and motions for depositions before an action or pending appeal, please see the General Requirements section below.
4. *Sequence and timing of discovery.* Except as provided in FL ST RCP Rule 1.280(b)(5) or unless the court upon motion for the convenience of parties and witnesses and in the interest of justice orders otherwise, methods of discovery may be used in any sequence, and the fact that a party is conducting discovery, whether by deposition or otherwise, shall not delay any other party's discovery. FL ST RCP Rule 1.280(e).
   a. *Close of discovery.* Except as otherwise provided by FL ST 7 J CIR CV-2003-002-SC or agreed to

by the parties in writing, discovery shall remain open until ten (10) days prior to docket sounding. FL ST 7 J CIR CV-2003-002-SC.

5. *Deposition transcripts.* A deposition transcript shall only be filed in a civil (including family, juvenile and probate) case if the hearing, or trial to which it relates, is scheduled to take place within thirty (30) days of the date the transcript is filed. FL ST 7 J CIR CV-2003-009-SC.

6. *Computation of time*

   a. *Generally.* Computation of time shall be governed by FL ST J ADMIN Rule 2.514. FL ST RCP Rule 1.090(a). The following rules apply in computing time periods specified in any rule of procedure, local rule, court order, or statute that does not specify a method of computing time. FL ST J ADMIN Rule 2.514(a).

      i. *Period stated in days or a longer unit.* When the period is stated in days or a longer unit of time (A) exclude the day of the event that triggers the period; (B) count every day, including intermediate Saturdays, Sundays, and legal holidays; and (C) include the last day of the period, but if the last day is a Saturday, Sunday, or legal holiday, or falls within any period of time extended through an order of the chief justice under FL ST J ADMIN Rule 2.205(a)(2)(B)(iv), the period continues to run until the end of the next day that is not a Saturday, Sunday, or legal holiday and does not fall within any period of time extended through an order of the chief justice. FL ST J ADMIN Rule 2.514(a)(1).

      ii. *Period stated in hours.* When the period is stated in hours (A) begin counting immediately on the occurrence of the event that triggers the period; (B) count every hour, including hours during intermediate Saturdays, Sundays, and legal holidays; and (C) if the period would end on a Saturday, Sunday, or legal holiday, or during any period of time extended through an order of the chief justice under FL ST J ADMIN Rule 2.205(a)(2)(B)(iv), the period continues to run until the same time on the next day that is not a Saturday, Sunday, or legal holiday and does not fall within any period of time extended through an order of the chief justice. FL ST J ADMIN Rule 2.514(a)(2).

      iii. *Period stated in days less than seven (7) days.* When the period stated in days is less than seven (7) days, intermediate Saturdays, Sundays, and legal holidays shall be excluded in the computation. FL ST J ADMIN Rule 2.514(a)(3).

      iv. *"Last day" defined.* Unless a different time is set by a statute, local rule, or court order, the last day ends (A) for electronic filing or for service by any means, at midnight; and (B) for filing by other means, when the clerk's office is scheduled to close. FL ST J ADMIN Rule 2.514(a)(4).

      v. *"Next day" defined.* The "next day" is determined by continuing to count forward when the period is measured after an event and backward when measured before an event. FL ST J ADMIN Rule 2.514(a)(5).

      vi. *"Legal holiday" defined.* "Legal holiday" means (A) the day set aside by FL ST § 110.117, for observing New Year's Day, Martin Luther King, Jr.'s Birthday, Memorial Day, Independence Day, Labor Day, Veterans' Day, Thanksgiving Day, the Friday after Thanksgiving Day, or Christmas Day, and (B) any day observed as a holiday by the clerk's office or as designated by the chief judge. FL ST J ADMIN Rule 2.514(a)(6).

   b. *Additional time after service by mail or e-mail.* When a party may or must act within a specified time after service and service is made by mail or e-mail, five (5) days are added after the period that would otherwise expire under FL ST J ADMIN Rule 2.514(a). FL ST J ADMIN Rule 2.514(b).

   c. *Enlargement.* When an act is required or allowed to be done at or within a specified time by order of court, by the Florida Rules of Civil Procedure, or by notice given thereunder, for cause shown the court at any time in its discretion (1) with or without notice, may order the period enlarged if request therefor is made before the expiration of the period originally prescribed or as extended by a previous order, or (2) upon motion made and notice after the expiration of the specified period, may permit the act to be done when failure to act was the result of excusable neglect, but it may not extend the time for making a motion for new trial, for rehearing, or to alter or amend a judgment; making a motion for relief from a judgment under FL ST RCP Rule 1.540(b); taking an appeal or filing a petition for certiorari; or making a motion for a directed verdict. FL ST RCP Rule 1.090(b).

d. *Unaffected by expiration of term.* The period of time provided for the doing of any act or the taking of any proceeding shall not be affected or limited by the continued existence or expiration of a term of court. The continued existence or expiration of a term of court in no way affects the power of a court to do any act or take any proceeding in any action which is or has been pending before it. FL ST RCP Rule 1.090(c).

C. General Requirements

1. *General provisions governing discovery*

a. *Discovery methods.* Parties may obtain discovery by one or more of the following methods: depositions upon oral examination or written questions; written interrogatories; production of documents or things or permission to enter upon land or other property for inspection and other purposes; physical and mental examinations; and requests for admission. Unless the court orders otherwise and under FL ST RCP Rule 1.280(c), the frequency of use of these methods is not limited, except as provided in FL ST RCP Rule 1.200, FL ST RCP Rule 1.340, and FL ST RCP Rule 1.370. FL ST RCP Rule 1.280(a).

b. *Scope of discovery.* Unless otherwise limited by order of the court in accordance with the Florida Rules of Civil Procedure, the scope of discovery is as follows:

i. *In general.* Parties may obtain discovery regarding any matter, not privileged, that is relevant to the subject matter of the pending action, whether it relates to the claim or defense of the party seeking discovery or the claim or defense of any other party, including the existence, description, nature, custody, condition, and location of any books, documents, or other tangible things and the identity and location of persons having knowledge of any discoverable matter. It is not ground for objection that the information sought will be inadmissible at the trial if the information sought appears reasonably calculated to lead to the discovery of admissible evidence. FL ST RCP Rule 1.280(b)(1).

ii. *Indemnity agreements.* A party may obtain discovery of the existence and contents of any agreement under which any person may be liable to satisfy part or all of a judgment that may be entered in the action or to indemnify or to reimburse a party for payments made to satisfy the judgment. Information concerning the agreement is not admissible in evidence at trial by reason of disclosure. FL ST RCP Rule 1.280(b)(2).

iii. *Electronically stored information.* A party may obtain discovery of electronically stored information in accordance with the Florida Rules of Civil Procedure. FL ST RCP Rule 1.280(b)(3).

iv. *Trial preparation; Materials.* Subject to the provisions of FL ST RCP Rule 1.280(b)(5), a party may obtain discovery of documents and tangible things otherwise discoverable under FL ST RCP Rule 1.280(b)(1) and prepared in anticipation of litigation or for trial by or for another party or by or for that party's representative, including that party's attorney, consultant, surety, indemnitor, insurer, or agent, only upon a showing that the party seeking discovery has need of the materials in the preparation of the case and is unable without undue hardship to obtain the substantial equivalent of the materials by other means. FL ST RCP Rule 1.280(b)(4).

- In ordering discovery of the materials when the required showing has been made, the court shall protect against disclosure of the mental impressions, conclusions, opinions, or legal theories of an attorney or other representative of a party concerning the litigation. FL ST RCP Rule 1.280(b)(4).
- Without the required showing a party may obtain a copy of a statement concerning the action or its subject matter previously made by that party. FL ST RCP Rule 1.280(b)(4).
- Upon request without the required showing a person not a party may obtain a copy of a statement concerning the action or its subject matter previously made by that person. If the request is refused, the person may move for an order to obtain a copy. The provisions of FL ST RCP Rule 1.380(a)(5) apply to the award of expenses incurred as a result of making the motion. FL ST RCP Rule 1.280(b)(4).
- For purposes of FL ST RCP Rule 1.280(b)(4), a statement previously made is a written

statement signed or otherwise adopted or approved by the person making it, or a stenographic, mechanical, electrical, or other recording or transcription of it that is a substantially verbatim recital of an oral statement by the person making it and contemporaneously recorded. FL ST RCP Rule 1.280(b)(4).

v. *Trial preparation; Experts.* Discovery of facts known and opinions held by experts, otherwise discoverable under the provisions of FL ST RCP Rule 1.280(b)(1) and acquired or developed in anticipation of litigation or for trial, may be obtained only as follows:

- By interrogatories a party may require any other party to identify each person whom the other party expects to call as an expert witness at trial and to state the subject matter on which the expert is expected to testify, and to state the substance of the facts and opinions to which the expert is expected to testify and a summary of the grounds for each opinion. FL ST RCP Rule 1.280(b)(5)(A)(i).
- Any person disclosed by interrogatories or otherwise as a person expected to be called as an expert witness at trial may be deposed in accordance with FL ST RCP Rule 1.390 without motion or order of court. FL ST RCP Rule 1.280(b)(5)(A)(ii).
- A party may obtain the following discovery regarding any person disclosed by interrogatories or otherwise as a person expected to be called as an expert witness at trial: The scope of employment in the pending case and the compensation for such service, FL ST RCP Rule 1.280(b)(5)(A)(iii)(1); The expert's general litigation experience, including the percentage of work performed for plaintiffs and defendants, FL ST RCP Rule 1.280(b)(5)(A)(iii)(2); The identity of other cases, within a reasonable time period, in which the expert has testified by deposition or at trial, FL ST RCP Rule 1.280(b)(5)(A)(iii)(3); An approximation of the portion of the expert's involvement as an expert witness, which may be based on the number of hours, percentage of hours, or percentage of earned income derived from serving as an expert witness; however, the expert shall not be required to disclose his or her earnings as an expert witness or income derived from other services. FL ST RCP Rule 1.280(b)(5)(A)(iii)(4).
- An expert may be required to produce financial and business records only under the most unusual or compelling circumstances and may not be compelled to compile or produce nonexistent documents. Upon motion, the court may order further discovery by other means, subject to such restrictions as to scope and other provisions pursuant to FL ST RCP Rule 1.280(b)(5)(C) concerning fees and expenses as the court may deem appropriate. FL ST RCP Rule 1.280(b)(5).
- A party may discover facts known or opinions held by an expert who has been retained or specially employed by another party in anticipation of litigation or preparation for trial and who is not expected to be called as a witness at trial, only as provided in FL ST RCP Rule 1.360(b) or upon a showing of exceptional circumstances under which it is impracticable for the party seeking discovery to obtain facts or opinions on the same subject by other means. FL ST RCP Rule 1.280(b)(5)(B).
- Unless manifest injustice would result, the court shall require that the party seeking discovery pay the expert a reasonable fee for time spent in responding to discovery under FL ST RCP Rule 1.280(b)(5)(A) and FL ST RCP Rule 1.280(b)(5)(B); and concerning discovery from an expert obtained under FL ST RCP Rule 1.280(b)(5)(A) the court may require, and concerning discovery obtained under FL ST RCP Rule 1.280(b)(5)(B) shall require, the party seeking discovery to pay the other party a fair part of the fees and expenses reasonably incurred by the latter party in obtaining facts and opinions from the expert. FL ST RCP Rule 1.280(b)(5)(C).
- As used in the Florida Rules of Civil Procedure an expert shall be an expert witness as defined in FL ST RCP Rule 1.390(a). FL ST RCP Rule 1.280(b)(5)(D).

vi. *Claims to privilege or protection.* When a party withholds information otherwise discoverable under the Florida Rules of Civil Procedure by claiming that it is privileged or subject to protection as trial preparation material, the party shall make the claim expressly and shall describe the nature of the documents, communications, or things not produced or disclosed in a manner that, without revealing information itself privileged or protected, will enable other parties to assess the applicability of the privilege or protection. FL ST RCP Rule 1.280(b)(6).

c. *Limitations on discovery of electronically stored information*

i. A person may object to discovery of electronically stored information from sources that the person identifies as not reasonably accessible because of burden or cost. On motion to compel discovery or for a protective order, the person from whom discovery is sought must show that the information sought or the format requested is not reasonably accessible because of undue burden or cost. If that showing is made, the court may nonetheless order the discovery from such sources or in such formats if the requesting party shows good cause. The court may specify conditions of the discovery, including ordering that some or all of the expenses incurred by the person from whom discovery is sought be paid by the party seeking the discovery. FL ST RCP Rule 1.280(d)(1).

ii. In determining any motion involving discovery of electronically stored information, the court must limit the frequency or extent of discovery otherwise allowed by the Florida Rules of Civil Procedure if it determines that (i) the discovery sought is unreasonably cumulative or duplicative, or can be obtained from another source or in another manner that is more convenient, less burdensome, or less expensive; or (ii) the burden or expense of the discovery outweighs its likely benefit, considering the needs of the case, the amount in controversy, the parties' resources, the importance of the issues at stake in the action, and the importance of the discovery in resolving the issues. FL ST RCP Rule 1.280(d)(2).

d. For information on inadvertent disclosure of privileged materials, see FL ST RCP Rule 1.285.

2. *Notice of deposition*

a. *Upon oral examination.* A party desiring to take the deposition of any person upon oral examination shall give reasonable notice in writing to every other party to the action. The notice shall state the time and place for taking the deposition and the name and address of each person to be examined, if known, and, if the name is not known, a general description sufficient to identify the person or the particular class or group to which the person belongs. If a subpoena duces tecum is to be served on the person to be examined, the designation of the materials to be produced under the subpoena shall be attached to or included in the notice. FL ST RCP Rule 1.310(b)(1).

b. *Upon written examination.* A party desiring to take a deposition upon written questions shall serve a notice stating: (1) the name and address of the person who is to answer them, if known, and, if the name is not known, a general description sufficient to identify the person or the particular class or group to which that person belongs, and (2) the name or descriptive title and address of the officer before whom the deposition is to be taken. FL ST RCP Rule 1.320(a).

3. *When leave of court required.* Leave of court, granted with or without notice, must be obtained only if the plaintiff seeks to take a deposition within thirty (30) days after service of the process and initial pleading upon any defendant, except that leave is not required if a defendant has served a notice of taking deposition or otherwise sought discovery. FL ST RCP Rule 1.310(a).

a. *Exceptions.* Leave of court is not required for the taking of a deposition by plaintiff if the notice states that the person to be examined is about to go out of the state and will be unavailable for examination unless a deposition is taken before expiration of the thirty (30) day period. If a party shows that when served with notice under FL ST RCP Rule 1.310(b) that party was unable through the exercise of diligence to obtain counsel to represent the party at the taking of the deposition, the deposition may not be used against that party. FL ST RCP Rule 1.310(b)(2).

b. *Persons in prison.* The deposition of a person confined in prison may be taken only by leave of court on such terms as the court prescribes. FL ST RCP Rule 1.310(a); FL ST RCP Rule 1.320(a).

4. *Deposition procedure*

a. *Who may take depositions.* Depositions may be taken before any notary public or judicial officer or before any officer authorized by the statutes of Florida to take acknowledgments or proof of executions of deeds or by any person appointed by the court in which the action is pending. FL ST RCP Rule 1.300(a).

i. *In foreign countries.* In a foreign country depositions may be taken: on notice before a person authorized to administer oaths in the place in which the examination is held, either by the law thereof or by the law of Florida or of the United States; before a person commissioned by the court, and a person so commissioned shall have the power by virtue of the commission to administer any necessary oath and take testimony; or pursuant to a letter rogatory. FL ST RCP Rule 1.300(b).

ii. *Selection by stipulation.* If the parties so stipulate in writing, depositions may be taken before any person at any time or place upon any notice and in any manner and when so taken may be used like other depositions. FL ST RCP Rule 1.300(c).

iii. *Persons disqualified.* Unless so stipulated by the parties, no deposition shall be taken before a person who is a relative, employee, attorney, or counsel of any of the parties, is a relative or employee of any of the parties' attorney or counsel, or is financially interested in the action. FL ST RCP Rule 1.300(d).

b. *Depositions before action*

i. *Petition.* A person who desires to perpetuate that person's own testimony or that of another person regarding any matter that may be cognizable in any Florida court may file a verified petition in the circuit court in the county of the residence of any expected adverse party. The petition shall be entitled in the name of the petitioner and shall show:

- That the petitioner expects to be a party to an action cognizable in a court of Florida, but is presently unable to bring the action;
- The subject matter of the expected action and the petitioner's interest therein;
- The facts which the petitioner desires to establish by the proposed testimony and the petitioner's reasons for desiring to perpetuate it;
- The names or a description of the persons the petitioner expects will be adverse parties and their addresses so far as known; and
- The names and addresses of the persons to be examined and the substance of the testimony which the petitioner expects to elicit from each; and shall ask for an order authorizing the petitioner to take the deposition of the persons to be examined named in the petition for the purpose of perpetuating their testimony. FL ST RCP Rule 1.290(a)(1).

ii. *Notice and service.* After submitting the petition, the petitioner must thereafter serve a notice upon each person named in the petition as an expected adverse party, together with a copy of the petition, stating that the petitioner will apply to the court at a time and place named therein for an order described in the petition. At least twenty (20) days before the date of hearing the notice shall be served either within or without the county in the manner provided by law for service of summons, but if such service cannot with due diligence be made upon any expected adverse party named in the petition, the court may make an order for service by publication or otherwise, and shall appoint an attorney for persons not served in the manner provided by law for service of summons who shall represent them, and if they are not otherwise represented, shall cross-examine the deponent. FL ST RCP Rule 1.290(a)(2).

iii. *Order and examination.* If the court is satisfied that the perpetuation of the testimony may prevent a failure or delay of justice, it shall make an order designating or describing the persons whose depositions may be taken and specifying the subject matter of the examination and whether the deposition shall be taken upon oral examination or written interrogatories. The deposition may then be taken in accordance with the rules governing depositions. FL ST RCP Rule 1.290(a)(3).

iv. *Use of deposition.* A deposition taken before an action and in accordance with the procedures above may be used in any action involving the same subject matter subsequently brought in any court. FL ST RCP Rule 1.290(a)(4).

c. *Depositions upon oral examination*

i. *Enlargement of time.* For cause shown the court may enlarge or shorten the time for taking the deposition. FL ST RCP Rule 1.310(b)(3).

ii. *Videotaped depositions.* Any deposition may be recorded by videotape without leave of the court or stipulation of the parties, provided the deposition is taken in accordance with the following:

- *Notice.* A party intending to videotape a deposition shall state in the notice that the deposition is to be videotaped and shall give the name and address of the operator. Any subpoena served on the person to be examined shall state the method or methods for recording the testimony. FL ST RCP Rule 1.310(b)(4)(A).
- *Stenographer.* Videotaped depositions shall also be recorded stenographically, unless all parties agree otherwise. FL ST RCP Rule 1.310(b)(4)(B).
- *Procedure.* At the beginning of the deposition, the officer before whom it is taken shall, on camera: (i) identify the style of the action, (ii) state the date, and (iii) swear the witness. FL ST RCP Rule 1.310(b)(4)(C).
- *Custody of tape and copies.* The attorney for the party requesting the videotaping of the deposition shall take custody of and be responsible for the safeguarding of the videotape, shall permit the viewing of it by the opposing party, and, if requested, shall provide a copy of the videotape at the expense of the party requesting the copy. FL ST RCP Rule 1.310(b)(4)(D).
- *Cost of videotaped depositions.* The party requesting the videotaping shall bear the initial cost of videotaping. FL ST RCP Rule 1.310(b)(4)(E).

iii. *Production of documents.* The notice to a party deponent may be accompanied by a request for the production of documents and tangible things at the taking of the deposition. The procedure of FL ST RCP Rule 1.350 shall apply to the request. FL ST RCP Rule 1.351 provides the exclusive procedure for obtaining documents or things by subpoena from nonparties without deposing the custodian or other person in possession of the documents. FL ST RCP Rule 1.310(b)(5).

iv. *Deposing organizations.* In the notice a party may name as the deponent a public or private corporation, a partnership or association, or a governmental agency, and designate with reasonable particularity the matters on which examination is requested. The organization so named shall designate one or more officers, directors, or managing agents, or other persons who consent to do so, to testify on its behalf and may state the matters on which each person designated will testify. The persons so designated shall testify about matters known or reasonably available to the organization. FL ST RCP Rule 1.310(b)(6).

v. *Depositions by telephone.* On motion the court may order that the testimony at a deposition be taken by telephone. The order may prescribe the manner in which the deposition will be taken. A party may also arrange for a stenographic transcription at that party's own initial expense. FL ST RCP Rule 1.310(b)(7).

vi. *Deposing a minor.* Any minor subpoenaed for testimony shall have the right to be accompanied by a parent or guardian at all times during the taking of testimony notwithstanding the invocation of the rule of sequestration of section FL ST § 90.616, except upon a showing that the presence of a parent or guardian is likely to have a material, negative impact on the credibility or accuracy of the minor's testimony, or that the interests of the parent or guardian are in actual or potential conflict with the interests of the minor. FL ST RCP Rule 1.310(b)(8).

vii. *Examination and cross-examination.* Examination and cross-examination of witnesses may proceed as permitted at the trial. FL ST RCP Rule 1.310(c).

viii. *Oath.* The officer before whom the deposition is to be taken shall put the witness on oath and shall personally, or by someone acting under the officer's direction and in the officer's presence, record the testimony of the witness, except that when a deposition is being taken by telephone, the witness shall be sworn by a person present with the witness who is qualified to administer an oath in that location. FL ST RCP Rule 1.310(c).

ix. *Record of examination.* The deposition testimony must be taken stenographically or recorded by any other means ordered. If requested by one of the parties, the testimony shall be transcribed at the initial cost of the requesting party and prompt notice of the request shall be given to all other parties. FL ST RCP Rule 1.310(c).

x. *Objections.* All objections made at time of the examination to the qualifications of the officer taking the deposition, the manner of taking it, the evidence presented, or the conduct of any party, and any other objection to the proceedings shall be noted by the officer upon the deposition. Any objection during a deposition shall be stated concisely and in a nonargumentative and nonsuggestive manner. A party may instruct a deponent not to answer only when necessary to preserve a privilege, to enforce a limitation on evidence directed by the court, or to present a motion under FL ST RCP Rule 1.310(d). FL ST RCP Rule 1.310(c).

- Otherwise, evidence objected to shall be taken subject to the objections. Instead of participating in the oral examination, parties may serve written questions in a sealed envelope on the party taking the deposition and that party shall transmit them to the officer, who shall propound them to the witness and record the answers verbatim. FL ST RCP Rule 1.310(c).

xi. *Motion to terminate or limit examination.* At any time during the taking of the deposition, on motion of a party or of the deponent and upon a showing that the examination is being conducted in bad faith or in such manner as unreasonably to annoy, embarrass, or oppress the deponent or party, or that improper objections and instructions to a deponent not to answer are being made, the court in which the action is pending or the circuit court where the deposition is being taken may order the officer conducting the examination to cease forthwith from taking the deposition or may limit the scope and manner of the taking of the deposition under the scope of permissible discovery. FL ST RCP Rule 1.310(d).

- If the order terminates the examination, it shall be resumed thereafter only upon the order of the court in which the action is pending. Upon demand of any party or the deponent, the taking of the deposition shall be suspended for the time necessary to make a motion for an order. FL ST RCP Rule 1.310(d).

xii. *Deponent review.* If the testimony is transcribed, the transcript shall be furnished to the witness for examination and shall be read to or by the witness unless the examination and reading are waived by the witness and by the parties. Any changes in form or substance that the witness wants to make shall be listed in writing by the officer with a statement of the reasons given by the witness for making the changes. The changes shall be attached to the transcript. It shall then be signed by the witness unless the parties waived the signing or the witness is ill, cannot be found, or refuses to sign. If the transcript is not signed by the witness within a reasonable time after it is furnished to the witness, the officer shall sign the transcript and state on the transcript the waiver, illness, absence of the witness, or refusal to sign with any reasons given. The deposition may then be used as fully as though signed unless the court holds that the reasons given for the refusal to sign require rejection of the deposition wholly or partly, on motion under FL ST RCP Rule 1.330(d)(4). FL ST RCP Rule 1.310(e).

xiii. *Certification and inspection.* If the deposition is transcribed, the officer shall certify on each copy of the deposition that the witness was duly sworn by the officer and that the deposition is a true record of the testimony given by the witness. Documents and things produced for inspection during the examination of the witness shall be marked for identification and annexed to and returned with the deposition upon the request of a party, and may be inspected and copied by any party, except that the person producing the materials may substitute copies to be marked for identification if that person affords to all parties fair opportunity to verify the copies by comparison with the originals. If the person producing the materials requests their return, the officer shall mark them, give each party an opportunity to inspect and copy them, and return them to the person producing them and the materials may then be used in the same manner as if annexed to and returned with the deposition. FL ST RCP Rule 1.310(f)(1).

xiv. *Copies.* Upon payment of reasonable charges, the officer shall furnish a copy of the deposition to any party or to the deponent. FL ST RCP Rule 1.310(f)(2). A party or witness who does not have a copy of the deposition may obtain it from the officer taking the deposition unless the court orders otherwise. If the deposition is obtained from a person other than the officer, the reasonable cost of reproducing the copies shall be paid to the person by the requesting party or witness. FL ST RCP Rule 1.310(g).

d. *Depositions upon written examination*

i. *Deposing an organization upon written examination.* A deposition upon written questions may be taken of a public or private corporation, a partnership or association, or a governmental agency in accordance with FL ST RCP Rule 1.310(b)(6). FL ST RCP Rule 1.320(a).

ii. *Cross, redirect, and recross questions.* Within thirty (30) days after the notice and written questions are served, a party may serve cross questions upon all other parties. Within ten (10) days after being served with cross questions, a party may serve redirect questions upon all other parties. Within ten (10) days after being served with redirect questions, a party may serve recross questions upon all other parties. The court may for cause shown enlarge or shorten the time. FL ST RCP Rule 1.320(a).

iii. *Procedure.* A copy of the notice and copies of all questions served shall be delivered by the party taking the depositions to the officer designated in the notice, who shall proceed promptly to take the testimony of the witness in the manner provided by FL ST RCP Rule 1.310(c), FL ST RCP Rule 1.310(e), and FL ST RCP Rule 1.310(f) in response to the questions and to prepare the deposition, attaching the copy of the notice and the questions received by the officer. The questions shall not be filed separately from the deposition unless a party seeks to have the court consider the questions before the questions are submitted to the witness. FL ST RCP Rule 1.320(b).

5. *Arbitration and mediation*

a. *Referral to arbitration and mediation.* Except as hereinafter provided or as otherwise prohibited by law, the presiding judge may enter an order referring all or any part of a contested civil matter to mediation or arbitration. The parties to any contested civil matter may file a written stipulation to mediate or arbitrate any issue between them at any time. Such stipulation shall be incorporated into the order of referral. FL ST RCP Rule 1.700(a).

b. *Arbitration*

i. *Exclusions.* A civil action shall be ordered to arbitration or arbitration in conjunction with mediation upon stipulation of the parties. A civil action may be ordered to arbitration or arbitration in conjunction with mediation upon motion of any party or by the court, if the judge determines the action to be of such a nature that arbitration could be of benefit to the litigants or the court. FL ST RCP Rule 1.800.

- Under no circumstances may the following categories of actions be referred to arbitration: (1) bond estreatures; (2) habeas corpus or other extraordinary writs; (3) bond validations; (4) civil or criminal contempt; (5) such other matters as may be specified by order of the chief judge in the circuit. FL ST RCP Rule 1.800.

ii. For more information regarding arbitration, please see FL ST RCP Rule 1.810; FL ST RCP Rule 1.820; FL ST RCP Rule 1.830; and FL ST 7 J CIR CV-2009-019-SC; and FL ST 7 J CIR CV-2003-002-SC(1)(c).

c. *Mediation.* For more information regarding mediation, please see FL ST RCP Rule 1.710; FL ST RCP Rule 1.720; FL ST RCP Rule 1.730; FL ST RCP Rule 1.750; FL ST 7 J CIR CV-2008-018-SC; and FL ST 7 J CIR CV-2003-002-SC(1).

6. *Rules of court*

a. *Rules of civil procedure.* The Florida Rules of Civil Procedure apply to all actions of a civil nature and all special statutory proceedings in the circuit courts and county courts except those to which the

Florida Probate Rules, the Florida Family Law Rules of Procedure, or the Small Claims Rules apply. FL ST RCP Rule 1.010.

i. The form, content, procedure, and time for pleading in all special statutory proceedings shall be as prescribed by the statutes governing the proceeding unless the Florida Rules of Civil Procedure specifically provide to the contrary. FL ST RCP Rule 1.010.

ii. The Florida Rules of Civil Procedure shall be construed to secure the just, speedy, and inexpensive determination of every action. FL ST RCP Rule 1.010.

b. *Rules of judicial administration.* The Florida Rules of Judicial Administration shall apply to administrative matters in all courts to which the Florida Rules of Judicial Administration are applicable by their terms. The Florida Rules of Judicial Administration shall be construed to secure the speedy and inexpensive determination of every proceeding to which they are applicable. The Florida Rules of Judicial Administration shall supersede all conflicting rules and statutes. FL ST J ADMIN Rule 2.110.

D. Documents

1. *Deposition upon oral or written examination*

a. *Required documents*

i. *Notice of deposition.* Please see the General Requirements section of this document for information on the content of a notice of deposition upon oral examination.

ii. *Certificate of service.* A certificate of service of the interrogatories shall be filed, giving the date of service and the name of the party to whom they were directed. FL ST RCP Rule 1.340(e). When any attorney certifies in substance: "I certify that a copy hereof has been furnished to (here insert name or names and addresses used for service) by (e-mail) (delivery) (mail) (fax) on .... (date) ....______________ Attorney" the certificate is taken as prima facie proof of such service in compliance with FL ST J ADMIN Rule 2.516. FL ST J ADMIN Rule 2.516(f).

b. *Supplemental documents*

i. *Motion for leave to take deposition.* See the Timing section for information on when leave is required.

ii. *Subpoena.* See the Timing section for requirements of when a subpoena is required.

iii. *Request for production of documents.* See the General Requirements section for further information.

iv. *Notice of filing of deposition transcript.* Deposition transcripts must be accompanied with a Notice of Filing of Deposition Transcript containing certification that the deposition is being filed for the purpose of being considered by the Court in a pending matter. The certification must specifically state the matter to be considered by the Court and the date and time of the hearing or other such proceeding. FL ST 7 J CIR CV-2003-009-SC.

E. Format

1. *Documents; Type and size.* Documents subject to the exceptions set forth in FL ST J ADMIN Rule 2.525(d) shall be filed on recycled paper measuring eight and one half by eleven (8 1/2 by 11) inches. For purposes of FL ST J ADMIN Rule 2.520, paper is recycled if it contains a minimum content of fifty (50) percent waste paper. Xerographic reduction of legal-size (eight and one half by fourteen (8 1/2 by 14) inches) documents to letter size (eight and one half by eleven (8 1/2 by 11) inches) is prohibited. All other documents filed by electronic transmission shall be filed in a format capable of being printed in a format consistent with the provisions of FL ST J ADMIN Rule 2.250. FL ST J ADMIN Rule 2.520(b).

a. *Exhibits.* Any exhibit or attachment filed with pleadings or papers may be filed in its original size. FL ST J ADMIN Rule 2.520(c).

b. *Recording space.* On all papers and documents prepared and filed by the court or by any party to a proceeding which are to be recorded in the public records of any county, including but not limited to final money judgments and notices of lis pendens, a three (3) inch by three (3) inch space at the top right-hand corner on the first page and a one (1) inch by three (3) inch space at the top right-hand corner on each subsequent page shall be left blank and reserved for use by the clerk of court. FL ST J ADMIN Rule 2.520(d).

i. *Exceptions to recording space.* Any papers or documents created by persons or entities over which the filing party has no control, including but not limited to wills, codicils, trusts, or other testamentary documents; documents prepared or executed by any public officer; documents prepared, executed, acknowledged, or proved outside of the State of Florida; or documents created by State or Federal government agencies, may be filed without the space required by FL ST J ADMIN Rule 2.520. FL ST J ADMIN Rule 2.520(e).

c. *Noncompliance.* No clerk of court is permitted to refuse to file any document or paper because of noncompliance with the Florida Rules of Judicial Administration. However, upon request of the clerk of court, noncomplying documents must be resubmitted in accordance with the formatting rules. FL ST J ADMIN Rule 2.520(f).

2. *Caption.* Every pleading, motion, order, judgment, or other paper shall have a caption containing the name of the court, the file number, and except for in rem proceedings, including forfeiture proceedings, the name of the first party on each side with an appropriate indication of other parties, and a designation identifying the party filing it and its nature or the nature of the order, as the case may be. In any in rem proceeding, every pleading, motion, order, judgment, or other paper shall have a caption containing the name of the court, the file number, the style "In re" (followed by the name or general description of the property), and a designation of the person or entity filing it and its nature or the nature of the order, as the case may be. In an in rem forfeiture proceeding, the style shall be "In re forfeiture of" (followed by the name of the general description of the property). All papers filed in the action shall be styled in such a manner as to indicate clearly the subject matter of the paper and the party requesting or obtaining relief. FL ST RCP Rule 1.100(c)(1).

a. *Volusia County eminent domain cases.* All orders, pleadings, motions and other papers will bear the initial case style. Documents intended to apply only to particular parcel(s) will indicate in their caption the parcel number(s) to which they apply and sufficient copies shall be provided to the Clerk of Court to allow the filing and docketing of each relevant paper in each parcel file. FL ST 7 J CIR CV-2000-011-VL(b).

3. *Writing and written defined.* Writing or written means a document containing information, an application, or a stipulation. FL ST RCP Rule 1.080(c).

4. *Rule abbreviations*

a. The Florida Rules of Civil Procedure and shall be abbreviated as Fla.R.Civ.P. FL ST RCP Rule 1.010.

b. The Florida Rules of Judicial Administration shall be abbreviated as Fla. R. Jud. Admin. FL ST J ADMIN Rule 2.110.

5. *Nonverification.* Except when otherwise specifically provided by the Florida Rules of Civil Procedure or an applicable statute, every pleading or other document of a party represented by an attorney need not be verified or accompanied by an affidavit. FL ST RCP Rule 1.030; FL ST J ADMIN Rule 2.515(a).

6. *Attorney signature*

a. *Attorney signature.* Every pleading and other document of a party represented by an attorney shall be signed by at least one (1) attorney of record in that attorney's individual name whose current record Florida Bar address, telephone number, including area code, primary e-mail address and secondary e-mail addresses, if any, and Florida Bar number shall be stated, and who shall be duly licensed to practice law in Florida or who shall have received permission to appear in the particular case as provided in FL ST J ADMIN Rule 2.510. FL ST J ADMIN Rule 2.515(a).

i. The attorney may be required by the court to give the address of, and to vouch for the attorney's authority to represent, the party. FL ST J ADMIN Rule 2.515(a).

ii. The signature of an attorney shall constitute a certificate by the attorney that the attorney has read the pleading or other document; that to the best of the attorney's knowledge, information, and belief there is good ground to support it; and that it is not interposed for delay. FL ST J ADMIN Rule 2.515(a).

iii. If a pleading is not signed or is signed with intent to defeat the purpose of FL ST J ADMIN Rule 2.515, it may be stricken and the action may proceed as though the pleading or other document had not been served. FL ST J ADMIN Rule 2.515(a).

b. *Pro se litigant signature.* A party who is not represented by an attorney shall sign any pleading or other paper and state the party's address and telephone number, including area code. FL ST J ADMIN Rule 2.515(b).

c. *Form of signature*

i. The signatures required on pleadings and documents by FL ST J ADMIN Rule 2.515(a) and FL ST J ADMIN Rule 2.515(b) may be:

- Original signatures;
- Original signatures that have been reproduced by electronic means, such as on electronically transmitted documents or photocopied documents;
- Electronic signatures using the "/s/," "s/," or "/s" formats by or at the direction of the person signing; or
- Any other signature format authorized by general law, so long as the clerk where the proceeding is pending has the capability of receiving and has obtained approval from the Supreme Court of Florida to accept pleadings and documents with that signature format. FL ST J ADMIN Rule 2.515(c)(1).

ii. An attorney, party, or other person who files a pleading or paper by electronic transmission that does not contain the original signature of that attorney, party, or other person shall file that identical pleading or paper in paper form containing an original signature of that attorney, party, or other person (hereinafter called the follow-up filing) immediately thereafter. The follow-up filing is not required if the Supreme Court of Florida has entered an order directing the clerk of court to discontinue accepting the follow-up filing. FL ST J ADMIN Rule 2.515(c)(2).

7. *Forms*

a. *Process.* The forms of process, notice of lis pendens, and notice of action provided in the Florida Rules of Civil Procedure are sufficient. Variations from the forms do not void process or notices that are otherwise sufficient. FL ST RCP Rule 1.900(a).

b. *Other forms.* The other forms provided in the Florida Rules of Civil Procedure are sufficient for the matters that are covered by them. So long as the substance is expressed without prolixity, the forms may be varied to meet the facts of a particular case. FL ST RCP Rule 1.900(b).

c. *Formal matters.* Captions, except for the designation of the paper, are omitted from the forms provided in the Florida Rules of Civil Procedure. A general form of caption is the first form provided. Signatures are omitted from pleadings and motions. FL ST RCP Rule 1.900(c).

8. *Notices to persons with disabilities.* All notices of court proceedings to be held in a public facility, and all process compelling appearance at such proceedings, shall include the following statement in bold face, fourteen (14) point Times New Roman or Courier font: "If you are a person with a disability who needs any accommodation in order to participate in this proceeding, you are entitled, at no cost to you, to the provision of certain assistance. Please contact [identify applicable court personnel by name, address, and telephone number] at least seven (7) days before your scheduled court appearance, or immediately upon receiving this notification if the time before the scheduled appearance is less than seven (7) days; if you are hearing or voice impaired, call 711." FL ST J ADMIN Rule 2.540(c)(1).

9. *Minimization of the filing of sensitive information*

a. *Limitations for court filings.* Unless authorized by FL ST J ADMIN Rule 2.425(b), statute, another rule of court, or the court orders otherwise, designated sensitive information filed with the court must be limited to the following format:

i. The initials of a person known to be a minor;

ii. The year of birth of a person's birth date;

iii. No portion of any: Social security number, Bank account number, Credit card account number, Charge account number, or Debit account number;

iv. The last four digits of any: Taxpayer identification number (TIN), Employee identification number, Driver's license number, Passport number, Telephone number, Financial account number, except as set forth in FL ST J ADMIN Rule 2.425(a)(3), Brokerage account number, Insurance policy account number, Loan account number, Customer account number, or Patient or health care number;

v. A truncated version of any: Email address, Computer user name, Password, or Personal identification number (PIN); and

vi. A truncated version of any other sensitive information as provided by court order. FL ST J ADMIN Rule 2.425(a).

b. *Exceptions.* FL ST J ADMIN Rule 2.425(a) does not apply to the following:

i. An account number which identifies the property alleged to be the subject of a proceeding;

ii. The record of an administrative or agency proceeding;

iii. The record in appellate or review proceedings;

iv. The birth date of a minor whenever the birth date is necessary for the court to establish or maintain subject matter jurisdiction;

v. The name of a minor in any order relating to parental responsibility, time-sharing, or child support;

vi. The name of a minor in any document or order affecting the minor's ownership of real property;

vii. The birth date of a party in a writ of attachment or notice to payor;

viii. In traffic and criminal proceedings: a pro se filing; a court filing that is related to a criminal matter or investigation and that is prepared before the filing of a criminal charge or is not filed as part of any docketed criminal case; an arrest or search warrant or any information in support thereof; a charging document and an affidavit or other documents filed in support of any charging document, including any driving records; a statement of particulars; discovery material introduced into evidence or otherwise filed with the court; and all information necessary for the proper issuance and execution of a subpoena duces tecum;

ix. Information used by the clerk for case maintenance purposes or the courts for case management purposes; and

x. Information which is relevant and material to an issue before the court. FL ST J ADMIN Rule 2.425(b).

c. *Remedies.* Upon motion by a party or interested person or sua sponte by the court, the court may order remedies, sanctions or both for a violation of FL ST J ADMIN Rule 2.425(a). Following notice and an opportunity to respond, the court may impose sanctions if such filing was not made in good faith. FL ST J ADMIN Rule 2.425(c).

d. *Motions not restricted.* FL ST J ADMIN Rule 2.425 does not restrict a party's right to move for protective order, to move to file documents under seal, or to request a determination of the confidentiality of records. FL ST J ADMIN Rule 2.425(d).

e. *Application.* FL ST J ADMIN Rule 2.425 does not affect the application of constitutional provisions, statutes, or rules of court regarding confidential information or access to public information. FL ST J ADMIN Rule 2.425(e).

F. Filing and Service Requirements

1. *Court filing of documents and discovery.* Information obtained during discovery shall not be filed with the court until such time as it is filed for good cause. The requirement of good cause is satisfied only where the filing of the information is allowed or required by another applicable rule of procedure or by court order.

All filings of discovery documents shall comply with FL ST J ADMIN Rule 2.425. The court shall have the authority to impose sanctions for violation of FL ST RCP Rule 1.280. FL ST RCP Rule 1.280(g).

a. *Filing of copies.* A copy of a deposition may be filed only under the following circumstances:

   i. It may be filed in compliance with FL ST J ADMIN Rule 2.425 and FL ST RCP Rule 1.280(f) by a party or the witness when the contents of the deposition must be considered by the court on any matter pending before the court. Prompt notice of the filing of the deposition shall be given to all parties unless notice is waived. A party filing the deposition shall furnish a copy of the deposition or the part being filed to other parties unless the party already has a copy. FL ST RCP Rule 1.310(f)(3)(A).

   ii. If the court determines that a deposition previously taken is necessary for the decision of a matter pending before the court, the court may order that a copy be filed by any party at the initial cost of the party, and the filing party shall comply with FL ST J ADMIN Rule 2.425 and FL ST RCP Rule 1.280(f). FL ST RCP Rule 1.310(f)(3)(B).

   iii. Deposition transcripts must be accompanied with a Notice of Filing of Deposition Transcript containing certification that the deposition is being filed for the purpose of being considered by the Court in a pending matter. The certification must specifically state the matter to be considered by the Court and the date and time of the hearing or other such proceeding. FL ST 7 J CIR CV-2003-009-SC.

2. *Filing requirements.* All original documents must be filed with the court either before service or immediately thereafter, unless otherwise provided for by general law or other rules. If the original of any bond or other document is not placed in the court file, a certified copy must be so placed by the clerk. FL ST J ADMIN Rule 2.516(d). All documents shall be filed in conformity with the requirements of FL ST J ADMIN Rule 2.525. FL ST RCP Rule 1.080(b). All documents filed in any court shall be filed by electronic transmission in accordance with FL ST J ADMIN Rule 2.525. "Documents" means pleadings, motions, petitions, memoranda, briefs, notices, exhibits, declarations, affidavits, orders, judgments, decrees, writs, opinions, and any other paper or writing submitted to a court. FL ST J ADMIN Rule 2.520(a). All documents that are court records, as defined in FL ST J ADMIN Rule 2.430(a)(1), must be filed by electronic transmission, provided that: (1) the clerk has the ability to accept and retain such documents; (2) the clerk or the chief judge of the circuit has requested permission to accept documents filed by electronic transmission; and (3) the supreme court has entered an order granting permission to the clerk to accept documents filed by electronic transmission. FL ST J ADMIN Rule 2.525(c)(1).

   a. *Definition.* "Electronic transmission of documents" means the sending of information by electronic signals to, by or from a court or clerk, which when received can be transformed and stored or transmitted on paper, microfilm, magnetic storage device, optical imaging system, CD-ROM, flash drive, other electronic data storage system, server, case maintenance system ("CM"), electronic court filing ("ECF") system, statewide or local electronic portal ("e-portal"), or other electronic record keeping system authorized by the supreme court in a format sufficient to communicate the information on the original document in a readable format. Electronic transmission of documents includes electronic mail ("e-mail") and any internet-based transmission procedure, and may include procedures allowing for documents to be signed or verified by electronic means. FL ST J ADMIN Rule 2.525(a).

      i. The filing of documents with the court as required by the Florida Rules of Judicial Administration must be made by filing them with the clerk in accordance with FL ST J ADMIN Rule 2.525, except that the judge may permit documents to be filed with the judge, in which event the judge must note the filing date before him or her on the documents and transmit them to the clerk. The date of filing is that shown on the face of the document by the judge's notation or the clerk's time stamp, whichever is earlier. FL ST J ADMIN Rule 2.516(e).

   b. *Application.* Any court or clerk of the court may accept the electronic transmission of documents for filing after the clerk, together with input from the chief judge of the circuit, has obtained approval of the procedures and program for doing so from the Supreme Court of Florida. FL ST J ADMIN Rule 2.525(b).

c. *Exceptions*

i. Paper documents and other submissions may be manually submitted to the clerk or court:

- When the clerk does not have the ability to accept and retain documents by electronic filing or has not had ECF Procedures approved by the supreme court;
- For filing by any self-represented party or any self-represented nonparty unless specific ECF Procedures provide a means to file documents electronically. However, any self-represented nonparty that is a governmental or public agency and any other agency, partnership, corporation, or business entity acting on behalf of any governmental or public agency may file documents by electronic transmission if such entity has the capability of filing documents electronically;
- For filing by attorneys excused from e-mail service in accordance with FL ST J ADMIN Rule 2.516(b);
- When submitting evidentiary exhibits or filing non-documentary materials;
- When the filing involves documents in excess of twenty-five (25) megabytes (25MB) in size. For such filings, documents may be transmitted using an electronic storage medium that the clerk has the ability to accept, which may include a CD-ROM, flash drive, or similar storage medium;
- When filed in open court, as permitted by the court;
- When paper filing is permitted by any approved statewide or local ECF procedures; and
- If any court determines that justice so requires. FL ST J ADMIN Rule 2.525(d).

ii. Any document in paper form submitted under FL ST J ADMIN Rule 2.525(d) is filed when it is received by the clerk or court and the clerk shall immediately thereafter convert any filed paper document to an electronic document. "Convert to an electronic document" means optically capturing an image of a paper document and using character recognition software to recover as much of the document's text as practicable and then indexing and storing the document in the official court file. FL ST J ADMIN Rule 2.525(c)(4).

iii. Any storage medium submitted under FL ST J ADMIN Rule 2.525(d)(5) is filed when received by the clerk or court and the clerk shall immediately thereafter transfer the electronic documents from the storage device to the official court file. FL ST J ADMIN Rule 2.525(c)(5).

iv. If the filer of any paper document authorized under FL ST J ADMIN Rule 2.525(d) provides a self-addressed, postage-paid envelope for return of the paper document after it is converted to electronic form by the clerk, the clerk shall place the paper document in the envelope and deposit it in the mail. Except when a paper document is required to be maintained, the clerk may recycle any filed paper document that is not to be returned to the filer. FL ST J ADMIN Rule 2.525(c)(6).

v. The clerk may convert any paper document filed before the effective date of FL ST J ADMIN Rule 2.525 to an electronic document. Unless the clerk is required to maintain the paper document, if the paper document has been converted to an electronic document by the clerk, the paper document is no longer part of the official court file and may be removed and recycled. FL ST J ADMIN Rule 2.525(c)(7).

d. *Official court file.* For information on what constitutes the official court file, please see FL ST J ADMIN Rule 2.525(c)(2), FL ST J ADMIN Rule 2.525(c)(3).

e. *Administration.* All attorneys, parties, or other persons using this rule to file documents are required to make arrangements with the court or clerk for the payment of any charges authorized by general law or the supreme court before filing any document by electronic transmission. FL ST J ADMIN Rule 2.525(f)(2).

f. *Filing date.* The filing date for an electronically transmitted document is the date and time that such filing is acknowledged by an electronic stamp or otherwise, pursuant to any procedure set forth in any ECF Procedures approved by the supreme court, or the date the last page of such filing is received by the court or clerk. FL ST J ADMIN Rule 2.525(f)(3).

g. *Accessibility.* All documents transmitted in any electronic form under FL ST J ADMIN Rule 2.525 must comply with the accessibility requirements of FL ST J ADMIN Rule 2.526. FL ST J ADMIN Rule 2.525(g).

3. *Service requirements.* Every pleading subsequent to the initial pleading, all orders, and every other document filed in the action must be served in conformity with the requirements of FL ST J ADMIN Rule 2.516. FL ST RCP Rule 1.080(a).

   a. *Service; When required.* Unless the court otherwise orders, or a statute or supreme court administrative order specifies a different means of service, every pleading subsequent to the initial pleading and every other document filed in any court proceeding, except applications for witness subpoenas and documents served by formal notice or required to be served in the manner provided for service of formal notice, must be served in accordance with FL ST J ADMIN Rule 2.516 on each party. No service need be made on parties against whom a default has been entered, except that pleadings asserting new or additional claims against them must be served in the manner provided for service of summons. FL ST J ADMIN Rule 2.516(a).

   b. *Service; How made.* When service is required or permitted to be made upon a party represented by an attorney, service must be made upon the attorney unless service upon the party is ordered by the court. FL ST J ADMIN Rule 2.516(b).

      i. *Service by electronic mail ("e-mail").* All documents required or permitted to be served on another party must be served by e-mail, unless FL ST J ADMIN Rule 2.516 otherwise provides. When, in addition to service by e-mail, the sender also utilizes another means of service provided for in FL ST J ADMIN Rule 2.516(b)(2), any differing time limits and other provisions applicable to that other means of service control. FL ST J ADMIN Rule 2.516(b)(1). Any document electronically transmitted to a court or clerk must also be served on all parties and interested persons in accordance with the applicable rules of court. FL ST J ADMIN Rule 2.525(e)(2).

         - *Service on attorneys.* Upon appearing in a proceeding, an attorney must serve a designation of a primary e-mail address and may designate no more than two (2) secondary e-mail addresses. Thereafter, service must be directed to all designated e-mail addresses in that proceeding. Every document filed by an attorney thereafter must include the primary e-mail address of that attorney and any secondary e-mail addresses. If an attorney does not designate any e-mail address for service, documents may be served on that attorney at the e-mail address on record with The Florida Bar. FL ST J ADMIN Rule 2.516(b)(1)(A).

         - *Exception to e-mail service on attorneys.* Service by an attorney on another attorney must be made by e-mail unless excused by the court. Upon motion by an attorney demonstrating that the attorney has no e-mail account and lacks access to the Internet at the attorney's office, the court may excuse the attorney from the requirements of e-mail service. Service on and by an attorney excused by the court from e-mail service must be by the means provided in FL ST J ADMIN Rule 2.516(b)(2). FL ST J ADMIN Rule 2.516(b)(1)(B).

         - *Service on and by parties not represented by an attorney.* Any party not represented by an attorney may serve a designation of a primary e-mail address and also may designate no more than two (2) secondary e-mail addresses to which service must be directed in that proceeding by the means provided in FL ST J ADMIN Rule 2.516(b)(1). If a party not represented by an attorney does not designate an e-mail address for service in a proceeding, service on and by that party must be by the means provided in FL ST J ADMIN Rule 2.516(b)(2). FL ST J ADMIN Rule 2.516(b)(1)(C).

         - *Time of service.* Service by e-mail is complete when it is sent. FL ST J ADMIN Rule 2.516(b)(1)(D). An e-mail is deemed served on the date it is sent. FL ST J ADMIN Rule 2.516(b)(1)(D)(i). If the sender learns that the e-mail did not reach the address of the person to be served, the sender must immediately send another copy by e-mail, or by a means authorized by FL ST J ADMIN Rule 2.516(b)(2). FL ST J ADMIN Rule 2.516(b)(1)(D)(ii). E-mail service is treated as service by mail for the computation of time. FL ST J ADMIN Rule 2.516(b)(1)(D)(iii).

ii. *Format of e-mail for service.* Service of a document by e-mail is made by attaching a copy of the document in PDF format to an e-mail sent to all addresses designated by the attorney or party. FL ST J ADMIN Rule 2.516(b)(1)(E).

- All documents served by e-mail must be attached to an e-mail message containing a subject line beginning with the words "SERVICE OF COURT DOCUMENT" in all capital letters, followed by the case number of the proceeding in which the documents are being served. FL ST J ADMIN Rule 2.516(b)(1)(E)(i).
- The body of the e-mail must identify the court in which the proceeding is pending, the case number, the name of the initial party on each side, the title of each document served with that e-mail, and the sender's name and telephone number. FL ST J ADMIN Rule 2.516(b)(1)(E)(ii).
- Any document served by e-mail may be signed by the "/s/" format, as long as the filed original is signed in accordance with the applicable rule of procedure. FL ST J ADMIN Rule 2.516(b)(1)(E)(iii).
- Any e-mail which, together with its attached documents, exceeds five megabytes (5MB) in size, must be divided and sent as separate e-mails, no one of which may exceed five megabytes (5MB) in size and each of which must be sequentially numbered in the subject line. FL ST J ADMIN Rule 2.516(b)(1)(E)(iv).

iii. *Service by other means.* In addition to, and not in lieu of, service by e-mail, service may also be made upon attorneys by any of the means specified in FL ST J ADMIN Rule 2.516(b)(2). Service on and by all parties who are not represented by an attorney and who do not designate an e-mail address, and on and by all attorneys excused from e-mail service, must be made by delivering a copy of the document or by mailing it to the party or attorney at their last known address or, if no address is known, by leaving it with the clerk of the court. Service by mail is complete upon mailing. Delivery of a copy within FL ST J ADMIN Rule 2.516 is complete upon:

- Handing it to the attorney or to the party,
- Leaving it at the attorney's or party's office with a clerk or other person in charge thereof,
- If there is no one in charge, leaving it in a conspicuous place therein,
- If the office is closed or the person to be served has no office, leaving it at the person's usual place of abode with some person of his or her family above fifteen (15) years of age and informing such person of the contents, or
- Transmitting it by facsimile to the attorney's or party's office with a cover sheet containing the sender's name, firm, address, telephone number, and facsimile number, and the number of pages transmitted. When service is made by facsimile, a copy must also be served by any other method permitted by FL ST J ADMIN Rule 2.516. Facsimile service occurs when transmission is complete. FL ST J ADMIN Rule 2.516(b)(2)(A) through FL ST J ADMIN Rule 2.516(b)(2)(E).
- Service by delivery after 5:00 p.m. must be deemed to have been made by mailing on the date of delivery. FL ST J ADMIN Rule 2.516(b)(2)(F).

c. *Service; Numerous defendants.* In actions when the parties are unusually numerous, the court may regulate the service contemplated by the Florida Rules of Judicial Administration on motion or on its own initiative in such manner as may be found to be just and reasonable. FL ST J ADMIN Rule 2.516(c).

d. *Service by clerk.* Service of notices and other documents required to be made by the clerk must also be done as provided in FL ST J ADMIN Rule 2.516(b). FL ST J ADMIN Rule 2.516(g).

G. Hearings

1. There is no hearing required or contemplated with regard to responses to requests for admission in the Florida Rules of Civil Procedure.

H. Forms

1. Official Notice of Deposition Forms for Florida

a. Caption. FL ST RCP Form 1.901.

2. Notice of Deposition Forms for Florida

a. Form for motion by plaintiff for leave to take deposition within 20-day period. FL-RCPF R 1.310(6).
b. Form for order on motion for leave to take deposition within 20-day period. FL-RCPF R 1.310(8).
c. Notice of examination; Time and place. FL-RCPF R 1.310(9).
d. Nonparty witness, subpoena required. FL-RCPF R 1.310(10).
e. Form for notice to take deposition on oral examination. FL-RCPF R 1.310(11).
f. Form for notice of taking multiple depositions. FL-RCPF R 1.310(11.1).
g. Form for notice of taking deposition and examination of documents. FL-RCPF R 1.310(12).
h. Form for notice of taking video deposition duces tecum. FL-RCPF R 1.310(13).
i. Form for motion to modify time for taking deposition. FL-RCPF R 1.310(14).
j. Form for motion to take deposition by telephone. FL-RCPF R 1.310(16).
k. Form for order permitting deposition by telephone. FL-RCPF R 1.310(17).
l. Form for notice of taking deposition by telephone. FL-RCPF R 1.310(18).
m. Form for notice of deposition upon written questions. FL-RCPF R 1.320(2).
n. Form of questions. FL-RCPF R 1.320(3).
o. Form of cross-questions. FL-RCPF R 1.320(4).
p. Form for objection to form of written questions. FL-RCPF R 1.320(6).

I. Checklist

(I) ❑ Matters to be considered by deposing party (oral depositions)
- (a) ❑ Required documents
  - (1) ❑ Notice of deposition
  - (2) ❑ Certificate of service
- (b) ❑ Supplemental documents
  - (1) ❑ Motion for leave to request deposition
  - (2) ❑ Subpoena
  - (3) ❑ Request for production of documents
- (c) ❑ Time for service of notice of deposition
  - (1) ❑ After commencement of action
  - (2) ❑ Within thirty (30) days after service of initial pleadings by leave of court only

(II) ❑ Matters to be considered by deponent (oral depositions)
- (a) ❑ Required documents
  - (1) ❑ Production of documents (if subpoenaed)

(III) ❑ Matters to be considered by deposing party (depositions by written questions)
- (a) ❑ Required documents
  - (1) ❑ Notice of deposition
  - (2) ❑ Written questions
  - (3) ❑ Certificate of service

(b) ❑ Supplemental documents

(1) ❑ Motion for leave to request deposition

(2) ❑ Subpoena

(3) ❑ Request for production of documents

(c) ❑ Time for service of direct and redirect questions

(1) ❑ Within ten (10) days after being served with cross questions, a party may serve redirect questions upon all other parties

(2) ❑ Objections to the form of the question must be served within the time for service of redirect questions or ten (10) days after service of recross questions

(IV) ❑ Matters to be considered by deponent (depositions by written questions)

(a) ❑ Required documents

(1) ❑ Cross questions, with certificate of service

(2) ❑ Recross questions with certificate of service

(b) ❑ Time for service of cross and recross questions

(1) ❑ Within thirty (30) days after the notice and written questions are served, a party may serve cross questions upon all other parties

(2) ❑ Within ten (10) days after being served with redirect questions, a party may serve recross questions upon all other parties

(3) ❑ Objections to the form of the questions must be served within the time for serving succeeding questions

NINTH JUDICIAL CIRCUIT

Pleadings
Complaint

Document Last Updated January 2013

A. Applicable Rules

1. *State rules*
   a. Nonverification of pleadings. FL ST RCP Rule 1.030.
   b. When action commenced. FL ST RCP Rule 1.050.
   c. Process. FL ST RCP Rule 1.070.
   d. Service and filing of pleadings, orders, and documents. FL ST RCP Rule 1.080.
   e. Time. FL ST RCP Rule 1.090.
   f. Pleadings and motions. FL ST RCP Rule 1.100; FL ST RCP Rule 1.110; FL ST RCP Rule 1.120; FL ST RCP Rule 1.130; FL ST RCP Rule 1.170; FL ST RCP Rule 1.430.
   g. Relief from judgment, decrees, or orders. FL ST RCP Rule 1.540.
   h. Forms. FL ST RCP Rule 1.900.
   i. Minimization of the filing of sensitive information. FL ST J ADMIN Rule 2.425.
   j. Retention of court records. FL ST J ADMIN Rule 2.430.
   k. Foreign attorneys. FL ST J ADMIN Rule 2.510.
   l. Signature of attorneys and parties. FL ST J ADMIN Rule 2.515.
   m. Paper. FL ST J ADMIN Rule 2.520.
   n. Electronic filing. FL ST J ADMIN Rule 2.525.
   o. Accessibility of information and technology. FL ST J ADMIN Rule 2.526.
   p. Requests for accommodations by persons with disabilities. FL ST J ADMIN Rule 2.540.
   q. Service. FL ST § 48.011; FL ST § 48.021; FL ST § 48.031; FL ST § 48.041; FL ST § 48.042; FL ST § 48.051; FL ST § 48.061; FL ST § 48.071; FL ST § 48.081; FL ST § 48.091; FL ST § 48.101; FL ST § 48.111; FL ST § 48.121; FL ST § 48.131; FL ST § 48.141; FL ST § 48.151; FL ST § 48.161; FL ST § 48.171; FL ST § 48.181; FL ST § 48.183; FL ST § 48.19; FL ST § 48.193; FL ST § 48.194; FL ST § 48.20; FL ST § 48.21; FL ST § 48.25; FL ST § 48.31; FL ST § 49.011; FL ST § 49.021; FL ST § 49.031; FL ST § 49.041; FL ST § 49.051; FL ST § 49.061; FL ST § 49.071; FL ST § 49.08; FL ST § 49.09; FL ST § 49.10; FL ST § 49.11; FL ST § 49.12; FL ST § 50.011; FL ST § 50.021; FL ST § 50.031; FL ST § 50.041; FL ST § 50.051; FL ST § 50.061.
   r. Fees. FL ST § 57.081; FL ST § 57.085; FL ST § 28.241; FL ST § 34.041.
2. *Local rules*
   a. Unrepresented (pro se) parties. FL ST 9 J CIR SECTION 7.
   b. Business court procedures. FL ST 9 J CIR ORANGE CIV SECTION 1.

B. Timing

1. *Commencement of an action.* Every action of a civil nature shall be deemed commenced when the complaint or petition is filed except that ancillary proceedings shall be deemed commenced when the writ is issued or the pleading setting forth the claim of the party initiating the action is filed. FL ST RCP Rule 1.050.
2. *Summons; Time limit.* If service of the initial process and initial pleading is not made upon a defendant

within one hundred twenty (120) days after filing of the initial pleading directed to that defendant the court, on its own initiative after notice or on motion, shall direct that service be effected within a specified time or shall dismiss the action without prejudice or drop that defendant as a party; provided that if the plaintiff shows good cause or excusable neglect for the failure, the court shall extend the time for service for an appropriate period. FL ST RCP Rule 1.070(j).

3. *Computation of time*
   a. *Generally.* Computation of time shall be governed by FL ST J ADMIN Rule 2.514. FL ST RCP Rule 1.090(a). The following rules apply in computing time periods specified in any rule of procedure, local rule, court order, or statute that does not specify a method of computing time. FL ST J ADMIN Rule 2.514(a).
      i. *Period stated in days or a longer unit.* When the period is stated in days or a longer unit of time (A) exclude the day of the event that triggers the period; (B) count every day, including intermediate Saturdays, Sundays, and legal holidays; and (C) include the last day of the period, but if the last day is a Saturday, Sunday, or legal holiday, or falls within any period of time extended through an order of the chief justice under FL ST J ADMIN Rule 2.205(a)(2)(B)(iv), the period continues to run until the end of the next day that is not a Saturday, Sunday, or legal holiday and does not fall within any period of time extended through an order of the chief justice. FL ST J ADMIN Rule 2.514(a)(1).
      ii. *Period stated in hours.* When the period is stated in hours (A) begin counting immediately on the occurrence of the event that triggers the period; (B) count every hour, including hours during intermediate Saturdays, Sundays, and legal holidays; and (C) if the period would end on a Saturday, Sunday, or legal holiday, or during any period of time extended through an order of the chief justice under FL ST J ADMIN Rule 2.205(a)(2)(B)(iv), the period continues to run until the same time on the next day that is not a Saturday, Sunday, or legal holiday and does not fall within any period of time extended through an order of the chief justice. FL ST J ADMIN Rule 2.514(a)(2).
      iii. *Period stated in days less than seven (7) days.* When the period stated in days is less than seven (7) days, intermediate Saturdays, Sundays, and legal holidays shall be excluded in the computation. FL ST J ADMIN Rule 2.514(a)(3).
      iv. *"Last day" defined.* Unless a different time is set by a statute, local rule, or court order, the last day ends (A) for electronic filing or for service by any means, at midnight; and (B) for filing by other means, when the clerk's office is scheduled to close. FL ST J ADMIN Rule 2.514(a)(4).
      v. *"Next day" defined.* The "next day" is determined by continuing to count forward when the period is measured after an event and backward when measured before an event. FL ST J ADMIN Rule 2.514(a)(5).
      vi. *"Legal holiday" defined.* "Legal holiday" means (A) the day set aside by FL ST § 110.117, for observing New Year's Day, Martin Luther King, Jr.'s Birthday, Memorial Day, Independence Day, Labor Day, Veterans' Day, Thanksgiving Day, the Friday after Thanksgiving Day, or Christmas Day, and (B) any day observed as a holiday by the clerk's office or as designated by the chief judge. FL ST J ADMIN Rule 2.514(a)(6).
   b. *Additional time after service by mail or e-mail.* When a party may or must act within a specified time after service and service is made by mail or e-mail, five (5) days are added after the period that would otherwise expire under FL ST J ADMIN Rule 2.514(a). FL ST J ADMIN Rule 2.514(b).
   c. *Enlargement.* When an act is required or allowed to be done at or within a specified time by order of court, by the Florida Rules of Civil Procedure, or by notice given thereunder, for cause shown the court at any time in its discretion (1) with or without notice, may order the period enlarged if request therefor is made before the expiration of the period originally prescribed or as extended by a previous order, or (2) upon motion made and notice after the expiration of the specified period, may permit the act to be done when failure to act was the result of excusable neglect, but it may not extend the time for making a motion for new trial, for rehearing, or to alter or amend a judgment; making a motion for relief from a judgment under FL ST RCP Rule 1.540(b); taking an appeal or filing a petition for certiorari; or making a motion for a directed verdict. FL ST RCP Rule 1.090(b).

d. *Unaffected by expiration of term.* The period of time provided for the doing of any act or the taking of any proceeding shall not be affected or limited by the continued existence or expiration of a term of court. The continued existence or expiration of a term of court in no way affects the power of a court to do any act or take any proceeding in any action which is or has been pending before it. FL ST RCP Rule 1.090(c).

C. General Requirements

1. *General rules of pleading*

a. *Claims for relief*

i. A pleading which sets forth a claim for relief, whether an original claim, counterclaim, crossclaim, or third-party claim, must state a cause of action and shall contain

- A short and plain statement of the grounds upon which the court's jurisdiction depends, unless the court already has jurisdiction and the claim needs no new grounds of jurisdiction to support it (For information regarding acts subjecting persons to jurisdiction, please see FL ST § 48.193),
- A short and plain statement of the ultimate facts showing that the pleader is entitled to relief, and
- A demand for judgment for the relief to which the pleader deems himself or herself entitled. FL ST RCP Rule 1.110(b).

ii. Relief in the alternative or of several different types may be demanded. Every complaint shall be considered to demand general relief. FL ST RCP Rule 1.110(b).

b. *Verification.* Except when otherwise specifically provided by these rules or an applicable statute, every pleading or other document of a party represented by an attorney need not be verified or accompanied by an affidavit. FL ST RCP Rule 1.030. When filing an action for foreclosure of a mortgage on residential real property the complaint shall be verified. When verification of a document is required, the document filed shall include an oath, affirmation, or the following statement: "Under penalty of perjury, I declare that I have read the foregoing, and the facts alleged therein are true and correct to the best of my knowledge and belief." FL ST RCP Rule 1.110(b).

c. *Separate statements.* All averments of claim or defense shall be made in consecutively numbered paragraphs, the contents of each of which shall be limited as far as practicable to a statement of a single set of circumstances, and a paragraph may be referred to by number in all subsequent pleadings. Each claim founded upon a separate transaction or occurrence and each defense other than denials shall be stated in a separate count or defense when a separation facilitates the clear presentation of the matter set forth. FL ST RCP Rule 1.110(f).

d. *Statements adopted by reference.* Statements in a pleading may be adopted by reference in a different part of the same pleading, in another pleading, or in any motion. FL ST RCP Rule 1.130(b).

e. *Joinder of causes of action; Consistency.* A pleader may set up in the same action as many claims or causes of action or defenses in the same right as the pleader has, and claims for relief may be stated in the alternative if separate items make up the cause of action, or if two (2) or more causes of action are joined. A party may also set forth two (2) or more statements of a claim or defense alternatively, either in one (1) count or defense or in separate counts or defenses. When two (2) or more statements are made in the alternative and one (1) of them, if made independently, would be sufficient, the pleading is not made insufficient by the insufficiency of one (1) or more of the alternative statements. A party may also state as many separate claims or defenses as that party has, regardless of consistency and whether based on legal or equitable grounds or both. All pleadings shall be construed so as to do substantial justice. FL ST RCP Rule 1.110(g).

f. *Subsequent pleadings.* When the nature of an action permits pleadings subsequent to final judgment and the jurisdiction of the court over the parties has not terminated, the initial pleading subsequent to final judgment shall be designated a supplemental complaint or petition. The action shall then proceed in the same manner and time as though the supplemental complaint or petition were the initial pleading in the action, including the issuance of any needed process. FL ST RCP Rule

1.110(h) shall not apply to proceedings that may be initiated by motion under the Florida Rules of Civil Procedure. FL ST RCP Rule 1.110(h).

g. *Pleading basis for service.* When service of process is to be made under statutes authorizing service on nonresidents of Florida, it is sufficient to plead the basis for service in the language of the statute without pleading the facts supporting service. FL ST RCP Rule 1.070(h).

h. *Forms of pleadings.* Forms of action and technical forms for seeking relief and of pleas, pleadings, or motions are abolished. FL ST RCP Rule 1.110(a).

2. *Complaint; Generally*

a. *Purpose.* The purpose of a complaint is to advise the court and the defendant of the nature of a cause of action asserted by the plaintiff. FL-PP § 2:12.

b. *Sufficiency of complaint.* A complaint will be found to be insufficient if it contains only general conclusory allegations unsupported by any facts. The test to determine whether a complaint is sufficient is whether, if the factual allegations of the complaint are established, the plaintiff will be legally or equitably entitled to the claimed relief. Pizzi v. Central Bank & Trust Co., 250 So.2d 895, 896 (Fla. 1971); Bowen v. G H C Properties, Limited, 251 So.2d 359, 361 (Fla. 1st DCA 1971); FL-PP § 2:12. In determining the sufficiency of the complaint to state a cause of action, all allegations of the complaint are taken as true, and possible affirmative defenses are not considered. Strickland v. Commerce Loan Co. of Jacksonville, 158 So.2d 814 (Fla. 1st DCA 1963); FL-PP § 2:12.

i. The issues for trial in Florida must be settled by the pleadings. The issues cannot be raised by discovery. FL-PRACPROC § 7:6.

ii. Causes of action may be pleaded alternatively in the same count or in different counts and against the same or different defendants as long as the joinder of parties is proper. FL-PRACPROC § 7:6.

iii. Each count must state a cause of action. Each independent cause of action should be pleaded in a separate count. FL-PRACPROC § 7:6.

iv. Incorporation by reference of all allegations from one count to another is not proper. Separate counts facilitate reference to the pleading in which they appear in other pleadings, motions or papers as well as the assertion of defenses against some, but not all, causes of action. Some defenses may not apply to the initial pleading as a whole. FL-PRACPROC § 7:6.

3. *Pleading special matters*

a. *Capacity.* It is not necessary to aver the capacity of a party to sue or be sued, the authority of a party to sue or be sued in a representative capacity, or the legal existence of an organized association of persons that is made a party, except to the extent required to show the jurisdiction of the court. The initial pleading served on behalf of a minor party shall specifically aver the age of the minor party. When a party desires to raise an issue as to the legal existence of any party, the capacity of any party to sue or be sued, or the authority of a party to sue or be sued in a representative capacity, that party shall do so by specific negative averment which shall include such supporting particulars as are peculiarly within the pleader's knowledge. FL ST RCP Rule 1.120(a).

b. *Fraud, mistake, condition of the mind.* In all averments of fraud or mistake, the circumstances constituting fraud or mistake shall be stated with such particularity as the circumstances may permit. Malice, intent, knowledge, mental attitude, and other condition of mind of a person may be averred generally. FL ST RCP Rule 1.120(b).

c. *Conditions precedent.* In pleading the performance or occurrence of conditions precedent, it is sufficient to aver generally that all conditions precedent have been performed or have occurred. A denial of performance or occurrence shall be made specifically and with particularity. FL ST RCP Rule 1.120(c).

d. *Official document or act.* In pleading an official document or official act it is sufficient to aver that the document was issued or the act done in compliance with law. FL ST RCP Rule 1.120(c).

e. *Judgment or decree.* In pleading a judgment or decree of a domestic or foreign court, a judicial or quasi-judicial tribunal, or a board or officer, it is sufficient to aver the judgment or decree without setting forth matter showing jurisdiction to render it. FL ST RCP Rule 1.120(e).

f. *Time and place.* For the purpose of testing the sufficiency of a pleading, averments of time and place are material and shall be considered like all other averments of material matter. FL ST RCP Rule 1.120(f).

g. *Special damage.* When items of special damage are claimed, they shall be specifically stated. FL ST RCP Rule 1.120(g).

4. *Parties*

a. *Parties generally.* Every action may be prosecuted in the name of the real party in interest, but a personal representative, administrator, guardian, trustee of an express trust, a party with whom or in whose name a contract has been made for the benefit of another, or a party expressly authorized by statute may sue in that person's own name without joining the party for whose benefit the action is brought. All persons having an interest in the subject of the action and in obtaining the relief demanded may join as plaintiffs and any person may be made a defendant who has or claims an interest adverse to the plaintiff. Any person may at any time be made a party if that person's presence is necessary or proper to a complete determination of the cause. Persons having a united interest may be joined on the same side as plaintiffs or defendants, and anyone who refuses to join may for such reason be made a defendant. FL ST RCP Rule 1.210(a).

b. *Minors or incompetent persons.* When a minor or incompetent person has a representative, such as a guardian or other like fiduciary, the representative may sue or defend on behalf of the minor or incompetent person. A minor or incompetent person who does not have a duly appointed representative may sue by next friend or by a guardian ad litem. The court shall appoint a guardian ad litem for a minor or incompetent person not otherwise represented in an action or shall make such other order as it deems proper for the protection of the minor or incompetent person. FL ST RCP Rule 1.210(b).

c. For survivor and substitution of parties information, please see FL ST RCP Rule 1.260.

5. *Counterclaims and crossclaims*

a. *Compulsory counterclaims.* A pleading shall state as a counterclaim any claim which at the time of serving the pleading the pleader has against any opposing party, provided it arises out of the transaction or occurrence that is the subject matter of the opposing party's claim and does not require for its adjudication the presence of third parties over whom the court cannot acquire jurisdiction. But the pleader need not state a claim if (1) at the time the action was commenced the claim was the subject of another pending action, or (2) the opposing party brought suit upon that party's claim by attachment or other process by which the court did not acquire jurisdiction to render a personal judgment on the claim and the pleader is not stating a counterclaim under this rule. FL ST RCP Rule 1.170(a).

b. *Permissive counterclaim.* A pleading may state as a counterclaim any claim against an opposing party not arising out of the transaction or occurrence that is the subject matter of the opposing party's claim. FL ST RCP Rule 1.170(b).

c. *Counterclaim exceeding opposing claim.* A counterclaim may or may not diminish or defeat the recovery sought by the opposing party. It may claim relief exceeding in amount or different in kind from that sought in the pleading of the opposing party. FL ST RCP Rule 1.170(c).

d. *Counterclaim against the State.* The Florida Rules of Civil Procedure shall not be construed to enlarge beyond the limits established by law the right to assert counterclaims or to claim credits against the state or any of its subdivisions or other governmental organizations thereof subject to suit or against a municipal corporation or against an officer, agency, or administrative board of the state. FL ST RCP Rule 1.170(d).

e. *Counterclaim maturing or acquired after pleading.* A claim which matured or was acquired by the pleader after serving the pleading may be presented as a counterclaim by supplemental pleading with the permission of the court. FL ST RCP Rule 1.170(e).

f. *Omitted counterclaim or crossclaim.* When a pleader fails to set up a counterclaim or crossclaim through oversight, inadvertence, or excusable neglect, or when justice requires, the pleader may set up the counterclaim or crossclaim by amendment with leave of the court. FL ST RCP Rule 1.170(f).

g. *Crossclaim against co-party.* A pleading may state as a crossclaim any claim by one party against a co-party arising out of the transaction or occurrence that is the subject matter of either the original action or a counterclaim therein, or relating to any property that is the subject matter of the original action. The crossclaim may include a claim that the party against whom it is asserted is or may be liable to the crossclaimant for all or part of a claim asserted in the action against the crossclaimant. Service of a crossclaim on a party who has appeared in the action shall be made pursuant to FL ST RCP Rule 1.080. Service of a crossclaim against a party who has not appeared in the action shall be made in the manner provided for service of summons. FL ST RCP Rule 1.170(g).

h. *Additional parties may be brought in.* When the presence of parties other than those to the original action is required to grant complete relief in the determination of a counterclaim or crossclaim, they shall be named in the counterclaim or crossclaim and be served with process and shall be parties to the action thereafter if jurisdiction of them can be obtained and their joinder will not deprive the court of jurisdiction of the action. FL ST RCP Rule 1.250(b) and FL ST RCP Rule 1.250(c) apply to parties brought in under FL ST RCP Rule 1.170(h). FL ST RCP Rule 1.170(h).

i. *Separate trials; Separate judgment.* If the court orders separate trials as provided in FL ST RCP Rule 1.270(b), judgment on a counterclaim or crossclaim may be rendered when the court has jurisdiction to do so even if a claim of the opposing party has been dismissed or otherwise disposed of. FL ST RCP Rule 1.170(i).

j. *Demand exceeding jurisdiction; Transfer of action.* If the demand of any counterclaim or crossclaim exceeds the jurisdiction of the court in which the action is pending, the action shall be transferred forthwith to the court of the same county having jurisdiction of the demand in the counterclaim or crossclaim with only such alterations in the pleadings as are essential. The court shall order the transfer of the action and the transmittal of all papers in it to the proper court if the party asserting the demand exceeding the jurisdiction deposits with the court having jurisdiction a sum sufficient to pay the clerk's service charge in the court to which the action is transferred at the time of filing the counterclaim or crossclaim. Thereupon the original papers and deposit shall be transmitted and filed with a certified copy of the order. The court to which the action is transferred shall have full power and jurisdiction over the demands of all parties. Failure to make the service charge deposit at the time the counterclaim or crossclaim is filed, or within such further time as the court may allow, shall reduce a claim for damages to an amount within the jurisdiction of the court where the action is pending and waive the claim in other cases. FL ST RCP Rule 1.170(j).

6. *Misjoinder and nonjoinder of parties*

a. *Misjoinder.* Misjoinder of parties is not a ground for dismissal of an action. Any claim against a party may be severed and proceeded with separately. FL ST RCP Rule 1.250(a).

b. *Dropping parties.* Parties may be dropped by an adverse party in the manner provided for voluntary dismissal in FL ST RCP Rule 1.420(a)(1) subject to the exception stated in FL ST RCP Rule 1.420. If notice of lis pendens has been filed in the action against a party so dropped, the notice of dismissal shall be recorded and cancels the notice of lis pendens without the necessity of a court order. Parties may be dropped by order of court on its own initiative or the motion of any party at any stage of the action on such terms as are just. FL ST RCP Rule 1.250(b).

c. *Adding parties.* Parties may be added once as a matter of course within the same time that pleadings can be so amended under FL ST RCP Rule 1.190(a). If amendment by leave of court or stipulation of the parties is permitted, parties may be added in the amended pleading without further order of court. Parties may be added by order of court on its own initiative or on motion of any party at any stage of the action and on such terms as are just. FL ST RCP Rule 1.250(c).

7. *Jury demand*

a. *Right preserved.* The right of trial by jury as declared by the Constitution or by statute shall be preserved to the parties inviolate. FL ST RCP Rule 1.430(a).

b. *Demand.* Any party may demand a trial by jury of any issue triable of right by a jury by serving upon the other party a demand therefor in writing at any time after commencement of the action and not later than ten (10) days after the service of the last pleading directed to such issue. The demand may be indorsed upon a pleading of the party. FL ST RCP Rule 1.430(b).

c. *Specification of issues.* In the demand a party may specify the issues that the party wishes so tried; otherwise, the party is deemed to demand trial by jury for all issues so triable. FL ST RCP Rule 1.430(c).

  i. If a party has demanded trial by jury for only some of the issues, any other party may serve a demand for trial by jury of any other or all of the issues triable by jury ten (10) days after service of the demand or such lesser time as the court may order. FL ST RCP Rule 1.430(c).

d. *Waiver.* A party who fails to serve a demand as required by FL ST RCP Rule 1.430 waives trial by jury. FL ST RCP Rule 1.430(d).

  i. If waived, a jury trial may not be granted without the consent of the parties, but the court may allow an amendment in the proceedings to demand a trial by jury or order a trial by jury on its own motion. FL ST RCP Rule 1.430(d).

  ii. A demand for trial by jury may not be withdrawn without the consent of the parties. FL ST RCP Rule 1.430(d).

8. *Arbitration and mediation*

a. *Referral to arbitration and mediation.* Except as hereinafter provided or as otherwise prohibited by law, the presiding judge may enter an order referring all or any part of a contested civil matter to mediation or arbitration. The parties to any contested civil matter may file a written stipulation to mediate or arbitrate any issue between them at any time. Such stipulation shall be incorporated into the order of referral. FL ST RCP Rule 1.700(a).

b. *Arbitration*

  i. *Exclusions.* A civil action shall be ordered to arbitration or arbitration in conjunction with mediation upon stipulation of the parties. A civil action may be ordered to arbitration or arbitration in conjunction with mediation upon motion of any party or by the court, if the judge determines the action to be of such a nature that arbitration could be of benefit to the litigants or the court. FL ST RCP Rule 1.800.

    - Under no circumstances may the following categories of actions be referred to arbitration: (1) bond estreatures; (2) habeas corpus or other extraordinary writs; (3) bond validations; (4) civil or criminal contempt; (5) such other matters as may be specified by order of the chief judge in the circuit. FL ST RCP Rule 1.800.

  ii. For more information regarding arbitration, please see FL ST RCP Rule 1.810; FL ST RCP Rule 1.820; FL ST RCP Rule 1.830.

c. *Mediation.* For more information regarding mediation, please see FL ST RCP Rule 1.710; FL ST RCP Rule 1.720; FL ST RCP Rule 1.730; and FL ST RCP Rule 1.750.

d. It is the policy of the Civil Division judges to maximize the use of alternative dispute resolution procedures. Except where prohibited by statute, mediation will be ordered in all cases where jury trial is requested and in selected cases which are to be tried non-jury. Also, selected cases will be referred for court-annexed non-binding arbitration through the Orange County Bar Association Arbitration Service. Counsel may move to dispense with or defer mediation or arbitration or move to modify the referral order for good cause. FL ST 9 J CIR SECTION 15.

9. *Rules of court*

a. *Rules of civil procedure.* The Florida Rules of Civil Procedure apply to all actions of a civil nature and all special statutory proceedings in the circuit courts and county courts except those to which the Florida Probate Rules, the Florida Family Law Rules of Procedure, or the Small Claims Rules apply. FL ST RCP Rule 1.010.

  i. The form, content, procedure, and time for pleading in all special statutory proceedings shall be as prescribed by the statutes governing the proceeding unless the Florida Rules of Civil Procedure specifically provide to the contrary. FL ST RCP Rule 1.010.

  ii. The Florida Rules of Civil Procedure shall be construed to secure the just, speedy, and inexpensive determination of every action. FL ST RCP Rule 1.010.

b. *Rules of judicial administration.* The Florida Rules of Judicial Administration shall apply to administrative matters in all courts to which the Florida Rules of Judicial Administration are applicable by their terms. The Florida Rules of Judicial Administration shall be construed to secure the speedy and inexpensive determination of every proceeding to which they are applicable. The Florida Rules of Judicial Administration shall supersede all conflicting rules and statutes. FL ST J ADMIN Rule 2.110.

c. *Business court procedures.* For rules specific to Business Court, please see FL ST 9 J CIR ORANGE CIV SECTION 1, et seq.

D. Documents

1. *Required documents*

a. *Summons.* Upon the commencement of the action, summons or other process authorized by law shall be issued forthwith by the clerk or judge under the clerk's or the judge's signature and the seal of the court and delivered for service without praecipe. FL ST RCP Rule 1.070(a).

b. *Complaint.* See the General Requirements section for the contents of the complaint.

i. *Notices to persons with disabilities.* See the Format section of this KeyRules document for further information.

c. *Civil cover sheet.* A civil cover sheet (FL ST RCP Form 1.997) shall be completed and filed with the clerk at the time an initial complaint or petition is filed by the party initiating the action. If the cover sheet is not filed, the clerk shall accept the complaint or petition for filing; but all proceedings in the action shall be abated until a properly executed cover sheet is completed and filed. The clerk shall complete the civil cover sheet for a party appearing pro se. FL ST RCP Rule 1.100(c)(2).

d. *Return of execution process by process server.* Each person who effects service of process shall note on a return-of-service form attached thereto, the date and time when it comes to hand, the date and time when it is served, the manner of service, the name of the person on whom it was served and, if the person is served in a representative capacity, the position occupied by the person. The return-of-service form must be signed by the person who effects the service of process. However, a person employed by a sheriff who effects the service of process may sign the return-of-service form using an electronic signature certified by the sheriff. FL ST § 48.21(1).

i. A failure to state the facts or to include the signature required by FL ST § 48.21(1) invalidates the service, but the return is amendable to state the facts or to include the signature at any time on application to the court from which the process issued. On amendment, service is as effective as if the return had originally stated the omitted facts or included the signature. A failure to state all the facts in or to include the signature on the return shall subject the person effecting service to a fine not exceeding $10, in the court's discretion. FL ST § 48.21(2).

e. *Filing fees.* Filing fees are due at the time a party files a pleading to initiate a proceeding or files a pleading for relief. FL ST § 28.241. For a fee schedule, see FL ST § 28.241.

2. *Supplemental documents*

a. *Exhibits.* All bonds, notes, bills of exchange, contracts, accounts, or documents upon which action may be brought or defense made, or a copy thereof or a copy of the portions thereof material to the pleadings, shall be incorporated in or attached to the pleading. No papers shall be unnecessarily annexed as exhibits. The pleadings shall contain no unnecessary recitals of deeds, documents, contracts, or other instruments. Any exhibit attached to a pleading shall be considered a part of the pleadings for all purposes. FL ST RCP Rule 1.130(a).

b. *Notice of constitutional question.* A party that files a pleading, written motion, or other paper drawing into question the constitutionality of a state statute or a county or municipal charter, ordinance, or franchise must promptly (1) file a notice of constitutional question stating the question and identifying the paper that raises it; and (2) serve the notice and the pleading, written motion, or other paper drawing into question the constitutionality of a state statute or a county or municipal charter, ordinance, or franchise on the Attorney General or the state attorney of the judicial circuit in which the action is pending, by either certified or registered mail. Service of the notice and pleading,

written motion, or other paper does not require joinder of the Attorney General or the state attorney as a party to the action. FL ST RCP Rule 1.071.

E. Format

1. *Documents; Type and size.* Documents subject to the exceptions set forth in FL ST J ADMIN Rule 2.525(d) shall be filed on recycled paper measuring eight and one half by eleven (8 1/2 by 11) inches. For purposes of FL ST J ADMIN Rule 2.520, paper is recycled if it contains a minimum content of fifty (50) percent waste paper. Xerographic reduction of legal-size (eight and one half by fourteen (8 1/2 by 14) inches) documents to letter size (eight and one half by eleven (8 1/2 by 11) inches) is prohibited. All other documents filed by electronic transmission shall be filed in a format capable of being printed in a format consistent with the provisions of FL ST J ADMIN Rule 2.250. FL ST J ADMIN Rule 2.520(b).
   a. *Exhibits.* Any exhibit or attachment filed with pleadings or papers may be filed in its original size. FL ST J ADMIN Rule 2.520(c).
   b. *Recording space.* On all papers and documents prepared and filed by the court or by any party to a proceeding which are to be recorded in the public records of any county, including but not limited to final money judgments and notices of lis pendens, a three (3) inch by three (3) inch space at the top right-hand corner on the first page and a one (1) inch by three (3) inch space at the top right-hand corner on each subsequent page shall be left blank and reserved for use by the clerk of court. FL ST J ADMIN Rule 2.520(d).
      i. *Exceptions to recording space.* Any papers or documents created by persons or entities over which the filing party has no control, including but not limited to wills, codicils, trusts, or other testamentary documents; documents prepared or executed by any public officer; documents prepared, executed, acknowledged, or proved outside of the State of Florida; or documents created by State or Federal government agencies, may be filed without the space required by FL ST J ADMIN Rule 2.520. FL ST J ADMIN Rule 2.520(e).
   c. *Noncompliance.* No clerk of court is permitted to refuse to file any document or paper because of noncompliance with the Florida Rules of Judicial Administration. However, upon request of the clerk of court, noncomplying documents must be resubmitted in accordance with the formatting rules. FL ST J ADMIN Rule 2.520(f).
2. *Caption.* Every pleading, motion, order, judgment, or other paper shall have a caption containing the name of the court, the file number, and except for in rem proceedings, including forfeiture proceedings, the name of the first party on each side with an appropriate indication of other parties, and a designation identifying the party filing it and its nature or the nature of the order, as the case may be. In any in rem proceeding, every pleading, motion, order, judgment, or other paper shall have a caption containing the name of the court, the file number, the style "In re" (followed by the name or general description of the property), and a designation of the person or entity filing it and its nature or the nature of the order, as the case may be. In an in rem forfeiture proceeding, the style shall be "In re forfeiture of" (followed by the name of the general description of the property). All papers filed in the action shall be styled in such a manner as to indicate clearly the subject matter of the paper and the party requesting or obtaining relief. FL ST RCP Rule 1.100(c)(1).
3. *Writing and written defined.* Writing or written means a document containing information, an application, or a stipulation. FL ST RCP Rule 1.080(c).
4. *Rule abbreviations*
   a. The Florida Rules of Civil Procedure and shall be abbreviated as Fla.R.Civ.P. FL ST RCP Rule 1.010.
   b. The Florida Rules of Judicial Administration shall be abbreviated as Fla. R. Jud. Admin. FL ST J ADMIN Rule 2.110.
5. *Nonverification.* Except when otherwise specifically provided by the Florida Rules of Civil Procedure or an applicable statute, every pleading or other document of a party represented by an attorney need not be verified or accompanied by an affidavit. FL ST RCP Rule 1.030; FL ST J ADMIN Rule 2.515(a).
6. *Unrepresented parties.* An unrepresented party must file his or her papers with the clerk and send copies

to other attorneys or unrepresented parties. All such papers must be typed double-spaced on plain white eight and a half by eleven (8 1/2 by 11) inch paper, with the name of the case and case number at the top and the party's mailing address, telephone number and FAX number, if any, below his or her signature at the end of the paper. Such unrepresented party must immediately notify the clerk and all other counsel or parties of record in writing of any change in mailing address or telephone or FAX number. Failure to promptly notify of change of address could result in a dismissal or default entered against such party. FL ST 9 J CIR SECTION 7(B)(5).

7. *Attorney signature*

   a. *Attorney signature.* Every pleading and other document of a party represented by an attorney shall be signed by at least one (1) attorney of record in that attorney's individual name whose current record Florida Bar address, telephone number, including area code, primary e-mail address and secondary e-mail addresses, if any, and Florida Bar number shall be stated, and who shall be duly licensed to practice law in Florida or who shall have received permission to appear in the particular case as provided in FL ST J ADMIN Rule 2.510. FL ST J ADMIN Rule 2.515(a).

      i. The attorney may be required by the court to give the address of, and to vouch for the attorney's authority to represent, the party. FL ST J ADMIN Rule 2.515(a).

      ii. The signature of an attorney shall constitute a certificate by the attorney that the attorney has read the pleading or other document; that to the best of the attorney's knowledge, information, and belief there is good ground to support it; and that it is not interposed for delay. FL ST J ADMIN Rule 2.515(a).

      iii. If a pleading is not signed or is signed with intent to defeat the purpose of FL ST J ADMIN Rule 2.515, it may be stricken and the action may proceed as though the pleading or other document had not been served. FL ST J ADMIN Rule 2.515(a).

   b. *Pro se litigant signature.* A party who is not represented by an attorney shall sign any pleading or other paper and state the party's address and telephone number, including area code. FL ST J ADMIN Rule 2.515(b).

   c. *Form of signature*

      i. The signatures required on pleadings and documents by FL ST J ADMIN Rule 2.515(a) and FL ST J ADMIN Rule 2.515(b) may be:

         - Original signatures;
         - Original signatures that have been reproduced by electronic means, such as on electronically transmitted documents or photocopied documents;
         - Electronic signatures using the "/s/," "s/," or "/s" formats by or at the direction of the person signing; or
         - Any other signature format authorized by general law, so long as the clerk where the proceeding is pending has the capability of receiving and has obtained approval from the Supreme Court of Florida to accept pleadings and documents with that signature format. FL ST J ADMIN Rule 2.515(c)(1).

      ii. An attorney, party, or other person who files a pleading or paper by electronic transmission that does not contain the original signature of that attorney, party, or other person shall file that identical pleading or paper in paper form containing an original signature of that attorney, party, or other person (hereinafter called the follow-up filing) immediately thereafter. The follow-up filing is not required if the Supreme Court of Florida has entered an order directing the clerk of court to discontinue accepting the follow-up filing. FL ST J ADMIN Rule 2.515(c)(2).

8. *Forms*

   a. *Process.* The forms of process, notice of lis pendens, and notice of action provided in the Florida Rules of Civil Procedure are sufficient. Variations from the forms do not void process or notices that are otherwise sufficient. FL ST RCP Rule 1.900(a).

   b. *Other forms.* The other forms provided in the Florida Rules of Civil Procedure are sufficient for the

matters that are covered by them. So long as the substance is expressed without prolixity, the forms may be varied to meet the facts of a particular case. FL ST RCP Rule 1.900(b).

c. *Formal matters.* Captions, except for the designation of the paper, are omitted from the forms provided in the Florida Rules of Civil Procedure. A general form of caption is the first form provided. Signatures are omitted from pleadings and motions. FL ST RCP Rule 1.900(c).

9. *Notices to persons with disabilities.* All notices of court proceedings to be held in a public facility, and all process compelling appearance at such proceedings, shall include the following statement in bold face, fourteen (14) point Times New Roman or Courier font: "If you are a person with a disability who needs any accommodation in order to participate in this proceeding, you are entitled, at no cost to you, to the provision of certain assistance. Please contact [identify applicable court personnel by name, address, and telephone number] at least seven (7) days before your scheduled court appearance, or immediately upon receiving this notification if the time before the scheduled appearance is less than seven (7) days; if you are hearing or voice impaired, call 711." FL ST J ADMIN Rule 2.540(c)(1).

10. *Minimization of the filing of sensitive information*

a. *Limitations for court filings.* Unless authorized by FL ST J ADMIN Rule 2.425(b), statute, another rule of court, or the court orders otherwise, designated sensitive information filed with the court must be limited to the following format:

i. The initials of a person known to be a minor;

ii. The year of birth of a person's birth date;

iii. No portion of any: Social security number, Bank account number, Credit card account number, Charge account number, or Debit account number;

iv. The last four digits of any: Taxpayer identification number (TIN), Employee identification number, Driver's license number, Passport number, Telephone number, Financial account number, except as set forth in FL ST J ADMIN Rule 2.425(a)(3), Brokerage account number, Insurance policy account number, Loan account number, Customer account number, or Patient or health care number;

v. A truncated version of any: Email address, Computer user name, Password, or Personal identification number (PIN); and

vi. A truncated version of any other sensitive information as provided by court order. FL ST J ADMIN Rule 2.425(a).

b. *Exceptions.* FL ST J ADMIN Rule 2.425(a) does not apply to the following:

i. An account number which identifies the property alleged to be the subject of a proceeding;

ii. The record of an administrative or agency proceeding;

iii. The record in appellate or review proceedings;

iv. The birth date of a minor whenever the birth date is necessary for the court to establish or maintain subject matter jurisdiction;

v. The name of a minor in any order relating to parental responsibility, time-sharing, or child support;

vi. The name of a minor in any document or order affecting the minor's ownership of real property;

vii. The birth date of a party in a writ of attachment or notice to payor;

viii. In traffic and criminal proceedings: a pro se filing; a court filing that is related to a criminal matter or investigation and that is prepared before the filing of a criminal charge or is not filed as part of any docketed criminal case; an arrest or search warrant or any information in support thereof; a charging document and an affidavit or other documents filed in support of any charging document, including any driving records; a statement of particulars; discovery material introduced into evidence or otherwise filed with the court; and all information necessary for the proper issuance and execution of a subpoena duces tecum;

ix. Information used by the clerk for case maintenance purposes or the courts for case management purposes; and

x. Information which is relevant and material to an issue before the court. FL ST J ADMIN Rule 2.425(b).

c. *Remedies.* Upon motion by a party or interested person or sua sponte by the court, the court may order remedies, sanctions or both for a violation of FL ST J ADMIN Rule 2.425(a). Following notice and an opportunity to respond, the court may impose sanctions if such filing was not made in good faith. FL ST J ADMIN Rule 2.425(c).

d. *Motions not restricted.* FL ST J ADMIN Rule 2.425 does not restrict a party's right to move for protective order, to move to file documents under seal, or to request a determination of the confidentiality of records. FL ST J ADMIN Rule 2.425(d).

e. *Application.* FL ST J ADMIN Rule 2.425 does not affect the application of constitutional provisions, statutes, or rules of court regarding confidential information or access to public information. FL ST J ADMIN Rule 2.425(e).

F. Filing and Service Requirements

1. *Filing requirements.* All documents filed in any court shall be filed by electronic transmission in accordance with FL ST J ADMIN Rule 2.525. "Documents" means pleadings, motions, petitions, memoranda, briefs, notices, exhibits, declarations, affidavits, orders, judgments, decrees, writs, opinions, and any other paper or writing submitted to a court. FL ST J ADMIN Rule 2.520(a). All documents that are court records, as defined in FL ST J ADMIN Rule 2.430(a)(1), must be filed by electronic transmission, provided that: (1) the clerk has the ability to accept and retain such documents; (2) the clerk or the chief judge of the circuit has requested permission to accept documents filed by electronic transmission; and (3) the supreme court has entered an order granting permission to the clerk to accept documents filed by electronic transmission. FL ST J ADMIN Rule 2.525(c)(1).

a. *Definition.* "Electronic transmission of documents" means the sending of information by electronic signals to, by or from a court or clerk, which when received can be transformed and stored or transmitted on paper, microfilm, magnetic storage device, optical imaging system, CD-ROM, flash drive, other electronic data storage system, server, case maintenance system ("CM"), electronic court filing ("ECF") system, statewide or local electronic portal ("e-portal"), or other electronic record keeping system authorized by the supreme court in a format sufficient to communicate the information on the original document in a readable format. Electronic transmission of documents includes electronic mail ("e-mail") and any internet-based transmission procedure, and may include procedures allowing for documents to be signed or verified by electronic means. FL ST J ADMIN Rule 2.525(a).

b. *Application.* Any court or clerk of the court may accept the electronic transmission of documents for filing after the clerk, together with input from the chief judge of the circuit, has obtained approval of the procedures and program for doing so from the Supreme Court of Florida. FL ST J ADMIN Rule 2.525(b).

c. *Exceptions*

i. Paper documents and other submissions may be manually submitted to the clerk or court:

- When the clerk does not have the ability to accept and retain documents by electronic filing or has not had ECF Procedures approved by the supreme court;
- For filing by any self-represented party or any self-represented nonparty unless specific ECF Procedures provide a means to file documents electronically. However, any self-represented nonparty that is a governmental or public agency and any other agency, partnership, corporation, or business entity acting on behalf of any governmental or public agency may file documents by electronic transmission if such entity has the capability of filing documents electronically;
- For filing by attorneys excused from e-mail service in accordance with FL ST J ADMIN Rule 2.516(b);
- When submitting evidentiary exhibits or filing non-documentary materials;
- When the filing involves documents in excess of twenty-five (25) megabytes (25MB) in

size. For such filings, documents may be transmitted using an electronic storage medium that the clerk has the ability to accept, which may include a CD-ROM, flash drive, or similar storage medium;

- When filed in open court, as permitted by the court;
- When paper filing is permitted by any approved statewide or local ECF procedures; and
- If any court determines that justice so requires. FL ST J ADMIN Rule 2.525(d).

ii. Any document in paper form submitted under FL ST J ADMIN Rule 2.525(d) is filed when it is received by the clerk or court and the clerk shall immediately thereafter convert any filed paper document to an electronic document. "Convert to an electronic document" means optically capturing an image of a paper document and using character recognition software to recover as much of the document's text as practicable and then indexing and storing the document in the official court file. FL ST J ADMIN Rule 2.525(c)(4).

iii. Any storage medium submitted under FL ST J ADMIN Rule 2.525(d)(5) is filed when received by the clerk or court and the clerk shall immediately thereafter transfer the electronic documents from the storage device to the official court file. FL ST J ADMIN Rule 2.525(c)(5).

iv. If the filer of any paper document authorized under FL ST J ADMIN Rule 2.525(d) provides a self-addressed, postage-paid envelope for return of the paper document after it is converted to electronic form by the clerk, the clerk shall place the paper document in the envelope and deposit it in the mail. Except when a paper document is required to be maintained, the clerk may recycle any filed paper document that is not to be returned to the filer. FL ST J ADMIN Rule 2.525(c)(6).

v. The clerk may convert any paper document filed before the effective date of FL ST J ADMIN Rule 2.525 to an electronic document. Unless the clerk is required to maintain the paper document, if the paper document has been converted to an electronic document by the clerk, the paper document is no longer part of the official court file and may be removed and recycled. FL ST J ADMIN Rule 2.525(c)(7).

d. *Unrepresented parties.* An unrepresented party must file his or her papers with the clerk and send copies to other attorneys or unrepresented parties. FL ST 9 J CIR SECTION 7(B)(5).

i. An unrepresented party may not communicate privately with the judge either by letter, telephone, in person or otherwise. FL ST 9 J CIR SECTION 7(B)(4).

ii. Copies of legal papers or other written materials should not be sent to the judge unless specifically requested by the judge or required by the local administrative procedures. Any unrequested or non-required papers or materials sent to a judge may not be read but may be returned to the sender or placed unread into the court file. FL ST 9 J CIR SECTION 7(B)(4).

e. *Official court file.* For information on what constitutes the official court file, please see FL ST J ADMIN Rule 2.525(c)(2), FL ST J ADMIN Rule 2.525(c)(3).

f. *Administration.* All attorneys, parties, or other persons using this rule to file documents are required to make arrangements with the court or clerk for the payment of any charges authorized by general law or the supreme court before filing any document by electronic transmission. FL ST J ADMIN Rule 2.525(f)(2).

g. *Filing date.* The filing date for an electronically transmitted document is the date and time that such filing is acknowledged by an electronic stamp or otherwise, pursuant to any procedure set forth in any ECF Procedures approved by the supreme court, or the date the last page of such filing is received by the court or clerk. FL ST J ADMIN Rule 2.525(f)(3).

h. *Accessibility.* All documents transmitted in any electronic form under FL ST J ADMIN Rule 2.525 must comply with the accessibility requirements of FL ST J ADMIN Rule 2.526. FL ST J ADMIN Rule 2.525(g).

2. *Service requirements*

a. *Papers to be served.* At the time of personal service of process a copy of the initial pleading shall be delivered to the party upon whom service is made. The date and hour of service shall be endorsed on the original process and all copies of it by the person making the service. The party seeking to effect personal service shall furnish the person making service with the necessary copies. When the service is made by publication, copies of the initial pleadings shall be furnished to the clerk and mailed by the clerk with the notice of action to all parties whose addresses are stated in the initial pleading or sworn statement. FL ST RCP Rule 1.070(e).

b. *Issuance of summons.* Upon the commencement of the action, summons or other process authorized by law shall be issued forthwith by the clerk or judge under the clerk's or the judge's signature and the seal of the court and delivered for service without praecipe. FL ST RCP Rule 1.070(a).

 i. *How directed.* Summons, subpoenas, and other process in civil actions run throughout the state. All process except subpoenas shall be directed to all and singular the sheriffs of the state. FL ST § 48.011.

 ii. *Service as to numerous defendants.* If there is more than one (1) defendant, the clerk or judge shall issue as many writs of process against the several defendants as may be directed by the plaintiff or the plaintiff's attorney. FL ST RCP Rule 1.070(c).

c. *Who may serve process.* Service of process may be made by an officer authorized by law to serve process, but the court may appoint any competent person not interested in the action to serve the process. When so appointed, the person serving process shall make proof of service by affidavit promptly and in any event within the time during which the person served must respond to the process. Failure to make proof of service shall not affect the validity of the service. When any process is returned not executed or returned improperly executed for any defendant, the party causing its issuance shall be entitled to such additional process against the unserved party as is required to effect service. FL ST RCP Rule 1.070(b).

 i. All process shall be served by the sheriff of the county where the person to be served is found, except initial nonenforceable civil process may be served by a special process server appointed by the sheriff as provided for in FL ST § 48.021 or by a certified process server as provided for in FL ST § 48.25 through FL ST § 48.31. FL ST § 48.021(1).

 ii. The sheriff of each county may, in his or her discretion, establish an approved list of natural persons designated as special process servers. FL ST § 48.021(2)(a). For more information regarding process servers, please see FL ST § 48.021(2).

 iii. A person serving process shall place, on the copy served, the date and time of service and his or her identification number and initials for all service of process. FL ST § 48.031(5).

d. *Service of process on Sunday*

 i. Service or execution on Sunday of any writ, process, warrant, order, or judgment is void and the person serving or executing, or causing it to be served or executed, is liable to the party aggrieved for damages for so doing as if he or she had done it without any process, writ, warrant, order, or judgment. FL ST § 48.20.

 ii. If affidavit is made by the person requesting service or execution that he or she has good reason to believe that any person liable to have any such writ, process, warrant, order, or judgment served on him or her intends to escape from this state under protection of Sunday, any officer furnished with an order authorizing service or execution by the trial court judge may serve or execute such writ, process, warrant, order, or judgment on Sunday, and it is as valid as if it had been done on any other day. FL ST § 48.20.

e. *Methods of service*

 i. *Service of process generally.* Service of original process is made by delivering a copy of it to the person to be served with a copy of the complaint, petition, or other initial pleading or paper or by leaving the copies at his or her usual place of abode with any person residing therein who is fifteen (15) years of age or older and informing the person of their contents. Minors who are or have been married shall be served as provided in FL ST § 48.031. FL ST § 48.031(1)(a).

 - Employers, when contacted by an individual authorized to make service of process, shall permit the authorized individual to make service on employees in a private area designated by the employer. FL ST § 48.031(1)(b).

- Substitute service may be made on the spouse of the person to be served at any place in the county, if the cause of action is not an adversary proceeding between the spouse and the person to be served, if the spouse requests such service, and if the spouse and person to be served are residing together in the same dwelling. FL ST § 48.031(2)(a).
- Substitute service may be made on an individual doing business as a sole proprietorship at his or her place of business, during regular business hours, by serving the person in charge of the business at the time of service if two (2) or more attempts to serve the owner have been made at the place of business. FL ST § 48.031(2)(b).
- If the only address for a person to be served, which is discoverable through public records, is a private mailbox, substitute service may be made by leaving a copy of the process with the person in charge of the private mailbox, but only if the process server determines that the person to be served maintains a mailbox at that location. FL ST § 48.031(6).

ii. *Service by mail.* A defendant may accept service of process by mail. FL ST RCP Rule 1.070(i). A plaintiff may notify any defendant of the commencement of the action and request that the defendant waive service of a summons. FL ST RCP Rule 1.070(i)(2).

- *Notice and request for waiver.* The notice and request shall: (1) be in writing and be addressed directly to the defendant, if an individual, or to an officer or managing or general agent of the defendant or other agent authorized by appointment or law to receive service of process; (2) be dispatched by certified mail, return receipt requested; (3) be accompanied by a copy of the complaint and shall identify the court in which it has been filed; (4) inform the defendant of the consequences of compliance and of failure to comply with the request; (5) state the date on which the request is sent; (6) allow the defendant twenty (20) days from the date on which the request is received to return the waiver, or, if the address of the defendant is outside of the United States, thirty (30) days from the date on which it is received to return the waiver; and (7) provide the defendant with an extra copy of the notice and request, including the waiver, as well as a prepaid means of compliance in writing. FL ST RCP Rule 1.070(i)(2).
- *Consequences of accepting/rejecting service by mail.* Acceptance of service of a complaint by mail does not thereby waive any objection to the venue or to the jurisdiction of the court over the person of the defendant. FL ST RCP Rule 1.070(i)(1). If a defendant fails to comply with a request for waiver within the time provided, the court shall impose the costs subsequently incurred in effecting service on the defendant unless good cause for the failure is shown. FL ST RCP Rule 1.070(i)(3). A defendant who, before being served with process, timely returns a waiver so requested is not required to respond to the complaint until sixty (60) days after the date the defendant received the request for waiver of service. For purposes of computing any time prescribed or allowed by the Florida Rules of Civil Procedure, service of process shall be deemed effected twenty (20) days before the time required to respond to the complaint. FL ST RCP Rule 1.070(i)(4). When the plaintiff files a waiver of service with the court, the action shall proceed, except as provided in FL ST RCP Rule 1.070(i)(4), as if a summons and complaint had been served at the time of filing the waiver, and no further proof of service shall be required. FL ST RCP Rule 1.070(i)(5).

iii. *Service on partnerships and limited partnerships*

- Process against a partnership shall be served on any partner and is as valid as if served on each individual partner. If a partner is not available during regular business hours to accept service on behalf of the partnership, he or she may designate an employee to accept such service. After one (1) attempt to serve a partner or designated employee has been made, process may be served on the person in charge of the partnership during regular business hours. After service on any partner, plaintiff may proceed to judgment and execution against that partner and the assets of the partnership. After service on a designated employee or other person in charge, plaintiff may proceed to judgment and execution against the partnership assets but not against the individual assets of any partner. FL ST § 48.061(1).

- Process against a domestic limited partnership may be served on any general partner or on the agent for service of process specified in its certificate of limited partnership or in its certificate as amended or restated and is as valid as if served on each individual member of the partnership. After service on a general partner or the agent, the plaintiff may proceed to judgment and execution against the limited partnership and all of the general partners individually. If a general partner cannot be found in this state and service cannot be made on an agent because of failure to maintain such an agent or because the agent cannot be found or served with the exercise of reasonable diligence, service of process may be effected by service upon the Secretary of State as agent of the limited partnership as provided for in FL ST § 48.181. Service of process may be made under FL ST § 48.071 and FL ST § 48.21 on limited partnerships. FL ST § 48.061(2).
- Process against a foreign limited partnership may be served on any general partner found in the state or on any agent for service of process specified in its application for registration and is as valid as if served on each individual member of the partnership. If a general partner cannot be found in this state and an agent for service of process has not been appointed or, if appointed, the agent's authority has been revoked or the agent cannot be found or served with the exercise of reasonable diligence, service of process may be effected by service upon the Secretary of State as agent of the limited partnership as provided for in FL ST § 48.181, or process may be served as provided in FL ST § 48.071 and FL ST § 48.21. FL ST § 48.061(3).

iv. *Service on corporation*

- Process against any private corporation, domestic or foreign, may be served: (1) on the president or vice president, or other head of the corporation; (2) in the absence of any person described in FL ST § 48.081(1)(a), on the cashier, treasurer, secretary, or general manager; (3) in the absence of any person described in FL ST § 48.081(1)(a) or FL ST § 48.081(1)(b), on any director; or (4) in the absence of any person described in FL ST § 48.081(1)(a), FL ST § 48.081(1)(b), or FL ST § 48.081(1)(c), on any officer or business agent residing in the state. FL ST § 48.081(1).
- If a foreign corporation has none of the foregoing officers or agents in this state, service may be made on any agent transacting business for it in this state. FL ST § 48.081(2).
- As an alternative to all of the foregoing, process may be served on the agent designated by the corporation under FL ST § 48.091. However, if service cannot be made on a registered agent because of failure to comply with FL ST § 48.091, service of process shall be permitted on any employee at the corporation's principal place of business or on any employee of the registered agent. FL ST § 48.081(3)(a). If the address provided for the registered agent, officer, director, or principal place of business is a residence or private mailbox, service on the corporation may be made by serving the registered agent, officer, or director in accordance with FL ST § 48.031. FL ST § 48.081(3)(b).
- FL ST § 48.081 does not apply to service of process on insurance companies. FL ST § 48.081(4).
- When a corporation engages in substantial and not isolated activities within this state, or has a business office within the state and is actually engaged in the transaction of business therefrom, service upon any officer or business agent while on corporate business within this state may personally be made, pursuant to FL ST § 48.081, and it is not necessary in such case that the action, suit, or proceeding against the corporation shall have arisen out of any transaction or operation connected with or incidental to the business being transacted within the state. FL ST § 48.081(5).
- For information regarding service on a dissolved corporation refer to FL ST § 48.101.

v. *Personal service outside state*

- Except as otherwise provided herein, service of process on persons outside of this state shall be made in the same manner as service within this state by any officer authorized to serve process in the state where the person is served. No order of court is required. An affidavit of the officer shall be filed, stating the time, manner, and place of service. The court may consider the affidavit, or any other competent evidence, in determining whether service has been properly made. Service of process on persons outside the United States may be required to conform to the provisions of the Hague Convention on the Service Abroad of Judicial and Extrajudicial Documents in Civil or Commercial Matters. FL ST § 48.194(1).

- For further information on service of process in an in rem or quasi in rem action refer to FL ST § 48.194(2); FL ST § 48.194(3); and FL ST § 48.194(4).

vi. *Method of substituted service on nonresident*

- When authorized by law, substituted service of process on a nonresident or a person who conceals his or her whereabouts by serving a public officer designated by law shall be made by leaving a copy of the process with a fee of eight dollars and seventy-five cents ($8.75) with the public officer or in his or her office or by mailing the copies by certified mail to the public officer with the fee. The service is sufficient service on a defendant who has appointed a public officer as his or her agent for the service of process. FL ST § 48.161(1).
- Notice of service and a copy of the process shall be sent forthwith by registered or certified mail by the plaintiff or his or her attorney to the defendant, and the defendant's return receipt and the affidavit of the plaintiff or his or her attorney of compliance shall be filed on or before the return day of the process or within such time as the court allows, or the notice and copy shall be served on the defendant, if found within the state, by an officer authorized to serve legal process, or if found without the state, by a sheriff or a deputy sheriff of any county of this state or any duly constituted public officer qualified to serve like process in the state or jurisdiction where the defendant is found. The officer's return showing service shall be filed on or before the return day of the process or within such time as the court allows. The public officer shall keep a record of all process served on him or her showing the day and hour of service. FL ST § 48.161(1).
- If any person on whom service of process is authorized under FL ST § 48.161(1) dies, service may be made on his or her administrator, executor, curator, or personal representative in the same manner. FL ST § 48.161(2).
- FL ST § 48.161 does not apply to persons on whom service is authorized under FL ST § 48.151. FL ST § 48.161(3).
- The public officer may designate some other person in his or her office to accept service. FL ST § 48.161(4).

vii. *Service by publication.* Service of process by publication may be made as provided by statute. FL ST RCP Rule 1.070(d). Service of process by publication is allowable in cases listed in FL ST § 49.011 and upon the parties listed in FL ST § 49.021.

- As a condition precedent to service by publication, a statement shall be filed in the action executed by the plaintiff, the plaintiff's agent or attorney, setting forth substantially the matters hereafter required, which statement may be contained in a verified pleading, or in an affidavit or other sworn statement. FL ST § 49.031(1). After the entry of a final judgment or decree in any action no sworn statement shall ever be held defective for failure to state a required fact if the fact otherwise appears from the record in the action. FL ST § 49.031(3).
- For the sworn statement requirements for service of process by publication refer to FL ST § 49.041; FL ST § 49.051; FL ST § 49.061; and FL ST § 49.071.
- On filing the sworn statement, and otherwise complying with the foregoing requirements, the plaintiff is entitled to have issued by the clerk or judge, not later than sixty (60) days after filing the sworn statement, a notice of action which notice shall set forth: (1) the

names of the known natural defendants; the names, status and description of the corporate defendants; a description of the unknown defendants who claim by, through, under or against a known party which may be described as "all parties claiming interests by, through, under or against (name of known party)" and a description of all unknown defendants which may be described as "all parties having or claiming to have any right, title or interest in the property herein described"; (2) the nature of the action or proceeding in short and simple terms (but neglect to do so is not jurisdictional); (3) the name of the court in which the action or proceeding was instituted and an abbreviated title of the case; (4) the description of real property, if any, proceeded against. FL ST § 49.08.

- For further information on service of process by publication refer to FL ST § 49.09; FL ST § 49.10; FL ST § 49.11; FL ST § 49.12; FL ST § 50.011; FL ST § 50.021; FL ST § 50.031; FL ST § 50.041; FL ST § 50.051; and FL ST § 50.061.

viii. *Service on agents of nonresidents doing business in the state.* When any natural person or partnership not residing or having a principal place of business in this state engages in business in this state, process may be served on the person who is in charge of any business in which the defendant is engaged within this state at the time of service, including agents soliciting orders for goods, wares, merchandise or services. FL ST § 48.071.

- Any process so served is as valid as if served personally on the nonresident person or partnership engaging in business in this state in any action against the person or partnership arising out of such business. FL ST § 48.071.
- A copy of such process with a notice of service on the person in charge of such business shall be sent forthwith to the nonresident person or partnership by registered or certified mail, return receipt requested. FL ST § 48.071.
- An affidavit of compliance with FL ST § 48.071 shall be filed before the return day or within such further time as the court may allow. FL ST § 48.071.

ix. *Service on nonresident engaging in business in state.* The acceptance by any person or persons, individually or associated together as a copartnership or any other form or type of association, who are residents of any other state or country, and all foreign corporations, and any person who is a resident of the state and who subsequently becomes a nonresident of the state or conceals his or her whereabouts, of the privilege extended by law to nonresidents and others to operate, conduct, engage in, or carry on a business or business venture in the state, or to have an office or agency in the state, constitutes an appointment by the persons and foreign corporations of the Secretary of State of the state as their agent on whom all process in any action or proceeding against them, or any of them, arising out of any transaction or operation connected with or incidental to the business or business venture may be served. The acceptance of the privilege is signification of the agreement of the persons and foreign corporations that the process against them which is so served is of the same validity as if served personally on the persons or foreign corporations. FL ST § 48.181(1).

- If a foreign corporation has a resident agent or officer in the state, process shall be served on the resident agent or officer. FL ST § 48.181(2).
- Any person, firm, or corporation which sells, consigns, or leases by any means whatsoever tangible or intangible personal property, through brokers, jobbers, wholesalers, or distributors to any person, firm, or corporation in this state is conclusively presumed to be both engaged in substantial and not isolated activities within this state and operating, conducting, engaging in, or carrying on a business or business venture in this state. FL ST § 48.181(3).

x. *Other service provisions:*

- Service on alien property custodian. FL ST § 48.131.
- Service on an incompetent person. FL ST § 48.042.
- Service on minor. FL ST § 48.041.
- Service on public agencies and officers. FL ST § 48.111.

- Service on the state. FL ST § 48.121.
- Service on a state prisoner. FL ST § 48.051.
- Service on labor unions. FL ST § 48.141.
- Service on statutory agents for certain persons. FL ST § 48.151.
- Service on nonresident motor vehicle owners. FL ST § 48.171.
- Service of process in action for possession of premises. FL ST § 48.183.
- Service on nonresidents operating aircraft or watercraft in the state. FL ST § 48.19.

f. *Crossclaims.* Service of a crossclaim on a party who has appeared in the action shall be made pursuant to FL ST RCP Rule 1.080. Service of a crossclaim against a party who has not appeared in the action shall be made in the manner provided for service of summons. FL ST RCP Rule 1.170(g).

g. *Fees.* The statutory compensation for making service shall not be increased by the simultaneous delivery or mailing of the copy of the initial pleading in conformity with FL ST RCP Rule 1.070. FL ST RCP Rule 1.070(g).

G. Hearings

1. There is no hearing required or contemplated in the Florida rules governing the complaint and service of summons.

H. Forms

1. Official Complaint and Summons Forms for Florida

a. Caption. FL ST RCP Form 1.901.
b. Summons. FL ST RCP Form 1.902.
c. Crossclaim summons. FL ST RCP Form 1.903.
d. Third-party summons. FL ST RCP Form 1.904.
e. Notice of action, constructive service, no property. FL ST RCP Form 1.919.
f. Notice of action, constructive service, property. FL ST RCP Form 1.920.
g. Third-party complaint; General form. FL ST RCP Form 1.948.
h. Civil cover sheet. FL ST RCP Form 1.997.
i. Fall-down negligence complaint. FL ST RCP Form 1.951.
j. Notice of compliance when constitutional challenge is brought. FL ST RCP Form 1.975.

2. Complaint Forms for Florida

a. Complaint for damages; General form. FL-PP § 2:17.
b. Complaint; Negligent infliction of personal injury. FL-PP § 2:19.
c. Complaint; Fall down negligence. FL-PP § 2:20.
d. Complaint; Professional negligence. FL-PP § 2:23.
e. Complaint; Breach of contract. FL-PP § 2:24.
f. Complaint; Breach of personal services contract. FL-PP § 2:25.
g. Summons; General form. FL-PRACFORM § 3:4.
h. Summons; Natural person. FL-PRACFORM § 3:5.
i. Complaint; Assault and battery. FL-PRACFORM § 4:9.
j. Complaint; Breach of contract, general form. FL-PRACFORM § 4:17.
k. Complaint; Civil rights. FL-PRACFORM § 4:23.
l. Complaint; Conversion. FL-PRACFORM § 4:30.
m. Complaint; Employment contract. FL-PRACFORM § 4:44.

n. Complaint; False imprisonment. FL-PRACFORM § 4:46.
o. Complaint; Fraud, misrepresentation. FL-PRACFORM § 4:62.
p. Complaint; Lease, by landlord. FL-PRACFORM § 4:86.
q. Complaint; Lease, by tenant. FL-PRACFORM § 4:87.
r. Complaint; Libel. FL-PRACFORM § 4:89.
s. Complaint; Life insurance policy. FL-PRACFORM § 4:90.
t. Complaint; Medical malpractice, negligence. FL-PRACFORM § 4:95.
u. Complaint; Negligence, automobile, driver. FL-PRACFORM § 4:101.
v. Complaint; Negligence, hospital. FL-PRACFORM § 4:104.

I. Checklist

(I) ❑ Matters to be considered by plaintiff
- (a) ❑ Required documents
  - (1) ❑ Summons
  - (2) ❑ Complaint
  - (3) ❑ Civil cover sheet
  - (4) ❑ Return of execution process by process server
  - (5) ❑ Filing fees
- (b) ❑ Supplemental documents
  - (1) ❑ Exhibits
  - (2) ❑ Notice of constitutional question
- (c) ❑ Time for filing and serving complaint
  - (1) ❑ Service of the initial process and initial pleading should be made upon a defendant within one hundred twenty (120) days after the filing of the complaint with the court

(II) ❑ Matters to be considered by defendant
- (a) ❑ Required documents
  - (1) ❑ Answer
  - (2) ❑ Certificate of service
- (b) ❑ Supplemental documents
  - (1) ❑ Exhibits
  - (2) ❑ Notice of constitutional question
- (c) ❑ Time for answer
  - (1) ❑ Unless a different time is prescribed in a statute of Florida, a defendant shall serve an answer within twenty (20) days after service of original process and the initial pleading on the defendant, or not later than the date fixed in a notice by publication
  - (2) ❑ A party served with a pleading stating a crossclaim against that party shall serve an answer to it within twenty (20) days after service on that party
  - (3) ❑ The plaintiff shall serve an answer to a counterclaim within twenty (20) days after service of the counterclaim
  - (4) ❑ A defendant who, before being served with process, timely returns a waiver so requested is not required to respond to the complaint until sixty (60) days after the date the defendant received the request for waiver of service; for purposes of computing any time prescribed or allowed by the Florida Rules of Civil Procedure, service of process shall be deemed effected twenty (20) days before the time required to respond to the complaint

(5) ❑ For timing requirements related to service on the state, service of motion impact, and responding when no responsive pleading is required, please see the Timing section of this document

Pleadings
Amended Complaint

Document Last Updated January 2013

A. Applicable Rules

1. *State rules*
   a. Nonverification of papers. FL ST RCP Rule 1.030.
   b. Process. FL ST RCP Rule 1.070.
   c. Service and filing of pleadings, orders, and documents. FL ST RCP Rule 1.080.
   d. Pleadings and motions. FL ST RCP Rule 1.100; FL ST RCP Rule 1.110; FL ST RCP Rule 1.120; FL ST RCP Rule 1.130; FL ST RCP Rule 1.190; FL ST § 48.193.
   e. Pretrial procedure. FL ST RCP Rule 1.200.
   f. Relief from judgment, decrees, or orders. FL ST RCP Rule 1.540.
   g. Forms. FL ST RCP Rule 1.900.
   h. Minimization of the filing of sensitive information. FL ST J ADMIN Rule 2.425.
   i. Retention of court records. FL ST J ADMIN Rule 2.430.
   j. Foreign attorneys. FL ST J ADMIN Rule 2.510.
   k. Signature of attorneys and parties. FL ST J ADMIN Rule 2.515.
   l. Paper. FL ST J ADMIN Rule 2.520.
   m. Electronic filing. FL ST J ADMIN Rule 2.525.
   n. Accessibility of information and technology. FL ST J ADMIN Rule 2.526.
   o. Requests for accommodations by persons with disabilities. FL ST J ADMIN Rule 2.540.
2. *Local rules*
   a. Unrepresented (pro se) parties. FL ST 9 J CIR SECTION 7.
   b. Business court procedures. FL ST 9 J CIR ORANGE CIV SECTION 1.

B. Timing

1. *Amendment as a matter of course.* A party may amend a pleading once as a matter of course at any time before a responsive pleading is served or, if the pleading is one to which no responsive pleading is permitted and the action has not been placed on the trial calendar, may so amend it at any time within twenty (20) days after it is served. FL ST RCP Rule 1.190(a).
2. *Amendment by leave of court.* Otherwise a party may amend a pleading only by leave of court or by written consent of the adverse party. Leave of court shall be given freely when justice so requires. FL ST RCP Rule 1.190(a).
3. *Amendments in furtherance of justice.* At any time in furtherance of justice, upon such terms as may be just, the court may permit any process, proceeding, pleading, or record to be amended or material supplemental matter to be set forth in an amended or supplemental pleading. At every stage of the action the court must disregard any error or defect in the proceedings which does not affect the substantial rights of the parties. FL ST RCP Rule 1.190(e).
4. *Response to amended pleading.* A party shall plead in response to an amended pleading within ten (10) days after service of the amended pleading unless the court otherwise orders. FL ST RCP Rule 1.190(a).

5. *Computation of time*

   a. *Generally.* Computation of time shall be governed by FL ST J ADMIN Rule 2.514. FL ST RCP Rule 1.090(a). The following rules apply in computing time periods specified in any rule of procedure, local rule, court order, or statute that does not specify a method of computing time. FL ST J ADMIN Rule 2.514(a).

      i. *Period stated in days or a longer unit.* When the period is stated in days or a longer unit of time (A) exclude the day of the event that triggers the period; (B) count every day, including intermediate Saturdays, Sundays, and legal holidays; and (C) include the last day of the period, but if the last day is a Saturday, Sunday, or legal holiday, or falls within any period of time extended through an order of the chief justice under FL ST J ADMIN Rule 2.205(a)(2)(B)(iv), the period continues to run until the end of the next day that is not a Saturday, Sunday, or legal holiday and does not fall within any period of time extended through an order of the chief justice. FL ST J ADMIN Rule 2.514(a)(1).

      ii. *Period stated in hours.* When the period is stated in hours (A) begin counting immediately on the occurrence of the event that triggers the period; (B) count every hour, including hours during intermediate Saturdays, Sundays, and legal holidays; and (C) if the period would end on a Saturday, Sunday, or legal holiday, or during any period of time extended through an order of the chief justice under FL ST J ADMIN Rule 2.205(a)(2)(B)(iv), the period continues to run until the same time on the next day that is not a Saturday, Sunday, or legal holiday and does not fall within any period of time extended through an order of the chief justice. FL ST J ADMIN Rule 2.514(a)(2).

      iii. *Period stated in days less than seven (7) days.* When the period stated in days is less than seven (7) days, intermediate Saturdays, Sundays, and legal holidays shall be excluded in the computation. FL ST J ADMIN Rule 2.514(a)(3).

      iv. *"Last day" defined.* Unless a different time is set by a statute, local rule, or court order, the last day ends (A) for electronic filing or for service by any means, at midnight; and (B) for filing by other means, when the clerk's office is scheduled to close. FL ST J ADMIN Rule 2.514(a)(4).

      v. *"Next day" defined.* The "next day" is determined by continuing to count forward when the period is measured after an event and backward when measured before an event. FL ST J ADMIN Rule 2.514(a)(5).

      vi. *"Legal holiday" defined.* "Legal holiday" means (A) the day set aside by FL ST § 110.117, for observing New Year's Day, Martin Luther King, Jr.'s Birthday, Memorial Day, Independence Day, Labor Day, Veterans' Day, Thanksgiving Day, the Friday after Thanksgiving Day, or Christmas Day, and (B) any day observed as a holiday by the clerk's office or as designated by the chief judge. FL ST J ADMIN Rule 2.514(a)(6).

   b. *Additional time after service by mail or e-mail.* When a party may or must act within a specified time after service and service is made by mail or e-mail, five (5) days are added after the period that would otherwise expire under FL ST J ADMIN Rule 2.514(a). FL ST J ADMIN Rule 2.514(b).

   c. *Enlargement.* When an act is required or allowed to be done at or within a specified time by order of court, by the Florida Rules of Civil Procedure, or by notice given thereunder, for cause shown the court at any time in its discretion (1) with or without notice, may order the period enlarged if request therefor is made before the expiration of the period originally prescribed or as extended by a previous order, or (2) upon motion made and notice after the expiration of the specified period, may permit the act to be done when failure to act was the result of excusable neglect, but it may not extend the time for making a motion for new trial, for rehearing, or to alter or amend a judgment; making a motion for relief from a judgment under FL ST RCP Rule 1.540(b); taking an appeal or filing a petition for certiorari; or making a motion for a directed verdict. FL ST RCP Rule 1.090(b).

   d. *Unaffected by expiration of term.* The period of time provided for the doing of any act or the taking of any proceeding shall not be affected or limited by the continued existence or expiration of a term of court. The continued existence or expiration of a term of court in no way affects the power of a court to do any act or take any proceeding in any action which is or has been pending before it. FL ST RCP Rule 1.090(c).

C. General Requirements

1. *Amendments.* A party may amend a pleading once as a matter of course at any time before a responsive pleading is served or, if the pleading is one to which no responsive pleading is permitted and the action has not been placed on the trial calendar, may so amend it at any time within twenty (20) days after it is served. Otherwise a party may amend a pleading only by leave of court or by written consent of the adverse party. Leave of court shall be freely given when justice so requires. FL ST RCP Rule 1.190(a).
   a. *Purpose of amendments.* Amendments can relate to the correction of mistakes, the insertion of jurisdictional averments, the correction or addition of verifications, the addition or substitution or striking out of parties, and generally the rectification of all formal defects in the pleading. The court can also allow amendments setting up an omitted counterclaim or cross-claim if the defendant failed to raise the claim through oversight, inadvertence, or excusable neglect. FL-PP § 2:151.
   b. *Amendment to a pleading/Amended pleading.* A significant difference exists between an amendment to a pleading and an amended pleading. An amendment to a pleading corrects, adds to or deletes from the pleading. An amended pleading is substituted for the former pleading and the former pleading ceases to have any effect. Dee v. Southern Brewing Company, 146 Fla. 588, 1 So.2d 562 (Fla. 1941); Shannon v. McBride, 105 So.2d 16 (Fla. 2d DCA 1958); Hughes v. Home Sav. of America, F.S.B., 675 So.2d 649 (Fla. 2d DCA 1996); FL-PRACPROC § 14:2.
   c. *Relation back of amendments.* When the claim or defense asserted in the amended pleading arose out of the conduct, transaction, or occurrence set forth or attempted to be set forth in the original pleading, the amendment shall relate back to the date of the original pleading. FL ST RCP Rule 1.190(c).
2. *General rules of pleading*
   a. *Claims for relief*
      i. A pleading which sets forth a claim for relief, whether an original claim, counterclaim, crossclaim, or third-party claim, must state a cause of action and shall contain
         - A short and plain statement of the grounds upon which the court's jurisdiction depends, unless the court already has jurisdiction and the claim needs no new grounds of jurisdiction to support it (For information regarding acts subjecting persons to jurisdiction, please see FL ST § 48.193),
         - A short and plain statement of the ultimate facts showing that the pleader is entitled to relief, and
         - A demand for judgment for the relief to which the pleader deems himself or herself entitled. FL ST RCP Rule 1.110(b).
      ii. Relief in the alternative or of several different types may be demanded. Every complaint shall be considered to demand general relief. FL ST RCP Rule 1.110(b).
   b. *Verification.* Except when otherwise specifically provided by these rules or an applicable statute, every pleading or other document of a party represented by an attorney need not be verified or accompanied by an affidavit. FL ST RCP Rule 1.030. When filing an action for foreclosure of a mortgage on residential real property the complaint shall be verified. When verification of a document is required, the document filed shall include an oath, affirmation, or the following statement: "Under penalty of perjury, I declare that I have read the foregoing, and the facts alleged therein are true and correct to the best of my knowledge and belief." FL ST RCP Rule 1.110(b).
   c. *Separate statements.* All averments of claim or defense shall be made in consecutively numbered paragraphs, the contents of each of which shall be limited as far as practicable to a statement of a single set of circumstances, and a paragraph may be referred to by number in all subsequent pleadings. Each claim founded upon a separate transaction or occurrence and each defense other than denials shall be stated in a separate count or defense when a separation facilitates the clear presentation of the matter set forth. FL ST RCP Rule 1.110(f).
   d. *Statements adopted by reference.* Statements in a pleading may be adopted by reference in a different part of the same pleading, in another pleading, or in any motion. FL ST RCP Rule 1.130(b).

e. *Joinder of causes of action; Consistency.* A pleader may set up in the same action as many claims or causes of action or defenses in the same right as the pleader has, and claims for relief may be stated in the alternative if separate items make up the cause of action, or if two (2) or more causes of action are joined. A party may also set forth two (2) or more statements of a claim or defense alternatively, either in one (1) count or defense or in separate counts or defenses. When two (2) or more statements are made in the alternative and one (1) of them, if made independently, would be sufficient, the pleading is not made insufficient by the insufficiency of one (1) or more of the alternative statements. A party may also state as many separate claims or defenses as that party has, regardless of consistency and whether based on legal or equitable grounds or both. All pleadings shall be construed so as to do substantial justice. FL ST RCP Rule 1.110(g).

f. *Subsequent pleadings.* When the nature of an action permits pleadings subsequent to final judgment and the jurisdiction of the court over the parties has not terminated, the initial pleading subsequent to final judgment shall be designated a supplemental complaint or petition. The action shall then proceed in the same manner and time as though the supplemental complaint or petition were the initial pleading in the action, including the issuance of any needed process. FL ST RCP Rule 1.110(h) shall not apply to proceedings that may be initiated by motion under the Florida Rules of Civil Procedure. FL ST RCP Rule 1.110(h).

g. *Pleading basis for service.* When service of process is to be made under statutes authorizing service on nonresidents of Florida, it is sufficient to plead the basis for service in the language of the statute without pleading the facts supporting service. FL ST RCP Rule 1.070(h).

h. *Forms of pleadings.* Forms of action and technical forms for seeking relief and of pleas, pleadings, or motions are abolished. FL ST RCP Rule 1.110(a).

3. *Complaint; Generally*

a. *Purpose.* The purpose of a complaint is to advise the court and the defendant of the nature of a cause of action asserted by the plaintiff. FL-PP § 2:12.

b. *Sufficiency of complaint.* A complaint will be found to be insufficient if it contains only general conclusory allegations unsupported by any facts. The test to determine whether a complaint is sufficient is whether, if the factual allegations of the complaint are established, the plaintiff will be legally or equitably entitled to the claimed relief. Pizzi v. Central Bank & Trust Co., 250 So.2d 895, 896 (Fla. 1971); Bowen v. G H C Properties, Limited, 251 So.2d 359, 361 (Fla. 1st DCA 1971); FL-PP § 2:12. In determining the sufficiency of the complaint to state a cause of action, all allegations of the complaint are taken as true, and possible affirmative defenses are not considered. Strickland v. Commerce Loan Co. of Jacksonville, 158 So.2d 814 (Fla. 1st DCA 1963); FL-PP § 2:12.

i. The issues for trial in Florida must be settled by the pleadings. The issues cannot be raised by discovery. FL-PRACPROC § 7:6.

ii. Causes of action may be pleaded alternatively in the same count or in different counts and against the same or different defendants as long as the joinder of parties is proper. FL-PRACPROC § 7:6.

iii. Each count must state a cause of action. Each independent cause of action should be pleaded in a separate count. FL-PRACPROC § 7:6.

iv. Incorporation by reference of all allegations from one count to another is not proper. Separate counts facilitate reference to the pleading in which they appear in other pleadings, motions or papers as well as the assertion of defenses against some, but not all, causes of action. Some defenses may not apply to the initial pleading as a whole. FL-PRACPROC § 7:6.

4. *Pleading special matters*

a. *Capacity.* It is not necessary to aver the capacity of a party to sue or be sued, the authority of a party to sue or be sued in a representative capacity, or the legal existence of an organized association of persons that is made a party, except to the extent required to show the jurisdiction of the court. The initial pleading served on behalf of a minor party shall specifically aver the age of the minor party. When a party desires to raise an issue as to the legal existence of any party, the capacity of any party to sue or be sued, or the authority of a party to sue or be sued in a representative capacity, that party shall do so by specific negative averment which shall include such supporting particulars as are peculiarly within the pleader's knowledge. FL ST RCP Rule 1.120(a).

b. *Fraud, mistake, condition of the mind.* In all averments of fraud or mistake, the circumstances constituting fraud or mistake shall be stated with such particularity as the circumstances may permit. Malice, intent, knowledge, mental attitude, and other condition of mind of a person may be averred generally. FL ST RCP Rule 1.120(b).

c. *Conditions precedent.* In pleading the performance or occurrence of conditions precedent, it is sufficient to aver generally that all conditions precedent have been performed or have occurred. A denial of performance or occurrence shall be made specifically and with particularity. FL ST RCP Rule 1.120(c).

d. *Official document or act.* In pleading an official document or official act it is sufficient to aver that the document was issued or the act done in compliance with law. FL ST RCP Rule 1.120(c).

e. *Judgment or decree.* In pleading a judgment or decree of a domestic or foreign court, a judicial or quasi-judicial tribunal, or a board or officer, it is sufficient to aver the judgment or decree without setting forth matter showing jurisdiction to render it. FL ST RCP Rule 1.120(e).

f. *Time and place.* For the purpose of testing the sufficiency of a pleading, averments of time and place are material and shall be considered like all other averments of material matter. FL ST RCP Rule 1.120(f).

g. *Special damage.* When items of special damage are claimed, they shall be specifically stated. FL ST RCP Rule 1.120(g).

5. *Parties*

a. *Parties generally.* Every action may be prosecuted in the name of the real party in interest, but a personal representative, administrator, guardian, trustee of an express trust, a party with whom or in whose name a contract has been made for the benefit of another, or a party expressly authorized by statute may sue in that person's own name without joining the party for whose benefit the action is brought. All persons having an interest in the subject of the action and in obtaining the relief demanded may join as plaintiffs and any person may be made a defendant who has or claims an interest adverse to the plaintiff. Any person may at any time be made a party if that person's presence is necessary or proper to a complete determination of the cause. Persons having a united interest may be joined on the same side as plaintiffs or defendants, and anyone who refuses to join may for such reason be made a defendant. FL ST RCP Rule 1.210(a).

b. *Minors or incompetent persons.* When a minor or incompetent person has a representative, such as a guardian or other like fiduciary, the representative may sue or defend on behalf of the minor or incompetent person. A minor or incompetent person who does not have a duly appointed representative may sue by next friend or by a guardian ad litem. The court shall appoint a guardian ad litem for a minor or incompetent person not otherwise represented in an action or shall make such other order as it deems proper for the protection of the minor or incompetent person. FL ST RCP Rule 1.210(b).

c. For survivor and substitution of parties information, please see FL ST RCP Rule 1.260.

6. *Counterclaims and crossclaims*

a. *Compulsory counterclaims.* A pleading shall state as a counterclaim any claim which at the time of serving the pleading the pleader has against any opposing party, provided it arises out of the transaction or occurrence that is the subject matter of the opposing party's claim and does not require for its adjudication the presence of third parties over whom the court cannot acquire jurisdiction. But the pleader need not state a claim if (1) at the time the action was commenced the claim was the subject of another pending action, or (2) the opposing party brought suit upon that party's claim by attachment or other process by which the court did not acquire jurisdiction to render a personal judgment on the claim and the pleader is not stating a counterclaim under this rule. FL ST RCP Rule 1.170(a).

b. *Permissive counterclaim.* A pleading may state as a counterclaim any claim against an opposing party not arising out of the transaction or occurrence that is the subject matter of the opposing party's claim. FL ST RCP Rule 1.170(b).

c. *Counterclaim exceeding opposing claim.* A counterclaim may or may not diminish or defeat the recovery sought by the opposing party. It may claim relief exceeding in amount or different in kind from that sought in the pleading of the opposing party. FL ST RCP Rule 1.170(c).

d. *Counterclaim against the State.* The Florida Rules of Civil Procedure shall not be construed to enlarge beyond the limits established by law the right to assert counterclaims or to claim credits against the state or any of its subdivisions or other governmental organizations thereof subject to suit or against a municipal corporation or against an officer, agency, or administrative board of the state. FL ST RCP Rule 1.170(d).

e. *Counterclaim maturing or acquired after pleading.* A claim which matured or was acquired by the pleader after serving the pleading may be presented as a counterclaim by supplemental pleading with the permission of the court. FL ST RCP Rule 1.170(e).

f. *Omitted counterclaim or crossclaim.* When a pleader fails to set up a counterclaim or crossclaim through oversight, inadvertence, or excusable neglect, or when justice requires, the pleader may set up the counterclaim or crossclaim by amendment with leave of the court. FL ST RCP Rule 1.170(f).

g. *Crossclaim against co-party.* A pleading may state as a crossclaim any claim by one party against a co-party arising out of the transaction or occurrence that is the subject matter of either the original action or a counterclaim therein, or relating to any property that is the subject matter of the original action. The crossclaim may include a claim that the party against whom it is asserted is or may be liable to the crossclaimant for all or part of a claim asserted in the action against the crossclaimant. Service of a crossclaim on a party who has appeared in the action shall be made pursuant to FL ST RCP Rule 1.080. Service of a crossclaim against a party who has not appeared in the action shall be made in the manner provided for service of summons. FL ST RCP Rule 1.170(g).

h. *Additional parties may be brought in.* When the presence of parties other than those to the original action is required to grant complete relief in the determination of a counterclaim or crossclaim, they shall be named in the counterclaim or crossclaim and be served with process and shall be parties to the action thereafter if jurisdiction of them can be obtained and their joinder will not deprive the court of jurisdiction of the action. FL ST RCP Rule 1.250(b) and FL ST RCP Rule 1.250(c) apply to parties brought in under FL ST RCP Rule 1.170(h). FL ST RCP Rule 1.170(h).

i. *Separate trials; Separate judgment.* If the court orders separate trials as provided in FL ST RCP Rule 1.270(b), judgment on a counterclaim or crossclaim may be rendered when the court has jurisdiction to do so even if a claim of the opposing party has been dismissed or otherwise disposed of. FL ST RCP Rule 1.170(i).

j. *Demand exceeding jurisdiction; Transfer of action.* If the demand of any counterclaim or crossclaim exceeds the jurisdiction of the court in which the action is pending, the action shall be transferred forthwith to the court of the same county having jurisdiction of the demand in the counterclaim or crossclaim with only such alterations in the pleadings as are essential. The court shall order the transfer of the action and the transmittal of all papers in it to the proper court if the party asserting the demand exceeding the jurisdiction deposits with the court having jurisdiction a sum sufficient to pay the clerk's service charge in the court to which the action is transferred at the time of filing the counterclaim or crossclaim. Thereupon the original papers and deposit shall be transmitted and filed with a certified copy of the order. The court to which the action is transferred shall have full power and jurisdiction over the demands of all parties. Failure to make the service charge deposit at the time the counterclaim or crossclaim is filed, or within such further time as the court may allow, shall reduce a claim for damages to an amount within the jurisdiction of the court where the action is pending and waive the claim in other cases. FL ST RCP Rule 1.170(j).

7. *Misjoinder and nonjoinder of parties*

a. *Misjoinder.* Misjoinder of parties is not a ground for dismissal of an action. Any claim against a party may be severed and proceeded with separately. FL ST RCP Rule 1.250(a).

b. *Dropping parties.* Parties may be dropped by an adverse party in the manner provided for voluntary dismissal in FL ST RCP Rule 1.420(a)(1) subject to the exception stated in FL ST RCP Rule 1.420. If notice of lis pendens has been filed in the action against a party so dropped, the notice of dismissal shall be recorded and cancels the notice of lis pendens without the necessity of a court order. Parties may be dropped by order of court on its own initiative or the motion of any party at any stage of the action on such terms as are just. FL ST RCP Rule 1.250(b).

c. *Adding parties.* Parties may be added once as a matter of course within the same time that pleadings can be so amended under FL ST RCP Rule 1.190(a). If amendment by leave of court or stipulation of the parties is permitted, parties may be added in the amended pleading without further order of court. Parties may be added by order of court on its own initiative or on motion of any party at any stage of the action and on such terms as are just. FL ST RCP Rule 1.250(c).

8. *Jury demand*
   a. *Right preserved.* The right of trial by jury as declared by the Constitution or by statute shall be preserved to the parties inviolate. FL ST RCP Rule 1.430(a).
   b. *Demand.* Any party may demand a trial by jury of any issue triable of right by a jury by serving upon the other party a demand therefor in writing at any time after commencement of the action and not later than ten (10) days after the service of the last pleading directed to such issue. The demand may be indorsed upon a pleading of the party. FL ST RCP Rule 1.430(b).
   c. *Specification of issues.* In the demand a party may specify the issues that the party wishes so tried; otherwise, the party is deemed to demand trial by jury for all issues so triable. FL ST RCP Rule 1.430(c).
      i. If a party has demanded trial by jury for only some of the issues, any other party may serve a demand for trial by jury of any other or all of the issues triable by jury ten (10) days after service of the demand or such lesser time as the court may order. FL ST RCP Rule 1.430(c).
   d. *Waiver.* A party who fails to serve a demand as required by FL ST RCP Rule 1.430 waives trial by jury. FL ST RCP Rule 1.430(d).
      i. If waived, a jury trial may not be granted without the consent of the parties, but the court may allow an amendment in the proceedings to demand a trial by jury or order a trial by jury on its own motion. FL ST RCP Rule 1.430(d).
      ii. A demand for trial by jury may not be withdrawn without the consent of the parties. FL ST RCP Rule 1.430(d).
9. *Arbitration and mediation*
   a. *Referral to arbitration and mediation.* Except as hereinafter provided or as otherwise prohibited by law, the presiding judge may enter an order referring all or any part of a contested civil matter to mediation or arbitration. The parties to any contested civil matter may file a written stipulation to mediate or arbitrate any issue between them at any time. Such stipulation shall be incorporated into the order of referral. FL ST RCP Rule 1.700(a).
   b. *Arbitration*
      i. *Exclusions.* A civil action shall be ordered to arbitration or arbitration in conjunction with mediation upon stipulation of the parties. A civil action may be ordered to arbitration or arbitration in conjunction with mediation upon motion of any party or by the court, if the judge determines the action to be of such a nature that arbitration could be of benefit to the litigants or the court. FL ST RCP Rule 1.800.
         - Under no circumstances may the following categories of actions be referred to arbitration: (1) bond estreatures; (2) habeas corpus or other extraordinary writs; (3) bond validations; (4) civil or criminal contempt; (5) such other matters as may be specified by order of the chief judge in the circuit. FL ST RCP Rule 1.800.
      ii. For more information regarding arbitration, please see FL ST RCP Rule 1.810; FL ST RCP Rule 1.820; FL ST RCP Rule 1.830.
   c. *Mediation.* For more information regarding mediation, please see FL ST RCP Rule 1.710; FL ST RCP Rule 1.720; FL ST RCP Rule 1.730; and FL ST RCP Rule 1.750.

d. It is the policy of the Civil Division judges to maximize the use of alternative dispute resolution procedures. Except where prohibited by statute, mediation will be ordered in all cases where jury trial is requested and in selected cases which are to be tried non-jury. Also, selected cases will be referred for court-annexed non-binding arbitration through the Orange County Bar Association Arbitration Service. Counsel may move to dispense with or defer mediation or arbitration or move to modify the referral order for good cause. FL ST 9 J CIR SECTION 15.

10. *Rules of court*

a. *Rules of civil procedure.* The Florida Rules of Civil Procedure apply to all actions of a civil nature and all special statutory proceedings in the circuit courts and county courts except those to which the Florida Probate Rules, the Florida Family Law Rules of Procedure, or the Small Claims Rules apply. FL ST RCP Rule 1.010.

i. The form, content, procedure, and time for pleading in all special statutory proceedings shall be as prescribed by the statutes governing the proceeding unless the Florida Rules of Civil Procedure specifically provide to the contrary. FL ST RCP Rule 1.010.

ii. The Florida Rules of Civil Procedure shall be construed to secure the just, speedy, and inexpensive determination of every action. FL ST RCP Rule 1.010.

b. *Rules of judicial administration.* The Florida Rules of Judicial Administration shall apply to administrative matters in all courts to which the Florida Rules of Judicial Administration are applicable by their terms. The Florida Rules of Judicial Administration shall be construed to secure the speedy and inexpensive determination of every proceeding to which they are applicable. The Florida Rules of Judicial Administration shall supersede all conflicting rules and statutes. FL ST J ADMIN Rule 2.110.

c. *Business court procedures.* For rules specific to Business Court, please see FL ST 9 J CIR ORANGE CIV SECTION 1, et seq.

D. Documents

1. *Required documents*

a. *Amended complaint.* See the General Requirements section of this document for the content of an amended complaint. If a party files a motion to amend a pleading, the party shall attach the proposed amended pleading to the motion. FL ST RCP Rule 1.190(a). See the KeyRules Florida Circuit Court Motion for Leave to Amend document for further information.

i. *Notices to persons with disabilities.* See the Format section of this KeyRules document for further information.

b. *Certificate of service.* When any attorney certifies in substance: "I certify that a copy hereof has been furnished to (here insert name or names and addresses used for service) by (e-mail) (delivery) (mail) (fax) on .... (date) ....________________ Attorney" the certificate is taken as prima facie proof of such service in compliance with FL ST J ADMIN Rule 2.516. FL ST J ADMIN Rule 2.516(f).

2. *Supplemental documents*

a. *Exhibits.* All bonds, notes, bills of exchange, contracts, accounts, or documents upon which action may be brought or defense made, or a copy thereof or a copy of the portions thereof material to the pleadings, shall be incorporated in or attached to the pleading. No papers shall be unnecessarily annexed as exhibits. The pleadings shall contain no unnecessary recitals of deeds, documents, contracts, or other instruments. Any exhibit attached to a pleading shall be considered a part of the pleadings for all purposes. FL ST RCP Rule 1.130(a).

b. *Notice of constitutional question.* A party that files a pleading, written motion, or other paper drawing into question the constitutionality of a state statute or a county or municipal charter, ordinance, or franchise must promptly (1) file a notice of constitutional question stating the question and identifying the paper that raises it; and (2) serve the notice and the pleading, written motion, or other paper drawing into question the constitutionality of a state statute or a county or municipal charter, ordinance, or franchise on the Attorney General or the state attorney of the judicial circuit in which the action is pending, by either certified or registered mail. Service of the notice and pleading,

written motion, or other paper does not require joinder of the Attorney General or the state attorney as a party to the action. FL ST RCP Rule 1.071.

E. Format

1. *Documents; Type and size.* Documents subject to the exceptions set forth in FL ST J ADMIN Rule 2.525(d) shall be filed on recycled paper measuring eight and one half by eleven (8 1/2 by 11) inches. For purposes of FL ST J ADMIN Rule 2.520, paper is recycled if it contains a minimum content of fifty (50) percent waste paper. Xerographic reduction of legal-size (eight and one half by fourteen (8 1/2 by 14) inches) documents to letter size (eight and one half by eleven (8 1/2 by 11) inches) is prohibited. All other documents filed by electronic transmission shall be filed in a format capable of being printed in a format consistent with the provisions of FL ST J ADMIN Rule 2.250. FL ST J ADMIN Rule 2.520(b).
    a. *Exhibits.* Any exhibit or attachment filed with pleadings or papers may be filed in its original size. FL ST J ADMIN Rule 2.520(c).
    b. *Recording space.* On all papers and documents prepared and filed by the court or by any party to a proceeding which are to be recorded in the public records of any county, including but not limited to final money judgments and notices of lis pendens, a three (3) inch by three (3) inch space at the top right-hand corner on the first page and a one (1) inch by three (3) inch space at the top right-hand corner on each subsequent page shall be left blank and reserved for use by the clerk of court. FL ST J ADMIN Rule 2.520(d).
        i. *Exceptions to recording space.* Any papers or documents created by persons or entities over which the filing party has no control, including but not limited to wills, codicils, trusts, or other testamentary documents; documents prepared or executed by any public officer; documents prepared, executed, acknowledged, or proved outside of the State of Florida; or documents created by State or Federal government agencies, may be filed without the space required by FL ST J ADMIN Rule 2.520. FL ST J ADMIN Rule 2.520(e).
    c. *Noncompliance.* No clerk of court is permitted to refuse to file any document or paper because of noncompliance with the Florida Rules of Judicial Administration. However, upon request of the clerk of court, noncomplying documents must be resubmitted in accordance with the formatting rules. FL ST J ADMIN Rule 2.520(f).
2. *Caption.* Every pleading, motion, order, judgment, or other paper shall have a caption containing the name of the court, the file number, and except for in rem proceedings, including forfeiture proceedings, the name of the first party on each side with an appropriate indication of other parties, and a designation identifying the party filing it and its nature or the nature of the order, as the case may be. In any in rem proceeding, every pleading, motion, order, judgment, or other paper shall have a caption containing the name of the court, the file number, the style "In re" (followed by the name or general description of the property), and a designation of the person or entity filing it and its nature or the nature of the order, as the case may be. In an in rem forfeiture proceeding, the style shall be "In re forfeiture of" (followed by the name of the general description of the property). All papers filed in the action shall be styled in such a manner as to indicate clearly the subject matter of the paper and the party requesting or obtaining relief. FL ST RCP Rule 1.100(c)(1).
3. *Writing and written defined.* Writing or written means a document containing information, an application, or a stipulation. FL ST RCP Rule 1.080(c).
4. *Rule abbreviations*
    a. The Florida Rules of Civil Procedure and shall be abbreviated as Fla.R.Civ.P. FL ST RCP Rule 1.010.
    b. The Florida Rules of Judicial Administration shall be abbreviated as Fla. R. Jud. Admin. FL ST J ADMIN Rule 2.110.
5. *Nonverification.* Except when otherwise specifically provided by the Florida Rules of Civil Procedure or an applicable statute, every pleading or other document of a party represented by an attorney need not be verified or accompanied by an affidavit. FL ST RCP Rule 1.030; FL ST J ADMIN Rule 2.515(a).
6. *Unrepresented parties.* An unrepresented party must file his or her papers with the clerk and send copies

to other attorneys or unrepresented parties. All such papers must be typed double-spaced on plain white eight and a half by eleven (8 1/2 by 11) inch paper, with the name of the case and case number at the top and the party's mailing address, telephone number and FAX number, if any, below his or her signature at the end of the paper. Such unrepresented party must immediately notify the clerk and all other counsel or parties of record in writing of any change in mailing address or telephone or FAX number. Failure to promptly notify of change of address could result in a dismissal or default entered against such party. FL ST 9 J CIR SECTION 7(B)(5).

7. *Attorney signature*
   a. *Attorney signature.* Every pleading and other document of a party represented by an attorney shall be signed by at least one (1) attorney of record in that attorney's individual name whose current record Florida Bar address, telephone number, including area code, primary e-mail address and secondary e-mail addresses, if any, and Florida Bar number shall be stated, and who shall be duly licensed to practice law in Florida or who shall have received permission to appear in the particular case as provided in FL ST J ADMIN Rule 2.510. FL ST J ADMIN Rule 2.515(a).
      i. The attorney may be required by the court to give the address of, and to vouch for the attorney's authority to represent, the party. FL ST J ADMIN Rule 2.515(a).
      ii. The signature of an attorney shall constitute a certificate by the attorney that the attorney has read the pleading or other document; that to the best of the attorney's knowledge, information, and belief there is good ground to support it; and that it is not interposed for delay. FL ST J ADMIN Rule 2.515(a).
      iii. If a pleading is not signed or is signed with intent to defeat the purpose of FL ST J ADMIN Rule 2.515, it may be stricken and the action may proceed as though the pleading or other document had not been served. FL ST J ADMIN Rule 2.515(a).
   b. *Pro se litigant signature.* A party who is not represented by an attorney shall sign any pleading or other paper and state the party's address and telephone number, including area code. FL ST J ADMIN Rule 2.515(b).
   c. *Form of signature*
      i. The signatures required on pleadings and documents by FL ST J ADMIN Rule 2.515(a) and FL ST J ADMIN Rule 2.515(b) may be:
         - Original signatures;
         - Original signatures that have been reproduced by electronic means, such as on electronically transmitted documents or photocopied documents;
         - Electronic signatures using the "/s/," "s/," or "/s" formats by or at the direction of the person signing; or
         - Any other signature format authorized by general law, so long as the clerk where the proceeding is pending has the capability of receiving and has obtained approval from the Supreme Court of Florida to accept pleadings and documents with that signature format. FL ST J ADMIN Rule 2.515(c)(1).
      ii. An attorney, party, or other person who files a pleading or paper by electronic transmission that does not contain the original signature of that attorney, party, or other person shall file that identical pleading or paper in paper form containing an original signature of that attorney, party, or other person (hereinafter called the follow-up filing) immediately thereafter. The follow-up filing is not required if the Supreme Court of Florida has entered an order directing the clerk of court to discontinue accepting the follow-up filing. FL ST J ADMIN Rule 2.515(c)(2).
8. *Forms*
   a. *Process.* The forms of process, notice of lis pendens, and notice of action provided in the Florida Rules of Civil Procedure are sufficient. Variations from the forms do not void process or notices that are otherwise sufficient. FL ST RCP Rule 1.900(a).
   b. *Other forms.* The other forms provided in the Florida Rules of Civil Procedure are sufficient for the

matters that are covered by them. So long as the substance is expressed without prolixity, the forms may be varied to meet the facts of a particular case. FL ST RCP Rule 1.900(b).

c. *Formal matters.* Captions, except for the designation of the paper, are omitted from the forms provided in the Florida Rules of Civil Procedure. A general form of caption is the first form provided. Signatures are omitted from pleadings and motions. FL ST RCP Rule 1.900(c).

9. *Notices to persons with disabilities.* All notices of court proceedings to be held in a public facility, and all process compelling appearance at such proceedings, shall include the following statement in bold face, fourteen (14) point Times New Roman or Courier font: "If you are a person with a disability who needs any accommodation in order to participate in this proceeding, you are entitled, at no cost to you, to the provision of certain assistance. Please contact [identify applicable court personnel by name, address, and telephone number] at least seven (7) days before your scheduled court appearance, or immediately upon receiving this notification if the time before the scheduled appearance is less than seven (7) days; if you are hearing or voice impaired, call 711." FL ST J ADMIN Rule 2.540(c)(1).

10. *Minimization of the filing of sensitive information*

a. *Limitations for court filings.* Unless authorized by FL ST J ADMIN Rule 2.425(b), statute, another rule of court, or the court orders otherwise, designated sensitive information filed with the court must be limited to the following format:

i. The initials of a person known to be a minor;

ii. The year of birth of a person's birth date;

iii. No portion of any: Social security number, Bank account number, Credit card account number, Charge account number, or Debit account number;

iv. The last four digits of any: Taxpayer identification number (TIN), Employee identification number, Driver's license number, Passport number, Telephone number, Financial account number, except as set forth in FL ST J ADMIN Rule 2.425(a)(3), Brokerage account number, Insurance policy account number, Loan account number, Customer account number, or Patient or health care number;

v. A truncated version of any: Email address, Computer user name, Password, or Personal identification number (PIN); and

vi. A truncated version of any other sensitive information as provided by court order. FL ST J ADMIN Rule 2.425(a).

b. *Exceptions.* FL ST J ADMIN Rule 2.425(a) does not apply to the following:

i. An account number which identifies the property alleged to be the subject of a proceeding;

ii. The record of an administrative or agency proceeding;

iii. The record in appellate or review proceedings;

iv. The birth date of a minor whenever the birth date is necessary for the court to establish or maintain subject matter jurisdiction;

v. The name of a minor in any order relating to parental responsibility, time-sharing, or child support;

vi. The name of a minor in any document or order affecting the minor's ownership of real property;

vii. The birth date of a party in a writ of attachment or notice to payor;

viii. In traffic and criminal proceedings: a pro se filing; a court filing that is related to a criminal matter or investigation and that is prepared before the filing of a criminal charge or is not filed as part of any docketed criminal case; an arrest or search warrant or any information in support thereof; a charging document and an affidavit or other documents filed in support of any charging document, including any driving records; a statement of particulars; discovery material introduced into evidence or otherwise filed with the court; and all information necessary for the proper issuance and execution of a subpoena duces tecum;

ix. Information used by the clerk for case maintenance purposes or the courts for case management purposes; and

x. Information which is relevant and material to an issue before the court. FL ST J ADMIN Rule 2.425(b).

c. *Remedies.* Upon motion by a party or interested person or sua sponte by the court, the court may order remedies, sanctions or both for a violation of FL ST J ADMIN Rule 2.425(a). Following notice and an opportunity to respond, the court may impose sanctions if such filing was not made in good faith. FL ST J ADMIN Rule 2.425(c).

d. *Motions not restricted.* FL ST J ADMIN Rule 2.425 does not restrict a party's right to move for protective order, to move to file documents under seal, or to request a determination of the confidentiality of records. FL ST J ADMIN Rule 2.425(d).

e. *Application.* FL ST J ADMIN Rule 2.425 does not affect the application of constitutional provisions, statutes, or rules of court regarding confidential information or access to public information. FL ST J ADMIN Rule 2.425(e).

F. Filing and Service Requirements

1. *Filing requirements.* All original documents must be filed with the court either before service or immediately thereafter, unless otherwise provided for by general law or other rules. If the original of any bond or other document is not placed in the court file, a certified copy must be so placed by the clerk. FL ST J ADMIN Rule 2.516(d). All documents shall be filed in conformity with the requirements of FL ST J ADMIN Rule 2.525. FL ST RCP Rule 1.080(b). All documents filed in any court shall be filed by electronic transmission in accordance with FL ST J ADMIN Rule 2.525. "Documents" means pleadings, motions, petitions, memoranda, briefs, notices, exhibits, declarations, affidavits, orders, judgments, decrees, writs, opinions, and any other paper or writing submitted to a court. FL ST J ADMIN Rule 2.520(a). All documents that are court records, as defined in FL ST J ADMIN Rule 2.430(a)(1), must be filed by electronic transmission, provided that: (1) the clerk has the ability to accept and retain such documents; (2) the clerk or the chief judge of the circuit has requested permission to accept documents filed by electronic transmission; and (3) the supreme court has entered an order granting permission to the clerk to accept documents filed by electronic transmission. FL ST J ADMIN Rule 2.525(c)(1).

a. *Definition.* "Electronic transmission of documents" means the sending of information by electronic signals to, by or from a court or clerk, which when received can be transformed and stored or transmitted on paper, microfilm, magnetic storage device, optical imaging system, CD-ROM, flash drive, other electronic data storage system, server, case maintenance system ("CM"), electronic court filing ("ECF") system, statewide or local electronic portal ("e-portal"), or other electronic record keeping system authorized by the supreme court in a format sufficient to communicate the information on the original document in a readable format. Electronic transmission of documents includes electronic mail ("e-mail") and any internet-based transmission procedure, and may include procedures allowing for documents to be signed or verified by electronic means. FL ST J ADMIN Rule 2.525(a).

i. The filing of documents with the court as required by the Florida Rules of Judicial Administration must be made by filing them with the clerk in accordance with FL ST J ADMIN Rule 2.525, except that the judge may permit documents to be filed with the judge, in which event the judge must note the filing date before him or her on the documents and transmit them to the clerk. The date of filing is that shown on the face of the document by the judge's notation or the clerk's time stamp, whichever is earlier. FL ST J ADMIN Rule 2.516(e).

b. *Application.* Any court or clerk of the court may accept the electronic transmission of documents for filing after the clerk, together with input from the chief judge of the circuit, has obtained approval of the procedures and program for doing so from the Supreme Court of Florida. FL ST J ADMIN Rule 2.525(b).

c. *Exceptions*

i. Paper documents and other submissions may be manually submitted to the clerk or court:

- When the clerk does not have the ability to accept and retain documents by electronic filing or has not had ECF Procedures approved by the supreme court;
- For filing by any self-represented party or any self-represented nonparty unless specific

ECF Procedures provide a means to file documents electronically. However, any self-represented nonparty that is a governmental or public agency and any other agency, partnership, corporation, or business entity acting on behalf of any governmental or public agency may file documents by electronic transmission if such entity has the capability of filing documents electronically;

- For filing by attorneys excused from e-mail service in accordance with FL ST J ADMIN Rule 2.516(b);
- When submitting evidentiary exhibits or filing non-documentary materials;
- When the filing involves documents in excess of twenty-five (25) megabytes (25MB) in size. For such filings, documents may be transmitted using an electronic storage medium that the clerk has the ability to accept, which may include a CD-ROM, flash drive, or similar storage medium;
- When filed in open court, as permitted by the court;
- When paper filing is permitted by any approved statewide or local ECF procedures; and
- If any court determines that justice so requires. FL ST J ADMIN Rule 2.525(d).

ii. Any document in paper form submitted under FL ST J ADMIN Rule 2.525(d) is filed when it is received by the clerk or court and the clerk shall immediately thereafter convert any filed paper document to an electronic document. "Convert to an electronic document" means optically capturing an image of a paper document and using character recognition software to recover as much of the document's text as practicable and then indexing and storing the document in the official court file. FL ST J ADMIN Rule 2.525(c)(4).

iii. Any storage medium submitted under FL ST J ADMIN Rule 2.525(d)(5) is filed when received by the clerk or court and the clerk shall immediately thereafter transfer the electronic documents from the storage device to the official court file. FL ST J ADMIN Rule 2.525(c)(5).

iv. If the filer of any paper document authorized under FL ST J ADMIN Rule 2.525(d) provides a self-addressed, postage-paid envelope for return of the paper document after it is converted to electronic form by the clerk, the clerk shall place the paper document in the envelope and deposit it in the mail. Except when a paper document is required to be maintained, the clerk may recycle any filed paper document that is not to be returned to the filer. FL ST J ADMIN Rule 2.525(c)(6).

v. The clerk may convert any paper document filed before the effective date of FL ST J ADMIN Rule 2.525 to an electronic document. Unless the clerk is required to maintain the paper document, if the paper document has been converted to an electronic document by the clerk, the paper document is no longer part of the official court file and may be removed and recycled. FL ST J ADMIN Rule 2.525(c)(7).

d. *Unrepresented parties.* An unrepresented party must file his or her papers with the clerk and send copies to other attorneys or unrepresented parties. FL ST 9 J CIR SECTION 7(B)(5).

i. An unrepresented party may not communicate privately with the judge either by letter, telephone, in person or otherwise. FL ST 9 J CIR SECTION 7(B)(4).

ii. Copies of legal papers or other written materials should not be sent to the judge unless specifically requested by the judge or required by the local administrative procedures. Any unrequested or non-required papers or materials sent to a judge may not be read but may be returned to the sender or placed unread into the court file. FL ST 9 J CIR SECTION 7(B)(4).

e. *Official court file.* For information on what constitutes the official court file, please see FL ST J ADMIN Rule 2.525(c)(2), FL ST J ADMIN Rule 2.525(c)(3).

f. *Administration.* All attorneys, parties, or other persons using this rule to file documents are required to make arrangements with the court or clerk for the payment of any charges authorized by general law or the supreme court before filing any document by electronic transmission. FL ST J ADMIN Rule 2.525(f)(2).

g. *Filing date.* The filing date for an electronically transmitted document is the date and time that such

filing is acknowledged by an electronic stamp or otherwise, pursuant to any procedure set forth in any ECF Procedures approved by the supreme court, or the date the last page of such filing is received by the court or clerk. FL ST J ADMIN Rule 2.525(f)(3).

h. *Accessibility.* All documents transmitted in any electronic form under FL ST J ADMIN Rule 2.525 must comply with the accessibility requirements of FL ST J ADMIN Rule 2.526. FL ST J ADMIN Rule 2.525(g).

2. *Service requirements.* Every pleading subsequent to the initial pleading, all orders, and every other document filed in the action must be served in conformity with the requirements of FL ST J ADMIN Rule 2.516. FL ST RCP Rule 1.080(a).

   a. *Service; When required.* Unless the court otherwise orders, or a statute or supreme court administrative order specifies a different means of service, every pleading subsequent to the initial pleading and every other document filed in any court proceeding, except applications for witness subpoenas and documents served by formal notice or required to be served in the manner provided for service of formal notice, must be served in accordance with FL ST J ADMIN Rule 2.516 on each party. No service need be made on parties against whom a default has been entered, except that pleadings asserting new or additional claims against them must be served in the manner provided for service of summons. FL ST J ADMIN Rule 2.516(a).

   b. *Service; How made.* When service is required or permitted to be made upon a party represented by an attorney, service must be made upon the attorney unless service upon the party is ordered by the court. FL ST J ADMIN Rule 2.516(b).

      i. *Service by electronic mail ("e-mail").* All documents required or permitted to be served on another party must be served by e-mail, unless FL ST J ADMIN Rule 2.516 otherwise provides. When, in addition to service by e-mail, the sender also utilizes another means of service provided for in FL ST J ADMIN Rule 2.516(b)(2), any differing time limits and other provisions applicable to that other means of service control. FL ST J ADMIN Rule 2.516(b)(1). Any document electronically transmitted to a court or clerk must also be served on all parties and interested persons in accordance with the applicable rules of court. FL ST J ADMIN Rule 2.525(e)(2).

         - *Service on attorneys.* Upon appearing in a proceeding, an attorney must serve a designation of a primary e-mail address and may designate no more than two (2) secondary e-mail addresses. Thereafter, service must be directed to all designated e-mail addresses in that proceeding. Every document filed by an attorney thereafter must include the primary e-mail address of that attorney and any secondary e-mail addresses. If an attorney does not designate any e-mail address for service, documents may be served on that attorney at the e-mail address on record with The Florida Bar. FL ST J ADMIN Rule 2.516(b)(1)(A).
         - *Exception to e-mail service on attorneys.* Service by an attorney on another attorney must be made by e-mail unless excused by the court. Upon motion by an attorney demonstrating that the attorney has no e-mail account and lacks access to the Internet at the attorney's office, the court may excuse the attorney from the requirements of e-mail service. Service on and by an attorney excused by the court from e-mail service must be by the means provided in FL ST J ADMIN Rule 2.516(b)(2). FL ST J ADMIN Rule 2.516(b)(1)(B).
         - *Service on and by parties not represented by an attorney.* Any party not represented by an attorney may serve a designation of a primary e-mail address and also may designate no more than two (2) secondary e-mail addresses to which service must be directed in that proceeding by the means provided in FL ST J ADMIN Rule 2.516(b)(1). If a party not represented by an attorney does not designate an e-mail address for service in a proceeding, service on and by that party must be by the means provided in FL ST J ADMIN Rule 2.516(b)(2). FL ST J ADMIN Rule 2.516(b)(1)(C).
         - *Time of service.* Service by e-mail is complete when it is sent. FL ST J ADMIN Rule 2.516(b)(1)(D). An e-mail is deemed served on the date it is sent. FL ST J ADMIN Rule 2.516(b)(1)(D)(i). If the sender learns that the e-mail did not reach the address of the person to be served, the sender must immediately send another copy by e-mail, or by a

means authorized by FL ST J ADMIN Rule 2.516(b)(2). FL ST J ADMIN Rule 2.516(b)(1)(D)(ii). E-mail service is treated as service by mail for the computation of time. FL ST J ADMIN Rule 2.516(b)(1)(D)(iii).

ii. *Format of e-mail for service.* Service of a document by e-mail is made by attaching a copy of the document in PDF format to an e-mail sent to all addresses designated by the attorney or party. FL ST J ADMIN Rule 2.516(b)(1)(E).

- All documents served by e-mail must be attached to an e-mail message containing a subject line beginning with the words "SERVICE OF COURT DOCUMENT" in all capital letters, followed by the case number of the proceeding in which the documents are being served. FL ST J ADMIN Rule 2.516(b)(1)(E)(i).
- The body of the e-mail must identify the court in which the proceeding is pending, the case number, the name of the initial party on each side, the title of each document served with that e-mail, and the sender's name and telephone number. FL ST J ADMIN Rule 2.516(b)(1)(E)(ii).
- Any document served by e-mail may be signed by the "/s/" format, as long as the filed original is signed in accordance with the applicable rule of procedure. FL ST J ADMIN Rule 2.516(b)(1)(E)(iii).
- Any e-mail which, together with its attached documents, exceeds five megabytes (5MB) in size, must be divided and sent as separate e-mails, no one of which may exceed five megabytes (5MB) in size and each of which must be sequentially numbered in the subject line. FL ST J ADMIN Rule 2.516(b)(1)(E)(iv).

iii. *Service by other means.* In addition to, and not in lieu of, service by e-mail, service may also be made upon attorneys by any of the means specified in FL ST J ADMIN Rule 2.516(b)(2). Service on and by all parties who are not represented by an attorney and who do not designate an e-mail address, and on and by all attorneys excused from e-mail service, must be made by delivering a copy of the document or by mailing it to the party or attorney at their last known address or, if no address is known, by leaving it with the clerk of the court. Service by mail is complete upon mailing. Delivery of a copy within FL ST J ADMIN Rule 2.516 is complete upon:

- Handing it to the attorney or to the party,
- Leaving it at the attorney's or party's office with a clerk or other person in charge thereof,
- If there is no one in charge, leaving it in a conspicuous place therein,
- If the office is closed or the person to be served has no office, leaving it at the person's usual place of abode with some person of his or her family above fifteen (15) years of age and informing such person of the contents, or
- Transmitting it by facsimile to the attorney's or party's office with a cover sheet containing the sender's name, firm, address, telephone number, and facsimile number, and the number of pages transmitted. When service is made by facsimile, a copy must also be served by any other method permitted by FL ST J ADMIN Rule 2.516. Facsimile service occurs when transmission is complete. FL ST J ADMIN Rule 2.516(b)(2)(A) through FL ST J ADMIN Rule 2.516(b)(2)(E).
- Service by delivery after 5:00 p.m. must be deemed to have been made by mailing on the date of delivery. FL ST J ADMIN Rule 2.516(b)(2)(F).

c. *Service; Numerous defendants.* In actions when the parties are unusually numerous, the court may regulate the service contemplated by the Florida Rules of Judicial Administration on motion or on its own initiative in such manner as may be found to be just and reasonable. FL ST J ADMIN Rule 2.516(c).

d. *Service by clerk.* Service of notices and other documents required to be made by the clerk must also be done as provided in FL ST J ADMIN Rule 2.516(b). FL ST J ADMIN Rule 2.516(g).

G. Hearings

1. The parties may be required to participate in pretrial proceedings to consider and determine the necessity or desirability of an amendment to a pleading. FL ST RCP Rule 1.200(b)(2); FL-PP § 2:151.

H. Forms

1. Official Amended Complaint Forms for Florida

a. Caption. FL ST RCP Form 1.901.

b. Notice of compliance when constitutional challenge is brought. FL ST RCP Form 1.975.

2. Amended Complaint Forms for Florida

a. Consent; Of party; To amendment of pleadings. FL-PP § 2:154.

b. Notice of amended complaint. 3 FLPRAC § 190.1.

c. Complaint for damages; General form. FL-PP § 2:17.

d. Complaint; Negligent infliction of personal injury. FL-PP § 2:19.

e. Complaint; Fall down negligence. FL-PP § 2:20.

f. Complaint; Mortgage foreclosure. FL-PP § 2:21.

g. Complaint; Implied warranty. FL-PP § 2:22.

h. Complaint; Professional negligence. FL-PP § 2:23.

i. Complaint; Breach of contract. FL-PP § 2:24.

j. Complaint; Breach of personal services contract. FL-PP § 2:25.

I. Checklist

(I) ❑ Matters to be considered by plaintiff

(a) ❑ Required documents

(1) ❑ Amended complaint

(2) ❑ Certificate of service

(b) ❑ Supplemental documents

(1) ❑ Exhibits

(2) ❑ Notice of constitutional question

(c) ❑ Timing

(1) ❑ A party may amend a pleading once as a matter of course at any time before a responsive pleading is served

(2) ❑ If the pleading is one to which no responsive pleading is permitted and the action has not been placed on the trial calendar, may so amend it at any time within twenty (20) days after it is served

Pleadings
Answer

Document Last Updated January 2013

A. Applicable Rules

1. *State rules*

a. Nonverification of pleadings. FL ST RCP Rule 1.030.

b. Process. FL ST RCP Rule 1.070.

c. Service and filing of pleadings, orders, and documents. FL ST RCP Rule 1.080.

d. Time. FL ST RCP Rule 1.090.

e. Pleadings and motions. FL ST RCP Rule 1.100; FL ST RCP Rule 1.110; FL ST RCP Rule 1.120; FL ST RCP Rule 1.130; FL ST RCP Rule 1.190; FL ST RCP Rule 1.430.

f. Defenses. FL ST RCP Rule 1.140.

g. Relief from judgment, decrees, or orders. FL ST RCP Rule 1.540.

h. Forms. FL ST RCP Rule 1.900.

i. Minimization of the filing of sensitive information. FL ST J ADMIN Rule 2.425.

j. Retention of court records. FL ST J ADMIN Rule 2.430.

k. Foreign attorneys. FL ST J ADMIN Rule 2.510.

l. Signature of attorneys and parties. FL ST J ADMIN Rule 2.515.

m. Paper. FL ST J ADMIN Rule 2.520.

n. Electronic filing. FL ST J ADMIN Rule 2.525.

o. Accessibility of information and technology. FL ST J ADMIN Rule 2.526.

p. Court reporting. FL ST J ADMIN Rule 2.535.

q. Requests for accommodations by persons with disabilities. FL ST J ADMIN Rule 2.540.

r. Waiver of sovereign immunity in tort actions; Recovery limits; Limitation on attorney fees; Statute of limitations; Exclusions; Indemnification; Risk management programs. FL ST § 768.28.

2. *Local rules*

a. Unrepresented (pro se) parties. FL ST 9 J CIR SECTION 7.

b. Business court procedures. FL ST 9 J CIR ORANGE CIV SECTION 1.

B. Timing

1. *General answer timing.* Unless a different time is prescribed in a statute of Florida, a defendant shall serve an answer within twenty (20) days after service of original process and the initial pleading on the defendant, or not later than the date fixed in a notice by publication. A party served with a pleading stating a crossclaim against that party shall serve an answer to it within twenty (20) days after service on that party. The plaintiff shall serve an answer to a counterclaim within twenty (20) days after service of the counterclaim. FL ST RCP Rule 1.140(a)(1).

a. *Waiver of service.* A defendant who, before being served with process, timely returns a waiver so requested is not required to respond to the complaint until sixty (60) days after the date the defendant received the request for waiver of service. For purposes of computing any time prescribed or allowed by the Florida Rules of Civil Procedure, service of process shall be deemed effected twenty (20) days before the time required to respond to the complaint. FL ST RCP Rule 1.070(i)(4).

b. *Service on the state.* Except when sued pursuant to FL ST § 768.28, the state of Florida, an agency of the state, or an officer or employee of the state sued in an official capacity shall serve an answer to the complaint or crossclaim, or a reply to a counterclaim, within forty (40) days after service. When sued pursuant to FL ST § 768.28, the Department of Financial Services or the defendant state agency shall have thirty (30) days from the date of service within which to serve an answer to the complaint or crossclaim or a reply to a counterclaim. FL ST RCP Rule 1.140(a)(2).

c. *Service of motion impact on time periods for service of answer.* The service of a motion under FL ST RCP Rule 1.140, except a motion for judgment on the pleadings or a motion to strike under FL ST RCP Rule 1.140(f), alters these periods of time so that if the court denies the motion or postpones its disposition until the trial on the merits, the responsive pleadings shall be served within ten (10) days after notice of the court's action or, if the court grants a motion for a more definite statement, the responsive pleadings shall be served within ten (10) days after service of the more definite statement unless a different time is fixed by the court in either case. FL ST RCP Rule 1.140(a)(3).

d. *Responding if pleading does not require a responsive pleading.* If a pleading sets forth a claim for relief to which the adverse party is not required to serve a responsive pleading, the adverse party may assert any defense in law or fact to that claim for relief at the trial, except that the objection of failure to state a legal defense in an answer or reply shall be asserted by motion to strike the defense within twenty (20) days after service of the answer or reply. FL ST RCP Rule 1.140(b).

2. *Computation of time*

    a. *Generally.* Computation of time shall be governed by FL ST J ADMIN Rule 2.514. FL ST RCP Rule 1.090(a). The following rules apply in computing time periods specified in any rule of procedure, local rule, court order, or statute that does not specify a method of computing time. FL ST J ADMIN Rule 2.514(a).

        i. *Period stated in days or a longer unit.* When the period is stated in days or a longer unit of time (A) exclude the day of the event that triggers the period; (B) count every day, including intermediate Saturdays, Sundays, and legal holidays; and (C) include the last day of the period, but if the last day is a Saturday, Sunday, or legal holiday, or falls within any period of time extended through an order of the chief justice under FL ST J ADMIN Rule 2.205(a)(2)(B)(iv), the period continues to run until the end of the next day that is not a Saturday, Sunday, or legal holiday and does not fall within any period of time extended through an order of the chief justice. FL ST J ADMIN Rule 2.514(a)(1).

        ii. *Period stated in hours.* When the period is stated in hours (A) begin counting immediately on the occurrence of the event that triggers the period; (B) count every hour, including hours during intermediate Saturdays, Sundays, and legal holidays; and (C) if the period would end on a Saturday, Sunday, or legal holiday, or during any period of time extended through an order of the chief justice under FL ST J ADMIN Rule 2.205(a)(2)(B)(iv), the period continues to run until the same time on the next day that is not a Saturday, Sunday, or legal holiday and does not fall within any period of time extended through an order of the chief justice. FL ST J ADMIN Rule 2.514(a)(2).

        iii. *Period stated in days less than seven (7) days.* When the period stated in days is less than seven (7) days, intermediate Saturdays, Sundays, and legal holidays shall be excluded in the computation. FL ST J ADMIN Rule 2.514(a)(3).

        iv. *"Last day" defined.* Unless a different time is set by a statute, local rule, or court order, the last day ends (A) for electronic filing or for service by any means, at midnight; and (B) for filing by other means, when the clerk's office is scheduled to close. FL ST J ADMIN Rule 2.514(a)(4).

        v. *"Next day" defined.* The "next day" is determined by continuing to count forward when the period is measured after an event and backward when measured before an event. FL ST J ADMIN Rule 2.514(a)(5).

        vi. *"Legal holiday" defined.* "Legal holiday" means (A) the day set aside by FL ST § 110.117, for observing New Year's Day, Martin Luther King, Jr.'s Birthday, Memorial Day, Independence Day, Labor Day, Veterans' Day, Thanksgiving Day, the Friday after Thanksgiving Day, or Christmas Day, and (B) any day observed as a holiday by the clerk's office or as designated by the chief judge. FL ST J ADMIN Rule 2.514(a)(6).

    b. *Additional time after service by mail or e-mail.* When a party may or must act within a specified time after service and service is made by mail or e-mail, five (5) days are added after the period that would otherwise expire under FL ST J ADMIN Rule 2.514(a). FL ST J ADMIN Rule 2.514(b).

    c. *Enlargement.* When an act is required or allowed to be done at or within a specified time by order of court, by the Florida Rules of Civil Procedure, or by notice given thereunder, for cause shown the court at any time in its discretion (1) with or without notice, may order the period enlarged if request therefor is made before the expiration of the period originally prescribed or as extended by a previous order, or (2) upon motion made and notice after the expiration of the specified period, may permit the act to be done when failure to act was the result of excusable neglect, but it may not extend the time for making a motion for new trial, for rehearing, or to alter or amend a judgment; making a motion for relief from a judgment under FL ST RCP Rule 1.540(b); taking an appeal or filing a petition for certiorari; or making a motion for a directed verdict. FL ST RCP Rule 1.090(b).

    d. *Unaffected by expiration of term.* The period of time provided for the doing of any act or the taking

of any proceeding shall not be affected or limited by the continued existence or expiration of a term of court. The continued existence or expiration of a term of court in no way affects the power of a court to do any act or take any proceeding in any action which is or has been pending before it. FL ST RCP Rule 1.090(c).

C. General Requirements

1. *General rules of pleading*
    a. *Claims for relief*
        i. A pleading which sets forth a claim for relief, whether an original claim, counterclaim, crossclaim, or third-party claim, must state a cause of action and shall contain
            - A short and plain statement of the grounds upon which the court's jurisdiction depends, unless the court already has jurisdiction and the claim needs no new grounds of jurisdiction to support it (For information regarding acts subjecting persons to jurisdiction, please see FL ST § 48.193),
            - A short and plain statement of the ultimate facts showing that the pleader is entitled to relief, and
            - A demand for judgment for the relief to which the pleader deems himself or herself entitled. FL ST RCP Rule 1.110(b).
        ii. Relief in the alternative or of several different types may be demanded. Every complaint shall be considered to demand general relief. FL ST RCP Rule 1.110(b).
    b. *Verification.* Except when otherwise specifically provided by these rules or an applicable statute, every pleading or other document of a party represented by an attorney need not be verified or accompanied by an affidavit. FL ST RCP Rule 1.030. When filing an action for foreclosure of a mortgage on residential real property the complaint shall be verified. When verification of a document is required, the document filed shall include an oath, affirmation, or the following statement: "Under penalty of perjury, I declare that I have read the foregoing, and the facts alleged therein are true and correct to the best of my knowledge and belief." FL ST RCP Rule 1.110(b).
    c. *Separate statements.* All averments of claim or defense shall be made in consecutively numbered paragraphs, the contents of each of which shall be limited as far as practicable to a statement of a single set of circumstances, and a paragraph may be referred to by number in all subsequent pleadings. Each claim founded upon a separate transaction or occurrence and each defense other than denials shall be stated in a separate count or defense when a separation facilitates the clear presentation of the matter set forth. FL ST RCP Rule 1.110(f).
    d. *Statements adopted by reference.* Statements in a pleading may be adopted by reference in a different part of the same pleading, in another pleading, or in any motion. FL ST RCP Rule 1.130(b).
    e. *Joinder of causes of action; Consistency.* A pleader may set up in the same action as many claims or causes of action or defenses in the same right as the pleader has, and claims for relief may be stated in the alternative if separate items make up the cause of action, or if two (2) or more causes of action are joined. A party may also set forth two (2) or more statements of a claim or defense alternatively, either in one (1) count or defense or in separate counts or defenses. When two (2) or more statements are made in the alternative and one (1) of them, if made independently, would be sufficient, the pleading is not made insufficient by the insufficiency of one (1) or more of the alternative statements. A party may also state as many separate claims or defenses as that party has, regardless of consistency and whether based on legal or equitable grounds or both. All pleadings shall be construed so as to do substantial justice. FL ST RCP Rule 1.110(g).
    f. *Subsequent pleadings.* When the nature of an action permits pleadings subsequent to final judgment and the jurisdiction of the court over the parties has not terminated, the initial pleading subsequent to final judgment shall be designated a supplemental complaint or petition. The action shall then proceed in the same manner and time as though the supplemental complaint or petition were the initial pleading in the action, including the issuance of any needed process. FL ST RCP Rule 1.110(h) shall not apply to proceedings that may be initiated by motion under the Florida Rules of Civil Procedure. FL ST RCP Rule 1.110(h).

g. *Pleading basis for service.* When service of process is to be made under statutes authorizing service on nonresidents of Florida, it is sufficient to plead the basis for service in the language of the statute without pleading the facts supporting service. FL ST RCP Rule 1.070(h).

h. *Forms of pleadings.* Forms of action and technical forms for seeking relief and of pleas, pleadings, or motions are abolished. FL ST RCP Rule 1.110(a).

2. *Answer; Generally.* An answer has three (3) functions. First, it must respond to each allegation of the preceding pleading by admitting, denying or alleging that the pleader is without knowledge of the allegation. Second, it must contain any affirmative defenses that the pleader is interposing to any cause of action alleged in the preceding pleading. Third, the answer may claim affirmative relief against the plaintiff or petitioner by a counterclaim or against a codefendant by a crossclaim. FL-PRACPROC § 11:1.

a. *Content.* In the answer a pleader shall state in short and plain terms the pleader's defenses to each claim asserted and shall admit or deny the averments on which the adverse party relies. If the defendant is without knowledge, the defendant shall so state and such statement shall operate as a denial. Denial shall fairly meet the substance of the averments denied. When a pleader intends in good faith to deny only a part of an averment, the pleader shall specify so much of it as is true and shall deny the remainder. Unless the pleader intends in good faith to controvert all of the averments of the preceding pleading, the pleader may make denials as specific denials of designated averments or may generally deny all of the averments except such designated averments as the pleader expressly admits, but when the pleader does so intend to controvert all of its averments, including averments of the grounds upon which the court's jurisdiction depends, the pleader may do so by general denial. FL ST RCP Rule 1.110(c).

b. *Form of answer.* An answer contains a caption, commencement, body, signature and certificate of service. The caption is the same as that of the initial pleading, except for the designation as one of the types of answer. The body of an answer should contain an admission, denial or plea of without knowledge to each allegation of the preceding pleading, except for the additional allegations in response to a general allegation of conditions precedent and the denial of capacity to sue. FL-PRACPROC § 11:3.

i. *Responding sequentially.* The best method of responding is to answer each paragraph sequentially, combining admissions, denials or pleas of without knowledge when the sequence permits. The admissions, denials and allegations of without knowledge should be stated first, followed separately by any affirmative defenses and then by any counterclaim or crossclaim. A third party complaint may be a part of the same paper, but it is not a part of the answer as is a counterclaim or crossclaim. Paragraphs are numbered consecutively throughout the pleading whether in the answer, counterclaim or crossclaim. Denials for the record only are improper. FL-PRACPROC § 11:3.

c. *Defenses*

i. *Generally.* Every defense in law or fact to a claim for relief in a pleading shall be asserted in the responsive pleading, if one is required, but the following defenses may be made by motion at the option of the pleader: (1) lack of jurisdiction over the subject matter, (2) lack of jurisdiction over the person, (3) improper venue, (4) insufficiency of process, (5) insufficiency of service of process, (6) failure to state a cause of action, and (7) failure to join indispensable parties. A motion making any of these defenses shall be made before pleading if a further pleading is permitted. FL ST RCP Rule 1.140(b).

- *Stated specifically.* The grounds on which any of the enumerated defenses are based and the substantial matters of law intended to be argued shall be stated specifically and with particularity in the responsive pleading or motion. FL ST RCP Rule 1.140(b).
- *Waiver.* Any ground not stated shall be deemed to be waived except any ground showing that the court lacks jurisdiction of the subject matter may be made at any time. No defense or objection is waived by being joined with other defenses or objections in a responsive pleading or motion. FL ST RCP Rule 1.140(b). A party waives all defenses and objections that the party does not present either by motion under FL ST RCP Rule 1.140(b), FL ST RCP Rule 1.140(e), or FL ST RCP Rule 1.140(f) or, if the party has made no motion, in a

responsive pleading except as provided in FL ST RCP Rule 1.140(h)(2). FL ST RCP Rule 1.140(h)(1). The defenses of failure to state a cause of action or a legal defense or to join an indispensable party may be raised by motion for judgment on the pleadings or at the trial on the merits in addition to being raised either in a motion under FL ST RCP Rule 1.140(b) or in the answer or reply. The defense of lack of jurisdiction of the subject matter may be raised at any time. FL ST RCP Rule 1.140(h)(2).

ii. *Affirmative defenses.* In pleading to a preceding pleading a party shall set forth affirmatively accord and satisfaction, arbitration and award, assumption of risk, contributory negligence, discharge in bankruptcy, duress, estoppel, failure of consideration, fraud, illegality, injury by fellow servant, laches, license, payment, release, res judicata, statute of frauds, statute of limitations, waiver, and any other matter constituting an avoidance or affirmative defense. When a party has mistakenly designated a defense as a counterclaim or a counterclaim as a defense, the court, on terms if justice so requires, shall treat the pleading as if there had been a proper designation. Affirmative defenses appearing on the face of a prior pleading may be asserted as grounds for a motion or defense under FL ST RCP Rule 1.140(b); provided this shall not limit amendments under FL ST RCP Rule 1.190 even if such ground is sustained. FL ST RCP Rule 1.110(d).

- *Format of defenses.* Affirmative defenses should be placed after the admissions, denials and allegations of without knowledge in the answer. All paragraphs must be numbered consecutively throughout the answer. If a defense is directed to only a part of a cause of action or to one or more, but not all, of several causes of action in the preceding pleading, the part or cause of action to which it is directed should be identified in the defense. Defenses should be identified by consecutive ordinal numbers such as "First Defense" and "Second Defense." FL-PRACPROC § 11:4.

iii. *Effect of failure to deny.* Averments in a pleading to which a responsive pleading is required, other than those as to the amount of damages, are admitted when not denied in the responsive pleading. Averments in a pleading to which no responsive pleading is required or permitted shall be taken as denied or avoided. FL ST RCP Rule 1.110(e). An admission in an answer binds the party and no proof is required. An admission does not extend beyond the scope of the allegation in the preceding pleading. FL-PRACPROC § 11:3.

3. *Pleading special matters*

a. *Capacity.* It is not necessary to aver the capacity of a party to sue or be sued, the authority of a party to sue or be sued in a representative capacity, or the legal existence of an organized association of persons that is made a party, except to the extent required to show the jurisdiction of the court. The initial pleading served on behalf of a minor party shall specifically aver the age of the minor party. When a party desires to raise an issue as to the legal existence of any party, the capacity of any party to sue or be sued, or the authority of a party to sue or be sued in a representative capacity, that party shall do so by specific negative averment which shall include such supporting particulars as are peculiarly within the pleader's knowledge. FL ST RCP Rule 1.120(a).

b. *Fraud, mistake, condition of the mind.* In all averments of fraud or mistake, the circumstances constituting fraud or mistake shall be stated with such particularity as the circumstances may permit. Malice, intent, knowledge, mental attitude, and other condition of mind of a person may be averred generally. FL ST RCP Rule 1.120(b).

c. *Conditions precedent.* In pleading the performance or occurrence of conditions precedent, it is sufficient to aver generally that all conditions precedent have been performed or have occurred. A denial of performance or occurrence shall be made specifically and with particularity. FL ST RCP Rule 1.120(c).

d. *Official document or act.* In pleading an official document or official act it is sufficient to aver that the document was issued or the act done in compliance with law. FL ST RCP Rule 1.120(c).

e. *Judgment or decree.* In pleading a judgment or decree of a domestic or foreign court, a judicial or quasi-judicial tribunal, or a board or officer, it is sufficient to aver the judgment or decree without setting forth matter showing jurisdiction to render it. FL ST RCP Rule 1.120(e).

f. *Time and place.* For the purpose of testing the sufficiency of a pleading, averments of time and place are material and shall be considered like all other averments of material matter. FL ST RCP Rule 1.120(f).

g. *Special damage.* When items of special damage are claimed, they shall be specifically stated. FL ST RCP Rule 1.120(g).

4. *Parties*

a. *Parties generally.* Every action may be prosecuted in the name of the real party in interest, but a personal representative, administrator, guardian, trustee of an express trust, a party with whom or in whose name a contract has been made for the benefit of another, or a party expressly authorized by statute may sue in that person's own name without joining the party for whose benefit the action is brought. All persons having an interest in the subject of the action and in obtaining the relief demanded may join as plaintiffs and any person may be made a defendant who has or claims an interest adverse to the plaintiff. Any person may at any time be made a party if that person's presence is necessary or proper to a complete determination of the cause. Persons having a united interest may be joined on the same side as plaintiffs or defendants, and anyone who refuses to join may for such reason be made a defendant. FL ST RCP Rule 1.210(a).

b. *Minors or incompetent persons.* When a minor or incompetent person has a representative, such as a guardian or other like fiduciary, the representative may sue or defend on behalf of the minor or incompetent person. A minor or incompetent person who does not have a duly appointed representative may sue by next friend or by a guardian ad litem. The court shall appoint a guardian ad litem for a minor or incompetent person not otherwise represented in an action or shall make such other order as it deems proper for the protection of the minor or incompetent person. FL ST RCP Rule 1.210(b).

c. For survivor and substitution of parties information, please see FL ST RCP Rule 1.260.

5. *Counterclaims and crossclaims*

a. *Compulsory counterclaims.* A pleading shall state as a counterclaim any claim which at the time of serving the pleading the pleader has against any opposing party, provided it arises out of the transaction or occurrence that is the subject matter of the opposing party's claim and does not require for its adjudication the presence of third parties over whom the court cannot acquire jurisdiction. But the pleader need not state a claim if (1) at the time the action was commenced the claim was the subject of another pending action, or (2) the opposing party brought suit upon that party's claim by attachment or other process by which the court did not acquire jurisdiction to render a personal judgment on the claim and the pleader is not stating a counterclaim under this rule. FL ST RCP Rule 1.170(a).

b. *Permissive counterclaim.* A pleading may state as a counterclaim any claim against an opposing party not arising out of the transaction or occurrence that is the subject matter of the opposing party's claim. FL ST RCP Rule 1.170(b).

c. *Counterclaim exceeding opposing claim.* A counterclaim may or may not diminish or defeat the recovery sought by the opposing party. It may claim relief exceeding in amount or different in kind from that sought in the pleading of the opposing party. FL ST RCP Rule 1.170(c).

d. *Counterclaim against the State.* The Florida Rules of Civil Procedure shall not be construed to enlarge beyond the limits established by law the right to assert counterclaims or to claim credits against the state or any of its subdivisions or other governmental organizations thereof subject to suit or against a municipal corporation or against an officer, agency, or administrative board of the state. FL ST RCP Rule 1.170(d).

e. *Counterclaim maturing or acquired after pleading.* A claim which matured or was acquired by the pleader after serving the pleading may be presented as a counterclaim by supplemental pleading with the permission of the court. FL ST RCP Rule 1.170(e).

f. *Omitted counterclaim or crossclaim.* When a pleader fails to set up a counterclaim or crossclaim through oversight, inadvertence, or excusable neglect, or when justice requires, the pleader may set up the counterclaim or crossclaim by amendment with leave of the court. FL ST RCP Rule 1.170(f).

g. *Crossclaim against co-party.* A pleading may state as a crossclaim any claim by one party against a co-party arising out of the transaction or occurrence that is the subject matter of either the original action or a counterclaim therein, or relating to any property that is the subject matter of the original action. The crossclaim may include a claim that the party against whom it is asserted is or may be liable to the crossclaimant for all or part of a claim asserted in the action against the crossclaimant. Service of a crossclaim on a party who has appeared in the action shall be made pursuant to FL ST RCP Rule 1.080. Service of a crossclaim against a party who has not appeared in the action shall be made in the manner provided for service of summons. FL ST RCP Rule 1.170(g).

h. *Additional parties may be brought in.* When the presence of parties other than those to the original action is required to grant complete relief in the determination of a counterclaim or crossclaim, they shall be named in the counterclaim or crossclaim and be served with process and shall be parties to the action thereafter if jurisdiction of them can be obtained and their joinder will not deprive the court of jurisdiction of the action. FL ST RCP Rule 1.250(b) and FL ST RCP Rule 1.250(c) apply to parties brought in under FL ST RCP Rule 1.170(h). FL ST RCP Rule 1.170(h).

i. *Separate trials; Separate judgment.* If the court orders separate trials as provided in FL ST RCP Rule 1.270(b), judgment on a counterclaim or crossclaim may be rendered when the court has jurisdiction to do so even if a claim of the opposing party has been dismissed or otherwise disposed of. FL ST RCP Rule 1.170(i).

j. *Demand exceeding jurisdiction; Transfer of action.* If the demand of any counterclaim or crossclaim exceeds the jurisdiction of the court in which the action is pending, the action shall be transferred forthwith to the court of the same county having jurisdiction of the demand in the counterclaim or crossclaim with only such alterations in the pleadings as are essential. The court shall order the transfer of the action and the transmittal of all papers in it to the proper court if the party asserting the demand exceeding the jurisdiction deposits with the court having jurisdiction a sum sufficient to pay the clerk's service charge in the court to which the action is transferred at the time of filing the counterclaim or crossclaim. Thereupon the original papers and deposit shall be transmitted and filed with a certified copy of the order. The court to which the action is transferred shall have full power and jurisdiction over the demands of all parties. Failure to make the service charge deposit at the time the counterclaim or crossclaim is filed, or within such further time as the court may allow, shall reduce a claim for damages to an amount within the jurisdiction of the court where the action is pending and waive the claim in other cases. FL ST RCP Rule 1.170(j).

6. *Misjoinder and nonjoinder of parties*

   a. *Misjoinder.* Misjoinder of parties is not a ground for dismissal of an action. Any claim against a party may be severed and proceeded with separately. FL ST RCP Rule 1.250(a).

   b. *Dropping parties.* Parties may be dropped by an adverse party in the manner provided for voluntary dismissal in FL ST RCP Rule 1.420(a)(1) subject to the exception stated in FL ST RCP Rule 1.420. If notice of lis pendens has been filed in the action against a party so dropped, the notice of dismissal shall be recorded and cancels the notice of lis pendens without the necessity of a court order. Parties may be dropped by order of court on its own initiative or the motion of any party at any stage of the action on such terms as are just. FL ST RCP Rule 1.250(b).

   c. *Adding parties.* Parties may be added once as a matter of course within the same time that pleadings can be so amended under FL ST RCP Rule 1.190(a). If amendment by leave of court or stipulation of the parties is permitted, parties may be added in the amended pleading without further order of court. Parties may be added by order of court on its own initiative or on motion of any party at any stage of the action and on such terms as are just. FL ST RCP Rule 1.250(c).

7. *Jury demand*

   a. *Right preserved.* The right of trial by jury as declared by the Constitution or by statute shall be preserved to the parties inviolate. FL ST RCP Rule 1.430(a).

   b. *Demand.* Any party may demand a trial by jury of any issue triable of right by a jury by serving upon the other party a demand therefor in writing at any time after commencement of the action and not later than ten (10) days after the service of the last pleading directed to such issue. The demand may be indorsed upon a pleading of the party. FL ST RCP Rule 1.430(b).

c. *Specification of issues.* In the demand a party may specify the issues that the party wishes so tried; otherwise, the party is deemed to demand trial by jury for all issues so triable. FL ST RCP Rule 1.430(c).

  i. If a party has demanded trial by jury for only some of the issues, any other party may serve a demand for trial by jury of any other or all of the issues triable by jury ten (10) days after service of the demand or such lesser time as the court may order. FL ST RCP Rule 1.430(c).

d. *Waiver.* A party who fails to serve a demand as required by FL ST RCP Rule 1.430 waives trial by jury. FL ST RCP Rule 1.430(d).

  i. If waived, a jury trial may not be granted without the consent of the parties, but the court may allow an amendment in the proceedings to demand a trial by jury or order a trial by jury on its own motion. FL ST RCP Rule 1.430(d).

  ii. A demand for trial by jury may not be withdrawn without the consent of the parties. FL ST RCP Rule 1.430(d).

8. *Arbitration and mediation*

  a. *Referral to arbitration and mediation.* Except as hereinafter provided or as otherwise prohibited by law, the presiding judge may enter an order referring all or any part of a contested civil matter to mediation or arbitration. The parties to any contested civil matter may file a written stipulation to mediate or arbitrate any issue between them at any time. Such stipulation shall be incorporated into the order of referral. FL ST RCP Rule 1.700(a).

  b. *Arbitration*

    i. *Exclusions.* A civil action shall be ordered to arbitration or arbitration in conjunction with mediation upon stipulation of the parties. A civil action may be ordered to arbitration or arbitration in conjunction with mediation upon motion of any party or by the court, if the judge determines the action to be of such a nature that arbitration could be of benefit to the litigants or the court. FL ST RCP Rule 1.800.

      - Under no circumstances may the following categories of actions be referred to arbitration: (1) bond estreatures; (2) habeas corpus or other extraordinary writs; (3) bond validations; (4) civil or criminal contempt; (5) such other matters as may be specified by order of the chief judge in the circuit. FL ST RCP Rule 1.800.

    ii. For more information regarding arbitration, please see FL ST RCP Rule 1.810; FL ST RCP Rule 1.820; FL ST RCP Rule 1.830.

  c. *Mediation.* For more information regarding mediation, please see FL ST RCP Rule 1.710; FL ST RCP Rule 1.720; FL ST RCP Rule 1.730; and FL ST RCP Rule 1.750.

  d. *Local arbitration policy.* It is the policy of the Civil Division judges to maximize the use of alternative dispute resolution procedures. Except where prohibited by statute, mediation will be ordered in all cases where jury trial is requested and in selected cases which are to be tried non-jury. Also, selected cases will be referred for court-annexed non-binding arbitration through the Orange County Bar Association Arbitration Service. Counsel may move to dispense with or defer mediation or arbitration or move to modify the referral order for good cause. FL ST 9 J CIR SECTION 15.

9. *Rules of court*

  a. *Rules of civil procedure.* The Florida Rules of Civil Procedure apply to all actions of a civil nature and all special statutory proceedings in the circuit courts and county courts except those to which the Florida Probate Rules, the Florida Family Law Rules of Procedure, or the Small Claims Rules apply. FL ST RCP Rule 1.010.

    i. The form, content, procedure, and time for pleading in all special statutory proceedings shall be as prescribed by the statutes governing the proceeding unless the Florida Rules of Civil Procedure specifically provide to the contrary. FL ST RCP Rule 1.010.

    ii. The Florida Rules of Civil Procedure shall be construed to secure the just, speedy, and inexpensive determination of every action. FL ST RCP Rule 1.010.

b. *Rules of judicial administration.* The Florida Rules of Judicial Administration shall apply to administrative matters in all courts to which the Florida Rules of Judicial Administration are applicable by their terms. The Florida Rules of Judicial Administration shall be construed to secure the speedy and inexpensive determination of every proceeding to which they are applicable. The Florida Rules of Judicial Administration shall supersede all conflicting rules and statutes. FL ST J ADMIN Rule 2.110.

c. *Business court procedures.* For rules specific to Business Court, please see FL ST 9 J CIR ORANGE CIV SECTION 1, et seq.

D. Documents

1. *Required documents*

   a. *Answer.* See the General Requirements section of this document for further information about the content of an answer.

      i. *Notices to persons with disabilities.* See the Format section of this KeyRules document for further information.

   b. *Certificate of service.* When any attorney certifies in substance: "I certify that a copy hereof has been furnished to (here insert name or names and addresses used for service) by (e-mail) (delivery) (mail) (fax) on .... (date) ....________________ Attorney" the certificate is taken as prima facie proof of such service in compliance with FL ST J ADMIN Rule 2.516. FL ST J ADMIN Rule 2.516(f).

2. *Supplemental documents*

   a. *Exhibits.* All bonds, notes, bills of exchange, contracts, accounts, or documents upon which action may be brought or defense made, or a copy thereof or a copy of the portions thereof material to the pleadings, shall be incorporated in or attached to the pleading. No papers shall be unnecessarily annexed as exhibits. The pleadings shall contain no unnecessary recitals of deeds, documents, contracts, or other instruments. Any exhibit attached to a pleading shall be considered a part of the pleadings for all purposes. FL ST RCP Rule 1.130(a).

   b. *Notice of constitutional question.* A party that files a pleading, written motion, or other paper drawing into question the constitutionality of a state statute or a county or municipal charter, ordinance, or franchise must promptly (1) file a notice of constitutional question stating the question and identifying the paper that raises it; and (2) serve the notice and the pleading, written motion, or other paper drawing into question the constitutionality of a state statute or a county or municipal charter, ordinance, or franchise on the Attorney General or the state attorney of the judicial circuit in which the action is pending, by either certified or registered mail. Service of the notice and pleading, written motion, or other paper does not require joinder of the Attorney General or the state attorney as a party to the action. FL ST RCP Rule 1.071.

E. Format

1. *Documents; Type and size.* Documents subject to the exceptions set forth in FL ST J ADMIN Rule 2.525(d) shall be filed on recycled paper measuring eight and one half by eleven (8 1/2 by 11) inches. For purposes of FL ST J ADMIN Rule 2.520, paper is recycled if it contains a minimum content of fifty (50) percent waste paper. Xerographic reduction of legal-size (eight and one half by fourteen (8 1/2 by 14) inches) documents to letter size (eight and one half by eleven (8 1/2 by 11) inches) is prohibited. All other documents filed by electronic transmission shall be filed in a format capable of being printed in a format consistent with the provisions of FL ST J ADMIN Rule 2.250. FL ST J ADMIN Rule 2.520(b).

   a. *Exhibits.* Any exhibit or attachment filed with pleadings or papers may be filed in its original size. FL ST J ADMIN Rule 2.520(c).

   b. *Recording space.* On all papers and documents prepared and filed by the court or by any party to a proceeding which are to be recorded in the public records of any county, including but not limited to final money judgments and notices of lis pendens, a three (3) inch by three (3) inch space at the top right-hand corner on the first page and a one (1) inch by three (3) inch space at the top right-hand corner on each subsequent page shall be left blank and reserved for use by the clerk of court. FL ST J ADMIN Rule 2.520(d).

      i. *Exceptions to recording space.* Any papers or documents created by persons or entities over

which the filing party has no control, including but not limited to wills, codicils, trusts, or other testamentary documents; documents prepared or executed by any public officer; documents prepared, executed, acknowledged, or proved outside of the State of Florida; or documents created by State or Federal government agencies, may be filed without the space required by FL ST J ADMIN Rule 2.520. FL ST J ADMIN Rule 2.520(e).

c. *Noncompliance.* No clerk of court is permitted to refuse to file any document or paper because of noncompliance with the Florida Rules of Judicial Administration. However, upon request of the clerk of court, noncomplying documents must be resubmitted in accordance with the formatting rules. FL ST J ADMIN Rule 2.520(f).

2. *Caption.* Every pleading, motion, order, judgment, or other paper shall have a caption containing the name of the court, the file number, and except for in rem proceedings, including forfeiture proceedings, the name of the first party on each side with an appropriate indication of other parties, and a designation identifying the party filing it and its nature or the nature of the order, as the case may be. In any in rem proceeding, every pleading, motion, order, judgment, or other paper shall have a caption containing the name of the court, the file number, the style "In re" (followed by the name or general description of the property), and a designation of the person or entity filing it and its nature or the nature of the order, as the case may be. In an in rem forfeiture proceeding, the style shall be "In re forfeiture of" (followed by the name of the general description of the property). All papers filed in the action shall be styled in such a manner as to indicate clearly the subject matter of the paper and the party requesting or obtaining relief. FL ST RCP Rule 1.100(c)(1).

3. *Writing and written defined.* Writing or written means a document containing information, an application, or a stipulation. FL ST RCP Rule 1.080(c).

4. *Rule abbreviations*

   a. The Florida Rules of Civil Procedure and shall be abbreviated as Fla.R.Civ.P. FL ST RCP Rule 1.010.

   b. The Florida Rules of Judicial Administration shall be abbreviated as Fla. R. Jud. Admin. FL ST J ADMIN Rule 2.110.

5. *Nonverification.* Except when otherwise specifically provided by the Florida Rules of Civil Procedure or an applicable statute, every pleading or other document of a party represented by an attorney need not be verified or accompanied by an affidavit. FL ST RCP Rule 1.030; FL ST J ADMIN Rule 2.515(a).

6. *Unrepresented parties.* An unrepresented party must file his or her papers with the clerk and send copies to other attorneys or unrepresented parties. All such papers must be typed double-spaced on plain white eight and a half by eleven (8 1/2 by 11) inch paper, with the name of the case and case number at the top and the party's mailing address, telephone number and FAX number, if any, below his or her signature at the end of the paper. Such unrepresented party must immediately notify the clerk and all other counsel or parties of record in writing of any change in mailing address or telephone or FAX number. Failure to promptly notify of change of address could result in a dismissal or default entered against such party. FL ST 9 J CIR SECTION 7(B)(5).

7. *Attorney signature*

   a. *Attorney signature.* Every pleading and other document of a party represented by an attorney shall be signed by at least one (1) attorney of record in that attorney's individual name whose current record Florida Bar address, telephone number, including area code, primary e-mail address and secondary e-mail addresses, if any, and Florida Bar number shall be stated, and who shall be duly licensed to practice law in Florida or who shall have received permission to appear in the particular case as provided in FL ST J ADMIN Rule 2.510. FL ST J ADMIN Rule 2.515(a).

      i. The attorney may be required by the court to give the address of, and to vouch for the attorney's authority to represent, the party. FL ST J ADMIN Rule 2.515(a).

      ii. The signature of an attorney shall constitute a certificate by the attorney that the attorney has read the pleading or other document; that to the best of the attorney's knowledge, information, and belief there is good ground to support it; and that it is not interposed for delay. FL ST J ADMIN Rule 2.515(a).

iii. If a pleading is not signed or is signed with intent to defeat the purpose of FL ST J ADMIN Rule 2.515, it may be stricken and the action may proceed as though the pleading or other document had not been served. FL ST J ADMIN Rule 2.515(a).

b. *Pro se litigant signature.* A party who is not represented by an attorney shall sign any pleading or other paper and state the party's address and telephone number, including area code. FL ST J ADMIN Rule 2.515(b).

c. *Form of signature*

i. The signatures required on pleadings and documents by FL ST J ADMIN Rule 2.515(a) and FL ST J ADMIN Rule 2.515(b) may be:

- Original signatures;
- Original signatures that have been reproduced by electronic means, such as on electronically transmitted documents or photocopied documents;
- Electronic signatures using the "/s/," "s/," or "/s" formats by or at the direction of the person signing; or
- Any other signature format authorized by general law, so long as the clerk where the proceeding is pending has the capability of receiving and has obtained approval from the Supreme Court of Florida to accept pleadings and documents with that signature format. FL ST J ADMIN Rule 2.515(c)(1).

ii. An attorney, party, or other person who files a pleading or paper by electronic transmission that does not contain the original signature of that attorney, party, or other person shall file that identical pleading or paper in paper form containing an original signature of that attorney, party, or other person (hereinafter called the follow-up filing) immediately thereafter. The follow-up filing is not required if the Supreme Court of Florida has entered an order directing the clerk of court to discontinue accepting the follow-up filing. FL ST J ADMIN Rule 2.515(c)(2).

8. *Forms*

a. *Process.* The forms of process, notice of lis pendens, and notice of action provided in the Florida Rules of Civil Procedure are sufficient. Variations from the forms do not void process or notices that are otherwise sufficient. FL ST RCP Rule 1.900(a).

b. *Other forms.* The other forms provided in the Florida Rules of Civil Procedure are sufficient for the matters that are covered by them. So long as the substance is expressed without prolixity, the forms may be varied to meet the facts of a particular case. FL ST RCP Rule 1.900(b).

c. *Formal matters.* Captions, except for the designation of the paper, are omitted from the forms provided in the Florida Rules of Civil Procedure. A general form of caption is the first form provided. Signatures are omitted from pleadings and motions. FL ST RCP Rule 1.900(c).

9. *Notices to persons with disabilities.* All notices of court proceedings to be held in a public facility, and all process compelling appearance at such proceedings, shall include the following statement in bold face, fourteen (14) point Times New Roman or Courier font: "If you are a person with a disability who needs any accommodation in order to participate in this proceeding, you are entitled, at no cost to you, to the provision of certain assistance. Please contact [identify applicable court personnel by name, address, and telephone number] at least seven (7) days before your scheduled court appearance, or immediately upon receiving this notification if the time before the scheduled appearance is less than seven (7) days; if you are hearing or voice impaired, call 711." FL ST J ADMIN Rule 2.540(c)(1).

10. *Minimization of the filing of sensitive information*

a. *Limitations for court filings.* Unless authorized by FL ST J ADMIN Rule 2.425(b), statute, another rule of court, or the court orders otherwise, designated sensitive information filed with the court must be limited to the following format:

i. The initials of a person known to be a minor;

ii. The year of birth of a person's birth date;

iii. No portion of any: Social security number, Bank account number, Credit card account number, Charge account number, or Debit account number;

iv. The last four digits of any: Taxpayer identification number (TIN), Employee identification number, Driver's license number, Passport number, Telephone number, Financial account number, except as set forth in FL ST J ADMIN Rule 2.425(a)(3), Brokerage account number, Insurance policy account number, Loan account number, Customer account number, or Patient or health care number;

v. A truncated version of any: Email address, Computer user name, Password, or Personal identification number (PIN); and

vi. A truncated version of any other sensitive information as provided by court order. FL ST J ADMIN Rule 2.425(a).

b. *Exceptions.* FL ST J ADMIN Rule 2.425(a) does not apply to the following:

i. An account number which identifies the property alleged to be the subject of a proceeding;

ii. The record of an administrative or agency proceeding;

iii. The record in appellate or review proceedings;

iv. The birth date of a minor whenever the birth date is necessary for the court to establish or maintain subject matter jurisdiction;

v. The name of a minor in any order relating to parental responsibility, time-sharing, or child support;

vi. The name of a minor in any document or order affecting the minor's ownership of real property;

vii. The birth date of a party in a writ of attachment or notice to payor;

viii. In traffic and criminal proceedings: a pro se filing; a court filing that is related to a criminal matter or investigation and that is prepared before the filing of a criminal charge or is not filed as part of any docketed criminal case; an arrest or search warrant or any information in support thereof; a charging document and an affidavit or other documents filed in support of any charging document, including any driving records; a statement of particulars; discovery material introduced into evidence or otherwise filed with the court; and all information necessary for the proper issuance and execution of a subpoena duces tecum;

ix. Information used by the clerk for case maintenance purposes or the courts for case management purposes; and

x. Information which is relevant and material to an issue before the court. FL ST J ADMIN Rule 2.425(b).

c. *Remedies.* Upon motion by a party or interested person or sua sponte by the court, the court may order remedies, sanctions or both for a violation of FL ST J ADMIN Rule 2.425(a). Following notice and an opportunity to respond, the court may impose sanctions if such filing was not made in good faith. FL ST J ADMIN Rule 2.425(c).

d. *Motions not restricted.* FL ST J ADMIN Rule 2.425 does not restrict a party's right to move for protective order, to move to file documents under seal, or to request a determination of the confidentiality of records. FL ST J ADMIN Rule 2.425(d).

e. *Application.* FL ST J ADMIN Rule 2.425 does not affect the application of constitutional provisions, statutes, or rules of court regarding confidential information or access to public information. FL ST J ADMIN Rule 2.425(e).

F. Filing and Service Requirements

1. *Filing requirements.* All original documents must be filed with the court either before service or immediately thereafter, unless otherwise provided for by general law or other rules. If the original of any bond or other document is not placed in the court file, a certified copy must be so placed by the clerk. FL ST J ADMIN Rule 2.516(d). All documents shall be filed in conformity with the requirements of FL ST J ADMIN Rule 2.525. FL ST RCP Rule 1.080(b). All documents filed in any court shall be filed by electronic transmission in accordance with FL ST J ADMIN Rule 2.525. "Documents" means pleadings, motions, petitions, memoranda, briefs, notices, exhibits, declarations, affidavits, orders, judgments, decrees, writs, opinions, and any other paper or writing submitted to a court. FL ST J ADMIN Rule

2.520(a). All documents that are court records, as defined in FL ST J ADMIN Rule 2.430(a)(1), must be filed by electronic transmission, provided that: (1) the clerk has the ability to accept and retain such documents; (2) the clerk or the chief judge of the circuit has requested permission to accept documents filed by electronic transmission; and (3) the supreme court has entered an order granting permission to the clerk to accept documents filed by electronic transmission. FL ST J ADMIN Rule 2.525(c)(1).

a. *Definition.* "Electronic transmission of documents" means the sending of information by electronic signals to, by or from a court or clerk, which when received can be transformed and stored or transmitted on paper, microfilm, magnetic storage device, optical imaging system, CD-ROM, flash drive, other electronic data storage system, server, case maintenance system ("CM"), electronic court filing ("ECF") system, statewide or local electronic portal ("e-portal"), or other electronic record keeping system authorized by the supreme court in a format sufficient to communicate the information on the original document in a readable format. Electronic transmission of documents includes electronic mail ("e-mail") and any internet-based transmission procedure, and may include procedures allowing for documents to be signed or verified by electronic means. FL ST J ADMIN Rule 2.525(a).

   i. The filing of documents with the court as required by the Florida Rules of Judicial Administration must be made by filing them with the clerk in accordance with FL ST J ADMIN Rule 2.525, except that the judge may permit documents to be filed with the judge, in which event the judge must note the filing date before him or her on the documents and transmit them to the clerk. The date of filing is that shown on the face of the document by the judge's notation or the clerk's time stamp, whichever is earlier. FL ST J ADMIN Rule 2.516(e).

b. *Application.* Any court or clerk of the court may accept the electronic transmission of documents for filing after the clerk, together with input from the chief judge of the circuit, has obtained approval of the procedures and program for doing so from the Supreme Court of Florida. FL ST J ADMIN Rule 2.525(b).

c. *Exceptions*

   i. Paper documents and other submissions may be manually submitted to the clerk or court:

      - When the clerk does not have the ability to accept and retain documents by electronic filing or has not had ECF Procedures approved by the supreme court;
      - For filing by any self-represented party or any self-represented nonparty unless specific ECF Procedures provide a means to file documents electronically. However, any self-represented nonparty that is a governmental or public agency and any other agency, partnership, corporation, or business entity acting on behalf of any governmental or public agency may file documents by electronic transmission if such entity has the capability of filing documents electronically;
      - For filing by attorneys excused from e-mail service in accordance with FL ST J ADMIN Rule 2.516(b);
      - When submitting evidentiary exhibits or filing non-documentary materials;
      - When the filing involves documents in excess of twenty-five (25) megabytes (25MB) in size. For such filings, documents may be transmitted using an electronic storage medium that the clerk has the ability to accept, which may include a CD-ROM, flash drive, or similar storage medium;
      - When filed in open court, as permitted by the court;
      - When paper filing is permitted by any approved statewide or local ECF procedures; and
      - If any court determines that justice so requires. FL ST J ADMIN Rule 2.525(d).

   ii. Any document in paper form submitted under FL ST J ADMIN Rule 2.525(d) is filed when it is received by the clerk or court and the clerk shall immediately thereafter convert any filed paper document to an electronic document. "Convert to an electronic document" means optically capturing an image of a paper document and using character recognition software to recover as much of the document's text as practicable and then indexing and storing the document in the official court file. FL ST J ADMIN Rule 2.525(c)(4).

iii. Any storage medium submitted under FL ST J ADMIN Rule 2.525(d)(5) is filed when received by the clerk or court and the clerk shall immediately thereafter transfer the electronic documents from the storage device to the official court file. FL ST J ADMIN Rule 2.525(c)(5).

iv. If the filer of any paper document authorized under FL ST J ADMIN Rule 2.525(d) provides a self-addressed, postage-paid envelope for return of the paper document after it is converted to electronic form by the clerk, the clerk shall place the paper document in the envelope and deposit it in the mail. Except when a paper document is required to be maintained, the clerk may recycle any filed paper document that is not to be returned to the filer. FL ST J ADMIN Rule 2.525(c)(6).

v. The clerk may convert any paper document filed before the effective date of FL ST J ADMIN Rule 2.525 to an electronic document. Unless the clerk is required to maintain the paper document, if the paper document has been converted to an electronic document by the clerk, the paper document is no longer part of the official court file and may be removed and recycled. FL ST J ADMIN Rule 2.525(c)(7).

d. *Unrepresented parties.* An unrepresented party must file his or her papers with the clerk and send copies to other attorneys or unrepresented parties. FL ST 9 J CIR SECTION 7(B)(5).

i. An unrepresented party may not communicate privately with the judge either by letter, telephone, in person or otherwise. FL ST 9 J CIR SECTION 7(B)(4).

ii. Copies of legal papers or other written materials should not be sent to the judge unless specifically requested by the judge or required by the local administrative procedures. Any unrequested or non-required papers or materials sent to a judge may not be read but may be returned to the sender or placed unread into the court file. FL ST 9 J CIR SECTION 7(B)(4).

e. *Official court file.* For information on what constitutes the official court file, please see FL ST J ADMIN Rule 2.525(c)(2), FL ST J ADMIN Rule 2.525(c)(3).

f. *Administration.* All attorneys, parties, or other persons using this rule to file documents are required to make arrangements with the court or clerk for the payment of any charges authorized by general law or the supreme court before filing any document by electronic transmission. FL ST J ADMIN Rule 2.525(f)(2).

g. *Filing date.* The filing date for an electronically transmitted document is the date and time that such filing is acknowledged by an electronic stamp or otherwise, pursuant to any procedure set forth in any ECF Procedures approved by the supreme court, or the date the last page of such filing is received by the court or clerk. FL ST J ADMIN Rule 2.525(f)(3).

h. *Accessibility.* All documents transmitted in any electronic form under FL ST J ADMIN Rule 2.525 must comply with the accessibility requirements of FL ST J ADMIN Rule 2.526. FL ST J ADMIN Rule 2.525(g).

2. *Service requirements.* Every pleading subsequent to the initial pleading, all orders, and every other document filed in the action must be served in conformity with the requirements of FL ST J ADMIN Rule 2.516. FL ST RCP Rule 1.080(a).

a. *Service; When required.* Unless the court otherwise orders, or a statute or supreme court administrative order specifies a different means of service, every pleading subsequent to the initial pleading and every other document filed in any court proceeding, except applications for witness subpoenas and documents served by formal notice or required to be served in the manner provided for service of formal notice, must be served in accordance with FL ST J ADMIN Rule 2.516 on each party. No service need be made on parties against whom a default has been entered, except that pleadings asserting new or additional claims against them must be served in the manner provided for service of summons. FL ST J ADMIN Rule 2.516(a).

i. Counsel who serves a memorandum or authority list first should also include a copy of the motion, any papers to which it is addressed, and the response, if any. In order for the judge to properly review a submission in advance, it must be received in the judge's office at least three (3) working days before the hearing. FL ST 9 J CIR SECTION 11(B).

b. *Service; How made.* When service is required or permitted to be made upon a party represented by

an attorney, service must be made upon the attorney unless service upon the party is ordered by the court. FL ST J ADMIN Rule 2.516(b).

i. *Service by electronic mail ("e-mail").* All documents required or permitted to be served on another party must be served by e-mail, unless FL ST J ADMIN Rule 2.516 otherwise provides. When, in addition to service by e-mail, the sender also utilizes another means of service provided for in FL ST J ADMIN Rule 2.516(b)(2), any differing time limits and other provisions applicable to that other means of service control. FL ST J ADMIN Rule 2.516(b)(1). Any document electronically transmitted to a court or clerk must also be served on all parties and interested persons in accordance with the applicable rules of court. FL ST J ADMIN Rule 2.525(e)(2).

- *Service on attorneys.* Upon appearing in a proceeding, an attorney must serve a designation of a primary e-mail address and may designate no more than two (2) secondary e-mail addresses. Thereafter, service must be directed to all designated e-mail addresses in that proceeding. Every document filed by an attorney thereafter must include the primary e-mail address of that attorney and any secondary e-mail addresses. If an attorney does not designate any e-mail address for service, documents may be served on that attorney at the e-mail address on record with The Florida Bar. FL ST J ADMIN Rule 2.516(b)(1)(A).
- *Exception to e-mail service on attorneys.* Service by an attorney on another attorney must be made by e-mail unless excused by the court. Upon motion by an attorney demonstrating that the attorney has no e-mail account and lacks access to the Internet at the attorney's office, the court may excuse the attorney from the requirements of e-mail service. Service on and by an attorney excused by the court from e-mail service must be by the means provided in FL ST J ADMIN Rule 2.516(b)(2). FL ST J ADMIN Rule 2.516(b)(1)(B).
- *Service on and by parties not represented by an attorney.* Any party not represented by an attorney may serve a designation of a primary e-mail address and also may designate no more than two (2) secondary e-mail addresses to which service must be directed in that proceeding by the means provided in FL ST J ADMIN Rule 2.516(b)(1). If a party not represented by an attorney does not designate an e-mail address for service in a proceeding, service on and by that party must be by the means provided in FL ST J ADMIN Rule 2.516(b)(2). FL ST J ADMIN Rule 2.516(b)(1)(C).
- *Time of service.* Service by e-mail is complete when it is sent. FL ST J ADMIN Rule 2.516(b)(1)(D). An e-mail is deemed served on the date it is sent. FL ST J ADMIN Rule 2.516(b)(1)(D)(i). If the sender learns that the e-mail did not reach the address of the person to be served, the sender must immediately send another copy by e-mail, or by a means authorized by FL ST J ADMIN Rule 2.516(b)(2). FL ST J ADMIN Rule 2.516(b)(1)(D)(ii). E-mail service is treated as service by mail for the computation of time. FL ST J ADMIN Rule 2.516(b)(1)(D)(iii).

ii. *Format of e-mail for service.* Service of a document by e-mail is made by attaching a copy of the document in PDF format to an e-mail sent to all addresses designated by the attorney or party. FL ST J ADMIN Rule 2.516(b)(1)(E).

- All documents served by e-mail must be attached to an e-mail message containing a subject line beginning with the words "SERVICE OF COURT DOCUMENT" in all capital letters, followed by the case number of the proceeding in which the documents are being served. FL ST J ADMIN Rule 2.516(b)(1)(E)(i).
- The body of the e-mail must identify the court in which the proceeding is pending, the case number, the name of the initial party on each side, the title of each document served with that e-mail, and the sender's name and telephone number. FL ST J ADMIN Rule 2.516(b)(1)(E)(ii).
- Any document served by e-mail may be signed by the "/s/" format, as long as the filed original is signed in accordance with the applicable rule of procedure. FL ST J ADMIN Rule 2.516(b)(1)(E)(iii).
- Any e-mail which, together with its attached documents, exceeds five megabytes (5MB) in

size, must be divided and sent as separate e-mails, no one of which may exceed five megabytes (5MB) in size and each of which must be sequentially numbered in the subject line. FL ST J ADMIN Rule 2.516(b)(1)(E)(iv).

iii. *Service by other means.* In addition to, and not in lieu of, service by e-mail, service may also be made upon attorneys by any of the means specified in FL ST J ADMIN Rule 2.516(b)(2). Service on and by all parties who are not represented by an attorney and who do not designate an e-mail address, and on and by all attorneys excused from e-mail service, must be made by delivering a copy of the document or by mailing it to the party or attorney at their last known address or, if no address is known, by leaving it with the clerk of the court. Service by mail is complete upon mailing. Delivery of a copy within FL ST J ADMIN Rule 2.516 is complete upon:

- Handing it to the attorney or to the party,
- Leaving it at the attorney's or party's office with a clerk or other person in charge thereof,
- If there is no one in charge, leaving it in a conspicuous place therein,
- If the office is closed or the person to be served has no office, leaving it at the person's usual place of abode with some person of his or her family above fifteen (15) years of age and informing such person of the contents, or
- Transmitting it by facsimile to the attorney's or party's office with a cover sheet containing the sender's name, firm, address, telephone number, and facsimile number, and the number of pages transmitted. When service is made by facsimile, a copy must also be served by any other method permitted by FL ST J ADMIN Rule 2.516. Facsimile service occurs when transmission is complete. FL ST J ADMIN Rule 2.516(b)(2)(A) through FL ST J ADMIN Rule 2.516(b)(2)(E).
- Service by delivery after 5:00 p.m. must be deemed to have been made by mailing on the date of delivery. FL ST J ADMIN Rule 2.516(b)(2)(F).

c. *Service; Numerous defendants.* In actions when the parties are unusually numerous, the court may regulate the service contemplated by the Florida Rules of Judicial Administration on motion or on its own initiative in such manner as may be found to be just and reasonable. FL ST J ADMIN Rule 2.516(c).

d. *Service by clerk.* Service of notices and other documents required to be made by the clerk must also be done as provided in FL ST J ADMIN Rule 2.516(b). FL ST J ADMIN Rule 2.516(g).

G. Hearings

1. *Preliminary hearings.* The defenses in FL ST RCP Rule 1.140(b)(1) through FL ST RCP Rule 1.140(b)(7), whether made in a pleading or by motion, and the motion for judgment in FL ST RCP Rule 1.140(c) shall be heard and determined before trial on application of any party unless the court orders that the hearing and determination shall be deferred until the trial. FL ST RCP Rule 1.140(d).

H. Forms

1. Official Answer Forms for Florida

a. Caption. FL ST RCP Form 1.901.

b. Crossclaim summons. FL ST RCP Form 1.903.

c. Third-party summons. FL ST RCP Form 1.904.

d. Defense; Statute of limitations. FL ST RCP Form 1.965.

e. Defense; Payment. FL ST RCP Form 1.966.

f. Defense; Accord and satisfaction. FL ST RCP Form 1.967.

g. Defense; Failure of consideration. FL ST RCP Form 1.968.

h. Defense; Statute of frauds. FL ST RCP Form 1.969.

i. Defense; Release. FL ST RCP Form 1.970.

j. Notice of compliance when constitutional challenge is brought. FL ST RCP Form 1.975.

2. Answer Forms for Florida

a. Answer; General form, traverses. FL-PRACFORM § 5:4.

b. Answer; General form, traverses and affirmative defenses. FL-PRACFORM § 5:6.

c. Answer; General form, traverses, affirmative defenses and counterclaim. FL-PRACFORM § 5:7.

d. Answer; General form, traverses, affirmative defenses, counterclaim and crossclaim. FL-PRACFORM § 5:8.

e. Answer; Affirmative defense, fraud. FL-PRACFORM § 5:43.

f. Answer; Affirmative defense, laches. FL-PRACFORM § 5:47.

g. Answer; Affirmative defense, misjoinder. FL-PRACFORM § 5:49.

h. Answer; Affirmative defense, misrepresentation. FL-PRACFORM § 5:50.

i. Answer; Affirmative defense, self defense. FL-PRACFORM § 5:64.

j. Answer; Denial of conditions precedent. FL-PRACFORM § 5:80.

k. General denial. FL-PP § 2:58.

l. General denial; With specified admissions. FL-PP § 2:59.

m. Admission with qualification. FL-PP § 2:60.

n. Conclusions of law not requiring denial. FL-PP § 2:61.

o. Defenses stated in the alternative. FL-PP § 2:62.

p. Denial as to part of allegation. FL-PP § 2:63.

q. Pleader as without knowledge as to truth of allegation. FL-PP § 2:64.

I. Checklist

(I) ❑ Matters to be considered by plaintiff

(a) ❑ Required documents

(1) ❑ Summons

(2) ❑ Complaint

(3) ❑ Civil cover sheet

(4) ❑ Return of execution process by process server

(5) ❑ Filing fees

(b) ❑ Supplemental documents

(1) ❑ Exhibits

(2) ❑ Notice of constitutional question

(c) ❑ Time for filing and serving complaint

(1) ❑ Service of the initial process and initial pleading should be made upon a defendant within one hundred twenty (120) days after the filing of the complaint with the court

(II) ❑ Matters to be considered by defendant

(a) ❑ Required documents

(1) ❑ Answer

(2) ❑ Certificate of service

(b) ❑ Supplemental documents

(1) ❑ Exhibits

(2) ❑ Notice of constitutional question

(c) ❑ Time for answer

(1) ❑ Unless a different time is prescribed in a statute of Florida, a defendant shall serve an answer within twenty (20) days after service of original process and the initial pleading on the defendant, or not later than the date fixed in a notice by publication

(2) ❑ A party served with a pleading stating a crossclaim against that party shall serve an answer to it within twenty (20) days after service on that party

(3) ❑ The plaintiff shall serve an answer to a counterclaim within twenty (20) days after service of the counterclaim

(4) ❑ A defendant who, before being served with process, timely returns a waiver so requested is not required to respond to the complaint until sixty (60) days after the date the defendant received the request for waiver of service; for purposes of computing any time prescribed or allowed by the Florida Rules of Civil Procedure, service of process shall be deemed effected twenty (20) days before the time required to respond to the complaint

(5) ❑ For timing requirements related to service on the state, service of motion impact, and responding when no responsive pleading is required, please see the Timing section of this document

Pleadings
Amended Answer

Document Last Updated January 2013

A. Applicable Rules

1. *State rules*

   a. Nonverification of papers. FL ST RCP Rule 1.030.

   b. Service and filing of pleadings, orders, and documents. FL ST RCP Rule 1.080.

   c. Time. FL ST RCP Rule 1.090.

   d. Pleadings and motions. FL ST RCP Rule 1.100; FL ST RCP Rule 1.110; FL ST RCP Rule 1.120; FL ST RCP Rule 1.130; FL ST RCP Rule 1.190.

   e. Defenses. FL ST RCP Rule 1.140.

   f. Pretrial procedure. FL ST RCP Rule 1.200.

   g. Relief from judgment, decrees, or orders. FL ST RCP Rule 1.540.

   h. Forms. FL ST RCP Rule 1.900.

   i. Minimization of the filing of sensitive information. FL ST J ADMIN Rule 2.425.

   j. Foreign attorneys. FL ST J ADMIN Rule 2.510.

   k. Signature of attorneys and parties. FL ST J ADMIN Rule 2.515.

   l. Paper. FL ST J ADMIN Rule 2.520.

   m. Electronic filing. FL ST J ADMIN Rule 2.525.

   n. Accessibility of information and technology. FL ST J ADMIN Rule 2.526.

   o. Court reporting. FL ST J ADMIN Rule 2.535.

   p. Requests for accommodations by persons with disabilities. FL ST J ADMIN Rule 2.540.

2. *Local rules*

   a. Unrepresented (pro se) parties. FL ST 9 J CIR SECTION 7.

   b. Business court procedures. FL ST 9 J CIR ORANGE CIV SECTION 1.

B. Timing

1. *Amendment as a matter of course.* A party may amend a pleading once as a matter of course at any time

before a responsive pleading is served or, if the pleading is one to which no responsive pleading is permitted and the action has not been placed on the trial calendar, may so amend it at any time within twenty (20) days after it is served. FL ST RCP Rule 1.190(a).

2. *Amendment by leave of court.* Otherwise a party may amend a pleading only by leave of court or by written consent of the adverse party. Leave of court shall be given freely when justice so requires. FL ST RCP Rule 1.190(a).
3. *Amendments in furtherance of justice.* At any time in furtherance of justice, upon such terms as may be just, the court may permit any process, proceeding, pleading, or record to be amended or material supplemental matter to be set forth in an amended or supplemental pleading. At every stage of the action the court must disregard any error or defect in the proceedings which does not affect the substantial rights of the parties. FL ST RCP Rule 1.190(e).
4. *Response to amended pleading.* A party shall plead in response to an amended pleading within ten (10) days after service of the amended pleading unless the court otherwise orders. FL ST RCP Rule 1.190(a).
5. *Computation of time*
   a. *Generally.* Computation of time shall be governed by FL ST J ADMIN Rule 2.514. FL ST RCP Rule 1.090(a). The following rules apply in computing time periods specified in any rule of procedure, local rule, court order, or statute that does not specify a method of computing time. FL ST J ADMIN Rule 2.514(a).
      i. *Period stated in days or a longer unit.* When the period is stated in days or a longer unit of time (A) exclude the day of the event that triggers the period; (B) count every day, including intermediate Saturdays, Sundays, and legal holidays; and (C) include the last day of the period, but if the last day is a Saturday, Sunday, or legal holiday, or falls within any period of time extended through an order of the chief justice under FL ST J ADMIN Rule 2.205(a)(2)(B)(iv), the period continues to run until the end of the next day that is not a Saturday, Sunday, or legal holiday and does not fall within any period of time extended through an order of the chief justice. FL ST J ADMIN Rule 2.514(a)(1).
      ii. *Period stated in hours.* When the period is stated in hours (A) begin counting immediately on the occurrence of the event that triggers the period; (B) count every hour, including hours during intermediate Saturdays, Sundays, and legal holidays; and (C) if the period would end on a Saturday, Sunday, or legal holiday, or during any period of time extended through an order of the chief justice under FL ST J ADMIN Rule 2.205(a)(2)(B)(iv), the period continues to run until the same time on the next day that is not a Saturday, Sunday, or legal holiday and does not fall within any period of time extended through an order of the chief justice. FL ST J ADMIN Rule 2.514(a)(2).
      iii. *Period stated in days less than seven (7) days.* When the period stated in days is less than seven (7) days, intermediate Saturdays, Sundays, and legal holidays shall be excluded in the computation. FL ST J ADMIN Rule 2.514(a)(3).
      iv. *"Last day" defined.* Unless a different time is set by a statute, local rule, or court order, the last day ends (A) for electronic filing or for service by any means, at midnight; and (B) for filing by other means, when the clerk's office is scheduled to close. FL ST J ADMIN Rule 2.514(a)(4).
      v. *"Next day" defined.* The "next day" is determined by continuing to count forward when the period is measured after an event and backward when measured before an event. FL ST J ADMIN Rule 2.514(a)(5).
      vi. *"Legal holiday" defined.* "Legal holiday" means (A) the day set aside by FL ST § 110.117, for observing New Year's Day, Martin Luther King, Jr.'s Birthday, Memorial Day, Independence Day, Labor Day, Veterans' Day, Thanksgiving Day, the Friday after Thanksgiving Day, or Christmas Day, and (B) any day observed as a holiday by the clerk's office or as designated by the chief judge. FL ST J ADMIN Rule 2.514(a)(6).
   b. *Additional time after service by mail or e-mail.* When a party may or must act within a specified time after service and service is made by mail or e-mail, five (5) days are added after the period that would otherwise expire under FL ST J ADMIN Rule 2.514(a). FL ST J ADMIN Rule 2.514(b).

c. *Enlargement.* When an act is required or allowed to be done at or within a specified time by order of court, by the Florida Rules of Civil Procedure, or by notice given thereunder, for cause shown the court at any time in its discretion (1) with or without notice, may order the period enlarged if request therefor is made before the expiration of the period originally prescribed or as extended by a previous order, or (2) upon motion made and notice after the expiration of the specified period, may permit the act to be done when failure to act was the result of excusable neglect, but it may not extend the time for making a motion for new trial, for rehearing, or to alter or amend a judgment; making a motion for relief from a judgment under FL ST RCP Rule 1.540(b); taking an appeal or filing a petition for certiorari; or making a motion for a directed verdict. FL ST RCP Rule 1.090(b).

d. *Unaffected by expiration of term.* The period of time provided for the doing of any act or the taking of any proceeding shall not be affected or limited by the continued existence or expiration of a term of court. The continued existence or expiration of a term of court in no way affects the power of a court to do any act or take any proceeding in any action which is or has been pending before it. FL ST RCP Rule 1.090(c).

C. General Requirements

1. *Amendments.* A party may amend a pleading once as a matter of course at any time before a responsive pleading is served or, if the pleading is one to which no responsive pleading is permitted and the action has not been placed on the trial calendar, may so amend it at any time within twenty (20) days after it is served. Otherwise a party may amend a pleading only by leave of court or by written consent of the adverse party. Leave of court shall be freely given when justice so requires. FL ST RCP Rule 1.190(a).

   a. *Purpose of amendments.* Amendments can relate to the correction of mistakes, the insertion of jurisdictional averments, the correction or addition of verifications, the addition or substitution or striking out of parties, and generally the rectification of all formal defects in the pleading. The court can also allow amendments setting up an omitted counterclaim or cross-claim if the defendant failed to raise the claim through oversight, inadvertence, or excusable neglect. FL-PP § 2:151.

   b. *Amendment to a pleading/Amended pleading.* A significant difference exists between an amendment to a pleading and an amended pleading. An amendment to a pleading corrects, adds to or deletes from the pleading. An amended pleading is substituted for the former pleading and the former pleading ceases to have any effect. Dee v. Southern Brewing Company, 146 Fla. 588, 1 So.2d 562 (Fla. 1941); Shannon v. McBride, 105 So.2d 16 (Fla. 2d DCA 1958); Hughes v. Home Sav. of America, F.S.B., 675 So.2d 649 (Fla. 2d DCA 1996); FL-PRACPROC § 14:2.

   c. *Relation back of amendments.* When the claim or defense asserted in the amended pleading arose out of the conduct, transaction, or occurrence set forth or attempted to be set forth in the original pleading, the amendment shall relate back to the date of the original pleading. FL ST RCP Rule 1.190(c).

2. *General rules of pleading*

   a. *Claims for relief*

      i. A pleading which sets forth a claim for relief, whether an original claim, counterclaim, crossclaim, or third-party claim, must state a cause of action and shall contain

         - A short and plain statement of the grounds upon which the court's jurisdiction depends, unless the court already has jurisdiction and the claim needs no new grounds of jurisdiction to support it (For information regarding acts subjecting persons to jurisdiction, please see FL ST § 48.193),
         - A short and plain statement of the ultimate facts showing that the pleader is entitled to relief, and
         - A demand for judgment for the relief to which the pleader deems himself or herself entitled. FL ST RCP Rule 1.110(b).

      ii. Relief in the alternative or of several different types may be demanded. Every complaint shall be considered to demand general relief. FL ST RCP Rule 1.110(b).

   b. *Verification.* Except when otherwise specifically provided by these rules or an applicable statute, every pleading or other document of a party represented by an attorney need not be verified or accompanied by an affidavit. FL ST RCP Rule 1.030. When filing an action for foreclosure of a mortgage on residential real property the complaint shall be verified. When verification of a document is required, the document filed shall include an oath, affirmation, or the following statement: "Under penalty of perjury, I declare that I have read the foregoing, and the facts alleged therein are true and correct to the best of my knowledge and belief." FL ST RCP Rule 1.110(b).

c. *Separate statements.* All averments of claim or defense shall be made in consecutively numbered paragraphs, the contents of each of which shall be limited as far as practicable to a statement of a single set of circumstances, and a paragraph may be referred to by number in all subsequent pleadings. Each claim founded upon a separate transaction or occurrence and each defense other than denials shall be stated in a separate count or defense when a separation facilitates the clear presentation of the matter set forth. FL ST RCP Rule 1.110(f).

d. *Statements adopted by reference.* Statements in a pleading may be adopted by reference in a different part of the same pleading, in another pleading, or in any motion. FL ST RCP Rule 1.130(b).

e. *Joinder of causes of action; Consistency.* A pleader may set up in the same action as many claims or causes of action or defenses in the same right as the pleader has, and claims for relief may be stated in the alternative if separate items make up the cause of action, or if two (2) or more causes of action are joined. A party may also set forth two (2) or more statements of a claim or defense alternatively, either in one (1) count or defense or in separate counts or defenses. When two (2) or more statements are made in the alternative and one (1) of them, if made independently, would be sufficient, the pleading is not made insufficient by the insufficiency of one (1) or more of the alternative statements. A party may also state as many separate claims or defenses as that party has, regardless of consistency and whether based on legal or equitable grounds or both. All pleadings shall be construed so as to do substantial justice. FL ST RCP Rule 1.110(g).

f. *Subsequent pleadings.* When the nature of an action permits pleadings subsequent to final judgment and the jurisdiction of the court over the parties has not terminated, the initial pleading subsequent to final judgment shall be designated a supplemental complaint or petition. The action shall then proceed in the same manner and time as though the supplemental complaint or petition were the initial pleading in the action, including the issuance of any needed process. FL ST RCP Rule 1.110(h) shall not apply to proceedings that may be initiated by motion under the Florida Rules of Civil Procedure. FL ST RCP Rule 1.110(h).

g. *Pleading basis for service.* When service of process is to be made under statutes authorizing service on nonresidents of Florida, it is sufficient to plead the basis for service in the language of the statute without pleading the facts supporting service. FL ST RCP Rule 1.070(h).

h. *Forms of pleadings.* Forms of action and technical forms for seeking relief and of pleas, pleadings, or motions are abolished. FL ST RCP Rule 1.110(a).

3. *Answer; Generally.* An answer has three (3) functions. First, it must respond to each allegation of the preceding pleading by admitting, denying or alleging that the pleader is without knowledge of the allegation. Second, it must contain any affirmative defenses that the pleader is interposing to any cause of action alleged in the preceding pleading. Third, the answer may claim affirmative relief against the plaintiff or petitioner by a counterclaim or against a codefendant by a crossclaim. FL-PRACPROC § 11:1.

a. *Content.* In the answer a pleader shall state in short and plain terms the pleader's defenses to each claim asserted and shall admit or deny the averments on which the adverse party relies. If the defendant is without knowledge, the defendant shall so state and such statement shall operate as a denial. Denial shall fairly meet the substance of the averments denied. When a pleader intends in good faith to deny only a part of an averment, the pleader shall specify so much of it as is true and shall deny the remainder. Unless the pleader intends in good faith to controvert all of the averments of the preceding pleading, the pleader may make denials as specific denials of designated averments or may generally deny all of the averments except such designated averments as the pleader expressly admits, but when the pleader does so intend to controvert all of its averments, including averments of the grounds upon which the court's jurisdiction depends, the pleader may do so by general denial. FL ST RCP Rule 1.110(c).

b. *Form of answer.* An answer contains a caption, commencement, body, signature and certificate of service. The caption is the same as that of the initial pleading, except for the designation as one of the types of answer. The body of an answer should contain an admission, denial or plea of without knowledge to each allegation of the preceding pleading, except for the additional allegations in response to a general allegation of conditions precedent and the denial of capacity to sue. FL-PRACPROC § 11:3.

   i. *Responding sequentially.* The best method of responding is to answer each paragraph sequentially, combining admissions, denials or pleas of without knowledge when the sequence permits. The admissions, denials and allegations of without knowledge should be stated first, followed separately by any affirmative defenses and then by any counterclaim or crossclaim. A third party complaint may be a part of the same paper, but it is not a part of the answer as is a counterclaim or crossclaim. Paragraphs are numbered consecutively throughout the pleading whether in the answer, counterclaim or crossclaim. Denials for the record only are improper. FL-PRACPROC § 11:3.

c. *Defenses*

   i. *Generally.* Every defense in law or fact to a claim for relief in a pleading shall be asserted in the responsive pleading, if one is required, but the following defenses may be made by motion at the option of the pleader: (1) lack of jurisdiction over the subject matter, (2) lack of jurisdiction over the person, (3) improper venue, (4) insufficiency of process, (5) insufficiency of service of process, (6) failure to state a cause of action, and (7) failure to join indispensable parties. A motion making any of these defenses shall be made before pleading if a further pleading is permitted. FL ST RCP Rule 1.140(b).

   - *Stated specifically.* The grounds on which any of the enumerated defenses are based and the substantial matters of law intended to be argued shall be stated specifically and with particularity in the responsive pleading or motion. FL ST RCP Rule 1.140(b).
   - *Waiver.* Any ground not stated shall be deemed to be waived except any ground showing that the court lacks jurisdiction of the subject matter may be made at any time. No defense or objection is waived by being joined with other defenses or objections in a responsive pleading or motion. FL ST RCP Rule 1.140(b). A party waives all defenses and objections that the party does not present either by motion under FL ST RCP Rule 1.140(b), FL ST RCP Rule 1.140(e), or FL ST RCP Rule 1.140(f) or, if the party has made no motion, in a responsive pleading except as provided in FL ST RCP Rule 1.140(h)(2). FL ST RCP Rule 1.140(h)(1). The defenses of failure to state a cause of action or a legal defense or to join an indispensable party may be raised by motion for judgment on the pleadings or at the trial on the merits in addition to being raised either in a motion under FL ST RCP Rule 1.140(b) or in the answer or reply. The defense of lack of jurisdiction of the subject matter may be raised at any time. FL ST RCP Rule 1.140(h)(2).

   ii. *Affirmative defenses.* In pleading to a preceding pleading a party shall set forth affirmatively accord and satisfaction, arbitration and award, assumption of risk, contributory negligence, discharge in bankruptcy, duress, estoppel, failure of consideration, fraud, illegality, injury by fellow servant, laches, license, payment, release, res judicata, statute of frauds, statute of limitations, waiver, and any other matter constituting an avoidance or affirmative defense. When a party has mistakenly designated a defense as a counterclaim or a counterclaim as a defense, the court, on terms if justice so requires, shall treat the pleading as if there had been a proper designation. Affirmative defenses appearing on the face of a prior pleading may be asserted as grounds for a motion or defense under FL ST RCP Rule 1.140(b); provided this shall not limit amendments under FL ST RCP Rule 1.190 even if such ground is sustained. FL ST RCP Rule 1.110(d).

   - *Format of defenses.* Affirmative defenses should be placed after the admissions, denials and allegations of without knowledge in the answer. All paragraphs must be numbered consecutively throughout the answer. If a defense is directed to only a part of a cause of action or to one or more, but not all, of several causes of action in the preceding pleading, the part or cause of action to which it is directed should be identified in the defense.

Defenses should be identified by consecutive ordinal numbers such as "First Defense" and "Second Defense." FL-PRACPROC § 11:4.

iii. *Effect of failure to deny.* Averments in a pleading to which a responsive pleading is required, other than those as to the amount of damages, are admitted when not denied in the responsive pleading. Averments in a pleading to which no responsive pleading is required or permitted shall be taken as denied or avoided. FL ST RCP Rule 1.110(e). An admission in an answer binds the party and no proof is required. An admission does not extend beyond the scope of the allegation in the preceding pleading. FL-PRACPROC § 11:3.

4. *Pleading special matters*

a. *Capacity.* It is not necessary to aver the capacity of a party to sue or be sued, the authority of a party to sue or be sued in a representative capacity, or the legal existence of an organized association of persons that is made a party, except to the extent required to show the jurisdiction of the court. The initial pleading served on behalf of a minor party shall specifically aver the age of the minor party. When a party desires to raise an issue as to the legal existence of any party, the capacity of any party to sue or be sued, or the authority of a party to sue or be sued in a representative capacity, that party shall do so by specific negative averment which shall include such supporting particulars as are peculiarly within the pleader's knowledge. FL ST RCP Rule 1.120(a).

b. *Fraud, mistake, condition of the mind.* In all averments of fraud or mistake, the circumstances constituting fraud or mistake shall be stated with such particularity as the circumstances may permit. Malice, intent, knowledge, mental attitude, and other condition of mind of a person may be averred generally. FL ST RCP Rule 1.120(b).

c. *Conditions precedent.* In pleading the performance or occurrence of conditions precedent, it is sufficient to aver generally that all conditions precedent have been performed or have occurred. A denial of performance or occurrence shall be made specifically and with particularity. FL ST RCP Rule 1.120(c).

d. *Official document or act.* In pleading an official document or official act it is sufficient to aver that the document was issued or the act done in compliance with law. FL ST RCP Rule 1.120(c).

e. *Judgment or decree.* In pleading a judgment or decree of a domestic or foreign court, a judicial or quasi-judicial tribunal, or a board or officer, it is sufficient to aver the judgment or decree without setting forth matter showing jurisdiction to render it. FL ST RCP Rule 1.120(e).

f. *Time and place.* For the purpose of testing the sufficiency of a pleading, averments of time and place are material and shall be considered like all other averments of material matter. FL ST RCP Rule 1.120(f).

g. *Special damage.* When items of special damage are claimed, they shall be specifically stated. FL ST RCP Rule 1.120(g).

5. *Parties*

a. *Parties generally.* Every action may be prosecuted in the name of the real party in interest, but a personal representative, administrator, guardian, trustee of an express trust, a party with whom or in whose name a contract has been made for the benefit of another, or a party expressly authorized by statute may sue in that person's own name without joining the party for whose benefit the action is brought. All persons having an interest in the subject of the action and in obtaining the relief demanded may join as plaintiffs and any person may be made a defendant who has or claims an interest adverse to the plaintiff. Any person may at any time be made a party if that person's presence is necessary or proper to a complete determination of the cause. Persons having a united interest may be joined on the same side as plaintiffs or defendants, and anyone who refuses to join may for such reason be made a defendant. FL ST RCP Rule 1.210(a).

b. *Minors or incompetent persons.* When a minor or incompetent person has a representative, such as a guardian or other like fiduciary, the representative may sue or defend on behalf of the minor or incompetent person. A minor or incompetent person who does not have a duly appointed representative may sue by next friend or by a guardian ad litem. The court shall appoint a guardian ad litem for a minor or incompetent person not otherwise represented in an action or shall make such other order as it deems proper for the protection of the minor or incompetent person. FL ST RCP Rule 1.210(b).

c. For survivor and substitution of parties information, please see FL ST RCP Rule 1.260.

6. *Counterclaims and crossclaims*

a. *Compulsory counterclaims.* A pleading shall state as a counterclaim any claim which at the time of serving the pleading the pleader has against any opposing party, provided it arises out of the transaction or occurrence that is the subject matter of the opposing party's claim and does not require for its adjudication the presence of third parties over whom the court cannot acquire jurisdiction. But the pleader need not state a claim if (1) at the time the action was commenced the claim was the subject of another pending action, or (2) the opposing party brought suit upon that party's claim by attachment or other process by which the court did not acquire jurisdiction to render a personal judgment on the claim and the pleader is not stating a counterclaim under this rule. FL ST RCP Rule 1.170(a).

b. *Permissive counterclaim.* A pleading may state as a counterclaim any claim against an opposing party not arising out of the transaction or occurrence that is the subject matter of the opposing party's claim. FL ST RCP Rule 1.170(b).

c. *Counterclaim exceeding opposing claim.* A counterclaim may or may not diminish or defeat the recovery sought by the opposing party. It may claim relief exceeding in amount or different in kind from that sought in the pleading of the opposing party. FL ST RCP Rule 1.170(c).

d. *Counterclaim against the State.* The Florida Rules of Civil Procedure shall not be construed to enlarge beyond the limits established by law the right to assert counterclaims or to claim credits against the state or any of its subdivisions or other governmental organizations thereof subject to suit or against a municipal corporation or against an officer, agency, or administrative board of the state. FL ST RCP Rule 1.170(d).

e. *Counterclaim maturing or acquired after pleading.* A claim which matured or was acquired by the pleader after serving the pleading may be presented as a counterclaim by supplemental pleading with the permission of the court. FL ST RCP Rule 1.170(e).

f. *Omitted counterclaim or crossclaim.* When a pleader fails to set up a counterclaim or crossclaim through oversight, inadvertence, or excusable neglect, or when justice requires, the pleader may set up the counterclaim or crossclaim by amendment with leave of the court. FL ST RCP Rule 1.170(f).

g. *Crossclaim against co-party.* A pleading may state as a crossclaim any claim by one party against a co-party arising out of the transaction or occurrence that is the subject matter of either the original action or a counterclaim therein, or relating to any property that is the subject matter of the original action. The crossclaim may include a claim that the party against whom it is asserted is or may be liable to the crossclaimant for all or part of a claim asserted in the action against the crossclaimant. Service of a crossclaim on a party who has appeared in the action shall be made pursuant to FL ST RCP Rule 1.080. Service of a crossclaim against a party who has not appeared in the action shall be made in the manner provided for service of summons. FL ST RCP Rule 1.170(g).

h. *Additional parties may be brought in.* When the presence of parties other than those to the original action is required to grant complete relief in the determination of a counterclaim or crossclaim, they shall be named in the counterclaim or crossclaim and be served with process and shall be parties to the action thereafter if jurisdiction of them can be obtained and their joinder will not deprive the court of jurisdiction of the action. FL ST RCP Rule 1.250(b) and FL ST RCP Rule 1.250(c) apply to parties brought in under FL ST RCP Rule 1.170(h). FL ST RCP Rule 1.170(h).

i. *Separate trials; Separate judgment.* If the court orders separate trials as provided in FL ST RCP Rule 1.270(b), judgment on a counterclaim or crossclaim may be rendered when the court has jurisdiction to do so even if a claim of the opposing party has been dismissed or otherwise disposed of. FL ST RCP Rule 1.170(i).

j. *Demand exceeding jurisdiction; Transfer of action.* If the demand of any counterclaim or crossclaim exceeds the jurisdiction of the court in which the action is pending, the action shall be transferred forthwith to the court of the same county having jurisdiction of the demand in the counterclaim or crossclaim with only such alterations in the pleadings as are essential. The court shall order the transfer of the action and the transmittal of all papers in it to the proper court if the party asserting the demand exceeding the jurisdiction deposits with the court having jurisdiction a sum sufficient to pay the clerk's service charge in the court to which the action is transferred at the time of filing the counterclaim or crossclaim. Thereupon the original papers and deposit shall be transmitted and filed with a certified copy of the order. The court to which the action is transferred shall have full power and jurisdiction over the demands of all parties. Failure to make the service charge deposit at the time the counterclaim or crossclaim is filed, or within such further time as the court may allow, shall reduce a claim for damages to an amount within the jurisdiction of the court where the action is pending and waive the claim in other cases. FL ST RCP Rule 1.170(j).

7. *Misjoinder and nonjoinder of parties*
   a. *Misjoinder.* Misjoinder of parties is not a ground for dismissal of an action. Any claim against a party may be severed and proceeded with separately. FL ST RCP Rule 1.250(a).
   b. *Dropping parties.* Parties may be dropped by an adverse party in the manner provided for voluntary dismissal in FL ST RCP Rule 1.420(a)(1) subject to the exception stated in FL ST RCP Rule 1.420. If notice of lis pendens has been filed in the action against a party so dropped, the notice of dismissal shall be recorded and cancels the notice of lis pendens without the necessity of a court order. Parties may be dropped by order of court on its own initiative or the motion of any party at any stage of the action on such terms as are just. FL ST RCP Rule 1.250(b).
   c. *Adding parties.* Parties may be added once as a matter of course within the same time that pleadings can be so amended under FL ST RCP Rule 1.190(a). If amendment by leave of court or stipulation of the parties is permitted, parties may be added in the amended pleading without further order of court. Parties may be added by order of court on its own initiative or on motion of any party at any stage of the action and on such terms as are just. FL ST RCP Rule 1.250(c).
8. *Jury demand*
   a. *Right preserved.* The right of trial by jury as declared by the Constitution or by statute shall be preserved to the parties inviolate. FL ST RCP Rule 1.430(a).
   b. *Demand.* Any party may demand a trial by jury of any issue triable of right by a jury by serving upon the other party a demand therefor in writing at any time after commencement of the action and not later than ten (10) days after the service of the last pleading directed to such issue. The demand may be indorsed upon a pleading of the party. FL ST RCP Rule 1.430(b).
   c. *Specification of issues.* In the demand a party may specify the issues that the party wishes so tried; otherwise, the party is deemed to demand trial by jury for all issues so triable. FL ST RCP Rule 1.430(c).
      i. If a party has demanded trial by jury for only some of the issues, any other party may serve a demand for trial by jury of any other or all of the issues triable by jury ten (10) days after service of the demand or such lesser time as the court may order. FL ST RCP Rule 1.430(c).
   d. *Waiver.* A party who fails to serve a demand as required by FL ST RCP Rule 1.430 waives trial by jury. FL ST RCP Rule 1.430(d).
      i. If waived, a jury trial may not be granted without the consent of the parties, but the court may allow an amendment in the proceedings to demand a trial by jury or order a trial by jury on its own motion. FL ST RCP Rule 1.430(d).
      ii. A demand for trial by jury may not be withdrawn without the consent of the parties. FL ST RCP Rule 1.430(d).
9. *Arbitration and mediation*
   a. *Referral to arbitration and mediation.* Except as hereinafter provided or as otherwise prohibited by law, the presiding judge may enter an order referring all or any part of a contested civil matter to mediation or arbitration. The parties to any contested civil matter may file a written stipulation to mediate or arbitrate any issue between them at any time. Such stipulation shall be incorporated into the order of referral. FL ST RCP Rule 1.700(a).

b. *Arbitration*

i. *Exclusions.* A civil action shall be ordered to arbitration or arbitration in conjunction with mediation upon stipulation of the parties. A civil action may be ordered to arbitration or arbitration in conjunction with mediation upon motion of any party or by the court, if the judge determines the action to be of such a nature that arbitration could be of benefit to the litigants or the court. FL ST RCP Rule 1.800.

- Under no circumstances may the following categories of actions be referred to arbitration: (1) bond estreatures; (2) habeas corpus or other extraordinary writs; (3) bond validations; (4) civil or criminal contempt; (5) such other matters as may be specified by order of the chief judge in the circuit. FL ST RCP Rule 1.800.

ii. For more information regarding arbitration, please see FL ST RCP Rule 1.810; FL ST RCP Rule 1.820; FL ST RCP Rule 1.830.

c. *Mediation.* For more information regarding mediation, please see FL ST RCP Rule 1.710; FL ST RCP Rule 1.720; FL ST RCP Rule 1.730; and FL ST RCP Rule 1.750.

d. It is the policy of the Civil Division judges to maximize the use of alternative dispute resolution procedures. Except where prohibited by statute, mediation will be ordered in all cases where jury trial is requested and in selected cases which are to be tried non-jury. Also, selected cases will be referred for court-annexed non-binding arbitration through the Orange County Bar Association Arbitration Service. Counsel may move to dispense with or defer mediation or arbitration or move to modify the referral order for good cause. FL ST 9 J CIR SECTION 15.

10. *Rules of court*

a. *Rules of civil procedure.* The Florida Rules of Civil Procedure apply to all actions of a civil nature and all special statutory proceedings in the circuit courts and county courts except those to which the Florida Probate Rules, the Florida Family Law Rules of Procedure, or the Small Claims Rules apply. FL ST RCP Rule 1.010.

i. The form, content, procedure, and time for pleading in all special statutory proceedings shall be as prescribed by the statutes governing the proceeding unless the Florida Rules of Civil Procedure specifically provide to the contrary. FL ST RCP Rule 1.010.

ii. The Florida Rules of Civil Procedure shall be construed to secure the just, speedy, and inexpensive determination of every action. FL ST RCP Rule 1.010.

b. *Rules of judicial administration.* The Florida Rules of Judicial Administration shall apply to administrative matters in all courts to which the Florida Rules of Judicial Administration are applicable by their terms. The Florida Rules of Judicial Administration shall be construed to secure the speedy and inexpensive determination of every proceeding to which they are applicable. The Florida Rules of Judicial Administration shall supersede all conflicting rules and statutes. FL ST J ADMIN Rule 2.110.

c. *Business court procedures.* For rules specific to Business Court, please see FL ST 9 J CIR ORANGE CIV SECTION 1, et seq.

D. Documents

1. *Required documents*

a. *Amended answer.* See the General Requirements section of this document for the content of an amended answer. If a party files a motion to amend a pleading, the party shall attach the proposed amended pleading to the motion. FL ST RCP Rule 1.190(a). See the KeyRules Florida Circuit Court Motion for Leave to Amend document for further information.

i. *Notices to persons with disabilities.* See the Format section of this KeyRules document for further information.

b. *Certificate of service.* When any attorney certifies in substance: "I certify that a copy hereof has been furnished to (here insert name or names and addresses used for service) by (e-mail) (delivery) (mail) (fax) on .... (date) ....______________ Attorney" the certificate is taken as prima facie proof of such service in compliance with FL ST J ADMIN Rule 2.516. FL ST J ADMIN Rule 2.516(f).

2. *Supplemental documents*

   a. *Exhibits.* All bonds, notes, bills of exchange, contracts, accounts, or documents upon which action may be brought or defense made, or a copy thereof or a copy of the portions thereof material to the pleadings, shall be incorporated in or attached to the pleading. No papers shall be unnecessarily annexed as exhibits. The pleadings shall contain no unnecessary recitals of deeds, documents, contracts, or other instruments. Any exhibit attached to a pleading shall be considered a part of the pleadings for all purposes. FL ST RCP Rule 1.130(a).

   b. *Notice of constitutional question.* A party that files a pleading, written motion, or other paper drawing into question the constitutionality of a state statute or a county or municipal charter, ordinance, or franchise must promptly (1) file a notice of constitutional question stating the question and identifying the paper that raises it; and (2) serve the notice and the pleading, written motion, or other paper drawing into question the constitutionality of a state statute or a county or municipal charter, ordinance, or franchise on the Attorney General or the state attorney of the judicial circuit in which the action is pending, by either certified or registered mail. Service of the notice and pleading, written motion, or other paper does not require joinder of the Attorney General or the state attorney as a party to the action. FL ST RCP Rule 1.071.

E. Format

1. *Documents; Type and size.* Documents subject to the exceptions set forth in FL ST J ADMIN Rule 2.525(d) shall be filed on recycled paper measuring eight and one half by eleven (8 1/2 by 11) inches. For purposes of FL ST J ADMIN Rule 2.520, paper is recycled if it contains a minimum content of fifty (50) percent waste paper. Xerographic reduction of legal-size (eight and one half by fourteen (8 1/2 by 14) inches) documents to letter size (eight and one half by eleven (8 1/2 by 11) inches) is prohibited. All other documents filed by electronic transmission shall be filed in a format capable of being printed in a format consistent with the provisions of FL ST J ADMIN Rule 2.250. FL ST J ADMIN Rule 2.520(b).

   a. *Exhibits.* Any exhibit or attachment filed with pleadings or papers may be filed in its original size. FL ST J ADMIN Rule 2.520(c).

   b. *Recording space.* On all papers and documents prepared and filed by the court or by any party to a proceeding which are to be recorded in the public records of any county, including but not limited to final money judgments and notices of lis pendens, a three (3) inch by three (3) inch space at the top right-hand corner on the first page and a one (1) inch by three (3) inch space at the top right-hand corner on each subsequent page shall be left blank and reserved for use by the clerk of court. FL ST J ADMIN Rule 2.520(d).

      i. *Exceptions to recording space.* Any papers or documents created by persons or entities over which the filing party has no control, including but not limited to wills, codicils, trusts, or other testamentary documents; documents prepared or executed by any public officer; documents prepared, executed, acknowledged, or proved outside of the State of Florida; or documents created by State or Federal government agencies, may be filed without the space required by FL ST J ADMIN Rule 2.520. FL ST J ADMIN Rule 2.520(e).

   c. *Noncompliance.* No clerk of court is permitted to refuse to file any document or paper because of noncompliance with the Florida Rules of Judicial Administration. However, upon request of the clerk of court, noncomplying documents must be resubmitted in accordance with the formatting rules. FL ST J ADMIN Rule 2.520(f).

2. *Caption.* Every pleading, motion, order, judgment, or other paper shall have a caption containing the name of the court, the file number, and except for in rem proceedings, including forfeiture proceedings, the name of the first party on each side with an appropriate indication of other parties, and a designation identifying the party filing it and its nature or the nature of the order, as the case may be. In any in rem proceeding, every pleading, motion, order, judgment, or other paper shall have a caption containing the name of the court, the file number, the style "In re" (followed by the name or general description of the property), and a designation of the person or entity filing it and its nature or the nature of the order, as the case may be. In an in rem forfeiture proceeding, the style shall be "In re forfeiture of" (followed by the name of the general description of the property). All papers filed in the action shall be styled in such a manner as to indicate clearly the subject matter of the paper and the party requesting or obtaining relief. FL ST RCP Rule 1.100(c)(1).

3. *Writing and written defined.* Writing or written means a document containing information, an application, or a stipulation. FL ST RCP Rule 1.080(c).
4. *Rule abbreviations*
    a. The Florida Rules of Civil Procedure and shall be abbreviated as Fla.R.Civ.P. FL ST RCP Rule 1.010.
    b. The Florida Rules of Judicial Administration shall be abbreviated as Fla. R. Jud. Admin. FL ST J ADMIN Rule 2.110.
5. *Nonverification.* Except when otherwise specifically provided by the Florida Rules of Civil Procedure or an applicable statute, every pleading or other document of a party represented by an attorney need not be verified or accompanied by an affidavit. FL ST RCP Rule 1.030; FL ST J ADMIN Rule 2.515(a).
6. *Unrepresented parties.* An unrepresented party must file his or her papers with the clerk and send copies to other attorneys or unrepresented parties. All such papers must be typed double-spaced on plain white eight and a half by eleven (8 1/2 by 11) inch paper, with the name of the case and case number at the top and the party's mailing address, telephone number and FAX number, if any, below his or her signature at the end of the paper. Such unrepresented party must immediately notify the clerk and all other counsel or parties of record in writing of any change in mailing address or telephone or FAX number. Failure to promptly notify of change of address could result in a dismissal or default entered against such party. FL ST 9 J CIR SECTION 7(B)(5).
7. *Attorney signature*
    a. *Attorney signature.* Every pleading and other document of a party represented by an attorney shall be signed by at least one (1) attorney of record in that attorney's individual name whose current record Florida Bar address, telephone number, including area code, primary e-mail address and secondary e-mail addresses, if any, and Florida Bar number shall be stated, and who shall be duly licensed to practice law in Florida or who shall have received permission to appear in the particular case as provided in FL ST J ADMIN Rule 2.510. FL ST J ADMIN Rule 2.515(a).
        i. The attorney may be required by the court to give the address of, and to vouch for the attorney's authority to represent, the party. FL ST J ADMIN Rule 2.515(a).
        ii. The signature of an attorney shall constitute a certificate by the attorney that the attorney has read the pleading or other document; that to the best of the attorney's knowledge, information, and belief there is good ground to support it; and that it is not interposed for delay. FL ST J ADMIN Rule 2.515(a).
        iii. If a pleading is not signed or is signed with intent to defeat the purpose of FL ST J ADMIN Rule 2.515, it may be stricken and the action may proceed as though the pleading or other document had not been served. FL ST J ADMIN Rule 2.515(a).
    b. *Pro se litigant signature.* A party who is not represented by an attorney shall sign any pleading or other paper and state the party's address and telephone number, including area code. FL ST J ADMIN Rule 2.515(b).
    c. *Form of signature*
        i. The signatures required on pleadings and documents by FL ST J ADMIN Rule 2.515(a) and FL ST J ADMIN Rule 2.515(b) may be:
            - Original signatures;
            - Original signatures that have been reproduced by electronic means, such as on electronically transmitted documents or photocopied documents;
            - Electronic signatures using the "/s/," "s/," or "/s" formats by or at the direction of the person signing; or
            - Any other signature format authorized by general law, so long as the clerk where the proceeding is pending has the capability of receiving and has obtained approval from the Supreme Court of Florida to accept pleadings and documents with that signature format. FL ST J ADMIN Rule 2.515(c)(1).

ii. An attorney, party, or other person who files a pleading or paper by electronic transmission that does not contain the original signature of that attorney, party, or other person shall file that identical pleading or paper in paper form containing an original signature of that attorney, party, or other person (hereinafter called the follow-up filing) immediately thereafter. The follow-up filing is not required if the Supreme Court of Florida has entered an order directing the clerk of court to discontinue accepting the follow-up filing. FL ST J ADMIN Rule 2.515(c)(2).

8. *Forms*

a. *Process.* The forms of process, notice of lis pendens, and notice of action provided in the Florida Rules of Civil Procedure are sufficient. Variations from the forms do not void process or notices that are otherwise sufficient. FL ST RCP Rule 1.900(a).

b. *Other forms.* The other forms provided in the Florida Rules of Civil Procedure are sufficient for the matters that are covered by them. So long as the substance is expressed without prolixity, the forms may be varied to meet the facts of a particular case. FL ST RCP Rule 1.900(b).

c. *Formal matters.* Captions, except for the designation of the paper, are omitted from the forms provided in the Florida Rules of Civil Procedure. A general form of caption is the first form provided. Signatures are omitted from pleadings and motions. FL ST RCP Rule 1.900(c).

9. *Notices to persons with disabilities.* All notices of court proceedings to be held in a public facility, and all process compelling appearance at such proceedings, shall include the following statement in bold face, fourteen (14) point Times New Roman or Courier font: "If you are a person with a disability who needs any accommodation in order to participate in this proceeding, you are entitled, at no cost to you, to the provision of certain assistance. Please contact [identify applicable court personnel by name, address, and telephone number] at least seven (7) days before your scheduled court appearance, or immediately upon receiving this notification if the time before the scheduled appearance is less than seven (7) days; if you are hearing or voice impaired, call 711." FL ST J ADMIN Rule 2.540(c)(1).

10. *Minimization of the filing of sensitive information*

a. *Limitations for court filings.* Unless authorized by FL ST J ADMIN Rule 2.425(b), statute, another rule of court, or the court orders otherwise, designated sensitive information filed with the court must be limited to the following format:

i. The initials of a person known to be a minor;

ii. The year of birth of a person's birth date;

iii. No portion of any: Social security number, Bank account number, Credit card account number, Charge account number, or Debit account number;

iv. The last four digits of any: Taxpayer identification number (TIN), Employee identification number, Driver's license number, Passport number, Telephone number, Financial account number, except as set forth in FL ST J ADMIN Rule 2.425(a)(3), Brokerage account number, Insurance policy account number, Loan account number, Customer account number, or Patient or health care number;

v. A truncated version of any: Email address, Computer user name, Password, or Personal identification number (PIN); and

vi. A truncated version of any other sensitive information as provided by court order. FL ST J ADMIN Rule 2.425(a).

b. *Exceptions.* FL ST J ADMIN Rule 2.425(a) does not apply to the following:

i. An account number which identifies the property alleged to be the subject of a proceeding;

ii. The record of an administrative or agency proceeding;

iii. The record in appellate or review proceedings;

iv. The birth date of a minor whenever the birth date is necessary for the court to establish or maintain subject matter jurisdiction;

v. The name of a minor in any order relating to parental responsibility, time-sharing, or child support;

vi. The name of a minor in any document or order affecting the minor's ownership of real property;

vii. The birth date of a party in a writ of attachment or notice to payor;

viii. In traffic and criminal proceedings: a pro se filing; a court filing that is related to a criminal matter or investigation and that is prepared before the filing of a criminal charge or is not filed as part of any docketed criminal case; an arrest or search warrant or any information in support thereof; a charging document and an affidavit or other documents filed in support of any charging document, including any driving records; a statement of particulars; discovery material introduced into evidence or otherwise filed with the court; and all information necessary for the proper issuance and execution of a subpoena duces tecum;

ix. Information used by the clerk for case maintenance purposes or the courts for case management purposes; and

x. Information which is relevant and material to an issue before the court. FL ST J ADMIN Rule 2.425(b).

c. *Remedies.* Upon motion by a party or interested person or sua sponte by the court, the court may order remedies, sanctions or both for a violation of FL ST J ADMIN Rule 2.425(a). Following notice and an opportunity to respond, the court may impose sanctions if such filing was not made in good faith. FL ST J ADMIN Rule 2.425(c).

d. *Motions not restricted.* FL ST J ADMIN Rule 2.425 does not restrict a party's right to move for protective order, to move to file documents under seal, or to request a determination of the confidentiality of records. FL ST J ADMIN Rule 2.425(d).

e. *Application.* FL ST J ADMIN Rule 2.425 does not affect the application of constitutional provisions, statutes, or rules of court regarding confidential information or access to public information. FL ST J ADMIN Rule 2.425(e).

F. Filing and Service Requirements

1. *Filing requirements.* All original documents must be filed with the court either before service or immediately thereafter, unless otherwise provided for by general law or other rules. If the original of any bond or other document is not placed in the court file, a certified copy must be so placed by the clerk. FL ST J ADMIN Rule 2.516(d). All documents shall be filed in conformity with the requirements of FL ST J ADMIN Rule 2.525. FL ST RCP Rule 1.080(b). All documents filed in any court shall be filed by electronic transmission in accordance with FL ST J ADMIN Rule 2.525. "Documents" means pleadings, motions, petitions, memoranda, briefs, notices, exhibits, declarations, affidavits, orders, judgments, decrees, writs, opinions, and any other paper or writing submitted to a court. FL ST J ADMIN Rule 2.520(a). All documents that are court records, as defined in FL ST J ADMIN Rule 2.430(a)(1), must be filed by electronic transmission, provided that: (1) the clerk has the ability to accept and retain such documents; (2) the clerk or the chief judge of the circuit has requested permission to accept documents filed by electronic transmission; and (3) the supreme court has entered an order granting permission to the clerk to accept documents filed by electronic transmission. FL ST J ADMIN Rule 2.525(c)(1).

a. *Definition.* "Electronic transmission of documents" means the sending of information by electronic signals to, by or from a court or clerk, which when received can be transformed and stored or transmitted on paper, microfilm, magnetic storage device, optical imaging system, CD-ROM, flash drive, other electronic data storage system, server, case maintenance system ("CM"), electronic court filing ("ECF") system, statewide or local electronic portal ("e-portal"), or other electronic record keeping system authorized by the supreme court in a format sufficient to communicate the information on the original document in a readable format. Electronic transmission of documents includes electronic mail ("e-mail") and any internet-based transmission procedure, and may include procedures allowing for documents to be signed or verified by electronic means. FL ST J ADMIN Rule 2.525(a).

i. The filing of documents with the court as required by the Florida Rules of Judicial Administration must be made by filing them with the clerk in accordance with FL ST J ADMIN Rule 2.525, except that the judge may permit documents to be filed with the judge, in which event the judge must note the filing date before him or her on the documents and transmit them to the

clerk. The date of filing is that shown on the face of the document by the judge's notation or the clerk's time stamp, whichever is earlier. FL ST J ADMIN Rule 2.516(e).

b. *Application.* Any court or clerk of the court may accept the electronic transmission of documents for filing after the clerk, together with input from the chief judge of the circuit, has obtained approval of the procedures and program for doing so from the Supreme Court of Florida. FL ST J ADMIN Rule 2.525(b).

c. *Exceptions*

   i. Paper documents and other submissions may be manually submitted to the clerk or court:

      - When the clerk does not have the ability to accept and retain documents by electronic filing or has not had ECF Procedures approved by the supreme court;
      - For filing by any self-represented party or any self-represented nonparty unless specific ECF Procedures provide a means to file documents electronically. However, any self-represented nonparty that is a governmental or public agency and any other agency, partnership, corporation, or business entity acting on behalf of any governmental or public agency may file documents by electronic transmission if such entity has the capability of filing documents electronically;
      - For filing by attorneys excused from e-mail service in accordance with FL ST J ADMIN Rule 2.516(b);
      - When submitting evidentiary exhibits or filing non-documentary materials;
      - When the filing involves documents in excess of twenty-five (25) megabytes (25MB) in size. For such filings, documents may be transmitted using an electronic storage medium that the clerk has the ability to accept, which may include a CD-ROM, flash drive, or similar storage medium;
      - When filed in open court, as permitted by the court;
      - When paper filing is permitted by any approved statewide or local ECF procedures; and
      - If any court determines that justice so requires. FL ST J ADMIN Rule 2.525(d).

   ii. Any document in paper form submitted under FL ST J ADMIN Rule 2.525(d) is filed when it is received by the clerk or court and the clerk shall immediately thereafter convert any filed paper document to an electronic document. "Convert to an electronic document" means optically capturing an image of a paper document and using character recognition software to recover as much of the document's text as practicable and then indexing and storing the document in the official court file. FL ST J ADMIN Rule 2.525(c)(4).

   iii. Any storage medium submitted under FL ST J ADMIN Rule 2.525(d)(5) is filed when received by the clerk or court and the clerk shall immediately thereafter transfer the electronic documents from the storage device to the official court file. FL ST J ADMIN Rule 2.525(c)(5).

   iv. If the filer of any paper document authorized under FL ST J ADMIN Rule 2.525(d) provides a self-addressed, postage-paid envelope for return of the paper document after it is converted to electronic form by the clerk, the clerk shall place the paper document in the envelope and deposit it in the mail. Except when a paper document is required to be maintained, the clerk may recycle any filed paper document that is not to be returned to the filer. FL ST J ADMIN Rule 2.525(c)(6).

   v. The clerk may convert any paper document filed before the effective date of FL ST J ADMIN Rule 2.525 to an electronic document. Unless the clerk is required to maintain the paper document, if the paper document has been converted to an electronic document by the clerk, the paper document is no longer part of the official court file and may be removed and recycled. FL ST J ADMIN Rule 2.525(c)(7).

d. *Unrepresented parties.* An unrepresented party must file his or her papers with the clerk and send copies to other attorneys or unrepresented parties. FL ST 9 J CIR SECTION 7(B)(5).

   i. An unrepresented party may not communicate privately with the judge either by letter, telephone, in person or otherwise. FL ST 9 J CIR SECTION 7(B)(4).

ii. Copies of legal papers or other written materials should not be sent to the judge unless specifically requested by the judge or required by the local administrative procedures. Any unrequested or non-required papers or materials sent to a judge may not be read but may be returned to the sender or placed unread into the court file. FL ST 9 J CIR SECTION 7(B)(4).

e. *Official court file.* For information on what constitutes the official court file, please see FL ST J ADMIN Rule 2.525(c)(2), FL ST J ADMIN Rule 2.525(c)(3).

f. *Administration.* All attorneys, parties, or other persons using this rule to file documents are required to make arrangements with the court or clerk for the payment of any charges authorized by general law or the supreme court before filing any document by electronic transmission. FL ST J ADMIN Rule 2.525(f)(2).

g. *Filing date.* The filing date for an electronically transmitted document is the date and time that such filing is acknowledged by an electronic stamp or otherwise, pursuant to any procedure set forth in any ECF Procedures approved by the supreme court, or the date the last page of such filing is received by the court or clerk. FL ST J ADMIN Rule 2.525(f)(3).

h. *Accessibility.* All documents transmitted in any electronic form under FL ST J ADMIN Rule 2.525 must comply with the accessibility requirements of FL ST J ADMIN Rule 2.526. FL ST J ADMIN Rule 2.525(g).

2. *Service requirements.* Every pleading subsequent to the initial pleading, all orders, and every other document filed in the action must be served in conformity with the requirements of FL ST J ADMIN Rule 2.516. FL ST RCP Rule 1.080(a).

a. *Service; When required.* Unless the court otherwise orders, or a statute or supreme court administrative order specifies a different means of service, every pleading subsequent to the initial pleading and every other document filed in any court proceeding, except applications for witness subpoenas and documents served by formal notice or required to be served in the manner provided for service of formal notice, must be served in accordance with FL ST J ADMIN Rule 2.516 on each party. No service need be made on parties against whom a default has been entered, except that pleadings asserting new or additional claims against them must be served in the manner provided for service of summons. FL ST J ADMIN Rule 2.516(a).

i. Counsel who serves a memorandum or authority list first should also include a copy of the motion, any papers to which it is addressed, and the response, if any. In order for the judge to properly review a submission in advance, it must be received in the judge's office at least three (3) working days before the hearing. FL ST 9 J CIR SECTION 11(B).

b. *Service; How made.* When service is required or permitted to be made upon a party represented by an attorney, service must be made upon the attorney unless service upon the party is ordered by the court. FL ST J ADMIN Rule 2.516(b).

i. *Service by electronic mail ("e-mail").* All documents required or permitted to be served on another party must be served by e-mail, unless FL ST J ADMIN Rule 2.516 otherwise provides. When, in addition to service by e-mail, the sender also utilizes another means of service provided for in FL ST J ADMIN Rule 2.516(b)(2), any differing time limits and other provisions applicable to that other means of service control. FL ST J ADMIN Rule 2.516(b)(1). Any document electronically transmitted to a court or clerk must also be served on all parties and interested persons in accordance with the applicable rules of court. FL ST J ADMIN Rule 2.525(e)(2).

- *Service on attorneys.* Upon appearing in a proceeding, an attorney must serve a designation of a primary e-mail address and may designate no more than two (2) secondary e-mail addresses. Thereafter, service must be directed to all designated e-mail addresses in that proceeding. Every document filed by an attorney thereafter must include the primary e-mail address of that attorney and any secondary e-mail addresses. If an attorney does not designate any e-mail address for service, documents may be served on that attorney at the e-mail address on record with The Florida Bar. FL ST J ADMIN Rule 2.516(b)(1)(A).

- *Exception to e-mail service on attorneys.* Service by an attorney on another attorney must

be made by e-mail unless excused by the court. Upon motion by an attorney demonstrating that the attorney has no e-mail account and lacks access to the Internet at the attorney's office, the court may excuse the attorney from the requirements of e-mail service. Service on and by an attorney excused by the court from e-mail service must be by the means provided in FL ST J ADMIN Rule 2.516(b)(2). FL ST J ADMIN Rule 2.516(b)(1)(B).

- *Service on and by parties not represented by an attorney.* Any party not represented by an attorney may serve a designation of a primary e-mail address and also may designate no more than two (2) secondary e-mail addresses to which service must be directed in that proceeding by the means provided in FL ST J ADMIN Rule 2.516(b)(1). If a party not represented by an attorney does not designate an e-mail address for service in a proceeding, service on and by that party must be by the means provided in FL ST J ADMIN Rule 2.516(b)(2). FL ST J ADMIN Rule 2.516(b)(1)(C).
- *Time of service.* Service by e-mail is complete when it is sent. FL ST J ADMIN Rule 2.516(b)(1)(D). An e-mail is deemed served on the date it is sent. FL ST J ADMIN Rule 2.516(b)(1)(D)(i). If the sender learns that the e-mail did not reach the address of the person to be served, the sender must immediately send another copy by e-mail, or by a means authorized by FL ST J ADMIN Rule 2.516(b)(2). FL ST J ADMIN Rule 2.516(b)(1)(D)(ii). E-mail service is treated as service by mail for the computation of time. FL ST J ADMIN Rule 2.516(b)(1)(D)(iii).

ii. *Format of e-mail for service.* Service of a document by e-mail is made by attaching a copy of the document in PDF format to an e-mail sent to all addresses designated by the attorney or party. FL ST J ADMIN Rule 2.516(b)(1)(E).

- All documents served by e-mail must be attached to an e-mail message containing a subject line beginning with the words "SERVICE OF COURT DOCUMENT" in all capital letters, followed by the case number of the proceeding in which the documents are being served. FL ST J ADMIN Rule 2.516(b)(1)(E)(i).
- The body of the e-mail must identify the court in which the proceeding is pending, the case number, the name of the initial party on each side, the title of each document served with that e-mail, and the sender's name and telephone number. FL ST J ADMIN Rule 2.516(b)(1)(E)(ii).
- Any document served by e-mail may be signed by the "/s/" format, as long as the filed original is signed in accordance with the applicable rule of procedure. FL ST J ADMIN Rule 2.516(b)(1)(E)(iii).
- Any e-mail which, together with its attached documents, exceeds five megabytes (5MB) in size, must be divided and sent as separate e-mails, no one of which may exceed five megabytes (5MB) in size and each of which must be sequentially numbered in the subject line. FL ST J ADMIN Rule 2.516(b)(1)(E)(iv).

iii. *Service by other means.* In addition to, and not in lieu of, service by e-mail, service may also be made upon attorneys by any of the means specified in FL ST J ADMIN Rule 2.516(b)(2). Service on and by all parties who are not represented by an attorney and who do not designate an e-mail address, and on and by all attorneys excused from e-mail service, must be made by delivering a copy of the document or by mailing it to the party or attorney at their last known address or, if no address is known, by leaving it with the clerk of the court. Service by mail is complete upon mailing. Delivery of a copy within FL ST J ADMIN Rule 2.516 is complete upon:

- Handing it to the attorney or to the party,
- Leaving it at the attorney's or party's office with a clerk or other person in charge thereof,
- If there is no one in charge, leaving it in a conspicuous place therein,
- If the office is closed or the person to be served has no office, leaving it at the person's usual place of abode with some person of his or her family above fifteen (15) years of age and informing such person of the contents, or

- Transmitting it by facsimile to the attorney's or party's office with a cover sheet containing the sender's name, firm, address, telephone number, and facsimile number, and the number of pages transmitted. When service is made by facsimile, a copy must also be served by any other method permitted by FL ST J ADMIN Rule 2.516. Facsimile service occurs when transmission is complete. FL ST J ADMIN Rule 2.516(b)(2)(A) through FL ST J ADMIN Rule 2.516(b)(2)(E).
- Service by delivery after 5:00 p.m. must be deemed to have been made by mailing on the date of delivery. FL ST J ADMIN Rule 2.516(b)(2)(F).

c. *Service; Numerous defendants.* In actions when the parties are unusually numerous, the court may regulate the service contemplated by the Florida Rules of Judicial Administration on motion or on its own initiative in such manner as may be found to be just and reasonable. FL ST J ADMIN Rule 2.516(c).

d. *Service by clerk.* Service of notices and other documents required to be made by the clerk must also be done as provided in FL ST J ADMIN Rule 2.516(b). FL ST J ADMIN Rule 2.516(g).

G. Hearings

1. The parties may be required to participate in pretrial proceedings to consider and determine the necessity or desirability of an amendment to a pleading. FL ST RCP Rule 1.200(b)(2); FL-PP § 2:151.

H. Forms

1. Official Amended Answer Forms for Florida

a. Caption. FL ST RCP Form 1.901.

b. Notice of compliance when constitutional challenge is brought. FL ST RCP Form 1.975.

2. Amended Answer Forms for Florida

a. Form for amendment to answer. FL-RCPF R 1.190(50).

b. Form for supplement to pleading. FL-RCPF R 1.190(102).

I. Checklist

(I) ❑ Matters to be considered by plaintiff

(a) ❑ Required documents

(1) ❑ Amended answer

(2) ❑ Certificate of service

(b) ❑ Supplemental documents

(1) ❑ Exhibits

(2) ❑ Notice of constitutional question

(c) ❑ Timing

(1) ❑ A party may amend a pleading once as a matter of course at any time before a responsive pleading is served

(2) ❑ If the pleading is one to which no responsive pleading is permitted and the action has not been placed on the trial calendar, may so amend it at any time within twenty (20) days after it is served

Motions, Oppositions and Replies
Motion to Strike

Document Last Updated January 2013

A. Applicable Rules

1. *State rules*

a. Rules of court. FL ST RCP Rule 1.010; FL ST J ADMIN Rule 2.110.

b. Nonverification of pleadings. FL ST RCP Rule 1.030.
c. Service and filing of pleadings, orders, and documents. FL ST RCP Rule 1.080.
d. Time. FL ST RCP Rule 1.090.
e. Pleadings and motions. FL ST RCP Rule 1.100.
f. Defenses. FL ST RCP Rule 1.140.
g. Sham pleadings. FL ST RCP Rule 1.150.
h. Motions. FL ST RCP Rule 1.160.
i. Relief from judgment, decrees, or orders. FL ST RCP Rule 1.540.
j. Mediation and arbitration. FL ST RCP Rule 1.700; FL ST RCP Rule 1.710; FL ST RCP Rule 1.720; FL ST RCP Rule 1.730; FL ST RCP Rule 1.750; FL ST RCP Rule 1.800; FL ST RCP Rule 1.810; FL ST RCP Rule 1.820; FL ST RCP Rule 1.830.
k. Forms. FL ST RCP Rule 1.900.
l. Minimization of the filing of sensitive information. FL ST J ADMIN Rule 2.425.
m. Retention of court records. FL ST J ADMIN Rule 2.430.
n. Foreign attorneys. FL ST J ADMIN Rule 2.510.
o. Signature of attorneys and parties. FL ST J ADMIN Rule 2.515.
p. Paper. FL ST J ADMIN Rule 2.520.
q. Electronic filing. FL ST J ADMIN Rule 2.525.
r. Accessibility of information and technology. FL ST J ADMIN Rule 2.526.
s. Communication equipment. FL ST J ADMIN Rule 2.530.
t. Court reporting. FL ST J ADMIN Rule 2.535.
u. Requests for accommodations by persons with disabilities. FL ST J ADMIN Rule 2.540.

2. *Local rules*
   a. Hearings. FL ST 9 J CIR SECTION 10.
   b. Motion practice generally. FL ST 9 J CIR SECTION 11.
   c. Orders and judgments. FL ST 9 J CIR SECTION 12.
   d. Alternative dispute resolution. FL ST 9 J CIR SECTION 15.
   e. Business court procedures. FL ST 9 J CIR ORANGE CIV SECTION 1.

B. Timing

1. *Motion to strike.* A party may move to strike or the court may strike redundant, immaterial, impertinent, or scandalous matter from any pleading at any time. FL ST RCP Rule 1.140(f).
2. *Motion to strike; Failure to state a legal defense.* If a pleading sets forth a claim for relief to which the adverse party is not required to serve a responsive pleading, the adverse party may assert any defense in law or fact to that claim for relief at the trial, except that the objection of failure to state a legal defense in an answer or reply shall be asserted by motion to strike the defense within twenty (20) days after service of the answer or reply. FL ST RCP Rule 1.140(b).
3. *Motion to strike; Sham pleadings.* If a party deems any pleading or part thereof filed by another party to be a sham, that party may move to strike the pleading or part thereof before the cause is set for trial. FL ST RCP Rule 1.150(a).
4. *General motion timing.* A copy of any written motion which may not be heard ex parte and a copy of the notice of the hearing thereof shall be served a reasonable time before the time specified for the hearing. FL ST RCP Rule 1.090(d).
   a. Each attorney shall utilize the courts web page under judicial automated calendaring system, for available hearing time and the judge's schedule before telephoning the Judicial Assistant. FL ST 9 J CIR SECTION 10(A)(1).

b. The hearing will be scheduled with the judge's judicial assistant. Written or fax notice must be received in opposing counsel's office at least four (4) working days before the hearing. FL ST 9 J CIR SECTION 10(A)(2).

   i. Counsel who serves a memorandum or authority list first should also include a copy of the motion, any papers to which it is addressed, and the response, if any. In order for the judge to properly review a submission in advance, it must be received in the judge's office at least three (3) working days before the hearing. FL ST 9 J CIR SECTION 11(B).

c. *Obtaining hearing times*

   i. If the motion is one which might be resolved by stipulation or agreed order, moving counsel must explore that possibility with opposing counsel before reserving hearing time. FL ST 9 J CIR SECTION 11(C)(1).

   ii. If at all possible, hearing time for complex motions or several motions to be heard at one time should be cleared with all affected counsel so as to avoid calendar conflicts. FL ST 9 J CIR SECTION 11(C)(1).

   iii. If hearing time cannot be coordinated with opposing counsel, attorneys shall appear at ex parte to resolve the issue. FL ST 9 J CIR SECTION 11(C)(1).

5. *Computation of time*

a. *Generally.* Computation of time shall be governed by FL ST J ADMIN Rule 2.514. FL ST RCP Rule 1.090(a). The following rules apply in computing time periods specified in any rule of procedure, local rule, court order, or statute that does not specify a method of computing time. FL ST J ADMIN Rule 2.514(a).

   i. *Period stated in days or a longer unit.* When the period is stated in days or a longer unit of time (A) exclude the day of the event that triggers the period; (B) count every day, including intermediate Saturdays, Sundays, and legal holidays; and (C) include the last day of the period, but if the last day is a Saturday, Sunday, or legal holiday, or falls within any period of time extended through an order of the chief justice under FL ST J ADMIN Rule 2.205(a)(2)(B)(iv), the period continues to run until the end of the next day that is not a Saturday, Sunday, or legal holiday and does not fall within any period of time extended through an order of the chief justice. FL ST J ADMIN Rule 2.514(a)(1).

   ii. *Period stated in hours.* When the period is stated in hours (A) begin counting immediately on the occurrence of the event that triggers the period; (B) count every hour, including hours during intermediate Saturdays, Sundays, and legal holidays; and (C) if the period would end on a Saturday, Sunday, or legal holiday, or during any period of time extended through an order of the chief justice under FL ST J ADMIN Rule 2.205(a)(2)(B)(iv), the period continues to run until the same time on the next day that is not a Saturday, Sunday, or legal holiday and does not fall within any period of time extended through an order of the chief justice. FL ST J ADMIN Rule 2.514(a)(2).

   iii. *Period stated in days less than seven (7) days.* When the period stated in days is less than seven (7) days, intermediate Saturdays, Sundays, and legal holidays shall be excluded in the computation. FL ST J ADMIN Rule 2.514(a)(3).

   iv. *"Last day" defined.* Unless a different time is set by a statute, local rule, or court order, the last day ends (A) for electronic filing or for service by any means, at midnight; and (B) for filing by other means, when the clerk's office is scheduled to close. FL ST J ADMIN Rule 2.514(a)(4).

   v. *"Next day" defined.* The "next day" is determined by continuing to count forward when the period is measured after an event and backward when measured before an event. FL ST J ADMIN Rule 2.514(a)(5).

   vi. *"Legal holiday" defined.* "Legal holiday" means (A) the day set aside by FL ST § 110.117, for observing New Year's Day, Martin Luther King, Jr.'s Birthday, Memorial Day, Independence Day, Labor Day, Veterans' Day, Thanksgiving Day, the Friday after Thanksgiving Day, or Christmas Day, and (B) any day observed as a holiday by the clerk's office or as designated by the chief judge. FL ST J ADMIN Rule 2.514(a)(6).

b. *Additional time after service by mail or e-mail.* When a party may or must act within a specified time after service and service is made by mail or e-mail, five (5) days are added after the period that would otherwise expire under FL ST J ADMIN Rule 2.514(a). FL ST J ADMIN Rule 2.514(b).

c. *Enlargement.* When an act is required or allowed to be done at or within a specified time by order of court, by the Florida Rules of Civil Procedure, or by notice given thereunder, for cause shown the court at any time in its discretion (1) with or without notice, may order the period enlarged if request therefor is made before the expiration of the period originally prescribed or as extended by a previous order, or (2) upon motion made and notice after the expiration of the specified period, may permit the act to be done when failure to act was the result of excusable neglect, but it may not extend the time for making a motion for new trial, for rehearing, or to alter or amend a judgment; making a motion for relief from a judgment under FL ST RCP Rule 1.540(b); taking an appeal or filing a petition for certiorari; or making a motion for a directed verdict. FL ST RCP Rule 1.090(b).

d. *Unaffected by expiration of term.* The period of time provided for the doing of any act or the taking of any proceeding shall not be affected or limited by the continued existence or expiration of a term of court. The continued existence or expiration of a term of court in no way affects the power of a court to do any act or take any proceeding in any action which is or has been pending before it. FL ST RCP Rule 1.090(c).

C. General Requirements

1. *Motions generally*

a. *Contents.* An application to the court for an order shall be by motion which shall be made in writing unless made during a hearing or trial, shall state with particularity the grounds therefor, and shall set forth the relief or order sought. The requirement of writing is fulfilled if the motion is stated in a written notice of the hearing of the motion. All notices of hearing shall specify each motion or other matter to be heard. FL ST RCP Rule 1.100(b).

b. *Particularity requirement.* The court considers a motion in the light of the substantive law, rule or statute to make its determination. Some rules require a statement of the grounds for a motion under the rule. Failure to give the grounds will result in denial of the motion. This should be the result in all situations when the ground for the motion is not inherent in the rule. FL-PRACPROC § 9:3. The requirement is nevertheless an important one, first because of the due process notice rights of the respondent, as well as for the assistance it provides to the court in its preparation for the hearing or, absent a hearing, for disposition. 4 FLPRAC R 1.100. Every written motion shall cite the particular rule or statute and/or leading case upon which the motion is based. FL ST 9 J CIR SECTION 11(A)(1).

2. *Motion to strike under FL ST RCP Rule 1.140.* Two (2) types of motion to strike are authorized by FL ST RCP Rule 1.140. One is used to eliminate immaterial, redundant, impertinent or scandalous allegations. The other is used to test the legal sufficiency of a defense. FL-PRACPROC § 10:6.

a. *Motion to strike to eliminate immaterial, redundant, impertinent or scandalous allegations*

i. As used in FL ST RCP Rule 1.140(f), redundant means allegations that are foreign to the issues or needless repetition of allegations. Immaterial means allegations having no essential or important relationship to the issues or unnecessary elaboration of material allegations. Impertinent means allegations that do not belong to the issue and are not necessary to it. Scandalous means unnecessary allegations censuring or accusing a party. FL-PRACPROC § 10:6.

ii. The motion can be made at any time and does not toll the time for pleading. FL-PRACPROC § 10:6.

iii. The motion reaches improper allegations of damages. When directed to an entire paragraph and any part of it is proper, the motion should be denied. Leave to amend should be granted after striking part of a pleading unless a proper amendment cannot be made. FL-PRACPROC § 10:6.

iv. The use of a motion to strike is not favored by the courts and the remedy is used sparingly. Florida courts have held that an allegation must be "wholly irrelevant" and that if there is some doubt it must be resolved in support of the pleading and against the party moving to strike. If any part of an allegation is relevant, then that part should not be stricken from the pleading. 5 FLPRAC § 7:30.

b. *Motion to strike the legal sufficiency of a defense*

i. The legal insufficiency of a defense alleged in an answer or reply is attacked by a motion to strike. It is the counterpart of a motion to dismiss for failure to state a cause of action directed to a pleading seeking affirmative relief. FL-PRACPROC § 10:7.

ii. A motion to strike a defense tests only the legal sufficiency of the defense, and it is reversible error for a trial court to strike the defense where evidence may be presented to support it. Burns v. Equilease Corp., 357 So.2d 786, 24, 24 U.C.C. Rep.Serv. 254 (Fla. 3d DCA 1978); 20 FLPRAC § 3:15.

3. *Sham pleadings.* If a party deems any pleading or part thereof filed by another party to be a sham, that party may move to strike the pleading or part thereof before the cause is set for trial and the court shall hear the motion, taking evidence of the respective parties, and if the motion is sustained, the pleading to which the motion is directed shall be stricken. Default and summary judgment on the merits may be entered in the discretion of the court or the court may permit additional pleadings to be filed for good cause shown. FL ST RCP Rule 1.150(a).

a. *Contents of motion.* The motion to strike shall be verified and shall set forth fully the facts on which the movant relies and may be supported by affidavit. No traverse of the motion shall be required. FL ST RCP Rule 1.150(b).

b. *Allegations supported by evidence.* The issue is not whether the allegations are material or proper, but whether the allegations are supported by evidence. 5 FLPRAC § 7:30.

4. *Arbitration and mediation*

a. *Referral to arbitration and mediation.* Except as hereinafter provided or as otherwise prohibited by law, the presiding judge may enter an order referring all or any part of a contested civil matter to mediation or arbitration. The parties to any contested civil matter may file a written stipulation to mediate or arbitrate any issue between them at any time. Such stipulation shall be incorporated into the order of referral. FL ST RCP Rule 1.700(a).

i. *Local arbitration policy.* It is the policy of the Civil Division judges to maximize the use of alternative dispute resolution procedures. Except where prohibited by statute, mediation will be ordered in all cases where jury trial is requested and in selected cases which are to be tried non-jury. Also, selected cases will be referred for court-annexed non-binding arbitration through the Orange County Bar Association Arbitration Service. Counsel may move to dispense with or defer mediation or arbitration or move to modify the referral order for good cause. FL ST 9 J CIR SECTION 15.

b. *Arbitration*

i. *Exclusions.* A civil action shall be ordered to arbitration or arbitration in conjunction with mediation upon stipulation of the parties. A civil action may be ordered to arbitration or arbitration in conjunction with mediation upon motion of any party or by the court, if the judge determines the action to be of such a nature that arbitration could be of benefit to the litigants or the court. FL ST RCP Rule 1.800.

- Under no circumstances may the following categories of actions be referred to arbitration: (1) bond estreatures; (2) habeas corpus or other extraordinary writs; (3) bond validations; (4) civil or criminal contempt; (5) such other matters as may be specified by order of the chief judge in the circuit. FL ST RCP Rule 1.800.

ii. For more information regarding arbitration, please see FL ST RCP Rule 1.810; FL ST RCP Rule 1.820; FL ST RCP Rule 1.830.

c. *Mediation.* For more information regarding mediation, please see FL ST RCP Rule 1.710; FL ST RCP Rule 1.720; FL ST RCP Rule 1.730; and FL ST RCP Rule 1.750.

5. *Rules of court*

a. *Rules of civil procedure.* The Florida Rules of Civil Procedure apply to all actions of a civil nature and all special statutory proceedings in the circuit courts and county courts except those to which the

Florida Probate Rules, the Florida Family Law Rules of Procedure, or the Small Claims Rules apply. FL ST RCP Rule 1.010.

i. The form, content, procedure, and time for pleading in all special statutory proceedings shall be as prescribed by the statutes governing the proceeding unless the Florida Rules of Civil Procedure specifically provide to the contrary. FL ST RCP Rule 1.010.

ii. The Florida Rules of Civil Procedure shall be construed to secure the just, speedy, and inexpensive determination of every action. FL ST RCP Rule 1.010.

b. *Rules of judicial administration.* The Florida Rules of Judicial Administration shall apply to administrative matters in all courts to which the Florida Rules of Judicial Administration are applicable by their terms. The Florida Rules of Judicial Administration shall be construed to secure the speedy and inexpensive determination of every proceeding to which they are applicable. The Florida Rules of Judicial Administration shall supersede all conflicting rules and statutes. FL ST J ADMIN Rule 2.110.

c. *Business court procedures.* For rules specific to Business Court, please see FL ST 9 J CIR ORANGE CIV SECTION 1, et seq.

D. Documents

1. *Required documents*

a. *Notice of hearing/Motion.* An application to the court for an order shall be by motion which shall be made in writing unless made during a hearing or trial, shall state with particularity the grounds therefor, and shall set forth the relief or order sought. The requirement of writing is fulfilled if the motion is stated in a written notice of the hearing of the motion. All notices of hearing shall specify each motion or other matter to be heard. FL ST RCP Rule 1.100(b).

i. *Notices to persons with disabilities.* See the Format section of this KeyRules document for further information.

ii. Every notice must specify the motions to be heard. A notice calling up "all pending motions" is insufficient. FL ST 9 J CIR SECTION 11(D)(1). Additional motions should not be "piggy-backed" by cross-notice unless counsel first confirms with opposing counsel and the judge's judicial assistant that there can be sufficient additional time reserved in which to hear them. FL ST 9 J CIR SECTION 11(D)(2).

b. *Certificate of service.* When any attorney certifies in substance: "I certify that a copy hereof has been furnished to (here insert name or names and addresses used for service) by (e-mail) (delivery) (mail) (fax) on .... (date) ....______________ Attorney" the certificate is taken as prima facie proof of such service in compliance with FL ST J ADMIN Rule 2.516. FL ST J ADMIN Rule 2.516(f).

2. *Supplemental documents*

a. *Proposed order.* The court may require that orders or judgments be prepared by a party, may require the party to furnish the court with stamped, addressed envelopes for service of the order or judgment, and may require that proposed orders and judgments be furnished to all parties before entry by the court of the order or judgment. FL ST J ADMIN Rule 2.516(h)(1).

i. Proposed orders and judgments will be prepared by the prevailing attorney unless the judge designates some other attorney or states that he or she will prepare the order or judgment. FL ST 9 J CIR SECTION 12(A)(1).

ii. When submitting proposed orders or judgments, counsel shall also include sufficient copies and self address stamped envelopes for all parties. FL ST 9 J CIR SECTION 12(A)(2).

iii. Moving counsel must present a proposed order with space for ruling left blank at the conclusion of the hearing and must serve conformed copies on all other counsel and unrepresented parties. FL ST 9 J CIR SECTION 10(A)(3).

iv. Unsigned orders or judgments should not be sent to the Clerk's office for transmission to the judge. FL ST 9 J CIR SECTION 12(D)(3).

b. *Legal memorandum.* Legal memorandums in support of or opposition to motions are optional. But if filed, counsel must furnish the judge with chambers copies of the memorandum and highlighted copies of primary legal authorities cited therein. FL ST 9 J CIR SECTION 11(B).

i. As an alternative to a memorandum, a list of primary legal authorities with highlighted copies attached may be submitted. Chambers copies and authority lists must be under cover letter referencing the case style and number and stating the date and time of the hearing. FL ST 9 J CIR SECTION 11(B).

c. *Notice of constitutional question.* A party that files a pleading, written motion, or other paper drawing into question the constitutionality of a state statute or a county or municipal charter, ordinance, or franchise must promptly (1) file a notice of constitutional question stating the question and identifying the paper that raises it; and (2) serve the notice and the pleading, written motion, or other paper drawing into question the constitutionality of a state statute or a county or municipal charter, ordinance, or franchise on the Attorney General or the state attorney of the judicial circuit in which the action is pending, by either certified or registered mail. Service of the notice and pleading, written motion, or other paper does not require joinder of the Attorney General or the state attorney as a party to the action. FL ST RCP Rule 1.071.

E. Format

1. *Documents; Type and size.* Documents subject to the exceptions set forth in FL ST J ADMIN Rule 2.525(d) shall be filed on recycled paper measuring eight and one half by eleven (8 1/2 by 11) inches. For purposes of FL ST J ADMIN Rule 2.520, paper is recycled if it contains a minimum content of fifty (50) percent waste paper. Xerographic reduction of legal-size (eight and one half by fourteen (8 1/2 by 14) inches) documents to letter size (eight and one half by eleven (8 1/2 by 11) inches) is prohibited. All other documents filed by electronic transmission shall be filed in a format capable of being printed in a format consistent with the provisions of FL ST J ADMIN Rule 2.250. FL ST J ADMIN Rule 2.520(b).

a. *Exhibits.* Any exhibit or attachment filed with pleadings or papers may be filed in its original size. FL ST J ADMIN Rule 2.520(c).

b. *Recording space.* On all papers and documents prepared and filed by the court or by any party to a proceeding which are to be recorded in the public records of any county, including but not limited to final money judgments and notices of lis pendens, a three (3) inch by three (3) inch space at the top right-hand corner on the first page and a one (1) inch by three (3) inch space at the top right-hand corner on each subsequent page shall be left blank and reserved for use by the clerk of court. FL ST J ADMIN Rule 2.520(d).

i. *Exceptions to recording space.* Any papers or documents created by persons or entities over which the filing party has no control, including but not limited to wills, codicils, trusts, or other testamentary documents; documents prepared or executed by any public officer; documents prepared, executed, acknowledged, or proved outside of the State of Florida; or documents created by State or Federal government agencies, may be filed without the space required by FL ST J ADMIN Rule 2.520. FL ST J ADMIN Rule 2.520(e).

c. *Noncompliance.* No clerk of court is permitted to refuse to file any document or paper because of noncompliance with the Florida Rules of Judicial Administration. However, upon request of the clerk of court, noncomplying documents must be resubmitted in accordance with the formatting rules. FL ST J ADMIN Rule 2.520(f).

d. *Proposed orders*

i. All orders will be on eight and a half by eleven (8 1/2 by 11) inch plain white paper (not lined or letterhead paper) and be double spaced. FL ST 9 J CIR SECTION 12(B)(1).

ii. The order must contain a title indicating what matter the order pertains to, e.g., "Order On Defendant Smith's Motion To Dismiss." FL ST 9 J CIR SECTION 12(B)(2).

iii. The preamble of the order should include the date of the hearing and what motions were heard. FL ST 9 J CIR SECTION 12(B)(3).

iv. The adjudication portion of the order should state what relief is ordered. Simply stating that "the motion is granted" without more is insufficient. FL ST 9 J CIR SECTION 12(B)(4).

v. The order should indicate the specific time period of any act ordered to be done and should state whether the time period runs from the date of the hearing or the date the order is signed or some other specified date. FL ST 9 J CIR SECTION 12(B)(5).

vi. The order should contain a full certificate of service with the complete names and addresses of the attorneys and unrepresented parties to be served. Merely showing "copies to" is insufficient. FL ST 9 J CIR SECTION 12(B)(6).

vii. If an order of dismissal is final (i.e., it disposes of the entire case) the title should contain the word "Final." When the order is not final but leaves other counts or claims against other defendants pending, it should so state in a separate paragraph. FL ST 9 J CIR SECTION 12(B)(7).

viii. When submitting stipulations, orders shall be by separate order, not attached to the stipulation. FL ST 9 J CIR SECTION 12(B)(8).

ix. Counsel preparing the Final Judgment or order should draft and circulate copies within two (2) working days of the ruling or jury verdict. If counsel preparing the Final Judgment or order gets approval as to form of the order from all counsel, the original with copies and envelopes should be sent directly to the judge with a cover letter stating all counsel agree to the form of the order or judgment. If other counsel objects to the form or cannot be reached for approval, counsel preparing the judgment or order shall notice a motion for entry of the order or judgment. If objecting counsel does not furnish the judge prior to or at the hearing with a proposed judgment or order version with copies under cover letter stating the reasons for the objection, all objections will be deemed waived. FL ST 9 J CIR SECTION 12(D).

2. *Caption.* Every pleading, motion, order, judgment, or other paper shall have a caption containing the name of the court, the file number, and except for in rem proceedings, including forfeiture proceedings, the name of the first party on each side with an appropriate indication of other parties, and a designation identifying the party filing it and its nature or the nature of the order, as the case may be. In any in rem proceeding, every pleading, motion, order, judgment, or other paper shall have a caption containing the name of the court, the file number, the style "In re" (followed by the name or general description of the property), and a designation of the person or entity filing it and its nature or the nature of the order, as the case may be. In an in rem forfeiture proceeding, the style shall be "In re forfeiture of" (followed by the name of the general description of the property). All papers filed in the action shall be styled in such a manner as to indicate clearly the subject matter of the paper and the party requesting or obtaining relief. FL ST RCP Rule 1.100(c)(1).

3. *Writing and written defined.* Writing or written means a document containing information, an application, or a stipulation. FL ST RCP Rule 1.080(c).

4. *Rule abbreviations*

   a. The Florida Rules of Civil Procedure and shall be abbreviated as Fla.R.Civ.P. FL ST RCP Rule 1.010.

   b. The Florida Rules of Judicial Administration shall be abbreviated as Fla. R. Jud. Admin. FL ST J ADMIN Rule 2.110.

5. *Nonverification.* Except when otherwise specifically provided by the Florida Rules of Civil Procedure or an applicable statute, every pleading or other document of a party represented by an attorney need not be verified or accompanied by an affidavit. FL ST RCP Rule 1.030; FL ST J ADMIN Rule 2.515(a).

6. *Unrepresented parties.* An unrepresented party must file his or her papers with the clerk and send copies to other attorneys or unrepresented parties. All such papers must be typed double-spaced on plain white eight and a half by eleven (8 1/2 by 11) inch paper, with the name of the case and case number at the top and the party's mailing address, telephone number and FAX number, if any, below his or her signature at the end of the paper. Such unrepresented party must immediately notify the clerk and all other counsel or parties of record in writing of any change in mailing address or telephone or FAX number. Failure to promptly notify of change of address could result in a dismissal or default entered against such party. FL ST 9 J CIR SECTION 7(B)(5).

7. *Attorney signature*

   a. *Attorney signature.* Every pleading and other document of a party represented by an attorney shall be

signed by at least one (1) attorney of record in that attorney's individual name whose current record Florida Bar address, telephone number, including area code, primary e-mail address and secondary e-mail addresses, if any, and Florida Bar number shall be stated, and who shall be duly licensed to practice law in Florida or who shall have received permission to appear in the particular case as provided in FL ST J ADMIN Rule 2.510. FL ST J ADMIN Rule 2.515(a).

i. The attorney may be required by the court to give the address of, and to vouch for the attorney's authority to represent, the party. FL ST J ADMIN Rule 2.515(a).

ii. The signature of an attorney shall constitute a certificate by the attorney that the attorney has read the pleading or other document; that to the best of the attorney's knowledge, information, and belief there is good ground to support it; and that it is not interposed for delay. FL ST J ADMIN Rule 2.515(a).

iii. If a pleading is not signed or is signed with intent to defeat the purpose of FL ST J ADMIN Rule 2.515, it may be stricken and the action may proceed as though the pleading or other document had not been served. FL ST J ADMIN Rule 2.515(a).

b. *Pro se litigant signature.* A party who is not represented by an attorney shall sign any pleading or other paper and state the party's address and telephone number, including area code. FL ST J ADMIN Rule 2.515(b).

c. *Form of signature*

i. The signatures required on pleadings and documents by FL ST J ADMIN Rule 2.515(a) and FL ST J ADMIN Rule 2.515(b) may be:

- Original signatures;
- Original signatures that have been reproduced by electronic means, such as on electronically transmitted documents or photocopied documents;
- Electronic signatures using the "/s/," "s/," or "/s" formats by or at the direction of the person signing; or
- Any other signature format authorized by general law, so long as the clerk where the proceeding is pending has the capability of receiving and has obtained approval from the Supreme Court of Florida to accept pleadings and documents with that signature format. FL ST J ADMIN Rule 2.515(c)(1).

ii. An attorney, party, or other person who files a pleading or paper by electronic transmission that does not contain the original signature of that attorney, party, or other person shall file that identical pleading or paper in paper form containing an original signature of that attorney, party, or other person (hereinafter called the follow-up filing) immediately thereafter. The follow-up filing is not required if the Supreme Court of Florida has entered an order directing the clerk of court to discontinue accepting the follow-up filing. FL ST J ADMIN Rule 2.515(c)(2).

8. *Forms*

a. *Process.* The forms of process, notice of lis pendens, and notice of action provided in the Florida Rules of Civil Procedure are sufficient. Variations from the forms do not void process or notices that are otherwise sufficient. FL ST RCP Rule 1.900(a).

b. *Other forms.* The other forms provided in the Florida Rules of Civil Procedure are sufficient for the matters that are covered by them. So long as the substance is expressed without prolixity, the forms may be varied to meet the facts of a particular case. FL ST RCP Rule 1.900(b).

c. *Formal matters.* Captions, except for the designation of the paper, are omitted from the forms provided in the Florida Rules of Civil Procedure. A general form of caption is the first form provided. Signatures are omitted from pleadings and motions. FL ST RCP Rule 1.900(c).

9. *Notices to persons with disabilities.* All notices of court proceedings to be held in a public facility, and all process compelling appearance at such proceedings, shall include the following statement in bold face, fourteen (14) point Times New Roman or Courier font: "If you are a person with a disability who needs any accommodation in order to participate in this proceeding, you are entitled, at no cost to you, to the

provision of certain assistance. Please contact [identify applicable court personnel by name, address, and telephone number] at least seven (7) days before your scheduled court appearance, or immediately upon receiving this notification if the time before the scheduled appearance is less than seven (7) days; if you are hearing or voice impaired, call 711." FL ST J ADMIN Rule 2.540(c)(1).

10. *Minimization of the filing of sensitive information*
    a. *Limitations for court filings.* Unless authorized by FL ST J ADMIN Rule 2.425(b), statute, another rule of court, or the court orders otherwise, designated sensitive information filed with the court must be limited to the following format:
        i. The initials of a person known to be a minor;
        ii. The year of birth of a person's birth date;
        iii. No portion of any: Social security number, Bank account number, Credit card account number, Charge account number, or Debit account number;
        iv. The last four digits of any: Taxpayer identification number (TIN), Employee identification number, Driver's license number, Passport number, Telephone number, Financial account number, except as set forth in FL ST J ADMIN Rule 2.425(a)(3), Brokerage account number, Insurance policy account number, Loan account number, Customer account number, or Patient or health care number;
        v. A truncated version of any: Email address, Computer user name, Password, or Personal identification number (PIN); and
        vi. A truncated version of any other sensitive information as provided by court order. FL ST J ADMIN Rule 2.425(a).
    b. *Exceptions.* FL ST J ADMIN Rule 2.425(a) does not apply to the following:
        i. An account number which identifies the property alleged to be the subject of a proceeding;
        ii. The record of an administrative or agency proceeding;
        iii. The record in appellate or review proceedings;
        iv. The birth date of a minor whenever the birth date is necessary for the court to establish or maintain subject matter jurisdiction;
        v. The name of a minor in any order relating to parental responsibility, time-sharing, or child support;
        vi. The name of a minor in any document or order affecting the minor's ownership of real property;
        vii. The birth date of a party in a writ of attachment or notice to payor;
        viii. In traffic and criminal proceedings: a pro se filing; a court filing that is related to a criminal matter or investigation and that is prepared before the filing of a criminal charge or is not filed as part of any docketed criminal case; an arrest or search warrant or any information in support thereof; a charging document and an affidavit or other documents filed in support of any charging document, including any driving records; a statement of particulars; discovery material introduced into evidence or otherwise filed with the court; and all information necessary for the proper issuance and execution of a subpoena duces tecum;
        ix. Information used by the clerk for case maintenance purposes or the courts for case management purposes; and
        x. Information which is relevant and material to an issue before the court. FL ST J ADMIN Rule 2.425(b).
    c. *Remedies.* Upon motion by a party or interested person or sua sponte by the court, the court may order remedies, sanctions or both for a violation of FL ST J ADMIN Rule 2.425(a). Following notice and an opportunity to respond, the court may impose sanctions if such filing was not made in good faith. FL ST J ADMIN Rule 2.425(c).
    d. *Motions not restricted.* FL ST J ADMIN Rule 2.425 does not restrict a party's right to move for

protective order, to move to file documents under seal, or to request a determination of the confidentiality of records. FL ST J ADMIN Rule 2.425(d).

e. *Application.* FL ST J ADMIN Rule 2.425 does not affect the application of constitutional provisions, statutes, or rules of court regarding confidential information or access to public information. FL ST J ADMIN Rule 2.425(e).

F. Filing and Service Requirements

1. *Filing requirements.* All original documents must be filed with the court either before service or immediately thereafter, unless otherwise provided for by general law or other rules. If the original of any bond or other document is not placed in the court file, a certified copy must be so placed by the clerk. FL ST J ADMIN Rule 2.516(d). All documents shall be filed in conformity with the requirements of FL ST J ADMIN Rule 2.525. FL ST RCP Rule 1.080(b). All documents filed in any court shall be filed by electronic transmission in accordance with FL ST J ADMIN Rule 2.525. "Documents" means pleadings, motions, petitions, memoranda, briefs, notices, exhibits, declarations, affidavits, orders, judgments, decrees, writs, opinions, and any other paper or writing submitted to a court. FL ST J ADMIN Rule 2.520(a). All documents that are court records, as defined in FL ST J ADMIN Rule 2.430(a)(1), must be filed by electronic transmission, provided that: (1) the clerk has the ability to accept and retain such documents; (2) the clerk or the chief judge of the circuit has requested permission to accept documents filed by electronic transmission; and (3) the supreme court has entered an order granting permission to the clerk to accept documents filed by electronic transmission. FL ST J ADMIN Rule 2.525(c)(1).

   a. *Definition.* "Electronic transmission of documents" means the sending of information by electronic signals to, by or from a court or clerk, which when received can be transformed and stored or transmitted on paper, microfilm, magnetic storage device, optical imaging system, CD-ROM, flash drive, other electronic data storage system, server, case maintenance system ("CM"), electronic court filing ("ECF") system, statewide or local electronic portal ("e-portal"), or other electronic record keeping system authorized by the supreme court in a format sufficient to communicate the information on the original document in a readable format. Electronic transmission of documents includes electronic mail ("e-mail") and any internet-based transmission procedure, and may include procedures allowing for documents to be signed or verified by electronic means. FL ST J ADMIN Rule 2.525(a).

      i. The filing of documents with the court as required by the Florida Rules of Judicial Administration must be made by filing them with the clerk in accordance with FL ST J ADMIN Rule 2.525, except that the judge may permit documents to be filed with the judge, in which event the judge must note the filing date before him or her on the documents and transmit them to the clerk. The date of filing is that shown on the face of the document by the judge's notation or the clerk's time stamp, whichever is earlier. FL ST J ADMIN Rule 2.516(e).

   b. *Application.* Any court or clerk of the court may accept the electronic transmission of documents for filing after the clerk, together with input from the chief judge of the circuit, has obtained approval of the procedures and program for doing so from the Supreme Court of Florida. FL ST J ADMIN Rule 2.525(b).

   c. *Exceptions*

      i. Paper documents and other submissions may be manually submitted to the clerk or court:

         - When the clerk does not have the ability to accept and retain documents by electronic filing or has not had ECF Procedures approved by the supreme court;
         - For filing by any self-represented party or any self-represented nonparty unless specific ECF Procedures provide a means to file documents electronically. However, any self-represented nonparty that is a governmental or public agency and any other agency, partnership, corporation, or business entity acting on behalf of any governmental or public agency may file documents by electronic transmission if such entity has the capability of filing documents electronically;
         - For filing by attorneys excused from e-mail service in accordance with FL ST J ADMIN Rule 2.516(b);

- When submitting evidentiary exhibits or filing non-documentary materials;
- When the filing involves documents in excess of twenty-five (25) megabytes (25MB) in size. For such filings, documents may be transmitted using an electronic storage medium that the clerk has the ability to accept, which may include a CD-ROM, flash drive, or similar storage medium;
- When filed in open court, as permitted by the court;
- When paper filing is permitted by any approved statewide or local ECF procedures; and
- If any court determines that justice so requires. FL ST J ADMIN Rule 2.525(d).

ii. Any document in paper form submitted under FL ST J ADMIN Rule 2.525(d) is filed when it is received by the clerk or court and the clerk shall immediately thereafter convert any filed paper document to an electronic document. "Convert to an electronic document" means optically capturing an image of a paper document and using character recognition software to recover as much of the document's text as practicable and then indexing and storing the document in the official court file. FL ST J ADMIN Rule 2.525(c)(4).

iii. Any storage medium submitted under FL ST J ADMIN Rule 2.525(d)(5) is filed when received by the clerk or court and the clerk shall immediately thereafter transfer the electronic documents from the storage device to the official court file. FL ST J ADMIN Rule 2.525(c)(5).

iv. If the filer of any paper document authorized under FL ST J ADMIN Rule 2.525(d) provides a self-addressed, postage-paid envelope for return of the paper document after it is converted to electronic form by the clerk, the clerk shall place the paper document in the envelope and deposit it in the mail. Except when a paper document is required to be maintained, the clerk may recycle any filed paper document that is not to be returned to the filer. FL ST J ADMIN Rule 2.525(c)(6).

v. The clerk may convert any paper document filed before the effective date of FL ST J ADMIN Rule 2.525 to an electronic document. Unless the clerk is required to maintain the paper document, if the paper document has been converted to an electronic document by the clerk, the paper document is no longer part of the official court file and may be removed and recycled. FL ST J ADMIN Rule 2.525(c)(7).

d. *Unrepresented parties.* An unrepresented party must file his or her papers with the clerk and send copies to other attorneys or unrepresented parties. FL ST 9 J CIR SECTION 7(B)(5).

i. An unrepresented party may not communicate privately with the judge either by letter, telephone, in person or otherwise. FL ST 9 J CIR SECTION 7(B)(4).

ii. Copies of legal papers or other written materials should not be sent to the judge unless specifically requested by the judge or required by the local administrative procedures. Any unrequested or non-required papers or materials sent to a judge may not be read but may be returned to the sender or placed unread into the court file. FL ST 9 J CIR SECTION 7(B)(4).

e. *Official court file.* For information on what constitutes the official court file, please see FL ST J ADMIN Rule 2.525(c)(2), FL ST J ADMIN Rule 2.525(c)(3).

f. *Administration.* All attorneys, parties, or other persons using this rule to file documents are required to make arrangements with the court or clerk for the payment of any charges authorized by general law or the supreme court before filing any document by electronic transmission. FL ST J ADMIN Rule 2.525(f)(2).

g. *Filing date.* The filing date for an electronically transmitted document is the date and time that such filing is acknowledged by an electronic stamp or otherwise, pursuant to any procedure set forth in any ECF Procedures approved by the supreme court, or the date the last page of such filing is received by the court or clerk. FL ST J ADMIN Rule 2.525(f)(3).

h. *Accessibility.* All documents transmitted in any electronic form under FL ST J ADMIN Rule 2.525 must comply with the accessibility requirements of FL ST J ADMIN Rule 2.526. FL ST J ADMIN Rule 2.525(g).

2. *Service requirements.* Every pleading subsequent to the initial pleading, all orders, and every other

document filed in the action must be served in conformity with the requirements of FL ST J ADMIN Rule 2.516. FL ST RCP Rule 1.080(a).

a. *Service; When required.* Unless the court otherwise orders, or a statute or supreme court administrative order specifies a different means of service, every pleading subsequent to the initial pleading and every other document filed in any court proceeding, except applications for witness subpoenas and documents served by formal notice or required to be served in the manner provided for service of formal notice, must be served in accordance with FL ST J ADMIN Rule 2.516 on each party. No service need be made on parties against whom a default has been entered, except that pleadings asserting new or additional claims against them must be served in the manner provided for service of summons. FL ST J ADMIN Rule 2.516(a).

    i. Counsel who serves a memorandum or authority list first should also include a copy of the motion, any papers to which it is addressed, and the response, if any. In order for the judge to properly review a submission in advance, it must be received in the judge's office at least three (3) working days before the hearing. FL ST 9 J CIR SECTION 11(B).

b. *Service; How made.* When service is required or permitted to be made upon a party represented by an attorney, service must be made upon the attorney unless service upon the party is ordered by the court. FL ST J ADMIN Rule 2.516(b).

    i. *Service by electronic mail ("e-mail").* All documents required or permitted to be served on another party must be served by e-mail, unless FL ST J ADMIN Rule 2.516 otherwise provides. When, in addition to service by e-mail, the sender also utilizes another means of service provided for in FL ST J ADMIN Rule 2.516(b)(2), any differing time limits and other provisions applicable to that other means of service control. FL ST J ADMIN Rule 2.516(b)(1). Any document electronically transmitted to a court or clerk must also be served on all parties and interested persons in accordance with the applicable rules of court. FL ST J ADMIN Rule 2.525(e)(2).

        - *Service on attorneys.* Upon appearing in a proceeding, an attorney must serve a designation of a primary e-mail address and may designate no more than two (2) secondary e-mail addresses. Thereafter, service must be directed to all designated e-mail addresses in that proceeding. Every document filed by an attorney thereafter must include the primary e-mail address of that attorney and any secondary e-mail addresses. If an attorney does not designate any e-mail address for service, documents may be served on that attorney at the e-mail address on record with The Florida Bar. FL ST J ADMIN Rule 2.516(b)(1)(A).

        - *Exception to e-mail service on attorneys.* Service by an attorney on another attorney must be made by e-mail unless excused by the court. Upon motion by an attorney demonstrating that the attorney has no e-mail account and lacks access to the Internet at the attorney's office, the court may excuse the attorney from the requirements of e-mail service. Service on and by an attorney excused by the court from e-mail service must be by the means provided in FL ST J ADMIN Rule 2.516(b)(2). FL ST J ADMIN Rule 2.516(b)(1)(B).

        - *Service on and by parties not represented by an attorney.* Any party not represented by an attorney may serve a designation of a primary e-mail address and also may designate no more than two (2) secondary e-mail addresses to which service must be directed in that proceeding by the means provided in FL ST J ADMIN Rule 2.516(b)(1). If a party not represented by an attorney does not designate an e-mail address for service in a proceeding, service on and by that party must be by the means provided in FL ST J ADMIN Rule 2.516(b)(2). FL ST J ADMIN Rule 2.516(b)(1)(C).

        - *Time of service.* Service by e-mail is complete when it is sent. FL ST J ADMIN Rule 2.516(b)(1)(D). An e-mail is deemed served on the date it is sent. FL ST J ADMIN Rule 2.516(b)(1)(D)(i). If the sender learns that the e-mail did not reach the address of the person to be served, the sender must immediately send another copy by e-mail, or by a means authorized by FL ST J ADMIN Rule 2.516(b)(2). FL ST J ADMIN Rule 2.516(b)(1)(D)(ii). E-mail service is treated as service by mail for the computation of time. FL ST J ADMIN Rule 2.516(b)(1)(D)(iii).

ii. *Format of e-mail for service.* Service of a document by e-mail is made by attaching a copy of the document in PDF format to an e-mail sent to all addresses designated by the attorney or party. FL ST J ADMIN Rule 2.516(b)(1)(E).

- All documents served by e-mail must be attached to an e-mail message containing a subject line beginning with the words "SERVICE OF COURT DOCUMENT" in all capital letters, followed by the case number of the proceeding in which the documents are being served. FL ST J ADMIN Rule 2.516(b)(1)(E)(i).
- The body of the e-mail must identify the court in which the proceeding is pending, the case number, the name of the initial party on each side, the title of each document served with that e-mail, and the sender's name and telephone number. FL ST J ADMIN Rule 2.516(b)(1)(E)(ii).
- Any document served by e-mail may be signed by the "/s/" format, as long as the filed original is signed in accordance with the applicable rule of procedure. FL ST J ADMIN Rule 2.516(b)(1)(E)(iii).
- Any e-mail which, together with its attached documents, exceeds five megabytes (5MB) in size, must be divided and sent as separate e-mails, no one of which may exceed five megabytes (5MB) in size and each of which must be sequentially numbered in the subject line. FL ST J ADMIN Rule 2.516(b)(1)(E)(iv).

iii. *Service by other means.* In addition to, and not in lieu of, service by e-mail, service may also be made upon attorneys by any of the means specified in FL ST J ADMIN Rule 2.516(b)(2). Service on and by all parties who are not represented by an attorney and who do not designate an e-mail address, and on and by all attorneys excused from e-mail service, must be made by delivering a copy of the document or by mailing it to the party or attorney at their last known address or, if no address is known, by leaving it with the clerk of the court. Service by mail is complete upon mailing. Delivery of a copy within FL ST J ADMIN Rule 2.516 is complete upon:

- Handing it to the attorney or to the party,
- Leaving it at the attorney's or party's office with a clerk or other person in charge thereof,
- If there is no one in charge, leaving it in a conspicuous place therein,
- If the office is closed or the person to be served has no office, leaving it at the person's usual place of abode with some person of his or her family above fifteen (15) years of age and informing such person of the contents, or
- Transmitting it by facsimile to the attorney's or party's office with a cover sheet containing the sender's name, firm, address, telephone number, and facsimile number, and the number of pages transmitted. When service is made by facsimile, a copy must also be served by any other method permitted by FL ST J ADMIN Rule 2.516. Facsimile service occurs when transmission is complete. FL ST J ADMIN Rule 2.516(b)(2)(A) through FL ST J ADMIN Rule 2.516(b)(2)(E).
- Service by delivery after 5:00 p.m. must be deemed to have been made by mailing on the date of delivery. FL ST J ADMIN Rule 2.516(b)(2)(F).

c. *Service; Numerous defendants.* In actions when the parties are unusually numerous, the court may regulate the service contemplated by the Florida Rules of Judicial Administration on motion or on its own initiative in such manner as may be found to be just and reasonable. FL ST J ADMIN Rule 2.516(c).

d. *Service by clerk.* Service of notices and other documents required to be made by the clerk must also be done as provided in FL ST J ADMIN Rule 2.516(b). FL ST J ADMIN Rule 2.516(g).

G. Hearings

1. *Regularly scheduled hearings*

a. *Available hearing time.* Each attorney shall utilize the courts web page under Judicial Automated

Calendaring System, for available hearing time and the judge's schedule before telephoning the judicial assistant. FL ST 9 J CIR SECTION 10(A)(1).

b. *Scheduling hearings.* The hearing will be scheduled with the judge's judicial assistant. Written or fax notice must be received in opposing counsel's office at least four (4) working days before the hearing. FL ST 9 J CIR SECTION 10(A)(2).

c. *Presentation of proposed order.* Moving counsel must present a proposed order with space for ruling left blank at the conclusion of the hearing and must serve conformed copies on all other counsel and unrepresented parties. FL ST 9 J CIR SECTION 10(A)(3).

2. *Uniform motion calendar*

a. *Contacting judge's office on short matters.* Counsel should contact the judge's office to ascertain whether short matters are heard by the specific division. FL ST 9 J CIR SECTION 10(C)(1).

b. *Motions suitable for hearing.* Types of motions suitable for hearing on the motion calendar are simple motions to dismiss complaints with only one or two counts, to strike one or two affirmative defenses, for more definite statement, to amend pleadings, to compel discovery, for protective order, objections to IME, etc. Complex motions, motions requiring testimony or motions for summary judgment (except uncontested mortgage foreclosures), or more than two motions to be heard at one time should not be scheduled on this calendar and will not be heard by the Court. FL ST 9 J CIR SECTION 10(C)(2).

3. *Other motion hearings.* All other motions should be specially set through the judge's judicial assistant for a date and time certain. Requests for hearing time in excess of one (1) hour will require special permission of the judge obtained through the judicial assistant or by personal appearance of counsel at ex parte time. FL ST 9 J CIR SECTION 10(D).

4. *Cancelling hearings.* Only the attorney who noticed it can cancel a hearing. If a hearing becomes unnecessary after it has been noticed, the judge's judicial assistant and all other counsel must be notified immediately and effectively that the hearing is canceled. FL ST 9 J CIR SECTION 11(E).

5. *Communication equipment*

a. *Definition.* Communication equipment means a conference telephone or other electronic device that permits all those appearing or participating to hear and speak to each other, provided that all conversation of all parties is audible to all persons present. FL ST J ADMIN Rule 2.530(a).

b. *Use by all parties.* A county or circuit court judge may, upon the court's own motion or upon the written request of a party, direct that communication equipment be used for a motion hearing, pretrial conference, or a status conference. A judge must give notice to the parties and consider any objections they may have to the use of communication equipment before directing that communication equipment be used. The decision to use communication equipment over the objection of parties will be in the sound discretion of the trial court, except as noted below. FL ST J ADMIN Rule 2.530(b).

i. Counsel or unrepresented parties may arrange through the judge's judicial assistant to appear by telephone at a scheduled time and date certain hearing. The published practices and procedures of the individual judge should be reviewed or if not available, the judge should be contacted to determine the policy on telephonic appearances. If two or more attorneys are to appear by telephone, one of them should arrange to connect the other attorney or attorneys on a conference call. FL ST 9 J CIR SECTION 10(E).

c. *Use only by requesting party.* A county or circuit court judge may, upon the written request of a party upon reasonable notice to all other parties, permit a requesting party to participate through communication equipment in a scheduled motion hearing; however, any such request (except in criminal, juvenile, and appellate proceedings) must be granted, absent a showing of good cause to deny the same, where the hearing is set for not longer than fifteen (15) minutes. FL ST J ADMIN Rule 2.530(c).

d. *Testimony*

i. *Generally.* A county or circuit court judge, general magistrate, special magistrate, or hearing officer may allow testimony to be taken through communication equipment if all parties consent or if permitted by another applicable rule of procedure. FL ST J ADMIN Rule 2.530(d)(1).

ii. *Procedure.* Any party desiring to present testimony through communication equipment shall, prior to the hearing or trial at which the testimony is to be presented, contact all parties to determine whether each party consents to this form of testimony. The party seeking to present the testimony shall move for permission to present testimony through communication equipment, which motion shall set forth good cause as to why the testimony should be allowed in this form. FL ST J ADMIN Rule 2.530(d)(2).

iii. *Oath.* Testimony may be taken through communication equipment only if a notary public or other person authorized to administer oaths in the witness's jurisdiction is present with the witness and administers the oath consistent with the laws of the jurisdiction. FL ST J ADMIN Rule 2.530(d)(3).

iv. *Confrontation rights.* In juvenile and criminal proceedings the defendant must make an informed waiver of any confrontation rights that may be abridged by the use of communication equipment. FL ST J ADMIN Rule 2.530(d)(4).

v. *Video testimony.* If the testimony to be presented utilizes video conferencing or comparable two-way visual capabilities, the court in its discretion may modify the procedures set forth in FL ST J ADMIN Rule 2.530 to accommodate the technology utilized. FL ST J ADMIN Rule 2.530(d)(5).

e. *Burden of expense.* The cost for the use of the communication equipment is the responsibility of the requesting party unless otherwise directed by the court. FL ST J ADMIN Rule 2.530(e).

H. Forms

1. Official Motion to Strike Forms for Florida

a. Caption. FL ST RCP Form 1.901.

b. Notice of compliance when constitutional challenge is brought. FL ST RCP Form 1.975.

2. Motion to Strike Forms for Florida

a. Motion to strike. FL-PP § 2:128.

b. Form for motion to strike. FL-RCPF R 1.140(802).

c. Form for motion to strike insufficient pleading. FL-RCPF R 1.140(803).

d. Form for motion to strike claim for business or financial losses. FL-RCPF R 1.140(804).

e. Motion; Strike, complaint signed by corporation. FL-PRACFORM § 7:176.

f. Motion; Strike, defenses. FL-PRACFORM § 7:177.

g. Motion; Strike, ejectment chain of title. FL-PRACFORM § 7:178.

h. Motion; Strike, pleading, departure. FL-PRACFORM § 7:180.

i. Motion; Strike, pleading, improper signature. FL-PRACFORM § 7:181.

j. Motion; Strike, sham pleading. FL-PRACFORM § 7:182.

k. Motion; Strike, sham, defenses, statute of limitations and failure of consideration. FL-PRACFORM § 7:183.

l. Motion; Strike, third party complaint. FL-PRACFORM § 7:184.

I. Checklist

(I) ❑ Matters to be considered by moving party

(a) ❑ Required documents

(1) ❑ Notice of hearing/Motion

(2) ❑ Certificate of service

- (b) ❑ Supplemental documents
  - (1) ❑ Proposed order
  - (2) ❑ Notice of constitutional question
- (c) ❑ Time for making motion
  - (1) ❑ A party may move to strike or the court may strike redundant, immaterial, impertinent, or scandalous matter from any pleading at any time
  - (2) ❑ If a pleading sets forth a claim for relief to which the adverse party is not required to serve a responsive pleading, the adverse party may assert any defense in law or fact to that claim for relief at the trial, except that the objection of failure to state a legal defense in an answer or reply shall be asserted by motion to strike the defense within twenty (20) days after service of the answer or reply
  - (3) ❑ If a party deems any pleading or part thereof filed by another party to be a sham, that party may move to strike the pleading or part thereof before the cause is set for trial
  - (4) ❑ A copy of any written motion which may not be heard ex parte and a copy of the notice of the hearing thereof shall be served a reasonable time before the time specified for the hearing

(II) ❑ Matters to be considered by opposing party

- (a) ❑ Required documents
  - (1) ❑ Response to motion
  - (2) ❑ Certificate of service
- (b) ❑ Supplemental documents
  - (1) ❑ Proposed order
  - (2) ❑ Notice of constitutional question
- (c) ❑ Time for service and filing of opposition
  - (1) ❑ No time specified for responding to a motion

Motions, Oppositions and Replies
Motion for Leave to Amend

Document Last Updated January 2013

A. Applicable Rules

1. *State rules*
   - a. Rules of court. FL ST RCP Rule 1.010; FL ST J ADMIN Rule 2.110.
   - b. Nonverification of pleadings. FL ST RCP Rule 1.030.
   - c. Process. FL ST RCP Rule 1.070.
   - d. Service and filing of pleadings, orders, and documents. FL ST RCP Rule 1.080.
   - e. Time. FL ST RCP Rule 1.090.
   - f. Pleadings and motions. FL ST RCP Rule 1.100.
   - g. Defenses. FL ST RCP Rule 1.140.
   - h. Motions. FL ST RCP Rule 1.160.
   - i. Amended and supplemental pleadings. FL ST RCP Rule 1.190.
   - j. Relief from judgment, decrees, or orders. FL ST RCP Rule 1.540.
   - k. Mediation and arbitration. FL ST RCP Rule 1.700; FL ST RCP Rule 1.710; FL ST RCP Rule 1.720; FL ST RCP Rule 1.730; FL ST RCP Rule 1.750; FL ST RCP Rule 1.800; FL ST RCP Rule 1.810; FL ST RCP Rule 1.820; FL ST RCP Rule 1.830.

l. Forms. FL ST RCP Rule 1.900.
m. Minimization of the filing of sensitive information. FL ST J ADMIN Rule 2.425.
n. Retention of court records. FL ST J ADMIN Rule 2.430.
o. Foreign attorneys. FL ST J ADMIN Rule 2.510.
p. Signature of attorneys and parties. FL ST J ADMIN Rule 2.515.
q. Paper. FL ST J ADMIN Rule 2.520.
r. Electronic filing. FL ST J ADMIN Rule 2.525.
s. Accessibility of information and technology. FL ST J ADMIN Rule 2.526.
t. Communication equipment. FL ST J ADMIN Rule 2.530.
u. Court reporting. FL ST J ADMIN Rule 2.535.
v. Requests for accommodations by persons with disabilities. FL ST J ADMIN Rule 2.540.

2. *Local rules*
   a. Hearings. FL ST 9 J CIR SECTION 10.
   b. Motion practice generally. FL ST 9 J CIR SECTION 11.
   c. Orders and judgments. FL ST 9 J CIR SECTION 12.
   d. Alternative dispute resolution. FL ST 9 J CIR SECTION 15.
   e. Business court procedures. FL ST 9 J CIR ORANGE CIV SECTION 1.

B. Timing

1. *Amended pleadings as a matter of course.* A party may amend a pleading once as a matter of course at any time before a responsive pleading is served or, if the pleading is one to which no responsive pleading is permitted and the action has not been placed on the trial calendar, may amend it at any time within twenty (20) days after it is served. Otherwise a party may amend a pleading only by leave of court or by written consent of the adverse party. FL ST RCP Rule 1.190(a).
2. *Amended pleadings with leave of court.* Leave of court shall be given freely when justice so requires. FL ST RCP Rule 1.190(a). Under the Florida Rules of Civil Procedure, there is no time limit as to when an amendment with leave of court may be sought. Amendments of the pleadings may be permitted, with the court's discretion, at any stage of the proceedings in furtherance of justice. McSwiggan v. Edson, 186 So.2d 13, 15 (Fla. 1966); FL-PP § 2:153. Nevertheless, the liberality in permitting amendment of pleadings diminishes as the case progresses to trial. Versen v. Versen, 347 So.2d 1047, 1050 (Fla. 4th DCA 1977); FL-PP § 2:153.
3. *Claims for punitive damages.* A motion for leave to amend a pleading to assert a claim for punitive damages can be filed separately and before the supporting evidence or proffer, but each shall be served on all parties at least twenty (20) days before the hearing. FL ST RCP Rule 1.190(f).
4. *Post motion for leave to amend*
   a. If the court permits or requires an amended or responsive pleading or a more definite statement, the pleading or statement shall be served within ten (10) days after notice of the court's action. FL ST RCP Rule 1.140(a)(4).
   b. When a motion for leave to amend with the attached proposed amended complaint is filed, the one hundred twenty (120) day period for service of amended complaints on the new party or parties shall begin upon the entry of an order granting leave to amend. FL ST RCP Rule 1.070(j).
5. *General motion timing.* A copy of any written motion which may not be heard ex parte and a copy of the notice of the hearing thereof shall be served a reasonable time before the time specified for the hearing. FL ST RCP Rule 1.090(d).
   a. Each attorney shall utilize the courts web page under Judicial Automated Calendaring System, for available hearing time and the judge's schedule before telephoning the judicial assistant. FL ST 9 J CIR SECTION 10(A)(1).

b. The hearing will be scheduled with the judge's judicial assistant. Written or fax notice must be received in opposing counsel's office at least four (4) working days before the hearing. FL ST 9 J CIR SECTION 10(A)(2).

   i. Counsel who serves a memorandum or authority list first should also include a copy of the motion, any papers to which it is addressed, and the response, if any. In order for the judge to properly review a submission in advance, it must be received in the judge's office at least three (3) working days before the hearing. FL ST 9 J CIR SECTION 11(B).

c. *Obtaining hearing times*

   i. If the motion is one which might be resolved by stipulation or agreed order, moving counsel must explore that possibility with opposing counsel before reserving hearing time. FL ST 9 J CIR SECTION 11(C)(1).

   ii. If at all possible, hearing time for complex motions or several motions to be heard at one time should be cleared with all affected counsel so as to avoid calendar conflicts. FL ST 9 J CIR SECTION 11(C)(1).

   iii. If hearing time cannot be coordinated with opposing counsel, attorneys shall appear at ex parte to resolve the issue. FL ST 9 J CIR SECTION 11(C)(1).

6. *Computation of time*

a. *Generally.* Computation of time shall be governed by FL ST J ADMIN Rule 2.514. FL ST RCP Rule 1.090(a). The following rules apply in computing time periods specified in any rule of procedure, local rule, court order, or statute that does not specify a method of computing time. FL ST J ADMIN Rule 2.514(a).

   i. *Period stated in days or a longer unit.* When the period is stated in days or a longer unit of time (A) exclude the day of the event that triggers the period; (B) count every day, including intermediate Saturdays, Sundays, and legal holidays; and (C) include the last day of the period, but if the last day is a Saturday, Sunday, or legal holiday, or falls within any period of time extended through an order of the chief justice under FL ST J ADMIN Rule 2.205(a)(2)(B)(iv), the period continues to run until the end of the next day that is not a Saturday, Sunday, or legal holiday and does not fall within any period of time extended through an order of the chief justice. FL ST J ADMIN Rule 2.514(a)(1).

   ii. *Period stated in hours.* When the period is stated in hours (A) begin counting immediately on the occurrence of the event that triggers the period; (B) count every hour, including hours during intermediate Saturdays, Sundays, and legal holidays; and (C) if the period would end on a Saturday, Sunday, or legal holiday, or during any period of time extended through an order of the chief justice under FL ST J ADMIN Rule 2.205(a)(2)(B)(iv), the period continues to run until the same time on the next day that is not a Saturday, Sunday, or legal holiday and does not fall within any period of time extended through an order of the chief justice. FL ST J ADMIN Rule 2.514(a)(2).

   iii. *Period stated in days less than seven (7) days.* When the period stated in days is less than seven (7) days, intermediate Saturdays, Sundays, and legal holidays shall be excluded in the computation. FL ST J ADMIN Rule 2.514(a)(3).

   iv. *"Last day" defined.* Unless a different time is set by a statute, local rule, or court order, the last day ends (A) for electronic filing or for service by any means, at midnight; and (B) for filing by other means, when the clerk's office is scheduled to close. FL ST J ADMIN Rule 2.514(a)(4).

   v. *"Next day" defined.* The "next day" is determined by continuing to count forward when the period is measured after an event and backward when measured before an event. FL ST J ADMIN Rule 2.514(a)(5).

   vi. *"Legal holiday" defined.* "Legal holiday" means (A) the day set aside by FL ST § 110.117, for observing New Year's Day, Martin Luther King, Jr.'s Birthday, Memorial Day, Independence Day, Labor Day, Veterans' Day, Thanksgiving Day, the Friday after Thanksgiving Day, or Christmas Day, and (B) any day observed as a holiday by the clerk's office or as designated by the chief judge. FL ST J ADMIN Rule 2.514(a)(6).

b. *Additional time after service by mail or e-mail.* When a party may or must act within a specified time after service and service is made by mail or e-mail, five (5) days are added after the period that would otherwise expire under FL ST J ADMIN Rule 2.514(a). FL ST J ADMIN Rule 2.514(b).

c. *Enlargement.* When an act is required or allowed to be done at or within a specified time by order of court, by the Florida Rules of Civil Procedure, or by notice given thereunder, for cause shown the court at any time in its discretion (1) with or without notice, may order the period enlarged if request therefor is made before the expiration of the period originally prescribed or as extended by a previous order, or (2) upon motion made and notice after the expiration of the specified period, may permit the act to be done when failure to act was the result of excusable neglect, but it may not extend the time for making a motion for new trial, for rehearing, or to alter or amend a judgment; making a motion for relief from a judgment under FL ST RCP Rule 1.540(b); taking an appeal or filing a petition for certiorari; or making a motion for a directed verdict. FL ST RCP Rule 1.090(b).

d. *Unaffected by expiration of term.* The period of time provided for the doing of any act or the taking of any proceeding shall not be affected or limited by the continued existence or expiration of a term of court. The continued existence or expiration of a term of court in no way affects the power of a court to do any act or take any proceeding in any action which is or has been pending before it. FL ST RCP Rule 1.090(c).

C. General Requirements

1. *Motions generally*

a. *Contents.* An application to the court for an order shall be by motion which shall be made in writing unless made during a hearing or trial, shall state with particularity the grounds therefor, and shall set forth the relief or order sought. The requirement of writing is fulfilled if the motion is stated in a written notice of the hearing of the motion. All notices of hearing shall specify each motion or other matter to be heard. FL ST RCP Rule 1.100(b).

b. *Particularity requirement.* The court considers a motion in the light of the substantive law, rule or statute to make its determination. Some rules require a statement of the grounds for a motion under the rule. Failure to give the grounds will result in denial of the motion. This should be the result in all situations when the ground for the motion is not inherent in the rule. FL-PRACPROC § 9:3. The requirement is nevertheless an important one, first because of the due process notice rights of the respondent, as well as for the assistance it provides to the court in its preparation for the hearing or, absent a hearing, for disposition. 4 FLPRAC R 1.100. Every written motion shall cite the particular rule or statute and/or leading case upon which the motion is based. FL ST 9 J CIR SECTION 11(A)(1).

2. *Motion for leave to amend.* Although the Florida Rules of Civil Procedure do not specify a procedure for obtaining leave to amend, it is usually accomplished by way of a motion. FL-PP § 2:153. At any time in furtherance of justice, upon such terms as may be just, the court may permit any process, proceeding, pleading, or record to be amended or material supplemental matter to be set forth in an amended or supplemental pleading. At every stage of the action the court must disregard any error or defect in the proceedings which does not affect the substantial rights of the parties. FL ST RCP Rule 1.190(e).

a. *Permissible amendments.* Amendments can relate to the correction of mistakes, the insertion of jurisdictional averments, the correction or addition of verifications, the addition or substitution or striking out of parties, and generally the rectification of all formal defects in the pleading. The court can also allow amendments setting up an omitted counterclaim or cross-claim if the defendant failed to raise the claim through oversight, inadvertence, or excusable neglect. FL-PP § 2:151.

b. *Amendments to conform with the evidence.* When issues not raised by the pleadings are tried by express or implied consent of the parties, they shall be treated in all respects as if they had been raised in the pleadings. Such amendment of the pleadings as may be necessary to cause them to conform to the evidence and to raise these issues may be made upon motion of any party at any time, even after judgment, but failure so to amend shall not affect the result of the trial of these issues. If the evidence is objected to at the trial on the ground that it is not within the issues made by the pleadings, the court may allow the pleadings to be amended to conform with the evidence and shall do so freely when the merits of the cause are more effectually presented thereby and the objecting party fails to satisfy the court that the admission of such evidence will prejudice the objecting party in maintaining an action or defense upon the merits. FL ST RCP Rule 1.190(b).

i. The courts have been extremely liberal in permitting amendments after trial to conform pleadings to the evidence where the issues were tried by the express or implied consent of the parties. Turner v. Long, 225 So.2d 434 (Fla. 1st DCA 1969); FL-PP § 2:152.

c. *Procedure for adding parties.* Parties may be added once as a matter of course within the same time that pleadings can be so amended. If amendment by leave of court or stipulation of the parties is permitted, parties may be added in the amended pleading without further order of court. Parties may be added by order of court on its own initiative or on motion of any party at any stage of the action and on such terms as are just. FL ST RCP Rule 1.250(c).

d. *Claims for punitive damages.* A motion for leave to amend a pleading to assert a claim for punitive damages shall make a reasonable showing by evidence in the record or evidence to be proffered by the claimant that provides a reasonable basis for recovery of such damages. The motion to amend can be filed separately and before the supporting evidence or proffer, but each shall be served on all parties at least twenty (20) days before the hearing. FL ST RCP Rule 1.190(f). Leave of court to amend the complaint must be obtained before a plaintiff may assert a punitive damages claim in the complaint. Failure to do so will result in the claims being dismissed or stricken. FL-PP § 2:151.

e. *Relation back of amendments.* When the claim or defense asserted in the amended pleading arose out of the conduct, transaction, or occurrence set forth or attempted to be set forth in the original pleading, the amendment shall relate back to the date of the original pleading. FL ST RCP Rule 1.190(c).

i. The doctrine of relation back becomes critical in applying the statute of limitations. For example, it has been held that the doctrine of relation back may not be utilized to circumvent the statute of limitations to permit an amendment where a claim could have been filed as an independent action but was not timely asserted and would otherwise be barred under the statute of limitations. Cox v. Seaboard Coast Line R. Co., 360 So.2d 8 (Fla. 2d DCA 1978); FL-PP § 2:152.

3. *Arbitration and mediation*

a. *Referral to arbitration and mediation.* Except as hereinafter provided or as otherwise prohibited by law, the presiding judge may enter an order referring all or any part of a contested civil matter to mediation or arbitration. The parties to any contested civil matter may file a written stipulation to mediate or arbitrate any issue between them at any time. Such stipulation shall be incorporated into the order of referral. FL ST RCP Rule 1.700(a).

i. *Local arbitration policy.* It is the policy of the Civil Division judges to maximize the use of alternative dispute resolution procedures. Except where prohibited by statute, mediation will be ordered in all cases where jury trial is requested and in selected cases which are to be tried non-jury. Also, selected cases will be referred for court-annexed non-binding arbitration through the Orange County Bar Association Arbitration Service. Counsel may move to dispense with or defer mediation or arbitration or move to modify the referral order for good cause. FL ST 9 J CIR SECTION 15.

b. *Arbitration*

i. *Exclusions.* A civil action shall be ordered to arbitration or arbitration in conjunction with mediation upon stipulation of the parties. A civil action may be ordered to arbitration or arbitration in conjunction with mediation upon motion of any party or by the court, if the judge determines the action to be of such a nature that arbitration could be of benefit to the litigants or the court. FL ST RCP Rule 1.800.

- Under no circumstances may the following categories of actions be referred to arbitration: (1) bond estreatures; (2) habeas corpus or other extraordinary writs; (3) bond validations; (4) civil or criminal contempt; (5) such other matters as may be specified by order of the chief judge in the circuit. FL ST RCP Rule 1.800.

ii. For more information regarding arbitration, please see FL ST RCP Rule 1.810; FL ST RCP Rule 1.820; FL ST RCP Rule 1.830.

c. *Mediation.* For more information regarding mediation, please see FL ST RCP Rule 1.710; FL ST RCP Rule 1.720; FL ST RCP Rule 1.730; and FL ST RCP Rule 1.750.

4. *Rules of court*

a. *Rules of civil procedure.* The Florida Rules of Civil Procedure apply to all actions of a civil nature and all special statutory proceedings in the circuit courts and county courts except those to which the Florida Probate Rules, the Florida Family Law Rules of Procedure, or the Small Claims Rules apply. FL ST RCP Rule 1.010.

i. The form, content, procedure, and time for pleading in all special statutory proceedings shall be as prescribed by the statutes governing the proceeding unless the Florida Rules of Civil Procedure specifically provide to the contrary. FL ST RCP Rule 1.010.

ii. The Florida Rules of Civil Procedure shall be construed to secure the just, speedy, and inexpensive determination of every action. FL ST RCP Rule 1.010.

b. *Rules of judicial administration.* The Florida Rules of Judicial Administration shall apply to administrative matters in all courts to which the Florida Rules of Judicial Administration are applicable by their terms. The Florida Rules of Judicial Administration shall be construed to secure the speedy and inexpensive determination of every proceeding to which they are applicable. The Florida Rules of Judicial Administration shall supersede all conflicting rules and statutes. FL ST J ADMIN Rule 2.110. For rules specific to Business Court, please see FL ST 9 J CIR ORANGE CIV SECTION 1, et seq.

c. *Business court procedures.* For rules specific to Business Court, please see FL ST 9 J CIR ORANGE CIV SECTION 1, et seq.

D. Documents

1. *Required documents*

a. *Notice of hearing/Motion.* An application to the court for an order shall be by motion which shall be made in writing unless made during a hearing or trial, shall state with particularity the grounds therefor, and shall set forth the relief or order sought. The requirement of writing is fulfilled if the motion is stated in a written notice of the hearing of the motion. All notices of hearing shall specify each motion or other matter to be heard. FL ST RCP Rule 1.100(b). A notice calling up "all pending motions" is insufficient. FL ST 9 J CIR SECTION 11(D)(1). Additional motions should not be "piggy-backed" by cross-notice unless counsel first confirms with opposing counsel and the judge's judicial assistant that there can be sufficient additional time reserved in which to hear them. FL ST 9 J CIR SECTION 11(D)(2).

i. *Notices to persons with disabilities.* See the Format section of this KeyRules document for further information.

b. *Proposed amended pleading.* The moving party shall attach the proposed amended pleading to the motion. FL ST RCP Rule 1.190(a).

c. *Certificate of service.* When any attorney certifies in substance: "I certify that a copy hereof has been furnished to (here insert name or names and addresses used for service) by (e-mail) (delivery) (mail) (fax) on .... (date) ....__________________ Attorney" the certificate is taken as prima facie proof of such service in compliance with FL ST J ADMIN Rule 2.516. FL ST J ADMIN Rule 2.516(f).

2. *Supplemental documents*

a. *Legal memorandum.* Legal memorandums in support of or opposition to motions are optional. But if filed, counsel must furnish the judge with chambers copies of the memorandum and highlighted copies of primary legal authorities cited therein. FL ST 9 J CIR SECTION 11(B).

i. As an alternative to a memorandum, a list of primary legal authorities with highlighted copies attached may be submitted. Chambers copies and authority lists must be under cover letter referencing the case style and number and stating the date and time of the hearing. FL ST 9 J CIR SECTION 11(B).

b. *Proposed order.* The court may require that orders or judgments be prepared by a party, may require the party to furnish the court with stamped, addressed envelopes for service of the order or judgment, and may require that proposed orders and judgments be furnished to all parties before entry by the court of the order or judgment. FL ST J ADMIN Rule 2.516(h)(1).

i. Proposed orders and judgments will be prepared by the prevailing attorney unless the judge designates some other attorney or states that he or she will prepare the order or judgment. FL ST 9 J CIR SECTION 12(A)(1).

ii. When submitting proposed orders or judgments, counsel shall also include sufficient copies and self address stamped envelopes for all parties. FL ST 9 J CIR SECTION 12(A)(2).

iii. Moving counsel must present a proposed order with space for ruling left blank at the conclusion of the hearing and must serve conformed copies on all other counsel and unrepresented parties. FL ST 9 J CIR SECTION 10(A)(3).

iv. Unsigned orders or judgments should not be sent to the Clerk's office for transmission to the judge. FL ST 9 J CIR SECTION 12(D)(3).

c. *Notice of constitutional question.* A party that files a pleading, written motion, or other paper drawing into question the constitutionality of a state statute or a county or municipal charter, ordinance, or franchise must promptly (1) file a notice of constitutional question stating the question and identifying the paper that raises it; and (2) serve the notice and the pleading, written motion, or other paper drawing into question the constitutionality of a state statute or a county or municipal charter, ordinance, or franchise on the Attorney General or the state attorney of the judicial circuit in which the action is pending, by either certified or registered mail. Service of the notice and pleading, written motion, or other paper does not require joinder of the Attorney General or the state attorney as a party to the action. FL ST RCP Rule 1.071.

E. Format

1. *Documents; Type and size.* Documents subject to the exceptions set forth in FL ST J ADMIN Rule 2.525(d) shall be filed on recycled paper measuring eight and one half by eleven (8 1/2 by 11) inches. For purposes of FL ST J ADMIN Rule 2.520, paper is recycled if it contains a minimum content of fifty (50) percent waste paper. Xerographic reduction of legal-size (eight and one half by fourteen (8 1/2 by 14) inches) documents to letter size (eight and one half by eleven (8 1/2 by 11) inches) is prohibited. All other documents filed by electronic transmission shall be filed in a format capable of being printed in a format consistent with the provisions of FL ST J ADMIN Rule 2.250. FL ST J ADMIN Rule 2.520(b).

a. *Exhibits.* Any exhibit or attachment filed with pleadings or papers may be filed in its original size. FL ST J ADMIN Rule 2.520(c).

b. *Recording space.* On all papers and documents prepared and filed by the court or by any party to a proceeding which are to be recorded in the public records of any county, including but not limited to final money judgments and notices of lis pendens, a three (3) inch by three (3) inch space at the top right-hand corner on the first page and a one (1) inch by three (3) inch space at the top right-hand corner on each subsequent page shall be left blank and reserved for use by the clerk of court. FL ST J ADMIN Rule 2.520(d).

i. *Exceptions to recording space.* Any papers or documents created by persons or entities over which the filing party has no control, including but not limited to wills, codicils, trusts, or other testamentary documents; documents prepared or executed by any public officer; documents prepared, executed, acknowledged, or proved outside of the State of Florida; or documents created by State or Federal government agencies, may be filed without the space required by FL ST J ADMIN Rule 2.520. FL ST J ADMIN Rule 2.520(e).

c. *Noncompliance.* No clerk of court is permitted to refuse to file any document or paper because of noncompliance with the Florida Rules of Judicial Administration. However, upon request of the clerk of court, noncomplying documents must be resubmitted in accordance with the formatting rules. FL ST J ADMIN Rule 2.520(f).

d. *Proposed orders*

i. All orders will be on eight and a half by eleven (8 1/2 by 11) inch plain white paper (not lined or letterhead paper) and be double spaced. FL ST 9 J CIR SECTION 12(B)(1).

ii. The order must contain a title indicating what matter the order pertains to, e.g., "Order On Defendant Smith's Motion To Dismiss." FL ST 9 J CIR SECTION 12(B)(2).

iii. The preamble of the order should include the date of the hearing and what motions were heard. FL ST 9 J CIR SECTION 12(B)(3).

iv. The adjudication portion of the order should state what relief is ordered. Simply stating that "the motion is granted" without more is insufficient. FL ST 9 J CIR SECTION 12(B)(4).

v. The order should indicate the specific time period of any act ordered to be done and should state whether the time period runs from the date of the hearing or the date the order is signed or some other specified date. FL ST 9 J CIR SECTION 12(B)(5).

vi. The order should contain a full certificate of service with the complete names and addresses of the attorneys and unrepresented parties to be served. Merely showing "copies to" is insufficient. FL ST 9 J CIR SECTION 12(B)(6).

vii. If an order of dismissal is final (i.e., it disposes of the entire case) the title should contain the word "Final." When the order is not final but leaves other counts or claims against other defendants pending, it should so state in a separate paragraph. FL ST 9 J CIR SECTION 12(B)(7).

viii. When submitting stipulations, orders shall be by separate order, not attached to the stipulation. FL ST 9 J CIR SECTION 12(B)(8).

ix. Counsel preparing the Final Judgment or order should draft and circulate copies within two (2) working days of the ruling or jury verdict. If counsel preparing the Final Judgment or order gets approval as to form of the order from all counsel, the original with copies and envelopes should be sent directly to the judge with a cover letter stating all counsel agree to the form of the order or judgment. If other counsel objects to the form or cannot be reached for approval, counsel preparing the judgment or order shall notice a motion for entry of the order or judgment. If objecting counsel does not furnish the judge prior to or at the hearing with a proposed judgment or order version with copies under cover letter stating the reasons for the objection, all objections will be deemed waived. Orders and judgments should not be submitted to the judge to hold waiting for an objection. FL ST 9 J CIR SECTION 12(D).

2. *Caption.* Every pleading, motion, order, judgment, or other paper shall have a caption containing the name of the court, the file number, and except for in rem proceedings, including forfeiture proceedings, the name of the first party on each side with an appropriate indication of other parties, and a designation identifying the party filing it and its nature or the nature of the order, as the case may be. In any in rem proceeding, every pleading, motion, order, judgment, or other paper shall have a caption containing the name of the court, the file number, the style "In re" (followed by the name or general description of the property), and a designation of the person or entity filing it and its nature or the nature of the order, as the case may be. In an in rem forfeiture proceeding, the style shall be "In re forfeiture of" (followed by the name of the general description of the property). All papers filed in the action shall be styled in such a manner as to indicate clearly the subject matter of the paper and the party requesting or obtaining relief. FL ST RCP Rule 1.100(c)(1).

3. *Writing and written defined.* Writing or written means a document containing information, an application, or a stipulation. FL ST RCP Rule 1.080(c).

4. *Rule abbreviations*

   a. The Florida Rules of Civil Procedure and shall be abbreviated as Fla.R.Civ.P. FL ST RCP Rule 1.010.

   b. The Florida Rules of Judicial Administration shall be abbreviated as Fla. R. Jud. Admin. FL ST J ADMIN Rule 2.110.

5. *Nonverification.* Except when otherwise specifically provided by the Florida Rules of Civil Procedure or an applicable statute, every pleading or other document of a party represented by an attorney need not be verified or accompanied by an affidavit. FL ST RCP Rule 1.030; FL ST J ADMIN Rule 2.515(a).

6. *Unrepresented parties.* An unrepresented party must file his or her papers with the clerk and send copies

to other attorneys or unrepresented parties. All such papers must be typed double-spaced on plain white eight and a half by eleven (8 1/2 by 11) inch paper, with the name of the case and case number at the top and the party's mailing address, telephone number and FAX number, if any, below his or her signature at the end of the paper. Such unrepresented party must immediately notify the clerk and all other counsel or parties of record in writing of any change in mailing address or telephone or FAX number. Failure to promptly notify of change of address could result in a dismissal or default entered against such party. FL ST 9 J CIR SECTION 7(B)(5).

7. *Attorney signature*
   a. *Attorney signature.* Every pleading and other document of a party represented by an attorney shall be signed by at least one (1) attorney of record in that attorney's individual name whose current record Florida Bar address, telephone number, including area code, primary e-mail address and secondary e-mail addresses, if any, and Florida Bar number shall be stated, and who shall be duly licensed to practice law in Florida or who shall have received permission to appear in the particular case as provided in FL ST J ADMIN Rule 2.510. FL ST J ADMIN Rule 2.515(a).
      i. The attorney may be required by the court to give the address of, and to vouch for the attorney's authority to represent, the party. FL ST J ADMIN Rule 2.515(a).
      ii. The signature of an attorney shall constitute a certificate by the attorney that the attorney has read the pleading or other document; that to the best of the attorney's knowledge, information, and belief there is good ground to support it; and that it is not interposed for delay. FL ST J ADMIN Rule 2.515(a).
      iii. If a pleading is not signed or is signed with intent to defeat the purpose of FL ST J ADMIN Rule 2.515, it may be stricken and the action may proceed as though the pleading or other document had not been served. FL ST J ADMIN Rule 2.515(a).
   b. *Pro se litigant signature.* A party who is not represented by an attorney shall sign any pleading or other paper and state the party's address and telephone number, including area code. FL ST J ADMIN Rule 2.515(b).
   c. *Form of signature*
      i. The signatures required on pleadings and documents by FL ST J ADMIN Rule 2.515(a) and FL ST J ADMIN Rule 2.515(b) may be:
         - Original signatures;
         - Original signatures that have been reproduced by electronic means, such as on electronically transmitted documents or photocopied documents;
         - Electronic signatures using the "/s/," "s/," or "/s" formats by or at the direction of the person signing; or
         - Any other signature format authorized by general law, so long as the clerk where the proceeding is pending has the capability of receiving and has obtained approval from the Supreme Court of Florida to accept pleadings and documents with that signature format. FL ST J ADMIN Rule 2.515(c)(1).
      ii. An attorney, party, or other person who files a pleading or paper by electronic transmission that does not contain the original signature of that attorney, party, or other person shall file that identical pleading or paper in paper form containing an original signature of that attorney, party, or other person (hereinafter called the follow-up filing) immediately thereafter. The follow-up filing is not required if the Supreme Court of Florida has entered an order directing the clerk of court to discontinue accepting the follow-up filing. FL ST J ADMIN Rule 2.515(c)(2).

8. *Forms*
   a. *Process.* The forms of process, notice of lis pendens, and notice of action provided in the Florida Rules of Civil Procedure are sufficient. Variations from the forms do not void process or notices that are otherwise sufficient. FL ST RCP Rule 1.900(a).
   b. *Other forms.* The other forms provided in the Florida Rules of Civil Procedure are sufficient for the

matters that are covered by them. So long as the substance is expressed without prolixity, the forms may be varied to meet the facts of a particular case. FL ST RCP Rule 1.900(b).

c. *Formal matters.* Captions, except for the designation of the paper, are omitted from the forms provided in the Florida Rules of Civil Procedure. A general form of caption is the first form provided. Signatures are omitted from pleadings and motions. FL ST RCP Rule 1.900(c).

9. *Notices to persons with disabilities.* All notices of court proceedings to be held in a public facility, and all process compelling appearance at such proceedings, shall include the following statement in bold face, fourteen (14) point Times New Roman or Courier font: "If you are a person with a disability who needs any accommodation in order to participate in this proceeding, you are entitled, at no cost to you, to the provision of certain assistance. Please contact [identify applicable court personnel by name, address, and telephone number] at least seven (7) days before your scheduled court appearance, or immediately upon receiving this notification if the time before the scheduled appearance is less than seven (7) days; if you are hearing or voice impaired, call 711." FL ST J ADMIN Rule 2.540(c)(1).

10. *Minimization of the filing of sensitive information*

   a. *Limitations for court filings.* Unless authorized by FL ST J ADMIN Rule 2.425(b), statute, another rule of court, or the court orders otherwise, designated sensitive information filed with the court must be limited to the following format:

      i. The initials of a person known to be a minor;

      ii. The year of birth of a person's birth date;

      iii. No portion of any: Social security number, Bank account number, Credit card account number, Charge account number, or Debit account number;

      iv. The last four digits of any: Taxpayer identification number (TIN), Employee identification number, Driver's license number, Passport number, Telephone number, Financial account number, except as set forth in FL ST J ADMIN Rule 2.425(a)(3), Brokerage account number, Insurance policy account number, Loan account number, Customer account number, or Patient or health care number;

      v. A truncated version of any: Email address, Computer user name, Password, or Personal identification number (PIN); and

      vi. A truncated version of any other sensitive information as provided by court order. FL ST J ADMIN Rule 2.425(a).

   b. *Exceptions.* FL ST J ADMIN Rule 2.425(a) does not apply to the following:

      i. An account number which identifies the property alleged to be the subject of a proceeding;

      ii. The record of an administrative or agency proceeding;

      iii. The record in appellate or review proceedings;

      iv. The birth date of a minor whenever the birth date is necessary for the court to establish or maintain subject matter jurisdiction;

      v. The name of a minor in any order relating to parental responsibility, time-sharing, or child support;

      vi. The name of a minor in any document or order affecting the minor's ownership of real property;

      vii. The birth date of a party in a writ of attachment or notice to payor;

      viii. In traffic and criminal proceedings: a pro se filing; a court filing that is related to a criminal matter or investigation and that is prepared before the filing of a criminal charge or is not filed as part of any docketed criminal case; an arrest or search warrant or any information in support thereof; a charging document and an affidavit or other documents filed in support of any charging document, including any driving records; a statement of particulars; discovery material introduced into evidence or otherwise filed with the court; and all information necessary for the proper issuance and execution of a subpoena duces tecum;

      ix. Information used by the clerk for case maintenance purposes or the courts for case management purposes; and

x. Information which is relevant and material to an issue before the court. FL ST J ADMIN Rule 2.425(b).

c. *Remedies.* Upon motion by a party or interested person or sua sponte by the court, the court may order remedies, sanctions or both for a violation of FL ST J ADMIN Rule 2.425(a). Following notice and an opportunity to respond, the court may impose sanctions if such filing was not made in good faith. FL ST J ADMIN Rule 2.425(c).

d. *Motions not restricted.* FL ST J ADMIN Rule 2.425 does not restrict a party's right to move for protective order, to move to file documents under seal, or to request a determination of the confidentiality of records. FL ST J ADMIN Rule 2.425(d).

e. *Application.* FL ST J ADMIN Rule 2.425 does not affect the application of constitutional provisions, statutes, or rules of court regarding confidential information or access to public information. FL ST J ADMIN Rule 2.425(e).

F. Filing and Service Requirements

1. *Filing requirements.* All original documents must be filed with the court either before service or immediately thereafter, unless otherwise provided for by general law or other rules. If the original of any bond or other document is not placed in the court file, a certified copy must be so placed by the clerk. FL ST J ADMIN Rule 2.516(d). All documents shall be filed in conformity with the requirements of FL ST J ADMIN Rule 2.525. FL ST RCP Rule 1.080(b). All documents filed in any court shall be filed by electronic transmission in accordance with FL ST J ADMIN Rule 2.525. "Documents" means pleadings, motions, petitions, memoranda, briefs, notices, exhibits, declarations, affidavits, orders, judgments, decrees, writs, opinions, and any other paper or writing submitted to a court. FL ST J ADMIN Rule 2.520(a). All documents that are court records, as defined in FL ST J ADMIN Rule 2.430(a)(1), must be filed by electronic transmission, provided that: (1) the clerk has the ability to accept and retain such documents; (2) the clerk or the chief judge of the circuit has requested permission to accept documents filed by electronic transmission; and (3) the supreme court has entered an order granting permission to the clerk to accept documents filed by electronic transmission. FL ST J ADMIN Rule 2.525(c)(1).

a. *Definition.* "Electronic transmission of documents" means the sending of information by electronic signals to, by or from a court or clerk, which when received can be transformed and stored or transmitted on paper, microfilm, magnetic storage device, optical imaging system, CD-ROM, flash drive, other electronic data storage system, server, case maintenance system ("CM"), electronic court filing ("ECF") system, statewide or local electronic portal ("e-portal"), or other electronic record keeping system authorized by the supreme court in a format sufficient to communicate the information on the original document in a readable format. Electronic transmission of documents includes electronic mail ("e-mail") and any internet-based transmission procedure, and may include procedures allowing for documents to be signed or verified by electronic means. FL ST J ADMIN Rule 2.525(a).

i. The filing of documents with the court as required by the Florida Rules of Judicial Administration must be made by filing them with the clerk in accordance with FL ST J ADMIN Rule 2.525, except that the judge may permit documents to be filed with the judge, in which event the judge must note the filing date before him or her on the documents and transmit them to the clerk. The date of filing is that shown on the face of the document by the judge's notation or the clerk's time stamp, whichever is earlier. FL ST J ADMIN Rule 2.516(e).

b. *Application.* Any court or clerk of the court may accept the electronic transmission of documents for filing after the clerk, together with input from the chief judge of the circuit, has obtained approval of the procedures and program for doing so from the Supreme Court of Florida. FL ST J ADMIN Rule 2.525(b).

c. *Exceptions*

i. Paper documents and other submissions may be manually submitted to the clerk or court:

- When the clerk does not have the ability to accept and retain documents by electronic filing or has not had ECF Procedures approved by the supreme court;
- For filing by any self-represented party or any self-represented nonparty unless specific

ECF Procedures provide a means to file documents electronically. However, any self-represented nonparty that is a governmental or public agency and any other agency, partnership, corporation, or business entity acting on behalf of any governmental or public agency may file documents by electronic transmission if such entity has the capability of filing documents electronically;

- For filing by attorneys excused from e-mail service in accordance with FL ST J ADMIN Rule 2.516(b);
- When submitting evidentiary exhibits or filing non-documentary materials;
- When the filing involves documents in excess of twenty-five (25) megabytes (25MB) in size. For such filings, documents may be transmitted using an electronic storage medium that the clerk has the ability to accept, which may include a CD-ROM, flash drive, or similar storage medium;
- When filed in open court, as permitted by the court;
- When paper filing is permitted by any approved statewide or local ECF procedures; and
- If any court determines that justice so requires. FL ST J ADMIN Rule 2.525(d).

ii. Any document in paper form submitted under FL ST J ADMIN Rule 2.525(d) is filed when it is received by the clerk or court and the clerk shall immediately thereafter convert any filed paper document to an electronic document. "Convert to an electronic document" means optically capturing an image of a paper document and using character recognition software to recover as much of the document's text as practicable and then indexing and storing the document in the official court file. FL ST J ADMIN Rule 2.525(c)(4).

iii. Any storage medium submitted under FL ST J ADMIN Rule 2.525(d)(5) is filed when received by the clerk or court and the clerk shall immediately thereafter transfer the electronic documents from the storage device to the official court file. FL ST J ADMIN Rule 2.525(c)(5).

iv. If the filer of any paper document authorized under FL ST J ADMIN Rule 2.525(d) provides a self-addressed, postage-paid envelope for return of the paper document after it is converted to electronic form by the clerk, the clerk shall place the paper document in the envelope and deposit it in the mail. Except when a paper document is required to be maintained, the clerk may recycle any filed paper document that is not to be returned to the filer. FL ST J ADMIN Rule 2.525(c)(6).

v. The clerk may convert any paper document filed before the effective date of FL ST J ADMIN Rule 2.525 to an electronic document. Unless the clerk is required to maintain the paper document, if the paper document has been converted to an electronic document by the clerk, the paper document is no longer part of the official court file and may be removed and recycled. FL ST J ADMIN Rule 2.525(c)(7).

d. *Unrepresented parties.* An unrepresented party must file his or her papers with the clerk and send copies to other attorneys or unrepresented parties. FL ST 9 J CIR SECTION 7(B)(5).

i. An unrepresented party may not communicate privately with the judge either by letter, telephone, in person or otherwise. FL ST 9 J CIR SECTION 7(B)(4).

ii. Copies of legal papers or other written materials should not be sent to the judge unless specifically requested by the judge or required by the local administrative procedures. Any unrequested or non-required papers or materials sent to a judge may not be read but may be returned to the sender or placed unread into the court file. FL ST 9 J CIR SECTION 7(B)(4).

e. *Official court file.* For information on what constitutes the official court file, please see FL ST J ADMIN Rule 2.525(c)(2), FL ST J ADMIN Rule 2.525(c)(3).

f. *Administration.* All attorneys, parties, or other persons using this rule to file documents are required to make arrangements with the court or clerk for the payment of any charges authorized by general law or the supreme court before filing any document by electronic transmission. FL ST J ADMIN Rule 2.525(f)(2).

g. *Filing date.* The filing date for an electronically transmitted document is the date and time that such

filing is acknowledged by an electronic stamp or otherwise, pursuant to any procedure set forth in any ECF Procedures approved by the supreme court, or the date the last page of such filing is received by the court or clerk. FL ST J ADMIN Rule 2.525(f)(3).

h. *Accessibility.* All documents transmitted in any electronic form under FL ST J ADMIN Rule 2.525 must comply with the accessibility requirements of FL ST J ADMIN Rule 2.526. FL ST J ADMIN Rule 2.525(g).

2. *Service requirements.* Every pleading subsequent to the initial pleading, all orders, and every other document filed in the action must be served in conformity with the requirements of FL ST J ADMIN Rule 2.516. FL ST RCP Rule 1.080(a).

a. *Service; When required.* Unless the court otherwise orders, or a statute or supreme court administrative order specifies a different means of service, every pleading subsequent to the initial pleading and every other document filed in any court proceeding, except applications for witness subpoenas and documents served by formal notice or required to be served in the manner provided for service of formal notice, must be served in accordance with FL ST J ADMIN Rule 2.516 on each party. No service need be made on parties against whom a default has been entered, except that pleadings asserting new or additional claims against them must be served in the manner provided for service of summons. FL ST J ADMIN Rule 2.516(a).

i. Counsel who serves a memorandum or authority list first should also include a copy of the motion, any papers to which it is addressed, and the response, if any. In order for the judge to properly review a submission in advance, it must be received in the judge's office at least three (3) working days before the hearing. FL ST 9 J CIR SECTION 11(B).

b. *Service; How made.* When service is required or permitted to be made upon a party represented by an attorney, service must be made upon the attorney unless service upon the party is ordered by the court. FL ST J ADMIN Rule 2.516(b).

i. *Service by electronic mail ("e-mail").* All documents required or permitted to be served on another party must be served by e-mail, unless FL ST J ADMIN Rule 2.516 otherwise provides. When, in addition to service by e-mail, the sender also utilizes another means of service provided for in FL ST J ADMIN Rule 2.516(b)(2), any differing time limits and other provisions applicable to that other means of service control. FL ST J ADMIN Rule 2.516(b)(1). Any document electronically transmitted to a court or clerk must also be served on all parties and interested persons in accordance with the applicable rules of court. FL ST J ADMIN Rule 2.525(e)(2).

- *Service on attorneys.* Upon appearing in a proceeding, an attorney must serve a designation of a primary e-mail address and may designate no more than two (2) secondary e-mail addresses. Thereafter, service must be directed to all designated e-mail addresses in that proceeding. Every document filed by an attorney thereafter must include the primary e-mail address of that attorney and any secondary e-mail addresses. If an attorney does not designate any e-mail address for service, documents may be served on that attorney at the e-mail address on record with The Florida Bar. FL ST J ADMIN Rule 2.516(b)(1)(A).
- *Exception to e-mail service on attorneys.* Service by an attorney on another attorney must be made by e-mail unless excused by the court. Upon motion by an attorney demonstrating that the attorney has no e-mail account and lacks access to the Internet at the attorney's office, the court may excuse the attorney from the requirements of e-mail service. Service on and by an attorney excused by the court from e-mail service must be by the means provided in FL ST J ADMIN Rule 2.516(b)(2). FL ST J ADMIN Rule 2.516(b)(1)(B).
- *Service on and by parties not represented by an attorney.* Any party not represented by an attorney may serve a designation of a primary e-mail address and also may designate no more than two (2) secondary e-mail addresses to which service must be directed in that proceeding by the means provided in FL ST J ADMIN Rule 2.516(b)(1). If a party not represented by an attorney does not designate an e-mail address for service in a proceeding, service on and by that party must be by the means provided in FL ST J ADMIN Rule 2.516(b)(2). FL ST J ADMIN Rule 2.516(b)(1)(C).

- *Time of service.* Service by e-mail is complete when it is sent. FL ST J ADMIN Rule 2.516(b)(1)(D). An e-mail is deemed served on the date it is sent. FL ST J ADMIN Rule 2.516(b)(1)(D)(i). If the sender learns that the e-mail did not reach the address of the person to be served, the sender must immediately send another copy by e-mail, or by a means authorized by FL ST J ADMIN Rule 2.516(b)(2). FL ST J ADMIN Rule 2.516(b)(1)(D)(ii). E-mail service is treated as service by mail for the computation of time. FL ST J ADMIN Rule 2.516(b)(1)(D)(iii).

ii. *Format of e-mail for service.* Service of a document by e-mail is made by attaching a copy of the document in PDF format to an e-mail sent to all addresses designated by the attorney or party. FL ST J ADMIN Rule 2.516(b)(1)(E).

- All documents served by e-mail must be attached to an e-mail message containing a subject line beginning with the words "SERVICE OF COURT DOCUMENT" in all capital letters, followed by the case number of the proceeding in which the documents are being served. FL ST J ADMIN Rule 2.516(b)(1)(E)(i).
- The body of the e-mail must identify the court in which the proceeding is pending, the case number, the name of the initial party on each side, the title of each document served with that e-mail, and the sender's name and telephone number. FL ST J ADMIN Rule 2.516(b)(1)(E)(ii).
- Any document served by e-mail may be signed by the "/s/" format, as long as the filed original is signed in accordance with the applicable rule of procedure. FL ST J ADMIN Rule 2.516(b)(1)(E)(iii).
- Any e-mail which, together with its attached documents, exceeds five megabytes (5MB) in size, must be divided and sent as separate e-mails, no one of which may exceed five megabytes (5MB) in size and each of which must be sequentially numbered in the subject line. FL ST J ADMIN Rule 2.516(b)(1)(E)(iv).

iii. *Service by other means.* In addition to, and not in lieu of, service by e-mail, service may also be made upon attorneys by any of the means specified in FL ST J ADMIN Rule 2.516(b)(2). Service on and by all parties who are not represented by an attorney and who do not designate an e-mail address, and on and by all attorneys excused from e-mail service, must be made by delivering a copy of the document or by mailing it to the party or attorney at their last known address or, if no address is known, by leaving it with the clerk of the court. Service by mail is complete upon mailing. Delivery of a copy within FL ST J ADMIN Rule 2.516 is complete upon:

- Handing it to the attorney or to the party,
- Leaving it at the attorney's or party's office with a clerk or other person in charge thereof,
- If there is no one in charge, leaving it in a conspicuous place therein,
- If the office is closed or the person to be served has no office, leaving it at the person's usual place of abode with some person of his or her family above fifteen (15) years of age and informing such person of the contents, or
- Transmitting it by facsimile to the attorney's or party's office with a cover sheet containing the sender's name, firm, address, telephone number, and facsimile number, and the number of pages transmitted. When service is made by facsimile, a copy must also be served by any other method permitted by FL ST J ADMIN Rule 2.516. Facsimile service occurs when transmission is complete. FL ST J ADMIN Rule 2.516(b)(2)(A) through FL ST J ADMIN Rule 2.516(b)(2)(E).
- Service by delivery after 5:00 p.m. must be deemed to have been made by mailing on the date of delivery. FL ST J ADMIN Rule 2.516(b)(2)(F).

c. *Service; Numerous defendants.* In actions when the parties are unusually numerous, the court may regulate the service contemplated by the Florida Rules of Judicial Administration on motion or on its own initiative in such manner as may be found to be just and reasonable. FL ST J ADMIN Rule 2.516(c).

d. *Service by clerk.* Service of notices and other documents required to be made by the clerk must also be done as provided in FL ST J ADMIN Rule 2.516(b). FL ST J ADMIN Rule 2.516(g).

G. Hearings

1. *Evidentiary hearing.* A motion by the defendant to dismiss or transfer on the ground of improper venue raises issues of fact which must be resolved by an evidentiary hearing, unless the complaint shows on its face that venue is improper. Kinetiks.Com, Inc. v. Sweeney, 789 So.2d 1221 (Fla. 1st DCA 2001); FLJUR VENUE § 100.

2. *Preliminary hearings.* The defense of improper venue, whether made in a pleading or by motion shall be heard and determined before trial on application of any party unless the court orders that the hearing and determination shall be deferred until the trial. FL ST RCP Rule 1.140(d).

3. *Regularly scheduled hearings*

   a. *Available hearing time.* Each attorney shall utilize the courts web page under Judicial Automated Calendaring System, for available hearing time and the judge's schedule before telephoning the judicial assistant. FL ST 9 J CIR SECTION 10(A)(1).

   b. *Scheduling hearings.* The hearing will be scheduled with the judge's judicial assistant. Written or fax notice must be received in opposing counsel's office at least four (4) working days before the hearing. FL ST 9 J CIR SECTION 10(A)(2).

   c. *Presentation of proposed order.* Moving counsel must present a proposed order with space for ruling left blank at the conclusion of the hearing and must serve conformed copies on all other counsel and unrepresented parties. FL ST 9 J CIR SECTION 10(A)(3).

4. *Uniform motion calendar*

   a. *Contacting judge's office on short matters.* Counsel should contact the judge's office to ascertain whether short matters are heard by the specific division. FL ST 9 J CIR SECTION 10(C)(1).

   b. *Motions suitable for hearing.* Types of motions suitable for hearing on the motion calendar are simple motions to dismiss complaints with only one or two counts, to strike one or two affirmative defenses, for more definite statement, to amend pleadings, to compel discovery, for protective order, objections to IME, etc. Complex motions, motions requiring testimony or motions for summary judgment (except uncontested mortgage foreclosures), or more than two motions to be heard at one time should not be scheduled on this calendar and will not be heard by the Court. FL ST 9 J CIR SECTION 10(C)(2).

5. *Other motion hearings.* All other motions should be specially set through the judge's judicial assistant for a date and time certain. Requests for hearing time in excess of one (1) hour will require special permission of the judge obtained through the judicial assistant or by personal appearance of counsel at ex parte time. FL ST 9 J CIR SECTION 10(D).

6. *Cancelling hearings.* Only the attorney who noticed it can cancel a hearing. If a hearing becomes unnecessary after it has been noticed, the judge's judicial assistant and all other counsel must be notified immediately and effectively that the hearing is canceled. FL ST 9 J CIR SECTION 11(E).

7. *Communication equipment*

   a. *Definition.* Communication equipment means a conference telephone or other electronic device that permits all those appearing or participating to hear and speak to each other, provided that all conversation of all parties is audible to all persons present. FL ST J ADMIN Rule 2.530(a).

   b. *Use by all parties.* A county or circuit court judge may, upon the court's own motion or upon the written request of a party, direct that communication equipment be used for a motion hearing, pretrial conference, or a status conference. A judge must give notice to the parties and consider any objections they may have to the use of communication equipment before directing that communication equipment be used. The decision to use communication equipment over the objection of parties will be in the sound discretion of the trial court, except as noted below. FL ST J ADMIN Rule 2.530(b).

   c. *Use only by requesting party.* A county or circuit court judge may, upon the written request of a party upon reasonable notice to all other parties, permit a requesting party to participate through communication equipment in a scheduled motion hearing; however, any such request (except in criminal, juvenile, and appellate proceedings) must be granted, absent a showing of good cause to deny the same, where the hearing is set for not longer than fifteen (15) minutes. FL ST J ADMIN Rule 2.530(c).

d. *Testimony*

   i. *Generally.* A county or circuit court judge, general magistrate, special magistrate, or hearing officer may allow testimony to be taken through communication equipment if all parties consent or if permitted by another applicable rule of procedure. FL ST J ADMIN Rule 2.530(d)(1).

   ii. *Procedure.* Any party desiring to present testimony through communication equipment shall, prior to the hearing or trial at which the testimony is to be presented, contact all parties to determine whether each party consents to this form of testimony. The party seeking to present the testimony shall move for permission to present testimony through communication equipment, which motion shall set forth good cause as to why the testimony should be allowed in this form. FL ST J ADMIN Rule 2.530(d)(2).

   iii. *Oath.* Testimony may be taken through communication equipment only if a notary public or other person authorized to administer oaths in the witness's jurisdiction is present with the witness and administers the oath consistent with the laws of the jurisdiction. FL ST J ADMIN Rule 2.530(d)(3).

   iv. *Confrontation rights.* In juvenile and criminal proceedings the defendant must make an informed waiver of any confrontation rights that may be abridged by the use of communication equipment. FL ST J ADMIN Rule 2.530(d)(4).

   v. *Video testimony.* If the testimony to be presented utilizes video conferencing or comparable two-way visual capabilities, the court in its discretion may modify the procedures set forth in FL ST J ADMIN Rule 2.530 to accommodate the technology utilized. FL ST J ADMIN Rule 2.530(d)(5).

e. *Burden of expense.* The cost for the use of the communication equipment is the responsibility of the requesting party unless otherwise directed by the court. FL ST J ADMIN Rule 2.530(e).

H. Forms

1. Official Motion for Leave to Amend Forms for Florida

a. Caption. FL ST RCP Form 1.901.

b. Notice of compliance when constitutional challenge is brought. FL ST RCP Form 1.975.

2. Motion for Leave to Amend Forms for Florida

a. Motion; For leave of court; To amend complaint. FL-PP § 2:155.

b. Motion; For leave of court ; To add claim for punitive damages. FL-PP § 2:156.

c. Motion; For leave of court; To amend complaint; To conform to evidence. FL-PP § 2:157.

d. Motion; For leave of court; To permit admission of evidence. FL-PP § 2:158.

e. Order; Granting leave to amend complaint. FL-PP § 2:163.

f. Order; Granting leave to amend complaint; To conform to evidence. FL-PP § 2:164.

g. Order; Granting leave to amend complaint; To permit admission of evidence. FL-PP § 2:165.

h. Form for motion for leave to amend complaint. FL-RCPF R 1.190(39).

i. Form for amendment to complaint with leave of court. FL-RCPF R 1.190(40).

j. Form for motion to amend amended complaint. FL-RCPF R 1.190(42).

k. Form for amendment to amended complaint (or second amended complaint). FL-RCPF R 1.190(43).

l. Form for motion to amend complaint to add count. FL-RCPF R 1.190(44).

I. Checklist

(I) ❑ Matters to be considered by moving party

(a) ❑ Required documents

(1) ❑ Notice of hearing/Motion

(2) ❑ Proposed amended pleading

(3) ❑ Certificate of service

(b) ❑ Supplemental documents

(1) ❑ Legal memorandum

(2) ❑ Proposed order

(3) ❑ Notice of constitutional question

(c) ❑ Time for making motion

(1) ❑ A party may amend a pleading once as a matter of course at any time before a responsive pleading is served or, if the pleading is one to which no responsive pleading is permitted and the action has not been placed on the trial calendar, may amend it at any time within twenty (20) days after it is served

(2) ❑ Under the Florida Rules of Civil Procedure, there is no time limit as to when an amendment with leave of court may be sought; amendments of the pleadings may be permitted, with the court's discretion, at any stage of the proceedings in furtherance of justice

(3) ❑ A motion for leave to amend a pleading to assert a claim for punitive damages can be filed separately and before the supporting evidence or proffer, but each shall be served on all parties at least twenty (20) days before the hearing

(4) ❑ A copy of any written motion which may not be heard ex parte and a copy of the notice of the hearing thereof shall be served a reasonable time before the time specified for the hearing

(II) ❑ Matters to be considered by opposing party

(a) ❑ Required documents

(1) ❑ Response to motion

(2) ❑ Certificate of service

(b) ❑ Supplemental documents

(1) ❑ Legal memorandum

(2) ❑ Proposed order

(3) ❑ Notice of constitutional question

(c) ❑ Time for service and filing of opposition

(1) ❑ No time specified for responding to a motion

Motions, Oppositions and Replies
Motion for Summary Judgment

Document Last Updated January 2013

A. Applicable Rules

1. *State rules*

a. Rules of court. FL ST RCP Rule 1.010; FL ST J ADMIN Rule 2.110.

b. Nonverification of pleadings. FL ST RCP Rule 1.030.

c. Service and filing of pleadings, orders, and documents. FL ST RCP Rule 1.080.

d. Time. FL ST RCP Rule 1.090.

e. Pleadings and motions. FL ST RCP Rule 1.100.

f. Motions. FL ST RCP Rule 1.160.

g. Summary judgment. FL ST RCP Rule 1.510.

h. Relief from judgment, decrees, or orders. FL ST RCP Rule 1.540.

i. Mediation and arbitration. FL ST RCP Rule 1.700; FL ST RCP Rule 1.710; FL ST RCP Rule 1.720; FL ST RCP Rule 1.730; FL ST RCP Rule 1.750; FL ST RCP Rule 1.800; FL ST RCP Rule 1.810; FL ST RCP Rule 1.820; FL ST RCP Rule 1.830.

j. Forms. FL ST RCP Rule 1.900.

k. Minimization of the filing of sensitive information. FL ST J ADMIN Rule 2.425.

l. Retention of court records. FL ST J ADMIN Rule 2.430.

m. Foreign attorneys. FL ST J ADMIN Rule 2.510..

n. Signature of attorneys and parties. FL ST J ADMIN Rule 2.515.

o. Paper. FL ST J ADMIN Rule 2.520.

p. Electronic filing. FL ST J ADMIN Rule 2.525.

q. Accessibility of information and technology. FL ST J ADMIN Rule 2.526.

r. Communication equipment. FL ST J ADMIN Rule 2.530.

s. Court reporting. FL ST J ADMIN Rule 2.535.

t. Requests for accommodations by persons with disabilities. FL ST J ADMIN Rule 2.540.

2. *Local rules*

a. Hearings. FL ST 9 J CIR SECTION 10.

b. Motion practice generally. FL ST 9 J CIR SECTION 11.

c. Orders and judgments. FL ST 9 J CIR SECTION 12.

d. Alternative dispute resolution. FL ST 9 J CIR SECTION 15.

e. Business court procedures. FL ST 9 J CIR ORANGE CIV SECTION 1.

B. Timing

1. *Motion for summary judgment*

a. *For the claimant.* A party seeking to recover upon a claim, counterclaim, crossclaim or third-party claim or to obtain a declaratory judgment may move for a summary judgment in that party's favor at any time after the expiration of twenty (20) days from the commencement of the action or after service of a motion for summary judgment by the adverse party. FL ST RCP Rule 1.510(a).

b. *For defending party.* A party against whom a claim, counterclaim, crossclaim, or third-party claim is asserted or a declaratory judgment is sought may move for a summary judgment in that party's favor as to all or any part thereof at any time with or without supporting affidavits. FL ST RCP Rule 1.510(b).

i. A defending party is not required to serve his responsive pleading before moving for summary judgment. He may make the motion at any time, setting out his defenses by affidavit, and thus effect a speedy termination of the action if no genuine issue exists as to any fact or facts pertaining to a defense that would defeat the claim. FL ST RCP Rule 1.510, notes.

2. *Service of motion.* The movant shall serve the motion for summary judgment at least twenty (20) days before the time fixed for the hearing, and shall also serve at that time a copy of any summary judgment evidence on which the movant relies that has not already been filed with the court. FL ST RCP Rule 1.510(c).

3. *General motion timing*

a. Each attorney shall utilize the courts web page under Judicial Automated Calendaring System, for available hearing time and the judge's schedule before telephoning the judicial assistant. FL ST 9 J CIR SECTION 10(A)(1).

b. The hearing will be scheduled with the judge's judicial assistant. Written or fax notice must be received in opposing counsel's office at least four (4) working days before the hearing. FL ST 9 J CIR SECTION 10(A)(2).

   i. Counsel who serves a memorandum or authority list first should also include a copy of the motion, any papers to which it is addressed, and the response, if any. In order for the judge to properly review a submission in advance, it must be received in the judge's office at least three (3) working days before the hearing. FL ST 9 J CIR SECTION 11(B).

c. *Obtaining hearing times*

   i. If the motion is one which might be resolved by stipulation or agreed order, moving counsel must explore that possibility with opposing counsel before reserving hearing time. FL ST 9 J CIR SECTION 11(C)(1).

   ii. If at all possible, hearing time for complex motions or several motions to be heard at one time should be cleared with all affected counsel so as to avoid calendar conflicts. FL ST 9 J CIR SECTION 11(C)(1).

   iii. If hearing time cannot be coordinated with opposing counsel, attorneys shall appear at ex parte to resolve the issue. FL ST 9 J CIR SECTION 11(C)(1).

4. *Computation of time*

a. *Generally.* Computation of time shall be governed by FL ST J ADMIN Rule 2.514. FL ST RCP Rule 1.090(a). The following rules apply in computing time periods specified in any rule of procedure, local rule, court order, or statute that does not specify a method of computing time. FL ST J ADMIN Rule 2.514(a).

   i. *Period stated in days or a longer unit.* When the period is stated in days or a longer unit of time (A) exclude the day of the event that triggers the period; (B) count every day, including intermediate Saturdays, Sundays, and legal holidays; and (C) include the last day of the period, but if the last day is a Saturday, Sunday, or legal holiday, or falls within any period of time extended through an order of the chief justice under FL ST J ADMIN Rule 2.205(a)(2)(B)(iv), the period continues to run until the end of the next day that is not a Saturday, Sunday, or legal holiday and does not fall within any period of time extended through an order of the chief justice. FL ST J ADMIN Rule 2.514(a)(1).

   ii. *Period stated in hours.* When the period is stated in hours (A) begin counting immediately on the occurrence of the event that triggers the period; (B) count every hour, including hours during intermediate Saturdays, Sundays, and legal holidays; and (C) if the period would end on a Saturday, Sunday, or legal holiday, or during any period of time extended through an order of the chief justice under FL ST J ADMIN Rule 2.205(a)(2)(B)(iv), the period continues to run until the same time on the next day that is not a Saturday, Sunday, or legal holiday and does not fall within any period of time extended through an order of the chief justice. FL ST J ADMIN Rule 2.514(a)(2).

   iii. *Period stated in days less than seven (7) days.* When the period stated in days is less than seven (7) days, intermediate Saturdays, Sundays, and legal holidays shall be excluded in the computation. FL ST J ADMIN Rule 2.514(a)(3).

   iv. *"Last day" defined.* Unless a different time is set by a statute, local rule, or court order, the last day ends (A) for electronic filing or for service by any means, at midnight; and (B) for filing by other means, when the clerk's office is scheduled to close. FL ST J ADMIN Rule 2.514(a)(4).

   v. *"Next day" defined.* The "next day" is determined by continuing to count forward when the period is measured after an event and backward when measured before an event. FL ST J ADMIN Rule 2.514(a)(5).

   vi. *"Legal holiday" defined.* "Legal holiday" means (A) the day set aside by FL ST § 110.117, for observing New Year's Day, Martin Luther King, Jr.'s Birthday, Memorial Day, Independence

Day, Labor Day, Veterans' Day, Thanksgiving Day, the Friday after Thanksgiving Day, or Christmas Day, and (B) any day observed as a holiday by the clerk's office or as designated by the chief judge. FL ST J ADMIN Rule 2.514(a)(6).

b. *Additional time after service by mail or e-mail.* When a party may or must act within a specified time after service and service is made by mail or e-mail, five (5) days are added after the period that would otherwise expire under FL ST J ADMIN Rule 2.514(a). FL ST J ADMIN Rule 2.514(b).

c. *Enlargement.* When an act is required or allowed to be done at or within a specified time by order of court, by the Florida Rules of Civil Procedure, or by notice given thereunder, for cause shown the court at any time in its discretion (1) with or without notice, may order the period enlarged if request therefor is made before the expiration of the period originally prescribed or as extended by a previous order, or (2) upon motion made and notice after the expiration of the specified period, may permit the act to be done when failure to act was the result of excusable neglect, but it may not extend the time for making a motion for new trial, for rehearing, or to alter or amend a judgment; making a motion for relief from a judgment under FL ST RCP Rule 1.540(b); taking an appeal or filing a petition for certiorari; or making a motion for a directed verdict. FL ST RCP Rule 1.090(b).

d. *Unaffected by expiration of term.* The period of time provided for the doing of any act or the taking of any proceeding shall not be affected or limited by the continued existence or expiration of a term of court. The continued existence or expiration of a term of court in no way affects the power of a court to do any act or take any proceeding in any action which is or has been pending before it. FL ST RCP Rule 1.090(c).

C. General Requirements

1. *Motions generally*

a. *Contents.* An application to the court for an order shall be by motion which shall be made in writing unless made during a hearing or trial, shall state with particularity the grounds therefor, and shall set forth the relief or order sought. The requirement of writing is fulfilled if the motion is stated in a written notice of the hearing of the motion. All notices of hearing shall specify each motion or other matter to be heard. FL ST RCP Rule 1.100(b).

b. *Particularity requirement.* The court considers a motion in the light of the substantive law, rule or statute to make its determination. Some rules require a statement of the grounds for a motion under the rule. Failure to give the grounds will result in denial of the motion. This should be the result in all situations when the ground for the motion is not inherent in the rule. FL-PRACPROC § 9:3. The requirement is nevertheless an important one, first because of the due process notice rights of the respondent, as well as for the assistance it provides to the court in its preparation for the hearing or, absent a hearing, for disposition. 4 FLPRAC R 1.100. Every written motion shall cite the particular rule or statute and/or leading case upon which the motion is based. FL ST 9 J CIR SECTION 11(A)(1).

2. *Summary judgment.* A party seeking to recover upon or defend against a claim, counterclaim, crossclaim, or third-party claim or to obtain a declaratory judgment may move for a summary judgment. FL ST RCP Rule 1.510(a); FL ST RCP Rule 1.510(b).

a. *General motion for summary judgment information*

i. *Contents of motion.* The motion shall state with particularity the grounds upon which it is based and the substantial matters of law to be argued and shall specifically identify any affidavits, answers to interrogatories, admissions, depositions, and other materials as would be admissible in evidence ("summary judgment evidence") on which the movant relies. FL ST RCP Rule 1.510(c).

ii. *Evidence relied upon.* The movant shall also serve at that time a copy of any summary judgment evidence on which the movant relies that has not already been filed with the court. FL ST RCP Rule 1.510(c).

iii. *Judgment as a matter of law.* The judgment sought shall be rendered forthwith if the pleadings and summary judgment evidence on file show that there is no genuine issue as to any material fact and that the moving party is entitled to a judgment as a matter of law. A summary judgment,

interlocutory in character, may be rendered on the issue of liability alone although there is a genuine issue as to the amount of damages. FL ST RCP Rule 1.510(c).

b. *Sham pleadings.* If a party deems any pleading or part thereof filed by another party to be a sham, that party may move to strike the pleading or part thereof before the cause is set for trial and the court shall hear the motion, taking evidence of the respective parties, and if the motion is sustained, the pleading to which the motion is directed shall be stricken. Default and summary judgment on the merits may be entered in the discretion of the court or the court may permit additional pleadings to be filed for good cause shown. FL ST RCP Rule 1.150(a).

c. *Burden of proof*

   i. The moving party in a motion for summary judgment has the initial burden of demonstrating the nonexistence of any genuine issue of fact. Landers v. Milton, 370 So.2d 368, 370 (Fla. 1979); Gardner v. Sabal Point Properties, Inc., 616 So.2d 1111, 1112 (Fla. 5th DCA 1993); FL-PP § 6:7.

   ii. If the record raises the slightest doubt that material issues could be present, that doubt must be resolved against the movant and the motion for summary judgment denied. Moore v. Morris, 475 So.2d 666, 668 (Fla. 1985); Henderson v. CSX Transportation, Inc., 617 So.2d 770 (Fla. 1st DCA 1993); Jones v. Directors Guild of America, Inc., 584 So.2d 1057 (Fla. 1st DCA 1991); FL-PP § 6:7.

   iii. Until the moving party meets the initial burden of showing there is no issue of material fact, the opposing party need do nothing. Holl v. Talcott, 191 So.2d 40, 43 (Fla. 1966); Spradley v. Stick, 622 So.2d 610 (Fla. 1st DCA 1993); FL-RCPF R 1.510(404).

   iv. When the movant has tendered competent evidence in support of its motion, the burden shifts to the nonmoving party to come forward with opposing evidence to show that a question of material fact exists. Landers v. Milton, 370 So.2d 368, 370 (Fla. 1979); Holl v. Talcott, 191 So.2d 40, 43-44 (Fla. 1966); Lenhal Realty, Inc. v. Transamerica Commercial Finance Corp., 615 So.2d 207 (Fla. 4th DCA 1993); FL-PP § 6:7.

d. *Affidavits*

   i. *Form of affidavits; Further testimony.* Supporting and opposing affidavits shall be made on personal knowledge, shall set forth such facts as would be admissible in evidence, and shall show affirmatively that the affiant is competent to testify to the matters stated. Sworn or certified copies of all papers or parts referred to in an affidavit shall be attached to or served with the affidavit. The court may permit affidavits to be supplemented or opposed by depositions, answers to interrogatories, or by further affidavits. FL ST RCP Rule 1.510(e).

   ii. *When affidavits are unavailable.* If it appears from the affidavits of a party opposing the motion that the party cannot for reasons stated present by affidavit facts essential to justify opposition, the court may refuse the application for judgment or may order a continuance to permit affidavits to be obtained or depositions to be taken or discovery to be had or may make such other order as is just. FL ST RCP Rule 1.510(f).

   iii. *Affidavits made in bad faith.* If it appears to the satisfaction of the court at any time that any of the affidavits presented pursuant to FL ST RCP Rule 1.510 are presented in bad faith or solely for the purpose of delay, the court shall forthwith order the party employing them to pay to the other party the amount of the reasonable expenses that the filing of the affidavits caused the other party to incur, including reasonable attorneys' fees, and any offending party or attorney may be adjudged guilty of contempt. FL ST RCP Rule 1.510(g).

e. *Case not fully adjudicated on motion.* On motion under FL ST RCP Rule 1.510 if judgment is not rendered upon the whole case or for all the relief asked and a trial or the taking of testimony and a final hearing is necessary, the court at the hearing of the motion, by examining the pleadings and the evidence before it and by interrogating counsel, shall ascertain, if practicable, what material facts exist without substantial controversy and what material facts are actually and in good faith controverted. FL ST RCP Rule 1.510(d).

   i. It shall thereupon make an order specifying the facts that appear without substantial contro-

versy, including the extent to which the amount of damages or other relief is not in controversy, and directing such further proceedings in the action as are just. FL ST RCP Rule 1.510(d).

ii. On the trial or final hearing of the action the facts so specified shall be deemed established, and the trial or final hearing shall be conducted accordingly. FL ST RCP Rule 1.510(d).

3. *Arbitration and mediation*

a. *Referral to arbitration and mediation.* Except as hereinafter provided or as otherwise prohibited by law, the presiding judge may enter an order referring all or any part of a contested civil matter to mediation or arbitration. The parties to any contested civil matter may file a written stipulation to mediate or arbitrate any issue between them at any time. Such stipulation shall be incorporated into the order of referral. FL ST RCP Rule 1.700(a).

i. *Local arbitration policy.* It is the policy of the Civil Division judges to maximize the use of alternative dispute resolution procedures. Except where prohibited by statute, mediation will be ordered in all cases where jury trial is requested and in selected cases which are to be tried non-jury. Also, selected cases will be referred for court-annexed non-binding arbitration through the Orange County Bar Association Arbitration Service. Counsel may move to dispense with or defer mediation or arbitration or move to modify the referral order for good cause. FL ST 9 J CIR SECTION 15.

b. *Arbitration*

i. *Exclusions.* A civil action shall be ordered to arbitration or arbitration in conjunction with mediation upon stipulation of the parties. A civil action may be ordered to arbitration or arbitration in conjunction with mediation upon motion of any party or by the court, if the judge determines the action to be of such a nature that arbitration could be of benefit to the litigants or the court. FL ST RCP Rule 1.800.

- Under no circumstances may the following categories of actions be referred to arbitration: (1) bond estreatures; (2) habeas corpus or other extraordinary writs; (3) bond validations; (4) civil or criminal contempt; (5) such other matters as may be specified by order of the chief judge in the circuit. FL ST RCP Rule 1.800.

ii. For more information regarding arbitration, please see FL ST RCP Rule 1.810; FL ST RCP Rule 1.820; FL ST RCP Rule 1.830.

c. *Mediation.* For more information regarding mediation, please see FL ST RCP Rule 1.710; FL ST RCP Rule 1.720; FL ST RCP Rule 1.730; and FL ST RCP Rule 1.750.

4. *Rules of court*

a. *Rules of civil procedure.* The Florida Rules of Civil Procedure apply to all actions of a civil nature and all special statutory proceedings in the circuit courts and county courts except those to which the Florida Probate Rules, the Florida Family Law Rules of Procedure, or the Small Claims Rules apply. FL ST RCP Rule 1.010.

i. The form, content, procedure, and time for pleading in all special statutory proceedings shall be as prescribed by the statutes governing the proceeding unless the Florida Rules of Civil Procedure specifically provide to the contrary. FL ST RCP Rule 1.010.

ii. The Florida Rules of Civil Procedure shall be construed to secure the just, speedy, and inexpensive determination of every action. FL ST RCP Rule 1.010.

b. *Rules of judicial administration.* The Florida Rules of Judicial Administration shall apply to administrative matters in all courts to which the Florida Rules of Judicial Administration are applicable by their terms. The Florida Rules of Judicial Administration shall be construed to secure the speedy and inexpensive determination of every proceeding to which they are applicable. The Florida Rules of Judicial Administration shall supersede all conflicting rules and statutes. FL ST J ADMIN Rule 2.110.

c. *Business court procedures.* For rules specific to Business Court, please see FL ST 9 J CIR ORANGE CIV SECTION 1, et seq.

D. Documents

1. *Required documents*

   a. *Notice of hearing/Motion.* An application to the court for an order shall be by motion which shall be made in writing unless made during a hearing or trial, shall state with particularity the grounds therefor, and shall set forth the relief or order sought. The requirement of writing is fulfilled if the motion is stated in a written notice of the hearing of the motion. All notices of hearing shall specify each motion or other matter to be heard. FL ST RCP Rule 1.100(b). A notice calling up "all pending motions" is insufficient. FL ST 9 J CIR SECTION 11(D)(1). Additional motions should not be "piggy-backed" by cross-notice unless counsel first confirms with opposing counsel and the judge's judicial assistant that there can be sufficient additional time reserved in which to hear them. FL ST 9 J CIR SECTION 11(D)(2).

      i. *Notices to persons with disabilities.* See the Format section of this KeyRules document for further information.

   b. *Certificate of service.* When any attorney certifies in substance: "I certify that a copy hereof has been furnished to (here insert name or names and addresses used for service) by (e-mail) (delivery) (mail) (fax) on .... (date) ....________________ Attorney" the certificate is taken as prima facie proof of such service in compliance with FL ST J ADMIN Rule 2.516. FL ST J ADMIN Rule 2.516(f).

2. *Supplemental documents*

   a. *Legal memorandum.* Legal memorandums in support of or opposition to motions are optional. But if filed, counsel must furnish the judge with chambers copies of the memorandum and highlighted copies of primary legal authorities cited therein. FL ST 9 J CIR SECTION 11(B).

      i. As an alternative to a memorandum, a list of primary legal authorities with highlighted copies attached may be submitted. Chambers copies and authority lists must be under cover letter referencing the case style and number and stating the date and time of the hearing. FL ST 9 J CIR SECTION 11(B).

   b. *Affidavits.* Supporting and opposing affidavits shall be made on personal knowledge, shall set forth such facts as would be admissible in evidence, and shall show affirmatively that the affiant is competent to testify to the matters stated therein. Sworn or certified copies of all papers or parts thereof referred to in an affidavit shall be attached thereto or served therewith. FL ST RCP Rule 1.510(e). For further information regarding affidavits made in the context of a motion for summary judgment see FL ST RCP Rule 1.510(e) through FL ST RCP Rule 1.510(g).

   c. *Other evidence.* The movant shall also serve at that time a copy of any summary judgment evidence on which the movant relies that has not already been filed with the court. FL ST RCP Rule 1.510(c).

   d. *Proposed order.* The court may require that orders or judgments be prepared by a party, may require the party to furnish the court with stamped, addressed envelopes for service of the order or judgment, and may require that proposed orders and judgments be furnished to all parties before entry by the court of the order or judgment. FL ST J ADMIN Rule 2.516(h)(1).

      i. Proposed orders and judgments will be prepared by the prevailing attorney unless the judge designates some other attorney or states that he or she will prepare the order or judgment. FL ST 9 J CIR SECTION 12(A)(1).

      ii. When submitting proposed orders or judgments, counsel shall also include sufficient copies and self address stamped envelopes for all parties. FL ST 9 J CIR SECTION 12(A)(2).

      iii. Moving counsel must present a proposed order with space for ruling left blank at the conclusion of the hearing and must serve conformed copies on all other counsel and unrepresented parties. FL ST 9 J CIR SECTION 10(A)(3).

      iv. Unsigned orders or judgments should not be sent to the Clerk's office for transmission to the judge. FL ST 9 J CIR SECTION 12(D)(3).

   e. *Notice of constitutional question.* A party that files a pleading, written motion, or other paper drawing into question the constitutionality of a state statute or a county or municipal charter, ordinance, or franchise must promptly (1) file a notice of constitutional question stating the question

and identifying the paper that raises it; and (2) serve the notice and the pleading, written motion, or other paper drawing into question the constitutionality of a state statute or a county or municipal charter, ordinance, or franchise on the Attorney General or the state attorney of the judicial circuit in which the action is pending, by either certified or registered mail. Service of the notice and pleading, written motion, or other paper does not require joinder of the Attorney General or the state attorney as a party to the action. FL ST RCP Rule 1.071.

E. Format

1. *Documents; Type and size.* Documents subject to the exceptions set forth in FL ST J ADMIN Rule 2.525(d) shall be filed on recycled paper measuring eight and one half by eleven (8 1/2 by 11) inches. For purposes of FL ST J ADMIN Rule 2.520, paper is recycled if it contains a minimum content of fifty (50) percent waste paper. Xerographic reduction of legal-size (eight and one half by fourteen (8 1/2 by 14) inches) documents to letter size (eight and one half by eleven (8 1/2 by 11) inches) is prohibited. All other documents filed by electronic transmission shall be filed in a format capable of being printed in a format consistent with the provisions of FL ST J ADMIN Rule 2.250. FL ST J ADMIN Rule 2.520(b).
    a. *Exhibits.* Any exhibit or attachment filed with pleadings or papers may be filed in its original size. FL ST J ADMIN Rule 2.520(c).
    b. *Recording space.* On all papers and documents prepared and filed by the court or by any party to a proceeding which are to be recorded in the public records of any county, including but not limited to final money judgments and notices of lis pendens, a three (3) inch by three (3) inch space at the top right-hand corner on the first page and a one (1) inch by three (3) inch space at the top right-hand corner on each subsequent page shall be left blank and reserved for use by the clerk of court. FL ST J ADMIN Rule 2.520(d).
        i. *Exceptions to recording space.* Any papers or documents created by persons or entities over which the filing party has no control, including but not limited to wills, codicils, trusts, or other testamentary documents; documents prepared or executed by any public officer; documents prepared, executed, acknowledged, or proved outside of the State of Florida; or documents created by State or Federal government agencies, may be filed without the space required by FL ST J ADMIN Rule 2.520. FL ST J ADMIN Rule 2.520(e).
    c. *Noncompliance.* No clerk of court is permitted to refuse to file any document or paper because of noncompliance with the Florida Rules of Judicial Administration. However, upon request of the clerk of court, noncomplying documents must be resubmitted in accordance with the formatting rules. FL ST J ADMIN Rule 2.520(f).
    d. *Proposed orders*
        i. All orders will be on eight and a half by eleven (8 1/2 by 11) inch plain white paper (not lined or letterhead paper) and be double spaced. FL ST 9 J CIR SECTION 12(B)(1).
        ii. The order must contain a title indicating what matter the order pertains to, e.g., "Order On Defendant Smith's Motion To Dismiss." FL ST 9 J CIR SECTION 12(B)(2).
        iii. The preamble of the order should include the date of the hearing and what motions were heard. FL ST 9 J CIR SECTION 12(B)(3).
        iv. The adjudication portion of the order should state what relief is ordered. Simply stating that "the motion is granted" without more is insufficient. FL ST 9 J CIR SECTION 12(B)(4).
        v. The order should indicate the specific time period of any act ordered to be done and should state whether the time period runs from the date of the hearing or the date the order is signed or some other specified date. FL ST 9 J CIR SECTION 12(B)(5).
        vi. The order should contain a full certificate of service with the complete names and addresses of the attorneys and unrepresented parties to be served. Merely showing "copies to" is insufficient. FL ST 9 J CIR SECTION 12(B)(6).
        vii. If an order of dismissal is final (i.e., it disposes of the entire case) the title should contain the word "Final." When the order is not final but leaves other counts or claims against other defendants pending, it should so state in a separate paragraph. FL ST 9 J CIR SECTION 12(B)(7).

viii. When submitting stipulations, orders shall be by separate order, not attached to the stipulation. FL ST 9 J CIR SECTION 12(B)(8).

ix. Counsel preparing the Final Judgment or order should draft and circulate copies within two (2) working days of the ruling or jury verdict. If counsel preparing the Final Judgment or order gets approval as to form of the order from all counsel, the original with copies and envelopes should be sent directly to the judge with a cover letter stating all counsel agree to the form of the order or judgment. If other counsel objects to the form or cannot be reached for approval, counsel preparing the judgment or order shall notice a motion for entry of the order or judgment. If objecting counsel does not furnish the judge prior to or at the hearing with a proposed judgment or order version with copies under cover letter stating the reasons for the objection, all objections will be deemed waived. Orders and judgments should not be submitted to the judge to hold waiting for an objection. FL ST 9 J CIR SECTION 12(D).

2. *Caption.* Every pleading, motion, order, judgment, or other paper shall have a caption containing the name of the court, the file number, and except for in rem proceedings, including forfeiture proceedings, the name of the first party on each side with an appropriate indication of other parties, and a designation identifying the party filing it and its nature or the nature of the order, as the case may be. In any in rem proceeding, every pleading, motion, order, judgment, or other paper shall have a caption containing the name of the court, the file number, the style "In re" (followed by the name or general description of the property), and a designation of the person or entity filing it and its nature or the nature of the order, as the case may be. In an in rem forfeiture proceeding, the style shall be "In re forfeiture of" (followed by the name of the general description of the property). All papers filed in the action shall be styled in such a manner as to indicate clearly the subject matter of the paper and the party requesting or obtaining relief. FL ST RCP Rule 1.100(c)(1).

3. *Writing and written defined.* Writing or written means a document containing information, an application, or a stipulation. FL ST RCP Rule 1.080(c).

4. *Rule abbreviations*

   a. The Florida Rules of Civil Procedure and shall be abbreviated as Fla.R.Civ.P. FL ST RCP Rule 1.010.

   b. The Florida Rules of Judicial Administration shall be abbreviated as Fla. R. Jud. Admin. FL ST J ADMIN Rule 2.110.

5. *Nonverification.* Except when otherwise specifically provided by the Florida Rules of Civil Procedure or an applicable statute, every pleading or other document of a party represented by an attorney need not be verified or accompanied by an affidavit. FL ST RCP Rule 1.030; FL ST J ADMIN Rule 2.515(a).

6. *Unrepresented parties.* An unrepresented party must file his or her papers with the clerk and send copies to other attorneys or unrepresented parties. All such papers must be typed double-spaced on plain white eight and a half by eleven (8 1/2 by 11) inch paper, with the name of the case and case number at the top and the party's mailing address, telephone number and FAX number, if any, below his or her signature at the end of the paper. Such unrepresented party must immediately notify the clerk and all other counsel or parties of record in writing of any change in mailing address or telephone or FAX number. Failure to promptly notify of change of address could result in a dismissal or default entered against such party. FL ST 9 J CIR SECTION 7(B)(5).

7. *Attorney signature*

   a. *Attorney signature.* Every pleading and other document of a party represented by an attorney shall be signed by at least one (1) attorney of record in that attorney's individual name whose current record Florida Bar address, telephone number, including area code, primary e-mail address and secondary e-mail addresses, if any, and Florida Bar number shall be stated, and who shall be duly licensed to practice law in Florida or who shall have received permission to appear in the particular case as provided in FL ST J ADMIN Rule 2.510. FL ST J ADMIN Rule 2.515(a).

      i. The attorney may be required by the court to give the address of, and to vouch for the attorney's authority to represent, the party. FL ST J ADMIN Rule 2.515(a).

      ii. The signature of an attorney shall constitute a certificate by the attorney that the attorney has read the pleading or other document; that to the best of the attorney's knowledge, information, and belief there is good ground to support it; and that it is not interposed for delay. FL ST J ADMIN Rule 2.515(a).

iii. If a pleading is not signed or is signed with intent to defeat the purpose of FL ST J ADMIN Rule 2.515, it may be stricken and the action may proceed as though the pleading or other document had not been served. FL ST J ADMIN Rule 2.515(a).

b. *Pro se litigant signature.* A party who is not represented by an attorney shall sign any pleading or other paper and state the party's address and telephone number, including area code. FL ST J ADMIN Rule 2.515(b).

c. *Form of signature*

i. The signatures required on pleadings and documents by FL ST J ADMIN Rule 2.515(a) and FL ST J ADMIN Rule 2.515(b) may be:

- Original signatures;
- Original signatures that have been reproduced by electronic means, such as on electronically transmitted documents or photocopied documents;
- Electronic signatures using the "/s/," "s/," or "/s" formats by or at the direction of the person signing; or
- Any other signature format authorized by general law, so long as the clerk where the proceeding is pending has the capability of receiving and has obtained approval from the Supreme Court of Florida to accept pleadings and documents with that signature format. FL ST J ADMIN Rule 2.515(c)(1).

ii. An attorney, party, or other person who files a pleading or paper by electronic transmission that does not contain the original signature of that attorney, party, or other person shall file that identical pleading or paper in paper form containing an original signature of that attorney, party, or other person (hereinafter called the follow-up filing) immediately thereafter. The follow-up filing is not required if the Supreme Court of Florida has entered an order directing the clerk of court to discontinue accepting the follow-up filing. FL ST J ADMIN Rule 2.515(c)(2).

8. *Forms*

a. *Process.* The forms of process, notice of lis pendens, and notice of action provided in the Florida Rules of Civil Procedure are sufficient. Variations from the forms do not void process or notices that are otherwise sufficient. FL ST RCP Rule 1.900(a).

b. *Other forms.* The other forms provided in the Florida Rules of Civil Procedure are sufficient for the matters that are covered by them. So long as the substance is expressed without prolixity, the forms may be varied to meet the facts of a particular case. FL ST RCP Rule 1.900(b).

c. *Formal matters.* Captions, except for the designation of the paper, are omitted from the forms provided in the Florida Rules of Civil Procedure. A general form of caption is the first form provided. Signatures are omitted from pleadings and motions. FL ST RCP Rule 1.900(c).

9. *Notices to persons with disabilities.* All notices of court proceedings to be held in a public facility, and all process compelling appearance at such proceedings, shall include the following statement in bold face, fourteen (14) point Times New Roman or Courier font: "If you are a person with a disability who needs any accommodation in order to participate in this proceeding, you are entitled, at no cost to you, to the provision of certain assistance. Please contact [identify applicable court personnel by name, address, and telephone number] at least seven (7) days before your scheduled court appearance, or immediately upon receiving this notification if the time before the scheduled appearance is less than seven (7) days; if you are hearing or voice impaired, call 711." FL ST J ADMIN Rule 2.540(c)(1).

10. *Minimization of the filing of sensitive information*

a. *Limitations for court filings.* Unless authorized by FL ST J ADMIN Rule 2.425(b), statute, another rule of court, or the court orders otherwise, designated sensitive information filed with the court must be limited to the following format:

i. The initials of a person known to be a minor;

- ii. The year of birth of a person's birth date;
- iii. No portion of any: Social security number, Bank account number, Credit card account number, Charge account number, or Debit account number;
- iv. The last four digits of any: Taxpayer identification number (TIN), Employee identification number, Driver's license number, Passport number, Telephone number, Financial account number, except as set forth in FL ST J ADMIN Rule 2.425(a)(3), Brokerage account number, Insurance policy account number, Loan account number, Customer account number, or Patient or health care number;
- v. A truncated version of any: Email address, Computer user name, Password, or Personal identification number (PIN); and
- vi. A truncated version of any other sensitive information as provided by court order. FL ST J ADMIN Rule 2.425(a).

b. *Exceptions.* FL ST J ADMIN Rule 2.425(a) does not apply to the following:

- i. An account number which identifies the property alleged to be the subject of a proceeding;
- ii. The record of an administrative or agency proceeding;
- iii. The record in appellate or review proceedings;
- iv. The birth date of a minor whenever the birth date is necessary for the court to establish or maintain subject matter jurisdiction;
- v. The name of a minor in any order relating to parental responsibility, time-sharing, or child support;
- vi. The name of a minor in any document or order affecting the minor's ownership of real property;
- vii. The birth date of a party in a writ of attachment or notice to payor;
- viii. In traffic and criminal proceedings: a pro se filing; a court filing that is related to a criminal matter or investigation and that is prepared before the filing of a criminal charge or is not filed as part of any docketed criminal case; an arrest or search warrant or any information in support thereof; a charging document and an affidavit or other documents filed in support of any charging document, including any driving records; a statement of particulars; discovery material introduced into evidence or otherwise filed with the court; and all information necessary for the proper issuance and execution of a subpoena duces tecum;
- ix. Information used by the clerk for case maintenance purposes or the courts for case management purposes; and
- x. Information which is relevant and material to an issue before the court. FL ST J ADMIN Rule 2.425(b).

c. *Remedies.* Upon motion by a party or interested person or sua sponte by the court, the court may order remedies, sanctions or both for a violation of FL ST J ADMIN Rule 2.425(a). Following notice and an opportunity to respond, the court may impose sanctions if such filing was not made in good faith. FL ST J ADMIN Rule 2.425(c).

d. *Motions not restricted.* FL ST J ADMIN Rule 2.425 does not restrict a party's right to move for protective order, to move to file documents under seal, or to request a determination of the confidentiality of records. FL ST J ADMIN Rule 2.425(d).

e. *Application.* FL ST J ADMIN Rule 2.425 does not affect the application of constitutional provisions, statutes, or rules of court regarding confidential information or access to public information. FL ST J ADMIN Rule 2.425(e).

F. Filing and Service Requirements

1. *Filing requirements.* All original documents must be filed with the court either before service or immediately thereafter, unless otherwise provided for by general law or other rules. If the original of any bond or other document is not placed in the court file, a certified copy must be so placed by the clerk. FL ST J ADMIN Rule 2.516(d). All documents shall be filed in conformity with the requirements of FL ST

J ADMIN Rule 2.525. FL ST RCP Rule 1.080(b). All documents filed in any court shall be filed by electronic transmission in accordance with FL ST J ADMIN Rule 2.525. "Documents" means pleadings, motions, petitions, memoranda, briefs, notices, exhibits, declarations, affidavits, orders, judgments, decrees, writs, opinions, and any other paper or writing submitted to a court. FL ST J ADMIN Rule 2.520(a). All documents that are court records, as defined in FL ST J ADMIN Rule 2.430(a)(1), must be filed by electronic transmission, provided that: (1) the clerk has the ability to accept and retain such documents; (2) the clerk or the chief judge of the circuit has requested permission to accept documents filed by electronic transmission; and (3) the supreme court has entered an order granting permission to the clerk to accept documents filed by electronic transmission. FL ST J ADMIN Rule 2.525(c)(1).

a. *Definition.* "Electronic transmission of documents" means the sending of information by electronic signals to, by or from a court or clerk, which when received can be transformed and stored or transmitted on paper, microfilm, magnetic storage device, optical imaging system, CD-ROM, flash drive, other electronic data storage system, server, case maintenance system ("CM"), electronic court filing ("ECF") system, statewide or local electronic portal ("e-portal"), or other electronic record keeping system authorized by the supreme court in a format sufficient to communicate the information on the original document in a readable format. Electronic transmission of documents includes electronic mail ("e-mail") and any internet-based transmission procedure, and may include procedures allowing for documents to be signed or verified by electronic means. FL ST J ADMIN Rule 2.525(a).
    i. The filing of documents with the court as required by the Florida Rules of Judicial Administration must be made by filing them with the clerk in accordance with FL ST J ADMIN Rule 2.525, except that the judge may permit documents to be filed with the judge, in which event the judge must note the filing date before him or her on the documents and transmit them to the clerk. The date of filing is that shown on the face of the document by the judge's notation or the clerk's time stamp, whichever is earlier. FL ST J ADMIN Rule 2.516(e).
b. *Application.* Any court or clerk of the court may accept the electronic transmission of documents for filing after the clerk, together with input from the chief judge of the circuit, has obtained approval of the procedures and program for doing so from the Supreme Court of Florida. FL ST J ADMIN Rule 2.525(b).
c. *Exceptions*
    i. Paper documents and other submissions may be manually submitted to the clerk or court:
        - When the clerk does not have the ability to accept and retain documents by electronic filing or has not had ECF Procedures approved by the supreme court;
        - For filing by any self-represented party or any self-represented nonparty unless specific ECF Procedures provide a means to file documents electronically. However, any self-represented nonparty that is a governmental or public agency and any other agency, partnership, corporation, or business entity acting on behalf of any governmental or public agency may file documents by electronic transmission if such entity has the capability of filing documents electronically;
        - For filing by attorneys excused from e-mail service in accordance with FL ST J ADMIN Rule 2.516(b);
        - When submitting evidentiary exhibits or filing non-documentary materials;
        - When the filing involves documents in excess of twenty-five (25) megabytes (25MB) in size. For such filings, documents may be transmitted using an electronic storage medium that the clerk has the ability to accept, which may include a CD-ROM, flash drive, or similar storage medium;
        - When filed in open court, as permitted by the court;
        - When paper filing is permitted by any approved statewide or local ECF procedures; and
        - If any court determines that justice so requires. FL ST J ADMIN Rule 2.525(d).
    ii. Any document in paper form submitted under FL ST J ADMIN Rule 2.525(d) is filed when it

is received by the clerk or court and the clerk shall immediately thereafter convert any filed paper document to an electronic document. "Convert to an electronic document" means optically capturing an image of a paper document and using character recognition software to recover as much of the document's text as practicable and then indexing and storing the document in the official court file. FL ST J ADMIN Rule 2.525(c)(4).

iii. Any storage medium submitted under FL ST J ADMIN Rule 2.525(d)(5) is filed when received by the clerk or court and the clerk shall immediately thereafter transfer the electronic documents from the storage device to the official court file. FL ST J ADMIN Rule 2.525(c)(5).

iv. If the filer of any paper document authorized under FL ST J ADMIN Rule 2.525(d) provides a self-addressed, postage-paid envelope for return of the paper document after it is converted to electronic form by the clerk, the clerk shall place the paper document in the envelope and deposit it in the mail. Except when a paper document is required to be maintained, the clerk may recycle any filed paper document that is not to be returned to the filer. FL ST J ADMIN Rule 2.525(c)(6).

v. The clerk may convert any paper document filed before the effective date of FL ST J ADMIN Rule 2.525 to an electronic document. Unless the clerk is required to maintain the paper document, if the paper document has been converted to an electronic document by the clerk, the paper document is no longer part of the official court file and may be removed and recycled. FL ST J ADMIN Rule 2.525(c)(7).

d. *Unrepresented parties.* An unrepresented party must file his or her papers with the clerk and send copies to other attorneys or unrepresented parties. FL ST 9 J CIR SECTION 7(B)(5).

i. An unrepresented party may not communicate privately with the judge either by letter, telephone, in person or otherwise. FL ST 9 J CIR SECTION 7(B)(4).

ii. Copies of legal papers or other written materials should not be sent to the judge unless specifically requested by the judge or required by the local administrative procedures. Any unrequested or non-required papers or materials sent to a judge may not be read but may be returned to the sender or placed unread into the court file. FL ST 9 J CIR SECTION 7(B)(4).

e. *Official court file.* For information on what constitutes the official court file, please see FL ST J ADMIN Rule 2.525(c)(2), FL ST J ADMIN Rule 2.525(c)(3).

f. *Administration.* All attorneys, parties, or other persons using this rule to file documents are required to make arrangements with the court or clerk for the payment of any charges authorized by general law or the supreme court before filing any document by electronic transmission. FL ST J ADMIN Rule 2.525(f)(2).

g. *Filing date.* The filing date for an electronically transmitted document is the date and time that such filing is acknowledged by an electronic stamp or otherwise, pursuant to any procedure set forth in any ECF Procedures approved by the supreme court, or the date the last page of such filing is received by the court or clerk. FL ST J ADMIN Rule 2.525(f)(3).

h. *Accessibility.* All documents transmitted in any electronic form under FL ST J ADMIN Rule 2.525 must comply with the accessibility requirements of FL ST J ADMIN Rule 2.526. FL ST J ADMIN Rule 2.525(g).

2. *Service requirements.* Every pleading subsequent to the initial pleading, all orders, and every other document filed in the action must be served in conformity with the requirements of FL ST J ADMIN Rule 2.516. FL ST RCP Rule 1.080(a).

a. *Service; When required.* Unless the court otherwise orders, or a statute or supreme court administrative order specifies a different means of service, every pleading subsequent to the initial pleading and every other document filed in any court proceeding, except applications for witness subpoenas and documents served by formal notice or required to be served in the manner provided for service of formal notice, must be served in accordance with FL ST J ADMIN Rule 2.516 on each party. No service need be made on parties against whom a default has been entered, except that pleadings asserting new or additional claims against them must be served in the manner provided for service of summons. FL ST J ADMIN Rule 2.516(a).

i. Counsel who serves a memorandum or authority list first should also include a copy of the motion, any papers to which it is addressed, and the response, if any. In order for the judge to properly review a submission in advance, it must be received in the judge's office at least three (3) working days before the hearing. FL ST 9 J CIR SECTION 11(B).

b. *Service; How made.* When service is required or permitted to be made upon a party represented by an attorney, service must be made upon the attorney unless service upon the party is ordered by the court. FL ST J ADMIN Rule 2.516(b).

   i. *Service by electronic mail ("e-mail").* All documents required or permitted to be served on another party must be served by e-mail, unless FL ST J ADMIN Rule 2.516 otherwise provides. When, in addition to service by e-mail, the sender also utilizes another means of service provided for in FL ST J ADMIN Rule 2.516(b)(2), any differing time limits and other provisions applicable to that other means of service control. FL ST J ADMIN Rule 2.516(b)(1). Any document electronically transmitted to a court or clerk must also be served on all parties and interested persons in accordance with the applicable rules of court. FL ST J ADMIN Rule 2.525(e)(2).

      - *Service on attorneys.* Upon appearing in a proceeding, an attorney must serve a designation of a primary e-mail address and may designate no more than two (2) secondary e-mail addresses. Thereafter, service must be directed to all designated e-mail addresses in that proceeding. Every document filed by an attorney thereafter must include the primary e-mail address of that attorney and any secondary e-mail addresses. If an attorney does not designate any e-mail address for service, documents may be served on that attorney at the e-mail address on record with The Florida Bar. FL ST J ADMIN Rule 2.516(b)(1)(A).
      - *Exception to e-mail service on attorneys.* Service by an attorney on another attorney must be made by e-mail unless excused by the court. Upon motion by an attorney demonstrating that the attorney has no e-mail account and lacks access to the Internet at the attorney's office, the court may excuse the attorney from the requirements of e-mail service. Service on and by an attorney excused by the court from e-mail service must be by the means provided in FL ST J ADMIN Rule 2.516(b)(2). FL ST J ADMIN Rule 2.516(b)(1)(B).
      - *Service on and by parties not represented by an attorney.* Any party not represented by an attorney may serve a designation of a primary e-mail address and also may designate no more than two (2) secondary e-mail addresses to which service must be directed in that proceeding by the means provided in FL ST J ADMIN Rule 2.516(b)(1). If a party not represented by an attorney does not designate an e-mail address for service in a proceeding, service on and by that party must be by the means provided in FL ST J ADMIN Rule 2.516(b)(2). FL ST J ADMIN Rule 2.516(b)(1)(C).
      - *Time of service.* Service by e-mail is complete when it is sent. FL ST J ADMIN Rule 2.516(b)(1)(D). An e-mail is deemed served on the date it is sent. FL ST J ADMIN Rule 2.516(b)(1)(D)(i). If the sender learns that the e-mail did not reach the address of the person to be served, the sender must immediately send another copy by e-mail, or by a means authorized by FL ST J ADMIN Rule 2.516(b)(2). FL ST J ADMIN Rule 2.516(b)(1)(D)(ii). E-mail service is treated as service by mail for the computation of time. FL ST J ADMIN Rule 2.516(b)(1)(D)(iii).

   ii. *Format of e-mail for service.* Service of a document by e-mail is made by attaching a copy of the document in PDF format to an e-mail sent to all addresses designated by the attorney or party. FL ST J ADMIN Rule 2.516(b)(1)(E).

      - All documents served by e-mail must be attached to an e-mail message containing a subject line beginning with the words "SERVICE OF COURT DOCUMENT" in all capital letters, followed by the case number of the proceeding in which the documents are being served. FL ST J ADMIN Rule 2.516(b)(1)(E)(i).
      - The body of the e-mail must identify the court in which the proceeding is pending, the case number, the name of the initial party on each side, the title of each document served with that e-mail, and the sender's name and telephone number. FL ST J ADMIN Rule 2.516(b)(1)(E)(ii).

- Any document served by e-mail may be signed by the "/s/" format, as long as the filed original is signed in accordance with the applicable rule of procedure. FL ST J ADMIN Rule 2.516(b)(1)(E)(iii).
- Any e-mail which, together with its attached documents, exceeds five megabytes (5MB) in size, must be divided and sent as separate e-mails, no one of which may exceed five megabytes (5MB) in size and each of which must be sequentially numbered in the subject line. FL ST J ADMIN Rule 2.516(b)(1)(E)(iv).

iii. *Service by other means.* In addition to, and not in lieu of, service by e-mail, service may also be made upon attorneys by any of the means specified in FL ST J ADMIN Rule 2.516(b)(2). Service on and by all parties who are not represented by an attorney and who do not designate an e-mail address, and on and by all attorneys excused from e-mail service, must be made by delivering a copy of the document or by mailing it to the party or attorney at their last known address or, if no address is known, by leaving it with the clerk of the court. Service by mail is complete upon mailing. Delivery of a copy within FL ST J ADMIN Rule 2.516 is complete upon:

- Handing it to the attorney or to the party,
- Leaving it at the attorney's or party's office with a clerk or other person in charge thereof,
- If there is no one in charge, leaving it in a conspicuous place therein,
- If the office is closed or the person to be served has no office, leaving it at the person's usual place of abode with some person of his or her family above fifteen (15) years of age and informing such person of the contents, or
- Transmitting it by facsimile to the attorney's or party's office with a cover sheet containing the sender's name, firm, address, telephone number, and facsimile number, and the number of pages transmitted. When service is made by facsimile, a copy must also be served by any other method permitted by FL ST J ADMIN Rule 2.516. Facsimile service occurs when transmission is complete. FL ST J ADMIN Rule 2.516(b)(2)(A) through FL ST J ADMIN Rule 2.516(b)(2)(E).
- Service by delivery after 5:00 p.m. must be deemed to have been made by mailing on the date of delivery. FL ST J ADMIN Rule 2.516(b)(2)(F).

c. *Service; Numerous defendants.* In actions when the parties are unusually numerous, the court may regulate the service contemplated by the Florida Rules of Judicial Administration on motion or on its own initiative in such manner as may be found to be just and reasonable. FL ST J ADMIN Rule 2.516(c).

d. *Service by clerk.* Service of notices and other documents required to be made by the clerk must also be done as provided in FL ST J ADMIN Rule 2.516(b). FL ST J ADMIN Rule 2.516(g).

G. Hearings

1. *Hearing on motion for summary judgment.* The summary judgment rule does not provide the trial court with discretion to decide whether a hearing is required. A failure to hold a hearing on a motion for summary judgment violates due process as well as rule of procedure governing summary judgment procedure. Kozich v. Hartford Ins. Co. of Midwest, 609 So.2d 147, 148 (Fla. 4th DCA 1992); FL-RCPF R 1.510(102).
2. *Summary judgment consideration at pretrial conference.* A summary judgment can be granted at the pretrial conference. The standard and procedure for granting summary judgment is the same at a pretrial conference as at other times. The notice time for a pretrial conference and for service of a motion for summary judgment is the same, so summary judgment can be entered at the conference if no genuine issue of material fact exists. FL-PRACPROC § 19:4.
3. *Uniform motion calendar*

a. *Contacting judge's office on short matters.* Counsel should contact the judge's office to ascertain whether short matters are heard by the specific division. FL ST 9 J CIR SECTION 10(C)(1).

b. *Motions suitable for hearing.* Types of motions suitable for hearing on the motion calendar are simple motions to dismiss complaints with only one or two counts, to strike one or two affirmative defenses, for more definite statement, to amend pleadings, to compel discovery, for protective order, objections to IME, etc. Complex motions, motions requiring testimony or motions for summary judgment (except uncontested mortgage foreclosures), or more than two motions to be heard at one time should not be scheduled on this calendar and will not be heard by the Court. FL ST 9 J CIR SECTION 10(C)(2).

4. *Other motion hearings.* All other motions should be specially set through the judge's judicial assistant for a date and time certain. Requests for hearing time in excess of one (1) hour will require special permission of the judge obtained through the judicial assistant or by personal appearance of counsel at ex parte time. FL ST 9 J CIR SECTION 10(D).

5. *Cancelling hearings.* Only the attorney who noticed it can cancel a hearing. If a hearing becomes unnecessary after it has been noticed, the judge's judicial assistant and all other counsel must be notified immediately and effectively that the hearing is canceled. FL ST 9 J CIR SECTION 11(E).

6. *Communication equipment*
   a. *Definition.* Communication equipment means a conference telephone or other electronic device that permits all those appearing or participating to hear and speak to each other, provided that all conversation of all parties is audible to all persons present. FL ST J ADMIN Rule 2.530(a).
   b. *Use by all parties.* A county or circuit court judge may, upon the court's own motion or upon the written request of a party, direct that communication equipment be used for a motion hearing, pretrial conference, or a status conference. A judge must give notice to the parties and consider any objections they may have to the use of communication equipment before directing that communication equipment be used. The decision to use communication equipment over the objection of parties will be in the sound discretion of the trial court, except as noted below. FL ST J ADMIN Rule 2.530(b).
   c. *Use only by requesting party.* A county or circuit court judge may, upon the written request of a party upon reasonable notice to all other parties, permit a requesting party to participate through communication equipment in a scheduled motion hearing; however, any such request (except in criminal, juvenile, and appellate proceedings) must be granted, absent a showing of good cause to deny the same, where the hearing is set for not longer than fifteen (15) minutes. FL ST J ADMIN Rule 2.530(c).
   d. *Testimony*
      i. *Generally.* A county or circuit court judge, general magistrate, special magistrate, or hearing officer may allow testimony to be taken through communication equipment if all parties consent or if permitted by another applicable rule of procedure. FL ST J ADMIN Rule 2.530(d)(1).
      ii. *Procedure.* Any party desiring to present testimony through communication equipment shall, prior to the hearing or trial at which the testimony is to be presented, contact all parties to determine whether each party consents to this form of testimony. The party seeking to present the testimony shall move for permission to present testimony through communication equipment, which motion shall set forth good cause as to why the testimony should be allowed in this form. FL ST J ADMIN Rule 2.530(d)(2).
      iii. *Oath.* Testimony may be taken through communication equipment only if a notary public or other person authorized to administer oaths in the witness's jurisdiction is present with the witness and administers the oath consistent with the laws of the jurisdiction. FL ST J ADMIN Rule 2.530(d)(3).
      iv. *Confrontation rights.* In juvenile and criminal proceedings the defendant must make an informed waiver of any confrontation rights that may be abridged by the use of communication equipment. FL ST J ADMIN Rule 2.530(d)(4).
      v. *Video testimony.* If the testimony to be presented utilizes video conferencing or comparable two-way visual capabilities, the court in its discretion may modify the procedures set forth in FL ST J ADMIN Rule 2.530 to accommodate the technology utilized. FL ST J ADMIN Rule 2.530(d)(5).

e. *Burden of expense.* The cost for the use of the communication equipment is the responsibility of the requesting party unless otherwise directed by the court. FL ST J ADMIN Rule 2.530(e).

H. Forms

1. Official Motion for Summary Judgment Forms for Florida

a. Caption. FL ST RCP Form 1.901.

b. Notice of compliance when constitutional challenge is brought. FL ST RCP Form 1.975.

2. Motion for Summary Judgment Forms for Florida

a. Motion for summary judgment; By plaintiff. FL-PP § 6:9.

b. Motion for summary judgment; By defendant. FL-PP § 6:10.

c. Affidavit; Supporting motion for summary judgment; By plaintiff's attorney. FL-PP § 6:11.

d. Affidavit; Opposing motion for summary judgment; By defendant's attorney. FL-PP § 6:12.

e. Affidavit; Opposing motion for summary judgment; By party; Inability to present facts. FL-PP § 6:13.

f. Order; Establishing uncontroverted facts and stating issues requiring further determination. FL-PP § 6:14.

g. Summary judgment. FL-PP § 6:15.

h. Motion; Summary judgment, by defendant. FL-PRACFORM § 7:190.

i. Motion; Summary judgment, by plaintiff. FL-PRACFORM § 7:191.

j. Motion; Summary judgment, partial, by defendant. FL-PRACFORM § 7:192.

k. Motion; Summary judgment, part of claim. FL-PRACFORM § 7:193.

l. Form for plaintiff's motion for summary judgment. FL-RCPF R 1.510(128).

m. Form for notice of motion for summary judgment by plaintiff. FL-RCPF R 1.510(129).

n. Form for notice of cross-motion for summary judgment by plaintiff. FL-RCPF R 1.510(130).

o. Form for order denying motion for summary judgment and specifying uncontroverted facts. FL-RCPF R 1.510(304).

p. Form for motion for partial summary judgment. FL-RCPF R 1.510(305).

q. Form for motion for partial summary judgment-affirmative defenses. FL-RCPF R 1.510(305.1).

I. Checklist

(I) ❑ Matters to be considered by moving party

(a) ❑ Required documents

(1) ❑ Notice of hearing/Motion

(2) ❑ Certificate of service

(b) ❑ Supplemental documents

(1) ❑ Legal memorandum

(2) ❑ Affidavits

(3) ❑ Other evidence

(4) ❑ Proposed order

(5) ❑ Notice of constitutional question

(c) ❑ Time for making motion

(1) ❑ By the plaintiff, after the expiration of twenty (20) days from the commencement of the action (claimant), or after service of a motion for summary judgment by the adverse party

(2) ❑ By the defending party at any time

(3) ❑ The motion for summary judgment must be served at least twenty (20) days before the time fixed for the hearing

(II) ❑ Matters to be considered by opposing party

(a) ❑ Required documents

(1) ❑ Response to motion

(2) ❑ Certificate of service

(b) ❑ Supplemental documents

(1) ❑ Legal memorandum

(2) ❑ Affidavits

(3) ❑ Notice of evidence relied upon

(4) ❑ Other evidence

(5) ❑ Proposed order

(6) ❑ Notice of constitutional question

(c) ❑ Time for service and filing of opposition

(1) ❑ The adverse party shall identify, by notice mailed to the movant's attorney at least five (5) days prior to the day of the hearing, or delivered no later than 5:00 p.m. two (2) business days prior to the day of the hearing, any summary judgment evidence on which the adverse party relies

(2) ❑ To the extent that summary judgment evidence has not already been filed with the court, the adverse party shall serve a copy on the movant by mail at least five (5) days prior to the day of the hearing, or by delivery to the movant's attorney no later than 5:00 p.m. two (2) business days prior to the day of hearing

Motions, Oppositions and Replies
Motion for Sanctions

Document Last Updated January 2013

A. Applicable Rules

1. *State rules*

a. Attorney's fee; Sanctions for raising unsupported claims or defenses; Exceptions; Service of motions; Damages for delay of litigation. FL ST § 57.105.

b. Administrative Procedure Act. FL ST § 120.50; FL ST § 120.52; FL ST § 120.68; FL ST § 120.81.

c. Offer of judgment and demand for judgment. FL ST § 768.79.

d. Proposals for settlement. FL ST RCP Rule 1.442.

e. Motions for costs and attorneys' fees. FL ST RCP Rule 1.525.

f. Rules of court. FL ST RCP Rule 1.010; FL ST J ADMIN Rule 2.110.

g. Nonverification of pleadings. FL ST RCP Rule 1.030.

h. Service and filing of pleadings, orders, and documents. FL ST RCP Rule 1.080.

i. Time. FL ST RCP Rule 1.090.

j. Pleadings and motions. FL ST RCP Rule 1.100.

k. Motions. FL ST RCP Rule 1.160.

l. Relief from judgment, decrees, or orders. FL ST RCP Rule 1.540.

m. Mediation and arbitration. FL ST RCP Rule 1.700; FL ST RCP Rule 1.710; FL ST RCP Rule 1.720;

FL ST RCP Rule 1.730; FL ST RCP Rule 1.750; FL ST RCP Rule 1.800; FL ST RCP Rule 1.810; FL ST RCP Rule 1.820; FL ST RCP Rule 1.830.

n. Forms. FL ST RCP Rule 1.900.

o. Minimization of the filing of sensitive information. FL ST J ADMIN Rule 2.425.

p. Retention of court records. FL ST J ADMIN Rule 2.430.

q. Foreign attorneys. FL ST J ADMIN Rule 2.510.

r. Signature of attorneys and parties. FL ST J ADMIN Rule 2.515.

s. Paper. FL ST J ADMIN Rule 2.520.

t. Electronic filing. FL ST J ADMIN Rule 2.525.

u. Accessibility of information and technology. FL ST J ADMIN Rule 2.526.

v. Communication equipment. FL ST J ADMIN Rule 2.530.

w. Court reporting. FL ST J ADMIN Rule 2.535.

x. Requests for accommodations by persons with disabilities. FL ST J ADMIN Rule 2.540.

2. *Local rules*

   a. Hearings. FL ST 9 J CIR SECTION 10.

   b. Motion practice generally. FL ST 9 J CIR SECTION 11.

   c. Orders and judgments. FL ST 9 J CIR SECTION 12.

   d. Alternative dispute resolution. FL ST 9 J CIR SECTION 15.

   e. Business court procedures. FL ST 9 J CIR ORANGE CIV SECTION 1.

B. Timing

1. *Motion for sanctions.* A motion by a party seeking sanctions under FL ST § 57.105 must be served but may not be filed with or presented to the court unless, within twenty one (21) days after service of the motion, the challenged paper, claim, defense, contention, allegation, or denial is not withdrawn or appropriately corrected. FL ST § 57.105(4).

2. *Sanctions in relation to proposals for settlement.* Any party seeking sanctions pursuant to applicable Florida law, based on the failure of the proposal's recipient to accept a proposal, shall do so by serving a motion in accordance with FL ST RCP Rule 1.525. FL ST RCP Rule 1.442(g). Any party seeking a judgment taxing costs, attorneys' fees, or both shall serve a motion no later than thirty (30) days after filing of the judgment, including a judgment of dismissal, or the service of a notice of voluntary dismissal, which judgment or notice concludes the action as to that party. FL ST RCP Rule 1.525.

3. *General motion timing.* A copy of any written motion which may not be heard ex parte and a copy of the notice of the hearing thereof shall be served a reasonable time before the time specified for the hearing. FL ST RCP Rule 1.090(d).

   a. Each attorney shall utilize the courts web page under Judicial Automated Calendaring System, for available hearing time and the judge's schedule before telephoning the judicial assistant. FL ST 9 J CIR SECTION 10(A)(1).

   b. The hearing will be scheduled with the judge's judicial assistant. Written or fax notice must be received in opposing counsel's office at least four (4) working days before the hearing. FL ST 9 J CIR SECTION 10(A)(2).

      i. Counsel who serves a memorandum or authority list first should also include a copy of the motion, any papers to which it is addressed, and the response, if any. In order for the judge to properly review a submission in advance, it must be received in the judge's office at least three (3) working days before the hearing. FL ST 9 J CIR SECTION 11(B).

   c. *Obtaining hearing times*

      i. If the motion is one which might be resolved by stipulation or agreed order, moving counsel must explore that possibility with opposing counsel before reserving hearing time. FL ST 9 J CIR SECTION 11(C)(1).

ii. If at all possible, hearing time for complex motions or several motions to be heard at one time should be cleared with all affected counsel so as to avoid calendar conflicts. FL ST 9 J CIR SECTION 11(C)(1).

iii. If hearing time cannot be coordinated with opposing counsel, attorneys shall appear at ex parte to resolve the issue. FL ST 9 J CIR SECTION 11(C)(1).

4. *Computation of time*

a. *Generally.* Computation of time shall be governed by FL ST J ADMIN Rule 2.514. FL ST RCP Rule 1.090(a). The following rules apply in computing time periods specified in any rule of procedure, local rule, court order, or statute that does not specify a method of computing time. FL ST J ADMIN Rule 2.514(a).

i. *Period stated in days or a longer unit.* When the period is stated in days or a longer unit of time (A) exclude the day of the event that triggers the period; (B) count every day, including intermediate Saturdays, Sundays, and legal holidays; and (C) include the last day of the period, but if the last day is a Saturday, Sunday, or legal holiday, or falls within any period of time extended through an order of the chief justice under FL ST J ADMIN Rule 2.205(a)(2)(B)(iv), the period continues to run until the end of the next day that is not a Saturday, Sunday, or legal holiday and does not fall within any period of time extended through an order of the chief justice. FL ST J ADMIN Rule 2.514(a)(1).

ii. *Period stated in hours.* When the period is stated in hours (A) begin counting immediately on the occurrence of the event that triggers the period; (B) count every hour, including hours during intermediate Saturdays, Sundays, and legal holidays; and (C) if the period would end on a Saturday, Sunday, or legal holiday, or during any period of time extended through an order of the chief justice under FL ST J ADMIN Rule 2.205(a)(2)(B)(iv), the period continues to run until the same time on the next day that is not a Saturday, Sunday, or legal holiday and does not fall within any period of time extended through an order of the chief justice. FL ST J ADMIN Rule 2.514(a)(2).

iii. *Period stated in days less than seven (7) days.* When the period stated in days is less than seven (7) days, intermediate Saturdays, Sundays, and legal holidays shall be excluded in the computation. FL ST J ADMIN Rule 2.514(a)(3).

iv. *"Last day" defined.* Unless a different time is set by a statute, local rule, or court order, the last day ends (A) for electronic filing or for service by any means, at midnight; and (B) for filing by other means, when the clerk's office is scheduled to close. FL ST J ADMIN Rule 2.514(a)(4).

v. *"Next day" defined.* The "next day" is determined by continuing to count forward when the period is measured after an event and backward when measured before an event. FL ST J ADMIN Rule 2.514(a)(5).

vi. *"Legal holiday" defined.* "Legal holiday" means (A) the day set aside by FL ST § 110.117, for observing New Year's Day, Martin Luther King, Jr.'s Birthday, Memorial Day, Independence Day, Labor Day, Veterans' Day, Thanksgiving Day, the Friday after Thanksgiving Day, or Christmas Day, and (B) any day observed as a holiday by the clerk's office or as designated by the chief judge. FL ST J ADMIN Rule 2.514(a)(6).

b. *Additional time after service by mail or e-mail.* When a party may or must act within a specified time after service and service is made by mail or e-mail, five (5) days are added after the period that would otherwise expire under FL ST J ADMIN Rule 2.514(a). FL ST J ADMIN Rule 2.514(b).

c. *Enlargement.* When an act is required or allowed to be done at or within a specified time by order of court, by the Florida Rules of Civil Procedure, or by notice given thereunder, for cause shown the court at any time in its discretion (1) with or without notice, may order the period enlarged if request therefor is made before the expiration of the period originally prescribed or as extended by a previous order, or (2) upon motion made and notice after the expiration of the specified period, may permit the act to be done when failure to act was the result of excusable neglect, but it may not extend the time for making a motion for new trial, for rehearing, or to alter or amend a judgment; making a motion for relief from a judgment under FL ST RCP Rule 1.540(b); taking an appeal or filing a petition for certiorari; or making a motion for a directed verdict. FL ST RCP Rule 1.090(b).

d. *Unaffected by expiration of term.* The period of time provided for the doing of any act or the taking of any proceeding shall not be affected or limited by the continued existence or expiration of a term of court. The continued existence or expiration of a term of court in no way affects the power of a court to do any act or take any proceeding in any action which is or has been pending before it. FL ST RCP Rule 1.090(c).

C. General Requirements

1. *Motions generally*

   a. *Contents.* An application to the court for an order shall be by motion which shall be made in writing unless made during a hearing or trial, shall state with particularity the grounds therefor, and shall set forth the relief or order sought. The requirement of writing is fulfilled if the motion is stated in a written notice of the hearing of the motion. All notices of hearing shall specify each motion or other matter to be heard. FL ST RCP Rule 1.100(b).

   b. *Particularity requirement.* The court considers a motion in the light of the substantive law, rule or statute to make its determination. Some rules require a statement of the grounds for a motion under the rule. Failure to give the grounds will result in denial of the motion. This should be the result in all situations when the ground for the motion is not inherent in the rule. FL-PRACPROC § 9:3. The requirement is nevertheless an important one, first because of the due process notice rights of the respondent, as well as for the assistance it provides to the court in its preparation for the hearing or, absent a hearing, for disposition. 4 FLPRAC R 1.100. Every written motion shall cite the particular rule or statute and/or leading case upon which the motion is based. FL ST 9 J CIR SECTION 11(A)(1).

2. *Motion for sanctions*

   a. *Sanctions for raising unsupported claims or defenses*

      i. *No material facts; No law supporting material facts.* Upon the court's initiative or motion of any party, the court shall award a reasonable attorney's fee, including prejudgment interest, to be paid to the prevailing party in equal amounts by the losing party and the losing party's attorney on any claim or defense at any time during a civil proceeding or action in which the court finds that the losing party or the losing party's attorney knew or should have known that a claim or defense when initially presented to the court or at any time before trial was not supported by the material facts necessary to establish the claim or defense; or would not be supported by the application of then-existing law to those material facts. FL ST § 57.105(1).

      ii. *Unreasonable delay.* At any time in any civil proceeding or action in which the moving party proves by a preponderance of the evidence that any action taken by the opposing party, including, but not limited to, the filing of any pleading or part thereof, the assertion of or response to any discovery demand, the assertion of any claim or defense, or the response to any request by any other party, was taken primarily for the purpose of unreasonable delay, the court shall award damages to the moving party for its reasonable expenses incurred in obtaining the order, which may include attorney's fees, and other loss resulting from the improper delay. FL ST § 57.105(2).

      iii. *Limit on monetary sanctions.* Notwithstanding FL ST § 57.105(1) and FL ST § 57.105(2), monetary sanctions may not be awarded:

         - Under FL ST § 57.105(1)(b) if the court determines that the claim or defense was initially presented to the court as a good faith argument for the extension, modification, or reversal of existing law or the establishment of new law, as it applied to the material facts, with a reasonable expectation of success. FL ST § 57.105(3)(a).
         - Under FL ST § 57.105(1)(a) or FL ST § 57.105(1)(b) against the losing party's attorney if he or she has acted in good faith, based on the representations of his or her client as to the existence of those material facts. FL ST § 57.105(3)(b).
         - Under FL ST § 57.105(1)(b) against a represented party. FL ST § 57.105(3)(c).
         - On the court's initiative under FL ST § 57.105(1) and FL ST § 57.105(2) unless sanctions

are awarded before a voluntary dismissal or settlement of the claims made by or against the party that is, or whose attorneys are, to be sanctioned. FL ST § 57.105(3)(d).

iv. *Other sanctions available.* The provisions of FL ST § 57.105 are supplemental to other sanctions or remedies available under law or under court rules. FL ST § 57.105(6).

v. *Fees provided for in contract.* If a contract contains a provision allowing attorney's fees to a party when he or she is required to take any action to enforce the contract, the court may also allow reasonable attorney's fees to the other party when that party prevails in any action, whether as plaintiff or defendant, with respect to the contract. FL ST § 57.105(7) applies to any contract entered into on or after October 1, 1988. FL ST § 57.105(7).

b. *Sanctions in relation to proposals for settlement*

i. *Generally.* Any party seeking sanctions pursuant to applicable Florida law, based on the failure of the proposal's recipient to accept a proposal, shall do so by serving a motion in accordance with FL ST RCP Rule 1.525. FL ST RCP Rule 1.442(g). Any party seeking a judgment taxing costs, attorneys' fees, or both shall serve a motion no later than thirty (30) days after filing of the judgment, including a judgment of dismissal, or the service of a notice of voluntary dismissal, which judgment or notice concludes the action as to that party. FL ST RCP Rule 1.525.

ii. *Motion after judgment, voluntary or involuntary dismissal.* Upon motion made by the offeror within thirty (30) days after the entry of judgment or after voluntary or involuntary dismissal, the court shall determine the following:

- If a defendant serves an offer which is not accepted by the plaintiff, and if the judgment obtained by the plaintiff is at least twenty-five (25%) percent less than the amount of the offer, the defendant shall be awarded reasonable costs, including investigative expenses, and attorney's fees, calculated in accordance with the guidelines promulgated by the Supreme Court, incurred from the date the offer was served, and the court shall set off such costs in attorney's fees against the award. When such costs and attorney's fees total more than the amount of the judgment, the court shall enter judgment for the defendant against the plaintiff for the amount of the costs and fees, less the amount of the award to the plaintiff. FL ST § 768.79(6)(a).
- If a plaintiff serves an offer which is not accepted by the defendant, and if the judgment obtained by the plaintiff is at least twenty-five (25%) percent more than the amount of the offer, the plaintiff shall be awarded reasonable costs, including investigative expenses, and attorney's fees, calculated in accordance with the guidelines promulgated by the Supreme Court, incurred from the date the offer was served. FL ST § 768.79(6)(b).
- For purposes of the determination required by FL ST § 768.79(6)(a), the term "judgment obtained" means the amount of the net judgment entered, plus any postoffer collateral source payments received or due as of the date of the judgment, plus any postoffer settlement amounts by which the verdict was reduced. For purposes of the determination required by FL ST § 768.79(6)(b), the term "judgment obtained" means the amount of the net judgment entered, plus any postoffer settlement amounts by which the verdict was reduced. FL ST § 768.79(6).

iii. For further information please see FL ST § 768.79 and FL ST RCP Rule 1.442.

3. *Arbitration and mediation*

a. *Referral to arbitration and mediation.* Except as hereinafter provided or as otherwise prohibited by law, the presiding judge may enter an order referring all or any part of a contested civil matter to mediation or arbitration. The parties to any contested civil matter may file a written stipulation to mediate or arbitrate any issue between them at any time. Such stipulation shall be incorporated into the order of referral. FL ST RCP Rule 1.700(a).

i. *Local arbitration policy.* It is the policy of the Civil Division judges to maximize the use of alternative dispute resolution procedures. Except where prohibited by statute, mediation will be ordered in all cases where jury trial is requested and in selected cases which are to be tried non-jury. Also, selected cases will be referred for court-annexed non-binding arbitration through the Orange County Bar Association Arbitration Service. Counsel may move to dispense with or defer mediation or arbitration or move to modify the referral order for good cause. FL ST 9 J CIR SECTION 15.

b. *Arbitration*

i. *Exclusions.* A civil action shall be ordered to arbitration or arbitration in conjunction with mediation upon stipulation of the parties. A civil action may be ordered to arbitration or arbitration in conjunction with mediation upon motion of any party or by the court, if the judge determines the action to be of such a nature that arbitration could be of benefit to the litigants or the court. FL ST RCP Rule 1.800.

- Under no circumstances may the following categories of actions be referred to arbitration: (1) bond estreatures; (2) habeas corpus or other extraordinary writs; (3) bond validations; (4) civil or criminal contempt; (5) such other matters as may be specified by order of the chief judge in the circuit. FL ST RCP Rule 1.800.

ii. For more information regarding arbitration, please see FL ST RCP Rule 1.810; FL ST RCP Rule 1.820; FL ST RCP Rule 1.830.

c. *Mediation.* For more information regarding mediation, please see FL ST RCP Rule 1.710; FL ST RCP Rule 1.720; FL ST RCP Rule 1.730; and FL ST RCP Rule 1.750.

4. *Rules of court*

a. *Rules of civil procedure.* The Florida Rules of Civil Procedure apply to all actions of a civil nature and all special statutory proceedings in the circuit courts and county courts except those to which the Florida Probate Rules, the Florida Family Law Rules of Procedure, or the Small Claims Rules apply. FL ST RCP Rule 1.010.

i. The form, content, procedure, and time for pleading in all special statutory proceedings shall be as prescribed by the statutes governing the proceeding unless the Florida Rules of Civil Procedure specifically provide to the contrary. FL ST RCP Rule 1.010.

ii. The Florida Rules of Civil Procedure shall be construed to secure the just, speedy, and inexpensive determination of every action. FL ST RCP Rule 1.010.

b. *Rules of judicial administration.* The Florida Rules of Judicial Administration shall apply to administrative matters in all courts to which the Florida Rules of Judicial Administration are applicable by their terms. The Florida Rules of Judicial Administration shall be construed to secure the speedy and inexpensive determination of every proceeding to which they are applicable. The Florida Rules of Judicial Administration shall supersede all conflicting rules and statutes. FL ST J ADMIN Rule 2.110.

c. *Business court procedures.* For rules specific to Business Court, please see FL ST 9 J CIR ORANGE CIV SECTION 1, et seq.

D. Documents

1. *Required documents*

a. *Notice of hearing/Motion.* An application to the court for an order shall be by motion which shall be made in writing unless made during a hearing or trial, shall state with particularity the grounds therefor, and shall set forth the relief or order sought. The requirement of writing is fulfilled if the motion is stated in a written notice of the hearing of the motion. All notices of hearing shall specify each motion or other matter to be heard. FL ST RCP Rule 1.100(b). A notice calling up "all pending motions" is insufficient. FL ST 9 J CIR SECTION 11(D)(1). Additional motions should not be "piggy-backed" by cross-notice unless counsel first confirms with opposing counsel and the judge's judicial assistant that there can be sufficient additional time reserved in which to hear them. FL ST 9 J CIR SECTION 11(D)(2).

i. *Notices to persons with disabilities.* See the Format section of this KeyRules document for further information.

b. *Certificate of service.* When any attorney certifies in substance: "I certify that a copy hereof has been furnished to (here insert name or names and addresses used for service) by (e-mail) (delivery) (mail) (fax) on .... (date) ....________ Attorney" the certificate is taken as prima facie proof of such service in compliance with FL ST J ADMIN Rule 2.516. FL ST J ADMIN Rule 2.516(f).

2. *Supplemental documents*

   a. *Legal memorandum.* Legal memorandums in support of or opposition to motions are optional. But if filed, counsel must furnish the judge with chambers copies of the memorandum and highlighted copies of primary legal authorities cited therein. FL ST 9 J CIR SECTION 11(B).

      i. As an alternative to a memorandum, a list of primary legal authorities with highlighted copies attached may be submitted. Chambers copies and authority lists must be under cover letter referencing the case style and number and stating the date and time of the hearing. FL ST 9 J CIR SECTION 11(B).

   b. *Proposed order.* The court may require that orders or judgments be prepared by a party, may require the party to furnish the court with stamped, addressed envelopes for service of the order or judgment, and may require that proposed orders and judgments be furnished to all parties before entry by the court of the order or judgment. FL ST J ADMIN Rule 2.516(h)(1).

      i. Proposed orders and judgments will be prepared by the prevailing attorney unless the judge designates some other attorney or states that he or she will prepare the order or judgment. FL ST 9 J CIR SECTION 12(A)(1).

      ii. When submitting proposed orders or judgments, counsel shall also include sufficient copies and self address stamped envelopes for all parties. FL ST 9 J CIR SECTION 12(A)(2).

      iii. Moving counsel must present a proposed order with space for ruling left blank at the conclusion of the hearing and must serve conformed copies on all other counsel and unrepresented parties. FL ST 9 J CIR SECTION 10(A)(3).

      iv. Unsigned orders or judgments should not be sent to the Clerk's office for transmission to the judge. FL ST 9 J CIR SECTION 12(D)(3).

   c. *Notice of constitutional question.* A party that files a pleading, written motion, or other paper drawing into question the constitutionality of a state statute or a county or municipal charter, ordinance, or franchise must promptly (1) file a notice of constitutional question stating the question and identifying the paper that raises it; and (2) serve the notice and the pleading, written motion, or other paper drawing into question the constitutionality of a state statute or a county or municipal charter, ordinance, or franchise on the Attorney General or the state attorney of the judicial circuit in which the action is pending, by either certified or registered mail. Service of the notice and pleading, written motion, or other paper does not require joinder of the Attorney General or the state attorney as a party to the action. FL ST RCP Rule 1.071.

E. Format

1. *Documents; Type and size.* Documents subject to the exceptions set forth in FL ST J ADMIN Rule 2.525(d) shall be filed on recycled paper measuring eight and one half by eleven (8 1/2 by 11) inches. For purposes of FL ST J ADMIN Rule 2.520, paper is recycled if it contains a minimum content of fifty (50) percent waste paper. Xerographic reduction of legal-size (eight and one half by fourteen (8 1/2 by 14) inches) documents to letter size (eight and one half by eleven (8 1/2 by 11) inches) is prohibited. All other documents filed by electronic transmission shall be filed in a format capable of being printed in a format consistent with the provisions of FL ST J ADMIN Rule 2.250. FL ST J ADMIN Rule 2.520(b).

   a. *Exhibits.* Any exhibit or attachment filed with pleadings or papers may be filed in its original size. FL ST J ADMIN Rule 2.520(c).

   b. *Recording space.* On all papers and documents prepared and filed by the court or by any party to a proceeding which are to be recorded in the public records of any county, including but not limited to final money judgments and notices of lis pendens, a three (3) inch by three (3) inch space at the top right-hand corner on the first page and a one (1) inch by three (3) inch space at the top right-hand corner on each subsequent page shall be left blank and reserved for use by the clerk of court. FL ST J ADMIN Rule 2.520(d).

      i. *Exceptions to recording space.* Any papers or documents created by persons or entities over

which the filing party has no control, including but not limited to wills, codicils, trusts, or other testamentary documents; documents prepared or executed by any public officer; documents prepared, executed, acknowledged, or proved outside of the State of Florida; or documents created by State or Federal government agencies, may be filed without the space required by FL ST J ADMIN Rule 2.520. FL ST J ADMIN Rule 2.520(e).

c. *Noncompliance.* No clerk of court is permitted to refuse to file any document or paper because of noncompliance with the Florida Rules of Judicial Administration. However, upon request of the clerk of court, noncomplying documents must be resubmitted in accordance with the formatting rules. FL ST J ADMIN Rule 2.520(f).

d. *Proposed orders*

   i. All orders will be on eight and a half by eleven (8 1/2 by 11) inch plain white paper (not lined or letterhead paper) and be double spaced. FL ST 9 J CIR SECTION 12(B)(1).

   ii. The order must contain a title indicating what matter the order pertains to, e.g., "Order On Defendant Smith's Motion To Dismiss." FL ST 9 J CIR SECTION 12(B)(2).

   iii. The preamble of the order should include the date of the hearing and what motions were heard. FL ST 9 J CIR SECTION 12(B)(3).

   iv. The adjudication portion of the order should state what relief is ordered. Simply stating that "the motion is granted" without more is insufficient. FL ST 9 J CIR SECTION 12(B)(4).

   v. The order should indicate the specific time period of any act ordered to be done and should state whether the time period runs from the date of the hearing or the date the order is signed or some other specified date. FL ST 9 J CIR SECTION 12(B)(5).

   vi. The order should contain a full certificate of service with the complete names and addresses of the attorneys and unrepresented parties to be served. Merely showing "copies to" is insufficient. FL ST 9 J CIR SECTION 12(B)(6).

   vii. If an order of dismissal is final (i.e., it disposes of the entire case) the title should contain the word "Final." When the order is not final but leaves other counts or claims against other defendants pending, it should so state in a separate paragraph. FL ST 9 J CIR SECTION 12(B)(7).

   viii. When submitting stipulations, orders shall be by separate order, not attached to the stipulation. FL ST 9 J CIR SECTION 12(B)(8).

   ix. Counsel preparing the Final Judgment or order should draft and circulate copies within two (2) working days of the ruling or jury verdict. If counsel preparing the Final Judgment or order gets approval as to form of the order from all counsel, the original with copies and envelopes should be sent directly to the judge with a cover letter stating all counsel agree to the form of the order or judgment. If other counsel objects to the form or cannot be reached for approval, counsel preparing the judgment or order shall notice a motion for entry of the order or judgment. If objecting counsel does not furnish the judge prior to or at the hearing with a proposed judgment or order version with copies under cover letter stating the reasons for the objection, all objections will be deemed waived. Orders and judgments should not be submitted to the judge to hold waiting for an objection. FL ST 9 J CIR SECTION 12(D).

2. *Caption.* Every pleading, motion, order, judgment, or other paper shall have a caption containing the name of the court, the file number, and except for in rem proceedings, including forfeiture proceedings, the name of the first party on each side with an appropriate indication of other parties, and a designation identifying the party filing it and its nature or the nature of the order, as the case may be. In any in rem proceeding, every pleading, motion, order, judgment, or other paper shall have a caption containing the name of the court, the file number, the style "In re" (followed by the name or general description of the property), and a designation of the person or entity filing it and its nature or the nature of the order, as the case may be. In an in rem forfeiture proceeding, the style shall be "In re forfeiture of" (followed by the name of the general description of the property). All papers filed in the action shall be styled in such a manner as to indicate clearly the subject matter of the paper and the party requesting or obtaining relief. FL ST RCP Rule 1.100(c)(1).

3. *Writing and written defined.* Writing or written means a document containing information, an application, or a stipulation. FL ST RCP Rule 1.080(c).
4. *Rule abbreviations*
    a. The Florida Rules of Civil Procedure and shall be abbreviated as Fla.R.Civ.P. FL ST RCP Rule 1.010.
    b. The Florida Rules of Judicial Administration shall be abbreviated as Fla. R. Jud. Admin. FL ST J ADMIN Rule 2.110.
5. *Nonverification.* Except when otherwise specifically provided by the Florida Rules of Civil Procedure or an applicable statute, every pleading or other document of a party represented by an attorney need not be verified or accompanied by an affidavit. FL ST RCP Rule 1.030; FL ST J ADMIN Rule 2.515(a).
6. *Unrepresented parties.* An unrepresented party must file his or her papers with the clerk and send copies to other attorneys or unrepresented parties. All such papers must be typed double-spaced on plain white eight and a half by eleven (8 1/2 by 11) inch paper, with the name of the case and case number at the top and the party's mailing address, telephone number and FAX number, if any, below his or her signature at the end of the paper. Such unrepresented party must immediately notify the clerk and all other counsel or parties of record in writing of any change in mailing address or telephone or FAX number. Failure to promptly notify of change of address could result in a dismissal or default entered against such party. FL ST 9 J CIR SECTION 7(B)(5).
7. *Attorney signature*
    a. *Attorney signature.* Every pleading and other document of a party represented by an attorney shall be signed by at least one (1) attorney of record in that attorney's individual name whose current record Florida Bar address, telephone number, including area code, primary e-mail address and secondary e-mail addresses, if any, and Florida Bar number shall be stated, and who shall be duly licensed to practice law in Florida or who shall have received permission to appear in the particular case as provided in FL ST J ADMIN Rule 2.510. FL ST J ADMIN Rule 2.515(a).
        i. The attorney may be required by the court to give the address of, and to vouch for the attorney's authority to represent, the party. FL ST J ADMIN Rule 2.515(a).
        ii. The signature of an attorney shall constitute a certificate by the attorney that the attorney has read the pleading or other document; that to the best of the attorney's knowledge, information, and belief there is good ground to support it; and that it is not interposed for delay. FL ST J ADMIN Rule 2.515(a).
        iii. If a pleading is not signed or is signed with intent to defeat the purpose of FL ST J ADMIN Rule 2.515, it may be stricken and the action may proceed as though the pleading or other document had not been served. FL ST J ADMIN Rule 2.515(a).
    b. *Pro se litigant signature.* A party who is not represented by an attorney shall sign any pleading or other paper and state the party's address and telephone number, including area code. FL ST J ADMIN Rule 2.515(b).
    c. *Form of signature*
        i. The signatures required on pleadings and documents by FL ST J ADMIN Rule 2.515(a) and FL ST J ADMIN Rule 2.515(b) may be:
            - Original signatures;
            - Original signatures that have been reproduced by electronic means, such as on electronically transmitted documents or photocopied documents;
            - Electronic signatures using the "/s/," "s/," or "/s" formats by or at the direction of the person signing; or
            - Any other signature format authorized by general law, so long as the clerk where the proceeding is pending has the capability of receiving and has obtained approval from the Supreme Court of Florida to accept pleadings and documents with that signature format. FL ST J ADMIN Rule 2.515(c)(1).

ii. An attorney, party, or other person who files a pleading or paper by electronic transmission that does not contain the original signature of that attorney, party, or other person shall file that identical pleading or paper in paper form containing an original signature of that attorney, party, or other person (hereinafter called the follow-up filing) immediately thereafter. The follow-up filing is not required if the Supreme Court of Florida has entered an order directing the clerk of court to discontinue accepting the follow-up filing. FL ST J ADMIN Rule 2.515(c)(2).

8. *Forms*

a. *Process.* The forms of process, notice of lis pendens, and notice of action provided in the Florida Rules of Civil Procedure are sufficient. Variations from the forms do not void process or notices that are otherwise sufficient. FL ST RCP Rule 1.900(a).

b. *Other forms.* The other forms provided in the Florida Rules of Civil Procedure are sufficient for the matters that are covered by them. So long as the substance is expressed without prolixity, the forms may be varied to meet the facts of a particular case. FL ST RCP Rule 1.900(b).

c. *Formal matters.* Captions, except for the designation of the paper, are omitted from the forms provided in the Florida Rules of Civil Procedure. A general form of caption is the first form provided. Signatures are omitted from pleadings and motions. FL ST RCP Rule 1.900(c).

9. *Notices to persons with disabilities.* All notices of court proceedings to be held in a public facility, and all process compelling appearance at such proceedings, shall include the following statement in bold face, fourteen (14) point Times New Roman or Courier font: "If you are a person with a disability who needs any accommodation in order to participate in this proceeding, you are entitled, at no cost to you, to the provision of certain assistance. Please contact [identify applicable court personnel by name, address, and telephone number] at least seven (7) days before your scheduled court appearance, or immediately upon receiving this notification if the time before the scheduled appearance is less than seven (7) days; if you are hearing or voice impaired, call 711." FL ST J ADMIN Rule 2.540(c)(1).

10. *Minimization of the filing of sensitive information*

a. *Limitations for court filings.* Unless authorized by FL ST J ADMIN Rule 2.425(b), statute, another rule of court, or the court orders otherwise, designated sensitive information filed with the court must be limited to the following format:

i. The initials of a person known to be a minor;

ii. The year of birth of a person's birth date;

iii. No portion of any: Social security number, Bank account number, Credit card account number, Charge account number, or Debit account number;

iv. The last four digits of any: Taxpayer identification number (TIN), Employee identification number, Driver's license number, Passport number, Telephone number, Financial account number, except as set forth in FL ST J ADMIN Rule 2.425(a)(3), Brokerage account number, Insurance policy account number, Loan account number, Customer account number, or Patient or health care number;

v. A truncated version of any: Email address, Computer user name, Password, or Personal identification number (PIN); and

vi. A truncated version of any other sensitive information as provided by court order. FL ST J ADMIN Rule 2.425(a).

b. *Exceptions.* FL ST J ADMIN Rule 2.425(a) does not apply to the following:

i. An account number which identifies the property alleged to be the subject of a proceeding;

ii. The record of an administrative or agency proceeding;

iii. The record in appellate or review proceedings;

iv. The birth date of a minor whenever the birth date is necessary for the court to establish or maintain subject matter jurisdiction;

v. The name of a minor in any order relating to parental responsibility, time-sharing, or child support;

vi. The name of a minor in any document or order affecting the minor's ownership of real property;

vii. The birth date of a party in a writ of attachment or notice to payor;

viii. In traffic and criminal proceedings: a pro se filing; a court filing that is related to a criminal matter or investigation and that is prepared before the filing of a criminal charge or is not filed as part of any docketed criminal case; an arrest or search warrant or any information in support thereof; a charging document and an affidavit or other documents filed in support of any charging document, including any driving records; a statement of particulars; discovery material introduced into evidence or otherwise filed with the court; and all information necessary for the proper issuance and execution of a subpoena duces tecum;

ix. Information used by the clerk for case maintenance purposes or the courts for case management purposes; and

x. Information which is relevant and material to an issue before the court. FL ST J ADMIN Rule 2.425(b).

c. *Remedies.* Upon motion by a party or interested person or sua sponte by the court, the court may order remedies, sanctions or both for a violation of FL ST J ADMIN Rule 2.425(a). Following notice and an opportunity to respond, the court may impose sanctions if such filing was not made in good faith. FL ST J ADMIN Rule 2.425(c).

d. *Motions not restricted.* FL ST J ADMIN Rule 2.425 does not restrict a party's right to move for protective order, to move to file documents under seal, or to request a determination of the confidentiality of records. FL ST J ADMIN Rule 2.425(d).

e. *Application.* FL ST J ADMIN Rule 2.425 does not affect the application of constitutional provisions, statutes, or rules of court regarding confidential information or access to public information. FL ST J ADMIN Rule 2.425(e).

F. Filing and Service Requirements

1. *Filing requirements.* All original documents must be filed with the court either before service or immediately thereafter, unless otherwise provided for by general law or other rules. If the original of any bond or other document is not placed in the court file, a certified copy must be so placed by the clerk. FL ST J ADMIN Rule 2.516(d). All documents shall be filed in conformity with the requirements of FL ST J ADMIN Rule 2.525. FL ST RCP Rule 1.080(b). All documents filed in any court shall be filed by electronic transmission in accordance with FL ST J ADMIN Rule 2.525. "Documents" means pleadings, motions, petitions, memoranda, briefs, notices, exhibits, declarations, affidavits, orders, judgments, decrees, writs, opinions, and any other paper or writing submitted to a court. FL ST J ADMIN Rule 2.520(a). All documents that are court records, as defined in FL ST J ADMIN Rule 2.430(a)(1), must be filed by electronic transmission, provided that: (1) the clerk has the ability to accept and retain such documents; (2) the clerk or the chief judge of the circuit has requested permission to accept documents filed by electronic transmission; and (3) the supreme court has entered an order granting permission to the clerk to accept documents filed by electronic transmission. FL ST J ADMIN Rule 2.525(c)(1).

a. *Definition.* "Electronic transmission of documents" means the sending of information by electronic signals to, by or from a court or clerk, which when received can be transformed and stored or transmitted on paper, microfilm, magnetic storage device, optical imaging system, CD-ROM, flash drive, other electronic data storage system, server, case maintenance system ("CM"), electronic court filing ("ECF") system, statewide or local electronic portal ("e-portal"), or other electronic record keeping system authorized by the supreme court in a format sufficient to communicate the information on the original document in a readable format. Electronic transmission of documents includes electronic mail ("e-mail") and any internet-based transmission procedure, and may include procedures allowing for documents to be signed or verified by electronic means. FL ST J ADMIN Rule 2.525(a).

i. The filing of documents with the court as required by the Florida Rules of Judicial Administration must be made by filing them with the clerk in accordance with FL ST J ADMIN Rule 2.525, except that the judge may permit documents to be filed with the judge, in which event the judge must note the filing date before him or her on the documents and transmit them to the

clerk. The date of filing is that shown on the face of the document by the judge's notation or the clerk's time stamp, whichever is earlier. FL ST J ADMIN Rule 2.516(e).

b. *Application.* Any court or clerk of the court may accept the electronic transmission of documents for filing after the clerk, together with input from the chief judge of the circuit, has obtained approval of the procedures and program for doing so from the Supreme Court of Florida. FL ST J ADMIN Rule 2.525(b).

c. *Exceptions*

   i. Paper documents and other submissions may be manually submitted to the clerk or court:

      - When the clerk does not have the ability to accept and retain documents by electronic filing or has not had ECF Procedures approved by the supreme court;
      - For filing by any self-represented party or any self-represented nonparty unless specific ECF Procedures provide a means to file documents electronically. However, any self-represented nonparty that is a governmental or public agency and any other agency, partnership, corporation, or business entity acting on behalf of any governmental or public agency may file documents by electronic transmission if such entity has the capability of filing documents electronically;
      - For filing by attorneys excused from e-mail service in accordance with FL ST J ADMIN Rule 2.516(b);
      - When submitting evidentiary exhibits or filing non-documentary materials;
      - When the filing involves documents in excess of twenty-five (25) megabytes (25MB) in size. For such filings, documents may be transmitted using an electronic storage medium that the clerk has the ability to accept, which may include a CD-ROM, flash drive, or similar storage medium;
      - When filed in open court, as permitted by the court;
      - When paper filing is permitted by any approved statewide or local ECF procedures; and
      - If any court determines that justice so requires. FL ST J ADMIN Rule 2.525(d).

   ii. Any document in paper form submitted under FL ST J ADMIN Rule 2.525(d) is filed when it is received by the clerk or court and the clerk shall immediately thereafter convert any filed paper document to an electronic document. "Convert to an electronic document" means optically capturing an image of a paper document and using character recognition software to recover as much of the document's text as practicable and then indexing and storing the document in the official court file. FL ST J ADMIN Rule 2.525(c)(4).

   iii. Any storage medium submitted under FL ST J ADMIN Rule 2.525(d)(5) is filed when received by the clerk or court and the clerk shall immediately thereafter transfer the electronic documents from the storage device to the official court file. FL ST J ADMIN Rule 2.525(c)(5).

   iv. If the filer of any paper document authorized under FL ST J ADMIN Rule 2.525(d) provides a self-addressed, postage-paid envelope for return of the paper document after it is converted to electronic form by the clerk, the clerk shall place the paper document in the envelope and deposit it in the mail. Except when a paper document is required to be maintained, the clerk may recycle any filed paper document that is not to be returned to the filer. FL ST J ADMIN Rule 2.525(c)(6).

   v. The clerk may convert any paper document filed before the effective date of FL ST J ADMIN Rule 2.525 to an electronic document. Unless the clerk is required to maintain the paper document, if the paper document has been converted to an electronic document by the clerk, the paper document is no longer part of the official court file and may be removed and recycled. FL ST J ADMIN Rule 2.525(c)(7).

d. *Unrepresented parties.* An unrepresented party must file his or her papers with the clerk and send copies to other attorneys or unrepresented parties. FL ST 9 J CIR SECTION 7(B)(5).

   i. An unrepresented party may not communicate privately with the judge either by letter, telephone, in person or otherwise. FL ST 9 J CIR SECTION 7(B)(4).

ii. Copies of legal papers or other written materials should not be sent to the judge unless specifically requested by the judge or required by the local administrative procedures. Any unrequested or non-required papers or materials sent to a judge may not be read but may be returned to the sender or placed unread into the court file. FL ST 9 J CIR SECTION 7(B)(4).

e. *Official court file.* For information on what constitutes the official court file, please see FL ST J ADMIN Rule 2.525(c)(2), FL ST J ADMIN Rule 2.525(c)(3).

f. *Administration.* All attorneys, parties, or other persons using this rule to file documents are required to make arrangements with the court or clerk for the payment of any charges authorized by general law or the supreme court before filing any document by electronic transmission. FL ST J ADMIN Rule 2.525(f)(2).

g. *Filing date.* The filing date for an electronically transmitted document is the date and time that such filing is acknowledged by an electronic stamp or otherwise, pursuant to any procedure set forth in any ECF Procedures approved by the supreme court, or the date the last page of such filing is received by the court or clerk. FL ST J ADMIN Rule 2.525(f)(3).

h. *Accessibility.* All documents transmitted in any electronic form under FL ST J ADMIN Rule 2.525 must comply with the accessibility requirements of FL ST J ADMIN Rule 2.526. FL ST J ADMIN Rule 2.525(g).

2. *Service requirements.* Every pleading subsequent to the initial pleading, all orders, and every other document filed in the action must be served in conformity with the requirements of FL ST J ADMIN Rule 2.516. FL ST RCP Rule 1.080(a).

a. *Service; When required.* Unless the court otherwise orders, or a statute or supreme court administrative order specifies a different means of service, every pleading subsequent to the initial pleading and every other document filed in any court proceeding, except applications for witness subpoenas and documents served by formal notice or required to be served in the manner provided for service of formal notice, must be served in accordance with FL ST J ADMIN Rule 2.516 on each party. No service need be made on parties against whom a default has been entered, except that pleadings asserting new or additional claims against them must be served in the manner provided for service of summons. FL ST J ADMIN Rule 2.516(a).

i. Counsel who serves a memorandum or authority list first should also include a copy of the motion, any papers to which it is addressed, and the response, if any. In order for the judge to properly review a submission in advance, it must be received in the judge's office at least three (3) working days before the hearing. FL ST 9 J CIR SECTION 11(B).

b. *Service; How made.* When service is required or permitted to be made upon a party represented by an attorney, service must be made upon the attorney unless service upon the party is ordered by the court. FL ST J ADMIN Rule 2.516(b).

i. *Service by electronic mail ("e-mail").* All documents required or permitted to be served on another party must be served by e-mail, unless FL ST J ADMIN Rule 2.516 otherwise provides. When, in addition to service by e-mail, the sender also utilizes another means of service provided for in FL ST J ADMIN Rule 2.516(b)(2), any differing time limits and other provisions applicable to that other means of service control. FL ST J ADMIN Rule 2.516(b)(1). Any document electronically transmitted to a court or clerk must also be served on all parties and interested persons in accordance with the applicable rules of court. FL ST J ADMIN Rule 2.525(e)(2).

- *Service on attorneys.* Upon appearing in a proceeding, an attorney must serve a designation of a primary e-mail address and may designate no more than two (2) secondary e-mail addresses. Thereafter, service must be directed to all designated e-mail addresses in that proceeding. Every document filed by an attorney thereafter must include the primary e-mail address of that attorney and any secondary e-mail addresses. If an attorney does not designate any e-mail address for service, documents may be served on that attorney at the e-mail address on record with The Florida Bar. FL ST J ADMIN Rule 2.516(b)(1)(A).
- *Exception to e-mail service on attorneys.* Service by an attorney on another attorney must

be made by e-mail unless excused by the court. Upon motion by an attorney demonstrating that the attorney has no e-mail account and lacks access to the Internet at the attorney's office, the court may excuse the attorney from the requirements of e-mail service. Service on and by an attorney excused by the court from e-mail service must be by the means provided in FL ST J ADMIN Rule 2.516(b)(2). FL ST J ADMIN Rule 2.516(b)(1)(B).

- *Service on and by parties not represented by an attorney.* Any party not represented by an attorney may serve a designation of a primary e-mail address and also may designate no more than two (2) secondary e-mail addresses to which service must be directed in that proceeding by the means provided in FL ST J ADMIN Rule 2.516(b)(1). If a party not represented by an attorney does not designate an e-mail address for service in a proceeding, service on and by that party must be by the means provided in FL ST J ADMIN Rule 2.516(b)(2). FL ST J ADMIN Rule 2.516(b)(1)(C).
- *Time of service.* Service by e-mail is complete when it is sent. FL ST J ADMIN Rule 2.516(b)(1)(D). An e-mail is deemed served on the date it is sent. FL ST J ADMIN Rule 2.516(b)(1)(D)(i). If the sender learns that the e-mail did not reach the address of the person to be served, the sender must immediately send another copy by e-mail, or by a means authorized by FL ST J ADMIN Rule 2.516(b)(2). FL ST J ADMIN Rule 2.516(b)(1)(D)(ii). E-mail service is treated as service by mail for the computation of time. FL ST J ADMIN Rule 2.516(b)(1)(D)(iii).

ii. *Format of e-mail for service.* Service of a document by e-mail is made by attaching a copy of the document in PDF format to an e-mail sent to all addresses designated by the attorney or party. FL ST J ADMIN Rule 2.516(b)(1)(E).

- All documents served by e-mail must be attached to an e-mail message containing a subject line beginning with the words "SERVICE OF COURT DOCUMENT" in all capital letters, followed by the case number of the proceeding in which the documents are being served. FL ST J ADMIN Rule 2.516(b)(1)(E)(i).
- The body of the e-mail must identify the court in which the proceeding is pending, the case number, the name of the initial party on each side, the title of each document served with that e-mail, and the sender's name and telephone number. FL ST J ADMIN Rule 2.516(b)(1)(E)(ii).
- Any document served by e-mail may be signed by the "/s/" format, as long as the filed original is signed in accordance with the applicable rule of procedure. FL ST J ADMIN Rule 2.516(b)(1)(E)(iii).
- Any e-mail which, together with its attached documents, exceeds five megabytes (5MB) in size, must be divided and sent as separate e-mails, no one of which may exceed five megabytes (5MB) in size and each of which must be sequentially numbered in the subject line. FL ST J ADMIN Rule 2.516(b)(1)(E)(iv).

iii. *Service by other means.* In addition to, and not in lieu of, service by e-mail, service may also be made upon attorneys by any of the means specified in FL ST J ADMIN Rule 2.516(b)(2). Service on and by all parties who are not represented by an attorney and who do not designate an e-mail address, and on and by all attorneys excused from e-mail service, must be made by delivering a copy of the document or by mailing it to the party or attorney at their last known address or, if no address is known, by leaving it with the clerk of the court. Service by mail is complete upon mailing. Delivery of a copy within FL ST J ADMIN Rule 2.516 is complete upon:

- Handing it to the attorney or to the party,
- Leaving it at the attorney's or party's office with a clerk or other person in charge thereof,
- If there is no one in charge, leaving it in a conspicuous place therein,
- If the office is closed or the person to be served has no office, leaving it at the person's usual place of abode with some person of his or her family above fifteen (15) years of age and informing such person of the contents, or

- Transmitting it by facsimile to the attorney's or party's office with a cover sheet containing the sender's name, firm, address, telephone number, and facsimile number, and the number of pages transmitted. When service is made by facsimile, a copy must also be served by any other method permitted by FL ST J ADMIN Rule 2.516. Facsimile service occurs when transmission is complete. FL ST J ADMIN Rule 2.516(b)(2)(A) through FL ST J ADMIN Rule 2.516(b)(2)(E).
- Service by delivery after 5:00 p.m. must be deemed to have been made by mailing on the date of delivery. FL ST J ADMIN Rule 2.516(b)(2)(F).

c. *Service; Numerous defendants.* In actions when the parties are unusually numerous, the court may regulate the service contemplated by the Florida Rules of Judicial Administration on motion or on its own initiative in such manner as may be found to be just and reasonable. FL ST J ADMIN Rule 2.516(c).

d. *Service by clerk.* Service of notices and other documents required to be made by the clerk must also be done as provided in FL ST J ADMIN Rule 2.516(b). FL ST J ADMIN Rule 2.516(g).

G. Hearings

1. *Uniform motion calendar*

   a. *Contacting judge's office on short matters.* Counsel should contact the judge's office to ascertain whether short matters are heard by the specific division. FL ST 9 J CIR SECTION 10(C)(1).

   b. *Motions suitable for hearing.* Types of motions suitable for hearing on the motion calendar are simple motions to dismiss complaints with only one or two counts, to strike one or two affirmative defenses, for more definite statement, to amend pleadings, to compel discovery, for protective order, objections to IME, etc. Complex motions, motions requiring testimony or motions for summary judgment (except uncontested mortgage foreclosures), or more than two motions to be heard at one time should not be scheduled on this calendar and will not be heard by the Court. FL ST 9 J CIR SECTION 10(C)(2).

2. *Other motion hearings.* All other motions should be specially set through the judge's judicial assistant for a date and time certain. Requests for hearing time in excess of one (1) hour will require special permission of the judge obtained through the judicial assistant or by personal appearance of counsel at ex parte time. FL ST 9 J CIR SECTION 10(D).

3. *Cancelling hearings.* Only the attorney who noticed it can cancel a hearing. If a hearing becomes unnecessary after it has been noticed, the judge's judicial assistant and all other counsel must be notified immediately and effectively that the hearing is canceled. FL ST 9 J CIR SECTION 11(E).

4. *Communication equipment*

   a. *Definition.* Communication equipment means a conference telephone or other electronic device that permits all those appearing or participating to hear and speak to each other, provided that all conversation of all parties is audible to all persons present. FL ST J ADMIN Rule 2.530(a).

   b. *Use by all parties.* A county or circuit court judge may, upon the court's own motion or upon the written request of a party, direct that communication equipment be used for a motion hearing, pretrial conference, or a status conference. A judge must give notice to the parties and consider any objections they may have to the use of communication equipment before directing that communication equipment be used. The decision to use communication equipment over the objection of parties will be in the sound discretion of the trial court, except as noted below. FL ST J ADMIN Rule 2.530(b).

   c. *Use only by requesting party.* A county or circuit court judge may, upon the written request of a party upon reasonable notice to all other parties, permit a requesting party to participate through communication equipment in a scheduled motion hearing; however, any such request (except in criminal, juvenile, and appellate proceedings) must be granted, absent a showing of good cause to deny the same, where the hearing is set for not longer than fifteen (15) minutes. FL ST J ADMIN Rule 2.530(c).

   d. *Testimony*

      i. *Generally.* A county or circuit court judge, general magistrate, special magistrate, or hearing officer may allow testimony to be taken through communication equipment if all parties consent or if permitted by another applicable rule of procedure. FL ST J ADMIN Rule 2.530(d)(1).

ii. *Procedure.* Any party desiring to present testimony through communication equipment shall, prior to the hearing or trial at which the testimony is to be presented, contact all parties to determine whether each party consents to this form of testimony. The party seeking to present the testimony shall move for permission to present testimony through communication equipment, which motion shall set forth good cause as to why the testimony should be allowed in this form. FL ST J ADMIN Rule 2.530(d)(2).

iii. *Oath.* Testimony may be taken through communication equipment only if a notary public or other person authorized to administer oaths in the witness's jurisdiction is present with the witness and administers the oath consistent with the laws of the jurisdiction. FL ST J ADMIN Rule 2.530(d)(3).

iv. *Confrontation rights.* In juvenile and criminal proceedings the defendant must make an informed waiver of any confrontation rights that may be abridged by the use of communication equipment. FL ST J ADMIN Rule 2.530(d)(4).

v. *Video testimony.* If the testimony to be presented utilizes video conferencing or comparable two-way visual capabilities, the court in its discretion may modify the procedures set forth in FL ST J ADMIN Rule 2.530 to accommodate the technology utilized. FL ST J ADMIN Rule 2.530(d)(5).

e. *Burden of expense.* The cost for the use of the communication equipment is the responsibility of the requesting party unless otherwise directed by the court. FL ST J ADMIN Rule 2.530(e)..

H. Forms

1. Official Motion for Sanctions Forms for Florida

a. Caption. FL ST RCP Form 1.901.

b. Notice of compliance when constitutional challenge is brought. FL ST RCP Form 1.975.

2. Motion for Sanctions Forms for Florida

a. Motion; By defendant; For sanctions for refusal of offer of judgment. FL-PP § 61:22.

b. Motion; Sanctions, proposal for settlement. FL-PRACFORM § 7:165.

I. Checklist

(I) ❑ Matters to be considered by moving party

(a) ❑ Required documents

(1) ❑ Notice of hearing/Motion

(2) ❑ Certificate of service

(b) ❑ Supplemental documents

(1) ❑ Legal memorandum

(2) ❑ Proposed order

(3) ❑ Notice of constitutional question

(c) ❑ Time for making motion

(1) ❑ A motion by a party seeking sanctions under FL ST § 57.105 must be served but may not be filed with or presented to the court unless, within twenty one (21) days after service of the motion, the challenged paper, claim, defense, contention, allegation, or denial is not withdrawn or appropriately corrected

(2) ❑ Any party seeking a judgment taxing costs, attorneys' fees, or both shall serve a motion no later than thirty (30) days after filing of the judgment, including a judgment of dismissal, or the service of a notice of voluntary dismissal

(3) ❑ A copy of any written motion which may not be heard ex parte and a copy of the notice of the hearing thereof shall be served a reasonable time before the time specified for the hearing

(II) ❑ Matters to be considered by opposing party

(a) ❑ Required documents

(1) ❑ Response to motion

(2) ❑ Certificate of service

(b) ❑ Supplemental documents

(1) ❑ Legal memorandum

(2) ❑ Proposed order

(3) ❑ Notice of constitutional question

(c) ❑ Time for service and filing of opposition

(1) ❑ No time specified for responding to a motion

Motions, Oppositions and Replies
Motion to Compel Discovery

Document Last Updated January 2013

A. Applicable Rules

1. *State rules*

a. Rules of court. FL ST RCP Rule 1.010; FL ST J ADMIN Rule 2.110.

b. Nonverification of pleadings. FL ST RCP Rule 1.030.

c. Service and filing of pleadings, orders, and documents. FL ST RCP Rule 1.080.

d. Time. FL ST RCP Rule 1.090.

e. Pleadings and motions. FL ST RCP Rule 1.100.

f. Motions. FL ST RCP Rule 1.160.

g. General provisions governing discovery. FL ST RCP Rule 1.280.

h. Depositions. FL ST RCP Rule 1.310; FL ST RCP Rule 1.320; FL ST FAM LAW Rule 12.310.

i. Interrogatories to parties. FL ST RCP Rule 1.340.

j. Production of documents and things and entry upon land for inspection and other purposes. FL ST RCP Rule 1.350.

k. Examination of persons. FL ST RCP Rule 1.360.

l. Failure to make discovery; Sanctions. FL ST RCP Rule 1.380.

m. Relief from judgment, decrees, or orders. FL ST RCP Rule 1.540.

n. Mediation and arbitration. FL ST RCP Rule 1.700; FL ST RCP Rule 1.710; FL ST RCP Rule 1.720; FL ST RCP Rule 1.730; FL ST RCP Rule 1.750; FL ST RCP Rule 1.800; FL ST RCP Rule 1.810; FL ST RCP Rule 1.820; FL ST RCP Rule 1.830.

o. Forms. FL ST RCP Rule 1.900.

p. Minimization of the filing of sensitive information. FL ST J ADMIN Rule 2.425.

q. Retention of court records. FL ST J ADMIN Rule 2.430.

r. Foreign attorneys. FL ST J ADMIN Rule 2.510.

s. Signature of attorneys and parties. FL ST J ADMIN Rule 2.515.

t. Paper. FL ST J ADMIN Rule 2.520.

u. Electronic filing. FL ST J ADMIN Rule 2.525.

v. Accessibility of information and technology. FL ST J ADMIN Rule 2.526.

w. Communication equipment. FL ST J ADMIN Rule 2.530.

x. Court reporting. FL ST J ADMIN Rule 2.535.

y. Requests for accommodations by persons with disabilities. FL ST J ADMIN Rule 2.540.

2. *Local rules*

a. Hearings. FL ST 9 J CIR SECTION 10.

b. Motion practice generally. FL ST 9 J CIR SECTION 11.

c. Orders and judgments. FL ST 9 J CIR SECTION 12.

d. General discovery guidelines. FL ST 9 J CIR SECTION 13.

e. Alternative dispute resolution. FL ST 9 J CIR SECTION 15.

f. Business court procedures. FL ST 9 J CIR ORANGE CIV SECTION 1.

B. Timing

1. *Motion to compel discovery.* Upon reasonable notice to other parties and all persons affected, a party may apply for an order compelling discovery. FL ST RCP Rule 1.380(a).

2. *General motion timing.* A copy of any written motion which may not be heard ex parte and a copy of the notice of the hearing thereof shall be served a reasonable time before the time specified for the hearing. FL ST RCP Rule 1.090(d).

a. Each attorney shall utilize the courts web page under Judicial Automated Calendaring System, for available hearing time and the judge's schedule before telephoning the judicial assistant. FL ST 9 J CIR SECTION 10(A)(1).

b. The hearing will be scheduled with the judge's judicial assistant. Written or fax notice must be received in opposing counsel's office at least four (4) working days before the hearing. FL ST 9 J CIR SECTION 10(A)(2).

i. Counsel who serves a memorandum or authority list first should also include a copy of the motion, any papers to which it is addressed, and the response, if any. In order for the judge to properly review a submission in advance, it must be received in the judge's office at least three (3) working days before the hearing. FL ST 9 J CIR SECTION 11(B).

c. *Obtaining hearing times*

i. If the motion is one which might be resolved by stipulation or agreed order, moving counsel must explore that possibility with opposing counsel before reserving hearing time. FL ST 9 J CIR SECTION 11(C)(1).

ii. If at all possible, hearing time for complex motions or several motions to be heard at one time should be cleared with all affected counsel so as to avoid calendar conflicts. FL ST 9 J CIR SECTION 11(C)(1).

iii. If hearing time cannot be coordinated with opposing counsel, attorneys shall appear at ex parte to resolve the issue. FL ST 9 J CIR SECTION 11(C)(1).

3. *Computation of time*

a. *Generally.* Computation of time shall be governed by FL ST J ADMIN Rule 2.514. FL ST RCP Rule 1.090(a). The following rules apply in computing time periods specified in any rule of procedure, local rule, court order, or statute that does not specify a method of computing time. FL ST J ADMIN Rule 2.514(a).

i. *Period stated in days or a longer unit.* When the period is stated in days or a longer unit of time (A) exclude the day of the event that triggers the period; (B) count every day, including intermediate Saturdays, Sundays, and legal holidays; and (C) include the last day of the period, but if the last day is a Saturday, Sunday, or legal holiday, or falls within any period of time extended through an order of the chief justice under FL ST J ADMIN Rule 2.205(a)(2)(B)(iv), the period continues to run until the end of the next day that is not a Saturday, Sunday, or legal holiday and does not fall within any period of time extended through an order of the chief justice. FL ST J ADMIN Rule 2.514(a)(1).

ii. *Period stated in hours.* When the period is stated in hours (A) begin counting immediately on the occurrence of the event that triggers the period; (B) count every hour, including hours during intermediate Saturdays, Sundays, and legal holidays; and (C) if the period would end on a Saturday, Sunday, or legal holiday, or during any period of time extended through an order of the chief justice under FL ST J ADMIN Rule 2.205(a)(2)(B)(iv), the period continues to run until the same time on the next day that is not a Saturday, Sunday, or legal holiday and does not fall within any period of time extended through an order of the chief justice. FL ST J ADMIN Rule 2.514(a)(2).

iii. *Period stated in days less than seven (7) days.* When the period stated in days is less than seven (7) days, intermediate Saturdays, Sundays, and legal holidays shall be excluded in the computation. FL ST J ADMIN Rule 2.514(a)(3).

iv. *"Last day" defined.* Unless a different time is set by a statute, local rule, or court order, the last day ends (A) for electronic filing or for service by any means, at midnight; and (B) for filing by other means, when the clerk's office is scheduled to close. FL ST J ADMIN Rule 2.514(a)(4).

v. *"Next day" defined.* The "next day" is determined by continuing to count forward when the period is measured after an event and backward when measured before an event. FL ST J ADMIN Rule 2.514(a)(5).

vi. *"Legal holiday" defined.* "Legal holiday" means (A) the day set aside by FL ST § 110.117, for observing New Year's Day, Martin Luther King, Jr.'s Birthday, Memorial Day, Independence Day, Labor Day, Veterans' Day, Thanksgiving Day, the Friday after Thanksgiving Day, or Christmas Day, and (B) any day observed as a holiday by the clerk's office or as designated by the chief judge. FL ST J ADMIN Rule 2.514(a)(6).

b. *Additional time after service by mail or e-mail.* When a party may or must act within a specified time after service and service is made by mail or e-mail, five (5) days are added after the period that would otherwise expire under FL ST J ADMIN Rule 2.514(a). FL ST J ADMIN Rule 2.514(b).

c. *Enlargement.* When an act is required or allowed to be done at or within a specified time by order of court, by the Florida Rules of Civil Procedure, or by notice given thereunder, for cause shown the court at any time in its discretion (1) with or without notice, may order the period enlarged if request therefor is made before the expiration of the period originally prescribed or as extended by a previous order, or (2) upon motion made and notice after the expiration of the specified period, may permit the act to be done when failure to act was the result of excusable neglect, but it may not extend the time for making a motion for new trial, for rehearing, or to alter or amend a judgment; making a motion for relief from a judgment under FL ST RCP Rule 1.540(b); taking an appeal or filing a petition for certiorari; or making a motion for a directed verdict. FL ST RCP Rule 1.090(b).

d. *Unaffected by expiration of term.* The period of time provided for the doing of any act or the taking of any proceeding shall not be affected or limited by the continued existence or expiration of a term of court. The continued existence or expiration of a term of court in no way affects the power of a court to do any act or take any proceeding in any action which is or has been pending before it. FL ST RCP Rule 1.090(c).

C. General Requirements

1. *Motions generally*

a. *Contents.* An application to the court for an order shall be by motion which shall be made in writing unless made during a hearing or trial, shall state with particularity the grounds therefor, and shall set forth the relief or order sought. The requirement of writing is fulfilled if the motion is stated in a written notice of the hearing of the motion. All notices of hearing shall specify each motion or other matter to be heard. FL ST RCP Rule 1.100(b).

b. *Particularity requirement.* The court considers a motion in the light of the substantive law, rule or

statute to make its determination. Some rules require a statement of the grounds for a motion under the rule. Failure to give the grounds will result in denial of the motion. This should be the result in all situations when the ground for the motion is not inherent in the rule. FL-PRACPROC § 9:3. The requirement is nevertheless an important one, first because of the due process notice rights of the respondent, as well as for the assistance it provides to the court in its preparation for the hearing or, absent a hearing, for disposition. 4 FLPRAC R 1.100. Every written motion shall cite the particular rule or statute and/or leading case upon which the motion is based. FL ST 9 J CIR SECTION 11(A)(1).

2. *Failure to make discovery; Types of available relief*
   a. Three categories. Three (3) categories of relief are available for failure to make discovery. FL-PRACPROC § 16:14.
      i. The first category is an order compelling discovery. This is obtained by a motion to compel discovery. The motion is made in the court in which the action is pending, except when a deposition is being taken out of the territorial jurisdiction of the court and protective relief is sought in accordance with FL ST RCP Rule 1.310(d) or when a deponent is not a party. When one of the exceptions occurs, the motion is made in the circuit court of the county where the deposition is being taken. FL-PRACPROC § 16:14.
      ii. The second category results from a failure to comply with an order to make discovery. The sanctions should not be applied until a hearing on the merits of the failure is held, including an opportunity to present evidence of explanation or mitigation. FL-PRACPROC § 16:14.
      iii. The third category is available: (1) if a party or a person designated by an organization to answer questions at a deposition fails to appear before the officer who is to take the deposition after being served with a proper notice; (2) fails to serve answers or objections to interrogatories after proper service of the interrogatories; or (3) a party fails to serve a response to a request for production, inspection and entry after proper service of the request. FL-PRACPROC § 16:14. For further information regarding discovery sanctions please see the KeyRules Motion for Discovery Sanctions documents.
3. *Motion for order compelling discovery*
   a. *Reasonable notice.* Upon reasonable notice to other parties and all persons affected, a party may apply for an order compelling discovery. FL ST RCP Rule 1.380(a).
   b. *Appropriate court.* An application for an order to a party may be made to the court in which the action is pending or in accordance with FL ST RCP Rule 1.310(d). An application for an order to a deponent who is not a party shall be made to the circuit court where the deposition is being taken. FL ST RCP Rule 1.380(a)(1).
   c. *Motion*
      i. *Grounds.* The discovering party may move for an order compelling an answer, or a designation or an order compelling inspection, or an order compelling an examination in accordance with the request:
         - If a deponent fails to answer a question propounded or submitted under FL ST RCP Rule 1.310 or FL ST RCP Rule 1.320;
         - Or a corporation or other entity fails to make a designation under FL ST RCP Rule 1.310(b)(6) or FL ST RCP Rule 1.320(a);
         - Or a party fails to answer an interrogatory submitted under FL ST RCP Rule 1.340;
         - Or if a party in response to a request for inspection submitted under FL ST RCP Rule 1.350 fails to respond that inspection will be permitted as requested or fails to permit inspection as requested;
         - Or if a party in response to a request for examination of a person submitted under FL ST RCP Rule 1.360(a) objects to the examination, fails to respond that the examination will be permitted as requested, or fails to submit to or to produce a person in that party's custody or legal control for examination. FL ST RCP Rule 1.380(a)(2).

ii. *Certification.* The motion must include a certification that the movant, in good faith, has conferred or attempted to confer with the person or party failing to make the discovery in an effort to secure the information or material without court action. FL ST RCP Rule 1.380(a)(2).

iii. *During deposition.* When taking a deposition on oral examination, the proponent of the question may complete or adjourn the examination before applying for an order. FL ST RCP Rule 1.380(a)(2).

iv. *Protective order.* If the court denies the motion in whole or in part, it may make such protective order as it would have been empowered to make on a motion made pursuant to FL ST RCP Rule 1.280(c). FL ST RCP Rule 1.380(a)(2).

d. *Evasive or incomplete answer.* For purposes of FL ST RCP Rule 1.380(a) an evasive or incomplete answer shall be treated as a failure to answer. FL ST RCP Rule 1.380(a)(3).

e. *Award of expenses of motion*

i. *Motion granted.* If the motion is granted and after opportunity for hearing, the court shall require the party or deponent whose conduct necessitated the motion or the party or counsel advising the conduct to pay to the moving party the reasonable expenses incurred in obtaining the order that may include attorneys' fees, unless the court finds that the movant failed to certify in the motion that a good faith effort was made to obtain the discovery without court action, that the opposition to the motion was justified, or that other circumstances make an award of expenses unjust. FL ST RCP Rule 1.380(a)(4).

ii. *Motion denied.* If the motion is denied and after opportunity for hearing, the court shall require the moving party to pay to the party or deponent who opposed the motion the reasonable expenses incurred in opposing the motion that may include attorneys' fees, unless the court finds that the making of the motion was substantially justified or that other circumstances make an award of expenses unjust. FL ST RCP Rule 1.380(a)(4).

iii. *Motion granted in part and denied in part.* If the motion is granted in part and denied in part, the court may apportion the reasonable expenses incurred as a result of making the motion among the parties and persons. FL ST RCP Rule 1.380(a)(4).

iv. *Electronically stored information; Sanctions for failure to preserve.* Absent exceptional circumstances, a court may not impose sanctions under these rules on a party for failing to provide electronically stored information lost as a result of the routine, good faith operation of an electronic information system. FL ST RCP Rule 1.380(e).

4. *Limitations on discovery of electronically stored information*

a. A person may object to discovery of electronically stored information from sources that the person identifies as not reasonably accessible because of burden or cost. On motion to compel discovery or for a protective order, the person from whom discovery is sought must show that the information sought or the format requested is not reasonably accessible because of undue burden or cost. If that showing is made, the court may nonetheless order the discovery from such sources or in such formats if the requesting party shows good cause. The court may specify conditions of the discovery, including ordering that some or all of the expenses incurred by the person from whom discovery is sought be paid by the party seeking the discovery. FL ST RCP Rule 1.280(d)(1).

b. In determining any motion involving discovery of electronically stored information, the court must limit the frequency or extent of discovery otherwise allowed by the Florida Rules of Civil Procedure if it determines that (i) the discovery sought is unreasonably cumulative or duplicative, or can be obtained from another source or in another manner that is more convenient, less burdensome, or less expensive; or (ii) the burden or expense of the discovery outweighs its likely benefit, considering the needs of the case, the amount in controversy, the parties' resources, the importance of the issues at stake in the action, and the importance of the discovery in resolving the issues. FL ST RCP Rule 1.280(d)(2).

5. *Arbitration and mediation*

a. *Referral to arbitration and mediation.* Except as hereinafter provided or as otherwise prohibited by

law, the presiding judge may enter an order referring all or any part of a contested civil matter to mediation or arbitration. The parties to any contested civil matter may file a written stipulation to mediate or arbitrate any issue between them at any time. Such stipulation shall be incorporated into the order of referral. FL ST RCP Rule 1.700(a).

i. *Local arbitration policy.* It is the policy of the Civil Division judges to maximize the use of alternative dispute resolution procedures. Except where prohibited by statute, mediation will be ordered in all cases where jury trial is requested and in selected cases which are to be tried non-jury. Also, selected cases will be referred for court-annexed non-binding arbitration through the Orange County Bar Association Arbitration Service. Counsel may move to dispense with or defer mediation or arbitration or move to modify the referral order for good cause. FL ST 9 J CIR SECTION 15.

b. *Arbitration*

i. *Exclusions.* A civil action shall be ordered to arbitration or arbitration in conjunction with mediation upon stipulation of the parties. A civil action may be ordered to arbitration or arbitration in conjunction with mediation upon motion of any party or by the court, if the judge determines the action to be of such a nature that arbitration could be of benefit to the litigants or the court. FL ST RCP Rule 1.800.

- Under no circumstances may the following categories of actions be referred to arbitration: (1) bond estreatures; (2) habeas corpus or other extraordinary writs; (3) bond validations; (4) civil or criminal contempt; (5) such other matters as may be specified by order of the chief judge in the circuit. FL ST RCP Rule 1.800.

ii. For more information regarding arbitration, please see FL ST RCP Rule 1.810; FL ST RCP Rule 1.820; FL ST RCP Rule 1.830.

c. *Mediation.* For more information regarding mediation, please see FL ST RCP Rule 1.710; FL ST RCP Rule 1.720; FL ST RCP Rule 1.730; and FL ST RCP Rule 1.750.

6. *Rules of court*

a. *Rules of civil procedure.* The Florida Rules of Civil Procedure apply to all actions of a civil nature and all special statutory proceedings in the circuit courts and county courts except those to which the Florida Probate Rules, the Florida Family Law Rules of Procedure, or the Small Claims Rules apply. FL ST RCP Rule 1.010.

i. The form, content, procedure, and time for pleading in all special statutory proceedings shall be as prescribed by the statutes governing the proceeding unless the Florida Rules of Civil Procedure specifically provide to the contrary. FL ST RCP Rule 1.010.

ii. The Florida Rules of Civil Procedure shall be construed to secure the just, speedy, and inexpensive determination of every action. FL ST RCP Rule 1.010.

b. *Rules of judicial administration.* The Florida Rules of Judicial Administration shall apply to administrative matters in all courts to which the Florida Rules of Judicial Administration are applicable by their terms. The Florida Rules of Judicial Administration shall be construed to secure the speedy and inexpensive determination of every proceeding to which they are applicable. The Florida Rules of Judicial Administration shall supersede all conflicting rules and statutes. FL ST J ADMIN Rule 2.110.

c. *Business court procedures.* For rules specific to Business Court, please see FL ST 9 J CIR ORANGE CIV SECTION 1, et seq.

D. Documents

1. *Required documents*

a. *Notice of hearing/Motion.* An application to the court for an order shall be by motion which shall be made in writing unless made during a hearing or trial, shall state with particularity the grounds therefor, and shall set forth the relief or order sought. The requirement of writing is fulfilled if the motion is stated in a written notice of the hearing of the motion. All notices of hearing shall specify each motion or other matter to be heard. FL ST RCP Rule 1.100(b). A notice calling up "all pending motions" is insufficient. FL ST 9 J CIR SECTION 11(D)(1). Additional motions should not be "piggy-backed" by cross-notice unless counsel first confirms with opposing counsel and the judge's judicial assistant that there can be sufficient additional time reserved in which to hear them. FL ST 9 J CIR SECTION 11(D)(2).

i. *Certification.* The motion must include a certification that the movant, in good faith, has conferred or attempted to confer with the person or party failing to make the discovery in an effort to secure the information or material without court action. FL ST RCP Rule 1.380(a)(2).

ii. *Notices to persons with disabilities.* See the Format section of this KeyRules document for further information.

b. *Certificate of service.* When any attorney certifies in substance: "I certify that a copy hereof has been furnished to (here insert name or names and addresses used for service) by (e-mail) (delivery) (mail) (fax) on .... (date) ....________________ Attorney" the certificate is taken as prima facie proof of such service in compliance with FL ST J ADMIN Rule 2.516. FL ST J ADMIN Rule 2.516(f).

2. *Supplemental documents*

a. *Legal memorandum.* Legal memorandums in support of or opposition to motions are optional. But if filed, counsel must furnish the judge with chambers copies of the memorandum and highlighted copies of primary legal authorities cited therein. FL ST 9 J CIR SECTION 11(B).

i. As an alternative to a memorandum, a list of primary legal authorities with highlighted copies attached may be submitted. Chambers copies and authority lists must be under cover letter referencing the case style and number and stating the date and time of the hearing. FL ST 9 J CIR SECTION 11(B).

b. *Proposed order.* The court may require that orders or judgments be prepared by a party, may require the party to furnish the court with stamped, addressed envelopes for service of the order or judgment, and may require that proposed orders and judgments be furnished to all parties before entry by the court of the order or judgment. FL ST J ADMIN Rule 2.516(h)(1).

i. Proposed orders and judgments will be prepared by the prevailing attorney unless the judge designates some other attorney or states that he or she will prepare the order or judgment. FL ST 9 J CIR SECTION 12(A)(1).

ii. When submitting proposed orders or judgments, counsel shall also include sufficient copies and self address stamped envelopes for all parties. FL ST 9 J CIR SECTION 12(A)(2).

iii. Moving counsel must present a proposed order with space for ruling left blank at the conclusion of the hearing and must serve conformed copies on all other counsel and unrepresented parties. FL ST 9 J CIR SECTION 10(A)(3).

iv. Unsigned orders or judgments should not be sent to the Clerk's office for transmission to the judge. FL ST 9 J CIR SECTION 12(D)(3).

c. *Notice of constitutional question.* A party that files a pleading, written motion, or other paper drawing into question the constitutionality of a state statute or a county or municipal charter, ordinance, or franchise must promptly (1) file a notice of constitutional question stating the question and identifying the paper that raises it; and (2) serve the notice and the pleading, written motion, or other paper drawing into question the constitutionality of a state statute or a county or municipal charter, ordinance, or franchise on the Attorney General or the state attorney of the judicial circuit in which the action is pending, by either certified or registered mail. Service of the notice and pleading, written motion, or other paper does not require joinder of the Attorney General or the state attorney as a party to the action. FL ST RCP Rule 1.071.

E. Format

1. *Documents; Type and size.* Documents subject to the exceptions set forth in FL ST J ADMIN Rule 2.525(d) shall be filed on recycled paper measuring eight and one half by eleven (8 1/2 by 11) inches. For purposes of FL ST J ADMIN Rule 2.520, paper is recycled if it contains a minimum content of fifty (50) percent waste paper. Xerographic reduction of legal-size (eight and one half by fourteen (8 1/2 by 14) inches) documents to letter size (eight and one half by eleven (8 1/2 by 11) inches) is prohibited. All other

documents filed by electronic transmission shall be filed in a format capable of being printed in a format consistent with the provisions of FL ST J ADMIN Rule 2.250. FL ST J ADMIN Rule 2.520(b).

a. *Exhibits.* Any exhibit or attachment filed with pleadings or papers may be filed in its original size. FL ST J ADMIN Rule 2.520(c).

b. *Recording space.* On all papers and documents prepared and filed by the court or by any party to a proceeding which are to be recorded in the public records of any county, including but not limited to final money judgments and notices of lis pendens, a three (3) inch by three (3) inch space at the top right-hand corner on the first page and a one (1) inch by three (3) inch space at the top right-hand corner on each subsequent page shall be left blank and reserved for use by the clerk of court. FL ST J ADMIN Rule 2.520(d).

   i. *Exceptions to recording space.* Any papers or documents created by persons or entities over which the filing party has no control, including but not limited to wills, codicils, trusts, or other testamentary documents; documents prepared or executed by any public officer; documents prepared, executed, acknowledged, or proved outside of the State of Florida; or documents created by State or Federal government agencies, may be filed without the space required by FL ST J ADMIN Rule 2.520. FL ST J ADMIN Rule 2.520(e).

c. *Noncompliance.* No clerk of court is permitted to refuse to file any document or paper because of noncompliance with the Florida Rules of Judicial Administration. However, upon request of the clerk of court, noncomplying documents must be resubmitted in accordance with the formatting rules. FL ST J ADMIN Rule 2.520(f).

d. *Proposed orders*

   i. All orders will be on eight and a half by eleven (8 1/2 by 11) inch plain white paper (not lined or letterhead paper) and be double spaced. FL ST 9 J CIR SECTION 12(B)(1).

   ii. The order must contain a title indicating what matter the order pertains to, e.g., "Order On Defendant Smith's Motion To Dismiss." FL ST 9 J CIR SECTION 12(B)(2).

   iii. The preamble of the order should include the date of the hearing and what motions were heard. FL ST 9 J CIR SECTION 12(B)(3).

   iv. The adjudication portion of the order should state what relief is ordered. Simply stating that "the motion is granted" without more is insufficient. FL ST 9 J CIR SECTION 12(B)(4).

   v. The order should indicate the specific time period of any act ordered to be done and should state whether the time period runs from the date of the hearing or the date the order is signed or some other specified date. FL ST 9 J CIR SECTION 12(B)(5).

   vi. The order should contain a full certificate of service with the complete names and addresses of the attorneys and unrepresented parties to be served. Merely showing "copies to" is insufficient. FL ST 9 J CIR SECTION 12(B)(6).

   vii. If an order of dismissal is final (i.e., it disposes of the entire case) the title should contain the word "Final." When the order is not final but leaves other counts or claims against other defendants pending, it should so state in a separate paragraph. FL ST 9 J CIR SECTION 12(B)(7).

   viii. When submitting stipulations, orders shall be by separate order, not attached to the stipulation. FL ST 9 J CIR SECTION 12(B)(8).

   ix. Counsel preparing the Final Judgment or order should draft and circulate copies within two (2) working days of the ruling or jury verdict. If counsel preparing the Final Judgment or order gets approval as to form of the order from all counsel, the original with copies and envelopes should be sent directly to the judge with a cover letter stating all counsel agree to the form of the order or judgment. If other counsel objects to the form or cannot be reached for approval, counsel preparing the judgment or order shall notice a motion for entry of the order or judgment. If objecting counsel does not furnish the judge prior to or at the hearing with a proposed judgment or order version with copies under cover letter stating the reasons for the objection, all objections will be deemed waived. Orders and judgments should not be submitted to the judge to hold waiting for an objection. FL ST 9 J CIR SECTION 12(D).

2. *Caption.* Every pleading, motion, order, judgment, or other paper shall have a caption containing the name of the court, the file number, and except for in rem proceedings, including forfeiture proceedings, the name of the first party on each side with an appropriate indication of other parties, and a designation identifying the party filing it and its nature or the nature of the order, as the case may be. In any in rem proceeding, every pleading, motion, order, judgment, or other paper shall have a caption containing the name of the court, the file number, the style "In re" (followed by the name or general description of the property), and a designation of the person or entity filing it and its nature or the nature of the order, as the case may be. In an in rem forfeiture proceeding, the style shall be "In re forfeiture of" (followed by the name of the general description of the property). All papers filed in the action shall be styled in such a manner as to indicate clearly the subject matter of the paper and the party requesting or obtaining relief. FL ST RCP Rule 1.100(c)(1).
3. *Writing and written defined.* Writing or written means a document containing information, an application, or a stipulation. FL ST RCP Rule 1.080(c).
4. *Rule abbreviations*
   a. The Florida Rules of Civil Procedure and shall be abbreviated as Fla.R.Civ.P. FL ST RCP Rule 1.010.
   b. The Florida Rules of Judicial Administration shall be abbreviated as Fla. R. Jud. Admin. FL ST J ADMIN Rule 2.110.
5. *Nonverification.* Except when otherwise specifically provided by the Florida Rules of Civil Procedure or an applicable statute, every pleading or other document of a party represented by an attorney need not be verified or accompanied by an affidavit. FL ST RCP Rule 1.030; FL ST J ADMIN Rule 2.515(a).
6. *Unrepresented parties.* An unrepresented party must file his or her papers with the clerk and send copies to other attorneys or unrepresented parties. All such papers must be typed double-spaced on plain white eight and a half by eleven (8 1/2 by 11) inch paper, with the name of the case and case number at the top and the party's mailing address, telephone number and FAX number, if any, below his or her signature at the end of the paper. Such unrepresented party must immediately notify the clerk and all other counsel or parties of record in writing of any change in mailing address or telephone or FAX number. Failure to promptly notify of change of address could result in a dismissal or default entered against such party. FL ST 9 J CIR SECTION 7(B)(5).
7. *Attorney signature*
   a. *Attorney signature.* Every pleading and other document of a party represented by an attorney shall be signed by at least one (1) attorney of record in that attorney's individual name whose current record Florida Bar address, telephone number, including area code, primary e-mail address and secondary e-mail addresses, if any, and Florida Bar number shall be stated, and who shall be duly licensed to practice law in Florida or who shall have received permission to appear in the particular case as provided in FL ST J ADMIN Rule 2.510. FL ST J ADMIN Rule 2.515(a).
      i. The attorney may be required by the court to give the address of, and to vouch for the attorney's authority to represent, the party. FL ST J ADMIN Rule 2.515(a).
      ii. The signature of an attorney shall constitute a certificate by the attorney that the attorney has read the pleading or other document; that to the best of the attorney's knowledge, information, and belief there is good ground to support it; and that it is not interposed for delay. FL ST J ADMIN Rule 2.515(a).
      iii. If a pleading is not signed or is signed with intent to defeat the purpose of FL ST J ADMIN Rule 2.515, it may be stricken and the action may proceed as though the pleading or other document had not been served. FL ST J ADMIN Rule 2.515(a).
   b. *Pro se litigant signature.* A party who is not represented by an attorney shall sign any pleading or other paper and state the party's address and telephone number, including area code. FL ST J ADMIN Rule 2.515(b).

c. *Form of signature*

i. The signatures required on pleadings and documents by FL ST J ADMIN Rule 2.515(a) and FL ST J ADMIN Rule 2.515(b) may be:

- Original signatures;
- Original signatures that have been reproduced by electronic means, such as on electronically transmitted documents or photocopied documents;
- Electronic signatures using the "/s/," "s/," or "/s" formats by or at the direction of the person signing; or
- Any other signature format authorized by general law, so long as the clerk where the proceeding is pending has the capability of receiving and has obtained approval from the Supreme Court of Florida to accept pleadings and documents with that signature format. FL ST J ADMIN Rule 2.515(c)(1).

ii. An attorney, party, or other person who files a pleading or paper by electronic transmission that does not contain the original signature of that attorney, party, or other person shall file that identical pleading or paper in paper form containing an original signature of that attorney, party, or other person (hereinafter called the follow-up filing) immediately thereafter. The follow-up filing is not required if the Supreme Court of Florida has entered an order directing the clerk of court to discontinue accepting the follow-up filing. FL ST J ADMIN Rule 2.515(c)(2).

8. *Forms*

a. *Process.* The forms of process, notice of lis pendens, and notice of action provided in the Florida Rules of Civil Procedure are sufficient. Variations from the forms do not void process or notices that are otherwise sufficient. FL ST RCP Rule 1.900(a).

b. *Other forms.* The other forms provided in the Florida Rules of Civil Procedure are sufficient for the matters that are covered by them. So long as the substance is expressed without prolixity, the forms may be varied to meet the facts of a particular case. FL ST RCP Rule 1.900(b).

c. *Formal matters.* Captions, except for the designation of the paper, are omitted from the forms provided in the Florida Rules of Civil Procedure. A general form of caption is the first form provided. Signatures are omitted from pleadings and motions. FL ST RCP Rule 1.900(c).

9. *Notices to persons with disabilities.* All notices of court proceedings to be held in a public facility, and all process compelling appearance at such proceedings, shall include the following statement in bold face, fourteen (14) point Times New Roman or Courier font: "If you are a person with a disability who needs any accommodation in order to participate in this proceeding, you are entitled, at no cost to you, to the provision of certain assistance. Please contact [identify applicable court personnel by name, address, and telephone number] at least seven (7) days before your scheduled court appearance, or immediately upon receiving this notification if the time before the scheduled appearance is less than seven (7) days; if you are hearing or voice impaired, call 711." FL ST J ADMIN Rule 2.540(c)(1).

10. *Minimization of the filing of sensitive information*

a. *Limitations for court filings.* Unless authorized by FL ST J ADMIN Rule 2.425(b), statute, another rule of court, or the court orders otherwise, designated sensitive information filed with the court must be limited to the following format:

i. The initials of a person known to be a minor;

ii. The year of birth of a person's birth date;

iii. No portion of any: Social security number, Bank account number, Credit card account number, Charge account number, or Debit account number;

iv. The last four digits of any: Taxpayer identification number (TIN), Employee identification number, Driver's license number, Passport number, Telephone number, Financial account number, except as set forth in FL ST J ADMIN Rule 2.425(a)(3), Brokerage account number, Insurance policy account number, Loan account number, Customer account number, or Patient or health care number;

v. A truncated version of any: Email address, Computer user name, Password, or Personal identification number (PIN); and

vi. A truncated version of any other sensitive information as provided by court order. FL ST J ADMIN Rule 2.425(a).

b. *Exceptions.* FL ST J ADMIN Rule 2.425(a) does not apply to the following:

i. An account number which identifies the property alleged to be the subject of a proceeding;

ii. The record of an administrative or agency proceeding;

iii. The record in appellate or review proceedings;

iv. The birth date of a minor whenever the birth date is necessary for the court to establish or maintain subject matter jurisdiction;

v. The name of a minor in any order relating to parental responsibility, time-sharing, or child support;

vi. The name of a minor in any document or order affecting the minor's ownership of real property;

vii. The birth date of a party in a writ of attachment or notice to payor;

viii. In traffic and criminal proceedings: a pro se filing; a court filing that is related to a criminal matter or investigation and that is prepared before the filing of a criminal charge or is not filed as part of any docketed criminal case; an arrest or search warrant or any information in support thereof; a charging document and an affidavit or other documents filed in support of any charging document, including any driving records; a statement of particulars; discovery material introduced into evidence or otherwise filed with the court; and all information necessary for the proper issuance and execution of a subpoena duces tecum;

ix. Information used by the clerk for case maintenance purposes or the courts for case management purposes; and

x. Information which is relevant and material to an issue before the court. FL ST J ADMIN Rule 2.425(b).

c. *Remedies.* Upon motion by a party or interested person or sua sponte by the court, the court may order remedies, sanctions or both for a violation of FL ST J ADMIN Rule 2.425(a). Following notice and an opportunity to respond, the court may impose sanctions if such filing was not made in good faith. FL ST J ADMIN Rule 2.425(c).

d. *Motions not restricted.* FL ST J ADMIN Rule 2.425 does not restrict a party's right to move for protective order, to move to file documents under seal, or to request a determination of the confidentiality of records. FL ST J ADMIN Rule 2.425(d).

e. *Application.* FL ST J ADMIN Rule 2.425 does not affect the application of constitutional provisions, statutes, or rules of court regarding confidential information or access to public information. FL ST J ADMIN Rule 2.425(e).

F. Filing and Service Requirements

1. *Filing requirements.* All original documents must be filed with the court either before service or immediately thereafter, unless otherwise provided for by general law or other rules. If the original of any bond or other document is not placed in the court file, a certified copy must be so placed by the clerk. FL ST J ADMIN Rule 2.516(d). All documents shall be filed in conformity with the requirements of FL ST J ADMIN Rule 2.525. FL ST RCP Rule 1.080(b). All documents filed in any court shall be filed by electronic transmission in accordance with FL ST J ADMIN Rule 2.525. "Documents" means pleadings, motions, petitions, memoranda, briefs, notices, exhibits, declarations, affidavits, orders, judgments, decrees, writs, opinions, and any other paper or writing submitted to a court. FL ST J ADMIN Rule 2.520(a). All documents that are court records, as defined in FL ST J ADMIN Rule 2.430(a)(1), must be filed by electronic transmission, provided that: (1) the clerk has the ability to accept and retain such documents; (2) the clerk or the chief judge of the circuit has requested permission to accept documents filed by electronic transmission; and (3) the supreme court has entered an order granting permission to the clerk to accept documents filed by electronic transmission. FL ST J ADMIN Rule 2.525(c)(1).

a. *Definition.* "Electronic transmission of documents" means the sending of information by electronic

signals to, by or from a court or clerk, which when received can be transformed and stored or transmitted on paper, microfilm, magnetic storage device, optical imaging system, CD-ROM, flash drive, other electronic data storage system, server, case maintenance system ("CM"), electronic court filing ("ECF") system, statewide or local electronic portal ("e-portal"), or other electronic record keeping system authorized by the supreme court in a format sufficient to communicate the information on the original document in a readable format. Electronic transmission of documents includes electronic mail ("e-mail") and any internet-based transmission procedure, and may include procedures allowing for documents to be signed or verified by electronic means. FL ST J ADMIN Rule 2.525(a).

i. The filing of documents with the court as required by the Florida Rules of Judicial Administration must be made by filing them with the clerk in accordance with FL ST J ADMIN Rule 2.525, except that the judge may permit documents to be filed with the judge, in which event the judge must note the filing date before him or her on the documents and transmit them to the clerk. The date of filing is that shown on the face of the document by the judge's notation or the clerk's time stamp, whichever is earlier. FL ST J ADMIN Rule 2.516(e).

b. *Application.* Any court or clerk of the court may accept the electronic transmission of documents for filing after the clerk, together with input from the chief judge of the circuit, has obtained approval of the procedures and program for doing so from the Supreme Court of Florida. FL ST J ADMIN Rule 2.525(b).

c. *Exceptions*

i. Paper documents and other submissions may be manually submitted to the clerk or court:

- When the clerk does not have the ability to accept and retain documents by electronic filing or has not had ECF Procedures approved by the supreme court;
- For filing by any self-represented party or any self-represented nonparty unless specific ECF Procedures provide a means to file documents electronically. However, any self-represented nonparty that is a governmental or public agency and any other agency, partnership, corporation, or business entity acting on behalf of any governmental or public agency may file documents by electronic transmission if such entity has the capability of filing documents electronically;
- For filing by attorneys excused from e-mail service in accordance with FL ST J ADMIN Rule 2.516(b);
- When submitting evidentiary exhibits or filing non-documentary materials;
- When the filing involves documents in excess of twenty-five (25) megabytes (25MB) in size. For such filings, documents may be transmitted using an electronic storage medium that the clerk has the ability to accept, which may include a CD-ROM, flash drive, or similar storage medium;
- When filed in open court, as permitted by the court;
- When paper filing is permitted by any approved statewide or local ECF procedures; and
- If any court determines that justice so requires. FL ST J ADMIN Rule 2.525(d).

ii. Any document in paper form submitted under FL ST J ADMIN Rule 2.525(d) is filed when it is received by the clerk or court and the clerk shall immediately thereafter convert any filed paper document to an electronic document. "Convert to an electronic document" means optically capturing an image of a paper document and using character recognition software to recover as much of the document's text as practicable and then indexing and storing the document in the official court file. FL ST J ADMIN Rule 2.525(c)(4).

iii. Any storage medium submitted under FL ST J ADMIN Rule 2.525(d)(5) is filed when received by the clerk or court and the clerk shall immediately thereafter transfer the electronic documents from the storage device to the official court file. FL ST J ADMIN Rule 2.525(c)(5).

iv. If the filer of any paper document authorized under FL ST J ADMIN Rule 2.525(d) provides a self-addressed, postage-paid envelope for return of the paper document after it is converted to

electronic form by the clerk, the clerk shall place the paper document in the envelope and deposit it in the mail. Except when a paper document is required to be maintained, the clerk may recycle any filed paper document that is not to be returned to the filer. FL ST J ADMIN Rule 2.525(c)(6).

v. The clerk may convert any paper document filed before the effective date of FL ST J ADMIN Rule 2.525 to an electronic document. Unless the clerk is required to maintain the paper document, if the paper document has been converted to an electronic document by the clerk, the paper document is no longer part of the official court file and may be removed and recycled. FL ST J ADMIN Rule 2.525(c)(7).

d. *Unrepresented parties.* An unrepresented party must file his or her papers with the clerk and send copies to other attorneys or unrepresented parties. FL ST 9 J CIR SECTION 7(B)(5).

i. An unrepresented party may not communicate privately with the judge either by letter, telephone, in person or otherwise. FL ST 9 J CIR SECTION 7(B)(4).

ii. Copies of legal papers or other written materials should not be sent to the judge unless specifically requested by the judge or required by the local administrative procedures. Any unrequested or non-required papers or materials sent to a judge may not be read but may be returned to the sender or placed unread into the court file. FL ST 9 J CIR SECTION 7(B)(4).

e. *Official court file.* For information on what constitutes the official court file, please see FL ST J ADMIN Rule 2.525(c)(2), FL ST J ADMIN Rule 2.525(c)(3).

f. *Administration.* All attorneys, parties, or other persons using this rule to file documents are required to make arrangements with the court or clerk for the payment of any charges authorized by general law or the supreme court before filing any document by electronic transmission. FL ST J ADMIN Rule 2.525(f)(2).

g. *Filing date.* The filing date for an electronically transmitted document is the date and time that such filing is acknowledged by an electronic stamp or otherwise, pursuant to any procedure set forth in any ECF Procedures approved by the supreme court, or the date the last page of such filing is received by the court or clerk. FL ST J ADMIN Rule 2.525(f)(3).

h. *Accessibility.* All documents transmitted in any electronic form under FL ST J ADMIN Rule 2.525 must comply with the accessibility requirements of FL ST J ADMIN Rule 2.526. FL ST J ADMIN Rule 2.525(g).

2. *Service requirements.* Every pleading subsequent to the initial pleading, all orders, and every other document filed in the action must be served in conformity with the requirements of FL ST J ADMIN Rule 2.516. FL ST RCP Rule 1.080(a).

a. *Service; When required.* Unless the court otherwise orders, or a statute or supreme court administrative order specifies a different means of service, every pleading subsequent to the initial pleading and every other document filed in any court proceeding, except applications for witness subpoenas and documents served by formal notice or required to be served in the manner provided for service of formal notice, must be served in accordance with FL ST J ADMIN Rule 2.516 on each party. No service need be made on parties against whom a default has been entered, except that pleadings asserting new or additional claims against them must be served in the manner provided for service of summons. FL ST J ADMIN Rule 2.516(a).

i. Counsel who serves a memorandum or authority list first should also include a copy of the motion, any papers to which it is addressed, and the response, if any. In order for the judge to properly review a submission in advance, it must be received in the judge's office at least three (3) working days before the hearing. FL ST 9 J CIR SECTION 11(B).

b. *Service; How made.* When service is required or permitted to be made upon a party represented by an attorney, service must be made upon the attorney unless service upon the party is ordered by the court. FL ST J ADMIN Rule 2.516(b).

i. *Service by electronic mail ("e-mail").* All documents required or permitted to be served on another party must be served by e-mail, unless FL ST J ADMIN Rule 2.516 otherwise provides.

When, in addition to service by e-mail, the sender also utilizes another means of service provided for in FL ST J ADMIN Rule 2.516(b)(2), any differing time limits and other provisions applicable to that other means of service control. FL ST J ADMIN Rule 2.516(b)(1). Any document electronically transmitted to a court or clerk must also be served on all parties and interested persons in accordance with the applicable rules of court. FL ST J ADMIN Rule 2.525(e)(2).

- *Service on attorneys.* Upon appearing in a proceeding, an attorney must serve a designation of a primary e-mail address and may designate no more than two (2) secondary e-mail addresses. Thereafter, service must be directed to all designated e-mail addresses in that proceeding. Every document filed by an attorney thereafter must include the primary e-mail address of that attorney and any secondary e-mail addresses. If an attorney does not designate any e-mail address for service, documents may be served on that attorney at the e-mail address on record with The Florida Bar. FL ST J ADMIN Rule 2.516(b)(1)(A).
- *Exception to e-mail service on attorneys.* Service by an attorney on another attorney must be made by e-mail unless excused by the court. Upon motion by an attorney demonstrating that the attorney has no e-mail account and lacks access to the Internet at the attorney's office, the court may excuse the attorney from the requirements of e-mail service. Service on and by an attorney excused by the court from e-mail service must be by the means provided in FL ST J ADMIN Rule 2.516(b)(2). FL ST J ADMIN Rule 2.516(b)(1)(B).
- *Service on and by parties not represented by an attorney.* Any party not represented by an attorney may serve a designation of a primary e-mail address and also may designate no more than two (2) secondary e-mail addresses to which service must be directed in that proceeding by the means provided in FL ST J ADMIN Rule 2.516(b)(1). If a party not represented by an attorney does not designate an e-mail address for service in a proceeding, service on and by that party must be by the means provided in FL ST J ADMIN Rule 2.516(b)(2). FL ST J ADMIN Rule 2.516(b)(1)(C).
- *Time of service.* Service by e-mail is complete when it is sent. FL ST J ADMIN Rule 2.516(b)(1)(D). An e-mail is deemed served on the date it is sent. FL ST J ADMIN Rule 2.516(b)(1)(D)(i). If the sender learns that the e-mail did not reach the address of the person to be served, the sender must immediately send another copy by e-mail, or by a means authorized by FL ST J ADMIN Rule 2.516(b)(2). FL ST J ADMIN Rule 2.516(b)(1)(D)(ii). E-mail service is treated as service by mail for the computation of time. FL ST J ADMIN Rule 2.516(b)(1)(D)(iii).

ii. *Format of e-mail for service.* Service of a document by e-mail is made by attaching a copy of the document in PDF format to an e-mail sent to all addresses designated by the attorney or party. FL ST J ADMIN Rule 2.516(b)(1)(E).

- All documents served by e-mail must be attached to an e-mail message containing a subject line beginning with the words "SERVICE OF COURT DOCUMENT" in all capital letters, followed by the case number of the proceeding in which the documents are being served. FL ST J ADMIN Rule 2.516(b)(1)(E)(i).
- The body of the e-mail must identify the court in which the proceeding is pending, the case number, the name of the initial party on each side, the title of each document served with that e-mail, and the sender's name and telephone number. FL ST J ADMIN Rule 2.516(b)(1)(E)(ii).
- Any document served by e-mail may be signed by the "/s/" format, as long as the filed original is signed in accordance with the applicable rule of procedure. FL ST J ADMIN Rule 2.516(b)(1)(E)(iii).
- Any e-mail which, together with its attached documents, exceeds five megabytes (5MB) in size, must be divided and sent as separate e-mails, no one of which may exceed five megabytes (5MB) in size and each of which must be sequentially numbered in the subject line. FL ST J ADMIN Rule 2.516(b)(1)(E)(iv).

iii. *Service by other means.* In addition to, and not in lieu of, service by e-mail, service may also be

made upon attorneys by any of the means specified in FL ST J ADMIN Rule 2.516(b)(2). Service on and by all parties who are not represented by an attorney and who do not designate an e-mail address, and on and by all attorneys excused from e-mail service, must be made by delivering a copy of the document or by mailing it to the party or attorney at their last known address or, if no address is known, by leaving it with the clerk of the court. Service by mail is complete upon mailing. Delivery of a copy within FL ST J ADMIN Rule 2.516 is complete upon:

- Handing it to the attorney or to the party,
- Leaving it at the attorney's or party's office with a clerk or other person in charge thereof,
- If there is no one in charge, leaving it in a conspicuous place therein,
- If the office is closed or the person to be served has no office, leaving it at the person's usual place of abode with some person of his or her family above fifteen (15) years of age and informing such person of the contents, or
- Transmitting it by facsimile to the attorney's or party's office with a cover sheet containing the sender's name, firm, address, telephone number, and facsimile number, and the number of pages transmitted. When service is made by facsimile, a copy must also be served by any other method permitted by FL ST J ADMIN Rule 2.516. Facsimile service occurs when transmission is complete. FL ST J ADMIN Rule 2.516(b)(2)(A) through FL ST J ADMIN Rule 2.516(b)(2)(E).
- Service by delivery after 5:00 p.m. must be deemed to have been made by mailing on the date of delivery. FL ST J ADMIN Rule 2.516(b)(2)(F).

c. *Service; Numerous defendants.* In actions when the parties are unusually numerous, the court may regulate the service contemplated by the Florida Rules of Judicial Administration on motion or on its own initiative in such manner as may be found to be just and reasonable. FL ST J ADMIN Rule 2.516(c).

d. *Service by clerk.* Service of notices and other documents required to be made by the clerk must also be done as provided in FL ST J ADMIN Rule 2.516(b). FL ST J ADMIN Rule 2.516(g).

G. Hearings

1. *Uniform motion calendar*

   a. *Contacting judge's office on short matters.* Counsel should contact the judge's office to ascertain whether short matters are heard by the specific division. FL ST 9 J CIR SECTION 10(C)(1).

   b. *Motions suitable for hearing.* Types of motions suitable for hearing on the motion calendar are simple motions to dismiss complaints with only one or two counts, to strike one or two affirmative defenses, for more definite statement, to amend pleadings, to compel discovery, for protective order, objections to IME, etc. Complex motions, motions requiring testimony or motions for summary judgment (except uncontested mortgage foreclosures), or more than two motions to be heard at one time should not be scheduled on this calendar and will not be heard by the Court. FL ST 9 J CIR SECTION 10(C)(2).

2. *Other motion hearings.* All other motions should be specially set through the judge's judicial assistant for a date and time certain. Requests for hearing time in excess of one (1) hour will require special permission of the judge obtained through the judicial assistant or by personal appearance of counsel at ex parte time. FL ST 9 J CIR SECTION 10(D).

3. *Cancelling hearings.* Only the attorney who noticed it can cancel a hearing. If a hearing becomes unnecessary after it has been noticed, the judge's judicial assistant and all other counsel must be notified immediately and effectively that the hearing is canceled. FL ST 9 J CIR SECTION 11(E).

4. *Communication equipment*

   a. *Definition.* Communication equipment means a conference telephone or other electronic device that permits all those appearing or participating to hear and speak to each other, provided that all conversation of all parties is audible to all persons present. FL ST J ADMIN Rule 2.530(a).

b. *Use by all parties.* A county or circuit court judge may, upon the court's own motion or upon the written request of a party, direct that communication equipment be used for a motion hearing, pretrial conference, or a status conference. A judge must give notice to the parties and consider any objections they may have to the use of communication equipment before directing that communication equipment be used. The decision to use communication equipment over the objection of parties will be in the sound discretion of the trial court, except as noted below. FL ST J ADMIN Rule 2.530(b).

c. *Use only by requesting party.* A county or circuit court judge may, upon the written request of a party upon reasonable notice to all other parties, permit a requesting party to participate through communication equipment in a scheduled motion hearing; however, any such request (except in criminal, juvenile, and appellate proceedings) must be granted, absent a showing of good cause to deny the same, where the hearing is set for not longer than fifteen (15) minutes. FL ST J ADMIN Rule 2.530(c).

d. *Testimony*

   i. *Generally.* A county or circuit court judge, general magistrate, special magistrate, or hearing officer may allow testimony to be taken through communication equipment if all parties consent or if permitted by another applicable rule of procedure. FL ST J ADMIN Rule 2.530(d)(1).

   ii. *Procedure.* Any party desiring to present testimony through communication equipment shall, prior to the hearing or trial at which the testimony is to be presented, contact all parties to determine whether each party consents to this form of testimony. The party seeking to present the testimony shall move for permission to present testimony through communication equipment, which motion shall set forth good cause as to why the testimony should be allowed in this form. FL ST J ADMIN Rule 2.530(d)(2).

   iii. *Oath.* Testimony may be taken through communication equipment only if a notary public or other person authorized to administer oaths in the witness's jurisdiction is present with the witness and administers the oath consistent with the laws of the jurisdiction. FL ST J ADMIN Rule 2.530(d)(3).

   iv. *Confrontation rights.* In juvenile and criminal proceedings the defendant must make an informed waiver of any confrontation rights that may be abridged by the use of communication equipment. FL ST J ADMIN Rule 2.530(d)(4).

   v. *Video testimony.* If the testimony to be presented utilizes video conferencing or comparable two-way visual capabilities, the court in its discretion may modify the procedures set forth in FL ST J ADMIN Rule 2.530 to accommodate the technology utilized. FL ST J ADMIN Rule 2.530(d)(5).

e. *Burden of expense.* The cost for the use of the communication equipment is the responsibility of the requesting party unless otherwise directed by the court. FL ST J ADMIN Rule 2.530(e).

H. Forms

1. Official Motion to Compel Discovery Forms for Florida

a. Caption. FL ST RCP Form 1.901.

b. Notice of compliance when constitutional challenge is brought. FL ST RCP Form 1.975.

2. Motion to Compel Discovery Forms for Florida

a. Motion to compel attendance and for sanctions. FL-PP § 3:160.

b. Motion; To compel answer to questions asked on oral examination or written questions. FL-PP § 3:161.

c. Order; Directing deponent to answer questions asked on oral examination; Costs and attorney fees to moving party. FL-PP § 3:162.

d. Order; Compelling answer to written questions. FL-PP § 3:163.

e. Motion; For order finding person in contempt of court; Refusal, after order, to answer question. FL-PP § 3:167.

f. Motion; For order compelling opposing party to pay expenses incurred in proving facts the party refused to admit. FL-PP § 3:168.

g. Motion; Compel discovery, deposition. FL-PRACFORM § 7:37.

h. Motion; Compel discovery, interrogatories. FL-PRACFORM § 7:38.

i. Form for motion to compel answer on deposition. FL-RCPF R 1.380(6).

j. Form for certificate of non-appearance at deposition. FL-RCPF R 1.380(7).

k. Form for notice of motion. FL-RCPF R 1.380(8).

l. Form for order on motion to compel answer. FL-RCPF R 1.380(9).

m. Form for notice and motion to compel. FL-RCPF R 1.380(10).

n. Form for order to compel discovery. FL-RCPF R 1.380(18).

o. Form for order to comply with discovery and answer interrogatories. FL-RCPF R 1.380(19).

I. Checklist

(I) ❑ Matters to be considered by moving party
- (a) ❑ Required documents
  - (1) ❑ Notice of hearing/Motion
  - (2) ❑ Certificate of service
- (b) ❑ Supplemental documents
  - (1) ❑ Legal memorandum
  - (2) ❑ Proposed order
  - (3) ❑ Notice of constitutional question
- (c) ❑ Time for making motion
  - (1) ❑ Upon reasonable notice to other parties and all persons affected, a party may apply for an order compelling discovery
  - (2) ❑ A copy of any written motion which may not be heard ex parte and a copy of the notice of the hearing thereof shall be served a reasonable time before the time specified for the hearing

(II) ❑ Matters to be considered by opposing party
- (a) ❑ Required documents
  - (1) ❑ Response to motion
  - (2) ❑ Certificate of service
- (b) ❑ Supplemental documents
  - (1) ❑ Legal memorandum
  - (2) ❑ Proposed order
  - (3) ❑ Notice of constitutional question
- (c) ❑ Time for service and filing of opposition
  - (1) ❑ No time specified for responding to a motion

Motions, Oppositions and Replies
Motion for Directed Verdict

Document Last Updated January 2013

A. Applicable Rules

1. *State rules*

a. Motion for a directed verdict. FL ST RCP Rule 1.480.

b. Rules of court. FL ST RCP Rule 1.010; FL ST J ADMIN Rule 2.110.
c. Nonverification of pleadings. FL ST RCP Rule 1.030.
d. Service and filing of pleadings, orders, and documents. FL ST RCP Rule 1.080.
e. Time. FL ST RCP Rule 1.090.
f. Pleadings and motions. FL ST RCP Rule 1.100.
g. Motions. FL ST RCP Rule 1.160.
h. Relief from judgment, decrees, or orders. FL ST RCP Rule 1.540.
i. Mediation and arbitration. FL ST RCP Rule 1.700; FL ST RCP Rule 1.710; FL ST RCP Rule 1.720; FL ST RCP Rule 1.730; FL ST RCP Rule 1.750; FL ST RCP Rule 1.800; FL ST RCP Rule 1.810; FL ST RCP Rule 1.820; FL ST RCP Rule 1.830.
j. Forms. FL ST RCP Rule 1.900.
k. Minimization of the filing of sensitive information. FL ST J ADMIN Rule 2.425.
l. Retention of court records. FL ST J ADMIN Rule 2.430.
m. Foreign attorneys. FL ST J ADMIN Rule 2.510.
n. Signature of attorneys and parties. FL ST J ADMIN Rule 2.515.
o. Paper. FL ST J ADMIN Rule 2.520.
p. Electronic filing. FL ST J ADMIN Rule 2.525.
q. Accessibility of information and technology. FL ST J ADMIN Rule 2.526.
r. Communication equipment. FL ST J ADMIN Rule 2.530.
s. Court reporting. FL ST J ADMIN Rule 2.535.
t. Requests for accommodations by persons with disabilities. FL ST J ADMIN Rule 2.540.

2. *Local rules*
   a. Hearings. FL ST 9 J CIR SECTION 10.
   b. Motion practice generally. FL ST 9 J CIR SECTION 11.
   c. Orders and judgments. FL ST 9 J CIR SECTION 12.
   d. Alternative dispute resolution. FL ST 9 J CIR SECTION 15.
   e. Business court procedures. FL ST 9 J CIR ORANGE CIV SECTION 1.

B. Timing

1. *Before a verdict is returned.* A directed verdict is available to the defendant at the close of the plaintiff's evidence or to either party at the close of all of the evidence. A verdict may be directed either by the court on its own motion or on the motion of counsel. FL ST RCP Rule 1.480(a); FL-PP § 5:83. The movant should be prepared to argue the motion immediately. FL-PRACPROC § 22:14.
2. *After a verdict is returned.* Within ten (10) days after the return of a verdict, a party who has timely moved for a directed verdict may serve a motion to enter judgment in accordance with the motion for a directed verdict. FL ST RCP Rule 1.480(b).
3. *No verdict is returned.* If a verdict was not returned, a party who has timely moved for a directed verdict may serve a motion for judgment in accordance with the motion for a directed verdict within ten (10) days after discharge of the jury. FL ST RCP Rule 1.480(b).
4. *General motion timing.* A copy of any written motion which may not be heard ex parte and a copy of the notice of the hearing thereof shall be served a reasonable time before the time specified for the hearing. FL ST RCP Rule 1.090(d).
   a. Each attorney shall utilize the courts web page under Judicial Automated Calendaring System, for available hearing time and the judge's schedule before telephoning the judicial assistant. FL ST 9 J CIR SECTION 10(A)(1).

b. The hearing will be scheduled with the judge's judicial assistant. Written or fax notice must be received in opposing counsel's office at least four (4) working days before the hearing. FL ST 9 J CIR SECTION 10(A)(2).

   i. Counsel who serves a memorandum or authority list first should also include a copy of the motion, any papers to which it is addressed, and the response, if any. In order for the judge to properly review a submission in advance, it must be received in the judge's office at least three (3) working days before the hearing. FL ST 9 J CIR SECTION 11(B).

c. *Obtaining hearing times*

   i. If the motion is one which might be resolved by stipulation or agreed order, moving counsel must explore that possibility with opposing counsel before reserving hearing time. FL ST 9 J CIR SECTION 11(C)(1).

   ii. If at all possible, hearing time for complex motions or several motions to be heard at one time should be cleared with all affected counsel so as to avoid calendar conflicts. FL ST 9 J CIR SECTION 11(C)(1).

   iii. If hearing time cannot be coordinated with opposing counsel, attorneys shall appear at ex parte to resolve the issue. FL ST 9 J CIR SECTION 11(C)(1).

5. *Computation of time*

   a. *Generally.* Computation of time shall be governed by FL ST J ADMIN Rule 2.514. FL ST RCP Rule 1.090(a). The following rules apply in computing time periods specified in any rule of procedure, local rule, court order, or statute that does not specify a method of computing time. FL ST J ADMIN Rule 2.514(a).

      i. *Period stated in days or a longer unit.* When the period is stated in days or a longer unit of time (A) exclude the day of the event that triggers the period; (B) count every day, including intermediate Saturdays, Sundays, and legal holidays; and (C) include the last day of the period, but if the last day is a Saturday, Sunday, or legal holiday, or falls within any period of time extended through an order of the chief justice under FL ST J ADMIN Rule 2.205(a)(2)(B)(iv), the period continues to run until the end of the next day that is not a Saturday, Sunday, or legal holiday and does not fall within any period of time extended through an order of the chief justice. FL ST J ADMIN Rule 2.514(a)(1).

      ii. *Period stated in hours.* When the period is stated in hours (A) begin counting immediately on the occurrence of the event that triggers the period; (B) count every hour, including hours during intermediate Saturdays, Sundays, and legal holidays; and (C) if the period would end on a Saturday, Sunday, or legal holiday, or during any period of time extended through an order of the chief justice under FL ST J ADMIN Rule 2.205(a)(2)(B)(iv), the period continues to run until the same time on the next day that is not a Saturday, Sunday, or legal holiday and does not fall within any period of time extended through an order of the chief justice. FL ST J ADMIN Rule 2.514(a)(2).

      iii. *Period stated in days less than seven (7) days.* When the period stated in days is less than seven (7) days, intermediate Saturdays, Sundays, and legal holidays shall be excluded in the computation. FL ST J ADMIN Rule 2.514(a)(3).

      iv. *"Last day" defined.* Unless a different time is set by a statute, local rule, or court order, the last day ends (A) for electronic filing or for service by any means, at midnight; and (B) for filing by other means, when the clerk's office is scheduled to close. FL ST J ADMIN Rule 2.514(a)(4).

      v. *"Next day" defined.* The "next day" is determined by continuing to count forward when the period is measured after an event and backward when measured before an event. FL ST J ADMIN Rule 2.514(a)(5).

      vi. *"Legal holiday" defined.* "Legal holiday" means (A) the day set aside by FL ST § 110.117, for observing New Year's Day, Martin Luther King, Jr.'s Birthday, Memorial Day, Independence Day, Labor Day, Veterans' Day, Thanksgiving Day, the Friday after Thanksgiving Day, or Christmas Day, and (B) any day observed as a holiday by the clerk's office or as designated by the chief judge. FL ST J ADMIN Rule 2.514(a)(6).

b. *Additional time after service by mail or e-mail.* When a party may or must act within a specified time after service and service is made by mail or e-mail, five (5) days are added after the period that would otherwise expire under FL ST J ADMIN Rule 2.514(a). FL ST J ADMIN Rule 2.514(b).

c. *Enlargement.* When an act is required or allowed to be done at or within a specified time by order of court, by the Florida Rules of Civil Procedure, or by notice given thereunder, for cause shown the court at any time in its discretion (1) with or without notice, may order the period enlarged if request therefor is made before the expiration of the period originally prescribed or as extended by a previous order, or (2) upon motion made and notice after the expiration of the specified period, may permit the act to be done when failure to act was the result of excusable neglect, but it may not extend the time for making a motion for new trial, for rehearing, or to alter or amend a judgment; making a motion for relief from a judgment under FL ST RCP Rule 1.540(b); taking an appeal or filing a petition for certiorari; or making a motion for a directed verdict. FL ST RCP Rule 1.090(b).

d. *Unaffected by expiration of term.* The period of time provided for the doing of any act or the taking of any proceeding shall not be affected or limited by the continued existence or expiration of a term of court. The continued existence or expiration of a term of court in no way affects the power of a court to do any act or take any proceeding in any action which is or has been pending before it. FL ST RCP Rule 1.090(c).

C. General Requirements

1. *Motions generally*

a. *Contents.* An application to the court for an order shall be by motion which shall be made in writing unless made during a hearing or trial, shall state with particularity the grounds therefor, and shall set forth the relief or order sought. The requirement of writing is fulfilled if the motion is stated in a written notice of the hearing of the motion. All notices of hearing shall specify each motion or other matter to be heard. FL ST RCP Rule 1.100(b).

b. *Particularity requirement.* The court considers a motion in the light of the substantive law, rule or statute to make its determination. Some rules require a statement of the grounds for a motion under the rule. Failure to give the grounds will result in denial of the motion. This should be the result in all situations when the ground for the motion is not inherent in the rule. FL-PRACPROC § 9:3. The requirement is nevertheless an important one, first because of the due process notice rights of the respondent, as well as for the assistance it provides to the court in its preparation for the hearing or, absent a hearing, for disposition. 4 FLPRAC R 1.100. Every written motion shall cite the particular rule or statute and/or leading case upon which the motion is based. FL ST 9 J CIR SECTION 11(A)(1).

2. *Motion for directed verdict*

a. *Effect of a motion for directed verdict.* A party who moves for a directed verdict at the close of the evidence offered by the adverse party may offer evidence in the event the motion is denied without having reserved the right to do so and to the same extent as if the motion had not been made. The denial of a motion for a directed verdict shall not operate to discharge the jury. A motion for a directed verdict shall state the specific grounds therefor. The order directing a verdict is effective without any assent of the jury. FL ST RCP Rule 1.480(a).

b. *Reservation of decision on motion.* When a motion for a directed verdict is denied or for any reason is not granted, the court is deemed to have submitted the action to the jury subject to a later determination of the legal questions raised by the motion. Within ten (10) days after the return of a verdict, a party who has timely moved for a directed verdict may serve a motion to set aside the verdict and any judgment entered thereon and to enter judgment in accordance with the motion for a directed verdict. If a verdict was not returned, a party who has timely moved for a directed verdict may serve a motion for judgment in accordance with the motion for a directed verdict within ten (10) days after discharge of the jury. FL ST RCP Rule 1.480(b).

c. *Joined with motion for new trial.* A motion for a new trial may be joined with a motion for directed verdict or a new trial may be requested in the alternative. If a verdict was returned, the court may allow the judgment to stand or may reopen the judgment and either order a new trial or direct the entry of judgment as if the requested verdict had been directed. If no verdict was returned, the court may direct the entry of judgment as if the requested verdict had been directed or may order a new trial. FL ST RCP Rule 1.480(c).

d. *General procedures on a motion for directed verdict*

   i. *Proper method.* The proper method of advocating that a party is entitled to prevail on a claim or defense as a matter of law is to make a motion for a directed verdict at the close of the evidence offered by the opposing party. The trial judge has authority to direct a verdict in favor of one party and against another, without submitting the case to the jury, if there is no other verdict the jury could lawfully return. 5 FLPRAC § 22:5.

   ii. *Directed verdict only in a jury trial.* A motion for directed verdict is proper only in a jury trial. The equivalent motion in nonjury trial is called a motion for involuntary dismissal. 5 FLPRAC § 22:5.

   iii. *Test for the sufficiency of the evidence.* A motion for directed verdict is used primarily to test the sufficiency of the evidence offered in support of a claim or defense. It may also be used to raise legal issues other than the sufficiency of the evidence, but that is less common because most pure issues of law can be resolved on a motion to dismiss or a motion for summary judgment before the case is set for trial. If there is no evidence to support a claim or defense, the trial judge has a duty to direct a verdict for the opposing party on that claim or defense. 5 FLPRAC § 22:5.

      - The trial judge must view all of the facts and factual inferences in a light most favorable to the party opposing the motion. 5 FLPRAC § 22:5.
      - The rule has often been stated by the Florida courts in the negative, that is, a motion for directed verdict should not be granted unless the court, after viewing the evidence and testimony in the light most favorable to the nonmoving party, determines that no reasonable jury could render a verdict for the nonmoving party. Under this rule, the trial judge may not direct a verdict against a party if there is any evidence upon which the jury could lawfully make a finding in favor of that party. 5 FLPRAC § 22:5.

3. *Arbitration and mediation*

a. *Referral to arbitration and mediation.* Except as hereinafter provided or as otherwise prohibited by law, the presiding judge may enter an order referring all or any part of a contested civil matter to mediation or arbitration. The parties to any contested civil matter may file a written stipulation to mediate or arbitrate any issue between them at any time. Such stipulation shall be incorporated into the order of referral. FL ST RCP Rule 1.700(a).

   i. *Local arbitration policy.* It is the policy of the Civil Division judges to maximize the use of alternative dispute resolution procedures. Except where prohibited by statute, mediation will be ordered in all cases where jury trial is requested and in selected cases which are to be tried non-jury. Also, selected cases will be referred for court-annexed non-binding arbitration through the Orange County Bar Association Arbitration Service. Counsel may move to dispense with or defer mediation or arbitration or move to modify the referral order for good cause. FL ST 9 J CIR SECTION 15.

b. *Arbitration*

   i. *Exclusions.* A civil action shall be ordered to arbitration or arbitration in conjunction with mediation upon stipulation of the parties. A civil action may be ordered to arbitration or arbitration in conjunction with mediation upon motion of any party or by the court, if the judge determines the action to be of such a nature that arbitration could be of benefit to the litigants or the court. FL ST RCP Rule 1.800.

      - Under no circumstances may the following categories of actions be referred to arbitration: (1) bond estreatures; (2) habeas corpus or other extraordinary writs; (3) bond validations; (4) civil or criminal contempt; (5) such other matters as may be specified by order of the chief judge in the circuit. FL ST RCP Rule 1.800.

   ii. For more information regarding arbitration, please see FL ST RCP Rule 1.810; FL ST RCP Rule 1.820; FL ST RCP Rule 1.830.

c. *Mediation.* For more information regarding mediation, please see FL ST RCP Rule 1.710; FL ST RCP Rule 1.720; FL ST RCP Rule 1.730; and FL ST RCP Rule 1.750.

4. *Rules of court*

a. *Rules of civil procedure.* The Florida Rules of Civil Procedure apply to all actions of a civil nature and all special statutory proceedings in the circuit courts and county courts except those to which the Florida Probate Rules, the Florida Family Law Rules of Procedure, or the Small Claims Rules apply. FL ST RCP Rule 1.010.

i. The form, content, procedure, and time for pleading in all special statutory proceedings shall be as prescribed by the statutes governing the proceeding unless the Florida Rules of Civil Procedure specifically provide to the contrary. FL ST RCP Rule 1.010.

ii. The Florida Rules of Civil Procedure shall be construed to secure the just, speedy, and inexpensive determination of every action. FL ST RCP Rule 1.010.

b. *Rules of judicial administration.* The Florida Rules of Judicial Administration shall apply to administrative matters in all courts to which the Florida Rules of Judicial Administration are applicable by their terms. The Florida Rules of Judicial Administration shall be construed to secure the speedy and inexpensive determination of every proceeding to which they are applicable. The Florida Rules of Judicial Administration shall supersede all conflicting rules and statutes. FL ST J ADMIN Rule 2.110.

c. *Business court procedures.* For rules specific to Business Court, please see FL ST 9 J CIR ORANGE CIV SECTION 1, et seq.

D. Documents

1. *Required documents*

a. *Notice of hearing/Motion.* An application to the court for an order shall be by motion which shall be made in writing unless made during a hearing or trial, shall state with particularity the grounds therefor, and shall set forth the relief or order sought. The requirement of writing is fulfilled if the motion is stated in a written notice of the hearing of the motion. All notices of hearing shall specify each motion or other matter to be heard. FL ST RCP Rule 1.100(b). A notice calling up "all pending motions" is insufficient. FL ST 9 J CIR SECTION 11(D)(1). Additional motions should not be "piggy-backed" by cross-notice unless counsel first confirms with opposing counsel and the judge's judicial assistant that there can be sufficient additional time reserved in which to hear them. FL ST 9 J CIR SECTION 11(D)(2).

i. *Notices to persons with disabilities.* See the Format section of this KeyRules document for further information.

b. *Certificate of service.* When any attorney certifies in substance: "I certify that a copy hereof has been furnished to (here insert name or names and addresses used for service) by (e-mail) (delivery) (mail) (fax) on .... (date) ....________________ Attorney" the certificate is taken as prima facie proof of such service in compliance with FL ST J ADMIN Rule 2.516. FL ST J ADMIN Rule 2.516(f).

2. *Supplemental documents*

a. *Legal memorandum.* Legal memorandums in support of or opposition to motions are optional. But if filed, counsel must furnish the judge with chambers copies of the memorandum and highlighted copies of primary legal authorities cited therein. FL ST 9 J CIR SECTION 11(B).

i. As an alternative to a memorandum, a list of primary legal authorities with highlighted copies attached may be submitted. Chambers copies and authority lists must be under cover letter referencing the case style and number and stating the date and time of the hearing. FL ST 9 J CIR SECTION 11(B).

b. *Proposed order.* The court may require that orders or judgments be prepared by a party, may require the party to furnish the court with stamped, addressed envelopes for service of the order or judgment, and may require that proposed orders and judgments be furnished to all parties before entry by the court of the order or judgment. FL ST J ADMIN Rule 2.516(h)(1).

i. Proposed orders and judgments will be prepared by the prevailing attorney unless the judge designates some other attorney or states that he or she will prepare the order or judgment. FL ST 9 J CIR SECTION 12(A)(1).

ii. When submitting proposed orders or judgments, counsel shall also include sufficient copies and self address stamped envelopes for all parties. FL ST 9 J CIR SECTION 12(A)(2).

iii. Moving counsel must present a proposed order with space for ruling left blank at the conclusion of the hearing and must serve conformed copies on all other counsel and unrepresented parties. FL ST 9 J CIR SECTION 10(A)(3).

iv. Unsigned orders or judgments should not be sent to the Clerk's office for transmission to the judge. FL ST 9 J CIR SECTION 12(D)(3).

c. *Notice of constitutional question.* A party that files a pleading, written motion, or other paper drawing into question the constitutionality of a state statute or a county or municipal charter, ordinance, or franchise must promptly (1) file a notice of constitutional question stating the question and identifying the paper that raises it; and (2) serve the notice and the pleading, written motion, or other paper drawing into question the constitutionality of a state statute or a county or municipal charter, ordinance, or franchise on the Attorney General or the state attorney of the judicial circuit in which the action is pending, by either certified or registered mail. Service of the notice and pleading, written motion, or other paper does not require joinder of the Attorney General or the state attorney as a party to the action. FL ST RCP Rule 1.071.

E. Format

1. *Documents; Type and size.* Documents subject to the exceptions set forth in FL ST J ADMIN Rule 2.525(d) shall be filed on recycled paper measuring eight and one half by eleven (8 1/2 by 11) inches. For purposes of FL ST J ADMIN Rule 2.520, paper is recycled if it contains a minimum content of fifty (50) percent waste paper. Xerographic reduction of legal-size (eight and one half by fourteen (8 1/2 by 14) inches) documents to letter size (eight and one half by eleven (8 1/2 by 11) inches) is prohibited. All other documents filed by electronic transmission shall be filed in a format capable of being printed in a format consistent with the provisions of FL ST J ADMIN Rule 2.250. FL ST J ADMIN Rule 2.520(b).

a. *Exhibits.* Any exhibit or attachment filed with pleadings or papers may be filed in its original size. FL ST J ADMIN Rule 2.520(c).

b. *Recording space.* On all papers and documents prepared and filed by the court or by any party to a proceeding which are to be recorded in the public records of any county, including but not limited to final money judgments and notices of lis pendens, a three (3) inch by three (3) inch space at the top right-hand corner on the first page and a one (1) inch by three (3) inch space at the top right-hand corner on each subsequent page shall be left blank and reserved for use by the clerk of court. FL ST J ADMIN Rule 2.520(d).

i. *Exceptions to recording space.* Any papers or documents created by persons or entities over which the filing party has no control, including but not limited to wills, codicils, trusts, or other testamentary documents; documents prepared or executed by any public officer; documents prepared, executed, acknowledged, or proved outside of the State of Florida; or documents created by State or Federal government agencies, may be filed without the space required by FL ST J ADMIN Rule 2.520. FL ST J ADMIN Rule 2.520(e).

c. *Noncompliance.* No clerk of court is permitted to refuse to file any document or paper because of noncompliance with the Florida Rules of Judicial Administration. However, upon request of the clerk of court, noncomplying documents must be resubmitted in accordance with the formatting rules. FL ST J ADMIN Rule 2.520(f).

d. *Proposed orders*

i. All orders will be on eight and a half by eleven (8 1/2 by 11) inch plain white paper (not lined or letterhead paper) and be double spaced. FL ST 9 J CIR SECTION 12(B)(1).

ii. The order must contain a title indicating what matter the order pertains to, e.g., "Order On Defendant Smith's Motion To Dismiss." FL ST 9 J CIR SECTION 12(B)(2).

iii. The preamble of the order should include the date of the hearing and what motions were heard. FL ST 9 J CIR SECTION 12(B)(3).

iv. The adjudication portion of the order should state what relief is ordered. Simply stating that "the motion is granted" without more is insufficient. FL ST 9 J CIR SECTION 12(B)(4).

v. The order should indicate the specific time period of any act ordered to be done and should state whether the time period runs from the date of the hearing or the date the order is signed or some other specified date. FL ST 9 J CIR SECTION 12(B)(5).

vi. The order should contain a full certificate of service with the complete names and addresses of the attorneys and unrepresented parties to be served. Merely showing "copies to" is insufficient. FL ST 9 J CIR SECTION 12(B)(6).

vii. If an order of dismissal is final (i.e., it disposes of the entire case) the title should contain the word "Final." When the order is not final but leaves other counts or claims against other defendants pending, it should so state in a separate paragraph. FL ST 9 J CIR SECTION 12(B)(7).

viii. When submitting stipulations, orders shall be by separate order, not attached to the stipulation. FL ST 9 J CIR SECTION 12(B)(8).

ix. Counsel preparing the Final Judgment or order should draft and circulate copies within two (2) working days of the ruling or jury verdict. If counsel preparing the Final Judgment or order gets approval as to form of the order from all counsel, the original with copies and envelopes should be sent directly to the judge with a cover letter stating all counsel agree to the form of the order or judgment. If other counsel objects to the form or cannot be reached for approval, counsel preparing the judgment or order shall notice a motion for entry of the order or judgment. If objecting counsel does not furnish the judge prior to or at the hearing with a proposed judgment or order version with copies under cover letter stating the reasons for the objection, all objections will be deemed waived. Orders and judgments should not be submitted to the judge to hold waiting for an objection. FL ST 9 J CIR SECTION 12(D).

2. *Caption.* Every pleading, motion, order, judgment, or other paper shall have a caption containing the name of the court, the file number, and except for in rem proceedings, including forfeiture proceedings, the name of the first party on each side with an appropriate indication of other parties, and a designation identifying the party filing it and its nature or the nature of the order, as the case may be. In any in rem proceeding, every pleading, motion, order, judgment, or other paper shall have a caption containing the name of the court, the file number, the style "In re" (followed by the name or general description of the property), and a designation of the person or entity filing it and its nature or the nature of the order, as the case may be. In an in rem forfeiture proceeding, the style shall be "In re forfeiture of" (followed by the name of the general description of the property). All papers filed in the action shall be styled in such a manner as to indicate clearly the subject matter of the paper and the party requesting or obtaining relief. FL ST RCP Rule 1.100(c)(1).

3. *Writing and written defined.* Writing or written means a document containing information, an application, or a stipulation. FL ST RCP Rule 1.080(c).

4. *Rule abbreviations*

   a. The Florida Rules of Civil Procedure and shall be abbreviated as Fla.R.Civ.P. FL ST RCP Rule 1.010.

   b. The Florida Rules of Judicial Administration shall be abbreviated as Fla. R. Jud. Admin. FL ST J ADMIN Rule 2.110.

5. *Nonverification.* Except when otherwise specifically provided by the Florida Rules of Civil Procedure or an applicable statute, every pleading or other document of a party represented by an attorney need not be verified or accompanied by an affidavit. FL ST RCP Rule 1.030; FL ST J ADMIN Rule 2.515(a).

6. *Unrepresented parties.* An unrepresented party must file his or her papers with the clerk and send copies to other attorneys or unrepresented parties. All such papers must be typed double-spaced on plain white eight and a half by eleven (8 1/2 by 11) inch paper, with the name of the case and case number at the top and the party's mailing address, telephone number and FAX number, if any, below his or her signature at the end of the paper. Such unrepresented party must immediately notify the clerk and all other counsel or parties of record in writing of any change in mailing address or telephone or FAX number. Failure to

promptly notify of change of address could result in a dismissal or default entered against such party. FL ST 9 J CIR SECTION 7(B)(5).

7. *Attorney signature*

   a. *Attorney signature.* Every pleading and other document of a party represented by an attorney shall be signed by at least one (1) attorney of record in that attorney's individual name whose current record Florida Bar address, telephone number, including area code, primary e-mail address and secondary e-mail addresses, if any, and Florida Bar number shall be stated, and who shall be duly licensed to practice law in Florida or who shall have received permission to appear in the particular case as provided in FL ST J ADMIN Rule 2.510. FL ST J ADMIN Rule 2.515(a).

      i. The attorney may be required by the court to give the address of, and to vouch for the attorney's authority to represent, the party. FL ST J ADMIN Rule 2.515(a).

      ii. The signature of an attorney shall constitute a certificate by the attorney that the attorney has read the pleading or other document; that to the best of the attorney's knowledge, information, and belief there is good ground to support it; and that it is not interposed for delay. FL ST J ADMIN Rule 2.515(a).

      iii. If a pleading is not signed or is signed with intent to defeat the purpose of FL ST J ADMIN Rule 2.515, it may be stricken and the action may proceed as though the pleading or other document had not been served. FL ST J ADMIN Rule 2.515(a).

   b. *Pro se litigant signature.* A party who is not represented by an attorney shall sign any pleading or other paper and state the party's address and telephone number, including area code. FL ST J ADMIN Rule 2.515(b).

   c. *Form of signature*

      i. The signatures required on pleadings and documents by FL ST J ADMIN Rule 2.515(a) and FL ST J ADMIN Rule 2.515(b) may be:

         - Original signatures;
         - Original signatures that have been reproduced by electronic means, such as on electronically transmitted documents or photocopied documents;
         - Electronic signatures using the "/s/," "s/," or "/s" formats by or at the direction of the person signing; or
         - Any other signature format authorized by general law, so long as the clerk where the proceeding is pending has the capability of receiving and has obtained approval from the Supreme Court of Florida to accept pleadings and documents with that signature format. FL ST J ADMIN Rule 2.515(c)(1).

      ii. An attorney, party, or other person who files a pleading or paper by electronic transmission that does not contain the original signature of that attorney, party, or other person shall file that identical pleading or paper in paper form containing an original signature of that attorney, party, or other person (hereinafter called the follow-up filing) immediately thereafter. The follow-up filing is not required if the Supreme Court of Florida has entered an order directing the clerk of court to discontinue accepting the follow-up filing. FL ST J ADMIN Rule 2.515(c)(2).

8. *Forms*

   a. *Process.* The forms of process, notice of lis pendens, and notice of action provided in the Florida Rules of Civil Procedure are sufficient. Variations from the forms do not void process or notices that are otherwise sufficient. FL ST RCP Rule 1.900(a).

   b. *Other forms.* The other forms provided in the Florida Rules of Civil Procedure are sufficient for the matters that are covered by them. So long as the substance is expressed without prolixity, the forms may be varied to meet the facts of a particular case. FL ST RCP Rule 1.900(b).

   c. *Formal matters.* Captions, except for the designation of the paper, are omitted from the forms provided in the Florida Rules of Civil Procedure. A general form of caption is the first form provided. Signatures are omitted from pleadings and motions. FL ST RCP Rule 1.900(c).

9. *Notices to persons with disabilities.* All notices of court proceedings to be held in a public facility, and all process compelling appearance at such proceedings, shall include the following statement in bold face, fourteen (14) point Times New Roman or Courier font: "If you are a person with a disability who needs any accommodation in order to participate in this proceeding, you are entitled, at no cost to you, to the provision of certain assistance. Please contact [identify applicable court personnel by name, address, and telephone number] at least seven (7) days before your scheduled court appearance, or immediately upon receiving this notification if the time before the scheduled appearance is less than seven (7) days; if you are hearing or voice impaired, call 711." FL ST J ADMIN Rule 2.540(c)(1).

10. *Minimization of the filing of sensitive information*
   a. *Limitations for court filings.* Unless authorized by FL ST J ADMIN Rule 2.425(b), statute, another rule of court, or the court orders otherwise, designated sensitive information filed with the court must be limited to the following format:
      i. The initials of a person known to be a minor;
      ii. The year of birth of a person's birth date;
      iii. No portion of any: Social security number, Bank account number, Credit card account number, Charge account number, or Debit account number;
      iv. The last four digits of any: Taxpayer identification number (TIN), Employee identification number, Driver's license number, Passport number, Telephone number, Financial account number, except as set forth in FL ST J ADMIN Rule 2.425(a)(3), Brokerage account number, Insurance policy account number, Loan account number, Customer account number, or Patient or health care number;
      v. A truncated version of any: Email address, Computer user name, Password, or Personal identification number (PIN); and
      vi. A truncated version of any other sensitive information as provided by court order. FL ST J ADMIN Rule 2.425(a).
   b. *Exceptions.* FL ST J ADMIN Rule 2.425(a) does not apply to the following:
      i. An account number which identifies the property alleged to be the subject of a proceeding;
      ii. The record of an administrative or agency proceeding;
      iii. The record in appellate or review proceedings;
      iv. The birth date of a minor whenever the birth date is necessary for the court to establish or maintain subject matter jurisdiction;
      v. The name of a minor in any order relating to parental responsibility, time-sharing, or child support;
      vi. The name of a minor in any document or order affecting the minor's ownership of real property;
      vii. The birth date of a party in a writ of attachment or notice to payor;
      viii. In traffic and criminal proceedings: a pro se filing; a court filing that is related to a criminal matter or investigation and that is prepared before the filing of a criminal charge or is not filed as part of any docketed criminal case; an arrest or search warrant or any information in support thereof; a charging document and an affidavit or other documents filed in support of any charging document, including any driving records; a statement of particulars; discovery material introduced into evidence or otherwise filed with the court; and all information necessary for the proper issuance and execution of a subpoena duces tecum;
      ix. Information used by the clerk for case maintenance purposes or the courts for case management purposes; and
      x. Information which is relevant and material to an issue before the court. FL ST J ADMIN Rule 2.425(b).
   c. *Remedies.* Upon motion by a party or interested person or sua sponte by the court, the court may order remedies, sanctions or both for a violation of FL ST J ADMIN Rule 2.425(a). Following notice

and an opportunity to respond, the court may impose sanctions if such filing was not made in good faith. FL ST J ADMIN Rule 2.425(c).

d. *Motions not restricted.* FL ST J ADMIN Rule 2.425 does not restrict a party's right to move for protective order, to move to file documents under seal, or to request a determination of the confidentiality of records. FL ST J ADMIN Rule 2.425(d).

e. *Application.* FL ST J ADMIN Rule 2.425 does not affect the application of constitutional provisions, statutes, or rules of court regarding confidential information or access to public information. FL ST J ADMIN Rule 2.425(e).

F. Filing and Service Requirements

1. *Filing requirements.* All original documents must be filed with the court either before service or immediately thereafter, unless otherwise provided for by general law or other rules. If the original of any bond or other document is not placed in the court file, a certified copy must be so placed by the clerk. FL ST J ADMIN Rule 2.516(d). All documents shall be filed in conformity with the requirements of FL ST J ADMIN Rule 2.525. FL ST RCP Rule 1.080(b). All documents filed in any court shall be filed by electronic transmission in accordance with FL ST J ADMIN Rule 2.525. "Documents" means pleadings, motions, petitions, memoranda, briefs, notices, exhibits, declarations, affidavits, orders, judgments, decrees, writs, opinions, and any other paper or writing submitted to a court. FL ST J ADMIN Rule 2.520(a). All documents that are court records, as defined in FL ST J ADMIN Rule 2.430(a)(1), must be filed by electronic transmission, provided that: (1) the clerk has the ability to accept and retain such documents; (2) the clerk or the chief judge of the circuit has requested permission to accept documents filed by electronic transmission; and (3) the supreme court has entered an order granting permission to the clerk to accept documents filed by electronic transmission. FL ST J ADMIN Rule 2.525(c)(1).

a. *Definition.* "Electronic transmission of documents" means the sending of information by electronic signals to, by or from a court or clerk, which when received can be transformed and stored or transmitted on paper, microfilm, magnetic storage device, optical imaging system, CD-ROM, flash drive, other electronic data storage system, server, case maintenance system ("CM"), electronic court filing ("ECF") system, statewide or local electronic portal ("e-portal"), or other electronic record keeping system authorized by the supreme court in a format sufficient to communicate the information on the original document in a readable format. Electronic transmission of documents includes electronic mail ("e-mail") and any internet-based transmission procedure, and may include procedures allowing for documents to be signed or verified by electronic means. FL ST J ADMIN Rule 2.525(a).

i. The filing of documents with the court as required by the Florida Rules of Judicial Administration must be made by filing them with the clerk in accordance with FL ST J ADMIN Rule 2.525, except that the judge may permit documents to be filed with the judge, in which event the judge must note the filing date before him or her on the documents and transmit them to the clerk. The date of filing is that shown on the face of the document by the judge's notation or the clerk's time stamp, whichever is earlier. FL ST J ADMIN Rule 2.516(e).

b. *Application.* Any court or clerk of the court may accept the electronic transmission of documents for filing after the clerk, together with input from the chief judge of the circuit, has obtained approval of the procedures and program for doing so from the Supreme Court of Florida. FL ST J ADMIN Rule 2.525(b).

c. *Exceptions*

i. Paper documents and other submissions may be manually submitted to the clerk or court:

- When the clerk does not have the ability to accept and retain documents by electronic filing or has not had ECF Procedures approved by the supreme court;
- For filing by any self-represented party or any self-represented nonparty unless specific ECF Procedures provide a means to file documents electronically. However, any self-represented nonparty that is a governmental or public agency and any other agency, partnership, corporation, or business entity acting on behalf of any governmental or public agency may file documents by electronic transmission if such entity has the capability of filing documents electronically;

- For filing by attorneys excused from e-mail service in accordance with FL ST J ADMIN Rule 2.516(b);
- When submitting evidentiary exhibits or filing non-documentary materials;
- When the filing involves documents in excess of twenty-five (25) megabytes (25MB) in size. For such filings, documents may be transmitted using an electronic storage medium that the clerk has the ability to accept, which may include a CD-ROM, flash drive, or similar storage medium;
- When filed in open court, as permitted by the court;
- When paper filing is permitted by any approved statewide or local ECF procedures; and
- If any court determines that justice so requires. FL ST J ADMIN Rule 2.525(d).

ii. Any document in paper form submitted under FL ST J ADMIN Rule 2.525(d) is filed when it is received by the clerk or court and the clerk shall immediately thereafter convert any filed paper document to an electronic document. "Convert to an electronic document" means optically capturing an image of a paper document and using character recognition software to recover as much of the document's text as practicable and then indexing and storing the document in the official court file. FL ST J ADMIN Rule 2.525(c)(4).

iii. Any storage medium submitted under FL ST J ADMIN Rule 2.525(d)(5) is filed when received by the clerk or court and the clerk shall immediately thereafter transfer the electronic documents from the storage device to the official court file. FL ST J ADMIN Rule 2.525(c)(5).

iv. If the filer of any paper document authorized under FL ST J ADMIN Rule 2.525(d) provides a self-addressed, postage-paid envelope for return of the paper document after it is converted to electronic form by the clerk, the clerk shall place the paper document in the envelope and deposit it in the mail. Except when a paper document is required to be maintained, the clerk may recycle any filed paper document that is not to be returned to the filer. FL ST J ADMIN Rule 2.525(c)(6).

v. The clerk may convert any paper document filed before the effective date of FL ST J ADMIN Rule 2.525 to an electronic document. Unless the clerk is required to maintain the paper document, if the paper document has been converted to an electronic document by the clerk, the paper document is no longer part of the official court file and may be removed and recycled. FL ST J ADMIN Rule 2.525(c)(7).

d. *Unrepresented parties.* An unrepresented party must file his or her papers with the clerk and send copies to other attorneys or unrepresented parties. FL ST 9 J CIR SECTION 7(B)(5).

i. An unrepresented party may not communicate privately with the judge either by letter, telephone, in person or otherwise. FL ST 9 J CIR SECTION 7(B)(4).

ii. Copies of legal papers or other written materials should not be sent to the judge unless specifically requested by the judge or required by the local administrative procedures. Any unrequested or non-required papers or materials sent to a judge may not be read but may be returned to the sender or placed unread into the court file. FL ST 9 J CIR SECTION 7(B)(4).

e. *Official court file.* For information on what constitutes the official court file, please see FL ST J ADMIN Rule 2.525(c)(2), FL ST J ADMIN Rule 2.525(c)(3).

f. *Administration.* All attorneys, parties, or other persons using this rule to file documents are required to make arrangements with the court or clerk for the payment of any charges authorized by general law or the supreme court before filing any document by electronic transmission. FL ST J ADMIN Rule 2.525(f)(2).

g. *Filing date.* The filing date for an electronically transmitted document is the date and time that such filing is acknowledged by an electronic stamp or otherwise, pursuant to any procedure set forth in any ECF Procedures approved by the supreme court, or the date the last page of such filing is received by the court or clerk. FL ST J ADMIN Rule 2.525(f)(3).

h. *Accessibility.* All documents transmitted in any electronic form under FL ST J ADMIN Rule 2.525

must comply with the accessibility requirements of FL ST J ADMIN Rule 2.526. FL ST J ADMIN Rule 2.525(g).

2. *Service requirements.* Every pleading subsequent to the initial pleading, all orders, and every other document filed in the action must be served in conformity with the requirements of FL ST J ADMIN Rule 2.516. FL ST RCP Rule 1.080(a).
   a. *Service; When required.* Unless the court otherwise orders, or a statute or supreme court administrative order specifies a different means of service, every pleading subsequent to the initial pleading and every other document filed in any court proceeding, except applications for witness subpoenas and documents served by formal notice or required to be served in the manner provided for service of formal notice, must be served in accordance with FL ST J ADMIN Rule 2.516 on each party. No service need be made on parties against whom a default has been entered, except that pleadings asserting new or additional claims against them must be served in the manner provided for service of summons. FL ST J ADMIN Rule 2.516(a).
      i. Counsel who serves a memorandum or authority list first should also include a copy of the motion, any papers to which it is addressed, and the response, if any. In order for the judge to properly review a submission in advance, it must be received in the judge's office at least three (3) working days before the hearing. FL ST 9 J CIR SECTION 11(B).
   b. *Service; How made.* When service is required or permitted to be made upon a party represented by an attorney, service must be made upon the attorney unless service upon the party is ordered by the court. FL ST J ADMIN Rule 2.516(b).
      i. *Service by electronic mail ("e-mail").* All documents required or permitted to be served on another party must be served by e-mail, unless FL ST J ADMIN Rule 2.516 otherwise provides. When, in addition to service by e-mail, the sender also utilizes another means of service provided for in FL ST J ADMIN Rule 2.516(b)(2), any differing time limits and other provisions applicable to that other means of service control. FL ST J ADMIN Rule 2.516(b)(1). Any document electronically transmitted to a court or clerk must also be served on all parties and interested persons in accordance with the applicable rules of court. FL ST J ADMIN Rule 2.525(e)(2).
         - *Service on attorneys.* Upon appearing in a proceeding, an attorney must serve a designation of a primary e-mail address and may designate no more than two (2) secondary e-mail addresses. Thereafter, service must be directed to all designated e-mail addresses in that proceeding. Every document filed by an attorney thereafter must include the primary e-mail address of that attorney and any secondary e-mail addresses. If an attorney does not designate any e-mail address for service, documents may be served on that attorney at the e-mail address on record with The Florida Bar. FL ST J ADMIN Rule 2.516(b)(1)(A).
         - *Exception to e-mail service on attorneys.* Service by an attorney on another attorney must be made by e-mail unless excused by the court. Upon motion by an attorney demonstrating that the attorney has no e-mail account and lacks access to the Internet at the attorney's office, the court may excuse the attorney from the requirements of e-mail service. Service on and by an attorney excused by the court from e-mail service must be by the means provided in FL ST J ADMIN Rule 2.516(b)(2). FL ST J ADMIN Rule 2.516(b)(1)(B).
         - *Service on and by parties not represented by an attorney.* Any party not represented by an attorney may serve a designation of a primary e-mail address and also may designate no more than two (2) secondary e-mail addresses to which service must be directed in that proceeding by the means provided in FL ST J ADMIN Rule 2.516(b)(1). If a party not represented by an attorney does not designate an e-mail address for service in a proceeding, service on and by that party must be by the means provided in FL ST J ADMIN Rule 2.516(b)(2). FL ST J ADMIN Rule 2.516(b)(1)(C).
         - *Time of service.* Service by e-mail is complete when it is sent. FL ST J ADMIN Rule 2.516(b)(1)(D). An e-mail is deemed served on the date it is sent. FL ST J ADMIN Rule 2.516(b)(1)(D)(i). If the sender learns that the e-mail did not reach the address of the person to be served, the sender must immediately send another copy by e-mail, or by a

means authorized by FL ST J ADMIN Rule 2.516(b)(2). FL ST J ADMIN Rule 2.516(b)(1)(D)(ii). E-mail service is treated as service by mail for the computation of time. FL ST J ADMIN Rule 2.516(b)(1)(D)(iii).

ii. *Format of e-mail for service.* Service of a document by e-mail is made by attaching a copy of the document in PDF format to an e-mail sent to all addresses designated by the attorney or party. FL ST J ADMIN Rule 2.516(b)(1)(E).

- All documents served by e-mail must be attached to an e-mail message containing a subject line beginning with the words "SERVICE OF COURT DOCUMENT" in all capital letters, followed by the case number of the proceeding in which the documents are being served. FL ST J ADMIN Rule 2.516(b)(1)(E)(i).
- The body of the e-mail must identify the court in which the proceeding is pending, the case number, the name of the initial party on each side, the title of each document served with that e-mail, and the sender's name and telephone number. FL ST J ADMIN Rule 2.516(b)(1)(E)(ii).
- Any document served by e-mail may be signed by the "/s/" format, as long as the filed original is signed in accordance with the applicable rule of procedure. FL ST J ADMIN Rule 2.516(b)(1)(E)(iii).
- Any e-mail which, together with its attached documents, exceeds five megabytes (5MB) in size, must be divided and sent as separate e-mails, no one of which may exceed five megabytes (5MB) in size and each of which must be sequentially numbered in the subject line. FL ST J ADMIN Rule 2.516(b)(1)(E)(iv).

iii. *Service by other means.* In addition to, and not in lieu of, service by e-mail, service may also be made upon attorneys by any of the means specified in FL ST J ADMIN Rule 2.516(b)(2). Service on and by all parties who are not represented by an attorney and who do not designate an e-mail address, and on and by all attorneys excused from e-mail service, must be made by delivering a copy of the document or by mailing it to the party or attorney at their last known address or, if no address is known, by leaving it with the clerk of the court. Service by mail is complete upon mailing. Delivery of a copy within FL ST J ADMIN Rule 2.516 is complete upon:

- Handing it to the attorney or to the party,
- Leaving it at the attorney's or party's office with a clerk or other person in charge thereof,
- If there is no one in charge, leaving it in a conspicuous place therein,
- If the office is closed or the person to be served has no office, leaving it at the person's usual place of abode with some person of his or her family above fifteen (15) years of age and informing such person of the contents, or
- Transmitting it by facsimile to the attorney's or party's office with a cover sheet containing the sender's name, firm, address, telephone number, and facsimile number, and the number of pages transmitted. When service is made by facsimile, a copy must also be served by any other method permitted by FL ST J ADMIN Rule 2.516. Facsimile service occurs when transmission is complete. FL ST J ADMIN Rule 2.516(b)(2)(A) through FL ST J ADMIN Rule 2.516(b)(2)(E).
- Service by delivery after 5:00 p.m. must be deemed to have been made by mailing on the date of delivery. FL ST J ADMIN Rule 2.516(b)(2)(F).

c. *Service; Numerous defendants.* In actions when the parties are unusually numerous, the court may regulate the service contemplated by the Florida Rules of Judicial Administration on motion or on its own initiative in such manner as may be found to be just and reasonable. FL ST J ADMIN Rule 2.516(c).

d. *Service by clerk.* Service of notices and other documents required to be made by the clerk must also be done as provided in FL ST J ADMIN Rule 2.516(b). FL ST J ADMIN Rule 2.516(g).

G. Hearings

1. *Uniform motion calendar*
    a. *Contacting judge's office on short matters.* Counsel should contact the judge's office to ascertain whether short matters are heard by the specific division. FL ST 9 J CIR SECTION 10(C)(1).
    b. *Motions suitable for hearing.* Types of motions suitable for hearing on the motion calendar are simple motions to dismiss complaints with only one or two counts, to strike one or two affirmative defenses, for more definite statement, to amend pleadings, to compel discovery, for protective order, objections to IME, etc. Complex motions, motions requiring testimony or motions for summary judgment (except uncontested mortgage foreclosures), or more than two motions to be heard at one time should not be scheduled on this calendar and will not be heard by the Court. FL ST 9 J CIR SECTION 10(C)(2).
2. *Other motion hearings.* All other motions should be specially set through the judge's judicial assistant for a date and time certain. Requests for hearing time in excess of one (1) hour will require special permission of the judge obtained through the judicial assistant or by personal appearance of counsel at ex parte time. FL ST 9 J CIR SECTION 10(D).
3. *Cancelling hearings.* Only the attorney who noticed it can cancel a hearing. If a hearing becomes unnecessary after it has been noticed, the judge's judicial assistant and all other counsel must be notified immediately and effectively that the hearing is canceled. FL ST 9 J CIR SECTION 11(E).
4. *Communication equipment*
    a. *Definition.* Communication equipment means a conference telephone or other electronic device that permits all those appearing or participating to hear and speak to each other, provided that all conversation of all parties is audible to all persons present. FL ST J ADMIN Rule 2.530(a).
    b. *Use by all parties.* A county or circuit court judge may, upon the court's own motion or upon the written request of a party, direct that communication equipment be used for a motion hearing, pretrial conference, or a status conference. A judge must give notice to the parties and consider any objections they may have to the use of communication equipment before directing that communication equipment be used. The decision to use communication equipment over the objection of parties will be in the sound discretion of the trial court, except as noted below. FL ST J ADMIN Rule 2.530(b).
    c. *Use only by requesting party.* A county or circuit court judge may, upon the written request of a party upon reasonable notice to all other parties, permit a requesting party to participate through communication equipment in a scheduled motion hearing; however, any such request (except in criminal, juvenile, and appellate proceedings) must be granted, absent a showing of good cause to deny the same, where the hearing is set for not longer than fifteen (15) minutes. FL ST J ADMIN Rule 2.530(c).
    d. *Testimony*
        i. *Generally.* A county or circuit court judge, general magistrate, special magistrate, or hearing officer may allow testimony to be taken through communication equipment if all parties consent or if permitted by another applicable rule of procedure. FL ST J ADMIN Rule 2.530(d)(1).
        ii. *Procedure.* Any party desiring to present testimony through communication equipment shall, prior to the hearing or trial at which the testimony is to be presented, contact all parties to determine whether each party consents to this form of testimony. The party seeking to present the testimony shall move for permission to present testimony through communication equipment, which motion shall set forth good cause as to why the testimony should be allowed in this form. FL ST J ADMIN Rule 2.530(d)(2).
        iii. *Oath.* Testimony may be taken through communication equipment only if a notary public or other person authorized to administer oaths in the witness's jurisdiction is present with the witness and administers the oath consistent with the laws of the jurisdiction. FL ST J ADMIN Rule 2.530(d)(3).

iv. *Confrontation rights.* In juvenile and criminal proceedings the defendant must make an informed waiver of any confrontation rights that may be abridged by the use of communication equipment. FL ST J ADMIN Rule 2.530(d)(4).

v. *Video testimony.* If the testimony to be presented utilizes video conferencing or comparable two-way visual capabilities, the court in its discretion may modify the procedures set forth in FL ST J ADMIN Rule 2.530 to accommodate the technology utilized. FL ST J ADMIN Rule 2.530(d)(5).

e. *Burden of expense.* The cost for the use of the communication equipment is the responsibility of the requesting party unless otherwise directed by the court. FL ST J ADMIN Rule 2.530(e).

H. Forms

1. Official Motion for Directed Verdict Forms for Florida

a. Caption. FL ST RCP Form 1.901.

b. Notice of compliance when constitutional challenge is brought. FL ST RCP Form 1.975.

2. Motion for Directed Verdict Forms for Florida

a. Motion; For directed verdict; At close of adverse party's evidence. FL-PP § 5:86.

b. Motion; For directed verdict; At close of all of evidence. FL-PP § 5:87.

c. Motion; Request to go to jury if motions by both parties are denied. FL-PP § 5:88.

d. Order; Granting defendant's motion for directed verdict; Insufficiency of plaintiff's evidence. FL-PP § 5:89.

e. Motion; Directed verdict, renewed. FL-PRACFORM § 7:62.

f. Form for motion for directed verdict at close of plaintiff's case. FL-RCPF R 1.480(24).

g. Form for motion for directed verdict at close of defendant's case. FL-RCPF R 1.480(25).

h. Form for motion to set aside verdict and enter directed verdict. FL-RCPF R 1.480(26).

I. Checklist

(I) ❑ Matters to be considered by moving party

(a) ❑ Required documents

(1) ❑ Notice of hearing/Motion

(2) ❑ Certificate of service

(b) ❑ Supplemental documents

(1) ❑ Legal memorandum

(2) ❑ Proposed order

(3) ❑ Notice of constitutional question

(c) ❑ Time for making motion

(1) ❑ Before a verdict is returned - A directed verdict is available to the defendant at the close of the plaintiff's evidence or to either party at the close of all of the evidence

(2) ❑ After a verdict is returned - Within ten (10) days after the return of a verdict, a party who has timely moved for a directed verdict may serve a motion to enter judgment in accordance with the motion for a directed verdict

(3) ❑ No verdict is returned - If a verdict was not returned, a party who has timely moved for a directed verdict may serve a motion for judgment in accordance with the motion for a directed verdict within ten (10) days after discharge of the jury

(4) ❑ General motion timing - A copy of any written motion which may not be heard ex parte and a copy of the notice of the hearing thereof shall be served a reasonable time before the time specified for the hearings

(II) ❑ Matters to be considered by opposing party
- (a) ❑ Required documents
  - (1) ❑ Response to motion
  - (2) ❑ Certificate of service
- (b) ❑ Supplemental documents
  - (1) ❑ Legal memorandum
  - (2) ❑ Proposed order
  - (3) ❑ Notice of constitutional question
- (c) ❑ Time for service and filing of opposition
  - (1) ❑ No time specified for responding to a motion

Requests, Notices and Applications
Request for Production of Documents

Document Last Updated January 2013

A. Applicable Rules

1. *State rules*
   - a. Nonverification of pleadings. FL ST RCP Rule 1.030.
   - b. Service and filing of pleadings, orders, and documents. FL ST RCP Rule 1.080.
   - c. Time. FL ST RCP Rule 1.090.
   - d. Pleadings and motions. FL ST RCP Rule 1.100.
   - e. Pretrial procedure. FL ST RCP Rule 1.200.
   - f. General provisions governing discovery. FL ST RCP Rule 1.280.
   - g. Depositions upon oral examination. FL ST RCP Rule 1.310.
   - h. Interrogatories to parties. FL ST RCP Rule 1.340.
   - i. Production of documents and things and entry upon land for inspection and other purposes. FL ST RCP Rule 1.350.
   - j. Production of documents and things without deposition. FL ST RCP Rule 1.351.
   - k. Examination of persons. FL ST RCP Rule 1.360.
   - l. Requests for admission. FL ST RCP Rule 1.370.
   - m. Failure to make discovery; Sanctions. FL ST RCP Rule 1.380.
   - n. Depositions of expert witnesses. FL ST RCP Rule 1.390.
   - o. Relief from judgment, decrees, or orders. FL ST RCP Rule 1.540.
   - p. Forms. FL ST RCP Rule 1.900.
   - q. Minimization of the filing of sensitive information. FL ST J ADMIN Rule 2.425.
   - r. Retention of court records. FL ST J ADMIN Rule 2.430.
   - s. Foreign attorneys. FL ST J ADMIN Rule 2.510.
   - t. Signature of attorneys and parties. FL ST J ADMIN Rule 2.515.
   - u. Paper. FL ST J ADMIN Rule 2.520.
   - v. Electronic filing. FL ST J ADMIN Rule 2.525.
   - w. Accessibility of information and technology. FL ST J ADMIN Rule 2.526.
   - x. Requests for accommodations by persons with disabilities. FL ST J ADMIN Rule 2.540.

2. *Local rules*
   a. Unrepresented (pro se) parties. FL ST 9 J CIR SECTION 7.
   b. General discovery guidelines. FL ST 9 J CIR SECTION 13.

B. Timing

1. *Request for production of documents.* Without leave of court the request may be served on the plaintiff after commencement of the action and on any other party with or after service of the process and initial pleading on that party. FL ST RCP Rule 1.350(b).
2. *Notice of intent to serve subpoena.* A party desiring production under FL ST RCP Rule 1.351 shall serve notice as provided in FL ST RCP Rule 1.080 on every other party of the intent to serve a subpoena under FL ST RCP Rule 1.351 at least ten (10) days before the subpoena is issued if service is by delivery and fifteen (15) days before the subpoena is issued if the service is by mail or e-mail. FL ST RCP Rule 1.351(b).
3. *Sequence and timing of discovery.* Except as provided in FL ST RCP Rule 1.280(b)(5) or unless the court upon motion for the convenience of parties and witnesses and in the interest of justice orders otherwise, methods of discovery may be used in any sequence, and the fact that a party is conducting discovery, whether by deposition or otherwise, shall not delay any other party's discovery. FL ST RCP Rule 1.280(e).
   a. *Timeliness.* The time limit specified in the rules and applicable orders must be observed. If additional time is needed, an extension must be sought before the time limit expires by stipulation, or failing that, by motion and order. FL ST 9 J CIR SECTION 13(B).
4. *Computation of time*
   a. *Generally.* Computation of time shall be governed by FL ST J ADMIN Rule 2.514. FL ST RCP Rule 1.090(a). The following rules apply in computing time periods specified in any rule of procedure, local rule, court order, or statute that does not specify a method of computing time. FL ST J ADMIN Rule 2.514(a).
      i. *Period stated in days or a longer unit.* When the period is stated in days or a longer unit of time (A) exclude the day of the event that triggers the period; (B) count every day, including intermediate Saturdays, Sundays, and legal holidays; and (C) include the last day of the period, but if the last day is a Saturday, Sunday, or legal holiday, or falls within any period of time extended through an order of the chief justice under FL ST J ADMIN Rule 2.205(a)(2)(B)(iv), the period continues to run until the end of the next day that is not a Saturday, Sunday, or legal holiday and does not fall within any period of time extended through an order of the chief justice. FL ST J ADMIN Rule 2.514(a)(1).
      ii. *Period stated in hours.* When the period is stated in hours (A) begin counting immediately on the occurrence of the event that triggers the period; (B) count every hour, including hours during intermediate Saturdays, Sundays, and legal holidays; and (C) if the period would end on a Saturday, Sunday, or legal holiday, or during any period of time extended through an order of the chief justice under FL ST J ADMIN Rule 2.205(a)(2)(B)(iv), the period continues to run until the same time on the next day that is not a Saturday, Sunday, or legal holiday and does not fall within any period of time extended through an order of the chief justice. FL ST J ADMIN Rule 2.514(a)(2).
      iii. *Period stated in days less than seven (7) days.* When the period stated in days is less than seven (7) days, intermediate Saturdays, Sundays, and legal holidays shall be excluded in the computation. FL ST J ADMIN Rule 2.514(a)(3).
      iv. *"Last day" defined.* Unless a different time is set by a statute, local rule, or court order, the last day ends (A) for electronic filing or for service by any means, at midnight; and (B) for filing by other means, when the clerk's office is scheduled to close. FL ST J ADMIN Rule 2.514(a)(4).
      v. *"Next day" defined.* The "next day" is determined by continuing to count forward when the period is measured after an event and backward when measured before an event. FL ST J ADMIN Rule 2.514(a)(5).

vi. *"Legal holiday" defined.* "Legal holiday" means (A) the day set aside by FL ST § 110.117, for observing New Year's Day, Martin Luther King, Jr.'s Birthday, Memorial Day, Independence Day, Labor Day, Veterans' Day, Thanksgiving Day, the Friday after Thanksgiving Day, or Christmas Day, and (B) any day observed as a holiday by the clerk's office or as designated by the chief judge. FL ST J ADMIN Rule 2.514(a)(6).

b. *Additional time after service by mail or e-mail.* When a party may or must act within a specified time after service and service is made by mail or e-mail, five (5) days are added after the period that would otherwise expire under FL ST J ADMIN Rule 2.514(a). FL ST J ADMIN Rule 2.514(b).

c. *Enlargement.* When an act is required or allowed to be done at or within a specified time by order of court, by the Florida Rules of Civil Procedure, or by notice given thereunder, for cause shown the court at any time in its discretion (1) with or without notice, may order the period enlarged if request therefor is made before the expiration of the period originally prescribed or as extended by a previous order, or (2) upon motion made and notice after the expiration of the specified period, may permit the act to be done when failure to act was the result of excusable neglect, but it may not extend the time for making a motion for new trial, for rehearing, or to alter or amend a judgment; making a motion for relief from a judgment under FL ST RCP Rule 1.540(b); taking an appeal or filing a petition for certiorari; or making a motion for a directed verdict. FL ST RCP Rule 1.090(b).

d. *Unaffected by expiration of term.* The period of time provided for the doing of any act or the taking of any proceeding shall not be affected or limited by the continued existence or expiration of a term of court. The continued existence or expiration of a term of court in no way affects the power of a court to do any act or take any proceeding in any action which is or has been pending before it. FL ST RCP Rule 1.090(c).

C. General Requirements

1. *General provisions governing discovery*

a. *Discovery methods.* Parties may obtain discovery by one or more of the following methods: depositions upon oral examination or written questions; written interrogatories; production of documents or things or permission to enter upon land or other property for inspection and other purposes; physical and mental examinations; and requests for admission. Unless the court orders otherwise and under FL ST RCP Rule 1.280(c), the frequency of use of these methods is not limited, except as provided in FL ST RCP Rule 1.200, FL ST RCP Rule 1.340, and FL ST RCP Rule 1.370. FL ST RCP Rule 1.280(a).

b. *Scope of discovery.* Unless otherwise limited by order of the court in accordance with the Florida Rules of Civil Procedure, the scope of discovery is as follows:

i. *In general.* Parties may obtain discovery regarding any matter, not privileged, that is relevant to the subject matter of the pending action, whether it relates to the claim or defense of the party seeking discovery or the claim or defense of any other party, including the existence, description, nature, custody, condition, and location of any books, documents, or other tangible things and the identity and location of persons having knowledge of any discoverable matter. It is not ground for objection that the information sought will be inadmissible at the trial if the information sought appears reasonably calculated to lead to the discovery of admissible evidence. FL ST RCP Rule 1.280(b)(1).

ii. *Indemnity agreements.* A party may obtain discovery of the existence and contents of any agreement under which any person may be liable to satisfy part or all of a judgment that may be entered in the action or to indemnify or to reimburse a party for payments made to satisfy the judgment. Information concerning the agreement is not admissible in evidence at trial by reason of disclosure. FL ST RCP Rule 1.280(b)(2).

iii. *Electronically stored information.* A party may obtain discovery of electronically stored information in accordance with the Florida Rules of Civil Procedure. FL ST RCP Rule 1.280(b)(3).

iv. *Trial preparation; Materials.* Subject to the provisions of FL ST RCP Rule 1.280(b)(5), a party may obtain discovery of documents and tangible things otherwise discoverable under FL ST

RCP Rule 1.280(b)(1) and prepared in anticipation of litigation or for trial by or for another party or by or for that party's representative, including that party's attorney, consultant, surety, indemnitor, insurer, or agent, only upon a showing that the party seeking discovery has need of the materials in the preparation of the case and is unable without undue hardship to obtain the substantial equivalent of the materials by other means. FL ST RCP Rule 1.280(b)(4).

- In ordering discovery of the materials when the required showing has been made, the court shall protect against disclosure of the mental impressions, conclusions, opinions, or legal theories of an attorney or other representative of a party concerning the litigation. FL ST RCP Rule 1.280(b)(4).
- Without the required showing a party may obtain a copy of a statement concerning the action or its subject matter previously made by that party. FL ST RCP Rule 1.280(b)(4).
- Upon request without the required showing a person not a party may obtain a copy of a statement concerning the action or its subject matter previously made by that person. If the request is refused, the person may move for an order to obtain a copy. The provisions of FL ST RCP Rule 1.380(a)(5) apply to the award of expenses incurred as a result of making the motion. FL ST RCP Rule 1.280(b)(4).
- For purposes of FL ST RCP Rule 1.280(b)(4), a statement previously made is a written statement signed or otherwise adopted or approved by the person making it, or a stenographic, mechanical, electrical, or other recording or transcription of it that is a substantially verbatim recital of an oral statement by the person making it and contemporaneously recorded. FL ST RCP Rule 1.280(b)(4).

v. *Trial preparation; Experts.* Discovery of facts known and opinions held by experts, otherwise discoverable under the provisions of FL ST RCP Rule 1.280(b)(1) and acquired or developed in anticipation of litigation or for trial, may be obtained only as follows:

- By interrogatories a party may require any other party to identify each person whom the other party expects to call as an expert witness at trial and to state the subject matter on which the expert is expected to testify, and to state the substance of the facts and opinions to which the expert is expected to testify and a summary of the grounds for each opinion. FL ST RCP Rule 1.280(b)(5)(A)(i).
- Any person disclosed by interrogatories or otherwise as a person expected to be called as an expert witness at trial may be deposed in accordance with FL ST RCP Rule 1.390 without motion or order of court. FL ST RCP Rule 1.280(b)(5)(A)(ii).
- A party may obtain the following discovery regarding any person disclosed by interrogatories or otherwise as a person expected to be called as an expert witness at trial: The scope of employment in the pending case and the compensation for such service, FL ST RCP Rule 1.280(b)(5)(A)(iii)(1); The expert's general litigation experience, including the percentage of work performed for plaintiffs and defendants, FL ST RCP Rule 1.280(b)(5)(A)(iii)(2); The identity of other cases, within a reasonable time period, in which the expert has testified by deposition or at trial, FL ST RCP Rule 1.280(b)(5)(A)(iii)(3); An approximation of the portion of the expert's involvement as an expert witness, which may be based on the number of hours, percentage of hours, or percentage of earned income derived from serving as an expert witness; however, the expert shall not be required to disclose his or her earnings as an expert witness or income derived from other services. FL ST RCP Rule 1.280(b)(5)(A)(iii)(4).
- An expert may be required to produce financial and business records only under the most unusual or compelling circumstances and may not be compelled to compile or produce nonexistent documents. Upon motion, the court may order further discovery by other means, subject to such restrictions as to scope and other provisions pursuant to FL ST RCP Rule 1.280(b)(5)(C) concerning fees and expenses as the court may deem appropriate. FL ST RCP Rule 1.280(b)(5).
- A party may discover facts known or opinions held by an expert who has been retained or

specially employed by another party in anticipation of litigation or preparation for trial and who is not expected to be called as a witness at trial, only as provided in FL ST RCP Rule 1.360(b) or upon a showing of exceptional circumstances under which it is impracticable for the party seeking discovery to obtain facts or opinions on the same subject by other means. FL ST RCP Rule 1.280(b)(5)(B).

- Unless manifest injustice would result, the court shall require that the party seeking discovery pay the expert a reasonable fee for time spent in responding to discovery under FL ST RCP Rule 1.280(b)(5)(A) and FL ST RCP Rule 1.280(b)(5)(B); and concerning discovery from an expert obtained under FL ST RCP Rule 1.280(b)(5)(A) the court may require, and concerning discovery obtained under FL ST RCP Rule 1.280(b)(5)(B) shall require, the party seeking discovery to pay the other party a fair part of the fees and expenses reasonably incurred by the latter party in obtaining facts and opinions from the expert. FL ST RCP Rule 1.280(b)(5)(C).
- As used in the Florida Rules of Civil Procedure an expert shall be an expert witness as defined in FL ST RCP Rule 1.390(a). FL ST RCP Rule 1.280(b)(5)(D).

vi. *Claims to privilege or protection.* When a party withholds information otherwise discoverable under the Florida Rules of Civil Procedure by claiming that it is privileged or subject to protection as trial preparation material, the party shall make the claim expressly and shall describe the nature of the documents, communications, or things not produced or disclosed in a manner that, without revealing information itself privileged or protected, will enable other parties to assess the applicability of the privilege or protection. FL ST RCP Rule 1.280(b)(6).

c. *Limitations on discovery of electronically stored information*

i. A person may object to discovery of electronically stored information from sources that the person identifies as not reasonably accessible because of burden or cost. On motion to compel discovery or for a protective order, the person from whom discovery is sought must show that the information sought or the format requested is not reasonably accessible because of undue burden or cost. If that showing is made, the court may nonetheless order the discovery from such sources or in such formats if the requesting party shows good cause. The court may specify conditions of the discovery, including ordering that some or all of the expenses incurred by the person from whom discovery is sought be paid by the party seeking the discovery. FL ST RCP Rule 1.280(d)(1).

ii. In determining any motion involving discovery of electronically stored information, the court must limit the frequency or extent of discovery otherwise allowed by the Florida Rules of Civil Procedure if it determines that (i) the discovery sought is unreasonably cumulative or duplicative, or can be obtained from another source or in another manner that is more convenient, less burdensome, or less expensive; or (ii) the burden or expense of the discovery outweighs its likely benefit, considering the needs of the case, the amount in controversy, the parties' resources, the importance of the issues at stake in the action, and the importance of the discovery in resolving the issues. FL ST RCP Rule 1.280(d)(2).

d. For information on inadvertent disclosure of privileged materials, see FL ST RCP Rule 1.285.

2. *Request for production of documents*

a. *Scope of request.* Any party may request any other party:

i. To produce and permit the party making the request, or someone acting in the requesting party's behalf, to inspect and copy any designated documents, including electronically stored information, writings, drawings, graphs, charts, photographs, phono-records, and other data compilations from which information can be obtained, translated, if necessary, by the party to whom the request is directed through detection devices into reasonably usable form, that constitute or contain matters within the scope of FL ST RCP Rule 1.280(b) and that are in the possession, custody, or control of the party to whom the request is directed;

ii. To inspect and copy, test, or sample any tangible things that constitute or contain matters within the scope of FL ST RCP Rule 1.280(b) and that are in the possession, custody, or control of the party to whom the request is directed; or

iii. To permit entry upon designated land or other property in the possession or control of the party upon whom the request is served for the purpose of inspection and measuring, surveying, photographing, testing, or sampling the property or any designated object or operation on it within the scope of FL ST RCP Rule 1.280(b). FL ST RCP Rule 1.350(a).

b. *Contents of request*

i. The request shall set forth the items to be inspected, either by individual item or category, and describe each item and category with reasonable particularity. The request shall specify a reasonable time, place, and manner of making the inspection or performing the related acts. FL ST RCP Rule 1.350(b).

ii. A request for electronically stored information may specify the form or forms in which electronically stored information is to be produced. If the responding party objects to a requested form, or if no form is specified in the request, the responding party must state the form or forms it intends to use. If a request for electronically stored information does not specify the form of production, the producing party must produce the information in a form or forms in which it is ordinarily maintained or in a reasonably usable form or forms. FL ST RCP Rule 1.350(b).

c. *Failure to respond to requests.* The party submitting the request may move for an order under FL ST RCP Rule 1.380 concerning any objection, failure to respond to the request, or any part of it, or failure to permit the inspection as requested. FL ST RCP Rule 1.350(b). Please see FL ST RCP Rule 1.380(d) and the KeyRules Motion to Compel Discovery documents for further information regarding compelling discovery and discovery sanctions.

i. *Response requirements.* For each item or category the response shall state that inspection and related activities will be permitted as requested unless the request is objected to, in which event the reasons for the objection shall be stated. If an objection is made to part of an item or category, the part shall be specified. When producing documents, the producing party shall either produce them as they are kept in the usual course of business or shall identify them to correspond with the categories in the request. If the responding party objects to a requested form (for electronic information), or if no form is specified in the request, the responding party must state the form or forms it intends to use. If a request for electronically stored information does not specify the form of production, the producing party must produce the information in a form or forms in which it is ordinarily maintained or in a reasonably usable form or forms. FL ST RCP Rule 1.350(b).

3. *Requests to a non-party*

a. *Independent action not prohibited.* FL ST RCP Rule 1.350 does not preclude an independent action against a person not a party for production of documents and things and permission to enter upon land. FL ST RCP Rule 1.350(c). FL ST RCP Rule 1.351 does not affect the right of any party to bring an independent action for production of documents and things or permission to enter upon land. FL ST RCP Rule 1.351(f).

b. *Scope.* A party may seek inspection and copying of any documents or things within the scope of FL ST RCP Rule 1.350(a) from a person who is not a party by issuance of a subpoena directing the production of the documents or things when the requesting party does not seek to depose the custodian or other person in possession of the documents or things. FL ST RCP Rule 1.351 provides the exclusive procedure for obtaining documents or things by subpoena from nonparties without deposing the custodian or other person in possession of the documents or things pursuant to FL ST RCP Rule 1.310. FL ST RCP Rule 1.351(a).

i. *Procedure.* The proposed subpoena shall be attached to the notice and shall state the time, place, and method for production of the documents or things, and the name and address of the person who is to produce the documents or things, if known, and if not known, a general description sufficient to identify the person or the particular class or group to which the person belongs; shall include a designation of the items to be produced; and shall state that the person who will be asked to produce the documents or things has the right to object to the production under FL ST RCP Rule 1.351 and that the person will not be required to surrender the documents or things. A copy of the notice and proposed subpoena shall not be furnished to the person upon whom the subpoena is to be served. If any party serves an objection to production under FL ST RCP Rule 1.351 within ten (10) days of service of the notice, the documents or things shall not be produced pending resolution of the objection in accordance with FL ST RCP Rule 1.351(d). FL ST RCP Rule 1.351(b).

ii. *Subpoena.* If no objection is made by a party under FL ST RCP Rule 1.351(b), an attorney of record in the action may issue a subpoena or the party desiring production shall deliver to the clerk for issuance a subpoena together with a certificate of counsel or pro se party that no timely objection has been received from any party, and the clerk shall issue the subpoena and deliver it to the party desiring production. FL ST RCP Rule 1.351(c).

- The subpoena shall be identical to the copy attached to the notice and shall specify that no testimony may be taken and shall require only production of the documents or things specified in it. FL ST RCP Rule 1.351(c).
- The subpoena may give the recipient an option to deliver or mail legible copies of the documents or things to the party serving the subpoena. FL ST RCP Rule 1.351(c).
- The person upon whom the subpoena is served may condition the preparation of copies on the payment in advance of the reasonable costs of preparing the copies. FL ST RCP Rule 1.351(c).
- The subpoena shall require production only in the county of the residence of the custodian or other person in possession of the documents or things or in the county where the documents or things are located or where the custodian or person in possession usually conducts business. FL ST RCP Rule 1.351(c).
- If the person upon whom the subpoena is served objects at any time before the production of the documents or things, the documents or things shall not be produced under FL ST RCP Rule 1.351, and relief may be obtained pursuant to FL ST RCP Rule 1.310. FL ST RCP Rule 1.351(c).

iii. *Ruling on objection.* If an objection is made by a party under FL ST RCP Rule 1.351(b), the party desiring production may file a motion with the court seeking a ruling on the objection or may proceed pursuant to FL ST RCP Rule 1.310. FL ST RCP Rule 1.351(d).

iv. *Copies furnished.* If the subpoena is complied with by delivery or mailing of copies as provided in FL ST RCP Rule 1.351(c), the party receiving the copies shall furnish a legible copy of each item furnished to any other party who requests it upon the payment of the reasonable cost of preparing the copies. FL ST RCP Rule 1.351(e).

4. *Arbitration and mediation*

a. *Referral to arbitration and mediation.* Except as hereinafter provided or as otherwise prohibited by law, the presiding judge may enter an order referring all or any part of a contested civil matter to mediation or arbitration. The parties to any contested civil matter may file a written stipulation to mediate or arbitrate any issue between them at any time. Such stipulation shall be incorporated into the order of referral. FL ST RCP Rule 1.700(a).

b. *Arbitration*

i. *Exclusions.* A civil action shall be ordered to arbitration or arbitration in conjunction with mediation upon stipulation of the parties. A civil action may be ordered to arbitration or arbitration in conjunction with mediation upon motion of any party or by the court, if the judge determines the action to be of such a nature that arbitration could be of benefit to the litigants or the court. FL ST RCP Rule 1.800.

- Under no circumstances may the following categories of actions be referred to arbitration: (1) bond estreatures; (2) habeas corpus or other extraordinary writs; (3) bond validations; (4) civil or criminal contempt; (5) such other matters as may be specified by order of the chief judge in the circuit. FL ST RCP Rule 1.800.

ii. For more information regarding arbitration, please see FL ST RCP Rule 1.810; FL ST RCP Rule 1.820; FL ST RCP Rule 1.830.

c. *Mediation.* For more information regarding mediation, please see FL ST RCP Rule 1.710; FL ST RCP Rule 1.720; FL ST RCP Rule 1.730; and FL ST RCP Rule 1.750.

d. *Local arbitration policy.* It is the policy of the Civil Division judges to maximize the use of alternative dispute resolution procedures. Except where prohibited by statute, mediation will be ordered in all cases where jury trial is requested and in selected cases which are to be tried non-jury. Also, selected cases will be referred for court-annexed non-binding arbitration through the Orange County Bar Association Arbitration Service. Counsel may move to dispense with or defer mediation or arbitration or move to modify the referral order for good cause. FL ST 9 J CIR SECTION 15.

5. *Rules of court*

a. *Rules of civil procedure.* The Florida Rules of Civil Procedure apply to all actions of a civil nature and all special statutory proceedings in the circuit courts and county courts except those to which the Florida Probate Rules, the Florida Family Law Rules of Procedure, or the Small Claims Rules apply. FL ST RCP Rule 1.010.

i. The form, content, procedure, and time for pleading in all special statutory proceedings shall be as prescribed by the statutes governing the proceeding unless the Florida Rules of Civil Procedure specifically provide to the contrary. FL ST RCP Rule 1.010.

ii. The Florida Rules of Civil Procedure shall be construed to secure the just, speedy, and inexpensive determination of every action. FL ST RCP Rule 1.010.

b. *Rules of judicial administration.* The Florida Rules of Judicial Administration shall apply to administrative matters in all courts to which the Florida Rules of Judicial Administration are applicable by their terms. The Florida Rules of Judicial Administration shall be construed to secure the speedy and inexpensive determination of every proceeding to which they are applicable. The Florida Rules of Judicial Administration shall supersede all conflicting rules and statutes. FL ST J ADMIN Rule 2.110.

c. *Business court procedures.* For rules specific to Business Court, please see FL ST 9 J CIR ORANGE CIV SECTION 1, et seq.

6. *Communication between counsel.* Counsel should be guided by courtesy, candor and common sense and conform to the Florida Rules of Civil Procedure and any applicable orders. In particular, counsel should have in mind the broad scope of discovery allowed by the Civil Rules of Procedure. Direct and informal communication between counsel is encouraged to facilitate discovery and resolve disputes. FL ST 9 J CIR SECTION 13(A).

D. Documents

1. *Required documents*

a. *Request for production.* Please see the General Requirements section of this document for more information on the contents of the request for production.

i. *Notices to persons with disabilities.* See the Format section of this KeyRules document for further information.

b. *Certificate of service.* A certificate of service of the interrogatories shall be filed, giving the date of service and the name of the party to whom they were directed. FL ST RCP Rule 1.340(e). When any attorney certifies in substance: "I certify that a copy hereof has been furnished to (here insert name or names and addresses used for service) by (e-mail) (delivery) (mail) (fax) on .... (date) ....______________ Attorney" the certificate is taken as prima facie proof of such service in compliance with FL ST J ADMIN Rule 2.516. FL ST J ADMIN Rule 2.516(f).

2. *Supplemental documents*

a. *Notice of intent to serve subpoena/Subpoena.* Please see the General Requirements section of this document for more information.

E. Format

1. *Documents; Type and size.* Documents subject to the exceptions set forth in FL ST J ADMIN Rule 2.525(d) shall be filed on recycled paper measuring eight and one half by eleven (8 1/2 by 11) inches. For

purposes of FL ST J ADMIN Rule 2.520, paper is recycled if it contains a minimum content of fifty (50) percent waste paper. Xerographic reduction of legal-size (eight and one half by fourteen (8 1/2 by 14) inches) documents to letter size (eight and one half by eleven (8 1/2 by 11) inches) is prohibited. All other documents filed by electronic transmission shall be filed in a format capable of being printed in a format consistent with the provisions of FL ST J ADMIN Rule 2.250. FL ST J ADMIN Rule 2.520(b).

a. *Exhibits.* Any exhibit or attachment filed with pleadings or papers may be filed in its original size. FL ST J ADMIN Rule 2.520(c).

b. *Recording space.* On all papers and documents prepared and filed by the court or by any party to a proceeding which are to be recorded in the public records of any county, including but not limited to final money judgments and notices of lis pendens, a three (3) inch by three (3) inch space at the top right-hand corner on the first page and a one (1) inch by three (3) inch space at the top right-hand corner on each subsequent page shall be left blank and reserved for use by the clerk of court. FL ST J ADMIN Rule 2.520(d).

   i. *Exceptions to recording space.* Any papers or documents created by persons or entities over which the filing party has no control, including but not limited to wills, codicils, trusts, or other testamentary documents; documents prepared or executed by any public officer; documents prepared, executed, acknowledged, or proved outside of the State of Florida; or documents created by State or Federal government agencies, may be filed without the space required by FL ST J ADMIN Rule 2.520. FL ST J ADMIN Rule 2.520(e).

c. *Noncompliance.* No clerk of court is permitted to refuse to file any document or paper because of noncompliance with the Florida Rules of Judicial Administration. However, upon request of the clerk of court, noncomplying documents must be resubmitted in accordance with the formatting rules. FL ST J ADMIN Rule 2.520(f).

d. *Proposed orders*

   i. All orders will be on eight and a half by eleven (8 1/2 by 11) inch plain white paper (not lined or letterhead paper) and be double spaced. FL ST 9 J CIR SECTION 12(B)(1).

   ii. The order must contain a title indicating what matter the order pertains to, e.g., "Order On Defendant Smith's Motion To Dismiss." FL ST 9 J CIR SECTION 12(B)(2).

   iii. The preamble of the order should include the date of the hearing and what motions were heard. FL ST 9 J CIR SECTION 12(B)(3).

   iv. The adjudication portion of the order should state what relief is ordered. Simply stating that "the motion is granted" without more is insufficient. FL ST 9 J CIR SECTION 12(B)(4).

   v. The order should indicate the specific time period of any act ordered to be done and should state whether the time period runs from the date of the hearing or the date the order is signed or some other specified date. FL ST 9 J CIR SECTION 12(B)(5).

   vi. The order should contain a full certificate of service with the complete names and addresses of the attorneys and unrepresented parties to be served. Merely showing "copies to" is insufficient. FL ST 9 J CIR SECTION 12(B)(6).

   vii. If an order of dismissal is final (i.e., it disposes of the entire case) the title should contain the word "Final." When the order is not final but leaves other counts or claims against other defendants pending, it should so state in a separate paragraph. FL ST 9 J CIR SECTION 12(B)(7).

   viii. When submitting stipulations, orders shall be by separate order, not attached to the stipulation. FL ST 9 J CIR SECTION 12(B)(8).

   ix. Counsel preparing the Final Judgment or order should draft and circulate copies within two (2) working days of the ruling or jury verdict. If counsel preparing the Final Judgment or order gets approval as to form of the order from all counsel, the original with copies and envelopes should be sent directly to the judge with a cover letter stating all counsel agree to the form of the order or judgment. If other counsel objects to the form or cannot be reached for approval, counsel preparing the judgment or order shall notice a motion for entry of the order or judgment. If objecting counsel does not furnish the judge prior to or at the hearing with a proposed judgment or order version with copies under cover letter stating the reasons for the objection, all objections will be deemed waived. Orders and judgments should not be submitted to the judge to hold waiting for an objection. FL ST 9 J CIR SECTION 12(D).

2. *Caption.* Every pleading, motion, order, judgment, or other paper shall have a caption containing the name of the court, the file number, and except for in rem proceedings, including forfeiture proceedings, the name of the first party on each side with an appropriate indication of other parties, and a designation identifying the party filing it and its nature or the nature of the order, as the case may be. In any in rem proceeding, every pleading, motion, order, judgment, or other paper shall have a caption containing the name of the court, the file number, the style "In re" (followed by the name or general description of the property), and a designation of the person or entity filing it and its nature or the nature of the order, as the case may be. In an in rem forfeiture proceeding, the style shall be "In re forfeiture of" (followed by the name of the general description of the property). All papers filed in the action shall be styled in such a manner as to indicate clearly the subject matter of the paper and the party requesting or obtaining relief. FL ST RCP Rule 1.100(c)(1).

3. *Writing and written defined.* Writing or written means a document containing information, an application, or a stipulation. FL ST RCP Rule 1.080(c).

4. *Rule abbreviations*

   a. The Florida Rules of Civil Procedure and shall be abbreviated as Fla.R.Civ.P. FL ST RCP Rule 1.010.

   b. The Florida Rules of Judicial Administration shall be abbreviated as Fla. R. Jud. Admin. FL ST J ADMIN Rule 2.110.

5. *Nonverification.* Except when otherwise specifically provided by the Florida Rules of Civil Procedure or an applicable statute, every pleading or other document of a party represented by an attorney need not be verified or accompanied by an affidavit. FL ST RCP Rule 1.030; FL ST J ADMIN Rule 2.515(a).

6. *Unrepresented parties.* An unrepresented party must file his or her papers with the clerk and send copies to other attorneys or unrepresented parties. All such papers must be typed double-spaced on plain white eight and a half by eleven (8 1/2 by 11) inch paper, with the name of the case and case number at the top and the party's mailing address, telephone number and FAX number, if any, below his or her signature at the end of the paper. Such unrepresented party must immediately notify the Clerk and all other counsel or parties of record in writing of any change in mailing address or telephone or FAX number. Failure to promptly notify of change of address could result in a dismissal or default entered against such party. FL ST 9 J CIR SECTION 7(B)(5).

7. *Attorney signature*

   a. *Attorney signature.* Every pleading and other document of a party represented by an attorney shall be signed by at least one (1) attorney of record in that attorney's individual name whose current record Florida Bar address, telephone number, including area code, primary e-mail address and secondary e-mail addresses, if any, and Florida Bar number shall be stated, and who shall be duly licensed to practice law in Florida or who shall have received permission to appear in the particular case as provided in FL ST J ADMIN Rule 2.510. FL ST J ADMIN Rule 2.515(a).

      i. The attorney may be required by the court to give the address of, and to vouch for the attorney's authority to represent, the party. FL ST J ADMIN Rule 2.515(a).

      ii. The signature of an attorney shall constitute a certificate by the attorney that the attorney has read the pleading or other document; that to the best of the attorney's knowledge, information, and belief there is good ground to support it; and that it is not interposed for delay. FL ST J ADMIN Rule 2.515(a).

      iii. If a pleading is not signed or is signed with intent to defeat the purpose of FL ST J ADMIN Rule 2.515, it may be stricken and the action may proceed as though the pleading or other document had not been served. FL ST J ADMIN Rule 2.515(a).

   b. *Pro se litigant signature.* A party who is not represented by an attorney shall sign any pleading or

other paper and state the party's address and telephone number, including area code. FL ST J ADMIN Rule 2.515(b).

c. *Form of signature*

i. The signatures required on pleadings and documents by FL ST J ADMIN Rule 2.515(a) and FL ST J ADMIN Rule 2.515(b) may be:

- Original signatures;
- Original signatures that have been reproduced by electronic means, such as on electronically transmitted documents or photocopied documents;
- Electronic signatures using the "/s/," "s/," or "/s" formats by or at the direction of the person signing; or
- Any other signature format authorized by general law, so long as the clerk where the proceeding is pending has the capability of receiving and has obtained approval from the Supreme Court of Florida to accept pleadings and documents with that signature format. FL ST J ADMIN Rule 2.515(c)(1).

ii. An attorney, party, or other person who files a pleading or paper by electronic transmission that does not contain the original signature of that attorney, party, or other person shall file that identical pleading or paper in paper form containing an original signature of that attorney, party, or other person (hereinafter called the follow-up filing) immediately thereafter. The follow-up filing is not required if the Supreme Court of Florida has entered an order directing the clerk of court to discontinue accepting the follow-up filing. FL ST J ADMIN Rule 2.515(c)(2).

8. *Forms*

a. *Process.* The forms of process, notice of lis pendens, and notice of action provided in the Florida Rules of Civil Procedure are sufficient. Variations from the forms do not void process or notices that are otherwise sufficient. FL ST RCP Rule 1.900(a).

b. *Other forms.* The other forms provided in the Florida Rules of Civil Procedure are sufficient for the matters that are covered by them. So long as the substance is expressed without prolixity, the forms may be varied to meet the facts of a particular case. FL ST RCP Rule 1.900(b).

c. *Formal matters.* Captions, except for the designation of the paper, are omitted from the forms provided in the Florida Rules of Civil Procedure. A general form of caption is the first form provided. Signatures are omitted from pleadings and motions. FL ST RCP Rule 1.900(c).

9. *Notices to persons with disabilities.* All notices of court proceedings to be held in a public facility, and all process compelling appearance at such proceedings, shall include the following statement in bold face, fourteen (14) point Times New Roman or Courier font: "If you are a person with a disability who needs any accommodation in order to participate in this proceeding, you are entitled, at no cost to you, to the provision of certain assistance. Please contact [identify applicable court personnel by name, address, and telephone number] at least seven (7) days before your scheduled court appearance, or immediately upon receiving this notification if the time before the scheduled appearance is less than seven (7) days; if you are hearing or voice impaired, call 711." FL ST J ADMIN Rule 2.540(c)(1).

10. *Minimization of the filing of sensitive information*

a. *Limitations for court filings.* Unless authorized by FL ST J ADMIN Rule 2.425(b), statute, another rule of court, or the court orders otherwise, designated sensitive information filed with the court must be limited to the following format:

i. The initials of a person known to be a minor;

ii. The year of birth of a person's birth date;

iii. No portion of any: Social security number, Bank account number, Credit card account number, Charge account number, or Debit account number;

iv. The last four digits of any: Taxpayer identification number (TIN), Employee identification number, Driver's license number, Passport number, Telephone number, Financial account number, except as set forth in FL ST J ADMIN Rule 2.425(a)(3), Brokerage account number,

Insurance policy account number, Loan account number, Customer account number, or Patient or health care number;

v. A truncated version of any: Email address, Computer user name, Password, or Personal identification number (PIN); and

vi. A truncated version of any other sensitive information as provided by court order. FL ST J ADMIN Rule 2.425(a).

b. *Exceptions.* FL ST J ADMIN Rule 2.425(a) does not apply to the following:

i. An account number which identifies the property alleged to be the subject of a proceeding;

ii. The record of an administrative or agency proceeding;

iii. The record in appellate or review proceedings;

iv. The birth date of a minor whenever the birth date is necessary for the court to establish or maintain subject matter jurisdiction;

v. The name of a minor in any order relating to parental responsibility, time-sharing, or child support;

vi. The name of a minor in any document or order affecting the minor's ownership of real property;

vii. The birth date of a party in a writ of attachment or notice to payor;

viii. In traffic and criminal proceedings: a pro se filing; a court filing that is related to a criminal matter or investigation and that is prepared before the filing of a criminal charge or is not filed as part of any docketed criminal case; an arrest or search warrant or any information in support thereof; a charging document and an affidavit or other documents filed in support of any charging document, including any driving records; a statement of particulars; discovery material introduced into evidence or otherwise filed with the court; and all information necessary for the proper issuance and execution of a subpoena duces tecum;

ix. Information used by the clerk for case maintenance purposes or the courts for case management purposes; and

x. Information which is relevant and material to an issue before the court. FL ST J ADMIN Rule 2.425(b).

c. *Remedies.* Upon motion by a party or interested person or sua sponte by the court, the court may order remedies, sanctions or both for a violation of FL ST J ADMIN Rule 2.425(a). Following notice and an opportunity to respond, the court may impose sanctions if such filing was not made in good faith. FL ST J ADMIN Rule 2.425(c).

d. *Motions not restricted.* FL ST J ADMIN Rule 2.425 does not restrict a party's right to move for protective order, to move to file documents under seal, or to request a determination of the confidentiality of records. FL ST J ADMIN Rule 2.425(d).

e. *Application.* FL ST J ADMIN Rule 2.425 does not affect the application of constitutional provisions, statutes, or rules of court regarding confidential information or access to public information. FL ST J ADMIN Rule 2.425(e).

F. Filing and Service Requirements

1. *Court filing of documents and discovery.* Information obtained during discovery shall not be filed with the court until such time as it is filed for good cause. The requirement of good cause is satisfied only where the filing of the information is allowed or required by another applicable rule of procedure or by court order. All filings of discovery documents shall comply with FL ST J ADMIN Rule 2.425. The court shall have the authority to impose sanctions for violation of FL ST RCP Rule 1.280. FL ST RCP Rule 1.280(g).

a. Unless required by the court, a party shall not file any of the documents or things produced with the response. Documents or things may be filed in compliance with FL ST J ADMIN Rule 2.425 and FL ST RCP Rule 1.280(g) when they should be considered by the court in determining a matter pending before the court. FL ST RCP Rule 1.350(d).

2. *Filing requirements.* All original documents must be filed with the court either before service or

immediately thereafter, unless otherwise provided for by general law or other rules. If the original of any bond or other document is not placed in the court file, a certified copy must be so placed by the clerk. FL ST J ADMIN Rule 2.516(d). All documents shall be filed in conformity with the requirements of FL ST J ADMIN Rule 2.525. FL ST RCP Rule 1.080(b). All documents filed in any court shall be filed by electronic transmission in accordance with FL ST J ADMIN Rule 2.525. "Documents" means pleadings, motions, petitions, memoranda, briefs, notices, exhibits, declarations, affidavits, orders, judgments, decrees, writs, opinions, and any other paper or writing submitted to a court. FL ST J ADMIN Rule 2.520(a). All documents that are court records, as defined in FL ST J ADMIN Rule 2.430(a)(1), must be filed by electronic transmission, provided that: (1) the clerk has the ability to accept and retain such documents; (2) the clerk or the chief judge of the circuit has requested permission to accept documents filed by electronic transmission; and (3) the supreme court has entered an order granting permission to the clerk to accept documents filed by electronic transmission. FL ST J ADMIN Rule 2.525(c)(1).

a. *Definition.* "Electronic transmission of documents" means the sending of information by electronic signals to, by or from a court or clerk, which when received can be transformed and stored or transmitted on paper, microfilm, magnetic storage device, optical imaging system, CD-ROM, flash drive, other electronic data storage system, server, case maintenance system ("CM"), electronic court filing ("ECF") system, statewide or local electronic portal ("e-portal"), or other electronic record keeping system authorized by the supreme court in a format sufficient to communicate the information on the original document in a readable format. Electronic transmission of documents includes electronic mail ("e-mail") and any internet-based transmission procedure, and may include procedures allowing for documents to be signed or verified by electronic means. FL ST J ADMIN Rule 2.525(a).

    i. The filing of documents with the court as required by the Florida Rules of Judicial Administration must be made by filing them with the clerk in accordance with FL ST J ADMIN Rule 2.525, except that the judge may permit documents to be filed with the judge, in which event the judge must note the filing date before him or her on the documents and transmit them to the clerk. The date of filing is that shown on the face of the document by the judge's notation or the clerk's time stamp, whichever is earlier. FL ST J ADMIN Rule 2.516(e).

b. *Application.* Any court or clerk of the court may accept the electronic transmission of documents for filing after the clerk, together with input from the chief judge of the circuit, has obtained approval of the procedures and program for doing so from the Supreme Court of Florida. FL ST J ADMIN Rule 2.525(b).

c. *Exceptions*

    i. Paper documents and other submissions may be manually submitted to the clerk or court:

        - When the clerk does not have the ability to accept and retain documents by electronic filing or has not had ECF Procedures approved by the supreme court;
        - For filing by any self-represented party or any self-represented nonparty unless specific ECF Procedures provide a means to file documents electronically. However, any self-represented nonparty that is a governmental or public agency and any other agency, partnership, corporation, or business entity acting on behalf of any governmental or public agency may file documents by electronic transmission if such entity has the capability of filing documents electronically;
        - For filing by attorneys excused from e-mail service in accordance with FL ST J ADMIN Rule 2.516(b);
        - When submitting evidentiary exhibits or filing non-documentary materials;
        - When the filing involves documents in excess of twenty-five (25) megabytes (25MB) in size. For such filings, documents may be transmitted using an electronic storage medium that the clerk has the ability to accept, which may include a CD-ROM, flash drive, or similar storage medium;
        - When filed in open court, as permitted by the court;
        - When paper filing is permitted by any approved statewide or local ECF procedures; and

- If any court determines that justice so requires. FL ST J ADMIN Rule 2.525(d).

ii. Any document in paper form submitted under FL ST J ADMIN Rule 2.525(d) is filed when it is received by the clerk or court and the clerk shall immediately thereafter convert any filed paper document to an electronic document. "Convert to an electronic document" means optically capturing an image of a paper document and using character recognition software to recover as much of the document's text as practicable and then indexing and storing the document in the official court file. FL ST J ADMIN Rule 2.525(c)(4).

iii. Any storage medium submitted under FL ST J ADMIN Rule 2.525(d)(5) is filed when received by the clerk or court and the clerk shall immediately thereafter transfer the electronic documents from the storage device to the official court file. FL ST J ADMIN Rule 2.525(c)(5).

iv. If the filer of any paper document authorized under FL ST J ADMIN Rule 2.525(d) provides a self-addressed, postage-paid envelope for return of the paper document after it is converted to electronic form by the clerk, the clerk shall place the paper document in the envelope and deposit it in the mail. Except when a paper document is required to be maintained, the clerk may recycle any filed paper document that is not to be returned to the filer. FL ST J ADMIN Rule 2.525(c)(6).

v. The clerk may convert any paper document filed before the effective date of FL ST J ADMIN Rule 2.525 to an electronic document. Unless the clerk is required to maintain the paper document, if the paper document has been converted to an electronic document by the clerk, the paper document is no longer part of the official court file and may be removed and recycled. FL ST J ADMIN Rule 2.525(c)(7).

d. *Official court file.* For information on what constitutes the official court file, please see FL ST J ADMIN Rule 2.525(c)(2), FL ST J ADMIN Rule 2.525(c)(3).

e. *Administration.* All attorneys, parties, or other persons using this rule to file documents are required to make arrangements with the court or clerk for the payment of any charges authorized by general law or the supreme court before filing any document by electronic transmission. FL ST J ADMIN Rule 2.525(f)(2).

f. *Filing date.* The filing date for an electronically transmitted document is the date and time that such filing is acknowledged by an electronic stamp or otherwise, pursuant to any procedure set forth in any ECF Procedures approved by the supreme court, or the date the last page of such filing is received by the court or clerk. FL ST J ADMIN Rule 2.525(f)(3).

g. *Accessibility.* All documents transmitted in any electronic form under FL ST J ADMIN Rule 2.525 must comply with the accessibility requirements of FL ST J ADMIN Rule 2.526. FL ST J ADMIN Rule 2.525(g).

h. *Unrepresented parties.* An unrepresented party must file his or her papers with the clerk and send copies to other attorneys or unrepresented parties. FL ST 9 J CIR SECTION 7(B)(5).

i. An unrepresented party may not communicate privately with the judge either by letter, telephone, in person or otherwise. FL ST 9 J CIR SECTION 7(B)(4).

ii. Copies of legal papers or other written materials should not be sent to the judge unless specifically requested by the judge or required by these administrative procedures. Any unrequested or non-required papers or materials sent to a judge may not be read but may be returned to the sender or placed unread into the court file. FL ST 9 J CIR SECTION 7(B)(4).

3. *Service requirements.* Every pleading subsequent to the initial pleading, all orders, and every other document filed in the action must be served in conformity with the requirements of FL ST J ADMIN Rule 2.516. FL ST RCP Rule 1.080(a).

a. *Service; When required.* Unless the court otherwise orders, or a statute or supreme court administrative order specifies a different means of service, every pleading subsequent to the initial pleading and every other document filed in any court proceeding, except applications for witness subpoenas and documents served by formal notice or required to be served in the manner provided for service of formal notice, must be served in accordance with FL ST J ADMIN Rule 2.516 on each party. No service need be made on parties against whom a default has been entered, except that pleadings asserting new or additional claims against them must be served in the manner provided for service of summons. FL ST J ADMIN Rule 2.516(a).

b. *Service; How made.* When service is required or permitted to be made upon a party represented by an attorney, service must be made upon the attorney unless service upon the party is ordered by the court. FL ST J ADMIN Rule 2.516(b).

   i. *Service by electronic mail ("e-mail").* All documents required or permitted to be served on another party must be served by e-mail, unless FL ST J ADMIN Rule 2.516 otherwise provides. When, in addition to service by e-mail, the sender also utilizes another means of service provided for in FL ST J ADMIN Rule 2.516(b)(2), any differing time limits and other provisions applicable to that other means of service control. FL ST J ADMIN Rule 2.516(b)(1). Any document electronically transmitted to a court or clerk must also be served on all parties and interested persons in accordance with the applicable rules of court. FL ST J ADMIN Rule 2.525(e)(2).

      - *Service on attorneys.* Upon appearing in a proceeding, an attorney must serve a designation of a primary e-mail address and may designate no more than two (2) secondary e-mail addresses. Thereafter, service must be directed to all designated e-mail addresses in that proceeding. Every document filed by an attorney thereafter must include the primary e-mail address of that attorney and any secondary e-mail addresses. If an attorney does not designate any e-mail address for service, documents may be served on that attorney at the e-mail address on record with The Florida Bar. FL ST J ADMIN Rule 2.516(b)(1)(A).
      - *Exception to e-mail service on attorneys.* Service by an attorney on another attorney must be made by e-mail unless excused by the court. Upon motion by an attorney demonstrating that the attorney has no e-mail account and lacks access to the Internet at the attorney's office, the court may excuse the attorney from the requirements of e-mail service. Service on and by an attorney excused by the court from e-mail service must be by the means provided in FL ST J ADMIN Rule 2.516(b)(2). FL ST J ADMIN Rule 2.516(b)(1)(B).
      - *Service on and by parties not represented by an attorney.* Any party not represented by an attorney may serve a designation of a primary e-mail address and also may designate no more than two (2) secondary e-mail addresses to which service must be directed in that proceeding by the means provided in FL ST J ADMIN Rule 2.516(b)(1). If a party not represented by an attorney does not designate an e-mail address for service in a proceeding, service on and by that party must be by the means provided in FL ST J ADMIN Rule 2.516(b)(2). FL ST J ADMIN Rule 2.516(b)(1)(C).
      - *Time of service.* Service by e-mail is complete when it is sent. FL ST J ADMIN Rule 2.516(b)(1)(D). An e-mail is deemed served on the date it is sent. FL ST J ADMIN Rule 2.516(b)(1)(D)(i). If the sender learns that the e-mail did not reach the address of the person to be served, the sender must immediately send another copy by e-mail, or by a means authorized by FL ST J ADMIN Rule 2.516(b)(2). FL ST J ADMIN Rule 2.516(b)(1)(D)(ii). E-mail service is treated as service by mail for the computation of time. FL ST J ADMIN Rule 2.516(b)(1)(D)(iii).

   ii. *Format of e-mail for service.* Service of a document by e-mail is made by attaching a copy of the document in PDF format to an e-mail sent to all addresses designated by the attorney or party. FL ST J ADMIN Rule 2.516(b)(1)(E).

      - All documents served by e-mail must be attached to an e-mail message containing a subject line beginning with the words "SERVICE OF COURT DOCUMENT" in all capital letters, followed by the case number of the proceeding in which the documents are being served. FL ST J ADMIN Rule 2.516(b)(1)(E)(i).
      - The body of the e-mail must identify the court in which the proceeding is pending, the case number, the name of the initial party on each side, the title of each document served with that e-mail, and the sender's name and telephone number. FL ST J ADMIN Rule 2.516(b)(1)(E)(ii).

- Any document served by e-mail may be signed by the "/s/" format, as long as the filed original is signed in accordance with the applicable rule of procedure. FL ST J ADMIN Rule 2.516(b)(1)(E)(iii).
- Any e-mail which, together with its attached documents, exceeds five megabytes (5MB) in size, must be divided and sent as separate e-mails, no one of which may exceed five megabytes (5MB) in size and each of which must be sequentially numbered in the subject line. FL ST J ADMIN Rule 2.516(b)(1)(E)(iv).

iii. *Service by other means.* In addition to, and not in lieu of, service by e-mail, service may also be made upon attorneys by any of the means specified in FL ST J ADMIN Rule 2.516(b)(2). Service on and by all parties who are not represented by an attorney and who do not designate an e-mail address, and on and by all attorneys excused from e-mail service, must be made by delivering a copy of the document or by mailing it to the party or attorney at their last known address or, if no address is known, by leaving it with the clerk of the court. Service by mail is complete upon mailing. Delivery of a copy within FL ST J ADMIN Rule 2.516 is complete upon:

- Handing it to the attorney or to the party,
- Leaving it at the attorney's or party's office with a clerk or other person in charge thereof,
- If there is no one in charge, leaving it in a conspicuous place therein,
- If the office is closed or the person to be served has no office, leaving it at the person's usual place of abode with some person of his or her family above fifteen (15) years of age and informing such person of the contents, or
- Transmitting it by facsimile to the attorney's or party's office with a cover sheet containing the sender's name, firm, address, telephone number, and facsimile number, and the number of pages transmitted. When service is made by facsimile, a copy must also be served by any other method permitted by FL ST J ADMIN Rule 2.516. Facsimile service occurs when transmission is complete. FL ST J ADMIN Rule 2.516(b)(2)(A) through FL ST J ADMIN Rule 2.516(b)(2)(E).
- Service by delivery after 5:00 p.m. must be deemed to have been made by mailing on the date of delivery. FL ST J ADMIN Rule 2.516(b)(2)(F).

c. *Service; Numerous defendants.* In actions when the parties are unusually numerous, the court may regulate the service contemplated by the Florida Rules of Judicial Administration on motion or on its own initiative in such manner as may be found to be just and reasonable. FL ST J ADMIN Rule 2.516(c).

d. *Service by clerk.* Service of notices and other documents required to be made by the clerk must also be done as provided in FL ST J ADMIN Rule 2.516(b). FL ST J ADMIN Rule 2.516(g).

G. Hearings

1. There is no hearing required or contemplated with regard to requests for production of documents in the Florida Rules of Civil Procedure.

H. Forms

1. Official Request for Production of Documents Forms for Florida

a. Caption. FL ST RCP Form 1.901.

b. Subpoena duces tecum for trial. FL ST RCP Form 1.911.

c. Notice of production from nonparty. FL ST RCP Form 1.921.

d. Subpoena duces tecum without deposition. FL ST RCP Form 1.922.

2. Florida Requests for Production of Documents Forms

a. Request for production; Documents. FL-PRACFORM § 8:29.

b. Request for inspection; Documents, deposition. FL-PRACFORM § 8:30.

c. Request for inspection; Tangible things. FL-PRACFORM § 8:31.
d. Request for entry; Real property. FL-PRACFORM § 8:32.
e. Request for production; Documents, response. FL-PRACFORM § 8:33.
f. Request for inspection; Response, tangible things. FL-PRACFORM § 8:34.
g. Request for entry; Response, land and buildings. FL-PRACFORM § 8:35.
h. Production of documents; Nonparty, notice. FL-PRACFORM § 8:36.
i. Production of documents; Nonparty, objection. FL-PRACFORM § 8:37.
j. Request; Production of documents for inspection and copying. FL-PP § 3:115.
k. Notice of request for production from nonparty. FL-PP § 3:116.
l. Request; For permission to enter on land; To inspect and photograph. FL-PP § 3:127.

I. Checklist

(I) ❑ Matters to be considered by requesting party
- (a) ❑ Required documents
  - (1) ❑ Request
  - (2) ❑ Certificate of service
- (b) ❑ Supplemental documents
  - (1) ❑ Notice of intent to serve subpoena/Subpoena
- (c) ❑ Time for request
  - (1) ❑ Without leave of court the request may be served on the plaintiff after commencement of the action and on any other party with or after service of the process and initial pleading on that party
  - (2) ❑ A party desiring production under FL ST RCP Rule 1.351 shall serve notice as provided in FL ST RCP Rule 1.080 on every other party of the intent to serve a subpoena under FL ST RCP Rule 1.351 at least ten (10) days before the subpoena is issued if service is by delivery and fifteen (15) days before the subpoena is issued if the service is by mail or e-mail

(II) ❑ Matters to be considered by responding party
- (a) ❑ Required documents
  - (1) ❑ Response to request
  - (2) ❑ Certificate of service
- (b) ❑ Supplemental documents
  - (1) ❑ Objections
- (c) ❑ Time for response
  - (1) ❑ The party to whom the request is directed shall serve a written response within thirty (30) days after service of the request, except that a defendant may serve a response within forty-five (45) days after service of the process and initial pleading on that defendant; the court may allow a shorter or longer time

Requests, Notices and Applications
Request for Admissions

Document Last Updated January 2013

A. Applicable Rules

1. *State rules*

a. Nonverification of pleadings. FL ST RCP Rule 1.030.

b. Service and filing of pleadings, orders, and documents. FL ST RCP Rule 1.080.
c. Time. FL ST RCP Rule 1.090.
d. Pleadings and motions. FL ST RCP Rule 1.100.
e. Pretrial procedure. FL ST RCP Rule 1.200.
f. General provisions governing discovery. FL ST RCP Rule 1.280.
g. Interrogatories to parties. FL ST RCP Rule 1.340.
h. Examination of persons. FL ST RCP Rule 1.360.
i. Requests for admission. FL ST RCP Rule 1.370.
j. Failure to make discovery; Sanctions. FL ST RCP Rule 1.380.
k. Depositions of expert witnesses. FL ST RCP Rule 1.390.
l. Relief from judgment, decrees, or orders. FL ST RCP Rule 1.540.
m. Forms. FL ST RCP Rule 1.900.
n. Minimization of the filing of sensitive information. FL ST J ADMIN Rule 2.425.
o. Retention of court records. FL ST J ADMIN Rule 2.430.
p. Foreign attorneys. FL ST J ADMIN Rule 2.510.
q. Signature of attorneys and parties. FL ST J ADMIN Rule 2.515.
r. Paper. FL ST J ADMIN Rule 2.520.
s. Electronic filing. FL ST J ADMIN Rule 2.525.
t. Accessibility of information and technology. FL ST J ADMIN Rule 2.526.
u. Requests for accommodations by persons with disabilities. FL ST J ADMIN Rule 2.540.

2. *Local rules*
   a. Unrepresented (pro se) parties. FL ST 9 J CIR SECTION 7.
   b. General discovery guidelines. FL ST 9 J CIR SECTION 13.

B. Timing

1. *Request for admission.* Without leave of court the request may be served upon the plaintiff after commencement of the action and upon any other party with or after service of the process and initial pleading upon that party. FL ST RCP Rule 1.370(a).
2. *Sequence and timing of discovery.* Except as provided in FL ST RCP Rule 1.280(b)(5) or unless the court upon motion for the convenience of parties and witnesses and in the interest of justice orders otherwise, methods of discovery may be used in any sequence, and the fact that a party is conducting discovery, whether by deposition or otherwise, shall not delay any other party's discovery. FL ST RCP Rule 1.280(e).
   a. *Timeliness.* The time limit specified in the rules and applicable orders must be observed. If additional time is needed, an extension must be sought before the time limit expires by stipulation, or failing that, by motion and order. FL ST 9 J CIR SECTION 13(B).
3. *Computation of time*
   a. *Generally.* Computation of time shall be governed by FL ST J ADMIN Rule 2.514. FL ST RCP Rule 1.090(a). The following rules apply in computing time periods specified in any rule of procedure, local rule, court order, or statute that does not specify a method of computing time. FL ST J ADMIN Rule 2.514(a).
      i. *Period stated in days or a longer unit.* When the period is stated in days or a longer unit of time (A) exclude the day of the event that triggers the period; (B) count every day, including intermediate Saturdays, Sundays, and legal holidays; and (C) include the last day of the period, but if the last day is a Saturday, Sunday, or legal holiday, or falls within any period of time extended through an order of the chief justice under FL ST J ADMIN Rule 2.205(a)(2)(B)(iv),

the period continues to run until the end of the next day that is not a Saturday, Sunday, or legal holiday and does not fall within any period of time extended through an order of the chief justice. FL ST J ADMIN Rule 2.514(a)(1).

ii. *Period stated in hours.* When the period is stated in hours (A) begin counting immediately on the occurrence of the event that triggers the period; (B) count every hour, including hours during intermediate Saturdays, Sundays, and legal holidays; and (C) if the period would end on a Saturday, Sunday, or legal holiday, or during any period of time extended through an order of the chief justice under FL ST J ADMIN Rule 2.205(a)(2)(B)(iv), the period continues to run until the same time on the next day that is not a Saturday, Sunday, or legal holiday and does not fall within any period of time extended through an order of the chief justice. FL ST J ADMIN Rule 2.514(a)(2).

iii. *Period stated in days less than seven (7) days.* When the period stated in days is less than seven (7) days, intermediate Saturdays, Sundays, and legal holidays shall be excluded in the computation. FL ST J ADMIN Rule 2.514(a)(3).

iv. *"Last day" defined.* Unless a different time is set by a statute, local rule, or court order, the last day ends (A) for electronic filing or for service by any means, at midnight; and (B) for filing by other means, when the clerk's office is scheduled to close. FL ST J ADMIN Rule 2.514(a)(4).

v. *"Next day" defined.* The "next day" is determined by continuing to count forward when the period is measured after an event and backward when measured before an event. FL ST J ADMIN Rule 2.514(a)(5).

vi. *"Legal holiday" defined.* "Legal holiday" means (A) the day set aside by FL ST § 110.117, for observing New Year's Day, Martin Luther King, Jr.'s Birthday, Memorial Day, Independence Day, Labor Day, Veterans' Day, Thanksgiving Day, the Friday after Thanksgiving Day, or Christmas Day, and (B) any day observed as a holiday by the clerk's office or as designated by the chief judge. FL ST J ADMIN Rule 2.514(a)(6).

b. *Additional time after service by mail or e-mail.* When a party may or must act within a specified time after service and service is made by mail or e-mail, five (5) days are added after the period that would otherwise expire under FL ST J ADMIN Rule 2.514(a). FL ST J ADMIN Rule 2.514(b).

c. *Enlargement.* When an act is required or allowed to be done at or within a specified time by order of court, by the Florida Rules of Civil Procedure, or by notice given thereunder, for cause shown the court at any time in its discretion (1) with or without notice, may order the period enlarged if request therefor is made before the expiration of the period originally prescribed or as extended by a previous order, or (2) upon motion made and notice after the expiration of the specified period, may permit the act to be done when failure to act was the result of excusable neglect, but it may not extend the time for making a motion for new trial, for rehearing, or to alter or amend a judgment; making a motion for relief from a judgment under FL ST RCP Rule 1.540(b); taking an appeal or filing a petition for certiorari; or making a motion for a directed verdict. FL ST RCP Rule 1.090(b).

d. *Unaffected by expiration of term.* The period of time provided for the doing of any act or the taking of any proceeding shall not be affected or limited by the continued existence or expiration of a term of court. The continued existence or expiration of a term of court in no way affects the power of a court to do any act or take any proceeding in any action which is or has been pending before it. FL ST RCP Rule 1.090(c).

C. General Requirements

1. *General provisions governing discovery*

a. *Discovery methods.* Parties may obtain discovery by one or more of the following methods: depositions upon oral examination or written questions; written interrogatories; production of documents or things or permission to enter upon land or other property for inspection and other purposes; physical and mental examinations; and requests for admission. Unless the court orders otherwise and under FL ST RCP Rule 1.280(c), the frequency of use of these methods is not limited, except as provided in FL ST RCP Rule 1.200, FL ST RCP Rule 1.340, and FL ST RCP Rule 1.370. FL ST RCP Rule 1.280(a).

b. *Scope of discovery.* Unless otherwise limited by order of the court in accordance with the Florida Rules of Civil Procedure, the scope of discovery is as follows:

i. *In general.* Parties may obtain discovery regarding any matter, not privileged, that is relevant to the subject matter of the pending action, whether it relates to the claim or defense of the party seeking discovery or the claim or defense of any other party, including the existence, description, nature, custody, condition, and location of any books, documents, or other tangible things and the identity and location of persons having knowledge of any discoverable matter. It is not ground for objection that the information sought will be inadmissible at the trial if the information sought appears reasonably calculated to lead to the discovery of admissible evidence. FL ST RCP Rule 1.280(b)(1).

ii. *Indemnity agreements.* A party may obtain discovery of the existence and contents of any agreement under which any person may be liable to satisfy part or all of a judgment that may be entered in the action or to indemnify or to reimburse a party for payments made to satisfy the judgment. Information concerning the agreement is not admissible in evidence at trial by reason of disclosure. FL ST RCP Rule 1.280(b)(2).

iii. *Electronically stored information.* A party may obtain discovery of electronically stored information in accordance with the Florida Rules of Civil Procedure. FL ST RCP Rule 1.280(b)(3).

iv. *Trial preparation; Materials.* Subject to the provisions of FL ST RCP Rule 1.280(b)(5), a party may obtain discovery of documents and tangible things otherwise discoverable under FL ST RCP Rule 1.280(b)(1) and prepared in anticipation of litigation or for trial by or for another party or by or for that party's representative, including that party's attorney, consultant, surety, indemnitor, insurer, or agent, only upon a showing that the party seeking discovery has need of the materials in the preparation of the case and is unable without undue hardship to obtain the substantial equivalent of the materials by other means. FL ST RCP Rule 1.280(b)(4).

- In ordering discovery of the materials when the required showing has been made, the court shall protect against disclosure of the mental impressions, conclusions, opinions, or legal theories of an attorney or other representative of a party concerning the litigation. FL ST RCP Rule 1.280(b)(4).
- Without the required showing a party may obtain a copy of a statement concerning the action or its subject matter previously made by that party. FL ST RCP Rule 1.280(b)(4).
- Upon request without the required showing a person not a party may obtain a copy of a statement concerning the action or its subject matter previously made by that person. If the request is refused, the person may move for an order to obtain a copy. The provisions of FL ST RCP Rule 1.380(a)(5) apply to the award of expenses incurred as a result of making the motion. FL ST RCP Rule 1.280(b)(4).
- For purposes of FL ST RCP Rule 1.280(b)(4), a statement previously made is a written statement signed or otherwise adopted or approved by the person making it, or a stenographic, mechanical, electrical, or other recording or transcription of it that is a substantially verbatim recital of an oral statement by the person making it and contemporaneously recorded. FL ST RCP Rule 1.280(b)(4).

v. *Trial preparation; Experts.* Discovery of facts known and opinions held by experts, otherwise discoverable under the provisions of FL ST RCP Rule 1.280(b)(1) and acquired or developed in anticipation of litigation or for trial, may be obtained only as follows:

- By interrogatories a party may require any other party to identify each person whom the other party expects to call as an expert witness at trial and to state the subject matter on which the expert is expected to testify, and to state the substance of the facts and opinions to which the expert is expected to testify and a summary of the grounds for each opinion. FL ST RCP Rule 1.280(b)(5)(A)(i).
- Any person disclosed by interrogatories or otherwise as a person expected to be called as an expert witness at trial may be deposed in accordance with FL ST RCP Rule 1.390 without motion or order of court. FL ST RCP Rule 1.280(b)(5)(A)(ii).

- A party may obtain the following discovery regarding any person disclosed by interrogatories or otherwise as a person expected to be called as an expert witness at trial: The scope of employment in the pending case and the compensation for such service, FL ST RCP Rule 1.280(b)(5)(A)(iii)(1); The expert's general litigation experience, including the percentage of work performed for plaintiffs and defendants, FL ST RCP Rule 1.280(b)(5)(A)(iii)(2); The identity of other cases, within a reasonable time period, in which the expert has testified by deposition or at trial, FL ST RCP Rule 1.280(b)(5)(A)(iii)(3); An approximation of the portion of the expert's involvement as an expert witness, which may be based on the number of hours, percentage of hours, or percentage of earned income derived from serving as an expert witness; however, the expert shall not be required to disclose his or her earnings as an expert witness or income derived from other services. FL ST RCP Rule 1.280(b)(5)(A)(iii)(4).
- An expert may be required to produce financial and business records only under the most unusual or compelling circumstances and may not be compelled to compile or produce nonexistent documents. Upon motion, the court may order further discovery by other means, subject to such restrictions as to scope and other provisions pursuant to FL ST RCP Rule 1.280(b)(5)(C) concerning fees and expenses as the court may deem appropriate. FL ST RCP Rule 1.280(b)(5).
- A party may discover facts known or opinions held by an expert who has been retained or specially employed by another party in anticipation of litigation or preparation for trial and who is not expected to be called as a witness at trial, only as provided in FL ST RCP Rule 1.360(b) or upon a showing of exceptional circumstances under which it is impracticable for the party seeking discovery to obtain facts or opinions on the same subject by other means. FL ST RCP Rule 1.280(b)(5)(B).
- Unless manifest injustice would result, the court shall require that the party seeking discovery pay the expert a reasonable fee for time spent in responding to discovery under FL ST RCP Rule 1.280(b)(5)(A) and FL ST RCP Rule 1.280(b)(5)(B); and concerning discovery from an expert obtained under FL ST RCP Rule 1.280(b)(5)(A) the court may require, and concerning discovery obtained under FL ST RCP Rule 1.280(b)(5)(B) shall require, the party seeking discovery to pay the other party a fair part of the fees and expenses reasonably incurred by the latter party in obtaining facts and opinions from the expert. FL ST RCP Rule 1.280(b)(5)(C).
- As used in the Florida Rules of Civil Procedure an expert shall be an expert witness as defined in FL ST RCP Rule 1.390(a). FL ST RCP Rule 1.280(b)(5)(D).

vi. *Claims to privilege or protection.* When a party withholds information otherwise discoverable under the Florida Rules of Civil Procedure by claiming that it is privileged or subject to protection as trial preparation material, the party shall make the claim expressly and shall describe the nature of the documents, communications, or things not produced or disclosed in a manner that, without revealing information itself privileged or protected, will enable other parties to assess the applicability of the privilege or protection. FL ST RCP Rule 1.280(b)(6).

c. *Limitations on discovery of electronically stored information*

i. A person may object to discovery of electronically stored information from sources that the person identifies as not reasonably accessible because of burden or cost. On motion to compel discovery or for a protective order, the person from whom discovery is sought must show that the information sought or the format requested is not reasonably accessible because of undue burden or cost. If that showing is made, the court may nonetheless order the discovery from such sources or in such formats if the requesting party shows good cause. The court may specify conditions of the discovery, including ordering that some or all of the expenses incurred by the person from whom discovery is sought be paid by the party seeking the discovery. FL ST RCP Rule 1.280(d)(1).

ii. In determining any motion involving discovery of electronically stored information, the court must limit the frequency or extent of discovery otherwise allowed by the Florida Rules of Civil

Procedure if it determines that (i) the discovery sought is unreasonably cumulative or duplicative, or can be obtained from another source or in another manner that is more convenient, less burdensome, or less expensive; or (ii) the burden or expense of the discovery outweighs its likely benefit, considering the needs of the case, the amount in controversy, the parties' resources, the importance of the issues at stake in the action, and the importance of the discovery in resolving the issues. FL ST RCP Rule 1.280(d)(2).

d. For information on inadvertent disclosure of privileged materials, see FL ST RCP Rule 1.285.

2. *Requests for admission.* It is an advantage to use requests for admission. The biggest advantage is that if an adversary denies a request for an admission and the denied matter is later proven to be true, the adversary may have to pay the costs of proving the genuineness of the document or the truth of the matter requested to be admitted. FL-PP § 3:143.

   a. *Scope.* A party may serve upon any other party a written request for the admission of the truth of any matters within the scope of FL ST RCP Rule 1.280(b) set forth in the request that relate to statements or opinions of fact or of the application of law to fact, including the genuineness of any documents described in the request. FL ST RCP Rule 1.370(a).

   b. *Copies of documents.* Copies of documents shall be served with the request unless they have been or are otherwise furnished or made available for inspection and copying. FL ST RCP Rule 1.370(a).

   c. *Number of requests.* The request for admission shall not exceed thirty (30) requests, including all subparts, unless the court permits a larger number on motion and notice and for good cause, or the parties propounding and responding to the requests stipulate to a larger number. Each matter of which an admission is requested shall be separately set forth. FL ST RCP Rule 1.370(a).

   d. *Sufficiency of responses.* The party who has requested the admissions may move to determine the sufficiency of the answers or objections. Unless the court determines that an objection is justified, it shall order that an answer be served. If the court determines that an answer does not comply with the requirements of this rule, it may order either that the matter is admitted or that an amended answer be served. Instead of these orders the court may determine that final disposition of the request be made at a pretrial conference or at a designated time before trial. The provisions of FL ST RCP Rule 1.380(a)(4) apply to the award of expenses incurred in relation to the motion. FL ST RCP Rule 1.370(a).

   e. *Effect of admission.* Any matter admitted under FL ST RCP Rule 1.370 is conclusively established unless the court on motion permits withdrawal or amendment of the admission. Subject to FL ST RCP Rule 1.200 governing amendment of a pretrial order, the court may permit withdrawal or amendment when the presentation of the merits of the action will be subserved by it and the party who obtained the admission fails to satisfy the court that withdrawal or amendment will prejudice that party in maintaining an action or defense on the merits. Any admission made by a party under this rule is for the purpose of the pending action only and is not an admission for any other purpose nor may it be used against that party in any other proceeding. FL ST RCP Rule 1.370(b).

   f. *Answer requirements.* The matter is admitted unless the party to whom the request is directed serves upon the party requesting the admission a written answer or objection addressed to the matter within thirty (30) days after service of the request or such shorter or longer time as the court may allow but, unless the court shortens the time, a defendant shall not be required to serve answers or objections before the expiration of forty-five (45) days after service of the process and initial pleading upon the defendant. If objection is made, the reasons shall be stated. The answer shall specifically deny the matter or set forth in detail the reasons why the answering party cannot truthfully admit or deny the matter. A denial shall fairly meet the substance of the requested admission, and when good faith requires that a party qualify an answer or deny only a part of the matter of which an admission is requested, the party shall specify so much of it as is true and qualify or deny the remainder. An answering party may not give lack of information or knowledge as a reason for failure to admit or deny unless that party states that that party has made reasonable inquiry and that the information known or readily obtainable by that party is insufficient to enable that party to admit or deny. A party who considers that a matter of which an admission has been requested presents a genuine issue for trial may not object to the request on that ground alone; the party may deny the matter or set forth reasons why the party cannot admit or deny it, subject to FL ST RCP Rule 1.380(c). FL ST RCP Rule 1.370(a).

3. *Arbitration and mediation*
   a. *Referral to arbitration and mediation.* Except as hereinafter provided or as otherwise prohibited by law, the presiding judge may enter an order referring all or any part of a contested civil matter to mediation or arbitration. The parties to any contested civil matter may file a written stipulation to mediate or arbitrate any issue between them at any time. Such stipulation shall be incorporated into the order of referral. FL ST RCP Rule 1.700(a).
   b. *Arbitration*
      i. *Exclusions.* A civil action shall be ordered to arbitration or arbitration in conjunction with mediation upon stipulation of the parties. A civil action may be ordered to arbitration or arbitration in conjunction with mediation upon motion of any party or by the court, if the judge determines the action to be of such a nature that arbitration could be of benefit to the litigants or the court. FL ST RCP Rule 1.800.
         - Under no circumstances may the following categories of actions be referred to arbitration: (1) bond estreatures; (2) habeas corpus or other extraordinary writs; (3) bond validations; (4) civil or criminal contempt; (5) such other matters as may be specified by order of the chief judge in the circuit. FL ST RCP Rule 1.800.
      ii. For more information regarding arbitration, please see FL ST RCP Rule 1.810; FL ST RCP Rule 1.820; FL ST RCP Rule 1.830.
   c. *Mediation.* For more information regarding mediation, please see FL ST RCP Rule 1.710; FL ST RCP Rule 1.720; FL ST RCP Rule 1.730; and FL ST RCP Rule 1.750.
   d. *Local arbitration policy.* It is the policy of the Civil Division judges to maximize the use of alternative dispute resolution procedures. Except where prohibited by statute, mediation will be ordered in all cases where jury trial is requested and in selected cases which are to be tried non-jury. Also, selected cases will be referred for court-annexed non-binding arbitration through the Orange County Bar Association Arbitration Service. Counsel may move to dispense with or defer mediation or arbitration or move to modify the referral order for good cause. FL ST 9 J CIR SECTION 15.
4. *Rules of court*
   a. *Rules of civil procedure.* The Florida Rules of Civil Procedure apply to all actions of a civil nature and all special statutory proceedings in the circuit courts and county courts except those to which the Florida Probate Rules, the Florida Family Law Rules of Procedure, or the Small Claims Rules apply. FL ST RCP Rule 1.010.
      i. The form, content, procedure, and time for pleading in all special statutory proceedings shall be as prescribed by the statutes governing the proceeding unless the Florida Rules of Civil Procedure specifically provide to the contrary. FL ST RCP Rule 1.010.
      ii. The Florida Rules of Civil Procedure shall be construed to secure the just, speedy, and inexpensive determination of every action. FL ST RCP Rule 1.010.
   b. *Rules of judicial administration.* The Florida Rules of Judicial Administration shall apply to administrative matters in all courts to which the Florida Rules of Judicial Administration are applicable by their terms. The Florida Rules of Judicial Administration shall be construed to secure the speedy and inexpensive determination of every proceeding to which they are applicable. The Florida Rules of Judicial Administration shall supersede all conflicting rules and statutes. FL ST J ADMIN Rule 2.110.
   c. *Business court procedures.* For rules specific to Business Court, please see FL ST 9 J CIR ORANGE CIV SECTION 1, et seq.
5. *Communication between counsel.* Counsel should be guided by courtesy, candor and common sense and conform to the Florida Rules of Civil Procedure and any applicable orders. In particular, counsel should have in mind the broad scope of discovery allowed by the Civil Rules of Procedure. Direct and informal communication between counsel is encouraged to facilitate discovery and resolve disputes. FL ST 9 J CIR SECTION 13(A).

D. Documents

1. *Required documents*

a. *Request for admission.* Please see the General Requirements section of this document for more information on the contents of the request for admission.

i. *Notices to persons with disabilities.* See the Format section of this KeyRules document for further information.

b. *Copies of documents.* Copies of documents shall be served with the request unless they have been or are otherwise furnished or made available for inspection and copying. FL ST RCP Rule 1.370(a).

c. *Certificate of service.* A certificate of service of the interrogatories shall be filed, giving the date of service and the name of the party to whom they were directed. FL ST RCP Rule 1.340(e). When any attorney certifies in substance: "I certify that a copy hereof has been furnished to (here insert name or names and addresses used for service) by (e-mail) (delivery) (mail) (fax) on .... (date) ....________________ Attorney" the certificate is taken as prima facie proof of such service in compliance with FL ST J ADMIN Rule 2.516. FL ST J ADMIN Rule 2.516(f).

E. Format

1. *Documents; Type and size.* Documents subject to the exceptions set forth in FL ST J ADMIN Rule 2.525(d) shall be filed on recycled paper measuring eight and one half by eleven (8 1/2 by 11) inches. For purposes of FL ST J ADMIN Rule 2.520, paper is recycled if it contains a minimum content of fifty (50) percent waste paper. Xerographic reduction of legal-size (eight and one half by fourteen (8 1/2 by 14) inches) documents to letter size (eight and one half by eleven (8 1/2 by 11) inches) is prohibited. All other documents filed by electronic transmission shall be filed in a format capable of being printed in a format consistent with the provisions of FL ST J ADMIN Rule 2.250. FL ST J ADMIN Rule 2.520(b).

a. *Exhibits.* Any exhibit or attachment filed with pleadings or papers may be filed in its original size. FL ST J ADMIN Rule 2.520(c).

b. *Recording space.* On all papers and documents prepared and filed by the court or by any party to a proceeding which are to be recorded in the public records of any county, including but not limited to final money judgments and notices of lis pendens, a three (3) inch by three (3) inch space at the top right-hand corner on the first page and a one (1) inch by three (3) inch space at the top right-hand corner on each subsequent page shall be left blank and reserved for use by the clerk of court. FL ST J ADMIN Rule 2.520(d).

i. *Exceptions to recording space.* Any papers or documents created by persons or entities over which the filing party has no control, including but not limited to wills, codicils, trusts, or other testamentary documents; documents prepared or executed by any public officer; documents prepared, executed, acknowledged, or proved outside of the State of Florida; or documents created by State or Federal government agencies, may be filed without the space required by FL ST J ADMIN Rule 2.520. FL ST J ADMIN Rule 2.520(e).

c. *Noncompliance.* No clerk of court is permitted to refuse to file any document or paper because of noncompliance with the Florida Rules of Judicial Administration. However, upon request of the clerk of court, noncomplying documents must be resubmitted in accordance with the formatting rules. FL ST J ADMIN Rule 2.520(f).

d. *Proposed orders*

i. All orders will be on eight and a half by eleven (8 1/2 by 11) inch plain white paper (not lined or letterhead paper) and be double spaced. FL ST 9 J CIR SECTION 12(B)(1).

ii. The order must contain a title indicating what matter the order pertains to, e.g., "Order On Defendant Smith's Motion To Dismiss." FL ST 9 J CIR SECTION 12(B)(2).

iii. The preamble of the order should include the date of the hearing and what motions were heard. FL ST 9 J CIR SECTION 12(B)(3).

iv. The adjudication portion of the order should state what relief is ordered. Simply stating that "the motion is granted" without more is insufficient. FL ST 9 J CIR SECTION 12(B)(4).

v. The order should indicate the specific time period of any act ordered to be done and should state whether the time period runs from the date of the hearing or the date the order is signed or some other specified date. FL ST 9 J CIR SECTION 12(B)(5).

vi. The order should contain a full certificate of service with the complete names and addresses of the attorneys and unrepresented parties to be served. Merely showing "copies to" is insufficient. FL ST 9 J CIR SECTION 12(B)(6).

vii. If an order of dismissal is final (i.e., it disposes of the entire case) the title should contain the word "Final." When the order is not final but leaves other counts or claims against other defendants pending, it should so state in a separate paragraph. FL ST 9 J CIR SECTION 12(B)(7).

viii. When submitting stipulations, orders shall be by separate order, not attached to the stipulation. FL ST 9 J CIR SECTION 12(B)(8).

ix. Counsel preparing the Final Judgment or order should draft and circulate copies within two (2) working days of the ruling or jury verdict. If counsel preparing the Final Judgment or order gets approval as to form of the order from all counsel, the original with copies and envelopes should be sent directly to the judge with a cover letter stating all counsel agree to the form of the order or judgment. If other counsel objects to the form or cannot be reached for approval, counsel preparing the judgment or order shall notice a motion for entry of the order or judgment. If objecting counsel does not furnish the judge prior to or at the hearing with a proposed judgment or order version with copies under cover letter stating the reasons for the objection, all objections will be deemed waived. Orders and judgments should not be submitted to the judge to hold waiting for an objection. FL ST 9 J CIR SECTION 12(D).

2. *Caption.* Every pleading, motion, order, judgment, or other paper shall have a caption containing the name of the court, the file number, and except for in rem proceedings, including forfeiture proceedings, the name of the first party on each side with an appropriate indication of other parties, and a designation identifying the party filing it and its nature or the nature of the order, as the case may be. In any in rem proceeding, every pleading, motion, order, judgment, or other paper shall have a caption containing the name of the court, the file number, the style "In re" (followed by the name or general description of the property), and a designation of the person or entity filing it and its nature or the nature of the order, as the case may be. In an in rem forfeiture proceeding, the style shall be "In re forfeiture of" (followed by the name of the general description of the property). All papers filed in the action shall be styled in such a manner as to indicate clearly the subject matter of the paper and the party requesting or obtaining relief. FL ST RCP Rule 1.100(c)(1).

3. *Writing and written defined.* Writing or written means a document containing information, an application, or a stipulation. FL ST RCP Rule 1.080(c).

4. *Rule abbreviations*

   a. The Florida Rules of Civil Procedure and shall be abbreviated as Fla.R.Civ.P. FL ST RCP Rule 1.010.

   b. The Florida Rules of Judicial Administration shall be abbreviated as Fla. R. Jud. Admin. FL ST J ADMIN Rule 2.110.

5. *Nonverification.* Except when otherwise specifically provided by the Florida Rules of Civil Procedure or an applicable statute, every pleading or other document of a party represented by an attorney need not be verified or accompanied by an affidavit. FL ST RCP Rule 1.030; FL ST J ADMIN Rule 2.515(a).

6. *Unrepresented parties.* An unrepresented party must file his or her papers with the clerk and send copies to other attorneys or unrepresented parties. All such papers must be typed double-spaced on plain white eight and a half by eleven (8 1/2 by 11) inch paper, with the name of the case and case number at the top and the party's mailing address, telephone number and FAX number, if any, below his or her signature at the end of the paper. Such unrepresented party must immediately notify the Clerk and all other counsel or parties of record in writing of any change in mailing address or telephone or FAX number. Failure to promptly notify of change of address could result in a dismissal or default entered against such party. FL ST 9 J CIR SECTION 7(B)(5).

7. *Attorney signature*
    a. *Attorney signature.* Every pleading and other document of a party represented by an attorney shall be signed by at least one (1) attorney of record in that attorney's individual name whose current record Florida Bar address, telephone number, including area code, primary e-mail address and secondary e-mail addresses, if any, and Florida Bar number shall be stated, and who shall be duly licensed to practice law in Florida or who shall have received permission to appear in the particular case as provided in FL ST J ADMIN Rule 2.510. FL ST J ADMIN Rule 2.515(a).
        i. The attorney may be required by the court to give the address of, and to vouch for the attorney's authority to represent, the party. FL ST J ADMIN Rule 2.515(a).
        ii. The signature of an attorney shall constitute a certificate by the attorney that the attorney has read the pleading or other document; that to the best of the attorney's knowledge, information, and belief there is good ground to support it; and that it is not interposed for delay. FL ST J ADMIN Rule 2.515(a).
        iii. If a pleading is not signed or is signed with intent to defeat the purpose of FL ST J ADMIN Rule 2.515, it may be stricken and the action may proceed as though the pleading or other document had not been served. FL ST J ADMIN Rule 2.515(a).
    b. *Pro se litigant signature.* A party who is not represented by an attorney shall sign any pleading or other paper and state the party's address and telephone number, including area code. FL ST J ADMIN Rule 2.515(b).
    c. *Form of signature*
        i. The signatures required on pleadings and documents by FL ST J ADMIN Rule 2.515(a) and FL ST J ADMIN Rule 2.515(b) may be:
            - Original signatures;
            - Original signatures that have been reproduced by electronic means, such as on electronically transmitted documents or photocopied documents;
            - Electronic signatures using the "/s/," "s/," or "/s" formats by or at the direction of the person signing; or
            - Any other signature format authorized by general law, so long as the clerk where the proceeding is pending has the capability of receiving and has obtained approval from the Supreme Court of Florida to accept pleadings and documents with that signature format. FL ST J ADMIN Rule 2.515(c)(1).
        ii. An attorney, party, or other person who files a pleading or paper by electronic transmission that does not contain the original signature of that attorney, party, or other person shall file that identical pleading or paper in paper form containing an original signature of that attorney, party, or other person (hereinafter called the follow-up filing) immediately thereafter. The follow-up filing is not required if the Supreme Court of Florida has entered an order directing the clerk of court to discontinue accepting the follow-up filing. FL ST J ADMIN Rule 2.515(c)(2).
8. *Forms*
    a. *Process.* The forms of process, notice of lis pendens, and notice of action provided in the Florida Rules of Civil Procedure are sufficient. Variations from the forms do not void process or notices that are otherwise sufficient. FL ST RCP Rule 1.900(a).
    b. *Other forms.* The other forms provided in the Florida Rules of Civil Procedure are sufficient for the matters that are covered by them. So long as the substance is expressed without prolixity, the forms may be varied to meet the facts of a particular case. FL ST RCP Rule 1.900(b).
    c. *Formal matters.* Captions, except for the designation of the paper, are omitted from the forms provided in the Florida Rules of Civil Procedure. A general form of caption is the first form provided. Signatures are omitted from pleadings and motions. FL ST RCP Rule 1.900(c).
9. *Notices to persons with disabilities.* All notices of court proceedings to be held in a public facility, and all process compelling appearance at such proceedings, shall include the following statement in bold face,

fourteen (14) point Times New Roman or Courier font: "If you are a person with a disability who needs any accommodation in order to participate in this proceeding, you are entitled, at no cost to you, to the provision of certain assistance. Please contact [identify applicable court personnel by name, address, and telephone number] at least seven (7) days before your scheduled court appearance, or immediately upon receiving this notification if the time before the scheduled appearance is less than seven (7) days; if you are hearing or voice impaired, call 711." FL ST J ADMIN Rule 2.540(c)(1).

10. *Minimization of the filing of sensitive information*

a. *Limitations for court filings.* Unless authorized by FL ST J ADMIN Rule 2.425(b), statute, another rule of court, or the court orders otherwise, designated sensitive information filed with the court must be limited to the following format:

i. The initials of a person known to be a minor;

ii. The year of birth of a person's birth date;

iii. No portion of any: Social security number, Bank account number, Credit card account number, Charge account number, or Debit account number;

iv. The last four digits of any: Taxpayer identification number (TIN), Employee identification number, Driver's license number, Passport number, Telephone number, Financial account number, except as set forth in FL ST J ADMIN Rule 2.425(a)(3), Brokerage account number, Insurance policy account number, Loan account number, Customer account number, or Patient or health care number;

v. A truncated version of any: Email address, Computer user name, Password, or Personal identification number (PIN); and

vi. A truncated version of any other sensitive information as provided by court order. FL ST J ADMIN Rule 2.425(a).

b. *Exceptions.* FL ST J ADMIN Rule 2.425(a) does not apply to the following:

i. An account number which identifies the property alleged to be the subject of a proceeding;

ii. The record of an administrative or agency proceeding;

iii. The record in appellate or review proceedings;

iv. The birth date of a minor whenever the birth date is necessary for the court to establish or maintain subject matter jurisdiction;

v. The name of a minor in any order relating to parental responsibility, time-sharing, or child support;

vi. The name of a minor in any document or order affecting the minor's ownership of real property;

vii. The birth date of a party in a writ of attachment or notice to payor;

viii. In traffic and criminal proceedings: a pro se filing; a court filing that is related to a criminal matter or investigation and that is prepared before the filing of a criminal charge or is not filed as part of any docketed criminal case; an arrest or search warrant or any information in support thereof; a charging document and an affidavit or other documents filed in support of any charging document, including any driving records; a statement of particulars; discovery material introduced into evidence or otherwise filed with the court; and all information necessary for the proper issuance and execution of a subpoena duces tecum;

ix. Information used by the clerk for case maintenance purposes or the courts for case management purposes; and

x. Information which is relevant and material to an issue before the court. FL ST J ADMIN Rule 2.425(b).

c. *Remedies.* Upon motion by a party or interested person or sua sponte by the court, the court may order remedies, sanctions or both for a violation of FL ST J ADMIN Rule 2.425(a). Following notice and an opportunity to respond, the court may impose sanctions if such filing was not made in good faith. FL ST J ADMIN Rule 2.425(c).

d. *Motions not restricted.* FL ST J ADMIN Rule 2.425 does not restrict a party's right to move for protective order, to move to file documents under seal, or to request a determination of the confidentiality of records. FL ST J ADMIN Rule 2.425(d).

e. *Application.* FL ST J ADMIN Rule 2.425 does not affect the application of constitutional provisions, statutes, or rules of court regarding confidential information or access to public information. FL ST J ADMIN Rule 2.425(e).

F. Filing and Service Requirements

1. *Court filing of documents and discovery.* Information obtained during discovery shall not be filed with the court until such time as it is filed for good cause. The requirement of good cause is satisfied only where the filing of the information is allowed or required by another applicable rule of procedure or by court order. All filings of discovery documents shall comply with FL ST J ADMIN Rule 2.425. The court shall have the authority to impose sanctions for violation of FL ST RCP Rule 1.280. FL ST RCP Rule 1.280(g).

2. *Filing requirements.* All original documents must be filed with the court either before service or immediately thereafter, unless otherwise provided for by general law or other rules. If the original of any bond or other document is not placed in the court file, a certified copy must be so placed by the clerk. FL ST J ADMIN Rule 2.516(d). All documents shall be filed in conformity with the requirements of FL ST J ADMIN Rule 2.525. FL ST RCP Rule 1.080(b). All documents filed in any court shall be filed by electronic transmission in accordance with FL ST J ADMIN Rule 2.525. "Documents" means pleadings, motions, petitions, memoranda, briefs, notices, exhibits, declarations, affidavits, orders, judgments, decrees, writs, opinions, and any other paper or writing submitted to a court. FL ST J ADMIN Rule 2.520(a). All documents that are court records, as defined in FL ST J ADMIN Rule 2.430(a)(1), must be filed by electronic transmission, provided that: (1) the clerk has the ability to accept and retain such documents; (2) the clerk or the chief judge of the circuit has requested permission to accept documents filed by electronic transmission; and (3) the supreme court has entered an order granting permission to the clerk to accept documents filed by electronic transmission. FL ST J ADMIN Rule 2.525(c)(1).

   a. *Definition.* "Electronic transmission of documents" means the sending of information by electronic signals to, by or from a court or clerk, which when received can be transformed and stored or transmitted on paper, microfilm, magnetic storage device, optical imaging system, CD-ROM, flash drive, other electronic data storage system, server, case maintenance system ("CM"), electronic court filing ("ECF") system, statewide or local electronic portal ("e-portal"), or other electronic record keeping system authorized by the supreme court in a format sufficient to communicate the information on the original document in a readable format. Electronic transmission of documents includes electronic mail ("e-mail") and any internet-based transmission procedure, and may include procedures allowing for documents to be signed or verified by electronic means. FL ST J ADMIN Rule 2.525(a).

      i. The filing of documents with the court as required by the Florida Rules of Judicial Administration must be made by filing them with the clerk in accordance with FL ST J ADMIN Rule 2.525, except that the judge may permit documents to be filed with the judge, in which event the judge must note the filing date before him or her on the documents and transmit them to the clerk. The date of filing is that shown on the face of the document by the judge's notation or the clerk's time stamp, whichever is earlier. FL ST J ADMIN Rule 2.516(e).

   b. *Application.* Any court or clerk of the court may accept the electronic transmission of documents for filing after the clerk, together with input from the chief judge of the circuit, has obtained approval of the procedures and program for doing so from the Supreme Court of Florida. FL ST J ADMIN Rule 2.525(b).

   c. *Exceptions*

      i. Paper documents and other submissions may be manually submitted to the clerk or court:

         - When the clerk does not have the ability to accept and retain documents by electronic filing or has not had ECF Procedures approved by the supreme court;
         - For filing by any self-represented party or any self-represented nonparty unless specific ECF Procedures provide a means to file documents electronically. However, any self-

represented nonparty that is a governmental or public agency and any other agency, partnership, corporation, or business entity acting on behalf of any governmental or public agency may file documents by electronic transmission if such entity has the capability of filing documents electronically;

- For filing by attorneys excused from e-mail service in accordance with FL ST J ADMIN Rule 2.516(b);
- When submitting evidentiary exhibits or filing non-documentary materials;
- When the filing involves documents in excess of twenty-five (25) megabytes (25MB) in size. For such filings, documents may be transmitted using an electronic storage medium that the clerk has the ability to accept, which may include a CD-ROM, flash drive, or similar storage medium;
- When filed in open court, as permitted by the court;
- When paper filing is permitted by any approved statewide or local ECF procedures; and
- If any court determines that justice so requires. FL ST J ADMIN Rule 2.525(d).

ii. Any document in paper form submitted under FL ST J ADMIN Rule 2.525(d) is filed when it is received by the clerk or court and the clerk shall immediately thereafter convert any filed paper document to an electronic document. "Convert to an electronic document" means optically capturing an image of a paper document and using character recognition software to recover as much of the document's text as practicable and then indexing and storing the document in the official court file. FL ST J ADMIN Rule 2.525(c)(4).

iii. Any storage medium submitted under FL ST J ADMIN Rule 2.525(d)(5) is filed when received by the clerk or court and the clerk shall immediately thereafter transfer the electronic documents from the storage device to the official court file. FL ST J ADMIN Rule 2.525(c)(5).

iv. If the filer of any paper document authorized under FL ST J ADMIN Rule 2.525(d) provides a self-addressed, postage-paid envelope for return of the paper document after it is converted to electronic form by the clerk, the clerk shall place the paper document in the envelope and deposit it in the mail. Except when a paper document is required to be maintained, the clerk may recycle any filed paper document that is not to be returned to the filer. FL ST J ADMIN Rule 2.525(c)(6).

v. The clerk may convert any paper document filed before the effective date of FL ST J ADMIN Rule 2.525 to an electronic document. Unless the clerk is required to maintain the paper document, if the paper document has been converted to an electronic document by the clerk, the paper document is no longer part of the official court file and may be removed and recycled. FL ST J ADMIN Rule 2.525(c)(7).

d. *Unrepresented parties.* An unrepresented party must file his or her papers with the clerk and send copies to other attorneys or unrepresented parties. FL ST 9 J CIR SECTION 7(B)(5).

i. An unrepresented party may not communicate privately with the judge either by letter, telephone, in person or otherwise. FL ST 9 J CIR SECTION 7(B)(4).

ii. Copies of legal papers or other written materials should not be sent to the judge unless specifically requested by the judge or required by the local administrative procedures. Any unrequested or non-required papers or materials sent to a judge may not be read but may be returned to the sender or placed unread into the court file. FL ST 9 J CIR SECTION 7(B)(4).

e. *Official court file.* For information on what constitutes the official court file, please see FL ST J ADMIN Rule 2.525(c)(2), FL ST J ADMIN Rule 2.525(c)(3).

f. *Administration.* All attorneys, parties, or other persons using this rule to file documents are required to make arrangements with the court or clerk for the payment of any charges authorized by general law or the supreme court before filing any document by electronic transmission. FL ST J ADMIN Rule 2.525(f)(2).

g. *Filing date.* The filing date for an electronically transmitted document is the date and time that such

filing is acknowledged by an electronic stamp or otherwise, pursuant to any procedure set forth in any ECF Procedures approved by the supreme court, or the date the last page of such filing is received by the court or clerk. FL ST J ADMIN Rule 2.525(f)(3).

h. *Accessibility.* All documents transmitted in any electronic form under FL ST J ADMIN Rule 2.525 must comply with the accessibility requirements of FL ST J ADMIN Rule 2.526. FL ST J ADMIN Rule 2.525(g).

3. *Service requirements.* Every pleading subsequent to the initial pleading, all orders, and every other document filed in the action must be served in conformity with the requirements of FL ST J ADMIN Rule 2.516. FL ST RCP Rule 1.080(a).

   a. *Service; When required.* Unless the court otherwise orders, or a statute or supreme court administrative order specifies a different means of service, every pleading subsequent to the initial pleading and every other document filed in any court proceeding, except applications for witness subpoenas and documents served by formal notice or required to be served in the manner provided for service of formal notice, must be served in accordance with FL ST J ADMIN Rule 2.516 on each party. No service need be made on parties against whom a default has been entered, except that pleadings asserting new or additional claims against them must be served in the manner provided for service of summons. FL ST J ADMIN Rule 2.516(a).

   b. *Service; How made.* When service is required or permitted to be made upon a party represented by an attorney, service must be made upon the attorney unless service upon the party is ordered by the court. FL ST J ADMIN Rule 2.516(b).

      i. *Service by electronic mail ("e-mail").* All documents required or permitted to be served on another party must be served by e-mail, unless FL ST J ADMIN Rule 2.516 otherwise provides. When, in addition to service by e-mail, the sender also utilizes another means of service provided for in FL ST J ADMIN Rule 2.516(b)(2), any differing time limits and other provisions applicable to that other means of service control. FL ST J ADMIN Rule 2.516(b)(1). Any document electronically transmitted to a court or clerk must also be served on all parties and interested persons in accordance with the applicable rules of court. FL ST J ADMIN Rule 2.525(e)(2).

         - *Service on attorneys.* Upon appearing in a proceeding, an attorney must serve a designation of a primary e-mail address and may designate no more than two (2) secondary e-mail addresses. Thereafter, service must be directed to all designated e-mail addresses in that proceeding. Every document filed by an attorney thereafter must include the primary e-mail address of that attorney and any secondary e-mail addresses. If an attorney does not designate any e-mail address for service, documents may be served on that attorney at the e-mail address on record with The Florida Bar. FL ST J ADMIN Rule 2.516(b)(1)(A).

         - *Exception to e-mail service on attorneys.* Service by an attorney on another attorney must be made by e-mail unless excused by the court. Upon motion by an attorney demonstrating that the attorney has no e-mail account and lacks access to the Internet at the attorney's office, the court may excuse the attorney from the requirements of e-mail service. Service on and by an attorney excused by the court from e-mail service must be by the means provided in FL ST J ADMIN Rule 2.516(b)(2). FL ST J ADMIN Rule 2.516(b)(1)(B).

         - *Service on and by parties not represented by an attorney.* Any party not represented by an attorney may serve a designation of a primary e-mail address and also may designate no more than two (2) secondary e-mail addresses to which service must be directed in that proceeding by the means provided in FL ST J ADMIN Rule 2.516(b)(1). If a party not represented by an attorney does not designate an e-mail address for service in a proceeding, service on and by that party must be by the means provided in FL ST J ADMIN Rule 2.516(b)(2). FL ST J ADMIN Rule 2.516(b)(1)(C).

         - *Time of service.* Service by e-mail is complete when it is sent. FL ST J ADMIN Rule 2.516(b)(1)(D). An e-mail is deemed served on the date it is sent. FL ST J ADMIN Rule 2.516(b)(1)(D)(i). If the sender learns that the e-mail did not reach the address of the person to be served, the sender must immediately send another copy by e-mail, or by a

means authorized by FL ST J ADMIN Rule 2.516(b)(2). FL ST J ADMIN Rule 2.516(b)(1)(D)(ii). E-mail service is treated as service by mail for the computation of time. FL ST J ADMIN Rule 2.516(b)(1)(D)(iii).

ii. *Format of e-mail for service.* Service of a document by e-mail is made by attaching a copy of the document in PDF format to an e-mail sent to all addresses designated by the attorney or party. FL ST J ADMIN Rule 2.516(b)(1)(E).

- All documents served by e-mail must be attached to an e-mail message containing a subject line beginning with the words "SERVICE OF COURT DOCUMENT" in all capital letters, followed by the case number of the proceeding in which the documents are being served. FL ST J ADMIN Rule 2.516(b)(1)(E)(i).
- The body of the e-mail must identify the court in which the proceeding is pending, the case number, the name of the initial party on each side, the title of each document served with that e-mail, and the sender's name and telephone number. FL ST J ADMIN Rule 2.516(b)(1)(E)(ii).
- Any document served by e-mail may be signed by the "/s/" format, as long as the filed original is signed in accordance with the applicable rule of procedure. FL ST J ADMIN Rule 2.516(b)(1)(E)(iii).
- Any e-mail which, together with its attached documents, exceeds five megabytes (5MB) in size, must be divided and sent as separate e-mails, no one of which may exceed five megabytes (5MB) in size and each of which must be sequentially numbered in the subject line. FL ST J ADMIN Rule 2.516(b)(1)(E)(iv).

iii. *Service by other means.* In addition to, and not in lieu of, service by e-mail, service may also be made upon attorneys by any of the means specified in FL ST J ADMIN Rule 2.516(b)(2). Service on and by all parties who are not represented by an attorney and who do not designate an e-mail address, and on and by all attorneys excused from e-mail service, must be made by delivering a copy of the document or by mailing it to the party or attorney at their last known address or, if no address is known, by leaving it with the clerk of the court. Service by mail is complete upon mailing. Delivery of a copy within FL ST J ADMIN Rule 2.516 is complete upon:

- Handing it to the attorney or to the party,
- Leaving it at the attorney's or party's office with a clerk or other person in charge thereof,
- If there is no one in charge, leaving it in a conspicuous place therein,
- If the office is closed or the person to be served has no office, leaving it at the person's usual place of abode with some person of his or her family above fifteen (15) years of age and informing such person of the contents, or
- Transmitting it by facsimile to the attorney's or party's office with a cover sheet containing the sender's name, firm, address, telephone number, and facsimile number, and the number of pages transmitted. When service is made by facsimile, a copy must also be served by any other method permitted by FL ST J ADMIN Rule 2.516. Facsimile service occurs when transmission is complete. FL ST J ADMIN Rule 2.516(b)(2)(A) through FL ST J ADMIN Rule 2.516(b)(2)(E).
- Service by delivery after 5:00 p.m. must be deemed to have been made by mailing on the date of delivery. FL ST J ADMIN Rule 2.516(b)(2)(F).

c. *Service; Numerous defendants.* In actions when the parties are unusually numerous, the court may regulate the service contemplated by the Florida Rules of Judicial Administration on motion or on its own initiative in such manner as may be found to be just and reasonable. FL ST J ADMIN Rule 2.516(c).

d. *Service by clerk.* Service of notices and other documents required to be made by the clerk must also be done as provided in FL ST J ADMIN Rule 2.516(b). FL ST J ADMIN Rule 2.516(g).

G. Hearings

1. There is no hearing required or contemplated with regard to requests for admission in the Florida Rules of Civil Procedure.

H. Forms

1. Official Request for Admissions Forms for Florida

a. Caption. FL ST RCP Form 1.901.

2. Request for Admissions Forms for Florida

a. Requests for admissions; Negligence, fall down. FL-PRACFORM § 8:41.

b. Requests for admissions; Promissory note. FL-PRACFORM § 8:42.

c. Requests for admissions; Open account. FL-PRACFORM § 8:43.

d. Requests for admissions; Mortgage foreclosure. FL-PRACFORM § 8:44.

e. Request for admissions; General form. FL-PP § 3:146.

f. Request for admissions; Facts and genuineness of documents. FL-PP § 3:147.

g. Motion; To determine sufficiency of reply to request for admissions. FL-PP § 3:152.

h. Form for request for admissions. FL-RCPF R 1.370(5).

i. Form for request for admissions (another form). FL-RCPF R 1.370(6).

j. Form for request for admissions served concurrently with interrogatories. FL-RCPF R 1.370(7).

k. Form for request for admissions as to factual situation and refinement of issues. FL-RCPF R 1.370(9).

l. Form for request to admit party uses electronic data storage. FL-RCPF R 1.370(10).

I. Checklist

(I) ❑ Matters to be considered by requesting party

- (a) ❑ Required documents
  - (1) ❑ Request
  - (2) ❑ Copies of documents
  - (3) ❑ Certificate of service
- (b) ❑ Time for request
  - (1) ❑ Without leave of court the request may be served upon the plaintiff after commencement of the action and upon any other party with or after service of the process and initial pleading upon that party

(II) ❑ Matters to be considered by responding party

- (a) ❑ Required documents
  - (1) ❑ Response to request
  - (2) ❑ Certificate of service
- (b) ❑ Time for response
  - (1) ❑ The party to whom the request is directed shall serve a written response within thirty (30) days after service of the request, except that a defendant may serve a response within forty-five (45) days after service of the process and initial pleading on that defendant

Requests, Notices and Applications
Notice of Deposition

Document Last Updated January 2013

A. Applicable Rules

1. *State rules*
   a. Pleadings and motions. FL ST RCP Rule 1.100.
   b. Depositions before action or pending appeal. FL ST RCP Rule 1.290.
   c. Persons before whom depositions may be taken. FL ST RCP Rule 1.300.
   d. Depositions upon oral examination. FL ST RCP Rule 1.310.
   e. Depositions upon written questions. FL ST RCP Rule 1.320.
   f. Use of depositions in court proceedings. FL ST RCP Rule 1.330.
   g. Nonverification of pleadings. FL ST RCP Rule 1.030.
   h. Service and filing of pleadings, orders, and documents. FL ST RCP Rule 1.080.
   i. Time. FL ST RCP Rule 1.090.
   j. General provisions governing discovery. FL ST RCP Rule 1.280.
   k. Failure to make discovery; Sanctions. FL ST RCP Rule 1.380.
   l. Depositions of expert witnesses. FL ST RCP Rule 1.390.
   m. Relief from judgment, decrees, or orders. FL ST RCP Rule 1.540.
   n. Forms. FL ST RCP Rule 1.900.
   o. Minimization of the filing of sensitive information. FL ST J ADMIN Rule 2.425.
   p. Retention of court records. FL ST J ADMIN Rule 2.430.
   q. Foreign attorneys. FL ST J ADMIN Rule 2.510.
   r. Signature of attorneys and parties. FL ST J ADMIN Rule 2.515.
   s. Paper. FL ST J ADMIN Rule 2.520.
   t. Electronic filing. FL ST J ADMIN Rule 2.525.
   u. Accessibility of information and technology. FL ST J ADMIN Rule 2.526.
   v. Requests for accommodations by persons with disabilities. FL ST J ADMIN Rule 2.540.
2. *Local rules*
   a. General discovery guidelines. FL ST 9 J CIR SECTION 13.
   b. Deposition guidelines. FL ST 9 J CIR SECTION 14.

B. Timing

1. *Depositions upon oral examination.* After commencement of the action any party may take the testimony of any person, including a party, by deposition upon oral examination. Leave of court, granted with or without notice, must be obtained only if the plaintiff seeks to take a deposition within thirty (30) days after service of the process and initial pleading upon any defendant, except that leave is not required (1) if a defendant has served a notice of taking deposition or otherwise sought discovery, or (2) if special notice is given as provided in FL ST RCP Rule 1.310(b)(2). The attendance of witnesses may be compelled by subpoena as provided in FL ST RCP Rule 1.410. The deposition of a person confined in prison may be taken only by leave of court on such terms as the court prescribes. FL ST RCP Rule 1.310(a). A party desiring to take the deposition of any person upon oral examination shall give reasonable notice in writing to every other party to the action. FL ST RCP Rule 1.310(b)(1).
2. *Depositions upon written questions.* After commencement of the action any party may take the testimony

of any person, including a party, by deposition upon written questions. The attendance of witnesses may be compelled by the use of subpoena as provided in FL ST RCP Rule 1.410. The deposition of a person confined in prison may be taken only by leave of court on such terms as the court prescribes. Within thrity (30) days after the notice and written questions are served, a party may serve cross questions upon all other parties. Within ten (10) days after being served with cross questions, a party may serve redirect questions upon all other parties. Within ten (10) days after being served with redirect questions, a party may serve recross questions upon all other parties. The court may for cause shown enlarge or shorten the time. FL ST RCP Rule 1.320(a).

3. *Depositions before action or pending appeal.* For information on petitions and motions for depositions before an action or pending appeal, please see the General Requirements section below.
4. *Sequence and timing of discovery.* Except as provided in FL ST RCP Rule 1.280(b)(5) or unless the court upon motion for the convenience of parties and witnesses and in the interest of justice orders otherwise, methods of discovery may be used in any sequence, and the fact that a party is conducting discovery, whether by deposition or otherwise, shall not delay any other party's discovery. FL ST RCP Rule 1.280(e).
   a. *Scheduling.* If the time for taking a deposition cannot be coordinated with other counsel in advance, at least ten (10) working days notice should be given. Note that it is often less expensive to bring the witness to the deposition (and for the parties to share the expense) than for the lawyers to travel. Likewise, a telephone deposition of a secondary witness will save expense. FL ST 9 J CIR SECTION 14(a).
5. *Computation of time*
   a. *Generally.* Computation of time shall be governed by FL ST J ADMIN Rule 2.514. FL ST RCP Rule 1.090(a). The following rules apply in computing time periods specified in any rule of procedure, local rule, court order, or statute that does not specify a method of computing time. FL ST J ADMIN Rule 2.514(a).
      i. *Period stated in days or a longer unit.* When the period is stated in days or a longer unit of time (A) exclude the day of the event that triggers the period; (B) count every day, including intermediate Saturdays, Sundays, and legal holidays; and (C) include the last day of the period, but if the last day is a Saturday, Sunday, or legal holiday, or falls within any period of time extended through an order of the chief justice under FL ST J ADMIN Rule 2.205(a)(2)(B)(iv), the period continues to run until the end of the next day that is not a Saturday, Sunday, or legal holiday and does not fall within any period of time extended through an order of the chief justice. FL ST J ADMIN Rule 2.514(a)(1).
      ii. *Period stated in hours.* When the period is stated in hours (A) begin counting immediately on the occurrence of the event that triggers the period; (B) count every hour, including hours during intermediate Saturdays, Sundays, and legal holidays; and (C) if the period would end on a Saturday, Sunday, or legal holiday, or during any period of time extended through an order of the chief justice under FL ST J ADMIN Rule 2.205(a)(2)(B)(iv), the period continues to run until the same time on the next day that is not a Saturday, Sunday, or legal holiday and does not fall within any period of time extended through an order of the chief justice. FL ST J ADMIN Rule 2.514(a)(2).
      iii. *Period stated in days less than seven (7) days.* When the period stated in days is less than seven (7) days, intermediate Saturdays, Sundays, and legal holidays shall be excluded in the computation. FL ST J ADMIN Rule 2.514(a)(3).
      iv. *"Last day" defined.* Unless a different time is set by a statute, local rule, or court order, the last day ends (A) for electronic filing or for service by any means, at midnight; and (B) for filing by other means, when the clerk's office is scheduled to close. FL ST J ADMIN Rule 2.514(a)(4).
      v. *"Next day" defined.* The "next day" is determined by continuing to count forward when the period is measured after an event and backward when measured before an event. FL ST J ADMIN Rule 2.514(a)(5).
      vi. *"Legal holiday" defined.* "Legal holiday" means (A) the day set aside by FL ST § 110.117, for

observing New Year's Day, Martin Luther King, Jr.'s Birthday, Memorial Day, Independence Day, Labor Day, Veterans' Day, Thanksgiving Day, the Friday after Thanksgiving Day, or Christmas Day, and (B) any day observed as a holiday by the clerk's office or as designated by the chief judge. FL ST J ADMIN Rule 2.514(a)(6).

b. *Additional time after service by mail or e-mail.* When a party may or must act within a specified time after service and service is made by mail or e-mail, five (5) days are added after the period that would otherwise expire under FL ST J ADMIN Rule 2.514(a). FL ST J ADMIN Rule 2.514(b).

c. *Enlargement.* When an act is required or allowed to be done at or within a specified time by order of court, by the Florida Rules of Civil Procedure, or by notice given thereunder, for cause shown the court at any time in its discretion (1) with or without notice, may order the period enlarged if request therefor is made before the expiration of the period originally prescribed or as extended by a previous order, or (2) upon motion made and notice after the expiration of the specified period, may permit the act to be done when failure to act was the result of excusable neglect, but it may not extend the time for making a motion for new trial, for rehearing, or to alter or amend a judgment; making a motion for relief from a judgment under FL ST RCP Rule 1.540(b); taking an appeal or filing a petition for certiorari; or making a motion for a directed verdict. FL ST RCP Rule 1.090(b).

d. *Unaffected by expiration of term.* The period of time provided for the doing of any act or the taking of any proceeding shall not be affected or limited by the continued existence or expiration of a term of court. The continued existence or expiration of a term of court in no way affects the power of a court to do any act or take any proceeding in any action which is or has been pending before it. FL ST RCP Rule 1.090(c).

C. General Requirements

1. *General provisions governing discovery*

a. *Discovery methods.* Parties may obtain discovery by one or more of the following methods: depositions upon oral examination or written questions; written interrogatories; production of documents or things or permission to enter upon land or other property for inspection and other purposes; physical and mental examinations; and requests for admission. Unless the court orders otherwise and under FL ST RCP Rule 1.280(c), the frequency of use of these methods is not limited, except as provided in FL ST RCP Rule 1.200, FL ST RCP Rule 1.340, and FL ST RCP Rule 1.370. FL ST RCP Rule 1.280(a).

b. *Scope of discovery.* Unless otherwise limited by order of the court in accordance with the Florida Rules of Civil Procedure, the scope of discovery is as follows:

i. *In general.* Parties may obtain discovery regarding any matter, not privileged, that is relevant to the subject matter of the pending action, whether it relates to the claim or defense of the party seeking discovery or the claim or defense of any other party, including the existence, description, nature, custody, condition, and location of any books, documents, or other tangible things and the identity and location of persons having knowledge of any discoverable matter. It is not ground for objection that the information sought will be inadmissible at the trial if the information sought appears reasonably calculated to lead to the discovery of admissible evidence. FL ST RCP Rule 1.280(b)(1).

ii. *Indemnity agreements.* A party may obtain discovery of the existence and contents of any agreement under which any person may be liable to satisfy part or all of a judgment that may be entered in the action or to indemnify or to reimburse a party for payments made to satisfy the judgment. Information concerning the agreement is not admissible in evidence at trial by reason of disclosure. FL ST RCP Rule 1.280(b)(2).

iii. *Electronically stored information.* A party may obtain discovery of electronically stored information in accordance with the Florida Rules of Civil Procedure. FL ST RCP Rule 1.280(b)(3).

iv. *Trial preparation; Materials.* Subject to the provisions of FL ST RCP Rule 1.280(b)(5), a party may obtain discovery of documents and tangible things otherwise discoverable under FL ST RCP Rule 1.280(b)(1) and prepared in anticipation of litigation or for trial by or for another party or by or for that party's representative, including that party's attorney, consultant, surety, indemnitor, insurer, or agent, only upon a showing that the party seeking discovery has need of the materials in the preparation of the case and is unable without undue hardship to obtain the substantial equivalent of the materials by other means. FL ST RCP Rule 1.280(b)(4).

- In ordering discovery of the materials when the required showing has been made, the court shall protect against disclosure of the mental impressions, conclusions, opinions, or legal theories of an attorney or other representative of a party concerning the litigation. FL ST RCP Rule 1.280(b)(4).
- Without the required showing a party may obtain a copy of a statement concerning the action or its subject matter previously made by that party. FL ST RCP Rule 1.280(b)(4).
- Upon request without the required showing a person not a party may obtain a copy of a statement concerning the action or its subject matter previously made by that person. If the request is refused, the person may move for an order to obtain a copy. The provisions of FL ST RCP Rule 1.380(a)(5) apply to the award of expenses incurred as a result of making the motion. FL ST RCP Rule 1.280(b)(4).
- For purposes of FL ST RCP Rule 1.280(b)(4), a statement previously made is a written statement signed or otherwise adopted or approved by the person making it, or a stenographic, mechanical, electrical, or other recording or transcription of it that is a substantially verbatim recital of an oral statement by the person making it and contemporaneously recorded. FL ST RCP Rule 1.280(b)(4).

v. *Trial preparation; Experts.* Discovery of facts known and opinions held by experts, otherwise discoverable under the provisions of FL ST RCP Rule 1.280(b)(1) and acquired or developed in anticipation of litigation or for trial, may be obtained only as follows:

- By interrogatories a party may require any other party to identify each person whom the other party expects to call as an expert witness at trial and to state the subject matter on which the expert is expected to testify, and to state the substance of the facts and opinions to which the expert is expected to testify and a summary of the grounds for each opinion. FL ST RCP Rule 1.280(b)(5)(A)(i).
- Any person disclosed by interrogatories or otherwise as a person expected to be called as an expert witness at trial may be deposed in accordance with FL ST RCP Rule 1.390 without motion or order of court. FL ST RCP Rule 1.280(b)(5)(A)(ii).
- A party may obtain the following discovery regarding any person disclosed by interrogatories or otherwise as a person expected to be called as an expert witness at trial: The scope of employment in the pending case and the compensation for such service, FL ST RCP Rule 1.280(b)(5)(A)(iii)(1); The expert's general litigation experience, including the percentage of work performed for plaintiffs and defendants, FL ST RCP Rule 1.280(b)(5)(A)(iii)(2); The identity of other cases, within a reasonable time period, in which the expert has testified by deposition or at trial, FL ST RCP Rule 1.280(b)(5)(A)(iii)(3); An approximation of the portion of the expert's involvement as an expert witness, which may be based on the number of hours, percentage of hours, or percentage of earned income derived from serving as an expert witness; however, the expert shall not be required to disclose his or her earnings as an expert witness or income derived from other services. FL ST RCP Rule 1.280(b)(5)(A)(iii)(4).
- An expert may be required to produce financial and business records only under the most unusual or compelling circumstances and may not be compelled to compile or produce nonexistent documents. Upon motion, the court may order further discovery by other means, subject to such restrictions as to scope and other provisions pursuant to FL ST RCP Rule 1.280(b)(5)(C) concerning fees and expenses as the court may deem appropriate. FL ST RCP Rule 1.280(b)(5).
- A party may discover facts known or opinions held by an expert who has been retained or specially employed by another party in anticipation of litigation or preparation for trial and

who is not expected to be called as a witness at trial, only as provided in FL ST RCP Rule 1.360(b) or upon a showing of exceptional circumstances under which it is impracticable for the party seeking discovery to obtain facts or opinions on the same subject by other means. FL ST RCP Rule 1.280(b)(5)(B).

- Unless manifest injustice would result, the court shall require that the party seeking discovery pay the expert a reasonable fee for time spent in responding to discovery under FL ST RCP Rule 1.280(b)(5)(A) and FL ST RCP Rule 1.280(b)(5)(B); and concerning discovery from an expert obtained under FL ST RCP Rule 1.280(b)(5)(A) the court may require, and concerning discovery obtained under FL ST RCP Rule 1.280(b)(5)(B) shall require, the party seeking discovery to pay the other party a fair part of the fees and expenses reasonably incurred by the latter party in obtaining facts and opinions from the expert. FL ST RCP Rule 1.280(b)(5)(C).
- As used in the Florida Rules of Civil Procedure an expert shall be an expert witness as defined in FL ST RCP Rule 1.390(a). FL ST RCP Rule 1.280(b)(5)(D).

vi. *Claims to privilege or protection.* When a party withholds information otherwise discoverable under the Florida Rules of Civil Procedure by claiming that it is privileged or subject to protection as trial preparation material, the party shall make the claim expressly and shall describe the nature of the documents, communications, or things not produced or disclosed in a manner that, without revealing information itself privileged or protected, will enable other parties to assess the applicability of the privilege or protection. FL ST RCP Rule 1.280(b)(6).

c. *Limitations on discovery of electronically stored information*

i. A person may object to discovery of electronically stored information from sources that the person identifies as not reasonably accessible because of burden or cost. On motion to compel discovery or for a protective order, the person from whom discovery is sought must show that the information sought or the format requested is not reasonably accessible because of undue burden or cost. If that showing is made, the court may nonetheless order the discovery from such sources or in such formats if the requesting party shows good cause. The court may specify conditions of the discovery, including ordering that some or all of the expenses incurred by the person from whom discovery is sought be paid by the party seeking the discovery. FL ST RCP Rule 1.280(d)(1).

ii. In determining any motion involving discovery of electronically stored information, the court must limit the frequency or extent of discovery otherwise allowed by the Florida Rules of Civil Procedure if it determines that (i) the discovery sought is unreasonably cumulative or duplicative, or can be obtained from another source or in another manner that is more convenient, less burdensome, or less expensive; or (ii) the burden or expense of the discovery outweighs its likely benefit, considering the needs of the case, the amount in controversy, the parties' resources, the importance of the issues at stake in the action, and the importance of the discovery in resolving the issues. FL ST RCP Rule 1.280(d)(2).

d. For information on inadvertent disclosure of privileged materials, see FL ST RCP Rule 1.285.

e. *Questioning.* Questions should be brief, clear and simple. Each question should deal with only a single point. Argumentative or unnecessary embarrassing questions are out of order. The purpose of a deposition is not to harass or intimidate, but simply to make a clear and unambiguous record of what the witness' testimony would be at trial or to locate other witnesses or admissible evidence. FL ST 9 J CIR SECTION 14(b).

f. *Multiple depositions of same witness.* Generally, a witness or party should be deposed only once in a given case. All counsel of record should be given notice of the deposition and an opportunity to examine. Counsel who fail to attend or fail to examine a witness after notice shall be deemed to have waived their right to depose the witness. A second deposition may be taken of a witness only upon stipulation of counsel or court order, and if allowed will generally be limited to new matters occurring after the first deposition. FL ST 9 J CIR SECTION 14(e).

2. *Notice of deposition*

a. *Upon oral examination.* A party desiring to take the deposition of any person upon oral examination shall give reasonable notice in writing to every other party to the action. The notice shall state the time and place for taking the deposition and the name and address of each person to be examined, if known, and, if the name is not known, a general description sufficient to identify the person or the particular class or group to which the person belongs. If a subpoena duces tecum is to be served on the person to be examined, the designation of the materials to be produced under the subpoena shall be attached to or included in the notice. FL ST RCP Rule 1.310(b)(1).

b. *Upon written examination.* A party desiring to take a deposition upon written questions shall serve a notice stating: (1) the name and address of the person who is to answer them, if known, and, if the name is not known, a general description sufficient to identify the person or the particular class or group to which that person belongs, and (2) the name or descriptive title and address of the officer before whom the deposition is to be taken. FL ST RCP Rule 1.320(a).

3. *When leave of court required.* Leave of court, granted with or without notice, must be obtained only if the plaintiff seeks to take a deposition within thirty (30) days after service of the process and initial pleading upon any defendant, except that leave is not required if a defendant has served a notice of taking deposition or otherwise sought discovery. FL ST RCP Rule 1.310(a)..

a. *Exceptions.* Leave of court is not required for the taking of a deposition by plaintiff if the notice states that the person to be examined is about to go out of the state and will be unavailable for examination unless a deposition is taken before expiration of the thirty (30) day period. If a party shows that when served with notice under FL ST RCP Rule 1.310(b) that party was unable through the exercise of diligence to obtain counsel to represent the party at the taking of the deposition, the deposition may not be used against that party. FL ST RCP Rule 1.310(b)(2).

b. *Persons in prison.* The deposition of a person confined in prison may be taken only by leave of court on such terms as the court prescribes. FL ST RCP Rule 1.310(a).

4. *Deposition procedure*

a. *Who may take depositions.* Depositions may be taken before any notary public or judicial officer or before any officer authorized by the statutes of Florida to take acknowledgments or proof of executions of deeds or by any person appointed by the court in which the action is pending. FL ST RCP Rule 1.300(a).

i. *In foreign countries.* In a foreign country depositions may be taken: on notice before a person authorized to administer oaths in the place in which the examination is held, either by the law thereof or by the law of Florida or of the United States; before a person commissioned by the court, and a person so commissioned shall have the power by virtue of the commission to administer any necessary oath and take testimony; or pursuant to a letter rogatory. FL ST RCP Rule 1.300(b).

ii. *Selection by stipulation.* If the parties so stipulate in writing, depositions may be taken before any person at any time or place upon any notice and in any manner and when so taken may be used like other depositions. FL ST RCP Rule 1.300(c).

iii. *Persons disqualified.* Unless so stipulated by the parties, no deposition shall be taken before a person who is a relative, employee, attorney, or counsel of any of the parties, is a relative or employee of any of the parties' attorney or counsel, or is financially interested in the action. FL ST RCP Rule 1.300(d).

b. *Depositions before action*

i. *Petition.* A person who desires to perpetuate that person's own testimony or that of another person regarding any matter that may be cognizable in any Florida court may file a verified petition in the circuit court in the county of the residence of any expected adverse party. The petition shall be entitled in the name of the petitioner and shall show:

- That the petitioner expects to be a party to an action cognizable in a court of Florida, but is presently unable to bring the action;
- The subject matter of the expected action and the petitioner's interest therein;
- The facts which the petitioner desires to establish by the proposed testimony and the petitioner's reasons for desiring to perpetuate it;

- The names or a description of the persons the petitioner expects will be adverse parties and their addresses so far as known; and
- The names and addresses of the persons to be examined and the substance of the testimony which the petitioner expects to elicit from each; and shall ask for an order authorizing the petitioner to take the deposition of the persons to be examined named in the petition for the purpose of perpetuating their testimony. FL ST RCP Rule 1.290(a)(1).

ii. *Notice and service.* After submitting the petition, the petitioner must thereafter serve a notice upon each person named in the petition as an expected adverse party, together with a copy of the petition, stating that the petitioner will apply to the court at a time and place named therein for an order described in the petition. At least twenty (20) days before the date of hearing the notice shall be served either within or without the county in the manner provided by law for service of summons, but if such service cannot with due diligence be made upon any expected adverse party named in the petition, the court may make an order for service by publication or otherwise, and shall appoint an attorney for persons not served in the manner provided by law for service of summons who shall represent them, and if they are not otherwise represented, shall cross-examine the deponent. FL ST RCP Rule 1.290(a)(2).

iii. *Order and examination.* If the court is satisfied that the perpetuation of the testimony may prevent a failure or delay of justice, it shall make an order designating or describing the persons whose depositions may be taken and specifying the subject matter of the examination and whether the deposition shall be taken upon oral examination or written interrogatories. The deposition may then be taken in accordance with the rules governing depositions. FL ST RCP Rule 1.290(a)(3).

iv. *Use of deposition.* A deposition taken before an action and in accordance with the procedures above may be used in any action involving the same subject matter subsequently brought in any court. FL ST RCP Rule 1.290(a)(4).

c. *Depositions upon oral examination*

i. *Enlargement of time.* For cause shown the court may enlarge or shorten the time for taking the deposition. FL ST RCP Rule 1.310(b)(3).

ii. *Videotaped depositions.* Any deposition may be recorded by videotape without leave of the court or stipulation of the parties, provided the deposition is taken in accordance with the following:

- *Notice.* A party intending to videotape a deposition shall state in the notice that the deposition is to be videotaped and shall give the name and address of the operator. Any subpoena served on the person to be examined shall state the method or methods for recording the testimony. FL ST RCP Rule 1.310(b)(4)(A).
- *Stenographer.* Videotaped depositions shall also be recorded stenographically, unless all parties agree otherwise. FL ST RCP Rule 1.310(b)(4)(B).
- *Procedure.* At the beginning of the deposition, the officer before whom it is taken shall, on camera: (i) identify the style of the action, (ii) state the date, and (iii) swear the witness. FL ST RCP Rule 1.310(b)(4)(C).
- *Custody of tape and copies.* The attorney for the party requesting the videotaping of the deposition shall take custody of and be responsible for the safeguarding of the videotape, shall permit the viewing of it by the opposing party, and, if requested, shall provide a copy of the videotape at the expense of the party requesting the copy. FL ST RCP Rule 1.310(b)(4)(D).
- *Cost of videotaped depositions.* The party requesting the videotaping shall bear the initial cost of videotaping. FL ST RCP Rule 1.310(b)(4)(E).

iii. *Production of documents.* The notice to a party deponent may be accompanied by a request for the production of documents and tangible things at the taking of the deposition. The procedure of FL ST RCP Rule 1.350 shall apply to the request. FL ST RCP Rule 1.351 provides the

exclusive procedure for obtaining documents or things by subpoena from nonparties without deposing the custodian or other person in possession of the documents. FL ST RCP Rule 1.310(b)(5).

iv. *Deposing organizations.* In the notice a party may name as the deponent a public or private corporation, a partnership or association, or a governmental agency, and designate with reasonable particularity the matters on which examination is requested. The organization so named shall designate one or more officers, directors, or managing agents, or other persons who consent to do so, to testify on its behalf and may state the matters on which each person designated will testify. The persons so designated shall testify about matters known or reasonably available to the organization. FL ST RCP Rule 1.310(b)(6).

v. *Depositions by telephone.* On motion the court may order that the testimony at a deposition be taken by telephone. The order may prescribe the manner in which the deposition will be taken. A party may also arrange for a stenographic transcription at that party's own initial expense. FL ST RCP Rule 1.310(b)(7).

vi. *Deposing a minor.* Any minor subpoenaed for testimony shall have the right to be accompanied by a parent or guardian at all times during the taking of testimony notwithstanding the invocation of the rule of sequestration of section FL ST § 90.616, except upon a showing that the presence of a parent or guardian is likely to have a material, negative impact on the credibility or accuracy of the minor's testimony, or that the interests of the parent or guardian are in actual or potential conflict with the interests of the minor. FL ST RCP Rule 1.310(b)(8).

vii. *Examination and cross-examination.* Examination and cross-examination of witnesses may proceed as permitted at the trial. FL ST RCP Rule 1.310(c).

viii. *Oath.* The officer before whom the deposition is to be taken shall put the witness on oath and shall personally, or by someone acting under the officer's direction and in the officer's presence, record the testimony of the witness, except that when a deposition is being taken by telephone, the witness shall be sworn by a person present with the witness who is qualified to administer an oath in that location. FL ST RCP Rule 1.310(c).

ix. *Record of examination.* The deposition testimony must be taken stenographically or recorded by any other means ordered. If requested by one of the parties, the testimony shall be transcribed at the initial cost of the requesting party and prompt notice of the request shall be given to all other parties. FL ST RCP Rule 1.310(c).

x. *Objections.* All objections made at time of the examination to the qualifications of the officer taking the deposition, the manner of taking it, the evidence presented, or the conduct of any party, and any other objection to the proceedings shall be noted by the officer upon the deposition. Any objection during a deposition shall be stated concisely and in a nonargumentative and nonsuggestive manner. A party may instruct a deponent not to answer only when necessary to preserve a privilege, to enforce a limitation on evidence directed by the court, or to present a motion under FL ST RCP Rule 1.310(d). FL ST RCP Rule 1.310(c).

- Otherwise, evidence objected to shall be taken subject to the objections. Instead of participating in the oral examination, parties may serve written questions in a sealed envelope on the party taking the deposition and that party shall transmit them to the officer, who shall propound them to the witness and record the answers verbatim. FL ST RCP Rule 1.310(c).

xi. *Motion to terminate or limit examination.* At any time during the taking of the deposition, on motion of a party or of the deponent and upon a showing that the examination is being conducted in bad faith or in such manner as unreasonably to annoy, embarrass, or oppress the deponent or party, or that improper objections and instructions to a deponent not to answer are being made, the court in which the action is pending or the circuit court where the deposition is being taken may order the officer conducting the examination to cease forthwith from taking the deposition or may limit the scope and manner of the taking of the deposition under the scope of permissible discovery. FL ST RCP Rule 1.310(d).

- If the order terminates the examination, it shall be resumed thereafter only upon the order of the court in which the action is pending. Upon demand of any party or the deponent, the taking of the deposition shall be suspended for the time necessary to make a motion for an order. FL ST RCP Rule 1.310(d).

xii. *Deponent review.* If the testimony is transcribed, the transcript shall be furnished to the witness for examination and shall be read to or by the witness unless the examination and reading are waived by the witness and by the parties. Any changes in form or substance that the witness wants to make shall be listed in writing by the officer with a statement of the reasons given by the witness for making the changes. The changes shall be attached to the transcript. It shall then be signed by the witness unless the parties waived the signing or the witness is ill, cannot be found, or refuses to sign. If the transcript is not signed by the witness within a reasonable time after it is furnished to the witness, the officer shall sign the transcript and state on the transcript the waiver, illness, absence of the witness, or refusal to sign with any reasons given. The deposition may then be used as fully as though signed unless the court holds that the reasons given for the refusal to sign require rejection of the deposition wholly or partly, on motion under FL ST RCP Rule 1.330(d)(4). FL ST RCP Rule 1.310(e).

xiii. *Certification and inspection.* If the deposition is transcribed, the officer shall certify on each copy of the deposition that the witness was duly sworn by the officer and that the deposition is a true record of the testimony given by the witness. Documents and things produced for inspection during the examination of the witness shall be marked for identification and annexed to and returned with the deposition upon the request of a party, and may be inspected and copied by any party, except that the person producing the materials may substitute copies to be marked for identification if that person affords to all parties fair opportunity to verify the copies by comparison with the originals. If the person producing the materials requests their return, the officer shall mark them, give each party an opportunity to inspect and copy them, and return them to the person producing them and the materials may then be used in the same manner as if annexed to and returned with the deposition. FL ST RCP Rule 1.310(f)(1).

xiv. *Copies.* Upon payment of reasonable charges, the officer shall furnish a copy of the deposition to any party or to the deponent. FL ST RCP Rule 1.310(f)(2). A party or witness who does not have a copy of the deposition may obtain it from the officer taking the deposition unless the court orders otherwise. If the deposition is obtained from a person other than the officer, the reasonable cost of reproducing the copies shall be paid to the person by the requesting party or witness. FL ST RCP Rule 1.310(g).

d. *Depositions upon written examination*

i. *Deposing an organization upon written examination.* A deposition upon written questions may be taken of a public or private corporation, a partnership or association, or a governmental agency in accordance with FL ST RCP Rule 1.310(b)(6). FL ST RCP Rule 1.320(a).

ii. *Cross, redirect, and recross questions.* Within thirty (30) days after the notice and written questions are served, a party may serve cross questions upon all other parties. Within ten (10) days after being served with cross questions, a party may serve redirect questions upon all other parties. Within ten (10) days after being served with redirect questions, a party may serve recross questions upon all other parties. The court may for cause shown enlarge or shorten the time. FL ST RCP Rule 1.320(a).

iii. *Procedure.* A copy of the notice and copies of all questions served shall be delivered by the party taking the depositions to the officer designated in the notice, who shall proceed promptly to take the testimony of the witness in the manner provided by FL ST RCP Rule 1.310(c), FL ST RCP Rule 1.310(e), and FL ST RCP Rule 1.310(f) in response to the questions and to prepare the deposition, attaching the copy of the notice and the questions received by the officer. The questions shall not be filed separately from the deposition unless a party seeks to have the court consider the questions before the questions are submitted to the witness. FL ST RCP Rule 1.320(b).

5. *Arbitration and mediation*

a. *Referral to arbitration and mediation.* Except as hereinafter provided or as otherwise prohibited by

law, the presiding judge may enter an order referring all or any part of a contested civil matter to mediation or arbitration. The parties to any contested civil matter may file a written stipulation to mediate or arbitrate any issue between them at any time. Such stipulation shall be incorporated into the order of referral. FL ST RCP Rule 1.700(a).

b. *Arbitration*

   i. *Exclusions.* A civil action shall be ordered to arbitration or arbitration in conjunction with mediation upon stipulation of the parties. A civil action may be ordered to arbitration or arbitration in conjunction with mediation upon motion of any party or by the court, if the judge determines the action to be of such a nature that arbitration could be of benefit to the litigants or the court. FL ST RCP Rule 1.800.

      - Under no circumstances may the following categories of actions be referred to arbitration: (1) bond estreatures; (2) habeas corpus or other extraordinary writs; (3) bond validations; (4) civil or criminal contempt; (5) such other matters as may be specified by order of the chief judge in the circuit. FL ST RCP Rule 1.800.

   ii. For more information regarding arbitration, please see FL ST RCP Rule 1.810; FL ST RCP Rule 1.820; FL ST RCP Rule 1.830.

c. *Mediation.* For more information regarding mediation, please see FL ST RCP Rule 1.710; FL ST RCP Rule 1.720; FL ST RCP Rule 1.730; and FL ST RCP Rule 1.750.

d. *Local arbitration policy.* It is the policy of the Civil Division judges to maximize the use of alternative dispute resolution procedures. Except where prohibited by statute, mediation will be ordered in all cases where jury trial is requested and in selected cases which are to be tried non-jury. Also, selected cases will be referred for court-annexed non-binding arbitration through the Orange County Bar Association Arbitration Service. Counsel may move to dispense with or defer mediation or arbitration or move to modify the referral order for good cause. FL ST 9 J CIR SECTION 15.

6. *Rules of court*

   a. *Rules of civil procedure.* The Florida Rules of Civil Procedure apply to all actions of a civil nature and all special statutory proceedings in the circuit courts and county courts except those to which the Florida Probate Rules, the Florida Family Law Rules of Procedure, or the Small Claims Rules apply. FL ST RCP Rule 1.010.

      i. The form, content, procedure, and time for pleading in all special statutory proceedings shall be as prescribed by the statutes governing the proceeding unless the Florida Rules of Civil Procedure specifically provide to the contrary. FL ST RCP Rule 1.010.

      ii. The Florida Rules of Civil Procedure shall be construed to secure the just, speedy, and inexpensive determination of every action. FL ST RCP Rule 1.010.

   b. *Rules of judicial administration.* The Florida Rules of Judicial Administration shall apply to administrative matters in all courts to which the Florida Rules of Judicial Administration are applicable by their terms. The Florida Rules of Judicial Administration shall be construed to secure the speedy and inexpensive determination of every proceeding to which they are applicable. The Florida Rules of Judicial Administration shall supersede all conflicting rules and statutes. FL ST J ADMIN Rule 2.110.

   c. *Business court procedures.* For rules specific to Business Court, please see FL ST 9 J CIR ORANGE CIV SECTION 1, et seq.

7. *Communication between counsel.* Counsel should be guided by courtesy, candor and common sense and conform to the Florida Rules of Civil Procedure and any applicable orders. In particular, counsel should have in mind the broad scope of discovery allowed by the Civil Rules of Procedure. Direct and informal communication between counsel is encouraged to facilitate discovery and resolve disputes. FL ST 9 J CIR SECTION 13(a).

D. Documents

1. *Deposition upon oral or written examination*
   a. *Required documents*
      i. *Notice of deposition.* Please see the General Requirements section of this document for information on the content of a notice of deposition upon oral examination.
      ii. *Certificate of service.* A certificate of service of the interrogatories shall be filed, giving the date of service and the name of the party to whom they were directed. FL ST RCP Rule 1.340(e). When any attorney certifies in substance: "I certify that a copy hereof has been furnished to (here insert name or names and addresses used for service) by (e-mail) (delivery) (mail) (fax) on .... (date) ....________________ Attorney" the certificate is taken as prima facie proof of such service in compliance with FL ST J ADMIN Rule 2.516. FL ST J ADMIN Rule 2.516(f).
   b. *Supplemental documents*
      i. *Motion for leave to take deposition.* See the Timing section for information on when leave is required.
      ii. *Subpoena.* See the Timing section for requirements of when a subpoena is required.
      iii. *Request for production of documents.* See the General Requirements section for further information.

E. Format

1. *Documents; Type and size.* Documents subject to the exceptions set forth in FL ST J ADMIN Rule 2.525(d) shall be filed on recycled paper measuring eight and one half by eleven (8 1/2 by 11) inches. For purposes of FL ST J ADMIN Rule 2.520, paper is recycled if it contains a minimum content of fifty (50) percent waste paper. Xerographic reduction of legal-size (eight and one half by fourteen (8 1/2 by 14) inches) documents to letter size (eight and one half by eleven (8 1/2 by 11) inches) is prohibited. All other documents filed by electronic transmission shall be filed in a format capable of being printed in a format consistent with the provisions of FL ST J ADMIN Rule 2.250. FL ST J ADMIN Rule 2.520(b).
   a. *Exhibits.* Any exhibit or attachment filed with pleadings or papers may be filed in its original size. FL ST J ADMIN Rule 2.520(c).
   b. *Recording space.* On all papers and documents prepared and filed by the court or by any party to a proceeding which are to be recorded in the public records of any county, including but not limited to final money judgments and notices of lis pendens, a three (3) inch by three (3) inch space at the top right-hand corner on the first page and a one (1) inch by three (3) inch space at the top right-hand corner on each subsequent page shall be left blank and reserved for use by the clerk of court. FL ST J ADMIN Rule 2.520(d).
      i. *Exceptions to recording space.* Any papers or documents created by persons or entities over which the filing party has no control, including but not limited to wills, codicils, trusts, or other testamentary documents; documents prepared or executed by any public officer; documents prepared, executed, acknowledged, or proved outside of the State of Florida; or documents created by State or Federal government agencies, may be filed without the space required by FL ST J ADMIN Rule 2.520. FL ST J ADMIN Rule 2.520(e).
   c. *Noncompliance.* No clerk of court is permitted to refuse to file any document or paper because of noncompliance with the Florida Rules of Judicial Administration. However, upon request of the clerk of court, noncomplying documents must be resubmitted in accordance with the formatting rules. FL ST J ADMIN Rule 2.520(f).
   d. *Proposed orders*
      i. All orders will be on eight and a half by eleven (8 1/2 by 11) inch plain white paper (not lined or letterhead paper) and be double spaced. FL ST 9 J CIR SECTION 12(B)(1).
      ii. The order must contain a title indicating what matter the order pertains to, e.g., "Order On Defendant Smith's Motion To Dismiss." FL ST 9 J CIR SECTION 12(B)(2).

iii. The preamble of the order should include the date of the hearing and what motions were heard. FL ST 9 J CIR SECTION 12(B)(3).

iv. The adjudication portion of the order should state what relief is ordered. Simply stating that "the motion is granted" without more is insufficient. FL ST 9 J CIR SECTION 12(B)(4).

v. The order should indicate the specific time period of any act ordered to be done and should state whether the time period runs from the date of the hearing or the date the order is signed or some other specified date. FL ST 9 J CIR SECTION 12(B)(5).

vi. The order should contain a full certificate of service with the complete names and addresses of the attorneys and unrepresented parties to be served. Merely showing "copies to" is insufficient. FL ST 9 J CIR SECTION 12(B)(6).

vii. If an order of dismissal is final (i.e., it disposes of the entire case) the title should contain the word "Final." When the order is not final but leaves other counts or claims against other defendants pending, it should so state in a separate paragraph. FL ST 9 J CIR SECTION 12(B)(7).

viii. When submitting stipulations, orders shall be by separate order, not attached to the stipulation. FL ST 9 J CIR SECTION 12(B)(8).

ix. Counsel preparing the Final Judgment or order should draft and circulate copies within two (2) working days of the ruling or jury verdict. If counsel preparing the Final Judgment or order gets approval as to form of the order from all counsel, the original with copies and envelopes should be sent directly to the judge with a cover letter stating all counsel agree to the form of the order or judgment. If other counsel objects to the form or cannot be reached for approval, counsel preparing the judgment or order shall notice a motion for entry of the order or judgment. If objecting counsel does not furnish the judge prior to or at the hearing with a proposed judgment or order version with copies under cover letter stating the reasons for the objection, all objections will be deemed waived. Orders and judgments should not be submitted to the judge to hold waiting for an objection. FL ST 9 J CIR SECTION 12(D).

2. *Caption.* Every pleading, motion, order, judgment, or other paper shall have a caption containing the name of the court, the file number, and except for in rem proceedings, including forfeiture proceedings, the name of the first party on each side with an appropriate indication of other parties, and a designation identifying the party filing it and its nature or the nature of the order, as the case may be. In any in rem proceeding, every pleading, motion, order, judgment, or other paper shall have a caption containing the name of the court, the file number, the style "In re" (followed by the name or general description of the property), and a designation of the person or entity filing it and its nature or the nature of the order, as the case may be. In an in rem forfeiture proceeding, the style shall be "In re forfeiture of" (followed by the name of the general description of the property). All papers filed in the action shall be styled in such a manner as to indicate clearly the subject matter of the paper and the party requesting or obtaining relief. FL ST RCP Rule 1.100(c)(1).

3. *Writing and written defined.* Writing or written means a document containing information, an application, or a stipulation. FL ST RCP Rule 1.080(c).

4. *Rule abbreviations*

   a. The Florida Rules of Civil Procedure and shall be abbreviated as Fla.R.Civ.P. FL ST RCP Rule 1.010.

   b. The Florida Rules of Judicial Administration shall be abbreviated as Fla. R. Jud. Admin. FL ST J ADMIN Rule 2.110.

5. *Nonverification.* Except when otherwise specifically provided by the Florida Rules of Civil Procedure or an applicable statute, every pleading or other document of a party represented by an attorney need not be verified or accompanied by an affidavit. FL ST RCP Rule 1.030; FL ST J ADMIN Rule 2.515(a).

6. *Unrepresented parties.* An unrepresented party must file his or her papers with the clerk and send copies to other attorneys or unrepresented parties. All such papers must be typed double-spaced on plain white eight and a half by eleven (8 1/2 by 11) inch paper, with the name of the case and case number at the top

and the party's mailing address, telephone number and FAX number, if any, below his or her signature at the end of the paper. Such unrepresented party must immediately notify the Clerk and all other counsel or parties of record in writing of any change in mailing address or telephone or FAX number. Failure to promptly notify of change of address could result in a dismissal or default entered against such party. FL ST 9 J CIR SECTION 7(B)(5).

7. *Attorney signature*
   a. *Attorney signature.* Every pleading and other document of a party represented by an attorney shall be signed by at least one (1) attorney of record in that attorney's individual name whose current record Florida Bar address, telephone number, including area code, primary e-mail address and secondary e-mail addresses, if any, and Florida Bar number shall be stated, and who shall be duly licensed to practice law in Florida or who shall have received permission to appear in the particular case as provided in FL ST J ADMIN Rule 2.510. FL ST J ADMIN Rule 2.515(a).
      i. The attorney may be required by the court to give the address of, and to vouch for the attorney's authority to represent, the party. FL ST J ADMIN Rule 2.515(a).
      ii. The signature of an attorney shall constitute a certificate by the attorney that the attorney has read the pleading or other document; that to the best of the attorney's knowledge, information, and belief there is good ground to support it; and that it is not interposed for delay. FL ST J ADMIN Rule 2.515(a).
      iii. If a pleading is not signed or is signed with intent to defeat the purpose of FL ST J ADMIN Rule 2.515, it may be stricken and the action may proceed as though the pleading or other document had not been served. FL ST J ADMIN Rule 2.515(a).
   b. *Pro se litigant signature.* A party who is not represented by an attorney shall sign any pleading or other paper and state the party's address and telephone number, including area code. FL ST J ADMIN Rule 2.515(b).
   c. *Form of signature*
      i. The signatures required on pleadings and documents by FL ST J ADMIN Rule 2.515(a) and FL ST J ADMIN Rule 2.515(b) may be:
         - Original signatures;
         - Original signatures that have been reproduced by electronic means, such as on electronically transmitted documents or photocopied documents;
         - Electronic signatures using the "/s/," "s/," or "/s" formats by or at the direction of the person signing; or
         - Any other signature format authorized by general law, so long as the clerk where the proceeding is pending has the capability of receiving and has obtained approval from the Supreme Court of Florida to accept pleadings and documents with that signature format. FL ST J ADMIN Rule 2.515(c)(1).
      ii. An attorney, party, or other person who files a pleading or paper by electronic transmission that does not contain the original signature of that attorney, party, or other person shall file that identical pleading or paper in paper form containing an original signature of that attorney, party, or other person (hereinafter called the follow-up filing) immediately thereafter. The follow-up filing is not required if the Supreme Court of Florida has entered an order directing the clerk of court to discontinue accepting the follow-up filing. FL ST J ADMIN Rule 2.515(c)(2).
8. *Forms*
   a. *Process.* The forms of process, notice of lis pendens, and notice of action provided in the Florida Rules of Civil Procedure are sufficient. Variations from the forms do not void process or notices that are otherwise sufficient. FL ST RCP Rule 1.900(a).
   b. *Other forms.* The other forms provided in the Florida Rules of Civil Procedure are sufficient for the matters that are covered by them. So long as the substance is expressed without prolixity, the forms may be varied to meet the facts of a particular case. FL ST RCP Rule 1.900(b).

c. *Formal matters.* Captions, except for the designation of the paper, are omitted from the forms provided in the Florida Rules of Civil Procedure. A general form of caption is the first form provided. Signatures are omitted from pleadings and motions. FL ST RCP Rule 1.900(c).

9. *Notices to persons with disabilities.* All notices of court proceedings to be held in a public facility, and all process compelling appearance at such proceedings, shall include the following statement in bold face, fourteen (14) point Times New Roman or Courier font: "If you are a person with a disability who needs any accommodation in order to participate in this proceeding, you are entitled, at no cost to you, to the provision of certain assistance. Please contact [identify applicable court personnel by name, address, and telephone number] at least seven (7) days before your scheduled court appearance, or immediately upon receiving this notification if the time before the scheduled appearance is less than seven (7) days; if you are hearing or voice impaired, call 711." FL ST J ADMIN Rule 2.540(c)(1).

10. *Minimization of the filing of sensitive information*

a. *Limitations for court filings.* Unless authorized by FL ST J ADMIN Rule 2.425(b), statute, another rule of court, or the court orders otherwise, designated sensitive information filed with the court must be limited to the following format:

i. The initials of a person known to be a minor;

ii. The year of birth of a person's birth date;

iii. No portion of any: Social security number, Bank account number, Credit card account number, Charge account number, or Debit account number;

iv. The last four digits of any: Taxpayer identification number (TIN), Employee identification number, Driver's license number, Passport number, Telephone number, Financial account number, except as set forth in FL ST J ADMIN Rule 2.425(a)(3), Brokerage account number, Insurance policy account number, Loan account number, Customer account number, or Patient or health care number;

v. A truncated version of any: Email address, Computer user name, Password, or Personal identification number (PIN); and

vi. A truncated version of any other sensitive information as provided by court order. FL ST J ADMIN Rule 2.425(a).

b. *Exceptions.* FL ST J ADMIN Rule 2.425(a) does not apply to the following:

i. An account number which identifies the property alleged to be the subject of a proceeding;

ii. The record of an administrative or agency proceeding;

iii. The record in appellate or review proceedings;

iv. The birth date of a minor whenever the birth date is necessary for the court to establish or maintain subject matter jurisdiction;

v. The name of a minor in any order relating to parental responsibility, time-sharing, or child support;

vi. The name of a minor in any document or order affecting the minor's ownership of real property;

vii. The birth date of a party in a writ of attachment or notice to payor;

viii. In traffic and criminal proceedings: a pro se filing; a court filing that is related to a criminal matter or investigation and that is prepared before the filing of a criminal charge or is not filed as part of any docketed criminal case; an arrest or search warrant or any information in support thereof; a charging document and an affidavit or other documents filed in support of any charging document, including any driving records; a statement of particulars; discovery material introduced into evidence or otherwise filed with the court; and all information necessary for the proper issuance and execution of a subpoena duces tecum;

ix. Information used by the clerk for case maintenance purposes or the courts for case management purposes; and

x. Information which is relevant and material to an issue before the court. FL ST J ADMIN Rule 2.425(b).

c. *Remedies.* Upon motion by a party or interested person or sua sponte by the court, the court may order remedies, sanctions or both for a violation of FL ST J ADMIN Rule 2.425(a). Following notice and an opportunity to respond, the court may impose sanctions if such filing was not made in good faith. FL ST J ADMIN Rule 2.425(c).

d. *Motions not restricted.* FL ST J ADMIN Rule 2.425 does not restrict a party's right to move for protective order, to move to file documents under seal, or to request a determination of the confidentiality of records. FL ST J ADMIN Rule 2.425(d).

e. *Application.* FL ST J ADMIN Rule 2.425 does not affect the application of constitutional provisions, statutes, or rules of court regarding confidential information or access to public information. FL ST J ADMIN Rule 2.425(e).

F. Filing and Service Requirements

1. *Court filing of documents and discovery.* Information obtained during discovery shall not be filed with the court until such time as it is filed for good cause. The requirement of good cause is satisfied only where the filing of the information is allowed or required by another applicable rule of procedure or by court order. All filings of discovery documents shall comply with FL ST J ADMIN Rule 2.425. The court shall have the authority to impose sanctions for violation of FL ST RCP Rule 1.280. FL ST RCP Rule 1.280(g).

   a. *Filing of copies.* Depositions are not be filed with the Clerk unless they are needed for a hearing or trial. FL ST 9 J CIR SECTION 13(c). A copy of a deposition may be filed only under the following circumstances:

      i. It may be filed in compliance with FL ST J ADMIN Rule 2.425 and FL ST RCP Rule 1.280(f) by a party or the witness when the contents of the deposition must be considered by the court on any matter pending before the court. Prompt notice of the filing of the deposition shall be given to all parties unless notice is waived. A party filing the deposition shall furnish a copy of the deposition or the part being filed to other parties unless the party already has a copy. FL ST RCP Rule 1.310(f)(3)(A).

      ii. If the court determines that a deposition previously taken is necessary for the decision of a matter pending before the court, the court may order that a copy be filed by any party at the initial cost of the party, and the filing party shall comply with FL ST J ADMIN Rule 2.425 and FL ST RCP Rule 1.280(f). FL ST RCP Rule 1.310(f)(3)(B).

2. *Filing requirements.* All original documents must be filed with the court either before service or immediately thereafter, unless otherwise provided for by general law or other rules. If the original of any bond or other document is not placed in the court file, a certified copy must be so placed by the clerk. FL ST J ADMIN Rule 2.516(d). All documents shall be filed in conformity with the requirements of FL ST J ADMIN Rule 2.525. FL ST RCP Rule 1.080(b). All documents filed in any court shall be filed by electronic transmission in accordance with FL ST J ADMIN Rule 2.525. "Documents" means pleadings, motions, petitions, memoranda, briefs, notices, exhibits, declarations, affidavits, orders, judgments, decrees, writs, opinions, and any other paper or writing submitted to a court. FL ST J ADMIN Rule 2.520(a). All documents that are court records, as defined in FL ST J ADMIN Rule 2.430(a)(1), must be filed by electronic transmission, provided that: (1) the clerk has the ability to accept and retain such documents; (2) the clerk or the chief judge of the circuit has requested permission to accept documents filed by electronic transmission; and (3) the supreme court has entered an order granting permission to the clerk to accept documents filed by electronic transmission. FL ST J ADMIN Rule 2.525(c)(1).

   a. *Definition.* "Electronic transmission of documents" means the sending of information by electronic signals to, by or from a court or clerk, which when received can be transformed and stored or transmitted on paper, microfilm, magnetic storage device, optical imaging system, CD-ROM, flash drive, other electronic data storage system, server, case maintenance system ("CM"), electronic court filing ("ECF") system, statewide or local electronic portal ("e-portal"), or other electronic record keeping system authorized by the supreme court in a format sufficient to communicate the information on the original document in a readable format. Electronic transmission of documents includes electronic mail ("e-mail") and any internet-based transmission procedure, and may include procedures allowing for documents to be signed or verified by electronic means. FL ST J ADMIN Rule 2.525(a).

      i. The filing of documents with the court as required by the Florida Rules of Judicial Adminis-

tration must be made by filing them with the clerk in accordance with FL ST J ADMIN Rule 2.525, except that the judge may permit documents to be filed with the judge, in which event the judge must note the filing date before him or her on the documents and transmit them to the clerk. The date of filing is that shown on the face of the document by the judge's notation or the clerk's time stamp, whichever is earlier. FL ST J ADMIN Rule 2.516(e).

b. *Application.* Any court or clerk of the court may accept the electronic transmission of documents for filing after the clerk, together with input from the chief judge of the circuit, has obtained approval of the procedures and program for doing so from the Supreme Court of Florida. FL ST J ADMIN Rule 2.525(b).

c. *Exceptions*

   i. Paper documents and other submissions may be manually submitted to the clerk or court:
      - When the clerk does not have the ability to accept and retain documents by electronic filing or has not had ECF Procedures approved by the supreme court;
      - For filing by any self-represented party or any self-represented nonparty unless specific ECF Procedures provide a means to file documents electronically. However, any self-represented nonparty that is a governmental or public agency and any other agency, partnership, corporation, or business entity acting on behalf of any governmental or public agency may file documents by electronic transmission if such entity has the capability of filing documents electronically;
      - For filing by attorneys excused from e-mail service in accordance with FL ST J ADMIN Rule 2.516(b);
      - When submitting evidentiary exhibits or filing non-documentary materials;
      - When the filing involves documents in excess of twenty-five (25) megabytes (25MB) in size. For such filings, documents may be transmitted using an electronic storage medium that the clerk has the ability to accept, which may include a CD-ROM, flash drive, or similar storage medium;
      - When filed in open court, as permitted by the court;
      - When paper filing is permitted by any approved statewide or local ECF procedures; and
      - If any court determines that justice so requires. FL ST J ADMIN Rule 2.525(d).

   ii. Any document in paper form submitted under FL ST J ADMIN Rule 2.525(d) is filed when it is received by the clerk or court and the clerk shall immediately thereafter convert any filed paper document to an electronic document. "Convert to an electronic document" means optically capturing an image of a paper document and using character recognition software to recover as much of the document's text as practicable and then indexing and storing the document in the official court file. FL ST J ADMIN Rule 2.525(c)(4).

   iii. Any storage medium submitted under FL ST J ADMIN Rule 2.525(d)(5) is filed when received by the clerk or court and the clerk shall immediately thereafter transfer the electronic documents from the storage device to the official court file. FL ST J ADMIN Rule 2.525(c)(5).

   iv. If the filer of any paper document authorized under FL ST J ADMIN Rule 2.525(d) provides a self-addressed, postage-paid envelope for return of the paper document after it is converted to electronic form by the clerk, the clerk shall place the paper document in the envelope and deposit it in the mail. Except when a paper document is required to be maintained, the clerk may recycle any filed paper document that is not to be returned to the filer. FL ST J ADMIN Rule 2.525(c)(6).

   v. The clerk may convert any paper document filed before the effective date of FL ST J ADMIN Rule 2.525 to an electronic document. Unless the clerk is required to maintain the paper document, if the paper document has been converted to an electronic document by the clerk, the paper document is no longer part of the official court file and may be removed and recycled. FL ST J ADMIN Rule 2.525(c)(7).

d. *Unrepresented parties.* An unrepresented party must file his or her papers with the clerk and send copies to other attorneys or unrepresented parties. FL ST 9 J CIR SECTION 7(B)(5).

   i. An unrepresented party may not communicate privately with the judge either by letter, telephone, in person or otherwise. FL ST 9 J CIR SECTION 7(B)(4).

   ii. Copies of legal papers or other written materials should not be sent to the judge unless specifically requested by the judge or required by the local administrative procedures. Any unrequested or non-required papers or materials sent to a judge may not be read but may be returned to the sender or placed unread into the court file. FL ST 9 J CIR SECTION 7(B)(4).

e. *Official court file.* For information on what constitutes the official court file, please see FL ST J ADMIN Rule 2.525(c)(2), FL ST J ADMIN Rule 2.525(c)(3).

f. *Administration.* All attorneys, parties, or other persons using this rule to file documents are required to make arrangements with the court or clerk for the payment of any charges authorized by general law or the supreme court before filing any document by electronic transmission. FL ST J ADMIN Rule 2.525(f)(2).

g. *Filing date.* The filing date for an electronically transmitted document is the date and time that such filing is acknowledged by an electronic stamp or otherwise, pursuant to any procedure set forth in any ECF Procedures approved by the supreme court, or the date the last page of such filing is received by the court or clerk. FL ST J ADMIN Rule 2.525(f)(3).

h. *Accessibility.* All documents transmitted in any electronic form under FL ST J ADMIN Rule 2.525 must comply with the accessibility requirements of FL ST J ADMIN Rule 2.526. FL ST J ADMIN Rule 2.525(g).

3. *Service requirements.* Every pleading subsequent to the initial pleading, all orders, and every other document filed in the action must be served in conformity with the requirements of FL ST J ADMIN Rule 2.516. FL ST RCP Rule 1.080(a).

   a. *Service; When required.* Unless the court otherwise orders, or a statute or supreme court administrative order specifies a different means of service, every pleading subsequent to the initial pleading and every other document filed in any court proceeding, except applications for witness subpoenas and documents served by formal notice or required to be served in the manner provided for service of formal notice, must be served in accordance with FL ST J ADMIN Rule 2.516 on each party. No service need be made on parties against whom a default has been entered, except that pleadings asserting new or additional claims against them must be served in the manner provided for service of summons. FL ST J ADMIN Rule 2.516(a).

   b. *Service; How made.* When service is required or permitted to be made upon a party represented by an attorney, service must be made upon the attorney unless service upon the party is ordered by the court. FL ST J ADMIN Rule 2.516(b).

      i. *Service by electronic mail ("e-mail").* All documents required or permitted to be served on another party must be served by e-mail, unless FL ST J ADMIN Rule 2.516 otherwise provides. When, in addition to service by e-mail, the sender also utilizes another means of service provided for in FL ST J ADMIN Rule 2.516(b)(2), any differing time limits and other provisions applicable to that other means of service control. FL ST J ADMIN Rule 2.516(b)(1). Any document electronically transmitted to a court or clerk must also be served on all parties and interested persons in accordance with the applicable rules of court. FL ST J ADMIN Rule 2.525(e)(2).

         - *Service on attorneys.* Upon appearing in a proceeding, an attorney must serve a designation of a primary e-mail address and may designate no more than two (2) secondary e-mail addresses. Thereafter, service must be directed to all designated e-mail addresses in that proceeding. Every document filed by an attorney thereafter must include the primary e-mail address of that attorney and any secondary e-mail addresses. If an attorney does not designate any e-mail address for service, documents may be served on that attorney at the e-mail address on record with The Florida Bar. FL ST J ADMIN Rule 2.516(b)(1)(A).

         - *Exception to e-mail service on attorneys.* Service by an attorney on another attorney must

be made by e-mail unless excused by the court. Upon motion by an attorney demonstrating that the attorney has no e-mail account and lacks access to the Internet at the attorney's office, the court may excuse the attorney from the requirements of e-mail service. Service on and by an attorney excused by the court from e-mail service must be by the means provided in FL ST J ADMIN Rule 2.516(b)(2). FL ST J ADMIN Rule 2.516(b)(1)(B).

- *Service on and by parties not represented by an attorney.* Any party not represented by an attorney may serve a designation of a primary e-mail address and also may designate no more than two (2) secondary e-mail addresses to which service must be directed in that proceeding by the means provided in FL ST J ADMIN Rule 2.516(b)(1). If a party not represented by an attorney does not designate an e-mail address for service in a proceeding, service on and by that party must be by the means provided in FL ST J ADMIN Rule 2.516(b)(2). FL ST J ADMIN Rule 2.516(b)(1)(C).
- *Time of service.* Service by e-mail is complete when it is sent. FL ST J ADMIN Rule 2.516(b)(1)(D). An e-mail is deemed served on the date it is sent. FL ST J ADMIN Rule 2.516(b)(1)(D)(i). If the sender learns that the e-mail did not reach the address of the person to be served, the sender must immediately send another copy by e-mail, or by a means authorized by FL ST J ADMIN Rule 2.516(b)(2). FL ST J ADMIN Rule 2.516(b)(1)(D)(ii). E-mail service is treated as service by mail for the computation of time. FL ST J ADMIN Rule 2.516(b)(1)(D)(iii).

ii. *Format of e-mail for service.* Service of a document by e-mail is made by attaching a copy of the document in PDF format to an e-mail sent to all addresses designated by the attorney or party. FL ST J ADMIN Rule 2.516(b)(1)(E).

- All documents served by e-mail must be attached to an e-mail message containing a subject line beginning with the words "SERVICE OF COURT DOCUMENT" in all capital letters, followed by the case number of the proceeding in which the documents are being served. FL ST J ADMIN Rule 2.516(b)(1)(E)(i).
- The body of the e-mail must identify the court in which the proceeding is pending, the case number, the name of the initial party on each side, the title of each document served with that e-mail, and the sender's name and telephone number. FL ST J ADMIN Rule 2.516(b)(1)(E)(ii).
- Any document served by e-mail may be signed by the "/s/" format, as long as the filed original is signed in accordance with the applicable rule of procedure. FL ST J ADMIN Rule 2.516(b)(1)(E)(iii).
- Any e-mail which, together with its attached documents, exceeds five megabytes (5MB) in size, must be divided and sent as separate e-mails, no one of which may exceed five megabytes (5MB) in size and each of which must be sequentially numbered in the subject line. FL ST J ADMIN Rule 2.516(b)(1)(E)(iv).

iii. *Service by other means.* In addition to, and not in lieu of, service by e-mail, service may also be made upon attorneys by any of the means specified in FL ST J ADMIN Rule 2.516(b)(2). Service on and by all parties who are not represented by an attorney and who do not designate an e-mail address, and on and by all attorneys excused from e-mail service, must be made by delivering a copy of the document or by mailing it to the party or attorney at their last known address or, if no address is known, by leaving it with the clerk of the court. Service by mail is complete upon mailing. Delivery of a copy within FL ST J ADMIN Rule 2.516 is complete upon:

- Handing it to the attorney or to the party,
- Leaving it at the attorney's or party's office with a clerk or other person in charge thereof,
- If there is no one in charge, leaving it in a conspicuous place therein,
- If the office is closed or the person to be served has no office, leaving it at the person's usual place of abode with some person of his or her family above fifteen (15) years of age and informing such person of the contents, or

- Transmitting it by facsimile to the attorney's or party's office with a cover sheet containing the sender's name, firm, address, telephone number, and facsimile number, and the number of pages transmitted. When service is made by facsimile, a copy must also be served by any other method permitted by FL ST J ADMIN Rule 2.516. Facsimile service occurs when transmission is complete. FL ST J ADMIN Rule 2.516(b)(2)(A) through FL ST J ADMIN Rule 2.516(b)(2)(E).
- Service by delivery after 5:00 p.m. must be deemed to have been made by mailing on the date of delivery. FL ST J ADMIN Rule 2.516(b)(2)(F).

c. *Service; Numerous defendants.* In actions when the parties are unusually numerous, the court may regulate the service contemplated by the Florida Rules of Judicial Administration on motion or on its own initiative in such manner as may be found to be just and reasonable. FL ST J ADMIN Rule 2.516(c).

d. *Service by clerk.* Service of notices and other documents required to be made by the clerk must also be done as provided in FL ST J ADMIN Rule 2.516(b). FL ST J ADMIN Rule 2.516(g).

G. Hearings

1. There is no hearing required or contemplated with regard to a notice of deposition for admission in the Florida Rules of Civil Procedure.

H. Forms

1. Florida Notice of Deposition Forms

a. Form for motion by plaintiff for leave to take deposition within 20-day period. FL-RCPF R 1.310(6).
b. Form for order on motion for leave to take deposition within 20-day period. FL-RCPF R 1.310(8).
c. Notice of examination; Time and place. FL-RCPF R 1.310(9).
d. Nonparty witness; Subpoena required. FL-RCPF R 1.310(10).
e. Form for notice to take deposition on oral examination. FL-RCPF R 1.310(11).
f. Form for notice of taking multiple depositions. FL-RCPF R 1.310(11.1).
g. Form for notice of taking deposition and examination of documents. FL-RCPF R 1.310(12).
h. Form for notice of taking video deposition duces tecum. FL-RCPF R 1.310(13).
i. Form for motion to modify time for taking deposition. FL-RCPF R 1.310(14).
j. Form for motion to take deposition by telephone. FL-RCPF R 1.310(16).
k. Form for order permitting deposition by telephone. FL-RCPF R 1.310(17).
l. Form for notice of taking deposition by telephone. FL-RCPF R 1.310(18).
m. Form for notice of deposition upon written questions. FL-RCPF R 1.320(2).
n. Form of questions. FL-RCPF R 1.320(3).
o. Form of cross-questions. FL-RCPF R 1.320(4).
p. Form for objection to form of written questions. FL-RCPF R 1.320(6).

I. Checklist

(I) ❑ Matters to be considered by deposing party (oral depositions)
- (a) ❑ Required documents
  - (1) ❑ Notice of deposition
  - (2) ❑ Certificate of service
- (b) ❑ Supplemental documents
  - (1) ❑ Motion for leave to request deposition
  - (2) ❑ Subpoena
  - (3) ❑ Request for production of documents

(c) ❑ Time for service of notice of deposition
  (1) ❑ After commencement of action
  (2) ❑ Within thirty (30) days after service of initial pleadings by leave of court only

(II) ❑ Matters to be considered by deponent (oral depositions)
(a) ❑ Required documents
  (1) ❑ Production of documents (if subpoenaed)

(III) ❑ Matters to be considered by deposing party (depositions by written questions)
(a) ❑ Required documents
  (1) ❑ Notice of deposition
  (2) ❑ Written questions
  (3) ❑ Certificate of service
(b) ❑ Supplemental documents
  (1) ❑ Motion for leave to request deposition
  (2) ❑ Subpoena
  (3) ❑ Request for production of documents
(c) ❑ Time for service of direct and redirect questions
  (1) ❑ Within ten (10) days after being served with cross questions, a party may serve redirect questions upon all other parties
  (2) ❑ Objections to the form of the question must be served within the time for service of redirect questions or ten (10) days after service of recross questions

(IV) ❑ Matters to be considered by deponent (depositions by written questions)
(a) ❑ Required documents
  (1) ❑ Cross questions, with certificate of service
  (2) ❑ Recross questions with certificate of service
(b) ❑ Time for service of cross and recross questions
  (1) ❑ Within thirty (30) days after the notice and written questions are served, a party may serve cross questions upon all other parties
  (2) ❑ Within ten (10) days after being served with redirect questions, a party may serve recross questions upon all other parties
  (3) ❑ Objections to the form of the questions must be served within the time for serving succeeding questions

ELEVENTH JUDICIAL CIRCUIT

Pleadings
Complaint

Document Last Updated January 2013

A. Applicable Rules

1. *State rules*
   a. Nonverification of pleadings. FL ST RCP Rule 1.030.
   b. When action commenced. FL ST RCP Rule 1.050.
   c. Process. FL ST RCP Rule 1.070.
   d. Service and filing of pleadings, orders, and documents. FL ST RCP Rule 1.080.
   e. Time. FL ST RCP Rule 1.090.
   f. Pleadings and motions. FL ST RCP Rule 1.100; FL ST RCP Rule 1.110; FL ST RCP Rule 1.120; FL ST RCP Rule 1.130; FL ST RCP Rule 1.170; FL ST RCP Rule 1.430.
   g. Relief from judgment, decrees, or orders. FL ST RCP Rule 1.540.
   h. Forms. FL ST RCP Rule 1.900.
   i. Minimization of the filing of sensitive information. FL ST J ADMIN Rule 2.425.
   j. Retention of court records. FL ST J ADMIN Rule 2.430.
   k. Foreign attorneys. FL ST J ADMIN Rule 2.510.
   l. Signature of attorneys and parties. FL ST J ADMIN Rule 2.515.
   m. Paper. FL ST J ADMIN Rule 2.520.
   n. Electronic filing. FL ST J ADMIN Rule 2.525.
   o. Accessibility of information and technology. FL ST J ADMIN Rule 2.526.
   p. Requests for accommodations by persons with disabilities. FL ST J ADMIN Rule 2.540.
   q. Service. FL ST § 48.011; FL ST § 48.021; FL ST § 48.031; FL ST § 48.041; FL ST § 48.042; FL ST § 48.051; FL ST § 48.061; FL ST § 48.071; FL ST § 48.081; FL ST § 48.091; FL ST § 48.101; FL ST § 48.194; FL ST § 48.111; FL ST § 48.121; FL ST § 48.131; FL ST § 48.141; FL ST § 48.151; FL ST § 48.161; FL ST § 48.171; FL ST § 48.181; FL ST § 48.183; FL ST § 48.19; FL ST § 48.193; FL ST § 48.194; FL ST § 48.20; FL ST § 48.21; FL ST § 48.25; FL ST § 48.31; FL ST § 49.011; FL ST § 49.021; FL ST § 49.031; FL ST § 49.041; FL ST § 49.051; FL ST § 49.061; FL ST § 49.071; FL ST § 49.08; FL ST § 49.09; FL ST § 49.10; FL ST § 49.11; FL ST § 49.12; FL ST § 50.011; FL ST § 50.021; FL ST § 50.031; FL ST § 50.041; FL ST § 50.051; FL ST § 50.061.
2. *Local rules*
   a. Establishment of 11th Circuit Homestead ACcess to Mediation Program ("CHAMP") for case management of residential foreclosure cases in the Eleventh Judicial Circuit of Florida. FL ST 11 J CIR 1-09-08.

B. Timing

1. *Commencement of an action.* Every action of a civil nature shall be deemed commenced when the complaint or petition is filed except that ancillary proceedings shall be deemed commenced when the writ is issued or the pleading setting forth the claim of the party initiating the action is filed. FL ST RCP Rule 1.050.
2. *Summons; Time limit.* If service of the initial process and initial pleading is not made upon a defendant

within one hundred twenty (120) days after filing of the initial pleading directed to that defendant the court, on its own initiative after notice or on motion, shall direct that service be effected within a specified time or shall dismiss the action without prejudice or drop that defendant as a party; provided that if the plaintiff shows good cause or excusable neglect for the failure, the court shall extend the time for service for an appropriate period. FL ST RCP Rule 1.070(j).

3. *Computation of time*
    a. *Generally.* Computation of time shall be governed by FL ST J ADMIN Rule 2.514. FL ST RCP Rule 1.090(a). The following rules apply in computing time periods specified in any rule of procedure, local rule, court order, or statute that does not specify a method of computing time. FL ST J ADMIN Rule 2.514(a).
        i. *Period stated in days or a longer unit.* When the period is stated in days or a longer unit of time (A) exclude the day of the event that triggers the period; (B) count every day, including intermediate Saturdays, Sundays, and legal holidays; and (C) include the last day of the period, but if the last day is a Saturday, Sunday, or legal holiday, or falls within any period of time extended through an order of the chief justice under FL ST J ADMIN Rule 2.205(a)(2)(B)(iv), the period continues to run until the end of the next day that is not a Saturday, Sunday, or legal holiday and does not fall within any period of time extended through an order of the chief justice. FL ST J ADMIN Rule 2.514(a)(1).
        ii. *Period stated in hours.* When the period is stated in hours (A) begin counting immediately on the occurrence of the event that triggers the period; (B) count every hour, including hours during intermediate Saturdays, Sundays, and legal holidays; and (C) if the period would end on a Saturday, Sunday, or legal holiday, or during any period of time extended through an order of the chief justice under FL ST J ADMIN Rule 2.205(a)(2)(B)(iv), the period continues to run until the same time on the next day that is not a Saturday, Sunday, or legal holiday and does not fall within any period of time extended through an order of the chief justice. FL ST J ADMIN Rule 2.514(a)(2).
        iii. *Period stated in days less than seven (7) days.* When the period stated in days is less than seven (7) days, intermediate Saturdays, Sundays, and legal holidays shall be excluded in the computation. FL ST J ADMIN Rule 2.514(a)(3).
        iv. *"Last day" defined.* Unless a different time is set by a statute, local rule, or court order, the last day ends (A) for electronic filing or for service by any means, at midnight; and (B) for filing by other means, when the clerk's office is scheduled to close. FL ST J ADMIN Rule 2.514(a)(4).
        v. *"Next day" defined.* The "next day" is determined by continuing to count forward when the period is measured after an event and backward when measured before an event. FL ST J ADMIN Rule 2.514(a)(5).
        vi. *"Legal holiday" defined.* "Legal holiday" means (A) the day set aside by FL ST § 110.117, for observing New Year's Day, Martin Luther King, Jr.'s Birthday, Memorial Day, Independence Day, Labor Day, Veterans' Day, Thanksgiving Day, the Friday after Thanksgiving Day, or Christmas Day, and (B) any day observed as a holiday by the clerk's office or as designated by the chief judge. FL ST J ADMIN Rule 2.514(a)(6).
    b. *Additional time after service by mail or e-mail.* When a party may or must act within a specified time after service and service is made by mail or e-mail, five (5) days are added after the period that would otherwise expire under FL ST J ADMIN Rule 2.514(a). FL ST J ADMIN Rule 2.514(b).
    c. *Enlargement.* When an act is required or allowed to be done at or within a specified time by order of court, by the Florida Rules of Civil Procedure, or by notice given thereunder, for cause shown the court at any time in its discretion (1) with or without notice, may order the period enlarged if request therefor is made before the expiration of the period originally prescribed or as extended by a previous order, or (2) upon motion made and notice after the expiration of the specified period, may permit the act to be done when failure to act was the result of excusable neglect, but it may not extend the time for making a motion for new trial, for rehearing, or to alter or amend a judgment; making a motion for relief from a judgment under FL ST RCP Rule 1.540(b); taking an appeal or filing a petition for certiorari; or making a motion for a directed verdict. FL ST RCP Rule 1.090(b).

d. *Unaffected by expiration of term.* The period of time provided for the doing of any act or the taking of any proceeding shall not be affected or limited by the continued existence or expiration of a term of court. The continued existence or expiration of a term of court in no way affects the power of a court to do any act or take any proceeding in any action which is or has been pending before it. FL ST RCP Rule 1.090(c).

C. General Requirements

1. *General rules of pleading*

a. *Claims for relief*

i. A pleading which sets forth a claim for relief, whether an original claim, counterclaim, crossclaim, or third-party claim, must state a cause of action and shall contain

- A short and plain statement of the grounds upon which the court's jurisdiction depends, unless the court already has jurisdiction and the claim needs no new grounds of jurisdiction to support it (For information regarding acts subjecting persons to jurisdiction, please see FL ST § 48.193),
- A short and plain statement of the ultimate facts showing that the pleader is entitled to relief, and
- A demand for judgment for the relief to which the pleader deems himself or herself entitled. FL ST RCP Rule 1.110(b).

ii. Relief in the alternative or of several different types may be demanded. Every complaint shall be considered to demand general relief. FL ST RCP Rule 1.110(b).

b. *Verification.* Except when otherwise specifically provided by these rules or an applicable statute, every pleading or other document of a party represented by an attorney need not be verified or accompanied by an affidavit. FL ST RCP Rule 1.030. When filing an action for foreclosure of a mortgage on residential real property the complaint shall be verified. When verification of a document is required, the document filed shall include an oath, affirmation, or the following statement: "Under penalty of perjury, I declare that I have read the foregoing, and the facts alleged therein are true and correct to the best of my knowledge and belief." FL ST RCP Rule 1.110(b).

c. *Separate statements.* All averments of claim or defense shall be made in consecutively numbered paragraphs, the contents of each of which shall be limited as far as practicable to a statement of a single set of circumstances, and a paragraph may be referred to by number in all subsequent pleadings. Each claim founded upon a separate transaction or occurrence and each defense other than denials shall be stated in a separate count or defense when a separation facilitates the clear presentation of the matter set forth. FL ST RCP Rule 1.110(f).

d. *Statements adopted by reference.* Statements in a pleading may be adopted by reference in a different part of the same pleading, in another pleading, or in any motion. FL ST RCP Rule 1.130(b).

e. *Joinder of causes of action; Consistency.* A pleader may set up in the same action as many claims or causes of action or defenses in the same right as the pleader has, and claims for relief may be stated in the alternative if separate items make up the cause of action, or if two (2) or more causes of action are joined. A party may also set forth two (2) or more statements of a claim or defense alternatively, either in one (1) count or defense or in separate counts or defenses. When two (2) or more statements are made in the alternative and one (1) of them, if made independently, would be sufficient, the pleading is not made insufficient by the insufficiency of one (1) or more of the alternative statements. A party may also state as many separate claims or defenses as that party has, regardless of consistency and whether based on legal or equitable grounds or both. All pleadings shall be construed so as to do substantial justice. FL ST RCP Rule 1.110(g).

f. *Subsequent pleadings.* When the nature of an action permits pleadings subsequent to final judgment and the jurisdiction of the court over the parties has not terminated, the initial pleading subsequent to final judgment shall be designated a supplemental complaint or petition. The action shall then proceed in the same manner and time as though the supplemental complaint or petition were the initial pleading in the action, including the issuance of any needed process. FL ST RCP Rule

1.110(h) shall not apply to proceedings that may be initiated by motion under the Florida Rules of Civil Procedure. FL ST RCP Rule 1.110(h).

g. *Pleading basis for service.* When service of process is to be made under statutes authorizing service on nonresidents of Florida, it is sufficient to plead the basis for service in the language of the statute without pleading the facts supporting service. FL ST RCP Rule 1.070(h).

h. *Forms of pleadings.* Forms of action and technical forms for seeking relief and of pleas, pleadings, or motions are abolished. FL ST RCP Rule 1.110(a).

2. *Complaint; Generally*

a. *Purpose.* The purpose of a complaint is to advise the court and the defendant of the nature of a cause of action asserted by the plaintiff. FL-PP § 2:12.

b. *Sufficiency of complaint.* A complaint will be found to be insufficient if it contains only general conclusory allegations unsupported by any facts. The test to determine whether a complaint is sufficient is whether, if the factual allegations of the complaint are established, the plaintiff will be legally or equitably entitled to the claimed relief. Pizzi v. Central Bank & Trust Co., 250 So.2d 895, 896 (Fla. 1971); Bowen v. G H C Properties, Limited, 251 So.2d 359, 361 (Fla. 1st DCA 1971); FL-PP § 2:12. In determining the sufficiency of the complaint to state a cause of action, all allegations of the complaint are taken as true, and possible affirmative defenses are not considered. Strickland v. Commerce Loan Co. of Jacksonville, 158 So.2d 814 (Fla. 1st DCA 1963); FL-PP § 2:12.

i. The issues for trial in Florida must be settled by the pleadings. The issues cannot be raised by discovery. FL-PRACPROC § 7:6.

ii. Causes of action may be pleaded alternatively in the same count or in different counts and against the same or different defendants as long as the joinder of parties is proper. FL-PRACPROC § 7:6.

iii. Each count must state a cause of action. Each independent cause of action should be pleaded in a separate count. FL-PRACPROC § 7:6.

iv. Incorporation by reference of all allegations from one count to another is not proper. Separate counts facilitate reference to the pleading in which they appear in other pleadings, motions or papers as well as the assertion of defenses against some, but not all, causes of action. Some defenses may not apply to the initial pleading as a whole. FL-PRACPROC § 7:6.

3. *Pleading special matters*

a. *Capacity.* It is not necessary to aver the capacity of a party to sue or be sued, the authority of a party to sue or be sued in a representative capacity, or the legal existence of an organized association of persons that is made a party, except to the extent required to show the jurisdiction of the court. The initial pleading served on behalf of a minor party shall specifically aver the age of the minor party. When a party desires to raise an issue as to the legal existence of any party, the capacity of any party to sue or be sued, or the authority of a party to sue or be sued in a representative capacity, that party shall do so by specific negative averment which shall include such supporting particulars as are peculiarly within the pleader's knowledge. FL ST RCP Rule 1.120(a).

b. *Fraud, mistake, condition of the mind.* In all averments of fraud or mistake, the circumstances constituting fraud or mistake shall be stated with such particularity as the circumstances may permit. Malice, intent, knowledge, mental attitude, and other condition of mind of a person may be averred generally. FL ST RCP Rule 1.120(b).

c. *Conditions precedent.* In pleading the performance or occurrence of conditions precedent, it is sufficient to aver generally that all conditions precedent have been performed or have occurred. A denial of performance or occurrence shall be made specifically and with particularity. FL ST RCP Rule 1.120(c).

d. *Official document or act.* In pleading an official document or official act it is sufficient to aver that the document was issued or the act done in compliance with law. FL ST RCP Rule 1.120(c).

e. *Judgment or decree.* In pleading a judgment or decree of a domestic or foreign court, a judicial or quasi-judicial tribunal, or a board or officer, it is sufficient to aver the judgment or decree without setting forth matter showing jurisdiction to render it. FL ST RCP Rule 1.120(e).

f. *Time and place.* For the purpose of testing the sufficiency of a pleading, averments of time and place are material and shall be considered like all other averments of material matter. FL ST RCP Rule 1.120(f).

g. *Special damage.* When items of special damage are claimed, they shall be specifically stated. FL ST RCP Rule 1.120(g).

4. *Parties*

a. *Parties generally.* Every action may be prosecuted in the name of the real party in interest, but a personal representative, administrator, guardian, trustee of an express trust, a party with whom or in whose name a contract has been made for the benefit of another, or a party expressly authorized by statute may sue in that person's own name without joining the party for whose benefit the action is brought. All persons having an interest in the subject of the action and in obtaining the relief demanded may join as plaintiffs and any person may be made a defendant who has or claims an interest adverse to the plaintiff. Any person may at any time be made a party if that person's presence is necessary or proper to a complete determination of the cause. Persons having a united interest may be joined on the same side as plaintiffs or defendants, and anyone who refuses to join may for such reason be made a defendant. FL ST RCP Rule 1.210(a).

b. *Minors or incompetent persons.* When a minor or incompetent person has a representative, such as a guardian or other like fiduciary, the representative may sue or defend on behalf of the minor or incompetent person. A minor or incompetent person who does not have a duly appointed representative may sue by next friend or by a guardian ad litem. The court shall appoint a guardian ad litem for a minor or incompetent person not otherwise represented in an action or shall make such other order as it deems proper for the protection of the minor or incompetent person. FL ST RCP Rule 1.210(b).

c. For survivor and substitution of parties information, please see FL ST RCP Rule 1.260.

5. *Counterclaims and crossclaims*

a. *Compulsory counterclaims.* A pleading shall state as a counterclaim any claim which at the time of serving the pleading the pleader has against any opposing party, provided it arises out of the transaction or occurrence that is the subject matter of the opposing party's claim and does not require for its adjudication the presence of third parties over whom the court cannot acquire jurisdiction. But the pleader need not state a claim if (1) at the time the action was commenced the claim was the subject of another pending action, or (2) the opposing party brought suit upon that party's claim by attachment or other process by which the court did not acquire jurisdiction to render a personal judgment on the claim and the pleader is not stating a counterclaim under this rule. FL ST RCP Rule 1.170(a).

b. *Permissive counterclaim.* A pleading may state as a counterclaim any claim against an opposing party not arising out of the transaction or occurrence that is the subject matter of the opposing party's claim. FL ST RCP Rule 1.170(b).

c. *Counterclaim exceeding opposing claim.* A counterclaim may or may not diminish or defeat the recovery sought by the opposing party. It may claim relief exceeding in amount or different in kind from that sought in the pleading of the opposing party. FL ST RCP Rule 1.170(c).

d. *Counterclaim against the State.* The Florida Rules of Civil Procedure shall not be construed to enlarge beyond the limits established by law the right to assert counterclaims or to claim credits against the state or any of its subdivisions or other governmental organizations thereof subject to suit or against a municipal corporation or against an officer, agency, or administrative board of the state. FL ST RCP Rule 1.170(d).

e. *Counterclaim maturing or acquired after pleading.* A claim which matured or was acquired by the pleader after serving the pleading may be presented as a counterclaim by supplemental pleading with the permission of the court. FL ST RCP Rule 1.170(e).

f. *Omitted counterclaim or crossclaim.* When a pleader fails to set up a counterclaim or crossclaim through oversight, inadvertence, or excusable neglect, or when justice requires, the pleader may set up the counterclaim or crossclaim by amendment with leave of the court. FL ST RCP Rule 1.170(f).

g. *Crossclaim against co-party.* A pleading may state as a crossclaim any claim by one party against a co-party arising out of the transaction or occurrence that is the subject matter of either the original action or a counterclaim therein, or relating to any property that is the subject matter of the original action. The crossclaim may include a claim that the party against whom it is asserted is or may be liable to the crossclaimant for all or part of a claim asserted in the action against the crossclaimant. Service of a crossclaim on a party who has appeared in the action shall be made pursuant to FL ST RCP Rule 1.080. Service of a crossclaim against a party who has not appeared in the action shall be made in the manner provided for service of summons. FL ST RCP Rule 1.170(g).

h. *Additional parties may be brought in.* When the presence of parties other than those to the original action is required to grant complete relief in the determination of a counterclaim or crossclaim, they shall be named in the counterclaim or crossclaim and be served with process and shall be parties to the action thereafter if jurisdiction of them can be obtained and their joinder will not deprive the court of jurisdiction of the action. FL ST RCP Rule 1.250(b) and FL ST RCP Rule 1.250(c) apply to parties brought in under FL ST RCP Rule 1.170(h). FL ST RCP Rule 1.170(h).

i. *Separate trials; Separate judgment.* If the court orders separate trials as provided in FL ST RCP Rule 1.270(b), judgment on a counterclaim or crossclaim may be rendered when the court has jurisdiction to do so even if a claim of the opposing party has been dismissed or otherwise disposed of. FL ST RCP Rule 1.170(i).

j. *Demand exceeding jurisdiction; Transfer of action.* If the demand of any counterclaim or crossclaim exceeds the jurisdiction of the court in which the action is pending, the action shall be transferred forthwith to the court of the same county having jurisdiction of the demand in the counterclaim or crossclaim with only such alterations in the pleadings as are essential. The court shall order the transfer of the action and the transmittal of all papers in it to the proper court if the party asserting the demand exceeding the jurisdiction deposits with the court having jurisdiction a sum sufficient to pay the clerk's service charge in the court to which the action is transferred at the time of filing the counterclaim or crossclaim. Thereupon the original papers and deposit shall be transmitted and filed with a certified copy of the order. The court to which the action is transferred shall have full power and jurisdiction over the demands of all parties. Failure to make the service charge deposit at the time the counterclaim or crossclaim is filed, or within such further time as the court may allow, shall reduce a claim for damages to an amount within the jurisdiction of the court where the action is pending and waive the claim in other cases. FL ST RCP Rule 1.170(j).

6. *Misjoinder and nonjoinder of parties*

a. *Misjoinder.* Misjoinder of parties is not a ground for dismissal of an action. Any claim against a party may be severed and proceeded with separately. FL ST RCP Rule 1.250(a).

b. *Dropping parties.* Parties may be dropped by an adverse party in the manner provided for voluntary dismissal in FL ST RCP Rule 1.420(a)(1) subject to the exception stated in FL ST RCP Rule 1.420. If notice of lis pendens has been filed in the action against a party so dropped, the notice of dismissal shall be recorded and cancels the notice of lis pendens without the necessity of a court order. Parties may be dropped by order of court on its own initiative or the motion of any party at any stage of the action on such terms as are just. FL ST RCP Rule 1.250(b).

c. *Adding parties.* Parties may be added once as a matter of course within the same time that pleadings can be so amended under FL ST RCP Rule 1.190(a). If amendment by leave of court or stipulation of the parties is permitted, parties may be added in the amended pleading without further order of court. Parties may be added by order of court on its own initiative or on motion of any party at any stage of the action and on such terms as are just. FL ST RCP Rule 1.250(c).

7. *Jury demand*

a. *Right preserved.* The right of trial by jury as declared by the Constitution or by statute shall be preserved to the parties inviolate. FL ST RCP Rule 1.430(a).

b. *Demand.* Any party may demand a trial by jury of any issue triable of right by a jury by serving upon the other party a demand therefor in writing at any time after commencement of the action and not later than ten (10) days after the service of the last pleading directed to such issue. The demand may be indorsed upon a pleading of the party. FL ST RCP Rule 1.430(b).

c. *Specification of issues.* In the demand a party may specify the issues that the party wishes so tried; otherwise, the party is deemed to demand trial by jury for all issues so triable. FL ST RCP Rule 1.430(c).

   i. If a party has demanded trial by jury for only some of the issues, any other party may serve a demand for trial by jury of any other or all of the issues triable by jury ten (10) days after service of the demand or such lesser time as the court may order. FL ST RCP Rule 1.430(c).

d. *Waiver.* A party who fails to serve a demand as required by FL ST RCP Rule 1.430 waives trial by jury. FL ST RCP Rule 1.430(d).

   i. If waived, a jury trial may not be granted without the consent of the parties, but the court may allow an amendment in the proceedings to demand a trial by jury or order a trial by jury on its own motion. FL ST RCP Rule 1.430(d).

   ii. A demand for trial by jury may not be withdrawn without the consent of the parties. FL ST RCP Rule 1.430(d).

8. *Arbitration and mediation*

   a. *Referral to arbitration and mediation.* Except as hereinafter provided or as otherwise prohibited by law, the presiding judge may enter an order referring all or any part of a contested civil matter to mediation or arbitration. The parties to any contested civil matter may file a written stipulation to mediate or arbitrate any issue between them at any time. Such stipulation shall be incorporated into the order of referral. FL ST RCP Rule 1.700(a).

      i. In all residential foreclosure actions involving homestead properties filed on or after May 1, 2009, unless a stipulation is specifically invoked by the parties in writing within five (5) days of service of the complaint on the main defendant, the parties are deemed to have stipulated to referral of the mediation to the Collins Center pursuant to FL ST RCP Rule 1.720(f). FL ST 11 J CIR 1-09-08(2); FL ST 11 J CIR 1-09-08(3). FL ST 11 J CIR 1-09-08 constitutes a formal referral to mediation pursuant to the Florida Rules of Civil Procedure. FL ST 11 J CIR 1-09-08(2).

      ii. For further information on referral to mediation, refer to FL ST 11 J CIR 1-09-08.

   b. *Arbitration*

      i. *Exclusions.* A civil action shall be ordered to arbitration or arbitration in conjunction with mediation upon stipulation of the parties. A civil action may be ordered to arbitration or arbitration in conjunction with mediation upon motion of any party or by the court, if the judge determines the action to be of such a nature that arbitration could be of benefit to the litigants or the court. FL ST RCP Rule 1.800.

         - Under no circumstances may the following categories of actions be referred to arbitration: (1) bond estreatures; (2) habeas corpus or other extraordinary writs; (3) bond validations; (4) civil or criminal contempt; (5) such other matters as may be specified by order of the chief judge in the circuit. FL ST RCP Rule 1.800.

      ii. For more information regarding arbitration, please see FL ST RCP Rule 1.810; FL ST RCP Rule 1.820; FL ST RCP Rule 1.830.

   c. *Mediation.* For more information regarding mediation, please see FL ST RCP Rule 1.710; FL ST RCP Rule 1.720; FL ST RCP Rule 1.730; and FL ST RCP Rule 1.750.

9. *Rules of court*

   a. *Rules of civil procedure.* The Florida Rules of Civil Procedure apply to all actions of a civil nature and all special statutory proceedings in the circuit courts and county courts except those to which the Florida Probate Rules, the Florida Family Law Rules of Procedure, or the Small Claims Rules apply. FL ST RCP Rule 1.010.

      i. The form, content, procedure, and time for pleading in all special statutory proceedings shall be as prescribed by the statutes governing the proceeding unless the Florida Rules of Civil Procedure specifically provide to the contrary. FL ST RCP Rule 1.010.

ii. The Florida Rules of Civil Procedure shall be construed to secure the just, speedy, and inexpensive determination of every action. FL ST RCP Rule 1.010.

b. *Rules of judicial administration.* The Florida Rules of Judicial Administration shall apply to administrative matters in all courts to which the Florida Rules of Judicial Administration are applicable by their terms. The Florida Rules of Judicial Administration shall be construed to secure the speedy and inexpensive determination of every proceeding to which they are applicable. The Florida Rules of Judicial Administration shall supersede all conflicting rules and statutes. FL ST J ADMIN Rule 2.110.

D. Documents

1. *Required documents*

a. *Summons.* Upon the commencement of the action, summons or other process authorized by law shall be issued forthwith by the clerk or judge under the clerk's or the judge's signature and the seal of the court and delivered for service without praecipe. FL ST RCP Rule 1.070(a).

b. *Complaint.* See the General Requirements section for the contents of the complaint.

i. *Notices to persons with disabilities.* See the Format section of this KeyRules document for further information.

c. *Civil cover sheet.* A civil cover sheet (FL ST RCP Form 1.997) shall be completed and filed with the clerk at the time an initial complaint or petition is filed by the party initiating the action. If the cover sheet is not filed, the clerk shall accept the complaint or petition for filing; but all proceedings in the action shall be abated until a properly executed cover sheet is completed and filed. The clerk shall complete the civil cover sheet for a party appearing pro se. FL ST RCP Rule 1.100(c)(2).

d. *Return of execution process by process server.* Each person who effects service of process shall note on a return-of-service form attached thereto, the date and time when it comes to hand, the date and time when it is served, the manner of service, the name of the person on whom it was served and, if the person is served in a representative capacity, the position occupied by the person. The return-of-service form must be signed by the person who effects the service of process. However, a person employed by a sheriff who effects the service of process may sign the return-of-service form using an electronic signature certified by the sheriff. FL ST § 48.21(1).

i. A failure to state the facts or to include the signature required by FL ST § 48.21(1) invalidates the service, but the return is amendable to state the facts or to include the signature at any time on application to the court from which the process issued. On amendment, service is as effective as if the return had originally stated the omitted facts or included the signature. A failure to state all the facts in or to include the signature on the return shall subject the person effecting service to a fine not exceeding $10, in the court's discretion. FL ST § 48.21(2).

e. *Filing fees.* Filing fees are due at the time a party files a pleading to initiate a proceeding or files a pleading for relief. FL ST § 28.241. For a fee schedule, see FL ST § 28.241.

2. *Supplemental documents*

a. *Exhibits.* All bonds, notes, bills of exchange, contracts, accounts, or documents upon which action may be brought or defense made, or a copy thereof or a copy of the portions thereof material to the pleadings, shall be incorporated in or attached to the pleading. No papers shall be unnecessarily annexed as exhibits. The pleadings shall contain no unnecessary recitals of deeds, documents, contracts, or other instruments. Any exhibit attached to a pleading shall be considered a part of the pleadings for all purposes. FL ST RCP Rule 1.130(a).

b. *Notice of constitutional question.* A party that files a pleading, written motion, or other paper drawing into question the constitutionality of a state statute or a county or municipal charter, ordinance, or franchise must promptly (1) file a notice of constitutional question stating the question and identifying the paper that raises it; and (2) serve the notice and the pleading, written motion, or other paper drawing into question the constitutionality of a state statute or a county or municipal charter, ordinance, or franchise on the Attorney General or the state attorney of the judicial circuit in which the action is pending, by either certified or registered mail. Service of the notice and pleading,

written motion, or other paper does not require joinder of the Attorney General or the state attorney as a party to the action. FL ST RCP Rule 1.071.

E. Format

1. *Documents; Type and size.* Documents subject to the exceptions set forth in FL ST J ADMIN Rule 2.525(d) shall be filed on recycled paper measuring eight and one half by eleven (8 1/2 by 11) inches. For purposes of FL ST J ADMIN Rule 2.520, paper is recycled if it contains a minimum content of fifty (50) percent waste paper. Xerographic reduction of legal-size (eight and one half by fourteen (8 1/2 by 14) inches) documents to letter size (eight and one half by eleven (8 1/2 by 11) inches) is prohibited. All other documents filed by electronic transmission shall be filed in a format capable of being printed in a format consistent with the provisions of FL ST J ADMIN Rule 2.250. FL ST J ADMIN Rule 2.520(b).

    a. *Exhibits.* Any exhibit or attachment filed with pleadings or papers may be filed in its original size. FL ST J ADMIN Rule 2.520(c).

    b. *Recording space.* On all papers and documents prepared and filed by the court or by any party to a proceeding which are to be recorded in the public records of any county, including but not limited to final money judgments and notices of lis pendens, a three (3) inch by three (3) inch space at the top right-hand corner on the first page and a one (1) inch by three (3) inch space at the top right-hand corner on each subsequent page shall be left blank and reserved for use by the clerk of court. FL ST J ADMIN Rule 2.520(d).

        i. *Exceptions to recording space.* Any papers or documents created by persons or entities over which the filing party has no control, including but not limited to wills, codicils, trusts, or other testamentary documents; documents prepared or executed by any public officer; documents prepared, executed, acknowledged, or proved outside of the State of Florida; or documents created by State or Federal government agencies, may be filed without the space required by FL ST J ADMIN Rule 2.520. FL ST J ADMIN Rule 2.520(e).

    c. *Noncompliance.* No clerk of court is permitted to refuse to file any document or paper because of noncompliance with the Florida Rules of Judicial Administration. However, upon request of the clerk of court, noncomplying documents must be resubmitted in accordance with the formatting rules. FL ST J ADMIN Rule 2.520(f).

2. *Caption.* Every pleading, motion, order, judgment, or other paper shall have a caption containing the name of the court, the file number, and except for in rem proceedings, including forfeiture proceedings, the name of the first party on each side with an appropriate indication of other parties, and a designation identifying the party filing it and its nature or the nature of the order, as the case may be. In any in rem proceeding, every pleading, motion, order, judgment, or other paper shall have a caption containing the name of the court, the file number, the style "In re" (followed by the name or general description of the property), and a designation of the person or entity filing it and its nature or the nature of the order, as the case may be. In an in rem forfeiture proceeding, the style shall be "In re forfeiture of" (followed by the name of the general description of the property). All papers filed in the action shall be styled in such a manner as to indicate clearly the subject matter of the paper and the party requesting or obtaining relief. FL ST RCP Rule 1.100(c)(1).

3. *Writing and written defined.* Writing or written means a document containing information, an application, or a stipulation. FL ST RCP Rule 1.080(c).

4. *Rule abbreviations*

    a. The Florida Rules of Civil Procedure and shall be abbreviated as Fla.R.Civ.P. FL ST RCP Rule 1.010.

    b. The Florida Rules of Judicial Administration shall be abbreviated as Fla. R. Jud. Admin. FL ST J ADMIN Rule 2.110.

5. *Nonverification.* Except when otherwise specifically provided by the Florida Rules of Civil Procedure or an applicable statute, every pleading or other document of a party represented by an attorney need not be verified or accompanied by an affidavit. FL ST RCP Rule 1.030; FL ST J ADMIN Rule 2.515(a).

6. *Attorney signature*

    a. *Attorney signature.* Every pleading and other document of a party represented by an attorney shall be

signed by at least one (1) attorney of record in that attorney's individual name whose current record Florida Bar address, telephone number, including area code, primary e-mail address and secondary e-mail addresses, if any, and Florida Bar number shall be stated, and who shall be duly licensed to practice law in Florida or who shall have received permission to appear in the particular case as provided in FL ST J ADMIN Rule 2.510. FL ST J ADMIN Rule 2.515(a).

i. The attorney may be required by the court to give the address of, and to vouch for the attorney's authority to represent, the party. FL ST J ADMIN Rule 2.515(a).

ii. The signature of an attorney shall constitute a certificate by the attorney that the attorney has read the pleading or other document; that to the best of the attorney's knowledge, information, and belief there is good ground to support it; and that it is not interposed for delay. FL ST J ADMIN Rule 2.515(a).

iii. If a pleading is not signed or is signed with intent to defeat the purpose of FL ST J ADMIN Rule 2.515, it may be stricken and the action may proceed as though the pleading or other document had not been served. FL ST J ADMIN Rule 2.515(a).

b. *Pro se litigant signature.* A party who is not represented by an attorney shall sign any pleading or other paper and state the party's address and telephone number, including area code. FL ST J ADMIN Rule 2.515(b).

c. *Form of signature*

i. The signatures required on pleadings and documents by FL ST J ADMIN Rule 2.515(a) and FL ST J ADMIN Rule 2.515(b) may be:

- Original signatures;
- Original signatures that have been reproduced by electronic means, such as on electronically transmitted documents or photocopied documents;
- Electronic signatures using the "/s/," "s/," or "/s" formats by or at the direction of the person signing; or
- Any other signature format authorized by general law, so long as the clerk where the proceeding is pending has the capability of receiving and has obtained approval from the Supreme Court of Florida to accept pleadings and documents with that signature format. FL ST J ADMIN Rule 2.515(c)(1).

ii. An attorney, party, or other person who files a pleading or paper by electronic transmission that does not contain the original signature of that attorney, party, or other person shall file that identical pleading or paper in paper form containing an original signature of that attorney, party, or other person (hereinafter called the follow-up filing) immediately thereafter. The follow-up filing is not required if the Supreme Court of Florida has entered an order directing the clerk of court to discontinue accepting the follow-up filing. FL ST J ADMIN Rule 2.515(c)(2).

7. *Forms*

a. *Process.* The forms of process, notice of lis pendens, and notice of action provided in the Florida Rules of Civil Procedure are sufficient. Variations from the forms do not void process or notices that are otherwise sufficient. FL ST RCP Rule 1.900(a).

b. *Other forms.* The other forms provided in the Florida Rules of Civil Procedure are sufficient for the matters that are covered by them. So long as the substance is expressed without prolixity, the forms may be varied to meet the facts of a particular case. FL ST RCP Rule 1.900(b).

c. *Formal matters.* Captions, except for the designation of the paper, are omitted from the forms provided in the Florida Rules of Civil Procedure. A general form of caption is the first form provided. Signatures are omitted from pleadings and motions. FL ST RCP Rule 1.900(c).

8. *Notices to persons with disabilities.* All notices of court proceedings to be held in a public facility, and all process compelling appearance at such proceedings, shall include the following statement in bold face, fourteen (14) point Times New Roman or Courier font: "If you are a person with a disability who needs any accommodation in order to participate in this proceeding, you are entitled, at no cost to you, to the

provision of certain assistance. Please contact [identify applicable court personnel by name, address, and telephone number] at least seven (7) days before your scheduled court appearance, or immediately upon receiving this notification if the time before the scheduled appearance is less than seven (7) days; if you are hearing or voice impaired, call 711." FL ST J ADMIN Rule 2.540(c)(1).

9. *Minimization of the filing of sensitive information*
   a. *Limitations for court filings.* Unless authorized by FL ST J ADMIN Rule 2.425(b), statute, another rule of court, or the court orders otherwise, designated sensitive information filed with the court must be limited to the following format:
      i. The initials of a person known to be a minor;
      ii. The year of birth of a person's birth date;
      iii. No portion of any: Social security number, Bank account number, Credit card account number, Charge account number, or Debit account number;
      iv. The last four digits of any: Taxpayer identification number (TIN), Employee identification number, Driver's license number, Passport number, Telephone number, Financial account number, except as set forth in FL ST J ADMIN Rule 2.425(a)(3), Brokerage account number, Insurance policy account number, Loan account number, Customer account number, or Patient or health care number;
      v. A truncated version of any: Email address, Computer user name, Password, or Personal identification number (PIN); and
      vi. A truncated version of any other sensitive information as provided by court order. FL ST J ADMIN Rule 2.425(a).
   b. *Exceptions.* FL ST J ADMIN Rule 2.425(a) does not apply to the following:
      i. An account number which identifies the property alleged to be the subject of a proceeding;
      ii. The record of an administrative or agency proceeding;
      iii. The record in appellate or review proceedings;
      iv. The birth date of a minor whenever the birth date is necessary for the court to establish or maintain subject matter jurisdiction;
      v. The name of a minor in any order relating to parental responsibility, time-sharing, or child support;
      vi. The name of a minor in any document or order affecting the minor's ownership of real property;
      vii. The birth date of a party in a writ of attachment or notice to payor;
      viii. In traffic and criminal proceedings: a pro se filing; a court filing that is related to a criminal matter or investigation and that is prepared before the filing of a criminal charge or is not filed as part of any docketed criminal case; an arrest or search warrant or any information in support thereof; a charging document and an affidavit or other documents filed in support of any charging document, including any driving records; a statement of particulars; discovery material introduced into evidence or otherwise filed with the court; and all information necessary for the proper issuance and execution of a subpoena duces tecum;
      ix. Information used by the clerk for case maintenance purposes or the courts for case management purposes; and
      x. Information which is relevant and material to an issue before the court. FL ST J ADMIN Rule 2.425(b).
   c. *Remedies.* Upon motion by a party or interested person or sua sponte by the court, the court may order remedies, sanctions or both for a violation of FL ST J ADMIN Rule 2.425(a). Following notice and an opportunity to respond, the court may impose sanctions if such filing was not made in good faith. FL ST J ADMIN Rule 2.425(c).
   d. *Motions not restricted.* FL ST J ADMIN Rule 2.425 does not restrict a party's right to move for

protective order, to move to file documents under seal, or to request a determination of the confidentiality of records. FL ST J ADMIN Rule 2.425(d).

e. *Application.* FL ST J ADMIN Rule 2.425 does not affect the application of constitutional provisions, statutes, or rules of court regarding confidential information or access to public information. FL ST J ADMIN Rule 2.425(e).

F. Filing and Service Requirements

1. *Filing requirements.* All documents filed in any court shall be filed by electronic transmission in accordance with FL ST J ADMIN Rule 2.525. "Documents" means pleadings, motions, petitions, memoranda, briefs, notices, exhibits, declarations, affidavits, orders, judgments, decrees, writs, opinions, and any other paper or writing submitted to a court. FL ST J ADMIN Rule 2.520(a). All documents that are court records, as defined in FL ST J ADMIN Rule 2.430(a)(1), must be filed by electronic transmission, provided that: (1) the clerk has the ability to accept and retain such documents; (2) the clerk or the chief judge of the circuit has requested permission to accept documents filed by electronic transmission; and (3) the supreme court has entered an order granting permission to the clerk to accept documents filed by electronic transmission. FL ST J ADMIN Rule 2.525(c)(1).

a. *Definition.* "Electronic transmission of documents" means the sending of information by electronic signals to, by or from a court or clerk, which when received can be transformed and stored or transmitted on paper, microfilm, magnetic storage device, optical imaging system, CD-ROM, flash drive, other electronic data storage system, server, case maintenance system ("CM"), electronic court filing ("ECF") system, statewide or local electronic portal ("e-portal"), or other electronic record keeping system authorized by the supreme court in a format sufficient to communicate the information on the original document in a readable format. Electronic transmission of documents includes electronic mail ("e-mail") and any internet-based transmission procedure, and may include procedures allowing for documents to be signed or verified by electronic means. FL ST J ADMIN Rule 2.525(a).

b. *Application.* Any court or clerk of the court may accept the electronic transmission of documents for filing after the clerk, together with input from the chief judge of the circuit, has obtained approval of the procedures and program for doing so from the Supreme Court of Florida. FL ST J ADMIN Rule 2.525(b).

c. *Exceptions*

i. Paper documents and other submissions may be manually submitted to the clerk or court:

- When the clerk does not have the ability to accept and retain documents by electronic filing or has not had ECF Procedures approved by the supreme court;
- For filing by any self-represented party or any self-represented nonparty unless specific ECF Procedures provide a means to file documents electronically. However, any self-represented nonparty that is a governmental or public agency and any other agency, partnership, corporation, or business entity acting on behalf of any governmental or public agency may file documents by electronic transmission if such entity has the capability of filing documents electronically;
- For filing by attorneys excused from e-mail service in accordance with FL ST J ADMIN Rule 2.516(b);
- When submitting evidentiary exhibits or filing non-documentary materials;
- When the filing involves documents in excess of twenty-five (25) megabytes (25MB) in size. For such filings, documents may be transmitted using an electronic storage medium that the clerk has the ability to accept, which may include a CD-ROM, flash drive, or similar storage medium;
- When filed in open court, as permitted by the court;
- When paper filing is permitted by any approved statewide or local ECF procedures; and
- If any court determines that justice so requires. FL ST J ADMIN Rule 2.525(d).

ii. Any document in paper form submitted under FL ST J ADMIN Rule 2.525(d) is filed when it

is received by the clerk or court and the clerk shall immediately thereafter convert any filed paper document to an electronic document. "Convert to an electronic document" means optically capturing an image of a paper document and using character recognition software to recover as much of the document's text as practicable and then indexing and storing the document in the official court file. FL ST J ADMIN Rule 2.525(c)(4).

iii. Any storage medium submitted under FL ST J ADMIN Rule 2.525(d)(5) is filed when received by the clerk or court and the clerk shall immediately thereafter transfer the electronic documents from the storage device to the official court file. FL ST J ADMIN Rule 2.525(c)(5).

iv. If the filer of any paper document authorized under FL ST J ADMIN Rule 2.525(d) provides a self-addressed, postage-paid envelope for return of the paper document after it is converted to electronic form by the clerk, the clerk shall place the paper document in the envelope and deposit it in the mail. Except when a paper document is required to be maintained, the clerk may recycle any filed paper document that is not to be returned to the filer. FL ST J ADMIN Rule 2.525(c)(6).

v. The clerk may convert any paper document filed before the effective date of FL ST J ADMIN Rule 2.525 to an electronic document. Unless the clerk is required to maintain the paper document, if the paper document has been converted to an electronic document by the clerk, the paper document is no longer part of the official court file and may be removed and recycled. FL ST J ADMIN Rule 2.525(c)(7).

d. *Official court file.* For information on what constitutes the official court file, please see FL ST J ADMIN Rule 2.525(c)(2), FL ST J ADMIN Rule 2.525(c)(3).

e. *Administration.* All attorneys, parties, or other persons using this rule to file documents are required to make arrangements with the court or clerk for the payment of any charges authorized by general law or the supreme court before filing any document by electronic transmission. FL ST J ADMIN Rule 2.525(f)(2).

f. *Filing date.* The filing date for an electronically transmitted document is the date and time that such filing is acknowledged by an electronic stamp or otherwise, pursuant to any procedure set forth in any ECF Procedures approved by the supreme court, or the date the last page of such filing is received by the court or clerk. FL ST J ADMIN Rule 2.525(f)(3).

g. *Accessibility.* All documents transmitted in any electronic form under FL ST J ADMIN Rule 2.525 must comply with the accessibility requirements of FL ST J ADMIN Rule 2.526. FL ST J ADMIN Rule 2.525(g).

2. *Service requirements*

a. *Papers to be served.* At the time of personal service of process a copy of the initial pleading shall be delivered to the party upon whom service is made. The date and hour of service shall be endorsed on the original process and all copies of it by the person making the service. The party seeking to effect personal service shall furnish the person making service with the necessary copies. When the service is made by publication, copies of the initial pleadings shall be furnished to the clerk and mailed by the clerk with the notice of action to all parties whose addresses are stated in the initial pleading or sworn statement. FL ST RCP Rule 1.070(e).

b. *Issuance of summons.* Upon the commencement of the action, summons or other process authorized by law shall be issued forthwith by the clerk or judge under the clerk's or the judge's signature and the seal of the court and delivered for service without praecipe. FL ST RCP Rule 1.070(a).

i. *How directed.* Summons, subpoenas, and other process in civil actions run throughout the state. All process except subpoenas shall be directed to all and singular the sheriffs of the state. FL ST § 48.011.

ii. *Service as to numerous defendants.* If there is more than one (1) defendant, the clerk or judge shall issue as many writs of process against the several defendants as may be directed by the plaintiff or the plaintiff's attorney. FL ST RCP Rule 1.070(c).

c. *Who may serve process.* Service of process may be made by an officer authorized by law to serve process, but the court may appoint any competent person not interested in the action to serve the process. When so appointed, the person serving process shall make proof of service by affidavit promptly and in any event within the time during which the person served must respond to the process. Failure to make proof of service shall not affect the validity of the service. When any process is returned not executed or returned improperly executed for any defendant, the party causing its issuance shall be entitled to such additional process against the unserved party as is required to effect service. FL ST RCP Rule 1.070(b).

i. All process shall be served by the sheriff of the county where the person to be served is found, except initial nonenforceable civil process may be served by a special process server appointed by the sheriff as provided for in FL ST § 48.021 or by a certified process server as provided for in FL ST § 48.25 through FL ST § 48.31. FL ST § 48.021(1).

ii. The sheriff of each county may, in his or her discretion, establish an approved list of natural persons designated as special process servers. FL ST § 48.021(2)(a). For more information regarding process servers, please see FL ST § 48.021(2).

iii. A person serving process shall place, on the copy served, the date and time of service and his or her identification number and initials for all service of process. FL ST § 48.031(5).

d. *Service of process on Sunday*

i. Service or execution on Sunday of any writ, process, warrant, order, or judgment is void and the person serving or executing, or causing it to be served or executed, is liable to the party aggrieved for damages for so doing as if he or she had done it without any process, writ, warrant, order, or judgment. FL ST § 48.20.

ii. If affidavit is made by the person requesting service or execution that he or she has good reason to believe that any person liable to have any such writ, process, warrant, order, or judgment served on him or her intends to escape from this state under protection of Sunday, any officer furnished with an order authorizing service or execution by the trial court judge may serve or execute such writ, process, warrant, order, or judgment on Sunday, and it is as valid as if it had been done on any other day. FL ST § 48.20.

e. *Methods of service*

i. *Service of process generally.* Service of original process is made by delivering a copy of it to the person to be served with a copy of the complaint, petition, or other initial pleading or paper or by leaving the copies at his or her usual place of abode with any person residing therein who is fifteen (15) years of age or older and informing the person of their contents. Minors who are or have been married shall be served as provided in FL ST § 48.031. FL ST § 48.031(1)(a).

- Employers, when contacted by an individual authorized to make service of process, shall permit the authorized individual to make service on employees in a private area designated by the employer. FL ST § 48.031(1)(b).
- Substitute service may be made on the spouse of the person to be served at any place in the county, if the cause of action is not an adversary proceeding between the spouse and the person to be served, if the spouse requests such service, and if the spouse and person to be served are residing together in the same dwelling. FL ST § 48.031(2)(a).
- Substitute service may be made on an individual doing business as a sole proprietorship at his or her place of business, during regular business hours, by serving the person in charge of the business at the time of service if two (2) or more attempts to serve the owner have been made at the place of business. FL ST § 48.031(2)(b).
- If the only address for a person to be served, which is discoverable through public records, is a private mailbox, substitute service may be made by leaving a copy of the process with the person in charge of the private mailbox, but only if the process server determines that the person to be served maintains a mailbox at that location. FL ST § 48.031(6).

ii. *Service by mail.* A defendant may accept service of process by mail. FL ST RCP Rule 1.070(i).

A plaintiff may notify any defendant of the commencement of the action and request that the defendant waive service of a summons. FL ST RCP Rule 1.070(i)(2).

- *Notice and request for waiver.* The notice and request shall: (1) be in writing and be addressed directly to the defendant, if an individual, or to an officer or managing or general agent of the defendant or other agent authorized by appointment or law to receive service of process; (2) be dispatched by certified mail, return receipt requested; (3) be accompanied by a copy of the complaint and shall identify the court in which it has been filed; (4) inform the defendant of the consequences of compliance and of failure to comply with the request; (5) state the date on which the request is sent; (6) allow the defendant twenty (20) days from the date on which the request is received to return the waiver, or, if the address of the defendant is outside of the United States, thirty (30) days from the date on which it is received to return the waiver; and (7) provide the defendant with an extra copy of the notice and request, including the waiver, as well as a prepaid means of compliance in writing. FL ST RCP Rule 1.070(i)(2).
- *Consequences of accepting/rejecting service by mail.* Acceptance of service of a complaint by mail does not thereby waive any objection to the venue or to the jurisdiction of the court over the person of the defendant. FL ST RCP Rule 1.070(i)(1). If a defendant fails to comply with a request for waiver within the time provided, the court shall impose the costs subsequently incurred in effecting service on the defendant unless good cause for the failure is shown. FL ST RCP Rule 1.070(i)(3). A defendant who, before being served with process, timely returns a waiver so requested is not required to respond to the complaint until sixty (60) days after the date the defendant received the request for waiver of service. For purposes of computing any time prescribed or allowed by the Florida Rules of Civil Procedure, service of process shall be deemed effected twenty (20) days before the time required to respond to the complaint. FL ST RCP Rule 1.070(i)(4). When the plaintiff files a waiver of service with the court, the action shall proceed, except as provided in FL ST RCP Rule 1.070(i)(4), as if a summons and complaint had been served at the time of filing the waiver, and no further proof of service shall be required. FL ST RCP Rule 1.070(i)(5).

iii. *Service on partnerships and limited partnerships*

- Process against a partnership shall be served on any partner and is as valid as if served on each individual partner. If a partner is not available during regular business hours to accept service on behalf of the partnership, he or she may designate an employee to accept such service. After one (1) attempt to serve a partner or designated employee has been made, process may be served on the person in charge of the partnership during regular business hours. After service on any partner, plaintiff may proceed to judgment and execution against that partner and the assets of the partnership. After service on a designated employee or other person in charge, plaintiff may proceed to judgment and execution against the partnership assets but not against the individual assets of any partner. FL ST § 48.061(1).
- Process against a domestic limited partnership may be served on any general partner or on the agent for service of process specified in its certificate of limited partnership or in its certificate as amended or restated and is as valid as if served on each individual member of the partnership. After service on a general partner or the agent, the plaintiff may proceed to judgment and execution against the limited partnership and all of the general partners individually. If a general partner cannot be found in this state and service cannot be made on an agent because of failure to maintain such an agent or because the agent cannot be found or served with the exercise of reasonable diligence, service of process may be effected by service upon the Secretary of State as agent of the limited partnership as provided for in FL ST § 48.181. Service of process may be made under FL ST § 48.071 and FL ST § 48.21 on limited partnerships. FL ST § 48.061(2).
- Process against a foreign limited partnership may be served on any general partner found in the state or on any agent for service of process specified in its application for registration

and is as valid as if served on each individual member of the partnership. If a general partner cannot be found in this state and an agent for service of process has not been appointed or, if appointed, the agent's authority has been revoked or the agent cannot be found or served with the exercise of reasonable diligence, service of process may be effected by service upon the Secretary of State as agent of the limited partnership as provided for in FL ST § 48.181, or process may be served as provided in FL ST § 48.071 and FL ST § 48.21. FL ST § 48.061(3).

iv. *Service on corporation*

- Process against any private corporation, domestic or foreign, may be served: (1) on the president or vice president, or other head of the corporation; (2) in the absence of any person described in FL ST § 48.081(1)(a), on the cashier, treasurer, secretary, or general manager; (3) in the absence of any person described in FL ST § 48.081(1)(a) or FL ST § 48.081(1)(b), on any director; or (4) in the absence of any person described in FL ST § 48.081(1)(a), FL ST § 48.081(1)(b), or FL ST § 48.081(1)(c), on any officer or business agent residing in the state. FL ST § 48.081(1).
- If a foreign corporation has none of the foregoing officers or agents in this state, service may be made on any agent transacting business for it in this state. FL ST § 48.081(2).
- As an alternative to all of the foregoing, process may be served on the agent designated by the corporation under FL ST § 48.091. However, if service cannot be made on a registered agent because of failure to comply with FL ST § 48.091, service of process shall be permitted on any employee at the corporation's principal place of business or on any employee of the registered agent. FL ST § 48.081(3)(a). If the address provided for the registered agent, officer, director, or principal place of business is a residence or private mailbox, service on the corporation may be made by serving the registered agent, officer, or director in accordance with FL ST § 48.031. FL ST § 48.081(3)(b).
- FL ST § 48.081 does not apply to service of process on insurance companies. FL ST § 48.081(4).
- When a corporation engages in substantial and not isolated activities within this state, or has a business office within the state and is actually engaged in the transaction of business therefrom, service upon any officer or business agent while on corporate business within this state may personally be made, pursuant to FL ST § 48.081, and it is not necessary in such case that the action, suit, or proceeding against the corporation shall have arisen out of any transaction or operation connected with or incidental to the business being transacted within the state. FL ST § 48.081(5).
- For information regarding service on a dissolved corporation refer to FL ST § 48.101.

v. *Personal service outside state*

- Except as otherwise provided herein, service of process on persons outside of this state shall be made in the same manner as service within this state by any officer authorized to serve process in the state where the person is served. No order of court is required. An affidavit of the officer shall be filed, stating the time, manner, and place of service. The court may consider the affidavit, or any other competent evidence, in determining whether service has been properly made. Service of process on persons outside the United States may be required to conform to the provisions of the Hague Convention on the Service Abroad of Judicial and Extrajudicial Documents in Civil or Commercial Matters. FL ST § 48.194(1).
- For further information on service of process in an in rem or quasi in rem action refer to FL ST § 48.194(2); FL ST § 48.194(3); and FL ST § 48.194(4).

vi. *Method of substituted service on nonresident*

- When authorized by law, substituted service of process on a nonresident or a person who conceals his or her whereabouts by serving a public officer designated by law shall be made by leaving a copy of the process with a fee of eight dollars and seventy-five cents

($8.75) with the public officer or in his or her office or by mailing the copies by certified mail to the public officer with the fee. The service is sufficient service on a defendant who has appointed a public officer as his or her agent for the service of process. FL ST § 48.161(1).

- Notice of service and a copy of the process shall be sent forthwith by registered or certified mail by the plaintiff or his or her attorney to the defendant, and the defendant's return receipt and the affidavit of the plaintiff or his or her attorney of compliance shall be filed on or before the return day of the process or within such time as the court allows, or the notice and copy shall be served on the defendant, if found within the state, by an officer authorized to serve legal process, or if found without the state, by a sheriff or a deputy sheriff of any county of this state or any duly constituted public officer qualified to serve like process in the state or jurisdiction where the defendant is found. The officer's return showing service shall be filed on or before the return day of the process or within such time as the court allows. The public officer shall keep a record of all process served on him or her showing the day and hour of service. FL ST § 48.161(1).
- If any person on whom service of process is authorized under FL ST § 48.161(1) dies, service may be made on his or her administrator, executor, curator, or personal representative in the same manner. FL ST § 48.161(2).
- FL ST § 48.161 does not apply to persons on whom service is authorized under FL ST § 48.151. FL ST § 48.161(3).
- The public officer may designate some other person in his or her office to accept service. FL ST § 48.161(4).

vii. *Service by publication.* Service of process by publication may be made as provided by statute. FL ST RCP Rule 1.070(d). Service of process by publication is allowable in cases listed in FL ST § 49.011 and upon the parties listed in FL ST § 49.021.

- As a condition precedent to service by publication, a statement shall be filed in the action executed by the plaintiff, the plaintiff's agent or attorney, setting forth substantially the matters hereafter required, which statement may be contained in a verified pleading, or in an affidavit or other sworn statement. FL ST § 49.031(1). After the entry of a final judgment or decree in any action no sworn statement shall ever be held defective for failure to state a required fact if the fact otherwise appears from the record in the action. FL ST § 49.031(3).
- For the sworn statement requirements for service of process by publication refer to FL ST § 49.041; FL ST § 49.051; FL ST § 49.061; and FL ST § 49.071.
- On filing the sworn statement, and otherwise complying with the foregoing requirements, the plaintiff is entitled to have issued by the clerk or judge, not later than sixty (60) days after filing the sworn statement, a notice of action which notice shall set forth: (1) the names of the known natural defendants; the names, status and description of the corporate defendants; a description of the unknown defendants who claim by, through, under or against a known party which may be described as "all parties claiming interests by, through, under or against (name of known party)" and a description of all unknown defendants which may be described as "all parties having or claiming to have any right, title or interest in the property herein described"; (2) the nature of the action or proceeding in short and simple terms (but neglect to do so is not jurisdictional); (3) the name of the court in which the action or proceeding was instituted and an abbreviated title of the case; (4) the description of real property, if any, proceeded against. FL ST § 49.08.
- For further information on service of process by publication refer to FL ST § 49.09; FL ST § 49.10; FL ST § 49.11; FL ST § 49.12; FL ST § 50.011; FL ST § 50.021; FL ST § 50.031; FL ST § 50.041; FL ST § 50.051; and FL ST § 50.061.

viii. *Service on agents of nonresidents doing business in the state.* When any natural person or partnership not residing or having a principal place of business in this state engages in business in this state, process may be served on the person who is in charge of any business in which the defendant is engaged within this state at the time of service, including agents soliciting orders for goods, wares, merchandise or services. FL ST § 48.071.

- Any process so served is as valid as if served personally on the nonresident person or partnership engaging in business in this state in any action against the person or partnership arising out of such business. FL ST § 48.071.
- A copy of such process with a notice of service on the person in charge of such business shall be sent forthwith to the nonresident person or partnership by registered or certified mail, return receipt requested. FL ST § 48.071.
- An affidavit of compliance with FL ST § 48.071 shall be filed before the return day or within such further time as the court may allow. FL ST § 48.071.

ix. *Service on nonresident engaging in business in state.* The acceptance by any person or persons, individually or associated together as a copartnership or any other form or type of association, who are residents of any other state or country, and all foreign corporations, and any person who is a resident of the state and who subsequently becomes a nonresident of the state or conceals his or her whereabouts, of the privilege extended by law to nonresidents and others to operate, conduct, engage in, or carry on a business or business venture in the state, or to have an office or agency in the state, constitutes an appointment by the persons and foreign corporations of the Secretary of State of the state as their agent on whom all process in any action or proceeding against them, or any of them, arising out of any transaction or operation connected with or incidental to the business or business venture may be served. The acceptance of the privilege is signification of the agreement of the persons and foreign corporations that the process against them which is so served is of the same validity as if served personally on the persons or foreign corporations. FL ST § 48.181(1).

- If a foreign corporation has a resident agent or officer in the state, process shall be served on the resident agent or officer. FL ST § 48.181(2).
- Any person, firm, or corporation which sells, consigns, or leases by any means whatsoever tangible or intangible personal property, through brokers, jobbers, wholesalers, or distributors to any person, firm, or corporation in this state is conclusively presumed to be both engaged in substantial and not isolated activities within this state and operating, conducting, engaging in, or carrying on a business or business venture in this state. FL ST § 48.181(3).

x. *Other service provisions:*

- Service on alien property custodian. FL ST § 48.131.
- Service on an incompetent person. FL ST § 48.042.
- Service on minor. FL ST § 48.041.
- Service on public agencies and officers. FL ST § 48.111.
- Service on the state. FL ST § 48.121.
- Service on a state prisoner. FL ST § 48.051.
- Service on labor unions. FL ST § 48.141.
- Service on statutory agents for certain persons. FL ST § 48.151.
- Service on nonresident motor vehicle owners. FL ST § 48.171.
- Service of process in action for possession of premises. FL ST § 48.183.
- Service on nonresidents operating aircraft or watercraft in the state. FL ST § 48.19.

f. *Crossclaims.* Service of a crossclaim on a party who has appeared in the action shall be made pursuant to FL ST RCP Rule 1.080. Service of a crossclaim against a party who has not appeared in the action shall be made in the manner provided for service of summons. FL ST RCP Rule 1.170(g).

g. *Fees.* The statutory compensation for making service shall not be increased by the simultaneous delivery or mailing of the copy of the initial pleading in conformity with FL ST RCP Rule 1.070. FL ST RCP Rule 1.070(g).

G. Hearings

1. There is no hearing required or contemplated in the Florida rules governing the complaint and service of summons.

H. Forms

1. Official Complaint Forms for Florida

a. Caption. FL ST RCP Form 1.901.

b. Summons. FL ST RCP Form 1.902.

c. Crossclaim summons. FL ST RCP Form 1.903.

d. Third-party summons. FL ST RCP Form 1.904.

e. Notice of action; Constructive service; No property. FL ST RCP Form 1.919.

f. Notice of action; Constructive service; Property. FL ST RCP Form 1.920.

g. Third-party complaint. FL ST RCP Form 1.948.

h. Civil cover sheet. FL ST RCP Form 1.997.

i. Fall-down negligence complaint. FL ST RCP Form 1.951.

j. Notice of compliance when constitutional challenge is brought. FL ST RCP Form 1.975.

2. Complaint Forms for Florida

a. Complaint for damages; General form. FL-PP § 2:17.

b. Complaint; Negligent infliction of personal injury. FL-PP § 2:19.

c. Complaint; Fall down negligence. FL-PP § 2:20.

d. Complaint; Professional negligence. FL-PP § 2:23.

e. Complaint; Breach of contract. FL-PP § 2:24.

f. Complaint; Breach of personal services contract. FL-PP § 2:25.

g. Summons; General form. FL-PRACFORM § 3:4.

h. Summons; Natural person. FL-PRACFORM § 3:5.

i. Complaint; Assault and battery. FL-PRACFORM § 4:9.

j. Complaint; Breach of contract, general form. FL-PRACFORM § 4:17.

k. Complaint; Civil rights. FL-PRACFORM § 4:23.

l. Complaint; Conversion. FL-PRACFORM § 4:30.

m. Complaint; Employment contract. FL-PRACFORM § 4:44.

n. Complaint; False imprisonment. FL-PRACFORM § 4:46.

o. Complaint; Fraud, misrepresentation. FL-PRACFORM § 4:62.

p. Complaint; Lease, by landlord. FL-PRACFORM § 4:86.

q. Complaint; Lease, by tenant. FL-PRACFORM § 4:87.

r. Complaint; Libel. FL-PRACFORM § 4:89.

s. Complaint; Life insurance policy. FL-PRACFORM § 4:90.

t. Complaint; Medical malpractice, negligence. FL-PRACFORM § 4:95.

u. Complaint; Negligence, automobile, driver. FL-PRACFORM § 4:101.

v. Complaint; Negligence, hospital. FL-PRACFORM § 4:104.

I. Checklist

(I) ❑ Matters to be considered by plaintiff
- (a) ❑ Required documents
  - (1) ❑ Summons
  - (2) ❑ Complaint
  - (3) ❑ Civil cover sheet
  - (4) ❑ Return of execution process by process server
  - (5) ❑ Filing fees
- (b) ❑ Supplemental documents
  - (1) ❑ Exhibits
  - (2) ❑ Notice of constitutional question
- (c) ❑ Time for filing and serving complaint
  - (1) ❑ Service of the initial process and initial pleading should be made upon a defendant within one hundred twenty (120) days after the filing of the complaint with the court

(II) ❑ Matters to be considered by defendant
- (a) ❑ Required documents
  - (1) ❑ Answer
  - (2) ❑ Certificate of service
- (b) ❑ Supplemental documents
  - (1) ❑ Exhibits
  - (2) ❑ Notice of constitutional question
- (c) ❑ Time for answer
  - (1) ❑ Unless a different time is prescribed in a statute of Florida, a defendant shall serve an answer within twenty (20) days after service of original process and the initial pleading on the defendant, or not later than the date fixed in a notice by publication
  - (2) ❑ A party served with a pleading stating a crossclaim against that party shall serve an answer to it within twenty (20) days after service on that party
  - (3) ❑ The plaintiff shall serve an answer to a counterclaim within twenty (20) days after service of the counterclaim
  - (4) ❑ A defendant who, before being served with process, timely returns a waiver so requested is not required to respond to the complaint until sixty (60) days after the date the defendant received the request for waiver of service; for purposes of computing any time prescribed or allowed by the Florida Rules of Civil Procedure, service of process shall be deemed effected twenty (20) days before the time required to respond to the complaint
  - (5) ❑ For timing requirements related to service on the state, service of motion impact, and responding when no responsive pleading is required, please see the Timing section of this document

Pleadings
Amended Complaint

Document Last Updated January 2013

A. Applicable Rules

1. *State rules*
   - a. Nonverification of papers. FL ST RCP Rule 1.030.

b. Process. FL ST RCP Rule 1.070.
c. Service and filing of pleadings, orders, and documents. FL ST RCP Rule 1.080.
d. Pleadings and motions. FL ST RCP Rule 1.100; FL ST RCP Rule 1.110; FL ST RCP Rule 1.120; FL ST RCP Rule 1.130; FL ST RCP Rule 1.190; FL ST § 48.193.
e. Pretrial procedure. FL ST RCP Rule 1.200.
f. Relief from judgment, decrees, or orders. FL ST RCP Rule 1.540.
g. Forms. FL ST RCP Rule 1.900.
h. Minimization of the filing of sensitive information. FL ST J ADMIN Rule 2.425.
i. Retention of court records. FL ST J ADMIN Rule 2.430.
j. Foreign attorneys. FL ST J ADMIN Rule 2.510.
k. Signature of attorneys and parties. FL ST J ADMIN Rule 2.515.
l. Paper. FL ST J ADMIN Rule 2.520.
m. Electronic filing. FL ST J ADMIN Rule 2.525.
n. Accessibility of information and technology. FL ST J ADMIN Rule 2.526.
o. Requests for accommodations by persons with disabilities. FL ST J ADMIN Rule 2.540.

2. *Local rules*
   a. Establishment of 11th Circuit Homestead Access to Mediation Program ("CHAMP") for case management of residential foreclosure cases in the Eleventh Judicial Circuit of Florida. FL ST 11 J CIR 1-09-08.

B. Timing

1. *Amendment as a matter of course.* A party may amend a pleading once as a matter of course at any time before a responsive pleading is served or, if the pleading is one to which no responsive pleading is permitted and the action has not been placed on the trial calendar, may so amend it at any time within twenty (20) days after it is served. FL ST RCP Rule 1.190(a).
2. *Amendment by leave of court.* Otherwise a party may amend a pleading only by leave of court or by written consent of the adverse party. Leave of court shall be given freely when justice so requires. FL ST RCP Rule 1.190(a).
3. *Amendments in furtherance of justice.* At any time in furtherance of justice, upon such terms as may be just, the court may permit any process, proceeding, pleading, or record to be amended or material supplemental matter to be set forth in an amended or supplemental pleading. At every stage of the action the court must disregard any error or defect in the proceedings which does not affect the substantial rights of the parties. FL ST RCP Rule 1.190(e).
4. *Response to amended pleading.* A party shall plead in response to an amended pleading within ten (10) days after service of the amended pleading unless the court otherwise orders. FL ST RCP Rule 1.190(a).
5. *Computation of time*
   a. *Generally.* Computation of time shall be governed by FL ST J ADMIN Rule 2.514. FL ST RCP Rule 1.090(a). The following rules apply in computing time periods specified in any rule of procedure, local rule, court order, or statute that does not specify a method of computing time. FL ST J ADMIN Rule 2.514(a).
      i. *Period stated in days or a longer unit.* When the period is stated in days or a longer unit of time (A) exclude the day of the event that triggers the period; (B) count every day, including intermediate Saturdays, Sundays, and legal holidays; and (C) include the last day of the period, but if the last day is a Saturday, Sunday, or legal holiday, or falls within any period of time extended through an order of the chief justice under FL ST J ADMIN Rule 2.205(a)(2)(B)(iv), the period continues to run until the end of the next day that is not a Saturday, Sunday, or legal holiday and does not fall within any period of time extended through an order of the chief justice. FL ST J ADMIN Rule 2.514(a)(1).

ii. *Period stated in hours.* When the period is stated in hours (A) begin counting immediately on the occurrence of the event that triggers the period; (B) count every hour, including hours during intermediate Saturdays, Sundays, and legal holidays; and (C) if the period would end on a Saturday, Sunday, or legal holiday, or during any period of time extended through an order of the chief justice under FL ST J ADMIN Rule 2.205(a)(2)(B)(iv), the period continues to run until the same time on the next day that is not a Saturday, Sunday, or legal holiday and does not fall within any period of time extended through an order of the chief justice. FL ST J ADMIN Rule 2.514(a)(2).

iii. *Period stated in days less than seven (7) days.* When the period stated in days is less than seven (7) days, intermediate Saturdays, Sundays, and legal holidays shall be excluded in the computation. FL ST J ADMIN Rule 2.514(a)(3).

iv. *"Last day" defined.* Unless a different time is set by a statute, local rule, or court order, the last day ends (A) for electronic filing or for service by any means, at midnight; and (B) for filing by other means, when the clerk's office is scheduled to close. FL ST J ADMIN Rule 2.514(a)(4).

v. *"Next day" defined.* The "next day" is determined by continuing to count forward when the period is measured after an event and backward when measured before an event. FL ST J ADMIN Rule 2.514(a)(5).

vi. *"Legal holiday" defined.* "Legal holiday" means (A) the day set aside by FL ST § 110.117, for observing New Year's Day, Martin Luther King, Jr.'s Birthday, Memorial Day, Independence Day, Labor Day, Veterans' Day, Thanksgiving Day, the Friday after Thanksgiving Day, or Christmas Day, and (B) any day observed as a holiday by the clerk's office or as designated by the chief judge. FL ST J ADMIN Rule 2.514(a)(6).

b. *Additional time after service by mail or e-mail.* When a party may or must act within a specified time after service and service is made by mail or e-mail, five (5) days are added after the period that would otherwise expire under FL ST J ADMIN Rule 2.514(a). FL ST J ADMIN Rule 2.514(b).

c. *Enlargement.* When an act is required or allowed to be done at or within a specified time by order of court, by the Florida Rules of Civil Procedure, or by notice given thereunder, for cause shown the court at any time in its discretion (1) with or without notice, may order the period enlarged if request therefor is made before the expiration of the period originally prescribed or as extended by a previous order, or (2) upon motion made and notice after the expiration of the specified period, may permit the act to be done when failure to act was the result of excusable neglect, but it may not extend the time for making a motion for new trial, for rehearing, or to alter or amend a judgment; making a motion for relief from a judgment under FL ST RCP Rule 1.540(b); taking an appeal or filing a petition for certiorari; or making a motion for a directed verdict. FL ST RCP Rule 1.090(b).

d. *Unaffected by expiration of term.* The period of time provided for the doing of any act or the taking of any proceeding shall not be affected or limited by the continued existence or expiration of a term of court. The continued existence or expiration of a term of court in no way affects the power of a court to do any act or take any proceeding in any action which is or has been pending before it. FL ST RCP Rule 1.090(c).

C. General Requirements

1. *Amendments.* A party may amend a pleading once as a matter of course at any time before a responsive pleading is served or, if the pleading is one to which no responsive pleading is permitted and the action has not been placed on the trial calendar, may so amend it at any time within twenty (20) days after it is served. Otherwise a party may amend a pleading only by leave of court or by written consent of the adverse party. Leave of court shall be freely given when justice so requires. FL ST RCP Rule 1.190(a).

a. *Purpose of amendments.* Amendments can relate to the correction of mistakes, the insertion of jurisdictional averments, the correction or addition of verifications, the addition or substitution or striking out of parties, and generally the rectification of all formal defects in the pleading. The court can also allow amendments setting up an omitted counterclaim or cross-claim if the defendant failed to raise the claim through oversight, inadvertence, or excusable neglect. FL-PP § 2:151.

b. *Amendment to a pleading/Amended pleading.* A significant difference exists between an amendment to a pleading and an amended pleading. An amendment to a pleading corrects, adds to or deletes from the pleading. An amended pleading is substituted for the former pleading and the former pleading ceases to have any effect. Dee v. Southern Brewing Company, 146 Fla. 588, 1 So.2d 562 (Fla. 1941); Shannon v. McBride, 105 So.2d 16 (Fla. 2d DCA 1958); Hughes v. Home Sav. of America, F.S.B., 675 So.2d 649 (Fla. 2d DCA 1996); FL-PRACPROC § 14:2.

c. *Relation back of amendments.* When the claim or defense asserted in the amended pleading arose out of the conduct, transaction, or occurrence set forth or attempted to be set forth in the original pleading, the amendment shall relate back to the date of the original pleading. FL ST RCP Rule 1.190(c).

2. *General rules of pleading*

   a. *Claims for relief*

      i. A pleading which sets forth a claim for relief, whether an original claim, counterclaim, crossclaim, or third-party claim, must state a cause of action and shall contain

         - A short and plain statement of the grounds upon which the court's jurisdiction depends, unless the court already has jurisdiction and the claim needs no new grounds of jurisdiction to support it (For information regarding acts subjecting persons to jurisdiction, please see FL ST § 48.193),
         - A short and plain statement of the ultimate facts showing that the pleader is entitled to relief, and
         - A demand for judgment for the relief to which the pleader deems himself or herself entitled. FL ST RCP Rule 1.110(b).

      ii. Relief in the alternative or of several different types may be demanded. Every complaint shall be considered to demand general relief. FL ST RCP Rule 1.110(b).

   b. *Verification.* Except when otherwise specifically provided by these rules or an applicable statute, every pleading or other document of a party represented by an attorney need not be verified or accompanied by an affidavit. FL ST RCP Rule 1.030. When filing an action for foreclosure of a mortgage on residential real property the complaint shall be verified. When verification of a document is required, the document filed shall include an oath, affirmation, or the following statement: "Under penalty of perjury, I declare that I have read the foregoing, and the facts alleged therein are true and correct to the best of my knowledge and belief." FL ST RCP Rule 1.110(b).

   c. *Separate statements.* All averments of claim or defense shall be made in consecutively numbered paragraphs, the contents of each of which shall be limited as far as practicable to a statement of a single set of circumstances, and a paragraph may be referred to by number in all subsequent pleadings. Each claim founded upon a separate transaction or occurrence and each defense other than denials shall be stated in a separate count or defense when a separation facilitates the clear presentation of the matter set forth. FL ST RCP Rule 1.110(f).

   d. *Statements adopted by reference.* Statements in a pleading may be adopted by reference in a different part of the same pleading, in another pleading, or in any motion. FL ST RCP Rule 1.130(b).

   e. *Joinder of causes of action; Consistency.* A pleader may set up in the same action as many claims or causes of action or defenses in the same right as the pleader has, and claims for relief may be stated in the alternative if separate items make up the cause of action, or if two (2) or more causes of action are joined. A party may also set forth two (2) or more statements of a claim or defense alternatively, either in one (1) count or defense or in separate counts or defenses. When two (2) or more statements are made in the alternative and one (1) of them, if made independently, would be sufficient, the pleading is not made insufficient by the insufficiency of one (1) or more of the alternative statements. A party may also state as many separate claims or defenses as that party has, regardless of consistency and whether based on legal or equitable grounds or both. All pleadings shall be construed so as to do substantial justice. FL ST RCP Rule 1.110(g).

   f. *Subsequent pleadings.* When the nature of an action permits pleadings subsequent to final judgment and the jurisdiction of the court over the parties has not terminated, the initial pleading subsequent to final judgment shall be designated a supplemental complaint or petition. The action shall then proceed in the same manner and time as though the supplemental complaint or petition were the initial pleading in the action, including the issuance of any needed process. FL ST RCP Rule 1.110(h) shall not apply to proceedings that may be initiated by motion under the Florida Rules of Civil Procedure. FL ST RCP Rule 1.110(h).

g. *Pleading basis for service.* When service of process is to be made under statutes authorizing service on nonresidents of Florida, it is sufficient to plead the basis for service in the language of the statute without pleading the facts supporting service. FL ST RCP Rule 1.070(h).

h. *Forms of pleadings.* Forms of action and technical forms for seeking relief and of pleas, pleadings, or motions are abolished. FL ST RCP Rule 1.110(a).

3. *Complaint; Generally*

a. *Purpose.* The purpose of a complaint is to advise the court and the defendant of the nature of a cause of action asserted by the plaintiff. FL-PP § 2:12.

b. *Sufficiency of complaint.* A complaint will be found to be insufficient if it contains only general conclusory allegations unsupported by any facts. The test to determine whether a complaint is sufficient is whether, if the factual allegations of the complaint are established, the plaintiff will be legally or equitably entitled to the claimed relief. Pizzi v. Central Bank & Trust Co., 250 So.2d 895, 896 (Fla. 1971); Bowen v. G H C Properties, Limited, 251 So.2d 359, 361 (Fla. 1st DCA 1971); FL-PP § 2:12. In determining the sufficiency of the complaint to state a cause of action, all allegations of the complaint are taken as true, and possible affirmative defenses are not considered. Strickland v. Commerce Loan Co. of Jacksonville, 158 So.2d 814 (Fla. 1st DCA 1963); FL-PP § 2:12.

i. The issues for trial in Florida must be settled by the pleadings. The issues cannot be raised by discovery. FL-PRACPROC § 7:6.

ii. Causes of action may be pleaded alternatively in the same count or in different counts and against the same or different defendants as long as the joinder of parties is proper. FL-PRACPROC § 7:6.

iii. Each count must state a cause of action. Each independent cause of action should be pleaded in a separate count. FL-PRACPROC § 7:6.

iv. Incorporation by reference of all allegations from one count to another is not proper. Separate counts facilitate reference to the pleading in which they appear in other pleadings, motions or papers as well as the assertion of defenses against some, but not all, causes of action. Some defenses may not apply to the initial pleading as a whole. FL-PRACPROC § 7:6.

4. *Pleading special matters*

a. *Capacity.* It is not necessary to aver the capacity of a party to sue or be sued, the authority of a party to sue or be sued in a representative capacity, or the legal existence of an organized association of persons that is made a party, except to the extent required to show the jurisdiction of the court. The initial pleading served on behalf of a minor party shall specifically aver the age of the minor party. When a party desires to raise an issue as to the legal existence of any party, the capacity of any party to sue or be sued, or the authority of a party to sue or be sued in a representative capacity, that party shall do so by specific negative averment which shall include such supporting particulars as are peculiarly within the pleader's knowledge. FL ST RCP Rule 1.120(a).

b. *Fraud, mistake, condition of the mind.* In all averments of fraud or mistake, the circumstances constituting fraud or mistake shall be stated with such particularity as the circumstances may permit. Malice, intent, knowledge, mental attitude, and other condition of mind of a person may be averred generally. FL ST RCP Rule 1.120(b).

c. *Conditions precedent.* In pleading the performance or occurrence of conditions precedent, it is sufficient to aver generally that all conditions precedent have been performed or have occurred. A denial of performance or occurrence shall be made specifically and with particularity. FL ST RCP Rule 1.120(c).

d. *Official document or act.* In pleading an official document or official act it is sufficient to aver that the document was issued or the act done in compliance with law. FL ST RCP Rule 1.120(c).

e. *Judgment or decree.* In pleading a judgment or decree of a domestic or foreign court, a judicial or quasi-judicial tribunal, or a board or officer, it is sufficient to aver the judgment or decree without setting forth matter showing jurisdiction to render it. FL ST RCP Rule 1.120(e).

f. *Time and place.* For the purpose of testing the sufficiency of a pleading, averments of time and place are material and shall be considered like all other averments of material matter. FL ST RCP Rule 1.120(f).

g. *Special damage.* When items of special damage are claimed, they shall be specifically stated. FL ST RCP Rule 1.120(g).

5. *Parties*

a. *Parties generally.* Every action may be prosecuted in the name of the real party in interest, but a personal representative, administrator, guardian, trustee of an express trust, a party with whom or in whose name a contract has been made for the benefit of another, or a party expressly authorized by statute may sue in that person's own name without joining the party for whose benefit the action is brought. All persons having an interest in the subject of the action and in obtaining the relief demanded may join as plaintiffs and any person may be made a defendant who has or claims an interest adverse to the plaintiff. Any person may at any time be made a party if that person's presence is necessary or proper to a complete determination of the cause. Persons having a united interest may be joined on the same side as plaintiffs or defendants, and anyone who refuses to join may for such reason be made a defendant. FL ST RCP Rule 1.210(a).

b. *Minors or incompetent persons.* When a minor or incompetent person has a representative, such as a guardian or other like fiduciary, the representative may sue or defend on behalf of the minor or incompetent person. A minor or incompetent person who does not have a duly appointed representative may sue by next friend or by a guardian ad litem. The court shall appoint a guardian ad litem for a minor or incompetent person not otherwise represented in an action or shall make such other order as it deems proper for the protection of the minor or incompetent person. FL ST RCP Rule 1.210(b).

c. For survivor and substitution of parties information, please see FL ST RCP Rule 1.260.

6. *Counterclaims and crossclaims*

a. *Compulsory counterclaims.* A pleading shall state as a counterclaim any claim which at the time of serving the pleading the pleader has against any opposing party, provided it arises out of the transaction or occurrence that is the subject matter of the opposing party's claim and does not require for its adjudication the presence of third parties over whom the court cannot acquire jurisdiction. But the pleader need not state a claim if (1) at the time the action was commenced the claim was the subject of another pending action, or (2) the opposing party brought suit upon that party's claim by attachment or other process by which the court did not acquire jurisdiction to render a personal judgment on the claim and the pleader is not stating a counterclaim under this rule. FL ST RCP Rule 1.170(a).

b. *Permissive counterclaim.* A pleading may state as a counterclaim any claim against an opposing party not arising out of the transaction or occurrence that is the subject matter of the opposing party's claim. FL ST RCP Rule 1.170(b).

c. *Counterclaim exceeding opposing claim.* A counterclaim may or may not diminish or defeat the recovery sought by the opposing party. It may claim relief exceeding in amount or different in kind from that sought in the pleading of the opposing party. FL ST RCP Rule 1.170(c).

d. *Counterclaim against the State.* The Florida Rules of Civil Procedure shall not be construed to enlarge beyond the limits established by law the right to assert counterclaims or to claim credits against the state or any of its subdivisions or other governmental organizations thereof subject to suit or against a municipal corporation or against an officer, agency, or administrative board of the state. FL ST RCP Rule 1.170(d).

e. *Counterclaim maturing or acquired after pleading.* A claim which matured or was acquired by the pleader after serving the pleading may be presented as a counterclaim by supplemental pleading with the permission of the court. FL ST RCP Rule 1.170(e).

f. *Omitted counterclaim or crossclaim.* When a pleader fails to set up a counterclaim or crossclaim through oversight, inadvertence, or excusable neglect, or when justice requires, the pleader may set up the counterclaim or crossclaim by amendment with leave of the court. FL ST RCP Rule 1.170(f).

g. *Crossclaim against co-party.* A pleading may state as a crossclaim any claim by one party against a co-party arising out of the transaction or occurrence that is the subject matter of either the original action or a counterclaim therein, or relating to any property that is the subject matter of the original action. The crossclaim may include a claim that the party against whom it is asserted is or may be liable to the crossclaimant for all or part of a claim asserted in the action against the crossclaimant. Service of a crossclaim on a party who has appeared in the action shall be made pursuant to FL ST RCP Rule 1.080. Service of a crossclaim against a party who has not appeared in the action shall be made in the manner provided for service of summons. FL ST RCP Rule 1.170(g).

h. *Additional parties may be brought in.* When the presence of parties other than those to the original action is required to grant complete relief in the determination of a counterclaim or crossclaim, they shall be named in the counterclaim or crossclaim and be served with process and shall be parties to the action thereafter if jurisdiction of them can be obtained and their joinder will not deprive the court of jurisdiction of the action. FL ST RCP Rule 1.250(b) and FL ST RCP Rule 1.250(c) apply to parties brought in under FL ST RCP Rule 1.170(h). FL ST RCP Rule 1.170(h).

i. *Separate trials; Separate judgment.* If the court orders separate trials as provided in FL ST RCP Rule 1.270(b), judgment on a counterclaim or crossclaim may be rendered when the court has jurisdiction to do so even if a claim of the opposing party has been dismissed or otherwise disposed of. FL ST RCP Rule 1.170(i).

j. *Demand exceeding jurisdiction; Transfer of action.* If the demand of any counterclaim or crossclaim exceeds the jurisdiction of the court in which the action is pending, the action shall be transferred forthwith to the court of the same county having jurisdiction of the demand in the counterclaim or crossclaim with only such alterations in the pleadings as are essential. The court shall order the transfer of the action and the transmittal of all papers in it to the proper court if the party asserting the demand exceeding the jurisdiction deposits with the court having jurisdiction a sum sufficient to pay the clerk's service charge in the court to which the action is transferred at the time of filing the counterclaim or crossclaim. Thereupon the original papers and deposit shall be transmitted and filed with a certified copy of the order. The court to which the action is transferred shall have full power and jurisdiction over the demands of all parties. Failure to make the service charge deposit at the time the counterclaim or crossclaim is filed, or within such further time as the court may allow, shall reduce a claim for damages to an amount within the jurisdiction of the court where the action is pending and waive the claim in other cases. FL ST RCP Rule 1.170(j).

7. *Misjoinder and nonjoinder of parties*

a. *Misjoinder.* Misjoinder of parties is not a ground for dismissal of an action. Any claim against a party may be severed and proceeded with separately. FL ST RCP Rule 1.250(a).

b. *Dropping parties.* Parties may be dropped by an adverse party in the manner provided for voluntary dismissal in FL ST RCP Rule 1.420(a)(1) subject to the exception stated in FL ST RCP Rule 1.420. If notice of lis pendens has been filed in the action against a party so dropped, the notice of dismissal shall be recorded and cancels the notice of lis pendens without the necessity of a court order. Parties may be dropped by order of court on its own initiative or the motion of any party at any stage of the action on such terms as are just. FL ST RCP Rule 1.250(b).

c. *Adding parties.* Parties may be added once as a matter of course within the same time that pleadings can be so amended under FL ST RCP Rule 1.190(a). If amendment by leave of court or stipulation of the parties is permitted, parties may be added in the amended pleading without further order of court. Parties may be added by order of court on its own initiative or on motion of any party at any stage of the action and on such terms as are just. FL ST RCP Rule 1.250(c).

8. *Jury demand*

a. *Right preserved.* The right of trial by jury as declared by the Constitution or by statute shall be preserved to the parties inviolate. FL ST RCP Rule 1.430(a).

b. *Demand.* Any party may demand a trial by jury of any issue triable of right by a jury by serving upon the other party a demand therefor in writing at any time after commencement of the action and not later than ten (10) days after the service of the last pleading directed to such issue. The demand may be indorsed upon a pleading of the party. FL ST RCP Rule 1.430(b).

c. *Specification of issues.* In the demand a party may specify the issues that the party wishes so tried; otherwise, the party is deemed to demand trial by jury for all issues so triable. FL ST RCP Rule 1.430(c).

   i. If a party has demanded trial by jury for only some of the issues, any other party may serve a demand for trial by jury of any other or all of the issues triable by jury ten (10) days after service of the demand or such lesser time as the court may order. FL ST RCP Rule 1.430(c).

d. *Waiver.* A party who fails to serve a demand as required by FL ST RCP Rule 1.430 waives trial by jury. FL ST RCP Rule 1.430(d).

   i. If waived, a jury trial may not be granted without the consent of the parties, but the court may allow an amendment in the proceedings to demand a trial by jury or order a trial by jury on its own motion. FL ST RCP Rule 1.430(d).

   ii. A demand for trial by jury may not be withdrawn without the consent of the parties. FL ST RCP Rule 1.430(d).

9. *Arbitration and mediation*

a. *Referral to arbitration and mediation.* Except as hereinafter provided or as otherwise prohibited by law, the presiding judge may enter an order referring all or any part of a contested civil matter to mediation or arbitration. The parties to any contested civil matter may file a written stipulation to mediate or arbitrate any issue between them at any time. Such stipulation shall be incorporated into the order of referral. FL ST RCP Rule 1.700(a).

   i. In all residential foreclosure actions involving homestead properties filed on or after May 1, 2009, unless a stipulation is specifically invoked by the parties in writing within five (5) days of service of the complaint on the main defendant, the parties are deemed to have stipulated to referral of the mediation to the Collins Center pursuant to FL ST RCP Rule 1.720(f). FL ST 11 J CIR 1-09-08(2); FL ST 11 J CIR 1-09-08(3). FL ST 11 J CIR 1-09-08 constitutes a formal referral to mediation pursuant to the Florida Rules of Civil Procedure. FL ST 11 J CIR 1-09-08(2).

   ii. For further information on referral to mediation, refer to FL ST 11 J CIR 1-09-08.

b. *Arbitration*

   i. *Exclusions.* A civil action shall be ordered to arbitration or arbitration in conjunction with mediation upon stipulation of the parties. A civil action may be ordered to arbitration or arbitration in conjunction with mediation upon motion of any party or by the court, if the judge determines the action to be of such a nature that arbitration could be of benefit to the litigants or the court. FL ST RCP Rule 1.800.

      - Under no circumstances may the following categories of actions be referred to arbitration: (1) bond estreatures; (2) habeas corpus or other extraordinary writs; (3) bond validations; (4) civil or criminal contempt; (5) such other matters as may be specified by order of the chief judge in the circuit. FL ST RCP Rule 1.800.

   ii. For more information regarding arbitration, please see FL ST RCP Rule 1.810; FL ST RCP Rule 1.820; FL ST RCP Rule 1.830.

c. *Mediation.* For more information regarding mediation, please see FL ST RCP Rule 1.710; FL ST RCP Rule 1.720; FL ST RCP Rule 1.730; and FL ST RCP Rule 1.750.

10. *Rules of court*

a. *Rules of civil procedure.* The Florida Rules of Civil Procedure apply to all actions of a civil nature and all special statutory proceedings in the circuit courts and county courts except those to which the

Florida Probate Rules, the Florida Family Law Rules of Procedure, or the Small Claims Rules apply. FL ST RCP Rule 1.010.

i. The form, content, procedure, and time for pleading in all special statutory proceedings shall be as prescribed by the statutes governing the proceeding unless the Florida Rules of Civil Procedure specifically provide to the contrary. FL ST RCP Rule 1.010.

ii. The Florida Rules of Civil Procedure shall be construed to secure the just, speedy, and inexpensive determination of every action. FL ST RCP Rule 1.010.

b. *Rules of judicial administration.* The Florida Rules of Judicial Administration shall apply to administrative matters in all courts to which the Florida Rules of Judicial Administration are applicable by their terms. The Florida Rules of Judicial Administration shall be construed to secure the speedy and inexpensive determination of every proceeding to which they are applicable. The Florida Rules of Judicial Administration shall supersede all conflicting rules and statutes. FL ST J ADMIN Rule 2.110.

D. Documents

1. *Required documents*

a. *Amended complaint.* See the General Requirements section of this document for the content of an amended complaint. If a party files a motion to amend a pleading, the party shall attach the proposed amended pleading to the motion. FL ST RCP Rule 1.190(a). See the KeyRules Florida Circuit Court Motion for Leave to Amend document for further information.

i. *Notices to persons with disabilities.* See the Format section of this KeyRules document for further information.

b. *Certificate of service.* When any attorney certifies in substance: "I certify that a copy hereof has been furnished to (here insert name or names and addresses used for service) by (e-mail) (delivery) (mail) (fax) on .... (date) ....________________ Attorney" the certificate is taken as prima facie proof of such service in compliance with FL ST J ADMIN Rule 2.516. FL ST J ADMIN Rule 2.516(f).

2. *Supplemental documents*

a. *Exhibits.* All bonds, notes, bills of exchange, contracts, accounts, or documents upon which action may be brought or defense made, or a copy thereof or a copy of the portions thereof material to the pleadings, shall be incorporated in or attached to the pleading. No papers shall be unnecessarily annexed as exhibits. The pleadings shall contain no unnecessary recitals of deeds, documents, contracts, or other instruments. Any exhibit attached to a pleading shall be considered a part of the pleadings for all purposes. FL ST RCP Rule 1.130(a).

b. *Notice of constitutional question.* A party that files a pleading, written motion, or other paper drawing into question the constitutionality of a state statute or a county or municipal charter, ordinance, or franchise must promptly (1) file a notice of constitutional question stating the question and identifying the paper that raises it; and (2) serve the notice and the pleading, written motion, or other paper drawing into question the constitutionality of a state statute or a county or municipal charter, ordinance, or franchise on the Attorney General or the state attorney of the judicial circuit in which the action is pending, by either certified or registered mail. Service of the notice and pleading, written motion, or other paper does not require joinder of the Attorney General or the state attorney as a party to the action. FL ST RCP Rule 1.071.

E. Format

1. *Documents; Type and size.* Documents subject to the exceptions set forth in FL ST J ADMIN Rule 2.525(d) shall be filed on recycled paper measuring eight and one half by eleven (8 1/2 by 11) inches. For purposes of FL ST J ADMIN Rule 2.520, paper is recycled if it contains a minimum content of fifty (50) percent waste paper. Xerographic reduction of legal-size (eight and one half by fourteen (8 1/2 by 14) inches) documents to letter size (eight and one half by eleven (8 1/2 by 11) inches) is prohibited. All other documents filed by electronic transmission shall be filed in a format capable of being printed in a format consistent with the provisions of FL ST J ADMIN Rule 2.250. FL ST J ADMIN Rule 2.520(b).

a. *Exhibits.* Any exhibit or attachment filed with pleadings or papers may be filed in its original size. FL ST J ADMIN Rule 2.520(c).

b. *Recording space.* On all papers and documents prepared and filed by the court or by any party to a proceeding which are to be recorded in the public records of any county, including but not limited to final money judgments and notices of lis pendens, a three (3) inch by three (3) inch space at the top right-hand corner on the first page and a one (1) inch by three (3) inch space at the top right-hand corner on each subsequent page shall be left blank and reserved for use by the clerk of court. FL ST J ADMIN Rule 2.520(d).

  i. *Exceptions to recording space.* Any papers or documents created by persons or entities over which the filing party has no control, including but not limited to wills, codicils, trusts, or other testamentary documents; documents prepared or executed by any public officer; documents prepared, executed, acknowledged, or proved outside of the State of Florida; or documents created by State or Federal government agencies, may be filed without the space required by FL ST J ADMIN Rule 2.520. FL ST J ADMIN Rule 2.520(e).

c. *Noncompliance.* No clerk of court is permitted to refuse to file any document or paper because of noncompliance with the Florida Rules of Judicial Administration. However, upon request of the clerk of court, noncomplying documents must be resubmitted in accordance with the formatting rules. FL ST J ADMIN Rule 2.520(f).

2. *Caption.* Every pleading, motion, order, judgment, or other paper shall have a caption containing the name of the court, the file number, and except for in rem proceedings, including forfeiture proceedings, the name of the first party on each side with an appropriate indication of other parties, and a designation identifying the party filing it and its nature or the nature of the order, as the case may be. In any in rem proceeding, every pleading, motion, order, judgment, or other paper shall have a caption containing the name of the court, the file number, the style "In re" (followed by the name or general description of the property), and a designation of the person or entity filing it and its nature or the nature of the order, as the case may be. In an in rem forfeiture proceeding, the style shall be "In re forfeiture of" (followed by the name of the general description of the property). All papers filed in the action shall be styled in such a manner as to indicate clearly the subject matter of the paper and the party requesting or obtaining relief. FL ST RCP Rule 1.100(c)(1).

3. *Writing and written defined.* Writing or written means a document containing information, an application, or a stipulation. FL ST RCP Rule 1.080(c).

4. *Rule abbreviations*

a. The Florida Rules of Civil Procedure and shall be abbreviated as Fla.R.Civ.P. FL ST RCP Rule 1.010.

b. The Florida Rules of Judicial Administration shall be abbreviated as Fla. R. Jud. Admin. FL ST J ADMIN Rule 2.110.

5. *Nonverification.* Except when otherwise specifically provided by the Florida Rules of Civil Procedure or an applicable statute, every pleading or other document of a party represented by an attorney need not be verified or accompanied by an affidavit. FL ST RCP Rule 1.030; FL ST J ADMIN Rule 2.515(a).

6. *Attorney signature*

a. *Attorney signature.* Every pleading and other document of a party represented by an attorney shall be signed by at least one (1) attorney of record in that attorney's individual name whose current record Florida Bar address, telephone number, including area code, primary e-mail address and secondary e-mail addresses, if any, and Florida Bar number shall be stated, and who shall be duly licensed to practice law in Florida or who shall have received permission to appear in the particular case as provided in FL ST J ADMIN Rule 2.510. FL ST J ADMIN Rule 2.515(a).

  i. The attorney may be required by the court to give the address of, and to vouch for the attorney's authority to represent, the party. FL ST J ADMIN Rule 2.515(a).

  ii. The signature of an attorney shall constitute a certificate by the attorney that the attorney has read the pleading or other document; that to the best of the attorney's knowledge, information, and belief there is good ground to support it; and that it is not interposed for delay. FL ST J ADMIN Rule 2.515(a).

  iii. If a pleading is not signed or is signed with intent to defeat the purpose of FL ST J ADMIN Rule

2.515, it may be stricken and the action may proceed as though the pleading or other document had not been served. FL ST J ADMIN Rule 2.515(a).

b. *Pro se litigant signature.* A party who is not represented by an attorney shall sign any pleading or other paper and state the party's address and telephone number, including area code. FL ST J ADMIN Rule 2.515(b).

c. *Form of signature*

   i. The signatures required on pleadings and documents by FL ST J ADMIN Rule 2.515(a) and FL ST J ADMIN Rule 2.515(b) may be:

   - Original signatures;
   - Original signatures that have been reproduced by electronic means, such as on electronically transmitted documents or photocopied documents;
   - Electronic signatures using the "/s/," "s/," or "/s" formats by or at the direction of the person signing; or
   - Any other signature format authorized by general law, so long as the clerk where the proceeding is pending has the capability of receiving and has obtained approval from the Supreme Court of Florida to accept pleadings and documents with that signature format. FL ST J ADMIN Rule 2.515(c)(1).

   ii. An attorney, party, or other person who files a pleading or paper by electronic transmission that does not contain the original signature of that attorney, party, or other person shall file that identical pleading or paper in paper form containing an original signature of that attorney, party, or other person (hereinafter called the follow-up filing) immediately thereafter. The follow-up filing is not required if the Supreme Court of Florida has entered an order directing the clerk of court to discontinue accepting the follow-up filing. FL ST J ADMIN Rule 2.515(c)(2).

7. *Forms*

a. *Process.* The forms of process, notice of lis pendens, and notice of action provided in the Florida Rules of Civil Procedure are sufficient. Variations from the forms do not void process or notices that are otherwise sufficient. FL ST RCP Rule 1.900(a).

b. *Other forms.* The other forms provided in the Florida Rules of Civil Procedure are sufficient for the matters that are covered by them. So long as the substance is expressed without prolixity, the forms may be varied to meet the facts of a particular case. FL ST RCP Rule 1.900(b).

c. *Formal matters.* Captions, except for the designation of the paper, are omitted from the forms provided in the Florida Rules of Civil Procedure. A general form of caption is the first form provided. Signatures are omitted from pleadings and motions. FL ST RCP Rule 1.900(c).

8. *Notices to persons with disabilities.* All notices of court proceedings to be held in a public facility, and all process compelling appearance at such proceedings, shall include the following statement in bold face, fourteen (14) point Times New Roman or Courier font: "If you are a person with a disability who needs any accommodation in order to participate in this proceeding, you are entitled, at no cost to you, to the provision of certain assistance. Please contact [identify applicable court personnel by name, address, and telephone number] at least seven (7) days before your scheduled court appearance, or immediately upon receiving this notification if the time before the scheduled appearance is less than seven (7) days; if you are hearing or voice impaired, call 711." FL ST J ADMIN Rule 2.540(c)(1).

9. *Minimization of the filing of sensitive information*

a. *Limitations for court filings.* Unless authorized by FL ST J ADMIN Rule 2.425(b), statute, another rule of court, or the court orders otherwise, designated sensitive information filed with the court must be limited to the following format:

   i. The initials of a person known to be a minor;

   ii. The year of birth of a person's birth date;

   iii. No portion of any: Social security number, Bank account number, Credit card account number, Charge account number, or Debit account number;

- iv. The last four digits of any: Taxpayer identification number (TIN), Employee identification number, Driver's license number, Passport number, Telephone number, Financial account number, except as set forth in FL ST J ADMIN Rule 2.425(a)(3), Brokerage account number, Insurance policy account number, Loan account number, Customer account number, or Patient or health care number;
- v. A truncated version of any: Email address, Computer user name, Password, or Personal identification number (PIN); and
- vi. A truncated version of any other sensitive information as provided by court order. FL ST J ADMIN Rule 2.425(a).

b. *Exceptions.* FL ST J ADMIN Rule 2.425(a) does not apply to the following:

- i. An account number which identifies the property alleged to be the subject of a proceeding;
- ii. The record of an administrative or agency proceeding;
- iii. The record in appellate or review proceedings;
- iv. The birth date of a minor whenever the birth date is necessary for the court to establish or maintain subject matter jurisdiction;
- v. The name of a minor in any order relating to parental responsibility, time-sharing, or child support;
- vi. The name of a minor in any document or order affecting the minor's ownership of real property;
- vii. The birth date of a party in a writ of attachment or notice to payor;
- viii. In traffic and criminal proceedings: a pro se filing; a court filing that is related to a criminal matter or investigation and that is prepared before the filing of a criminal charge or is not filed as part of any docketed criminal case; an arrest or search warrant or any information in support thereof; a charging document and an affidavit or other documents filed in support of any charging document, including any driving records; a statement of particulars; discovery material introduced into evidence or otherwise filed with the court; and all information necessary for the proper issuance and execution of a subpoena duces tecum;
- ix. Information used by the clerk for case maintenance purposes or the courts for case management purposes; and
- x. Information which is relevant and material to an issue before the court. FL ST J ADMIN Rule 2.425(b).

c. *Remedies.* Upon motion by a party or interested person or sua sponte by the court, the court may order remedies, sanctions or both for a violation of FL ST J ADMIN Rule 2.425(a). Following notice and an opportunity to respond, the court may impose sanctions if such filing was not made in good faith. FL ST J ADMIN Rule 2.425(c).

d. *Motions not restricted.* FL ST J ADMIN Rule 2.425 does not restrict a party's right to move for protective order, to move to file documents under seal, or to request a determination of the confidentiality of records. FL ST J ADMIN Rule 2.425(d).

e. *Application.* FL ST J ADMIN Rule 2.425 does not affect the application of constitutional provisions, statutes, or rules of court regarding confidential information or access to public information. FL ST J ADMIN Rule 2.425(e).

F. Filing and Service Requirements

1. *Filing requirements.* All original documents must be filed with the court either before service or immediately thereafter, unless otherwise provided for by general law or other rules. If the original of any bond or other document is not placed in the court file, a certified copy must be so placed by the clerk. FL ST J ADMIN Rule 2.516(d). All documents shall be filed in conformity with the requirements of FL ST J ADMIN Rule 2.525. FL ST RCP Rule 1.080(b). All documents filed in any court shall be filed by electronic transmission in accordance with FL ST J ADMIN Rule 2.525. "Documents" means pleadings, motions, petitions, memoranda, briefs, notices, exhibits, declarations, affidavits, orders, judgments, decrees, writs, opinions, and any other paper or writing submitted to a court. FL ST J ADMIN Rule

2.520(a). All documents that are court records, as defined in FL ST J ADMIN Rule 2.430(a)(1), must be filed by electronic transmission, provided that: (1) the clerk has the ability to accept and retain such documents; (2) the clerk or the chief judge of the circuit has requested permission to accept documents filed by electronic transmission; and (3) the supreme court has entered an order granting permission to the clerk to accept documents filed by electronic transmission. FL ST J ADMIN Rule 2.525(c)(1).

a. *Definition.* "Electronic transmission of documents" means the sending of information by electronic signals to, by or from a court or clerk, which when received can be transformed and stored or transmitted on paper, microfilm, magnetic storage device, optical imaging system, CD-ROM, flash drive, other electronic data storage system, server, case maintenance system ("CM"), electronic court filing ("ECF") system, statewide or local electronic portal ("e-portal"), or other electronic record keeping system authorized by the supreme court in a format sufficient to communicate the information on the original document in a readable format. Electronic transmission of documents includes electronic mail ("e-mail") and any internet-based transmission procedure, and may include procedures allowing for documents to be signed or verified by electronic means. FL ST J ADMIN Rule 2.525(a).

    i. The filing of documents with the court as required by the Florida Rules of Judicial Administration must be made by filing them with the clerk in accordance with FL ST J ADMIN Rule 2.525, except that the judge may permit documents to be filed with the judge, in which event the judge must note the filing date before him or her on the documents and transmit them to the clerk. The date of filing is that shown on the face of the document by the judge's notation or the clerk's time stamp, whichever is earlier. FL ST J ADMIN Rule 2.516(e).

b. *Application.* Any court or clerk of the court may accept the electronic transmission of documents for filing after the clerk, together with input from the chief judge of the circuit, has obtained approval of the procedures and program for doing so from the Supreme Court of Florida. FL ST J ADMIN Rule 2.525(b).

c. *Exceptions*

    i. Paper documents and other submissions may be manually submitted to the clerk or court:

        - When the clerk does not have the ability to accept and retain documents by electronic filing or has not had ECF Procedures approved by the supreme court;
        - For filing by any self-represented party or any self-represented nonparty unless specific ECF Procedures provide a means to file documents electronically. However, any self-represented nonparty that is a governmental or public agency and any other agency, partnership, corporation, or business entity acting on behalf of any governmental or public agency may file documents by electronic transmission if such entity has the capability of filing documents electronically;
        - For filing by attorneys excused from e-mail service in accordance with FL ST J ADMIN Rule 2.516(b);
        - When submitting evidentiary exhibits or filing non-documentary materials;
        - When the filing involves documents in excess of twenty-five (25) megabytes (25MB) in size. For such filings, documents may be transmitted using an electronic storage medium that the clerk has the ability to accept, which may include a CD-ROM, flash drive, or similar storage medium;
        - When filed in open court, as permitted by the court;
        - When paper filing is permitted by any approved statewide or local ECF procedures; and
        - If any court determines that justice so requires. FL ST J ADMIN Rule 2.525(d).

    ii. Any document in paper form submitted under FL ST J ADMIN Rule 2.525(d) is filed when it is received by the clerk or court and the clerk shall immediately thereafter convert any filed paper document to an electronic document. "Convert to an electronic document" means optically capturing an image of a paper document and using character recognition software to recover as much of the document's text as practicable and then indexing and storing the document in the official court file. FL ST J ADMIN Rule 2.525(c)(4).

iii. Any storage medium submitted under FL ST J ADMIN Rule 2.525(d)(5) is filed when received by the clerk or court and the clerk shall immediately thereafter transfer the electronic documents from the storage device to the official court file. FL ST J ADMIN Rule 2.525(c)(5).

iv. If the filer of any paper document authorized under FL ST J ADMIN Rule 2.525(d) provides a self-addressed, postage-paid envelope for return of the paper document after it is converted to electronic form by the clerk, the clerk shall place the paper document in the envelope and deposit it in the mail. Except when a paper document is required to be maintained, the clerk may recycle any filed paper document that is not to be returned to the filer. FL ST J ADMIN Rule 2.525(c)(6).

v. The clerk may convert any paper document filed before the effective date of FL ST J ADMIN Rule 2.525 to an electronic document. Unless the clerk is required to maintain the paper document, if the paper document has been converted to an electronic document by the clerk, the paper document is no longer part of the official court file and may be removed and recycled. FL ST J ADMIN Rule 2.525(c)(7).

d. *Official court file.* For information on what constitutes the official court file, please see FL ST J ADMIN Rule 2.525(c)(2), FL ST J ADMIN Rule 2.525(c)(3).

e. *Administration.* All attorneys, parties, or other persons using this rule to file documents are required to make arrangements with the court or clerk for the payment of any charges authorized by general law or the supreme court before filing any document by electronic transmission. FL ST J ADMIN Rule 2.525(f)(2).

f. *Filing date.* The filing date for an electronically transmitted document is the date and time that such filing is acknowledged by an electronic stamp or otherwise, pursuant to any procedure set forth in any ECF Procedures approved by the supreme court, or the date the last page of such filing is received by the court or clerk. FL ST J ADMIN Rule 2.525(f)(3).

g. *Accessibility.* All documents transmitted in any electronic form under FL ST J ADMIN Rule 2.525 must comply with the accessibility requirements of FL ST J ADMIN Rule 2.526. FL ST J ADMIN Rule 2.525(g).

2. *Service requirements.* Every pleading subsequent to the initial pleading, all orders, and every other document filed in the action must be served in conformity with the requirements of FL ST J ADMIN Rule 2.516. FL ST RCP Rule 1.080(a).

a. *Service; When required.* Unless the court otherwise orders, or a statute or supreme court administrative order specifies a different means of service, every pleading subsequent to the initial pleading and every other document filed in any court proceeding, except applications for witness subpoenas and documents served by formal notice or required to be served in the manner provided for service of formal notice, must be served in accordance with FL ST J ADMIN Rule 2.516 on each party. No service need be made on parties against whom a default has been entered, except that pleadings asserting new or additional claims against them must be served in the manner provided for service of summons. FL ST J ADMIN Rule 2.516(a).

b. *Service; How made.* When service is required or permitted to be made upon a party represented by an attorney, service must be made upon the attorney unless service upon the party is ordered by the court. FL ST J ADMIN Rule 2.516(b).

i. *Service by electronic mail ("e-mail").* All documents required or permitted to be served on another party must be served by e-mail, unless FL ST J ADMIN Rule 2.516 otherwise provides. When, in addition to service by e-mail, the sender also utilizes another means of service provided for in FL ST J ADMIN Rule 2.516(b)(2), any differing time limits and other provisions applicable to that other means of service control. FL ST J ADMIN Rule 2.516(b)(1). Any document electronically transmitted to a court or clerk must also be served on all parties and interested persons in accordance with the applicable rules of court. FL ST J ADMIN Rule 2.525(e)(2).

- *Service on attorneys.* Upon appearing in a proceeding, an attorney must serve a designation of a primary e-mail address and may designate no more than two (2) secondary e-mail

addresses. Thereafter, service must be directed to all designated e-mail addresses in that proceeding. Every document filed by an attorney thereafter must include the primary e-mail address of that attorney and any secondary e-mail addresses. If an attorney does not designate any e-mail address for service, documents may be served on that attorney at the e-mail address on record with The Florida Bar. FL ST J ADMIN Rule 2.516(b)(1)(A).

- *Exception to e-mail service on attorneys.* Service by an attorney on another attorney must be made by e-mail unless excused by the court. Upon motion by an attorney demonstrating that the attorney has no e-mail account and lacks access to the Internet at the attorney's office, the court may excuse the attorney from the requirements of e-mail service. Service on and by an attorney excused by the court from e-mail service must be by the means provided in FL ST J ADMIN Rule 2.516(b)(2). FL ST J ADMIN Rule 2.516(b)(1)(B).
- *Service on and by parties not represented by an attorney.* Any party not represented by an attorney may serve a designation of a primary e-mail address and also may designate no more than two (2) secondary e-mail addresses to which service must be directed in that proceeding by the means provided in FL ST J ADMIN Rule 2.516(b)(1). If a party not represented by an attorney does not designate an e-mail address for service in a proceeding, service on and by that party must be by the means provided in FL ST J ADMIN Rule 2.516(b)(2). FL ST J ADMIN Rule 2.516(b)(1)(C).
- *Time of service.* Service by e-mail is complete when it is sent. FL ST J ADMIN Rule 2.516(b)(1)(D). An e-mail is deemed served on the date it is sent. FL ST J ADMIN Rule 2.516(b)(1)(D)(i). If the sender learns that the e-mail did not reach the address of the person to be served, the sender must immediately send another copy by e-mail, or by a means authorized by FL ST J ADMIN Rule 2.516(b)(2). FL ST J ADMIN Rule 2.516(b)(1)(D)(ii). E-mail service is treated as service by mail for the computation of time. FL ST J ADMIN Rule 2.516(b)(1)(D)(iii).

ii. *Format of e-mail for service.* Service of a document by e-mail is made by attaching a copy of the document in PDF format to an e-mail sent to all addresses designated by the attorney or party. FL ST J ADMIN Rule 2.516(b)(1)(E).

- All documents served by e-mail must be attached to an e-mail message containing a subject line beginning with the words "SERVICE OF COURT DOCUMENT" in all capital letters, followed by the case number of the proceeding in which the documents are being served. FL ST J ADMIN Rule 2.516(b)(1)(E)(i).
- The body of the e-mail must identify the court in which the proceeding is pending, the case number, the name of the initial party on each side, the title of each document served with that e-mail, and the sender's name and telephone number. FL ST J ADMIN Rule 2.516(b)(1)(E)(ii).
- Any document served by e-mail may be signed by the "/s/" format, as long as the filed original is signed in accordance with the applicable rule of procedure. FL ST J ADMIN Rule 2.516(b)(1)(E)(iii).
- Any e-mail which, together with its attached documents, exceeds five megabytes (5MB) in size, must be divided and sent as separate e-mails, no one of which may exceed five megabytes (5MB) in size and each of which must be sequentially numbered in the subject line. FL ST J ADMIN Rule 2.516(b)(1)(E)(iv).

iii. *Service by other means.* In addition to, and not in lieu of, service by e-mail, service may also be made upon attorneys by any of the means specified in FL ST J ADMIN Rule 2.516(b)(2). Service on and by all parties who are not represented by an attorney and who do not designate an e-mail address, and on and by all attorneys excused from e-mail service, must be made by delivering a copy of the document or by mailing it to the party or attorney at their last known address or, if no address is known, by leaving it with the clerk of the court. Service by mail is complete upon mailing. Delivery of a copy within FL ST J ADMIN Rule 2.516 is complete upon:

- Handing it to the attorney or to the party,

- Leaving it at the attorney's or party's office with a clerk or other person in charge thereof,
- If there is no one in charge, leaving it in a conspicuous place therein,
- If the office is closed or the person to be served has no office, leaving it at the person's usual place of abode with some person of his or her family above fifteen (15) years of age and informing such person of the contents, or
- Transmitting it by facsimile to the attorney's or party's office with a cover sheet containing the sender's name, firm, address, telephone number, and facsimile number, and the number of pages transmitted. When service is made by facsimile, a copy must also be served by any other method permitted by FL ST J ADMIN Rule 2.516. Facsimile service occurs when transmission is complete. FL ST J ADMIN Rule 2.516(b)(2)(A) through FL ST J ADMIN Rule 2.516(b)(2)(E).
- Service by delivery after 5:00 p.m. must be deemed to have been made by mailing on the date of delivery. FL ST J ADMIN Rule 2.516(b)(2)(F).

c. *Service; Numerous defendants.* In actions when the parties are unusually numerous, the court may regulate the service contemplated by the Florida Rules of Judicial Administration on motion or on its own initiative in such manner as may be found to be just and reasonable. FL ST J ADMIN Rule 2.516(c).

d. *Service by clerk.* Service of notices and other documents required to be made by the clerk must also be done as provided in FL ST J ADMIN Rule 2.516(b). FL ST J ADMIN Rule 2.516(g).

G. Hearings

1. The parties may be required to participate in pretrial proceedings to consider and determine the necessity or desirability of an amendment to a pleading. FL ST RCP Rule 1.200(b)(2); FL-PP § 2:151.

H. Forms

1. Official Amended Complaint Forms for Florida

a. Caption. FL ST RCP Form 1.901.

b. Notice of compliance when constitutional challenge is brought. FL ST RCP Form 1.975.

2. Amended Complaint Forms for Florida

a. Consent; Of party; To amendment of pleadings. FL-PP § 2:154.

b. Notice of amended complaint. 3 FLPRAC § 190.1.

c. Complaint for damages; General form. FL-PP § 2:17.

d. Complaint; Negligent infliction of personal injury. FL-PP § 2:19.

e. Complaint; Fall-down negligence. FL-PP § 2:20.

f. Complaint; Mortgage foreclosure. FL-PP § 2:21.

g. Complaint; Implied warranty. FL-PP § 2:22.

h. Complaint; Professional negligence. FL-PP § 2:23.

i. Complaint; Breach of contract. FL-PP § 2:24.

j. Complaint; Breach of personal services contract. FL-PP § 2:25.

I. Checklist

(I) ❑ Matters to be considered by plaintiff

(a) ❑ Required documents

(1) ❑ Amended complaint

(2) ❑ Certificate of service

(b) ❑ Supplemental documents

(1) ❑ Exhibits

(2) ❑ Notice of constitutional question

(c) ❑ Timing

(1) ❑ A party may amend a pleading once as a matter of course at any time before a responsive pleading is served

(2) ❑ If the pleading is one to which no responsive pleading is permitted and the action has not been placed on the trial calendar, may so amend it at any time within twenty (20) days after it is served

Pleadings
Answer

Document Last Updated January 2013

A. Applicable Rules

1. *State rules*

   a. Nonverification of pleadings. FL ST RCP Rule 1.030.

   b. Process. FL ST RCP Rule 1.070.

   c. Service and filing of pleadings, orders, and documents. FL ST RCP Rule 1.080.

   d. Time. FL ST RCP Rule 1.090.

   e. Pleadings and motions. FL ST RCP Rule 1.100; FL ST RCP Rule 1.110; FL ST RCP Rule 1.120; FL ST RCP Rule 1.130; FL ST RCP Rule 1.190; FL ST RCP Rule 1.430.

   f. Defenses. FL ST RCP Rule 1.140.

   g. Relief from judgment, decrees, or orders. FL ST RCP Rule 1.540.

   h. Forms. FL ST RCP Rule 1.900.

   i. Minimization of the filing of sensitive information. FL ST J ADMIN Rule 2.425.

   j. Retention of court records. FL ST J ADMIN Rule 2.430.

   k. Foreign attorneys. FL ST J ADMIN Rule 2.510.

   l. Signature of attorneys and parties. FL ST J ADMIN Rule 2.515.

   m. Paper. FL ST J ADMIN Rule 2.520.

   n. Electronic filing. FL ST J ADMIN Rule 2.525.

   o. Accessibility of information and technology. FL ST J ADMIN Rule 2.526.

   p. Court reporting. FL ST J ADMIN Rule 2.535.

   q. Requests for accommodations by persons with disabilities. FL ST J ADMIN Rule 2.540.

   r. Waiver of sovereign immunity in tort actions; Recovery limits; Limitation on attorney fees; Statute of limitations; Exclusions; Indemnification; Risk management programs. FL ST § 768.28.

2. *Local rules*

   a. Establishment of 11th Circuit Homestead Access to Mediation Program ("CHAMP") for case management of residential foreclosure cases in the Eleventh Judicial Circuit of Florida. FL ST 11 J CIR 1-09-08.

B. Timing

1. *General answer timing.* Unless a different time is prescribed in a statute of Florida, a defendant shall serve an answer within twenty (20) days after service of original process and the initial pleading on the defendant, or not later than the date fixed in a notice by publication. A party served with a pleading stating a crossclaim against that party shall serve an answer to it within twenty (20) days after service on that

party. The plaintiff shall serve an answer to a counterclaim within twenty (20) days after service of the counterclaim. FL ST RCP Rule 1.140(a)(1).

a. *Waiver of service.* A defendant who, before being served with process, timely returns a waiver so requested is not required to respond to the complaint until sixty (60) days after the date the defendant received the request for waiver of service. For purposes of computing any time prescribed or allowed by the Florida Rules of Civil Procedure, service of process shall be deemed effected twenty (20) days before the time required to respond to the complaint. FL ST RCP Rule 1.070(i)(4).

b. *Service on the state.* Except when sued pursuant to FL ST § 768.28, the state of Florida, an agency of the state, or an officer or employee of the state sued in an official capacity shall serve an answer to the complaint or crossclaim, or a reply to a counterclaim, within forty (40) days after service. When sued pursuant to FL ST § 768.28, the Department of Financial Services or the defendant state agency shall have thirty (30) days from the date of service within which to serve an answer to the complaint or crossclaim or a reply to a counterclaim. FL ST RCP Rule 1.140(a)(2).

c. *Service of motion impact on time periods for service of answer.* The service of a motion under FL ST RCP Rule 1.140, except a motion for judgment on the pleadings or a motion to strike under FL ST RCP Rule 1.140(f), alters these periods of time so that if the court denies the motion or postpones its disposition until the trial on the merits, the responsive pleadings shall be served within ten (10) days after notice of the court's action or, if the court grants a motion for a more definite statement, the responsive pleadings shall be served within ten (10) days after service of the more definite statement unless a different time is fixed by the court in either case. FL ST RCP Rule 1.140(a)(3).

d. *Responding if pleading does not require a responsive pleading.* If a pleading sets forth a claim for relief to which the adverse party is not required to serve a responsive pleading, the adverse party may assert any defense in law or fact to that claim for relief at the trial, except that the objection of failure to state a legal defense in an answer or reply shall be asserted by motion to strike the defense within twenty (20) days after service of the answer or reply. FL ST RCP Rule 1.140(b).

2. *Computation of time*

a. *Generally.* Computation of time shall be governed by FL ST J ADMIN Rule 2.514. FL ST RCP Rule 1.090(a). The following rules apply in computing time periods specified in any rule of procedure, local rule, court order, or statute that does not specify a method of computing time. FL ST J ADMIN Rule 2.514(a).

i. *Period stated in days or a longer unit.* When the period is stated in days or a longer unit of time (A) exclude the day of the event that triggers the period; (B) count every day, including intermediate Saturdays, Sundays, and legal holidays; and (C) include the last day of the period, but if the last day is a Saturday, Sunday, or legal holiday, or falls within any period of time extended through an order of the chief justice under FL ST J ADMIN Rule 2.205(a)(2)(B)(iv), the period continues to run until the end of the next day that is not a Saturday, Sunday, or legal holiday and does not fall within any period of time extended through an order of the chief justice. FL ST J ADMIN Rule 2.514(a)(1).

ii. *Period stated in hours.* When the period is stated in hours (A) begin counting immediately on the occurrence of the event that triggers the period; (B) count every hour, including hours during intermediate Saturdays, Sundays, and legal holidays; and (C) if the period would end on a Saturday, Sunday, or legal holiday, or during any period of time extended through an order of the chief justice under FL ST J ADMIN Rule 2.205(a)(2)(B)(iv), the period continues to run until the same time on the next day that is not a Saturday, Sunday, or legal holiday and does not fall within any period of time extended through an order of the chief justice. FL ST J ADMIN Rule 2.514(a)(2).

iii. *Period stated in days less than seven (7) days.* When the period stated in days is less than seven (7) days, intermediate Saturdays, Sundays, and legal holidays shall be excluded in the computation. FL ST J ADMIN Rule 2.514(a)(3).

iv. *"Last day" defined.* Unless a different time is set by a statute, local rule, or court order, the last day ends (A) for electronic filing or for service by any means, at midnight; and (B) for filing by other means, when the clerk's office is scheduled to close. FL ST J ADMIN Rule 2.514(a)(4).

v. *"Next day" defined.* The "next day" is determined by continuing to count forward when the period is measured after an event and backward when measured before an event. FL ST J ADMIN Rule 2.514(a)(5).

vi. *"Legal holiday" defined.* "Legal holiday" means (A) the day set aside by FL ST § 110.117, for observing New Year's Day, Martin Luther King, Jr.'s Birthday, Memorial Day, Independence Day, Labor Day, Veterans' Day, Thanksgiving Day, the Friday after Thanksgiving Day, or Christmas Day, and (B) any day observed as a holiday by the clerk's office or as designated by the chief judge. FL ST J ADMIN Rule 2.514(a)(6).

b. *Additional time after service by mail or e-mail.* When a party may or must act within a specified time after service and service is made by mail or e-mail, five (5) days are added after the period that would otherwise expire under FL ST J ADMIN Rule 2.514(a). FL ST J ADMIN Rule 2.514(b).

c. *Enlargement.* When an act is required or allowed to be done at or within a specified time by order of court, by the Florida Rules of Civil Procedure, or by notice given thereunder, for cause shown the court at any time in its discretion (1) with or without notice, may order the period enlarged if request therefor is made before the expiration of the period originally prescribed or as extended by a previous order, or (2) upon motion made and notice after the expiration of the specified period, may permit the act to be done when failure to act was the result of excusable neglect, but it may not extend the time for making a motion for new trial, for rehearing, or to alter or amend a judgment; making a motion for relief from a judgment under FL ST RCP Rule 1.540(b); taking an appeal or filing a petition for certiorari; or making a motion for a directed verdict. FL ST RCP Rule 1.090(b).

d. *Unaffected by expiration of term.* The period of time provided for the doing of any act or the taking of any proceeding shall not be affected or limited by the continued existence or expiration of a term of court. The continued existence or expiration of a term of court in no way affects the power of a court to do any act or take any proceeding in any action which is or has been pending before it. FL ST RCP Rule 1.090(c).

C. General Requirements

1. *General rules of pleading*

a. *Claims for relief*

i. A pleading which sets forth a claim for relief, whether an original claim, counterclaim, crossclaim, or third-party claim, must state a cause of action and shall contain

- A short and plain statement of the grounds upon which the court's jurisdiction depends, unless the court already has jurisdiction and the claim needs no new grounds of jurisdiction to support it (For information regarding acts subjecting persons to jurisdiction, please see FL ST § 48.193),
- A short and plain statement of the ultimate facts showing that the pleader is entitled to relief, and
- A demand for judgment for the relief to which the pleader deems himself or herself entitled. FL ST RCP Rule 1.110(b).

ii. Relief in the alternative or of several different types may be demanded. Every complaint shall be considered to demand general relief. FL ST RCP Rule 1.110(b).

b. *Verification.* Except when otherwise specifically provided by these rules or an applicable statute, every pleading or other document of a party represented by an attorney need not be verified or accompanied by an affidavit. FL ST RCP Rule 1.030. When filing an action for foreclosure of a mortgage on residential real property the complaint shall be verified. When verification of a document is required, the document filed shall include an oath, affirmation, or the following statement: "Under penalty of perjury, I declare that I have read the foregoing, and the facts alleged therein are true and correct to the best of my knowledge and belief." FL ST RCP Rule 1.110(b).

c. *Separate statements.* All averments of claim or defense shall be made in consecutively numbered paragraphs, the contents of each of which shall be limited as far as practicable to a statement of a single set of circumstances, and a paragraph may be referred to by number in all subsequent pleadings. Each claim founded upon a separate transaction or occurrence and each defense other than denials shall be stated in a separate count or defense when a separation facilitates the clear presentation of the matter set forth. FL ST RCP Rule 1.110(f).

d. *Statements adopted by reference.* Statements in a pleading may be adopted by reference in a different part of the same pleading, in another pleading, or in any motion. FL ST RCP Rule 1.130(b).

e. *Joinder of causes of action; Consistency.* A pleader may set up in the same action as many claims or causes of action or defenses in the same right as the pleader has, and claims for relief may be stated in the alternative if separate items make up the cause of action, or if two (2) or more causes of action are joined. A party may also set forth two (2) or more statements of a claim or defense alternatively, either in one (1) count or defense or in separate counts or defenses. When two (2) or more statements are made in the alternative and one (1) of them, if made independently, would be sufficient, the pleading is not made insufficient by the insufficiency of one (1) or more of the alternative statements. A party may also state as many separate claims or defenses as that party has, regardless of consistency and whether based on legal or equitable grounds or both. All pleadings shall be construed so as to do substantial justice. FL ST RCP Rule 1.110(g).

f. *Subsequent pleadings.* When the nature of an action permits pleadings subsequent to final judgment and the jurisdiction of the court over the parties has not terminated, the initial pleading subsequent to final judgment shall be designated a supplemental complaint or petition. The action shall then proceed in the same manner and time as though the supplemental complaint or petition were the initial pleading in the action, including the issuance of any needed process. FL ST RCP Rule 1.110(h) shall not apply to proceedings that may be initiated by motion under the Florida Rules of Civil Procedure. FL ST RCP Rule 1.110(h).

g. *Pleading basis for service.* When service of process is to be made under statutes authorizing service on nonresidents of Florida, it is sufficient to plead the basis for service in the language of the statute without pleading the facts supporting service. FL ST RCP Rule 1.070(h).

h. *Forms of pleadings.* Forms of action and technical forms for seeking relief and of pleas, pleadings, or motions are abolished. FL ST RCP Rule 1.110(a).

2. *Answer; Generally.* An answer has three (3) functions. First, it must respond to each allegation of the preceding pleading by admitting, denying or alleging that the pleader is without knowledge of the allegation. Second, it must contain any affirmative defenses that the pleader is interposing to any cause of action alleged in the preceding pleading. Third, the answer may claim affirmative relief against the plaintiff or petitioner by a counterclaim or against a codefendant by a crossclaim. FL-PRACPROC § 11:1.

   a. *Content.* In the answer a pleader shall state in short and plain terms the pleader's defenses to each claim asserted and shall admit or deny the averments on which the adverse party relies. If the defendant is without knowledge, the defendant shall so state and such statement shall operate as a denial. Denial shall fairly meet the substance of the averments denied. When a pleader intends in good faith to deny only a part of an averment, the pleader shall specify so much of it as is true and shall deny the remainder. Unless the pleader intends in good faith to controvert all of the averments of the preceding pleading, the pleader may make denials as specific denials of designated averments or may generally deny all of the averments except such designated averments as the pleader expressly admits, but when the pleader does so intend to controvert all of its averments, including averments of the grounds upon which the court's jurisdiction depends, the pleader may do so by general denial. FL ST RCP Rule 1.110(c).

   b. *Form of answer.* An answer contains a caption, commencement, body, signature and certificate of service. The caption is the same as that of the initial pleading, except for the designation as one of the types of answer. The body of an answer should contain an admission, denial or plea of without knowledge to each allegation of the preceding pleading, except for the additional allegations in response to a general allegation of conditions precedent and the denial of capacity to sue. FL-PRACPROC § 11:3.

      i. *Responding sequentially.* The best method of responding is to answer each paragraph sequentially, combining admissions, denials or pleas of without knowledge when the sequence permits. The admissions, denials and allegations of without knowledge should be stated first, followed separately by any affirmative defenses and then by any counterclaim or crossclaim. A third party complaint may be a part of the same paper, but it is not a part of the answer as is a counterclaim or crossclaim. Paragraphs are numbered consecutively throughout the pleading whether in the answer, counterclaim or crossclaim. Denials for the record only are improper. FL-PRACPROC § 11:3.

c. *Defenses*

i. *Generally.* Every defense in law or fact to a claim for relief in a pleading shall be asserted in the responsive pleading, if one is required, but the following defenses may be made by motion at the option of the pleader: (1) lack of jurisdiction over the subject matter, (2) lack of jurisdiction over the person, (3) improper venue, (4) insufficiency of process, (5) insufficiency of service of process, (6) failure to state a cause of action, and (7) failure to join indispensable parties. A motion making any of these defenses shall be made before pleading if a further pleading is permitted. FL ST RCP Rule 1.140(b).

- *Stated specifically.* The grounds on which any of the enumerated defenses are based and the substantial matters of law intended to be argued shall be stated specifically and with particularity in the responsive pleading or motion. FL ST RCP Rule 1.140(b).
- *Waiver.* Any ground not stated shall be deemed to be waived except any ground showing that the court lacks jurisdiction of the subject matter may be made at any time. No defense or objection is waived by being joined with other defenses or objections in a responsive pleading or motion. FL ST RCP Rule 1.140(b). A party waives all defenses and objections that the party does not present either by motion under FL ST RCP Rule 1.140(b), FL ST RCP Rule 1.140(e), or FL ST RCP Rule 1.140(f) or, if the party has made no motion, in a responsive pleading except as provided in FL ST RCP Rule 1.140(h)(2). FL ST RCP Rule 1.140(h)(1). The defenses of failure to state a cause of action or a legal defense or to join an indispensable party may be raised by motion for judgment on the pleadings or at the trial on the merits in addition to being raised either in a motion under FL ST RCP Rule 1.140(b) or in the answer or reply. The defense of lack of jurisdiction of the subject matter may be raised at any time. FL ST RCP Rule 1.140(h)(2).

ii. *Affirmative defenses.* In pleading to a preceding pleading a party shall set forth affirmatively accord and satisfaction, arbitration and award, assumption of risk, contributory negligence, discharge in bankruptcy, duress, estoppel, failure of consideration, fraud, illegality, injury by fellow servant, laches, license, payment, release, res judicata, statute of frauds, statute of limitations, waiver, and any other matter constituting an avoidance or affirmative defense. When a party has mistakenly designated a defense as a counterclaim or a counterclaim as a defense, the court, on terms if justice so requires, shall treat the pleading as if there had been a proper designation. Affirmative defenses appearing on the face of a prior pleading may be asserted as grounds for a motion or defense under FL ST RCP Rule 1.140(b); provided this shall not limit amendments under FL ST RCP Rule 1.190 even if such ground is sustained. FL ST RCP Rule 1.110(d).

- *Format of defenses.* Affirmative defenses should be placed after the admissions, denials and allegations of without knowledge in the answer. All paragraphs must be numbered consecutively throughout the answer. If a defense is directed to only a part of a cause of action or to one or more, but not all, of several causes of action in the preceding pleading, the part or cause of action to which it is directed should be identified in the defense. Defenses should be identified by consecutive ordinal numbers such as "First Defense" and "Second Defense." FL-PRACPROC § 11:4.

iii. *Effect of failure to deny.* Averments in a pleading to which a responsive pleading is required, other than those as to the amount of damages, are admitted when not denied in the responsive pleading. Averments in a pleading to which no responsive pleading is required or permitted shall be taken as denied or avoided. FL ST RCP Rule 1.110(e). An admission in an answer binds the party and no proof is required. An admission does not extend beyond the scope of the allegation in the preceding pleading. FL-PRACPROC § 11:3.

3. *Pleading special matters*
   a. *Capacity.* It is not necessary to aver the capacity of a party to sue or be sued, the authority of a party to sue or be sued in a representative capacity, or the legal existence of an organized association of persons that is made a party, except to the extent required to show the jurisdiction of the court. The initial pleading served on behalf of a minor party shall specifically aver the age of the minor party. When a party desires to raise an issue as to the legal existence of any party, the capacity of any party to sue or sued, or the authority of a party to sue or be sued in a representative capacity, that party shall do so by specific negative averment which shall include such supporting particulars as are peculiarly within the pleader's knowledge. FL ST RCP Rule 1.120(a).
   b. *Fraud, mistake, condition of the mind.* In all averments of fraud or mistake, the circumstances constituting fraud or mistake shall be stated with such particularity as the circumstances may permit. Malice, intent, knowledge, mental attitude, and other condition of mind of a person may be averred generally. FL ST RCP Rule 1.120(b).
   c. *Conditions precedent.* In pleading the performance or occurrence of conditions precedent, it is sufficient to aver generally that all conditions precedent have been performed or have occurred. A denial of performance or occurrence shall be made specifically and with particularity. FL ST RCP Rule 1.120(c).
   d. *Official document or act.* In pleading an official document or official act it is sufficient to aver that the document was issued or the act done in compliance with law. FL ST RCP Rule 1.120(c).
   e. *Judgment or decree.* In pleading a judgment or decree of a domestic or foreign court, a judicial or quasi-judicial tribunal, or a board or officer, it is sufficient to aver the judgment or decree without setting forth matter showing jurisdiction to render it. FL ST RCP Rule 1.120(e).
   f. *Time and place.* For the purpose of testing the sufficiency of a pleading, averments of time and place are material and shall be considered like all other averments of material matter. FL ST RCP Rule 1.120(f).
   g. *Special damage.* When items of special damage are claimed, they shall be specifically stated. FL ST RCP Rule 1.120(g).
4. *Parties*
   a. *Parties generally.* Every action may be prosecuted in the name of the real party in interest, but a personal representative, administrator, guardian, trustee of an express trust, a party with whom or in whose name a contract has been made for the benefit of another, or a party expressly authorized by statute may sue in that person's own name without joining the party for whose benefit the action is brought. All persons having an interest in the subject of the action and in obtaining the relief demanded may join as plaintiffs and any person may be made a defendant who has or claims an interest adverse to the plaintiff. Any person may at any time be made a party if that person's presence is necessary or proper to a complete determination of the cause. Persons having a united interest may be joined on the same side as plaintiffs or defendants, and anyone who refuses to join may for such reason be made a defendant. FL ST RCP Rule 1.210(a).
   b. *Minors or incompetent persons.* When a minor or incompetent person has a representative, such as a guardian or other like fiduciary, the representative may sue or defend on behalf of the minor or incompetent person. A minor or incompetent person who does not have a duly appointed representative may sue by next friend or by a guardian ad litem. The court shall appoint a guardian ad litem for a minor or incompetent person not otherwise represented in an action or shall make such other order as it deems proper for the protection of the minor or incompetent person. FL ST RCP Rule 1.210(b).
   c. For survivor and substitution of parties information, please see FL ST RCP Rule 1.260.
5. *Counterclaims and crossclaims*
   a. *Compulsory counterclaims.* A pleading shall state as a counterclaim any claim which at the time of serving the pleading the pleader has against any opposing party, provided it arises out of the transaction or occurrence that is the subject matter of the opposing party's claim and does not require

for its adjudication the presence of third parties over whom the court cannot acquire jurisdiction. But the pleader need not state a claim if (1) at the time the action was commenced the claim was the subject of another pending action, or (2) the opposing party brought suit upon that party's claim by attachment or other process by which the court did not acquire jurisdiction to render a personal judgment on the claim and the pleader is not stating a counterclaim under this rule. FL ST RCP Rule 1.170(a).

b. *Permissive counterclaim.* A pleading may state as a counterclaim any claim against an opposing party not arising out of the transaction or occurrence that is the subject matter of the opposing party's claim. FL ST RCP Rule 1.170(b).

c. *Counterclaim exceeding opposing claim.* A counterclaim may or may not diminish or defeat the recovery sought by the opposing party. It may claim relief exceeding in amount or different in kind from that sought in the pleading of the opposing party. FL ST RCP Rule 1.170(c).

d. *Counterclaim against the State.* The Florida Rules of Civil Procedure shall not be construed to enlarge beyond the limits established by law the right to assert counterclaims or to claim credits against the state or any of its subdivisions or other governmental organizations thereof subject to suit or against a municipal corporation or against an officer, agency, or administrative board of the state. FL ST RCP Rule 1.170(d).

e. *Counterclaim maturing or acquired after pleading.* A claim which matured or was acquired by the pleader after serving the pleading may be presented as a counterclaim by supplemental pleading with the permission of the court. FL ST RCP Rule 1.170(e).

f. *Omitted counterclaim or crossclaim.* When a pleader fails to set up a counterclaim or crossclaim through oversight, inadvertence, or excusable neglect, or when justice requires, the pleader may set up the counterclaim or crossclaim by amendment with leave of the court. FL ST RCP Rule 1.170(f).

g. *Crossclaim against co-party.* A pleading may state as a crossclaim any claim by one party against a co-party arising out of the transaction or occurrence that is the subject matter of either the original action or a counterclaim therein, or relating to any property that is the subject matter of the original action. The crossclaim may include a claim that the party against whom it is asserted is or may be liable to the crossclaimant for all or part of a claim asserted in the action against the crossclaimant. Service of a crossclaim on a party who has appeared in the action shall be made pursuant to FL ST RCP Rule 1.080. Service of a crossclaim against a party who has not appeared in the action shall be made in the manner provided for service of summons. FL ST RCP Rule 1.170(g).

h. *Additional parties may be brought in.* When the presence of parties other than those to the original action is required to grant complete relief in the determination of a counterclaim or crossclaim, they shall be named in the counterclaim or crossclaim and be served with process and shall be parties to the action thereafter if jurisdiction of them can be obtained and their joinder will not deprive the court of jurisdiction of the action. FL ST RCP Rule 1.250(b) and FL ST RCP Rule 1.250(c) apply to parties brought in under FL ST RCP Rule 1.170(h). FL ST RCP Rule 1.170(h).

i. *Separate trials; Separate judgment.* If the court orders separate trials as provided in FL ST RCP Rule 1.270(b), judgment on a counterclaim or crossclaim may be rendered when the court has jurisdiction to do so even if a claim of the opposing party has been dismissed or otherwise disposed of. FL ST RCP Rule 1.170(i).

j. *Demand exceeding jurisdiction; Transfer of action.* If the demand of any counterclaim or crossclaim exceeds the jurisdiction of the court in which the action is pending, the action shall be transferred forthwith to the court of the same county having jurisdiction of the demand in the counterclaim or crossclaim with only such alterations in the pleadings as are essential. The court shall order the transfer of the action and the transmittal of all papers in it to the proper court if the party asserting the demand exceeding the jurisdiction deposits with the court having jurisdiction a sum sufficient to pay the clerk's service charge in the court to which the action is transferred at the time of filing the counterclaim or crossclaim. Thereupon the original papers and deposit shall be transmitted and filed with a certified copy of the order. The court to which the action is transferred shall have full power and jurisdiction over the demands of all parties. Failure to make the service charge deposit at the time the counterclaim or crossclaim is filed, or within such further time as the court may allow, shall reduce a claim for damages to an amount within the jurisdiction of the court where the action is pending and waive the claim in other cases. FL ST RCP Rule 1.170(j).

6. *Misjoinder and nonjoinder of parties*
   a. *Misjoinder.* Misjoinder of parties is not a ground for dismissal of an action. Any claim against a party may be severed and proceeded with separately. FL ST RCP Rule 1.250(a).
   b. *Dropping parties.* Parties may be dropped by an adverse party in the manner provided for voluntary dismissal in FL ST RCP Rule 1.420(a)(1) subject to the exception stated in FL ST RCP Rule 1.420. If notice of lis pendens has been filed in the action against a party so dropped, the notice of dismissal shall be recorded and cancels the notice of lis pendens without the necessity of a court order. Parties may be dropped by order of court on its own initiative or the motion of any party at any stage of the action on such terms as are just. FL ST RCP Rule 1.250(b).
   c. *Adding parties.* Parties may be added once as a matter of course within the same time that pleadings can be so amended under FL ST RCP Rule 1.190(a). If amendment by leave of court or stipulation of the parties is permitted, parties may be added in the amended pleading without further order of court. Parties may be added by order of court on its own initiative or on motion of any party at any stage of the action and on such terms as are just. FL ST RCP Rule 1.250(c).
7. *Jury demand*
   a. *Right preserved.* The right of trial by jury as declared by the Constitution or by statute shall be preserved to the parties inviolate. FL ST RCP Rule 1.430(a).
   b. *Demand.* Any party may demand a trial by jury of any issue triable of right by a jury by serving upon the other party a demand therefor in writing at any time after commencement of the action and not later than ten (10) days after the service of the last pleading directed to such issue. The demand may be indorsed upon a pleading of the party. FL ST RCP Rule 1.430(b).
   c. *Specification of issues.* In the demand a party may specify the issues that the party wishes so tried; otherwise, the party is deemed to demand trial by jury for all issues so triable. FL ST RCP Rule 1.430(c).
      i. If a party has demanded trial by jury for only some of the issues, any other party may serve a demand for trial by jury of any other or all of the issues triable by jury ten (10) days after service of the demand or such lesser time as the court may order. FL ST RCP Rule 1.430(c).
   d. *Waiver.* A party who fails to serve a demand as required by FL ST RCP Rule 1.430 waives trial by jury. FL ST RCP Rule 1.430(d).
      i. If waived, a jury trial may not be granted without the consent of the parties, but the court may allow an amendment in the proceedings to demand a trial by jury or order a trial by jury on its own motion. FL ST RCP Rule 1.430(d).
      ii. A demand for trial by jury may not be withdrawn without the consent of the parties. FL ST RCP Rule 1.430(d).
8. *Arbitration and mediation*
   a. *Referral to arbitration and mediation.* Except as hereinafter provided or as otherwise prohibited by law, the presiding judge may enter an order referring all or any part of a contested civil matter to mediation or arbitration. The parties to any contested civil matter may file a written stipulation to mediate or arbitrate any issue between them at any time. Such stipulation shall be incorporated into the order of referral. FL ST RCP Rule 1.700(a).
      i. In all residential foreclosure actions involving homestead properties filed on or after May 1, 2009, unless a stipulation is specifically invoked by the parties in writing within five (5) days of service of the complaint on the main defendant, the parties are deemed to have stipulated to referral of the mediation to the Collins Center pursuant to FL ST RCP Rule 1.720(f). FL ST 11 J CIR 1-09-08(2); FL ST 11 J CIR 1-09-08(3). FL ST 11 J CIR 1-09-08 constitutes a formal referral to mediation pursuant to the Florida Rules of Civil Procedure. FL ST 11 J CIR 1-09-08(2).
      ii. For further information on referral to mediation, refer to FL ST 11 J CIR 1-09-08.

b. *Arbitration*

i. *Exclusions.* A civil action shall be ordered to arbitration or arbitration in conjunction with mediation upon stipulation of the parties. A civil action may be ordered to arbitration or arbitration in conjunction with mediation upon motion of any party or by the court, if the judge determines the action to be of such a nature that arbitration could be of benefit to the litigants or the court. FL ST RCP Rule 1.800.

- Under no circumstances may the following categories of actions be referred to arbitration: (1) bond estreatures; (2) habeas corpus or other extraordinary writs; (3) bond validations; (4) civil or criminal contempt; (5) such other matters as may be specified by order of the chief judge in the circuit. FL ST RCP Rule 1.800.

ii. For more information regarding arbitration, please see FL ST RCP Rule 1.810; FL ST RCP Rule 1.820; FL ST RCP Rule 1.830.

c. *Mediation.* For more information regarding mediation, please see FL ST RCP Rule 1.710; FL ST RCP Rule 1.720; FL ST RCP Rule 1.730; and FL ST RCP Rule 1.750.

9. *Rules of court*

a. *Rules of civil procedure.* The Florida Rules of Civil Procedure apply to all actions of a civil nature and all special statutory proceedings in the circuit courts and county courts except those to which the Florida Probate Rules, the Florida Family Law Rules of Procedure, or the Small Claims Rules apply. FL ST RCP Rule 1.010.

i. The form, content, procedure, and time for pleading in all special statutory proceedings shall be as prescribed by the statutes governing the proceeding unless the Florida Rules of Civil Procedure specifically provide to the contrary. FL ST RCP Rule 1.010.

ii. The Florida Rules of Civil Procedure shall be construed to secure the just, speedy, and inexpensive determination of every action. FL ST RCP Rule 1.010.

b. *Rules of judicial administration.* The Florida Rules of Judicial Administration shall apply to administrative matters in all courts to which the Florida Rules of Judicial Administration are applicable by their terms. The Florida Rules of Judicial Administration shall be construed to secure the speedy and inexpensive determination of every proceeding to which they are applicable. The Florida Rules of Judicial Administration shall supersede all conflicting rules and statutes. FL ST J ADMIN Rule 2.110.

D. Documents

1. *Required documents*

a. *Answer.* See the General Requirements section of this document for further information about the content of an answer.

i. *Notices to persons with disabilities.* See the Format section of this KeyRules document for further information.

b. *Certificate of service.* When any attorney certifies in substance: "I certify that a copy hereof has been furnished to (here insert name or names and addresses used for service) by (e-mail) (delivery) (mail) (fax) on .... (date) ....________________ Attorney" the certificate is taken as prima facie proof of such service in compliance with FL ST J ADMIN Rule 2.516. FL ST J ADMIN Rule 2.516(f).

2. *Supplemental documents*

a. *Exhibits.* All bonds, notes, bills of exchange, contracts, accounts, or documents upon which action may be brought or defense made, or a copy thereof or a copy of the portions thereof material to the pleadings, shall be incorporated in or attached to the pleading. No papers shall be unnecessarily annexed as exhibits. The pleadings shall contain no unnecessary recitals of deeds, documents, contracts, or other instruments. Any exhibit attached to a pleading shall be considered a part of the pleadings for all purposes. FL ST RCP Rule 1.130(a).

b. *Notice of constitutional question.* A party that files a pleading, written motion, or other paper drawing into question the constitutionality of a state statute or a county or municipal charter,

ordinance, or franchise must promptly (1) file a notice of constitutional question stating the question and identifying the paper that raises it; and (2) serve the notice and the pleading, written motion, or other paper drawing into question the constitutionality of a state statute or a county or municipal charter, ordinance, or franchise on the Attorney General or the state attorney of the judicial circuit in which the action is pending, by either certified or registered mail. Service of the notice and pleading, written motion, or other paper does not require joinder of the Attorney General or the state attorney as a party to the action. FL ST RCP Rule 1.071.

E. Format

1. *Documents; Type and size.* Documents subject to the exceptions set forth in FL ST J ADMIN Rule 2.525(d) shall be filed on recycled paper measuring eight and one half by eleven (8 1/2 by 11) inches. For purposes of FL ST J ADMIN Rule 2.520, paper is recycled if it contains a minimum content of fifty (50) percent waste paper. Xerographic reduction of legal-size (eight and one half by fourteen (8 1/2 by 14) inches) documents to letter size (eight and one half by eleven (8 1/2 by 11) inches) is prohibited. All other documents filed by electronic transmission shall be filed in a format capable of being printed in a format consistent with the provisions of FL ST J ADMIN Rule 2.250. FL ST J ADMIN Rule 2.520(b).
   a. *Exhibits.* Any exhibit or attachment filed with pleadings or papers may be filed in its original size. FL ST J ADMIN Rule 2.520(c).
   b. *Recording space.* On all papers and documents prepared and filed by the court or by any party to a proceeding which are to be recorded in the public records of any county, including but not limited to final money judgments and notices of lis pendens, a three (3) inch by three (3) inch space at the top right-hand corner on the first page and a one (1) inch by three (3) inch space at the top right-hand corner on each subsequent page shall be left blank and reserved for use by the clerk of court. FL ST J ADMIN Rule 2.520(d).
      i. *Exceptions to recording space.* Any papers or documents created by persons or entities over which the filing party has no control, including but not limited to wills, codicils, trusts, or other testamentary documents; documents prepared or executed by any public officer; documents prepared, executed, acknowledged, or proved outside of the State of Florida; or documents created by State or Federal government agencies, may be filed without the space required by FL ST J ADMIN Rule 2.520. FL ST J ADMIN Rule 2.520(e).
   c. *Noncompliance.* No clerk of court is permitted to refuse to file any document or paper because of noncompliance with the Florida Rules of Judicial Administration. However, upon request of the clerk of court, noncomplying documents must be resubmitted in accordance with the formatting rules. FL ST J ADMIN Rule 2.520(f).
2. *Caption.* Every pleading, motion, order, judgment, or other paper shall have a caption containing the name of the court, the file number, and except for in rem proceedings, including forfeiture proceedings, the name of the first party on each side with an appropriate indication of other parties, and a designation identifying the party filing it and its nature or the nature of the order, as the case may be. In any in rem proceeding, every pleading, motion, order, judgment, or other paper shall have a caption containing the name of the court, the file number, the style "In re" (followed by the name or general description of the property), and a designation of the person or entity filing it and its nature or the nature of the order, as the case may be. In an in rem forfeiture proceeding, the style shall be "In re forfeiture of" (followed by the name of the general description of the property). All papers filed in the action shall be styled in such a manner as to indicate clearly the subject matter of the paper and the party requesting or obtaining relief. FL ST RCP Rule 1.100(c)(1).
3. *Writing and written defined.* Writing or written means a document containing information, an application, or a stipulation. FL ST RCP Rule 1.080(c).
4. *Rule abbreviations*
   a. The Florida Rules of Civil Procedure and shall be abbreviated as Fla.R.Civ.P. FL ST RCP Rule 1.010.
   b. The Florida Rules of Judicial Administration shall be abbreviated as Fla. R. Jud. Admin. FL ST J ADMIN Rule 2.110.

5. *Nonverification.* Except when otherwise specifically provided by the Florida Rules of Civil Procedure or an applicable statute, every pleading or other document of a party represented by an attorney need not be verified or accompanied by an affidavit. FL ST RCP Rule 1.030; FL ST J ADMIN Rule 2.515(a).
6. *Attorney signature*
   a. *Attorney signature.* Every pleading and other document of a party represented by an attorney shall be signed by at least one (1) attorney of record in that attorney's individual name whose current record Florida Bar address, telephone number, including area code, primary e-mail address and secondary e-mail addresses, if any, and Florida Bar number shall be stated, and who shall be duly licensed to practice law in Florida or who shall have received permission to appear in the particular case as provided in FL ST J ADMIN Rule 2.510. FL ST J ADMIN Rule 2.515(a).
      i. The attorney may be required by the court to give the address of, and to vouch for the attorney's authority to represent, the party. FL ST J ADMIN Rule 2.515(a).
      ii. The signature of an attorney shall constitute a certificate by the attorney that the attorney has read the pleading or other document; that to the best of the attorney's knowledge, information, and belief there is good ground to support it; and that it is not interposed for delay. FL ST J ADMIN Rule 2.515(a).
      iii. If a pleading is not signed or is signed with intent to defeat the purpose of FL ST J ADMIN Rule 2.515, it may be stricken and the action may proceed as though the pleading or other document had not been served. FL ST J ADMIN Rule 2.515(a).
   b. *Pro se litigant signature.* A party who is not represented by an attorney shall sign any pleading or other paper and state the party's address and telephone number, including area code. FL ST J ADMIN Rule 2.515(b).
   c. *Form of signature*
      i. The signatures required on pleadings and documents by FL ST J ADMIN Rule 2.515(a) and FL ST J ADMIN Rule 2.515(b) may be:
         - Original signatures;
         - Original signatures that have been reproduced by electronic means, such as on electronically transmitted documents or photocopied documents;
         - Electronic signatures using the "/s/," "s/," or "/s" formats by or at the direction of the person signing; or
         - Any other signature format authorized by general law, so long as the clerk where the proceeding is pending has the capability of receiving and has obtained approval from the Supreme Court of Florida to accept pleadings and documents with that signature format. FL ST J ADMIN Rule 2.515(c)(1).
      ii. An attorney, party, or other person who files a pleading or paper by electronic transmission that does not contain the original signature of that attorney, party, or other person shall file that identical pleading or paper in paper form containing an original signature of that attorney, party, or other person (hereinafter called the follow-up filing) immediately thereafter. The follow-up filing is not required if the Supreme Court of Florida has entered an order directing the clerk of court to discontinue accepting the follow-up filing. FL ST J ADMIN Rule 2.515(c)(2).
7. *Forms*
   a. *Process.* The forms of process, notice of lis pendens, and notice of action provided in the Florida Rules of Civil Procedure are sufficient. Variations from the forms do not void process or notices that are otherwise sufficient. FL ST RCP Rule 1.900(a).
   b. *Other forms.* The other forms provided in the Florida Rules of Civil Procedure are sufficient for the matters that are covered by them. So long as the substance is expressed without prolixity, the forms may be varied to meet the facts of a particular case. FL ST RCP Rule 1.900(b).
   c. *Formal matters.* Captions, except for the designation of the paper, are omitted from the forms provided in the Florida Rules of Civil Procedure. A general form of caption is the first form provided. Signatures are omitted from pleadings and motions. FL ST RCP Rule 1.900(c).

8. *Notices to persons with disabilities.* All notices of court proceedings to be held in a public facility, and all process compelling appearance at such proceedings, shall include the following statement in bold face, fourteen (14) point Times New Roman or Courier font: "If you are a person with a disability who needs any accommodation in order to participate in this proceeding, you are entitled, at no cost to you, to the provision of certain assistance. Please contact [identify applicable court personnel by name, address, and telephone number] at least seven (7) days before your scheduled court appearance, or immediately upon receiving this notification if the time before the scheduled appearance is less than seven (7) days; if you are hearing or voice impaired, call 711." FL ST J ADMIN Rule 2.540(c)(1).
9. *Minimization of the filing of sensitive information*
   a. *Limitations for court filings.* Unless authorized by FL ST J ADMIN Rule 2.425(b), statute, another rule of court, or the court orders otherwise, designated sensitive information filed with the court must be limited to the following format:
      i. The initials of a person known to be a minor;
      ii. The year of birth of a person's birth date;
      iii. No portion of any: Social security number, Bank account number, Credit card account number, Charge account number, or Debit account number;
      iv. The last four digits of any: Taxpayer identification number (TIN), Employee identification number, Driver's license number, Passport number, Telephone number, Financial account number, except as set forth in FL ST J ADMIN Rule 2.425(a)(3), Brokerage account number, Insurance policy account number, Loan account number, Customer account number, or Patient or health care number;
      v. A truncated version of any: Email address, Computer user name, Password, or Personal identification number (PIN); and
      vi. A truncated version of any other sensitive information as provided by court order. FL ST J ADMIN Rule 2.425(a).
   b. *Exceptions.* FL ST J ADMIN Rule 2.425(a) does not apply to the following:
      i. An account number which identifies the property alleged to be the subject of a proceeding;
      ii. The record of an administrative or agency proceeding;
      iii. The record in appellate or review proceedings;
      iv. The birth date of a minor whenever the birth date is necessary for the court to establish or maintain subject matter jurisdiction;
      v. The name of a minor in any order relating to parental responsibility, time-sharing, or child support;
      vi. The name of a minor in any document or order affecting the minor's ownership of real property;
      vii. The birth date of a party in a writ of attachment or notice to payor;
      viii. In traffic and criminal proceedings: a pro se filing; a court filing that is related to a criminal matter or investigation and that is prepared before the filing of a criminal charge or is not filed as part of any docketed criminal case; an arrest or search warrant or any information in support thereof; a charging document and an affidavit or other documents filed in support of any charging document, including any driving records; a statement of particulars; discovery material introduced into evidence or otherwise filed with the court; and all information necessary for the proper issuance and execution of a subpoena duces tecum;
      ix. Information used by the clerk for case maintenance purposes or the courts for case management purposes; and
      x. Information which is relevant and material to an issue before the court. FL ST J ADMIN Rule 2.425(b).
   c. *Remedies.* Upon motion by a party or interested person or sua sponte by the court, the court may order remedies, sanctions or both for a violation of FL ST J ADMIN Rule 2.425(a). Following notice

and an opportunity to respond, the court may impose sanctions if such filing was not made in good faith. FL ST J ADMIN Rule 2.425(c).

d. *Motions not restricted.* FL ST J ADMIN Rule 2.425 does not restrict a party's right to move for protective order, to move to file documents under seal, or to request a determination of the confidentiality of records. FL ST J ADMIN Rule 2.425(d).

e. *Application.* FL ST J ADMIN Rule 2.425 does not affect the application of constitutional provisions, statutes, or rules of court regarding confidential information or access to public information. FL ST J ADMIN Rule 2.425(e).

F. Filing and Service Requirements

1. *Filing requirements.* All original documents must be filed with the court either before service or immediately thereafter, unless otherwise provided for by general law or other rules. If the original of any bond or other document is not placed in the court file, a certified copy must be so placed by the clerk. FL ST J ADMIN Rule 2.516(d). All documents shall be filed in conformity with the requirements of FL ST J ADMIN Rule 2.525. FL ST RCP Rule 1.080(b). All documents filed in any court shall be filed by electronic transmission in accordance with FL ST J ADMIN Rule 2.525. "Documents" means pleadings, motions, petitions, memoranda, briefs, notices, exhibits, declarations, affidavits, orders, judgments, decrees, writs, opinions, and any other paper or writing submitted to a court. FL ST J ADMIN Rule 2.520(a). All documents that are court records, as defined in FL ST J ADMIN Rule 2.430(a)(1), must be filed by electronic transmission, provided that: (1) the clerk has the ability to accept and retain such documents; (2) the clerk or the chief judge of the circuit has requested permission to accept documents filed by electronic transmission; and (3) the supreme court has entered an order granting permission to the clerk to accept documents filed by electronic transmission. FL ST J ADMIN Rule 2.525(c)(1).

a. *Definition.* "Electronic transmission of documents" means the sending of information by electronic signals to, by or from a court or clerk, which when received can be transformed and stored or transmitted on paper, microfilm, magnetic storage device, optical imaging system, CD-ROM, flash drive, other electronic data storage system, server, case maintenance system ("CM"), electronic court filing ("ECF") system, statewide or local electronic portal ("e-portal"), or other electronic record keeping system authorized by the supreme court in a format sufficient to communicate the information on the original document in a readable format. Electronic transmission of documents includes electronic mail ("e-mail") and any internet-based transmission procedure, and may include procedures allowing for documents to be signed or verified by electronic means. FL ST J ADMIN Rule 2.525(a).

i. The filing of documents with the court as required by the Florida Rules of Judicial Administration must be made by filing them with the clerk in accordance with FL ST J ADMIN Rule 2.525, except that the judge may permit documents to be filed with the judge, in which event the judge must note the filing date before him or her on the documents and transmit them to the clerk. The date of filing is that shown on the face of the document by the judge's notation or the clerk's time stamp, whichever is earlier. FL ST J ADMIN Rule 2.516(e).

b. *Application.* Any court or clerk of the court may accept the electronic transmission of documents for filing after the clerk, together with input from the chief judge of the circuit, has obtained approval of the procedures and program for doing so from the Supreme Court of Florida. FL ST J ADMIN Rule 2.525(b).

c. *Exceptions*

i. Paper documents and other submissions may be manually submitted to the clerk or court:

- When the clerk does not have the ability to accept and retain documents by electronic filing or has not had ECF Procedures approved by the supreme court;
- For filing by any self-represented party or any self-represented nonparty unless specific ECF Procedures provide a means to file documents electronically. However, any self-represented nonparty that is a governmental or public agency and any other agency, partnership, corporation, or business entity acting on behalf of any governmental or public agency may file documents by electronic transmission if such entity has the capability of filing documents electronically;

- For filing by attorneys excused from e-mail service in accordance with FL ST J ADMIN Rule 2.516(b);
- When submitting evidentiary exhibits or filing non-documentary materials;
- When the filing involves documents in excess of twenty-five (25) megabytes (25MB) in size. For such filings, documents may be transmitted using an electronic storage medium that the clerk has the ability to accept, which may include a CD-ROM, flash drive, or similar storage medium;
- When filed in open court, as permitted by the court;
- When paper filing is permitted by any approved statewide or local ECF procedures; and
- If any court determines that justice so requires. FL ST J ADMIN Rule 2.525(d).

ii. Any document in paper form submitted under FL ST J ADMIN Rule 2.525(d) is filed when it is received by the clerk or court and the clerk shall immediately thereafter convert any filed paper document to an electronic document. "Convert to an electronic document" means optically capturing an image of a paper document and using character recognition software to recover as much of the document's text as practicable and then indexing and storing the document in the official court file. FL ST J ADMIN Rule 2.525(c)(4).

iii. Any storage medium submitted under FL ST J ADMIN Rule 2.525(d)(5) is filed when received by the clerk or court and the clerk shall immediately thereafter transfer the electronic documents from the storage device to the official court file. FL ST J ADMIN Rule 2.525(c)(5).

iv. If the filer of any paper document authorized under FL ST J ADMIN Rule 2.525(d) provides a self-addressed, postage-paid envelope for return of the paper document after it is converted to electronic form by the clerk, the clerk shall place the paper document in the envelope and deposit it in the mail. Except when a paper document is required to be maintained, the clerk may recycle any filed paper document that is not to be returned to the filer. FL ST J ADMIN Rule 2.525(c)(6).

v. The clerk may convert any paper document filed before the effective date of FL ST J ADMIN Rule 2.525 to an electronic document. Unless the clerk is required to maintain the paper document, if the paper document has been converted to an electronic document by the clerk, the paper document is no longer part of the official court file and may be removed and recycled. FL ST J ADMIN Rule 2.525(c)(7).

d. *Official court file.* For information on what constitutes the official court file, please see FL ST J ADMIN Rule 2.525(c)(2), FL ST J ADMIN Rule 2.525(c)(3).

e. *Administration.* All attorneys, parties, or other persons using this rule to file documents are required to make arrangements with the court or clerk for the payment of any charges authorized by general law or the supreme court before filing any document by electronic transmission. FL ST J ADMIN Rule 2.525(f)(2).

f. *Filing date.* The filing date for an electronically transmitted document is the date and time that such filing is acknowledged by an electronic stamp or otherwise, pursuant to any procedure set forth in any ECF Procedures approved by the supreme court, or the date the last page of such filing is received by the court or clerk. FL ST J ADMIN Rule 2.525(f)(3).

g. *Accessibility.* All documents transmitted in any electronic form under FL ST J ADMIN Rule 2.525 must comply with the accessibility requirements of FL ST J ADMIN Rule 2.526. FL ST J ADMIN Rule 2.525(g).

2. *Service requirements.* Every pleading subsequent to the initial pleading, all orders, and every other document filed in the action must be served in conformity with the requirements of FL ST J ADMIN Rule 2.516. FL ST RCP Rule 1.080(a).

a. *Service; When required.* Unless the court otherwise orders, or a statute or supreme court administrative order specifies a different means of service, every pleading subsequent to the initial pleading and every other document filed in any court proceeding, except applications for witness subpoenas and documents served by formal notice or required to be served in the manner provided for service

of formal notice, must be served in accordance with FL ST J ADMIN Rule 2.516 on each party. No service need be made on parties against whom a default has been entered, except that pleadings asserting new or additional claims against them must be served in the manner provided for service of summons. FL ST J ADMIN Rule 2.516(a).

b. *Service; How made.* When service is required or permitted to be made upon a party represented by an attorney, service must be made upon the attorney unless service upon the party is ordered by the court. FL ST J ADMIN Rule 2.516(b).

   i. *Service by electronic mail ("e-mail").* All documents required or permitted to be served on another party must be served by e-mail, unless FL ST J ADMIN Rule 2.516 otherwise provides. When, in addition to service by e-mail, the sender also utilizes another means of service provided for in FL ST J ADMIN Rule 2.516(b)(2), any differing time limits and other provisions applicable to that other means of service control. FL ST J ADMIN Rule 2.516(b)(1). Any document electronically transmitted to a court or clerk must also be served on all parties and interested persons in accordance with the applicable rules of court. FL ST J ADMIN Rule 2.525(e)(2).

      - *Service on attorneys.* Upon appearing in a proceeding, an attorney must serve a designation of a primary e-mail address and may designate no more than two (2) secondary e-mail addresses. Thereafter, service must be directed to all designated e-mail addresses in that proceeding. Every document filed by an attorney thereafter must include the primary e-mail address of that attorney and any secondary e-mail addresses. If an attorney does not designate any e-mail address for service, documents may be served on that attorney at the e-mail address on record with The Florida Bar. FL ST J ADMIN Rule 2.516(b)(1)(A).

      - *Exception to e-mail service on attorneys.* Service by an attorney on another attorney must be made by e-mail unless excused by the court. Upon motion by an attorney demonstrating that the attorney has no e-mail account and lacks access to the Internet at the attorney's office, the court may excuse the attorney from the requirements of e-mail service. Service on and by an attorney excused by the court from e-mail service must be by the means provided in FL ST J ADMIN Rule 2.516(b)(2). FL ST J ADMIN Rule 2.516(b)(1)(B).

      - *Service on and by parties not represented by an attorney.* Any party not represented by an attorney may serve a designation of a primary e-mail address and also may designate no more than two (2) secondary e-mail addresses to which service must be directed in that proceeding by the means provided in FL ST J ADMIN Rule 2.516(b)(1). If a party not represented by an attorney does not designate an e-mail address for service in a proceeding, service on and by that party must be by the means provided in FL ST J ADMIN Rule 2.516(b)(2). FL ST J ADMIN Rule 2.516(b)(1)(C).

      - *Time of service.* Service by e-mail is complete when it is sent. FL ST J ADMIN Rule 2.516(b)(1)(D). An e-mail is deemed served on the date it is sent. FL ST J ADMIN Rule 2.516(b)(1)(D)(i). If the sender learns that the e-mail did not reach the address of the person to be served, the sender must immediately send another copy by e-mail, or by a means authorized by FL ST J ADMIN Rule 2.516(b)(2). FL ST J ADMIN Rule 2.516(b)(1)(D)(ii). E-mail service is treated as service by mail for the computation of time. FL ST J ADMIN Rule 2.516(b)(1)(D)(iii).

   ii. *Format of e-mail for service.* Service of a document by e-mail is made by attaching a copy of the document in PDF format to an e-mail sent to all addresses designated by the attorney or party. FL ST J ADMIN Rule 2.516(b)(1)(E).

      - All documents served by e-mail must be attached to an e-mail message containing a subject line beginning with the words "SERVICE OF COURT DOCUMENT" in all capital letters, followed by the case number of the proceeding in which the documents are being served. FL ST J ADMIN Rule 2.516(b)(1)(E)(i).

      - The body of the e-mail must identify the court in which the proceeding is pending, the case number, the name of the initial party on each side, the title of each document served with that e-mail, and the sender's name and telephone number. FL ST J ADMIN Rule 2.516(b)(1)(E)(ii).

- Any document served by e-mail may be signed by the "/s/" format, as long as the filed original is signed in accordance with the applicable rule of procedure. FL ST J ADMIN Rule 2.516(b)(1)(E)(iii).
- Any e-mail which, together with its attached documents, exceeds five megabytes (5MB) in size, must be divided and sent as separate e-mails, no one of which may exceed five megabytes (5MB) in size and each of which must be sequentially numbered in the subject line. FL ST J ADMIN Rule 2.516(b)(1)(E)(iv).

iii. *Service by other means.* In addition to, and not in lieu of, service by e-mail, service may also be made upon attorneys by any of the means specified in FL ST J ADMIN Rule 2.516(b)(2). Service on and by all parties who are not represented by an attorney and who do not designate an e-mail address, and on and by all attorneys excused from e-mail service, must be made by delivering a copy of the document or by mailing it to the party or attorney at their last known address or, if no address is known, by leaving it with the clerk of the court. Service by mail is complete upon mailing. Delivery of a copy within FL ST J ADMIN Rule 2.516 is complete upon:

- Handing it to the attorney or to the party,
- Leaving it at the attorney's or party's office with a clerk or other person in charge thereof,
- If there is no one in charge, leaving it in a conspicuous place therein,
- If the office is closed or the person to be served has no office, leaving it at the person's usual place of abode with some person of his or her family above fifteen (15) years of age and informing such person of the contents, or
- Transmitting it by facsimile to the attorney's or party's office with a cover sheet containing the sender's name, firm, address, telephone number, and facsimile number, and the number of pages transmitted. When service is made by facsimile, a copy must also be served by any other method permitted by FL ST J ADMIN Rule 2.516. Facsimile service occurs when transmission is complete. FL ST J ADMIN Rule 2.516(b)(2)(A) through FL ST J ADMIN Rule 2.516(b)(2)(E).
- Service by delivery after 5:00 p.m. must be deemed to have been made by mailing on the date of delivery. FL ST J ADMIN Rule 2.516(b)(2)(F).

c. *Service; Numerous defendants.* In actions when the parties are unusually numerous, the court may regulate the service contemplated by the Florida Rules of Judicial Administration on motion or on its own initiative in such manner as may be found to be just and reasonable. FL ST J ADMIN Rule 2.516(c).

d. *Service by clerk.* Service of notices and other documents required to be made by the clerk must also be done as provided in FL ST J ADMIN Rule 2.516(b). FL ST J ADMIN Rule 2.516(g).

G. Hearings

1. *Preliminary hearings.* The defenses in FL ST RCP Rule 1.140(b)(1) through FL ST RCP Rule 1.140(b)(7), whether made in a pleading or by motion, and the motion for judgment in FL ST RCP Rule 1.140(c) shall be heard and determined before trial on application of any party unless the court orders that the hearing and determination shall be deferred until the trial. FL ST RCP Rule 1.140(d).

H. Forms

1. Official Answer Forms for Florida

a. Caption. FL ST RCP Form 1.901.

b. Crossclaim summons. FL ST RCP Form 1.903.

c. Third-party summons. FL ST RCP Form 1.904.

d. Defense; Statute of limitations. FL ST RCP Form 1.965.

e. Defense; Payment. FL ST RCP Form 1.966.

f. Defense; Accord and satisfaction. FL ST RCP Form 1.967.

g. Defense; Failure of consideration. FL ST RCP Form 1.968.
h. Defense; Statute of frauds. FL ST RCP Form 1.969.
i. Defense; Release. FL ST RCP Form 1.970.
j. Notice of compliance when constitutional challenge is brought. FL ST RCP Form 1.975.

2. Answer Forms for Florida

a. Answer; General form, traverses. FL-PRACFORM § 5:4.
b. Answer; General form, traverses and affirmative defenses. FL-PRACFORM § 5:6.
c. Answer; General form, traverses, affirmative defenses and counterclaim. FL-PRACFORM § 5:7.
d. Answer; General form, traverses, affirmative defenses, counterclaim and crossclaim. FL-PRACFORM § 5:8.
e. Answer; Affirmative defense, fraud. FL-PRACFORM § 5:43.
f. Answer; Affirmative defense, laches. FL-PRACFORM § 5:47.
g. Answer; Affirmative defense, misjoinder. FL-PRACFORM § 5:49.
h. Answer; Affirmative defense, misrepresentation. FL-PRACFORM § 5:50.
i. Answer; Affirmative defense, self defense. FL-PRACFORM § 5:64.
j. Answer; Denial of conditions precedent. FL-PRACFORM § 5:80.
k. General denial. FL-PP § 2:58.
l. General denial; With specified admissions. FL-PP § 2:59.
m. Admission with qualification. FL-PP § 2:60.
n. Conclusions of law not requiring denial. FL-PP § 2:61.
o. Defenses stated in the alternative. FL-PP § 2:62.
p. Denial as to part of allegation. FL-PP § 2:63.
q. Pleader as without knowledge as to truth of allegation. FL-PP § 2:64.

I. Checklist

(I) ❑ Matters to be considered by plaintiff
- (a) ❑ Required documents
  - (1) ❑ Summons
  - (2) ❑ Complaint
  - (3) ❑ Civil cover sheet
  - (4) ❑ Return of execution process by process server
  - (5) ❑ Filing fees
- (b) ❑ Supplemental documents
  - (1) ❑ Exhibits
  - (2) ❑ Notice of constitutional question
- (c) ❑ Time for filing and serving complaint
  - (1) ❑ Service of the initial process and initial pleading should be made upon a defendant within one hundred twenty (120) days after the filing of the complaint with the court

(II) ❑ Matters to be considered by defendant
- (a) ❑ Required documents
  - (1) ❑ Answer
  - (2) ❑ Certificate of service

(b) ❑ Supplemental documents
  (1) ❑ Exhibits
  (2) ❑ Notice of constitutional question
(c) ❑ Time for answer
  (1) ❑ Unless a different time is prescribed in a statute of Florida, a defendant shall serve an answer within twenty (20) days after service of original process and the initial pleading on the defendant, or not later than the date fixed in a notice by publication
  (2) ❑ A party served with a pleading stating a crossclaim against that party shall serve an answer to it within twenty (20) days after service on that party
  (3) ❑ The plaintiff shall serve an answer to a counterclaim within twenty (20) days after service of the counterclaim
  (4) ❑ A defendant who, before being served with process, timely returns a waiver so requested is not required to respond to the complaint until sixty (60) days after the date the defendant received the request for waiver of service; for purposes of computing any time prescribed or allowed by the Florida Rules of Civil Procedure, service of process shall be deemed effected twenty (20) days before the time required to respond to the complaint
  (5) ❑ For timing requirements related to service on the state, service of motion impact, and responding when no responsive pleading is required, please see the Timing section of this document

Pleadings
Amended Answer

Document Last Updated January 2013

A. Applicable Rules

1. *State rules*
   a. Nonverification of papers. FL ST RCP Rule 1.030.
   b. Service and filing of pleadings, orders, and documents. FL ST RCP Rule 1.080.
   c. Time. FL ST RCP Rule 1.090.
   d. Pleadings and motions. FL ST RCP Rule 1.100; FL ST RCP Rule 1.110; FL ST RCP Rule 1.120; FL ST RCP Rule 1.130; FL ST RCP Rule 1.190.
   e. Defenses. FL ST RCP Rule 1.140.
   f. Pretrial procedure. FL ST RCP Rule 1.200.
   g. Relief from judgment, decrees, or orders. FL ST RCP Rule 1.540.
   h. Forms. FL ST RCP Rule 1.900.
   i. Minimization of the filing of sensitive information. FL ST J ADMIN Rule 2.425.
   j. Foreign attorneys. FL ST J ADMIN Rule 2.510.
   k. Signature of attorneys and parties. FL ST J ADMIN Rule 2.515.
   l. Paper. FL ST J ADMIN Rule 2.520.
   m. Electronic filing. FL ST J ADMIN Rule 2.525.
   n. Accessibility of information and technology. FL ST J ADMIN Rule 2.526.
   o. Court reporting. FL ST J ADMIN Rule 2.535.
   p. Requests for accommodations by persons with disabilities. FL ST J ADMIN Rule 2.540.
2. *Local rules*
   a. Establishment of 11th Circuit Homestead Access to Mediation Program ("CHAMP") for case

management of residential foreclosure cases in the Eleventh Judicial Circuit of Florida. FL ST 11 J CIR 1-09-08.

B. Timing

1. *Amendment as a matter of course.* A party may amend a pleading once as a matter of course at any time before a responsive pleading is served or, if the pleading is one to which no responsive pleading is permitted and the action has not been placed on the trial calendar, may so amend it at any time within twenty (20) days after it is served. FL ST RCP Rule 1.190(a).
2. *Amendment by leave of court.* Otherwise a party may amend a pleading only by leave of court or by written consent of the adverse party. Leave of court shall be given freely when justice so requires. FL ST RCP Rule 1.190(a).
3. *Amendments in furtherance of justice.* At any time in furtherance of justice, upon such terms as may be just, the court may permit any process, proceeding, pleading, or record to be amended or material supplemental matter to be set forth in an amended or supplemental pleading. At every stage of the action the court must disregard any error or defect in the proceedings which does not affect the substantial rights of the parties. FL ST RCP Rule 1.190(e).
4. *Response to amended pleading.* A party shall plead in response to an amended pleading within ten (10) days after service of the amended pleading unless the court otherwise orders. FL ST RCP Rule 1.190(a).
5. *Computation of time*
    a. *Generally.* Computation of time shall be governed by FL ST J ADMIN Rule 2.514. FL ST RCP Rule 1.090(a). The following rules apply in computing time periods specified in any rule of procedure, local rule, court order, or statute that does not specify a method of computing time. FL ST J ADMIN Rule 2.514(a).
        i. *Period stated in days or a longer unit.* When the period is stated in days or a longer unit of time (A) exclude the day of the event that triggers the period; (B) count every day, including intermediate Saturdays, Sundays, and legal holidays; and (C) include the last day of the period, but if the last day is a Saturday, Sunday, or legal holiday, or falls within any period of time extended through an order of the chief justice under FL ST J ADMIN Rule 2.205(a)(2)(B)(iv), the period continues to run until the end of the next day that is not a Saturday, Sunday, or legal holiday and does not fall within any period of time extended through an order of the chief justice. FL ST J ADMIN Rule 2.514(a)(1).
        ii. *Period stated in hours.* When the period is stated in hours (A) begin counting immediately on the occurrence of the event that triggers the period; (B) count every hour, including hours during intermediate Saturdays, Sundays, and legal holidays; and (C) if the period would end on a Saturday, Sunday, or legal holiday, or during any period of time extended through an order of the chief justice under FL ST J ADMIN Rule 2.205(a)(2)(B)(iv), the period continues to run until the same time on the next day that is not a Saturday, Sunday, or legal holiday and does not fall within any period of time extended through an order of the chief justice. FL ST J ADMIN Rule 2.514(a)(2).
        iii. *Period stated in days less than seven (7) days.* When the period stated in days is less than seven (7) days, intermediate Saturdays, Sundays, and legal holidays shall be excluded in the computation. FL ST J ADMIN Rule 2.514(a)(3).
        iv. *"Last day" defined.* Unless a different time is set by a statute, local rule, or court order, the last day ends (A) for electronic filing or for service by any means, at midnight; and (B) for filing by other means, when the clerk's office is scheduled to close. FL ST J ADMIN Rule 2.514(a)(4).
        v. *"Next day" defined.* The "next day" is determined by continuing to count forward when the period is measured after an event and backward when measured before an event. FL ST J ADMIN Rule 2.514(a)(5).
        vi. *"Legal holiday" defined.* "Legal holiday" means (A) the day set aside by FL ST § 110.117, for observing New Year's Day, Martin Luther King, Jr.'s Birthday, Memorial Day, Independence Day, Labor Day, Veterans' Day, Thanksgiving Day, the Friday after Thanksgiving Day, or

Christmas Day, and (B) any day observed as a holiday by the clerk's office or as designated by the chief judge. FL ST J ADMIN Rule 2.514(a)(6).

b. *Additional time after service by mail or e-mail.* When a party may or must act within a specified time after service and service is made by mail or e-mail, five (5) days are added after the period that would otherwise expire under FL ST J ADMIN Rule 2.514(a). FL ST J ADMIN Rule 2.514(b).

c. *Enlargement.* When an act is required or allowed to be done at or within a specified time by order of court, by the Florida Rules of Civil Procedure, or by notice given thereunder, for cause shown the court at any time in its discretion (1) with or without notice, may order the period enlarged if request therefor is made before the expiration of the period originally prescribed or as extended by a previous order, or (2) upon motion made and notice after the expiration of the specified period, may permit the act to be done when failure to act was the result of excusable neglect, but it may not extend the time for making a motion for new trial, for rehearing, or to alter or amend a judgment; making a motion for relief from a judgment under FL ST RCP Rule 1.540(b); taking an appeal or filing a petition for certiorari; or making a motion for a directed verdict. FL ST RCP Rule 1.090(b).

d. *Unaffected by expiration of term.* The period of time provided for the doing of any act or the taking of any proceeding shall not be affected or limited by the continued existence or expiration of a term of court. The continued existence or expiration of a term of court in no way affects the power of a court to do any act or take any proceeding in any action which is or has been pending before it. FL ST RCP Rule 1.090(c).

C. General Requirements

1. *Amendments.* A party may amend a pleading once as a matter of course at any time before a responsive pleading is served or, if the pleading is one to which no responsive pleading is permitted and the action has not been placed on the trial calendar, may so amend it at any time within twenty (20) days after it is served. Otherwise a party may amend a pleading only by leave of court or by written consent of the adverse party. Leave of court shall be freely given when justice so requires. FL ST RCP Rule 1.190(a).

   a. *Purpose of amendments.* Amendments can relate to the correction of mistakes, the insertion of jurisdictional averments, the correction or addition of verifications, the addition or substitution or striking out of parties, and generally the rectification of all formal defects in the pleading. The court can also allow amendments setting up an omitted counterclaim or cross-claim if the defendant failed to raise the claim through oversight, inadvertence, or excusable neglect. FL-PP § 2:151.

   b. *Amendment to a pleading/Amended pleading.* A significant difference exists between an amendment to a pleading and an amended pleading. An amendment to a pleading corrects, adds to or deletes from the pleading. An amended pleading is substituted for the former pleading and the former pleading ceases to have any effect. Dee v. Southern Brewing Company, 146 Fla. 588, 1 So.2d 562 (Fla. 1941); Shannon v. McBride, 105 So.2d 16 (Fla. 2d DCA 1958); Hughes v. Home Sav. of America, F.S.B., 675 So.2d 649 (Fla. 2d DCA 1996); FL-PRACPROC § 14:2.

   c. *Relation back of amendments.* When the claim or defense asserted in the amended pleading arose out of the conduct, transaction, or occurrence set forth or attempted to be set forth in the original pleading, the amendment shall relate back to the date of the original pleading. FL ST RCP Rule 1.190(c).

2. *General rules of pleading*

   a. *Claims for relief*

      i. A pleading which sets forth a claim for relief, whether an original claim, counterclaim, crossclaim, or third-party claim, must state a cause of action and shall contain

         - A short and plain statement of the grounds upon which the court's jurisdiction depends, unless the court already has jurisdiction and the claim needs no new grounds of jurisdiction to support it (For information regarding acts subjecting persons to jurisdiction, please see FL ST § 48.193),
         - A short and plain statement of the ultimate facts showing that the pleader is entitled to relief, and

- A demand for judgment for the relief to which the pleader deems himself or herself entitled. FL ST RCP Rule 1.110(b).

ii. Relief in the alternative or of several different types may be demanded. Every complaint shall be considered to demand general relief. FL ST RCP Rule 1.110(b).

b. *Verification.* Except when otherwise specifically provided by these rules or an applicable statute, every pleading or other document of a party represented by an attorney need not be verified or accompanied by an affidavit. FL ST RCP Rule 1.030. When filing an action for foreclosure of a mortgage on residential real property the complaint shall be verified. When verification of a document is required, the document filed shall include an oath, affirmation, or the following statement: "Under penalty of perjury, I declare that I have read the foregoing, and the facts alleged therein are true and correct to the best of my knowledge and belief." FL ST RCP Rule 1.110(b).

c. *Separate statements.* All averments of claim or defense shall be made in consecutively numbered paragraphs, the contents of each of which shall be limited as far as practicable to a statement of a single set of circumstances, and a paragraph may be referred to by number in all subsequent pleadings. Each claim founded upon a separate transaction or occurrence and each defense other than denials shall be stated in a separate count or defense when a separation facilitates the clear presentation of the matter set forth. FL ST RCP Rule 1.110(f).

d. *Statements adopted by reference.* Statements in a pleading may be adopted by reference in a different part of the same pleading, in another pleading, or in any motion. FL ST RCP Rule 1.130(b).

e. *Joinder of causes of action; Consistency.* A pleader may set up in the same action as many claims or causes of action or defenses in the same right as the pleader has, and claims for relief may be stated in the alternative if separate items make up the cause of action, or if two (2) or more causes of action are joined. A party may also set forth two (2) or more statements of a claim or defense alternatively, either in one (1) count or defense or in separate counts or defenses. When two (2) or more statements are made in the alternative and one (1) of them, if made independently, would be sufficient, the pleading is not made insufficient by the insufficiency of one (1) or more of the alternative statements. A party may also state as many separate claims or defenses as that party has, regardless of consistency and whether based on legal or equitable grounds or both. All pleadings shall be construed so as to do substantial justice. FL ST RCP Rule 1.110(g).

f. *Subsequent pleadings.* When the nature of an action permits pleadings subsequent to final judgment and the jurisdiction of the court over the parties has not terminated, the initial pleading subsequent to final judgment shall be designated a supplemental complaint or petition. The action shall then proceed in the same manner and time as though the supplemental complaint or petition were the initial pleading in the action, including the issuance of any needed process. FL ST RCP Rule 1.110(h) shall not apply to proceedings that may be initiated by motion under the Florida Rules of Civil Procedure. FL ST RCP Rule 1.110(h).

g. *Pleading basis for service.* When service of process is to be made under statutes authorizing service on nonresidents of Florida, it is sufficient to plead the basis for service in the language of the statute without pleading the facts supporting service. FL ST RCP Rule 1.070(h).

h. *Forms of pleadings.* Forms of action and technical forms for seeking relief and of pleas, pleadings, or motions are abolished. FL ST RCP Rule 1.110(a).

3. *Answer; Generally.* An answer has three (3) functions. First, it must respond to each allegation of the preceding pleading by admitting, denying or alleging that the pleader is without knowledge of the allegation. Second, it must contain any affirmative defenses that the pleader is interposing to any cause of action alleged in the preceding pleading. Third, the answer may claim affirmative relief against the plaintiff or petitioner by a counterclaim or against a codefendant by a crossclaim. FL-PRACPROC § 11:1.

a. *Content.* In the answer a pleader shall state in short and plain terms the pleader's defenses to each claim asserted and shall admit or deny the averments on which the adverse party relies. If the defendant is without knowledge, the defendant shall so state and such statement shall operate as a denial. Denial shall fairly meet the substance of the averments denied. When a pleader intends in good faith to deny only a part of an averment, the pleader shall specify so much of it as is true and

shall deny the remainder. Unless the pleader intends in good faith to controvert all of the averments of the preceding pleading, the pleader may make denials as specific denials of designated averments or may generally deny all of the averments except such designated averments as the pleader expressly admits, but when the pleader does so intend to controvert all of its averments, including averments of the grounds upon which the court's jurisdiction depends, the pleader may do so by general denial. FL ST RCP Rule 1.110(c).

b. *Form of answer.* An answer contains a caption, commencement, body, signature and certificate of service. The caption is the same as that of the initial pleading, except for the designation as one of the types of answer. The body of an answer should contain an admission, denial or plea of without knowledge to each allegation of the preceding pleading, except for the additional allegations in response to a general allegation of conditions precedent and the denial of capacity to sue. FL-PRACPROC § 11:3.

   i. *Responding sequentially.* The best method of responding is to answer each paragraph sequentially, combining admissions, denials or pleas of without knowledge when the sequence permits. The admissions, denials and allegations of without knowledge should be stated first, followed separately by any affirmative defenses and then by any counterclaim or crossclaim. A third party complaint may be a part of the same paper, but it is not a part of the answer as is a counterclaim or crossclaim. Paragraphs are numbered consecutively throughout the pleading whether in the answer, counterclaim or crossclaim. Denials for the record only are improper. FL-PRACPROC § 11:3.

c. *Defenses*

   i. *Generally.* Every defense in law or fact to a claim for relief in a pleading shall be asserted in the responsive pleading, if one is required, but the following defenses may be made by motion at the option of the pleader: (1) lack of jurisdiction over the subject matter, (2) lack of jurisdiction over the person, (3) improper venue, (4) insufficiency of process, (5) insufficiency of service of process, (6) failure to state a cause of action, and (7) failure to join indispensable parties. A motion making any of these defenses shall be made before pleading if a further pleading is permitted. FL ST RCP Rule 1.140(b).

      - *Stated specifically.* The grounds on which any of the enumerated defenses are based and the substantial matters of law intended to be argued shall be stated specifically and with particularity in the responsive pleading or motion. FL ST RCP Rule 1.140(b).
      - *Waiver.* Any ground not stated shall be deemed to be waived except any ground showing that the court lacks jurisdiction of the subject matter may be made at any time. No defense or objection is waived by being joined with other defenses or objections in a responsive pleading or motion. FL ST RCP Rule 1.140(b). A party waives all defenses and objections that the party does not present either by motion under FL ST RCP Rule 1.140(b), FL ST RCP Rule 1.140(e), or FL ST RCP Rule 1.140(f) or, if the party has made no motion, in a responsive pleading except as provided in FL ST RCP Rule 1.140(h)(2). FL ST RCP Rule 1.140(h)(1). The defenses of failure to state a cause of action or a legal defense or to join an indispensable party may be raised by motion for judgment on the pleadings or at the trial on the merits in addition to being raised either in a motion under FL ST RCP Rule 1.140(b) or in the answer or reply. The defense of lack of jurisdiction of the subject matter may be raised at any time. FL ST RCP Rule 1.140(h)(2).

   ii. *Affirmative defenses.* In pleading to a preceding pleading a party shall set forth affirmatively accord and satisfaction, arbitration and award, assumption of risk, contributory negligence, discharge in bankruptcy, duress, estoppel, failure of consideration, fraud, illegality, injury by fellow servant, laches, license, payment, release, res judicata, statute of frauds, statute of limitations, waiver, and any other matter constituting an avoidance or affirmative defense. When a party has mistakenly designated a defense as a counterclaim or a counterclaim as a defense, the court, on terms if justice so requires, shall treat the pleading as if there had been a proper designation. Affirmative defenses appearing on the face of a prior pleading may be asserted as grounds for a motion or defense under FL ST RCP Rule 1.140(b); provided this shall

not limit amendments under FL ST RCP Rule 1.190 even if such ground is sustained. FL ST RCP Rule 1.110(d).

- *Format of defenses.* Affirmative defenses should be placed after the admissions, denials and allegations of without knowledge in the answer. All paragraphs must be numbered consecutively throughout the answer. If a defense is directed to only a part of a cause of action or to one or more, but not all, of several causes of action in the preceding pleading, the part or cause of action to which it is directed should be identified in the defense. Defenses should be identified by consecutive ordinal numbers such as "First Defense" and "Second Defense." FL-PRACPROC § 11:4.

iii. *Effect of failure to deny.* Averments in a pleading to which a responsive pleading is required, other than those as to the amount of damages, are admitted when not denied in the responsive pleading. Averments in a pleading to which no responsive pleading is required or permitted shall be taken as denied or avoided. FL ST RCP Rule 1.110(e). An admission in an answer binds the party and no proof is required. An admission does not extend beyond the scope of the allegation in the preceding pleading. FL-PRACPROC § 11:3.

4. *Pleading special matters*

a. *Capacity.* It is not necessary to aver the capacity of a party to sue or be sued, the authority of a party to sue or be sued in a representative capacity, or the legal existence of an organized association of persons that is made a party, except to the extent required to show the jurisdiction of the court. The initial pleading served on behalf of a minor party shall specifically aver the age of the minor party. When a party desires to raise an issue as to the legal existence of any party, the capacity of any party to sue or be sued, or the authority of a party to sue or be sued in a representative capacity, that party shall do so by specific negative averment which shall include such supporting particulars as are peculiarly within the pleader's knowledge. FL ST RCP Rule 1.120(a).

b. *Fraud, mistake, condition of the mind.* In all averments of fraud or mistake, the circumstances constituting fraud or mistake shall be stated with such particularity as the circumstances may permit. Malice, intent, knowledge, mental attitude, and other condition of mind of a person may be averred generally. FL ST RCP Rule 1.120(b).

c. *Conditions precedent.* In pleading the performance or occurrence of conditions precedent, it is sufficient to aver generally that all conditions precedent have been performed or have occurred. A denial of performance or occurrence shall be made specifically and with particularity. FL ST RCP Rule 1.120(c).

d. *Official document or act.* In pleading an official document or official act it is sufficient to aver that the document was issued or the act done in compliance with law. FL ST RCP Rule 1.120(c).

e. *Judgment or decree.* In pleading a judgment or decree of a domestic or foreign court, a judicial or quasi-judicial tribunal, or a board or officer, it is sufficient to aver the judgment or decree without setting forth matter showing jurisdiction to render it. FL ST RCP Rule 1.120(e).

f. *Time and place.* For the purpose of testing the sufficiency of a pleading, averments of time and place are material and shall be considered like all other averments of material matter. FL ST RCP Rule 1.120(f).

g. *Special damage.* When items of special damage are claimed, they shall be specifically stated. FL ST RCP Rule 1.120(g).

5. *Parties*

a. *Parties generally.* Every action may be prosecuted in the name of the real party in interest, but a personal representative, administrator, guardian, trustee of an express trust, a party with whom or in whose name a contract has been made for the benefit of another, or a party expressly authorized by statute may sue in that person's own name without joining the party for whose benefit the action is brought. All persons having an interest in the subject of the action and in obtaining the relief demanded may join as plaintiffs and any person may be made a defendant who has or claims an interest adverse to the plaintiff. Any person may at any time be made a party if that person's presence is necessary or proper to a complete determination of the cause. Persons having a united interest may

be joined on the same side as plaintiffs or defendants, and anyone who refuses to join may for such reason be made a defendant. FL ST RCP Rule 1.210(a).

b. *Minors or incompetent persons.* When a minor or incompetent person has a representative, such as a guardian or other like fiduciary, the representative may sue or defend on behalf of the minor or incompetent person. A minor or incompetent person who does not have a duly appointed representative may sue by next friend or by a guardian ad litem. The court shall appoint a guardian ad litem for a minor or incompetent person not otherwise represented in an action or shall make such other order as it deems proper for the protection of the minor or incompetent person. FL ST RCP Rule 1.210(b).

c. For survivor and substitution of parties information, please see FL ST RCP Rule 1.260.

6. *Counterclaims and crossclaims*

a. *Compulsory counterclaims.* A pleading shall state as a counterclaim any claim which at the time of serving the pleading the pleader has against any opposing party, provided it arises out of the transaction or occurrence that is the subject matter of the opposing party's claim and does not require for its adjudication the presence of third parties over whom the court cannot acquire jurisdiction. But the pleader need not state a claim if (1) at the time the action was commenced the claim was the subject of another pending action, or (2) the opposing party brought suit upon that party's claim by attachment or other process by which the court did not acquire jurisdiction to render a personal judgment on the claim and the pleader is not stating a counterclaim under this rule. FL ST RCP Rule 1.170(a).

b. *Permissive counterclaim.* A pleading may state as a counterclaim any claim against an opposing party not arising out of the transaction or occurrence that is the subject matter of the opposing party's claim. FL ST RCP Rule 1.170(b).

c. *Counterclaim exceeding opposing claim.* A counterclaim may or may not diminish or defeat the recovery sought by the opposing party. It may claim relief exceeding in amount or different in kind from that sought in the pleading of the opposing party. FL ST RCP Rule 1.170(c).

d. *Counterclaim against the State.* The Florida Rules of Civil Procedure shall not be construed to enlarge beyond the limits established by law the right to assert counterclaims or to claim credits against the state or any of its subdivisions or other governmental organizations thereof subject to suit or against a municipal corporation or against an officer, agency, or administrative board of the state. FL ST RCP Rule 1.170(d).

e. *Counterclaim maturing or acquired after pleading.* A claim which matured or was acquired by the pleader after serving the pleading may be presented as a counterclaim by supplemental pleading with the permission of the court. FL ST RCP Rule 1.170(e).

f. *Omitted counterclaim or crossclaim.* When a pleader fails to set up a counterclaim or crossclaim through oversight, inadvertence, or excusable neglect, or when justice requires, the pleader may set up the counterclaim or crossclaim by amendment with leave of the court. FL ST RCP Rule 1.170(f).

g. *Crossclaim against co-party.* A pleading may state as a crossclaim any claim by one party against a co-party arising out of the transaction or occurrence that is the subject matter of either the original action or a counterclaim therein, or relating to any property that is the subject matter of the original action. The crossclaim may include a claim that the party against whom it is asserted is or may be liable to the crossclaimant for all or part of a claim asserted in the action against the crossclaimant. Service of a crossclaim on a party who has appeared in the action shall be made pursuant to FL ST RCP Rule 1.080. Service of a crossclaim against a party who has not appeared in the action shall be made in the manner provided for service of summons. FL ST RCP Rule 1.170(g).

h. *Additional parties may be brought in.* When the presence of parties other than those to the original action is required to grant complete relief in the determination of a counterclaim or crossclaim, they shall be named in the counterclaim or crossclaim and be served with process and shall be parties to the action thereafter if jurisdiction of them can be obtained and their joinder will not deprive the court of jurisdiction of the action. FL ST RCP Rule 1.250(b) and FL ST RCP Rule 1.250(c) apply to parties brought in under FL ST RCP Rule 1.170(h). FL ST RCP Rule 1.170(h).

i. *Separate trials; Separate judgment.* If the court orders separate trials as provided in FL ST RCP Rule 1.270(b), judgment on a counterclaim or crossclaim may be rendered when the court has jurisdiction to do so even if a claim of the opposing party has been dismissed or otherwise disposed of. FL ST RCP Rule 1.170(i).

j. *Demand exceeding jurisdiction; Transfer of action.* If the demand of any counterclaim or crossclaim exceeds the jurisdiction of the court in which the action is pending, the action shall be transferred forthwith to the court of the same county having jurisdiction of the demand in the counterclaim or crossclaim with only such alterations in the pleadings as are essential. The court shall order the transfer of the action and the transmittal of all papers in it to the proper court if the party asserting the demand exceeding the jurisdiction deposits with the court having jurisdiction a sum sufficient to pay the clerk's service charge in the court to which the action is transferred at the time of filing the counterclaim or crossclaim. Thereupon the original papers and deposit shall be transmitted and filed with a certified copy of the order. The court to which the action is transferred shall have full power and jurisdiction over the demands of all parties. Failure to make the service charge deposit at the time the counterclaim or crossclaim is filed, or within such further time as the court may allow, shall reduce a claim for damages to an amount within the jurisdiction of the court where the action is pending and waive the claim in other cases. FL ST RCP Rule 1.170(j).

7. *Misjoinder and nonjoinder of parties*

a. *Misjoinder.* Misjoinder of parties is not a ground for dismissal of an action. Any claim against a party may be severed and proceeded with separately. FL ST RCP Rule 1.250(a).

b. *Dropping parties.* Parties may be dropped by an adverse party in the manner provided for voluntary dismissal in FL ST RCP Rule 1.420(a)(1) subject to the exception stated in FL ST RCP Rule 1.420. If notice of lis pendens has been filed in the action against a party so dropped, the notice of dismissal shall be recorded and cancels the notice of lis pendens without the necessity of a court order. Parties may be dropped by order of court on its own initiative or the motion of any party at any stage of the action on such terms as are just. FL ST RCP Rule 1.250(b).

c. *Adding parties.* Parties may be added once as a matter of course within the same time that pleadings can be so amended under FL ST RCP Rule 1.190(a). If amendment by leave of court or stipulation of the parties is permitted, parties may be added in the amended pleading without further order of court. Parties may be added by order of court on its own initiative or on motion of any party at any stage of the action and on such terms as are just. FL ST RCP Rule 1.250(c).

8. *Jury demand*

a. *Right preserved.* The right of trial by jury as declared by the Constitution or by statute shall be preserved to the parties inviolate. FL ST RCP Rule 1.430(a).

b. *Demand.* Any party may demand a trial by jury of any issue triable of right by a jury by serving upon the other party a demand therefor in writing at any time after commencement of the action and not later than ten (10) days after the service of the last pleading directed to such issue. The demand may be indorsed upon a pleading of the party. FL ST RCP Rule 1.430(b).

c. *Specification of issues.* In the demand a party may specify the issues that the party wishes so tried; otherwise, the party is deemed to demand trial by jury for all issues so triable. FL ST RCP Rule 1.430(c).

  i. If a party has demanded trial by jury for only some of the issues, any other party may serve a demand for trial by jury of any other or all of the issues triable by jury ten (10) days after service of the demand or such lesser time as the court may order. FL ST RCP Rule 1.430(c).

d. *Waiver.* A party who fails to serve a demand as required by FL ST RCP Rule 1.430 waives trial by jury. FL ST RCP Rule 1.430(d).

  i. If waived, a jury trial may not be granted without the consent of the parties, but the court may allow an amendment in the proceedings to demand a trial by jury or order a trial by jury on its own motion. FL ST RCP Rule 1.430(d).

  ii. A demand for trial by jury may not be withdrawn without the consent of the parties. FL ST RCP Rule 1.430(d).

9. *Arbitration and mediation*

   a. *Referral to arbitration and mediation.* Except as hereinafter provided or as otherwise prohibited by law, the presiding judge may enter an order referring all or any part of a contested civil matter to mediation or arbitration. The parties to any contested civil matter may file a written stipulation to mediate or arbitrate any issue between them at any time. Such stipulation shall be incorporated into the order of referral. FL ST RCP Rule 1.700(a).

      i. In all residential foreclosure actions involving homestead properties filed on or after May 1, 2009, unless a stipulation is specifically invoked by the parties in writing within five (5) days of service of the complaint on the main defendant, the parties are deemed to have stipulated to referral of the mediation to the Collins Center pursuant to FL ST RCP Rule 1.720(f). FL ST 11 J CIR 1-09-08(2); FL ST 11 J CIR 1-09-08(3). FL ST 11 J CIR 1-09-08 constitutes a formal referral to mediation pursuant to the Florida Rules of Civil Procedure. FL ST 11 J CIR 1-09-08(2).

      ii. For further information on referral to mediation, refer to FL ST 11 J CIR 1-09-08.

   b. *Arbitration*

      i. *Exclusions.* A civil action shall be ordered to arbitration or arbitration in conjunction with mediation upon stipulation of the parties. A civil action may be ordered to arbitration or arbitration in conjunction with mediation upon motion of any party or by the court, if the judge determines the action to be of such a nature that arbitration could be of benefit to the litigants or the court. FL ST RCP Rule 1.800.

         - Under no circumstances may the following categories of actions be referred to arbitration: (1) bond estreatures; (2) habeas corpus or other extraordinary writs; (3) bond validations; (4) civil or criminal contempt; (5) such other matters as may be specified by order of the chief judge in the circuit. FL ST RCP Rule 1.800.

      ii. For more information regarding arbitration, please see FL ST RCP Rule 1.810; FL ST RCP Rule 1.820; FL ST RCP Rule 1.830.

   c. *Mediation.* For more information regarding mediation, please see FL ST RCP Rule 1.710; FL ST RCP Rule 1.720; FL ST RCP Rule 1.730; and FL ST RCP Rule 1.750.

10. *Rules of court*

   a. *Rules of civil procedure.* The Florida Rules of Civil Procedure apply to all actions of a civil nature and all special statutory proceedings in the circuit courts and county courts except those to which the Florida Probate Rules, the Florida Family Law Rules of Procedure, or the Small Claims Rules apply. FL ST RCP Rule 1.010.

      i. The form, content, procedure, and time for pleading in all special statutory proceedings shall be as prescribed by the statutes governing the proceeding unless the Florida Rules of Civil Procedure specifically provide to the contrary. FL ST RCP Rule 1.010.

      ii. The Florida Rules of Civil Procedure shall be construed to secure the just, speedy, and inexpensive determination of every action. FL ST RCP Rule 1.010.

   b. *Rules of judicial administration.* The Florida Rules of Judicial Administration shall apply to administrative matters in all courts to which the Florida Rules of Judicial Administration are applicable by their terms. The Florida Rules of Judicial Administration shall be construed to secure the speedy and inexpensive determination of every proceeding to which they are applicable. The Florida Rules of Judicial Administration shall supersede all conflicting rules and statutes. FL ST J ADMIN Rule 2.110.

D. Documents

1. *Required documents*

   a. *Amended answer.* See the General Requirements section of this document for the content of an amended answer. If a party files a motion to amend a pleading, the party shall attach the proposed amended pleading to the motion. FL ST RCP Rule 1.190(a). See the KeyRules Florida Circuit Court Motion for Leave to Amend document for further information.

i. *Notices to persons with disabilities.* See the Format section of this KeyRules document for further information.

b. *Certificate of service.* When any attorney certifies in substance: "I certify that a copy hereof has been furnished to (here insert name or names and addresses used for service) by (e-mail) (delivery) (mail) (fax) on .... (date) ....________________ Attorney" the certificate is taken as prima facie proof of such service in compliance with FL ST J ADMIN Rule 2.516. FL ST J ADMIN Rule 2.516(f).

2. *Supplemental documents*

a. *Exhibits.* All bonds, notes, bills of exchange, contracts, accounts, or documents upon which action may be brought or defense made, or a copy thereof or a copy of the portions thereof material to the pleadings, shall be incorporated in or attached to the pleading. No papers shall be unnecessarily annexed as exhibits. The pleadings shall contain no unnecessary recitals of deeds, documents, contracts, or other instruments. Any exhibit attached to a pleading shall be considered a part of the pleadings for all purposes. FL ST RCP Rule 1.130(a).

b. *Notice of constitutional question.* A party that files a pleading, written motion, or other paper drawing into question the constitutionality of a state statute or a county or municipal charter, ordinance, or franchise must promptly (1) file a notice of constitutional question stating the question and identifying the paper that raises it; and (2) serve the notice and the pleading, written motion, or other paper drawing into question the constitutionality of a state statute or a county or municipal charter, ordinance, or franchise on the Attorney General or the state attorney of the judicial circuit in which the action is pending, by either certified or registered mail. Service of the notice and pleading, written motion, or other paper does not require joinder of the Attorney General or the state attorney as a party to the action. FL ST RCP Rule 1.071.

E. Format

1. *Documents; Type and size.* Documents subject to the exceptions set forth in FL ST J ADMIN Rule 2.525(d) shall be filed on recycled paper measuring eight and one half by eleven (8 1/2 by 11) inches. For purposes of FL ST J ADMIN Rule 2.520, paper is recycled if it contains a minimum content of fifty (50) percent waste paper. Xerographic reduction of legal-size (eight and one half by fourteen (8 1/2 by 14) inches) documents to letter size (eight and one half by eleven (8 1/2 by 11) inches) is prohibited. All other documents filed by electronic transmission shall be filed in a format capable of being printed in a format consistent with the provisions of FL ST J ADMIN Rule 2.250. FL ST J ADMIN Rule 2.520(b).

a. *Exhibits.* Any exhibit or attachment filed with pleadings or papers may be filed in its original size. FL ST J ADMIN Rule 2.520(c).

b. *Recording space.* On all papers and documents prepared and filed by the court or by any party to a proceeding which are to be recorded in the public records of any county, including but not limited to final money judgments and notices of lis pendens, a three (3) inch by three (3) inch space at the top right-hand corner on the first page and a one (1) inch by three (3) inch space at the top right-hand corner on each subsequent page shall be left blank and reserved for use by the clerk of court. FL ST J ADMIN Rule 2.520(d).

i. *Exceptions to recording space.* Any papers or documents created by persons or entities over which the filing party has no control, including but not limited to wills, codicils, trusts, or other testamentary documents; documents prepared or executed by any public officer; documents prepared, executed, acknowledged, or proved outside of the State of Florida; or documents created by State or Federal government agencies, may be filed without the space required by FL ST J ADMIN Rule 2.520. FL ST J ADMIN Rule 2.520(e).

c. *Noncompliance.* No clerk of court is permitted to refuse to file any document or paper because of noncompliance with the Florida Rules of Judicial Administration. However, upon request of the clerk of court, noncomplying documents must be resubmitted in accordance with the formatting rules. FL ST J ADMIN Rule 2.520(f).

2. *Caption.* Every pleading, motion, order, judgment, or other paper shall have a caption containing the

name of the court, the file number, and except for in rem proceedings, including forfeiture proceedings, the name of the first party on each side with an appropriate indication of other parties, and a designation identifying the party filing it and its nature or the nature of the order, as the case may be. In any in rem proceeding, every pleading, motion, order, judgment, or other paper shall have a caption containing the name of the court, the file number, the style "In re" (followed by the name or general description of the property), and a designation of the person or entity filing it and its nature or the nature of the order, as the case may be. In an in rem forfeiture proceeding, the style shall be "In re forfeiture of" (followed by the name of the general description of the property). All papers filed in the action shall be styled in such a manner as to indicate clearly the subject matter of the paper and the party requesting or obtaining relief. FL ST RCP Rule 1.100(c)(1).

3. *Writing and written defined.* Writing or written means a document containing information, an application, or a stipulation. FL ST RCP Rule 1.080(c).
4. *Rule abbreviations*
   a. The Florida Rules of Civil Procedure and shall be abbreviated as Fla.R.Civ.P. FL ST RCP Rule 1.010.
   b. The Florida Rules of Judicial Administration shall be abbreviated as Fla. R. Jud. Admin. FL ST J ADMIN Rule 2.110.
5. *Nonverification.* Except when otherwise specifically provided by the Florida Rules of Civil Procedure or an applicable statute, every pleading or other document of a party represented by an attorney need not be verified or accompanied by an affidavit. FL ST RCP Rule 1.030; FL ST J ADMIN Rule 2.515(a).
6. *Attorney signature*
   a. *Attorney signature.* Every pleading and other document of a party represented by an attorney shall be signed by at least one (1) attorney of record in that attorney's individual name whose current record Florida Bar address, telephone number, including area code, primary e-mail address and secondary e-mail addresses, if any, and Florida Bar number shall be stated, and who shall be duly licensed to practice law in Florida or who shall have received permission to appear in the particular case as provided in FL ST J ADMIN Rule 2.510. FL ST J ADMIN Rule 2.515(a).
      i. The attorney may be required by the court to give the address of, and to vouch for the attorney's authority to represent, the party. FL ST J ADMIN Rule 2.515(a).
      ii. The signature of an attorney shall constitute a certificate by the attorney that the attorney has read the pleading or other document; that to the best of the attorney's knowledge, information, and belief there is good ground to support it; and that it is not interposed for delay. FL ST J ADMIN Rule 2.515(a).
      iii. If a pleading is not signed or is signed with intent to defeat the purpose of FL ST J ADMIN Rule 2.515, it may be stricken and the action may proceed as though the pleading or other document had not been served. FL ST J ADMIN Rule 2.515(a).
   b. *Pro se litigant signature.* A party who is not represented by an attorney shall sign any pleading or other paper and state the party's address and telephone number, including area code. FL ST J ADMIN Rule 2.515(b).
   c. *Form of signature*
      i. The signatures required on pleadings and documents by FL ST J ADMIN Rule 2.515(a) and FL ST J ADMIN Rule 2.515(b) may be:
         - Original signatures;
         - Original signatures that have been reproduced by electronic means, such as on electronically transmitted documents or photocopied documents;
         - Electronic signatures using the "/s/," "s/," or "/s" formats by or at the direction of the person signing; or
         - Any other signature format authorized by general law, so long as the clerk where the proceeding is pending has the capability of receiving and has obtained approval from the

Supreme Court of Florida to accept pleadings and documents with that signature format. FL ST J ADMIN Rule 2.515(c)(1).

ii. An attorney, party, or other person who files a pleading or paper by electronic transmission that does not contain the original signature of that attorney, party, or other person shall file that identical pleading or paper in paper form containing an original signature of that attorney, party, or other person (hereinafter called the follow-up filing) immediately thereafter. The follow-up filing is not required if the Supreme Court of Florida has entered an order directing the clerk of court to discontinue accepting the follow-up filing. FL ST J ADMIN Rule 2.515(c)(2).

7. *Forms*

a. *Process.* The forms of process, notice of lis pendens, and notice of action provided in the Florida Rules of Civil Procedure are sufficient. Variations from the forms do not void process or notices that are otherwise sufficient. FL ST RCP Rule 1.900(a).

b. *Other forms.* The other forms provided in the Florida Rules of Civil Procedure are sufficient for the matters that are covered by them. So long as the substance is expressed without prolixity, the forms may be varied to meet the facts of a particular case. FL ST RCP Rule 1.900(b).

c. *Formal matters.* Captions, except for the designation of the paper, are omitted from the forms provided in the Florida Rules of Civil Procedure. A general form of caption is the first form provided. Signatures are omitted from pleadings and motions. FL ST RCP Rule 1.900(c).

8. *Notices to persons with disabilities.* All notices of court proceedings to be held in a public facility, and all process compelling appearance at such proceedings, shall include the following statement in bold face, fourteen (14) point Times New Roman or Courier font: "If you are a person with a disability who needs any accommodation in order to participate in this proceeding, you are entitled, at no cost to you, to the provision of certain assistance. Please contact [identify applicable court personnel by name, address, and telephone number] at least seven (7) days before your scheduled court appearance, or immediately upon receiving this notification if the time before the scheduled appearance is less than seven (7) days; if you are hearing or voice impaired, call 711." FL ST J ADMIN Rule 2.540(c)(1).

9. *Minimization of the filing of sensitive information*

a. *Limitations for court filings.* Unless authorized by FL ST J ADMIN Rule 2.425(b), statute, another rule of court, or the court orders otherwise, designated sensitive information filed with the court must be limited to the following format:

i. The initials of a person known to be a minor;

ii. The year of birth of a person's birth date;

iii. No portion of any: Social security number, Bank account number, Credit card account number, Charge account number, or Debit account number;

iv. The last four digits of any: Taxpayer identification number (TIN), Employee identification number, Driver's license number, Passport number, Telephone number, Financial account number, except as set forth in FL ST J ADMIN Rule 2.425(a)(3), Brokerage account number, Insurance policy account number, Loan account number, Customer account number, or Patient or health care number;

v. A truncated version of any: Email address, Computer user name, Password, or Personal identification number (PIN); and

vi. A truncated version of any other sensitive information as provided by court order. FL ST J ADMIN Rule 2.425(a).

b. *Exceptions.* FL ST J ADMIN Rule 2.425(a) does not apply to the following:

i. An account number which identifies the property alleged to be the subject of a proceeding;

ii. The record of an administrative or agency proceeding;

iii. The record in appellate or review proceedings;

iv. The birth date of a minor whenever the birth date is necessary for the court to establish or maintain subject matter jurisdiction;

v. The name of a minor in any order relating to parental responsibility, time-sharing, or child support;

vi. The name of a minor in any document or order affecting the minor's ownership of real property;

vii. The birth date of a party in a writ of attachment or notice to payor;

viii. In traffic and criminal proceedings: a pro se filing; a court filing that is related to a criminal matter or investigation and that is prepared before the filing of a criminal charge or is not filed as part of any docketed criminal case; an arrest or search warrant or any information in support thereof; a charging document and an affidavit or other documents filed in support of any charging document, including any driving records; a statement of particulars; discovery material introduced into evidence or otherwise filed with the court; and all information necessary for the proper issuance and execution of a subpoena duces tecum;

ix. Information used by the clerk for case maintenance purposes or the courts for case management purposes; and

x. Information which is relevant and material to an issue before the court. FL ST J ADMIN Rule 2.425(b).

c. *Remedies.* Upon motion by a party or interested person or sua sponte by the court, the court may order remedies, sanctions or both for a violation of FL ST J ADMIN Rule 2.425(a). Following notice and an opportunity to respond, the court may impose sanctions if such filing was not made in good faith. FL ST J ADMIN Rule 2.425(c).

d. *Motions not restricted.* FL ST J ADMIN Rule 2.425 does not restrict a party's right to move for protective order, to move to file documents under seal, or to request a determination of the confidentiality of records. FL ST J ADMIN Rule 2.425(d).

e. *Application.* FL ST J ADMIN Rule 2.425 does not affect the application of constitutional provisions, statutes, or rules of court regarding confidential information or access to public information. FL ST J ADMIN Rule 2.425(e).

F. Filing and Service Requirements

1. *Filing requirements.* All original documents must be filed with the court either before service or immediately thereafter, unless otherwise provided for by general law or other rules. If the original of any bond or other document is not placed in the court file, a certified copy must be so placed by the clerk. FL ST J ADMIN Rule 2.516(d). All documents shall be filed in conformity with the requirements of FL ST J ADMIN Rule 2.525. FL ST RCP Rule 1.080(b). All documents filed in any court shall be filed by electronic transmission in accordance with FL ST J ADMIN Rule 2.525. "Documents" means pleadings, motions, petitions, memoranda, briefs, notices, exhibits, declarations, affidavits, orders, judgments, decrees, writs, opinions, and any other paper or writing submitted to a court. FL ST J ADMIN Rule 2.520(a). All documents that are court records, as defined in FL ST J ADMIN Rule 2.430(a)(1), must be filed by electronic transmission, provided that: (1) the clerk has the ability to accept and retain such documents; (2) the clerk or the chief judge of the circuit has requested permission to accept documents filed by electronic transmission; and (3) the supreme court has entered an order granting permission to the clerk to accept documents filed by electronic transmission. FL ST J ADMIN Rule 2.525(c)(1).

a. *Definition.* "Electronic transmission of documents" means the sending of information by electronic signals to, by or from a court or clerk, which when received can be transformed and stored or transmitted on paper, microfilm, magnetic storage device, optical imaging system, CD-ROM, flash drive, other electronic data storage system, server, case maintenance system ("CM"), electronic court filing ("ECF") system, statewide or local electronic portal ("e-portal"), or other electronic record keeping system authorized by the supreme court in a format sufficient to communicate the information on the original document in a readable format. Electronic transmission of documents includes electronic mail ("e-mail") and any internet-based transmission procedure, and may include procedures allowing for documents to be signed or verified by electronic means. FL ST J ADMIN Rule 2.525(a).

i. The filing of documents with the court as required by the Florida Rules of Judicial Administration must be made by filing them with the clerk in accordance with FL ST J ADMIN Rule

2.525, except that the judge may permit documents to be filed with the judge, in which event the judge must note the filing date before him or her on the documents and transmit them to the clerk. The date of filing is that shown on the face of the document by the judge's notation or the clerk's time stamp, whichever is earlier. FL ST J ADMIN Rule 2.516(e).

b. *Application.* Any court or clerk of the court may accept the electronic transmission of documents for filing after the clerk, together with input from the chief judge of the circuit, has obtained approval of the procedures and program for doing so from the Supreme Court of Florida. FL ST J ADMIN Rule 2.525(b).

c. *Exceptions*

   i. Paper documents and other submissions may be manually submitted to the clerk or court:
      - When the clerk does not have the ability to accept and retain documents by electronic filing or has not had ECF Procedures approved by the supreme court;
      - For filing by any self-represented party or any self-represented nonparty unless specific ECF Procedures provide a means to file documents electronically. However, any self-represented nonparty that is a governmental or public agency and any other agency, partnership, corporation, or business entity acting on behalf of any governmental or public agency may file documents by electronic transmission if such entity has the capability of filing documents electronically;
      - For filing by attorneys excused from e-mail service in accordance with FL ST J ADMIN Rule 2.516(b);
      - When submitting evidentiary exhibits or filing non-documentary materials;
      - When the filing involves documents in excess of twenty-five (25) megabytes (25MB) in size. For such filings, documents may be transmitted using an electronic storage medium that the clerk has the ability to accept, which may include a CD-ROM, flash drive, or similar storage medium;
      - When filed in open court, as permitted by the court;
      - When paper filing is permitted by any approved statewide or local ECF procedures; and
      - If any court determines that justice so requires. FL ST J ADMIN Rule 2.525(d).

   ii. Any document in paper form submitted under FL ST J ADMIN Rule 2.525(d) is filed when it is received by the clerk or court and the clerk shall immediately thereafter convert any filed paper document to an electronic document. "Convert to an electronic document" means optically capturing an image of a paper document and using character recognition software to recover as much of the document's text as practicable and then indexing and storing the document in the official court file. FL ST J ADMIN Rule 2.525(c)(4).

   iii. Any storage medium submitted under FL ST J ADMIN Rule 2.525(d)(5) is filed when received by the clerk or court and the clerk shall immediately thereafter transfer the electronic documents from the storage device to the official court file. FL ST J ADMIN Rule 2.525(c)(5).

   iv. If the filer of any paper document authorized under FL ST J ADMIN Rule 2.525(d) provides a self-addressed, postage-paid envelope for return of the paper document after it is converted to electronic form by the clerk, the clerk shall place the paper document in the envelope and deposit it in the mail. Except when a paper document is required to be maintained, the clerk may recycle any filed paper document that is not to be returned to the filer. FL ST J ADMIN Rule 2.525(c)(6).

   v. The clerk may convert any paper document filed before the effective date of FL ST J ADMIN Rule 2.525 to an electronic document. Unless the clerk is required to maintain the paper document, if the paper document has been converted to an electronic document by the clerk, the paper document is no longer part of the official court file and may be removed and recycled. FL ST J ADMIN Rule 2.525(c)(7).

d. *Official court file.* For information on what constitutes the official court file, please see FL ST J ADMIN Rule 2.525(c)(2), FL ST J ADMIN Rule 2.525(c)(3).

e. *Administration.* All attorneys, parties, or other persons using this rule to file documents are required to make arrangements with the court or clerk for the payment of any charges authorized by general law or the supreme court before filing any document by electronic transmission. FL ST J ADMIN Rule 2.525(f)(2).

f. *Filing date.* The filing date for an electronically transmitted document is the date and time that such filing is acknowledged by an electronic stamp or otherwise, pursuant to any procedure set forth in any ECF Procedures approved by the supreme court, or the date the last page of such filing is received by the court or clerk. FL ST J ADMIN Rule 2.525(f)(3).

g. *Accessibility.* All documents transmitted in any electronic form under FL ST J ADMIN Rule 2.525 must comply with the accessibility requirements of FL ST J ADMIN Rule 2.526. FL ST J ADMIN Rule 2.525(g).

2. *Service requirements.* Every pleading subsequent to the initial pleading, all orders, and every other document filed in the action must be served in conformity with the requirements of FL ST J ADMIN Rule 2.516. FL ST RCP Rule 1.080(a).

   a. *Service; When required.* Unless the court otherwise orders, or a statute or supreme court administrative order specifies a different means of service, every pleading subsequent to the initial pleading and every other document filed in any court proceeding, except applications for witness subpoenas and documents served by formal notice or required to be served in the manner provided for service of formal notice, must be served in accordance with FL ST J ADMIN Rule 2.516 on each party. No service need be made on parties against whom a default has been entered, except that pleadings asserting new or additional claims against them must be served in the manner provided for service of summons. FL ST J ADMIN Rule 2.516(a).

   b. *Service; How made.* When service is required or permitted to be made upon a party represented by an attorney, service must be made upon the attorney unless service upon the party is ordered by the court. FL ST J ADMIN Rule 2.516(b).

      i. *Service by electronic mail ("e-mail").* All documents required or permitted to be served on another party must be served by e-mail, unless FL ST J ADMIN Rule 2.516 otherwise provides. When, in addition to service by e-mail, the sender also utilizes another means of service provided for in FL ST J ADMIN Rule 2.516(b)(2), any differing time limits and other provisions applicable to that other means of service control. FL ST J ADMIN Rule 2.516(b)(1). Any document electronically transmitted to a court or clerk must also be served on all parties and interested persons in accordance with the applicable rules of court. FL ST J ADMIN Rule 2.525(e)(2).

         - *Service on attorneys.* Upon appearing in a proceeding, an attorney must serve a designation of a primary e-mail address and may designate no more than two (2) secondary e-mail addresses. Thereafter, service must be directed to all designated e-mail addresses in that proceeding. Every document filed by an attorney thereafter must include the primary e-mail address of that attorney and any secondary e-mail addresses. If an attorney does not designate any e-mail address for service, documents may be served on that attorney at the e-mail address on record with The Florida Bar. FL ST J ADMIN Rule 2.516(b)(1)(A).

         - *Exception to e-mail service on attorneys.* Service by an attorney on another attorney must be made by e-mail unless excused by the court. Upon motion by an attorney demonstrating that the attorney has no e-mail account and lacks access to the Internet at the attorney's office, the court may excuse the attorney from the requirements of e-mail service. Service on and by an attorney excused by the court from e-mail service must be by the means provided in FL ST J ADMIN Rule 2.516(b)(2). FL ST J ADMIN Rule 2.516(b)(1)(B).

         - *Service on and by parties not represented by an attorney.* Any party not represented by an attorney may serve a designation of a primary e-mail address and also may designate no more than two (2) secondary e-mail addresses to which service must be directed in that proceeding by the means provided in FL ST J ADMIN Rule 2.516(b)(1). If a party not represented by an attorney does not designate an e-mail address for service in a proceeding, service on and by that party must be by the means provided in FL ST J ADMIN Rule 2.516(b)(2). FL ST J ADMIN Rule 2.516(b)(1)(C).

- *Time of service.* Service by e-mail is complete when it is sent. FL ST J ADMIN Rule 2.516(b)(1)(D). An e-mail is deemed served on the date it is sent. FL ST J ADMIN Rule 2.516(b)(1)(D)(i). If the sender learns that the e-mail did not reach the address of the person to be served, the sender must immediately send another copy by e-mail, or by a means authorized by FL ST J ADMIN Rule 2.516(b)(2). FL ST J ADMIN Rule 2.516(b)(1)(D)(ii). E-mail service is treated as service by mail for the computation of time. FL ST J ADMIN Rule 2.516(b)(1)(D)(iii).

ii. *Format of e-mail for service.* Service of a document by e-mail is made by attaching a copy of the document in PDF format to an e-mail sent to all addresses designated by the attorney or party. FL ST J ADMIN Rule 2.516(b)(1)(E).

- All documents served by e-mail must be attached to an e-mail message containing a subject line beginning with the words "SERVICE OF COURT DOCUMENT" in all capital letters, followed by the case number of the proceeding in which the documents are being served. FL ST J ADMIN Rule 2.516(b)(1)(E)(i).
- The body of the e-mail must identify the court in which the proceeding is pending, the case number, the name of the initial party on each side, the title of each document served with that e-mail, and the sender's name and telephone number. FL ST J ADMIN Rule 2.516(b)(1)(E)(ii).
- Any document served by e-mail may be signed by the "/s/" format, as long as the filed original is signed in accordance with the applicable rule of procedure. FL ST J ADMIN Rule 2.516(b)(1)(E)(iii).
- Any e-mail which, together with its attached documents, exceeds five megabytes (5MB) in size, must be divided and sent as separate e-mails, no one of which may exceed five megabytes (5MB) in size and each of which must be sequentially numbered in the subject line. FL ST J ADMIN Rule 2.516(b)(1)(E)(iv).

iii. *Service by other means.* In addition to, and not in lieu of, service by e-mail, service may also be made upon attorneys by any of the means specified in FL ST J ADMIN Rule 2.516(b)(2). Service on and by all parties who are not represented by an attorney and who do not designate an e-mail address, and on and by all attorneys excused from e-mail service, must be made by delivering a copy of the document or by mailing it to the party or attorney at their last known address or, if no address is known, by leaving it with the clerk of the court. Service by mail is complete upon mailing. Delivery of a copy within FL ST J ADMIN Rule 2.516 is complete upon:

- Handing it to the attorney or to the party,
- Leaving it at the attorney's or party's office with a clerk or other person in charge thereof,
- If there is no one in charge, leaving it in a conspicuous place therein,
- If the office is closed or the person to be served has no office, leaving it at the person's usual place of abode with some person of his or her family above fifteen (15) years of age and informing such person of the contents, or
- Transmitting it by facsimile to the attorney's or party's office with a cover sheet containing the sender's name, firm, address, telephone number, and facsimile number, and the number of pages transmitted. When service is made by facsimile, a copy must also be served by any other method permitted by FL ST J ADMIN Rule 2.516. Facsimile service occurs when transmission is complete. FL ST J ADMIN Rule 2.516(b)(2)(A) through FL ST J ADMIN Rule 2.516(b)(2)(E).
- Service by delivery after 5:00 p.m. must be deemed to have been made by mailing on the date of delivery. FL ST J ADMIN Rule 2.516(b)(2)(F).

c. *Service; Numerous defendants.* In actions when the parties are unusually numerous, the court may regulate the service contemplated by the Florida Rules of Judicial Administration on motion or on its own initiative in such manner as may be found to be just and reasonable. FL ST J ADMIN Rule 2.516(c).

d. *Service by clerk.* Service of notices and other documents required to be made by the clerk must also be done as provided in FL ST J ADMIN Rule 2.516(b). FL ST J ADMIN Rule 2.516(g).

G. Hearings

1. The parties may be required to participate in pretrial proceedings to consider and determine the necessity or desirability of an amendment to a pleading. FL ST RCP Rule 1.200(b)(2); FL-PP § 2:151.

H. Forms

1. Official Amended Answer Forms for Florida

a. Caption. FL ST RCP Form 1.901.

b. Notice of compliance when constitutional challenge is brought. FL ST RCP Form 1.975.

2. Amended Answer Forms for Florida

a. Form for amendment to answer. FL-RCPF R 1.190(50).

b. Form for supplement to pleading. FL-RCPF R 1.190(102).

I. Checklist

(I) ❑ Matters to be considered by plaintiff

(a) ❑ Required documents

(1) ❑ Amended answer

(2) ❑ Certificate of service

(b) ❑ Supplemental documents

(1) ❑ Exhibits

(2) ❑ Notice of constitutional question

(c) ❑ Timing

(1) ❑ A party may amend a pleading once as a matter of course at any time before a responsive pleading is served

(2) ❑ If the pleading is one to which no responsive pleading is permitted and the action has not been placed on the trial calendar, may so amend it at any time within twenty (20) days after it is served

Motions, Oppositions and Replies
Motion to Strike

Document Last Updated January 2013

A. Applicable Rules

1. *State rules*

a. Rules of court. FL ST RCP Rule 1.010; FL ST J ADMIN Rule 2.110.

b. Nonverification of pleadings. FL ST RCP Rule 1.030.

c. Service and filing of pleadings, orders, and documents. FL ST RCP Rule 1.080.

d. Time. FL ST RCP Rule 1.090.

e. Pleadings and motions. FL ST RCP Rule 1.100.

f. Defenses. FL ST RCP Rule 1.140.

g. Sham pleadings. FL ST RCP Rule 1.150.

h. Motions. FL ST RCP Rule 1.160.

i. Relief from judgment, decrees, or orders. FL ST RCP Rule 1.540.

j. Mediation and arbitration. FL ST RCP Rule 1.700; FL ST RCP Rule 1.710; FL ST RCP Rule 1.720;

FL ST RCP Rule 1.730; FL ST RCP Rule 1.750; FL ST RCP Rule 1.800; FL ST RCP Rule 1.810; FL ST RCP Rule 1.820; FL ST RCP Rule 1.830.

k. Forms. FL ST RCP Rule 1.900.

l. Minimization of the filing of sensitive information. FL ST J ADMIN Rule 2.425.

m. Retention of court records. FL ST J ADMIN Rule 2.430.

n. Foreign attorneys. FL ST J ADMIN Rule 2.510.

o. Signature of attorneys and parties. FL ST J ADMIN Rule 2.515.

p. Paper. FL ST J ADMIN Rule 2.520.

q. Electronic filing. FL ST J ADMIN Rule 2.525.

r. Accessibility of information and technology. FL ST J ADMIN Rule 2.526.

s. Communication equipment. FL ST J ADMIN Rule 2.530.

t. Court reporting. FL ST J ADMIN Rule 2.535.

u. Requests for accommodations by persons with disabilities. FL ST J ADMIN Rule 2.540.

2. *Local rules*

a. Establishment of 11th Circuit Homestead Access to Mediation Program ("CHAMP") for case management of residential foreclosure cases in the Eleventh Judicial Circuit of Florida. FL ST 11 J CIR 1-09-08.

b. Enlargement and expansion of the current pilot project for electronic submissions of courtesy copies for uniform motion calendar and requests for special set hearings, emergency motions, and proposed orders. FL ST 11 J CIR 1-09-13-A1.

B. Timing

1. *Motion to strike.* A party may move to strike or the court may strike redundant, immaterial, impertinent, or scandalous matter from any pleading at any time. FL ST RCP Rule 1.140(f).

2. *Motion to strike; Failure to state a legal defense.* If a pleading sets forth a claim for relief to which the adverse party is not required to serve a responsive pleading, the adverse party may assert any defense in law or fact to that claim for relief at the trial, except that the objection of failure to state a legal defense in an answer or reply shall be asserted by motion to strike the defense within twenty (20) days after service of the answer or reply. FL ST RCP Rule 1.140(b).

3. *Motion to strike; Sham pleadings.* If a party deems any pleading or part thereof filed by another party to be a sham, that party may move to strike the pleading or part thereof before the cause is set for trial. FL ST RCP Rule 1.150(a).

4. *General motion timing.* A copy of any written motion which may not be heard ex parte and a copy of the notice of the hearing thereof shall be served a reasonable time before the time specified for the hearing. FL ST RCP Rule 1.090(d).

5. *Computation of time*

a. *Generally.* Computation of time shall be governed by FL ST J ADMIN Rule 2.514. FL ST RCP Rule 1.090(a). The following rules apply in computing time periods specified in any rule of procedure, local rule, court order, or statute that does not specify a method of computing time. FL ST J ADMIN Rule 2.514(a).

i. *Period stated in days or a longer unit.* When the period is stated in days or a longer unit of time (A) exclude the day of the event that triggers the period; (B) count every day, including intermediate Saturdays, Sundays, and legal holidays; and (C) include the last day of the period, but if the last day is a Saturday, Sunday, or legal holiday, or falls within any period of time extended through an order of the chief justice under FL ST J ADMIN Rule 2.205(a)(2)(B)(iv), the period continues to run until the end of the next day that is not a Saturday, Sunday, or legal holiday and does not fall within any period of time extended through an order of the chief justice. FL ST J ADMIN Rule 2.514(a)(1).

ii. *Period stated in hours.* When the period is stated in hours (A) begin counting immediately on the occurrence of the event that triggers the period; (B) count every hour, including hours during intermediate Saturdays, Sundays, and legal holidays; and (C) if the period would end on a Saturday, Sunday, or legal holiday, or during any period of time extended through an order of the chief justice under FL ST J ADMIN Rule 2.205(a)(2)(B)(iv), the period continues to run until the same time on the next day that is not a Saturday, Sunday, or legal holiday and does not fall within any period of time extended through an order of the chief justice. FL ST J ADMIN Rule 2.514(a)(2).

iii. *Period stated in days less than seven (7) days.* When the period stated in days is less than seven (7) days, intermediate Saturdays, Sundays, and legal holidays shall be excluded in the computation. FL ST J ADMIN Rule 2.514(a)(3).

iv. *"Last day" defined.* Unless a different time is set by a statute, local rule, or court order, the last day ends (A) for electronic filing or for service by any means, at midnight; and (B) for filing by other means, when the clerk's office is scheduled to close. FL ST J ADMIN Rule 2.514(a)(4).

v. *"Next day" defined.* The "next day" is determined by continuing to count forward when the period is measured after an event and backward when measured before an event. FL ST J ADMIN Rule 2.514(a)(5).

vi. *"Legal holiday" defined.* "Legal holiday" means (A) the day set aside by FL ST § 110.117, for observing New Year's Day, Martin Luther King, Jr.'s Birthday, Memorial Day, Independence Day, Labor Day, Veterans' Day, Thanksgiving Day, the Friday after Thanksgiving Day, or Christmas Day, and (B) any day observed as a holiday by the clerk's office or as designated by the chief judge. FL ST J ADMIN Rule 2.514(a)(6).

b. *Additional time after service by mail or e-mail.* When a party may or must act within a specified time after service and service is made by mail or e-mail, five (5) days are added after the period that would otherwise expire under FL ST J ADMIN Rule 2.514(a). FL ST J ADMIN Rule 2.514(b).

c. *Enlargement.* When an act is required or allowed to be done at or within a specified time by order of court, by the Florida Rules of Civil Procedure, or by notice given thereunder, for cause shown the court at any time in its discretion (1) with or without notice, may order the period enlarged if request therefor is made before the expiration of the period originally prescribed or as extended by a previous order, or (2) upon motion made and notice after the expiration of the specified period, may permit the act to be done when failure to act was the result of excusable neglect, but it may not extend the time for making a motion for new trial, for rehearing, or to alter or amend a judgment; making a motion for relief from a judgment under FL ST RCP Rule 1.540(b); taking an appeal or filing a petition for certiorari; or making a motion for a directed verdict. FL ST RCP Rule 1.090(b).

d. *Unaffected by expiration of term.* The period of time provided for the doing of any act or the taking of any proceeding shall not be affected or limited by the continued existence or expiration of a term of court. The continued existence or expiration of a term of court in no way affects the power of a court to do any act or take any proceeding in any action which is or has been pending before it. FL ST RCP Rule 1.090(c).

C. General Requirements

1. *Motions generally*

a. *Contents.* An application to the court for an order shall be by motion which shall be made in writing unless made during a hearing or trial, shall state with particularity the grounds therefor, and shall set forth the relief or order sought. The requirement of writing is fulfilled if the motion is stated in a written notice of the hearing of the motion. All notices of hearing shall specify each motion or other matter to be heard. FL ST RCP Rule 1.100(b).

b. *Particularity requirement.* The court considers a motion in the light of the substantive law, rule or statute to make its determination. Some rules require a statement of the grounds for a motion under the rule. Failure to give the grounds will result in denial of the motion. This should be the result in all situations when the ground for the motion is not inherent in the rule. FL-PRACPROC § 9:3. The requirement is nevertheless an important one, first because of the due process notice rights of the respondent, as well as for the assistance it provides to the court in its preparation for the hearing or, absent a hearing, for disposition. 4 FLPRAC R 1.100.

2. *Motion to strike under FL ST RCP Rule 1.140.* Two (2) types of motion to strike are authorized by FL ST RCP Rule 1.140. One is used to eliminate immaterial, redundant, impertinent or scandalous allegations. The other is used to test the legal sufficiency of a defense. FL-PRACPROC § 10:6.
   a. *Motion to strike to eliminate immaterial, redundant, impertinent or scandalous allegations*
      i. As used in FL ST RCP Rule 1.140(f), redundant means allegations that are foreign to the issues or needless repetition of allegations. Immaterial means allegations having no essential or important relationship to the issues or unnecessary elaboration of material allegations. Impertinent means allegations that do not belong to the issue and are not necessary to it. Scandalous means unnecessary allegations censuring or accusing a party. FL-PRACPROC § 10:6.
      ii. The motion can be made at any time and does not toll the time for pleading. FL-PRACPROC § 10:6.
      iii. The motion reaches improper allegations of damages. When directed to an entire paragraph and any part of it is proper, the motion should be denied. Leave to amend should be granted after striking part of a pleading unless a proper amendment cannot be made. FL-PRACPROC § 10:6.
      iv. The use of a motion to strike is not favored by the courts and the remedy is used sparingly. Florida courts have held that an allegation must be "wholly irrelevant" and that if there is some doubt it must be resolved in support of the pleading and against the party moving to strike. If any part of an allegation is relevant, then that part should not be stricken from the pleading. 5 FLPRAC § 7:30.
   b. *Motion to strike the legal sufficiency of a defense*
      i. The legal insufficiency of a defense alleged in an answer or reply is attacked by a motion to strike. It is the counterpart of a motion to dismiss for failure to state a cause of action directed to a pleading seeking affirmative relief. FL-PRACPROC § 10:7.
      ii. A motion to strike a defense tests only the legal sufficiency of the defense, and it is reversible error for a trial court to strike the defense where evidence may be presented to support it. Burns v. Equilease Corp., 357 So.2d 786, 24, 24 U.C.C. Rep.Serv. 254 (Fla. 3d DCA 1978); 20 FLPRAC § 3:15.
3. *Sham pleadings.* If a party deems any pleading or part thereof filed by another party to be a sham, that party may move to strike the pleading or part thereof before the cause is set for trial and the court shall hear the motion, taking evidence of the respective parties, and if the motion is sustained, the pleading to which the motion is directed shall be stricken. Default and summary judgment on the merits may be entered in the discretion of the court or the court may permit additional pleadings to be filed for good cause shown. FL ST RCP Rule 1.150(a).
   a. *Contents of motion.* The motion to strike shall be verified and shall set forth fully the facts on which the movant relies and may be supported by affidavit. No traverse of the motion shall be required. FL ST RCP Rule 1.150(b).
   b. *Allegations supported by evidence.* The issue is not whether the allegations are material or proper, but whether the allegations are supported by evidence. 5 FLPRAC § 7:30.
4. *Arbitration and mediation*
   a. *Referral to arbitration and mediation.* Except as hereinafter provided or as otherwise prohibited by law, the presiding judge may enter an order referring all or any part of a contested civil matter to mediation or arbitration. The parties to any contested civil matter may file a written stipulation to mediate or arbitrate any issue between them at any time. Such stipulation shall be incorporated into the order of referral. FL ST RCP Rule 1.700(a).
      i. In all residential foreclosure actions involving homestead properties filed on or after May 1, 2009, unless a stipulation is specifically invoked by the parties in writing within five (5) days of service of the complaint on the main defendant, the parties are deemed to have stipulated to referral of the mediation to the Collins Center pursuant to FL ST RCP Rule 1.720(f). FL ST 11

J CIR 1-09-08(2); FL ST 11 J CIR 1-09-08(3). FL ST 11 J CIR 1-09-08 constitutes a formal referral to mediation pursuant to the Florida Rules of Civil Procedure. FL ST 11 J CIR 1-09-08(2).

ii. For further information on referral to mediation, refer to FL ST 11 J CIR 1-09-08.

b. *Arbitration*

i. *Exclusions.* A civil action shall be ordered to arbitration or arbitration in conjunction with mediation upon stipulation of the parties. A civil action may be ordered to arbitration or arbitration in conjunction with mediation upon motion of any party or by the court, if the judge determines the action to be of such a nature that arbitration could be of benefit to the litigants or the court. FL ST RCP Rule 1.800.

- Under no circumstances may the following categories of actions be referred to arbitration: (1) bond estreatures; (2) habeas corpus or other extraordinary writs; (3) bond validations; (4) civil or criminal contempt; (5) such other matters as may be specified by order of the chief judge in the circuit. FL ST RCP Rule 1.800.

ii. For more information regarding arbitration, please see FL ST RCP Rule 1.810; FL ST RCP Rule 1.820; FL ST RCP Rule 1.830.

c. *Mediation.* For more information regarding mediation, please see FL ST RCP Rule 1.710; FL ST RCP Rule 1.720; FL ST RCP Rule 1.730; and FL ST RCP Rule 1.750.

5. *Rules of court*

a. *Rules of civil procedure.* The Florida Rules of Civil Procedure apply to all actions of a civil nature and all special statutory proceedings in the circuit courts and county courts except those to which the Florida Probate Rules, the Florida Family Law Rules of Procedure, or the Small Claims Rules apply. FL ST RCP Rule 1.010.

i. The form, content, procedure, and time for pleading in all special statutory proceedings shall be as prescribed by the statutes governing the proceeding unless the Florida Rules of Civil Procedure specifically provide to the contrary. FL ST RCP Rule 1.010.

ii. The Florida Rules of Civil Procedure shall be construed to secure the just, speedy, and inexpensive determination of every action. FL ST RCP Rule 1.010.

b. *Rules of judicial administration.* The Florida Rules of Judicial Administration shall apply to administrative matters in all courts to which the Florida Rules of Judicial Administration are applicable by their terms. The Florida Rules of Judicial Administration shall be construed to secure the speedy and inexpensive determination of every proceeding to which they are applicable. The Florida Rules of Judicial Administration shall supersede all conflicting rules and statutes. FL ST J ADMIN Rule 2.110.

D. Documents

1. *Required documents*

a. *Notice of hearing/Motion.* An application to the court for an order shall be by motion which shall be made in writing unless made during a hearing or trial, shall state with particularity the grounds therefor, and shall set forth the relief or order sought. The requirement of writing is fulfilled if the motion is stated in a written notice of the hearing of the motion. All notices of hearing shall specify each motion or other matter to be heard. FL ST RCP Rule 1.100(b).

i. *Notices to persons with disabilities.* See the Format section of this KeyRules document for further information.

b. *Certificate of service.* When any attorney certifies in substance: "I certify that a copy hereof has been furnished to (here insert name or names and addresses used for service) by (e-mail) (delivery) (mail) (fax) on .... (date) ....______________ Attorney" the certificate is taken as prima facie proof of such service in compliance with FL ST J ADMIN Rule 2.516. FL ST J ADMIN Rule 2.516(f).

2. *Supplemental documents*

a. *Proposed order.* The court may require that orders or judgments be prepared by a party, may require

the party to furnish the court with stamped, addressed envelopes for service of the order or judgment, and may require that proposed orders and judgments be furnished to all parties before entry by the court of the order or judgment. FL ST J ADMIN Rule 2.516(h)(1). For additional information on the submission of proposed orders, refer to FL ST 11 J CIR 1-09-13-A1(e).

b. *Notice of constitutional question.* A party that files a pleading, written motion, or other paper drawing into question the constitutionality of a state statute or a county or municipal charter, ordinance, or franchise must promptly (1) file a notice of constitutional question stating the question and identifying the paper that raises it; and (2) serve the notice and the pleading, written motion, or other paper drawing into question the constitutionality of a state statute or a county or municipal charter, ordinance, or franchise on the Attorney General or the state attorney of the judicial circuit in which the action is pending, by either certified or registered mail. Service of the notice and pleading, written motion, or other paper does not require joinder of the Attorney General or the state attorney as a party to the action. FL ST RCP Rule 1.071.

E. Format

1. *Documents; Type and size.* Documents subject to the exceptions set forth in FL ST J ADMIN Rule 2.525(d) shall be filed on recycled paper measuring eight and one half by eleven (8 1/2 by 11) inches. For purposes of FL ST J ADMIN Rule 2.520, paper is recycled if it contains a minimum content of fifty (50) percent waste paper. Xerographic reduction of legal-size (eight and one half by fourteen (8 1/2 by 14) inches) documents to letter size (eight and one half by eleven (8 1/2 by 11) inches) is prohibited. All other documents filed by electronic transmission shall be filed in a format capable of being printed in a format consistent with the provisions of FL ST J ADMIN Rule 2.250. FL ST J ADMIN Rule 2.520(b).

   a. *Exhibits.* Any exhibit or attachment filed with pleadings or papers may be filed in its original size. FL ST J ADMIN Rule 2.520(c).

   b. *Recording space.* On all papers and documents prepared and filed by the court or by any party to a proceeding which are to be recorded in the public records of any county, including but not limited to final money judgments and notices of lis pendens, a three (3) inch by three (3) inch space at the top right-hand corner on the first page and a one (1) inch by three (3) inch space at the top right-hand corner on each subsequent page shall be left blank and reserved for use by the clerk of court. FL ST J ADMIN Rule 2.520(d).

      i. *Exceptions to recording space.* Any papers or documents created by persons or entities over which the filing party has no control, including but not limited to wills, codicils, trusts, or other testamentary documents; documents prepared or executed by any public officer; documents prepared, executed, acknowledged, or proved outside of the State of Florida; or documents created by State or Federal government agencies, may be filed without the space required by FL ST J ADMIN Rule 2.520. FL ST J ADMIN Rule 2.520(e).

   c. *Noncompliance.* No clerk of court is permitted to refuse to file any document or paper because of noncompliance with the Florida Rules of Judicial Administration. However, upon request of the clerk of court, noncomplying documents must be resubmitted in accordance with the formatting rules. FL ST J ADMIN Rule 2.520(f).

   d. *Format of electronically filed documents.* Hyperlinks in the attachments, (not in the body of the email) are encouraged just as are submissions in Microsoft Word format. Electronic versions submitted in WordPerfect will be converted by the Court to Microsoft Word and there is no guarantee that the document will be converted without error. FL ST 11 J CIR 1-09-13-A1(4)(b)(v).

2. *Caption.* Every pleading, motion, order, judgment, or other paper shall have a caption containing the name of the court, the file number, and except for in rem proceedings, including forfeiture proceedings, the name of the first party on each side with an appropriate indication of other parties, and a designation identifying the party filing it and its nature or the nature of the order, as the case may be. In any in rem proceeding, every pleading, motion, order, judgment, or other paper shall have a caption containing the name of the court, the file number, the style "In re" (followed by the name or general description of the property), and a designation of the person or entity filing it and its nature or the nature of the order, as the case may be. In an in rem forfeiture proceeding, the style shall be "In re forfeiture of" (followed by the name of the general description of the property). All papers filed in the action shall be styled in such a

manner as to indicate clearly the subject matter of the paper and the party requesting or obtaining relief. FL ST RCP Rule 1.100(c)(1).

a. *Caption of electronically filed documents.* All submitted documents shall be titled with the Court Case Number and the name/type of document using the following format: two (2) digit year followed by a hyphen with the sequential case number (e.g., 09-1; 91-12; 08-123; 07-1234; or 09-12345). Do not use zeros after the hyphen to fill in the sequential case number. FL ST 11 J CIR 1-09-13-A1(4)(a).

3. *Writing and written defined.* Writing or written means a document containing information, an application, or a stipulation. FL ST RCP Rule 1.080(c).

4. *Rule abbreviations*

a. The Florida Rules of Civil Procedure and shall be abbreviated as Fla.R.Civ.P. FL ST RCP Rule 1.010.

b. The Florida Rules of Judicial Administration shall be abbreviated as Fla. R. Jud. Admin. FL ST J ADMIN Rule 2.110.

5. *Nonverification.* Except when otherwise specifically provided by the Florida Rules of Civil Procedure or an applicable statute, every pleading or other document of a party represented by an attorney need not be verified or accompanied by an affidavit. FL ST RCP Rule 1.030; FL ST J ADMIN Rule 2.515(a).

6. *Attorney signature*

a. *Attorney signature.* Every pleading and other document of a party represented by an attorney shall be signed by at least one (1) attorney of record in that attorney's individual name whose current record Florida Bar address, telephone number, including area code, primary e-mail address and secondary e-mail addresses, if any, and Florida Bar number shall be stated, and who shall be duly licensed to practice law in Florida or who shall have received permission to appear in the particular case as provided in FL ST J ADMIN Rule 2.510. FL ST J ADMIN Rule 2.515(a).

i. The attorney may be required by the court to give the address of, and to vouch for the attorney's authority to represent, the party. FL ST J ADMIN Rule 2.515(a).

ii. The signature of an attorney shall constitute a certificate by the attorney that the attorney has read the pleading or other document; that to the best of the attorney's knowledge, information, and belief there is good ground to support it; and that it is not interposed for delay. FL ST J ADMIN Rule 2.515(a).

iii. If a pleading is not signed or is signed with intent to defeat the purpose of FL ST J ADMIN Rule 2.515, it may be stricken and the action may proceed as though the pleading or other document had not been served. FL ST J ADMIN Rule 2.515(a).

b. *Pro se litigant signature.* A party who is not represented by an attorney shall sign any pleading or other paper and state the party's address and telephone number, including area code. FL ST J ADMIN Rule 2.515(b).

c. *Form of signature*

i. The signatures required on pleadings and documents by FL ST J ADMIN Rule 2.515(a) and FL ST J ADMIN Rule 2.515(b) may be:

- Original signatures;
- Original signatures that have been reproduced by electronic means, such as on electronically transmitted documents or photocopied documents;
- Electronic signatures using the "/s/," "s/," or "/s" formats by or at the direction of the person signing; or
- Any other signature format authorized by general law, so long as the clerk where the proceeding is pending has the capability of receiving and has obtained approval from the Supreme Court of Florida to accept pleadings and documents with that signature format. FL ST J ADMIN Rule 2.515(c)(1).

ii. An attorney, party, or other person who files a pleading or paper by electronic transmission that

does not contain the original signature of that attorney, party, or other person shall file that identical pleading or paper in paper form containing an original signature of that attorney, party, or other person (hereinafter called the follow-up filing) immediately thereafter. The follow-up filing is not required if the Supreme Court of Florida has entered an order directing the clerk of court to discontinue accepting the follow-up filing. FL ST J ADMIN Rule 2.515(c)(2).

7. *Forms*
   a. *Process.* The forms of process, notice of lis pendens, and notice of action provided in the Florida Rules of Civil Procedure are sufficient. Variations from the forms do not void process or notices that are otherwise sufficient. FL ST RCP Rule 1.900(a).
   b. *Other forms.* The other forms provided in the Florida Rules of Civil Procedure are sufficient for the matters that are covered by them. So long as the substance is expressed without prolixity, the forms may be varied to meet the facts of a particular case. FL ST RCP Rule 1.900(b).
   c. *Formal matters.* Captions, except for the designation of the paper, are omitted from the forms provided in the Florida Rules of Civil Procedure. A general form of caption is the first form provided. Signatures are omitted from pleadings and motions. FL ST RCP Rule 1.900(c).
8. *Notices to persons with disabilities.* All notices of court proceedings to be held in a public facility, and all process compelling appearance at such proceedings, shall include the following statement in bold face, fourteen (14) point Times New Roman or Courier font: "If you are a person with a disability who needs any accommodation in order to participate in this proceeding, you are entitled, at no cost to you, to the provision of certain assistance. Please contact [identify applicable court personnel by name, address, and telephone number] at least seven (7) days before your scheduled court appearance, or immediately upon receiving this notification if the time before the scheduled appearance is less than seven (7) days; if you are hearing or voice impaired, call 711." FL ST J ADMIN Rule 2.540(c)(1).
9. *Minimization of the filing of sensitive information*
   a. *Limitations for court filings.* Unless authorized by FL ST J ADMIN Rule 2.425(b), statute, another rule of court, or the court orders otherwise, designated sensitive information filed with the court must be limited to the following format:
      i. The initials of a person known to be a minor;
      ii. The year of birth of a person's birth date;
      iii. No portion of any: Social security number, Bank account number, Credit card account number, Charge account number, or Debit account number;
      iv. The last four digits of any: Taxpayer identification number (TIN), Employee identification number, Driver's license number, Passport number, Telephone number, Financial account number, except as set forth in FL ST J ADMIN Rule 2.425(a)(3), Brokerage account number, Insurance policy account number, Loan account number, Customer account number, or Patient or health care number;
      v. A truncated version of any: Email address, Computer user name, Password, or Personal identification number (PIN); and
      vi. A truncated version of any other sensitive information as provided by court order. FL ST J ADMIN Rule 2.425(a).
   b. *Exceptions.* FL ST J ADMIN Rule 2.425(a) does not apply to the following:
      i. An account number which identifies the property alleged to be the subject of a proceeding;
      ii. The record of an administrative or agency proceeding;
      iii. The record in appellate or review proceedings;
      iv. The birth date of a minor whenever the birth date is necessary for the court to establish or maintain subject matter jurisdiction;
      v. The name of a minor in any order relating to parental responsibility, time-sharing, or child support;

vi. The name of a minor in any document or order affecting the minor's ownership of real property;

vii. The birth date of a party in a writ of attachment or notice to payor;

viii. In traffic and criminal proceedings: a pro se filing; a court filing that is related to a criminal matter or investigation and that is prepared before the filing of a criminal charge or is not filed as part of any docketed criminal case; an arrest or search warrant or any information in support thereof; a charging document and an affidavit or other documents filed in support of any charging document, including any driving records; a statement of particulars; discovery material introduced into evidence or otherwise filed with the court; and all information necessary for the proper issuance and execution of a subpoena duces tecum;

ix. Information used by the clerk for case maintenance purposes or the courts for case management purposes; and

x. Information which is relevant and material to an issue before the court. FL ST J ADMIN Rule 2.425(b).

c. *Remedies.* Upon motion by a party or interested person or sua sponte by the court, the court may order remedies, sanctions or both for a violation of FL ST J ADMIN Rule 2.425(a). Following notice and an opportunity to respond, the court may impose sanctions if such filing was not made in good faith. FL ST J ADMIN Rule 2.425(c).

d. *Motions not restricted.* FL ST J ADMIN Rule 2.425 does not restrict a party's right to move for protective order, to move to file documents under seal, or to request a determination of the confidentiality of records. FL ST J ADMIN Rule 2.425(d).

e. *Application.* FL ST J ADMIN Rule 2.425 does not affect the application of constitutional provisions, statutes, or rules of court regarding confidential information or access to public information. FL ST J ADMIN Rule 2.425(e).

F. Filing and Service Requirements

1. *Filing requirements.* All original documents must be filed with the court either before service or immediately thereafter, unless otherwise provided for by general law or other rules. If the original of any bond or other document is not placed in the court file, a certified copy must be so placed by the clerk. FL ST J ADMIN Rule 2.516(d). All documents shall be filed in conformity with the requirements of FL ST J ADMIN Rule 2.525. FL ST RCP Rule 1.080(b). All documents filed in any court shall be filed by electronic transmission in accordance with FL ST J ADMIN Rule 2.525. "Documents" means pleadings, motions, petitions, memoranda, briefs, notices, exhibits, declarations, affidavits, orders, judgments, decrees, writs, opinions, and any other paper or writing submitted to a court. FL ST J ADMIN Rule 2.520(a). All documents that are court records, as defined in FL ST J ADMIN Rule 2.430(a)(1), must be filed by electronic transmission, provided that: (1) the clerk has the ability to accept and retain such documents; (2) the clerk or the chief judge of the circuit has requested permission to accept documents filed by electronic transmission; and (3) the supreme court has entered an order granting permission to the clerk to accept documents filed by electronic transmission. FL ST J ADMIN Rule 2.525(c)(1).

   a. *Definition.* "Electronic transmission of documents" means the sending of information by electronic signals to, by or from a court or clerk, which when received can be transformed and stored or transmitted on paper, microfilm, magnetic storage device, optical imaging system, CD-ROM, flash drive, other electronic data storage system, server, case maintenance system ("CM"), electronic court filing ("ECF") system, statewide or local electronic portal ("e-portal"), or other electronic record keeping system authorized by the supreme court in a format sufficient to communicate the information on the original document in a readable format. Electronic transmission of documents includes electronic mail ("e-mail") and any internet-based transmission procedure, and may include procedures allowing for documents to be signed or verified by electronic means. FL ST J ADMIN Rule 2.525(a).

      i. The filing of documents with the court as required by the Florida Rules of Judicial Administration must be made by filing them with the clerk in accordance with FL ST J ADMIN Rule 2.525, except that the judge may permit documents to be filed with the judge, in which event the judge must note the filing date before him or her on the documents and transmit them to the

clerk. The date of filing is that shown on the face of the document by the judge's notation or the clerk's time stamp, whichever is earlier. FL ST J ADMIN Rule 2.516(e).

b. *Application.* Any court or clerk of the court may accept the electronic transmission of documents for filing after the clerk, together with input from the chief judge of the circuit, has obtained approval of the procedures and program for doing so from the Supreme Court of Florida. FL ST J ADMIN Rule 2.525(b).
   i. *E-filing mandatory.* All attorneys of record shall be required to follow the protocol set forth in FL ST 11 J CIR 1-09-13-A1(4). FL ST 11 J CIR 1-09-13-A1(3).

c. *Exceptions*
   i. Paper documents and other submissions may be manually submitted to the clerk or court:
      - When the clerk does not have the ability to accept and retain documents by electronic filing or has not had ECF Procedures approved by the supreme court;
      - For filing by any self-represented party or any self-represented nonparty unless specific ECF Procedures provide a means to file documents electronically. However, any self-represented nonparty that is a governmental or public agency and any other agency, partnership, corporation, or business entity acting on behalf of any governmental or public agency may file documents by electronic transmission if such entity has the capability of filing documents electronically;
      - For filing by attorneys excused from e-mail service in accordance with FL ST J ADMIN Rule 2.516(b);
      - When submitting evidentiary exhibits or filing non-documentary materials;
      - When the filing involves documents in excess of twenty-five (25) megabytes (25MB) in size. For such filings, documents may be transmitted using an electronic storage medium that the clerk has the ability to accept, which may include a CD-ROM, flash drive, or similar storage medium;
      - When filed in open court, as permitted by the court;
      - When paper filing is permitted by any approved statewide or local ECF procedures; and
      - If any court determines that justice so requires. FL ST J ADMIN Rule 2.525(d).
   ii. Any document in paper form submitted under FL ST J ADMIN Rule 2.525(d) is filed when it is received by the clerk or court and the clerk shall immediately thereafter convert any filed paper document to an electronic document. "Convert to an electronic document" means optically capturing an image of a paper document and using character recognition software to recover as much of the document's text as practicable and then indexing and storing the document in the official court file. FL ST J ADMIN Rule 2.525(c)(4).
   iii. Any storage medium submitted under FL ST J ADMIN Rule 2.525(d)(5) is filed when received by the clerk or court and the clerk shall immediately thereafter transfer the electronic documents from the storage device to the official court file. FL ST J ADMIN Rule 2.525(c)(5).
   iv. If the filer of any paper document authorized under FL ST J ADMIN Rule 2.525(d) provides a self-addressed, postage-paid envelope for return of the paper document after it is converted to electronic form by the clerk, the clerk shall place the paper document in the envelope and deposit it in the mail. Except when a paper document is required to be maintained, the clerk may recycle any filed paper document that is not to be returned to the filer. FL ST J ADMIN Rule 2.525(c)(6).
   v. The clerk may convert any paper document filed before the effective date of FL ST J ADMIN Rule 2.525 to an electronic document. Unless the clerk is required to maintain the paper document, if the paper document has been converted to an electronic document by the clerk, the paper document is no longer part of the official court file and may be removed and recycled. FL ST J ADMIN Rule 2.525(c)(7).

d. *Official court file.* For information on what constitutes the official court file, please see FL ST J ADMIN Rule 2.525(c)(2), FL ST J ADMIN Rule 2.525(c)(3).

e. *Administration.* All attorneys, parties, or other persons using this rule to file documents are required to make arrangements with the court or clerk for the payment of any charges authorized by general law or the supreme court before filing any document by electronic transmission. FL ST J ADMIN Rule 2.525(f)(2).

f. *Filing date.* The filing date for an electronically transmitted document is the date and time that such filing is acknowledged by an electronic stamp or otherwise, pursuant to any procedure set forth in any ECF Procedures approved by the supreme court, or the date the last page of such filing is received by the court or clerk. FL ST J ADMIN Rule 2.525(f)(3).

g. *Accessibility.* All documents transmitted in any electronic form under FL ST J ADMIN Rule 2.525 must comply with the accessibility requirements of FL ST J ADMIN Rule 2.526. FL ST J ADMIN Rule 2.525(g).

2. *Service requirements.* Every pleading subsequent to the initial pleading, all orders, and every other document filed in the action must be served in conformity with the requirements of FL ST J ADMIN Rule 2.516. FL ST RCP Rule 1.080(a).

a. *Service; When required.* Unless the court otherwise orders, or a statute or supreme court administrative order specifies a different means of service, every pleading subsequent to the initial pleading and every other document filed in any court proceeding, except applications for witness subpoenas and documents served by formal notice or required to be served in the manner provided for service of formal notice, must be served in accordance with FL ST J ADMIN Rule 2.516 on each party. No service need be made on parties against whom a default has been entered, except that pleadings asserting new or additional claims against them must be served in the manner provided for service of summons. FL ST J ADMIN Rule 2.516(a).

b. *Service; How made.* When service is required or permitted to be made upon a party represented by an attorney, service must be made upon the attorney unless service upon the party is ordered by the court. FL ST J ADMIN Rule 2.516(b).

i. *Service by electronic mail ("e-mail").* All documents required or permitted to be served on another party must be served by e-mail, unless FL ST J ADMIN Rule 2.516 otherwise provides. When, in addition to service by e-mail, the sender also utilizes another means of service provided for in FL ST J ADMIN Rule 2.516(b)(2), any differing time limits and other provisions applicable to that other means of service control. FL ST J ADMIN Rule 2.516(b)(1). Any document electronically transmitted to a court or clerk must also be served on all parties and interested persons in accordance with the applicable rules of court. FL ST J ADMIN Rule 2.525(e)(2).

- *Service on attorneys.* Upon appearing in a proceeding, an attorney must serve a designation of a primary e-mail address and may designate no more than two (2) secondary e-mail addresses. Thereafter, service must be directed to all designated e-mail addresses in that proceeding. Every document filed by an attorney thereafter must include the primary e-mail address of that attorney and any secondary e-mail addresses. If an attorney does not designate any e-mail address for service, documents may be served on that attorney at the e-mail address on record with The Florida Bar. FL ST J ADMIN Rule 2.516(b)(1)(A).

- *Exception to e-mail service on attorneys.* Service by an attorney on another attorney must be made by e-mail unless excused by the court. Upon motion by an attorney demonstrating that the attorney has no e-mail account and lacks access to the Internet at the attorney's office, the court may excuse the attorney from the requirements of e-mail service. Service on and by an attorney excused by the court from e-mail service must be by the means provided in FL ST J ADMIN Rule 2.516(b)(2). FL ST J ADMIN Rule 2.516(b)(1)(B).

- *Service on and by parties not represented by an attorney.* Any party not represented by an attorney may serve a designation of a primary e-mail address and also may designate no more than two (2) secondary e-mail addresses to which service must be directed in that proceeding by the means provided in FL ST J ADMIN Rule 2.516(b)(1). If a party not represented by an attorney does not designate an e-mail address for service in a proceeding, service on and by that party must be by the means provided in FL ST J ADMIN Rule 2.516(b)(2). FL ST J ADMIN Rule 2.516(b)(1)(C).

- *Time of service.* Service by e-mail is complete when it is sent. FL ST J ADMIN Rule 2.516(b)(1)(D). An e-mail is deemed served on the date it is sent. FL ST J ADMIN Rule 2.516(b)(1)(D)(i). If the sender learns that the e-mail did not reach the address of the person to be served, the sender must immediately send another copy by e-mail, or by a means authorized by FL ST J ADMIN Rule 2.516(b)(2). FL ST J ADMIN Rule 2.516(b)(1)(D)(ii). E-mail service is treated as service by mail for the computation of time. FL ST J ADMIN Rule 2.516(b)(1)(D)(iii).
- *Specifics of e-mail filing.* In addition to providing proper service pursuant to FL ST RCP Rule 1.080(b), courtesy copies of the Motion and Memorandum of Law for the Uniform Motion Calendar (e.g., Notice of Hearing, Motions, Exhibits, submitted case law, and other hearing specific documents) must be electronically attached to an email using either Microsoft Word or WordPerfect format (not as a PDF document) and sent via email to (a) The Court at its designated e-mail address; (b) Opposing counsel at their fax number as provided to The Florida Bar (see The Florida Bar's website and then click on "Find a Lawyer") or any other fax number provided on a Pleading, Motion to Quash Service, Motion to Dismiss Complaint or Notice of Appearance, whichever is most recent; and (c) Pro se parties at their last known fax number or any other fax number provided on a Pleading, Motion to Quash Service, Motion to Dismiss Complaint or Notice of Appearance, whichever is most recent. FL ST 11 J CIR 1-09-13-A1(4)(b)(i).
- *E-mail subject line.* The subject line of the email must contain only the numeric motion calendar hearing date using the following format: mm/dd/yy (two (2) digit month forward slash; two (2) digit day forward slash; two (2) digit year). For example: 06/15/10. FL ST 11 J CIR 1-09-13-A1(4)(b)(iii).

ii. *Format of e-mail for service.* Service of a document by e-mail is made by attaching a copy of the document in PDF format to an e-mail sent to all addresses designated by the attorney or party. FL ST J ADMIN Rule 2.516(b)(1)(E).

- All documents served by e-mail must be attached to an e-mail message containing a subject line beginning with the words "SERVICE OF COURT DOCUMENT" in all capital letters, followed by the case number of the proceeding in which the documents are being served. FL ST J ADMIN Rule 2.516(b)(1)(E)(i).
- The body of the e-mail must identify the court in which the proceeding is pending, the case number, the name of the initial party on each side, the title of each document served with that e-mail, and the sender's name and telephone number. FL ST J ADMIN Rule 2.516(b)(1)(E)(ii).
- Any document served by e-mail may be signed by the "/s/" format, as long as the filed original is signed in accordance with the applicable rule of procedure. FL ST J ADMIN Rule 2.516(b)(1)(E)(iii).
- Any e-mail which, together with its attached documents, exceeds five megabytes (5MB) in size, must be divided and sent as separate e-mails, no one of which may exceed five megabytes (5MB) in size and each of which must be sequentially numbered in the subject line. FL ST J ADMIN Rule 2.516(b)(1)(E)(iv).

iii. *Service by other means.* In addition to, and not in lieu of, service by e-mail, service may also be made upon attorneys by any of the means specified in FL ST J ADMIN Rule 2.516(b)(2). Service on and by all parties who are not represented by an attorney and who do not designate an e-mail address, and on and by all attorneys excused from e-mail service, must be made by delivering a copy of the document or by mailing it to the party or attorney at their last known address or, if no address is known, by leaving it with the clerk of the court. Service by mail is complete upon mailing. Delivery of a copy within FL ST J ADMIN Rule 2.516 is complete upon:

- Handing it to the attorney or to the party,
- Leaving it at the attorney's or party's office with a clerk or other person in charge thereof,

- If there is no one in charge, leaving it in a conspicuous place therein,
- If the office is closed or the person to be served has no office, leaving it at the person's usual place of abode with some person of his or her family above fifteen (15) years of age and informing such person of the contents, or
- Transmitting it by facsimile to the attorney's or party's office with a cover sheet containing the sender's name, firm, address, telephone number, and facsimile number, and the number of pages transmitted. When service is made by facsimile, a copy must also be served by any other method permitted by FL ST J ADMIN Rule 2.516. Facsimile service occurs when transmission is complete. FL ST J ADMIN Rule 2.516(b)(2)(A) through FL ST J ADMIN Rule 2.516(b)(2)(E).
- Service by delivery after 5:00 p.m. must be deemed to have been made by mailing on the date of delivery. FL ST J ADMIN Rule 2.516(b)(2)(F).
- If a scheduling attorney or a scheduling pro se party does not have a fax number, then a courtesy copy of Motions and Proposed orders must be sent as an attachment to the service of process required pursuant to FL ST RCP Rule 1.080(b). FL ST 11 J CIR 1-09-13-A1(4)(b)(ii).

c. *Service; Numerous defendants.* In actions when the parties are unusually numerous, the court may regulate the service contemplated by the Florida Rules of Judicial Administration on motion or on its own initiative in such manner as may be found to be just and reasonable. FL ST J ADMIN Rule 2.516(c).

d. *Service by clerk.* Service of notices and other documents required to be made by the clerk must also be done as provided in FL ST J ADMIN Rule 2.516(b). FL ST J ADMIN Rule 2.516(g).

G. Hearings

1. *Communication equipment*

a. *Definition.* Communication equipment means a conference telephone or other electronic device that permits all those appearing or participating to hear and speak to each other, provided that all conversation of all parties is audible to all persons present. FL ST J ADMIN Rule 2.530(a).

b. *Use by all parties.* A county or circuit court judge may, upon the court's own motion or upon the written request of a party, direct that communication equipment be used for a motion hearing, pretrial conference, or a status conference. A judge must give notice to the parties and consider any objections they may have to the use of communication equipment before directing that communication equipment be used. The decision to use communication equipment over the objection of parties will be in the sound discretion of the trial court, except as noted below. FL ST J ADMIN Rule 2.530(b).

c. *Use only by requesting party.* A county or circuit court judge may, upon the written request of a party upon reasonable notice to all other parties, permit a requesting party to participate through communication equipment in a scheduled motion hearing; however, any such request (except in criminal, juvenile, and appellate proceedings) must be granted, absent a showing of good cause to deny the same, where the hearing is set for not longer than fifteen (15) minutes. FL ST J ADMIN Rule 2.530(c).

d. *Testimony*

i. *Generally.* A county or circuit court judge, general magistrate, special magistrate, or hearing officer may allow testimony to be taken through communication equipment if all parties consent or if permitted by another applicable rule of procedure. FL ST J ADMIN Rule 2.530(d)(1).

ii. *Procedure.* Any party desiring to present testimony through communication equipment shall, prior to the hearing or trial at which the testimony is to be presented, contact all parties to determine whether each party consents to this form of testimony. The party seeking to present the testimony shall move for permission to present testimony through communication equipment, which motion shall set forth good cause as to why the testimony should be allowed in this form. FL ST J ADMIN Rule 2.530(d)(2).

iii. *Oath.* Testimony may be taken through communication equipment only if a notary public or other person authorized to administer oaths in the witness's jurisdiction is present with the witness and administers the oath consistent with the laws of the jurisdiction. FL ST J ADMIN Rule 2.530(d)(3).

iv. *Confrontation rights.* In juvenile and criminal proceedings the defendant must make an informed waiver of any confrontation rights that may be abridged by the use of communication equipment. FL ST J ADMIN Rule 2.530(d)(4).

v. *Video testimony.* If the testimony to be presented utilizes video conferencing or comparable two-way visual capabilities, the court in its discretion may modify the procedures set forth in FL ST J ADMIN Rule 2.530 to accommodate the technology utilized. FL ST J ADMIN Rule 2.530(d)(5).

e. *Burden of expense.* The cost for the use of the communication equipment is the responsibility of the requesting party unless otherwise directed by the court. FL ST J ADMIN Rule 2.530(e).

2. *Time allotted for hearing.* Each party may set only one five (5) minute motion per case. Multiple motions must be specially set or set on different motion calendars (one five (5) minute motion per party per case), so as not to encroach on the time the Court is allotting for other litigants/attorneys. Consequently, the parties are advised to use good faith efforts to resolve the issues set forth in the motion prior to the setting of a motion; coordinate the date and time of the hearing; and confirm that the hearing shall require no more than five (5) minutes (if the hearing will require more than five (5) minutes, then it must be a Special Set Hearing). FL ST 11 J CIR 1-09-13-A1(4)(b)(i). For information on Special Set Hearings, refer to FL ST 11 J CIR 1-09-13-A1(4)(c).

3. *Hearing cancellation policy.* Should any scheduled hearing become unnecessary or have to be cancelled, the scheduling attorney or scheduling pro se party shall immediately, but, not later than by Noon on the business day prior to the hearing date and time, send an email to the court's designated e-mail address regarding the cancellation of the Motion Calendar hearing with an electronically attached Notice of Cancellation formatted in the same manner (using Microsoft Word or Word Perfect) as the email that scheduled the Motion Calendar hearing and in the same manner as the Motions and Notices. FL ST 11 J CIR 1-09-13-A1(4)(b)(vii).

H. Forms

1. Official Motion to Strike Forms for Florida

a. Caption. FL ST RCP Form 1.901.

b. Notice of compliance when constitutional challenge is brought. FL ST RCP Form 1.975.

2. Motion to Strike Forms for Florida

a. Motion to strike. FL-PP § 2:128.

b. Form for motion to strike. FL-RCPF R 1.140(802).

c. Form for motion to strike insufficient pleading. FL-RCPF R 1.140(803).

d. Form for motion to strike claim for business or financial losses. FL-RCPF R 1.140(804).

e. Motion; Strike, complaint signed by corporation. FL-PRACFORM § 7:176.

f. Motion; Strike, defenses. FL-PRACFORM § 7:177.

g. Motion; Strike, ejectment chain of title. FL-PRACFORM § 7:178.

h. Motion; Strike, pleading, departure. FL-PRACFORM § 7:180.

i. Motion; Strike, pleading, improper signature. FL-PRACFORM § 7:181.

j. Motion; Strike, sham pleading. FL-PRACFORM § 7:182.

k. Motion; Strike, sham, defenses, statute of limitations and failure of consideration. FL-PRACFORM § 7:183.

l. Motion; Strike, third party complaint. FL-PRACFORM § 7:184.

I. Checklist

- (I) ❑ Matters to be considered by moving party
  - (a) ❑ Required documents
    - (1) ❑ Notice of hearing/Motion
    - (2) ❑ Certificate of service
  - (b) ❑ Supplemental documents
    - (1) ❑ Proposed order
    - (2) ❑ Notice of constitutional question
  - (c) ❑ Time for making motion
    - (1) ❑ A party may move to strike or the court may strike redundant, immaterial, impertinent, or scandalous matter from any pleading at any time
    - (2) ❑ If a pleading sets forth a claim for relief to which the adverse party is not required to serve a responsive pleading, the adverse party may assert any defense in law or fact to that claim for relief at the trial, except that the objection of failure to state a legal defense in an answer or reply shall be asserted by motion to strike the defense within twenty (20) days after service of the answer or reply
    - (3) ❑ If a party deems any pleading or part thereof filed by another party to be a sham, that party may move to strike the pleading or part thereof before the cause is set for trial
    - (4) ❑ A copy of any written motion which may not be heard ex parte and a copy of the notice of the hearing thereof shall be served a reasonable time before the time specified for the hearing
- (II) ❑ Matters to be considered by opposing party
  - (a) ❑ Required documents
    - (1) ❑ Response to motion
    - (2) ❑ Certificate of service
  - (b) ❑ Supplemental documents
    - (1) ❑ Proposed order
    - (2) ❑ Notice of constitutional question
  - (c) ❑ Time for service and filing of opposition
    - (1) ❑ No time specified for responding to a motion

Motions, Oppositions and Replies
Motion for Leave to Amend

Document Last Updated January 2013

A. Applicable Rules

1. *State rules*
   - a. Rules of court. FL ST RCP Rule 1.010; FL ST J ADMIN Rule 2.110.
   - b. Nonverification of pleadings. FL ST RCP Rule 1.030.
   - c. Process. FL ST RCP Rule 1.070.
   - d. Service and filing of pleadings, orders, and documents. FL ST RCP Rule 1.080.
   - e. Time. FL ST RCP Rule 1.090.
   - f. Pleadings and motions. FL ST RCP Rule 1.100.
   - g. Defenses. FL ST RCP Rule 1.140.

h. Motions. FL ST RCP Rule 1.160.

i. Amended and supplemental pleadings. FL ST RCP Rule 1.190.

j. Relief from judgment, decrees, or orders. FL ST RCP Rule 1.540.

k. Mediation and arbitration. FL ST RCP Rule 1.700; FL ST RCP Rule 1.710; FL ST RCP Rule 1.720; FL ST RCP Rule 1.730; FL ST RCP Rule 1.750; FL ST RCP Rule 1.800; FL ST RCP Rule 1.810; FL ST RCP Rule 1.820; FL ST RCP Rule 1.830.

l. Forms. FL ST RCP Rule 1.900.

m. Minimization of the filing of sensitive information. FL ST J ADMIN Rule 2.425.

n. Retention of court records. FL ST J ADMIN Rule 2.430.

o. Foreign attorneys. FL ST J ADMIN Rule 2.510.

p. Signature of attorneys and parties. FL ST J ADMIN Rule 2.515.

q. Paper. FL ST J ADMIN Rule 2.520.

r. Electronic filing. FL ST J ADMIN Rule 2.525.

s. Accessibility of information and technology. FL ST J ADMIN Rule 2.526.

t. Communication equipment. FL ST J ADMIN Rule 2.530.

u. Court reporting. FL ST J ADMIN Rule 2.535.

v. Requests for accommodations by persons with disabilities. FL ST J ADMIN Rule 2.540.

2. *Local rules*

a. Establishment of 11th Circuit Homestead Access to Mediation Program ("CHAMP") for case management of residential foreclosure cases in the Eleventh Judicial Circuit of Florida. FL ST 11 J CIR 1-09-08.

b. Enlargement and expansion of the current pilot project for electronic submissions of courtesy copies for uniform motion calendar and requests for special set hearings, emergency motions, and proposed orders. FL ST 11 J CIR 1-09-13-A1.

B. Timing

1. *Amended pleadings as a matter of course.* A party may amend a pleading once as a matter of course at any time before a responsive pleading is served or, if the pleading is one to which no responsive pleading is permitted and the action has not been placed on the trial calendar, may amend it at any time within twenty (20) days after it is served. Otherwise a party may amend a pleading only by leave of court or by written consent of the adverse party. FL ST RCP Rule 1.190(a).

2. *Amended pleadings with leave of court.* Leave of court shall be given freely when justice so requires. FL ST RCP Rule 1.190(a). Under the Florida Rules of Civil Procedure, there is no time limit as to when an amendment with leave of court may be sought. Amendments of the pleadings may be permitted, with the court's discretion, at any stage of the proceedings in furtherance of justice. McSwiggan v. Edson, 186 So.2d 13, 15 (Fla. 1966); FL-PP § 2:153. Nevertheless, the liberality in permitting amendment of pleadings diminishes as the case progresses to trial. Versen v. Versen, 347 So.2d 1047, 1050 (Fla. 4th DCA 1977); FL-PP § 2:153.

3. *Claims for punitive damages.* A motion for leave to amend a pleading to assert a claim for punitive damages can be filed separately and before the supporting evidence or proffer, but each shall be served on all parties at least twenty (20) days before the hearing. FL ST RCP Rule 1.190(f).

4. *Post motion for leave to amend*

a. If the court permits or requires an amended or responsive pleading or a more definite statement, the pleading or statement shall be served within ten (10) days after notice of the court's action. FL ST RCP Rule 1.140(a)(4).

b. When a motion for leave to amend with the attached proposed amended complaint is filed, the one hundred twenty (120) day period for service of amended complaints on the new party or parties shall begin upon the entry of an order granting leave to amend. FL ST RCP Rule 1.070(j).

5. *General motion timing.* A copy of any written motion which may not be heard ex parte and a copy of the notice of the hearing thereof shall be served a reasonable time before the time specified for the hearing. FL ST RCP Rule 1.090(d).
6. *Computation of time*
   a. *Generally.* Computation of time shall be governed by FL ST J ADMIN Rule 2.514. FL ST RCP Rule 1.090(a). The following rules apply in computing time periods specified in any rule of procedure, local rule, court order, or statute that does not specify a method of computing time. FL ST J ADMIN Rule 2.514(a).
      i. *Period stated in days or a longer unit.* When the period is stated in days or a longer unit of time (A) exclude the day of the event that triggers the period; (B) count every day, including intermediate Saturdays, Sundays, and legal holidays; and (C) include the last day of the period, but if the last day is a Saturday, Sunday, or legal holiday, or falls within any period of time extended through an order of the chief justice under FL ST J ADMIN Rule 2.205(a)(2)(B)(iv), the period continues to run until the end of the next day that is not a Saturday, Sunday, or legal holiday and does not fall within any period of time extended through an order of the chief justice. FL ST J ADMIN Rule 2.514(a)(1).
      ii. *Period stated in hours.* When the period is stated in hours (A) begin counting immediately on the occurrence of the event that triggers the period; (B) count every hour, including hours during intermediate Saturdays, Sundays, and legal holidays; and (C) if the period would end on a Saturday, Sunday, or legal holiday, or during any period of time extended through an order of the chief justice under FL ST J ADMIN Rule 2.205(a)(2)(B)(iv), the period continues to run until the same time on the next day that is not a Saturday, Sunday, or legal holiday and does not fall within any period of time extended through an order of the chief justice. FL ST J ADMIN Rule 2.514(a)(2).
      iii. *Period stated in days less than seven (7) days.* When the period stated in days is less than seven (7) days, intermediate Saturdays, Sundays, and legal holidays shall be excluded in the computation. FL ST J ADMIN Rule 2.514(a)(3).
      iv. *"Last day" defined.* Unless a different time is set by a statute, local rule, or court order, the last day ends (A) for electronic filing or for service by any means, at midnight; and (B) for filing by other means, when the clerk's office is scheduled to close. FL ST J ADMIN Rule 2.514(a)(4).
      v. *"Next day" defined.* The "next day" is determined by continuing to count forward when the period is measured after an event and backward when measured before an event. FL ST J ADMIN Rule 2.514(a)(5).
      vi. *"Legal holiday" defined.* "Legal holiday" means (A) the day set aside by FL ST § 110.117, for observing New Year's Day, Martin Luther King, Jr.'s Birthday, Memorial Day, Independence Day, Labor Day, Veterans' Day, Thanksgiving Day, the Friday after Thanksgiving Day, or Christmas Day, and (B) any day observed as a holiday by the clerk's office or as designated by the chief judge. FL ST J ADMIN Rule 2.514(a)(6).
   b. *Additional time after service by mail or e-mail.* When a party may or must act within a specified time after service and service is made by mail or e-mail, five (5) days are added after the period that would otherwise expire under FL ST J ADMIN Rule 2.514(a). FL ST J ADMIN Rule 2.514(b).
   c. *Enlargement.* When an act is required or allowed to be done at or within a specified time by order of court, by the Florida Rules of Civil Procedure, or by notice given thereunder, for cause shown the court at any time in its discretion (1) with or without notice, may order the period enlarged if request therefor is made before the expiration of the period originally prescribed or as extended by a previous order, or (2) upon motion made and notice after the expiration of the specified period, may permit the act to be done when failure to act was the result of excusable neglect, but it may not extend the time for making a motion for new trial, for rehearing, or to alter or amend a judgment; making a motion for relief from a judgment under FL ST RCP Rule 1.540(b); taking an appeal or filing a petition for certiorari; or making a motion for a directed verdict. FL ST RCP Rule 1.090(b).
   d. *Unaffected by expiration of term.* The period of time provided for the doing of any act or the taking

of any proceeding shall not be affected or limited by the continued existence or expiration of a term of court. The continued existence or expiration of a term of court in no way affects the power of a court to do any act or take any proceeding in any action which is or has been pending before it. FL ST RCP Rule 1.090(c).

C. General Requirements

1. *Motions generally*
   a. *Contents.* An application to the court for an order shall be by motion which shall be made in writing unless made during a hearing or trial, shall state with particularity the grounds therefor, and shall set forth the relief or order sought. The requirement of writing is fulfilled if the motion is stated in a written notice of the hearing of the motion. All notices of hearing shall specify each motion or other matter to be heard. FL ST RCP Rule 1.100(b).
   b. *Particularity requirement.* The court considers a motion in the light of the substantive law, rule or statute to make its determination. Some rules require a statement of the grounds for a motion under the rule. Failure to give the grounds will result in denial of the motion. This should be the result in all situations when the ground for the motion is not inherent in the rule. FL-PRACPROC § 9:3. The requirement is nevertheless an important one, first because of the due process notice rights of the respondent, as well as for the assistance it provides to the court in its preparation for the hearing or, absent a hearing, for disposition. 4 FLPRAC R 1.100.
2. *Motion for leave to amend.* Although the Florida Rules of Civil Procedure do not specify a procedure for obtaining leave to amend, it is usually accomplished by way of a motion. FL-PP § 2:153. At any time in furtherance of justice, upon such terms as may be just, the court may permit any process, proceeding, pleading, or record to be amended or material supplemental matter to be set forth in an amended or supplemental pleading. At every stage of the action the court must disregard any error or defect in the proceedings which does not affect the substantial rights of the parties. FL ST RCP Rule 1.190(e).
   a. *Permissible amendments.* Amendments can relate to the correction of mistakes, the insertion of jurisdictional averments, the correction or addition of verifications, the addition or substitution or striking out of parties, and generally the rectification of all formal defects in the pleading. The court can also allow amendments setting up an omitted counterclaim or cross-claim if the defendant failed to raise the claim through oversight, inadvertence, or excusable neglect. FL-PP § 2:151.
   b. *Amendments to conform with the evidence.* When issues not raised by the pleadings are tried by express or implied consent of the parties, they shall be treated in all respects as if they had been raised in the pleadings. Such amendment of the pleadings as may be necessary to cause them to conform to the evidence and to raise these issues may be made upon motion of any party at any time, even after judgment, but failure so to amend shall not affect the result of the trial of these issues. If the evidence is objected to at the trial on the ground that it is not within the issues made by the pleadings, the court may allow the pleadings to be amended to conform with the evidence and shall do so freely when the merits of the cause are more effectually presented thereby and the objecting party fails to satisfy the court that the admission of such evidence will prejudice the objecting party in maintaining an action or defense upon the merits. FL ST RCP Rule 1.190(b).
      i. The courts have been extremely liberal in permitting amendments after trial to conform pleadings to the evidence where the issues were tried by the express or implied consent of the parties. Turner v. Long, 225 So.2d 434 (Fla. 1st DCA 1969); FL-PP § 2:152.
   c. *Procedure for adding parties.* Parties may be added once as a matter of course within the same time that pleadings can be so amended. If amendment by leave of court or stipulation of the parties is permitted, parties may be added in the amended pleading without further order of court. Parties may be added by order of court on its own initiative or on motion of any party at any stage of the action and on such terms as are just. FL ST RCP Rule 1.250(c).
   d. *Claims for punitive damages.* A motion for leave to amend a pleading to assert a claim for punitive damages shall make a reasonable showing by evidence in the record or evidence to be proffered by the claimant that provides a reasonable basis for recovery of such damages. The motion to amend can be filed separately and before the supporting evidence or proffer, but each shall be served on all

parties at least twenty (20) days before the hearing. FL ST RCP Rule 1.190(f). Leave of court to amend the complaint must be obtained before a plaintiff may assert a punitive damages claim in the complaint. Failure to do so will result in the claims being dismissed or stricken. FL-PP § 2:151.

e. *Relation back of amendments.* When the claim or defense asserted in the amended pleading arose out of the conduct, transaction, or occurrence set forth or attempted to be set forth in the original pleading, the amendment shall relate back to the date of the original pleading. FL ST RCP Rule 1.190(c).

   i. The doctrine of relation back becomes critical in applying the statute of limitations. For example, it has been held that the doctrine of relation back may not be utilized to circumvent the statute of limitations to permit an amendment where a claim could have been filed as an independent action but was not timely asserted and would otherwise be barred under the statute of limitations. Cox v. Seaboard Coast Line R. Co., 360 So.2d 8 (Fla. 2d DCA 1978); FL-PP § 2:152.

3. *Arbitration and mediation*

   a. *Referral to arbitration and mediation.* Except as hereinafter provided or as otherwise prohibited by law, the presiding judge may enter an order referring all or any part of a contested civil matter to mediation or arbitration. The parties to any contested civil matter may file a written stipulation to mediate or arbitrate any issue between them at any time. Such stipulation shall be incorporated into the order of referral. FL ST RCP Rule 1.700(a).

      i. In all residential foreclosure actions involving homestead properties filed on or after May 1, 2009, unless a stipulation is specifically invoked by the parties in writing within five (5) days of service of the complaint on the main defendant, the parties are deemed to have stipulated to referral of the mediation to the Collins Center pursuant to FL ST RCP Rule 1.720(f). FL ST 11 J CIR 1-09-08(2); FL ST 11 J CIR 1-09-08(3). FL ST 11 J CIR 1-09-08 constitutes a formal referral to mediation pursuant to the Florida Rules of Civil Procedure. FL ST 11 J CIR 1-09-08(2).

      ii. For further information on referral to mediation, refer to FL ST 11 J CIR 1-09-08.

   b. *Arbitration*

      i. *Exclusions.* A civil action shall be ordered to arbitration or arbitration in conjunction with mediation upon stipulation of the parties. A civil action may be ordered to arbitration or arbitration in conjunction with mediation upon motion of any party or by the court, if the judge determines the action to be of such a nature that arbitration could be of benefit to the litigants or the court. FL ST RCP Rule 1.800.

         - Under no circumstances may the following categories of actions be referred to arbitration: (1) bond estreatures; (2) habeas corpus or other extraordinary writs; (3) bond validations; (4) civil or criminal contempt; (5) such other matters as may be specified by order of the chief judge in the circuit. FL ST RCP Rule 1.800.

      ii. For more information regarding arbitration, please see FL ST RCP Rule 1.810; FL ST RCP Rule 1.820; FL ST RCP Rule 1.830.

   c. *Mediation.* For more information regarding mediation, please see FL ST RCP Rule 1.710; FL ST RCP Rule 1.720; FL ST RCP Rule 1.730; and FL ST RCP Rule 1.750.

4. *Rules of court*

   a. *Rules of civil procedure.* The Florida Rules of Civil Procedure apply to all actions of a civil nature and all special statutory proceedings in the circuit courts and county courts except those to which the Florida Probate Rules, the Florida Family Law Rules of Procedure, or the Small Claims Rules apply. FL ST RCP Rule 1.010.

      i. The form, content, procedure, and time for pleading in all special statutory proceedings shall be as prescribed by the statutes governing the proceeding unless the Florida Rules of Civil Procedure specifically provide to the contrary. FL ST RCP Rule 1.010.

      ii. The Florida Rules of Civil Procedure shall be construed to secure the just, speedy, and inexpensive determination of every action. FL ST RCP Rule 1.010.

b. *Rules of judicial administration.* The Florida Rules of Judicial Administration shall apply to administrative matters in all courts to which the Florida Rules of Judicial Administration are applicable by their terms. The Florida Rules of Judicial Administration shall be construed to secure the speedy and inexpensive determination of every proceeding to which they are applicable. The Florida Rules of Judicial Administration shall supersede all conflicting rules and statutes. FL ST J ADMIN Rule 2.110.

D. Documents

1. *Required documents*

a. *Notice of hearing/Motion.* An application to the court for an order shall be by motion which shall be made in writing unless made during a hearing or trial, shall state with particularity the grounds therefor, and shall set forth the relief or order sought. The requirement of writing is fulfilled if the motion is stated in a written notice of the hearing of the motion. All notices of hearing shall specify each motion or other matter to be heard. FL ST RCP Rule 1.100(b).

i. *Notices to persons with disabilities.* See the Format section of this KeyRules document for further information.

b. *Proposed amended pleading.* The moving party shall attach the proposed amended pleading to the motion. FL ST RCP Rule 1.190(a).

c. *Certificate of service.* When any attorney certifies in substance: "I certify that a copy hereof has been furnished to (here insert name or names and addresses used for service) by (e-mail) (delivery) (mail) (fax) on .... (date) ....______________ Attorney" the certificate is taken as prima facie proof of such service in compliance with FL ST J ADMIN Rule 2.516. FL ST J ADMIN Rule 2.516(f).

2. *Supplemental documents*

a. *Proposed order.* The court may require that orders or judgments be prepared by a party, may require the party to furnish the court with stamped, addressed envelopes for service of the order or judgment, and may require that proposed orders and judgments be furnished to all parties before entry by the court of the order or judgment. FL ST J ADMIN Rule 2.516(h)(1). For additional information on the submission of proposed orders, refer to FL ST 11 J CIR 1-09-13-A1(e).

b. *Notice of constitutional question.* A party that files a pleading, written motion, or other paper drawing into question the constitutionality of a state statute or a county or municipal charter, ordinance, or franchise must promptly (1) file a notice of constitutional question stating the question and identifying the paper that raises it; and (2) serve the notice and the pleading, written motion, or other paper drawing into question the constitutionality of a state statute or a county or municipal charter, ordinance, or franchise on the Attorney General or the state attorney of the judicial circuit in which the action is pending, by either certified or registered mail. Service of the notice and pleading, written motion, or other paper does not require joinder of the Attorney General or the state attorney as a party to the action. FL ST RCP Rule 1.071.

E. Format

1. *Documents; Type and size.* Documents subject to the exceptions set forth in FL ST J ADMIN Rule 2.525(d) shall be filed on recycled paper measuring eight and one half by eleven (8 1/2 by 11) inches. For purposes of FL ST J ADMIN Rule 2.520, paper is recycled if it contains a minimum content of fifty (50) percent waste paper. Xerographic reduction of legal-size (eight and one half by fourteen (8 1/2 by 14) inches) documents to letter size (eight and one half by eleven (8 1/2 by 11) inches) is prohibited. All other documents filed by electronic transmission shall be filed in a format capable of being printed in a format consistent with the provisions of FL ST J ADMIN Rule 2.250. FL ST J ADMIN Rule 2.520(b).

a. *Exhibits.* Any exhibit or attachment filed with pleadings or papers may be filed in its original size. FL ST J ADMIN Rule 2.520(c).

b. *Recording space.* On all papers and documents prepared and filed by the court or by any party to a proceeding which are to be recorded in the public records of any county, including but not limited to final money judgments and notices of lis pendens, a three (3) inch by three (3) inch space at the top right-hand corner on the first page and a one (1) inch by three (3) inch space at the top right-hand

corner on each subsequent page shall be left blank and reserved for use by the clerk of court. FL ST J ADMIN Rule 2.520(d).

   i. *Exceptions to recording space.* Any papers or documents created by persons or entities over which the filing party has no control, including but not limited to wills, codicils, trusts, or other testamentary documents; documents prepared or executed by any public officer; documents prepared, executed, acknowledged, or proved outside of the State of Florida; or documents created by State or Federal government agencies, may be filed without the space required by FL ST J ADMIN Rule 2.520. FL ST J ADMIN Rule 2.520(e).

c. *Noncompliance.* No clerk of court is permitted to refuse to file any document or paper because of noncompliance with the Florida Rules of Judicial Administration. However, upon request of the clerk of court, noncomplying documents must be resubmitted in accordance with the formatting rules. FL ST J ADMIN Rule 2.520(f).

d. *Format of electronically filed documents.* Hyperlinks in the attachments, (not in the body of the email) are encouraged just as are submissions in Microsoft Word format. Electronic versions submitted in WordPerfect will be converted by the Court to Microsoft Word and there is no guarantee that the document will be converted without error. FL ST 11 J CIR 1-09-13-A1(4)(b)(v).

2. *Caption.* Every pleading, motion, order, judgment, or other paper shall have a caption containing the name of the court, the file number, and except for in rem proceedings, including forfeiture proceedings, the name of the first party on each side with an appropriate indication of other parties, and a designation identifying the party filing it and its nature or the nature of the order, as the case may be. In any in rem proceeding, every pleading, motion, order, judgment, or other paper shall have a caption containing the name of the court, the file number, the style "In re" (followed by the name or general description of the property), and a designation of the person or entity filing it and its nature or the nature of the order, as the case may be. In an in rem forfeiture proceeding, the style shall be "In re forfeiture of" (followed by the name of the general description of the property). All papers filed in the action shall be styled in such a manner as to indicate clearly the subject matter of the paper and the party requesting or obtaining relief. FL ST RCP Rule 1.100(c)(1).

   a. *Caption of electronically filed documents.* All submitted documents shall be titled with the Court Case Number and the name/type of document using the following format: two (2) digit year followed by a hyphen with the sequential case number (e.g., 09-1; 91-12; 08-123; 07-1234; or 09-12345). Do not use zeros after the hyphen to fill in the sequential case number. FL ST 11 J CIR 1-09-13-A1(4)(a).

3. *Writing and written defined.* Writing or written means a document containing information, an application, or a stipulation. FL ST RCP Rule 1.080(c).

4. *Rule abbreviations*

   a. The Florida Rules of Civil Procedure and shall be abbreviated as Fla.R.Civ.P. FL ST RCP Rule 1.010.

   b. The Florida Rules of Judicial Administration shall be abbreviated as Fla. R. Jud. Admin. FL ST J ADMIN Rule 2.110.

5. *Nonverification.* Except when otherwise specifically provided by the Florida Rules of Civil Procedure or an applicable statute, every pleading or other document of a party represented by an attorney need not be verified or accompanied by an affidavit. FL ST RCP Rule 1.030; FL ST J ADMIN Rule 2.515(a).

6. *Attorney signature*

   a. *Attorney signature.* Every pleading and other document of a party represented by an attorney shall be signed by at least one (1) attorney of record in that attorney's individual name whose current record Florida Bar address, telephone number, including area code, primary e-mail address and secondary e-mail addresses, if any, and Florida Bar number shall be stated, and who shall be duly licensed to practice law in Florida or who shall have received permission to appear in the particular case as provided in FL ST J ADMIN Rule 2.510. FL ST J ADMIN Rule 2.515(a).

      i. The attorney may be required by the court to give the address of, and to vouch for the attorney's authority to represent, the party. FL ST J ADMIN Rule 2.515(a).

ii. The signature of an attorney shall constitute a certificate by the attorney that the attorney has read the pleading or other document; that to the best of the attorney's knowledge, information, and belief there is good ground to support it; and that it is not interposed for delay. FL ST J ADMIN Rule 2.515(a).

iii. If a pleading is not signed or is signed with intent to defeat the purpose of FL ST J ADMIN Rule 2.515, it may be stricken and the action may proceed as though the pleading or other document had not been served. FL ST J ADMIN Rule 2.515(a).

b. *Pro se litigant signature.* A party who is not represented by an attorney shall sign any pleading or other paper and state the party's address and telephone number, including area code. FL ST J ADMIN Rule 2.515(b).

c. *Form of signature*

i. The signatures required on pleadings and documents by FL ST J ADMIN Rule 2.515(a) and FL ST J ADMIN Rule 2.515(b) may be:

- Original signatures;
- Original signatures that have been reproduced by electronic means, such as on electronically transmitted documents or photocopied documents;
- Electronic signatures using the "/s/," "s/," or "/s" formats by or at the direction of the person signing; or
- Any other signature format authorized by general law, so long as the clerk where the proceeding is pending has the capability of receiving and has obtained approval from the Supreme Court of Florida to accept pleadings and documents with that signature format. FL ST J ADMIN Rule 2.515(c)(1).

ii. An attorney, party, or other person who files a pleading or paper by electronic transmission that does not contain the original signature of that attorney, party, or other person shall file that identical pleading or paper in paper form containing an original signature of that attorney, party, or other person (hereinafter called the follow-up filing) immediately thereafter. The follow-up filing is not required if the Supreme Court of Florida has entered an order directing the clerk of court to discontinue accepting the follow-up filing. FL ST J ADMIN Rule 2.515(c)(2).

7. *Forms*

a. *Process.* The forms of process, notice of lis pendens, and notice of action provided in the Florida Rules of Civil Procedure are sufficient. Variations from the forms do not void process or notices that are otherwise sufficient. FL ST RCP Rule 1.900(a).

b. *Other forms.* The other forms provided in the Florida Rules of Civil Procedure are sufficient for the matters that are covered by them. So long as the substance is expressed without prolixity, the forms may be varied to meet the facts of a particular case. FL ST RCP Rule 1.900(b).

c. *Formal matters.* Captions, except for the designation of the paper, are omitted from the forms provided in the Florida Rules of Civil Procedure. A general form of caption is the first form provided. Signatures are omitted from pleadings and motions. FL ST RCP Rule 1.900(c).

8. *Notices to persons with disabilities.* All notices of court proceedings to be held in a public facility, and all process compelling appearance at such proceedings, shall include the following statement in bold face, fourteen (14) point Times New Roman or Courier font: "If you are a person with a disability who needs any accommodation in order to participate in this proceeding, you are entitled, at no cost to you, to the provision of certain assistance. Please contact [identify applicable court personnel by name, address, and telephone number] at least seven (7) days before your scheduled court appearance, or immediately upon receiving this notification if the time before the scheduled appearance is less than seven (7) days; if you are hearing or voice impaired, call 711." FL ST J ADMIN Rule 2.540(c)(1).

9. *Minimization of the filing of sensitive information*

a. *Limitations for court filings.* Unless authorized by FL ST J ADMIN Rule 2.425(b), statute, another

rule of court, or the court orders otherwise, designated sensitive information filed with the court must be limited to the following format:

i. The initials of a person known to be a minor;

ii. The year of birth of a person's birth date;

iii. No portion of any: Social security number, Bank account number, Credit card account number, Charge account number, or Debit account number;

iv. The last four digits of any: Taxpayer identification number (TIN), Employee identification number, Driver's license number, Passport number, Telephone number, Financial account number, except as set forth in FL ST J ADMIN Rule 2.425(a)(3), Brokerage account number, Insurance policy account number, Loan account number, Customer account number, or Patient or health care number;

v. A truncated version of any: Email address, Computer user name, Password, or Personal identification number (PIN); and

vi. A truncated version of any other sensitive information as provided by court order. FL ST J ADMIN Rule 2.425(a).

b. *Exceptions.* FL ST J ADMIN Rule 2.425(a) does not apply to the following:

i. An account number which identifies the property alleged to be the subject of a proceeding;

ii. The record of an administrative or agency proceeding;

iii. The record in appellate or review proceedings;

iv. The birth date of a minor whenever the birth date is necessary for the court to establish or maintain subject matter jurisdiction;

v. The name of a minor in any order relating to parental responsibility, time-sharing, or child support;

vi. The name of a minor in any document or order affecting the minor's ownership of real property;

vii. The birth date of a party in a writ of attachment or notice to payor;

viii. In traffic and criminal proceedings: a pro se filing; a court filing that is related to a criminal matter or investigation and that is prepared before the filing of a criminal charge or is not filed as part of any docketed criminal case; an arrest or search warrant or any information in support thereof; a charging document and an affidavit or other documents filed in support of any charging document, including any driving records; a statement of particulars; discovery material introduced into evidence or otherwise filed with the court; and all information necessary for the proper issuance and execution of a subpoena duces tecum;

ix. Information used by the clerk for case maintenance purposes or the courts for case management purposes; and

x. Information which is relevant and material to an issue before the court. FL ST J ADMIN Rule 2.425(b).

c. *Remedies.* Upon motion by a party or interested person or sua sponte by the court, the court may order remedies, sanctions or both for a violation of FL ST J ADMIN Rule 2.425(a). Following notice and an opportunity to respond, the court may impose sanctions if such filing was not made in good faith. FL ST J ADMIN Rule 2.425(c).

d. *Motions not restricted.* FL ST J ADMIN Rule 2.425 does not restrict a party's right to move for protective order, to move to file documents under seal, or to request a determination of the confidentiality of records. FL ST J ADMIN Rule 2.425(d).

e. *Application.* FL ST J ADMIN Rule 2.425 does not affect the application of constitutional provisions, statutes, or rules of court regarding confidential information or access to public information. FL ST J ADMIN Rule 2.425(e).

F. Filing and Service Requirements

1. *Filing requirements.* All original documents must be filed with the court either before service or

immediately thereafter, unless otherwise provided for by general law or other rules. If the original of any bond or other document is not placed in the court file, a certified copy must be so placed by the clerk. FL ST J ADMIN Rule 2.516(d). All documents shall be filed in conformity with the requirements of FL ST J ADMIN Rule 2.525. FL ST RCP Rule 1.080(b). All documents filed in any court shall be filed by electronic transmission in accordance with FL ST J ADMIN Rule 2.525. "Documents" means pleadings, motions, petitions, memoranda, briefs, notices, exhibits, declarations, affidavits, orders, judgments, decrees, writs, opinions, and any other paper or writing submitted to a court. FL ST J ADMIN Rule 2.520(a). All documents that are court records, as defined in FL ST J ADMIN Rule 2.430(a)(1), must be filed by electronic transmission, provided that: (1) the clerk has the ability to accept and retain such documents; (2) the clerk or the chief judge of the circuit has requested permission to accept documents filed by electronic transmission; and (3) the supreme court has entered an order granting permission to the clerk to accept documents filed by electronic transmission. FL ST J ADMIN Rule 2.525(c)(1).

a. *Definition.* "Electronic transmission of documents" means the sending of information by electronic signals to, by or from a court or clerk, which when received can be transformed and stored or transmitted on paper, microfilm, magnetic storage device, optical imaging system, CD-ROM, flash drive, other electronic data storage system, server, case maintenance system ("CM"), electronic court filing ("ECF") system, statewide or local electronic portal ("e-portal"), or other electronic record keeping system authorized by the supreme court in a format sufficient to communicate the information on the original document in a readable format. Electronic transmission of documents includes electronic mail ("e-mail") and any internet-based transmission procedure, and may include procedures allowing for documents to be signed or verified by electronic means. FL ST J ADMIN Rule 2.525(a).

    i. The filing of documents with the court as required by the Florida Rules of Judicial Administration must be made by filing them with the clerk in accordance with FL ST J ADMIN Rule 2.525, except that the judge may permit documents to be filed with the judge, in which event the judge must note the filing date before him or her on the documents and transmit them to the clerk. The date of filing is that shown on the face of the document by the judge's notation or the clerk's time stamp, whichever is earlier. FL ST J ADMIN Rule 2.516(e).

b. *Application.* Any court or clerk of the court may accept the electronic transmission of documents for filing after the clerk, together with input from the chief judge of the circuit, has obtained approval of the procedures and program for doing so from the Supreme Court of Florida. FL ST J ADMIN Rule 2.525(b).

    i. *E-filing mandatory.* All attorneys of record shall be required to follow the protocol set forth in FL ST 11 J CIR 1-09-13-A1(4). FL ST 11 J CIR 1-09-13-A1(3).

c. *Exceptions*

    i. Paper documents and other submissions may be manually submitted to the clerk or court:

        - When the clerk does not have the ability to accept and retain documents by electronic filing or has not had ECF Procedures approved by the supreme court;
        - For filing by any self-represented party or any self-represented nonparty unless specific ECF Procedures provide a means to file documents electronically. However, any self-represented nonparty that is a governmental or public agency and any other agency, partnership, corporation, or business entity acting on behalf of any governmental or public agency may file documents by electronic transmission if such entity has the capability of filing documents electronically;
        - For filing by attorneys excused from e-mail service in accordance with FL ST J ADMIN Rule 2.516(b);
        - When submitting evidentiary exhibits or filing non-documentary materials;
        - When the filing involves documents in excess of twenty-five (25) megabytes (25MB) in size. For such filings, documents may be transmitted using an electronic storage medium that the clerk has the ability to accept, which may include a CD-ROM, flash drive, or similar storage medium;

- When filed in open court, as permitted by the court;
- When paper filing is permitted by any approved statewide or local ECF procedures; and
- If any court determines that justice so requires. FL ST J ADMIN Rule 2.525(d).

ii. Any document in paper form submitted under FL ST J ADMIN Rule 2.525(d) is filed when it is received by the clerk or court and the clerk shall immediately thereafter convert any filed paper document to an electronic document. "Convert to an electronic document" means optically capturing an image of a paper document and using character recognition software to recover as much of the document's text as practicable and then indexing and storing the document in the official court file. FL ST J ADMIN Rule 2.525(c)(4).

iii. Any storage medium submitted under FL ST J ADMIN Rule 2.525(d)(5) is filed when received by the clerk or court and the clerk shall immediately thereafter transfer the electronic documents from the storage device to the official court file. FL ST J ADMIN Rule 2.525(c)(5).

iv. If the filer of any paper document authorized under FL ST J ADMIN Rule 2.525(d) provides a self-addressed, postage-paid envelope for return of the paper document after it is converted to electronic form by the clerk, the clerk shall place the paper document in the envelope and deposit it in the mail. Except when a paper document is required to be maintained, the clerk may recycle any filed paper document that is not to be returned to the filer. FL ST J ADMIN Rule 2.525(c)(6).

v. The clerk may convert any paper document filed before the effective date of FL ST J ADMIN Rule 2.525 to an electronic document. Unless the clerk is required to maintain the paper document, if the paper document has been converted to an electronic document by the clerk, the paper document is no longer part of the official court file and may be removed and recycled. FL ST J ADMIN Rule 2.525(c)(7).

d. *Official court file.* For information on what constitutes the official court file, please see FL ST J ADMIN Rule 2.525(c)(2), FL ST J ADMIN Rule 2.525(c)(3).

e. *Administration.* All attorneys, parties, or other persons using this rule to file documents are required to make arrangements with the court or clerk for the payment of any charges authorized by general law or the supreme court before filing any document by electronic transmission. FL ST J ADMIN Rule 2.525(f)(2).

f. *Filing date.* The filing date for an electronically transmitted document is the date and time that such filing is acknowledged by an electronic stamp or otherwise, pursuant to any procedure set forth in any ECF Procedures approved by the supreme court, or the date the last page of such filing is received by the court or clerk. FL ST J ADMIN Rule 2.525(f)(3).

g. *Accessibility.* All documents transmitted in any electronic form under FL ST J ADMIN Rule 2.525 must comply with the accessibility requirements of FL ST J ADMIN Rule 2.526. FL ST J ADMIN Rule 2.525(g).

2. *Service requirements.* Every pleading subsequent to the initial pleading, all orders, and every other document filed in the action must be served in conformity with the requirements of FL ST J ADMIN Rule 2.516. FL ST RCP Rule 1.080(a).

a. *Service; When required.* Unless the court otherwise orders, or a statute or supreme court administrative order specifies a different means of service, every pleading subsequent to the initial pleading and every other document filed in any court proceeding, except applications for witness subpoenas and documents served by formal notice or required to be served in the manner provided for service of formal notice, must be served in accordance with FL ST J ADMIN Rule 2.516 on each party. No service need be made on parties against whom a default has been entered, except that pleadings asserting new or additional claims against them must be served in the manner provided for service of summons. FL ST J ADMIN Rule 2.516(a).

b. *Service; How made.* When service is required or permitted to be made upon a party represented by an attorney, service must be made upon the attorney unless service upon the party is ordered by the court. FL ST J ADMIN Rule 2.516(b).

i. *Service by electronic mail ("e-mail").* All documents required or permitted to be served on

another party must be served by e-mail, unless FL ST J ADMIN Rule 2.516 otherwise provides. When, in addition to service by e-mail, the sender also utilizes another means of service provided for in FL ST J ADMIN Rule 2.516(b)(2), any differing time limits and other provisions applicable to that other means of service control. FL ST J ADMIN Rule 2.516(b)(1). Any document electronically transmitted to a court or clerk must also be served on all parties and interested persons in accordance with the applicable rules of court. FL ST J ADMIN Rule 2.525(e)(2).

- *Service on attorneys.* Upon appearing in a proceeding, an attorney must serve a designation of a primary e-mail address and may designate no more than two (2) secondary e-mail addresses. Thereafter, service must be directed to all designated e-mail addresses in that proceeding. Every document filed by an attorney thereafter must include the primary e-mail address of that attorney and any secondary e-mail addresses. If an attorney does not designate any e-mail address for service, documents may be served on that attorney at the e-mail address on record with The Florida Bar. FL ST J ADMIN Rule 2.516(b)(1)(A).
- *Exception to e-mail service on attorneys.* Service by an attorney on another attorney must be made by e-mail unless excused by the court. Upon motion by an attorney demonstrating that the attorney has no e-mail account and lacks access to the Internet at the attorney's office, the court may excuse the attorney from the requirements of e-mail service. Service on and by an attorney excused by the court from e-mail service must be by the means provided in FL ST J ADMIN Rule 2.516(b)(2). FL ST J ADMIN Rule 2.516(b)(1)(B).
- *Service on and by parties not represented by an attorney.* Any party not represented by an attorney may serve a designation of a primary e-mail address and also may designate no more than two (2) secondary e-mail addresses to which service must be directed in that proceeding by the means provided in FL ST J ADMIN Rule 2.516(b)(1). If a party not represented by an attorney does not designate an e-mail address for service in a proceeding, service on and by that party must be by the means provided in FL ST J ADMIN Rule 2.516(b)(2). FL ST J ADMIN Rule 2.516(b)(1)(C).
- *Time of service.* Service by e-mail is complete when it is sent. FL ST J ADMIN Rule 2.516(b)(1)(D). An e-mail is deemed served on the date it is sent. FL ST J ADMIN Rule 2.516(b)(1)(D)(i). If the sender learns that the e-mail did not reach the address of the person to be served, the sender must immediately send another copy by e-mail, or by a means authorized by FL ST J ADMIN Rule 2.516(b)(2). FL ST J ADMIN Rule 2.516(b)(1)(D)(ii). E-mail service is treated as service by mail for the computation of time. FL ST J ADMIN Rule 2.516(b)(1)(D)(iii).
- *Specifics of e-mail filing.* In addition to providing proper service pursuant to FL ST RCP Rule 1.080(b), courtesy copies of the Motion and Memorandum of Law for the Uniform Motion Calendar (e.g., Notice of Hearing, Motions, Exhibits, submitted case law, and other hearing specific documents) must be electronically attached to an email using either Microsoft Word or WordPerfect format (not as a PDF document) and sent via email to (a) The Court at its designated e-mail address; (b) Opposing counsel at their fax number as provided to The Florida Bar (see The Florida Bar's website and then click on "Find a Lawyer") or any other fax number provided on a Pleading, Motion to Quash Service, Motion to Dismiss Complaint or Notice of Appearance, whichever is most recent; and (c) Pro se parties at their last known fax number or any other fax number provided on a Pleading, Motion to Quash Service, Motion to Dismiss Complaint or Notice of Appearance, whichever is most recent. FL ST 11 J CIR 1-09-13-A1(4)(b)(i).
- *E-mail subject line.* The subject line of the email must contain only the numeric motion calendar hearing date using the following format: mm/dd/yy (two (2) digit month forward slash; two (2) digit day forward slash; two (2) digit year). For example: 06/15/10. FL ST 11 J CIR 1-09-13-A1(4)(b)(iii).

ii. *Format of e-mail for service.* Service of a document by e-mail is made by attaching a copy of the document in PDF format to an e-mail sent to all addresses designated by the attorney or party. FL ST J ADMIN Rule 2.516(b)(1)(E).

- All documents served by e-mail must be attached to an e-mail message containing a

subject line beginning with the words "SERVICE OF COURT DOCUMENT" in all capital letters, followed by the case number of the proceeding in which the documents are being served. FL ST J ADMIN Rule 2.516(b)(1)(E)(i).

- The body of the e-mail must identify the court in which the proceeding is pending, the case number, the name of the initial party on each side, the title of each document served with that e-mail, and the sender's name and telephone number. FL ST J ADMIN Rule 2.516(b)(1)(E)(ii).
- Any document served by e-mail may be signed by the "/s/" format, as long as the filed original is signed in accordance with the applicable rule of procedure. FL ST J ADMIN Rule 2.516(b)(1)(E)(iii).
- Any e-mail which, together with its attached documents, exceeds five megabytes (5MB) in size, must be divided and sent as separate e-mails, no one of which may exceed five megabytes (5MB) in size and each of which must be sequentially numbered in the subject line. FL ST J ADMIN Rule 2.516(b)(1)(E)(iv).

iii. *Service by other means.* In addition to, and not in lieu of, service by e-mail, service may also be made upon attorneys by any of the means specified in FL ST J ADMIN Rule 2.516(b)(2). Service on and by all parties who are not represented by an attorney and who do not designate an e-mail address, and on and by all attorneys excused from e-mail service, must be made by delivering a copy of the document or by mailing it to the party or attorney at their last known address or, if no address is known, by leaving it with the clerk of the court. Service by mail is complete upon mailing. Delivery of a copy within FL ST J ADMIN Rule 2.516 is complete upon:

- Handing it to the attorney or to the party,
- Leaving it at the attorney's or party's office with a clerk or other person in charge thereof,
- If there is no one in charge, leaving it in a conspicuous place therein,
- If the office is closed or the person to be served has no office, leaving it at the person's usual place of abode with some person of his or her family above fifteen (15) years of age and informing such person of the contents, or
- Transmitting it by facsimile to the attorney's or party's office with a cover sheet containing the sender's name, firm, address, telephone number, and facsimile number, and the number of pages transmitted. When service is made by facsimile, a copy must also be served by any other method permitted by FL ST J ADMIN Rule 2.516. Facsimile service occurs when transmission is complete. FL ST J ADMIN Rule 2.516(b)(2)(A) through FL ST J ADMIN Rule 2.516(b)(2)(E).
- Service by delivery after 5:00 p.m. must be deemed to have been made by mailing on the date of delivery. FL ST J ADMIN Rule 2.516(b)(2)(F).
- If a scheduling attorney or a scheduling pro se party does not have a fax number, then a courtesy copy of Motions and Proposed orders must be sent as an attachment to the service of process required pursuant to FL ST RCP Rule 1.080(b). FL ST 11 J CIR 1-09-13-A1(4)(b)(ii).

c. *Service; Numerous defendants.* In actions when the parties are unusually numerous, the court may regulate the service contemplated by the Florida Rules of Judicial Administration on motion or on its own initiative in such manner as may be found to be just and reasonable. FL ST J ADMIN Rule 2.516(c).

d. *Service by clerk.* Service of notices and other documents required to be made by the clerk must also be done as provided in FL ST J ADMIN Rule 2.516(b). FL ST J ADMIN Rule 2.516(g).

G. Hearings

1. *Communication equipment*

a. *Definition.* Communication equipment means a conference telephone or other electronic device that permits all those appearing or participating to hear and speak to each other, provided that all conversation of all parties is audible to all persons present. FL ST J ADMIN Rule 2.530(a).

b. *Use by all parties.* A county or circuit court judge may, upon the court's own motion or upon the written request of a party, direct that communication equipment be used for a motion hearing, pretrial conference, or a status conference. A judge must give notice to the parties and consider any objections they may have to the use of communication equipment before directing that communication equipment be used. The decision to use communication equipment over the objection of parties will be in the sound discretion of the trial court, except as noted below. FL ST J ADMIN Rule 2.530(b).

c. *Use only by requesting party.* A county or circuit court judge may, upon the written request of a party upon reasonable notice to all other parties, permit a requesting party to participate through communication equipment in a scheduled motion hearing; however, any such request (except in criminal, juvenile, and appellate proceedings) must be granted, absent a showing of good cause to deny the same, where the hearing is set for not longer than fifteen (15) minutes. FL ST J ADMIN Rule 2.530(c).

d. *Testimony*

   i. *Generally.* A county or circuit court judge, general magistrate, special magistrate, or hearing officer may allow testimony to be taken through communication equipment if all parties consent or if permitted by another applicable rule of procedure. FL ST J ADMIN Rule 2.530(d)(1).

   ii. *Procedure.* Any party desiring to present testimony through communication equipment shall, prior to the hearing or trial at which the testimony is to be presented, contact all parties to determine whether each party consents to this form of testimony. The party seeking to present the testimony shall move for permission to present testimony through communication equipment, which motion shall set forth good cause as to why the testimony should be allowed in this form. FL ST J ADMIN Rule 2.530(d)(2).

   iii. *Oath.* Testimony may be taken through communication equipment only if a notary public or other person authorized to administer oaths in the witness's jurisdiction is present with the witness and administers the oath consistent with the laws of the jurisdiction. FL ST J ADMIN Rule 2.530(d)(3).

   iv. *Confrontation rights.* In juvenile and criminal proceedings the defendant must make an informed waiver of any confrontation rights that may be abridged by the use of communication equipment. FL ST J ADMIN Rule 2.530(d)(4).

   v. *Video testimony.* If the testimony to be presented utilizes video conferencing or comparable two-way visual capabilities, the court in its discretion may modify the procedures set forth in FL ST J ADMIN Rule 2.530 to accommodate the technology utilized. FL ST J ADMIN Rule 2.530(d)(5).

e. *Burden of expense.* The cost for the use of the communication equipment is the responsibility of the requesting party unless otherwise directed by the court. FL ST J ADMIN Rule 2.530(e).

2. *Time allotted for hearing.* Each party may set only one five (5) minute motion per case. Multiple motions must be specially set or set on different motion calendars (one five (5) minute motion per party per case), so as not to encroach on the time the Court is allotting for other litigants/attorneys. Consequently, the parties are advised to use good faith efforts to resolve the issues set forth in the motion prior to the setting of a motion; coordinate the date and time of the hearing; and confirm that the hearing shall require no more than five (5) minutes (if the hearing will require more than five (5) minutes, then it must be a Special Set Hearing). FL ST 11 J CIR 1-09-13-A1(4)(b)(i). For information on Special Set Hearings, refer to FL ST 11 J CIR 1-09-13-A1(4)(c).

3. *Hearing cancellation policy.* Should any scheduled hearing become unnecessary or have to be cancelled, the scheduling attorney or scheduling pro se party shall immediately, but, not later than by Noon on the business day prior to the hearing date and time, send an email to the court's designated e-mail address regarding the cancellation of the Motion Calendar hearing with an electronically attached Notice of

Cancellation formatted in the same manner (using Microsoft Word or Word Perfect) as the email that scheduled the Motion Calendar hearing and in the same manner as the Motions and Notices. FL ST 11 J CIR 1-09-13-A1(4)(b)(vii).

H. Forms

1. Official Motion for Leave to Amend Forms for Florida

a. Caption. FL ST RCP Form 1.901.

b. Notice of compliance when constitutional challenge is brought. FL ST RCP Form 1.975.

2. Motion for Leave to Amend Forms for Florida

a. Motion; For leave of court; To amend complaint. FL-PP § 2:155.

b. Motion; For leave of court; To add claim for punitive damages. FL-PP § 2:156.

c. Motion; For leave of court; To amend complaint; To conform to evidence. FL-PP § 2:157.

d. Motion; For leave of court; To permit admission of evidence. FL-PP § 2:158.

e. Order; Granting leave to amend complaint. FL-PP § 2:163.

f. Order; Granting leave to amend complaint; To conform to evidence. FL-PP § 2:164.

g. Order; Granting leave to amend complaint; To permit admission of evidence. FL-PP § 2:165.

h. Form for motion for leave to amend complaint. FL-RCPF R 1.190(39).

i. Form for amendment to complaint with leave of court. FL-RCPF R 1.190(40).

j. Form for motion to amend amended complaint. FL-RCPF R 1.190(42).

k. Form for amendment to amended complaint (or second amended complaint). FL-RCPF R 1.190(43).

l. Form for motion to amend complaint to add count. FL-RCPF R 1.190(44).

I. Checklist

(I) ❑ Matters to be considered by moving party

(a) ❑ Required documents

(1) ❑ Notice of hearing/Motion

(2) ❑ Proposed amended pleading

(3) ❑ Certificate of service

(b) ❑ Supplemental documents

(1) ❑ Proposed order

(2) ❑ Notice of constitutional question

(c) ❑ Time for making motion

(1) ❑ A party may amend a pleading once as a matter of course at any time before a responsive pleading is served or, if the pleading is one to which no responsive pleading is permitted and the action has not been placed on the trial calendar, may amend it at any time within twenty (20) days after it is served

(2) ❑ Under the Florida Rules of Civil Procedure, there is no time limit as to when an amendment with leave of court may be sought; amendments of the pleadings may be permitted, with the court's discretion, at any stage of the proceedings in furtherance of justice

(3) ❑ A motion for leave to amend a pleading to assert a claim for punitive damages can be filed separately and before the supporting evidence or proffer, but each shall be served on all parties at least twenty (20) days before the hearing

(4) ❑ A copy of any written motion which may not be heard ex parte and a copy of the notice of the hearing thereof shall be served a reasonable time before the time specified for the hearing

(II) ❑ Matters to be considered by opposing party
- (a) ❑ Required documents
  - (1) ❑ Response to motion
  - (2) ❑ Certificate of service
- (b) ❑ Supplemental documents
  - (1) ❑ Proposed order
  - (2) ❑ Notice of constitutional question
- (c) ❑ Time for service and filing of opposition
  - (1) ❑ No time specified for responding to a motion

Motions, Oppositions and Replies
Motion for Summary Judgment

Document Last Updated January 2013

A. Applicable Rules

1. *State rules*
   - a. Rules of court. FL ST RCP Rule 1.010; FL ST J ADMIN Rule 2.110.
   - b. Nonverification of pleadings. FL ST RCP Rule 1.030.
   - c. Service and filing of pleadings, orders, and documents. FL ST RCP Rule 1.080.
   - d. Time. FL ST RCP Rule 1.090.
   - e. Pleadings and motions. FL ST RCP Rule 1.100.
   - f. Motions. FL ST RCP Rule 1.160.
   - g. Summary judgment. FL ST RCP Rule 1.510.
   - h. Relief from judgment, decrees, or orders. FL ST RCP Rule 1.540.
   - i. Mediation and arbitration. FL ST RCP Rule 1.700; FL ST RCP Rule 1.710; FL ST RCP Rule 1.720; FL ST RCP Rule 1.730; FL ST RCP Rule 1.750; FL ST RCP Rule 1.800; FL ST RCP Rule 1.810; FL ST RCP Rule 1.820; FL ST RCP Rule 1.830.
   - j. Forms. FL ST RCP Rule 1.900.
   - k. Minimization of the filing of sensitive information. FL ST J ADMIN Rule 2.425.
   - l. Retention of court records. FL ST J ADMIN Rule 2.430.
   - m. Foreign attorneys. FL ST J ADMIN Rule 2.510.
   - n. Signature of attorneys and parties. FL ST J ADMIN Rule 2.515.
   - o. Paper. FL ST J ADMIN Rule 2.520.
   - p. Electronic filing. FL ST J ADMIN Rule 2.525.
   - q. Accessibility of information and technology. FL ST J ADMIN Rule 2.526.
   - r. Communication equipment. FL ST J ADMIN Rule 2.530.
   - s. Court reporting. FL ST J ADMIN Rule 2.535.
   - t. Requests for accommodations by persons with disabilities. FL ST J ADMIN Rule 2.540.
2. *Local rules*
   - a. Establishment of 11th Circuit Homestead Access to Mediation Program ("CHAMP") for case management of residential foreclosure cases in the Eleventh Judicial Circuit of Florida. FL ST 11 J CIR 1-09-08.

b. Enlargement and expansion of the current pilot project for electronic submissions of courtesy copies for uniform motion calendar and requests for special set hearings, emergency motions, and proposed orders. FL ST 11 J CIR 1-09-13-A1.

B. Timing

1. *Motion for summary judgment*
   a. *For the claimant.* A party seeking to recover upon a claim, counterclaim, crossclaim or third-party claim or to obtain a declaratory judgment may move for a summary judgment in that party's favor at any time after the expiration of twenty (20) days from the commencement of the action or after service of a motion for summary judgment by the adverse party. FL ST RCP Rule 1.510(a).
   b. *For defending party.* A party against whom a claim, counterclaim, crossclaim, or third-party claim is asserted or a declaratory judgment is sought may move for a summary judgment in that party's favor as to all or any part thereof at any time with or without supporting affidavits. FL ST RCP Rule 1.510(b).
      i. A defending party is not required to serve his responsive pleading before moving for summary judgment. He may make the motion at any time, setting out his defenses by affidavit, and thus effect a speedy termination of the action if no genuine issue exists as to any fact or facts pertaining to a defense that would defeat the claim. FL ST RCP Rule 1.510, notes.
2. *Service of motion.* The movant shall serve the motion for summary judgment at least twenty (20) days before the time fixed for the hearing, and shall also serve at that time a copy of any summary judgment evidence on which the movant relies that has not already been filed with the court. FL ST RCP Rule 1.510(c).
3. *Computation of time*
   a. *Generally.* Computation of time shall be governed by FL ST J ADMIN Rule 2.514. FL ST RCP Rule 1.090(a). The following rules apply in computing time periods specified in any rule of procedure, local rule, court order, or statute that does not specify a method of computing time. FL ST J ADMIN Rule 2.514(a).
      i. *Period stated in days or a longer unit.* When the period is stated in days or a longer unit of time (A) exclude the day of the event that triggers the period; (B) count every day, including intermediate Saturdays, Sundays, and legal holidays; and (C) include the last day of the period, but if the last day is a Saturday, Sunday, or legal holiday, or falls within any period of time extended through an order of the chief justice under FL ST J ADMIN Rule 2.205(a)(2)(B)(iv), the period continues to run until the end of the next day that is not a Saturday, Sunday, or legal holiday and does not fall within any period of time extended through an order of the chief justice. FL ST J ADMIN Rule 2.514(a)(1).
      ii. *Period stated in hours.* When the period is stated in hours (A) begin counting immediately on the occurrence of the event that triggers the period; (B) count every hour, including hours during intermediate Saturdays, Sundays, and legal holidays; and (C) if the period would end on a Saturday, Sunday, or legal holiday, or during any period of time extended through an order of the chief justice under FL ST J ADMIN Rule 2.205(a)(2)(B)(iv), the period continues to run until the same time on the next day that is not a Saturday, Sunday, or legal holiday and does not fall within any period of time extended through an order of the chief justice. FL ST J ADMIN Rule 2.514(a)(2).
      iii. *Period stated in days less than seven (7) days.* When the period stated in days is less than seven (7) days, intermediate Saturdays, Sundays, and legal holidays shall be excluded in the computation. FL ST J ADMIN Rule 2.514(a)(3).
      iv. *"Last day" defined.* Unless a different time is set by a statute, local rule, or court order, the last day ends (A) for electronic filing or for service by any means, at midnight; and (B) for filing by other means, when the clerk's office is scheduled to close. FL ST J ADMIN Rule 2.514(a)(4).
      v. *"Next day" defined.* The "next day" is determined by continuing to count forward when the period is measured after an event and backward when measured before an event. FL ST J ADMIN Rule 2.514(a)(5).

vi. *"Legal holiday" defined.* "Legal holiday" means (A) the day set aside by FL ST § 110.117, for observing New Year's Day, Martin Luther King, Jr.'s Birthday, Memorial Day, Independence Day, Labor Day, Veterans' Day, Thanksgiving Day, the Friday after Thanksgiving Day, or Christmas Day, and (B) any day observed as a holiday by the clerk's office or as designated by the chief judge. FL ST J ADMIN Rule 2.514(a)(6).

b. *Additional time after service by mail or e-mail.* When a party may or must act within a specified time after service and service is made by mail or e-mail, five (5) days are added after the period that would otherwise expire under FL ST J ADMIN Rule 2.514(a). FL ST J ADMIN Rule 2.514(b).

c. *Enlargement.* When an act is required or allowed to be done at or within a specified time by order of court, by the Florida Rules of Civil Procedure, or by notice given thereunder, for cause shown the court at any time in its discretion (1) with or without notice, may order the period enlarged if request therefor is made before the expiration of the period originally prescribed or as extended by a previous order, or (2) upon motion made and notice after the expiration of the specified period, may permit the act to be done when failure to act was the result of excusable neglect, but it may not extend the time for making a motion for new trial, for rehearing, or to alter or amend a judgment; making a motion for relief from a judgment under FL ST RCP Rule 1.540(b); taking an appeal or filing a petition for certiorari; or making a motion for a directed verdict. FL ST RCP Rule 1.090(b).

d. *Unaffected by expiration of term.* The period of time provided for the doing of any act or the taking of any proceeding shall not be affected or limited by the continued existence or expiration of a term of court. The continued existence or expiration of a term of court in no way affects the power of a court to do any act or take any proceeding in any action which is or has been pending before it. FL ST RCP Rule 1.090(c).

C. General Requirements

1. *Motions generally*

a. *Contents.* An application to the court for an order shall be by motion which shall be made in writing unless made during a hearing or trial, shall state with particularity the grounds therefor, and shall set forth the relief or order sought. The requirement of writing is fulfilled if the motion is stated in a written notice of the hearing of the motion. All notices of hearing shall specify each motion or other matter to be heard. FL ST RCP Rule 1.100(b).

b. *Particularity requirement.* The court considers a motion in the light of the substantive law, rule or statute to make its determination. Some rules require a statement of the grounds for a motion under the rule. Failure to give the grounds will result in denial of the motion. This should be the result in all situations when the ground for the motion is not inherent in the rule. FL-PRACPROC § 9:3. The requirement is nevertheless an important one, first because of the due process notice rights of the respondent, as well as for the assistance it provides to the court in its preparation for the hearing or, absent a hearing, for disposition. 4 FLPRAC R 1.100.

2. *Summary judgment.* A party seeking to recover upon or defend against a claim, counterclaim, crossclaim, or third-party claim or to obtain a declaratory judgment may move for a summary judgment. FL ST RCP Rule 1.510(a); FL ST RCP Rule 1.510(b).

a. *General motion for summary judgment information*

i. *Contents of motion.* The motion shall state with particularity the grounds upon which it is based and the substantial matters of law to be argued and shall specifically identify any affidavits, answers to interrogatories, admissions, depositions, and other materials as would be admissible in evidence ("summary judgment evidence") on which the movant relies. FL ST RCP Rule 1.510(c).

ii. *Evidence relied upon.* The movant shall also serve at that time a copy of any summary judgment evidence on which the movant relies that has not already been filed with the court. FL ST RCP Rule 1.510(c).

iii. *Judgment as a matter of law.* The judgment sought shall be rendered forthwith if the pleadings and summary judgment evidence on file show that there is no genuine issue as to any material fact and that the moving party is entitled to a judgment as a matter of law. A summary judgment,

interlocutory in character, may be rendered on the issue of liability alone although there is a genuine issue as to the amount of damages. FL ST RCP Rule 1.510(c).

b. *Sham pleadings.* If a party deems any pleading or part thereof filed by another party to be a sham, that party may move to strike the pleading or part thereof before the cause is set for trial and the court shall hear the motion, taking evidence of the respective parties, and if the motion is sustained, the pleading to which the motion is directed shall be stricken. Default and summary judgment on the merits may be entered in the discretion of the court or the court may permit additional pleadings to be filed for good cause shown. FL ST RCP Rule 1.150(a).

c. *Burden of proof*

   i. The moving party in a motion for summary judgment has the initial burden of demonstrating the nonexistence of any genuine issue of fact. Landers v. Milton, 370 So.2d 368, 370 (Fla. 1979); Gardner v. Sabal Point Properties, Inc., 616 So.2d 1111, 1112 (Fla. 5th DCA 1993); FL-PP § 6:7.

   ii. If the record raises the slightest doubt that material issues could be present, that doubt must be resolved against the movant and the motion for summary judgment denied. Moore v. Morris, 475 So.2d 666, 668 (Fla. 1985); Henderson v. CSX Transportation, Inc., 617 So.2d 770 (Fla. 1st DCA 1993); Jones v. Directors Guild of America, Inc., 584 So.2d 1057 (Fla. 1st DCA 1991); FL-PP § 6:7.

   iii. Until the moving party meets the initial burden of showing there is no issue of material fact, the opposing party need do nothing. Holl v. Talcott, 191 So.2d 40, 43 (Fla. 1966); Spradley v. Stick, 622 So.2d 610 (Fla. 1st DCA 1993); FL-RCPF R 1.510(404).

   iv. When the movant has tendered competent evidence in support of its motion, the burden shifts to the nonmoving party to come forward with opposing evidence to show that a question of material fact exists. Landers v. Milton, 370 So.2d 368, 370 (Fla. 1979); Holl v. Talcott, 191 So.2d 40, 43-44 (Fla. 1966); Lenhal Realty, Inc. v. Transamerica Commercial Finance Corp., 615 So.2d 207 (Fla. 4th DCA 1993); FL-PP § 6:7.

d. *Affidavits*

   i. *Form of affidavits; Further testimony.* Supporting and opposing affidavits shall be made on personal knowledge, shall set forth such facts as would be admissible in evidence, and shall show affirmatively that the affiant is competent to testify to the matters stated. Sworn or certified copies of all papers or parts referred to in an affidavit shall be attached to or served with the affidavit. The court may permit affidavits to be supplemented or opposed by depositions, answers to interrogatories, or by further affidavits. FL ST RCP Rule 1.510(e).

   ii. *When affidavits are unavailable.* If it appears from the affidavits of a party opposing the motion that the party cannot for reasons stated present by affidavit facts essential to justify opposition, the court may refuse the application for judgment or may order a continuance to permit affidavits to be obtained or depositions to be taken or discovery to be had or may make such other order as is just. FL ST RCP Rule 1.510(f).

   iii. *Affidavits made in bad faith.* If it appears to the satisfaction of the court at any time that any of the affidavits presented pursuant to FL ST RCP Rule 1.510 are presented in bad faith or solely for the purpose of delay, the court shall forthwith order the party employing them to pay to the other party the amount of the reasonable expenses that the filing of the affidavits caused the other party to incur, including reasonable attorneys' fees, and any offending party or attorney may be adjudged guilty of contempt. FL ST RCP Rule 1.510(g).

e. *Case not fully adjudicated on motion.* On motion under FL ST RCP Rule 1.510 if judgment is not rendered upon the whole case or for all the relief asked and a trial or the taking of testimony and a final hearing is necessary, the court at the hearing of the motion, by examining the pleadings and the evidence before it and by interrogating counsel, shall ascertain, if practicable, what material facts exist without substantial controversy and what material facts are actually and in good faith controverted. FL ST RCP Rule 1.510(d).

   i. It shall thereupon make an order specifying the facts that appear without substantial contro-

versy, including the extent to which the amount of damages or other relief is not in controversy, and directing such further proceedings in the action as are just. FL ST RCP Rule 1.510(d).

ii. On the trial or final hearing of the action the facts so specified shall be deemed established, and the trial or final hearing shall be conducted accordingly. FL ST RCP Rule 1.510(d).

3. *Arbitration and mediation*

a. *Referral to arbitration and mediation.* Except as hereinafter provided or as otherwise prohibited by law, the presiding judge may enter an order referring all or any part of a contested civil matter to mediation or arbitration. The parties to any contested civil matter may file a written stipulation to mediate or arbitrate any issue between them at any time. Such stipulation shall be incorporated into the order of referral. FL ST RCP Rule 1.700(a).

i. In all residential foreclosure actions involving homestead properties filed on or after May 1, 2009, unless a stipulation is specifically invoked by the parties in writing within five (5) days of service of the complaint on the main defendant, the parties are deemed to have stipulated to referral of the mediation to the Collins Center pursuant to FL ST RCP Rule 1.720(f). FL ST 11 J CIR 1-09-08(2); FL ST 11 J CIR 1-09-08(3). FL ST 11 J CIR 1-09-08 constitutes a formal referral to mediation pursuant to the Florida Rules of Civil Procedure. FL ST 11 J CIR 1-09-08(2).

ii. For further information on referral to mediation, refer to FL ST 11 J CIR 1-09-08.

b. *Arbitration*

i. *Exclusions.* A civil action shall be ordered to arbitration or arbitration in conjunction with mediation upon stipulation of the parties. A civil action may be ordered to arbitration or arbitration in conjunction with mediation upon motion of any party or by the court, if the judge determines the action to be of such a nature that arbitration could be of benefit to the litigants or the court. FL ST RCP Rule 1.800.

- Under no circumstances may the following categories of actions be referred to arbitration: (1) bond estreatures; (2) habeas corpus or other extraordinary writs; (3) bond validations; (4) civil or criminal contempt; (5) such other matters as may be specified by order of the chief judge in the circuit. FL ST RCP Rule 1.800.

ii. For more information regarding arbitration, please see FL ST RCP Rule 1.810; FL ST RCP Rule 1.820; FL ST RCP Rule 1.830.

c. *Mediation.* For more information regarding mediation, please see FL ST RCP Rule 1.710; FL ST RCP Rule 1.720; FL ST RCP Rule 1.730; and FL ST RCP Rule 1.750.

4. *Rules of court*

a. *Rules of civil procedure.* The Florida Rules of Civil Procedure apply to all actions of a civil nature and all special statutory proceedings in the circuit courts and county courts except those to which the Florida Probate Rules, the Florida Family Law Rules of Procedure, or the Small Claims Rules apply. FL ST RCP Rule 1.010.

i. The form, content, procedure, and time for pleading in all special statutory proceedings shall be as prescribed by the statutes governing the proceeding unless the Florida Rules of Civil Procedure specifically provide to the contrary. FL ST RCP Rule 1.010.

ii. The Florida Rules of Civil Procedure shall be construed to secure the just, speedy, and inexpensive determination of every action. FL ST RCP Rule 1.010.

b. *Rules of judicial administration.* The Florida Rules of Judicial Administration shall apply to administrative matters in all courts to which the Florida Rules of Judicial Administration are applicable by their terms. The Florida Rules of Judicial Administration shall be construed to secure the speedy and inexpensive determination of every proceeding to which they are applicable. The Florida Rules of Judicial Administration shall supersede all conflicting rules and statutes. FL ST J ADMIN Rule 2.110.

D. Documents

1. *Required documents*

   a. *Notice of hearing/Motion.* An application to the court for an order shall be by motion which shall be made in writing unless made during a hearing or trial, shall state with particularity the grounds therefor, and shall set forth the relief or order sought. The requirement of writing is fulfilled if the motion is stated in a written notice of the hearing of the motion. All notices of hearing shall specify each motion or other matter to be heard. FL ST RCP Rule 1.100(b).

      i. *Notices to persons with disabilities.* See the Format section of this KeyRules document for further information.

   b. *Certificate of service.* When any attorney certifies in substance: "I certify that a copy hereof has been furnished to (here insert name or names and addresses used for service) by (e-mail) (delivery) (mail) (fax) on .... (date) ....________________ Attorney" the certificate is taken as prima facie proof of such service in compliance with FL ST J ADMIN Rule 2.516. FL ST J ADMIN Rule 2.516(f).

2. *Supplemental documents*

   a. *Affidavits.* Supporting and opposing affidavits shall be made on personal knowledge, shall set forth such facts as would be admissible in evidence, and shall show affirmatively that the affiant is competent to testify to the matters stated therein. Sworn or certified copies of all papers or parts thereof referred to in an affidavit shall be attached thereto or served therewith. FL ST RCP Rule 1.510(e). For further information regarding affidavits made in the context of a motion for summary judgment see FL ST RCP Rule 1.510(e) through FL ST RCP Rule 1.510(g).

   b. *Other evidence.* The movant shall also serve at that time a copy of any summary judgment evidence on which the movant relies that has not already been filed with the court. FL ST RCP Rule 1.510(c).

   c. *Proposed order.* The court may require that orders or judgments be prepared by a party, may require the party to furnish the court with stamped, addressed envelopes for service of the order or judgment, and may require that proposed orders and judgments be furnished to all parties before entry by the court of the order or judgment. FL ST J ADMIN Rule 2.516(h)(1). For additional information on the submission of proposed orders, refer to FL ST 11 J CIR 1-09-13-A1(e).

   d. *Notice of constitutional question.* A party that files a pleading, written motion, or other paper drawing into question the constitutionality of a state statute or a county or municipal charter, ordinance, or franchise must promptly (1) file a notice of constitutional question stating the question and identifying the paper that raises it; and (2) serve the notice and the pleading, written motion, or other paper drawing into question the constitutionality of a state statute or a county or municipal charter, ordinance, or franchise on the Attorney General or the state attorney of the judicial circuit in which the action is pending, by either certified or registered mail. Service of the notice and pleading, written motion, or other paper does not require joinder of the Attorney General or the state attorney as a party to the action. FL ST RCP Rule 1.071.

E. Format

1. *Documents; Type and size.* Documents subject to the exceptions set forth in FL ST J ADMIN Rule 2.525(d) shall be filed on recycled paper measuring eight and one half by eleven (8 1/2 by 11) inches. For purposes of FL ST J ADMIN Rule 2.520, paper is recycled if it contains a minimum content of fifty (50) percent waste paper. Xerographic reduction of legal-size (eight and one half by fourteen (8 1/2 by 14) inches) documents to letter size (eight and one half by eleven (8 1/2 by 11) inches) is prohibited. All other documents filed by electronic transmission shall be filed in a format capable of being printed in a format consistent with the provisions of FL ST J ADMIN Rule 2.250. FL ST J ADMIN Rule 2.520(b).

   a. *Exhibits.* Any exhibit or attachment filed with pleadings or papers may be filed in its original size. FL ST J ADMIN Rule 2.520(c).

   b. *Recording space.* On all papers and documents prepared and filed by the court or by any party to a proceeding which are to be recorded in the public records of any county, including but not limited to final money judgments and notices of lis pendens, a three (3) inch by three (3) inch space at the top right-hand corner on the first page and a one (1) inch by three (3) inch space at the top right-hand

corner on each subsequent page shall be left blank and reserved for use by the clerk of court. FL ST J ADMIN Rule 2.520(d).

i. *Exceptions to recording space.* Any papers or documents created by persons or entities over which the filing party has no control, including but not limited to wills, codicils, trusts, or other testamentary documents; documents prepared or executed by any public officer; documents prepared, executed, acknowledged, or proved outside of the State of Florida; or documents created by State or Federal government agencies, may be filed without the space required by FL ST J ADMIN Rule 2.520. FL ST J ADMIN Rule 2.520(e).

c. *Noncompliance.* No clerk of court is permitted to refuse to file any document or paper because of noncompliance with the Florida Rules of Judicial Administration. However, upon request of the clerk of court, noncomplying documents must be resubmitted in accordance with the formatting rules. FL ST J ADMIN Rule 2.520(f).

d. *Format of electronically filed documents.* Hyperlinks in the attachments, (not in the body of the email) are encouraged just as are submissions in Microsoft Word format. Electronic versions submitted in WordPerfect will be converted by the Court to Microsoft Word and there is no guarantee that the document will be converted without error. FL ST 11 J CIR 1-09-13-A1(4)(b)(v).

2. *Caption.* Every pleading, motion, order, judgment, or other paper shall have a caption containing the name of the court, the file number, and except for in rem proceedings, including forfeiture proceedings, the name of the first party on each side with an appropriate indication of other parties, and a designation identifying the party filing it and its nature or the nature of the order, as the case may be. In any in rem proceeding, every pleading, motion, order, judgment, or other paper shall have a caption containing the name of the court, the file number, the style "In re" (followed by the name or general description of the property), and a designation of the person or entity filing it and its nature or the nature of the order, as the case may be. In an in rem forfeiture proceeding, the style shall be "In re forfeiture of" (followed by the name of the general description of the property). All papers filed in the action shall be styled in such a manner as to indicate clearly the subject matter of the paper and the party requesting or obtaining relief. FL ST RCP Rule 1.100(c)(1).

a. *Caption of electronically filed documents.* All submitted documents shall be titled with the Court Case Number and the name/type of document using the following format: two (2) digit year followed by a hyphen with the sequential case number (e.g., 09-1; 91-12; 08-123; 07-1234; or 09-12345). Do not use zeros after the hyphen to fill in the sequential case number. FL ST 11 J CIR 1-09-13-A1(4)(a).

3. *Writing and written defined.* Writing or written means a document containing information, an application, or a stipulation. FL ST RCP Rule 1.080(c).

4. *Rule abbreviations*

a. The Florida Rules of Civil Procedure and shall be abbreviated as Fla.R.Civ.P. FL ST RCP Rule 1.010.

b. The Florida Rules of Judicial Administration shall be abbreviated as Fla. R. Jud. Admin. FL ST J ADMIN Rule 2.110.

5. *Nonverification.* Except when otherwise specifically provided by the Florida Rules of Civil Procedure or an applicable statute, every pleading or other document of a party represented by an attorney need not be verified or accompanied by an affidavit. FL ST RCP Rule 1.030; FL ST J ADMIN Rule 2.515(a).

6. *Attorney signature*

a. *Attorney signature.* Every pleading and other document of a party represented by an attorney shall be signed by at least one (1) attorney of record in that attorney's individual name whose current record Florida Bar address, telephone number, including area code, primary e-mail address and secondary e-mail addresses, if any, and Florida Bar number shall be stated, and who shall be duly licensed to practice law in Florida or who shall have received permission to appear in the particular case as provided in FL ST J ADMIN Rule 2.510. FL ST J ADMIN Rule 2.515(a).

i. The attorney may be required by the court to give the address of, and to vouch for the attorney's authority to represent, the party. FL ST J ADMIN Rule 2.515(a).

ii. The signature of an attorney shall constitute a certificate by the attorney that the attorney has read the pleading or other document; that to the best of the attorney's knowledge, information, and belief there is good ground to support it; and that it is not interposed for delay. FL ST J ADMIN Rule 2.515(a).

iii. If a pleading is not signed or is signed with intent to defeat the purpose of FL ST J ADMIN Rule 2.515, it may be stricken and the action may proceed as though the pleading or other document had not been served. FL ST J ADMIN Rule 2.515(a).

b. *Pro se litigant signature.* A party who is not represented by an attorney shall sign any pleading or other paper and state the party's address and telephone number, including area code. FL ST J ADMIN Rule 2.515(b).

c. *Form of signature*

i. The signatures required on pleadings and documents by FL ST J ADMIN Rule 2.515(a) and FL ST J ADMIN Rule 2.515(b) may be:

- Original signatures;
- Original signatures that have been reproduced by electronic means, such as on electronically transmitted documents or photocopied documents;
- Electronic signatures using the "/s/," "s/," or "/s" formats by or at the direction of the person signing; or
- Any other signature format authorized by general law, so long as the clerk where the proceeding is pending has the capability of receiving and has obtained approval from the Supreme Court of Florida to accept pleadings and documents with that signature format. FL ST J ADMIN Rule 2.515(c)(1).

ii. An attorney, party, or other person who files a pleading or paper by electronic transmission that does not contain the original signature of that attorney, party, or other person shall file that identical pleading or paper in paper form containing an original signature of that attorney, party, or other person (hereinafter called the follow-up filing) immediately thereafter. The follow-up filing is not required if the Supreme Court of Florida has entered an order directing the clerk of court to discontinue accepting the follow-up filing. FL ST J ADMIN Rule 2.515(c)(2).

7. *Forms*

a. *Process.* The forms of process, notice of lis pendens, and notice of action provided in the Florida Rules of Civil Procedure are sufficient. Variations from the forms do not void process or notices that are otherwise sufficient. FL ST RCP Rule 1.900(a).

b. *Other forms.* The other forms provided in the Florida Rules of Civil Procedure are sufficient for the matters that are covered by them. So long as the substance is expressed without prolixity, the forms may be varied to meet the facts of a particular case. FL ST RCP Rule 1.900(b).

c. *Formal matters.* Captions, except for the designation of the paper, are omitted from the forms provided in the Florida Rules of Civil Procedure. A general form of caption is the first form provided. Signatures are omitted from pleadings and motions. FL ST RCP Rule 1.900(c).

8. *Notices to persons with disabilities.* All notices of court proceedings to be held in a public facility, and all process compelling appearance at such proceedings, shall include the following statement in bold face, fourteen (14) point Times New Roman or Courier font: "If you are a person with a disability who needs any accommodation in order to participate in this proceeding, you are entitled, at no cost to you, to the provision of certain assistance. Please contact [identify applicable court personnel by name, address, and telephone number] at least seven (7) days before your scheduled court appearance, or immediately upon receiving this notification if the time before the scheduled appearance is less than seven (7) days; if you are hearing or voice impaired, call 711." FL ST J ADMIN Rule 2.540(c)(1).

9. *Minimization of the filing of sensitive information*

a. *Limitations for court filings.* Unless authorized by FL ST J ADMIN Rule 2.425(b), statute, another

rule of court, or the court orders otherwise, designated sensitive information filed with the court must be limited to the following format:

i. The initials of a person known to be a minor;

ii. The year of birth of a person's birth date;

iii. No portion of any: Social security number, Bank account number, Credit card account number, Charge account number, or Debit account number;

iv. The last four digits of any: Taxpayer identification number (TIN), Employee identification number, Driver's license number, Passport number, Telephone number, Financial account number, except as set forth in FL ST J ADMIN Rule 2.425(a)(3), Brokerage account number, Insurance policy account number, Loan account number, Customer account number, or Patient or health care number;

v. A truncated version of any: Email address, Computer user name, Password, or Personal identification number (PIN); and

vi. A truncated version of any other sensitive information as provided by court order. FL ST J ADMIN Rule 2.425(a).

b. *Exceptions.* FL ST J ADMIN Rule 2.425(a) does not apply to the following:

i. An account number which identifies the property alleged to be the subject of a proceeding;

ii. The record of an administrative or agency proceeding;

iii. The record in appellate or review proceedings;

iv. The birth date of a minor whenever the birth date is necessary for the court to establish or maintain subject matter jurisdiction;

v. The name of a minor in any order relating to parental responsibility, time-sharing, or child support;

vi. The name of a minor in any document or order affecting the minor's ownership of real property;

vii. The birth date of a party in a writ of attachment or notice to payor;

viii. In traffic and criminal proceedings: a pro se filing; a court filing that is related to a criminal matter or investigation and that is prepared before the filing of a criminal charge or is not filed as part of any docketed criminal case; an arrest or search warrant or any information in support thereof; a charging document and an affidavit or other documents filed in support of any charging document, including any driving records; a statement of particulars; discovery material introduced into evidence or otherwise filed with the court; and all information necessary for the proper issuance and execution of a subpoena duces tecum;

ix. Information used by the clerk for case maintenance purposes or the courts for case management purposes; and

x. Information which is relevant and material to an issue before the court. FL ST J ADMIN Rule 2.425(b).

c. *Remedies.* Upon motion by a party or interested person or sua sponte by the court, the court may order remedies, sanctions or both for a violation of FL ST J ADMIN Rule 2.425(a). Following notice and an opportunity to respond, the court may impose sanctions if such filing was not made in good faith. FL ST J ADMIN Rule 2.425(c).

d. *Motions not restricted.* FL ST J ADMIN Rule 2.425 does not restrict a party's right to move for protective order, to move to file documents under seal, or to request a determination of the confidentiality of records. FL ST J ADMIN Rule 2.425(d).

e. *Application.* FL ST J ADMIN Rule 2.425 does not affect the application of constitutional provisions, statutes, or rules of court regarding confidential information or access to public information. FL ST J ADMIN Rule 2.425(e).

F. Filing and Service Requirements

1. *Filing requirements.* All original documents must be filed with the court either before service or

immediately thereafter, unless otherwise provided for by general law or other rules. If the original of any bond or other document is not placed in the court file, a certified copy must be so placed by the clerk. FL ST J ADMIN Rule 2.516(d). All documents shall be filed in conformity with the requirements of FL ST J ADMIN Rule 2.525. FL ST RCP Rule 1.080(b). All documents filed in any court shall be filed by electronic transmission in accordance with FL ST J ADMIN Rule 2.525. "Documents" means pleadings, motions, petitions, memoranda, briefs, notices, exhibits, declarations, affidavits, orders, judgments, decrees, writs, opinions, and any other paper or writing submitted to a court. FL ST J ADMIN Rule 2.520(a). All documents that are court records, as defined in FL ST J ADMIN Rule 2.430(a)(1), must be filed by electronic transmission, provided that: (1) the clerk has the ability to accept and retain such documents; (2) the clerk or the chief judge of the circuit has requested permission to accept documents filed by electronic transmission; and (3) the supreme court has entered an order granting permission to the clerk to accept documents filed by electronic transmission. FL ST J ADMIN Rule 2.525(c)(1).

a. *Definition.* "Electronic transmission of documents" means the sending of information by electronic signals to, by or from a court or clerk, which when received can be transformed and stored or transmitted on paper, microfilm, magnetic storage device, optical imaging system, CD-ROM, flash drive, other electronic data storage system, server, case maintenance system ("CM"), electronic court filing ("ECF") system, statewide or local electronic portal ("e-portal"), or other electronic record keeping system authorized by the supreme court in a format sufficient to communicate the information on the original document in a readable format. Electronic transmission of documents includes electronic mail ("e-mail") and any internet-based transmission procedure, and may include procedures allowing for documents to be signed or verified by electronic means. FL ST J ADMIN Rule 2.525(a).
    i. The filing of documents with the court as required by the Florida Rules of Judicial Administration must be made by filing them with the clerk in accordance with FL ST J ADMIN Rule 2.525, except that the judge may permit documents to be filed with the judge, in which event the judge must note the filing date before him or her on the documents and transmit them to the clerk. The date of filing is that shown on the face of the document by the judge's notation or the clerk's time stamp, whichever is earlier. FL ST J ADMIN Rule 2.516(e).
b. *Application.* Any court or clerk of the court may accept the electronic transmission of documents for filing after the clerk, together with input from the chief judge of the circuit, has obtained approval of the procedures and program for doing so from the Supreme Court of Florida. FL ST J ADMIN Rule 2.525(b).
    i. *E-filing mandatory.* All attorneys of record shall be required to follow the protocol set forth in FL ST 11 J CIR 1-09-13-A1(4). FL ST 11 J CIR 1-09-13-A1(3).
c. *Exceptions*
    i. Paper documents and other submissions may be manually submitted to the clerk or court:
        - When the clerk does not have the ability to accept and retain documents by electronic filing or has not had ECF Procedures approved by the supreme court;
        - For filing by any self-represented party or any self-represented nonparty unless specific ECF Procedures provide a means to file documents electronically. However, any self-represented nonparty that is a governmental or public agency and any other agency, partnership, corporation, or business entity acting on behalf of any governmental or public agency may file documents by electronic transmission if such entity has the capability of filing documents electronically;
        - For filing by attorneys excused from e-mail service in accordance with FL ST J ADMIN Rule 2.516(b);
        - When submitting evidentiary exhibits or filing non-documentary materials;
        - When the filing involves documents in excess of twenty-five (25) megabytes (25MB) in size. For such filings, documents may be transmitted using an electronic storage medium that the clerk has the ability to accept, which may include a CD-ROM, flash drive, or similar storage medium;

- When filed in open court, as permitted by the court;
- When paper filing is permitted by any approved statewide or local ECF procedures; and
- If any court determines that justice so requires. FL ST J ADMIN Rule 2.525(d).

ii. Any document in paper form submitted under FL ST J ADMIN Rule 2.525(d) is filed when it is received by the clerk or court and the clerk shall immediately thereafter convert any filed paper document to an electronic document. "Convert to an electronic document" means optically capturing an image of a paper document and using character recognition software to recover as much of the document's text as practicable and then indexing and storing the document in the official court file. FL ST J ADMIN Rule 2.525(c)(4).

iii. Any storage medium submitted under FL ST J ADMIN Rule 2.525(d)(5) is filed when received by the clerk or court and the clerk shall immediately thereafter transfer the electronic documents from the storage device to the official court file. FL ST J ADMIN Rule 2.525(c)(5).

iv. If the filer of any paper document authorized under FL ST J ADMIN Rule 2.525(d) provides a self-addressed, postage-paid envelope for return of the paper document after it is converted to electronic form by the clerk, the clerk shall place the paper document in the envelope and deposit it in the mail. Except when a paper document is required to be maintained, the clerk may recycle any filed paper document that is not to be returned to the filer. FL ST J ADMIN Rule 2.525(c)(6).

v. The clerk may convert any paper document filed before the effective date of FL ST J ADMIN Rule 2.525 to an electronic document. Unless the clerk is required to maintain the paper document, if the paper document has been converted to an electronic document by the clerk, the paper document is no longer part of the official court file and may be removed and recycled. FL ST J ADMIN Rule 2.525(c)(7).

d. *Official court file.* For information on what constitutes the official court file, please see FL ST J ADMIN Rule 2.525(c)(2), FL ST J ADMIN Rule 2.525(c)(3).

e. *Administration.* All attorneys, parties, or other persons using this rule to file documents are required to make arrangements with the court or clerk for the payment of any charges authorized by general law or the supreme court before filing any document by electronic transmission. FL ST J ADMIN Rule 2.525(f)(2).

f. *Filing date.* The filing date for an electronically transmitted document is the date and time that such filing is acknowledged by an electronic stamp or otherwise, pursuant to any procedure set forth in any ECF Procedures approved by the supreme court, or the date the last page of such filing is received by the court or clerk. FL ST J ADMIN Rule 2.525(f)(3).

g. *Accessibility.* All documents transmitted in any electronic form under FL ST J ADMIN Rule 2.525 must comply with the accessibility requirements of FL ST J ADMIN Rule 2.526. FL ST J ADMIN Rule 2.525(g).

2. *Service requirements.* Every pleading subsequent to the initial pleading, all orders, and every other document filed in the action must be served in conformity with the requirements of FL ST J ADMIN Rule 2.516. FL ST RCP Rule 1.080(a).

a. *Service; When required.* Unless the court otherwise orders, or a statute or supreme court administrative order specifies a different means of service, every pleading subsequent to the initial pleading and every other document filed in any court proceeding, except applications for witness subpoenas and documents served by formal notice or required to be served in the manner provided for service of formal notice, must be served in accordance with FL ST J ADMIN Rule 2.516 on each party. No service need be made on parties against whom a default has been entered, except that pleadings asserting new or additional claims against them must be served in the manner provided for service of summons. FL ST J ADMIN Rule 2.516(a).

b. *Service; How made.* When service is required or permitted to be made upon a party represented by an attorney, service must be made upon the attorney unless service upon the party is ordered by the court. FL ST J ADMIN Rule 2.516(b).

i. *Service by electronic mail ("e-mail").* All documents required or permitted to be served on

another party must be served by e-mail, unless FL ST J ADMIN Rule 2.516 otherwise provides. When, in addition to service by e-mail, the sender also utilizes another means of service provided for in FL ST J ADMIN Rule 2.516(b)(2), any differing time limits and other provisions applicable to that other means of service control. FL ST J ADMIN Rule 2.516(b)(1). Any document electronically transmitted to a court or clerk must also be served on all parties and interested persons in accordance with the applicable rules of court. FL ST J ADMIN Rule 2.525(e)(2).

- *Service on attorneys.* Upon appearing in a proceeding, an attorney must serve a designation of a primary e-mail address and may designate no more than two (2) secondary e-mail addresses. Thereafter, service must be directed to all designated e-mail addresses in that proceeding. Every document filed by an attorney thereafter must include the primary e-mail address of that attorney and any secondary e-mail addresses. If an attorney does not designate any e-mail address for service, documents may be served on that attorney at the e-mail address on record with The Florida Bar. FL ST J ADMIN Rule 2.516(b)(1)(A).
- *Exception to e-mail service on attorneys.* Service by an attorney on another attorney must be made by e-mail unless excused by the court. Upon motion by an attorney demonstrating that the attorney has no e-mail account and lacks access to the Internet at the attorney's office, the court may excuse the attorney from the requirements of e-mail service. Service on and by an attorney excused by the court from e-mail service must be by the means provided in FL ST J ADMIN Rule 2.516(b)(2). FL ST J ADMIN Rule 2.516(b)(1)(B).
- *Service on and by parties not represented by an attorney.* Any party not represented by an attorney may serve a designation of a primary e-mail address and also may designate no more than two (2) secondary e-mail addresses to which service must be directed in that proceeding by the means provided in FL ST J ADMIN Rule 2.516(b)(1). If a party not represented by an attorney does not designate an e-mail address for service in a proceeding, service on and by that party must be by the means provided in FL ST J ADMIN Rule 2.516(b)(2). FL ST J ADMIN Rule 2.516(b)(1)(C).
- *Time of service.* Service by e-mail is complete when it is sent. FL ST J ADMIN Rule 2.516(b)(1)(D). An e-mail is deemed served on the date it is sent. FL ST J ADMIN Rule 2.516(b)(1)(D)(i). If the sender learns that the e-mail did not reach the address of the person to be served, the sender must immediately send another copy by e-mail, or by a means authorized by FL ST J ADMIN Rule 2.516(b)(2). FL ST J ADMIN Rule 2.516(b)(1)(D)(ii). E-mail service is treated as service by mail for the computation of time. FL ST J ADMIN Rule 2.516(b)(1)(D)(iii).
- *Specifics of e-mail filing.* In addition to providing proper service pursuant to FL ST RCP Rule 1.080(b), courtesy copies of the Motion and Memorandum of Law for the Uniform Motion Calendar (e.g., Notice of Hearing, Motions, Exhibits, submitted case law, and other hearing specific documents) must be electronically attached to an email using either Microsoft Word or WordPerfect format (not as a PDF document) and sent via email to (a) The Court at its designated e-mail address; (b) Opposing counsel at their fax number as provided to The Florida Bar (see The Florida Bar's website and then click on "Find a Lawyer") or any other fax number provided on a Pleading, Motion to Quash Service, Motion to Dismiss Complaint or Notice of Appearance, whichever is most recent; and (c) Pro se parties at their last known fax number or any other fax number provided on a Pleading, Motion to Quash Service, Motion to Dismiss Complaint or Notice of Appearance, whichever is most recent. FL ST 11 J CIR 1-09-13-A1(4)(b)(i).
- *E-mail subject line.* The subject line of the email must contain only the numeric motion calendar hearing date using the following format: mm/dd/yy (two (2) digit month forward slash; two (2) digit day forward slash; two (2) digit year). For example: 06/15/10. FL ST 11 J CIR 1-09-13-A1(4)(b)(iii).

ii. *Format of e-mail for service.* Service of a document by e-mail is made by attaching a copy of the document in PDF format to an e-mail sent to all addresses designated by the attorney or party. FL ST J ADMIN Rule 2.516(b)(1)(E).

- All documents served by e-mail must be attached to an e-mail message containing a

subject line beginning with the words "SERVICE OF COURT DOCUMENT" in all capital letters, followed by the case number of the proceeding in which the documents are being served. FL ST J ADMIN Rule 2.516(b)(1)(E)(i).

- The body of the e-mail must identify the court in which the proceeding is pending, the case number, the name of the initial party on each side, the title of each document served with that e-mail, and the sender's name and telephone number. FL ST J ADMIN Rule 2.516(b)(1)(E)(ii).
- Any document served by e-mail may be signed by the "/s/" format, as long as the filed original is signed in accordance with the applicable rule of procedure. FL ST J ADMIN Rule 2.516(b)(1)(E)(iii).
- Any e-mail which, together with its attached documents, exceeds five megabytes (5MB) in size, must be divided and sent as separate e-mails, no one of which may exceed five megabytes (5MB) in size and each of which must be sequentially numbered in the subject line. FL ST J ADMIN Rule 2.516(b)(1)(E)(iv).

iii. *Service by other means.* In addition to, and not in lieu of, service by e-mail, service may also be made upon attorneys by any of the means specified in FL ST J ADMIN Rule 2.516(b)(2). Service on and by all parties who are not represented by an attorney and who do not designate an e-mail address, and on and by all attorneys excused from e-mail service, must be made by delivering a copy of the document or by mailing it to the party or attorney at their last known address or, if no address is known, by leaving it with the clerk of the court. Service by mail is complete upon mailing. Delivery of a copy within FL ST J ADMIN Rule 2.516 is complete upon:

- Handing it to the attorney or to the party,
- Leaving it at the attorney's or party's office with a clerk or other person in charge thereof,
- If there is no one in charge, leaving it in a conspicuous place therein,
- If the office is closed or the person to be served has no office, leaving it at the person's usual place of abode with some person of his or her family above fifteen (15) years of age and informing such person of the contents, or
- Transmitting it by facsimile to the attorney's or party's office with a cover sheet containing the sender's name, firm, address, telephone number, and facsimile number, and the number of pages transmitted. When service is made by facsimile, a copy must also be served by any other method permitted by FL ST J ADMIN Rule 2.516. Facsimile service occurs when transmission is complete. FL ST J ADMIN Rule 2.516(b)(2)(A) through FL ST J ADMIN Rule 2.516(b)(2)(E).
- Service by delivery after 5:00 p.m. must be deemed to have been made by mailing on the date of delivery. FL ST J ADMIN Rule 2.516(b)(2)(F).
- If a scheduling attorney or a scheduling pro se party does not have a fax number, then a courtesy copy of Motions and Proposed orders must be sent as an attachment to the service of process required pursuant to FL ST RCP Rule 1.080(b). FL ST 11 J CIR 1-09-13-A1(4)(b)(ii).

c. *Service; Numerous defendants.* In actions when the parties are unusually numerous, the court may regulate the service contemplated by the Florida Rules of Judicial Administration on motion or on its own initiative in such manner as may be found to be just and reasonable. FL ST J ADMIN Rule 2.516(c).

d. *Service by clerk.* Service of notices and other documents required to be made by the clerk must also be done as provided in FL ST J ADMIN Rule 2.516(b). FL ST J ADMIN Rule 2.516(g).

G. Hearings

1. *Hearing on motion for summary judgment.* The summary judgment rule does not provide the trial court with discretion to decide whether a hearing is required. A failure to hold a hearing on a motion for summary judgment violates due process as well as rule of procedure governing summary judgment

procedure. Kozich v. Hartford Ins. Co. of Midwest, 609 So.2d 147, 148 (Fla. 4th DCA 1992); FL-RCPF R 1.510(102).

2. *Summary judgment consideration at pretrial conference.* A summary judgment can be granted at the pretrial conference. The standard and procedure for granting summary judgment is the same at a pretrial conference as at other times. The notice time for a pretrial conference and for service of a motion for summary judgment is the same, so summary judgment can be entered at the conference if no genuine issue of material fact exists. FL-PRACPROC § 19:4.

3. *Communication equipment*

   a. *Definition.* Communication equipment means a conference telephone or other electronic device that permits all those appearing or participating to hear and speak to each other, provided that all conversation of all parties is audible to all persons present. FL ST J ADMIN Rule 2.530(a).

   b. *Use by all parties.* A county or circuit court judge may, upon the court's own motion or upon the written request of a party, direct that communication equipment be used for a motion hearing, pretrial conference, or a status conference. A judge must give notice to the parties and consider any objections they may have to the use of communication equipment before directing that communication equipment be used. The decision to use communication equipment over the objection of parties will be in the sound discretion of the trial court, except as noted below. FL ST J ADMIN Rule 2.530(b).

   c. *Use only by requesting party.* A county or circuit court judge may, upon the written request of a party upon reasonable notice to all other parties, permit a requesting party to participate through communication equipment in a scheduled motion hearing; however, any such request (except in criminal, juvenile, and appellate proceedings) must be granted, absent a showing of good cause to deny the same, where the hearing is set for not longer than fifteen (15) minutes. FL ST J ADMIN Rule 2.530(c).

   d. *Testimony*

      i. *Generally.* A county or circuit court judge, general magistrate, special magistrate, or hearing officer may allow testimony to be taken through communication equipment if all parties consent or if permitted by another applicable rule of procedure. FL ST J ADMIN Rule 2.530(d)(1).

      ii. *Procedure.* Any party desiring to present testimony through communication equipment shall, prior to the hearing or trial at which the testimony is to be presented, contact all parties to determine whether each party consents to this form of testimony. The party seeking to present the testimony shall move for permission to present testimony through communication equipment, which motion shall set forth good cause as to why the testimony should be allowed in this form. FL ST J ADMIN Rule 2.530(d)(2).

      iii. *Oath.* Testimony may be taken through communication equipment only if a notary public or other person authorized to administer oaths in the witness's jurisdiction is present with the witness and administers the oath consistent with the laws of the jurisdiction. FL ST J ADMIN Rule 2.530(d)(3).

      iv. *Confrontation rights.* In juvenile and criminal proceedings the defendant must make an informed waiver of any confrontation rights that may be abridged by the use of communication equipment. FL ST J ADMIN Rule 2.530(d)(4).

      v. *Video testimony.* If the testimony to be presented utilizes video conferencing or comparable two-way visual capabilities, the court in its discretion may modify the procedures set forth in FL ST J ADMIN Rule 2.530 to accommodate the technology utilized. FL ST J ADMIN Rule 2.530(d)(5).

   e. *Burden of expense.* The cost for the use of the communication equipment is the responsibility of the requesting party unless otherwise directed by the court. FL ST J ADMIN Rule 2.530(e).

4. *Time allotted for hearing.* Each party may set only one five (5) minute motion per case. Multiple motions must be specially set or set on different motion calendars (one five (5) minute motion per party per case),

so as not to encroach on the time the Court is allotting for other litigants/attorneys. Consequently, the parties are advised to use good faith efforts to resolve the issues set forth in the motion prior to the setting of a motion; coordinate the date and time of the hearing; and confirm that the hearing shall require no more than five (5) minutes (if the hearing will require more than five (5) minutes, then it must be a Special Set Hearing). FL ST 11 J CIR 1-09-13-A1(4)(b)(i). For information on Special Set Hearings, refer to FL ST 11 J CIR 1-09-13-A1(4)(c).

5. *Hearing cancellation policy.* Should any scheduled hearing become unnecessary or have to be cancelled, the scheduling attorney or scheduling pro se party shall immediately, but, not later than by Noon on the business day prior to the hearing date and time, send an email to the court's designated e-mail address regarding the cancellation of the Motion Calendar hearing with an electronically attached Notice of Cancellation formatted in the same manner (using Microsoft Word or Word Perfect) as the email that scheduled the Motion Calendar hearing and in the same manner as the Motions and Notices. FL ST 11 J CIR 1-09-13-A1(4)(b)(vii).

H. Forms

1. Official Motion for Summary Judgment Forms for Florida

a. Caption. FL ST RCP Form 1.901.

b. Notice of compliance when constitutional challenge is brought. FL ST RCP Form 1.975.

2. Motion for Summary Judgment Forms for Florida

a. Motion for summary judgment; By plaintiff. FL-PP § 6:9.

b. Motion for summary judgment; By defendant. FL-PP § 6:10.

c. Affidavit; Supporting motion for summary judgment; By plaintiff's attorney. FL-PP § 6:11.

d. Affidavit; Opposing motion for summary judgment; By defendant's attorney. FL-PP § 6:12.

e. Affidavit; Opposing motion for summary judgment; By party; Inability to present facts. FL-PP § 6:13.

f. Order; Establishing uncontroverted facts and stating issues requiring further determination. FL-PP § 6:14.

g. Summary judgment. FL-PP § 6:15.

h. Motion; Summary judgment, by defendant. FL-PRACFORM § 7:190.

i. Motion; Summary judgment, by plaintiff. FL-PRACFORM § 7:191.

j. Motion; Summary judgment, partial, by defendant. FL-PRACFORM § 7:192.

k. Motion; Summary judgment, part of claim. FL-PRACFORM § 7:193.

l. Form for plaintiff's motion for summary judgment. FL-RCPF R 1.510(128).

m. Form for notice of motion for summary judgment by plaintiff. FL-RCPF R 1.510(129).

n. Form for notice of cross-motion for summary judgment by plaintiff. FL-RCPF R 1.510(130).

o. Form for order denying motion for summary judgment and specifying uncontroverted facts. FL-RCPF R 1.510(304).

p. Form for motion for partial summary judgment. FL-RCPF R 1.510(305).

q. Form for motion for partial summary judgment; Affirmative defenses. FL-RCPF R 1.510(305.1).

I. Checklist

(I) ❑ Matters to be considered by moving party

(a) ❑ Required documents

(1) ❑ Notice of hearing/Motion

(2) ❑ Certificate of service

(b) ❑ Supplemental documents

(1) ❑ Affidavits

- (2) ❑ Other evidence
- (3) ❑ Proposed order
- (4) ❑ Notice of constitutional question

(c) ❑ Time for making motion

- (1) ❑ By the plaintiff, after the expiration of twenty (20) days from the commencement of the action (claimant), or after service of a motion for summary judgment by the adverse party
- (2) ❑ By the defending party at any time
- (3) ❑ The motion for summary judgment must be served at least twenty (20) days before the time fixed for the hearing

(II) ❑ Matters to be considered by opposing party

(a) ❑ Required documents

- (1) ❑ Response to motion
- (2) ❑ Certificate of service

(b) ❑ Supplemental documents

- (1) ❑ Affidavits
- (2) ❑ Notice of evidence relied upon
- (3) ❑ Other evidence
- (4) ❑ Proposed order
- (5) ❑ Notice of constitutional question

(c) ❑ Time for service and filing of opposition

- (1) ❑ The adverse party shall identify, by notice mailed to the movant's attorney at least five (5) days prior to the day of the hearing, or delivered no later than 5:00 p.m. two (2) business days prior to the day of the hearing, any summary judgment evidence on which the adverse party relies
- (2) ❑ To the extent that summary judgment evidence has not already been filed with the court, the adverse party shall serve a copy on the movant by mail at least five (5) days prior to the day of the hearing, or by delivery to the movant's attorney no later than 5:00 p.m. two (2) business days prior to the day of hearing

Motions, Oppositions and Replies
Motion for Sanctions

Document Last Updated January 2013

A. Applicable Rules

1. *State rules*

   a. Attorney's fee; Sanctions for raising unsupported claims or defenses; Exceptions; Service of motions; Damages for delay of litigation. FL ST § 57.105.

   b. Administrative Procedure Act. FL ST § 120.50; FL ST § 120.52; FL ST § 120.68; FL ST § 120.81.

   c. Offer of judgment and demand for judgment. FL ST § 768.79.

   d. Proposals for settlement. FL ST RCP Rule 1.442.

   e. Motions for costs and attorneys' fees. FL ST RCP Rule 1.525.

   f. Rules of court. FL ST RCP Rule 1.010; FL ST J ADMIN Rule 2.110.

   g. Nonverification of pleadings. FL ST RCP Rule 1.030.

   h. Service and filing of pleadings, orders, and documents. FL ST RCP Rule 1.080.

i. Time. FL ST RCP Rule 1.090.

j. Pleadings and motions. FL ST RCP Rule 1.100.

k. Motions. FL ST RCP Rule 1.160.

l. Relief from judgment, decrees, or orders. FL ST RCP Rule 1.540.

m. Mediation and arbitration. FL ST RCP Rule 1.700; FL ST RCP Rule 1.710; FL ST RCP Rule 1.720; FL ST RCP Rule 1.730; FL ST RCP Rule 1.750; FL ST RCP Rule 1.800; FL ST RCP Rule 1.810; FL ST RCP Rule 1.820; FL ST RCP Rule 1.830.

n. Forms. FL ST RCP Rule 1.900.

o. Minimization of the filing of sensitive information. FL ST J ADMIN Rule 2.425.

p. Retention of court records. FL ST J ADMIN Rule 2.430.

q. Foreign attorneys. FL ST J ADMIN Rule 2.510.

r. Signature of attorneys and parties. FL ST J ADMIN Rule 2.515.

s. Paper. FL ST J ADMIN Rule 2.520.

t. Electronic filing. FL ST J ADMIN Rule 2.525.

u. Accessibility of information and technology. FL ST J ADMIN Rule 2.526.

v. Communication equipment. FL ST J ADMIN Rule 2.530.

w. Court reporting. FL ST J ADMIN Rule 2.535.

x. Requests for accommodations by persons with disabilities. FL ST J ADMIN Rule 2.540.

2. *Local rules*

   a. Establishment of 11th Circuit Homestead Access to Mediation Program ("CHAMP") for case management of residential foreclosure cases in the Eleventh Judicial Circuit of Florida. FL ST 11 J CIR 1-09-08.

   b. Enlargement and expansion of the current pilot project for electronic submissions of courtesy copies for uniform motion calendar and requests for special set hearings, emergency motions, and proposed orders. FL ST 11 J CIR 1-09-13-A1.

B. Timing

1. *Motion for sanctions.* A motion by a party seeking sanctions under FL ST § 57.105 must be served but may not be filed with or presented to the court unless, within twenty one (21) days after service of the motion, the challenged paper, claim, defense, contention, allegation, or denial is not withdrawn or appropriately corrected. FL ST § 57.105(4).

2. *Sanctions in relation to proposals for settlement.* Any party seeking sanctions pursuant to applicable Florida law, based on the failure of the proposal's recipient to accept a proposal, shall do so by serving a motion in accordance with FL ST RCP Rule 1.525. FL ST RCP Rule 1.442(g). Any party seeking a judgment taxing costs, attorneys' fees, or both shall serve a motion no later than thirty (30) days after filing of the judgment, including a judgment of dismissal, or the service of a notice of voluntary dismissal, which judgment or notice concludes the action as to that party. FL ST RCP Rule 1.525.

3. *General motion timing.* A copy of any written motion which may not be heard ex parte and a copy of the notice of the hearing thereof shall be served a reasonable time before the time specified for the hearing. FL ST RCP Rule 1.090(d).

4. *Computation of time*

   a. *Generally.* Computation of time shall be governed by FL ST J ADMIN Rule 2.514. FL ST RCP Rule 1.090(a). The following rules apply in computing time periods specified in any rule of procedure, local rule, court order, or statute that does not specify a method of computing time. FL ST J ADMIN Rule 2.514(a).

      i. *Period stated in days or a longer unit.* When the period is stated in days or a longer unit of time (A) exclude the day of the event that triggers the period; (B) count every day, including intermediate Saturdays, Sundays, and legal holidays; and (C) include the last day of the period, but if the last day is a Saturday, Sunday, or legal holiday, or falls within any period of time extended through an order of the chief justice under FL ST J ADMIN Rule 2.205(a)(2)(B)(iv), the period continues to run until the end of the next day that is not a Saturday, Sunday, or legal holiday and does not fall within any period of time extended through an order of the chief justice. FL ST J ADMIN Rule 2.514(a)(1).

ii. *Period stated in hours.* When the period is stated in hours (A) begin counting immediately on the occurrence of the event that triggers the period; (B) count every hour, including hours during intermediate Saturdays, Sundays, and legal holidays; and (C) if the period would end on a Saturday, Sunday, or legal holiday, or during any period of time extended through an order of the chief justice under FL ST J ADMIN Rule 2.205(a)(2)(B)(iv), the period continues to run until the same time on the next day that is not a Saturday, Sunday, or legal holiday and does not fall within any period of time extended through an order of the chief justice. FL ST J ADMIN Rule 2.514(a)(2).

iii. *Period stated in days less than seven (7) days.* When the period stated in days is less than seven (7) days, intermediate Saturdays, Sundays, and legal holidays shall be excluded in the computation. FL ST J ADMIN Rule 2.514(a)(3).

iv. *"Last day" defined.* Unless a different time is set by a statute, local rule, or court order, the last day ends (A) for electronic filing or for service by any means, at midnight; and (B) for filing by other means, when the clerk's office is scheduled to close. FL ST J ADMIN Rule 2.514(a)(4).

v. *"Next day" defined.* The "next day" is determined by continuing to count forward when the period is measured after an event and backward when measured before an event. FL ST J ADMIN Rule 2.514(a)(5).

vi. *"Legal holiday" defined.* "Legal holiday" means (A) the day set aside by FL ST § 110.117, for observing New Year's Day, Martin Luther King, Jr.'s Birthday, Memorial Day, Independence Day, Labor Day, Veterans' Day, Thanksgiving Day, the Friday after Thanksgiving Day, or Christmas Day, and (B) any day observed as a holiday by the clerk's office or as designated by the chief judge. FL ST J ADMIN Rule 2.514(a)(6).

b. *Additional time after service by mail or e-mail.* When a party may or must act within a specified time after service and service is made by mail or e-mail, five (5) days are added after the period that would otherwise expire under FL ST J ADMIN Rule 2.514(a). FL ST J ADMIN Rule 2.514(b).

c. *Enlargement.* When an act is required or allowed to be done at or within a specified time by order of court, by the Florida Rules of Civil Procedure, or by notice given thereunder, for cause shown the court at any time in its discretion (1) with or without notice, may order the period enlarged if request therefor is made before the expiration of the period originally prescribed or as extended by a previous order, or (2) upon motion made and notice after the expiration of the specified period, may permit the act to be done when failure to act was the result of excusable neglect, but it may not extend the time for making a motion for new trial, for rehearing, or to alter or amend a judgment; making a motion for relief from a judgment under FL ST RCP Rule 1.540(b); taking an appeal or filing a petition for certiorari; or making a motion for a directed verdict. FL ST RCP Rule 1.090(b).

d. *Unaffected by expiration of term.* The period of time provided for the doing of any act or the taking of any proceeding shall not be affected or limited by the continued existence or expiration of a term of court. The continued existence or expiration of a term of court in no way affects the power of a court to do any act or take any proceeding in any action which is or has been pending before it. FL ST RCP Rule 1.090(c).

C. General Requirements

1. *Motions generally*

a. *Contents.* An application to the court for an order shall be by motion which shall be made in writing unless made during a hearing or trial, shall state with particularity the grounds therefor, and shall set forth the relief or order sought. The requirement of writing is fulfilled if the motion is stated in a written notice of the hearing of the motion. All notices of hearing shall specify each motion or other matter to be heard. FL ST RCP Rule 1.100(b).

b. *Particularity requirement.* The court considers a motion in the light of the substantive law, rule or statute to make its determination. Some rules require a statement of the grounds for a motion under the rule. Failure to give the grounds will result in denial of the motion. This should be the result in all situations when the ground for the motion is not inherent in the rule. FL-PRACPROC § 9:3. The requirement is nevertheless an important one, first because of the due process notice rights of the respondent, as well as for the assistance it provides to the court in its preparation for the hearing or, absent a hearing, for disposition. 4 FLPRAC R 1.100.

2. *Motion for sanctions*

   a. *Sanctions for raising unsupported claims or defenses*

      i. *No material facts; No law supporting material facts.* Upon the court's initiative or motion of any party, the court shall award a reasonable attorney's fee, including prejudgment interest, to be paid to the prevailing party in equal amounts by the losing party and the losing party's attorney on any claim or defense at any time during a civil proceeding or action in which the court finds that the losing party or the losing party's attorney knew or should have known that a claim or defense when initially presented to the court or at any time before trial was not supported by the material facts necessary to establish the claim or defense; or would not be supported by the application of then-existing law to those material facts. FL ST § 57.105(1).

      ii. *Unreasonable delay.* At any time in any civil proceeding or action in which the moving party proves by a preponderance of the evidence that any action taken by the opposing party, including, but not limited to, the filing of any pleading or part thereof, the assertion of or response to any discovery demand, the assertion of any claim or defense, or the response to any request by any other party, was taken primarily for the purpose of unreasonable delay, the court shall award damages to the moving party for its reasonable expenses incurred in obtaining the order, which may include attorney's fees, and other loss resulting from the improper delay. FL ST § 57.105(2).

      iii. *Limit on monetary sanctions.* Notwithstanding FL ST § 57.105(1) and FL ST § 57.105(2), monetary sanctions may not be awarded:

         - Under FL ST § 57.105(1)(b) if the court determines that the claim or defense was initially presented to the court as a good faith argument for the extension, modification, or reversal of existing law or the establishment of new law, as it applied to the material facts, with a reasonable expectation of success. FL ST § 57.105(3)(a).
         - Under FL ST § 57.105(1)(a) or FL ST § 57.105(1)(b) against the losing party's attorney if he or she has acted in good faith, based on the representations of his or her client as to the existence of those material facts. FL ST § 57.105(3)(b).
         - Under FL ST § 57.105(1)(b) against a represented party. FL ST § 57.105(3)(c).
         - On the court's initiative under FL ST § 57.105(1) and FL ST § 57.105(2) unless sanctions are awarded before a voluntary dismissal or settlement of the claims made by or against the party that is, or whose attorneys are, to be sanctioned. FL ST § 57.105(3)(d).

      iv. *Other sanctions available.* The provisions of FL ST § 57.105 are supplemental to other sanctions or remedies available under law or under court rules. FL ST § 57.105(6).

      v. *Fees provided for in contract.* If a contract contains a provision allowing attorney's fees to a party when he or she is required to take any action to enforce the contract, the court may also allow reasonable attorney's fees to the other party when that party prevails in any action, whether as plaintiff or defendant, with respect to the contract. FL ST § 57.105(7) applies to any contract entered into on or after October 1, 1988. FL ST § 57.105(7).

   b. *Sanctions in relation to proposals for settlement*

      i. *Generally.* Any party seeking sanctions pursuant to applicable Florida law, based on the failure of the proposal's recipient to accept a proposal, shall do so by serving a motion in accordance with FL ST RCP Rule 1.525. FL ST RCP Rule 1.442(g). Any party seeking a judgment taxing costs, attorneys' fees, or both shall serve a motion no later than thirty (30) days after filing of the judgment, including a judgment of dismissal, or the service of a notice of voluntary dismissal, which judgment or notice concludes the action as to that party. FL ST RCP Rule 1.525.

ii. *Motion after judgment, voluntary or involuntary dismissal.* Upon motion made by the offeror within thirty (30) days after the entry of judgment or after voluntary or involuntary dismissal, the court shall determine the following:

- If a defendant serves an offer which is not accepted by the plaintiff, and if the judgment obtained by the plaintiff is at least twenty-five (25%) percent less than the amount of the offer, the defendant shall be awarded reasonable costs, including investigative expenses, and attorney's fees, calculated in accordance with the guidelines promulgated by the Supreme Court, incurred from the date the offer was served, and the court shall set off such costs in attorney's fees against the award. When such costs and attorney's fees total more than the amount of the judgment, the court shall enter judgment for the defendant against the plaintiff for the amount of the costs and fees, less the amount of the award to the plaintiff. FL ST § 768.79(6)(a).
- If a plaintiff serves an offer which is not accepted by the defendant, and if the judgment obtained by the plaintiff is at least twenty-five (25%) percent more than the amount of the offer, the plaintiff shall be awarded reasonable costs, including investigative expenses, and attorney's fees, calculated in accordance with the guidelines promulgated by the Supreme Court, incurred from the date the offer was served. FL ST § 768.79(6)(b).
- For purposes of the determination required by FL ST § 768.79(6)(a), the term "judgment obtained" means the amount of the net judgment entered, plus any postoffer collateral source payments received or due as of the date of the judgment, plus any postoffer settlement amounts by which the verdict was reduced. For purposes of the determination required by FL ST § 768.79(6)(b), the term "judgment obtained" means the amount of the net judgment entered, plus any postoffer settlement amounts by which the verdict was reduced. FL ST § 768.79(6).

iii. For further information please see FL ST § 768.79 and FL ST RCP Rule 1.442.

3. *Arbitration and mediation*

a. *Referral to arbitration and mediation.* Except as hereinafter provided or as otherwise prohibited by law, the presiding judge may enter an order referring all or any part of a contested civil matter to mediation or arbitration. The parties to any contested civil matter may file a written stipulation to mediate or arbitrate any issue between them at any time. Such stipulation shall be incorporated into the order of referral. FL ST RCP Rule 1.700(a).

i. In all residential foreclosure actions involving homestead properties filed on or after May 1, 2009, unless a stipulation is specifically invoked by the parties in writing within five (5) days of service of the complaint on the main defendant, the parties are deemed to have stipulated to referral of the mediation to the Collins Center pursuant to FL ST RCP Rule 1.720(f). FL ST 11 J CIR 1-09-08(2); FL ST 11 J CIR 1-09-08(3). FL ST 11 J CIR 1-09-08 constitutes a formal referral to mediation pursuant to the Florida Rules of Civil Procedure. FL ST 11 J CIR 1-09-08(2).

ii. For further information on referral to mediation, refer to FL ST 11 J CIR 1-09-08.

b. *Arbitration*

i. *Exclusions.* A civil action shall be ordered to arbitration or arbitration in conjunction with mediation upon stipulation of the parties. A civil action may be ordered to arbitration or arbitration in conjunction with mediation upon motion of any party or by the court, if the judge determines the action to be of such a nature that arbitration could be of benefit to the litigants or the court. FL ST RCP Rule 1.800.

- Under no circumstances may the following categories of actions be referred to arbitration: (1) bond estreatures; (2) habeas corpus or other extraordinary writs; (3) bond validations; (4) civil or criminal contempt; (5) such other matters as may be specified by order of the chief judge in the circuit. FL ST RCP Rule 1.800.

ii. For more information regarding arbitration, please see FL ST RCP Rule 1.810; FL ST RCP Rule 1.820; FL ST RCP Rule 1.830.

c. *Mediation.* For more information regarding mediation, please see FL ST RCP Rule 1.710; FL ST RCP Rule 1.720; FL ST RCP Rule 1.730; and FL ST RCP Rule 1.750.

4. *Rules of court*

a. *Rules of civil procedure.* The Florida Rules of Civil Procedure apply to all actions of a civil nature and all special statutory proceedings in the circuit courts and county courts except those to which the Florida Probate Rules, the Florida Family Law Rules of Procedure, or the Small Claims Rules apply. FL ST RCP Rule 1.010.

i. The form, content, procedure, and time for pleading in all special statutory proceedings shall be as prescribed by the statutes governing the proceeding unless the Florida Rules of Civil Procedure specifically provide to the contrary. FL ST RCP Rule 1.010.

ii. The Florida Rules of Civil Procedure shall be construed to secure the just, speedy, and inexpensive determination of every action. FL ST RCP Rule 1.010.

b. *Rules of judicial administration.* The Florida Rules of Judicial Administration shall apply to administrative matters in all courts to which the Florida Rules of Judicial Administration are applicable by their terms. The Florida Rules of Judicial Administration shall be construed to secure the speedy and inexpensive determination of every proceeding to which they are applicable. The Florida Rules of Judicial Administration shall supersede all conflicting rules and statutes. FL ST J ADMIN Rule 2.110.

D. Documents

1. *Required documents*

a. *Notice of hearing/Motion.* An application to the court for an order shall be by motion which shall be made in writing unless made during a hearing or trial, shall state with particularity the grounds therefor, and shall set forth the relief or order sought. The requirement of writing is fulfilled if the motion is stated in a written notice of the hearing of the motion. All notices of hearing shall specify each motion or other matter to be heard. FL ST RCP Rule 1.100(b).

i. *Notices to persons with disabilities.* See the Format section of this KeyRules document for further information.

b. *Certificate of service.* When any attorney certifies in substance: "I certify that a copy hereof has been furnished to (here insert name or names and addresses used for service) by (e-mail) (delivery) (mail) (fax) on .... (date) ....________________ Attorney" the certificate is taken as prima facie proof of such service in compliance with FL ST J ADMIN Rule 2.516. FL ST J ADMIN Rule 2.516(f).

2. *Supplemental documents*

a. *Proposed order.* The court may require that orders or judgments be prepared by a party, may require the party to furnish the court with stamped, addressed envelopes for service of the order or judgment, and may require that proposed orders and judgments be furnished to all parties before entry by the court of the order or judgment. FL ST J ADMIN Rule 2.516(h)(1). For additional information on the submission of proposed orders, refer to FL ST 11 J CIR 1-09-13-A1(e).

b. *Notice of constitutional question.* A party that files a pleading, written motion, or other paper drawing into question the constitutionality of a state statute or a county or municipal charter, ordinance, or franchise must promptly (1) file a notice of constitutional question stating the question and identifying the paper that raises it; and (2) serve the notice and the pleading, written motion, or other paper drawing into question the constitutionality of a state statute or a county or municipal charter, ordinance, or franchise on the Attorney General or the state attorney of the judicial circuit in which the action is pending, by either certified or registered mail. Service of the notice and pleading, written motion, or other paper does not require joinder of the Attorney General or the state attorney as a party to the action. FL ST RCP Rule 1.071.

E. Format

1. *Documents; Type and size.* Documents subject to the exceptions set forth in FL ST J ADMIN Rule

2.525(d) shall be filed on recycled paper measuring eight and one half by eleven (8 1/2 by 11) inches. For purposes of FL ST J ADMIN Rule 2.520, paper is recycled if it contains a minimum content of fifty (50) percent waste paper. Xerographic reduction of legal-size (eight and one half by fourteen (8 1/2 by 14) inches) documents to letter size (eight and one half by eleven (8 1/2 by 11) inches) is prohibited. All other documents filed by electronic transmission shall be filed in a format capable of being printed in a format consistent with the provisions of FL ST J ADMIN Rule 2.250. FL ST J ADMIN Rule 2.520(b).

a. *Exhibits.* Any exhibit or attachment filed with pleadings or papers may be filed in its original size. FL ST J ADMIN Rule 2.520(c).

b. *Recording space.* On all papers and documents prepared and filed by the court or by any party to a proceeding which are to be recorded in the public records of any county, including but not limited to final money judgments and notices of lis pendens, a three (3) inch by three (3) inch space at the top right-hand corner on the first page and a one (1) inch by three (3) inch space at the top right-hand corner on each subsequent page shall be left blank and reserved for use by the clerk of court. FL ST J ADMIN Rule 2.520(d).

i. *Exceptions to recording space.* Any papers or documents created by persons or entities over which the filing party has no control, including but not limited to wills, codicils, trusts, or other testamentary documents; documents prepared or executed by any public officer; documents prepared, executed, acknowledged, or proved outside of the State of Florida; or documents created by State or Federal government agencies, may be filed without the space required by FL ST J ADMIN Rule 2.520. FL ST J ADMIN Rule 2.520(e).

c. *Noncompliance.* No clerk of court is permitted to refuse to file any document or paper because of noncompliance with the Florida Rules of Judicial Administration. However, upon request of the clerk of court, noncomplying documents must be resubmitted in accordance with the formatting rules. FL ST J ADMIN Rule 2.520(f).

d. *Format of electronically filed documents.* Hyperlinks in the attachments, (not in the body of the email) are encouraged just as are submissions in Microsoft Word format. Electronic versions submitted in WordPerfect will be converted by the Court to Microsoft Word and there is no guarantee that the document will be converted without error. FL ST 11 J CIR 1-09-13-A1(4)(b)(v).

2. *Caption.* Every pleading, motion, order, judgment, or other paper shall have a caption containing the name of the court, the file number, and except for in rem proceedings, including forfeiture proceedings, the name of the first party on each side with an appropriate indication of other parties, and a designation identifying the party filing it and its nature or the nature of the order, as the case may be. In any in rem proceeding, every pleading, motion, order, judgment, or other paper shall have a caption containing the name of the court, the file number, the style "In re" (followed by the name or general description of the property), and a designation of the person or entity filing it and its nature or the nature of the order, as the case may be. In an in rem forfeiture proceeding, the style shall be "In re forfeiture of" (followed by the name of the general description of the property). All papers filed in the action shall be styled in such a manner as to indicate clearly the subject matter of the paper and the party requesting or obtaining relief. FL ST RCP Rule 1.100(c)(1).

a. *Caption of electronically filed documents.* All submitted documents shall be titled with the Court Case Number and the name/type of document using the following format: two (2) digit year followed by a hyphen with the sequential case number (e.g., 09-1; 91-12; 08-123; 07-1234; or 09-12345). Do not use zeros after the hyphen to fill in the sequential case number. FL ST 11 J CIR 1-09-13-A1(4)(a).

3. *Writing and written defined.* Writing or written means a document containing information, an application, or a stipulation. FL ST RCP Rule 1.080(c).

4. *Rule abbreviations*

a. The Florida Rules of Civil Procedure and shall be abbreviated as Fla.R.Civ.P. FL ST RCP Rule 1.010.

b. The Florida Rules of Judicial Administration shall be abbreviated as Fla. R. Jud. Admin. FL ST J ADMIN Rule 2.110.

5. *Nonverification.* Except when otherwise specifically provided by the Florida Rules of Civil Procedure or

an applicable statute, every pleading or other document of a party represented by an attorney need not be verified or accompanied by an affidavit. FL ST RCP Rule 1.030; FL ST J ADMIN Rule 2.515(a).

6. *Attorney signature*

   a. *Attorney signature.* Every pleading and other document of a party represented by an attorney shall be signed by at least one (1) attorney of record in that attorney's individual name whose current record Florida Bar address, telephone number, including area code, primary e-mail address and secondary e-mail addresses, if any, and Florida Bar number shall be stated, and who shall be duly licensed to practice law in Florida or who shall have received permission to appear in the particular case as provided in FL ST J ADMIN Rule 2.510. FL ST J ADMIN Rule 2.515(a).

      i. The attorney may be required by the court to give the address of, and to vouch for the attorney's authority to represent, the party. FL ST J ADMIN Rule 2.515(a).

      ii. The signature of an attorney shall constitute a certificate by the attorney that the attorney has read the pleading or other document; that to the best of the attorney's knowledge, information, and belief there is good ground to support it; and that it is not interposed for delay. FL ST J ADMIN Rule 2.515(a).

      iii. If a pleading is not signed or is signed with intent to defeat the purpose of FL ST J ADMIN Rule 2.515, it may be stricken and the action may proceed as though the pleading or other document had not been served. FL ST J ADMIN Rule 2.515(a).

   b. *Pro se litigant signature.* A party who is not represented by an attorney shall sign any pleading or other paper and state the party's address and telephone number, including area code. FL ST J ADMIN Rule 2.515(b).

   c. *Form of signature*

      i. The signatures required on pleadings and documents by FL ST J ADMIN Rule 2.515(a) and FL ST J ADMIN Rule 2.515(b) may be:

         - Original signatures;
         - Original signatures that have been reproduced by electronic means, such as on electronically transmitted documents or photocopied documents;
         - Electronic signatures using the "/s/," "s/," or "/s" formats by or at the direction of the person signing; or
         - Any other signature format authorized by general law, so long as the clerk where the proceeding is pending has the capability of receiving and has obtained approval from the Supreme Court of Florida to accept pleadings and documents with that signature format. FL ST J ADMIN Rule 2.515(c)(1).

      ii. An attorney, party, or other person who files a pleading or paper by electronic transmission that does not contain the original signature of that attorney, party, or other person shall file that identical pleading or paper in paper form containing an original signature of that attorney, party, or other person (hereinafter called the follow-up filing) immediately thereafter. The follow-up filing is not required if the Supreme Court of Florida has entered an order directing the clerk of court to discontinue accepting the follow-up filing. FL ST J ADMIN Rule 2.515(c)(2).

7. *Forms*

   a. *Process.* The forms of process, notice of lis pendens, and notice of action provided in the Florida Rules of Civil Procedure are sufficient. Variations from the forms do not void process or notices that are otherwise sufficient. FL ST RCP Rule 1.900(a).

   b. *Other forms.* The other forms provided in the Florida Rules of Civil Procedure are sufficient for the matters that are covered by them. So long as the substance is expressed without prolixity, the forms may be varied to meet the facts of a particular case. FL ST RCP Rule 1.900(b).

   c. *Formal matters.* Captions, except for the designation of the paper, are omitted from the forms provided in the Florida Rules of Civil Procedure. A general form of caption is the first form provided. Signatures are omitted from pleadings and motions. FL ST RCP Rule 1.900(c).

8. *Notices to persons with disabilities.* All notices of court proceedings to be held in a public facility, and all process compelling appearance at such proceedings, shall include the following statement in bold face, fourteen (14) point Times New Roman or Courier font: "If you are a person with a disability who needs any accommodation in order to participate in this proceeding, you are entitled, at no cost to you, to the provision of certain assistance. Please contact [identify applicable court personnel by name, address, and telephone number] at least seven (7) days before your scheduled court appearance, or immediately upon receiving this notification if the time before the scheduled appearance is less than seven (7) days; if you are hearing or voice impaired, call 711." FL ST J ADMIN Rule 2.540(c)(1).
9. *Minimization of the filing of sensitive information*
   a. *Limitations for court filings.* Unless authorized by FL ST J ADMIN Rule 2.425(b), statute, another rule of court, or the court orders otherwise, designated sensitive information filed with the court must be limited to the following format:
      i. The initials of a person known to be a minor;
      ii. The year of birth of a person's birth date;
      iii. No portion of any: Social security number, Bank account number, Credit card account number, Charge account number, or Debit account number;
      iv. The last four digits of any: Taxpayer identification number (TIN), Employee identification number, Driver's license number, Passport number, Telephone number, Financial account number, except as set forth in FL ST J ADMIN Rule 2.425(a)(3), Brokerage account number, Insurance policy account number, Loan account number, Customer account number, or Patient or health care number;
      v. A truncated version of any: Email address, Computer user name, Password, or Personal identification number (PIN); and
      vi. A truncated version of any other sensitive information as provided by court order. FL ST J ADMIN Rule 2.425(a).
   b. *Exceptions.* FL ST J ADMIN Rule 2.425(a) does not apply to the following:
      i. An account number which identifies the property alleged to be the subject of a proceeding;
      ii. The record of an administrative or agency proceeding;
      iii. The record in appellate or review proceedings;
      iv. The birth date of a minor whenever the birth date is necessary for the court to establish or maintain subject matter jurisdiction;
      v. The name of a minor in any order relating to parental responsibility, time-sharing, or child support;
      vi. The name of a minor in any document or order affecting the minor's ownership of real property;
      vii. The birth date of a party in a writ of attachment or notice to payor;
      viii. In traffic and criminal proceedings: a pro se filing; a court filing that is related to a criminal matter or investigation and that is prepared before the filing of a criminal charge or is not filed as part of any docketed criminal case; an arrest or search warrant or any information in support thereof; a charging document and an affidavit or other documents filed in support of any charging document, including any driving records; a statement of particulars; discovery material introduced into evidence or otherwise filed with the court; and all information necessary for the proper issuance and execution of a subpoena duces tecum;
      ix. Information used by the clerk for case maintenance purposes or the courts for case management purposes; and
      x. Information which is relevant and material to an issue before the court. FL ST J ADMIN Rule 2.425(b).
   c. *Remedies.* Upon motion by a party or interested person or sua sponte by the court, the court may order remedies, sanctions or both for a violation of FL ST J ADMIN Rule 2.425(a). Following notice

and an opportunity to respond, the court may impose sanctions if such filing was not made in good faith. FL ST J ADMIN Rule 2.425(c).

d. *Motions not restricted.* FL ST J ADMIN Rule 2.425 does not restrict a party's right to move for protective order, to move to file documents under seal, or to request a determination of the confidentiality of records. FL ST J ADMIN Rule 2.425(d).

e. *Application.* FL ST J ADMIN Rule 2.425 does not affect the application of constitutional provisions, statutes, or rules of court regarding confidential information or access to public information. FL ST J ADMIN Rule 2.425(e).

F. Filing and Service Requirements

1. *Filing requirements.* All original documents must be filed with the court either before service or immediately thereafter, unless otherwise provided for by general law or other rules. If the original of any bond or other document is not placed in the court file, a certified copy must be so placed by the clerk. FL ST J ADMIN Rule 2.516(d). All documents shall be filed in conformity with the requirements of FL ST J ADMIN Rule 2.525. FL ST RCP Rule 1.080(b). All documents filed in any court shall be filed by electronic transmission in accordance with FL ST J ADMIN Rule 2.525. "Documents" means pleadings, motions, petitions, memoranda, briefs, notices, exhibits, declarations, affidavits, orders, judgments, decrees, writs, opinions, and any other paper or writing submitted to a court. FL ST J ADMIN Rule 2.520(a). All documents that are court records, as defined in FL ST J ADMIN Rule 2.430(a)(1), must be filed by electronic transmission, provided that: (1) the clerk has the ability to accept and retain such documents; (2) the clerk or the chief judge of the circuit has requested permission to accept documents filed by electronic transmission; and (3) the supreme court has entered an order granting permission to the clerk to accept documents filed by electronic transmission. FL ST J ADMIN Rule 2.525(c)(1).

a. *Definition.* "Electronic transmission of documents" means the sending of information by electronic signals to, by or from a court or clerk, which when received can be transformed and stored or transmitted on paper, microfilm, magnetic storage device, optical imaging system, CD-ROM, flash drive, other electronic data storage system, server, case maintenance system ("CM"), electronic court filing ("ECF") system, statewide or local electronic portal ("e-portal"), or other electronic record keeping system authorized by the supreme court in a format sufficient to communicate the information on the original document in a readable format. Electronic transmission of documents includes electronic mail ("e-mail") and any internet-based transmission procedure, and may include procedures allowing for documents to be signed or verified by electronic means. FL ST J ADMIN Rule 2.525(a).

i. The filing of documents with the court as required by the Florida Rules of Judicial Administration must be made by filing them with the clerk in accordance with FL ST J ADMIN Rule 2.525, except that the judge may permit documents to be filed with the judge, in which event the judge must note the filing date before him or her on the documents and transmit them to the clerk. The date of filing is that shown on the face of the document by the judge's notation or the clerk's time stamp, whichever is earlier. FL ST J ADMIN Rule 2.516(e).

b. *Application.* Any court or clerk of the court may accept the electronic transmission of documents for filing after the clerk, together with input from the chief judge of the circuit, has obtained approval of the procedures and program for doing so from the Supreme Court of Florida. FL ST J ADMIN Rule 2.525(b).

i. *E-filing mandatory.* All attorneys of record shall be required to follow the protocol set forth in FL ST 11 J CIR 1-09-13-A1(4). FL ST 11 J CIR 1-09-13-A1(3).

c. *Exceptions*

i. Paper documents and other submissions may be manually submitted to the clerk or court:

- When the clerk does not have the ability to accept and retain documents by electronic filing or has not had ECF Procedures approved by the supreme court;
- For filing by any self-represented party or any self-represented nonparty unless specific ECF Procedures provide a means to file documents electronically. However, any self-represented nonparty that is a governmental or public agency and any other agency,

partnership, corporation, or business entity acting on behalf of any governmental or public agency may file documents by electronic transmission if such entity has the capability of filing documents electronically;

- For filing by attorneys excused from e-mail service in accordance with FL ST J ADMIN Rule 2.516(b);
- When submitting evidentiary exhibits or filing non-documentary materials;
- When the filing involves documents in excess of twenty-five (25) megabytes (25MB) in size. For such filings, documents may be transmitted using an electronic storage medium that the clerk has the ability to accept, which may include a CD-ROM, flash drive, or similar storage medium;
- When filed in open court, as permitted by the court;
- When paper filing is permitted by any approved statewide or local ECF procedures; and
- If any court determines that justice so requires. FL ST J ADMIN Rule 2.525(d).

ii. Any document in paper form submitted under FL ST J ADMIN Rule 2.525(d) is filed when it is received by the clerk or court and the clerk shall immediately thereafter convert any filed paper document to an electronic document. "Convert to an electronic document" means optically capturing an image of a paper document and using character recognition software to recover as much of the document's text as practicable and then indexing and storing the document in the official court file. FL ST J ADMIN Rule 2.525(c)(4).

iii. Any storage medium submitted under FL ST J ADMIN Rule 2.525(d)(5) is filed when received by the clerk or court and the clerk shall immediately thereafter transfer the electronic documents from the storage device to the official court file. FL ST J ADMIN Rule 2.525(c)(5).

iv. If the filer of any paper document authorized under FL ST J ADMIN Rule 2.525(d) provides a self-addressed, postage-paid envelope for return of the paper document after it is converted to electronic form by the clerk, the clerk shall place the paper document in the envelope and deposit it in the mail. Except when a paper document is required to be maintained, the clerk may recycle any filed paper document that is not to be returned to the filer. FL ST J ADMIN Rule 2.525(c)(6).

v. The clerk may convert any paper document filed before the effective date of FL ST J ADMIN Rule 2.525 to an electronic document. Unless the clerk is required to maintain the paper document, if the paper document has been converted to an electronic document by the clerk, the paper document is no longer part of the official court file and may be removed and recycled. FL ST J ADMIN Rule 2.525(c)(7).

d. *Official court file.* For information on what constitutes the official court file, please see FL ST J ADMIN Rule 2.525(c)(2), FL ST J ADMIN Rule 2.525(c)(3).

e. *Administration.* All attorneys, parties, or other persons using this rule to file documents are required to make arrangements with the court or clerk for the payment of any charges authorized by general law or the supreme court before filing any document by electronic transmission. FL ST J ADMIN Rule 2.525(f)(2).

f. *Filing date.* The filing date for an electronically transmitted document is the date and time that such filing is acknowledged by an electronic stamp or otherwise, pursuant to any procedure set forth in any ECF Procedures approved by the supreme court, or the date the last page of such filing is received by the court or clerk. FL ST J ADMIN Rule 2.525(f)(3).

g. *Accessibility.* All documents transmitted in any electronic form under FL ST J ADMIN Rule 2.525 must comply with the accessibility requirements of FL ST J ADMIN Rule 2.526. FL ST J ADMIN Rule 2.525(g).

2. *Service requirements.* Every pleading subsequent to the initial pleading, all orders, and every other document filed in the action must be served in conformity with the requirements of FL ST J ADMIN Rule 2.516. FL ST RCP Rule 1.080(a).

a. *Service; When required.* Unless the court otherwise orders, or a statute or supreme court adminis-

trative order specifies a different means of service, every pleading subsequent to the initial pleading and every other document filed in any court proceeding, except applications for witness subpoenas and documents served by formal notice or required to be served in the manner provided for service of formal notice, must be served in accordance with FL ST J ADMIN Rule 2.516 on each party. No service need be made on parties against whom a default has been entered, except that pleadings asserting new or additional claims against them must be served in the manner provided for service of summons. FL ST J ADMIN Rule 2.516(a).

b. *Service; How made.* When service is required or permitted to be made upon a party represented by an attorney, service must be made upon the attorney unless service upon the party is ordered by the court. FL ST J ADMIN Rule 2.516(b).

   i. *Service by electronic mail ("e-mail").* All documents required or permitted to be served on another party must be served by e-mail, unless FL ST J ADMIN Rule 2.516 otherwise provides. When, in addition to service by e-mail, the sender also utilizes another means of service provided for in FL ST J ADMIN Rule 2.516(b)(2), any differing time limits and other provisions applicable to that other means of service control. FL ST J ADMIN Rule 2.516(b)(1). Any document electronically transmitted to a court or clerk must also be served on all parties and interested persons in accordance with the applicable rules of court. FL ST J ADMIN Rule 2.525(e)(2).

      - *Service on attorneys.* Upon appearing in a proceeding, an attorney must serve a designation of a primary e-mail address and may designate no more than two (2) secondary e-mail addresses. Thereafter, service must be directed to all designated e-mail addresses in that proceeding. Every document filed by an attorney thereafter must include the primary e-mail address of that attorney and any secondary e-mail addresses. If an attorney does not designate any e-mail address for service, documents may be served on that attorney at the e-mail address on record with The Florida Bar. FL ST J ADMIN Rule 2.516(b)(1)(A).

      - *Exception to e-mail service on attorneys.* Service by an attorney on another attorney must be made by e-mail unless excused by the court. Upon motion by an attorney demonstrating that the attorney has no e-mail account and lacks access to the Internet at the attorney's office, the court may excuse the attorney from the requirements of e-mail service. Service on and by an attorney excused by the court from e-mail service must be by the means provided in FL ST J ADMIN Rule 2.516(b)(2). FL ST J ADMIN Rule 2.516(b)(1)(B).

      - *Service on and by parties not represented by an attorney.* Any party not represented by an attorney may serve a designation of a primary e-mail address and also may designate no more than two (2) secondary e-mail addresses to which service must be directed in that proceeding by the means provided in FL ST J ADMIN Rule 2.516(b)(1). If a party not represented by an attorney does not designate an e-mail address for service in a proceeding, service on and by that party must be by the means provided in FL ST J ADMIN Rule 2.516(b)(2). FL ST J ADMIN Rule 2.516(b)(1)(C).

      - *Time of service.* Service by e-mail is complete when it is sent. FL ST J ADMIN Rule 2.516(b)(1)(D). An e-mail is deemed served on the date it is sent. FL ST J ADMIN Rule 2.516(b)(1)(D)(i). If the sender learns that the e-mail did not reach the address of the person to be served, the sender must immediately send another copy by e-mail, or by a means authorized by FL ST J ADMIN Rule 2.516(b)(2). FL ST J ADMIN Rule 2.516(b)(1)(D)(ii). E-mail service is treated as service by mail for the computation of time. FL ST J ADMIN Rule 2.516(b)(1)(D)(iii).

      - *Specifics of e-mail filing.* In addition to providing proper service pursuant to FL ST RCP Rule 1.080(b), courtesy copies of the Motion and Memorandum of Law for the Uniform Motion Calendar (e.g., Notice of Hearing, Motions, Exhibits, submitted case law, and other hearing specific documents) must be electronically attached to an email using either Microsoft Word or WordPerfect format (not as a PDF document) and sent via email to (a) The Court at its designated e-mail address; (b) Opposing counsel at their fax number as provided to The Florida Bar (see The Florida Bar's website and then click on "Find a Lawyer") or any other fax number provided on a Pleading, Motion to Quash Service,

Motion to Dismiss Complaint or Notice of Appearance, whichever is most recent; and (c) Pro se parties at their last known fax number or any other fax number provided on a Pleading, Motion to Quash Service, Motion to Dismiss Complaint or Notice of Appearance, whichever is most recent. FL ST 11 J CIR 1-09-13-A1(4)(b)(i).

- *E-mail subject line.* The subject line of the email must contain only the numeric motion calendar hearing date using the following format: mm/dd/yy (two (2) digit month forward slash; two (2) digit day forward slash; two (2) digit year). For example: 06/15/10. FL ST 11 J CIR 1-09-13-A1(4)(b)(iii).

ii. *Format of e-mail for service.* Service of a document by e-mail is made by attaching a copy of the document in PDF format to an e-mail sent to all addresses designated by the attorney or party. FL ST J ADMIN Rule 2.516(b)(1)(E).

- All documents served by e-mail must be attached to an e-mail message containing a subject line beginning with the words "SERVICE OF COURT DOCUMENT" in all capital letters, followed by the case number of the proceeding in which the documents are being served. FL ST J ADMIN Rule 2.516(b)(1)(E)(i).
- The body of the e-mail must identify the court in which the proceeding is pending, the case number, the name of the initial party on each side, the title of each document served with that e-mail, and the sender's name and telephone number. FL ST J ADMIN Rule 2.516(b)(1)(E)(ii).
- Any document served by e-mail may be signed by the "/s/" format, as long as the filed original is signed in accordance with the applicable rule of procedure. FL ST J ADMIN Rule 2.516(b)(1)(E)(iii).
- Any e-mail which, together with its attached documents, exceeds five megabytes (5MB) in size, must be divided and sent as separate e-mails, no one of which may exceed five megabytes (5MB) in size and each of which must be sequentially numbered in the subject line. FL ST J ADMIN Rule 2.516(b)(1)(E)(iv).

iii. *Service by other means.* In addition to, and not in lieu of, service by e-mail, service may also be made upon attorneys by any of the means specified in FL ST J ADMIN Rule 2.516(b)(2). Service on and by all parties who are not represented by an attorney and who do not designate an e-mail address, and on and by all attorneys excused from e-mail service, must be made by delivering a copy of the document or by mailing it to the party or attorney at their last known address or, if no address is known, by leaving it with the clerk of the court. Service by mail is complete upon mailing. Delivery of a copy within FL ST J ADMIN Rule 2.516 is complete upon:

- Handing it to the attorney or to the party,
- Leaving it at the attorney's or party's office with a clerk or other person in charge thereof,
- If there is no one in charge, leaving it in a conspicuous place therein,
- If the office is closed or the person to be served has no office, leaving it at the person's usual place of abode with some person of his or her family above fifteen (15) years of age and informing such person of the contents, or
- Transmitting it by facsimile to the attorney's or party's office with a cover sheet containing the sender's name, firm, address, telephone number, and facsimile number, and the number of pages transmitted. When service is made by facsimile, a copy must also be served by any other method permitted by FL ST J ADMIN Rule 2.516. Facsimile service occurs when transmission is complete. FL ST J ADMIN Rule 2.516(b)(2)(A) through FL ST J ADMIN Rule 2.516(b)(2)(E).
- Service by delivery after 5:00 p.m. must be deemed to have been made by mailing on the date of delivery. FL ST J ADMIN Rule 2.516(b)(2)(F).
- If a scheduling attorney or a scheduling pro se party does not have a fax number, then a courtesy copy of Motions and Proposed orders must be sent as an attachment to the service

of process required pursuant to FL ST RCP Rule 1.080(b). FL ST 11 J CIR 1-09-13-A1(4)(b)(ii).

c. *Service; Numerous defendants.* In actions when the parties are unusually numerous, the court may regulate the service contemplated by the Florida Rules of Judicial Administration on motion or on its own initiative in such manner as may be found to be just and reasonable. FL ST J ADMIN Rule 2.516(c).

d. *Service by clerk.* Service of notices and other documents required to be made by the clerk must also be done as provided in FL ST J ADMIN Rule 2.516(b). FL ST J ADMIN Rule 2.516(g).

G. Hearings

1. *Communication equipment*

a. *Definition.* Communication equipment means a conference telephone or other electronic device that permits all those appearing or participating to hear and speak to each other, provided that all conversation of all parties is audible to all persons present. FL ST J ADMIN Rule 2.530(a).

b. *Use by all parties.* A county or circuit court judge may, upon the court's own motion or upon the written request of a party, direct that communication equipment be used for a motion hearing, pretrial conference, or a status conference. A judge must give notice to the parties and consider any objections they may have to the use of communication equipment before directing that communication equipment be used. The decision to use communication equipment over the objection of parties will be in the sound discretion of the trial court, except as noted below. FL ST J ADMIN Rule 2.530(b).

c. *Use only by requesting party.* A county or circuit court judge may, upon the written request of a party upon reasonable notice to all other parties, permit a requesting party to participate through communication equipment in a scheduled motion hearing; however, any such request (except in criminal, juvenile, and appellate proceedings) must be granted, absent a showing of good cause to deny the same, where the hearing is set for not longer than fifteen (15) minutes. FL ST J ADMIN Rule 2.530(c).

d. *Testimony*

i. *Generally.* A county or circuit court judge, general magistrate, special magistrate, or hearing officer may allow testimony to be taken through communication equipment if all parties consent or if permitted by another applicable rule of procedure. FL ST J ADMIN Rule 2.530(d)(1).

ii. *Procedure.* Any party desiring to present testimony through communication equipment shall, prior to the hearing or trial at which the testimony is to be presented, contact all parties to determine whether each party consents to this form of testimony. The party seeking to present the testimony shall move for permission to present testimony through communication equipment, which motion shall set forth good cause as to why the testimony should be allowed in this form. FL ST J ADMIN Rule 2.530(d)(2).

iii. *Oath.* Testimony may be taken through communication equipment only if a notary public or other person authorized to administer oaths in the witness's jurisdiction is present with the witness and administers the oath consistent with the laws of the jurisdiction. FL ST J ADMIN Rule 2.530(d)(3).

iv. *Confrontation rights.* In juvenile and criminal proceedings the defendant must make an informed waiver of any confrontation rights that may be abridged by the use of communication equipment. FL ST J ADMIN Rule 2.530(d)(4).

v. *Video testimony.* If the testimony to be presented utilizes video conferencing or comparable two-way visual capabilities, the court in its discretion may modify the procedures set forth in FL ST J ADMIN Rule 2.530 to accommodate the technology utilized. FL ST J ADMIN Rule 2.530(d)(5).

e. *Burden of expense.* The cost for the use of the communication equipment is the responsibility of the requesting party unless otherwise directed by the court. FL ST J ADMIN Rule 2.530(e).

2. *Time allotted for hearing.* Each party may set only one five (5) minute motion per case. Multiple motions must be specially set or set on different motion calendars (one five (5) minute motion per party per case), so as not to encroach on the time the Court is allotting for other litigants/attorneys. Consequently, the parties are advised to use good faith efforts to resolve the issues set forth in the motion prior to the setting of a motion; coordinate the date and time of the hearing; and confirm that the hearing shall require no more than five (5) minutes (if the hearing will require more than five (5) minutes, then it must be a Special Set Hearing). FL ST 11 J CIR 1-09-13-A1(4)(b)(i). For information on Special Set Hearings, refer to FL ST 11 J CIR 1-09-13-A1(4)(c).
3. *Hearing cancellation policy.* Should any scheduled hearing become unnecessary or have to be cancelled, the scheduling attorney or scheduling pro se party shall immediately, but, not later than by Noon on the business day prior to the hearing date and time, send an email to the court's designated e-mail address regarding the cancellation of the Motion Calendar hearing with an electronically attached Notice of Cancellation formatted in the same manner (using Microsoft Word or Word Perfect) as the email that scheduled the Motion Calendar hearing and in the same manner as the Motions and Notices. FL ST 11 J CIR 1-09-13-A1(4)(b)(vii).

H. Forms

1. Official Motion for Sanctions Forms for Florida

a. Caption. FL ST RCP Form 1.901.

b. Notice of compliance when constitutional challenge is brought. FL ST RCP Form 1.975.

2. Motion for Sanctions Forms for Florida

a. Motion; By defendant; For sanctions for refusal of offer of judgment. FL-PP § 61:22.

b. Motion; Sanctions, proposal for settlement. FL-PRACFORM § 7:165.

I. Checklist

(I) ❑ Matters to be considered by moving party
- (a) ❑ Required documents
  - (1) ❑ Notice of hearing/Motion
  - (2) ❑ Certificate of service
- (b) ❑ Supplemental documents
  - (1) ❑ Proposed order
  - (2) ❑ Notice of constitutional question
- (c) ❑ Time for making motion
  - (1) ❑ A motion by a party seeking sanctions under FL ST § 57.105 must be served but may not be filed with or presented to the court unless, within twenty one (21) days after service of the motion, the challenged paper, claim, defense, contention, allegation, or denial is not withdrawn or appropriately corrected
  - (2) ❑ Any party seeking a judgment taxing costs, attorneys' fees, or both shall serve a motion no later than thirty (30) days after filing of the judgment, including a judgment of dismissal, or the service of a notice of voluntary dismissal
  - (3) ❑ A copy of any written motion which may not be heard ex parte and a copy of the notice of the hearing thereof shall be served a reasonable time before the time specified for the hearing

(II) ❑ Matters to be considered by opposing party
- (a) ❑ Required documents
  - (1) ❑ Response to motion
  - (2) ❑ Certificate of service
- (b) ❑ Supplemental documents
  - (1) ❑ Proposed order

(2) ❑ Notice of constitutional question

(c) ❑ Time for service and filing of opposition

(1) ❑ No time specified for responding to a motion

Motions, Oppositions and Replies
Motion to Compel Discovery

Document Last Updated January 2013

A. Applicable Rules

1. *State rules*
   a. Rules of court. FL ST RCP Rule 1.010; FL ST J ADMIN Rule 2.110.
   b. Nonverification of pleadings. FL ST RCP Rule 1.030.
   c. Service and filing of pleadings, orders, and documents. FL ST RCP Rule 1.080.
   d. Time. FL ST RCP Rule 1.090.
   e. Pleadings and motions. FL ST RCP Rule 1.100.
   f. Motions. FL ST RCP Rule 1.160.
   g. General provisions governing discovery. FL ST RCP Rule 1.280.
   h. Depositions. FL ST RCP Rule 1.310; FL ST RCP Rule 1.320; FL ST FAM LAW Rule 12.310.
   i. Interrogatories to parties. FL ST RCP Rule 1.340.
   j. Production of documents and things and entry upon land for inspection and other purposes. FL ST RCP Rule 1.350.
   k. Examination of persons. FL ST RCP Rule 1.360.
   l. Failure to make discovery; Sanctions. FL ST RCP Rule 1.380.
   m. Relief from judgment, decrees, or orders. FL ST RCP Rule 1.540.
   n. Mediation and arbitration. FL ST RCP Rule 1.700; FL ST RCP Rule 1.710; FL ST RCP Rule 1.720; FL ST RCP Rule 1.730; FL ST RCP Rule 1.750; FL ST RCP Rule 1.800; FL ST RCP Rule 1.810; FL ST RCP Rule 1.820; FL ST RCP Rule 1.830.
   o. Forms. FL ST RCP Rule 1.900.
   p. Minimization of the filing of sensitive information. FL ST J ADMIN Rule 2.425.
   q. Retention of court records. FL ST J ADMIN Rule 2.430.
   r. Foreign attorneys. FL ST J ADMIN Rule 2.510.
   s. Signature of attorneys and parties. FL ST J ADMIN Rule 2.515.
   t. Paper. FL ST J ADMIN Rule 2.520.
   u. Electronic filing. FL ST J ADMIN Rule 2.525.
   v. Accessibility of information and technology. FL ST J ADMIN Rule 2.526.
   w. Communication equipment. FL ST J ADMIN Rule 2.530.
   x. Court reporting. FL ST J ADMIN Rule 2.535.
   y. Requests for accommodations by persons with disabilities. FL ST J ADMIN Rule 2.540.
2. *Local rules*
   a. Establishment of 11th Circuit Homestead Access to Mediation Program ("CHAMP") for case management of residential foreclosure cases in the Eleventh Judicial Circuit of Florida. FL ST 11 J CIR 1-09-08.
   b. Enlargement and expansion of the current pilot project for electronic submissions of courtesy copies

for uniform motion calendar and requests for special set hearings, emergency motions, and proposed orders. FL ST 11 J CIR 1-09-13-A1.

c. Ex parte motions to compel discovery in civil actions. FL ST 11 J CIR 1-06-09.

B. Timing

1. *Motion to compel discovery.* Upon reasonable notice to other parties and all persons affected, a party may apply for an order compelling discovery. FL ST RCP Rule 1.380(a).
2. *General motion timing.* A copy of any written motion which may not be heard ex parte and a copy of the notice of the hearing thereof shall be served a reasonable time before the time specified for the hearing. FL ST RCP Rule 1.090(d).
3. *Computation of time*
   a. *Generally.* Computation of time shall be governed by FL ST J ADMIN Rule 2.514. FL ST RCP Rule 1.090(a). The following rules apply in computing time periods specified in any rule of procedure, local rule, court order, or statute that does not specify a method of computing time. FL ST J ADMIN Rule 2.514(a).
      i. *Period stated in days or a longer unit.* When the period is stated in days or a longer unit of time (A) exclude the day of the event that triggers the period; (B) count every day, including intermediate Saturdays, Sundays, and legal holidays; and (C) include the last day of the period, but if the last day is a Saturday, Sunday, or legal holiday, or falls within any period of time extended through an order of the chief justice under FL ST J ADMIN Rule 2.205(a)(2)(B)(iv), the period continues to run until the end of the next day that is not a Saturday, Sunday, or legal holiday and does not fall within any period of time extended through an order of the chief justice. FL ST J ADMIN Rule 2.514(a)(1).
      ii. *Period stated in hours.* When the period is stated in hours (A) begin counting immediately on the occurrence of the event that triggers the period; (B) count every hour, including hours during intermediate Saturdays, Sundays, and legal holidays; and (C) if the period would end on a Saturday, Sunday, or legal holiday, or during any period of time extended through an order of the chief justice under FL ST J ADMIN Rule 2.205(a)(2)(B)(iv), the period continues to run until the same time on the next day that is not a Saturday, Sunday, or legal holiday and does not fall within any period of time extended through an order of the chief justice. FL ST J ADMIN Rule 2.514(a)(2).
      iii. *Period stated in days less than seven (7) days.* When the period stated in days is less than seven (7) days, intermediate Saturdays, Sundays, and legal holidays shall be excluded in the computation. FL ST J ADMIN Rule 2.514(a)(3).
      iv. *"Last day" defined.* Unless a different time is set by a statute, local rule, or court order, the last day ends (A) for electronic filing or for service by any means, at midnight; and (B) for filing by other means, when the clerk's office is scheduled to close. FL ST J ADMIN Rule 2.514(a)(4).
      v. *"Next day" defined.* The "next day" is determined by continuing to count forward when the period is measured after an event and backward when measured before an event. FL ST J ADMIN Rule 2.514(a)(5).
      vi. *"Legal holiday" defined.* "Legal holiday" means (A) the day set aside by FL ST § 110.117, for observing New Year's Day, Martin Luther King, Jr.'s Birthday, Memorial Day, Independence Day, Labor Day, Veterans' Day, Thanksgiving Day, the Friday after Thanksgiving Day, or Christmas Day, and (B) any day observed as a holiday by the clerk's office or as designated by the chief judge. FL ST J ADMIN Rule 2.514(a)(6).

   b. *Additional time after service by mail or e-mail.* When a party may or must act within a specified time after service and service is made by mail or e-mail, five (5) days are added after the period that would otherwise expire under FL ST J ADMIN Rule 2.514(a). FL ST J ADMIN Rule 2.514(b).
   c. *Enlargement.* When an act is required or allowed to be done at or within a specified time by order of court, by the Florida Rules of Civil Procedure, or by notice given thereunder, for cause shown the court at any time in its discretion (1) with or without notice, may order the period enlarged if request

therefor is made before the expiration of the period originally prescribed or as extended by a previous order, or (2) upon motion made and notice after the expiration of the specified period, may permit the act to be done when failure to act was the result of excusable neglect, but it may not extend the time for making a motion for new trial, for rehearing, or to alter or amend a judgment; making a motion for relief from a judgment under FL ST RCP Rule 1.540(b); taking an appeal or filing a petition for certiorari; or making a motion for a directed verdict. FL ST RCP Rule 1.090(b).

d. *Unaffected by expiration of term.* The period of time provided for the doing of any act or the taking of any proceeding shall not be affected or limited by the continued existence or expiration of a term of court. The continued existence or expiration of a term of court in no way affects the power of a court to do any act or take any proceeding in any action which is or has been pending before it. FL ST RCP Rule 1.090(c).

C. General Requirements

1. *Motions generally*

   a. *Contents.* An application to the court for an order shall be by motion which shall be made in writing unless made during a hearing or trial, shall state with particularity the grounds therefor, and shall set forth the relief or order sought. The requirement of writing is fulfilled if the motion is stated in a written notice of the hearing of the motion. All notices of hearing shall specify each motion or other matter to be heard. FL ST RCP Rule 1.100(b).

   b. *Particularity requirement.* The court considers a motion in the light of the substantive law, rule or statute to make its determination. Some rules require a statement of the grounds for a motion under the rule. Failure to give the grounds will result in denial of the motion. This should be the result in all situations when the ground for the motion is not inherent in the rule. FL-PRACPROC § 9:3. The requirement is nevertheless an important one, first because of the due process notice rights of the respondent, as well as for the assistance it provides to the court in its preparation for the hearing or, absent a hearing, for disposition. 4 FLPRAC R 1.100.

2. *Failure to make discovery; Types of available relief.* Three (3) categories of relief are available for failure to make discovery. FL-PRACPROC § 16:14.

   a. The first category is an order compelling discovery. This is obtained by a motion to compel discovery. The motion is made in the court in which the action is pending, except when a deposition is being taken out of the territorial jurisdiction of the court and protective relief is sought in accordance with FL ST RCP Rule 1.310(d) or when a deponent is not a party. When one of the exceptions occurs, the motion is made in the circuit court of the county where the deposition is being taken. FL-PRACPROC § 16:14.

   b. The second category results from a failure to comply with an order to make discovery. The sanctions should not be applied until a hearing on the merits of the failure is held, including an opportunity to present evidence of explanation or mitigation. FL-PRACPROC § 16:14.

   c. The third category is available: (1) if a party or a person designated by an organization to answer questions at a deposition fails to appear before the officer who is to take the deposition after being served with a proper notice; (2) fails to serve answers or objections to interrogatories after proper service of the interrogatories; or (3) a party fails to serve a response to a request for production, inspection and entry after proper service of the request. FL-PRACPROC § 16:14. For further information regarding discovery sanctions please see the KeyRules Motion for Discovery Sanctions documents.

3. *Motion for order compelling discovery*

   a. *Reasonable notice.* Upon reasonable notice to other parties and all persons affected, a party may apply for an order compelling discovery. FL ST RCP Rule 1.380(a).

   b. *Appropriate court.* An application for an order to a party may be made to the court in which the action is pending or in accordance with FL ST RCP Rule 1.310(d). An application for an order to a deponent who is not a party shall be made to the circuit court where the deposition is being taken. FL ST RCP Rule 1.380(a)(1).

c. *Motion*

i. *Grounds.* The discovering party may move for an order compelling an answer, or a designation or an order compelling inspection, or an order compelling an examination in accordance with the request:

- If a deponent fails to answer a question propounded or submitted under FL ST RCP Rule 1.310 or FL ST RCP Rule 1.320;
- Or a corporation or other entity fails to make a designation under FL ST RCP Rule 1.310(b)(6) or FL ST RCP Rule 1.320(a);
- Or a party fails to answer an interrogatory submitted under FL ST RCP Rule 1.340;
- Or if a party in response to a request for inspection submitted under FL ST RCP Rule 1.350 fails to respond that inspection will be permitted as requested or fails to permit inspection as requested;
- Or if a party in response to a request for examination of a person submitted under FL ST RCP Rule 1.360(a) objects to the examination, fails to respond that the examination will be permitted as requested, or fails to submit to or to produce a person in that party's custody or legal control for examination. FL ST RCP Rule 1.380(a)(2).

ii. *Certification.* The motion must include a certification that the movant, in good faith, has conferred or attempted to confer with the person or party failing to make the discovery in an effort to secure the information or material without court action. FL ST RCP Rule 1.380(a)(2).

iii. *During deposition.* When taking a deposition on oral examination, the proponent of the question may complete or adjourn the examination before applying for an order. FL ST RCP Rule 1.380(a)(2).

iv. *Protective order.* If the court denies the motion in whole or in part, it may make such protective order as it would have been empowered to make on a motion made pursuant to FL ST RCP Rule 1.280(c). FL ST RCP Rule 1.380(a)(2).

d. *Evasive or incomplete answer.* For purposes of FL ST RCP Rule 1.380(a) an evasive or incomplete answer shall be treated as a failure to answer. FL ST RCP Rule 1.380(a)(3).

e. *Award of expenses of motion*

i. *Motion granted.* If the motion is granted and after opportunity for hearing, the court shall require the party or deponent whose conduct necessitated the motion or the party or counsel advising the conduct to pay to the moving party the reasonable expenses incurred in obtaining the order that may include attorneys' fees, unless the court finds that the movant failed to certify in the motion that a good faith effort was made to obtain the discovery without court action, that the opposition to the motion was justified, or that other circumstances make an award of expenses unjust. FL ST RCP Rule 1.380(a)(4).

ii. *Motion denied.* If the motion is denied and after opportunity for hearing, the court shall require the moving party to pay to the party or deponent who opposed the motion the reasonable expenses incurred in opposing the motion that may include attorneys' fees, unless the court finds that the making of the motion was substantially justified or that other circumstances make an award of expenses unjust. FL ST RCP Rule 1.380(a)(4).

iii. *Motion granted in part and denied in part.* If the motion is granted in part and denied in part, the court may apportion the reasonable expenses incurred as a result of making the motion among the parties and persons. FL ST RCP Rule 1.380(a)(4).

iv. *Electronically stored information; Sanctions for failure to preserve.* Absent exceptional circumstances, a court may not impose sanctions under these rules on a party for failing to provide electronically stored information lost as a result of the routine, good faith operation of an electronic information system. FL ST RCP Rule 1.380(e).

4. *Limitations on discovery of electronically stored information*

a. A person may object to discovery of electronically stored information from sources that the person identifies as not reasonably accessible because of burden or cost. On motion to compel discovery or for a protective order, the person from whom discovery is sought must show that the information sought or the format requested is not reasonably accessible because of undue burden or cost. If that showing is made, the court may nonetheless order the discovery from such sources or in such formats if the requesting party shows good cause. The court may specify conditions of the discovery, including ordering that some or all of the expenses incurred by the person from whom discovery is sought be paid by the party seeking the discovery. FL ST RCP Rule 1.280(d)(1).

b. In determining any motion involving discovery of electronically stored information, the court must limit the frequency or extent of discovery otherwise allowed by the Florida Rules of Civil Procedure if it determines that (i) the discovery sought is unreasonably cumulative or duplicative, or can be obtained from another source or in another manner that is more convenient, less burdensome, or less expensive; or (ii) the burden or expense of the discovery outweighs its likely benefit, considering the needs of the case, the amount in controversy, the parties' resources, the importance of the issues at stake in the action, and the importance of the discovery in resolving the issues. FL ST RCP Rule 1.280(d)(2).

5. *Ex parte motion to compel*

a. *Brining the motion ex parte.* A motion to compel discovery ex parte in a civil action may be submitted to the Court if the moving party has complied with the following procedures:

i. The moving party must serve the motion on the opposing party at least seven (7) days prior to the submission of the order to the Court. FL ST 11 J CIR 1-06-09(1)(a).

ii. The motion must include the following:

- The nature of the discovery and the date upon which the discovery was propounded and due;
- That there has been a complete failure to respond or object to discovery, and the non-moving party has failed to request an extension of time to respond to discovery; and
- That the moving party has otherwise complied with FL ST RCP Rule 1.380(a)(2), certifying that he has conferred, or attempted to confer, with the person or party failing to make the discovery in an effort to secure the information or material without court action. FL ST 11 J CIR 1-06-09(1)(b).

b. *Submission of ex parte order.* In the event that the non-moving party fails to provide the requested discovery, fails to object to discovery, or fails to request an extension of time to respond to the discovery within seven (7) days of service of the motion, the moving party may submit an ex parte order to the court. FL ST 11 J CIR 1-06-09(2).

c. *Effect of ex parte order.* In entering the ex parte order, the court may direct that the non-moving party comply with the outstanding discovery request within ten (10) days or such other time, within the discretion of the Court. The court may also, in its discretion, order that the non-moving party pay costs and/or attorney's fees, if appropriate. FL ST 11 J CIR 1-06-09(3).

6. *Arbitration and mediation*

a. *Referral to arbitration and mediation.* Except as hereinafter provided or as otherwise prohibited by law, the presiding judge may enter an order referring all or any part of a contested civil matter to mediation or arbitration. The parties to any contested civil matter may file a written stipulation to mediate or arbitrate any issue between them at any time. Such stipulation shall be incorporated into the order of referral. FL ST RCP Rule 1.700(a).

i. In all residential foreclosure actions involving homestead properties filed on or after May 1, 2009, unless a stipulation is specifically invoked by the parties in writing within five (5) days of service of the complaint on the main defendant, the parties are deemed to have stipulated to referral of the mediation to the Collins Center pursuant to FL ST RCP Rule 1.720(f). FL ST 11 J CIR 1-09-08(2); FL ST 11 J CIR 1-09-08(3). FL ST 11 J CIR 1-09-08 constitutes a formal referral to mediation pursuant to the Florida Rules of Civil Procedure. FL ST 11 J CIR 1-09-08(2).

ii. For further information on referral to mediation, refer to FL ST 11 J CIR 1-09-08.

b. *Arbitration*

i. *Exclusions.* A civil action shall be ordered to arbitration or arbitration in conjunction with mediation upon stipulation of the parties. A civil action may be ordered to arbitration or arbitration in conjunction with mediation upon motion of any party or by the court, if the judge determines the action to be of such a nature that arbitration could be of benefit to the litigants or the court. FL ST RCP Rule 1.800.

- Under no circumstances may the following categories of actions be referred to arbitration: (1) bond estreatures; (2) habeas corpus or other extraordinary writs; (3) bond validations; (4) civil or criminal contempt; (5) such other matters as may be specified by order of the chief judge in the circuit. FL ST RCP Rule 1.800.

ii. For more information regarding arbitration, please see FL ST RCP Rule 1.810; FL ST RCP Rule 1.820; FL ST RCP Rule 1.830.

c. *Mediation.* For more information regarding mediation, please see FL ST RCP Rule 1.710; FL ST RCP Rule 1.720; FL ST RCP Rule 1.730; and FL ST RCP Rule 1.750.

7. *Rules of court*

a. *Rules of civil procedure.* The Florida Rules of Civil Procedure apply to all actions of a civil nature and all special statutory proceedings in the circuit courts and county courts except those to which the Florida Probate Rules, the Florida Family Law Rules of Procedure, or the Small Claims Rules apply. FL ST RCP Rule 1.010.

i. The form, content, procedure, and time for pleading in all special statutory proceedings shall be as prescribed by the statutes governing the proceeding unless the Florida Rules of Civil Procedure specifically provide to the contrary. FL ST RCP Rule 1.010.

ii. The Florida Rules of Civil Procedure shall be construed to secure the just, speedy, and inexpensive determination of every action. FL ST RCP Rule 1.010.

b. *Rules of judicial administration.* The Florida Rules of Judicial Administration shall apply to administrative matters in all courts to which the Florida Rules of Judicial Administration are applicable by their terms. The Florida Rules of Judicial Administration shall be construed to secure the speedy and inexpensive determination of every proceeding to which they are applicable. The Florida Rules of Judicial Administration shall supersede all conflicting rules and statutes. FL ST J ADMIN Rule 2.110.

D. Documents

1. *Required documents*

a. *Notice of hearing/Motion.* An application to the court for an order shall be by motion which shall be made in writing unless made during a hearing or trial, shall state with particularity the grounds therefor, and shall set forth the relief or order sought. The requirement of writing is fulfilled if the motion is stated in a written notice of the hearing of the motion. All notices of hearing shall specify each motion or other matter to be heard. FL ST RCP Rule 1.100(b).

i. *Certification.* The motion must include a certification that the movant, in good faith, has conferred or attempted to confer with the person or party failing to make the discovery in an effort to secure the information or material without court action. FL ST RCP Rule 1.380(a)(2).

ii. *Notices to persons with disabilities.* See the Format section of this KeyRules document for further information.

b. *Certificate of service.* When any attorney certifies in substance: "I certify that a copy hereof has been furnished to (here insert name or names and addresses used for service) by (e-mail) (delivery) (mail) (fax) on .... (date) ....________________ Attorney" the certificate is taken as prima facie proof of such service in compliance with FL ST J ADMIN Rule 2.516. FL ST J ADMIN Rule 2.516(f).

2. *Supplemental documents*

a. *Proposed order.* The court may require that orders or judgments be prepared by a party, may require

the party to furnish the court with stamped, addressed envelopes for service of the order or judgment, and may require that proposed orders and judgments be furnished to all parties before entry by the court of the order or judgment. FL ST J ADMIN Rule 2.516(h)(1). For additional information on the submission of proposed orders, refer to FL ST 11 J CIR 1-09-13-A1(e).

b. *Notice of constitutional question.* A party that files a pleading, written motion, or other paper drawing into question the constitutionality of a state statute or a county or municipal charter, ordinance, or franchise must promptly (1) file a notice of constitutional question stating the question and identifying the paper that raises it; and (2) serve the notice and the pleading, written motion, or other paper drawing into question the constitutionality of a state statute or a county or municipal charter, ordinance, or franchise on the Attorney General or the state attorney of the judicial circuit in which the action is pending, by either certified or registered mail. Service of the notice and pleading, written motion, or other paper does not require joinder of the Attorney General or the state attorney as a party to the action. FL ST RCP Rule 1.071.

E. Format

1. *Documents; Type and size.* Documents subject to the exceptions set forth in FL ST J ADMIN Rule 2.525(d) shall be filed on recycled paper measuring eight and one half by eleven (8 1/2 by 11) inches. For purposes of FL ST J ADMIN Rule 2.520, paper is recycled if it contains a minimum content of fifty (50) percent waste paper. Xerographic reduction of legal-size (eight and one half by fourteen (8 1/2 by 14) inches) documents to letter size (eight and one half by eleven (8 1/2 by 11) inches) is prohibited. All other documents filed by electronic transmission shall be filed in a format capable of being printed in a format consistent with the provisions of FL ST J ADMIN Rule 2.250. FL ST J ADMIN Rule 2.520(b).

   a. *Exhibits.* Any exhibit or attachment filed with pleadings or papers may be filed in its original size. FL ST J ADMIN Rule 2.520(c).

   b. *Recording space.* On all papers and documents prepared and filed by the court or by any party to a proceeding which are to be recorded in the public records of any county, including but not limited to final money judgments and notices of lis pendens, a three (3) inch by three (3) inch space at the top right-hand corner on the first page and a one (1) inch by three (3) inch space at the top right-hand corner on each subsequent page shall be left blank and reserved for use by the clerk of court. FL ST J ADMIN Rule 2.520(d).

      i. *Exceptions to recording space.* Any papers or documents created by persons or entities over which the filing party has no control, including but not limited to wills, codicils, trusts, or other testamentary documents; documents prepared or executed by any public officer; documents prepared, executed, acknowledged, or proved outside of the State of Florida; or documents created by State or Federal government agencies, may be filed without the space required by FL ST J ADMIN Rule 2.520. FL ST J ADMIN Rule 2.520(e).

   c. *Noncompliance.* No clerk of court is permitted to refuse to file any document or paper because of noncompliance with the Florida Rules of Judicial Administration. However, upon request of the clerk of court, noncomplying documents must be resubmitted in accordance with the formatting rules. FL ST J ADMIN Rule 2.520(f).

   d. *Format of electronically filed documents.* Hyperlinks in the attachments, (not in the body of the email) are encouraged just as are submissions in Microsoft Word format. Electronic versions submitted in WordPerfect will be converted by the Court to Microsoft Word and there is no guarantee that the document will be converted without error. FL ST 11 J CIR 1-09-13-A1(4)(b)(v).

2. *Caption.* Every pleading, motion, order, judgment, or other paper shall have a caption containing the name of the court, the file number, and except for in rem proceedings, including forfeiture proceedings, the name of the first party on each side with an appropriate indication of other parties, and a designation identifying the party filing it and its nature or the nature of the order, as the case may be. In any in rem proceeding, every pleading, motion, order, judgment, or other paper shall have a caption containing the name of the court, the file number, the style "In re" (followed by the name or general description of the property), and a designation of the person or entity filing it and its nature or the nature of the order, as the case may be. In an in rem forfeiture proceeding, the style shall be "In re forfeiture of" (followed by the name of the general description of the property). All papers filed in the action shall be styled in such a

manner as to indicate clearly the subject matter of the paper and the party requesting or obtaining relief. FL ST RCP Rule 1.100(c)(1).

a. *Caption of electronically filed documents.* All submitted documents shall be titled with the Court Case Number and the name/type of document using the following format: two (2) digit year followed by a hyphen with the sequential case number (e.g., 09-1; 91-12; 08-123; 07-1234; or 09-12345). Do not use zeros after the hyphen to fill in the sequential case number. FL ST 11 J CIR 1-09-13-A1(4)(a).

3. *Writing and written defined.* Writing or written means a document containing information, an application, or a stipulation. FL ST RCP Rule 1.080(c).

4. *Rule abbreviations*

   a. The Florida Rules of Civil Procedure and shall be abbreviated as Fla.R.Civ.P. FL ST RCP Rule 1.010.

   b. The Florida Rules of Judicial Administration shall be abbreviated as Fla. R. Jud. Admin. FL ST J ADMIN Rule 2.110.

5. *Nonverification.* Except when otherwise specifically provided by the Florida Rules of Civil Procedure or an applicable statute, every pleading or other document of a party represented by an attorney need not be verified or accompanied by an affidavit. FL ST RCP Rule 1.030; FL ST J ADMIN Rule 2.515(a).

6. *Attorney signature*

   a. *Attorney signature.* Every pleading and other document of a party represented by an attorney shall be signed by at least one (1) attorney of record in that attorney's individual name whose current record Florida Bar address, telephone number, including area code, primary e-mail address and secondary e-mail addresses, if any, and Florida Bar number shall be stated, and who shall be duly licensed to practice law in Florida or who shall have received permission to appear in the particular case as provided in FL ST J ADMIN Rule 2.510. FL ST J ADMIN Rule 2.515(a).

      i. The attorney may be required by the court to give the address of, and to vouch for the attorney's authority to represent, the party. FL ST J ADMIN Rule 2.515(a).

      ii. The signature of an attorney shall constitute a certificate by the attorney that the attorney has read the pleading or other document; that to the best of the attorney's knowledge, information, and belief there is good ground to support it; and that it is not interposed for delay. FL ST J ADMIN Rule 2.515(a).

      iii. If a pleading is not signed or is signed with intent to defeat the purpose of FL ST J ADMIN Rule 2.515, it may be stricken and the action may proceed as though the pleading or other document had not been served. FL ST J ADMIN Rule 2.515(a).

   b. *Pro se litigant signature.* A party who is not represented by an attorney shall sign any pleading or other paper and state the party's address and telephone number, including area code. FL ST J ADMIN Rule 2.515(b).

   c. *Form of signature*

      i. The signatures required on pleadings and documents by FL ST J ADMIN Rule 2.515(a) and FL ST J ADMIN Rule 2.515(b) may be:

         - Original signatures;
         - Original signatures that have been reproduced by electronic means, such as on electronically transmitted documents or photocopied documents;
         - Electronic signatures using the "/s/," "s/," or "/s" formats by or at the direction of the person signing; or
         - Any other signature format authorized by general law, so long as the clerk where the proceeding is pending has the capability of receiving and has obtained approval from the Supreme Court of Florida to accept pleadings and documents with that signature format. FL ST J ADMIN Rule 2.515(c)(1).

      ii. An attorney, party, or other person who files a pleading or paper by electronic transmission that

does not contain the original signature of that attorney, party, or other person shall file that identical pleading or paper in paper form containing an original signature of that attorney, party, or other person (hereinafter called the follow-up filing) immediately thereafter. The follow-up filing is not required if the Supreme Court of Florida has entered an order directing the clerk of court to discontinue accepting the follow-up filing. FL ST J ADMIN Rule 2.515(c)(2).

7. *Forms*
   a. *Process.* The forms of process, notice of lis pendens, and notice of action provided in the Florida Rules of Civil Procedure are sufficient. Variations from the forms do not void process or notices that are otherwise sufficient. FL ST RCP Rule 1.900(a).
   b. *Other forms.* The other forms provided in the Florida Rules of Civil Procedure are sufficient for the matters that are covered by them. So long as the substance is expressed without prolixity, the forms may be varied to meet the facts of a particular case. FL ST RCP Rule 1.900(b).
   c. *Formal matters.* Captions, except for the designation of the paper, are omitted from the forms provided in the Florida Rules of Civil Procedure. A general form of caption is the first form provided. Signatures are omitted from pleadings and motions. FL ST RCP Rule 1.900(c).
8. *Notices to persons with disabilities.* All notices of court proceedings to be held in a public facility, and all process compelling appearance at such proceedings, shall include the following statement in bold face, fourteen (14) point Times New Roman or Courier font: "If you are a person with a disability who needs any accommodation in order to participate in this proceeding, you are entitled, at no cost to you, to the provision of certain assistance. Please contact [identify applicable court personnel by name, address, and telephone number] at least seven (7) days before your scheduled court appearance, or immediately upon receiving this notification if the time before the scheduled appearance is less than seven (7) days; if you are hearing or voice impaired, call 711." FL ST J ADMIN Rule 2.540(c)(1).
9. *Minimization of the filing of sensitive information*
   a. *Limitations for court filings.* Unless authorized by FL ST J ADMIN Rule 2.425(b), statute, another rule of court, or the court orders otherwise, designated sensitive information filed with the court must be limited to the following format:
      i. The initials of a person known to be a minor;
      ii. The year of birth of a person's birth date;
      iii. No portion of any: Social security number, Bank account number, Credit card account number, Charge account number, or Debit account number;
      iv. The last four digits of any: Taxpayer identification number (TIN), Employee identification number, Driver's license number, Passport number, Telephone number, Financial account number, except as set forth in FL ST J ADMIN Rule 2.425(a)(3), Brokerage account number, Insurance policy account number, Loan account number, Customer account number, or Patient or health care number;
      v. A truncated version of any: Email address, Computer user name, Password, or Personal identification number (PIN); and
      vi. A truncated version of any other sensitive information as provided by court order. FL ST J ADMIN Rule 2.425(a).
   b. *Exceptions.* FL ST J ADMIN Rule 2.425(a) does not apply to the following:
      i. An account number which identifies the property alleged to be the subject of a proceeding;
      ii. The record of an administrative or agency proceeding;
      iii. The record in appellate or review proceedings;
      iv. The birth date of a minor whenever the birth date is necessary for the court to establish or maintain subject matter jurisdiction;
      v. The name of a minor in any order relating to parental responsibility, time-sharing, or child support;

vi. The name of a minor in any document or order affecting the minor's ownership of real property;

vii. The birth date of a party in a writ of attachment or notice to payor;

viii. In traffic and criminal proceedings: a pro se filing; a court filing that is related to a criminal matter or investigation and that is prepared before the filing of a criminal charge or is not filed as part of any docketed criminal case; an arrest or search warrant or any information in support thereof; a charging document and an affidavit or other documents filed in support of any charging document, including any driving records; a statement of particulars; discovery material introduced into evidence or otherwise filed with the court; and all information necessary for the proper issuance and execution of a subpoena duces tecum;

ix. Information used by the clerk for case maintenance purposes or the courts for case management purposes; and

x. Information which is relevant and material to an issue before the court. FL ST J ADMIN Rule 2.425(b).

c. *Remedies.* Upon motion by a party or interested person or sua sponte by the court, the court may order remedies, sanctions or both for a violation of FL ST J ADMIN Rule 2.425(a). Following notice and an opportunity to respond, the court may impose sanctions if such filing was not made in good faith. FL ST J ADMIN Rule 2.425(c).

d. *Motions not restricted.* FL ST J ADMIN Rule 2.425 does not restrict a party's right to move for protective order, to move to file documents under seal, or to request a determination of the confidentiality of records. FL ST J ADMIN Rule 2.425(d).

e. *Application.* FL ST J ADMIN Rule 2.425 does not affect the application of constitutional provisions, statutes, or rules of court regarding confidential information or access to public information. FL ST J ADMIN Rule 2.425(e).

F. Filing and Service Requirements

1. *Filing requirements.* All original documents must be filed with the court either before service or immediately thereafter, unless otherwise provided for by general law or other rules. If the original of any bond or other document is not placed in the court file, a certified copy must be so placed by the clerk. FL ST J ADMIN Rule 2.516(d). All documents shall be filed in conformity with the requirements of FL ST J ADMIN Rule 2.525. FL ST RCP Rule 1.080(b). All documents filed in any court shall be filed by electronic transmission in accordance with FL ST J ADMIN Rule 2.525. "Documents" means pleadings, motions, petitions, memoranda, briefs, notices, exhibits, declarations, affidavits, orders, judgments, decrees, writs, opinions, and any other paper or writing submitted to a court. FL ST J ADMIN Rule 2.520(a). All documents that are court records, as defined in FL ST J ADMIN Rule 2.430(a)(1), must be filed by electronic transmission, provided that: (1) the clerk has the ability to accept and retain such documents; (2) the clerk or the chief judge of the circuit has requested permission to accept documents filed by electronic transmission; and (3) the supreme court has entered an order granting permission to the clerk to accept documents filed by electronic transmission. FL ST J ADMIN Rule 2.525(c)(1).

a. *Definition.* "Electronic transmission of documents" means the sending of information by electronic signals to, by or from a court or clerk, which when received can be transformed and stored or transmitted on paper, microfilm, magnetic storage device, optical imaging system, CD-ROM, flash drive, other electronic data storage system, server, case maintenance system ("CM"), electronic court filing ("ECF") system, statewide or local electronic portal ("e-portal"), or other electronic record keeping system authorized by the supreme court in a format sufficient to communicate the information on the original document in a readable format. Electronic transmission of documents includes electronic mail ("e-mail") and any internet-based transmission procedure, and may include procedures allowing for documents to be signed or verified by electronic means. FL ST J ADMIN Rule 2.525(a).

i. The filing of documents with the court as required by the Florida Rules of Judicial Administration must be made by filing them with the clerk in accordance with FL ST J ADMIN Rule 2.525, except that the judge may permit documents to be filed with the judge, in which event the judge must note the filing date before him or her on the documents and transmit them to the

clerk. The date of filing is that shown on the face of the document by the judge's notation or the clerk's time stamp, whichever is earlier. FL ST J ADMIN Rule 2.516(e).

b. *Application.* Any court or clerk of the court may accept the electronic transmission of documents for filing after the clerk, together with input from the chief judge of the circuit, has obtained approval of the procedures and program for doing so from the Supreme Court of Florida. FL ST J ADMIN Rule 2.525(b).

   i. *E-filing mandatory.* All attorneys of record shall be required to follow the protocol set forth in FL ST 11 J CIR 1-09-13-A1(4). FL ST 11 J CIR 1-09-13-A1(3).

c. *Exceptions*

   i. Paper documents and other submissions may be manually submitted to the clerk or court:

      - When the clerk does not have the ability to accept and retain documents by electronic filing or has not had ECF Procedures approved by the supreme court;
      - For filing by any self-represented party or any self-represented nonparty unless specific ECF Procedures provide a means to file documents electronically. However, any self-represented nonparty that is a governmental or public agency and any other agency, partnership, corporation, or business entity acting on behalf of any governmental or public agency may file documents by electronic transmission if such entity has the capability of filing documents electronically;
      - For filing by attorneys excused from e-mail service in accordance with FL ST J ADMIN Rule 2.516(b);
      - When submitting evidentiary exhibits or filing non-documentary materials;
      - When the filing involves documents in excess of twenty-five (25) megabytes (25MB) in size. For such filings, documents may be transmitted using an electronic storage medium that the clerk has the ability to accept, which may include a CD-ROM, flash drive, or similar storage medium;
      - When filed in open court, as permitted by the court;
      - When paper filing is permitted by any approved statewide or local ECF procedures; and
      - If any court determines that justice so requires. FL ST J ADMIN Rule 2.525(d).

   ii. Any document in paper form submitted under FL ST J ADMIN Rule 2.525(d) is filed when it is received by the clerk or court and the clerk shall immediately thereafter convert any filed paper document to an electronic document. "Convert to an electronic document" means optically capturing an image of a paper document and using character recognition software to recover as much of the document's text as practicable and then indexing and storing the document in the official court file. FL ST J ADMIN Rule 2.525(c)(4).

   iii. Any storage medium submitted under FL ST J ADMIN Rule 2.525(d)(5) is filed when received by the clerk or court and the clerk shall immediately thereafter transfer the electronic documents from the storage device to the official court file. FL ST J ADMIN Rule 2.525(c)(5).

   iv. If the filer of any paper document authorized under FL ST J ADMIN Rule 2.525(d) provides a self-addressed, postage-paid envelope for return of the paper document after it is converted to electronic form by the clerk, the clerk shall place the paper document in the envelope and deposit it in the mail. Except when a paper document is required to be maintained, the clerk may recycle any filed paper document that is not to be returned to the filer. FL ST J ADMIN Rule 2.525(c)(6).

   v. The clerk may convert any paper document filed before the effective date of FL ST J ADMIN Rule 2.525 to an electronic document. Unless the clerk is required to maintain the paper document, if the paper document has been converted to an electronic document by the clerk, the paper document is no longer part of the official court file and may be removed and recycled. FL ST J ADMIN Rule 2.525(c)(7).

d. *Official court file.* For information on what constitutes the official court file, please see FL ST J ADMIN Rule 2.525(c)(2), FL ST J ADMIN Rule 2.525(c)(3).

e. *Administration.* All attorneys, parties, or other persons using this rule to file documents are required to make arrangements with the court or clerk for the payment of any charges authorized by general law or the supreme court before filing any document by electronic transmission. FL ST J ADMIN Rule 2.525(f)(2).

f. *Filing date.* The filing date for an electronically transmitted document is the date and time that such filing is acknowledged by an electronic stamp or otherwise, pursuant to any procedure set forth in any ECF Procedures approved by the supreme court, or the date the last page of such filing is received by the court or clerk. FL ST J ADMIN Rule 2.525(f)(3).

g. *Accessibility.* All documents transmitted in any electronic form under FL ST J ADMIN Rule 2.525 must comply with the accessibility requirements of FL ST J ADMIN Rule 2.526. FL ST J ADMIN Rule 2.525(g).

2. *Service requirements.* Every pleading subsequent to the initial pleading, all orders, and every other document filed in the action must be served in conformity with the requirements of FL ST J ADMIN Rule 2.516. FL ST RCP Rule 1.080(a).

a. *Service; When required.* Unless the court otherwise orders, or a statute or supreme court administrative order specifies a different means of service, every pleading subsequent to the initial pleading and every other document filed in any court proceeding, except applications for witness subpoenas and documents served by formal notice or required to be served in the manner provided for service of formal notice, must be served in accordance with FL ST J ADMIN Rule 2.516 on each party. No service need be made on parties against whom a default has been entered, except that pleadings asserting new or additional claims against them must be served in the manner provided for service of summons. FL ST J ADMIN Rule 2.516(a).

b. *Service; How made.* When service is required or permitted to be made upon a party represented by an attorney, service must be made upon the attorney unless service upon the party is ordered by the court. FL ST J ADMIN Rule 2.516(b).

i. *Service by electronic mail ("e-mail").* All documents required or permitted to be served on another party must be served by e-mail, unless FL ST J ADMIN Rule 2.516 otherwise provides. When, in addition to service by e-mail, the sender also utilizes another means of service provided for in FL ST J ADMIN Rule 2.516(b)(2), any differing time limits and other provisions applicable to that other means of service control. FL ST J ADMIN Rule 2.516(b)(1). Any document electronically transmitted to a court or clerk must also be served on all parties and interested persons in accordance with the applicable rules of court. FL ST J ADMIN Rule 2.525(e)(2).

- *Service on attorneys.* Upon appearing in a proceeding, an attorney must serve a designation of a primary e-mail address and may designate no more than two (2) secondary e-mail addresses. Thereafter, service must be directed to all designated e-mail addresses in that proceeding. Every document filed by an attorney thereafter must include the primary e-mail address of that attorney and any secondary e-mail addresses. If an attorney does not designate any e-mail address for service, documents may be served on that attorney at the e-mail address on record with The Florida Bar. FL ST J ADMIN Rule 2.516(b)(1)(A).

- *Exception to e-mail service on attorneys.* Service by an attorney on another attorney must be made by e-mail unless excused by the court. Upon motion by an attorney demonstrating that the attorney has no e-mail account and lacks access to the Internet at the attorney's office, the court may excuse the attorney from the requirements of e-mail service. Service on and by an attorney excused by the court from e-mail service must be by the means provided in FL ST J ADMIN Rule 2.516(b)(2). FL ST J ADMIN Rule 2.516(b)(1)(B).

- *Service on and by parties not represented by an attorney.* Any party not represented by an attorney may serve a designation of a primary e-mail address and also may designate no more than two (2) secondary e-mail addresses to which service must be directed in that proceeding by the means provided in FL ST J ADMIN Rule 2.516(b)(1). If a party not represented by an attorney does not designate an e-mail address for service in a proceeding, service on and by that party must be by the means provided in FL ST J ADMIN Rule 2.516(b)(2). FL ST J ADMIN Rule 2.516(b)(1)(C).

- *Time of service.* Service by e-mail is complete when it is sent. FL ST J ADMIN Rule 2.516(b)(1)(D). An e-mail is deemed served on the date it is sent. FL ST J ADMIN Rule 2.516(b)(1)(D)(i). If the sender learns that the e-mail did not reach the address of the person to be served, the sender must immediately send another copy by e-mail, or by a means authorized by FL ST J ADMIN Rule 2.516(b)(2). FL ST J ADMIN Rule 2.516(b)(1)(D)(ii). E-mail service is treated as service by mail for the computation of time. FL ST J ADMIN Rule 2.516(b)(1)(D)(iii).
- *Specifics of e-mail filing.* In addition to providing proper service pursuant to FL ST RCP Rule 1.080(b), courtesy copies of the Motion and Memorandum of Law for the Uniform Motion Calendar (e.g., Notice of Hearing, Motions, Exhibits, submitted case law, and other hearing specific documents) must be electronically attached to an email using either Microsoft Word or WordPerfect format (not as a PDF document) and sent via email to (a) The Court at its designated e-mail address; (b) Opposing counsel at their fax number as provided to The Florida Bar (see The Florida Bar's website and then click on "Find a Lawyer") or any other fax number provided on a Pleading, Motion to Quash Service, Motion to Dismiss Complaint or Notice of Appearance, whichever is most recent; and (c) Pro se parties at their last known fax number or any other fax number provided on a Pleading, Motion to Quash Service, Motion to Dismiss Complaint or Notice of Appearance, whichever is most recent. FL ST 11 J CIR 1-09-13-A1(4)(b)(i).
- *E-mail subject line.* The subject line of the email must contain only the numeric motion calendar hearing date using the following format: mm/dd/yy (two (2) digit month forward slash; two (2) digit day forward slash; two (2) digit year). For example: 06/15/10. FL ST 11 J CIR 1-09-13-A1(4)(b)(iii).

ii. *Format of e-mail for service.* Service of a document by e-mail is made by attaching a copy of the document in PDF format to an e-mail sent to all addresses designated by the attorney or party. FL ST J ADMIN Rule 2.516(b)(1)(E).

- All documents served by e-mail must be attached to an e-mail message containing a subject line beginning with the words "SERVICE OF COURT DOCUMENT" in all capital letters, followed by the case number of the proceeding in which the documents are being served. FL ST J ADMIN Rule 2.516(b)(1)(E)(i).
- The body of the e-mail must identify the court in which the proceeding is pending, the case number, the name of the initial party on each side, the title of each document served with that e-mail, and the sender's name and telephone number. FL ST J ADMIN Rule 2.516(b)(1)(E)(ii).
- Any document served by e-mail may be signed by the "/s/" format, as long as the filed original is signed in accordance with the applicable rule of procedure. FL ST J ADMIN Rule 2.516(b)(1)(E)(iii).
- Any e-mail which, together with its attached documents, exceeds five megabytes (5MB) in size, must be divided and sent as separate e-mails, no one of which may exceed five megabytes (5MB) in size and each of which must be sequentially numbered in the subject line. FL ST J ADMIN Rule 2.516(b)(1)(E)(iv).

iii. *Service by other means.* In addition to, and not in lieu of, service by e-mail, service may also be made upon attorneys by any of the means specified in FL ST J ADMIN Rule 2.516(b)(2). Service on and by all parties who are not represented by an attorney and who do not designate an e-mail address, and on and by all attorneys excused from e-mail service, must be made by delivering a copy of the document or by mailing it to the party or attorney at their last known address or, if no address is known, by leaving it with the clerk of the court. Service by mail is complete upon mailing. Delivery of a copy within FL ST J ADMIN Rule 2.516 is complete upon:

- Handing it to the attorney or to the party,
- Leaving it at the attorney's or party's office with a clerk or other person in charge thereof,

- If there is no one in charge, leaving it in a conspicuous place therein,
- If the office is closed or the person to be served has no office, leaving it at the person's usual place of abode with some person of his or her family above fifteen (15) years of age and informing such person of the contents, or
- Transmitting it by facsimile to the attorney's or party's office with a cover sheet containing the sender's name, firm, address, telephone number, and facsimile number, and the number of pages transmitted. When service is made by facsimile, a copy must also be served by any other method permitted by FL ST J ADMIN Rule 2.516. Facsimile service occurs when transmission is complete. FL ST J ADMIN Rule 2.516(b)(2)(A) through FL ST J ADMIN Rule 2.516(b)(2)(E).
- Service by delivery after 5:00 p.m. must be deemed to have been made by mailing on the date of delivery. FL ST J ADMIN Rule 2.516(b)(2)(F).
- If a scheduling attorney or a scheduling pro se party does not have a fax number, then a courtesy copy of Motions and Proposed orders must be sent as an attachment to the service of process required pursuant to FL ST RCP Rule 1.080(b). FL ST 11 J CIR 1-09-13-A1(4)(b)(ii).

c. *Service; Numerous defendants.* In actions when the parties are unusually numerous, the court may regulate the service contemplated by the Florida Rules of Judicial Administration on motion or on its own initiative in such manner as may be found to be just and reasonable. FL ST J ADMIN Rule 2.516(c).

d. *Service by clerk.* Service of notices and other documents required to be made by the clerk must also be done as provided in FL ST J ADMIN Rule 2.516(b). FL ST J ADMIN Rule 2.516(g).

G. Hearings

1. *Communication equipment*

a. *Definition.* Communication equipment means a conference telephone or other electronic device that permits all those appearing or participating to hear and speak to each other, provided that all conversation of all parties is audible to all persons present. FL ST J ADMIN Rule 2.530(a).

b. *Use by all parties.* A county or circuit court judge may, upon the court's own motion or upon the written request of a party, direct that communication equipment be used for a motion hearing, pretrial conference, or a status conference. A judge must give notice to the parties and consider any objections they may have to the use of communication equipment before directing that communication equipment be used. The decision to use communication equipment over the objection of parties will be in the sound discretion of the trial court, except as noted below. FL ST J ADMIN Rule 2.530(b).

c. *Use only by requesting party.* A county or circuit court judge may, upon the written request of a party upon reasonable notice to all other parties, permit a requesting party to participate through communication equipment in a scheduled motion hearing; however, any such request (except in criminal, juvenile, and appellate proceedings) must be granted, absent a showing of good cause to deny the same, where the hearing is set for not longer than fifteen (15) minutes. FL ST J ADMIN Rule 2.530(c).

d. *Testimony*

i. *Generally.* A county or circuit court judge, general magistrate, special magistrate, or hearing officer may allow testimony to be taken through communication equipment if all parties consent or if permitted by another applicable rule of procedure. FL ST J ADMIN Rule 2.530(d)(1).

ii. *Procedure.* Any party desiring to present testimony through communication equipment shall, prior to the hearing or trial at which the testimony is to be presented, contact all parties to determine whether each party consents to this form of testimony. The party seeking to present the testimony shall move for permission to present testimony through communication equipment, which motion shall set forth good cause as to why the testimony should be allowed in this form. FL ST J ADMIN Rule 2.530(d)(2).

iii. *Oath.* Testimony may be taken through communication equipment only if a notary public or other person authorized to administer oaths in the witness's jurisdiction is present with the witness and administers the oath consistent with the laws of the jurisdiction. FL ST J ADMIN Rule 2.530(d)(3).

iv. *Confrontation rights.* In juvenile and criminal proceedings the defendant must make an informed waiver of any confrontation rights that may be abridged by the use of communication equipment. FL ST J ADMIN Rule 2.530(d)(4).

v. *Video testimony.* If the testimony to be presented utilizes video conferencing or comparable two-way visual capabilities, the court in its discretion may modify the procedures set forth in FL ST J ADMIN Rule 2.530 to accommodate the technology utilized. FL ST J ADMIN Rule 2.530(d)(5).

e. *Burden of expense.* The cost for the use of the communication equipment is the responsibility of the requesting party unless otherwise directed by the court. FL ST J ADMIN Rule 2.530(e).

2. *Time allotted for hearing.* Each party may set only one five (5) minute motion per case. Multiple motions must be specially set or set on different motion calendars (one five (5) minute motion per party per case), so as not to encroach on the time the Court is allotting for other litigants/attorneys. Consequently, the parties are advised to use good faith efforts to resolve the issues set forth in the motion prior to the setting of a motion; coordinate the date and time of the hearing; and confirm that the hearing shall require no more than five (5) minutes (if the hearing will require more than five (5) minutes, then it must be a Special Set Hearing). FL ST 11 J CIR 1-09-13-A1(4)(b)(i). For information on Special Set Hearings, refer to FL ST 11 J CIR 1-09-13-A1(4)(c).

3. *Hearing cancellation policy.* Should any scheduled hearing become unnecessary or have to be cancelled, the scheduling attorney or scheduling pro se party shall immediately, but, not later than by Noon on the business day prior to the hearing date and time, send an email to the court's designated e-mail address regarding the cancellation of the Motion Calendar hearing with an electronically attached Notice of Cancellation formatted in the same manner (using Microsoft Word or Word Perfect) as the email that scheduled the Motion Calendar hearing and in the same manner as the Motions and Notices. FL ST 11 J CIR 1-09-13-A1(4)(b)(vii).

H. Forms

1. Official Motion to Compel Discovery Forms for Florida

a. Caption. FL ST RCP Form 1.901.

b. Notice of compliance when constitutional challenge is brought. FL ST RCP Form 1.975.

2. Motion to Compel Discovery Forms for Florida

a. Motion to compel attendance and for sanctions. FL-PP § 3:160.

b. Motion; To compel answer to questions asked on oral examination or written questions. FL-PP § 3:161.

c. Order; Directing deponent to answer questions asked on oral examination; Costs and attorney fees to moving party. FL-PP § 3:162.

d. Order; Compelling answer to written questions. FL-PP § 3:163.

e. Motion; For order finding person in contempt of court; Refusal, after order, to answer question. FL-PP § 3:167.

f. Motion; For order compelling opposing party to pay expenses incurred in proving facts the party refused to admit. FL-PP § 3:168.

g. Motion; Compel discovery, deposition. FL-PRACFORM § 7:37.

h. Motion; Compel discovery, interrogatories. FL-PRACFORM § 7:38.

i. Form for motion to compel answer on deposition. FL-RCPF R 1.380(6).

j. Form for certificate of non-appearance at deposition. FL-RCPF R 1.380(7).

k. Form for notice of motion. FL-RCPF R 1.380(8).

l. Form for order on motion to compel answer. FL-RCPF R 1.380(9).
m. Form for notice and motion to compel. FL-RCPF R 1.380(10).
n. Form for order to compel discovery. FL-RCPF R 1.380(18).
o. Form for order to comply with discovery and answer interrogatories. FL-RCPF R 1.380(19).

I. Checklist

(I) ❑ Matters to be considered by moving party
- (a) ❑ Required documents
  - (1) ❑ Notice of hearing/Motion
  - (2) ❑ Certificate of service
- (b) ❑ Supplemental documents
  - (1) ❑ Proposed order
  - (2) ❑ Notice of constitutional question
- (c) ❑ Time for making motion
  - (1) ❑ Upon reasonable notice to other parties and all persons affected, a party may apply for an order compelling discovery
  - (2) ❑ A copy of any written motion which may not be heard ex parte and a copy of the notice of the hearing thereof shall be served a reasonable time before the time specified for the hearing

(II) ❑ Matters to be considered by opposing party
- (a) ❑ Required documents
  - (1) ❑ Response to motion
  - (2) ❑ Certificate of service
- (b) ❑ Supplemental documents
  - (1) ❑ Proposed order
  - (2) ❑ Notice of constitutional question
- (c) ❑ Time for service and filing of opposition
  - (1) ❑ No time specified for responding to a motion

Motions, Oppositions and Replies
Motion for Directed Verdict

Document Last Updated January 2013

A. Applicable Rules

1. *State rules*
   - a. Motion for a directed verdict. FL ST RCP Rule 1.480.
   - b. Rules of court. FL ST RCP Rule 1.010; FL ST J ADMIN Rule 2.110.
   - c. Nonverification of pleadings. FL ST RCP Rule 1.030.
   - d. Service and filing of pleadings, orders, and documents. FL ST RCP Rule 1.080.
   - e. Time. FL ST RCP Rule 1.090.
   - f. Pleadings and motions. FL ST RCP Rule 1.100.
   - g. Motions. FL ST RCP Rule 1.160.
   - h. Relief from judgment, decrees, or orders. FL ST RCP Rule 1.540.
   - i. Mediation and arbitration. FL ST RCP Rule 1.700; FL ST RCP Rule 1.710; FL ST RCP Rule 1.720;

FL ST RCP Rule 1.730; FL ST RCP Rule 1.750; FL ST RCP Rule 1.800; FL ST RCP Rule 1.810; FL ST RCP Rule 1.820; FL ST RCP Rule 1.830.

j. Forms. FL ST RCP Rule 1.900.

k. Minimization of the filing of sensitive information. FL ST J ADMIN Rule 2.425.

l. Retention of court records. FL ST J ADMIN Rule 2.430.

m. Foreign attorneys. FL ST J ADMIN Rule 2.510.

n. Signature of attorneys and parties. FL ST J ADMIN Rule 2.515.

o. Paper. FL ST J ADMIN Rule 2.520.

p. Electronic filing. FL ST J ADMIN Rule 2.525.

q. Accessibility of information and technology. FL ST J ADMIN Rule 2.526.

r. Communication equipment. FL ST J ADMIN Rule 2.530.

s. Court reporting. FL ST J ADMIN Rule 2.535.

t. Requests for accommodations by persons with disabilities. FL ST J ADMIN Rule 2.540.

2. *Local rules*

a. Establishment of 11th Circuit Homestead Access to Mediation Program ("CHAMP") for case management of residential foreclosure cases in the Eleventh Judicial Circuit of Florida. FL ST 11 J CIR 1-09-08.

b. Enlargement and expansion of the current pilot project for electronic submissions of courtesy copies for uniform motion calendar and requests for special set hearings, emergency motions, and proposed orders. FL ST 11 J CIR 1-09-13-A1.

B. Timing

1. *Before a verdict is returned.* A directed verdict is available to the defendant at the close of the plaintiff's evidence or to either party at the close of all of the evidence. A verdict may be directed either by the court on its own motion or on the motion of counsel. FL ST RCP Rule 1.480(a); FL-PP § 5:83. The movant should be prepared to argue the motion immediately. FL-PRACPROC § 22:14.

2. *After a verdict is returned.* Within ten (10) days after the return of a verdict, a party who has timely moved for a directed verdict may serve a motion to enter judgment in accordance with the motion for a directed verdict. FL ST RCP Rule 1.480(b).

3. *No verdict is returned.* If a verdict was not returned, a party who has timely moved for a directed verdict may serve a motion for judgment in accordance with the motion for a directed verdict within ten (10) days after discharge of the jury. FL ST RCP Rule 1.480(b).

4. *General motion timing.* A copy of any written motion which may not be heard ex parte and a copy of the notice of the hearing thereof shall be served a reasonable time before the time specified for the hearing. FL ST RCP Rule 1.090(d).

5. *Computation of time*

a. *Generally.* Computation of time shall be governed by FL ST J ADMIN Rule 2.514. FL ST RCP Rule 1.090(a). The following rules apply in computing time periods specified in any rule of procedure, local rule, court order, or statute that does not specify a method of computing time. FL ST J ADMIN Rule 2.514(a).

i. *Period stated in days or a longer unit.* When the period is stated in days or a longer unit of time (A) exclude the day of the event that triggers the period; (B) count every day, including intermediate Saturdays, Sundays, and legal holidays; and (C) include the last day of the period, but if the last day is a Saturday, Sunday, or legal holiday, or falls within any period of time extended through an order of the chief justice under FL ST J ADMIN Rule 2.205(a)(2)(B)(iv), the period continues to run until the end of the next day that is not a Saturday, Sunday, or legal holiday and does not fall within any period of time extended through an order of the chief justice. FL ST J ADMIN Rule 2.514(a)(1).

ii. *Period stated in hours.* When the period is stated in hours (A) begin counting immediately on the occurrence of the event that triggers the period; (B) count every hour, including hours during intermediate Saturdays, Sundays, and legal holidays; and (C) if the period would end on a Saturday, Sunday, or legal holiday, or during any period of time extended through an order of the chief justice under FL ST J ADMIN Rule 2.205(a)(2)(B)(iv), the period continues to run until the same time on the next day that is not a Saturday, Sunday, or legal holiday and does not fall within any period of time extended through an order of the chief justice. FL ST J ADMIN Rule 2.514(a)(2).

iii. *Period stated in days less than seven (7) days.* When the period stated in days is less than seven (7) days, intermediate Saturdays, Sundays, and legal holidays shall be excluded in the computation. FL ST J ADMIN Rule 2.514(a)(3).

iv. *"Last day" defined.* Unless a different time is set by a statute, local rule, or court order, the last day ends (A) for electronic filing or for service by any means, at midnight; and (B) for filing by other means, when the clerk's office is scheduled to close. FL ST J ADMIN Rule 2.514(a)(4).

v. *"Next day" defined.* The "next day" is determined by continuing to count forward when the period is measured after an event and backward when measured before an event. FL ST J ADMIN Rule 2.514(a)(5).

vi. *"Legal holiday" defined.* "Legal holiday" means (A) the day set aside by FL ST § 110.117, for observing New Year's Day, Martin Luther King, Jr.'s Birthday, Memorial Day, Independence Day, Labor Day, Veterans' Day, Thanksgiving Day, the Friday after Thanksgiving Day, or Christmas Day, and (B) any day observed as a holiday by the clerk's office or as designated by the chief judge. FL ST J ADMIN Rule 2.514(a)(6).

b. *Additional time after service by mail or e-mail.* When a party may or must act within a specified time after service and service is made by mail or e-mail, five (5) days are added after the period that would otherwise expire under FL ST J ADMIN Rule 2.514(a). FL ST J ADMIN Rule 2.514(b).

c. *Enlargement.* When an act is required or allowed to be done at or within a specified time by order of court, by the Florida Rules of Civil Procedure, or by notice given thereunder, for cause shown the court at any time in its discretion (1) with or without notice, may order the period enlarged if request therefor is made before the expiration of the period originally prescribed or as extended by a previous order, or (2) upon motion made and notice after the expiration of the specified period, may permit the act to be done when failure to act was the result of excusable neglect, but it may not extend the time for making a motion for new trial, for rehearing, or to alter or amend a judgment; making a motion for relief from a judgment under FL ST RCP Rule 1.540(b); taking an appeal or filing a petition for certiorari; or making a motion for a directed verdict. FL ST RCP Rule 1.090(b).

d. *Unaffected by expiration of term.* The period of time provided for the doing of any act or the taking of any proceeding shall not be affected or limited by the continued existence or expiration of a term of court. The continued existence or expiration of a term of court in no way affects the power of a court to do any act or take any proceeding in any action which is or has been pending before it. FL ST RCP Rule 1.090(c).

C. General Requirements

1. *Motions generally*

a. *Contents.* An application to the court for an order shall be by motion which shall be made in writing unless made during a hearing or trial, shall state with particularity the grounds therefor, and shall set forth the relief or order sought. The requirement of writing is fulfilled if the motion is stated in a written notice of the hearing of the motion. All notices of hearing shall specify each motion or other matter to be heard. FL ST RCP Rule 1.100(b).

b. *Particularity requirement.* The court considers a motion in the light of the substantive law, rule or statute to make its determination. Some rules require a statement of the grounds for a motion under the rule. Failure to give the grounds will result in denial of the motion. This should be the result in all situations when the ground for the motion is not inherent in the rule. FL-PRACPROC § 9:3. The requirement is nevertheless an important one, first because of the due process notice rights of the respondent, as well as for the assistance it provides to the court in its preparation for the hearing or, absent a hearing, for disposition. 4 FLPRAC R 1.100.

2. *Motion for directed verdict*
    a. *Effect of a motion for directed verdict.* A party who moves for a directed verdict at the close of the evidence offered by the adverse party may offer evidence in the event the motion is denied without having reserved the right to do so and to the same extent as if the motion had not been made. The denial of a motion for a directed verdict shall not operate to discharge the jury. A motion for a directed verdict shall state the specific grounds therefor. The order directing a verdict is effective without any assent of the jury. FL ST RCP Rule 1.480(a).
    b. *Reservation of decision on motion.* When a motion for a directed verdict is denied or for any reason is not granted, the court is deemed to have submitted the action to the jury subject to a later determination of the legal questions raised by the motion. Within ten (10) days after the return of a verdict, a party who has timely moved for a directed verdict may serve a motion to set aside the verdict and any judgment entered thereon and to enter judgment in accordance with the motion for a directed verdict. If a verdict was not returned, a party who has timely moved for a directed verdict may serve a motion for judgment in accordance with the motion for a directed verdict within ten (10) days after discharge of the jury. FL ST RCP Rule 1.480(b).
    c. *Joined with motion for new trial.* A motion for a new trial may be joined with a motion for directed verdict or a new trial may be requested in the alternative. If a verdict was returned, the court may allow the judgment to stand or may reopen the judgment and either order a new trial or direct the entry of judgment as if the requested verdict had been directed. If no verdict was returned, the court may direct the entry of judgment as if the requested verdict had been directed or may order a new trial. FL ST RCP Rule 1.480(c).
    d. *General procedures on a motion for directed verdict*
        i. *Proper method.* The proper method of advocating that a party is entitled to prevail on a claim or defense as a matter of law is to make a motion for a directed verdict at the close of the evidence offered by the opposing party. The trial judge has authority to direct a verdict in favor of one party and against another, without submitting the case to the jury, if there is no other verdict the jury could lawfully return. 5 FLPRAC § 22:5.
        ii. *Directed verdict only in a jury trial.* A motion for directed verdict is proper only in a jury trial. The equivalent motion in nonjury trial is called a motion for involuntary dismissal. 5 FLPRAC § 22:5.
        iii. *Test for the sufficiency of the evidence.* A motion for directed verdict is used primarily to test the sufficiency of the evidence offered in support of a claim or defense. It may also be used to raise legal issues other than the sufficiency of the evidence, but that is less common because most pure issues of law can be resolved on a motion to dismiss or a motion for summary judgment before the case is set for trial. If there is no evidence to support a claim or defense, the trial judge has a duty to direct a verdict for the opposing party on that claim or defense. 5 FLPRAC § 22:5.
            - The trial judge must view all of the facts and factual inferences in a light most favorable to the party opposing the motion. 5 FLPRAC § 22:5.
            - The rule has often been stated by the Florida courts in the negative, that is, a motion for directed verdict should not be granted unless the court, after viewing the evidence and testimony in the light most favorable to the nonmoving party, determines that no reasonable jury could render a verdict for the nonmoving party. Under this rule, the trial judge may not direct a verdict against a party if there is any evidence upon which the jury could lawfully make a finding in favor of that party. 5 FLPRAC § 22:5.

3. *Arbitration and mediation*
    a. *Referral to arbitration and mediation.* Except as hereinafter provided or as otherwise prohibited by law, the presiding judge may enter an order referring all or any part of a contested civil matter to mediation or arbitration. The parties to any contested civil matter may file a written stipulation to

mediate or arbitrate any issue between them at any time. Such stipulation shall be incorporated into the order of referral. FL ST RCP Rule 1.700(a).

i. In all residential foreclosure actions involving homestead properties filed on or after May 1, 2009, unless a stipulation is specifically invoked by the parties in writing within five (5) days of service of the complaint on the main defendant, the parties are deemed to have stipulated to referral of the mediation to the Collins Center pursuant to FL ST RCP Rule 1.720(f). FL ST 11 J CIR 1-09-08(2); FL ST 11 J CIR 1-09-08(3). FL ST 11 J CIR 1-09-08 constitutes a formal referral to mediation pursuant to the Florida Rules of Civil Procedure. FL ST 11 J CIR 1-09-08(2).

ii. For further information on referral to mediation, refer to FL ST 11 J CIR 1-09-08.

b. *Arbitration*

i. *Exclusions.* A civil action shall be ordered to arbitration or arbitration in conjunction with mediation upon stipulation of the parties. A civil action may be ordered to arbitration or arbitration in conjunction with mediation upon motion of any party or by the court, if the judge determines the action to be of such a nature that arbitration could be of benefit to the litigants or the court. FL ST RCP Rule 1.800.

- Under no circumstances may the following categories of actions be referred to arbitration: (1) bond estreatures; (2) habeas corpus or other extraordinary writs; (3) bond validations; (4) civil or criminal contempt; (5) such other matters as may be specified by order of the chief judge in the circuit. FL ST RCP Rule 1.800.

ii. For more information regarding arbitration, please see FL ST RCP Rule 1.810; FL ST RCP Rule 1.820; FL ST RCP Rule 1.830.

c. *Mediation.* For more information regarding mediation, please see FL ST RCP Rule 1.710; FL ST RCP Rule 1.720; FL ST RCP Rule 1.730; and FL ST RCP Rule 1.750.

4. *Rules of court*

a. *Rules of civil procedure.* The Florida Rules of Civil Procedure apply to all actions of a civil nature and all special statutory proceedings in the circuit courts and county courts except those to which the Florida Probate Rules, the Florida Family Law Rules of Procedure, or the Small Claims Rules apply. FL ST RCP Rule 1.010.

i. The form, content, procedure, and time for pleading in all special statutory proceedings shall be as prescribed by the statutes governing the proceeding unless the Florida Rules of Civil Procedure specifically provide to the contrary. FL ST RCP Rule 1.010.

ii. The Florida Rules of Civil Procedure shall be construed to secure the just, speedy, and inexpensive determination of every action. FL ST RCP Rule 1.010.

b. *Rules of judicial administration.* The Florida Rules of Judicial Administration shall apply to administrative matters in all courts to which the Florida Rules of Judicial Administration are applicable by their terms. The Florida Rules of Judicial Administration shall be construed to secure the speedy and inexpensive determination of every proceeding to which they are applicable. The Florida Rules of Judicial Administration shall supersede all conflicting rules and statutes. FL ST J ADMIN Rule 2.110.

D. Documents

1. *Required documents*

a. *Notice of hearing/Motion.* An application to the court for an order shall be by motion which shall be made in writing unless made during a hearing or trial, shall state with particularity the grounds therefor, and shall set forth the relief or order sought. The requirement of writing is fulfilled if the motion is stated in a written notice of the hearing of the motion. All notices of hearing shall specify each motion or other matter to be heard. FL ST RCP Rule 1.100(b).

i. *Notices to persons with disabilities.* See the Format section of this KeyRules document for further information.

b. *Certificate of service.* When any attorney certifies in substance: "I certify that a copy hereof has been furnished to (here insert name or names and addresses used for service) by (e-mail) (delivery) (mail) (fax) on .... (date) ....______________ Attorney" the certificate is taken as prima facie proof of such service in compliance with FL ST J ADMIN Rule 2.516. FL ST J ADMIN Rule 2.516(f).

2. *Supplemental documents*

a. *Proposed order.* The court may require that orders or judgments be prepared by a party, may require the party to furnish the court with stamped, addressed envelopes for service of the order or judgment, and may require that proposed orders and judgments be furnished to all parties before entry by the court of the order or judgment. FL ST J ADMIN Rule 2.516(h)(1). For additional information on the submission of proposed orders, refer to FL ST 11 J CIR 1-09-13-A1(e).

b. *Notice of constitutional question.* A party that files a pleading, written motion, or other paper drawing into question the constitutionality of a state statute or a county or municipal charter, ordinance, or franchise must promptly (1) file a notice of constitutional question stating the question and identifying the paper that raises it; and (2) serve the notice and the pleading, written motion, or other paper drawing into question the constitutionality of a state statute or a county or municipal charter, ordinance, or franchise on the Attorney General or the state attorney of the judicial circuit in which the action is pending, by either certified or registered mail. Service of the notice and pleading, written motion, or other paper does not require joinder of the Attorney General or the state attorney as a party to the action. FL ST RCP Rule 1.071.

E. Format

1. *Documents; Type and size.* Documents subject to the exceptions set forth in FL ST J ADMIN Rule 2.525(d) shall be filed on recycled paper measuring eight and one half by eleven (8 1/2 by 11) inches. For purposes of FL ST J ADMIN Rule 2.520, paper is recycled if it contains a minimum content of fifty (50) percent waste paper. Xerographic reduction of legal-size (eight and one half by fourteen (8 1/2 by 14) inches) documents to letter size (eight and one half by eleven (8 1/2 by 11) inches) is prohibited. All other documents filed by electronic transmission shall be filed in a format capable of being printed in a format consistent with the provisions of FL ST J ADMIN Rule 2.250. FL ST J ADMIN Rule 2.520(b).

a. *Exhibits.* Any exhibit or attachment filed with pleadings or papers may be filed in its original size. FL ST J ADMIN Rule 2.520(c).

b. *Recording space.* On all papers and documents prepared and filed by the court or by any party to a proceeding which are to be recorded in the public records of any county, including but not limited to final money judgments and notices of lis pendens, a three (3) inch by three (3) inch space at the top right-hand corner on the first page and a one (1) inch by three (3) inch space at the top right-hand corner on each subsequent page shall be left blank and reserved for use by the clerk of court. FL ST J ADMIN Rule 2.520(d).

i. *Exceptions to recording space.* Any papers or documents created by persons or entities over which the filing party has no control, including but not limited to wills, codicils, trusts, or other testamentary documents; documents prepared or executed by any public officer; documents prepared, executed, acknowledged, or proved outside of the State of Florida; or documents created by State or Federal government agencies, may be filed without the space required by FL ST J ADMIN Rule 2.520. FL ST J ADMIN Rule 2.520(e).

c. *Noncompliance.* No clerk of court is permitted to refuse to file any document or paper because of noncompliance with the Florida Rules of Judicial Administration. However, upon request of the clerk of court, noncomplying documents must be resubmitted in accordance with the formatting rules. FL ST J ADMIN Rule 2.520(f).

d. *Format of electronically filed documents.* Hyperlinks in the attachments, (not in the body of the email) are encouraged just as are submissions in Microsoft Word format. Electronic versions submitted in WordPerfect will be converted by the Court to Microsoft Word and there is no guarantee that the document will be converted without error. FL ST 11 J CIR 1-09-13-A1(4)(b)(v).

2. *Caption.* Every pleading, motion, order, judgment, or other paper shall have a caption containing the name of the court, the file number, and except for in rem proceedings, including forfeiture proceedings,

the name of the first party on each side with an appropriate indication of other parties, and a designation identifying the party filing it and its nature or the nature of the order, as the case may be. In any in rem proceeding, every pleading, motion, order, judgment, or other paper shall have a caption containing the name of the court, the file number, the style "In re" (followed by the name or general description of the property), and a designation of the person or entity filing it and its nature or the nature of the order, as the case may be. In an in rem forfeiture proceeding, the style shall be "In re forfeiture of" (followed by the name of the general description of the property). All papers filed in the action shall be styled in such a manner as to indicate clearly the subject matter of the paper and the party requesting or obtaining relief. FL ST RCP Rule 1.100(c)(1).

a. *Caption of electronically filed documents.* All submitted documents shall be titled with the Court Case Number and the name/type of document using the following format: two (2) digit year followed by a hyphen with the sequential case number (e.g., 09-1; 91-12; 08-123; 07-1234; or 09-12345). Do not use zeros after the hyphen to fill in the sequential case number. FL ST 11 J CIR 1-09-13-A1(4)(a).

3. *Writing and written defined.* Writing or written means a document containing information, an application, or a stipulation. FL ST RCP Rule 1.080(c).

4. *Rule abbreviations*

   a. The Florida Rules of Civil Procedure and shall be abbreviated as Fla.R.Civ.P. FL ST RCP Rule 1.010.

   b. The Florida Rules of Judicial Administration shall be abbreviated as Fla. R. Jud. Admin. FL ST J ADMIN Rule 2.110.

5. *Nonverification.* Except when otherwise specifically provided by the Florida Rules of Civil Procedure or an applicable statute, every pleading or other document of a party represented by an attorney need not be verified or accompanied by an affidavit. FL ST RCP Rule 1.030; FL ST J ADMIN Rule 2.515(a).

6. *Attorney signature*

   a. *Attorney signature.* Every pleading and other document of a party represented by an attorney shall be signed by at least one (1) attorney of record in that attorney's individual name whose current record Florida Bar address, telephone number, including area code, primary e-mail address and secondary e-mail addresses, if any, and Florida Bar number shall be stated, and who shall be duly licensed to practice law in Florida or who shall have received permission to appear in the particular case as provided in FL ST J ADMIN Rule 2.510. FL ST J ADMIN Rule 2.515(a).

      i. The attorney may be required by the court to give the address of, and to vouch for the attorney's authority to represent, the party. FL ST J ADMIN Rule 2.515(a).

      ii. The signature of an attorney shall constitute a certificate by the attorney that the attorney has read the pleading or other document; that to the best of the attorney's knowledge, information, and belief there is good ground to support it; and that it is not interposed for delay. FL ST J ADMIN Rule 2.515(a).

      iii. If a pleading is not signed or is signed with intent to defeat the purpose of FL ST J ADMIN Rule 2.515, it may be stricken and the action may proceed as though the pleading or other document had not been served. FL ST J ADMIN Rule 2.515(a).

   b. *Pro se litigant signature.* A party who is not represented by an attorney shall sign any pleading or other paper and state the party's address and telephone number, including area code. FL ST J ADMIN Rule 2.515(b).

   c. *Form of signature*

      i. The signatures required on pleadings and documents by FL ST J ADMIN Rule 2.515(a) and FL ST J ADMIN Rule 2.515(b) may be:

         - Original signatures;
         - Original signatures that have been reproduced by electronic means, such as on electronically transmitted documents or photocopied documents;
         - Electronic signatures using the "/s/," "s/," or "/s" formats by or at the direction of the person signing; or

- Any other signature format authorized by general law, so long as the clerk where the proceeding is pending has the capability of receiving and has obtained approval from the Supreme Court of Florida to accept pleadings and documents with that signature format. FL ST J ADMIN Rule 2.515(c)(1).

ii. An attorney, party, or other person who files a pleading or paper by electronic transmission that does not contain the original signature of that attorney, party, or other person shall file that identical pleading or paper in paper form containing an original signature of that attorney, party, or other person (hereinafter called the follow-up filing) immediately thereafter. The follow-up filing is not required if the Supreme Court of Florida has entered an order directing the clerk of court to discontinue accepting the follow-up filing. FL ST J ADMIN Rule 2.515(c)(2).

7. *Forms*
   a. *Process.* The forms of process, notice of lis pendens, and notice of action provided in the Florida Rules of Civil Procedure are sufficient. Variations from the forms do not void process or notices that are otherwise sufficient. FL ST RCP Rule 1.900(a).
   b. *Other forms.* The other forms provided in the Florida Rules of Civil Procedure are sufficient for the matters that are covered by them. So long as the substance is expressed without prolixity, the forms may be varied to meet the facts of a particular case. FL ST RCP Rule 1.900(b).
   c. *Formal matters.* Captions, except for the designation of the paper, are omitted from the forms provided in the Florida Rules of Civil Procedure. A general form of caption is the first form provided. Signatures are omitted from pleadings and motions. FL ST RCP Rule 1.900(c).
8. *Notices to persons with disabilities.* All notices of court proceedings to be held in a public facility, and all process compelling appearance at such proceedings, shall include the following statement in bold face, fourteen (14) point Times New Roman or Courier font: "If you are a person with a disability who needs any accommodation in order to participate in this proceeding, you are entitled, at no cost to you, to the provision of certain assistance. Please contact [identify applicable court personnel by name, address, and telephone number] at least seven (7) days before your scheduled court appearance, or immediately upon receiving this notification if the time before the scheduled appearance is less than seven (7) days; if you are hearing or voice impaired, call 711." FL ST J ADMIN Rule 2.540(c)(1).
9. *Minimization of the filing of sensitive information*
   a. *Limitations for court filings.* Unless authorized by FL ST J ADMIN Rule 2.425(b), statute, another rule of court, or the court orders otherwise, designated sensitive information filed with the court must be limited to the following format:
      i. The initials of a person known to be a minor;
      ii. The year of birth of a person's birth date;
      iii. No portion of any: Social security number, Bank account number, Credit card account number, Charge account number, or Debit account number;
      iv. The last four digits of any: Taxpayer identification number (TIN), Employee identification number, Driver's license number, Passport number, Telephone number, Financial account number, except as set forth in FL ST J ADMIN Rule 2.425(a)(3), Brokerage account number, Insurance policy account number, Loan account number, Customer account number, or Patient or health care number;
      v. A truncated version of any: Email address, Computer user name, Password, or Personal identification number (PIN); and
      vi. A truncated version of any other sensitive information as provided by court order. FL ST J ADMIN Rule 2.425(a).
   b. *Exceptions.* FL ST J ADMIN Rule 2.425(a) does not apply to the following:
      i. An account number which identifies the property alleged to be the subject of a proceeding;
      ii. The record of an administrative or agency proceeding;
      iii. The record in appellate or review proceedings;

iv. The birth date of a minor whenever the birth date is necessary for the court to establish or maintain subject matter jurisdiction;

v. The name of a minor in any order relating to parental responsibility, time-sharing, or child support;

vi. The name of a minor in any document or order affecting the minor's ownership of real property;

vii. The birth date of a party in a writ of attachment or notice to payor;

viii. In traffic and criminal proceedings: a pro se filing; a court filing that is related to a criminal matter or investigation and that is prepared before the filing of a criminal charge or is not filed as part of any docketed criminal case; an arrest or search warrant or any information in support thereof; a charging document and an affidavit or other documents filed in support of any charging document, including any driving records; a statement of particulars; discovery material introduced into evidence or otherwise filed with the court; and all information necessary for the proper issuance and execution of a subpoena duces tecum;

ix. Information used by the clerk for case maintenance purposes or the courts for case management purposes; and

x. Information which is relevant and material to an issue before the court. FL ST J ADMIN Rule 2.425(b).

c. *Remedies.* Upon motion by a party or interested person or sua sponte by the court, the court may order remedies, sanctions or both for a violation of FL ST J ADMIN Rule 2.425(a). Following notice and an opportunity to respond, the court may impose sanctions if such filing was not made in good faith. FL ST J ADMIN Rule 2.425(c).

d. *Motions not restricted.* FL ST J ADMIN Rule 2.425 does not restrict a party's right to move for protective order, to move to file documents under seal, or to request a determination of the confidentiality of records. FL ST J ADMIN Rule 2.425(d).

e. *Application.* FL ST J ADMIN Rule 2.425 does not affect the application of constitutional provisions, statutes, or rules of court regarding confidential information or access to public information. FL ST J ADMIN Rule 2.425(e).

F. Filing and Service Requirements

1. *Filing requirements.* All original documents must be filed with the court either before service or immediately thereafter, unless otherwise provided for by general law or other rules. If the original of any bond or other document is not placed in the court file, a certified copy must be so placed by the clerk. FL ST J ADMIN Rule 2.516(d). All documents shall be filed in conformity with the requirements of FL ST J ADMIN Rule 2.525. FL ST RCP Rule 1.080(b). All documents filed in any court shall be filed by electronic transmission in accordance with FL ST J ADMIN Rule 2.525. "Documents" means pleadings, motions, petitions, memoranda, briefs, notices, exhibits, declarations, affidavits, orders, judgments, decrees, writs, opinions, and any other paper or writing submitted to a court. FL ST J ADMIN Rule 2.520(a). All documents that are court records, as defined in FL ST J ADMIN Rule 2.430(a)(1), must be filed by electronic transmission, provided that: (1) the clerk has the ability to accept and retain such documents; (2) the clerk or the chief judge of the circuit has requested permission to accept documents filed by electronic transmission; and (3) the supreme court has entered an order granting permission to the clerk to accept documents filed by electronic transmission. FL ST J ADMIN Rule 2.525(c)(1).

a. *Definition.* "Electronic transmission of documents" means the sending of information by electronic signals to, by or from a court or clerk, which when received can be transformed and stored or transmitted on paper, microfilm, magnetic storage device, optical imaging system, CD-ROM, flash drive, other electronic data storage system, server, case maintenance system ("CM"), electronic court filing ("ECF") system, statewide or local electronic portal ("e-portal"), or other electronic record keeping system authorized by the supreme court in a format sufficient to communicate the information on the original document in a readable format. Electronic transmission of documents includes electronic mail ("e-mail") and any internet-based transmission procedure, and may include procedures allowing for documents to be signed or verified by electronic means. FL ST J ADMIN Rule 2.525(a).

i. The filing of documents with the court as required by the Florida Rules of Judicial Adminis-

tration must be made by filing them with the clerk in accordance with FL ST J ADMIN Rule 2.525, except that the judge may permit documents to be filed with the judge, in which event the judge must note the filing date before him or her on the documents and transmit them to the clerk. The date of filing is that shown on the face of the document by the judge's notation or the clerk's time stamp, whichever is earlier. FL ST J ADMIN Rule 2.516(e).

b. *Application.* Any court or clerk of the court may accept the electronic transmission of documents for filing after the clerk, together with input from the chief judge of the circuit, has obtained approval of the procedures and program for doing so from the Supreme Court of Florida. FL ST J ADMIN Rule 2.525(b).

   i. *E-filing mandatory.* All attorneys of record shall be required to follow the protocol set forth in FL ST 11 J CIR 1-09-13-A1(4). FL ST 11 J CIR 1-09-13-A1(3).

c. *Exceptions*

   i. Paper documents and other submissions may be manually submitted to the clerk or court:

      - When the clerk does not have the ability to accept and retain documents by electronic filing or has not had ECF Procedures approved by the supreme court;
      - For filing by any self-represented party or any self-represented nonparty unless specific ECF Procedures provide a means to file documents electronically. However, any self-represented nonparty that is a governmental or public agency and any other agency, partnership, corporation, or business entity acting on behalf of any governmental or public agency may file documents by electronic transmission if such entity has the capability of filing documents electronically;
      - For filing by attorneys excused from e-mail service in accordance with FL ST J ADMIN Rule 2.516(b);
      - When submitting evidentiary exhibits or filing non-documentary materials;
      - When the filing involves documents in excess of twenty-five (25) megabytes (25MB) in size. For such filings, documents may be transmitted using an electronic storage medium that the clerk has the ability to accept, which may include a CD-ROM, flash drive, or similar storage medium;
      - When filed in open court, as permitted by the court;
      - When paper filing is permitted by any approved statewide or local ECF procedures; and
      - If any court determines that justice so requires. FL ST J ADMIN Rule 2.525(d).

   ii. Any document in paper form submitted under FL ST J ADMIN Rule 2.525(d) is filed when it is received by the clerk or court and the clerk shall immediately thereafter convert any filed paper document to an electronic document. "Convert to an electronic document" means optically capturing an image of a paper document and using character recognition software to recover as much of the document's text as practicable and then indexing and storing the document in the official court file. FL ST J ADMIN Rule 2.525(c)(4).

   iii. Any storage medium submitted under FL ST J ADMIN Rule 2.525(d)(5) is filed when received by the clerk or court and the clerk shall immediately thereafter transfer the electronic documents from the storage device to the official court file. FL ST J ADMIN Rule 2.525(c)(5).

   iv. If the filer of any paper document authorized under FL ST J ADMIN Rule 2.525(d) provides a self-addressed, postage-paid envelope for return of the paper document after it is converted to electronic form by the clerk, the clerk shall place the paper document in the envelope and deposit it in the mail. Except when a paper document is required to be maintained, the clerk may recycle any filed paper document that is not to be returned to the filer. FL ST J ADMIN Rule 2.525(c)(6).

   v. The clerk may convert any paper document filed before the effective date of FL ST J ADMIN Rule 2.525 to an electronic document. Unless the clerk is required to maintain the paper document, if the paper document has been converted to an electronic document by the clerk, the paper document is no longer part of the official court file and may be removed and recycled. FL ST J ADMIN Rule 2.525(c)(7).

d. *Official court file.* For information on what constitutes the official court file, please see FL ST J ADMIN Rule 2.525(c)(2), FL ST J ADMIN Rule 2.525(c)(3).

e. *Administration.* All attorneys, parties, or other persons using this rule to file documents are required to make arrangements with the court or clerk for the payment of any charges authorized by general law or the supreme court before filing any document by electronic transmission. FL ST J ADMIN Rule 2.525(f)(2).

f. *Filing date.* The filing date for an electronically transmitted document is the date and time that such filing is acknowledged by an electronic stamp or otherwise, pursuant to any procedure set forth in any ECF Procedures approved by the supreme court, or the date the last page of such filing is received by the court or clerk. FL ST J ADMIN Rule 2.525(f)(3).

g. *Accessibility.* All documents transmitted in any electronic form under FL ST J ADMIN Rule 2.525 must comply with the accessibility requirements of FL ST J ADMIN Rule 2.526. FL ST J ADMIN Rule 2.525(g).

2. *Service requirements.* Every pleading subsequent to the initial pleading, all orders, and every other document filed in the action must be served in conformity with the requirements of FL ST J ADMIN Rule 2.516. FL ST RCP Rule 1.080(a).

a. *Service; When required.* Unless the court otherwise orders, or a statute or supreme court administrative order specifies a different means of service, every pleading subsequent to the initial pleading and every other document filed in any court proceeding, except applications for witness subpoenas and documents served by formal notice or required to be served in the manner provided for service of formal notice, must be served in accordance with FL ST J ADMIN Rule 2.516 on each party. No service need be made on parties against whom a default has been entered, except that pleadings asserting new or additional claims against them must be served in the manner provided for service of summons. FL ST J ADMIN Rule 2.516(a).

b. *Service; How made.* When service is required or permitted to be made upon a party represented by an attorney, service must be made upon the attorney unless service upon the party is ordered by the court. FL ST J ADMIN Rule 2.516(b).

i. *Service by electronic mail ("e-mail").* All documents required or permitted to be served on another party must be served by e-mail, unless FL ST J ADMIN Rule 2.516 otherwise provides. When, in addition to service by e-mail, the sender also utilizes another means of service provided for in FL ST J ADMIN Rule 2.516(b)(2), any differing time limits and other provisions applicable to that other means of service control. FL ST J ADMIN Rule 2.516(b)(1). Any document electronically transmitted to a court or clerk must also be served on all parties and interested persons in accordance with the applicable rules of court. FL ST J ADMIN Rule 2.525(e)(2).

- *Service on attorneys.* Upon appearing in a proceeding, an attorney must serve a designation of a primary e-mail address and may designate no more than two (2) secondary e-mail addresses. Thereafter, service must be directed to all designated e-mail addresses in that proceeding. Every document filed by an attorney thereafter must include the primary e-mail address of that attorney and any secondary e-mail addresses. If an attorney does not designate any e-mail address for service, documents may be served on that attorney at the e-mail address on record with The Florida Bar. FL ST J ADMIN Rule 2.516(b)(1)(A).

- *Exception to e-mail service on attorneys.* Service by an attorney on another attorney must be made by e-mail unless excused by the court. Upon motion by an attorney demonstrating that the attorney has no e-mail account and lacks access to the Internet at the attorney's office, the court may excuse the attorney from the requirements of e-mail service. Service on and by an attorney excused by the court from e-mail service must be by the means provided in FL ST J ADMIN Rule 2.516(b)(2). FL ST J ADMIN Rule 2.516(b)(1)(B).

- *Service on and by parties not represented by an attorney.* Any party not represented by an attorney may serve a designation of a primary e-mail address and also may designate no more than two (2) secondary e-mail addresses to which service must be directed in that proceeding by the means provided in FL ST J ADMIN Rule 2.516(b)(1). If a party not represented by an attorney does not designate an e-mail address for service in a proceeding, service on and by that party must be by the means provided in FL ST J ADMIN Rule 2.516(b)(2). FL ST J ADMIN Rule 2.516(b)(1)(C).

- *Time of service.* Service by e-mail is complete when it is sent. FL ST J ADMIN Rule 2.516(b)(1)(D). An e-mail is deemed served on the date it is sent. FL ST J ADMIN Rule 2.516(b)(1)(D)(i). If the sender learns that the e-mail did not reach the address of the person to be served, the sender must immediately send another copy by e-mail, or by a means authorized by FL ST J ADMIN Rule 2.516(b)(2). FL ST J ADMIN Rule 2.516(b)(1)(D)(ii). E-mail service is treated as service by mail for the computation of time. FL ST J ADMIN Rule 2.516(b)(1)(D)(iii).
- *Specifics of e-mail filing.* In addition to providing proper service pursuant to FL ST RCP Rule 1.080(b), courtesy copies of the Motion and Memorandum of Law for the Uniform Motion Calendar (e.g., Notice of Hearing, Motions, Exhibits, submitted case law, and other hearing specific documents) must be electronically attached to an email using either Microsoft Word or WordPerfect format (not as a PDF document) and sent via email to (a) The Court at its designated e-mail address; (b) Opposing counsel at their fax number as provided to The Florida Bar (see The Florida Bar's website and then click on "Find a Lawyer") or any other fax number provided on a Pleading, Motion to Quash Service, Motion to Dismiss Complaint or Notice of Appearance, whichever is most recent; and (c) Pro se parties at their last known fax number or any other fax number provided on a Pleading, Motion to Quash Service, Motion to Dismiss Complaint or Notice of Appearance, whichever is most recent. FL ST 11 J CIR 1-09-13-A1(4)(b)(i).
- *E-mail subject line.* The subject line of the email must contain only the numeric motion calendar hearing date using the following format: mm/dd/yy (two (2) digit month forward slash; two (2) digit day forward slash; two (2) digit year). For example: 06/15/10. FL ST 11 J CIR 1-09-13-A1(4)(b)(iii).

ii. *Format of e-mail for service.* Service of a document by e-mail is made by attaching a copy of the document in PDF format to an e-mail sent to all addresses designated by the attorney or party. FL ST J ADMIN Rule 2.516(b)(1)(E).

- All documents served by e-mail must be attached to an e-mail message containing a subject line beginning with the words "SERVICE OF COURT DOCUMENT" in all capital letters, followed by the case number of the proceeding in which the documents are being served. FL ST J ADMIN Rule 2.516(b)(1)(E)(i).
- The body of the e-mail must identify the court in which the proceeding is pending, the case number, the name of the initial party on each side, the title of each document served with that e-mail, and the sender's name and telephone number. FL ST J ADMIN Rule 2.516(b)(1)(E)(ii).
- Any document served by e-mail may be signed by the "/s/" format, as long as the filed original is signed in accordance with the applicable rule of procedure. FL ST J ADMIN Rule 2.516(b)(1)(E)(iii).
- Any e-mail which, together with its attached documents, exceeds five megabytes (5MB) in size, must be divided and sent as separate e-mails, no one of which may exceed five megabytes (5MB) in size and each of which must be sequentially numbered in the subject line. FL ST J ADMIN Rule 2.516(b)(1)(E)(iv).

iii. *Service by other means.* In addition to, and not in lieu of, service by e-mail, service may also be made upon attorneys by any of the means specified in FL ST J ADMIN Rule 2.516(b)(2). Service on and by all parties who are not represented by an attorney and who do not designate an e-mail address, and on and by all attorneys excused from e-mail service, must be made by delivering a copy of the document or by mailing it to the party or attorney at their last known address or, if no address is known, by leaving it with the clerk of the court. Service by mail is complete upon mailing. Delivery of a copy within FL ST J ADMIN Rule 2.516 is complete upon:

- Handing it to the attorney or to the party,
- Leaving it at the attorney's or party's office with a clerk or other person in charge thereof,
- If there is no one in charge, leaving it in a conspicuous place therein,
- If the office is closed or the person to be served has no office, leaving it at the person's usual place of abode with some person of his or her family above fifteen (15) years of age and informing such person of the contents, or
- Transmitting it by facsimile to the attorney's or party's office with a cover sheet containing the sender's name, firm, address, telephone number, and facsimile number, and the number of pages transmitted. When service is made by facsimile, a copy must also be served by any other method permitted by FL ST J ADMIN Rule 2.516. Facsimile service occurs when transmission is complete. FL ST J ADMIN Rule 2.516(b)(2)(A) through FL ST J ADMIN Rule 2.516(b)(2)(E).
- Service by delivery after 5:00 p.m. must be deemed to have been made by mailing on the date of delivery. FL ST J ADMIN Rule 2.516(b)(2)(F).
- If a scheduling attorney or a scheduling pro se party does not have a fax number, then a courtesy copy of Motions and Proposed orders must be sent as an attachment to the service of process required pursuant to FL ST RCP Rule 1.080(b). FL ST 11 J CIR 1-09-13-A1(4)(b)(ii).

c. *Service; Numerous defendants.* In actions when the parties are unusually numerous, the court may regulate the service contemplated by the Florida Rules of Judicial Administration on motion or on its own initiative in such manner as may be found to be just and reasonable. FL ST J ADMIN Rule 2.516(c).

d. *Service by clerk.* Service of notices and other documents required to be made by the clerk must also be done as provided in FL ST J ADMIN Rule 2.516(b). FL ST J ADMIN Rule 2.516(g).

G. Hearings

1. *Communication equipment*

a. *Definition.* Communication equipment means a conference telephone or other electronic device that permits all those appearing or participating to hear and speak to each other, provided that all conversation of all parties is audible to all persons present. FL ST J ADMIN Rule 2.530(a).

b. *Use by all parties.* A county or circuit court judge may, upon the court's own motion or upon the written request of a party, direct that communication equipment be used for a motion hearing, pretrial conference, or a status conference. A judge must give notice to the parties and consider any objections they may have to the use of communication equipment before directing that communication equipment be used. The decision to use communication equipment over the objection of parties will be in the sound discretion of the trial court, except as noted below. FL ST J ADMIN Rule 2.530(b).

c. *Use only by requesting party.* A county or circuit court judge may, upon the written request of a party upon reasonable notice to all other parties, permit a requesting party to participate through communication equipment in a scheduled motion hearing; however, any such request (except in criminal, juvenile, and appellate proceedings) must be granted, absent a showing of good cause to deny the same, where the hearing is set for not longer than fifteen (15) minutes. FL ST J ADMIN Rule 2.530(c).

d. *Testimony*

i. *Generally.* A county or circuit court judge, general magistrate, special magistrate, or hearing officer may allow testimony to be taken through communication equipment if all parties consent or if permitted by another applicable rule of procedure. FL ST J ADMIN Rule 2.530(d)(1).

ii. *Procedure.* Any party desiring to present testimony through communication equipment shall, prior to the hearing or trial at which the testimony is to be presented, contact all parties to determine whether each party consents to this form of testimony. The party seeking to present the testimony shall move for permission to present testimony through communication equipment, which motion shall set forth good cause as to why the testimony should be allowed in this form. FL ST J ADMIN Rule 2.530(d)(2).

iii. *Oath.* Testimony may be taken through communication equipment only if a notary public or other person authorized to administer oaths in the witness's jurisdiction is present with the witness and administers the oath consistent with the laws of the jurisdiction. FL ST J ADMIN Rule 2.530(d)(3).

iv. *Confrontation rights.* In juvenile and criminal proceedings the defendant must make an informed waiver of any confrontation rights that may be abridged by the use of communication equipment. FL ST J ADMIN Rule 2.530(d)(4).

v. *Video testimony.* If the testimony to be presented utilizes video conferencing or comparable two-way visual capabilities, the court in its discretion may modify the procedures set forth in FL ST J ADMIN Rule 2.530 to accommodate the technology utilized. FL ST J ADMIN Rule 2.530(d)(5).

e. *Burden of expense.* The cost for the use of the communication equipment is the responsibility of the requesting party unless otherwise directed by the court. FL ST J ADMIN Rule 2.530(e).

2. *Time allotted for hearing.* Each party may set only one five (5) minute motion per case. Multiple motions must be specially set or set on different motion calendars (one five (5) minute motion per party per case), so as not to encroach on the time the Court is allotting for other litigants/attorneys. Consequently, the parties are advised to use good faith efforts to resolve the issues set forth in the motion prior to the setting of a motion; coordinate the date and time of the hearing; and confirm that the hearing shall require no more than five (5) minutes (if the hearing will require more than five (5) minutes, then it must be a Special Set Hearing). FL ST 11 J CIR 1-09-13-A1(4)(b)(i). For information on Special Set Hearings, refer to FL ST 11 J CIR 1-09-13-A1(4)(c).

3. *Hearing cancellation policy.* Should any scheduled hearing become unnecessary or have to be cancelled, the scheduling attorney or scheduling pro se party shall immediately, but, not later than by Noon on the business day prior to the hearing date and time, send an email to the court's designated e-mail address regarding the cancellation of the Motion Calendar hearing with an electronically attached Notice of Cancellation formatted in the same manner (using Microsoft Word or Word Perfect) as the email that scheduled the Motion Calendar hearing and in the same manner as the Motions and Notices. FL ST 11 J CIR 1-09-13-A1(4)(b)(vii).

H. Forms

1. Official Motion for Directed Verdict Forms for Florida

a. Caption. FL ST RCP Form 1.901.

b. Notice of compliance when constitutional challenge is brought. FL ST RCP Form 1.975.

2. Motion for Directed Verdict Forms for Florida

a. Motion; For directed verdict; At close of adverse party's evidence. FL-PP § 5:86.

b. Motion; For directed verdict; At close of all of evidence. FL-PP § 5:87.

c. Motion; Request to go to jury if motions by both parties are denied. FL-PP § 5:88.

d. Order; Granting defendant's motion for directed verdict; Insufficiency of plaintiff's evidence. FL-PP § 5:89.

e. Motion; Directed verdict, renewed. FL-PRACFORM § 7:62.

f. Form for motion for directed verdict at close of plaintiff's case. FL-RCPF R 1.480(24).

g. Form for motion for directed verdict at close of defendant's case. FL-RCPF R 1.480(25).

h. Form for motion to set aside verdict and enter directed verdict. FL-RCPF R 1.480(26).

I. Checklist

(I) ❑ Matters to be considered by moving party

(a) ❑ Required documents

(1) ❑ Notice of hearing/Motion

(2) ❑ Certificate of service

(b) ❑ Supplemental documents

(1) ❑ Proposed order

(2) ❑ Notice of constitutional question

(c) ❑ Time for making motion

(1) ❑ Before a verdict is returned - A directed verdict is available to the defendant at the close of the plaintiff's evidence or to either party at the close of all of the evidence

(2) ❑ After a verdict is returned - Within ten (10) days after the return of a verdict, a party who has timely moved for a directed verdict may serve a motion to enter judgment in accordance with the motion for a directed verdict

(3) ❑ No verdict is returned - If a verdict was not returned, a party who has timely moved for a directed verdict may serve a motion for judgment in accordance with the motion for a directed verdict within ten (10) days after discharge of the jury

(4) ❑ General motion timing - A copy of any written motion which may not be heard ex parte and a copy of the notice of the hearing thereof shall be served a reasonable time before the time specified for the hearing

(II) ❑ Matters to be considered by opposing party

(a) ❑ Required documents

(1) ❑ Response to motion

(2) ❑ Certificate of service

(b) ❑ Supplemental documents

(1) ❑ Proposed order

(2) ❑ Notice of constitutional question

(c) ❑ Time for service and filing of opposition

(1) ❑ No time specified for responding to a motion

Requests, Notices and Applications
Request for Production of Documents

Document Last Updated January 2013

A. Applicable Rules

1. *State rules*

a. Nonverification of pleadings. FL ST RCP Rule 1.030.

b. Service and filing of pleadings, orders, and documents. FL ST RCP Rule 1.080.

c. Time. FL ST RCP Rule 1.090.

d. Pleadings and motions. FL ST RCP Rule 1.100.

e. Pretrial procedure. FL ST RCP Rule 1.200.

f. General provisions governing discovery. FL ST RCP Rule 1.280.

g. Depositions upon oral examination. FL ST RCP Rule 1.310.

h. Interrogatories to parties. FL ST RCP Rule 1.340.

i. Production of documents and things and entry upon land for inspection and other purposes. FL ST RCP Rule 1.350.

j. Production of documents and things without deposition. FL ST RCP Rule 1.351.

k. Examination of persons. FL ST RCP Rule 1.360.

l. Requests for admission. FL ST RCP Rule 1.370.

m. Failure to make discovery; Sanctions. FL ST RCP Rule 1.380.

n. Depositions of expert witnesses. FL ST RCP Rule 1.390.

o. Relief from judgment, decrees, or orders. FL ST RCP Rule 1.540.

p. Forms. FL ST RCP Rule 1.900.

q. Minimization of the filing of sensitive information. FL ST J ADMIN Rule 2.425.

r. Retention of court records. FL ST J ADMIN Rule 2.430.

s. Foreign attorneys. FL ST J ADMIN Rule 2.510.

t. Signature of attorneys and parties. FL ST J ADMIN Rule 2.515.

u. Paper. FL ST J ADMIN Rule 2.520.

v. Electronic filing. FL ST J ADMIN Rule 2.525.

w. Accessibility of information and technology. FL ST J ADMIN Rule 2.526.

x. Requests for accommodations by persons with disabilities. FL ST J ADMIN Rule 2.540.

2. *Local rules*

a. Establishment of 11th Circuit Homestead Access to Mediation Program ("CHAMP") for case management of residential foreclosure cases in the Eleventh Judicial Circuit of Florida. FL ST 11 J CIR 1-09-08.

b. Enlargement and expansion of the current pilot project for electronic submissions of courtesy copies for uniform motion calendar and requests for special set hearings, emergency motions, and proposed orders. FL ST 11 J CIR 1-09-13-A1.

B. Timing

1. *Request for production of documents.* Without leave of court the request may be served on the plaintiff after commencement of the action and on any other party with or after service of the process and initial pleading on that party. FL ST RCP Rule 1.350(b).

2. *Notice of intent to serve subpoena.* A party desiring production under FL ST RCP Rule 1.351 shall serve notice as provided in FL ST RCP Rule 1.080 on every other party of the intent to serve a subpoena under FL ST RCP Rule 1.351 at least ten (10) days before the subpoena is issued if service is by delivery and fifteen (15) days before the subpoena is issued if the service is by mail or e-mail. FL ST RCP Rule 1.351(b).

3. *Sequence and timing of discovery.* Except as provided in FL ST RCP Rule 1.280(b)(5) or unless the court upon motion for the convenience of parties and witnesses and in the interest of justice orders otherwise, methods of discovery may be used in any sequence, and the fact that a party is conducting discovery, whether by deposition or otherwise, shall not delay any other party's discovery. FL ST RCP Rule 1.280(e).

4. *Computation of time*

a. *Generally.* Computation of time shall be governed by FL ST J ADMIN Rule 2.514. FL ST RCP Rule 1.090(a). The following rules apply in computing time periods specified in any rule of procedure, local rule, court order, or statute that does not specify a method of computing time. FL ST J ADMIN Rule 2.514(a).

i. *Period stated in days or a longer unit.* When the period is stated in days or a longer unit of time (A) exclude the day of the event that triggers the period; (B) count every day, including intermediate Saturdays, Sundays, and legal holidays; and (C) include the last day of the period, but if the last day is a Saturday, Sunday, or legal holiday, or falls within any period of time extended through an order of the chief justice under FL ST J ADMIN Rule 2.205(a)(2)(B)(iv), the period continues to run until the end of the next day that is not a Saturday, Sunday, or legal holiday and does not fall within any period of time extended through an order of the chief justice. FL ST J ADMIN Rule 2.514(a)(1).

ii. *Period stated in hours.* When the period is stated in hours (A) begin counting immediately on the occurrence of the event that triggers the period; (B) count every hour, including hours during intermediate Saturdays, Sundays, and legal holidays; and (C) if the period would end on a Saturday, Sunday, or legal holiday, or during any period of time extended through an order of the chief justice under FL ST J ADMIN Rule 2.205(a)(2)(B)(iv), the period continues to run until the same time on the next day that is not a Saturday, Sunday, or legal holiday and does not fall within any period of time extended through an order of the chief justice. FL ST J ADMIN Rule 2.514(a)(2).

iii. *Period stated in days less than seven (7) days.* When the period stated in days is less than seven (7) days, intermediate Saturdays, Sundays, and legal holidays shall be excluded in the computation. FL ST J ADMIN Rule 2.514(a)(3).

iv. *"Last day" defined.* Unless a different time is set by a statute, local rule, or court order, the last day ends (A) for electronic filing or for service by any means, at midnight; and (B) for filing by other means, when the clerk's office is scheduled to close. FL ST J ADMIN Rule 2.514(a)(4).

v. *"Next day" defined.* The "next day" is determined by continuing to count forward when the period is measured after an event and backward when measured before an event. FL ST J ADMIN Rule 2.514(a)(5).

vi. *"Legal holiday" defined.* "Legal holiday" means (A) the day set aside by FL ST § 110.117, for observing New Year's Day, Martin Luther King, Jr.'s Birthday, Memorial Day, Independence Day, Labor Day, Veterans' Day, Thanksgiving Day, the Friday after Thanksgiving Day, or Christmas Day, and (B) any day observed as a holiday by the clerk's office or as designated by the chief judge. FL ST J ADMIN Rule 2.514(a)(6).

b. *Additional time after service by mail or e-mail.* When a party may or must act within a specified time after service and service is made by mail or e-mail, five (5) days are added after the period that would otherwise expire under FL ST J ADMIN Rule 2.514(a). FL ST J ADMIN Rule 2.514(b).

c. *Enlargement.* When an act is required or allowed to be done at or within a specified time by order of court, by the Florida Rules of Civil Procedure, or by notice given thereunder, for cause shown the court at any time in its discretion (1) with or without notice, may order the period enlarged if request therefor is made before the expiration of the period originally prescribed or as extended by a previous order, or (2) upon motion made and notice after the expiration of the specified period, may permit the act to be done when failure to act was the result of excusable neglect, but it may not extend the time for making a motion for new trial, for rehearing, or to alter or amend a judgment; making a motion for relief from a judgment under FL ST RCP Rule 1.540(b); taking an appeal or filing a petition for certiorari; or making a motion for a directed verdict. FL ST RCP Rule 1.090(b).

d. *Unaffected by expiration of term.* The period of time provided for the doing of any act or the taking of any proceeding shall not be affected or limited by the continued existence or expiration of a term of court. The continued existence or expiration of a term of court in no way affects the power of a court to do any act or take any proceeding in any action which is or has been pending before it. FL ST RCP Rule 1.090(c).

C. General Requirements

1. *General provisions governing discovery*

a. *Discovery methods.* Parties may obtain discovery by one or more of the following methods: depositions upon oral examination or written questions; written interrogatories; production of documents or things or permission to enter upon land or other property for inspection and other purposes; physical and mental examinations; and requests for admission. Unless the court orders otherwise and under FL ST RCP Rule 1.280(c), the frequency of use of these methods is not limited, except as provided in FL ST RCP Rule 1.200, FL ST RCP Rule 1.340, and FL ST RCP Rule 1.370. FL ST RCP Rule 1.280(a).

b. *Scope of discovery.* Unless otherwise limited by order of the court in accordance with the Florida Rules of Civil Procedure, the scope of discovery is as follows:

   i. *In general.* Parties may obtain discovery regarding any matter, not privileged, that is relevant to the subject matter of the pending action, whether it relates to the claim or defense of the party seeking discovery or the claim or defense of any other party, including the existence, description, nature, custody, condition, and location of any books, documents, or other tangible things and the identity and location of persons having knowledge of any discoverable matter. It is not ground for objection that the information sought will be inadmissible at the trial if the information sought appears reasonably calculated to lead to the discovery of admissible evidence. FL ST RCP Rule 1.280(b)(1).

   ii. *Indemnity agreements.* A party may obtain discovery of the existence and contents of any agreement under which any person may be liable to satisfy part or all of a judgment that may be entered in the action or to indemnify or to reimburse a party for payments made to satisfy the judgment. Information concerning the agreement is not admissible in evidence at trial by reason of disclosure. FL ST RCP Rule 1.280(b)(2).

   iii. *Electronically stored information.* A party may obtain discovery of electronically stored information in accordance with the Florida Rules of Civil Procedure. FL ST RCP Rule 1.280(b)(3).

   iv. *Trial preparation; Materials.* Subject to the provisions of FL ST RCP Rule 1.280(b)(5), a party may obtain discovery of documents and tangible things otherwise discoverable under FL ST RCP Rule 1.280(b)(1) and prepared in anticipation of litigation or for trial by or for another party or by or for that party's representative, including that party's attorney, consultant, surety, indemnitor, insurer, or agent, only upon a showing that the party seeking discovery has need of the materials in the preparation of the case and is unable without undue hardship to obtain the substantial equivalent of the materials by other means. FL ST RCP Rule 1.280(b)(4).

      - In ordering discovery of the materials when the required showing has been made, the court shall protect against disclosure of the mental impressions, conclusions, opinions, or legal theories of an attorney or other representative of a party concerning the litigation. FL ST RCP Rule 1.280(b)(4).
      - Without the required showing a party may obtain a copy of a statement concerning the action or its subject matter previously made by that party. FL ST RCP Rule 1.280(b)(4).
      - Upon request without the required showing a person not a party may obtain a copy of a statement concerning the action or its subject matter previously made by that person. If the request is refused, the person may move for an order to obtain a copy. The provisions of FL ST RCP Rule 1.380(a)(5) apply to the award of expenses incurred as a result of making the motion. FL ST RCP Rule 1.280(b)(4).
      - For purposes of FL ST RCP Rule 1.280(b)(4), a statement previously made is a written statement signed or otherwise adopted or approved by the person making it, or a stenographic, mechanical, electrical, or other recording or transcription of it that is a substantially verbatim recital of an oral statement by the person making it and contemporaneously recorded. FL ST RCP Rule 1.280(b)(4).

   v. *Trial preparation; Experts.* Discovery of facts known and opinions held by experts, otherwise discoverable under the provisions of FL ST RCP Rule 1.280(b)(1) and acquired or developed in anticipation of litigation or for trial, may be obtained only as follows:

      - By interrogatories a party may require any other party to identify each person whom the other party expects to call as an expert witness at trial and to state the subject matter on which the expert is expected to testify, and to state the substance of the facts and opinions to which the expert is expected to testify and a summary of the grounds for each opinion. FL ST RCP Rule 1.280(b)(5)(A)(i).

- Any person disclosed by interrogatories or otherwise as a person expected to be called as an expert witness at trial may be deposed in accordance with FL ST RCP Rule 1.390 without motion or order of court. FL ST RCP Rule 1.280(b)(5)(A)(ii).
- A party may obtain the following discovery regarding any person disclosed by interrogatories or otherwise as a person expected to be called as an expert witness at trial: The scope of employment in the pending case and the compensation for such service, FL ST RCP Rule 1.280(b)(5)(A)(iii)(1); The expert's general litigation experience, including the percentage of work performed for plaintiffs and defendants, FL ST RCP Rule 1.280(b)(5)(A)(iii)(2); The identity of other cases, within a reasonable time period, in which the expert has testified by deposition or at trial, FL ST RCP Rule 1.280(b)(5)(A)(iii)(3); An approximation of the portion of the expert's involvement as an expert witness, which may be based on the number of hours, percentage of hours, or percentage of earned income derived from serving as an expert witness; however, the expert shall not be required to disclose his or her earnings as an expert witness or income derived from other services. FL ST RCP Rule 1.280(b)(5)(A)(iii)(4).
- An expert may be required to produce financial and business records only under the most unusual or compelling circumstances and may not be compelled to compile or produce nonexistent documents. Upon motion, the court may order further discovery by other means, subject to such restrictions as to scope and other provisions pursuant to FL ST RCP Rule 1.280(b)(5)(C) concerning fees and expenses as the court may deem appropriate. FL ST RCP Rule 1.280(b)(5).
- A party may discover facts known or opinions held by an expert who has been retained or specially employed by another party in anticipation of litigation or preparation for trial and who is not expected to be called as a witness at trial, only as provided in FL ST RCP Rule 1.360(b) or upon a showing of exceptional circumstances under which it is impracticable for the party seeking discovery to obtain facts or opinions on the same subject by other means. FL ST RCP Rule 1.280(b)(5)(B).
- Unless manifest injustice would result, the court shall require that the party seeking discovery pay the expert a reasonable fee for time spent in responding to discovery under FL ST RCP Rule 1.280(b)(5)(A) and FL ST RCP Rule 1.280(b)(5)(B); and concerning discovery from an expert obtained under FL ST RCP Rule 1.280(b)(5)(A) the court may require, and concerning discovery obtained under FL ST RCP Rule 1.280(b)(5)(B) shall require, the party seeking discovery to pay the other party a fair part of the fees and expenses reasonably incurred by the latter party in obtaining facts and opinions from the expert. FL ST RCP Rule 1.280(b)(5)(C).
- As used in the Florida Rules of Civil Procedure an expert shall be an expert witness as defined in FL ST RCP Rule 1.390(a). FL ST RCP Rule 1.280(b)(5)(D).

vi. *Claims to privilege or protection.* When a party withholds information otherwise discoverable under the Florida Rules of Civil Procedure by claiming that it is privileged or subject to protection as trial preparation material, the party shall make the claim expressly and shall describe the nature of the documents, communications, or things not produced or disclosed in a manner that, without revealing information itself privileged or protected, will enable other parties to assess the applicability of the privilege or protection. FL ST RCP Rule 1.280(b)(6).

c. *Limitations on discovery of electronically stored information*

i. A person may object to discovery of electronically stored information from sources that the person identifies as not reasonably accessible because of burden or cost. On motion to compel discovery or for a protective order, the person from whom discovery is sought must show that the information sought or the format requested is not reasonably accessible because of undue burden or cost. If that showing is made, the court may nonetheless order the discovery from such sources or in such formats if the requesting party shows good cause. The court may specify conditions of the discovery, including ordering that some or all of the expenses incurred by the person from whom discovery is sought be paid by the party seeking the discovery. FL ST RCP Rule 1.280(d)(1).

ii. In determining any motion involving discovery of electronically stored information, the court must limit the frequency or extent of discovery otherwise allowed by the Florida Rules of Civil Procedure if it determines that (i) the discovery sought is unreasonably cumulative or duplicative, or can be obtained from another source or in another manner that is more convenient, less burdensome, or less expensive; or (ii) the burden or expense of the discovery outweighs its likely benefit, considering the needs of the case, the amount in controversy, the parties' resources, the importance of the issues at stake in the action, and the importance of the discovery in resolving the issues. FL ST RCP Rule 1.280(d)(2).

d. For information on inadvertent disclosure of privileged materials, see FL ST RCP Rule 1.285.

2. *Request for production of documents*

a. *Scope of request.* Any party may request any other party:

i. To produce and permit the party making the request, or someone acting in the requesting party's behalf, to inspect and copy any designated documents, including electronically stored information, writings, drawings, graphs, charts, photographs, phono-records, and other data compilations from which information can be obtained, translated, if necessary, by the party to whom the request is directed through detection devices into reasonably usable form, that constitute or contain matters within the scope of FL ST RCP Rule 1.280(b) and that are in the possession, custody, or control of the party to whom the request is directed;

ii. To inspect and copy, test, or sample any tangible things that constitute or contain matters within the scope of FL ST RCP Rule 1.280(b) and that are in the possession, custody, or control of the party to whom the request is directed; or

iii. To permit entry upon designated land or other property in the possession or control of the party upon whom the request is served for the purpose of inspection and measuring, surveying, photographing, testing, or sampling the property or any designated object or operation on it within the scope of FL ST RCP Rule 1.280(b). FL ST RCP Rule 1.350(a).

b. *Contents of request*

i. The request shall set forth the items to be inspected, either by individual item or category, and describe each item and category with reasonable particularity. The request shall specify a reasonable time, place, and manner of making the inspection or performing the related acts. FL ST RCP Rule 1.350(b).

ii. A request for electronically stored information may specify the form or forms in which electronically stored information is to be produced. If the responding party objects to a requested form, or if no form is specified in the request, the responding party must state the form or forms it intends to use. If a request for electronically stored information does not specify the form of production, the producing party must produce the information in a form or forms in which it is ordinarily maintained or in a reasonably usable form or forms. FL ST RCP Rule 1.350(b).

c. *Failure to respond to requests.* The party submitting the request may move for an order under FL ST RCP Rule 1.380 concerning any objection, failure to respond to the request, or any part of it, or failure to permit the inspection as requested. FL ST RCP Rule 1.350(b). Please see FL ST RCP Rule 1.380(d) and the KeyRules Motion to Compel Discovery documents for further information regarding compelling discovery and discovery sanctions.

i. *Response requirements.* For each item or category the response shall state that inspection and related activities will be permitted as requested unless the request is objected to, in which event the reasons for the objection shall be stated. If an objection is made to part of an item or category, the part shall be specified. When producing documents, the producing party shall either produce them as they are kept in the usual course of business or shall identify them to correspond with the categories in the request. If the responding party objects to a requested form (for electronic information), or if no form is specified in the request, the responding party must state the form or forms it intends to use. If a request for electronically stored information does not specify the form of production, the producing party must produce the information in a form or forms in which it is ordinarily maintained or in a reasonably usable form or forms. FL ST RCP Rule 1.350(b).

3. *Requests to a non-party*
    a. *Independent action not prohibited.* FL ST RCP Rule 1.350 does not preclude an independent action against a person not a party for production of documents and things and permission to enter upon land. FL ST RCP Rule 1.350(c). FL ST RCP Rule 1.351 does not affect the right of any party to bring an independent action for production of documents and things or permission to enter upon land. FL ST RCP Rule 1.351(f).
    b. *Scope.* A party may seek inspection and copying of any documents or things within the scope of FL ST RCP Rule 1.350(a) from a person who is not a party by issuance of a subpoena directing the production of the documents or things when the requesting party does not seek to depose the custodian or other person in possession of the documents or things. FL ST RCP Rule 1.351 provides the exclusive procedure for obtaining documents or things by subpoena from nonparties without deposing the custodian or other person in possession of the documents or things pursuant to FL ST RCP Rule 1.310. FL ST RCP Rule 1.351(a).
        i. *Procedure.* The proposed subpoena shall be attached to the notice and shall state the time, place, and method for production of the documents or things, and the name and address of the person who is to produce the documents or things, if known, and if not known, a general description sufficient to identify the person or the particular class or group to which the person belongs; shall include a designation of the items to be produced; and shall state that the person who will be asked to produce the documents or things has the right to object to the production under FL ST RCP Rule 1.351 and that the person will not be required to surrender the documents or things. A copy of the notice and proposed subpoena shall not be furnished to the person upon whom the subpoena is to be served. If any party serves an objection to production under FL ST RCP Rule 1.351 within ten (10) days of service of the notice, the documents or things shall not be produced pending resolution of the objection in accordance with FL ST RCP Rule 1.351(d). FL ST RCP Rule 1.351(b).
        ii. *Subpoena.* If no objection is made by a party under FL ST RCP Rule 1.351(b), an attorney of record in the action may issue a subpoena or the party desiring production shall deliver to the clerk for issuance a subpoena together with a certificate of counsel or pro se party that no timely objection has been received from any party, and the clerk shall issue the subpoena and deliver it to the party desiring production. FL ST RCP Rule 1.351(c).
            - The subpoena shall be identical to the copy attached to the notice and shall specify that no testimony may be taken and shall require only production of the documents or things specified in it. FL ST RCP Rule 1.351(c).
            - The subpoena may give the recipient an option to deliver or mail legible copies of the documents or things to the party serving the subpoena. FL ST RCP Rule 1.351(c).
            - The person upon whom the subpoena is served may condition the preparation of copies on the payment in advance of the reasonable costs of preparing the copies. FL ST RCP Rule 1.351(c).
            - The subpoena shall require production only in the county of the residence of the custodian or other person in possession of the documents or things or in the county where the documents or things are located or where the custodian or person in possession usually conducts business. FL ST RCP Rule 1.351(c).
            - If the person upon whom the subpoena is served objects at any time before the production of the documents or things, the documents or things shall not be produced under FL ST RCP Rule 1.351, and relief may be obtained pursuant to FL ST RCP Rule 1.310. FL ST RCP Rule 1.351(c).
        iii. *Ruling on objection.* If an objection is made by a party under FL ST RCP Rule 1.351(b), the party desiring production may file a motion with the court seeking a ruling on the objection or may proceed pursuant to FL ST RCP Rule 1.310. FL ST RCP Rule 1.351(d).

iv. *Copies furnished.* If the subpoena is complied with by delivery or mailing of copies as provided in FL ST RCP Rule 1.351(c), the party receiving the copies shall furnish a legible copy of each item furnished to any other party who requests it upon the payment of the reasonable cost of preparing the copies. FL ST RCP Rule 1.351(e).

4. *Arbitration and mediation*

a. *Referral to arbitration and mediation.* Except as hereinafter provided or as otherwise prohibited by law, the presiding judge may enter an order referring all or any part of a contested civil matter to mediation or arbitration. The parties to any contested civil matter may file a written stipulation to mediate or arbitrate any issue between them at any time. Such stipulation shall be incorporated into the order of referral. FL ST RCP Rule 1.700(a).

i. In all residential foreclosure actions involving homestead properties filed on or after May 1, 2009, unless a stipulation is specifically invoked by the parties in writing within five (5) days of service of the complaint on the main defendant, the parties are deemed to have stipulated to referral of the mediation to the Collins Center pursuant to FL ST RCP Rule 1.720(f). FL ST 11 J CIR 1-09-08(2); FL ST 11 J CIR 1-09-08(3). FL ST 11 J CIR 1-09-08 constitutes a formal referral to mediation pursuant to the Florida Rules of Civil Procedure. FL ST 11 J CIR 1-09-08(2).

ii. For further information on referral to mediation, refer to FL ST 11 J CIR 1-09-08.

b. *Arbitration*

i. *Exclusions.* A civil action shall be ordered to arbitration or arbitration in conjunction with mediation upon stipulation of the parties. A civil action may be ordered to arbitration or arbitration in conjunction with mediation upon motion of any party or by the court, if the judge determines the action to be of such a nature that arbitration could be of benefit to the litigants or the court. FL ST RCP Rule 1.800.

- Under no circumstances may the following categories of actions be referred to arbitration: (1) bond estreatures; (2) habeas corpus or other extraordinary writs; (3) bond validations; (4) civil or criminal contempt; (5) such other matters as may be specified by order of the chief judge in the circuit. FL ST RCP Rule 1.800.

ii. For more information regarding arbitration, please see FL ST RCP Rule 1.810; FL ST RCP Rule 1.820; FL ST RCP Rule 1.830.

c. *Mediation.* For more information regarding mediation, please see FL ST RCP Rule 1.710; FL ST RCP Rule 1.720; FL ST RCP Rule 1.730; and FL ST RCP Rule 1.750.

5. *Rules of court*

a. *Rules of civil procedure.* The Florida Rules of Civil Procedure apply to all actions of a civil nature and all special statutory proceedings in the circuit courts and county courts except those to which the Florida Probate Rules, the Florida Family Law Rules of Procedure, or the Small Claims Rules apply. FL ST RCP Rule 1.010.

i. The form, content, procedure, and time for pleading in all special statutory proceedings shall be as prescribed by the statutes governing the proceeding unless the Florida Rules of Civil Procedure specifically provide to the contrary. FL ST RCP Rule 1.010.

ii. The Florida Rules of Civil Procedure shall be construed to secure the just, speedy, and inexpensive determination of every action. FL ST RCP Rule 1.010.

b. *Rules of judicial administration.* The Florida Rules of Judicial Administration shall apply to administrative matters in all courts to which the Florida Rules of Judicial Administration are applicable by their terms. The Florida Rules of Judicial Administration shall be construed to secure the speedy and inexpensive determination of every proceeding to which they are applicable. The Florida Rules of Judicial Administration shall supersede all conflicting rules and statutes. FL ST J ADMIN Rule 2.110.

D. Documents

1. *Required documents*

   a. *Request for production.* Please see the General Requirements section of this document for more information on the contents of the request for production.

      i. *Notices to persons with disabilities.* See the Format section of this KeyRules document for further information.

   b. *Certificate of service.* A certificate of service of the interrogatories shall be filed, giving the date of service and the name of the party to whom they were directed. FL ST RCP Rule 1.340(e). When any attorney certifies in substance: "I certify that a copy hereof has been furnished to (here insert name or names and addresses used for service) by (e-mail) (delivery) (mail) (fax) on .... (date) ....________________ Attorney" the certificate is taken as prima facie proof of such service in compliance with FL ST J ADMIN Rule 2.516. FL ST J ADMIN Rule 2.516(f).

2. *Supplemental documents*

   a. *Notice of intent to serve subpoena/Subpoena.* Please see the General Requirements section of this document for more information.

E. Format

1. *Documents; Type and size.* Documents subject to the exceptions set forth in FL ST J ADMIN Rule 2.525(d) shall be filed on recycled paper measuring eight and one half by eleven (8 1/2 by 11) inches. For purposes of FL ST J ADMIN Rule 2.520, paper is recycled if it contains a minimum content of fifty (50) percent waste paper. Xerographic reduction of legal-size (eight and one half by fourteen (8 1/2 by 14) inches) documents to letter size (eight and one half by eleven (8 1/2 by 11) inches) is prohibited. All other documents filed by electronic transmission shall be filed in a format capable of being printed in a format consistent with the provisions of FL ST J ADMIN Rule 2.250. FL ST J ADMIN Rule 2.520(b).

   a. *Exhibits.* Any exhibit or attachment filed with pleadings or papers may be filed in its original size. FL ST J ADMIN Rule 2.520(c).

   b. *Recording space.* On all papers and documents prepared and filed by the court or by any party to a proceeding which are to be recorded in the public records of any county, including but not limited to final money judgments and notices of lis pendens, a three (3) inch by three (3) inch space at the top right-hand corner on the first page and a one (1) inch by three (3) inch space at the top right-hand corner on each subsequent page shall be left blank and reserved for use by the clerk of court. FL ST J ADMIN Rule 2.520(d).

      i. *Exceptions to recording space.* Any papers or documents created by persons or entities over which the filing party has no control, including but not limited to wills, codicils, trusts, or other testamentary documents; documents prepared or executed by any public officer; documents prepared, executed, acknowledged, or proved outside of the State of Florida; or documents created by State or Federal government agencies, may be filed without the space required by FL ST J ADMIN Rule 2.520. FL ST J ADMIN Rule 2.520(e).

   c. *Noncompliance.* No clerk of court is permitted to refuse to file any document or paper because of noncompliance with the Florida Rules of Judicial Administration. However, upon request of the clerk of court, noncomplying documents must be resubmitted in accordance with the formatting rules. FL ST J ADMIN Rule 2.520(f).

2. *Caption.* Every pleading, motion, order, judgment, or other paper shall have a caption containing the name of the court, the file number, and except for in rem proceedings, including forfeiture proceedings, the name of the first party on each side with an appropriate indication of other parties, and a designation identifying the party filing it and its nature or the nature of the order, as the case may be. In any in rem proceeding, every pleading, motion, order, judgment, or other paper shall have a caption containing the name of the court, the file number, the style "In re" (followed by the name or general description of the property), and a designation of the person or entity filing it and its nature or the nature of the order, as the case may be. In an in rem forfeiture proceeding, the style shall be "In re forfeiture of" (followed by the name of the general description of the property). All papers filed in the action shall be styled in such a

manner as to indicate clearly the subject matter of the paper and the party requesting or obtaining relief. FL ST RCP Rule 1.100(c)(1).

3. *Writing and written defined.* Writing or written means a document containing information, an application, or a stipulation. FL ST RCP Rule 1.080(c).
4. *Rule abbreviations*
   a. The Florida Rules of Civil Procedure and shall be abbreviated as Fla.R.Civ.P. FL ST RCP Rule 1.010.
   b. The Florida Rules of Judicial Administration shall be abbreviated as Fla. R. Jud. Admin. FL ST J ADMIN Rule 2.110.
5. *Nonverification.* Except when otherwise specifically provided by the Florida Rules of Civil Procedure or an applicable statute, every pleading or other document of a party represented by an attorney need not be verified or accompanied by an affidavit. FL ST RCP Rule 1.030; FL ST J ADMIN Rule 2.515(a).
6. *Attorney signature*
   a. *Attorney signature.* Every pleading and other document of a party represented by an attorney shall be signed by at least one (1) attorney of record in that attorney's individual name whose current record Florida Bar address, telephone number, including area code, primary e-mail address and secondary e-mail addresses, if any, and Florida Bar number shall be stated, and who shall be duly licensed to practice law in Florida or who shall have received permission to appear in the particular case as provided in FL ST J ADMIN Rule 2.510. FL ST J ADMIN Rule 2.515(a).
      i. The attorney may be required by the court to give the address of, and to vouch for the attorney's authority to represent, the party. FL ST J ADMIN Rule 2.515(a).
      ii. The signature of an attorney shall constitute a certificate by the attorney that the attorney has read the pleading or other document; that to the best of the attorney's knowledge, information, and belief there is good ground to support it; and that it is not interposed for delay. FL ST J ADMIN Rule 2.515(a).
      iii. If a pleading is not signed or is signed with intent to defeat the purpose of FL ST J ADMIN Rule 2.515, it may be stricken and the action may proceed as though the pleading or other document had not been served. FL ST J ADMIN Rule 2.515(a).
   b. *Pro se litigant signature.* A party who is not represented by an attorney shall sign any pleading or other paper and state the party's address and telephone number, including area code. FL ST J ADMIN Rule 2.515(b).
   c. *Form of signature*
      i. The signatures required on pleadings and documents by FL ST J ADMIN Rule 2.515(a) and FL ST J ADMIN Rule 2.515(b) may be:
         - Original signatures;
         - Original signatures that have been reproduced by electronic means, such as on electronically transmitted documents or photocopied documents;
         - Electronic signatures using the "/s/," "s/," or "/s" formats by or at the direction of the person signing; or
         - Any other signature format authorized by general law, so long as the clerk where the proceeding is pending has the capability of receiving and has obtained approval from the Supreme Court of Florida to accept pleadings and documents with that signature format. FL ST J ADMIN Rule 2.515(c)(1).
      ii. An attorney, party, or other person who files a pleading or paper by electronic transmission that does not contain the original signature of that attorney, party, or other person shall file that identical pleading or paper in paper form containing an original signature of that attorney, party, or other person (hereinafter called the follow-up filing) immediately thereafter. The follow-up filing is not required if the Supreme Court of Florida has entered an order directing the clerk of court to discontinue accepting the follow-up filing. FL ST J ADMIN Rule 2.515(c)(2).

7. *Forms*
   a. *Process.* The forms of process, notice of lis pendens, and notice of action provided in the Florida Rules of Civil Procedure are sufficient. Variations from the forms do not void process or notices that are otherwise sufficient. FL ST RCP Rule 1.900(a).
   b. *Other forms.* The other forms provided in the Florida Rules of Civil Procedure are sufficient for the matters that are covered by them. So long as the substance is expressed without prolixity, the forms may be varied to meet the facts of a particular case. FL ST RCP Rule 1.900(b).
   c. *Formal matters.* Captions, except for the designation of the paper, are omitted from the forms provided in the Florida Rules of Civil Procedure. A general form of caption is the first form provided. Signatures are omitted from pleadings and motions. FL ST RCP Rule 1.900(c).
8. *Notices to persons with disabilities.* All notices of court proceedings to be held in a public facility, and all process compelling appearance at such proceedings, shall include the following statement in bold face, fourteen (14) point Times New Roman or Courier font: "If you are a person with a disability who needs any accommodation in order to participate in this proceeding, you are entitled, at no cost to you, to the provision of certain assistance. Please contact [identify applicable court personnel by name, address, and telephone number] at least seven (7) days before your scheduled court appearance, or immediately upon receiving this notification if the time before the scheduled appearance is less than seven (7) days; if you are hearing or voice impaired, call 711." FL ST J ADMIN Rule 2.540(c)(1).
9. *Minimization of the filing of sensitive information*
   a. *Limitations for court filings.* Unless authorized by FL ST J ADMIN Rule 2.425(b), statute, another rule of court, or the court orders otherwise, designated sensitive information filed with the court must be limited to the following format:
      i. The initials of a person known to be a minor;
      ii. The year of birth of a person's birth date;
      iii. No portion of any: Social security number, Bank account number, Credit card account number, Charge account number, or Debit account number;
      iv. The last four digits of any: Taxpayer identification number (TIN), Employee identification number, Driver's license number, Passport number, Telephone number, Financial account number, except as set forth in FL ST J ADMIN Rule 2.425(a)(3), Brokerage account number, Insurance policy account number, Loan account number, Customer account number, or Patient or health care number;
      v. A truncated version of any: Email address, Computer user name, Password, or Personal identification number (PIN); and
      vi. A truncated version of any other sensitive information as provided by court order. FL ST J ADMIN Rule 2.425(a).
   b. *Exceptions.* FL ST J ADMIN Rule 2.425(a) does not apply to the following:
      i. An account number which identifies the property alleged to be the subject of a proceeding;
      ii. The record of an administrative or agency proceeding;
      iii. The record in appellate or review proceedings;
      iv. The birth date of a minor whenever the birth date is necessary for the court to establish or maintain subject matter jurisdiction;
      v. The name of a minor in any order relating to parental responsibility, time-sharing, or child support;
      vi. The name of a minor in any document or order affecting the minor's ownership of real property;
      vii. The birth date of a party in a writ of attachment or notice to payor;
      viii. In traffic and criminal proceedings: a pro se filing; a court filing that is related to a criminal matter or investigation and that is prepared before the filing of a criminal charge or is not filed

as part of any docketed criminal case; an arrest or search warrant or any information in support thereof; a charging document and an affidavit or other documents filed in support of any charging document, including any driving records; a statement of particulars; discovery material introduced into evidence or otherwise filed with the court; and all information necessary for the proper issuance and execution of a subpoena duces tecum;

ix. Information used by the clerk for case maintenance purposes or the courts for case management purposes; and

x. Information which is relevant and material to an issue before the court. FL ST J ADMIN Rule 2.425(b).

c. *Remedies.* Upon motion by a party or interested person or sua sponte by the court, the court may order remedies, sanctions or both for a violation of FL ST J ADMIN Rule 2.425(a). Following notice and an opportunity to respond, the court may impose sanctions if such filing was not made in good faith. FL ST J ADMIN Rule 2.425(c).

d. *Motions not restricted.* FL ST J ADMIN Rule 2.425 does not restrict a party's right to move for protective order, to move to file documents under seal, or to request a determination of the confidentiality of records. FL ST J ADMIN Rule 2.425(d).

e. *Application.* FL ST J ADMIN Rule 2.425 does not affect the application of constitutional provisions, statutes, or rules of court regarding confidential information or access to public information. FL ST J ADMIN Rule 2.425(e).

F. Filing and Service Requirements

1. *Court filing of documents and discovery.* Information obtained during discovery shall not be filed with the court until such time as it is filed for good cause. The requirement of good cause is satisfied only where the filing of the information is allowed or required by another applicable rule of procedure or by court order. All filings of discovery documents shall comply with FL ST J ADMIN Rule 2.425. The court shall have the authority to impose sanctions for violation of FL ST RCP Rule 1.280. FL ST RCP Rule 1.280(g).

a. Unless required by the court, a party shall not file any of the documents or things produced with the response. Documents or things may be filed in compliance with FL ST J ADMIN Rule 2.425 and FL ST RCP Rule 1.280(g) when they should be considered by the court in determining a matter pending before the court. FL ST RCP Rule 1.350(d).

2. *Filing requirements.* All original documents must be filed with the court either before service or immediately thereafter, unless otherwise provided for by general law or other rules. If the original of any bond or other document is not placed in the court file, a certified copy must be so placed by the clerk. FL ST J ADMIN Rule 2.516(d). All documents shall be filed in conformity with the requirements of FL ST J ADMIN Rule 2.525. FL ST RCP Rule 1.080(b). All documents filed in any court shall be filed by electronic transmission in accordance with FL ST J ADMIN Rule 2.525. "Documents" means pleadings, motions, petitions, memoranda, briefs, notices, exhibits, declarations, affidavits, orders, judgments, decrees, writs, opinions, and any other paper or writing submitted to a court. FL ST J ADMIN Rule 2.520(a). All documents that are court records, as defined in FL ST J ADMIN Rule 2.430(a)(1), must be filed by electronic transmission, provided that: (1) the clerk has the ability to accept and retain such documents; (2) the clerk or the chief judge of the circuit has requested permission to accept documents filed by electronic transmission; and (3) the supreme court has entered an order granting permission to the clerk to accept documents filed by electronic transmission. FL ST J ADMIN Rule 2.525(c)(1).

a. *Definition.* "Electronic transmission of documents" means the sending of information by electronic signals to, by or from a court or clerk, which when received can be transformed and stored or transmitted on paper, microfilm, magnetic storage device, optical imaging system, CD-ROM, flash drive, other electronic data storage system, server, case maintenance system ("CM"), electronic court filing ("ECF") system, statewide or local electronic portal ("e-portal"), or other electronic record keeping system authorized by the supreme court in a format sufficient to communicate the information on the original document in a readable format. Electronic transmission of documents includes electronic mail ("e-mail") and any internet-based transmission procedure, and may include procedures allowing for documents to be signed or verified by electronic means. FL ST J ADMIN Rule 2.525(a).

i. The filing of documents with the court as required by the Florida Rules of Judicial Adminis-

tration must be made by filing them with the clerk in accordance with FL ST J ADMIN Rule 2.525, except that the judge may permit documents to be filed with the judge, in which event the judge must note the filing date before him or her on the documents and transmit them to the clerk. The date of filing is that shown on the face of the document by the judge's notation or the clerk's time stamp, whichever is earlier. FL ST J ADMIN Rule 2.516(e).

b. *Application.* Any court or clerk of the court may accept the electronic transmission of documents for filing after the clerk, together with input from the chief judge of the circuit, has obtained approval of the procedures and program for doing so from the Supreme Court of Florida. FL ST J ADMIN Rule 2.525(b).

c. *Exceptions*

   i. Paper documents and other submissions may be manually submitted to the clerk or court:

      - When the clerk does not have the ability to accept and retain documents by electronic filing or has not had ECF Procedures approved by the supreme court;
      - For filing by any self-represented party or any self-represented nonparty unless specific ECF Procedures provide a means to file documents electronically. However, any self-represented nonparty that is a governmental or public agency and any other agency, partnership, corporation, or business entity acting on behalf of any governmental or public agency may file documents by electronic transmission if such entity has the capability of filing documents electronically;
      - For filing by attorneys excused from e-mail service in accordance with FL ST J ADMIN Rule 2.516(b);
      - When submitting evidentiary exhibits or filing non-documentary materials;
      - When the filing involves documents in excess of twenty-five (25) megabytes (25MB) in size. For such filings, documents may be transmitted using an electronic storage medium that the clerk has the ability to accept, which may include a CD-ROM, flash drive, or similar storage medium;
      - When filed in open court, as permitted by the court;
      - When paper filing is permitted by any approved statewide or local ECF procedures; and
      - If any court determines that justice so requires. FL ST J ADMIN Rule 2.525(d).

   ii. Any document in paper form submitted under FL ST J ADMIN Rule 2.525(d) is filed when it is received by the clerk or court and the clerk shall immediately thereafter convert any filed paper document to an electronic document. "Convert to an electronic document" means optically capturing an image of a paper document and using character recognition software to recover as much of the document's text as practicable and then indexing and storing the document in the official court file. FL ST J ADMIN Rule 2.525(c)(4).

   iii. Any storage medium submitted under FL ST J ADMIN Rule 2.525(d)(5) is filed when received by the clerk or court and the clerk shall immediately thereafter transfer the electronic documents from the storage device to the official court file. FL ST J ADMIN Rule 2.525(c)(5).

   iv. If the filer of any paper document authorized under FL ST J ADMIN Rule 2.525(d) provides a self-addressed, postage-paid envelope for return of the paper document after it is converted to electronic form by the clerk, the clerk shall place the paper document in the envelope and deposit it in the mail. Except when a paper document is required to be maintained, the clerk may recycle any filed paper document that is not to be returned to the filer. FL ST J ADMIN Rule 2.525(c)(6).

   v. The clerk may convert any paper document filed before the effective date of FL ST J ADMIN Rule 2.525 to an electronic document. Unless the clerk is required to maintain the paper document, if the paper document has been converted to an electronic document by the clerk, the paper document is no longer part of the official court file and may be removed and recycled. FL ST J ADMIN Rule 2.525(c)(7).

d. *Official court file.* For information on what constitutes the official court file, please see FL ST J ADMIN Rule 2.525(c)(2), FL ST J ADMIN Rule 2.525(c)(3).

e. *Administration.* All attorneys, parties, or other persons using this rule to file documents are required to make arrangements with the court or clerk for the payment of any charges authorized by general law or the supreme court before filing any document by electronic transmission. FL ST J ADMIN Rule 2.525(f)(2).

f. *Filing date.* The filing date for an electronically transmitted document is the date and time that such filing is acknowledged by an electronic stamp or otherwise, pursuant to any procedure set forth in any ECF Procedures approved by the supreme court, or the date the last page of such filing is received by the court or clerk. FL ST J ADMIN Rule 2.525(f)(3).

g. *Accessibility.* All documents transmitted in any electronic form under FL ST J ADMIN Rule 2.525 must comply with the accessibility requirements of FL ST J ADMIN Rule 2.526. FL ST J ADMIN Rule 2.525(g).

3. *Service requirements.* Every pleading subsequent to the initial pleading, all orders, and every other document filed in the action must be served in conformity with the requirements of FL ST J ADMIN Rule 2.516. FL ST RCP Rule 1.080(a).

a. *Service; When required.* Unless the court otherwise orders, or a statute or supreme court administrative order specifies a different means of service, every pleading subsequent to the initial pleading and every other document filed in any court proceeding, except applications for witness subpoenas and documents served by formal notice or required to be served in the manner provided for service of formal notice, must be served in accordance with FL ST J ADMIN Rule 2.516 on each party. No service need be made on parties against whom a default has been entered, except that pleadings asserting new or additional claims against them must be served in the manner provided for service of summons. FL ST J ADMIN Rule 2.516(a).

b. *Service; How made.* When service is required or permitted to be made upon a party represented by an attorney, service must be made upon the attorney unless service upon the party is ordered by the court. FL ST J ADMIN Rule 2.516(b).

i. *Service by electronic mail ("e-mail").* All documents required or permitted to be served on another party must be served by e-mail, unless FL ST J ADMIN Rule 2.516 otherwise provides. When, in addition to service by e-mail, the sender also utilizes another means of service provided for in FL ST J ADMIN Rule 2.516(b)(2), any differing time limits and other provisions applicable to that other means of service control. FL ST J ADMIN Rule 2.516(b)(1). Any document electronically transmitted to a court or clerk must also be served on all parties and interested persons in accordance with the applicable rules of court. FL ST J ADMIN Rule 2.525(e)(2).

- *Service on attorneys.* Upon appearing in a proceeding, an attorney must serve a designation of a primary e-mail address and may designate no more than two (2) secondary e-mail addresses. Thereafter, service must be directed to all designated e-mail addresses in that proceeding. Every document filed by an attorney thereafter must include the primary e-mail address of that attorney and any secondary e-mail addresses. If an attorney does not designate any e-mail address for service, documents may be served on that attorney at the e-mail address on record with The Florida Bar. FL ST J ADMIN Rule 2.516(b)(1)(A).

- *Exception to e-mail service on attorneys.* Service by an attorney on another attorney must be made by e-mail unless excused by the court. Upon motion by an attorney demonstrating that the attorney has no e-mail account and lacks access to the Internet at the attorney's office, the court may excuse the attorney from the requirements of e-mail service. Service on and by an attorney excused by the court from e-mail service must be by the means provided in FL ST J ADMIN Rule 2.516(b)(2). FL ST J ADMIN Rule 2.516(b)(1)(B).

- *Service on and by parties not represented by an attorney.* Any party not represented by an attorney may serve a designation of a primary e-mail address and also may designate no more than two (2) secondary e-mail addresses to which service must be directed in that proceeding by the means provided in FL ST J ADMIN Rule 2.516(b)(1). If a party not represented by an attorney does not designate an e-mail address for service in a proceeding, service on and by that party must be by the means provided in FL ST J ADMIN Rule 2.516(b)(2). FL ST J ADMIN Rule 2.516(b)(1)(C).

- *Time of service.* Service by e-mail is complete when it is sent. FL ST J ADMIN Rule 2.516(b)(1)(D). An e-mail is deemed served on the date it is sent. FL ST J ADMIN Rule 2.516(b)(1)(D)(i). If the sender learns that the e-mail did not reach the address of the person to be served, the sender must immediately send another copy by e-mail, or by a means authorized by FL ST J ADMIN Rule 2.516(b)(2). FL ST J ADMIN Rule 2.516(b)(1)(D)(ii). E-mail service is treated as service by mail for the computation of time. FL ST J ADMIN Rule 2.516(b)(1)(D)(iii).

ii. *Format of e-mail for service.* Service of a document by e-mail is made by attaching a copy of the document in PDF format to an e-mail sent to all addresses designated by the attorney or party. FL ST J ADMIN Rule 2.516(b)(1)(E).

- All documents served by e-mail must be attached to an e-mail message containing a subject line beginning with the words "SERVICE OF COURT DOCUMENT" in all capital letters, followed by the case number of the proceeding in which the documents are being served. FL ST J ADMIN Rule 2.516(b)(1)(E)(i).
- The body of the e-mail must identify the court in which the proceeding is pending, the case number, the name of the initial party on each side, the title of each document served with that e-mail, and the sender's name and telephone number. FL ST J ADMIN Rule 2.516(b)(1)(E)(ii).
- Any document served by e-mail may be signed by the "/s/" format, as long as the filed original is signed in accordance with the applicable rule of procedure. FL ST J ADMIN Rule 2.516(b)(1)(E)(iii).
- Any e-mail which, together with its attached documents, exceeds five megabytes (5MB) in size, must be divided and sent as separate e-mails, no one of which may exceed five megabytes (5MB) in size and each of which must be sequentially numbered in the subject line. FL ST J ADMIN Rule 2.516(b)(1)(E)(iv).

iii. *Service by other means.* In addition to, and not in lieu of, service by e-mail, service may also be made upon attorneys by any of the means specified in FL ST J ADMIN Rule 2.516(b)(2). Service on and by all parties who are not represented by an attorney and who do not designate an e-mail address, and on and by all attorneys excused from e-mail service, must be made by delivering a copy of the document or by mailing it to the party or attorney at their last known address or, if no address is known, by leaving it with the clerk of the court. Service by mail is complete upon mailing. Delivery of a copy within FL ST J ADMIN Rule 2.516 is complete upon:

- Handing it to the attorney or to the party,
- Leaving it at the attorney's or party's office with a clerk or other person in charge thereof,
- If there is no one in charge, leaving it in a conspicuous place therein,
- If the office is closed or the person to be served has no office, leaving it at the person's usual place of abode with some person of his or her family above fifteen (15) years of age and informing such person of the contents, or
- Transmitting it by facsimile to the attorney's or party's office with a cover sheet containing the sender's name, firm, address, telephone number, and facsimile number, and the number of pages transmitted. When service is made by facsimile, a copy must also be served by any other method permitted by FL ST J ADMIN Rule 2.516. Facsimile service occurs when transmission is complete. FL ST J ADMIN Rule 2.516(b)(2)(A) through FL ST J ADMIN Rule 2.516(b)(2)(E).
- Service by delivery after 5:00 p.m. must be deemed to have been made by mailing on the date of delivery. FL ST J ADMIN Rule 2.516(b)(2)(F).

c. *Service; Numerous defendants.* In actions when the parties are unusually numerous, the court may regulate the service contemplated by the Florida Rules of Judicial Administration on motion or on its own initiative in such manner as may be found to be just and reasonable. FL ST J ADMIN Rule 2.516(c).

d. *Service by clerk.* Service of notices and other documents required to be made by the clerk must also be done as provided in FL ST J ADMIN Rule 2.516(b). FL ST J ADMIN Rule 2.516(g).

G. Hearings

1. There is no hearing required or contemplated with regard to requests for production of documents in the Florida Rules of Civil Procedure.

H. Forms

1. Official Request for Production of Documents Forms for Florida

a. Caption. FL ST RCP Form 1.901.

b. Subpoena duces tecum for trial. FL ST RCP Form 1.911.

c. Notice of production from nonparty. FL ST RCP Form 1.921.

d. Subpoena duces tecum without deposition. FL ST RCP Form 1.922.

2. Request for Production of Documents Forms for Florida

a. Request for production; Documents. FL-PRACFORM § 8:29.

b. Request for inspection; Documents, deposition. FL-PRACFORM § 8:30.

c. Request for inspection; Tangible things. FL-PRACFORM § 8:31.

d. Request for entry; Real property. FL-PRACFORM § 8:32.

e. Request for production; Documents, response. FL-PRACFORM § 8:33.

f. Request for inspection; Response, tangible things. FL-PRACFORM § 8:34.

g. Request for entry; Response, land and buildings. FL-PRACFORM § 8:35.

h. Production of documents; Nonparty, notice. FL-PRACFORM § 8:36.

i. Production of documents; Nonparty, objection. FL-PRACFORM § 8:37.

j. Request; Production of documents for inspection and copying. FL-PP § 3:115.

k. Notice of request for production from nonparty. FL-PP § 3:116.

l. Request; For permission to enter on land; To inspect and photograph. FL-PP § 3:127.

I. Checklist

(I) ❑ Matters to be considered by requesting party

(a) ❑ Required documents

(1) ❑ Request

(2) ❑ Certificate of service

(b) ❑ Supplemental documents

(1) ❑ Notice of intent to serve subpoena/Subpoena

(c) ❑ Time for request

(1) ❑ Without leave of court the request may be served on the plaintiff after commencement of the action and on any other party with or after service of the process and initial pleading on that party

(2) ❑ A party desiring production under FL ST RCP Rule 1.351 shall serve notice as provided in FL ST RCP Rule 1.080 on every other party of the intent to serve a subpoena under FL ST RCP Rule 1.351 at least ten (10) days before the subpoena is issued if service is by delivery and fifteen (15) days before the subpoena is issued if the service is by mail or e-mail

(II) ❑ Matters to be considered by responding party

(a) ❑ Required documents

(1) ❑ Response to request

(2) ❑ Certificate of service

(b) ❑ Supplemental documents

(1) ❑ Objections

(c) ❑ Time for response

(1) ❑ The party to whom the request is directed shall serve a written response within thirty (30) days after service of the request, except that a defendant may serve a response within forty-five (45) days after service of the process and initial pleading on that defendant; the court may allow a shorter or longer time

Requests, Notices and Applications
Request for Admissions

Document Last Updated January 2013

A. Applicable Rules

1. *State rules*
   a. Nonverification of pleadings. FL ST RCP Rule 1.030.
   b. Service and filing of pleadings, orders, and documents. FL ST RCP Rule 1.080.
   c. Time. FL ST RCP Rule 1.090.
   d. Pleadings and motions. FL ST RCP Rule 1.100.
   e. Pretrial procedure. FL ST RCP Rule 1.200.
   f. General provisions governing discovery. FL ST RCP Rule 1.280.
   g. Interrogatories to parties. FL ST RCP Rule 1.340.
   h. Examination of persons. FL ST RCP Rule 1.360.
   i. Requests for admission. FL ST RCP Rule 1.370.
   j. Failure to make discovery; Sanctions. FL ST RCP Rule 1.380.
   k. Depositions of expert witnesses. FL ST RCP Rule 1.390.
   l. Relief from judgment, decrees, or orders. FL ST RCP Rule 1.540.
   m. Forms. FL ST RCP Rule 1.900.
   n. Minimization of the filing of sensitive information. FL ST J ADMIN Rule 2.425.
   o. Retention of court records. FL ST J ADMIN Rule 2.430.
   p. Foreign attorneys. FL ST J ADMIN Rule 2.510.
   q. Signature of attorneys and parties. FL ST J ADMIN Rule 2.515.
   r. Paper. FL ST J ADMIN Rule 2.520.
   s. Electronic filing. FL ST J ADMIN Rule 2.525.
   t. Accessibility of information and technology. FL ST J ADMIN Rule 2.526.
   u. Requests for accommodations by persons with disabilities. FL ST J ADMIN Rule 2.540.
2. *Local rules*
   a. Establishment of 11th Circuit Homestead Access to Mediation Program ("CHAMP") for case management of residential foreclosure cases in the Eleventh Judicial Circuit of Florida. FL ST 11 J CIR 1-09-08.
   b. Enlargement and expansion of the current pilot project for electronic submissions of courtesy copies for uniform motion calendar and requests for special set hearings, emergency motions, and proposed orders. FL ST 11 J CIR 1-09-13-A1.

B. Timing

1. *Request for admission.* Without leave of court the request may be served upon the plaintiff after

commencement of the action and upon any other party with or after service of the process and initial pleading upon that party. FL ST RCP Rule 1.370(a).

2. *Sequence and timing of discovery.* Except as provided in FL ST RCP Rule 1.280(b)(5) or unless the court upon motion for the convenience of parties and witnesses and in the interest of justice orders otherwise, methods of discovery may be used in any sequence, and the fact that a party is conducting discovery, whether by deposition or otherwise, shall not delay any other party's discovery. FL ST RCP Rule 1.280(e).

3. *Computation of time*

   a. *Generally.* Computation of time shall be governed by FL ST J ADMIN Rule 2.514. FL ST RCP Rule 1.090(a). The following rules apply in computing time periods specified in any rule of procedure, local rule, court order, or statute that does not specify a method of computing time. FL ST J ADMIN Rule 2.514(a).

      i. *Period stated in days or a longer unit.* When the period is stated in days or a longer unit of time (A) exclude the day of the event that triggers the period; (B) count every day, including intermediate Saturdays, Sundays, and legal holidays; and (C) include the last day of the period, but if the last day is a Saturday, Sunday, or legal holiday, or falls within any period of time extended through an order of the chief justice under FL ST J ADMIN Rule 2.205(a)(2)(B)(iv), the period continues to run until the end of the next day that is not a Saturday, Sunday, or legal holiday and does not fall within any period of time extended through an order of the chief justice. FL ST J ADMIN Rule 2.514(a)(1).

      ii. *Period stated in hours.* When the period is stated in hours (A) begin counting immediately on the occurrence of the event that triggers the period; (B) count every hour, including hours during intermediate Saturdays, Sundays, and legal holidays; and (C) if the period would end on a Saturday, Sunday, or legal holiday, or during any period of time extended through an order of the chief justice under FL ST J ADMIN Rule 2.205(a)(2)(B)(iv), the period continues to run until the same time on the next day that is not a Saturday, Sunday, or legal holiday and does not fall within any period of time extended through an order of the chief justice. FL ST J ADMIN Rule 2.514(a)(2).

      iii. *Period stated in days less than seven (7) days.* When the period stated in days is less than seven (7) days, intermediate Saturdays, Sundays, and legal holidays shall be excluded in the computation. FL ST J ADMIN Rule 2.514(a)(3).

      iv. *"Last day" defined.* Unless a different time is set by a statute, local rule, or court order, the last day ends (A) for electronic filing or for service by any means, at midnight; and (B) for filing by other means, when the clerk's office is scheduled to close. FL ST J ADMIN Rule 2.514(a)(4).

      v. *"Next day" defined.* The "next day" is determined by continuing to count forward when the period is measured after an event and backward when measured before an event. FL ST J ADMIN Rule 2.514(a)(5).

      vi. *"Legal holiday" defined.* "Legal holiday" means (A) the day set aside by FL ST § 110.117, for observing New Year's Day, Martin Luther King, Jr.'s Birthday, Memorial Day, Independence Day, Labor Day, Veterans' Day, Thanksgiving Day, the Friday after Thanksgiving Day, or Christmas Day, and (B) any day observed as a holiday by the clerk's office or as designated by the chief judge. FL ST J ADMIN Rule 2.514(a)(6).

   b. *Additional time after service by mail or e-mail.* When a party may or must act within a specified time after service and service is made by mail or e-mail, five (5) days are added after the period that would otherwise expire under FL ST J ADMIN Rule 2.514(a). FL ST J ADMIN Rule 2.514(b).

   c. *Enlargement.* When an act is required or allowed to be done at or within a specified time by order of court, by the Florida Rules of Civil Procedure, or by notice given thereunder, for cause shown the court at any time in its discretion (1) with or without notice, may order the period enlarged if request therefor is made before the expiration of the period originally prescribed or as extended by a previous order, or (2) upon motion made and notice after the expiration of the specified period, may permit the act to be done when failure to act was the result of excusable neglect, but it may not extend the time for making a motion for new trial, for rehearing, or to alter or amend a judgment; making a motion for relief from a judgment under FL ST RCP Rule 1.540(b); taking an appeal or filing a petition for certiorari; or making a motion for a directed verdict. FL ST RCP Rule 1.090(b).

d. *Unaffected by expiration of term.* The period of time provided for the doing of any act or the taking of any proceeding shall not be affected or limited by the continued existence or expiration of a term of court. The continued existence or expiration of a term of court in no way affects the power of a court to do any act or take any proceeding in any action which is or has been pending before it. FL ST RCP Rule 1.090(c).

C. General Requirements

1. *General provisions governing discovery*

a. *Discovery methods.* Parties may obtain discovery by one or more of the following methods: depositions upon oral examination or written questions; written interrogatories; production of documents or things or permission to enter upon land or other property for inspection and other purposes; physical and mental examinations; and requests for admission. Unless the court orders otherwise and under FL ST RCP Rule 1.280(c), the frequency of use of these methods is not limited, except as provided in FL ST RCP Rule 1.200, FL ST RCP Rule 1.340, and FL ST RCP Rule 1.370. FL ST RCP Rule 1.280(a).

b. *Scope of discovery.* Unless otherwise limited by order of the court in accordance with the Florida Rules of Civil Procedure, the scope of discovery is as follows:

i. *In general.* Parties may obtain discovery regarding any matter, not privileged, that is relevant to the subject matter of the pending action, whether it relates to the claim or defense of the party seeking discovery or the claim or defense of any other party, including the existence, description, nature, custody, condition, and location of any books, documents, or other tangible things and the identity and location of persons having knowledge of any discoverable matter. It is not ground for objection that the information sought will be inadmissible at the trial if the information sought appears reasonably calculated to lead to the discovery of admissible evidence. FL ST RCP Rule 1.280(b)(1).

ii. *Indemnity agreements.* A party may obtain discovery of the existence and contents of any agreement under which any person may be liable to satisfy part or all of a judgment that may be entered in the action or to indemnify or to reimburse a party for payments made to satisfy the judgment. Information concerning the agreement is not admissible in evidence at trial by reason of disclosure. FL ST RCP Rule 1.280(b)(2).

iii. *Electronically stored information.* A party may obtain discovery of electronically stored information in accordance with the Florida Rules of Civil Procedure. FL ST RCP Rule 1.280(b)(3).

iv. *Trial preparation; Materials.* Subject to the provisions of FL ST RCP Rule 1.280(b)(5), a party may obtain discovery of documents and tangible things otherwise discoverable under FL ST RCP Rule 1.280(b)(1) and prepared in anticipation of litigation or for trial by or for another party or by or for that party's representative, including that party's attorney, consultant, surety, indemnitor, insurer, or agent, only upon a showing that the party seeking discovery has need of the materials in the preparation of the case and is unable without undue hardship to obtain the substantial equivalent of the materials by other means. FL ST RCP Rule 1.280(b)(4).

- In ordering discovery of the materials when the required showing has been made, the court shall protect against disclosure of the mental impressions, conclusions, opinions, or legal theories of an attorney or other representative of a party concerning the litigation. FL ST RCP Rule 1.280(b)(4).
- Without the required showing a party may obtain a copy of a statement concerning the action or its subject matter previously made by that party. FL ST RCP Rule 1.280(b)(4).
- Upon request without the required showing a person not a party may obtain a copy of a statement concerning the action or its subject matter previously made by that person. If the request is refused, the person may move for an order to obtain a copy. The provisions of FL

ST RCP Rule 1.380(a)(5) apply to the award of expenses incurred as a result of making the motion. FL ST RCP Rule 1.280(b)(4).

- For purposes of FL ST RCP Rule 1.280(b)(4), a statement previously made is a written statement signed or otherwise adopted or approved by the person making it, or a stenographic, mechanical, electrical, or other recording or transcription of it that is a substantially verbatim recital of an oral statement by the person making it and contemporaneously recorded. FL ST RCP Rule 1.280(b)(4).

v. *Trial preparation; Experts.* Discovery of facts known and opinions held by experts, otherwise discoverable under the provisions of FL ST RCP Rule 1.280(b)(1) and acquired or developed in anticipation of litigation or for trial, may be obtained only as follows:

- By interrogatories a party may require any other party to identify each person whom the other party expects to call as an expert witness at trial and to state the subject matter on which the expert is expected to testify, and to state the substance of the facts and opinions to which the expert is expected to testify and a summary of the grounds for each opinion. FL ST RCP Rule 1.280(b)(5)(A)(i).
- Any person disclosed by interrogatories or otherwise as a person expected to be called as an expert witness at trial may be deposed in accordance with FL ST RCP Rule 1.390 without motion or order of court. FL ST RCP Rule 1.280(b)(5)(A)(ii).
- A party may obtain the following discovery regarding any person disclosed by interrogatories or otherwise as a person expected to be called as an expert witness at trial: The scope of employment in the pending case and the compensation for such service, FL ST RCP Rule 1.280(b)(5)(A)(iii)(1); The expert's general litigation experience, including the percentage of work performed for plaintiffs and defendants, FL ST RCP Rule 1.280(b)(5)(A)(iii)(2); The identity of other cases, within a reasonable time period, in which the expert has testified by deposition or at trial, FL ST RCP Rule 1.280(b)(5)(A)(iii)(3); An approximation of the portion of the expert's involvement as an expert witness, which may be based on the number of hours, percentage of hours, or percentage of earned income derived from serving as an expert witness; however, the expert shall not be required to disclose his or her earnings as an expert witness or income derived from other services. FL ST RCP Rule 1.280(b)(5)(A)(iii)(4).
- An expert may be required to produce financial and business records only under the most unusual or compelling circumstances and may not be compelled to compile or produce nonexistent documents. Upon motion, the court may order further discovery by other means, subject to such restrictions as to scope and other provisions pursuant to FL ST RCP Rule 1.280(b)(5)(C) concerning fees and expenses as the court may deem appropriate. FL ST RCP Rule 1.280(b)(5).
- A party may discover facts known or opinions held by an expert who has been retained or specially employed by another party in anticipation of litigation or preparation for trial and who is not expected to be called as a witness at trial, only as provided in FL ST RCP Rule 1.360(b) or upon a showing of exceptional circumstances under which it is impracticable for the party seeking discovery to obtain facts or opinions on the same subject by other means. FL ST RCP Rule 1.280(b)(5)(B).
- Unless manifest injustice would result, the court shall require that the party seeking discovery pay the expert a reasonable fee for time spent in responding to discovery under FL ST RCP Rule 1.280(b)(5)(A) and FL ST RCP Rule 1.280(b)(5)(B); and concerning discovery from an expert obtained under FL ST RCP Rule 1.280(b)(5)(A) the court may require, and concerning discovery obtained under FL ST RCP Rule 1.280(b)(5)(B) shall require, the party seeking discovery to pay the other party a fair part of the fees and expenses reasonably incurred by the latter party in obtaining facts and opinions from the expert. FL ST RCP Rule 1.280(b)(5)(C).
- As used in the Florida Rules of Civil Procedure an expert shall be an expert witness as defined in FL ST RCP Rule 1.390(a). FL ST RCP Rule 1.280(b)(5)(D).

vi. *Claims to privilege or protection.* When a party withholds information otherwise discoverable under the Florida Rules of Civil Procedure by claiming that it is privileged or subject to protection as trial preparation material, the party shall make the claim expressly and shall describe the nature of the documents, communications, or things not produced or disclosed in a manner that, without revealing information itself privileged or protected, will enable other parties to assess the applicability of the privilege or protection. FL ST RCP Rule 1.280(b)(6).

c. *Limitations on discovery of electronically stored information*

i. A person may object to discovery of electronically stored information from sources that the person identifies as not reasonably accessible because of burden or cost. On motion to compel discovery or for a protective order, the person from whom discovery is sought must show that the information sought or the format requested is not reasonably accessible because of undue burden or cost. If that showing is made, the court may nonetheless order the discovery from such sources or in such formats if the requesting party shows good cause. The court may specify conditions of the discovery, including ordering that some or all of the expenses incurred by the person from whom discovery is sought be paid by the party seeking the discovery. FL ST RCP Rule 1.280(d)(1).

ii. In determining any motion involving discovery of electronically stored information, the court must limit the frequency or extent of discovery otherwise allowed by the Florida Rules of Civil Procedure if it determines that (i) the discovery sought is unreasonably cumulative or duplicative, or can be obtained from another source or in another manner that is more convenient, less burdensome, or less expensive; or (ii) the burden or expense of the discovery outweighs its likely benefit, considering the needs of the case, the amount in controversy, the parties' resources, the importance of the issues at stake in the action, and the importance of the discovery in resolving the issues. FL ST RCP Rule 1.280(d)(2).

d. For information on inadvertent disclosure of privileged materials, see FL ST RCP Rule 1.285.

2. *Requests for admission.* It is an advantage to use requests for admission. The biggest advantage is that if an adversary denies a request for an admission and the denied matter is later proven to be true, the adversary may have to pay the costs of proving the genuineness of the document or the truth of the matter requested to be admitted. FL-PP § 3:143.

a. *Scope.* A party may serve upon any other party a written request for the admission of the truth of any matters within the scope of FL ST RCP Rule 1.280(b) set forth in the request that relate to statements or opinions of fact or of the application of law to fact, including the genuineness of any documents described in the request. FL ST RCP Rule 1.370(a).

b. *Copies of documents.* Copies of documents shall be served with the request unless they have been or are otherwise furnished or made available for inspection and copying. FL ST RCP Rule 1.370(a).

c. *Number of requests.* The request for admission shall not exceed thirty (30) requests, including all subparts, unless the court permits a larger number on motion and notice and for good cause, or the parties propounding and responding to the requests stipulate to a larger number. Each matter of which an admission is requested shall be separately set forth. FL ST RCP Rule 1.370(a).

d. *Sufficiency of responses.* The party who has requested the admissions may move to determine the sufficiency of the answers or objections. Unless the court determines that an objection is justified, it shall order that an answer be served. If the court determines that an answer does not comply with the requirements of this rule, it may order either that the matter is admitted or that an amended answer be served. Instead of these orders the court may determine that final disposition of the request be made at a pretrial conference or at a designated time before trial. The provisions of FL ST RCP Rule 1.380(a)(4) apply to the award of expenses incurred in relation to the motion. FL ST RCP Rule 1.370(a).

e. *Effect of admission.* Any matter admitted under FL ST RCP Rule 1.370 is conclusively established unless the court on motion permits withdrawal or amendment of the admission. Subject to FL ST RCP Rule 1.200 governing amendment of a pretrial order, the court may permit withdrawal or amendment when the presentation of the merits of the action will be subserved by it and the party who obtained the admission fails to satisfy the court that withdrawal or amendment will prejudice that party in maintaining an action or defense on the merits. Any admission made by a party under this rule is for the purpose of the pending action only and is not an admission for any other purpose nor may it be used against that party in any other proceeding. FL ST RCP Rule 1.370(b).

f. *Answer requirements.* The matter is admitted unless the party to whom the request is directed serves upon the party requesting the admission a written answer or objection addressed to the matter within thirty (30) days after service of the request or such shorter or longer time as the court may allow but, unless the court shortens the time, a defendant shall not be required to serve answers or objections before the expiration of forty-five (45) days after service of the process and initial pleading upon the defendant. If objection is made, the reasons shall be stated. The answer shall specifically deny the matter or set forth in detail the reasons why the answering party cannot truthfully admit or deny the matter. A denial shall fairly meet the substance of the requested admission, and when good faith requires that a party qualify an answer or deny only a part of the matter of which an admission is requested, the party shall specify so much of it as is true and qualify or deny the remainder. An answering party may not give lack of information or knowledge as a reason for failure to admit or deny unless that party states that that party has made reasonable inquiry and that the information known or readily obtainable by that party is insufficient to enable that party to admit or deny. A party who considers that a matter of which an admission has been requested presents a genuine issue for trial may not object to the request on that ground alone; the party may deny the matter or set forth reasons why the party cannot admit or deny it, subject to FL ST RCP Rule 1.380(c). FL ST RCP Rule 1.370(a).

3. *Arbitration and mediation*

a. *Referral to arbitration and mediation.* Except as hereinafter provided or as otherwise prohibited by law, the presiding judge may enter an order referring all or any part of a contested civil matter to mediation or arbitration. The parties to any contested civil matter may file a written stipulation to mediate or arbitrate any issue between them at any time. Such stipulation shall be incorporated into the order of referral. FL ST RCP Rule 1.700(a).

i. In all residential foreclosure actions involving homestead properties filed on or after May 1, 2009, unless a stipulation is specifically invoked by the parties in writing within five (5) days of service of the complaint on the main defendant, the parties are deemed to have stipulated to referral of the mediation to the Collins Center pursuant to FL ST RCP Rule 1.720(f). FL ST 11 J CIR 1-09-08(2); FL ST 11 J CIR 1-09-08(3). FL ST 11 J CIR 1-09-08 constitutes a formal referral to mediation pursuant to the Florida Rules of Civil Procedure. FL ST 11 J CIR 1-09-08(2).

ii. For further information on referral to mediation, refer to FL ST 11 J CIR 1-09-08.

b. *Arbitration*

i. *Exclusions.* A civil action shall be ordered to arbitration or arbitration in conjunction with mediation upon stipulation of the parties. A civil action may be ordered to arbitration or arbitration in conjunction with mediation upon motion of any party or by the court, if the judge determines the action to be of such a nature that arbitration could be of benefit to the litigants or the court. FL ST RCP Rule 1.800.

- Under no circumstances may the following categories of actions be referred to arbitration: (1) bond estreatures; (2) habeas corpus or other extraordinary writs; (3) bond validations; (4) civil or criminal contempt; (5) such other matters as may be specified by order of the chief judge in the circuit. FL ST RCP Rule 1.800.

ii. For more information regarding arbitration, please see FL ST RCP Rule 1.810; FL ST RCP Rule 1.820; FL ST RCP Rule 1.830.

c. *Mediation.* For more information regarding mediation, please see FL ST RCP Rule 1.710; FL ST RCP Rule 1.720; FL ST RCP Rule 1.730; and FL ST RCP Rule 1.750.

4. *Rules of court*

a. *Rules of civil procedure.* The Florida Rules of Civil Procedure apply to all actions of a civil nature

and all special statutory proceedings in the circuit courts and county courts except those to which the Florida Probate Rules, the Florida Family Law Rules of Procedure, or the Small Claims Rules apply. FL ST RCP Rule 1.010.

i. The form, content, procedure, and time for pleading in all special statutory proceedings shall be as prescribed by the statutes governing the proceeding unless the Florida Rules of Civil Procedure specifically provide to the contrary. FL ST RCP Rule 1.010.

ii. The Florida Rules of Civil Procedure shall be construed to secure the just, speedy, and inexpensive determination of every action. FL ST RCP Rule 1.010.

b. *Rules of judicial administration.* The Florida Rules of Judicial Administration shall apply to administrative matters in all courts to which the Florida Rules of Judicial Administration are applicable by their terms. The Florida Rules of Judicial Administration shall be construed to secure the speedy and inexpensive determination of every proceeding to which they are applicable. The Florida Rules of Judicial Administration shall supersede all conflicting rules and statutes. FL ST J ADMIN Rule 2.110.

D. Documents

1. *Required documents*

a. *Request for admission.* Please see the General Requirements section of this document for more information on the contents of the request for admission.

i. *Notices to persons with disabilities.* See the Format section of this KeyRules document for further information.

b. *Copies of documents.* Copies of documents shall be served with the request unless they have been or are otherwise furnished or made available for inspection and copying. FL ST RCP Rule 1.370(a).

c. *Certificate of service.* A certificate of service of the interrogatories shall be filed, giving the date of service and the name of the party to whom they were directed. FL ST RCP Rule 1.340(e). When any attorney certifies in substance: "I certify that a copy hereof has been furnished to (here insert name or names and addresses used for service) by (e-mail) (delivery) (mail) (fax) on .... (date) ....__________________ Attorney" the certificate is taken as prima facie proof of such service in compliance with FL ST J ADMIN Rule 2.516. FL ST J ADMIN Rule 2.516(f).

E. Format

1. *Documents; Type and size.* Documents subject to the exceptions set forth in FL ST J ADMIN Rule 2.525(d) shall be filed on recycled paper measuring eight and one half by eleven (8 1/2 by 11) inches. For purposes of FL ST J ADMIN Rule 2.520, paper is recycled if it contains a minimum content of fifty (50) percent waste paper. Xerographic reduction of legal-size (eight and one half by fourteen (8 1/2 by 14) inches) documents to letter size (eight and one half by eleven (8 1/2 by 11) inches) is prohibited. All other documents filed by electronic transmission shall be filed in a format capable of being printed in a format consistent with the provisions of FL ST J ADMIN Rule 2.250. FL ST J ADMIN Rule 2.520(b).

a. *Exhibits.* Any exhibit or attachment filed with pleadings or papers may be filed in its original size. FL ST J ADMIN Rule 2.520(c).

b. *Recording space.* On all papers and documents prepared and filed by the court or by any party to a proceeding which are to be recorded in the public records of any county, including but not limited to final money judgments and notices of lis pendens, a three (3) inch by three (3) inch space at the top right-hand corner on the first page and a one (1) inch by three (3) inch space at the top right-hand corner on each subsequent page shall be left blank and reserved for use by the clerk of court. FL ST J ADMIN Rule 2.520(d).

i. *Exceptions to recording space.* Any papers or documents created by persons or entities over which the filing party has no control, including but not limited to wills, codicils, trusts, or other testamentary documents; documents prepared or executed by any public officer; documents prepared, executed, acknowledged, or proved outside of the State of Florida; or documents created by State or Federal government agencies, may be filed without the space required by FL ST J ADMIN Rule 2.520. FL ST J ADMIN Rule 2.520(e).

c. *Noncompliance.* No clerk of court is permitted to refuse to file any document or paper because of noncompliance with the Florida Rules of Judicial Administration. However, upon request of the clerk of court, noncomplying documents must be resubmitted in accordance with the formatting rules. FL ST J ADMIN Rule 2.520(f).

2. *Caption.* Every pleading, motion, order, judgment, or other paper shall have a caption containing the name of the court, the file number, and except for in rem proceedings, including forfeiture proceedings, the name of the first party on each side with an appropriate indication of other parties, and a designation identifying the party filing it and its nature or the nature of the order, as the case may be. In any in rem proceeding, every pleading, motion, order, judgment, or other paper shall have a caption containing the name of the court, the file number, the style "In re" (followed by the name or general description of the property), and a designation of the person or entity filing it and its nature or the nature of the order, as the case may be. In an in rem forfeiture proceeding, the style shall be "In re forfeiture of" (followed by the name of the general description of the property). All papers filed in the action shall be styled in such a manner as to indicate clearly the subject matter of the paper and the party requesting or obtaining relief. FL ST RCP Rule 1.100(c)(1).

3. *Writing and written defined.* Writing or written means a document containing information, an application, or a stipulation. FL ST RCP Rule 1.080(c).

4. *Rule abbreviations*

   a. The Florida Rules of Civil Procedure and shall be abbreviated as Fla.R.Civ.P. FL ST RCP Rule 1.010.

   b. The Florida Rules of Judicial Administration shall be abbreviated as Fla. R. Jud. Admin. FL ST J ADMIN Rule 2.110.

5. *Nonverification.* Except when otherwise specifically provided by the Florida Rules of Civil Procedure or an applicable statute, every pleading or other document of a party represented by an attorney need not be verified or accompanied by an affidavit. FL ST RCP Rule 1.030; FL ST J ADMIN Rule 2.515(a).

6. *Attorney signature*

   a. *Attorney signature.* Every pleading and other document of a party represented by an attorney shall be signed by at least one (1) attorney of record in that attorney's individual name whose current record Florida Bar address, telephone number, including area code, primary e-mail address and secondary e-mail addresses, if any, and Florida Bar number shall be stated, and who shall be duly licensed to practice law in Florida or who shall have received permission to appear in the particular case as provided in FL ST J ADMIN Rule 2.510. FL ST J ADMIN Rule 2.515(a).

      i. The attorney may be required by the court to give the address of, and to vouch for the attorney's authority to represent, the party. FL ST J ADMIN Rule 2.515(a).

      ii. The signature of an attorney shall constitute a certificate by the attorney that the attorney has read the pleading or other document; that to the best of the attorney's knowledge, information, and belief there is good ground to support it; and that it is not interposed for delay. FL ST J ADMIN Rule 2.515(a).

      iii. If a pleading is not signed or is signed with intent to defeat the purpose of FL ST J ADMIN Rule 2.515, it may be stricken and the action may proceed as though the pleading or other document had not been served. FL ST J ADMIN Rule 2.515(a).

   b. *Pro se litigant signature.* A party who is not represented by an attorney shall sign any pleading or other paper and state the party's address and telephone number, including area code. FL ST J ADMIN Rule 2.515(b).

   c. *Form of signature*

      i. The signatures required on pleadings and documents by FL ST J ADMIN Rule 2.515(a) and FL ST J ADMIN Rule 2.515(b) may be:

         - Original signatures;
         - Original signatures that have been reproduced by electronic means, such as on electronically transmitted documents or photocopied documents;

- Electronic signatures using the "/s/," "s/," or "/s" formats by or at the direction of the person signing; or
- Any other signature format authorized by general law, so long as the clerk where the proceeding is pending has the capability of receiving and has obtained approval from the Supreme Court of Florida to accept pleadings and documents with that signature format. FL ST J ADMIN Rule 2.515(c)(1).

ii. An attorney, party, or other person who files a pleading or paper by electronic transmission that does not contain the original signature of that attorney, party, or other person shall file that identical pleading or paper in paper form containing an original signature of that attorney, party, or other person (hereinafter called the follow-up filing) immediately thereafter. The follow-up filing is not required if the Supreme Court of Florida has entered an order directing the clerk of court to discontinue accepting the follow-up filing. FL ST J ADMIN Rule 2.515(c)(2).

7. *Forms*

a. *Process.* The forms of process, notice of lis pendens, and notice of action provided in the Florida Rules of Civil Procedure are sufficient. Variations from the forms do not void process or notices that are otherwise sufficient. FL ST RCP Rule 1.900(a).

b. *Other forms.* The other forms provided in the Florida Rules of Civil Procedure are sufficient for the matters that are covered by them. So long as the substance is expressed without prolixity, the forms may be varied to meet the facts of a particular case. FL ST RCP Rule 1.900(b).

c. *Formal matters.* Captions, except for the designation of the paper, are omitted from the forms provided in the Florida Rules of Civil Procedure. A general form of caption is the first form provided. Signatures are omitted from pleadings and motions. FL ST RCP Rule 1.900(c).

8. *Notices to persons with disabilities.* All notices of court proceedings to be held in a public facility, and all process compelling appearance at such proceedings, shall include the following statement in bold face, fourteen (14) point Times New Roman or Courier font: "If you are a person with a disability who needs any accommodation in order to participate in this proceeding, you are entitled, at no cost to you, to the provision of certain assistance. Please contact [identify applicable court personnel by name, address, and telephone number] at least seven (7) days before your scheduled court appearance, or immediately upon receiving this notification if the time before the scheduled appearance is less than seven (7) days; if you are hearing or voice impaired, call 711." FL ST J ADMIN Rule 2.540(c)(1).

9. *Minimization of the filing of sensitive information*

a. *Limitations for court filings.* Unless authorized by FL ST J ADMIN Rule 2.425(b), statute, another rule of court, or the court orders otherwise, designated sensitive information filed with the court must be limited to the following format:

i. The initials of a person known to be a minor;

ii. The year of birth of a person's birth date;

iii. No portion of any: Social security number, Bank account number, Credit card account number, Charge account number, or Debit account number;

iv. The last four digits of any: Taxpayer identification number (TIN), Employee identification number, Driver's license number, Passport number, Telephone number, Financial account number, except as set forth in FL ST J ADMIN Rule 2.425(a)(3), Brokerage account number, Insurance policy account number, Loan account number, Customer account number, or Patient or health care number;

v. A truncated version of any: Email address, Computer user name, Password, or Personal identification number (PIN); and

vi. A truncated version of any other sensitive information as provided by court order. FL ST J ADMIN Rule 2.425(a).

b. *Exceptions.* FL ST J ADMIN Rule 2.425(a) does not apply to the following:

i. An account number which identifies the property alleged to be the subject of a proceeding;

ii. The record of an administrative or agency proceeding;

iii. The record in appellate or review proceedings;

iv. The birth date of a minor whenever the birth date is necessary for the court to establish or maintain subject matter jurisdiction;

v. The name of a minor in any order relating to parental responsibility, time-sharing, or child support;

vi. The name of a minor in any document or order affecting the minor's ownership of real property;

vii. The birth date of a party in a writ of attachment or notice to payor;

viii. In traffic and criminal proceedings: a pro se filing; a court filing that is related to a criminal matter or investigation and that is prepared before the filing of a criminal charge or is not filed as part of any docketed criminal case; an arrest or search warrant or any information in support thereof; a charging document and an affidavit or other documents filed in support of any charging document, including any driving records; a statement of particulars; discovery material introduced into evidence or otherwise filed with the court; and all information necessary for the proper issuance and execution of a subpoena duces tecum;

ix. Information used by the clerk for case maintenance purposes or the courts for case management purposes; and

x. Information which is relevant and material to an issue before the court. FL ST J ADMIN Rule 2.425(b).

c. *Remedies.* Upon motion by a party or interested person or sua sponte by the court, the court may order remedies, sanctions or both for a violation of FL ST J ADMIN Rule 2.425(a). Following notice and an opportunity to respond, the court may impose sanctions if such filing was not made in good faith. FL ST J ADMIN Rule 2.425(c).

d. *Motions not restricted.* FL ST J ADMIN Rule 2.425 does not restrict a party's right to move for protective order, to move to file documents under seal, or to request a determination of the confidentiality of records. FL ST J ADMIN Rule 2.425(d).

e. *Application.* FL ST J ADMIN Rule 2.425 does not affect the application of constitutional provisions, statutes, or rules of court regarding confidential information or access to public information. FL ST J ADMIN Rule 2.425(e).

F. Filing and Service Requirements

1. *Court filing of documents and discovery.* Information obtained during discovery shall not be filed with the court until such time as it is filed for good cause. The requirement of good cause is satisfied only where the filing of the information is allowed or required by another applicable rule of procedure or by court order. All filings of discovery documents shall comply with FL ST J ADMIN Rule 2.425. The court shall have the authority to impose sanctions for violation of FL ST RCP Rule 1.280. FL ST RCP Rule 1.280(g).

2. *Filing requirements.* All original documents must be filed with the court either before service or immediately thereafter, unless otherwise provided for by general law or other rules. If the original of any bond or other document is not placed in the court file, a certified copy must be so placed by the clerk. FL ST J ADMIN Rule 2.516(d). All documents shall be filed in conformity with the requirements of FL ST J ADMIN Rule 2.525. FL ST RCP Rule 1.080(b). All documents filed in any court shall be filed by electronic transmission in accordance with FL ST J ADMIN Rule 2.525. "Documents" means pleadings, motions, petitions, memoranda, briefs, notices, exhibits, declarations, affidavits, orders, judgments, decrees, writs, opinions, and any other paper or writing submitted to a court. FL ST J ADMIN Rule 2.520(a). All documents that are court records, as defined in FL ST J ADMIN Rule 2.430(a)(1), must be filed by electronic transmission, provided that: (1) the clerk has the ability to accept and retain such documents; (2) the clerk or the chief judge of the circuit has requested permission to accept documents filed by electronic transmission; and (3) the supreme court has entered an order granting permission to the clerk to accept documents filed by electronic transmission. FL ST J ADMIN Rule 2.525(c)(1).

a. *Definition.* "Electronic transmission of documents" means the sending of information by electronic signals to, by or from a court or clerk, which when received can be transformed and stored or

transmitted on paper, microfilm, magnetic storage device, optical imaging system, CD-ROM, flash drive, other electronic data storage system, server, case maintenance system ("CM"), electronic court filing ("ECF") system, statewide or local electronic portal ("e-portal"), or other electronic record keeping system authorized by the supreme court in a format sufficient to communicate the information on the original document in a readable format. Electronic transmission of documents includes electronic mail ("e-mail") and any internet-based transmission procedure, and may include procedures allowing for documents to be signed or verified by electronic means. FL ST J ADMIN Rule 2.525(a).

i. The filing of documents with the court as required by the Florida Rules of Judicial Administration must be made by filing them with the clerk in accordance with FL ST J ADMIN Rule 2.525, except that the judge may permit documents to be filed with the judge, in which event the judge must note the filing date before him or her on the documents and transmit them to the clerk. The date of filing is that shown on the face of the document by the judge's notation or the clerk's time stamp, whichever is earlier. FL ST J ADMIN Rule 2.516(e).

b. *Application.* Any court or clerk of the court may accept the electronic transmission of documents for filing after the clerk, together with input from the chief judge of the circuit, has obtained approval of the procedures and program for doing so from the Supreme Court of Florida. FL ST J ADMIN Rule 2.525(b).

c. *Exceptions*

i. Paper documents and other submissions may be manually submitted to the clerk or court:

- When the clerk does not have the ability to accept and retain documents by electronic filing or has not had ECF Procedures approved by the supreme court;
- For filing by any self-represented party or any self-represented nonparty unless specific ECF Procedures provide a means to file documents electronically. However, any self-represented nonparty that is a governmental or public agency and any other agency, partnership, corporation, or business entity acting on behalf of any governmental or public agency may file documents by electronic transmission if such entity has the capability of filing documents electronically;
- For filing by attorneys excused from e-mail service in accordance with FL ST J ADMIN Rule 2.516(b);
- When submitting evidentiary exhibits or filing non-documentary materials;
- When the filing involves documents in excess of twenty-five (25) megabytes (25MB) in size. For such filings, documents may be transmitted using an electronic storage medium that the clerk has the ability to accept, which may include a CD-ROM, flash drive, or similar storage medium;
- When filed in open court, as permitted by the court;
- When paper filing is permitted by any approved statewide or local ECF procedures; and
- If any court determines that justice so requires. FL ST J ADMIN Rule 2.525(d).

ii. Any document in paper form submitted under FL ST J ADMIN Rule 2.525(d) is filed when it is received by the clerk or court and the clerk shall immediately thereafter convert any filed paper document to an electronic document. "Convert to an electronic document" means optically capturing an image of a paper document and using character recognition software to recover as much of the document's text as practicable and then indexing and storing the document in the official court file. FL ST J ADMIN Rule 2.525(c)(4).

iii. Any storage medium submitted under FL ST J ADMIN Rule 2.525(d)(5) is filed when received by the clerk or court and the clerk shall immediately thereafter transfer the electronic documents from the storage device to the official court file. FL ST J ADMIN Rule 2.525(c)(5).

iv. If the filer of any paper document authorized under FL ST J ADMIN Rule 2.525(d) provides a self-addressed, postage-paid envelope for return of the paper document after it is converted to electronic form by the clerk, the clerk shall place the paper document in the envelope and

deposit it in the mail. Except when a paper document is required to be maintained, the clerk may recycle any filed paper document that is not to be returned to the filer. FL ST J ADMIN Rule 2.525(c)(6).

v. The clerk may convert any paper document filed before the effective date of FL ST J ADMIN Rule 2.525 to an electronic document. Unless the clerk is required to maintain the paper document, if the paper document has been converted to an electronic document by the clerk, the paper document is no longer part of the official court file and may be removed and recycled. FL ST J ADMIN Rule 2.525(c)(7).

d. *Official court file.* For information on what constitutes the official court file, please see FL ST J ADMIN Rule 2.525(c)(2), FL ST J ADMIN Rule 2.525(c)(3).

e. *Administration.* All attorneys, parties, or other persons using this rule to file documents are required to make arrangements with the court or clerk for the payment of any charges authorized by general law or the supreme court before filing any document by electronic transmission. FL ST J ADMIN Rule 2.525(f)(2).

f. *Filing date.* The filing date for an electronically transmitted document is the date and time that such filing is acknowledged by an electronic stamp or otherwise, pursuant to any procedure set forth in any ECF Procedures approved by the supreme court, or the date the last page of such filing is received by the court or clerk. FL ST J ADMIN Rule 2.525(f)(3).

g. *Accessibility.* All documents transmitted in any electronic form under FL ST J ADMIN Rule 2.525 must comply with the accessibility requirements of FL ST J ADMIN Rule 2.526. FL ST J ADMIN Rule 2.525(g).

3. *Service requirements.* Every pleading subsequent to the initial pleading, all orders, and every other document filed in the action must be served in conformity with the requirements of FL ST J ADMIN Rule 2.516. FL ST RCP Rule 1.080(a).

a. *Service; When required.* Unless the court otherwise orders, or a statute or supreme court administrative order specifies a different means of service, every pleading subsequent to the initial pleading and every other document filed in any court proceeding, except applications for witness subpoenas and documents served by formal notice or required to be served in the manner provided for service of formal notice, must be served in accordance with FL ST J ADMIN Rule 2.516 on each party. No service need be made on parties against whom a default has been entered, except that pleadings asserting new or additional claims against them must be served in the manner provided for service of summons. FL ST J ADMIN Rule 2.516(a).

b. *Service; How made.* When service is required or permitted to be made upon a party represented by an attorney, service must be made upon the attorney unless service upon the party is ordered by the court. FL ST J ADMIN Rule 2.516(b).

i. *Service by electronic mail ("e-mail").* All documents required or permitted to be served on another party must be served by e-mail, unless FL ST J ADMIN Rule 2.516 otherwise provides. When, in addition to service by e-mail, the sender also utilizes another means of service provided for in FL ST J ADMIN Rule 2.516(b)(2), any differing time limits and other provisions applicable to that other means of service control. FL ST J ADMIN Rule 2.516(b)(1). Any document electronically transmitted to a court or clerk must also be served on all parties and interested persons in accordance with the applicable rules of court. FL ST J ADMIN Rule 2.525(e)(2).

- *Service on attorneys.* Upon appearing in a proceeding, an attorney must serve a designation of a primary e-mail address and may designate no more than two (2) secondary e-mail addresses. Thereafter, service must be directed to all designated e-mail addresses in that proceeding. Every document filed by an attorney thereafter must include the primary e-mail address of that attorney and any secondary e-mail addresses. If an attorney does not designate any e-mail address for service, documents may be served on that attorney at the e-mail address on record with The Florida Bar. FL ST J ADMIN Rule 2.516(b)(1)(A).
- *Exception to e-mail service on attorneys.* Service by an attorney on another attorney must

be made by e-mail unless excused by the court. Upon motion by an attorney demonstrating that the attorney has no e-mail account and lacks access to the Internet at the attorney's office, the court may excuse the attorney from the requirements of e-mail service. Service on and by an attorney excused by the court from e-mail service must be by the means provided in FL ST J ADMIN Rule 2.516(b)(2). FL ST J ADMIN Rule 2.516(b)(1)(B).

- *Service on and by parties not represented by an attorney.* Any party not represented by an attorney may serve a designation of a primary e-mail address and also may designate no more than two (2) secondary e-mail addresses to which service must be directed in that proceeding by the means provided in FL ST J ADMIN Rule 2.516(b)(1). If a party not represented by an attorney does not designate an e-mail address for service in a proceeding, service on and by that party must be by the means provided in FL ST J ADMIN Rule 2.516(b)(2). FL ST J ADMIN Rule 2.516(b)(1)(C).
- *Time of service.* Service by e-mail is complete when it is sent. FL ST J ADMIN Rule 2.516(b)(1)(D). An e-mail is deemed served on the date it is sent. FL ST J ADMIN Rule 2.516(b)(1)(D)(i). If the sender learns that the e-mail did not reach the address of the person to be served, the sender must immediately send another copy by e-mail, or by a means authorized by FL ST J ADMIN Rule 2.516(b)(2). FL ST J ADMIN Rule 2.516(b)(1)(D)(ii). E-mail service is treated as service by mail for the computation of time. FL ST J ADMIN Rule 2.516(b)(1)(D)(iii).

ii. *Format of e-mail for service.* Service of a document by e-mail is made by attaching a copy of the document in PDF format to an e-mail sent to all addresses designated by the attorney or party. FL ST J ADMIN Rule 2.516(b)(1)(E).

- All documents served by e-mail must be attached to an e-mail message containing a subject line beginning with the words "SERVICE OF COURT DOCUMENT" in all capital letters, followed by the case number of the proceeding in which the documents are being served. FL ST J ADMIN Rule 2.516(b)(1)(E)(i).
- The body of the e-mail must identify the court in which the proceeding is pending, the case number, the name of the initial party on each side, the title of each document served with that e-mail, and the sender's name and telephone number. FL ST J ADMIN Rule 2.516(b)(1)(E)(ii).
- Any document served by e-mail may be signed by the "/s/" format, as long as the filed original is signed in accordance with the applicable rule of procedure. FL ST J ADMIN Rule 2.516(b)(1)(E)(iii).
- Any e-mail which, together with its attached documents, exceeds five megabytes (5MB) in size, must be divided and sent as separate e-mails, no one of which may exceed five megabytes (5MB) in size and each of which must be sequentially numbered in the subject line. FL ST J ADMIN Rule 2.516(b)(1)(E)(iv).

iii. *Service by other means.* In addition to, and not in lieu of, service by e-mail, service may also be made upon attorneys by any of the means specified in FL ST J ADMIN Rule 2.516(b)(2). Service on and by all parties who are not represented by an attorney and who do not designate an e-mail address, and on and by all attorneys excused from e-mail service, must be made by delivering a copy of the document or by mailing it to the party or attorney at their last known address or, if no address is known, by leaving it with the clerk of the court. Service by mail is complete upon mailing. Delivery of a copy within FL ST J ADMIN Rule 2.516 is complete upon:

- Handing it to the attorney or to the party,
- Leaving it at the attorney's or party's office with a clerk or other person in charge thereof,
- If there is no one in charge, leaving it in a conspicuous place therein,
- If the office is closed or the person to be served has no office, leaving it at the person's usual place of abode with some person of his or her family above fifteen (15) years of age and informing such person of the contents, or

- Transmitting it by facsimile to the attorney's or party's office with a cover sheet containing the sender's name, firm, address, telephone number, and facsimile number, and the number of pages transmitted. When service is made by facsimile, a copy must also be served by any other method permitted by FL ST J ADMIN Rule 2.516. Facsimile service occurs when transmission is complete. FL ST J ADMIN Rule 2.516(b)(2)(A) through FL ST J ADMIN Rule 2.516(b)(2)(E).
- Service by delivery after 5:00 p.m. must be deemed to have been made by mailing on the date of delivery. FL ST J ADMIN Rule 2.516(b)(2)(F).

c. *Service; Numerous defendants.* In actions when the parties are unusually numerous, the court may regulate the service contemplated by the Florida Rules of Judicial Administration on motion or on its own initiative in such manner as may be found to be just and reasonable. FL ST J ADMIN Rule 2.516(c).

d. *Service by clerk.* Service of notices and other documents required to be made by the clerk must also be done as provided in FL ST J ADMIN Rule 2.516(b). FL ST J ADMIN Rule 2.516(g).

G. Hearings

1. There is no hearing required or contemplated with regard to requests for admission in the Florida Rules of Civil Procedure.

H. Forms

1. Official Request for Admissions Forms for Florida

a. Caption. FL ST RCP Form 1.901.

2. Request for Admissions Forms for Florida

a. Requests for admissions; Negligence, fall down. FL-PRACFORM § 8:41.

b. Requests for admissions; Promissory note. FL-PRACFORM § 8:42.

c. Requests for admissions; Open account. FL-PRACFORM § 8:43.

d. Requests for admissions; Mortgage foreclosure. FL-PRACFORM § 8:44.

e. Request for admissions; General form. FL-PP § 3:146.

f. Request for admissions; Facts and genuineness of documents. FL-PP § 3:147.

g. Motion; To determine sufficiency of reply to request for admissions. FL-PP § 3:152.

h. Form for request for admissions. FL-RCPF R 1.370(5).

i. Form for request for admissions (another form). FL-RCPF R 1.370(6).

j. Form for request for admissions served concurrently with interrogatories. FL-RCPF R 1.370(7).

k. Form for response to request for admissions. FL-RCPF R 1.370(8).

l. Form for request for admissions as to factual situation and refinement of issues. FL-RCPF R 1.370(9).

m. Form for request to admit party uses electronic data storage. FL-RCPF R 1.370(10).

I. Checklist

(I) ❑ Matters to be considered by requesting party

(a) ❑ Required documents

(1) ❑ Request

(2) ❑ Copies of documents

(3) ❑ Certificate of service

(b) ❑ Time for request

(1) ❑ Without leave of court the request may be served upon the plaintiff after commencement of the action and upon any other party with or after service of the process and initial pleading upon that party

(II) ❑ Matters to be considered by responding party

(a) ❑ Required documents

(1) ❑ Response to request

(2) ❑ Certificate of service

(b) ❑ Time for response

(1) ❑ The party to whom the request is directed shall serve a written response within thirty (30) days after service of the request, except that a defendant may serve a response within forty-five (45) days after service of the process and initial pleading on that defendant

Requests, Notices and Applications
Notice of Deposition

Document Last Updated January 2013

A. Applicable Rules

1. *State rules*

a. Pleadings and motions. FL ST RCP Rule 1.100.

b. Depositions before action or pending appeal. FL ST RCP Rule 1.290.

c. Persons before whom depositions may be taken. FL ST RCP Rule 1.300.

d. Depositions upon oral examination. FL ST RCP Rule 1.310.

e. Depositions upon written questions. FL ST RCP Rule 1.320.

f. Use of depositions in court proceedings. FL ST RCP Rule 1.330.

g. Nonverification of pleadings. FL ST RCP Rule 1.030.

h. Service and filing of pleadings, orders, and documents. FL ST RCP Rule 1.080.

i. Time. FL ST RCP Rule 1.090.

j. General provisions governing discovery. FL ST RCP Rule 1.280.

k. Failure to make discovery; Sanctions. FL ST RCP Rule 1.380.

l. Depositions of expert witnesses. FL ST RCP Rule 1.390.

m. Relief from judgment, decrees, or orders. FL ST RCP Rule 1.540.

n. Forms. FL ST RCP Rule 1.900.

o. Minimization of the filing of sensitive information. FL ST J ADMIN Rule 2.425.

p. Retention of court records. FL ST J ADMIN Rule 2.430.

q. Foreign attorneys. FL ST J ADMIN Rule 2.510.

r. Signature of attorneys and parties. FL ST J ADMIN Rule 2.515.

s. Paper. FL ST J ADMIN Rule 2.520.

t. Electronic filing. FL ST J ADMIN Rule 2.525.

u. Accessibility of information and technology. FL ST J ADMIN Rule 2.526.

v. Notices to persons with disabilities. FL ST J ADMIN Rule 2.540.

2. *Local rules*

a. Establishment of 11th Circuit Homestead Access to Mediation Program ("CHAMP") for case management of residential foreclosure cases in the Eleventh Judicial Circuit of Florida. FL ST 11 J CIR 1-09-08.

b. Enlargement and expansion of the current pilot project for electronic submissions of courtesy copies for uniform motion calendar and requests for special set hearings, emergency motions, and proposed orders. FL ST 11 J CIR 1-09-13-A1.

B. Timing

1. *Depositions upon oral examination.* After commencement of the action any party may take the testimony of any person, including a party, by deposition upon oral examination. Leave of court, granted with or without notice, must be obtained only if the plaintiff seeks to take a deposition within thirty (30) days after service of the process and initial pleading upon any defendant, except that leave is not required (1) if a defendant has served a notice of taking deposition or otherwise sought discovery, or (2) if special notice is given as provided in FL ST RCP Rule 1.310(b)(2). The attendance of witnesses may be compelled by subpoena as provided in FL ST RCP Rule 1.410. The deposition of a person confined in prison may be taken only by leave of court on such terms as the court prescribes. FL ST RCP Rule 1.310(a). A party desiring to take the deposition of any person upon oral examination shall give reasonable notice in writing to every other party to the action. FL ST RCP Rule 1.310(b)(1).
2. *Depositions upon written questions.* After commencement of the action any party may take the testimony of any person, including a party, by deposition upon written questions. The attendance of witnesses may be compelled by the use of subpoena as provided in FL ST RCP Rule 1.410. The deposition of a person confined in prison may be taken only by leave of court on such terms as the court prescribes. Within thrity (30) days after the notice and written questions are served, a party may serve cross questions upon all other parties. Within ten (10) days after being served with cross questions, a party may serve redirect questions upon all other parties. Within ten (10) days after being served with redirect questions, a party may serve recross questions upon all other parties. The court may for cause shown enlarge or shorten the time. FL ST RCP Rule 1.320(a).
3. *Depositions before action or pending appeal.* For information on petitions and motions for depositions before an action or pending appeal, please see the General Requirements section below.
4. *Sequence and timing of discovery.* Except as provided in FL ST RCP Rule 1.280(b)(5) or unless the court upon motion for the convenience of parties and witnesses and in the interest of justice orders otherwise, methods of discovery may be used in any sequence, and the fact that a party is conducting discovery, whether by deposition or otherwise, shall not delay any other party's discovery. FL ST RCP Rule 1.280(e).
5. *Computation of time*
    a. *Generally.* Computation of time shall be governed by FL ST J ADMIN Rule 2.514. FL ST RCP Rule 1.090(a). The following rules apply in computing time periods specified in any rule of procedure, local rule, court order, or statute that does not specify a method of computing time. FL ST J ADMIN Rule 2.514(a).
        i. *Period stated in days or a longer unit.* When the period is stated in days or a longer unit of time (A) exclude the day of the event that triggers the period; (B) count every day, including intermediate Saturdays, Sundays, and legal holidays; and (C) include the last day of the period, but if the last day is a Saturday, Sunday, or legal holiday, or falls within any period of time extended through an order of the chief justice under FL ST J ADMIN Rule 2.205(a)(2)(B)(iv), the period continues to run until the end of the next day that is not a Saturday, Sunday, or legal holiday and does not fall within any period of time extended through an order of the chief justice. FL ST J ADMIN Rule 2.514(a)(1).
        ii. *Period stated in hours.* When the period is stated in hours (A) begin counting immediately on the occurrence of the event that triggers the period; (B) count every hour, including hours during intermediate Saturdays, Sundays, and legal holidays; and (C) if the period would end on a Saturday, Sunday, or legal holiday, or during any period of time extended through an order of the chief justice under FL ST J ADMIN Rule 2.205(a)(2)(B)(iv), the period continues to run until the same time on the next day that is not a Saturday, Sunday, or legal holiday and does not fall within any period of time extended through an order of the chief justice. FL ST J ADMIN Rule 2.514(a)(2).
        iii. *Period stated in days less than seven (7) days.* When the period stated in days is less than seven

(7) days, intermediate Saturdays, Sundays, and legal holidays shall be excluded in the computation. FL ST J ADMIN Rule 2.514(a)(3).

iv. *"Last day" defined.* Unless a different time is set by a statute, local rule, or court order, the last day ends (A) for electronic filing or for service by any means, at midnight; and (B) for filing by other means, when the clerk's office is scheduled to close. FL ST J ADMIN Rule 2.514(a)(4).

v. *"Next day" defined.* The "next day" is determined by continuing to count forward when the period is measured after an event and backward when measured before an event. FL ST J ADMIN Rule 2.514(a)(5).

vi. *"Legal holiday" defined.* "Legal holiday" means (A) the day set aside by FL ST § 110.117, for observing New Year's Day, Martin Luther King, Jr.'s Birthday, Memorial Day, Independence Day, Labor Day, Veterans' Day, Thanksgiving Day, the Friday after Thanksgiving Day, or Christmas Day, and (B) any day observed as a holiday by the clerk's office or as designated by the chief judge. FL ST J ADMIN Rule 2.514(a)(6).

b. *Additional time after service by mail or e-mail.* When a party may or must act within a specified time after service and service is made by mail or e-mail, five (5) days are added after the period that would otherwise expire under FL ST J ADMIN Rule 2.514(a). FL ST J ADMIN Rule 2.514(b).

c. *Enlargement.* When an act is required or allowed to be done at or within a specified time by order of court, by the Florida Rules of Civil Procedure, or by notice given thereunder, for cause shown the court at any time in its discretion (1) with or without notice, may order the period enlarged if request therefor is made before the expiration of the period originally prescribed or as extended by a previous order, or (2) upon motion made and notice after the expiration of the specified period, may permit the act to be done when failure to act was the result of excusable neglect, but it may not extend the time for making a motion for new trial, for rehearing, or to alter or amend a judgment; making a motion for relief from a judgment under FL ST RCP Rule 1.540(b); taking an appeal or filing a petition for certiorari; or making a motion for a directed verdict. FL ST RCP Rule 1.090(b).

d. *Unaffected by expiration of term.* The period of time provided for the doing of any act or the taking of any proceeding shall not be affected or limited by the continued existence or expiration of a term of court. The continued existence or expiration of a term of court in no way affects the power of a court to do any act or take any proceeding in any action which is or has been pending before it. FL ST RCP Rule 1.090(c).

C. General Requirements

1. *General provisions governing discovery*

a. *Discovery methods.* Parties may obtain discovery by one or more of the following methods: depositions upon oral examination or written questions; written interrogatories; production of documents or things or permission to enter upon land or other property for inspection and other purposes; physical and mental examinations; and requests for admission. Unless the court orders otherwise and under FL ST RCP Rule 1.280(c), the frequency of use of these methods is not limited, except as provided in FL ST RCP Rule 1.200, FL ST RCP Rule 1.340, and FL ST RCP Rule 1.370. FL ST RCP Rule 1.280(a).

b. *Scope of discovery.* Unless otherwise limited by order of the court in accordance with the Florida Rules of Civil Procedure, the scope of discovery is as follows:

i. *In general.* Parties may obtain discovery regarding any matter, not privileged, that is relevant to the subject matter of the pending action, whether it relates to the claim or defense of the party seeking discovery or the claim or defense of any other party, including the existence, description, nature, custody, condition, and location of any books, documents, or other tangible things and the identity and location of persons having knowledge of any discoverable matter. It is not ground for objection that the information sought will be inadmissible at the trial if the information sought appears reasonably calculated to lead to the discovery of admissible evidence. FL ST RCP Rule 1.280(b)(1).

ii. *Indemnity agreements.* A party may obtain discovery of the existence and contents of any agreement under which any person may be liable to satisfy part or all of a judgment that may be entered in the action or to indemnify or to reimburse a party for payments made to satisfy the judgment. Information concerning the agreement is not admissible in evidence at trial by reason of disclosure. FL ST RCP Rule 1.280(b)(2).

iii. *Electronically stored information.* A party may obtain discovery of electronically stored information in accordance with the Florida Rules of Civil Procedure. FL ST RCP Rule 1.280(b)(3).

iv. *Trial preparation; Materials.* Subject to the provisions of FL ST RCP Rule 1.280(b)(5), a party may obtain discovery of documents and tangible things otherwise discoverable under FL ST RCP Rule 1.280(b)(1) and prepared in anticipation of litigation or for trial by or for another party or by or for that party's representative, including that party's attorney, consultant, surety, indemnitor, insurer, or agent, only upon a showing that the party seeking discovery has need of the materials in the preparation of the case and is unable without undue hardship to obtain the substantial equivalent of the materials by other means. FL ST RCP Rule 1.280(b)(4).

- In ordering discovery of the materials when the required showing has been made, the court shall protect against disclosure of the mental impressions, conclusions, opinions, or legal theories of an attorney or other representative of a party concerning the litigation. FL ST RCP Rule 1.280(b)(4).
- Without the required showing a party may obtain a copy of a statement concerning the action or its subject matter previously made by that party. FL ST RCP Rule 1.280(b)(4).
- Upon request without the required showing a person not a party may obtain a copy of a statement concerning the action or its subject matter previously made by that person. If the request is refused, the person may move for an order to obtain a copy. The provisions of FL ST RCP Rule 1.380(a)(5) apply to the award of expenses incurred as a result of making the motion. FL ST RCP Rule 1.280(b)(4).
- For purposes of FL ST RCP Rule 1.280(b)(4), a statement previously made is a written statement signed or otherwise adopted or approved by the person making it, or a stenographic, mechanical, electrical, or other recording or transcription of it that is a substantially verbatim recital of an oral statement by the person making it and contemporaneously recorded. FL ST RCP Rule 1.280(b)(4).

v. *Trial preparation; Experts.* Discovery of facts known and opinions held by experts, otherwise discoverable under the provisions of FL ST RCP Rule 1.280(b)(1) and acquired or developed in anticipation of litigation or for trial, may be obtained only as follows:

- By interrogatories a party may require any other party to identify each person whom the other party expects to call as an expert witness at trial and to state the subject matter on which the expert is expected to testify, and to state the substance of the facts and opinions to which the expert is expected to testify and a summary of the grounds for each opinion. FL ST RCP Rule 1.280(b)(5)(A)(i).
- Any person disclosed by interrogatories or otherwise as a person expected to be called as an expert witness at trial may be deposed in accordance with FL ST RCP Rule 1.390 without motion or order of court. FL ST RCP Rule 1.280(b)(5)(A)(ii).
- A party may obtain the following discovery regarding any person disclosed by interrogatories or otherwise as a person expected to be called as an expert witness at trial: The scope of employment in the pending case and the compensation for such service, FL ST RCP Rule 1.280(b)(5)(A)(iii)(1); The expert's general litigation experience, including the percentage of work performed for plaintiffs and defendants, FL ST RCP Rule 1.280(b)(5)(A)(iii)(2); The identity of other cases, within a reasonable time period, in which the expert has testified by deposition or at trial, FL ST RCP Rule 1.280(b)(5)(A)(iii)(3); An approximation of the portion of the expert's involvement as an expert witness, which may be based on the number of hours, percentage of hours, or percentage of earned income derived from serving as an expert witness; however, the expert shall not be required to disclose his or her earnings as an expert witness or income derived from other services. FL ST RCP Rule 1.280(b)(5)(A)(iii)(4).

- An expert may be required to produce financial and business records only under the most unusual or compelling circumstances and may not be compelled to compile or produce nonexistent documents. Upon motion, the court may order further discovery by other means, subject to such restrictions as to scope and other provisions pursuant to FL ST RCP Rule 1.280(b)(5)(C) concerning fees and expenses as the court may deem appropriate. FL ST RCP Rule 1.280(b)(5).
- A party may discover facts known or opinions held by an expert who has been retained or specially employed by another party in anticipation of litigation or preparation for trial and who is not expected to be called as a witness at trial, only as provided in FL ST RCP Rule 1.360(b) or upon a showing of exceptional circumstances under which it is impracticable for the party seeking discovery to obtain facts or opinions on the same subject by other means. FL ST RCP Rule 1.280(b)(5)(B).
- Unless manifest injustice would result, the court shall require that the party seeking discovery pay the expert a reasonable fee for time spent in responding to discovery under FL ST RCP Rule 1.280(b)(5)(A) and FL ST RCP Rule 1.280(b)(5)(B); and concerning discovery from an expert obtained under FL ST RCP Rule 1.280(b)(5)(A) the court may require, and concerning discovery obtained under FL ST RCP Rule 1.280(b)(5)(B) shall require, the party seeking discovery to pay the other party a fair part of the fees and expenses reasonably incurred by the latter party in obtaining facts and opinions from the expert. FL ST RCP Rule 1.280(b)(5)(C).
- As used in the Florida Rules of Civil Procedure an expert shall be an expert witness as defined in FL ST RCP Rule 1.390(a). FL ST RCP Rule 1.280(b)(5)(D).

vi. *Claims to privilege or protection.* When a party withholds information otherwise discoverable under the Florida Rules of Civil Procedure by claiming that it is privileged or subject to protection as trial preparation material, the party shall make the claim expressly and shall describe the nature of the documents, communications, or things not produced or disclosed in a manner that, without revealing information itself privileged or protected, will enable other parties to assess the applicability of the privilege or protection. FL ST RCP Rule 1.280(b)(6).

c. *Limitations on discovery of electronically stored information*

i. A person may object to discovery of electronically stored information from sources that the person identifies as not reasonably accessible because of burden or cost. On motion to compel discovery or for a protective order, the person from whom discovery is sought must show that the information sought or the format requested is not reasonably accessible because of undue burden or cost. If that showing is made, the court may nonetheless order the discovery from such sources or in such formats if the requesting party shows good cause. The court may specify conditions of the discovery, including ordering that some or all of the expenses incurred by the person from whom discovery is sought be paid by the party seeking the discovery. FL ST RCP Rule 1.280(d)(1).

ii. In determining any motion involving discovery of electronically stored information, the court must limit the frequency or extent of discovery otherwise allowed by the Florida Rules of Civil Procedure if it determines that (i) the discovery sought is unreasonably cumulative or duplicative, or can be obtained from another source or in another manner that is more convenient, less burdensome, or less expensive; or (ii) the burden or expense of the discovery outweighs its likely benefit, considering the needs of the case, the amount in controversy, the parties' resources, the importance of the issues at stake in the action, and the importance of the discovery in resolving the issues. FL ST RCP Rule 1.280(d)(2).

d. For information on inadvertent disclosure of privileged materials, see FL ST RCP Rule 1.285.

2. *Notice of deposition*

a. *Upon oral examination.* A party desiring to take the deposition of any person upon oral examination shall give reasonable notice in writing to every other party to the action. The notice shall state the time and place for taking the deposition and the name and address of each person to be examined, if known, and, if the name is not known, a general description sufficient to identify the person or the particular class or group to which the person belongs. If a subpoena duces tecum is to be served on the person to be examined, the designation of the materials to be produced under the subpoena shall be attached to or included in the notice. FL ST RCP Rule 1.310(b)(1).

b. *Upon written examination.* A party desiring to take a deposition upon written questions shall serve a notice stating: (1) the name and address of the person who is to answer them, if known, and, if the name is not known, a general description sufficient to identify the person or the particular class or group to which that person belongs, and (2) the name or descriptive title and address of the officer before whom the deposition is to be taken. FL ST RCP Rule 1.320(a).

3. *When leave of court required.* Leave of court, granted with or without notice, must be obtained only if the plaintiff seeks to take a deposition within thirty (30) days after service of the process and initial pleading upon any defendant, except that leave is not required if a defendant has served a notice of taking deposition or otherwise sought discovery. FL ST RCP Rule 1.310(a).

a. *Exceptions.* Leave of court is not required for the taking of a deposition by plaintiff if the notice states that the person to be examined is about to go out of the state and will be unavailable for examination unless a deposition is taken before expiration of the thirty (30) day period. If a party shows that when served with notice under FL ST RCP Rule 1.310(b) that party was unable through the exercise of diligence to obtain counsel to represent the party at the taking of the deposition, the deposition may not be used against that party. FL ST RCP Rule 1.310(b)(2).

b. *Persons in prison.* The deposition of a person confined in prison may be taken only by leave of court on such terms as the court prescribes. FL ST RCP Rule 1.310(a); FL ST RCP Rule 1.320(a).

4. *Deposition procedure*

a. *Who may take depositions.* Depositions may be taken before any notary public or judicial officer or before any officer authorized by the statutes of Florida to take acknowledgments or proof of executions of deeds or by any person appointed by the court in which the action is pending. FL ST RCP Rule 1.300(a).

i. *In foreign countries.* In a foreign country depositions may be taken: on notice before a person authorized to administer oaths in the place in which the examination is held, either by the law thereof or by the law of Florida or of the United States; before a person commissioned by the court, and a person so commissioned shall have the power by virtue of the commission to administer any necessary oath and take testimony; or pursuant to a letter rogatory. FL ST RCP Rule 1.300(b).

ii. *Selection by stipulation.* If the parties so stipulate in writing, depositions may be taken before any person at any time or place upon any notice and in any manner and when so taken may be used like other depositions. FL ST RCP Rule 1.300(c).

iii. *Persons disqualified.* Unless so stipulated by the parties, no deposition shall be taken before a person who is a relative, employee, attorney, or counsel of any of the parties, is a relative or employee of any of the parties' attorney or counsel, or is financially interested in the action. FL ST RCP Rule 1.300(d).

b. *Depositions before action*

i. *Petition.* A person who desires to perpetuate that person's own testimony or that of another person regarding any matter that may be cognizable in any Florida court may file a verified petition in the circuit court in the county of the residence of any expected adverse party. The petition shall be entitled in the name of the petitioner and shall show:

- That the petitioner expects to be a party to an action cognizable in a court of Florida, but is presently unable to bring the action;
- The subject matter of the expected action and the petitioner's interest therein;
- The facts which the petitioner desires to establish by the proposed testimony and the petitioner's reasons for desiring to perpetuate it;
- The names or a description of the persons the petitioner expects will be adverse parties and their addresses so far as known; and

- The names and addresses of the persons to be examined and the substance of the testimony which the petitioner expects to elicit from each; and shall ask for an order authorizing the petitioner to take the deposition of the persons to be examined named in the petition for the purpose of perpetuating their testimony. FL ST RCP Rule 1.290(a)(1).

ii. *Notice and service.* After submitting the petition, the petitioner must thereafter serve a notice upon each person named in the petition as an expected adverse party, together with a copy of the petition, stating that the petitioner will apply to the court at a time and place named therein for an order described in the petition. At least twenty (20) days before the date of hearing the notice shall be served either within or without the county in the manner provided by law for service of summons, but if such service cannot with due diligence be made upon any expected adverse party named in the petition, the court may make an order for service by publication or otherwise, and shall appoint an attorney for persons not served in the manner provided by law for service of summons who shall represent them, and if they are not otherwise represented, shall cross-examine the deponent. FL ST RCP Rule 1.290(a)(2).

iii. *Order and examination.* If the court is satisfied that the perpetuation of the testimony may prevent a failure or delay of justice, it shall make an order designating or describing the persons whose depositions may be taken and specifying the subject matter of the examination and whether the deposition shall be taken upon oral examination or written interrogatories. The deposition may then be taken in accordance with the rules governing depositions. FL ST RCP Rule 1.290(a)(3).

iv. *Use of deposition.* A deposition taken before an action and in accordance with the procedures above may be used in any action involving the same subject matter subsequently brought in any court. FL ST RCP Rule 1.290(a)(4).

c. *Depositions upon oral examination*

i. *Enlargement of time.* For cause shown the court may enlarge or shorten the time for taking the deposition. FL ST RCP Rule 1.310(b)(3).

ii. *Videotaped depositions.* Any deposition may be recorded by videotape without leave of the court or stipulation of the parties, provided the deposition is taken in accordance with the following:

- *Notice.* A party intending to videotape a deposition shall state in the notice that the deposition is to be videotaped and shall give the name and address of the operator. Any subpoena served on the person to be examined shall state the method or methods for recording the testimony. FL ST RCP Rule 1.310(b)(4)(A).
- *Stenographer.* Videotaped depositions shall also be recorded stenographically, unless all parties agree otherwise. FL ST RCP Rule 1.310(b)(4)(B).
- *Procedure.* At the beginning of the deposition, the officer before whom it is taken shall, on camera: (i) identify the style of the action, (ii) state the date, and (iii) swear the witness. FL ST RCP Rule 1.310(b)(4)(C).
- *Custody of tape and copies.* The attorney for the party requesting the videotaping of the deposition shall take custody of and be responsible for the safeguarding of the videotape, shall permit the viewing of it by the opposing party, and, if requested, shall provide a copy of the videotape at the expense of the party requesting the copy. FL ST RCP Rule 1.310(b)(4)(D).
- *Cost of videotaped depositions.* The party requesting the videotaping shall bear the initial cost of videotaping. FL ST RCP Rule 1.310(b)(4)(E).

iii. *Production of documents.* The notice to a party deponent may be accompanied by a request for the production of documents and tangible things at the taking of the deposition. The procedure of FL ST RCP Rule 1.350 shall apply to the request. FL ST RCP Rule 1.351 provides the exclusive procedure for obtaining documents or things by subpoena from nonparties without deposing the custodian or other person in possession of the documents. FL ST RCP Rule 1.310(b)(5).

iv. *Deposing organizations.* In the notice a party may name as the deponent a public or private corporation, a partnership or association, or a governmental agency, and designate with reasonable particularity the matters on which examination is requested. The organization so named shall designate one or more officers, directors, or managing agents, or other persons who consent to do so, to testify on its behalf and may state the matters on which each person designated will testify. The persons so designated shall testify about matters known or reasonably available to the organization. FL ST RCP Rule 1.310(b)(6).

v. *Depositions by telephone.* On motion the court may order that the testimony at a deposition be taken by telephone. The order may prescribe the manner in which the deposition will be taken. A party may also arrange for a stenographic transcription at that party's own initial expense. FL ST RCP Rule 1.310(b)(7).

vi. *Deposing a minor.* Any minor subpoenaed for testimony shall have the right to be accompanied by a parent or guardian at all times during the taking of testimony notwithstanding the invocation of the rule of sequestration of section FL ST § 90.616, except upon a showing that the presence of a parent or guardian is likely to have a material, negative impact on the credibility or accuracy of the minor's testimony, or that the interests of the parent or guardian are in actual or potential conflict with the interests of the minor. FL ST RCP Rule 1.310(b)(8).

vii. *Examination and cross-examination.* Examination and cross-examination of witnesses may proceed as permitted at the trial. FL ST RCP Rule 1.310(c).

viii. *Oath.* The officer before whom the deposition is to be taken shall put the witness on oath and shall personally, or by someone acting under the officer's direction and in the officer's presence, record the testimony of the witness, except that when a deposition is being taken by telephone, the witness shall be sworn by a person present with the witness who is qualified to administer an oath in that location. FL ST RCP Rule 1.310(c).

ix. *Record of examination.* The deposition testimony must be taken stenographically or recorded by any other means ordered. If requested by one of the parties, the testimony shall be transcribed at the initial cost of the requesting party and prompt notice of the request shall be given to all other parties. FL ST RCP Rule 1.310(c).

x. *Objections.* All objections made at time of the examination to the qualifications of the officer taking the deposition, the manner of taking it, the evidence presented, or the conduct of any party, and any other objection to the proceedings shall be noted by the officer upon the deposition. Any objection during a deposition shall be stated concisely and in a nonargumentative and nonsuggestive manner. A party may instruct a deponent not to answer only when necessary to preserve a privilege, to enforce a limitation on evidence directed by the court, or to present a motion under FL ST RCP Rule 1.310(d). FL ST RCP Rule 1.310(c).

- Otherwise, evidence objected to shall be taken subject to the objections. Instead of participating in the oral examination, parties may serve written questions in a sealed envelope on the party taking the deposition and that party shall transmit them to the officer, who shall propound them to the witness and record the answers verbatim. FL ST RCP Rule 1.310(c).

xi. *Motion to terminate or limit examination.* At any time during the taking of the deposition, on motion of a party or of the deponent and upon a showing that the examination is being conducted in bad faith or in such manner as unreasonably to annoy, embarrass, or oppress the deponent or party, or that improper objections and instructions to a deponent not to answer are being made, the court in which the action is pending or the circuit court where the deposition is being taken may order the officer conducting the examination to cease forthwith from taking the deposition or may limit the scope and manner of the taking of the deposition under the scope of permissible discovery. FL ST RCP Rule 1.310(d).

- If the order terminates the examination, it shall be resumed thereafter only upon the order of the court in which the action is pending. Upon demand of any party or the deponent, the taking of the deposition shall be suspended for the time necessary to make a motion for an order. FL ST RCP Rule 1.310(d).

xii. *Deponent review.* If the testimony is transcribed, the transcript shall be furnished to the witness for examination and shall be read to or by the witness unless the examination and reading are waived by the witness and by the parties. Any changes in form or substance that the witness wants to make shall be listed in writing by the officer with a statement of the reasons given by the witness for making the changes. The changes shall be attached to the transcript. It shall then be signed by the witness unless the parties waived the signing or the witness is ill, cannot be found, or refuses to sign. If the transcript is not signed by the witness within a reasonable time after it is furnished to the witness, the officer shall sign the transcript and state on the transcript the waiver, illness, absence of the witness, or refusal to sign with any reasons given. The deposition may then be used as fully as though signed unless the court holds that the reasons given for the refusal to sign require rejection of the deposition wholly or partly, on motion under FL ST RCP Rule 1.330(d)(4). FL ST RCP Rule 1.310(e).

xiii. *Certification and inspection.* If the deposition is transcribed, the officer shall certify on each copy of the deposition that the witness was duly sworn by the officer and that the deposition is a true record of the testimony given by the witness. Documents and things produced for inspection during the examination of the witness shall be marked for identification and annexed to and returned with the deposition upon the request of a party, and may be inspected and copied by any party, except that the person producing the materials may substitute copies to be marked for identification if that person affords to all parties fair opportunity to verify the copies by comparison with the originals. If the person producing the materials requests their return, the officer shall mark them, give each party an opportunity to inspect and copy them, and return them to the person producing them and the materials may then be used in the same manner as if annexed to and returned with the deposition. FL ST RCP Rule 1.310(f)(1).

xiv. *Copies.* Upon payment of reasonable charges, the officer shall furnish a copy of the deposition to any party or to the deponent. FL ST RCP Rule 1.310(f)(2). A party or witness who does not have a copy of the deposition may obtain it from the officer taking the deposition unless the court orders otherwise. If the deposition is obtained from a person other than the officer, the reasonable cost of reproducing the copies shall be paid to the person by the requesting party or witness. FL ST RCP Rule 1.310(g).

d. *Depositions upon written examination*

i. *Deposing an organization upon written examination.* A deposition upon written questions may be taken of a public or private corporation, a partnership or association, or a governmental agency in accordance with FL ST RCP Rule 1.310(b)(6). FL ST RCP Rule 1.320(a).

ii. *Cross, redirect, and recross questions.* Within thirty (30) days after the notice and written questions are served, a party may serve cross questions upon all other parties. Within ten (10) days after being served with cross questions, a party may serve redirect questions upon all other parties. Within ten (10) days after being served with redirect questions, a party may serve recross questions upon all other parties. The court may for cause shown enlarge or shorten the time. FL ST RCP Rule 1.320(a).

iii. *Procedure.* A copy of the notice and copies of all questions served shall be delivered by the party taking the depositions to the officer designated in the notice, who shall proceed promptly to take the testimony of the witness in the manner provided by FL ST RCP Rule 1.310(c), FL ST RCP Rule 1.310(e), and FL ST RCP Rule 1.310(f) in response to the questions and to prepare the deposition, attaching the copy of the notice and the questions received by the officer. The questions shall not be filed separately from the deposition unless a party seeks to have the court consider the questions before the questions are submitted to the witness. FL ST RCP Rule 1.320(b).

5. *Arbitration and mediation*

a. *Referral to arbitration and mediation.* Except as hereinafter provided or as otherwise prohibited by law, the presiding judge may enter an order referring all or any part of a contested civil matter to mediation or arbitration. The parties to any contested civil matter may file a written stipulation to

mediate or arbitrate any issue between them at any time. Such stipulation shall be incorporated into the order of referral. FL ST RCP Rule 1.700(a).

i. In all residential foreclosure actions involving homestead properties filed on or after May 1, 2009, unless a stipulation is specifically invoked by the parties in writing within five (5) days of service of the complaint on the main defendant, the parties are deemed to have stipulated to referral of the mediation to the Collins Center pursuant to FL ST RCP Rule 1.720(f). FL ST 11 J CIR 1-09-08(2); FL ST 11 J CIR 1-09-08(3). FL ST 11 J CIR 1-09-08 constitutes a formal referral to mediation pursuant to the Florida Rules of Civil Procedure. FL ST 11 J CIR 1-09-08(2).

ii. For further information on referral to mediation, refer to FL ST 11 J CIR 1-09-08.

b. *Arbitration*

i. *Exclusions.* A civil action shall be ordered to arbitration or arbitration in conjunction with mediation upon stipulation of the parties. A civil action may be ordered to arbitration or arbitration in conjunction with mediation upon motion of any party or by the court, if the judge determines the action to be of such a nature that arbitration could be of benefit to the litigants or the court. FL ST RCP Rule 1.800.

- Under no circumstances may the following categories of actions be referred to arbitration: (1) bond estreatures; (2) habeas corpus or other extraordinary writs; (3) bond validations; (4) civil or criminal contempt; (5) such other matters as may be specified by order of the chief judge in the circuit. FL ST RCP Rule 1.800.

ii. For more information regarding arbitration, please see FL ST RCP Rule 1.810; FL ST RCP Rule 1.820; FL ST RCP Rule 1.830.

c. *Mediation.* For more information regarding mediation, please see FL ST RCP Rule 1.710; FL ST RCP Rule 1.720; FL ST RCP Rule 1.730; and FL ST RCP Rule 1.750.

6. *Rules of court*

a. *Rules of civil procedure.* The Florida Rules of Civil Procedure apply to all actions of a civil nature and all special statutory proceedings in the circuit courts and county courts except those to which the Florida Probate Rules, the Florida Family Law Rules of Procedure, or the Small Claims Rules apply. FL ST RCP Rule 1.010.

i. The form, content, procedure, and time for pleading in all special statutory proceedings shall be as prescribed by the statutes governing the proceeding unless the Florida Rules of Civil Procedure specifically provide to the contrary. FL ST RCP Rule 1.010.

ii. The Florida Rules of Civil Procedure shall be construed to secure the just, speedy, and inexpensive determination of every action. FL ST RCP Rule 1.010.

b. *Rules of judicial administration.* The Florida Rules of Judicial Administration shall apply to administrative matters in all courts to which the Florida Rules of Judicial Administration are applicable by their terms. The Florida Rules of Judicial Administration shall be construed to secure the speedy and inexpensive determination of every proceeding to which they are applicable. The Florida Rules of Judicial Administration shall supersede all conflicting rules and statutes. FL ST J ADMIN Rule 2.110.

D. Documents

1. *Deposition upon oral or written examination*

a. *Required documents*

i. *Notice of deposition.* Please see the General Requirements section of this document for information on the content of a notice of deposition upon oral examination.

ii. *Certificate of service.* A certificate of service of the interrogatories shall be filed, giving the date of service and the name of the party to whom they were directed. FL ST RCP Rule 1.340(e). When any attorney certifies in substance: "I certify that a copy hereof has been furnished to (here insert name or names and addresses used for service) by (e-mail) (delivery) (mail) (fax) on .... (date) ....__________________ Attorney" the certificate is taken as prima facie proof of such service in compliance with FL ST J ADMIN Rule 2.516. FL ST J ADMIN Rule 2.516(f).

b. *Supplemental documents*

   i. *Motion for leave to take deposition.* See the Timing section for information on when leave is required.

   ii. *Subpoena.* See the Timing section for requirements of when a subpoena is required.

   iii. *Request for production of documents.* See the General Requirements section for further information.

E. Format

1. *Documents; Type and size.* Documents subject to the exceptions set forth in FL ST J ADMIN Rule 2.525(d) shall be filed on recycled paper measuring eight and one half by eleven (8 1/2 by 11) inches. For purposes of FL ST J ADMIN Rule 2.520, paper is recycled if it contains a minimum content of fifty (50) percent waste paper. Xerographic reduction of legal-size (eight and one half by fourteen (8 1/2 by 14) inches) documents to letter size (eight and one half by eleven (8 1/2 by 11) inches) is prohibited. All other documents filed by electronic transmission shall be filed in a format capable of being printed in a format consistent with the provisions of FL ST J ADMIN Rule 2.250. FL ST J ADMIN Rule 2.520(b).

   a. *Exhibits.* Any exhibit or attachment filed with pleadings or papers may be filed in its original size. FL ST J ADMIN Rule 2.520(c).

   b. *Recording space.* On all papers and documents prepared and filed by the court or by any party to a proceeding which are to be recorded in the public records of any county, including but not limited to final money judgments and notices of lis pendens, a three (3) inch by three (3) inch space at the top right-hand corner on the first page and a one (1) inch by three (3) inch space at the top right-hand corner on each subsequent page shall be left blank and reserved for use by the clerk of court. FL ST J ADMIN Rule 2.520(d).

      i. *Exceptions to recording space.* Any papers or documents created by persons or entities over which the filing party has no control, including but not limited to wills, codicils, trusts, or other testamentary documents; documents prepared or executed by any public officer; documents prepared, executed, acknowledged, or proved outside of the State of Florida; or documents created by State or Federal government agencies, may be filed without the space required by FL ST J ADMIN Rule 2.520. FL ST J ADMIN Rule 2.520(e).

   c. *Noncompliance.* No clerk of court is permitted to refuse to file any document or paper because of noncompliance with the Florida Rules of Judicial Administration. However, upon request of the clerk of court, noncomplying documents must be resubmitted in accordance with the formatting rules. FL ST J ADMIN Rule 2.520(f).

2. *Caption.* Every pleading, motion, order, judgment, or other paper shall have a caption containing the name of the court, the file number, and except for in rem proceedings, including forfeiture proceedings, the name of the first party on each side with an appropriate indication of other parties, and a designation identifying the party filing it and its nature or the nature of the order, as the case may be. In any in rem proceeding, every pleading, motion, order, judgment, or other paper shall have a caption containing the name of the court, the file number, the style "In re" (followed by the name or general description of the property), and a designation of the person or entity filing it and its nature or the nature of the order, as the case may be. In an in rem forfeiture proceeding, the style shall be "In re forfeiture of" (followed by the name of the general description of the property). All papers filed in the action shall be styled in such a manner as to indicate clearly the subject matter of the paper and the party requesting or obtaining relief. FL ST RCP Rule 1.100(c)(1).

3. *Writing and written defined.* Writing or written means a document containing information, an application, or a stipulation. FL ST RCP Rule 1.080(c).

4. *Rule abbreviations*

   a. The Florida Rules of Civil Procedure and shall be abbreviated as Fla.R.Civ.P. FL ST RCP Rule 1.010.

b. The Florida Rules of Judicial Administration shall be abbreviated as Fla. R. Jud. Admin. FL ST J ADMIN Rule 2.110.

5. *Nonverification.* Except when otherwise specifically provided by the Florida Rules of Civil Procedure or an applicable statute, every pleading or other document of a party represented by an attorney need not be verified or accompanied by an affidavit. FL ST RCP Rule 1.030; FL ST J ADMIN Rule 2.515(a).

6. *Attorney signature*

   a. *Attorney signature.* Every pleading and other document of a party represented by an attorney shall be signed by at least one (1) attorney of record in that attorney's individual name whose current record Florida Bar address, telephone number, including area code, primary e-mail address and secondary e-mail addresses, if any, and Florida Bar number shall be stated, and who shall be duly licensed to practice law in Florida or who shall have received permission to appear in the particular case as provided in FL ST J ADMIN Rule 2.510. FL ST J ADMIN Rule 2.515(a).

      i. The attorney may be required by the court to give the address of, and to vouch for the attorney's authority to represent, the party. FL ST J ADMIN Rule 2.515(a).

      ii. The signature of an attorney shall constitute a certificate by the attorney that the attorney has read the pleading or other document; that to the best of the attorney's knowledge, information, and belief there is good ground to support it; and that it is not interposed for delay. FL ST J ADMIN Rule 2.515(a).

      iii. If a pleading is not signed or is signed with intent to defeat the purpose of FL ST J ADMIN Rule 2.515, it may be stricken and the action may proceed as though the pleading or other document had not been served. FL ST J ADMIN Rule 2.515(a).

   b. *Pro se litigant signature.* A party who is not represented by an attorney shall sign any pleading or other paper and state the party's address and telephone number, including area code. FL ST J ADMIN Rule 2.515(b).

   c. *Form of signature*

      i. The signatures required on pleadings and documents by FL ST J ADMIN Rule 2.515(a) and FL ST J ADMIN Rule 2.515(b) may be:

         - Original signatures;
         - Original signatures that have been reproduced by electronic means, such as on electronically transmitted documents or photocopied documents;
         - Electronic signatures using the "/s/," "s/," or "/s" formats by or at the direction of the person signing; or
         - Any other signature format authorized by general law, so long as the clerk where the proceeding is pending has the capability of receiving and has obtained approval from the Supreme Court of Florida to accept pleadings and documents with that signature format. FL ST J ADMIN Rule 2.515(c)(1).

      ii. An attorney, party, or other person who files a pleading or paper by electronic transmission that does not contain the original signature of that attorney, party, or other person shall file that identical pleading or paper in paper form containing an original signature of that attorney, party, or other person (hereinafter called the follow-up filing) immediately thereafter. The follow-up filing is not required if the Supreme Court of Florida has entered an order directing the clerk of court to discontinue accepting the follow-up filing. FL ST J ADMIN Rule 2.515(c)(2).

7. *Forms*

   a. *Process.* The forms of process, notice of lis pendens, and notice of action provided in the Florida Rules of Civil Procedure are sufficient. Variations from the forms do not void process or notices that are otherwise sufficient. FL ST RCP Rule 1.900(a).

   b. *Other forms.* The other forms provided in the Florida Rules of Civil Procedure are sufficient for the matters that are covered by them. So long as the substance is expressed without prolixity, the forms may be varied to meet the facts of a particular case. FL ST RCP Rule 1.900(b).

c. *Formal matters.* Captions, except for the designation of the paper, are omitted from the forms provided in the Florida Rules of Civil Procedure. A general form of caption is the first form provided. Signatures are omitted from pleadings and motions. FL ST RCP Rule 1.900(c).

8. *Notices to persons with disabilities.* All notices of court proceedings to be held in a public facility, and all process compelling appearance at such proceedings, shall include the following statement in bold face, fourteen (14) point Times New Roman or Courier font: "If you are a person with a disability who needs any accommodation in order to participate in this proceeding, you are entitled, at no cost to you, to the provision of certain assistance. Please contact [identify applicable court personnel by name, address, and telephone number] at least seven (7) days before your scheduled court appearance, or immediately upon receiving this notification if the time before the scheduled appearance is less than seven (7) days; if you are hearing or voice impaired, call 711." FL ST J ADMIN Rule 2.540(c)(1).

9. *Minimization of the filing of sensitive information*

a. *Limitations for court filings.* Unless authorized by FL ST J ADMIN Rule 2.425(b), statute, another rule of court, or the court orders otherwise, designated sensitive information filed with the court must be limited to the following format:

i. The initials of a person known to be a minor;

ii. The year of birth of a person's birth date;

iii. No portion of any: Social security number, Bank account number, Credit card account number, Charge account number, or Debit account number;

iv. The last four digits of any: Taxpayer identification number (TIN), Employee identification number, Driver's license number, Passport number, Telephone number, Financial account number, except as set forth in FL ST J ADMIN Rule 2.425(a)(3), Brokerage account number, Insurance policy account number, Loan account number, Customer account number, or Patient or health care number;

v. A truncated version of any: Email address, Computer user name, Password, or Personal identification number (PIN); and

vi. A truncated version of any other sensitive information as provided by court order. FL ST J ADMIN Rule 2.425(a).

b. *Exceptions.* FL ST J ADMIN Rule 2.425(a) does not apply to the following:

i. An account number which identifies the property alleged to be the subject of a proceeding;

ii. The record of an administrative or agency proceeding;

iii. The record in appellate or review proceedings;

iv. The birth date of a minor whenever the birth date is necessary for the court to establish or maintain subject matter jurisdiction;

v. The name of a minor in any order relating to parental responsibility, time-sharing, or child support;

vi. The name of a minor in any document or order affecting the minor's ownership of real property;

vii. The birth date of a party in a writ of attachment or notice to payor;

viii. In traffic and criminal proceedings: a pro se filing; a court filing that is related to a criminal matter or investigation and that is prepared before the filing of a criminal charge or is not filed as part of any docketed criminal case; an arrest or search warrant or any information in support thereof; a charging document and an affidavit or other documents filed in support of any charging document, including any driving records; a statement of particulars; discovery material introduced into evidence or otherwise filed with the court; and all information necessary for the proper issuance and execution of a subpoena duces tecum;

ix. Information used by the clerk for case maintenance purposes or the courts for case management purposes; and

x. Information which is relevant and material to an issue before the court. FL ST J ADMIN Rule 2.425(b).

c. *Remedies.* Upon motion by a party or interested person or sua sponte by the court, the court may order remedies, sanctions or both for a violation of FL ST J ADMIN Rule 2.425(a). Following notice and an opportunity to respond, the court may impose sanctions if such filing was not made in good faith. FL ST J ADMIN Rule 2.425(c).

d. *Motions not restricted.* FL ST J ADMIN Rule 2.425 does not restrict a party's right to move for protective order, to move to file documents under seal, or to request a determination of the confidentiality of records. FL ST J ADMIN Rule 2.425(d).

e. *Application.* FL ST J ADMIN Rule 2.425 does not affect the application of constitutional provisions, statutes, or rules of court regarding confidential information or access to public information. FL ST J ADMIN Rule 2.425(e).

F. Filing and Service Requirements

1. *Court filing of documents and discovery.* Information obtained during discovery shall not be filed with the court until such time as it is filed for good cause. The requirement of good cause is satisfied only where the filing of the information is allowed or required by another applicable rule of procedure or by court order. All filings of discovery documents shall comply with FL ST J ADMIN Rule 2.425. The court shall have the authority to impose sanctions for violation of FL ST RCP Rule 1.280. FL ST RCP Rule 1.280(g).

   a. *Filing of copies.* A copy of a deposition may be filed only under the following circumstances:

      i. It may be filed in compliance with FL ST J ADMIN Rule 2.425 and FL ST RCP Rule 1.280(f) by a party or the witness when the contents of the deposition must be considered by the court on any matter pending before the court. Prompt notice of the filing of the deposition shall be given to all parties unless notice is waived. A party filing the deposition shall furnish a copy of the deposition or the part being filed to other parties unless the party already has a copy. FL ST RCP Rule 1.310(f)(3)(A).

      ii. If the court determines that a deposition previously taken is necessary for the decision of a matter pending before the court, the court may order that a copy be filed by any party at the initial cost of the party, and the filing party shall comply with FL ST J ADMIN Rule 2.425 and FL ST RCP Rule 1.280(f). FL ST RCP Rule 1.310(f)(3)(B).

2. *Filing requirements.* All original documents must be filed with the court either before service or immediately thereafter, unless otherwise provided for by general law or other rules. If the original of any bond or other document is not placed in the court file, a certified copy must be so placed by the clerk. FL ST J ADMIN Rule 2.516(d). All documents shall be filed in conformity with the requirements of FL ST J ADMIN Rule 2.525. FL ST RCP Rule 1.080(b). All documents filed in any court shall be filed by electronic transmission in accordance with FL ST J ADMIN Rule 2.525. "Documents" means pleadings, motions, petitions, memoranda, briefs, notices, exhibits, declarations, affidavits, orders, judgments, decrees, writs, opinions, and any other paper or writing submitted to a court. FL ST J ADMIN Rule 2.520(a). All documents that are court records, as defined in FL ST J ADMIN Rule 2.430(a)(1), must be filed by electronic transmission, provided that: (1) the clerk has the ability to accept and retain such documents; (2) the clerk or the chief judge of the circuit has requested permission to accept documents filed by electronic transmission; and (3) the supreme court has entered an order granting permission to the clerk to accept documents filed by electronic transmission. FL ST J ADMIN Rule 2.525(c)(1).

   a. *Definition.* "Electronic transmission of documents" means the sending of information by electronic signals to, by or from a court or clerk, which when received can be transformed and stored or transmitted on paper, microfilm, magnetic storage device, optical imaging system, CD-ROM, flash drive, other electronic data storage system, server, case maintenance system ("CM"), electronic court filing ("ECF") system, statewide or local electronic portal ("e-portal"), or other electronic record keeping system authorized by the supreme court in a format sufficient to communicate the information on the original document in a readable format. Electronic transmission of documents includes electronic mail ("e-mail") and any internet-based transmission procedure, and may include procedures allowing for documents to be signed or verified by electronic means. FL ST J ADMIN Rule 2.525(a).

      i. The filing of documents with the court as required by the Florida Rules of Judicial Adminis-

tration must be made by filing them with the clerk in accordance with FL ST J ADMIN Rule 2.525, except that the judge may permit documents to be filed with the judge, in which event the judge must note the filing date before him or her on the documents and transmit them to the clerk. The date of filing is that shown on the face of the document by the judge's notation or the clerk's time stamp, whichever is earlier. FL ST J ADMIN Rule 2.516(e).

b. *Application.* Any court or clerk of the court may accept the electronic transmission of documents for filing after the clerk, together with input from the chief judge of the circuit, has obtained approval of the procedures and program for doing so from the Supreme Court of Florida. FL ST J ADMIN Rule 2.525(b).

c. *Exceptions*

   i. Paper documents and other submissions may be manually submitted to the clerk or court:
      - When the clerk does not have the ability to accept and retain documents by electronic filing or has not had ECF Procedures approved by the supreme court;
      - For filing by any self-represented party or any self-represented nonparty unless specific ECF Procedures provide a means to file documents electronically. However, any self-represented nonparty that is a governmental or public agency and any other agency, partnership, corporation, or business entity acting on behalf of any governmental or public agency may file documents by electronic transmission if such entity has the capability of filing documents electronically;
      - For filing by attorneys excused from e-mail service in accordance with FL ST J ADMIN Rule 2.516(b);
      - When submitting evidentiary exhibits or filing non-documentary materials;
      - When the filing involves documents in excess of twenty-five (25) megabytes (25MB) in size. For such filings, documents may be transmitted using an electronic storage medium that the clerk has the ability to accept, which may include a CD-ROM, flash drive, or similar storage medium;
      - When filed in open court, as permitted by the court;
      - When paper filing is permitted by any approved statewide or local ECF procedures; and
      - If any court determines that justice so requires. FL ST J ADMIN Rule 2.525(d).

   ii. Any document in paper form submitted under FL ST J ADMIN Rule 2.525(d) is filed when it is received by the clerk or court and the clerk shall immediately thereafter convert any filed paper document to an electronic document. "Convert to an electronic document" means optically capturing an image of a paper document and using character recognition software to recover as much of the document's text as practicable and then indexing and storing the document in the official court file. FL ST J ADMIN Rule 2.525(c)(4).

   iii. Any storage medium submitted under FL ST J ADMIN Rule 2.525(d)(5) is filed when received by the clerk or court and the clerk shall immediately thereafter transfer the electronic documents from the storage device to the official court file. FL ST J ADMIN Rule 2.525(c)(5).

   iv. If the filer of any paper document authorized under FL ST J ADMIN Rule 2.525(d) provides a self-addressed, postage-paid envelope for return of the paper document after it is converted to electronic form by the clerk, the clerk shall place the paper document in the envelope and deposit it in the mail. Except when a paper document is required to be maintained, the clerk may recycle any filed paper document that is not to be returned to the filer. FL ST J ADMIN Rule 2.525(c)(6).

   v. The clerk may convert any paper document filed before the effective date of FL ST J ADMIN Rule 2.525 to an electronic document. Unless the clerk is required to maintain the paper document, if the paper document has been converted to an electronic document by the clerk, the paper document is no longer part of the official court file and may be removed and recycled. FL ST J ADMIN Rule 2.525(c)(7).

d. *Official court file.* For information on what constitutes the official court file, please see FL ST J ADMIN Rule 2.525(c)(2), FL ST J ADMIN Rule 2.525(c)(3).

e. *Administration.* All attorneys, parties, or other persons using this rule to file documents are required to make arrangements with the court or clerk for the payment of any charges authorized by general law or the supreme court before filing any document by electronic transmission. FL ST J ADMIN Rule 2.525(f)(2).

f. *Filing date.* The filing date for an electronically transmitted document is the date and time that such filing is acknowledged by an electronic stamp or otherwise, pursuant to any procedure set forth in any ECF Procedures approved by the supreme court, or the date the last page of such filing is received by the court or clerk. FL ST J ADMIN Rule 2.525(f)(3).

g. *Accessibility.* All documents transmitted in any electronic form under FL ST J ADMIN Rule 2.525 must comply with the accessibility requirements of FL ST J ADMIN Rule 2.526. FL ST J ADMIN Rule 2.525(g).

3. *Service requirements.* Every pleading subsequent to the initial pleading, all orders, and every other document filed in the action must be served in conformity with the requirements of FL ST J ADMIN Rule 2.516. FL ST RCP Rule 1.080(a).

   a. *Service; When required.* Unless the court otherwise orders, or a statute or supreme court administrative order specifies a different means of service, every pleading subsequent to the initial pleading and every other document filed in any court proceeding, except applications for witness subpoenas and documents served by formal notice or required to be served in the manner provided for service of formal notice, must be served in accordance with FL ST J ADMIN Rule 2.516 on each party. No service need be made on parties against whom a default has been entered, except that pleadings asserting new or additional claims against them must be served in the manner provided for service of summons. FL ST J ADMIN Rule 2.516(a).

   b. *Service; How made.* When service is required or permitted to be made upon a party represented by an attorney, service must be made upon the attorney unless service upon the party is ordered by the court. FL ST J ADMIN Rule 2.516(b).

      i. *Service by electronic mail ("e-mail").* All documents required or permitted to be served on another party must be served by e-mail, unless FL ST J ADMIN Rule 2.516 otherwise provides. When, in addition to service by e-mail, the sender also utilizes another means of service provided for in FL ST J ADMIN Rule 2.516(b)(2), any differing time limits and other provisions applicable to that other means of service control. FL ST J ADMIN Rule 2.516(b)(1). Any document electronically transmitted to a court or clerk must also be served on all parties and interested persons in accordance with the applicable rules of court. FL ST J ADMIN Rule 2.525(e)(2).

         - *Service on attorneys.* Upon appearing in a proceeding, an attorney must serve a designation of a primary e-mail address and may designate no more than two (2) secondary e-mail addresses. Thereafter, service must be directed to all designated e-mail addresses in that proceeding. Every document filed by an attorney thereafter must include the primary e-mail address of that attorney and any secondary e-mail addresses. If an attorney does not designate any e-mail address for service, documents may be served on that attorney at the e-mail address on record with The Florida Bar. FL ST J ADMIN Rule 2.516(b)(1)(A).

         - *Exception to e-mail service on attorneys.* Service by an attorney on another attorney must be made by e-mail unless excused by the court. Upon motion by an attorney demonstrating that the attorney has no e-mail account and lacks access to the Internet at the attorney's office, the court may excuse the attorney from the requirements of e-mail service. Service on and by an attorney excused by the court from e-mail service must be by the means provided in FL ST J ADMIN Rule 2.516(b)(2). FL ST J ADMIN Rule 2.516(b)(1)(B).

         - *Service on and by parties not represented by an attorney.* Any party not represented by an attorney may serve a designation of a primary e-mail address and also may designate no more than two (2) secondary e-mail addresses to which service must be directed in that proceeding by the means provided in FL ST J ADMIN Rule 2.516(b)(1). If a party not represented by an attorney does not designate an e-mail address for service in a proceeding, service on and by that party must be by the means provided in FL ST J ADMIN Rule 2.516(b)(2). FL ST J ADMIN Rule 2.516(b)(1)(C).

- *Time of service.* Service by e-mail is complete when it is sent. FL ST J ADMIN Rule 2.516(b)(1)(D). An e-mail is deemed served on the date it is sent. FL ST J ADMIN Rule 2.516(b)(1)(D)(i). If the sender learns that the e-mail did not reach the address of the person to be served, the sender must immediately send another copy by e-mail, or by a means authorized by FL ST J ADMIN Rule 2.516(b)(2). FL ST J ADMIN Rule 2.516(b)(1)(D)(ii). E-mail service is treated as service by mail for the computation of time. FL ST J ADMIN Rule 2.516(b)(1)(D)(iii).

ii. *Format of e-mail for service.* Service of a document by e-mail is made by attaching a copy of the document in PDF format to an e-mail sent to all addresses designated by the attorney or party. FL ST J ADMIN Rule 2.516(b)(1)(E).

- All documents served by e-mail must be attached to an e-mail message containing a subject line beginning with the words "SERVICE OF COURT DOCUMENT" in all capital letters, followed by the case number of the proceeding in which the documents are being served. FL ST J ADMIN Rule 2.516(b)(1)(E)(i).
- The body of the e-mail must identify the court in which the proceeding is pending, the case number, the name of the initial party on each side, the title of each document served with that e-mail, and the sender's name and telephone number. FL ST J ADMIN Rule 2.516(b)(1)(E)(ii).
- Any document served by e-mail may be signed by the "/s/" format, as long as the filed original is signed in accordance with the applicable rule of procedure. FL ST J ADMIN Rule 2.516(b)(1)(E)(iii).
- Any e-mail which, together with its attached documents, exceeds five megabytes (5MB) in size, must be divided and sent as separate e-mails, no one of which may exceed five megabytes (5MB) in size and each of which must be sequentially numbered in the subject line. FL ST J ADMIN Rule 2.516(b)(1)(E)(iv).

iii. *Service by other means.* In addition to, and not in lieu of, service by e-mail, service may also be made upon attorneys by any of the means specified in FL ST J ADMIN Rule 2.516(b)(2). Service on and by all parties who are not represented by an attorney and who do not designate an e-mail address, and on and by all attorneys excused from e-mail service, must be made by delivering a copy of the document or by mailing it to the party or attorney at their last known address or, if no address is known, by leaving it with the clerk of the court. Service by mail is complete upon mailing. Delivery of a copy within FL ST J ADMIN Rule 2.516 is complete upon:

- Handing it to the attorney or to the party,
- Leaving it at the attorney's or party's office with a clerk or other person in charge thereof,
- If there is no one in charge, leaving it in a conspicuous place therein,
- If the office is closed or the person to be served has no office, leaving it at the person's usual place of abode with some person of his or her family above fifteen (15) years of age and informing such person of the contents, or
- Transmitting it by facsimile to the attorney's or party's office with a cover sheet containing the sender's name, firm, address, telephone number, and facsimile number, and the number of pages transmitted. When service is made by facsimile, a copy must also be served by any other method permitted by FL ST J ADMIN Rule 2.516. Facsimile service occurs when transmission is complete. FL ST J ADMIN Rule 2.516(b)(2)(A) through FL ST J ADMIN Rule 2.516(b)(2)(E).
- Service by delivery after 5:00 p.m. must be deemed to have been made by mailing on the date of delivery. FL ST J ADMIN Rule 2.516(b)(2)(F).

c. *Service; Numerous defendants.* In actions when the parties are unusually numerous, the court may regulate the service contemplated by the Florida Rules of Judicial Administration on motion or on its own initiative in such manner as may be found to be just and reasonable. FL ST J ADMIN Rule 2.516(c).

d. *Service by clerk.* Service of notices and other documents required to be made by the clerk must also be done as provided in FL ST J ADMIN Rule 2.516(b). FL ST J ADMIN Rule 2.516(g).

G. Hearings

1. There is no hearing required or contemplated with regard to responses to requests for admission in the Florida Rules of Civil Procedure.

H. Forms

1. Official Notice of Deposition Forms for Florida

a. Caption. FL ST RCP Form 1.901.

2. Notice of Deposition Forms for Florida

a. Form for motion by plaintiff for leave to take deposition within 20-day period. FL-RCPF R 1.310(6).

b. Form for order on motion for leave to take deposition within 20-day period. FL-RCPF R 1.310(8).

c. Notice of examination; Time and place. FL-RCPF R 1.310(9).

d. Nonparty witness, subpoena required. FL-RCPF R 1.310(10).

e. Form for notice to take deposition on oral examination. FL-RCPF R 1.310(11).

f. Form for notice of taking multiple depositions. FL-RCPF R 1.310(11.1).

g. Form for notice of taking deposition and examination of documents. FL-RCPF R 1.310(12).

h. Form for notice of taking video deposition duces tecum. FL-RCPF R 1.310(13).

i. Form for motion to modify time for taking deposition. FL-RCPF R 1.310(14).

j. Form for motion to take deposition by telephone. FL-RCPF R 1.310(16).

k. Form for order permitting deposition by telephone. FL-RCPF R 1.310(17).

l. Form for notice of taking deposition by telephone. FL-RCPF R 1.310(18).

m. Form for notice of deposition upon written questions. FL-RCPF R 1.320(2).

n. Form of questions. FL-RCPF R 1.320(3).

o. Form of cross-questions. FL-RCPF R 1.320(4).

p. Form for objection to form of written questions. FL-RCPF R 1.320(6).

I. Checklist

(I) ❑ Matters to be considered by deposing party (oral depositions)
- (a) ❑ Required documents
  - (1) ❑ Notice of deposition
  - (2) ❑ Certificate of service
- (b) ❑ Supplemental documents
  - (1) ❑ Motion for leave to request deposition
  - (2) ❑ Subpoena
  - (3) ❑ Request for production of documents
- (c) ❑ Time for service of notice of deposition
  - (1) ❑ After commencement of action
  - (2) ❑ Within thirty (30) days after service of initial pleadings by leave of court only

(II) ❑ Matters to be considered by deponent (oral depositions)
- (a) ❑ Required documents
  - (1) ❑ Production of documents (if subpoenaed)

(III) ❑ Matters to be considered by deposing party (depositions by written questions)

(a) ❑ Required documents

(1) ❑ Notice of deposition

(2) ❑ Written questions

(3) ❑ Certificate of service

(b) ❑ Supplemental documents

(1) ❑ Motion for leave to request deposition

(2) ❑ Subpoena

(3) ❑ Request for production of documents

(c) ❑ Time for service of direct and redirect questions

(1) ❑ Within ten (10) days after being served with cross questions, a party may serve redirect questions upon all other parties

(2) ❑ Objections to the form of the question must be served within the time for service of redirect questions or ten (10) days after service of recross questions

(IV) ❑ Matters to be considered by deponent (depositions by written questions)

(a) ❑ Required documents

(1) ❑ Cross questions, with certificate of service

(2) ❑ Recross questions with certificate of service

(b) ❑ Time for service of cross and recross questions

(1) ❑ Within thirty (30) days after the notice and written questions are served, a party may serve cross questions upon all other parties

(2) ❑ Within ten (10) days after being served with redirect questions, a party may serve recross questions upon all other parties

(3) ❑ Objections to the form of the questions must be served within the time for serving succeeding questions

SEVENTEENTH JUDICIAL CIRCUIT

Pleadings
Complaint

Document Last Updated January 2013

A. Applicable Rules

1. *State rules*
    a. Nonverification of pleadings. FL ST RCP Rule 1.030.
    b. When action commenced. FL ST RCP Rule 1.050.
    c. Process. FL ST RCP Rule 1.070.
    d. Constitutional challenge to state statute or county or municipal charter, ordinance, or franchise; Notice by party. FL ST RCP Rule 1.071.
    e. Service and filing of pleadings, orders, and documents. FL ST RCP Rule 1.080.
    f. Time. FL ST RCP Rule 1.090.
    g. Pleadings and motions. FL ST RCP Rule 1.100; FL ST RCP Rule 1.110; FL ST RCP Rule 1.120; FL ST RCP Rule 1.130; FL ST RCP Rule 1.170; FL ST RCP Rule 1.430.
    h. Relief from judgment, decrees or orders. FL ST RCP Rule 1.540.
    i. Forms. FL ST RCP Rule 1.900.
    j. Retention of court records. FL ST J ADMIN Rule 2.430.
    k. Foreign attorneys. FL ST J ADMIN Rule 2.510.
    l. Signature of attorneys and parties. FL ST J ADMIN Rule 2.515.
    m. Paper. FL ST J ADMIN Rule 2.520.
    n. Electronic filing. FL ST J ADMIN Rule 2.525.
    o. Requests for accommodations by persons with disabilities. FL ST J ADMIN Rule 2.540.
    p. Service. FL ST § 48.011; FL ST § 48.021; FL ST § 48.031; FL ST § 48.041; FL ST § 48.042; FL ST § 48.051; FL ST § 48.061; FL ST § 48.071; FL ST § 48.081; FL ST § 48.091; FL ST § 48.101; FL ST § 48.111; FL ST § 48.121; FL ST § 48.131; FL ST § 48.141; FL ST § 48.151; FL ST § 48.161; FL ST § 48.171; FL ST § 48.181; FL ST § 48.183; FL ST § 48.19; FL ST § 48.193; FL ST § 48.194; FL ST § 48.20; FL ST § 48.21; FL ST § 48.25; FL ST § 48.31; FL ST § 49.011; FL ST § 49.021; FL ST § 49.031; FL ST § 49.041; FL ST § 49.051; FL ST § 49.061; FL ST § 49.071; FL ST § 49.08; FL ST § 49.09; FL ST § 49.10; FL ST § 49.11; FL ST § 49.12; FL ST § 50.011; FL ST § 50.021; FL ST § 50.031; FL ST § 50.041; FL ST § 50.051; FL ST § 50.061.
    q. Minimization of the filing of sensitive information. FL ST J ADMIN Rule 2.425.
    r. Accessibility of information and technology. FL ST J ADMIN Rule 2.526.
2. *Local rules*
    a. Standards of professional courtesy. FL ST 17 J CIR I-94-O-1.
    b. Administrative order authorizing the filing of pleadings or papers at any office of the clerk of court. FL ST 17 J CIR 2008-153-GEN.
    c. Administrative order regarding provision of ADA accommodations. FL ST 17 J CIR 2010-49-GEN.
    d. Administrative order designating record newspaper. FL ST 17 J CIR 2012-21-GEN.
    e. Administrative order establishing electronic filing procedures for the civil division. FL ST 17 J CIR 2012-16-CIV.

B. Timing

1. *Commencement of an action.* Every action of a civil nature shall be deemed commenced when the complaint or petition is filed except that ancillary proceedings shall be deemed commenced when the writ is issued or the pleading setting forth the claim of the party initiating the action is filed. FL ST RCP Rule 1.050.

2. *Summons; Time limit.* If service of the initial process and initial pleading is not made upon a defendant within one hundred twenty (120) days after filing of the initial pleading directed to that defendant the court, on its own initiative after notice or on motion, shall direct that service be effected within a specified time or shall dismiss the action without prejudice or drop that defendant as a party; provided that if the plaintiff shows good cause or excusable neglect for the failure, the court shall extend the time for service for an appropriate period. FL ST RCP Rule 1.070(j).

3. *Standard of professional conduct; Scheduling*
   a. Attorneys should endeavor to provide opposing counsel, parties, witnesses, and other affected persons, sufficient notice of depositions, hearings and other proceedings, except upon agreement of course, in an emergency, or in other circumstances compelling more expedited scheduling. As a general rule, actual notice should be no less than five (5) business days for instate depositions, ten (10) business days for out-of-state depositions and four (4) business days for hearings. FL ST 17 J CIR I-94-O-1(I)(1).
   b. Attorneys should communicate with opposing counsel prior to scheduling depositions, hearings and other proceedings, in an effort to schedule them at times that are mutually convenient for all interested persons. Further, sufficient time should be reserved to permit a complete presentation by counsel for all parties. FL ST 17 J CIR I-94-O-1(I)(2).
   c. Attorneys should notify opposing counsel, the court, and others affected, of scheduling conflicts as soon as they become apparent. Further, attorneys should cooperate with one another regarding all reasonable rescheduling requests that do not prejudice their clients or unduly delay a proceeding. FL ST 17 J CIR I-94-O-1(I)(3).
   d. Attorneys should promptly notify the court or other tribunal of any resolution between the parties that renders a scheduled court appearance unnecessary or otherwise moot. FL ST 17 J CIR I-94-O-1(I)(4).
   e. Attorneys should grant reasonable requests by opposing counsel for extensions of time within which to respond to pleadings, discovery, and other matters when such an extension will not prejudice their client or unduly delay a proceeding. FL ST 17 J CIR I-94-O-1(I)(5).

4. *Timing considerations when filing electronically.* The filing date of an efiled document is when the last page is received by the Clerk. The electronic filing of a document does not modify any filing deadlines as required by law, rule of procedure, or court order. FL ST 17 J CIR 2012-16-CIV.

5. *Computation of time*
   a. *Generally.* Computation of time shall be governed by FL ST J ADMIN Rule 2.514. FL ST RCP Rule 1.090(a). The following rules apply in computing time periods specified in any rule of procedure, local rule, court order, or statute that does not specify a method of computing time. FL ST J ADMIN Rule 2.514(a).
      i. *Period stated in days or a longer unit.* When the period is stated in days or a longer unit of time (A) exclude the day of the event that triggers the period; (B) count every day, including intermediate Saturdays, Sundays, and legal holidays; and (C) include the last day of the period, but if the last day is a Saturday, Sunday, or legal holiday, or falls within any period of time extended through an order of the chief justice under FL ST J ADMIN Rule 2.205(a)(2)(B)(iv), the period continues to run until the end of the next day that is not a Saturday, Sunday, or legal holiday and does not fall within any period of time extended through an order of the chief justice. FL ST J ADMIN Rule 2.514(a)(1).
      ii. *Period stated in hours.* When the period is stated in hours (A) begin counting immediately on the occurrence of the event that triggers the period; (B) count every hour, including hours

during intermediate Saturdays, Sundays, and legal holidays; and (C) if the period would end on a Saturday, Sunday, or legal holiday, or during any period of time extended through an order of the chief justice under FL ST J ADMIN Rule 2.205(a)(2)(B)(iv), the period continues to run until the same time on the next day that is not a Saturday, Sunday, or legal holiday and does not fall within any period of time extended through an order of the chief justice. FL ST J ADMIN Rule 2.514(a)(2).

iii. *Period stated in days less than seven (7) days.* When the period stated in days is less than seven (7) days, intermediate Saturdays, Sundays, and legal holidays shall be excluded in the computation. FL ST J ADMIN Rule 2.514(a)(3).

iv. *"Last day" defined.* Unless a different time is set by a statute, local rule, or court order, the last day ends (A) for electronic filing or for service by any means, at midnight; and (B) for filing by other means, when the clerk's office is scheduled to close. FL ST J ADMIN Rule 2.514(a)(4).

v. *"Next day" defined.* The "next day" is determined by continuing to count forward when the period is measured after an event and backward when measured before an event. FL ST J ADMIN Rule 2.514(a)(5).

vi. *"Legal holiday" defined.* "Legal holiday" means (A) the day set aside by FL ST § 110.117, for observing New Year's Day, Martin Luther King, Jr.'s Birthday, Memorial Day, Independence Day, Labor Day, Veterans' Day, Thanksgiving Day, the Friday after Thanksgiving Day, or Christmas Day, and (B) any day observed as a holiday by the clerk's office or as designated by the chief judge. FL ST J ADMIN Rule 2.514(a)(6).

b. *Additional time after service by mail or e-mail.* When a party may or must act within a specified time after service and service is made by mail or e-mail, five (5) days are added after the period that would otherwise expire under FL ST J ADMIN Rule 2.514(a). FL ST J ADMIN Rule 2.514(b).

c. *Enlargement.* When an act is required or allowed to be done at or within a specified time by order of court, by the Florida Rules of Civil Procedure, or by notice given thereunder, for cause shown the court at any time in its discretion (1) with or without notice, may order the period enlarged if request therefor is made before the expiration of the period originally prescribed or as extended by a previous order, or (2) upon motion made and notice after the expiration of the specified period, may permit the act to be done when failure to act was the result of excusable neglect, but it may not extend the time for making a motion for new trial, for rehearing, or to alter or amend a judgment; making a motion for relief from a judgment under FL ST RCP Rule 1.540(b); taking an appeal or filing a petition for certiorari; or making a motion for a directed verdict. FL ST RCP Rule 1.090(b).

d. *Unaffected by expiration of term.* The period of time provided for the doing of any act or the taking of any proceeding shall not be affected or limited by the continued existence or expiration of a term of court. The continued existence or expiration of a term of court in no way affects the power of a court to do any act or take any proceeding in any action which is or has been pending before it. FL ST RCP Rule 1.090(c).

C. General Requirements

1. *General rules of pleading*

a. *Claims for relief*

i. A pleading which sets forth a claim for relief, whether an original claim, counterclaim, crossclaim, or third-party claim, must state a cause of action and shall contain

- A short and plain statement of the grounds upon which the court's jurisdiction depends, unless the court already has jurisdiction and the claim needs no new grounds of jurisdiction to support it (For information regarding acts subjecting persons to jurisdiction, please see FL ST § 48.193),
- A short and plain statement of the ultimate facts showing that the pleader is entitled to relief, and
- A demand for judgment for the relief to which the pleader deems himself or herself entitled. FL ST RCP Rule 1.110(b).

ii. Relief in the alternative or of several different types may be demanded. Every complaint shall be considered to demand general relief. FL ST RCP Rule 1.110(b).

b. *Verification.* Except when otherwise specifically provided by these rules or an applicable statute, every pleading or other document of a party represented by an attorney need not be verified or accompanied by an affidavit. FL ST RCP Rule 1.030. When filing an action for foreclosure of a mortgage on residential real property the complaint shall be verified. When verification of a document is required, the document filed shall include an oath, affirmation, or the following statement: "Under penalty of perjury, I declare that I have read the foregoing, and the facts alleged therein are true and correct to the best of my knowledge and belief." FL ST RCP Rule 1.110(b).

c. *Separate statements.* All averments of claim or defense shall be made in consecutively numbered paragraphs, the contents of each of which shall be limited as far as practicable to a statement of a single set of circumstances, and a paragraph may be referred to by number in all subsequent pleadings. Each claim founded upon a separate transaction or occurrence and each defense other than denials shall be stated in a separate count or defense when a separation facilitates the clear presentation of the matter set forth. FL ST RCP Rule 1.110(f).

d. *Statements adopted by reference.* Statements in a pleading may be adopted by reference in a different part of the same pleading, in another pleading, or in any motion. FL ST RCP Rule 1.130(b).

e. *Joinder of causes of action; Consistency.* A pleader may set up in the same action as many claims or causes of action or defenses in the same right as the pleader has, and claims for relief may be stated in the alternative if separate items make up the cause of action, or if two (2) or more causes of action are joined. A party may also set forth two (2) or more statements of a claim or defense alternatively, either in one (1) count or defense or in separate counts or defenses. When two (2) or more statements are made in the alternative and one (1) of them, if made independently, would be sufficient, the pleading is not made insufficient by the insufficiency of one (1) or more of the alternative statements. A party may also state as many separate claims or defenses as that party has, regardless of consistency and whether based on legal or equitable grounds or both. All pleadings shall be construed so as to do substantial justice. FL ST RCP Rule 1.110(g).

f. *Subsequent pleadings.* When the nature of an action permits pleadings subsequent to final judgment and the jurisdiction of the court over the parties has not terminated, the initial pleading subsequent to final judgment shall be designated a supplemental complaint or petition. The action shall then proceed in the same manner and time as though the supplemental complaint or petition were the initial pleading in the action, including the issuance of any needed process. FL ST RCP Rule 1.110(h) shall not apply to proceedings that may be initiated by motion under the Florida Rules of Civil Procedure. FL ST RCP Rule 1.110(h).

g. *Pleading basis for service.* When service of process is to be made under statutes authorizing service on nonresidents of Florida, it is sufficient to plead the basis for service in the language of the statute without pleading the facts supporting service. FL ST RCP Rule 1.070(h).

h. *Forms of pleadings.* Forms of action and technical forms for seeking relief and of pleas, pleadings, or motions are abolished. FL ST RCP Rule 1.110(a).

2. *Complaint; Generally*

a. *Purpose.* The purpose of a complaint is to advise the court and the defendant of the nature of a cause of action asserted by the plaintiff. FL-PP § 2:12.

b. *Sufficiency of complaint.* A complaint will be found to be insufficient if it contains only general conclusory allegations unsupported by any facts. The test to determine whether a complaint is sufficient is whether, if the factual allegations of the complaint are established, the plaintiff will be legally or equitably entitled to the claimed relief. Pizzi v. Central Bank & Trust Co., 250 So.2d 895, 896 (Fla. 1971); Bowen v. G H C Properties, Limited, 251 So.2d 359, 361 (Fla. 1st DCA 1971); FL-PP § 2:12. In determining the sufficiency of the complaint to state a cause of action, all allegations of the complaint are taken as true, and possible affirmative defenses are not considered. Strickland v. Commerce Loan Co. of Jacksonville, 158 So.2d 814 (Fla. 1st DCA 1963); FL-PP § 2:12.

i. The issues for trial in Florida must be settled by the pleadings. The issues cannot be raised by discovery. FL-PRACPROC § 7:6.

ii. Causes of action may be pleaded alternatively in the same count or in different counts and against the same or different defendants as long as the joinder of parties is proper. FL-PRACPROC § 7:6.

iii. Each count must state a cause of action. Each independent cause of action should be pleaded in a separate count. FL-PRACPROC § 7:6.

iv. Incorporation by reference of all allegations from one count to another is not proper. Separate counts facilitate reference to the pleading in which they appear in other pleadings, motions or papers as well as the assertion of defenses against some, but not all, causes of action. Some defenses may not apply to the initial pleading as a whole. FL-PRACPROC § 7:6.

3. *Pleading special matters*

a. *Capacity.* It is not necessary to aver the capacity of a party to sue or be sued, the authority of a party to sue or be sued in a representative capacity, or the legal existence of an organized association of persons that is made a party, except to the extent required to show the jurisdiction of the court. The initial pleading served on behalf of a minor party shall specifically aver the age of the minor party. When a party desires to raise an issue as to the legal existence of any party, the capacity of any party to sue or be sued, or the authority of a party to sue or be sued in a representative capacity, that party shall do so by specific negative averment which shall include such supporting particulars as are peculiarly within the pleader's knowledge. FL ST RCP Rule 1.120(a).

b. *Fraud, mistake, condition of the mind.* In all averments of fraud or mistake, the circumstances constituting fraud or mistake shall be stated with such particularity as the circumstances may permit. Malice, intent, knowledge, mental attitude, and other condition of mind of a person may be averred generally. FL ST RCP Rule 1.120(b).

c. *Conditions precedent.* In pleading the performance or occurrence of conditions precedent, it is sufficient to aver generally that all conditions precedent have been performed or have occurred. A denial of performance or occurrence shall be made specifically and with particularity. FL ST RCP Rule 1.120(c).

d. *Official document or act.* In pleading an official document or official act it is sufficient to aver that the document was issued or the act done in compliance with law. FL ST RCP Rule 1.120(c).

e. *Judgment or decree.* In pleading a judgment or decree of a domestic or foreign court, a judicial or quasi-judicial tribunal, or a board or officer, it is sufficient to aver the judgment or decree without setting forth matter showing jurisdiction to render it. FL ST RCP Rule 1.120(e).

f. *Time and place.* For the purpose of testing the sufficiency of a pleading, averments of time and place are material and shall be considered like all other averments of material matter. FL ST RCP Rule 1.120(f).

g. *Special damage.* When items of special damage are claimed, they shall be specifically stated. FL ST RCP Rule 1.120(g).

4. *Parties*

a. *Parties generally.* Every action may be prosecuted in the name of the real party in interest, but a personal representative, administrator, guardian, trustee of an express trust, a party with whom or in whose name a contract has been made for the benefit of another, or a party expressly authorized by statute may sue in that person's own name without joining the party for whose benefit the action is brought. All persons having an interest in the subject of the action and in obtaining the relief demanded may join as plaintiffs and any person may be made a defendant who has or claims an interest adverse to the plaintiff. Any person may at any time be made a party if that person's presence is necessary or proper to a complete determination of the cause. Persons having a united interest may be joined on the same side as plaintiffs or defendants, and anyone who refuses to join may for such reason be made a defendant. FL ST RCP Rule 1.210(a).

b. *Minors or incompetent persons.* When a minor or incompetent person has a representative, such as a guardian or other like fiduciary, the representative may sue or defend on behalf of the minor or incompetent person. A minor or incompetent person who does not have a duly appointed representative may sue by next friend or by a guardian ad litem. The court shall appoint a guardian ad litem for a minor or incompetent person not otherwise represented in an action or shall make such other order as it deems proper for the protection of the minor or incompetent person. FL ST RCP Rule 1.210(b).

c. For survivor and substitution of parties information, please see FL ST RCP Rule 1.260.

5. *Counterclaims and crossclaims*

a. *Compulsory counterclaims.* A pleading shall state as a counterclaim any claim which at the time of serving the pleading the pleader has against any opposing party, provided it arises out of the transaction or occurrence that is the subject matter of the opposing party's claim and does not require for its adjudication the presence of third parties over whom the court cannot acquire jurisdiction. But the pleader need not state a claim if (1) at the time the action was commenced the claim was the subject of another pending action, or (2) the opposing party brought suit upon that party's claim by attachment or other process by which the court did not acquire jurisdiction to render a personal judgment on the claim and the pleader is not stating a counterclaim under this rule. FL ST RCP Rule 1.170(a).

b. *Permissive counterclaim.* A pleading may state as a counterclaim any claim against an opposing party not arising out of the transaction or occurrence that is the subject matter of the opposing party's claim. FL ST RCP Rule 1.170(b).

c. *Counterclaim exceeding opposing claim.* A counterclaim may or may not diminish or defeat the recovery sought by the opposing party. It may claim relief exceeding in amount or different in kind from that sought in the pleading of the opposing party. FL ST RCP Rule 1.170(c).

d. *Counterclaim against the State.* The Florida Rules of Civil Procedure shall not be construed to enlarge beyond the limits established by law the right to assert counterclaims or to claim credits against the state or any of its subdivisions or other governmental organizations thereof subject to suit or against a municipal corporation or against an officer, agency, or administrative board of the state. FL ST RCP Rule 1.170(d).

e. *Counterclaim maturing or acquired after pleading.* A claim which matured or was acquired by the pleader after serving the pleading may be presented as a counterclaim by supplemental pleading with the permission of the court. FL ST RCP Rule 1.170(e).

f. *Omitted counterclaim or crossclaim.* When a pleader fails to set up a counterclaim or crossclaim through oversight, inadvertence, or excusable neglect, or when justice requires, the pleader may set up the counterclaim or crossclaim by amendment with leave of the court. FL ST RCP Rule 1.170(f).

g. *Crossclaim against co-party.* A pleading may state as a crossclaim any claim by one party against a co-party arising out of the transaction or occurrence that is the subject matter of either the original action or a counterclaim therein, or relating to any property that is the subject matter of the original action. The crossclaim may include a claim that the party against whom it is asserted is or may be liable to the crossclaimant for all or part of a claim asserted in the action against the crossclaimant. Service of a crossclaim on a party who has appeared in the action shall be made pursuant to FL ST RCP Rule 1.080. Service of a crossclaim against a party who has not appeared in the action shall be made in the manner provided for service of summons. FL ST RCP Rule 1.170(g).

h. *Additional parties may be brought in.* When the presence of parties other than those to the original action is required to grant complete relief in the determination of a counterclaim or crossclaim, they shall be named in the counterclaim or crossclaim and be served with process and shall be parties to the action thereafter if jurisdiction of them can be obtained and their joinder will not deprive the court of jurisdiction of the action. FL ST RCP Rule 1.250(b) and FL ST RCP Rule 1.250(c) apply to parties brought in under FL ST RCP Rule 1.170(h). FL ST RCP Rule 1.170(h).

i. *Separate trials; Separate judgment.* If the court orders separate trials as provided in FL ST RCP Rule 1.270(b), judgment on a counterclaim or crossclaim may be rendered when the court has jurisdiction to do so even if a claim of the opposing party has been dismissed or otherwise disposed of. FL ST RCP Rule 1.170(i).

j. *Demand exceeding jurisdiction; Transfer of action.* If the demand of any counterclaim or crossclaim exceeds the jurisdiction of the court in which the action is pending, the action shall be transferred forthwith to the court of the same county having jurisdiction of the demand in the counterclaim or crossclaim with only such alterations in the pleadings as are essential. The court shall order the transfer of the action and the transmittal of all papers in it to the proper court if the party asserting the demand exceeding the jurisdiction deposits with the court having jurisdiction a sum sufficient to pay the clerk's service charge in the court to which the action is transferred at the time of filing the counterclaim or crossclaim. Thereupon the original papers and deposit shall be transmitted and filed with a certified copy of the order. The court to which the action is transferred shall have full power and jurisdiction over the demands of all parties. Failure to make the service charge deposit at the time the counterclaim or crossclaim is filed, or within such further time as the court may allow, shall reduce a claim for damages to an amount within the jurisdiction of the court where the action is pending and waive the claim in other cases. FL ST RCP Rule 1.170(j).

6. *Misjoinder and nonjoinder of parties*
    a. *Misjoinder.* Misjoinder of parties is not a ground for dismissal of an action. Any claim against a party may be severed and proceeded with separately. FL ST RCP Rule 1.250(a).
    b. *Dropping parties.* Parties may be dropped by an adverse party in the manner provided for voluntary dismissal in FL ST RCP Rule 1.420(a)(1) subject to the exception stated in FL ST RCP Rule 1.420. If notice of lis pendens has been filed in the action against a party so dropped, the notice of dismissal shall be recorded and cancels the notice of lis pendens without the necessity of a court order. Parties may be dropped by order of court on its own initiative or the motion of any party at any stage of the action on such terms as are just. FL ST RCP Rule 1.250(b).
    c. *Adding parties.* Parties may be added once as a matter of course within the same time that pleadings can be so amended under FL ST RCP Rule 1.190(a). If amendment by leave of court or stipulation of the parties is permitted, parties may be added in the amended pleading without further order of court. Parties may be added by order of court on its own initiative or on motion of any party at any stage of the action and on such terms as are just. FL ST RCP Rule 1.250(c).
7. *Jury demand*
    a. *Right preserved.* The right of trial by jury as declared by the Constitution or by statute shall be preserved to the parties inviolate. FL ST RCP Rule 1.430(a).
    b. *Demand.* Any party may demand a trial by jury of any issue triable of right by a jury by serving upon the other party a demand therefor in writing at any time after commencement of the action and not later than ten (10) days after the service of the last pleading directed to such issue. The demand may be indorsed upon a pleading of the party. FL ST RCP Rule 1.430(b).
    c. *Specification of issues.* In the demand a party may specify the issues that the party wishes so tried; otherwise, the party is deemed to demand trial by jury for all issues so triable. FL ST RCP Rule 1.430(c).
        i. If a party has demanded trial by jury for only some of the issues, any other party may serve a demand for trial by jury of any other or all of the issues triable by jury ten (10) days after service of the demand or such lesser time as the court may order. FL ST RCP Rule 1.430(c).
    d. *Waiver.* A party who fails to serve a demand as required by FL ST RCP Rule 1.430 waives trial by jury. FL ST RCP Rule 1.430(d).
        i. If waived, a jury trial may not be granted without the consent of the parties, but the court may allow an amendment in the proceedings to demand a trial by jury or order a trial by jury on its own motion. FL ST RCP Rule 1.430(d).
        ii. A demand for trial by jury may not be withdrawn without the consent of the parties. FL ST RCP Rule 1.430(d).
8. *Arbitration and mediation*
    a. *Referral to arbitration and mediation.* Except as hereinafter provided or as otherwise prohibited by law, the presiding judge may enter an order referring all or any part of a contested civil matter to mediation or arbitration. The parties to any contested civil matter may file a written stipulation to

mediate or arbitrate any issue between them at any time. Such stipulation shall be incorporated into the order of referral. FL ST RCP Rule 1.700(a).

b. *Arbitration*

i. *Exclusions.* A civil action shall be ordered to arbitration or arbitration in conjunction with mediation upon stipulation of the parties. A civil action may be ordered to arbitration or arbitration in conjunction with mediation upon motion of any party or by the court, if the judge determines the action to be of such a nature that arbitration could be of benefit to the litigants or the court. FL ST RCP Rule 1.800.

- Under no circumstances may the following categories of actions be referred to arbitration: (1) bond estreatures; (2) habeas corpus or other extraordinary writs; (3) bond validations; (4) civil or criminal contempt; (5) such other matters as may be specified by order of the chief judge in the circuit. FL ST RCP Rule 1.800.

ii. For more information regarding arbitration, please see FL ST RCP Rule 1.810; FL ST RCP Rule 1.820; FL ST RCP Rule 1.830.

c. *Mediation.* For more information regarding mediation, please see FL ST RCP Rule 1.710; FL ST RCP Rule 1.720; FL ST RCP Rule 1.730; and FL ST RCP Rule 1.750.

9. *Rules of court*

a. *Rules of civil procedure.* The Florida Rules of Civil Procedure apply to all actions of a civil nature and all special statutory proceedings in the circuit courts and county courts except those to which the Florida Probate Rules, the Florida Family Law Rules of Procedure, or the Small Claims Rules apply. FL ST RCP Rule 1.010.

i. The form, content, procedure, and time for pleading in all special statutory proceedings shall be as prescribed by the statutes governing the proceeding unless the Florida Rules of Civil Procedure specifically provide to the contrary. FL ST RCP Rule 1.010.

ii. The Florida Rules of Civil Procedure shall be construed to secure the just, speedy, and inexpensive determination of every action. FL ST RCP Rule 1.010.

b. *Rules of judicial administration.* The Florida Rules of Judicial Administration shall apply to administrative matters in all courts to which the Florida Rules of Judicial Administration are applicable by their terms. The Florida Rules of Judicial Administration shall be construed to secure the speedy and inexpensive determination of every proceeding to which they are applicable. The Florida Rules of Judicial Administration shall supersede all conflicting rules and statutes. FL ST J ADMIN Rule 2.110.

D. Documents

1. *Required documents*

a. *Summons.* Upon the commencement of the action, summons or other process authorized by law shall be issued forthwith by the clerk or judge under the clerk's or the judge's signature and the seal of the court and delivered for service without praecipe. FL ST RCP Rule 1.070(a).

b. *Complaint.* See the General Requirements section for the contents of the complaint.

i. *Notices to persons with disabilities.* See the Format section of this KeyRules document for further information.

c. *Civil cover sheet.* A civil cover sheet (FL ST RCP Form 1.997) shall be completed and filed with the clerk at the time an initial complaint or petition is filed by the party initiating the action. If the cover sheet is not filed, the clerk shall accept the complaint or petition for filing; but all proceedings in the action shall be abated until a properly executed cover sheet is completed and filed. The clerk shall complete the civil cover sheet for a party appearing pro se. FL ST RCP Rule 1.100(c)(2).

d. *Return of execution process by process server.* Each person who effects service of process shall note on a return-of-service form attached thereto, the date and time when it comes to hand, the date and time when it is served, the manner of service, the name of the person on whom it was served and, if the person is served in a representative capacity, the position occupied by the person. The return-of-service form must be signed by the person who effects the service of process. However, a person employed by a sheriff who effects the service of process may sign the return-of-service form using an electronic signature certified by the sheriff. FL ST § 48.21(1).

i. A failure to state the facts or to include the signature required by FL ST § 48.21(1) invalidates the service, but the return is amendable to state the facts or to include the signature at any time on application to the court from which the process issued. On amendment, service is as effective as if the return had originally stated the omitted facts or included the signature. A failure to state all the facts in or to include the signature on the return shall subject the person effecting service to a fine not exceeding $10, in the court's discretion. FL ST § 48.21(2).

e. *Filing fees.* Filing fees are due at the time a party files a pleading to initiate a proceeding or files a pleading for relief. FL ST § 28.241. For a fee schedule, see FL ST § 28.241.

2. *Supplemental documents*

a. *Exhibits.* All bonds, notes, bills of exchange, contracts, accounts, or documents upon which action may be brought or defense made, or a copy thereof or a copy of the portions thereof material to the pleadings, shall be incorporated in or attached to the pleading. No papers shall be unnecessarily annexed as exhibits. The pleadings shall contain no unnecessary recitals of deeds, documents, contracts, or other instruments. Any exhibit attached to a pleading shall be considered a part of the pleadings for all purposes. FL ST RCP Rule 1.130(a).

b. *Notice of constitutional question.* A party that files a pleading, written motion, or other paper drawing into question the constitutionality of a state statute or a county or municipal charter, ordinance, or franchise must promptly (1) file a notice of constitutional question stating the question and identifying the paper that raises it; and (2) serve the notice and the pleading, written motion, or other paper drawing into question the constitutionality of a state statute or a county or municipal charter, ordinance, or franchise on the Attorney General or the state attorney of the judicial circuit in which the action is pending, by either certified or registered mail. Service of the notice and pleading, written motion, or other paper does not require joinder of the Attorney General or the state attorney as a party to the action. FL ST RCP Rule 1.071.

E. Format

1. *Documents; Type and size.* Documents subject to the exceptions set forth in FL ST J ADMIN Rule 2.525(d) shall be filed on recycled paper measuring eight and one half by eleven (8 1/2 by 11) inches. For purposes of FL ST J ADMIN Rule 2.520, paper is recycled if it contains a minimum content of fifty (50) percent waste paper. Xerographic reduction of legal-size (eight and one half by fourteen (8 1/2 by 14) inches) documents to letter size (eight and one half by eleven (8 1/2 by 11) inches) is prohibited. All other documents filed by electronic transmission shall be filed in a format capable of being printed in a format consistent with the provisions of FL ST J ADMIN Rule 2.250. FL ST J ADMIN Rule 2.520(b).

a. *Exhibits.* Any exhibit or attachment filed with pleadings or papers may be filed in its original size. FL ST J ADMIN Rule 2.520(c).

b. *Recording space.* On all papers and documents prepared and filed by the court or by any party to a proceeding which are to be recorded in the public records of any county, including but not limited to final money judgments and notices of lis pendens, a three (3) inch by three (3) inch space at the top right-hand corner on the first page and a one (1) inch by three (3) inch space at the top right-hand corner on each subsequent page shall be left blank and reserved for use by the clerk of court. FL ST J ADMIN Rule 2.520(d).

i. *Exceptions to recording space.* Any papers or documents created by persons or entities over which the filing party has no control, including but not limited to wills, codicils, trusts, or other testamentary documents; documents prepared or executed by any public officer; documents prepared, executed, acknowledged, or proved outside of the State of Florida; or documents created by State or Federal government agencies, may be filed without the space required by FL ST J ADMIN Rule 2.520. FL ST J ADMIN Rule 2.520(e).

c. *Noncompliance.* No clerk of court is permitted to refuse to file any document or paper because of noncompliance with the Florida Rules of Judicial Administration. However, upon request of the

clerk of court, noncomplying documents must be resubmitted in accordance with the formatting rules. FL ST J ADMIN Rule 2.520(f).

2. *Caption.* Every pleading, motion, order, judgment, or other paper shall have a caption containing the name of the court, the file number, and except for in rem proceedings, including forfeiture proceedings, the name of the first party on each side with an appropriate indication of other parties, and a designation identifying the party filing it and its nature or the nature of the order, as the case may be. In any in rem proceeding, every pleading, motion, order, judgment, or other paper shall have a caption containing the name of the court, the file number, the style "In re" (followed by the name or general description of the property), and a designation of the person or entity filing it and its nature or the nature of the order, as the case may be. In an in rem forfeiture proceeding, the style shall be "In re forfeiture of" (followed by the name of the general description of the property). All papers filed in the action shall be styled in such a manner as to indicate clearly the subject matter of the paper and the party requesting or obtaining relief. FL ST RCP Rule 1.100(c)(1).

3. *Writing and written defined.* Writing or written means a document containing information, an application, or a stipulation. FL ST RCP Rule 1.080(c).

4. *Rule abbreviations*

    a. The Florida Rules of Civil Procedure and shall be abbreviated as Fla.R.Civ.P. FL ST RCP Rule 1.010.

    b. The Florida Rules of Judicial Administration shall be abbreviated as Fla. R. Jud. Admin. FL ST J ADMIN Rule 2.110.

5. *Nonverification.* Except when otherwise specifically provided by the Florida Rules of Civil Procedure or an applicable statute, every pleading or other document of a party represented by an attorney need not be verified or accompanied by an affidavit. FL ST RCP Rule 1.030; FL ST J ADMIN Rule 2.515(a).

6. *Attorney signature*

    a. *Attorney signature.* Every pleading and other document of a party represented by an attorney shall be signed by at least one (1) attorney of record in that attorney's individual name whose current record Florida Bar address, telephone number, including area code, primary e-mail address and secondary e-mail addresses, if any, and Florida Bar number shall be stated, and who shall be duly licensed to practice law in Florida or who shall have received permission to appear in the particular case as provided in FL ST J ADMIN Rule 2.510. FL ST J ADMIN Rule 2.515(a).

        i. The attorney may be required by the court to give the address of, and to vouch for the attorney's authority to represent, the party. FL ST J ADMIN Rule 2.515(a).

        ii. The signature of an attorney shall constitute a certificate by the attorney that the attorney has read the pleading or other document; that to the best of the attorney's knowledge, information, and belief there is good ground to support it; and that it is not interposed for delay. FL ST J ADMIN Rule 2.515(a).

        iii. If a pleading is not signed or is signed with intent to defeat the purpose of FL ST J ADMIN Rule 2.515, it may be stricken and the action may proceed as though the pleading or other document had not been served. FL ST J ADMIN Rule 2.515(a).

    b. *Pro se litigant signature.* A party who is not represented by an attorney shall sign any pleading or other paper and state the party's address and telephone number, including area code. FL ST J ADMIN Rule 2.515(b).

    c. *Form of signature*

        i. The signatures required on pleadings and documents by FL ST J ADMIN Rule 2.515(a) and FL ST J ADMIN Rule 2.515(b) may be:

            - Original signatures;
            - Original signatures that have been reproduced by electronic means, such as on electronically transmitted documents or photocopied documents;
            - Electronic signatures using the "/s/," "s/," or "/s" formats by or at the direction of the person signing; or

- Any other signature format authorized by general law, so long as the clerk where the proceeding is pending has the capability of receiving and has obtained approval from the Supreme Court of Florida to accept pleadings and documents with that signature format. FL ST J ADMIN Rule 2.515(c)(1).

ii. An attorney, party, or other person who files a pleading or paper by electronic transmission that does not contain the original signature of that attorney, party, or other person shall file that identical pleading or paper in paper form containing an original signature of that attorney, party, or other person (hereinafter called the follow-up filing) immediately thereafter. The follow-up filing is not required if the Supreme Court of Florida has entered an order directing the clerk of court to discontinue accepting the follow-up filing. FL ST J ADMIN Rule 2.515(c)(2).

iii. The placement of a "/s/" or the image of a signature by an attorney or party or affected non-party signature line on an electronically filed document shall be accepted as the signature and shall verify to the Court the filer is in possession of the originally executed document. Notwithstanding the manner in which an electronic document is signed the originally executed pleading or paper shall be maintained in the filer's possession for a minimum of one (1) year after final disposition and time for appeal of the case. The originally executed document shall be produced for filing or inspection as directed by the Court. FL ST 17 J CIR 2012-16-CIV.

7. *Forms*

a. *Process.* The forms of process, notice of lis pendens, and notice of action provided in the Florida Rules of Civil Procedure are sufficient. Variations from the forms do not void process or notices that are otherwise sufficient. FL ST RCP Rule 1.900(a).

b. *Other forms.* The other forms provided in the Florida Rules of Civil Procedure are sufficient for the matters that are covered by them. So long as the substance is expressed without prolixity, the forms may be varied to meet the facts of a particular case. FL ST RCP Rule 1.900(b).

c. *Formal matters.* Captions, except for the designation of the paper, are omitted from the forms provided in the Florida Rules of Civil Procedure. A general form of caption is the first form provided. Signatures are omitted from pleadings and motions. FL ST RCP Rule 1.900(c).

8. *Notices to persons with disabilities.* All notices of court proceedings to be held in a public facility, and all process compelling appearance at such proceedings, shall include the following statement in bold face, fourteen (14) point Times New Roman or Courier font: "If you are a person with a disability who needs any accommodation in order to participate in this proceeding, you are entitled, at no cost to you, to the provision of certain assistance. Please contact [identify applicable court personnel by name, address, and telephone number] at least seven (7) days before your scheduled court appearance, or immediately upon receiving this notification if the time before the scheduled appearance is less than seven (7) days; if you are hearing or voice impaired, call 711." FL ST J ADMIN Rule 2.540(c)(1). For further information, please see FL ST 17 J CIR 2010-49-GEN.

9. *Minimization of the filing of sensitive information*

a. *Limitations for court filings.* Unless authorized by FL ST J ADMIN Rule 2.425(b), statute, another rule of court, or the court orders otherwise, designated sensitive information filed with the court must be limited to the following format:

i. The initials of a person known to be a minor;

ii. The year of birth of a person's birth date;

iii. No portion of any: Social security number, Bank account number, Credit card account number, Charge account number, or Debit account number;

iv. The last four digits of any: Taxpayer identification number (TIN), Employee identification number, Driver's license number, Passport number, Telephone number, Financial account number, except as set forth in FL ST J ADMIN Rule 2.425(a)(3), Brokerage account number, Insurance policy account number, Loan account number, Customer account number, or Patient or health care number;

v. A truncated version of any: Email address, Computer user name, Password, or Personal identification number (PIN); and

vi. A truncated version of any other sensitive information as provided by court order. FL ST J ADMIN Rule 2.425(a).

b. *Exceptions.* FL ST J ADMIN Rule 2.425(a) does not apply to the following:

i. An account number which identifies the property alleged to be the subject of a proceeding;

ii. The record of an administrative or agency proceeding;

iii. The record in appellate or review proceedings;

iv. The birth date of a minor whenever the birth date is necessary for the court to establish or maintain subject matter jurisdiction;

v. The name of a minor in any order relating to parental responsibility, time-sharing, or child support;

vi. The name of a minor in any document or order affecting the minor's ownership of real property;

vii. The birth date of a party in a writ of attachment or notice to payor;

viii. In traffic and criminal proceedings: a pro se filing; a court filing that is related to a criminal matter or investigation and that is prepared before the filing of a criminal charge or is not filed as part of any docketed criminal case; an arrest or search warrant or any information in support thereof; a charging document and an affidavit or other documents filed in support of any charging document, including any driving records; a statement of particulars; discovery material introduced into evidence or otherwise filed with the court; and all information necessary for the proper issuance and execution of a subpoena duces tecum;

ix. Information used by the clerk for case maintenance purposes or the courts for case management purposes; and

x. Information which is relevant and material to an issue before the court. FL ST J ADMIN Rule 2.425(b).

c. *Remedies.* Upon motion by a party or interested person or sua sponte by the court, the court may order remedies, sanctions or both for a violation of FL ST J ADMIN Rule 2.425(a). Following notice and an opportunity to respond, the court may impose sanctions if such filing was not made in good faith. FL ST J ADMIN Rule 2.425(c).

d. *Motions not restricted.* FL ST J ADMIN Rule 2.425 does not restrict a party's right to move for protective order, to move to file documents under seal, or to request a determination of the confidentiality of records. FL ST J ADMIN Rule 2.425(d).

e. *Application.* FL ST J ADMIN Rule 2.425 does not affect the application of constitutional provisions, statutes, or rules of court regarding confidential information or access to public information. FL ST J ADMIN Rule 2.425(e).

F. Filing and Service Requirements

1. *Filing requirements.* All documents filed in any court shall be filed by electronic transmission in accordance with FL ST J ADMIN Rule 2.525. "Documents" means pleadings, motions, petitions, memoranda, briefs, notices, exhibits, declarations, affidavits, orders, judgments, decrees, writs, opinions, and any other paper or writing submitted to a court. FL ST J ADMIN Rule 2.520(a). All documents that are court records, as defined in FL ST J ADMIN Rule 2.430(a)(1), must be filed by electronic transmission, provided that: (1) the clerk has the ability to accept and retain such documents; (2) the clerk or the chief judge of the circuit has requested permission to accept documents filed by electronic transmission; and (3) the supreme court has entered an order granting permission to the clerk to accept documents filed by electronic transmission. FL ST J ADMIN Rule 2.525(c)(1).

a. *Definition.* "Electronic transmission of documents" means the sending of information by electronic signals to, by or from a court or clerk, which when received can be transformed and stored or transmitted on paper, microfilm, magnetic storage device, optical imaging system, CD-ROM, flash drive, other electronic data storage system, server, case maintenance system ("CM"), electronic court filing ("ECF") system, statewide or local electronic portal ("e-portal"), or other electronic record keeping system authorized by the supreme court in a format sufficient to communicate the information on the original document in a readable format. Electronic transmission of documents includes electronic mail ("e-mail") and any internet-based transmission procedure, and may include procedures allowing for documents to be signed or verified by electronic means. FL ST J ADMIN Rule 2.525(a).

b. *Application.* Any court or clerk of the court may accept the electronic transmission of documents for filing after the clerk, together with input from the chief judge of the circuit, has obtained approval of the procedures and program for doing so from the Supreme Court of Florida. FL ST J ADMIN Rule 2.525(b).

c. *Exceptions*

   i. Paper documents and other submissions may be manually submitted to the clerk or court:
      - When the clerk does not have the ability to accept and retain documents by electronic filing or has not had ECF Procedures approved by the supreme court;
      - For filing by any self-represented party or any self-represented nonparty unless specific ECF Procedures provide a means to file documents electronically. However, any self-represented nonparty that is a governmental or public agency and any other agency, partnership, corporation, or business entity acting on behalf of any governmental or public agency may file documents by electronic transmission if such entity has the capability of filing documents electronically;
      - For filing by attorneys excused from e-mail service in accordance with FL ST J ADMIN Rule 2.516(b);
      - When submitting evidentiary exhibits or filing non-documentary materials;
      - When the filing involves documents in excess of twenty-five (25) megabytes (25MB) in size. For such filings, documents may be transmitted using an electronic storage medium that the clerk has the ability to accept, which may include a CD-ROM, flash drive, or similar storage medium;
      - When filed in open court, as permitted by the court;
      - When paper filing is permitted by any approved statewide or local ECF procedures; and
      - If any court determines that justice so requires. FL ST J ADMIN Rule 2.525(d).

   ii. Any document in paper form submitted under FL ST J ADMIN Rule 2.525(d) is filed when it is received by the clerk or court and the clerk shall immediately thereafter convert any filed paper document to an electronic document. "Convert to an electronic document" means optically capturing an image of a paper document and using character recognition software to recover as much of the document's text as practicable and then indexing and storing the document in the official court file. FL ST J ADMIN Rule 2.525(c)(4).

   iii. Any storage medium submitted under FL ST J ADMIN Rule 2.525(d)(5) is filed when received by the clerk or court and the clerk shall immediately thereafter transfer the electronic documents from the storage device to the official court file. FL ST J ADMIN Rule 2.525(c)(5).

   iv. If the filer of any paper document authorized under FL ST J ADMIN Rule 2.525(d) provides a self-addressed, postage-paid envelope for return of the paper document after it is converted to electronic form by the clerk, the clerk shall place the paper document in the envelope and deposit it in the mail. Except when a paper document is required to be maintained, the clerk may recycle any filed paper document that is not to be returned to the filer. FL ST J ADMIN Rule 2.525(c)(6).

   v. The clerk may convert any paper document filed before the effective date of FL ST J ADMIN Rule 2.525 to an electronic document. Unless the clerk is required to maintain the paper document, if the paper document has been converted to an electronic document by the clerk, the paper document is no longer part of the official court file and may be removed and recycled. FL ST J ADMIN Rule 2.525(c)(7).

d. *Official court file.* For information on what constitutes the official court file, please see FL ST J ADMIN Rule 2.525(c)(2), FL ST J ADMIN Rule 2.525(c)(3).

e. *Administration.* All attorneys, parties, or other persons using this rule to file documents are required to make arrangements with the court or clerk for the payment of any charges authorized by general law or the supreme court before filing any document by electronic transmission. FL ST J ADMIN Rule 2.525(f)(2).

f. *Filing date.* The filing date for an electronically transmitted document is the date and time that such filing is acknowledged by an electronic stamp or otherwise, pursuant to any procedure set forth in any ECF Procedures approved by the supreme court, or the date the last page of such filing is received by the court or clerk. FL ST J ADMIN Rule 2.525(f)(3).

g. *Accessibility.* All documents transmitted in any electronic form under FL ST J ADMIN Rule 2.525 must comply with the accessibility requirements of FL ST J ADMIN Rule 2.526. FL ST J ADMIN Rule 2.525(g).

h. *Provisions for electronic filing in the Seventeenth Circuit.* Attorneys may electronically file pleadings and papers on existing cases in circuit civil divisions 1, 7, 9, 19, 26 and 27. The following documents may be scanned and efiled; however, the original must be filed with the Clerk: Documents ordered by the Court; and original documents required by law or rule of procedure to be filed with the Clerk. Self represented individuals shall file pleadings and papers with the Clerk. The Clerk within twenty four (24) hours of receipt of an electronic document shall either accept or reject the electronic document for filing and send electronic notice to the filer. FL ST 17 J CIR 2012-16-CIV.

i. *Technical failures.* If a document filed electronically is not received due to: an error in the transmission of the document to the Clerk or any vendor of the Clerk to provide electronic court record filing services which is unknown to an attorney or party or affected non party, or a failure to process the electronic document when received by the Clerk or rejection by the Clerk, or any other technical problems experienced by the attorney or party or affected non party, the Court may, after an evidentiary hearing and upon satisfactory proof, enter an order permitting the document to be filed nunc pro tunc to the date it was first attempted to be sent electronically. FL ST 17 J CIR 2012-16-CIV.

j. *Filing of pleadings or papers at any office of the clerk of court.* The Clerk of Courts, commencing November 3, 2008, shall accept for filing, at the central courthouse, north satellite courthouse, south satellite courthouse, and west satellite courthouse any pleading or motion or other document for filing in the court file from any attorney or party for an existing case except as otherwise set forth. FL ST 17 J CIR 2008-153-GEN. See FL ST 17 J CIR 2008-153-GEN for specific exceptions.

2. *Service requirements*

a. *Papers to be served.* At the time of personal service of process a copy of the initial pleading shall be delivered to the party upon whom service is made. The date and hour of service shall be endorsed on the original process and all copies of it by the person making the service. The party seeking to effect personal service shall furnish the person making service with the necessary copies. When the service is made by publication, copies of the initial pleadings shall be furnished to the clerk and mailed by the clerk with the notice of action to all parties whose addresses are stated in the initial pleading or sworn statement. FL ST RCP Rule 1.070(e).

b. *Issuance of summons.* Upon the commencement of the action, summons or other process authorized by law shall be issued forthwith by the clerk or judge under the clerk's or the judge's signature and the seal of the court and delivered for service without praecipe. FL ST RCP Rule 1.070(a).

i. *How directed.* Summons, subpoenas, and other process in civil actions run throughout the state. All process except subpoenas shall be directed to all and singular the sheriffs of the state. FL ST § 48.011.

ii. *Service as to numerous defendants.* If there is more than one (1) defendant, the clerk or judge shall issue as many writs of process against the several defendants as may be directed by the plaintiff or the plaintiff's attorney. FL ST RCP Rule 1.070(c).

c. *Who may serve process.* Service of process may be made by an officer authorized by law to serve process, but the court may appoint any competent person not interested in the action to serve the process. When so appointed, the person serving process shall make proof of service by affidavit promptly and in any event within the time during which the person served must respond to the process. Failure to make proof of service shall not affect the validity of the service. When any process is returned not executed or returned improperly executed for any defendant, the party causing its issuance shall be entitled to such additional process against the unserved party as is required to effect service. FL ST RCP Rule 1.070(b).

i. All process shall be served by the sheriff of the county where the person to be served is found, except initial nonenforceable civil process may be served by a special process server appointed by the sheriff as provided for in FL ST § 48.021 or by a certified process server as provided for in FL ST § 48.25 through FL ST § 48.31. FL ST § 48.021(1).

ii. The sheriff of each county may, in his or her discretion, establish an approved list of natural persons designated as special process servers. FL ST § 48.021(2)(a). For more information regarding process servers, please see FL ST § 48.021(2).

iii. A person serving process shall place, on the copy served, the date and time of service and his or her identification number and initials for all service of process. FL ST § 48.031(5).

d. *Service of process on Sunday*

i. Service or execution on Sunday of any writ, process, warrant, order, or judgment is void and the person serving or executing, or causing it to be served or executed, is liable to the party aggrieved for damages for so doing as if he or she had done it without any process, writ, warrant, order, or judgment. FL ST § 48.20.

ii. If affidavit is made by the person requesting service or execution that he or she has good reason to believe that any person liable to have any such writ, process, warrant, order, or judgment served on him or her intends to escape from this state under protection of Sunday, any officer furnished with an order authorizing service or execution by the trial court judge may serve or execute such writ, process, warrant, order, or judgment on Sunday, and it is as valid as if it had been done on any other day. FL ST § 48.20.

e. *Methods of service*

i. *Service of process generally.* Service of original process is made by delivering a copy of it to the person to be served with a copy of the complaint, petition, or other initial pleading or paper or by leaving the copies at his or her usual place of abode with any person residing therein who is fifteen (15) years of age or older and informing the person of their contents. Minors who are or have been married shall be served as provided in FL ST § 48.031. FL ST § 48.031(1)(a).

- Employers, when contacted by an individual authorized to make service of process, shall permit the authorized individual to make service on employees in a private area designated by the employer. FL ST § 48.031(1)(b).
- Substitute service may be made on the spouse of the person to be served at any place in the county, if the cause of action is not an adversary proceeding between the spouse and the person to be served, if the spouse requests such service, and if the spouse and person to be served are residing together in the same dwelling. FL ST § 48.031(2)(a).
- Substitute service may be made on an individual doing business as a sole proprietorship at his or her place of business, during regular business hours, by serving the person in charge of the business at the time of service if two (2) or more attempts to serve the owner have been made at the place of business. FL ST § 48.031(2)(b).
- If the only address for a person to be served, which is discoverable through public records, is a private mailbox, substitute service may be made by leaving a copy of the process with the person in charge of the private mailbox, but only if the process server determines that the person to be served maintains a mailbox at that location. FL ST § 48.031(6).

ii. *Service by mail.* A defendant may accept service of process by mail. FL ST RCP Rule 1.070(i). A plaintiff may notify any defendant of the commencement of the action and request that the defendant waive service of a summons. FL ST RCP Rule 1.070(i)(2).

- *Notice and request for waiver.* The notice and request shall: (1) be in writing and be addressed directly to the defendant, if an individual, or to an officer or managing or general agent of the defendant or other agent authorized by appointment or law to receive service of process; (2) be dispatched by certified mail, return receipt requested; (3) be accompanied by a copy of the complaint and shall identify the court in which it has been filed; (4) inform the defendant of the consequences of compliance and of failure to comply with the request; (5) state the date on which the request is sent; (6) allow the defendant twenty (20) days from the date on which the request is received to return the waiver, or, if the address of the defendant is outside of the United States, thirty (30) days from the date on which it is received to return the waiver; and (7) provide the defendant with an extra copy of the notice and request, including the waiver, as well as a prepaid means of compliance in writing. FL ST RCP Rule 1.070(i)(2).

- *Consequences of accepting/rejecting service by mail.* Acceptance of service of a complaint by mail does not thereby waive any objection to the venue or to the jurisdiction of the court over the person of the defendant. FL ST RCP Rule 1.070(i)(1). If a defendant fails to comply with a request for waiver within the time provided, the court shall impose the costs subsequently incurred in effecting service on the defendant unless good cause for the failure is shown. FL ST RCP Rule 1.070(i)(3). A defendant who, before being served with process, timely returns a waiver so requested is not required to respond to the complaint until sixty (60) days after the date the defendant received the request for waiver of service. For purposes of computing any time prescribed or allowed by the Florida Rules of Civil Procedure, service of process shall be deemed effected twenty (20) days before the time required to respond to the complaint. FL ST RCP Rule 1.070(i)(4). When the plaintiff files a waiver of service with the court, the action shall proceed, except as provided in FL ST RCP Rule 1.070(i)(4), as if a summons and complaint had been served at the time of filing the waiver, and no further proof of service shall be required. FL ST RCP Rule 1.070(i)(5).

iii. *Service on partnerships and limited partnerships*

- Process against a partnership shall be served on any partner and is as valid as if served on each individual partner. If a partner is not available during regular business hours to accept service on behalf of the partnership, he or she may designate an employee to accept such service. After one (1) attempt to serve a partner or designated employee has been made, process may be served on the person in charge of the partnership during regular business hours. After service on any partner, plaintiff may proceed to judgment and execution against that partner and the assets of the partnership. After service on a designated employee or other person in charge, plaintiff may proceed to judgment and execution against the partnership assets but not against the individual assets of any partner. FL ST § 48.061(1).
- Process against a domestic limited partnership may be served on any general partner or on the agent for service of process specified in its certificate of limited partnership or in its certificate as amended or restated and is as valid as if served on each individual member of the partnership. After service on a general partner or the agent, the plaintiff may proceed to judgment and execution against the limited partnership and all of the general partners individually. If a general partner cannot be found in this state and service cannot be made on an agent because of failure to maintain such an agent or because the agent cannot be found or served with the exercise of reasonable diligence, service of process may be effected by service upon the Secretary of State as agent of the limited partnership as provided for in FL ST § 48.181. Service of process may be made under FL ST § 48.071 and FL ST § 48.21 on limited partnerships. FL ST § 48.061(2).
- Process against a foreign limited partnership may be served on any general partner found in the state or on any agent for service of process specified in its application for registration and is as valid as if served on each individual member of the partnership. If a general partner cannot be found in this state and an agent for service of process has not been appointed or, if appointed, the agent's authority has been revoked or the agent cannot be

found or served with the exercise of reasonable diligence, service of process may be effected by service upon the Secretary of State as agent of the limited partnership as provided for in FL ST § 48.181, or process may be served as provided in FL ST § 48.071 and FL ST § 48.21. FL ST § 48.061(3).

iv. *Service on corporation*

- Process against any private corporation, domestic or foreign, may be served: (1) on the president or vice president, or other head of the corporation; (2) in the absence of any person described in FL ST § 48.081(1)(a), on the cashier, treasurer, secretary, or general manager; (3) in the absence of any person described in FL ST § 48.081(1)(a) or FL ST § 48.081(1)(b), on any director; or (4) in the absence of any person described in FL ST § 48.081(1)(a), FL ST § 48.081(1)(b), or FL ST § 48.081(1)(c), on any officer or business agent residing in the state. FL ST § 48.081(1).
- If a foreign corporation has none of the foregoing officers or agents in this state, service may be made on any agent transacting business for it in this state. FL ST § 48.081(2).
- As an alternative to all of the foregoing, process may be served on the agent designated by the corporation under FL ST § 48.091. However, if service cannot be made on a registered agent because of failure to comply with FL ST § 48.091, service of process shall be permitted on any employee at the corporation's principal place of business or on any employee of the registered agent. FL ST § 48.081(3)(a). If the address provided for the registered agent, officer, director, or principal place of business is a residence or private mailbox, service on the corporation may be made by serving the registered agent, officer, or director in accordance with FL ST § 48.031. FL ST § 48.081(3)(b).
- FL ST § 48.081 does not apply to service of process on insurance companies. FL ST § 48.081(4).
- When a corporation engages in substantial and not isolated activities within this state, or has a business office within the state and is actually engaged in the transaction of business therefrom, service upon any officer or business agent while on corporate business within this state may personally be made, pursuant to FL ST § 48.081, and it is not necessary in such case that the action, suit, or proceeding against the corporation shall have arisen out of any transaction or operation connected with or incidental to the business being transacted within the state. FL ST § 48.081(5).
- For information regarding service on a dissolved corporation refer to FL ST § 48.101.

v. *Personal service outside state*

- Except as otherwise provided herein, service of process on persons outside of this state shall be made in the same manner as service within this state by any officer authorized to serve process in the state where the person is served. No order of court is required. An affidavit of the officer shall be filed, stating the time, manner, and place of service. The court may consider the affidavit, or any other competent evidence, in determining whether service has been properly made. Service of process on persons outside the United States may be required to conform to the provisions of the Hague Convention on the Service Abroad of Judicial and Extrajudicial Documents in Civil or Commercial Matters. FL ST § 48.194(1).
- For further information on service of process in an in rem or quasi in rem action refer to FL ST § 48.194(2); FL ST § 48.194(3); and FL ST § 48.194(4).

vi. *Method of substituted service on nonresident*

- When authorized by law, substituted service of process on a nonresident or a person who conceals his or her whereabouts by serving a public officer designated by law shall be made by leaving a copy of the process with a fee of eight dollars and seventy-five cents ($8.75) with the public officer or in his or her office or by mailing the copies by certified mail to the public officer with the fee. The service is sufficient service on a defendant who has appointed a public officer as his or her agent for the service of process. FL ST § 48.161(1).

- Notice of service and a copy of the process shall be sent forthwith by registered or certified mail by the plaintiff or his or her attorney to the defendant, and the defendant's return receipt and the affidavit of the plaintiff or his or her attorney of compliance shall be filed on or before the return day of the process or within such time as the court allows, or the notice and copy shall be served on the defendant, if found within the state, by an officer authorized to serve legal process, or if found without the state, by a sheriff or a deputy sheriff of any county of this state or any duly constituted public officer qualified to serve like process in the state or jurisdiction where the defendant is found. The officer's return showing service shall be filed on or before the return day of the process or within such time as the court allows. The public officer shall keep a record of all process served on him or her showing the day and hour of service. FL ST § 48.161(1).
- If any person on whom service of process is authorized under FL ST § 48.161(1) dies, service may be made on his or her administrator, executor, curator, or personal representative in the same manner. FL ST § 48.161(2).
- FL ST § 48.161 does not apply to persons on whom service is authorized under FL ST § 48.151. FL ST § 48.161(3).
- The public officer may designate some other person in his or her office to accept service. FL ST § 48.161(4).

vii. *Service by publication.* Service of process by publication may be made as provided by statute. FL ST RCP Rule 1.070(d). Service of process by publication is allowable in cases listed in FL ST § 49.011 and upon the parties listed in FL ST § 49.021.

- As a condition precedent to service by publication, a statement shall be filed in the action executed by the plaintiff, the plaintiff's agent or attorney, setting forth substantially the matters hereafter required, which statement may be contained in a verified pleading, or in an affidavit or other sworn statement. FL ST § 49.031(1). After the entry of a final judgment or decree in any action no sworn statement shall ever be held defective for failure to state a required fact if the fact otherwise appears from the record in the action. FL ST § 49.031(3).
- For the sworn statement requirements for service of process by publication refer to FL ST § 49.041; FL ST § 49.051; FL ST § 49.061; and FL ST § 49.071.
- On filing the sworn statement, and otherwise complying with the foregoing requirements, the plaintiff is entitled to have issued by the clerk or judge, not later than sixty (60) days after filing the sworn statement, a notice of action which notice shall set forth: (1) the names of the known natural defendants; the names, status and description of the corporate defendants; a description of the unknown defendants who claim by, through, under or against a known party which may be described as "all parties claiming interests by, through, under or against (name of known party)" and a description of all unknown defendants which may be described as "all parties having or claiming to have any right, title or interest in the property herein described"; (2) the nature of the action or proceeding in short and simple terms (but neglect to do so is not jurisdictional); (3) the name of the court in which the action or proceeding was instituted and an abbreviated title of the case; (4) the description of real property, if any, proceeded against. FL ST § 49.08.
- For further information on service of process by publication refer to FL ST § 49.09; FL ST § 49.10; FL ST § 49.11; FL ST § 49.12; FL ST § 50.011; FL ST § 50.021; FL ST § 50.031; FL ST § 50.041; FL ST § 50.051; FL ST § 50.061; and FL ST 17 J CIR 2012-21-GEN.

viii. *Service on agents of nonresidents doing business in the state.* When any natural person or partnership not residing or having a principal place of business in this state engages in business in this state, process may be served on the person who is in charge of any business in which the defendant is engaged within this state at the time of service, including agents soliciting orders for goods, wares, merchandise or services. FL ST § 48.071.

- Any process so served is as valid as if served personally on the nonresident person or partnership engaging in business in this state in any action against the person or partnership arising out of such business. FL ST § 48.071.

- A copy of such process with a notice of service on the person in charge of such business shall be sent forthwith to the nonresident person or partnership by registered or certified mail, return receipt requested. FL ST § 48.071.
- An affidavit of compliance with FL ST § 48.071 shall be filed before the return day or within such further time as the court may allow. FL ST § 48.071.

ix. *Service on nonresident engaging in business in state.* The acceptance by any person or persons, individually or associated together as a copartnership or any other form or type of association, who are residents of any other state or country, and all foreign corporations, and any person who is a resident of the state and who subsequently becomes a nonresident of the state or conceals his or her whereabouts, of the privilege extended by law to nonresidents and others to operate, conduct, engage in, or carry on a business or business venture in the state, or to have an office or agency in the state, constitutes an appointment by the persons and foreign corporations of the Secretary of State of the state as their agent on whom all process in any action or proceeding against them, or any of them, arising out of any transaction or operation connected with or incidental to the business or business venture may be served. The acceptance of the privilege is signification of the agreement of the persons and foreign corporations that the process against them which is so served is of the same validity as if served personally on the persons or foreign corporations. FL ST § 48.181(1).

- If a foreign corporation has a resident agent or officer in the state, process shall be served on the resident agent or officer. FL ST § 48.181(2).
- Any person, firm, or corporation which sells, consigns, or leases by any means whatsoever tangible or intangible personal property, through brokers, jobbers, wholesalers, or distributors to any person, firm, or corporation in this state is conclusively presumed to be both engaged in substantial and not isolated activities within this state and operating, conducting, engaging in, or carrying on a business or business venture in this state. FL ST § 48.181(3).

x. *Other service provisions:*

- Service on alien property custodian. FL ST § 48.131.
- Service on an incompetent person. FL ST § 48.042.
- Service on minor. FL ST § 48.041.
- Service on public agencies and officers. FL ST § 48.111.
- Service on the state. FL ST § 48.121.
- Service on a state prisoner. FL ST § 48.051.
- Service on labor unions. FL ST § 48.141.
- Service on statutory agents for certain persons. FL ST § 48.151.
- Service on nonresident motor vehicle owners. FL ST § 48.171.
- Service of process in action for possession of premises. FL ST § 48.183.
- Service on nonresidents operating aircraft or watercraft in the state. FL ST § 48.19.

f. *Crossclaims.* Service of a crossclaim on a party who has appeared in the action shall be made pursuant to FL ST RCP Rule 1.080. Service of a crossclaim against a party who has not appeared in the action shall be made in the manner provided for service of summons. FL ST RCP Rule 1.170(g).

g. *Fees.* The statutory compensation for making service shall not be increased by the simultaneous delivery or mailing of the copy of the initial pleading in conformity with FL ST RCP Rule 1.070. FL ST RCP Rule 1.070(g).

G. Hearings

1. There is no hearing required or contemplated in the Florida rules governing the complaint and service of summons.

H. Forms

1. Official Complaint Forms for Florida

a. Caption. FL ST RCP Form 1.901.
b. Summons. FL ST RCP Form 1.902.
c. Crossclaim summons. FL ST RCP Form 1.903.
d. Third-party summons. FL ST RCP Form 1.904.
e. Notice of action; Constructive service; No property. FL ST RCP Form 1.919.
f. Notice of action, Constructive service; Property. FL ST RCP Form 1.920.
g. Third-party complaint. FL ST RCP Form 1.948.
h. Notice of compliance when constitutional challenge is brought. FL ST RCP Form 1.975.
i. Fall-down negligence complaint. FL ST RCP Form 1.951.
j. Civil cover sheet. FL ST RCP Form 1.997.

2. Complaint Forms for Florida

a. Complaint for damages; General form. FL-PP § 2:17.
b. Complaint; Negligent infliction of personal injury. FL-PP § 2:19.
c. Complaint; Fall-down negligence. FL-PP § 2:20.
d. Complaint; Professional negligence. FL-PP § 2:23.
e. Complaint; Breach of contract. FL-PP § 2:24.
f. Complaint; Breach of personal services contract. FL-PP § 2:25.
g. Summons; General form. FL-PRACFORM § 3:4.
h. Summons; Natural person. FL-PRACFORM § 3:5.
i. Complaint; Assault and battery. FL-PRACFORM § 4:9.
j. Complaint; Breach of contract, general form. FL-PRACFORM § 4:17.
k. Complaint; Civil rights. FL-PRACFORM § 4:23.
l. Complaint; Conversion. FL-PRACFORM § 4:30.
m. Complaint; Employment contract. FL-PRACFORM § 4:44.
n. Complaint; False imprisonment. FL-PRACFORM § 4:46.
o. Complaint; Fraud, misrepresentation. FL-PRACFORM § 4:62.
p. Complaint; Lease, by landlord. FL-PRACFORM § 4:86.
q. Complaint; Lease, by tenant. FL-PRACFORM § 4:87.
r. Complaint; Libel. FL-PRACFORM § 4:89.
s. Complaint; Life insurance policy. FL-PRACFORM § 4:90.
t. Complaint; Medical malpractice, negligence. FL-PRACFORM § 4:95.
u. Complaint; Negligence, automobile, driver. FL-PRACFORM § 4:101.
v. Complaint; Negligence, hospital. FL-PRACFORM § 4:104.

I. Checklist

(I) ❑ Matters to be considered by plaintiff
  (a) ❑ Required documents
    (1) ❑ Summons
    (2) ❑ Complaint
    (3) ❑ Civil cover sheet

(4) ❑ Return of execution process by process server

(5) ❑ Filing fees

(b) ❑ Supplemental documents

(1) ❑ Exhibits

(2) ❑ Notice of constitutional question

(c) ❑ Time for filing and serving complaint

(1) ❑ Service of the initial process and initial pleading should be made upon a defendant within one hundred twenty (120) days after the filing of the complaint with the court

(II) ❑ Matters to be considered by defendant

(a) ❑ Required documents

(1) ❑ Answer

(2) ❑ Certificate of service

(b) ❑ Supplemental documents

(1) ❑ Exhibits

(2) ❑ Notice of constitutional question

(c) ❑ Time for answer

(1) ❑ Unless a different time is prescribed in a statute of Florida, a defendant shall serve an answer within twenty (20) days after service of original process and the initial pleading on the defendant, or not later than the date fixed in a notice by publication

(2) ❑ A party served with a pleading stating a crossclaim against that party shall serve an answer to it within twenty (20) days after service on that party

(3) ❑ The plaintiff shall serve an answer to a counterclaim within twenty (20) days after service of the counterclaim

(4) ❑ A defendant who, before being served with process, timely returns a waiver so requested is not required to respond to the complaint until sixty (60) days after the date the defendant received the request for waiver of service; for purposes of computing any time prescribed or allowed by the Florida Rules of Civil Procedure, service of process shall be deemed effected twenty (20) days before the time required to respond to the complaint

(5) ❑ For timing requirements related to service on the state, service of motion impact, and responding when no responsive pleading is required, please see the Timing section of this document

Pleadings
Amended Complaint

Document Last Updated January 2013

A. Applicable Rules

1. *State rules*

a. Nonverification of papers. FL ST RCP Rule 1.030.

b. Process. FL ST RCP Rule 1.070.

c. Constitutional challenge to state statute or county or municipal charter, ordinance, or franchise; Notice by party. FL ST RCP Rule 1.071.

d. Service and filing of pleadings, orders, and documents. FL ST RCP Rule 1.080.

e. Pleadings and motions. FL ST RCP Rule 1.100; FL ST RCP Rule 1.110; FL ST RCP Rule 1.120; FL ST RCP Rule 1.130; FL ST RCP Rule 1.190; FL ST § 48.193.

f. Pretrial procedure. FL ST RCP Rule 1.200.
g. Relief from judgment, decrees or orders. FL ST RCP Rule 1.540.
h. Forms. FL ST RCP Rule 1.900.
i. Retention of court records. FL ST J ADMIN Rule 2.430.
j. Foreign attorneys. FL ST J ADMIN Rule 2.510.
k. Signature of attorneys and parties. FL ST J ADMIN Rule 2.515.
l. Paper. FL ST J ADMIN Rule 2.520.
m. Electronic filing. FL ST J ADMIN Rule 2.525.
n. Requests for accommodations by persons with disabilities. FL ST J ADMIN Rule 2.540.
o. Minimization of the filing of sensitive information. FL ST J ADMIN Rule 2.425.
p. Accessibility of information and technology. FL ST J ADMIN Rule 2.526.

2. *Local rules*
   a. Standards of professional courtesy. FL ST 17 J CIR I-94-O-1.
   b. Administrative order authorizing the filing of pleadings or papers at any office of the clerk of court. FL ST 17 J CIR 2008-153-GEN.
   c. Administrative order regarding provision of ADA accommodations. FL ST 17 J CIR 2010-49-GEN.
   d. Administrative order establishing electronic filing procedures for the civil division. FL ST 17 J CIR 2012-16-CIV.

B. Timing

1. *Amendment as a matter of course.* A party may amend a pleading once as a matter of course at any time before a responsive pleading is served or, if the pleading is one to which no responsive pleading is permitted and the action has not been placed on the trial calendar, may so amend it at any time within twenty (20) days after it is served. FL ST RCP Rule 1.190(a).
2. *Amendment by leave of court.* Otherwise a party may amend a pleading only by leave of court or by written consent of the adverse party. Leave of court shall be given freely when justice so requires. FL ST RCP Rule 1.190(a).
3. *Amendments in furtherance of justice.* At any time in furtherance of justice, upon such terms as may be just, the court may permit any process, proceeding, pleading, or record to be amended or material supplemental matter to be set forth in an amended or supplemental pleading. At every stage of the action the court must disregard any error or defect in the proceedings which does not affect the substantial rights of the parties. FL ST RCP Rule 1.190(e).
4. *Response to amended pleading.* A party shall plead in response to an amended pleading within ten (10) days after service of the amended pleading unless the court otherwise orders. FL ST RCP Rule 1.190(a).
5. *Standard of professional conduct; Scheduling*
   a. Attorneys should endeavor to provide opposing counsel, parties, witnesses, and other affected persons, sufficient notice of depositions, hearings and other proceedings, except upon agreement of course, in an emergency, or in other circumstances compelling more expedited scheduling. As a general rule, actual notice should be no less than five (5) business days for instate depositions, ten (10) business days for out-of-state depositions and four (4) business days for hearings. FL ST 17 J CIR I-94-O-1(I)(1).
   b. Attorneys should communicate with opposing counsel prior to scheduling depositions, hearings and other proceedings, in an effort to schedule them at times that are mutually convenient for all interested persons. Further, sufficient time should be reserved to permit a complete presentation by counsel for all parties. FL ST 17 J CIR I-94-O-1(I)(2).
   c. Attorneys should notify opposing counsel, the court, and others affected, of scheduling conflicts as soon as they become apparent. Further, attorneys should cooperate with one another regarding all

reasonable rescheduling requests that do not prejudice their clients or unduly delay a proceeding. FL ST 17 J CIR I-94-O-1(I)(3).

d. Attorneys should promptly notify the court or other tribunal of any resolution between the parties that renders a scheduled court appearance unnecessary or otherwise moot. FL ST 17 J CIR I-94-O-1(I)(4).

e. Attorneys should grant reasonable requests by opposing counsel for extensions of time within which to respond to pleadings, discovery, and other matters when such an extension will not prejudice their client or unduly delay a proceeding. FL ST 17 J CIR I-94-O-1(I)(5).

6. *Timing considerations when filing electronically.* The filing date of an efiled document is when the last page is received by the Clerk. The electronic filing of a document does not modify any filing deadlines as required by law, rule of procedure, or court order. FL ST 17 J CIR 2012-16-CIV.

7. *Computation of time*

a. *Generally.* Computation of time shall be governed by FL ST J ADMIN Rule 2.514. FL ST RCP Rule 1.090(a). The following rules apply in computing time periods specified in any rule of procedure, local rule, court order, or statute that does not specify a method of computing time. FL ST J ADMIN Rule 2.514(a).

i. *Period stated in days or a longer unit.* When the period is stated in days or a longer unit of time (A) exclude the day of the event that triggers the period; (B) count every day, including intermediate Saturdays, Sundays, and legal holidays; and (C) include the last day of the period, but if the last day is a Saturday, Sunday, or legal holiday, or falls within any period of time extended through an order of the chief justice under FL ST J ADMIN Rule 2.205(a)(2)(B)(iv), the period continues to run until the end of the next day that is not a Saturday, Sunday, or legal holiday and does not fall within any period of time extended through an order of the chief justice. FL ST J ADMIN Rule 2.514(a)(1).

ii. *Period stated in hours.* When the period is stated in hours (A) begin counting immediately on the occurrence of the event that triggers the period; (B) count every hour, including hours during intermediate Saturdays, Sundays, and legal holidays; and (C) if the period would end on a Saturday, Sunday, or legal holiday, or during any period of time extended through an order of the chief justice under FL ST J ADMIN Rule 2.205(a)(2)(B)(iv), the period continues to run until the same time on the next day that is not a Saturday, Sunday, or legal holiday and does not fall within any period of time extended through an order of the chief justice. FL ST J ADMIN Rule 2.514(a)(2).

iii. *Period stated in days less than seven (7) days.* When the period stated in days is less than seven (7) days, intermediate Saturdays, Sundays, and legal holidays shall be excluded in the computation. FL ST J ADMIN Rule 2.514(a)(3).

iv. *"Last day" defined.* Unless a different time is set by a statute, local rule, or court order, the last day ends (A) for electronic filing or for service by any means, at midnight; and (B) for filing by other means, when the clerk's office is scheduled to close. FL ST J ADMIN Rule 2.514(a)(4).

v. *"Next day" defined.* The "next day" is determined by continuing to count forward when the period is measured after an event and backward when measured before an event. FL ST J ADMIN Rule 2.514(a)(5).

vi. *"Legal holiday" defined.* "Legal holiday" means (A) the day set aside by FL ST § 110.117, for observing New Year's Day, Martin Luther King, Jr.'s Birthday, Memorial Day, Independence Day, Labor Day, Veterans' Day, Thanksgiving Day, the Friday after Thanksgiving Day, or Christmas Day, and (B) any day observed as a holiday by the clerk's office or as designated by the chief judge. FL ST J ADMIN Rule 2.514(a)(6).

b. *Additional time after service by mail or e-mail.* When a party may or must act within a specified time after service and service is made by mail or e-mail, five (5) days are added after the period that would otherwise expire under FL ST J ADMIN Rule 2.514(a). FL ST J ADMIN Rule 2.514(b).

c. *Enlargement.* When an act is required or allowed to be done at or within a specified time by order of court, by the Florida Rules of Civil Procedure, or by notice given thereunder, for cause shown the court at any time in its discretion (1) with or without notice, may order the period enlarged if request therefor is made before the expiration of the period originally prescribed or as extended by a previous order, or (2) upon motion made and notice after the expiration of the specified period, may permit the act to be done when failure to act was the result of excusable neglect, but it may not extend the time for making a motion for new trial, for rehearing, or to alter or amend a judgment; making a motion for relief from a judgment under FL ST RCP Rule 1.540(b); taking an appeal or filing a petition for certiorari; or making a motion for a directed verdict. FL ST RCP Rule 1.090(b).

d. *Unaffected by expiration of term.* The period of time provided for the doing of any act or the taking of any proceeding shall not be affected or limited by the continued existence or expiration of a term of court. The continued existence or expiration of a term of court in no way affects the power of a court to do any act or take any proceeding in any action which is or has been pending before it. FL ST RCP Rule 1.090(c).

C. General Requirements

1. *Amendments.* A party may amend a pleading once as a matter of course at any time before a responsive pleading is served or, if the pleading is one to which no responsive pleading is permitted and the action has not been placed on the trial calendar, may so amend it at any time within twenty (20) days after it is served. Otherwise a party may amend a pleading only by leave of court or by written consent of the adverse party. Leave of court shall be freely given when justice so requires. FL ST RCP Rule 1.190(a).

   a. *Purpose of amendments.* Amendments can relate to the correction of mistakes, the insertion of jurisdictional averments, the correction or addition of verifications, the addition or substitution or striking out of parties, and generally the rectification of all formal defects in the pleading. The court can also allow amendments setting up an omitted counterclaim or cross-claim if the defendant failed to raise the claim through oversight, inadvertence, or excusable neglect. FL-PP § 2:151.

   b. *Amendment to a pleading/Amended pleading.* A significant difference exists between an amendment to a pleading and an amended pleading. An amendment to a pleading corrects, adds to or deletes from the pleading. An amended pleading is substituted for the former pleading and the former pleading ceases to have any effect. Dee v. Southern Brewing Company, 146 Fla. 588, 1 So.2d 562 (Fla. 1941); Shannon v. McBride, 105 So.2d 16 (Fla. 2d DCA 1958); Hughes v. Home Sav. of America, F.S.B., 675 So.2d 649 (Fla. 2d DCA 1996); FL-PRACPROC § 14:2.

   c. *Relation back of amendments.* When the claim or defense asserted in the amended pleading arose out of the conduct, transaction, or occurrence set forth or attempted to be set forth in the original pleading, the amendment shall relate back to the date of the original pleading. FL ST RCP Rule 1.190(c).

2. *General rules of pleading*

   a. *Claims for relief*

      i. A pleading which sets forth a claim for relief, whether an original claim, counterclaim, crossclaim, or third-party claim, must state a cause of action and shall contain

         - A short and plain statement of the grounds upon which the court's jurisdiction depends, unless the court already has jurisdiction and the claim needs no new grounds of jurisdiction to support it (For information regarding acts subjecting persons to jurisdiction, please see FL ST § 48.193),

         - A short and plain statement of the ultimate facts showing that the pleader is entitled to relief, and

         - A demand for judgment for the relief to which the pleader deems himself or herself entitled. FL ST RCP Rule 1.110(b).

      ii. Relief in the alternative or of several different types may be demanded. Every complaint shall be considered to demand general relief. FL ST RCP Rule 1.110(b).

   b. *Verification.* Except when otherwise specifically provided by these rules or an applicable statute, every pleading or other document of a party represented by an attorney need not be verified or accompanied by an affidavit. FL ST RCP Rule 1.030. When filing an action for foreclosure of a mortgage on residential real property the complaint shall be verified. When verification of a document is required, the document filed shall include an oath, affirmation, or the following statement: "Under penalty of perjury, I declare that I have read the foregoing, and the facts alleged therein are true and correct to the best of my knowledge and belief." FL ST RCP Rule 1.110(b).

c. *Separate statements.* All averments of claim or defense shall be made in consecutively numbered paragraphs, the contents of each of which shall be limited as far as practicable to a statement of a single set of circumstances, and a paragraph may be referred to by number in all subsequent pleadings. Each claim founded upon a separate transaction or occurrence and each defense other than denials shall be stated in a separate count or defense when a separation facilitates the clear presentation of the matter set forth. FL ST RCP Rule 1.110(f).

d. *Statements adopted by reference.* Statements in a pleading may be adopted by reference in a different part of the same pleading, in another pleading, or in any motion. FL ST RCP Rule 1.130(b).

e. *Joinder of causes of action; Consistency.* A pleader may set up in the same action as many claims or causes of action or defenses in the same right as the pleader has, and claims for relief may be stated in the alternative if separate items make up the cause of action, or if two (2) or more causes of action are joined. A party may also set forth two (2) or more statements of a claim or defense alternatively, either in one (1) count or defense or in separate counts or defenses. When two (2) or more statements are made in the alternative and one (1) of them, if made independently, would be sufficient, the pleading is not made insufficient by the insufficiency of one (1) or more of the alternative statements. A party may also state as many separate claims or defenses as that party has, regardless of consistency and whether based on legal or equitable grounds or both. All pleadings shall be construed so as to do substantial justice. FL ST RCP Rule 1.110(g).

f. *Subsequent pleadings.* When the nature of an action permits pleadings subsequent to final judgment and the jurisdiction of the court over the parties has not terminated, the initial pleading subsequent to final judgment shall be designated a supplemental complaint or petition. The action shall then proceed in the same manner and time as though the supplemental complaint or petition were the initial pleading in the action, including the issuance of any needed process. FL ST RCP Rule 1.110(h) shall not apply to proceedings that may be initiated by motion under the Florida Rules of Civil Procedure. FL ST RCP Rule 1.110(h).

g. *Pleading basis for service.* When service of process is to be made under statutes authorizing service on nonresidents of Florida, it is sufficient to plead the basis for service in the language of the statute without pleading the facts supporting service. FL ST RCP Rule 1.070(h).

h. *Forms of pleadings.* Forms of action and technical forms for seeking relief and of pleas, pleadings, or motions are abolished. FL ST RCP Rule 1.110(a).

3. *Complaint; Generally*

a. *Purpose.* The purpose of a complaint is to advise the court and the defendant of the nature of a cause of action asserted by the plaintiff. FL-PP § 2:12.

b. *Sufficiency of complaint.* A complaint will be found to be insufficient if it contains only general conclusory allegations unsupported by any facts. The test to determine whether a complaint is sufficient is whether, if the factual allegations of the complaint are established, the plaintiff will be legally or equitably entitled to the claimed relief. Pizzi v. Central Bank & Trust Co., 250 So.2d 895, 896 (Fla. 1971); Bowen v. G H C Properties, Limited, 251 So.2d 359, 361 (Fla. 1st DCA 1971); FL-PP § 2:12. In determining the sufficiency of the complaint to state a cause of action, all allegations of the complaint are taken as true, and possible affirmative defenses are not considered. Strickland v. Commerce Loan Co. of Jacksonville, 158 So.2d 814 (Fla. 1st DCA 1963); FL-PP § 2:12.

i. The issues for trial in Florida must be settled by the pleadings. The issues cannot be raised by discovery. FL-PRACPROC § 7:6.

ii. Causes of action may be pleaded alternatively in the same count or in different counts and against the same or different defendants as long as the joinder of parties is proper. FL-PRACPROC § 7:6.

   iii. Each count must state a cause of action. Each independent cause of action should be pleaded in a separate count. FL-PRACPROC § 7:6.

   iv. Incorporation by reference of all allegations from one count to another is not proper. Separate counts facilitate reference to the pleading in which they appear in other pleadings, motions or papers as well as the assertion of defenses against some, but not all, causes of action. Some defenses may not apply to the initial pleading as a whole. FL-PRACPROC § 7:6.

4. *Pleading special matters*

   a. *Capacity.* It is not necessary to aver the capacity of a party to sue or be sued, the authority of a party to sue or be sued in a representative capacity, or the legal existence of an organized association of persons that is made a party, except to the extent required to show the jurisdiction of the court. The initial pleading served on behalf of a minor party shall specifically aver the age of the minor party. When a party desires to raise an issue as to the legal existence of any party, the capacity of any party to sue or be sued, or the authority of a party to sue or be sued in a representative capacity, that party shall do so by specific negative averment which shall include such supporting particulars as are peculiarly within the pleader's knowledge. FL ST RCP Rule 1.120(a).

   b. *Fraud, mistake, condition of the mind.* In all averments of fraud or mistake, the circumstances constituting fraud or mistake shall be stated with such particularity as the circumstances may permit. Malice, intent, knowledge, mental attitude, and other condition of mind of a person may be averred generally. FL ST RCP Rule 1.120(b).

   c. *Conditions precedent.* In pleading the performance or occurrence of conditions precedent, it is sufficient to aver generally that all conditions precedent have been performed or have occurred. A denial of performance or occurrence shall be made specifically and with particularity. FL ST RCP Rule 1.120(c).

   d. *Official document or act.* In pleading an official document or official act it is sufficient to aver that the document was issued or the act done in compliance with law. FL ST RCP Rule 1.120(c).

   e. *Judgment or decree.* In pleading a judgment or decree of a domestic or foreign court, a judicial or quasi-judicial tribunal, or a board or officer, it is sufficient to aver the judgment or decree without setting forth matter showing jurisdiction to render it. FL ST RCP Rule 1.120(e).

   f. *Time and place.* For the purpose of testing the sufficiency of a pleading, averments of time and place are material and shall be considered like all other averments of material matter. FL ST RCP Rule 1.120(f).

   g. *Special damage.* When items of special damage are claimed, they shall be specifically stated. FL ST RCP Rule 1.120(g).

5. *Parties*

   a. *Parties generally.* Every action may be prosecuted in the name of the real party in interest, but a personal representative, administrator, guardian, trustee of an express trust, a party with whom or in whose name a contract has been made for the benefit of another, or a party expressly authorized by statute may sue in that person's own name without joining the party for whose benefit the action is brought. All persons having an interest in the subject of the action and in obtaining the relief demanded may join as plaintiffs and any person may be made a defendant who has or claims an interest adverse to the plaintiff. Any person may at any time be made a party if that person's presence is necessary or proper to a complete determination of the cause. Persons having a united interest may be joined on the same side as plaintiffs or defendants, and anyone who refuses to join may for such reason be made a defendant. FL ST RCP Rule 1.210(a).

   b. *Minors or incompetent persons.* When a minor or incompetent person has a representative, such as a guardian or other like fiduciary, the representative may sue or defend on behalf of the minor or incompetent person. A minor or incompetent person who does not have a duly appointed representative may sue by next friend or by a guardian ad litem. The court shall appoint a guardian ad litem for a minor or incompetent person not otherwise represented in an action or shall make such other order as it deems proper for the protection of the minor or incompetent person. FL ST RCP Rule 1.210(b).

c. For survivor and substitution of parties information, please see FL ST RCP Rule 1.260.

6. *Counterclaims and crossclaims*

   a. *Compulsory counterclaims.* A pleading shall state as a counterclaim any claim which at the time of serving the pleading the pleader has against any opposing party, provided it arises out of the transaction or occurrence that is the subject matter of the opposing party's claim and does not require for its adjudication the presence of third parties over whom the court cannot acquire jurisdiction. But the pleader need not state a claim if (1) at the time the action was commenced the claim was the subject of another pending action, or (2) the opposing party brought suit upon that party's claim by attachment or other process by which the court did not acquire jurisdiction to render a personal judgment on the claim and the pleader is not stating a counterclaim under this rule. FL ST RCP Rule 1.170(a).

   b. *Permissive counterclaim.* A pleading may state as a counterclaim any claim against an opposing party not arising out of the transaction or occurrence that is the subject matter of the opposing party's claim. FL ST RCP Rule 1.170(b).

   c. *Counterclaim exceeding opposing claim.* A counterclaim may or may not diminish or defeat the recovery sought by the opposing party. It may claim relief exceeding in amount or different in kind from that sought in the pleading of the opposing party. FL ST RCP Rule 1.170(c).

   d. *Counterclaim against the State.* The Florida Rules of Civil Procedure shall not be construed to enlarge beyond the limits established by law the right to assert counterclaims or to claim credits against the state or any of its subdivisions or other governmental organizations thereof subject to suit or against a municipal corporation or against an officer, agency, or administrative board of the state. FL ST RCP Rule 1.170(d).

   e. *Counterclaim maturing or acquired after pleading.* A claim which matured or was acquired by the pleader after serving the pleading may be presented as a counterclaim by supplemental pleading with the permission of the court. FL ST RCP Rule 1.170(e).

   f. *Omitted counterclaim or crossclaim.* When a pleader fails to set up a counterclaim or crossclaim through oversight, inadvertence, or excusable neglect, or when justice requires, the pleader may set up the counterclaim or crossclaim by amendment with leave of the court. FL ST RCP Rule 1.170(f).

   g. *Crossclaim against co-party.* A pleading may state as a crossclaim any claim by one party against a co-party arising out of the transaction or occurrence that is the subject matter of either the original action or a counterclaim therein, or relating to any property that is the subject matter of the original action. The crossclaim may include a claim that the party against whom it is asserted is or may be liable to the crossclaimant for all or part of a claim asserted in the action against the crossclaimant. Service of a crossclaim on a party who has appeared in the action shall be made pursuant to FL ST RCP Rule 1.080. Service of a crossclaim against a party who has not appeared in the action shall be made in the manner provided for service of summons. FL ST RCP Rule 1.170(g).

   h. *Additional parties may be brought in.* When the presence of parties other than those to the original action is required to grant complete relief in the determination of a counterclaim or crossclaim, they shall be named in the counterclaim or crossclaim and be served with process and shall be parties to the action thereafter if jurisdiction of them can be obtained and their joinder will not deprive the court of jurisdiction of the action. FL ST RCP Rule 1.250(b) and FL ST RCP Rule 1.250(c) apply to parties brought in under FL ST RCP Rule 1.170(h). FL ST RCP Rule 1.170(h).

   i. *Separate trials; Separate judgment.* If the court orders separate trials as provided in FL ST RCP Rule 1.270(b), judgment on a counterclaim or crossclaim may be rendered when the court has jurisdiction to do so even if a claim of the opposing party has been dismissed or otherwise disposed of. FL ST RCP Rule 1.170(i).

   j. *Demand exceeding jurisdiction; Transfer of action.* If the demand of any counterclaim or crossclaim exceeds the jurisdiction of the court in which the action is pending, the action shall be transferred forthwith to the court of the same county having jurisdiction of the demand in the counterclaim or crossclaim with only such alterations in the pleadings as are essential. The court shall order the transfer of the action and the transmittal of all papers in it to the proper court if the party asserting the demand exceeding the jurisdiction deposits with the court having jurisdiction a sum sufficient to pay the clerk's service charge in the court to which the action is transferred at the time of filing the counterclaim or crossclaim. Thereupon the original papers and deposit shall be transmitted and filed with a certified copy of the order. The court to which the action is transferred shall have full power and jurisdiction over the demands of all parties. Failure to make the service charge deposit at the time the counterclaim or crossclaim is filed, or within such further time as the court may allow, shall reduce a claim for damages to an amount within the jurisdiction of the court where the action is pending and waive the claim in other cases. FL ST RCP Rule 1.170(j).

7. *Misjoinder and nonjoinder of parties*
   a. *Misjoinder.* Misjoinder of parties is not a ground for dismissal of an action. Any claim against a party may be severed and proceeded with separately. FL ST RCP Rule 1.250(a).
   b. *Dropping parties.* Parties may be dropped by an adverse party in the manner provided for voluntary dismissal in FL ST RCP Rule 1.420(a)(1) subject to the exception stated in FL ST RCP Rule 1.420. If notice of lis pendens has been filed in the action against a party so dropped, the notice of dismissal shall be recorded and cancels the notice of lis pendens without the necessity of a court order. Parties may be dropped by order of court on its own initiative or the motion of any party at any stage of the action on such terms as are just. FL ST RCP Rule 1.250(b).
   c. *Adding parties.* Parties may be added once as a matter of course within the same time that pleadings can be so amended under FL ST RCP Rule 1.190(a). If amendment by leave of court or stipulation of the parties is permitted, parties may be added in the amended pleading without further order of court. Parties may be added by order of court on its own initiative or on motion of any party at any stage of the action and on such terms as are just. FL ST RCP Rule 1.250(c).
8. *Jury demand*
   a. *Right preserved.* The right of trial by jury as declared by the Constitution or by statute shall be preserved to the parties inviolate. FL ST RCP Rule 1.430(a).
   b. *Demand.* Any party may demand a trial by jury of any issue triable of right by a jury by serving upon the other party a demand therefor in writing at any time after commencement of the action and not later than ten (10) days after the service of the last pleading directed to such issue. The demand may be indorsed upon a pleading of the party. FL ST RCP Rule 1.430(b).
   c. *Specification of issues.* In the demand a party may specify the issues that the party wishes so tried; otherwise, the party is deemed to demand trial by jury for all issues so triable. FL ST RCP Rule 1.430(c).
      i. If a party has demanded trial by jury for only some of the issues, any other party may serve a demand for trial by jury of any other or all of the issues triable by jury ten (10) days after service of the demand or such lesser time as the court may order. FL ST RCP Rule 1.430(c).
   d. *Waiver.* A party who fails to serve a demand as required by FL ST RCP Rule 1.430 waives trial by jury. FL ST RCP Rule 1.430(d).
      i. If waived, a jury trial may not be granted without the consent of the parties, but the court may allow an amendment in the proceedings to demand a trial by jury or order a trial by jury on its own motion. FL ST RCP Rule 1.430(d).
      ii. A demand for trial by jury may not be withdrawn without the consent of the parties. FL ST RCP Rule 1.430(d).
9. *Arbitration and mediation*
   a. *Referral to arbitration and mediation.* Except as hereinafter provided or as otherwise prohibited by law, the presiding judge may enter an order referring all or any part of a contested civil matter to mediation or arbitration. The parties to any contested civil matter may file a written stipulation to mediate or arbitrate any issue between them at any time. Such stipulation shall be incorporated into the order of referral. FL ST RCP Rule 1.700(a).
   b. *Arbitration*
      i. *Exclusions.* A civil action shall be ordered to arbitration or arbitration in conjunction with

mediation upon stipulation of the parties. A civil action may be ordered to arbitration or arbitration in conjunction with mediation upon motion of any party or by the court, if the judge determines the action to be of such a nature that arbitration could be of benefit to the litigants or the court. FL ST RCP Rule 1.800.

- Under no circumstances may the following categories of actions be referred to arbitration: (1) bond estreatures; (2) habeas corpus or other extraordinary writs; (3) bond validations; (4) civil or criminal contempt; (5) such other matters as may be specified by order of the chief judge in the circuit. FL ST RCP Rule 1.800.

ii. For more information regarding arbitration, please see FL ST RCP Rule 1.810; FL ST RCP Rule 1.820; FL ST RCP Rule 1.830.

c. *Mediation.* For more information regarding mediation, please see FL ST RCP Rule 1.710; FL ST RCP Rule 1.720; FL ST RCP Rule 1.730; and FL ST RCP Rule 1.750.

10. *Rules of court*

a. *Rules of civil procedure.* The Florida Rules of Civil Procedure apply to all actions of a civil nature and all special statutory proceedings in the circuit courts and county courts except those to which the Florida Probate Rules, the Florida Family Law Rules of Procedure, or the Small Claims Rules apply. FL ST RCP Rule 1.010.

i. The form, content, procedure, and time for pleading in all special statutory proceedings shall be as prescribed by the statutes governing the proceeding unless the Florida Rules of Civil Procedure specifically provide to the contrary. FL ST RCP Rule 1.010.

ii. The Florida Rules of Civil Procedure shall be construed to secure the just, speedy, and inexpensive determination of every action. FL ST RCP Rule 1.010.

b. *Rules of judicial administration.* The Florida Rules of Judicial Administration shall apply to administrative matters in all courts to which the Florida Rules of Judicial Administration are applicable by their terms. The Florida Rules of Judicial Administration shall be construed to secure the speedy and inexpensive determination of every proceeding to which they are applicable. The Florida Rules of Judicial Administration shall supersede all conflicting rules and statutes. FL ST J ADMIN Rule 2.110.

D. Documents

1. *Required documents*

a. *Amended complaint.* See the General Requirements section of this document for the content of an amended complaint. If a party files a motion to amend a pleading, the party shall attach the proposed amended pleading to the motion. FL ST RCP Rule 1.190(a). See the KeyRules Florida Circuit Court Motion for Leave to Amend document for further information.

i. *Notices to persons with disabilities.* See the Format section of this KeyRules document for further information.

b. *Certificate of service.* When any attorney certifies in substance: "I certify that a copy hereof has been furnished to (here insert name or names and addresses used for service) by (e-mail) (delivery) (mail) (fax) on .... (date) ....______________ Attorney" the certificate is taken as prima facie proof of such service in compliance with FL ST J ADMIN Rule 2.516. FL ST J ADMIN Rule 2.516(f).

2. *Supplemental documents*

a. *Exhibits.* All bonds, notes, bills of exchange, contracts, accounts, or documents upon which action may be brought or defense made, or a copy thereof or a copy of the portions thereof material to the pleadings, shall be incorporated in or attached to the pleading. No papers shall be unnecessarily annexed as exhibits. The pleadings shall contain no unnecessary recitals of deeds, documents, contracts, or other instruments. Any exhibit attached to a pleading shall be considered a part of the pleadings for all purposes. FL ST RCP Rule 1.130(a).

b. *Notice of constitutional question.* A party that files a pleading, written motion, or other paper drawing into question the constitutionality of a state statute or a county or municipal charter,

ordinance, or franchise must promptly (1) file a notice of constitutional question stating the question and identifying the paper that raises it; and (2) serve the notice and the pleading, written motion, or other paper drawing into question the constitutionality of a state statute or a county or municipal charter, ordinance, or franchise on the Attorney General or the state attorney of the judicial circuit in which the action is pending, by either certified or registered mail. Service of the notice and pleading, written motion, or other paper does not require joinder of the Attorney General or the state attorney as a party to the action. FL ST RCP Rule 1.071.

E. Format

1. *Documents; Type and size.* Documents subject to the exceptions set forth in FL ST J ADMIN Rule 2.525(d) shall be filed on recycled paper measuring eight and one half by eleven (8 1/2 by 11) inches. For purposes of FL ST J ADMIN Rule 2.520, paper is recycled if it contains a minimum content of fifty (50) percent waste paper. Xerographic reduction of legal-size (eight and one half by fourteen (8 1/2 by 14) inches) documents to letter size (eight and one half by eleven (8 1/2 by 11) inches) is prohibited. All other documents filed by electronic transmission shall be filed in a format capable of being printed in a format consistent with the provisions of FL ST J ADMIN Rule 2.250. FL ST J ADMIN Rule 2.520(b).
    a. *Exhibits.* Any exhibit or attachment filed with pleadings or papers may be filed in its original size. FL ST J ADMIN Rule 2.520(c).
    b. *Recording space.* On all papers and documents prepared and filed by the court or by any party to a proceeding which are to be recorded in the public records of any county, including but not limited to final money judgments and notices of lis pendens, a three (3) inch by three (3) inch space at the top right-hand corner on the first page and a one (1) inch by three (3) inch space at the top right-hand corner on each subsequent page shall be left blank and reserved for use by the clerk of court. FL ST J ADMIN Rule 2.520(d).
        i. *Exceptions to recording space.* Any papers or documents created by persons or entities over which the filing party has no control, including but not limited to wills, codicils, trusts, or other testamentary documents; documents prepared or executed by any public officer; documents prepared, executed, acknowledged, or proved outside of the State of Florida; or documents created by State or Federal government agencies, may be filed without the space required by FL ST J ADMIN Rule 2.520. FL ST J ADMIN Rule 2.520(e).
    c. *Noncompliance.* No clerk of court is permitted to refuse to file any document or paper because of noncompliance with the Florida Rules of Judicial Administration. However, upon request of the clerk of court, noncomplying documents must be resubmitted in accordance with the formatting rules. FL ST J ADMIN Rule 2.520(f).
2. *Caption.* Every pleading, motion, order, judgment, or other paper shall have a caption containing the name of the court, the file number, and except for in rem proceedings, including forfeiture proceedings, the name of the first party on each side with an appropriate indication of other parties, and a designation identifying the party filing it and its nature or the nature of the order, as the case may be. In any in rem proceeding, every pleading, motion, order, judgment, or other paper shall have a caption containing the name of the court, the file number, the style "In re" (followed by the name or general description of the property), and a designation of the person or entity filing it and its nature or the nature of the order, as the case may be. In an in rem forfeiture proceeding, the style shall be "In re forfeiture of" (followed by the name of the general description of the property). All papers filed in the action shall be styled in such a manner as to indicate clearly the subject matter of the paper and the party requesting or obtaining relief. FL ST RCP Rule 1.100(c)(1).
3. *Writing and written defined.* Writing or written means a document containing information, an application, or a stipulation. FL ST RCP Rule 1.080(c).
4. *Rule abbreviations*
    a. The Florida Rules of Civil Procedure and shall be abbreviated as Fla.R.Civ.P. FL ST RCP Rule 1.010.
    b. The Florida Rules of Judicial Administration shall be abbreviated as Fla. R. Jud. Admin. FL ST J ADMIN Rule 2.110.

5. *Nonverification.* Except when otherwise specifically provided by the Florida Rules of Civil Procedure or an applicable statute, every pleading or other document of a party represented by an attorney need not be verified or accompanied by an affidavit. FL ST RCP Rule 1.030; FL ST J ADMIN Rule 2.515(a).
6. *Attorney signature*
   a. *Attorney signature.* Every pleading and other document of a party represented by an attorney shall be signed by at least one (1) attorney of record in that attorney's individual name whose current record Florida Bar address, telephone number, including area code, primary e-mail address and secondary e-mail addresses, if any, and Florida Bar number shall be stated, and who shall be duly licensed to practice law in Florida or who shall have received permission to appear in the particular case as provided in FL ST J ADMIN Rule 2.510. FL ST J ADMIN Rule 2.515(a).
      i. The attorney may be required by the court to give the address of, and to vouch for the attorney's authority to represent, the party. FL ST J ADMIN Rule 2.515(a).
      ii. The signature of an attorney shall constitute a certificate by the attorney that the attorney has read the pleading or other document; that to the best of the attorney's knowledge, information, and belief there is good ground to support it; and that it is not interposed for delay. FL ST J ADMIN Rule 2.515(a).
      iii. If a pleading is not signed or is signed with intent to defeat the purpose of FL ST J ADMIN Rule 2.515, it may be stricken and the action may proceed as though the pleading or other document had not been served. FL ST J ADMIN Rule 2.515(a).
   b. *Pro se litigant signature.* A party who is not represented by an attorney shall sign any pleading or other paper and state the party's address and telephone number, including area code. FL ST J ADMIN Rule 2.515(b).
   c. *Form of signature*
      i. The signatures required on pleadings and documents by FL ST J ADMIN Rule 2.515(a) and FL ST J ADMIN Rule 2.515(b) may be:
         - Original signatures;
         - Original signatures that have been reproduced by electronic means, such as on electronically transmitted documents or photocopied documents;
         - Electronic signatures using the "/s/," "s/," or "/s" formats by or at the direction of the person signing; or
         - Any other signature format authorized by general law, so long as the clerk where the proceeding is pending has the capability of receiving and has obtained approval from the Supreme Court of Florida to accept pleadings and documents with that signature format. FL ST J ADMIN Rule 2.515(c)(1).
      ii. An attorney, party, or other person who files a pleading or paper by electronic transmission that does not contain the original signature of that attorney, party, or other person shall file that identical pleading or paper in paper form containing an original signature of that attorney, party, or other person (hereinafter called the follow-up filing) immediately thereafter. The follow-up filing is not required if the Supreme Court of Florida has entered an order directing the clerk of court to discontinue accepting the follow-up filing. FL ST J ADMIN Rule 2.515(c)(2).
      iii. The placement of a "/s/" or the image of a signature by an attorney or party or affected non-party signature line on an electronically filed document shall be accepted as the signature and shall verify to the Court the filer is in possession of the originally executed document. Notwithstanding the manner in which an electronic document is signed the originally executed pleading or paper shall be maintained in the filer's possession for a minimum of one (1) year after final disposition and time for appeal of the case. The originally executed document shall be produced for filing or inspection as directed by the Court. FL ST 17 J CIR 2012-16-CIV.
7. *Forms*
   a. *Process.* The forms of process, notice of lis pendens, and notice of action provided in the Florida

Rules of Civil Procedure are sufficient. Variations from the forms do not void process or notices that are otherwise sufficient. FL ST RCP Rule 1.900(a).

b. *Other forms.* The other forms provided in the Florida Rules of Civil Procedure are sufficient for the matters that are covered by them. So long as the substance is expressed without prolixity, the forms may be varied to meet the facts of a particular case. FL ST RCP Rule 1.900(b).

c. *Formal matters.* Captions, except for the designation of the paper, are omitted from the forms provided in the Florida Rules of Civil Procedure. A general form of caption is the first form provided. Signatures are omitted from pleadings and motions. FL ST RCP Rule 1.900(c).

8. *Notices to persons with disabilities.* All notices of court proceedings to be held in a public facility, and all process compelling appearance at such proceedings, shall include the following statement in bold face, fourteen (14) point Times New Roman or Courier font: "If you are a person with a disability who needs any accommodation in order to participate in this proceeding, you are entitled, at no cost to you, to the provision of certain assistance. Please contact [identify applicable court personnel by name, address, and telephone number] at least seven (7) days before your scheduled court appearance, or immediately upon receiving this notification if the time before the scheduled appearance is less than seven (7) days; if you are hearing or voice impaired, call 711." FL ST J ADMIN Rule 2.540(c)(1). For further information, please see FL ST 17 J CIR 2010-49-GEN.

9. *Minimization of the filing of sensitive information*

a. *Limitations for court filings.* Unless authorized by FL ST J ADMIN Rule 2.425(b), statute, another rule of court, or the court orders otherwise, designated sensitive information filed with the court must be limited to the following format:

i. The initials of a person known to be a minor;

ii. The year of birth of a person's birth date;

iii. No portion of any: Social security number, Bank account number, Credit card account number, Charge account number, or Debit account number;

iv. The last four digits of any: Taxpayer identification number (TIN), Employee identification number, Driver's license number, Passport number, Telephone number, Financial account number, except as set forth in FL ST J ADMIN Rule 2.425(a)(3), Brokerage account number, Insurance policy account number, Loan account number, Customer account number, or Patient or health care number;

v. A truncated version of any: Email address, Computer user name, Password, or Personal identification number (PIN); and

vi. A truncated version of any other sensitive information as provided by court order. FL ST J ADMIN Rule 2.425(a).

b. *Exceptions.* FL ST J ADMIN Rule 2.425(a) does not apply to the following:

i. An account number which identifies the property alleged to be the subject of a proceeding;

ii. The record of an administrative or agency proceeding;

iii. The record in appellate or review proceedings;

iv. The birth date of a minor whenever the birth date is necessary for the court to establish or maintain subject matter jurisdiction;

v. The name of a minor in any order relating to parental responsibility, time-sharing, or child support;

vi. The name of a minor in any document or order affecting the minor's ownership of real property;

vii. The birth date of a party in a writ of attachment or notice to payor;

viii. In traffic and criminal proceedings: a pro se filing; a court filing that is related to a criminal matter or investigation and that is prepared before the filing of a criminal charge or is not filed as part of any docketed criminal case; an arrest or search warrant or any information in support thereof; a charging document and an affidavit or other documents filed in support of any

charging document, including any driving records; a statement of particulars; discovery material introduced into evidence or otherwise filed with the court; and all information necessary for the proper issuance and execution of a subpoena duces tecum;

ix. Information used by the clerk for case maintenance purposes or the courts for case management purposes; and

x. Information which is relevant and material to an issue before the court. FL ST J ADMIN Rule 2.425(b).

c. *Remedies.* Upon motion by a party or interested person or sua sponte by the court, the court may order remedies, sanctions or both for a violation of FL ST J ADMIN Rule 2.425(a). Following notice and an opportunity to respond, the court may impose sanctions if such filing was not made in good faith. FL ST J ADMIN Rule 2.425(c).

d. *Motions not restricted.* FL ST J ADMIN Rule 2.425 does not restrict a party's right to move for protective order, to move to file documents under seal, or to request a determination of the confidentiality of records. FL ST J ADMIN Rule 2.425(d).

e. *Application.* FL ST J ADMIN Rule 2.425 does not affect the application of constitutional provisions, statutes, or rules of court regarding confidential information or access to public information. FL ST J ADMIN Rule 2.425(e).

F. Filing and Service Requirements

1. *Filing requirements.* All original documents must be filed with the court either before service or immediately thereafter, unless otherwise provided for by general law or other rules. If the original of any bond or other document is not placed in the court file, a certified copy must be so placed by the clerk. FL ST J ADMIN Rule 2.516(d). All documents shall be filed in conformity with the requirements of FL ST J ADMIN Rule 2.525. FL ST RCP Rule 1.080(b). All documents filed in any court shall be filed by electronic transmission in accordance with FL ST J ADMIN Rule 2.525. "Documents" means pleadings, motions, petitions, memoranda, briefs, notices, exhibits, declarations, affidavits, orders, judgments, decrees, writs, opinions, and any other paper or writing submitted to a court. FL ST J ADMIN Rule 2.520(a). All documents that are court records, as defined in FL ST J ADMIN Rule 2.430(a)(1), must be filed by electronic transmission, provided that: (1) the clerk has the ability to accept and retain such documents; (2) the clerk or the chief judge of the circuit has requested permission to accept documents filed by electronic transmission; and (3) the supreme court has entered an order granting permission to the clerk to accept documents filed by electronic transmission. FL ST J ADMIN Rule 2.525(c)(1).

a. *Definition.* "Electronic transmission of documents" means the sending of information by electronic signals to, by or from a court or clerk, which when received can be transformed and stored or transmitted on paper, microfilm, magnetic storage device, optical imaging system, CD-ROM, flash drive, other electronic data storage system, server, case maintenance system ("CM"), electronic court filing ("ECF") system, statewide or local electronic portal ("e-portal"), or other electronic record keeping system authorized by the supreme court in a format sufficient to communicate the information on the original document in a readable format. Electronic transmission of documents includes electronic mail ("e-mail") and any internet-based transmission procedure, and may include procedures allowing for documents to be signed or verified by electronic means. FL ST J ADMIN Rule 2.525(a).

i. The filing of documents with the court as required by the Florida Rules of Judicial Administration must be made by filing them with the clerk in accordance with FL ST J ADMIN Rule 2.525, except that the judge may permit documents to be filed with the judge, in which event the judge must note the filing date before him or her on the documents and transmit them to the clerk. The date of filing is that shown on the face of the document by the judge's notation or the clerk's time stamp, whichever is earlier. FL ST J ADMIN Rule 2.516(e).

b. *Application.* Any court or clerk of the court may accept the electronic transmission of documents for filing after the clerk, together with input from the chief judge of the circuit, has obtained approval of the procedures and program for doing so from the Supreme Court of Florida. FL ST J ADMIN Rule 2.525(b).

c. *Exceptions*

i. Paper documents and other submissions may be manually submitted to the clerk or court:

- When the clerk does not have the ability to accept and retain documents by electronic filing or has not had ECF Procedures approved by the supreme court;
- For filing by any self-represented party or any self-represented nonparty unless specific ECF Procedures provide a means to file documents electronically. However, any self-represented nonparty that is a governmental or public agency and any other agency, partnership, corporation, or business entity acting on behalf of any governmental or public agency may file documents by electronic transmission if such entity has the capability of filing documents electronically;
- For filing by attorneys excused from e-mail service in accordance with FL ST J ADMIN Rule 2.516(b);
- When submitting evidentiary exhibits or filing non-documentary materials;
- When the filing involves documents in excess of twenty-five (25) megabytes (25MB) in size. For such filings, documents may be transmitted using an electronic storage medium that the clerk has the ability to accept, which may include a CD-ROM, flash drive, or similar storage medium;
- When filed in open court, as permitted by the court;
- When paper filing is permitted by any approved statewide or local ECF procedures; and
- If any court determines that justice so requires. FL ST J ADMIN Rule 2.525(d).

ii. Any document in paper form submitted under FL ST J ADMIN Rule 2.525(d) is filed when it is received by the clerk or court and the clerk shall immediately thereafter convert any filed paper document to an electronic document. "Convert to an electronic document" means optically capturing an image of a paper document and using character recognition software to recover as much of the document's text as practicable and then indexing and storing the document in the official court file. FL ST J ADMIN Rule 2.525(c)(4).

iii. Any storage medium submitted under FL ST J ADMIN Rule 2.525(d)(5) is filed when received by the clerk or court and the clerk shall immediately thereafter transfer the electronic documents from the storage device to the official court file. FL ST J ADMIN Rule 2.525(c)(5).

iv. If the filer of any paper document authorized under FL ST J ADMIN Rule 2.525(d) provides a self-addressed, postage-paid envelope for return of the paper document after it is converted to electronic form by the clerk, the clerk shall place the paper document in the envelope and deposit it in the mail. Except when a paper document is required to be maintained, the clerk may recycle any filed paper document that is not to be returned to the filer. FL ST J ADMIN Rule 2.525(c)(6).

v. The clerk may convert any paper document filed before the effective date of FL ST J ADMIN Rule 2.525 to an electronic document. Unless the clerk is required to maintain the paper document, if the paper document has been converted to an electronic document by the clerk, the paper document is no longer part of the official court file and may be removed and recycled. FL ST J ADMIN Rule 2.525(c)(7).

d. *Official court file.* For information on what constitutes the official court file, please see FL ST J ADMIN Rule 2.525(c)(2), FL ST J ADMIN Rule 2.525(c)(3).

e. *Administration.* All attorneys, parties, or other persons using this rule to file documents are required to make arrangements with the court or clerk for the payment of any charges authorized by general law or the supreme court before filing any document by electronic transmission. FL ST J ADMIN Rule 2.525(f)(2).

f. *Filing date.* The filing date for an electronically transmitted document is the date and time that such filing is acknowledged by an electronic stamp or otherwise, pursuant to any procedure set forth in any ECF Procedures approved by the supreme court, or the date the last page of such filing is received by the court or clerk. FL ST J ADMIN Rule 2.525(f)(3).

g. *Accessibility.* All documents transmitted in any electronic form under FL ST J ADMIN Rule 2.525 must comply with the accessibility requirements of FL ST J ADMIN Rule 2.526. FL ST J ADMIN Rule 2.525(g).

h. *Provisions for electronic filing in the Seventeenth Circuit.* Attorneys may electronically file pleadings and papers on existing cases in circuit civil divisions 1, 7, 9, 19, 26 and 27. The following documents may be scanned and efiled; however, the original must be filed with the Clerk: Documents ordered by the Court; and original documents required by law or rule of procedure to be filed with the Clerk. Self represented individuals shall file pleadings and papers with the Clerk. The Clerk within twenty four (24) hours of receipt of an electronic document shall either accept or reject the electronic document for filing and send electronic notice to the filer. FL ST 17 J CIR 2012-16-CIV.

i. *Technical failures.* If a document filed electronically is not received due to: an error in the transmission of the document to the Clerk or any vendor of the Clerk to provide electronic court record filing services which is unknown to an attorney or party or affected non party, or a failure to process the electronic document when received by the Clerk or rejection by the Clerk, or any other technical problems experienced by the attorney or party or affected non party, the Court may, after an evidentiary hearing and upon satisfactory proof, enter an order permitting the document to be filed nunc pro tunc to the date it was first attempted to be sent electronically. FL ST 17 J CIR 2012-16-CIV.

j. *Filing of pleadings or papers at any office of the clerk of court.* The Clerk of Courts, commencing November 3, 2008, shall accept for filing, at the central courthouse, north satellite courthouse, south satellite courthouse, and west satellite courthouse any pleading or motion or other document for filing in the court file from any attorney or party for an existing case except as otherwise set forth. FL ST 17 J CIR 2008-153-GEN. See FL ST 17 J CIR 2008-153-GEN for specific exceptions.

2. *Service requirements.* Every pleading subsequent to the initial pleading, all orders, and every other document filed in the action must be served in conformity with the requirements of FL ST J ADMIN Rule 2.516. FL ST RCP Rule 1.080(a).

   a. *Service; When required.* Unless the court otherwise orders, or a statute or supreme court administrative order specifies a different means of service, every pleading subsequent to the initial pleading and every other document filed in any court proceeding, except applications for witness subpoenas and documents served by formal notice or required to be served in the manner provided for service of formal notice, must be served in accordance with FL ST J ADMIN Rule 2.516 on each party. No service need be made on parties against whom a default has been entered, except that pleadings asserting new or additional claims against them must be served in the manner provided for service of summons. FL ST J ADMIN Rule 2.516(a).

   b. *Service; How made.* When service is required or permitted to be made upon a party represented by an attorney, service must be made upon the attorney unless service upon the party is ordered by the court. FL ST J ADMIN Rule 2.516(b).

      i. *Service by electronic mail ("e-mail").* All documents required or permitted to be served on another party must be served by e-mail, unless FL ST J ADMIN Rule 2.516 otherwise provides. When, in addition to service by e-mail, the sender also utilizes another means of service provided for in FL ST J ADMIN Rule 2.516(b)(2), any differing time limits and other provisions applicable to that other means of service control. FL ST J ADMIN Rule 2.516(b)(1). Any document electronically transmitted to a court or clerk must also be served on all parties and interested persons in accordance with the applicable rules of court. FL ST J ADMIN Rule 2.525(e)(2).

         - *Service on attorneys.* Upon appearing in a proceeding, an attorney must serve a designation of a primary e-mail address and may designate no more than two (2) secondary e-mail addresses. Thereafter, service must be directed to all designated e-mail addresses in that proceeding. Every document filed by an attorney thereafter must include the primary e-mail address of that attorney and any secondary e-mail addresses. If an attorney does not designate any e-mail address for service, documents may be served on that attorney at the e-mail address on record with The Florida Bar. FL ST J ADMIN Rule 2.516(b)(1)(A).

- *Exception to e-mail service on attorneys.* Service by an attorney on another attorney must be made by e-mail unless excused by the court. Upon motion by an attorney demonstrating that the attorney has no e-mail account and lacks access to the Internet at the attorney's office, the court may excuse the attorney from the requirements of e-mail service. Service on and by an attorney excused by the court from e-mail service must be by the means provided in FL ST J ADMIN Rule 2.516(b)(2). FL ST J ADMIN Rule 2.516(b)(1)(B).
- *Service on and by parties not represented by an attorney.* Any party not represented by an attorney may serve a designation of a primary e-mail address and also may designate no more than two (2) secondary e-mail addresses to which service must be directed in that proceeding by the means provided in FL ST J ADMIN Rule 2.516(b)(1). If a party not represented by an attorney does not designate an e-mail address for service in a proceeding, service on and by that party must be by the means provided in FL ST J ADMIN Rule 2.516(b)(2). FL ST J ADMIN Rule 2.516(b)(1)(C).
- *Time of service.* Service by e-mail is complete when it is sent. FL ST J ADMIN Rule 2.516(b)(1)(D). An e-mail is deemed served on the date it is sent. FL ST J ADMIN Rule 2.516(b)(1)(D)(i). If the sender learns that the e-mail did not reach the address of the person to be served, the sender must immediately send another copy by e-mail, or by a means authorized by FL ST J ADMIN Rule 2.516(b)(2). FL ST J ADMIN Rule 2.516(b)(1)(D)(ii). E-mail service is treated as service by mail for the computation of time. FL ST J ADMIN Rule 2.516(b)(1)(D)(iii).

ii. *Format of e-mail for service.* Service of a document by e-mail is made by attaching a copy of the document in PDF format to an e-mail sent to all addresses designated by the attorney or party. FL ST J ADMIN Rule 2.516(b)(1)(E).

- All documents served by e-mail must be attached to an e-mail message containing a subject line beginning with the words "SERVICE OF COURT DOCUMENT" in all capital letters, followed by the case number of the proceeding in which the documents are being served. FL ST J ADMIN Rule 2.516(b)(1)(E)(i).
- The body of the e-mail must identify the court in which the proceeding is pending, the case number, the name of the initial party on each side, the title of each document served with that e-mail, and the sender's name and telephone number. FL ST J ADMIN Rule 2.516(b)(1)(E)(ii).
- Any document served by e-mail may be signed by the "/s/" format, as long as the filed original is signed in accordance with the applicable rule of procedure. FL ST J ADMIN Rule 2.516(b)(1)(E)(iii).
- Any e-mail which, together with its attached documents, exceeds five megabytes (5MB) in size, must be divided and sent as separate e-mails, no one of which may exceed five megabytes (5MB) in size and each of which must be sequentially numbered in the subject line. FL ST J ADMIN Rule 2.516(b)(1)(E)(iv).

iii. *Service by other means.* In addition to, and not in lieu of, service by e-mail, service may also be made upon attorneys by any of the means specified in FL ST J ADMIN Rule 2.516(b)(2). Service on and by all parties who are not represented by an attorney and who do not designate an e-mail address, and on and by all attorneys excused from e-mail service, must be made by delivering a copy of the document or by mailing it to the party or attorney at their last known address or, if no address is known, by leaving it with the clerk of the court. Service by mail is complete upon mailing. Delivery of a copy within FL ST J ADMIN Rule 2.516 is complete upon:

- Handing it to the attorney or to the party,
- Leaving it at the attorney's or party's office with a clerk or other person in charge thereof,
- If there is no one in charge, leaving it in a conspicuous place therein,
- If the office is closed or the person to be served has no office, leaving it at the person's usual place of abode with some person of his or her family above fifteen (15) years of age and informing such person of the contents, or

- Transmitting it by facsimile to the attorney's or party's office with a cover sheet containing the sender's name, firm, address, telephone number, and facsimile number, and the number of pages transmitted. When service is made by facsimile, a copy must also be served by any other method permitted by FL ST J ADMIN Rule 2.516. Facsimile service occurs when transmission is complete. FL ST J ADMIN Rule 2.516(b)(2)(A) through FL ST J ADMIN Rule 2.516(b)(2)(E).
- Service by delivery after 5:00 p.m. must be deemed to have been made by mailing on the date of delivery. FL ST J ADMIN Rule 2.516(b)(2)(F).

c. *Service; Numerous defendants.* In actions when the parties are unusually numerous, the court may regulate the service contemplated by the Florida Rules of Judicial Administration on motion or on its own initiative in such manner as may be found to be just and reasonable. FL ST J ADMIN Rule 2.516(c).

d. *Service by clerk.* Service of notices and other documents required to be made by the clerk must also be done as provided in FL ST J ADMIN Rule 2.516(b). FL ST J ADMIN Rule 2.516(g).

G. Hearings

1. The parties may be required to participate in pretrial proceedings to consider and determine the necessity or desirability of an amendment to a pleading. FL ST RCP Rule 1.200(b)(2); FL-PP § 2:151.

H. Forms

1. Official Amended Complaint Forms for Florida

a. Caption. FL ST RCP Form 1.901.

b. Notice of compliance when constitutional challenge is brought. FL ST RCP Form 1.975.

2. Amended Complaint Forms for Florida

a. Consent; Of party; To amendment of pleadings. FL-PP § 2:154.

b. Notice of amended complaint. 3 FLPRAC § 190.1.

c. Complaint for damages; General form. FL-PP § 2:17.

d. Complaint; Negligent infliction of personal injury. FL-PP § 2:19.

e. Complaint; Fall down negligence. FL-PP § 2:20.

f. Complaint; Mortgage foreclosure. FL-PP § 2:21.

g. Complaint; Implied warranty. FL-PP § 2:22.

h. Complaint; Professional negligence. FL-PP § 2:23.

i. Complaint; Breach of contract. FL-PP § 2:24.

j. Complaint; Breach of personal services contract. FL-PP § 2:25.

I. Checklist

(I) ❑ Matters to be considered by plaintiff

(a) ❑ Required documents

(1) ❑ Amended complaint

(2) ❑ Certificate of service

(b) ❑ Supplemental documents

(1) ❑ Exhibits

(2) ❑ Notice of constitutional question

(c) ❑ Timing

(1) ❑ A party may amend a pleading once as a matter of course at any time before a responsive pleading is served

(2) ❑ If the pleading is one to which no responsive pleading is permitted and the action has not

been placed on the trial calendar, may so amend it at any time within twenty (20) days after it is served

Pleadings
Answer

Document Last Updated January 2013

A. Applicable Rules

1. *State rules*
   a. Nonverification of pleadings. FL ST RCP Rule 1.030.
   b. Process. FL ST RCP Rule 1.070.
   c. Constitutional challenge to state statute or county or municipal charter, ordinance, or franchise; Notice by party. FL ST RCP Rule 1.071.
   d. Service and filing of pleadings, orders, and documents. FL ST RCP Rule 1.080.
   e. Time. FL ST RCP Rule 1.090.
   f. Pleadings and motions. FL ST RCP Rule 1.100; FL ST RCP Rule 1.110; FL ST RCP Rule 1.120; FL ST RCP Rule 1.130; FL ST RCP Rule 1.190; FL ST RCP Rule 1.430.
   g. Defenses. FL ST RCP Rule 1.140.
   h. Relief from judgment, decrees or orders. FL ST RCP Rule 1.540.
   i. Forms. FL ST RCP Rule 1.900.
   j. Retention of court records. FL ST J ADMIN Rule 2.430.
   k. Foreign attorneys. FL ST J ADMIN Rule 2.510.
   l. Signature of attorneys and parties. FL ST J ADMIN Rule 2.515.
   m. Paper. FL ST J ADMIN Rule 2.520.
   n. Electronic filing. FL ST J ADMIN Rule 2.525.
   o. Court reporting. FL ST J ADMIN Rule 2.535.
   p. Requests for accommodations by persons with disabilities. FL ST J ADMIN Rule 2.540.
   q. Waiver of sovereign immunity in tort actions; Recovery limits; Limitation on attorney fees; Statute of limitations; Exclusions; Indemnification; Risk management programs. FL ST § 768.28.
   r. Minimization of the filing of sensitive information. FL ST J ADMIN Rule 2.425.
   s. Accessibility of information and technology. FL ST J ADMIN Rule 2.526.
2. *Local rules*
   a. Standards of professional courtesy. FL ST 17 J CIR I-94-O-1.
   b. Administrative order authorizing the filing of pleadings or papers at any office of the clerk of court. FL ST 17 J CIR 2008-153-GEN.
   c. Administrative order regarding provision of ADA accommodations. FL ST 17 J CIR 2010-49-GEN.
   d. Administrative order establishing electronic filing procedures for the civil division. FL ST 17 J CIR 2012-16-CIV.

B. Timing

1. *General answer timing.* Unless a different time is prescribed in a statute of Florida, a defendant shall serve an answer within twenty (20) days after service of original process and the initial pleading on the defendant, or not later than the date fixed in a notice by publication. A party served with a pleading stating a crossclaim against that party shall serve an answer to it within twenty (20) days after service on that

party. The plaintiff shall serve an answer to a counterclaim within twenty (20) days after service of the counterclaim. FL ST RCP Rule 1.140(a)(1).

a. *Waiver of service.* A defendant who, before being served with process, timely returns a waiver so requested is not required to respond to the complaint until sixty (60) days after the date the defendant received the request for waiver of service. For purposes of computing any time prescribed or allowed by the Florida Rules of Civil Procedure, service of process shall be deemed effected twenty (20) days before the time required to respond to the complaint. FL ST RCP Rule 1.070(i)(4).

b. *Service on the state.* Except when sued pursuant to FL ST § 768.28, the state of Florida, an agency of the state, or an officer or employee of the state sued in an official capacity shall serve an answer to the complaint or crossclaim, or a reply to a counterclaim, within forty (40) days after service. When sued pursuant to FL ST § 768.28, the Department of Financial Services or the defendant state agency shall have thirty (30) days from the date of service within which to serve an answer to the complaint or crossclaim or a reply to a counterclaim. FL ST RCP Rule 1.140(a)(2).

c. *Service of motion impact on time periods for service of answer.* The service of a motion under FL ST RCP Rule 1.140, except a motion for judgment on the pleadings or a motion to strike under FL ST RCP Rule 1.140(f), alters these periods of time so that if the court denies the motion or postpones its disposition until the trial on the merits, the responsive pleadings shall be served within ten (10) days after notice of the court's action or, if the court grants a motion for a more definite statement, the responsive pleadings shall be served within ten (10) days after service of the more definite statement unless a different time is fixed by the court in either case. FL ST RCP Rule 1.140(a)(3).

d. *Responding if pleading does not require a responsive pleading.* If a pleading sets forth a claim for relief to which the adverse party is not required to serve a responsive pleading, the adverse party may assert any defense in law or fact to that claim for relief at the trial, except that the objection of failure to state a legal defense in an answer or reply shall be asserted by motion to strike the defense within twenty (20) days after service of the answer or reply. FL ST RCP Rule 1.140(b).

2. *Standard of professional conduct; Scheduling*

a. Attorneys should endeavor to provide opposing counsel, parties, witnesses, and other affected persons, sufficient notice of depositions, hearings and other proceedings, except upon agreement of course, in an emergency, or in other circumstances compelling more expedited scheduling. As a general rule, actual notice should be no less than five (5) business days for instate depositions, ten (10) business days for out-of-state depositions and four (4) business days for hearings. FL ST 17 J CIR I-94-O-1(I)(1).

b. Attorneys should communicate with opposing counsel prior to scheduling depositions, hearings and other proceedings, in an effort to schedule them at times that are mutually convenient for all interested persons. Further, sufficient time should be reserved to permit a complete presentation by counsel for all parties. FL ST 17 J CIR I-94-O-1(I)(2).

c. Attorneys should notify opposing counsel, the court, and others affected, of scheduling conflicts as soon as they become apparent. Further, attorneys should cooperate with one another regarding all reasonable rescheduling requests that do not prejudice their clients or unduly delay a proceeding. FL ST 17 J CIR I-94-O-1(I)(3).

d. Attorneys should promptly notify the court or other tribunal of any resolution between the parties that renders a scheduled court appearance unnecessary or otherwise moot. FL ST 17 J CIR I-94-O-1(I)(4).

e. Attorneys should grant reasonable requests by opposing counsel for extensions of time within which to respond to pleadings, discovery, and other matters when such an extension will not prejudice their client or unduly delay a proceeding. FL ST 17 J CIR I-94-O-1(I)(5).

3. *Timing considerations when filing electronically.* The filing date of an efiled document is when the last page is received by the Clerk. The electronic filing of a document does not modify any filing deadlines as required by law, rule of procedure, or court order. FL ST 17 J CIR 2012-16-CIV.

4. *Computation of time*

a. *Generally.* Computation of time shall be governed by FL ST J ADMIN Rule 2.514. FL ST RCP Rule

1.090(a). The following rules apply in computing time periods specified in any rule of procedure, local rule, court order, or statute that does not specify a method of computing time. FL ST J ADMIN Rule 2.514(a).

i. *Period stated in days or a longer unit.* When the period is stated in days or a longer unit of time (A) exclude the day of the event that triggers the period; (B) count every day, including intermediate Saturdays, Sundays, and legal holidays; and (C) include the last day of the period, but if the last day is a Saturday, Sunday, or legal holiday, or falls within any period of time extended through an order of the chief justice under FL ST J ADMIN Rule 2.205(a)(2)(B)(iv), the period continues to run until the end of the next day that is not a Saturday, Sunday, or legal holiday and does not fall within any period of time extended through an order of the chief justice. FL ST J ADMIN Rule 2.514(a)(1).

ii. *Period stated in hours.* When the period is stated in hours (A) begin counting immediately on the occurrence of the event that triggers the period; (B) count every hour, including hours during intermediate Saturdays, Sundays, and legal holidays; and (C) if the period would end on a Saturday, Sunday, or legal holiday, or during any period of time extended through an order of the chief justice under FL ST J ADMIN Rule 2.205(a)(2)(B)(iv), the period continues to run until the same time on the next day that is not a Saturday, Sunday, or legal holiday and does not fall within any period of time extended through an order of the chief justice. FL ST J ADMIN Rule 2.514(a)(2).

iii. *Period stated in days less than seven (7) days.* When the period stated in days is less than seven (7) days, intermediate Saturdays, Sundays, and legal holidays shall be excluded in the computation. FL ST J ADMIN Rule 2.514(a)(3).

iv. *"Last day" defined.* Unless a different time is set by a statute, local rule, or court order, the last day ends (A) for electronic filing or for service by any means, at midnight; and (B) for filing by other means, when the clerk's office is scheduled to close. FL ST J ADMIN Rule 2.514(a)(4).

v. *"Next day" defined.* The "next day" is determined by continuing to count forward when the period is measured after an event and backward when measured before an event. FL ST J ADMIN Rule 2.514(a)(5).

vi. *"Legal holiday" defined.* "Legal holiday" means (A) the day set aside by FL ST § 110.117, for observing New Year's Day, Martin Luther King, Jr.'s Birthday, Memorial Day, Independence Day, Labor Day, Veterans' Day, Thanksgiving Day, the Friday after Thanksgiving Day, or Christmas Day, and (B) any day observed as a holiday by the clerk's office or as designated by the chief judge. FL ST J ADMIN Rule 2.514(a)(6).

b. *Additional time after service by mail or e-mail.* When a party may or must act within a specified time after service and service is made by mail or e-mail, five (5) days are added after the period that would otherwise expire under FL ST J ADMIN Rule 2.514(a). FL ST J ADMIN Rule 2.514(b).

c. *Enlargement.* When an act is required or allowed to be done at or within a specified time by order of court, by the Florida Rules of Civil Procedure, or by notice given thereunder, for cause shown the court at any time in its discretion (1) with or without notice, may order the period enlarged if request therefor is made before the expiration of the period originally prescribed or as extended by a previous order, or (2) upon motion made and notice after the expiration of the specified period, may permit the act to be done when failure to act was the result of excusable neglect, but it may not extend the time for making a motion for new trial, for rehearing, or to alter or amend a judgment; making a motion for relief from a judgment under FL ST RCP Rule 1.540(b); taking an appeal or filing a petition for certiorari; or making a motion for a directed verdict. FL ST RCP Rule 1.090(b).

d. *Unaffected by expiration of term.* The period of time provided for the doing of any act or the taking of any proceeding shall not be affected or limited by the continued existence or expiration of a term of court. The continued existence or expiration of a term of court in no way affects the power of a court to do any act or take any proceeding in any action which is or has been pending before it. FL ST RCP Rule 1.090(c).

C. General Requirements

1. *General rules of pleading*

   a. *Claims for relief*

      i. A pleading which sets forth a claim for relief, whether an original claim, counterclaim, crossclaim, or third-party claim, must state a cause of action and shall contain

         - A short and plain statement of the grounds upon which the court's jurisdiction depends, unless the court already has jurisdiction and the claim needs no new grounds of jurisdiction to support it (For information regarding acts subjecting persons to jurisdiction, please see FL ST § 48.193),
         - A short and plain statement of the ultimate facts showing that the pleader is entitled to relief, and
         - A demand for judgment for the relief to which the pleader deems himself or herself entitled. FL ST RCP Rule 1.110(b).

      ii. Relief in the alternative or of several different types may be demanded. Every complaint shall be considered to demand general relief. FL ST RCP Rule 1.110(b).

   b. *Verification.* Except when otherwise specifically provided by these rules or an applicable statute, every pleading or other document of a party represented by an attorney need not be verified or accompanied by an affidavit. FL ST RCP Rule 1.030. When filing an action for foreclosure of a mortgage on residential real property the complaint shall be verified. When verification of a document is required, the document filed shall include an oath, affirmation, or the following statement: "Under penalty of perjury, I declare that I have read the foregoing, and the facts alleged therein are true and correct to the best of my knowledge and belief." FL ST RCP Rule 1.110(b).

   c. *Separate statements.* All averments of claim or defense shall be made in consecutively numbered paragraphs, the contents of each of which shall be limited as far as practicable to a statement of a single set of circumstances, and a paragraph may be referred to by number in all subsequent pleadings. Each claim founded upon a separate transaction or occurrence and each defense other than denials shall be stated in a separate count or defense when a separation facilitates the clear presentation of the matter set forth. FL ST RCP Rule 1.110(f).

   d. *Statements adopted by reference.* Statements in a pleading may be adopted by reference in a different part of the same pleading, in another pleading, or in any motion. FL ST RCP Rule 1.130(b).

   e. *Joinder of causes of action; Consistency.* A pleader may set up in the same action as many claims or causes of action or defenses in the same right as the pleader has, and claims for relief may be stated in the alternative if separate items make up the cause of action, or if two (2) or more causes of action are joined. A party may also set forth two (2) or more statements of a claim or defense alternatively, either in one (1) count or defense or in separate counts or defenses. When two (2) or more statements are made in the alternative and one (1) of them, if made independently, would be sufficient, the pleading is not made insufficient by the insufficiency of one (1) or more of the alternative statements. A party may also state as many separate claims or defenses as that party has, regardless of consistency and whether based on legal or equitable grounds or both. All pleadings shall be construed so as to do substantial justice. FL ST RCP Rule 1.110(g).

   f. *Subsequent pleadings.* When the nature of an action permits pleadings subsequent to final judgment and the jurisdiction of the court over the parties has not terminated, the initial pleading subsequent to final judgment shall be designated a supplemental complaint or petition. The action shall then proceed in the same manner and time as though the supplemental complaint or petition were the initial pleading in the action, including the issuance of any needed process. FL ST RCP Rule 1.110(h) shall not apply to proceedings that may be initiated by motion under the Florida Rules of Civil Procedure. FL ST RCP Rule 1.110(h).

   g. *Pleading basis for service.* When service of process is to be made under statutes authorizing service on nonresidents of Florida, it is sufficient to plead the basis for service in the language of the statute without pleading the facts supporting service. FL ST RCP Rule 1.070(h).

h. *Forms of pleadings.* Forms of action and technical forms for seeking relief and of pleas, pleadings, or motions are abolished. FL ST RCP Rule 1.110(a).

2. *Answer; Generally.* An answer has three (3) functions. First, it must respond to each allegation of the preceding pleading by admitting, denying or alleging that the pleader is without knowledge of the allegation. Second, it must contain any affirmative defenses that the pleader is interposing to any cause of action alleged in the preceding pleading. Third, the answer may claim affirmative relief against the plaintiff or petitioner by a counterclaim or against a codefendant by a crossclaim. FL-PRACPROC § 11:1.

a. *Content.* In the answer a pleader shall state in short and plain terms the pleader's defenses to each claim asserted and shall admit or deny the averments on which the adverse party relies. If the defendant is without knowledge, the defendant shall so state and such statement shall operate as a denial. Denial shall fairly meet the substance of the averments denied. When a pleader intends in good faith to deny only a part of an averment, the pleader shall specify so much of it as is true and shall deny the remainder. Unless the pleader intends in good faith to controvert all of the averments of the preceding pleading, the pleader may make denials as specific denials of designated averments or may generally deny all of the averments except such designated averments as the pleader expressly admits, but when the pleader does so intend to controvert all of its averments, including averments of the grounds upon which the court's jurisdiction depends, the pleader may do so by general denial. FL ST RCP Rule 1.110(c).

b. *Form of answer.* An answer contains a caption, commencement, body, signature and certificate of service. The caption is the same as that of the initial pleading, except for the designation as one of the types of answer. The body of an answer should contain an admission, denial or plea of without knowledge to each allegation of the preceding pleading, except for the additional allegations in response to a general allegation of conditions precedent and the denial of capacity to sue. FL-PRACPROC § 11:3.

i. *Responding sequentially.* The best method of responding is to answer each paragraph sequentially, combining admissions, denials or pleas of without knowledge when the sequence permits. The admissions, denials and allegations of without knowledge should be stated first, followed separately by any affirmative defenses and then by any counterclaim or crossclaim. A third party complaint may be a part of the same paper, but it is not a part of the answer as is a counterclaim or crossclaim. Paragraphs are numbered consecutively throughout the pleading whether in the answer, counterclaim or crossclaim. Denials for the record only are improper. FL-PRACPROC § 11:3.

c. *Defenses*

i. *Generally.* Every defense in law or fact to a claim for relief in a pleading shall be asserted in the responsive pleading, if one is required, but the following defenses may be made by motion at the option of the pleader: (1) lack of jurisdiction over the subject matter, (2) lack of jurisdiction over the person, (3) improper venue, (4) insufficiency of process, (5) insufficiency of service of process, (6) failure to state a cause of action, and (7) failure to join indispensable parties. A motion making any of these defenses shall be made before pleading if a further pleading is permitted. FL ST RCP Rule 1.140(b).

- *Stated specifically.* The grounds on which any of the enumerated defenses are based and the substantial matters of law intended to be argued shall be stated specifically and with particularity in the responsive pleading or motion. FL ST RCP Rule 1.140(b).
- *Waiver.* Any ground not stated shall be deemed to be waived except any ground showing that the court lacks jurisdiction of the subject matter may be made at any time. No defense or objection is waived by being joined with other defenses or objections in a responsive pleading or motion. FL ST RCP Rule 1.140(b). A party waives all defenses and objections that the party does not present either by motion under FL ST RCP Rule 1.140(b), FL ST RCP Rule 1.140(e), or FL ST RCP Rule 1.140(f) or, if the party has made no motion, in a responsive pleading except as provided in FL ST RCP Rule 1.140(h)(2). FL ST RCP Rule 1.140(h)(1). The defenses of failure to state a cause of action or a legal defense or to join an indispensable party may be raised by motion for judgment on the pleadings or at the

trial on the merits in addition to being raised either in a motion under FL ST RCP Rule 1.140(b) or in the answer or reply. The defense of lack of jurisdiction of the subject matter may be raised at any time. FL ST RCP Rule 1.140(h)(2).

ii. *Affirmative defenses.* In pleading to a preceding pleading a party shall set forth affirmatively accord and satisfaction, arbitration and award, assumption of risk, contributory negligence, discharge in bankruptcy, duress, estoppel, failure of consideration, fraud, illegality, injury by fellow servant, laches, license, payment, release, res judicata, statute of frauds, statute of limitations, waiver, and any other matter constituting an avoidance or affirmative defense. When a party has mistakenly designated a defense as a counterclaim or a counterclaim as a defense, the court, on terms if justice so requires, shall treat the pleading as if there had been a proper designation. Affirmative defenses appearing on the face of a prior pleading may be asserted as grounds for a motion or defense under FL ST RCP Rule 1.140(b); provided this shall not limit amendments under FL ST RCP Rule 1.190 even if such ground is sustained. FL ST RCP Rule 1.110(d).

- *Format of defenses.* Affirmative defenses should be placed after the admissions, denials and allegations of without knowledge in the answer. All paragraphs must be numbered consecutively throughout the answer. If a defense is directed to only a part of a cause of action or to one or more, but not all, of several causes of action in the preceding pleading, the part or cause of action to which it is directed should be identified in the defense. Defenses should be identified by consecutive ordinal numbers such as "First Defense" and "Second Defense." FL-PRACPROC § 11:4.

iii. *Effect of failure to deny.* Averments in a pleading to which a responsive pleading is required, other than those as to the amount of damages, are admitted when not denied in the responsive pleading. Averments in a pleading to which no responsive pleading is required or permitted shall be taken as denied or avoided. FL ST RCP Rule 1.110(e). An admission in an answer binds the party and no proof is required. An admission does not extend beyond the scope of the allegation in the preceding pleading. FL-PRACPROC § 11:3.

3. *Pleading special matters*

a. *Capacity.* It is not necessary to aver the capacity of a party to sue or be sued, the authority of a party to sue or be sued in a representative capacity, or the legal existence of an organized association of persons that is made a party, except to the extent required to show the jurisdiction of the court. The initial pleading served on behalf of a minor party shall specifically aver the age of the minor party. When a party desires to raise an issue as to the legal existence of any party, the capacity of any party to sue or be sued, or the authority of a party to sue or be sued in a representative capacity, that party shall do so by specific negative averment which shall include such supporting particulars as are peculiarly within the pleader's knowledge. FL ST RCP Rule 1.120(a).

b. *Fraud, mistake, condition of the mind.* In all averments of fraud or mistake, the circumstances constituting fraud or mistake shall be stated with such particularity as the circumstances may permit. Malice, intent, knowledge, mental attitude, and other condition of mind of a person may be averred generally. FL ST RCP Rule 1.120(b).

c. *Conditions precedent.* In pleading the performance or occurrence of conditions precedent, it is sufficient to aver generally that all conditions precedent have been performed or have occurred. A denial of performance or occurrence shall be made specifically and with particularity. FL ST RCP Rule 1.120(c).

d. *Official document or act.* In pleading an official document or official act it is sufficient to aver that the document was issued or the act done in compliance with law. FL ST RCP Rule 1.120(c).

e. *Judgment or decree.* In pleading a judgment or decree of a domestic or foreign court, a judicial or quasi-judicial tribunal, or a board or officer, it is sufficient to aver the judgment or decree without setting forth matter showing jurisdiction to render it. FL ST RCP Rule 1.120(e).

f. *Time and place.* For the purpose of testing the sufficiency of a pleading, averments of time and place are material and shall be considered like all other averments of material matter. FL ST RCP Rule 1.120(f).

g. *Special damage.* When items of special damage are claimed, they shall be specifically stated. FL ST RCP Rule 1.120(g).

4. *Parties*

a. *Parties generally.* Every action may be prosecuted in the name of the real party in interest, but a personal representative, administrator, guardian, trustee of an express trust, a party with whom or in whose name a contract has been made for the benefit of another, or a party expressly authorized by statute may sue in that person's own name without joining the party for whose benefit the action is brought. All persons having an interest in the subject of the action and in obtaining the relief demanded may join as plaintiffs and any person may be made a defendant who has or claims an interest adverse to the plaintiff. Any person may at any time be made a party if that person's presence is necessary or proper to a complete determination of the cause. Persons having a united interest may be joined on the same side as plaintiffs or defendants, and anyone who refuses to join may for such reason be made a defendant. FL ST RCP Rule 1.210(a).

b. *Minors or incompetent persons.* When a minor or incompetent person has a representative, such as a guardian or other like fiduciary, the representative may sue or defend on behalf of the minor or incompetent person. A minor or incompetent person who does not have a duly appointed representative may sue by next friend or by a guardian ad litem. The court shall appoint a guardian ad litem for a minor or incompetent person not otherwise represented in an action or shall make such other order as it deems proper for the protection of the minor or incompetent person. FL ST RCP Rule 1.210(b).

c. For survivor and substitution of parties information, please see FL ST RCP Rule 1.260.

5. *Counterclaims and crossclaims*

a. *Compulsory counterclaims.* A pleading shall state as a counterclaim any claim which at the time of serving the pleading the pleader has against any opposing party, provided it arises out of the transaction or occurrence that is the subject matter of the opposing party's claim and does not require for its adjudication the presence of third parties over whom the court cannot acquire jurisdiction. But the pleader need not state a claim if (1) at the time the action was commenced the claim was the subject of another pending action, or (2) the opposing party brought suit upon that party's claim by attachment or other process by which the court did not acquire jurisdiction to render a personal judgment on the claim and the pleader is not stating a counterclaim under this rule. FL ST RCP Rule 1.170(a).

b. *Permissive counterclaim.* A pleading may state as a counterclaim any claim against an opposing party not arising out of the transaction or occurrence that is the subject matter of the opposing party's claim. FL ST RCP Rule 1.170(b).

c. *Counterclaim exceeding opposing claim.* A counterclaim may or may not diminish or defeat the recovery sought by the opposing party. It may claim relief exceeding in amount or different in kind from that sought in the pleading of the opposing party. FL ST RCP Rule 1.170(c).

d. *Counterclaim against the State.* The Florida Rules of Civil Procedure shall not be construed to enlarge beyond the limits established by law the right to assert counterclaims or to claim credits against the state or any of its subdivisions or other governmental organizations thereof subject to suit or against a municipal corporation or against an officer, agency, or administrative board of the state. FL ST RCP Rule 1.170(d).

e. *Counterclaim maturing or acquired after pleading.* A claim which matured or was acquired by the pleader after serving the pleading may be presented as a counterclaim by supplemental pleading with the permission of the court. FL ST RCP Rule 1.170(e).

f. *Omitted counterclaim or crossclaim.* When a pleader fails to set up a counterclaim or crossclaim through oversight, inadvertence, or excusable neglect, or when justice requires, the pleader may set up the counterclaim or crossclaim by amendment with leave of the court. FL ST RCP Rule 1.170(f).

g. *Crossclaim against co-party.* A pleading may state as a crossclaim any claim by one party against a co-party arising out of the transaction or occurrence that is the subject matter of either the original action or a counterclaim therein, or relating to any property that is the subject matter of the original action. The crossclaim may include a claim that the party against whom it is asserted is or may be liable to the crossclaimant for all or part of a claim asserted in the action against the crossclaimant. Service of a crossclaim on a party who has appeared in the action shall be made pursuant to FL ST RCP Rule 1.080. Service of a crossclaim against a party who has not appeared in the action shall be made in the manner provided for service of summons. FL ST RCP Rule 1.170(g).

h. *Additional parties may be brought in.* When the presence of parties other than those to the original action is required to grant complete relief in the determination of a counterclaim or crossclaim, they shall be named in the counterclaim or crossclaim and be served with process and shall be parties to the action thereafter if jurisdiction of them can be obtained and their joinder will not deprive the court of jurisdiction of the action. FL ST RCP Rule 1.250(b) and FL ST RCP Rule 1.250(c) apply to parties brought in under FL ST RCP Rule 1.170(h). FL ST RCP Rule 1.170(h).

i. *Separate trials; Separate judgment.* If the court orders separate trials as provided in FL ST RCP Rule 1.270(b), judgment on a counterclaim or crossclaim may be rendered when the court has jurisdiction to do so even if a claim of the opposing party has been dismissed or otherwise disposed of. FL ST RCP Rule 1.170(i).

j. *Demand exceeding jurisdiction; Transfer of action.* If the demand of any counterclaim or crossclaim exceeds the jurisdiction of the court in which the action is pending, the action shall be transferred forthwith to the court of the same county having jurisdiction of the demand in the counterclaim or crossclaim with only such alterations in the pleadings as are essential. The court shall order the transfer of the action and the transmittal of all papers in it to the proper court if the party asserting the demand exceeding the jurisdiction deposits with the court having jurisdiction a sum sufficient to pay the clerk's service charge in the court to which the action is transferred at the time of filing the counterclaim or crossclaim. Thereupon the original papers and deposit shall be transmitted and filed with a certified copy of the order. The court to which the action is transferred shall have full power and jurisdiction over the demands of all parties. Failure to make the service charge deposit at the time the counterclaim or crossclaim is filed, or within such further time as the court may allow, shall reduce a claim for damages to an amount within the jurisdiction of the court where the action is pending and waive the claim in other cases. FL ST RCP Rule 1.170(j).

6. *Misjoinder and nonjoinder of parties*

   a. *Misjoinder.* Misjoinder of parties is not a ground for dismissal of an action. Any claim against a party may be severed and proceeded with separately. FL ST RCP Rule 1.250(a).

   b. *Dropping parties.* Parties may be dropped by an adverse party in the manner provided for voluntary dismissal in FL ST RCP Rule 1.420(a)(1) subject to the exception stated in FL ST RCP Rule 1.420. If notice of lis pendens has been filed in the action against a party so dropped, the notice of dismissal shall be recorded and cancels the notice of lis pendens without the necessity of a court order. Parties may be dropped by order of court on its own initiative or the motion of any party at any stage of the action on such terms as are just. FL ST RCP Rule 1.250(b).

   c. *Adding parties.* Parties may be added once as a matter of course within the same time that pleadings can be so amended under FL ST RCP Rule 1.190(a). If amendment by leave of court or stipulation of the parties is permitted, parties may be added in the amended pleading without further order of court. Parties may be added by order of court on its own initiative or on motion of any party at any stage of the action and on such terms as are just. FL ST RCP Rule 1.250(c).

7. *Jury demand*

   a. *Right preserved.* The right of trial by jury as declared by the Constitution or by statute shall be preserved to the parties inviolate. FL ST RCP Rule 1.430(a).

   b. *Demand.* Any party may demand a trial by jury of any issue triable of right by a jury by serving upon the other party a demand therefor in writing at any time after commencement of the action and not later than ten (10) days after the service of the last pleading directed to such issue. The demand may be indorsed upon a pleading of the party. FL ST RCP Rule 1.430(b).

   c. *Specification of issues.* In the demand a party may specify the issues that the party wishes so tried;

otherwise, the party is deemed to demand trial by jury for all issues so triable. FL ST RCP Rule 1.430(c).

i. If a party has demanded trial by jury for only some of the issues, any other party may serve a demand for trial by jury of any other or all of the issues triable by jury ten (10) days after service of the demand or such lesser time as the court may order. FL ST RCP Rule 1.430(c).

d. *Waiver.* A party who fails to serve a demand as required by FL ST RCP Rule 1.430 waives trial by jury. FL ST RCP Rule 1.430(d).

i. If waived, a jury trial may not be granted without the consent of the parties, but the court may allow an amendment in the proceedings to demand a trial by jury or order a trial by jury on its own motion. FL ST RCP Rule 1.430(d).

ii. A demand for trial by jury may not be withdrawn without the consent of the parties. FL ST RCP Rule 1.430(d).

8. *Arbitration and mediation*

a. *Referral to arbitration and mediation.* Except as hereinafter provided or as otherwise prohibited by law, the presiding judge may enter an order referring all or any part of a contested civil matter to mediation or arbitration. The parties to any contested civil matter may file a written stipulation to mediate or arbitrate any issue between them at any time. Such stipulation shall be incorporated into the order of referral. FL ST RCP Rule 1.700(a).

b. *Arbitration*

i. *Exclusions.* A civil action shall be ordered to arbitration or arbitration in conjunction with mediation upon stipulation of the parties. A civil action may be ordered to arbitration or arbitration in conjunction with mediation upon motion of any party or by the court, if the judge determines the action to be of such a nature that arbitration could be of benefit to the litigants or the court. FL ST RCP Rule 1.800.

- Under no circumstances may the following categories of actions be referred to arbitration: (1) bond estreatures; (2) habeas corpus or other extraordinary writs; (3) bond validations; (4) civil or criminal contempt; (5) such other matters as may be specified by order of the chief judge in the circuit. FL ST RCP Rule 1.800.

ii. For more information regarding arbitration, please see FL ST RCP Rule 1.810; FL ST RCP Rule 1.820; FL ST RCP Rule 1.830.

c. *Mediation.* For more information regarding mediation, please see FL ST RCP Rule 1.710; FL ST RCP Rule 1.720; FL ST RCP Rule 1.730; and FL ST RCP Rule 1.750.

9. *Rules of court*

a. *Rules of civil procedure.* The Florida Rules of Civil Procedure apply to all actions of a civil nature and all special statutory proceedings in the circuit courts and county courts except those to which the Florida Probate Rules, the Florida Family Law Rules of Procedure, or the Small Claims Rules apply. FL ST RCP Rule 1.010.

i. The form, content, procedure, and time for pleading in all special statutory proceedings shall be as prescribed by the statutes governing the proceeding unless the Florida Rules of Civil Procedure specifically provide to the contrary. FL ST RCP Rule 1.010.

ii. The Florida Rules of Civil Procedure shall be construed to secure the just, speedy, and inexpensive determination of every action. FL ST RCP Rule 1.010.

b. *Rules of judicial administration.* The Florida Rules of Judicial Administration shall apply to administrative matters in all courts to which the Florida Rules of Judicial Administration are applicable by their terms. The Florida Rules of Judicial Administration shall be construed to secure the speedy and inexpensive determination of every proceeding to which they are applicable. The Florida Rules of Judicial Administration shall supersede all conflicting rules and statutes. FL ST J ADMIN Rule 2.110.

D. Documents

1. *Required documents*

   a. *Answer.* See the General Requirements section of this document for further information about the content of an answer.

      i. *Notices to persons with disabilities.* See the Format section of this KeyRules document for further information.

   b. *Certificate of service.* When any attorney certifies in substance: "I certify that a copy hereof has been furnished to (here insert name or names and addresses used for service) by (e-mail) (delivery) (mail) (fax) on .... (date) ...._________________ Attorney" the certificate is taken as prima facie proof of such service in compliance with FL ST J ADMIN Rule 2.516. FL ST J ADMIN Rule 2.516(f).

2. *Supplemental documents*

   a. *Exhibits.* All bonds, notes, bills of exchange, contracts, accounts, or documents upon which action may be brought or defense made, or a copy thereof or a copy of the portions thereof material to the pleadings, shall be incorporated in or attached to the pleading. No papers shall be unnecessarily annexed as exhibits. The pleadings shall contain no unnecessary recitals of deeds, documents, contracts, or other instruments. Any exhibit attached to a pleading shall be considered a part of the pleadings for all purposes. FL ST RCP Rule 1.130(a).

   b. *Notice of constitutional question.* A party that files a pleading, written motion, or other paper drawing into question the constitutionality of a state statute or a county or municipal charter, ordinance, or franchise must promptly (1) file a notice of constitutional question stating the question and identifying the paper that raises it; and (2) serve the notice and the pleading, written motion, or other paper drawing into question the constitutionality of a state statute or a county or municipal charter, ordinance, or franchise on the Attorney General or the state attorney of the judicial circuit in which the action is pending, by either certified or registered mail. Service of the notice and pleading, written motion, or other paper does not require joinder of the Attorney General or the state attorney as a party to the action. FL ST RCP Rule 1.071.

E. Format

1. *Documents; Type and size.* Documents subject to the exceptions set forth in FL ST J ADMIN Rule 2.525(d) shall be filed on recycled paper measuring eight and one half by eleven (8 1/2 by 11) inches. For purposes of FL ST J ADMIN Rule 2.520, paper is recycled if it contains a minimum content of fifty (50) percent waste paper. Xerographic reduction of legal-size (eight and one half by fourteen (8 1/2 by 14) inches) documents to letter size (eight and one half by eleven (8 1/2 by 11) inches) is prohibited. All other documents filed by electronic transmission shall be filed in a format capable of being printed in a format consistent with the provisions of FL ST J ADMIN Rule 2.250. FL ST J ADMIN Rule 2.520(b).

   a. *Exhibits.* Any exhibit or attachment filed with pleadings or papers may be filed in its original size. FL ST J ADMIN Rule 2.520(c).

   b. *Recording space.* On all papers and documents prepared and filed by the court or by any party to a proceeding which are to be recorded in the public records of any county, including but not limited to final money judgments and notices of lis pendens, a three (3) inch by three (3) inch space at the top right-hand corner on the first page and a one (1) inch by three (3) inch space at the top right-hand corner on each subsequent page shall be left blank and reserved for use by the clerk of court. FL ST J ADMIN Rule 2.520(d).

      i. *Exceptions to recording space.* Any papers or documents created by persons or entities over which the filing party has no control, including but not limited to wills, codicils, trusts, or other testamentary documents; documents prepared or executed by any public officer; documents prepared, executed, acknowledged, or proved outside of the State of Florida; or documents created by State or Federal government agencies, may be filed without the space required by FL ST J ADMIN Rule 2.520. FL ST J ADMIN Rule 2.520(e).

   c. *Noncompliance.* No clerk of court is permitted to refuse to file any document or paper because of noncompliance with the Florida Rules of Judicial Administration. However, upon request of the

clerk of court, noncomplying documents must be resubmitted in accordance with the formatting rules. FL ST J ADMIN Rule 2.520(f).

2. *Caption.* Every pleading, motion, order, judgment, or other paper shall have a caption containing the name of the court, the file number, and except for in rem proceedings, including forfeiture proceedings, the name of the first party on each side with an appropriate indication of other parties, and a designation identifying the party filing it and its nature or the nature of the order, as the case may be. In any in rem proceeding, every pleading, motion, order, judgment, or other paper shall have a caption containing the name of the court, the file number, the style "In re" (followed by the name or general description of the property), and a designation of the person or entity filing it and its nature or the nature of the order, as the case may be. In an in rem forfeiture proceeding, the style shall be "In re forfeiture of" (followed by the name of the general description of the property). All papers filed in the action shall be styled in such a manner as to indicate clearly the subject matter of the paper and the party requesting or obtaining relief. FL ST RCP Rule 1.100(c)(1).
3. *Writing and written defined.* Writing or written means a document containing information, an application, or a stipulation. FL ST RCP Rule 1.080(c).
4. *Rule abbreviations*
   a. The Florida Rules of Civil Procedure and shall be abbreviated as Fla.R.Civ.P. FL ST RCP Rule 1.010.
   b. The Florida Rules of Judicial Administration shall be abbreviated as Fla. R. Jud. Admin. FL ST J ADMIN Rule 2.110.
5. *Nonverification.* Except when otherwise specifically provided by the Florida Rules of Civil Procedure or an applicable statute, every pleading or other document of a party represented by an attorney need not be verified or accompanied by an affidavit. FL ST RCP Rule 1.030; FL ST J ADMIN Rule 2.515(a).
6. *Attorney signature*
   a. *Attorney signature.* Every pleading and other document of a party represented by an attorney shall be signed by at least one (1) attorney of record in that attorney's individual name whose current record Florida Bar address, telephone number, including area code, primary e-mail address and secondary e-mail addresses, if any, and Florida Bar number shall be stated, and who shall be duly licensed to practice law in Florida or who shall have received permission to appear in the particular case as provided in FL ST J ADMIN Rule 2.510. FL ST J ADMIN Rule 2.515(a).
      i. The attorney may be required by the court to give the address of, and to vouch for the attorney's authority to represent, the party. FL ST J ADMIN Rule 2.515(a).
      ii. The signature of an attorney shall constitute a certificate by the attorney that the attorney has read the pleading or other document; that to the best of the attorney's knowledge, information, and belief there is good ground to support it; and that it is not interposed for delay. FL ST J ADMIN Rule 2.515(a).
      iii. If a pleading is not signed or is signed with intent to defeat the purpose of FL ST J ADMIN Rule 2.515, it may be stricken and the action may proceed as though the pleading or other document had not been served. FL ST J ADMIN Rule 2.515(a).
   b. *Pro se litigant signature.* A party who is not represented by an attorney shall sign any pleading or other paper and state the party's address and telephone number, including area code. FL ST J ADMIN Rule 2.515(b).
   c. *Form of signature*
      i. The signatures required on pleadings and documents by FL ST J ADMIN Rule 2.515(a) and FL ST J ADMIN Rule 2.515(b) may be:
         - Original signatures;
         - Original signatures that have been reproduced by electronic means, such as on electronically transmitted documents or photocopied documents;
         - Electronic signatures using the "/s/," "s/," or "/s" formats by or at the direction of the person signing; or

- Any other signature format authorized by general law, so long as the clerk where the proceeding is pending has the capability of receiving and has obtained approval from the Supreme Court of Florida to accept pleadings and documents with that signature format. FL ST J ADMIN Rule 2.515(c)(1).

ii. An attorney, party, or other person who files a pleading or paper by electronic transmission that does not contain the original signature of that attorney, party, or other person shall file that identical pleading or paper in paper form containing an original signature of that attorney, party, or other person (hereinafter called the follow-up filing) immediately thereafter. The follow-up filing is not required if the Supreme Court of Florida has entered an order directing the clerk of court to discontinue accepting the follow-up filing. FL ST J ADMIN Rule 2.515(c)(2).

iii. The placement of a "/s/" or the image of a signature by an attorney or party or affected non-party signature line on an electronically filed document shall be accepted as the signature and shall verify to the Court the filer is in possession of the originally executed document. Notwithstanding the manner in which an electronic document is signed the originally executed pleading or paper shall be maintained in the filer's possession for a minimum of one (1) year after final disposition and time for appeal of the case. The originally executed document shall be produced for filing or inspection as directed by the Court. FL ST 17 J CIR 2012-16-CIV.

7. *Forms*

a. *Process.* The forms of process, notice of lis pendens, and notice of action provided in the Florida Rules of Civil Procedure are sufficient. Variations from the forms do not void process or notices that are otherwise sufficient. FL ST RCP Rule 1.900(a).

b. *Other forms.* The other forms provided in the Florida Rules of Civil Procedure are sufficient for the matters that are covered by them. So long as the substance is expressed without prolixity, the forms may be varied to meet the facts of a particular case. FL ST RCP Rule 1.900(b).

c. *Formal matters.* Captions, except for the designation of the paper, are omitted from the forms provided in the Florida Rules of Civil Procedure. A general form of caption is the first form provided. Signatures are omitted from pleadings and motions. FL ST RCP Rule 1.900(c).

8. *Notices to persons with disabilities.* All notices of court proceedings to be held in a public facility, and all process compelling appearance at such proceedings, shall include the following statement in bold face, fourteen (14) point Times New Roman or Courier font: "If you are a person with a disability who needs any accommodation in order to participate in this proceeding, you are entitled, at no cost to you, to the provision of certain assistance. Please contact [identify applicable court personnel by name, address, and telephone number] at least seven (7) days before your scheduled court appearance, or immediately upon receiving this notification if the time before the scheduled appearance is less than seven (7) days; if you are hearing or voice impaired, call 711." FL ST J ADMIN Rule 2.540(c)(1). For further information, please see FL ST 17 J CIR 2010-49-GEN.

9. *Minimization of the filing of sensitive information*

a. *Limitations for court filings.* Unless authorized by FL ST J ADMIN Rule 2.425(b), statute, another rule of court, or the court orders otherwise, designated sensitive information filed with the court must be limited to the following format:

i. The initials of a person known to be a minor;

ii. The year of birth of a person's birth date;

iii. No portion of any: Social security number, Bank account number, Credit card account number, Charge account number, or Debit account number;

iv. The last four digits of any: Taxpayer identification number (TIN), Employee identification number, Driver's license number, Passport number, Telephone number, Financial account number, except as set forth in FL ST J ADMIN Rule 2.425(a)(3), Brokerage account number, Insurance policy account number, Loan account number, Customer account number, or Patient or health care number;

v. A truncated version of any: Email address, Computer user name, Password, or Personal identification number (PIN); and

vi. A truncated version of any other sensitive information as provided by court order. FL ST J ADMIN Rule 2.425(a).

b. *Exceptions.* FL ST J ADMIN Rule 2.425(a) does not apply to the following:

i. An account number which identifies the property alleged to be the subject of a proceeding;

ii. The record of an administrative or agency proceeding;

iii. The record in appellate or review proceedings;

iv. The birth date of a minor whenever the birth date is necessary for the court to establish or maintain subject matter jurisdiction;

v. The name of a minor in any order relating to parental responsibility, time-sharing, or child support;

vi. The name of a minor in any document or order affecting the minor's ownership of real property;

vii. The birth date of a party in a writ of attachment or notice to payor;

viii. In traffic and criminal proceedings: a pro se filing; a court filing that is related to a criminal matter or investigation and that is prepared before the filing of a criminal charge or is not filed as part of any docketed criminal case; an arrest or search warrant or any information in support thereof; a charging document and an affidavit or other documents filed in support of any charging document, including any driving records; a statement of particulars; discovery material introduced into evidence or otherwise filed with the court; and all information necessary for the proper issuance and execution of a subpoena duces tecum;

ix. Information used by the clerk for case maintenance purposes or the courts for case management purposes; and

x. Information which is relevant and material to an issue before the court. FL ST J ADMIN Rule 2.425(b).

c. *Remedies.* Upon motion by a party or interested person or sua sponte by the court, the court may order remedies, sanctions or both for a violation of FL ST J ADMIN Rule 2.425(a). Following notice and an opportunity to respond, the court may impose sanctions if such filing was not made in good faith. FL ST J ADMIN Rule 2.425(c).

d. *Motions not restricted.* FL ST J ADMIN Rule 2.425 does not restrict a party's right to move for protective order, to move to file documents under seal, or to request a determination of the confidentiality of records. FL ST J ADMIN Rule 2.425(d).

e. *Application.* FL ST J ADMIN Rule 2.425 does not affect the application of constitutional provisions, statutes, or rules of court regarding confidential information or access to public information. FL ST J ADMIN Rule 2.425(e).

F. Filing and Service Requirements

1. *Filing requirements.* All original documents must be filed with the court either before service or immediately thereafter, unless otherwise provided for by general law or other rules. If the original of any bond or other document is not placed in the court file, a certified copy must be so placed by the clerk. FL ST J ADMIN Rule 2.516(d). All documents shall be filed in conformity with the requirements of FL ST J ADMIN Rule 2.525. FL ST RCP Rule 1.080(b). All documents filed in any court shall be filed by electronic transmission in accordance with FL ST J ADMIN Rule 2.525. "Documents" means pleadings, motions, petitions, memoranda, briefs, notices, exhibits, declarations, affidavits, orders, judgments, decrees, writs, opinions, and any other paper or writing submitted to a court. FL ST J ADMIN Rule 2.520(a). All documents that are court records, as defined in FL ST J ADMIN Rule 2.430(a)(1), must be filed by electronic transmission, provided that: (1) the clerk has the ability to accept and retain such documents; (2) the clerk or the chief judge of the circuit has requested permission to accept documents filed by electronic transmission; and (3) the supreme court has entered an order granting permission to the clerk to accept documents filed by electronic transmission. FL ST J ADMIN Rule 2.525(c)(1).

a. *Definition.* "Electronic transmission of documents" means the sending of information by electronic signals to, by or from a court or clerk, which when received can be transformed and stored or

transmitted on paper, microfilm, magnetic storage device, optical imaging system, CD-ROM, flash drive, other electronic data storage system, server, case maintenance system ("CM"), electronic court filing ("ECF") system, statewide or local electronic portal ("e-portal"), or other electronic record keeping system authorized by the supreme court in a format sufficient to communicate the information on the original document in a readable format. Electronic transmission of documents includes electronic mail ("e-mail") and any internet-based transmission procedure, and may include procedures allowing for documents to be signed or verified by electronic means. FL ST J ADMIN Rule 2.525(a).

i. The filing of documents with the court as required by the Florida Rules of Judicial Administration must be made by filing them with the clerk in accordance with FL ST J ADMIN Rule 2.525, except that the judge may permit documents to be filed with the judge, in which event the judge must note the filing date before him or her on the documents and transmit them to the clerk. The date of filing is that shown on the face of the document by the judge's notation or the clerk's time stamp, whichever is earlier. FL ST J ADMIN Rule 2.516(e).

b. *Application.* Any court or clerk of the court may accept the electronic transmission of documents for filing after the clerk, together with input from the chief judge of the circuit, has obtained approval of the procedures and program for doing so from the Supreme Court of Florida. FL ST J ADMIN Rule 2.525(b).

c. *Exceptions*

i. Paper documents and other submissions may be manually submitted to the clerk or court:

- When the clerk does not have the ability to accept and retain documents by electronic filing or has not had ECF Procedures approved by the supreme court;
- For filing by any self-represented party or any self-represented nonparty unless specific ECF Procedures provide a means to file documents electronically. However, any self-represented nonparty that is a governmental or public agency and any other agency, partnership, corporation, or business entity acting on behalf of any governmental or public agency may file documents by electronic transmission if such entity has the capability of filing documents electronically;
- For filing by attorneys excused from e-mail service in accordance with FL ST J ADMIN Rule 2.516(b);
- When submitting evidentiary exhibits or filing non-documentary materials;
- When the filing involves documents in excess of twenty-five (25) megabytes (25MB) in size. For such filings, documents may be transmitted using an electronic storage medium that the clerk has the ability to accept, which may include a CD-ROM, flash drive, or similar storage medium;
- When filed in open court, as permitted by the court;
- When paper filing is permitted by any approved statewide or local ECF procedures; and
- If any court determines that justice so requires. FL ST J ADMIN Rule 2.525(d).

ii. Any document in paper form submitted under FL ST J ADMIN Rule 2.525(d) is filed when it is received by the clerk or court and the clerk shall immediately thereafter convert any filed paper document to an electronic document. "Convert to an electronic document" means optically capturing an image of a paper document and using character recognition software to recover as much of the document's text as practicable and then indexing and storing the document in the official court file. FL ST J ADMIN Rule 2.525(c)(4).

iii. Any storage medium submitted under FL ST J ADMIN Rule 2.525(d)(5) is filed when received by the clerk or court and the clerk shall immediately thereafter transfer the electronic documents from the storage device to the official court file. FL ST J ADMIN Rule 2.525(c)(5).

iv. If the filer of any paper document authorized under FL ST J ADMIN Rule 2.525(d) provides a self-addressed, postage-paid envelope for return of the paper document after it is converted to electronic form by the clerk, the clerk shall place the paper document in the envelope and

deposit it in the mail. Except when a paper document is required to be maintained, the clerk may recycle any filed paper document that is not to be returned to the filer. FL ST J ADMIN Rule 2.525(c)(6).

v. The clerk may convert any paper document filed before the effective date of FL ST J ADMIN Rule 2.525 to an electronic document. Unless the clerk is required to maintain the paper document, if the paper document has been converted to an electronic document by the clerk, the paper document is no longer part of the official court file and may be removed and recycled. FL ST J ADMIN Rule 2.525(c)(7).

d. *Official court file.* For information on what constitutes the official court file, please see FL ST J ADMIN Rule 2.525(c)(2), FL ST J ADMIN Rule 2.525(c)(3).

e. *Administration.* All attorneys, parties, or other persons using this rule to file documents are required to make arrangements with the court or clerk for the payment of any charges authorized by general law or the supreme court before filing any document by electronic transmission. FL ST J ADMIN Rule 2.525(f)(2).

f. *Filing date.* The filing date for an electronically transmitted document is the date and time that such filing is acknowledged by an electronic stamp or otherwise, pursuant to any procedure set forth in any ECF Procedures approved by the supreme court, or the date the last page of such filing is received by the court or clerk. FL ST J ADMIN Rule 2.525(f)(3).

g. *Accessibility.* All documents transmitted in any electronic form under FL ST J ADMIN Rule 2.525 must comply with the accessibility requirements of FL ST J ADMIN Rule 2.526. FL ST J ADMIN Rule 2.525(g).

h. *Provisions for electronic filing in the Seventeenth Circuit.* Attorneys may electronically file pleadings and papers on existing cases in circuit civil divisions 1, 7, 9, 19, 26 and 27. The following documents may be scanned and efiled; however, the original must be filed with the Clerk: Documents ordered by the Court; and original documents required by law or rule of procedure to be filed with the Clerk. Self represented individuals shall file pleadings and papers with the Clerk. The Clerk within twenty four (24) hours of receipt of an electronic document shall either accept or reject the electronic document for filing and send electronic notice to the filer. FL ST 17 J CIR 2012-16-CIV.

i. *Technical failures.* If a document filed electronically is not received due to: an error in the transmission of the document to the Clerk or any vendor of the Clerk to provide electronic court record filing services which is unknown to an attorney or party or affected non party, or a failure to process the electronic document when received by the Clerk or rejection by the Clerk, or any other technical problems experienced by the attorney or party or affected non party, the Court may, after an evidentiary hearing and upon satisfactory proof, enter an order permitting the document to be filed nunc pro tunc to the date it was first attempted to be sent electronically. FL ST 17 J CIR 2012-16-CIV.

j. *Filing of pleadings or papers at any office of the clerk of court.* The Clerk of Courts, commencing November 3, 2008, shall accept for filing, at the central courthouse, north satellite courthouse, south satellite courthouse, and west satellite courthouse any pleading or motion or other document for filing in the court file from any attorney or party for an existing case except as otherwise set forth. FL ST 17 J CIR 2008-153-GEN. See FL ST 17 J CIR 2008-153-GEN for specific exceptions.

2. *Service requirements.* Every pleading subsequent to the initial pleading, all orders, and every other document filed in the action must be served in conformity with the requirements of FL ST J ADMIN Rule 2.516. FL ST RCP Rule 1.080(a).

a. *Service; When required.* Unless the court otherwise orders, or a statute or supreme court administrative order specifies a different means of service, every pleading subsequent to the initial pleading and every other document filed in any court proceeding, except applications for witness subpoenas and documents served by formal notice or required to be served in the manner provided for service of formal notice, must be served in accordance with FL ST J ADMIN Rule 2.516 on each party. No service need be made on parties against whom a default has been entered, except that pleadings asserting new or additional claims against them must be served in the manner provided for service of summons. FL ST J ADMIN Rule 2.516(a).

b. *Service; How made.* When service is required or permitted to be made upon a party represented by an attorney, service must be made upon the attorney unless service upon the party is ordered by the court. FL ST J ADMIN Rule 2.516(b).

   i. *Service by electronic mail ("e-mail").* All documents required or permitted to be served on another party must be served by e-mail, unless FL ST J ADMIN Rule 2.516 otherwise provides. When, in addition to service by e-mail, the sender also utilizes another means of service provided for in FL ST J ADMIN Rule 2.516(b)(2), any differing time limits and other provisions applicable to that other means of service control. FL ST J ADMIN Rule 2.516(b)(1). Any document electronically transmitted to a court or clerk must also be served on all parties and interested persons in accordance with the applicable rules of court. FL ST J ADMIN Rule 2.525(e)(2).

      - *Service on attorneys.* Upon appearing in a proceeding, an attorney must serve a designation of a primary e-mail address and may designate no more than two (2) secondary e-mail addresses. Thereafter, service must be directed to all designated e-mail addresses in that proceeding. Every document filed by an attorney thereafter must include the primary e-mail address of that attorney and any secondary e-mail addresses. If an attorney does not designate any e-mail address for service, documents may be served on that attorney at the e-mail address on record with The Florida Bar. FL ST J ADMIN Rule 2.516(b)(1)(A).

      - *Exception to e-mail service on attorneys.* Service by an attorney on another attorney must be made by e-mail unless excused by the court. Upon motion by an attorney demonstrating that the attorney has no e-mail account and lacks access to the Internet at the attorney's office, the court may excuse the attorney from the requirements of e-mail service. Service on and by an attorney excused by the court from e-mail service must be by the means provided in FL ST J ADMIN Rule 2.516(b)(2). FL ST J ADMIN Rule 2.516(b)(1)(B).

      - *Service on and by parties not represented by an attorney.* Any party not represented by an attorney may serve a designation of a primary e-mail address and also may designate no more than two (2) secondary e-mail addresses to which service must be directed in that proceeding by the means provided in FL ST J ADMIN Rule 2.516(b)(1). If a party not represented by an attorney does not designate an e-mail address for service in a proceeding, service on and by that party must be by the means provided in FL ST J ADMIN Rule 2.516(b)(2). FL ST J ADMIN Rule 2.516(b)(1)(C).

      - *Time of service.* Service by e-mail is complete when it is sent. FL ST J ADMIN Rule 2.516(b)(1)(D). An e-mail is deemed served on the date it is sent. FL ST J ADMIN Rule 2.516(b)(1)(D)(i). If the sender learns that the e-mail did not reach the address of the person to be served, the sender must immediately send another copy by e-mail, or by a means authorized by FL ST J ADMIN Rule 2.516(b)(2). FL ST J ADMIN Rule 2.516(b)(1)(D)(ii). E-mail service is treated as service by mail for the computation of time. FL ST J ADMIN Rule 2.516(b)(1)(D)(iii).

   ii. *Format of e-mail for service.* Service of a document by e-mail is made by attaching a copy of the document in PDF format to an e-mail sent to all addresses designated by the attorney or party. FL ST J ADMIN Rule 2.516(b)(1)(E).

      - All documents served by e-mail must be attached to an e-mail message containing a subject line beginning with the words "SERVICE OF COURT DOCUMENT" in all capital letters, followed by the case number of the proceeding in which the documents are being served. FL ST J ADMIN Rule 2.516(b)(1)(E)(i).

      - The body of the e-mail must identify the court in which the proceeding is pending, the case number, the name of the initial party on each side, the title of each document served with that e-mail, and the sender's name and telephone number. FL ST J ADMIN Rule 2.516(b)(1)(E)(ii).

      - Any document served by e-mail may be signed by the "/s/" format, as long as the filed original is signed in accordance with the applicable rule of procedure. FL ST J ADMIN Rule 2.516(b)(1)(E)(iii).

- Any e-mail which, together with its attached documents, exceeds five megabytes (5MB) in size, must be divided and sent as separate e-mails, no one of which may exceed five megabytes (5MB) in size and each of which must be sequentially numbered in the subject line. FL ST J ADMIN Rule 2.516(b)(1)(E)(iv).

iii. *Service by other means.* In addition to, and not in lieu of, service by e-mail, service may also be made upon attorneys by any of the means specified in FL ST J ADMIN Rule 2.516(b)(2). Service on and by all parties who are not represented by an attorney and who do not designate an e-mail address, and on and by all attorneys excused from e-mail service, must be made by delivering a copy of the document or by mailing it to the party or attorney at their last known address or, if no address is known, by leaving it with the clerk of the court. Service by mail is complete upon mailing. Delivery of a copy within FL ST J ADMIN Rule 2.516 is complete upon:

- Handing it to the attorney or to the party,
- Leaving it at the attorney's or party's office with a clerk or other person in charge thereof,
- If there is no one in charge, leaving it in a conspicuous place therein,
- If the office is closed or the person to be served has no office, leaving it at the person's usual place of abode with some person of his or her family above fifteen (15) years of age and informing such person of the contents, or
- Transmitting it by facsimile to the attorney's or party's office with a cover sheet containing the sender's name, firm, address, telephone number, and facsimile number, and the number of pages transmitted. When service is made by facsimile, a copy must also be served by any other method permitted by FL ST J ADMIN Rule 2.516. Facsimile service occurs when transmission is complete. FL ST J ADMIN Rule 2.516(b)(2)(A) through FL ST J ADMIN Rule 2.516(b)(2)(E).
- Service by delivery after 5:00 p.m. must be deemed to have been made by mailing on the date of delivery. FL ST J ADMIN Rule 2.516(b)(2)(F).

c. *Service; Numerous defendants.* In actions when the parties are unusually numerous, the court may regulate the service contemplated by the Florida Rules of Judicial Administration on motion or on its own initiative in such manner as may be found to be just and reasonable. FL ST J ADMIN Rule 2.516(c).

d. *Service by clerk.* Service of notices and other documents required to be made by the clerk must also be done as provided in FL ST J ADMIN Rule 2.516(b). FL ST J ADMIN Rule 2.516(g).

G. Hearings

1. *Preliminary hearings.* The defenses in FL ST RCP Rule 1.140(b)(1) through FL ST RCP Rule 1.140(b)(7), whether made in a pleading or by motion, and the motion for judgment in FL ST RCP Rule 1.140(c) shall be heard and determined before trial on application of any party unless the court orders that the hearing and determination shall be deferred until the trial. FL ST RCP Rule 1.140(d).

2. *Communication equipment*

a. *Definition.* Communication equipment means a conference telephone or other electronic device that permits all those appearing or participating to hear and speak to each other, provided that all conversation of all parties is audible to all persons present. FL ST J ADMIN Rule 2.530(a).

b. *Use by all parties.* A county or circuit court judge may, upon the court's own motion or upon the written request of a party, direct that communication equipment be used for a motion hearing, pretrial conference, or a status conference. A judge must give notice to the parties and consider any objections they may have to the use of communication equipment before directing that communication equipment be used. The decision to use communication equipment over the objection of parties will be in the sound discretion of the trial court, except as noted below. FL ST J ADMIN Rule 2.530(b).

c. *Use only by requesting party.* A county or circuit court judge may, upon the written request of a party upon reasonable notice to all other parties, permit a requesting party to participate through communication equipment in a scheduled motion hearing; however, any such request (except in criminal, juvenile, and appellate proceedings) must be granted, absent a showing of good cause to deny the same, where the hearing is set for not longer than fifteen (15) minutes. FL ST J ADMIN Rule 2.530(c).

d. *Testimony*

   i. *Generally.* A county or circuit court judge, general magistrate, special magistrate, or hearing officer may allow testimony to be taken through communication equipment if all parties consent or if permitted by another applicable rule of procedure. FL ST J ADMIN Rule 2.530(d)(1).

   ii. *Procedure.* Any party desiring to present testimony through communication equipment shall, prior to the hearing or trial at which the testimony is to be presented, contact all parties to determine whether each party consents to this form of testimony. The party seeking to present the testimony shall move for permission to present testimony through communication equipment, which motion shall set forth good cause as to why the testimony should be allowed in this form. FL ST J ADMIN Rule 2.530(d)(2).

   iii. *Oath.* Testimony may be taken through communication equipment only if a notary public or other person authorized to administer oaths in the witness's jurisdiction is present with the witness and administers the oath consistent with the laws of the jurisdiction. FL ST J ADMIN Rule 2.530(d)(3).

   iv. *Confrontation rights.* In juvenile and criminal proceedings the defendant must make an informed waiver of any confrontation rights that may be abridged by the use of communication equipment. FL ST J ADMIN Rule 2.530(d)(4).

   v. *Video testimony.* If the testimony to be presented utilizes video conferencing or comparable two-way visual capabilities, the court in its discretion may modify the procedures set forth in FL ST J ADMIN Rule 2.530 to accommodate the technology utilized. FL ST J ADMIN Rule 2.530(d)(5).

e. *Burden of expense.* The cost for the use of the communication equipment is the responsibility of the requesting party unless otherwise directed by the court. FL ST J ADMIN Rule 2.530(e).

3. *Uniform motion calendar.* The Circuit Judges of the general civil/family division (excluding juvenile/dependency) shall maintain a uniform motion calendar from 8:45 A.M. to 9:30 A.M., Monday through Thursday. The motion calendar shall end PROMPTLY at 9:30 A.M. All parties shall be prepared to proceed at 8:45 A.M., and if one party fails to timely appear, the matter may proceed on the merits in his/her absence. FL ST 17 J CIR LOCAL RULE NO. 10A(1).

4. *Noticed motion limitation.* No more than two (2) motions may be noticed for each case on any given day except by leave of court. FL ST 17 J CIR LOCAL RULE NO. 10A(4).

5. *Ex parte and non-evidentiary motion.* Ex parte matters, non-evidentiary motions, and uncontested proceedings for adoptions, or dissolution may be heard on the uniform motion calendar, provided such matters can be conducted in five (5) minutes equally allocated among the parties and the moving party shall so certify as specified in FL ST 17 J CIR LOCAL RULE NO. 10A(3). FL ST 17 J CIR LOCAL RULE NO. 10A(6).

6. *Good faith effort to resolve issues.* Prior to appearing before the court, the parties shall discuss the issues raised in the pending motion, and both parties shall be prepared to certify at the hearing they have made a good faith effort to resolve the issues. FL ST 17 J CIR LOCAL RULE NO. 10A(7).

7. *Re-noticing hearings.* When the motion calendar has been filled, the judge's office shall notify the party noticing any hearings which cannot be reached. The noticing party shall call opposing counsel and re-notice the hearing. FL ST 17 J CIR LOCAL RULE NO. 10A(9).

8. *Hearing cancellation.* Motion calendar hearings may be canceled by the attorney who set the hearing. FL ST 17 J CIR LOCAL RULE NO. 10A(10).

9. *Other motion calendars.* Hearing officers/general masters shall conduct a motion calendar, the dates and times of which shall be determined by the hearing officer/general master or by administrative order. FL ST 17 J CIR LOCAL RULE NO. 10A(11).

10. *Sanctions.* Failure to comply with the procedures designated in the above paragraphs may result in the hearing being stricken from the docket or such other sanctions as the court deems appropriate. FL ST 17 J CIR LOCAL RULE NO. 10A(12).

H. Forms

1. Official Answer Forms for Florida

a. Caption. FL ST RCP Form 1.901.

b. Crossclaim summons. FL ST RCP Form 1.903.

c. Third-party summons. FL ST RCP Form 1.904.

d. Defense; Statute of limitations. FL ST RCP Form 1.965.

e. Defense; Payment. FL ST RCP Form 1.966.

f. Defense; Accord and satisfaction. FL ST RCP Form 1.967.

g. Defense; Failure of consideration. FL ST RCP Form 1.968.

h. Defense; Statute of frauds. FL ST RCP Form 1.969.

i. Defense; Release. FL ST RCP Form 1.970.

j. Notice of compliance when constitutional challenge is brought. FL ST RCP Form 1.975.

2. Answer Forms for Florida

a. Answer; General form, traverses. FL-PRACFORM § 5:4.

b. Answer; General form, traverses and affirmative defenses. FL-PRACFORM § 5:6.

c. Answer; General form, traverses, affirmative defenses and counterclaim. FL-PRACFORM § 5:7.

d. Answer; General form, traverses, affirmative defenses, counterclaim and crossclaim. FL-PRACFORM § 5:8.

e. Answer; Affirmative defense, fraud. FL-PRACFORM § 5:43.

f. Answer; Affirmative defense, laches. FL-PRACFORM § 5:47.

g. Answer; Affirmative defense, misjoinder. FL-PRACFORM § 5:49.

h. Answer; Affirmative defense, misrepresentation. FL-PRACFORM § 5:50.

i. Answer; Affirmative defense, self defense. FL-PRACFORM § 5:64.

j. Answer; Denial of conditions precedent. FL-PRACFORM § 5:80.

k. General denial. FL-PP § 2:58.

l. General denial; With specified admissions. FL-PP § 2:59.

m. Admission with qualification. FL-PP § 2:60.

n. Conclusions of law not requiring denial. FL-PP § 2:61.

o. Defenses stated in the alternative. FL-PP § 2:62.

p. Denial as to part of allegation. FL-PP § 2:63.

q. Pleader as without knowledge as to truth of allegation. FL-PP § 2:64.

I. Checklist

(I) ❑ Matters to be considered by plaintiff

(a) ❑ Required documents

(1) ❑ Summons

(2) ❑ Complaint

(3) ❑ Civil cover sheet

(4) ❑ Return of execution process by process server

(5) ❑ Filing fees

(b) ❑ Supplemental documents

(1) ❑ Exhibits

(2) ❑ Notice of constitutional question

(c) ❑ Time for filing and serving complaint

(1) ❑ Service of the initial process and initial pleading should be made upon a defendant within one hundred twenty (120) days after the filing of the complaint with the court

(II) ❑ Matters to be considered by defendant

(a) ❑ Required documents

(1) ❑ Answer

(2) ❑ Certificate of service

(b) ❑ Supplemental documents

(1) ❑ Exhibits

(2) ❑ Notice of constitutional question

(c) ❑ Time for answer

(1) ❑ Unless a different time is prescribed in a statute of Florida, a defendant shall serve an answer within twenty (20) days after service of original process and the initial pleading on the defendant, or not later than the date fixed in a notice by publication

(2) ❑ A party served with a pleading stating a crossclaim against that party shall serve an answer to it within twenty (20) days after service on that party

(3) ❑ The plaintiff shall serve an answer to a counterclaim within twenty (20) days after service of the counterclaim

(4) ❑ A defendant who, before being served with process, timely returns a waiver so requested is not required to respond to the complaint until sixty (60) days after the date the defendant received the request for waiver of service; for purposes of computing any time prescribed or allowed by the Florida Rules of Civil Procedure, service of process shall be deemed effected twenty (20) days before the time required to respond to the complaint

(5) ❑ For timing requirements related to service on the state, service of motion impact, and responding when no responsive pleading is required, please see the Timing section of this document

Pleadings
Amended Answer

Document Last Updated January 2013

A. Applicable Rules

1. *State rules*

a. Nonverification of papers. FL ST RCP Rule 1.030.

b. Constitutional challenge to state statute or county or municipal charter, ordinance, or franchise; Notice by party. FL ST RCP Rule 1.071.

c. Service and filing of pleadings, orders, and documents. FL ST RCP Rule 1.080.

d. Time. FL ST RCP Rule 1.090.

e. Pleadings and motions. FL ST RCP Rule 1.100; FL ST RCP Rule 1.110; FL ST RCP Rule 1.120; FL ST RCP Rule 1.130; FL ST RCP Rule 1.190.

f. Defenses. FL ST RCP Rule 1.140.

g. Pretrial procedure. FL ST RCP Rule 1.200.

h. Relief from judgment, decrees or orders. FL ST RCP Rule 1.540.
i. Forms. FL ST RCP Rule 1.900.
j. Foreign attorneys. FL ST J ADMIN Rule 2.510.
k. Signature of attorneys and parties. FL ST J ADMIN Rule 2.515.
l. Paper. FL ST J ADMIN Rule 2.520.
m. Electronic filing. FL ST J ADMIN Rule 2.525.
n. Court reporting. FL ST J ADMIN Rule 2.535.
o. Requests for accommodations by persons with disabilities. FL ST J ADMIN Rule 2.540.
p. Minimization of the filing of sensitive information. FL ST J ADMIN Rule 2.425.
q. Accessibility of information and technology. FL ST J ADMIN Rule 2.526.

2. *Local rules*
   a. Standards of professional courtesy. FL ST 17 J CIR I-94-O-1.
   b. Administrative order authorizing the filing of pleadings or papers at any office of the clerk of court. FL ST 17 J CIR 2008-153-GEN.
   c. Administrative order regarding provision of ADA accommodations. FL ST 17 J CIR 2010-49-GEN.
   d. Administrative order establishing electronic filing procedures for the civil division. FL ST 17 J CIR 2012-16-CIV.

B. Timing

1. *Amendment as a matter of course.* A party may amend a pleading once as a matter of course at any time before a responsive pleading is served or, if the pleading is one to which no responsive pleading is permitted and the action has not been placed on the trial calendar, may so amend it at any time within twenty (20) days after it is served. FL ST RCP Rule 1.190(a).
2. *Amendment by leave of court.* Otherwise a party may amend a pleading only by leave of court or by written consent of the adverse party. Leave of court shall be given freely when justice so requires. FL ST RCP Rule 1.190(a).
3. *Amendments in furtherance of justice.* At any time in furtherance of justice, upon such terms as may be just, the court may permit any process, proceeding, pleading, or record to be amended or material supplemental matter to be set forth in an amended or supplemental pleading. At every stage of the action the court must disregard any error or defect in the proceedings which does not affect the substantial rights of the parties. FL ST RCP Rule 1.190(e).
4. *Response to amended pleading.* A party shall plead in response to an amended pleading within ten (10) days after service of the amended pleading unless the court otherwise orders. FL ST RCP Rule 1.190(a).
5. *Standard of professional conduct; Scheduling*
   a. Attorneys should endeavor to provide opposing counsel, parties, witnesses, and other affected persons, sufficient notice of depositions, hearings and other proceedings, except upon agreement of course, in an emergency, or in other circumstances compelling more expedited scheduling. As a general rule, actual notice should be no less than five (5) business days for instate depositions, ten (10) business days for out-of-state depositions and four (4) business days for hearings. FL ST 17 J CIR I-94-O-1(I)(1).
   b. Attorneys should communicate with opposing counsel prior to scheduling depositions, hearings and other proceedings, in an effort to schedule them at times that are mutually convenient for all interested persons. Further, sufficient time should be reserved to permit a complete presentation by counsel for all parties. FL ST 17 J CIR I-94-O-1(I)(2).
   c. Attorneys should notify opposing counsel, the court, and others affected, of scheduling conflicts as soon as they become apparent. Further, attorneys should cooperate with one another regarding all reasonable rescheduling requests that do not prejudice their clients or unduly delay a proceeding. FL ST 17 J CIR I-94-O-1(I)(3).

d. Attorneys should promptly notify the court or other tribunal of any resolution between the parties that renders a scheduled court appearance unnecessary or otherwise moot. FL ST 17 J CIR I-94-O-1(I)(4).

e. Attorneys should grant reasonable requests by opposing counsel for extensions of time within which to respond to pleadings, discovery, and other matters when such an extension will not prejudice their client or unduly delay a proceeding. FL ST 17 J CIR I-94-O-1(I)(5).

6. *Timing considerations when filing electronically.* The filing date of an efiled document is when the last page is received by the Clerk. The electronic filing of a document does not modify any filing deadlines as required by law, rule of procedure, or court order. FL ST 17 J CIR 2012-16-CIV.

7. *Computation of time*

a. *Generally.* Computation of time shall be governed by FL ST J ADMIN Rule 2.514. FL ST RCP Rule 1.090(a). The following rules apply in computing time periods specified in any rule of procedure, local rule, court order, or statute that does not specify a method of computing time. FL ST J ADMIN Rule 2.514(a).

i. *Period stated in days or a longer unit.* When the period is stated in days or a longer unit of time (A) exclude the day of the event that triggers the period; (B) count every day, including intermediate Saturdays, Sundays, and legal holidays; and (C) include the last day of the period, but if the last day is a Saturday, Sunday, or legal holiday, or falls within any period of time extended through an order of the chief justice under FL ST J ADMIN Rule 2.205(a)(2)(B)(iv), the period continues to run until the end of the next day that is not a Saturday, Sunday, or legal holiday and does not fall within any period of time extended through an order of the chief justice. FL ST J ADMIN Rule 2.514(a)(1).

ii. *Period stated in hours.* When the period is stated in hours (A) begin counting immediately on the occurrence of the event that triggers the period; (B) count every hour, including hours during intermediate Saturdays, Sundays, and legal holidays; and (C) if the period would end on a Saturday, Sunday, or legal holiday, or during any period of time extended through an order of the chief justice under FL ST J ADMIN Rule 2.205(a)(2)(B)(iv), the period continues to run until the same time on the next day that is not a Saturday, Sunday, or legal holiday and does not fall within any period of time extended through an order of the chief justice. FL ST J ADMIN Rule 2.514(a)(2).

iii. *Period stated in days less than seven (7) days.* When the period stated in days is less than seven (7) days, intermediate Saturdays, Sundays, and legal holidays shall be excluded in the computation. FL ST J ADMIN Rule 2.514(a)(3).

iv. *"Last day" defined.* Unless a different time is set by a statute, local rule, or court order, the last day ends (A) for electronic filing or for service by any means, at midnight; and (B) for filing by other means, when the clerk's office is scheduled to close. FL ST J ADMIN Rule 2.514(a)(4).

v. *"Next day" defined.* The "next day" is determined by continuing to count forward when the period is measured after an event and backward when measured before an event. FL ST J ADMIN Rule 2.514(a)(5).

vi. *"Legal holiday" defined.* "Legal holiday" means (A) the day set aside by FL ST § 110.117, for observing New Year's Day, Martin Luther King, Jr.'s Birthday, Memorial Day, Independence Day, Labor Day, Veterans' Day, Thanksgiving Day, the Friday after Thanksgiving Day, or Christmas Day, and (B) any day observed as a holiday by the clerk's office or as designated by the chief judge. FL ST J ADMIN Rule 2.514(a)(6).

b. *Additional time after service by mail or e-mail.* When a party may or must act within a specified time after service and service is made by mail or e-mail, five (5) days are added after the period that would otherwise expire under FL ST J ADMIN Rule 2.514(a). FL ST J ADMIN Rule 2.514(b).

c. *Enlargement.* When an act is required or allowed to be done at or within a specified time by order of court, by the Florida Rules of Civil Procedure, or by notice given thereunder, for cause shown the court at any time in its discretion (1) with or without notice, may order the period enlarged if request therefor is made before the expiration of the period originally prescribed or as extended by a previous

order, or (2) upon motion made and notice after the expiration of the specified period, may permit the act to be done when failure to act was the result of excusable neglect, but it may not extend the time for making a motion for new trial, for rehearing, or to alter or amend a judgment; making a motion for relief from a judgment under FL ST RCP Rule 1.540(b); taking an appeal or filing a petition for certiorari; or making a motion for a directed verdict. FL ST RCP Rule 1.090(b).

d. *Unaffected by expiration of term.* The period of time provided for the doing of any act or the taking of any proceeding shall not be affected or limited by the continued existence or expiration of a term of court. The continued existence or expiration of a term of court in no way affects the power of a court to do any act or take any proceeding in any action which is or has been pending before it. FL ST RCP Rule 1.090(c).

C. General Requirements

1. *Amendments.* A party may amend a pleading once as a matter of course at any time before a responsive pleading is served or, if the pleading is one to which no responsive pleading is permitted and the action has not been placed on the trial calendar, may so amend it at any time within twenty (20) days after it is served. Otherwise a party may amend a pleading only by leave of court or by written consent of the adverse party. Leave of court shall be freely given when justice so requires. FL ST RCP Rule 1.190(a).

   a. *Purpose of amendments.* Amendments can relate to the correction of mistakes, the insertion of jurisdictional averments, the correction or addition of verifications, the addition or substitution or striking out of parties, and generally the rectification of all formal defects in the pleading. The court can also allow amendments setting up an omitted counterclaim or cross-claim if the defendant failed to raise the claim through oversight, inadvertence, or excusable neglect. FL-PP § 2:151.

   b. *Amendment to a pleading/Amended pleading.* A significant difference exists between an amendment to a pleading and an amended pleading. An amendment to a pleading corrects, adds to or deletes from the pleading. An amended pleading is substituted for the former pleading and the former pleading ceases to have any effect. Dee v. Southern Brewing Company, 146 Fla. 588, 1 So.2d 562 (Fla. 1941); Shannon v. McBride, 105 So.2d 16 (Fla. 2d DCA 1958); Hughes v. Home Sav. of America, F.S.B., 675 So.2d 649 (Fla. 2d DCA 1996); FL-PRACPROC § 14:2.

   c. *Relation back of amendments.* When the claim or defense asserted in the amended pleading arose out of the conduct, transaction, or occurrence set forth or attempted to be set forth in the original pleading, the amendment shall relate back to the date of the original pleading. FL ST RCP Rule 1.190(c).

2. *General rules of pleading*

   a. *Claims for relief*

      i. A pleading which sets forth a claim for relief, whether an original claim, counterclaim, crossclaim, or third-party claim, must state a cause of action and shall contain

         - A short and plain statement of the grounds upon which the court's jurisdiction depends, unless the court already has jurisdiction and the claim needs no new grounds of jurisdiction to support it (For information regarding acts subjecting persons to jurisdiction, please see FL ST § 48.193),

         - A short and plain statement of the ultimate facts showing that the pleader is entitled to relief, and

         - A demand for judgment for the relief to which the pleader deems himself or herself entitled. FL ST RCP Rule 1.110(b).

      ii. Relief in the alternative or of several different types may be demanded. Every complaint shall be considered to demand general relief. FL ST RCP Rule 1.110(b).

   b. *Verification.* Except when otherwise specifically provided by these rules or an applicable statute, every pleading or other document of a party represented by an attorney need not be verified or accompanied by an affidavit. FL ST RCP Rule 1.030. When filing an action for foreclosure of a mortgage on residential real property the complaint shall be verified. When verification of a document is required, the document filed shall include an oath, affirmation, or the following statement: "Under penalty of perjury, I declare that I have read the foregoing, and the facts alleged therein are true and correct to the best of my knowledge and belief." FL ST RCP Rule 1.110(b).

c. *Separate statements.* All averments of claim or defense shall be made in consecutively numbered paragraphs, the contents of each of which shall be limited as far as practicable to a statement of a single set of circumstances, and a paragraph may be referred to by number in all subsequent pleadings. Each claim founded upon a separate transaction or occurrence and each defense other than denials shall be stated in a separate count or defense when a separation facilitates the clear presentation of the matter set forth. FL ST RCP Rule 1.110(f).

d. *Statements adopted by reference.* Statements in a pleading may be adopted by reference in a different part of the same pleading, in another pleading, or in any motion. FL ST RCP Rule 1.130(b).

e. *Joinder of causes of action; Consistency.* A pleader may set up in the same action as many claims or causes of action or defenses in the same right as the pleader has, and claims for relief may be stated in the alternative if separate items make up the cause of action, or if two (2) or more causes of action are joined. A party may also set forth two (2) or more statements of a claim or defense alternatively, either in one (1) count or defense or in separate counts or defenses. When two (2) or more statements are made in the alternative and one (1) of them, if made independently, would be sufficient, the pleading is not made insufficient by the insufficiency of one (1) or more of the alternative statements. A party may also state as many separate claims or defenses as that party has, regardless of consistency and whether based on legal or equitable grounds or both. All pleadings shall be construed so as to do substantial justice. FL ST RCP Rule 1.110(g).

f. *Subsequent pleadings.* When the nature of an action permits pleadings subsequent to final judgment and the jurisdiction of the court over the parties has not terminated, the initial pleading subsequent to final judgment shall be designated a supplemental complaint or petition. The action shall then proceed in the same manner and time as though the supplemental complaint or petition were the initial pleading in the action, including the issuance of any needed process. FL ST RCP Rule 1.110(h) shall not apply to proceedings that may be initiated by motion under the Florida Rules of Civil Procedure. FL ST RCP Rule 1.110(h).

g. *Pleading basis for service.* When service of process is to be made under statutes authorizing service on nonresidents of Florida, it is sufficient to plead the basis for service in the language of the statute without pleading the facts supporting service. FL ST RCP Rule 1.070(h).

h. *Forms of pleadings.* Forms of action and technical forms for seeking relief and of pleas, pleadings, or motions are abolished. FL ST RCP Rule 1.110(a).

3. *Answer; Generally.* An answer has three (3) functions. First, it must respond to each allegation of the preceding pleading by admitting, denying or alleging that the pleader is without knowledge of the allegation. Second, it must contain any affirmative defenses that the pleader is interposing to any cause of action alleged in the preceding pleading. Third, the answer may claim affirmative relief against the plaintiff or petitioner by a counterclaim or against a codefendant by a crossclaim. FL-PRACPROC § 11:1.

a. *Content.* In the answer a pleader shall state in short and plain terms the pleader's defenses to each claim asserted and shall admit or deny the averments on which the adverse party relies. If the defendant is without knowledge, the defendant shall so state and such statement shall operate as a denial. Denial shall fairly meet the substance of the averments denied. When a pleader intends in good faith to deny only a part of an averment, the pleader shall specify so much of it as is true and shall deny the remainder. Unless the pleader intends in good faith to controvert all of the averments of the preceding pleading, the pleader may make denials as specific denials of designated averments or may generally deny all of the averments except such designated averments as the pleader expressly admits, but when the pleader does so intend to controvert all of its averments, including averments of the grounds upon which the court's jurisdiction depends, the pleader may do so by general denial. FL ST RCP Rule 1.110(c).

b. *Form of answer.* An answer contains a caption, commencement, body, signature and certificate of service. The caption is the same as that of the initial pleading, except for the designation as one of the types of answer. The body of an answer should contain an admission, denial or plea of without knowledge to each allegation of the preceding pleading, except for the additional allegations in response to a general allegation of conditions precedent and the denial of capacity to sue. FL-PRACPROC § 11:3.

i. *Responding sequentially.* The best method of responding is to answer each paragraph sequentially, combining admissions, denials or pleas of without knowledge when the sequence permits. The admissions, denials and allegations of without knowledge should be stated first, followed separately by any affirmative defenses and then by any counterclaim or crossclaim. A third party complaint may be a part of the same paper, but it is not a part of the answer as is a counterclaim or crossclaim. Paragraphs are numbered consecutively throughout the pleading whether in the answer, counterclaim or crossclaim. Denials for the record only are improper. FL-PRACPROC § 11:3.

c. *Defenses*

i. *Generally.* Every defense in law or fact to a claim for relief in a pleading shall be asserted in the responsive pleading, if one is required, but the following defenses may be made by motion at the option of the pleader: (1) lack of jurisdiction over the subject matter, (2) lack of jurisdiction over the person, (3) improper venue, (4) insufficiency of process, (5) insufficiency of service of process, (6) failure to state a cause of action, and (7) failure to join indispensable parties. A motion making any of these defenses shall be made before pleading if a further pleading is permitted. FL ST RCP Rule 1.140(b).

- *Stated specifically.* The grounds on which any of the enumerated defenses are based and the substantial matters of law intended to be argued shall be stated specifically and with particularity in the responsive pleading or motion. FL ST RCP Rule 1.140(b).
- *Waiver.* Any ground not stated shall be deemed to be waived except any ground showing that the court lacks jurisdiction of the subject matter may be made at any time. No defense or objection is waived by being joined with other defenses or objections in a responsive pleading or motion. FL ST RCP Rule 1.140(b). A party waives all defenses and objections that the party does not present either by motion under FL ST RCP Rule 1.140(b), FL ST RCP Rule 1.140(e), or FL ST RCP Rule 1.140(f) or, if the party has made no motion, in a responsive pleading except as provided in FL ST RCP Rule 1.140(h)(2). FL ST RCP Rule 1.140(h)(1). The defenses of failure to state a cause of action or a legal defense or to join an indispensable party may be raised by motion for judgment on the pleadings or at the trial on the merits in addition to being raised either in a motion under FL ST RCP Rule 1.140(b) or in the answer or reply. The defense of lack of jurisdiction of the subject matter may be raised at any time. FL ST RCP Rule 1.140(h)(2).

ii. *Affirmative defenses.* In pleading to a preceding pleading a party shall set forth affirmatively accord and satisfaction, arbitration and award, assumption of risk, contributory negligence, discharge in bankruptcy, duress, estoppel, failure of consideration, fraud, illegality, injury by fellow servant, laches, license, payment, release, res judicata, statute of frauds, statute of limitations, waiver, and any other matter constituting an avoidance or affirmative defense. When a party has mistakenly designated a defense as a counterclaim or a counterclaim as a defense, the court, on terms if justice so requires, shall treat the pleading as if there had been a proper designation. Affirmative defenses appearing on the face of a prior pleading may be asserted as grounds for a motion or defense under FL ST RCP Rule 1.140(b); provided this shall not limit amendments under FL ST RCP Rule 1.190 even if such ground is sustained. FL ST RCP Rule 1.110(d).

- *Format of defenses.* Affirmative defenses should be placed after the admissions, denials and allegations of without knowledge in the answer. All paragraphs must be numbered consecutively throughout the answer. If a defense is directed to only a part of a cause of action or to one or more, but not all, of several causes of action in the preceding pleading, the part or cause of action to which it is directed should be identified in the defense. Defenses should be identified by consecutive ordinal numbers such as "First Defense" and "Second Defense." FL-PRACPROC § 11:4.

iii. *Effect of failure to deny.* Averments in a pleading to which a responsive pleading is required,

other than those as to the amount of damages, are admitted when not denied in the responsive pleading. Averments in a pleading to which no responsive pleading is required or permitted shall be taken as denied or avoided. FL ST RCP Rule 1.110(e). An admission in an answer binds the party and no proof is required. An admission does not extend beyond the scope of the allegation in the preceding pleading. FL-PRACPROC § 11:3.

4. *Pleading special matters*

   a. *Capacity.* It is not necessary to aver the capacity of a party to sue or be sued, the authority of a party to sue or be sued in a representative capacity, or the legal existence of an organized association of persons that is made a party, except to the extent required to show the jurisdiction of the court. The initial pleading served on behalf of a minor party shall specifically aver the age of the minor party. When a party desires to raise an issue as to the legal existence of any party, the capacity of any party to sue or be sued, or the authority of a party to sue or be sued in a representative capacity, that party shall do so by specific negative averment which shall include such supporting particulars as are peculiarly within the pleader's knowledge. FL ST RCP Rule 1.120(a).

   b. *Fraud, mistake, condition of the mind.* In all averments of fraud or mistake, the circumstances constituting fraud or mistake shall be stated with such particularity as the circumstances may permit. Malice, intent, knowledge, mental attitude, and other condition of mind of a person may be averred generally. FL ST RCP Rule 1.120(b).

   c. *Conditions precedent.* In pleading the performance or occurrence of conditions precedent, it is sufficient to aver generally that all conditions precedent have been performed or have occurred. A denial of performance or occurrence shall be made specifically and with particularity. FL ST RCP Rule 1.120(c).

   d. *Official document or act.* In pleading an official document or official act it is sufficient to aver that the document was issued or the act done in compliance with law. FL ST RCP Rule 1.120(c).

   e. *Judgment or decree.* In pleading a judgment or decree of a domestic or foreign court, a judicial or quasi-judicial tribunal, or a board or officer, it is sufficient to aver the judgment or decree without setting forth matter showing jurisdiction to render it. FL ST RCP Rule 1.120(e).

   f. *Time and place.* For the purpose of testing the sufficiency of a pleading, averments of time and place are material and shall be considered like all other averments of material matter. FL ST RCP Rule 1.120(f).

   g. *Special damage.* When items of special damage are claimed, they shall be specifically stated. FL ST RCP Rule 1.120(g).

5. *Parties*

   a. *Parties generally.* Every action may be prosecuted in the name of the real party in interest, but a personal representative, administrator, guardian, trustee of an express trust, a party with whom or in whose name a contract has been made for the benefit of another, or a party expressly authorized by statute may sue in that person's own name without joining the party for whose benefit the action is brought. All persons having an interest in the subject of the action and in obtaining the relief demanded may join as plaintiffs and any person may be made a defendant who has or claims an interest adverse to the plaintiff. Any person may at any time be made a party if that person's presence is necessary or proper to a complete determination of the cause. Persons having a united interest may be joined on the same side as plaintiffs or defendants, and anyone who refuses to join may for such reason be made a defendant. FL ST RCP Rule 1.210(a).

   b. *Minors or incompetent persons.* When a minor or incompetent person has a representative, such as a guardian or other like fiduciary, the representative may sue or defend on behalf of the minor or incompetent person. A minor or incompetent person who does not have a duly appointed representative may sue by next friend or by a guardian ad litem. The court shall appoint a guardian ad litem for a minor or incompetent person not otherwise represented in an action or shall make such other order as it deems proper for the protection of the minor or incompetent person. FL ST RCP Rule 1.210(b).

   c. For survivor and substitution of parties information, please see FL ST RCP Rule 1.260.

6. *Counterclaims and crossclaims*

   a. *Compulsory counterclaims.* A pleading shall state as a counterclaim any claim which at the time of serving the pleading the pleader has against any opposing party, provided it arises out of the transaction or occurrence that is the subject matter of the opposing party's claim and does not require for its adjudication the presence of third parties over whom the court cannot acquire jurisdiction. But the pleader need not state a claim if (1) at the time the action was commenced the claim was the subject of another pending action, or (2) the opposing party brought suit upon that party's claim by attachment or other process by which the court did not acquire jurisdiction to render a personal judgment on the claim and the pleader is not stating a counterclaim under this rule. FL ST RCP Rule 1.170(a).

   b. *Permissive counterclaim.* A pleading may state as a counterclaim any claim against an opposing party not arising out of the transaction or occurrence that is the subject matter of the opposing party's claim. FL ST RCP Rule 1.170(b).

   c. *Counterclaim exceeding opposing claim.* A counterclaim may or may not diminish or defeat the recovery sought by the opposing party. It may claim relief exceeding in amount or different in kind from that sought in the pleading of the opposing party. FL ST RCP Rule 1.170(c).

   d. *Counterclaim against the State.* The Florida Rules of Civil Procedure shall not be construed to enlarge beyond the limits established by law the right to assert counterclaims or to claim credits against the state or any of its subdivisions or other governmental organizations thereof subject to suit or against a municipal corporation or against an officer, agency, or administrative board of the state. FL ST RCP Rule 1.170(d).

   e. *Counterclaim maturing or acquired after pleading.* A claim which matured or was acquired by the pleader after serving the pleading may be presented as a counterclaim by supplemental pleading with the permission of the court. FL ST RCP Rule 1.170(e).

   f. *Omitted counterclaim or crossclaim.* When a pleader fails to set up a counterclaim or crossclaim through oversight, inadvertence, or excusable neglect, or when justice requires, the pleader may set up the counterclaim or crossclaim by amendment with leave of the court. FL ST RCP Rule 1.170(f).

   g. *Crossclaim against co-party.* A pleading may state as a crossclaim any claim by one party against a co-party arising out of the transaction or occurrence that is the subject matter of either the original action or a counterclaim therein, or relating to any property that is the subject matter of the original action. The crossclaim may include a claim that the party against whom it is asserted is or may be liable to the crossclaimant for all or part of a claim asserted in the action against the crossclaimant. Service of a crossclaim on a party who has appeared in the action shall be made pursuant to FL ST RCP Rule 1.080. Service of a crossclaim against a party who has not appeared in the action shall be made in the manner provided for service of summons. FL ST RCP Rule 1.170(g).

   h. *Additional parties may be brought in.* When the presence of parties other than those to the original action is required to grant complete relief in the determination of a counterclaim or crossclaim, they shall be named in the counterclaim or crossclaim and be served with process and shall be parties to the action thereafter if jurisdiction of them can be obtained and their joinder will not deprive the court of jurisdiction of the action. FL ST RCP Rule 1.250(b) and FL ST RCP Rule 1.250(c) apply to parties brought in under FL ST RCP Rule 1.170(h). FL ST RCP Rule 1.170(h).

   i. *Separate trials; Separate judgment.* If the court orders separate trials as provided in FL ST RCP Rule 1.270(b), judgment on a counterclaim or crossclaim may be rendered when the court has jurisdiction to do so even if a claim of the opposing party has been dismissed or otherwise disposed of. FL ST RCP Rule 1.170(i).

   j. *Demand exceeding jurisdiction; Transfer of action.* If the demand of any counterclaim or crossclaim exceeds the jurisdiction of the court in which the action is pending, the action shall be transferred forthwith to the court of the same county having jurisdiction of the demand in the counterclaim or crossclaim with only such alterations in the pleadings as are essential. The court shall order the transfer of the action and the transmittal of all papers in it to the proper court if the party asserting the demand exceeding the jurisdiction deposits with the court having jurisdiction a sum sufficient to pay

the clerk's service charge in the court to which the action is transferred at the time of filing the counterclaim or crossclaim. Thereupon the original papers and deposit shall be transmitted and filed with a certified copy of the order. The court to which the action is transferred shall have full power and jurisdiction over the demands of all parties. Failure to make the service charge deposit at the time the counterclaim or crossclaim is filed, or within such further time as the court may allow, shall reduce a claim for damages to an amount within the jurisdiction of the court where the action is pending and waive the claim in other cases. FL ST RCP Rule 1.170(j).

7. *Misjoinder and nonjoinder of parties*
   a. *Misjoinder.* Misjoinder of parties is not a ground for dismissal of an action. Any claim against a party may be severed and proceeded with separately. FL ST RCP Rule 1.250(a).
   b. *Dropping parties.* Parties may be dropped by an adverse party in the manner provided for voluntary dismissal in FL ST RCP Rule 1.420(a)(1) subject to the exception stated in FL ST RCP Rule 1.420. If notice of lis pendens has been filed in the action against a party so dropped, the notice of dismissal shall be recorded and cancels the notice of lis pendens without the necessity of a court order. Parties may be dropped by order of court on its own initiative or the motion of any party at any stage of the action on such terms as are just. FL ST RCP Rule 1.250(b).
   c. *Adding parties.* Parties may be added once as a matter of course within the same time that pleadings can be so amended under FL ST RCP Rule 1.190(a). If amendment by leave of court or stipulation of the parties is permitted, parties may be added in the amended pleading without further order of court. Parties may be added by order of court on its own initiative or on motion of any party at any stage of the action and on such terms as are just. FL ST RCP Rule 1.250(c).
8. *Jury demand*
   a. *Right preserved.* The right of trial by jury as declared by the Constitution or by statute shall be preserved to the parties inviolate. FL ST RCP Rule 1.430(a).
   b. *Demand.* Any party may demand a trial by jury of any issue triable of right by a jury by serving upon the other party a demand therefor in writing at any time after commencement of the action and not later than ten (10) days after the service of the last pleading directed to such issue. The demand may be indorsed upon a pleading of the party. FL ST RCP Rule 1.430(b).
   c. *Specification of issues.* In the demand a party may specify the issues that the party wishes so tried; otherwise, the party is deemed to demand trial by jury for all issues so triable. FL ST RCP Rule 1.430(c).
      i. If a party has demanded trial by jury for only some of the issues, any other party may serve a demand for trial by jury of any other or all of the issues triable by jury ten (10) days after service of the demand or such lesser time as the court may order. FL ST RCP Rule 1.430(c).
   d. *Waiver.* A party who fails to serve a demand as required by FL ST RCP Rule 1.430 waives trial by jury. FL ST RCP Rule 1.430(d).
      i. If waived, a jury trial may not be granted without the consent of the parties, but the court may allow an amendment in the proceedings to demand a trial by jury or order a trial by jury on its own motion. FL ST RCP Rule 1.430(d).
      ii. A demand for trial by jury may not be withdrawn without the consent of the parties. FL ST RCP Rule 1.430(d).
9. *Arbitration and mediation*
   a. *Referral to arbitration and mediation.* Except as hereinafter provided or as otherwise prohibited by law, the presiding judge may enter an order referring all or any part of a contested civil matter to mediation or arbitration. The parties to any contested civil matter may file a written stipulation to mediate or arbitrate any issue between them at any time. Such stipulation shall be incorporated into the order of referral. FL ST RCP Rule 1.700(a).
   b. *Arbitration*
      i. *Exclusions.* A civil action shall be ordered to arbitration or arbitration in conjunction with

mediation upon stipulation of the parties. A civil action may be ordered to arbitration or arbitration in conjunction with mediation upon motion of any party or by the court, if the judge determines the action to be of such a nature that arbitration could be of benefit to the litigants or the court. FL ST RCP Rule 1.800.

- Under no circumstances may the following categories of actions be referred to arbitration: (1) bond estreatures; (2) habeas corpus or other extraordinary writs; (3) bond validations; (4) civil or criminal contempt; (5) such other matters as may be specified by order of the chief judge in the circuit. FL ST RCP Rule 1.800.

ii. For more information regarding arbitration, please see FL ST RCP Rule 1.810; FL ST RCP Rule 1.820; FL ST RCP Rule 1.830.

c. *Mediation.* For more information regarding mediation, please see FL ST RCP Rule 1.710; FL ST RCP Rule 1.720; FL ST RCP Rule 1.730; and FL ST RCP Rule 1.750.

10. *Rules of court*

a. *Rules of civil procedure.* The Florida Rules of Civil Procedure apply to all actions of a civil nature and all special statutory proceedings in the circuit courts and county courts except those to which the Florida Probate Rules, the Florida Family Law Rules of Procedure, or the Small Claims Rules apply. FL ST RCP Rule 1.010.

i. The form, content, procedure, and time for pleading in all special statutory proceedings shall be as prescribed by the statutes governing the proceeding unless the Florida Rules of Civil Procedure specifically provide to the contrary. FL ST RCP Rule 1.010.

ii. The Florida Rules of Civil Procedure shall be construed to secure the just, speedy, and inexpensive determination of every action. FL ST RCP Rule 1.010.

b. *Rules of judicial administration.* The Florida Rules of Judicial Administration shall apply to administrative matters in all courts to which the Florida Rules of Judicial Administration are applicable by their terms. The Florida Rules of Judicial Administration shall be construed to secure the speedy and inexpensive determination of every proceeding to which they are applicable. The Florida Rules of Judicial Administration shall supersede all conflicting rules and statutes. FL ST J ADMIN Rule 2.110.

D. Documents

1. *Required documents*

a. *Amended answer.* See the General Requirements section of this document for the content of an amended answer. If a party files a motion to amend a pleading, the party shall attach the proposed amended pleading to the motion. FL ST RCP Rule 1.190(a). See the KeyRules Florida Circuit Court Motion for Leave to Amend document for further information.

i. *Notices to persons with disabilities.* See the Format section of this KeyRules document for further information.

b. *Certificate of service.* When any attorney certifies in substance: "I certify that a copy hereof has been furnished to (here insert name or names and addresses used for service) by (e-mail) (delivery) (mail) (fax) on .... (date) ....________________ Attorney" the certificate is taken as prima facie proof of such service in compliance with FL ST J ADMIN Rule 2.516. FL ST J ADMIN Rule 2.516(f).

2. *Supplemental documents*

a. *Exhibits.* All bonds, notes, bills of exchange, contracts, accounts, or documents upon which action may be brought or defense made, or a copy thereof or a copy of the portions thereof material to the pleadings, shall be incorporated in or attached to the pleading. No papers shall be unnecessarily annexed as exhibits. The pleadings shall contain no unnecessary recitals of deeds, documents, contracts, or other instruments. Any exhibit attached to a pleading shall be considered a part of the pleadings for all purposes. FL ST RCP Rule 1.130(a).

b. *Notice of constitutional question.* A party that files a pleading, written motion, or other paper drawing into question the constitutionality of a state statute or a county or municipal charter,

ordinance, or franchise must promptly (1) file a notice of constitutional question stating the question and identifying the paper that raises it; and (2) serve the notice and the pleading, written motion, or other paper drawing into question the constitutionality of a state statute or a county or municipal charter, ordinance, or franchise on the Attorney General or the state attorney of the judicial circuit in which the action is pending, by either certified or registered mail. Service of the notice and pleading, written motion, or other paper does not require joinder of the Attorney General or the state attorney as a party to the action. FL ST RCP Rule 1.071.

E. Format

1. *Documents; Type and size.* Documents subject to the exceptions set forth in FL ST J ADMIN Rule 2.525(d) shall be filed on recycled paper measuring eight and one half by eleven (8 1/2 by 11) inches. For purposes of FL ST J ADMIN Rule 2.520, paper is recycled if it contains a minimum content of fifty (50) percent waste paper. Xerographic reduction of legal-size (eight and one half by fourteen (8 1/2 by 14) inches) documents to letter size (eight and one half by eleven (8 1/2 by 11) inches) is prohibited. All other documents filed by electronic transmission shall be filed in a format capable of being printed in a format consistent with the provisions of FL ST J ADMIN Rule 2.250. FL ST J ADMIN Rule 2.520(b).
    a. *Exhibits.* Any exhibit or attachment filed with pleadings or papers may be filed in its original size. FL ST J ADMIN Rule 2.520(c).
    b. *Recording space.* On all papers and documents prepared and filed by the court or by any party to a proceeding which are to be recorded in the public records of any county, including but not limited to final money judgments and notices of lis pendens, a three (3) inch by three (3) inch space at the top right-hand corner on the first page and a one (1) inch by three (3) inch space at the top right-hand corner on each subsequent page shall be left blank and reserved for use by the clerk of court. FL ST J ADMIN Rule 2.520(d).
        i. *Exceptions to recording space.* Any papers or documents created by persons or entities over which the filing party has no control, including but not limited to wills, codicils, trusts, or other testamentary documents; documents prepared or executed by any public officer; documents prepared, executed, acknowledged, or proved outside of the State of Florida; or documents created by State or Federal government agencies, may be filed without the space required by FL ST J ADMIN Rule 2.520. FL ST J ADMIN Rule 2.520(e).
    c. *Noncompliance.* No clerk of court is permitted to refuse to file any document or paper because of noncompliance with the Florida Rules of Judicial Administration. However, upon request of the clerk of court, noncomplying documents must be resubmitted in accordance with the formatting rules. FL ST J ADMIN Rule 2.520(f).
2. *Caption.* Every pleading, motion, order, judgment, or other paper shall have a caption containing the name of the court, the file number, and except for in rem proceedings, including forfeiture proceedings, the name of the first party on each side with an appropriate indication of other parties, and a designation identifying the party filing it and its nature or the nature of the order, as the case may be. In any in rem proceeding, every pleading, motion, order, judgment, or other paper shall have a caption containing the name of the court, the file number, the style "In re" (followed by the name or general description of the property), and a designation of the person or entity filing it and its nature or the nature of the order, as the case may be. In an in rem forfeiture proceeding, the style shall be "In re forfeiture of" (followed by the name of the general description of the property). All papers filed in the action shall be styled in such a manner as to indicate clearly the subject matter of the paper and the party requesting or obtaining relief. FL ST RCP Rule 1.100(c)(1).
3. *Writing and written defined.* Writing or written means a document containing information, an application, or a stipulation. FL ST RCP Rule 1.080(c).
4. *Rule abbreviations*
    a. The Florida Rules of Civil Procedure and shall be abbreviated as Fla.R.Civ.P. FL ST RCP Rule 1.010.
    b. The Florida Rules of Judicial Administration shall be abbreviated as Fla. R. Jud. Admin. FL ST J ADMIN Rule 2.110.

5. *Nonverification.* Except when otherwise specifically provided by the Florida Rules of Civil Procedure or an applicable statute, every pleading or other document of a party represented by an attorney need not be verified or accompanied by an affidavit. FL ST RCP Rule 1.030; FL ST J ADMIN Rule 2.515(a).
6. *Attorney signature*
   a. *Attorney signature.* Every pleading and other document of a party represented by an attorney shall be signed by at least one (1) attorney of record in that attorney's individual name whose current record Florida Bar address, telephone number, including area code, primary e-mail address and secondary e-mail addresses, if any, and Florida Bar number shall be stated, and who shall be duly licensed to practice law in Florida or who shall have received permission to appear in the particular case as provided in FL ST J ADMIN Rule 2.510. FL ST J ADMIN Rule 2.515(a).
      i. The attorney may be required by the court to give the address of, and to vouch for the attorney's authority to represent, the party. FL ST J ADMIN Rule 2.515(a).
      ii. The signature of an attorney shall constitute a certificate by the attorney that the attorney has read the pleading or other document; that to the best of the attorney's knowledge, information, and belief there is good ground to support it; and that it is not interposed for delay. FL ST J ADMIN Rule 2.515(a).
      iii. If a pleading is not signed or is signed with intent to defeat the purpose of FL ST J ADMIN Rule 2.515, it may be stricken and the action may proceed as though the pleading or other document had not been served. FL ST J ADMIN Rule 2.515(a).
   b. *Pro se litigant signature.* A party who is not represented by an attorney shall sign any pleading or other paper and state the party's address and telephone number, including area code. FL ST J ADMIN Rule 2.515(b).
   c. *Form of signature*
      i. The signatures required on pleadings and documents by FL ST J ADMIN Rule 2.515(a) and FL ST J ADMIN Rule 2.515(b) may be:
         - Original signatures;
         - Original signatures that have been reproduced by electronic means, such as on electronically transmitted documents or photocopied documents;
         - Electronic signatures using the "/s/," "s/," or "/s" formats by or at the direction of the person signing; or
         - Any other signature format authorized by general law, so long as the clerk where the proceeding is pending has the capability of receiving and has obtained approval from the Supreme Court of Florida to accept pleadings and documents with that signature format. FL ST J ADMIN Rule 2.515(c)(1).
      ii. An attorney, party, or other person who files a pleading or paper by electronic transmission that does not contain the original signature of that attorney, party, or other person shall file that identical pleading or paper in paper form containing an original signature of that attorney, party, or other person (hereinafter called the follow-up filing) immediately thereafter. The follow-up filing is not required if the Supreme Court of Florida has entered an order directing the clerk of court to discontinue accepting the follow-up filing. FL ST J ADMIN Rule 2.515(c)(2).
      iii. The placement of a "/s/" or the image of a signature by an attorney or party or affected non-party signature line on an electronically filed document shall be accepted as the signature and shall verify to the Court the filer is in possession of the originally executed document. Notwithstanding the manner in which an electronic document is signed the originally executed pleading or paper shall be maintained in the filer's possession for a minimum of one (1) year after final disposition and time for appeal of the case. The originally executed document shall be produced for filing or inspection as directed by the Court. FL ST 17 J CIR 2012-16-CIV.
7. *Forms*
   a. *Process.* The forms of process, notice of lis pendens, and notice of action provided in the Florida

Rules of Civil Procedure are sufficient. Variations from the forms do not void process or notices that are otherwise sufficient. FL ST RCP Rule 1.900(a).

b. *Other forms.* The other forms provided in the Florida Rules of Civil Procedure are sufficient for the matters that are covered by them. So long as the substance is expressed without prolixity, the forms may be varied to meet the facts of a particular case. FL ST RCP Rule 1.900(b).

c. *Formal matters.* Captions, except for the designation of the paper, are omitted from the forms provided in the Florida Rules of Civil Procedure. A general form of caption is the first form provided. Signatures are omitted from pleadings and motions. FL ST RCP Rule 1.900(c).

8. *Notices to persons with disabilities.* All notices of court proceedings to be held in a public facility, and all process compelling appearance at such proceedings, shall include the following statement in bold face, fourteen (14) point Times New Roman or Courier font: "If you are a person with a disability who needs any accommodation in order to participate in this proceeding, you are entitled, at no cost to you, to the provision of certain assistance. Please contact [identify applicable court personnel by name, address, and telephone number] at least seven (7) days before your scheduled court appearance, or immediately upon receiving this notification if the time before the scheduled appearance is less than seven (7) days; if you are hearing or voice impaired, call 711." FL ST J ADMIN Rule 2.540(c)(1). For further information, please see FL ST 17 J CIR 2010-49-GEN.

9. *Minimization of the filing of sensitive information*

a. *Limitations for court filings.* Unless authorized by FL ST J ADMIN Rule 2.425(b), statute, another rule of court, or the court orders otherwise, designated sensitive information filed with the court must be limited to the following format:

i. The initials of a person known to be a minor;

ii. The year of birth of a person's birth date;

iii. No portion of any: Social security number, Bank account number, Credit card account number, Charge account number, or Debit account number;

iv. The last four digits of any: Taxpayer identification number (TIN), Employee identification number, Driver's license number, Passport number, Telephone number, Financial account number, except as set forth in FL ST J ADMIN Rule 2.425(a)(3), Brokerage account number, Insurance policy account number, Loan account number, Customer account number, or Patient or health care number;

v. A truncated version of any: Email address, Computer user name, Password, or Personal identification number (PIN); and

vi. A truncated version of any other sensitive information as provided by court order. FL ST J ADMIN Rule 2.425(a).

b. *Exceptions.* FL ST J ADMIN Rule 2.425(a) does not apply to the following:

i. An account number which identifies the property alleged to be the subject of a proceeding;

ii. The record of an administrative or agency proceeding;

iii. The record in appellate or review proceedings;

iv. The birth date of a minor whenever the birth date is necessary for the court to establish or maintain subject matter jurisdiction;

v. The name of a minor in any order relating to parental responsibility, time-sharing, or child support;

vi. The name of a minor in any document or order affecting the minor's ownership of real property;

vii. The birth date of a party in a writ of attachment or notice to payor;

viii. In traffic and criminal proceedings: a pro se filing; a court filing that is related to a criminal matter or investigation and that is prepared before the filing of a criminal charge or is not filed as part of any docketed criminal case; an arrest or search warrant or any information in support thereof; a charging document and an affidavit or other documents filed in support of any

charging document, including any driving records; a statement of particulars; discovery material introduced into evidence or otherwise filed with the court; and all information necessary for the proper issuance and execution of a subpoena duces tecum;

ix. Information used by the clerk for case maintenance purposes or the courts for case management purposes; and

x. Information which is relevant and material to an issue before the court. FL ST J ADMIN Rule 2.425(b).

c. *Remedies.* Upon motion by a party or interested person or sua sponte by the court, the court may order remedies, sanctions or both for a violation of FL ST J ADMIN Rule 2.425(a). Following notice and an opportunity to respond, the court may impose sanctions if such filing was not made in good faith. FL ST J ADMIN Rule 2.425(c).

d. *Motions not restricted.* FL ST J ADMIN Rule 2.425 does not restrict a party's right to move for protective order, to move to file documents under seal, or to request a determination of the confidentiality of records. FL ST J ADMIN Rule 2.425(d).

e. *Application.* FL ST J ADMIN Rule 2.425 does not affect the application of constitutional provisions, statutes, or rules of court regarding confidential information or access to public information. FL ST J ADMIN Rule 2.425(e).

F. Filing and Service Requirements

1. *Filing requirements.* All original documents must be filed with the court either before service or immediately thereafter, unless otherwise provided for by general law or other rules. If the original of any bond or other document is not placed in the court file, a certified copy must be so placed by the clerk. FL ST J ADMIN Rule 2.516(d). All documents shall be filed in conformity with the requirements of FL ST J ADMIN Rule 2.525. FL ST RCP Rule 1.080(b). All documents filed in any court shall be filed by electronic transmission in accordance with FL ST J ADMIN Rule 2.525. "Documents" means pleadings, motions, petitions, memoranda, briefs, notices, exhibits, declarations, affidavits, orders, judgments, decrees, writs, opinions, and any other paper or writing submitted to a court. FL ST J ADMIN Rule 2.520(a). All documents that are court records, as defined in FL ST J ADMIN Rule 2.430(a)(1), must be filed by electronic transmission, provided that: (1) the clerk has the ability to accept and retain such documents; (2) the clerk or the chief judge of the circuit has requested permission to accept documents filed by electronic transmission; and (3) the supreme court has entered an order granting permission to the clerk to accept documents filed by electronic transmission. FL ST J ADMIN Rule 2.525(c)(1).

a. *Definition.* "Electronic transmission of documents" means the sending of information by electronic signals to, by or from a court or clerk, which when received can be transformed and stored or transmitted on paper, microfilm, magnetic storage device, optical imaging system, CD-ROM, flash drive, other electronic data storage system, server, case maintenance system ("CM"), electronic court filing ("ECF") system, statewide or local electronic portal ("e-portal"), or other electronic record keeping system authorized by the supreme court in a format sufficient to communicate the information on the original document in a readable format. Electronic transmission of documents includes electronic mail ("e-mail") and any internet-based transmission procedure, and may include procedures allowing for documents to be signed or verified by electronic means. FL ST J ADMIN Rule 2.525(a).

i. The filing of documents with the court as required by the Florida Rules of Judicial Administration must be made by filing them with the clerk in accordance with FL ST J ADMIN Rule 2.525, except that the judge may permit documents to be filed with the judge, in which event the judge must note the filing date before him or her on the documents and transmit them to the clerk. The date of filing is that shown on the face of the document by the judge's notation or the clerk's time stamp, whichever is earlier. FL ST J ADMIN Rule 2.516(e).

b. *Application.* Any court or clerk of the court may accept the electronic transmission of documents for filing after the clerk, together with input from the chief judge of the circuit, has obtained approval of the procedures and program for doing so from the Supreme Court of Florida. FL ST J ADMIN Rule 2.525(b).

c. *Exceptions*
   i. Paper documents and other submissions may be manually submitted to the clerk or court:
      - When the clerk does not have the ability to accept and retain documents by electronic filing or has not had ECF Procedures approved by the supreme court;
      - For filing by any self-represented party or any self-represented nonparty unless specific ECF Procedures provide a means to file documents electronically. However, any self-represented nonparty that is a governmental or public agency and any other agency, partnership, corporation, or business entity acting on behalf of any governmental or public agency may file documents by electronic transmission if such entity has the capability of filing documents electronically;
      - For filing by attorneys excused from e-mail service in accordance with FL ST J ADMIN Rule 2.516(b);
      - When submitting evidentiary exhibits or filing non-documentary materials;
      - When the filing involves documents in excess of twenty-five (25) megabytes (25MB) in size. For such filings, documents may be transmitted using an electronic storage medium that the clerk has the ability to accept, which may include a CD-ROM, flash drive, or similar storage medium;
      - When filed in open court, as permitted by the court;
      - When paper filing is permitted by any approved statewide or local ECF procedures; and
      - If any court determines that justice so requires. FL ST J ADMIN Rule 2.525(d).
   ii. Any document in paper form submitted under FL ST J ADMIN Rule 2.525(d) is filed when it is received by the clerk or court and the clerk shall immediately thereafter convert any filed paper document to an electronic document. "Convert to an electronic document" means optically capturing an image of a paper document and using character recognition software to recover as much of the document's text as practicable and then indexing and storing the document in the official court file. FL ST J ADMIN Rule 2.525(c)(4).
   iii. Any storage medium submitted under FL ST J ADMIN Rule 2.525(d)(5) is filed when received by the clerk or court and the clerk shall immediately thereafter transfer the electronic documents from the storage device to the official court file. FL ST J ADMIN Rule 2.525(c)(5).
   iv. If the filer of any paper document authorized under FL ST J ADMIN Rule 2.525(d) provides a self-addressed, postage-paid envelope for return of the paper document after it is converted to electronic form by the clerk, the clerk shall place the paper document in the envelope and deposit it in the mail. Except when a paper document is required to be maintained, the clerk may recycle any filed paper document that is not to be returned to the filer. FL ST J ADMIN Rule 2.525(c)(6).
   v. The clerk may convert any paper document filed before the effective date of FL ST J ADMIN Rule 2.525 to an electronic document. Unless the clerk is required to maintain the paper document, if the paper document has been converted to an electronic document by the clerk, the paper document is no longer part of the official court file and may be removed and recycled. FL ST J ADMIN Rule 2.525(c)(7).

d. *Official court file.* For information on what constitutes the official court file, please see FL ST J ADMIN Rule 2.525(c)(2), FL ST J ADMIN Rule 2.525(c)(3).

e. *Administration.* All attorneys, parties, or other persons using this rule to file documents are required to make arrangements with the court or clerk for the payment of any charges authorized by general law or the supreme court before filing any document by electronic transmission. FL ST J ADMIN Rule 2.525(f)(2).

f. *Filing date.* The filing date for an electronically transmitted document is the date and time that such filing is acknowledged by an electronic stamp or otherwise, pursuant to any procedure set forth in any ECF Procedures approved by the supreme court, or the date the last page of such filing is received by the court or clerk. FL ST J ADMIN Rule 2.525(f)(3).

g. *Accessibility.* All documents transmitted in any electronic form under FL ST J ADMIN Rule 2.525 must comply with the accessibility requirements of FL ST J ADMIN Rule 2.526. FL ST J ADMIN Rule 2.525(g).

h. *Provisions for electronic filing in the Seventeenth Circuit.* Attorneys may electronically file pleadings and papers on existing cases in circuit civil divisions 1, 7, 9, 19, 26 and 27. The following documents may be scanned and efiled; however, the original must be filed with the Clerk: Documents ordered by the Court; and original documents required by law or rule of procedure to be filed with the Clerk. Self represented individuals shall file pleadings and papers with the Clerk. The Clerk within twenty four (24) hours of receipt of an electronic document shall either accept or reject the electronic document for filing and send electronic notice to the filer. FL ST 17 J CIR 2012-16-CIV.

i. *Technical failures.* If a document filed electronically is not received due to: an error in the transmission of the document to the Clerk or any vendor of the Clerk to provide electronic court record filing services which is unknown to an attorney or party or affected non party, or a failure to process the electronic document when received by the Clerk or rejection by the Clerk, or any other technical problems experienced by the attorney or party or affected non party, the Court may, after an evidentiary hearing and upon satisfactory proof, enter an order permitting the document to be filed nunc pro tunc to the date it was first attempted to be sent electronically. FL ST 17 J CIR 2012-16-CIV.

j. *Filing of pleadings or papers at any office of the clerk of court.* The Clerk of Courts, commencing November 3, 2008, shall accept for filing, at the central courthouse, north satellite courthouse, south satellite courthouse, and west satellite courthouse any pleading or motion or other document for filing in the court file from any attorney or party for an existing case except as otherwise set forth. FL ST 17 J CIR 2008-153-GEN. See FL ST 17 J CIR 2008-153-GEN for specific exceptions.

2. *Service requirements.* Every pleading subsequent to the initial pleading, all orders, and every other document filed in the action must be served in conformity with the requirements of FL ST J ADMIN Rule 2.516. FL ST RCP Rule 1.080(a).

a. *Service; When required.* Unless the court otherwise orders, or a statute or supreme court administrative order specifies a different means of service, every pleading subsequent to the initial pleading and every other document filed in any court proceeding, except applications for witness subpoenas and documents served by formal notice or required to be served in the manner provided for service of formal notice, must be served in accordance with FL ST J ADMIN Rule 2.516 on each party. No service need be made on parties against whom a default has been entered, except that pleadings asserting new or additional claims against them must be served in the manner provided for service of summons. FL ST J ADMIN Rule 2.516(a).

b. *Service; How made.* When service is required or permitted to be made upon a party represented by an attorney, service must be made upon the attorney unless service upon the party is ordered by the court. FL ST J ADMIN Rule 2.516(b).

i. *Service by electronic mail ("e-mail").* All documents required or permitted to be served on another party must be served by e-mail, unless FL ST J ADMIN Rule 2.516 otherwise provides. When, in addition to service by e-mail, the sender also utilizes another means of service provided for in FL ST J ADMIN Rule 2.516(b)(2), any differing time limits and other provisions applicable to that other means of service control. FL ST J ADMIN Rule 2.516(b)(1). Any document electronically transmitted to a court or clerk must also be served on all parties and interested persons in accordance with the applicable rules of court. FL ST J ADMIN Rule 2.525(e)(2).

- *Service on attorneys.* Upon appearing in a proceeding, an attorney must serve a designation of a primary e-mail address and may designate no more than two (2) secondary e-mail addresses. Thereafter, service must be directed to all designated e-mail addresses in that proceeding. Every document filed by an attorney thereafter must include the primary e-mail address of that attorney and any secondary e-mail addresses. If an attorney does not designate any e-mail address for service, documents may be served on that attorney at the e-mail address on record with The Florida Bar. FL ST J ADMIN Rule 2.516(b)(1)(A).

- *Exception to e-mail service on attorneys.* Service by an attorney on another attorney must be made by e-mail unless excused by the court. Upon motion by an attorney demonstrating that the attorney has no e-mail account and lacks access to the Internet at the attorney's office, the court may excuse the attorney from the requirements of e-mail service. Service on and by an attorney excused by the court from e-mail service must be by the means provided in FL ST J ADMIN Rule 2.516(b)(2). FL ST J ADMIN Rule 2.516(b)(1)(B).
- *Service on and by parties not represented by an attorney.* Any party not represented by an attorney may serve a designation of a primary e-mail address and also may designate no more than two (2) secondary e-mail addresses to which service must be directed in that proceeding by the means provided in FL ST J ADMIN Rule 2.516(b)(1). If a party not represented by an attorney does not designate an e-mail address for service in a proceeding, service on and by that party must be by the means provided in FL ST J ADMIN Rule 2.516(b)(2). FL ST J ADMIN Rule 2.516(b)(1)(C).
- *Time of service.* Service by e-mail is complete when it is sent. FL ST J ADMIN Rule 2.516(b)(1)(D). An e-mail is deemed served on the date it is sent. FL ST J ADMIN Rule 2.516(b)(1)(D)(i). If the sender learns that the e-mail did not reach the address of the person to be served, the sender must immediately send another copy by e-mail, or by a means authorized by FL ST J ADMIN Rule 2.516(b)(2). FL ST J ADMIN Rule 2.516(b)(1)(D)(ii). E-mail service is treated as service by mail for the computation of time. FL ST J ADMIN Rule 2.516(b)(1)(D)(iii).

ii. *Format of e-mail for service.* Service of a document by e-mail is made by attaching a copy of the document in PDF format to an e-mail sent to all addresses designated by the attorney or party. FL ST J ADMIN Rule 2.516(b)(1)(E).

- All documents served by e-mail must be attached to an e-mail message containing a subject line beginning with the words "SERVICE OF COURT DOCUMENT" in all capital letters, followed by the case number of the proceeding in which the documents are being served. FL ST J ADMIN Rule 2.516(b)(1)(E)(i).
- The body of the e-mail must identify the court in which the proceeding is pending, the case number, the name of the initial party on each side, the title of each document served with that e-mail, and the sender's name and telephone number. FL ST J ADMIN Rule 2.516(b)(1)(E)(ii).
- Any document served by e-mail may be signed by the "/s/" format, as long as the filed original is signed in accordance with the applicable rule of procedure. FL ST J ADMIN Rule 2.516(b)(1)(E)(iii).
- Any e-mail which, together with its attached documents, exceeds five megabytes (5MB) in size, must be divided and sent as separate e-mails, no one of which may exceed five megabytes (5MB) in size and each of which must be sequentially numbered in the subject line. FL ST J ADMIN Rule 2.516(b)(1)(E)(iv).

iii. *Service by other means.* In addition to, and not in lieu of, service by e-mail, service may also be made upon attorneys by any of the means specified in FL ST J ADMIN Rule 2.516(b)(2). Service on and by all parties who are not represented by an attorney and who do not designate an e-mail address, and on and by all attorneys excused from e-mail service, must be made by delivering a copy of the document or by mailing it to the party or attorney at their last known address or, if no address is known, by leaving it with the clerk of the court. Service by mail is complete upon mailing. Delivery of a copy within FL ST J ADMIN Rule 2.516 is complete upon:

- Handing it to the attorney or to the party,
- Leaving it at the attorney's or party's office with a clerk or other person in charge thereof,
- If there is no one in charge, leaving it in a conspicuous place therein,
- If the office is closed or the person to be served has no office, leaving it at the person's usual place of abode with some person of his or her family above fifteen (15) years of age and informing such person of the contents, or

- Transmitting it by facsimile to the attorney's or party's office with a cover sheet containing the sender's name, firm, address, telephone number, and facsimile number, and the number of pages transmitted. When service is made by facsimile, a copy must also be served by any other method permitted by FL ST J ADMIN Rule 2.516. Facsimile service occurs when transmission is complete. FL ST J ADMIN Rule 2.516(b)(2)(A) through FL ST J ADMIN Rule 2.516(b)(2)(E).
- Service by delivery after 5:00 p.m. must be deemed to have been made by mailing on the date of delivery. FL ST J ADMIN Rule 2.516(b)(2)(F).

c. *Service; Numerous defendants.* In actions when the parties are unusually numerous, the court may regulate the service contemplated by the Florida Rules of Judicial Administration on motion or on its own initiative in such manner as may be found to be just and reasonable. FL ST J ADMIN Rule 2.516(c).

d. *Service by clerk.* Service of notices and other documents required to be made by the clerk must also be done as provided in FL ST J ADMIN Rule 2.516(b). FL ST J ADMIN Rule 2.516(g).

G. Hearings

1. The parties may be required to participate in pretrial proceedings to consider and determine the necessity or desirability of an amendment to a pleading. FL ST RCP Rule 1.200(b)(2); FL-PP § 2:151.

H. Forms

1. Official Amended Answer Forms for Florida

a. Caption. FL ST RCP Form 1.901.

b. Notice of compliance when constitutional challenge is brought. FL ST RCP Form 1.975.

2. Amended Answer Forms for Florida

a. Form for amendment to answer. FL-RCPF R 1.190(50).

b. Form for supplement to pleading. FL-RCPF R 1.190(102).

I. Checklist

(I) ❑ Matters to be considered by plaintiff
- (a) ❑ Required documents
  - (1) ❑ Amended answer
  - (2) ❑ Certificate of service
- (b) ❑ Supplemental documents
  - (1) ❑ Exhibits
  - (2) ❑ Notice of constitutional question
- (c) ❑ Timing
  - (1) ❑ A party may amend a pleading once as a matter of course at any time before a responsive pleading is served
  - (2) ❑ If the pleading is one to which no responsive pleading is permitted and the action has not been placed on the trial calendar, may so amend it at any time within twenty (20) days after it is served

Motions, Oppositions and Replies
Motion to Strike

Document Last Updated January 2013

A. Applicable Rules

1. *State rules*

a. Rules of court. FL ST RCP Rule 1.010; FL ST J ADMIN Rule 2.110.

b. Nonverification of pleadings. FL ST RCP Rule 1.030.
c. Service and filing of pleadings, orders, and documents. FL ST RCP Rule 1.080.
d. Time. FL ST RCP Rule 1.090.
e. Pleadings and motions. FL ST RCP Rule 1.100.
f. Defenses. FL ST RCP Rule 1.140.
g. Sham pleadings. FL ST RCP Rule 1.150.
h. Motions. FL ST RCP Rule 1.160.
i. Relief from judgment, decrees or orders. FL ST RCP Rule 1.540.
j. Mediation and arbitration. FL ST RCP Rule 1.700; FL ST RCP Rule 1.710; FL ST RCP Rule 1.720; FL ST RCP Rule 1.730; FL ST RCP Rule 1.750; FL ST RCP Rule 1.800; FL ST RCP Rule 1.810; FL ST RCP Rule 1.820; FL ST RCP Rule 1.830.
k. Forms. FL ST RCP Rule 1.900.
l. Retention of court records. FL ST J ADMIN Rule 2.430.
m. Foreign attorneys. FL ST J ADMIN Rule 2.510.
n. Signature of attorneys and parties. FL ST J ADMIN Rule 2.515.
o. Paper. FL ST J ADMIN Rule 2.520.
p. Electronic filing. FL ST J ADMIN Rule 2.525.
q. Communication equipment. FL ST J ADMIN Rule 2.530.
r. Court reporting. FL ST J ADMIN Rule 2.535.
s. Requests for accommodations by persons with disabilities. FL ST J ADMIN Rule 2.540.
t. Minimization of the filing of sensitive information. FL ST J ADMIN Rule 2.425.
u. Accessibility of information and technology. FL ST J ADMIN Rule 2.526.

2. *Local rules*
   a. Orders for signature; Civil division. FL ST 17 J CIR LOCAL RULE NO. 8.
   b. Uniform motion calendar ex parte motions to compel discovery, and special set hearings. FL ST 17 J CIR LOCAL RULE NO. 10A.
   c. Standards of professional courtesy. FL ST 17 J CIR I-94-O-1.
   d. Administrative order authorizing the filing of pleadings or papers at any office of the clerk of court. FL ST 17 J CIR 2008-153-GEN.
   e. Administrative order regarding provision of ADA accommodations. FL ST 17 J CIR 2010-49-GEN.
   f. Administrative order establishing electronic filing procedures for the civil division. FL ST 17 J CIR 2012-16-CIV.

B. Timing

1. *Motion to strike.* A party may move to strike or the court may strike redundant, immaterial, impertinent, or scandalous matter from any pleading at any time. FL ST RCP Rule 1.140(f).
2. *Motion to strike; Failure to state a legal defense.* If a pleading sets forth a claim for relief to which the adverse party is not required to serve a responsive pleading, the adverse party may assert any defense in law or fact to that claim for relief at the trial, except that the objection of failure to state a legal defense in an answer or reply shall be asserted by motion to strike the defense within twenty (20) days after service of the answer or reply. FL ST RCP Rule 1.140(b).
3. *Motion to strike; Sham pleadings.* If a party deems any pleading or part thereof filed by another party to be a sham, that party may move to strike the pleading or part thereof before the cause is set for trial. FL ST RCP Rule 1.150(a).
4. *General motion timing.* A copy of any written motion which may not be heard ex parte and a copy of the

notice of the hearing thereof shall be served a reasonable time before the time specified for the hearing. FL ST RCP Rule 1.090(d). Copies of the notice of hearing, the motion, and any pleading or interrogatories to which the motion is addressed shall be in the hands of the Judicial Assistant and opposing party at least four (4) working days in advance of the hearing. The original notice shall be filed with the Clerk. FL ST 17 J CIR LOCAL RULE NO. 10A(5).

5. *Standard of professional conduct; Scheduling*
   a. Attorneys should endeavor to provide opposing counsel, parties, witnesses, and other affected persons, sufficient notice of depositions, hearings and other proceedings, except upon agreement of course, in an emergency, or in other circumstances compelling more expedited scheduling. As a general rule, actual notice should be no less than five (5) business days for instate depositions, ten (10) business days for out-of-state depositions and four (4) business days for hearings. FL ST 17 J CIR I-94-O-1(I)(1).
   b. Attorneys should communicate with opposing counsel prior to scheduling depositions, hearings and other proceedings, in an effort to schedule them at times that are mutually convenient for all interested persons. Further, sufficient time should be reserved to permit a complete presentation by counsel for all parties. FL ST 17 J CIR I-94-O-1(I)(2).
   c. Attorneys should notify opposing counsel, the court, and others affected, of scheduling conflicts as soon as they become apparent. Further, attorneys should cooperate with one another regarding all reasonable rescheduling requests that do not prejudice their clients or unduly delay a proceeding. FL ST 17 J CIR I-94-O-1(I)(3).
   d. Attorneys should promptly notify the court or other tribunal of any resolution between the parties that renders a scheduled court appearance unnecessary or otherwise moot. FL ST 17 J CIR I-94-O-1(I)(4).
   e. Attorneys should grant reasonable requests by opposing counsel for extensions of time within which to respond to pleadings, discovery, and other matters when such an extension will not prejudice their client or unduly delay a proceeding. FL ST 17 J CIR I-94-O-1(I)(5).
6. *Timing considerations when filing electronically.* The filing date of an efiled document is when the last page is received by the Clerk. The electronic filing of a document does not modify any filing deadlines as required by law, rule of procedure, or court order. FL ST 17 J CIR 2012-16-CIV.
7. *Computation of time*
   a. *Generally.* Computation of time shall be governed by FL ST J ADMIN Rule 2.514. FL ST RCP Rule 1.090(a). The following rules apply in computing time periods specified in any rule of procedure, local rule, court order, or statute that does not specify a method of computing time. FL ST J ADMIN Rule 2.514(a).
      i. *Period stated in days or a longer unit.* When the period is stated in days or a longer unit of time (A) exclude the day of the event that triggers the period; (B) count every day, including intermediate Saturdays, Sundays, and legal holidays; and (C) include the last day of the period, but if the last day is a Saturday, Sunday, or legal holiday, or falls within any period of time extended through an order of the chief justice under FL ST J ADMIN Rule 2.205(a)(2)(B)(iv), the period continues to run until the end of the next day that is not a Saturday, Sunday, or legal holiday and does not fall within any period of time extended through an order of the chief justice. FL ST J ADMIN Rule 2.514(a)(1).
      ii. *Period stated in hours.* When the period is stated in hours (A) begin counting immediately on the occurrence of the event that triggers the period; (B) count every hour, including hours during intermediate Saturdays, Sundays, and legal holidays; and (C) if the period would end on a Saturday, Sunday, or legal holiday, or during any period of time extended through an order of the chief justice under FL ST J ADMIN Rule 2.205(a)(2)(B)(iv), the period continues to run until the same time on the next day that is not a Saturday, Sunday, or legal holiday and does not fall within any period of time extended through an order of the chief justice. FL ST J ADMIN Rule 2.514(a)(2).
      iii. *Period stated in days less than seven (7) days.* When the period stated in days is less than seven

(7) days, intermediate Saturdays, Sundays, and legal holidays shall be excluded in the computation. FL ST J ADMIN Rule 2.514(a)(3).

iv. *"Last day" defined.* Unless a different time is set by a statute, local rule, or court order, the last day ends (A) for electronic filing or for service by any means, at midnight; and (B) for filing by other means, when the clerk's office is scheduled to close. FL ST J ADMIN Rule 2.514(a)(4).

v. *"Next day" defined.* The "next day" is determined by continuing to count forward when the period is measured after an event and backward when measured before an event. FL ST J ADMIN Rule 2.514(a)(5).

vi. *"Legal holiday" defined.* "Legal holiday" means (A) the day set aside by FL ST § 110.117, for observing New Year's Day, Martin Luther King, Jr.'s Birthday, Memorial Day, Independence Day, Labor Day, Veterans' Day, Thanksgiving Day, the Friday after Thanksgiving Day, or Christmas Day, and (B) any day observed as a holiday by the clerk's office or as designated by the chief judge. FL ST J ADMIN Rule 2.514(a)(6).

b. *Additional time after service by mail or e-mail.* When a party may or must act within a specified time after service and service is made by mail or e-mail, five (5) days are added after the period that would otherwise expire under FL ST J ADMIN Rule 2.514(a). FL ST J ADMIN Rule 2.514(b).

c. *Enlargement.* When an act is required or allowed to be done at or within a specified time by order of court, by the Florida Rules of Civil Procedure, or by notice given thereunder, for cause shown the court at any time in its discretion (1) with or without notice, may order the period enlarged if request therefor is made before the expiration of the period originally prescribed or as extended by a previous order, or (2) upon motion made and notice after the expiration of the specified period, may permit the act to be done when failure to act was the result of excusable neglect, but it may not extend the time for making a motion for new trial, for rehearing, or to alter or amend a judgment; making a motion for relief from a judgment under FL ST RCP Rule 1.540(b); taking an appeal or filing a petition for certiorari; or making a motion for a directed verdict. FL ST RCP Rule 1.090(b).

d. *Unaffected by expiration of term.* The period of time provided for the doing of any act or the taking of any proceeding shall not be affected or limited by the continued existence or expiration of a term of court. The continued existence or expiration of a term of court in no way affects the power of a court to do any act or take any proceeding in any action which is or has been pending before it. FL ST RCP Rule 1.090(c).

C. General Requirements

1. *Motions generally*

a. *Contents.* An application to the court for an order shall be by motion which shall be made in writing unless made during a hearing or trial, shall state with particularity the grounds therefor, and shall set forth the relief or order sought. The requirement of writing is fulfilled if the motion is stated in a written notice of the hearing of the motion. All notices of hearing shall specify each motion or other matter to be heard. FL ST RCP Rule 1.100(b).

b. *Particularity requirement.* The court considers a motion in the light of the substantive law, rule or statute to make its determination. Some rules require a statement of the grounds for a motion under the rule. Failure to give the grounds will result in denial of the motion. This should be the result in all situations when the ground for the motion is not inherent in the rule. FL-PRACPROC § 9:3. The requirement is nevertheless an important one, first because of the due process notice rights of the respondent, as well as for the assistance it provides to the court in its preparation for the hearing or, absent a hearing, for disposition. 4 FLPRAC R 1.100.

2. *Motion to strike under FL ST RCP Rule 1.140.* Two (2) types of motion to strike are authorized by FL ST RCP Rule 1.140. One is used to eliminate immaterial, redundant, impertinent or scandalous allegations. The other is used to test the legal sufficiency of a defense. FL-PRACPROC § 10:6.

a. *Motion to strike to eliminate immaterial, redundant, impertinent or scandalous allegations*

i. As used in FL ST RCP Rule 1.140(f), redundant means allegations that are foreign to the issues or needless repetition of allegations. Immaterial means allegations having no essential or important relationship to the issues or unnecessary elaboration of material allegations. Impertinent means allegations that do not belong to the issue and are not necessary to it. Scandalous means unnecessary allegations censuring or accusing a party. FL-PRACPROC § 10:6.

ii. The motion can be made at any time and does not toll the time for pleading. FL-PRACPROC § 10:6.

iii. The motion reaches improper allegations of damages. When directed to an entire paragraph and any part of it is proper, the motion should be denied. Leave to amend should be granted after striking part of a pleading unless a proper amendment cannot be made. FL-PRACPROC § 10:6.

iv. The use of a motion to strike is not favored by the courts and the remedy is used sparingly. Florida courts have held that an allegation must be "wholly irrelevant" and that if there is some doubt it must be resolved in support of the pleading and against the party moving to strike. If any part of an allegation is relevant, then that part should not be stricken from the pleading. 5 FLPRAC § 7:30.

b. *Motion to strike the legal sufficiency of a defense*

i. The legal insufficiency of a defense alleged in an answer or reply is attacked by a motion to strike. It is the counterpart of a motion to dismiss for failure to state a cause of action directed to a pleading seeking affirmative relief. FL-PRACPROC § 10:7.

ii. A motion to strike a defense tests only the legal sufficiency of the defense, and it is reversible error for a trial court to strike the defense where evidence may be presented to support it. Burns v. Equilease Corp., 357 So.2d 786, 24, 24 U.C.C. Rep.Serv. 254 (Fla. 3d DCA 1978); 20 FLPRAC § 3:15.

3. *Sham pleadings.* If a party deems any pleading or part thereof filed by another party to be a sham, that party may move to strike the pleading or part thereof before the cause is set for trial and the court shall hear the motion, taking evidence of the respective parties, and if the motion is sustained, the pleading to which the motion is directed shall be stricken. Default and summary judgment on the merits may be entered in the discretion of the court or the court may permit additional pleadings to be filed for good cause shown. FL ST RCP Rule 1.150(a).

a. *Contents of motion.* The motion to strike shall be verified and shall set forth fully the facts on which the movant relies and may be supported by affidavit. No traverse of the motion shall be required. FL ST RCP Rule 1.150(b).

b. *Allegations supported by evidence.* The issue is not whether the allegations are material or proper, but whether the allegations are supported by evidence. 5 FLPRAC § 7:30.

4. *Arbitration and mediation*

a. *Referral to arbitration and mediation.* Except as hereinafter provided or as otherwise prohibited by law, the presiding judge may enter an order referring all or any part of a contested civil matter to mediation or arbitration. The parties to any contested civil matter may file a written stipulation to mediate or arbitrate any issue between them at any time. Such stipulation shall be incorporated into the order of referral. FL ST RCP Rule 1.700(a).

b. *Arbitration*

i. *Exclusions.* A civil action shall be ordered to arbitration or arbitration in conjunction with mediation upon stipulation of the parties. A civil action may be ordered to arbitration or arbitration in conjunction with mediation upon motion of any party or by the court, if the judge determines the action to be of such a nature that arbitration could be of benefit to the litigants or the court. FL ST RCP Rule 1.800.

- Under no circumstances may the following categories of actions be referred to arbitration: (1) bond estreatures; (2) habeas corpus or other extraordinary writs; (3) bond validations; (4) civil or criminal contempt; (5) such other matters as may be specified by order of the chief judge in the circuit. FL ST RCP Rule 1.800.

ii. For more information regarding arbitration, please see FL ST RCP Rule 1.810; FL ST RCP Rule 1.820; FL ST RCP Rule 1.830.

c. *Mediation.* For more information regarding mediation, please see FL ST RCP Rule 1.710; FL ST RCP Rule 1.720; FL ST RCP Rule 1.730; and FL ST RCP Rule 1.750.

5. *Rules of court*

a. *Rules of civil procedure.* The Florida Rules of Civil Procedure apply to all actions of a civil nature and all special statutory proceedings in the circuit courts and county courts except those to which the Florida Probate Rules, the Florida Family Law Rules of Procedure, or the Small Claims Rules apply. FL ST RCP Rule 1.010.

i. The form, content, procedure, and time for pleading in all special statutory proceedings shall be as prescribed by the statutes governing the proceeding unless the Florida Rules of Civil Procedure specifically provide to the contrary. FL ST RCP Rule 1.010.

ii. The Florida Rules of Civil Procedure shall be construed to secure the just, speedy, and inexpensive determination of every action. FL ST RCP Rule 1.010.

b. *Rules of judicial administration.* The Florida Rules of Judicial Administration shall apply to administrative matters in all courts to which the Florida Rules of Judicial Administration are applicable by their terms. The Florida Rules of Judicial Administration shall be construed to secure the speedy and inexpensive determination of every proceeding to which they are applicable. The Florida Rules of Judicial Administration shall supersede all conflicting rules and statutes. FL ST J ADMIN Rule 2.110.

D. Documents

1. *Required documents*

a. *Notice of hearing/Motion.* An application to the court for an order shall be by motion which shall be made in writing unless made during a hearing or trial, shall state with particularity the grounds therefor, and shall set forth the relief or order sought. The requirement of writing is fulfilled if the motion is stated in a written notice of the hearing of the motion. All notices of hearing shall specify each motion or other matter to be heard. FL ST RCP Rule 1.100(b).

i. *Notices to persons with disabilities.* See the Format section of this KeyRules document for further information.

b. *Good faith certification.* Prior to setting a matter on the motion calendar, the party or attorney noticing the motion shall attempt to resolve the matter and shall certify the good faith attempt to resolve. FL ST 17 J CIR LOCAL RULE NO. 10A(2). To comply, every party or attorney setting a motion for hearing shall execute the following certification: I hereby certify that A) I have made a good faith attempt to resolve this matter prior to my noticing this motion for hearing, and B) the issues before the Court may be heard and resolved by the court within five (5) minutes. FL ST 17 J CIR LOCAL RULE NO. 10A(3).

c. *Certificate of service.* When any attorney certifies in substance: "I certify that a copy hereof has been furnished to (here insert name or names and addresses used for service) by (e-mail) (delivery) (mail) (fax) on .... (date) ....______________ Attorney" the certificate is taken as prima facie proof of such service in compliance with FL ST J ADMIN Rule 2.516. FL ST J ADMIN Rule 2.516(f).

2. *Supplemental documents*

a. *Proposed order, copies, stamped envelopes.* The court may require that orders or judgments be prepared by a party, may require the party to furnish the court with stamped, addressed envelopes for service of the order or judgment, and may require that proposed orders and judgments be furnished to all parties before entry by the court of the order or judgment. FL ST J ADMIN Rule 2.516(h)(1).

i. A party submitting an order or judgment shall furnish the Court with sufficient copies together with stamped envelopes addressed to all parties entitled to receive a copy. Proposed orders or judgments must be furnished opposing counsel prior to submission to the court. Proposed orders or judgments must be titled to conform with the motion to which it refers. Language in the order or judgment not agreed as conforming to the court's pronouncement shall be brought to the attention of the court. The proposed order shall indicate date of the hearing on which the order is predicated. Attorneys for the movant shall have at Motion Calendar Hearings all proposed orders and judgments together with the appropriate stamped envelopes where applicable. Unless the Court directs otherwise, proposed orders on non-Motion Calendar Hearings must be prepared by the prevailing or designated counsel and submitted to the Court for consideration within forty-eight (48) hours after said hearing. Copies of all such orders, after entry, shall be conformed and mailed by the Clerk of Court, or the judge's secretary, within forty-eight (48) hours. FL ST 17 J CIR LOCAL RULE NO. 8. Any party requesting relief shall furnish the court with a prepared form of order and sufficient copies with stamped addressed envelopes for all parties. FL ST 17 J CIR LOCAL RULE NO. 10A(8).

ii. Attorneys should draft proposed orders promptly and the orders should fairly and adequately represent the ruling of the court. Attorneys should promptly provide, either orally or in writing, proposed orders to opposing counsel for approval. Opposing counsel should then promptly communicate any objections and at that time, the drafting attorney should immediately submit a copy of the proposed order to the court and advise the court as to whether or not it has been approved by opposing counsel. FL ST 17 J CIR I-94-O-1(IV)(3).

b. *Notice of constitutional question.* A party that files a pleading, written motion, or other paper drawing into question the constitutionality of a state statute or a county or municipal charter, ordinance, or franchise must promptly (1) file a notice of constitutional question stating the question and identifying the paper that raises it; and (2) serve the notice and the pleading, written motion, or other paper drawing into question the constitutionality of a state statute or a county or municipal charter, ordinance, or franchise on the Attorney General or the state attorney of the judicial circuit in which the action is pending, by either certified or registered mail. Service of the notice and pleading, written motion, or other paper does not require joinder of the Attorney General or the state attorney as a party to the action. FL ST RCP Rule 1.071.

E. Format

1. *Documents; Type and size.* Documents subject to the exceptions set forth in FL ST J ADMIN Rule 2.525(d) shall be filed on recycled paper measuring eight and one half by eleven (8 1/2 by 11) inches. For purposes of FL ST J ADMIN Rule 2.520, paper is recycled if it contains a minimum content of fifty (50) percent waste paper. Xerographic reduction of legal-size (eight and one half by fourteen (8 1/2 by 14) inches) documents to letter size (eight and one half by eleven (8 1/2 by 11) inches) is prohibited. All other documents filed by electronic transmission shall be filed in a format capable of being printed in a format consistent with the provisions of FL ST J ADMIN Rule 2.250. FL ST J ADMIN Rule 2.520(b).

   a. *Exhibits.* Any exhibit or attachment filed with pleadings or papers may be filed in its original size. FL ST J ADMIN Rule 2.520(c).

   b. *Recording space.* On all papers and documents prepared and filed by the court or by any party to a proceeding which are to be recorded in the public records of any county, including but not limited to final money judgments and notices of lis pendens, a three (3) inch by three (3) inch space at the top right-hand corner on the first page and a one (1) inch by three (3) inch space at the top right-hand corner on each subsequent page shall be left blank and reserved for use by the clerk of court. FL ST J ADMIN Rule 2.520(d).

      i. *Exceptions to recording space.* Any papers or documents created by persons or entities over which the filing party has no control, including but not limited to wills, codicils, trusts, or other testamentary documents; documents prepared or executed by any public officer; documents prepared, executed, acknowledged, or proved outside of the State of Florida; or documents created by State or Federal government agencies, may be filed without the space required by FL ST J ADMIN Rule 2.520. FL ST J ADMIN Rule 2.520(e).

   c. *Noncompliance.* No clerk of court is permitted to refuse to file any document or paper because of noncompliance with the Florida Rules of Judicial Administration. However, upon request of the clerk of court, noncomplying documents must be resubmitted in accordance with the formatting rules. FL ST J ADMIN Rule 2.520(f).

2. *Caption.* Every pleading, motion, order, judgment, or other paper shall have a caption containing the name of the court, the file number, and except for in rem proceedings, including forfeiture proceedings, the name of the first party on each side with an appropriate indication of other parties, and a designation

identifying the party filing it and its nature or the nature of the order, as the case may be. In any in rem proceeding, every pleading, motion, order, judgment, or other paper shall have a caption containing the name of the court, the file number, the style "In re" (followed by the name or general description of the property), and a designation of the person or entity filing it and its nature or the nature of the order, as the case may be. In an in rem forfeiture proceeding, the style shall be "In re forfeiture of" (followed by the name of the general description of the property). All papers filed in the action shall be styled in such a manner as to indicate clearly the subject matter of the paper and the party requesting or obtaining relief. FL ST RCP Rule 1.100(c)(1).

3. *Writing and written defined.* Writing or written means a document containing information, an application, or a stipulation. FL ST RCP Rule 1.080(c).
4. *Rule abbreviations*
    a. The Florida Rules of Civil Procedure and shall be abbreviated as Fla.R.Civ.P. FL ST RCP Rule 1.010.
    b. The Florida Rules of Judicial Administration shall be abbreviated as Fla. R. Jud. Admin. FL ST J ADMIN Rule 2.110.
5. *Nonverification.* Except when otherwise specifically provided by the Florida Rules of Civil Procedure or an applicable statute, every pleading or other document of a party represented by an attorney need not be verified or accompanied by an affidavit. FL ST RCP Rule 1.030; FL ST J ADMIN Rule 2.515(a).
6. *Attorney signature*
    a. *Attorney signature.* Every pleading and other document of a party represented by an attorney shall be signed by at least one (1) attorney of record in that attorney's individual name whose current record Florida Bar address, telephone number, including area code, primary e-mail address and secondary e-mail addresses, if any, and Florida Bar number shall be stated, and who shall be duly licensed to practice law in Florida or who shall have received permission to appear in the particular case as provided in FL ST J ADMIN Rule 2.510. FL ST J ADMIN Rule 2.515(a).
        i. The attorney may be required by the court to give the address of, and to vouch for the attorney's authority to represent, the party. FL ST J ADMIN Rule 2.515(a).
        ii. The signature of an attorney shall constitute a certificate by the attorney that the attorney has read the pleading or other document; that to the best of the attorney's knowledge, information, and belief there is good ground to support it; and that it is not interposed for delay. FL ST J ADMIN Rule 2.515(a).
        iii. If a pleading is not signed or is signed with intent to defeat the purpose of FL ST J ADMIN Rule 2.515, it may be stricken and the action may proceed as though the pleading or other document had not been served. FL ST J ADMIN Rule 2.515(a).
    b. *Pro se litigant signature.* A party who is not represented by an attorney shall sign any pleading or other paper and state the party's address and telephone number, including area code. FL ST J ADMIN Rule 2.515(b).
    c. *Form of signature*
        i. The signatures required on pleadings and documents by FL ST J ADMIN Rule 2.515(a) and FL ST J ADMIN Rule 2.515(b) may be:
            - Original signatures;
            - Original signatures that have been reproduced by electronic means, such as on electronically transmitted documents or photocopied documents;
            - Electronic signatures using the "/s/," "s/," or "/s" formats by or at the direction of the person signing; or
            - Any other signature format authorized by general law, so long as the clerk where the proceeding is pending has the capability of receiving and has obtained approval from the Supreme Court of Florida to accept pleadings and documents with that signature format. FL ST J ADMIN Rule 2.515(c)(1).

ii. An attorney, party, or other person who files a pleading or paper by electronic transmission that does not contain the original signature of that attorney, party, or other person shall file that identical pleading or paper in paper form containing an original signature of that attorney, party, or other person (hereinafter called the follow-up filing) immediately thereafter. The follow-up filing is not required if the Supreme Court of Florida has entered an order directing the clerk of court to discontinue accepting the follow-up filing. FL ST J ADMIN Rule 2.515(c)(2).

iii. The placement of a "/s/" or the image of a signature by an attorney or party or affected non-party signature line on an electronically filed document shall be accepted as the signature and shall verify to the Court the filer is in possession of the originally executed document. Notwithstanding the manner in which an electronic document is signed the originally executed pleading or paper shall be maintained in the filer's possession for a minimum of one (1) year after final disposition and time for appeal of the case. The originally executed document shall be produced for filing or inspection as directed by the Court. FL ST 17 J CIR 2012-16-CIV.

7. *Forms*

a. *Process.* The forms of process, notice of lis pendens, and notice of action provided in the Florida Rules of Civil Procedure are sufficient. Variations from the forms do not void process or notices that are otherwise sufficient. FL ST RCP Rule 1.900(a).

b. *Other forms.* The other forms provided in the Florida Rules of Civil Procedure are sufficient for the matters that are covered by them. So long as the substance is expressed without prolixity, the forms may be varied to meet the facts of a particular case. FL ST RCP Rule 1.900(b).

c. *Formal matters.* Captions, except for the designation of the paper, are omitted from the forms provided in the Florida Rules of Civil Procedure. A general form of caption is the first form provided. Signatures are omitted from pleadings and motions. FL ST RCP Rule 1.900(c).

8. *Notices to persons with disabilities.* All notices of court proceedings to be held in a public facility, and all process compelling appearance at such proceedings, shall include the following statement in bold face, fourteen (14) point Times New Roman or Courier font: "If you are a person with a disability who needs any accommodation in order to participate in this proceeding, you are entitled, at no cost to you, to the provision of certain assistance. Please contact [identify applicable court personnel by name, address, and telephone number] at least seven (7) days before your scheduled court appearance, or immediately upon receiving this notification if the time before the scheduled appearance is less than seven (7) days; if you are hearing or voice impaired, call 711." FL ST J ADMIN Rule 2.540(c)(1). For further information, please see FL ST 17 J CIR 2010-49-GEN.

9. *Minimization of the filing of sensitive information*

a. *Limitations for court filings.* Unless authorized by FL ST J ADMIN Rule 2.425(b), statute, another rule of court, or the court orders otherwise, designated sensitive information filed with the court must be limited to the following format:

i. The initials of a person known to be a minor;

ii. The year of birth of a person's birth date;

iii. No portion of any: Social security number, Bank account number, Credit card account number, Charge account number, or Debit account number;

iv. The last four digits of any: Taxpayer identification number (TIN), Employee identification number, Driver's license number, Passport number, Telephone number, Financial account number, except as set forth in FL ST J ADMIN Rule 2.425(a)(3), Brokerage account number, Insurance policy account number, Loan account number, Customer account number, or Patient or health care number;

v. A truncated version of any: Email address, Computer user name, Password, or Personal identification number (PIN); and

vi. A truncated version of any other sensitive information as provided by court order. FL ST J ADMIN Rule 2.425(a).

b. *Exceptions.* FL ST J ADMIN Rule 2.425(a) does not apply to the following:

i. An account number which identifies the property alleged to be the subject of a proceeding;

ii. The record of an administrative or agency proceeding;

iii. The record in appellate or review proceedings;

iv. The birth date of a minor whenever the birth date is necessary for the court to establish or maintain subject matter jurisdiction;

v. The name of a minor in any order relating to parental responsibility, time-sharing, or child support;

vi. The name of a minor in any document or order affecting the minor's ownership of real property;

vii. The birth date of a party in a writ of attachment or notice to payor;

viii. In traffic and criminal proceedings: a pro se filing; a court filing that is related to a criminal matter or investigation and that is prepared before the filing of a criminal charge or is not filed as part of any docketed criminal case; an arrest or search warrant or any information in support thereof; a charging document and an affidavit or other documents filed in support of any charging document, including any driving records; a statement of particulars; discovery material introduced into evidence or otherwise filed with the court; and all information necessary for the proper issuance and execution of a subpoena duces tecum;

ix. Information used by the clerk for case maintenance purposes or the courts for case management purposes; and

x. Information which is relevant and material to an issue before the court. FL ST J ADMIN Rule 2.425(b).

c. *Remedies.* Upon motion by a party or interested person or sua sponte by the court, the court may order remedies, sanctions or both for a violation of FL ST J ADMIN Rule 2.425(a). Following notice and an opportunity to respond, the court may impose sanctions if such filing was not made in good faith. FL ST J ADMIN Rule 2.425(c).

d. *Motions not restricted.* FL ST J ADMIN Rule 2.425 does not restrict a party's right to move for protective order, to move to file documents under seal, or to request a determination of the confidentiality of records. FL ST J ADMIN Rule 2.425(d).

e. *Application.* FL ST J ADMIN Rule 2.425 does not affect the application of constitutional provisions, statutes, or rules of court regarding confidential information or access to public information. FL ST J ADMIN Rule 2.425(e).

F. Filing and Service Requirements

1. *Filing requirements.* All original documents must be filed with the court either before service or immediately thereafter, unless otherwise provided for by general law or other rules. If the original of any bond or other document is not placed in the court file, a certified copy must be so placed by the clerk. FL ST J ADMIN Rule 2.516(d). All documents shall be filed in conformity with the requirements of FL ST J ADMIN Rule 2.525. FL ST RCP Rule 1.080(b). All documents filed in any court shall be filed by electronic transmission in accordance with FL ST J ADMIN Rule 2.525. "Documents" means pleadings, motions, petitions, memoranda, briefs, notices, exhibits, declarations, affidavits, orders, judgments, decrees, writs, opinions, and any other paper or writing submitted to a court. FL ST J ADMIN Rule 2.520(a). All documents that are court records, as defined in FL ST J ADMIN Rule 2.430(a)(1), must be filed by electronic transmission, provided that: (1) the clerk has the ability to accept and retain such documents; (2) the clerk or the chief judge of the circuit has requested permission to accept documents filed by electronic transmission; and (3) the supreme court has entered an order granting permission to the clerk to accept documents filed by electronic transmission. FL ST J ADMIN Rule 2.525(c)(1).

a. *Definition.* "Electronic transmission of documents" means the sending of information by electronic signals to, by or from a court or clerk, which when received can be transformed and stored or transmitted on paper, microfilm, magnetic storage device, optical imaging system, CD-ROM, flash drive, other electronic data storage system, server, case maintenance system ("CM"), electronic court filing ("ECF") system, statewide or local electronic portal ("e-portal"), or other electronic record keeping system authorized by the supreme court in a format sufficient to communicate the information on the original document in a readable format. Electronic transmission of documents

includes electronic mail ("e-mail") and any internet-based transmission procedure, and may include procedures allowing for documents to be signed or verified by electronic means. FL ST J ADMIN Rule 2.525(a).

i. The filing of documents with the court as required by the Florida Rules of Judicial Administration must be made by filing them with the clerk in accordance with FL ST J ADMIN Rule 2.525, except that the judge may permit documents to be filed with the judge, in which event the judge must note the filing date before him or her on the documents and transmit them to the clerk. The date of filing is that shown on the face of the document by the judge's notation or the clerk's time stamp, whichever is earlier. FL ST J ADMIN Rule 2.516(e).

b. *Application.* Any court or clerk of the court may accept the electronic transmission of documents for filing after the clerk, together with input from the chief judge of the circuit, has obtained approval of the procedures and program for doing so from the Supreme Court of Florida. FL ST J ADMIN Rule 2.525(b).

c. *Exceptions*

i. Paper documents and other submissions may be manually submitted to the clerk or court:

- When the clerk does not have the ability to accept and retain documents by electronic filing or has not had ECF Procedures approved by the supreme court;
- For filing by any self-represented party or any self-represented nonparty unless specific ECF Procedures provide a means to file documents electronically. However, any self-represented nonparty that is a governmental or public agency and any other agency, partnership, corporation, or business entity acting on behalf of any governmental or public agency may file documents by electronic transmission if such entity has the capability of filing documents electronically;
- For filing by attorneys excused from e-mail service in accordance with FL ST J ADMIN Rule 2.516(b);
- When submitting evidentiary exhibits or filing non-documentary materials;
- When the filing involves documents in excess of twenty-five (25) megabytes (25MB) in size. For such filings, documents may be transmitted using an electronic storage medium that the clerk has the ability to accept, which may include a CD-ROM, flash drive, or similar storage medium;
- When filed in open court, as permitted by the court;
- When paper filing is permitted by any approved statewide or local ECF procedures; and
- If any court determines that justice so requires. FL ST J ADMIN Rule 2.525(d).

ii. Any document in paper form submitted under FL ST J ADMIN Rule 2.525(d) is filed when it is received by the clerk or court and the clerk shall immediately thereafter convert any filed paper document to an electronic document. "Convert to an electronic document" means optically capturing an image of a paper document and using character recognition software to recover as much of the document's text as practicable and then indexing and storing the document in the official court file. FL ST J ADMIN Rule 2.525(c)(4).

iii. Any storage medium submitted under FL ST J ADMIN Rule 2.525(d)(5) is filed when received by the clerk or court and the clerk shall immediately thereafter transfer the electronic documents from the storage device to the official court file. FL ST J ADMIN Rule 2.525(c)(5).

iv. If the filer of any paper document authorized under FL ST J ADMIN Rule 2.525(d) provides a self-addressed, postage-paid envelope for return of the paper document after it is converted to electronic form by the clerk, the clerk shall place the paper document in the envelope and deposit it in the mail. Except when a paper document is required to be maintained, the clerk may recycle any filed paper document that is not to be returned to the filer. FL ST J ADMIN Rule 2.525(c)(6).

v. The clerk may convert any paper document filed before the effective date of FL ST J ADMIN

Rule 2.525 to an electronic document. Unless the clerk is required to maintain the paper document, if the paper document has been converted to an electronic document by the clerk, the paper document is no longer part of the official court file and may be removed and recycled. FL ST J ADMIN Rule 2.525(c)(7).

d. *Official court file.* For information on what constitutes the official court file, please see FL ST J ADMIN Rule 2.525(c)(2), FL ST J ADMIN Rule 2.525(c)(3).

e. *Administration.* All attorneys, parties, or other persons using this rule to file documents are required to make arrangements with the court or clerk for the payment of any charges authorized by general law or the supreme court before filing any document by electronic transmission. FL ST J ADMIN Rule 2.525(f)(2).

f. *Filing date.* The filing date for an electronically transmitted document is the date and time that such filing is acknowledged by an electronic stamp or otherwise, pursuant to any procedure set forth in any ECF Procedures approved by the supreme court, or the date the last page of such filing is received by the court or clerk. FL ST J ADMIN Rule 2.525(f)(3).

g. *Accessibility.* All documents transmitted in any electronic form under FL ST J ADMIN Rule 2.525 must comply with the accessibility requirements of FL ST J ADMIN Rule 2.526. FL ST J ADMIN Rule 2.525(g).

h. *Provisions for electronic filing in the Seventeenth Circuit.* Attorneys may electronically file pleadings and papers on existing cases in circuit civil divisions 1, 7, 9, 19, 26 and 27. The following documents may be scanned and efiled; however, the original must be filed with the Clerk: Documents ordered by the Court; and original documents required by law or rule of procedure to be filed with the Clerk. Self represented individuals shall file pleadings and papers with the Clerk. The Clerk within twenty four (24) hours of receipt of an electronic document shall either accept or reject the electronic document for filing and send electronic notice to the filer. FL ST 17 J CIR 2012-16-CIV.

i. *Technical failures.* If a document filed electronically is not received due to: an error in the transmission of the document to the Clerk or any vendor of the Clerk to provide electronic court record filing services which is unknown to an attorney or party or affected non party, or a failure to process the electronic document when received by the Clerk or rejection by the Clerk, or any other technical problems experienced by the attorney or party or affected non party, the Court may, after an evidentiary hearing and upon satisfactory proof, enter an order permitting the document to be filed nunc pro tunc to the date it was first attempted to be sent electronically. FL ST 17 J CIR 2012-16-CIV.

j. *Filing of pleadings or papers at any office of the clerk of court.* The Clerk of Courts, commencing November 3, 2008, shall accept for filing, at the central courthouse, north satellite courthouse, south satellite courthouse, and west satellite courthouse any pleading or motion or other document for filing in the court file from any attorney or party for an existing case except as otherwise set forth. FL ST 17 J CIR 2008-153-GEN. See FL ST 17 J CIR 2008-153-GEN for specific exceptions.

2. *Service requirements.* Every pleading subsequent to the initial pleading, all orders, and every other document filed in the action must be served in conformity with the requirements of FL ST J ADMIN Rule 2.516. FL ST RCP Rule 1.080(a).

   a. *Service; When required.* Unless the court otherwise orders, or a statute or supreme court administrative order specifies a different means of service, every pleading subsequent to the initial pleading and every other document filed in any court proceeding, except applications for witness subpoenas and documents served by formal notice or required to be served in the manner provided for service of formal notice, must be served in accordance with FL ST J ADMIN Rule 2.516 on each party. No service need be made on parties against whom a default has been entered, except that pleadings asserting new or additional claims against them must be served in the manner provided for service of summons. FL ST J ADMIN Rule 2.516(a).

   b. *Service; How made.* When service is required or permitted to be made upon a party represented by an attorney, service must be made upon the attorney unless service upon the party is ordered by the court. FL ST J ADMIN Rule 2.516(b).

      i. *Service by electronic mail ("e-mail").* All documents required or permitted to be served on

another party must be served by e-mail, unless FL ST J ADMIN Rule 2.516 otherwise provides. When, in addition to service by e-mail, the sender also utilizes another means of service provided for in FL ST J ADMIN Rule 2.516(b)(2), any differing time limits and other provisions applicable to that other means of service control. FL ST J ADMIN Rule 2.516(b)(1). Any document electronically transmitted to a court or clerk must also be served on all parties and interested persons in accordance with the applicable rules of court. FL ST J ADMIN Rule 2.525(e)(2).

- *Service on attorneys.* Upon appearing in a proceeding, an attorney must serve a designation of a primary e-mail address and may designate no more than two (2) secondary e-mail addresses. Thereafter, service must be directed to all designated e-mail addresses in that proceeding. Every document filed by an attorney thereafter must include the primary e-mail address of that attorney and any secondary e-mail addresses. If an attorney does not designate any e-mail address for service, documents may be served on that attorney at the e-mail address on record with The Florida Bar. FL ST J ADMIN Rule 2.516(b)(1)(A).
- *Exception to e-mail service on attorneys.* Service by an attorney on another attorney must be made by e-mail unless excused by the court. Upon motion by an attorney demonstrating that the attorney has no e-mail account and lacks access to the Internet at the attorney's office, the court may excuse the attorney from the requirements of e-mail service. Service on and by an attorney excused by the court from e-mail service must be by the means provided in FL ST J ADMIN Rule 2.516(b)(2). FL ST J ADMIN Rule 2.516(b)(1)(B).
- *Service on and by parties not represented by an attorney.* Any party not represented by an attorney may serve a designation of a primary e-mail address and also may designate no more than two (2) secondary e-mail addresses to which service must be directed in that proceeding by the means provided in FL ST J ADMIN Rule 2.516(b)(1). If a party not represented by an attorney does not designate an e-mail address for service in a proceeding, service on and by that party must be by the means provided in FL ST J ADMIN Rule 2.516(b)(2). FL ST J ADMIN Rule 2.516(b)(1)(C).
- *Time of service.* Service by e-mail is complete when it is sent. FL ST J ADMIN Rule 2.516(b)(1)(D). An e-mail is deemed served on the date it is sent. FL ST J ADMIN Rule 2.516(b)(1)(D)(i). If the sender learns that the e-mail did not reach the address of the person to be served, the sender must immediately send another copy by e-mail, or by a means authorized by FL ST J ADMIN Rule 2.516(b)(2). FL ST J ADMIN Rule 2.516(b)(1)(D)(ii). E-mail service is treated as service by mail for the computation of time. FL ST J ADMIN Rule 2.516(b)(1)(D)(iii).

ii. *Format of e-mail for service.* Service of a document by e-mail is made by attaching a copy of the document in PDF format to an e-mail sent to all addresses designated by the attorney or party. FL ST J ADMIN Rule 2.516(b)(1)(E).

- All documents served by e-mail must be attached to an e-mail message containing a subject line beginning with the words "SERVICE OF COURT DOCUMENT" in all capital letters, followed by the case number of the proceeding in which the documents are being served. FL ST J ADMIN Rule 2.516(b)(1)(E)(i).
- The body of the e-mail must identify the court in which the proceeding is pending, the case number, the name of the initial party on each side, the title of each document served with that e-mail, and the sender's name and telephone number. FL ST J ADMIN Rule 2.516(b)(1)(E)(ii).
- Any document served by e-mail may be signed by the "/s/" format, as long as the filed original is signed in accordance with the applicable rule of procedure. FL ST J ADMIN Rule 2.516(b)(1)(E)(iii).
- Any e-mail which, together with its attached documents, exceeds five megabytes (5MB) in size, must be divided and sent as separate e-mails, no one of which may exceed five megabytes (5MB) in size and each of which must be sequentially numbered in the subject line. FL ST J ADMIN Rule 2.516(b)(1)(E)(iv).

iii. *Servic by other means.* In addition to, and not in lieu of, service by e-mail, service may also be made upon attorneys by any of the means specified in FL ST J ADMIN Rule 2.516(b)(2). Service on and by all parties who are not represented by an attorney and who do not designate an e-mail address, and on and by all attorneys excused from e-mail service, must be made by delivering a copy of the document or by mailing it to the party or attorney at their last known address or, if no address is known, by leaving it with the clerk of the court. Service by mail is complete upon mailing. Delivery of a copy within FL ST J ADMIN Rule 2.516 is complete upon:

- Handing it to the attorney or to the party,
- Leaving it at the attorney's or party's office with a clerk or other person in charge thereof,
- If there is no one in charge, leaving it in a conspicuous place therein,
- If the office is closed or the person to be served has no office, leaving it at the person's usual place of abode with some person of his or her family above fifteen (15) years of age and informing such person of the contents, or
- Transmitting it by facsimile to the attorney's or party's office with a cover sheet containing the sender's name, firm, address, telephone number, and facsimile number, and the number of pages transmitted. When service is made by facsimile, a copy must also be served by any other method permitted by FL ST J ADMIN Rule 2.516. Facsimile service occurs when transmission is complete. FL ST J ADMIN Rule 2.516(b)(2)(A) through FL ST J ADMIN Rule 2.516(b)(2)(E).
- Service by delivery after 5:00 p.m. must be deemed to have been made by mailing on the date of delivery. FL ST J ADMIN Rule 2.516(b)(2)(F).

c. *Service; Numerous defendants.* In actions when the parties are unusually numerous, the court may regulate the service contemplated by the Florida Rules of Judicial Administration on motion or on its own initiative in such manner as may be found to be just and reasonable. FL ST J ADMIN Rule 2.516(c).

d. *Service by clerk.* Service of notices and other documents required to be made by the clerk must also be done as provided in FL ST J ADMIN Rule 2.516(b). FL ST J ADMIN Rule 2.516(g).

G. Hearings

1. *Communication equipment*

a. *Definition.* Communication equipment means a conference telephone or other electronic device that permits all those appearing or participating to hear and speak to each other, provided that all conversation of all parties is audible to all persons present. FL ST J ADMIN Rule 2.530(a).

b. *Use by all parties.* A county or circuit court judge may, upon the court's own motion or upon the written request of a party, direct that communication equipment be used for a motion hearing, pretrial conference, or a status conference. A judge must give notice to the parties and consider any objections they may have to the use of communication equipment before directing that communication equipment be used. The decision to use communication equipment over the objection of parties will be in the sound discretion of the trial court, except as noted below. FL ST J ADMIN Rule 2.530(b).

c. *Use only by requesting party.* A county or circuit court judge may, upon the written request of a party upon reasonable notice to all other parties, permit a requesting party to participate through communication equipment in a scheduled motion hearing; however, any such request (except in criminal, juvenile, and appellate proceedings) must be granted, absent a showing of good cause to deny the same, where the hearing is set for not longer than fifteen (15) minutes. FL ST J ADMIN Rule 2.530(c).

d. *Testimony*

i. *Generally.* A county or circuit court judge, general magistrate, special magistrate, or hearing officer may allow testimony to be taken through communication equipment if all parties consent or if permitted by another applicable rule of procedure. FL ST J ADMIN Rule 2.530(d)(1).

ii. *Procedure.* Any party desiring to present testimony through communication equipment shall, prior to the hearing or trial at which the testimony is to be presented, contact all parties to determine whether each party consents to this form of testimony. The party seeking to present the testimony shall move for permission to present testimony through communication equipment, which motion shall set forth good cause as to why the testimony should be allowed in this form. FL ST J ADMIN Rule 2.530(d)(2).

iii. *Oath.* Testimony may be taken through communication equipment only if a notary public or other person authorized to administer oaths in the witness's jurisdiction is present with the witness and administers the oath consistent with the laws of the jurisdiction. FL ST J ADMIN Rule 2.530(d)(3).

iv. *Confrontation rights.* In juvenile and criminal proceedings the defendant must make an informed waiver of any confrontation rights that may be abridged by the use of communication equipment. FL ST J ADMIN Rule 2.530(d)(4).

v. *Video testimony.* If the testimony to be presented utilizes video conferencing or comparable two-way visual capabilities, the court in its discretion may modify the procedures set forth in FL ST J ADMIN Rule 2.530 to accommodate the technology utilized. FL ST J ADMIN Rule 2.530(d)(5).

e. *Burden of expense.* The cost for the use of the communication equipment is the responsibility of the requesting party unless otherwise directed by the court. FL ST J ADMIN Rule 2.530(e).

2. *Uniform motion calendar.* The Circuit Judges of the general civil/family division (excluding juvenile/dependency) shall maintain a uniform motion calendar from 8:45 A.M. to 9:30 A.M., Monday through Thursday. The motion calendar shall end PROMPTLY at 9:30 A.M. All parties shall be prepared to proceed at 8:45 A.M., and if one party fails to timely appear, the matter may proceed on the merits in his/her absence. FL ST 17 J CIR LOCAL RULE NO. 10A(1).

3. *Noticed motion limitation.* No more than two (2) motions may be noticed for each case on any given day except by leave of court. FL ST 17 J CIR LOCAL RULE NO. 10A(4).

4. *Ex parte and non-evidentiary motion.* Ex parte matters, non-evidentiary motions, and uncontested proceedings for adoptions, or dissolution may be heard on the uniform motion calendar, provided such matters can be conducted in five (5) minutes equally allocated among the parties and the moving party shall so certify as specified in FL ST 17 J CIR LOCAL RULE NO. 10A(3). FL ST 17 J CIR LOCAL RULE NO. 10A(6).

5. *Good faith effort to resolve issues.* Prior to appearing before the court, the parties shall discuss the issues raised in the pending motion, and both parties shall be prepared to certify at the hearing they have made a good faith effort to resolve the issues. FL ST 17 J CIR LOCAL RULE NO. 10A(7).

6. *Re-noticing hearings.* When the motion calendar has been filled, the judge's office shall notify the party noticing any hearings which cannot be reached. The noticing party shall call opposing counsel and re-notice the hearing. FL ST 17 J CIR LOCAL RULE NO. 10A(9).

7. *Hearing cancellation.* Motion calendar hearings may be canceled by the attorney who set the hearing. FL ST 17 J CIR LOCAL RULE NO. 10A(10).

8. *Other motion calendars.* Hearing officers/general masters shall conduct a motion calendar, the dates and times of which shall be determined by the hearing officer/general master or by administrative order. FL ST 17 J CIR LOCAL RULE NO. 10A(11).

9. *Sanctions.* Failure to comply with the procedures designated in the above paragraphs may result in the hearing being stricken from the docket or such other sanctions as the court deems appropriate. FL ST 17 J CIR LOCAL RULE NO. 10A(12).

H. Forms

1. Official Motion to Strike Forms for Florida

a. Caption. FL ST RCP Form 1.901.

b. Notice of compliance when constitutional challenge is brought. FL ST RCP Form 1.975.

2. Motion to Strike Forms for Florida

a. Motion to strike. FL-PP § 2:128.

b. Form for motion to strike. FL-RCPF R 1.140(802).

c. Form for motion to strike insufficient pleading. FL-RCPF R 1.140(803).

d. Form for motion to strike claim for business or financial losses. FL-RCPF R 1.140(804).

e. Motion; Strike, complaint signed by corporation. FL-PRACFORM § 7:176.

f. Motion; Strike, defenses. FL-PRACFORM § 7:177.

g. Motion; Strike, ejectment chain of title. FL-PRACFORM § 7:178.

h. Motion; Strike, pleading, departure. FL-PRACFORM § 7:180.

i. Motion; Strike, pleading, improper signature. FL-PRACFORM § 7:181.

j. Motion; Strike, sham pleading. FL-PRACFORM § 7:182.

k. Motion; Strike, sham, defenses, statute of limitations and failure of consideration. FL-PRACFORM § 7:183.

l. Motion; Strike, third party complaint. FL-PRACFORM § 7:184.

I. Checklist

(I) ❑ Matters to be considered by moving party

(a) ❑ Required documents

(1) ❑ Notice of hearing/Motion

(2) ❑ Good faith certificate

(3) ❑ Certificate of service

(b) ❑ Supplemental documents

(1) ❑ Proposed order, copies, stamped envelopes

(2) ❑ Notice of constitutional question

(c) ❑ Time for making motion

(1) ❑ A party may move to strike or the court may strike redundant, immaterial, impertinent, or scandalous matter from any pleading at any time

(2) ❑ If a pleading sets forth a claim for relief to which the adverse party is not required to serve a responsive pleading, the adverse party may assert any defense in law or fact to that claim for relief at the trial, except that the objection of failure to state a legal defense in an answer or reply shall be asserted by motion to strike the defense within twenty (20) days after service of the answer or reply

(3) ❑ If a party deems any pleading or part thereof filed by another party to be a sham, that party may move to strike the pleading or part thereof before the cause is set for trial

(4) ❑ A copy of any written motion which may not be heard ex parte and a copy of the notice of the hearing thereof shall be served a reasonable time before the time specified for the hearing

(5) ❑ Copies of the notice of hearing, the motion, and any pleading or interrogatories to which the motion is addressed shall be in the hands of the Judicial Assistant and opposing party at least four (4) working days in advance of the hearing

(II) ❑ Matters to be considered by opposing party

(a) ❑ Required documents

(1) ❑ Response to motion

(2) ❑ Certificate of service

(b) ❑ Supplemental documents

(1) ❑ Proposed order, copies, stamped envelopes

(2) ❑ Notice of constitutional question

(c) ❑ Time for service and filing of opposition

(1) ❑ No time specified for responding to a motion

Motions, Oppositions and Replies
Motion for Leave to Amend

Document Last Updated January 2013

A. Applicable Rules

1. *State rules*
   a. Rules of court. FL ST RCP Rule 1.010; FL ST J ADMIN Rule 2.110.
   b. Nonverification of pleadings. FL ST RCP Rule 1.030.
   c. Process. FL ST RCP Rule 1.070.
   d. Service and filing of pleadings, orders, and documents. FL ST RCP Rule 1.080.
   e. Time. FL ST RCP Rule 1.090.
   f. Pleadings and motions. FL ST RCP Rule 1.100.
   g. Defenses. FL ST RCP Rule 1.140.
   h. Motions. FL ST RCP Rule 1.160.
   i. Amended and supplemental pleadings. FL ST RCP Rule 1.190.
   j. Relief from judgment, decrees or orders. FL ST RCP Rule 1.540.
   k. Mediation and arbitration. FL ST RCP Rule 1.700; FL ST RCP Rule 1.710; FL ST RCP Rule 1.720; FL ST RCP Rule 1.730; FL ST RCP Rule 1.750; FL ST RCP Rule 1.800; FL ST RCP Rule 1.810; FL ST RCP Rule 1.820; FL ST RCP Rule 1.830.
   l. Forms. FL ST RCP Rule 1.900.
   m. Retention of court records. FL ST J ADMIN Rule 2.430.
   n. Foreign attorneys. FL ST J ADMIN Rule 2.510..
   o. Signature of attorneys and parties. FL ST J ADMIN Rule 2.515.
   p. Paper. FL ST J ADMIN Rule 2.520.
   q. Electronic filing. FL ST J ADMIN Rule 2.525.
   r. Communication equipment. FL ST J ADMIN Rule 2.530.
   s. Court reporting. FL ST J ADMIN Rule 2.535.
   t. Requests for accommodations by persons with disabilities. FL ST J ADMIN Rule 2.540.
   u. Minimization of the filing of sensitive information. FL ST J ADMIN Rule 2.425.
   v. Accessibility of information and technology. FL ST J ADMIN Rule 2.526.
2. *Local rules*
   a. Orders for signature; Civil division. FL ST 17 J CIR LOCAL RULE NO. 8.
   b. Uniform motion calendar ex parte motions to compel discovery, and special set hearings. FL ST 17 J CIR LOCAL RULE NO. 10A.
   c. Standards of professional courtesy. FL ST 17 J CIR I-94-O-1.
   d. Administrative order authorizing the filing of pleadings or papers at any office of the clerk of court. FL ST 17 J CIR 2008-153-GEN.
   e. Administrative order regarding provision of ADA accommodations. FL ST 17 J CIR 2010-49-GEN.

f. Administrative order establishing electronic filing procedures for the civil division. FL ST 17 J CIR 2012-16-CIV.

B. Timing

1. *Amended pleadings as a matter of course.* A party may amend a pleading once as a matter of course at any time before a responsive pleading is served or, if the pleading is one to which no responsive pleading is permitted and the action has not been placed on the trial calendar, may amend it at any time within twenty (20) days after it is served. Otherwise a party may amend a pleading only by leave of court or by written consent of the adverse party. FL ST RCP Rule 1.190(a).
2. *Amended pleadings with leave of court.* Leave of court shall be given freely when justice so requires. FL ST RCP Rule 1.190(a). Under the Florida Rules of Civil Procedure, there is no time limit as to when an amendment with leave of court may be sought. Amendments of the pleadings may be permitted, with the court's discretion, at any stage of the proceedings in furtherance of justice. McSwiggan v. Edson, 186 So.2d 13, 15 (Fla. 1966); FL-PP § 2:153. Nevertheless, the liberality in permitting amendment of pleadings diminishes as the case progresses to trial. Versen v. Versen, 347 So.2d 1047, 1050 (Fla. 4th DCA 1977); FL-PP § 2:153.
3. *Claims for punitive damages.* A motion for leave to amend a pleading to assert a claim for punitive damages can be filed separately and before the supporting evidence or proffer, but each shall be served on all parties at least twenty (20) days before the hearing. FL ST RCP Rule 1.190(f).
4. *Post motion for leave to amend*
   a. If the court permits or requires an amended or responsive pleading or a more definite statement, the pleading or statement shall be served within ten (10) days after notice of the court's action. FL ST RCP Rule 1.140(a)(4).
   b. When a motion for leave to amend with the attached proposed amended complaint is filed, the one hundred twenty (120) day period for service of amended complaints on the new party or parties shall begin upon the entry of an order granting leave to amend. FL ST RCP Rule 1.070(j).
5. *General motion timing.* A copy of any written motion which may not be heard ex parte and a copy of the notice of the hearing thereof shall be served a reasonable time before the time specified for the hearing. FL ST RCP Rule 1.090(d). Copies of the notice of hearing, the motion, and any pleading or interrogatories to which the motion is addressed shall be in the hands of the Judicial Assistant and opposing party at least four (4) working days in advance of the hearing. The original notice shall be filed with the Clerk. FL ST 17 J CIR LOCAL RULE NO. 10A(5).
6. *Standard of professional conduct; Scheduling*
   a. Attorneys should endeavor to provide opposing counsel, parties, witnesses, and other affected persons, sufficient notice of depositions, hearings and other proceedings, except upon agreement of course, in an emergency, or in other circumstances compelling more expedited scheduling. As a general rule, actual notice should be no less than five (5) business days for instate depositions, ten (10) business days for out-of-state depositions and four (4) business days for hearings. FL ST 17 J CIR I-94-O-1(I)(1).
   b. Attorneys should communicate with opposing counsel prior to scheduling depositions, hearings and other proceedings, in an effort to schedule them at times that are mutually convenient for all interested persons. Further, sufficient time should be reserved to permit a complete presentation by counsel for all parties. FL ST 17 J CIR I-94-O-1(I)(2).
   c. Attorneys should notify opposing counsel, the court, and others affected, of scheduling conflicts as soon as they become apparent. Further, attorneys should cooperate with one another regarding all reasonable rescheduling requests that do not prejudice their clients or unduly delay a proceeding. FL ST 17 J CIR I-94-O-1(I)(3).
   d. Attorneys should promptly notify the court or other tribunal of any resolution between the parties that renders a scheduled court appearance unnecessary or otherwise moot. FL ST 17 J CIR I-94-O-1(I)(4).
   e. Attorneys should grant reasonable requests by opposing counsel for extensions of time within which

to respond to pleadings, discovery, and other matters when such an extension will not prejudice their client or unduly delay a proceeding. FL ST 17 J CIR I-94-O-1(I)(5).

7. *Timing considerations when filing electronically.* The filing date of an efiled document is when the last page is received by the Clerk. The electronic filing of a document does not modify any filing deadlines as required by law, rule of procedure, or court order. FL ST 17 J CIR 2012-16-CIV.

8. *Computation of time*

   a. *Generally.* Computation of time shall be governed by FL ST J ADMIN Rule 2.514. FL ST RCP Rule 1.090(a). The following rules apply in computing time periods specified in any rule of procedure, local rule, court order, or statute that does not specify a method of computing time. FL ST J ADMIN Rule 2.514(a).

      i. *Period stated in days or a longer unit.* When the period is stated in days or a longer unit of time (A) exclude the day of the event that triggers the period; (B) count every day, including intermediate Saturdays, Sundays, and legal holidays; and (C) include the last day of the period, but if the last day is a Saturday, Sunday, or legal holiday, or falls within any period of time extended through an order of the chief justice under FL ST J ADMIN Rule 2.205(a)(2)(B)(iv), the period continues to run until the end of the next day that is not a Saturday, Sunday, or legal holiday and does not fall within any period of time extended through an order of the chief justice. FL ST J ADMIN Rule 2.514(a)(1).

      ii. *Period stated in hours.* When the period is stated in hours (A) begin counting immediately on the occurrence of the event that triggers the period; (B) count every hour, including hours during intermediate Saturdays, Sundays, and legal holidays; and (C) if the period would end on a Saturday, Sunday, or legal holiday, or during any period of time extended through an order of the chief justice under FL ST J ADMIN Rule 2.205(a)(2)(B)(iv), the period continues to run until the same time on the next day that is not a Saturday, Sunday, or legal holiday and does not fall within any period of time extended through an order of the chief justice. FL ST J ADMIN Rule 2.514(a)(2).

      iii. *Period stated in days less than seven (7) days.* When the period stated in days is less than seven (7) days, intermediate Saturdays, Sundays, and legal holidays shall be excluded in the computation. FL ST J ADMIN Rule 2.514(a)(3).

      iv. *"Last day" defined.* Unless a different time is set by a statute, local rule, or court order, the last day ends (A) for electronic filing or for service by any means, at midnight; and (B) for filing by other means, when the clerk's office is scheduled to close. FL ST J ADMIN Rule 2.514(a)(4).

      v. *"Next day" defined.* The "next day" is determined by continuing to count forward when the period is measured after an event and backward when measured before an event. FL ST J ADMIN Rule 2.514(a)(5).

      vi. *"Legal holiday" defined.* "Legal holiday" means (A) the day set aside by FL ST § 110.117, for observing New Year's Day, Martin Luther King, Jr.'s Birthday, Memorial Day, Independence Day, Labor Day, Veterans' Day, Thanksgiving Day, the Friday after Thanksgiving Day, or Christmas Day, and (B) any day observed as a holiday by the clerk's office or as designated by the chief judge. FL ST J ADMIN Rule 2.514(a)(6).

   b. *Additional time after service by mail or e-mail.* When a party may or must act within a specified time after service and service is made by mail or e-mail, five (5) days are added after the period that would otherwise expire under FL ST J ADMIN Rule 2.514(a). FL ST J ADMIN Rule 2.514(b).

   c. *Enlargement.* When an act is required or allowed to be done at or within a specified time by order of court, by the Florida Rules of Civil Procedure, or by notice given thereunder, for cause shown the court at any time in its discretion (1) with or without notice, may order the period enlarged if request therefor is made before the expiration of the period originally prescribed or as extended by a previous order, or (2) upon motion made and notice after the expiration of the specified period, may permit the act to be done when failure to act was the result of excusable neglect, but it may not extend the time for making a motion for new trial, for rehearing, or to alter or amend a judgment; making a motion for relief from a judgment under FL ST RCP Rule 1.540(b); taking an appeal or filing a petition for certiorari; or making a motion for a directed verdict. FL ST RCP Rule 1.090(b).

d. *Unaffected by expiration of term.* The period of time provided for the doing of any act or the taking of any proceeding shall not be affected or limited by the continued existence or expiration of a term of court. The continued existence or expiration of a term of court in no way affects the power of a court to do any act or take any proceeding in any action which is or has been pending before it. FL ST RCP Rule 1.090(c).

C. General Requirements

1. *Motions generally*

   a. *Contents.* An application to the court for an order shall be by motion which shall be made in writing unless made during a hearing or trial, shall state with particularity the grounds therefor, and shall set forth the relief or order sought. The requirement of writing is fulfilled if the motion is stated in a written notice of the hearing of the motion. All notices of hearing shall specify each motion or other matter to be heard. FL ST RCP Rule 1.100(b).

   b. *Particularity requirement.* The court considers a motion in the light of the substantive law, rule or statute to make its determination. Some rules require a statement of the grounds for a motion under the rule. Failure to give the grounds will result in denial of the motion. This should be the result in all situations when the ground for the motion is not inherent in the rule. FL-PRACPROC § 9:3. The requirement is nevertheless an important one, first because of the due process notice rights of the respondent, as well as for the assistance it provides to the court in its preparation for the hearing or, absent a hearing, for disposition. 4 FLPRAC R 1.100.

2. *Motion for leave to amend.* Although the Florida Rules of Civil Procedure do not specify a procedure for obtaining leave to amend, it is usually accomplished by way of a motion. FL-PP § 2:153. At any time in furtherance of justice, upon such terms as may be just, the court may permit any process, proceeding, pleading, or record to be amended or material supplemental matter to be set forth in an amended or supplemental pleading. At every stage of the action the court must disregard any error or defect in the proceedings which does not affect the substantial rights of the parties. FL ST RCP Rule 1.190(e).

   a. *Permissible amendments.* Amendments can relate to the correction of mistakes, the insertion of jurisdictional averments, the correction or addition of verifications, the addition or substitution or striking out of parties, and generally the rectification of all formal defects in the pleading. The court can also allow amendments setting up an omitted counterclaim or cross-claim if the defendant failed to raise the claim through oversight, inadvertence, or excusable neglect. FL-PP § 2:151.

   b. *Amendments to conform with the evidence.* When issues not raised by the pleadings are tried by express or implied consent of the parties, they shall be treated in all respects as if they had been raised in the pleadings. Such amendment of the pleadings as may be necessary to cause them to conform to the evidence and to raise these issues may be made upon motion of any party at any time, even after judgment, but failure so to amend shall not affect the result of the trial of these issues. If the evidence is objected to at the trial on the ground that it is not within the issues made by the pleadings, the court may allow the pleadings to be amended to conform with the evidence and shall do so freely when the merits of the cause are more effectually presented thereby and the objecting party fails to satisfy the court that the admission of such evidence will prejudice the objecting party in maintaining an action or defense upon the merits. FL ST RCP Rule 1.190(b).

      i. The courts have been extremely liberal in permitting amendments after trial to conform pleadings to the evidence where the issues were tried by the express or implied consent of the parties. Turner v. Long, 225 So.2d 434 (Fla. 1st DCA 1969); FL-PP § 2:152.

   c. *Procedure for adding parties.* Parties may be added once as a matter of course within the same time that pleadings can be so amended. If amendment by leave of court or stipulation of the parties is permitted, parties may be added in the amended pleading without further order of court. Parties may be added by order of court on its own initiative or on motion of any party at any stage of the action and on such terms as are just. FL ST RCP Rule 1.250(c).

   d. *Claims for punitive damages.* A motion for leave to amend a pleading to assert a claim for punitive damages shall make a reasonable showing by evidence in the record or evidence to be proffered by the claimant that provides a reasonable basis for recovery of such damages. The motion to amend can be filed separately and before the supporting evidence or proffer, but each shall be served on all parties at least twenty (20) days before the hearing. FL ST RCP Rule 1.190(f). Leave of court to amend the complaint must be obtained before a plaintiff may assert a punitive damages claim in the complaint. Failure to do so will result in the claims being dismissed or stricken. FL-PP § 2:151.

e. *Relation back of amendments.* When the claim or defense asserted in the amended pleading arose out of the conduct, transaction, or occurrence set forth or attempted to be set forth in the original pleading, the amendment shall relate back to the date of the original pleading. FL ST RCP Rule 1.190(c).

    i. The doctrine of relation back becomes critical in applying the statute of limitations. For example, it has been held that the doctrine of relation back may not be utilized to circumvent the statute of limitations to permit an amendment where a claim could have been filed as an independent action but was not timely asserted and would otherwise be barred under the statute of limitations. Cox v. Seaboard Coast Line R. Co., 360 So.2d 8 (Fla. 2d DCA 1978); FL-PP § 2:152.

3. *Arbitration and mediation*

    a. *Referral to arbitration and mediation.* Except as hereinafter provided or as otherwise prohibited by law, the presiding judge may enter an order referring all or any part of a contested civil matter to mediation or arbitration. The parties to any contested civil matter may file a written stipulation to mediate or arbitrate any issue between them at any time. Such stipulation shall be incorporated into the order of referral. FL ST RCP Rule 1.700(a).

    b. *Arbitration*

        i. *Exclusions.* A civil action shall be ordered to arbitration or arbitration in conjunction with mediation upon stipulation of the parties. A civil action may be ordered to arbitration or arbitration in conjunction with mediation upon motion of any party or by the court, if the judge determines the action to be of such a nature that arbitration could be of benefit to the litigants or the court. FL ST RCP Rule 1.800.

            - Under no circumstances may the following categories of actions be referred to arbitration: (1) bond estreatures; (2) habeas corpus or other extraordinary writs; (3) bond validations; (4) civil or criminal contempt; (5) such other matters as may be specified by order of the chief judge in the circuit. FL ST RCP Rule 1.800.

        ii. For more information regarding arbitration, please see FL ST RCP Rule 1.810; FL ST RCP Rule 1.820; FL ST RCP Rule 1.830.

    c. *Mediation.* For more information regarding mediation, please see FL ST RCP Rule 1.710; FL ST RCP Rule 1.720; FL ST RCP Rule 1.730; and FL ST RCP Rule 1.750.

4. *Rules of court*

    a. *Rules of civil procedure.* The Florida Rules of Civil Procedure apply to all actions of a civil nature and all special statutory proceedings in the circuit courts and county courts except those to which the Florida Probate Rules, the Florida Family Law Rules of Procedure, or the Small Claims Rules apply. FL ST RCP Rule 1.010.

        i. The form, content, procedure, and time for pleading in all special statutory proceedings shall be as prescribed by the statutes governing the proceeding unless the Florida Rules of Civil Procedure specifically provide to the contrary. FL ST RCP Rule 1.010.

        ii. The Florida Rules of Civil Procedure shall be construed to secure the just, speedy, and inexpensive determination of every action. FL ST RCP Rule 1.010.

    b. *Rules of judicial administration.* The Florida Rules of Judicial Administration shall apply to administrative matters in all courts to which the Florida Rules of Judicial Administration are applicable by their terms. The Florida Rules of Judicial Administration shall be construed to secure the speedy and inexpensive determination of every proceeding to which they are applicable. The Florida Rules of Judicial Administration shall supersede all conflicting rules and statutes. FL ST J ADMIN Rule 2.110.

D. Documents

1. *Required documents*

   a. *Notice of hearing/Motion.* An application to the court for an order shall be by motion which shall be made in writing unless made during a hearing or trial, shall state with particularity the grounds therefor, and shall set forth the relief or order sought. The requirement of writing is fulfilled if the motion is stated in a written notice of the hearing of the motion. All notices of hearing shall specify each motion or other matter to be heard. FL ST RCP Rule 1.100(b).

      i. *Notices to persons with disabilities.* See the Format section of this KeyRules document for further information.

   b. *Proposed amended pleading.* The moving party shall attach the proposed amended pleading to the motion. FL ST RCP Rule 1.190(a).

   c. *Good faith certification.* Prior to setting a matter on the motion calendar, the party or attorney noticing the motion shall attempt to resolve the matter and shall certify the good faith attempt to resolve. FL ST 17 J CIR LOCAL RULE NO. 10A(2). To comply, every party or attorney setting a motion for hearing shall execute the following certification: I hereby certify that A) I have made a good faith attempt to resolve this matter prior to my noticing this motion for hearing, and B) the issues before the Court may be heard and resolved by the court within five (5) minutes. FL ST 17 J CIR LOCAL RULE NO. 10A(3).

   d. *Certificate of service.* When any attorney certifies in substance: "I certify that a copy hereof has been furnished to (here insert name or names and addresses used for service) by (e-mail) (delivery) (mail) (fax) on .... (date) ....______________ Attorney" the certificate is taken as prima facie proof of such service in compliance with FL ST J ADMIN Rule 2.516. FL ST J ADMIN Rule 2.516(f).

2. *Supplemental documents*

   a. *Proposed order, copies, stamped envelopes.* The court may require that orders or judgments be prepared by a party, may require the party to furnish the court with stamped, addressed envelopes for service of the order or judgment, and may require that proposed orders and judgments be furnished to all parties before entry by the court of the order or judgment. FL ST J ADMIN Rule 2.516(h)(1).

      i. A party submitting an order or judgment shall furnish the Court with sufficient copies together with stamped envelopes addressed to all parties entitled to receive a copy. Proposed orders or judgments must be furnished opposing counsel prior to submission to the court. Proposed orders or judgments must be titled to conform with the motion to which it refers. Language in the order or judgment not agreed as conforming to the court's pronouncement shall be brought to the attention of the court. The proposed order shall indicate date of the hearing on which the order is predicated. Attorneys for the movant shall have at Motion Calendar Hearings all proposed orders and judgments together with the appropriate stamped envelopes where applicable. Unless the Court directs otherwise, proposed orders on non-Motion Calendar Hearings must be prepared by the prevailing or designated counsel and submitted to the Court for consideration within forty-eight (48) hours after said hearing. Copies of all such orders, after entry, shall be conformed and mailed by the Clerk of Court, or the judge's secretary, within forty-eight (48) hours. FL ST 17 J CIR LOCAL RULE NO. 8. Any party requesting relief shall furnish the court with a prepared form of order and sufficient copies with stamped addressed envelopes for all parties. FL ST 17 J CIR LOCAL RULE NO. 10A(8).

      ii. Attorneys should draft proposed orders promptly and the orders should fairly and adequately represent the ruling of the court. Attorneys should promptly provide, either orally or in writing, proposed orders to opposing counsel for approval. Opposing counsel should then promptly communicate any objections and at that time, the drafting attorney should immediately submit a copy of the proposed order to the court and advise the court as to whether or not it has been approved by opposing counsel. FL ST 17 J CIR I-94-O-1(IV)(3).

   b. *Notice of constitutional question.* A party that files a pleading, written motion, or other paper drawing into question the constitutionality of a state statute or a county or municipal charter, ordinance, or franchise must promptly (1) file a notice of constitutional question stating the question

and identifying the paper that raises it; and (2) serve the notice and the pleading, written motion, or other paper drawing into question the constitutionality of a state statute or a county or municipal charter, ordinance, or franchise on the Attorney General or the state attorney of the judicial circuit in which the action is pending, by either certified or registered mail. Service of the notice and pleading, written motion, or other paper does not require joinder of the Attorney General or the state attorney as a party to the action. FL ST RCP Rule 1.071.

E. Format

1. *Documents; Type and size.* Documents subject to the exceptions set forth in FL ST J ADMIN Rule 2.525(d) shall be filed on recycled paper measuring eight and one half by eleven (8 1/2 by 11) inches. For purposes of FL ST J ADMIN Rule 2.520, paper is recycled if it contains a minimum content of fifty (50) percent waste paper. Xerographic reduction of legal-size (eight and one half by fourteen (8 1/2 by 14) inches) documents to letter size (eight and one half by eleven (8 1/2 by 11) inches) is prohibited. All other documents filed by electronic transmission shall be filed in a format capable of being printed in a format consistent with the provisions of FL ST J ADMIN Rule 2.250. FL ST J ADMIN Rule 2.520(b).
   a. *Exhibits.* Any exhibit or attachment filed with pleadings or papers may be filed in its original size. FL ST J ADMIN Rule 2.520(c).
   b. *Recording space.* On all papers and documents prepared and filed by the court or by any party to a proceeding which are to be recorded in the public records of any county, including but not limited to final money judgments and notices of lis pendens, a three (3) inch by three (3) inch space at the top right-hand corner on the first page and a one (1) inch by three (3) inch space at the top right-hand corner on each subsequent page shall be left blank and reserved for use by the clerk of court. FL ST J ADMIN Rule 2.520(d).
      i. *Exceptions to recording space.* Any papers or documents created by persons or entities over which the filing party has no control, including but not limited to wills, codicils, trusts, or other testamentary documents; documents prepared or executed by any public officer; documents prepared, executed, acknowledged, or proved outside of the State of Florida; or documents created by State or Federal government agencies, may be filed without the space required by FL ST J ADMIN Rule 2.520. FL ST J ADMIN Rule 2.520(e).
   c. *Noncompliance.* No clerk of court is permitted to refuse to file any document or paper because of noncompliance with the Florida Rules of Judicial Administration. However, upon request of the clerk of court, noncomplying documents must be resubmitted in accordance with the formatting rules. FL ST J ADMIN Rule 2.520(f).
2. *Caption.* Every pleading, motion, order, judgment, or other paper shall have a caption containing the name of the court, the file number, and except for in rem proceedings, including forfeiture proceedings, the name of the first party on each side with an appropriate indication of other parties, and a designation identifying the party filing it and its nature or the nature of the order, as the case may be. In any in rem proceeding, every pleading, motion, order, judgment, or other paper shall have a caption containing the name of the court, the file number, the style "In re" (followed by the name or general description of the property), and a designation of the person or entity filing it and its nature or the nature of the order, as the case may be. In an in rem forfeiture proceeding, the style shall be "In re forfeiture of" (followed by the name of the general description of the property). All papers filed in the action shall be styled in such a manner as to indicate clearly the subject matter of the paper and the party requesting or obtaining relief. FL ST RCP Rule 1.100(c)(1).
3. *Writing and written defined.* Writing or written means a document containing information, an application, or a stipulation. FL ST RCP Rule 1.080(c).
4. *Rule abbreviations*
   a. The Florida Rules of Civil Procedure and shall be abbreviated as Fla.R.Civ.P. FL ST RCP Rule 1.010.
   b. The Florida Rules of Judicial Administration shall be abbreviated as Fla. R. Jud. Admin. FL ST J ADMIN Rule 2.110.
5. *Nonverification.* Except when otherwise specifically provided by the Florida Rules of Civil Procedure or

an applicable statute, every pleading or other document of a party represented by an attorney need not be verified or accompanied by an affidavit. FL ST RCP Rule 1.030; FL ST J ADMIN Rule 2.515(a).

6. *Attorney signature*

   a. *Attorney signature.* Every pleading and other document of a party represented by an attorney shall be signed by at least one (1) attorney of record in that attorney's individual name whose current record Florida Bar address, telephone number, including area code, primary e-mail address and secondary e-mail addresses, if any, and Florida Bar number shall be stated, and who shall be duly licensed to practice law in Florida or who shall have received permission to appear in the particular case as provided in FL ST J ADMIN Rule 2.510. FL ST J ADMIN Rule 2.515(a).

      i. The attorney may be required by the court to give the address of, and to vouch for the attorney's authority to represent, the party. FL ST J ADMIN Rule 2.515(a).

      ii. The signature of an attorney shall constitute a certificate by the attorney that the attorney has read the pleading or other document; that to the best of the attorney's knowledge, information, and belief there is good ground to support it; and that it is not interposed for delay. FL ST J ADMIN Rule 2.515(a).

      iii. If a pleading is not signed or is signed with intent to defeat the purpose of FL ST J ADMIN Rule 2.515, it may be stricken and the action may proceed as though the pleading or other document had not been served. FL ST J ADMIN Rule 2.515(a).

   b. *Pro se litigant signature.* A party who is not represented by an attorney shall sign any pleading or other paper and state the party's address and telephone number, including area code. FL ST J ADMIN Rule 2.515(b).

   c. *Form of signature*

      i. The signatures required on pleadings and documents by FL ST J ADMIN Rule 2.515(a) and FL ST J ADMIN Rule 2.515(b) may be:

         - Original signatures;
         - Original signatures that have been reproduced by electronic means, such as on electronically transmitted documents or photocopied documents;
         - Electronic signatures using the "/s/," "s/," or "/s" formats by or at the direction of the person signing; or
         - Any other signature format authorized by general law, so long as the clerk where the proceeding is pending has the capability of receiving and has obtained approval from the Supreme Court of Florida to accept pleadings and documents with that signature format. FL ST J ADMIN Rule 2.515(c)(1).

      ii. An attorney, party, or other person who files a pleading or paper by electronic transmission that does not contain the original signature of that attorney, party, or other person shall file that identical pleading or paper in paper form containing an original signature of that attorney, party, or other person (hereinafter called the follow-up filing) immediately thereafter. The follow-up filing is not required if the Supreme Court of Florida has entered an order directing the clerk of court to discontinue accepting the follow-up filing. FL ST J ADMIN Rule 2.515(c)(2).

      iii. The placement of a "/s/" or the image of a signature by an attorney or party or affected non-party signature line on an electronically filed document shall be accepted as the signature and shall verify to the Court the filer is in possession of the originally executed document. Notwithstanding the manner in which an electronic document is signed the originally executed pleading or paper shall be maintained in the filer's possession for a minimum of one (1) year after final disposition and time for appeal of the case. The originally executed document shall be produced for filing or inspection as directed by the Court. FL ST 17 J CIR 2012-16-CIV.

7. *Forms*

   a. *Process.* The forms of process, notice of lis pendens, and notice of action provided in the Florida Rules of Civil Procedure are sufficient. Variations from the forms do not void process or notices that are otherwise sufficient. FL ST RCP Rule 1.900(a).

b. *Other forms.* The other forms provided in the Florida Rules of Civil Procedure are sufficient for the matters that are covered by them. So long as the substance is expressed without prolixity, the forms may be varied to meet the facts of a particular case. FL ST RCP Rule 1.900(b).

c. *Formal matters.* Captions, except for the designation of the paper, are omitted from the forms provided in the Florida Rules of Civil Procedure. A general form of caption is the first form provided. Signatures are omitted from pleadings and motions. FL ST RCP Rule 1.900(c).

8. *Notices to persons with disabilities.* All notices of court proceedings to be held in a public facility, and all process compelling appearance at such proceedings, shall include the following statement in bold face, fourteen (14) point Times New Roman or Courier font: "If you are a person with a disability who needs any accommodation in order to participate in this proceeding, you are entitled, at no cost to you, to the provision of certain assistance. Please contact [identify applicable court personnel by name, address, and telephone number] at least seven (7) days before your scheduled court appearance, or immediately upon receiving this notification if the time before the scheduled appearance is less than seven (7) days; if you are hearing or voice impaired, call 711." FL ST J ADMIN Rule 2.540(c)(1). For further information, please see FL ST 17 J CIR 2010-49-GEN.

9. *Minimization of the filing of sensitive information*

a. *Limitations for court filings.* Unless authorized by FL ST J ADMIN Rule 2.425(b), statute, another rule of court, or the court orders otherwise, designated sensitive information filed with the court must be limited to the following format:

i. The initials of a person known to be a minor;

ii. The year of birth of a person's birth date;

iii. No portion of any: Social security number, Bank account number, Credit card account number, Charge account number, or Debit account number;

iv. The last four digits of any: Taxpayer identification number (TIN), Employee identification number, Driver's license number, Passport number, Telephone number, Financial account number, except as set forth in FL ST J ADMIN Rule 2.425(a)(3), Brokerage account number, Insurance policy account number, Loan account number, Customer account number, or Patient or health care number;

v. A truncated version of any: Email address, Computer user name, Password, or Personal identification number (PIN); and

vi. A truncated version of any other sensitive information as provided by court order. FL ST J ADMIN Rule 2.425(a).

b. *Exceptions.* FL ST J ADMIN Rule 2.425(a) does not apply to the following:

i. An account number which identifies the property alleged to be the subject of a proceeding;

ii. The record of an administrative or agency proceeding;

iii. The record in appellate or review proceedings;

iv. The birth date of a minor whenever the birth date is necessary for the court to establish or maintain subject matter jurisdiction;

v. The name of a minor in any order relating to parental responsibility, time-sharing, or child support;

vi. The name of a minor in any document or order affecting the minor's ownership of real property;

vii. The birth date of a party in a writ of attachment or notice to payor;

viii. In traffic and criminal proceedings: a pro se filing; a court filing that is related to a criminal matter or investigation and that is prepared before the filing of a criminal charge or is not filed as part of any docketed criminal case; an arrest or search warrant or any information in support thereof; a charging document and an affidavit or other documents filed in support of any charging document, including any driving records; a statement of particulars; discovery material introduced into evidence or otherwise filed with the court; and all information necessary for the proper issuance and execution of a subpoena duces tecum;

ix. Information used by the clerk for case maintenance purposes or the courts for case management purposes; and

x. Information which is relevant and material to an issue before the court. FL ST J ADMIN Rule 2.425(b).

c. *Remedies.* Upon motion by a party or interested person or sua sponte by the court, the court may order remedies, sanctions or both for a violation of FL ST J ADMIN Rule 2.425(a). Following notice and an opportunity to respond, the court may impose sanctions if such filing was not made in good faith. FL ST J ADMIN Rule 2.425(c).

d. *Motions not restricted.* FL ST J ADMIN Rule 2.425 does not restrict a party's right to move for protective order, to move to file documents under seal, or to request a determination of the confidentiality of records. FL ST J ADMIN Rule 2.425(d).

e. *Application.* FL ST J ADMIN Rule 2.425 does not affect the application of constitutional provisions, statutes, or rules of court regarding confidential information or access to public information. FL ST J ADMIN Rule 2.425(e).

F. Filing and Service Requirements

1. *Filing requirements.* All original documents must be filed with the court either before service or immediately thereafter, unless otherwise provided for by general law or other rules. If the original of any bond or other document is not placed in the court file, a certified copy must be so placed by the clerk. FL ST J ADMIN Rule 2.516(d). All documents shall be filed in conformity with the requirements of FL ST J ADMIN Rule 2.525. FL ST RCP Rule 1.080(b). All documents filed in any court shall be filed by electronic transmission in accordance with FL ST J ADMIN Rule 2.525. "Documents" means pleadings, motions, petitions, memoranda, briefs, notices, exhibits, declarations, affidavits, orders, judgments, decrees, writs, opinions, and any other paper or writing submitted to a court. FL ST J ADMIN Rule 2.520(a). All documents that are court records, as defined in FL ST J ADMIN Rule 2.430(a)(1), must be filed by electronic transmission, provided that: (1) the clerk has the ability to accept and retain such documents; (2) the clerk or the chief judge of the circuit has requested permission to accept documents filed by electronic transmission; and (3) the supreme court has entered an order granting permission to the clerk to accept documents filed by electronic transmission. FL ST J ADMIN Rule 2.525(c)(1).

a. *Definition.* "Electronic transmission of documents" means the sending of information by electronic signals to, by or from a court or clerk, which when received can be transformed and stored or transmitted on paper, microfilm, magnetic storage device, optical imaging system, CD-ROM, flash drive, other electronic data storage system, server, case maintenance system ("CM"), electronic court filing ("ECF") system, statewide or local electronic portal ("e-portal"), or other electronic record keeping system authorized by the supreme court in a format sufficient to communicate the information on the original document in a readable format. Electronic transmission of documents includes electronic mail ("e-mail") and any internet-based transmission procedure, and may include procedures allowing for documents to be signed or verified by electronic means. FL ST J ADMIN Rule 2.525(a).

i. The filing of documents with the court as required by the Florida Rules of Judicial Administration must be made by filing them with the clerk in accordance with FL ST J ADMIN Rule 2.525, except that the judge may permit documents to be filed with the judge, in which event the judge must note the filing date before him or her on the documents and transmit them to the clerk. The date of filing is that shown on the face of the document by the judge's notation or the clerk's time stamp, whichever is earlier. FL ST J ADMIN Rule 2.516(e).

b. *Application.* Any court or clerk of the court may accept the electronic transmission of documents for filing after the clerk, together with input from the chief judge of the circuit, has obtained approval of the procedures and program for doing so from the Supreme Court of Florida. FL ST J ADMIN Rule 2.525(b).

c. *Exceptions*

i. Paper documents and other submissions may be manually submitted to the clerk or court:

- When the clerk does not have the ability to accept and retain documents by electronic filing or has not had ECF Procedures approved by the supreme court;

- For filing by any self-represented party or any self-represented nonparty unless specific ECF Procedures provide a means to file documents electronically. However, any self-represented nonparty that is a governmental or public agency and any other agency, partnership, corporation, or business entity acting on behalf of any governmental or public agency may file documents by electronic transmission if such entity has the capability of filing documents electronically;
- For filing by attorneys excused from e-mail service in accordance with FL ST J ADMIN Rule 2.516(b);
- When submitting evidentiary exhibits or filing non-documentary materials;
- When the filing involves documents in excess of twenty-five (25) megabytes (25MB) in size. For such filings, documents may be transmitted using an electronic storage medium that the clerk has the ability to accept, which may include a CD-ROM, flash drive, or similar storage medium;
- When filed in open court, as permitted by the court;
- When paper filing is permitted by any approved statewide or local ECF procedures; and
- If any court determines that justice so requires. FL ST J ADMIN Rule 2.525(d).

ii. Any document in paper form submitted under FL ST J ADMIN Rule 2.525(d) is filed when it is received by the clerk or court and the clerk shall immediately thereafter convert any filed paper document to an electronic document. "Convert to an electronic document" means optically capturing an image of a paper document and using character recognition software to recover as much of the document's text as practicable and then indexing and storing the document in the official court file. FL ST J ADMIN Rule 2.525(c)(4).

iii. Any storage medium submitted under FL ST J ADMIN Rule 2.525(d)(5) is filed when received by the clerk or court and the clerk shall immediately thereafter transfer the electronic documents from the storage device to the official court file. FL ST J ADMIN Rule 2.525(c)(5).

iv. If the filer of any paper document authorized under FL ST J ADMIN Rule 2.525(d) provides a self-addressed, postage-paid envelope for return of the paper document after it is converted to electronic form by the clerk, the clerk shall place the paper document in the envelope and deposit it in the mail. Except when a paper document is required to be maintained, the clerk may recycle any filed paper document that is not to be returned to the filer. FL ST J ADMIN Rule 2.525(c)(6).

v. The clerk may convert any paper document filed before the effective date of FL ST J ADMIN Rule 2.525 to an electronic document. Unless the clerk is required to maintain the paper document, if the paper document has been converted to an electronic document by the clerk, the paper document is no longer part of the official court file and may be removed and recycled. FL ST J ADMIN Rule 2.525(c)(7).

d. *Official court file.* For information on what constitutes the official court file, please see FL ST J ADMIN Rule 2.525(c)(2), FL ST J ADMIN Rule 2.525(c)(3).

e. *Administration.* All attorneys, parties, or other persons using this rule to file documents are required to make arrangements with the court or clerk for the payment of any charges authorized by general law or the supreme court before filing any document by electronic transmission. FL ST J ADMIN Rule 2.525(f)(2).

f. *Filing date.* The filing date for an electronically transmitted document is the date and time that such filing is acknowledged by an electronic stamp or otherwise, pursuant to any procedure set forth in any ECF Procedures approved by the supreme court, or the date the last page of such filing is received by the court or clerk. FL ST J ADMIN Rule 2.525(f)(3).

g. *Accessibility.* All documents transmitted in any electronic form under FL ST J ADMIN Rule 2.525 must comply with the accessibility requirements of FL ST J ADMIN Rule 2.526. FL ST J ADMIN Rule 2.525(g).

h. *Provisions for electronic filing in the Seventeenth Circuit.* Attorneys may electronically file plead-

ings and papers on existing cases in circuit civil divisions 1, 7, 9, 19, 26 and 27. The following documents may be scanned and efiled; however, the original must be filed with the Clerk: Documents ordered by the Court; and original documents required by law or rule of procedure to be filed with the Clerk. Self represented individuals shall file pleadings and papers with the Clerk. The Clerk within twenty four (24) hours of receipt of an electronic document shall either accept or reject the electronic document for filing and send electronic notice to the filer. FL ST 17 J CIR 2012-16-CIV.

i. *Technical failures.* If a document filed electronically is not received due to: an error in the transmission of the document to the Clerk or any vendor of the Clerk to provide electronic court record filing services which is unknown to an attorney or party or affected non party, or a failure to process the electronic document when received by the Clerk or rejection by the Clerk, or any other technical problems experienced by the attorney or party or affected non party, the Court may, after an evidentiary hearing and upon satisfactory proof, enter an order permitting the document to be filed nunc pro tunc to the date it was first attempted to be sent electronically. FL ST 17 J CIR 2012-16-CIV.

j. *Filing of pleadings or papers at any office of the clerk of court.* The Clerk of Courts, commencing November 3, 2008, shall accept for filing, at the central courthouse, north satellite courthouse, south satellite courthouse, and west satellite courthouse any pleading or motion or other document for filing in the court file from any attorney or party for an existing case except as otherwise set forth. FL ST 17 J CIR 2008-153-GEN. See FL ST 17 J CIR 2008-153-GEN for specific exceptions.

2. *Service requirements.* Every pleading subsequent to the initial pleading, all orders, and every other document filed in the action must be served in conformity with the requirements of FL ST J ADMIN Rule 2.516. FL ST RCP Rule 1.080(a).

   a. *Service; When required.* Unless the court otherwise orders, or a statute or supreme court administrative order specifies a different means of service, every pleading subsequent to the initial pleading and every other document filed in any court proceeding, except applications for witness subpoenas and documents served by formal notice or required to be served in the manner provided for service of formal notice, must be served in accordance with FL ST J ADMIN Rule 2.516 on each party. No service need be made on parties against whom a default has been entered, except that pleadings asserting new or additional claims against them must be served in the manner provided for service of summons. FL ST J ADMIN Rule 2.516(a).

   b. *Service; How made.* When service is required or permitted to be made upon a party represented by an attorney, service must be made upon the attorney unless service upon the party is ordered by the court. FL ST J ADMIN Rule 2.516(b).

      i. *Service by electronic mail ("e-mail").* All documents required or permitted to be served on another party must be served by e-mail, unless FL ST J ADMIN Rule 2.516 otherwise provides. When, in addition to service by e-mail, the sender also utilizes another means of service provided for in FL ST J ADMIN Rule 2.516(b)(2), any differing time limits and other provisions applicable to that other means of service control. FL ST J ADMIN Rule 2.516(b)(1). Any document electronically transmitted to a court or clerk must also be served on all parties and interested persons in accordance with the applicable rules of court. FL ST J ADMIN Rule 2.525(e)(2).

         - *Service on attorneys.* Upon appearing in a proceeding, an attorney must serve a designation of a primary e-mail address and may designate no more than two (2) secondary e-mail addresses. Thereafter, service must be directed to all designated e-mail addresses in that proceeding. Every document filed by an attorney thereafter must include the primary e-mail address of that attorney and any secondary e-mail addresses. If an attorney does not designate any e-mail address for service, documents may be served on that attorney at the e-mail address on record with The Florida Bar. FL ST J ADMIN Rule 2.516(b)(1)(A).

         - *Exception to e-mail service on attorneys.* Service by an attorney on another attorney must be made by e-mail unless excused by the court. Upon motion by an attorney demonstrating that the attorney has no e-mail account and lacks access to the Internet at the attorney's office, the court may excuse the attorney from the requirements of e-mail service. Service

on and by an attorney excused by the court from e-mail service must be by the means provided in FL ST J ADMIN Rule 2.516(b)(2). FL ST J ADMIN Rule 2.516(b)(1)(B).

- *Service on and by parties not represented by an attorney.* Any party not represented by an attorney may serve a designation of a primary e-mail address and also may designate no more than two (2) secondary e-mail addresses to which service must be directed in that proceeding by the means provided in FL ST J ADMIN Rule 2.516(b)(1). If a party not represented by an attorney does not designate an e-mail address for service in a proceeding, service on and by that party must be by the means provided in FL ST J ADMIN Rule 2.516(b)(2). FL ST J ADMIN Rule 2.516(b)(1)(C).
- *Time of service.* Service by e-mail is complete when it is sent. FL ST J ADMIN Rule 2.516(b)(1)(D). An e-mail is deemed served on the date it is sent. FL ST J ADMIN Rule 2.516(b)(1)(D)(i). If the sender learns that the e-mail did not reach the address of the person to be served, the sender must immediately send another copy by e-mail, or by a means authorized by FL ST J ADMIN Rule 2.516(b)(2). FL ST J ADMIN Rule 2.516(b)(1)(D)(ii). E-mail service is treated as service by mail for the computation of time. FL ST J ADMIN Rule 2.516(b)(1)(D)(iii).

ii. *Format of e-mail for service.* Service of a document by e-mail is made by attaching a copy of the document in PDF format to an e-mail sent to all addresses designated by the attorney or party. FL ST J ADMIN Rule 2.516(b)(1)(E).

- All documents served by e-mail must be attached to an e-mail message containing a subject line beginning with the words "SERVICE OF COURT DOCUMENT" in all capital letters, followed by the case number of the proceeding in which the documents are being served. FL ST J ADMIN Rule 2.516(b)(1)(E)(i).
- The body of the e-mail must identify the court in which the proceeding is pending, the case number, the name of the initial party on each side, the title of each document served with that e-mail, and the sender's name and telephone number. FL ST J ADMIN Rule 2.516(b)(1)(E)(ii).
- Any document served by e-mail may be signed by the "/s/" format, as long as the filed original is signed in accordance with the applicable rule of procedure. FL ST J ADMIN Rule 2.516(b)(1)(E)(iii).
- Any e-mail which, together with its attached documents, exceeds five megabytes (5MB) in size, must be divided and sent as separate e-mails, no one of which may exceed five megabytes (5MB) in size and each of which must be sequentially numbered in the subject line. FL ST J ADMIN Rule 2.516(b)(1)(E)(iv).

iii. *Service by other means.* In addition to, and not in lieu of, service by e-mail, service may also be made upon attorneys by any of the means specified in FL ST J ADMIN Rule 2.516(b)(2). Service on and by all parties who are not represented by an attorney and who do not designate an e-mail address, and on and by all attorneys excused from e-mail service, must be made by delivering a copy of the document or by mailing it to the party or attorney at their last known address or, if no address is known, by leaving it with the clerk of the court. Service by mail is complete upon mailing. Delivery of a copy within FL ST J ADMIN Rule 2.516 is complete upon:

- Handing it to the attorney or to the party,
- Leaving it at the attorney's or party's office with a clerk or other person in charge thereof,
- If there is no one in charge, leaving it in a conspicuous place therein,
- If the office is closed or the person to be served has no office, leaving it at the person's usual place of abode with some person of his or her family above fifteen (15) years of age and informing such person of the contents, or
- Transmitting it by facsimile to the attorney's or party's office with a cover sheet containing the sender's name, firm, address, telephone number, and facsimile number, and the

number of pages transmitted. When service is made by facsimile, a copy must also be served by any other method permitted by FL ST J ADMIN Rule 2.516. Facsimile service occurs when transmission is complete. FL ST J ADMIN Rule 2.516(b)(2)(A) through FL ST J ADMIN Rule 2.516(b)(2)(E).

- Service by delivery after 5:00 p.m. must be deemed to have been made by mailing on the date of delivery. FL ST J ADMIN Rule 2.516(b)(2)(F).

c. *Service; Numerous defendants.* In actions when the parties are unusually numerous, the court may regulate the service contemplated by the Florida Rules of Judicial Administration on motion or on its own initiative in such manner as may be found to be just and reasonable. FL ST J ADMIN Rule 2.516(c).

d. *Service by clerk.* Service of notices and other documents required to be made by the clerk must also be done as provided in FL ST J ADMIN Rule 2.516(b). FL ST J ADMIN Rule 2.516(g).

G. Hearings

1. *Communication equipment*

a. *Definition.* Communication equipment means a conference telephone or other electronic device that permits all those appearing or participating to hear and speak to each other, provided that all conversation of all parties is audible to all persons present. FL ST J ADMIN Rule 2.530(a).

b. *Use by all parties.* A county or circuit court judge may, upon the court's own motion or upon the written request of a party, direct that communication equipment be used for a motion hearing, pretrial conference, or a status conference. A judge must give notice to the parties and consider any objections they may have to the use of communication equipment before directing that communication equipment be used. The decision to use communication equipment over the objection of parties will be in the sound discretion of the trial court, except as noted below. FL ST J ADMIN Rule 2.530(b).

c. *Use only by requesting party.* A county or circuit court judge may, upon the written request of a party upon reasonable notice to all other parties, permit a requesting party to participate through communication equipment in a scheduled motion hearing; however, any such request (except in criminal, juvenile, and appellate proceedings) must be granted, absent a showing of good cause to deny the same, where the hearing is set for not longer than fifteen (15) minutes. FL ST J ADMIN Rule 2.530(c).

d. *Testimony*

i. *Generally.* A county or circuit court judge, general magistrate, special magistrate, or hearing officer may allow testimony to be taken through communication equipment if all parties consent or if permitted by another applicable rule of procedure. FL ST J ADMIN Rule 2.530(d)(1).

ii. *Procedure.* Any party desiring to present testimony through communication equipment shall, prior to the hearing or trial at which the testimony is to be presented, contact all parties to determine whether each party consents to this form of testimony. The party seeking to present the testimony shall move for permission to present testimony through communication equipment, which motion shall set forth good cause as to why the testimony should be allowed in this form. FL ST J ADMIN Rule 2.530(d)(2).

iii. *Oath.* Testimony may be taken through communication equipment only if a notary public or other person authorized to administer oaths in the witness's jurisdiction is present with the witness and administers the oath consistent with the laws of the jurisdiction. FL ST J ADMIN Rule 2.530(d)(3).

iv. *Confrontation rights.* In juvenile and criminal proceedings the defendant must make an informed waiver of any confrontation rights that may be abridged by the use of communication equipment. FL ST J ADMIN Rule 2.530(d)(4).

v. *Video testimony.* If the testimony to be presented utilizes video conferencing or comparable two-way visual capabilities, the court in its discretion may modify the procedures set forth in

FL ST J ADMIN Rule 2.530 to accommodate the technology utilized. FL ST J ADMIN Rule 2.530(d)(5).

e. *Burden of expense.* The cost for the use of the communication equipment is the responsibility of the requesting party unless otherwise directed by the court. FL ST J ADMIN Rule 2.530(e).

2. *Uniform motion calendar.* The Circuit Judges of the general civil/family division (excluding juvenile/dependency) shall maintain a uniform motion calendar from 8:45 A.M. to 9:30 A.M., Monday through Thursday. The motion calendar shall end PROMPTLY at 9:30 A.M. All parties shall be prepared to proceed at 8:45 A.M., and if one party fails to timely appear, the matter may proceed on the merits in his/her absence. FL ST 17 J CIR LOCAL RULE NO. 10A(1).
3. *Noticed motion limitation.* No more than two (2) motions may be noticed for each case on any given day except by leave of court. FL ST 17 J CIR LOCAL RULE NO. 10A(4).
4. *Ex parte and non-evidentiary motion.* Ex parte matters, non-evidentiary motions, and uncontested proceedings for adoptions, or dissolution may be heard on the uniform motion calendar, provided such matters can be conducted in five (5) minutes equally allocated among the parties and the moving party shall so certify as specified in FL ST 17 J CIR LOCAL RULE NO. 10A(3). FL ST 17 J CIR LOCAL RULE NO. 10A(6).
5. *Good faith effort to resolve issues.* Prior to appearing before the court, the parties shall discuss the issues raised in the pending motion, and both parties shall be prepared to certify at the hearing they have made a good faith effort to resolve the issues. FL ST 17 J CIR LOCAL RULE NO. 10A(7).
6. *Re-noticing hearings.* When the motion calendar has been filled, the judge's office shall notify the party noticing any hearings which cannot be reached. The noticing party shall call opposing counsel and re-notice the hearing. FL ST 17 J CIR LOCAL RULE NO. 10A(9).
7. *Hearing cancellation.* Motion calendar hearings may be canceled by the attorney who set the hearing. FL ST 17 J CIR LOCAL RULE NO. 10A(10).
8. *Other motion calendars.* Hearing officers/general masters shall conduct a motion calendar, the dates and times of which shall be determined by the hearing officer/general master or by administrative order. FL ST 17 J CIR LOCAL RULE NO. 10A(11).
9. *Sanctions.* Failure to comply with the procedures designated in the above paragraphs may result in the hearing being stricken from the docket or such other sanctions as the court deems appropriate. FL ST 17 J CIR LOCAL RULE NO. 10A(12).

H. Forms

1. Official Motion for Leave to Amend Forms for Florida

a. Caption. FL ST RCP Form 1.901.

b. Notice of compliance when constitutional challenge is brought. FL ST RCP Form 1.975.

2. Motion for Leave to Amend Forms for Florida

a. Motion; For leave of court; To amend complaint. FL-PP § 2:155.

b. Motion; For leave of court; To add claim for punitive damages. FL-PP § 2:156.

c. Motion; For leave of court; To amend complaint; To conform to evidence. FL-PP § 2:157.

d. Motion; For leave of court; To permit admission of evidence. FL-PP § 2:158.

e. Order; Granting leave to amend complaint. FL-PP § 2:163.

f. Order; Granting leave to amend complaint; To conform to evidence. FL-PP § 2:164.

g. Order; Granting leave to amend complaint; To permit admission of evidence. FL-PP § 2:165.

h. Form for motion for leave to amend complaint. FL-RCPF R 1.190(39).

i. Form for amendment to complaint with leave of court. FL-RCPF R 1.190(40).

j. Form for motion to amend amended complaint. FL-RCPF R 1.190(42).

k. Form for amendment to amended complaint (or second amended complaint). FL-RCPF R 1.190(43).

l. Form for motion to amend complaint to add count. FL-RCPF R 1.190(44).

I. Checklist

(I) ❑ Matters to be considered by moving party

(a) ❑ Required documents

(1) ❑ Notice of hearing/Motion

(2) ❑ Proposed amended pleading

(3) ❑ Good faith certificate

(4) ❑ Certificate of service

(b) ❑ Supplemental documents

(1) ❑ Proposed order, copies, stamped envelopes

(2) ❑ Notice of constitutional question

(c) ❑ Time for making motion

(1) ❑ A party may amend a pleading once as a matter of course at any time before a responsive pleading is served or, if the pleading is one to which no responsive pleading is permitted and the action has not been placed on the trial calendar, may amend it at any time within twenty (20) days after it is served

(2) ❑ Under the Florida Rules of Civil Procedure, there is no time limit as to when an amendment with leave of court may be sought; amendments of the pleadings may be permitted, with the court's discretion, at any stage of the proceedings in furtherance of justice

(3) ❑ A motion for leave to amend a pleading to assert a claim for punitive damages can be filed separately and before the supporting evidence or proffer, but each shall be served on all parties at least twenty (20) days before the hearing

(4) ❑ A copy of any written motion which may not be heard ex parte and a copy of the notice of the hearing thereof shall be served a reasonable time before the time specified for the hearing

(5) ❑ Copies of the notice of hearing, the motion, and any pleading or interrogatories to which the motion is addressed shall be in the hands of the Judicial Assistant and opposing party at least four (4) working days in advance of the hearing

(II) ❑ Matters to be considered by opposing party

(a) ❑ Required documents

(1) ❑ Response to motion

(2) ❑ Certificate of service

(b) ❑ Supplemental documents

(1) ❑ Proposed order, copies, stamped envelopes

(2) ❑ Notice of constitutional question

(c) ❑ Time for service and filing of opposition

(1) ❑ No time specified for responding to a motion

Motions, Oppositions and Replies
Motion for Summary Judgment

Document Last Updated January 2013

A. Applicable Rules

1. *State rules*

a. Rules of court. FL ST RCP Rule 1.010; FL ST J ADMIN Rule 2.110.

b. Nonverification of pleadings. FL ST RCP Rule 1.030.

c. Service and filing of pleadings, orders, and documents. FL ST RCP Rule 1.080.

d. Time. FL ST RCP Rule 1.090.

e. Pleadings and motions. FL ST RCP Rule 1.100.

f. Motions. FL ST RCP Rule 1.160.

g. Summary judgment. FL ST RCP Rule 1.510.

h. Relief from judgment, decrees or orders. FL ST RCP Rule 1.540.

i. Mediation and arbitration. FL ST RCP Rule 1.700; FL ST RCP Rule 1.710; FL ST RCP Rule 1.720; FL ST RCP Rule 1.730; FL ST RCP Rule 1.750; FL ST RCP Rule 1.800; FL ST RCP Rule 1.810; FL ST RCP Rule 1.820; FL ST RCP Rule 1.830.

j. Forms. FL ST RCP Rule 1.900.

k. Retention of court records. FL ST J ADMIN Rule 2.430.

l. Foreign attorneys. FL ST J ADMIN Rule 2.510.

m. Signature of attorneys and parties. FL ST J ADMIN Rule 2.515.

n. Paper. FL ST J ADMIN Rule 2.520.

o. Electronic filing. FL ST J ADMIN Rule 2.525.

p. Communication equipment. FL ST J ADMIN Rule 2.530.

q. Court reporting. FL ST J ADMIN Rule 2.535.

r. Requests for accommodations by persons with disabilities. FL ST J ADMIN Rule 2.540.

s. Minimization of the filing of sensitive information. FL ST J ADMIN Rule 2.425.

t. Accessibility of information and technology. FL ST J ADMIN Rule 2.526.

2. *Local rules*

a. Orders for signature; Civil division. FL ST 17 J CIR LOCAL RULE NO. 8.

b. Uniform motion calendar ex parte motions to compel discovery, and special set hearings. FL ST 17 J CIR LOCAL RULE NO. 10A.

c. Standards of professional courtesy. FL ST 17 J CIR I-94-O-1.

d. Administrative order authorizing the filing of pleadings or papers at any office of the clerk of court. FL ST 17 J CIR 2008-153-GEN.

e. Administrative order regarding provision of ADA accommodations. FL ST 17 J CIR 2010-49-GEN.

f. Administrative order establishing electronic filing procedures for the civil division. FL ST 17 J CIR 2012-16-CIV.

B. Timing

1. *Motion for summary judgment*

a. *For the claimant.* A party seeking to recover upon a claim, counterclaim, crossclaim or third-party claim or to obtain a declaratory judgment may move for a summary judgment in that party's favor at any time after the expiration of twenty (20) days from the commencement of the action or after service of a motion for summary judgment by the adverse party. FL ST RCP Rule 1.510(a).

b. *For defending party.* A party against whom a claim, counterclaim, crossclaim, or third-party claim is asserted or a declaratory judgment is sought may move for a summary judgment in that party's favor as to all or any part thereof at any time with or without supporting affidavits. FL ST RCP Rule 1.510(b).

i. A defending party is not required to serve his responsive pleading before moving for summary judgment. He may make the motion at any time, setting out his defenses by affidavit, and thus effect a speedy termination of the action if no genuine issue exists as to any fact or facts pertaining to a defense that would defeat the claim. FL ST RCP Rule 1.510, notes.

2. *Service of motion.* The movant shall serve the motion for summary judgment at least twenty (20) days before the time fixed for the hearing, and shall also serve at that time a copy of any summary judgment evidence on which the movant relies that has not already been filed with the court. FL ST RCP Rule 1.510(c).
3. *Standard of professional conduct; Scheduling*
   a. Attorneys should endeavor to provide opposing counsel, parties, witnesses, and other affected persons, sufficient notice of depositions, hearings and other proceedings, except upon agreement of course, in an emergency, or in other circumstances compelling more expedited scheduling. As a general rule, actual notice should be no less than five (5) business days for instate depositions, ten (10) business days for out-of-state depositions and four (4) business days for hearings. FL ST 17 J CIR I-94-O-1(I)(1).
   b. Attorneys should communicate with opposing counsel prior to scheduling depositions, hearings and other proceedings, in an effort to schedule them at times that are mutually convenient for all interested persons. Further, sufficient time should be reserved to permit a complete presentation by counsel for all parties. FL ST 17 J CIR I-94-O-1(I)(2).
   c. Attorneys should notify opposing counsel, the court, and others affected, of scheduling conflicts as soon as they become apparent. Further, attorneys should cooperate with one another regarding all reasonable rescheduling requests that do not prejudice their clients or unduly delay a proceeding. FL ST 17 J CIR I-94-O-1(I)(3).
   d. Attorneys should promptly notify the court or other tribunal of any resolution between the parties that renders a scheduled court appearance unnecessary or otherwise moot. FL ST 17 J CIR I-94-O-1(I)(4).
   e. Attorneys should grant reasonable requests by opposing counsel for extensions of time within which to respond to pleadings, discovery, and other matters when such an extension will not prejudice their client or unduly delay a proceeding. FL ST 17 J CIR I-94-O-1(I)(5).
4. *Timing considerations when filing electronically.* The filing date of an efiled document is when the last page is received by the Clerk. The electronic filing of a document does not modify any filing deadlines as required by law, rule of procedure, or court order. FL ST 17 J CIR 2012-16-CIV.
5. *Computation of time*
   a. *Generally.* Computation of time shall be governed by FL ST J ADMIN Rule 2.514. FL ST RCP Rule 1.090(a). The following rules apply in computing time periods specified in any rule of procedure, local rule, court order, or statute that does not specify a method of computing time. FL ST J ADMIN Rule 2.514(a).
      i. *Period stated in days or a longer unit.* When the period is stated in days or a longer unit of time (A) exclude the day of the event that triggers the period; (B) count every day, including intermediate Saturdays, Sundays, and legal holidays; and (C) include the last day of the period, but if the last day is a Saturday, Sunday, or legal holiday, or falls within any period of time extended through an order of the chief justice under FL ST J ADMIN Rule 2.205(a)(2)(B)(iv), the period continues to run until the end of the next day that is not a Saturday, Sunday, or legal holiday and does not fall within any period of time extended through an order of the chief justice. FL ST J ADMIN Rule 2.514(a)(1).
      ii. *Period stated in hours.* When the period is stated in hours (A) begin counting immediately on the occurrence of the event that triggers the period; (B) count every hour, including hours during intermediate Saturdays, Sundays, and legal holidays; and (C) if the period would end on a Saturday, Sunday, or legal holiday, or during any period of time extended through an order of the chief justice under FL ST J ADMIN Rule 2.205(a)(2)(B)(iv), the period continues to run until the same time on the next day that is not a Saturday, Sunday, or legal holiday and does not fall within any period of time extended through an order of the chief justice. FL ST J ADMIN Rule 2.514(a)(2).
      iii. *Period stated in days less than seven (7) days.* When the period stated in days is less than seven (7) days, intermediate Saturdays, Sundays, and legal holidays shall be excluded in the computation. FL ST J ADMIN Rule 2.514(a)(3).

iv. *"Last day" defined.* Unless a different time is set by a statute, local rule, or court order, the last day ends (A) for electronic filing or for service by any means, at midnight; and (B) for filing by other means, when the clerk's office is scheduled to close. FL ST J ADMIN Rule 2.514(a)(4).

v. *"Next day" defined.* The "next day" is determined by continuing to count forward when the period is measured after an event and backward when measured before an event. FL ST J ADMIN Rule 2.514(a)(5).

vi. *"Legal holiday" defined.* "Legal holiday" means (A) the day set aside by FL ST § 110.117, for observing New Year's Day, Martin Luther King, Jr.'s Birthday, Memorial Day, Independence Day, Labor Day, Veterans' Day, Thanksgiving Day, the Friday after Thanksgiving Day, or Christmas Day, and (B) any day observed as a holiday by the clerk's office or as designated by the chief judge. FL ST J ADMIN Rule 2.514(a)(6).

b. *Additional time after service by mail or e-mail.* When a party may or must act within a specified time after service and service is made by mail or e-mail, five (5) days are added after the period that would otherwise expire under FL ST J ADMIN Rule 2.514(a). FL ST J ADMIN Rule 2.514(b).

c. *Enlargement.* When an act is required or allowed to be done at or within a specified time by order of court, by the Florida Rules of Civil Procedure, or by notice given thereunder, for cause shown the court at any time in its discretion (1) with or without notice, may order the period enlarged if request therefor is made before the expiration of the period originally prescribed or as extended by a previous order, or (2) upon motion made and notice after the expiration of the specified period, may permit the act to be done when failure to act was the result of excusable neglect, but it may not extend the time for making a motion for new trial, for rehearing, or to alter or amend a judgment; making a motion for relief from a judgment under FL ST RCP Rule 1.540(b); taking an appeal or filing a petition for certiorari; or making a motion for a directed verdict. FL ST RCP Rule 1.090(b).

d. *Unaffected by expiration of term.* The period of time provided for the doing of any act or the taking of any proceeding shall not be affected or limited by the continued existence or expiration of a term of court. The continued existence or expiration of a term of court in no way affects the power of a court to do any act or take any proceeding in any action which is or has been pending before it. FL ST RCP Rule 1.090(c).

C. General Requirements

1. *Motions generally*

a. *Contents.* An application to the court for an order shall be by motion which shall be made in writing unless made during a hearing or trial, shall state with particularity the grounds therefor, and shall set forth the relief or order sought. The requirement of writing is fulfilled if the motion is stated in a written notice of the hearing of the motion. All notices of hearing shall specify each motion or other matter to be heard. FL ST RCP Rule 1.100(b).

b. *Particularity requirement.* The court considers a motion in the light of the substantive law, rule or statute to make its determination. Some rules require a statement of the grounds for a motion under the rule. Failure to give the grounds will result in denial of the motion. This should be the result in all situations when the ground for the motion is not inherent in the rule. FL-PRACPROC § 9:3. The requirement is nevertheless an important one, first because of the due process notice rights of the respondent, as well as for the assistance it provides to the court in its preparation for the hearing or, absent a hearing, for disposition. 4 FLPRAC R 1.100.

2. *Summary judgment.* A party seeking to recover upon or defend against a claim, counterclaim, crossclaim, or third-party claim or to obtain a declaratory judgment may move for a summary judgment. FL ST RCP Rule 1.510(a); FL ST RCP Rule 1.510(b).

a. *General motion for summary judgment information*

i. *Contents of motion.* The motion shall state with particularity the grounds upon which it is based and the substantial matters of law to be argued and shall specifically identify any affidavits, answers to interrogatories, admissions, depositions, and other materials as would be admissible in evidence ("summary judgment evidence") on which the movant relies. FL ST RCP Rule 1.510(c).

   ii. *Evidence relied upon.* The movant shall also serve at that time a copy of any summary judgment evidence on which the movant relies that has not already been filed with the court. FL ST RCP Rule 1.510(c).

   iii. *Judgment as a matter of law.* The judgment sought shall be rendered forthwith if the pleadings and summary judgment evidence on file show that there is no genuine issue as to any material fact and that the moving party is entitled to a judgment as a matter of law. A summary judgment, interlocutory in character, may be rendered on the issue of liability alone although there is a genuine issue as to the amount of damages. FL ST RCP Rule 1.510(c).

b. *Sham pleadings.* If a party deems any pleading or part thereof filed by another party to be a sham, that party may move to strike the pleading or part thereof before the cause is set for trial and the court shall hear the motion, taking evidence of the respective parties, and if the motion is sustained, the pleading to which the motion is directed shall be stricken. Default and summary judgment on the merits may be entered in the discretion of the court or the court may permit additional pleadings to be filed for good cause shown. FL ST RCP Rule 1.150(a).

c. *Burden of proof*

   i. The moving party in a motion for summary judgment has the initial burden of demonstrating the nonexistence of any genuine issue of fact. Landers v. Milton, 370 So.2d 368, 370 (Fla. 1979); Gardner v. Sabal Point Properties, Inc., 616 So.2d 1111, 1112 (Fla. 5th DCA 1993); FL-PP § 6:7.

   ii. If the record raises the slightest doubt that material issues could be present, that doubt must be resolved against the movant and the motion for summary judgment denied. Moore v. Morris, 475 So.2d 666, 668 (Fla. 1985); Henderson v. CSX Transportation, Inc., 617 So.2d 770 (Fla. 1st DCA 1993); Jones v. Directors Guild of America, Inc., 584 So.2d 1057 (Fla. 1st DCA 1991); FL-PP § 6:7.

   iii. Until the moving party meets the initial burden of showing there is no issue of material fact, the opposing party need do nothing. Holl v. Talcott, 191 So.2d 40, 43 (Fla. 1966); Spradley v. Stick, 622 So.2d 610 (Fla. 1st DCA 1993); FL-RCPF R 1.510(404).

   iv. When the movant has tendered competent evidence in support of its motion, the burden shifts to the nonmoving party to come forward with opposing evidence to show that a question of material fact exists. Landers v. Milton, 370 So.2d 368, 370 (Fla. 1979); Holl v. Talcott, 191 So.2d 40, 43-44 (Fla. 1966); Lenhal Realty, Inc. v. Transamerica Commercial Finance Corp., 615 So.2d 207 (Fla. 4th DCA 1993); FL-PP § 6:7.

d. *Affidavits*

   i. *Form of affidavits; Further testimony.* Supporting and opposing affidavits shall be made on personal knowledge, shall set forth such facts as would be admissible in evidence, and shall show affirmatively that the affiant is competent to testify to the matters stated. Sworn or certified copies of all papers or parts referred to in an affidavit shall be attached to or served with the affidavit. The court may permit affidavits to be supplemented or opposed by depositions, answers to interrogatories, or by further affidavits. FL ST RCP Rule 1.510(e).

   ii. *When affidavits are unavailable.* If it appears from the affidavits of a party opposing the motion that the party cannot for reasons stated present by affidavit facts essential to justify opposition, the court may refuse the application for judgment or may order a continuance to permit affidavits to be obtained or depositions to be taken or discovery to be had or may make such other order as is just. FL ST RCP Rule 1.510(f).

   iii. *Affidavits made in bad faith.* If it appears to the satisfaction of the court at any time that any of the affidavits presented pursuant to FL ST RCP Rule 1.510 are presented in bad faith or solely for the purpose of delay, the court shall forthwith order the party employing them to pay to the other party the amount of the reasonable expenses that the filing of the affidavits caused the other party to incur, including reasonable attorneys' fees, and any offending party or attorney may be adjudged guilty of contempt. FL ST RCP Rule 1.510(g).

e. *Case not fully adjudicated on motion.* On motion under FL ST RCP Rule 1.510 if judgment is not rendered upon the whole case or for all the relief asked and a trial or the taking of testimony and a final hearing is necessary, the court at the hearing of the motion, by examining the pleadings and the evidence before it and by interrogating counsel, shall ascertain, if practicable, what material facts exist without substantial controversy and what material facts are actually and in good faith controverted. FL ST RCP Rule 1.510(d).

i. It shall thereupon make an order specifying the facts that appear without substantial controversy, including the extent to which the amount of damages or other relief is not in controversy, and directing such further proceedings in the action as are just. FL ST RCP Rule 1.510(d).

ii. On the trial or final hearing of the action the facts so specified shall be deemed established, and the trial or final hearing shall be conducted accordingly. FL ST RCP Rule 1.510(d).

3. *Arbitration and mediation*

a. *Referral to arbitration and mediation.* Except as hereinafter provided or as otherwise prohibited by law, the presiding judge may enter an order referring all or any part of a contested civil matter to mediation or arbitration. The parties to any contested civil matter may file a written stipulation to mediate or arbitrate any issue between them at any time. Such stipulation shall be incorporated into the order of referral. FL ST RCP Rule 1.700(a).

b. *Arbitration*

i. *Exclusions.* A civil action shall be ordered to arbitration or arbitration in conjunction with mediation upon stipulation of the parties. A civil action may be ordered to arbitration or arbitration in conjunction with mediation upon motion of any party or by the court, if the judge determines the action to be of such a nature that arbitration could be of benefit to the litigants or the court. FL ST RCP Rule 1.800.

- Under no circumstances may the following categories of actions be referred to arbitration: (1) bond estreatures; (2) habeas corpus or other extraordinary writs; (3) bond validations; (4) civil or criminal contempt; (5) such other matters as may be specified by order of the chief judge in the circuit. FL ST RCP Rule 1.800.

ii. For more information regarding arbitration, please see FL ST RCP Rule 1.810; FL ST RCP Rule 1.820; FL ST RCP Rule 1.830.

c. *Mediation.* For more information regarding mediation, please see FL ST RCP Rule 1.710; FL ST RCP Rule 1.720; FL ST RCP Rule 1.730; and FL ST RCP Rule 1.750.

4. *Rules of court*

a. *Rules of civil procedure.* The Florida Rules of Civil Procedure apply to all actions of a civil nature and all special statutory proceedings in the circuit courts and county courts except those to which the Florida Probate Rules, the Florida Family Law Rules of Procedure, or the Small Claims Rules apply. FL ST RCP Rule 1.010.

i. The form, content, procedure, and time for pleading in all special statutory proceedings shall be as prescribed by the statutes governing the proceeding unless the Florida Rules of Civil Procedure specifically provide to the contrary. FL ST RCP Rule 1.010.

ii. The Florida Rules of Civil Procedure shall be construed to secure the just, speedy, and inexpensive determination of every action. FL ST RCP Rule 1.010.

b. *Rules of judicial administration.* The Florida Rules of Judicial Administration shall apply to administrative matters in all courts to which the Florida Rules of Judicial Administration are applicable by their terms. The Florida Rules of Judicial Administration shall be construed to secure the speedy and inexpensive determination of every proceeding to which they are applicable. The Florida Rules of Judicial Administration shall supersede all conflicting rules and statutes. FL ST J ADMIN Rule 2.110.

D. Documents

1. *Required documents*

a. *Notice of hearing/Motion.* An application to the court for an order shall be by motion which shall be

made in writing unless made during a hearing or trial, shall state with particularity the grounds therefor, and shall set forth the relief or order sought. The requirement of writing is fulfilled if the motion is stated in a written notice of the hearing of the motion. All notices of hearing shall specify each motion or other matter to be heard. FL ST RCP Rule 1.100(b).

i. *Notices to persons with disabilities.* See the Format section of this KeyRules document for further information.

b. *Good faith certification.* Prior to setting a matter on the motion calendar, the party or attorney noticing the motion shall attempt to resolve the matter and shall certify the good faith attempt to resolve. FL ST 17 J CIR LOCAL RULE NO. 10A(2). To comply, every party or attorney setting a motion for hearing shall execute the following certification: I hereby certify that A) I have made a good faith attempt to resolve this matter prior to my noticing this motion for hearing, and B) the issues before the Court may be heard and resolved by the court within five (5) minutes. FL ST 17 J CIR LOCAL RULE NO. 10A(3).

c. *Certificate of service.* When any attorney certifies in substance: "I certify that a copy hereof has been furnished to (here insert name or names and addresses used for service) by (e-mail) (delivery) (mail) (fax) on .... (date) ....______________ Attorney" the certificate is taken as prima facie proof of such service in compliance with FL ST J ADMIN Rule 2.516. FL ST J ADMIN Rule 2.516(f).

2. *Supplemental documents*

a. *Affidavits.* Supporting and opposing affidavits shall be made on personal knowledge, shall set forth such facts as would be admissible in evidence, and shall show affirmatively that the affiant is competent to testify to the matters stated therein. Sworn or certified copies of all papers or parts thereof referred to in an affidavit shall be attached thereto or served therewith. FL ST RCP Rule 1.510(e). For further information regarding affidavits made in the context of a motion for summary judgment see FL ST RCP Rule 1.510(e) through FL ST RCP Rule 1.510(g).

b. *Other evidence.* The movant shall also serve at that time a copy of any summary judgment evidence on which the movant relies that has not already been filed with the court. FL ST RCP Rule 1.510(c).

c. *Proposed order, copies, stamped envelopes.* The court may require that orders or judgments be prepared by a party, may require the party to furnish the court with stamped, addressed envelopes for service of the order or judgment, and may require that proposed orders and judgments be furnished to all parties before entry by the court of the order or judgment. FL ST J ADMIN Rule 2.516(h)(1).

i. A party submitting an order or judgment shall furnish the Court with sufficient copies together with stamped envelopes addressed to all parties entitled to receive a copy. Proposed orders or judgments must be furnished opposing counsel prior to submission to the court. Proposed orders or judgments must be titled to conform with the motion to which it refers. Language in the order or judgment not agreed as conforming to the court's pronouncement shall be brought to the attention of the court. The proposed order shall indicate date of the hearing on which the order is predicated. Attorneys for the movant shall have at Motion Calendar Hearings all proposed orders and judgments together with the appropriate stamped envelopes where applicable. Unless the Court directs otherwise, proposed orders on non-Motion Calendar Hearings must be prepared by the prevailing or designated counsel and submitted to the Court for consideration within forty-eight (48) hours after said hearing. Copies of all such orders, after entry, shall be conformed and mailed by the Clerk of Court, or the judge's secretary, within forty-eight (48) hours. FL ST 17 J CIR LOCAL RULE NO. 8. Any party requesting relief shall furnish the court with a prepared form of order and sufficient copies with stamped addressed envelopes for all parties. FL ST 17 J CIR LOCAL RULE NO. 10A(8).

ii. Attorneys should draft proposed orders promptly and the orders should fairly and adequately represent the ruling of the court. Attorneys should promptly provide, either orally or in writing, proposed orders to opposing counsel for approval. Opposing counsel should then promptly communicate any objections and at that time, the drafting attorney should immediately submit a copy of the proposed order to the court and advise the court as to whether or not it has been approved by opposing counsel. FL ST 17 J CIR I-94-O-1(IV)(3).

d. *Notice of constitutional question.* A party that files a pleading, written motion, or other paper drawing into question the constitutionality of a state statute or a county or municipal charter, ordinance, or franchise must promptly (1) file a notice of constitutional question stating the question and identifying the paper that raises it; and (2) serve the notice and the pleading, written motion, or other paper drawing into question the constitutionality of a state statute or a county or municipal charter, ordinance, or franchise on the Attorney General or the state attorney of the judicial circuit in which the action is pending, by either certified or registered mail. Service of the notice and pleading, written motion, or other paper does not require joinder of the Attorney General or the state attorney as a party to the action. FL ST RCP Rule 1.071.

E. Format

1. *Documents; Type and size.* Documents subject to the exceptions set forth in FL ST J ADMIN Rule 2.525(d) shall be filed on recycled paper measuring eight and one half by eleven (8 1/2 by 11) inches. For purposes of FL ST J ADMIN Rule 2.520, paper is recycled if it contains a minimum content of fifty (50) percent waste paper. Xerographic reduction of legal-size (eight and one half by fourteen (8 1/2 by 14) inches) documents to letter size (eight and one half by eleven (8 1/2 by 11) inches) is prohibited. All other documents filed by electronic transmission shall be filed in a format capable of being printed in a format consistent with the provisions of FL ST J ADMIN Rule 2.250. FL ST J ADMIN Rule 2.520(b).
   a. *Exhibits.* Any exhibit or attachment filed with pleadings or papers may be filed in its original size. FL ST J ADMIN Rule 2.520(c).
   b. *Recording space.* On all papers and documents prepared and filed by the court or by any party to a proceeding which are to be recorded in the public records of any county, including but not limited to final money judgments and notices of lis pendens, a three (3) inch by three (3) inch space at the top right-hand corner on the first page and a one (1) inch by three (3) inch space at the top right-hand corner on each subsequent page shall be left blank and reserved for use by the clerk of court. FL ST J ADMIN Rule 2.520(d).
      i. *Exceptions to recording space.* Any papers or documents created by persons or entities over which the filing party has no control, including but not limited to wills, codicils, trusts, or other testamentary documents; documents prepared or executed by any public officer; documents prepared, executed, acknowledged, or proved outside of the State of Florida; or documents created by State or Federal government agencies, may be filed without the space required by FL ST J ADMIN Rule 2.520. FL ST J ADMIN Rule 2.520(e).
   c. *Noncompliance.* No clerk of court is permitted to refuse to file any document or paper because of noncompliance with the Florida Rules of Judicial Administration. However, upon request of the clerk of court, noncomplying documents must be resubmitted in accordance with the formatting rules. FL ST J ADMIN Rule 2.520(f).
2. *Caption.* Every pleading, motion, order, judgment, or other paper shall have a caption containing the name of the court, the file number, and except for in rem proceedings, including forfeiture proceedings, the name of the first party on each side with an appropriate indication of other parties, and a designation identifying the party filing it and its nature or the nature of the order, as the case may be. In any in rem proceeding, every pleading, motion, order, judgment, or other paper shall have a caption containing the name of the court, the file number, the style "In re" (followed by the name or general description of the property), and a designation of the person or entity filing it and its nature or the nature of the order, as the case may be. In an in rem forfeiture proceeding, the style shall be "In re forfeiture of" (followed by the name of the general description of the property). All papers filed in the action shall be styled in such a manner as to indicate clearly the subject matter of the paper and the party requesting or obtaining relief. FL ST RCP Rule 1.100(c)(1).
3. *Writing and written defined.* Writing or written means a document containing information, an application, or a stipulation. FL ST RCP Rule 1.080(c).
4. *Rule abbreviations*
   a. The Florida Rules of Civil Procedure and shall be abbreviated as Fla.R.Civ.P. FL ST RCP Rule 1.010.
   b. The Florida Rules of Judicial Administration shall be abbreviated as Fla. R. Jud. Admin. FL ST J ADMIN Rule 2.110.

5. *Nonverification.* Except when otherwise specifically provided by the Florida Rules of Civil Procedure or an applicable statute, every pleading or other document of a party represented by an attorney need not be verified or accompanied by an affidavit. FL ST RCP Rule 1.030; FL ST J ADMIN Rule 2.515(a).
6. *Attorney signature*
    a. *Attorney signature.* Every pleading and other document of a party represented by an attorney shall be signed by at least one (1) attorney of record in that attorney's individual name whose current record Florida Bar address, telephone number, including area code, primary e-mail address and secondary e-mail addresses, if any, and Florida Bar number shall be stated, and who shall be duly licensed to practice law in Florida or who shall have received permission to appear in the particular case as provided in FL ST J ADMIN Rule 2.510. FL ST J ADMIN Rule 2.515(a).
        i. The attorney may be required by the court to give the address of, and to vouch for the attorney's authority to represent, the party. FL ST J ADMIN Rule 2.515(a).
        ii. The signature of an attorney shall constitute a certificate by the attorney that the attorney has read the pleading or other document; that to the best of the attorney's knowledge, information, and belief there is good ground to support it; and that it is not interposed for delay. FL ST J ADMIN Rule 2.515(a).
        iii. If a pleading is not signed or is signed with intent to defeat the purpose of FL ST J ADMIN Rule 2.515, it may be stricken and the action may proceed as though the pleading or other document had not been served. FL ST J ADMIN Rule 2.515(a).
    b. *Pro se litigant signature.* A party who is not represented by an attorney shall sign any pleading or other paper and state the party's address and telephone number, including area code. FL ST J ADMIN Rule 2.515(b).
    c. *Form of signature*
        i. The signatures required on pleadings and documents by FL ST J ADMIN Rule 2.515(a) and FL ST J ADMIN Rule 2.515(b) may be:
            - Original signatures;
            - Original signatures that have been reproduced by electronic means, such as on electronically transmitted documents or photocopied documents;
            - Electronic signatures using the "/s/," "s/," or "/s" formats by or at the direction of the person signing; or
            - Any other signature format authorized by general law, so long as the clerk where the proceeding is pending has the capability of receiving and has obtained approval from the Supreme Court of Florida to accept pleadings and documents with that signature format. FL ST J ADMIN Rule 2.515(c)(1).
        ii. An attorney, party, or other person who files a pleading or paper by electronic transmission that does not contain the original signature of that attorney, party, or other person shall file that identical pleading or paper in paper form containing an original signature of that attorney, party, or other person (hereinafter called the follow-up filing) immediately thereafter. The follow-up filing is not required if the Supreme Court of Florida has entered an order directing the clerk of court to discontinue accepting the follow-up filing. FL ST J ADMIN Rule 2.515(c)(2).
        iii. The placement of a "/s/" or the image of a signature by an attorney or party or affected non-party signature line on an electronically filed document shall be accepted as the signature and shall verify to the Court the filer is in possession of the originally executed document. Notwithstanding the manner in which an electronic document is signed the originally executed pleading or paper shall be maintained in the filer's possession for a minimum of one (1) year after final disposition and time for appeal of the case. The originally executed document shall be produced for filing or inspection as directed by the Court. FL ST 17 J CIR 2012-16-CIV.
7. *Forms*
    a. *Process.* The forms of process, notice of lis pendens, and notice of action provided in the Florida

Rules of Civil Procedure are sufficient. Variations from the forms do not void process or notices that are otherwise sufficient. FL ST RCP Rule 1.900(a).

b. *Other forms.* The other forms provided in the Florida Rules of Civil Procedure are sufficient for the matters that are covered by them. So long as the substance is expressed without prolixity, the forms may be varied to meet the facts of a particular case. FL ST RCP Rule 1.900(b).

c. *Formal matters.* Captions, except for the designation of the paper, are omitted from the forms provided in the Florida Rules of Civil Procedure. A general form of caption is the first form provided. Signatures are omitted from pleadings and motions. FL ST RCP Rule 1.900(c).

8. *Notices to persons with disabilities.* All notices of court proceedings to be held in a public facility, and all process compelling appearance at such proceedings, shall include the following statement in bold face, fourteen (14) point Times New Roman or Courier font: "If you are a person with a disability who needs any accommodation in order to participate in this proceeding, you are entitled, at no cost to you, to the provision of certain assistance. Please contact [identify applicable court personnel by name, address, and telephone number] at least seven (7) days before your scheduled court appearance, or immediately upon receiving this notification if the time before the scheduled appearance is less than seven (7) days; if you are hearing or voice impaired, call 711." FL ST J ADMIN Rule 2.540(c)(1). For further information, please see FL ST 17 J CIR 2010-49-GEN.

9. *Minimization of the filing of sensitive information*

a. *Limitations for court filings.* Unless authorized by FL ST J ADMIN Rule 2.425(b), statute, another rule of court, or the court orders otherwise, designated sensitive information filed with the court must be limited to the following format:

i. The initials of a person known to be a minor;

ii. The year of birth of a person's birth date;

iii. No portion of any: Social security number, Bank account number, Credit card account number, Charge account number, or Debit account number;

iv. The last four digits of any: Taxpayer identification number (TIN), Employee identification number, Driver's license number, Passport number, Telephone number, Financial account number, except as set forth in FL ST J ADMIN Rule 2.425(a)(3), Brokerage account number, Insurance policy account number, Loan account number, Customer account number, or Patient or health care number;

v. A truncated version of any: Email address, Computer user name, Password, or Personal identification number (PIN); and

vi. A truncated version of any other sensitive information as provided by court order. FL ST J ADMIN Rule 2.425(a).

b. *Exceptions.* FL ST J ADMIN Rule 2.425(a) does not apply to the following:

i. An account number which identifies the property alleged to be the subject of a proceeding;

ii. The record of an administrative or agency proceeding;

iii. The record in appellate or review proceedings;

iv. The birth date of a minor whenever the birth date is necessary for the court to establish or maintain subject matter jurisdiction;

v. The name of a minor in any order relating to parental responsibility, time-sharing, or child support;

vi. The name of a minor in any document or order affecting the minor's ownership of real property;

vii. The birth date of a party in a writ of attachment or notice to payor;

viii. In traffic and criminal proceedings: a pro se filing; a court filing that is related to a criminal matter or investigation and that is prepared before the filing of a criminal charge or is not filed as part of any docketed criminal case; an arrest or search warrant or any information in support thereof; a charging document and an affidavit or other documents filed in support of any

charging document, including any driving records; a statement of particulars; discovery material introduced into evidence or otherwise filed with the court; and all information necessary for the proper issuance and execution of a subpoena duces tecum;

ix. Information used by the clerk for case maintenance purposes or the courts for case management purposes; and

x. Information which is relevant and material to an issue before the court. FL ST J ADMIN Rule 2.425(b).

c. *Remedies.* Upon motion by a party or interested person or sua sponte by the court, the court may order remedies, sanctions or both for a violation of FL ST J ADMIN Rule 2.425(a). Following notice and an opportunity to respond, the court may impose sanctions if such filing was not made in good faith. FL ST J ADMIN Rule 2.425(c).

d. *Motions not restricted.* FL ST J ADMIN Rule 2.425 does not restrict a party's right to move for protective order, to move to file documents under seal, or to request a determination of the confidentiality of records. FL ST J ADMIN Rule 2.425(d).

e. *Application.* FL ST J ADMIN Rule 2.425 does not affect the application of constitutional provisions, statutes, or rules of court regarding confidential information or access to public information. FL ST J ADMIN Rule 2.425(e).

F. Filing and Service Requirements

1. *Filing requirements.* All original documents must be filed with the court either before service or immediately thereafter, unless otherwise provided for by general law or other rules. If the original of any bond or other document is not placed in the court file, a certified copy must be so placed by the clerk. FL ST J ADMIN Rule 2.516(d). All documents shall be filed in conformity with the requirements of FL ST J ADMIN Rule 2.525. FL ST RCP Rule 1.080(b). All documents filed in any court shall be filed by electronic transmission in accordance with FL ST J ADMIN Rule 2.525. "Documents" means pleadings, motions, petitions, memoranda, briefs, notices, exhibits, declarations, affidavits, orders, judgments, decrees, writs, opinions, and any other paper or writing submitted to a court. FL ST J ADMIN Rule 2.520(a). All documents that are court records, as defined in FL ST J ADMIN Rule 2.430(a)(1), must be filed by electronic transmission, provided that: (1) the clerk has the ability to accept and retain such documents; (2) the clerk or the chief judge of the circuit has requested permission to accept documents filed by electronic transmission; and (3) the supreme court has entered an order granting permission to the clerk to accept documents filed by electronic transmission. FL ST J ADMIN Rule 2.525(c)(1).

a. *Definition.* "Electronic transmission of documents" means the sending of information by electronic signals to, by or from a court or clerk, which when received can be transformed and stored or transmitted on paper, microfilm, magnetic storage device, optical imaging system, CD-ROM, flash drive, other electronic data storage system, server, case maintenance system ("CM"), electronic court filing ("ECF") system, statewide or local electronic portal ("e-portal"), or other electronic record keeping system authorized by the supreme court in a format sufficient to communicate the information on the original document in a readable format. Electronic transmission of documents includes electronic mail ("e-mail") and any internet-based transmission procedure, and may include procedures allowing for documents to be signed or verified by electronic means. FL ST J ADMIN Rule 2.525(a).

i. The filing of documents with the court as required by the Florida Rules of Judicial Administration must be made by filing them with the clerk in accordance with FL ST J ADMIN Rule 2.525, except that the judge may permit documents to be filed with the judge, in which event the judge must note the filing date before him or her on the documents and transmit them to the clerk. The date of filing is that shown on the face of the document by the judge's notation or the clerk's time stamp, whichever is earlier. FL ST J ADMIN Rule 2.516(e).

b. *Application.* Any court or clerk of the court may accept the electronic transmission of documents for filing after the clerk, together with input from the chief judge of the circuit, has obtained approval of the procedures and program for doing so from the Supreme Court of Florida. FL ST J ADMIN Rule 2.525(b).

c. *Exceptions*

   i. Paper documents and other submissions may be manually submitted to the clerk or court:

      - When the clerk does not have the ability to accept and retain documents by electronic filing or has not had ECF Procedures approved by the supreme court;
      - For filing by any self-represented party or any self-represented nonparty unless specific ECF Procedures provide a means to file documents electronically. However, any self-represented nonparty that is a governmental or public agency and any other agency, partnership, corporation, or business entity acting on behalf of any governmental or public agency may file documents by electronic transmission if such entity has the capability of filing documents electronically;
      - For filing by attorneys excused from e-mail service in accordance with FL ST J ADMIN Rule 2.516(b);
      - When submitting evidentiary exhibits or filing non-documentary materials;
      - When the filing involves documents in excess of twenty-five (25) megabytes (25MB) in size. For such filings, documents may be transmitted using an electronic storage medium that the clerk has the ability to accept, which may include a CD-ROM, flash drive, or similar storage medium;
      - When filed in open court, as permitted by the court;
      - When paper filing is permitted by any approved statewide or local ECF procedures; and
      - If any court determines that justice so requires. FL ST J ADMIN Rule 2.525(d).

   ii. Any document in paper form submitted under FL ST J ADMIN Rule 2.525(d) is filed when it is received by the clerk or court and the clerk shall immediately thereafter convert any filed paper document to an electronic document. "Convert to an electronic document" means optically capturing an image of a paper document and using character recognition software to recover as much of the document's text as practicable and then indexing and storing the document in the official court file. FL ST J ADMIN Rule 2.525(c)(4).

   iii. Any storage medium submitted under FL ST J ADMIN Rule 2.525(d)(5) is filed when received by the clerk or court and the clerk shall immediately thereafter transfer the electronic documents from the storage device to the official court file. FL ST J ADMIN Rule 2.525(c)(5).

   iv. If the filer of any paper document authorized under FL ST J ADMIN Rule 2.525(d) provides a self-addressed, postage-paid envelope for return of the paper document after it is converted to electronic form by the clerk, the clerk shall place the paper document in the envelope and deposit it in the mail. Except when a paper document is required to be maintained, the clerk may recycle any filed paper document that is not to be returned to the filer. FL ST J ADMIN Rule 2.525(c)(6).

   v. The clerk may convert any paper document filed before the effective date of FL ST J ADMIN Rule 2.525 to an electronic document. Unless the clerk is required to maintain the paper document, if the paper document has been converted to an electronic document by the clerk, the paper document is no longer part of the official court file and may be removed and recycled. FL ST J ADMIN Rule 2.525(c)(7).

d. *Official court file.* For information on what constitutes the official court file, please see FL ST J ADMIN Rule 2.525(c)(2), FL ST J ADMIN Rule 2.525(c)(3).

e. *Administration.* All attorneys, parties, or other persons using this rule to file documents are required to make arrangements with the court or clerk for the payment of any charges authorized by general law or the supreme court before filing any document by electronic transmission. FL ST J ADMIN Rule 2.525(f)(2).

f. *Filing date.* The filing date for an electronically transmitted document is the date and time that such filing is acknowledged by an electronic stamp or otherwise, pursuant to any procedure set forth in any ECF Procedures approved by the supreme court, or the date the last page of such filing is received by the court or clerk. FL ST J ADMIN Rule 2.525(f)(3).

g. *Accessibility.* All documents transmitted in any electronic form under FL ST J ADMIN Rule 2.525 must comply with the accessibility requirements of FL ST J ADMIN Rule 2.526. FL ST J ADMIN Rule 2.525(g).

h. *Provisions for electronic filing in the Seventeenth Circuit.* Attorneys may electronically file pleadings and papers on existing cases in circuit civil divisions 1, 7, 9, 19, 26 and 27. The following documents may be scanned and efiled; however, the original must be filed with the Clerk: Documents ordered by the Court; and original documents required by law or rule of procedure to be filed with the Clerk. Self represented individuals shall file pleadings and papers with the Clerk. The Clerk within twenty four (24) hours of receipt of an electronic document shall either accept or reject the electronic document for filing and send electronic notice to the filer. FL ST 17 J CIR 2012-16-CIV.

i. *Technical failures.* If a document filed electronically is not received due to: an error in the transmission of the document to the Clerk or any vendor of the Clerk to provide electronic court record filing services which is unknown to an attorney or party or affected non party, or a failure to process the electronic document when received by the Clerk or rejection by the Clerk, or any other technical problems experienced by the attorney or party or affected non party, the Court may, after an evidentiary hearing and upon satisfactory proof, enter an order permitting the document to be filed nunc pro tunc to the date it was first attempted to be sent electronically. FL ST 17 J CIR 2012-16-CIV.

j. *Filing of pleadings or papers at any office of the clerk of court.* The Clerk of Courts, commencing November 3, 2008, shall accept for filing, at the central courthouse, north satellite courthouse, south satellite courthouse, and west satellite courthouse any pleading or motion or other document for filing in the court file from any attorney or party for an existing case except as otherwise set forth. FL ST 17 J CIR 2008-153-GEN. See FL ST 17 J CIR 2008-153-GEN for specific exceptions.

2. *Service requirements.* Every pleading subsequent to the initial pleading, all orders, and every other document filed in the action must be served in conformity with the requirements of FL ST J ADMIN Rule 2.516. FL ST RCP Rule 1.080(a).

   a. *Service; When required.* Unless the court otherwise orders, or a statute or supreme court administrative order specifies a different means of service, every pleading subsequent to the initial pleading and every other document filed in any court proceeding, except applications for witness subpoenas and documents served by formal notice or required to be served in the manner provided for service of formal notice, must be served in accordance with FL ST J ADMIN Rule 2.516 on each party. No service need be made on parties against whom a default has been entered, except that pleadings asserting new or additional claims against them must be served in the manner provided for service of summons. FL ST J ADMIN Rule 2.516(a).

   b. *Service; How made.* When service is required or permitted to be made upon a party represented by an attorney, service must be made upon the attorney unless service upon the party is ordered by the court. FL ST J ADMIN Rule 2.516(b).

      i. *Service by electronic mail ("e-mail").* All documents required or permitted to be served on another party must be served by e-mail, unless FL ST J ADMIN Rule 2.516 otherwise provides. When, in addition to service by e-mail, the sender also utilizes another means of service provided for in FL ST J ADMIN Rule 2.516(b)(2), any differing time limits and other provisions applicable to that other means of service control. FL ST J ADMIN Rule 2.516(b)(1). Any document electronically transmitted to a court or clerk must also be served on all parties and interested persons in accordance with the applicable rules of court. FL ST J ADMIN Rule 2.525(e)(2).

         - *Service on attorneys.* Upon appearing in a proceeding, an attorney must serve a designation of a primary e-mail address and may designate no more than two (2) secondary e-mail addresses. Thereafter, service must be directed to all designated e-mail addresses in that proceeding. Every document filed by an attorney thereafter must include the primary e-mail address of that attorney and any secondary e-mail addresses. If an attorney does not designate any e-mail address for service, documents may be served on that attorney at the e-mail address on record with The Florida Bar. FL ST J ADMIN Rule 2.516(b)(1)(A).

- *Exception to e-mail service on attorneys.* Service by an attorney on another attorney must be made by e-mail unless excused by the court. Upon motion by an attorney demonstrating that the attorney has no e-mail account and lacks access to the Internet at the attorney's office, the court may excuse the attorney from the requirements of e-mail service. Service on and by an attorney excused by the court from e-mail service must be by the means provided in FL ST J ADMIN Rule 2.516(b)(2). FL ST J ADMIN Rule 2.516(b)(1)(B).
- *Service on and by parties not represented by an attorney.* Any party not represented by an attorney may serve a designation of a primary e-mail address and also may designate no more than two (2) secondary e-mail addresses to which service must be directed in that proceeding by the means provided in FL ST J ADMIN Rule 2.516(b)(1). If a party not represented by an attorney does not designate an e-mail address for service in a proceeding, service on and by that party must be by the means provided in FL ST J ADMIN Rule 2.516(b)(2). FL ST J ADMIN Rule 2.516(b)(1)(C).
- *Time of service.* Service by e-mail is complete when it is sent. FL ST J ADMIN Rule 2.516(b)(1)(D). An e-mail is deemed served on the date it is sent. FL ST J ADMIN Rule 2.516(b)(1)(D)(i). If the sender learns that the e-mail did not reach the address of the person to be served, the sender must immediately send another copy by e-mail, or by a means authorized by FL ST J ADMIN Rule 2.516(b)(2). FL ST J ADMIN Rule 2.516(b)(1)(D)(ii). E-mail service is treated as service by mail for the computation of time. FL ST J ADMIN Rule 2.516(b)(1)(D)(iii).

ii. *Format of e-mail for service.* Service of a document by e-mail is made by attaching a copy of the document in PDF format to an e-mail sent to all addresses designated by the attorney or party. FL ST J ADMIN Rule 2.516(b)(1)(E).

- All documents served by e-mail must be attached to an e-mail message containing a subject line beginning with the words "SERVICE OF COURT DOCUMENT" in all capital letters, followed by the case number of the proceeding in which the documents are being served. FL ST J ADMIN Rule 2.516(b)(1)(E)(i).
- The body of the e-mail must identify the court in which the proceeding is pending, the case number, the name of the initial party on each side, the title of each document served with that e-mail, and the sender's name and telephone number. FL ST J ADMIN Rule 2.516(b)(1)(E)(ii).
- Any document served by e-mail may be signed by the "/s/" format, as long as the filed original is signed in accordance with the applicable rule of procedure. FL ST J ADMIN Rule 2.516(b)(1)(E)(iii).
- Any e-mail which, together with its attached documents, exceeds five megabytes (5MB) in size, must be divided and sent as separate e-mails, no one of which may exceed five megabytes (5MB) in size and each of which must be sequentially numbered in the subject line. FL ST J ADMIN Rule 2.516(b)(1)(E)(iv).

iii. *Service by other means.* In addition to, and not in lieu of, service by e-mail, service may also be made upon attorneys by any of the means specified in FL ST J ADMIN Rule 2.516(b)(2). Service on and by all parties who are not represented by an attorney and who do not designate an e-mail address, and on and by all attorneys excused from e-mail service, must be made by delivering a copy of the document or by mailing it to the party or attorney at their last known address or, if no address is known, by leaving it with the clerk of the court. Service by mail is complete upon mailing. Delivery of a copy within FL ST J ADMIN Rule 2.516 is complete upon:

- Handing it to the attorney or to the party,
- Leaving it at the attorney's or party's office with a clerk or other person in charge thereof,
- If there is no one in charge, leaving it in a conspicuous place therein,
- If the office is closed or the person to be served has no office, leaving it at the person's usual place of abode with some person of his or her family above fifteen (15) years of age and informing such person of the contents, or

- Transmitting it by facsimile to the attorney's or party's office with a cover sheet containing the sender's name, firm, address, telephone number, and facsimile number, and the number of pages transmitted. When service is made by facsimile, a copy must also be served by any other method permitted by FL ST J ADMIN Rule 2.516. Facsimile service occurs when transmission is complete. FL ST J ADMIN Rule 2.516(b)(2)(A) through FL ST J ADMIN Rule 2.516(b)(2)(E).
- Service by delivery after 5:00 p.m. must be deemed to have been made by mailing on the date of delivery. FL ST J ADMIN Rule 2.516(b)(2)(F).

c. *Service; Numerous defendants.* In actions when the parties are unusually numerous, the court may regulate the service contemplated by the Florida Rules of Judicial Administration on motion or on its own initiative in such manner as may be found to be just and reasonable. FL ST J ADMIN Rule 2.516(c).

d. *Service by clerk.* Service of notices and other documents required to be made by the clerk must also be done as provided in FL ST J ADMIN Rule 2.516(b). FL ST J ADMIN Rule 2.516(g).

G. Hearings

1. *Hearing on motion for summary judgment.* The summary judgment rule does not provide the trial court with discretion to decide whether a hearing is required. A failure to hold a hearing on a motion for summary judgment violates due process as well as rule of procedure governing summary judgment procedure. Kozich v. Hartford Ins. Co. of Midwest, 609 So.2d 147, 148 (Fla. 4th DCA 1992); FL-RCPF R 1.510(102).

2. *Summary judgment consideration at pretrial conference.* A summary judgment can be granted at the pretrial conference. The standard and procedure for granting summary judgment is the same at a pretrial conference as at other times. The notice time for a pretrial conference and for service of a motion for summary judgment is the same, so summary judgment can be entered at the conference if no genuine issue of material fact exists. FL-PRACPROC § 19:4.

3. *Communication equipment*

a. *Definition.* Communication equipment means a conference telephone or other electronic device that permits all those appearing or participating to hear and speak to each other, provided that all conversation of all parties is audible to all persons present. FL ST J ADMIN Rule 2.530(a).

b. *Use by all parties.* A county or circuit court judge may, upon the court's own motion or upon the written request of a party, direct that communication equipment be used for a motion hearing, pretrial conference, or a status conference. A judge must give notice to the parties and consider any objections they may have to the use of communication equipment before directing that communication equipment be used. The decision to use communication equipment over the objection of parties will be in the sound discretion of the trial court, except as noted below. FL ST J ADMIN Rule 2.530(b).

c. *Use only by requesting party.* A county or circuit court judge may, upon the written request of a party upon reasonable notice to all other parties, permit a requesting party to participate through communication equipment in a scheduled motion hearing; however, any such request (except in criminal, juvenile, and appellate proceedings) must be granted, absent a showing of good cause to deny the same, where the hearing is set for not longer than fifteen (15) minutes. FL ST J ADMIN Rule 2.530(c).

d. *Testimony*

i. *Generally.* A county or circuit court judge, general magistrate, special magistrate, or hearing officer may allow testimony to be taken through communication equipment if all parties consent or if permitted by another applicable rule of procedure. FL ST J ADMIN Rule 2.530(d)(1).

ii. *Procedure.* Any party desiring to present testimony through communication equipment shall, prior to the hearing or trial at which the testimony is to be presented, contact all parties to determine whether each party consents to this form of testimony. The party seeking to present the testimony shall move for permission to present testimony through communication equipment, which motion shall set forth good cause as to why the testimony should be allowed in this form. FL ST J ADMIN Rule 2.530(d)(2).

iii. *Oath.* Testimony may be taken through communication equipment only if a notary public or other person authorized to administer oaths in the witness's jurisdiction is present with the witness and administers the oath consistent with the laws of the jurisdiction. FL ST J ADMIN Rule 2.530(d)(3).

iv. *Confrontation rights.* In juvenile and criminal proceedings the defendant must make an informed waiver of any confrontation rights that may be abridged by the use of communication equipment. FL ST J ADMIN Rule 2.530(d)(4).

v. *Video testimony.* If the testimony to be presented utilizes video conferencing or comparable two-way visual capabilities, the court in its discretion may modify the procedures set forth in FL ST J ADMIN Rule 2.530 to accommodate the technology utilized. FL ST J ADMIN Rule 2.530(d)(5).

e. *Burden of expense.* The cost for the use of the communication equipment is the responsibility of the requesting party unless otherwise directed by the court. FL ST J ADMIN Rule 2.530(e).

4. *Uniform motion calendar.* The Circuit Judges of the general civil/family division (excluding juvenile/dependency) shall maintain a uniform motion calendar from 8:45 A.M. to 9:30 A.M., Monday through Thursday. The motion calendar shall end PROMPTLY at 9:30 A.M. All parties shall be prepared to proceed at 8:45 A.M., and if one party fails to timely appear, the matter may proceed on the merits in his/her absence. FL ST 17 J CIR LOCAL RULE NO. 10A(1).

5. *Noticed motion limitation.* No more than two (2) motions may be noticed for each case on any given day except by leave of court. FL ST 17 J CIR LOCAL RULE NO. 10A(4).

6. *Ex parte and non-evidentiary motion.* Ex parte matters, non-evidentiary motions, and uncontested proceedings for adoptions, or dissolution may be heard on the uniform motion calendar, provided such matters can be conducted in five (5) minutes equally allocated among the parties and the moving party shall so certify as specified in FL ST 17 J CIR LOCAL RULE NO. 10A(3). FL ST 17 J CIR LOCAL RULE NO. 10A(6).

7. *Good faith effort to resolve issues.* Prior to appearing before the court, the parties shall discuss the issues raised in the pending motion, and both parties shall be prepared to certify at the hearing they have made a good faith effort to resolve the issues. FL ST 17 J CIR LOCAL RULE NO. 10A(7).

8. *Re-noticing hearings.* When the motion calendar has been filled, the judge's office shall notify the party noticing any hearings which cannot be reached. The noticing party shall call opposing counsel and re-notice the hearing. FL ST 17 J CIR LOCAL RULE NO. 10A(9).

9. *Hearing cancellation.* Motion calendar hearings may be canceled by the attorney who set the hearing. FL ST 17 J CIR LOCAL RULE NO. 10A(10).

10. *Other motion calendars.* Hearing officers/general masters shall conduct a motion calendar, the dates and times of which shall be determined by the hearing officer/general master or by administrative order. FL ST 17 J CIR LOCAL RULE NO. 10A(11).

11. *Sanctions.* Failure to comply with the procedures designated in the above paragraphs may result in the hearing being stricken from the docket or such other sanctions as the court deems appropriate. FL ST 17 J CIR LOCAL RULE NO. 10A(12).

H. Forms

1. Official Motion for Summary Judgment Forms for Florida

a. Caption. FL ST RCP Form 1.901.

b. Notice of compliance when constitutional challenge is brought. FL ST RCP Form 1.975.

2. Motion for Summary Judgment Forms for Florida

a. Motion for summary judgment; By plaintiff. FL-PP § 6:9.

b. Motion for summary judgment; By defendant. FL-PP § 6:10.

c. Affidavit; Supporting motion for summary judgment; By plaintiff's attorney. FL-PP § 6:11.
d. Affidavit; Opposing motion for summary judgment; By defendant's attorney. FL-PP § 6:12.
e. Affidavit; Opposing motion for summary judgment; By party; Inability to present facts. FL-PP § 6:13.
f. Order; Establishing uncontroverted facts and stating issues requiring further determination. FL-PP § 6:14.
g. Summary judgment. FL-PP § 6:15.
h. Motion; Summary judgment, by defendant. FL-PRACFORM § 7:190.
i. Motion; Summary judgment, by plaintiff. FL-PRACFORM § 7:191.
j. Motion; Summary judgment, partial, by defendant. FL-PRACFORM § 7:192.
k. Motion; Summary judgment, part of claim. FL-PRACFORM § 7:193.
l. Form for plaintiff's motion for summary judgment. FL-RCPF R 1.510(128).
m. Form for notice of motion for summary judgment by plaintiff. FL-RCPF R 1.510(129).
n. Form for notice of cross-motion for summary judgment by plaintiff. FL-RCPF R 1.510(130).
o. Form for order denying motion for summary judgment and specifying uncontroverted facts. FL-RCPF R 1.510(304).
p. Form for motion for partial summary judgment. FL-RCPF R 1.510(305).
q. Form for motion for partial summary judgment; Affirmative defenses. FL-RCPF R 1.510(305.1).

I. Checklist

(I) ❑ Matters to be considered by moving party
- (a) ❑ Required documents
  - (1) ❑ Notice of hearing/Motion
  - (2) ❑ Good faith certificate
  - (3) ❑ Certificate of service
- (b) ❑ Supplemental documents
  - (1) ❑ Affidavits
  - (2) ❑ Other evidence
  - (3) ❑ Proposed order
  - (4) ❑ Notice of constitutional question
- (c) ❑ Time for making motion
  - (1) ❑ By the plaintiff, after the expiration of twenty (20) days from the commencement of the action (claimant), or after service of a motion for summary judgment by the adverse party
  - (2) ❑ By the defending party at any time
  - (3) ❑ The motion for summary judgment must be served at least twenty (20) days before the time fixed for the hearing

(II) ❑ Matters to be considered by opposing party
- (a) ❑ Required documents
  - (1) ❑ Response to motion
  - (2) ❑ Certificate of service
- (b) ❑ Supplemental documents
  - (1) ❑ Affidavits
  - (2) ❑ Notice of evidence relied upon

(3) ❑ Other evidence

(4) ❑ Proposed order

(5) ❑ Notice of constitutional question

(c) ❑ Time for service and filing of opposition

(1) ❑ The adverse party shall identify, by notice mailed to the movant's attorney at least five (5) days prior to the day of the hearing, or delivered no later than 5:00 p.m. two (2) business days prior to the day of the hearing, any summary judgment evidence on which the adverse party relies

(2) ❑ To the extent that summary judgment evidence has not already been filed with the court, the adverse party shall serve a copy on the movant by mail at least five (5) days prior to the day of the hearing, or by delivery to the movant's attorney no later than 5:00 p.m. two (2) business days prior to the day of hearing

Motions, Oppositions and Replies
Motion for Sanctions

Document Last Updated January 2013

A. Applicable Rules

1. *State rules*

a. Attorney's fee; Sanctions for raising unsupported claims or defenses; Exceptions; Service of motions; Damages for delay of litigation. FL ST § 57.105.

b. Offer of judgment and demand for judgment. FL ST § 768.79.

c. Proposals for settlement. FL ST RCP Rule 1.442.

d. Motions for costs and attorneys' fees. FL ST RCP Rule 1.525.

e. Rules of court. FL ST RCP Rule 1.010; FL ST J ADMIN Rule 2.110.

f. Nonverification of pleadings. FL ST RCP Rule 1.030.

g. Service and filing of pleadings, orders, and documents. FL ST RCP Rule 1.080.

h. Time. FL ST RCP Rule 1.090.

i. Pleadings and motions. FL ST RCP Rule 1.100.

j. Motions. FL ST RCP Rule 1.160.

k. Relief from judgment, decrees or orders. FL ST RCP Rule 1.540.

l. Mediation and arbitration. FL ST RCP Rule 1.700; FL ST RCP Rule 1.710; FL ST RCP Rule 1.720; FL ST RCP Rule 1.730; FL ST RCP Rule 1.750; FL ST RCP Rule 1.800; FL ST RCP Rule 1.810; FL ST RCP Rule 1.820; FL ST RCP Rule 1.830.

m. Forms. FL ST RCP Rule 1.900.

n. Retention of court records. FL ST J ADMIN Rule 2.430.

o. Foreign attorneys. FL ST J ADMIN Rule 2.510..

p. Signature of attorneys and parties. FL ST J ADMIN Rule 2.515.

q. Paper. FL ST J ADMIN Rule 2.520.

r. Electronic filing. FL ST J ADMIN Rule 2.525.

s. Communication equipment. FL ST J ADMIN Rule 2.530.

t. Court reporting. FL ST J ADMIN Rule 2.535.

u. Requests for accommodations by persons with disabilities. FL ST J ADMIN Rule 2.540.

v. Minimization of the filing of sensitive information. FL ST J ADMIN Rule 2.425.

- w. Accessibility of information and technology. FL ST J ADMIN Rule 2.526.
- x. Administrative Procedure Act. FL ST § 120.50; FL ST § 120.52; FL ST § 120.68; FL ST § 120.81.

2. *Local rules*
   - a. Orders for signature; Civil division. FL ST 17 J CIR LOCAL RULE NO. 8.
   - b. Uniform motion calendar ex parte motions to compel discovery, and special set hearings. FL ST 17 J CIR LOCAL RULE NO. 10A.
   - c. Standards of professional courtesy. FL ST 17 J CIR I-94-O-1.
   - d. Administrative order authorizing the filing of pleadings or papers at any office of the clerk of court. FL ST 17 J CIR 2008-153-GEN.
   - e. Administrative order regarding provision of ADA accommodations. FL ST 17 J CIR 2010-49-GEN.
   - f. Administrative order establishing electronic filing procedures for the civil division. FL ST 17 J CIR 2012-16-CIV.

B. Timing

1. *Motion for sanctions.* A motion by a party seeking sanctions under FL ST § 57.105 must be served but may not be filed with or presented to the court unless, within twenty one (21) days after service of the motion, the challenged paper, claim, defense, contention, allegation, or denial is not withdrawn or appropriately corrected. FL ST § 57.105(4).
2. *Sanctions in relation to proposals for settlement.* Any party seeking sanctions pursuant to applicable Florida law, based on the failure of the proposal's recipient to accept a proposal, shall do so by serving a motion in accordance with FL ST RCP Rule 1.525. FL ST RCP Rule 1.442(g). Any party seeking a judgment taxing costs, attorneys' fees, or both shall serve a motion no later than thirty (30) days after filing of the judgment, including a judgment of dismissal, or the service of a notice of voluntary dismissal, which judgment or notice concludes the action as to that party. FL ST RCP Rule 1.525.
3. *General motion timing.* A copy of any written motion which may not be heard ex parte and a copy of the notice of the hearing thereof shall be served a reasonable time before the time specified for the hearing. FL ST RCP Rule 1.090(d). Copies of the notice of hearing, the motion, and any pleading or interrogatories to which the motion is addressed shall be in the hands of the Judicial Assistant and opposing party at least four (4) working days in advance of the hearing. The original notice shall be filed with the Clerk. FL ST 17 J CIR LOCAL RULE NO. 10A(5).
4. *Standard of professional conduct; Scheduling*
   - a. Attorneys should endeavor to provide opposing counsel, parties, witnesses, and other affected persons, sufficient notice of depositions, hearings and other proceedings, except upon agreement of course, in an emergency, or in other circumstances compelling more expedited scheduling. As a general rule, actual notice should be no less than five (5) business days for instate depositions, ten (10) business days for out-of-state depositions and four (4) business days for hearings. FL ST 17 J CIR I-94-O-1(I)(1).
   - b. Attorneys should communicate with opposing counsel prior to scheduling depositions, hearings and other proceedings, in an effort to schedule them at times that are mutually convenient for all interested persons. Further, sufficient time should be reserved to permit a complete presentation by counsel for all parties. FL ST 17 J CIR I-94-O-1(I)(2).
   - c. Attorneys should notify opposing counsel, the court, and others affected, of scheduling conflicts as soon as they become apparent. Further, attorneys should cooperate with one another regarding all reasonable rescheduling requests that do not prejudice their clients or unduly delay a proceeding. FL ST 17 J CIR I-94-O-1(I)(3).
   - d. Attorneys should promptly notify the court or other tribunal of any resolution between the parties that renders a scheduled court appearance unnecessary or otherwise moot. FL ST 17 J CIR I-94-O-1(I)(4).
   - e. Attorneys should grant reasonable requests by opposing counsel for extensions of time within which to respond to pleadings, discovery, and other matters when such an extension will not prejudice their client or unduly delay a proceeding. FL ST 17 J CIR I-94-O-1(I)(5).

5. *Timing considerations when filing electronically.* The filing date of an efiled document is when the last page is received by the Clerk. The electronic filing of a document does not modify any filing deadlines as required by law, rule of procedure, or court order. FL ST 17 J CIR 2012-16-CIV.
6. *Computation of time*
   a. *Generally.* Computation of time shall be governed by FL ST J ADMIN Rule 2.514. FL ST RCP Rule 1.090(a). The following rules apply in computing time periods specified in any rule of procedure, local rule, court order, or statute that does not specify a method of computing time. FL ST J ADMIN Rule 2.514(a).
      i. *Period stated in days or a longer unit.* When the period is stated in days or a longer unit of time (A) exclude the day of the event that triggers the period; (B) count every day, including intermediate Saturdays, Sundays, and legal holidays; and (C) include the last day of the period, but if the last day is a Saturday, Sunday, or legal holiday, or falls within any period of time extended through an order of the chief justice under FL ST J ADMIN Rule 2.205(a)(2)(B)(iv), the period continues to run until the end of the next day that is not a Saturday, Sunday, or legal holiday and does not fall within any period of time extended through an order of the chief justice. FL ST J ADMIN Rule 2.514(a)(1).
      ii. *Period stated in hours.* When the period is stated in hours (A) begin counting immediately on the occurrence of the event that triggers the period; (B) count every hour, including hours during intermediate Saturdays, Sundays, and legal holidays; and (C) if the period would end on a Saturday, Sunday, or legal holiday, or during any period of time extended through an order of the chief justice under FL ST J ADMIN Rule 2.205(a)(2)(B)(iv), the period continues to run until the same time on the next day that is not a Saturday, Sunday, or legal holiday and does not fall within any period of time extended through an order of the chief justice. FL ST J ADMIN Rule 2.514(a)(2).
      iii. *Period stated in days less than seven (7) days.* When the period stated in days is less than seven (7) days, intermediate Saturdays, Sundays, and legal holidays shall be excluded in the computation. FL ST J ADMIN Rule 2.514(a)(3).
      iv. *"Last day" defined.* Unless a different time is set by a statute, local rule, or court order, the last day ends (A) for electronic filing or for service by any means, at midnight; and (B) for filing by other means, when the clerk's office is scheduled to close. FL ST J ADMIN Rule 2.514(a)(4).
      v. *"Next day" defined.* The "next day" is determined by continuing to count forward when the period is measured after an event and backward when measured before an event. FL ST J ADMIN Rule 2.514(a)(5).
      vi. *"Legal holiday" defined.* "Legal holiday" means (A) the day set aside by FL ST § 110.117, for observing New Year's Day, Martin Luther King, Jr.'s Birthday, Memorial Day, Independence Day, Labor Day, Veterans' Day, Thanksgiving Day, the Friday after Thanksgiving Day, or Christmas Day, and (B) any day observed as a holiday by the clerk's office or as designated by the chief judge. FL ST J ADMIN Rule 2.514(a)(6).
   b. *Additional time after service by mail or e-mail.* When a party may or must act within a specified time after service and service is made by mail or e-mail, five (5) days are added after the period that would otherwise expire under FL ST J ADMIN Rule 2.514(a). FL ST J ADMIN Rule 2.514(b).
   c. *Enlargement.* When an act is required or allowed to be done at or within a specified time by order of court, by the Florida Rules of Civil Procedure, or by notice given thereunder, for cause shown the court at any time in its discretion (1) with or without notice, may order the period enlarged if request therefor is made before the expiration of the period originally prescribed or as extended by a previous order, or (2) upon motion made and notice after the expiration of the specified period, may permit the act to be done when failure to act was the result of excusable neglect, but it may not extend the time for making a motion for new trial, for rehearing, or to alter or amend a judgment; making a motion for relief from a judgment under FL ST RCP Rule 1.540(b); taking an appeal or filing a petition for certiorari; or making a motion for a directed verdict. FL ST RCP Rule 1.090(b).
   d. *Unaffected by expiration of term.* The period of time provided for the doing of any act or the taking

of any proceeding shall not be affected or limited by the continued existence or expiration of a term of court. The continued existence or expiration of a term of court in no way affects the power of a court to do any act or take any proceeding in any action which is or has been pending before it. FL ST RCP Rule 1.090(c).

C. General Requirements

1. *Motions generally*

   a. *Contents.* An application to the court for an order shall be by motion which shall be made in writing unless made during a hearing or trial, shall state with particularity the grounds therefor, and shall set forth the relief or order sought. The requirement of writing is fulfilled if the motion is stated in a written notice of the hearing of the motion. All notices of hearing shall specify each motion or other matter to be heard. FL ST RCP Rule 1.100(b).

   b. *Particularity requirement.* The court considers a motion in the light of the substantive law, rule or statute to make its determination. Some rules require a statement of the grounds for a motion under the rule. Failure to give the grounds will result in denial of the motion. This should be the result in all situations when the ground for the motion is not inherent in the rule. FL-PRACPROC § 9:3. The requirement is nevertheless an important one, first because of the due process notice rights of the respondent, as well as for the assistance it provides to the court in its preparation for the hearing or, absent a hearing, for disposition. 4 FLPRAC R 1.100.

2. *Motion for sanctions*

   a. *Sanctions for raising unsupported claims or defenses*

      i. *No material facts; No law supporting material facts.* Upon the court's initiative or motion of any party, the court shall award a reasonable attorney's fee, including prejudgment interest, to be paid to the prevailing party in equal amounts by the losing party and the losing party's attorney on any claim or defense at any time during a civil proceeding or action in which the court finds that the losing party or the losing party's attorney knew or should have known that a claim or defense when initially presented to the court or at any time before trial was not supported by the material facts necessary to establish the claim or defense; or would not be supported by the application of then-existing law to those material facts. FL ST § 57.105(1).

      ii. *Unreasonable delay.* At any time in any civil proceeding or action in which the moving party proves by a preponderance of the evidence that any action taken by the opposing party, including, but not limited to, the filing of any pleading or part thereof, the assertion of or response to any discovery demand, the assertion of any claim or defense, or the response to any request by any other party, was taken primarily for the purpose of unreasonable delay, the court shall award damages to the moving party for its reasonable expenses incurred in obtaining the order, which may include attorney's fees, and other loss resulting from the improper delay. FL ST § 57.105(2).

      iii. *Limit on monetary sanctions.* Notwithstanding FL ST § 57.105(1) and FL ST § 57.105(2), monetary sanctions may not be awarded:

         - Under FL ST § 57.105(1)(b) if the court determines that the claim or defense was initially presented to the court as a good faith argument for the extension, modification, or reversal of existing law or the establishment of new law, as it applied to the material facts, with a reasonable expectation of success. FL ST § 57.105(3)(a).
         - Under FL ST § 57.105(1)(a) or FL ST § 57.105(1)(b) against the losing party's attorney if he or she has acted in good faith, based on the representations of his or her client as to the existence of those material facts. FL ST § 57.105(3)(b).
         - Under FL ST § 57.105(1)(b) against a represented party. FL ST § 57.105(3)(c).
         - On the court's initiative under FL ST § 57.105(1) and FL ST § 57.105(2) unless sanctions are awarded before a voluntary dismissal or settlement of the claims made by or against the party that is, or whose attorneys are, to be sanctioned. FL ST § 57.105(3)(d).

      iv. *Other sanctions available.* The provisions of FL ST § 57.105 are supplemental to other sanctions or remedies available under law or under court rules. FL ST § 57.105(6).

v. *Fees provided for in contract.* If a contract contains a provision allowing attorney's fees to a party when he or she is required to take any action to enforce the contract, the court may also allow reasonable attorney's fees to the other party when that party prevails in any action, whether as plaintiff or defendant, with respect to the contract. FL ST § 57.105(7) applies to any contract entered into on or after October 1, 1988. FL ST § 57.105(7).

b. *Sanctions in relation to proposals for settlement*

i. *Generally.* Any party seeking sanctions pursuant to applicable Florida law, based on the failure of the proposal's recipient to accept a proposal, shall do so by serving a motion in accordance with FL ST RCP Rule 1.525. FL ST RCP Rule 1.442(g). Any party seeking a judgment taxing costs, attorneys' fees, or both shall serve a motion no later than thirty (30) days after filing of the judgment, including a judgment of dismissal, or the service of a notice of voluntary dismissal, which judgment or notice concludes the action as to that party. FL ST RCP Rule 1.525.

ii. *Motion after judgment, voluntary or involuntary dismissal.* Upon motion made by the offeror within thirty (30) days after the entry of judgment or after voluntary or involuntary dismissal, the court shall determine the following:

- If a defendant serves an offer which is not accepted by the plaintiff, and if the judgment obtained by the plaintiff is at least twenty-five (25%) percent less than the amount of the offer, the defendant shall be awarded reasonable costs, including investigative expenses, and attorney's fees, calculated in accordance with the guidelines promulgated by the Supreme Court, incurred from the date the offer was served, and the court shall set off such costs in attorney's fees against the award. When such costs and attorney's fees total more than the amount of the judgment, the court shall enter judgment for the defendant against the plaintiff for the amount of the costs and fees, less the amount of the award to the plaintiff. FL ST § 768.79(6)(a).
- If a plaintiff serves an offer which is not accepted by the defendant, and if the judgment obtained by the plaintiff is at least twenty-five (25%) percent more than the amount of the offer, the plaintiff shall be awarded reasonable costs, including investigative expenses, and attorney's fees, calculated in accordance with the guidelines promulgated by the Supreme Court, incurred from the date the offer was served. FL ST § 768.79(6)(b).
- For purposes of the determination required by FL ST § 768.79(6)(a), the term "judgment obtained" means the amount of the net judgment entered, plus any postoffer collateral source payments received or due as of the date of the judgment, plus any postoffer settlement amounts by which the verdict was reduced. For purposes of the determination required by FL ST § 768.79(6)(b), the term "judgment obtained" means the amount of the net judgment entered, plus any postoffer settlement amounts by which the verdict was reduced. FL ST § 768.79(6).

iii. For further information please see FL ST § 768.79 and FL ST RCP Rule 1.442.

3. *Arbitration and mediation*

a. *Referral to arbitration and mediation.* Except as hereinafter provided or as otherwise prohibited by law, the presiding judge may enter an order referring all or any part of a contested civil matter to mediation or arbitration. The parties to any contested civil matter may file a written stipulation to mediate or arbitrate any issue between them at any time. Such stipulation shall be incorporated into the order of referral. FL ST RCP Rule 1.700(a).

b. *Arbitration*

i. *Exclusions.* A civil action shall be ordered to arbitration or arbitration in conjunction with mediation upon stipulation of the parties. A civil action may be ordered to arbitration or arbitration in conjunction with mediation upon motion of any party or by the court, if the judge determines the action to be of such a nature that arbitration could be of benefit to the litigants or the court. FL ST RCP Rule 1.800.

- Under no circumstances may the following categories of actions be referred to arbitration: (1) bond estreatures; (2) habeas corpus or other extraordinary writs; (3) bond validations;

(4) civil or criminal contempt; (5) such other matters as may be specified by order of the chief judge in the circuit. FL ST RCP Rule 1.800.

ii. For more information regarding arbitration, please see FL ST RCP Rule 1.810; FL ST RCP Rule 1.820; FL ST RCP Rule 1.830.

c. *Mediation.* For more information regarding mediation, please see FL ST RCP Rule 1.710; FL ST RCP Rule 1.720; FL ST RCP Rule 1.730; and FL ST RCP Rule 1.750.

4. *Rules of court*

a. *Rules of civil procedure.* The Florida Rules of Civil Procedure apply to all actions of a civil nature and all special statutory proceedings in the circuit courts and county courts except those to which the Florida Probate Rules, the Florida Family Law Rules of Procedure, or the Small Claims Rules apply. FL ST RCP Rule 1.010.

i. The form, content, procedure, and time for pleading in all special statutory proceedings shall be as prescribed by the statutes governing the proceeding unless the Florida Rules of Civil Procedure specifically provide to the contrary. FL ST RCP Rule 1.010.

ii. The Florida Rules of Civil Procedure shall be construed to secure the just, speedy, and inexpensive determination of every action. FL ST RCP Rule 1.010.

b. *Rules of judicial administration.* The Florida Rules of Judicial Administration shall apply to administrative matters in all courts to which the Florida Rules of Judicial Administration are applicable by their terms. The Florida Rules of Judicial Administration shall be construed to secure the speedy and inexpensive determination of every proceeding to which they are applicable. The Florida Rules of Judicial Administration shall supersede all conflicting rules and statutes. FL ST J ADMIN Rule 2.110.

D. Documents

1. *Required documents*

a. *Notice of hearing/Motion.* An application to the court for an order shall be by motion which shall be made in writing unless made during a hearing or trial, shall state with particularity the grounds therefor, and shall set forth the relief or order sought. The requirement of writing is fulfilled if the motion is stated in a written notice of the hearing of the motion. All notices of hearing shall specify each motion or other matter to be heard. FL ST RCP Rule 1.100(b).

i. *Notices to persons with disabilities.* See the Format section of this KeyRules document for further information.

b. *Good faith certification.* Prior to setting a matter on the motion calendar, the party or attorney noticing the motion shall attempt to resolve the matter and shall certify the good faith attempt to resolve. FL ST 17 J CIR LOCAL RULE NO. 10A(2). To comply, every party or attorney setting a motion for hearing shall execute the following certification: I hereby certify that A) I have made a good faith attempt to resolve this matter prior to my noticing this motion for hearing, and B) the issues before the Court may be heard and resolved by the court within five (5) minutes. FL ST 17 J CIR LOCAL RULE NO. 10A(3).

c. *Certificate of service.* When any attorney certifies in substance: "I certify that a copy hereof has been furnished to (here insert name or names and addresses used for service) by (e-mail) (delivery) (mail) (fax) on .... (date) ....________________ Attorney" the certificate is taken as prima facie proof of such service in compliance with FL ST J ADMIN Rule 2.516. FL ST J ADMIN Rule 2.516(f).

2. *Supplemental documents*

a. *Proposed order, copies, stamped envelopes.* The court may require that orders or judgments be prepared by a party, may require the party to furnish the court with stamped, addressed envelopes for service of the order or judgment, and may require that proposed orders and judgments be furnished to all parties before entry by the court of the order or judgment. FL ST J ADMIN Rule 2.516(h)(1).

i. A party submitting an order or judgment shall furnish the Court with sufficient copies together with stamped envelopes addressed to all parties entitled to receive a copy. Proposed orders or judgments must be furnished opposing counsel prior to submission to the court. Proposed orders or judgments must be titled to conform with the motion to which it refers. Language in the order or judgment not agreed as conforming to the court's pronouncement shall be brought to the attention of the court. The proposed order shall indicate date of the hearing on which the order is predicated. Attorneys for the movant shall have at Motion Calendar Hearings all proposed orders and judgments together with the appropriate stamped envelopes where applicable. Unless the Court directs otherwise, proposed orders on non-Motion Calendar Hearings must be prepared by the prevailing or designated counsel and submitted to the Court for consideration within forty-eight (48) hours after said hearing. Copies of all such orders, after entry, shall be conformed and mailed by the Clerk of Court, or the judge's secretary, within forty-eight (48) hours. FL ST 17 J CIR LOCAL RULE NO. 8. Any party requesting relief shall furnish the court with a prepared form of order and sufficient copies with stamped addressed envelopes for all parties. FL ST 17 J CIR LOCAL RULE NO. 10A(8).

ii. Attorneys should draft proposed orders promptly and the orders should fairly and adequately represent the ruling of the court. Attorneys should promptly provide, either orally or in writing, proposed orders to opposing counsel for approval. Opposing counsel should then promptly communicate any objections and at that time, the drafting attorney should immediately submit a copy of the proposed order to the court and advise the court as to whether or not it has been approved by opposing counsel. FL ST 17 J CIR I-94-O-1(IV)(3).

b. *Notice of constitutional question.* A party that files a pleading, written motion, or other paper drawing into question the constitutionality of a state statute or a county or municipal charter, ordinance, or franchise must promptly (1) file a notice of constitutional question stating the question and identifying the paper that raises it; and (2) serve the notice and the pleading, written motion, or other paper drawing into question the constitutionality of a state statute or a county or municipal charter, ordinance, or franchise on the Attorney General or the state attorney of the judicial circuit in which the action is pending, by either certified or registered mail. Service of the notice and pleading, written motion, or other paper does not require joinder of the Attorney General or the state attorney as a party to the action. FL ST RCP Rule 1.071.

E. Format

1. *Documents; Type and size.* Documents subject to the exceptions set forth in FL ST J ADMIN Rule 2.525(d) shall be filed on recycled paper measuring eight and one half by eleven (8 1/2 by 11) inches. For purposes of FL ST J ADMIN Rule 2.520, paper is recycled if it contains a minimum content of fifty (50) percent waste paper. Xerographic reduction of legal-size (eight and one half by fourteen (8 1/2 by 14) inches) documents to letter size (eight and one half by eleven (8 1/2 by 11) inches) is prohibited. All other documents filed by electronic transmission shall be filed in a format capable of being printed in a format consistent with the provisions of FL ST J ADMIN Rule 2.250. FL ST J ADMIN Rule 2.520(b).

   a. *Exhibits.* Any exhibit or attachment filed with pleadings or papers may be filed in its original size. FL ST J ADMIN Rule 2.520(c).

   b. *Recording space.* On all papers and documents prepared and filed by the court or by any party to a proceeding which are to be recorded in the public records of any county, including but not limited to final money judgments and notices of lis pendens, a three (3) inch by three (3) inch space at the top right-hand corner on the first page and a one (1) inch by three (3) inch space at the top right-hand corner on each subsequent page shall be left blank and reserved for use by the clerk of court. FL ST J ADMIN Rule 2.520(d).

      i. *Exceptions to recording space.* Any papers or documents created by persons or entities over which the filing party has no control, including but not limited to wills, codicils, trusts, or other testamentary documents; documents prepared or executed by any public officer; documents prepared, executed, acknowledged, or proved outside of the State of Florida; or documents created by State or Federal government agencies, may be filed without the space required by FL ST J ADMIN Rule 2.520. FL ST J ADMIN Rule 2.520(e).

   c. *Noncompliance.* No clerk of court is permitted to refuse to file any document or paper because of noncompliance with the Florida Rules of Judicial Administration. However, upon request of the

clerk of court, noncomplying documents must be resubmitted in accordance with the formatting rules. FL ST J ADMIN Rule 2.520(f).

2. *Caption.* Every pleading, motion, order, judgment, or other paper shall have a caption containing the name of the court, the file number, and except for in rem proceedings, including forfeiture proceedings, the name of the first party on each side with an appropriate indication of other parties, and a designation identifying the party filing it and its nature or the nature of the order, as the case may be. In any in rem proceeding, every pleading, motion, order, judgment, or other paper shall have a caption containing the name of the court, the file number, the style "In re" (followed by the name or general description of the property), and a designation of the person or entity filing it and its nature or the nature of the order, as the case may be. In an in rem forfeiture proceeding, the style shall be "In re forfeiture of" (followed by the name of the general description of the property). All papers filed in the action shall be styled in such a manner as to indicate clearly the subject matter of the paper and the party requesting or obtaining relief. FL ST RCP Rule 1.100(c)(1).

3. *Writing and written defined.* Writing or written means a document containing information, an application, or a stipulation. FL ST RCP Rule 1.080(c).

4. *Rule abbreviations*

   a. The Florida Rules of Civil Procedure and shall be abbreviated as Fla.R.Civ.P. FL ST RCP Rule 1.010.

   b. The Florida Rules of Judicial Administration shall be abbreviated as Fla. R. Jud. Admin. FL ST J ADMIN Rule 2.110.

5. *Nonverification.* Except when otherwise specifically provided by the Florida Rules of Civil Procedure or an applicable statute, every pleading or other document of a party represented by an attorney need not be verified or accompanied by an affidavit. FL ST RCP Rule 1.030; FL ST J ADMIN Rule 2.515(a).

6. *Attorney signature*

   a. *Attorney signature.* Every pleading and other document of a party represented by an attorney shall be signed by at least one (1) attorney of record in that attorney's individual name whose current record Florida Bar address, telephone number, including area code, primary e-mail address and secondary e-mail addresses, if any, and Florida Bar number shall be stated, and who shall be duly licensed to practice law in Florida or who shall have received permission to appear in the particular case as provided in FL ST J ADMIN Rule 2.510. FL ST J ADMIN Rule 2.515(a).

      i. The attorney may be required by the court to give the address of, and to vouch for the attorney's authority to represent, the party. FL ST J ADMIN Rule 2.515(a).

      ii. The signature of an attorney shall constitute a certificate by the attorney that the attorney has read the pleading or other document; that to the best of the attorney's knowledge, information, and belief there is good ground to support it; and that it is not interposed for delay. FL ST J ADMIN Rule 2.515(a).

      iii. If a pleading is not signed or is signed with intent to defeat the purpose of FL ST J ADMIN Rule 2.515, it may be stricken and the action may proceed as though the pleading or other document had not been served. FL ST J ADMIN Rule 2.515(a).

   b. *Pro se litigant signature.* A party who is not represented by an attorney shall sign any pleading or other paper and state the party's address and telephone number, including area code. FL ST J ADMIN Rule 2.515(b).

   c. *Form of signature*

      i. The signatures required on pleadings and documents by FL ST J ADMIN Rule 2.515(a) and FL ST J ADMIN Rule 2.515(b) may be:

         - Original signatures;
         - Original signatures that have been reproduced by electronic means, such as on electronically transmitted documents or photocopied documents;
         - Electronic signatures using the "/s/," "s/," or "/s" formats by or at the direction of the person signing; or

- Any other signature format authorized by general law, so long as the clerk where the proceeding is pending has the capability of receiving and has obtained approval from the Supreme Court of Florida to accept pleadings and documents with that signature format. FL ST J ADMIN Rule 2.515(c)(1).

ii. An attorney, party, or other person who files a pleading or paper by electronic transmission that does not contain the original signature of that attorney, party, or other person shall file that identical pleading or paper in paper form containing an original signature of that attorney, party, or other person (hereinafter called the follow-up filing) immediately thereafter. The follow-up filing is not required if the Supreme Court of Florida has entered an order directing the clerk of court to discontinue accepting the follow-up filing. FL ST J ADMIN Rule 2.515(c)(2).

iii. The placement of a "/s/" or the image of a signature by an attorney or party or affected non-party signature line on an electronically filed document shall be accepted as the signature and shall verify to the Court the filer is in possession of the originally executed document. Notwithstanding the manner in which an electronic document is signed the originally executed pleading or paper shall be maintained in the filer's possession for a minimum of one (1) year after final disposition and time for appeal of the case. The originally executed document shall be produced for filing or inspection as directed by the Court. FL ST 17 J CIR 2012-16-CIV.

7. *Forms*

a. *Process.* The forms of process, notice of lis pendens, and notice of action provided in the Florida Rules of Civil Procedure are sufficient. Variations from the forms do not void process or notices that are otherwise sufficient. FL ST RCP Rule 1.900(a).

b. *Other forms.* The other forms provided in the Florida Rules of Civil Procedure are sufficient for the matters that are covered by them. So long as the substance is expressed without prolixity, the forms may be varied to meet the facts of a particular case. FL ST RCP Rule 1.900(b).

c. *Formal matters.* Captions, except for the designation of the paper, are omitted from the forms provided in the Florida Rules of Civil Procedure. A general form of caption is the first form provided. Signatures are omitted from pleadings and motions. FL ST RCP Rule 1.900(c).

8. *Notices to persons with disabilities.* All notices of court proceedings to be held in a public facility, and all process compelling appearance at such proceedings, shall include the following statement in bold face, fourteen (14) point Times New Roman or Courier font: "If you are a person with a disability who needs any accommodation in order to participate in this proceeding, you are entitled, at no cost to you, to the provision of certain assistance. Please contact [identify applicable court personnel by name, address, and telephone number] at least seven (7) days before your scheduled court appearance, or immediately upon receiving this notification if the time before the scheduled appearance is less than seven (7) days; if you are hearing or voice impaired, call 711." FL ST J ADMIN Rule 2.540(c)(1). For further information, please see FL ST 17 J CIR 2010-49-GEN.

9. *Minimization of the filing of sensitive information*

a. *Limitations for court filings.* Unless authorized by FL ST J ADMIN Rule 2.425(b), statute, another rule of court, or the court orders otherwise, designated sensitive information filed with the court must be limited to the following format:

i. The initials of a person known to be a minor;

ii. The year of birth of a person's birth date;

iii. No portion of any: Social security number, Bank account number, Credit card account number, Charge account number, or Debit account number;

iv. The last four digits of any: Taxpayer identification number (TIN), Employee identification number, Driver's license number, Passport number, Telephone number, Financial account number, except as set forth in FL ST J ADMIN Rule 2.425(a)(3), Brokerage account number, Insurance policy account number, Loan account number, Customer account number, or Patient or health care number;

v. A truncated version of any: Email address, Computer user name, Password, or Personal identification number (PIN); and

vi. A truncated version of any other sensitive information as provided by court order. FL ST J ADMIN Rule 2.425(a).

b. *Exceptions.* FL ST J ADMIN Rule 2.425(a) does not apply to the following:

i. An account number which identifies the property alleged to be the subject of a proceeding;

ii. The record of an administrative or agency proceeding;

iii. The record in appellate or review proceedings;

iv. The birth date of a minor whenever the birth date is necessary for the court to establish or maintain subject matter jurisdiction;

v. The name of a minor in any order relating to parental responsibility, time-sharing, or child support;

vi. The name of a minor in any document or order affecting the minor's ownership of real property;

vii. The birth date of a party in a writ of attachment or notice to payor;

viii. In traffic and criminal proceedings: a pro se filing; a court filing that is related to a criminal matter or investigation and that is prepared before the filing of a criminal charge or is not filed as part of any docketed criminal case; an arrest or search warrant or any information in support thereof; a charging document and an affidavit or other documents filed in support of any charging document, including any driving records; a statement of particulars; discovery material introduced into evidence or otherwise filed with the court; and all information necessary for the proper issuance and execution of a subpoena duces tecum;

ix. Information used by the clerk for case maintenance purposes or the courts for case management purposes; and

x. Information which is relevant and material to an issue before the court. FL ST J ADMIN Rule 2.425(b).

c. *Remedies.* Upon motion by a party or interested person or sua sponte by the court, the court may order remedies, sanctions or both for a violation of FL ST J ADMIN Rule 2.425(a). Following notice and an opportunity to respond, the court may impose sanctions if such filing was not made in good faith. FL ST J ADMIN Rule 2.425(c).

d. *Motions not restricted.* FL ST J ADMIN Rule 2.425 does not restrict a party's right to move for protective order, to move to file documents under seal, or to request a determination of the confidentiality of records. FL ST J ADMIN Rule 2.425(d).

e. *Application.* FL ST J ADMIN Rule 2.425 does not affect the application of constitutional provisions, statutes, or rules of court regarding confidential information or access to public information. FL ST J ADMIN Rule 2.425(e).

F. Filing and Service Requirements

1. *Filing requirements.* All original documents must be filed with the court either before service or immediately thereafter, unless otherwise provided for by general law or other rules. If the original of any bond or other document is not placed in the court file, a certified copy must be so placed by the clerk. FL ST J ADMIN Rule 2.516(d). All documents shall be filed in conformity with the requirements of FL ST J ADMIN Rule 2.525. FL ST RCP Rule 1.080(b). All documents filed in any court shall be filed by electronic transmission in accordance with FL ST J ADMIN Rule 2.525. "Documents" means pleadings, motions, petitions, memoranda, briefs, notices, exhibits, declarations, affidavits, orders, judgments, decrees, writs, opinions, and any other paper or writing submitted to a court. FL ST J ADMIN Rule 2.520(a). All documents that are court records, as defined in FL ST J ADMIN Rule 2.430(a)(1), must be filed by electronic transmission, provided that: (1) the clerk has the ability to accept and retain such documents; (2) the clerk or the chief judge of the circuit has requested permission to accept documents filed by electronic transmission; and (3) the supreme court has entered an order granting permission to the clerk to accept documents filed by electronic transmission. FL ST J ADMIN Rule 2.525(c)(1).

a. *Definition.* "Electronic transmission of documents" means the sending of information by electronic signals to, by or from a court or clerk, which when received can be transformed and stored or

transmitted on paper, microfilm, magnetic storage device, optical imaging system, CD-ROM, flash drive, other electronic data storage system, server, case maintenance system ("CM"), electronic court filing ("ECF") system, statewide or local electronic portal ("e-portal"), or other electronic record keeping system authorized by the supreme court in a format sufficient to communicate the information on the original document in a readable format. Electronic transmission of documents includes electronic mail ("e-mail") and any internet-based transmission procedure, and may include procedures allowing for documents to be signed or verified by electronic means. FL ST J ADMIN Rule 2.525(a).

i. The filing of documents with the court as required by the Florida Rules of Judicial Administration must be made by filing them with the clerk in accordance with FL ST J ADMIN Rule 2.525, except that the judge may permit documents to be filed with the judge, in which event the judge must note the filing date before him or her on the documents and transmit them to the clerk. The date of filing is that shown on the face of the document by the judge's notation or the clerk's time stamp, whichever is earlier. FL ST J ADMIN Rule 2.516(e).

b. *Application.* Any court or clerk of the court may accept the electronic transmission of documents for filing after the clerk, together with input from the chief judge of the circuit, has obtained approval of the procedures and program for doing so from the Supreme Court of Florida. FL ST J ADMIN Rule 2.525(b).

c. *Exceptions*

i. Paper documents and other submissions may be manually submitted to the clerk or court:

- When the clerk does not have the ability to accept and retain documents by electronic filing or has not had ECF Procedures approved by the supreme court;
- For filing by any self-represented party or any self-represented nonparty unless specific ECF Procedures provide a means to file documents electronically. However, any self-represented nonparty that is a governmental or public agency and any other agency, partnership, corporation, or business entity acting on behalf of any governmental or public agency may file documents by electronic transmission if such entity has the capability of filing documents electronically;
- For filing by attorneys excused from e-mail service in accordance with FL ST J ADMIN Rule 2.516(b);
- When submitting evidentiary exhibits or filing non-documentary materials;
- When the filing involves documents in excess of twenty-five (25) megabytes (25MB) in size. For such filings, documents may be transmitted using an electronic storage medium that the clerk has the ability to accept, which may include a CD-ROM, flash drive, or similar storage medium;
- When filed in open court, as permitted by the court;
- When paper filing is permitted by any approved statewide or local ECF procedures; and
- If any court determines that justice so requires. FL ST J ADMIN Rule 2.525(d).

ii. Any document in paper form submitted under FL ST J ADMIN Rule 2.525(d) is filed when it is received by the clerk or court and the clerk shall immediately thereafter convert any filed paper document to an electronic document. "Convert to an electronic document" means optically capturing an image of a paper document and using character recognition software to recover as much of the document's text as practicable and then indexing and storing the document in the official court file. FL ST J ADMIN Rule 2.525(c)(4).

iii. Any storage medium submitted under FL ST J ADMIN Rule 2.525(d)(5) is filed when received by the clerk or court and the clerk shall immediately thereafter transfer the electronic documents from the storage device to the official court file. FL ST J ADMIN Rule 2.525(c)(5).

iv. If the filer of any paper document authorized under FL ST J ADMIN Rule 2.525(d) provides a self-addressed, postage-paid envelope for return of the paper document after it is converted to electronic form by the clerk, the clerk shall place the paper document in the envelope and

deposit it in the mail. Except when a paper document is required to be maintained, the clerk may recycle any filed paper document that is not to be returned to the filer. FL ST J ADMIN Rule 2.525(c)(6).

v. The clerk may convert any paper document filed before the effective date of FL ST J ADMIN Rule 2.525 to an electronic document. Unless the clerk is required to maintain the paper document, if the paper document has been converted to an electronic document by the clerk, the paper document is no longer part of the official court file and may be removed and recycled. FL ST J ADMIN Rule 2.525(c)(7).

d. *Official court file.* For information on what constitutes the official court file, please see FL ST J ADMIN Rule 2.525(c)(2), FL ST J ADMIN Rule 2.525(c)(3).

e. *Administration.* All attorneys, parties, or other persons using this rule to file documents are required to make arrangements with the court or clerk for the payment of any charges authorized by general law or the supreme court before filing any document by electronic transmission. FL ST J ADMIN Rule 2.525(f)(2).

f. *Filing date.* The filing date for an electronically transmitted document is the date and time that such filing is acknowledged by an electronic stamp or otherwise, pursuant to any procedure set forth in any ECF Procedures approved by the supreme court, or the date the last page of such filing is received by the court or clerk. FL ST J ADMIN Rule 2.525(f)(3).

g. *Accessibility.* All documents transmitted in any electronic form under FL ST J ADMIN Rule 2.525 must comply with the accessibility requirements of FL ST J ADMIN Rule 2.526. FL ST J ADMIN Rule 2.525(g).

h. *Provisions for electronic filing in the Seventeenth Circuit.* Attorneys may electronically file pleadings and papers on existing cases in circuit civil divisions 1, 7, 9, 19, 26 and 27. The following documents may be scanned and efiled; however, the original must be filed with the Clerk: Documents ordered by the Court; and original documents required by law or rule of procedure to be filed with the Clerk. Self represented individuals shall file pleadings and papers with the Clerk. The Clerk within twenty four (24) hours of receipt of an electronic document shall either accept or reject the electronic document for filing and send electronic notice to the filer. FL ST 17 J CIR 2012-16-CIV.

i. *Technical failures.* If a document filed electronically is not received due to: an error in the transmission of the document to the Clerk or any vendor of the Clerk to provide electronic court record filing services which is unknown to an attorney or party or affected non party, or a failure to process the electronic document when received by the Clerk or rejection by the Clerk, or any other technical problems experienced by the attorney or party or affected non party, the Court may, after an evidentiary hearing and upon satisfactory proof, enter an order permitting the document to be filed nunc pro tunc to the date it was first attempted to be sent electronically. FL ST 17 J CIR 2012-16-CIV.

j. *Filing of pleadings or papers at any office of the clerk of court.* The Clerk of Courts, commencing November 3, 2008, shall accept for filing, at the central courthouse, north satellite courthouse, south satellite courthouse, and west satellite courthouse any pleading or motion or other document for filing in the court file from any attorney or party for an existing case except as otherwise set forth. FL ST 17 J CIR 2008-153-GEN. See FL ST 17 J CIR 2008-153-GEN for specific exceptions.

2. *Service requirements.* Every pleading subsequent to the initial pleading, all orders, and every other document filed in the action must be served in conformity with the requirements of FL ST J ADMIN Rule 2.516. FL ST RCP Rule 1.080(a).

a. *Service; When required.* Unless the court otherwise orders, or a statute or supreme court administrative order specifies a different means of service, every pleading subsequent to the initial pleading and every other document filed in any court proceeding, except applications for witness subpoenas and documents served by formal notice or required to be served in the manner provided for service of formal notice, must be served in accordance with FL ST J ADMIN Rule 2.516 on each party. No service need be made on parties against whom a default has been entered, except that pleadings asserting new or additional claims against them must be served in the manner provided for service of summons. FL ST J ADMIN Rule 2.516(a).

b. *Service; How made.* When service is required or permitted to be made upon a party represented by an attorney, service must be made upon the attorney unless service upon the party is ordered by the court. FL ST J ADMIN Rule 2.516(b).

   i. *Service by electronic mail ("e-mail").* All documents required or permitted to be served on another party must be served by e-mail, unless FL ST J ADMIN Rule 2.516 otherwise provides. When, in addition to service by e-mail, the sender also utilizes another means of service provided for in FL ST J ADMIN Rule 2.516(b)(2), any differing time limits and other provisions applicable to that other means of service control. FL ST J ADMIN Rule 2.516(b)(1). Any document electronically transmitted to a court or clerk must also be served on all parties and interested persons in accordance with the applicable rules of court. FL ST J ADMIN Rule 2.525(e)(2).

      - *Service on attorneys.* Upon appearing in a proceeding, an attorney must serve a designation of a primary e-mail address and may designate no more than two (2) secondary e-mail addresses. Thereafter, service must be directed to all designated e-mail addresses in that proceeding. Every document filed by an attorney thereafter must include the primary e-mail address of that attorney and any secondary e-mail addresses. If an attorney does not designate any e-mail address for service, documents may be served on that attorney at the e-mail address on record with The Florida Bar. FL ST J ADMIN Rule 2.516(b)(1)(A).

      - *Exception to e-mail service on attorneys.* Service by an attorney on another attorney must be made by e-mail unless excused by the court. Upon motion by an attorney demonstrating that the attorney has no e-mail account and lacks access to the Internet at the attorney's office, the court may excuse the attorney from the requirements of e-mail service. Service on and by an attorney excused by the court from e-mail service must be by the means provided in FL ST J ADMIN Rule 2.516(b)(2). FL ST J ADMIN Rule 2.516(b)(1)(B).

      - *Service on and by parties not represented by an attorney.* Any party not represented by an attorney may serve a designation of a primary e-mail address and also may designate no more than two (2) secondary e-mail addresses to which service must be directed in that proceeding by the means provided in FL ST J ADMIN Rule 2.516(b)(1). If a party not represented by an attorney does not designate an e-mail address for service in a proceeding, service on and by that party must be by the means provided in FL ST J ADMIN Rule 2.516(b)(2). FL ST J ADMIN Rule 2.516(b)(1)(C).

      - *Time of service.* Service by e-mail is complete when it is sent. FL ST J ADMIN Rule 2.516(b)(1)(D). An e-mail is deemed served on the date it is sent. FL ST J ADMIN Rule 2.516(b)(1)(D)(i). If the sender learns that the e-mail did not reach the address of the person to be served, the sender must immediately send another copy by e-mail, or by a means authorized by FL ST J ADMIN Rule 2.516(b)(2). FL ST J ADMIN Rule 2.516(b)(1)(D)(ii). E-mail service is treated as service by mail for the computation of time. FL ST J ADMIN Rule 2.516(b)(1)(D)(iii).

   ii. *Format of e-mail for service.* Service of a document by e-mail is made by attaching a copy of the document in PDF format to an e-mail sent to all addresses designated by the attorney or party. FL ST J ADMIN Rule 2.516(b)(1)(E).

      - All documents served by e-mail must be attached to an e-mail message containing a subject line beginning with the words "SERVICE OF COURT DOCUMENT" in all capital letters, followed by the case number of the proceeding in which the documents are being served. FL ST J ADMIN Rule 2.516(b)(1)(E)(i).

      - The body of the e-mail must identify the court in which the proceeding is pending, the case number, the name of the initial party on each side, the title of each document served with that e-mail, and the sender's name and telephone number. FL ST J ADMIN Rule 2.516(b)(1)(E)(ii).

      - Any document served by e-mail may be signed by the "/s/" format, as long as the filed original is signed in accordance with the applicable rule of procedure. FL ST J ADMIN Rule 2.516(b)(1)(E)(iii).

- Any e-mail which, together with its attached documents, exceeds five megabytes (5MB) in size, must be divided and sent as separate e-mails, no one of which may exceed five megabytes (5MB) in size and each of which must be sequentially numbered in the subject line. FL ST J ADMIN Rule 2.516(b)(1)(E)(iv).

iii. *Service by other means.* In addition to, and not in lieu of, service by e-mail, service may also be made upon attorneys by any of the means specified in FL ST J ADMIN Rule 2.516(b)(2). Service on and by all parties who are not represented by an attorney and who do not designate an e-mail address, and on and by all attorneys excused from e-mail service, must be made by delivering a copy of the document or by mailing it to the party or attorney at their last known address or, if no address is known, by leaving it with the clerk of the court. Service by mail is complete upon mailing. Delivery of a copy within FL ST J ADMIN Rule 2.516 is complete upon:

- Handing it to the attorney or to the party,
- Leaving it at the attorney's or party's office with a clerk or other person in charge thereof,
- If there is no one in charge, leaving it in a conspicuous place therein,
- If the office is closed or the person to be served has no office, leaving it at the person's usual place of abode with some person of his or her family above fifteen (15) years of age and informing such person of the contents, or
- Transmitting it by facsimile to the attorney's or party's office with a cover sheet containing the sender's name, firm, address, telephone number, and facsimile number, and the number of pages transmitted. When service is made by facsimile, a copy must also be served by any other method permitted by FL ST J ADMIN Rule 2.516. Facsimile service occurs when transmission is complete. FL ST J ADMIN Rule 2.516(b)(2)(A) through FL ST J ADMIN Rule 2.516(b)(2)(E).
- Service by delivery after 5:00 p.m. must be deemed to have been made by mailing on the date of delivery. FL ST J ADMIN Rule 2.516(b)(2)(F).

c. *Service; Numerous defendants.* In actions when the parties are unusually numerous, the court may regulate the service contemplated by the Florida Rules of Judicial Administration on motion or on its own initiative in such manner as may be found to be just and reasonable. FL ST J ADMIN Rule 2.516(c).

d. *Service by clerk.* Service of notices and other documents required to be made by the clerk must also be done as provided in FL ST J ADMIN Rule 2.516(b). FL ST J ADMIN Rule 2.516(g).

G. Hearings

1. *Communication equipment*

a. *Definition.* Communication equipment means a conference telephone or other electronic device that permits all those appearing or participating to hear and speak to each other, provided that all conversation of all parties is audible to all persons present. FL ST J ADMIN Rule 2.530(a).

b. *Use by all parties.* A county or circuit court judge may, upon the court's own motion or upon the written request of a party, direct that communication equipment be used for a motion hearing, pretrial conference, or a status conference. A judge must give notice to the parties and consider any objections they may have to the use of communication equipment before directing that communication equipment be used. The decision to use communication equipment over the objection of parties will be in the sound discretion of the trial court, except as noted below. FL ST J ADMIN Rule 2.530(b).

c. *Use only by requesting party.* A county or circuit court judge may, upon the written request of a party upon reasonable notice to all other parties, permit a requesting party to participate through communication equipment in a scheduled motion hearing; however, any such request (except in criminal, juvenile, and appellate proceedings) must be granted, absent a showing of good cause to deny the same, where the hearing is set for not longer than fifteen (15) minutes. FL ST J ADMIN Rule 2.530(c).

d. *Testimony*
   i. *Generally.* A county or circuit court judge, general magistrate, special magistrate, or hearing officer may allow testimony to be taken through communication equipment if all parties consent or if permitted by another applicable rule of procedure. FL ST J ADMIN Rule 2.530(d)(1).
   ii. *Procedure.* Any party desiring to present testimony through communication equipment shall, prior to the hearing or trial at which the testimony is to be presented, contact all parties to determine whether each party consents to this form of testimony. The party seeking to present the testimony shall move for permission to present testimony through communication equipment, which motion shall set forth good cause as to why the testimony should be allowed in this form. FL ST J ADMIN Rule 2.530(d)(2).
   iii. *Oath.* Testimony may be taken through communication equipment only if a notary public or other person authorized to administer oaths in the witness's jurisdiction is present with the witness and administers the oath consistent with the laws of the jurisdiction. FL ST J ADMIN Rule 2.530(d)(3).
   iv. *Confrontation rights.* In juvenile and criminal proceedings the defendant must make an informed waiver of any confrontation rights that may be abridged by the use of communication equipment. FL ST J ADMIN Rule 2.530(d)(4).
   v. *Video testimony.* If the testimony to be presented utilizes video conferencing or comparable two-way visual capabilities, the court in its discretion may modify the procedures set forth in FL ST J ADMIN Rule 2.530 to accommodate the technology utilized. FL ST J ADMIN Rule 2.530(d)(5).

e. *Burden of expense.* The cost for the use of the communication equipment is the responsibility of the requesting party unless otherwise directed by the court. FL ST J ADMIN Rule 2.530(e).

2. *Uniform motion calendar.* The Circuit Judges of the general civil/family division (excluding juvenile/dependency) shall maintain a uniform motion calendar from 8:45 A.M. to 9:30 A.M., Monday through Thursday. The motion calendar shall end PROMPTLY at 9:30 A.M. All parties shall be prepared to proceed at 8:45 A.M., and if one party fails to timely appear, the matter may proceed on the merits in his/her absence. FL ST 17 J CIR LOCAL RULE NO. 10A(1).
3. *Noticed motion limitation.* No more than two (2) motions may be noticed for each case on any given day except by leave of court. FL ST 17 J CIR LOCAL RULE NO. 10A(4).
4. *Ex parte and non-evidentiary motion.* Ex parte matters, non-evidentiary motions, and uncontested proceedings for adoptions, or dissolution may be heard on the uniform motion calendar, provided such matters can be conducted in five (5) minutes equally allocated among the parties and the moving party shall so certify as specified in FL ST 17 J CIR LOCAL RULE NO. 10A(3). FL ST 17 J CIR LOCAL RULE NO. 10A(6).
5. *Good faith effort to resolve issues.* Prior to appearing before the court, the parties shall discuss the issues raised in the pending motion, and both parties shall be prepared to certify at the hearing they have made a good faith effort to resolve the issues. FL ST 17 J CIR LOCAL RULE NO. 10A(7).
6. *Re-noticing hearings.* When the motion calendar has been filled, the judge's office shall notify the party noticing any hearings which cannot be reached. The noticing party shall call opposing counsel and re-notice the hearing. FL ST 17 J CIR LOCAL RULE NO. 10A(9).
7. *Hearing cancellation.* Motion calendar hearings may be canceled by the attorney who set the hearing. FL ST 17 J CIR LOCAL RULE NO. 10A(10).
8. *Other motion calendars.* Hearing officers/general masters shall conduct a motion calendar, the dates and times of which shall be determined by the hearing officer/general master or by administrative order. FL ST 17 J CIR LOCAL RULE NO. 10A(11).
9. *Sanctions.* Failure to comply with the procedures designated in the above paragraphs may result in the hearing being stricken from the docket or such other sanctions as the court deems appropriate. FL ST 17 J CIR LOCAL RULE NO. 10A(12).

H. Forms

1. Official Motion for Sanctions Forms for Florida

a. Caption. FL ST RCP Form 1.901.

b. Notice of compliance when constitutional challenge is brought. FL ST RCP Form 1.975.

2. Motion for Sanctions Forms for Florida

a. Motion; By defendant; For sanctions for refusal of offer of judgment. FL-PP § 61:22.

b. Motion; Sanctions, proposal for settlement. FL-PRACFORM § 7:165.

I. Checklist

(I) ❑ Matters to be considered by moving party
- (a) ❑ Required documents
  - (1) ❑ Notice of hearing/Motion
  - (2) ❑ Good faith certificate
  - (3) ❑ Certificate of service
- (b) ❑ Supplemental documents
  - (1) ❑ Proposed order, copies, stamped envelopes
  - (2) ❑ Notice of constitutional question
- (c) ❑ Time for making motion
  - (1) ❑ A motion by a party seeking sanctions under FL ST § 57.105 must be served but may not be filed with or presented to the court unless, within twenty one (21) days after service of the motion, the challenged paper, claim, defense, contention, allegation, or denial is not withdrawn or appropriately corrected
  - (2) ❑ Any party seeking a judgment taxing costs, attorneys' fees, or both shall serve a motion no later than thirty (30) days after filing of the judgment, including a judgment of dismissal, or the service of a notice of voluntary dismissal
  - (3) ❑ A copy of any written motion which may not be heard ex parte and a copy of the notice of the hearing thereof shall be served a reasonable time before the time specified for the hearing
  - (4) ❑ Copies of the notice of hearing, the motion, and any pleading or interrogatories to which the motion is addressed shall be in the hands of the Judicial Assistant and opposing party at least four (4) working days in advance of the hearing

(II) ❑ Matters to be considered by opposing party
- (a) ❑ Required documents
  - (1) ❑ Response to motion
  - (2) ❑ Certificate of service
- (b) ❑ Supplemental documents
  - (1) ❑ Proposed order, copies, stamped envelopes
  - (2) ❑ Notice of constitutional question
- (c) ❑ Time for service and filing of opposition
  - (1) ❑ No time specified for responding to a motion

Motions, Oppositions and Replies
Motion to Compel Discovery

Document Last Updated January 2013

A. Applicable Rules

1. *State rules*
   a. Rules of court. FL ST RCP Rule 1.010; FL ST J ADMIN Rule 2.110.
   b. Nonverification of pleadings. FL ST RCP Rule 1.030.
   c. Service and filing of pleadings, orders, and documents. FL ST RCP Rule 1.080.
   d. Time. FL ST RCP Rule 1.090.
   e. Pleadings and motions. FL ST RCP Rule 1.100.
   f. Motions. FL ST RCP Rule 1.160.
   g. General provisions governing discovery. FL ST RCP Rule 1.280.
   h. Depositions. FL ST RCP Rule 1.310; FL ST RCP Rule 1.320; FL ST FAM LAW Rule 12.310.
   i. Interrogatories to parties. FL ST RCP Rule 1.340.
   j. Production of documents and things and entry upon land for inspection and other purposes. FL ST RCP Rule 1.350.
   k. Examination of persons. FL ST RCP Rule 1.360.
   l. Failure to make discovery; Sanctions. FL ST RCP Rule 1.380.
   m. Relief from judgment, decrees or orders. FL ST RCP Rule 1.540.
   n. Mediation and arbitration. FL ST RCP Rule 1.700; FL ST RCP Rule 1.710; FL ST RCP Rule 1.720; FL ST RCP Rule 1.730; FL ST RCP Rule 1.750; FL ST RCP Rule 1.800; FL ST RCP Rule 1.810; FL ST RCP Rule 1.820; FL ST RCP Rule 1.830.
   o. Forms. FL ST RCP Rule 1.900.
   p. Retention of court records. FL ST J ADMIN Rule 2.430.
   q. Foreign attorneys. FL ST J ADMIN Rule 2.510.
   r. Signature of attorneys and parties. FL ST J ADMIN Rule 2.515.
   s. Paper. FL ST J ADMIN Rule 2.520.
   t. Electronic filing. FL ST J ADMIN Rule 2.525.
   u. Communication equipment. FL ST J ADMIN Rule 2.530.
   v. Court reporting. FL ST J ADMIN Rule 2.535.
   w. Requests for accommodations by persons with disabilities. FL ST J ADMIN Rule 2.540.
   x. Minimization of the filing of sensitive information. FL ST J ADMIN Rule 2.425.
   y. Accessibility of information and technology. FL ST J ADMIN Rule 2.526.
2. *Local rules*
   a. Orders for signature; Civil division. FL ST 17 J CIR LOCAL RULE NO. 8.
   b. Uniform motion calendar ex parte motions to compel discovery, and special set hearings. FL ST 17 J CIR LOCAL RULE NO. 10A.
   c. Standards of professional courtesy. FL ST 17 J CIR I-94-O-1.
   d. Administrative order authorizing the filing of pleadings or papers at any office of the clerk of court. FL ST 17 J CIR 2008-153-GEN.
   e. Administrative order regarding provision of ADA accommodations. FL ST 17 J CIR 2010-49-GEN.

f. Administrative order establishing electronic filing procedures for the civil division. FL ST 17 J CIR 2012-16-CIV.

B. Timing

1. *Motion to compel discovery.* Upon reasonable notice to other parties and all persons affected, a party may apply for an order compelling discovery. FL ST RCP Rule 1.380(a).
2. *Ex parte order requiring compliance.* When a motion to compel alleges a complete failure to respond or object to discovery, and there has been no request for extension, an ex parte order may be entered requiring compliance with the original discovery demand within ten (10) days of the signing of the order. Movant shall submit the proposed order and the envelopes. Sanctions may be imposed if discovery is not completed within ten (10) days from the date of the ex parte order is entered necessitating a hearing on a motion to compel, or if a party fails to appear for a properly noticed hearing on a motion to compel. FL ST 17 J CIR LOCAL RULE NO. 10A(13).
3. *General motion timing.* A copy of any written motion which may not be heard ex parte and a copy of the notice of the hearing thereof shall be served a reasonable time before the time specified for the hearing. FL ST RCP Rule 1.090(d). Copies of the notice of hearing, the motion, and any pleading or interrogatories to which the motion is addressed shall be in the hands of the Judicial Assistant and opposing party at least four (4) working days in advance of the hearing. The original notice shall be filed with the Clerk. FL ST 17 J CIR LOCAL RULE NO. 10A(5).
4. *Standard of professional conduct; Scheduling*
   a. Attorneys should endeavor to provide opposing counsel, parties, witnesses, and other affected persons, sufficient notice of depositions, hearings and other proceedings, except upon agreement of course, in an emergency, or in other circumstances compelling more expedited scheduling. As a general rule, actual notice should be no less than five (5) business days for instate depositions, ten (10) business days for out-of-state depositions and four (4) business days for hearings. FL ST 17 J CIR I-94-O-1(I)(1).
   b. Attorneys should communicate with opposing counsel prior to scheduling depositions, hearings and other proceedings, in an effort to schedule them at times that are mutually convenient for all interested persons. Further, sufficient time should be reserved to permit a complete presentation by counsel for all parties. FL ST 17 J CIR I-94-O-1(I)(2).
   c. Attorneys should notify opposing counsel, the court, and others affected, of scheduling conflicts as soon as they become apparent. Further, attorneys should cooperate with one another regarding all reasonable rescheduling requests that do not prejudice their clients or unduly delay a proceeding. FL ST 17 J CIR I-94-O-1(I)(3).
   d. Attorneys should promptly notify the court or other tribunal of any resolution between the parties that renders a scheduled court appearance unnecessary or otherwise moot. FL ST 17 J CIR I-94-O-1(I)(4).
   e. Attorneys should grant reasonable requests by opposing counsel for extensions of time within which to respond to pleadings, discovery, and other matters when such an extension will not prejudice their client or unduly delay a proceeding. FL ST 17 J CIR I-94-O-1(I)(5).
5. *Timing considerations when filing electronically.* The filing date of an efiled document is when the last page is received by the Clerk. The electronic filing of a document does not modify any filing deadlines as required by law, rule of procedure, or court order. FL ST 17 J CIR 2012-16-CIV.
6. *Computation of time*
   a. *Generally.* Computation of time shall be governed by FL ST J ADMIN Rule 2.514. FL ST RCP Rule 1.090(a). The following rules apply in computing time periods specified in any rule of procedure, local rule, court order, or statute that does not specify a method of computing time. FL ST J ADMIN Rule 2.514(a).
      i. *Period stated in days or a longer unit.* When the period is stated in days or a longer unit of time (A) exclude the day of the event that triggers the period; (B) count every day, including intermediate Saturdays, Sundays, and legal holidays; and (C) include the last day of the period,

but if the last day is a Saturday, Sunday, or legal holiday, or falls within any period of time extended through an order of the chief justice under FL ST J ADMIN Rule 2.205(a)(2)(B)(iv), the period continues to run until the end of the next day that is not a Saturday, Sunday, or legal holiday and does not fall within any period of time extended through an order of the chief justice. FL ST J ADMIN Rule 2.514(a)(1).

ii. *Period stated in hours.* When the period is stated in hours (A) begin counting immediately on the occurrence of the event that triggers the period; (B) count every hour, including hours during intermediate Saturdays, Sundays, and legal holidays; and (C) if the period would end on a Saturday, Sunday, or legal holiday, or during any period of time extended through an order of the chief justice under FL ST J ADMIN Rule 2.205(a)(2)(B)(iv), the period continues to run until the same time on the next day that is not a Saturday, Sunday, or legal holiday and does not fall within any period of time extended through an order of the chief justice. FL ST J ADMIN Rule 2.514(a)(2).

iii. *Period stated in days less than seven (7) days.* When the period stated in days is less than seven (7) days, intermediate Saturdays, Sundays, and legal holidays shall be excluded in the computation. FL ST J ADMIN Rule 2.514(a)(3).

iv. *"Last day" defined.* Unless a different time is set by a statute, local rule, or court order, the last day ends (A) for electronic filing or for service by any means, at midnight; and (B) for filing by other means, when the clerk's office is scheduled to close. FL ST J ADMIN Rule 2.514(a)(4).

v. *"Next day" defined.* The "next day" is determined by continuing to count forward when the period is measured after an event and backward when measured before an event. FL ST J ADMIN Rule 2.514(a)(5).

vi. *"Legal holiday" defined.* "Legal holiday" means (A) the day set aside by FL ST § 110.117, for observing New Year's Day, Martin Luther King, Jr.'s Birthday, Memorial Day, Independence Day, Labor Day, Veterans' Day, Thanksgiving Day, the Friday after Thanksgiving Day, or Christmas Day, and (B) any day observed as a holiday by the clerk's office or as designated by the chief judge. FL ST J ADMIN Rule 2.514(a)(6).

b. *Additional time after service by mail or e-mail.* When a party may or must act within a specified time after service and service is made by mail or e-mail, five (5) days are added after the period that would otherwise expire under FL ST J ADMIN Rule 2.514(a). FL ST J ADMIN Rule 2.514(b).

c. *Enlargement.* When an act is required or allowed to be done at or within a specified time by order of court, by the Florida Rules of Civil Procedure, or by notice given thereunder, for cause shown the court at any time in its discretion (1) with or without notice, may order the period enlarged if request therefor is made before the expiration of the period originally prescribed or as extended by a previous order, or (2) upon motion made and notice after the expiration of the specified period, may permit the act to be done when failure to act was the result of excusable neglect, but it may not extend the time for making a motion for new trial, for rehearing, or to alter or amend a judgment; making a motion for relief from a judgment under FL ST RCP Rule 1.540(b); taking an appeal or filing a petition for certiorari; or making a motion for a directed verdict. FL ST RCP Rule 1.090(b).

d. *Unaffected by expiration of term.* The period of time provided for the doing of any act or the taking of any proceeding shall not be affected or limited by the continued existence or expiration of a term of court. The continued existence or expiration of a term of court in no way affects the power of a court to do any act or take any proceeding in any action which is or has been pending before it. FL ST RCP Rule 1.090(c).

C. General Requirements

1. *Motions generally*

a. *Contents.* An application to the court for an order shall be by motion which shall be made in writing unless made during a hearing or trial, shall state with particularity the grounds therefor, and shall set forth the relief or order sought. The requirement of writing is fulfilled if the motion is stated in a written notice of the hearing of the motion. All notices of hearing shall specify each motion or other matter to be heard. FL ST RCP Rule 1.100(b).

b. *Particularity requirement.* The court considers a motion in the light of the substantive law, rule or statute to make its determination. Some rules require a statement of the grounds for a motion under the rule. Failure to give the grounds will result in denial of the motion. This should be the result in all situations when the ground for the motion is not inherent in the rule. FL-PRACPROC § 9:3. The requirement is nevertheless an important one, first because of the due process notice rights of the respondent, as well as for the assistance it provides to the court in its preparation for the hearing or, absent a hearing, for disposition. 4 FLPRAC R 1.100.

2. *Failure to make discovery; Types of available relief.* Three (3) categories of relief are available for failure to make discovery. FL-PRACPROC § 16:14.

   a. The first category is an order compelling discovery. This is obtained by a motion to compel discovery. The motion is made in the court in which the action is pending, except when a deposition is being taken out of the territorial jurisdiction of the court and protective relief is sought in accordance with FL ST RCP Rule 1.310(d) or when a deponent is not a party. When one of the exceptions occurs, the motion is made in the circuit court of the county where the deposition is being taken. FL-PRACPROC § 16:14.

   b. The second category results from a failure to comply with an order to make discovery. The sanctions should not be applied until a hearing on the merits of the failure is held, including an opportunity to present evidence of explanation or mitigation. FL-PRACPROC § 16:14.

   c. The third category is available: (1) if a party or a person designated by an organization to answer questions at a deposition fails to appear before the officer who is to take the deposition after being served with a proper notice; (2) fails to serve answers or objections to interrogatories after proper service of the interrogatories; or (3) a party fails to serve a response to a request for production, inspection and entry after proper service of the request. FL-PRACPROC § 16:14. For further information regarding discovery sanctions please see the KeyRules Motion for Discovery Sanctions documents.

3. *Motion for order compelling discovery*

   a. *Reasonable notice.* Upon reasonable notice to other parties and all persons affected, a party may apply for an order compelling discovery. FL ST RCP Rule 1.380(a).

   b. *Appropriate court.* An application for an order to a party may be made to the court in which the action is pending or in accordance with FL ST RCP Rule 1.310(d). An application for an order to a deponent who is not a party shall be made to the circuit court where the deposition is being taken. FL ST RCP Rule 1.380(a)(1).

   c. *Motion*

      i. *Grounds.* The discovering party may move for an order compelling an answer, or a designation or an order compelling inspection, or an order compelling an examination in accordance with the request:

         - If a deponent fails to answer a question propounded or submitted under FL ST RCP Rule 1.310 or FL ST RCP Rule 1.320;
         - Or a corporation or other entity fails to make a designation under FL ST RCP Rule 1.310(b)(6) or FL ST RCP Rule 1.320(a);
         - Or a party fails to answer an interrogatory submitted under FL ST RCP Rule 1.340;
         - Or if a party in response to a request for inspection submitted under FL ST RCP Rule 1.350 fails to respond that inspection will be permitted as requested or fails to permit inspection as requested;
         - Or if a party in response to a request for examination of a person submitted under FL ST RCP Rule 1.360(a) objects to the examination, fails to respond that the examination will be permitted as requested, or fails to submit to or to produce a person in that party's custody or legal control for examination. FL ST RCP Rule 1.380(a)(2).

      ii. *Certification.* The motion must include a certification that the movant, in good faith, has conferred or attempted to confer with the person or party failing to make the discovery in an effort to secure the information or material without court action. FL ST RCP Rule 1.380(a)(2).

iii. *During deposition.* When taking a deposition on oral examination, the proponent of the question may complete or adjourn the examination before applying for an order. FL ST RCP Rule 1.380(a)(2).

iv. *Protective order.* If the court denies the motion in whole or in part, it may make such protective order as it would have been empowered to make on a motion made pursuant to FL ST RCP Rule 1.280(c). FL ST RCP Rule 1.380(a)(2).

d. *Evasive or incomplete answer.* For purposes of FL ST RCP Rule 1.380(a) an evasive or incomplete answer shall be treated as a failure to answer. FL ST RCP Rule 1.380(a)(3).

e. *Award of expenses of motion*

i. *Motion granted.* If the motion is granted and after opportunity for hearing, the court shall require the party or deponent whose conduct necessitated the motion or the party or counsel advising the conduct to pay to the moving party the reasonable expenses incurred in obtaining the order that may include attorneys' fees, unless the court finds that the movant failed to certify in the motion that a good faith effort was made to obtain the discovery without court action, that the opposition to the motion was justified, or that other circumstances make an award of expenses unjust. FL ST RCP Rule 1.380(a)(4).

ii. *Motion denied.* If the motion is denied and after opportunity for hearing, the court shall require the moving party to pay to the party or deponent who opposed the motion the reasonable expenses incurred in opposing the motion that may include attorneys' fees, unless the court finds that the making of the motion was substantially justified or that other circumstances make an award of expenses unjust. FL ST RCP Rule 1.380(a)(4).

iii. *Motion granted in part and denied in part.* If the motion is granted in part and denied in part, the court may apportion the reasonable expenses incurred as a result of making the motion among the parties and persons. FL ST RCP Rule 1.380(a)(4).

iv. *Electronically stored information; Sanctions for failure to preserve.* Absent exceptional circumstances, a court may not impose sanctions under these rules on a party for failing to provide electronically stored information lost as a result of the routine, good faith operation of an electronic information system. FL ST RCP Rule 1.380(e).

4. *Limitations on discovery of electronically stored information*

a. A person may object to discovery of electronically stored information from sources that the person identifies as not reasonably accessible because of burden or cost. On motion to compel discovery or for a protective order, the person from whom discovery is sought must show that the information sought or the format requested is not reasonably accessible because of undue burden or cost. If that showing is made, the court may nonetheless order the discovery from such sources or in such formats if the requesting party shows good cause. The court may specify conditions of the discovery, including ordering that some or all of the expenses incurred by the person from whom discovery is sought be paid by the party seeking the discovery. FL ST RCP Rule 1.280(d)(1).

b. In determining any motion involving discovery of electronically stored information, the court must limit the frequency or extent of discovery otherwise allowed by the Florida Rules of Civil Procedure if it determines that (i) the discovery sought is unreasonably cumulative or duplicative, or can be obtained from another source or in another manner that is more convenient, less burdensome, or less expensive; or (ii) the burden or expense of the discovery outweighs its likely benefit, considering the needs of the case, the amount in controversy, the parties' resources, the importance of the issues at stake in the action, and the importance of the discovery in resolving the issues. FL ST RCP Rule 1.280(d)(2).

5. *Arbitration and mediation*

a. *Referral to arbitration and mediation.* Except as hereinafter provided or as otherwise prohibited by law, the presiding judge may enter an order referring all or any part of a contested civil matter to mediation or arbitration. The parties to any contested civil matter may file a written stipulation to mediate or arbitrate any issue between them at any time. Such stipulation shall be incorporated into the order of referral. FL ST RCP Rule 1.700(a).

b. *Arbitration*

i. *Exclusions.* A civil action shall be ordered to arbitration or arbitration in conjunction with mediation upon stipulation of the parties. A civil action may be ordered to arbitration or arbitration in conjunction with mediation upon motion of any party or by the court, if the judge determines the action to be of such a nature that arbitration could be of benefit to the litigants or the court. FL ST RCP Rule 1.800.

- Under no circumstances may the following categories of actions be referred to arbitration: (1) bond estreatures; (2) habeas corpus or other extraordinary writs; (3) bond validations; (4) civil or criminal contempt; (5) such other matters as may be specified by order of the chief judge in the circuit. FL ST RCP Rule 1.800.

ii. For more information regarding arbitration, please see FL ST RCP Rule 1.810; FL ST RCP Rule 1.820; FL ST RCP Rule 1.830.

c. *Mediation.* For more information regarding mediation, please see FL ST RCP Rule 1.710; FL ST RCP Rule 1.720; FL ST RCP Rule 1.730; and FL ST RCP Rule 1.750.

6. *Rules of court*

a. *Rules of civil procedure.* The Florida Rules of Civil Procedure apply to all actions of a civil nature and all special statutory proceedings in the circuit courts and county courts except those to which the Florida Probate Rules, the Florida Family Law Rules of Procedure, or the Small Claims Rules apply. FL ST RCP Rule 1.010.

i. The form, content, procedure, and time for pleading in all special statutory proceedings shall be as prescribed by the statutes governing the proceeding unless the Florida Rules of Civil Procedure specifically provide to the contrary. FL ST RCP Rule 1.010.

ii. The Florida Rules of Civil Procedure shall be construed to secure the just, speedy, and inexpensive determination of every action. FL ST RCP Rule 1.010.

b. *Rules of judicial administration.* The Florida Rules of Judicial Administration shall apply to administrative matters in all courts to which the Florida Rules of Judicial Administration are applicable by their terms. The Florida Rules of Judicial Administration shall be construed to secure the speedy and inexpensive determination of every proceeding to which they are applicable. The Florida Rules of Judicial Administration shall supersede all conflicting rules and statutes. FL ST J ADMIN Rule 2.110.

D. Documents

1. *Required documents*

a. *Notice of hearing/Motion.* An application to the court for an order shall be by motion which shall be made in writing unless made during a hearing or trial, shall state with particularity the grounds therefor, and shall set forth the relief or order sought. The requirement of writing is fulfilled if the motion is stated in a written notice of the hearing of the motion. All notices of hearing shall specify each motion or other matter to be heard. FL ST RCP Rule 1.100(b).

i. *Certification.* The motion must include a certification that the movant, in good faith, has conferred or attempted to confer with the person or party failing to make the discovery in an effort to secure the information or material without court action. FL ST RCP Rule 1.380(a)(2).

ii. *Notices to persons with disabilities.* See the Format section of this KeyRules document for further information.

b. *Good faith certification.* Prior to setting a matter on the motion calendar, the party or attorney noticing the motion shall attempt to resolve the matter and shall certify the good faith attempt to resolve. FL ST 17 J CIR LOCAL RULE NO. 10A(2). To comply, every party or attorney setting a motion for hearing shall execute the following certification: I hereby certify that A) I have made a good faith attempt to resolve this matter prior to my noticing this motion for hearing, and B) the issues before the Court may be heard and resolved by the court within five (5) minutes. FL ST 17 J CIR LOCAL RULE NO. 10A(3).

c. *Certificate of service.* When any attorney certifies in substance: "I certify that a copy hereof has been furnished to (here insert name or names and addresses used for service) by (e-mail) (delivery) (mail) (fax) on .... (date) ....________________ Attorney" the certificate is taken as prima facie proof of such service in compliance with FL ST J ADMIN Rule 2.516. FL ST J ADMIN Rule 2.516(f).

2. *Supplemental documents*
   a. *Proposed order, copies, stamped envelopes.* The court may require that orders or judgments be prepared by a party, may require the party to furnish the court with stamped, addressed envelopes for service of the order or judgment, and may require that proposed orders and judgments be furnished to all parties before entry by the court of the order or judgment. FL ST J ADMIN Rule 2.516(h)(1).
      i. A party submitting an order or judgment shall furnish the Court with sufficient copies together with stamped envelopes addressed to all parties entitled to receive a copy. Proposed orders or judgments must be furnished opposing counsel prior to submission to the court. Proposed orders or judgments must be titled to conform with the motion to which it refers. Language in the order or judgment not agreed as conforming to the court's pronouncement shall be brought to the attention of the court. The proposed order shall indicate date of the hearing on which the order is predicated. Attorneys for the movant shall have at Motion Calendar Hearings all proposed orders and judgments together with the appropriate stamped envelopes where applicable. Unless the Court directs otherwise, proposed orders on non-Motion Calendar Hearings must be prepared by the prevailing or designated counsel and submitted to the Court for consideration within forty-eight (48) hours after said hearing. Copies of all such orders, after entry, shall be conformed and mailed by the Clerk of Court, or the judge's secretary, within forty-eight (48) hours. FL ST 17 J CIR LOCAL RULE NO. 8. Any party requesting relief shall furnish the court with a prepared form of order and sufficient copies with stamped addressed envelopes for all parties. FL ST 17 J CIR LOCAL RULE NO. 10A(8).
      ii. Attorneys should draft proposed orders promptly and the orders should fairly and adequately represent the ruling of the court. Attorneys should promptly provide, either orally or in writing, proposed orders to opposing counsel for approval. Opposing counsel should then promptly communicate any objections and at that time, the drafting attorney should immediately submit a copy of the proposed order to the court and advise the court as to whether or not it has been approved by opposing counsel. FL ST 17 J CIR I-94-O-1(IV)(3).
   b. *Notice of constitutional question.* A party that files a pleading, written motion, or other paper drawing into question the constitutionality of a state statute or a county or municipal charter, ordinance, or franchise must promptly (1) file a notice of constitutional question stating the question and identifying the paper that raises it; and (2) serve the notice and the pleading, written motion, or other paper drawing into question the constitutionality of a state statute or a county or municipal charter, ordinance, or franchise on the Attorney General or the state attorney of the judicial circuit in which the action is pending, by either certified or registered mail. Service of the notice and pleading, written motion, or other paper does not require joinder of the Attorney General or the state attorney as a party to the action. FL ST RCP Rule 1.071.

E. Format

1. *Documents; Type and size.* Documents subject to the exceptions set forth in FL ST J ADMIN Rule 2.525(d) shall be filed on recycled paper measuring eight and one half by eleven (8 1/2 by 11) inches. For purposes of FL ST J ADMIN Rule 2.520, paper is recycled if it contains a minimum content of fifty (50) percent waste paper. Xerographic reduction of legal-size (eight and one half by fourteen (8 1/2 by 14) inches) documents to letter size (eight and one half by eleven (8 1/2 by 11) inches) is prohibited. All other documents filed by electronic transmission shall be filed in a format capable of being printed in a format consistent with the provisions of FL ST J ADMIN Rule 2.250. FL ST J ADMIN Rule 2.520(b).
   a. *Exhibits.* Any exhibit or attachment filed with pleadings or papers may be filed in its original size. FL ST J ADMIN Rule 2.520(c).
   b. *Recording space.* On all papers and documents prepared and filed by the court or by any party to a proceeding which are to be recorded in the public records of any county, including but not limited to final money judgments and notices of lis pendens, a three (3) inch by three (3) inch space at the top right-hand corner on the first page and a one (1) inch by three (3) inch space at the top right-hand

corner on each subsequent page shall be left blank and reserved for use by the clerk of court. FL ST J ADMIN Rule 2.520(d).

i. *Exceptions to recording space.* Any papers or documents created by persons or entities over which the filing party has no control, including but not limited to wills, codicils, trusts, or other testamentary documents; documents prepared or executed by any public officer; documents prepared, executed, acknowledged, or proved outside of the State of Florida; or documents created by State or Federal government agencies, may be filed without the space required by FL ST J ADMIN Rule 2.520. FL ST J ADMIN Rule 2.520(e).

c. *Noncompliance.* No clerk of court is permitted to refuse to file any document or paper because of noncompliance with the Florida Rules of Judicial Administration. However, upon request of the clerk of court, noncomplying documents must be resubmitted in accordance with the formatting rules. FL ST J ADMIN Rule 2.520(f).

2. *Caption.* Every pleading, motion, order, judgment, or other paper shall have a caption containing the name of the court, the file number, and except for in rem proceedings, including forfeiture proceedings, the name of the first party on each side with an appropriate indication of other parties, and a designation identifying the party filing it and its nature or the nature of the order, as the case may be. In any in rem proceeding, every pleading, motion, order, judgment, or other paper shall have a caption containing the name of the court, the file number, the style "In re" (followed by the name or general description of the property), and a designation of the person or entity filing it and its nature or the nature of the order, as the case may be. In an in rem forfeiture proceeding, the style shall be "In re forfeiture of" (followed by the name of the general description of the property). All papers filed in the action shall be styled in such a manner as to indicate clearly the subject matter of the paper and the party requesting or obtaining relief. FL ST RCP Rule 1.100(c)(1).

3. *Writing and written defined.* Writing or written means a document containing information, an application, or a stipulation. FL ST RCP Rule 1.080(c).

4. *Rule abbreviations*

a. The Florida Rules of Civil Procedure and shall be abbreviated as Fla.R.Civ.P. FL ST RCP Rule 1.010.

b. The Florida Rules of Judicial Administration shall be abbreviated as Fla. R. Jud. Admin. FL ST J ADMIN Rule 2.110.

5. *Nonverification.* Except when otherwise specifically provided by the Florida Rules of Civil Procedure or an applicable statute, every pleading or other document of a party represented by an attorney need not be verified or accompanied by an affidavit. FL ST RCP Rule 1.030; FL ST J ADMIN Rule 2.515(a).

6. *Attorney signature*

a. *Attorney signature.* Every pleading and other document of a party represented by an attorney shall be signed by at least one (1) attorney of record in that attorney's individual name whose current record Florida Bar address, telephone number, including area code, primary e-mail address and secondary e-mail addresses, if any, and Florida Bar number shall be stated, and who shall be duly licensed to practice law in Florida or who shall have received permission to appear in the particular case as provided in FL ST J ADMIN Rule 2.510. FL ST J ADMIN Rule 2.515(a).

i. The attorney may be required by the court to give the address of, and to vouch for the attorney's authority to represent, the party. FL ST J ADMIN Rule 2.515(a).

ii. The signature of an attorney shall constitute a certificate by the attorney that the attorney has read the pleading or other document; that to the best of the attorney's knowledge, information, and belief there is good ground to support it; and that it is not interposed for delay. FL ST J ADMIN Rule 2.515(a).

iii. If a pleading is not signed or is signed with intent to defeat the purpose of FL ST J ADMIN Rule 2.515, it may be stricken and the action may proceed as though the pleading or other document had not been served. FL ST J ADMIN Rule 2.515(a).

b. *Pro se litigant signature.* A party who is not represented by an attorney shall sign any pleading or

other paper and state the party's address and telephone number, including area code. FL ST J ADMIN Rule 2.515(b).

c. *Form of signature*

i. The signatures required on pleadings and documents by FL ST J ADMIN Rule 2.515(a) and FL ST J ADMIN Rule 2.515(b) may be:

- Original signatures;
- Original signatures that have been reproduced by electronic means, such as on electronically transmitted documents or photocopied documents;
- Electronic signatures using the "/s/," "s/," or "/s" formats by or at the direction of the person signing; or
- Any other signature format authorized by general law, so long as the clerk where the proceeding is pending has the capability of receiving and has obtained approval from the Supreme Court of Florida to accept pleadings and documents with that signature format. FL ST J ADMIN Rule 2.515(c)(1).

ii. An attorney, party, or other person who files a pleading or paper by electronic transmission that does not contain the original signature of that attorney, party, or other person shall file that identical pleading or paper in paper form containing an original signature of that attorney, party, or other person (hereinafter called the follow-up filing) immediately thereafter. The follow-up filing is not required if the Supreme Court of Florida has entered an order directing the clerk of court to discontinue accepting the follow-up filing. FL ST J ADMIN Rule 2.515(c)(2).

iii. The placement of a "/s/" or the image of a signature by an attorney or party or affected non-party signature line on an electronically filed document shall be accepted as the signature and shall verify to the Court the filer is in possession of the originally executed document. Notwithstanding the manner in which an electronic document is signed the originally executed pleading or paper shall be maintained in the filer's possession for a minimum of one (1) year after final disposition and time for appeal of the case. The originally executed document shall be produced for filing or inspection as directed by the Court. FL ST 17 J CIR 2012-16-CIV.

7. *Forms*

a. *Process.* The forms of process, notice of lis pendens, and notice of action provided in the Florida Rules of Civil Procedure are sufficient. Variations from the forms do not void process or notices that are otherwise sufficient. FL ST RCP Rule 1.900(a).

b. *Other forms.* The other forms provided in the Florida Rules of Civil Procedure are sufficient for the matters that are covered by them. So long as the substance is expressed without prolixity, the forms may be varied to meet the facts of a particular case. FL ST RCP Rule 1.900(b).

c. *Formal matters.* Captions, except for the designation of the paper, are omitted from the forms provided in the Florida Rules of Civil Procedure. A general form of caption is the first form provided. Signatures are omitted from pleadings and motions. FL ST RCP Rule 1.900(c).

8. *Notices to persons with disabilities.* All notices of court proceedings to be held in a public facility, and all process compelling appearance at such proceedings, shall include the following statement in bold face, fourteen (14) point Times New Roman or Courier font: "If you are a person with a disability who needs any accommodation in order to participate in this proceeding, you are entitled, at no cost to you, to the provision of certain assistance. Please contact [identify applicable court personnel by name, address, and telephone number] at least seven (7) days before your scheduled court appearance, or immediately upon receiving this notification if the time before the scheduled appearance is less than seven (7) days; if you are hearing or voice impaired, call 711." FL ST J ADMIN Rule 2.540(c)(1). For further information, please see FL ST 17 J CIR 2010-49-GEN.

9. *Minimization of the filing of sensitive information*

a. *Limitations for court filings.* Unless authorized by FL ST J ADMIN Rule 2.425(b), statute, another rule of court, or the court orders otherwise, designated sensitive information filed with the court must be limited to the following format:

i. The initials of a person known to be a minor;

ii. The year of birth of a person's birth date;

iii. No portion of any: Social security number, Bank account number, Credit card account number, Charge account number, or Debit account number;

iv. The last four digits of any: Taxpayer identification number (TIN), Employee identification number, Driver's license number, Passport number, Telephone number, Financial account number, except as set forth in FL ST J ADMIN Rule 2.425(a)(3), Brokerage account number, Insurance policy account number, Loan account number, Customer account number, or Patient or health care number;

v. A truncated version of any: Email address, Computer user name, Password, or Personal identification number (PIN); and

vi. A truncated version of any other sensitive information as provided by court order. FL ST J ADMIN Rule 2.425(a).

b. *Exceptions.* FL ST J ADMIN Rule 2.425(a) does not apply to the following:

i. An account number which identifies the property alleged to be the subject of a proceeding;

ii. The record of an administrative or agency proceeding;

iii. The record in appellate or review proceedings;

iv. The birth date of a minor whenever the birth date is necessary for the court to establish or maintain subject matter jurisdiction;

v. The name of a minor in any order relating to parental responsibility, time-sharing, or child support;

vi. The name of a minor in any document or order affecting the minor's ownership of real property;

vii. The birth date of a party in a writ of attachment or notice to payor;

viii. In traffic and criminal proceedings: a pro se filing; a court filing that is related to a criminal matter or investigation and that is prepared before the filing of a criminal charge or is not filed as part of any docketed criminal case; an arrest or search warrant or any information in support thereof; a charging document and an affidavit or other documents filed in support of any charging document, including any driving records; a statement of particulars; discovery material introduced into evidence or otherwise filed with the court; and all information necessary for the proper issuance and execution of a subpoena duces tecum;

ix. Information used by the clerk for case maintenance purposes or the courts for case management purposes; and

x. Information which is relevant and material to an issue before the court. FL ST J ADMIN Rule 2.425(b).

c. *Remedies.* Upon motion by a party or interested person or sua sponte by the court, the court may order remedies, sanctions or both for a violation of FL ST J ADMIN Rule 2.425(a). Following notice and an opportunity to respond, the court may impose sanctions if such filing was not made in good faith. FL ST J ADMIN Rule 2.425(c).

d. *Motions not restricted.* FL ST J ADMIN Rule 2.425 does not restrict a party's right to move for protective order, to move to file documents under seal, or to request a determination of the confidentiality of records. FL ST J ADMIN Rule 2.425(d).

e. *Application.* FL ST J ADMIN Rule 2.425 does not affect the application of constitutional provisions, statutes, or rules of court regarding confidential information or access to public information. FL ST J ADMIN Rule 2.425(e).

F. Filing and Service Requirements

1. *Filing requirements.* All original documents must be filed with the court either before service or immediately thereafter, unless otherwise provided for by general law or other rules. If the original of any bond or other document is not placed in the court file, a certified copy must be so placed by the clerk. FL ST J ADMIN Rule 2.516(d). All documents shall be filed in conformity with the requirements of FL ST

J ADMIN Rule 2.525. FL ST RCP Rule 1.080(b). All documents filed in any court shall be filed by electronic transmission in accordance with FL ST J ADMIN Rule 2.525. "Documents" means pleadings, motions, petitions, memoranda, briefs, notices, exhibits, declarations, affidavits, orders, judgments, decrees, writs, opinions, and any other paper or writing submitted to a court. FL ST J ADMIN Rule 2.520(a). All documents that are court records, as defined in FL ST J ADMIN Rule 2.430(a)(1), must be filed by electronic transmission, provided that: (1) the clerk has the ability to accept and retain such documents; (2) the clerk or the chief judge of the circuit has requested permission to accept documents filed by electronic transmission; and (3) the supreme court has entered an order granting permission to the clerk to accept documents filed by electronic transmission. FL ST J ADMIN Rule 2.525(c)(1).

a. *Definition.* "Electronic transmission of documents" means the sending of information by electronic signals to, by or from a court or clerk, which when received can be transformed and stored or transmitted on paper, microfilm, magnetic storage device, optical imaging system, CD-ROM, flash drive, other electronic data storage system, server, case maintenance system ("CM"), electronic court filing ("ECF") system, statewide or local electronic portal ("e-portal"), or other electronic record keeping system authorized by the supreme court in a format sufficient to communicate the information on the original document in a readable format. Electronic transmission of documents includes electronic mail ("e-mail") and any internet-based transmission procedure, and may include procedures allowing for documents to be signed or verified by electronic means. FL ST J ADMIN Rule 2.525(a).

   i. The filing of documents with the court as required by the Florida Rules of Judicial Administration must be made by filing them with the clerk in accordance with FL ST J ADMIN Rule 2.525, except that the judge may permit documents to be filed with the judge, in which event the judge must note the filing date before him or her on the documents and transmit them to the clerk. The date of filing is that shown on the face of the document by the judge's notation or the clerk's time stamp, whichever is earlier. FL ST J ADMIN Rule 2.516(e).

b. *Application.* Any court or clerk of the court may accept the electronic transmission of documents for filing after the clerk, together with input from the chief judge of the circuit, has obtained approval of the procedures and program for doing so from the Supreme Court of Florida. FL ST J ADMIN Rule 2.525(b).

c. *Exceptions*

   i. Paper documents and other submissions may be manually submitted to the clerk or court:

      - When the clerk does not have the ability to accept and retain documents by electronic filing or has not had ECF Procedures approved by the supreme court;
      - For filing by any self-represented party or any self-represented nonparty unless specific ECF Procedures provide a means to file documents electronically. However, any self-represented nonparty that is a governmental or public agency and any other agency, partnership, corporation, or business entity acting on behalf of any governmental or public agency may file documents by electronic transmission if such entity has the capability of filing documents electronically;
      - For filing by attorneys excused from e-mail service in accordance with FL ST J ADMIN Rule 2.516(b);
      - When submitting evidentiary exhibits or filing non-documentary materials;
      - When the filing involves documents in excess of twenty-five (25) megabytes (25MB) in size. For such filings, documents may be transmitted using an electronic storage medium that the clerk has the ability to accept, which may include a CD-ROM, flash drive, or similar storage medium;
      - When filed in open court, as permitted by the court;
      - When paper filing is permitted by any approved statewide or local ECF procedures; and
      - If any court determines that justice so requires. FL ST J ADMIN Rule 2.525(d).

   ii. Any document in paper form submitted under FL ST J ADMIN Rule 2.525(d) is filed when it

is received by the clerk or court and the clerk shall immediately thereafter convert any filed paper document to an electronic document. "Convert to an electronic document" means optically capturing an image of a paper document and using character recognition software to recover as much of the document's text as practicable and then indexing and storing the document in the official court file. FL ST J ADMIN Rule 2.525(c)(4).

iii. Any storage medium submitted under FL ST J ADMIN Rule 2.525(d)(5) is filed when received by the clerk or court and the clerk shall immediately thereafter transfer the electronic documents from the storage device to the official court file. FL ST J ADMIN Rule 2.525(c)(5).

iv. If the filer of any paper document authorized under FL ST J ADMIN Rule 2.525(d) provides a self-addressed, postage-paid envelope for return of the paper document after it is converted to electronic form by the clerk, the clerk shall place the paper document in the envelope and deposit it in the mail. Except when a paper document is required to be maintained, the clerk may recycle any filed paper document that is not to be returned to the filer. FL ST J ADMIN Rule 2.525(c)(6).

v. The clerk may convert any paper document filed before the effective date of FL ST J ADMIN Rule 2.525 to an electronic document. Unless the clerk is required to maintain the paper document, if the paper document has been converted to an electronic document by the clerk, the paper document is no longer part of the official court file and may be removed and recycled. FL ST J ADMIN Rule 2.525(c)(7).

d. *Official court file.* For information on what constitutes the official court file, please see FL ST J ADMIN Rule 2.525(c)(2), FL ST J ADMIN Rule 2.525(c)(3).

e. *Administration.* All attorneys, parties, or other persons using this rule to file documents are required to make arrangements with the court or clerk for the payment of any charges authorized by general law or the supreme court before filing any document by electronic transmission. FL ST J ADMIN Rule 2.525(f)(2).

f. *Filing date.* The filing date for an electronically transmitted document is the date and time that such filing is acknowledged by an electronic stamp or otherwise, pursuant to any procedure set forth in any ECF Procedures approved by the supreme court, or the date the last page of such filing is received by the court or clerk. FL ST J ADMIN Rule 2.525(f)(3).

g. *Accessibility.* All documents transmitted in any electronic form under FL ST J ADMIN Rule 2.525 must comply with the accessibility requirements of FL ST J ADMIN Rule 2.526. FL ST J ADMIN Rule 2.525(g).

h. *Provisions for electronic filing in the Seventeenth Circuit.* Attorneys may electronically file pleadings and papers on existing cases in circuit civil divisions 1, 7, 9, 19, 26 and 27. The following documents may be scanned and efiled; however, the original must be filed with the Clerk: Documents ordered by the Court; and original documents required by law or rule of procedure to be filed with the Clerk. Self represented individuals shall file pleadings and papers with the Clerk. The Clerk within twenty four (24) hours of receipt of an electronic document shall either accept or reject the electronic document for filing and send electronic notice to the filer. FL ST 17 J CIR 2012-16-CIV.

i. *Technical failures.* If a document filed electronically is not received due to: an error in the transmission of the document to the Clerk or any vendor of the Clerk to provide electronic court record filing services which is unknown to an attorney or party or affected non party, or a failure to process the electronic document when received by the Clerk or rejection by the Clerk, or any other technical problems experienced by the attorney or party or affected non party, the Court may, after an evidentiary hearing and upon satisfactory proof, enter an order permitting the document to be filed nunc pro tunc to the date it was first attempted to be sent electronically. FL ST 17 J CIR 2012-16-CIV.

j. *Filing of pleadings or papers at any office of the clerk of court.* The Clerk of Courts, commencing November 3, 2008, shall accept for filing, at the central courthouse, north satellite courthouse, south satellite courthouse, and west satellite courthouse any pleading or motion or other document for filing in the court file from any attorney or party for an existing case except as otherwise set forth. FL ST 17 J CIR 2008-153-GEN. See FL ST 17 J CIR 2008-153-GEN for specific exceptions.

2. *Service requirements.* Every pleading subsequent to the initial pleading, all orders, and every other document filed in the action must be served in conformity with the requirements of FL ST J ADMIN Rule 2.516. FL ST RCP Rule 1.080(a).

   a. *Service; When required.* Unless the court otherwise orders, or a statute or supreme court administrative order specifies a different means of service, every pleading subsequent to the initial pleading and every other document filed in any court proceeding, except applications for witness subpoenas and documents served by formal notice or required to be served in the manner provided for service of formal notice, must be served in accordance with FL ST J ADMIN Rule 2.516 on each party. No service need be made on parties against whom a default has been entered, except that pleadings asserting new or additional claims against them must be served in the manner provided for service of summons. FL ST J ADMIN Rule 2.516(a).

   b. *Service; How made.* When service is required or permitted to be made upon a party represented by an attorney, service must be made upon the attorney unless service upon the party is ordered by the court. FL ST J ADMIN Rule 2.516(b).

      i. *Service by electronic mail ("e-mail").* All documents required or permitted to be served on another party must be served by e-mail, unless FL ST J ADMIN Rule 2.516 otherwise provides. When, in addition to service by e-mail, the sender also utilizes another means of service provided for in FL ST J ADMIN Rule 2.516(b)(2), any differing time limits and other provisions applicable to that other means of service control. FL ST J ADMIN Rule 2.516(b)(1). Any document electronically transmitted to a court or clerk must also be served on all parties and interested persons in accordance with the applicable rules of court. FL ST J ADMIN Rule 2.525(e)(2).

         - *Service on attorneys.* Upon appearing in a proceeding, an attorney must serve a designation of a primary e-mail address and may designate no more than two (2) secondary e-mail addresses. Thereafter, service must be directed to all designated e-mail addresses in that proceeding. Every document filed by an attorney thereafter must include the primary e-mail address of that attorney and any secondary e-mail addresses. If an attorney does not designate any e-mail address for service, documents may be served on that attorney at the e-mail address on record with The Florida Bar. FL ST J ADMIN Rule 2.516(b)(1)(A).

         - *Exception to e-mail service on attorneys.* Service by an attorney on another attorney must be made by e-mail unless excused by the court. Upon motion by an attorney demonstrating that the attorney has no e-mail account and lacks access to the Internet at the attorney's office, the court may excuse the attorney from the requirements of e-mail service. Service on and by an attorney excused by the court from e-mail service must be by the means provided in FL ST J ADMIN Rule 2.516(b)(2). FL ST J ADMIN Rule 2.516(b)(1)(B).

         - *Service on and by parties not represented by an attorney.* Any party not represented by an attorney may serve a designation of a primary e-mail address and also may designate no more than two (2) secondary e-mail addresses to which service must be directed in that proceeding by the means provided in FL ST J ADMIN Rule 2.516(b)(1). If a party not represented by an attorney does not designate an e-mail address for service in a proceeding, service on and by that party must be by the means provided in FL ST J ADMIN Rule 2.516(b)(2). FL ST J ADMIN Rule 2.516(b)(1)(C).

         - *Time of service.* Service by e-mail is complete when it is sent. FL ST J ADMIN Rule 2.516(b)(1)(D). An e-mail is deemed served on the date it is sent. FL ST J ADMIN Rule 2.516(b)(1)(D)(i). If the sender learns that the e-mail did not reach the address of the person to be served, the sender must immediately send another copy by e-mail, or by a means authorized by FL ST J ADMIN Rule 2.516(b)(2). FL ST J ADMIN Rule 2.516(b)(1)(D)(ii). E-mail service is treated as service by mail for the computation of time. FL ST J ADMIN Rule 2.516(b)(1)(D)(iii).

      ii. *Format of e-mail for service.* Service of a document by e-mail is made by attaching a copy of the document in PDF format to an e-mail sent to all addresses designated by the attorney or party. FL ST J ADMIN Rule 2.516(b)(1)(E).

         - All documents served by e-mail must be attached to an e-mail message containing a

subject line beginning with the words "SERVICE OF COURT DOCUMENT" in all capital letters, followed by the case number of the proceeding in which the documents are being served. FL ST J ADMIN Rule 2.516(b)(1)(E)(i).

- The body of the e-mail must identify the court in which the proceeding is pending, the case number, the name of the initial party on each side, the title of each document served with that e-mail, and the sender's name and telephone number. FL ST J ADMIN Rule 2.516(b)(1)(E)(ii).
- Any document served by e-mail may be signed by the "/s/" format, as long as the filed original is signed in accordance with the applicable rule of procedure. FL ST J ADMIN Rule 2.516(b)(1)(E)(iii).
- Any e-mail which, together with its attached documents, exceeds five megabytes (5MB) in size, must be divided and sent as separate e-mails, no one of which may exceed five megabytes (5MB) in size and each of which must be sequentially numbered in the subject line. FL ST J ADMIN Rule 2.516(b)(1)(E)(iv).

iii. *Service by other means.* In addition to, and not in lieu of, service by e-mail, service may also be made upon attorneys by any of the means specified in FL ST J ADMIN Rule 2.516(b)(2). Service on and by all parties who are not represented by an attorney and who do not designate an e-mail address, and on and by all attorneys excused from e-mail service, must be made by delivering a copy of the document or by mailing it to the party or attorney at their last known address or, if no address is known, by leaving it with the clerk of the court. Service by mail is complete upon mailing. Delivery of a copy within FL ST J ADMIN Rule 2.516 is complete upon:

- Handing it to the attorney or to the party,
- Leaving it at the attorney's or party's office with a clerk or other person in charge thereof,
- If there is no one in charge, leaving it in a conspicuous place therein,
- If the office is closed or the person to be served has no office, leaving it at the person's usual place of abode with some person of his or her family above fifteen (15) years of age and informing such person of the contents, or
- Transmitting it by facsimile to the attorney's or party's office with a cover sheet containing the sender's name, firm, address, telephone number, and facsimile number, and the number of pages transmitted. When service is made by facsimile, a copy must also be served by any other method permitted by FL ST J ADMIN Rule 2.516. Facsimile service occurs when transmission is complete. FL ST J ADMIN Rule 2.516(b)(2)(A) through FL ST J ADMIN Rule 2.516(b)(2)(E).
- Service by delivery after 5:00 p.m. must be deemed to have been made by mailing on the date of delivery. FL ST J ADMIN Rule 2.516(b)(2)(F).

c. *Service; Numerous defendants.* In actions when the parties are unusually numerous, the court may regulate the service contemplated by the Florida Rules of Judicial Administration on motion or on its own initiative in such manner as may be found to be just and reasonable. FL ST J ADMIN Rule 2.516(c).

d. *Service by clerk.* Service of notices and other documents required to be made by the clerk must also be done as provided in FL ST J ADMIN Rule 2.516(b). FL ST J ADMIN Rule 2.516(g).

G. Hearings

1. *Communication equipment*

a. *Definition.* Communication equipment means a conference telephone or other electronic device that permits all those appearing or participating to hear and speak to each other, provided that all conversation of all parties is audible to all persons present. FL ST J ADMIN Rule 2.530(a).

b. *Use by all parties.* A county or circuit court judge may, upon the court's own motion or upon the written request of a party, direct that communication equipment be used for a motion hearing, pretrial conference, or a status conference. A judge must give notice to the parties and consider any objections they may have to the use of communication equipment before directing that communication equipment be used. The decision to use communication equipment over the objection of parties will be in the sound discretion of the trial court, except as noted below. FL ST J ADMIN Rule 2.530(b).

c. *Use only by requesting party.* A county or circuit court judge may, upon the written request of a party upon reasonable notice to all other parties, permit a requesting party to participate through communication equipment in a scheduled motion hearing; however, any such request (except in criminal, juvenile, and appellate proceedings) must be granted, absent a showing of good cause to deny the same, where the hearing is set for not longer than fifteen (15) minutes. FL ST J ADMIN Rule 2.530(c).

d. *Testimony*

   i. *Generally.* A county or circuit court judge, general magistrate, special magistrate, or hearing officer may allow testimony to be taken through communication equipment if all parties consent or if permitted by another applicable rule of procedure. FL ST J ADMIN Rule 2.530(d)(1).

   ii. *Procedure.* Any party desiring to present testimony through communication equipment shall, prior to the hearing or trial at which the testimony is to be presented, contact all parties to determine whether each party consents to this form of testimony. The party seeking to present the testimony shall move for permission to present testimony through communication equipment, which motion shall set forth good cause as to why the testimony should be allowed in this form. FL ST J ADMIN Rule 2.530(d)(2).

   iii. *Oath.* Testimony may be taken through communication equipment only if a notary public or other person authorized to administer oaths in the witness's jurisdiction is present with the witness and administers the oath consistent with the laws of the jurisdiction. FL ST J ADMIN Rule 2.530(d)(3).

   iv. *Confrontation rights.* In juvenile and criminal proceedings the defendant must make an informed waiver of any confrontation rights that may be abridged by the use of communication equipment. FL ST J ADMIN Rule 2.530(d)(4).

   v. *Video testimony.* If the testimony to be presented utilizes video conferencing or comparable two-way visual capabilities, the court in its discretion may modify the procedures set forth in FL ST J ADMIN Rule 2.530 to accommodate the technology utilized. FL ST J ADMIN Rule 2.530(d)(5).

e. *Burden of expense.* The cost for the use of the communication equipment is the responsibility of the requesting party unless otherwise directed by the court. FL ST J ADMIN Rule 2.530(e).

2. *Uniform motion calendar.* The Circuit Judges of the general civil/family division (excluding juvenile/dependency) shall maintain a uniform motion calendar from 8:45 A.M. to 9:30 A.M., Monday through Thursday. The motion calendar shall end PROMPTLY at 9:30 A.M. All parties shall be prepared to proceed at 8:45 A.M., and if one party fails to timely appear, the matter may proceed on the merits in his/her absence. FL ST 17 J CIR LOCAL RULE NO. 10A(1).

3. *Noticed motion limitation.* No more than two (2) motions may be noticed for each case on any given day except by leave of court. FL ST 17 J CIR LOCAL RULE NO. 10A(4).

4. *Ex parte and non-evidentiary motion.* Ex parte matters, non-evidentiary motions, and uncontested proceedings for adoptions, or dissolution may be heard on the uniform motion calendar, provided such matters can be conducted in five (5) minutes equally allocated among the parties and the moving party shall so certify as specified in FL ST 17 J CIR LOCAL RULE NO. 10A(3). FL ST 17 J CIR LOCAL RULE NO. 10A(6).

5. *Good faith effort to resolve issues.* Prior to appearing before the court, the parties shall discuss the issues raised in the pending motion, and both parties shall be prepared to certify at the hearing they have made a good faith effort to resolve the issues. FL ST 17 J CIR LOCAL RULE NO. 10A(7).

6. *Re-noticing hearings.* When the motion calendar has been filled, the judge's office shall notify the party

noticing any hearings which cannot be reached. The noticing party shall call opposing counsel and re-notice the hearing. FL ST 17 J CIR LOCAL RULE NO. 10A(9).

7. *Hearing cancellation.* Motion calendar hearings may be canceled by the attorney who set the hearing. FL ST 17 J CIR LOCAL RULE NO. 10A(10).

8. *Other motion calendars.* Hearing officers/general masters shall conduct a motion calendar, the dates and times of which shall be determined by the hearing officer/general master or by administrative order. FL ST 17 J CIR LOCAL RULE NO. 10A(11).

9. *Sanctions.* Failure to comply with the procedures designated in the above paragraphs may result in the hearing being stricken from the docket or such other sanctions as the court deems appropriate. FL ST 17 J CIR LOCAL RULE NO. 10A(12).

H. Forms

1. Official Motion to Compel Discovery Forms for Florida

a. Caption. FL ST RCP Form 1.901.

b. Notice of compliance when constitutional challenge is brought. FL ST RCP Form 1.975.

2. Motion to Compel Discovery Forms for Florida

a. Motion to compel attendance and for sanctions. FL-PP § 3:160.

b. Motion; To compel answer to questions asked on oral examination or written questions. FL-PP § 3:161.

c. Order; Directing deponent to answer questions asked on oral examination; Costs and attorney fees to moving party. FL-PP § 3:162.

d. Order; Compelling answer to written questions. FL-PP § 3:163.

e. Motion; For order finding person in contempt of court; Refusal, after order, to answer question. FL-PP § 3:167.

f. Motion; For order compelling opposing party to pay expenses incurred in proving facts the party refused to admit. FL-PP § 3:168.

g. Motion; Compel discovery, deposition. FL-PRACFORM § 7:37.

h. Motion; Compel discovery, interrogatories. FL-PRACFORM § 7:38.

i. Form for motion to compel answer on deposition. FL-RCPF R 1.380(6).

j. Form for certificate of non-appearance at deposition. FL-RCPF R 1.380(7).

k. Form for notice of motion. FL-RCPF R 1.380(8).

l. Form for order on motion to compel answer. FL-RCPF R 1.380(9).

m. Form for notice and motion to compel. FL-RCPF R 1.380(10).

n. Form for order to compel discovery. FL-RCPF R 1.380(18).

o. Form for order to comply with discovery and answer interrogatories. FL-RCPF R 1.380(19).

I. Checklist

(I) ❑ Matters to be considered by moving party

(a) ❑ Required documents

(1) ❑ Notice of hearing/Motion

(2) ❑ Good faith certificate

(3) ❑ Certificate of service

(b) ❑ Supplemental documents

(1) ❑ Proposed order, copies, stamped envelopes

(2) ❑ Notice of constitutional question

(c) ❑ Time for making motion

(1) ❑ Upon reasonable notice to other parties and all persons affected, a party may apply for an order compelling discovery

(2) ❑ A copy of any written motion which may not be heard ex parte and a copy of the notice of the hearing thereof shall be served a reasonable time before the time specified for the hearing

(3) ❑ Copies of the notice of hearing, the motion, and any pleading or interrogatories to which the motion is addressed shall be in the hands of the Judicial Assistant and opposing party at least four (4) working days in advance of the hearing

(II) ❑ Matters to be considered by opposing party

(a) ❑ Required documents

(1) ❑ Response to motion

(2) ❑ Certificate of service

(b) ❑ Supplemental documents

(1) ❑ Proposed order, copies, stamped envelopes

(2) ❑ Notice of constitutional question

(c) ❑ Time for service and filing of opposition

(1) ❑ No time specified for responding to a motion

Motions, Oppositions and Replies
Motion for Directed Verdict

Document Last Updated January 2013

A. Applicable Rules

1. *State rules*

a. Motion for a directed verdict. FL ST RCP Rule 1.480.

b. Rules of court. FL ST RCP Rule 1.010; FL ST J ADMIN Rule 2.110.

c. Nonverification of pleadings. FL ST RCP Rule 1.030.

d. Service and filing of pleadings, orders, and documents. FL ST RCP Rule 1.080.

e. Time. FL ST RCP Rule 1.090.

f. Pleadings and motions. FL ST RCP Rule 1.100.

g. Motions. FL ST RCP Rule 1.160.

h. Relief from judgment, decrees or orders. FL ST RCP Rule 1.540.

i. Mediation and arbitration. FL ST RCP Rule 1.700; FL ST RCP Rule 1.710; FL ST RCP Rule 1.720; FL ST RCP Rule 1.730; FL ST RCP Rule 1.750; FL ST RCP Rule 1.800; FL ST RCP Rule 1.810; FL ST RCP Rule 1.820; FL ST RCP Rule 1.830.

j. Forms. FL ST RCP Rule 1.900.

k. Retention of court records. FL ST J ADMIN Rule 2.430.

l. Foreign attorneys. FL ST J ADMIN Rule 2.510.

m. Signature of attorneys and parties. FL ST J ADMIN Rule 2.515.

n. Paper. FL ST J ADMIN Rule 2.520.

o. Electronic filing. FL ST J ADMIN Rule 2.525.

p. Communication equipment. FL ST J ADMIN Rule 2.530.

q. Court reporting. FL ST J ADMIN Rule 2.535.

r. Requests for accommodations by persons with disabilities. FL ST J ADMIN Rule 2.540.

s. Minimization of the filing of sensitive information. FL ST J ADMIN Rule 2.425.

t. Accessibility of information and technology. FL ST J ADMIN Rule 2.526.

2. *Local rules*

a. Orders for signature; Civil division. FL ST 17 J CIR LOCAL RULE NO. 8.

b. Uniform motion calendar ex parte motions to compel discovery, and special set hearings. FL ST 17 J CIR LOCAL RULE NO. 10A.

c. Standards of professional courtesy. FL ST 17 J CIR I-94-O-1.

d. Administrative order authorizing the filing of pleadings or papers at any office of the clerk of court. FL ST 17 J CIR 2008-153-GEN.

e. Administrative order regarding provision of ADA accommodations. FL ST 17 J CIR 2010-49-GEN.

f. Administrative order establishing electronic filing procedures for the civil division. FL ST 17 J CIR 2012-16-CIV.

B. Timing

1. *Before a verdict is returned.* A directed verdict is available to the defendant at the close of the plaintiff's evidence or to either party at the close of all of the evidence. A verdict may be directed either by the court on its own motion or on the motion of counsel. FL ST RCP Rule 1.480(a); FL-PP § 5:83. The movant should be prepared to argue the motion immediately. FL-PRACPROC § 22:14.

2. *After a verdict is returned.* Within ten (10) days after the return of a verdict, a party who has timely moved for a directed verdict may serve a motion to enter judgment in accordance with the motion for a directed verdict. FL ST RCP Rule 1.480(b).

3. *No verdict is returned.* If a verdict was not returned, a party who has timely moved for a directed verdict may serve a motion for judgment in accordance with the motion for a directed verdict within ten (10) days after discharge of the jury. FL ST RCP Rule 1.480(b).

4. *General motion timing.* A copy of any written motion which may not be heard ex parte and a copy of the notice of the hearing thereof shall be served a reasonable time before the time specified for the hearing. FL ST RCP Rule 1.090(d). Copies of the notice of hearing, the motion, and any pleading or interrogatories to which the motion is addressed shall be in the hands of the Judicial Assistant and opposing party at least four (4) working days in advance of the hearing. The original notice shall be filed with the Clerk. FL ST 17 J CIR LOCAL RULE NO. 10A(5).

5. *Standard of professional conduct; Scheduling*

a. Attorneys should endeavor to provide opposing counsel, parties, witnesses, and other affected persons, sufficient notice of depositions, hearings and other proceedings, except upon agreement of course, in an emergency, or in other circumstances compelling more expedited scheduling. As a general rule, actual notice should be no less than five (5) business days for instate depositions, ten (10) business days for out-of-state depositions and four (4) business days for hearings. FL ST 17 J CIR I-94-O-1(I)(1).

b. Attorneys should communicate with opposing counsel prior to scheduling depositions, hearings and other proceedings, in an effort to schedule them at times that are mutually convenient for all interested persons. Further, sufficient time should be reserved to permit a complete presentation by counsel for all parties. FL ST 17 J CIR I-94-O-1(I)(2).

c. Attorneys should notify opposing counsel, the court, and others affected, of scheduling conflicts as soon as they become apparent. Further, attorneys should cooperate with one another regarding all reasonable rescheduling requests that do not prejudice their clients or unduly delay a proceeding. FL ST 17 J CIR I-94-O-1(I)(3).

d. Attorneys should promptly notify the court or other tribunal of any resolution between the parties that renders a scheduled court appearance unnecessary or otherwise moot. FL ST 17 J CIR I-94-O-1(I)(4).

e. Attorneys should grant reasonable requests by opposing counsel for extensions of time within which to respond to pleadings, discovery, and other matters when such an extension will not prejudice their client or unduly delay a proceeding. FL ST 17 J CIR I-94-O-1(I)(5).

6. *Timing considerations when filing electronically.* The filing date of an efiled document is when the last page is received by the Clerk. The electronic filing of a document does not modify any filing deadlines as required by law, rule of procedure, or court order. FL ST 17 J CIR 2012-16-CIV.

7. *Computation of time*

a. *Generally.* Computation of time shall be governed by FL ST J ADMIN Rule 2.514. FL ST RCP Rule 1.090(a). The following rules apply in computing time periods specified in any rule of procedure, local rule, court order, or statute that does not specify a method of computing time. FL ST J ADMIN Rule 2.514(a).

i. *Period stated in days or a longer unit.* When the period is stated in days or a longer unit of time (A) exclude the day of the event that triggers the period; (B) count every day, including intermediate Saturdays, Sundays, and legal holidays; and (C) include the last day of the period, but if the last day is a Saturday, Sunday, or legal holiday, or falls within any period of time extended through an order of the chief justice under FL ST J ADMIN Rule 2.205(a)(2)(B)(iv), the period continues to run until the end of the next day that is not a Saturday, Sunday, or legal holiday and does not fall within any period of time extended through an order of the chief justice. FL ST J ADMIN Rule 2.514(a)(1).

ii. *Period stated in hours.* When the period is stated in hours (A) begin counting immediately on the occurrence of the event that triggers the period; (B) count every hour, including hours during intermediate Saturdays, Sundays, and legal holidays; and (C) if the period would end on a Saturday, Sunday, or legal holiday, or during any period of time extended through an order of the chief justice under FL ST J ADMIN Rule 2.205(a)(2)(B)(iv), the period continues to run until the same time on the next day that is not a Saturday, Sunday, or legal holiday and does not fall within any period of time extended through an order of the chief justice. FL ST J ADMIN Rule 2.514(a)(2).

iii. *Period stated in days less than seven (7) days.* When the period stated in days is less than seven (7) days, intermediate Saturdays, Sundays, and legal holidays shall be excluded in the computation. FL ST J ADMIN Rule 2.514(a)(3).

iv. *"Last day" defined.* Unless a different time is set by a statute, local rule, or court order, the last day ends (A) for electronic filing or for service by any means, at midnight; and (B) for filing by other means, when the clerk's office is scheduled to close. FL ST J ADMIN Rule 2.514(a)(4).

v. *"Next day" defined.* The "next day" is determined by continuing to count forward when the period is measured after an event and backward when measured before an event. FL ST J ADMIN Rule 2.514(a)(5).

vi. *"Legal holiday" defined.* "Legal holiday" means (A) the day set aside by FL ST § 110.117, for observing New Year's Day, Martin Luther King, Jr.'s Birthday, Memorial Day, Independence Day, Labor Day, Veterans' Day, Thanksgiving Day, the Friday after Thanksgiving Day, or Christmas Day, and (B) any day observed as a holiday by the clerk's office or as designated by the chief judge. FL ST J ADMIN Rule 2.514(a)(6).

b. *Additional time after service by mail or e-mail.* When a party may or must act within a specified time after service and service is made by mail or e-mail, five (5) days are added after the period that would otherwise expire under FL ST J ADMIN Rule 2.514(a). FL ST J ADMIN Rule 2.514(b).

c. *Enlargement.* When an act is required or allowed to be done at or within a specified time by order of court, by the Florida Rules of Civil Procedure, or by notice given thereunder, for cause shown the court at any time in its discretion (1) with or without notice, may order the period enlarged if request therefor is made before the expiration of the period originally prescribed or as extended by a previous order, or (2) upon motion made and notice after the expiration of the specified period, may permit the act to be done when failure to act was the result of excusable neglect, but it may not extend the time for making a motion for new trial, for rehearing, or to alter or amend a judgment; making a motion for relief from a judgment under FL ST RCP Rule 1.540(b); taking an appeal or filing a petition for certiorari; or making a motion for a directed verdict. FL ST RCP Rule 1.090(b).

d. *Unaffected by expiration of term.* The period of time provided for the doing of any act or the taking of any proceeding shall not be affected or limited by the continued existence or expiration of a term of court. The continued existence or expiration of a term of court in no way affects the power of a court to do any act or take any proceeding in any action which is or has been pending before it. FL ST RCP Rule 1.090(c).

C. General Requirements

1. *Motions generally*

a. *Contents.* An application to the court for an order shall be by motion which shall be made in writing unless made during a hearing or trial, shall state with particularity the grounds therefor, and shall set forth the relief or order sought. The requirement of writing is fulfilled if the motion is stated in a written notice of the hearing of the motion. All notices of hearing shall specify each motion or other matter to be heard. FL ST RCP Rule 1.100(b).

b. *Particularity requirement.* The court considers a motion in the light of the substantive law, rule or statute to make its determination. Some rules require a statement of the grounds for a motion under the rule. Failure to give the grounds will result in denial of the motion. This should be the result in all situations when the ground for the motion is not inherent in the rule. FL-PRACPROC § 9:3. The requirement is nevertheless an important one, first because of the due process notice rights of the respondent, as well as for the assistance it provides to the court in its preparation for the hearing or, absent a hearing, for disposition. 4 FLPRAC R 1.100.

2. *Motion for directed verdict*

a. *Effect of a motion for directed verdict.* A party who moves for a directed verdict at the close of the evidence offered by the adverse party may offer evidence in the event the motion is denied without having reserved the right to do so and to the same extent as if the motion had not been made. The denial of a motion for a directed verdict shall not operate to discharge the jury. A motion for a directed verdict shall state the specific grounds therefor. The order directing a verdict is effective without any assent of the jury. FL ST RCP Rule 1.480(a).

b. *Reservation of decision on motion.* When a motion for a directed verdict is denied or for any reason is not granted, the court is deemed to have submitted the action to the jury subject to a later determination of the legal questions raised by the motion. Within ten (10) days after the return of a verdict, a party who has timely moved for a directed verdict may serve a motion to set aside the verdict and any judgment entered thereon and to enter judgment in accordance with the motion for a directed verdict. If a verdict was not returned, a party who has timely moved for a directed verdict may serve a motion for judgment in accordance with the motion for a directed verdict within ten (10) days after discharge of the jury. FL ST RCP Rule 1.480(b).

c. *Joined with motion for new trial.* A motion for a new trial may be joined with a motion for directed verdict or a new trial may be requested in the alternative. If a verdict was returned, the court may allow the judgment to stand or may reopen the judgment and either order a new trial or direct the entry of judgment as if the requested verdict had been directed. If no verdict was returned, the court may direct the entry of judgment as if the requested verdict had been directed or may order a new trial. FL ST RCP Rule 1.480(c).

d. *General procedures on a motion for directed verdict*

i. *Proper method.* The proper method of advocating that a party is entitled to prevail on a claim or defense as a matter of law is to make a motion for a directed verdict at the close of the evidence offered by the opposing party. The trial judge has authority to direct a verdict in favor of one party and against another, without submitting the case to the jury, if there is no other verdict the jury could lawfully return. 5 FLPRAC § 22:5.

ii. *Directed verdict only in a jury trial.* A motion for directed verdict is proper only in a jury trial. The equivalent motion in nonjury trial is called a motion for involuntary dismissal. 5 FLPRAC § 22:5.

iii. *Test for the sufficiency of the evidence.* A motion for directed verdict is used primarily to test the sufficiency of the evidence offered in support of a claim or defense. It may also be used to raise legal issues other than the sufficiency of the evidence, but that is less common because most pure issues of law can be resolved on a motion to dismiss or a motion for summary judgment before the case is set for trial. If there is no evidence to support a claim or defense, the trial judge has a duty to direct a verdict for the opposing party on that claim or defense. 5 FLPRAC § 22:5.

- The trial judge must view all of the facts and factual inferences in a light most favorable to the party opposing the motion. 5 FLPRAC § 22:5.
- The rule has often been stated by the Florida courts in the negative, that is, a motion for directed verdict should not be granted unless the court, after viewing the evidence and testimony in the light most favorable to the nonmoving party, determines that no reasonable jury could render a verdict for the nonmoving party. Under this rule, the trial judge may not direct a verdict against a party if there is any evidence upon which the jury could lawfully make a finding in favor of that party. 5 FLPRAC § 22:5.

3. *Arbitration and mediation*

a. *Referral to arbitration and mediation.* Except as hereinafter provided or as otherwise prohibited by law, the presiding judge may enter an order referring all or any part of a contested civil matter to mediation or arbitration. The parties to any contested civil matter may file a written stipulation to mediate or arbitrate any issue between them at any time. Such stipulation shall be incorporated into the order of referral. FL ST RCP Rule 1.700(a).

b. *Arbitration*

i. *Exclusions.* A civil action shall be ordered to arbitration or arbitration in conjunction with mediation upon stipulation of the parties. A civil action may be ordered to arbitration or arbitration in conjunction with mediation upon motion of any party or by the court, if the judge determines the action to be of such a nature that arbitration could be of benefit to the litigants or the court. FL ST RCP Rule 1.800.

- Under no circumstances may the following categories of actions be referred to arbitration: (1) bond estreatures; (2) habeas corpus or other extraordinary writs; (3) bond validations; (4) civil or criminal contempt; (5) such other matters as may be specified by order of the chief judge in the circuit. FL ST RCP Rule 1.800.

ii. For more information regarding arbitration, please see FL ST RCP Rule 1.810; FL ST RCP Rule 1.820; FL ST RCP Rule 1.830.

c. *Mediation.* For more information regarding mediation, please see FL ST RCP Rule 1.710; FL ST RCP Rule 1.720; FL ST RCP Rule 1.730; and FL ST RCP Rule 1.750.

4. *Rules of court*

a. *Rules of civil procedure.* The Florida Rules of Civil Procedure apply to all actions of a civil nature and all special statutory proceedings in the circuit courts and county courts except those to which the Florida Probate Rules, the Florida Family Law Rules of Procedure, or the Small Claims Rules apply. FL ST RCP Rule 1.010.

i. The form, content, procedure, and time for pleading in all special statutory proceedings shall be as prescribed by the statutes governing the proceeding unless the Florida Rules of Civil Procedure specifically provide to the contrary. FL ST RCP Rule 1.010.

ii. The Florida Rules of Civil Procedure shall be construed to secure the just, speedy, and inexpensive determination of every action. FL ST RCP Rule 1.010.

b. *Rules of judicial administration.* The Florida Rules of Judicial Administration shall apply to administrative matters in all courts to which the Florida Rules of Judicial Administration are applicable by their terms. The Florida Rules of Judicial Administration shall be construed to secure the speedy and inexpensive determination of every proceeding to which they are applicable. The Florida Rules of Judicial Administration shall supersede all conflicting rules and statutes. FL ST J ADMIN Rule 2.110.

D. Documents

1. *Required documents*

   a. *Notice of hearing/Motion.* An application to the court for an order shall be by motion which shall be made in writing unless made during a hearing or trial, shall state with particularity the grounds therefor, and shall set forth the relief or order sought. The requirement of writing is fulfilled if the motion is stated in a written notice of the hearing of the motion. All notices of hearing shall specify each motion or other matter to be heard. FL ST RCP Rule 1.100(b).

      i. *Notices to persons with disabilities.* See the Format section of this KeyRules document for further information.

   b. *Good faith certification.* Prior to setting a matter on the motion calendar, the party or attorney noticing the motion shall attempt to resolve the matter and shall certify the good faith attempt to resolve. FL ST 17 J CIR LOCAL RULE NO. 10A(2). To comply, every party or attorney setting a motion for hearing shall execute the following certification: I hereby certify that A) I have made a good faith attempt to resolve this matter prior to my noticing this motion for hearing, and B) the issues before the Court may be heard and resolved by the court within five (5) minutes. FL ST 17 J CIR LOCAL RULE NO. 10A(3).

   c. *Certificate of service.* When any attorney certifies in substance: "I certify that a copy hereof has been furnished to (here insert name or names and addresses used for service) by (e-mail) (delivery) (mail) (fax) on .... (date) ....________________ Attorney" the certificate is taken as prima facie proof of such service in compliance with FL ST J ADMIN Rule 2.516. FL ST J ADMIN Rule 2.516(f).

2. *Supplemental documents*

   a. *Proposed order, copies, stamped envelopes.* The court may require that orders or judgments be prepared by a party, may require the party to furnish the court with stamped, addressed envelopes for service of the order or judgment, and may require that proposed orders and judgments be furnished to all parties before entry by the court of the order or judgment. FL ST J ADMIN Rule 2.516(h)(1).

      i. A party submitting an order or judgment shall furnish the Court with sufficient copies together with stamped envelopes addressed to all parties entitled to receive a copy. Proposed orders or judgments must be furnished opposing counsel prior to submission to the court. Proposed orders or judgments must be titled to conform with the motion to which it refers. Language in the order or judgment not agreed as conforming to the court's pronouncement shall be brought to the attention of the court. The proposed order shall indicate date of the hearing on which the order is predicated. Attorneys for the movant shall have at Motion Calendar Hearings all proposed orders and judgments together with the appropriate stamped envelopes where applicable. Unless the Court directs otherwise, proposed orders on non-Motion Calendar Hearings must be prepared by the prevailing or designated counsel and submitted to the Court for consideration within forty-eight (48) hours after said hearing. Copies of all such orders, after entry, shall be conformed and mailed by the Clerk of Court, or the judge's secretary, within forty-eight (48) hours. FL ST 17 J CIR LOCAL RULE NO. 8. Any party requesting relief shall furnish the court with a prepared form of order and sufficient copies with stamped addressed envelopes for all parties. FL ST 17 J CIR LOCAL RULE NO. 10A(8).

      ii. Attorneys should draft proposed orders promptly and the orders should fairly and adequately represent the ruling of the court. Attorneys should promptly provide, either orally or in writing, proposed orders to opposing counsel for approval. Opposing counsel should then promptly communicate any objections and at that time, the drafting attorney should immediately submit a copy of the proposed order to the court and advise the court as to whether or not it has been approved by opposing counsel. FL ST 17 J CIR I-94-O-1(IV)(3).

   b. *Notice of constitutional question.* A party that files a pleading, written motion, or other paper drawing into question the constitutionality of a state statute or a county or municipal charter, ordinance, or franchise must promptly (1) file a notice of constitutional question stating the question and identifying the paper that raises it; and (2) serve the notice and the pleading, written motion, or other paper drawing into question the constitutionality of a state statute or a county or municipal charter, ordinance, or franchise on the Attorney General or the state attorney of the judicial circuit in which the action is pending, by either certified or registered mail. Service of the notice and pleading, written motion, or other paper does not require joinder of the Attorney General or the state attorney as a party to the action. FL ST RCP Rule 1.071.

E. Format

1. *Documents; Type and size.* Documents subject to the exceptions set forth in FL ST J ADMIN Rule 2.525(d) shall be filed on recycled paper measuring eight and one half by eleven (8 1/2 by 11) inches. For purposes of FL ST J ADMIN Rule 2.520, paper is recycled if it contains a minimum content of fifty (50) percent waste paper. Xerographic reduction of legal-size (eight and one half by fourteen (8 1/2 by 14) inches) documents to letter size (eight and one half by eleven (8 1/2 by 11) inches) is prohibited. All other documents filed by electronic transmission shall be filed in a format capable of being printed in a format consistent with the provisions of FL ST J ADMIN Rule 2.250. FL ST J ADMIN Rule 2.520(b).
    a. *Exhibits.* Any exhibit or attachment filed with pleadings or papers may be filed in its original size. FL ST J ADMIN Rule 2.520(c).
    b. *Recording space.* On all papers and documents prepared and filed by the court or by any party to a proceeding which are to be recorded in the public records of any county, including but not limited to final money judgments and notices of lis pendens, a three (3) inch by three (3) inch space at the top right-hand corner on the first page and a one (1) inch by three (3) inch space at the top right-hand corner on each subsequent page shall be left blank and reserved for use by the clerk of court. FL ST J ADMIN Rule 2.520(d).
        i. *Exceptions to recording space.* Any papers or documents created by persons or entities over which the filing party has no control, including but not limited to wills, codicils, trusts, or other testamentary documents; documents prepared or executed by any public officer; documents prepared, executed, acknowledged, or proved outside of the State of Florida; or documents created by State or Federal government agencies, may be filed without the space required by FL ST J ADMIN Rule 2.520. FL ST J ADMIN Rule 2.520(e).
    c. *Noncompliance.* No clerk of court is permitted to refuse to file any document or paper because of noncompliance with the Florida Rules of Judicial Administration. However, upon request of the clerk of court, noncomplying documents must be resubmitted in accordance with the formatting rules. FL ST J ADMIN Rule 2.520(f).
2. *Caption.* Every pleading, motion, order, judgment, or other paper shall have a caption containing the name of the court, the file number, and except for in rem proceedings, including forfeiture proceedings, the name of the first party on each side with an appropriate indication of other parties, and a designation identifying the party filing it and its nature or the nature of the order, as the case may be. In any in rem proceeding, every pleading, motion, order, judgment, or other paper shall have a caption containing the name of the court, the file number, the style "In re" (followed by the name or general description of the property), and a designation of the person or entity filing it and its nature or the nature of the order, as the case may be. In an in rem forfeiture proceeding, the style shall be "In re forfeiture of" (followed by the name of the general description of the property). All papers filed in the action shall be styled in such a manner as to indicate clearly the subject matter of the paper and the party requesting or obtaining relief. FL ST RCP Rule 1.100(c)(1).
3. *Writing and written defined.* Writing or written means a document containing information, an application, or a stipulation. FL ST RCP Rule 1.080(c).
4. *Rule abbreviations*
    a. The Florida Rules of Civil Procedure and shall be abbreviated as Fla.R.Civ.P. FL ST RCP Rule 1.010.
    b. The Florida Rules of Judicial Administration shall be abbreviated as Fla. R. Jud. Admin. FL ST J ADMIN Rule 2.110.
5. *Nonverification.* Except when otherwise specifically provided by the Florida Rules of Civil Procedure or an applicable statute, every pleading or other document of a party represented by an attorney need not be verified or accompanied by an affidavit. FL ST RCP Rule 1.030; FL ST J ADMIN Rule 2.515(a).

6. *Attorney signature*
   a. *Attorney signature.* Every pleading and other document of a party represented by an attorney shall be signed by at least one (1) attorney of record in that attorney's individual name whose current record Florida Bar address, telephone number, including area code, primary e-mail address and secondary e-mail addresses, if any, and Florida Bar number shall be stated, and who shall be duly licensed to practice law in Florida or who shall have received permission to appear in the particular case as provided in FL ST J ADMIN Rule 2.510. FL ST J ADMIN Rule 2.515(a).
      i. The attorney may be required by the court to give the address of, and to vouch for the attorney's authority to represent, the party. FL ST J ADMIN Rule 2.515(a).
      ii. The signature of an attorney shall constitute a certificate by the attorney that the attorney has read the pleading or other document; that to the best of the attorney's knowledge, information, and belief there is good ground to support it; and that it is not interposed for delay. FL ST J ADMIN Rule 2.515(a).
      iii. If a pleading is not signed or is signed with intent to defeat the purpose of FL ST J ADMIN Rule 2.515, it may be stricken and the action may proceed as though the pleading or other document had not been served. FL ST J ADMIN Rule 2.515(a).
   b. *Pro se litigant signature.* A party who is not represented by an attorney shall sign any pleading or other paper and state the party's address and telephone number, including area code. FL ST J ADMIN Rule 2.515(b).
   c. *Form of signature*
      i. The signatures required on pleadings and documents by FL ST J ADMIN Rule 2.515(a) and FL ST J ADMIN Rule 2.515(b) may be:
         - Original signatures;
         - Original signatures that have been reproduced by electronic means, such as on electronically transmitted documents or photocopied documents;
         - Electronic signatures using the "/s/," "s/," or "/s" formats by or at the direction of the person signing; or
         - Any other signature format authorized by general law, so long as the clerk where the proceeding is pending has the capability of receiving and has obtained approval from the Supreme Court of Florida to accept pleadings and documents with that signature format. FL ST J ADMIN Rule 2.515(c)(1).
      ii. An attorney, party, or other person who files a pleading or paper by electronic transmission that does not contain the original signature of that attorney, party, or other person shall file that identical pleading or paper in paper form containing an original signature of that attorney, party, or other person (hereinafter called the follow-up filing) immediately thereafter. The follow-up filing is not required if the Supreme Court of Florida has entered an order directing the clerk of court to discontinue accepting the follow-up filing. FL ST J ADMIN Rule 2.515(c)(2).
      iii. The placement of a "/s/" or the image of a signature by an attorney or party or affected non-party signature line on an electronically filed document shall be accepted as the signature and shall verify to the Court the filer is in possession of the originally executed document. Notwithstanding the manner in which an electronic document is signed the originally executed pleading or paper shall be maintained in the filer's possession for a minimum of one (1) year after final disposition and time for appeal of the case. The originally executed document shall be produced for filing or inspection as directed by the Court. FL ST 17 J CIR 2012-16-CIV.
7. *Forms*
   a. *Process.* The forms of process, notice of lis pendens, and notice of action provided in the Florida Rules of Civil Procedure are sufficient. Variations from the forms do not void process or notices that are otherwise sufficient. FL ST RCP Rule 1.900(a).
   b. *Other forms.* The other forms provided in the Florida Rules of Civil Procedure are sufficient for the

matters that are covered by them. So long as the substance is expressed without prolixity, the forms may be varied to meet the facts of a particular case. FL ST RCP Rule 1.900(b).

c. *Formal matters.* Captions, except for the designation of the paper, are omitted from the forms provided in the Florida Rules of Civil Procedure. A general form of caption is the first form provided. Signatures are omitted from pleadings and motions. FL ST RCP Rule 1.900(c).

8. *Notices to persons with disabilities.* All notices of court proceedings to be held in a public facility, and all process compelling appearance at such proceedings, shall include the following statement in bold face, fourteen (14) point Times New Roman or Courier font: "If you are a person with a disability who needs any accommodation in order to participate in this proceeding, you are entitled, at no cost to you, to the provision of certain assistance. Please contact [identify applicable court personnel by name, address, and telephone number] at least seven (7) days before your scheduled court appearance, or immediately upon receiving this notification if the time before the scheduled appearance is less than seven (7) days; if you are hearing or voice impaired, call 711." FL ST J ADMIN Rule 2.540(c)(1). For further information, please see FL ST 17 J CIR 2010-49-GEN.

9. *Minimization of the filing of sensitive information*

a. *Limitations for court filings.* Unless authorized by FL ST J ADMIN Rule 2.425(b), statute, another rule of court, or the court orders otherwise, designated sensitive information filed with the court must be limited to the following format:

i. The initials of a person known to be a minor;

ii. The year of birth of a person's birth date;

iii. No portion of any: Social security number, Bank account number, Credit card account number, Charge account number, or Debit account number;

iv. The last four digits of any: Taxpayer identification number (TIN), Employee identification number, Driver's license number, Passport number, Telephone number, Financial account number, except as set forth in FL ST J ADMIN Rule 2.425(a)(3), Brokerage account number, Insurance policy account number, Loan account number, Customer account number, or Patient or health care number;

v. A truncated version of any: Email address, Computer user name, Password, or Personal identification number (PIN); and

vi. A truncated version of any other sensitive information as provided by court order. FL ST J ADMIN Rule 2.425(a).

b. *Exceptions.* FL ST J ADMIN Rule 2.425(a) does not apply to the following:

i. An account number which identifies the property alleged to be the subject of a proceeding;

ii. The record of an administrative or agency proceeding;

iii. The record in appellate or review proceedings;

iv. The birth date of a minor whenever the birth date is necessary for the court to establish or maintain subject matter jurisdiction;

v. The name of a minor in any order relating to parental responsibility, time-sharing, or child support;

vi. The name of a minor in any document or order affecting the minor's ownership of real property;

vii. The birth date of a party in a writ of attachment or notice to payor;

viii. In traffic and criminal proceedings: a pro se filing; a court filing that is related to a criminal matter or investigation and that is prepared before the filing of a criminal charge or is not filed as part of any docketed criminal case; an arrest or search warrant or any information in support thereof; a charging document and an affidavit or other documents filed in support of any charging document, including any driving records; a statement of particulars; discovery material introduced into evidence or otherwise filed with the court; and all information necessary for the proper issuance and execution of a subpoena duces tecum;

ix. Information used by the clerk for case maintenance purposes or the courts for case management purposes; and

x. Information which is relevant and material to an issue before the court. FL ST J ADMIN Rule 2.425(b).

c. *Remedies.* Upon motion by a party or interested person or sua sponte by the court, the court may order remedies, sanctions or both for a violation of FL ST J ADMIN Rule 2.425(a). Following notice and an opportunity to respond, the court may impose sanctions if such filing was not made in good faith. FL ST J ADMIN Rule 2.425(c).

d. *Motions not restricted.* FL ST J ADMIN Rule 2.425 does not restrict a party's right to move for protective order, to move to file documents under seal, or to request a determination of the confidentiality of records. FL ST J ADMIN Rule 2.425(d).

e. *Application.* FL ST J ADMIN Rule 2.425 does not affect the application of constitutional provisions, statutes, or rules of court regarding confidential information or access to public information. FL ST J ADMIN Rule 2.425(e).

F. Filing and Service Requirements

1. *Filing requirements.* All original documents must be filed with the court either before service or immediately thereafter, unless otherwise provided for by general law or other rules. If the original of any bond or other document is not placed in the court file, a certified copy must be so placed by the clerk. FL ST J ADMIN Rule 2.516(d). All documents shall be filed in conformity with the requirements of FL ST J ADMIN Rule 2.525. FL ST RCP Rule 1.080(b). All documents filed in any court shall be filed by electronic transmission in accordance with FL ST J ADMIN Rule 2.525. "Documents" means pleadings, motions, petitions, memoranda, briefs, notices, exhibits, declarations, affidavits, orders, judgments, decrees, writs, opinions, and any other paper or writing submitted to a court. FL ST J ADMIN Rule 2.520(a). All documents that are court records, as defined in FL ST J ADMIN Rule 2.430(a)(1), must be filed by electronic transmission, provided that: (1) the clerk has the ability to accept and retain such documents; (2) the clerk or the chief judge of the circuit has requested permission to accept documents filed by electronic transmission; and (3) the supreme court has entered an order granting permission to the clerk to accept documents filed by electronic transmission. FL ST J ADMIN Rule 2.525(c)(1).

a. *Definition.* "Electronic transmission of documents" means the sending of information by electronic signals to, by or from a court or clerk, which when received can be transformed and stored or transmitted on paper, microfilm, magnetic storage device, optical imaging system, CD-ROM, flash drive, other electronic data storage system, server, case maintenance system ("CM"), electronic court filing ("ECF") system, statewide or local electronic portal ("e-portal"), or other electronic record keeping system authorized by the supreme court in a format sufficient to communicate the information on the original document in a readable format. Electronic transmission of documents includes electronic mail ("e-mail") and any internet-based transmission procedure, and may include procedures allowing for documents to be signed or verified by electronic means. FL ST J ADMIN Rule 2.525(a).

i. The filing of documents with the court as required by the Florida Rules of Judicial Administration must be made by filing them with the clerk in accordance with FL ST J ADMIN Rule 2.525, except that the judge may permit documents to be filed with the judge, in which event the judge must note the filing date before him or her on the documents and transmit them to the clerk. The date of filing is that shown on the face of the document by the judge's notation or the clerk's time stamp, whichever is earlier. FL ST J ADMIN Rule 2.516(e).

b. *Application.* Any court or clerk of the court may accept the electronic transmission of documents for filing after the clerk, together with input from the chief judge of the circuit, has obtained approval of the procedures and program for doing so from the Supreme Court of Florida. FL ST J ADMIN Rule 2.525(b).

c. *Exceptions*

i. Paper documents and other submissions may be manually submitted to the clerk or court:

- When the clerk does not have the ability to accept and retain documents by electronic filing or has not had ECF Procedures approved by the supreme court;

- For filing by any self-represented party or any self-represented nonparty unless specific ECF Procedures provide a means to file documents electronically. However, any self-represented nonparty that is a governmental or public agency and any other agency, partnership, corporation, or business entity acting on behalf of any governmental or public agency may file documents by electronic transmission if such entity has the capability of filing documents electronically;
- For filing by attorneys excused from e-mail service in accordance with FL ST J ADMIN Rule 2.516(b);
- When submitting evidentiary exhibits or filing non-documentary materials;
- When the filing involves documents in excess of twenty-five (25) megabytes (25MB) in size. For such filings, documents may be transmitted using an electronic storage medium that the clerk has the ability to accept, which may include a CD-ROM, flash drive, or similar storage medium;
- When filed in open court, as permitted by the court;
- When paper filing is permitted by any approved statewide or local ECF procedures; and
- If any court determines that justice so requires. FL ST J ADMIN Rule 2.525(d).

ii. Any document in paper form submitted under FL ST J ADMIN Rule 2.525(d) is filed when it is received by the clerk or court and the clerk shall immediately thereafter convert any filed paper document to an electronic document. "Convert to an electronic document" means optically capturing an image of a paper document and using character recognition software to recover as much of the document's text as practicable and then indexing and storing the document in the official court file. FL ST J ADMIN Rule 2.525(c)(4).

iii. Any storage medium submitted under FL ST J ADMIN Rule 2.525(d)(5) is filed when received by the clerk or court and the clerk shall immediately thereafter transfer the electronic documents from the storage device to the official court file. FL ST J ADMIN Rule 2.525(c)(5).

iv. If the filer of any paper document authorized under FL ST J ADMIN Rule 2.525(d) provides a self-addressed, postage-paid envelope for return of the paper document after it is converted to electronic form by the clerk, the clerk shall place the paper document in the envelope and deposit it in the mail. Except when a paper document is required to be maintained, the clerk may recycle any filed paper document that is not to be returned to the filer. FL ST J ADMIN Rule 2.525(c)(6).

v. The clerk may convert any paper document filed before the effective date of FL ST J ADMIN Rule 2.525 to an electronic document. Unless the clerk is required to maintain the paper document, if the paper document has been converted to an electronic document by the clerk, the paper document is no longer part of the official court file and may be removed and recycled. FL ST J ADMIN Rule 2.525(c)(7).

d. *Official court file.* For information on what constitutes the official court file, please see FL ST J ADMIN Rule 2.525(c)(2), FL ST J ADMIN Rule 2.525(c)(3).

e. *Administration.* All attorneys, parties, or other persons using this rule to file documents are required to make arrangements with the court or clerk for the payment of any charges authorized by general law or the supreme court before filing any document by electronic transmission. FL ST J ADMIN Rule 2.525(f)(2).

f. *Filing date.* The filing date for an electronically transmitted document is the date and time that such filing is acknowledged by an electronic stamp or otherwise, pursuant to any procedure set forth in any ECF Procedures approved by the supreme court, or the date the last page of such filing is received by the court or clerk. FL ST J ADMIN Rule 2.525(f)(3).

g. *Accessibility.* All documents transmitted in any electronic form under FL ST J ADMIN Rule 2.525 must comply with the accessibility requirements of FL ST J ADMIN Rule 2.526. FL ST J ADMIN Rule 2.525(g).

h. *Provisions for electronic filing in the Seventeenth Circuit.* Attorneys may electronically file plead-

ings and papers on existing cases in circuit civil divisions 1, 7, 9, 19, 26 and 27. The following documents may be scanned and efiled; however, the original must be filed with the Clerk: Documents ordered by the Court; and original documents required by law or rule of procedure to be filed with the Clerk. Self represented individuals shall file pleadings and papers with the Clerk. The Clerk within twenty four (24) hours of receipt of an electronic document shall either accept or reject the electronic document for filing and send electronic notice to the filer. FL ST 17 J CIR 2012-16-CIV.

i. *Technical failures.* If a document filed electronically is not received due to: an error in the transmission of the document to the Clerk or any vendor of the Clerk to provide electronic court record filing services which is unknown to an attorney or party or affected non party, or a failure to process the electronic document when received by the Clerk or rejection by the Clerk, or any other technical problems experienced by the attorney or party or affected non party, the Court may, after an evidentiary hearing and upon satisfactory proof, enter an order permitting the document to be filed nunc pro tunc to the date it was first attempted to be sent electronically. FL ST 17 J CIR 2012-16-CIV.

j. *Filing of pleadings or papers at any office of the clerk of court.* The Clerk of Courts, commencing November 3, 2008, shall accept for filing, at the central courthouse, north satellite courthouse, south satellite courthouse, and west satellite courthouse any pleading or motion or other document for filing in the court file from any attorney or party for an existing case except as otherwise set forth. FL ST 17 J CIR 2008-153-GEN. See FL ST 17 J CIR 2008-153-GEN for specific exceptions.

2. *Service requirements.* Every pleading subsequent to the initial pleading, all orders, and every other document filed in the action must be served in conformity with the requirements of FL ST J ADMIN Rule 2.516. FL ST RCP Rule 1.080(a).

a. *Service; When required.* Unless the court otherwise orders, or a statute or supreme court administrative order specifies a different means of service, every pleading subsequent to the initial pleading and every other document filed in any court proceeding, except applications for witness subpoenas and documents served by formal notice or required to be served in the manner provided for service of formal notice, must be served in accordance with FL ST J ADMIN Rule 2.516 on each party. No service need be made on parties against whom a default has been entered, except that pleadings asserting new or additional claims against them must be served in the manner provided for service of summons. FL ST J ADMIN Rule 2.516(a).

b. *Service; How made.* When service is required or permitted to be made upon a party represented by an attorney, service must be made upon the attorney unless service upon the party is ordered by the court. FL ST J ADMIN Rule 2.516(b).

i. *Service by electronic mail ("e-mail").* All documents required or permitted to be served on another party must be served by e-mail, unless FL ST J ADMIN Rule 2.516 otherwise provides. When, in addition to service by e-mail, the sender also utilizes another means of service provided for in FL ST J ADMIN Rule 2.516(b)(2), any differing time limits and other provisions applicable to that other means of service control. FL ST J ADMIN Rule 2.516(b)(1). Any document electronically transmitted to a court or clerk must also be served on all parties and interested persons in accordance with the applicable rules of court. FL ST J ADMIN Rule 2.525(e)(2).

- *Service on attorneys.* Upon appearing in a proceeding, an attorney must serve a designation of a primary e-mail address and may designate no more than two (2) secondary e-mail addresses. Thereafter, service must be directed to all designated e-mail addresses in that proceeding. Every document filed by an attorney thereafter must include the primary e-mail address of that attorney and any secondary e-mail addresses. If an attorney does not designate any e-mail address for service, documents may be served on that attorney at the e-mail address on record with The Florida Bar. FL ST J ADMIN Rule 2.516(b)(1)(A).

- *Exception to e-mail service on attorneys.* Service by an attorney on another attorney must be made by e-mail unless excused by the court. Upon motion by an attorney demonstrating that the attorney has no e-mail account and lacks access to the Internet at the attorney's office, the court may excuse the attorney from the requirements of e-mail service. Service

on and by an attorney excused by the court from e-mail service must be by the means provided in FL ST J ADMIN Rule 2.516(b)(2). FL ST J ADMIN Rule 2.516(b)(1)(B).

- *Service on and by parties not represented by an attorney.* Any party not represented by an attorney may serve a designation of a primary e-mail address and also may designate no more than two (2) secondary e-mail addresses to which service must be directed in that proceeding by the means provided in FL ST J ADMIN Rule 2.516(b)(1). If a party not represented by an attorney does not designate an e-mail address for service in a proceeding, service on and by that party must be by the means provided in FL ST J ADMIN Rule 2.516(b)(2). FL ST J ADMIN Rule 2.516(b)(1)(C).
- *Time of service.* Service by e-mail is complete when it is sent. FL ST J ADMIN Rule 2.516(b)(1)(D). An e-mail is deemed served on the date it is sent. FL ST J ADMIN Rule 2.516(b)(1)(D)(i). If the sender learns that the e-mail did not reach the address of the person to be served, the sender must immediately send another copy by e-mail, or by a means authorized by FL ST J ADMIN Rule 2.516(b)(2). FL ST J ADMIN Rule 2.516(b)(1)(D)(ii). E-mail service is treated as service by mail for the computation of time. FL ST J ADMIN Rule 2.516(b)(1)(D)(iii).

ii. *Format of e-mail for service.* Service of a document by e-mail is made by attaching a copy of the document in PDF format to an e-mail sent to all addresses designated by the attorney or party. FL ST J ADMIN Rule 2.516(b)(1)(E).

- All documents served by e-mail must be attached to an e-mail message containing a subject line beginning with the words "SERVICE OF COURT DOCUMENT" in all capital letters, followed by the case number of the proceeding in which the documents are being served. FL ST J ADMIN Rule 2.516(b)(1)(E)(i).
- The body of the e-mail must identify the court in which the proceeding is pending, the case number, the name of the initial party on each side, the title of each document served with that e-mail, and the sender's name and telephone number. FL ST J ADMIN Rule 2.516(b)(1)(E)(ii).
- Any document served by e-mail may be signed by the "/s/" format, as long as the filed original is signed in accordance with the applicable rule of procedure. FL ST J ADMIN Rule 2.516(b)(1)(E)(iii).
- Any e-mail which, together with its attached documents, exceeds five megabytes (5MB) in size, must be divided and sent as separate e-mails, no one of which may exceed five megabytes (5MB) in size and each of which must be sequentially numbered in the subject line. FL ST J ADMIN Rule 2.516(b)(1)(E)(iv).

iii. *Service by other means.* In addition to, and not in lieu of, service by e-mail, service may also be made upon attorneys by any of the means specified in FL ST J ADMIN Rule 2.516(b)(2). Service on and by all parties who are not represented by an attorney and who do not designate an e-mail address, and on and by all attorneys excused from e-mail service, must be made by delivering a copy of the document or by mailing it to the party or attorney at their last known address or, if no address is known, by leaving it with the clerk of the court. Service by mail is complete upon mailing. Delivery of a copy within FL ST J ADMIN Rule 2.516 is complete upon:

- Handing it to the attorney or to the party,
- Leaving it at the attorney's or party's office with a clerk or other person in charge thereof,
- If there is no one in charge, leaving it in a conspicuous place therein,
- If the office is closed or the person to be served has no office, leaving it at the person's usual place of abode with some person of his or her family above fifteen (15) years of age and informing such person of the contents, or
- Transmitting it by facsimile to the attorney's or party's office with a cover sheet containing the sender's name, firm, address, telephone number, and facsimile number, and the

number of pages transmitted. When service is made by facsimile, a copy must also be served by any other method permitted by FL ST J ADMIN Rule 2.516. Facsimile service occurs when transmission is complete. FL ST J ADMIN Rule 2.516(b)(2)(A) through FL ST J ADMIN Rule 2.516(b)(2)(E).

- Service by delivery after 5:00 p.m. must be deemed to have been made by mailing on the date of delivery. FL ST J ADMIN Rule 2.516(b)(2)(F).

c. *Service; Numerous defendants.* In actions when the parties are unusually numerous, the court may regulate the service contemplated by the Florida Rules of Judicial Administration on motion or on its own initiative in such manner as may be found to be just and reasonable. FL ST J ADMIN Rule 2.516(c).

d. *Service by clerk.* Service of notices and other documents required to be made by the clerk must also be done as provided in FL ST J ADMIN Rule 2.516(b). FL ST J ADMIN Rule 2.516(g).

G. Hearings

1. *Communication equipment*

a. *Definition.* Communication equipment means a conference telephone or other electronic device that permits all those appearing or participating to hear and speak to each other, provided that all conversation of all parties is audible to all persons present. FL ST J ADMIN Rule 2.530(a).

b. *Use by all parties.* A county or circuit court judge may, upon the court's own motion or upon the written request of a party, direct that communication equipment be used for a motion hearing, pretrial conference, or a status conference. A judge must give notice to the parties and consider any objections they may have to the use of communication equipment before directing that communication equipment be used. The decision to use communication equipment over the objection of parties will be in the sound discretion of the trial court, except as noted below. FL ST J ADMIN Rule 2.530(b).

c. *Use only by requesting party.* A county or circuit court judge may, upon the written request of a party upon reasonable notice to all other parties, permit a requesting party to participate through communication equipment in a scheduled motion hearing; however, any such request (except in criminal, juvenile, and appellate proceedings) must be granted, absent a showing of good cause to deny the same, where the hearing is set for not longer than fifteen (15) minutes. FL ST J ADMIN Rule 2.530(c).

d. *Testimony*

i. *Generally.* A county or circuit court judge, general magistrate, special magistrate, or hearing officer may allow testimony to be taken through communication equipment if all parties consent or if permitted by another applicable rule of procedure. FL ST J ADMIN Rule 2.530(d)(1).

ii. *Procedure.* Any party desiring to present testimony through communication equipment shall, prior to the hearing or trial at which the testimony is to be presented, contact all parties to determine whether each party consents to this form of testimony. The party seeking to present the testimony shall move for permission to present testimony through communication equipment, which motion shall set forth good cause as to why the testimony should be allowed in this form. FL ST J ADMIN Rule 2.530(d)(2).

iii. *Oath.* Testimony may be taken through communication equipment only if a notary public or other person authorized to administer oaths in the witness's jurisdiction is present with the witness and administers the oath consistent with the laws of the jurisdiction. FL ST J ADMIN Rule 2.530(d)(3).

iv. *Confrontation rights.* In juvenile and criminal proceedings the defendant must make an informed waiver of any confrontation rights that may be abridged by the use of communication equipment. FL ST J ADMIN Rule 2.530(d)(4).

v. *Video testimony.* If the testimony to be presented utilizes video conferencing or comparable two-way visual capabilities, the court in its discretion may modify the procedures set forth in

FL ST J ADMIN Rule 2.530 to accommodate the technology utilized. FL ST J ADMIN Rule 2.530(d)(5).

e. *Burden of expense.* The cost for the use of the communication equipment is the responsibility of the requesting party unless otherwise directed by the court. FL ST J ADMIN Rule 2.530(e).

2. *Uniform motion calendar.* The Circuit Judges of the general civil/family division (excluding juvenile/dependency) shall maintain a uniform motion calendar from 8:45 A.M. to 9:30 A.M., Monday through Thursday. The motion calendar shall end PROMPTLY at 9:30 A.M. All parties shall be prepared to proceed at 8:45 A.M., and if one party fails to timely appear, the matter may proceed on the merits in his/her absence. FL ST 17 J CIR LOCAL RULE NO. 10A(1).
3. *Noticed motion limitation.* No more than two (2) motions may be noticed for each case on any given day except by leave of court. FL ST 17 J CIR LOCAL RULE NO. 10A(4).
4. *Ex parte and non-evidentiary motion.* Ex parte matters, non-evidentiary motions, and uncontested proceedings for adoptions, or dissolution may be heard on the uniform motion calendar, provided such matters can be conducted in five (5) minutes equally allocated among the parties and the moving party shall so certify as specified in FL ST 17 J CIR LOCAL RULE NO. 10A(3). FL ST 17 J CIR LOCAL RULE NO. 10A(6).
5. *Good faith effort to resolve issues.* Prior to appearing before the court, the parties shall discuss the issues raised in the pending motion, and both parties shall be prepared to certify at the hearing they have made a good faith effort to resolve the issues. FL ST 17 J CIR LOCAL RULE NO. 10A(7).
6. *Re-noticing hearings.* When the motion calendar has been filled, the judge's office shall notify the party noticing any hearings which cannot be reached. The noticing party shall call opposing counsel and re-notice the hearing. FL ST 17 J CIR LOCAL RULE NO. 10A(9).
7. *Hearing cancellation.* Motion calendar hearings may be canceled by the attorney who set the hearing. FL ST 17 J CIR LOCAL RULE NO. 10A(10).
8. *Other motion calendars.* Hearing officers/general masters shall conduct a motion calendar, the dates and times of which shall be determined by the hearing officer/general master or by administrative order. FL ST 17 J CIR LOCAL RULE NO. 10A(11).
9. *Sanctions.* Failure to comply with the procedures designated in the above paragraphs may result in the hearing being stricken from the docket or such other sanctions as the court deems appropriate. FL ST 17 J CIR LOCAL RULE NO. 10A(12).

H. Forms

1. Official Motion for Directed Verdict Forms for Florida

a. Caption. FL ST RCP Form 1.901.

b. Notice of compliance when constitutional challenge is brought. FL ST RCP Form 1.975.

2. Motion for Directed Verdict Forms for Florida

a. Motion; For directed verdict; At close of adverse party's evidence. FL-PP § 5:86.

b. Motion; For directed verdict; At close of all of evidence. FL-PP § 5:87.

c. Motion; Request to go to jury if motions by both parties are denied. FL-PP § 5:88.

d. Order; Granting defendant's motion for directed verdict; Insufficiency of plaintiff's evidence. FL-PP § 5:89.

e. Motion; Directed verdict, renewed. FL-PRACFORM § 7:62.

f. Form for motion for directed verdict at close of plaintiff's case. FL-RCPF R 1.480(24).

g. Form for motion for directed verdict at close of defendant's case. FL-RCPF R 1.480(25).

h. Form for motion to set aside verdict and enter directed verdict. FL-RCPF R 1.480(26).

I. Checklist

(I) ❑ Matters to be considered by moving party

(a) ❑ Required documents

(1) ❑ Notice of hearing/Motion

(2) ❑ Good faith certificate

(3) ❑ Certificate of service

(b) ❑ Supplemental documents

(1) ❑ Proposed order, copies, stamped envelopes

(2) ❑ Notice of constitutional question

(c) ❑ Time for making motion

(1) ❑ Before a verdict is returned - A directed verdict is available to the defendant at the close of the plaintiff's evidence or to either party at the close of all of the evidence

(2) ❑ After a verdict is returned - Within ten (10) days after the return of a verdict, a party who has timely moved for a directed verdict may serve a motion to enter judgment in accordance with the motion for a directed verdict

(3) ❑ No verdict is returned - If a verdict was not returned, a party who has timely moved for a directed verdict may serve a motion for judgment in accordance with the motion for a directed verdict within ten (10) days after discharge of the jury

(4) ❑ General motion timing - A copy of any written motion which may not be heard ex parte and a copy of the notice of the hearing thereof shall be served a reasonable time before the time specified for the hearing; copies of the notice of hearing, the motion, and any pleading or interrogatories to which the motion is addressed shall be in the hands of the Judicial Assistant and opposing party at least four (4) working days in advance of the hearing

(II) ❑ Matters to be considered by opposing party

(a) ❑ Required documents

(1) ❑ Response to motion

(2) ❑ Certificate of service

(b) ❑ Supplemental documents

(1) ❑ Proposed order, copies, stamped envelopes

(2) ❑ Notice of constitutional question

(c) ❑ Time for service and filing of opposition

(1) ❑ No time specified for responding to a motion

Requests, Notices and Applications
Request for Production of Documents

Document Last Updated January 2013

A. Applicable Rules

1. *State rules*

a. Nonverification of pleadings. FL ST RCP Rule 1.030.

b. Service and filing of pleadings, orders, and documents. FL ST RCP Rule 1.080.

c. Time. FL ST RCP Rule 1.090.

d. Pleadings and motions. FL ST RCP Rule 1.100.

e. Pretrial procedure. FL ST RCP Rule 1.200.

f. General provisions governing discovery. FL ST RCP Rule 1.280.

g. Depositions upon oral examination. FL ST RCP Rule 1.310.

h. Interrogatories to parties. FL ST RCP Rule 1.340.

i. Production of documents and things and entry upon land for inspection and other purposes. FL ST RCP Rule 1.350.

j. Production of documents and things without deposition. FL ST RCP Rule 1.351.

k. Examination of persons. FL ST RCP Rule 1.360.

l. Requests for admission. FL ST RCP Rule 1.370.

m. Failure to make discovery; Sanctions. FL ST RCP Rule 1.380.

n. Depositions of expert witnesses. FL ST RCP Rule 1.390.

o. Relief from judgment, decrees or orders. FL ST RCP Rule 1.540.

p. Forms. FL ST RCP Rule 1.900.

q. Retention of court records. FL ST J ADMIN Rule 2.430.

r. Foreign attorneys. FL ST J ADMIN Rule 2.510.

s. Signature of attorneys and parties. FL ST J ADMIN Rule 2.515.

t. Paper. FL ST J ADMIN Rule 2.520.

u. Electronic filing. FL ST J ADMIN Rule 2.525.

v. Requests for accommodations by persons with disabilities. FL ST J ADMIN Rule 2.540.

w. Minimization of the filing of sensitive information. FL ST J ADMIN Rule 2.425.

x. Accessibility of information and technology. FL ST J ADMIN Rule 2.526.

2. *Local rules*

a. Standards of professional courtesy. FL ST 17 J CIR I-94-O-1.

b. Administrative order authorizing the filing of pleadings or papers at any office of the clerk of court. FL ST 17 J CIR 2008-153-GEN.

c. Administrative order regarding provision of ADA accommodations. FL ST 17 J CIR 2010-49-GEN.

d. Administrative order establishing electronic filing procedures for the civil division. FL ST 17 J CIR 2012-16-CIV.

B. Timing

1. *Request for production of documents.* Without leave of court the request may be served on the plaintiff after commencement of the action and on any other party with or after service of the process and initial pleading on that party. FL ST RCP Rule 1.350(b).

2. *Notice of intent to serve subpoena.* A party desiring production under FL ST RCP Rule 1.351 shall serve notice as provided in FL ST RCP Rule 1.080 on every other party of the intent to serve a subpoena under FL ST RCP Rule 1.351 at least ten (10) days before the subpoena is issued if service is by delivery and fifteen (15) days before the subpoena is issued if the service is by mail or e-mail. FL ST RCP Rule 1.351(b).

3. *Sequence and timing of discovery.* Except as provided in FL ST RCP Rule 1.280(b)(5) or unless the court upon motion for the convenience of parties and witnesses and in the interest of justice orders otherwise, methods of discovery may be used in any sequence, and the fact that a party is conducting discovery, whether by deposition or otherwise, shall not delay any other party's discovery. FL ST RCP Rule 1.280(e).

4. *Standard of professional conduct; Scheduling*

a. Attorneys should endeavor to provide opposing counsel, parties, witnesses, and other affected persons, sufficient notice of depositions, hearings and other proceedings, except upon agreement of course, in an emergency, or in other circumstances compelling more expedited scheduling. As a general rule, actual notice should be no less than five (5) business days for instate depositions, ten (10) business days for out-of-state depositions and four (4) business days for hearings. FL ST 17 J CIR I-94-O-1(I)(1).

b. Attorneys should communicate with opposing counsel prior to scheduling depositions, hearings and other proceedings, in an effort to schedule them at times that are mutually convenient for all interested persons. Further, sufficient time should be reserved to permit a complete presentation by counsel for all parties. FL ST 17 J CIR I-94-O-1(I)(2).

c. Attorneys should notify opposing counsel, the court, and others affected, of scheduling conflicts as soon as they become apparent. Further, attorneys should cooperate with one another regarding all reasonable rescheduling requests that do not prejudice their clients or unduly delay a proceeding. FL ST 17 J CIR I-94-O-1(I)(3).

d. Attorneys should promptly notify the court or other tribunal of any resolution between the parties that renders a scheduled court appearance unnecessary or otherwise moot. FL ST 17 J CIR I-94-O-1(I)(4).

e. Attorneys should grant reasonable requests by opposing counsel for extensions of time within which to respond to pleadings, discovery, and other matters when such an extension will not prejudice their client or unduly delay a proceeding. FL ST 17 J CIR I-94-O-1(I)(5).

5. *Timing considerations when filing electronically.* The filing date of an efiled document is when the last page is received by the Clerk. The electronic filing of a document does not modify any filing deadlines as required by law, rule of procedure, or court order. FL ST 17 J CIR 2012-16-CIV.

6. *Computation of time*

a. *Generally.* Computation of time shall be governed by FL ST J ADMIN Rule 2.514. FL ST RCP Rule 1.090(a). The following rules apply in computing time periods specified in any rule of procedure, local rule, court order, or statute that does not specify a method of computing time. FL ST J ADMIN Rule 2.514(a).

i. *Period stated in days or a longer unit.* When the period is stated in days or a longer unit of time (A) exclude the day of the event that triggers the period; (B) count every day, including intermediate Saturdays, Sundays, and legal holidays; and (C) include the last day of the period, but if the last day is a Saturday, Sunday, or legal holiday, or falls within any period of time extended through an order of the chief justice under FL ST J ADMIN Rule 2.205(a)(2)(B)(iv), the period continues to run until the end of the next day that is not a Saturday, Sunday, or legal holiday and does not fall within any period of time extended through an order of the chief justice. FL ST J ADMIN Rule 2.514(a)(1).

ii. *Period stated in hours.* When the period is stated in hours (A) begin counting immediately on the occurrence of the event that triggers the period; (B) count every hour, including hours during intermediate Saturdays, Sundays, and legal holidays; and (C) if the period would end on a Saturday, Sunday, or legal holiday, or during any period of time extended through an order of the chief justice under FL ST J ADMIN Rule 2.205(a)(2)(B)(iv), the period continues to run until the same time on the next day that is not a Saturday, Sunday, or legal holiday and does not fall within any period of time extended through an order of the chief justice. FL ST J ADMIN Rule 2.514(a)(2).

iii. *Period stated in days less than seven (7) days.* When the period stated in days is less than seven (7) days, intermediate Saturdays, Sundays, and legal holidays shall be excluded in the computation. FL ST J ADMIN Rule 2.514(a)(3).

iv. *"Last day" defined.* Unless a different time is set by a statute, local rule, or court order, the last day ends (A) for electronic filing or for service by any means, at midnight; and (B) for filing by other means, when the clerk's office is scheduled to close. FL ST J ADMIN Rule 2.514(a)(4).

v. *"Next day" defined.* The "next day" is determined by continuing to count forward when the period is measured after an event and backward when measured before an event. FL ST J ADMIN Rule 2.514(a)(5).

vi. *"Legal holiday" defined.* "Legal holiday" means (A) the day set aside by FL ST § 110.117, for

observing New Year's Day, Martin Luther King, Jr.'s Birthday, Memorial Day, Independence Day, Labor Day, Veterans' Day, Thanksgiving Day, the Friday after Thanksgiving Day, or Christmas Day, and (B) any day observed as a holiday by the clerk's office or as designated by the chief judge. FL ST J ADMIN Rule 2.514(a)(6).

b. *Additional time after service by mail or e-mail.* When a party may or must act within a specified time after service and service is made by mail or e-mail, five (5) days are added after the period that would otherwise expire under FL ST J ADMIN Rule 2.514(a). FL ST J ADMIN Rule 2.514(b).

c. *Enlargement.* When an act is required or allowed to be done at or within a specified time by order of court, by the Florida Rules of Civil Procedure, or by notice given thereunder, for cause shown the court at any time in its discretion (1) with or without notice, may order the period enlarged if request therefor is made before the expiration of the period originally prescribed or as extended by a previous order, or (2) upon motion made and notice after the expiration of the specified period, may permit the act to be done when failure to act was the result of excusable neglect, but it may not extend the time for making a motion for new trial, for rehearing, or to alter or amend a judgment; making a motion for relief from a judgment under FL ST RCP Rule 1.540(b); taking an appeal or filing a petition for certiorari; or making a motion for a directed verdict. FL ST RCP Rule 1.090(b).

d. *Unaffected by expiration of term.* The period of time provided for the doing of any act or the taking of any proceeding shall not be affected or limited by the continued existence or expiration of a term of court. The continued existence or expiration of a term of court in no way affects the power of a court to do any act or take any proceeding in any action which is or has been pending before it. FL ST RCP Rule 1.090(c).

C. General Requirements

1. *General provisions governing discovery*

a. *Discovery methods.* Parties may obtain discovery by one or more of the following methods: depositions upon oral examination or written questions; written interrogatories; production of documents or things or permission to enter upon land or other property for inspection and other purposes; physical and mental examinations; and requests for admission. Unless the court orders otherwise and under FL ST RCP Rule 1.280(c), the frequency of use of these methods is not limited, except as provided in FL ST RCP Rule 1.200, FL ST RCP Rule 1.340, and FL ST RCP Rule 1.370. FL ST RCP Rule 1.280(a).

b. *Scope of discovery.* Unless otherwise limited by order of the court in accordance with the Florida Rules of Civil Procedure, the scope of discovery is as follows:

i. *In general.* Parties may obtain discovery regarding any matter, not privileged, that is relevant to the subject matter of the pending action, whether it relates to the claim or defense of the party seeking discovery or the claim or defense of any other party, including the existence, description, nature, custody, condition, and location of any books, documents, or other tangible things and the identity and location of persons having knowledge of any discoverable matter. It is not ground for objection that the information sought will be inadmissible at the trial if the information sought appears reasonably calculated to lead to the discovery of admissible evidence. FL ST RCP Rule 1.280(b)(1).

ii. *Indemnity agreements.* A party may obtain discovery of the existence and contents of any agreement under which any person may be liable to satisfy part or all of a judgment that may be entered in the action or to indemnify or to reimburse a party for payments made to satisfy the judgment. Information concerning the agreement is not admissible in evidence at trial by reason of disclosure. FL ST RCP Rule 1.280(b)(2).

iii. *Electronically stored information.* A party may obtain discovery of electronically stored information in accordance with the Florida Rules of Civil Procedure. FL ST RCP Rule 1.280(b)(3).

iv. *Trial preparation; Materials.* Subject to the provisions of FL ST RCP Rule 1.280(b)(5), a party may obtain discovery of documents and tangible things otherwise discoverable under FL ST RCP Rule 1.280(b)(1) and prepared in anticipation of litigation or for trial by or for another party or by or for that party's representative, including that party's attorney, consultant, surety, indemnitor, insurer, or agent, only upon a showing that the party seeking discovery has need of the materials in the preparation of the case and is unable without undue hardship to obtain the substantial equivalent of the materials by other means. FL ST RCP Rule 1.280(b)(4).

- In ordering discovery of the materials when the required showing has been made, the court shall protect against disclosure of the mental impressions, conclusions, opinions, or legal theories of an attorney or other representative of a party concerning the litigation. FL ST RCP Rule 1.280(b)(4).
- Without the required showing a party may obtain a copy of a statement concerning the action or its subject matter previously made by that party. FL ST RCP Rule 1.280(b)(4).
- Upon request without the required showing a person not a party may obtain a copy of a statement concerning the action or its subject matter previously made by that person. If the request is refused, the person may move for an order to obtain a copy. The provisions of FL ST RCP Rule 1.380(a)(5) apply to the award of expenses incurred as a result of making the motion. FL ST RCP Rule 1.280(b)(4).
- For purposes of FL ST RCP Rule 1.280(b)(4), a statement previously made is a written statement signed or otherwise adopted or approved by the person making it, or a stenographic, mechanical, electrical, or other recording or transcription of it that is a substantially verbatim recital of an oral statement by the person making it and contemporaneously recorded. FL ST RCP Rule 1.280(b)(4).

v. *Trial preparation; Experts.* Discovery of facts known and opinions held by experts, otherwise discoverable under the provisions of FL ST RCP Rule 1.280(b)(1) and acquired or developed in anticipation of litigation or for trial, may be obtained only as follows:

- By interrogatories a party may require any other party to identify each person whom the other party expects to call as an expert witness at trial and to state the subject matter on which the expert is expected to testify, and to state the substance of the facts and opinions to which the expert is expected to testify and a summary of the grounds for each opinion. FL ST RCP Rule 1.280(b)(5)(A)(i).
- Any person disclosed by interrogatories or otherwise as a person expected to be called as an expert witness at trial may be deposed in accordance with FL ST RCP Rule 1.390 without motion or order of court. FL ST RCP Rule 1.280(b)(5)(A)(ii).
- A party may obtain the following discovery regarding any person disclosed by interrogatories or otherwise as a person expected to be called as an expert witness at trial: The scope of employment in the pending case and the compensation for such service, FL ST RCP Rule 1.280(b)(5)(A)(iii)(1); The expert's general litigation experience, including the percentage of work performed for plaintiffs and defendants, FL ST RCP Rule 1.280(b)(5)(A)(iii)(2); The identity of other cases, within a reasonable time period, in which the expert has testified by deposition or at trial, FL ST RCP Rule 1.280(b)(5)(A)(iii)(3); An approximation of the portion of the expert's involvement as an expert witness, which may be based on the number of hours, percentage of hours, or percentage of earned income derived from serving as an expert witness; however, the expert shall not be required to disclose his or her earnings as an expert witness or income derived from other services. FL ST RCP Rule 1.280(b)(5)(A)(iii)(4).
- An expert may be required to produce financial and business records only under the most unusual or compelling circumstances and may not be compelled to compile or produce nonexistent documents. Upon motion, the court may order further discovery by other means, subject to such restrictions as to scope and other provisions pursuant to FL ST RCP Rule 1.280(b)(5)(C) concerning fees and expenses as the court may deem appropriate. FL ST RCP Rule 1.280(b)(5).
- A party may discover facts known or opinions held by an expert who has been retained or specially employed by another party in anticipation of litigation or preparation for trial and

who is not expected to be called as a witness at trial, only as provided in FL ST RCP Rule 1.360(b) or upon a showing of exceptional circumstances under which it is impracticable for the party seeking discovery to obtain facts or opinions on the same subject by other means. FL ST RCP Rule 1.280(b)(5)(B).

- Unless manifest injustice would result, the court shall require that the party seeking discovery pay the expert a reasonable fee for time spent in responding to discovery under FL ST RCP Rule 1.280(b)(5)(A) and FL ST RCP Rule 1.280(b)(5)(B); and concerning discovery from an expert obtained under FL ST RCP Rule 1.280(b)(5)(A) the court may require, and concerning discovery obtained under FL ST RCP Rule 1.280(b)(5)(B) shall require, the party seeking discovery to pay the other party a fair part of the fees and expenses reasonably incurred by the latter party in obtaining facts and opinions from the expert. FL ST RCP Rule 1.280(b)(5)(C).
- As used in the Florida Rules of Civil Procedure an expert shall be an expert witness as defined in FL ST RCP Rule 1.390(a). FL ST RCP Rule 1.280(b)(5)(D).

vi. *Claims to privilege or protection.* When a party withholds information otherwise discoverable under the Florida Rules of Civil Procedure by claiming that it is privileged or subject to protection as trial preparation material, the party shall make the claim expressly and shall describe the nature of the documents, communications, or things not produced or disclosed in a manner that, without revealing information itself privileged or protected, will enable other parties to assess the applicability of the privilege or protection. FL ST RCP Rule 1.280(b)(6).

c. *Limitations on discovery of electronically stored information*

i. A person may object to discovery of electronically stored information from sources that the person identifies as not reasonably accessible because of burden or cost. On motion to compel discovery or for a protective order, the person from whom discovery is sought must show that the information sought or the format requested is not reasonably accessible because of undue burden or cost. If that showing is made, the court may nonetheless order the discovery from such sources or in such formats if the requesting party shows good cause. The court may specify conditions of the discovery, including ordering that some or all of the expenses incurred by the person from whom discovery is sought be paid by the party seeking the discovery. FL ST RCP Rule 1.280(d)(1).

ii. In determining any motion involving discovery of electronically stored information, the court must limit the frequency or extent of discovery otherwise allowed by the Florida Rules of Civil Procedure if it determines that (i) the discovery sought is unreasonably cumulative or duplicative, or can be obtained from another source or in another manner that is more convenient, less burdensome, or less expensive; or (ii) the burden or expense of the discovery outweighs its likely benefit, considering the needs of the case, the amount in controversy, the parties' resources, the importance of the issues at stake in the action, and the importance of the discovery in resolving the issues. FL ST RCP Rule 1.280(d)(2).

d. *Standards of professional conduct; Discovery*

i. Attorneys should pursue discovery requests that are reasonably related to the matter at issue. Attorneys should not use discovery for the purpose of harassing, embarrassing or causing the adversary to incur unnecessary expenses. FL ST 17 J CIR I-94-O-1(II)(1).

ii. Attorneys should not use discovery for the purpose of causing undue delay or obtaining unfair advantage. FL ST 17 J CIR I-94-O-1(II)(2).

iii. Attorneys should ensure that responses to reasonable discovery requests are timely, organized, complete and consistent with the obvious intent of the request. For example, a response to a request to produce should refer to each of the items in the request and should refer to each set of documents as separately marked exhibits. FL ST 17 J CIR I-94-O-1(II)(3).

e. For information on inadvertent disclosure of privileged materials, see FL ST RCP Rule 1.285.

2. *Request for production of documents*
    a. *Scope of request.* Any party may request any other party:
        i. To produce and permit the party making the request, or someone acting in the requesting party's behalf, to inspect and copy any designated documents, including electronically stored information, writings, drawings, graphs, charts, photographs, phono-records, and other data compilations from which information can be obtained, translated, if necessary, by the party to whom the request is directed through detection devices into reasonably usable form, that constitute or contain matters within the scope of FL ST RCP Rule 1.280(b) and that are in the possession, custody, or control of the party to whom the request is directed;
        ii. To inspect and copy, test, or sample any tangible things that constitute or contain matters within the scope of FL ST RCP Rule 1.280(b) and that are in the possession, custody, or control of the party to whom the request is directed; or
        iii. To permit entry upon designated land or other property in the possession or control of the party upon whom the request is served for the purpose of inspection and measuring, surveying, photographing, testing, or sampling the property or any designated object or operation on it within the scope of FL ST RCP Rule 1.280(b). FL ST RCP Rule 1.350(a).
    b. *Contents of request*
        i. The request shall set forth the items to be inspected, either by individual item or category, and describe each item and category with reasonable particularity. The request shall specify a reasonable time, place, and manner of making the inspection or performing the related acts. FL ST RCP Rule 1.350(b).
        ii. A request for electronically stored information may specify the form or forms in which electronically stored information is to be produced. If the responding party objects to a requested form, or if no form is specified in the request, the responding party must state the form or forms it intends to use. If a request for electronically stored information does not specify the form of production, the producing party must produce the information in a form or forms in which it is ordinarily maintained or in a reasonably usable form or forms. FL ST RCP Rule 1.350(b).
    c. *Failure to respond to requests.* The party submitting the request may move for an order under FL ST RCP Rule 1.380 concerning any objection, failure to respond to the request, or any part of it, or failure to permit the inspection as requested. FL ST RCP Rule 1.350(b). Please see FL ST RCP Rule 1.380(d) and the KeyRules Motion to Compel Discovery documents for further information regarding compelling discovery and discovery sanctions.
        i. *Response requirements.* For each item or category the response shall state that inspection and related activities will be permitted as requested unless the request is objected to, in which event the reasons for the objection shall be stated. If an objection is made to part of an item or category, the part shall be specified. When producing documents, the producing party shall either produce them as they are kept in the usual course of business or shall identify them to correspond with the categories in the request. If the responding party objects to a requested form (for electronic information), or if no form is specified in the request, the responding party must state the form or forms it intends to use. If a request for electronically stored information does not specify the form of production, the producing party must produce the information in a form or forms in which it is ordinarily maintained or in a reasonably usable form or forms. FL ST RCP Rule 1.350(b).
3. *Requests to a non-party*
    a. *Independent action not prohibited.* FL ST RCP Rule 1.350 does not preclude an independent action against a person not a party for production of documents and things and permission to enter upon land. FL ST RCP Rule 1.350(c). FL ST RCP Rule 1.351 does not affect the right of any party to bring an independent action for production of documents and things or permission to enter upon land. FL ST RCP Rule 1.351(f).
    b. *Scope.* A party may seek inspection and copying of any documents or things within the scope of FL

ST RCP Rule 1.350(a) from a person who is not a party by issuance of a subpoena directing the production of the documents or things when the requesting party does not seek to depose the custodian or other person in possession of the documents or things. FL ST RCP Rule 1.351 provides the exclusive procedure for obtaining documents or things by subpoena from nonparties without deposing the custodian or other person in possession of the documents or things pursuant to FL ST RCP Rule 1.310. FL ST RCP Rule 1.351(a).

i. *Procedure.* The proposed subpoena shall be attached to the notice and shall state the time, place, and method for production of the documents or things, and the name and address of the person who is to produce the documents or things, if known, and if not known, a general description sufficient to identify the person or the particular class or group to which the person belongs; shall include a designation of the items to be produced; and shall state that the person who will be asked to produce the documents or things has the right to object to the production under FL ST RCP Rule 1.351 and that the person will not be required to surrender the documents or things. A copy of the notice and proposed subpoena shall not be furnished to the person upon whom the subpoena is to be served. If any party serves an objection to production under FL ST RCP Rule 1.351 within ten (10) days of service of the notice, the documents or things shall not be produced pending resolution of the objection in accordance with FL ST RCP Rule 1.351(d). FL ST RCP Rule 1.351(b).

ii. *Subpoena.* If no objection is made by a party under FL ST RCP Rule 1.351(b), an attorney of record in the action may issue a subpoena or the party desiring production shall deliver to the clerk for issuance a subpoena together with a certificate of counsel or pro se party that no timely objection has been received from any party, and the clerk shall issue the subpoena and deliver it to the party desiring production. FL ST RCP Rule 1.351(c).

- The subpoena shall be identical to the copy attached to the notice and shall specify that no testimony may be taken and shall require only production of the documents or things specified in it. FL ST RCP Rule 1.351(c).
- The subpoena may give the recipient an option to deliver or mail legible copies of the documents or things to the party serving the subpoena. FL ST RCP Rule 1.351(c).
- The person upon whom the subpoena is served may condition the preparation of copies on the payment in advance of the reasonable costs of preparing the copies. FL ST RCP Rule 1.351(c).
- The subpoena shall require production only in the county of the residence of the custodian or other person in possession of the documents or things or in the county where the documents or things are located or where the custodian or person in possession usually conducts business. FL ST RCP Rule 1.351(c).
- If the person upon whom the subpoena is served objects at any time before the production of the documents or things, the documents or things shall not be produced under FL ST RCP Rule 1.351, and relief may be obtained pursuant to FL ST RCP Rule 1.310. FL ST RCP Rule 1.351(c).

iii. *Ruling on objection.* If an objection is made by a party under FL ST RCP Rule 1.351(b), the party desiring production may file a motion with the court seeking a ruling on the objection or may proceed pursuant to FL ST RCP Rule 1.310. FL ST RCP Rule 1.351(d).

iv. *Copies furnished.* If the subpoena is complied with by delivery or mailing of copies as provided in FL ST RCP Rule 1.351(c), the party receiving the copies shall furnish a legible copy of each item furnished to any other party who requests it upon the payment of the reasonable cost of preparing the copies. FL ST RCP Rule 1.351(e).

4. *Arbitration and mediation*

a. *Referral to arbitration and mediation.* Except as hereinafter provided or as otherwise prohibited by law, the presiding judge may enter an order referring all or any part of a contested civil matter to mediation or arbitration. The parties to any contested civil matter may file a written stipulation to mediate or arbitrate any issue between them at any time. Such stipulation shall be incorporated into the order of referral. FL ST RCP Rule 1.700(a).

b. *Arbitration*

i. *Exclusions.* A civil action shall be ordered to arbitration or arbitration in conjunction with mediation upon stipulation of the parties. A civil action may be ordered to arbitration or arbitration in conjunction with mediation upon motion of any party or by the court, if the judge determines the action to be of such a nature that arbitration could be of benefit to the litigants or the court. FL ST RCP Rule 1.800.

- Under no circumstances may the following categories of actions be referred to arbitration: (1) bond estreatures; (2) habeas corpus or other extraordinary writs; (3) bond validations; (4) civil or criminal contempt; (5) such other matters as may be specified by order of the chief judge in the circuit. FL ST RCP Rule 1.800.

ii. For more information regarding arbitration, please see FL ST RCP Rule 1.810; FL ST RCP Rule 1.820; FL ST RCP Rule 1.830.

c. *Mediation.* For more information regarding mediation, please see FL ST RCP Rule 1.710; FL ST RCP Rule 1.720; FL ST RCP Rule 1.730; and FL ST RCP Rule 1.750.

5. *Rules of court*

a. *Rules of civil procedure.* The Florida Rules of Civil Procedure apply to all actions of a civil nature and all special statutory proceedings in the circuit courts and county courts except those to which the Florida Probate Rules, the Florida Family Law Rules of Procedure, or the Small Claims Rules apply. FL ST RCP Rule 1.010.

i. The form, content, procedure, and time for pleading in all special statutory proceedings shall be as prescribed by the statutes governing the proceeding unless the Florida Rules of Civil Procedure specifically provide to the contrary. FL ST RCP Rule 1.010.

ii. The Florida Rules of Civil Procedure shall be construed to secure the just, speedy, and inexpensive determination of every action. FL ST RCP Rule 1.010.

b. *Rules of judicial administration.* The Florida Rules of Judicial Administration shall apply to administrative matters in all courts to which the Florida Rules of Judicial Administration are applicable by their terms. The Florida Rules of Judicial Administration shall be construed to secure the speedy and inexpensive determination of every proceeding to which they are applicable. The Florida Rules of Judicial Administration shall supersede all conflicting rules and statutes. FL ST J ADMIN Rule 2.110.

D. Documents

1. *Required documents*

a. *Request for production.* Please see the General Requirements section of this document for more information on the contents of the request for production.

i. *Notices to persons with disabilities.* See the Format section of this KeyRules document for further information.

b. *Certificate of service.* A certificate of service of the interrogatories shall be filed, giving the date of service and the name of the party to whom they were directed. FL ST RCP Rule 1.340(e). When any attorney certifies in substance: "I certify that a copy hereof has been furnished to (here insert name or names and addresses used for service) by (e-mail) (delivery) (mail) (fax) on .... (date) ....________________ Attorney" the certificate is taken as prima facie proof of such service in compliance with FL ST J ADMIN Rule 2.516. FL ST J ADMIN Rule 2.516(f).

2. *Supplemental documents*

a. *Notice of intent to serve subpoena/Subpoena.* Please see the General Requirements section of this document for more information.

E. Format

1. *Documents; Type and size.* Documents subject to the exceptions set forth in FL ST J ADMIN Rule 2.525(d) shall be filed on recycled paper measuring eight and one half by eleven (8 1/2 by 11) inches. For purposes of FL ST J ADMIN Rule 2.520, paper is recycled if it contains a minimum content of fifty (50)

percent waste paper. Xerographic reduction of legal-size (eight and one half by fourteen (8 1/2 by 14) inches) documents to letter size (eight and one half by eleven (8 1/2 by 11) inches) is prohibited. All other documents filed by electronic transmission shall be filed in a format capable of being printed in a format consistent with the provisions of FL ST J ADMIN Rule 2.250. FL ST J ADMIN Rule 2.520(b).

a. *Exhibits.* Any exhibit or attachment filed with pleadings or papers may be filed in its original size. FL ST J ADMIN Rule 2.520(c).

b. *Recording space.* On all papers and documents prepared and filed by the court or by any party to a proceeding which are to be recorded in the public records of any county, including but not limited to final money judgments and notices of lis pendens, a three (3) inch by three (3) inch space at the top right-hand corner on the first page and a one (1) inch by three (3) inch space at the top right-hand corner on each subsequent page shall be left blank and reserved for use by the clerk of court. FL ST J ADMIN Rule 2.520(d).

    i. *Exceptions to recording space.* Any papers or documents created by persons or entities over which the filing party has no control, including but not limited to wills, codicils, trusts, or other testamentary documents; documents prepared or executed by any public officer; documents prepared, executed, acknowledged, or proved outside of the State of Florida; or documents created by State or Federal government agencies, may be filed without the space required by FL ST J ADMIN Rule 2.520. FL ST J ADMIN Rule 2.520(e).

c. *Noncompliance.* No clerk of court is permitted to refuse to file any document or paper because of noncompliance with the Florida Rules of Judicial Administration. However, upon request of the clerk of court, noncomplying documents must be resubmitted in accordance with the formatting rules. FL ST J ADMIN Rule 2.520(f).

2. *Caption.* Every pleading, motion, order, judgment, or other paper shall have a caption containing the name of the court, the file number, and except for in rem proceedings, including forfeiture proceedings, the name of the first party on each side with an appropriate indication of other parties, and a designation identifying the party filing it and its nature or the nature of the order, as the case may be. In any in rem proceeding, every pleading, motion, order, judgment, or other paper shall have a caption containing the name of the court, the file number, the style "In re" (followed by the name or general description of the property), and a designation of the person or entity filing it and its nature or the nature of the order, as the case may be. In an in rem forfeiture proceeding, the style shall be "In re forfeiture of" (followed by the name of the general description of the property). All papers filed in the action shall be styled in such a manner as to indicate clearly the subject matter of the paper and the party requesting or obtaining relief. FL ST RCP Rule 1.100(c)(1).

3. *Writing and written defined.* Writing or written means a document containing information, an application, or a stipulation. FL ST RCP Rule 1.080(c).

4. *Rule abbreviations*

    a. The Florida Rules of Civil Procedure and shall be abbreviated as Fla.R.Civ.P. FL ST RCP Rule 1.010.

    b. The Florida Rules of Judicial Administration shall be abbreviated as Fla. R. Jud. Admin. FL ST J ADMIN Rule 2.110.

5. *Nonverification.* Except when otherwise specifically provided by the Florida Rules of Civil Procedure or an applicable statute, every pleading or other document of a party represented by an attorney need not be verified or accompanied by an affidavit. FL ST RCP Rule 1.030; FL ST J ADMIN Rule 2.515(a).

6. *Attorney signature*

    a. *Attorney signature.* Every pleading and other document of a party represented by an attorney shall be signed by at least one (1) attorney of record in that attorney's individual name whose current record Florida Bar address, telephone number, including area code, primary e-mail address and secondary e-mail addresses, if any, and Florida Bar number shall be stated, and who shall be duly licensed to practice law in Florida or who shall have received permission to appear in the particular case as provided in FL ST J ADMIN Rule 2.510. FL ST J ADMIN Rule 2.515(a).

        i. The attorney may be required by the court to give the address of, and to vouch for the attorney's authority to represent, the party. FL ST J ADMIN Rule 2.515(a).

ii. The signature of an attorney shall constitute a certificate by the attorney that the attorney has read the pleading or other document; that to the best of the attorney's knowledge, information, and belief there is good ground to support it; and that it is not interposed for delay. FL ST J ADMIN Rule 2.515(a).

iii. If a pleading is not signed or is signed with intent to defeat the purpose of FL ST J ADMIN Rule 2.515, it may be stricken and the action may proceed as though the pleading or other document had not been served. FL ST J ADMIN Rule 2.515(a).

b. *Pro se litigant signature.* A party who is not represented by an attorney shall sign any pleading or other paper and state the party's address and telephone number, including area code. FL ST J ADMIN Rule 2.515(b).

c. *Form of signature*

i. The signatures required on pleadings and documents by FL ST J ADMIN Rule 2.515(a) and FL ST J ADMIN Rule 2.515(b) may be:

- Original signatures;
- Original signatures that have been reproduced by electronic means, such as on electronically transmitted documents or photocopied documents;
- Electronic signatures using the "/s/," "s/," or "/s" formats by or at the direction of the person signing; or
- Any other signature format authorized by general law, so long as the clerk where the proceeding is pending has the capability of receiving and has obtained approval from the Supreme Court of Florida to accept pleadings and documents with that signature format. FL ST J ADMIN Rule 2.515(c)(1).

ii. An attorney, party, or other person who files a pleading or paper by electronic transmission that does not contain the original signature of that attorney, party, or other person shall file that identical pleading or paper in paper form containing an original signature of that attorney, party, or other person (hereinafter called the follow-up filing) immediately thereafter. The follow-up filing is not required if the Supreme Court of Florida has entered an order directing the clerk of court to discontinue accepting the follow-up filing. FL ST J ADMIN Rule 2.515(c)(2).

iii. The placement of a "/s/" or the image of a signature by an attorney or party or affected non-party signature line on an electronically filed document shall be accepted as the signature and shall verify to the Court the filer is in possession of the originally executed document. Notwithstanding the manner in which an electronic document is signed the originally executed pleading or paper shall be maintained in the filer's possession for a minimum of one (1) year after final disposition and time for appeal of the case. The originally executed document shall be produced for filing or inspection as directed by the Court. FL ST 17 J CIR 2012-16-CIV.

7. *Forms*

a. *Process.* The forms of process, notice of lis pendens, and notice of action provided in the Florida Rules of Civil Procedure are sufficient. Variations from the forms do not void process or notices that are otherwise sufficient. FL ST RCP Rule 1.900(a).

b. *Other forms.* The other forms provided in the Florida Rules of Civil Procedure are sufficient for the matters that are covered by them. So long as the substance is expressed without prolixity, the forms may be varied to meet the facts of a particular case. FL ST RCP Rule 1.900(b).

c. *Formal matters.* Captions, except for the designation of the paper, are omitted from the forms provided in the Florida Rules of Civil Procedure. A general form of caption is the first form provided. Signatures are omitted from pleadings and motions. FL ST RCP Rule 1.900(c).

8. *Notices to persons with disabilities.* All notices of court proceedings to be held in a public facility, and all process compelling appearance at such proceedings, shall include the following statement in bold face, fourteen (14) point Times New Roman or Courier font: "If you are a person with a disability who needs any accommodation in order to participate in this proceeding, you are entitled, at no cost to you, to the provision of certain assistance. Please contact [identify applicable court personnel by name, address, and

telephone number] at least seven (7) days before your scheduled court appearance, or immediately upon receiving this notification if the time before the scheduled appearance is less than seven (7) days; if you are hearing or voice impaired, call 711." FL ST J ADMIN Rule 2.540(c)(1). For further information, please see FL ST 17 J CIR 2010-49-GEN.

9. *Minimization of the filing of sensitive information*
   a. *Limitations for court filings.* Unless authorized by FL ST J ADMIN Rule 2.425(b), statute, another rule of court, or the court orders otherwise, designated sensitive information filed with the court must be limited to the following format:
      i. The initials of a person known to be a minor;
      ii. The year of birth of a person's birth date;
      iii. No portion of any: Social security number, Bank account number, Credit card account number, Charge account number, or Debit account number;
      iv. The last four digits of any: Taxpayer identification number (TIN), Employee identification number, Driver's license number, Passport number, Telephone number, Financial account number, except as set forth in FL ST J ADMIN Rule 2.425(a)(3), Brokerage account number, Insurance policy account number, Loan account number, Customer account number, or Patient or health care number;
      v. A truncated version of any: Email address, Computer user name, Password, or Personal identification number (PIN); and
      vi. A truncated version of any other sensitive information as provided by court order. FL ST J ADMIN Rule 2.425(a).
   b. *Exceptions.* FL ST J ADMIN Rule 2.425(a) does not apply to the following:
      i. An account number which identifies the property alleged to be the subject of a proceeding;
      ii. The record of an administrative or agency proceeding;
      iii. The record in appellate or review proceedings;
      iv. The birth date of a minor whenever the birth date is necessary for the court to establish or maintain subject matter jurisdiction;
      v. The name of a minor in any order relating to parental responsibility, time-sharing, or child support;
      vi. The name of a minor in any document or order affecting the minor's ownership of real property;
      vii. The birth date of a party in a writ of attachment or notice to payor;
      viii. In traffic and criminal proceedings: a pro se filing; a court filing that is related to a criminal matter or investigation and that is prepared before the filing of a criminal charge or is not filed as part of any docketed criminal case; an arrest or search warrant or any information in support thereof; a charging document and an affidavit or other documents filed in support of any charging document, including any driving records; a statement of particulars; discovery material introduced into evidence or otherwise filed with the court; and all information necessary for the proper issuance and execution of a subpoena duces tecum;
      ix. Information used by the clerk for case maintenance purposes or the courts for case management purposes; and
      x. Information which is relevant and material to an issue before the court. FL ST J ADMIN Rule 2.425(b).
   c. *Remedies.* Upon motion by a party or interested person or sua sponte by the court, the court may order remedies, sanctions or both for a violation of FL ST J ADMIN Rule 2.425(a). Following notice and an opportunity to respond, the court may impose sanctions if such filing was not made in good faith. FL ST J ADMIN Rule 2.425(c).
   d. *Motions not restricted.* FL ST J ADMIN Rule 2.425 does not restrict a party's right to move for

protective order, to move to file documents under seal, or to request a determination of the confidentiality of records. FL ST J ADMIN Rule 2.425(d).

e. *Application.* FL ST J ADMIN Rule 2.425 does not affect the application of constitutional provisions, statutes, or rules of court regarding confidential information or access to public information. FL ST J ADMIN Rule 2.425(e).

F. Filing and Service Requirements

1. *Court filing of documents and discovery.* Information obtained during discovery shall not be filed with the court until such time as it is filed for good cause. The requirement of good cause is satisfied only where the filing of the information is allowed or required by another applicable rule of procedure or by court order. All filings of discovery documents shall comply with FL ST J ADMIN Rule 2.425. The court shall have the authority to impose sanctions for violation of FL ST RCP Rule 1.280. FL ST RCP Rule 1.280(g).
   a. Unless required by the court, a party shall not file any of the documents or things produced with the response. Documents or things may be filed in compliance with FL ST J ADMIN Rule 2.425 and FL ST RCP Rule 1.280(g) when they should be considered by the court in determining a matter pending before the court. FL ST RCP Rule 1.350(d).
2. *Filing requirements.* All original documents must be filed with the court either before service or immediately thereafter, unless otherwise provided for by general law or other rules. If the original of any bond or other document is not placed in the court file, a certified copy must be so placed by the clerk. FL ST J ADMIN Rule 2.516(d). All documents shall be filed in conformity with the requirements of FL ST J ADMIN Rule 2.525. FL ST RCP Rule 1.080(b). All documents filed in any court shall be filed by electronic transmission in accordance with FL ST J ADMIN Rule 2.525. "Documents" means pleadings, motions, petitions, memoranda, briefs, notices, exhibits, declarations, affidavits, orders, judgments, decrees, writs, opinions, and any other paper or writing submitted to a court. FL ST J ADMIN Rule 2.520(a). All documents that are court records, as defined in FL ST J ADMIN Rule 2.430(a)(1), must be filed by electronic transmission, provided that: (1) the clerk has the ability to accept and retain such documents; (2) the clerk or the chief judge of the circuit has requested permission to accept documents filed by electronic transmission; and (3) the supreme court has entered an order granting permission to the clerk to accept documents filed by electronic transmission. FL ST J ADMIN Rule 2.525(c)(1).
   a. *Definition.* "Electronic transmission of documents" means the sending of information by electronic signals to, by or from a court or clerk, which when received can be transformed and stored or transmitted on paper, microfilm, magnetic storage device, optical imaging system, CD-ROM, flash drive, other electronic data storage system, server, case maintenance system ("CM"), electronic court filing ("ECF") system, statewide or local electronic portal ("e-portal"), or other electronic record keeping system authorized by the supreme court in a format sufficient to communicate the information on the original document in a readable format. Electronic transmission of documents includes electronic mail ("e-mail") and any internet-based transmission procedure, and may include procedures allowing for documents to be signed or verified by electronic means. FL ST J ADMIN Rule 2.525(a).
      i. The filing of documents with the court as required by the Florida Rules of Judicial Administration must be made by filing them with the clerk in accordance with FL ST J ADMIN Rule 2.525, except that the judge may permit documents to be filed with the judge, in which event the judge must note the filing date before him or her on the documents and transmit them to the clerk. The date of filing is that shown on the face of the document by the judge's notation or the clerk's time stamp, whichever is earlier. FL ST J ADMIN Rule 2.516(e).
   b. *Application.* Any court or clerk of the court may accept the electronic transmission of documents for filing after the clerk, together with input from the chief judge of the circuit, has obtained approval of the procedures and program for doing so from the Supreme Court of Florida. FL ST J ADMIN Rule 2.525(b).
   c. *Exceptions*
      i. Paper documents and other submissions may be manually submitted to the clerk or court:
         - When the clerk does not have the ability to accept and retain documents by electronic filing or has not had ECF Procedures approved by the supreme court;

- For filing by any self-represented party or any self-represented nonparty unless specific ECF Procedures provide a means to file documents electronically. However, any self-represented nonparty that is a governmental or public agency and any other agency, partnership, corporation, or business entity acting on behalf of any governmental or public agency may file documents by electronic transmission if such entity has the capability of filing documents electronically;
- For filing by attorneys excused from e-mail service in accordance with FL ST J ADMIN Rule 2.516(b);
- When submitting evidentiary exhibits or filing non-documentary materials;
- When the filing involves documents in excess of twenty-five (25) megabytes (25MB) in size. For such filings, documents may be transmitted using an electronic storage medium that the clerk has the ability to accept, which may include a CD-ROM, flash drive, or similar storage medium;
- When filed in open court, as permitted by the court;
- When paper filing is permitted by any approved statewide or local ECF procedures; and
- If any court determines that justice so requires. FL ST J ADMIN Rule 2.525(d).

ii. Any document in paper form submitted under FL ST J ADMIN Rule 2.525(d) is filed when it is received by the clerk or court and the clerk shall immediately thereafter convert any filed paper document to an electronic document. "Convert to an electronic document" means optically capturing an image of a paper document and using character recognition software to recover as much of the document's text as practicable and then indexing and storing the document in the official court file. FL ST J ADMIN Rule 2.525(c)(4).

iii. Any storage medium submitted under FL ST J ADMIN Rule 2.525(d)(5) is filed when received by the clerk or court and the clerk shall immediately thereafter transfer the electronic documents from the storage device to the official court file. FL ST J ADMIN Rule 2.525(c)(5).

iv. If the filer of any paper document authorized under FL ST J ADMIN Rule 2.525(d) provides a self-addressed, postage-paid envelope for return of the paper document after it is converted to electronic form by the clerk, the clerk shall place the paper document in the envelope and deposit it in the mail. Except when a paper document is required to be maintained, the clerk may recycle any filed paper document that is not to be returned to the filer. FL ST J ADMIN Rule 2.525(c)(6).

v. The clerk may convert any paper document filed before the effective date of FL ST J ADMIN Rule 2.525 to an electronic document. Unless the clerk is required to maintain the paper document, if the paper document has been converted to an electronic document by the clerk, the paper document is no longer part of the official court file and may be removed and recycled. FL ST J ADMIN Rule 2.525(c)(7).

d. *Official court file.* For information on what constitutes the official court file, please see FL ST J ADMIN Rule 2.525(c)(2), FL ST J ADMIN Rule 2.525(c)(3).

e. *Administration.* All attorneys, parties, or other persons using this rule to file documents are required to make arrangements with the court or clerk for the payment of any charges authorized by general law or the supreme court before filing any document by electronic transmission. FL ST J ADMIN Rule 2.525(f)(2).

f. *Filing date.* The filing date for an electronically transmitted document is the date and time that such filing is acknowledged by an electronic stamp or otherwise, pursuant to any procedure set forth in any ECF Procedures approved by the supreme court, or the date the last page of such filing is received by the court or clerk. FL ST J ADMIN Rule 2.525(f)(3).

g. *Accessibility.* All documents transmitted in any electronic form under FL ST J ADMIN Rule 2.525 must comply with the accessibility requirements of FL ST J ADMIN Rule 2.526. FL ST J ADMIN Rule 2.525(g).

h. *Provisions for electronic filing in the Seventeenth Circuit.* Attorneys may electronically file plead-

ings and papers on existing cases in circuit civil divisions 1, 7, 9, 19, 26 and 27. The following documents may be scanned and efiled; however, the original must be filed with the Clerk: Documents ordered by the Court; and original documents required by law or rule of procedure to be filed with the Clerk. Self represented individuals shall file pleadings and papers with the Clerk. The Clerk within twenty four (24) hours of receipt of an electronic document shall either accept or reject the electronic document for filing and send electronic notice to the filer. FL ST 17 J CIR 2012-16-CIV.

i. *Technical failures.* If a document filed electronically is not received due to: an error in the transmission of the document to the Clerk or any vendor of the Clerk to provide electronic court record filing services which is unknown to an attorney or party or affected non party, or a failure to process the electronic document when received by the Clerk or rejection by the Clerk, or any other technical problems experienced by the attorney or party or affected non party, the Court may, after an evidentiary hearing and upon satisfactory proof, enter an order permitting the document to be filed nunc pro tunc to the date it was first attempted to be sent electronically. FL ST 17 J CIR 2012-16-CIV.

j. *Filing of pleadings or papers at any office of the clerk of court.* The Clerk of Courts, commencing November 3, 2008, shall accept for filing, at the central courthouse, north satellite courthouse, south satellite courthouse, and west satellite courthouse any pleading or motion or other document for filing in the court file from any attorney or party for an existing case except as otherwise set forth. FL ST 17 J CIR 2008-153-GEN. See FL ST 17 J CIR 2008-153-GEN for specific exceptions.

3. *Service requirements.* Every pleading subsequent to the initial pleading, all orders, and every other document filed in the action must be served in conformity with the requirements of FL ST J ADMIN Rule 2.516. FL ST RCP Rule 1.080(a).

   a. *Service; When required.* Unless the court otherwise orders, or a statute or supreme court administrative order specifies a different means of service, every pleading subsequent to the initial pleading and every other document filed in any court proceeding, except applications for witness subpoenas and documents served by formal notice or required to be served in the manner provided for service of formal notice, must be served in accordance with FL ST J ADMIN Rule 2.516 on each party. No service need be made on parties against whom a default has been entered, except that pleadings asserting new or additional claims against them must be served in the manner provided for service of summons. FL ST J ADMIN Rule 2.516(a).

   b. *Service; How made.* When service is required or permitted to be made upon a party represented by an attorney, service must be made upon the attorney unless service upon the party is ordered by the court. FL ST J ADMIN Rule 2.516(b).

      i. *Service by electronic mail ("e-mail").* All documents required or permitted to be served on another party must be served by e-mail, unless FL ST J ADMIN Rule 2.516 otherwise provides. When, in addition to service by e-mail, the sender also utilizes another means of service provided for in FL ST J ADMIN Rule 2.516(b)(2), any differing time limits and other provisions applicable to that other means of service control. FL ST J ADMIN Rule 2.516(b)(1). Any document electronically transmitted to a court or clerk must also be served on all parties and interested persons in accordance with the applicable rules of court. FL ST J ADMIN Rule 2.525(e)(2).

         - *Service on attorneys.* Upon appearing in a proceeding, an attorney must serve a designation of a primary e-mail address and may designate no more than two (2) secondary e-mail addresses. Thereafter, service must be directed to all designated e-mail addresses in that proceeding. Every document filed by an attorney thereafter must include the primary e-mail address of that attorney and any secondary e-mail addresses. If an attorney does not designate any e-mail address for service, documents may be served on that attorney at the e-mail address on record with The Florida Bar. FL ST J ADMIN Rule 2.516(b)(1)(A).

         - *Exception to e-mail service on attorneys.* Service by an attorney on another attorney must be made by e-mail unless excused by the court. Upon motion by an attorney demonstrating that the attorney has no e-mail account and lacks access to the Internet at the attorney's office, the court may excuse the attorney from the requirements of e-mail service. Service

on and by an attorney excused by the court from e-mail service must be by the means provided in FL ST J ADMIN Rule 2.516(b)(2). FL ST J ADMIN Rule 2.516(b)(1)(B).

- *Service on and by parties not represented by an attorney.* Any party not represented by an attorney may serve a designation of a primary e-mail address and also may designate no more than two (2) secondary e-mail addresses to which service must be directed in that proceeding by the means provided in FL ST J ADMIN Rule 2.516(b)(1). If a party not represented by an attorney does not designate an e-mail address for service in a proceeding, service on and by that party must be by the means provided in FL ST J ADMIN Rule 2.516(b)(2). FL ST J ADMIN Rule 2.516(b)(1)(C).
- *Time of service.* Service by e-mail is complete when it is sent. FL ST J ADMIN Rule 2.516(b)(1)(D). An e-mail is deemed served on the date it is sent. FL ST J ADMIN Rule 2.516(b)(1)(D)(i). If the sender learns that the e-mail did not reach the address of the person to be served, the sender must immediately send another copy by e-mail, or by a means authorized by FL ST J ADMIN Rule 2.516(b)(2). FL ST J ADMIN Rule 2.516(b)(1)(D)(ii). E-mail service is treated as service by mail for the computation of time. FL ST J ADMIN Rule 2.516(b)(1)(D)(iii).

ii. *Format of e-mail for service.* Service of a document by e-mail is made by attaching a copy of the document in PDF format to an e-mail sent to all addresses designated by the attorney or party. FL ST J ADMIN Rule 2.516(b)(1)(E).

- All documents served by e-mail must be attached to an e-mail message containing a subject line beginning with the words "SERVICE OF COURT DOCUMENT" in all capital letters, followed by the case number of the proceeding in which the documents are being served. FL ST J ADMIN Rule 2.516(b)(1)(E)(i).
- The body of the e-mail must identify the court in which the proceeding is pending, the case number, the name of the initial party on each side, the title of each document served with that e-mail, and the sender's name and telephone number. FL ST J ADMIN Rule 2.516(b)(1)(E)(ii).
- Any document served by e-mail may be signed by the "/s/" format, as long as the filed original is signed in accordance with the applicable rule of procedure. FL ST J ADMIN Rule 2.516(b)(1)(E)(iii).
- Any e-mail which, together with its attached documents, exceeds five megabytes (5MB) in size, must be divided and sent as separate e-mails, no one of which may exceed five megabytes (5MB) in size and each of which must be sequentially numbered in the subject line. FL ST J ADMIN Rule 2.516(b)(1)(E)(iv).

iii. *Service by other means.* In addition to, and not in lieu of, service by e-mail, service may also be made upon attorneys by any of the means specified in FL ST J ADMIN Rule 2.516(b)(2). Service on and by all parties who are not represented by an attorney and who do not designate an e-mail address, and on and by all attorneys excused from e-mail service, must be made by delivering a copy of the document or by mailing it to the party or attorney at their last known address or, if no address is known, by leaving it with the clerk of the court. Service by mail is complete upon mailing. Delivery of a copy within FL ST J ADMIN Rule 2.516 is complete upon:

- Handing it to the attorney or to the party,
- Leaving it at the attorney's or party's office with a clerk or other person in charge thereof,
- If there is no one in charge, leaving it in a conspicuous place therein,
- If the office is closed or the person to be served has no office, leaving it at the person's usual place of abode with some person of his or her family above fifteen (15) years of age and informing such person of the contents, or
- Transmitting it by facsimile to the attorney's or party's office with a cover sheet containing the sender's name, firm, address, telephone number, and facsimile number, and the

number of pages transmitted. When service is made by facsimile, a copy must also be served by any other method permitted by FL ST J ADMIN Rule 2.516. Facsimile service occurs when transmission is complete. FL ST J ADMIN Rule 2.516(b)(2)(A) through FL ST J ADMIN Rule 2.516(b)(2)(E).

- Service by delivery after 5:00 p.m. must be deemed to have been made by mailing on the date of delivery. FL ST J ADMIN Rule 2.516(b)(2)(F).

c. *Service; Numerous defendants.* In actions when the parties are unusually numerous, the court may regulate the service contemplated by the Florida Rules of Judicial Administration on motion or on its own initiative in such manner as may be found to be just and reasonable. FL ST J ADMIN Rule 2.516(c).

d. *Service by clerk.* Service of notices and other documents required to be made by the clerk must also be done as provided in FL ST J ADMIN Rule 2.516(b). FL ST J ADMIN Rule 2.516(g).

G. Hearings

1. There is no hearing required or contemplated with regard to requests for production of documents in the Florida Rules of Civil Procedure.

H. Forms

1. Official Request for Production of Documents Forms for Florida

a. Caption. FL ST RCP Form 1.901.

b. Subpoena duces tecum for trial. FL ST RCP Form 1.911.

c. Notice of production from non-party. FL ST RCP Form 1.921.

d. Subpoena duces tecum without deposition. FL ST RCP Form 1.922.

2. Florida Requests for Production of Documents Forms

a. Request for production; Documents. FL-PRACFORM § 8:29.

b. Request for inspection; Documents, deposition. FL-PRACFORM § 8:30.

c. Request for inspection; Tangible things. FL-PRACFORM § 8:31.

d. Request for entry; Real property. FL-PRACFORM § 8:32.

e. Request for production; Documents, response. FL-PRACFORM § 8:33.

f. Request for inspection; Response, tangible things. FL-PRACFORM § 8:34.

g. Request for entry; Response, land and buildings. FL-PRACFORM § 8:35.

h. Production of documents; Nonparty, notice. FL-PRACFORM § 8:36.

i. Production of documents; Nonparty, objection. FL-PRACFORM § 8:37.

j. Request; Production of documents for inspection and copying. FL-PP § 3:115.

k. Notice of request for production from non-party. FL-PP § 3:116.

l. Request; For permission to enter on land; To inspect and photograph. FL-PP § 3:127.

I. Checklist

(I) ❑ Matters to be considered by requesting party

(a) ❑ Required documents

(1) ❑ Request

(2) ❑ Certificate of service

(b) ❑ Supplemental documents

(1) ❑ Notice of intent to serve subpoena/Subpoena

(c) ❑ Time for request

(1) ❑ Without leave of court the request may be served on the plaintiff after commencement of the

action and on any other party with or after service of the process and initial pleading on that party

(2) ❑ A party desiring production under FL ST RCP Rule 1.351 shall serve notice as provided in FL ST RCP Rule 1.080 on every other party of the intent to serve a subpoena under FL ST RCP Rule 1.351 at least ten (10) days before the subpoena is issued if service is by delivery and fifteen (15) days before the subpoena is issued if the service is by mail or e-mail

(II) ❑ Matters to be considered by responding party

(a) ❑ Required documents

(1) ❑ Response to request

(2) ❑ Certificate of service

(b) ❑ Supplemental documents

(1) ❑ Objections

(c) ❑ Time for response

(1) ❑ The party to whom the request is directed shall serve a written response within thirty (30) days after service of the request, except that a defendant may serve a response within forty-five (45) days after service of the process and initial pleading on that defendant; the court may allow a shorter or longer time

Requests, Notices and Applications
Request for Admissions

Document Last Updated January 2013

A. Applicable Rules

1. *State rules*

a. Nonverification of pleadings. FL ST RCP Rule 1.030.

b. Service and filing of pleadings, orders, and documents. FL ST RCP Rule 1.080.

c. Time. FL ST RCP Rule 1.090.

d. Pleadings and motions. FL ST RCP Rule 1.100.

e. Pretrial procedure. FL ST RCP Rule 1.200.

f. General provisions governing discovery. FL ST RCP Rule 1.280.

g. Interrogatories to parties. FL ST RCP Rule 1.340.

h. Examination of persons. FL ST RCP Rule 1.360.

i. Requests for admission. FL ST RCP Rule 1.370.

j. Failure to make discovery; Sanctions. FL ST RCP Rule 1.380.

k. Depositions of expert witnesses. FL ST RCP Rule 1.390.

l. Relief from judgment, decrees or orders. FL ST RCP Rule 1.540.

m. Forms. FL ST RCP Rule 1.900.

n. Retention of court records. FL ST J ADMIN Rule 2.430.

o. Foreign attorneys. FL ST J ADMIN Rule 2.510.

p. Signature of attorneys and parties. FL ST J ADMIN Rule 2.515.

q. Paper. FL ST J ADMIN Rule 2.520.

r. Electronic filing. FL ST J ADMIN Rule 2.525.

s. Requests for accommodations by persons with disabilities. FL ST J ADMIN Rule 2.540.

t. Minimization of the filing of sensitive information. FL ST J ADMIN Rule 2.425.

u. Accessibility of information and technology. FL ST J ADMIN Rule 2.526.

2. *Local rules*

a. Standards of professional courtesy. FL ST 17 J CIR I-94-O-1.

b. Administrative order authorizing the filing of pleadings or papers at any office of the clerk of court. FL ST 17 J CIR 2008-153-GEN.

c. Administrative order regarding provision of ADA accommodations. FL ST 17 J CIR 2010-49-GEN.

d. Administrative order establishing electronic filing procedures for the civil division. FL ST 17 J CIR 2012-16-CIV.

B. Timing

1. *Request for admission.* Without leave of court the request may be served upon the plaintiff after commencement of the action and upon any other party with or after service of the process and initial pleading upon that party. FL ST RCP Rule 1.370(a).

2. *Sequence and timing of discovery.* Except as provided in FL ST RCP Rule 1.280(b)(5) or unless the court upon motion for the convenience of parties and witnesses and in the interest of justice orders otherwise, methods of discovery may be used in any sequence, and the fact that a party is conducting discovery, whether by deposition or otherwise, shall not delay any other party's discovery. FL ST RCP Rule 1.280(e).

3. *Standard of professional conduct; Scheduling*

a. Attorneys should endeavor to provide opposing counsel, parties, witnesses, and other affected persons, sufficient notice of depositions, hearings and other proceedings, except upon agreement of course, in an emergency, or in other circumstances compelling more expedited scheduling. As a general rule, actual notice should be no less than five (5) business days for instate depositions, ten (10) business days for out-of-state depositions and four (4) business days for hearings. FL ST 17 J CIR I-94-O-1(I)(1).

b. Attorneys should communicate with opposing counsel prior to scheduling depositions, hearings and other proceedings, in an effort to schedule them at times that are mutually convenient for all interested persons. Further, sufficient time should be reserved to permit a complete presentation by counsel for all parties. FL ST 17 J CIR I-94-O-1(I)(2).

c. Attorneys should notify opposing counsel, the court, and others affected, of scheduling conflicts as soon as they become apparent. Further, attorneys should cooperate with one another regarding all reasonable rescheduling requests that do not prejudice their clients or unduly delay a proceeding. FL ST 17 J CIR I-94-O-1(I)(3).

d. Attorneys should promptly notify the court or other tribunal of any resolution between the parties that renders a scheduled court appearance unnecessary or otherwise moot. FL ST 17 J CIR I-94-O-1(I)(4).

e. Attorneys should grant reasonable requests by opposing counsel for extensions of time within which to respond to pleadings, discovery, and other matters when such an extension will not prejudice their client or unduly delay a proceeding. FL ST 17 J CIR I-94-O-1(I)(5).

4. *Timing considerations when filing electronically.* The filing date of an efiled document is when the last page is received by the Clerk. The electronic filing of a document does not modify any filing deadlines as required by law, rule of procedure, or court order. FL ST 17 J CIR 2012-16-CIV.

5. *Computation of time*

a. *Generally.* Computation of time shall be governed by FL ST J ADMIN Rule 2.514. FL ST RCP Rule 1.090(a). The following rules apply in computing time periods specified in any rule of procedure, local rule, court order, or statute that does not specify a method of computing time. FL ST J ADMIN Rule 2.514(a).

i. *Period stated in days or a longer unit.* When the period is stated in days or a longer unit of time

(A) exclude the day of the event that triggers the period; (B) count every day, including intermediate Saturdays, Sundays, and legal holidays; and (C) include the last day of the period, but if the last day is a Saturday, Sunday, or legal holiday, or falls within any period of time extended through an order of the chief justice under FL ST J ADMIN Rule 2.205(a)(2)(B)(iv), the period continues to run until the end of the next day that is not a Saturday, Sunday, or legal holiday and does not fall within any period of time extended through an order of the chief justice. FL ST J ADMIN Rule 2.514(a)(1).

ii. *Period stated in hours.* When the period is stated in hours (A) begin counting immediately on the occurrence of the event that triggers the period; (B) count every hour, including hours during intermediate Saturdays, Sundays, and legal holidays; and (C) if the period would end on a Saturday, Sunday, or legal holiday, or during any period of time extended through an order of the chief justice under FL ST J ADMIN Rule 2.205(a)(2)(B)(iv), the period continues to run until the same time on the next day that is not a Saturday, Sunday, or legal holiday and does not fall within any period of time extended through an order of the chief justice. FL ST J ADMIN Rule 2.514(a)(2).

iii. *Period stated in days less than seven (7) days.* When the period stated in days is less than seven (7) days, intermediate Saturdays, Sundays, and legal holidays shall be excluded in the computation. FL ST J ADMIN Rule 2.514(a)(3).

iv. *"Last day" defined.* Unless a different time is set by a statute, local rule, or court order, the last day ends (A) for electronic filing or for service by any means, at midnight; and (B) for filing by other means, when the clerk's office is scheduled to close. FL ST J ADMIN Rule 2.514(a)(4).

v. *"Next day" defined.* The "next day" is determined by continuing to count forward when the period is measured after an event and backward when measured before an event. FL ST J ADMIN Rule 2.514(a)(5).

vi. *"Legal holiday" defined.* "Legal holiday" means (A) the day set aside by FL ST § 110.117, for observing New Year's Day, Martin Luther King, Jr.'s Birthday, Memorial Day, Independence Day, Labor Day, Veterans' Day, Thanksgiving Day, the Friday after Thanksgiving Day, or Christmas Day, and (B) any day observed as a holiday by the clerk's office or as designated by the chief judge. FL ST J ADMIN Rule 2.514(a)(6).

b. *Additional time after service by mail or e-mail.* When a party may or must act within a specified time after service and service is made by mail or e-mail, five (5) days are added after the period that would otherwise expire under FL ST J ADMIN Rule 2.514(a). FL ST J ADMIN Rule 2.514(b).

c. *Enlargement.* When an act is required or allowed to be done at or within a specified time by order of court, by the Florida Rules of Civil Procedure, or by notice given thereunder, for cause shown the court at any time in its discretion (1) with or without notice, may order the period enlarged if request therefor is made before the expiration of the period originally prescribed or as extended by a previous order, or (2) upon motion made and notice after the expiration of the specified period, may permit the act to be done when failure to act was the result of excusable neglect, but it may not extend the time for making a motion for new trial, for rehearing, or to alter or amend a judgment; making a motion for relief from a judgment under FL ST RCP Rule 1.540(b); taking an appeal or filing a petition for certiorari; or making a motion for a directed verdict. FL ST RCP Rule 1.090(b).

d. *Unaffected by expiration of term.* The period of time provided for the doing of any act or the taking of any proceeding shall not be affected or limited by the continued existence or expiration of a term of court. The continued existence or expiration of a term of court in no way affects the power of a court to do any act or take any proceeding in any action which is or has been pending before it. FL ST RCP Rule 1.090(c).

C. General Requirements

1. *General provisions governing discovery*

a. *Discovery methods.* Parties may obtain discovery by one or more of the following methods: depositions upon oral examination or written questions; written interrogatories; production of documents or things or permission to enter upon land or other property for inspection and other purposes; physical and mental examinations; and requests for admission. Unless the court orders otherwise and under FL ST RCP Rule 1.280(c), the frequency of use of these methods is not limited, except as provided in FL ST RCP Rule 1.200, FL ST RCP Rule 1.340, and FL ST RCP Rule 1.370. FL ST RCP Rule 1.280(a).

b. *Scope of discovery.* Unless otherwise limited by order of the court in accordance with the Florida Rules of Civil Procedure, the scope of discovery is as follows:

   i. *In general.* Parties may obtain discovery regarding any matter, not privileged, that is relevant to the subject matter of the pending action, whether it relates to the claim or defense of the party seeking discovery or the claim or defense of any other party, including the existence, description, nature, custody, condition, and location of any books, documents, or other tangible things and the identity and location of persons having knowledge of any discoverable matter. It is not ground for objection that the information sought will be inadmissible at the trial if the information sought appears reasonably calculated to lead to the discovery of admissible evidence. FL ST RCP Rule 1.280(b)(1).

   ii. *Indemnity agreements.* A party may obtain discovery of the existence and contents of any agreement under which any person may be liable to satisfy part or all of a judgment that may be entered in the action or to indemnify or to reimburse a party for payments made to satisfy the judgment. Information concerning the agreement is not admissible in evidence at trial by reason of disclosure. FL ST RCP Rule 1.280(b)(2).

   iii. *Electronically stored information.* A party may obtain discovery of electronically stored information in accordance with the Florida Rules of Civil Procedure. FL ST RCP Rule 1.280(b)(3).

   iv. *Trial preparation; Materials.* Subject to the provisions of FL ST RCP Rule 1.280(b)(5), a party may obtain discovery of documents and tangible things otherwise discoverable under FL ST RCP Rule 1.280(b)(1) and prepared in anticipation of litigation or for trial by or for another party or by or for that party's representative, including that party's attorney, consultant, surety, indemnitor, insurer, or agent, only upon a showing that the party seeking discovery has need of the materials in the preparation of the case and is unable without undue hardship to obtain the substantial equivalent of the materials by other means. FL ST RCP Rule 1.280(b)(4).

      - In ordering discovery of the materials when the required showing has been made, the court shall protect against disclosure of the mental impressions, conclusions, opinions, or legal theories of an attorney or other representative of a party concerning the litigation. FL ST RCP Rule 1.280(b)(4).
      - Without the required showing a party may obtain a copy of a statement concerning the action or its subject matter previously made by that party. FL ST RCP Rule 1.280(b)(4).
      - Upon request without the required showing a person not a party may obtain a copy of a statement concerning the action or its subject matter previously made by that person. If the request is refused, the person may move for an order to obtain a copy. The provisions of FL ST RCP Rule 1.380(a)(5) apply to the award of expenses incurred as a result of making the motion. FL ST RCP Rule 1.280(b)(4).
      - For purposes of FL ST RCP Rule 1.280(b)(4), a statement previously made is a written statement signed or otherwise adopted or approved by the person making it, or a stenographic, mechanical, electrical, or other recording or transcription of it that is a substantially verbatim recital of an oral statement by the person making it and contemporaneously recorded. FL ST RCP Rule 1.280(b)(4).

   v. *Trial preparation; Experts.* Discovery of facts known and opinions held by experts, otherwise discoverable under the provisions of FL ST RCP Rule 1.280(b)(1) and acquired or developed in anticipation of litigation or for trial, may be obtained only as follows:

      - By interrogatories a party may require any other party to identify each person whom the other party expects to call as an expert witness at trial and to state the subject matter on which the expert is expected to testify, and to state the substance of the facts and opinions

to which the expert is expected to testify and a summary of the grounds for each opinion. FL ST RCP Rule 1.280(b)(5)(A)(i).

- Any person disclosed by interrogatories or otherwise as a person expected to be called as an expert witness at trial may be deposed in accordance with FL ST RCP Rule 1.390 without motion or order of court. FL ST RCP Rule 1.280(b)(5)(A)(ii).
- A party may obtain the following discovery regarding any person disclosed by interrogatories or otherwise as a person expected to be called as an expert witness at trial: The scope of employment in the pending case and the compensation for such service, FL ST RCP Rule 1.280(b)(5)(A)(iii)(1); The expert's general litigation experience, including the percentage of work performed for plaintiffs and defendants, FL ST RCP Rule 1.280(b)(5)(A)(iii)(2); The identity of other cases, within a reasonable time period, in which the expert has testified by deposition or at trial, FL ST RCP Rule 1.280(b)(5)(A)(iii)(3); An approximation of the portion of the expert's involvement as an expert witness, which may be based on the number of hours, percentage of hours, or percentage of earned income derived from serving as an expert witness; however, the expert shall not be required to disclose his or her earnings as an expert witness or income derived from other services. FL ST RCP Rule 1.280(b)(5)(A)(iii)(4).
- An expert may be required to produce financial and business records only under the most unusual or compelling circumstances and may not be compelled to compile or produce nonexistent documents. Upon motion, the court may order further discovery by other means, subject to such restrictions as to scope and other provisions pursuant to FL ST RCP Rule 1.280(b)(5)(C) concerning fees and expenses as the court may deem appropriate. FL ST RCP Rule 1.280(b)(5).
- A party may discover facts known or opinions held by an expert who has been retained or specially employed by another party in anticipation of litigation or preparation for trial and who is not expected to be called as a witness at trial, only as provided in FL ST RCP Rule 1.360(b) or upon a showing of exceptional circumstances under which it is impracticable for the party seeking discovery to obtain facts or opinions on the same subject by other means. FL ST RCP Rule 1.280(b)(5)(B).
- Unless manifest injustice would result, the court shall require that the party seeking discovery pay the expert a reasonable fee for time spent in responding to discovery under FL ST RCP Rule 1.280(b)(5)(A) and FL ST RCP Rule 1.280(b)(5)(B); and concerning discovery from an expert obtained under FL ST RCP Rule 1.280(b)(5)(A) the court may require, and concerning discovery obtained under FL ST RCP Rule 1.280(b)(5)(B) shall require, the party seeking discovery to pay the other party a fair part of the fees and expenses reasonably incurred by the latter party in obtaining facts and opinions from the expert. FL ST RCP Rule 1.280(b)(5)(C).
- As used in the Florida Rules of Civil Procedure an expert shall be an expert witness as defined in FL ST RCP Rule 1.390(a). FL ST RCP Rule 1.280(b)(5)(D).

vi. *Claims to privilege or protection.* When a party withholds information otherwise discoverable under the Florida Rules of Civil Procedure by claiming that it is privileged or subject to protection as trial preparation material, the party shall make the claim expressly and shall describe the nature of the documents, communications, or things not produced or disclosed in a manner that, without revealing information itself privileged or protected, will enable other parties to assess the applicability of the privilege or protection. FL ST RCP Rule 1.280(b)(6).

c. *Limitations on discovery of electronically stored information*

i. A person may object to discovery of electronically stored information from sources that the person identifies as not reasonably accessible because of burden or cost. On motion to compel discovery or for a protective order, the person from whom discovery is sought must show that the information sought or the format requested is not reasonably accessible because of undue burden or cost. If that showing is made, the court may nonetheless order the discovery from such sources or in such formats if the requesting party shows good cause. The court may specify

conditions of the discovery, including ordering that some or all of the expenses incurred by the person from whom discovery is sought be paid by the party seeking the discovery. FL ST RCP Rule 1.280(d)(1).

ii. In determining any motion involving discovery of electronically stored information, the court must limit the frequency or extent of discovery otherwise allowed by the Florida Rules of Civil Procedure if it determines that (i) the discovery sought is unreasonably cumulative or duplicative, or can be obtained from another source or in another manner that is more convenient, less burdensome, or less expensive; or (ii) the burden or expense of the discovery outweighs its likely benefit, considering the needs of the case, the amount in controversy, the parties' resources, the importance of the issues at stake in the action, and the importance of the discovery in resolving the issues. FL ST RCP Rule 1.280(d)(2).

d. *Standards of professional conduct; Discovery*

i. Attorneys should pursue discovery requests that are reasonably related to the matter at issue. Attorneys should not use discovery for the purpose of harassing, embarrassing or causing the adversary to incur unnecessary expenses. FL ST 17 J CIR I-94-O-1(II)(1).

ii. Attorneys should not use discovery for the purpose of causing undue delay or obtaining unfair advantage. FL ST 17 J CIR I-94-O-1(II)(2).

iii. Attorneys should ensure that responses to reasonable discovery requests are timely, organized, complete and consistent with the obvious intent of the request. For example, a response to a request to produce should refer to each of the items in the request and should refer to each set of documents as separately marked exhibits. FL ST 17 J CIR I-94-O-1(II)(3).

e. For information on inadvertent disclosure of privileged materials, see FL ST RCP Rule 1.285.

2. *Requests for admission.* It is an advantage to use requests for admission. The biggest advantage is that if an adversary denies a request for an admission and the denied matter is later proven to be true, the adversary may have to pay the costs of proving the genuineness of the document or the truth of the matter requested to be admitted. FL-PP § 3:143.

a. *Scope.* A party may serve upon any other party a written request for the admission of the truth of any matters within the scope of FL ST RCP Rule 1.280(b) set forth in the request that relate to statements or opinions of fact or of the application of law to fact, including the genuineness of any documents described in the request. FL ST RCP Rule 1.370(a).

b. *Copies of documents.* Copies of documents shall be served with the request unless they have been or are otherwise furnished or made available for inspection and copying. FL ST RCP Rule 1.370(a).

c. *Number of requests.* The request for admission shall not exceed thirty (30) requests, including all subparts, unless the court permits a larger number on motion and notice and for good cause, or the parties propounding and responding to the requests stipulate to a larger number. Each matter of which an admission is requested shall be separately set forth. FL ST RCP Rule 1.370(a).

d. *Sufficiency of responses.* The party who has requested the admissions may move to determine the sufficiency of the answers or objections. Unless the court determines that an objection is justified, it shall order that an answer be served. If the court determines that an answer does not comply with the requirements of this rule, it may order either that the matter is admitted or that an amended answer be served. Instead of these orders the court may determine that final disposition of the request be made at a pretrial conference or at a designated time before trial. The provisions of FL ST RCP Rule 1.380(a)(4) apply to the award of expenses incurred in relation to the motion. FL ST RCP Rule 1.370(a).

e. *Effect of admission.* Any matter admitted under FL ST RCP Rule 1.370 is conclusively established unless the court on motion permits withdrawal or amendment of the admission. Subject to FL ST RCP Rule 1.200 governing amendment of a pretrial order, the court may permit withdrawal or amendment when the presentation of the merits of the action will be subserved by it and the party who obtained the admission fails to satisfy the court that withdrawal or amendment will prejudice that party in maintaining an action or defense on the merits. Any admission made by a party under this rule is for the purpose of the pending action only and is not an admission for any other purpose nor may it be used against that party in any other proceeding. FL ST RCP Rule 1.370(b).

f. *Answer requirements.* The matter is admitted unless the party to whom the request is directed serves upon the party requesting the admission a written answer or objection addressed to the matter within thirty (30) days after service of the request or such shorter or longer time as the court may allow but, unless the court shortens the time, a defendant shall not be required to serve answers or objections before the expiration of forty-five (45) days after service of the process and initial pleading upon the defendant. If objection is made, the reasons shall be stated. The answer shall specifically deny the matter or set forth in detail the reasons why the answering party cannot truthfully admit or deny the matter. A denial shall fairly meet the substance of the requested admission, and when good faith requires that a party qualify an answer or deny only a part of the matter of which an admission is requested, the party shall specify so much of it as is true and qualify or deny the remainder. An answering party may not give lack of information or knowledge as a reason for failure to admit or deny unless that party states that that party has made reasonable inquiry and that the information known or readily obtainable by that party is insufficient to enable that party to admit or deny. A party who considers that a matter of which an admission has been requested presents a genuine issue for trial may not object to the request on that ground alone; the party may deny the matter or set forth reasons why the party cannot admit or deny it, subject to FL ST RCP Rule 1.380(c). FL ST RCP Rule 1.370(a).

3. *Arbitration and mediation*

   a. *Referral to arbitration and mediation.* Except as hereinafter provided or as otherwise prohibited by law, the presiding judge may enter an order referring all or any part of a contested civil matter to mediation or arbitration. The parties to any contested civil matter may file a written stipulation to mediate or arbitrate any issue between them at any time. Such stipulation shall be incorporated into the order of referral. FL ST RCP Rule 1.700(a).

   b. *Arbitration*

      i. *Exclusions.* A civil action shall be ordered to arbitration or arbitration in conjunction with mediation upon stipulation of the parties. A civil action may be ordered to arbitration or arbitration in conjunction with mediation upon motion of any party or by the court, if the judge determines the action to be of such a nature that arbitration could be of benefit to the litigants or the court. FL ST RCP Rule 1.800.

         - Under no circumstances may the following categories of actions be referred to arbitration: (1) bond estreatures; (2) habeas corpus or other extraordinary writs; (3) bond validations; (4) civil or criminal contempt; (5) such other matters as may be specified by order of the chief judge in the circuit. FL ST RCP Rule 1.800.

      ii. For more information regarding arbitration, please see FL ST RCP Rule 1.810; FL ST RCP Rule 1.820; FL ST RCP Rule 1.830.

   c. *Mediation.* For more information regarding mediation, please see FL ST RCP Rule 1.710; FL ST RCP Rule 1.720; FL ST RCP Rule 1.730; and FL ST RCP Rule 1.750.

4. *Rules of court*

   a. *Rules of civil procedure.* The Florida Rules of Civil Procedure apply to all actions of a civil nature and all special statutory proceedings in the circuit courts and county courts except those to which the Florida Probate Rules, the Florida Family Law Rules of Procedure, or the Small Claims Rules apply. FL ST RCP Rule 1.010.

      i. The form, content, procedure, and time for pleading in all special statutory proceedings shall be as prescribed by the statutes governing the proceeding unless the Florida Rules of Civil Procedure specifically provide to the contrary. FL ST RCP Rule 1.010.

      ii. The Florida Rules of Civil Procedure shall be construed to secure the just, speedy, and inexpensive determination of every action. FL ST RCP Rule 1.010.

   b. *Rules of judicial administration.* The Florida Rules of Judicial Administration shall apply to administrative matters in all courts to which the Florida Rules of Judicial Administration are applicable by their terms. The Florida Rules of Judicial Administration shall be construed to secure the speedy and inexpensive determination of every proceeding to which they are applicable. The

Florida Rules of Judicial Administration shall supersede all conflicting rules and statutes. FL ST J ADMIN Rule 2.110.

D. Documents

1. *Required documents*

   a. *Request for admission.* Please see the General Requirements section of this document for more information on the contents of the request for admission.

      i. *Notices to persons with disabilities.* See the Format section of this KeyRules document for further information.

   b. *Copies of documents.* Copies of documents shall be served with the request unless they have been or are otherwise furnished or made available for inspection and copying. FL ST RCP Rule 1.370(a).

   c. *Certificate of service.* A certificate of service of the interrogatories shall be filed, giving the date of service and the name of the party to whom they were directed. FL ST RCP Rule 1.340(e). When any attorney certifies in substance: "I certify that a copy hereof has been furnished to (here insert name or names and addresses used for service) by (e-mail) (delivery) (mail) (fax) on .... (date) ....________________ Attorney" the certificate is taken as prima facie proof of such service in compliance with FL ST J ADMIN Rule 2.516. FL ST J ADMIN Rule 2.516(f).

E. Format

1. *Documents; Type and size.* Documents subject to the exceptions set forth in FL ST J ADMIN Rule 2.525(d) shall be filed on recycled paper measuring eight and one half by eleven (8 1/2 by 11) inches. For purposes of FL ST J ADMIN Rule 2.520, paper is recycled if it contains a minimum content of fifty (50) percent waste paper. Xerographic reduction of legal-size (eight and one half by fourteen (8 1/2 by 14) inches) documents to letter size (eight and one half by eleven (8 1/2 by 11) inches) is prohibited. All other documents filed by electronic transmission shall be filed in a format capable of being printed in a format consistent with the provisions of FL ST J ADMIN Rule 2.250. FL ST J ADMIN Rule 2.520(b).

   a. *Exhibits.* Any exhibit or attachment filed with pleadings or papers may be filed in its original size. FL ST J ADMIN Rule 2.520(c).

   b. *Recording space.* On all papers and documents prepared and filed by the court or by any party to a proceeding which are to be recorded in the public records of any county, including but not limited to final money judgments and notices of lis pendens, a three (3) inch by three (3) inch space at the top right-hand corner on the first page and a one (1) inch by three (3) inch space at the top right-hand corner on each subsequent page shall be left blank and reserved for use by the clerk of court. FL ST J ADMIN Rule 2.520(d).

      i. *Exceptions to recording space.* Any papers or documents created by persons or entities over which the filing party has no control, including but not limited to wills, codicils, trusts, or other testamentary documents; documents prepared or executed by any public officer; documents prepared, executed, acknowledged, or proved outside of the State of Florida; or documents created by State or Federal government agencies, may be filed without the space required by FL ST J ADMIN Rule 2.520. FL ST J ADMIN Rule 2.520(e).

   c. *Noncompliance.* No clerk of court is permitted to refuse to file any document or paper because of noncompliance with the Florida Rules of Judicial Administration. However, upon request of the clerk of court, noncomplying documents must be resubmitted in accordance with the formatting rules. FL ST J ADMIN Rule 2.520(f).

2. *Caption.* Every pleading, motion, order, judgment, or other paper shall have a caption containing the name of the court, the file number, and except for in rem proceedings, including forfeiture proceedings, the name of the first party on each side with an appropriate indication of other parties, and a designation identifying the party filing it and its nature or the nature of the order, as the case may be. In any in rem proceeding, every pleading, motion, order, judgment, or other paper shall have a caption containing the name of the court, the file number, the style "In re" (followed by the name or general description of the property), and a designation of the person or entity filing it and its nature or the nature of the order, as the case may be. In an in rem forfeiture proceeding, the style shall be "In re forfeiture of" (followed by the

name of the general description of the property). All papers filed in the action shall be styled in such a manner as to indicate clearly the subject matter of the paper and the party requesting or obtaining relief. FL ST RCP Rule 1.100(c)(1).

3. *Writing and written defined.* Writing or written means a document containing information, an application, or a stipulation. FL ST RCP Rule 1.080(c).
4. *Rule abbreviations*
   a. The Florida Rules of Civil Procedure and shall be abbreviated as Fla.R.Civ.P. FL ST RCP Rule 1.010.
   b. The Florida Rules of Judicial Administration shall be abbreviated as Fla. R. Jud. Admin. FL ST J ADMIN Rule 2.110.
5. *Nonverification.* Except when otherwise specifically provided by the Florida Rules of Civil Procedure or an applicable statute, every pleading or other document of a party represented by an attorney need not be verified or accompanied by an affidavit. FL ST RCP Rule 1.030; FL ST J ADMIN Rule 2.515(a).
6. *Attorney signature*
   a. *Attorney signature.* Every pleading and other document of a party represented by an attorney shall be signed by at least one (1) attorney of record in that attorney's individual name whose current record Florida Bar address, telephone number, including area code, primary e-mail address and secondary e-mail addresses, if any, and Florida Bar number shall be stated, and who shall be duly licensed to practice law in Florida or who shall have received permission to appear in the particular case as provided in FL ST J ADMIN Rule 2.510. FL ST J ADMIN Rule 2.515(a).
      i. The attorney may be required by the court to give the address of, and to vouch for the attorney's authority to represent, the party. FL ST J ADMIN Rule 2.515(a).
      ii. The signature of an attorney shall constitute a certificate by the attorney that the attorney has read the pleading or other document; that to the best of the attorney's knowledge, information, and belief there is good ground to support it; and that it is not interposed for delay. FL ST J ADMIN Rule 2.515(a).
      iii. If a pleading is not signed or is signed with intent to defeat the purpose of FL ST J ADMIN Rule 2.515, it may be stricken and the action may proceed as though the pleading or other document had not been served. FL ST J ADMIN Rule 2.515(a).
   b. *Pro se litigant signature.* A party who is not represented by an attorney shall sign any pleading or other paper and state the party's address and telephone number, including area code. FL ST J ADMIN Rule 2.515(b).
   c. *Form of signature*
      i. The signatures required on pleadings and documents by FL ST J ADMIN Rule 2.515(a) and FL ST J ADMIN Rule 2.515(b) may be:
         - Original signatures;
         - Original signatures that have been reproduced by electronic means, such as on electronically transmitted documents or photocopied documents;
         - Electronic signatures using the "/s/," "s/," or "/s" formats by or at the direction of the person signing; or
         - Any other signature format authorized by general law, so long as the clerk where the proceeding is pending has the capability of receiving and has obtained approval from the Supreme Court of Florida to accept pleadings and documents with that signature format. FL ST J ADMIN Rule 2.515(c)(1).
      ii. An attorney, party, or other person who files a pleading or paper by electronic transmission that does not contain the original signature of that attorney, party, or other person shall file that identical pleading or paper in paper form containing an original signature of that attorney, party, or other person (hereinafter called the follow-up filing) immediately thereafter. The follow-up filing is not required if the Supreme Court of Florida has entered an order directing the clerk of court to discontinue accepting the follow-up filing. FL ST J ADMIN Rule 2.515(c)(2).

iii. The placement of a "/s/" or the image of a signature by an attorney or party or affected non-party signature line on an electronically filed document shall be accepted as the signature and shall verify to the Court the filer is in possession of the originally executed document. Notwithstanding the manner in which an electronic document is signed the originally executed pleading or paper shall be maintained in the filer's possession for a minimum of one (1) year after final disposition and time for appeal of the case. The originally executed document shall be produced for filing or inspection as directed by the Court. FL ST 17 J CIR 2012-16-CIV.

7. *Forms*

a. *Process.* The forms of process, notice of lis pendens, and notice of action provided in the Florida Rules of Civil Procedure are sufficient. Variations from the forms do not void process or notices that are otherwise sufficient. FL ST RCP Rule 1.900(a).

b. *Other forms.* The other forms provided in the Florida Rules of Civil Procedure are sufficient for the matters that are covered by them. So long as the substance is expressed without prolixity, the forms may be varied to meet the facts of a particular case. FL ST RCP Rule 1.900(b).

c. *Formal matters.* Captions, except for the designation of the paper, are omitted from the forms provided in the Florida Rules of Civil Procedure. A general form of caption is the first form provided. Signatures are omitted from pleadings and motions. FL ST RCP Rule 1.900(c).

8. *Notices to persons with disabilities.* All notices of court proceedings to be held in a public facility, and all process compelling appearance at such proceedings, shall include the following statement in bold face, fourteen (14) point Times New Roman or Courier font: "If you are a person with a disability who needs any accommodation in order to participate in this proceeding, you are entitled, at no cost to you, to the provision of certain assistance. Please contact [identify applicable court personnel by name, address, and telephone number] at least seven (7) days before your scheduled court appearance, or immediately upon receiving this notification if the time before the scheduled appearance is less than seven (7) days; if you are hearing or voice impaired, call 711." FL ST J ADMIN Rule 2.540(c)(1). For further information, please see FL ST 17 J CIR 2010-49-GEN.

9. *Minimization of the filing of sensitive information*

a. *Limitations for court filings.* Unless authorized by FL ST J ADMIN Rule 2.425(b), statute, another rule of court, or the court orders otherwise, designated sensitive information filed with the court must be limited to the following format:

i. The initials of a person known to be a minor;

ii. The year of birth of a person's birth date;

iii. No portion of any: Social security number, Bank account number, Credit card account number, Charge account number, or Debit account number;

iv. The last four digits of any: Taxpayer identification number (TIN), Employee identification number, Driver's license number, Passport number, Telephone number, Financial account number, except as set forth in FL ST J ADMIN Rule 2.425(a)(3), Brokerage account number, Insurance policy account number, Loan account number, Customer account number, or Patient or health care number;

v. A truncated version of any: Email address, Computer user name, Password, or Personal identification number (PIN); and

vi. A truncated version of any other sensitive information as provided by court order. FL ST J ADMIN Rule 2.425(a).

b. *Exceptions.* FL ST J ADMIN Rule 2.425(a) does not apply to the following:

i. An account number which identifies the property alleged to be the subject of a proceeding;

ii. The record of an administrative or agency proceeding;

iii. The record in appellate or review proceedings;

iv. The birth date of a minor whenever the birth date is necessary for the court to establish or maintain subject matter jurisdiction;

v. The name of a minor in any order relating to parental responsibility, time-sharing, or child support;

vi. The name of a minor in any document or order affecting the minor's ownership of real property;

vii. The birth date of a party in a writ of attachment or notice to payor;

viii. In traffic and criminal proceedings: a pro se filing; a court filing that is related to a criminal matter or investigation and that is prepared before the filing of a criminal charge or is not filed as part of any docketed criminal case; an arrest or search warrant or any information in support thereof; a charging document and an affidavit or other documents filed in support of any charging document, including any driving records; a statement of particulars; discovery material introduced into evidence or otherwise filed with the court; and all information necessary for the proper issuance and execution of a subpoena duces tecum;

ix. Information used by the clerk for case maintenance purposes or the courts for case management purposes; and

x. Information which is relevant and material to an issue before the court. FL ST J ADMIN Rule 2.425(b).

c. *Remedies.* Upon motion by a party or interested person or sua sponte by the court, the court may order remedies, sanctions or both for a violation of FL ST J ADMIN Rule 2.425(a). Following notice and an opportunity to respond, the court may impose sanctions if such filing was not made in good faith. FL ST J ADMIN Rule 2.425(c).

d. *Motions not restricted.* FL ST J ADMIN Rule 2.425 does not restrict a party's right to move for protective order, to move to file documents under seal, or to request a determination of the confidentiality of records. FL ST J ADMIN Rule 2.425(d).

e. *Application.* FL ST J ADMIN Rule 2.425 does not affect the application of constitutional provisions, statutes, or rules of court regarding confidential information or access to public information. FL ST J ADMIN Rule 2.425(e).

F. Filing and Service Requirements

1. *Court filing of documents and discovery.* Information obtained during discovery shall not be filed with the court until such time as it is filed for good cause. The requirement of good cause is satisfied only where the filing of the information is allowed or required by another applicable rule of procedure or by court order. All filings of discovery documents shall comply with FL ST J ADMIN Rule 2.425. The court shall have the authority to impose sanctions for violation of FL ST RCP Rule 1.280. FL ST RCP Rule 1.280(g).

2. *Filing requirements.* All original documents must be filed with the court either before service or immediately thereafter, unless otherwise provided for by general law or other rules. If the original of any bond or other document is not placed in the court file, a certified copy must be so placed by the clerk. FL ST J ADMIN Rule 2.516(d). All documents shall be filed in conformity with the requirements of FL ST J ADMIN Rule 2.525. FL ST RCP Rule 1.080(b). All documents filed in any court shall be filed by electronic transmission in accordance with FL ST J ADMIN Rule 2.525. "Documents" means pleadings, motions, petitions, memoranda, briefs, notices, exhibits, declarations, affidavits, orders, judgments, decrees, writs, opinions, and any other paper or writing submitted to a court. FL ST J ADMIN Rule 2.520(a). All documents that are court records, as defined in FL ST J ADMIN Rule 2.430(a)(1), must be filed by electronic transmission, provided that: (1) the clerk has the ability to accept and retain such documents; (2) the clerk or the chief judge of the circuit has requested permission to accept documents filed by electronic transmission; and (3) the supreme court has entered an order granting permission to the clerk to accept documents filed by electronic transmission. FL ST J ADMIN Rule 2.525(c)(1).

a. *Definition.* "Electronic transmission of documents" means the sending of information by electronic signals to, by or from a court or clerk, which when received can be transformed and stored or transmitted on paper, microfilm, magnetic storage device, optical imaging system, CD-ROM, flash drive, other electronic data storage system, server, case maintenance system ("CM"), electronic court filing ("ECF") system, statewide or local electronic portal ("e-portal"), or other electronic record keeping system authorized by the supreme court in a format sufficient to communicate the information on the original document in a readable format. Electronic transmission of documents

includes electronic mail ("e-mail") and any internet-based transmission procedure, and may include procedures allowing for documents to be signed or verified by electronic means. FL ST J ADMIN Rule 2.525(a).

i. The filing of documents with the court as required by the Florida Rules of Judicial Administration must be made by filing them with the clerk in accordance with FL ST J ADMIN Rule 2.525, except that the judge may permit documents to be filed with the judge, in which event the judge must note the filing date before him or her on the documents and transmit them to the clerk. The date of filing is that shown on the face of the document by the judge's notation or the clerk's time stamp, whichever is earlier. FL ST J ADMIN Rule 2.516(e).

b. *Application.* Any court or clerk of the court may accept the electronic transmission of documents for filing after the clerk, together with input from the chief judge of the circuit, has obtained approval of the procedures and program for doing so from the Supreme Court of Florida. FL ST J ADMIN Rule 2.525(b).

c. *Exceptions*

i. Paper documents and other submissions may be manually submitted to the clerk or court:

- When the clerk does not have the ability to accept and retain documents by electronic filing or has not had ECF Procedures approved by the supreme court;
- For filing by any self-represented party or any self-represented nonparty unless specific ECF Procedures provide a means to file documents electronically. However, any self-represented nonparty that is a governmental or public agency and any other agency, partnership, corporation, or business entity acting on behalf of any governmental or public agency may file documents by electronic transmission if such entity has the capability of filing documents electronically;
- For filing by attorneys excused from e-mail service in accordance with FL ST J ADMIN Rule 2.516(b);
- When submitting evidentiary exhibits or filing non-documentary materials;
- When the filing involves documents in excess of twenty-five (25) megabytes (25MB) in size. For such filings, documents may be transmitted using an electronic storage medium that the clerk has the ability to accept, which may include a CD-ROM, flash drive, or similar storage medium;
- When filed in open court, as permitted by the court;
- When paper filing is permitted by any approved statewide or local ECF procedures; and
- If any court determines that justice so requires. FL ST J ADMIN Rule 2.525(d).

ii. Any document in paper form submitted under FL ST J ADMIN Rule 2.525(d) is filed when it is received by the clerk or court and the clerk shall immediately thereafter convert any filed paper document to an electronic document. "Convert to an electronic document" means optically capturing an image of a paper document and using character recognition software to recover as much of the document's text as practicable and then indexing and storing the document in the official court file. FL ST J ADMIN Rule 2.525(c)(4).

iii. Any storage medium submitted under FL ST J ADMIN Rule 2.525(d)(5) is filed when received by the clerk or court and the clerk shall immediately thereafter transfer the electronic documents from the storage device to the official court file. FL ST J ADMIN Rule 2.525(c)(5).

iv. If the filer of any paper document authorized under FL ST J ADMIN Rule 2.525(d) provides a self-addressed, postage-paid envelope for return of the paper document after it is converted to electronic form by the clerk, the clerk shall place the paper document in the envelope and deposit it in the mail. Except when a paper document is required to be maintained, the clerk may recycle any filed paper document that is not to be returned to the filer. FL ST J ADMIN Rule 2.525(c)(6).

v. The clerk may convert any paper document filed before the effective date of FL ST J ADMIN

Rule 2.525 to an electronic document. Unless the clerk is required to maintain the paper document, if the paper document has been converted to an electronic document by the clerk, the paper document is no longer part of the official court file and may be removed and recycled. FL ST J ADMIN Rule 2.525(c)(7).

d. *Official court file.* For information on what constitutes the official court file, please see FL ST J ADMIN Rule 2.525(c)(2), FL ST J ADMIN Rule 2.525(c)(3).

e. *Administration.* All attorneys, parties, or other persons using this rule to file documents are required to make arrangements with the court or clerk for the payment of any charges authorized by general law or the supreme court before filing any document by electronic transmission. FL ST J ADMIN Rule 2.525(f)(2).

f. *Filing date.* The filing date for an electronically transmitted document is the date and time that such filing is acknowledged by an electronic stamp or otherwise, pursuant to any procedure set forth in any ECF Procedures approved by the supreme court, or the date the last page of such filing is received by the court or clerk. FL ST J ADMIN Rule 2.525(f)(3).

g. *Accessibility.* All documents transmitted in any electronic form under FL ST J ADMIN Rule 2.525 must comply with the accessibility requirements of FL ST J ADMIN Rule 2.526. FL ST J ADMIN Rule 2.525(g).

h. *Provisions for electronic filing in the Seventeenth Circuit.* Attorneys may electronically file pleadings and papers on existing cases in circuit civil divisions 1, 7, 9, 19, 26 and 27. The following documents may be scanned and efiled; however, the original must be filed with the Clerk: Documents ordered by the Court; and original documents required by law or rule of procedure to be filed with the Clerk. Self represented individuals shall file pleadings and papers with the Clerk. The Clerk within twenty four (24) hours of receipt of an electronic document shall either accept or reject the electronic document for filing and send electronic notice to the filer. FL ST 17 J CIR 2012-16-CIV.

i. *Technical failures.* If a document filed electronically is not received due to: an error in the transmission of the document to the Clerk or any vendor of the Clerk to provide electronic court record filing services which is unknown to an attorney or party or affected non party, or a failure to process the electronic document when received by the Clerk or rejection by the Clerk, or any other technical problems experienced by the attorney or party or affected non party, the Court may, after an evidentiary hearing and upon satisfactory proof, enter an order permitting the document to be filed nunc pro tunc to the date it was first attempted to be sent electronically. FL ST 17 J CIR 2012-16-CIV.

j. *Filing of pleadings or papers at any office of the clerk of court.* The Clerk of Courts, commencing November 3, 2008, shall accept for filing, at the central courthouse, north satellite courthouse, south satellite courthouse, and west satellite courthouse any pleading or motion or other document for filing in the court file from any attorney or party for an existing case except as otherwise set forth. FL ST 17 J CIR 2008-153-GEN. See FL ST 17 J CIR 2008-153-GEN for specific exceptions.

3. *Service requirements.* Every pleading subsequent to the initial pleading, all orders, and every other document filed in the action must be served in conformity with the requirements of FL ST J ADMIN Rule 2.516. FL ST RCP Rule 1.080(a).

a. *Service; When required.* Unless the court otherwise orders, or a statute or supreme court administrative order specifies a different means of service, every pleading subsequent to the initial pleading and every other document filed in any court proceeding, except applications for witness subpoenas and documents served by formal notice or required to be served in the manner provided for service of formal notice, must be served in accordance with FL ST J ADMIN Rule 2.516 on each party. No service need be made on parties against whom a default has been entered, except that pleadings asserting new or additional claims against them must be served in the manner provided for service of summons. FL ST J ADMIN Rule 2.516(a).

b. *Service; How made.* When service is required or permitted to be made upon a party represented by an attorney, service must be made upon the attorney unless service upon the party is ordered by the court. FL ST J ADMIN Rule 2.516(b).

i. *Service by electronic mail ("e-mail").* All documents required or permitted to be served on

another party must be served by e-mail, unless FL ST J ADMIN Rule 2.516 otherwise provides. When, in addition to service by e-mail, the sender also utilizes another means of service provided for in FL ST J ADMIN Rule 2.516(b)(2), any differing time limits and other provisions applicable to that other means of service control. FL ST J ADMIN Rule 2.516(b)(1). Any document electronically transmitted to a court or clerk must also be served on all parties and interested persons in accordance with the applicable rules of court. FL ST J ADMIN Rule 2.525(e)(2).

- *Service on attorneys.* Upon appearing in a proceeding, an attorney must serve a designation of a primary e-mail address and may designate no more than two (2) secondary e-mail addresses. Thereafter, service must be directed to all designated e-mail addresses in that proceeding. Every document filed by an attorney thereafter must include the primary e-mail address of that attorney and any secondary e-mail addresses. If an attorney does not designate any e-mail address for service, documents may be served on that attorney at the e-mail address on record with The Florida Bar. FL ST J ADMIN Rule 2.516(b)(1)(A).
- *Exception to e-mail service on attorneys.* Service by an attorney on another attorney must be made by e-mail unless excused by the court. Upon motion by an attorney demonstrating that the attorney has no e-mail account and lacks access to the Internet at the attorney's office, the court may excuse the attorney from the requirements of e-mail service. Service on and by an attorney excused by the court from e-mail service must be by the means provided in FL ST J ADMIN Rule 2.516(b)(2). FL ST J ADMIN Rule 2.516(b)(1)(B).
- *Service on and by parties not represented by an attorney.* Any party not represented by an attorney may serve a designation of a primary e-mail address and also may designate no more than two (2) secondary e-mail addresses to which service must be directed in that proceeding by the means provided in FL ST J ADMIN Rule 2.516(b)(1). If a party not represented by an attorney does not designate an e-mail address for service in a proceeding, service on and by that party must be by the means provided in FL ST J ADMIN Rule 2.516(b)(2). FL ST J ADMIN Rule 2.516(b)(1)(C).
- *Time of service.* Service by e-mail is complete when it is sent. FL ST J ADMIN Rule 2.516(b)(1)(D). An e-mail is deemed served on the date it is sent. FL ST J ADMIN Rule 2.516(b)(1)(D)(i). If the sender learns that the e-mail did not reach the address of the person to be served, the sender must immediately send another copy by e-mail, or by a means authorized by FL ST J ADMIN Rule 2.516(b)(2). FL ST J ADMIN Rule 2.516(b)(1)(D)(ii). E-mail service is treated as service by mail for the computation of time. FL ST J ADMIN Rule 2.516(b)(1)(D)(iii).

ii. *Format of e-mail for service.* Service of a document by e-mail is made by attaching a copy of the document in PDF format to an e-mail sent to all addresses designated by the attorney or party. FL ST J ADMIN Rule 2.516(b)(1)(E).

- All documents served by e-mail must be attached to an e-mail message containing a subject line beginning with the words "SERVICE OF COURT DOCUMENT" in all capital letters, followed by the case number of the proceeding in which the documents are being served. FL ST J ADMIN Rule 2.516(b)(1)(E)(i).
- The body of the e-mail must identify the court in which the proceeding is pending, the case number, the name of the initial party on each side, the title of each document served with that e-mail, and the sender's name and telephone number. FL ST J ADMIN Rule 2.516(b)(1)(E)(ii).
- Any document served by e-mail may be signed by the "/s/" format, as long as the filed original is signed in accordance with the applicable rule of procedure. FL ST J ADMIN Rule 2.516(b)(1)(E)(iii).
- Any e-mail which, together with its attached documents, exceeds five megabytes (5MB) in size, must be divided and sent as separate e-mails, no one of which may exceed five megabytes (5MB) in size and each of which must be sequentially numbered in the subject line. FL ST J ADMIN Rule 2.516(b)(1)(E)(iv).

iii. *Service by other means.* In addition to, and not in lieu of, service by e-mail, service may also be made upon attorneys by any of the means specified in FL ST J ADMIN Rule 2.516(b)(2). Service on and by all parties who are not represented by an attorney and who do not designate an e-mail address, and on and by all attorneys excused from e-mail service, must be made by delivering a copy of the document or by mailing it to the party or attorney at their last known address or, if no address is known, by leaving it with the clerk of the court. Service by mail is complete upon mailing. Delivery of a copy within FL ST J ADMIN Rule 2.516 is complete upon:

- Handing it to the attorney or to the party,
- Leaving it at the attorney's or party's office with a clerk or other person in charge thereof,
- If there is no one in charge, leaving it in a conspicuous place therein,
- If the office is closed or the person to be served has no office, leaving it at the person's usual place of abode with some person of his or her family above fifteen (15) years of age and informing such person of the contents, or
- Transmitting it by facsimile to the attorney's or party's office with a cover sheet containing the sender's name, firm, address, telephone number, and facsimile number, and the number of pages transmitted. When service is made by facsimile, a copy must also be served by any other method permitted by FL ST J ADMIN Rule 2.516. Facsimile service occurs when transmission is complete. FL ST J ADMIN Rule 2.516(b)(2)(A) through FL ST J ADMIN Rule 2.516(b)(2)(E).
- Service by delivery after 5:00 p.m. must be deemed to have been made by mailing on the date of delivery. FL ST J ADMIN Rule 2.516(b)(2)(F).

c. *Service; Numerous defendants.* In actions when the parties are unusually numerous, the court may regulate the service contemplated by the Florida Rules of Judicial Administration on motion or on its own initiative in such manner as may be found to be just and reasonable. FL ST J ADMIN Rule 2.516(c).

d. *Service by clerk.* Service of notices and other documents required to be made by the clerk must also be done as provided in FL ST J ADMIN Rule 2.516(b). FL ST J ADMIN Rule 2.516(g).

G. Hearings

1. There is no hearing required or contemplated with regard to requests for admission in the Florida Rules of Civil Procedure.

H. Forms

1. Official Request for Admissions Forms for Florida

a. Caption. FL ST RCP Form 1.901.

2. Request for Admissions Forms for Florida

a. Requests for admissions; Negligence, fall down. FL-PRACFORM § 8:41.

b. Requests for admissions; Promissory note. FL-PRACFORM § 8:42.

c. Requests for admissions; Open account. FL-PRACFORM § 8:43.

d. Requests for admissions; Mortgage foreclosure. FL-PRACFORM § 8:44.

e. Request for admissions; General form. FL-PP § 3:146.

f. Request for admissions; Facts and genuineness of documents. FL-PP § 3:147.

g. Motion; To determine sufficiency of reply to request for admissions. FL-PP § 3:152.

h. Form for request for admissions. FL-RCPF R 1.370(5).

i. Form for request for admissions (another form). FL-RCPF R 1.370(6).

j. Form for request for admissions served concurrently with interrogatories. FL-RCPF R 1.370(7).

k. Form for request for admissions as to factual situation and refinement of issues. FL-RCPF R 1.370(9).

l. Form for request to admit party uses electronic data storage. FL-RCPF R 1.370(10).

I. Checklist

(I) ❑ Matters to be considered by requesting party

(a) ❑ Required documents

(1) ❑ Request

(2) ❑ Copies of documents

(3) ❑ Certificate of service

(b) ❑ Time for request

(1) ❑ Without leave of court the request may be served upon the plaintiff after commencement of the action and upon any other party with or after service of the process and initial pleading upon that party

(II) ❑ Matters to be considered by responding party

(a) ❑ Required documents

(1) ❑ Response to request

(2) ❑ Certificate of service

(b) ❑ Time for response

(1) ❑ The party to whom the request is directed shall serve a written response within thirty (30) days after service of the request, except that a defendant may serve a response within forty-five (45) days after service of the process and initial pleading on that defendant

Requests, Notices and Applications
Notice of Deposition

Document Last Updated January 2013

A. Applicable Rules

1. *State rules*

a. Pleadings and motions. FL ST RCP Rule 1.100.

b. Depositions before action or pending appeal. FL ST RCP Rule 1.290.

c. Persons before whom depositions may be taken. FL ST RCP Rule 1.300.

d. Depositions upon oral examination. FL ST RCP Rule 1.310.

e. Depositions upon written questions. FL ST RCP Rule 1.320.

f. Use of depositions in court proceedings. FL ST RCP Rule 1.330.

g. Nonverification of pleadings. FL ST RCP Rule 1.030.

h. Service and filing of pleadings, orders, and documents. FL ST RCP Rule 1.080.

i. Time. FL ST RCP Rule 1.090.

j. General provisions governing discovery. FL ST RCP Rule 1.280.

k. Failure to make discovery; Sanctions. FL ST RCP Rule 1.380.

l. Depositions of expert witnesses. FL ST RCP Rule 1.390.

m. Relief from judgment, decrees or orders. FL ST RCP Rule 1.540.

n. Forms. FL ST RCP Rule 1.900.

o. Retention of court records. FL ST J ADMIN Rule 2.430.

p. Foreign attorneys. FL ST J ADMIN Rule 2.510..

q. Signature of attorneys and parties. FL ST J ADMIN Rule 2.515.
r. Paper. FL ST J ADMIN Rule 2.520.
s. Electronic filing. FL ST J ADMIN Rule 2.525.
t. Requests for accommodations by persons with disabilities. FL ST J ADMIN Rule 2.540.
u. Minimization of the filing of sensitive information. FL ST J ADMIN Rule 2.425.
v. Accessibility of information and technology. FL ST J ADMIN Rule 2.526.
w. Production of documents and things without deposition. FL ST RCP Rule 1.351.

2. *Local rules*
   a. Standards of professional courtesy. FL ST 17 J CIR I-94-O-1.
   b. Administrative order authorizing the filing of pleadings or papers at any office of the clerk of court. FL ST 17 J CIR 2008-153-GEN.
   c. Administrative order regarding provision of ADA accommodations. FL ST 17 J CIR 2010-49-GEN.
   d. Administrative order establishing electronic filing procedures for the civil division. FL ST 17 J CIR 2012-16-CIV.

B. Timing

1. *Depositions upon oral examination.* After commencement of the action any party may take the testimony of any person, including a party, by deposition upon oral examination. Leave of court, granted with or without notice, must be obtained only if the plaintiff seeks to take a deposition within thirty (30) days after service of the process and initial pleading upon any defendant, except that leave is not required (1) if a defendant has served a notice of taking deposition or otherwise sought discovery, or (2) if special notice is given as provided in FL ST RCP Rule 1.310(b)(2). The attendance of witnesses may be compelled by subpoena as provided in FL ST RCP Rule 1.410. The deposition of a person confined in prison may be taken only by leave of court on such terms as the court prescribes. FL ST RCP Rule 1.310(a). A party desiring to take the deposition of any person upon oral examination shall give reasonable notice in writing to every other party to the action. FL ST RCP Rule 1.310(b)(1).

2. *Depositions upon written questions.* After commencement of the action any party may take the testimony of any person, including a party, by deposition upon written questions. The attendance of witnesses may be compelled by the use of subpoena as provided in FL ST RCP Rule 1.410. The deposition of a person confined in prison may be taken only by leave of court on such terms as the court prescribes. Within thrity (30) days after the notice and written questions are served, a party may serve cross questions upon all other parties. Within ten (10) days after being served with cross questions, a party may serve redirect questions upon all other parties. Within ten (10) days after being served with redirect questions, a party may serve recross questions upon all other parties. The court may for cause shown enlarge or shorten the time. FL ST RCP Rule 1.320(a).

3. *Depositions before action or pending appeal.* For information on petitions and motions for depositions before an action or pending appeal, please see the General Requirements section below.

4. *Sequence and timing of discovery.* Except as provided in FL ST RCP Rule 1.280(b)(5) or unless the court upon motion for the convenience of parties and witnesses and in the interest of justice orders otherwise, methods of discovery may be used in any sequence, and the fact that a party is conducting discovery, whether by deposition or otherwise, shall not delay any other party's discovery. FL ST RCP Rule 1.280(e).

5. *Standard of professional conduct; Scheduling*
   a. Attorneys should endeavor to provide opposing counsel, parties, witnesses, and other affected persons, sufficient notice of depositions, hearings and other proceedings, except upon agreement of course, in an emergency, or in other circumstances compelling more expedited scheduling. As a general rule, actual notice should be no less than five (5) business days for instate depositions, ten (10) business days for out-of-state depositions and four (4) business days for hearings. FL ST 17 J CIR I-94-O-1(I)(1).
   b. Attorneys should communicate with opposing counsel prior to scheduling depositions, hearings and

other proceedings, in an effort to schedule them at times that are mutually convenient for all interested persons. Further, sufficient time should be reserved to permit a complete presentation by counsel for all parties. FL ST 17 J CIR I-94-O-1(I)(2).

c. Attorneys should notify opposing counsel, the court, and others affected, of scheduling conflicts as soon as they become apparent. Further, attorneys should cooperate with one another regarding all reasonable rescheduling requests that do not prejudice their clients or unduly delay a proceeding. FL ST 17 J CIR I-94-O-1(I)(3).

d. Attorneys should promptly notify the court or other tribunal of any resolution between the parties that renders a scheduled court appearance unnecessary or otherwise moot. FL ST 17 J CIR I-94-O-1(I)(4).

e. Attorneys should grant reasonable requests by opposing counsel for extensions of time within which to respond to pleadings, discovery, and other matters when such an extension will not prejudice their client or unduly delay a proceeding. FL ST 17 J CIR I-94-O-1(I)(5).

6. *Timing considerations when filing electronically.* The filing date of an efiled document is when the last page is received by the Clerk. The electronic filing of a document does not modify any filing deadlines as required by law, rule of procedure, or court order. FL ST 17 J CIR 2012-16-CIV.

7. *Computation of time*

a. *Generally.* Computation of time shall be governed by FL ST J ADMIN Rule 2.514. FL ST RCP Rule 1.090(a). The following rules apply in computing time periods specified in any rule of procedure, local rule, court order, or statute that does not specify a method of computing time. FL ST J ADMIN Rule 2.514(a).

i. *Period stated in days or a longer unit.* When the period is stated in days or a longer unit of time (A) exclude the day of the event that triggers the period; (B) count every day, including intermediate Saturdays, Sundays, and legal holidays; and (C) include the last day of the period, but if the last day is a Saturday, Sunday, or legal holiday, or falls within any period of time extended through an order of the chief justice under FL ST J ADMIN Rule 2.205(a)(2)(B)(iv), the period continues to run until the end of the next day that is not a Saturday, Sunday, or legal holiday and does not fall within any period of time extended through an order of the chief justice. FL ST J ADMIN Rule 2.514(a)(1).

ii. *Period stated in hours.* When the period is stated in hours (A) begin counting immediately on the occurrence of the event that triggers the period; (B) count every hour, including hours during intermediate Saturdays, Sundays, and legal holidays; and (C) if the period would end on a Saturday, Sunday, or legal holiday, or during any period of time extended through an order of the chief justice under FL ST J ADMIN Rule 2.205(a)(2)(B)(iv), the period continues to run until the same time on the next day that is not a Saturday, Sunday, or legal holiday and does not fall within any period of time extended through an order of the chief justice. FL ST J ADMIN Rule 2.514(a)(2).

iii. *Period stated in days less than seven (7) days.* When the period stated in days is less than seven (7) days, intermediate Saturdays, Sundays, and legal holidays shall be excluded in the computation. FL ST J ADMIN Rule 2.514(a)(3).

iv. *"Last day" defined.* Unless a different time is set by a statute, local rule, or court order, the last day ends (A) for electronic filing or for service by any means, at midnight; and (B) for filing by other means, when the clerk's office is scheduled to close. FL ST J ADMIN Rule 2.514(a)(4).

v. *"Next day" defined.* The "next day" is determined by continuing to count forward when the period is measured after an event and backward when measured before an event. FL ST J ADMIN Rule 2.514(a)(5).

vi. *"Legal holiday" defined.* "Legal holiday" means (A) the day set aside by FL ST § 110.117, for observing New Year's Day, Martin Luther King, Jr.'s Birthday, Memorial Day, Independence Day, Labor Day, Veterans' Day, Thanksgiving Day, the Friday after Thanksgiving Day, or Christmas Day, and (B) any day observed as a holiday by the clerk's office or as designated by the chief judge. FL ST J ADMIN Rule 2.514(a)(6).

b. *Additional time after service by mail or e-mail.* When a party may or must act within a specified time after service and service is made by mail or e-mail, five (5) days are added after the period that would otherwise expire under FL ST J ADMIN Rule 2.514(a). FL ST J ADMIN Rule 2.514(b).

c. *Enlargement.* When an act is required or allowed to be done at or within a specified time by order of court, by the Florida Rules of Civil Procedure, or by notice given thereunder, for cause shown the court at any time in its discretion (1) with or without notice, may order the period enlarged if request therefor is made before the expiration of the period originally prescribed or as extended by a previous order, or (2) upon motion made and notice after the expiration of the specified period, may permit the act to be done when failure to act was the result of excusable neglect, but it may not extend the time for making a motion for new trial, for rehearing, or to alter or amend a judgment; making a motion for relief from a judgment under FL ST RCP Rule 1.540(b); taking an appeal or filing a petition for certiorari; or making a motion for a directed verdict. FL ST RCP Rule 1.090(b).

d. *Unaffected by expiration of term.* The period of time provided for the doing of any act or the taking of any proceeding shall not be affected or limited by the continued existence or expiration of a term of court. The continued existence or expiration of a term of court in no way affects the power of a court to do any act or take any proceeding in any action which is or has been pending before it. FL ST RCP Rule 1.090(c).

C. General Requirements

1. *General provisions governing discovery*

a. *Discovery methods.* Parties may obtain discovery by one or more of the following methods: depositions upon oral examination or written questions; written interrogatories; production of documents or things or permission to enter upon land or other property for inspection and other purposes; physical and mental examinations; and requests for admission. Unless the court orders otherwise and under FL ST RCP Rule 1.280(c), the frequency of use of these methods is not limited, except as provided in FL ST RCP Rule 1.200, FL ST RCP Rule 1.340, and FL ST RCP Rule 1.370. FL ST RCP Rule 1.280(a).

b. *Scope of discovery.* Unless otherwise limited by order of the court in accordance with the Florida Rules of Civil Procedure, the scope of discovery is as follows:

i. *In general.* Parties may obtain discovery regarding any matter, not privileged, that is relevant to the subject matter of the pending action, whether it relates to the claim or defense of the party seeking discovery or the claim or defense of any other party, including the existence, description, nature, custody, condition, and location of any books, documents, or other tangible things and the identity and location of persons having knowledge of any discoverable matter. It is not ground for objection that the information sought will be inadmissible at the trial if the information sought appears reasonably calculated to lead to the discovery of admissible evidence. FL ST RCP Rule 1.280(b)(1).

ii. *Indemnity agreements.* A party may obtain discovery of the existence and contents of any agreement under which any person may be liable to satisfy part or all of a judgment that may be entered in the action or to indemnify or to reimburse a party for payments made to satisfy the judgment. Information concerning the agreement is not admissible in evidence at trial by reason of disclosure. FL ST RCP Rule 1.280(b)(2).

iii. *Electronically stored information.* A party may obtain discovery of electronically stored information in accordance with the Florida Rules of Civil Procedure. FL ST RCP Rule 1.280(b)(3).

iv. *Trial preparation; Materials.* Subject to the provisions of FL ST RCP Rule 1.280(b)(5), a party may obtain discovery of documents and tangible things otherwise discoverable under FL ST RCP Rule 1.280(b)(1) and prepared in anticipation of litigation or for trial by or for another party or by or for that party's representative, including that party's attorney, consultant, surety, indemnitor, insurer, or agent, only upon a showing that the party seeking discovery has need of the materials in the preparation of the case and is unable without undue hardship to obtain the substantial equivalent of the materials by other means. FL ST RCP Rule 1.280(b)(4).

- In ordering discovery of the materials when the required showing has been made, the court shall protect against disclosure of the mental impressions, conclusions, opinions, or legal theories of an attorney or other representative of a party concerning the litigation. FL ST RCP Rule 1.280(b)(4).

- Without the required showing a party may obtain a copy of a statement concerning the action or its subject matter previously made by that party. FL ST RCP Rule 1.280(b)(4).
- Upon request without the required showing a person not a party may obtain a copy of a statement concerning the action or its subject matter previously made by that person. If the request is refused, the person may move for an order to obtain a copy. The provisions of FL ST RCP Rule 1.380(a)(5) apply to the award of expenses incurred as a result of making the motion. FL ST RCP Rule 1.280(b)(4).
- For purposes of FL ST RCP Rule 1.280(b)(4), a statement previously made is a written statement signed or otherwise adopted or approved by the person making it, or a stenographic, mechanical, electrical, or other recording or transcription of it that is a substantially verbatim recital of an oral statement by the person making it and contemporaneously recorded. FL ST RCP Rule 1.280(b)(4).

v. *Trial preparation; Experts.* Discovery of facts known and opinions held by experts, otherwise discoverable under the provisions of FL ST RCP Rule 1.280(b)(1) and acquired or developed in anticipation of litigation or for trial, may be obtained only as follows:

- By interrogatories a party may require any other party to identify each person whom the other party expects to call as an expert witness at trial and to state the subject matter on which the expert is expected to testify, and to state the substance of the facts and opinions to which the expert is expected to testify and a summary of the grounds for each opinion. FL ST RCP Rule 1.280(b)(5)(A)(i).
- Any person disclosed by interrogatories or otherwise as a person expected to be called as an expert witness at trial may be deposed in accordance with FL ST RCP Rule 1.390 without motion or order of court. FL ST RCP Rule 1.280(b)(5)(A)(ii).
- A party may obtain the following discovery regarding any person disclosed by interrogatories or otherwise as a person expected to be called as an expert witness at trial: The scope of employment in the pending case and the compensation for such service, FL ST RCP Rule 1.280(b)(5)(A)(iii)(1); The expert's general litigation experience, including the percentage of work performed for plaintiffs and defendants, FL ST RCP Rule 1.280(b)(5)(A)(iii)(2); The identity of other cases, within a reasonable time period, in which the expert has testified by deposition or at trial, FL ST RCP Rule 1.280(b)(5)(A)(iii)(3); An approximation of the portion of the expert's involvement as an expert witness, which may be based on the number of hours, percentage of hours, or percentage of earned income derived from serving as an expert witness; however, the expert shall not be required to disclose his or her earnings as an expert witness or income derived from other services. FL ST RCP Rule 1.280(b)(5)(A)(iii)(4).
- An expert may be required to produce financial and business records only under the most unusual or compelling circumstances and may not be compelled to compile or produce nonexistent documents. Upon motion, the court may order further discovery by other means, subject to such restrictions as to scope and other provisions pursuant to FL ST RCP Rule 1.280(b)(5)(C) concerning fees and expenses as the court may deem appropriate. FL ST RCP Rule 1.280(b)(5).
- A party may discover facts known or opinions held by an expert who has been retained or specially employed by another party in anticipation of litigation or preparation for trial and who is not expected to be called as a witness at trial, only as provided in FL ST RCP Rule 1.360(b) or upon a showing of exceptional circumstances under which it is impracticable for the party seeking discovery to obtain facts or opinions on the same subject by other means. FL ST RCP Rule 1.280(b)(5)(B).
- Unless manifest injustice would result, the court shall require that the party seeking

discovery pay the expert a reasonable fee for time spent in responding to discovery under FL ST RCP Rule 1.280(b)(5)(A) and FL ST RCP Rule 1.280(b)(5)(B); and concerning discovery from an expert obtained under FL ST RCP Rule 1.280(b)(5)(A) the court may require, and concerning discovery obtained under FL ST RCP Rule 1.280(b)(5)(B) shall require, the party seeking discovery to pay the other party a fair part of the fees and expenses reasonably incurred by the latter party in obtaining facts and opinions from the expert. FL ST RCP Rule 1.280(b)(5)(C).

- As used in the Florida Rules of Civil Procedure an expert shall be an expert witness as defined in FL ST RCP Rule 1.390(a). FL ST RCP Rule 1.280(b)(5)(D).

vi. *Claims to privilege or protection.* When a party withholds information otherwise discoverable under the Florida Rules of Civil Procedure by claiming that it is privileged or subject to protection as trial preparation material, the party shall make the claim expressly and shall describe the nature of the documents, communications, or things not produced or disclosed in a manner that, without revealing information itself privileged or protected, will enable other parties to assess the applicability of the privilege or protection. FL ST RCP Rule 1.280(b)(6).

c. *Limitations on discovery of electronically stored information*

i. A person may object to discovery of electronically stored information from sources that the person identifies as not reasonably accessible because of burden or cost. On motion to compel discovery or for a protective order, the person from whom discovery is sought must show that the information sought or the format requested is not reasonably accessible because of undue burden or cost. If that showing is made, the court may nonetheless order the discovery from such sources or in such formats if the requesting party shows good cause. The court may specify conditions of the discovery, including ordering that some or all of the expenses incurred by the person from whom discovery is sought be paid by the party seeking the discovery. FL ST RCP Rule 1.280(d)(1).

ii. In determining any motion involving discovery of electronically stored information, the court must limit the frequency or extent of discovery otherwise allowed by the Florida Rules of Civil Procedure if it determines that (i) the discovery sought is unreasonably cumulative or duplicative, or can be obtained from another source or in another manner that is more convenient, less burdensome, or less expensive; or (ii) the burden or expense of the discovery outweighs its likely benefit, considering the needs of the case, the amount in controversy, the parties' resources, the importance of the issues at stake in the action, and the importance of the discovery in resolving the issues. FL ST RCP Rule 1.280(d)(2).

d. *Standards of professional conduct; Discovery*

i. Attorneys should pursue discovery requests that are reasonably related to the matter at issue. Attorneys should not use discovery for the purpose of harassing, embarrassing or causing the adversary to incur unnecessary expenses. FL ST 17 J CIR I-94-O-1(II)(1).

ii. Attorneys should not use discovery for the purpose of causing undue delay or obtaining unfair advantage. FL ST 17 J CIR I-94-O-1(II)(2).

iii. Attorneys should ensure that responses to reasonable discovery requests are timely, organized, complete and consistent with the obvious intent of the request. For example, a response to a request to produce should refer to each of the items in the request and should refer to each set of documents as separately marked exhibits. FL ST 17 J CIR I-94-O-1(II)(3).

e. For information on inadvertent disclosure of privileged materials, see FL ST RCP Rule 1.285.

2. *Notice of deposition*

a. *Upon oral examination.* A party desiring to take the deposition of any person upon oral examination shall give reasonable notice in writing to every other party to the action. The notice shall state the time and place for taking the deposition and the name and address of each person to be examined, if known, and, if the name is not known, a general description sufficient to identify the person or the particular class or group to which the person belongs. If a subpoena duces tecum is to be served on the person to be examined, the designation of the materials to be produced under the subpoena shall be attached to or included in the notice. FL ST RCP Rule 1.310(b)(1).

b. *Upon written examination.* A party desiring to take a deposition upon written questions shall serve a notice stating: (1) the name and address of the person who is to answer them, if known, and, if the name is not known, a general description sufficient to identify the person or the particular class or group to which that person belongs, and (2) the name or descriptive title and address of the officer before whom the deposition is to be taken. FL ST RCP Rule 1.320(a).

3. *When leave of court required.* Leave of court, granted with or without notice, must be obtained only if the plaintiff seeks to take a deposition within thirty (30) days after service of the process and initial pleading upon any defendant, except that leave is not required if a defendant has served a notice of taking deposition or otherwise sought discovery. FL ST RCP Rule 1.310(a).

a. *Exceptions.* Leave of court is not required for the taking of a deposition by plaintiff if the notice states that the person to be examined is about to go out of the state and will be unavailable for examination unless a deposition is taken before expiration of the thirty (30) day period. If a party shows that when served with notice under FL ST RCP Rule 1.310(b) that party was unable through the exercise of diligence to obtain counsel to represent the party at the taking of the deposition, the deposition may not be used against that party. FL ST RCP Rule 1.310(b)(2).

b. *Persons in prison.* The deposition of a person confined in prison may be taken only by leave of court on such terms as the court prescribes. FL ST RCP Rule 1.310(a); FL ST RCP Rule 1.320(a).

4. *Deposition procedure*

a. *Who may take depositions.* Depositions may be taken before any notary public or judicial officer or before any officer authorized by the statutes of Florida to take acknowledgments or proof of executions of deeds or by any person appointed by the court in which the action is pending. FL ST RCP Rule 1.300(a).

i. *In foreign countries.* In a foreign country depositions may be taken: on notice before a person authorized to administer oaths in the place in which the examination is held, either by the law thereof or by the law of Florida or of the United States; before a person commissioned by the court, and a person so commissioned shall have the power by virtue of the commission to administer any necessary oath and take testimony; or pursuant to a letter rogatory. FL ST RCP Rule 1.300(b).

ii. *Selection by stipulation.* If the parties so stipulate in writing, depositions may be taken before any person at any time or place upon any notice and in any manner and when so taken may be used like other depositions. FL ST RCP Rule 1.300(c).

iii. *Persons disqualified.* Unless so stipulated by the parties, no deposition shall be taken before a person who is a relative, employee, attorney, or counsel of any of the parties, is a relative or employee of any of the parties' attorney or counsel, or is financially interested in the action. FL ST RCP Rule 1.300(d).

b. *Depositions before action*

i. *Petition.* A person who desires to perpetuate that person's own testimony or that of another person regarding any matter that may be cognizable in any Florida court may file a verified petition in the circuit court in the county of the residence of any expected adverse party. The petition shall be entitled in the name of the petitioner and shall show:

- That the petitioner expects to be a party to an action cognizable in a court of Florida, but is presently unable to bring the action;
- The subject matter of the expected action and the petitioner's interest therein;
- The facts which the petitioner desires to establish by the proposed testimony and the petitioner's reasons for desiring to perpetuate it;
- The names or a description of the persons the petitioner expects will be adverse parties and their addresses so far as known; and
- The names and addresses of the persons to be examined and the substance of the testimony which the petitioner expects to elicit from each; and shall ask for an order authorizing the petitioner to take the deposition of the persons to be examined named in the petition for the purpose of perpetuating their testimony. FL ST RCP Rule 1.290(a)(1).

ii. *Notice and service.* After submitting the petition, the petitioner must thereafter serve a notice upon each person named in the petition as an expected adverse party, together with a copy of the petition, stating that the petitioner will apply to the court at a time and place named therein for an order described in the petition. At least twenty (20) days before the date of hearing the notice shall be served either within or without the county in the manner provided by law for service of summons, but if such service cannot with due diligence be made upon any expected adverse party named in the petition, the court may make an order for service by publication or otherwise, and shall appoint an attorney for persons not served in the manner provided by law for service of summons who shall represent them, and if they are not otherwise represented, shall cross-examine the deponent. FL ST RCP Rule 1.290(a)(2).

iii. *Order and examination.* If the court is satisfied that the perpetuation of the testimony may prevent a failure or delay of justice, it shall make an order designating or describing the persons whose depositions may be taken and specifying the subject matter of the examination and whether the deposition shall be taken upon oral examination or written interrogatories. The deposition may then be taken in accordance with the rules governing depositions. FL ST RCP Rule 1.290(a)(3).

iv. *Use of deposition.* A deposition taken before an action and in accordance with the procedures above may be used in any action involving the same subject matter subsequently brought in any court. FL ST RCP Rule 1.290(a)(4).

c. *Depositions upon oral examination*

i. *Enlargement of time.* For cause shown the court may enlarge or shorten the time for taking the deposition. FL ST RCP Rule 1.310(b)(3).

ii. *Videotaped depositions.* Any deposition may be recorded by videotape without leave of the court or stipulation of the parties, provided the deposition is taken in accordance with the following:

- *Notice.* A party intending to videotape a deposition shall state in the notice that the deposition is to be videotaped and shall give the name and address of the operator. Any subpoena served on the person to be examined shall state the method or methods for recording the testimony. FL ST RCP Rule 1.310(b)(4)(A).
- *Stenographer.* Videotaped depositions shall also be recorded stenographically, unless all parties agree otherwise. FL ST RCP Rule 1.310(b)(4)(B).
- *Procedure.* At the beginning of the deposition, the officer before whom it is taken shall, on camera: (i) identify the style of the action, (ii) state the date, and (iii) swear the witness. FL ST RCP Rule 1.310(b)(4)(C).
- *Custody of tape and copies.* The attorney for the party requesting the videotaping of the deposition shall take custody of and be responsible for the safeguarding of the videotape, shall permit the viewing of it by the opposing party, and, if requested, shall provide a copy of the videotape at the expense of the party requesting the copy. FL ST RCP Rule 1.310(b)(4)(D).
- *Cost of videotaped depositions.* The party requesting the videotaping shall bear the initial cost of videotaping. FL ST RCP Rule 1.310(b)(4)(E).

iii. *Production of documents.* The notice to a party deponent may be accompanied by a request for the production of documents and tangible things at the taking of the deposition. The procedure of FL ST RCP Rule 1.350 shall apply to the request. FL ST RCP Rule 1.351 provides the exclusive procedure for obtaining documents or things by subpoena from nonparties without deposing the custodian or other person in possession of the documents. FL ST RCP Rule 1.310(b)(5).

iv. *Deposing organizations.* In the notice a party may name as the deponent a public or private corporation, a partnership or association, or a governmental agency, and designate with reasonable particularity the matters on which examination is requested. The organization so named shall designate one or more officers, directors, or managing agents, or other persons who consent to do so, to testify on its behalf and may state the matters on which each person designated will testify. The persons so designated shall testify about matters known or reasonably available to the organization. FL ST RCP Rule 1.310(b)(6).

v. *Depositions by telephone.* On motion the court may order that the testimony at a deposition be taken by telephone. The order may prescribe the manner in which the deposition will be taken. A party may also arrange for a stenographic transcription at that party's own initial expense. FL ST RCP Rule 1.310(b)(7).

vi. *Deposing a minor.* Any minor subpoenaed for testimony shall have the right to be accompanied by a parent or guardian at all times during the taking of testimony notwithstanding the invocation of the rule of sequestration of section FL ST § 90.616, except upon a showing that the presence of a parent or guardian is likely to have a material, negative impact on the credibility or accuracy of the minor's testimony, or that the interests of the parent or guardian are in actual or potential conflict with the interests of the minor. FL ST RCP Rule 1.310(b)(8).

vii. *Examination and cross-examination.* Examination and cross-examination of witnesses may proceed as permitted at the trial. FL ST RCP Rule 1.310(c).

viii. *Oath.* The officer before whom the deposition is to be taken shall put the witness on oath and shall personally, or by someone acting under the officer's direction and in the officer's presence, record the testimony of the witness, except that when a deposition is being taken by telephone, the witness shall be sworn by a person present with the witness who is qualified to administer an oath in that location. FL ST RCP Rule 1.310(c).

ix. *Record of examination.* The deposition testimony must be taken stenographically or recorded by any other means ordered. If requested by one of the parties, the testimony shall be transcribed at the initial cost of the requesting party and prompt notice of the request shall be given to all other parties. FL ST RCP Rule 1.310(c).

x. *Objections.* All objections made at time of the examination to the qualifications of the officer taking the deposition, the manner of taking it, the evidence presented, or the conduct of any party, and any other objection to the proceedings shall be noted by the officer upon the deposition. Any objection during a deposition shall be stated concisely and in a nonargumentative and nonsuggestive manner. A party may instruct a deponent not to answer only when necessary to preserve a privilege, to enforce a limitation on evidence directed by the court, or to present a motion under FL ST RCP Rule 1.310(d). FL ST RCP Rule 1.310(c).

- Otherwise, evidence objected to shall be taken subject to the objections. Instead of participating in the oral examination, parties may serve written questions in a sealed envelope on the party taking the deposition and that party shall transmit them to the officer, who shall propound them to the witness and record the answers verbatim. FL ST RCP Rule 1.310(c).

xi. *Motion to terminate or limit examination.* At any time during the taking of the deposition, on motion of a party or of the deponent and upon a showing that the examination is being conducted in bad faith or in such manner as unreasonably to annoy, embarrass, or oppress the deponent or party, or that improper objections and instructions to a deponent not to answer are being made, the court in which the action is pending or the circuit court where the deposition is being taken may order the officer conducting the examination to cease forthwith from taking the deposition or may limit the scope and manner of the taking of the deposition under the scope of permissible discovery. FL ST RCP Rule 1.310(d).

- If the order terminates the examination, it shall be resumed thereafter only upon the order of the court in which the action is pending. Upon demand of any party or the deponent, the taking of the deposition shall be suspended for the time necessary to make a motion for an order. FL ST RCP Rule 1.310(d).

xii. *Deponent review.* If the testimony is transcribed, the transcript shall be furnished to the witness for examination and shall be read to or by the witness unless the examination and reading are waived by the witness and by the parties. Any changes in form or substance that the witness wants to make shall be listed in writing by the officer with a statement of the reasons given by the witness for making the changes. The changes shall be attached to the transcript. It shall then be signed by the witness unless the parties waived the signing or the witness is ill, cannot be found, or refuses to sign. If the transcript is not signed by the witness within a reasonable time after it is furnished to the witness, the officer shall sign the transcript and state on the transcript the waiver, illness, absence of the witness, or refusal to sign with any reasons given. The deposition may then be used as fully as though signed unless the court holds that the reasons given for the refusal to sign require rejection of the deposition wholly or partly, on motion under FL ST RCP Rule 1.330(d)(4). FL ST RCP Rule 1.310(e).

xiii. *Certification and inspection.* If the deposition is transcribed, the officer shall certify on each copy of the deposition that the witness was duly sworn by the officer and that the deposition is a true record of the testimony given by the witness. Documents and things produced for inspection during the examination of the witness shall be marked for identification and annexed to and returned with the deposition upon the request of a party, and may be inspected and copied by any party, except that the person producing the materials may substitute copies to be marked for identification if that person affords to all parties fair opportunity to verify the copies by comparison with the originals. If the person producing the materials requests their return, the officer shall mark them, give each party an opportunity to inspect and copy them, and return them to the person producing them and the materials may then be used in the same manner as if annexed to and returned with the deposition. FL ST RCP Rule 1.310(f)(1).

xiv. *Copies.* Upon payment of reasonable charges, the officer shall furnish a copy of the deposition to any party or to the deponent. FL ST RCP Rule 1.310(f)(2). A party or witness who does not have a copy of the deposition may obtain it from the officer taking the deposition unless the court orders otherwise. If the deposition is obtained from a person other than the officer, the reasonable cost of reproducing the copies shall be paid to the person by the requesting party or witness. FL ST RCP Rule 1.310(g).

d. *Depositions upon written examination*

i. *Deposing an organization upon written examination.* A deposition upon written questions may be taken of a public or private corporation, a partnership or association, or a governmental agency in accordance with FL ST RCP Rule 1.310(b)(6). FL ST RCP Rule 1.320(a).

ii. *Cross, redirect, and recross questions.* Within thirty (30) days after the notice and written questions are served, a party may serve cross questions upon all other parties. Within ten (10) days after being served with cross questions, a party may serve redirect questions upon all other parties. Within ten (10) days after being served with redirect questions, a party may serve recross questions upon all other parties. The court may for cause shown enlarge or shorten the time. FL ST RCP Rule 1.320(a).

iii. *Procedure.* A copy of the notice and copies of all questions served shall be delivered by the party taking the depositions to the officer designated in the notice, who shall proceed promptly to take the testimony of the witness in the manner provided by FL ST RCP Rule 1.310(c), FL ST RCP Rule 1.310(e), and FL ST RCP Rule 1.310(f) in response to the questions and to prepare the deposition, attaching the copy of the notice and the questions received by the officer. The questions shall not be filed separately from the deposition unless a party seeks to have the court consider the questions before the questions are submitted to the witness. FL ST RCP Rule 1.320(b).

5. *Arbitration and mediation*

a. *Referral to arbitration and mediation.* Except as hereinafter provided or as otherwise prohibited by law, the presiding judge may enter an order referring all or any part of a contested civil matter to mediation or arbitration. The parties to any contested civil matter may file a written stipulation to mediate or arbitrate any issue between them at any time. Such stipulation shall be incorporated into the order of referral. FL ST RCP Rule 1.700(a).

b. *Arbitration*

i. *Exclusions.* A civil action shall be ordered to arbitration or arbitration in conjunction with

mediation upon stipulation of the parties. A civil action may be ordered to arbitration or arbitration in conjunction with mediation upon motion of any party or by the court, if the judge determines the action to be of such a nature that arbitration could be of benefit to the litigants or the court. FL ST RCP Rule 1.800.

- Under no circumstances may the following categories of actions be referred to arbitration: (1) bond estreatures; (2) habeas corpus or other extraordinary writs; (3) bond validations; (4) civil or criminal contempt; (5) such other matters as may be specified by order of the chief judge in the circuit. FL ST RCP Rule 1.800.

ii. For more information regarding arbitration, please see FL ST RCP Rule 1.810; FL ST RCP Rule 1.820; FL ST RCP Rule 1.830.

c. *Mediation.* For more information regarding mediation, please see FL ST RCP Rule 1.710; FL ST RCP Rule 1.720; FL ST RCP Rule 1.730; and FL ST RCP Rule 1.750.

6. *Rules of court*

a. *Rules of civil procedure.* The Florida Rules of Civil Procedure apply to all actions of a civil nature and all special statutory proceedings in the circuit courts and county courts except those to which the Florida Probate Rules, the Florida Family Law Rules of Procedure, or the Small Claims Rules apply. FL ST RCP Rule 1.010.

i. The form, content, procedure, and time for pleading in all special statutory proceedings shall be as prescribed by the statutes governing the proceeding unless the Florida Rules of Civil Procedure specifically provide to the contrary. FL ST RCP Rule 1.010.

ii. The Florida Rules of Civil Procedure shall be construed to secure the just, speedy, and inexpensive determination of every action. FL ST RCP Rule 1.010.

b. *Rules of judicial administration.* The Florida Rules of Judicial Administration shall apply to administrative matters in all courts to which the Florida Rules of Judicial Administration are applicable by their terms. The Florida Rules of Judicial Administration shall be construed to secure the speedy and inexpensive determination of every proceeding to which they are applicable. The Florida Rules of Judicial Administration shall supersede all conflicting rules and statutes. FL ST J ADMIN Rule 2.110.

D. Documents

1. *Deposition upon oral or written examination*

a. *Required documents*

i. *Notice of deposition.* Please see the General Requirements section of this document for information on the content of a notice of deposition upon oral examination.

ii. *Certificate of service.* A certificate of service of the interrogatories shall be filed, giving the date of service and the name of the party to whom they were directed. FL ST RCP Rule 1.340(e). When any attorney certifies in substance: "I certify that a copy hereof has been furnished to (here insert name or names and addresses used for service) by (e-mail) (delivery) (mail) (fax) on .... (date) ....______________ Attorney" the certificate is taken as prima facie proof of such service in compliance with FL ST J ADMIN Rule 2.516. FL ST J ADMIN Rule 2.516(f).

b. *Supplemental documents*

i. *Motion for leave to take deposition.* See the Timing section for information on when leave is required.

ii. *Subpoena.* See the Timing section for requirements of when a subpoena is required.

iii. *Request for production of documents.* See the General Requirements section for further information.

E. Format

1. *Documents; Type and size.* Documents subject to the exceptions set forth in FL ST J ADMIN Rule

2.525(d) shall be filed on recycled paper measuring eight and one half by eleven (8 1/2 by 11) inches. For purposes of FL ST J ADMIN Rule 2.520, paper is recycled if it contains a minimum content of fifty (50) percent waste paper. Xerographic reduction of legal-size (eight and one half by fourteen (8 1/2 by 14) inches) documents to letter size (eight and one half by eleven (8 1/2 by 11) inches) is prohibited. All other documents filed by electronic transmission shall be filed in a format capable of being printed in a format consistent with the provisions of FL ST J ADMIN Rule 2.250. FL ST J ADMIN Rule 2.520(b).

a. *Exhibits.* Any exhibit or attachment filed with pleadings or papers may be filed in its original size. FL ST J ADMIN Rule 2.520(c).

b. *Recording space.* On all papers and documents prepared and filed by the court or by any party to a proceeding which are to be recorded in the public records of any county, including but not limited to final money judgments and notices of lis pendens, a three (3) inch by three (3) inch space at the top right-hand corner on the first page and a one (1) inch by three (3) inch space at the top right-hand corner on each subsequent page shall be left blank and reserved for use by the clerk of court. FL ST J ADMIN Rule 2.520(d).

   i. *Exceptions to recording space.* Any papers or documents created by persons or entities over which the filing party has no control, including but not limited to wills, codicils, trusts, or other testamentary documents; documents prepared or executed by any public officer; documents prepared, executed, acknowledged, or proved outside of the State of Florida; or documents created by State or Federal government agencies, may be filed without the space required by FL ST J ADMIN Rule 2.520. FL ST J ADMIN Rule 2.520(e).

c. *Noncompliance.* No clerk of court is permitted to refuse to file any document or paper because of noncompliance with the Florida Rules of Judicial Administration. However, upon request of the clerk of court, noncomplying documents must be resubmitted in accordance with the formatting rules. FL ST J ADMIN Rule 2.520(f).

2. *Caption.* Every pleading, motion, order, judgment, or other paper shall have a caption containing the name of the court, the file number, and except for in rem proceedings, including forfeiture proceedings, the name of the first party on each side with an appropriate indication of other parties, and a designation identifying the party filing it and its nature or the nature of the order, as the case may be. In any in rem proceeding, every pleading, motion, order, judgment, or other paper shall have a caption containing the name of the court, the file number, the style "In re" (followed by the name or general description of the property), and a designation of the person or entity filing it and its nature or the nature of the order, as the case may be. In an in rem forfeiture proceeding, the style shall be "In re forfeiture of" (followed by the name of the general description of the property). All papers filed in the action shall be styled in such a manner as to indicate clearly the subject matter of the paper and the party requesting or obtaining relief. FL ST RCP Rule 1.100(c)(1).

3. *Writing and written defined.* Writing or written means a document containing information, an application, or a stipulation. FL ST RCP Rule 1.080(c).

4. *Rule abbreviations*

   a. The Florida Rules of Civil Procedure and shall be abbreviated as Fla.R.Civ.P. FL ST RCP Rule 1.010.

   b. The Florida Rules of Judicial Administration shall be abbreviated as Fla. R. Jud. Admin. FL ST J ADMIN Rule 2.110.

5. *Nonverification.* Except when otherwise specifically provided by the Florida Rules of Civil Procedure or an applicable statute, every pleading or other document of a party represented by an attorney need not be verified or accompanied by an affidavit. FL ST RCP Rule 1.030; FL ST J ADMIN Rule 2.515(a).

6. *Attorney signature*

   a. *Attorney signature.* Every pleading and other document of a party represented by an attorney shall be signed by at least one (1) attorney of record in that attorney's individual name whose current record Florida Bar address, telephone number, including area code, primary e-mail address and secondary e-mail addresses, if any, and Florida Bar number shall be stated, and who shall be duly licensed to

practice law in Florida or who shall have received permission to appear in the particular case as provided in FL ST J ADMIN Rule 2.510. FL ST J ADMIN Rule 2.515(a).

i. The attorney may be required by the court to give the address of, and to vouch for the attorney's authority to represent, the party. FL ST J ADMIN Rule 2.515(a).

ii. The signature of an attorney shall constitute a certificate by the attorney that the attorney has read the pleading or other document; that to the best of the attorney's knowledge, information, and belief there is good ground to support it; and that it is not interposed for delay. FL ST J ADMIN Rule 2.515(a).

iii. If a pleading is not signed or is signed with intent to defeat the purpose of FL ST J ADMIN Rule 2.515, it may be stricken and the action may proceed as though the pleading or other document had not been served. FL ST J ADMIN Rule 2.515(a).

b. *Pro se litigant signature.* A party who is not represented by an attorney shall sign any pleading or other paper and state the party's address and telephone number, including area code. FL ST J ADMIN Rule 2.515(b).

c. *Form of signature*

i. The signatures required on pleadings and documents by FL ST J ADMIN Rule 2.515(a) and FL ST J ADMIN Rule 2.515(b) may be:

- Original signatures;
- Original signatures that have been reproduced by electronic means, such as on electronically transmitted documents or photocopied documents;
- Electronic signatures using the "/s/," "s/," or "/s" formats by or at the direction of the person signing; or
- Any other signature format authorized by general law, so long as the clerk where the proceeding is pending has the capability of receiving and has obtained approval from the Supreme Court of Florida to accept pleadings and documents with that signature format. FL ST J ADMIN Rule 2.515(c)(1).

ii. An attorney, party, or other person who files a pleading or paper by electronic transmission that does not contain the original signature of that attorney, party, or other person shall file that identical pleading or paper in paper form containing an original signature of that attorney, party, or other person (hereinafter called the follow-up filing) immediately thereafter. The follow-up filing is not required if the Supreme Court of Florida has entered an order directing the clerk of court to discontinue accepting the follow-up filing. FL ST J ADMIN Rule 2.515(c)(2).

iii. The placement of a "/s/" or the image of a signature by an attorney or party or affected non-party signature line on an electronically filed document shall be accepted as the signature and shall verify to the Court the filer is in possession of the originally executed document. Notwithstanding the manner in which an electronic document is signed the originally executed pleading or paper shall be maintained in the filer's possession for a minimum of one (1) year after final disposition and time for appeal of the case. The originally executed document shall be produced for filing or inspection as directed by the Court. FL ST 17 J CIR 2012-16-CIV.

7. *Forms*

a. *Process.* The forms of process, notice of lis pendens, and notice of action provided in the Florida Rules of Civil Procedure are sufficient. Variations from the forms do not void process or notices that are otherwise sufficient. FL ST RCP Rule 1.900(a).

b. *Other forms.* The other forms provided in the Florida Rules of Civil Procedure are sufficient for the matters that are covered by them. So long as the substance is expressed without prolixity, the forms may be varied to meet the facts of a particular case. FL ST RCP Rule 1.900(b).

c. *Formal matters.* Captions, except for the designation of the paper, are omitted from the forms provided in the Florida Rules of Civil Procedure. A general form of caption is the first form provided. Signatures are omitted from pleadings and motions. FL ST RCP Rule 1.900(c).

8. *Notices to persons with disabilities.* All notices of court proceedings to be held in a public facility, and all process compelling appearance at such proceedings, shall include the following statement in bold face, fourteen (14) point Times New Roman or Courier font: "If you are a person with a disability who needs any accommodation in order to participate in this proceeding, you are entitled, at no cost to you, to the provision of certain assistance. Please contact [identify applicable court personnel by name, address, and telephone number] at least seven (7) days before your scheduled court appearance, or immediately upon receiving this notification if the time before the scheduled appearance is less than seven (7) days; if you are hearing or voice impaired, call 711." FL ST J ADMIN Rule 2.540(c)(1). For further information, please see FL ST 17 J CIR 2010-49-GEN.
9. *Minimization of the filing of sensitive information*
    a. *Limitations for court filings.* Unless authorized by FL ST J ADMIN Rule 2.425(b), statute, another rule of court, or the court orders otherwise, designated sensitive information filed with the court must be limited to the following format:
        i. The initials of a person known to be a minor;
        ii. The year of birth of a person's birth date;
        iii. No portion of any: Social security number, Bank account number, Credit card account number, Charge account number, or Debit account number;
        iv. The last four digits of any: Taxpayer identification number (TIN), Employee identification number, Driver's license number, Passport number, Telephone number, Financial account number, except as set forth in FL ST J ADMIN Rule 2.425(a)(3), Brokerage account number, Insurance policy account number, Loan account number, Customer account number, or Patient or health care number;
        v. A truncated version of any: Email address, Computer user name, Password, or Personal identification number (PIN); and
        vi. A truncated version of any other sensitive information as provided by court order. FL ST J ADMIN Rule 2.425(a).
    b. *Exceptions.* FL ST J ADMIN Rule 2.425(a) does not apply to the following:
        i. An account number which identifies the property alleged to be the subject of a proceeding;
        ii. The record of an administrative or agency proceeding;
        iii. The record in appellate or review proceedings;
        iv. The birth date of a minor whenever the birth date is necessary for the court to establish or maintain subject matter jurisdiction;
        v. The name of a minor in any order relating to parental responsibility, time-sharing, or child support;
        vi. The name of a minor in any document or order affecting the minor's ownership of real property;
        vii. The birth date of a party in a writ of attachment or notice to payor;
        viii. In traffic and criminal proceedings: a pro se filing; a court filing that is related to a criminal matter or investigation and that is prepared before the filing of a criminal charge or is not filed as part of any docketed criminal case; an arrest or search warrant or any information in support thereof; a charging document and an affidavit or other documents filed in support of any charging document, including any driving records; a statement of particulars; discovery material introduced into evidence or otherwise filed with the court; and all information necessary for the proper issuance and execution of a subpoena duces tecum;
        ix. Information used by the clerk for case maintenance purposes or the courts for case management purposes; and
        x. Information which is relevant and material to an issue before the court. FL ST J ADMIN Rule 2.425(b).
    c. *Remedies.* Upon motion by a party or interested person or sua sponte by the court, the court may

order remedies, sanctions or both for a violation of FL ST J ADMIN Rule 2.425(a). Following notice and an opportunity to respond, the court may impose sanctions if such filing was not made in good faith. FL ST J ADMIN Rule 2.425(c).

d. *Motions not restricted.* FL ST J ADMIN Rule 2.425 does not restrict a party's right to move for protective order, to move to file documents under seal, or to request a determination of the confidentiality of records. FL ST J ADMIN Rule 2.425(d).

e. *Application.* FL ST J ADMIN Rule 2.425 does not affect the application of constitutional provisions, statutes, or rules of court regarding confidential information or access to public information. FL ST J ADMIN Rule 2.425(e).

F. Filing and Service Requirements

1. *Court filing of documents and discovery.* Information obtained during discovery shall not be filed with the court until such time as it is filed for good cause. The requirement of good cause is satisfied only where the filing of the information is allowed or required by another applicable rule of procedure or by court order. All filings of discovery documents shall comply with FL ST J ADMIN Rule 2.425. The court shall have the authority to impose sanctions for violation of FL ST RCP Rule 1.280. FL ST RCP Rule 1.280(g).

   a. *Filing of copies.* A copy of a deposition may be filed only under the following circumstances:

      i. It may be filed in compliance with FL ST J ADMIN Rule 2.425 and FL ST RCP Rule 1.280(f) by a party or the witness when the contents of the deposition must be considered by the court on any matter pending before the court. Prompt notice of the filing of the deposition shall be given to all parties unless notice is waived. A party filing the deposition shall furnish a copy of the deposition or the part being filed to other parties unless the party already has a copy. FL ST RCP Rule 1.310(f)(3)(A).

      ii. If the court determines that a deposition previously taken is necessary for the decision of a matter pending before the court, the court may order that a copy be filed by any party at the initial cost of the party, and the filing party shall comply with FL ST J ADMIN Rule 2.425 and FL ST RCP Rule 1.280(f). FL ST RCP Rule 1.310(f)(3)(B).

2. *Filing requirements.* All original documents must be filed with the court either before service or immediately thereafter, unless otherwise provided for by general law or other rules. If the original of any bond or other document is not placed in the court file, a certified copy must be so placed by the clerk. FL ST J ADMIN Rule 2.516(d). All documents shall be filed in conformity with the requirements of FL ST J ADMIN Rule 2.525. FL ST RCP Rule 1.080(b). All documents filed in any court shall be filed by electronic transmission in accordance with FL ST J ADMIN Rule 2.525. "Documents" means pleadings, motions, petitions, memoranda, briefs, notices, exhibits, declarations, affidavits, orders, judgments, decrees, writs, opinions, and any other paper or writing submitted to a court. FL ST J ADMIN Rule 2.520(a). All documents that are court records, as defined in FL ST J ADMIN Rule 2.430(a)(1), must be filed by electronic transmission, provided that: (1) the clerk has the ability to accept and retain such documents; (2) the clerk or the chief judge of the circuit has requested permission to accept documents filed by electronic transmission; and (3) the supreme court has entered an order granting permission to the clerk to accept documents filed by electronic transmission. FL ST J ADMIN Rule 2.525(c)(1).

   a. *Definition.* "Electronic transmission of documents" means the sending of information by electronic signals to, by or from a court or clerk, which when received can be transformed and stored or transmitted on paper, microfilm, magnetic storage device, optical imaging system, CD-ROM, flash drive, other electronic data storage system, server, case maintenance system ("CM"), electronic court filing ("ECF") system, statewide or local electronic portal ("e-portal"), or other electronic record keeping system authorized by the supreme court in a format sufficient to communicate the information on the original document in a readable format. Electronic transmission of documents includes electronic mail ("e-mail") and any internet-based transmission procedure, and may include procedures allowing for documents to be signed or verified by electronic means. FL ST J ADMIN Rule 2.525(a).

      i. The filing of documents with the court as required by the Florida Rules of Judicial Administration must be made by filing them with the clerk in accordance with FL ST J ADMIN Rule

2.525, except that the judge may permit documents to be filed with the judge, in which event the judge must note the filing date before him or her on the documents and transmit them to the clerk. The date of filing is that shown on the face of the document by the judge's notation or the clerk's time stamp, whichever is earlier. FL ST J ADMIN Rule 2.516(e).

b. *Application.* Any court or clerk of the court may accept the electronic transmission of documents for filing after the clerk, together with input from the chief judge of the circuit, has obtained approval of the procedures and program for doing so from the Supreme Court of Florida. FL ST J ADMIN Rule 2.525(b).

c. *Exceptions*

   i. Paper documents and other submissions may be manually submitted to the clerk or court:

      - When the clerk does not have the ability to accept and retain documents by electronic filing or has not had ECF Procedures approved by the supreme court;
      - For filing by any self-represented party or any self-represented nonparty unless specific ECF Procedures provide a means to file documents electronically. However, any self-represented nonparty that is a governmental or public agency and any other agency, partnership, corporation, or business entity acting on behalf of any governmental or public agency may file documents by electronic transmission if such entity has the capability of filing documents electronically;
      - For filing by attorneys excused from e-mail service in accordance with FL ST J ADMIN Rule 2.516(b);
      - When submitting evidentiary exhibits or filing non-documentary materials;
      - When the filing involves documents in excess of twenty-five (25) megabytes (25MB) in size. For such filings, documents may be transmitted using an electronic storage medium that the clerk has the ability to accept, which may include a CD-ROM, flash drive, or similar storage medium;
      - When filed in open court, as permitted by the court;
      - When paper filing is permitted by any approved statewide or local ECF procedures; and
      - If any court determines that justice so requires. FL ST J ADMIN Rule 2.525(d).

   ii. Any document in paper form submitted under FL ST J ADMIN Rule 2.525(d) is filed when it is received by the clerk or court and the clerk shall immediately thereafter convert any filed paper document to an electronic document. "Convert to an electronic document" means optically capturing an image of a paper document and using character recognition software to recover as much of the document's text as practicable and then indexing and storing the document in the official court file. FL ST J ADMIN Rule 2.525(c)(4).

   iii. Any storage medium submitted under FL ST J ADMIN Rule 2.525(d)(5) is filed when received by the clerk or court and the clerk shall immediately thereafter transfer the electronic documents from the storage device to the official court file. FL ST J ADMIN Rule 2.525(c)(5).

   iv. If the filer of any paper document authorized under FL ST J ADMIN Rule 2.525(d) provides a self-addressed, postage-paid envelope for return of the paper document after it is converted to electronic form by the clerk, the clerk shall place the paper document in the envelope and deposit it in the mail. Except when a paper document is required to be maintained, the clerk may recycle any filed paper document that is not to be returned to the filer. FL ST J ADMIN Rule 2.525(c)(6).

   v. The clerk may convert any paper document filed before the effective date of FL ST J ADMIN Rule 2.525 to an electronic document. Unless the clerk is required to maintain the paper document, if the paper document has been converted to an electronic document by the clerk, the paper document is no longer part of the official court file and may be removed and recycled. FL ST J ADMIN Rule 2.525(c)(7).

d. *Official court file.* For information on what constitutes the official court file, please see FL ST J ADMIN Rule 2.525(c)(2), FL ST J ADMIN Rule 2.525(c)(3).

e. *Administration.* All attorneys, parties, or other persons using this rule to file documents are required to make arrangements with the court or clerk for the payment of any charges authorized by general law or the supreme court before filing any document by electronic transmission. FL ST J ADMIN Rule 2.525(f)(2).

f. *Filing date.* The filing date for an electronically transmitted document is the date and time that such filing is acknowledged by an electronic stamp or otherwise, pursuant to any procedure set forth in any ECF Procedures approved by the supreme court, or the date the last page of such filing is received by the court or clerk. FL ST J ADMIN Rule 2.525(f)(3).

g. *Accessibility.* All documents transmitted in any electronic form under FL ST J ADMIN Rule 2.525 must comply with the accessibility requirements of FL ST J ADMIN Rule 2.526. FL ST J ADMIN Rule 2.525(g).

h. *Provisions for electronic filing in the Seventeenth Circuit.* Attorneys may electronically file pleadings and papers on existing cases in circuit civil divisions 1, 7, 9, 19, 26 and 27. The following documents may be scanned and efiled; however, the original must be filed with the Clerk: Documents ordered by the Court; and original documents required by law or rule of procedure to be filed with the Clerk. Self represented individuals shall file pleadings and papers with the Clerk. The Clerk within twenty four (24) hours of receipt of an electronic document shall either accept or reject the electronic document for filing and send electronic notice to the filer. FL ST 17 J CIR 2012-16-CIV.

i. *Technical failures.* If a document filed electronically is not received due to: an error in the transmission of the document to the Clerk or any vendor of the Clerk to provide electronic court record filing services which is unknown to an attorney or party or affected non party, or a failure to process the electronic document when received by the Clerk or rejection by the Clerk, or any other technical problems experienced by the attorney or party or affected non party, the Court may, after an evidentiary hearing and upon satisfactory proof, enter an order permitting the document to be filed nunc pro tunc to the date it was first attempted to be sent electronically. FL ST 17 J CIR 2012-16-CIV.

j. *Filing of pleadings or papers at any office of the clerk of court.* The Clerk of Courts, commencing November 3, 2008, shall accept for filing, at the central courthouse, north satellite courthouse, south satellite courthouse, and west satellite courthouse any pleading or motion or other document for filing in the court file from any attorney or party for an existing case except as otherwise set forth. FL ST 17 J CIR 2008-153-GEN. See FL ST 17 J CIR 2008-153-GEN for specific exceptions.

3. *Service requirements.* Every pleading subsequent to the initial pleading, all orders, and every other document filed in the action must be served in conformity with the requirements of FL ST J ADMIN Rule 2.516. FL ST RCP Rule 1.080(a).

   a. *Service; When required.* Unless the court otherwise orders, or a statute or supreme court administrative order specifies a different means of service, every pleading subsequent to the initial pleading and every other document filed in any court proceeding, except applications for witness subpoenas and documents served by formal notice or required to be served in the manner provided for service of formal notice, must be served in accordance with FL ST J ADMIN Rule 2.516 on each party. No service need be made on parties against whom a default has been entered, except that pleadings asserting new or additional claims against them must be served in the manner provided for service of summons. FL ST J ADMIN Rule 2.516(a).

   b. *Service; How made.* When service is required or permitted to be made upon a party represented by an attorney, service must be made upon the attorney unless service upon the party is ordered by the court. FL ST J ADMIN Rule 2.516(b).

      i. *Service by electronic mail ("e-mail").* All documents required or permitted to be served on another party must be served by e-mail, unless FL ST J ADMIN Rule 2.516 otherwise provides. When, in addition to service by e-mail, the sender also utilizes another means of service provided for in FL ST J ADMIN Rule 2.516(b)(2), any differing time limits and other provisions applicable to that other means of service control. FL ST J ADMIN Rule 2.516(b)(1). Any document electronically transmitted to a court or clerk must also be served on all parties and interested persons in accordance with the applicable rules of court. FL ST J ADMIN Rule 2.525(e)(2).

- *Service on attorneys.* Upon appearing in a proceeding, an attorney must serve a designation of a primary e-mail address and may designate no more than two (2) secondary e-mail addresses. Thereafter, service must be directed to all designated e-mail addresses in that proceeding. Every document filed by an attorney thereafter must include the primary e-mail address of that attorney and any secondary e-mail addresses. If an attorney does not designate any e-mail address for service, documents may be served on that attorney at the e-mail address on record with The Florida Bar. FL ST J ADMIN Rule 2.516(b)(1)(A).
- *Exception to e-mail service on attorneys.* Service by an attorney on another attorney must be made by e-mail unless excused by the court. Upon motion by an attorney demonstrating that the attorney has no e-mail account and lacks access to the Internet at the attorney's office, the court may excuse the attorney from the requirements of e-mail service. Service on and by an attorney excused by the court from e-mail service must be by the means provided in FL ST J ADMIN Rule 2.516(b)(2). FL ST J ADMIN Rule 2.516(b)(1)(B).
- *Service on and by parties not represented by an attorney.* Any party not represented by an attorney may serve a designation of a primary e-mail address and also may designate no more than two (2) secondary e-mail addresses to which service must be directed in that proceeding by the means provided in FL ST J ADMIN Rule 2.516(b)(1). If a party not represented by an attorney does not designate an e-mail address for service in a proceeding, service on and by that party must be by the means provided in FL ST J ADMIN Rule 2.516(b)(2). FL ST J ADMIN Rule 2.516(b)(1)(C).
- *Time of service.* Service by e-mail is complete when it is sent. FL ST J ADMIN Rule 2.516(b)(1)(D). An e-mail is deemed served on the date it is sent. FL ST J ADMIN Rule 2.516(b)(1)(D)(i). If the sender learns that the e-mail did not reach the address of the person to be served, the sender must immediately send another copy by e-mail, or by a means authorized by FL ST J ADMIN Rule 2.516(b)(2). FL ST J ADMIN Rule 2.516(b)(1)(D)(ii). E-mail service is treated as service by mail for the computation of time. FL ST J ADMIN Rule 2.516(b)(1)(D)(iii).

ii. *Format of e-mail for service.* Service of a document by e-mail is made by attaching a copy of the document in PDF format to an e-mail sent to all addresses designated by the attorney or party. FL ST J ADMIN Rule 2.516(b)(1)(E).

- All documents served by e-mail must be attached to an e-mail message containing a subject line beginning with the words "SERVICE OF COURT DOCUMENT" in all capital letters, followed by the case number of the proceeding in which the documents are being served. FL ST J ADMIN Rule 2.516(b)(1)(E)(i).
- The body of the e-mail must identify the court in which the proceeding is pending, the case number, the name of the initial party on each side, the title of each document served with that e-mail, and the sender's name and telephone number. FL ST J ADMIN Rule 2.516(b)(1)(E)(ii).
- Any document served by e-mail may be signed by the "/s/" format, as long as the filed original is signed in accordance with the applicable rule of procedure. FL ST J ADMIN Rule 2.516(b)(1)(E)(iii).
- Any e-mail which, together with its attached documents, exceeds five megabytes (5MB) in size, must be divided and sent as separate e-mails, no one of which may exceed five megabytes (5MB) in size and each of which must be sequentially numbered in the subject line. FL ST J ADMIN Rule 2.516(b)(1)(E)(iv).

iii. *Service by other means.* In addition to, and not in lieu of, service by e-mail, service may also be made upon attorneys by any of the means specified in FL ST J ADMIN Rule 2.516(b)(2). Service on and by all parties who are not represented by an attorney and who do not designate an e-mail address, and on and by all attorneys excused from e-mail service, must be made by delivering a copy of the document or by mailing it to the party or attorney at their last known address or, if no address is known, by leaving it with the clerk of the court. Service by mail is complete upon mailing. Delivery of a copy within FL ST J ADMIN Rule 2.516 is complete upon:

- Handing it to the attorney or to the party,
- Leaving it at the attorney's or party's office with a clerk or other person in charge thereof,
- If there is no one in charge, leaving it in a conspicuous place therein,
- If the office is closed or the person to be served has no office, leaving it at the person's usual place of abode with some person of his or her family above fifteen (15) years of age and informing such person of the contents, or
- Transmitting it by facsimile to the attorney's or party's office with a cover sheet containing the sender's name, firm, address, telephone number, and facsimile number, and the number of pages transmitted. When service is made by facsimile, a copy must also be served by any other method permitted by FL ST J ADMIN Rule 2.516. Facsimile service occurs when transmission is complete. FL ST J ADMIN Rule 2.516(b)(2)(A) through FL ST J ADMIN Rule 2.516(b)(2)(E).
- Service by delivery after 5:00 p.m. must be deemed to have been made by mailing on the date of delivery. FL ST J ADMIN Rule 2.516(b)(2)(F).

c. *Service; Numerous defendants.* In actions when the parties are unusually numerous, the court may regulate the service contemplated by the Florida Rules of Judicial Administration on motion or on its own initiative in such manner as may be found to be just and reasonable. FL ST J ADMIN Rule 2.516(c).

d. *Service by clerk.* Service of notices and other documents required to be made by the clerk must also be done as provided in FL ST J ADMIN Rule 2.516(b). FL ST J ADMIN Rule 2.516(g).

G. Hearings

1. There is no hearing required or contemplated with regard to responses to requests for admission in the Florida Rules of Civil Procedure.

H. Forms

1. Official Notice of Deposition Forms

a. Caption. FL ST RCP Form 1.901.

2. Florida Notice of Deposition Forms

a. Form for motion by plaintiff for leave to take deposition within 20-day period. FL-RCPF R 1.310(6).
b. Form for order on motion for leave to take deposition within 20-day period. FL-RCPF R 1.310(8).
c. Notice of examination; Time and place. FL-RCPF R 1.310(9).
d. Nonparty witness, subpoena required. FL-RCPF R 1.310(10).
e. Form for notice to take deposition on oral examination. FL-RCPF R 1.310(11).
f. Form for notice of taking multiple depositions. FL-RCPF R 1.310(11.1).
g. Form for notice of taking deposition and examination of documents. FL-RCPF R 1.310(12).
h. Form for notice of taking video deposition duces tecum. FL-RCPF R 1.310(13).
i. Form for motion to modify time for taking deposition. FL-RCPF R 1.310(14).
j. Form for motion to take deposition by telephone. FL-RCPF R 1.310(16).
k. Form for order permitting deposition by telephone. FL-RCPF R 1.310(17).
l. Form for notice of taking deposition by telephone. FL-RCPF R 1.310(18).
m. Form for notice of deposition upon written questions. FL-RCPF R 1.320(2).
n. Form of questions. FL-RCPF R 1.320(3).

o. Form of cross-questions. FL-RCPF R 1.320(4).

p. Form for objection to form of written questions. FL-RCPF R 1.320(6).

I. Checklist

(I) ❑ Matters to be considered by deposing party (oral depositions)

- (a) ❑ Required documents
  - (1) ❑ Notice of deposition
  - (2) ❑ Certificate of service
- (b) ❑ Supplemental documents
  - (1) ❑ Motion for leave to request deposition
  - (2) ❑ Subpoena
  - (3) ❑ Request for production of documents
- (c) ❑ Time for service of notice of deposition
  - (1) ❑ After commencement of action
  - (2) ❑ Within thirty (30) days after service of initial pleadings by leave of court only

(II) ❑ Matters to be considered by deponent (oral depositions)

- (a) ❑ Required documents
  - (1) ❑ Production of documents (if subpoenaed)

(III) ❑ Matters to be considered by deposing party (depositions by written questions)

- (a) ❑ Required documents
  - (1) ❑ Notice of deposition
  - (2) ❑ Written questions
  - (3) ❑ Certificate of service
- (b) ❑ Supplemental documents
  - (1) ❑ Motion for leave to request deposition
  - (2) ❑ Subpoena
  - (3) ❑ Request for production of documents
- (c) ❑ Time for service of direct and redirect questions
  - (1) ❑ Within ten (10) days after being served with cross questions, a party may serve redirect questions upon all other parties
  - (2) ❑ Objections to the form of the question must be served within the time for service of redirect questions or ten (10) days after service of recross questions

(IV) ❑ Matters to be considered by deponent (depositions by written questions)

- (a) ❑ Required documents
  - (1) ❑ Cross questions, with certificate of service
  - (2) ❑ Recross questions with certificate of service
- (b) ❑ Time for service of cross and recross questions
  - (1) ❑ Within thirty (30) days after the notice and written questions are served, a party may serve cross questions upon all other parties
  - (2) ❑ Within ten (10) days after being served with redirect questions, a party may serve recross questions upon all other parties
  - (3) ❑ Objections to the form of the questions must be served within the time for serving succeeding questions

TWENTIETH JUDICIAL CIRCUIT

Pleadings
Complaint

Document Last Updated January 2013

A. Applicable Rules

1. *State rules*
    a. Nonverification of pleadings. FL ST RCP Rule 1.030.
    b. When action commenced. FL ST RCP Rule 1.050.
    c. Process. FL ST RCP Rule 1.070.
    d. Service and filing of pleadings, orders, and documents. FL ST RCP Rule 1.080.
    e. Time. FL ST RCP Rule 1.090.
    f. Pleadings and motions. FL ST RCP Rule 1.100; FL ST RCP Rule 1.110; FL ST RCP Rule 1.120; FL ST RCP Rule 1.130; FL ST RCP Rule 1.170; FL ST RCP Rule 1.430.
    g. Relief from judgment, decrees, or orders. FL ST RCP Rule 1.540.
    h. Forms. FL ST RCP Rule 1.900.
    i. Minimization of the filing of sensitive information. FL ST J ADMIN Rule 2.425.
    j. Retention of court records. FL ST J ADMIN Rule 2.430.
    k. Foreign attorneys. FL ST J ADMIN Rule 2.510.
    l. Signature of attorneys and parties. FL ST J ADMIN Rule 2.515.
    m. Paper. FL ST J ADMIN Rule 2.520.
    n. Electronic filing. FL ST J ADMIN Rule 2.525.
    o. Accessibility of information and technology. FL ST J ADMIN Rule 2.526.
    p. Requests for accommodations by persons with disabilities. FL ST J ADMIN Rule 2.540.
    q. Case management. FL ST J ADMIN Rule 2.545.
    r. Service. FL ST § 48.011; FL ST § 48.021; FL ST § 48.031; FL ST § 48.041; FL ST § 48.042; FL ST § 48.051; FL ST § 48.061; FL ST § 48.071; FL ST § 48.081; FL ST § 48.091; FL ST § 48.101; FL ST § 48.111; FL ST § 48.121; FL ST § 48.131; FL ST § 48.141; FL ST § 48.151; FL ST § 48.161; FL ST § 48.171; FL ST § 48.181; FL ST § 48.183; FL ST § 48.19; FL ST § 48.193; FL ST § 48.194; FL ST § 48.20; FL ST § 48.21; FL ST § 48.25; FL ST § 48.31; FL ST § 49.011; FL ST § 49.021; FL ST § 49.031; FL ST § 49.041; FL ST § 49.051; FL ST § 49.061; FL ST § 49.071; FL ST § 49.08; FL ST § 49.09; FL ST § 49.10; FL ST § 49.11; FL ST § 49.12; FL ST § 50.011; FL ST § 50.021; FL ST § 50.031; FL ST § 50.041; FL ST § 50.051; FL ST § 50.061.
2. *Local rules*
    a. Exclusions from mediation. FL ST 20 J CIR 1.9.
    b. Establishment and implementation of civil case management plan. FL ST 20 J CIR 1.13.
    c. Size of paper. FL ST 20 J CIR 2.9.
    d. Americans with Disabilities Act; Notification of court proceedings. FL ST 20 J CIR 2.15.
    e. Standards of professional courtesy and conduct and establishment of peer review program. FL ST 20 J CIR 2.20.

B. Timing

1. *Commencement of an action.* Every action of a civil nature shall be deemed commenced when the

complaint or petition is filed except that ancillary proceedings shall be deemed commenced when the writ is issued or the pleading setting forth the claim of the party initiating the action is filed. FL ST RCP Rule 1.050.

2. *Summons; Time limit.* If service of the initial process and initial pleading is not made upon a defendant within one hundred twenty (120) days after filing of the initial pleading directed to that defendant the court, on its own initiative after notice or on motion, shall direct that service be effected within a specified time or shall dismiss the action without prejudice or drop that defendant as a party; provided that if the plaintiff shows good cause or excusable neglect for the failure, the court shall extend the time for service for an appropriate period. FL ST RCP Rule 1.070(j).

3. *Computation of time*

   a. *Generally.* Computation of time shall be governed by FL ST J ADMIN Rule 2.514. FL ST RCP Rule 1.090(a). The following rules apply in computing time periods specified in any rule of procedure, local rule, court order, or statute that does not specify a method of computing time. FL ST J ADMIN Rule 2.514(a).

      i. *Period stated in days or a longer unit.* When the period is stated in days or a longer unit of time (A) exclude the day of the event that triggers the period; (B) count every day, including intermediate Saturdays, Sundays, and legal holidays; and (C) include the last day of the period, but if the last day is a Saturday, Sunday, or legal holiday, or falls within any period of time extended through an order of the chief justice under FL ST J ADMIN Rule 2.205(a)(2)(B)(iv), the period continues to run until the end of the next day that is not a Saturday, Sunday, or legal holiday and does not fall within any period of time extended through an order of the chief justice. FL ST J ADMIN Rule 2.514(a)(1).

      ii. *Period stated in hours.* When the period is stated in hours (A) begin counting immediately on the occurrence of the event that triggers the period; (B) count every hour, including hours during intermediate Saturdays, Sundays, and legal holidays; and (C) if the period would end on a Saturday, Sunday, or legal holiday, or during any period of time extended through an order of the chief justice under FL ST J ADMIN Rule 2.205(a)(2)(B)(iv), the period continues to run until the same time on the next day that is not a Saturday, Sunday, or legal holiday and does not fall within any period of time extended through an order of the chief justice. FL ST J ADMIN Rule 2.514(a)(2).

      iii. *Period stated in days less than seven (7) days.* When the period stated in days is less than seven (7) days, intermediate Saturdays, Sundays, and legal holidays shall be excluded in the computation. FL ST J ADMIN Rule 2.514(a)(3).

      iv. *"Last day" defined.* Unless a different time is set by a statute, local rule, or court order, the last day ends (A) for electronic filing or for service by any means, at midnight; and (B) for filing by other means, when the clerk's office is scheduled to close. FL ST J ADMIN Rule 2.514(a)(4).

      v. *"Next day" defined.* The "next day" is determined by continuing to count forward when the period is measured after an event and backward when measured before an event. FL ST J ADMIN Rule 2.514(a)(5).

      vi. *"Legal holiday" defined.* "Legal holiday" means (A) the day set aside by FL ST § 110.117, for observing New Year's Day, Martin Luther King, Jr.'s Birthday, Memorial Day, Independence Day, Labor Day, Veterans' Day, Thanksgiving Day, the Friday after Thanksgiving Day, or Christmas Day, and (B) any day observed as a holiday by the clerk's office or as designated by the chief judge. FL ST J ADMIN Rule 2.514(a)(6).

   b. *Additional time after service by mail or e-mail.* When a party may or must act within a specified time after service and service is made by mail or e-mail, five (5) days are added after the period that would otherwise expire under FL ST J ADMIN Rule 2.514(a). FL ST J ADMIN Rule 2.514(b).

   c. *Enlargement.* When an act is required or allowed to be done at or within a specified time by order of court, by the Florida Rules of Civil Procedure, or by notice given thereunder, for cause shown the court at any time in its discretion (1) with or without notice, may order the period enlarged if request therefor is made before the expiration of the period originally prescribed or as extended by a previous

order, or (2) upon motion made and notice after the expiration of the specified period, may permit the act to be done when failure to act was the result of excusable neglect, but it may not extend the time for making a motion for new trial, for rehearing, or to alter or amend a judgment; making a motion for relief from a judgment under FL ST RCP Rule 1.540(b); taking an appeal or filing a petition for certiorari; or making a motion for a directed verdict. FL ST RCP Rule 1.090(b).

d. *Unaffected by expiration of term.* The period of time provided for the doing of any act or the taking of any proceeding shall not be affected or limited by the continued existence or expiration of a term of court. The continued existence or expiration of a term of court in no way affects the power of a court to do any act or take any proceeding in any action which is or has been pending before it. FL ST RCP Rule 1.090(c).

C. General Requirements

1. *General rules of pleading*

   a. *Claims for relief*

      i. A pleading which sets forth a claim for relief, whether an original claim, counterclaim, crossclaim, or third-party claim, must state a cause of action and shall contain

         - A short and plain statement of the grounds upon which the court's jurisdiction depends, unless the court already has jurisdiction and the claim needs no new grounds of jurisdiction to support it (For information regarding acts subjecting persons to jurisdiction, please see FL ST § 48.193),
         - A short and plain statement of the ultimate facts showing that the pleader is entitled to relief, and
         - A demand for judgment for the relief to which the pleader deems himself or herself entitled. FL ST RCP Rule 1.110(b).

      ii. Relief in the alternative or of several different types may be demanded. Every complaint shall be considered to demand general relief. FL ST RCP Rule 1.110(b).

   b. *Verification.* Except when otherwise specifically provided by these rules or an applicable statute, every pleading or other document of a party represented by an attorney need not be verified or accompanied by an affidavit. FL ST RCP Rule 1.030. When filing an action for foreclosure of a mortgage on residential real property the complaint shall be verified. When verification of a document is required, the document filed shall include an oath, affirmation, or the following statement: "Under penalty of perjury, I declare that I have read the foregoing, and the facts alleged therein are true and correct to the best of my knowledge and belief." FL ST RCP Rule 1.110(b).

   c. *Separate statements.* All averments of claim or defense shall be made in consecutively numbered paragraphs, the contents of each of which shall be limited as far as practicable to a statement of a single set of circumstances, and a paragraph may be referred to by number in all subsequent pleadings. Each claim founded upon a separate transaction or occurrence and each defense other than denials shall be stated in a separate count or defense when a separation facilitates the clear presentation of the matter set forth. FL ST RCP Rule 1.110(f).

   d. *Statements adopted by reference.* Statements in a pleading may be adopted by reference in a different part of the same pleading, in another pleading, or in any motion. FL ST RCP Rule 1.130(b).

   e. *Joinder of causes of action; Consistency.* A pleader may set up in the same action as many claims or causes of action or defenses in the same right as the pleader has, and claims for relief may be stated in the alternative if separate items make up the cause of action, or if two (2) or more causes of action are joined. A party may also set forth two (2) or more statements of a claim or defense alternatively, either in one (1) count or defense or in separate counts or defenses. When two (2) or more statements are made in the alternative and one (1) of them, if made independently, would be sufficient, the pleading is not made insufficient by the insufficiency of one (1) or more of the alternative statements. A party may also state as many separate claims or defenses as that party has, regardless of consistency and whether based on legal or equitable grounds or both. All pleadings shall be construed so as to do substantial justice. FL ST RCP Rule 1.110(g).

f. *Subsequent pleadings.* When the nature of an action permits pleadings subsequent to final judgment and the jurisdiction of the court over the parties has not terminated, the initial pleading subsequent to final judgment shall be designated a supplemental complaint or petition. The action shall then proceed in the same manner and time as though the supplemental complaint or petition were the initial pleading in the action, including the issuance of any needed process. FL ST RCP Rule 1.110(h) shall not apply to proceedings that may be initiated by motion under the Florida Rules of Civil Procedure. FL ST RCP Rule 1.110(h).

g. *Pleading basis for service.* When service of process is to be made under statutes authorizing service on nonresidents of Florida, it is sufficient to plead the basis for service in the language of the statute without pleading the facts supporting service. FL ST RCP Rule 1.070(h).

h. *Forms of pleadings.* Forms of action and technical forms for seeking relief and of pleas, pleadings, or motions are abolished. FL ST RCP Rule 1.110(a).

2. *Complaint; Generally*

a. *Purpose.* The purpose of a complaint is to advise the court and the defendant of the nature of a cause of action asserted by the plaintiff. FL-PP § 2:12.

b. *Sufficiency of complaint.* A complaint will be found to be insufficient if it contains only general conclusory allegations unsupported by any facts. The test to determine whether a complaint is sufficient is whether, if the factual allegations of the complaint are established, the plaintiff will be legally or equitably entitled to the claimed relief. Pizzi v. Central Bank & Trust Co., 250 So.2d 895, 896 (Fla. 1971); Bowen v. G H C Properties, Limited, 251 So.2d 359, 361 (Fla. 1st DCA 1971); FL-PP § 2:12. In determining the sufficiency of the complaint to state a cause of action, all allegations of the complaint are taken as true, and possible affirmative defenses are not considered. Strickland v. Commerce Loan Co. of Jacksonville, 158 So.2d 814 (Fla. 1st DCA 1963); FL-PP § 2:12.

i. The issues for trial in Florida must be settled by the pleadings. The issues cannot be raised by discovery. FL-PRACPROC § 7:6.

ii. Causes of action may be pleaded alternatively in the same count or in different counts and against the same or different defendants as long as the joinder of parties is proper. FL-PRACPROC § 7:6.

iii. Each count must state a cause of action. Each independent cause of action should be pleaded in a separate count. FL-PRACPROC § 7:6.

iv. Incorporation by reference of all allegations from one count to another is not proper. Separate counts facilitate reference to the pleading in which they appear in other pleadings, motions or papers as well as the assertion of defenses against some, but not all, causes of action. Some defenses may not apply to the initial pleading as a whole. FL-PRACPROC § 7:6.

3. *Pleading special matters*

a. *Capacity.* It is not necessary to aver the capacity of a party to sue or be sued, the authority of a party to sue or be sued in a representative capacity, or the legal existence of an organized association of persons that is made a party, except to the extent required to show the jurisdiction of the court. The initial pleading served on behalf of a minor party shall specifically aver the age of the minor party. When a party desires to raise an issue as to the legal existence of any party, the capacity of any party to sue or be sued, or the authority of a party to sue or be sued in a representative capacity, that party shall do so by specific negative averment which shall include such supporting particulars as are peculiarly within the pleader's knowledge. FL ST RCP Rule 1.120(a).

b. *Fraud, mistake, condition of the mind.* In all averments of fraud or mistake, the circumstances constituting fraud or mistake shall be stated with such particularity as the circumstances may permit. Malice, intent, knowledge, mental attitude, and other condition of mind of a person may be averred generally. FL ST RCP Rule 1.120(b).

c. *Conditions precedent.* In pleading the performance or occurrence of conditions precedent, it is sufficient to aver generally that all conditions precedent have been performed or have occurred. A denial of performance or occurrence shall be made specifically and with particularity. FL ST RCP Rule 1.120(c).

d. *Official document or act.* In pleading an official document or official act it is sufficient to aver that the document was issued or the act done in compliance with law. FL ST RCP Rule 1.120(c).

e. *Judgment or decree.* In pleading a judgment or decree of a domestic or foreign court, a judicial or quasi-judicial tribunal, or a board or officer, it is sufficient to aver the judgment or decree without setting forth matter showing jurisdiction to render it. FL ST RCP Rule 1.120(e).

f. *Time and place.* For the purpose of testing the sufficiency of a pleading, averments of time and place are material and shall be considered like all other averments of material matter. FL ST RCP Rule 1.120(f).

g. *Special damage.* When items of special damage are claimed, they shall be specifically stated. FL ST RCP Rule 1.120(g).

4. *Parties*

a. *Parties generally.* Every action may be prosecuted in the name of the real party in interest, but a personal representative, administrator, guardian, trustee of an express trust, a party with whom or in whose name a contract has been made for the benefit of another, or a party expressly authorized by statute may sue in that person's own name without joining the party for whose benefit the action is brought. All persons having an interest in the subject of the action and in obtaining the relief demanded may join as plaintiffs and any person may be made a defendant who has or claims an interest adverse to the plaintiff. Any person may at any time be made a party if that person's presence is necessary or proper to a complete determination of the cause. Persons having a united interest may be joined on the same side as plaintiffs or defendants, and anyone who refuses to join may for such reason be made a defendant. FL ST RCP Rule 1.210(a).

b. *Minors or incompetent persons.* When a minor or incompetent person has a representative, such as a guardian or other like fiduciary, the representative may sue or defend on behalf of the minor or incompetent person. A minor or incompetent person who does not have a duly appointed representative may sue by next friend or by a guardian ad litem. The court shall appoint a guardian ad litem for a minor or incompetent person not otherwise represented in an action or shall make such other order as it deems proper for the protection of the minor or incompetent person. FL ST RCP Rule 1.210(b).

c. For survivor and substitution of parties information, please see FL ST RCP Rule 1.260.

5. *Counterclaims and crossclaims*

a. *Compulsory counterclaims.* A pleading shall state as a counterclaim any claim which at the time of serving the pleading the pleader has against any opposing party, provided it arises out of the transaction or occurrence that is the subject matter of the opposing party's claim and does not require for its adjudication the presence of third parties over whom the court cannot acquire jurisdiction. But the pleader need not state a claim if (1) at the time the action was commenced the claim was the subject of another pending action, or (2) the opposing party brought suit upon that party's claim by attachment or other process by which the court did not acquire jurisdiction to render a personal judgment on the claim and the pleader is not stating a counterclaim under this rule. FL ST RCP Rule 1.170(a).

b. *Permissive counterclaim.* A pleading may state as a counterclaim any claim against an opposing party not arising out of the transaction or occurrence that is the subject matter of the opposing party's claim. FL ST RCP Rule 1.170(b).

c. *Counterclaim exceeding opposing claim.* A counterclaim may or may not diminish or defeat the recovery sought by the opposing party. It may claim relief exceeding in amount or different in kind from that sought in the pleading of the opposing party. FL ST RCP Rule 1.170(c).

d. *Counterclaim against the State.* The Florida Rules of Civil Procedure shall not be construed to enlarge beyond the limits established by law the right to assert counterclaims or to claim credits against the state or any of its subdivisions or other governmental organizations thereof subject to suit or against a municipal corporation or against an officer, agency, or administrative board of the state. FL ST RCP Rule 1.170(d).

e. *Counterclaim maturing or acquired after pleading.* A claim which matured or was acquired by the

pleader after serving the pleading may be presented as a counterclaim by supplemental pleading with the permission of the court. FL ST RCP Rule 1.170(e).

f. *Omitted counterclaim or crossclaim.* When a pleader fails to set up a counterclaim or crossclaim through oversight, inadvertence, or excusable neglect, or when justice requires, the pleader may set up the counterclaim or crossclaim by amendment with leave of the court. FL ST RCP Rule 1.170(f).

g. *Crossclaim against co-party.* A pleading may state as a crossclaim any claim by one party against a co-party arising out of the transaction or occurrence that is the subject matter of either the original action or a counterclaim therein, or relating to any property that is the subject matter of the original action. The crossclaim may include a claim that the party against whom it is asserted is or may be liable to the crossclaimant for all or part of a claim asserted in the action against the crossclaimant. Service of a crossclaim on a party who has appeared in the action shall be made pursuant to FL ST RCP Rule 1.080. Service of a crossclaim against a party who has not appeared in the action shall be made in the manner provided for service of summons. FL ST RCP Rule 1.170(g).

h. *Additional parties may be brought in.* When the presence of parties other than those to the original action is required to grant complete relief in the determination of a counterclaim or crossclaim, they shall be named in the counterclaim or crossclaim and be served with process and shall be parties to the action thereafter if jurisdiction of them can be obtained and their joinder will not deprive the court of jurisdiction of the action. FL ST RCP Rule 1.250(b) and FL ST RCP Rule 1.250(c) apply to parties brought in under FL ST RCP Rule 1.170(h). FL ST RCP Rule 1.170(h).

i. *Separate trials; Separate judgment.* If the court orders separate trials as provided in FL ST RCP Rule 1.270(b), judgment on a counterclaim or crossclaim may be rendered when the court has jurisdiction to do so even if a claim of the opposing party has been dismissed or otherwise disposed of. FL ST RCP Rule 1.170(i).

j. *Demand exceeding jurisdiction; Transfer of action.* If the demand of any counterclaim or crossclaim exceeds the jurisdiction of the court in which the action is pending, the action shall be transferred forthwith to the court of the same county having jurisdiction of the demand in the counterclaim or crossclaim with only such alterations in the pleadings as are essential. The court shall order the transfer of the action and the transmittal of all papers in it to the proper court if the party asserting the demand exceeding the jurisdiction deposits with the court having jurisdiction a sum sufficient to pay the clerk's service charge in the court to which the action is transferred at the time of filing the counterclaim or crossclaim. Thereupon the original papers and deposit shall be transmitted and filed with a certified copy of the order. The court to which the action is transferred shall have full power and jurisdiction over the demands of all parties. Failure to make the service charge deposit at the time the counterclaim or crossclaim is filed, or within such further time as the court may allow, shall reduce a claim for damages to an amount within the jurisdiction of the court where the action is pending and waive the claim in other cases. FL ST RCP Rule 1.170(j).

6. *Misjoinder and nonjoinder of parties*

a. *Misjoinder.* Misjoinder of parties is not a ground for dismissal of an action. Any claim against a party may be severed and proceeded with separately. FL ST RCP Rule 1.250(a).

b. *Dropping parties.* Parties may be dropped by an adverse party in the manner provided for voluntary dismissal in FL ST RCP Rule 1.420(a)(1) subject to the exception stated in FL ST RCP Rule 1.420. If notice of lis pendens has been filed in the action against a party so dropped, the notice of dismissal shall be recorded and cancels the notice of lis pendens without the necessity of a court order. Parties may be dropped by order of court on its own initiative or the motion of any party at any stage of the action on such terms as are just. FL ST RCP Rule 1.250(b).

c. *Adding parties.* Parties may be added once as a matter of course within the same time that pleadings can be so amended under FL ST RCP Rule 1.190(a). If amendment by leave of court or stipulation of the parties is permitted, parties may be added in the amended pleading without further order of court. Parties may be added by order of court on its own initiative or on motion of any party at any stage of the action and on such terms as are just. FL ST RCP Rule 1.250(c).

7. *Jury demand*

a. *Right preserved.* The right of trial by jury as declared by the Constitution or by statute shall be preserved to the parties inviolate. FL ST RCP Rule 1.430(a).

b. *Demand.* Any party may demand a trial by jury of any issue triable of right by a jury by serving upon the other party a demand therefor in writing at any time after commencement of the action and not later than ten (10) days after the service of the last pleading directed to such issue. The demand may be indorsed upon a pleading of the party. FL ST RCP Rule 1.430(b).

c. *Specification of issues.* In the demand a party may specify the issues that the party wishes so tried; otherwise, the party is deemed to demand trial by jury for all issues so triable. FL ST RCP Rule 1.430(c).

   i. If a party has demanded trial by jury for only some of the issues, any other party may serve a demand for trial by jury of any other or all of the issues triable by jury ten (10) days after service of the demand or such lesser time as the court may order. FL ST RCP Rule 1.430(c).

d. *Waiver.* A party who fails to serve a demand as required by FL ST RCP Rule 1.430 waives trial by jury. FL ST RCP Rule 1.430(d).

   i. If waived, a jury trial may not be granted without the consent of the parties, but the court may allow an amendment in the proceedings to demand a trial by jury or order a trial by jury on its own motion. FL ST RCP Rule 1.430(d).

   ii. A demand for trial by jury may not be withdrawn without the consent of the parties. FL ST RCP Rule 1.430(d).

8. *Arbitration and mediation.* Attorneys are encouraged to utilize arbitration, mediation or other forms of alternative dispute resolution if economically feasible. FL ST 20 J CIR 2.20(IV)(N)(3).

   a. *Referral to arbitration and mediation.* Except as hereinafter provided or as otherwise prohibited by law, the presiding judge may enter an order referring all or any part of a contested civil matter to mediation or arbitration. The parties to any contested civil matter may file a written stipulation to mediate or arbitrate any issue between them at any time. Such stipulation shall be incorporated into the order of referral. FL ST RCP Rule 1.700(a).

   b. *Arbitration*

      i. *Exclusions.* A civil action shall be ordered to arbitration or arbitration in conjunction with mediation upon stipulation of the parties. A civil action may be ordered to arbitration or arbitration in conjunction with mediation upon motion of any party or by the court, if the judge determines the action to be of such a nature that arbitration could be of benefit to the litigants or the court. FL ST RCP Rule 1.800.

         - Under no circumstances may the following categories of actions be referred to arbitration: (1) bond estreatures; (2) habeas corpus or other extraordinary writs; (3) bond validations; (4) civil or criminal contempt; (5) such other matters as may be specified by order of the chief judge in the circuit. FL ST RCP Rule 1.800.

      ii. For more information regarding arbitration, please see FL ST RCP Rule 1.810; FL ST RCP Rule 1.820; FL ST RCP Rule 1.830.

   c. *Mediation.* For more information regarding mediation, please see FL ST RCP Rule 1.710; FL ST RCP Rule 1.720; FL ST RCP Rule 1.730; FL ST RCP Rule 1.750; and FL ST 20 J CIR 1.9.

9. *Rules of court*

   a. *Rules of civil procedure.* The Florida Rules of Civil Procedure apply to all actions of a civil nature and all special statutory proceedings in the circuit courts and county courts except those to which the Florida Probate Rules, the Florida Family Law Rules of Procedure, or the Small Claims Rules apply. FL ST RCP Rule 1.010.

      i. The form, content, procedure, and time for pleading in all special statutory proceedings shall be as prescribed by the statutes governing the proceeding unless the Florida Rules of Civil Procedure specifically provide to the contrary. FL ST RCP Rule 1.010.

      ii. The Florida Rules of Civil Procedure shall be construed to secure the just, speedy, and inexpensive determination of every action. FL ST RCP Rule 1.010.

   b. *Rules of judicial administration.* The Florida Rules of Judicial Administration shall apply to

administrative matters in all courts to which the Florida Rules of Judicial Administration are applicable by their terms. The Florida Rules of Judicial Administration shall be construed to secure the speedy and inexpensive determination of every proceeding to which they are applicable. The Florida Rules of Judicial Administration shall supersede all conflicting rules and statutes. FL ST J ADMIN Rule 2.110.

10. *Civil case management plan.* There is established within the Twentieth Judicial Circuit a Civil Case Management Plan applicable to circuit civil cases, which will be administered by the Administrative Office of the Courts through direction of the Circuit Administrative Judges in each county for the implementation of enhanced case management procedures and guidelines for the timely and efficient processing of circuit civil cases and reduction in the pending backlog of civil cases. FL ST 20 J CIR 1.13.

    a. The basis for the Civil Case Management Plan is included in FL ST 20 J CIR 1.13, identified in Attachment A as the "Civil Differentiated Case Management (DCM) Procedures and Backlog Reduction Plan," and is incorporated as if fully set forth in FL ST 20 J CIR 1.13. The Civil Case Management Plan is to be used as a model for the purpose of establishing time standards, improving the courts ability to provide early and continuous management of civil cases as required by FL ST J ADMIN Rule 2.545, and to promote uniformity of practice throughout the Twentieth Judicial Circuit. FL ST 20 J CIR 1.13.

    b. Full implementation of the Civil DCM Case Management Procedures (Attachment A), including all uniform circuitwide procedures and forms, shall apply to all civil cases filed in Lee and Collier counties, effective January 1, 2011. Even though full implementation may be delayed in Charlotte, Hendry, and Glades counties, all civil time standards and goals, and the use of civil Case Managers and Magistrates to assist trial judges in the process of civil case management and backlog reduction programs, shall be effective circuitwide immediately. FL ST 20 J CIR 1.13.

    c. For more information on the civil case management plan, refer to the specific county website and/or see FL ST 20 J CIR 1.13.

D. Documents

1. *Required documents*

    a. *Summons.* Upon the commencement of the action, summons or other process authorized by law shall be issued forthwith by the clerk or judge under the clerk's or the judge's signature and the seal of the court and delivered for service without praecipe. FL ST RCP Rule 1.070(a).

    b. *Complaint.* See the General Requirements section for the contents of the complaint.

        i. *Notices to persons with disabilities.* See the Format section of this KeyRules document for further information.

    c. *Civil cover sheet.* A civil cover sheet (FL ST RCP Form 1.997) shall be completed and filed with the clerk at the time an initial complaint or petition is filed by the party initiating the action. If the cover sheet is not filed, the clerk shall accept the complaint or petition for filing; but all proceedings in the action shall be abated until a properly executed cover sheet is completed and filed. The clerk shall complete the civil cover sheet for a party appearing pro se. FL ST RCP Rule 1.100(c)(2).

    d. *Return of execution process by process server.* Each person who effects service of process shall note on a return-of-service form attached thereto, the date and time when it comes to hand, the date and time when it is served, the manner of service, the name of the person on whom it was served and, if the person is served in a representative capacity, the position occupied by the person. The return-of-service form must be signed by the person who effects the service of process. However, a person employed by a sheriff who effects the service of process may sign the return-of-service form using an electronic signature certified by the sheriff. FL ST § 48.21(1).

        i. A failure to state the facts or to include the signature required by FL ST § 48.21(1) invalidates the service, but the return is amendable to state the facts or to include the signature at any time on application to the court from which the process issued. On amendment, service is as effective as if the return had originally stated the omitted facts or included the signature. A failure to state all the facts in or to include the signature on the return shall subject the person effecting service to a fine not exceeding $10, in the court's discretion. FL ST § 48.21(2).

e. *Filing fees.* Filing fees are due at the time a party files a pleading to initiate a proceeding or files a pleading for relief. FL ST § 28.241. For a fee schedule, see FL ST § 28.241.

2. *Supplemental documents*

a. *Exhibits.* All bonds, notes, bills of exchange, contracts, accounts, or documents upon which action may be brought or defense made, or a copy thereof or a copy of the portions thereof material to the pleadings, shall be incorporated in or attached to the pleading. No papers shall be unnecessarily annexed as exhibits. The pleadings shall contain no unnecessary recitals of deeds, documents, contracts, or other instruments. Any exhibit attached to a pleading shall be considered a part of the pleadings for all purposes. FL ST RCP Rule 1.130(a).

b. *Notice of constitutional question.* A party that files a pleading, written motion, or other paper drawing into question the constitutionality of a state statute or a county or municipal charter, ordinance, or franchise must promptly (1) file a notice of constitutional question stating the question and identifying the paper that raises it; and (2) serve the notice and the pleading, written motion, or other paper drawing into question the constitutionality of a state statute or a county or municipal charter, ordinance, or franchise on the Attorney General or the state attorney of the judicial circuit in which the action is pending, by either certified or registered mail. Service of the notice and pleading, written motion, or other paper does not require joinder of the Attorney General or the state attorney as a party to the action. FL ST RCP Rule 1.071.

E. Format

1. *Documents; Type and size.* Documents subject to the exceptions set forth in FL ST J ADMIN Rule 2.525(d) shall be filed on recycled paper measuring eight and one half by eleven (8 1/2 by 11) inches. For purposes of FL ST J ADMIN Rule 2.520, paper is recycled if it contains a minimum content of fifty (50) percent waste paper. Xerographic reduction of legal-size (eight and one half by fourteen (8 1/2 by 14) inches) documents to letter size (eight and one half by eleven (8 1/2 by 11) inches) is prohibited. All other documents filed by electronic transmission shall be filed in a format capable of being printed in a format consistent with the provisions of FL ST J ADMIN Rule 2.250. FL ST J ADMIN Rule 2.520(b); FL ST 20 J CIR 2.9.

a. *Exhibits.* Any exhibit or attachment filed with pleadings or papers may be filed in its original size. FL ST J ADMIN Rule 2.520(c); FL ST 20 J CIR 2.9.

b. *Recording space.* On all papers and documents prepared and filed by the court or by any party to a proceeding which are to be recorded in the public records of any county, including but not limited to final money judgments and notices of lis pendens, a three (3) inch by three (3) inch space at the top right-hand corner on the first page and a one (1) inch by three (3) inch space at the top right-hand corner on each subsequent page shall be left blank and reserved for use by the clerk of court. FL ST J ADMIN Rule 2.520(d).

i. *Exceptions to recording space.* Any papers or documents created by persons or entities over which the filing party has no control, including but not limited to wills, codicils, trusts, or other testamentary documents; documents prepared or executed by any public officer; documents prepared, executed, acknowledged, or proved outside of the State of Florida; or documents created by State or Federal government agencies, may be filed without the space required by FL ST J ADMIN Rule 2.520. FL ST J ADMIN Rule 2.520(e).

c. *Noncompliance.* No clerk of court is permitted to refuse to file any document or paper because of noncompliance with the Florida Rules of Judicial Administration. However, upon request of the clerk of court, noncomplying documents must be resubmitted in accordance with the formatting rules. FL ST J ADMIN Rule 2.520(f).

i. When time of filing is critical, the Clerk shall accept pleadings, motions, petitions, briefs, notices, orders, judgments, decrees, opinions, or other papers or official documents on other than eight and one half by eleven (8 1/2 by 11) inch paper but shall then require that the document be resubmitted to comply with FL ST J ADMIN Rule 2.520. FL ST 20 J CIR 2.9.

2. *Caption.* Every pleading, motion, order, judgment, or other paper shall have a caption containing the name of the court, the file number, and except for in rem proceedings, including forfeiture proceedings,

the name of the first party on each side with an appropriate indication of other parties, and a designation identifying the party filing it and its nature or the nature of the order, as the case may be. In any in rem proceeding, every pleading, motion, order, judgment, or other paper shall have a caption containing the name of the court, the file number, the style "In re" (followed by the name or general description of the property), and a designation of the person or entity filing it and its nature or the nature of the order, as the case may be. In an in rem forfeiture proceeding, the style shall be "In re forfeiture of" (followed by the name of the general description of the property). All papers filed in the action shall be styled in such a manner as to indicate clearly the subject matter of the paper and the party requesting or obtaining relief. FL ST RCP Rule 1.100(c)(1).

3. *Writing and written defined.* Writing or written means a document containing information, an application, or a stipulation. FL ST RCP Rule 1.080(c).
4. *Rule abbreviations*
   a. The Florida Rules of Civil Procedure and shall be abbreviated as Fla.R.Civ.P. FL ST RCP Rule 1.010.
   b. The Florida Rules of Judicial Administration shall be abbreviated as Fla. R. Jud. Admin. FL ST J ADMIN Rule 2.110.
5. *Nonverification.* Except when otherwise specifically provided by the Florida Rules of Civil Procedure or an applicable statute, every pleading or other document of a party represented by an attorney need not be verified or accompanied by an affidavit. FL ST RCP Rule 1.030; FL ST J ADMIN Rule 2.515(a).
6. *Attorney signature*
   a. *Attorney signature.* Every pleading and other document of a party represented by an attorney shall be signed by at least one (1) attorney of record in that attorney's individual name whose current record Florida Bar address, telephone number, including area code, primary e-mail address and secondary e-mail addresses, if any, and Florida Bar number shall be stated, and who shall be duly licensed to practice law in Florida or who shall have received permission to appear in the particular case as provided in FL ST J ADMIN Rule 2.510. FL ST J ADMIN Rule 2.515(a).
      i. The attorney may be required by the court to give the address of, and to vouch for the attorney's authority to represent, the party. FL ST J ADMIN Rule 2.515(a).
      ii. The signature of an attorney shall constitute a certificate by the attorney that the attorney has read the pleading or other document; that to the best of the attorney's knowledge, information, and belief there is good ground to support it; and that it is not interposed for delay. FL ST J ADMIN Rule 2.515(a).
      iii. If a pleading is not signed or is signed with intent to defeat the purpose of FL ST J ADMIN Rule 2.515, it may be stricken and the action may proceed as though the pleading or other document had not been served. FL ST J ADMIN Rule 2.515(a).
   b. *Pro se litigant signature.* A party who is not represented by an attorney shall sign any pleading or other paper and state the party's address and telephone number, including area code. FL ST J ADMIN Rule 2.515(b).
   c. *Form of signature*
      i. The signatures required on pleadings and documents by FL ST J ADMIN Rule 2.515(a) and FL ST J ADMIN Rule 2.515(b) may be:
         - Original signatures;
         - Original signatures that have been reproduced by electronic means, such as on electronically transmitted documents or photocopied documents;
         - Electronic signatures using the "/s/," "s/," or "/s" formats by or at the direction of the person signing; or
         - Any other signature format authorized by general law, so long as the clerk where the proceeding is pending has the capability of receiving and has obtained approval from the Supreme Court of Florida to accept pleadings and documents with that signature format. FL ST J ADMIN Rule 2.515(c)(1).

ii. An attorney, party, or other person who files a pleading or paper by electronic transmission that does not contain the original signature of that attorney, party, or other person shall file that identical pleading or paper in paper form containing an original signature of that attorney, party, or other person (hereinafter called the follow-up filing) immediately thereafter. The follow-up filing is not required if the Supreme Court of Florida has entered an order directing the clerk of court to discontinue accepting the follow-up filing. FL ST J ADMIN Rule 2.515(c)(2).

7. *Forms*
   a. *Process.* The forms of process, notice of lis pendens, and notice of action provided in the Florida Rules of Civil Procedure are sufficient. Variations from the forms do not void process or notices that are otherwise sufficient. FL ST RCP Rule 1.900(a).
   b. *Other forms.* The other forms provided in the Florida Rules of Civil Procedure are sufficient for the matters that are covered by them. So long as the substance is expressed without prolixity, the forms may be varied to meet the facts of a particular case. FL ST RCP Rule 1.900(b).
   c. *Formal matters.* Captions, except for the designation of the paper, are omitted from the forms provided in the Florida Rules of Civil Procedure. A general form of caption is the first form provided. Signatures are omitted from pleadings and motions. FL ST RCP Rule 1.900(c).
8. *Notices to persons with disabilities.* All notices of court proceedings to be held in a public facility, and all process compelling appearance at such proceedings, shall include the following statement in bold face, fourteen (14) point Times New Roman or Courier font: "If you are a person with a disability who needs any accommodation in order to participate in this proceeding, you are entitled, at no cost to you, to the provision of certain assistance. Please contact [identify applicable court personnel by name, address, and telephone number] at least seven (7) days before your scheduled court appearance, or immediately upon receiving this notification if the time before the scheduled appearance is less than seven (7) days; if you are hearing or voice impaired, call 711." FL ST J ADMIN Rule 2.540(c)(1). For more information, see FL ST 20 J CIR 2.15.
9. *Minimization of the filing of sensitive information*
   a. *Limitations for court filings.* Unless authorized by FL ST J ADMIN Rule 2.425(b), statute, another rule of court, or the court orders otherwise, designated sensitive information filed with the court must be limited to the following format:
      i. The initials of a person known to be a minor;
      ii. The year of birth of a person's birth date;
      iii. No portion of any: Social security number, Bank account number, Credit card account number, Charge account number, or Debit account number;
      iv. The last four digits of any: Taxpayer identification number (TIN), Employee identification number, Driver's license number, Passport number, Telephone number, Financial account number, except as set forth in FL ST J ADMIN Rule 2.425(a)(3), Brokerage account number, Insurance policy account number, Loan account number, Customer account number, or Patient or health care number;
      v. A truncated version of any: Email address, Computer user name, Password, or Personal identification number (PIN); and
      vi. A truncated version of any other sensitive information as provided by court order. FL ST J ADMIN Rule 2.425(a).
   b. *Exceptions.* FL ST J ADMIN Rule 2.425(a) does not apply to the following:
      i. An account number which identifies the property alleged to be the subject of a proceeding;
      ii. The record of an administrative or agency proceeding;
      iii. The record in appellate or review proceedings;
      iv. The birth date of a minor whenever the birth date is necessary for the court to establish or maintain subject matter jurisdiction;
      v. The name of a minor in any order relating to parental responsibility, time-sharing, or child support;

vi. The name of a minor in any document or order affecting the minor's ownership of real property;

vii. The birth date of a party in a writ of attachment or notice to payor;

viii. In traffic and criminal proceedings: a pro se filing; a court filing that is related to a criminal matter or investigation and that is prepared before the filing of a criminal charge or is not filed as part of any docketed criminal case; an arrest or search warrant or any information in support thereof; a charging document and an affidavit or other documents filed in support of any charging document, including any driving records; a statement of particulars; discovery material introduced into evidence or otherwise filed with the court; and all information necessary for the proper issuance and execution of a subpoena duces tecum;

ix. Information used by the clerk for case maintenance purposes or the courts for case management purposes; and

x. Information which is relevant and material to an issue before the court. FL ST J ADMIN Rule 2.425(b).

c. *Remedies.* Upon motion by a party or interested person or sua sponte by the court, the court may order remedies, sanctions or both for a violation of FL ST J ADMIN Rule 2.425(a). Following notice and an opportunity to respond, the court may impose sanctions if such filing was not made in good faith. FL ST J ADMIN Rule 2.425(c).

d. *Motions not restricted.* FL ST J ADMIN Rule 2.425 does not restrict a party's right to move for protective order, to move to file documents under seal, or to request a determination of the confidentiality of records. FL ST J ADMIN Rule 2.425(d).

e. *Application.* FL ST J ADMIN Rule 2.425 does not affect the application of constitutional provisions, statutes, or rules of court regarding confidential information or access to public information. FL ST J ADMIN Rule 2.425(e).

F. Filing and Service Requirements

1. *Filing requirements.* All documents filed in any court shall be filed by electronic transmission in accordance with FL ST J ADMIN Rule 2.525. "Documents" means pleadings, motions, petitions, memoranda, briefs, notices, exhibits, declarations, affidavits, orders, judgments, decrees, writs, opinions, and any other paper or writing submitted to a court. FL ST J ADMIN Rule 2.520(a). All documents that are court records, as defined in FL ST J ADMIN Rule 2.430(a)(1), must be filed by electronic transmission, provided that: (1) the clerk has the ability to accept and retain such documents; (2) the clerk or the chief judge of the circuit has requested permission to accept documents filed by electronic transmission; and (3) the supreme court has entered an order granting permission to the clerk to accept documents filed by electronic transmission. FL ST J ADMIN Rule 2.525(c)(1).

a. *Definition.* "Electronic transmission of documents" means the sending of information by electronic signals to, by or from a court or clerk, which when received can be transformed and stored or transmitted on paper, microfilm, magnetic storage device, optical imaging system, CD-ROM, flash drive, other electronic data storage system, server, case maintenance system ("CM"), electronic court filing ("ECF") system, statewide or local electronic portal ("e-portal"), or other electronic record keeping system authorized by the supreme court in a format sufficient to communicate the information on the original document in a readable format. Electronic transmission of documents includes electronic mail ("e-mail") and any internet-based transmission procedure, and may include procedures allowing for documents to be signed or verified by electronic means. FL ST J ADMIN Rule 2.525(a).

b. *Application.* Any court or clerk of the court may accept the electronic transmission of documents for filing after the clerk, together with input from the chief judge of the circuit, has obtained approval of the procedures and program for doing so from the Supreme Court of Florida. FL ST J ADMIN Rule 2.525(b).

c. *Exceptions*

i. Paper documents and other submissions may be manually submitted to the clerk or court:

- When the clerk does not have the ability to accept and retain documents by electronic filing or has not had ECF Procedures approved by the supreme court;

- For filing by any self-represented party or any self-represented nonparty unless specific ECF Procedures provide a means to file documents electronically. However, any self-represented nonparty that is a governmental or public agency and any other agency, partnership, corporation, or business entity acting on behalf of any governmental or public agency may file documents by electronic transmission if such entity has the capability of filing documents electronically;
- For filing by attorneys excused from e-mail service in accordance with FL ST J ADMIN Rule 2.516(b);
- When submitting evidentiary exhibits or filing non-documentary materials;
- When the filing involves documents in excess of twenty-five (25) megabytes (25MB) in size. For such filings, documents may be transmitted using an electronic storage medium that the clerk has the ability to accept, which may include a CD-ROM, flash drive, or similar storage medium;
- When filed in open court, as permitted by the court;
- When paper filing is permitted by any approved statewide or local ECF procedures; and
- If any court determines that justice so requires. FL ST J ADMIN Rule 2.525(d).

ii. Any document in paper form submitted under FL ST J ADMIN Rule 2.525(d) is filed when it is received by the clerk or court and the clerk shall immediately thereafter convert any filed paper document to an electronic document. "Convert to an electronic document" means optically capturing an image of a paper document and using character recognition software to recover as much of the document's text as practicable and then indexing and storing the document in the official court file. FL ST J ADMIN Rule 2.525(c)(4).

iii. Any storage medium submitted under FL ST J ADMIN Rule 2.525(d)(5) is filed when received by the clerk or court and the clerk shall immediately thereafter transfer the electronic documents from the storage device to the official court file. FL ST J ADMIN Rule 2.525(c)(5).

iv. If the filer of any paper document authorized under FL ST J ADMIN Rule 2.525(d) provides a self-addressed, postage-paid envelope for return of the paper document after it is converted to electronic form by the clerk, the clerk shall place the paper document in the envelope and deposit it in the mail. Except when a paper document is required to be maintained, the clerk may recycle any filed paper document that is not to be returned to the filer. FL ST J ADMIN Rule 2.525(c)(6).

v. The clerk may convert any paper document filed before the effective date of FL ST J ADMIN Rule 2.525 to an electronic document. Unless the clerk is required to maintain the paper document, if the paper document has been converted to an electronic document by the clerk, the paper document is no longer part of the official court file and may be removed and recycled. FL ST J ADMIN Rule 2.525(c)(7).

d. *Official court file.* For information on what constitutes the official court file, please see FL ST J ADMIN Rule 2.525(c)(2), FL ST J ADMIN Rule 2.525(c)(3).

e. *Administration.* All attorneys, parties, or other persons using this rule to file documents are required to make arrangements with the court or clerk for the payment of any charges authorized by general law or the supreme court before filing any document by electronic transmission. FL ST J ADMIN Rule 2.525(f)(2).

f. *Filing date.* The filing date for an electronically transmitted document is the date and time that such filing is acknowledged by an electronic stamp or otherwise, pursuant to any procedure set forth in any ECF Procedures approved by the supreme court, or the date the last page of such filing is received by the court or clerk. FL ST J ADMIN Rule 2.525(f)(3).

g. *Accessibility.* All documents transmitted in any electronic form under FL ST J ADMIN Rule 2.525 must comply with the accessibility requirements of FL ST J ADMIN Rule 2.526. FL ST J ADMIN Rule 2.525(g).

2. *Service requirements*

a. *Papers to be served.* At the time of personal service of process a copy of the initial pleading shall be delivered to the party upon whom service is made. The date and hour of service shall be endorsed on the original process and all copies of it by the person making the service. The party seeking to effect personal service shall furnish the person making service with the necessary copies. When the service is made by publication, copies of the initial pleadings shall be furnished to the clerk and mailed by the clerk with the notice of action to all parties whose addresses are stated in the initial pleading or sworn statement. FL ST RCP Rule 1.070(e).

i. *Copies of court submissions.* Copies of any submissions to the court (such as correspondence, memoranda of law, motions, case law, etc.) should simultaneously be provided to opposing counsel by substantially the same method of delivery by which they are provided to the court. For example, if a memorandum of law is hand-delivered to the court, at substantially the same time a copy should be hand-delivered or faxed to opposing counsel. FL ST 20 J CIR 2.20(IV)(J)(4).

b. *Issuance of summons.* Upon the commencement of the action, summons or other process authorized by law shall be issued forthwith by the clerk or judge under the clerk's or the judge's signature and the seal of the court and delivered for service without praecipe. FL ST RCP Rule 1.070(a).

i. *How directed.* Summons, subpoenas, and other process in civil actions run throughout the state. All process except subpoenas shall be directed to all and singular the sheriffs of the state. FL ST § 48.011.

ii. *Service as to numerous defendants.* If there is more than one (1) defendant, the clerk or judge shall issue as many writs of process against the several defendants as may be directed by the plaintiff or the plaintiff's attorney. FL ST RCP Rule 1.070(c).

c. *Who may serve process.* Service of process may be made by an officer authorized by law to serve process, but the court may appoint any competent person not interested in the action to serve the process. When so appointed, the person serving process shall make proof of service by affidavit promptly and in any event within the time during which the person served must respond to the process. Failure to make proof of service shall not affect the validity of the service. When any process is returned not executed or returned improperly executed for any defendant, the party causing its issuance shall be entitled to such additional process against the unserved party as is required to effect service. FL ST RCP Rule 1.070(b).

i. All process shall be served by the sheriff of the county where the person to be served is found, except initial nonenforceable civil process may be served by a special process server appointed by the sheriff as provided for in FL ST § 48.021 or by a certified process server as provided for in FL ST § 48.25 through FL ST § 48.31. FL ST § 48.021(1).

ii. The sheriff of each county may, in his or her discretion, establish an approved list of natural persons designated as special process servers. FL ST § 48.021(2)(a). For more information regarding process servers, please see FL ST § 48.021(2).

iii. A person serving process shall place, on the copy served, the date and time of service and his or her identification number and initials for all service of process. FL ST § 48.031(5).

d. *Service of process on Sunday*

i. Service or execution on Sunday of any writ, process, warrant, order, or judgment is void and the person serving or executing, or causing it to be served or executed, is liable to the party aggrieved for damages for so doing as if he or she had done it without any process, writ, warrant, order, or judgment. FL ST § 48.20.

ii. If affidavit is made by the person requesting service or execution that he or she has good reason to believe that any person liable to have any such writ, process, warrant, order, or judgment served on him or her intends to escape from this state under protection of Sunday, any officer furnished with an order authorizing service or execution by the trial court judge may serve or execute such writ, process, warrant, order, or judgment on Sunday, and it is as valid as if it had been done on any other day. FL ST § 48.20.

e. *Service; Generally.* The timing and manner of service should not be used to the disadvantage of the party receiving the papers. FL ST 20 J CIR 2.20(IV)(C)(1).

i. Papers and memoranda of law should not be served at court appearances without advance notice to opposing counsel and should not be served so close to a court appearance so as to inhibit the ability of opposing counsel to prepare for that appearance or to respond to the papers. Should the attorney do so, the court is urged to take appropriate action in response, including continuing the matter to allow opposing counsel to prepare and respond. FL ST 20 J CIR 2.20(IV)(C)(2).

ii. Papers should not be served in order to take advantage of an opponent's known absence from the office or at a time or in a manner designed to inconvenience an adversary, such as late on Friday afternoon or the day preceding a secular or religious holiday. FL ST 20 J CIR 2.20(IV)(C)(3).

iii. Service should be made personally or by courtesy copy facsimile transmission when it is likely that service by mail, even when allowed, will prejudice the opposing party or will not provide the opposing party with a reasonable time to respond. FL ST 20 J CIR 2.20(IV)(C)(4).

f. *Methods of service*

i. *Service of process generally.* Service of original process is made by delivering a copy of it to the person to be served with a copy of the complaint, petition, or other initial pleading or paper or by leaving the copies at his or her usual place of abode with any person residing therein who is fifteen (15) years of age or older and informing the person of their contents. Minors who are or have been married shall be served as provided in FL ST § 48.031. FL ST § 48.031(1)(a).

- Employers, when contacted by an individual authorized to make service of process, shall permit the authorized individual to make service on employees in a private area designated by the employer. FL ST § 48.031(1)(b).
- Substitute service may be made on the spouse of the person to be served at any place in the county, if the cause of action is not an adversary proceeding between the spouse and the person to be served, if the spouse requests such service, and if the spouse and person to be served are residing together in the same dwelling. FL ST § 48.031(2)(a).
- Substitute service may be made on an individual doing business as a sole proprietorship at his or her place of business, during regular business hours, by serving the person in charge of the business at the time of service if two (2) or more attempts to serve the owner have been made at the place of business. FL ST § 48.031(2)(b).
- If the only address for a person to be served, which is discoverable through public records, is a private mailbox, substitute service may be made by leaving a copy of the process with the person in charge of the private mailbox, but only if the process server determines that the person to be served maintains a mailbox at that location. FL ST § 48.031(6).

ii. *Service by mail.* A defendant may accept service of process by mail. FL ST RCP Rule 1.070(i). A plaintiff may notify any defendant of the commencement of the action and request that the defendant waive service of a summons. FL ST RCP Rule 1.070(i)(2).

- *Notice and request for waiver.* The notice and request shall: (1) be in writing and be addressed directly to the defendant, if an individual, or to an officer or managing or general agent of the defendant or other agent authorized by appointment or law to receive service of process; (2) be dispatched by certified mail, return receipt requested; (3) be accompanied by a copy of the complaint and shall identify the court in which it has been filed; (4) inform the defendant of the consequences of compliance and of failure to comply with the request; (5) state the date on which the request is sent; (6) allow the defendant twenty (20) days from the date on which the request is received to return the waiver, or, if the address of the defendant is outside of the United States, thirty (30) days from the date on which it is received to return the waiver; and (7) provide the defendant with an extra copy of the notice and request, including the waiver, as well as a prepaid means of compliance in writing. FL ST RCP Rule 1.070(i)(2).
- *Consequences of accepting/rejecting service by mail.* Acceptance of service of a complaint by mail does not thereby waive any objection to the venue or to the jurisdiction of the court over the person of the defendant. FL ST RCP Rule 1.070(i)(1). If a defendant

fails to comply with a request for waiver within the time provided, the court shall impose the costs subsequently incurred in effecting service on the defendant unless good cause for the failure is shown. FL ST RCP Rule 1.070(i)(3). A defendant who, before being served with process, timely returns a waiver so requested is not required to respond to the complaint until sixty (60) days after the date the defendant received the request for waiver of service. For purposes of computing any time prescribed or allowed by the Florida Rules of Civil Procedure, service of process shall be deemed effected twenty (20) days before the time required to respond to the complaint. FL ST RCP Rule 1.070(i)(4). When the plaintiff files a waiver of service with the court, the action shall proceed, except as provided in FL ST RCP Rule 1.070(i)(4), as if a summons and complaint had been served at the time of filing the waiver, and no further proof of service shall be required. FL ST RCP Rule 1.070(i)(5).

iii. *Service on partnerships and limited partnerships*

- Process against a partnership shall be served on any partner and is as valid as if served on each individual partner. If a partner is not available during regular business hours to accept service on behalf of the partnership, he or she may designate an employee to accept such service. After one (1) attempt to serve a partner or designated employee has been made, process may be served on the person in charge of the partnership during regular business hours. After service on any partner, plaintiff may proceed to judgment and execution against that partner and the assets of the partnership. After service on a designated employee or other person in charge, plaintiff may proceed to judgment and execution against the partnership assets but not against the individual assets of any partner. FL ST § 48.061(1).
- Process against a domestic limited partnership may be served on any general partner or on the agent for service of process specified in its certificate of limited partnership or in its certificate as amended or restated and is as valid as if served on each individual member of the partnership. After service on a general partner or the agent, the plaintiff may proceed to judgment and execution against the limited partnership and all of the general partners individually. If a general partner cannot be found in this state and service cannot be made on an agent because of failure to maintain such an agent or because the agent cannot be found or served with the exercise of reasonable diligence, service of process may be effected by service upon the Secretary of State as agent of the limited partnership as provided for in FL ST § 48.181. Service of process may be made under FL ST § 48.071 and FL ST § 48.21 on limited partnerships. FL ST § 48.061(2).
- Process against a foreign limited partnership may be served on any general partner found in the state or on any agent for service of process specified in its application for registration and is as valid as if served on each individual member of the partnership. If a general partner cannot be found in this state and an agent for service of process has not been appointed or, if appointed, the agent's authority has been revoked or the agent cannot be found or served with the exercise of reasonable diligence, service of process may be effected by service upon the Secretary of State as agent of the limited partnership as provided for in FL ST § 48.181, or process may be served as provided in FL ST § 48.071 and FL ST § 48.21. FL ST § 48.061(3).

iv. *Service on corporation*

- Process against any private corporation, domestic or foreign, may be served: (1) on the president or vice president, or other head of the corporation; (2) in the absence of any person described in FL ST § 48.081(1)(a), on the cashier, treasurer, secretary, or general manager; (3) in the absence of any person described in FL ST § 48.081(1)(a) or FL ST § 48.081(1)(b), on any director; or (4) in the absence of any person described in FL ST § 48.081(1)(a), FL ST § 48.081(1)(b), or FL ST § 48.081(1)(c), on any officer or business agent residing in the state. FL ST § 48.081(1).
- If a foreign corporation has none of the foregoing officers or agents in this state, service may be made on any agent transacting business for it in this state. FL ST § 48.081(2).

- As an alternative to all of the foregoing, process may be served on the agent designated by the corporation under FL ST § 48.091. However, if service cannot be made on a registered agent because of failure to comply with FL ST § 48.091, service of process shall be permitted on any employee at the corporation's principal place of business or on any employee of the registered agent. FL ST § 48.081(3)(a). If the address provided for the registered agent, officer, director, or principal place of business is a residence or private mailbox, service on the corporation may be made by serving the registered agent, officer, or director in accordance with FL ST § 48.031. FL ST § 48.081(3)(b).
- FL ST § 48.081 does not apply to service of process on insurance companies. FL ST § 48.081(4).
- When a corporation engages in substantial and not isolated activities within this state, or has a business office within the state and is actually engaged in the transaction of business therefrom, service upon any officer or business agent while on corporate business within this state may personally be made, pursuant to FL ST § 48.081, and it is not necessary in such case that the action, suit, or proceeding against the corporation shall have arisen out of any transaction or operation connected with or incidental to the business being transacted within the state. FL ST § 48.081(5).
- For information regarding service on a dissolved corporation refer to FL ST § 48.101.

v. *Personal service outside state*

- Except as otherwise provided herein, service of process on persons outside of this state shall be made in the same manner as service within this state by any officer authorized to serve process in the state where the person is served. No order of court is required. An affidavit of the officer shall be filed, stating the time, manner, and place of service. The court may consider the affidavit, or any other competent evidence, in determining whether service has been properly made. Service of process on persons outside the United States may be required to conform to the provisions of the Hague Convention on the Service Abroad of Judicial and Extrajudicial Documents in Civil or Commercial Matters. FL ST § 48.194(1).
- For further information on service of process in an in rem or quasi in rem action refer to FL ST § 48.194(2); FL ST § 48.194(3); and FL ST § 48.194(4).

vi. *Method of substituted service on nonresident*

- When authorized by law, substituted service of process on a nonresident or a person who conceals his or her whereabouts by serving a public officer designated by law shall be made by leaving a copy of the process with a fee of eight dollars and seventy-five cents ($8.75) with the public officer or in his or her office or by mailing the copies by certified mail to the public officer with the fee. The service is sufficient service on a defendant who has appointed a public officer as his or her agent for the service of process. FL ST § 48.161(1).
- Notice of service and a copy of the process shall be sent forthwith by registered or certified mail by the plaintiff or his or her attorney to the defendant, and the defendant's return receipt and the affidavit of the plaintiff or his or her attorney of compliance shall be filed on or before the return day of the process or within such time as the court allows, or the notice and copy shall be served on the defendant, if found within the state, by an officer authorized to serve legal process, or if found without the state, by a sheriff or a deputy sheriff of any county of this state or any duly constituted public officer qualified to serve like process in the state or jurisdiction where the defendant is found. The officer's return showing service shall be filed on or before the return day of the process or within such time as the court allows. The public officer shall keep a record of all process served on him or her showing the day and hour of service. FL ST § 48.161(1).
- If any person on whom service of process is authorized under FL ST § 48.161(1) dies, service may be made on his or her administrator, executor, curator, or personal representative in the same manner. FL ST § 48.161(2).

- FL ST § 48.161 does not apply to persons on whom service is authorized under FL ST § 48.151. FL ST § 48.161(3).
- The public officer may designate some other person in his or her office to accept service. FL ST § 48.161(4).

vii. *Service by publication.* Service of process by publication may be made as provided by statute. FL ST RCP Rule 1.070(d). Service of process by publication is allowable in cases listed in FL ST § 49.011 and upon the parties listed in FL ST § 49.021.

- As a condition precedent to service by publication, a statement shall be filed in the action executed by the plaintiff, the plaintiff's agent or attorney, setting forth substantially the matters hereafter required, which statement may be contained in a verified pleading, or in an affidavit or other sworn statement. FL ST § 49.031(1). After the entry of a final judgment or decree in any action no sworn statement shall ever be held defective for failure to state a required fact if the fact otherwise appears from the record in the action. FL ST § 49.031(3).
- For the sworn statement requirements for service of process by publication refer to FL ST § 49.041; FL ST § 49.051; FL ST § 49.061; and FL ST § 49.071.
- On filing the sworn statement, and otherwise complying with the foregoing requirements, the plaintiff is entitled to have issued by the clerk or judge, not later than sixty (60) days after filing the sworn statement, a notice of action which notice shall set forth: (1) the names of the known natural defendants; the names, status and description of the corporate defendants; a description of the unknown defendants who claim by, through, under or against a known party which may be described as "all parties claiming interests by, through, under or against (name of known party)" and a description of all unknown defendants which may be described as "all parties having or claiming to have any right, title or interest in the property herein described"; (2) the nature of the action or proceeding in short and simple terms (but neglect to do so is not jurisdictional); (3) the name of the court in which the action or proceeding was instituted and an abbreviated title of the case; (4) the description of real property, if any, proceeded against. FL ST § 49.08.
- For further information on service of process by publication refer to FL ST § 49.09; FL ST § 49.10; FL ST § 49.11; FL ST § 49.12; FL ST § 50.011; FL ST § 50.021; FL ST § 50.031; FL ST § 50.041; FL ST § 50.051; and FL ST § 50.061.

viii. *Service on agents of nonresidents doing business in the state.* When any natural person or partnership not residing or having a principal place of business in this state engages in business in this state, process may be served on the person who is in charge of any business in which the defendant is engaged within this state at the time of service, including agents soliciting orders for goods, wares, merchandise or services. FL ST § 48.071.

- Any process so served is as valid as if served personally on the nonresident person or partnership engaging in business in this state in any action against the person or partnership arising out of such business. FL ST § 48.071.
- A copy of such process with a notice of service on the person in charge of such business shall be sent forthwith to the nonresident person or partnership by registered or certified mail, return receipt requested. FL ST § 48.071.
- An affidavit of compliance with FL ST § 48.071 shall be filed before the return day or within such further time as the court may allow. FL ST § 48.071.

ix. *Service on nonresident engaging in business in state.* The acceptance by any person or persons, individually or associated together as a copartnership or any other form or type of association, who are residents of any other state or country, and all foreign corporations, and any person who is a resident of the state and who subsequently becomes a nonresident of the state or conceals his or her whereabouts, of the privilege extended by law to nonresidents and others to operate, conduct, engage in, or carry on a business or business venture in the state, or to have an office or agency in the state, constitutes an appointment by the persons and foreign corporations of the

Secretary of State of the state as their agent on whom all process in any action or proceeding against them, or any of them, arising out of any transaction or operation connected with or incidental to the business or business venture may be served. The acceptance of the privilege is signification of the agreement of the persons and foreign corporations that the process against them which is so served is of the same validity as if served personally on the persons or foreign corporations. FL ST § 48.181(1).

- If a foreign corporation has a resident agent or officer in the state, process shall be served on the resident agent or officer. FL ST § 48.181(2).
- Any person, firm, or corporation which sells, consigns, or leases by any means whatsoever tangible or intangible personal property, through brokers, jobbers, wholesalers, or distributors to any person, firm, or corporation in this state is conclusively presumed to be both engaged in substantial and not isolated activities within this state and operating, conducting, engaging in, or carrying on a business or business venture in this state. FL ST § 48.181(3).

x. *Other service provisions:*

- Service on alien property custodian. FL ST § 48.131.
- Service on an incompetent person. FL ST § 48.042.
- Service on minor. FL ST § 48.041.
- Service on public agencies and officers. FL ST § 48.111.
- Service on the state. FL ST § 48.121.
- Service on a state prisoner. FL ST § 48.051.
- Service on labor unions. FL ST § 48.141.
- Service on statutory agents for certain persons. FL ST § 48.151.
- Service on nonresident motor vehicle owners. FL ST § 48.171.
- Service of process in action for possession of premises. FL ST § 48.183.
- Service on nonresidents operating aircraft or watercraft in the state. FL ST § 48.19.

g. *Crossclaims.* Service of a crossclaim on a party who has appeared in the action shall be made pursuant to FL ST RCP Rule 1.080. Service of a crossclaim against a party who has not appeared in the action shall be made in the manner provided for service of summons. FL ST RCP Rule 1.170(g).

h. *Fees.* The statutory compensation for making service shall not be increased by the simultaneous delivery or mailing of the copy of the initial pleading in conformity with FL ST RCP Rule 1.070. FL ST RCP Rule 1.070(g).

G. Hearings

1. There is no hearing required or contemplated in the Florida rules governing the complaint and service of summons.

H. Forms

1. Official Complaint Forms for Florida

a. Caption. FL ST RCP Form 1.901.

b. Summons. FL ST RCP Form 1.902.

c. Crossclaim summons. FL ST RCP Form 1.903.

d. Third-party summons. FL ST RCP Form 1.904.

e. Notice of action, constructive service, no property. FL ST RCP Form 1.919.

f. Notice of action, constructive service, property. FL ST RCP Form 1.920.

g. Third-party complaint. FL ST RCP Form 1.948.

h. Civil cover sheet. FL ST RCP Form 1.997.

i. Fall-down negligence complaint. FL ST RCP Form 1.951.

j. Notice of compliance when constitutional challenge is brought. FL ST RCP Form 1.975.

2. Complaint Forms for Florida

a. Complaint for damages; General form. FL-PP § 2:17.

b. Complaint; Negligent infliction of personal injury. FL-PP § 2:19.

c. Complaint; Fall down negligence. FL-PP § 2:20.

d. Complaint; Professional negligence. FL-PP § 2:23.

e. Complaint; Breach of contract. FL-PP § 2:24.

f. Complaint; Breach of personal services contract. FL-PP § 2:25.

g. Summons; General form. FL-PRACFORM § 3:4.

h. Summons; Natural person. FL-PRACFORM § 3:5.

i. Complaint; Assault and battery. FL-PRACFORM § 4:9.

j. Complaint; Breach of contract, general form. FL-PRACFORM § 4:17.

k. Complaint; Civil rights. FL-PRACFORM § 4:23.

l. Complaint; Conversion. FL-PRACFORM § 4:30.

m. Complaint; Employment contract. FL-PRACFORM § 4:44.

n. Complaint; False imprisonment. FL-PRACFORM § 4:46.

o. Complaint; Fraud, misrepresentation. FL-PRACFORM § 4:62.

p. Complaint; Lease, by landlord. FL-PRACFORM § 4:86.

q. Complaint; Lease, by tenant. FL-PRACFORM § 4:87.

r. Complaint; Libel. FL-PRACFORM § 4:89.

s. Complaint; Life insurance policy. FL-PRACFORM § 4:90.

t. Complaint; Medical malpractice, negligence. FL-PRACFORM § 4:95.

u. Complaint; Negligence, automobile, driver. FL-PRACFORM § 4:101.

v. Complaint; Negligence, hospital. FL-PRACFORM § 4:104.

I. Checklist

(I) ❑ Matters to be considered by plaintiff

(a) ❑ Required documents

(1) ❑ Summons

(2) ❑ Complaint

(3) ❑ Civil cover sheet

(4) ❑ Return of execution process by process server

(5) ❑ Filing fees

(b) ❑ Supplemental documents

(1) ❑ Exhibits

(2) ❑ Notice of constitutional question

(c) ❑ Time for filing and serving complaint

(1) ❑ Service of the initial process and initial pleading should be made upon a defendant within one hundred twenty (120) days after the filing of the complaint with the court

(II) ❑ Matters to be considered by defendant

(a) ❑ Required documents

(1) ❑ Answer

(2) ❑ Certificate of service

(b) ❑ Supplemental documents

(1) ❑ Exhibits

(2) ❑ Notice of constitutional question

(c) ❑ Time for answer

(1) ❑ Unless a different time is prescribed in a statute of Florida, a defendant shall serve an answer within twenty (20) days after service of original process and the initial pleading on the defendant, or not later than the date fixed in a notice by publication

(2) ❑ A party served with a pleading stating a crossclaim against that party shall serve an answer to it within twenty (20) days after service on that party

(3) ❑ The plaintiff shall serve an answer to a counterclaim within twenty (20) days after service of the counterclaim

(4) ❑ A defendant who, before being served with process, timely returns a waiver so requested is not required to respond to the complaint until sixty (60) days after the date the defendant received the request for waiver of service; for purposes of computing any time prescribed or allowed by the Florida Rules of Civil Procedure, service of process shall be deemed effected twenty (20) days before the time required to respond to the complaint

(5) ❑ For timing requirements related to service on the state, service of motion impact, and responding when no responsive pleading is required, please see the Timing section of this document

Pleadings
Amended Complaint

Document Last Updated January 2013

A. Applicable Rules

1. *State rules*

a. Nonverification of papers. FL ST RCP Rule 1.030.

b. Process. FL ST RCP Rule 1.070.

c. Service and filing of pleadings, orders, and documents. FL ST RCP Rule 1.080.

d. Pleadings and motions. FL ST RCP Rule 1.100; FL ST RCP Rule 1.110; FL ST RCP Rule 1.120; FL ST RCP Rule 1.130; FL ST RCP Rule 1.190; FL ST § 48.193.

e. Pretrial procedure. FL ST RCP Rule 1.200.

f. Relief from judgment, decrees, or orders. FL ST RCP Rule 1.540.

g. Forms. FL ST RCP Rule 1.900.

h. Minimization of the filing of sensitive information. FL ST J ADMIN Rule 2.425.

i. Retention of court records. FL ST J ADMIN Rule 2.430.

j. Foreign attorneys. FL ST J ADMIN Rule 2.510.

k. Signature of attorneys and parties. FL ST J ADMIN Rule 2.515.

l. Paper. FL ST J ADMIN Rule 2.520.

m. Electronic filing. FL ST J ADMIN Rule 2.525.

n. Accessibility of information and technology. FL ST J ADMIN Rule 2.526.

o. Requests for accommodations by persons with disabilities. FL ST J ADMIN Rule 2.540.

p. Case management. FL ST J ADMIN Rule 2.545.

2. *Local rules*
   a. Exclusions from mediation. FL ST 20 J CIR 1.9.
   b. Establishment and implementation of civil case management plan. FL ST 20 J CIR 1.13.
   c. Size of paper. FL ST 20 J CIR 2.9.
   d. Americans with Disabilities Act; Notification of court proceedings. FL ST 20 J CIR 2.15.
   e. Standards of professional courtesy and conduct and establishment of peer review program. FL ST 20 J CIR 2.20.

B. Timing

1. *Amendment as a matter of course.* A party may amend a pleading once as a matter of course at any time before a responsive pleading is served or, if the pleading is one to which no responsive pleading is permitted and the action has not been placed on the trial calendar, may so amend it at any time within twenty (20) days after it is served. FL ST RCP Rule 1.190(a).
2. *Amendment by leave of court.* Otherwise a party may amend a pleading only by leave of court or by written consent of the adverse party. Leave of court shall be given freely when justice so requires. FL ST RCP Rule 1.190(a).
3. *Amendments in furtherance of justice.* At any time in furtherance of justice, upon such terms as may be just, the court may permit any process, proceeding, pleading, or record to be amended or material supplemental matter to be set forth in an amended or supplemental pleading. At every stage of the action the court must disregard any error or defect in the proceedings which does not affect the substantial rights of the parties. FL ST RCP Rule 1.190(e).
4. *Response to amended pleading.* A party shall plead in response to an amended pleading within ten (10) days after service of the amended pleading unless the court otherwise orders. FL ST RCP Rule 1.190(a).
5. *Computation of time*
   a. *Generally.* Computation of time shall be governed by FL ST J ADMIN Rule 2.514. FL ST RCP Rule 1.090(a). The following rules apply in computing time periods specified in any rule of procedure, local rule, court order, or statute that does not specify a method of computing time. FL ST J ADMIN Rule 2.514(a).
      i. *Period stated in days or a longer unit.* When the period is stated in days or a longer unit of time (A) exclude the day of the event that triggers the period; (B) count every day, including intermediate Saturdays, Sundays, and legal holidays; and (C) include the last day of the period, but if the last day is a Saturday, Sunday, or legal holiday, or falls within any period of time extended through an order of the chief justice under FL ST J ADMIN Rule 2.205(a)(2)(B)(iv), the period continues to run until the end of the next day that is not a Saturday, Sunday, or legal holiday and does not fall within any period of time extended through an order of the chief justice. FL ST J ADMIN Rule 2.514(a)(1).
      ii. *Period stated in hours.* When the period is stated in hours (A) begin counting immediately on the occurrence of the event that triggers the period; (B) count every hour, including hours during intermediate Saturdays, Sundays, and legal holidays; and (C) if the period would end on a Saturday, Sunday, or legal holiday, or during any period of time extended through an order of the chief justice under FL ST J ADMIN Rule 2.205(a)(2)(B)(iv), the period continues to run until the same time on the next day that is not a Saturday, Sunday, or legal holiday and does not fall within any period of time extended through an order of the chief justice. FL ST J ADMIN Rule 2.514(a)(2).
      iii. *Period stated in days less than seven (7) days.* When the period stated in days is less than seven (7) days, intermediate Saturdays, Sundays, and legal holidays shall be excluded in the computation. FL ST J ADMIN Rule 2.514(a)(3).
      iv. *"Last day" defined.* Unless a different time is set by a statute, local rule, or court order, the last day ends (A) for electronic filing or for service by any means, at midnight; and (B) for filing by other means, when the clerk's office is scheduled to close. FL ST J ADMIN Rule 2.514(a)(4).

v. *"Next day" defined.* The "next day" is determined by continuing to count forward when the period is measured after an event and backward when measured before an event. FL ST J ADMIN Rule 2.514(a)(5).

vi. *"Legal holiday" defined.* "Legal holiday" means (A) the day set aside by FL ST § 110.117, for observing New Year's Day, Martin Luther King, Jr.'s Birthday, Memorial Day, Independence Day, Labor Day, Veterans' Day, Thanksgiving Day, the Friday after Thanksgiving Day, or Christmas Day, and (B) any day observed as a holiday by the clerk's office or as designated by the chief judge. FL ST J ADMIN Rule 2.514(a)(6).

b. *Additional time after service by mail or e-mail.* When a party may or must act within a specified time after service and service is made by mail or e-mail, five (5) days are added after the period that would otherwise expire under FL ST J ADMIN Rule 2.514(a). FL ST J ADMIN Rule 2.514(b).

c. *Enlargement.* When an act is required or allowed to be done at or within a specified time by order of court, by the Florida Rules of Civil Procedure, or by notice given thereunder, for cause shown the court at any time in its discretion (1) with or without notice, may order the period enlarged if request therefor is made before the expiration of the period originally prescribed or as extended by a previous order, or (2) upon motion made and notice after the expiration of the specified period, may permit the act to be done when failure to act was the result of excusable neglect, but it may not extend the time for making a motion for new trial, for rehearing, or to alter or amend a judgment; making a motion for relief from a judgment under FL ST RCP Rule 1.540(b); taking an appeal or filing a petition for certiorari; or making a motion for a directed verdict. FL ST RCP Rule 1.090(b).

d. *Unaffected by expiration of term.* The period of time provided for the doing of any act or the taking of any proceeding shall not be affected or limited by the continued existence or expiration of a term of court. The continued existence or expiration of a term of court in no way affects the power of a court to do any act or take any proceeding in any action which is or has been pending before it. FL ST RCP Rule 1.090(c).

C. General Requirements

1. *Amendments.* A party may amend a pleading once as a matter of course at any time before a responsive pleading is served or, if the pleading is one to which no responsive pleading is permitted and the action has not been placed on the trial calendar, may so amend it at any time within twenty (20) days after it is served. Otherwise a party may amend a pleading only by leave of court or by written consent of the adverse party. Leave of court shall be freely given when justice so requires. FL ST RCP Rule 1.190(a).

a. *Purpose of amendments.* Amendments can relate to the correction of mistakes, the insertion of jurisdictional averments, the correction or addition of verifications, the addition or substitution or striking out of parties, and generally the rectification of all formal defects in the pleading. The court can also allow amendments setting up an omitted counterclaim or cross-claim if the defendant failed to raise the claim through oversight, inadvertence, or excusable neglect. FL-PP § 2:151.

b. *Amendment to a pleading/Amended pleading.* A significant difference exists between an amendment to a pleading and an amended pleading. An amendment to a pleading corrects, adds to or deletes from the pleading. An amended pleading is substituted for the former pleading and the former pleading ceases to have any effect. Dee v. Southern Brewing Company, 146 Fla. 588, 1 So.2d 562 (Fla. 1941); Shannon v. McBride, 105 So.2d 16 (Fla. 2d DCA 1958); Hughes v. Home Sav. of America, F.S.B., 675 So.2d 649 (Fla. 2d DCA 1996); FL-PRACPROC § 14:2.

c. *Relation back of amendments.* When the claim or defense asserted in the amended pleading arose out of the conduct, transaction, or occurrence set forth or attempted to be set forth in the original pleading, the amendment shall relate back to the date of the original pleading. FL ST RCP Rule 1.190(c).

2. *General rules of pleading*

a. *Claims for relief*

i. A pleading which sets forth a claim for relief, whether an original claim, counterclaim, crossclaim, or third-party claim, must state a cause of action and shall contain

- A short and plain statement of the grounds upon which the court's jurisdiction depends, unless the court already has jurisdiction and the claim needs no new grounds of jurisdiction to support it (For information regarding acts subjecting persons to jurisdiction, please see FL ST § 48.193),

- A short and plain statement of the ultimate facts showing that the pleader is entitled to relief, and
- A demand for judgment for the relief to which the pleader deems himself or herself entitled. FL ST RCP Rule 1.110(b).

ii. Relief in the alternative or of several different types may be demanded. Every complaint shall be considered to demand general relief. FL ST RCP Rule 1.110(b).

b. *Verification.* Except when otherwise specifically provided by these rules or an applicable statute, every pleading or other document of a party represented by an attorney need not be verified or accompanied by an affidavit. FL ST RCP Rule 1.030. When filing an action for foreclosure of a mortgage on residential real property the complaint shall be verified. When verification of a document is required, the document filed shall include an oath, affirmation, or the following statement: "Under penalty of perjury, I declare that I have read the foregoing, and the facts alleged therein are true and correct to the best of my knowledge and belief." FL ST RCP Rule 1.110(b).

c. *Separate statements.* All averments of claim or defense shall be made in consecutively numbered paragraphs, the contents of each of which shall be limited as far as practicable to a statement of a single set of circumstances, and a paragraph may be referred to by number in all subsequent pleadings. Each claim founded upon a separate transaction or occurrence and each defense other than denials shall be stated in a separate count or defense when a separation facilitates the clear presentation of the matter set forth. FL ST RCP Rule 1.110(f).

d. *Statements adopted by reference.* Statements in a pleading may be adopted by reference in a different part of the same pleading, in another pleading, or in any motion. FL ST RCP Rule 1.130(b).

e. *Joinder of causes of action; Consistency.* A pleader may set up in the same action as many claims or causes of action or defenses in the same right as the pleader has, and claims for relief may be stated in the alternative if separate items make up the cause of action, or if two (2) or more causes of action are joined. A party may also set forth two (2) or more statements of a claim or defense alternatively, either in one (1) count or defense or in separate counts or defenses. When two (2) or more statements are made in the alternative and one (1) of them, if made independently, would be sufficient, the pleading is not made insufficient by the insufficiency of one (1) or more of the alternative statements. A party may also state as many separate claims or defenses as that party has, regardless of consistency and whether based on legal or equitable grounds or both. All pleadings shall be construed so as to do substantial justice. FL ST RCP Rule 1.110(g).

f. *Subsequent pleadings.* When the nature of an action permits pleadings subsequent to final judgment and the jurisdiction of the court over the parties has not terminated, the initial pleading subsequent to final judgment shall be designated a supplemental complaint or petition. The action shall then proceed in the same manner and time as though the supplemental complaint or petition were the initial pleading in the action, including the issuance of any needed process. FL ST RCP Rule 1.110(h) shall not apply to proceedings that may be initiated by motion under the Florida Rules of Civil Procedure. FL ST RCP Rule 1.110(h).

g. *Pleading basis for service.* When service of process is to be made under statutes authorizing service on nonresidents of Florida, it is sufficient to plead the basis for service in the language of the statute without pleading the facts supporting service. FL ST RCP Rule 1.070(h).

h. *Forms of pleadings.* Forms of action and technical forms for seeking relief and of pleas, pleadings, or motions are abolished. FL ST RCP Rule 1.110(a).

3. *Complaint; Generally*

a. *Purpose.* The purpose of a complaint is to advise the court and the defendant of the nature of a cause of action asserted by the plaintiff. FL-PP § 2:12.

b. *Sufficiency of complaint.* A complaint will be found to be insufficient if it contains only general conclusory allegations unsupported by any facts. The test to determine whether a complaint is sufficient is whether, if the factual allegations of the complaint are established, the plaintiff will be legally or equitably entitled to the claimed relief. Pizzi v. Central Bank & Trust Co., 250 So.2d 895, 896 (Fla. 1971); Bowen v. G H C Properties, Limited, 251 So.2d 359, 361 (Fla. 1st DCA 1971); FL-PP § 2:12. In determining the sufficiency of the complaint to state a cause of action, all allegations of the complaint are taken as true, and possible affirmative defenses are not considered. Strickland v. Commerce Loan Co. of Jacksonville, 158 So.2d 814 (Fla. 1st DCA 1963); FL-PP § 2:12.

i. The issues for trial in Florida must be settled by the pleadings. The issues cannot be raised by discovery. FL-PRACPROC § 7:6.

ii. Causes of action may be pleaded alternatively in the same count or in different counts and against the same or different defendants as long as the joinder of parties is proper. FL-PRACPROC § 7:6.

iii. Each count must state a cause of action. Each independent cause of action should be pleaded in a separate count. FL-PRACPROC § 7:6.

iv. Incorporation by reference of all allegations from one count to another is not proper. Separate counts facilitate reference to the pleading in which they appear in other pleadings, motions or papers as well as the assertion of defenses against some, but not all, causes of action. Some defenses may not apply to the initial pleading as a whole. FL-PRACPROC § 7:6.

4. *Pleading special matters*

a. *Capacity.* It is not necessary to aver the capacity of a party to sue or be sued, the authority of a party to sue or be sued in a representative capacity, or the legal existence of an organized association of persons that is made a party, except to the extent required to show the jurisdiction of the court. The initial pleading served on behalf of a minor party shall specifically aver the age of the minor party. When a party desires to raise an issue as to the legal existence of any party, the capacity of any party to sue or be sued, or the authority of a party to sue or be sued in a representative capacity, that party shall do so by specific negative averment which shall include such supporting particulars as are peculiarly within the pleader's knowledge. FL ST RCP Rule 1.120(a).

b. *Fraud, mistake, condition of the mind.* In all averments of fraud or mistake, the circumstances constituting fraud or mistake shall be stated with such particularity as the circumstances may permit. Malice, intent, knowledge, mental attitude, and other condition of mind of a person may be averred generally. FL ST RCP Rule 1.120(b).

c. *Conditions precedent.* In pleading the performance or occurrence of conditions precedent, it is sufficient to aver generally that all conditions precedent have been performed or have occurred. A denial of performance or occurrence shall be made specifically and with particularity. FL ST RCP Rule 1.120(c).

d. *Official document or act.* In pleading an official document or official act it is sufficient to aver that the document was issued or the act done in compliance with law. FL ST RCP Rule 1.120(c).

e. *Judgment or decree.* In pleading a judgment or decree of a domestic or foreign court, a judicial or quasi-judicial tribunal, or a board or officer, it is sufficient to aver the judgment or decree without setting forth matter showing jurisdiction to render it. FL ST RCP Rule 1.120(e).

f. *Time and place.* For the purpose of testing the sufficiency of a pleading, averments of time and place are material and shall be considered like all other averments of material matter. FL ST RCP Rule 1.120(f).

g. *Special damage.* When items of special damage are claimed, they shall be specifically stated. FL ST RCP Rule 1.120(g).

5. *Parties*

a. *Parties generally.* Every action may be prosecuted in the name of the real party in interest, but a personal representative, administrator, guardian, trustee of an express trust, a party with whom or in whose name a contract has been made for the benefit of another, or a party expressly authorized by statute may sue in that person's own name without joining the party for whose benefit the action is brought. All persons having an interest in the subject of the action and in obtaining the relief demanded may join as plaintiffs and any person may be made a defendant who has or claims an interest adverse to the plaintiff. Any person may at any time be made a party if that person's presence is necessary or proper to a complete determination of the cause. Persons having a united interest may be joined on the same side as plaintiffs or defendants, and anyone who refuses to join may for such reason be made a defendant. FL ST RCP Rule 1.210(a).

b. *Minors or incompetent persons.* When a minor or incompetent person has a representative, such as a guardian or other like fiduciary, the representative may sue or defend on behalf of the minor or incompetent person. A minor or incompetent person who does not have a duly appointed representative may sue by next friend or by a guardian ad litem. The court shall appoint a guardian ad litem for a minor or incompetent person not otherwise represented in an action or shall make such other order as it deems proper for the protection of the minor or incompetent person. FL ST RCP Rule 1.210(b).

c. For survivor and substitution of parties information, please see FL ST RCP Rule 1.260.

6. *Counterclaims and crossclaims*

a. *Compulsory counterclaims.* A pleading shall state as a counterclaim any claim which at the time of serving the pleading the pleader has against any opposing party, provided it arises out of the transaction or occurrence that is the subject matter of the opposing party's claim and does not require for its adjudication the presence of third parties over whom the court cannot acquire jurisdiction. But the pleader need not state a claim if (1) at the time the action was commenced the claim was the subject of another pending action, or (2) the opposing party brought suit upon that party's claim by attachment or other process by which the court did not acquire jurisdiction to render a personal judgment on the claim and the pleader is not stating a counterclaim under this rule. FL ST RCP Rule 1.170(a).

b. *Permissive counterclaim.* A pleading may state as a counterclaim any claim against an opposing party not arising out of the transaction or occurrence that is the subject matter of the opposing party's claim. FL ST RCP Rule 1.170(b).

c. *Counterclaim exceeding opposing claim.* A counterclaim may or may not diminish or defeat the recovery sought by the opposing party. It may claim relief exceeding in amount or different in kind from that sought in the pleading of the opposing party. FL ST RCP Rule 1.170(c).

d. *Counterclaim against the State.* The Florida Rules of Civil Procedure shall not be construed to enlarge beyond the limits established by law the right to assert counterclaims or to claim credits against the state or any of its subdivisions or other governmental organizations thereof subject to suit or against a municipal corporation or against an officer, agency, or administrative board of the state. FL ST RCP Rule 1.170(d).

e. *Counterclaim maturing or acquired after pleading.* A claim which matured or was acquired by the pleader after serving the pleading may be presented as a counterclaim by supplemental pleading with the permission of the court. FL ST RCP Rule 1.170(e).

f. *Omitted counterclaim or crossclaim.* When a pleader fails to set up a counterclaim or crossclaim through oversight, inadvertence, or excusable neglect, or when justice requires, the pleader may set up the counterclaim or crossclaim by amendment with leave of the court. FL ST RCP Rule 1.170(f).

g. *Crossclaim against co-party.* A pleading may state as a crossclaim any claim by one party against a co-party arising out of the transaction or occurrence that is the subject matter of either the original action or a counterclaim therein, or relating to any property that is the subject matter of the original action. The crossclaim may include a claim that the party against whom it is asserted is or may be liable to the crossclaimant for all or part of a claim asserted in the action against the crossclaimant. Service of a crossclaim on a party who has appeared in the action shall be made pursuant to FL ST RCP Rule 1.080. Service of a crossclaim against a party who has not appeared in the action shall be made in the manner provided for service of summons. FL ST RCP Rule 1.170(g).

h. *Additional parties may be brought in.* When the presence of parties other than those to the original action is required to grant complete relief in the determination of a counterclaim or crossclaim, they shall be named in the counterclaim or crossclaim and be served with process and shall be parties to the action thereafter if jurisdiction of them can be obtained and their joinder will not deprive the court of jurisdiction of the action. FL ST RCP Rule 1.250(b) and FL ST RCP Rule 1.250(c) apply to parties brought in under FL ST RCP Rule 1.170(h). FL ST RCP Rule 1.170(h).

i. *Separate trials; Separate judgment.* If the court orders separate trials as provided in FL ST RCP Rule 1.270(b), judgment on a counterclaim or crossclaim may be rendered when the court has jurisdiction to do so even if a claim of the opposing party has been dismissed or otherwise disposed of. FL ST RCP Rule 1.170(i).

j. *Demand exceeding jurisdiction; Transfer of action.* If the demand of any counterclaim or crossclaim exceeds the jurisdiction of the court in which the action is pending, the action shall be transferred forthwith to the court of the same county having jurisdiction of the demand in the counterclaim or crossclaim with only such alterations in the pleadings as are essential. The court shall order the transfer of the action and the transmittal of all papers in it to the proper court if the party asserting the demand exceeding the jurisdiction deposits with the court having jurisdiction a sum sufficient to pay the clerk's service charge in the court to which the action is transferred at the time of filing the counterclaim or crossclaim. Thereupon the original papers and deposit shall be transmitted and filed with a certified copy of the order. The court to which the action is transferred shall have full power and jurisdiction over the demands of all parties. Failure to make the service charge deposit at the time the counterclaim or crossclaim is filed, or within such further time as the court may allow, shall reduce a claim for damages to an amount within the jurisdiction of the court where the action is pending and waive the claim in other cases. FL ST RCP Rule 1.170(j).

7. *Misjoinder and nonjoinder of parties*

   a. *Misjoinder.* Misjoinder of parties is not a ground for dismissal of an action. Any claim against a party may be severed and proceeded with separately. FL ST RCP Rule 1.250(a).

   b. *Dropping parties.* Parties may be dropped by an adverse party in the manner provided for voluntary dismissal in FL ST RCP Rule 1.420(a)(1) subject to the exception stated in FL ST RCP Rule 1.420. If notice of lis pendens has been filed in the action against a party so dropped, the notice of dismissal shall be recorded and cancels the notice of lis pendens without the necessity of a court order. Parties may be dropped by order of court on its own initiative or the motion of any party at any stage of the action on such terms as are just. FL ST RCP Rule 1.250(b).

   c. *Adding parties.* Parties may be added once as a matter of course within the same time that pleadings can be so amended under FL ST RCP Rule 1.190(a). If amendment by leave of court or stipulation of the parties is permitted, parties may be added in the amended pleading without further order of court. Parties may be added by order of court on its own initiative or on motion of any party at any stage of the action and on such terms as are just. FL ST RCP Rule 1.250(c).

8. *Jury demand*

   a. *Right preserved.* The right of trial by jury as declared by the Constitution or by statute shall be preserved to the parties inviolate. FL ST RCP Rule 1.430(a).

   b. *Demand.* Any party may demand a trial by jury of any issue triable of right by a jury by serving upon the other party a demand therefor in writing at any time after commencement of the action and not later than ten (10) days after the service of the last pleading directed to such issue. The demand may be indorsed upon a pleading of the party. FL ST RCP Rule 1.430(b).

   c. *Specification of issues.* In the demand a party may specify the issues that the party wishes so tried; otherwise, the party is deemed to demand trial by jury for all issues so triable. FL ST RCP Rule 1.430(c).

      i. If a party has demanded trial by jury for only some of the issues, any other party may serve a demand for trial by jury of any other or all of the issues triable by jury ten (10) days after service of the demand or such lesser time as the court may order. FL ST RCP Rule 1.430(c).

   d. *Waiver.* A party who fails to serve a demand as required by FL ST RCP Rule 1.430 waives trial by jury. FL ST RCP Rule 1.430(d).

      i. If waived, a jury trial may not be granted without the consent of the parties, but the court may allow an amendment in the proceedings to demand a trial by jury or order a trial by jury on its own motion. FL ST RCP Rule 1.430(d).

ii. A demand for trial by jury may not be withdrawn without the consent of the parties. FL ST RCP Rule 1.430(d).

9. *Arbitration and mediation.* Attorneys are encouraged to utilize arbitration, mediation or other forms of alternative dispute resolution if economically feasible. FL ST 20 J CIR 2.20(IV)(N)(3).

a. *Referral to arbitration and mediation.* Except as hereinafter provided or as otherwise prohibited by law, the presiding judge may enter an order referring all or any part of a contested civil matter to mediation or arbitration. The parties to any contested civil matter may file a written stipulation to mediate or arbitrate any issue between them at any time. Such stipulation shall be incorporated into the order of referral. FL ST RCP Rule 1.700(a).

b. *Arbitration*

i. *Exclusions.* A civil action shall be ordered to arbitration or arbitration in conjunction with mediation upon stipulation of the parties. A civil action may be ordered to arbitration or arbitration in conjunction with mediation upon motion of any party or by the court, if the judge determines the action to be of such a nature that arbitration could be of benefit to the litigants or the court. FL ST RCP Rule 1.800.

- Under no circumstances may the following categories of actions be referred to arbitration: (1) bond estreatures; (2) habeas corpus or other extraordinary writs; (3) bond validations; (4) civil or criminal contempt; (5) such other matters as may be specified by order of the chief judge in the circuit. FL ST RCP Rule 1.800.

ii. For more information regarding arbitration, please see FL ST RCP Rule 1.810; FL ST RCP Rule 1.820; FL ST RCP Rule 1.830.

c. *Mediation.* For more information regarding mediation, please see FL ST RCP Rule 1.710; FL ST RCP Rule 1.720; FL ST RCP Rule 1.730; FL ST RCP Rule 1.750; and FL ST 20 J CIR 1.9.

10. *Rules of court*

a. *Rules of civil procedure.* The Florida Rules of Civil Procedure apply to all actions of a civil nature and all special statutory proceedings in the circuit courts and county courts except those to which the Florida Probate Rules, the Florida Family Law Rules of Procedure, or the Small Claims Rules apply. FL ST RCP Rule 1.010.

i. The form, content, procedure, and time for pleading in all special statutory proceedings shall be as prescribed by the statutes governing the proceeding unless the Florida Rules of Civil Procedure specifically provide to the contrary. FL ST RCP Rule 1.010.

ii. The Florida Rules of Civil Procedure shall be construed to secure the just, speedy, and inexpensive determination of every action. FL ST RCP Rule 1.010.

b. *Rules of judicial administration.* The Florida Rules of Judicial Administration shall apply to administrative matters in all courts to which the Florida Rules of Judicial Administration are applicable by their terms. The Florida Rules of Judicial Administration shall be construed to secure the speedy and inexpensive determination of every proceeding to which they are applicable. The Florida Rules of Judicial Administration shall supersede all conflicting rules and statutes. FL ST J ADMIN Rule 2.110.

11. *Civil case management plan.* There is established within the Twentieth Judicial Circuit a Civil Case Management Plan applicable to circuit civil cases, which will be administered by the Administrative Office of the Courts through direction of the Circuit Administrative Judges in each county for the implementation of enhanced case management procedures and guidelines for the timely and efficient processing of circuit civil cases and reduction in the pending backlog of civil cases. FL ST 20 J CIR 1.13.

a. The basis for the Civil Case Management Plan is included in FL ST 20 J CIR 1.13, identified in Attachment A as the "Civil Differentiated Case Management (DCM) Procedures and Backlog Reduction Plan," and is incorporated as if fully set forth in FL ST 20 J CIR 1.13. The Civil Case Management Plan is to be used as a model for the purpose of establishing time standards, improving the courts ability to provide early and continuous management of civil cases as required by FL ST J ADMIN Rule 2.545, and to promote uniformity of practice throughout the Twentieth Judicial Circuit. FL ST 20 J CIR 1.13.

b. Full implementation of the Civil DCM Case Management Procedures (Attachment A), including all uniform circuitwide procedures and forms, shall apply to all civil cases filed in Lee and Collier counties, effective January 1, 2011. Even though full implementation may be delayed in Charlotte, Hendry, and Glades counties, all civil time standards and goals, and the use of civil Case Managers and Magistrates to assist trial judges in the process of civil case management and backlog reduction programs, shall be effective circuitwide immediately. FL ST 20 J CIR 1.13.

c. For more information on the civil case management plan, refer to the specific county website and/or see FL ST 20 J CIR 1.13.

D. Documents

1. *Required documents*

a. *Amended complaint.* See the General Requirements section of this document for the content of an amended complaint. If a party files a motion to amend a pleading, the party shall attach the proposed amended pleading to the motion. FL ST RCP Rule 1.190(a). See the KeyRules Florida Circuit Court Motion for Leave to Amend document for further information.

i. *Notices to persons with disabilities.* See the Format section of this KeyRules document for further information.

b. *Certificate of service.* When any attorney certifies in substance: "I certify that a copy hereof has been furnished to (here insert name or names and addresses used for service) by (e-mail) (delivery) (mail) (fax) on .... (date) ....________________ Attorney" the certificate is taken as prima facie proof of such service in compliance with FL ST J ADMIN Rule 2.516. FL ST J ADMIN Rule 2.516(f).

2. *Supplemental documents*

a. *Exhibits.* All bonds, notes, bills of exchange, contracts, accounts, or documents upon which action may be brought or defense made, or a copy thereof or a copy of the portions thereof material to the pleadings, shall be incorporated in or attached to the pleading. No papers shall be unnecessarily annexed as exhibits. The pleadings shall contain no unnecessary recitals of deeds, documents, contracts, or other instruments. Any exhibit attached to a pleading shall be considered a part of the pleadings for all purposes. FL ST RCP Rule 1.130(a).

b. *Notice of constitutional question.* A party that files a pleading, written motion, or other paper drawing into question the constitutionality of a state statute or a county or municipal charter, ordinance, or franchise must promptly (1) file a notice of constitutional question stating the question and identifying the paper that raises it; and (2) serve the notice and the pleading, written motion, or other paper drawing into question the constitutionality of a state statute or a county or municipal charter, ordinance, or franchise on the Attorney General or the state attorney of the judicial circuit in which the action is pending, by either certified or registered mail. Service of the notice and pleading, written motion, or other paper does not require joinder of the Attorney General or the state attorney as a party to the action. FL ST RCP Rule 1.071.

E. Format

1. *Documents; Type and size.* Documents subject to the exceptions set forth in FL ST J ADMIN Rule 2.525(d) shall be filed on recycled paper measuring eight and one half by eleven (8 1/2 by 11) inches. For purposes of FL ST J ADMIN Rule 2.520, paper is recycled if it contains a minimum content of fifty (50) percent waste paper. Xerographic reduction of legal-size (eight and one half by fourteen (8 1/2 by 14) inches) documents to letter size (eight and one half by eleven (8 1/2 by 11) inches) is prohibited. All other documents filed by electronic transmission shall be filed in a format capable of being printed in a format consistent with the provisions of FL ST J ADMIN Rule 2.250. FL ST J ADMIN Rule 2.520(b); FL ST 20 J CIR 2.9.

a. *Exhibits.* Any exhibit or attachment filed with pleadings or papers may be filed in its original size. FL ST J ADMIN Rule 2.520(c); FL ST 20 J CIR 2.9.

b. *Recording space.* On all papers and documents prepared and filed by the court or by any party to a proceeding which are to be recorded in the public records of any county, including but not limited to final money judgments and notices of lis pendens, a three (3) inch by three (3) inch space at the top right-hand corner on the first page and a one (1) inch by three (3) inch space at the top right-hand corner on each subsequent page shall be left blank and reserved for use by the clerk of court. FL ST J ADMIN Rule 2.520(d).

i. *Exceptions to recording space.* Any papers or documents created by persons or entities over which the filing party has no control, including but not limited to wills, codicils, trusts, or other testamentary documents; documents prepared or executed by any public officer; documents prepared, executed, acknowledged, or proved outside of the State of Florida; or documents created by State or Federal government agencies, may be filed without the space required by FL ST J ADMIN Rule 2.520. FL ST J ADMIN Rule 2.520(e).

c. *Noncompliance.* No clerk of court is permitted to refuse to file any document or paper because of noncompliance with the Florida Rules of Judicial Administration. However, upon request of the clerk of court, noncomplying documents must be resubmitted in accordance with the formatting rules. FL ST J ADMIN Rule 2.520(f).

i. When time of filing is critical, the Clerk shall accept pleadings, motions, petitions, briefs, notices, orders, judgments, decrees, opinions, or other papers or official documents on other than eight and one half by eleven (8 1/2 by 11) inch paper but shall then require that the document be resubmitted to comply with FL ST J ADMIN Rule 2.520. FL ST 20 J CIR 2.9.

2. *Caption.* Every pleading, motion, order, judgment, or other paper shall have a caption containing the name of the court, the file number, and except for in rem proceedings, including forfeiture proceedings, the name of the first party on each side with an appropriate indication of other parties, and a designation identifying the party filing it and its nature or the nature of the order, as the case may be. In any in rem proceeding, every pleading, motion, order, judgment, or other paper shall have a caption containing the name of the court, the file number, the style "In re" (followed by the name or general description of the property), and a designation of the person or entity filing it and its nature or the nature of the order, as the case may be. In an in rem forfeiture proceeding, the style shall be "In re forfeiture of" (followed by the name of the general description of the property). All papers filed in the action shall be styled in such a manner as to indicate clearly the subject matter of the paper and the party requesting or obtaining relief. FL ST RCP Rule 1.100(c)(1).

3. *Writing and written defined.* Writing or written means a document containing information, an application, or a stipulation. FL ST RCP Rule 1.080(c).

4. *Rule abbreviations*

a. The Florida Rules of Civil Procedure and shall be abbreviated as Fla.R.Civ.P. FL ST RCP Rule 1.010.

b. The Florida Rules of Judicial Administration shall be abbreviated as Fla. R. Jud. Admin. FL ST J ADMIN Rule 2.110.

5. *Nonverification.* Except when otherwise specifically provided by the Florida Rules of Civil Procedure or an applicable statute, every pleading or other document of a party represented by an attorney need not be verified or accompanied by an affidavit. FL ST RCP Rule 1.030; FL ST J ADMIN Rule 2.515(a).

6. *Attorney signature*

a. *Attorney signature.* Every pleading and other document of a party represented by an attorney shall be signed by at least one (1) attorney of record in that attorney's individual name whose current record Florida Bar address, telephone number, including area code, primary e-mail address and secondary e-mail addresses, if any, and Florida Bar number shall be stated, and who shall be duly licensed to practice law in Florida or who shall have received permission to appear in the particular case as provided in FL ST J ADMIN Rule 2.510. FL ST J ADMIN Rule 2.515(a).

i. The attorney may be required by the court to give the address of, and to vouch for the attorney's authority to represent, the party. FL ST J ADMIN Rule 2.515(a).

ii. The signature of an attorney shall constitute a certificate by the attorney that the attorney has read the pleading or other document; that to the best of the attorney's knowledge, information, and belief there is good ground to support it; and that it is not interposed for delay. FL ST J ADMIN Rule 2.515(a).

iii. If a pleading is not signed or is signed with intent to defeat the purpose of FL ST J ADMIN Rule 2.515, it may be stricken and the action may proceed as though the pleading or other document had not been served. FL ST J ADMIN Rule 2.515(a).

b. *Pro se litigant signature.* A party who is not represented by an attorney shall sign any pleading or other paper and state the party's address and telephone number, including area code. FL ST J ADMIN Rule 2.515(b).

c. *Form of signature*

i. The signatures required on pleadings and documents by FL ST J ADMIN Rule 2.515(a) and FL ST J ADMIN Rule 2.515(b) may be:

- Original signatures;
- Original signatures that have been reproduced by electronic means, such as on electronically transmitted documents or photocopied documents;
- Electronic signatures using the "/s/," "s/," or "/s" formats by or at the direction of the person signing; or
- Any other signature format authorized by general law, so long as the clerk where the proceeding is pending has the capability of receiving and has obtained approval from the Supreme Court of Florida to accept pleadings and documents with that signature format. FL ST J ADMIN Rule 2.515(c)(1).

ii. An attorney, party, or other person who files a pleading or paper by electronic transmission that does not contain the original signature of that attorney, party, or other person shall file that identical pleading or paper in paper form containing an original signature of that attorney, party, or other person (hereinafter called the follow-up filing) immediately thereafter. The follow-up filing is not required if the Supreme Court of Florida has entered an order directing the clerk of court to discontinue accepting the follow-up filing. FL ST J ADMIN Rule 2.515(c)(2).

7. *Forms*

a. *Process.* The forms of process, notice of lis pendens, and notice of action provided in the Florida Rules of Civil Procedure are sufficient. Variations from the forms do not void process or notices that are otherwise sufficient. FL ST RCP Rule 1.900(a).

b. *Other forms.* The other forms provided in the Florida Rules of Civil Procedure are sufficient for the matters that are covered by them. So long as the substance is expressed without prolixity, the forms may be varied to meet the facts of a particular case. FL ST RCP Rule 1.900(b).

c. *Formal matters.* Captions, except for the designation of the paper, are omitted from the forms provided in the Florida Rules of Civil Procedure. A general form of caption is the first form provided. Signatures are omitted from pleadings and motions. FL ST RCP Rule 1.900(c).

8. *Notices to persons with disabilities.* All notices of court proceedings to be held in a public facility, and all process compelling appearance at such proceedings, shall include the following statement in bold face, fourteen (14) point Times New Roman or Courier font: "If you are a person with a disability who needs any accommodation in order to participate in this proceeding, you are entitled, at no cost to you, to the provision of certain assistance. Please contact [identify applicable court personnel by name, address, and telephone number] at least seven (7) days before your scheduled court appearance, or immediately upon receiving this notification if the time before the scheduled appearance is less than seven (7) days; if you are hearing or voice impaired, call 711." FL ST J ADMIN Rule 2.540(c)(1). For more information, see FL ST 20 J CIR 2.15.

9. *Minimization of the filing of sensitive information*

a. *Limitations for court filings.* Unless authorized by FL ST J ADMIN Rule 2.425(b), statute, another

rule of court, or the court orders otherwise, designated sensitive information filed with the court must be limited to the following format:

i. The initials of a person known to be a minor;

ii. The year of birth of a person's birth date;

iii. No portion of any: Social security number, Bank account number, Credit card account number, Charge account number, or Debit account number;

iv. The last four digits of any: Taxpayer identification number (TIN), Employee identification number, Driver's license number, Passport number, Telephone number, Financial account number, except as set forth in FL ST J ADMIN Rule 2.425(a)(3), Brokerage account number, Insurance policy account number, Loan account number, Customer account number, or Patient or health care number;

v. A truncated version of any: Email address, Computer user name, Password, or Personal identification number (PIN); and

vi. A truncated version of any other sensitive information as provided by court order. FL ST J ADMIN Rule 2.425(a).

b. *Exceptions.* FL ST J ADMIN Rule 2.425(a) does not apply to the following:

i. An account number which identifies the property alleged to be the subject of a proceeding;

ii. The record of an administrative or agency proceeding;

iii. The record in appellate or review proceedings;

iv. The birth date of a minor whenever the birth date is necessary for the court to establish or maintain subject matter jurisdiction;

v. The name of a minor in any order relating to parental responsibility, time-sharing, or child support;

vi. The name of a minor in any document or order affecting the minor's ownership of real property;

vii. The birth date of a party in a writ of attachment or notice to payor;

viii. In traffic and criminal proceedings: a pro se filing; a court filing that is related to a criminal matter or investigation and that is prepared before the filing of a criminal charge or is not filed as part of any docketed criminal case; an arrest or search warrant or any information in support thereof; a charging document and an affidavit or other documents filed in support of any charging document, including any driving records; a statement of particulars; discovery material introduced into evidence or otherwise filed with the court; and all information necessary for the proper issuance and execution of a subpoena duces tecum;

ix. Information used by the clerk for case maintenance purposes or the courts for case management purposes; and

x. Information which is relevant and material to an issue before the court. FL ST J ADMIN Rule 2.425(b).

c. *Remedies.* Upon motion by a party or interested person or sua sponte by the court, the court may order remedies, sanctions or both for a violation of FL ST J ADMIN Rule 2.425(a). Following notice and an opportunity to respond, the court may impose sanctions if such filing was not made in good faith. FL ST J ADMIN Rule 2.425(c).

d. *Motions not restricted.* FL ST J ADMIN Rule 2.425 does not restrict a party's right to move for protective order, to move to file documents under seal, or to request a determination of the confidentiality of records. FL ST J ADMIN Rule 2.425(d).

e. *Application.* FL ST J ADMIN Rule 2.425 does not affect the application of constitutional provisions, statutes, or rules of court regarding confidential information or access to public information. FL ST J ADMIN Rule 2.425(e).

F. Filing and Service Requirements

1. *Filing requirements.* All original documents must be filed with the court either before service or

immediately thereafter, unless otherwise provided for by general law or other rules. If the original of any bond or other document is not placed in the court file, a certified copy must be so placed by the clerk. FL ST J ADMIN Rule 2.516(d). All documents shall be filed in conformity with the requirements of FL ST J ADMIN Rule 2.525. FL ST RCP Rule 1.080(b). All documents filed in any court shall be filed by electronic transmission in accordance with FL ST J ADMIN Rule 2.525. "Documents" means pleadings, motions, petitions, memoranda, briefs, notices, exhibits, declarations, affidavits, orders, judgments, decrees, writs, opinions, and any other paper or writing submitted to a court. FL ST J ADMIN Rule 2.520(a). All documents that are court records, as defined in FL ST J ADMIN Rule 2.430(a)(1), must be filed by electronic transmission, provided that: (1) the clerk has the ability to accept and retain such documents; (2) the clerk or the chief judge of the circuit has requested permission to accept documents filed by electronic transmission; and (3) the supreme court has entered an order granting permission to the clerk to accept documents filed by electronic transmission. FL ST J ADMIN Rule 2.525(c)(1).

a. *Definition.* "Electronic transmission of documents" means the sending of information by electronic signals to, by or from a court or clerk, which when received can be transformed and stored or transmitted on paper, microfilm, magnetic storage device, optical imaging system, CD-ROM, flash drive, other electronic data storage system, server, case maintenance system ("CM"), electronic court filing ("ECF") system, statewide or local electronic portal ("e-portal"), or other electronic record keeping system authorized by the supreme court in a format sufficient to communicate the information on the original document in a readable format. Electronic transmission of documents includes electronic mail ("e-mail") and any internet-based transmission procedure, and may include procedures allowing for documents to be signed or verified by electronic means. FL ST J ADMIN Rule 2.525(a).
    i. The filing of documents with the court as required by the Florida Rules of Judicial Administration must be made by filing them with the clerk in accordance with FL ST J ADMIN Rule 2.525, except that the judge may permit documents to be filed with the judge, in which event the judge must note the filing date before him or her on the documents and transmit them to the clerk. The date of filing is that shown on the face of the document by the judge's notation or the clerk's time stamp, whichever is earlier. FL ST J ADMIN Rule 2.516(e).
b. *Application.* Any court or clerk of the court may accept the electronic transmission of documents for filing after the clerk, together with input from the chief judge of the circuit, has obtained approval of the procedures and program for doing so from the Supreme Court of Florida. FL ST J ADMIN Rule 2.525(b).
c. *Exceptions*
    i. Paper documents and other submissions may be manually submitted to the clerk or court:
        - When the clerk does not have the ability to accept and retain documents by electronic filing or has not had ECF Procedures approved by the supreme court;
        - For filing by any self-represented party or any self-represented nonparty unless specific ECF Procedures provide a means to file documents electronically. However, any self-represented nonparty that is a governmental or public agency and any other agency, partnership, corporation, or business entity acting on behalf of any governmental or public agency may file documents by electronic transmission if such entity has the capability of filing documents electronically;
        - For filing by attorneys excused from e-mail service in accordance with FL ST J ADMIN Rule 2.516(b);
        - When submitting evidentiary exhibits or filing non-documentary materials;
        - When the filing involves documents in excess of twenty-five (25) megabytes (25MB) in size. For such filings, documents may be transmitted using an electronic storage medium that the clerk has the ability to accept, which may include a CD-ROM, flash drive, or similar storage medium;
        - When filed in open court, as permitted by the court;
        - When paper filing is permitted by any approved statewide or local ECF procedures; and

- If any court determines that justice so requires. FL ST J ADMIN Rule 2.525(d).

ii. Any document in paper form submitted under FL ST J ADMIN Rule 2.525(d) is filed when it is received by the clerk or court and the clerk shall immediately thereafter convert any filed paper document to an electronic document. "Convert to an electronic document" means optically capturing an image of a paper document and using character recognition software to recover as much of the document's text as practicable and then indexing and storing the document in the official court file. FL ST J ADMIN Rule 2.525(c)(4).

iii. Any storage medium submitted under FL ST J ADMIN Rule 2.525(d)(5) is filed when received by the clerk or court and the clerk shall immediately thereafter transfer the electronic documents from the storage device to the official court file. FL ST J ADMIN Rule 2.525(c)(5).

iv. If the filer of any paper document authorized under FL ST J ADMIN Rule 2.525(d) provides a self-addressed, postage-paid envelope for return of the paper document after it is converted to electronic form by the clerk, the clerk shall place the paper document in the envelope and deposit it in the mail. Except when a paper document is required to be maintained, the clerk may recycle any filed paper document that is not to be returned to the filer. FL ST J ADMIN Rule 2.525(c)(6).

v. The clerk may convert any paper document filed before the effective date of FL ST J ADMIN Rule 2.525 to an electronic document. Unless the clerk is required to maintain the paper document, if the paper document has been converted to an electronic document by the clerk, the paper document is no longer part of the official court file and may be removed and recycled. FL ST J ADMIN Rule 2.525(c)(7).

d. *Official court file.* For information on what constitutes the official court file, please see FL ST J ADMIN Rule 2.525(c)(2), FL ST J ADMIN Rule 2.525(c)(3).

e. *Administration.* All attorneys, parties, or other persons using this rule to file documents are required to make arrangements with the court or clerk for the payment of any charges authorized by general law or the supreme court before filing any document by electronic transmission. FL ST J ADMIN Rule 2.525(f)(2).

f. *Filing date.* The filing date for an electronically transmitted document is the date and time that such filing is acknowledged by an electronic stamp or otherwise, pursuant to any procedure set forth in any ECF Procedures approved by the supreme court, or the date the last page of such filing is received by the court or clerk. FL ST J ADMIN Rule 2.525(f)(3).

g. *Accessibility.* All documents transmitted in any electronic form under FL ST J ADMIN Rule 2.525 must comply with the accessibility requirements of FL ST J ADMIN Rule 2.526. FL ST J ADMIN Rule 2.525(g).

2. *Service requirements.* Every pleading subsequent to the initial pleading, all orders, and every other document filed in the action must be served in conformity with the requirements of FL ST J ADMIN Rule 2.516. FL ST RCP Rule 1.080(a).

a. *Service; Generally.* The timing and manner of service should not be used to the disadvantage of the party receiving the papers. FL ST 20 J CIR 2.20(IV)(C)(1).

i. Papers and memoranda of law should not be served at court appearances without advance notice to opposing counsel and should not be served so close to a court appearance so as to inhibit the ability of opposing counsel to prepare for that appearance or to respond to the papers. Should the attorney do so, the court is urged to take appropriate action in response, including continuing the matter to allow opposing counsel to prepare and respond. FL ST 20 J CIR 2.20(IV)(C)(2).

ii. Papers should not be served in order to take advantage of an opponent's known absence from the office or at a time or in a manner designed to inconvenience an adversary, such as late on Friday afternoon or the day preceding a secular or religious holiday. FL ST 20 J CIR 2.20(IV)(C)(3).

iii. Service should be made personally or by courtesy copy facsimile transmission when it is likely that service by mail, even when allowed, will prejudice the opposing party or will not provide the opposing party with a reasonable time to respond. FL ST 20 J CIR 2.20(IV)(C)(4).

b. *Service; When required.* Unless the court otherwise orders, or a statute or supreme court administrative order specifies a different means of service, every pleading subsequent to the initial pleading and every other document filed in any court proceeding, except applications for witness subpoenas and documents served by formal notice or required to be served in the manner provided for service of formal notice, must be served in accordance with FL ST J ADMIN Rule 2.516 on each party. No service need be made on parties against whom a default has been entered, except that pleadings asserting new or additional claims against them must be served in the manner provided for service of summons. FL ST J ADMIN Rule 2.516(a).

   i. *Copies of court submissions.* Copies of any submissions to the court (such as correspondence, memoranda of law, motions, case law, etc.) should simultaneously be provided to opposing counsel by substantially the same method of delivery by which they are provided to the court. For example, if a memorandum of law is hand-delivered to the court, at substantially the same time a copy should be hand-delivered or faxed to opposing counsel. FL ST 20 J CIR 2.20(IV)(J)(4).

c. *Service; How made.* When service is required or permitted to be made upon a party represented by an attorney, service must be made upon the attorney unless service upon the party is ordered by the court. FL ST J ADMIN Rule 2.516(b).

   i. *Service by electronic mail ("e-mail").* All documents required or permitted to be served on another party must be served by e-mail, unless FL ST J ADMIN Rule 2.516 otherwise provides. When, in addition to service by e-mail, the sender also utilizes another means of service provided for in FL ST J ADMIN Rule 2.516(b)(2), any differing time limits and other provisions applicable to that other means of service control. FL ST J ADMIN Rule 2.516(b)(1). Any document electronically transmitted to a court or clerk must also be served on all parties and interested persons in accordance with the applicable rules of court. FL ST J ADMIN Rule 2.525(e)(2).

      - *Service on attorneys.* Upon appearing in a proceeding, an attorney must serve a designation of a primary e-mail address and may designate no more than two (2) secondary e-mail addresses. Thereafter, service must be directed to all designated e-mail addresses in that proceeding. Every document filed by an attorney thereafter must include the primary e-mail address of that attorney and any secondary e-mail addresses. If an attorney does not designate any e-mail address for service, documents may be served on that attorney at the e-mail address on record with The Florida Bar. FL ST J ADMIN Rule 2.516(b)(1)(A).

      - *Exception to e-mail service on attorneys.* Service by an attorney on another attorney must be made by e-mail unless excused by the court. Upon motion by an attorney demonstrating that the attorney has no e-mail account and lacks access to the Internet at the attorney's office, the court may excuse the attorney from the requirements of e-mail service. Service on and by an attorney excused by the court from e-mail service must be by the means provided in FL ST J ADMIN Rule 2.516(b)(2). FL ST J ADMIN Rule 2.516(b)(1)(B).

      - *Service on and by parties not represented by an attorney.* Any party not represented by an attorney may serve a designation of a primary e-mail address and also may designate no more than two (2) secondary e-mail addresses to which service must be directed in that proceeding by the means provided in FL ST J ADMIN Rule 2.516(b)(1). If a party not represented by an attorney does not designate an e-mail address for service in a proceeding, service on and by that party must be by the means provided in FL ST J ADMIN Rule 2.516(b)(2). FL ST J ADMIN Rule 2.516(b)(1)(C).

      - *Time of service.* Service by e-mail is complete when it is sent. FL ST J ADMIN Rule 2.516(b)(1)(D). An e-mail is deemed served on the date it is sent. FL ST J ADMIN Rule 2.516(b)(1)(D)(i). If the sender learns that the e-mail did not reach the address of the person to be served, the sender must immediately send another copy by e-mail, or by a means authorized by FL ST J ADMIN Rule 2.516(b)(2). FL ST J ADMIN Rule

2.516(b)(1)(D)(ii). E-mail service is treated as service by mail for the computation of time. FL ST J ADMIN Rule 2.516(b)(1)(D)(iii).

ii. *Format of e-mail for service.* Service of a document by e-mail is made by attaching a copy of the document in PDF format to an e-mail sent to all addresses designated by the attorney or party. FL ST J ADMIN Rule 2.516(b)(1)(E).

- All documents served by e-mail must be attached to an e-mail message containing a subject line beginning with the words "SERVICE OF COURT DOCUMENT" in all capital letters, followed by the case number of the proceeding in which the documents are being served. FL ST J ADMIN Rule 2.516(b)(1)(E)(i).
- The body of the e-mail must identify the court in which the proceeding is pending, the case number, the name of the initial party on each side, the title of each document served with that e-mail, and the sender's name and telephone number. FL ST J ADMIN Rule 2.516(b)(1)(E)(ii).
- Any document served by e-mail may be signed by the "/s/" format, as long as the filed original is signed in accordance with the applicable rule of procedure. FL ST J ADMIN Rule 2.516(b)(1)(E)(iii).
- Any e-mail which, together with its attached documents, exceeds five megabytes (5MB) in size, must be divided and sent as separate e-mails, no one of which may exceed five megabytes (5MB) in size and each of which must be sequentially numbered in the subject line. FL ST J ADMIN Rule 2.516(b)(1)(E)(iv).

iii. *Service by other means.* In addition to, and not in lieu of, service by e-mail, service may also be made upon attorneys by any of the means specified in FL ST J ADMIN Rule 2.516(b)(2). Service on and by all parties who are not represented by an attorney and who do not designate an e-mail address, and on and by all attorneys excused from e-mail service, must be made by delivering a copy of the document or by mailing it to the party or attorney at their last known address or, if no address is known, by leaving it with the clerk of the court. Service by mail is complete upon mailing. Delivery of a copy within FL ST J ADMIN Rule 2.516 is complete upon:

- Handing it to the attorney or to the party,
- Leaving it at the attorney's or party's office with a clerk or other person in charge thereof,
- If there is no one in charge, leaving it in a conspicuous place therein,
- If the office is closed or the person to be served has no office, leaving it at the person's usual place of abode with some person of his or her family above fifteen (15) years of age and informing such person of the contents, or
- Transmitting it by facsimile to the attorney's or party's office with a cover sheet containing the sender's name, firm, address, telephone number, and facsimile number, and the number of pages transmitted. When service is made by facsimile, a copy must also be served by any other method permitted by FL ST J ADMIN Rule 2.516. Facsimile service occurs when transmission is complete. FL ST J ADMIN Rule 2.516(b)(2)(A) through FL ST J ADMIN Rule 2.516(b)(2)(E).
- Service by delivery after 5:00 p.m. must be deemed to have been made by mailing on the date of delivery. FL ST J ADMIN Rule 2.516(b)(2)(F).

d. *Service; Numerous defendants.* In actions when the parties are unusually numerous, the court may regulate the service contemplated by the Florida Rules of Judicial Administration on motion or on its own initiative in such manner as may be found to be just and reasonable. FL ST J ADMIN Rule 2.516(c).

e. *Service by clerk.* Service of notices and other documents required to be made by the clerk must also be done as provided in FL ST J ADMIN Rule 2.516(b). FL ST J ADMIN Rule 2.516(g).

G. Hearings

1. The parties may be required to participate in pretrial proceedings to consider and determine the necessity or desirability of an amendment to a pleading. FL ST RCP Rule 1.200(b)(2); FL-PP § 2:151.

H. Forms

1. Official Amended Complaint Forms for Florida

a. Caption. FL ST RCP Form 1.901.

b. Notice of compliance when constitutional challenge is brought. FL ST RCP Form 1.975.

2. Amended Complaint Forms for Florida

a. Consent; Of party; To amendment of pleadings. FL-PP § 2:154.

b. Notice of amended complaint. 3 FLPRAC § 190.1.

c. Complaint for damages; General form. FL-PP § 2:17.

d. Complaint; Negligent infliction of personal injury. FL-PP § 2:19.

e. Complaint; Fall down negligence. FL-PP § 2:20.

f. Complaint; Mortgage foreclosure. FL-PP § 2:21.

g. Complaint; Implied warranty. FL-PP § 2:22.

h. Complaint; Professional negligence. FL-PP § 2:23.

i. Complaint; Breach of contract. FL-PP § 2:24.

j. Complaint; Breach of personal services contract. FL-PP § 2:25.

I. Checklist

(I) ❑ Matters to be considered by plaintiff

- (a) ❑ Required documents
  - (1) ❑ Amended complaint
  - (2) ❑ Certificate of service
- (b) ❑ Supplemental documents
  - (1) ❑ Exhibits
  - (2) ❑ Notice of constitutional question
- (c) ❑ Timing
  - (1) ❑ A party may amend a pleading once as a matter of course at any time before a responsive pleading is served
  - (2) ❑ If the pleading is one to which no responsive pleading is permitted and the action has not been placed on the trial calendar, may so amend it at any time within twenty (20) days after it is served

Pleadings
Answer

Document Last Updated January 2013

A. Applicable Rules

1. *State rules*

a. Nonverification of pleadings. FL ST RCP Rule 1.030.

b. Process. FL ST RCP Rule 1.070.

c. Service and filing of pleadings, orders, and documents. FL ST RCP Rule 1.080.

d. Time. FL ST RCP Rule 1.090.

e. Pleadings and motions. FL ST RCP Rule 1.100; FL ST RCP Rule 1.110; FL ST RCP Rule 1.120; FL ST RCP Rule 1.130; FL ST RCP Rule 1.190; FL ST RCP Rule 1.430.

f. Defenses. FL ST RCP Rule 1.140.
g. Relief from judgment, decrees, or orders. FL ST RCP Rule 1.540.
h. Forms. FL ST RCP Rule 1.900.
i. Minimization of the filing of sensitive information. FL ST J ADMIN Rule 2.425.
j. Retention of court records. FL ST J ADMIN Rule 2.430.
k. Foreign attorneys. FL ST J ADMIN Rule 2.510.
l. Signature of attorneys and parties. FL ST J ADMIN Rule 2.515.
m. Paper. FL ST J ADMIN Rule 2.520.
n. Electronic filing. FL ST J ADMIN Rule 2.525.
o. Accessibility of information and technology. FL ST J ADMIN Rule 2.526.
p. Court reporting. FL ST J ADMIN Rule 2.535.
q. Requests for accommodations by persons with disabilities. FL ST J ADMIN Rule 2.540.
r. Case management. FL ST J ADMIN Rule 2.545.
s. Waiver of sovereign immunity in tort actions; Recovery limits; Limitation on attorney fees; Statute of limitations; Exclusions; Indemnification; Risk management programs. FL ST § 768.28.

2. *Local rules*
   a. Exclusions from mediation. FL ST 20 J CIR 1.9.
   b. Establishment and implementation of civil case management plan. FL ST 20 J CIR 1.13.
   c. Size of paper. FL ST 20 J CIR 2.9.
   d. Americans with Disabilities Act; Notification of court proceedings. FL ST 20 J CIR 2.15.
   e. Standards of professional courtesy and conduct and establishment of peer review program. FL ST 20 J CIR 2.20.

B. Timing

1. *General answer timing.* Unless a different time is prescribed in a statute of Florida, a defendant shall serve an answer within twenty (20) days after service of original process and the initial pleading on the defendant, or not later than the date fixed in a notice by publication. A party served with a pleading stating a crossclaim against that party shall serve an answer to it within twenty (20) days after service on that party. The plaintiff shall serve an answer to a counterclaim within twenty (20) days after service of the counterclaim. FL ST RCP Rule 1.140(a)(1).
   a. *Waiver of service.* A defendant who, before being served with process, timely returns a waiver so requested is not required to respond to the complaint until sixty (60) days after the date the defendant received the request for waiver of service. For purposes of computing any time prescribed or allowed by the Florida Rules of Civil Procedure, service of process shall be deemed effected twenty (20) days before the time required to respond to the complaint. FL ST RCP Rule 1.070(i)(4).
   b. *Service on the state.* Except when sued pursuant to FL ST § 768.28, the state of Florida, an agency of the state, or an officer or employee of the state sued in an official capacity shall serve an answer to the complaint or crossclaim, or a reply to a counterclaim, within forty (40) days after service. When sued pursuant to FL ST § 768.28, the Department of Financial Services or the defendant state agency shall have thirty (30) days from the date of service within which to serve an answer to the complaint or crossclaim or a reply to a counterclaim. FL ST RCP Rule 1.140(a)(2).
   c. *Service of motion impact on time periods for service of answer.* The service of a motion under FL ST RCP Rule 1.140, except a motion for judgment on the pleadings or a motion to strike under FL ST RCP Rule 1.140(f), alters these periods of time so that if the court denies the motion or postpones its disposition until the trial on the merits, the responsive pleadings shall be served within ten (10) days after notice of the court's action or, if the court grants a motion for a more definite statement, the responsive pleadings shall be served within ten (10) days after service of the more definite statement unless a different time is fixed by the court in either case. FL ST RCP Rule 1.140(a)(3).

d. *Responding if pleading does not require a responsive pleading.* If a pleading sets forth a claim for relief to which the adverse party is not required to serve a responsive pleading, the adverse party may assert any defense in law or fact to that claim for relief at the trial, except that the objection of failure to state a legal defense in an answer or reply shall be asserted by motion to strike the defense within twenty (20) days after service of the answer or reply. FL ST RCP Rule 1.140(b).

2. *Computation of time*

a. *Generally.* Computation of time shall be governed by FL ST J ADMIN Rule 2.514. FL ST RCP Rule 1.090(a). The following rules apply in computing time periods specified in any rule of procedure, local rule, court order, or statute that does not specify a method of computing time. FL ST J ADMIN Rule 2.514(a).

i. *Period stated in days or a longer unit.* When the period is stated in days or a longer unit of time (A) exclude the day of the event that triggers the period; (B) count every day, including intermediate Saturdays, Sundays, and legal holidays; and (C) include the last day of the period, but if the last day is a Saturday, Sunday, or legal holiday, or falls within any period of time extended through an order of the chief justice under FL ST J ADMIN Rule 2.205(a)(2)(B)(iv), the period continues to run until the end of the next day that is not a Saturday, Sunday, or legal holiday and does not fall within any period of time extended through an order of the chief justice. FL ST J ADMIN Rule 2.514(a)(1).

ii. *Period stated in hours.* When the period is stated in hours (A) begin counting immediately on the occurrence of the event that triggers the period; (B) count every hour, including hours during intermediate Saturdays, Sundays, and legal holidays; and (C) if the period would end on a Saturday, Sunday, or legal holiday, or during any period of time extended through an order of the chief justice under FL ST J ADMIN Rule 2.205(a)(2)(B)(iv), the period continues to run until the same time on the next day that is not a Saturday, Sunday, or legal holiday and does not fall within any period of time extended through an order of the chief justice. FL ST J ADMIN Rule 2.514(a)(2).

iii. *Period stated in days less than seven (7) days.* When the period stated in days is less than seven (7) days, intermediate Saturdays, Sundays, and legal holidays shall be excluded in the computation. FL ST J ADMIN Rule 2.514(a)(3).

iv. *"Last day" defined.* Unless a different time is set by a statute, local rule, or court order, the last day ends (A) for electronic filing or for service by any means, at midnight; and (B) for filing by other means, when the clerk's office is scheduled to close. FL ST J ADMIN Rule 2.514(a)(4).

v. *"Next day" defined.* The "next day" is determined by continuing to count forward when the period is measured after an event and backward when measured before an event. FL ST J ADMIN Rule 2.514(a)(5).

vi. *"Legal holiday" defined.* "Legal holiday" means (A) the day set aside by FL ST § 110.117, for observing New Year's Day, Martin Luther King, Jr.'s Birthday, Memorial Day, Independence Day, Labor Day, Veterans' Day, Thanksgiving Day, the Friday after Thanksgiving Day, or Christmas Day, and (B) any day observed as a holiday by the clerk's office or as designated by the chief judge. FL ST J ADMIN Rule 2.514(a)(6).

b. *Additional time after service by mail or e-mail.* When a party may or must act within a specified time after service and service is made by mail or e-mail, five (5) days are added after the period that would otherwise expire under FL ST J ADMIN Rule 2.514(a). FL ST J ADMIN Rule 2.514(b).

c. *Enlargement.* When an act is required or allowed to be done at or within a specified time by order of court, by the Florida Rules of Civil Procedure, or by notice given thereunder, for cause shown the court at any time in its discretion (1) with or without notice, may order the period enlarged if request therefor is made before the expiration of the period originally prescribed or as extended by a previous order, or (2) upon motion made and notice after the expiration of the specified period, may permit the act to be done when failure to act was the result of excusable neglect, but it may not extend the time for making a motion for new trial, for rehearing, or to alter or amend a judgment; making a motion for relief from a judgment under FL ST RCP Rule 1.540(b); taking an appeal or filing a petition for certiorari; or making a motion for a directed verdict. FL ST RCP Rule 1.090(b).

d. *Unaffected by expiration of term.* The period of time provided for the doing of any act or the taking of any proceeding shall not be affected or limited by the continued existence or expiration of a term of court. The continued existence or expiration of a term of court in no way affects the power of a court to do any act or take any proceeding in any action which is or has been pending before it. FL ST RCP Rule 1.090(c).

C. General Requirements

1. *General rules of pleading*

a. *Claims for relief*

i. A pleading which sets forth a claim for relief, whether an original claim, counterclaim, crossclaim, or third-party claim, must state a cause of action and shall contain

- A short and plain statement of the grounds upon which the court's jurisdiction depends, unless the court already has jurisdiction and the claim needs no new grounds of jurisdiction to support it (For information regarding acts subjecting persons to jurisdiction, please see FL ST § 48.193),
- A short and plain statement of the ultimate facts showing that the pleader is entitled to relief, and
- A demand for judgment for the relief to which the pleader deems himself or herself entitled. FL ST RCP Rule 1.110(b).

ii. Relief in the alternative or of several different types may be demanded. Every complaint shall be considered to demand general relief. FL ST RCP Rule 1.110(b).

b. *Verification.* Except when otherwise specifically provided by these rules or an applicable statute, every pleading or other document of a party represented by an attorney need not be verified or accompanied by an affidavit. FL ST RCP Rule 1.030. When filing an action for foreclosure of a mortgage on residential real property the complaint shall be verified. When verification of a document is required, the document filed shall include an oath, affirmation, or the following statement: "Under penalty of perjury, I declare that I have read the foregoing, and the facts alleged therein are true and correct to the best of my knowledge and belief." FL ST RCP Rule 1.110(b).

c. *Separate statements.* All averments of claim or defense shall be made in consecutively numbered paragraphs, the contents of each of which shall be limited as far as practicable to a statement of a single set of circumstances, and a paragraph may be referred to by number in all subsequent pleadings. Each claim founded upon a separate transaction or occurrence and each defense other than denials shall be stated in a separate count or defense when a separation facilitates the clear presentation of the matter set forth. FL ST RCP Rule 1.110(f).

d. *Statements adopted by reference.* Statements in a pleading may be adopted by reference in a different part of the same pleading, in another pleading, or in any motion. FL ST RCP Rule 1.130(b).

e. *Joinder of causes of action; Consistency.* A pleader may set up in the same action as many claims or causes of action or defenses in the same right as the pleader has, and claims for relief may be stated in the alternative if separate items make up the cause of action, or if two (2) or more causes of action are joined. A party may also set forth two (2) or more statements of a claim or defense alternatively, either in one (1) count or defense or in separate counts or defenses. When two (2) or more statements are made in the alternative and one (1) of them, if made independently, would be sufficient, the pleading is not made insufficient by the insufficiency of one (1) or more of the alternative statements. A party may also state as many separate claims or defenses as that party has, regardless of consistency and whether based on legal or equitable grounds or both. All pleadings shall be construed so as to do substantial justice. FL ST RCP Rule 1.110(g).

f. *Subsequent pleadings.* When the nature of an action permits pleadings subsequent to final judgment and the jurisdiction of the court over the parties has not terminated, the initial pleading subsequent to final judgment shall be designated a supplemental complaint or petition. The action shall then proceed in the same manner and time as though the supplemental complaint or petition were the initial pleading in the action, including the issuance of any needed process. FL ST RCP Rule

1.110(h) shall not apply to proceedings that may be initiated by motion under the Florida Rules of Civil Procedure. FL ST RCP Rule 1.110(h).

g. *Pleading basis for service.* When service of process is to be made under statutes authorizing service on nonresidents of Florida, it is sufficient to plead the basis for service in the language of the statute without pleading the facts supporting service. FL ST RCP Rule 1.070(h).

h. *Forms of pleadings.* Forms of action and technical forms for seeking relief and of pleas, pleadings, or motions are abolished. FL ST RCP Rule 1.110(a).

2. *Answer; Generally.* An answer has three (3) functions. First, it must respond to each allegation of the preceding pleading by admitting, denying or alleging that the pleader is without knowledge of the allegation. Second, it must contain any affirmative defenses that the pleader is interposing to any cause of action alleged in the preceding pleading. Third, the answer may claim affirmative relief against the plaintiff or petitioner by a counterclaim or against a codefendant by a crossclaim. FL-PRACPROC § 11:1.

a. *Content.* In the answer a pleader shall state in short and plain terms the pleader's defenses to each claim asserted and shall admit or deny the averments on which the adverse party relies. If the defendant is without knowledge, the defendant shall so state and such statement shall operate as a denial. Denial shall fairly meet the substance of the averments denied. When a pleader intends in good faith to deny only a part of an averment, the pleader shall specify so much of it as is true and shall deny the remainder. Unless the pleader intends in good faith to controvert all of the averments of the preceding pleading, the pleader may make denials as specific denials of designated averments or may generally deny all of the averments except such designated averments as the pleader expressly admits, but when the pleader does so intend to controvert all of its averments, including averments of the grounds upon which the court's jurisdiction depends, the pleader may do so by general denial. FL ST RCP Rule 1.110(c).

b. *Form of answer.* An answer contains a caption, commencement, body, signature and certificate of service. The caption is the same as that of the initial pleading, except for the designation as one of the types of answer. The body of an answer should contain an admission, denial or plea of without knowledge to each allegation of the preceding pleading, except for the additional allegations in response to a general allegation of conditions precedent and the denial of capacity to sue. FL-PRACPROC § 11:3.

i. *Responding sequentially.* The best method of responding is to answer each paragraph sequentially, combining admissions, denials or pleas of without knowledge when the sequence permits. The admissions, denials and allegations of without knowledge should be stated first, followed separately by any affirmative defenses and then by any counterclaim or crossclaim. A third party complaint may be a part of the same paper, but it is not a part of the answer as is a counterclaim or crossclaim. Paragraphs are numbered consecutively throughout the pleading whether in the answer, counterclaim or crossclaim. Denials for the record only are improper. FL-PRACPROC § 11:3.

c. *Defenses*

i. *Generally.* Every defense in law or fact to a claim for relief in a pleading shall be asserted in the responsive pleading, if one is required, but the following defenses may be made by motion at the option of the pleader: (1) lack of jurisdiction over the subject matter, (2) lack of jurisdiction over the person, (3) improper venue, (4) insufficiency of process, (5) insufficiency of service of process, (6) failure to state a cause of action, and (7) failure to join indispensable parties. A motion making any of these defenses shall be made before pleading if a further pleading is permitted. FL ST RCP Rule 1.140(b).

- *Stated specifically.* The grounds on which any of the enumerated defenses are based and the substantial matters of law intended to be argued shall be stated specifically and with particularity in the responsive pleading or motion. FL ST RCP Rule 1.140(b).
- *Waiver.* Any ground not stated shall be deemed to be waived except any ground showing that the court lacks jurisdiction of the subject matter may be made at any time. No defense or objection is waived by being joined with other defenses or objections in a responsive

pleading or motion. FL ST RCP Rule 1.140(b). A party waives all defenses and objections that the party does not present either by motion under FL ST RCP Rule 1.140(b), FL ST RCP Rule 1.140(e), or FL ST RCP Rule 1.140(f) or, if the party has made no motion, in a responsive pleading except as provided in FL ST RCP Rule 1.140(h)(2). FL ST RCP Rule 1.140(h)(1). The defenses of failure to state a cause of action or a legal defense or to join an indispensable party may be raised by motion for judgment on the pleadings or at the trial on the merits in addition to being raised either in a motion under FL ST RCP Rule 1.140(b) or in the answer or reply. The defense of lack of jurisdiction of the subject matter may be raised at any time. FL ST RCP Rule 1.140(h)(2).

ii. *Affirmative defenses.* In pleading to a preceding pleading a party shall set forth affirmatively accord and satisfaction, arbitration and award, assumption of risk, contributory negligence, discharge in bankruptcy, duress, estoppel, failure of consideration, fraud, illegality, injury by fellow servant, laches, license, payment, release, res judicata, statute of frauds, statute of limitations, waiver, and any other matter constituting an avoidance or affirmative defense. When a party has mistakenly designated a defense as a counterclaim or a counterclaim as a defense, the court, on terms if justice so requires, shall treat the pleading as if there had been a proper designation. Affirmative defenses appearing on the face of a prior pleading may be asserted as grounds for a motion or defense under FL ST RCP Rule 1.140(b); provided this shall not limit amendments under FL ST RCP Rule 1.190 even if such ground is sustained. FL ST RCP Rule 1.110(d).

- *Format of defenses.* Affirmative defenses should be placed after the admissions, denials and allegations of without knowledge in the answer. All paragraphs must be numbered consecutively throughout the answer. If a defense is directed to only a part of a cause of action or to one or more, but not all, of several causes of action in the preceding pleading, the part or cause of action to which it is directed should be identified in the defense. Defenses should be identified by consecutive ordinal numbers such as "First Defense" and "Second Defense." FL-PRACPROC § 11:4.

iii. *Effect of failure to deny.* Averments in a pleading to which a responsive pleading is required, other than those as to the amount of damages, are admitted when not denied in the responsive pleading. Averments in a pleading to which no responsive pleading is required or permitted shall be taken as denied or avoided. FL ST RCP Rule 1.110(e). An admission in an answer binds the party and no proof is required. An admission does not extend beyond the scope of the allegation in the preceding pleading. FL-PRACPROC § 11:3.

3. *Pleading special matters*

a. *Capacity.* It is not necessary to aver the capacity of a party to sue or be sued, the authority of a party to sue or be sued in a representative capacity, or the legal existence of an organized association of persons that is made a party, except to the extent required to show the jurisdiction of the court. The initial pleading served on behalf of a minor party shall specifically aver the age of the minor party. When a party desires to raise an issue as to the legal existence of any party, the capacity of any party to sue or be sued, or the authority of a party to sue or be sued in a representative capacity, that party shall do so by specific negative averment which shall include such supporting particulars as are peculiarly within the pleader's knowledge. FL ST RCP Rule 1.120(a).

b. *Fraud, mistake, condition of the mind.* In all averments of fraud or mistake, the circumstances constituting fraud or mistake shall be stated with such particularity as the circumstances may permit. Malice, intent, knowledge, mental attitude, and other condition of mind of a person may be averred generally. FL ST RCP Rule 1.120(b).

c. *Conditions precedent.* In pleading the performance or occurrence of conditions precedent, it is sufficient to aver generally that all conditions precedent have been performed or have occurred. A denial of performance or occurrence shall be made specifically and with particularity. FL ST RCP Rule 1.120(c).

d. *Official document or act.* In pleading an official document or official act it is sufficient to aver that the document was issued or the act done in compliance with law. FL ST RCP Rule 1.120(c).

e. *Judgment or decree.* In pleading a judgment or decree of a domestic or foreign court, a judicial or quasi-judicial tribunal, or a board or officer, it is sufficient to aver the judgment or decree without setting forth matter showing jurisdiction to render it. FL ST RCP Rule 1.120(e).

f. *Time and place.* For the purpose of testing the sufficiency of a pleading, averments of time and place are material and shall be considered like all other averments of material matter. FL ST RCP Rule 1.120(f).

g. *Special damage.* When items of special damage are claimed, they shall be specifically stated. FL ST RCP Rule 1.120(g).

4. *Parties*

a. *Parties generally.* Every action may be prosecuted in the name of the real party in interest, but a personal representative, administrator, guardian, trustee of an express trust, a party with whom or in whose name a contract has been made for the benefit of another, or a party expressly authorized by statute may sue in that person's own name without joining the party for whose benefit the action is brought. All persons having an interest in the subject of the action and in obtaining the relief demanded may join as plaintiffs and any person may be made a defendant who has or claims an interest adverse to the plaintiff. Any person may at any time be made a party if that person's presence is necessary or proper to a complete determination of the cause. Persons having a united interest may be joined on the same side as plaintiffs or defendants, and anyone who refuses to join may for such reason be made a defendant. FL ST RCP Rule 1.210(a).

b. *Minors or incompetent persons.* When a minor or incompetent person has a representative, such as a guardian or other like fiduciary, the representative may sue or defend on behalf of the minor or incompetent person. A minor or incompetent person who does not have a duly appointed representative may sue by next friend or by a guardian ad litem. The court shall appoint a guardian ad litem for a minor or incompetent person not otherwise represented in an action or shall make such other order as it deems proper for the protection of the minor or incompetent person. FL ST RCP Rule 1.210(b).

c. For survivor and substitution of parties information, please see FL ST RCP Rule 1.260.

5. *Counterclaims and crossclaims*

a. *Compulsory counterclaims.* A pleading shall state as a counterclaim any claim which at the time of serving the pleading the pleader has against any opposing party, provided it arises out of the transaction or occurrence that is the subject matter of the opposing party's claim and does not require for its adjudication the presence of third parties over whom the court cannot acquire jurisdiction. But the pleader need not state a claim if (1) at the time the action was commenced the claim was the subject of another pending action, or (2) the opposing party brought suit upon that party's claim by attachment or other process by which the court did not acquire jurisdiction to render a personal judgment on the claim and the pleader is not stating a counterclaim under this rule. FL ST RCP Rule 1.170(a).

b. *Permissive counterclaim.* A pleading may state as a counterclaim any claim against an opposing party not arising out of the transaction or occurrence that is the subject matter of the opposing party's claim. FL ST RCP Rule 1.170(b).

c. *Counterclaim exceeding opposing claim.* A counterclaim may or may not diminish or defeat the recovery sought by the opposing party. It may claim relief exceeding in amount or different in kind from that sought in the pleading of the opposing party. FL ST RCP Rule 1.170(c).

d. *Counterclaim against the State.* The Florida Rules of Civil Procedure shall not be construed to enlarge beyond the limits established by law the right to assert counterclaims or to claim credits against the state or any of its subdivisions or other governmental organizations thereof subject to suit or against a municipal corporation or against an officer, agency, or administrative board of the state. FL ST RCP Rule 1.170(d).

e. *Counterclaim maturing or acquired after pleading.* A claim which matured or was acquired by the pleader after serving the pleading may be presented as a counterclaim by supplemental pleading with the permission of the court. FL ST RCP Rule 1.170(e).

f. *Omitted counterclaim or crossclaim.* When a pleader fails to set up a counterclaim or crossclaim through oversight, inadvertence, or excusable neglect, or when justice requires, the pleader may set up the counterclaim or crossclaim by amendment with leave of the court. FL ST RCP Rule 1.170(f).

g. *Crossclaim against co-party.* A pleading may state as a crossclaim any claim by one party against a co-party arising out of the transaction or occurrence that is the subject matter of either the original action or a counterclaim therein, or relating to any property that is the subject matter of the original action. The crossclaim may include a claim that the party against whom it is asserted is or may be liable to the crossclaimant for all or part of a claim asserted in the action against the crossclaimant. Service of a crossclaim on a party who has appeared in the action shall be made pursuant to FL ST RCP Rule 1.080. Service of a crossclaim against a party who has not appeared in the action shall be made in the manner provided for service of summons. FL ST RCP Rule 1.170(g).

h. *Additional parties may be brought in.* When the presence of parties other than those to the original action is required to grant complete relief in the determination of a counterclaim or crossclaim, they shall be named in the counterclaim or crossclaim and be served with process and shall be parties to the action thereafter if jurisdiction of them can be obtained and their joinder will not deprive the court of jurisdiction of the action. FL ST RCP Rule 1.250(b) and FL ST RCP Rule 1.250(c) apply to parties brought in under FL ST RCP Rule 1.170(h). FL ST RCP Rule 1.170(h).

i. *Separate trials; Separate judgment.* If the court orders separate trials as provided in FL ST RCP Rule 1.270(b), judgment on a counterclaim or crossclaim may be rendered when the court has jurisdiction to do so even if a claim of the opposing party has been dismissed or otherwise disposed of. FL ST RCP Rule 1.170(i).

j. *Demand exceeding jurisdiction; Transfer of action.* If the demand of any counterclaim or crossclaim exceeds the jurisdiction of the court in which the action is pending, the action shall be transferred forthwith to the court of the same county having jurisdiction of the demand in the counterclaim or crossclaim with only such alterations in the pleadings as are essential. The court shall order the transfer of the action and the transmittal of all papers in it to the proper court if the party asserting the demand exceeding the jurisdiction deposits with the court having jurisdiction a sum sufficient to pay the clerk's service charge in the court to which the action is transferred at the time of filing the counterclaim or crossclaim. Thereupon the original papers and deposit shall be transmitted and filed with a certified copy of the order. The court to which the action is transferred shall have full power and jurisdiction over the demands of all parties. Failure to make the service charge deposit at the time the counterclaim or crossclaim is filed, or within such further time as the court may allow, shall reduce a claim for damages to an amount within the jurisdiction of the court where the action is pending and waive the claim in other cases. FL ST RCP Rule 1.170(j).

6. *Misjoinder and nonjoinder of parties*

a. *Misjoinder.* Misjoinder of parties is not a ground for dismissal of an action. Any claim against a party may be severed and proceeded with separately. FL ST RCP Rule 1.250(a).

b. *Dropping parties.* Parties may be dropped by an adverse party in the manner provided for voluntary dismissal in FL ST RCP Rule 1.420(a)(1) subject to the exception stated in FL ST RCP Rule 1.420. If notice of lis pendens has been filed in the action against a party so dropped, the notice of dismissal shall be recorded and cancels the notice of lis pendens without the necessity of a court order. Parties may be dropped by order of court on its own initiative or the motion of any party at any stage of the action on such terms as are just. FL ST RCP Rule 1.250(b).

c. *Adding parties.* Parties may be added once as a matter of course within the same time that pleadings can be so amended under FL ST RCP Rule 1.190(a). If amendment by leave of court or stipulation of the parties is permitted, parties may be added in the amended pleading without further order of court. Parties may be added by order of court on its own initiative or on motion of any party at any stage of the action and on such terms as are just. FL ST RCP Rule 1.250(c).

7. *Jury demand*

a. *Right preserved.* The right of trial by jury as declared by the Constitution or by statute shall be preserved to the parties inviolate. FL ST RCP Rule 1.430(a).

b. *Demand.* Any party may demand a trial by jury of any issue triable of right by a jury by serving upon the other party a demand therefor in writing at any time after commencement of the action and not later than ten (10) days after the service of the last pleading directed to such issue. The demand may be indorsed upon a pleading of the party. FL ST RCP Rule 1.430(b).

c. *Specification of issues.* In the demand a party may specify the issues that the party wishes so tried; otherwise, the party is deemed to demand trial by jury for all issues so triable. FL ST RCP Rule 1.430(c).

   i. If a party has demanded trial by jury for only some of the issues, any other party may serve a demand for trial by jury of any other or all of the issues triable by jury ten (10) days after service of the demand or such lesser time as the court may order. FL ST RCP Rule 1.430(c).

d. *Waiver.* A party who fails to serve a demand as required by FL ST RCP Rule 1.430 waives trial by jury. FL ST RCP Rule 1.430(d).

   i. If waived, a jury trial may not be granted without the consent of the parties, but the court may allow an amendment in the proceedings to demand a trial by jury or order a trial by jury on its own motion. FL ST RCP Rule 1.430(d).

   ii. A demand for trial by jury may not be withdrawn without the consent of the parties. FL ST RCP Rule 1.430(d).

8. *Arbitration and mediation.* Attorneys are encouraged to utilize arbitration, mediation or other forms of alternative dispute resolution if economically feasible. FL ST 20 J CIR 2.20(IV)(N)(3).

   a. *Referral to arbitration and mediation.* Except as hereinafter provided or as otherwise prohibited by law, the presiding judge may enter an order referring all or any part of a contested civil matter to mediation or arbitration. The parties to any contested civil matter may file a written stipulation to mediate or arbitrate any issue between them at any time. Such stipulation shall be incorporated into the order of referral. FL ST RCP Rule 1.700(a).

   b. *Arbitration*

      i. *Exclusions.* A civil action shall be ordered to arbitration or arbitration in conjunction with mediation upon stipulation of the parties. A civil action may be ordered to arbitration or arbitration in conjunction with mediation upon motion of any party or by the court, if the judge determines the action to be of such a nature that arbitration could be of benefit to the litigants or the court. FL ST RCP Rule 1.800.

         - Under no circumstances may the following categories of actions be referred to arbitration: (1) bond estreatures; (2) habeas corpus or other extraordinary writs; (3) bond validations; (4) civil or criminal contempt; (5) such other matters as may be specified by order of the chief judge in the circuit. FL ST RCP Rule 1.800.

      ii. For more information regarding arbitration, please see FL ST RCP Rule 1.810; FL ST RCP Rule 1.820; FL ST RCP Rule 1.830.

   c. *Mediation.* For more information regarding mediation, please see FL ST RCP Rule 1.710; FL ST RCP Rule 1.720; FL ST RCP Rule 1.730; FL ST RCP Rule 1.750; and FL ST 20 J CIR 1.9.

9. *Rules of court*

   a. *Rules of civil procedure.* The Florida Rules of Civil Procedure apply to all actions of a civil nature and all special statutory proceedings in the circuit courts and county courts except those to which the Florida Probate Rules, the Florida Family Law Rules of Procedure, or the Small Claims Rules apply. FL ST RCP Rule 1.010.

      i. The form, content, procedure, and time for pleading in all special statutory proceedings shall be as prescribed by the statutes governing the proceeding unless the Florida Rules of Civil Procedure specifically provide to the contrary. FL ST RCP Rule 1.010.

      ii. The Florida Rules of Civil Procedure shall be construed to secure the just, speedy, and inexpensive determination of every action. FL ST RCP Rule 1.010.

   b. *Rules of judicial administration.* The Florida Rules of Judicial Administration shall apply to

administrative matters in all courts to which the Florida Rules of Judicial Administration are applicable by their terms. The Florida Rules of Judicial Administration shall be construed to secure the speedy and inexpensive determination of every proceeding to which they are applicable. The Florida Rules of Judicial Administration shall supersede all conflicting rules and statutes. FL ST J ADMIN Rule 2.110.

10. *Civil case management plan.* There is established within the Twentieth Judicial Circuit a Civil Case Management Plan applicable to circuit civil cases, which will be administered by the Administrative Office of the Courts through direction of the Circuit Administrative Judges in each county for the implementation of enhanced case management procedures and guidelines for the timely and efficient processing of circuit civil cases and reduction in the pending backlog of civil cases. FL ST 20 J CIR 1.13.
    a. The basis for the Civil Case Management Plan is included in FL ST 20 J CIR 1.13, identified in Attachment A as the "Civil Differentiated Case Management (DCM) Procedures and Backlog Reduction Plan," and is incorporated as if fully set forth in FL ST 20 J CIR 1.13. The Civil Case Management Plan is to be used as a model for the purpose of establishing time standards, improving the courts ability to provide early and continuous management of civil cases as required by FL ST J ADMIN Rule 2.545, and to promote uniformity of practice throughout the Twentieth Judicial Circuit. FL ST 20 J CIR 1.13.
    b. Full implementation of the Civil DCM Case Management Procedures (Attachment A), including all uniform circuitwide procedures and forms, shall apply to all civil cases filed in Lee and Collier counties, effective January 1, 2011. Even though full implementation may be delayed in Charlotte, Hendry, and Glades counties, all civil time standards and goals, and the use of civil Case Managers and Magistrates to assist trial judges in the process of civil case management and backlog reduction programs, shall be effective circuitwide immediately. FL ST 20 J CIR 1.13.
    c. For more information on the civil case management plan, refer to the specific county website and/or see FL ST 20 J CIR 1.13.

D. Documents

1. *Required documents*
    a. *Answer.* See the General Requirements section of this document for further information about the content of an answer.
        i. *Notices to persons with disabilities.* See the Format section of this KeyRules document for further information.
    b. *Certificate of service.* When any attorney certifies in substance: "I certify that a copy hereof has been furnished to (here insert name or names and addresses used for service) by (e-mail) (delivery) (mail) (fax) on .... (date) ....________________ Attorney" the certificate is taken as prima facie proof of such service in compliance with FL ST J ADMIN Rule 2.516. FL ST J ADMIN Rule 2.516(f).
2. *Supplemental documents*
    a. *Exhibits.* All bonds, notes, bills of exchange, contracts, accounts, or documents upon which action may be brought or defense made, or a copy thereof or a copy of the portions thereof material to the pleadings, shall be incorporated in or attached to the pleading. No papers shall be unnecessarily annexed as exhibits. The pleadings shall contain no unnecessary recitals of deeds, documents, contracts, or other instruments. Any exhibit attached to a pleading shall be considered a part of the pleadings for all purposes. FL ST RCP Rule 1.130(a).
    b. *Notice of constitutional question.* A party that files a pleading, written motion, or other paper drawing into question the constitutionality of a state statute or a county or municipal charter, ordinance, or franchise must promptly (1) file a notice of constitutional question stating the question and identifying the paper that raises it; and (2) serve the notice and the pleading, written motion, or other paper drawing into question the constitutionality of a state statute or a county or municipal charter, ordinance, or franchise on the Attorney General or the state attorney of the judicial circuit in which the action is pending, by either certified or registered mail. Service of the notice and pleading, written motion, or other paper does not require joinder of the Attorney General or the state attorney as a party to the action. FL ST RCP Rule 1.071.

E. Format

1. *Documents; Type and size.* Documents subject to the exceptions set forth in FL ST J ADMIN Rule 2.525(d) shall be filed on recycled paper measuring eight and one half by eleven (8 1/2 by 11) inches. For purposes of FL ST J ADMIN Rule 2.520, paper is recycled if it contains a minimum content of fifty (50) percent waste paper. Xerographic reduction of legal-size (eight and one half by fourteen (8 1/2 by 14) inches) documents to letter size (eight and one half by eleven (8 1/2 by 11) inches) is prohibited. All other documents filed by electronic transmission shall be filed in a format capable of being printed in a format consistent with the provisions of FL ST J ADMIN Rule 2.250. FL ST J ADMIN Rule 2.520(b); FL ST 20 J CIR 2.9.
   a. *Exhibits.* Any exhibit or attachment filed with pleadings or papers may be filed in its original size. FL ST J ADMIN Rule 2.520(c); FL ST 20 J CIR 2.9.
   b. *Recording space.* On all papers and documents prepared and filed by the court or by any party to a proceeding which are to be recorded in the public records of any county, including but not limited to final money judgments and notices of lis pendens, a three (3) inch by three (3) inch space at the top right-hand corner on the first page and a one (1) inch by three (3) inch space at the top right-hand corner on each subsequent page shall be left blank and reserved for use by the clerk of court. FL ST J ADMIN Rule 2.520(d).
      i. *Exceptions to recording space.* Any papers or documents created by persons or entities over which the filing party has no control, including but not limited to wills, codicils, trusts, or other testamentary documents; documents prepared or executed by any public officer; documents prepared, executed, acknowledged, or proved outside of the State of Florida; or documents created by State or Federal government agencies, may be filed without the space required by FL ST J ADMIN Rule 2.520. FL ST J ADMIN Rule 2.520(e).
   c. *Noncompliance.* No clerk of court is permitted to refuse to file any document or paper because of noncompliance with the Florida Rules of Judicial Administration. However, upon request of the clerk of court, noncomplying documents must be resubmitted in accordance with the formatting rules. FL ST J ADMIN Rule 2.520(f).
      i. When time of filing is critical, the Clerk shall accept pleadings, motions, petitions, briefs, notices, orders, judgments, decrees, opinions, or other papers or official documents on other than eight and one half by eleven (8 1/2 by 11) inch paper but shall then require that the document be resubmitted to comply with FL ST J ADMIN Rule 2.520. FL ST 20 J CIR 2.9.
2. *Caption.* Every pleading, motion, order, judgment, or other paper shall have a caption containing the name of the court, the file number, and except for in rem proceedings, including forfeiture proceedings, the name of the first party on each side with an appropriate indication of other parties, and a designation identifying the party filing it and its nature or the nature of the order, as the case may be. In any in rem proceeding, every pleading, motion, order, judgment, or other paper shall have a caption containing the name of the court, the file number, the style "In re" (followed by the name or general description of the property), and a designation of the person or entity filing it and its nature or the nature of the order, as the case may be. In an in rem forfeiture proceeding, the style shall be "In re forfeiture of" (followed by the name of the general description of the property). All papers filed in the action shall be styled in such a manner as to indicate clearly the subject matter of the paper and the party requesting or obtaining relief. FL ST RCP Rule 1.100(c)(1).
3. *Writing and written defined.* Writing or written means a document containing information, an application, or a stipulation. FL ST RCP Rule 1.080(c).
4. *Rule abbreviations*
   a. The Florida Rules of Civil Procedure and shall be abbreviated as Fla.R.Civ.P. FL ST RCP Rule 1.010.
   b. The Florida Rules of Judicial Administration shall be abbreviated as Fla. R. Jud. Admin. FL ST J ADMIN Rule 2.110.
5. *Nonverification.* Except when otherwise specifically provided by the Florida Rules of Civil Procedure or an applicable statute, every pleading or other document of a party represented by an attorney need not be verified or accompanied by an affidavit. FL ST RCP Rule 1.030; FL ST J ADMIN Rule 2.515(a).

6. *Attorney signature*

   a. *Attorney signature.* Every pleading and other document of a party represented by an attorney shall be signed by at least one (1) attorney of record in that attorney's individual name whose current record Florida Bar address, telephone number, including area code, primary e-mail address and secondary e-mail addresses, if any, and Florida Bar number shall be stated, and who shall be duly licensed to practice law in Florida or who shall have received permission to appear in the particular case as provided in FL ST J ADMIN Rule 2.510. FL ST J ADMIN Rule 2.515(a).

      i. The attorney may be required by the court to give the address of, and to vouch for the attorney's authority to represent, the party. FL ST J ADMIN Rule 2.515(a).

      ii. The signature of an attorney shall constitute a certificate by the attorney that the attorney has read the pleading or other document; that to the best of the attorney's knowledge, information, and belief there is good ground to support it; and that it is not interposed for delay. FL ST J ADMIN Rule 2.515(a).

      iii. If a pleading is not signed or is signed with intent to defeat the purpose of FL ST J ADMIN Rule 2.515, it may be stricken and the action may proceed as though the pleading or other document had not been served. FL ST J ADMIN Rule 2.515(a).

   b. *Pro se litigant signature.* A party who is not represented by an attorney shall sign any pleading or other paper and state the party's address and telephone number, including area code. FL ST J ADMIN Rule 2.515(b).

   c. *Form of signature*

      i. The signatures required on pleadings and documents by FL ST J ADMIN Rule 2.515(a) and FL ST J ADMIN Rule 2.515(b) may be:

         - Original signatures;
         - Original signatures that have been reproduced by electronic means, such as on electronically transmitted documents or photocopied documents;
         - Electronic signatures using the "/s/," "s/," or "/s" formats by or at the direction of the person signing; or
         - Any other signature format authorized by general law, so long as the clerk where the proceeding is pending has the capability of receiving and has obtained approval from the Supreme Court of Florida to accept pleadings and documents with that signature format. FL ST J ADMIN Rule 2.515(c)(1).

      ii. An attorney, party, or other person who files a pleading or paper by electronic transmission that does not contain the original signature of that attorney, party, or other person shall file that identical pleading or paper in paper form containing an original signature of that attorney, party, or other person (hereinafter called the follow-up filing) immediately thereafter. The follow-up filing is not required if the Supreme Court of Florida has entered an order directing the clerk of court to discontinue accepting the follow-up filing. FL ST J ADMIN Rule 2.515(c)(2).

7. *Forms*

   a. *Process.* The forms of process, notice of lis pendens, and notice of action provided in the Florida Rules of Civil Procedure are sufficient. Variations from the forms do not void process or notices that are otherwise sufficient. FL ST RCP Rule 1.900(a).

   b. *Other forms.* The other forms provided in the Florida Rules of Civil Procedure are sufficient for the matters that are covered by them. So long as the substance is expressed without prolixity, the forms may be varied to meet the facts of a particular case. FL ST RCP Rule 1.900(b).

   c. *Formal matters.* Captions, except for the designation of the paper, are omitted from the forms provided in the Florida Rules of Civil Procedure. A general form of caption is the first form provided. Signatures are omitted from pleadings and motions. FL ST RCP Rule 1.900(c).

8. *Notices to persons with disabilities.* All notices of court proceedings to be held in a public facility, and all process compelling appearance at such proceedings, shall include the following statement in bold face,

fourteen (14) point Times New Roman or Courier font: "If you are a person with a disability who needs any accommodation in order to participate in this proceeding, you are entitled, at no cost to you, to the provision of certain assistance. Please contact [identify applicable court personnel by name, address, and telephone number] at least seven (7) days before your scheduled court appearance, or immediately upon receiving this notification if the time before the scheduled appearance is less than seven (7) days; if you are hearing or voice impaired, call 711." FL ST J ADMIN Rule 2.540(c)(1). For more information, see FL ST 20 J CIR 2.15.

9. *Minimization of the filing of sensitive information*
   a. *Limitations for court filings.* Unless authorized by FL ST J ADMIN Rule 2.425(b), statute, another rule of court, or the court orders otherwise, designated sensitive information filed with the court must be limited to the following format:
      i. The initials of a person known to be a minor;
      ii. The year of birth of a person's birth date;
      iii. No portion of any: Social security number, Bank account number, Credit card account number, Charge account number, or Debit account number;
      iv. The last four digits of any: Taxpayer identification number (TIN), Employee identification number, Driver's license number, Passport number, Telephone number, Financial account number, except as set forth in FL ST J ADMIN Rule 2.425(a)(3), Brokerage account number, Insurance policy account number, Loan account number, Customer account number, or Patient or health care number;
      v. A truncated version of any: Email address, Computer user name, Password, or Personal identification number (PIN); and
      vi. A truncated version of any other sensitive information as provided by court order. FL ST J ADMIN Rule 2.425(a).
   b. *Exceptions.* FL ST J ADMIN Rule 2.425(a) does not apply to the following:
      i. An account number which identifies the property alleged to be the subject of a proceeding;
      ii. The record of an administrative or agency proceeding;
      iii. The record in appellate or review proceedings;
      iv. The birth date of a minor whenever the birth date is necessary for the court to establish or maintain subject matter jurisdiction;
      v. The name of a minor in any order relating to parental responsibility, time-sharing, or child support;
      vi. The name of a minor in any document or order affecting the minor's ownership of real property;
      vii. The birth date of a party in a writ of attachment or notice to payor;
      viii. In traffic and criminal proceedings: a pro se filing; a court filing that is related to a criminal matter or investigation and that is prepared before the filing of a criminal charge or is not filed as part of any docketed criminal case; an arrest or search warrant or any information in support thereof; a charging document and an affidavit or other documents filed in support of any charging document, including any driving records; a statement of particulars; discovery material introduced into evidence or otherwise filed with the court; and all information necessary for the proper issuance and execution of a subpoena duces tecum;
      ix. Information used by the clerk for case maintenance purposes or the courts for case management purposes; and
      x. Information which is relevant and material to an issue before the court. FL ST J ADMIN Rule 2.425(b).
   c. *Remedies.* Upon motion by a party or interested person or sua sponte by the court, the court may order remedies, sanctions or both for a violation of FL ST J ADMIN Rule 2.425(a). Following notice and an opportunity to respond, the court may impose sanctions if such filing was not made in good faith. FL ST J ADMIN Rule 2.425(c).

d. *Motions not restricted.* FL ST J ADMIN Rule 2.425 does not restrict a party's right to move for protective order, to move to file documents under seal, or to request a determination of the confidentiality of records. FL ST J ADMIN Rule 2.425(d).

e. *Application.* FL ST J ADMIN Rule 2.425 does not affect the application of constitutional provisions, statutes, or rules of court regarding confidential information or access to public information. FL ST J ADMIN Rule 2.425(e).

F. Filing and Service Requirements

1. *Filing requirements.* All original documents must be filed with the court either before service or immediately thereafter, unless otherwise provided for by general law or other rules. If the original of any bond or other document is not placed in the court file, a certified copy must be so placed by the clerk. FL ST J ADMIN Rule 2.516(d). All documents shall be filed in conformity with the requirements of FL ST J ADMIN Rule 2.525. FL ST RCP Rule 1.080(b). All documents filed in any court shall be filed by electronic transmission in accordance with FL ST J ADMIN Rule 2.525. "Documents" means pleadings, motions, petitions, memoranda, briefs, notices, exhibits, declarations, affidavits, orders, judgments, decrees, writs, opinions, and any other paper or writing submitted to a court. FL ST J ADMIN Rule 2.520(a). All documents that are court records, as defined in FL ST J ADMIN Rule 2.430(a)(1), must be filed by electronic transmission, provided that: (1) the clerk has the ability to accept and retain such documents; (2) the clerk or the chief judge of the circuit has requested permission to accept documents filed by electronic transmission; and (3) the supreme court has entered an order granting permission to the clerk to accept documents filed by electronic transmission. FL ST J ADMIN Rule 2.525(c)(1).

   a. *Definition.* "Electronic transmission of documents" means the sending of information by electronic signals to, by or from a court or clerk, which when received can be transformed and stored or transmitted on paper, microfilm, magnetic storage device, optical imaging system, CD-ROM, flash drive, other electronic data storage system, server, case maintenance system ("CM"), electronic court filing ("ECF") system, statewide or local electronic portal ("e-portal"), or other electronic record keeping system authorized by the supreme court in a format sufficient to communicate the information on the original document in a readable format. Electronic transmission of documents includes electronic mail ("e-mail") and any internet-based transmission procedure, and may include procedures allowing for documents to be signed or verified by electronic means. FL ST J ADMIN Rule 2.525(a).

      i. The filing of documents with the court as required by the Florida Rules of Judicial Administration must be made by filing them with the clerk in accordance with FL ST J ADMIN Rule 2.525, except that the judge may permit documents to be filed with the judge, in which event the judge must note the filing date before him or her on the documents and transmit them to the clerk. The date of filing is that shown on the face of the document by the judge's notation or the clerk's time stamp, whichever is earlier. FL ST J ADMIN Rule 2.516(e).

   b. *Application.* Any court or clerk of the court may accept the electronic transmission of documents for filing after the clerk, together with input from the chief judge of the circuit, has obtained approval of the procedures and program for doing so from the Supreme Court of Florida. FL ST J ADMIN Rule 2.525(b).

   c. *Exceptions*

      i. Paper documents and other submissions may be manually submitted to the clerk or court:

         - When the clerk does not have the ability to accept and retain documents by electronic filing or has not had ECF Procedures approved by the supreme court;
         - For filing by any self-represented party or any self-represented nonparty unless specific ECF Procedures provide a means to file documents electronically. However, any self-represented nonparty that is a governmental or public agency and any other agency, partnership, corporation, or business entity acting on behalf of any governmental or public agency may file documents by electronic transmission if such entity has the capability of filing documents electronically;
         - For filing by attorneys excused from e-mail service in accordance with FL ST J ADMIN Rule 2.516(b);

- When submitting evidentiary exhibits or filing non-documentary materials;
- When the filing involves documents in excess of twenty-five (25) megabytes (25MB) in size. For such filings, documents may be transmitted using an electronic storage medium that the clerk has the ability to accept, which may include a CD-ROM, flash drive, or similar storage medium;
- When filed in open court, as permitted by the court;
- When paper filing is permitted by any approved statewide or local ECF procedures; and
- If any court determines that justice so requires. FL ST J ADMIN Rule 2.525(d).

ii. Any document in paper form submitted under FL ST J ADMIN Rule 2.525(d) is filed when it is received by the clerk or court and the clerk shall immediately thereafter convert any filed paper document to an electronic document. "Convert to an electronic document" means optically capturing an image of a paper document and using character recognition software to recover as much of the document's text as practicable and then indexing and storing the document in the official court file. FL ST J ADMIN Rule 2.525(c)(4).

iii. Any storage medium submitted under FL ST J ADMIN Rule 2.525(d)(5) is filed when received by the clerk or court and the clerk shall immediately thereafter transfer the electronic documents from the storage device to the official court file. FL ST J ADMIN Rule 2.525(c)(5).

iv. If the filer of any paper document authorized under FL ST J ADMIN Rule 2.525(d) provides a self-addressed, postage-paid envelope for return of the paper document after it is converted to electronic form by the clerk, the clerk shall place the paper document in the envelope and deposit it in the mail. Except when a paper document is required to be maintained, the clerk may recycle any filed paper document that is not to be returned to the filer. FL ST J ADMIN Rule 2.525(c)(6).

v. The clerk may convert any paper document filed before the effective date of FL ST J ADMIN Rule 2.525 to an electronic document. Unless the clerk is required to maintain the paper document, if the paper document has been converted to an electronic document by the clerk, the paper document is no longer part of the official court file and may be removed and recycled. FL ST J ADMIN Rule 2.525(c)(7).

d. *Official court file.* For information on what constitutes the official court file, please see FL ST J ADMIN Rule 2.525(c)(2), FL ST J ADMIN Rule 2.525(c)(3).

e. *Administration.* All attorneys, parties, or other persons using this rule to file documents are required to make arrangements with the court or clerk for the payment of any charges authorized by general law or the supreme court before filing any document by electronic transmission. FL ST J ADMIN Rule 2.525(f)(2).

f. *Filing date.* The filing date for an electronically transmitted document is the date and time that such filing is acknowledged by an electronic stamp or otherwise, pursuant to any procedure set forth in any ECF Procedures approved by the supreme court, or the date the last page of such filing is received by the court or clerk. FL ST J ADMIN Rule 2.525(f)(3).

g. *Accessibility.* All documents transmitted in any electronic form under FL ST J ADMIN Rule 2.525 must comply with the accessibility requirements of FL ST J ADMIN Rule 2.526. FL ST J ADMIN Rule 2.525(g).

2. *Service requirements.* Every pleading subsequent to the initial pleading, all orders, and every other document filed in the action must be served in conformity with the requirements of FL ST J ADMIN Rule 2.516. FL ST RCP Rule 1.080(a).

a. *Service; Generally.* The timing and manner of service should not be used to the disadvantage of the party receiving the papers. FL ST 20 J CIR 2.20(IV)(C)(1).

i. Papers and memoranda of law should not be served at court appearances without advance notice to opposing counsel and should not be served so close to a court appearance so as to inhibit the ability of opposing counsel to prepare for that appearance or to respond to the papers. Should the attorney do so, the court is urged to take appropriate action in response, including

continuing the matter to allow opposing counsel to prepare and respond. FL ST 20 J CIR 2.20(IV)(C)(2).

ii. Papers should not be served in order to take advantage of an opponent's known absence from the office or at a time or in a manner designed to inconvenience an adversary, such as late on Friday afternoon or the day preceding a secular or religious holiday. FL ST 20 J CIR 2.20(IV)(C)(3).

iii. Service should be made personally or by courtesy copy facsimile transmission when it is likely that service by mail, even when allowed, will prejudice the opposing party or will not provide the opposing party with a reasonable time to respond. FL ST 20 J CIR 2.20(IV)(C)(4).

b. *Service; When required.* Unless the court otherwise orders, or a statute or supreme court administrative order specifies a different means of service, every pleading subsequent to the initial pleading and every other document filed in any court proceeding, except applications for witness subpoenas and documents served by formal notice or required to be served in the manner provided for service of formal notice, must be served in accordance with FL ST J ADMIN Rule 2.516 on each party. No service need be made on parties against whom a default has been entered, except that pleadings asserting new or additional claims against them must be served in the manner provided for service of summons. FL ST J ADMIN Rule 2.516(a).

i. *Copies of court submissions.* Copies of any submissions to the court (such as correspondence, memoranda of law, motions, case law, etc.) should simultaneously be provided to opposing counsel by substantially the same method of delivery by which they are provided to the court. For example, if a memorandum of law is hand-delivered to the court, at substantially the same time a copy should be hand-delivered or faxed to opposing counsel. FL ST 20 J CIR 2.20(IV)(J)(4).

c. *Service; How made.* When service is required or permitted to be made upon a party represented by an attorney, service must be made upon the attorney unless service upon the party is ordered by the court. FL ST J ADMIN Rule 2.516(b).

i. *Service by electronic mail ("e-mail").* All documents required or permitted to be served on another party must be served by e-mail, unless FL ST J ADMIN Rule 2.516 otherwise provides. When, in addition to service by e-mail, the sender also utilizes another means of service provided for in FL ST J ADMIN Rule 2.516(b)(2), any differing time limits and other provisions applicable to that other means of service control. FL ST J ADMIN Rule 2.516(b)(1). Any document electronically transmitted to a court or clerk must also be served on all parties and interested persons in accordance with the applicable rules of court. FL ST J ADMIN Rule 2.525(e)(2).

- *Service on attorneys.* Upon appearing in a proceeding, an attorney must serve a designation of a primary e-mail address and may designate no more than two (2) secondary e-mail addresses. Thereafter, service must be directed to all designated e-mail addresses in that proceeding. Every document filed by an attorney thereafter must include the primary e-mail address of that attorney and any secondary e-mail addresses. If an attorney does not designate any e-mail address for service, documents may be served on that attorney at the e-mail address on record with The Florida Bar. FL ST J ADMIN Rule 2.516(b)(1)(A).
- *Exception to e-mail service on attorneys.* Service by an attorney on another attorney must be made by e-mail unless excused by the court. Upon motion by an attorney demonstrating that the attorney has no e-mail account and lacks access to the Internet at the attorney's office, the court may excuse the attorney from the requirements of e-mail service. Service on and by an attorney excused by the court from e-mail service must be by the means provided in FL ST J ADMIN Rule 2.516(b)(2). FL ST J ADMIN Rule 2.516(b)(1)(B).
- *Service on and by parties not represented by an attorney.* Any party not represented by an attorney may serve a designation of a primary e-mail address and also may designate no more than two (2) secondary e-mail addresses to which service must be directed in that proceeding by the means provided in FL ST J ADMIN Rule 2.516(b)(1). If a party not represented by an attorney does not designate an e-mail address for service in a proceed-

ing, service on and by that party must be by the means provided in FL ST J ADMIN Rule 2.516(b)(2). FL ST J ADMIN Rule 2.516(b)(1)(C).

- *Time of service.* Service by e-mail is complete when it is sent. FL ST J ADMIN Rule 2.516(b)(1)(D). An e-mail is deemed served on the date it is sent. FL ST J ADMIN Rule 2.516(b)(1)(D)(i). If the sender learns that the e-mail did not reach the address of the person to be served, the sender must immediately send another copy by e-mail, or by a means authorized by FL ST J ADMIN Rule 2.516(b)(2). FL ST J ADMIN Rule 2.516(b)(1)(D)(ii). E-mail service is treated as service by mail for the computation of time. FL ST J ADMIN Rule 2.516(b)(1)(D)(iii).

ii. *Format of e-mail for service.* Service of a document by e-mail is made by attaching a copy of the document in PDF format to an e-mail sent to all addresses designated by the attorney or party. FL ST J ADMIN Rule 2.516(b)(1)(E).

- All documents served by e-mail must be attached to an e-mail message containing a subject line beginning with the words "SERVICE OF COURT DOCUMENT" in all capital letters, followed by the case number of the proceeding in which the documents are being served. FL ST J ADMIN Rule 2.516(b)(1)(E)(i).
- The body of the e-mail must identify the court in which the proceeding is pending, the case number, the name of the initial party on each side, the title of each document served with that e-mail, and the sender's name and telephone number. FL ST J ADMIN Rule 2.516(b)(1)(E)(ii).
- Any document served by e-mail may be signed by the "/s/" format, as long as the filed original is signed in accordance with the applicable rule of procedure. FL ST J ADMIN Rule 2.516(b)(1)(E)(iii).
- Any e-mail which, together with its attached documents, exceeds five megabytes (5MB) in size, must be divided and sent as separate e-mails, no one of which may exceed five megabytes (5MB) in size and each of which must be sequentially numbered in the subject line. FL ST J ADMIN Rule 2.516(b)(1)(E)(iv).

iii. *Service by other means.* In addition to, and not in lieu of, service by e-mail, service may also be made upon attorneys by any of the means specified in FL ST J ADMIN Rule 2.516(b)(2). Service on and by all parties who are not represented by an attorney and who do not designate an e-mail address, and on and by all attorneys excused from e-mail service, must be made by delivering a copy of the document or by mailing it to the party or attorney at their last known address or, if no address is known, by leaving it with the clerk of the court. Service by mail is complete upon mailing. Delivery of a copy within FL ST J ADMIN Rule 2.516 is complete upon:

- Handing it to the attorney or to the party,
- Leaving it at the attorney's or party's office with a clerk or other person in charge thereof,
- If there is no one in charge, leaving it in a conspicuous place therein,
- If the office is closed or the person to be served has no office, leaving it at the person's usual place of abode with some person of his or her family above fifteen (15) years of age and informing such person of the contents, or
- Transmitting it by facsimile to the attorney's or party's office with a cover sheet containing the sender's name, firm, address, telephone number, and facsimile number, and the number of pages transmitted. When service is made by facsimile, a copy must also be served by any other method permitted by FL ST J ADMIN Rule 2.516. Facsimile service occurs when transmission is complete. FL ST J ADMIN Rule 2.516(b)(2)(A) through FL ST J ADMIN Rule 2.516(b)(2)(E).
- Service by delivery after 5:00 p.m. must be deemed to have been made by mailing on the date of delivery. FL ST J ADMIN Rule 2.516(b)(2)(F).

d. *Service; Numerous defendants.* In actions when the parties are unusually numerous, the court may

regulate the service contemplated by the Florida Rules of Judicial Administration on motion or on its own initiative in such manner as may be found to be just and reasonable. FL ST J ADMIN Rule 2.516(c).

e. *Service by clerk.* Service of notices and other documents required to be made by the clerk must also be done as provided in FL ST J ADMIN Rule 2.516(b). FL ST J ADMIN Rule 2.516(g).

G. Hearings

1. There is no hearing required or contemplated in the Florida rules governing the answer.

H. Forms

1. Official Answer Forms for Florida

a. Caption. FL ST RCP Form 1.901.

b. Crossclaim summons. FL ST RCP Form 1.903.

c. Third-party summons. FL ST RCP Form 1.904.

d. Defense; Statute of limitations. FL ST RCP Form 1.965.

e. Defense; Payment. FL ST RCP Form 1.966.

f. Defense; Accord and satisfaction. FL ST RCP Form 1.967.

g. Defense; Failure of consideration. FL ST RCP Form 1.968.

h. Defense; Statute of frauds. FL ST RCP Form 1.969.

i. Defense; Release. FL ST RCP Form 1.970.

j. Notice of compliance when constitutional challenge is brought. FL ST RCP Form 1.975.

2. Answer Forms for Florida

a. Answer; General form, traverses. FL-PRACFORM § 5:4.

b. Answer; General form, traverses and affirmative defenses. FL-PRACFORM § 5:6.

c. Answer; General form, traverses, affirmative defenses and counterclaim. FL-PRACFORM § 5:7.

d. Answer; General form, traverses, affirmative defenses, counterclaim and crossclaim. FL-PRACFORM § 5:8.

e. Answer; Affirmative defense, fraud. FL-PRACFORM § 5:43.

f. Answer; Affirmative defense, laches. FL-PRACFORM § 5:47.

g. Answer; Affirmative defense, misjoinder. FL-PRACFORM § 5:49.

h. Answer; Affirmative defense, misrepresentation. FL-PRACFORM § 5:50.

i. Answer; Affirmative defense, self defense. FL-PRACFORM § 5:64.

j. Answer; Denial of conditions precedent. FL-PRACFORM § 5:80.

k. General denial. FL-PP § 2:58.

l. General denial; With specified admissions. FL-PP § 2:59.

m. Admission with qualification. FL-PP § 2:60.

n. Conclusions of law not requiring denial. FL-PP § 2:61.

o. Defenses stated in the alternative. FL-PP § 2:62.

p. Denial as to part of allegation. FL-PP § 2:63.

q. Pleader as without knowledge as to truth of allegation. FL-PP § 2:64.

I. Checklist

(I) ❑ Matters to be considered by plaintiff

(a) ❑ Required documents

(1) ❑ Summons

(2) ❑ Complaint

(3) ❑ Civil cover sheet

(4) ❑ Return of execution process by process server

(5) ❑ Filing fees

(b) ❑ Supplemental documents

(1) ❑ Exhibits

(2) ❑ Notice of constitutional question

(c) ❑ Time for filing and serving complaint

(1) ❑ Service of the initial process and initial pleading should be made upon a defendant within one hundred twenty (120) days after the filing of the complaint with the court

(II) ❑ Matters to be considered by defendant

(a) ❑ Required documents

(1) ❑ Answer

(2) ❑ Certificate of service

(b) ❑ Supplemental documents

(1) ❑ Exhibits

(2) ❑ Notice of constitutional question

(c) ❑ Time for answer

(1) ❑ Unless a different time is prescribed in a statute of Florida, a defendant shall serve an answer within twenty (20) days after service of original process and the initial pleading on the defendant, or not later than the date fixed in a notice by publication

(2) ❑ A party served with a pleading stating a crossclaim against that party shall serve an answer to it within twenty (20) days after service on that party

(3) ❑ The plaintiff shall serve an answer to a counterclaim within twenty (20) days after service of the counterclaim

(4) ❑ A defendant who, before being served with process, timely returns a waiver so requested is not required to respond to the complaint until sixty (60) days after the date the defendant received the request for waiver of service; for purposes of computing any time prescribed or allowed by the Florida Rules of Civil Procedure, service of process shall be deemed effected twenty (20) days before the time required to respond to the complaint

(5) ❑ For timing requirements related to service on the state, service of motion impact, and responding when no responsive pleading is required, please see the Timing section of this document

Pleadings
Amended Answer

Document Last Updated January 2013

A. Applicable Rules

1. *State rules*

   a. Nonverification of papers. FL ST RCP Rule 1.030.

   b. Service and filing of pleadings, orders, and documents. FL ST RCP Rule 1.080.

   c. Time. FL ST RCP Rule 1.090.

   d. Pleadings and motions. FL ST RCP Rule 1.100; FL ST RCP Rule 1.110; FL ST RCP Rule 1.120; FL ST RCP Rule 1.130; FL ST RCP Rule 1.190.

e. Defenses. FL ST RCP Rule 1.140.
f. Pretrial procedure. FL ST RCP Rule 1.200.
g. Relief from judgment. FL ST RCP Rule 1.540.
h. Forms. FL ST RCP Rule 1.900.
i. Minimization of the filing of sensitive information. FL ST J ADMIN Rule 2.425.
j. Foreign attorneys. FL ST J ADMIN Rule 2.510.
k. Signature of attorneys and parties. FL ST J ADMIN Rule 2.515.
l. Paper. FL ST J ADMIN Rule 2.520.
m. Electronic filing. FL ST J ADMIN Rule 2.525.
n. Accessibility of information and technology. FL ST J ADMIN Rule 2.526.
o. Court reporting. FL ST J ADMIN Rule 2.535.
p. Requests for accommodations by persons with disabilities. FL ST J ADMIN Rule 2.540.
q. Case management. FL ST J ADMIN Rule 2.545.

2. *Local rules*
   a. Exclusions from mediation. FL ST 20 J CIR 1.9.
   b. Establishment and implementation of civil case management plan. FL ST 20 J CIR 1.13.
   c. Size of paper. FL ST 20 J CIR 2.9.
   d. Americans with Disabilities Act; Notification of court proceedings. FL ST 20 J CIR 2.15.
   e. Standards of professional courtesy and conduct and establishment of peer review program. FL ST 20 J CIR 2.20.

B. Timing

1. *Amendment as a matter of course.* A party may amend a pleading once as a matter of course at any time before a responsive pleading is served or, if the pleading is one to which no responsive pleading is permitted and the action has not been placed on the trial calendar, may so amend it at any time within twenty (20) days after it is served. FL ST RCP Rule 1.190(a).
2. *Amendment by leave of court.* Otherwise a party may amend a pleading only by leave of court or by written consent of the adverse party. Leave of court shall be given freely when justice so requires. FL ST RCP Rule 1.190(a).
3. *Amendments in furtherance of justice.* At any time in furtherance of justice, upon such terms as may be just, the court may permit any process, proceeding, pleading, or record to be amended or material supplemental matter to be set forth in an amended or supplemental pleading. At every stage of the action the court must disregard any error or defect in the proceedings which does not affect the substantial rights of the parties. FL ST RCP Rule 1.190(e).
4. *Response to amended pleading.* A party shall plead in response to an amended pleading within ten (10) days after service of the amended pleading unless the court otherwise orders. FL ST RCP Rule 1.190(a).
5. *Computation of time*
   a. *Generally.* Computation of time shall be governed by FL ST J ADMIN Rule 2.514. FL ST RCP Rule 1.090(a). The following rules apply in computing time periods specified in any rule of procedure, local rule, court order, or statute that does not specify a method of computing time. FL ST J ADMIN Rule 2.514(a).
      i. *Period stated in days or a longer unit.* When the period is stated in days or a longer unit of time (A) exclude the day of the event that triggers the period; (B) count every day, including intermediate Saturdays, Sundays, and legal holidays; and (C) include the last day of the period, but if the last day is a Saturday, Sunday, or legal holiday, or falls within any period of time extended through an order of the chief justice under FL ST J ADMIN Rule 2.205(a)(2)(B)(iv), the period continues to run until the end of the next day that is not a Saturday, Sunday, or legal

holiday and does not fall within any period of time extended through an order of the chief justice. FL ST J ADMIN Rule 2.514(a)(1).

ii. *Period stated in hours.* When the period is stated in hours (A) begin counting immediately on the occurrence of the event that triggers the period; (B) count every hour, including hours during intermediate Saturdays, Sundays, and legal holidays; and (C) if the period would end on a Saturday, Sunday, or legal holiday, or during any period of time extended through an order of the chief justice under FL ST J ADMIN Rule 2.205(a)(2)(B)(iv), the period continues to run until the same time on the next day that is not a Saturday, Sunday, or legal holiday and does not fall within any period of time extended through an order of the chief justice. FL ST J ADMIN Rule 2.514(a)(2).

iii. *Period stated in days less than seven (7) days.* When the period stated in days is less than seven (7) days, intermediate Saturdays, Sundays, and legal holidays shall be excluded in the computation. FL ST J ADMIN Rule 2.514(a)(3).

iv. *"Last day" defined.* Unless a different time is set by a statute, local rule, or court order, the last day ends (A) for electronic filing or for service by any means, at midnight; and (B) for filing by other means, when the clerk's office is scheduled to close. FL ST J ADMIN Rule 2.514(a)(4).

v. *"Next day" defined.* The "next day" is determined by continuing to count forward when the period is measured after an event and backward when measured before an event. FL ST J ADMIN Rule 2.514(a)(5).

vi. *"Legal holiday" defined.* "Legal holiday" means (A) the day set aside by FL ST § 110.117, for observing New Year's Day, Martin Luther King, Jr.'s Birthday, Memorial Day, Independence Day, Labor Day, Veterans' Day, Thanksgiving Day, the Friday after Thanksgiving Day, or Christmas Day, and (B) any day observed as a holiday by the clerk's office or as designated by the chief judge. FL ST J ADMIN Rule 2.514(a)(6).

b. *Additional time after service by mail or e-mail.* When a party may or must act within a specified time after service and service is made by mail or e-mail, five (5) days are added after the period that would otherwise expire under FL ST J ADMIN Rule 2.514(a). FL ST J ADMIN Rule 2.514(b).

c. *Enlargement.* When an act is required or allowed to be done at or within a specified time by order of court, by the Florida Rules of Civil Procedure, or by notice given thereunder, for cause shown the court at any time in its discretion (1) with or without notice, may order the period enlarged if request therefor is made before the expiration of the period originally prescribed or as extended by a previous order, or (2) upon motion made and notice after the expiration of the specified period, may permit the act to be done when failure to act was the result of excusable neglect, but it may not extend the time for making a motion for new trial, for rehearing, or to alter or amend a judgment; making a motion for relief from a judgment under FL ST RCP Rule 1.540(b); taking an appeal or filing a petition for certiorari; or making a motion for a directed verdict. FL ST RCP Rule 1.090(b).

d. *Unaffected by expiration of term.* The period of time provided for the doing of any act or the taking of any proceeding shall not be affected or limited by the continued existence or expiration of a term of court. The continued existence or expiration of a term of court in no way affects the power of a court to do any act or take any proceeding in any action which is or has been pending before it. FL ST RCP Rule 1.090(c).

C. General Requirements

1. *Amendments.* A party may amend a pleading once as a matter of course at any time before a responsive pleading is served or, if the pleading is one to which no responsive pleading is permitted and the action has not been placed on the trial calendar, may so amend it at any time within twenty (20) days after it is served. Otherwise a party may amend a pleading only by leave of court or by written consent of the adverse party. Leave of court shall be freely given when justice so requires. FL ST RCP Rule 1.190(a).

a. *Purpose of amendments.* Amendments can relate to the correction of mistakes, the insertion of jurisdictional averments, the correction or addition of verifications, the addition or substitution or striking out of parties, and generally the rectification of all formal defects in the pleading. The court can also allow amendments setting up an omitted counterclaim or cross-claim if the defendant failed to raise the claim through oversight, inadvertence, or excusable neglect. FL-PP § 2:151.

b. *Amendment to a pleading/Amended pleading.* A significant difference exists between an amendment to a pleading and an amended pleading. An amendment to a pleading corrects, adds to or deletes from the pleading. An amended pleading is substituted for the former pleading and the former pleading ceases to have any effect. Dee v. Southern Brewing Company, 146 Fla. 588, 1 So.2d 562 (Fla. 1941); Shannon v. McBride, 105 So.2d 16 (Fla. 2d DCA 1958); Hughes v. Home Sav. of America, F.S.B., 675 So.2d 649 (Fla. 2d DCA 1996); FL-PRACPROC § 14:2.

c. *Relation back of amendments.* When the claim or defense asserted in the amended pleading arose out of the conduct, transaction, or occurrence set forth or attempted to be set forth in the original pleading, the amendment shall relate back to the date of the original pleading. FL ST RCP Rule 1.190(c).

2. *General rules of pleading*

a. *Claims for relief*

i. A pleading which sets forth a claim for relief, whether an original claim, counterclaim, crossclaim, or third-party claim, must state a cause of action and shall contain

- A short and plain statement of the grounds upon which the court's jurisdiction depends, unless the court already has jurisdiction and the claim needs no new grounds of jurisdiction to support it (For information regarding acts subjecting persons to jurisdiction, please see FL ST § 48.193),
- A short and plain statement of the ultimate facts showing that the pleader is entitled to relief, and
- A demand for judgment for the relief to which the pleader deems himself or herself entitled. FL ST RCP Rule 1.110(b).

ii. Relief in the alternative or of several different types may be demanded. Every complaint shall be considered to demand general relief. FL ST RCP Rule 1.110(b).

b. *Verification.* Except when otherwise specifically provided by these rules or an applicable statute, every pleading or other document of a party represented by an attorney need not be verified or accompanied by an affidavit. FL ST RCP Rule 1.030. When filing an action for foreclosure of a mortgage on residential real property the complaint shall be verified. When verification of a document is required, the document filed shall include an oath, affirmation, or the following statement: "Under penalty of perjury, I declare that I have read the foregoing, and the facts alleged therein are true and correct to the best of my knowledge and belief." FL ST RCP Rule 1.110(b).

c. *Separate statements.* All averments of claim or defense shall be made in consecutively numbered paragraphs, the contents of each of which shall be limited as far as practicable to a statement of a single set of circumstances, and a paragraph may be referred to by number in all subsequent pleadings. Each claim founded upon a separate transaction or occurrence and each defense other than denials shall be stated in a separate count or defense when a separation facilitates the clear presentation of the matter set forth. FL ST RCP Rule 1.110(f).

d. *Statements adopted by reference.* Statements in a pleading may be adopted by reference in a different part of the same pleading, in another pleading, or in any motion. FL ST RCP Rule 1.130(b).

e. *Joinder of causes of action; Consistency.* A pleader may set up in the same action as many claims or causes of action or defenses in the same right as the pleader has, and claims for relief may be stated in the alternative if separate items make up the cause of action, or if two (2) or more causes of action are joined. A party may also set forth two (2) or more statements of a claim or defense alternatively, either in one (1) count or defense or in separate counts or defenses. When two (2) or more statements are made in the alternative and one (1) of them, if made independently, would be sufficient, the pleading is not made insufficient by the insufficiency of one (1) or more of the alternative statements. A party may also state as many separate claims or defenses as that party has, regardless of consistency and whether based on legal or equitable grounds or both. All pleadings shall be construed so as to do substantial justice. FL ST RCP Rule 1.110(g).

f. *Subsequent pleadings.* When the nature of an action permits pleadings subsequent to final judgment and the jurisdiction of the court over the parties has not terminated, the initial pleading subsequent to final judgment shall be designated a supplemental complaint or petition. The action shall then proceed in the same manner and time as though the supplemental complaint or petition were the initial pleading in the action, including the issuance of any needed process. FL ST RCP Rule 1.110(h) shall not apply to proceedings that may be initiated by motion under the Florida Rules of Civil Procedure. FL ST RCP Rule 1.110(h).

g. *Pleading basis for service.* When service of process is to be made under statutes authorizing service on nonresidents of Florida, it is sufficient to plead the basis for service in the language of the statute without pleading the facts supporting service. FL ST RCP Rule 1.070(h).

h. *Forms of pleadings.* Forms of action and technical forms for seeking relief and of pleas, pleadings, or motions are abolished. FL ST RCP Rule 1.110(a).

3. *Answer; Generally.* An answer has three (3) functions. First, it must respond to each allegation of the preceding pleading by admitting, denying or alleging that the pleader is without knowledge of the allegation. Second, it must contain any affirmative defenses that the pleader is interposing to any cause of action alleged in the preceding pleading. Third, the answer may claim affirmative relief against the plaintiff or petitioner by a counterclaim or against a codefendant by a crossclaim. FL-PRACPROC § 11:1.

   a. *Content.* In the answer a pleader shall state in short and plain terms the pleader's defenses to each claim asserted and shall admit or deny the averments on which the adverse party relies. If the defendant is without knowledge, the defendant shall so state and such statement shall operate as a denial. Denial shall fairly meet the substance of the averments denied. When a pleader intends in good faith to deny only a part of an averment, the pleader shall specify so much of it as is true and shall deny the remainder. Unless the pleader intends in good faith to controvert all of the averments of the preceding pleading, the pleader may make denials as specific denials of designated averments or may generally deny all of the averments except such designated averments as the pleader expressly admits, but when the pleader does so intend to controvert all of its averments, including averments of the grounds upon which the court's jurisdiction depends, the pleader may do so by general denial. FL ST RCP Rule 1.110(c).

   b. *Form of answer.* An answer contains a caption, commencement, body, signature and certificate of service. The caption is the same as that of the initial pleading, except for the designation as one of the types of answer. The body of an answer should contain an admission, denial or plea of without knowledge to each allegation of the preceding pleading, except for the additional allegations in response to a general allegation of conditions precedent and the denial of capacity to sue. FL-PRACPROC § 11:3.

      i. *Responding sequentially.* The best method of responding is to answer each paragraph sequentially, combining admissions, denials or pleas of without knowledge when the sequence permits. The admissions, denials and allegations of without knowledge should be stated first, followed separately by any affirmative defenses and then by any counterclaim or crossclaim. A third party complaint may be a part of the same paper, but it is not a part of the answer as is a counterclaim or crossclaim. Paragraphs are numbered consecutively throughout the pleading whether in the answer, counterclaim or crossclaim. Denials for the record only are improper. FL-PRACPROC § 11:3.

   c. *Defenses*

      i. *Generally.* Every defense in law or fact to a claim for relief in a pleading shall be asserted in the responsive pleading, if one is required, but the following defenses may be made by motion at the option of the pleader: (1) lack of jurisdiction over the subject matter, (2) lack of jurisdiction over the person, (3) improper venue, (4) insufficiency of process, (5) insufficiency of service of process, (6) failure to state a cause of action, and (7) failure to join indispensable parties. A motion making any of these defenses shall be made before pleading if a further pleading is permitted. FL ST RCP Rule 1.140(b).

         - *Stated specifically.* The grounds on which any of the enumerated defenses are based and the substantial matters of law intended to be argued shall be stated specifically and with particularity in the responsive pleading or motion. FL ST RCP Rule 1.140(b).

- *Waiver.* Any ground not stated shall be deemed to be waived except any ground showing that the court lacks jurisdiction of the subject matter may be made at any time. No defense or objection is waived by being joined with other defenses or objections in a responsive pleading or motion. FL ST RCP Rule 1.140(b). A party waives all defenses and objections that the party does not present either by motion under FL ST RCP Rule 1.140(b), FL ST RCP Rule 1.140(e), or FL ST RCP Rule 1.140(f) or, if the party has made no motion, in a responsive pleading except as provided in FL ST RCP Rule 1.140(h)(2). FL ST RCP Rule 1.140(h)(1). The defenses of failure to state a cause of action or a legal defense or to join an indispensable party may be raised by motion for judgment on the pleadings or at the trial on the merits in addition to being raised either in a motion under FL ST RCP Rule 1.140(b) or in the answer or reply. The defense of lack of jurisdiction of the subject matter may be raised at any time. FL ST RCP Rule 1.140(h)(2).

ii. *Affirmative defenses.* In pleading to a preceding pleading a party shall set forth affirmatively accord and satisfaction, arbitration and award, assumption of risk, contributory negligence, discharge in bankruptcy, duress, estoppel, failure of consideration, fraud, illegality, injury by fellow servant, laches, license, payment, release, res judicata, statute of frauds, statute of limitations, waiver, and any other matter constituting an avoidance or affirmative defense. When a party has mistakenly designated a defense as a counterclaim or a counterclaim as a defense, the court, on terms if justice so requires, shall treat the pleading as if there had been a proper designation. Affirmative defenses appearing on the face of a prior pleading may be asserted as grounds for a motion or defense under FL ST RCP Rule 1.140(b); provided this shall not limit amendments under FL ST RCP Rule 1.190 even if such ground is sustained. FL ST RCP Rule 1.110(d).

- *Format of defenses.* Affirmative defenses should be placed after the admissions, denials and allegations of without knowledge in the answer. All paragraphs must be numbered consecutively throughout the answer. If a defense is directed to only a part of a cause of action or to one or more, but not all, of several causes of action in the preceding pleading, the part or cause of action to which it is directed should be identified in the defense. Defenses should be identified by consecutive ordinal numbers such as "First Defense" and "Second Defense." FL-PRACPROC § 11:4.

iii. *Effect of failure to deny.* Averments in a pleading to which a responsive pleading is required, other than those as to the amount of damages, are admitted when not denied in the responsive pleading. Averments in a pleading to which no responsive pleading is required or permitted shall be taken as denied or avoided. FL ST RCP Rule 1.110(e). An admission in an answer binds the party and no proof is required. An admission does not extend beyond the scope of the allegation in the preceding pleading. FL-PRACPROC § 11:3.

4. *Pleading special matters*

a. *Capacity.* It is not necessary to aver the capacity of a party to sue or be sued, the authority of a party to sue or be sued in a representative capacity, or the legal existence of an organized association of persons that is made a party, except to the extent required to show the jurisdiction of the court. The initial pleading served on behalf of a minor party shall specifically aver the age of the minor party. When a party desires to raise an issue as to the legal existence of any party, the capacity of any party to sue or be sued, or the authority of a party to sue or be sued in a representative capacity, that party shall do so by specific negative averment which shall include such supporting particulars as are peculiarly within the pleader's knowledge. FL ST RCP Rule 1.120(a).

b. *Fraud, mistake, condition of the mind.* In all averments of fraud or mistake, the circumstances constituting fraud or mistake shall be stated with such particularity as the circumstances may permit. Malice, intent, knowledge, mental attitude, and other condition of mind of a person may be averred generally. FL ST RCP Rule 1.120(b).

c. *Conditions precedent.* In pleading the performance or occurrence of conditions precedent, it is sufficient to aver generally that all conditions precedent have been performed or have occurred. A denial of performance or occurrence shall be made specifically and with particularity. FL ST RCP Rule 1.120(c).

d. *Official document or act.* In pleading an official document or official act it is sufficient to aver that the document was issued or the act done in compliance with law. FL ST RCP Rule 1.120(c).

e. *Judgment or decree.* In pleading a judgment or decree of a domestic or foreign court, a judicial or quasi-judicial tribunal, or a board or officer, it is sufficient to aver the judgment or decree without setting forth matter showing jurisdiction to render it. FL ST RCP Rule 1.120(e).

f. *Time and place.* For the purpose of testing the sufficiency of a pleading, averments of time and place are material and shall be considered like all other averments of material matter. FL ST RCP Rule 1.120(f).

g. *Special damage.* When items of special damage are claimed, they shall be specifically stated. FL ST RCP Rule 1.120(g).

5. *Parties*

a. *Parties generally.* Every action may be prosecuted in the name of the real party in interest, but a personal representative, administrator, guardian, trustee of an express trust, a party with whom or in whose name a contract has been made for the benefit of another, or a party expressly authorized by statute may sue in that person's own name without joining the party for whose benefit the action is brought. All persons having an interest in the subject of the action and in obtaining the relief demanded may join as plaintiffs and any person may be made a defendant who has or claims an interest adverse to the plaintiff. Any person may at any time be made a party if that person's presence is necessary or proper to a complete determination of the cause. Persons having a united interest may be joined on the same side as plaintiffs or defendants, and anyone who refuses to join may for such reason be made a defendant. FL ST RCP Rule 1.210(a).

b. *Minors or incompetent persons.* When a minor or incompetent person has a representative, such as a guardian or other like fiduciary, the representative may sue or defend on behalf of the minor or incompetent person. A minor or incompetent person who does not have a duly appointed representative may sue by next friend or by a guardian ad litem. The court shall appoint a guardian ad litem for a minor or incompetent person not otherwise represented in an action or shall make such other order as it deems proper for the protection of the minor or incompetent person. FL ST RCP Rule 1.210(b).

c. For survivor and substitution of parties information, please see FL ST RCP Rule 1.260.

6. *Counterclaims and crossclaims*

a. *Compulsory counterclaims.* A pleading shall state as a counterclaim any claim which at the time of serving the pleading the pleader has against any opposing party, provided it arises out of the transaction or occurrence that is the subject matter of the opposing party's claim and does not require for its adjudication the presence of third parties over whom the court cannot acquire jurisdiction. But the pleader need not state a claim if (1) at the time the action was commenced the claim was the subject of another pending action, or (2) the opposing party brought suit upon that party's claim by attachment or other process by which the court did not acquire jurisdiction to render a personal judgment on the claim and the pleader is not stating a counterclaim under this rule. FL ST RCP Rule 1.170(a).

b. *Permissive counterclaim.* A pleading may state as a counterclaim any claim against an opposing party not arising out of the transaction or occurrence that is the subject matter of the opposing party's claim. FL ST RCP Rule 1.170(b).

c. *Counterclaim exceeding opposing claim.* A counterclaim may or may not diminish or defeat the recovery sought by the opposing party. It may claim relief exceeding in amount or different in kind from that sought in the pleading of the opposing party. FL ST RCP Rule 1.170(c).

d. *Counterclaim against the State.* The Florida Rules of Civil Procedure shall not be construed to enlarge beyond the limits established by law the right to assert counterclaims or to claim credits against the state or any of its subdivisions or other governmental organizations thereof subject to suit or against a municipal corporation or against an officer, agency, or administrative board of the state. FL ST RCP Rule 1.170(d).

e. *Counterclaim maturing or acquired after pleading.* A claim which matured or was acquired by the

pleader after serving the pleading may be presented as a counterclaim by supplemental pleading with the permission of the court. FL ST RCP Rule 1.170(e).

f. *Omitted counterclaim or crossclaim.* When a pleader fails to set up a counterclaim or crossclaim through oversight, inadvertence, or excusable neglect, or when justice requires, the pleader may set up the counterclaim or crossclaim by amendment with leave of the court. FL ST RCP Rule 1.170(f).

g. *Crossclaim against co-party.* A pleading may state as a crossclaim any claim by one party against a co-party arising out of the transaction or occurrence that is the subject matter of either the original action or a counterclaim therein, or relating to any property that is the subject matter of the original action. The crossclaim may include a claim that the party against whom it is asserted is or may be liable to the crossclaimant for all or part of a claim asserted in the action against the crossclaimant. Service of a crossclaim on a party who has appeared in the action shall be made pursuant to FL ST RCP Rule 1.080. Service of a crossclaim against a party who has not appeared in the action shall be made in the manner provided for service of summons. FL ST RCP Rule 1.170(g).

h. *Additional parties may be brought in.* When the presence of parties other than those to the original action is required to grant complete relief in the determination of a counterclaim or crossclaim, they shall be named in the counterclaim or crossclaim and be served with process and shall be parties to the action thereafter if jurisdiction of them can be obtained and their joinder will not deprive the court of jurisdiction of the action. FL ST RCP Rule 1.250(b) and FL ST RCP Rule 1.250(c) apply to parties brought in under FL ST RCP Rule 1.170(h). FL ST RCP Rule 1.170(h).

i. *Separate trials; Separate judgment.* If the court orders separate trials as provided in FL ST RCP Rule 1.270(b), judgment on a counterclaim or crossclaim may be rendered when the court has jurisdiction to do so even if a claim of the opposing party has been dismissed or otherwise disposed of. FL ST RCP Rule 1.170(i).

j. *Demand exceeding jurisdiction; Transfer of action.* If the demand of any counterclaim or crossclaim exceeds the jurisdiction of the court in which the action is pending, the action shall be transferred forthwith to the court of the same county having jurisdiction of the demand in the counterclaim or crossclaim with only such alterations in the pleadings as are essential. The court shall order the transfer of the action and the transmittal of all papers in it to the proper court if the party asserting the demand exceeding the jurisdiction deposits with the court having jurisdiction a sum sufficient to pay the clerk's service charge in the court to which the action is transferred at the time of filing the counterclaim or crossclaim. Thereupon the original papers and deposit shall be transmitted and filed with a certified copy of the order. The court to which the action is transferred shall have full power and jurisdiction over the demands of all parties. Failure to make the service charge deposit at the time the counterclaim or crossclaim is filed, or within such further time as the court may allow, shall reduce a claim for damages to an amount within the jurisdiction of the court where the action is pending and waive the claim in other cases. FL ST RCP Rule 1.170(j).

7. *Misjoinder and nonjoinder of parties*

a. *Misjoinder.* Misjoinder of parties is not a ground for dismissal of an action. Any claim against a party may be severed and proceeded with separately. FL ST RCP Rule 1.250(a).

b. *Dropping parties.* Parties may be dropped by an adverse party in the manner provided for voluntary dismissal in FL ST RCP Rule 1.420(a)(1) subject to the exception stated in FL ST RCP Rule 1.420. If notice of lis pendens has been filed in the action against a party so dropped, the notice of dismissal shall be recorded and cancels the notice of lis pendens without the necessity of a court order. Parties may be dropped by order of court on its own initiative or the motion of any party at any stage of the action on such terms as are just. FL ST RCP Rule 1.250(b).

c. *Adding parties.* Parties may be added once as a matter of course within the same time that pleadings can be so amended under FL ST RCP Rule 1.190(a). If amendment by leave of court or stipulation of the parties is permitted, parties may be added in the amended pleading without further order of court. Parties may be added by order of court on its own initiative or on motion of any party at any stage of the action and on such terms as are just. FL ST RCP Rule 1.250(c).

8. *Jury demand*

a. *Right preserved.* The right of trial by jury as declared by the Constitution or by statute shall be preserved to the parties inviolate. FL ST RCP Rule 1.430(a).

b. *Demand.* Any party may demand a trial by jury of any issue triable of right by a jury by serving upon the other party a demand therefor in writing at any time after commencement of the action and not later than ten (10) days after the service of the last pleading directed to such issue. The demand may be indorsed upon a pleading of the party. FL ST RCP Rule 1.430(b).

c. *Specification of issues.* In the demand a party may specify the issues that the party wishes so tried; otherwise, the party is deemed to demand trial by jury for all issues so triable. FL ST RCP Rule 1.430(c).

   i. If a party has demanded trial by jury for only some of the issues, any other party may serve a demand for trial by jury of any other or all of the issues triable by jury ten (10) days after service of the demand or such lesser time as the court may order. FL ST RCP Rule 1.430(c).

d. *Waiver.* A party who fails to serve a demand as required by FL ST RCP Rule 1.430 waives trial by jury. FL ST RCP Rule 1.430(d).

   i. If waived, a jury trial may not be granted without the consent of the parties, but the court may allow an amendment in the proceedings to demand a trial by jury or order a trial by jury on its own motion. FL ST RCP Rule 1.430(d).

   ii. A demand for trial by jury may not be withdrawn without the consent of the parties. FL ST RCP Rule 1.430(d).

9. *Arbitration and mediation.* Attorneys are encouraged to utilize arbitration, mediation or other forms of alternative dispute resolution if economically feasible. FL ST 20 J CIR 2.20(IV)(N)(3).

   a. *Referral to arbitration and mediation.* Except as hereinafter provided or as otherwise prohibited by law, the presiding judge may enter an order referring all or any part of a contested civil matter to mediation or arbitration. The parties to any contested civil matter may file a written stipulation to mediate or arbitrate any issue between them at any time. Such stipulation shall be incorporated into the order of referral. FL ST RCP Rule 1.700(a).

   b. *Arbitration*

      i. *Exclusions.* A civil action shall be ordered to arbitration or arbitration in conjunction with mediation upon stipulation of the parties. A civil action may be ordered to arbitration or arbitration in conjunction with mediation upon motion of any party or by the court, if the judge determines the action to be of such a nature that arbitration could be of benefit to the litigants or the court. FL ST RCP Rule 1.800.

         - Under no circumstances may the following categories of actions be referred to arbitration: (1) bond estreatures; (2) habeas corpus or other extraordinary writs; (3) bond validations; (4) civil or criminal contempt; (5) such other matters as may be specified by order of the chief judge in the circuit. FL ST RCP Rule 1.800.

      ii. For more information regarding arbitration, please see FL ST RCP Rule 1.810; FL ST RCP Rule 1.820; FL ST RCP Rule 1.830.

   c. *Mediation.* For more information regarding mediation, please see FL ST RCP Rule 1.710; FL ST RCP Rule 1.720; FL ST RCP Rule 1.730; FL ST RCP Rule 1.750; and FL ST 20 J CIR 1.9.

10. *Rules of court*

   a. *Rules of civil procedure.* The Florida Rules of Civil Procedure apply to all actions of a civil nature and all special statutory proceedings in the circuit courts and county courts except those to which the Florida Probate Rules, the Florida Family Law Rules of Procedure, or the Small Claims Rules apply. FL ST RCP Rule 1.010.

      i. The form, content, procedure, and time for pleading in all special statutory proceedings shall be as prescribed by the statutes governing the proceeding unless the Florida Rules of Civil Procedure specifically provide to the contrary. FL ST RCP Rule 1.010.

      ii. The Florida Rules of Civil Procedure shall be construed to secure the just, speedy, and inexpensive determination of every action. FL ST RCP Rule 1.010.

   b. *Rules of judicial administration.* The Florida Rules of Judicial Administration shall apply to

administrative matters in all courts to which the Florida Rules of Judicial Administration are applicable by their terms. The Florida Rules of Judicial Administration shall be construed to secure the speedy and inexpensive determination of every proceeding to which they are applicable. The Florida Rules of Judicial Administration shall supersede all conflicting rules and statutes. FL ST J ADMIN Rule 2.110.

11. *Civil case management plan.* There is established within the Twentieth Judicial Circuit a Civil Case Management Plan applicable to circuit civil cases, which will be administered by the Administrative Office of the Courts through direction of the Circuit Administrative Judges in each county for the implementation of enhanced case management procedures and guidelines for the timely and efficient processing of circuit civil cases and reduction in the pending backlog of civil cases. FL ST 20 J CIR 1.13.
    a. The basis for the Civil Case Management Plan is included in FL ST 20 J CIR 1.13, identified in Attachment A as the "Civil Differentiated Case Management (DCM) Procedures and Backlog Reduction Plan," and is incorporated as if fully set forth in FL ST 20 J CIR 1.13. The Civil Case Management Plan is to be used as a model for the purpose of establishing time standards, improving the courts ability to provide early and continuous management of civil cases as required by FL ST J ADMIN Rule 2.545, and to promote uniformity of practice throughout the Twentieth Judicial Circuit. FL ST 20 J CIR 1.13.
    b. Full implementation of the Civil DCM Case Management Procedures (Attachment A), including all uniform circuitwide procedures and forms, shall apply to all civil cases filed in Lee and Collier counties, effective January 1, 2011. Even though full implementation may be delayed in Charlotte, Hendry, and Glades counties, all civil time standards and goals, and the use of civil Case Managers and Magistrates to assist trial judges in the process of civil case management and backlog reduction programs, shall be effective circuitwide immediately. FL ST 20 J CIR 1.13.
    c. For more information on the civil case management plan, refer to the specific county website and/or see FL ST 20 J CIR 1.13.

D. Documents

1. *Required documents*
    a. *Amended answer.* See the General Requirements section of this document for the content of an amended answer. If a party files a motion to amend a pleading, the party shall attach the proposed amended pleading to the motion. FL ST RCP Rule 1.190(a). See the KeyRules Florida Circuit Court Motion for Leave to Amend document for further information.
        i. *Notices to persons with disabilities.* See the Format section of this KeyRules document for further information.
    b. *Certificate of service.* When any attorney certifies in substance: "I certify that a copy hereof has been furnished to (here insert name or names and addresses used for service) by (e-mail) (delivery) (mail) (fax) on .... (date) ....________________ Attorney" the certificate is taken as prima facie proof of such service in compliance with FL ST J ADMIN Rule 2.516. FL ST J ADMIN Rule 2.516(f).
2. *Supplemental documents*
    a. *Exhibits.* All bonds, notes, bills of exchange, contracts, accounts, or documents upon which action may be brought or defense made, or a copy thereof or a copy of the portions thereof material to the pleadings, shall be incorporated in or attached to the pleading. No papers shall be unnecessarily annexed as exhibits. The pleadings shall contain no unnecessary recitals of deeds, documents, contracts, or other instruments. Any exhibit attached to a pleading shall be considered a part of the pleadings for all purposes. FL ST RCP Rule 1.130(a).
    b. *Notice of constitutional question.* A party that files a pleading, written motion, or other paper drawing into question the constitutionality of a state statute or a county or municipal charter, ordinance, or franchise must promptly (1) file a notice of constitutional question stating the question and identifying the paper that raises it; and (2) serve the notice and the pleading, written motion, or other paper drawing into question the constitutionality of a state statute or a county or municipal charter, ordinance, or franchise on the Attorney General or the state attorney of the judicial circuit in which the action is pending, by either certified or registered mail. Service of the notice and pleading,

written motion, or other paper does not require joinder of the Attorney General or the state attorney as a party to the action. FL ST RCP Rule 1.071.

E. Format

1. *Documents; Type and size.* Documents subject to the exceptions set forth in FL ST J ADMIN Rule 2.525(d) shall be filed on recycled paper measuring eight and one half by eleven (8 1/2 by 11) inches. For purposes of FL ST J ADMIN Rule 2.520, paper is recycled if it contains a minimum content of fifty (50) percent waste paper. Xerographic reduction of legal-size (eight and one half by fourteen (8 1/2 by 14) inches) documents to letter size (eight and one half by eleven (8 1/2 by 11) inches) is prohibited. All other documents filed by electronic transmission shall be filed in a format capable of being printed in a format consistent with the provisions of FL ST J ADMIN Rule 2.250. FL ST J ADMIN Rule 2.520(b); FL ST 20 J CIR 2.9.
   a. *Exhibits.* Any exhibit or attachment filed with pleadings or papers may be filed in its original size. FL ST J ADMIN Rule 2.520(c); FL ST 20 J CIR 2.9.
   b. *Recording space.* On all papers and documents prepared and filed by the court or by any party to a proceeding which are to be recorded in the public records of any county, including but not limited to final money judgments and notices of lis pendens, a three (3) inch by three (3) inch space at the top right-hand corner on the first page and a one (1) inch by three (3) inch space at the top right-hand corner on each subsequent page shall be left blank and reserved for use by the clerk of court. FL ST J ADMIN Rule 2.520(d).
      i. *Exceptions to recording space.* Any papers or documents created by persons or entities over which the filing party has no control, including but not limited to wills, codicils, trusts, or other testamentary documents; documents prepared or executed by any public officer; documents prepared, executed, acknowledged, or proved outside of the State of Florida; or documents created by State or Federal government agencies, may be filed without the space required by FL ST J ADMIN Rule 2.520. FL ST J ADMIN Rule 2.520(e).
   c. *Noncompliance.* No clerk of court is permitted to refuse to file any document or paper because of noncompliance with the Florida Rules of Judicial Administration. However, upon request of the clerk of court, noncomplying documents must be resubmitted in accordance with the formatting rules. FL ST J ADMIN Rule 2.520(f).
      i. When time of filing is critical, the Clerk shall accept pleadings, motions, petitions, briefs, notices, orders, judgments, decrees, opinions, or other papers or official documents on other than eight and one half by eleven (8 1/2 by 11) inch paper but shall then require that the document be resubmitted to comply with FL ST J ADMIN Rule 2.520. FL ST 20 J CIR 2.9.
2. *Caption.* Every pleading, motion, order, judgment, or other paper shall have a caption containing the name of the court, the file number, and except for in rem proceedings, including forfeiture proceedings, the name of the first party on each side with an appropriate indication of other parties, and a designation identifying the party filing it and its nature or the nature of the order, as the case may be. In any in rem proceeding, every pleading, motion, order, judgment, or other paper shall have a caption containing the name of the court, the file number, the style "In re" (followed by the name or general description of the property), and a designation of the person or entity filing it and its nature or the nature of the order, as the case may be. In an in rem forfeiture proceeding, the style shall be "In re forfeiture of" (followed by the name of the general description of the property). All papers filed in the action shall be styled in such a manner as to indicate clearly the subject matter of the paper and the party requesting or obtaining relief. FL ST RCP Rule 1.100(c)(1).
3. *Writing and written defined.* Writing or written means a document containing information, an application, or a stipulation. FL ST RCP Rule 1.080(c).
4. *Rule abbreviations*
   a. The Florida Rules of Civil Procedure and shall be abbreviated as Fla.R.Civ.P. FL ST RCP Rule 1.010.
   b. The Florida Rules of Judicial Administration shall be abbreviated as Fla. R. Jud. Admin. FL ST J ADMIN Rule 2.110.

5. *Nonverification.* Except when otherwise specifically provided by the Florida Rules of Civil Procedure or an applicable statute, every pleading or other document of a party represented by an attorney need not be verified or accompanied by an affidavit. FL ST RCP Rule 1.030; FL ST J ADMIN Rule 2.515(a).
6. *Attorney signature*
   a. *Attorney signature.* Every pleading and other document of a party represented by an attorney shall be signed by at least one (1) attorney of record in that attorney's individual name whose current record Florida Bar address, telephone number, including area code, primary e-mail address and secondary e-mail addresses, if any, and Florida Bar number shall be stated, and who shall be duly licensed to practice law in Florida or who shall have received permission to appear in the particular case as provided in FL ST J ADMIN Rule 2.510. FL ST J ADMIN Rule 2.515(a).
      i. The attorney may be required by the court to give the address of, and to vouch for the attorney's authority to represent, the party. FL ST J ADMIN Rule 2.515(a).
      ii. The signature of an attorney shall constitute a certificate by the attorney that the attorney has read the pleading or other document; that to the best of the attorney's knowledge, information, and belief there is good ground to support it; and that it is not interposed for delay. FL ST J ADMIN Rule 2.515(a).
      iii. If a pleading is not signed or is signed with intent to defeat the purpose of FL ST J ADMIN Rule 2.515, it may be stricken and the action may proceed as though the pleading or other document had not been served. FL ST J ADMIN Rule 2.515(a).
   b. *Pro se litigant signature.* A party who is not represented by an attorney shall sign any pleading or other paper and state the party's address and telephone number, including area code. FL ST J ADMIN Rule 2.515(b).
   c. *Form of signature*
      i. The signatures required on pleadings and documents by FL ST J ADMIN Rule 2.515(a) and FL ST J ADMIN Rule 2.515(b) may be:
         - Original signatures;
         - Original signatures that have been reproduced by electronic means, such as on electronically transmitted documents or photocopied documents;
         - Electronic signatures using the "/s/," "s/," or "/s" formats by or at the direction of the person signing; or
         - Any other signature format authorized by general law, so long as the clerk where the proceeding is pending has the capability of receiving and has obtained approval from the Supreme Court of Florida to accept pleadings and documents with that signature format. FL ST J ADMIN Rule 2.515(c)(1).
      ii. An attorney, party, or other person who files a pleading or paper by electronic transmission that does not contain the original signature of that attorney, party, or other person shall file that identical pleading or paper in paper form containing an original signature of that attorney, party, or other person (hereinafter called the follow-up filing) immediately thereafter. The follow-up filing is not required if the Supreme Court of Florida has entered an order directing the clerk of court to discontinue accepting the follow-up filing. FL ST J ADMIN Rule 2.515(c)(2).
7. *Forms*
   a. *Process.* The forms of process, notice of lis pendens, and notice of action provided in the Florida Rules of Civil Procedure are sufficient. Variations from the forms do not void process or notices that are otherwise sufficient. FL ST RCP Rule 1.900(a).
   b. *Other forms.* The other forms provided in the Florida Rules of Civil Procedure are sufficient for the matters that are covered by them. So long as the substance is expressed without prolixity, the forms may be varied to meet the facts of a particular case. FL ST RCP Rule 1.900(b).
   c. *Formal matters.* Captions, except for the designation of the paper, are omitted from the forms provided in the Florida Rules of Civil Procedure. A general form of caption is the first form provided. Signatures are omitted from pleadings and motions. FL ST RCP Rule 1.900(c).

8. *Notices to persons with disabilities.* All notices of court proceedings to be held in a public facility, and all process compelling appearance at such proceedings, shall include the following statement in bold face, fourteen (14) point Times New Roman or Courier font: "If you are a person with a disability who needs any accommodation in order to participate in this proceeding, you are entitled, at no cost to you, to the provision of certain assistance. Please contact [identify applicable court personnel by name, address, and telephone number] at least seven (7) days before your scheduled court appearance, or immediately upon receiving this notification if the time before the scheduled appearance is less than seven (7) days; if you are hearing or voice impaired, call 711." FL ST J ADMIN Rule 2.540(c)(1). For more information, see FL ST 20 J CIR 2.15.
9. *Minimization of the filing of sensitive information*
    a. *Limitations for court filings.* Unless authorized by FL ST J ADMIN Rule 2.425(b), statute, another rule of court, or the court orders otherwise, designated sensitive information filed with the court must be limited to the following format:
        i. The initials of a person known to be a minor;
        ii. The year of birth of a person's birth date;
        iii. No portion of any: Social security number, Bank account number, Credit card account number, Charge account number, or Debit account number;
        iv. The last four digits of any: Taxpayer identification number (TIN), Employee identification number, Driver's license number, Passport number, Telephone number, Financial account number, except as set forth in FL ST J ADMIN Rule 2.425(a)(3), Brokerage account number, Insurance policy account number, Loan account number, Customer account number, or Patient or health care number;
        v. A truncated version of any: Email address, Computer user name, Password, or Personal identification number (PIN); and
        vi. A truncated version of any other sensitive information as provided by court order. FL ST J ADMIN Rule 2.425(a).
    b. *Exceptions.* FL ST J ADMIN Rule 2.425(a) does not apply to the following:
        i. An account number which identifies the property alleged to be the subject of a proceeding;
        ii. The record of an administrative or agency proceeding;
        iii. The record in appellate or review proceedings;
        iv. The birth date of a minor whenever the birth date is necessary for the court to establish or maintain subject matter jurisdiction;
        v. The name of a minor in any order relating to parental responsibility, time-sharing, or child support;
        vi. The name of a minor in any document or order affecting the minor's ownership of real property;
        vii. The birth date of a party in a writ of attachment or notice to payor;
        viii. In traffic and criminal proceedings: a pro se filing; a court filing that is related to a criminal matter or investigation and that is prepared before the filing of a criminal charge or is not filed as part of any docketed criminal case; an arrest or search warrant or any information in support thereof; a charging document and an affidavit or other documents filed in support of any charging document, including any driving records; a statement of particulars; discovery material introduced into evidence or otherwise filed with the court; and all information necessary for the proper issuance and execution of a subpoena duces tecum;
        ix. Information used by the clerk for case maintenance purposes or the courts for case management purposes; and
        x. Information which is relevant and material to an issue before the court. FL ST J ADMIN Rule 2.425(b).
    c. *Remedies.* Upon motion by a party or interested person or sua sponte by the court, the court may

order remedies, sanctions or both for a violation of FL ST J ADMIN Rule 2.425(a). Following notice and an opportunity to respond, the court may impose sanctions if such filing was not made in good faith. FL ST J ADMIN Rule 2.425(c).

d. *Motions not restricted.* FL ST J ADMIN Rule 2.425 does not restrict a party's right to move for protective order, to move to file documents under seal, or to request a determination of the confidentiality of records. FL ST J ADMIN Rule 2.425(d).

e. *Application.* FL ST J ADMIN Rule 2.425 does not affect the application of constitutional provisions, statutes, or rules of court regarding confidential information or access to public information. FL ST J ADMIN Rule 2.425(e).

F. Filing and Service Requirements

1. *Filing requirements.* All original documents must be filed with the court either before service or immediately thereafter, unless otherwise provided for by general law or other rules. If the original of any bond or other document is not placed in the court file, a certified copy must be so placed by the clerk. FL ST J ADMIN Rule 2.516(d). All documents shall be filed in conformity with the requirements of FL ST J ADMIN Rule 2.525. FL ST RCP Rule 1.080(b). All documents filed in any court shall be filed by electronic transmission in accordance with FL ST J ADMIN Rule 2.525. "Documents" means pleadings, motions, petitions, memoranda, briefs, notices, exhibits, declarations, affidavits, orders, judgments, decrees, writs, opinions, and any other paper or writing submitted to a court. FL ST J ADMIN Rule 2.520(a). All documents that are court records, as defined in FL ST J ADMIN Rule 2.430(a)(1), must be filed by electronic transmission, provided that: (1) the clerk has the ability to accept and retain such documents; (2) the clerk or the chief judge of the circuit has requested permission to accept documents filed by electronic transmission; and (3) the supreme court has entered an order granting permission to the clerk to accept documents filed by electronic transmission. FL ST J ADMIN Rule 2.525(c)(1).

   a. *Definition.* "Electronic transmission of documents" means the sending of information by electronic signals to, by or from a court or clerk, which when received can be transformed and stored or transmitted on paper, microfilm, magnetic storage device, optical imaging system, CD-ROM, flash drive, other electronic data storage system, server, case maintenance system ("CM"), electronic court filing ("ECF") system, statewide or local electronic portal ("e-portal"), or other electronic record keeping system authorized by the supreme court in a format sufficient to communicate the information on the original document in a readable format. Electronic transmission of documents includes electronic mail ("e-mail") and any internet-based transmission procedure, and may include procedures allowing for documents to be signed or verified by electronic means. FL ST J ADMIN Rule 2.525(a).

      i. The filing of documents with the court as required by the Florida Rules of Judicial Administration must be made by filing them with the clerk in accordance with FL ST J ADMIN Rule 2.525, except that the judge may permit documents to be filed with the judge, in which event the judge must note the filing date before him or her on the documents and transmit them to the clerk. The date of filing is that shown on the face of the document by the judge's notation or the clerk's time stamp, whichever is earlier. FL ST J ADMIN Rule 2.516(e).

   b. *Application.* Any court or clerk of the court may accept the electronic transmission of documents for filing after the clerk, together with input from the chief judge of the circuit, has obtained approval of the procedures and program for doing so from the Supreme Court of Florida. FL ST J ADMIN Rule 2.525(b).

   c. *Exceptions*

      i. Paper documents and other submissions may be manually submitted to the clerk or court:

         - When the clerk does not have the ability to accept and retain documents by electronic filing or has not had ECF Procedures approved by the supreme court;
         - For filing by any self-represented party or any self-represented nonparty unless specific ECF Procedures provide a means to file documents electronically. However, any self-represented nonparty that is a governmental or public agency and any other agency, partnership, corporation, or business entity acting on behalf of any governmental or public

agency may file documents by electronic transmission if such entity has the capability of filing documents electronically;

- For filing by attorneys excused from e-mail service in accordance with FL ST J ADMIN Rule 2.516(b);
- When submitting evidentiary exhibits or filing non-documentary materials;
- When the filing involves documents in excess of twenty-five (25) megabytes (25MB) in size. For such filings, documents may be transmitted using an electronic storage medium that the clerk has the ability to accept, which may include a CD-ROM, flash drive, or similar storage medium;
- When filed in open court, as permitted by the court;
- When paper filing is permitted by any approved statewide or local ECF procedures; and
- If any court determines that justice so requires. FL ST J ADMIN Rule 2.525(d).

ii. Any document in paper form submitted under FL ST J ADMIN Rule 2.525(d) is filed when it is received by the clerk or court and the clerk shall immediately thereafter convert any filed paper document to an electronic document. "Convert to an electronic document" means optically capturing an image of a paper document and using character recognition software to recover as much of the document's text as practicable and then indexing and storing the document in the official court file. FL ST J ADMIN Rule 2.525(c)(4).

iii. Any storage medium submitted under FL ST J ADMIN Rule 2.525(d)(5) is filed when received by the clerk or court and the clerk shall immediately thereafter transfer the electronic documents from the storage device to the official court file. FL ST J ADMIN Rule 2.525(c)(5).

iv. If the filer of any paper document authorized under FL ST J ADMIN Rule 2.525(d) provides a self-addressed, postage-paid envelope for return of the paper document after it is converted to electronic form by the clerk, the clerk shall place the paper document in the envelope and deposit it in the mail. Except when a paper document is required to be maintained, the clerk may recycle any filed paper document that is not to be returned to the filer. FL ST J ADMIN Rule 2.525(c)(6).

v. The clerk may convert any paper document filed before the effective date of FL ST J ADMIN Rule 2.525 to an electronic document. Unless the clerk is required to maintain the paper document, if the paper document has been converted to an electronic document by the clerk, the paper document is no longer part of the official court file and may be removed and recycled. FL ST J ADMIN Rule 2.525(c)(7).

d. *Official court file.* For information on what constitutes the official court file, please see FL ST J ADMIN Rule 2.525(c)(2), FL ST J ADMIN Rule 2.525(c)(3).

e. *Administration.* All attorneys, parties, or other persons using this rule to file documents are required to make arrangements with the court or clerk for the payment of any charges authorized by general law or the supreme court before filing any document by electronic transmission. FL ST J ADMIN Rule 2.525(f)(2).

f. *Filing date.* The filing date for an electronically transmitted document is the date and time that such filing is acknowledged by an electronic stamp or otherwise, pursuant to any procedure set forth in any ECF Procedures approved by the supreme court, or the date the last page of such filing is received by the court or clerk. FL ST J ADMIN Rule 2.525(f)(3).

g. *Accessibility.* All documents transmitted in any electronic form under FL ST J ADMIN Rule 2.525 must comply with the accessibility requirements of FL ST J ADMIN Rule 2.526. FL ST J ADMIN Rule 2.525(g).

2. *Service requirements.* Every pleading subsequent to the initial pleading, all orders, and every other

document filed in the action must be served in conformity with the requirements of FL ST J ADMIN Rule 2.516. FL ST RCP Rule 1.080(a).

a. *Service; Generally.* The timing and manner of service should not be used to the disadvantage of the party receiving the papers. FL ST 20 J CIR 2.20(IV)(C)(1).

   i. Papers and memoranda of law should not be served at court appearances without advance notice to opposing counsel and should not be served so close to a court appearance so as to inhibit the ability of opposing counsel to prepare for that appearance or to respond to the papers. Should the attorney do so, the court is urged to take appropriate action in response, including continuing the matter to allow opposing counsel to prepare and respond. FL ST 20 J CIR 2.20(IV)(C)(2).

   ii. Papers should not be served in order to take advantage of an opponent's known absence from the office or at a time or in a manner designed to inconvenience an adversary, such as late on Friday afternoon or the day preceding a secular or religious holiday. FL ST 20 J CIR 2.20(IV)(C)(3).

   iii. Service should be made personally or by courtesy copy facsimile transmission when it is likely that service by mail, even when allowed, will prejudice the opposing party or will not provide the opposing party with a reasonable time to respond. FL ST 20 J CIR 2.20(IV)(C)(4).

b. *Service; When required.* Unless the court otherwise orders, or a statute or supreme court administrative order specifies a different means of service, every pleading subsequent to the initial pleading and every other document filed in any court proceeding, except applications for witness subpoenas and documents served by formal notice or required to be served in the manner provided for service of formal notice, must be served in accordance with FL ST J ADMIN Rule 2.516 on each party. No service need be made on parties against whom a default has been entered, except that pleadings asserting new or additional claims against them must be served in the manner provided for service of summons. FL ST J ADMIN Rule 2.516(a).

   i. *Copies of court submissions.* Copies of any submissions to the court (such as correspondence, memoranda of law, motions, case law, etc.) should simultaneously be provided to opposing counsel by substantially the same method of delivery by which they are provided to the court. For example, if a memorandum of law is hand-delivered to the court, at substantially the same time a copy should be hand-delivered or faxed to opposing counsel. FL ST 20 J CIR 2.20(IV)(J)(4).

c. *Service; How made.* When service is required or permitted to be made upon a party represented by an attorney, service must be made upon the attorney unless service upon the party is ordered by the court. FL ST J ADMIN Rule 2.516(b).

   i. *Service by electronic mail ("e-mail").* All documents required or permitted to be served on another party must be served by e-mail, unless FL ST J ADMIN Rule 2.516 otherwise provides. When, in addition to service by e-mail, the sender also utilizes another means of service provided for in FL ST J ADMIN Rule 2.516(b)(2), any differing time limits and other provisions applicable to that other means of service control. FL ST J ADMIN Rule 2.516(b)(1). Any document electronically transmitted to a court or clerk must also be served on all parties and interested persons in accordance with the applicable rules of court. FL ST J ADMIN Rule 2.525(e)(2).

      - *Service on attorneys.* Upon appearing in a proceeding, an attorney must serve a designation of a primary e-mail address and may designate no more than two (2) secondary e-mail addresses. Thereafter, service must be directed to all designated e-mail addresses in that proceeding. Every document filed by an attorney thereafter must include the primary e-mail address of that attorney and any secondary e-mail addresses. If an attorney does not designate any e-mail address for service, documents may be served on that attorney at the e-mail address on record with The Florida Bar. FL ST J ADMIN Rule 2.516(b)(1)(A).
      - *Exception to e-mail service on attorneys.* Service by an attorney on another attorney must be made by e-mail unless excused by the court. Upon motion by an attorney demonstrating

that the attorney has no e-mail account and lacks access to the Internet at the attorney's office, the court may excuse the attorney from the requirements of e-mail service. Service on and by an attorney excused by the court from e-mail service must be by the means provided in FL ST J ADMIN Rule 2.516(b)(2). FL ST J ADMIN Rule 2.516(b)(1)(B).

- *Service on and by parties not represented by an attorney.* Any party not represented by an attorney may serve a designation of a primary e-mail address and also may designate no more than two (2) secondary e-mail addresses to which service must be directed in that proceeding by the means provided in FL ST J ADMIN Rule 2.516(b)(1). If a party not represented by an attorney does not designate an e-mail address for service in a proceeding, service on and by that party must be by the means provided in FL ST J ADMIN Rule 2.516(b)(2). FL ST J ADMIN Rule 2.516(b)(1)(C).
- *Time of service.* Service by e-mail is complete when it is sent. FL ST J ADMIN Rule 2.516(b)(1)(D). An e-mail is deemed served on the date it is sent. FL ST J ADMIN Rule 2.516(b)(1)(D)(i). If the sender learns that the e-mail did not reach the address of the person to be served, the sender must immediately send another copy by e-mail, or by a means authorized by FL ST J ADMIN Rule 2.516(b)(2). FL ST J ADMIN Rule 2.516(b)(1)(D)(ii). E-mail service is treated as service by mail for the computation of time. FL ST J ADMIN Rule 2.516(b)(1)(D)(iii).

ii. *Format of e-mail for service.* Service of a document by e-mail is made by attaching a copy of the document in PDF format to an e-mail sent to all addresses designated by the attorney or party. FL ST J ADMIN Rule 2.516(b)(1)(E).

- All documents served by e-mail must be attached to an e-mail message containing a subject line beginning with the words "SERVICE OF COURT DOCUMENT" in all capital letters, followed by the case number of the proceeding in which the documents are being served. FL ST J ADMIN Rule 2.516(b)(1)(E)(i).
- The body of the e-mail must identify the court in which the proceeding is pending, the case number, the name of the initial party on each side, the title of each document served with that e-mail, and the sender's name and telephone number. FL ST J ADMIN Rule 2.516(b)(1)(E)(ii).
- Any document served by e-mail may be signed by the "/s/" format, as long as the filed original is signed in accordance with the applicable rule of procedure. FL ST J ADMIN Rule 2.516(b)(1)(E)(iii).
- Any e-mail which, together with its attached documents, exceeds five megabytes (5MB) in size, must be divided and sent as separate e-mails, no one of which may exceed five megabytes (5MB) in size and each of which must be sequentially numbered in the subject line. FL ST J ADMIN Rule 2.516(b)(1)(E)(iv).

iii. *Service by other means.* In addition to, and not in lieu of, service by e-mail, service may also be made upon attorneys by any of the means specified in FL ST J ADMIN Rule 2.516(b)(2). Service on and by all parties who are not represented by an attorney and who do not designate an e-mail address, and on and by all attorneys excused from e-mail service, must be made by delivering a copy of the document or by mailing it to the party or attorney at their last known address or, if no address is known, by leaving it with the clerk of the court. Service by mail is complete upon mailing. Delivery of a copy within FL ST J ADMIN Rule 2.516 is complete upon:

- Handing it to the attorney or to the party,
- Leaving it at the attorney's or party's office with a clerk or other person in charge thereof,
- If there is no one in charge, leaving it in a conspicuous place therein,
- If the office is closed or the person to be served has no office, leaving it at the person's usual place of abode with some person of his or her family above fifteen (15) years of age and informing such person of the contents, or
- Transmitting it by facsimile to the attorney's or party's office with a cover sheet containing

the sender's name, firm, address, telephone number, and facsimile number, and the number of pages transmitted. When service is made by facsimile, a copy must also be served by any other method permitted by FL ST J ADMIN Rule 2.516. Facsimile service occurs when transmission is complete. FL ST J ADMIN Rule 2.516(b)(2)(A) through FL ST J ADMIN Rule 2.516(b)(2)(E).

- Service by delivery after 5:00 p.m. must be deemed to have been made by mailing on the date of delivery. FL ST J ADMIN Rule 2.516(b)(2)(F).

d. *Service; Numerous defendants.* In actions when the parties are unusually numerous, the court may regulate the service contemplated by the Florida Rules of Judicial Administration on motion or on its own initiative in such manner as may be found to be just and reasonable. FL ST J ADMIN Rule 2.516(c).

e. *Service by clerk.* Service of notices and other documents required to be made by the clerk must also be done as provided in FL ST J ADMIN Rule 2.516(b). FL ST J ADMIN Rule 2.516(g).

G. Hearings

1. The parties may be required to participate in pretrial proceedings to consider and determine the necessity or desirability of an amendment to a pleading. FL ST RCP Rule 1.200(b)(2); FL-PP § 2:151.

H. Forms

1. Official Amended Answer Forms for Florida

a. Caption. FL ST RCP Form 1.901.

b. Notice of compliance when constitutional challenge is brought. FL ST RCP Form 1.975.

2. Amended Answer Forms for Florida

a. Form for amendment to answer. FL-RCPF R 1.190(50).

b. Form for supplement to pleading. FL-RCPF R 1.190(102).

I. Checklist

(I) ❑ Matters to be considered by plaintiff

(a) ❑ Required documents

(1) ❑ Amended answer

(2) ❑ Certificate of service

(b) ❑ Supplemental documents

(1) ❑ Exhibits

(2) ❑ Notice of constitutional question

(c) ❑ Timing

(1) ❑ A party may amend a pleading once as a matter of course at any time before a responsive pleading is served

(2) ❑ If the pleading is one to which no responsive pleading is permitted and the action has not been placed on the trial calendar, may so amend it at any time within twenty (20) days after it is served

Motions, Oppositions and Replies
Motion to Strike

Document Last Updated January 2013

A. Applicable Rules

1. *State rules*

a. Rules of court. FL ST RCP Rule 1.010; FL ST J ADMIN Rule 2.110.

b. Nonverification of pleadings. FL ST RCP Rule 1.030.
c. Service and filing of pleadings, orders, and documents. FL ST RCP Rule 1.080.
d. Time. FL ST RCP Rule 1.090.
e. Pleadings and motions. FL ST RCP Rule 1.100.
f. Defenses. FL ST RCP Rule 1.140.
g. Sham pleadings. FL ST RCP Rule 1.150.
h. Motions. FL ST RCP Rule 1.160.
i. Relief from judgment, decrees, or orders. FL ST RCP Rule 1.540.
j. Mediation and arbitration. FL ST RCP Rule 1.700; FL ST RCP Rule 1.710; FL ST RCP Rule 1.720; FL ST RCP Rule 1.730; FL ST RCP Rule 1.750; FL ST RCP Rule 1.800; FL ST RCP Rule 1.810; FL ST RCP Rule 1.820; FL ST RCP Rule 1.830.
k. Forms. FL ST RCP Rule 1.900.
l. Minimization of the filing of sensitive information. FL ST J ADMIN Rule 2.425.
m. Retention of court records. FL ST J ADMIN Rule 2.430.
n. Foreign attorneys. FL ST J ADMIN Rule 2.510.
o. Signature of attorneys and parties. FL ST J ADMIN Rule 2.515.
p. Paper. FL ST J ADMIN Rule 2.520.
q. Electronic filing. FL ST J ADMIN Rule 2.525.
r. Accessibility of information and technology. FL ST J ADMIN Rule 2.526.
s. Communication equipment. FL ST J ADMIN Rule 2.530.
t. Court reporting. FL ST J ADMIN Rule 2.535.
u. Requests for accommodations by persons with disabilities. FL ST J ADMIN Rule 2.540.
v. Case management. FL ST J ADMIN Rule 2.545.

2. *Local rules*
   a. Exclusions from mediation. FL ST 20 J CIR 1.9.
   b. Establishment and implementation of civil case management plan. FL ST 20 J CIR 1.13.
   c. Size of paper. FL ST 20 J CIR 2.9.
   d. Telephonic motion hearings set for not longer than fifteen minutes in circuit and county civil cases. FL ST 20 J CIR 1.10.
   e. Americans with Disabilities Act; Notification of court proceedings. FL ST 20 J CIR 2.15.
   f. Standards of professional courtesy and conduct and establishment of peer review program. FL ST 20 J CIR 2.20.

B. Timing

1. *Motion to strike.* A party may move to strike or the court may strike redundant, immaterial, impertinent, or scandalous matter from any pleading at any time. FL ST RCP Rule 1.140(f).
2. *Motion to strike; Failure to state a legal defense.* If a pleading sets forth a claim for relief to which the adverse party is not required to serve a responsive pleading, the adverse party may assert any defense in law or fact to that claim for relief at the trial, except that the objection of failure to state a legal defense in an answer or reply shall be asserted by motion to strike the defense within twenty (20) days after service of the answer or reply. FL ST RCP Rule 1.140(b).
3. *Motion to strike; Sham pleadings.* If a party deems any pleading or part thereof filed by another party to be a sham, that party may move to strike the pleading or part thereof before the cause is set for trial. FL ST RCP Rule 1.150(a).
4. *General motion timing.* A copy of any written motion which may not be heard ex parte and a copy of the

notice of the hearing thereof shall be served a reasonable time before the time specified for the hearing. FL ST RCP Rule 1.090(d).

a. *Notice of hearing.* Except in emergency situations, attorneys should provide opposing counsel, parties, witnesses, and other affected persons, sufficient notice of depositions, hearings and other proceedings. FL ST 20 J CIR 2.20(IV)(B)(1). Attorneys should notify opposing counsel of any hearing time reserved as soon as practicable. FL ST 20 J CIR 2.20(IV)(B)(3). When hearing time is obtained, attorneys should promptly prepare and serve all counsel of record with notice of the hearing. Do not delay in providing such notice. FL ST 20 J CIR 2.20(IV)(B)(4).

  i. As a general rule, notice should be provided (not including time for service) no less than five (5) business days for hearings. FL ST 20 J CIR 2.20(IV)(B)(1).

5. *Notice and request to participate in telephonic motion hearing.* Notice by the requesting party must be provided by mailing a copy of the written request at least five (5) days prior to the day of the hearing, or by delivering a copy of the written request to the other parties or, if represented by counsel, to the other parties' attorney(s) no later than 5:00 p.m. two (2) business days prior to the day of the hearing. FL ST 20 J CIR 1.10. Refer to the Hearings section of this document for more information.

6. *Computation of time*

a. *Generally.* Computation of time shall be governed by FL ST J ADMIN Rule 2.514. FL ST RCP Rule 1.090(a). The following rules apply in computing time periods specified in any rule of procedure, local rule, court order, or statute that does not specify a method of computing time. FL ST J ADMIN Rule 2.514(a).

  i. *Period stated in days or a longer unit.* When the period is stated in days or a longer unit of time (A) exclude the day of the event that triggers the period; (B) count every day, including intermediate Saturdays, Sundays, and legal holidays; and (C) include the last day of the period, but if the last day is a Saturday, Sunday, or legal holiday, or falls within any period of time extended through an order of the chief justice under FL ST J ADMIN Rule 2.205(a)(2)(B)(iv), the period continues to run until the end of the next day that is not a Saturday, Sunday, or legal holiday and does not fall within any period of time extended through an order of the chief justice. FL ST J ADMIN Rule 2.514(a)(1).

  ii. *Period stated in hours.* When the period is stated in hours (A) begin counting immediately on the occurrence of the event that triggers the period; (B) count every hour, including hours during intermediate Saturdays, Sundays, and legal holidays; and (C) if the period would end on a Saturday, Sunday, or legal holiday, or during any period of time extended through an order of the chief justice under FL ST J ADMIN Rule 2.205(a)(2)(B)(iv), the period continues to run until the same time on the next day that is not a Saturday, Sunday, or legal holiday and does not fall within any period of time extended through an order of the chief justice. FL ST J ADMIN Rule 2.514(a)(2).

  iii. *Period stated in days less than seven (7) days.* When the period stated in days is less than seven (7) days, intermediate Saturdays, Sundays, and legal holidays shall be excluded in the computation. FL ST J ADMIN Rule 2.514(a)(3).

  iv. *"Last day" defined.* Unless a different time is set by a statute, local rule, or court order, the last day ends (A) for electronic filing or for service by any means, at midnight; and (B) for filing by other means, when the clerk's office is scheduled to close. FL ST J ADMIN Rule 2.514(a)(4).

  v. *"Next day" defined.* The "next day" is determined by continuing to count forward when the period is measured after an event and backward when measured before an event. FL ST J ADMIN Rule 2.514(a)(5).

  vi. *"Legal holiday" defined.* "Legal holiday" means (A) the day set aside by FL ST § 110.117, for observing New Year's Day, Martin Luther King, Jr.'s Birthday, Memorial Day, Independence Day, Labor Day, Veterans' Day, Thanksgiving Day, the Friday after Thanksgiving Day, or Christmas Day, and (B) any day observed as a holiday by the clerk's office or as designated by the chief judge. FL ST J ADMIN Rule 2.514(a)(6).

b. *Additional time after service by mail or e-mail.* When a party may or must act within a specified time after service and service is made by mail or e-mail, five (5) days are added after the period that would otherwise expire under FL ST J ADMIN Rule 2.514(a). FL ST J ADMIN Rule 2.514(b).

c. *Enlargement.* When an act is required or allowed to be done at or within a specified time by order of court, by the Florida Rules of Civil Procedure, or by notice given thereunder, for cause shown the court at any time in its discretion (1) with or without notice, may order the period enlarged if request therefor is made before the expiration of the period originally prescribed or as extended by a previous order, or (2) upon motion made and notice after the expiration of the specified period, may permit the act to be done when failure to act was the result of excusable neglect, but it may not extend the time for making a motion for new trial, for rehearing, or to alter or amend a judgment; making a motion for relief from a judgment under FL ST RCP Rule 1.540(b); taking an appeal or filing a petition for certiorari; or making a motion for a directed verdict. FL ST RCP Rule 1.090(b).

d. *Unaffected by expiration of term.* The period of time provided for the doing of any act or the taking of any proceeding shall not be affected or limited by the continued existence or expiration of a term of court. The continued existence or expiration of a term of court in no way affects the power of a court to do any act or take any proceeding in any action which is or has been pending before it. FL ST RCP Rule 1.090(c).

C. General Requirements

1. *Motions generally*

a. *Contents.* An application to the court for an order shall be by motion which shall be made in writing unless made during a hearing or trial, shall state with particularity the grounds therefor, and shall set forth the relief or order sought. The requirement of writing is fulfilled if the motion is stated in a written notice of the hearing of the motion. All notices of hearing shall specify each motion or other matter to be heard. FL ST RCP Rule 1.100(b).

i. *Notice of hearing.* The notice of hearing should indicate on its face whether the date and time have been coordinated with opposing counsel. If the attorney has been unable to coordinate the hearing with opposing counsel, the notice should state the specific good faith efforts the attorney undertook to coordinate or why coordination was not obtained. FL ST 20 J CIR 2.20(IV)(B)(5).

b. *Particularity requirement.* The court considers a motion in the light of the substantive law, rule or statute to make its determination. Some rules require a statement of the grounds for a motion under the rule. Failure to give the grounds will result in denial of the motion. This should be the result in all situations when the ground for the motion is not inherent in the rule. FL-PRACPROC § 9:3. The requirement is nevertheless an important one, first because of the due process notice rights of the respondent, as well as for the assistance it provides to the court in its preparation for the hearing or, absent a hearing, for disposition. 4 FLPRAC R 1.100.

2. *Conference with opposing counsel.* Attorneys should, whenever possible, prior to filing or upon receiving a motion, contact opposing counsel to determine if the matter can be resolved in whole or in part. This may alleviate the need for a hearing on the motion or allow submission of an agreed order in lieu of a hearing. FL ST 20 J CIR 2.20(IV)(L)(2).

a. *Conference required.* Except in emergency situations, before filing any motion in a civil case, except a motion for injunctive relief, for judgment on the pleadings, for summary judgment, to dismiss or to permit maintenance of a class action, to dismiss for failure to state a cause of action, to dismiss for lack of prosecution, or to otherwise involuntarily dismiss an action, the moving party shall confer with counsel for the opposing party in a good faith effort to resolve the issues raised by the motion, and shall file with the motion a statement certifying that the moving counsel has conferred with opposing counsel and that counsel have been unable to agree on the resolution of the motion. FL ST 20 J CIR 2.20(IV)(I)(2).

3. *Motion to strike under FL ST RCP Rule 1.140.* Two (2) types of motion to strike are authorized by FL ST RCP Rule 1.140. One is used to eliminate immaterial, redundant, impertinent or scandalous allegations. The other is used to test the legal sufficiency of a defense. FL-PRACPROC § 10:6.

a. *Motion to strike to eliminate immaterial, redundant, impertinent or scandalous allegations*

i. As used in FL ST RCP Rule 1.140(f), redundant means allegations that are foreign to the issues or needless repetition of allegations. Immaterial means allegations having no essential or important relationship to the issues or unnecessary elaboration of material allegations. Impertinent means allegations that do not belong to the issue and are not necessary to it. Scandalous means unnecessary allegations censuring or accusing a party. FL-PRACPROC § 10:6.

ii. The motion can be made at any time and does not toll the time for pleading. FL-PRACPROC § 10:6.

iii. The motion reaches improper allegations of damages. When directed to an entire paragraph and any part of it is proper, the motion should be denied. Leave to amend should be granted after striking part of a pleading unless a proper amendment cannot be made. FL-PRACPROC § 10:6.

iv. The use of a motion to strike is not favored by the courts and the remedy is used sparingly. Florida courts have held that an allegation must be "wholly irrelevant" and that if there is some doubt it must be resolved in support of the pleading and against the party moving to strike. If any part of an allegation is relevant, then that part should not be stricken from the pleading. 5 FLPRAC § 7:30.

b. *Motion to strike the legal sufficiency of a defense*

i. The legal insufficiency of a defense alleged in an answer or reply is attacked by a motion to strike. It is the counterpart of a motion to dismiss for failure to state a cause of action directed to a pleading seeking affirmative relief. FL-PRACPROC § 10:7.

ii. A motion to strike a defense tests only the legal sufficiency of the defense, and it is reversible error for a trial court to strike the defense where evidence may be presented to support it. Burns v. Equilease Corp., 357 So.2d 786, 24, 24 U.C.C. Rep.Serv. 254 (Fla. 3d DCA 1978); 20 FLPRAC § 3:15.

4. *Sham pleadings.* If a party deems any pleading or part thereof filed by another party to be a sham, that party may move to strike the pleading or part thereof before the cause is set for trial and the court shall hear the motion, taking evidence of the respective parties, and if the motion is sustained, the pleading to which the motion is directed shall be stricken. Default and summary judgment on the merits may be entered in the discretion of the court or the court may permit additional pleadings to be filed for good cause shown. FL ST RCP Rule 1.150(a).

a. *Contents of motion.* The motion to strike shall be verified and shall set forth fully the facts on which the movant relies and may be supported by affidavit. No traverse of the motion shall be required. FL ST RCP Rule 1.150(b).

b. *Allegations supported by evidence.* The issue is not whether the allegations are material or proper, but whether the allegations are supported by evidence. 5 FLPRAC § 7:30.

5. *Arbitration and mediation.* Attorneys are encouraged to utilize arbitration, mediation or other forms of alternative dispute resolution if economically feasible. FL ST 20 J CIR 2.20(IV)(N)(3).

a. *Referral to arbitration and mediation.* Except as hereinafter provided or as otherwise prohibited by law, the presiding judge may enter an order referring all or any part of a contested civil matter to mediation or arbitration. The parties to any contested civil matter may file a written stipulation to mediate or arbitrate any issue between them at any time. Such stipulation shall be incorporated into the order of referral. FL ST RCP Rule 1.700(a).

b. *Arbitration*

i. *Exclusions.* A civil action shall be ordered to arbitration or arbitration in conjunction with mediation upon stipulation of the parties. A civil action may be ordered to arbitration or arbitration in conjunction with mediation upon motion of any party or by the court, if the judge determines the action to be of such a nature that arbitration could be of benefit to the litigants or the court. FL ST RCP Rule 1.800.

- Under no circumstances may the following categories of actions be referred to arbitration: (1) bond estreatures; (2) habeas corpus or other extraordinary writs; (3) bond validations; (4) civil or criminal contempt; (5) such other matters as may be specified by order of the chief judge in the circuit. FL ST RCP Rule 1.800.

ii. For more information regarding arbitration, please see FL ST RCP Rule 1.810; FL ST RCP Rule 1.820; FL ST RCP Rule 1.830.

c. *Mediation.* For more information regarding mediation, please see FL ST RCP Rule 1.710; FL ST RCP Rule 1.720; FL ST RCP Rule 1.730; FL ST RCP Rule 1.750; and FL ST 20 J CIR 1.9.

6. *Rules of court*

a. *Rules of civil procedure.* The Florida Rules of Civil Procedure apply to all actions of a civil nature and all special statutory proceedings in the circuit courts and county courts except those to which the Florida Probate Rules, the Florida Family Law Rules of Procedure, or the Small Claims Rules apply. FL ST RCP Rule 1.010.

i. The form, content, procedure, and time for pleading in all special statutory proceedings shall be as prescribed by the statutes governing the proceeding unless the Florida Rules of Civil Procedure specifically provide to the contrary. FL ST RCP Rule 1.010.

ii. The Florida Rules of Civil Procedure shall be construed to secure the just, speedy, and inexpensive determination of every action. FL ST RCP Rule 1.010.

b. *Rules of judicial administration.* The Florida Rules of Judicial Administration shall apply to administrative matters in all courts to which the Florida Rules of Judicial Administration are applicable by their terms. The Florida Rules of Judicial Administration shall be construed to secure the speedy and inexpensive determination of every proceeding to which they are applicable. The Florida Rules of Judicial Administration shall supersede all conflicting rules and statutes. FL ST J ADMIN Rule 2.110.

7. *Civil case management plan.* There is established within the Twentieth Judicial Circuit a Civil Case Management Plan applicable to circuit civil cases, which will be administered by the Administrative Office of the Courts through direction of the Circuit Administrative Judges in each county for the implementation of enhanced case management procedures and guidelines for the timely and efficient processing of circuit civil cases and reduction in the pending backlog of civil cases. FL ST 20 J CIR 1.13.

a. The basis for the Civil Case Management Plan is included in FL ST 20 J CIR 1.13, identified in Attachment A as the "Civil Differentiated Case Management (DCM) Procedures and Backlog Reduction Plan," and is incorporated as if fully set forth in FL ST 20 J CIR 1.13. The Civil Case Management Plan is to be used as a model for the purpose of establishing time standards, improving the courts ability to provide early and continuous management of civil cases as required by FL ST J ADMIN Rule 2.545, and to promote uniformity of practice throughout the Twentieth Judicial Circuit. FL ST 20 J CIR 1.13.

b. Full implementation of the Civil DCM Case Management Procedures (Attachment A), including all uniform circuitwide procedures and forms, shall apply to all civil cases filed in Lee and Collier counties, effective January 1, 2011. Even though full implementation may be delayed in Charlotte, Hendry, and Glades counties, all civil time standards and goals, and the use of civil Case Managers and Magistrates to assist trial judges in the process of civil case management and backlog reduction programs, shall be effective circuitwide immediately. FL ST 20 J CIR 1.13.

c. For more information on the civil case management plan, refer to the specific county website and/or see FL ST 20 J CIR 1.13.

D. Documents

1. *Required documents*

a. *Notice of hearing/Motion.* An application to the court for an order shall be by motion which shall be made in writing unless made during a hearing or trial, shall state with particularity the grounds therefor, and shall set forth the relief or order sought. The requirement of writing is fulfilled if the motion is stated in a written notice of the hearing of the motion. All notices of hearing shall specify each motion or other matter to be heard. FL ST RCP Rule 1.100(b). Refer to the General Requirements section of this document for more information on the notice of hearing.

i. *Notices to persons with disabilities.* See the Format section of this KeyRules document for further information.

b. *Certification.* Except in emergency situations, before filing any motion in a civil case, except a motion for injunctive relief, for judgment on the pleadings, for summary judgment, to dismiss or to permit maintenance of a class action, to dismiss for failure to state a cause of action, to dismiss for lack of prosecution, or to otherwise involuntarily dismiss an action, the moving party shall confer with counsel for the opposing party in a good faith effort to resolve the issues raised by the motion, and shall file with the motion a statement certifying that the moving counsel has conferred with opposing counsel and that counsel have been unable to agree on the resolution of the motion. FL ST 20 J CIR 2.20(IV)(I)(2).

c. *Certificate of service.* When any attorney certifies in substance: "I certify that a copy hereof has been furnished to (here insert name or names and addresses used for service) by (e-mail) (delivery) (mail) (fax) on .... (date) ....________________ Attorney" the certificate is taken as prima facie proof of such service in compliance with FL ST J ADMIN Rule 2.516. FL ST J ADMIN Rule 2.516(f).

2. *Supplemental documents*

 a. *Proposed order.* The court may require that orders or judgments be prepared by a party, may require the party to furnish the court with stamped, addressed envelopes for service of the order or judgment, and may require that proposed orders and judgments be furnished to all parties before entry by the court of the order or judgment. FL ST J ADMIN Rule 2.516(h)(1).

  i. Unless otherwise instructed by the court, or agreed to by counsel, all proposed orders shall be provided to other counsel with a reasonable time for approval or comment prior to submission to the court. Opposing counsel should promptly communicate any objections thereto. Thereafter, the drafting attorney should promptly submit a copy of the proposed order to the court and advise the court as to whether or not it has been approved by opposing counsel. FL ST 20 J CIR 2.20(IV)(I)(4).

  ii. Orders prepared by counsel must fairly and adequately represent the ruling of the court, and counsel shall make a good faith effort to agree upon the form of the order prior to submitting it to the court. Attorneys should not submit controverted orders to the court with a copy to opposing counsel for "objections within ______ days". Courts prefer to know that the order is either agreed upon or opposed. FL ST 20 J CIR 2.20(IV)(I)(5).

  iii. Attorneys should not use post-hearing submissions of proposed orders as a guise to reargue the merits of the matter. FL ST 20 J CIR 2.20(IV)(I)(6).

  iv. If asked by the court to prepare an order, counsel should furnish a copy of the order, and any transmitted letter, to opposing counsel at the time the material is submitted to the court. FL ST 20 J CIR 2.20(IV)(J)(4).

 b. *Notice of constitutional question.* A party that files a pleading, written motion, or other paper drawing into question the constitutionality of a state statute or a county or municipal charter, ordinance, or franchise must promptly (1) file a notice of constitutional question stating the question and identifying the paper that raises it; and (2) serve the notice and the pleading, written motion, or other paper drawing into question the constitutionality of a state statute or a county or municipal charter, ordinance, or franchise on the Attorney General or the state attorney of the judicial circuit in which the action is pending, by either certified or registered mail. Service of the notice and pleading, written motion, or other paper does not require joinder of the Attorney General or the state attorney as a party to the action. FL ST RCP Rule 1.071.

 c. *Notice and request to participate in telephonic motion hearing.* In instances where a civil motion hearing is scheduled for not longer than fifteen (15) minutes, a party may file a written request to participate via conference or speaker telephone, or other applicable communication equipment, and shall provide notice to the Court and the parties to the motion. FL ST 20 J CIR 1.10. Refer to the Timing and Hearings sections of this document for more information.

E. Format

1. *Documents; Type and size.* Documents subject to the exceptions set forth in FL ST J ADMIN Rule 2.525(d) shall be filed on recycled paper measuring eight and one half by eleven (8 1/2 by 11) inches. For purposes of FL ST J ADMIN Rule 2.520, paper is recycled if it contains a minimum content of fifty (50)

percent waste paper. Xerographic reduction of legal-size (eight and one half by fourteen (8 1/2 by 14) inches) documents to letter size (eight and one half by eleven (8 1/2 by 11) inches) is prohibited. All other documents filed by electronic transmission shall be filed in a format capable of being printed in a format consistent with the provisions of FL ST J ADMIN Rule 2.250. FL ST J ADMIN Rule 2.520(b); FL ST 20 J CIR 2.9.

a. *Exhibits.* Any exhibit or attachment filed with pleadings or papers may be filed in its original size. FL ST J ADMIN Rule 2.520(c); FL ST 20 J CIR 2.9.

b. *Recording space.* On all papers and documents prepared and filed by the court or by any party to a proceeding which are to be recorded in the public records of any county, including but not limited to final money judgments and notices of lis pendens, a three (3) inch by three (3) inch space at the top right-hand corner on the first page and a one (1) inch by three (3) inch space at the top right-hand corner on each subsequent page shall be left blank and reserved for use by the clerk of court. FL ST J ADMIN Rule 2.520(d).

i. *Exceptions to recording space.* Any papers or documents created by persons or entities over which the filing party has no control, including but not limited to wills, codicils, trusts, or other testamentary documents; documents prepared or executed by any public officer; documents prepared, executed, acknowledged, or proved outside of the State of Florida; or documents created by State or Federal government agencies, may be filed without the space required by FL ST J ADMIN Rule 2.520. FL ST J ADMIN Rule 2.520(e).

c. *Noncompliance.* No clerk of court is permitted to refuse to file any document or paper because of noncompliance with the Florida Rules of Judicial Administration. However, upon request of the clerk of court, noncomplying documents must be resubmitted in accordance with the formatting rules. FL ST J ADMIN Rule 2.520(f).

i. When time of filing is critical, the Clerk shall accept pleadings, motions, petitions, briefs, notices, orders, judgments, decrees, opinions, or other papers or official documents on other than eight and one half by eleven (8 1/2 by 11) inch paper but shall then require that the document be resubmitted to comply with FL ST J ADMIN Rule 2.520. FL ST 20 J CIR 2.9.

2. *Caption.* Every pleading, motion, order, judgment, or other paper shall have a caption containing the name of the court, the file number, and except for in rem proceedings, including forfeiture proceedings, the name of the first party on each side with an appropriate indication of other parties, and a designation identifying the party filing it and its nature or the nature of the order, as the case may be. In any in rem proceeding, every pleading, motion, order, judgment, or other paper shall have a caption containing the name of the court, the file number, the style "In re" (followed by the name or general description of the property), and a designation of the person or entity filing it and its nature or the nature of the order, as the case may be. In an in rem forfeiture proceeding, the style shall be "In re forfeiture of" (followed by the name of the general description of the property). All papers filed in the action shall be styled in such a manner as to indicate clearly the subject matter of the paper and the party requesting or obtaining relief. FL ST RCP Rule 1.100(c)(1).

3. *Writing and written defined.* Writing or written means a document containing information, an application, or a stipulation. FL ST RCP Rule 1.080(c).

4. *Rule abbreviations*

a. The Florida Rules of Civil Procedure and shall be abbreviated as Fla.R.Civ.P. FL ST RCP Rule 1.010.

b. The Florida Rules of Judicial Administration shall be abbreviated as Fla. R. Jud. Admin. FL ST J ADMIN Rule 2.110.

5. *Nonverification.* Except when otherwise specifically provided by the Florida Rules of Civil Procedure or an applicable statute, every pleading or other document of a party represented by an attorney need not be verified or accompanied by an affidavit. FL ST RCP Rule 1.030; FL ST J ADMIN Rule 2.515(a).

6. *Attorney signature*

a. *Attorney signature.* Every pleading and other document of a party represented by an attorney shall be

signed by at least one (1) attorney of record in that attorney's individual name whose current record Florida Bar address, telephone number, including area code, primary e-mail address and secondary e-mail addresses, if any, and Florida Bar number shall be stated, and who shall be duly licensed to practice law in Florida or who shall have received permission to appear in the particular case as provided in FL ST J ADMIN Rule 2.510. FL ST J ADMIN Rule 2.515(a).

i. The attorney may be required by the court to give the address of, and to vouch for the attorney's authority to represent, the party. FL ST J ADMIN Rule 2.515(a).

ii. The signature of an attorney shall constitute a certificate by the attorney that the attorney has read the pleading or other document; that to the best of the attorney's knowledge, information, and belief there is good ground to support it; and that it is not interposed for delay. FL ST J ADMIN Rule 2.515(a).

iii. If a pleading is not signed or is signed with intent to defeat the purpose of FL ST J ADMIN Rule 2.515, it may be stricken and the action may proceed as though the pleading or other document had not been served. FL ST J ADMIN Rule 2.515(a).

b. *Pro se litigant signature.* A party who is not represented by an attorney shall sign any pleading or other paper and state the party's address and telephone number, including area code. FL ST J ADMIN Rule 2.515(b).

c. *Form of signature*

i. The signatures required on pleadings and documents by FL ST J ADMIN Rule 2.515(a) and FL ST J ADMIN Rule 2.515(b) may be:

- Original signatures;
- Original signatures that have been reproduced by electronic means, such as on electronically transmitted documents or photocopied documents;
- Electronic signatures using the "/s/," "s/," or "/s" formats by or at the direction of the person signing; or
- Any other signature format authorized by general law, so long as the clerk where the proceeding is pending has the capability of receiving and has obtained approval from the Supreme Court of Florida to accept pleadings and documents with that signature format. FL ST J ADMIN Rule 2.515(c)(1).

ii. An attorney, party, or other person who files a pleading or paper by electronic transmission that does not contain the original signature of that attorney, party, or other person shall file that identical pleading or paper in paper form containing an original signature of that attorney, party, or other person (hereinafter called the follow-up filing) immediately thereafter. The follow-up filing is not required if the Supreme Court of Florida has entered an order directing the clerk of court to discontinue accepting the follow-up filing. FL ST J ADMIN Rule 2.515(c)(2).

7. *Forms*

a. *Process.* The forms of process, notice of lis pendens, and notice of action provided in the Florida Rules of Civil Procedure are sufficient. Variations from the forms do not void process or notices that are otherwise sufficient. FL ST RCP Rule 1.900(a).

b. *Other forms.* The other forms provided in the Florida Rules of Civil Procedure are sufficient for the matters that are covered by them. So long as the substance is expressed without prolixity, the forms may be varied to meet the facts of a particular case. FL ST RCP Rule 1.900(b).

c. *Formal matters.* Captions, except for the designation of the paper, are omitted from the forms provided in the Florida Rules of Civil Procedure. A general form of caption is the first form provided. Signatures are omitted from pleadings and motions. FL ST RCP Rule 1.900(c).

8. *Notices to persons with disabilities.* All notices of court proceedings to be held in a public facility, and all process compelling appearance at such proceedings, shall include the following statement in bold face, fourteen (14) point Times New Roman or Courier font: "If you are a person with a disability who needs any accommodation in order to participate in this proceeding, you are entitled, at no cost to you, to the

provision of certain assistance. Please contact [identify applicable court personnel by name, address, and telephone number] at least seven (7) days before your scheduled court appearance, or immediately upon receiving this notification if the time before the scheduled appearance is less than seven (7) days; if you are hearing or voice impaired, call 711." FL ST J ADMIN Rule 2.540(c)(1). For more information, see FL ST 20 J CIR 2.15.

9. *Minimization of the filing of sensitive information*
   a. *Limitations for court filings.* Unless authorized by FL ST J ADMIN Rule 2.425(b), statute, another rule of court, or the court orders otherwise, designated sensitive information filed with the court must be limited to the following format:
      i. The initials of a person known to be a minor;
      ii. The year of birth of a person's birth date;
      iii. No portion of any: Social security number, Bank account number, Credit card account number, Charge account number, or Debit account number;
      iv. The last four digits of any: Taxpayer identification number (TIN), Employee identification number, Driver's license number, Passport number, Telephone number, Financial account number, except as set forth in FL ST J ADMIN Rule 2.425(a)(3), Brokerage account number, Insurance policy account number, Loan account number, Customer account number, or Patient or health care number;
      v. A truncated version of any: Email address, Computer user name, Password, or Personal identification number (PIN); and
      vi. A truncated version of any other sensitive information as provided by court order. FL ST J ADMIN Rule 2.425(a).
   b. *Exceptions.* FL ST J ADMIN Rule 2.425(a) does not apply to the following:
      i. An account number which identifies the property alleged to be the subject of a proceeding;
      ii. The record of an administrative or agency proceeding;
      iii. The record in appellate or review proceedings;
      iv. The birth date of a minor whenever the birth date is necessary for the court to establish or maintain subject matter jurisdiction;
      v. The name of a minor in any order relating to parental responsibility, time-sharing, or child support;
      vi. The name of a minor in any document or order affecting the minor's ownership of real property;
      vii. The birth date of a party in a writ of attachment or notice to payor;
      viii. In traffic and criminal proceedings: a pro se filing; a court filing that is related to a criminal matter or investigation and that is prepared before the filing of a criminal charge or is not filed as part of any docketed criminal case; an arrest or search warrant or any information in support thereof; a charging document and an affidavit or other documents filed in support of any charging document, including any driving records; a statement of particulars; discovery material introduced into evidence or otherwise filed with the court; and all information necessary for the proper issuance and execution of a subpoena duces tecum;
      ix. Information used by the clerk for case maintenance purposes or the courts for case management purposes; and
      x. Information which is relevant and material to an issue before the court. FL ST J ADMIN Rule 2.425(b).
   c. *Remedies.* Upon motion by a party or interested person or sua sponte by the court, the court may order remedies, sanctions or both for a violation of FL ST J ADMIN Rule 2.425(a). Following notice and an opportunity to respond, the court may impose sanctions if such filing was not made in good faith. FL ST J ADMIN Rule 2.425(c).
   d. *Motions not restricted.* FL ST J ADMIN Rule 2.425 does not restrict a party's right to move for

protective order, to move to file documents under seal, or to request a determination of the confidentiality of records. FL ST J ADMIN Rule 2.425(d).

e. *Application.* FL ST J ADMIN Rule 2.425 does not affect the application of constitutional provisions, statutes, or rules of court regarding confidential information or access to public information. FL ST J ADMIN Rule 2.425(e).

F. Filing and Service Requirements

1. *Filing requirements.* All original documents must be filed with the court either before service or immediately thereafter, unless otherwise provided for by general law or other rules. If the original of any bond or other document is not placed in the court file, a certified copy must be so placed by the clerk. FL ST J ADMIN Rule 2.516(d). All documents shall be filed in conformity with the requirements of FL ST J ADMIN Rule 2.525. FL ST RCP Rule 1.080(b). All documents filed in any court shall be filed by electronic transmission in accordance with FL ST J ADMIN Rule 2.525. "Documents" means pleadings, motions, petitions, memoranda, briefs, notices, exhibits, declarations, affidavits, orders, judgments, decrees, writs, opinions, and any other paper or writing submitted to a court. FL ST J ADMIN Rule 2.520(a). All documents that are court records, as defined in FL ST J ADMIN Rule 2.430(a)(1), must be filed by electronic transmission, provided that: (1) the clerk has the ability to accept and retain such documents; (2) the clerk or the chief judge of the circuit has requested permission to accept documents filed by electronic transmission; and (3) the supreme court has entered an order granting permission to the clerk to accept documents filed by electronic transmission. FL ST J ADMIN Rule 2.525(c)(1).

a. *Definition.* "Electronic transmission of documents" means the sending of information by electronic signals to, by or from a court or clerk, which when received can be transformed and stored or transmitted on paper, microfilm, magnetic storage device, optical imaging system, CD-ROM, flash drive, other electronic data storage system, server, case maintenance system ("CM"), electronic court filing ("ECF") system, statewide or local electronic portal ("e-portal"), or other electronic record keeping system authorized by the supreme court in a format sufficient to communicate the information on the original document in a readable format. Electronic transmission of documents includes electronic mail ("e-mail") and any internet-based transmission procedure, and may include procedures allowing for documents to be signed or verified by electronic means. FL ST J ADMIN Rule 2.525(a).

i. The filing of documents with the court as required by the Florida Rules of Judicial Administration must be made by filing them with the clerk in accordance with FL ST J ADMIN Rule 2.525, except that the judge may permit documents to be filed with the judge, in which event the judge must note the filing date before him or her on the documents and transmit them to the clerk. The date of filing is that shown on the face of the document by the judge's notation or the clerk's time stamp, whichever is earlier. FL ST J ADMIN Rule 2.516(e).

b. *Application.* Any court or clerk of the court may accept the electronic transmission of documents for filing after the clerk, together with input from the chief judge of the circuit, has obtained approval of the procedures and program for doing so from the Supreme Court of Florida. FL ST J ADMIN Rule 2.525(b).

c. *Exceptions*

i. Paper documents and other submissions may be manually submitted to the clerk or court:

- When the clerk does not have the ability to accept and retain documents by electronic filing or has not had ECF Procedures approved by the supreme court;
- For filing by any self-represented party or any self-represented nonparty unless specific ECF Procedures provide a means to file documents electronically. However, any self-represented nonparty that is a governmental or public agency and any other agency, partnership, corporation, or business entity acting on behalf of any governmental or public agency may file documents by electronic transmission if such entity has the capability of filing documents electronically;
- For filing by attorneys excused from e-mail service in accordance with FL ST J ADMIN Rule 2.516(b);

- When submitting evidentiary exhibits or filing non-documentary materials;
- When the filing involves documents in excess of twenty-five (25) megabytes (25MB) in size. For such filings, documents may be transmitted using an electronic storage medium that the clerk has the ability to accept, which may include a CD-ROM, flash drive, or similar storage medium;
- When filed in open court, as permitted by the court;
- When paper filing is permitted by any approved statewide or local ECF procedures; and
- If any court determines that justice so requires. FL ST J ADMIN Rule 2.525(d).

ii. Any document in paper form submitted under FL ST J ADMIN Rule 2.525(d) is filed when it is received by the clerk or court and the clerk shall immediately thereafter convert any filed paper document to an electronic document. "Convert to an electronic document" means optically capturing an image of a paper document and using character recognition software to recover as much of the document's text as practicable and then indexing and storing the document in the official court file. FL ST J ADMIN Rule 2.525(c)(4).

iii. Any storage medium submitted under FL ST J ADMIN Rule 2.525(d)(5) is filed when received by the clerk or court and the clerk shall immediately thereafter transfer the electronic documents from the storage device to the official court file. FL ST J ADMIN Rule 2.525(c)(5).

iv. If the filer of any paper document authorized under FL ST J ADMIN Rule 2.525(d) provides a self-addressed, postage-paid envelope for return of the paper document after it is converted to electronic form by the clerk, the clerk shall place the paper document in the envelope and deposit it in the mail. Except when a paper document is required to be maintained, the clerk may recycle any filed paper document that is not to be returned to the filer. FL ST J ADMIN Rule 2.525(c)(6).

v. The clerk may convert any paper document filed before the effective date of FL ST J ADMIN Rule 2.525 to an electronic document. Unless the clerk is required to maintain the paper document, if the paper document has been converted to an electronic document by the clerk, the paper document is no longer part of the official court file and may be removed and recycled. FL ST J ADMIN Rule 2.525(c)(7).

d. *Official court file.* For information on what constitutes the official court file, please see FL ST J ADMIN Rule 2.525(c)(2), FL ST J ADMIN Rule 2.525(c)(3).

e. *Administration.* All attorneys, parties, or other persons using this rule to file documents are required to make arrangements with the court or clerk for the payment of any charges authorized by general law or the supreme court before filing any document by electronic transmission. FL ST J ADMIN Rule 2.525(f)(2).

f. *Filing date.* The filing date for an electronically transmitted document is the date and time that such filing is acknowledged by an electronic stamp or otherwise, pursuant to any procedure set forth in any ECF Procedures approved by the supreme court, or the date the last page of such filing is received by the court or clerk. FL ST J ADMIN Rule 2.525(f)(3).

g. *Accessibility.* All documents transmitted in any electronic form under FL ST J ADMIN Rule 2.525 must comply with the accessibility requirements of FL ST J ADMIN Rule 2.526. FL ST J ADMIN Rule 2.525(g).

2. *Service requirements.* Every pleading subsequent to the initial pleading, all orders, and every other document filed in the action must be served in conformity with the requirements of FL ST J ADMIN Rule 2.516. FL ST RCP Rule 1.080(a).

a. *Service; Generally.* The timing and manner of service should not be used to the disadvantage of the party receiving the papers. FL ST 20 J CIR 2.20(IV)(C)(1).

i. Papers and memoranda of law should not be served at court appearances without advance notice to opposing counsel and should not be served so close to a court appearance so as to inhibit the ability of opposing counsel to prepare for that appearance or to respond to the papers. Should the attorney do so, the court is urged to take appropriate action in response, including

continuing the matter to allow opposing counsel to prepare and respond. FL ST 20 J CIR 2.20(IV)(C)(2).

ii. Papers should not be served in order to take advantage of an opponent's known absence from the office or at a time or in a manner designed to inconvenience an adversary, such as late on Friday afternoon or the day preceding a secular or religious holiday. FL ST 20 J CIR 2.20(IV)(C)(3).

iii. Service should be made personally or by courtesy copy facsimile transmission when it is likely that service by mail, even when allowed, will prejudice the opposing party or will not provide the opposing party with a reasonable time to respond. FL ST 20 J CIR 2.20(IV)(C)(4).

b. *Service; When required.* Unless the court otherwise orders, or a statute or supreme court administrative order specifies a different means of service, every pleading subsequent to the initial pleading and every other document filed in any court proceeding, except applications for witness subpoenas and documents served by formal notice or required to be served in the manner provided for service of formal notice, must be served in accordance with FL ST J ADMIN Rule 2.516 on each party. No service need be made on parties against whom a default has been entered, except that pleadings asserting new or additional claims against them must be served in the manner provided for service of summons. FL ST J ADMIN Rule 2.516(a).

i. *Copies of court submissions.* Copies of any submissions to the court (such as correspondence, memoranda of law, motions, case law, etc.) should simultaneously be provided to opposing counsel by substantially the same method of delivery by which they are provided to the court. For example, if a memorandum of law is hand-delivered to the court, at substantially the same time a copy should be hand-delivered or faxed to opposing counsel. FL ST 20 J CIR 2.20(IV)(J)(4).

c. *Service; How made.* When service is required or permitted to be made upon a party represented by an attorney, service must be made upon the attorney unless service upon the party is ordered by the court. FL ST J ADMIN Rule 2.516(b).

i. *Service by electronic mail ("e-mail").* All documents required or permitted to be served on another party must be served by e-mail, unless FL ST J ADMIN Rule 2.516 otherwise provides. When, in addition to service by e-mail, the sender also utilizes another means of service provided for in FL ST J ADMIN Rule 2.516(b)(2), any differing time limits and other provisions applicable to that other means of service control. FL ST J ADMIN Rule 2.516(b)(1). Any document electronically transmitted to a court or clerk must also be served on all parties and interested persons in accordance with the applicable rules of court. FL ST J ADMIN Rule 2.525(e)(2).

- *Service on attorneys.* Upon appearing in a proceeding, an attorney must serve a designation of a primary e-mail address and may designate no more than two (2) secondary e-mail addresses. Thereafter, service must be directed to all designated e-mail addresses in that proceeding. Every document filed by an attorney thereafter must include the primary e-mail address of that attorney and any secondary e-mail addresses. If an attorney does not designate any e-mail address for service, documents may be served on that attorney at the e-mail address on record with The Florida Bar. FL ST J ADMIN Rule 2.516(b)(1)(A).
- *Exception to e-mail service on attorneys.* Service by an attorney on another attorney must be made by e-mail unless excused by the court. Upon motion by an attorney demonstrating that the attorney has no e-mail account and lacks access to the Internet at the attorney's office, the court may excuse the attorney from the requirements of e-mail service. Service on and by an attorney excused by the court from e-mail service must be by the means provided in FL ST J ADMIN Rule 2.516(b)(2). FL ST J ADMIN Rule 2.516(b)(1)(B).
- *Service on and by parties not represented by an attorney.* Any party not represented by an attorney may serve a designation of a primary e-mail address and also may designate no more than two (2) secondary e-mail addresses to which service must be directed in that proceeding by the means provided in FL ST J ADMIN Rule 2.516(b)(1). If a party not represented by an attorney does not designate an e-mail address for service in a proceed-

ing, service on and by that party must be by the means provided in FL ST J ADMIN Rule 2.516(b)(2). FL ST J ADMIN Rule 2.516(b)(1)(C).

- *Time of service.* Service by e-mail is complete when it is sent. FL ST J ADMIN Rule 2.516(b)(1)(D). An e-mail is deemed served on the date it is sent. FL ST J ADMIN Rule 2.516(b)(1)(D)(i). If the sender learns that the e-mail did not reach the address of the person to be served, the sender must immediately send another copy by e-mail, or by a means authorized by FL ST J ADMIN Rule 2.516(b)(2). FL ST J ADMIN Rule 2.516(b)(1)(D)(ii). E-mail service is treated as service by mail for the computation of time. FL ST J ADMIN Rule 2.516(b)(1)(D)(iii).

ii. *Format of e-mail for service.* Service of a document by e-mail is made by attaching a copy of the document in PDF format to an e-mail sent to all addresses designated by the attorney or party. FL ST J ADMIN Rule 2.516(b)(1)(E).

- All documents served by e-mail must be attached to an e-mail message containing a subject line beginning with the words "SERVICE OF COURT DOCUMENT" in all capital letters, followed by the case number of the proceeding in which the documents are being served. FL ST J ADMIN Rule 2.516(b)(1)(E)(i).
- The body of the e-mail must identify the court in which the proceeding is pending, the case number, the name of the initial party on each side, the title of each document served with that e-mail, and the sender's name and telephone number. FL ST J ADMIN Rule 2.516(b)(1)(E)(ii).
- Any document served by e-mail may be signed by the "/s/" format, as long as the filed original is signed in accordance with the applicable rule of procedure. FL ST J ADMIN Rule 2.516(b)(1)(E)(iii).
- Any e-mail which, together with its attached documents, exceeds five megabytes (5MB) in size, must be divided and sent as separate e-mails, no one of which may exceed five megabytes (5MB) in size and each of which must be sequentially numbered in the subject line. FL ST J ADMIN Rule 2.516(b)(1)(E)(iv).

iii. *Service by other means.* In addition to, and not in lieu of, service by e-mail, service may also be made upon attorneys by any of the means specified in FL ST J ADMIN Rule 2.516(b)(2). Service on and by all parties who are not represented by an attorney and who do not designate an e-mail address, and on and by all attorneys excused from e-mail service, must be made by delivering a copy of the document or by mailing it to the party or attorney at their last known address or, if no address is known, by leaving it with the clerk of the court. Service by mail is complete upon mailing. Delivery of a copy within FL ST J ADMIN Rule 2.516 is complete upon:

- Handing it to the attorney or to the party,
- Leaving it at the attorney's or party's office with a clerk or other person in charge thereof,
- If there is no one in charge, leaving it in a conspicuous place therein,
- If the office is closed or the person to be served has no office, leaving it at the person's usual place of abode with some person of his or her family above fifteen (15) years of age and informing such person of the contents, or
- Transmitting it by facsimile to the attorney's or party's office with a cover sheet containing the sender's name, firm, address, telephone number, and facsimile number, and the number of pages transmitted. When service is made by facsimile, a copy must also be served by any other method permitted by FL ST J ADMIN Rule 2.516. Facsimile service occurs when transmission is complete. FL ST J ADMIN Rule 2.516(b)(2)(A) through FL ST J ADMIN Rule 2.516(b)(2)(E).
- Service by delivery after 5:00 p.m. must be deemed to have been made by mailing on the date of delivery. FL ST J ADMIN Rule 2.516(b)(2)(F).

d. *Service; Numerous defendants.* In actions when the parties are unusually numerous, the court may

regulate the service contemplated by the Florida Rules of Judicial Administration on motion or on its own initiative in such manner as may be found to be just and reasonable. FL ST J ADMIN Rule 2.516(c).

e. *Service by clerk.* Service of notices and other documents required to be made by the clerk must also be done as provided in FL ST J ADMIN Rule 2.516(b). FL ST J ADMIN Rule 2.516(g).

G. Hearings

1. *Scheduling.* Before setting a motion for hearing, counsel should make a good faith effort to resolve the issue with opposing counsel. FL ST 20 J CIR 2.20(IV)(I)(1). Except in emergency situations, attorneys should make a good faith effort to communicate with opposing counsel prior to scheduling depositions, hearings and other proceedings, so as to schedule them at times that are mutually convenient for all interested persons. Further, a sufficient time should be reserved to permit a complete presentation by counsel for all parties. FL ST 20 J CIR 2.20(IV)(B)(1). Attorneys should not use the hearing time obtained by opposing counsel for other motion practice. FL ST 20 J CIR 2.20(IV)(B)(6).

   a. *Notice.* Counsel should notify opposing counsel of dates and times obtained from the court for future hearings on the same day that the hearing date is obtained from the court, or as soon as practicable thereafter. FL ST 20 J CIR 2.20(IV)(J)(3).

   b. *Scheduling conflict.* Attorneys should notify opposing counsel, the court, and others affected, of scheduling conflicts as soon as they become apparent. Further, attorneys should cooperate with one another regarding all reasonable rescheduling requests that do not prejudice their clients or unduly delay a proceeding. FL ST 20 J CIR 2.20(IV)(B)(7).

      i. Attorneys should call potential scheduling problems to the attention of those affected, including the court, as soon as they become apparent and should avoid last minute cancellations. FL ST 20 J CIR 2.20(IV)(B)(12).

   c. *Notice to court when appearance is unnecessary.* Attorneys should promptly notify the court or other tribunal of any resolution between the parties that renders a scheduled court appearance unnecessary. FL ST 20 J CIR 2.20(IV)(B)(8).

2. *Communication equipment*

   a. *Definition.* Communication equipment means a conference telephone or other electronic device that permits all those appearing or participating to hear and speak to each other, provided that all conversation of all parties is audible to all persons present. FL ST J ADMIN Rule 2.530(a).

   b. *Use by all parties.* A county or circuit court judge may, upon the court's own motion or upon the written request of a party, direct that communication equipment be used for a motion hearing, pretrial conference, or a status conference. A judge must give notice to the parties and consider any objections they may have to the use of communication equipment before directing that communication equipment be used. The decision to use communication equipment over the objection of parties will be in the sound discretion of the trial court, except as noted below. FL ST J ADMIN Rule 2.530(b).

   c. *Use only by requesting party.* A county or circuit court judge may, upon the written request of a party upon reasonable notice to all other parties, permit a requesting party to participate through communication equipment in a scheduled motion hearing; however, any such request (except in criminal, juvenile, and appellate proceedings) must be granted, absent a showing of good cause to deny the same, where the hearing is set for not longer than fifteen (15) minutes. FL ST J ADMIN Rule 2.530(c).

   d. *Testimony*

      i. *Generally.* A county or circuit court judge, general magistrate, special magistrate, or hearing officer may allow testimony to be taken through communication equipment if all parties consent or if permitted by another applicable rule of procedure. FL ST J ADMIN Rule 2.530(d)(1).

      ii. *Procedure.* Any party desiring to present testimony through communication equipment shall, prior to the hearing or trial at which the testimony is to be presented, contact all parties to

determine whether each party consents to this form of testimony. The party seeking to present the testimony shall move for permission to present testimony through communication equipment, which motion shall set forth good cause as to why the testimony should be allowed in this form. FL ST J ADMIN Rule 2.530(d)(2).

iii. *Oath.* Testimony may be taken through communication equipment only if a notary public or other person authorized to administer oaths in the witness's jurisdiction is present with the witness and administers the oath consistent with the laws of the jurisdiction. FL ST J ADMIN Rule 2.530(d)(3).

iv. *Confrontation rights.* In juvenile and criminal proceedings the defendant must make an informed waiver of any confrontation rights that may be abridged by the use of communication equipment. FL ST J ADMIN Rule 2.530(d)(4).

v. *Video testimony.* If the testimony to be presented utilizes video conferencing or comparable two-way visual capabilities, the court in its discretion may modify the procedures set forth in FL ST J ADMIN Rule 2.530 to accommodate the technology utilized. FL ST J ADMIN Rule 2.530(d)(5).

e. *Burden of expense.* The cost for the use of the communication equipment is the responsibility of the requesting party unless otherwise directed by the court. FL ST J ADMIN Rule 2.530(e).

3. *Telephonic non-evidentiary motion hearings set for not longer than fifteen (15) minutes.* FL ST 20 J CIR 1.10 specifically addresses non-evidentiary civil motion hearings set for not longer than fifteen (15) minutes. It is not intended to limit or address requests for telephonic hearings which are otherwise governed by FL ST J ADMIN Rule 2.071. FL ST 20 J CIR 1.10. [Editor's note: FL ST J ADMIN Rule 2.071 was renumbered as FL ST J ADMIN Rule 2.530]. Evidentiary hearings are exempted from the application of FL ST 20 J CIR 1.10. FL ST 20 J CIR 1.10.

a. In instances where a civil motion hearing is scheduled for not longer than fifteen (15) minutes, a party may file a written request to participate via conference or speaker telephone, or other applicable communication equipment, and shall provide notice to the Court and the parties to the motion. FL ST 20 J CIR 1.10. Refer to the Timing section of this document for information on when the notice must be given and when request must be served.

b. The requesting party shall be responsible for contacting the trial judge's Judicial Assistant and ensuring that appropriate arrangements have been made to permit participation through conference or speaker telephone, or other applicable communication equipment, on the scheduled date and time. It shall be at the discretion of the trial judge as to whether the requesting party shall be responsible for initiating the telephone or communication connection or whether the Court shall be responsible for initiating the telephone or communication connection. FL ST 20 J CIR 1.10(3).

c. Absent a showing of good cause, and in accordance with FL ST J ADMIN Rule 2.071(c), the trial judge shall grant the request and make reasonable accommodations to permit the requesting party's participation through conference or speaker telephone, or other applicable communication equipment. FL ST 20 J CIR 1.10. [Editor's note: FL ST J ADMIN Rule 2.071 was renumbered as FL ST J ADMIN Rule 2.530(c)].

d. To the extent that any provision of FL ST 20 J CIR 1.10 may be construed as being in conflict with any law, statute, or rule, the law, statute, or rule shall prevail. FL ST 20 J CIR 1.10.

H. Forms

1. Official Motion to Strike Forms for Florida

a. Caption. FL ST RCP Form 1.901.

b. Notice of compliance when constitutional challenge is brought. FL ST RCP Form 1.975.

2. Motion to Strike Forms for Florida

a. Motion to strike. FL-PP § 2:128.

b. Form for motion to strike. FL-RCPF R 1.140(802).

c. Form for motion to strike insufficient pleading. FL-RCPF R 1.140(803).

d. Form for motion to strike claim for business or financial losses. FL-RCPF R 1.140(804).
e. Motion; Strike, complaint signed by corporation. FL-PRACFORM § 7:176.
f. Motion; Strike, defenses. FL-PRACFORM § 7:177.
g. Motion; Strike, ejectment chain of title. FL-PRACFORM § 7:178.
h. Motion; Strike, pleading, departure. FL-PRACFORM § 7:180.
i. Motion; Strike, pleading, improper signature. FL-PRACFORM § 7:181.
j. Motion; Strike, sham pleading. FL-PRACFORM § 7:182.
k. Motion; Strike, sham, defenses, statute of limitations and failure of consideration. FL-PRACFORM § 7:183.
l. Motion; Strike, third party complaint. FL-PRACFORM § 7:184.

I. Checklist

(I) ❑ Matters to be considered by moving party
- (a) ❑ Required documents
  - (1) ❑ Notice of hearing/Motion
  - (2) ❑ Certification
  - (3) ❑ Certificate of service
- (b) ❑ Supplemental documents
  - (1) ❑ Proposed order
  - (2) ❑ Notice of constitutional question
  - (3) ❑ Notice and request to participate in telephonic motion hearing
- (c) ❑ Time for making motion
  - (1) ❑ A party may move to strike or the court may strike redundant, immaterial, impertinent, or scandalous matter from any pleading at any time
  - (2) ❑ If a pleading sets forth a claim for relief to which the adverse party is not required to serve a responsive pleading, the adverse party may assert any defense in law or fact to that claim for relief at the trial, except that the objection of failure to state a legal defense in an answer or reply shall be asserted by motion to strike the defense within twenty (20) days after service of the answer or reply
  - (3) ❑ If a party deems any pleading or part thereof filed by another party to be a sham, that party may move to strike the pleading or part thereof before the cause is set for trial
  - (4) ❑ A copy of any written motion which may not be heard ex parte and a copy of the notice of the hearing thereof shall be served a reasonable time before the time specified for the hearing; as a general rule, notice should be provided (not including time for service) no less than five (5) business days for hearings

(II) ❑ Matters to be considered by opposing party
- (a) ❑ Required documents
  - (1) ❑ Response to motion
  - (2) ❑ Certificate of service
- (b) ❑ Supplemental documents
  - (1) ❑ Proposed order
  - (2) ❑ Notice of constitutional question
  - (3) ❑ Notice and request to participate in telephonic motion hearing
- (c) ❑ Time for service and filing of opposition
  - (1) ❑ No time specified for responding to a motion

(2) ❑ Notice and request to participate in telephonic motion hearing: Notice by the requesting party must be provided by mailing a copy of the written request at least five (5) days prior to the day of the hearing, or by delivering a copy of the written request to the other parties or, if represented by counsel, to the other parties' attorney(s) no later than 5:00 p.m. two (2) business days prior to the day of the hearing

Motions, Oppositions and Replies
Motion for Leave to Amend

Document Last Updated January 2013

A. Applicable Rules

1. *State rules*
   a. Rules of court. FL ST RCP Rule 1.010; FL ST J ADMIN Rule 2.110.
   b. Nonverification of pleadings. FL ST RCP Rule 1.030.
   c. Process. FL ST RCP Rule 1.070.
   d. Service and filing of pleadings, orders, and documents. FL ST RCP Rule 1.080.
   e. Time. FL ST RCP Rule 1.090.
   f. Pleadings and motions. FL ST RCP Rule 1.100.
   g. Defenses. FL ST RCP Rule 1.140.
   h. Motions. FL ST RCP Rule 1.160.
   i. Amended and supplemental pleadings. FL ST RCP Rule 1.190.
   j. Relief from judgment, decrees, or orders. FL ST RCP Rule 1.540.
   k. Mediation and arbitration. FL ST RCP Rule 1.700; FL ST RCP Rule 1.710; FL ST RCP Rule 1.720; FL ST RCP Rule 1.730; FL ST RCP Rule 1.750; FL ST RCP Rule 1.800; FL ST RCP Rule 1.810; FL ST RCP Rule 1.820; FL ST RCP Rule 1.830.
   l. Forms. FL ST RCP Rule 1.900.
   m. Minimization of the filing of sensitive information. FL ST J ADMIN Rule 2.425.
   n. Retention of court records. FL ST J ADMIN Rule 2.430.
   o. Foreign attorneys. FL ST J ADMIN Rule 2.510.
   p. Signature of attorneys and parties. FL ST J ADMIN Rule 2.515.
   q. Paper. FL ST J ADMIN Rule 2.520.
   r. Electronic filing. FL ST J ADMIN Rule 2.525.
   s. Accessibility of information and technology. FL ST J ADMIN Rule 2.526.
   t. Communication equipment. FL ST J ADMIN Rule 2.530.
   u. Court reporting. FL ST J ADMIN Rule 2.535.
   v. Requests for accommodations by persons with disabilities. FL ST J ADMIN Rule 2.540.
   w. Case management. FL ST J ADMIN Rule 2.545.
2. *Local rules*
   a. Exclusions from mediation. FL ST 20 J CIR 1.9.
   b. Establishment and implementation of civil case management plan. FL ST 20 J CIR 1.13.
   c. Size of paper. FL ST 20 J CIR 2.9.
   d. Telephonic motion hearings set for not longer than fifteen minutes in circuit and county civil cases. FL ST 20 J CIR 1.10.

e. Americans with Disabilities Act; Notification of court proceedings. FL ST 20 J CIR 2.15.

f. Standards of professional courtesy and conduct and establishment of peer review program. FL ST 20 J CIR 2.20.

B. Timing

1. *Amended pleadings as a matter of course.* A party may amend a pleading once as a matter of course at any time before a responsive pleading is served or, if the pleading is one to which no responsive pleading is permitted and the action has not been placed on the trial calendar, may amend it at any time within twenty (20) days after it is served. Otherwise a party may amend a pleading only by leave of court or by written consent of the adverse party. FL ST RCP Rule 1.190(a).

2. *Amended pleadings with leave of court.* Leave of court shall be given freely when justice so requires. FL ST RCP Rule 1.190(a). Under the Florida Rules of Civil Procedure, there is no time limit as to when an amendment with leave of court may be sought. Amendments of the pleadings may be permitted, with the court's discretion, at any stage of the proceedings in furtherance of justice. McSwiggan v. Edson, 186 So.2d 13, 15 (Fla. 1966); FL-PP § 2:153. Nevertheless, the liberality in permitting amendment of pleadings diminishes as the case progresses to trial. Versen v. Versen, 347 So.2d 1047, 1050 (Fla. 4th DCA 1977); FL-PP § 2:153.

3. *Claims for punitive damages.* A motion for leave to amend a pleading to assert a claim for punitive damages can be filed separately and before the supporting evidence or proffer, but each shall be served on all parties at least twenty (20) days before the hearing. FL ST RCP Rule 1.190(f).

4. *Post motion for leave to amend*

   a. If the court permits or requires an amended or responsive pleading or a more definite statement, the pleading or statement shall be served within ten (10) days after notice of the court's action. FL ST RCP Rule 1.140(a)(4).

   b. When a motion for leave to amend with the attached proposed amended complaint is filed, the one hundred twenty (120) day period for service of amended complaints on the new party or parties shall begin upon the entry of an order granting leave to amend. FL ST RCP Rule 1.070(j).

5. *General motion timing.* A copy of any written motion which may not be heard ex parte and a copy of the notice of the hearing thereof shall be served a reasonable time before the time specified for the hearing. FL ST RCP Rule 1.090(d).

   a. *Notice of hearing.* Except in emergency situations, attorneys should provide opposing counsel, parties, witnesses, and other affected persons, sufficient notice of depositions, hearings and other proceedings. FL ST 20 J CIR 2.20(IV)(B)(1). Attorneys should notify opposing counsel of any hearing time reserved as soon as practicable. FL ST 20 J CIR 2.20(IV)(B)(3). When hearing time is obtained, attorneys should promptly prepare and serve all counsel of record with notice of the hearing. Do not delay in providing such notice. FL ST 20 J CIR 2.20(IV)(B)(4).

      i. As a general rule, notice should be provided (not including time for service) no less than five (5) business days for hearings. FL ST 20 J CIR 2.20(IV)(B)(1).

6. *Notice and request to participate in telephonic motion hearing.* Notice by the requesting party must be provided by mailing a copy of the written request at least five (5) days prior to the day of the hearing, or by delivering a copy of the written request to the other parties or, if represented by counsel, to the other parties' attorney(s) no later than 5:00 p.m. two (2) business days prior to the day of the hearing. FL ST 20 J CIR 1.10. Refer to the Hearings section of this document for more information.

7. *Computation of time*

   a. *Generally.* Computation of time shall be governed by FL ST J ADMIN Rule 2.514. FL ST RCP Rule 1.090(a). The following rules apply in computing time periods specified in any rule of procedure, local rule, court order, or statute that does not specify a method of computing time. FL ST J ADMIN Rule 2.514(a).

      i. *Period stated in days or a longer unit.* When the period is stated in days or a longer unit of time (A) exclude the day of the event that triggers the period; (B) count every day, including intermediate Saturdays, Sundays, and legal holidays; and (C) include the last day of the period,

but if the last day is a Saturday, Sunday, or legal holiday, or falls within any period of time extended through an order of the chief justice under FL ST J ADMIN Rule 2.205(a)(2)(B)(iv), the period continues to run until the end of the next day that is not a Saturday, Sunday, or legal holiday and does not fall within any period of time extended through an order of the chief justice. FL ST J ADMIN Rule 2.514(a)(1).

ii. *Period stated in hours.* When the period is stated in hours (A) begin counting immediately on the occurrence of the event that triggers the period; (B) count every hour, including hours during intermediate Saturdays, Sundays, and legal holidays; and (C) if the period would end on a Saturday, Sunday, or legal holiday, or during any period of time extended through an order of the chief justice under FL ST J ADMIN Rule 2.205(a)(2)(B)(iv), the period continues to run until the same time on the next day that is not a Saturday, Sunday, or legal holiday and does not fall within any period of time extended through an order of the chief justice. FL ST J ADMIN Rule 2.514(a)(2).

iii. *Period stated in days less than seven (7) days.* When the period stated in days is less than seven (7) days, intermediate Saturdays, Sundays, and legal holidays shall be excluded in the computation. FL ST J ADMIN Rule 2.514(a)(3).

iv. *"Last day" defined.* Unless a different time is set by a statute, local rule, or court order, the last day ends (A) for electronic filing or for service by any means, at midnight; and (B) for filing by other means, when the clerk's office is scheduled to close. FL ST J ADMIN Rule 2.514(a)(4).

v. *"Next day" defined.* The "next day" is determined by continuing to count forward when the period is measured after an event and backward when measured before an event. FL ST J ADMIN Rule 2.514(a)(5).

vi. *"Legal holiday" defined.* "Legal holiday" means (A) the day set aside by FL ST § 110.117, for observing New Year's Day, Martin Luther King, Jr.'s Birthday, Memorial Day, Independence Day, Labor Day, Veterans' Day, Thanksgiving Day, the Friday after Thanksgiving Day, or Christmas Day, and (B) any day observed as a holiday by the clerk's office or as designated by the chief judge. FL ST J ADMIN Rule 2.514(a)(6).

b. *Additional time after service by mail or e-mail.* When a party may or must act within a specified time after service and service is made by mail or e-mail, five (5) days are added after the period that would otherwise expire under FL ST J ADMIN Rule 2.514(a). FL ST J ADMIN Rule 2.514(b).

c. *Enlargement.* When an act is required or allowed to be done at or within a specified time by order of court, by the Florida Rules of Civil Procedure, or by notice given thereunder, for cause shown the court at any time in its discretion (1) with or without notice, may order the period enlarged if request therefor is made before the expiration of the period originally prescribed or as extended by a previous order, or (2) upon motion made and notice after the expiration of the specified period, may permit the act to be done when failure to act was the result of excusable neglect, but it may not extend the time for making a motion for new trial, for rehearing, or to alter or amend a judgment; making a motion for relief from a judgment under FL ST RCP Rule 1.540(b); taking an appeal or filing a petition for certiorari; or making a motion for a directed verdict. FL ST RCP Rule 1.090(b).

d. *Unaffected by expiration of term.* The period of time provided for the doing of any act or the taking of any proceeding shall not be affected or limited by the continued existence or expiration of a term of court. The continued existence or expiration of a term of court in no way affects the power of a court to do any act or take any proceeding in any action which is or has been pending before it. FL ST RCP Rule 1.090(c).

C. General Requirements

1. *Motions generally*

a. *Contents.* An application to the court for an order shall be by motion which shall be made in writing unless made during a hearing or trial, shall state with particularity the grounds therefor, and shall set forth the relief or order sought. The requirement of writing is fulfilled if the motion is stated in a written notice of the hearing of the motion. All notices of hearing shall specify each motion or other matter to be heard. FL ST RCP Rule 1.100(b).

i. *Notice of hearing.* The notice of hearing should indicate on its face whether the date and time have been coordinated with opposing counsel. If the attorney has been unable to coordinate the hearing with opposing counsel, the notice should state the specific good faith efforts the attorney undertook to coordinate or why coordination was not obtained. FL ST 20 J CIR 2.20(IV)(B)(5).

b. *Particularity requirement.* The court considers a motion in the light of the substantive law, rule or statute to make its determination. Some rules require a statement of the grounds for a motion under the rule. Failure to give the grounds will result in denial of the motion. This should be the result in all situations when the ground for the motion is not inherent in the rule. FL-PRACPROC § 9:3. The requirement is nevertheless an important one, first because of the due process notice rights of the respondent, as well as for the assistance it provides to the court in its preparation for the hearing or, absent a hearing, for disposition. 4 FLPRAC R 1.100.

2. *Conference with opposing counsel.* Attorneys should, whenever possible, prior to filing or upon receiving a motion, contact opposing counsel to determine if the matter can be resolved in whole or in part. This may alleviate the need for a hearing on the motion or allow submission of an agreed order in lieu of a hearing. FL ST 20 J CIR 2.20(IV)(L)(2).

   a. *Conference required.* Except in emergency situations, before filing any motion in a civil case, except a motion for injunctive relief, for judgment on the pleadings, for summary judgment, to dismiss or to permit maintenance of a class action, to dismiss for failure to state a cause of action, to dismiss for lack of prosecution, or to otherwise involuntarily dismiss an action, the moving party shall confer with counsel for the opposing party in a good faith effort to resolve the issues raised by the motion, and shall file with the motion a statement certifying that the moving counsel has conferred with opposing counsel and that counsel have been unable to agree on the resolution of the motion. FL ST 20 J CIR 2.20(IV)(I)(2).

3. *Motion for leave to amend.* Although the Florida Rules of Civil Procedure do not specify a procedure for obtaining leave to amend, it is usually accomplished by way of a motion. FL-PP § 2:153. At any time in furtherance of justice, upon such terms as may be just, the court may permit any process, proceeding, pleading, or record to be amended or material supplemental matter to be set forth in an amended or supplemental pleading. At every stage of the action the court must disregard any error or defect in the proceedings which does not affect the substantial rights of the parties. FL ST RCP Rule 1.190(e).

   a. *Permissible amendments.* Amendments can relate to the correction of mistakes, the insertion of jurisdictional averments, the correction or addition of verifications, the addition or substitution or striking out of parties, and generally the rectification of all formal defects in the pleading. The court can also allow amendments setting up an omitted counterclaim or cross-claim if the defendant failed to raise the claim through oversight, inadvertence, or excusable neglect. FL-PP § 2:151.

   b. *Amendments to conform with the evidence.* When issues not raised by the pleadings are tried by express or implied consent of the parties, they shall be treated in all respects as if they had been raised in the pleadings. Such amendment of the pleadings as may be necessary to cause them to conform to the evidence and to raise these issues may be made upon motion of any party at any time, even after judgment, but failure so to amend shall not affect the result of the trial of these issues. If the evidence is objected to at the trial on the ground that it is not within the issues made by the pleadings, the court may allow the pleadings to be amended to conform with the evidence and shall do so freely when the merits of the cause are more effectually presented thereby and the objecting party fails to satisfy the court that the admission of such evidence will prejudice the objecting party in maintaining an action or defense upon the merits. FL ST RCP Rule 1.190(b).

      i. The courts have been extremely liberal in permitting amendments after trial to conform pleadings to the evidence where the issues were tried by the express or implied consent of the parties. Turner v. Long, 225 So.2d 434 (Fla. 1st DCA 1969); FL-PP § 2:152.

   c. *Procedure for adding parties.* Parties may be added once as a matter of course within the same time that pleadings can be so amended. If amendment by leave of court or stipulation of the parties is permitted, parties may be added in the amended pleading without further order of court. Parties may be added by order of court on its own initiative or on motion of any party at any stage of the action and on such terms as are just. FL ST RCP Rule 1.250(c).

   d. *Claims for punitive damages.* A motion for leave to amend a pleading to assert a claim for punitive damages shall make a reasonable showing by evidence in the record or evidence to be proffered by the claimant that provides a reasonable basis for recovery of such damages. The motion to amend can be filed separately and before the supporting evidence or proffer, but each shall be served on all parties at least twenty (20) days before the hearing. FL ST RCP Rule 1.190(f). Leave of court to amend the complaint must be obtained before a plaintiff may assert a punitive damages claim in the complaint. Failure to do so will result in the claims being dismissed or stricken. FL-PP § 2:151.

e. *Relation back of amendments.* When the claim or defense asserted in the amended pleading arose out of the conduct, transaction, or occurrence set forth or attempted to be set forth in the original pleading, the amendment shall relate back to the date of the original pleading. FL ST RCP Rule 1.190(c).

i. The doctrine of relation back becomes critical in applying the statute of limitations. For example, it has been held that the doctrine of relation back may not be utilized to circumvent the statute of limitations to permit an amendment where a claim could have been filed as an independent action but was not timely asserted and would otherwise be barred under the statute of limitations. Cox v. Seaboard Coast Line R. Co., 360 So.2d 8 (Fla. 2d DCA 1978); FL-PP § 2:152.

4. *Arbitration and mediation.* Attorneys are encouraged to utilize arbitration, mediation or other forms of alternative dispute resolution if economically feasible. FL ST 20 J CIR 2.20(IV)(N)(3).

a. *Referral to arbitration and mediation.* Except as hereinafter provided or as otherwise prohibited by law, the presiding judge may enter an order referring all or any part of a contested civil matter to mediation or arbitration. The parties to any contested civil matter may file a written stipulation to mediate or arbitrate any issue between them at any time. Such stipulation shall be incorporated into the order of referral. FL ST RCP Rule 1.700(a).

b. *Arbitration*

i. *Exclusions.* A civil action shall be ordered to arbitration or arbitration in conjunction with mediation upon stipulation of the parties. A civil action may be ordered to arbitration or arbitration in conjunction with mediation upon motion of any party or by the court, if the judge determines the action to be of such a nature that arbitration could be of benefit to the litigants or the court. FL ST RCP Rule 1.800.

- Under no circumstances may the following categories of actions be referred to arbitration: (1) bond estreatures; (2) habeas corpus or other extraordinary writs; (3) bond validations; (4) civil or criminal contempt; (5) such other matters as may be specified by order of the chief judge in the circuit. FL ST RCP Rule 1.800.

ii. For more information regarding arbitration, please see FL ST RCP Rule 1.810; FL ST RCP Rule 1.820; FL ST RCP Rule 1.830.

c. *Mediation.* For more information regarding mediation, please see FL ST RCP Rule 1.710; FL ST RCP Rule 1.720; FL ST RCP Rule 1.730; FL ST RCP Rule 1.750; and FL ST 20 J CIR 1.9.

5. *Rules of court*

a. *Rules of civil procedure.* The Florida Rules of Civil Procedure apply to all actions of a civil nature and all special statutory proceedings in the circuit courts and county courts except those to which the Florida Probate Rules, the Florida Family Law Rules of Procedure, or the Small Claims Rules apply. FL ST RCP Rule 1.010.

i. The form, content, procedure, and time for pleading in all special statutory proceedings shall be as prescribed by the statutes governing the proceeding unless the Florida Rules of Civil Procedure specifically provide to the contrary. FL ST RCP Rule 1.010.

ii. The Florida Rules of Civil Procedure shall be construed to secure the just, speedy, and inexpensive determination of every action. FL ST RCP Rule 1.010.

b. *Rules of judicial administration.* The Florida Rules of Judicial Administration shall apply to administrative matters in all courts to which the Florida Rules of Judicial Administration are applicable by their terms. The Florida Rules of Judicial Administration shall be construed to secure

the speedy and inexpensive determination of every proceeding to which they are applicable. The Florida Rules of Judicial Administration shall supersede all conflicting rules and statutes. FL ST J ADMIN Rule 2.110.

6. *Civil case management plan.* There is established within the Twentieth Judicial Circuit a Civil Case Management Plan applicable to circuit civil cases, which will be administered by the Administrative Office of the Courts through direction of the Circuit Administrative Judges in each county for the implementation of enhanced case management procedures and guidelines for the timely and efficient processing of circuit civil cases and reduction in the pending backlog of civil cases. FL ST 20 J CIR 1.13.
   a. The basis for the Civil Case Management Plan is included in FL ST 20 J CIR 1.13, identified in Attachment A as the "Civil Differentiated Case Management (DCM) Procedures and Backlog Reduction Plan," and is incorporated as if fully set forth in FL ST 20 J CIR 1.13. The Civil Case Management Plan is to be used as a model for the purpose of establishing time standards, improving the courts ability to provide early and continuous management of civil cases as required by FL ST J ADMIN Rule 2.545, and to promote uniformity of practice throughout the Twentieth Judicial Circuit. FL ST 20 J CIR 1.13.
   b. Full implementation of the Civil DCM Case Management Procedures (Attachment A), including all uniform circuitwide procedures and forms, shall apply to all civil cases filed in Lee and Collier counties, effective January 1, 2011. Even though full implementation may be delayed in Charlotte, Hendry, and Glades counties, all civil time standards and goals, and the use of civil Case Managers and Magistrates to assist trial judges in the process of civil case management and backlog reduction programs, shall be effective circuitwide immediately. FL ST 20 J CIR 1.13.
   c. For more information on the civil case management plan, refer to the specific county website and/or see FL ST 20 J CIR 1.13.

D. Documents

1. *Required documents*
   a. *Notice of hearing/Motion.* An application to the court for an order shall be by motion which shall be made in writing unless made during a hearing or trial, shall state with particularity the grounds therefor, and shall set forth the relief or order sought. The requirement of writing is fulfilled if the motion is stated in a written notice of the hearing of the motion. All notices of hearing shall specify each motion or other matter to be heard. FL ST RCP Rule 1.100(b). Refer to the General Requirements section of this document for more information on the notice of hearing.
      i. *Notices to persons with disabilities.* See the Format section of this KeyRules document for further information.
   b. *Certification.* Except in emergency situations, before filing any motion in a civil case, except a motion for injunctive relief, for judgment on the pleadings, for summary judgment, to dismiss or to permit maintenance of a class action, to dismiss for failure to state a cause of action, to dismiss for lack of prosecution, or to otherwise involuntarily dismiss an action, the moving party shall confer with counsel for the opposing party in a good faith effort to resolve the issues raised by the motion, and shall file with the motion a statement certifying that the moving counsel has conferred with opposing counsel and that counsel have been unable to agree on the resolution of the motion. FL ST 20 J CIR 2.20(IV)(I)(2).
   c. *Proposed amended pleading.* The moving party shall attach the proposed amended pleading to the motion. FL ST RCP Rule 1.190(a).
   d. *Certificate of service.* When any attorney certifies in substance: "I certify that a copy hereof has been furnished to (here insert name or names and addresses used for service) by (e-mail) (delivery) (mail) (fax) on .... (date) ....________________ Attorney" the certificate is taken as prima facie proof of such service in compliance with FL ST J ADMIN Rule 2.516. FL ST J ADMIN Rule 2.516(f).
2. *Supplemental documents*
   a. *Proposed order.* The court may require that orders or judgments be prepared by a party, may require the party to furnish the court with stamped, addressed envelopes for service of the order or judgment,

and may require that proposed orders and judgments be furnished to all parties before entry by the court of the order or judgment. FL ST J ADMIN Rule 2.516(h)(1).

i. Unless otherwise instructed by the court, or agreed to by counsel, all proposed orders shall be provided to other counsel with a reasonable time for approval or comment prior to submission to the court. Opposing counsel should promptly communicate any objections thereto. Thereafter, the drafting attorney should promptly submit a copy of the proposed order to the court and advise the court as to whether or not it has been approved by opposing counsel. FL ST 20 J CIR 2.20(IV)(I)(4).

ii. Orders prepared by counsel must fairly and adequately represent the ruling of the court, and counsel shall make a good faith effort to agree upon the form of the order prior to submitting it to the court. Attorneys should not submit controverted orders to the court with a copy to opposing counsel for "objections within ______ days". Courts prefer to know that the order is either agreed upon or opposed. FL ST 20 J CIR 2.20(IV)(I)(5).

iii. Attorneys should not use post-hearing submissions of proposed orders as a guise to reargue the merits of the matter. FL ST 20 J CIR 2.20(IV)(I)(6).

iv. If asked by the court to prepare an order, counsel should furnish a copy of the order, and any transmitted letter, to opposing counsel at the time the material is submitted to the court. FL ST 20 J CIR 2.20(IV)(J)(4).

b. *Notice of constitutional question.* A party that files a pleading, written motion, or other paper drawing into question the constitutionality of a state statute or a county or municipal charter, ordinance, or franchise must promptly (1) file a notice of constitutional question stating the question and identifying the paper that raises it; and (2) serve the notice and the pleading, written motion, or other paper drawing into question the constitutionality of a state statute or a county or municipal charter, ordinance, or franchise on the Attorney General or the state attorney of the judicial circuit in which the action is pending, by either certified or registered mail. Service of the notice and pleading, written motion, or other paper does not require joinder of the Attorney General or the state attorney as a party to the action. FL ST RCP Rule 1.071.

c. *Notice and request to participate in telephonic motion hearing.* In instances where a civil motion hearing is scheduled for not longer than fifteen (15) minutes, a party may file a written request to participate via conference or speaker telephone, or other applicable communication equipment, and shall provide notice to the Court and the parties to the motion. FL ST 20 J CIR 1.10. Refer to the Timing and Hearings sections of this document for more information.

E. Format

1. *Documents; Type and size.* Documents subject to the exceptions set forth in FL ST J ADMIN Rule 2.525(d) shall be filed on recycled paper measuring eight and one half by eleven (8 1/2 by 11) inches. For purposes of FL ST J ADMIN Rule 2.520, paper is recycled if it contains a minimum content of fifty (50) percent waste paper. Xerographic reduction of legal-size (eight and one half by fourteen (8 1/2 by 14) inches) documents to letter size (eight and one half by eleven (8 1/2 by 11) inches) is prohibited. All other documents filed by electronic transmission shall be filed in a format capable of being printed in a format consistent with the provisions of FL ST J ADMIN Rule 2.250. FL ST J ADMIN Rule 2.520(b); FL ST 20 J CIR 2.9.

a. *Exhibits.* Any exhibit or attachment filed with pleadings or papers may be filed in its original size. FL ST J ADMIN Rule 2.520(c); FL ST 20 J CIR 2.9.

b. *Recording space.* On all papers and documents prepared and filed by the court or by any party to a proceeding which are to be recorded in the public records of any county, including but not limited to final money judgments and notices of lis pendens, a three (3) inch by three (3) inch space at the top right-hand corner on the first page and a one (1) inch by three (3) inch space at the top right-hand corner on each subsequent page shall be left blank and reserved for use by the clerk of court. FL ST J ADMIN Rule 2.520(d).

i. *Exceptions to recording space.* Any papers or documents created by persons or entities over which the filing party has no control, including but not limited to wills, codicils, trusts, or other testamentary documents; documents prepared or executed by any public officer; documents prepared, executed, acknowledged, or proved outside of the State of Florida; or documents created by State or Federal government agencies, may be filed without the space required by FL ST J ADMIN Rule 2.520. FL ST J ADMIN Rule 2.520(e).

c. *Noncompliance.* No clerk of court is permitted to refuse to file any document or paper because of noncompliance with the Florida Rules of Judicial Administration. However, upon request of the clerk of court, noncomplying documents must be resubmitted in accordance with the formatting rules. FL ST J ADMIN Rule 2.520(f).

   i. When time of filing is critical, the Clerk shall accept pleadings, motions, petitions, briefs, notices, orders, judgments, decrees, opinions, or other papers or official documents on other than eight and one half by eleven (8 1/2 by 11) inch paper but shall then require that the document be resubmitted to comply with FL ST J ADMIN Rule 2.520. FL ST 20 J CIR 2.9.

2. *Caption.* Every pleading, motion, order, judgment, or other paper shall have a caption containing the name of the court, the file number, and except for in rem proceedings, including forfeiture proceedings, the name of the first party on each side with an appropriate indication of other parties, and a designation identifying the party filing it and its nature or the nature of the order, as the case may be. In any in rem proceeding, every pleading, motion, order, judgment, or other paper shall have a caption containing the name of the court, the file number, the style "In re" (followed by the name or general description of the property), and a designation of the person or entity filing it and its nature or the nature of the order, as the case may be. In an in rem forfeiture proceeding, the style shall be "In re forfeiture of" (followed by the name of the general description of the property). All papers filed in the action shall be styled in such a manner as to indicate clearly the subject matter of the paper and the party requesting or obtaining relief. FL ST RCP Rule 1.100(c)(1).

3. *Writing and written defined.* Writing or written means a document containing information, an application, or a stipulation. FL ST RCP Rule 1.080(c).

4. *Rule abbreviations*

   a. The Florida Rules of Civil Procedure and shall be abbreviated as Fla.R.Civ.P. FL ST RCP Rule 1.010.

   b. The Florida Rules of Judicial Administration shall be abbreviated as Fla. R. Jud. Admin. FL ST J ADMIN Rule 2.110.

5. *Nonverification.* Except when otherwise specifically provided by the Florida Rules of Civil Procedure or an applicable statute, every pleading or other document of a party represented by an attorney need not be verified or accompanied by an affidavit. FL ST RCP Rule 1.030; FL ST J ADMIN Rule 2.515(a).

6. *Attorney signature*

   a. *Attorney signature.* Every pleading and other document of a party represented by an attorney shall be signed by at least one (1) attorney of record in that attorney's individual name whose current record Florida Bar address, telephone number, including area code, primary e-mail address and secondary e-mail addresses, if any, and Florida Bar number shall be stated, and who shall be duly licensed to practice law in Florida or who shall have received permission to appear in the particular case as provided in FL ST J ADMIN Rule 2.510. FL ST J ADMIN Rule 2.515(a).

      i. The attorney may be required by the court to give the address of, and to vouch for the attorney's authority to represent, the party. FL ST J ADMIN Rule 2.515(a).

      ii. The signature of an attorney shall constitute a certificate by the attorney that the attorney has read the pleading or other document; that to the best of the attorney's knowledge, information, and belief there is good ground to support it; and that it is not interposed for delay. FL ST J ADMIN Rule 2.515(a).

      iii. If a pleading is not signed or is signed with intent to defeat the purpose of FL ST J ADMIN Rule 2.515, it may be stricken and the action may proceed as though the pleading or other document had not been served. FL ST J ADMIN Rule 2.515(a).

   b. *Pro se litigant signature.* A party who is not represented by an attorney shall sign any pleading or

other paper and state the party's address and telephone number, including area code. FL ST J ADMIN Rule 2.515(b).

c. *Form of signature*

   i. The signatures required on pleadings and documents by FL ST J ADMIN Rule 2.515(a) and FL ST J ADMIN Rule 2.515(b) may be:

      - Original signatures;
      - Original signatures that have been reproduced by electronic means, such as on electronically transmitted documents or photocopied documents;
      - Electronic signatures using the "/s/," "s/," or "/s" formats by or at the direction of the person signing; or
      - Any other signature format authorized by general law, so long as the clerk where the proceeding is pending has the capability of receiving and has obtained approval from the Supreme Court of Florida to accept pleadings and documents with that signature format. FL ST J ADMIN Rule 2.515(c)(1).

   ii. An attorney, party, or other person who files a pleading or paper by electronic transmission that does not contain the original signature of that attorney, party, or other person shall file that identical pleading or paper in paper form containing an original signature of that attorney, party, or other person (hereinafter called the follow-up filing) immediately thereafter. The follow-up filing is not required if the Supreme Court of Florida has entered an order directing the clerk of court to discontinue accepting the follow-up filing. FL ST J ADMIN Rule 2.515(c)(2).

7. *Forms*

   a. *Process.* The forms of process, notice of lis pendens, and notice of action provided in the Florida Rules of Civil Procedure are sufficient. Variations from the forms do not void process or notices that are otherwise sufficient. FL ST RCP Rule 1.900(a).

   b. *Other forms.* The other forms provided in the Florida Rules of Civil Procedure are sufficient for the matters that are covered by them. So long as the substance is expressed without prolixity, the forms may be varied to meet the facts of a particular case. FL ST RCP Rule 1.900(b).

   c. *Formal matters.* Captions, except for the designation of the paper, are omitted from the forms provided in the Florida Rules of Civil Procedure. A general form of caption is the first form provided. Signatures are omitted from pleadings and motions. FL ST RCP Rule 1.900(c).

8. *Notices to persons with disabilities.* All notices of court proceedings to be held in a public facility, and all process compelling appearance at such proceedings, shall include the following statement in bold face, fourteen (14) point Times New Roman or Courier font: "If you are a person with a disability who needs any accommodation in order to participate in this proceeding, you are entitled, at no cost to you, to the provision of certain assistance. Please contact [identify applicable court personnel by name, address, and telephone number] at least seven (7) days before your scheduled court appearance, or immediately upon receiving this notification if the time before the scheduled appearance is less than seven (7) days; if you are hearing or voice impaired, call 711." FL ST J ADMIN Rule 2.540(c)(1). For more information, see FL ST 20 J CIR 2.15.

9. *Minimization of the filing of sensitive information*

   a. *Limitations for court filings.* Unless authorized by FL ST J ADMIN Rule 2.425(b), statute, another rule of court, or the court orders otherwise, designated sensitive information filed with the court must be limited to the following format:

      i. The initials of a person known to be a minor;

      ii. The year of birth of a person's birth date;

      iii. No portion of any: Social security number, Bank account number, Credit card account number, Charge account number, or Debit account number;

      iv. The last four digits of any: Taxpayer identification number (TIN), Employee identification number, Driver's license number, Passport number, Telephone number, Financial account

number, except as set forth in FL ST J ADMIN Rule 2.425(a)(3), Brokerage account number, Insurance policy account number, Loan account number, Customer account number, or Patient or health care number;

v. A truncated version of any: Email address, Computer user name, Password, or Personal identification number (PIN); and

vi. A truncated version of any other sensitive information as provided by court order. FL ST J ADMIN Rule 2.425(a).

b. *Exceptions.* FL ST J ADMIN Rule 2.425(a) does not apply to the following:

i. An account number which identifies the property alleged to be the subject of a proceeding;

ii. The record of an administrative or agency proceeding;

iii. The record in appellate or review proceedings;

iv. The birth date of a minor whenever the birth date is necessary for the court to establish or maintain subject matter jurisdiction;

v. The name of a minor in any order relating to parental responsibility, time-sharing, or child support;

vi. The name of a minor in any document or order affecting the minor's ownership of real property;

vii. The birth date of a party in a writ of attachment or notice to payor;

viii. In traffic and criminal proceedings: a pro se filing; a court filing that is related to a criminal matter or investigation and that is prepared before the filing of a criminal charge or is not filed as part of any docketed criminal case; an arrest or search warrant or any information in support thereof; a charging document and an affidavit or other documents filed in support of any charging document, including any driving records; a statement of particulars; discovery material introduced into evidence or otherwise filed with the court; and all information necessary for the proper issuance and execution of a subpoena duces tecum;

ix. Information used by the clerk for case maintenance purposes or the courts for case management purposes; and

x. Information which is relevant and material to an issue before the court. FL ST J ADMIN Rule 2.425(b).

c. *Remedies.* Upon motion by a party or interested person or sua sponte by the court, the court may order remedies, sanctions or both for a violation of FL ST J ADMIN Rule 2.425(a). Following notice and an opportunity to respond, the court may impose sanctions if such filing was not made in good faith. FL ST J ADMIN Rule 2.425(c).

d. *Motions not restricted.* FL ST J ADMIN Rule 2.425 does not restrict a party's right to move for protective order, to move to file documents under seal, or to request a determination of the confidentiality of records. FL ST J ADMIN Rule 2.425(d).

e. *Application.* FL ST J ADMIN Rule 2.425 does not affect the application of constitutional provisions, statutes, or rules of court regarding confidential information or access to public information. FL ST J ADMIN Rule 2.425(e).

F. Filing and Service Requirements

1. *Filing requirements.* All original documents must be filed with the court either before service or immediately thereafter, unless otherwise provided for by general law or other rules. If the original of any bond or other document is not placed in the court file, a certified copy must be so placed by the clerk. FL ST J ADMIN Rule 2.516(d). All documents shall be filed in conformity with the requirements of FL ST J ADMIN Rule 2.525. FL ST RCP Rule 1.080(b). All documents filed in any court shall be filed by electronic transmission in accordance with FL ST J ADMIN Rule 2.525. "Documents" means pleadings, motions, petitions, memoranda, briefs, notices, exhibits, declarations, affidavits, orders, judgments, decrees, writs, opinions, and any other paper or writing submitted to a court. FL ST J ADMIN Rule 2.520(a). All documents that are court records, as defined in FL ST J ADMIN Rule 2.430(a)(1), must be filed by electronic transmission, provided that: (1) the clerk has the ability to accept and retain such

documents; (2) the clerk or the chief judge of the circuit has requested permission to accept documents filed by electronic transmission; and (3) the supreme court has entered an order granting permission to the clerk to accept documents filed by electronic transmission. FL ST J ADMIN Rule 2.525(c)(1).

a. *Definition.* "Electronic transmission of documents" means the sending of information by electronic signals to, by or from a court or clerk, which when received can be transformed and stored or transmitted on paper, microfilm, magnetic storage device, optical imaging system, CD-ROM, flash drive, other electronic data storage system, server, case maintenance system ("CM"), electronic court filing ("ECF") system, statewide or local electronic portal ("e-portal"), or other electronic record keeping system authorized by the supreme court in a format sufficient to communicate the information on the original document in a readable format. Electronic transmission of documents includes electronic mail ("e-mail") and any internet-based transmission procedure, and may include procedures allowing for documents to be signed or verified by electronic means. FL ST J ADMIN Rule 2.525(a).

   i. The filing of documents with the court as required by the Florida Rules of Judicial Administration must be made by filing them with the clerk in accordance with FL ST J ADMIN Rule 2.525, except that the judge may permit documents to be filed with the judge, in which event the judge must note the filing date before him or her on the documents and transmit them to the clerk. The date of filing is that shown on the face of the document by the judge's notation or the clerk's time stamp, whichever is earlier. FL ST J ADMIN Rule 2.516(e).

b. *Application.* Any court or clerk of the court may accept the electronic transmission of documents for filing after the clerk, together with input from the chief judge of the circuit, has obtained approval of the procedures and program for doing so from the Supreme Court of Florida. FL ST J ADMIN Rule 2.525(b).

c. *Exceptions*

   i. Paper documents and other submissions may be manually submitted to the clerk or court:

      - When the clerk does not have the ability to accept and retain documents by electronic filing or has not had ECF Procedures approved by the supreme court;
      - For filing by any self-represented party or any self-represented nonparty unless specific ECF Procedures provide a means to file documents electronically. However, any self-represented nonparty that is a governmental or public agency and any other agency, partnership, corporation, or business entity acting on behalf of any governmental or public agency may file documents by electronic transmission if such entity has the capability of filing documents electronically;
      - For filing by attorneys excused from e-mail service in accordance with FL ST J ADMIN Rule 2.516(b);
      - When submitting evidentiary exhibits or filing non-documentary materials;
      - When the filing involves documents in excess of twenty-five (25) megabytes (25MB) in size. For such filings, documents may be transmitted using an electronic storage medium that the clerk has the ability to accept, which may include a CD-ROM, flash drive, or similar storage medium;
      - When filed in open court, as permitted by the court;
      - When paper filing is permitted by any approved statewide or local ECF procedures; and
      - If any court determines that justice so requires. FL ST J ADMIN Rule 2.525(d).

   ii. Any document in paper form submitted under FL ST J ADMIN Rule 2.525(d) is filed when it is received by the clerk or court and the clerk shall immediately thereafter convert any filed paper document to an electronic document. "Convert to an electronic document" means optically capturing an image of a paper document and using character recognition software to recover as much of the document's text as practicable and then indexing and storing the document in the official court file. FL ST J ADMIN Rule 2.525(c)(4).

   iii. Any storage medium submitted under FL ST J ADMIN Rule 2.525(d)(5) is filed when received

by the clerk or court and the clerk shall immediately thereafter transfer the electronic documents from the storage device to the official court file. FL ST J ADMIN Rule 2.525(c)(5).

iv. If the filer of any paper document authorized under FL ST J ADMIN Rule 2.525(d) provides a self-addressed, postage-paid envelope for return of the paper document after it is converted to electronic form by the clerk, the clerk shall place the paper document in the envelope and deposit it in the mail. Except when a paper document is required to be maintained, the clerk may recycle any filed paper document that is not to be returned to the filer. FL ST J ADMIN Rule 2.525(c)(6).

v. The clerk may convert any paper document filed before the effective date of FL ST J ADMIN Rule 2.525 to an electronic document. Unless the clerk is required to maintain the paper document, if the paper document has been converted to an electronic document by the clerk, the paper document is no longer part of the official court file and may be removed and recycled. FL ST J ADMIN Rule 2.525(c)(7).

d. *Official court file.* For information on what constitutes the official court file, please see FL ST J ADMIN Rule 2.525(c)(2), FL ST J ADMIN Rule 2.525(c)(3).

e. *Administration.* All attorneys, parties, or other persons using this rule to file documents are required to make arrangements with the court or clerk for the payment of any charges authorized by general law or the supreme court before filing any document by electronic transmission. FL ST J ADMIN Rule 2.525(f)(2).

f. *Filing date.* The filing date for an electronically transmitted document is the date and time that such filing is acknowledged by an electronic stamp or otherwise, pursuant to any procedure set forth in any ECF Procedures approved by the supreme court, or the date the last page of such filing is received by the court or clerk. FL ST J ADMIN Rule 2.525(f)(3).

g. *Accessibility.* All documents transmitted in any electronic form under FL ST J ADMIN Rule 2.525 must comply with the accessibility requirements of FL ST J ADMIN Rule 2.526. FL ST J ADMIN Rule 2.525(g).

2. *Service requirements.* Every pleading subsequent to the initial pleading, all orders, and every other document filed in the action must be served in conformity with the requirements of FL ST J ADMIN Rule 2.516. FL ST RCP Rule 1.080(a).

a. *Service; Generally.* The timing and manner of service should not be used to the disadvantage of the party receiving the papers. FL ST 20 J CIR 2.20(IV)(C)(1).

i. Papers and memoranda of law should not be served at court appearances without advance notice to opposing counsel and should not be served so close to a court appearance so as to inhibit the ability of opposing counsel to prepare for that appearance or to respond to the papers. Should the attorney do so, the court is urged to take appropriate action in response, including continuing the matter to allow opposing counsel to prepare and respond. FL ST 20 J CIR 2.20(IV)(C)(2).

ii. Papers should not be served in order to take advantage of an opponent's known absence from the office or at a time or in a manner designed to inconvenience an adversary, such as late on Friday afternoon or the day preceding a secular or religious holiday. FL ST 20 J CIR 2.20(IV)(C)(3).

iii. Service should be made personally or by courtesy copy facsimile transmission when it is likely that service by mail, even when allowed, will prejudice the opposing party or will not provide the opposing party with a reasonable time to respond. FL ST 20 J CIR 2.20(IV)(C)(4).

b. *Service; When required.* Unless the court otherwise orders, or a statute or supreme court administrative order specifies a different means of service, every pleading subsequent to the initial pleading and every other document filed in any court proceeding, except applications for witness subpoenas and documents served by formal notice or required to be served in the manner provided for service of formal notice, must be served in accordance with FL ST J ADMIN Rule 2.516 on each party. No service need be made on parties against whom a default has been entered, except that pleadings asserting new or additional claims against them must be served in the manner provided for service of summons. FL ST J ADMIN Rule 2.516(a).

i. *Copies of court submissions.* Copies of any submissions to the court (such as correspondence, memoranda of law, motions, case law, etc.) should simultaneously be provided to opposing counsel by substantially the same method of delivery by which they are provided to the court. For example, if a memorandum of law is hand-delivered to the court, at substantially the same time a copy should be hand-delivered or faxed to opposing counsel. FL ST 20 J CIR 2.20(IV)(J)(4).

c. *Service; How made.* When service is required or permitted to be made upon a party represented by an attorney, service must be made upon the attorney unless service upon the party is ordered by the court. FL ST J ADMIN Rule 2.516(b).

i. *Service by electronic mail ("e-mail").* All documents required or permitted to be served on another party must be served by e-mail, unless FL ST J ADMIN Rule 2.516 otherwise provides. When, in addition to service by e-mail, the sender also utilizes another means of service provided for in FL ST J ADMIN Rule 2.516(b)(2), any differing time limits and other provisions applicable to that other means of service control. FL ST J ADMIN Rule 2.516(b)(1). Any document electronically transmitted to a court or clerk must also be served on all parties and interested persons in accordance with the applicable rules of court. FL ST J ADMIN Rule 2.525(e)(2).

- *Service on attorneys.* Upon appearing in a proceeding, an attorney must serve a designation of a primary e-mail address and may designate no more than two (2) secondary e-mail addresses. Thereafter, service must be directed to all designated e-mail addresses in that proceeding. Every document filed by an attorney thereafter must include the primary e-mail address of that attorney and any secondary e-mail addresses. If an attorney does not designate any e-mail address for service, documents may be served on that attorney at the e-mail address on record with The Florida Bar. FL ST J ADMIN Rule 2.516(b)(1)(A).
- *Exception to e-mail service on attorneys.* Service by an attorney on another attorney must be made by e-mail unless excused by the court. Upon motion by an attorney demonstrating that the attorney has no e-mail account and lacks access to the Internet at the attorney's office, the court may excuse the attorney from the requirements of e-mail service. Service on and by an attorney excused by the court from e-mail service must be by the means provided in FL ST J ADMIN Rule 2.516(b)(2). FL ST J ADMIN Rule 2.516(b)(1)(B).
- *Service on and by parties not represented by an attorney.* Any party not represented by an attorney may serve a designation of a primary e-mail address and also may designate no more than two (2) secondary e-mail addresses to which service must be directed in that proceeding by the means provided in FL ST J ADMIN Rule 2.516(b)(1). If a party not represented by an attorney does not designate an e-mail address for service in a proceeding, service on and by that party must be by the means provided in FL ST J ADMIN Rule 2.516(b)(2). FL ST J ADMIN Rule 2.516(b)(1)(C).
- *Time of service.* Service by e-mail is complete when it is sent. FL ST J ADMIN Rule 2.516(b)(1)(D). An e-mail is deemed served on the date it is sent. FL ST J ADMIN Rule 2.516(b)(1)(D)(i). If the sender learns that the e-mail did not reach the address of the person to be served, the sender must immediately send another copy by e-mail, or by a means authorized by FL ST J ADMIN Rule 2.516(b)(2). FL ST J ADMIN Rule 2.516(b)(1)(D)(ii). E-mail service is treated as service by mail for the computation of time. FL ST J ADMIN Rule 2.516(b)(1)(D)(iii).

ii. *Format of e-mail for service.* Service of a document by e-mail is made by attaching a copy of the document in PDF format to an e-mail sent to all addresses designated by the attorney or party. FL ST J ADMIN Rule 2.516(b)(1)(E).

- All documents served by e-mail must be attached to an e-mail message containing a subject line beginning with the words "SERVICE OF COURT DOCUMENT" in all capital letters, followed by the case number of the proceeding in which the documents are being served. FL ST J ADMIN Rule 2.516(b)(1)(E)(i).

- The body of the e-mail must identify the court in which the proceeding is pending, the case number, the name of the initial party on each side, the title of each document served with that e-mail, and the sender's name and telephone number. FL ST J ADMIN Rule 2.516(b)(1)(E)(ii).
- Any document served by e-mail may be signed by the "/s/" format, as long as the filed original is signed in accordance with the applicable rule of procedure. FL ST J ADMIN Rule 2.516(b)(1)(E)(iii).
- Any e-mail which, together with its attached documents, exceeds five megabytes (5MB) in size, must be divided and sent as separate e-mails, no one of which may exceed five megabytes (5MB) in size and each of which must be sequentially numbered in the subject line. FL ST J ADMIN Rule 2.516(b)(1)(E)(iv).

iii. *Service by other means.* In addition to, and not in lieu of, service by e-mail, service may also be made upon attorneys by any of the means specified in FL ST J ADMIN Rule 2.516(b)(2). Service on and by all parties who are not represented by an attorney and who do not designate an e-mail address, and on and by all attorneys excused from e-mail service, must be made by delivering a copy of the document or by mailing it to the party or attorney at their last known address or, if no address is known, by leaving it with the clerk of the court. Service by mail is complete upon mailing. Delivery of a copy within FL ST J ADMIN Rule 2.516 is complete upon:

- Handing it to the attorney or to the party,
- Leaving it at the attorney's or party's office with a clerk or other person in charge thereof,
- If there is no one in charge, leaving it in a conspicuous place therein,
- If the office is closed or the person to be served has no office, leaving it at the person's usual place of abode with some person of his or her family above fifteen (15) years of age and informing such person of the contents, or
- Transmitting it by facsimile to the attorney's or party's office with a cover sheet containing the sender's name, firm, address, telephone number, and facsimile number, and the number of pages transmitted. When service is made by facsimile, a copy must also be served by any other method permitted by FL ST J ADMIN Rule 2.516. Facsimile service occurs when transmission is complete. FL ST J ADMIN Rule 2.516(b)(2)(A) through FL ST J ADMIN Rule 2.516(b)(2)(E).
- Service by delivery after 5:00 p.m. must be deemed to have been made by mailing on the date of delivery. FL ST J ADMIN Rule 2.516(b)(2)(F).

d. *Service; Numerous defendants.* In actions when the parties are unusually numerous, the court may regulate the service contemplated by the Florida Rules of Judicial Administration on motion or on its own initiative in such manner as may be found to be just and reasonable. FL ST J ADMIN Rule 2.516(c).

e. *Service by clerk.* Service of notices and other documents required to be made by the clerk must also be done as provided in FL ST J ADMIN Rule 2.516(b). FL ST J ADMIN Rule 2.516(g).

G. Hearings

1. *Scheduling.* Before setting a motion for hearing, counsel should make a good faith effort to resolve the issue with opposing counsel. FL ST 20 J CIR 2.20(IV)(I)(1). Except in emergency situations, attorneys should make a good faith effort to communicate with opposing counsel prior to scheduling depositions, hearings and other proceedings, so as to schedule them at times that are mutually convenient for all interested persons. Further, a sufficient time should be reserved to permit a complete presentation by counsel for all parties. FL ST 20 J CIR 2.20(IV)(B)(1). Attorneys should not use the hearing time obtained by opposing counsel for other motion practice. FL ST 20 J CIR 2.20(IV)(B)(6).

   a. *Notice.* Counsel should notify opposing counsel of dates and times obtained from the court for future hearings on the same day that the hearing date is obtained from the court, or as soon as practicable thereafter. FL ST 20 J CIR 2.20(IV)(J)(3).

b. *Scheduling conflict.* Attorneys should notify opposing counsel, the court, and others affected, of scheduling conflicts as soon as they become apparent. Further, attorneys should cooperate with one another regarding all reasonable rescheduling requests that do not prejudice their clients or unduly delay a proceeding. FL ST 20 J CIR 2.20(IV)(B)(7).

  i. Attorneys should call potential scheduling problems to the attention of those affected, including the court, as soon as they become apparent and should avoid last minute cancellations. FL ST 20 J CIR 2.20(IV)(B)(12).

c. *Notice to court when appearance is unnecessary.* Attorneys should promptly notify the court or other tribunal of any resolution between the parties that renders a scheduled court appearance unnecessary. FL ST 20 J CIR 2.20(IV)(B)(8).

2. *Communication equipment*

a. *Definition.* Communication equipment means a conference telephone or other electronic device that permits all those appearing or participating to hear and speak to each other, provided that all conversation of all parties is audible to all persons present. FL ST J ADMIN Rule 2.530(a).

b. *Use by all parties.* A county or circuit court judge may, upon the court's own motion or upon the written request of a party, direct that communication equipment be used for a motion hearing, pretrial conference, or a status conference. A judge must give notice to the parties and consider any objections they may have to the use of communication equipment before directing that communication equipment be used. The decision to use communication equipment over the objection of parties will be in the sound discretion of the trial court, except as noted below. FL ST J ADMIN Rule 2.530(b).

c. *Use only by requesting party.* A county or circuit court judge may, upon the written request of a party upon reasonable notice to all other parties, permit a requesting party to participate through communication equipment in a scheduled motion hearing; however, any such request (except in criminal, juvenile, and appellate proceedings) must be granted, absent a showing of good cause to deny the same, where the hearing is set for not longer than fifteen (15) minutes. FL ST J ADMIN Rule 2.530(c).

d. *Testimony*

  i. *Generally.* A county or circuit court judge, general magistrate, special magistrate, or hearing officer may allow testimony to be taken through communication equipment if all parties consent or if permitted by another applicable rule of procedure. FL ST J ADMIN Rule 2.530(d)(1).

  ii. *Procedure.* Any party desiring to present testimony through communication equipment shall, prior to the hearing or trial at which the testimony is to be presented, contact all parties to determine whether each party consents to this form of testimony. The party seeking to present the testimony shall move for permission to present testimony through communication equipment, which motion shall set forth good cause as to why the testimony should be allowed in this form. FL ST J ADMIN Rule 2.530(d)(2).

  iii. *Oath.* Testimony may be taken through communication equipment only if a notary public or other person authorized to administer oaths in the witness's jurisdiction is present with the witness and administers the oath consistent with the laws of the jurisdiction. FL ST J ADMIN Rule 2.530(d)(3).

  iv. *Confrontation rights.* In juvenile and criminal proceedings the defendant must make an informed waiver of any confrontation rights that may be abridged by the use of communication equipment. FL ST J ADMIN Rule 2.530(d)(4).

  v. *Video testimony.* If the testimony to be presented utilizes video conferencing or comparable two-way visual capabilities, the court in its discretion may modify the procedures set forth in FL ST J ADMIN Rule 2.530 to accommodate the technology utilized. FL ST J ADMIN Rule 2.530(d)(5).

e. *Burden of expense.* The cost for the use of the communication equipment is the responsibility of the requesting party unless otherwise directed by the court. FL ST J ADMIN Rule 2.530(e).

3. *Telephonic non-evidentiary motion hearings set for not longer than fifteen (15) minutes.* FL ST 20 J CIR 1.10 specifically addresses non-evidentiary civil motion hearings set for not longer than fifteen (15) minutes. It is not intended to limit or address requests for telephonic hearings which are otherwise governed by FL ST J ADMIN Rule 2.071. FL ST 20 J CIR 1.10. [Editor's note: FL ST J ADMIN Rule 2.071 was renumbered as FL ST J ADMIN Rule 2.530]. Evidentiary hearings are exempted from the application of FL ST 20 J CIR 1.10. FL ST 20 J CIR 1.10.
   a. In instances where a civil motion hearing is scheduled for not longer than fifteen (15) minutes, a party may file a written request to participate via conference or speaker telephone, or other applicable communication equipment, and shall provide notice to the Court and the parties to the motion. FL ST 20 J CIR 1.10. Refer to the Timing section of this document for information on when the notice must be given and when request must be served.
   b. The requesting party shall be responsible for contacting the trial judge's Judicial Assistant and ensuring that appropriate arrangements have been made to permit participation through conference or speaker telephone, or other applicable communication equipment, on the scheduled date and time. It shall be at the discretion of the trial judge as to whether the requesting party shall be responsible for initiating the telephone or communication connection or whether the Court shall be responsible for initiating the telephone or communication connection. FL ST 20 J CIR 1.10(3).
   c. Absent a showing of good cause, and in accordance with FL ST J ADMIN Rule 2.071(c), the trial judge shall grant the request and make reasonable accommodations to permit the requesting party's participation through conference or speaker telephone, or other applicable communication equipment. FL ST 20 J CIR 1.10. [Editor's note: FL ST J ADMIN Rule 2.071 was renumbered as FL ST J ADMIN Rule 2.530(c)].
   d. To the extent that any provision of FL ST 20 J CIR 1.10 may be construed as being in conflict with any law, statute, or rule, the law, statute, or rule shall prevail. FL ST 20 J CIR 1.10.

H. Forms

1. Official Motion for Leave to Amend Forms for Florida

a. Caption. FL ST RCP Form 1.901.
b. Notice of compliance when constitutional challenge is brought. FL ST RCP Form 1.975.

2. Motion for Leave to Amend Forms for Florida

a. Motion; For leave of court; To amend complaint. FL-PP § 2:155.
b. Motion; For leave of court ; To add claim for punitive damages. FL-PP § 2:156.
c. Motion; For leave of court; To amend complaint; To conform to evidence. FL-PP § 2:157.
d. Motion; For leave of court; To permit admission of evidence. FL-PP § 2:158.
e. Order; Granting leave to amend complaint. FL-PP § 2:163.
f. Order; Granting leave to amend complaint; To conform to evidence. FL-PP § 2:164.
g. Order; Granting leave to amend complaint; To permit admission of evidence. FL-PP § 2:165.
h. Form for motion for leave to amend complaint. FL-RCPF R 1.190(39).
i. Form for amendment to complaint with leave of court. FL-RCPF R 1.190(40).
j. Form for motion to amend amended complaint. FL-RCPF R 1.190(42).
k. Form for amendment to amended complaint (or second amended complaint). FL-RCPF R 1.190(43).
l. Form for motion to amend complaint to add count. FL-RCPF R 1.190(44).

I. Checklist

(I) ❑ Matters to be considered by moving party
   (a) ❑ Required documents
      (1) ❑ Notice of hearing/Motion
      (2) ❑ Certification

- (3) ❑ Proposed amended pleading
- (4) ❑ Certificate of service

(b) ❑ Supplemental documents

- (1) ❑ Proposed order
- (2) ❑ Notice of constitutional question
- (3) ❑ Notice and request to participate in telephonic motion hearing

(c) ❑ Time for making motion

- (1) ❑ A party may amend a pleading once as a matter of course at any time before a responsive pleading is served or, if the pleading is one to which no responsive pleading is permitted and the action has not been placed on the trial calendar, may amend it at any time within twenty (20) days after it is served
- (2) ❑ Under the Florida Rules of Civil Procedure, there is no time limit as to when an amendment with leave of court may be sought; amendments of the pleadings may be permitted, with the court's discretion, at any stage of the proceedings in furtherance of justice
- (3) ❑ A motion for leave to amend a pleading to assert a claim for punitive damages can be filed separately and before the supporting evidence or proffer, but each shall be served on all parties at least twenty (20) days before the hearing
- (4) ❑ A copy of any written motion which may not be heard ex parte and a copy of the notice of the hearing thereof shall be served a reasonable time before the time specified for the hearing; as a general rule, notice should be provided (not including time for service) no less than five (5) business days for hearings
- (5) ❑ Notice and request to participate in telephonic motion hearing: Notice by the requesting party must be provided by mailing a copy of the written request at least five (5) days prior to the day of the hearing, or by delivering a copy of the written request to the other parties or, if represented by counsel, to the other parties' attorney(s) no later than 5:00 p.m. two (2) business days prior to the day of the hearing

(II) ❑ Matters to be considered by opposing party

(a) ❑ Required documents

- (1) ❑ Response to motion
- (2) ❑ Certificate of service

(b) ❑ Supplemental documents

- (1) ❑ Proposed order
- (2) ❑ Notice of constitutional question
- (3) ❑ Notice and request to participate in telephonic motion hearing

(c) ❑ Time for service and filing of opposition

- (1) ❑ No time specified for responding to a motion
- (2) ❑ Notice and request to participate in telephonic motion hearing: Notice by the requesting party must be provided by mailing a copy of the written request at least five (5) days prior to the day of the hearing, or by delivering a copy of the written request to the other parties or, if represented by counsel, to the other parties' attorney(s) no later than 5:00 p.m. two (2) business days prior to the day of the hearing

Motions, Oppositions and Replies
Motion for Summary Judgment

Document Last Updated January 2013

A. Applicable Rules

1. *State rules*
   a. Rules of court. FL ST RCP Rule 1.010; FL ST J ADMIN Rule 2.110.
   b. Nonverification of pleadings. FL ST RCP Rule 1.030.
   c. Service and filing of pleadings, orders, and documents. FL ST RCP Rule 1.080.
   d. Time. FL ST RCP Rule 1.090.
   e. Pleadings and motions. FL ST RCP Rule 1.100.
   f. Motions. FL ST RCP Rule 1.160.
   g. Summary judgment. FL ST RCP Rule 1.510.
   h. Relief from judgment, decrees, or orders. FL ST RCP Rule 1.540.
   i. Mediation and arbitration. FL ST RCP Rule 1.700; FL ST RCP Rule 1.710; FL ST RCP Rule 1.720; FL ST RCP Rule 1.730; FL ST RCP Rule 1.750; FL ST RCP Rule 1.800; FL ST RCP Rule 1.810; FL ST RCP Rule 1.820; FL ST RCP Rule 1.830.
   j. Forms. FL ST RCP Rule 1.900.
   k. Minimization of the filing of sensitive information. FL ST J ADMIN Rule 2.425.
   l. Retention of court records. FL ST J ADMIN Rule 2.430.
   m. Foreign attorneys. FL ST J ADMIN Rule 2.510.
   n. Signature of attorneys and parties. FL ST J ADMIN Rule 2.515.
   o. Paper. FL ST J ADMIN Rule 2.520.
   p. Electronic filing. FL ST J ADMIN Rule 2.525.
   q. Accessibility of information and technology. FL ST J ADMIN Rule 2.526.
   r. Communication equipment. FL ST J ADMIN Rule 2.530.
   s. Court reporting. FL ST J ADMIN Rule 2.535.
   t. Requests for accommodations by persons with disabilities. FL ST J ADMIN Rule 2.540.
   u. Case management. FL ST J ADMIN Rule 2.545.
2. *Local rules*
   a. Exclusions from mediation. FL ST 20 J CIR 1.9.
   b. Establishment and implementation of civil case management plan. FL ST 20 J CIR 1.13.
   c. Size of paper. FL ST 20 J CIR 2.9.
   d. Telephonic motion hearings set for not longer than fifteen minutes in circuit and county civil cases. FL ST 20 J CIR 1.10.
   e. Americans with Disabilities Act; Notification of court proceedings. FL ST 20 J CIR 2.15.
   f. Standards of professional courtesy and conduct and establishment of peer review program. FL ST 20 J CIR 2.20.

B. Timing

1. *Motion for summary judgment*
   a. *For the claimant.* A party seeking to recover upon a claim, counterclaim, crossclaim or third-party claim or to obtain a declaratory judgment may move for a summary judgment in that party's favor at

any time after the expiration of twenty (20) days from the commencement of the action or after service of a motion for summary judgment by the adverse party. FL ST RCP Rule 1.510(a).

b. *For defending party.* A party against whom a claim, counterclaim, crossclaim, or third-party claim is asserted or a declaratory judgment is sought may move for a summary judgment in that party's favor as to all or any part thereof at any time with or without supporting affidavits. FL ST RCP Rule 1.510(b).

   i. A defending party is not required to serve his responsive pleading before moving for summary judgment. He may make the motion at any time, setting out his defenses by affidavit, and thus effect a speedy termination of the action if no genuine issue exists as to any fact or facts pertaining to a defense that would defeat the claim. FL ST RCP Rule 1.510, notes.

2. *Service of motion.* The movant shall serve the motion for summary judgment at least twenty (20) days before the time fixed for the hearing, and shall also serve at that time a copy of any summary judgment evidence on which the movant relies that has not already been filed with the court. FL ST RCP Rule 1.510(c).

   a. *Notice of hearing.* Except in emergency situations, attorneys should provide opposing counsel, parties, witnesses, and other affected persons, sufficient notice of depositions, hearings and other proceedings. FL ST 20 J CIR 2.20(IV)(B)(1). Attorneys should notify opposing counsel of any hearing time reserved as soon as practicable. FL ST 20 J CIR 2.20(IV)(B)(3). When hearing time is obtained, attorneys should promptly prepare and serve all counsel of record with notice of the hearing. Do not delay in providing such notice. FL ST 20 J CIR 2.20(IV)(B)(4).

3. *Notice and request to participate in telephonic motion hearing.* Notice by the requesting party must be provided by mailing a copy of the written request at least five (5) days prior to the day of the hearing, or by delivering a copy of the written request to the other parties or, if represented by counsel, to the other parties' attorney(s) no later than 5:00 p.m. two (2) business days prior to the day of the hearing. FL ST 20 J CIR 1.10. Refer to the Hearings section of this document for more information.

4. *Computation of time*

   a. *Generally.* Computation of time shall be governed by FL ST J ADMIN Rule 2.514. FL ST RCP Rule 1.090(a). The following rules apply in computing time periods specified in any rule of procedure, local rule, court order, or statute that does not specify a method of computing time. FL ST J ADMIN Rule 2.514(a).

      i. *Period stated in days or a longer unit.* When the period is stated in days or a longer unit of time (A) exclude the day of the event that triggers the period; (B) count every day, including intermediate Saturdays, Sundays, and legal holidays; and (C) include the last day of the period, but if the last day is a Saturday, Sunday, or legal holiday, or falls within any period of time extended through an order of the chief justice under FL ST J ADMIN Rule 2.205(a)(2)(B)(iv), the period continues to run until the end of the next day that is not a Saturday, Sunday, or legal holiday and does not fall within any period of time extended through an order of the chief justice. FL ST J ADMIN Rule 2.514(a)(1).

      ii. *Period stated in hours.* When the period is stated in hours (A) begin counting immediately on the occurrence of the event that triggers the period; (B) count every hour, including hours during intermediate Saturdays, Sundays, and legal holidays; and (C) if the period would end on a Saturday, Sunday, or legal holiday, or during any period of time extended through an order of the chief justice under FL ST J ADMIN Rule 2.205(a)(2)(B)(iv), the period continues to run until the same time on the next day that is not a Saturday, Sunday, or legal holiday and does not fall within any period of time extended through an order of the chief justice. FL ST J ADMIN Rule 2.514(a)(2).

      iii. *Period stated in days less than seven (7) days.* When the period stated in days is less than seven (7) days, intermediate Saturdays, Sundays, and legal holidays shall be excluded in the computation. FL ST J ADMIN Rule 2.514(a)(3).

      iv. *"Last day" defined.* Unless a different time is set by a statute, local rule, or court order, the last day ends (A) for electronic filing or for service by any means, at midnight; and (B) for filing by other means, when the clerk's office is scheduled to close. FL ST J ADMIN Rule 2.514(a)(4).

v. *"Next day" defined.* The "next day" is determined by continuing to count forward when the period is measured after an event and backward when measured before an event. FL ST J ADMIN Rule 2.514(a)(5).

vi. *"Legal holiday" defined.* "Legal holiday" means (A) the day set aside by FL ST § 110.117, for observing New Year's Day, Martin Luther King, Jr.'s Birthday, Memorial Day, Independence Day, Labor Day, Veterans' Day, Thanksgiving Day, the Friday after Thanksgiving Day, or Christmas Day, and (B) any day observed as a holiday by the clerk's office or as designated by the chief judge. FL ST J ADMIN Rule 2.514(a)(6).

b. *Additional time after service by mail or e-mail.* When a party may or must act within a specified time after service and service is made by mail or e-mail, five (5) days are added after the period that would otherwise expire under FL ST J ADMIN Rule 2.514(a). FL ST J ADMIN Rule 2.514(b).

c. *Enlargement.* When an act is required or allowed to be done at or within a specified time by order of court, by the Florida Rules of Civil Procedure, or by notice given thereunder, for cause shown the court at any time in its discretion (1) with or without notice, may order the period enlarged if request therefor is made before the expiration of the period originally prescribed or as extended by a previous order, or (2) upon motion made and notice after the expiration of the specified period, may permit the act to be done when failure to act was the result of excusable neglect, but it may not extend the time for making a motion for new trial, for rehearing, or to alter or amend a judgment; making a motion for relief from a judgment under FL ST RCP Rule 1.540(b); taking an appeal or filing a petition for certiorari; or making a motion for a directed verdict. FL ST RCP Rule 1.090(b).

d. *Unaffected by expiration of term.* The period of time provided for the doing of any act or the taking of any proceeding shall not be affected or limited by the continued existence or expiration of a term of court. The continued existence or expiration of a term of court in no way affects the power of a court to do any act or take any proceeding in any action which is or has been pending before it. FL ST RCP Rule 1.090(c).

C. General Requirements

1. *Motions generally*

a. *Contents.* An application to the court for an order shall be by motion which shall be made in writing unless made during a hearing or trial, shall state with particularity the grounds therefor, and shall set forth the relief or order sought. The requirement of writing is fulfilled if the motion is stated in a written notice of the hearing of the motion. All notices of hearing shall specify each motion or other matter to be heard. FL ST RCP Rule 1.100(b).

i. *Notice of hearing.* The notice of hearing should indicate on its face whether the date and time have been coordinated with opposing counsel. If the attorney has been unable to coordinate the hearing with opposing counsel, the notice should state the specific good faith efforts the attorney undertook to coordinate or why coordination was not obtained. FL ST 20 J CIR 2.20(IV)(B)(5).

b. *Particularity requirement.* The court considers a motion in the light of the substantive law, rule or statute to make its determination. Some rules require a statement of the grounds for a motion under the rule. Failure to give the grounds will result in denial of the motion. This should be the result in all situations when the ground for the motion is not inherent in the rule. FL-PRACPROC § 9:3. The requirement is nevertheless an important one, first because of the due process notice rights of the respondent, as well as for the assistance it provides to the court in its preparation for the hearing or, absent a hearing, for disposition. 4 FLPRAC R 1.100.

2. *Conference with opposing counsel.* Attorneys should, whenever possible, prior to filing or upon receiving a motion, contact opposing counsel to determine if the matter can be resolved in whole or in part. This may alleviate the need for a hearing on the motion or allow submission of an agreed order in lieu of a hearing. FL ST 20 J CIR 2.20(IV)(L)(2).

3. *Summary judgment.* A party seeking to recover upon or defend against a claim, counterclaim, crossclaim, or third-party claim or to obtain a declaratory judgment may move for a summary judgment. FL ST RCP Rule 1.510(a); FL ST RCP Rule 1.510(b).

a. *General motion for summary judgment information*

i. *Contents of motion.* The motion shall state with particularity the grounds upon which it is based and the substantial matters of law to be argued and shall specifically identify any affidavits, answers to interrogatories, admissions, depositions, and other materials as would be admissible in evidence ("summary judgment evidence") on which the movant relies. FL ST RCP Rule 1.510(c).

ii. *Evidence relied upon.* The movant shall also serve at that time a copy of any summary judgment evidence on which the movant relies that has not already been filed with the court. FL ST RCP Rule 1.510(c).

iii. *Judgment as a matter of law.* The judgment sought shall be rendered forthwith if the pleadings and summary judgment evidence on file show that there is no genuine issue as to any material fact and that the moving party is entitled to a judgment as a matter of law. A summary judgment, interlocutory in character, may be rendered on the issue of liability alone although there is a genuine issue as to the amount of damages. FL ST RCP Rule 1.510(c).

b. *Sham pleadings.* If a party deems any pleading or part thereof filed by another party to be a sham, that party may move to strike the pleading or part thereof before the cause is set for trial and the court shall hear the motion, taking evidence of the respective parties, and if the motion is sustained, the pleading to which the motion is directed shall be stricken. Default and summary judgment on the merits may be entered in the discretion of the court or the court may permit additional pleadings to be filed for good cause shown. FL ST RCP Rule 1.150(a).

c. *Burden of proof*

i. The moving party in a motion for summary judgment has the initial burden of demonstrating the nonexistence of any genuine issue of fact. Landers v. Milton, 370 So.2d 368, 370 (Fla. 1979); Gardner v. Sabal Point Properties, Inc., 616 So.2d 1111, 1112 (Fla. 5th DCA 1993); FL-PP § 6:7.

ii. If the record raises the slightest doubt that material issues could be present, that doubt must be resolved against the movant and the motion for summary judgment denied. Moore v. Morris, 475 So.2d 666, 668 (Fla. 1985); Henderson v. CSX Transportation, Inc., 617 So.2d 770 (Fla. 1st DCA 1993); Jones v. Directors Guild of America, Inc., 584 So.2d 1057 (Fla. 1st DCA 1991); FL-PP § 6:7.

iii. Until the moving party meets the initial burden of showing there is no issue of material fact, the opposing party need do nothing. Holl v. Talcott, 191 So.2d 40, 43 (Fla. 1966); Spradley v. Stick, 622 So.2d 610 (Fla. 1st DCA 1993); FL-RCPF R 1.510(404).

iv. When the movant has tendered competent evidence in support of its motion, the burden shifts to the nonmoving party to come forward with opposing evidence to show that a question of material fact exists. Landers v. Milton, 370 So.2d 368, 370 (Fla. 1979); Holl v. Talcott, 191 So.2d 40, 43-44 (Fla. 1966); Lenhal Realty, Inc. v. Transamerica Commercial Finance Corp., 615 So.2d 207 (Fla. 4th DCA 1993); FL-PP § 6:7.

d. *Affidavits*

i. *Form of affidavits; Further testimony.* Supporting and opposing affidavits shall be made on personal knowledge, shall set forth such facts as would be admissible in evidence, and shall show affirmatively that the affiant is competent to testify to the matters stated. Sworn or certified copies of all papers or parts referred to in an affidavit shall be attached to or served with the affidavit. The court may permit affidavits to be supplemented or opposed by depositions, answers to interrogatories, or by further affidavits. FL ST RCP Rule 1.510(e).

ii. *When affidavits are unavailable.* If it appears from the affidavits of a party opposing the motion that the party cannot for reasons stated present by affidavit facts essential to justify opposition, the court may refuse the application for judgment or may order a continuance to permit affidavits to be obtained or depositions to be taken or discovery to be had or may make such other order as is just. FL ST RCP Rule 1.510(f).

iii. *Affidavits made in bad faith.* If it appears to the satisfaction of the court at any time that any of the affidavits presented pursuant to FL ST RCP Rule 1.510 are presented in bad faith or solely for the purpose of delay, the court shall forthwith order the party employing them to pay to the other party the amount of the reasonable expenses that the filing of the affidavits caused the other party to incur, including reasonable attorneys' fees, and any offending party or attorney may be adjudged guilty of contempt. FL ST RCP Rule 1.510(g).

e. *Case not fully adjudicated on motion.* On motion under FL ST RCP Rule 1.510 if judgment is not rendered upon the whole case or for all the relief asked and a trial or the taking of testimony and a final hearing is necessary, the court at the hearing of the motion, by examining the pleadings and the evidence before it and by interrogating counsel, shall ascertain, if practicable, what material facts exist without substantial controversy and what material facts are actually and in good faith controverted. FL ST RCP Rule 1.510(d).

   i. It shall thereupon make an order specifying the facts that appear without substantial controversy, including the extent to which the amount of damages or other relief is not in controversy, and directing such further proceedings in the action as are just. FL ST RCP Rule 1.510(d).

   ii. On the trial or final hearing of the action the facts so specified shall be deemed established, and the trial or final hearing shall be conducted accordingly. FL ST RCP Rule 1.510(d).

4. *Arbitration and mediation.* Attorneys are encouraged to utilize arbitration, mediation or other forms of alternative dispute resolution if economically feasible. FL ST 20 J CIR 2.20(IV)(N)(3).

   a. *Referral to arbitration and mediation.* Except as hereinafter provided or as otherwise prohibited by law, the presiding judge may enter an order referring all or any part of a contested civil matter to mediation or arbitration. The parties to any contested civil matter may file a written stipulation to mediate or arbitrate any issue between them at any time. Such stipulation shall be incorporated into the order of referral. FL ST RCP Rule 1.700(a).

   b. *Arbitration*

      i. *Exclusions.* A civil action shall be ordered to arbitration or arbitration in conjunction with mediation upon stipulation of the parties. A civil action may be ordered to arbitration or arbitration in conjunction with mediation upon motion of any party or by the court, if the judge determines the action to be of such a nature that arbitration could be of benefit to the litigants or the court. FL ST RCP Rule 1.800.

         - Under no circumstances may the following categories of actions be referred to arbitration: (1) bond estreatures; (2) habeas corpus or other extraordinary writs; (3) bond validations; (4) civil or criminal contempt; (5) such other matters as may be specified by order of the chief judge in the circuit. FL ST RCP Rule 1.800.

      ii. For more information regarding arbitration, please see FL ST RCP Rule 1.810; FL ST RCP Rule 1.820; FL ST RCP Rule 1.830.

   c. *Mediation.* For more information regarding mediation, please see FL ST RCP Rule 1.710; FL ST RCP Rule 1.720; FL ST RCP Rule 1.730; FL ST RCP Rule 1.750; and FL ST 20 J CIR 1.9.

5. *Rules of court*

   a. *Rules of civil procedure.* The Florida Rules of Civil Procedure apply to all actions of a civil nature and all special statutory proceedings in the circuit courts and county courts except those to which the Florida Probate Rules, the Florida Family Law Rules of Procedure, or the Small Claims Rules apply. FL ST RCP Rule 1.010.

      i. The form, content, procedure, and time for pleading in all special statutory proceedings shall be as prescribed by the statutes governing the proceeding unless the Florida Rules of Civil Procedure specifically provide to the contrary. FL ST RCP Rule 1.010.

      ii. The Florida Rules of Civil Procedure shall be construed to secure the just, speedy, and inexpensive determination of every action. FL ST RCP Rule 1.010.

   b. *Rules of judicial administration.* The Florida Rules of Judicial Administration shall apply to administrative matters in all courts to which the Florida Rules of Judicial Administration are applicable by their terms. The Florida Rules of Judicial Administration shall be construed to secure the speedy and inexpensive determination of every proceeding to which they are applicable. The Florida Rules of Judicial Administration shall supersede all conflicting rules and statutes. FL ST J ADMIN Rule 2.110.

6. *Civil case management plan.* There is established within the Twentieth Judicial Circuit a Civil Case Management Plan applicable to circuit civil cases, which will be administered by the Administrative Office of the Courts through direction of the Circuit Administrative Judges in each county for the implementation of enhanced case management procedures and guidelines for the timely and efficient processing of circuit civil cases and reduction in the pending backlog of civil cases. FL ST 20 J CIR 1.13.
   a. The basis for the Civil Case Management Plan is included in FL ST 20 J CIR 1.13, identified in Attachment A as the "Civil Differentiated Case Management (DCM) Procedures and Backlog Reduction Plan," and is incorporated as if fully set forth in FL ST 20 J CIR 1.13. The Civil Case Management Plan is to be used as a model for the purpose of establishing time standards, improving the courts ability to provide early and continuous management of civil cases as required by FL ST J ADMIN Rule 2.545, and to promote uniformity of practice throughout the Twentieth Judicial Circuit. FL ST 20 J CIR 1.13.
   b. Full implementation of the Civil DCM Case Management Procedures (Attachment A), including all uniform circuitwide procedures and forms, shall apply to all civil cases filed in Lee and Collier counties, effective January 1, 2011. Even though full implementation may be delayed in Charlotte, Hendry, and Glades counties, all civil time standards and goals, and the use of civil Case Managers and Magistrates to assist trial judges in the process of civil case management and backlog reduction programs, shall be effective circuitwide immediately. FL ST 20 J CIR 1.13.
   c. For more information on the civil case management plan, refer to the specific county website and/or see FL ST 20 J CIR 1.13.

D. Documents

1. *Required documents*
   a. *Notice of hearing/Motion.* An application to the court for an order shall be by motion which shall be made in writing unless made during a hearing or trial, shall state with particularity the grounds therefor, and shall set forth the relief or order sought. The requirement of writing is fulfilled if the motion is stated in a written notice of the hearing of the motion. All notices of hearing shall specify each motion or other matter to be heard. FL ST RCP Rule 1.100(b). Refer to the General Requirements section of this document for more information on the notice of hearing.
      i. *Notices to persons with disabilities.* See the Format section of this KeyRules document for further information.
   b. *Certificate of service.* When any attorney certifies in substance: "I certify that a copy hereof has been furnished to (here insert name or names and addresses used for service) by (e-mail) (delivery) (mail) (fax) on .... (date) ....______________ Attorney" the certificate is taken as prima facie proof of such service in compliance with FL ST J ADMIN Rule 2.516. FL ST J ADMIN Rule 2.516(f).
2. *Supplemental documents*
   a. *Affidavits.* Supporting and opposing affidavits shall be made on personal knowledge, shall set forth such facts as would be admissible in evidence, and shall show affirmatively that the affiant is competent to testify to the matters stated therein. Sworn or certified copies of all papers or parts thereof referred to in an affidavit shall be attached thereto or served therewith. FL ST RCP Rule 1.510(e). For further information regarding affidavits made in the context of a motion for summary judgment see FL ST RCP Rule 1.510(e) through FL ST RCP Rule 1.510(g).
   b. *Other evidence.* The movant shall also serve at that time a copy of any summary judgment evidence on which the movant relies that has not already been filed with the court. FL ST RCP Rule 1.510(c).
   c. *Proposed order.* The court may require that orders or judgments be prepared by a party, may require the party to furnish the court with stamped, addressed envelopes for service of the order or judgment, and may require that proposed orders and judgments be furnished to all parties before entry by the court of the order or judgment. FL ST J ADMIN Rule 2.516(h)(1).
      i. Unless otherwise instructed by the court, or agreed to by counsel, all proposed orders shall be provided to other counsel with a reasonable time for approval or comment prior to submission to the court. Opposing counsel should promptly communicate any objections thereto. There-

after, the drafting attorney should promptly submit a copy of the proposed order to the court and advise the court as to whether or not it has been approved by opposing counsel. FL ST 20 J CIR 2.20(IV)(I)(4).

ii. Orders prepared by counsel must fairly and adequately represent the ruling of the court, and counsel shall make a good faith effort to agree upon the form of the order prior to submitting it to the court. Attorneys should not submit controverted orders to the court with a copy to opposing counsel for "objections within ______ days". Courts prefer to know that the order is either agreed upon or opposed. FL ST 20 J CIR 2.20(IV)(I)(5).

iii. Attorneys should not use post-hearing submissions of proposed orders as a guise to reargue the merits of the matter. FL ST 20 J CIR 2.20(IV)(I)(6).

iv. If asked by the court to prepare an order, counsel should furnish a copy of the order, and any transmitted letter, to opposing counsel at the time the material is submitted to the court. FL ST 20 J CIR 2.20(IV)(J)(4).

d. *Notice of constitutional question.* A party that files a pleading, written motion, or other paper drawing into question the constitutionality of a state statute or a county or municipal charter, ordinance, or franchise must promptly (1) file a notice of constitutional question stating the question and identifying the paper that raises it; and (2) serve the notice and the pleading, written motion, or other paper drawing into question the constitutionality of a state statute or a county or municipal charter, ordinance, or franchise on the Attorney General or the state attorney of the judicial circuit in which the action is pending, by either certified or registered mail. Service of the notice and pleading, written motion, or other paper does not require joinder of the Attorney General or the state attorney as a party to the action. FL ST RCP Rule 1.071.

e. *Notice and request to participate in telephonic motion hearing.* In instances where a civil motion hearing is scheduled for not longer than fifteen (15) minutes, a party may file a written request to participate via conference or speaker telephone, or other applicable communication equipment, and shall provide notice to the Court and the parties to the motion. FL ST 20 J CIR 1.10. Refer to the Timing and Hearings sections of this document for more information.

E. Format

1. *Documents; Type and size.* Documents subject to the exceptions set forth in FL ST J ADMIN Rule 2.525(d) shall be filed on recycled paper measuring eight and one half by eleven (8 1/2 by 11) inches. For purposes of FL ST J ADMIN Rule 2.520, paper is recycled if it contains a minimum content of fifty (50) percent waste paper. Xerographic reduction of legal-size (eight and one half by fourteen (8 1/2 by 14) inches) documents to letter size (eight and one half by eleven (8 1/2 by 11) inches) is prohibited. All other documents filed by electronic transmission shall be filed in a format capable of being printed in a format consistent with the provisions of FL ST J ADMIN Rule 2.250. FL ST J ADMIN Rule 2.520(b); FL ST 20 J CIR 2.9.

a. *Exhibits.* Any exhibit or attachment filed with pleadings or papers may be filed in its original size. FL ST J ADMIN Rule 2.520(c); FL ST 20 J CIR 2.9.

b. *Recording space.* On all papers and documents prepared and filed by the court or by any party to a proceeding which are to be recorded in the public records of any county, including but not limited to final money judgments and notices of lis pendens, a three (3) inch by three (3) inch space at the top right-hand corner on the first page and a one (1) inch by three (3) inch space at the top right-hand corner on each subsequent page shall be left blank and reserved for use by the clerk of court. FL ST J ADMIN Rule 2.520(d).

i. *Exceptions to recording space.* Any papers or documents created by persons or entities over which the filing party has no control, including but not limited to wills, codicils, trusts, or other testamentary documents; documents prepared or executed by any public officer; documents prepared, executed, acknowledged, or proved outside of the State of Florida; or documents created by State or Federal government agencies, may be filed without the space required by FL ST J ADMIN Rule 2.520. FL ST J ADMIN Rule 2.520(e).

c. *Noncompliance.* No clerk of court is permitted to refuse to file any document or paper because of noncompliance with the Florida Rules of Judicial Administration. However, upon request of the clerk of court, noncomplying documents must be resubmitted in accordance with the formatting rules. FL ST J ADMIN Rule 2.520(f).

i. When time of filing is critical, the Clerk shall accept pleadings, motions, petitions, briefs, notices, orders, judgments, decrees, opinions, or other papers or official documents on other than eight and one half by eleven (8 1/2 by 11) inch paper but shall then require that the document be resubmitted to comply with FL ST J ADMIN Rule 2.520. FL ST 20 J CIR 2.9.

2. *Caption.* Every pleading, motion, order, judgment, or other paper shall have a caption containing the name of the court, the file number, and except for in rem proceedings, including forfeiture proceedings, the name of the first party on each side with an appropriate indication of other parties, and a designation identifying the party filing it and its nature or the nature of the order, as the case may be. In any in rem proceeding, every pleading, motion, order, judgment, or other paper shall have a caption containing the name of the court, the file number, the style "In re" (followed by the name or general description of the property), and a designation of the person or entity filing it and its nature or the nature of the order, as the case may be. In an in rem forfeiture proceeding, the style shall be "In re forfeiture of" (followed by the name of the general description of the property). All papers filed in the action shall be styled in such a manner as to indicate clearly the subject matter of the paper and the party requesting or obtaining relief. FL ST RCP Rule 1.100(c)(1).

3. *Writing and written defined.* Writing or written means a document containing information, an application, or a stipulation. FL ST RCP Rule 1.080(c).

4. *Rule abbreviations*

   a. The Florida Rules of Civil Procedure and shall be abbreviated as Fla.R.Civ.P. FL ST RCP Rule 1.010.

   b. The Florida Rules of Judicial Administration shall be abbreviated as Fla. R. Jud. Admin. FL ST J ADMIN Rule 2.110.

5. *Nonverification.* Except when otherwise specifically provided by the Florida Rules of Civil Procedure or an applicable statute, every pleading or other document of a party represented by an attorney need not be verified or accompanied by an affidavit. FL ST RCP Rule 1.030; FL ST J ADMIN Rule 2.515(a).

6. *Attorney signature*

   a. *Attorney signature.* Every pleading and other document of a party represented by an attorney shall be signed by at least one (1) attorney of record in that attorney's individual name whose current record Florida Bar address, telephone number, including area code, primary e-mail address and secondary e-mail addresses, if any, and Florida Bar number shall be stated, and who shall be duly licensed to practice law in Florida or who shall have received permission to appear in the particular case as provided in FL ST J ADMIN Rule 2.510. FL ST J ADMIN Rule 2.515(a).

      i. The attorney may be required by the court to give the address of, and to vouch for the attorney's authority to represent, the party. FL ST J ADMIN Rule 2.515(a).

      ii. The signature of an attorney shall constitute a certificate by the attorney that the attorney has read the pleading or other document; that to the best of the attorney's knowledge, information, and belief there is good ground to support it; and that it is not interposed for delay. FL ST J ADMIN Rule 2.515(a).

      iii. If a pleading is not signed or is signed with intent to defeat the purpose of FL ST J ADMIN Rule 2.515, it may be stricken and the action may proceed as though the pleading or other document had not been served. FL ST J ADMIN Rule 2.515(a).

   b. *Pro se litigant signature.* A party who is not represented by an attorney shall sign any pleading or other paper and state the party's address and telephone number, including area code. FL ST J ADMIN Rule 2.515(b).

   c. *Form of signature*

      i. The signatures required on pleadings and documents by FL ST J ADMIN Rule 2.515(a) and FL ST J ADMIN Rule 2.515(b) may be:

         - Original signatures;

- Original signatures that have been reproduced by electronic means, such as on electronically transmitted documents or photocopied documents;
- Electronic signatures using the "/s/," "s/," or "/s" formats by or at the direction of the person signing; or
- Any other signature format authorized by general law, so long as the clerk where the proceeding is pending has the capability of receiving and has obtained approval from the Supreme Court of Florida to accept pleadings and documents with that signature format. FL ST J ADMIN Rule 2.515(c)(1).

ii. An attorney, party, or other person who files a pleading or paper by electronic transmission that does not contain the original signature of that attorney, party, or other person shall file that identical pleading or paper in paper form containing an original signature of that attorney, party, or other person (hereinafter called the follow-up filing) immediately thereafter. The follow-up filing is not required if the Supreme Court of Florida has entered an order directing the clerk of court to discontinue accepting the follow-up filing. FL ST J ADMIN Rule 2.515(c)(2).

7. *Forms*

a. *Process.* The forms of process, notice of lis pendens, and notice of action provided in the Florida Rules of Civil Procedure are sufficient. Variations from the forms do not void process or notices that are otherwise sufficient. FL ST RCP Rule 1.900(a).

b. *Other forms.* The other forms provided in the Florida Rules of Civil Procedure are sufficient for the matters that are covered by them. So long as the substance is expressed without prolixity, the forms may be varied to meet the facts of a particular case. FL ST RCP Rule 1.900(b).

c. *Formal matters.* Captions, except for the designation of the paper, are omitted from the forms provided in the Florida Rules of Civil Procedure. A general form of caption is the first form provided. Signatures are omitted from pleadings and motions. FL ST RCP Rule 1.900(c).

8. *Notices to persons with disabilities.* All notices of court proceedings to be held in a public facility, and all process compelling appearance at such proceedings, shall include the following statement in bold face, fourteen (14) point Times New Roman or Courier font: "If you are a person with a disability who needs any accommodation in order to participate in this proceeding, you are entitled, at no cost to you, to the provision of certain assistance. Please contact [identify applicable court personnel by name, address, and telephone number] at least seven (7) days before your scheduled court appearance, or immediately upon receiving this notification if the time before the scheduled appearance is less than seven (7) days; if you are hearing or voice impaired, call 711." FL ST J ADMIN Rule 2.540(c)(1). For more information, see FL ST 20 J CIR 2.15.

9. *Minimization of the filing of sensitive information*

a. *Limitations for court filings.* Unless authorized by FL ST J ADMIN Rule 2.425(b), statute, another rule of court, or the court orders otherwise, designated sensitive information filed with the court must be limited to the following format:

i. The initials of a person known to be a minor;

ii. The year of birth of a person's birth date;

iii. No portion of any: Social security number, Bank account number, Credit card account number, Charge account number, or Debit account number;

iv. The last four digits of any: Taxpayer identification number (TIN), Employee identification number, Driver's license number, Passport number, Telephone number, Financial account number, except as set forth in FL ST J ADMIN Rule 2.425(a)(3), Brokerage account number, Insurance policy account number, Loan account number, Customer account number, or Patient or health care number;

v. A truncated version of any: Email address, Computer user name, Password, or Personal identification number (PIN); and

vi. A truncated version of any other sensitive information as provided by court order. FL ST J ADMIN Rule 2.425(a).

b. *Exceptions.* FL ST J ADMIN Rule 2.425(a) does not apply to the following:
   i. An account number which identifies the property alleged to be the subject of a proceeding;
   ii. The record of an administrative or agency proceeding;
   iii. The record in appellate or review proceedings;
   iv. The birth date of a minor whenever the birth date is necessary for the court to establish or maintain subject matter jurisdiction;
   v. The name of a minor in any order relating to parental responsibility, time-sharing, or child support;
   vi. The name of a minor in any document or order affecting the minor's ownership of real property;
   vii. The birth date of a party in a writ of attachment or notice to payor;
   viii. In traffic and criminal proceedings: a pro se filing; a court filing that is related to a criminal matter or investigation and that is prepared before the filing of a criminal charge or is not filed as part of any docketed criminal case; an arrest or search warrant or any information in support thereof; a charging document and an affidavit or other documents filed in support of any charging document, including any driving records; a statement of particulars; discovery material introduced into evidence or otherwise filed with the court; and all information necessary for the proper issuance and execution of a subpoena duces tecum;
   ix. Information used by the clerk for case maintenance purposes or the courts for case management purposes; and
   x. Information which is relevant and material to an issue before the court. FL ST J ADMIN Rule 2.425(b).

c. *Remedies.* Upon motion by a party or interested person or sua sponte by the court, the court may order remedies, sanctions or both for a violation of FL ST J ADMIN Rule 2.425(a). Following notice and an opportunity to respond, the court may impose sanctions if such filing was not made in good faith. FL ST J ADMIN Rule 2.425(c).

d. *Motions not restricted.* FL ST J ADMIN Rule 2.425 does not restrict a party's right to move for protective order, to move to file documents under seal, or to request a determination of the confidentiality of records. FL ST J ADMIN Rule 2.425(d).

e. *Application.* FL ST J ADMIN Rule 2.425 does not affect the application of constitutional provisions, statutes, or rules of court regarding confidential information or access to public information. FL ST J ADMIN Rule 2.425(e).

F. Filing and Service Requirements

1. *Filing requirements.* All original documents must be filed with the court either before service or immediately thereafter, unless otherwise provided for by general law or other rules. If the original of any bond or other document is not placed in the court file, a certified copy must be so placed by the clerk. FL ST J ADMIN Rule 2.516(d). All documents shall be filed in conformity with the requirements of FL ST J ADMIN Rule 2.525. FL ST RCP Rule 1.080(b). All documents filed in any court shall be filed by electronic transmission in accordance with FL ST J ADMIN Rule 2.525. "Documents" means pleadings, motions, petitions, memoranda, briefs, notices, exhibits, declarations, affidavits, orders, judgments, decrees, writs, opinions, and any other paper or writing submitted to a court. FL ST J ADMIN Rule 2.520(a). All documents that are court records, as defined in FL ST J ADMIN Rule 2.430(a)(1), must be filed by electronic transmission, provided that: (1) the clerk has the ability to accept and retain such documents; (2) the clerk or the chief judge of the circuit has requested permission to accept documents filed by electronic transmission; and (3) the supreme court has entered an order granting permission to the clerk to accept documents filed by electronic transmission. FL ST J ADMIN Rule 2.525(c)(1).

   a. *Definition.* "Electronic transmission of documents" means the sending of information by electronic signals to, by or from a court or clerk, which when received can be transformed and stored or transmitted on paper, microfilm, magnetic storage device, optical imaging system, CD-ROM, flash drive, other electronic data storage system, server, case maintenance system ("CM"), electronic

court filing ("ECF") system, statewide or local electronic portal ("e-portal"), or other electronic record keeping system authorized by the supreme court in a format sufficient to communicate the information on the original document in a readable format. Electronic transmission of documents includes electronic mail ("e-mail") and any internet-based transmission procedure, and may include procedures allowing for documents to be signed or verified by electronic means. FL ST J ADMIN Rule 2.525(a).

i. The filing of documents with the court as required by the Florida Rules of Judicial Administration must be made by filing them with the clerk in accordance with FL ST J ADMIN Rule 2.525, except that the judge may permit documents to be filed with the judge, in which event the judge must note the filing date before him or her on the documents and transmit them to the clerk. The date of filing is that shown on the face of the document by the judge's notation or the clerk's time stamp, whichever is earlier. FL ST J ADMIN Rule 2.516(e).

b. *Application.* Any court or clerk of the court may accept the electronic transmission of documents for filing after the clerk, together with input from the chief judge of the circuit, has obtained approval of the procedures and program for doing so from the Supreme Court of Florida. FL ST J ADMIN Rule 2.525(b).

c. *Exceptions*

i. Paper documents and other submissions may be manually submitted to the clerk or court:

- When the clerk does not have the ability to accept and retain documents by electronic filing or has not had ECF Procedures approved by the supreme court;
- For filing by any self-represented party or any self-represented nonparty unless specific ECF Procedures provide a means to file documents electronically. However, any self-represented nonparty that is a governmental or public agency and any other agency, partnership, corporation, or business entity acting on behalf of any governmental or public agency may file documents by electronic transmission if such entity has the capability of filing documents electronically;
- For filing by attorneys excused from e-mail service in accordance with FL ST J ADMIN Rule 2.516(b);
- When submitting evidentiary exhibits or filing non-documentary materials;
- When the filing involves documents in excess of twenty-five (25) megabytes (25MB) in size. For such filings, documents may be transmitted using an electronic storage medium that the clerk has the ability to accept, which may include a CD-ROM, flash drive, or similar storage medium;
- When filed in open court, as permitted by the court;
- When paper filing is permitted by any approved statewide or local ECF procedures; and
- If any court determines that justice so requires. FL ST J ADMIN Rule 2.525(d).

ii. Any document in paper form submitted under FL ST J ADMIN Rule 2.525(d) is filed when it is received by the clerk or court and the clerk shall immediately thereafter convert any filed paper document to an electronic document. "Convert to an electronic document" means optically capturing an image of a paper document and using character recognition software to recover as much of the document's text as practicable and then indexing and storing the document in the official court file. FL ST J ADMIN Rule 2.525(c)(4).

iii. Any storage medium submitted under FL ST J ADMIN Rule 2.525(d)(5) is filed when received by the clerk or court and the clerk shall immediately thereafter transfer the electronic documents from the storage device to the official court file. FL ST J ADMIN Rule 2.525(c)(5).

iv. If the filer of any paper document authorized under FL ST J ADMIN Rule 2.525(d) provides a self-addressed, postage-paid envelope for return of the paper document after it is converted to electronic form by the clerk, the clerk shall place the paper document in the envelope and deposit it in the mail. Except when a paper document is required to be maintained, the clerk may recycle any filed paper document that is not to be returned to the filer. FL ST J ADMIN Rule 2.525(c)(6).

v. The clerk may convert any paper document filed before the effective date of FL ST J ADMIN Rule 2.525 to an electronic document. Unless the clerk is required to maintain the paper document, if the paper document has been converted to an electronic document by the clerk, the paper document is no longer part of the official court file and may be removed and recycled. FL ST J ADMIN Rule 2.525(c)(7).

d. *Official court file.* For information on what constitutes the official court file, please see FL ST J ADMIN Rule 2.525(c)(2), FL ST J ADMIN Rule 2.525(c)(3).

e. *Administration.* All attorneys, parties, or other persons using this rule to file documents are required to make arrangements with the court or clerk for the payment of any charges authorized by general law or the supreme court before filing any document by electronic transmission. FL ST J ADMIN Rule 2.525(f)(2).

f. *Filing date.* The filing date for an electronically transmitted document is the date and time that such filing is acknowledged by an electronic stamp or otherwise, pursuant to any procedure set forth in any ECF Procedures approved by the supreme court, or the date the last page of such filing is received by the court or clerk. FL ST J ADMIN Rule 2.525(f)(3).

g. *Accessibility.* All documents transmitted in any electronic form under FL ST J ADMIN Rule 2.525 must comply with the accessibility requirements of FL ST J ADMIN Rule 2.526. FL ST J ADMIN Rule 2.525(g).

2. *Service requirements.* Every pleading subsequent to the initial pleading, all orders, and every other document filed in the action must be served in conformity with the requirements of FL ST J ADMIN Rule 2.516. FL ST RCP Rule 1.080(a).

a. *Service; Generally.* The timing and manner of service should not be used to the disadvantage of the party receiving the papers. FL ST 20 J CIR 2.20(IV)(C)(1).

i. Papers and memoranda of law should not be served at court appearances without advance notice to opposing counsel and should not be served so close to a court appearance so as to inhibit the ability of opposing counsel to prepare for that appearance or to respond to the papers. Should the attorney do so, the court is urged to take appropriate action in response, including continuing the matter to allow opposing counsel to prepare and respond. FL ST 20 J CIR 2.20(IV)(C)(2).

ii. Papers should not be served in order to take advantage of an opponent's known absence from the office or at a time or in a manner designed to inconvenience an adversary, such as late on Friday afternoon or the day preceding a secular or religious holiday. FL ST 20 J CIR 2.20(IV)(C)(3).

iii. Service should be made personally or by courtesy copy facsimile transmission when it is likely that service by mail, even when allowed, will prejudice the opposing party or will not provide the opposing party with a reasonable time to respond. FL ST 20 J CIR 2.20(IV)(C)(4).

b. *Service; When required.* Unless the court otherwise orders, or a statute or supreme court administrative order specifies a different means of service, every pleading subsequent to the initial pleading and every other document filed in any court proceeding, except applications for witness subpoenas and documents served by formal notice or required to be served in the manner provided for service of formal notice, must be served in accordance with FL ST J ADMIN Rule 2.516 on each party. No service need be made on parties against whom a default has been entered, except that pleadings asserting new or additional claims against them must be served in the manner provided for service of summons. FL ST J ADMIN Rule 2.516(a).

i. *Copies of court submissions.* Copies of any submissions to the court (such as correspondence, memoranda of law, motions, case law, etc.) should simultaneously be provided to opposing counsel by substantially the same method of delivery by which they are provided to the court. For example, if a memorandum of law is hand-delivered to the court, at substantially the same time a copy should be hand-delivered or faxed to opposing counsel. FL ST 20 J CIR 2.20(IV)(J)(4).

c. *Service; How made.* When service is required or permitted to be made upon a party represented by

an attorney, service must be made upon the attorney unless service upon the party is ordered by the court. FL ST J ADMIN Rule 2.516(b).

i. *Service by electronic mail ("e-mail").* All documents required or permitted to be served on another party must be served by e-mail, unless FL ST J ADMIN Rule 2.516 otherwise provides. When, in addition to service by e-mail, the sender also utilizes another means of service provided for in FL ST J ADMIN Rule 2.516(b)(2), any differing time limits and other provisions applicable to that other means of service control. FL ST J ADMIN Rule 2.516(b)(1). Any document electronically transmitted to a court or clerk must also be served on all parties and interested persons in accordance with the applicable rules of court. FL ST J ADMIN Rule 2.525(e)(2).

- *Service on attorneys.* Upon appearing in a proceeding, an attorney must serve a designation of a primary e-mail address and may designate no more than two (2) secondary e-mail addresses. Thereafter, service must be directed to all designated e-mail addresses in that proceeding. Every document filed by an attorney thereafter must include the primary e-mail address of that attorney and any secondary e-mail addresses. If an attorney does not designate any e-mail address for service, documents may be served on that attorney at the e-mail address on record with The Florida Bar. FL ST J ADMIN Rule 2.516(b)(1)(A).
- *Exception to e-mail service on attorneys.* Service by an attorney on another attorney must be made by e-mail unless excused by the court. Upon motion by an attorney demonstrating that the attorney has no e-mail account and lacks access to the Internet at the attorney's office, the court may excuse the attorney from the requirements of e-mail service. Service on and by an attorney excused by the court from e-mail service must be by the means provided in FL ST J ADMIN Rule 2.516(b)(2). FL ST J ADMIN Rule 2.516(b)(1)(B).
- *Service on and by parties not represented by an attorney.* Any party not represented by an attorney may serve a designation of a primary e-mail address and also may designate no more than two (2) secondary e-mail addresses to which service must be directed in that proceeding by the means provided in FL ST J ADMIN Rule 2.516(b)(1). If a party not represented by an attorney does not designate an e-mail address for service in a proceeding, service on and by that party must be by the means provided in FL ST J ADMIN Rule 2.516(b)(2). FL ST J ADMIN Rule 2.516(b)(1)(C).
- *Time of service.* Service by e-mail is complete when it is sent. FL ST J ADMIN Rule 2.516(b)(1)(D). An e-mail is deemed served on the date it is sent. FL ST J ADMIN Rule 2.516(b)(1)(D)(i). If the sender learns that the e-mail did not reach the address of the person to be served, the sender must immediately send another copy by e-mail, or by a means authorized by FL ST J ADMIN Rule 2.516(b)(2). FL ST J ADMIN Rule 2.516(b)(1)(D)(ii). E-mail service is treated as service by mail for the computation of time. FL ST J ADMIN Rule 2.516(b)(1)(D)(iii).

ii. *Format of e-mail for service.* Service of a document by e-mail is made by attaching a copy of the document in PDF format to an e-mail sent to all addresses designated by the attorney or party. FL ST J ADMIN Rule 2.516(b)(1)(E).

- All documents served by e-mail must be attached to an e-mail message containing a subject line beginning with the words "SERVICE OF COURT DOCUMENT" in all capital letters, followed by the case number of the proceeding in which the documents are being served. FL ST J ADMIN Rule 2.516(b)(1)(E)(i).
- The body of the e-mail must identify the court in which the proceeding is pending, the case number, the name of the initial party on each side, the title of each document served with that e-mail, and the sender's name and telephone number. FL ST J ADMIN Rule 2.516(b)(1)(E)(ii).
- Any document served by e-mail may be signed by the "/s/" format, as long as the filed original is signed in accordance with the applicable rule of procedure. FL ST J ADMIN Rule 2.516(b)(1)(E)(iii).
- Any e-mail which, together with its attached documents, exceeds five megabytes (5MB) in

size, must be divided and sent as separate e-mails, no one of which may exceed five megabytes (5MB) in size and each of which must be sequentially numbered in the subject line. FL ST J ADMIN Rule 2.516(b)(1)(E)(iv).

iii. *Service by other means.* In addition to, and not in lieu of, service by e-mail, service may also be made upon attorneys by any of the means specified in FL ST J ADMIN Rule 2.516(b)(2). Service on and by all parties who are not represented by an attorney and who do not designate an e-mail address, and on and by all attorneys excused from e-mail service, must be made by delivering a copy of the document or by mailing it to the party or attorney at their last known address or, if no address is known, by leaving it with the clerk of the court. Service by mail is complete upon mailing. Delivery of a copy within FL ST J ADMIN Rule 2.516 is complete upon:

- Handing it to the attorney or to the party,
- Leaving it at the attorney's or party's office with a clerk or other person in charge thereof,
- If there is no one in charge, leaving it in a conspicuous place therein,
- If the office is closed or the person to be served has no office, leaving it at the person's usual place of abode with some person of his or her family above fifteen (15) years of age and informing such person of the contents, or
- Transmitting it by facsimile to the attorney's or party's office with a cover sheet containing the sender's name, firm, address, telephone number, and facsimile number, and the number of pages transmitted. When service is made by facsimile, a copy must also be served by any other method permitted by FL ST J ADMIN Rule 2.516. Facsimile service occurs when transmission is complete. FL ST J ADMIN Rule 2.516(b)(2)(A) through FL ST J ADMIN Rule 2.516(b)(2)(E).
- Service by delivery after 5:00 p.m. must be deemed to have been made by mailing on the date of delivery. FL ST J ADMIN Rule 2.516(b)(2)(F).

d. *Service; Numerous defendants.* In actions when the parties are unusually numerous, the court may regulate the service contemplated by the Florida Rules of Judicial Administration on motion or on its own initiative in such manner as may be found to be just and reasonable. FL ST J ADMIN Rule 2.516(c).

e. *Service by clerk.* Service of notices and other documents required to be made by the clerk must also be done as provided in FL ST J ADMIN Rule 2.516(b). FL ST J ADMIN Rule 2.516(g).

G. Hearings

1. *Hearing on motion for summary judgment.* The summary judgment rule does not provide the trial court with discretion to decide whether a hearing is required. A failure to hold a hearing on a motion for summary judgment violates due process as well as rule of procedure governing summary judgment procedure. Kozich v. Hartford Ins. Co. of Midwest, 609 So.2d 147, 148 (Fla. 4th DCA 1992); FL-RCPF R 1.510(102).
2. *Summary judgment consideration at pretrial conference.* A summary judgment can be granted at the pretrial conference. The standard and procedure for granting summary judgment is the same at a pretrial conference as at other times. The notice time for a pretrial conference and for service of a motion for summary judgment is the same, so summary judgment can be entered at the conference if no genuine issue of material fact exists. FL-PRACPROC § 19:4.
3. *Scheduling.* Before setting a motion for hearing, counsel should make a good faith effort to resolve the issue with opposing counsel. FL ST 20 J CIR 2.20(IV)(I)(1). Except in emergency situations, attorneys should make a good faith effort to communicate with opposing counsel prior to scheduling depositions, hearings and other proceedings, so as to schedule them at times that are mutually convenient for all interested persons. Further, a sufficient time should be reserved to permit a complete presentation by counsel for all parties. FL ST 20 J CIR 2.20(IV)(B)(1). Attorneys should not use the hearing time obtained by opposing counsel for other motion practice. FL ST 20 J CIR 2.20(IV)(B)(6).

a. *Notice.* Counsel should notify opposing counsel of dates and times obtained from the court for future hearings on the same day that the hearing date is obtained from the court, or as soon as practicable thereafter. FL ST 20 J CIR 2.20(IV)(J)(3).

b. *Scheduling conflict.* Attorneys should notify opposing counsel, the court, and others affected, of scheduling conflicts as soon as they become apparent. Further, attorneys should cooperate with one another regarding all reasonable rescheduling requests that do not prejudice their clients or unduly delay a proceeding. FL ST 20 J CIR 2.20(IV)(B)(7).

   i. Attorneys should call potential scheduling problems to the attention of those affected, including the court, as soon as they become apparent and should avoid last minute cancellations. FL ST 20 J CIR 2.20(IV)(B)(12).

c. *Notice to court when appearance is unnecessary.* Attorneys should promptly notify the court or other tribunal of any resolution between the parties that renders a scheduled court appearance unnecessary. FL ST 20 J CIR 2.20(IV)(B)(8).

4. *Communication equipment*

a. *Definition.* Communication equipment means a conference telephone or other electronic device that permits all those appearing or participating to hear and speak to each other, provided that all conversation of all parties is audible to all persons present. FL ST J ADMIN Rule 2.530(a).

b. *Use by all parties.* A county or circuit court judge may, upon the court's own motion or upon the written request of a party, direct that communication equipment be used for a motion hearing, pretrial conference, or a status conference. A judge must give notice to the parties and consider any objections they may have to the use of communication equipment before directing that communication equipment be used. The decision to use communication equipment over the objection of parties will be in the sound discretion of the trial court, except as noted below. FL ST J ADMIN Rule 2.530(b).

c. *Use only by requesting party.* A county or circuit court judge may, upon the written request of a party upon reasonable notice to all other parties, permit a requesting party to participate through communication equipment in a scheduled motion hearing; however, any such request (except in criminal, juvenile, and appellate proceedings) must be granted, absent a showing of good cause to deny the same, where the hearing is set for not longer than fifteen (15) minutes. FL ST J ADMIN Rule 2.530(c).

d. *Testimony*

   i. *Generally.* A county or circuit court judge, general magistrate, special magistrate, or hearing officer may allow testimony to be taken through communication equipment if all parties consent or if permitted by another applicable rule of procedure. FL ST J ADMIN Rule 2.530(d)(1).

   ii. *Procedure.* Any party desiring to present testimony through communication equipment shall, prior to the hearing or trial at which the testimony is to be presented, contact all parties to determine whether each party consents to this form of testimony. The party seeking to present the testimony shall move for permission to present testimony through communication equipment, which motion shall set forth good cause as to why the testimony should be allowed in this form. FL ST J ADMIN Rule 2.530(d)(2).

   iii. *Oath.* Testimony may be taken through communication equipment only if a notary public or other person authorized to administer oaths in the witness's jurisdiction is present with the witness and administers the oath consistent with the laws of the jurisdiction. FL ST J ADMIN Rule 2.530(d)(3).

   iv. *Confrontation rights.* In juvenile and criminal proceedings the defendant must make an informed waiver of any confrontation rights that may be abridged by the use of communication equipment. FL ST J ADMIN Rule 2.530(d)(4).

   v. *Video testimony.* If the testimony to be presented utilizes video conferencing or comparable two-way visual capabilities, the court in its discretion may modify the procedures set forth in FL ST J ADMIN Rule 2.530 to accommodate the technology utilized. FL ST J ADMIN Rule 2.530(d)(5).

e. *Burden of expense.* The cost for the use of the communication equipment is the responsibility of the requesting party unless otherwise directed by the court. FL ST J ADMIN Rule 2.530(e).

5. *Telephonic non-evidentiary motion hearings set for not longer than fifteen (15) minutes.* FL ST 20 J CIR 1.10 specifically addresses non-evidentiary civil motion hearings set for not longer than fifteen (15) minutes. It is not intended to limit or address requests for telephonic hearings which are otherwise governed by FL ST J ADMIN Rule 2.071. FL ST 20 J CIR 1.10. [Editor's note: FL ST J ADMIN Rule 2.071 was renumbered as FL ST J ADMIN Rule 2.530]. Evidentiary hearings are exempted from the application of FL ST 20 J CIR 1.10. FL ST 20 J CIR 1.10.

a. In instances where a civil motion hearing is scheduled for not longer than fifteen (15) minutes, a party may file a written request to participate via conference or speaker telephone, or other applicable communication equipment, and shall provide notice to the Court and the parties to the motion. FL ST 20 J CIR 1.10. Refer to the Timing section of this document for information on when the notice must be given and when request must be served.

b. The requesting party shall be responsible for contacting the trial judge's Judicial Assistant and ensuring that appropriate arrangements have been made to permit participation through conference or speaker telephone, or other applicable communication equipment, on the scheduled date and time. It shall be at the discretion of the trial judge as to whether the requesting party shall be responsible for initiating the telephone or communication connection or whether the Court shall be responsible for initiating the telephone or communication connection. FL ST 20 J CIR 1.10(3).

c. Absent a showing of good cause, and in accordance with FL ST J ADMIN Rule 2.071(c), the trial judge shall grant the request and make reasonable accommodations to permit the requesting party's participation through conference or speaker telephone, or other applicable communication equipment. FL ST 20 J CIR 1.10. [Editor's note: FL ST J ADMIN Rule 2.071 was renumbered as FL ST J ADMIN Rule 2.530(c)].

d. To the extent that any provision of FL ST 20 J CIR 1.10 may be construed as being in conflict with any law, statute, or rule, the law, statute, or rule shall prevail. FL ST 20 J CIR 1.10.

H. Forms

1. Official Motion for Summary Judgment Forms for Florida

a. Caption. FL ST RCP Form 1.901.

b. Notice of compliance when constitutional challenge is brought. FL ST RCP Form 1.975.

2. Motion for Summary Judgment Forms for Florida

a. Motion for summary judgment; By plaintiff. FL-PP § 6:9.

b. Motion for summary judgment; By defendant. FL-PP § 6:10.

c. Affidavit; Supporting motion for summary judgment; By plaintiff's attorney. FL-PP § 6:11.

d. Affidavit; Opposing motion for summary judgment; By defendant's attorney. FL-PP § 6:12.

e. Affidavit; Opposing motion for summary judgment; By party; Inability to present facts. FL-PP § 6:13.

f. Order; Establishing uncontroverted facts and stating issues requiring further determination. FL-PP § 6:14.

g. Summary judgment. FL-PP § 6:15.

h. Motion; Summary judgment, by defendant. FL-PRACFORM § 7:190.

i. Motion; Summary judgment, by plaintiff. FL-PRACFORM § 7:191.

j. Motion; Summary judgment, partial, by defendant. FL-PRACFORM § 7:192.

k. Motion; Summary judgment, part of claim. FL-PRACFORM § 7:193.

l. Form for plaintiff's motion for summary judgment. FL-RCPF R 1.510(128).

m. Form for notice of motion for summary judgment by plaintiff. FL-RCPF R 1.510(129).

n. Form for notice of cross-motion for summary judgment by plaintiff. FL-RCPF R 1.510(130).

o. Form for order denying motion for summary judgment and specifying uncontroverted facts. FL-RCPF R 1.510(304).

p. Form for motion for partial summary judgment. FL-RCPF R 1.510(305).

q. Form for motion for partial summary judgment; Affirmative defenses. FL-RCPF R 1.510(305.1).

I. Checklist

(I) ❑ Matters to be considered by moving party

(a) ❑ Required documents

(1) ❑ Notice of hearing/Motion

(2) ❑ Certificate of service

(b) ❑ Supplemental documents

(1) ❑ Affidavits

(2) ❑ Other evidence

(3) ❑ Proposed order

(4) ❑ Notice of constitutional question

(5) ❑ Notice and request to participate in telephonic motion hearing

(c) ❑ Time for making motion

(1) ❑ By the plaintiff, after the expiration of twenty (20) days from the commencement of the action (claimant), or after service of a motion for summary judgment by the adverse party

(2) ❑ By the defending party at any time

(3) ❑ The motion for summary judgment must be served at least twenty (20) days before the time fixed for the hearing

(4) ❑ As a general rule, notice should be provided (not including time for service) no less than five (5) business days for hearings

(5) ❑ Notice and request to participate in telephonic motion hearing: Notice by the requesting party must be provided by mailing a copy of the written request at least five (5) days prior to the day of the hearing, or by delivering a copy of the written request to the other parties or, if represented by counsel, to the other parties' attorney(s) no later than 5:00 p.m. two (2) business days prior to the day of the hearing

(II) ❑ Matters to be considered by opposing party

(a) ❑ Required documents

(1) ❑ Response to motion

(2) ❑ Certificate of service

(b) ❑ Supplemental documents

(1) ❑ Affidavits

(2) ❑ Notice of evidence relied upon

(3) ❑ Other evidence

(4) ❑ Proposed order

(5) ❑ Notice of constitutional question

(6) ❑ Notice and request to participate in telephonic motion hearing

(c) ❑ Time for service and filing of opposition

(1) ❑ The adverse party shall identify, by notice mailed to the movant's attorney at least five (5) days prior to the day of the hearing, or delivered no later than 5:00 p.m. two (2) business days prior to the day of the hearing, any summary judgment evidence on which the adverse party relies

(2) ❑ To the extent that summary judgment evidence has not already been filed with the court, the adverse party shall serve a copy on the movant by mail at least five (5) days prior to the day of the hearing, or by delivery to the movant's attorney no later than 5:00 p.m. two (2) business days prior to the day of hearing

(3) ❑ Notice and request to participate in telephonic motion hearing: Notice by the requesting party must be provided by mailing a copy of the written request at least five (5) days prior to the day of the hearing, or by delivering a copy of the written request to the other parties or, if represented by counsel, to the other parties' attorney(s) no later than 5:00 p.m. two (2) business days prior to the day of the hearing

Motions, Oppositions and Replies
Motion for Sanctions

Document Last Updated January 2013

A. Applicable Rules

1. *State rules*
   a. Attorney's fee; Sanctions for raising unsupported claims or defenses; Exceptions; Service of motions; Damages for delay of litigation. FL ST § 57.105.
   b. Administrative Procedure Act. FL ST § 120.50; FL ST § 120.52; FL ST § 120.68; FL ST § 120.81.
   c. Offer of judgment and demand for judgment. FL ST § 768.79.
   d. Proposals for settlement. FL ST RCP Rule 1.442.
   e. Motions for costs and attorneys' fees. FL ST RCP Rule 1.525.
   f. Rules of court. FL ST RCP Rule 1.010; FL ST J ADMIN Rule 2.110.
   g. Nonverification of pleadings. FL ST RCP Rule 1.030.
   h. Service and filing of pleadings, orders, and documents. FL ST RCP Rule 1.080.
   i. Time. FL ST RCP Rule 1.090.
   j. Pleadings and motions. FL ST RCP Rule 1.100.
   k. Motions. FL ST RCP Rule 1.160.
   l. Relief from judgment, decrees, or orders. FL ST RCP Rule 1.540.
   m. Mediation and arbitration. FL ST RCP Rule 1.700; FL ST RCP Rule 1.710; FL ST RCP Rule 1.720; FL ST RCP Rule 1.730; FL ST RCP Rule 1.750; FL ST RCP Rule 1.800; FL ST RCP Rule 1.810; FL ST RCP Rule 1.820; FL ST RCP Rule 1.830.
   n. Forms. FL ST RCP Rule 1.900.
   o. Minimization of the filing of sensitive information. FL ST J ADMIN Rule 2.425.
   p. Retention of court records. FL ST J ADMIN Rule 2.430.
   q. Foreign attorneys. FL ST J ADMIN Rule 2.510.
   r. Signature of attorneys and parties. FL ST J ADMIN Rule 2.515.
   s. Paper. FL ST J ADMIN Rule 2.520.
   t. Electronic filing. FL ST J ADMIN Rule 2.525.
   u. Accessibility of information and technology. FL ST J ADMIN Rule 2.526.
   v. Communication equipment. FL ST J ADMIN Rule 2.530.
   w. Court reporting. FL ST J ADMIN Rule 2.535.
   x. Requests for accommodations by persons with disabilities. FL ST J ADMIN Rule 2.540.
   y. Case management. FL ST J ADMIN Rule 2.545.

2. *Local rules*
   a. Exclusions from mediation. FL ST 20 J CIR 1.9.
   b. Establishment and implementation of civil case management plan. FL ST 20 J CIR 1.13.
   c. Size of paper. FL ST 20 J CIR 2.9.
   d. Telephonic motion hearings set for not longer than fifteen minutes in circuit and county civil cases. FL ST 20 J CIR 1.10.
   e. Americans with Disabilities Act; Notification of court proceedings. FL ST 20 J CIR 2.15.
   f. Standards of professional courtesy and conduct and establishment of peer review program. FL ST 20 J CIR 2.20.

B. Timing

1. *Motion for sanctions.* A motion by a party seeking sanctions under FL ST § 57.105 must be served but may not be filed with or presented to the court unless, within twenty one (21) days after service of the motion, the challenged paper, claim, defense, contention, allegation, or denial is not withdrawn or appropriately corrected. FL ST § 57.105(4).
2. *Sanctions in relation to proposals for settlement.* Any party seeking sanctions pursuant to applicable Florida law, based on the failure of the proposal's recipient to accept a proposal, shall do so by serving a motion in accordance with FL ST RCP Rule 1.525. FL ST RCP Rule 1.442(g). Any party seeking a judgment taxing costs, attorneys' fees, or both shall serve a motion no later than thirty (30) days after filing of the judgment, including a judgment of dismissal, or the service of a notice of voluntary dismissal, which judgment or notice concludes the action as to that party. FL ST RCP Rule 1.525.
3. *General motion timing.* A copy of any written motion which may not be heard ex parte and a copy of the notice of the hearing thereof shall be served a reasonable time before the time specified for the hearing. FL ST RCP Rule 1.090(d).
   a. *Notice of hearing.* Except in emergency situations, attorneys should provide opposing counsel, parties, witnesses, and other affected persons, sufficient notice of depositions, hearings and other proceedings. FL ST 20 J CIR 2.20(IV)(B)(1). Attorneys should notify opposing counsel of any hearing time reserved as soon as practicable. FL ST 20 J CIR 2.20(IV)(B)(3). When hearing time is obtained, attorneys should promptly prepare and serve all counsel of record with notice of the hearing. Do not delay in providing such notice. FL ST 20 J CIR 2.20(IV)(B)(4).
      i. As a general rule, notice should be provided (not including time for service) no less than five (5) business days for hearings. FL ST 20 J CIR 2.20(IV)(B)(1).
4. *Notice and request to participate in telephonic motion hearing.* Notice by the requesting party must be provided by mailing a copy of the written request at least five (5) days prior to the day of the hearing, or by delivering a copy of the written request to the other parties or, if represented by counsel, to the other parties' attorney(s) no later than 5:00 p.m. two (2) business days prior to the day of the hearing. FL ST 20 J CIR 1.10. Refer to the Hearings section of this document for more information.
5. *Computation of time*
   a. *Generally.* Computation of time shall be governed by FL ST J ADMIN Rule 2.514. FL ST RCP Rule 1.090(a). The following rules apply in computing time periods specified in any rule of procedure, local rule, court order, or statute that does not specify a method of computing time. FL ST J ADMIN Rule 2.514(a).
      i. *Period stated in days or a longer unit.* When the period is stated in days or a longer unit of time (A) exclude the day of the event that triggers the period; (B) count every day, including intermediate Saturdays, Sundays, and legal holidays; and (C) include the last day of the period, but if the last day is a Saturday, Sunday, or legal holiday, or falls within any period of time extended through an order of the chief justice under FL ST J ADMIN Rule 2.205(a)(2)(B)(iv), the period continues to run until the end of the next day that is not a Saturday, Sunday, or legal holiday and does not fall within any period of time extended through an order of the chief justice. FL ST J ADMIN Rule 2.514(a)(1).

ii. *Period stated in hours.* When the period is stated in hours (A) begin counting immediately on the occurrence of the event that triggers the period; (B) count every hour, including hours during intermediate Saturdays, Sundays, and legal holidays; and (C) if the period would end on a Saturday, Sunday, or legal holiday, or during any period of time extended through an order of the chief justice under FL ST J ADMIN Rule 2.205(a)(2)(B)(iv), the period continues to run until the same time on the next day that is not a Saturday, Sunday, or legal holiday and does not fall within any period of time extended through an order of the chief justice. FL ST J ADMIN Rule 2.514(a)(2).

iii. *Period stated in days less than seven (7) days.* When the period stated in days is less than seven (7) days, intermediate Saturdays, Sundays, and legal holidays shall be excluded in the computation. FL ST J ADMIN Rule 2.514(a)(3).

iv. *"Last day" defined.* Unless a different time is set by a statute, local rule, or court order, the last day ends (A) for electronic filing or for service by any means, at midnight; and (B) for filing by other means, when the clerk's office is scheduled to close. FL ST J ADMIN Rule 2.514(a)(4).

v. *"Next day" defined.* The "next day" is determined by continuing to count forward when the period is measured after an event and backward when measured before an event. FL ST J ADMIN Rule 2.514(a)(5).

vi. *"Legal holiday" defined.* "Legal holiday" means (A) the day set aside by FL ST § 110.117, for observing New Year's Day, Martin Luther King, Jr.'s Birthday, Memorial Day, Independence Day, Labor Day, Veterans' Day, Thanksgiving Day, the Friday after Thanksgiving Day, or Christmas Day, and (B) any day observed as a holiday by the clerk's office or as designated by the chief judge. FL ST J ADMIN Rule 2.514(a)(6).

b. *Additional time after service by mail or e-mail.* When a party may or must act within a specified time after service and service is made by mail or e-mail, five (5) days are added after the period that would otherwise expire under FL ST J ADMIN Rule 2.514(a). FL ST J ADMIN Rule 2.514(b).

c. *Enlargement.* When an act is required or allowed to be done at or within a specified time by order of court, by the Florida Rules of Civil Procedure, or by notice given thereunder, for cause shown the court at any time in its discretion (1) with or without notice, may order the period enlarged if request therefor is made before the expiration of the period originally prescribed or as extended by a previous order, or (2) upon motion made and notice after the expiration of the specified period, may permit the act to be done when failure to act was the result of excusable neglect, but it may not extend the time for making a motion for new trial, for rehearing, or to alter or amend a judgment; making a motion for relief from a judgment under FL ST RCP Rule 1.540(b); taking an appeal or filing a petition for certiorari; or making a motion for a directed verdict. FL ST RCP Rule 1.090(b).

d. *Unaffected by expiration of term.* The period of time provided for the doing of any act or the taking of any proceeding shall not be affected or limited by the continued existence or expiration of a term of court. The continued existence or expiration of a term of court in no way affects the power of a court to do any act or take any proceeding in any action which is or has been pending before it. FL ST RCP Rule 1.090(c).

C. General Requirements

1. *Motions generally*

a. *Contents.* An application to the court for an order shall be by motion which shall be made in writing unless made during a hearing or trial, shall state with particularity the grounds therefor, and shall set forth the relief or order sought. The requirement of writing is fulfilled if the motion is stated in a written notice of the hearing of the motion. All notices of hearing shall specify each motion or other matter to be heard. FL ST RCP Rule 1.100(b).

i. *Notice of hearing.* The notice of hearing should indicate on its face whether the date and time have been coordinated with opposing counsel. If the attorney has been unable to coordinate the hearing with opposing counsel, the notice should state the specific good faith efforts the attorney undertook to coordinate or why coordination was not obtained. FL ST 20 J CIR 2.20(IV)(B)(5).

b. *Particularity requirement.* The court considers a motion in the light of the substantive law, rule or

statute to make its determination. Some rules require a statement of the grounds for a motion under the rule. Failure to give the grounds will result in denial of the motion. This should be the result in all situations when the ground for the motion is not inherent in the rule. FL-PRACPROC § 9:3. The requirement is nevertheless an important one, first because of the due process notice rights of the respondent, as well as for the assistance it provides to the court in its preparation for the hearing or, absent a hearing, for disposition. 4 FLPRAC R 1.100.

2. *Conference with opposing counsel.* Attorneys should, whenever possible, prior to filing or upon receiving a motion, contact opposing counsel to determine if the matter can be resolved in whole or in part. This may alleviate the need for a hearing on the motion or allow submission of an agreed order in lieu of a hearing. FL ST 20 J CIR 2.20(IV)(L)(2).
    a. *Conference required.* Except in emergency situations, before filing any motion in a civil case, except a motion for injunctive relief, for judgment on the pleadings, for summary judgment, to dismiss or to permit maintenance of a class action, to dismiss for failure to state a cause of action, to dismiss for lack of prosecution, or to otherwise involuntarily dismiss an action, the moving party shall confer with counsel for the opposing party in a good faith effort to resolve the issues raised by the motion, and shall file with the motion a statement certifying that the moving counsel has conferred with opposing counsel and that counsel have been unable to agree on the resolution of the motion. FL ST 20 J CIR 2.20(IV)(I)(2).
3. *Motion for sanctions*
    a. *Sanctions for raising unsupported claims or defenses*
        i. *No material facts; No law supporting material facts.* Upon the court's initiative or motion of any party, the court shall award a reasonable attorney's fee, including prejudgment interest, to be paid to the prevailing party in equal amounts by the losing party and the losing party's attorney on any claim or defense at any time during a civil proceeding or action in which the court finds that the losing party or the losing party's attorney knew or should have known that a claim or defense when initially presented to the court or at any time before trial was not supported by the material facts necessary to establish the claim or defense; or would not be supported by the application of then-existing law to those material facts. FL ST § 57.105(1).
        ii. *Unreasonable delay.* At any time in any civil proceeding or action in which the moving party proves by a preponderance of the evidence that any action taken by the opposing party, including, but not limited to, the filing of any pleading or part thereof, the assertion of or response to any discovery demand, the assertion of any claim or defense, or the response to any request by any other party, was taken primarily for the purpose of unreasonable delay, the court shall award damages to the moving party for its reasonable expenses incurred in obtaining the order, which may include attorney's fees, and other loss resulting from the improper delay. FL ST § 57.105(2).
        iii. *Limit on monetary sanctions.* Notwithstanding FL ST § 57.105(1) and FL ST § 57.105(2), monetary sanctions may not be awarded:
            - Under FL ST § 57.105(1)(b) if the court determines that the claim or defense was initially presented to the court as a good faith argument for the extension, modification, or reversal of existing law or the establishment of new law, as it applied to the material facts, with a reasonable expectation of success. FL ST § 57.105(3)(a).
            - Under FL ST § 57.105(1)(a) or FL ST § 57.105(1)(b) against the losing party's attorney if he or she has acted in good faith, based on the representations of his or her client as to the existence of those material facts. FL ST § 57.105(3)(b).
            - Under FL ST § 57.105(1)(b) against a represented party. FL ST § 57.105(3)(c).
            - On the court's initiative under FL ST § 57.105(1) and FL ST § 57.105(2) unless sanctions are awarded before a voluntary dismissal or settlement of the claims made by or against the party that is, or whose attorneys are, to be sanctioned. FL ST § 57.105(3)(d).
        iv. *Other sanctions available.* The provisions of FL ST § 57.105 are supplemental to other sanctions or remedies available under law or under court rules. FL ST § 57.105(6).

v. *Fees provided for in contract.* If a contract contains a provision allowing attorney's fees to a party when he or she is required to take any action to enforce the contract, the court may also allow reasonable attorney's fees to the other party when that party prevails in any action, whether as plaintiff or defendant, with respect to the contract. FL ST § 57.105(7) applies to any contract entered into on or after October 1, 1988. FL ST § 57.105(7).

b. *Sanctions in relation to proposals for settlement*

i. *Generally.* Any party seeking sanctions pursuant to applicable Florida law, based on the failure of the proposal's recipient to accept a proposal, shall do so by serving a motion in accordance with FL ST RCP Rule 1.525. FL ST RCP Rule 1.442(g). Any party seeking a judgment taxing costs, attorneys' fees, or both shall serve a motion no later than thirty (30) days after filing of the judgment, including a judgment of dismissal, or the service of a notice of voluntary dismissal, which judgment or notice concludes the action as to that party. FL ST RCP Rule 1.525.

ii. *Motion after judgment, voluntary or involuntary dismissal.* Upon motion made by the offeror within thirty (30) days after the entry of judgment or after voluntary or involuntary dismissal, the court shall determine the following:

- If a defendant serves an offer which is not accepted by the plaintiff, and if the judgment obtained by the plaintiff is at least twenty-five (25%) percent less than the amount of the offer, the defendant shall be awarded reasonable costs, including investigative expenses, and attorney's fees, calculated in accordance with the guidelines promulgated by the Supreme Court, incurred from the date the offer was served, and the court shall set off such costs in attorney's fees against the award. When such costs and attorney's fees total more than the amount of the judgment, the court shall enter judgment for the defendant against the plaintiff for the amount of the costs and fees, less the amount of the award to the plaintiff. FL ST § 768.79(6)(a).
- If a plaintiff serves an offer which is not accepted by the defendant, and if the judgment obtained by the plaintiff is at least twenty-five (25%) percent more than the amount of the offer, the plaintiff shall be awarded reasonable costs, including investigative expenses, and attorney's fees, calculated in accordance with the guidelines promulgated by the Supreme Court, incurred from the date the offer was served. FL ST § 768.79(6)(b).
- For purposes of the determination required by FL ST § 768.79(6)(a), the term "judgment obtained" means the amount of the net judgment entered, plus any postoffer collateral source payments received or due as of the date of the judgment, plus any postoffer settlement amounts by which the verdict was reduced. For purposes of the determination required by FL ST § 768.79(6)(b), the term "judgment obtained" means the amount of the net judgment entered, plus any postoffer settlement amounts by which the verdict was reduced. FL ST § 768.79(6).

iii. For further information please see FL ST § 768.79 and FL ST RCP Rule 1.442.

4. *Arbitration and mediation.* Attorneys are encouraged to utilize arbitration, mediation or other forms of alternative dispute resolution if economically feasible. FL ST 20 J CIR 2.20(IV)(N)(3).

a. *Referral to arbitration and mediation.* Except as hereinafter provided or as otherwise prohibited by law, the presiding judge may enter an order referring all or any part of a contested civil matter to mediation or arbitration. The parties to any contested civil matter may file a written stipulation to mediate or arbitrate any issue between them at any time. Such stipulation shall be incorporated into the order of referral. FL ST RCP Rule 1.700(a).

b. *Arbitration*

i. *Exclusions.* A civil action shall be ordered to arbitration or arbitration in conjunction with mediation upon stipulation of the parties. A civil action may be ordered to arbitration or arbitration in conjunction with mediation upon motion of any party or by the court, if the judge determines the action to be of such a nature that arbitration could be of benefit to the litigants or the court. FL ST RCP Rule 1.800.

- Under no circumstances may the following categories of actions be referred to arbitration:

(1) bond estreatures; (2) habeas corpus or other extraordinary writs; (3) bond validations; (4) civil or criminal contempt; (5) such other matters as may be specified by order of the chief judge in the circuit. FL ST RCP Rule 1.800.

ii. For more information regarding arbitration, please see FL ST RCP Rule 1.810; FL ST RCP Rule 1.820; FL ST RCP Rule 1.830.

c. *Mediation.* For more information regarding mediation, please see FL ST RCP Rule 1.710; FL ST RCP Rule 1.720; FL ST RCP Rule 1.730; FL ST RCP Rule 1.750; and FL ST 20 J CIR 1.9.

5. *Rules of court*

a. *Rules of civil procedure.* The Florida Rules of Civil Procedure apply to all actions of a civil nature and all special statutory proceedings in the circuit courts and county courts except those to which the Florida Probate Rules, the Florida Family Law Rules of Procedure, or the Small Claims Rules apply. FL ST RCP Rule 1.010.

i. The form, content, procedure, and time for pleading in all special statutory proceedings shall be as prescribed by the statutes governing the proceeding unless the Florida Rules of Civil Procedure specifically provide to the contrary. FL ST RCP Rule 1.010.

ii. The Florida Rules of Civil Procedure shall be construed to secure the just, speedy, and inexpensive determination of every action. FL ST RCP Rule 1.010.

b. *Rules of judicial administration.* The Florida Rules of Judicial Administration shall apply to administrative matters in all courts to which the Florida Rules of Judicial Administration are applicable by their terms. The Florida Rules of Judicial Administration shall be construed to secure the speedy and inexpensive determination of every proceeding to which they are applicable. The Florida Rules of Judicial Administration shall supersede all conflicting rules and statutes. FL ST J ADMIN Rule 2.110.

6. *Civil case management plan.* There is established within the Twentieth Judicial Circuit a Civil Case Management Plan applicable to circuit civil cases, which will be administered by the Administrative Office of the Courts through direction of the Circuit Administrative Judges in each county for the implementation of enhanced case management procedures and guidelines for the timely and efficient processing of circuit civil cases and reduction in the pending backlog of civil cases. FL ST 20 J CIR 1.13.

a. The basis for the Civil Case Management Plan is included in FL ST 20 J CIR 1.13, identified in Attachment A as the "Civil Differentiated Case Management (DCM) Procedures and Backlog Reduction Plan," and is incorporated as if fully set forth in FL ST 20 J CIR 1.13. The Civil Case Management Plan is to be used as a model for the purpose of establishing time standards, improving the courts ability to provide early and continuous management of civil cases as required by FL ST J ADMIN Rule 2.545, and to promote uniformity of practice throughout the Twentieth Judicial Circuit. FL ST 20 J CIR 1.13.

b. Full implementation of the Civil DCM Case Management Procedures (Attachment A), including all uniform circuitwide procedures and forms, shall apply to all civil cases filed in Lee and Collier counties, effective January 1, 2011. Even though full implementation may be delayed in Charlotte, Hendry, and Glades counties, all civil time standards and goals, and the use of civil Case Managers and Magistrates to assist trial judges in the process of civil case management and backlog reduction programs, shall be effective circuitwide immediately. FL ST 20 J CIR 1.13.

c. For more information on the civil case management plan, refer to the specific county website and/or see FL ST 20 J CIR 1.13.

D. Documents

1. *Required documents*

a. *Notice of hearing/Motion.* An application to the court for an order shall be by motion which shall be made in writing unless made during a hearing or trial, shall state with particularity the grounds therefor, and shall set forth the relief or order sought. The requirement of writing is fulfilled if the motion is stated in a written notice of the hearing of the motion. All notices of hearing shall specify each motion or other matter to be heard. FL ST RCP Rule 1.100(b). Refer to the General Requirements section of this document for more information on the notice of hearing.

i. *Notices to persons with disabilities.* See the Format section of this KeyRules document for further information.

b. *Certification.* Except in emergency situations, before filing any motion in a civil case, except a motion for injunctive relief, for judgment on the pleadings, for summary judgment, to dismiss or to permit maintenance of a class action, to dismiss for failure to state a cause of action, to dismiss for lack of prosecution, or to otherwise involuntarily dismiss an action, the moving party shall confer with counsel for the opposing party in a good faith effort to resolve the issues raised by the motion, and shall file with the motion a statement certifying that the moving counsel has conferred with opposing counsel and that counsel have been unable to agree on the resolution of the motion. FL ST 20 J CIR 2.20(IV)(I)(2).

c. *Certificate of service.* When any attorney certifies in substance: "I certify that a copy hereof has been furnished to (here insert name or names and addresses used for service) by (e-mail) (delivery) (mail) (fax) on .... (date) ....______________ Attorney" the certificate is taken as prima facie proof of such service in compliance with FL ST J ADMIN Rule 2.516. FL ST J ADMIN Rule 2.516(f).

2. *Supplemental documents*

a. *Proposed order.* The court may require that orders or judgments be prepared by a party, may require the party to furnish the court with stamped, addressed envelopes for service of the order or judgment, and may require that proposed orders and judgments be furnished to all parties before entry by the court of the order or judgment. FL ST J ADMIN Rule 2.516(h)(1).

i. Unless otherwise instructed by the court, or agreed to by counsel, all proposed orders shall be provided to other counsel with a reasonable time for approval or comment prior to submission to the court. Opposing counsel should promptly communicate any objections thereto. Thereafter, the drafting attorney should promptly submit a copy of the proposed order to the court and advise the court as to whether or not it has been approved by opposing counsel. FL ST 20 J CIR 2.20(IV)(I)(4).

ii. Orders prepared by counsel must fairly and adequately represent the ruling of the court, and counsel shall make a good faith effort to agree upon the form of the order prior to submitting it to the court. Attorneys should not submit controverted orders to the court with a copy to opposing counsel for "objections within ______ days". Courts prefer to know that the order is either agreed upon or opposed. FL ST 20 J CIR 2.20(IV)(I)(5).

iii. Attorneys should not use post-hearing submissions of proposed orders as a guise to reargue the merits of the matter. FL ST 20 J CIR 2.20(IV)(I)(6).

iv. If asked by the court to prepare an order, counsel should furnish a copy of the order, and any transmitted letter, to opposing counsel at the time the material is submitted to the court. FL ST 20 J CIR 2.20(IV)(J)(4).

b. *Notice of constitutional question.* A party that files a pleading, written motion, or other paper drawing into question the constitutionality of a state statute or a county or municipal charter, ordinance, or franchise must promptly (1) file a notice of constitutional question stating the question and identifying the paper that raises it; and (2) serve the notice and the pleading, written motion, or other paper drawing into question the constitutionality of a state statute or a county or municipal charter, ordinance, or franchise on the Attorney General or the state attorney of the judicial circuit in which the action is pending, by either certified or registered mail. Service of the notice and pleading, written motion, or other paper does not require joinder of the Attorney General or the state attorney as a party to the action. FL ST RCP Rule 1.071.

c. *Notice and request to participate in telephonic motion hearing.* In instances where a civil motion hearing is scheduled for not longer than fifteen (15) minutes, a party may file a written request to participate via conference or speaker telephone, or other applicable communication equipment, and shall provide notice to the Court and the parties to the motion. FL ST 20 J CIR 1.10. Refer to the Timing and Hearings sections of this document for more information.

E. Format

1. *Documents; Type and size.* Documents subject to the exceptions set forth in FL ST J ADMIN Rule 2.525(d) shall be filed on recycled paper measuring eight and one half by eleven (8 1/2 by 11) inches. For purposes of FL ST J ADMIN Rule 2.520, paper is recycled if it contains a minimum content of fifty (50) percent waste paper. Xerographic reduction of legal-size (eight and one half by fourteen (8 1/2 by 14) inches) documents to letter size (eight and one half by eleven (8 1/2 by 11) inches) is prohibited. All other documents filed by electronic transmission shall be filed in a format capable of being printed in a format consistent with the provisions of FL ST J ADMIN Rule 2.250. FL ST J ADMIN Rule 2.520(b); FL ST 20 J CIR 2.9.
    a. *Exhibits.* Any exhibit or attachment filed with pleadings or papers may be filed in its original size. FL ST J ADMIN Rule 2.520(c); FL ST 20 J CIR 2.9.
    b. *Recording space.* On all papers and documents prepared and filed by the court or by any party to a proceeding which are to be recorded in the public records of any county, including but not limited to final money judgments and notices of lis pendens, a three (3) inch by three (3) inch space at the top right-hand corner on the first page and a one (1) inch by three (3) inch space at the top right-hand corner on each subsequent page shall be left blank and reserved for use by the clerk of court. FL ST J ADMIN Rule 2.520(d).
        i. *Exceptions to recording space.* Any papers or documents created by persons or entities over which the filing party has no control, including but not limited to wills, codicils, trusts, or other testamentary documents; documents prepared or executed by any public officer; documents prepared, executed, acknowledged, or proved outside of the State of Florida; or documents created by State or Federal government agencies, may be filed without the space required by FL ST J ADMIN Rule 2.520. FL ST J ADMIN Rule 2.520(e).
    c. *Noncompliance.* No clerk of court is permitted to refuse to file any document or paper because of noncompliance with the Florida Rules of Judicial Administration. However, upon request of the clerk of court, noncomplying documents must be resubmitted in accordance with the formatting rules. FL ST J ADMIN Rule 2.520(f).
        i. When time of filing is critical, the Clerk shall accept pleadings, motions, petitions, briefs, notices, orders, judgments, decrees, opinions, or other papers or official documents on other than eight and one half by eleven (8 1/2 by 11) inch paper but shall then require that the document be resubmitted to comply with FL ST J ADMIN Rule 2.520. FL ST 20 J CIR 2.9.
2. *Caption.* Every pleading, motion, order, judgment, or other paper shall have a caption containing the name of the court, the file number, and except for in rem proceedings, including forfeiture proceedings, the name of the first party on each side with an appropriate indication of other parties, and a designation identifying the party filing it and its nature or the nature of the order, as the case may be. In any in rem proceeding, every pleading, motion, order, judgment, or other paper shall have a caption containing the name of the court, the file number, the style "In re" (followed by the name or general description of the property), and a designation of the person or entity filing it and its nature or the nature of the order, as the case may be. In an in rem forfeiture proceeding, the style shall be "In re forfeiture of" (followed by the name of the general description of the property). All papers filed in the action shall be styled in such a manner as to indicate clearly the subject matter of the paper and the party requesting or obtaining relief. FL ST RCP Rule 1.100(c)(1).
3. *Writing and written defined.* Writing or written means a document containing information, an application, or a stipulation. FL ST RCP Rule 1.080(c).
4. *Rule abbreviations*
    a. The Florida Rules of Civil Procedure and shall be abbreviated as Fla.R.Civ.P. FL ST RCP Rule 1.010.
    b. The Florida Rules of Judicial Administration shall be abbreviated as Fla. R. Jud. Admin. FL ST J ADMIN Rule 2.110.
5. *Nonverification.* Except when otherwise specifically provided by the Florida Rules of Civil Procedure or an applicable statute, every pleading or other document of a party represented by an attorney need not be verified or accompanied by an affidavit. FL ST RCP Rule 1.030; FL ST J ADMIN Rule 2.515(a).

6. *Attorney signature*

   a. *Attorney signature.* Every pleading and other document of a party represented by an attorney shall be signed by at least one (1) attorney of record in that attorney's individual name whose current record Florida Bar address, telephone number, including area code, primary e-mail address and secondary e-mail addresses, if any, and Florida Bar number shall be stated, and who shall be duly licensed to practice law in Florida or who shall have received permission to appear in the particular case as provided in FL ST J ADMIN Rule 2.510. FL ST J ADMIN Rule 2.515(a).

      i. The attorney may be required by the court to give the address of, and to vouch for the attorney's authority to represent, the party. FL ST J ADMIN Rule 2.515(a).

      ii. The signature of an attorney shall constitute a certificate by the attorney that the attorney has read the pleading or other document; that to the best of the attorney's knowledge, information, and belief there is good ground to support it; and that it is not interposed for delay. FL ST J ADMIN Rule 2.515(a).

      iii. If a pleading is not signed or is signed with intent to defeat the purpose of FL ST J ADMIN Rule 2.515, it may be stricken and the action may proceed as though the pleading or other document had not been served. FL ST J ADMIN Rule 2.515(a).

   b. *Pro se litigant signature.* A party who is not represented by an attorney shall sign any pleading or other paper and state the party's address and telephone number, including area code. FL ST J ADMIN Rule 2.515(b).

   c. *Form of signature*

      i. The signatures required on pleadings and documents by FL ST J ADMIN Rule 2.515(a) and FL ST J ADMIN Rule 2.515(b) may be:

         - Original signatures;
         - Original signatures that have been reproduced by electronic means, such as on electronically transmitted documents or photocopied documents;
         - Electronic signatures using the "/s/," "s/," or "/s" formats by or at the direction of the person signing; or
         - Any other signature format authorized by general law, so long as the clerk where the proceeding is pending has the capability of receiving and has obtained approval from the Supreme Court of Florida to accept pleadings and documents with that signature format. FL ST J ADMIN Rule 2.515(c)(1).

      ii. An attorney, party, or other person who files a pleading or paper by electronic transmission that does not contain the original signature of that attorney, party, or other person shall file that identical pleading or paper in paper form containing an original signature of that attorney, party, or other person (hereinafter called the follow-up filing) immediately thereafter. The follow-up filing is not required if the Supreme Court of Florida has entered an order directing the clerk of court to discontinue accepting the follow-up filing. FL ST J ADMIN Rule 2.515(c)(2).

7. *Forms*

   a. *Process.* The forms of process, notice of lis pendens, and notice of action provided in the Florida Rules of Civil Procedure are sufficient. Variations from the forms do not void process or notices that are otherwise sufficient. FL ST RCP Rule 1.900(a).

   b. *Other forms.* The other forms provided in the Florida Rules of Civil Procedure are sufficient for the matters that are covered by them. So long as the substance is expressed without prolixity, the forms may be varied to meet the facts of a particular case. FL ST RCP Rule 1.900(b).

   c. *Formal matters.* Captions, except for the designation of the paper, are omitted from the forms provided in the Florida Rules of Civil Procedure. A general form of caption is the first form provided. Signatures are omitted from pleadings and motions. FL ST RCP Rule 1.900(c).

8. *Notices to persons with disabilities.* All notices of court proceedings to be held in a public facility, and all process compelling appearance at such proceedings, shall include the following statement in bold face,

fourteen (14) point Times New Roman or Courier font: "If you are a person with a disability who needs any accommodation in order to participate in this proceeding, you are entitled, at no cost to you, to the provision of certain assistance. Please contact [identify applicable court personnel by name, address, and telephone number] at least seven (7) days before your scheduled court appearance, or immediately upon receiving this notification if the time before the scheduled appearance is less than seven (7) days; if you are hearing or voice impaired, call 711." FL ST J ADMIN Rule 2.540(c)(1). For more information, see FL ST 20 J CIR 2.15.

9. *Minimization of the filing of sensitive information*
   a. *Limitations for court filings.* Unless authorized by FL ST J ADMIN Rule 2.425(b), statute, another rule of court, or the court orders otherwise, designated sensitive information filed with the court must be limited to the following format:
      i. The initials of a person known to be a minor;
      ii. The year of birth of a person's birth date;
      iii. No portion of any: Social security number, Bank account number, Credit card account number, Charge account number, or Debit account number;
      iv. The last four digits of any: Taxpayer identification number (TIN), Employee identification number, Driver's license number, Passport number, Telephone number, Financial account number, except as set forth in FL ST J ADMIN Rule 2.425(a)(3), Brokerage account number, Insurance policy account number, Loan account number, Customer account number, or Patient or health care number;
      v. A truncated version of any: Email address, Computer user name, Password, or Personal identification number (PIN); and
      vi. A truncated version of any other sensitive information as provided by court order. FL ST J ADMIN Rule 2.425(a).
   b. *Exceptions.* FL ST J ADMIN Rule 2.425(a) does not apply to the following:
      i. An account number which identifies the property alleged to be the subject of a proceeding;
      ii. The record of an administrative or agency proceeding;
      iii. The record in appellate or review proceedings;
      iv. The birth date of a minor whenever the birth date is necessary for the court to establish or maintain subject matter jurisdiction;
      v. The name of a minor in any order relating to parental responsibility, time-sharing, or child support;
      vi. The name of a minor in any document or order affecting the minor's ownership of real property;
      vii. The birth date of a party in a writ of attachment or notice to payor;
      viii. In traffic and criminal proceedings: a pro se filing; a court filing that is related to a criminal matter or investigation and that is prepared before the filing of a criminal charge or is not filed as part of any docketed criminal case; an arrest or search warrant or any information in support thereof; a charging document and an affidavit or other documents filed in support of any charging document, including any driving records; a statement of particulars; discovery material introduced into evidence or otherwise filed with the court; and all information necessary for the proper issuance and execution of a subpoena duces tecum;
      ix. Information used by the clerk for case maintenance purposes or the courts for case management purposes; and
      x. Information which is relevant and material to an issue before the court. FL ST J ADMIN Rule 2.425(b).
   c. *Remedies.* Upon motion by a party or interested person or sua sponte by the court, the court may order remedies, sanctions or both for a violation of FL ST J ADMIN Rule 2.425(a). Following notice and an opportunity to respond, the court may impose sanctions if such filing was not made in good faith. FL ST J ADMIN Rule 2.425(c).

d. *Motions not restricted.* FL ST J ADMIN Rule 2.425 does not restrict a party's right to move for protective order, to move to file documents under seal, or to request a determination of the confidentiality of records. FL ST J ADMIN Rule 2.425(d).

e. *Application.* FL ST J ADMIN Rule 2.425 does not affect the application of constitutional provisions, statutes, or rules of court regarding confidential information or access to public information. FL ST J ADMIN Rule 2.425(e).

F. Filing and Service Requirements

1. *Filing requirements.* All original documents must be filed with the court either before service or immediately thereafter, unless otherwise provided for by general law or other rules. If the original of any bond or other document is not placed in the court file, a certified copy must be so placed by the clerk. FL ST J ADMIN Rule 2.516(d). All documents shall be filed in conformity with the requirements of FL ST J ADMIN Rule 2.525. FL ST RCP Rule 1.080(b). All documents filed in any court shall be filed by electronic transmission in accordance with FL ST J ADMIN Rule 2.525. "Documents" means pleadings, motions, petitions, memoranda, briefs, notices, exhibits, declarations, affidavits, orders, judgments, decrees, writs, opinions, and any other paper or writing submitted to a court. FL ST J ADMIN Rule 2.520(a). All documents that are court records, as defined in FL ST J ADMIN Rule 2.430(a)(1), must be filed by electronic transmission, provided that: (1) the clerk has the ability to accept and retain such documents; (2) the clerk or the chief judge of the circuit has requested permission to accept documents filed by electronic transmission; and (3) the supreme court has entered an order granting permission to the clerk to accept documents filed by electronic transmission. FL ST J ADMIN Rule 2.525(c)(1).

a. *Definition.* "Electronic transmission of documents" means the sending of information by electronic signals to, by or from a court or clerk, which when received can be transformed and stored or transmitted on paper, microfilm, magnetic storage device, optical imaging system, CD-ROM, flash drive, other electronic data storage system, server, case maintenance system ("CM"), electronic court filing ("ECF") system, statewide or local electronic portal ("e-portal"), or other electronic record keeping system authorized by the supreme court in a format sufficient to communicate the information on the original document in a readable format. Electronic transmission of documents includes electronic mail ("e-mail") and any internet-based transmission procedure, and may include procedures allowing for documents to be signed or verified by electronic means. FL ST J ADMIN Rule 2.525(a).

i. The filing of documents with the court as required by the Florida Rules of Judicial Administration must be made by filing them with the clerk in accordance with FL ST J ADMIN Rule 2.525, except that the judge may permit documents to be filed with the judge, in which event the judge must note the filing date before him or her on the documents and transmit them to the clerk. The date of filing is that shown on the face of the document by the judge's notation or the clerk's time stamp, whichever is earlier. FL ST J ADMIN Rule 2.516(e).

b. *Application.* Any court or clerk of the court may accept the electronic transmission of documents for filing after the clerk, together with input from the chief judge of the circuit, has obtained approval of the procedures and program for doing so from the Supreme Court of Florida. FL ST J ADMIN Rule 2.525(b).

c. *Exceptions*

i. Paper documents and other submissions may be manually submitted to the clerk or court:

- When the clerk does not have the ability to accept and retain documents by electronic filing or has not had ECF Procedures approved by the supreme court;
- For filing by any self-represented party or any self-represented nonparty unless specific ECF Procedures provide a means to file documents electronically. However, any self-represented nonparty that is a governmental or public agency and any other agency, partnership, corporation, or business entity acting on behalf of any governmental or public agency may file documents by electronic transmission if such entity has the capability of filing documents electronically;
- For filing by attorneys excused from e-mail service in accordance with FL ST J ADMIN Rule 2.516(b);

- When submitting evidentiary exhibits or filing non-documentary materials;
- When the filing involves documents in excess of twenty-five (25) megabytes (25MB) in size. For such filings, documents may be transmitted using an electronic storage medium that the clerk has the ability to accept, which may include a CD-ROM, flash drive, or similar storage medium;
- When filed in open court, as permitted by the court;
- When paper filing is permitted by any approved statewide or local ECF procedures; and
- If any court determines that justice so requires. FL ST J ADMIN Rule 2.525(d).

ii. Any document in paper form submitted under FL ST J ADMIN Rule 2.525(d) is filed when it is received by the clerk or court and the clerk shall immediately thereafter convert any filed paper document to an electronic document. "Convert to an electronic document" means optically capturing an image of a paper document and using character recognition software to recover as much of the document's text as practicable and then indexing and storing the document in the official court file. FL ST J ADMIN Rule 2.525(c)(4).

iii. Any storage medium submitted under FL ST J ADMIN Rule 2.525(d)(5) is filed when received by the clerk or court and the clerk shall immediately thereafter transfer the electronic documents from the storage device to the official court file. FL ST J ADMIN Rule 2.525(c)(5).

iv. If the filer of any paper document authorized under FL ST J ADMIN Rule 2.525(d) provides a self-addressed, postage-paid envelope for return of the paper document after it is converted to electronic form by the clerk, the clerk shall place the paper document in the envelope and deposit it in the mail. Except when a paper document is required to be maintained, the clerk may recycle any filed paper document that is not to be returned to the filer. FL ST J ADMIN Rule 2.525(c)(6).

v. The clerk may convert any paper document filed before the effective date of FL ST J ADMIN Rule 2.525 to an electronic document. Unless the clerk is required to maintain the paper document, if the paper document has been converted to an electronic document by the clerk, the paper document is no longer part of the official court file and may be removed and recycled. FL ST J ADMIN Rule 2.525(c)(7).

d. *Official court file.* For information on what constitutes the official court file, please see FL ST J ADMIN Rule 2.525(c)(2), FL ST J ADMIN Rule 2.525(c)(3).

e. *Administration.* All attorneys, parties, or other persons using this rule to file documents are required to make arrangements with the court or clerk for the payment of any charges authorized by general law or the supreme court before filing any document by electronic transmission. FL ST J ADMIN Rule 2.525(f)(2).

f. *Filing date.* The filing date for an electronically transmitted document is the date and time that such filing is acknowledged by an electronic stamp or otherwise, pursuant to any procedure set forth in any ECF Procedures approved by the supreme court, or the date the last page of such filing is received by the court or clerk. FL ST J ADMIN Rule 2.525(f)(3).

g. *Accessibility.* All documents transmitted in any electronic form under FL ST J ADMIN Rule 2.525 must comply with the accessibility requirements of FL ST J ADMIN Rule 2.526. FL ST J ADMIN Rule 2.525(g).

2. *Service requirements.* Every pleading subsequent to the initial pleading, all orders, and every other document filed in the action must be served in conformity with the requirements of FL ST J ADMIN Rule 2.516. FL ST RCP Rule 1.080(a).

a. *Service; Generally.* The timing and manner of service should not be used to the disadvantage of the party receiving the papers. FL ST 20 J CIR 2.20(IV)(C)(1).

i. Papers and memoranda of law should not be served at court appearances without advance notice to opposing counsel and should not be served so close to a court appearance so as to inhibit the ability of opposing counsel to prepare for that appearance or to respond to the papers. Should the attorney do so, the court is urged to take appropriate action in response, including

continuing the matter to allow opposing counsel to prepare and respond. FL ST 20 J CIR 2.20(IV)(C)(2).

ii. Papers should not be served in order to take advantage of an opponent's known absence from the office or at a time or in a manner designed to inconvenience an adversary, such as late on Friday afternoon or the day preceding a secular or religious holiday. FL ST 20 J CIR 2.20(IV)(C)(3).

iii. Service should be made personally or by courtesy copy facsimile transmission when it is likely that service by mail, even when allowed, will prejudice the opposing party or will not provide the opposing party with a reasonable time to respond. FL ST 20 J CIR 2.20(IV)(C)(4).

b. *Service; When required.* Unless the court otherwise orders, or a statute or supreme court administrative order specifies a different means of service, every pleading subsequent to the initial pleading and every other document filed in any court proceeding, except applications for witness subpoenas and documents served by formal notice or required to be served in the manner provided for service of formal notice, must be served in accordance with FL ST J ADMIN Rule 2.516 on each party. No service need be made on parties against whom a default has been entered, except that pleadings asserting new or additional claims against them must be served in the manner provided for service of summons. FL ST J ADMIN Rule 2.516(a).

i. *Copies of court submissions.* Copies of any submissions to the court (such as correspondence, memoranda of law, motions, case law, etc.) should simultaneously be provided to opposing counsel by substantially the same method of delivery by which they are provided to the court. For example, if a memorandum of law is hand-delivered to the court, at substantially the same time a copy should be hand-delivered or faxed to opposing counsel. FL ST 20 J CIR 2.20(IV)(J)(4).

c. *Service; How made.* When service is required or permitted to be made upon a party represented by an attorney, service must be made upon the attorney unless service upon the party is ordered by the court. FL ST J ADMIN Rule 2.516(b).

i. *Service by electronic mail ("e-mail").* All documents required or permitted to be served on another party must be served by e-mail, unless FL ST J ADMIN Rule 2.516 otherwise provides. When, in addition to service by e-mail, the sender also utilizes another means of service provided for in FL ST J ADMIN Rule 2.516(b)(2), any differing time limits and other provisions applicable to that other means of service control. FL ST J ADMIN Rule 2.516(b)(1). Any document electronically transmitted to a court or clerk must also be served on all parties and interested persons in accordance with the applicable rules of court. FL ST J ADMIN Rule 2.525(e)(2).

- *Service on attorneys.* Upon appearing in a proceeding, an attorney must serve a designation of a primary e-mail address and may designate no more than two (2) secondary e-mail addresses. Thereafter, service must be directed to all designated e-mail addresses in that proceeding. Every document filed by an attorney thereafter must include the primary e-mail address of that attorney and any secondary e-mail addresses. If an attorney does not designate any e-mail address for service, documents may be served on that attorney at the e-mail address on record with The Florida Bar. FL ST J ADMIN Rule 2.516(b)(1)(A).
- *Exception to e-mail service on attorneys.* Service by an attorney on another attorney must be made by e-mail unless excused by the court. Upon motion by an attorney demonstrating that the attorney has no e-mail account and lacks access to the Internet at the attorney's office, the court may excuse the attorney from the requirements of e-mail service. Service on and by an attorney excused by the court from e-mail service must be by the means provided in FL ST J ADMIN Rule 2.516(b)(2). FL ST J ADMIN Rule 2.516(b)(1)(B).
- *Service on and by parties not represented by an attorney.* Any party not represented by an attorney may serve a designation of a primary e-mail address and also may designate no more than two (2) secondary e-mail addresses to which service must be directed in that proceeding by the means provided in FL ST J ADMIN Rule 2.516(b)(1). If a party not represented by an attorney does not designate an e-mail address for service in a proceed-

ing, service on and by that party must be by the means provided in FL ST J ADMIN Rule 2.516(b)(2). FL ST J ADMIN Rule 2.516(b)(1)(C).

- *Time of service.* Service by e-mail is complete when it is sent. FL ST J ADMIN Rule 2.516(b)(1)(D). An e-mail is deemed served on the date it is sent. FL ST J ADMIN Rule 2.516(b)(1)(D)(i). If the sender learns that the e-mail did not reach the address of the person to be served, the sender must immediately send another copy by e-mail, or by a means authorized by FL ST J ADMIN Rule 2.516(b)(2). FL ST J ADMIN Rule 2.516(b)(1)(D)(ii). E-mail service is treated as service by mail for the computation of time. FL ST J ADMIN Rule 2.516(b)(1)(D)(iii).

ii. *Format of e-mail for service.* Service of a document by e-mail is made by attaching a copy of the document in PDF format to an e-mail sent to all addresses designated by the attorney or party. FL ST J ADMIN Rule 2.516(b)(1)(E).

- All documents served by e-mail must be attached to an e-mail message containing a subject line beginning with the words "SERVICE OF COURT DOCUMENT" in all capital letters, followed by the case number of the proceeding in which the documents are being served. FL ST J ADMIN Rule 2.516(b)(1)(E)(i).
- The body of the e-mail must identify the court in which the proceeding is pending, the case number, the name of the initial party on each side, the title of each document served with that e-mail, and the sender's name and telephone number. FL ST J ADMIN Rule 2.516(b)(1)(E)(ii).
- Any document served by e-mail may be signed by the "/s/" format, as long as the filed original is signed in accordance with the applicable rule of procedure. FL ST J ADMIN Rule 2.516(b)(1)(E)(iii).
- Any e-mail which, together with its attached documents, exceeds five megabytes (5MB) in size, must be divided and sent as separate e-mails, no one of which may exceed five megabytes (5MB) in size and each of which must be sequentially numbered in the subject line. FL ST J ADMIN Rule 2.516(b)(1)(E)(iv).

iii. *Service by other means.* In addition to, and not in lieu of, service by e-mail, service may also be made upon attorneys by any of the means specified in FL ST J ADMIN Rule 2.516(b)(2). Service on and by all parties who are not represented by an attorney and who do not designate an e-mail address, and on and by all attorneys excused from e-mail service, must be made by delivering a copy of the document or by mailing it to the party or attorney at their last known address or, if no address is known, by leaving it with the clerk of the court. Service by mail is complete upon mailing. Delivery of a copy within FL ST J ADMIN Rule 2.516 is complete upon:

- Handing it to the attorney or to the party,
- Leaving it at the attorney's or party's office with a clerk or other person in charge thereof,
- If there is no one in charge, leaving it in a conspicuous place therein,
- If the office is closed or the person to be served has no office, leaving it at the person's usual place of abode with some person of his or her family above fifteen (15) years of age and informing such person of the contents, or
- Transmitting it by facsimile to the attorney's or party's office with a cover sheet containing the sender's name, firm, address, telephone number, and facsimile number, and the number of pages transmitted. When service is made by facsimile, a copy must also be served by any other method permitted by FL ST J ADMIN Rule 2.516. Facsimile service occurs when transmission is complete. FL ST J ADMIN Rule 2.516(b)(2)(A) through FL ST J ADMIN Rule 2.516(b)(2)(E).
- Service by delivery after 5:00 p.m. must be deemed to have been made by mailing on the date of delivery. FL ST J ADMIN Rule 2.516(b)(2)(F).

d. *Service; Numerous defendants.* In actions when the parties are unusually numerous, the court may

regulate the service contemplated by the Florida Rules of Judicial Administration on motion or on its own initiative in such manner as may be found to be just and reasonable. FL ST J ADMIN Rule 2.516(c).

e. *Service by clerk.* Service of notices and other documents required to be made by the clerk must also be done as provided in FL ST J ADMIN Rule 2.516(b). FL ST J ADMIN Rule 2.516(g).

G. Hearings

1. *Scheduling.* Before setting a motion for hearing, counsel should make a good faith effort to resolve the issue with opposing counsel. FL ST 20 J CIR 2.20(IV)(I)(1). Except in emergency situations, attorneys should make a good faith effort to communicate with opposing counsel prior to scheduling depositions, hearings and other proceedings, so as to schedule them at times that are mutually convenient for all interested persons. Further, a sufficient time should be reserved to permit a complete presentation by counsel for all parties. FL ST 20 J CIR 2.20(IV)(B)(1). Attorneys should not use the hearing time obtained by opposing counsel for other motion practice. FL ST 20 J CIR 2.20(IV)(B)(6).

   a. *Notice.* Counsel should notify opposing counsel of dates and times obtained from the court for future hearings on the same day that the hearing date is obtained from the court, or as soon as practicable thereafter. FL ST 20 J CIR 2.20(IV)(J)(3).

   b. *Scheduling conflict.* Attorneys should notify opposing counsel, the court, and others affected, of scheduling conflicts as soon as they become apparent. Further, attorneys should cooperate with one another regarding all reasonable rescheduling requests that do not prejudice their clients or unduly delay a proceeding. FL ST 20 J CIR 2.20(IV)(B)(7).

      i. Attorneys should call potential scheduling problems to the attention of those affected, including the court, as soon as they become apparent and should avoid last minute cancellations. FL ST 20 J CIR 2.20(IV)(B)(12).

   c. *Notice to court when appearance is unnecessary.* Attorneys should promptly notify the court or other tribunal of any resolution between the parties that renders a scheduled court appearance unnecessary. FL ST 20 J CIR 2.20(IV)(B)(8).

2. *Communication equipment*

   a. *Definition.* Communication equipment means a conference telephone or other electronic device that permits all those appearing or participating to hear and speak to each other, provided that all conversation of all parties is audible to all persons present. FL ST J ADMIN Rule 2.530(a).

   b. *Use by all parties.* A county or circuit court judge may, upon the court's own motion or upon the written request of a party, direct that communication equipment be used for a motion hearing, pretrial conference, or a status conference. A judge must give notice to the parties and consider any objections they may have to the use of communication equipment before directing that communication equipment be used. The decision to use communication equipment over the objection of parties will be in the sound discretion of the trial court, except as noted below. FL ST J ADMIN Rule 2.530(b).

   c. *Use only by requesting party.* A county or circuit court judge may, upon the written request of a party upon reasonable notice to all other parties, permit a requesting party to participate through communication equipment in a scheduled motion hearing; however, any such request (except in criminal, juvenile, and appellate proceedings) must be granted, absent a showing of good cause to deny the same, where the hearing is set for not longer than fifteen (15) minutes. FL ST J ADMIN Rule 2.530(c).

   d. *Testimony*

      i. *Generally.* A county or circuit court judge, general magistrate, special magistrate, or hearing officer may allow testimony to be taken through communication equipment if all parties consent or if permitted by another applicable rule of procedure. FL ST J ADMIN Rule 2.530(d)(1).

      ii. *Procedure.* Any party desiring to present testimony through communication equipment shall, prior to the hearing or trial at which the testimony is to be presented, contact all parties to

determine whether each party consents to this form of testimony. The party seeking to present the testimony shall move for permission to present testimony through communication equipment, which motion shall set forth good cause as to why the testimony should be allowed in this form. FL ST J ADMIN Rule 2.530(d)(2).

iii. *Oath.* Testimony may be taken through communication equipment only if a notary public or other person authorized to administer oaths in the witness's jurisdiction is present with the witness and administers the oath consistent with the laws of the jurisdiction. FL ST J ADMIN Rule 2.530(d)(3).

iv. *Confrontation rights.* In juvenile and criminal proceedings the defendant must make an informed waiver of any confrontation rights that may be abridged by the use of communication equipment. FL ST J ADMIN Rule 2.530(d)(4).

v. *Video testimony.* If the testimony to be presented utilizes video conferencing or comparable two-way visual capabilities, the court in its discretion may modify the procedures set forth in FL ST J ADMIN Rule 2.530 to accommodate the technology utilized. FL ST J ADMIN Rule 2.530(d)(5).

e. *Burden of expense.* The cost for the use of the communication equipment is the responsibility of the requesting party unless otherwise directed by the court. FL ST J ADMIN Rule 2.530(e).

3. *Telephonic non-evidentiary motion hearings set for not longer than fifteen (15) minutes.* FL ST 20 J CIR 1.10 specifically addresses non-evidentiary civil motion hearings set for not longer than fifteen (15) minutes. It is not intended to limit or address requests for telephonic hearings which are otherwise governed by FL ST J ADMIN Rule 2.071. FL ST 20 J CIR 1.10. [Editor's note: FL ST J ADMIN Rule 2.071 was renumbered as FL ST J ADMIN Rule 2.530]. Evidentiary hearings are exempted from the application of FL ST 20 J CIR 1.10. FL ST 20 J CIR 1.10.

a. In instances where a civil motion hearing is scheduled for not longer than fifteen (15) minutes, a party may file a written request to participate via conference or speaker telephone, or other applicable communication equipment, and shall provide notice to the Court and the parties to the motion. FL ST 20 J CIR 1.10. Refer to the Timing section of this document for information on when the notice must be given and when request must be served.

b. The requesting party shall be responsible for contacting the trial judge's Judicial Assistant and ensuring that appropriate arrangements have been made to permit participation through conference or speaker telephone, or other applicable communication equipment, on the scheduled date and time. It shall be at the discretion of the trial judge as to whether the requesting party shall be responsible for initiating the telephone or communication connection or whether the Court shall be responsible for initiating the telephone or communication connection. FL ST 20 J CIR 1.10(3).

c. Absent a showing of good cause, and in accordance with FL ST J ADMIN Rule 2.071(c), the trial judge shall grant the request and make reasonable accommodations to permit the requesting party's participation through conference or speaker telephone, or other applicable communication equipment. FL ST 20 J CIR 1.10. [Editor's note: FL ST J ADMIN Rule 2.071 was renumbered as FL ST J ADMIN Rule 2.530(c)].

d. To the extent that any provision of FL ST 20 J CIR 1.10 may be construed as being in conflict with any law, statute, or rule, the law, statute, or rule shall prevail. FL ST 20 J CIR 1.10.

H. Forms

1. Official Motion for Sanctions Forms for Florida

a. Caption. FL ST RCP Form 1.901.

b. Notice of compliance when constitutional challenge is brought. FL ST RCP Form 1.975.

2. Motion for Sanctions Forms for Florida

a. Motion; By defendant; For sanctions for refusal of offer of judgment. FL-PP § 61:22.

b. Motion; Sanctions, proposal for settlement. FL-PRACFORM § 7:165.

I. Checklist

(I) ❑ Matters to be considered by moving party

(a) ❑ Required documents

(1) ❑ Notice of hearing/Motion

(2) ❑ Certification

(3) ❑ Certificate of service

(b) ❑ Supplemental documents

(1) ❑ Proposed order

(2) ❑ Notice of constitutional question

(3) ❑ Notice and request to participate in telephonic motion hearing

(c) ❑ Time for making motion

(1) ❑ A motion by a party seeking sanctions under FL ST § 57.105 must be served but may not be filed with or presented to the court unless, within twenty one (21) days after service of the motion, the challenged paper, claim, defense, contention, allegation, or denial is not withdrawn or appropriately corrected

(2) ❑ Any party seeking a judgment taxing costs, attorneys' fees, or both shall serve a motion no later than thirty (30) days after filing of the judgment, including a judgment of dismissal, or the service of a notice of voluntary dismissal

(3) ❑ A copy of any written motion which may not be heard ex parte and a copy of the notice of the hearing thereof shall be served a reasonable time before the time specified for the hearing; as a general rule, notice should be provided (not including time for service) no less than five (5) business days for hearings

(4) ❑ Notice and request to participate in telephonic motion hearing: Notice by the requesting party must be provided by mailing a copy of the written request at least five (5) days prior to the day of the hearing, or by delivering a copy of the written request to the other parties or, if represented by counsel, to the other parties' attorney(s) no later than 5:00 p.m. two (2) business days prior to the day of the hearing

(II) ❑ Matters to be considered by opposing party

(a) ❑ Required documents

(1) ❑ Response to motion

(2) ❑ Certificate of service

(b) ❑ Supplemental documents

(1) ❑ Proposed order

(2) ❑ Notice of constitutional question

(3) ❑ Notice and request to participate in telephonic motion hearing

(c) ❑ Time for service and filing of opposition

(1) ❑ No time specified for responding to a motion

(2) ❑ Notice and request to participate in telephonic motion hearing: Notice by the requesting party must be provided by mailing a copy of the written request at least five (5) days prior to the day of the hearing, or by delivering a copy of the written request to the other parties or, if represented by counsel, to the other parties' attorney(s) no later than 5:00 p.m. two (2) business days prior to the day of the hearing

Motions, Oppositions and Replies
Motion to Compel Discovery

Document Last Updated January 2013

A. Applicable Rules

1. *State rules*
   a. Rules of court. FL ST RCP Rule 1.010; FL ST J ADMIN Rule 2.110.
   b. Nonverification of pleadings. FL ST RCP Rule 1.030.
   c. Service and filing of pleadings, orders, and documents. FL ST RCP Rule 1.080.
   d. Time. FL ST RCP Rule 1.090.
   e. Pleadings and motions. FL ST RCP Rule 1.100.
   f. Motions. FL ST RCP Rule 1.160.
   g. General provisions governing discovery. FL ST RCP Rule 1.280.
   h. Depositions. FL ST RCP Rule 1.310; FL ST RCP Rule 1.320; FL ST FAM LAW Rule 12.310.
   i. Interrogatories to parties. FL ST RCP Rule 1.340.
   j. Production of documents and things and entry upon land for inspection and other purposes. FL ST RCP Rule 1.350.
   k. Examination of persons. FL ST RCP Rule 1.360.
   l. Failure to make discovery; Sanctions. FL ST RCP Rule 1.380.
   m. Relief from judgment, decrees, or orders. FL ST RCP Rule 1.540.
   n. Mediation and arbitration. FL ST RCP Rule 1.700; FL ST RCP Rule 1.710; FL ST RCP Rule 1.720; FL ST RCP Rule 1.730; FL ST RCP Rule 1.750; FL ST RCP Rule 1.800; FL ST RCP Rule 1.810; FL ST RCP Rule 1.820; FL ST RCP Rule 1.830.
   o. Forms. FL ST RCP Rule 1.900.
   p. Minimization of the filing of sensitive information. FL ST J ADMIN Rule 2.425.
   q. Retention of court records. FL ST J ADMIN Rule 2.430.
   r. Foreign attorneys. FL ST J ADMIN Rule 2.510.
   s. Signature of attorneys and parties. FL ST J ADMIN Rule 2.515.
   t. Paper. FL ST J ADMIN Rule 2.520.
   u. Electronic filing. FL ST J ADMIN Rule 2.525.
   v. Accessibility of information and technology. FL ST J ADMIN Rule 2.526.
   w. Communication equipment. FL ST J ADMIN Rule 2.530.
   x. Court reporting. FL ST J ADMIN Rule 2.535.
   y. Requests for accommodations by persons with disabilities. FL ST J ADMIN Rule 2.540.
   z. Case management. FL ST J ADMIN Rule 2.545.
2. *Local rules*
   a. Exclusions from mediation. FL ST 20 J CIR 1.9.
   b. Establishment and implementation of civil case management plan. FL ST 20 J CIR 1.13.
   c. Size of paper. FL ST 20 J CIR 2.9.
   d. Telephonic motion hearings set for not longer than fifteen minutes in circuit and county civil cases. FL ST 20 J CIR 1.10.
   e. Americans with Disabilities Act; Notification of court proceedings. FL ST 20 J CIR 2.15.

f. Standards of professional courtesy and conduct and establishment of peer review program. FL ST 20 J CIR 2.20.

B. Timing

1. *Motion to compel discovery.* Upon reasonable notice to other parties and all persons affected, a party may apply for an order compelling discovery. FL ST RCP Rule 1.380(a).
2. *General motion timing.* A copy of any written motion which may not be heard ex parte and a copy of the notice of the hearing thereof shall be served a reasonable time before the time specified for the hearing. FL ST RCP Rule 1.090(d).
   a. *Notice of hearing.* Except in emergency situations, attorneys should provide opposing counsel, parties, witnesses, and other affected persons, sufficient notice of depositions, hearings and other proceedings. FL ST 20 J CIR 2.20(IV)(B)(1). Attorneys should notify opposing counsel of any hearing time reserved as soon as practicable. FL ST 20 J CIR 2.20(IV)(B)(3). When hearing time is obtained, attorneys should promptly prepare and serve all counsel of record with notice of the hearing. Do not delay in providing such notice. FL ST 20 J CIR 2.20(IV)(B)(4).
      i. As a general rule, notice should be provided (not including time for service) no less than five (5) business days for hearings. FL ST 20 J CIR 2.20(IV)(B)(1).
3. *Notice and request to participate in telephonic motion hearing.* Notice by the requesting party must be provided by mailing a copy of the written request at least five (5) days prior to the day of the hearing, or by delivering a copy of the written request to the other parties or, if represented by counsel, to the other parties' attorney(s) no later than 5:00 p.m. two (2) business days prior to the day of the hearing. FL ST 20 J CIR 1.10. Refer to the Hearings section of this document for more information.
4. *Computation of time*
   a. *Generally.* Computation of time shall be governed by FL ST J ADMIN Rule 2.514. FL ST RCP Rule 1.090(a). The following rules apply in computing time periods specified in any rule of procedure, local rule, court order, or statute that does not specify a method of computing time. FL ST J ADMIN Rule 2.514(a).
      i. *Period stated in days or a longer unit.* When the period is stated in days or a longer unit of time (A) exclude the day of the event that triggers the period; (B) count every day, including intermediate Saturdays, Sundays, and legal holidays; and (C) include the last day of the period, but if the last day is a Saturday, Sunday, or legal holiday, or falls within any period of time extended through an order of the chief justice under FL ST J ADMIN Rule 2.205(a)(2)(B)(iv), the period continues to run until the end of the next day that is not a Saturday, Sunday, or legal holiday and does not fall within any period of time extended through an order of the chief justice. FL ST J ADMIN Rule 2.514(a)(1).
      ii. *Period stated in hours.* When the period is stated in hours (A) begin counting immediately on the occurrence of the event that triggers the period; (B) count every hour, including hours during intermediate Saturdays, Sundays, and legal holidays; and (C) if the period would end on a Saturday, Sunday, or legal holiday, or during any period of time extended through an order of the chief justice under FL ST J ADMIN Rule 2.205(a)(2)(B)(iv), the period continues to run until the same time on the next day that is not a Saturday, Sunday, or legal holiday and does not fall within any period of time extended through an order of the chief justice. FL ST J ADMIN Rule 2.514(a)(2).
      iii. *Period stated in days less than seven (7) days.* When the period stated in days is less than seven (7) days, intermediate Saturdays, Sundays, and legal holidays shall be excluded in the computation. FL ST J ADMIN Rule 2.514(a)(3).
      iv. *"Last day" defined.* Unless a different time is set by a statute, local rule, or court order, the last day ends (A) for electronic filing or for service by any means, at midnight; and (B) for filing by other means, when the clerk's office is scheduled to close. FL ST J ADMIN Rule 2.514(a)(4).
      v. *"Next day" defined.* The "next day" is determined by continuing to count forward when the period is measured after an event and backward when measured before an event. FL ST J ADMIN Rule 2.514(a)(5).

vi. *"Legal holiday" defined.* "Legal holiday" means (A) the day set aside by FL ST § 110.117, for observing New Year's Day, Martin Luther King, Jr.'s Birthday, Memorial Day, Independence Day, Labor Day, Veterans' Day, Thanksgiving Day, the Friday after Thanksgiving Day, or Christmas Day, and (B) any day observed as a holiday by the clerk's office or as designated by the chief judge. FL ST J ADMIN Rule 2.514(a)(6).

b. *Additional time after service by mail or e-mail.* When a party may or must act within a specified time after service and service is made by mail or e-mail, five (5) days are added after the period that would otherwise expire under FL ST J ADMIN Rule 2.514(a). FL ST J ADMIN Rule 2.514(b).

c. *Enlargement.* When an act is required or allowed to be done at or within a specified time by order of court, by the Florida Rules of Civil Procedure, or by notice given thereunder, for cause shown the court at any time in its discretion (1) with or without notice, may order the period enlarged if request therefor is made before the expiration of the period originally prescribed or as extended by a previous order, or (2) upon motion made and notice after the expiration of the specified period, may permit the act to be done when failure to act was the result of excusable neglect, but it may not extend the time for making a motion for new trial, for rehearing, or to alter or amend a judgment; making a motion for relief from a judgment under FL ST RCP Rule 1.540(b); taking an appeal or filing a petition for certiorari; or making a motion for a directed verdict. FL ST RCP Rule 1.090(b).

d. *Unaffected by expiration of term.* The period of time provided for the doing of any act or the taking of any proceeding shall not be affected or limited by the continued existence or expiration of a term of court. The continued existence or expiration of a term of court in no way affects the power of a court to do any act or take any proceeding in any action which is or has been pending before it. FL ST RCP Rule 1.090(c).

C. General Requirements

1. *Motions generally*

a. *Contents.* An application to the court for an order shall be by motion which shall be made in writing unless made during a hearing or trial, shall state with particularity the grounds therefor, and shall set forth the relief or order sought. The requirement of writing is fulfilled if the motion is stated in a written notice of the hearing of the motion. All notices of hearing shall specify each motion or other matter to be heard. FL ST RCP Rule 1.100(b).

i. *Notice of hearing.* The notice of hearing should indicate on its face whether the date and time have been coordinated with opposing counsel. If the attorney has been unable to coordinate the hearing with opposing counsel, the notice should state the specific good faith efforts the attorney undertook to coordinate or why coordination was not obtained. FL ST 20 J CIR 2.20(IV)(B)(5).

b. *Particularity requirement.* The court considers a motion in the light of the substantive law, rule or statute to make its determination. Some rules require a statement of the grounds for a motion under the rule. Failure to give the grounds will result in denial of the motion. This should be the result in all situations when the ground for the motion is not inherent in the rule. FL-PRACPROC § 9:3. The requirement is nevertheless an important one, first because of the due process notice rights of the respondent, as well as for the assistance it provides to the court in its preparation for the hearing or, absent a hearing, for disposition. 4 FLPRAC R 1.100.

2. *Conference with opposing counsel.* Attorneys should, whenever possible, prior to filing or upon receiving a motion, contact opposing counsel to determine if the matter can be resolved in whole or in part. This may alleviate the need for a hearing on the motion or allow submission of an agreed order in lieu of a hearing. FL ST 20 J CIR 2.20(IV)(L)(2).

a. *Conference required.* Except in emergency situations, before filing any motion in a civil case, except a motion for injunctive relief, for judgment on the pleadings, for summary judgment, to dismiss or to permit maintenance of a class action, to dismiss for failure to state a cause of action, to dismiss for lack of prosecution, or to otherwise involuntarily dismiss an action, the moving party shall confer with counsel for the opposing party in a good faith effort to resolve the issues raised by the motion, and shall file with the motion a statement certifying that the moving counsel has conferred with opposing counsel and that counsel have been unable to agree on the resolution of the motion. FL ST 20 J CIR 2.20(IV)(I)(2).

3. *Failure to make discovery; Types of available relief.* Three (3) categories of relief are available for failure to make discovery. FL-PRACPROC § 16:14.
   a. The first category is an order compelling discovery. This is obtained by a motion to compel discovery. The motion is made in the court in which the action is pending, except when a deposition is being taken out of the territorial jurisdiction of the court and protective relief is sought in accordance with FL ST RCP Rule 1.310(d) or when a deponent is not a party. When one of the exceptions occurs, the motion is made in the circuit court of the county where the deposition is being taken. FL-PRACPROC § 16:14.
   b. The second category results from a failure to comply with an order to make discovery. The sanctions should not be applied until a hearing on the merits of the failure is held, including an opportunity to present evidence of explanation or mitigation. FL-PRACPROC § 16:14.
   c. The third category is available: (1) if a party or a person designated by an organization to answer questions at a deposition fails to appear before the officer who is to take the deposition after being served with a proper notice; (2) fails to serve answers or objections to interrogatories after proper service of the interrogatories; or (3) a party fails to serve a response to a request for production, inspection and entry after proper service of the request. FL-PRACPROC § 16:14. For further information regarding discovery sanctions please see the KeyRules Motion for Discovery Sanctions documents.
4. *Motion for order compelling discovery*
   a. *Reasonable notice.* Upon reasonable notice to other parties and all persons affected, a party may apply for an order compelling discovery. FL ST RCP Rule 1.380(a).
   b. *Appropriate court.* An application for an order to a party may be made to the court in which the action is pending or in accordance with FL ST RCP Rule 1.310(d). An application for an order to a deponent who is not a party shall be made to the circuit court where the deposition is being taken. FL ST RCP Rule 1.380(a)(1).
   c. *Motion*
      i. *Grounds.* The discovering party may move for an order compelling an answer, or a designation or an order compelling inspection, or an order compelling an examination in accordance with the request:
         - If a deponent fails to answer a question propounded or submitted under FL ST RCP Rule 1.310 or FL ST RCP Rule 1.320;
         - Or a corporation or other entity fails to make a designation under FL ST RCP Rule 1.310(b)(6) or FL ST RCP Rule 1.320(a);
         - Or a party fails to answer an interrogatory submitted under FL ST RCP Rule 1.340;
         - Or if a party in response to a request for inspection submitted under FL ST RCP Rule 1.350 fails to respond that inspection will be permitted as requested or fails to permit inspection as requested;
         - Or if a party in response to a request for examination of a person submitted under FL ST RCP Rule 1.360(a) objects to the examination, fails to respond that the examination will be permitted as requested, or fails to submit to or to produce a person in that party's custody or legal control for examination. FL ST RCP Rule 1.380(a)(2).
      ii. *Certification.* Prior to filing a motion to compel or for protective order, attorneys should confer with opposing counsel in a good faith effort to resolve the issues raised. FL ST 20 J CIR 2.20(IV)(E)(5). The motion must include a certification that the movant, in good faith, has conferred or attempted to confer with the person or party failing to make the discovery in an effort to secure the information or material without court action. FL ST RCP Rule 1.380(a)(2); FL ST 20 J CIR 2.20(IV)(E)(5).
      iii. *During deposition.* When taking a deposition on oral examination, the proponent of the question may complete or adjourn the examination before applying for an order. FL ST RCP Rule 1.380(a)(2).

iv. *Protective order.* If the court denies the motion in whole or in part, it may make such protective order as it would have been empowered to make on a motion made pursuant to FL ST RCP Rule 1.280(c). FL ST RCP Rule 1.380(a)(2).

d. *Evasive or incomplete answer.* For purposes of FL ST RCP Rule 1.380(a) an evasive or incomplete answer shall be treated as a failure to answer. FL ST RCP Rule 1.380(a)(3).

e. *Award of expenses of motion*

i. *Motion granted.* If the motion is granted and after opportunity for hearing, the court shall require the party or deponent whose conduct necessitated the motion or the party or counsel advising the conduct to pay to the moving party the reasonable expenses incurred in obtaining the order that may include attorneys' fees, unless the court finds that the movant failed to certify in the motion that a good faith effort was made to obtain the discovery without court action, that the opposition to the motion was justified, or that other circumstances make an award of expenses unjust. FL ST RCP Rule 1.380(a)(4).

ii. *Motion denied.* If the motion is denied and after opportunity for hearing, the court shall require the moving party to pay to the party or deponent who opposed the motion the reasonable expenses incurred in opposing the motion that may include attorneys' fees, unless the court finds that the making of the motion was substantially justified or that other circumstances make an award of expenses unjust. FL ST RCP Rule 1.380(a)(4).

iii. *Motion granted in part and denied in part.* If the motion is granted in part and denied in part, the court may apportion the reasonable expenses incurred as a result of making the motion among the parties and persons. FL ST RCP Rule 1.380(a)(4).

iv. *Electronically stored information; Sanctions for failure to preserve.* Absent exceptional circumstances, a court may not impose sanctions under these rules on a party for failing to provide electronically stored information lost as a result of the routine, good faith operation of an electronic information system. FL ST RCP Rule 1.380(e).

5. *Limitations on discovery of electronically stored information*

a. A person may object to discovery of electronically stored information from sources that the person identifies as not reasonably accessible because of burden or cost. On motion to compel discovery or for a protective order, the person from whom discovery is sought must show that the information sought or the format requested is not reasonably accessible because of undue burden or cost. If that showing is made, the court may nonetheless order the discovery from such sources or in such formats if the requesting party shows good cause. The court may specify conditions of the discovery, including ordering that some or all of the expenses incurred by the person from whom discovery is sought be paid by the party seeking the discovery. FL ST RCP Rule 1.280(d)(1).

b. In determining any motion involving discovery of electronically stored information, the court must limit the frequency or extent of discovery otherwise allowed by the Florida Rules of Civil Procedure if it determines that (i) the discovery sought is unreasonably cumulative or duplicative, or can be obtained from another source or in another manner that is more convenient, less burdensome, or less expensive; or (ii) the burden or expense of the discovery outweighs its likely benefit, considering the needs of the case, the amount in controversy, the parties' resources, the importance of the issues at stake in the action, and the importance of the discovery in resolving the issues. FL ST RCP Rule 1.280(d)(2).

6. *Arbitration and mediation.* Attorneys are encouraged to utilize arbitration, mediation or other forms of alternative dispute resolution if economically feasible. FL ST 20 J CIR 2.20(IV)(N)(3).

a. *Referral to arbitration and mediation.* Except as hereinafter provided or as otherwise prohibited by law, the presiding judge may enter an order referring all or any part of a contested civil matter to mediation or arbitration. The parties to any contested civil matter may file a written stipulation to mediate or arbitrate any issue between them at any time. Such stipulation shall be incorporated into the order of referral. FL ST RCP Rule 1.700(a).

b. *Arbitration*

i. *Exclusions.* A civil action shall be ordered to arbitration or arbitration in conjunction with

mediation upon stipulation of the parties. A civil action may be ordered to arbitration or arbitration in conjunction with mediation upon motion of any party or by the court, if the judge determines the action to be of such a nature that arbitration could be of benefit to the litigants or the court. FL ST RCP Rule 1.800.

- Under no circumstances may the following categories of actions be referred to arbitration: (1) bond estreatures; (2) habeas corpus or other extraordinary writs; (3) bond validations; (4) civil or criminal contempt; (5) such other matters as may be specified by order of the chief judge in the circuit. FL ST RCP Rule 1.800.

ii. For more information regarding arbitration, please see FL ST RCP Rule 1.810; FL ST RCP Rule 1.820; FL ST RCP Rule 1.830.

c. *Mediation.* For more information regarding mediation, please see FL ST RCP Rule 1.710; FL ST RCP Rule 1.720; FL ST RCP Rule 1.730; FL ST RCP Rule 1.750; and FL ST 20 J CIR 1.9.

7. *Rules of court*

a. *Rules of civil procedure.* The Florida Rules of Civil Procedure apply to all actions of a civil nature and all special statutory proceedings in the circuit courts and county courts except those to which the Florida Probate Rules, the Florida Family Law Rules of Procedure, or the Small Claims Rules apply. FL ST RCP Rule 1.010.

i. The form, content, procedure, and time for pleading in all special statutory proceedings shall be as prescribed by the statutes governing the proceeding unless the Florida Rules of Civil Procedure specifically provide to the contrary. FL ST RCP Rule 1.010.

ii. The Florida Rules of Civil Procedure shall be construed to secure the just, speedy, and inexpensive determination of every action. FL ST RCP Rule 1.010.

b. *Rules of judicial administration.* The Florida Rules of Judicial Administration shall apply to administrative matters in all courts to which the Florida Rules of Judicial Administration are applicable by their terms. The Florida Rules of Judicial Administration shall be construed to secure the speedy and inexpensive determination of every proceeding to which they are applicable. The Florida Rules of Judicial Administration shall supersede all conflicting rules and statutes. FL ST J ADMIN Rule 2.110.

8. *Civil case management plan.* There is established within the Twentieth Judicial Circuit a Civil Case Management Plan applicable to circuit civil cases, which will be administered by the Administrative Office of the Courts through direction of the Circuit Administrative Judges in each county for the implementation of enhanced case management procedures and guidelines for the timely and efficient processing of circuit civil cases and reduction in the pending backlog of civil cases. FL ST 20 J CIR 1.13.

a. The basis for the Civil Case Management Plan is included in FL ST 20 J CIR 1.13, identified in Attachment A as the "Civil Differentiated Case Management (DCM) Procedures and Backlog Reduction Plan," and is incorporated as if fully set forth in FL ST 20 J CIR 1.13. The Civil Case Management Plan is to be used as a model for the purpose of establishing time standards, improving the courts ability to provide early and continuous management of civil cases as required by FL ST J ADMIN Rule 2.545, and to promote uniformity of practice throughout the Twentieth Judicial Circuit. FL ST 20 J CIR 1.13.

b. Full implementation of the Civil DCM Case Management Procedures (Attachment A), including all uniform circuitwide procedures and forms, shall apply to all civil cases filed in Lee and Collier counties, effective January 1, 2011. Even though full implementation may be delayed in Charlotte, Hendry, and Glades counties, all civil time standards and goals, and the use of civil Case Managers and Magistrates to assist trial judges in the process of civil case management and backlog reduction programs, shall be effective circuitwide immediately. FL ST 20 J CIR 1.13.

c. For more information on the civil case management plan, refer to the specific county website and/or see FL ST 20 J CIR 1.13.

D. Documents

1. *Required documents*

a. *Notice of hearing/Motion.* An application to the court for an order shall be by motion which shall be

made in writing unless made during a hearing or trial, shall state with particularity the grounds therefor, and shall set forth the relief or order sought. The requirement of writing is fulfilled if the motion is stated in a written notice of the hearing of the motion. All notices of hearing shall specify each motion or other matter to be heard. FL ST RCP Rule 1.100(b). Refer to the General Requirements section of this document for more information on the notice of hearing.

i. *Certification.* The motion must include a certification that the movant, in good faith, has conferred or attempted to confer with the person or party failing to make the discovery in an effort to secure the information or material without court action. FL ST RCP Rule 1.380(a)(2); FL ST 20 J CIR 2.20(IV)(E)(5).

ii. *Notices to persons with disabilities.* See the Format section of this KeyRules document for further information.

b. *Certification.* Except in emergency situations, before filing any motion in a civil case, except a motion for injunctive relief, for judgment on the pleadings, for summary judgment, to dismiss or to permit maintenance of a class action, to dismiss for failure to state a cause of action, to dismiss for lack of prosecution, or to otherwise involuntarily dismiss an action, the moving party shall confer with counsel for the opposing party in a good faith effort to resolve the issues raised by the motion, and shall file with the motion a statement certifying that the moving counsel has conferred with opposing counsel and that counsel have been unable to agree on the resolution of the motion. FL ST 20 J CIR 2.20(IV)(I)(2).

c. *Certificate of service.* When any attorney certifies in substance: "I certify that a copy hereof has been furnished to (here insert name or names and addresses used for service) by (e-mail) (delivery) (mail) (fax) on .... (date) ....________________ Attorney" the certificate is taken as prima facie proof of such service in compliance with FL ST J ADMIN Rule 2.516. FL ST J ADMIN Rule 2.516(f).

2. *Supplemental documents*

a. *Proposed order.* The court may require that orders or judgments be prepared by a party, may require the party to furnish the court with stamped, addressed envelopes for service of the order or judgment, and may require that proposed orders and judgments be furnished to all parties before entry by the court of the order or judgment. FL ST J ADMIN Rule 2.516(h)(1).

i. Unless otherwise instructed by the court, or agreed to by counsel, all proposed orders shall be provided to other counsel with a reasonable time for approval or comment prior to submission to the court. Opposing counsel should promptly communicate any objections thereto. Thereafter, the drafting attorney should promptly submit a copy of the proposed order to the court and advise the court as to whether or not it has been approved by opposing counsel. FL ST 20 J CIR 2.20(IV)(I)(4).

ii. Orders prepared by counsel must fairly and adequately represent the ruling of the court, and counsel shall make a good faith effort to agree upon the form of the order prior to submitting it to the court. Attorneys should not submit controverted orders to the court with a copy to opposing counsel for "objections within ______ days". Courts prefer to know that the order is either agreed upon or opposed. FL ST 20 J CIR 2.20(IV)(I)(5).

iii. Attorneys should not use post-hearing submissions of proposed orders as a guise to reargue the merits of the matter. FL ST 20 J CIR 2.20(IV)(I)(6).

iv. If asked by the court to prepare an order, counsel should furnish a copy of the order, and any transmitted letter, to opposing counsel at the time the material is submitted to the court. FL ST 20 J CIR 2.20(IV)(J)(4).

b. *Notice of constitutional question.* A party that files a pleading, written motion, or other paper drawing into question the constitutionality of a state statute or a county or municipal charter, ordinance, or franchise must promptly (1) file a notice of constitutional question stating the question and identifying the paper that raises it; and (2) serve the notice and the pleading, written motion, or other paper drawing into question the constitutionality of a state statute or a county or municipal charter, ordinance, or franchise on the Attorney General or the state attorney of the judicial circuit in which the action is pending, by either certified or registered mail. Service of the notice and pleading,

written motion, or other paper does not require joinder of the Attorney General or the state attorney as a party to the action. FL ST RCP Rule 1.071.

c. *Notice and request to participate in telephonic motion hearing.* In instances where a civil motion hearing is scheduled for not longer than fifteen (15) minutes, a party may file a written request to participate via conference or speaker telephone, or other applicable communication equipment, and shall provide notice to the Court and the parties to the motion. FL ST 20 J CIR 1.10. Refer to the Timing and Hearings sections of this document for more information.

E. Format

1. *Documents; Type and size.* Documents subject to the exceptions set forth in FL ST J ADMIN Rule 2.525(d) shall be filed on recycled paper measuring eight and one half by eleven (8 1/2 by 11) inches. For purposes of FL ST J ADMIN Rule 2.520, paper is recycled if it contains a minimum content of fifty (50) percent waste paper. Xerographic reduction of legal-size (eight and one half by fourteen (8 1/2 by 14) inches) documents to letter size (eight and one half by eleven (8 1/2 by 11) inches) is prohibited. All other documents filed by electronic transmission shall be filed in a format capable of being printed in a format consistent with the provisions of FL ST J ADMIN Rule 2.250. FL ST J ADMIN Rule 2.520(b); FL ST 20 J CIR 2.9.

   a. *Exhibits.* Any exhibit or attachment filed with pleadings or papers may be filed in its original size. FL ST J ADMIN Rule 2.520(c); FL ST 20 J CIR 2.9.

   b. *Recording space.* On all papers and documents prepared and filed by the court or by any party to a proceeding which are to be recorded in the public records of any county, including but not limited to final money judgments and notices of lis pendens, a three (3) inch by three (3) inch space at the top right-hand corner on the first page and a one (1) inch by three (3) inch space at the top right-hand corner on each subsequent page shall be left blank and reserved for use by the clerk of court. FL ST J ADMIN Rule 2.520(d).

      i. *Exceptions to recording space.* Any papers or documents created by persons or entities over which the filing party has no control, including but not limited to wills, codicils, trusts, or other testamentary documents; documents prepared or executed by any public officer; documents prepared, executed, acknowledged, or proved outside of the State of Florida; or documents created by State or Federal government agencies, may be filed without the space required by FL ST J ADMIN Rule 2.520. FL ST J ADMIN Rule 2.520(e).

   c. *Noncompliance.* No clerk of court is permitted to refuse to file any document or paper because of noncompliance with the Florida Rules of Judicial Administration. However, upon request of the clerk of court, noncomplying documents must be resubmitted in accordance with the formatting rules. FL ST J ADMIN Rule 2.520(f).

      i. When time of filing is critical, the Clerk shall accept pleadings, motions, petitions, briefs, notices, orders, judgments, decrees, opinions, or other papers or official documents on other than eight and one half by eleven (8 1/2 by 11) inch paper but shall then require that the document be resubmitted to comply with FL ST J ADMIN Rule 2.520. FL ST 20 J CIR 2.9.

2. *Caption.* Every pleading, motion, order, judgment, or other paper shall have a caption containing the name of the court, the file number, and except for in rem proceedings, including forfeiture proceedings, the name of the first party on each side with an appropriate indication of other parties, and a designation identifying the party filing it and its nature or the nature of the order, as the case may be. In any in rem proceeding, every pleading, motion, order, judgment, or other paper shall have a caption containing the name of the court, the file number, the style "In re" (followed by the name or general description of the property), and a designation of the person or entity filing it and its nature or the nature of the order, as the case may be. In an in rem forfeiture proceeding, the style shall be "In re forfeiture of" (followed by the name of the general description of the property). All papers filed in the action shall be styled in such a manner as to indicate clearly the subject matter of the paper and the party requesting or obtaining relief. FL ST RCP Rule 1.100(c)(1).

3. *Writing and written defined.* Writing or written means a document containing information, an application, or a stipulation. FL ST RCP Rule 1.080(c).

4. *Rule abbreviations*
   a. The Florida Rules of Civil Procedure and shall be abbreviated as Fla.R.Civ.P. FL ST RCP Rule 1.010.
   b. The Florida Rules of Judicial Administration shall be abbreviated as Fla. R. Jud. Admin. FL ST J ADMIN Rule 2.110.
5. *Nonverification.* Except when otherwise specifically provided by the Florida Rules of Civil Procedure or an applicable statute, every pleading or other document of a party represented by an attorney need not be verified or accompanied by an affidavit. FL ST RCP Rule 1.030; FL ST J ADMIN Rule 2.515(a).
6. *Attorney signature*
   a. *Attorney signature.* Every pleading and other document of a party represented by an attorney shall be signed by at least one (1) attorney of record in that attorney's individual name whose current record Florida Bar address, telephone number, including area code, primary e-mail address and secondary e-mail addresses, if any, and Florida Bar number shall be stated, and who shall be duly licensed to practice law in Florida or who shall have received permission to appear in the particular case as provided in FL ST J ADMIN Rule 2.510. FL ST J ADMIN Rule 2.515(a).
      i. The attorney may be required by the court to give the address of, and to vouch for the attorney's authority to represent, the party. FL ST J ADMIN Rule 2.515(a).
      ii. The signature of an attorney shall constitute a certificate by the attorney that the attorney has read the pleading or other document; that to the best of the attorney's knowledge, information, and belief there is good ground to support it; and that it is not interposed for delay. FL ST J ADMIN Rule 2.515(a).
      iii. If a pleading is not signed or is signed with intent to defeat the purpose of FL ST J ADMIN Rule 2.515, it may be stricken and the action may proceed as though the pleading or other document had not been served. FL ST J ADMIN Rule 2.515(a).
   b. *Pro se litigant signature.* A party who is not represented by an attorney shall sign any pleading or other paper and state the party's address and telephone number, including area code. FL ST J ADMIN Rule 2.515(b).
   c. *Form of signature*
      i. The signatures required on pleadings and documents by FL ST J ADMIN Rule 2.515(a) and FL ST J ADMIN Rule 2.515(b) may be:
         - Original signatures;
         - Original signatures that have been reproduced by electronic means, such as on electronically transmitted documents or photocopied documents;
         - Electronic signatures using the "/s/," "s/," or "/s" formats by or at the direction of the person signing; or
         - Any other signature format authorized by general law, so long as the clerk where the proceeding is pending has the capability of receiving and has obtained approval from the Supreme Court of Florida to accept pleadings and documents with that signature format. FL ST J ADMIN Rule 2.515(c)(1).
      ii. An attorney, party, or other person who files a pleading or paper by electronic transmission that does not contain the original signature of that attorney, party, or other person shall file that identical pleading or paper in paper form containing an original signature of that attorney, party, or other person (hereinafter called the follow-up filing) immediately thereafter. The follow-up filing is not required if the Supreme Court of Florida has entered an order directing the clerk of court to discontinue accepting the follow-up filing. FL ST J ADMIN Rule 2.515(c)(2).
7. *Forms*
   a. *Process.* The forms of process, notice of lis pendens, and notice of action provided in the Florida Rules of Civil Procedure are sufficient. Variations from the forms do not void process or notices that are otherwise sufficient. FL ST RCP Rule 1.900(a).

b. *Other forms.* The other forms provided in the Florida Rules of Civil Procedure are sufficient for the matters that are covered by them. So long as the substance is expressed without prolixity, the forms may be varied to meet the facts of a particular case. FL ST RCP Rule 1.900(b).

c. *Formal matters.* Captions, except for the designation of the paper, are omitted from the forms provided in the Florida Rules of Civil Procedure. A general form of caption is the first form provided. Signatures are omitted from pleadings and motions. FL ST RCP Rule 1.900(c).

8. *Notices to persons with disabilities.* All notices of court proceedings to be held in a public facility, and all process compelling appearance at such proceedings, shall include the following statement in bold face, fourteen (14) point Times New Roman or Courier font: "If you are a person with a disability who needs any accommodation in order to participate in this proceeding, you are entitled, at no cost to you, to the provision of certain assistance. Please contact [identify applicable court personnel by name, address, and telephone number] at least seven (7) days before your scheduled court appearance, or immediately upon receiving this notification if the time before the scheduled appearance is less than seven (7) days; if you are hearing or voice impaired, call 711." FL ST J ADMIN Rule 2.540(c)(1). For more information, see FL ST 20 J CIR 2.15.

9. *Minimization of the filing of sensitive information*

a. *Limitations for court filings.* Unless authorized by FL ST J ADMIN Rule 2.425(b), statute, another rule of court, or the court orders otherwise, designated sensitive information filed with the court must be limited to the following format:

i. The initials of a person known to be a minor;

ii. The year of birth of a person's birth date;

iii. No portion of any: Social security number, Bank account number, Credit card account number, Charge account number, or Debit account number;

iv. The last four digits of any: Taxpayer identification number (TIN), Employee identification number, Driver's license number, Passport number, Telephone number, Financial account number, except as set forth in FL ST J ADMIN Rule 2.425(a)(3), Brokerage account number, Insurance policy account number, Loan account number, Customer account number, or Patient or health care number;

v. A truncated version of any: Email address, Computer user name, Password, or Personal identification number (PIN); and

vi. A truncated version of any other sensitive information as provided by court order. FL ST J ADMIN Rule 2.425(a).

b. *Exceptions.* FL ST J ADMIN Rule 2.425(a) does not apply to the following:

i. An account number which identifies the property alleged to be the subject of a proceeding;

ii. The record of an administrative or agency proceeding;

iii. The record in appellate or review proceedings;

iv. The birth date of a minor whenever the birth date is necessary for the court to establish or maintain subject matter jurisdiction;

v. The name of a minor in any order relating to parental responsibility, time-sharing, or child support;

vi. The name of a minor in any document or order affecting the minor's ownership of real property;

vii. The birth date of a party in a writ of attachment or notice to payor;

viii. In traffic and criminal proceedings: a pro se filing; a court filing that is related to a criminal matter or investigation and that is prepared before the filing of a criminal charge or is not filed as part of any docketed criminal case; an arrest or search warrant or any information in support thereof; a charging document and an affidavit or other documents filed in support of any charging document, including any driving records; a statement of particulars; discovery material introduced into evidence or otherwise filed with the court; and all information necessary for the proper issuance and execution of a subpoena duces tecum;

ix. Information used by the clerk for case maintenance purposes or the courts for case management purposes; and

x. Information which is relevant and material to an issue before the court. FL ST J ADMIN Rule 2.425(b).

c. *Remedies.* Upon motion by a party or interested person or sua sponte by the court, the court may order remedies, sanctions or both for a violation of FL ST J ADMIN Rule 2.425(a). Following notice and an opportunity to respond, the court may impose sanctions if such filing was not made in good faith. FL ST J ADMIN Rule 2.425(c).

d. *Motions not restricted.* FL ST J ADMIN Rule 2.425 does not restrict a party's right to move for protective order, to move to file documents under seal, or to request a determination of the confidentiality of records. FL ST J ADMIN Rule 2.425(d).

e. *Application.* FL ST J ADMIN Rule 2.425 does not affect the application of constitutional provisions, statutes, or rules of court regarding confidential information or access to public information. FL ST J ADMIN Rule 2.425(e).

F. Filing and Service Requirements

1. *Filing requirements.* All original documents must be filed with the court either before service or immediately thereafter, unless otherwise provided for by general law or other rules. If the original of any bond or other document is not placed in the court file, a certified copy must be so placed by the clerk. FL ST J ADMIN Rule 2.516(d). All documents shall be filed in conformity with the requirements of FL ST J ADMIN Rule 2.525. FL ST RCP Rule 1.080(b). All documents filed in any court shall be filed by electronic transmission in accordance with FL ST J ADMIN Rule 2.525. "Documents" means pleadings, motions, petitions, memoranda, briefs, notices, exhibits, declarations, affidavits, orders, judgments, decrees, writs, opinions, and any other paper or writing submitted to a court. FL ST J ADMIN Rule 2.520(a). All documents that are court records, as defined in FL ST J ADMIN Rule 2.430(a)(1), must be filed by electronic transmission, provided that: (1) the clerk has the ability to accept and retain such documents; (2) the clerk or the chief judge of the circuit has requested permission to accept documents filed by electronic transmission; and (3) the supreme court has entered an order granting permission to the clerk to accept documents filed by electronic transmission. FL ST J ADMIN Rule 2.525(c)(1).

a. *Definition.* "Electronic transmission of documents" means the sending of information by electronic signals to, by or from a court or clerk, which when received can be transformed and stored or transmitted on paper, microfilm, magnetic storage device, optical imaging system, CD-ROM, flash drive, other electronic data storage system, server, case maintenance system ("CM"), electronic court filing ("ECF") system, statewide or local electronic portal ("e-portal"), or other electronic record keeping system authorized by the supreme court in a format sufficient to communicate the information on the original document in a readable format. Electronic transmission of documents includes electronic mail ("e-mail") and any internet-based transmission procedure, and may include procedures allowing for documents to be signed or verified by electronic means. FL ST J ADMIN Rule 2.525(a).

i. The filing of documents with the court as required by the Florida Rules of Judicial Administration must be made by filing them with the clerk in accordance with FL ST J ADMIN Rule 2.525, except that the judge may permit documents to be filed with the judge, in which event the judge must note the filing date before him or her on the documents and transmit them to the clerk. The date of filing is that shown on the face of the document by the judge's notation or the clerk's time stamp, whichever is earlier. FL ST J ADMIN Rule 2.516(e).

b. *Application.* Any court or clerk of the court may accept the electronic transmission of documents for filing after the clerk, together with input from the chief judge of the circuit, has obtained approval of the procedures and program for doing so from the Supreme Court of Florida. FL ST J ADMIN Rule 2.525(b).

c. *Exceptions*

i. Paper documents and other submissions may be manually submitted to the clerk or court:

- When the clerk does not have the ability to accept and retain documents by electronic filing or has not had ECF Procedures approved by the supreme court;

- For filing by any self-represented party or any self-represented nonparty unless specific ECF Procedures provide a means to file documents electronically. However, any self-represented nonparty that is a governmental or public agency and any other agency, partnership, corporation, or business entity acting on behalf of any governmental or public agency may file documents by electronic transmission if such entity has the capability of filing documents electronically;
- For filing by attorneys excused from e-mail service in accordance with FL ST J ADMIN Rule 2.516(b);
- When submitting evidentiary exhibits or filing non-documentary materials;
- When the filing involves documents in excess of twenty-five (25) megabytes (25MB) in size. For such filings, documents may be transmitted using an electronic storage medium that the clerk has the ability to accept, which may include a CD-ROM, flash drive, or similar storage medium;
- When filed in open court, as permitted by the court;
- When paper filing is permitted by any approved statewide or local ECF procedures; and
- If any court determines that justice so requires. FL ST J ADMIN Rule 2.525(d).

ii. Any document in paper form submitted under FL ST J ADMIN Rule 2.525(d) is filed when it is received by the clerk or court and the clerk shall immediately thereafter convert any filed paper document to an electronic document. "Convert to an electronic document" means optically capturing an image of a paper document and using character recognition software to recover as much of the document's text as practicable and then indexing and storing the document in the official court file. FL ST J ADMIN Rule 2.525(c)(4).

iii. Any storage medium submitted under FL ST J ADMIN Rule 2.525(d)(5) is filed when received by the clerk or court and the clerk shall immediately thereafter transfer the electronic documents from the storage device to the official court file. FL ST J ADMIN Rule 2.525(c)(5).

iv. If the filer of any paper document authorized under FL ST J ADMIN Rule 2.525(d) provides a self-addressed, postage-paid envelope for return of the paper document after it is converted to electronic form by the clerk, the clerk shall place the paper document in the envelope and deposit it in the mail. Except when a paper document is required to be maintained, the clerk may recycle any filed paper document that is not to be returned to the filer. FL ST J ADMIN Rule 2.525(c)(6).

v. The clerk may convert any paper document filed before the effective date of FL ST J ADMIN Rule 2.525 to an electronic document. Unless the clerk is required to maintain the paper document, if the paper document has been converted to an electronic document by the clerk, the paper document is no longer part of the official court file and may be removed and recycled. FL ST J ADMIN Rule 2.525(c)(7).

d. *Official court file.* For information on what constitutes the official court file, please see FL ST J ADMIN Rule 2.525(c)(2), FL ST J ADMIN Rule 2.525(c)(3).

e. *Administration.* All attorneys, parties, or other persons using this rule to file documents are required to make arrangements with the court or clerk for the payment of any charges authorized by general law or the supreme court before filing any document by electronic transmission. FL ST J ADMIN Rule 2.525(f)(2).

f. *Filing date.* The filing date for an electronically transmitted document is the date and time that such filing is acknowledged by an electronic stamp or otherwise, pursuant to any procedure set forth in any ECF Procedures approved by the supreme court, or the date the last page of such filing is received by the court or clerk. FL ST J ADMIN Rule 2.525(f)(3).

g. *Accessibility.* All documents transmitted in any electronic form under FL ST J ADMIN Rule 2.525 must comply with the accessibility requirements of FL ST J ADMIN Rule 2.526. FL ST J ADMIN Rule 2.525(g).

2. *Service requirements.* Every pleading subsequent to the initial pleading, all orders, and every other

document filed in the action must be served in conformity with the requirements of FL ST J ADMIN Rule 2.516. FL ST RCP Rule 1.080(a).

a. *Service; Generally.* The timing and manner of service should not be used to the disadvantage of the party receiving the papers. FL ST 20 J CIR 2.20(IV)(C)(1).
   i. Papers and memoranda of law should not be served at court appearances without advance notice to opposing counsel and should not be served so close to a court appearance so as to inhibit the ability of opposing counsel to prepare for that appearance or to respond to the papers. Should the attorney do so, the court is urged to take appropriate action in response, including continuing the matter to allow opposing counsel to prepare and respond. FL ST 20 J CIR 2.20(IV)(C)(2).
   ii. Papers should not be served in order to take advantage of an opponent's known absence from the office or at a time or in a manner designed to inconvenience an adversary, such as late on Friday afternoon or the day preceding a secular or religious holiday. FL ST 20 J CIR 2.20(IV)(C)(3).
   iii. Service should be made personally or by courtesy copy facsimile transmission when it is likely that service by mail, even when allowed, will prejudice the opposing party or will not provide the opposing party with a reasonable time to respond. FL ST 20 J CIR 2.20(IV)(C)(4).

b. *Service; When required.* Unless the court otherwise orders, or a statute or supreme court administrative order specifies a different means of service, every pleading subsequent to the initial pleading and every other document filed in any court proceeding, except applications for witness subpoenas and documents served by formal notice or required to be served in the manner provided for service of formal notice, must be served in accordance with FL ST J ADMIN Rule 2.516 on each party. No service need be made on parties against whom a default has been entered, except that pleadings asserting new or additional claims against them must be served in the manner provided for service of summons. FL ST J ADMIN Rule 2.516(a).
   i. *Copies of court submissions.* Copies of any submissions to the court (such as correspondence, memoranda of law, motions, case law, etc.) should simultaneously be provided to opposing counsel by substantially the same method of delivery by which they are provided to the court. For example, if a memorandum of law is hand-delivered to the court, at substantially the same time a copy should be hand-delivered or faxed to opposing counsel. FL ST 20 J CIR 2.20(IV)(J)(4).

c. *Service; How made.* When service is required or permitted to be made upon a party represented by an attorney, service must be made upon the attorney unless service upon the party is ordered by the court. FL ST J ADMIN Rule 2.516(b).
   i. *Service by electronic mail ("e-mail").* All documents required or permitted to be served on another party must be served by e-mail, unless FL ST J ADMIN Rule 2.516 otherwise provides. When, in addition to service by e-mail, the sender also utilizes another means of service provided for in FL ST J ADMIN Rule 2.516(b)(2), any differing time limits and other provisions applicable to that other means of service control. FL ST J ADMIN Rule 2.516(b)(1). Any document electronically transmitted to a court or clerk must also be served on all parties and interested persons in accordance with the applicable rules of court. FL ST J ADMIN Rule 2.525(e)(2).
      - *Service on attorneys.* Upon appearing in a proceeding, an attorney must serve a designation of a primary e-mail address and may designate no more than two (2) secondary e-mail addresses. Thereafter, service must be directed to all designated e-mail addresses in that proceeding. Every document filed by an attorney thereafter must include the primary e-mail address of that attorney and any secondary e-mail addresses. If an attorney does not designate any e-mail address for service, documents may be served on that attorney at the e-mail address on record with The Florida Bar. FL ST J ADMIN Rule 2.516(b)(1)(A).
      - *Exception to e-mail service on attorneys.* Service by an attorney on another attorney must be made by e-mail unless excused by the court. Upon motion by an attorney demonstrating

that the attorney has no e-mail account and lacks access to the Internet at the attorney's office, the court may excuse the attorney from the requirements of e-mail service. Service on and by an attorney excused by the court from e-mail service must be by the means provided in FL ST J ADMIN Rule 2.516(b)(2). FL ST J ADMIN Rule 2.516(b)(1)(B).

- *Service on and by parties not represented by an attorney.* Any party not represented by an attorney may serve a designation of a primary e-mail address and also may designate no more than two (2) secondary e-mail addresses to which service must be directed in that proceeding by the means provided in FL ST J ADMIN Rule 2.516(b)(1). If a party not represented by an attorney does not designate an e-mail address for service in a proceeding, service on and by that party must be by the means provided in FL ST J ADMIN Rule 2.516(b)(2). FL ST J ADMIN Rule 2.516(b)(1)(C).
- *Time of service.* Service by e-mail is complete when it is sent. FL ST J ADMIN Rule 2.516(b)(1)(D). An e-mail is deemed served on the date it is sent. FL ST J ADMIN Rule 2.516(b)(1)(D)(i). If the sender learns that the e-mail did not reach the address of the person to be served, the sender must immediately send another copy by e-mail, or by a means authorized by FL ST J ADMIN Rule 2.516(b)(2). FL ST J ADMIN Rule 2.516(b)(1)(D)(ii). E-mail service is treated as service by mail for the computation of time. FL ST J ADMIN Rule 2.516(b)(1)(D)(iii).

ii. *Format of e-mail for service.* Service of a document by e-mail is made by attaching a copy of the document in PDF format to an e-mail sent to all addresses designated by the attorney or party. FL ST J ADMIN Rule 2.516(b)(1)(E).

- All documents served by e-mail must be attached to an e-mail message containing a subject line beginning with the words "SERVICE OF COURT DOCUMENT" in all capital letters, followed by the case number of the proceeding in which the documents are being served. FL ST J ADMIN Rule 2.516(b)(1)(E)(i).
- The body of the e-mail must identify the court in which the proceeding is pending, the case number, the name of the initial party on each side, the title of each document served with that e-mail, and the sender's name and telephone number. FL ST J ADMIN Rule 2.516(b)(1)(E)(ii).
- Any document served by e-mail may be signed by the "/s/" format, as long as the filed original is signed in accordance with the applicable rule of procedure. FL ST J ADMIN Rule 2.516(b)(1)(E)(iii).
- Any e-mail which, together with its attached documents, exceeds five megabytes (5MB) in size, must be divided and sent as separate e-mails, no one of which may exceed five megabytes (5MB) in size and each of which must be sequentially numbered in the subject line. FL ST J ADMIN Rule 2.516(b)(1)(E)(iv).

iii. *Service by other means.* In addition to, and not in lieu of, service by e-mail, service may also be made upon attorneys by any of the means specified in FL ST J ADMIN Rule 2.516(b)(2). Service on and by all parties who are not represented by an attorney and who do not designate an e-mail address, and on and by all attorneys excused from e-mail service, must be made by delivering a copy of the document or by mailing it to the party or attorney at their last known address or, if no address is known, by leaving it with the clerk of the court. Service by mail is complete upon mailing. Delivery of a copy within FL ST J ADMIN Rule 2.516 is complete upon:

- Handing it to the attorney or to the party,
- Leaving it at the attorney's or party's office with a clerk or other person in charge thereof,
- If there is no one in charge, leaving it in a conspicuous place therein,
- If the office is closed or the person to be served has no office, leaving it at the person's usual place of abode with some person of his or her family above fifteen (15) years of age and informing such person of the contents, or
- Transmitting it by facsimile to the attorney's or party's office with a cover sheet containing

the sender's name, firm, address, telephone number, and facsimile number, and the number of pages transmitted. When service is made by facsimile, a copy must also be served by any other method permitted by FL ST J ADMIN Rule 2.516. Facsimile service occurs when transmission is complete. FL ST J ADMIN Rule 2.516(b)(2)(A) through FL ST J ADMIN Rule 2.516(b)(2)(E).

- Service by delivery after 5:00 p.m. must be deemed to have been made by mailing on the date of delivery. FL ST J ADMIN Rule 2.516(b)(2)(F).

d. *Service; Numerous defendants.* In actions when the parties are unusually numerous, the court may regulate the service contemplated by the Florida Rules of Judicial Administration on motion or on its own initiative in such manner as may be found to be just and reasonable. FL ST J ADMIN Rule 2.516(c).

e. *Service by clerk.* Service of notices and other documents required to be made by the clerk must also be done as provided in FL ST J ADMIN Rule 2.516(b). FL ST J ADMIN Rule 2.516(g).

G. Hearings

1. *Scheduling.* Before setting a motion for hearing, counsel should make a good faith effort to resolve the issue with opposing counsel. FL ST 20 J CIR 2.20(IV)(I)(1). Except in emergency situations, attorneys should make a good faith effort to communicate with opposing counsel prior to scheduling depositions, hearings and other proceedings, so as to schedule them at times that are mutually convenient for all interested persons. Further, a sufficient time should be reserved to permit a complete presentation by counsel for all parties. FL ST 20 J CIR 2.20(IV)(B)(1). Attorneys should not use the hearing time obtained by opposing counsel for other motion practice. FL ST 20 J CIR 2.20(IV)(B)(6).

   a. *Notice.* Counsel should notify opposing counsel of dates and times obtained from the court for future hearings on the same day that the hearing date is obtained from the court, or as soon as practicable thereafter. FL ST 20 J CIR 2.20(IV)(J)(3).

   b. *Scheduling conflict.* Attorneys should notify opposing counsel, the court, and others affected, of scheduling conflicts as soon as they become apparent. Further, attorneys should cooperate with one another regarding all reasonable rescheduling requests that do not prejudice their clients or unduly delay a proceeding. FL ST 20 J CIR 2.20(IV)(B)(7).

      i. Attorneys should call potential scheduling problems to the attention of those affected, including the court, as soon as they become apparent and should avoid last minute cancellations. FL ST 20 J CIR 2.20(IV)(B)(12).

   c. *Notice to court when appearance is unnecessary.* Attorneys should promptly notify the court or other tribunal of any resolution between the parties that renders a scheduled court appearance unnecessary. FL ST 20 J CIR 2.20(IV)(B)(8).

2. *Communication equipment*

   a. *Definition.* Communication equipment means a conference telephone or other electronic device that permits all those appearing or participating to hear and speak to each other, provided that all conversation of all parties is audible to all persons present. FL ST J ADMIN Rule 2.530(a).

   b. *Use by all parties.* A county or circuit court judge may, upon the court's own motion or upon the written request of a party, direct that communication equipment be used for a motion hearing, pretrial conference, or a status conference. A judge must give notice to the parties and consider any objections they may have to the use of communication equipment before directing that communication equipment be used. The decision to use communication equipment over the objection of parties will be in the sound discretion of the trial court, except as noted below. FL ST J ADMIN Rule 2.530(b).

   c. *Use only by requesting party.* A county or circuit court judge may, upon the written request of a party upon reasonable notice to all other parties, permit a requesting party to participate through communication equipment in a scheduled motion hearing; however, any such request (except in criminal, juvenile, and appellate proceedings) must be granted, absent a showing of good cause to deny the same, where the hearing is set for not longer than fifteen (15) minutes. FL ST J ADMIN Rule 2.530(c).

d. *Testimony*

i. *Generally.* A county or circuit court judge, general magistrate, special magistrate, or hearing officer may allow testimony to be taken through communication equipment if all parties consent or if permitted by another applicable rule of procedure. FL ST J ADMIN Rule 2.530(d)(1).

ii. *Procedure.* Any party desiring to present testimony through communication equipment shall, prior to the hearing or trial at which the testimony is to be presented, contact all parties to determine whether each party consents to this form of testimony. The party seeking to present the testimony shall move for permission to present testimony through communication equipment, which motion shall set forth good cause as to why the testimony should be allowed in this form. FL ST J ADMIN Rule 2.530(d)(2).

iii. *Oath.* Testimony may be taken through communication equipment only if a notary public or other person authorized to administer oaths in the witness's jurisdiction is present with the witness and administers the oath consistent with the laws of the jurisdiction. FL ST J ADMIN Rule 2.530(d)(3).

iv. *Confrontation rights.* In juvenile and criminal proceedings the defendant must make an informed waiver of any confrontation rights that may be abridged by the use of communication equipment. FL ST J ADMIN Rule 2.530(d)(4).

v. *Video testimony.* If the testimony to be presented utilizes video conferencing or comparable two-way visual capabilities, the court in its discretion may modify the procedures set forth in FL ST J ADMIN Rule 2.530 to accommodate the technology utilized. FL ST J ADMIN Rule 2.530(d)(5).

e. *Burden of expense.* The cost for the use of the communication equipment is the responsibility of the requesting party unless otherwise directed by the court. FL ST J ADMIN Rule 2.530(e).

3. *Telephonic non-evidentiary motion hearings set for not longer than fifteen (15) minutes.* FL ST 20 J CIR 1.10 specifically addresses non-evidentiary civil motion hearings set for not longer than fifteen (15) minutes. It is not intended to limit or address requests for telephonic hearings which are otherwise governed by FL ST J ADMIN Rule 2.071. FL ST 20 J CIR 1.10. [Editor's note: FL ST J ADMIN Rule 2.071 was renumbered as FL ST J ADMIN Rule 2.530]. Evidentiary hearings are exempted from the application of FL ST 20 J CIR 1.10. FL ST 20 J CIR 1.10.

a. In instances where a civil motion hearing is scheduled for not longer than fifteen (15) minutes, a party may file a written request to participate via conference or speaker telephone, or other applicable communication equipment, and shall provide notice to the Court and the parties to the motion. FL ST 20 J CIR 1.10. Refer to the Timing section of this document for information on when the notice must be given and when request must be served.

b. The requesting party shall be responsible for contacting the trial judge's Judicial Assistant and ensuring that appropriate arrangements have been made to permit participation through conference or speaker telephone, or other applicable communication equipment, on the scheduled date and time. It shall be at the discretion of the trial judge as to whether the requesting party shall be responsible for initiating the telephone or communication connection or whether the Court shall be responsible for initiating the telephone or communication connection. FL ST 20 J CIR 1.10(3).

c. Absent a showing of good cause, and in accordance with FL ST J ADMIN Rule 2.071(c), the trial judge shall grant the request and make reasonable accommodations to permit the requesting party's participation through conference or speaker telephone, or other applicable communication equipment. FL ST 20 J CIR 1.10. [Editor's note: FL ST J ADMIN Rule 2.071 was renumbered as FL ST J ADMIN Rule 2.530(c)].

d. To the extent that any provision of FL ST 20 J CIR 1.10 may be construed as being in conflict with any law, statute, or rule, the law, statute, or rule shall prevail. FL ST 20 J CIR 1.10.

H. Forms

1. Official Motion to Compel Discovery Forms for Florida

a. Caption. FL ST RCP Form 1.901.

b. Notice of compliance when constitutional challenge is brought. FL ST RCP Form 1.975.

2. Motion to Compel Discovery Forms for Florida

a. Motion to compel attendance and for sanctions. FL-PP § 3:160.

b. Motion; To compel answer to questions asked on oral examination or written questions. FL-PP § 3:161.

c. Order; Directing deponent to answer questions asked on oral examination; Costs and attorney fees to moving party. FL-PP § 3:162.

d. Order; Compelling answer to written questions. FL-PP § 3:163.

e. Motion; For order finding person in contempt of court; Refusal, after order, to answer question. FL-PP § 3:167.

f. Motion; For order compelling opposing party to pay expenses incurred in proving facts the party refused to admit. FL-PP § 3:168.

g. Motion; Compel discovery, deposition. FL-PRACFORM § 7:37.

h. Motion; Compel discovery, interrogatories. FL-PRACFORM § 7:38.

i. Form for motion to compel answer on deposition. FL-RCPF R 1.380(6).

j. Form for certificate of non-appearance at deposition. FL-RCPF R 1.380(7).

k. Form for notice of motion. FL-RCPF R 1.380(8).

l. Form for order on motion to compel answer. FL-RCPF R 1.380(9).

m. Form for notice and motion to compel. FL-RCPF R 1.380(10).

n. Form for order to compel discovery. FL-RCPF R 1.380(18).

o. Form for order to comply with discovery and answer interrogatories. FL-RCPF R 1.380(19).

I. Checklist

(I) ❑ Matters to be considered by moving party

(a) ❑ Required documents

(1) ❑ Notice of hearing/Motion

(2) ❑ Certification

(3) ❑ Certificate of service

(b) ❑ Supplemental documents

(1) ❑ Proposed order

(2) ❑ Notice of constitutional question

(3) ❑ Notice and request to participate in telephonic motion hearing

(c) ❑ Time for making motion

(1) ❑ Upon reasonable notice to other parties and all persons affected, a party may apply for an order compelling discovery

(2) ❑ A copy of any written motion which may not be heard ex parte and a copy of the notice of the hearing thereof shall be served a reasonable time before the time specified for the hearing; as a general rule, notice should be provided (not including time for service) no less than five (5) business days for hearings

(3) ❑ Notice and request to participate in telephonic motion hearing: Notice by the requesting party must be provided by mailing a copy of the written request at least five (5) days prior to the day of the hearing, or by delivering a copy of the written request to the other parties or, if represented by counsel, to the other parties' attorney(s) no later than 5:00 p.m. two (2) business days prior to the day of the hearing

(II) ❑ Matters to be considered by opposing party

(a) ❑ Required documents

(1) ❑ Response to motion

(2) ❑ Certificate of service

(b) ❑ Supplemental documents

(1) ❑ Proposed order

(2) ❑ Notice of constitutional question

(3) ❑ Notice and request to participate in telephonic motion hearing

(c) ❑ Time for service and filing of opposition

(1) ❑ No time specified for responding to a motion

(2) ❑ Notice and request to participate in telephonic motion hearing: Notice by the requesting party must be provided by mailing a copy of the written request at least five (5) days prior to the day of the hearing, or by delivering a copy of the written request to the other parties or, if represented by counsel, to the other parties' attorney(s) no later than 5:00 p.m. two (2) business days prior to the day of the hearing

Motions, Oppositions and Replies
Motion for Directed Verdict

Document Last Updated January 2013

A. Applicable Rules

1. *State rules*

a. Motion for a directed verdict. FL ST RCP Rule 1.480.

b. Rules of court. FL ST RCP Rule 1.010; FL ST J ADMIN Rule 2.110.

c. Nonverification of pleadings. FL ST RCP Rule 1.030.

d. Service and filing of pleadings, orders, and documents. FL ST RCP Rule 1.080.

e. Time. FL ST RCP Rule 1.090.

f. Pleadings and motions. FL ST RCP Rule 1.100.

g. Motions. FL ST RCP Rule 1.160.

h. Relief from judgment, decrees, or orders. FL ST RCP Rule 1.540.

i. Mediation and arbitration. FL ST RCP Rule 1.700; FL ST RCP Rule 1.710; FL ST RCP Rule 1.720; FL ST RCP Rule 1.730; FL ST RCP Rule 1.750; FL ST RCP Rule 1.800; FL ST RCP Rule 1.810; FL ST RCP Rule 1.820; FL ST RCP Rule 1.830.

j. Forms. FL ST RCP Rule 1.900.

k. Minimization of the filing of sensitive information. FL ST J ADMIN Rule 2.425.

l. Retention of court records. FL ST J ADMIN Rule 2.430.

m. Foreign attorneys. FL ST J ADMIN Rule 2.510.

n. Signature of attorneys and parties. FL ST J ADMIN Rule 2.515.

o. Paper. FL ST J ADMIN Rule 2.520.

p. Electronic filing. FL ST J ADMIN Rule 2.525.

q. Accessibility of information and technology. FL ST J ADMIN Rule 2.526.

r. Communication equipment. FL ST J ADMIN Rule 2.530.

s. Court reporting. FL ST J ADMIN Rule 2.535.

t. Requests for accommodations by persons with disabilities. FL ST J ADMIN Rule 2.540.
u. Case management. FL ST J ADMIN Rule 2.545.

2. *Local rules*
   a. Exclusions from mediation. FL ST 20 J CIR 1.9.
   b. Establishment and implementation of civil case management plan. FL ST 20 J CIR 1.13.
   c. Size of paper. FL ST 20 J CIR 2.9.
   d. Telephonic motion hearings set for not longer than fifteen minutes in circuit and county civil cases. FL ST 20 J CIR 1.10.
   e. Americans with Disabilities Act; Notification of court proceedings. FL ST 20 J CIR 2.15.
   f. Standards of professional courtesy and conduct and establishment of peer review program. FL ST 20 J CIR 2.20.

B. Timing

1. *Before a verdict is returned.* A directed verdict is available to the defendant at the close of the plaintiff's evidence or to either party at the close of all of the evidence. A verdict may be directed either by the court on its own motion or on the motion of counsel. FL ST RCP Rule 1.480(a); FL-PP § 5:83. The movant should be prepared to argue the motion immediately. FL-PRACPROC § 22:14.
2. *After a verdict is returned.* Within ten (10) days after the return of a verdict, a party who has timely moved for a directed verdict may serve a motion to enter judgment in accordance with the motion for a directed verdict. FL ST RCP Rule 1.480(b).
3. *No verdict is returned.* If a verdict was not returned, a party who has timely moved for a directed verdict may serve a motion for judgment in accordance with the motion for a directed verdict within ten (10) days after discharge of the jury. FL ST RCP Rule 1.480(b).
4. *General motion timing.* A copy of any written motion which may not be heard ex parte and a copy of the notice of the hearing thereof shall be served a reasonable time before the time specified for the hearing. FL ST RCP Rule 1.090(d).
   a. *Notice of hearing.* Except in emergency situations, attorneys should provide opposing counsel, parties, witnesses, and other affected persons, sufficient notice of depositions, hearings and other proceedings. FL ST 20 J CIR 2.20(IV)(B)(1). Attorneys should notify opposing counsel of any hearing time reserved as soon as practicable. FL ST 20 J CIR 2.20(IV)(B)(3). When hearing time is obtained, attorneys should promptly prepare and serve all counsel of record with notice of the hearing. Do not delay in providing such notice. FL ST 20 J CIR 2.20(IV)(B)(4).
      i. As a general rule, notice should be provided (not including time for service) no less than five (5) business days for hearings. FL ST 20 J CIR 2.20(IV)(B)(1).
5. *Notice and request to participate in telephonic motion hearing.* Notice by the requesting party must be provided by mailing a copy of the written request at least five (5) days prior to the day of the hearing, or by delivering a copy of the written request to the other parties or, if represented by counsel, to the other parties' attorney(s) no later than 5:00 p.m. two (2) business days prior to the day of the hearing. FL ST 20 J CIR 1.10. Refer to the Hearings section of this document for more information.
6. *Computation of time*
   a. *Generally.* Computation of time shall be governed by FL ST J ADMIN Rule 2.514. FL ST RCP Rule 1.090(a). The following rules apply in computing time periods specified in any rule of procedure, local rule, court order, or statute that does not specify a method of computing time. FL ST J ADMIN Rule 2.514(a).
      i. *Period stated in days or a longer unit.* When the period is stated in days or a longer unit of time (A) exclude the day of the event that triggers the period; (B) count every day, including intermediate Saturdays, Sundays, and legal holidays; and (C) include the last day of the period, but if the last day is a Saturday, Sunday, or legal holiday, or falls within any period of time extended through an order of the chief justice under FL ST J ADMIN Rule 2.205(a)(2)(B)(iv),

the period continues to run until the end of the next day that is not a Saturday, Sunday, or legal holiday and does not fall within any period of time extended through an order of the chief justice. FL ST J ADMIN Rule 2.514(a)(1).

ii. *Period stated in hours.* When the period is stated in hours (A) begin counting immediately on the occurrence of the event that triggers the period; (B) count every hour, including hours during intermediate Saturdays, Sundays, and legal holidays; and (C) if the period would end on a Saturday, Sunday, or legal holiday, or during any period of time extended through an order of the chief justice under FL ST J ADMIN Rule 2.205(a)(2)(B)(iv), the period continues to run until the same time on the next day that is not a Saturday, Sunday, or legal holiday and does not fall within any period of time extended through an order of the chief justice. FL ST J ADMIN Rule 2.514(a)(2).

iii. *Period stated in days less than seven (7) days.* When the period stated in days is less than seven (7) days, intermediate Saturdays, Sundays, and legal holidays shall be excluded in the computation. FL ST J ADMIN Rule 2.514(a)(3).

iv. *"Last day" defined.* Unless a different time is set by a statute, local rule, or court order, the last day ends (A) for electronic filing or for service by any means, at midnight; and (B) for filing by other means, when the clerk's office is scheduled to close. FL ST J ADMIN Rule 2.514(a)(4).

v. *"Next day" defined.* The "next day" is determined by continuing to count forward when the period is measured after an event and backward when measured before an event. FL ST J ADMIN Rule 2.514(a)(5).

vi. *"Legal holiday" defined.* "Legal holiday" means (A) the day set aside by FL ST § 110.117, for observing New Year's Day, Martin Luther King, Jr.'s Birthday, Memorial Day, Independence Day, Labor Day, Veterans' Day, Thanksgiving Day, the Friday after Thanksgiving Day, or Christmas Day, and (B) any day observed as a holiday by the clerk's office or as designated by the chief judge. FL ST J ADMIN Rule 2.514(a)(6).

b. *Additional time after service by mail or e-mail.* When a party may or must act within a specified time after service and service is made by mail or e-mail, five (5) days are added after the period that would otherwise expire under FL ST J ADMIN Rule 2.514(a). FL ST J ADMIN Rule 2.514(b).

c. *Enlargement.* When an act is required or allowed to be done at or within a specified time by order of court, by the Florida Rules of Civil Procedure, or by notice given thereunder, for cause shown the court at any time in its discretion (1) with or without notice, may order the period enlarged if request therefor is made before the expiration of the period originally prescribed or as extended by a previous order, or (2) upon motion made and notice after the expiration of the specified period, may permit the act to be done when failure to act was the result of excusable neglect, but it may not extend the time for making a motion for new trial, for rehearing, or to alter or amend a judgment; making a motion for relief from a judgment under FL ST RCP Rule 1.540(b); taking an appeal or filing a petition for certiorari; or making a motion for a directed verdict. FL ST RCP Rule 1.090(b).

d. *Unaffected by expiration of term.* The period of time provided for the doing of any act or the taking of any proceeding shall not be affected or limited by the continued existence or expiration of a term of court. The continued existence or expiration of a term of court in no way affects the power of a court to do any act or take any proceeding in any action which is or has been pending before it. FL ST RCP Rule 1.090(c).

C. General Requirements

1. *Motions generally*

a. *Contents.* An application to the court for an order shall be by motion which shall be made in writing unless made during a hearing or trial, shall state with particularity the grounds therefor, and shall set forth the relief or order sought. The requirement of writing is fulfilled if the motion is stated in a written notice of the hearing of the motion. All notices of hearing shall specify each motion or other matter to be heard. FL ST RCP Rule 1.100(b).

i. *Notice of hearing.* The notice of hearing should indicate on its face whether the date and time have been coordinated with opposing counsel. If the attorney has been unable to coordinate the hearing with opposing counsel, the notice should state the specific good faith efforts the attorney undertook to coordinate or why coordination was not obtained. FL ST 20 J CIR 2.20(IV)(B)(5).

b. *Particularity requirement.* The court considers a motion in the light of the substantive law, rule or statute to make its determination. Some rules require a statement of the grounds for a motion under the rule. Failure to give the grounds will result in denial of the motion. This should be the result in all situations when the ground for the motion is not inherent in the rule. FL-PRACPROC § 9:3. The requirement is nevertheless an important one, first because of the due process notice rights of the respondent, as well as for the assistance it provides to the court in its preparation for the hearing or, absent a hearing, for disposition. 4 FLPRAC R 1.100.

2. *Conference with opposing counsel.* Attorneys should, whenever possible, prior to filing or upon receiving a motion, contact opposing counsel to determine if the matter can be resolved in whole or in part. This may alleviate the need for a hearing on the motion or allow submission of an agreed order in lieu of a hearing. FL ST 20 J CIR 2.20(IV)(L)(2).

a. *Conference required.* Except in emergency situations, before filing any motion in a civil case, except a motion for injunctive relief, for judgment on the pleadings, for summary judgment, to dismiss or to permit maintenance of a class action, to dismiss for failure to state a cause of action, to dismiss for lack of prosecution, or to otherwise involuntarily dismiss an action, the moving party shall confer with counsel for the opposing party in a good faith effort to resolve the issues raised by the motion, and shall file with the motion a statement certifying that the moving counsel has conferred with opposing counsel and that counsel have been unable to agree on the resolution of the motion. FL ST 20 J CIR 2.20(IV)(I)(2).

3. *Motion for directed verdict*

a. *Effect of a motion for directed verdict.* A party who moves for a directed verdict at the close of the evidence offered by the adverse party may offer evidence in the event the motion is denied without having reserved the right to do so and to the same extent as if the motion had not been made. The denial of a motion for a directed verdict shall not operate to discharge the jury. A motion for a directed verdict shall state the specific grounds therefor. The order directing a verdict is effective without any assent of the jury. FL ST RCP Rule 1.480(a).

b. *Reservation of decision on motion.* When a motion for a directed verdict is denied or for any reason is not granted, the court is deemed to have submitted the action to the jury subject to a later determination of the legal questions raised by the motion. Within ten (10) days after the return of a verdict, a party who has timely moved for a directed verdict may serve a motion to set aside the verdict and any judgment entered thereon and to enter judgment in accordance with the motion for a directed verdict. If a verdict was not returned, a party who has timely moved for a directed verdict may serve a motion for judgment in accordance with the motion for a directed verdict within ten (10) days after discharge of the jury. FL ST RCP Rule 1.480(b).

c. *Joined with motion for new trial.* A motion for a new trial may be joined with a motion for directed verdict or a new trial may be requested in the alternative. If a verdict was returned, the court may allow the judgment to stand or may reopen the judgment and either order a new trial or direct the entry of judgment as if the requested verdict had been directed. If no verdict was returned, the court may direct the entry of judgment as if the requested verdict had been directed or may order a new trial. FL ST RCP Rule 1.480(c).

d. *General procedures on a motion for directed verdict*

i. *Proper method.* The proper method of advocating that a party is entitled to prevail on a claim or defense as a matter of law is to make a motion for a directed verdict at the close of the evidence offered by the opposing party. The trial judge has authority to direct a verdict in favor of one party and against another, without submitting the case to the jury, if there is no other verdict the jury could lawfully return. 5 FLPRAC § 22:5.

ii. *Directed verdict only in a jury trial.* A motion for directed verdict is proper only in a jury trial. The equivalent motion in nonjury trial is called a motion for involuntary dismissal. 5 FLPRAC § 22:5.

iii. *Test for the sufficiency of the evidence.* A motion for directed verdict is used primarily to test the sufficiency of the evidence offered in support of a claim or defense. It may also be used to raise legal issues other than the sufficiency of the evidence, but that is less common because most pure issues of law can be resolved on a motion to dismiss or a motion for summary judgment before the case is set for trial. If there is no evidence to support a claim or defense, the trial judge has a duty to direct a verdict for the opposing party on that claim or defense. 5 FLPRAC § 22:5.

- The trial judge must view all of the facts and factual inferences in a light most favorable to the party opposing the motion. 5 FLPRAC § 22:5.
- The rule has often been stated by the Florida courts in the negative, that is, a motion for directed verdict should not be granted unless the court, after viewing the evidence and testimony in the light most favorable to the nonmoving party, determines that no reasonable jury could render a verdict for the nonmoving party. Under this rule, the trial judge may not direct a verdict against a party if there is any evidence upon which the jury could lawfully make a finding in favor of that party. 5 FLPRAC § 22:5.

4. *Arbitration and mediation.* Attorneys are encouraged to utilize arbitration, mediation or other forms of alternative dispute resolution if economically feasible. FL ST 20 J CIR 2.20(IV)(N)(3).

a. *Referral to arbitration and mediation.* Except as hereinafter provided or as otherwise prohibited by law, the presiding judge may enter an order referring all or any part of a contested civil matter to mediation or arbitration. The parties to any contested civil matter may file a written stipulation to mediate or arbitrate any issue between them at any time. Such stipulation shall be incorporated into the order of referral. FL ST RCP Rule 1.700(a).

b. *Arbitration*

i. *Exclusions.* A civil action shall be ordered to arbitration or arbitration in conjunction with mediation upon stipulation of the parties. A civil action may be ordered to arbitration or arbitration in conjunction with mediation upon motion of any party or by the court, if the judge determines the action to be of such a nature that arbitration could be of benefit to the litigants or the court. FL ST RCP Rule 1.800.

- Under no circumstances may the following categories of actions be referred to arbitration: (1) bond estreatures; (2) habeas corpus or other extraordinary writs; (3) bond validations; (4) civil or criminal contempt; (5) such other matters as may be specified by order of the chief judge in the circuit. FL ST RCP Rule 1.800.

ii. For more information regarding arbitration, please see FL ST RCP Rule 1.810; FL ST RCP Rule 1.820; FL ST RCP Rule 1.830.

c. *Mediation.* For more information regarding mediation, please see FL ST RCP Rule 1.710; FL ST RCP Rule 1.720; FL ST RCP Rule 1.730; FL ST RCP Rule 1.750; and FL ST 20 J CIR 1.9.

5. *Rules of court*

a. *Rules of civil procedure.* The Florida Rules of Civil Procedure apply to all actions of a civil nature and all special statutory proceedings in the circuit courts and county courts except those to which the Florida Probate Rules, the Florida Family Law Rules of Procedure, or the Small Claims Rules apply. FL ST RCP Rule 1.010.

i. The form, content, procedure, and time for pleading in all special statutory proceedings shall be as prescribed by the statutes governing the proceeding unless the Florida Rules of Civil Procedure specifically provide to the contrary. FL ST RCP Rule 1.010.

ii. The Florida Rules of Civil Procedure shall be construed to secure the just, speedy, and inexpensive determination of every action. FL ST RCP Rule 1.010.

b. *Rules of judicial administration.* The Florida Rules of Judicial Administration shall apply to administrative matters in all courts to which the Florida Rules of Judicial Administration are applicable by their terms. The Florida Rules of Judicial Administration shall be construed to secure the speedy and inexpensive determination of every proceeding to which they are applicable. The Florida Rules of Judicial Administration shall supersede all conflicting rules and statutes. FL ST J ADMIN Rule 2.110.

6. *Civil case management plan.* There is established within the Twentieth Judicial Circuit a Civil Case Management Plan applicable to circuit civil cases, which will be administered by the Administrative Office of the Courts through direction of the Circuit Administrative Judges in each county for the implementation of enhanced case management procedures and guidelines for the timely and efficient processing of circuit civil cases and reduction in the pending backlog of civil cases. FL ST 20 J CIR 1.13.
   a. The basis for the Civil Case Management Plan is included in FL ST 20 J CIR 1.13, identified in Attachment A as the "Civil Differentiated Case Management (DCM) Procedures and Backlog Reduction Plan," and is incorporated as if fully set forth in FL ST 20 J CIR 1.13. The Civil Case Management Plan is to be used as a model for the purpose of establishing time standards, improving the courts ability to provide early and continuous management of civil cases as required by FL ST J ADMIN Rule 2.545, and to promote uniformity of practice throughout the Twentieth Judicial Circuit. FL ST 20 J CIR 1.13.
   b. Full implementation of the Civil DCM Case Management Procedures (Attachment A), including all uniform circuitwide procedures and forms, shall apply to all civil cases filed in Lee and Collier counties, effective January 1, 2011. Even though full implementation may be delayed in Charlotte, Hendry, and Glades counties, all civil time standards and goals, and the use of civil Case Managers and Magistrates to assist trial judges in the process of civil case management and backlog reduction programs, shall be effective circuitwide immediately. FL ST 20 J CIR 1.13.
   c. For more information on the civil case management plan, refer to the specific county website and/or see FL ST 20 J CIR 1.13.

D. Documents

1. *Required documents*
   a. *Notice of hearing/Motion.* An application to the court for an order shall be by motion which shall be made in writing unless made during a hearing or trial, shall state with particularity the grounds therefor, and shall set forth the relief or order sought. The requirement of writing is fulfilled if the motion is stated in a written notice of the hearing of the motion. All notices of hearing shall specify each motion or other matter to be heard. FL ST RCP Rule 1.100(b). Refer to the General Requirements section of this document for more information on the notice of hearing.
      i. *Notices to persons with disabilities.* See the Format section of this KeyRules document for further information.
   b. *Certification.* Except in emergency situations, before filing any motion in a civil case, except a motion for injunctive relief, for judgment on the pleadings, for summary judgment, to dismiss or to permit maintenance of a class action, to dismiss for failure to state a cause of action, to dismiss for lack of prosecution, or to otherwise involuntarily dismiss an action, the moving party shall confer with counsel for the opposing party in a good faith effort to resolve the issues raised by the motion, and shall file with the motion a statement certifying that the moving counsel has conferred with opposing counsel and that counsel have been unable to agree on the resolution of the motion. FL ST 20 J CIR 2.20(IV)(I)(2).
   c. *Certificate of service.* When any attorney certifies in substance: "I certify that a copy hereof has been furnished to (here insert name or names and addresses used for service) by (e-mail) (delivery) (mail) (fax) on .... (date) ....______________ Attorney" the certificate is taken as prima facie proof of such service in compliance with FL ST J ADMIN Rule 2.516. FL ST J ADMIN Rule 2.516(f).
2. *Supplemental documents*
   a. *Proposed order.* The court may require that orders or judgments be prepared by a party, may require the party to furnish the court with stamped, addressed envelopes for service of the order or judgment, and may require that proposed orders and judgments be furnished to all parties before entry by the court of the order or judgment. FL ST J ADMIN Rule 2.516(h)(1).
      i. Unless otherwise instructed by the court, or agreed to by counsel, all proposed orders shall be provided to other counsel with a reasonable time for approval or comment prior to submission to the court. Opposing counsel should promptly communicate any objections thereto. Thereafter, the drafting attorney should promptly submit a copy of the proposed order to the court and

advise the court as to whether or not it has been approved by opposing counsel. FL ST 20 J CIR 2.20(IV)(I)(4).

ii. Orders prepared by counsel must fairly and adequately represent the ruling of the court, and counsel shall make a good faith effort to agree upon the form of the order prior to submitting it to the court. Attorneys should not submit controverted orders to the court with a copy to opposing counsel for "objections within ______ days". Courts prefer to know that the order is either agreed upon or opposed. FL ST 20 J CIR 2.20(IV)(I)(5).

iii. Attorneys should not use post-hearing submissions of proposed orders as a guise to reargue the merits of the matter. FL ST 20 J CIR 2.20(IV)(I)(6).

iv. If asked by the court to prepare an order, counsel should furnish a copy of the order, and any transmitted letter, to opposing counsel at the time the material is submitted to the court. FL ST 20 J CIR 2.20(IV)(J)(4).

b. *Notice of constitutional question.* A party that files a pleading, written motion, or other paper drawing into question the constitutionality of a state statute or a county or municipal charter, ordinance, or franchise must promptly (1) file a notice of constitutional question stating the question and identifying the paper that raises it; and (2) serve the notice and the pleading, written motion, or other paper drawing into question the constitutionality of a state statute or a county or municipal charter, ordinance, or franchise on the Attorney General or the state attorney of the judicial circuit in which the action is pending, by either certified or registered mail. Service of the notice and pleading, written motion, or other paper does not require joinder of the Attorney General or the state attorney as a party to the action. FL ST RCP Rule 1.071.

c. *Notice and request to participate in telephonic motion hearing.* In instances where a civil motion hearing is scheduled for not longer than fifteen (15) minutes, a party may file a written request to participate via conference or speaker telephone, or other applicable communication equipment, and shall provide notice to the Court and the parties to the motion. FL ST 20 J CIR 1.10. Refer to the Timing and Hearings sections of this document for more information.

E. Format

1. *Documents; Type and size.* Documents subject to the exceptions set forth in FL ST J ADMIN Rule 2.525(d) shall be filed on recycled paper measuring eight and one half by eleven (8 1/2 by 11) inches. For purposes of FL ST J ADMIN Rule 2.520, paper is recycled if it contains a minimum content of fifty (50) percent waste paper. Xerographic reduction of legal-size (eight and one half by fourteen (8 1/2 by 14) inches) documents to letter size (eight and one half by eleven (8 1/2 by 11) inches) is prohibited. All other documents filed by electronic transmission shall be filed in a format capable of being printed in a format consistent with the provisions of FL ST J ADMIN Rule 2.250. FL ST J ADMIN Rule 2.520(b); FL ST 20 J CIR 2.9.

a. *Exhibits.* Any exhibit or attachment filed with pleadings or papers may be filed in its original size. FL ST J ADMIN Rule 2.520(c); FL ST 20 J CIR 2.9.

b. *Recording space.* On all papers and documents prepared and filed by the court or by any party to a proceeding which are to be recorded in the public records of any county, including but not limited to final money judgments and notices of lis pendens, a three (3) inch by three (3) inch space at the top right-hand corner on the first page and a one (1) inch by three (3) inch space at the top right-hand corner on each subsequent page shall be left blank and reserved for use by the clerk of court. FL ST J ADMIN Rule 2.520(d).

i. *Exceptions to recording space.* Any papers or documents created by persons or entities over which the filing party has no control, including but not limited to wills, codicils, trusts, or other testamentary documents; documents prepared or executed by any public officer; documents prepared, executed, acknowledged, or proved outside of the State of Florida; or documents created by State or Federal government agencies, may be filed without the space required by FL ST J ADMIN Rule 2.520. FL ST J ADMIN Rule 2.520(e).

c. *Noncompliance.* No clerk of court is permitted to refuse to file any document or paper because of noncompliance with the Florida Rules of Judicial Administration. However, upon request of the

clerk of court, noncomplying documents must be resubmitted in accordance with the formatting rules. FL ST J ADMIN Rule 2.520(f).

i. When time of filing is critical, the Clerk shall accept pleadings, motions, petitions, briefs, notices, orders, judgments, decrees, opinions, or other papers or official documents on other than eight and one half by eleven (8 1/2 by 11) inch paper but shall then require that the document be resubmitted to comply with FL ST J ADMIN Rule 2.520. FL ST 20 J CIR 2.9.

2. *Caption.* Every pleading, motion, order, judgment, or other paper shall have a caption containing the name of the court, the file number, and except for in rem proceedings, including forfeiture proceedings, the name of the first party on each side with an appropriate indication of other parties, and a designation identifying the party filing it and its nature or the nature of the order, as the case may be. In any in rem proceeding, every pleading, motion, order, judgment, or other paper shall have a caption containing the name of the court, the file number, the style "In re" (followed by the name or general description of the property), and a designation of the person or entity filing it and its nature or the nature of the order, as the case may be. In an in rem forfeiture proceeding, the style shall be "In re forfeiture of" (followed by the name of the general description of the property). All papers filed in the action shall be styled in such a manner as to indicate clearly the subject matter of the paper and the party requesting or obtaining relief. FL ST RCP Rule 1.100(c)(1).

3. *Writing and written defined.* Writing or written means a document containing information, an application, or a stipulation. FL ST RCP Rule 1.080(c).

4. *Rule abbreviations*

a. The Florida Rules of Civil Procedure and shall be abbreviated as Fla.R.Civ.P. FL ST RCP Rule 1.010.

b. The Florida Rules of Judicial Administration shall be abbreviated as Fla. R. Jud. Admin. FL ST J ADMIN Rule 2.110.

5. *Nonverification.* Except when otherwise specifically provided by the Florida Rules of Civil Procedure or an applicable statute, every pleading or other document of a party represented by an attorney need not be verified or accompanied by an affidavit. FL ST RCP Rule 1.030; FL ST J ADMIN Rule 2.515(a).

6. *Attorney signature*

a. *Attorney signature.* Every pleading and other document of a party represented by an attorney shall be signed by at least one (1) attorney of record in that attorney's individual name whose current record Florida Bar address, telephone number, including area code, primary e-mail address and secondary e-mail addresses, if any, and Florida Bar number shall be stated, and who shall be duly licensed to practice law in Florida or who shall have received permission to appear in the particular case as provided in FL ST J ADMIN Rule 2.510. FL ST J ADMIN Rule 2.515(a).

i. The attorney may be required by the court to give the address of, and to vouch for the attorney's authority to represent, the party. FL ST J ADMIN Rule 2.515(a).

ii. The signature of an attorney shall constitute a certificate by the attorney that the attorney has read the pleading or other document; that to the best of the attorney's knowledge, information, and belief there is good ground to support it; and that it is not interposed for delay. FL ST J ADMIN Rule 2.515(a).

iii. If a pleading is not signed or is signed with intent to defeat the purpose of FL ST J ADMIN Rule 2.515, it may be stricken and the action may proceed as though the pleading or other document had not been served. FL ST J ADMIN Rule 2.515(a).

b. *Pro se litigant signature.* A party who is not represented by an attorney shall sign any pleading or other paper and state the party's address and telephone number, including area code. FL ST J ADMIN Rule 2.515(b).

c. *Form of signature*

i. The signatures required on pleadings and documents by FL ST J ADMIN Rule 2.515(a) and FL ST J ADMIN Rule 2.515(b) may be:

- Original signatures;

- Original signatures that have been reproduced by electronic means, such as on electronically transmitted documents or photocopied documents;
- Electronic signatures using the "/s/," "s/," or "/s" formats by or at the direction of the person signing; or
- Any other signature format authorized by general law, so long as the clerk where the proceeding is pending has the capability of receiving and has obtained approval from the Supreme Court of Florida to accept pleadings and documents with that signature format. FL ST J ADMIN Rule 2.515(c)(1).

ii. An attorney, party, or other person who files a pleading or paper by electronic transmission that does not contain the original signature of that attorney, party, or other person shall file that identical pleading or paper in paper form containing an original signature of that attorney, party, or other person (hereinafter called the follow-up filing) immediately thereafter. The follow-up filing is not required if the Supreme Court of Florida has entered an order directing the clerk of court to discontinue accepting the follow-up filing. FL ST J ADMIN Rule 2.515(c)(2).

7. *Forms*

a. *Process.* The forms of process, notice of lis pendens, and notice of action provided in the Florida Rules of Civil Procedure are sufficient. Variations from the forms do not void process or notices that are otherwise sufficient. FL ST RCP Rule 1.900(a).

b. *Other forms.* The other forms provided in the Florida Rules of Civil Procedure are sufficient for the matters that are covered by them. So long as the substance is expressed without prolixity, the forms may be varied to meet the facts of a particular case. FL ST RCP Rule 1.900(b).

c. *Formal matters.* Captions, except for the designation of the paper, are omitted from the forms provided in the Florida Rules of Civil Procedure. A general form of caption is the first form provided. Signatures are omitted from pleadings and motions. FL ST RCP Rule 1.900(c).

8. *Notices to persons with disabilities.* All notices of court proceedings to be held in a public facility, and all process compelling appearance at such proceedings, shall include the following statement in bold face, fourteen (14) point Times New Roman or Courier font: "If you are a person with a disability who needs any accommodation in order to participate in this proceeding, you are entitled, at no cost to you, to the provision of certain assistance. Please contact [identify applicable court personnel by name, address, and telephone number] at least seven (7) days before your scheduled court appearance, or immediately upon receiving this notification if the time before the scheduled appearance is less than seven (7) days; if you are hearing or voice impaired, call 711." FL ST J ADMIN Rule 2.540(c)(1). For more information, see FL ST 20 J CIR 2.15.

9. *Minimization of the filing of sensitive information*

a. *Limitations for court filings.* Unless authorized by FL ST J ADMIN Rule 2.425(b), statute, another rule of court, or the court orders otherwise, designated sensitive information filed with the court must be limited to the following format:

i. The initials of a person known to be a minor;

ii. The year of birth of a person's birth date;

iii. No portion of any: Social security number, Bank account number, Credit card account number, Charge account number, or Debit account number;

iv. The last four digits of any: Taxpayer identification number (TIN), Employee identification number, Driver's license number, Passport number, Telephone number, Financial account number, except as set forth in FL ST J ADMIN Rule 2.425(a)(3), Brokerage account number, Insurance policy account number, Loan account number, Customer account number, or Patient or health care number;

v. A truncated version of any: Email address, Computer user name, Password, or Personal identification number (PIN); and

vi. A truncated version of any other sensitive information as provided by court order. FL ST J ADMIN Rule 2.425(a).

b. *Exceptions.* FL ST J ADMIN Rule 2.425(a) does not apply to the following:
   i. An account number which identifies the property alleged to be the subject of a proceeding;
   ii. The record of an administrative or agency proceeding;
   iii. The record in appellate or review proceedings;
   iv. The birth date of a minor whenever the birth date is necessary for the court to establish or maintain subject matter jurisdiction;
   v. The name of a minor in any order relating to parental responsibility, time-sharing, or child support;
   vi. The name of a minor in any document or order affecting the minor's ownership of real property;
   vii. The birth date of a party in a writ of attachment or notice to payor;
   viii. In traffic and criminal proceedings: a pro se filing; a court filing that is related to a criminal matter or investigation and that is prepared before the filing of a criminal charge or is not filed as part of any docketed criminal case; an arrest or search warrant or any information in support thereof; a charging document and an affidavit or other documents filed in support of any charging document, including any driving records; a statement of particulars; discovery material introduced into evidence or otherwise filed with the court; and all information necessary for the proper issuance and execution of a subpoena duces tecum;
   ix. Information used by the clerk for case maintenance purposes or the courts for case management purposes; and
   x. Information which is relevant and material to an issue before the court. FL ST J ADMIN Rule 2.425(b).

c. *Remedies.* Upon motion by a party or interested person or sua sponte by the court, the court may order remedies, sanctions or both for a violation of FL ST J ADMIN Rule 2.425(a). Following notice and an opportunity to respond, the court may impose sanctions if such filing was not made in good faith. FL ST J ADMIN Rule 2.425(c).

d. *Motions not restricted.* FL ST J ADMIN Rule 2.425 does not restrict a party's right to move for protective order, to move to file documents under seal, or to request a determination of the confidentiality of records. FL ST J ADMIN Rule 2.425(d).

e. *Application.* FL ST J ADMIN Rule 2.425 does not affect the application of constitutional provisions, statutes, or rules of court regarding confidential information or access to public information. FL ST J ADMIN Rule 2.425(e).

F. Filing and Service Requirements

1. *Filing requirements.* All original documents must be filed with the court either before service or immediately thereafter, unless otherwise provided for by general law or other rules. If the original of any bond or other document is not placed in the court file, a certified copy must be so placed by the clerk. FL ST J ADMIN Rule 2.516(d). All documents shall be filed in conformity with the requirements of FL ST J ADMIN Rule 2.525. FL ST RCP Rule 1.080(b). All documents filed in any court shall be filed by electronic transmission in accordance with FL ST J ADMIN Rule 2.525. "Documents" means pleadings, motions, petitions, memoranda, briefs, notices, exhibits, declarations, affidavits, orders, judgments, decrees, writs, opinions, and any other paper or writing submitted to a court. FL ST J ADMIN Rule 2.520(a). All documents that are court records, as defined in FL ST J ADMIN Rule 2.430(a)(1), must be filed by electronic transmission, provided that: (1) the clerk has the ability to accept and retain such documents; (2) the clerk or the chief judge of the circuit has requested permission to accept documents filed by electronic transmission; and (3) the supreme court has entered an order granting permission to the clerk to accept documents filed by electronic transmission. FL ST J ADMIN Rule 2.525(c)(1).

   a. *Definition.* "Electronic transmission of documents" means the sending of information by electronic signals to, by or from a court or clerk, which when received can be transformed and stored or transmitted on paper, microfilm, magnetic storage device, optical imaging system, CD-ROM, flash drive, other electronic data storage system, server, case maintenance system ("CM"), electronic

court filing ("ECF") system, statewide or local electronic portal ("e-portal"), or other electronic record keeping system authorized by the supreme court in a format sufficient to communicate the information on the original document in a readable format. Electronic transmission of documents includes electronic mail ("e-mail") and any internet-based transmission procedure, and may include procedures allowing for documents to be signed or verified by electronic means. FL ST J ADMIN Rule 2.525(a).

i. The filing of documents with the court as required by the Florida Rules of Judicial Administration must be made by filing them with the clerk in accordance with FL ST J ADMIN Rule 2.525, except that the judge may permit documents to be filed with the judge, in which event the judge must note the filing date before him or her on the documents and transmit them to the clerk. The date of filing is that shown on the face of the document by the judge's notation or the clerk's time stamp, whichever is earlier. FL ST J ADMIN Rule 2.516(e).

b. *Application.* Any court or clerk of the court may accept the electronic transmission of documents for filing after the clerk, together with input from the chief judge of the circuit, has obtained approval of the procedures and program for doing so from the Supreme Court of Florida. FL ST J ADMIN Rule 2.525(b).

c. *Exceptions*

i. Paper documents and other submissions may be manually submitted to the clerk or court:

- When the clerk does not have the ability to accept and retain documents by electronic filing or has not had ECF Procedures approved by the supreme court;
- For filing by any self-represented party or any self-represented nonparty unless specific ECF Procedures provide a means to file documents electronically. However, any self-represented nonparty that is a governmental or public agency and any other agency, partnership, corporation, or business entity acting on behalf of any governmental or public agency may file documents by electronic transmission if such entity has the capability of filing documents electronically;
- For filing by attorneys excused from e-mail service in accordance with FL ST J ADMIN Rule 2.516(b);
- When submitting evidentiary exhibits or filing non-documentary materials;
- When the filing involves documents in excess of twenty-five (25) megabytes (25MB) in size. For such filings, documents may be transmitted using an electronic storage medium that the clerk has the ability to accept, which may include a CD-ROM, flash drive, or similar storage medium;
- When filed in open court, as permitted by the court;
- When paper filing is permitted by any approved statewide or local ECF procedures; and
- If any court determines that justice so requires. FL ST J ADMIN Rule 2.525(d).

ii. Any document in paper form submitted under FL ST J ADMIN Rule 2.525(d) is filed when it is received by the clerk or court and the clerk shall immediately thereafter convert any filed paper document to an electronic document. "Convert to an electronic document" means optically capturing an image of a paper document and using character recognition software to recover as much of the document's text as practicable and then indexing and storing the document in the official court file. FL ST J ADMIN Rule 2.525(c)(4).

iii. Any storage medium submitted under FL ST J ADMIN Rule 2.525(d)(5) is filed when received by the clerk or court and the clerk shall immediately thereafter transfer the electronic documents from the storage device to the official court file. FL ST J ADMIN Rule 2.525(c)(5).

iv. If the filer of any paper document authorized under FL ST J ADMIN Rule 2.525(d) provides a self-addressed, postage-paid envelope for return of the paper document after it is converted to electronic form by the clerk, the clerk shall place the paper document in the envelope and deposit it in the mail. Except when a paper document is required to be maintained, the clerk may recycle any filed paper document that is not to be returned to the filer. FL ST J ADMIN Rule 2.525(c)(6).

v. The clerk may convert any paper document filed before the effective date of FL ST J ADMIN Rule 2.525 to an electronic document. Unless the clerk is required to maintain the paper document, if the paper document has been converted to an electronic document by the clerk, the paper document is no longer part of the official court file and may be removed and recycled. FL ST J ADMIN Rule 2.525(c)(7).

d. *Official court file.* For information on what constitutes the official court file, please see FL ST J ADMIN Rule 2.525(c)(2), FL ST J ADMIN Rule 2.525(c)(3).

e. *Administration.* All attorneys, parties, or other persons using this rule to file documents are required to make arrangements with the court or clerk for the payment of any charges authorized by general law or the supreme court before filing any document by electronic transmission. FL ST J ADMIN Rule 2.525(f)(2).

f. *Filing date.* The filing date for an electronically transmitted document is the date and time that such filing is acknowledged by an electronic stamp or otherwise, pursuant to any procedure set forth in any ECF Procedures approved by the supreme court, or the date the last page of such filing is received by the court or clerk. FL ST J ADMIN Rule 2.525(f)(3).

g. *Accessibility.* All documents transmitted in any electronic form under FL ST J ADMIN Rule 2.525 must comply with the accessibility requirements of FL ST J ADMIN Rule 2.526. FL ST J ADMIN Rule 2.525(g).

2. *Service requirements.* Every pleading subsequent to the initial pleading, all orders, and every other document filed in the action must be served in conformity with the requirements of FL ST J ADMIN Rule 2.516. FL ST RCP Rule 1.080(a).

a. *Service; Generally.* The timing and manner of service should not be used to the disadvantage of the party receiving the papers. FL ST 20 J CIR 2.20(IV)(C)(1).

i. Papers and memoranda of law should not be served at court appearances without advance notice to opposing counsel and should not be served so close to a court appearance so as to inhibit the ability of opposing counsel to prepare for that appearance or to respond to the papers. Should the attorney do so, the court is urged to take appropriate action in response, including continuing the matter to allow opposing counsel to prepare and respond. FL ST 20 J CIR 2.20(IV)(C)(2).

ii. Papers should not be served in order to take advantage of an opponent's known absence from the office or at a time or in a manner designed to inconvenience an adversary, such as late on Friday afternoon or the day preceding a secular or religious holiday. FL ST 20 J CIR 2.20(IV)(C)(3).

iii. Service should be made personally or by courtesy copy facsimile transmission when it is likely that service by mail, even when allowed, will prejudice the opposing party or will not provide the opposing party with a reasonable time to respond. FL ST 20 J CIR 2.20(IV)(C)(4).

b. *Service; When required.* Unless the court otherwise orders, or a statute or supreme court administrative order specifies a different means of service, every pleading subsequent to the initial pleading and every other document filed in any court proceeding, except applications for witness subpoenas and documents served by formal notice or required to be served in the manner provided for service of formal notice, must be served in accordance with FL ST J ADMIN Rule 2.516 on each party. No service need be made on parties against whom a default has been entered, except that pleadings asserting new or additional claims against them must be served in the manner provided for service of summons. FL ST J ADMIN Rule 2.516(a).

i. *Copies of court submissions.* Copies of any submissions to the court (such as correspondence, memoranda of law, motions, case law, etc.) should simultaneously be provided to opposing counsel by substantially the same method of delivery by which they are provided to the court. For example, if a memorandum of law is hand-delivered to the court, at substantially the same time a copy should be hand-delivered or faxed to opposing counsel. FL ST 20 J CIR 2.20(IV)(J)(4).

c. *Service; How made.* When service is required or permitted to be made upon a party represented by

an attorney, service must be made upon the attorney unless service upon the party is ordered by the court. FL ST J ADMIN Rule 2.516(b).

i. *Service by electronic mail ("e-mail").* All documents required or permitted to be served on another party must be served by e-mail, unless FL ST J ADMIN Rule 2.516 otherwise provides. When, in addition to service by e-mail, the sender also utilizes another means of service provided for in FL ST J ADMIN Rule 2.516(b)(2), any differing time limits and other provisions applicable to that other means of service control. FL ST J ADMIN Rule 2.516(b)(1). Any document electronically transmitted to a court or clerk must also be served on all parties and interested persons in accordance with the applicable rules of court. FL ST J ADMIN Rule 2.525(e)(2).

- *Service on attorneys.* Upon appearing in a proceeding, an attorney must serve a designation of a primary e-mail address and may designate no more than two (2) secondary e-mail addresses. Thereafter, service must be directed to all designated e-mail addresses in that proceeding. Every document filed by an attorney thereafter must include the primary e-mail address of that attorney and any secondary e-mail addresses. If an attorney does not designate any e-mail address for service, documents may be served on that attorney at the e-mail address on record with The Florida Bar. FL ST J ADMIN Rule 2.516(b)(1)(A).
- *Exception to e-mail service on attorneys.* Service by an attorney on another attorney must be made by e-mail unless excused by the court. Upon motion by an attorney demonstrating that the attorney has no e-mail account and lacks access to the Internet at the attorney's office, the court may excuse the attorney from the requirements of e-mail service. Service on and by an attorney excused by the court from e-mail service must be by the means provided in FL ST J ADMIN Rule 2.516(b)(2). FL ST J ADMIN Rule 2.516(b)(1)(B).
- *Service on and by parties not represented by an attorney.* Any party not represented by an attorney may serve a designation of a primary e-mail address and also may designate no more than two (2) secondary e-mail addresses to which service must be directed in that proceeding by the means provided in FL ST J ADMIN Rule 2.516(b)(1). If a party not represented by an attorney does not designate an e-mail address for service in a proceeding, service on and by that party must be by the means provided in FL ST J ADMIN Rule 2.516(b)(2). FL ST J ADMIN Rule 2.516(b)(1)(C).
- *Time of service.* Service by e-mail is complete when it is sent. FL ST J ADMIN Rule 2.516(b)(1)(D). An e-mail is deemed served on the date it is sent. FL ST J ADMIN Rule 2.516(b)(1)(D)(i). If the sender learns that the e-mail did not reach the address of the person to be served, the sender must immediately send another copy by e-mail, or by a means authorized by FL ST J ADMIN Rule 2.516(b)(2). FL ST J ADMIN Rule 2.516(b)(1)(D)(ii). E-mail service is treated as service by mail for the computation of time. FL ST J ADMIN Rule 2.516(b)(1)(D)(iii).

ii. *Format of e-mail for service.* Service of a document by e-mail is made by attaching a copy of the document in PDF format to an e-mail sent to all addresses designated by the attorney or party. FL ST J ADMIN Rule 2.516(b)(1)(E).

- All documents served by e-mail must be attached to an e-mail message containing a subject line beginning with the words "SERVICE OF COURT DOCUMENT" in all capital letters, followed by the case number of the proceeding in which the documents are being served. FL ST J ADMIN Rule 2.516(b)(1)(E)(i).
- The body of the e-mail must identify the court in which the proceeding is pending, the case number, the name of the initial party on each side, the title of each document served with that e-mail, and the sender's name and telephone number. FL ST J ADMIN Rule 2.516(b)(1)(E)(ii).
- Any document served by e-mail may be signed by the "/s/" format, as long as the filed original is signed in accordance with the applicable rule of procedure. FL ST J ADMIN Rule 2.516(b)(1)(E)(iii).
- Any e-mail which, together with its attached documents, exceeds five megabytes (5MB) in

size, must be divided and sent as separate e-mails, no one of which may exceed five megabytes (5MB) in size and each of which must be sequentially numbered in the subject line. FL ST J ADMIN Rule 2.516(b)(1)(E)(iv).

iii. *Service by other means.* In addition to, and not in lieu of, service by e-mail, service may also be made upon attorneys by any of the means specified in FL ST J ADMIN Rule 2.516(b)(2). Service on and by all parties who are not represented by an attorney and who do not designate an e-mail address, and on and by all attorneys excused from e-mail service, must be made by delivering a copy of the document or by mailing it to the party or attorney at their last known address or, if no address is known, by leaving it with the clerk of the court. Service by mail is complete upon mailing. Delivery of a copy within FL ST J ADMIN Rule 2.516 is complete upon:

- Handing it to the attorney or to the party,
- Leaving it at the attorney's or party's office with a clerk or other person in charge thereof,
- If there is no one in charge, leaving it in a conspicuous place therein,
- If the office is closed or the person to be served has no office, leaving it at the person's usual place of abode with some person of his or her family above fifteen (15) years of age and informing such person of the contents, or
- Transmitting it by facsimile to the attorney's or party's office with a cover sheet containing the sender's name, firm, address, telephone number, and facsimile number, and the number of pages transmitted. When service is made by facsimile, a copy must also be served by any other method permitted by FL ST J ADMIN Rule 2.516. Facsimile service occurs when transmission is complete. FL ST J ADMIN Rule 2.516(b)(2)(A) through FL ST J ADMIN Rule 2.516(b)(2)(E).
- Service by delivery after 5:00 p.m. must be deemed to have been made by mailing on the date of delivery. FL ST J ADMIN Rule 2.516(b)(2)(F).

d. *Service; Numerous defendants.* In actions when the parties are unusually numerous, the court may regulate the service contemplated by the Florida Rules of Judicial Administration on motion or on its own initiative in such manner as may be found to be just and reasonable. FL ST J ADMIN Rule 2.516(c).

e. *Service by clerk.* Service of notices and other documents required to be made by the clerk must also be done as provided in FL ST J ADMIN Rule 2.516(b). FL ST J ADMIN Rule 2.516(g).

G. Hearings

1. *Scheduling.* Before setting a motion for hearing, counsel should make a good faith effort to resolve the issue with opposing counsel. FL ST 20 J CIR 2.20(IV)(I)(1). Except in emergency situations, attorneys should make a good faith effort to communicate with opposing counsel prior to scheduling depositions, hearings and other proceedings, so as to schedule them at times that are mutually convenient for all interested persons. Further, a sufficient time should be reserved to permit a complete presentation by counsel for all parties. FL ST 20 J CIR 2.20(IV)(B)(1). Attorneys should not use the hearing time obtained by opposing counsel for other motion practice. FL ST 20 J CIR 2.20(IV)(B)(6).

a. *Notice.* Counsel should notify opposing counsel of dates and times obtained from the court for future hearings on the same day that the hearing date is obtained from the court, or as soon as practicable thereafter. FL ST 20 J CIR 2.20(IV)(J)(3).

b. *Scheduling conflict.* Attorneys should notify opposing counsel, the court, and others affected, of scheduling conflicts as soon as they become apparent. Further, attorneys should cooperate with one another regarding all reasonable rescheduling requests that do not prejudice their clients or unduly delay a proceeding. FL ST 20 J CIR 2.20(IV)(B)(7).

i. Attorneys should call potential scheduling problems to the attention of those affected, including the court, as soon as they become apparent and should avoid last minute cancellations. FL ST 20 J CIR 2.20(IV)(B)(12).

c. *Notice to court when appearance is unnecessary.* Attorneys should promptly notify the court or other tribunal of any resolution between the parties that renders a scheduled court appearance unnecessary. FL ST 20 J CIR 2.20(IV)(B)(8).

2. *Communication equipment*

   a. *Definition.* Communication equipment means a conference telephone or other electronic device that permits all those appearing or participating to hear and speak to each other, provided that all conversation of all parties is audible to all persons present. FL ST J ADMIN Rule 2.530(a).

   b. *Use by all parties.* A county or circuit court judge may, upon the court's own motion or upon the written request of a party, direct that communication equipment be used for a motion hearing, pretrial conference, or a status conference. A judge must give notice to the parties and consider any objections they may have to the use of communication equipment before directing that communication equipment be used. The decision to use communication equipment over the objection of parties will be in the sound discretion of the trial court, except as noted below. FL ST J ADMIN Rule 2.530(b).

   c. *Use only by requesting party.* A county or circuit court judge may, upon the written request of a party upon reasonable notice to all other parties, permit a requesting party to participate through communication equipment in a scheduled motion hearing; however, any such request (except in criminal, juvenile, and appellate proceedings) must be granted, absent a showing of good cause to deny the same, where the hearing is set for not longer than fifteen (15) minutes. FL ST J ADMIN Rule 2.530(c).

   d. *Testimony*

      i. *Generally.* A county or circuit court judge, general magistrate, special magistrate, or hearing officer may allow testimony to be taken through communication equipment if all parties consent or if permitted by another applicable rule of procedure. FL ST J ADMIN Rule 2.530(d)(1).

      ii. *Procedure.* Any party desiring to present testimony through communication equipment shall, prior to the hearing or trial at which the testimony is to be presented, contact all parties to determine whether each party consents to this form of testimony. The party seeking to present the testimony shall move for permission to present testimony through communication equipment, which motion shall set forth good cause as to why the testimony should be allowed in this form. FL ST J ADMIN Rule 2.530(d)(2).

      iii. *Oath.* Testimony may be taken through communication equipment only if a notary public or other person authorized to administer oaths in the witness's jurisdiction is present with the witness and administers the oath consistent with the laws of the jurisdiction. FL ST J ADMIN Rule 2.530(d)(3).

      iv. *Confrontation rights.* In juvenile and criminal proceedings the defendant must make an informed waiver of any confrontation rights that may be abridged by the use of communication equipment. FL ST J ADMIN Rule 2.530(d)(4).

      v. *Video testimony.* If the testimony to be presented utilizes video conferencing or comparable two-way visual capabilities, the court in its discretion may modify the procedures set forth in FL ST J ADMIN Rule 2.530 to accommodate the technology utilized. FL ST J ADMIN Rule 2.530(d)(5).

   e. *Burden of expense.* The cost for the use of the communication equipment is the responsibility of the requesting party unless otherwise directed by the court. FL ST J ADMIN Rule 2.530(e).

3. *Telephonic non-evidentiary motion hearings set for not longer than fifteen (15) minutes.* FL ST 20 J CIR 1.10 specifically addresses non-evidentiary civil motion hearings set for not longer than fifteen (15) minutes. It is not intended to limit or address requests for telephonic hearings which are otherwise governed by FL ST J ADMIN Rule 2.071. FL ST 20 J CIR 1.10. [Editor's note: FL ST J ADMIN Rule 2.071 was renumbered as FL ST J ADMIN Rule 2.530]. Evidentiary hearings are exempted from the application of FL ST 20 J CIR 1.10. FL ST 20 J CIR 1.10.

   a. In instances where a civil motion hearing is scheduled for not longer than fifteen (15) minutes, a party may file a written request to participate via conference or speaker telephone, or other applicable communication equipment, and shall provide notice to the Court and the parties to the motion. FL ST 20 J CIR 1.10. Refer to the Timing section of this document for information on when the notice must be given and when request must be served.

b. The requesting party shall be responsible for contacting the trial judge's Judicial Assistant and ensuring that appropriate arrangements have been made to permit participation through conference or speaker telephone, or other applicable communication equipment, on the scheduled date and time. It shall be at the discretion of the trial judge as to whether the requesting party shall be responsible for initiating the telephone or communication connection or whether the Court shall be responsible for initiating the telephone or communication connection. FL ST 20 J CIR 1.10(3).

c. Absent a showing of good cause, and in accordance with FL ST J ADMIN Rule 2.071(c), the trial judge shall grant the request and make reasonable accommodations to permit the requesting party's participation through conference or speaker telephone, or other applicable communication equipment. FL ST 20 J CIR 1.10. [Editor's note: FL ST J ADMIN Rule 2.071 was renumbered as FL ST J ADMIN Rule 2.530(c)].

d. To the extent that any provision of FL ST 20 J CIR 1.10 may be construed as being in conflict with any law, statute, or rule, the law, statute, or rule shall prevail. FL ST 20 J CIR 1.10.

H. Forms

1. Official Motion for Directed Verdict Forms for Florida

a. Caption. FL ST RCP Form 1.901.

b. Notice of compliance when constitutional challenge is brought. FL ST RCP Form 1.975.

2. Motion for Directed Verdict Forms for Florida

a. Motion; For directed verdict; At close of adverse party's evidence. FL-PP § 5:86.

b. Motion; For directed verdict; At close of all of evidence. FL-PP § 5:87.

c. Motion; Request to go to jury if motions by both parties are denied. FL-PP § 5:88.

d. Order; Granting defendant's motion for directed verdict; Insufficiency of plaintiff's evidence. FL-PP § 5:89.

e. Motion; Directed verdict, renewed. FL-PRACFORM § 7:62.

f. Form for motion for directed verdict at close of plaintiff's case. FL-RCPF R 1.480(24).

g. Form for motion for directed verdict at close of defendant's case. FL-RCPF R 1.480(25).

h. Form for motion to set aside verdict and enter directed verdict. FL-RCPF R 1.480(26).

I. Checklist

(I) ❑ Matters to be considered by moving party

(a) ❑ Required documents

(1) ❑ Notice of hearing/Motion

(2) ❑ Certification

(3) ❑ Certificate of service

(b) ❑ Supplemental documents

(1) ❑ Proposed order

(2) ❑ Notice of constitutional question

(3) ❑ Notice and request to participate in telephonic motion hearing

(c) ❑ Time for making motion

(1) ❑ Before a verdict is returned - A directed verdict is available to the defendant at the close of the plaintiff's evidence or to either party at the close of all of the evidence

(2) ❑ After a verdict is returned - Within ten (10) days after the return of a verdict, a party who has

timely moved for a directed verdict may serve a motion to enter judgment in accordance with the motion for a directed verdict

(3) ❑ No verdict is returned - If a verdict was not returned, a party who has timely moved for a directed verdict may serve a motion for judgment in accordance with the motion for a directed verdict within ten (10) days after discharge of the jury

(4) ❑ General motion timing - A copy of any written motion which may not be heard ex parte and a copy of the notice of the hearing thereof shall be served a reasonable time before the time specified for the hearing; as a general rule, notice should be provided (not including time for service) no less than five (5) business days for hearings

(5) ❑ Notice and request to participate in telephonic motion hearing: Notice by the requesting party must be provided by mailing a copy of the written request at least five (5) days prior to the day of the hearing, or by delivering a copy of the written request to the other parties or, if represented by counsel, to the other parties' attorney(s) no later than 5:00 p.m. two (2) business days prior to the day of the hearing

(II) ❑ Matters to be considered by opposing party

(a) ❑ Required documents

(1) ❑ Response to motion

(2) ❑ Certificate of service

(b) ❑ Supplemental documents

(1) ❑ Proposed order

(2) ❑ Notice of constitutional question

(3) ❑ Notice and request to participate in telephonic motion hearing

(c) ❑ Time for service and filing of opposition

(1) ❑ No time specified for responding to a motion

(2) ❑ Notice and request to participate in telephonic motion hearing: Notice by the requesting party must be provided by mailing a copy of the written request at least five (5) days prior to the day of the hearing, or by delivering a copy of the written request to the other parties or, if represented by counsel, to the other parties' attorney(s) no later than 5:00 p.m. two (2) business days prior to the day of the hearing

Requests, Notices and Applications
Request for Production of Documents

Document Last Updated January 2013

A. Applicable Rules

1. *State rules*

a. Nonverification of pleadings. FL ST RCP Rule 1.030.

b. Service and filing of pleadings, orders, and documents. FL ST RCP Rule 1.080.

c. Time. FL ST RCP Rule 1.090.

d. Pleadings and motions. FL ST RCP Rule 1.100.

e. Pretrial procedure. FL ST RCP Rule 1.200.

f. General provisions governing discovery. FL ST RCP Rule 1.280.

g. Depositions upon oral examination. FL ST RCP Rule 1.310.

h. Interrogatories to parties. FL ST RCP Rule 1.340.

i. Production of documents and things and entry upon land for inspection and other purposes. FL ST RCP Rule 1.350.

j. Production of documents and things without deposition. FL ST RCP Rule 1.351.
k. Examination of persons. FL ST RCP Rule 1.360.
l. Requests for admission. FL ST RCP Rule 1.370.
m. Failure to make discovery; Sanctions. FL ST RCP Rule 1.380.
n. Depositions of expert witnesses. FL ST RCP Rule 1.390.
o. Relief from judgment, decrees, or orders. FL ST RCP Rule 1.540.
p. Forms. FL ST RCP Rule 1.900.
q. Minimization of the filing of sensitive information. FL ST J ADMIN Rule 2.425.
r. Retention of court records. FL ST J ADMIN Rule 2.430.
s. Foreign attorneys. FL ST J ADMIN Rule 2.510.
t. Signature of attorneys and parties. FL ST J ADMIN Rule 2.515.
u. Paper. FL ST J ADMIN Rule 2.520.
v. Electronic filing. FL ST J ADMIN Rule 2.525.
w. Accessibility of information and technology. FL ST J ADMIN Rule 2.526.
x. Notices to persons with disabilities. FL ST J ADMIN Rule 2.540.
y. Case management. FL ST J ADMIN Rule 2.545.

2. *Local rules*
   a. Exclusions from mediation. FL ST 20 J CIR 1.9.
   b. Establishment and implementation of civil case management plan. FL ST 20 J CIR 1.13.
   c. Size of paper. FL ST 20 J CIR 2.9.
   d. Americans with Disabilities Act; Notification of court proceedings. FL ST 20 J CIR 2.15.
   e. Standards of professional courtesy and conduct and establishment of peer review program. FL ST 20 J CIR 2.20.

B. Timing

1. *Request for production of documents.* Without leave of court the request may be served on the plaintiff after commencement of the action and on any other party with or after service of the process and initial pleading on that party. FL ST RCP Rule 1.350(b).
2. *Notice of intent to serve subpoena.* A party desiring production under FL ST RCP Rule 1.351 shall serve notice as provided in FL ST RCP Rule 1.080 on every other party of the intent to serve a subpoena under FL ST RCP Rule 1.351 at least ten (10) days before the subpoena is issued if service is by delivery and fifteen (15) days before the subpoena is issued if the service is by mail or e-mail. FL ST RCP Rule 1.351(b).
3. *Sequence and timing of discovery.* Except as provided in FL ST RCP Rule 1.280(b)(5) or unless the court upon motion for the convenience of parties and witnesses and in the interest of justice orders otherwise, methods of discovery may be used in any sequence, and the fact that a party is conducting discovery, whether by deposition or otherwise, shall not delay any other party's discovery. FL ST RCP Rule 1.280(e).
4. *Computation of time*
   a. *Generally.* Computation of time shall be governed by FL ST J ADMIN Rule 2.514. FL ST RCP Rule 1.090(a). The following rules apply in computing time periods specified in any rule of procedure, local rule, court order, or statute that does not specify a method of computing time. FL ST J ADMIN Rule 2.514(a).
      i. *Period stated in days or a longer unit.* When the period is stated in days or a longer unit of time (A) exclude the day of the event that triggers the period; (B) count every day, including intermediate Saturdays, Sundays, and legal holidays; and (C) include the last day of the period,

but if the last day is a Saturday, Sunday, or legal holiday, or falls within any period of time extended through an order of the chief justice under FL ST J ADMIN Rule 2.205(a)(2)(B)(iv), the period continues to run until the end of the next day that is not a Saturday, Sunday, or legal holiday and does not fall within any period of time extended through an order of the chief justice. FL ST J ADMIN Rule 2.514(a)(1).

ii. *Period stated in hours.* When the period is stated in hours (A) begin counting immediately on the occurrence of the event that triggers the period; (B) count every hour, including hours during intermediate Saturdays, Sundays, and legal holidays; and (C) if the period would end on a Saturday, Sunday, or legal holiday, or during any period of time extended through an order of the chief justice under FL ST J ADMIN Rule 2.205(a)(2)(B)(iv), the period continues to run until the same time on the next day that is not a Saturday, Sunday, or legal holiday and does not fall within any period of time extended through an order of the chief justice. FL ST J ADMIN Rule 2.514(a)(2).

iii. *Period stated in days less than seven (7) days.* When the period stated in days is less than seven (7) days, intermediate Saturdays, Sundays, and legal holidays shall be excluded in the computation. FL ST J ADMIN Rule 2.514(a)(3).

iv. *"Last day" defined.* Unless a different time is set by a statute, local rule, or court order, the last day ends (A) for electronic filing or for service by any means, at midnight; and (B) for filing by other means, when the clerk's office is scheduled to close. FL ST J ADMIN Rule 2.514(a)(4).

v. *"Next day" defined.* The "next day" is determined by continuing to count forward when the period is measured after an event and backward when measured before an event. FL ST J ADMIN Rule 2.514(a)(5).

vi. *"Legal holiday" defined.* "Legal holiday" means (A) the day set aside by FL ST § 110.117, for observing New Year's Day, Martin Luther King, Jr.'s Birthday, Memorial Day, Independence Day, Labor Day, Veterans' Day, Thanksgiving Day, the Friday after Thanksgiving Day, or Christmas Day, and (B) any day observed as a holiday by the clerk's office or as designated by the chief judge. FL ST J ADMIN Rule 2.514(a)(6).

b. *Additional time after service by mail or e-mail.* When a party may or must act within a specified time after service and service is made by mail or e-mail, five (5) days are added after the period that would otherwise expire under FL ST J ADMIN Rule 2.514(a). FL ST J ADMIN Rule 2.514(b).

c. *Enlargement.* When an act is required or allowed to be done at or within a specified time by order of court, by the Florida Rules of Civil Procedure, or by notice given thereunder, for cause shown the court at any time in its discretion (1) with or without notice, may order the period enlarged if request therefor is made before the expiration of the period originally prescribed or as extended by a previous order, or (2) upon motion made and notice after the expiration of the specified period, may permit the act to be done when failure to act was the result of excusable neglect, but it may not extend the time for making a motion for new trial, for rehearing, or to alter or amend a judgment; making a motion for relief from a judgment under FL ST RCP Rule 1.540(b); taking an appeal or filing a petition for certiorari; or making a motion for a directed verdict. FL ST RCP Rule 1.090(b).

d. *Unaffected by expiration of term.* The period of time provided for the doing of any act or the taking of any proceeding shall not be affected or limited by the continued existence or expiration of a term of court. The continued existence or expiration of a term of court in no way affects the power of a court to do any act or take any proceeding in any action which is or has been pending before it. FL ST RCP Rule 1.090(c).

C. General Requirements

1. *General provisions governing discovery*

a. *Discovery methods.* Parties may obtain discovery by one or more of the following methods: depositions upon oral examination or written questions; written interrogatories; production of documents or things or permission to enter upon land or other property for inspection and other purposes; physical and mental examinations; and requests for admission. Unless the court orders otherwise and under FL ST RCP Rule 1.280(c), the frequency of use of these methods is not limited, except as provided in FL ST RCP Rule 1.200, FL ST RCP Rule 1.340, and FL ST RCP Rule 1.370. FL ST RCP Rule 1.280(a).

b. *Scope of discovery.* Unless otherwise limited by order of the court in accordance with the Florida Rules of Civil Procedure, the scope of discovery is as follows:

   i. *In general.* Parties may obtain discovery regarding any matter, not privileged, that is relevant to the subject matter of the pending action, whether it relates to the claim or defense of the party seeking discovery or the claim or defense of any other party, including the existence, description, nature, custody, condition, and location of any books, documents, or other tangible things and the identity and location of persons having knowledge of any discoverable matter. It is not ground for objection that the information sought will be inadmissible at the trial if the information sought appears reasonably calculated to lead to the discovery of admissible evidence. FL ST RCP Rule 1.280(b)(1).

      - Attorneys should pursue discovery requests that are reasonably related to the matter at issue. FL ST 20 J CIR 2.20(IV)(E)(1).

   ii. *Indemnity agreements.* A party may obtain discovery of the existence and contents of any agreement under which any person may be liable to satisfy part or all of a judgment that may be entered in the action or to indemnify or to reimburse a party for payments made to satisfy the judgment. Information concerning the agreement is not admissible in evidence at trial by reason of disclosure. FL ST RCP Rule 1.280(b)(2).

   iii. *Electronically stored information.* A party may obtain discovery of electronically stored information in accordance with the Florida Rules of Civil Procedure. FL ST RCP Rule 1.280(b)(3).

   iv. *Trial preparation; Materials.* Subject to the provisions of FL ST RCP Rule 1.280(b)(5), a party may obtain discovery of documents and tangible things otherwise discoverable under FL ST RCP Rule 1.280(b)(1) and prepared in anticipation of litigation or for trial by or for another party or by or for that party's representative, including that party's attorney, consultant, surety, indemnitor, insurer, or agent, only upon a showing that the party seeking discovery has need of the materials in the preparation of the case and is unable without undue hardship to obtain the substantial equivalent of the materials by other means. FL ST RCP Rule 1.280(b)(4).

      - In ordering discovery of the materials when the required showing has been made, the court shall protect against disclosure of the mental impressions, conclusions, opinions, or legal theories of an attorney or other representative of a party concerning the litigation. FL ST RCP Rule 1.280(b)(4).
      - Without the required showing a party may obtain a copy of a statement concerning the action or its subject matter previously made by that party. FL ST RCP Rule 1.280(b)(4).
      - Upon request without the required showing a person not a party may obtain a copy of a statement concerning the action or its subject matter previously made by that person. If the request is refused, the person may move for an order to obtain a copy. The provisions of FL ST RCP Rule 1.380(a)(5) apply to the award of expenses incurred as a result of making the motion. FL ST RCP Rule 1.280(b)(4).
      - For purposes of FL ST RCP Rule 1.280(b)(4), a statement previously made is a written statement signed or otherwise adopted or approved by the person making it, or a stenographic, mechanical, electrical, or other recording or transcription of it that is a substantially verbatim recital of an oral statement by the person making it and contemporaneously recorded. FL ST RCP Rule 1.280(b)(4).

   v. *Trial preparation; Experts.* Discovery of facts known and opinions held by experts, otherwise discoverable under the provisions of FL ST RCP Rule 1.280(b)(1) and acquired or developed in anticipation of litigation or for trial, may be obtained only as follows:

      - By interrogatories a party may require any other party to identify each person whom the other party expects to call as an expert witness at trial and to state the subject matter on which the expert is expected to testify, and to state the substance of the facts and opinions

to which the expert is expected to testify and a summary of the grounds for each opinion. FL ST RCP Rule 1.280(b)(5)(A)(i).

- Any person disclosed by interrogatories or otherwise as a person expected to be called as an expert witness at trial may be deposed in accordance with FL ST RCP Rule 1.390 without motion or order of court. FL ST RCP Rule 1.280(b)(5)(A)(ii).
- A party may obtain the following discovery regarding any person disclosed by interrogatories or otherwise as a person expected to be called as an expert witness at trial: The scope of employment in the pending case and the compensation for such service, FL ST RCP Rule 1.280(b)(5)(A)(iii)(1); The expert's general litigation experience, including the percentage of work performed for plaintiffs and defendants, FL ST RCP Rule 1.280(b)(5)(A)(iii)(2); The identity of other cases, within a reasonable time period, in which the expert has testified by deposition or at trial, FL ST RCP Rule 1.280(b)(5)(A)(iii)(3); An approximation of the portion of the expert's involvement as an expert witness, which may be based on the number of hours, percentage of hours, or percentage of earned income derived from serving as an expert witness; however, the expert shall not be required to disclose his or her earnings as an expert witness or income derived from other services. FL ST RCP Rule 1.280(b)(5)(A)(iii)(4).
- An expert may be required to produce financial and business records only under the most unusual or compelling circumstances and may not be compelled to compile or produce nonexistent documents. Upon motion, the court may order further discovery by other means, subject to such restrictions as to scope and other provisions pursuant to FL ST RCP Rule 1.280(b)(5)(C) concerning fees and expenses as the court may deem appropriate. FL ST RCP Rule 1.280(b)(5).
- A party may discover facts known or opinions held by an expert who has been retained or specially employed by another party in anticipation of litigation or preparation for trial and who is not expected to be called as a witness at trial, only as provided in FL ST RCP Rule 1.360(b) or upon a showing of exceptional circumstances under which it is impracticable for the party seeking discovery to obtain facts or opinions on the same subject by other means. FL ST RCP Rule 1.280(b)(5)(B).
- Unless manifest injustice would result, the court shall require that the party seeking discovery pay the expert a reasonable fee for time spent in responding to discovery under FL ST RCP Rule 1.280(b)(5)(A) and FL ST RCP Rule 1.280(b)(5)(B); and concerning discovery from an expert obtained under FL ST RCP Rule 1.280(b)(5)(A) the court may require, and concerning discovery obtained under FL ST RCP Rule 1.280(b)(5)(B) shall require, the party seeking discovery to pay the other party a fair part of the fees and expenses reasonably incurred by the latter party in obtaining facts and opinions from the expert. FL ST RCP Rule 1.280(b)(5)(C).
- As used in the Florida Rules of Civil Procedure an expert shall be an expert witness as defined in FL ST RCP Rule 1.390(a). FL ST RCP Rule 1.280(b)(5)(D).

vi. *Claims to privilege or protection.* When a party withholds information otherwise discoverable under the Florida Rules of Civil Procedure by claiming that it is privileged or subject to protection as trial preparation material, the party shall make the claim expressly and shall describe the nature of the documents, communications, or things not produced or disclosed in a manner that, without revealing information itself privileged or protected, will enable other parties to assess the applicability of the privilege or protection. FL ST RCP Rule 1.280(b)(6).

c. *Limitations on discovery of electronically stored information*

i. A person may object to discovery of electronically stored information from sources that the person identifies as not reasonably accessible because of burden or cost. On motion to compel discovery or for a protective order, the person from whom discovery is sought must show that the information sought or the format requested is not reasonably accessible because of undue burden or cost. If that showing is made, the court may nonetheless order the discovery from such sources or in such formats if the requesting party shows good cause. The court may specify

conditions of the discovery, including ordering that some or all of the expenses incurred by the person from whom discovery is sought be paid by the party seeking the discovery. FL ST RCP Rule 1.280(d)(1).

ii. In determining any motion involving discovery of electronically stored information, the court must limit the frequency or extent of discovery otherwise allowed by the Florida Rules of Civil Procedure if it determines that (i) the discovery sought is unreasonably cumulative or duplicative, or can be obtained from another source or in another manner that is more convenient, less burdensome, or less expensive; or (ii) the burden or expense of the discovery outweighs its likely benefit, considering the needs of the case, the amount in controversy, the parties' resources, the importance of the issues at stake in the action, and the importance of the discovery in resolving the issues. FL ST RCP Rule 1.280(d)(2).

d. *Use of discovery.* Attorneys should not use discovery for the purpose of causing undue delay or obtaining unfair advantage. FL ST 20 J CIR 2.20(IV)(E)(2). Attorneys should use discovery to ascertain information, to perpetuate testimony, or to obtain documents or things necessary for the prosecution or defense of an action. Attorneys should never use discovery as a means of harassment, intimidation or to impose an inordinate burden or expense. FL ST 20 J CIR 2.20(IV)(E)(3).

e. For information on inadvertent disclosure of privileged materials, see FL ST RCP Rule 1.285.

2. *Request for production of documents*

a. *Scope of request.* Demands for document production should not be so broad as to encompass documents clearly not relevant to the subject matter of the case. FL ST 20 J CIR 2.20(IV)(G)(1). Any party may request any other party:

i. To produce and permit the party making the request, or someone acting in the requesting party's behalf, to inspect and copy any designated documents, including electronically stored information, writings, drawings, graphs, charts, photographs, phono-records, and other data compilations from which information can be obtained, translated, if necessary, by the party to whom the request is directed through detection devices into reasonably usable form, that constitute or contain matters within the scope of FL ST RCP Rule 1.280(b) and that are in the possession, custody, or control of the party to whom the request is directed;

ii. To inspect and copy, test, or sample any tangible things that constitute or contain matters within the scope of FL ST RCP Rule 1.280(b) and that are in the possession, custody, or control of the party to whom the request is directed; or

iii. To permit entry upon designated land or other property in the possession or control of the party upon whom the request is served for the purpose of inspection and measuring, surveying, photographing, testing, or sampling the property or any designated object or operation on it within the scope of FL ST RCP Rule 1.280(b). FL ST RCP Rule 1.350(a).

b. *Contents of request*

i. The request shall set forth the items to be inspected, either by individual item or category, and describe each item and category with reasonable particularity. The request shall specify a reasonable time, place, and manner of making the inspection or performing the related acts. FL ST RCP Rule 1.350(b).

ii. A request for electronically stored information may specify the form or forms in which electronically stored information is to be produced. If the responding party objects to a requested form, or if no form is specified in the request, the responding party must state the form or forms it intends to use. If a request for electronically stored information does not specify the form of production, the producing party must produce the information in a form or forms in which it is ordinarily maintained or in a reasonably usable form or forms. FL ST RCP Rule 1.350(b).

c. *Failure to respond to requests.* The party submitting the request may move for an order under FL ST RCP Rule 1.380 concerning any objection, failure to respond to the request, or any part of it, or failure to permit the inspection as requested. FL ST RCP Rule 1.350(b). Please see FL ST RCP Rule

1.380(d) and the KeyRules Motion to Compel Discovery documents for further information regarding compelling discovery and discovery sanctions.

i. *Response requirements.* For each item or category the response shall state that inspection and related activities will be permitted as requested unless the request is objected to, in which event the reasons for the objection shall be stated. If an objection is made to part of an item or category, the part shall be specified. When producing documents, the producing party shall either produce them as they are kept in the usual course of business or shall identify them to correspond with the categories in the request. If the responding party objects to a requested form (for electronic information), or if no form is specified in the request, the responding party must state the form or forms it intends to use. If a request for electronically stored information does not specify the form of production, the producing party must produce the information in a form or forms in which it is ordinarily maintained or in a reasonably usable form or forms. FL ST RCP Rule 1.350(b).

- In responding to document demands, counsel should not strain to interpret the request in an artificially restrictive manner just to avoid disclosure. FL ST 20 J CIR 2.20(G)(2).
- Documents should be withheld on the grounds of privilege only where appropriate. FL ST 20 J CIR 2.20(G)(3).
- Counsel should not produce documents in a disorganized or unintelligible fashion, or in a way calculated to hide or obscure the existence of other relevant documents. FL ST 20 J CIR 2.20(G)(4).
- Document production should not be delayed to prevent opposing counsel from inspecting documents prior to scheduled depositions or for an improper tactical reason. FL ST 20 J CIR 2.20(G)(5).

3. *Requests to a non-party*

a. *Independent action not prohibited.* FL ST RCP Rule 1.350 does not preclude an independent action against a person not a party for production of documents and things and permission to enter upon land. FL ST RCP Rule 1.350(c). FL ST RCP Rule 1.351 does not affect the right of any party to bring an independent action for production of documents and things or permission to enter upon land. FL ST RCP Rule 1.351(f).

b. *Scope.* A party may seek inspection and copying of any documents or things within the scope of FL ST RCP Rule 1.350(a) from a person who is not a party by issuance of a subpoena directing the production of the documents or things when the requesting party does not seek to depose the custodian or other person in possession of the documents or things. FL ST RCP Rule 1.351 provides the exclusive procedure for obtaining documents or things by subpoena from nonparties without deposing the custodian or other person in possession of the documents or things pursuant to FL ST RCP Rule 1.310. FL ST RCP Rule 1.351(a).

i. *Procedure.* The proposed subpoena shall be attached to the notice and shall state the time, place, and method for production of the documents or things, and the name and address of the person who is to produce the documents or things, if known, and if not known, a general description sufficient to identify the person or the particular class or group to which the person belongs; shall include a designation of the items to be produced; and shall state that the person who will be asked to produce the documents or things has the right to object to the production under FL ST RCP Rule 1.351 and that the person will not be required to surrender the documents or things. A copy of the notice and proposed subpoena shall not be furnished to the person upon whom the subpoena is to be served. If any party serves an objection to production under FL ST RCP Rule 1.351 within ten (10) days of service of the notice, the documents or things shall not be produced pending resolution of the objection in accordance with FL ST RCP Rule 1.351(d). FL ST RCP Rule 1.351(b).

ii. *Subpoena.* If no objection is made by a party under FL ST RCP Rule 1.351(b), an attorney of record in the action may issue a subpoena or the party desiring production shall deliver to the clerk for issuance a subpoena together with a certificate of counsel or pro se party that no timely objection has been received from any party, and the clerk shall issue the subpoena and deliver it to the party desiring production. FL ST RCP Rule 1.351(c).

- The subpoena shall be identical to the copy attached to the notice and shall specify that no testimony may be taken and shall require only production of the documents or things specified in it. FL ST RCP Rule 1.351(c).
- The subpoena may give the recipient an option to deliver or mail legible copies of the documents or things to the party serving the subpoena. FL ST RCP Rule 1.351(c).
- The person upon whom the subpoena is served may condition the preparation of copies on the payment in advance of the reasonable costs of preparing the copies. FL ST RCP Rule 1.351(c).
- The subpoena shall require production only in the county of the residence of the custodian or other person in possession of the documents or things or in the county where the documents or things are located or where the custodian or person in possession usually conducts business. FL ST RCP Rule 1.351(c).
- If the person upon whom the subpoena is served objects at any time before the production of the documents or things, the documents or things shall not be produced under FL ST RCP Rule 1.351, and relief may be obtained pursuant to FL ST RCP Rule 1.310. FL ST RCP Rule 1.351(c).

iii. *Ruling on objection.* If an objection is made by a party under FL ST RCP Rule 1.351(b), the party desiring production may file a motion with the court seeking a ruling on the objection or may proceed pursuant to FL ST RCP Rule 1.310. FL ST RCP Rule 1.351(d).

iv. *Copies furnished.* If the subpoena is complied with by delivery or mailing of copies as provided in FL ST RCP Rule 1.351(c), the party receiving the copies shall furnish a legible copy of each item furnished to any other party who requests it upon the payment of the reasonable cost of preparing the copies. FL ST RCP Rule 1.351(e).

4. *Arbitration and mediation.* Attorneys are encouraged to utilize arbitration, mediation or other forms of alternative dispute resolution if economically feasible. FL ST 20 J CIR 2.20(IV)(N)(3).

a. *Referral to arbitration and mediation.* Except as hereinafter provided or as otherwise prohibited by law, the presiding judge may enter an order referring all or any part of a contested civil matter to mediation or arbitration. The parties to any contested civil matter may file a written stipulation to mediate or arbitrate any issue between them at any time. Such stipulation shall be incorporated into the order of referral. FL ST RCP Rule 1.700(a).

b. *Arbitration*

i. *Exclusions.* A civil action shall be ordered to arbitration or arbitration in conjunction with mediation upon stipulation of the parties. A civil action may be ordered to arbitration or arbitration in conjunction with mediation upon motion of any party or by the court, if the judge determines the action to be of such a nature that arbitration could be of benefit to the litigants or the court. FL ST RCP Rule 1.800.

- Under no circumstances may the following categories of actions be referred to arbitration: (1) bond estreatures; (2) habeas corpus or other extraordinary writs; (3) bond validations; (4) civil or criminal contempt; (5) such other matters as may be specified by order of the chief judge in the circuit. FL ST RCP Rule 1.800.

ii. For more information regarding arbitration, please see FL ST RCP Rule 1.810; FL ST RCP Rule 1.820; FL ST RCP Rule 1.830.

c. *Mediation.* For more information regarding mediation, please see FL ST RCP Rule 1.710; FL ST RCP Rule 1.720; FL ST RCP Rule 1.730; FL ST RCP Rule 1.750; and FL ST 20 J CIR 1.9.

5. *Rules of court*

a. *Rules of civil procedure.* The Florida Rules of Civil Procedure apply to all actions of a civil nature and all special statutory proceedings in the circuit courts and county courts except those to which the

Florida Probate Rules, the Florida Family Law Rules of Procedure, or the Small Claims Rules apply. FL ST RCP Rule 1.010.

i. The form, content, procedure, and time for pleading in all special statutory proceedings shall be as prescribed by the statutes governing the proceeding unless the Florida Rules of Civil Procedure specifically provide to the contrary. FL ST RCP Rule 1.010.

ii. The Florida Rules of Civil Procedure shall be construed to secure the just, speedy, and inexpensive determination of every action. FL ST RCP Rule 1.010.

b. *Rules of judicial administration.* The Florida Rules of Judicial Administration shall apply to administrative matters in all courts to which the Florida Rules of Judicial Administration are applicable by their terms. The Florida Rules of Judicial Administration shall be construed to secure the speedy and inexpensive determination of every proceeding to which they are applicable. The Florida Rules of Judicial Administration shall supersede all conflicting rules and statutes. FL ST J ADMIN Rule 2.110.

6. *Civil case management plan.* There is established within the Twentieth Judicial Circuit a Civil Case Management Plan applicable to circuit civil cases, which will be administered by the Administrative Office of the Courts through direction of the Circuit Administrative Judges in each county for the implementation of enhanced case management procedures and guidelines for the timely and efficient processing of circuit civil cases and reduction in the pending backlog of civil cases. FL ST 20 J CIR 1.13.

a. The basis for the Civil Case Management Plan is included in FL ST 20 J CIR 1.13, identified in Attachment A as the "Civil Differentiated Case Management (DCM) Procedures and Backlog Reduction Plan," and is incorporated as if fully set forth in FL ST 20 J CIR 1.13. The Civil Case Management Plan is to be used as a model for the purpose of establishing time standards, improving the courts ability to provide early and continuous management of civil cases as required by FL ST J ADMIN Rule 2.545, and to promote uniformity of practice throughout the Twentieth Judicial Circuit. FL ST 20 J CIR 1.13.

b. Full implementation of the Civil DCM Case Management Procedures (Attachment A), including all uniform circuitwide procedures and forms, shall apply to all civil cases filed in Lee and Collier counties, effective January 1, 2011. Even though full implementation may be delayed in Charlotte, Hendry, and Glades counties, all civil time standards and goals, and the use of civil Case Managers and Magistrates to assist trial judges in the process of civil case management and backlog reduction programs, shall be effective circuitwide immediately. FL ST 20 J CIR 1.13.

c. For more information on the civil case management plan, refer to the specific county website and/or see FL ST 20 J CIR 1.13.

D. Documents

1. *Required documents*

a. *Request for production.* Please see the General Requirements section of this document for more information on the contents of the request for production.

i. *Notices to persons with disabilities.* See the Format section of this KeyRules document for further information.

b. *Certificate of service.* A certificate of service of the interrogatories shall be filed, giving the date of service and the name of the party to whom they were directed. FL ST RCP Rule 1.340(e). When any attorney certifies in substance: "I certify that a copy hereof has been furnished to (here insert name or names and addresses used for service) by (e-mail) (delivery) (mail) (fax) on .... (date) ....______________ Attorney" the certificate is taken as prima facie proof of such service in compliance with FL ST J ADMIN Rule 2.516. FL ST J ADMIN Rule 2.516(f).

2. *Supplemental documents*

a. *Notice of intent to serve subpoena/Subpoena.* Please see the General Requirements section of this document for more information.

E. Format

1. *Documents; Type and size.* Documents subject to the exceptions set forth in FL ST J ADMIN Rule

2.525(d) shall be filed on recycled paper measuring eight and one half by eleven (8 1/2 by 11) inches. For purposes of FL ST J ADMIN Rule 2.520, paper is recycled if it contains a minimum content of fifty (50) percent waste paper. Xerographic reduction of legal-size (eight and one half by fourteen (8 1/2 by 14) inches) documents to letter size (eight and one half by eleven (8 1/2 by 11) inches) is prohibited. All other documents filed by electronic transmission shall be filed in a format capable of being printed in a format consistent with the provisions of FL ST J ADMIN Rule 2.250. FL ST J ADMIN Rule 2.520(b); FL ST 20 J CIR 2.9.

a. *Exhibits.* Any exhibit or attachment filed with pleadings or papers may be filed in its original size. FL ST J ADMIN Rule 2.520(c); FL ST 20 J CIR 2.9.

b. *Recording space.* On all papers and documents prepared and filed by the court or by any party to a proceeding which are to be recorded in the public records of any county, including but not limited to final money judgments and notices of lis pendens, a three (3) inch by three (3) inch space at the top right-hand corner on the first page and a one (1) inch by three (3) inch space at the top right-hand corner on each subsequent page shall be left blank and reserved for use by the clerk of court. FL ST J ADMIN Rule 2.520(d).

   i. *Exceptions to recording space.* Any papers or documents created by persons or entities over which the filing party has no control, including but not limited to wills, codicils, trusts, or other testamentary documents; documents prepared or executed by any public officer; documents prepared, executed, acknowledged, or proved outside of the State of Florida; or documents created by State or Federal government agencies, may be filed without the space required by FL ST J ADMIN Rule 2.520. FL ST J ADMIN Rule 2.520(e).

c. *Noncompliance.* No clerk of court is permitted to refuse to file any document or paper because of noncompliance with the Florida Rules of Judicial Administration. However, upon request of the clerk of court, noncomplying documents must be resubmitted in accordance with the formatting rules. FL ST J ADMIN Rule 2.520(f).

   i. When time of filing is critical, the Clerk shall accept pleadings, motions, petitions, briefs, notices, orders, judgments, decrees, opinions, or other papers or official documents on other than eight and one half by eleven (8 1/2 by 11) inch paper but shall then require that the document be resubmitted to comply with FL ST J ADMIN Rule 2.520. FL ST 20 J CIR 2.9.

2. *Caption.* Every pleading, motion, order, judgment, or other paper shall have a caption containing the name of the court, the file number, and except for in rem proceedings, including forfeiture proceedings, the name of the first party on each side with an appropriate indication of other parties, and a designation identifying the party filing it and its nature or the nature of the order, as the case may be. In any in rem proceeding, every pleading, motion, order, judgment, or other paper shall have a caption containing the name of the court, the file number, the style "In re" (followed by the name or general description of the property), and a designation of the person or entity filing it and its nature or the nature of the order, as the case may be. In an in rem forfeiture proceeding, the style shall be "In re forfeiture of" (followed by the name of the general description of the property). All papers filed in the action shall be styled in such a manner as to indicate clearly the subject matter of the paper and the party requesting or obtaining relief. FL ST RCP Rule 1.100(c)(1).

3. *Writing and written defined.* Writing or written means a document containing information, an application, or a stipulation. FL ST RCP Rule 1.080(c).

4. *Rule abbreviations*

   a. The Florida Rules of Civil Procedure and shall be abbreviated as Fla.R.Civ.P. FL ST RCP Rule 1.010.

   b. The Florida Rules of Judicial Administration shall be abbreviated as Fla. R. Jud. Admin. FL ST J ADMIN Rule 2.110.

5. *Nonverification.* Except when otherwise specifically provided by the Florida Rules of Civil Procedure or an applicable statute, every pleading or other document of a party represented by an attorney need not be verified or accompanied by an affidavit. FL ST RCP Rule 1.030; FL ST J ADMIN Rule 2.515(a).

6. *Attorney signature*

   a. *Attorney signature.* Every pleading and other document of a party represented by an attorney shall be

signed by at least one (1) attorney of record in that attorney's individual name whose current record Florida Bar address, telephone number, including area code, primary e-mail address and secondary e-mail addresses, if any, and Florida Bar number shall be stated, and who shall be duly licensed to practice law in Florida or who shall have received permission to appear in the particular case as provided in FL ST J ADMIN Rule 2.510. FL ST J ADMIN Rule 2.515(a).

i. The attorney may be required by the court to give the address of, and to vouch for the attorney's authority to represent, the party. FL ST J ADMIN Rule 2.515(a).

ii. The signature of an attorney shall constitute a certificate by the attorney that the attorney has read the pleading or other document; that to the best of the attorney's knowledge, information, and belief there is good ground to support it; and that it is not interposed for delay. FL ST J ADMIN Rule 2.515(a).

iii. If a pleading is not signed or is signed with intent to defeat the purpose of FL ST J ADMIN Rule 2.515, it may be stricken and the action may proceed as though the pleading or other document had not been served. FL ST J ADMIN Rule 2.515(a).

b. *Pro se litigant signature.* A party who is not represented by an attorney shall sign any pleading or other paper and state the party's address and telephone number, including area code. FL ST J ADMIN Rule 2.515(b).

c. *Form of signature*

i. The signatures required on pleadings and documents by FL ST J ADMIN Rule 2.515(a) and FL ST J ADMIN Rule 2.515(b) may be:

- Original signatures;
- Original signatures that have been reproduced by electronic means, such as on electronically transmitted documents or photocopied documents;
- Electronic signatures using the "/s/," "s/," or "/s" formats by or at the direction of the person signing; or
- Any other signature format authorized by general law, so long as the clerk where the proceeding is pending has the capability of receiving and has obtained approval from the Supreme Court of Florida to accept pleadings and documents with that signature format. FL ST J ADMIN Rule 2.515(c)(1).

ii. An attorney, party, or other person who files a pleading or paper by electronic transmission that does not contain the original signature of that attorney, party, or other person shall file that identical pleading or paper in paper form containing an original signature of that attorney, party, or other person (hereinafter called the follow-up filing) immediately thereafter. The follow-up filing is not required if the Supreme Court of Florida has entered an order directing the clerk of court to discontinue accepting the follow-up filing. FL ST J ADMIN Rule 2.515(c)(2).

7. *Forms*

a. *Process.* The forms of process, notice of lis pendens, and notice of action provided in the Florida Rules of Civil Procedure are sufficient. Variations from the forms do not void process or notices that are otherwise sufficient. FL ST RCP Rule 1.900(a).

b. *Other forms.* The other forms provided in the Florida Rules of Civil Procedure are sufficient for the matters that are covered by them. So long as the substance is expressed without prolixity, the forms may be varied to meet the facts of a particular case. FL ST RCP Rule 1.900(b).

c. *Formal matters.* Captions, except for the designation of the paper, are omitted from the forms provided in the Florida Rules of Civil Procedure. A general form of caption is the first form provided. Signatures are omitted from pleadings and motions. FL ST RCP Rule 1.900(c).

8. *Notices to persons with disabilities.* All notices of court proceedings to be held in a public facility, and all process compelling appearance at such proceedings, shall include the following statement in bold face, fourteen (14) point Times New Roman or Courier font: "If you are a person with a disability who needs any accommodation in order to participate in this proceeding, you are entitled, at no cost to you, to the

provision of certain assistance. Please contact [identify applicable court personnel by name, address, and telephone number] at least seven (7) days before your scheduled court appearance, or immediately upon receiving this notification if the time before the scheduled appearance is less than seven (7) days; if you are hearing or voice impaired, call 711." FL ST J ADMIN Rule 2.540(c)(1). For more information, see FL ST 20 J CIR 2.15.

9. *Minimization of the filing of sensitive information*

   a. *Limitations for court filings.* Unless authorized by FL ST J ADMIN Rule 2.425(b), statute, another rule of court, or the court orders otherwise, designated sensitive information filed with the court must be limited to the following format:

      i. The initials of a person known to be a minor;

      ii. The year of birth of a person's birth date;

      iii. No portion of any: Social security number, Bank account number, Credit card account number, Charge account number, or Debit account number;

      iv. The last four digits of any: Taxpayer identification number (TIN), Employee identification number, Driver's license number, Passport number, Telephone number, Financial account number, except as set forth in FL ST J ADMIN Rule 2.425(a)(3), Brokerage account number, Insurance policy account number, Loan account number, Customer account number, or Patient or health care number;

      v. A truncated version of any: Email address, Computer user name, Password, or Personal identification number (PIN); and

      vi. A truncated version of any other sensitive information as provided by court order. FL ST J ADMIN Rule 2.425(a).

   b. *Exceptions.* FL ST J ADMIN Rule 2.425(a) does not apply to the following:

      i. An account number which identifies the property alleged to be the subject of a proceeding;

      ii. The record of an administrative or agency proceeding;

      iii. The record in appellate or review proceedings;

      iv. The birth date of a minor whenever the birth date is necessary for the court to establish or maintain subject matter jurisdiction;

      v. The name of a minor in any order relating to parental responsibility, time-sharing, or child support;

      vi. The name of a minor in any document or order affecting the minor's ownership of real property;

      vii. The birth date of a party in a writ of attachment or notice to payor;

      viii. In traffic and criminal proceedings: a pro se filing; a court filing that is related to a criminal matter or investigation and that is prepared before the filing of a criminal charge or is not filed as part of any docketed criminal case; an arrest or search warrant or any information in support thereof; a charging document and an affidavit or other documents filed in support of any charging document, including any driving records; a statement of particulars; discovery material introduced into evidence or otherwise filed with the court; and all information necessary for the proper issuance and execution of a subpoena duces tecum;

      ix. Information used by the clerk for case maintenance purposes or the courts for case management purposes; and

      x. Information which is relevant and material to an issue before the court. FL ST J ADMIN Rule 2.425(b).

   c. *Remedies.* Upon motion by a party or interested person or sua sponte by the court, the court may order remedies, sanctions or both for a violation of FL ST J ADMIN Rule 2.425(a). Following notice and an opportunity to respond, the court may impose sanctions if such filing was not made in good faith. FL ST J ADMIN Rule 2.425(c).

   d. *Motions not restricted.* FL ST J ADMIN Rule 2.425 does not restrict a party's right to move for

protective order, to move to file documents under seal, or to request a determination of the confidentiality of records. FL ST J ADMIN Rule 2.425(d).

e. *Application.* FL ST J ADMIN Rule 2.425 does not affect the application of constitutional provisions, statutes, or rules of court regarding confidential information or access to public information. FL ST J ADMIN Rule 2.425(e).

F. Filing and Service Requirements

1. *Court filing of documents and discovery.* Information obtained during discovery shall not be filed with the court until such time as it is filed for good cause. The requirement of good cause is satisfied only where the filing of the information is allowed or required by another applicable rule of procedure or by court order. All filings of discovery documents shall comply with FL ST J ADMIN Rule 2.425. The court shall have the authority to impose sanctions for violation of FL ST RCP Rule 1.280. FL ST RCP Rule 1.280(g).

   a. Unless required by the court, a party shall not file any of the documents or things produced with the response. Documents or things may be filed in compliance with FL ST J ADMIN Rule 2.425 and FL ST RCP Rule 1.280(g) when they should be considered by the court in determining a matter pending before the court. FL ST RCP Rule 1.350(d).

2. *Filing requirements.* All original documents must be filed with the court either before service or immediately thereafter, unless otherwise provided for by general law or other rules. If the original of any bond or other document is not placed in the court file, a certified copy must be so placed by the clerk. FL ST J ADMIN Rule 2.516(d). All documents shall be filed in conformity with the requirements of FL ST J ADMIN Rule 2.525. FL ST RCP Rule 1.080(b). All documents filed in any court shall be filed by electronic transmission in accordance with FL ST J ADMIN Rule 2.525. "Documents" means pleadings, motions, petitions, memoranda, briefs, notices, exhibits, declarations, affidavits, orders, judgments, decrees, writs, opinions, and any other paper or writing submitted to a court. FL ST J ADMIN Rule 2.520(a). All documents that are court records, as defined in FL ST J ADMIN Rule 2.430(a)(1), must be filed by electronic transmission, provided that: (1) the clerk has the ability to accept and retain such documents; (2) the clerk or the chief judge of the circuit has requested permission to accept documents filed by electronic transmission; and (3) the supreme court has entered an order granting permission to the clerk to accept documents filed by electronic transmission. FL ST J ADMIN Rule 2.525(c)(1).

   a. *Definition.* "Electronic transmission of documents" means the sending of information by electronic signals to, by or from a court or clerk, which when received can be transformed and stored or transmitted on paper, microfilm, magnetic storage device, optical imaging system, CD-ROM, flash drive, other electronic data storage system, server, case maintenance system ("CM"), electronic court filing ("ECF") system, statewide or local electronic portal ("e-portal"), or other electronic record keeping system authorized by the supreme court in a format sufficient to communicate the information on the original document in a readable format. Electronic transmission of documents includes electronic mail ("e-mail") and any internet-based transmission procedure, and may include procedures allowing for documents to be signed or verified by electronic means. FL ST J ADMIN Rule 2.525(a).

      i. The filing of documents with the court as required by the Florida Rules of Judicial Administration must be made by filing them with the clerk in accordance with FL ST J ADMIN Rule 2.525, except that the judge may permit documents to be filed with the judge, in which event the judge must note the filing date before him or her on the documents and transmit them to the clerk. The date of filing is that shown on the face of the document by the judge's notation or the clerk's time stamp, whichever is earlier. FL ST J ADMIN Rule 2.516(e).

   b. *Application.* Any court or clerk of the court may accept the electronic transmission of documents for filing after the clerk, together with input from the chief judge of the circuit, has obtained approval of the procedures and program for doing so from the Supreme Court of Florida. FL ST J ADMIN Rule 2.525(b).

   c. *Exceptions*

      i. Paper documents and other submissions may be manually submitted to the clerk or court:

         - When the clerk does not have the ability to accept and retain documents by electronic filing or has not had ECF Procedures approved by the supreme court;

- For filing by any self-represented party or any self-represented nonparty unless specific ECF Procedures provide a means to file documents electronically. However, any self-represented nonparty that is a governmental or public agency and any other agency, partnership, corporation, or business entity acting on behalf of any governmental or public agency may file documents by electronic transmission if such entity has the capability of filing documents electronically;
- For filing by attorneys excused from e-mail service in accordance with FL ST J ADMIN Rule 2.516(b);
- When submitting evidentiary exhibits or filing non-documentary materials;
- When the filing involves documents in excess of twenty-five (25) megabytes (25MB) in size. For such filings, documents may be transmitted using an electronic storage medium that the clerk has the ability to accept, which may include a CD-ROM, flash drive, or similar storage medium;
- When filed in open court, as permitted by the court;
- When paper filing is permitted by any approved statewide or local ECF procedures; and
- If any court determines that justice so requires. FL ST J ADMIN Rule 2.525(d).

ii. Any document in paper form submitted under FL ST J ADMIN Rule 2.525(d) is filed when it is received by the clerk or court and the clerk shall immediately thereafter convert any filed paper document to an electronic document. "Convert to an electronic document" means optically capturing an image of a paper document and using character recognition software to recover as much of the document's text as practicable and then indexing and storing the document in the official court file. FL ST J ADMIN Rule 2.525(c)(4).

iii. Any storage medium submitted under FL ST J ADMIN Rule 2.525(d)(5) is filed when received by the clerk or court and the clerk shall immediately thereafter transfer the electronic documents from the storage device to the official court file. FL ST J ADMIN Rule 2.525(c)(5).

iv. If the filer of any paper document authorized under FL ST J ADMIN Rule 2.525(d) provides a self-addressed, postage-paid envelope for return of the paper document after it is converted to electronic form by the clerk, the clerk shall place the paper document in the envelope and deposit it in the mail. Except when a paper document is required to be maintained, the clerk may recycle any filed paper document that is not to be returned to the filer. FL ST J ADMIN Rule 2.525(c)(6).

v. The clerk may convert any paper document filed before the effective date of FL ST J ADMIN Rule 2.525 to an electronic document. Unless the clerk is required to maintain the paper document, if the paper document has been converted to an electronic document by the clerk, the paper document is no longer part of the official court file and may be removed and recycled. FL ST J ADMIN Rule 2.525(c)(7).

d. *Official court file.* For information on what constitutes the official court file, please see FL ST J ADMIN Rule 2.525(c)(2), FL ST J ADMIN Rule 2.525(c)(3).

e. *Administration.* All attorneys, parties, or other persons using this rule to file documents are required to make arrangements with the court or clerk for the payment of any charges authorized by general law or the supreme court before filing any document by electronic transmission. FL ST J ADMIN Rule 2.525(f)(2).

f. *Filing date.* The filing date for an electronically transmitted document is the date and time that such filing is acknowledged by an electronic stamp or otherwise, pursuant to any procedure set forth in any ECF Procedures approved by the supreme court, or the date the last page of such filing is received by the court or clerk. FL ST J ADMIN Rule 2.525(f)(3).

g. *Accessibility.* All documents transmitted in any electronic form under FL ST J ADMIN Rule 2.525 must comply with the accessibility requirements of FL ST J ADMIN Rule 2.526. FL ST J ADMIN Rule 2.525(g).

3. *Service requirements.* Every pleading subsequent to the initial pleading, all orders, and every other

document filed in the action must be served in conformity with the requirements of FL ST J ADMIN Rule 2.516. FL ST RCP Rule 1.080(a).

a. *Service; Generally.* The timing and manner of service should not be used to the disadvantage of the party receiving the papers. FL ST 20 J CIR 2.20(IV)(C)(1).

   i. Papers and memoranda of law should not be served at court appearances without advance notice to opposing counsel and should not be served so close to a court appearance so as to inhibit the ability of opposing counsel to prepare for that appearance or to respond to the papers. Should the attorney do so, the court is urged to take appropriate action in response, including continuing the matter to allow opposing counsel to prepare and respond. FL ST 20 J CIR 2.20(IV)(C)(2).

   ii. Papers should not be served in order to take advantage of an opponent's known absence from the office or at a time or in a manner designed to inconvenience an adversary, such as late on Friday afternoon or the day preceding a secular or religious holiday. FL ST 20 J CIR 2.20(IV)(C)(3).

   iii. Service should be made personally or by courtesy copy facsimile transmission when it is likely that service by mail, even when allowed, will prejudice the opposing party or will not provide the opposing party with a reasonable time to respond. FL ST 20 J CIR 2.20(IV)(C)(4).

b. *Service; When required.* Unless the court otherwise orders, or a statute or supreme court administrative order specifies a different means of service, every pleading subsequent to the initial pleading and every other document filed in any court proceeding, except applications for witness subpoenas and documents served by formal notice or required to be served in the manner provided for service of formal notice, must be served in accordance with FL ST J ADMIN Rule 2.516 on each party. No service need be made on parties against whom a default has been entered, except that pleadings asserting new or additional claims against them must be served in the manner provided for service of summons. FL ST J ADMIN Rule 2.516(a).

   i. *Copies of court submissions.* Copies of any submissions to the court (such as correspondence, memoranda of law, motions, case law, etc.) should simultaneously be provided to opposing counsel by substantially the same method of delivery by which they are provided to the court. For example, if a memorandum of law is hand-delivered to the court, at substantially the same time a copy should be hand-delivered or faxed to opposing counsel. FL ST 20 J CIR 2.20(IV)(J)(4).

c. *Service; How made.* When service is required or permitted to be made upon a party represented by an attorney, service must be made upon the attorney unless service upon the party is ordered by the court. FL ST J ADMIN Rule 2.516(b).

   i. *Service by electronic mail ("e-mail").* All documents required or permitted to be served on another party must be served by e-mail, unless FL ST J ADMIN Rule 2.516 otherwise provides. When, in addition to service by e-mail, the sender also utilizes another means of service provided for in FL ST J ADMIN Rule 2.516(b)(2), any differing time limits and other provisions applicable to that other means of service control. FL ST J ADMIN Rule 2.516(b)(1). Any document electronically transmitted to a court or clerk must also be served on all parties and interested persons in accordance with the applicable rules of court. FL ST J ADMIN Rule 2.525(e)(2).

      - *Service on attorneys.* Upon appearing in a proceeding, an attorney must serve a designation of a primary e-mail address and may designate no more than two (2) secondary e-mail addresses. Thereafter, service must be directed to all designated e-mail addresses in that proceeding. Every document filed by an attorney thereafter must include the primary e-mail address of that attorney and any secondary e-mail addresses. If an attorney does not designate any e-mail address for service, documents may be served on that attorney at the e-mail address on record with The Florida Bar. FL ST J ADMIN Rule 2.516(b)(1)(A).

      - *Exception to e-mail service on attorneys.* Service by an attorney on another attorney must be made by e-mail unless excused by the court. Upon motion by an attorney demonstrating

that the attorney has no e-mail account and lacks access to the Internet at the attorney's office, the court may excuse the attorney from the requirements of e-mail service. Service on and by an attorney excused by the court from e-mail service must be by the means provided in FL ST J ADMIN Rule 2.516(b)(2). FL ST J ADMIN Rule 2.516(b)(1)(B).

- *Service on and by parties not represented by an attorney.* Any party not represented by an attorney may serve a designation of a primary e-mail address and also may designate no more than two (2) secondary e-mail addresses to which service must be directed in that proceeding by the means provided in FL ST J ADMIN Rule 2.516(b)(1). If a party not represented by an attorney does not designate an e-mail address for service in a proceeding, service on and by that party must be by the means provided in FL ST J ADMIN Rule 2.516(b)(2). FL ST J ADMIN Rule 2.516(b)(1)(C).
- *Time of service.* Service by e-mail is complete when it is sent. FL ST J ADMIN Rule 2.516(b)(1)(D). An e-mail is deemed served on the date it is sent. FL ST J ADMIN Rule 2.516(b)(1)(D)(i). If the sender learns that the e-mail did not reach the address of the person to be served, the sender must immediately send another copy by e-mail, or by a means authorized by FL ST J ADMIN Rule 2.516(b)(2). FL ST J ADMIN Rule 2.516(b)(1)(D)(ii). E-mail service is treated as service by mail for the computation of time. FL ST J ADMIN Rule 2.516(b)(1)(D)(iii).

ii. *Format of e-mail for service.* Service of a document by e-mail is made by attaching a copy of the document in PDF format to an e-mail sent to all addresses designated by the attorney or party. FL ST J ADMIN Rule 2.516(b)(1)(E).

- All documents served by e-mail must be attached to an e-mail message containing a subject line beginning with the words "SERVICE OF COURT DOCUMENT" in all capital letters, followed by the case number of the proceeding in which the documents are being served. FL ST J ADMIN Rule 2.516(b)(1)(E)(i).
- The body of the e-mail must identify the court in which the proceeding is pending, the case number, the name of the initial party on each side, the title of each document served with that e-mail, and the sender's name and telephone number. FL ST J ADMIN Rule 2.516(b)(1)(E)(ii).
- Any document served by e-mail may be signed by the "/s/" format, as long as the filed original is signed in accordance with the applicable rule of procedure. FL ST J ADMIN Rule 2.516(b)(1)(E)(iii).
- Any e-mail which, together with its attached documents, exceeds five megabytes (5MB) in size, must be divided and sent as separate e-mails, no one of which may exceed five megabytes (5MB) in size and each of which must be sequentially numbered in the subject line. FL ST J ADMIN Rule 2.516(b)(1)(E)(iv).

iii. *Service by other means.* In addition to, and not in lieu of, service by e-mail, service may also be made upon attorneys by any of the means specified in FL ST J ADMIN Rule 2.516(b)(2). Service on and by all parties who are not represented by an attorney and who do not designate an e-mail address, and on and by all attorneys excused from e-mail service, must be made by delivering a copy of the document or by mailing it to the party or attorney at their last known address or, if no address is known, by leaving it with the clerk of the court. Service by mail is complete upon mailing. Delivery of a copy within FL ST J ADMIN Rule 2.516 is complete upon:

- Handing it to the attorney or to the party,
- Leaving it at the attorney's or party's office with a clerk or other person in charge thereof,
- If there is no one in charge, leaving it in a conspicuous place therein,
- If the office is closed or the person to be served has no office, leaving it at the person's usual place of abode with some person of his or her family above fifteen (15) years of age and informing such person of the contents, or
- Transmitting it by facsimile to the attorney's or party's office with a cover sheet containing

the sender's name, firm, address, telephone number, and facsimile number, and the number of pages transmitted. When service is made by facsimile, a copy must also be served by any other method permitted by FL ST J ADMIN Rule 2.516. Facsimile service occurs when transmission is complete. FL ST J ADMIN Rule 2.516(b)(2)(A) through FL ST J ADMIN Rule 2.516(b)(2)(E).

- Service by delivery after 5:00 p.m. must be deemed to have been made by mailing on the date of delivery. FL ST J ADMIN Rule 2.516(b)(2)(F).

d. *Service; Numerous defendants.* In actions when the parties are unusually numerous, the court may regulate the service contemplated by the Florida Rules of Judicial Administration on motion or on its own initiative in such manner as may be found to be just and reasonable. FL ST J ADMIN Rule 2.516(c).

e. *Service by clerk.* Service of notices and other documents required to be made by the clerk must also be done as provided in FL ST J ADMIN Rule 2.516(b). FL ST J ADMIN Rule 2.516(g).

G. Hearings

1. There is no hearing required or contemplated with regard to requests for production of documents in the Florida Rules of Civil Procedure.

H. Forms

1. Official Request for Production of Documents Forms for Florida

a. Caption. FL ST RCP Form 1.901.

b. Subpoena duces tecum for trial. FL ST RCP Form 1.911.

c. Notice of production from nonparty. FL ST RCP Form 1.921.

d. Subpoena duces tecum without deposition. FL ST RCP Form 1.922.

2. Request for Production of Documents Forms for Florida

a. Request for production; Documents. FL-PRACFORM § 8:29.

b. Request for inspection; Documents, deposition. FL-PRACFORM § 8:30.

c. Request for inspection; Tangible things. FL-PRACFORM § 8:31.

d. Request for entry; Real property. FL-PRACFORM § 8:32.

e. Request for production; Documents, response. FL-PRACFORM § 8:33.

f. Request for inspection; Response, tangible things. FL-PRACFORM § 8:34.

g. Request for entry; Response, land and buildings. FL-PRACFORM § 8:35.

h. Production of documents; Nonparty, notice. FL-PRACFORM § 8:36.

i. Production of documents; Nonparty, objection. FL-PRACFORM § 8:37.

j. Request; Production of documents for inspection and copying. FL-PP § 3:115.

k. Notice of request for production from nonparty. FL-PP § 3:116.

l. Request; For permission to enter on land; To inspect and photograph. FL-PP § 3:127.

I. Checklist

(I) ❑ Matters to be considered by requesting party

(a) ❑ Required documents

(1) ❑ Request

(2) ❑ Certificate of service

(b) ❑ Supplemental documents

(1) ❑ Notice of intent to serve subpoena/Subpoena

(c) ❑ Time for request

(1) ❑ Without leave of court the request may be served on the plaintiff after commencement of the

action and on any other party with or after service of the process and initial pleading on that party

(2) ❑ A party desiring production under FL ST RCP Rule 1.351 shall serve notice as provided in FL ST RCP Rule 1.080 on every other party of the intent to serve a subpoena under FL ST RCP Rule 1.351 at least ten (10) days before the subpoena is issued if service is by delivery and fifteen (15) days before the subpoena is issued if the service is by mail or e-mail

(II) ❑ Matters to be considered by responding party

(a) ❑ Required documents

(1) ❑ Response to request

(2) ❑ Certificate of service

(b) ❑ Supplemental documents

(1) ❑ Objections

(c) ❑ Time for response

(1) ❑ The party to whom the request is directed shall serve a written response within thirty (30) days after service of the request, except that a defendant may serve a response within forty-five (45) days after service of the process and initial pleading on that defendant; the court may allow a shorter or longer time

Requests, Notices and Applications
Request for Admissions

Document Last Updated January 2013

A. Applicable Rules

1. *State rules*

a. Nonverification of pleadings. FL ST RCP Rule 1.030.

b. Service and filing of pleadings, orders, and documents. FL ST RCP Rule 1.080.

c. Time. FL ST RCP Rule 1.090.

d. Pleadings and motions. FL ST RCP Rule 1.100.

e. Pretrial procedure. FL ST RCP Rule 1.200.

f. General provisions governing discovery. FL ST RCP Rule 1.280.

g. Interrogatories to parties. FL ST RCP Rule 1.340.

h. Examination of persons. FL ST RCP Rule 1.360.

i. Requests for admission. FL ST RCP Rule 1.370.

j. Failure to make discovery; Sanctions. FL ST RCP Rule 1.380.

k. Depositions of expert witnesses. FL ST RCP Rule 1.390.

l. Relief from judgment, decrees, or orders. FL ST RCP Rule 1.540.

m. Forms. FL ST RCP Rule 1.900.

n. Minimization of the filing of sensitive information. FL ST J ADMIN Rule 2.425.

o. Retention of court records. FL ST J ADMIN Rule 2.430.

p. Foreign attorneys. FL ST J ADMIN Rule 2.510.

q. Signature of attorneys and parties. FL ST J ADMIN Rule 2.515.

r. Paper. FL ST J ADMIN Rule 2.520.

s. Electronic filing. FL ST J ADMIN Rule 2.525.

   t. Accessibility of information and technology. FL ST J ADMIN Rule 2.526.
   u. Requests for accommodations by persons with disabilities. FL ST J ADMIN Rule 2.540.
   v. Case management. FL ST J ADMIN Rule 2.545.

2. *Local rules*
   a. Exclusions from mediation. FL ST 20 J CIR 1.9.
   b. Establishment and implementation of civil case management plan. FL ST 20 J CIR 1.13.
   c. Size of paper. FL ST 20 J CIR 2.9.
   d. Americans with Disabilities Act; Notification of court proceedings. FL ST 20 J CIR 2.15.
   e. Standards of professional courtesy and conduct and establishment of peer review program. FL ST 20 J CIR 2.20.

B. Timing

1. *Request for admission.* Without leave of court the request may be served upon the plaintiff after commencement of the action and upon any other party with or after service of the process and initial pleading upon that party. FL ST RCP Rule 1.370(a).
2. *Sequence and timing of discovery.* Except as provided in FL ST RCP Rule 1.280(b)(5) or unless the court upon motion for the convenience of parties and witnesses and in the interest of justice orders otherwise, methods of discovery may be used in any sequence, and the fact that a party is conducting discovery, whether by deposition or otherwise, shall not delay any other party's discovery. FL ST RCP Rule 1.280(e).
3. *Computation of time*
   a. *Generally.* Computation of time shall be governed by FL ST J ADMIN Rule 2.514. FL ST RCP Rule 1.090(a). The following rules apply in computing time periods specified in any rule of procedure, local rule, court order, or statute that does not specify a method of computing time. FL ST J ADMIN Rule 2.514(a).
      i. *Period stated in days or a longer unit.* When the period is stated in days or a longer unit of time (A) exclude the day of the event that triggers the period; (B) count every day, including intermediate Saturdays, Sundays, and legal holidays; and (C) include the last day of the period, but if the last day is a Saturday, Sunday, or legal holiday, or falls within any period of time extended through an order of the chief justice under FL ST J ADMIN Rule 2.205(a)(2)(B)(iv), the period continues to run until the end of the next day that is not a Saturday, Sunday, or legal holiday and does not fall within any period of time extended through an order of the chief justice. FL ST J ADMIN Rule 2.514(a)(1).
      ii. *Period stated in hours.* When the period is stated in hours (A) begin counting immediately on the occurrence of the event that triggers the period; (B) count every hour, including hours during intermediate Saturdays, Sundays, and legal holidays; and (C) if the period would end on a Saturday, Sunday, or legal holiday, or during any period of time extended through an order of the chief justice under FL ST J ADMIN Rule 2.205(a)(2)(B)(iv), the period continues to run until the same time on the next day that is not a Saturday, Sunday, or legal holiday and does not fall within any period of time extended through an order of the chief justice. FL ST J ADMIN Rule 2.514(a)(2).
      iii. *Period stated in days less than seven (7) days.* When the period stated in days is less than seven (7) days, intermediate Saturdays, Sundays, and legal holidays shall be excluded in the computation. FL ST J ADMIN Rule 2.514(a)(3).
      iv. *"Last day" defined.* Unless a different time is set by a statute, local rule, or court order, the last day ends (A) for electronic filing or for service by any means, at midnight; and (B) for filing by other means, when the clerk's office is scheduled to close. FL ST J ADMIN Rule 2.514(a)(4).
      v. *"Next day" defined.* The "next day" is determined by continuing to count forward when the period is measured after an event and backward when measured before an event. FL ST J ADMIN Rule 2.514(a)(5).

vi. *"Legal holiday" defined.* "Legal holiday" means (A) the day set aside by FL ST § 110.117, for observing New Year's Day, Martin Luther King, Jr.'s Birthday, Memorial Day, Independence Day, Labor Day, Veterans' Day, Thanksgiving Day, the Friday after Thanksgiving Day, or Christmas Day, and (B) any day observed as a holiday by the clerk's office or as designated by the chief judge. FL ST J ADMIN Rule 2.514(a)(6).

b. *Additional time after service by mail or e-mail.* When a party may or must act within a specified time after service and service is made by mail or e-mail, five (5) days are added after the period that would otherwise expire under FL ST J ADMIN Rule 2.514(a). FL ST J ADMIN Rule 2.514(b).

c. *Enlargement.* When an act is required or allowed to be done at or within a specified time by order of court, by the Florida Rules of Civil Procedure, or by notice given thereunder, for cause shown the court at any time in its discretion (1) with or without notice, may order the period enlarged if request therefor is made before the expiration of the period originally prescribed or as extended by a previous order, or (2) upon motion made and notice after the expiration of the specified period, may permit the act to be done when failure to act was the result of excusable neglect, but it may not extend the time for making a motion for new trial, for rehearing, or to alter or amend a judgment; making a motion for relief from a judgment under FL ST RCP Rule 1.540(b); taking an appeal or filing a petition for certiorari; or making a motion for a directed verdict. FL ST RCP Rule 1.090(b).

d. *Unaffected by expiration of term.* The period of time provided for the doing of any act or the taking of any proceeding shall not be affected or limited by the continued existence or expiration of a term of court. The continued existence or expiration of a term of court in no way affects the power of a court to do any act or take any proceeding in any action which is or has been pending before it. FL ST RCP Rule 1.090(c).

C. General Requirements

1. *General provisions governing discovery*

a. *Discovery methods.* Parties may obtain discovery by one or more of the following methods: depositions upon oral examination or written questions; written interrogatories; production of documents or things or permission to enter upon land or other property for inspection and other purposes; physical and mental examinations; and requests for admission. Unless the court orders otherwise and under FL ST RCP Rule 1.280(c), the frequency of use of these methods is not limited, except as provided in FL ST RCP Rule 1.200, FL ST RCP Rule 1.340, and FL ST RCP Rule 1.370. FL ST RCP Rule 1.280(a).

b. *Scope of discovery.* Unless otherwise limited by order of the court in accordance with the Florida Rules of Civil Procedure, the scope of discovery is as follows:

i. *In general.* Parties may obtain discovery regarding any matter, not privileged, that is relevant to the subject matter of the pending action, whether it relates to the claim or defense of the party seeking discovery or the claim or defense of any other party, including the existence, description, nature, custody, condition, and location of any books, documents, or other tangible things and the identity and location of persons having knowledge of any discoverable matter. It is not ground for objection that the information sought will be inadmissible at the trial if the information sought appears reasonably calculated to lead to the discovery of admissible evidence. FL ST RCP Rule 1.280(b)(1).

- Attorneys should pursue discovery requests that are reasonably related to the matter at issue. FL ST 20 J CIR 2.20(IV)(E)(1).

ii. *Indemnity agreements.* A party may obtain discovery of the existence and contents of any agreement under which any person may be liable to satisfy part or all of a judgment that may be entered in the action or to indemnify or to reimburse a party for payments made to satisfy the judgment. Information concerning the agreement is not admissible in evidence at trial by reason of disclosure. FL ST RCP Rule 1.280(b)(2).

iii. *Electronically stored information.* A party may obtain discovery of electronically stored information in accordance with the Florida Rules of Civil Procedure. FL ST RCP Rule 1.280(b)(3).

iv. *Trial preparation; Materials.* Subject to the provisions of FL ST RCP Rule 1.280(b)(5), a party may obtain discovery of documents and tangible things otherwise discoverable under FL ST RCP Rule 1.280(b)(1) and prepared in anticipation of litigation or for trial by or for another party or by or for that party's representative, including that party's attorney, consultant, surety, indemnitor, insurer, or agent, only upon a showing that the party seeking discovery has need of the materials in the preparation of the case and is unable without undue hardship to obtain the substantial equivalent of the materials by other means. FL ST RCP Rule 1.280(b)(4).

- In ordering discovery of the materials when the required showing has been made, the court shall protect against disclosure of the mental impressions, conclusions, opinions, or legal theories of an attorney or other representative of a party concerning the litigation. FL ST RCP Rule 1.280(b)(4).
- Without the required showing a party may obtain a copy of a statement concerning the action or its subject matter previously made by that party. FL ST RCP Rule 1.280(b)(4).
- Upon request without the required showing a person not a party may obtain a copy of a statement concerning the action or its subject matter previously made by that person. If the request is refused, the person may move for an order to obtain a copy. The provisions of FL ST RCP Rule 1.380(a)(5) apply to the award of expenses incurred as a result of making the motion. FL ST RCP Rule 1.280(b)(4).
- For purposes of FL ST RCP Rule 1.280(b)(4), a statement previously made is a written statement signed or otherwise adopted or approved by the person making it, or a stenographic, mechanical, electrical, or other recording or transcription of it that is a substantially verbatim recital of an oral statement by the person making it and contemporaneously recorded. FL ST RCP Rule 1.280(b)(4).

v. *Trial preparation; Experts.* Discovery of facts known and opinions held by experts, otherwise discoverable under the provisions of FL ST RCP Rule 1.280(b)(1) and acquired or developed in anticipation of litigation or for trial, may be obtained only as follows:

- By interrogatories a party may require any other party to identify each person whom the other party expects to call as an expert witness at trial and to state the subject matter on which the expert is expected to testify, and to state the substance of the facts and opinions to which the expert is expected to testify and a summary of the grounds for each opinion. FL ST RCP Rule 1.280(b)(5)(A)(i).
- Any person disclosed by interrogatories or otherwise as a person expected to be called as an expert witness at trial may be deposed in accordance with FL ST RCP Rule 1.390 without motion or order of court. FL ST RCP Rule 1.280(b)(5)(A)(ii).
- A party may obtain the following discovery regarding any person disclosed by interrogatories or otherwise as a person expected to be called as an expert witness at trial: The scope of employment in the pending case and the compensation for such service, FL ST RCP Rule 1.280(b)(5)(A)(iii)(1); The expert's general litigation experience, including the percentage of work performed for plaintiffs and defendants, FL ST RCP Rule 1.280(b)(5)(A)(iii)(2); The identity of other cases, within a reasonable time period, in which the expert has testified by deposition or at trial, FL ST RCP Rule 1.280(b)(5)(A)(iii)(3); An approximation of the portion of the expert's involvement as an expert witness, which may be based on the number of hours, percentage of hours, or percentage of earned income derived from serving as an expert witness; however, the expert shall not be required to disclose his or her earnings as an expert witness or income derived from other services. FL ST RCP Rule 1.280(b)(5)(A)(iii)(4).
- An expert may be required to produce financial and business records only under the most unusual or compelling circumstances and may not be compelled to compile or produce nonexistent documents. Upon motion, the court may order further discovery by other means, subject to such restrictions as to scope and other provisions pursuant to FL ST RCP Rule 1.280(b)(5)(C) concerning fees and expenses as the court may deem appropriate. FL ST RCP Rule 1.280(b)(5).

- A party may discover facts known or opinions held by an expert who has been retained or specially employed by another party in anticipation of litigation or preparation for trial and who is not expected to be called as a witness at trial, only as provided in FL ST RCP Rule 1.360(b) or upon a showing of exceptional circumstances under which it is impracticable for the party seeking discovery to obtain facts or opinions on the same subject by other means. FL ST RCP Rule 1.280(b)(5)(B).
- Unless manifest injustice would result, the court shall require that the party seeking discovery pay the expert a reasonable fee for time spent in responding to discovery under FL ST RCP Rule 1.280(b)(5)(A) and FL ST RCP Rule 1.280(b)(5)(B); and concerning discovery from an expert obtained under FL ST RCP Rule 1.280(b)(5)(A) the court may require, and concerning discovery obtained under FL ST RCP Rule 1.280(b)(5)(B) shall require, the party seeking discovery to pay the other party a fair part of the fees and expenses reasonably incurred by the latter party in obtaining facts and opinions from the expert. FL ST RCP Rule 1.280(b)(5)(C).
- As used in the Florida Rules of Civil Procedure an expert shall be an expert witness as defined in FL ST RCP Rule 1.390(a). FL ST RCP Rule 1.280(b)(5)(D).

vi. *Claims to privilege or protection.* When a party withholds information otherwise discoverable under the Florida Rules of Civil Procedure by claiming that it is privileged or subject to protection as trial preparation material, the party shall make the claim expressly and shall describe the nature of the documents, communications, or things not produced or disclosed in a manner that, without revealing information itself privileged or protected, will enable other parties to assess the applicability of the privilege or protection. FL ST RCP Rule 1.280(b)(6).

c. *Limitations on discovery of electronically stored information*

i. A person may object to discovery of electronically stored information from sources that the person identifies as not reasonably accessible because of burden or cost. On motion to compel discovery or for a protective order, the person from whom discovery is sought must show that the information sought or the format requested is not reasonably accessible because of undue burden or cost. If that showing is made, the court may nonetheless order the discovery from such sources or in such formats if the requesting party shows good cause. The court may specify conditions of the discovery, including ordering that some or all of the expenses incurred by the person from whom discovery is sought be paid by the party seeking the discovery. FL ST RCP Rule 1.280(d)(1).

ii. In determining any motion involving discovery of electronically stored information, the court must limit the frequency or extent of discovery otherwise allowed by the Florida Rules of Civil Procedure if it determines that (i) the discovery sought is unreasonably cumulative or duplicative, or can be obtained from another source or in another manner that is more convenient, less burdensome, or less expensive; or (ii) the burden or expense of the discovery outweighs its likely benefit, considering the needs of the case, the amount in controversy, the parties' resources, the importance of the issues at stake in the action, and the importance of the discovery in resolving the issues. FL ST RCP Rule 1.280(d)(2).

d. *Use of discovery.* Attorneys should not use discovery for the purpose of causing undue delay or obtaining unfair advantage. FL ST 20 J CIR 2.20(IV)(E)(2). Attorneys should use discovery to ascertain information, to perpetuate testimony, or to obtain documents or things necessary for the prosecution or defense of an action. Attorneys should never use discovery as a means of harassment, intimidation or to impose an inordinate burden or expense. FL ST 20 J CIR 2.20(IV)(E)(3).

e. For information on inadvertent disclosure of privileged materials, see FL ST RCP Rule 1.285.

2. *Requests for admission.* It is an advantage to use requests for admission. The biggest advantage is that if an adversary denies a request for an admission and the denied matter is later proven to be true, the adversary may have to pay the costs of proving the genuineness of the document or the truth of the matter requested to be admitted. FL-PP § 3:143.

a. *Scope.* A party may serve upon any other party a written request for the admission of the truth of any matters within the scope of FL ST RCP Rule 1.280(b) set forth in the request that relate to statements or opinions of fact or of the application of law to fact, including the genuineness of any documents described in the request. FL ST RCP Rule 1.370(a).

b. *Copies of documents.* Copies of documents shall be served with the request unless they have been or are otherwise furnished or made available for inspection and copying. FL ST RCP Rule 1.370(a).

c. *Number of requests.* The request for admission shall not exceed thirty (30) requests, including all subparts, unless the court permits a larger number on motion and notice and for good cause, or the parties propounding and responding to the requests stipulate to a larger number. Each matter of which an admission is requested shall be separately set forth. FL ST RCP Rule 1.370(a).

d. *Sufficiency of responses.* The party who has requested the admissions may move to determine the sufficiency of the answers or objections. Unless the court determines that an objection is justified, it shall order that an answer be served. If the court determines that an answer does not comply with the requirements of this rule, it may order either that the matter is admitted or that an amended answer be served. Instead of these orders the court may determine that final disposition of the request be made at a pretrial conference or at a designated time before trial. The provisions of FL ST RCP Rule 1.380(a)(4) apply to the award of expenses incurred in relation to the motion. FL ST RCP Rule 1.370(a).

e. *Effect of admission.* Any matter admitted under FL ST RCP Rule 1.370 is conclusively established unless the court on motion permits withdrawal or amendment of the admission. Subject to FL ST RCP Rule 1.200 governing amendment of a pretrial order, the court may permit withdrawal or amendment when the presentation of the merits of the action will be subserved by it and the party who obtained the admission fails to satisfy the court that withdrawal or amendment will prejudice that party in maintaining an action or defense on the merits. Any admission made by a party under this rule is for the purpose of the pending action only and is not an admission for any other purpose nor may it be used against that party in any other proceeding. FL ST RCP Rule 1.370(b).

f. *Answer requirements.* The matter is admitted unless the party to whom the request is directed serves upon the party requesting the admission a written answer or objection addressed to the matter within thirty (30) days after service of the request or such shorter or longer time as the court may allow but, unless the court shortens the time, a defendant shall not be required to serve answers or objections before the expiration of forty-five (45) days after service of the process and initial pleading upon the defendant. If objection is made, the reasons shall be stated. The answer shall specifically deny the matter or set forth in detail the reasons why the answering party cannot truthfully admit or deny the matter. A denial shall fairly meet the substance of the requested admission, and when good faith requires that a party qualify an answer or deny only a part of the matter of which an admission is requested, the party shall specify so much of it as is true and qualify or deny the remainder. An answering party may not give lack of information or knowledge as a reason for failure to admit or deny unless that party states that that party has made reasonable inquiry and that the information known or readily obtainable by that party is insufficient to enable that party to admit or deny. A party who considers that a matter of which an admission has been requested presents a genuine issue for trial may not object to the request on that ground alone; the party may deny the matter or set forth reasons why the party cannot admit or deny it, subject to FL ST RCP Rule 1.380(c). FL ST RCP Rule 1.370(a).

3. *Arbitration and mediation.* Attorneys are encouraged to utilize arbitration, mediation or other forms of alternative dispute resolution if economically feasible. FL ST 20 J CIR 2.20(IV)(N)(3).

a. *Referral to arbitration and mediation.* Except as hereinafter provided or as otherwise prohibited by law, the presiding judge may enter an order referring all or any part of a contested civil matter to mediation or arbitration. The parties to any contested civil matter may file a written stipulation to mediate or arbitrate any issue between them at any time. Such stipulation shall be incorporated into the order of referral. FL ST RCP Rule 1.700(a).

b. *Arbitration*

i. *Exclusions.* A civil action shall be ordered to arbitration or arbitration in conjunction with mediation upon stipulation of the parties. A civil action may be ordered to arbitration or arbitration in conjunction with mediation upon motion of any party or by the court, if the judge determines the action to be of such a nature that arbitration could be of benefit to the litigants or the court. FL ST RCP Rule 1.800.

- Under no circumstances may the following categories of actions be referred to arbitration: (1) bond estreatures; (2) habeas corpus or other extraordinary writs; (3) bond validations; (4) civil or criminal contempt; (5) such other matters as may be specified by order of the chief judge in the circuit. FL ST RCP Rule 1.800.

ii. For more information regarding arbitration, please see FL ST RCP Rule 1.810; FL ST RCP Rule 1.820; FL ST RCP Rule 1.830.

c. *Mediation.* For more information regarding mediation, please see FL ST RCP Rule 1.710; FL ST RCP Rule 1.720; FL ST RCP Rule 1.730; FL ST RCP Rule 1.750; and FL ST 20 J CIR 1.9.

4. *Rules of court*

a. *Rules of civil procedure.* The Florida Rules of Civil Procedure apply to all actions of a civil nature and all special statutory proceedings in the circuit courts and county courts except those to which the Florida Probate Rules, the Florida Family Law Rules of Procedure, or the Small Claims Rules apply. FL ST RCP Rule 1.010.

i. The form, content, procedure, and time for pleading in all special statutory proceedings shall be as prescribed by the statutes governing the proceeding unless the Florida Rules of Civil Procedure specifically provide to the contrary. FL ST RCP Rule 1.010.

ii. The Florida Rules of Civil Procedure shall be construed to secure the just, speedy, and inexpensive determination of every action. FL ST RCP Rule 1.010.

b. *Rules of judicial administration.* The Florida Rules of Judicial Administration shall apply to administrative matters in all courts to which the Florida Rules of Judicial Administration are applicable by their terms. The Florida Rules of Judicial Administration shall be construed to secure the speedy and inexpensive determination of every proceeding to which they are applicable. The Florida Rules of Judicial Administration shall supersede all conflicting rules and statutes. FL ST J ADMIN Rule 2.110.

5. *Civil case management plan.* There is established within the Twentieth Judicial Circuit a Civil Case Management Plan applicable to circuit civil cases, which will be administered by the Administrative Office of the Courts through direction of the Circuit Administrative Judges in each county for the implementation of enhanced case management procedures and guidelines for the timely and efficient processing of circuit civil cases and reduction in the pending backlog of civil cases. FL ST 20 J CIR 1.13.

a. The basis for the Civil Case Management Plan is included in FL ST 20 J CIR 1.13, identified in Attachment A as the "Civil Differentiated Case Management (DCM) Procedures and Backlog Reduction Plan," and is incorporated as if fully set forth in FL ST 20 J CIR 1.13. The Civil Case Management Plan is to be used as a model for the purpose of establishing time standards, improving the courts ability to provide early and continuous management of civil cases as required by FL ST J ADMIN Rule 2.545, and to promote uniformity of practice throughout the Twentieth Judicial Circuit. FL ST 20 J CIR 1.13.

b. Full implementation of the Civil DCM Case Management Procedures (Attachment A), including all uniform circuitwide procedures and forms, shall apply to all civil cases filed in Lee and Collier counties, effective January 1, 2011. Even though full implementation may be delayed in Charlotte, Hendry, and Glades counties, all civil time standards and goals, and the use of civil Case Managers and Magistrates to assist trial judges in the process of civil case management and backlog reduction programs, shall be effective circuitwide immediately. FL ST 20 J CIR 1.13.

c. For more information on the civil case management plan, refer to the specific county website and/or see FL ST 20 J CIR 1.13.

D. Documents

1. *Required documents*

   a. *Request for admission.* Please see the General Requirements section of this document for more information on the contents of the request for admission.

      i. *Notices to persons with disabilities.* See the Format section of this KeyRules document for further information.

   b. *Copies of documents.* Copies of documents shall be served with the request unless they have been or are otherwise furnished or made available for inspection and copying. FL ST RCP Rule 1.370(a).

   c. *Certificate of service.* A certificate of service of the interrogatories shall be filed, giving the date of service and the name of the party to whom they were directed. FL ST RCP Rule 1.340(e). When any attorney certifies in substance: "I certify that a copy hereof has been furnished to (here insert name or names and addresses used for service) by (e-mail) (delivery) (mail) (fax) on .... (date) ....______________ Attorney" the certificate is taken as prima facie proof of such service in compliance with FL ST J ADMIN Rule 2.516. FL ST J ADMIN Rule 2.516(f).

E. Format

1. *Documents; Type and size.* Documents subject to the exceptions set forth in FL ST J ADMIN Rule 2.525(d) shall be filed on recycled paper measuring eight and one half by eleven (8 1/2 by 11) inches. For purposes of FL ST J ADMIN Rule 2.520, paper is recycled if it contains a minimum content of fifty (50) percent waste paper. Xerographic reduction of legal-size (eight and one half by fourteen (8 1/2 by 14) inches) documents to letter size (eight and one half by eleven (8 1/2 by 11) inches) is prohibited. All other documents filed by electronic transmission shall be filed in a format capable of being printed in a format consistent with the provisions of FL ST J ADMIN Rule 2.250. FL ST J ADMIN Rule 2.520(b); FL ST 20 J CIR 2.9.

   a. *Exhibits.* Any exhibit or attachment filed with pleadings or papers may be filed in its original size. FL ST J ADMIN Rule 2.520(c); FL ST 20 J CIR 2.9.

   b. *Recording space.* On all papers and documents prepared and filed by the court or by any party to a proceeding which are to be recorded in the public records of any county, including but not limited to final money judgments and notices of lis pendens, a three (3) inch by three (3) inch space at the top right-hand corner on the first page and a one (1) inch by three (3) inch space at the top right-hand corner on each subsequent page shall be left blank and reserved for use by the clerk of court. FL ST J ADMIN Rule 2.520(d).

      i. *Exceptions to recording space.* Any papers or documents created by persons or entities over which the filing party has no control, including but not limited to wills, codicils, trusts, or other testamentary documents; documents prepared or executed by any public officer; documents prepared, executed, acknowledged, or proved outside of the State of Florida; or documents created by State or Federal government agencies, may be filed without the space required by FL ST J ADMIN Rule 2.520. FL ST J ADMIN Rule 2.520(e).

   c. *Noncompliance.* No clerk of court is permitted to refuse to file any document or paper because of noncompliance with the Florida Rules of Judicial Administration. However, upon request of the clerk of court, noncomplying documents must be resubmitted in accordance with the formatting rules. FL ST J ADMIN Rule 2.520(f).

      i. When time of filing is critical, the Clerk shall accept pleadings, motions, petitions, briefs, notices, orders, judgments, decrees, opinions, or other papers or official documents on other than eight and one half by eleven (8 1/2 by 11) inch paper but shall then require that the document be resubmitted to comply with FL ST J ADMIN Rule 2.520. FL ST 20 J CIR 2.9.

2. *Caption.* Every pleading, motion, order, judgment, or other paper shall have a caption containing the name of the court, the file number, and except for in rem proceedings, including forfeiture proceedings, the name of the first party on each side with an appropriate indication of other parties, and a designation identifying the party filing it and its nature or the nature of the order, as the case may be. In any in rem proceeding, every pleading, motion, order, judgment, or other paper shall have a caption containing the

name of the court, the file number, the style "In re" (followed by the name or general description of the property), and a designation of the person or entity filing it and its nature or the nature of the order, as the case may be. In an in rem forfeiture proceeding, the style shall be "In re forfeiture of" (followed by the name of the general description of the property). All papers filed in the action shall be styled in such a manner as to indicate clearly the subject matter of the paper and the party requesting or obtaining relief. FL ST RCP Rule 1.100(c)(1).

3. *Writing and written defined.* Writing or written means a document containing information, an application, or a stipulation. FL ST RCP Rule 1.080(c).
4. *Rule abbreviations*
   a. The Florida Rules of Civil Procedure and shall be abbreviated as Fla.R.Civ.P. FL ST RCP Rule 1.010.
   b. The Florida Rules of Judicial Administration shall be abbreviated as Fla. R. Jud. Admin. FL ST J ADMIN Rule 2.110.
5. *Nonverification.* Except when otherwise specifically provided by the Florida Rules of Civil Procedure or an applicable statute, every pleading or other document of a party represented by an attorney need not be verified or accompanied by an affidavit. FL ST RCP Rule 1.030; FL ST J ADMIN Rule 2.515(a).
6. *Attorney signature*
   a. *Attorney signature.* Every pleading and other document of a party represented by an attorney shall be signed by at least one (1) attorney of record in that attorney's individual name whose current record Florida Bar address, telephone number, including area code, primary e-mail address and secondary e-mail addresses, if any, and Florida Bar number shall be stated, and who shall be duly licensed to practice law in Florida or who shall have received permission to appear in the particular case as provided in FL ST J ADMIN Rule 2.510. FL ST J ADMIN Rule 2.515(a).
      i. The attorney may be required by the court to give the address of, and to vouch for the attorney's authority to represent, the party. FL ST J ADMIN Rule 2.515(a).
      ii. The signature of an attorney shall constitute a certificate by the attorney that the attorney has read the pleading or other document; that to the best of the attorney's knowledge, information, and belief there is good ground to support it; and that it is not interposed for delay. FL ST J ADMIN Rule 2.515(a).
      iii. If a pleading is not signed or is signed with intent to defeat the purpose of FL ST J ADMIN Rule 2.515, it may be stricken and the action may proceed as though the pleading or other document had not been served. FL ST J ADMIN Rule 2.515(a).
   b. *Pro se litigant signature.* A party who is not represented by an attorney shall sign any pleading or other paper and state the party's address and telephone number, including area code. FL ST J ADMIN Rule 2.515(b).
   c. *Form of signature*
      i. The signatures required on pleadings and documents by FL ST J ADMIN Rule 2.515(a) and FL ST J ADMIN Rule 2.515(b) may be:
         - Original signatures;
         - Original signatures that have been reproduced by electronic means, such as on electronically transmitted documents or photocopied documents;
         - Electronic signatures using the "/s/," "s/," or "/s" formats by or at the direction of the person signing; or
         - Any other signature format authorized by general law, so long as the clerk where the proceeding is pending has the capability of receiving and has obtained approval from the Supreme Court of Florida to accept pleadings and documents with that signature format. FL ST J ADMIN Rule 2.515(c)(1).
      ii. An attorney, party, or other person who files a pleading or paper by electronic transmission that does not contain the original signature of that attorney, party, or other person shall file that

identical pleading or paper in paper form containing an original signature of that attorney, party, or other person (hereinafter called the follow-up filing) immediately thereafter. The follow-up filing is not required if the Supreme Court of Florida has entered an order directing the clerk of court to discontinue accepting the follow-up filing. FL ST J ADMIN Rule 2.515(c)(2).

7. *Forms*

   a. *Process.* The forms of process, notice of lis pendens, and notice of action provided in the Florida Rules of Civil Procedure are sufficient. Variations from the forms do not void process or notices that are otherwise sufficient. FL ST RCP Rule 1.900(a).

   b. *Other forms.* The other forms provided in the Florida Rules of Civil Procedure are sufficient for the matters that are covered by them. So long as the substance is expressed without prolixity, the forms may be varied to meet the facts of a particular case. FL ST RCP Rule 1.900(b).

   c. *Formal matters.* Captions, except for the designation of the paper, are omitted from the forms provided in the Florida Rules of Civil Procedure. A general form of caption is the first form provided. Signatures are omitted from pleadings and motions. FL ST RCP Rule 1.900(c).

8. *Notices to persons with disabilities.* All notices of court proceedings to be held in a public facility, and all process compelling appearance at such proceedings, shall include the following statement in bold face, fourteen (14) point Times New Roman or Courier font: "If you are a person with a disability who needs any accommodation in order to participate in this proceeding, you are entitled, at no cost to you, to the provision of certain assistance. Please contact [identify applicable court personnel by name, address, and telephone number] at least seven (7) days before your scheduled court appearance, or immediately upon receiving this notification if the time before the scheduled appearance is less than seven (7) days; if you are hearing or voice impaired, call 711." FL ST J ADMIN Rule 2.540(c)(1). For more information, see FL ST 20 J CIR 2.15.

9. *Minimization of the filing of sensitive information*

   a. *Limitations for court filings.* Unless authorized by FL ST J ADMIN Rule 2.425(b), statute, another rule of court, or the court orders otherwise, designated sensitive information filed with the court must be limited to the following format:

      i. The initials of a person known to be a minor;

      ii. The year of birth of a person's birth date;

      iii. No portion of any: Social security number, Bank account number, Credit card account number, Charge account number, or Debit account number;

      iv. The last four digits of any: Taxpayer identification number (TIN), Employee identification number, Driver's license number, Passport number, Telephone number, Financial account number, except as set forth in FL ST J ADMIN Rule 2.425(a)(3), Brokerage account number, Insurance policy account number, Loan account number, Customer account number, or Patient or health care number;

      v. A truncated version of any: Email address, Computer user name, Password, or Personal identification number (PIN); and

      vi. A truncated version of any other sensitive information as provided by court order. FL ST J ADMIN Rule 2.425(a).

   b. *Exceptions.* FL ST J ADMIN Rule 2.425(a) does not apply to the following:

      i. An account number which identifies the property alleged to be the subject of a proceeding;

      ii. The record of an administrative or agency proceeding;

      iii. The record in appellate or review proceedings;

      iv. The birth date of a minor whenever the birth date is necessary for the court to establish or maintain subject matter jurisdiction;

      v. The name of a minor in any order relating to parental responsibility, time-sharing, or child support;

vi. The name of a minor in any document or order affecting the minor's ownership of real property;

vii. The birth date of a party in a writ of attachment or notice to payor;

viii. In traffic and criminal proceedings: a pro se filing; a court filing that is related to a criminal matter or investigation and that is prepared before the filing of a criminal charge or is not filed as part of any docketed criminal case; an arrest or search warrant or any information in support thereof; a charging document and an affidavit or other documents filed in support of any charging document, including any driving records; a statement of particulars; discovery material introduced into evidence or otherwise filed with the court; and all information necessary for the proper issuance and execution of a subpoena duces tecum;

ix. Information used by the clerk for case maintenance purposes or the courts for case management purposes; and

x. Information which is relevant and material to an issue before the court. FL ST J ADMIN Rule 2.425(b).

c. *Remedies.* Upon motion by a party or interested person or sua sponte by the court, the court may order remedies, sanctions or both for a violation of FL ST J ADMIN Rule 2.425(a). Following notice and an opportunity to respond, the court may impose sanctions if such filing was not made in good faith. FL ST J ADMIN Rule 2.425(c).

d. *Motions not restricted.* FL ST J ADMIN Rule 2.425 does not restrict a party's right to move for protective order, to move to file documents under seal, or to request a determination of the confidentiality of records. FL ST J ADMIN Rule 2.425(d).

e. *Application.* FL ST J ADMIN Rule 2.425 does not affect the application of constitutional provisions, statutes, or rules of court regarding confidential information or access to public information. FL ST J ADMIN Rule 2.425(e).

F. Filing and Service Requirements

1. *Court filing of documents and discovery.* Information obtained during discovery shall not be filed with the court until such time as it is filed for good cause. The requirement of good cause is satisfied only where the filing of the information is allowed or required by another applicable rule of procedure or by court order. All filings of discovery documents shall comply with FL ST J ADMIN Rule 2.425. The court shall have the authority to impose sanctions for violation of FL ST RCP Rule 1.280. FL ST RCP Rule 1.280(g).

2. *Filing requirements.* All original documents must be filed with the court either before service or immediately thereafter, unless otherwise provided for by general law or other rules. If the original of any bond or other document is not placed in the court file, a certified copy must be so placed by the clerk. FL ST J ADMIN Rule 2.516(d). All documents shall be filed in conformity with the requirements of FL ST J ADMIN Rule 2.525. FL ST RCP Rule 1.080(b). All documents filed in any court shall be filed by electronic transmission in accordance with FL ST J ADMIN Rule 2.525. "Documents" means pleadings, motions, petitions, memoranda, briefs, notices, exhibits, declarations, affidavits, orders, judgments, decrees, writs, opinions, and any other paper or writing submitted to a court. FL ST J ADMIN Rule 2.520(a). All documents that are court records, as defined in FL ST J ADMIN Rule 2.430(a)(1), must be filed by electronic transmission, provided that: (1) the clerk has the ability to accept and retain such documents; (2) the clerk or the chief judge of the circuit has requested permission to accept documents filed by electronic transmission; and (3) the supreme court has entered an order granting permission to the clerk to accept documents filed by electronic transmission. FL ST J ADMIN Rule 2.525(c)(1).

a. *Definition.* "Electronic transmission of documents" means the sending of information by electronic signals to, by or from a court or clerk, which when received can be transformed and stored or transmitted on paper, microfilm, magnetic storage device, optical imaging system, CD-ROM, flash drive, other electronic data storage system, server, case maintenance system ("CM"), electronic court filing ("ECF") system, statewide or local electronic portal ("e-portal"), or other electronic record keeping system authorized by the supreme court in a format sufficient to communicate the information on the original document in a readable format. Electronic transmission of documents includes electronic mail ("e-mail") and any internet-based transmission procedure, and may include procedures allowing for documents to be signed or verified by electronic means. FL ST J ADMIN Rule 2.525(a).

i. The filing of documents with the court as required by the Florida Rules of Judicial Administration must be made by filing them with the clerk in accordance with FL ST J ADMIN Rule 2.525, except that the judge may permit documents to be filed with the judge, in which event the judge must note the filing date before him or her on the documents and transmit them to the clerk. The date of filing is that shown on the face of the document by the judge's notation or the clerk's time stamp, whichever is earlier. FL ST J ADMIN Rule 2.516(e).

b. *Application.* Any court or clerk of the court may accept the electronic transmission of documents for filing after the clerk, together with input from the chief judge of the circuit, has obtained approval of the procedures and program for doing so from the Supreme Court of Florida. FL ST J ADMIN Rule 2.525(b).

c. *Exceptions*

i. Paper documents and other submissions may be manually submitted to the clerk or court:

- When the clerk does not have the ability to accept and retain documents by electronic filing or has not had ECF Procedures approved by the supreme court;
- For filing by any self-represented party or any self-represented nonparty unless specific ECF Procedures provide a means to file documents electronically. However, any self-represented nonparty that is a governmental or public agency and any other agency, partnership, corporation, or business entity acting on behalf of any governmental or public agency may file documents by electronic transmission if such entity has the capability of filing documents electronically;
- For filing by attorneys excused from e-mail service in accordance with FL ST J ADMIN Rule 2.516(b);
- When submitting evidentiary exhibits or filing non-documentary materials;
- When the filing involves documents in excess of twenty-five (25) megabytes (25MB) in size. For such filings, documents may be transmitted using an electronic storage medium that the clerk has the ability to accept, which may include a CD-ROM, flash drive, or similar storage medium;
- When filed in open court, as permitted by the court;
- When paper filing is permitted by any approved statewide or local ECF procedures; and
- If any court determines that justice so requires. FL ST J ADMIN Rule 2.525(d).

ii. Any document in paper form submitted under FL ST J ADMIN Rule 2.525(d) is filed when it is received by the clerk or court and the clerk shall immediately thereafter convert any filed paper document to an electronic document. "Convert to an electronic document" means optically capturing an image of a paper document and using character recognition software to recover as much of the document's text as practicable and then indexing and storing the document in the official court file. FL ST J ADMIN Rule 2.525(c)(4).

iii. Any storage medium submitted under FL ST J ADMIN Rule 2.525(d)(5) is filed when received by the clerk or court and the clerk shall immediately thereafter transfer the electronic documents from the storage device to the official court file. FL ST J ADMIN Rule 2.525(c)(5).

iv. If the filer of any paper document authorized under FL ST J ADMIN Rule 2.525(d) provides a self-addressed, postage-paid envelope for return of the paper document after it is converted to electronic form by the clerk, the clerk shall place the paper document in the envelope and deposit it in the mail. Except when a paper document is required to be maintained, the clerk may recycle any filed paper document that is not to be returned to the filer. FL ST J ADMIN Rule 2.525(c)(6).

v. The clerk may convert any paper document filed before the effective date of FL ST J ADMIN Rule 2.525 to an electronic document. Unless the clerk is required to maintain the paper document, if the paper document has been converted to an electronic document by the clerk, the paper document is no longer part of the official court file and may be removed and recycled. FL ST J ADMIN Rule 2.525(c)(7).

d. *Official court file.* For information on what constitutes the official court file, please see FL ST J ADMIN Rule 2.525(c)(2), FL ST J ADMIN Rule 2.525(c)(3).

e. *Administration.* All attorneys, parties, or other persons using this rule to file documents are required to make arrangements with the court or clerk for the payment of any charges authorized by general law or the supreme court before filing any document by electronic transmission. FL ST J ADMIN Rule 2.525(f)(2).

f. *Filing date.* The filing date for an electronically transmitted document is the date and time that such filing is acknowledged by an electronic stamp or otherwise, pursuant to any procedure set forth in any ECF Procedures approved by the supreme court, or the date the last page of such filing is received by the court or clerk. FL ST J ADMIN Rule 2.525(f)(3).

g. *Accessibility.* All documents transmitted in any electronic form under FL ST J ADMIN Rule 2.525 must comply with the accessibility requirements of FL ST J ADMIN Rule 2.526. FL ST J ADMIN Rule 2.525(g).

3. *Service requirements.* Every pleading subsequent to the initial pleading, all orders, and every other document filed in the action must be served in conformity with the requirements of FL ST J ADMIN Rule 2.516. FL ST RCP Rule 1.080(a).

a. *Service; Generally.* The timing and manner of service should not be used to the disadvantage of the party receiving the papers. FL ST 20 J CIR 2.20(IV)(C)(1).

i. Papers and memoranda of law should not be served at court appearances without advance notice to opposing counsel and should not be served so close to a court appearance so as to inhibit the ability of opposing counsel to prepare for that appearance or to respond to the papers. Should the attorney do so, the court is urged to take appropriate action in response, including continuing the matter to allow opposing counsel to prepare and respond. FL ST 20 J CIR 2.20(IV)(C)(2).

ii. Papers should not be served in order to take advantage of an opponent's known absence from the office or at a time or in a manner designed to inconvenience an adversary, such as late on Friday afternoon or the day preceding a secular or religious holiday. FL ST 20 J CIR 2.20(IV)(C)(3).

iii. Service should be made personally or by courtesy copy facsimile transmission when it is likely that service by mail, even when allowed, will prejudice the opposing party or will not provide the opposing party with a reasonable time to respond. FL ST 20 J CIR 2.20(IV)(C)(4).

b. *Service; When required.* Unless the court otherwise orders, or a statute or supreme court administrative order specifies a different means of service, every pleading subsequent to the initial pleading and every other document filed in any court proceeding, except applications for witness subpoenas and documents served by formal notice or required to be served in the manner provided for service of formal notice, must be served in accordance with FL ST J ADMIN Rule 2.516 on each party. No service need be made on parties against whom a default has been entered, except that pleadings asserting new or additional claims against them must be served in the manner provided for service of summons. FL ST J ADMIN Rule 2.516(a).

i. *Copies of court submissions.* Copies of any submissions to the court (such as correspondence, memoranda of law, motions, case law, etc.) should simultaneously be provided to opposing counsel by substantially the same method of delivery by which they are provided to the court. For example, if a memorandum of law is hand-delivered to the court, at substantially the same time a copy should be hand-delivered or faxed to opposing counsel. FL ST 20 J CIR 2.20(IV)(J)(4).

c. *Service; How made.* When service is required or permitted to be made upon a party represented by an attorney, service must be made upon the attorney unless service upon the party is ordered by the court. FL ST J ADMIN Rule 2.516(b).

i. *Service by electronic mail ("e-mail").* All documents required or permitted to be served on

another party must be served by e-mail, unless FL ST J ADMIN Rule 2.516 otherwise provides. When, in addition to service by e-mail, the sender also utilizes another means of service provided for in FL ST J ADMIN Rule 2.516(b)(2), any differing time limits and other provisions applicable to that other means of service control. FL ST J ADMIN Rule 2.516(b)(1). Any document electronically transmitted to a court or clerk must also be served on all parties and interested persons in accordance with the applicable rules of court. FL ST J ADMIN Rule 2.525(e)(2).

- *Service on attorneys.* Upon appearing in a proceeding, an attorney must serve a designation of a primary e-mail address and may designate no more than two (2) secondary e-mail addresses. Thereafter, service must be directed to all designated e-mail addresses in that proceeding. Every document filed by an attorney thereafter must include the primary e-mail address of that attorney and any secondary e-mail addresses. If an attorney does not designate any e-mail address for service, documents may be served on that attorney at the e-mail address on record with The Florida Bar. FL ST J ADMIN Rule 2.516(b)(1)(A).
- *Exception to e-mail service on attorneys.* Service by an attorney on another attorney must be made by e-mail unless excused by the court. Upon motion by an attorney demonstrating that the attorney has no e-mail account and lacks access to the Internet at the attorney's office, the court may excuse the attorney from the requirements of e-mail service. Service on and by an attorney excused by the court from e-mail service must be by the means provided in FL ST J ADMIN Rule 2.516(b)(2). FL ST J ADMIN Rule 2.516(b)(1)(B).
- *Service on and by parties not represented by an attorney.* Any party not represented by an attorney may serve a designation of a primary e-mail address and also may designate no more than two (2) secondary e-mail addresses to which service must be directed in that proceeding by the means provided in FL ST J ADMIN Rule 2.516(b)(1). If a party not represented by an attorney does not designate an e-mail address for service in a proceeding, service on and by that party must be by the means provided in FL ST J ADMIN Rule 2.516(b)(2). FL ST J ADMIN Rule 2.516(b)(1)(C).
- *Time of service.* Service by e-mail is complete when it is sent. FL ST J ADMIN Rule 2.516(b)(1)(D). An e-mail is deemed served on the date it is sent. FL ST J ADMIN Rule 2.516(b)(1)(D)(i). If the sender learns that the e-mail did not reach the address of the person to be served, the sender must immediately send another copy by e-mail, or by a means authorized by FL ST J ADMIN Rule 2.516(b)(2). FL ST J ADMIN Rule 2.516(b)(1)(D)(ii). E-mail service is treated as service by mail for the computation of time. FL ST J ADMIN Rule 2.516(b)(1)(D)(iii).

ii. *Format of e-mail for service.* Service of a document by e-mail is made by attaching a copy of the document in PDF format to an e-mail sent to all addresses designated by the attorney or party. FL ST J ADMIN Rule 2.516(b)(1)(E).

- All documents served by e-mail must be attached to an e-mail message containing a subject line beginning with the words "SERVICE OF COURT DOCUMENT" in all capital letters, followed by the case number of the proceeding in which the documents are being served. FL ST J ADMIN Rule 2.516(b)(1)(E)(i).
- The body of the e-mail must identify the court in which the proceeding is pending, the case number, the name of the initial party on each side, the title of each document served with that e-mail, and the sender's name and telephone number. FL ST J ADMIN Rule 2.516(b)(1)(E)(ii).
- Any document served by e-mail may be signed by the "/s/" format, as long as the filed original is signed in accordance with the applicable rule of procedure. FL ST J ADMIN Rule 2.516(b)(1)(E)(iii).
- Any e-mail which, together with its attached documents, exceeds five megabytes (5MB) in size, must be divided and sent as separate e-mails, no one of which may exceed five megabytes (5MB) in size and each of which must be sequentially numbered in the subject line. FL ST J ADMIN Rule 2.516(b)(1)(E)(iv).

iii. *Service by other means.* In addition to, and not in lieu of, service by e-mail, service may also be made upon attorneys by any of the means specified in FL ST J ADMIN Rule 2.516(b)(2). Service on and by all parties who are not represented by an attorney and who do not designate an e-mail address, and on and by all attorneys excused from e-mail service, must be made by delivering a copy of the document or by mailing it to the party or attorney at their last known address or, if no address is known, by leaving it with the clerk of the court. Service by mail is complete upon mailing. Delivery of a copy within FL ST J ADMIN Rule 2.516 is complete upon:

- Handing it to the attorney or to the party,
- Leaving it at the attorney's or party's office with a clerk or other person in charge thereof,
- If there is no one in charge, leaving it in a conspicuous place therein,
- If the office is closed or the person to be served has no office, leaving it at the person's usual place of abode with some person of his or her family above fifteen (15) years of age and informing such person of the contents, or
- Transmitting it by facsimile to the attorney's or party's office with a cover sheet containing the sender's name, firm, address, telephone number, and facsimile number, and the number of pages transmitted. When service is made by facsimile, a copy must also be served by any other method permitted by FL ST J ADMIN Rule 2.516. Facsimile service occurs when transmission is complete. FL ST J ADMIN Rule 2.516(b)(2)(A) through FL ST J ADMIN Rule 2.516(b)(2)(E).
- Service by delivery after 5:00 p.m. must be deemed to have been made by mailing on the date of delivery. FL ST J ADMIN Rule 2.516(b)(2)(F).

d. *Service; Numerous defendants.* In actions when the parties are unusually numerous, the court may regulate the service contemplated by the Florida Rules of Judicial Administration on motion or on its own initiative in such manner as may be found to be just and reasonable. FL ST J ADMIN Rule 2.516(c).

e. *Service by clerk.* Service of notices and other documents required to be made by the clerk must also be done as provided in FL ST J ADMIN Rule 2.516(b). FL ST J ADMIN Rule 2.516(g).

G. Hearings

1. There is no hearing required or contemplated with regard to requests for admission in the Florida Rules of Civil Procedure.

H. Forms

1. Official Request for Admissions Forms for Florida

a. Caption. FL ST RCP Form 1.901.

2. Request for Admissions Forms for Florida

a. Requests for admissions; Negligence, fall down. FL-PRACFORM § 8:41.

b. Requests for admissions; Promissory note. FL-PRACFORM § 8:42.

c. Requests for admissions; Open account. FL-PRACFORM § 8:43.

d. Requests for admissions; Mortgage foreclosure. FL-PRACFORM § 8:44.

e. Request for admissions; General form. FL-PP § 3:146.

f. Request for admissions; Facts and genuineness of documents. FL-PP § 3:147.

g. Motion; To determine sufficiency of reply to request for admissions. FL-PP § 3:152.

h. Form for request for admissions. FL-RCPF R 1.370(5).

i. Form for request for admissions (another form). FL-RCPF R 1.370(6).

j. Form for request for admissions served concurrently with interrogatories. FL-RCPF R 1.370(7).

k. Form for request for admissions as to factual situation and refinement of issues. FL-RCPF R 1.370(9).

l. Form for request to admit party uses electronic data storage. FL-RCPF R 1.370(10).

I. Checklist

(I) ❑ Matters to be considered by requesting party

(a) ❑ Required documents

(1) ❑ Request

(2) ❑ Copies of documents

(3) ❑ Certificate of service

(b) ❑ Time for request

(1) ❑ Without leave of court the request may be served upon the plaintiff after commencement of the action and upon any other party with or after service of the process and initial pleading upon that party

(II) ❑ Matters to be considered by responding party

(a) ❑ Required documents

(1) ❑ Response to request

(2) ❑ Certificate of service

(b) ❑ Time for response

(1) ❑ The party to whom the request is directed shall serve a written response within thirty (30) days after service of the request, except that a defendant may serve a response within forty-five (45) days after service of the process and initial pleading on that defendant

Requests, Notices and Applications
Notice of Deposition

Document Last Updated January 2013

A. Applicable Rules

1. *State rules*

a. Pleadings and motions. FL ST RCP Rule 1.100.

b. Depositions before action or pending appeal. FL ST RCP Rule 1.290.

c. Persons before whom depositions may be taken. FL ST RCP Rule 1.300.

d. Depositions upon oral examination. FL ST RCP Rule 1.310.

e. Depositions upon written questions. FL ST RCP Rule 1.320.

f. Use of depositions in court proceedings. FL ST RCP Rule 1.330.

g. Nonverification of pleadings. FL ST RCP Rule 1.030.

h. Service and filing of pleadings, orders, and documents. FL ST RCP Rule 1.080.

i. Time. FL ST RCP Rule 1.090.

j. General provisions governing discovery. FL ST RCP Rule 1.280.

k. Failure to make discovery; Sanctions. FL ST RCP Rule 1.380.

l. Depositions of expert witnesses. FL ST RCP Rule 1.390.

m. Relief from judgment, decrees, or orders. FL ST RCP Rule 1.540.

n. Forms. FL ST RCP Rule 1.900.

o. Minimization of the filing of sensitive information. FL ST J ADMIN Rule 2.425.

p. Retention of court records. FL ST J ADMIN Rule 2.430.

q. Foreign attorneys. FL ST J ADMIN Rule 2.510.
r. Signature of attorneys and parties. FL ST J ADMIN Rule 2.515.
s. Paper. FL ST J ADMIN Rule 2.520.
t. Electronic filing. FL ST J ADMIN Rule 2.525.
u. Accessibility of information and technology. FL ST J ADMIN Rule 2.526.
v. Notices to persons with disabilities. FL ST J ADMIN Rule 2.540.
w. Case management. FL ST J ADMIN Rule 2.545.

2. *Local rules*
   a. Exclusions from mediation. FL ST 20 J CIR 1.9.
   b. Establishment and implementation of civil case management plan. FL ST 20 J CIR 1.13.
   c. Size of paper. FL ST 20 J CIR 2.9.
   d. Americans with Disabilities Act; Notification of court proceedings. FL ST 20 J CIR 2.15.
   e. Standards of professional courtesy and conduct and establishment of peer review program. FL ST 20 J CIR 2.20.

B. Timing

1. *Depositions upon oral examination.* After commencement of the action any party may take the testimony of any person, including a party, by deposition upon oral examination. Leave of court, granted with or without notice, must be obtained only if the plaintiff seeks to take a deposition within thirty (30) days after service of the process and initial pleading upon any defendant, except that leave is not required (1) if a defendant has served a notice of taking deposition or otherwise sought discovery, or (2) if special notice is given as provided in FL ST RCP Rule 1.310(b)(2). The attendance of witnesses may be compelled by subpoena as provided in FL ST RCP Rule 1.410. The deposition of a person confined in prison may be taken only by leave of court on such terms as the court prescribes. FL ST RCP Rule 1.310(a). A party desiring to take the deposition of any person upon oral examination shall give reasonable notice in writing to every other party to the action. FL ST RCP Rule 1.310(b)(1).
2. *Depositions upon written questions.* After commencement of the action any party may take the testimony of any person, including a party, by deposition upon written questions. The attendance of witnesses may be compelled by the use of subpoena as provided in FL ST RCP Rule 1.410. The deposition of a person confined in prison may be taken only by leave of court on such terms as the court prescribes. Within thrity (30) days after the notice and written questions are served, a party may serve cross questions upon all other parties. Within ten (10) days after being served with cross questions, a party may serve redirect questions upon all other parties. Within ten (10) days after being served with redirect questions, a party may serve recross questions upon all other parties. The court may for cause shown enlarge or shorten the time. FL ST RCP Rule 1.320(a).
3. *Depositions before action or pending appeal.* For information on petitions and motions for depositions before an action or pending appeal, please see the General Requirements section below.
4. *General notice of deposition timing.* Except in emergency situations, attorneys should provide opposing counsel, parties, witnesses, and other affected persons, sufficient notice of depositions, hearings and other proceedings. FL ST 20 J CIR 2.20(IV)(B)(1).
   a. As a general rule, notice should be provided (not including time for service) no less than five (5) business days for instate depositions, and ten (10) business days for out-of-state depositions. FL ST 20 J CIR 2.20(IV)(B)(1).
5. *Sequence and timing of discovery.* Except as provided in FL ST RCP Rule 1.280(b)(5) or unless the court upon motion for the convenience of parties and witnesses and in the interest of justice orders otherwise, methods of discovery may be used in any sequence, and the fact that a party is conducting discovery, whether by deposition or otherwise, shall not delay any other party's discovery. FL ST RCP Rule 1.280(e).
6. *Computation of time*
   a. *Generally.* Computation of time shall be governed by FL ST J ADMIN Rule 2.514. FL ST RCP Rule

1.090(a). The following rules apply in computing time periods specified in any rule of procedure, local rule, court order, or statute that does not specify a method of computing time. FL ST J ADMIN Rule 2.514(a).

i. *Period stated in days or a longer unit.* When the period is stated in days or a longer unit of time (A) exclude the day of the event that triggers the period; (B) count every day, including intermediate Saturdays, Sundays, and legal holidays; and (C) include the last day of the period, but if the last day is a Saturday, Sunday, or legal holiday, or falls within any period of time extended through an order of the chief justice under FL ST J ADMIN Rule 2.205(a)(2)(B)(iv), the period continues to run until the end of the next day that is not a Saturday, Sunday, or legal holiday and does not fall within any period of time extended through an order of the chief justice. FL ST J ADMIN Rule 2.514(a)(1).

ii. *Period stated in hours.* When the period is stated in hours (A) begin counting immediately on the occurrence of the event that triggers the period; (B) count every hour, including hours during intermediate Saturdays, Sundays, and legal holidays; and (C) if the period would end on a Saturday, Sunday, or legal holiday, or during any period of time extended through an order of the chief justice under FL ST J ADMIN Rule 2.205(a)(2)(B)(iv), the period continues to run until the same time on the next day that is not a Saturday, Sunday, or legal holiday and does not fall within any period of time extended through an order of the chief justice. FL ST J ADMIN Rule 2.514(a)(2).

iii. *Period stated in days less than seven (7) days.* When the period stated in days is less than seven (7) days, intermediate Saturdays, Sundays, and legal holidays shall be excluded in the computation. FL ST J ADMIN Rule 2.514(a)(3).

iv. *"Last day" defined.* Unless a different time is set by a statute, local rule, or court order, the last day ends (A) for electronic filing or for service by any means, at midnight; and (B) for filing by other means, when the clerk's office is scheduled to close. FL ST J ADMIN Rule 2.514(a)(4).

v. *"Next day" defined.* The "next day" is determined by continuing to count forward when the period is measured after an event and backward when measured before an event. FL ST J ADMIN Rule 2.514(a)(5).

vi. *"Legal holiday" defined.* "Legal holiday" means (A) the day set aside by FL ST § 110.117, for observing New Year's Day, Martin Luther King, Jr.'s Birthday, Memorial Day, Independence Day, Labor Day, Veterans' Day, Thanksgiving Day, the Friday after Thanksgiving Day, or Christmas Day, and (B) any day observed as a holiday by the clerk's office or as designated by the chief judge. FL ST J ADMIN Rule 2.514(a)(6).

b. *Additional time after service by mail or e-mail.* When a party may or must act within a specified time after service and service is made by mail or e-mail, five (5) days are added after the period that would otherwise expire under FL ST J ADMIN Rule 2.514(a). FL ST J ADMIN Rule 2.514(b).

c. *Enlargement.* When an act is required or allowed to be done at or within a specified time by order of court, by the Florida Rules of Civil Procedure, or by notice given thereunder, for cause shown the court at any time in its discretion (1) with or without notice, may order the period enlarged if request therefor is made before the expiration of the period originally prescribed or as extended by a previous order, or (2) upon motion made and notice after the expiration of the specified period, may permit the act to be done when failure to act was the result of excusable neglect, but it may not extend the time for making a motion for new trial, for rehearing, or to alter or amend a judgment; making a motion for relief from a judgment under FL ST RCP Rule 1.540(b); taking an appeal or filing a petition for certiorari; or making a motion for a directed verdict. FL ST RCP Rule 1.090(b).

d. *Unaffected by expiration of term.* The period of time provided for the doing of any act or the taking of any proceeding shall not be affected or limited by the continued existence or expiration of a term of court. The continued existence or expiration of a term of court in no way affects the power of a court to do any act or take any proceeding in any action which is or has been pending before it. FL ST RCP Rule 1.090(c).

C. General Requirements

1. *General provisions governing discovery*
   a. *Discovery methods.* Parties may obtain discovery by one or more of the following methods: depositions upon oral examination or written questions; written interrogatories; production of documents or things or permission to enter upon land or other property for inspection and other purposes; physical and mental examinations; and requests for admission. Unless the court orders otherwise and under FL ST RCP Rule 1.280(c), the frequency of use of these methods is not limited, except as provided in FL ST RCP Rule 1.200, FL ST RCP Rule 1.340, and FL ST RCP Rule 1.370. FL ST RCP Rule 1.280(a).
   b. *Scope of discovery.* Unless otherwise limited by order of the court in accordance with the Florida Rules of Civil Procedure, the scope of discovery is as follows:
      i. *In general.* Parties may obtain discovery regarding any matter, not privileged, that is relevant to the subject matter of the pending action, whether it relates to the claim or defense of the party seeking discovery or the claim or defense of any other party, including the existence, description, nature, custody, condition, and location of any books, documents, or other tangible things and the identity and location of persons having knowledge of any discoverable matter. It is not ground for objection that the information sought will be inadmissible at the trial if the information sought appears reasonably calculated to lead to the discovery of admissible evidence. FL ST RCP Rule 1.280(b)(1).
         - Attorneys should pursue discovery requests that are reasonably related to the matter at issue. FL ST 20 J CIR 2.20(IV)(E)(1).
      ii. *Indemnity agreements.* A party may obtain discovery of the existence and contents of any agreement under which any person may be liable to satisfy part or all of a judgment that may be entered in the action or to indemnify or to reimburse a party for payments made to satisfy the judgment. Information concerning the agreement is not admissible in evidence at trial by reason of disclosure. FL ST RCP Rule 1.280(b)(2).
      iii. *Electronically stored information.* A party may obtain discovery of electronically stored information in accordance with the Florida Rules of Civil Procedure. FL ST RCP Rule 1.280(b)(3).
      iv. *Trial preparation; Materials.* Subject to the provisions of FL ST RCP Rule 1.280(b)(5), a party may obtain discovery of documents and tangible things otherwise discoverable under FL ST RCP Rule 1.280(b)(1) and prepared in anticipation of litigation or for trial by or for another party or by or for that party's representative, including that party's attorney, consultant, surety, indemnitor, insurer, or agent, only upon a showing that the party seeking discovery has need of the materials in the preparation of the case and is unable without undue hardship to obtain the substantial equivalent of the materials by other means. FL ST RCP Rule 1.280(b)(4).
         - In ordering discovery of the materials when the required showing has been made, the court shall protect against disclosure of the mental impressions, conclusions, opinions, or legal theories of an attorney or other representative of a party concerning the litigation. FL ST RCP Rule 1.280(b)(4).
         - Without the required showing a party may obtain a copy of a statement concerning the action or its subject matter previously made by that party. FL ST RCP Rule 1.280(b)(4).
         - Upon request without the required showing a person not a party may obtain a copy of a statement concerning the action or its subject matter previously made by that person. If the request is refused, the person may move for an order to obtain a copy. The provisions of FL ST RCP Rule 1.380(a)(5) apply to the award of expenses incurred as a result of making the motion. FL ST RCP Rule 1.280(b)(4).
         - For purposes of FL ST RCP Rule 1.280(b)(4), a statement previously made is a written statement signed or otherwise adopted or approved by the person making it, or a stenographic, mechanical, electrical, or other recording or transcription of it that is a substantially verbatim recital of an oral statement by the person making it and contemporaneously recorded. FL ST RCP Rule 1.280(b)(4).

v. *Trial preparation; Experts.* Discovery of facts known and opinions held by experts, otherwise discoverable under the provisions of FL ST RCP Rule 1.280(b)(1) and acquired or developed in anticipation of litigation or for trial, may be obtained only as follows:

- By interrogatories a party may require any other party to identify each person whom the other party expects to call as an expert witness at trial and to state the subject matter on which the expert is expected to testify, and to state the substance of the facts and opinions to which the expert is expected to testify and a summary of the grounds for each opinion. FL ST RCP Rule 1.280(b)(5)(A)(i).
- Any person disclosed by interrogatories or otherwise as a person expected to be called as an expert witness at trial may be deposed in accordance with FL ST RCP Rule 1.390 without motion or order of court. FL ST RCP Rule 1.280(b)(5)(A)(ii).
- A party may obtain the following discovery regarding any person disclosed by interrogatories or otherwise as a person expected to be called as an expert witness at trial: The scope of employment in the pending case and the compensation for such service, FL ST RCP Rule 1.280(b)(5)(A)(iii)(1); The expert's general litigation experience, including the percentage of work performed for plaintiffs and defendants, FL ST RCP Rule 1.280(b)(5)(A)(iii)(2); The identity of other cases, within a reasonable time period, in which the expert has testified by deposition or at trial, FL ST RCP Rule 1.280(b)(5)(A)(iii)(3); An approximation of the portion of the expert's involvement as an expert witness, which may be based on the number of hours, percentage of hours, or percentage of earned income derived from serving as an expert witness; however, the expert shall not be required to disclose his or her earnings as an expert witness or income derived from other services. FL ST RCP Rule 1.280(b)(5)(A)(iii)(4).
- An expert may be required to produce financial and business records only under the most unusual or compelling circumstances and may not be compelled to compile or produce nonexistent documents. Upon motion, the court may order further discovery by other means, subject to such restrictions as to scope and other provisions pursuant to FL ST RCP Rule 1.280(b)(5)(C) concerning fees and expenses as the court may deem appropriate. FL ST RCP Rule 1.280(b)(5).
- A party may discover facts known or opinions held by an expert who has been retained or specially employed by another party in anticipation of litigation or preparation for trial and who is not expected to be called as a witness at trial, only as provided in FL ST RCP Rule 1.360(b) or upon a showing of exceptional circumstances under which it is impracticable for the party seeking discovery to obtain facts or opinions on the same subject by other means. FL ST RCP Rule 1.280(b)(5)(B).
- Unless manifest injustice would result, the court shall require that the party seeking discovery pay the expert a reasonable fee for time spent in responding to discovery under FL ST RCP Rule 1.280(b)(5)(A) and FL ST RCP Rule 1.280(b)(5)(B); and concerning discovery from an expert obtained under FL ST RCP Rule 1.280(b)(5)(A) the court may require, and concerning discovery obtained under FL ST RCP Rule 1.280(b)(5)(B) shall require, the party seeking discovery to pay the other party a fair part of the fees and expenses reasonably incurred by the latter party in obtaining facts and opinions from the expert. FL ST RCP Rule 1.280(b)(5)(C).
- As used in the Florida Rules of Civil Procedure an expert shall be an expert witness as defined in FL ST RCP Rule 1.390(a). FL ST RCP Rule 1.280(b)(5)(D).

vi. *Claims to privilege or protection.* When a party withholds information otherwise discoverable under the Florida Rules of Civil Procedure by claiming that it is privileged or subject to protection as trial preparation material, the party shall make the claim expressly and shall describe the nature of the documents, communications, or things not produced or disclosed in a manner that, without revealing information itself privileged or protected, will enable other parties to assess the applicability of the privilege or protection. FL ST RCP Rule 1.280(b)(6).

c. *Limitations on discovery of electronically stored information*

i. A person may object to discovery of electronically stored information from sources that the person identifies as not reasonably accessible because of burden or cost. On motion to compel discovery or for a protective order, the person from whom discovery is sought must show that the information sought or the format requested is not reasonably accessible because of undue burden or cost. If that showing is made, the court may nonetheless order the discovery from such sources or in such formats if the requesting party shows good cause. The court may specify conditions of the discovery, including ordering that some or all of the expenses incurred by the person from whom discovery is sought be paid by the party seeking the discovery. FL ST RCP Rule 1.280(d)(1).

ii. In determining any motion involving discovery of electronically stored information, the court must limit the frequency or extent of discovery otherwise allowed by the Florida Rules of Civil Procedure if it determines that (i) the discovery sought is unreasonably cumulative or duplicative, or can be obtained from another source or in another manner that is more convenient, less burdensome, or less expensive; or (ii) the burden or expense of the discovery outweighs its likely benefit, considering the needs of the case, the amount in controversy, the parties' resources, the importance of the issues at stake in the action, and the importance of the discovery in resolving the issues. FL ST RCP Rule 1.280(d)(2).

d. *Use of discovery.* Attorneys should not use discovery for the purpose of causing undue delay or obtaining unfair advantage. FL ST 20 J CIR 2.20(IV)(E)(2). Attorneys should use discovery to ascertain information, to perpetuate testimony, or to obtain documents or things necessary for the prosecution or defense of an action. Attorneys should never use discovery as a means of harassment, intimidation or to impose an inordinate burden or expense. FL ST 20 J CIR 2.20(IV)(E)(3).

e. For information on inadvertent disclosure of privileged materials, see FL ST RCP Rule 1.285.

2. *Notice of deposition*

a. *Upon oral examination.* A party desiring to take the deposition of any person upon oral examination shall give reasonable notice in writing to every other party to the action. The notice shall state the time and place for taking the deposition and the name and address of each person to be examined, if known, and, if the name is not known, a general description sufficient to identify the person or the particular class or group to which the person belongs. If a subpoena duces tecum is to be served on the person to be examined, the designation of the materials to be produced under the subpoena shall be attached to or included in the notice. FL ST RCP Rule 1.310(b)(1).

b. *Upon written examination.* A party desiring to take a deposition upon written questions shall serve a notice stating: (1) the name and address of the person who is to answer them, if known, and, if the name is not known, a general description sufficient to identify the person or the particular class or group to which that person belongs, and (2) the name or descriptive title and address of the officer before whom the deposition is to be taken. FL ST RCP Rule 1.320(a).

3. *When leave of court required.* Leave of court, granted with or without notice, must be obtained only if the plaintiff seeks to take a deposition within thirty (30) days after service of the process and initial pleading upon any defendant, except that leave is not required if a defendant has served a notice of taking deposition or otherwise sought discovery. FL ST RCP Rule 1.310(a).

a. *Exceptions.* Leave of court is not required for the taking of a deposition by plaintiff if the notice states that the person to be examined is about to go out of the state and will be unavailable for examination unless a deposition is taken before expiration of the thirty (30) day period. If a party shows that when served with notice under FL ST RCP Rule 1.310(b) that party was unable through the exercise of diligence to obtain counsel to represent the party at the taking of the deposition, the deposition may not be used against that party. FL ST RCP Rule 1.310(b)(2).

b. *Persons in prison.* The deposition of a person confined in prison may be taken only by leave of court on such terms as the court prescribes. FL ST RCP Rule 1.310(a); FL ST RCP Rule 1.320(a).

4. *Deposition procedure*

a. *Scheduling.* Except in emergency situations, attorneys should make a good faith effort to communicate with opposing counsel prior to scheduling depositions, hearings and other proceedings, so as to schedule them at times that are mutually convenient for all interested persons. Further, a sufficient time should be reserved to permit a complete presentation by counsel for all parties. FL ST 20 J CIR 2.20(IV)(B)(1).

i. *Generally.* When scheduling a deposition, attorneys should make a good faith effort to schedule enough time to complete the deposition without adjournment, unless otherwise stipulated with opposing counsel. FL ST 20 J CIR 2.20(IV)(B)(1).

- In scheduling depositions, reasonable consideration should be given to accommodating schedules of opposing counsel and of the deponent, where it is possible to do so without prejudicing the client's rights. FL ST 20 J CIR 2.20(IV)(F)(1).
- When a deposition is noticed by another party in the reasonably near future, counsel should ordinarily not notice another deposition for an earlier date without the agreement of opposing counsel. FL ST 20 J CIR 2.20(IV)(F)(2).

ii. *Scheduling conflict.* Attorneys should call potential scheduling problems to the attention of those affected, including the court, as soon as they become apparent and should avoid last minute cancellations. FL ST 20 J CIR 2.20(IV)(B)(12). Attorneys should notify opposing counsel, the court, and others affected, of scheduling conflicts as soon as they become apparent. FL ST 20 J CIR 2.20(IV)(B)(7). Further, attorneys should cooperate with one another regarding all reasonable rescheduling requests that do not prejudice their clients or unduly delay a proceeding. FL ST 20 J CIR 2.20(IV)(B)(7).

- Attorneys should make requests for scheduling changes only when necessary and should not request reschedulings, cancellations, extensions or postponements solely for the purpose of delay or obtaining unfair advantage. FL ST 20 J CIR 2.20(IV)(B)(13).
- Counsel should not attempt to delay a deposition for dilatory purposes. Delays should occur only if necessary to meet real scheduling problems. FL ST 20 J CIR 2.20(IV)(F)(3).

b. *Who may take depositions.* Depositions may be taken before any notary public or judicial officer or before any officer authorized by the statutes of Florida to take acknowledgments or proof of executions of deeds or by any person appointed by the court in which the action is pending. FL ST RCP Rule 1.300(a).

i. *In foreign countries.* In a foreign country depositions may be taken: on notice before a person authorized to administer oaths in the place in which the examination is held, either by the law thereof or by the law of Florida or of the United States; before a person commissioned by the court, and a person so commissioned shall have the power by virtue of the commission to administer any necessary oath and take testimony; or pursuant to a letter rogatory. FL ST RCP Rule 1.300(b).

ii. *Selection by stipulation.* If the parties so stipulate in writing, depositions may be taken before any person at any time or place upon any notice and in any manner and when so taken may be used like other depositions. FL ST RCP Rule 1.300(c).

iii. *Persons disqualified.* Unless so stipulated by the parties, no deposition shall be taken before a person who is a relative, employee, attorney, or counsel of any of the parties, is a relative or employee of any of the parties' attorney or counsel, or is financially interested in the action. FL ST RCP Rule 1.300(d).

c. *Depositions before action*

i. *Petition.* A person who desires to perpetuate that person's own testimony or that of another person regarding any matter that may be cognizable in any Florida court may file a verified petition in the circuit court in the county of the residence of any expected adverse party. The petition shall be entitled in the name of the petitioner and shall show:

- That the petitioner expects to be a party to an action cognizable in a court of Florida, but is presently unable to bring the action;
- The subject matter of the expected action and the petitioner's interest therein;
- The facts which the petitioner desires to establish by the proposed testimony and the petitioner's reasons for desiring to perpetuate it;

- The names or a description of the persons the petitioner expects will be adverse parties and their addresses so far as known; and
- The names and addresses of the persons to be examined and the substance of the testimony which the petitioner expects to elicit from each; and shall ask for an order authorizing the petitioner to take the deposition of the persons to be examined named in the petition for the purpose of perpetuating their testimony. FL ST RCP Rule 1.290(a)(1).

ii. *Notice and service.* After submitting the petition, the petitioner must thereafter serve a notice upon each person named in the petition as an expected adverse party, together with a copy of the petition, stating that the petitioner will apply to the court at a time and place named therein for an order described in the petition. At least twenty (20) days before the date of hearing the notice shall be served either within or without the county in the manner provided by law for service of summons, but if such service cannot with due diligence be made upon any expected adverse party named in the petition, the court may make an order for service by publication or otherwise, and shall appoint an attorney for persons not served in the manner provided by law for service of summons who shall represent them, and if they are not otherwise represented, shall cross-examine the deponent. FL ST RCP Rule 1.290(a)(2).

iii. *Order and examination.* If the court is satisfied that the perpetuation of the testimony may prevent a failure or delay of justice, it shall make an order designating or describing the persons whose depositions may be taken and specifying the subject matter of the examination and whether the deposition shall be taken upon oral examination or written interrogatories. The deposition may then be taken in accordance with the rules governing depositions. FL ST RCP Rule 1.290(a)(3).

iv. *Use of deposition.* A deposition taken before an action and in accordance with the procedures above may be used in any action involving the same subject matter subsequently brought in any court. FL ST RCP Rule 1.290(a)(4).

d. *Depositions upon oral examination*

i. *Enlargement of time.* For cause shown the court may enlarge or shorten the time for taking the deposition. FL ST RCP Rule 1.310(b)(3).

ii. *Videotaped depositions.* Any deposition may be recorded by videotape without leave of the court or stipulation of the parties, provided the deposition is taken in accordance with the following:

- *Notice.* A party intending to videotape a deposition shall state in the notice that the deposition is to be videotaped and shall give the name and address of the operator. Any subpoena served on the person to be examined shall state the method or methods for recording the testimony. FL ST RCP Rule 1.310(b)(4)(A).
- *Stenographer.* Videotaped depositions shall also be recorded stenographically, unless all parties agree otherwise. FL ST RCP Rule 1.310(b)(4)(B).
- *Procedure.* At the beginning of the deposition, the officer before whom it is taken shall, on camera: (i) identify the style of the action, (ii) state the date, and (iii) swear the witness. FL ST RCP Rule 1.310(b)(4)(C).
- *Custody of tape and copies.* The attorney for the party requesting the videotaping of the deposition shall take custody of and be responsible for the safeguarding of the videotape, shall permit the viewing of it by the opposing party, and, if requested, shall provide a copy of the videotape at the expense of the party requesting the copy. FL ST RCP Rule 1.310(b)(4)(D).
- *Cost of videotaped depositions.* The party requesting the videotaping shall bear the initial cost of videotaping. FL ST RCP Rule 1.310(b)(4)(E).

iii. *Production of documents.* The notice to a party deponent may be accompanied by a request for the production of documents and tangible things at the taking of the deposition. The procedure of FL ST RCP Rule 1.350 shall apply to the request. FL ST RCP Rule 1.351 provides the

exclusive procedure for obtaining documents or things by subpoena from nonparties without deposing the custodian or other person in possession of the documents. FL ST RCP Rule 1.310(b)(5).

iv. *Deposing organizations.* In the notice a party may name as the deponent a public or private corporation, a partnership or association, or a governmental agency, and designate with reasonable particularity the matters on which examination is requested. The organization so named shall designate one or more officers, directors, or managing agents, or other persons who consent to do so, to testify on its behalf and may state the matters on which each person designated will testify. The persons so designated shall testify about matters known or reasonably available to the organization. FL ST RCP Rule 1.310(b)(6).

v. *Depositions by telephone.* On motion the court may order that the testimony at a deposition be taken by telephone. The order may prescribe the manner in which the deposition will be taken. A party may also arrange for a stenographic transcription at that party's own initial expense. FL ST RCP Rule 1.310(b)(7).

vi. *Deposing a minor.* Any minor subpoenaed for testimony shall have the right to be accompanied by a parent or guardian at all times during the taking of testimony notwithstanding the invocation of the rule of sequestration of section FL ST § 90.616, except upon a showing that the presence of a parent or guardian is likely to have a material, negative impact on the credibility or accuracy of the minor's testimony, or that the interests of the parent or guardian are in actual or potential conflict with the interests of the minor. FL ST RCP Rule 1.310(b)(8).

vii. *Examination and cross-examination.* Examination and cross-examination of witnesses may proceed as permitted at the trial. FL ST RCP Rule 1.310(c).

viii. *Oath.* The officer before whom the deposition is to be taken shall put the witness on oath and shall personally, or by someone acting under the officer's direction and in the officer's presence, record the testimony of the witness, except that when a deposition is being taken by telephone, the witness shall be sworn by a person present with the witness who is qualified to administer an oath in that location. FL ST RCP Rule 1.310(c).

ix. *Conduct.* Counsel should not inquire into a deponent's personal affairs or finances or question a deponent's integrity where such inquiry is irrelevant to the subject matter of the deposition. FL ST 20 J CIR 2.20(IV)(F)(4).

- Counsel should not conduct questioning in a manner intended to harass the witness, such as by repeating questions after they have been answered, by raising the questioner's voice, by pointing at or standing over the witness, or by appearing angry at the witness. FL ST 20 J CIR 2.20(IV)(F)(5).
- Counsel should not interrupt the answer of the witness once the question has been asked because the answer is not the one which counsel was seeking or the answer is not responsive to the question. The witness should be allowed to finish his or her answer. FL ST 20 J CIR 2.20(IV)(F)(6).
- While a question is pending, counsel should not, through objections or otherwise, coach the deponent or suggest answers. Should any lawyer do so, the courts are urged to sanction such practices. FL ST 20 J CIR 2.20(IV)(F)(8).
- Counsel for all parties should refrain from self-serving speeches during depositions. FL ST 20 J CIR 2.20(IV)(F)(9).
- Counsel should not engage in any conduct during a deposition that would not be allowed in the presence of a judicial officer. FL ST 20 J CIR 2.20(IV)(F)(10).

x. *Record of examination.* The deposition testimony must be taken stenographically or recorded by any other means ordered. If requested by one of the parties, the testimony shall be transcribed at the initial cost of the requesting party and prompt notice of the request shall be given to all other parties. FL ST RCP Rule 1.310(c).

xi. *Objections.* All objections made at time of the examination to the qualifications of the officer taking the deposition, the manner of taking it, the evidence presented, or the conduct of any party, and any other objection to the proceedings shall be noted by the officer upon the deposition. Any objection during a deposition shall be stated concisely and in a nonargumentative and nonsuggestive manner. A party may instruct a deponent not to answer only when necessary to preserve a privilege, to enforce a limitation on evidence directed by the court, or to present a motion under FL ST RCP Rule 1.310(d). FL ST RCP Rule 1.310(c).

- Otherwise, evidence objected to shall be taken subject to the objections. Instead of participating in the oral examination, parties may serve written questions in a sealed envelope on the party taking the deposition and that party shall transmit them to the officer, who shall propound them to the witness and record the answers verbatim. FL ST RCP Rule 1.310(c).
- Counsel defending a deposition should limit objections to those that are well founded and permitted by the Florida Rules of Civil Procedure or applicable case law. Counsel should bear in mind that most objections are preserved and need to be interposed only when the form of a question is defective or privileged information is sought. When objecting to the form of a question, counsel should simply state "I object to the form of the question." The grounds should not be stated unless asked for by the examining attorney. When the grounds are then stated they should be stated succinctly. FL ST 20 J CIR 2.20(IV)(F)(7).

xii. *Motion to terminate or limit examination.* At any time during the taking of the deposition, on motion of a party or of the deponent and upon a showing that the examination is being conducted in bad faith or in such manner as unreasonably to annoy, embarrass, or oppress the deponent or party, or that improper objections and instructions to a deponent not to answer are being made, the court in which the action is pending or the circuit court where the deposition is being taken may order the officer conducting the examination to cease forthwith from taking the deposition or may limit the scope and manner of the taking of the deposition under the scope of permissible discovery. FL ST RCP Rule 1.310(d).

- If the order terminates the examination, it shall be resumed thereafter only upon the order of the court in which the action is pending. Upon demand of any party or the deponent, the taking of the deposition shall be suspended for the time necessary to make a motion for an order. FL ST RCP Rule 1.310(d).

xiii. *Deponent review.* If the testimony is transcribed, the transcript shall be furnished to the witness for examination and shall be read to or by the witness unless the examination and reading are waived by the witness and by the parties. Any changes in form or substance that the witness wants to make shall be listed in writing by the officer with a statement of the reasons given by the witness for making the changes. The changes shall be attached to the transcript. It shall then be signed by the witness unless the parties waived the signing or the witness is ill, cannot be found, or refuses to sign. If the transcript is not signed by the witness within a reasonable time after it is furnished to the witness, the officer shall sign the transcript and state on the transcript the waiver, illness, absence of the witness, or refusal to sign with any reasons given. The deposition may then be used as fully as though signed unless the court holds that the reasons given for the refusal to sign require rejection of the deposition wholly or partly, on motion under FL ST RCP Rule 1.330(d)(4). FL ST RCP Rule 1.310(e).

xiv. *Certification and inspection.* If the deposition is transcribed, the officer shall certify on each copy of the deposition that the witness was duly sworn by the officer and that the deposition is a true record of the testimony given by the witness. Documents and things produced for inspection during the examination of the witness shall be marked for identification and annexed to and returned with the deposition upon the request of a party, and may be inspected and copied by any party, except that the person producing the materials may substitute copies to be marked for identification if that person affords to all parties fair opportunity to verify the copies by comparison with the originals. If the person producing the materials requests their return, the officer shall mark them, give each party an opportunity to inspect and copy them, and return them to the person producing them and the materials may then be used in the same manner as if annexed to and returned with the deposition. FL ST RCP Rule 1.310(f)(1).

xv. *Copies.* Upon payment of reasonable charges, the officer shall furnish a copy of the deposition to any party or to the deponent. FL ST RCP Rule 1.310(f)(2). A party or witness who does not have a copy of the deposition may obtain it from the officer taking the deposition unless the court orders otherwise. If the deposition is obtained from a person other than the officer, the reasonable cost of reproducing the copies shall be paid to the person by the requesting party or witness. FL ST RCP Rule 1.310(g).

e. *Depositions upon written examination*

i. *Deposing an organization upon written examination.* A deposition upon written questions may be taken of a public or private corporation, a partnership or association, or a governmental agency in accordance with FL ST RCP Rule 1.310(b)(6). FL ST RCP Rule 1.320(a).

ii. *Cross, redirect, and recross questions.* Within thirty (30) days after the notice and written questions are served, a party may serve cross questions upon all other parties. Within ten (10) days after being served with cross questions, a party may serve redirect questions upon all other parties. Within ten (10) days after being served with redirect questions, a party may serve recross questions upon all other parties. The court may for cause shown enlarge or shorten the time. FL ST RCP Rule 1.320(a).

iii. *Procedure.* A copy of the notice and copies of all questions served shall be delivered by the party taking the depositions to the officer designated in the notice, who shall proceed promptly to take the testimony of the witness in the manner provided by FL ST RCP Rule 1.310(c), FL ST RCP Rule 1.310(e), and FL ST RCP Rule 1.310(f) in response to the questions and to prepare the deposition, attaching the copy of the notice and the questions received by the officer. The questions shall not be filed separately from the deposition unless a party seeks to have the court consider the questions before the questions are submitted to the witness. FL ST RCP Rule 1.320(b).

5. *Arbitration and mediation.* Attorneys are encouraged to utilize arbitration, mediation or other forms of alternative dispute resolution if economically feasible. FL ST 20 J CIR 2.20(IV)(N)(3).

a. *Referral to arbitration and mediation.* Except as hereinafter provided or as otherwise prohibited by law, the presiding judge may enter an order referring all or any part of a contested civil matter to mediation or arbitration. The parties to any contested civil matter may file a written stipulation to mediate or arbitrate any issue between them at any time. Such stipulation shall be incorporated into the order of referral. FL ST RCP Rule 1.700(a).

b. *Arbitration*

i. *Exclusions.* A civil action shall be ordered to arbitration or arbitration in conjunction with mediation upon stipulation of the parties. A civil action may be ordered to arbitration or arbitration in conjunction with mediation upon motion of any party or by the court, if the judge determines the action to be of such a nature that arbitration could be of benefit to the litigants or the court. FL ST RCP Rule 1.800.

- Under no circumstances may the following categories of actions be referred to arbitration: (1) bond estreatures; (2) habeas corpus or other extraordinary writs; (3) bond validations; (4) civil or criminal contempt; (5) such other matters as may be specified by order of the chief judge in the circuit. FL ST RCP Rule 1.800.

ii. For more information regarding arbitration, please see FL ST RCP Rule 1.810; FL ST RCP Rule 1.820; FL ST RCP Rule 1.830.

c. *Mediation.* For more information regarding mediation, please see FL ST RCP Rule 1.710; FL ST RCP Rule 1.720; FL ST RCP Rule 1.730; FL ST RCP Rule 1.750; and FL ST 20 J CIR 1.9.

6. *Rules of court*

a. *Rules of civil procedure.* The Florida Rules of Civil Procedure apply to all actions of a civil nature and all special statutory proceedings in the circuit courts and county courts except those to which the Florida Probate Rules, the Florida Family Law Rules of Procedure, or the Small Claims Rules apply. FL ST RCP Rule 1.010.

i. The form, content, procedure, and time for pleading in all special statutory proceedings shall be

as prescribed by the statutes governing the proceeding unless the Florida Rules of Civil Procedure specifically provide to the contrary. FL ST RCP Rule 1.010.

ii. The Florida Rules of Civil Procedure shall be construed to secure the just, speedy, and inexpensive determination of every action. FL ST RCP Rule 1.010.

b. *Rules of judicial administration.* The Florida Rules of Judicial Administration shall apply to administrative matters in all courts to which the Florida Rules of Judicial Administration are applicable by their terms. The Florida Rules of Judicial Administration shall be construed to secure the speedy and inexpensive determination of every proceeding to which they are applicable. The Florida Rules of Judicial Administration shall supersede all conflicting rules and statutes. FL ST J ADMIN Rule 2.110.

7. *Civil case management plan.* There is established within the Twentieth Judicial Circuit a Civil Case Management Plan applicable to circuit civil cases, which will be administered by the Administrative Office of the Courts through direction of the Circuit Administrative Judges in each county for the implementation of enhanced case management procedures and guidelines for the timely and efficient processing of circuit civil cases and reduction in the pending backlog of civil cases. FL ST 20 J CIR 1.13.

a. The basis for the Civil Case Management Plan is included in FL ST 20 J CIR 1.13, identified in Attachment A as the "Civil Differentiated Case Management (DCM) Procedures and Backlog Reduction Plan," and is incorporated as if fully set forth in FL ST 20 J CIR 1.13. The Civil Case Management Plan is to be used as a model for the purpose of establishing time standards, improving the courts ability to provide early and continuous management of civil cases as required by FL ST J ADMIN Rule 2.545, and to promote uniformity of practice throughout the Twentieth Judicial Circuit. FL ST 20 J CIR 1.13.

b. Full implementation of the Civil DCM Case Management Procedures (Attachment A), including all uniform circuitwide procedures and forms, shall apply to all civil cases filed in Lee and Collier counties, effective January 1, 2011. Even though full implementation may be delayed in Charlotte, Hendry, and Glades counties, all civil time standards and goals, and the use of civil Case Managers and Magistrates to assist trial judges in the process of civil case management and backlog reduction programs, shall be effective circuitwide immediately. FL ST 20 J CIR 1.13.

c. For more information on the civil case management plan, refer to the specific county website and/or see FL ST 20 J CIR 1.13.

D. Documents

1. *Deposition upon oral or written examination*

a. *Required documents*

i. *Notice of deposition.* Please see the General Requirements section of this document for information on the content of a notice of deposition upon oral examination.

ii. *Certificate of service.* A certificate of service of the interrogatories shall be filed, giving the date of service and the name of the party to whom they were directed. FL ST RCP Rule 1.340(e). When any attorney certifies in substance: "I certify that a copy hereof has been furnished to (here insert name or names and addresses used for service) by (e-mail) (delivery) (mail) (fax) on .... (date) ....________________ Attorney" the certificate is taken as prima facie proof of such service in compliance with FL ST J ADMIN Rule 2.516. FL ST J ADMIN Rule 2.516(f).

b. *Supplemental documents*

i. *Motion for leave to take deposition.* See the Timing section for information on when leave is required.

ii. *Subpoena.* See the Timing section for requirements of when a subpoena is required.

iii. *Request for production of documents.* See the General Requirements section for further information.

E. Format

1. *Documents; Type and size.* Documents subject to the exceptions set forth in FL ST J ADMIN Rule

2.525(d) shall be filed on recycled paper measuring eight and one half by eleven (8 1/2 by 11) inches. For purposes of FL ST J ADMIN Rule 2.520, paper is recycled if it contains a minimum content of fifty (50) percent waste paper. Xerographic reduction of legal-size (eight and one half by fourteen (8 1/2 by 14) inches) documents to letter size (eight and one half by eleven (8 1/2 by 11) inches) is prohibited. All other documents filed by electronic transmission shall be filed in a format capable of being printed in a format consistent with the provisions of FL ST J ADMIN Rule 2.250. FL ST J ADMIN Rule 2.520(b); FL ST 20 J CIR 2.9.

a. *Exhibits.* Any exhibit or attachment filed with pleadings or papers may be filed in its original size. FL ST J ADMIN Rule 2.520(c); FL ST 20 J CIR 2.9.

b. *Recording space.* On all papers and documents prepared and filed by the court or by any party to a proceeding which are to be recorded in the public records of any county, including but not limited to final money judgments and notices of lis pendens, a three (3) inch by three (3) inch space at the top right-hand corner on the first page and a one (1) inch by three (3) inch space at the top right-hand corner on each subsequent page shall be left blank and reserved for use by the clerk of court. FL ST J ADMIN Rule 2.520(d).

   i. *Exceptions to recording space.* Any papers or documents created by persons or entities over which the filing party has no control, including but not limited to wills, codicils, trusts, or other testamentary documents; documents prepared or executed by any public officer; documents prepared, executed, acknowledged, or proved outside of the State of Florida; or documents created by State or Federal government agencies, may be filed without the space required by FL ST J ADMIN Rule 2.520. FL ST J ADMIN Rule 2.520(e).

c. *Noncompliance.* No clerk of court is permitted to refuse to file any document or paper because of noncompliance with the Florida Rules of Judicial Administration. However, upon request of the clerk of court, noncomplying documents must be resubmitted in accordance with the formatting rules. FL ST J ADMIN Rule 2.520(f).

   i. When time of filing is critical, the Clerk shall accept pleadings, motions, petitions, briefs, notices, orders, judgments, decrees, opinions, or other papers or official documents on other than eight and one half by eleven (8 1/2 by 11) inch paper but shall then require that the document be resubmitted to comply with FL ST J ADMIN Rule 2.520. FL ST 20 J CIR 2.9.

2. *Caption.* Every pleading, motion, order, judgment, or other paper shall have a caption containing the name of the court, the file number, and except for in rem proceedings, including forfeiture proceedings, the name of the first party on each side with an appropriate indication of other parties, and a designation identifying the party filing it and its nature or the nature of the order, as the case may be. In any in rem proceeding, every pleading, motion, order, judgment, or other paper shall have a caption containing the name of the court, the file number, the style "In re" (followed by the name or general description of the property), and a designation of the person or entity filing it and its nature or the nature of the order, as the case may be. In an in rem forfeiture proceeding, the style shall be "In re forfeiture of" (followed by the name of the general description of the property). All papers filed in the action shall be styled in such a manner as to indicate clearly the subject matter of the paper and the party requesting or obtaining relief. FL ST RCP Rule 1.100(c)(1).

3. *Writing and written defined.* Writing or written means a document containing information, an application, or a stipulation. FL ST RCP Rule 1.080(c).

4. *Rule abbreviations*

   a. The Florida Rules of Civil Procedure and shall be abbreviated as Fla.R.Civ.P. FL ST RCP Rule 1.010.

   b. The Florida Rules of Judicial Administration shall be abbreviated as Fla. R. Jud. Admin. FL ST J ADMIN Rule 2.110.

5. *Nonverification.* Except when otherwise specifically provided by the Florida Rules of Civil Procedure or an applicable statute, every pleading or other document of a party represented by an attorney need not be verified or accompanied by an affidavit. FL ST RCP Rule 1.030; FL ST J ADMIN Rule 2.515(a).

6. *Attorney signature*

   a. *Attorney signature.* Every pleading and other document of a party represented by an attorney shall be

signed by at least one (1) attorney of record in that attorney's individual name whose current record Florida Bar address, telephone number, including area code, primary e-mail address and secondary e-mail addresses, if any, and Florida Bar number shall be stated, and who shall be duly licensed to practice law in Florida or who shall have received permission to appear in the particular case as provided in FL ST J ADMIN Rule 2.510. FL ST J ADMIN Rule 2.515(a).

i. The attorney may be required by the court to give the address of, and to vouch for the attorney's authority to represent, the party. FL ST J ADMIN Rule 2.515(a).

ii. The signature of an attorney shall constitute a certificate by the attorney that the attorney has read the pleading or other document; that to the best of the attorney's knowledge, information, and belief there is good ground to support it; and that it is not interposed for delay. FL ST J ADMIN Rule 2.515(a).

iii. If a pleading is not signed or is signed with intent to defeat the purpose of FL ST J ADMIN Rule 2.515, it may be stricken and the action may proceed as though the pleading or other document had not been served. FL ST J ADMIN Rule 2.515(a).

b. *Pro se litigant signature.* A party who is not represented by an attorney shall sign any pleading or other paper and state the party's address and telephone number, including area code. FL ST J ADMIN Rule 2.515(b).

c. *Form of signature*

i. The signatures required on pleadings and documents by FL ST J ADMIN Rule 2.515(a) and FL ST J ADMIN Rule 2.515(b) may be:

- Original signatures;
- Original signatures that have been reproduced by electronic means, such as on electronically transmitted documents or photocopied documents;
- Electronic signatures using the "/s/," "s/," or "/s" formats by or at the direction of the person signing; or
- Any other signature format authorized by general law, so long as the clerk where the proceeding is pending has the capability of receiving and has obtained approval from the Supreme Court of Florida to accept pleadings and documents with that signature format. FL ST J ADMIN Rule 2.515(c)(1).

ii. An attorney, party, or other person who files a pleading or paper by electronic transmission that does not contain the original signature of that attorney, party, or other person shall file that identical pleading or paper in paper form containing an original signature of that attorney, party, or other person (hereinafter called the follow-up filing) immediately thereafter. The follow-up filing is not required if the Supreme Court of Florida has entered an order directing the clerk of court to discontinue accepting the follow-up filing. FL ST J ADMIN Rule 2.515(c)(2).

7. *Forms*

a. *Process.* The forms of process, notice of lis pendens, and notice of action provided in the Florida Rules of Civil Procedure are sufficient. Variations from the forms do not void process or notices that are otherwise sufficient. FL ST RCP Rule 1.900(a).

b. *Other forms.* The other forms provided in the Florida Rules of Civil Procedure are sufficient for the matters that are covered by them. So long as the substance is expressed without prolixity, the forms may be varied to meet the facts of a particular case. FL ST RCP Rule 1.900(b).

c. *Formal matters.* Captions, except for the designation of the paper, are omitted from the forms provided in the Florida Rules of Civil Procedure. A general form of caption is the first form provided. Signatures are omitted from pleadings and motions. FL ST RCP Rule 1.900(c).

8. *Notices to persons with disabilities.* All notices of court proceedings to be held in a public facility, and all process compelling appearance at such proceedings, shall include the following statement in bold face, fourteen (14) point Times New Roman or Courier font: "If you are a person with a disability who needs any accommodation in order to participate in this proceeding, you are entitled, at no cost to you, to the

provision of certain assistance. Please contact [identify applicable court personnel by name, address, and telephone number] at least seven (7) days before your scheduled court appearance, or immediately upon receiving this notification if the time before the scheduled appearance is less than seven (7) days; if you are hearing or voice impaired, call 711." FL ST J ADMIN Rule 2.540(c)(1). For more information, see FL ST 20 J CIR 2.15.

9. *Minimization of the filing of sensitive information*
   a. *Limitations for court filings.* Unless authorized by FL ST J ADMIN Rule 2.425(b), statute, another rule of court, or the court orders otherwise, designated sensitive information filed with the court must be limited to the following format:
      i. The initials of a person known to be a minor;
      ii. The year of birth of a person's birth date;
      iii. No portion of any: Social security number, Bank account number, Credit card account number, Charge account number, or Debit account number;
      iv. The last four digits of any: Taxpayer identification number (TIN), Employee identification number, Driver's license number, Passport number, Telephone number, Financial account number, except as set forth in FL ST J ADMIN Rule 2.425(a)(3), Brokerage account number, Insurance policy account number, Loan account number, Customer account number, or Patient or health care number;
      v. A truncated version of any: Email address, Computer user name, Password, or Personal identification number (PIN); and
      vi. A truncated version of any other sensitive information as provided by court order. FL ST J ADMIN Rule 2.425(a).
   b. *Exceptions.* FL ST J ADMIN Rule 2.425(a) does not apply to the following:
      i. An account number which identifies the property alleged to be the subject of a proceeding;
      ii. The record of an administrative or agency proceeding;
      iii. The record in appellate or review proceedings;
      iv. The birth date of a minor whenever the birth date is necessary for the court to establish or maintain subject matter jurisdiction;
      v. The name of a minor in any order relating to parental responsibility, time-sharing, or child support;
      vi. The name of a minor in any document or order affecting the minor's ownership of real property;
      vii. The birth date of a party in a writ of attachment or notice to payor;
      viii. In traffic and criminal proceedings: a pro se filing; a court filing that is related to a criminal matter or investigation and that is prepared before the filing of a criminal charge or is not filed as part of any docketed criminal case; an arrest or search warrant or any information in support thereof; a charging document and an affidavit or other documents filed in support of any charging document, including any driving records; a statement of particulars; discovery material introduced into evidence or otherwise filed with the court; and all information necessary for the proper issuance and execution of a subpoena duces tecum;
      ix. Information used by the clerk for case maintenance purposes or the courts for case management purposes; and
      x. Information which is relevant and material to an issue before the court. FL ST J ADMIN Rule 2.425(b).
   c. *Remedies.* Upon motion by a party or interested person or sua sponte by the court, the court may order remedies, sanctions or both for a violation of FL ST J ADMIN Rule 2.425(a). Following notice and an opportunity to respond, the court may impose sanctions if such filing was not made in good faith. FL ST J ADMIN Rule 2.425(c).
   d. *Motions not restricted.* FL ST J ADMIN Rule 2.425 does not restrict a party's right to move for

protective order, to move to file documents under seal, or to request a determination of the confidentiality of records. FL ST J ADMIN Rule 2.425(d).

e. *Application.* FL ST J ADMIN Rule 2.425 does not affect the application of constitutional provisions, statutes, or rules of court regarding confidential information or access to public information. FL ST J ADMIN Rule 2.425(e).

F. Filing and Service Requirements

1. *Court filing of documents and discovery.* Information obtained during discovery shall not be filed with the court until such time as it is filed for good cause. The requirement of good cause is satisfied only where the filing of the information is allowed or required by another applicable rule of procedure or by court order. All filings of discovery documents shall comply with FL ST J ADMIN Rule 2.425. The court shall have the authority to impose sanctions for violation of FL ST RCP Rule 1.280. FL ST RCP Rule 1.280(g).

   a. *Filing of copies.* A copy of a deposition may be filed only under the following circumstances:

      i. It may be filed in compliance with FL ST J ADMIN Rule 2.425 and FL ST RCP Rule 1.280(f) by a party or the witness when the contents of the deposition must be considered by the court on any matter pending before the court. Prompt notice of the filing of the deposition shall be given to all parties unless notice is waived. A party filing the deposition shall furnish a copy of the deposition or the part being filed to other parties unless the party already has a copy. FL ST RCP Rule 1.310(f)(3)(A).

      ii. If the court determines that a deposition previously taken is necessary for the decision of a matter pending before the court, the court may order that a copy be filed by any party at the initial cost of the party, and the filing party shall comply with FL ST J ADMIN Rule 2.425 and FL ST RCP Rule 1.280(f). FL ST RCP Rule 1.310(f)(3)(B).

2. *Filing requirements.* All original documents must be filed with the court either before service or immediately thereafter, unless otherwise provided for by general law or other rules. If the original of any bond or other document is not placed in the court file, a certified copy must be so placed by the clerk. FL ST J ADMIN Rule 2.516(d). All documents shall be filed in conformity with the requirements of FL ST J ADMIN Rule 2.525. FL ST RCP Rule 1.080(b). All documents filed in any court shall be filed by electronic transmission in accordance with FL ST J ADMIN Rule 2.525. "Documents" means pleadings, motions, petitions, memoranda, briefs, notices, exhibits, declarations, affidavits, orders, judgments, decrees, writs, opinions, and any other paper or writing submitted to a court. FL ST J ADMIN Rule 2.520(a). All documents that are court records, as defined in FL ST J ADMIN Rule 2.430(a)(1), must be filed by electronic transmission, provided that: (1) the clerk has the ability to accept and retain such documents; (2) the clerk or the chief judge of the circuit has requested permission to accept documents filed by electronic transmission; and (3) the supreme court has entered an order granting permission to the clerk to accept documents filed by electronic transmission. FL ST J ADMIN Rule 2.525(c)(1).

   a. *Definition.* "Electronic transmission of documents" means the sending of information by electronic signals to, by or from a court or clerk, which when received can be transformed and stored or transmitted on paper, microfilm, magnetic storage device, optical imaging system, CD-ROM, flash drive, other electronic data storage system, server, case maintenance system ("CM"), electronic court filing ("ECF") system, statewide or local electronic portal ("e-portal"), or other electronic record keeping system authorized by the supreme court in a format sufficient to communicate the information on the original document in a readable format. Electronic transmission of documents includes electronic mail ("e-mail") and any internet-based transmission procedure, and may include procedures allowing for documents to be signed or verified by electronic means. FL ST J ADMIN Rule 2.525(a).

      i. The filing of documents with the court as required by the Florida Rules of Judicial Administration must be made by filing them with the clerk in accordance with FL ST J ADMIN Rule 2.525, except that the judge may permit documents to be filed with the judge, in which event the judge must note the filing date before him or her on the documents and transmit them to the clerk. The date of filing is that shown on the face of the document by the judge's notation or the clerk's time stamp, whichever is earlier. FL ST J ADMIN Rule 2.516(e).

   b. *Application.* Any court or clerk of the court may accept the electronic transmission of documents for

filing after the clerk, together with input from the chief judge of the circuit, has obtained approval of the procedures and program for doing so from the Supreme Court of Florida. FL ST J ADMIN Rule 2.525(b).

c. *Exceptions*

i. Paper documents and other submissions may be manually submitted to the clerk or court:

- When the clerk does not have the ability to accept and retain documents by electronic filing or has not had ECF Procedures approved by the supreme court;
- For filing by any self-represented party or any self-represented nonparty unless specific ECF Procedures provide a means to file documents electronically. However, any self-represented nonparty that is a governmental or public agency and any other agency, partnership, corporation, or business entity acting on behalf of any governmental or public agency may file documents by electronic transmission if such entity has the capability of filing documents electronically;
- For filing by attorneys excused from e-mail service in accordance with FL ST J ADMIN Rule 2.516(b);
- When submitting evidentiary exhibits or filing non-documentary materials;
- When the filing involves documents in excess of twenty-five (25) megabytes (25MB) in size. For such filings, documents may be transmitted using an electronic storage medium that the clerk has the ability to accept, which may include a CD-ROM, flash drive, or similar storage medium;
- When filed in open court, as permitted by the court;
- When paper filing is permitted by any approved statewide or local ECF procedures; and
- If any court determines that justice so requires. FL ST J ADMIN Rule 2.525(d).

ii. Any document in paper form submitted under FL ST J ADMIN Rule 2.525(d) is filed when it is received by the clerk or court and the clerk shall immediately thereafter convert any filed paper document to an electronic document. "Convert to an electronic document" means optically capturing an image of a paper document and using character recognition software to recover as much of the document's text as practicable and then indexing and storing the document in the official court file. FL ST J ADMIN Rule 2.525(c)(4).

iii. Any storage medium submitted under FL ST J ADMIN Rule 2.525(d)(5) is filed when received by the clerk or court and the clerk shall immediately thereafter transfer the electronic documents from the storage device to the official court file. FL ST J ADMIN Rule 2.525(c)(5).

iv. If the filer of any paper document authorized under FL ST J ADMIN Rule 2.525(d) provides a self-addressed, postage-paid envelope for return of the paper document after it is converted to electronic form by the clerk, the clerk shall place the paper document in the envelope and deposit it in the mail. Except when a paper document is required to be maintained, the clerk may recycle any filed paper document that is not to be returned to the filer. FL ST J ADMIN Rule 2.525(c)(6).

v. The clerk may convert any paper document filed before the effective date of FL ST J ADMIN Rule 2.525 to an electronic document. Unless the clerk is required to maintain the paper document, if the paper document has been converted to an electronic document by the clerk, the paper document is no longer part of the official court file and may be removed and recycled. FL ST J ADMIN Rule 2.525(c)(7).

d. *Official court file.* For information on what constitutes the official court file, please see FL ST J ADMIN Rule 2.525(c)(2), FL ST J ADMIN Rule 2.525(c)(3).

e. *Administration.* All attorneys, parties, or other persons using this rule to file documents are required to make arrangements with the court or clerk for the payment of any charges authorized by general law or the supreme court before filing any document by electronic transmission. FL ST J ADMIN Rule 2.525(f)(2).

f. *Filing date.* The filing date for an electronically transmitted document is the date and time that such filing is acknowledged by an electronic stamp or otherwise, pursuant to any procedure set forth in any ECF Procedures approved by the supreme court, or the date the last page of such filing is received by the court or clerk. FL ST J ADMIN Rule 2.525(f)(3).

g. *Accessibility.* All documents transmitted in any electronic form under FL ST J ADMIN Rule 2.525 must comply with the accessibility requirements of FL ST J ADMIN Rule 2.526. FL ST J ADMIN Rule 2.525(g).

3. *Service requirements.* Every pleading subsequent to the initial pleading, all orders, and every other document filed in the action must be served in conformity with the requirements of FL ST J ADMIN Rule 2.516. FL ST RCP Rule 1.080(a).

a. *Service; Generally.* The timing and manner of service should not be used to the disadvantage of the party receiving the papers. FL ST 20 J CIR 2.20(IV)(C)(1).

i. Papers and memoranda of law should not be served at court appearances without advance notice to opposing counsel and should not be served so close to a court appearance so as to inhibit the ability of opposing counsel to prepare for that appearance or to respond to the papers. Should the attorney do so, the court is urged to take appropriate action in response, including continuing the matter to allow opposing counsel to prepare and respond. FL ST 20 J CIR 2.20(IV)(C)(2).

ii. Papers should not be served in order to take advantage of an opponent's known absence from the office or at a time or in a manner designed to inconvenience an adversary, such as late on Friday afternoon or the day preceding a secular or religious holiday. FL ST 20 J CIR 2.20(IV)(C)(3).

iii. Service should be made personally or by courtesy copy facsimile transmission when it is likely that service by mail, even when allowed, will prejudice the opposing party or will not provide the opposing party with a reasonable time to respond. FL ST 20 J CIR 2.20(IV)(C)(4).

b. *Service; When required.* Unless the court otherwise orders, or a statute or supreme court administrative order specifies a different means of service, every pleading subsequent to the initial pleading and every other document filed in any court proceeding, except applications for witness subpoenas and documents served by formal notice or required to be served in the manner provided for service of formal notice, must be served in accordance with FL ST J ADMIN Rule 2.516 on each party. No service need be made on parties against whom a default has been entered, except that pleadings asserting new or additional claims against them must be served in the manner provided for service of summons. FL ST J ADMIN Rule 2.516(a).

i. *Copies of court submissions.* Copies of any submissions to the court (such as correspondence, memoranda of law, motions, case law, etc.) should simultaneously be provided to opposing counsel by substantially the same method of delivery by which they are provided to the court. For example, if a memorandum of law is hand-delivered to the court, at substantially the same time a copy should be hand-delivered or faxed to opposing counsel. FL ST 20 J CIR 2.20(IV)(J)(4).

c. *Service; How made.* When service is required or permitted to be made upon a party represented by an attorney, service must be made upon the attorney unless service upon the party is ordered by the court. FL ST J ADMIN Rule 2.516(b).

i. *Service by electronic mail ("e-mail").* All documents required or permitted to be served on another party must be served by e-mail, unless FL ST J ADMIN Rule 2.516 otherwise provides. When, in addition to service by e-mail, the sender also utilizes another means of service provided for in FL ST J ADMIN Rule 2.516(b)(2), any differing time limits and other provisions applicable to that other means of service control. FL ST J ADMIN Rule 2.516(b)(1). Any document electronically transmitted to a court or clerk must also be served on all parties and interested persons in accordance with the applicable rules of court. FL ST J ADMIN Rule 2.525(e)(2).

- *Service on attorneys.* Upon appearing in a proceeding, an attorney must serve a designation of a primary e-mail address and may designate no more than two (2) secondary e-mail addresses. Thereafter, service must be directed to all designated e-mail addresses in that proceeding. Every document filed by an attorney thereafter must include the primary e-mail address of that attorney and any secondary e-mail addresses. If an attorney does not designate any e-mail address for service, documents may be served on that attorney at the e-mail address on record with The Florida Bar. FL ST J ADMIN Rule 2.516(b)(1)(A).

- *Exception to e-mail service on attorneys.* Service by an attorney on another attorney must be made by e-mail unless excused by the court. Upon motion by an attorney demonstrating that the attorney has no e-mail account and lacks access to the Internet at the attorney's office, the court may excuse the attorney from the requirements of e-mail service. Service on and by an attorney excused by the court from e-mail service must be by the means provided in FL ST J ADMIN Rule 2.516(b)(2). FL ST J ADMIN Rule 2.516(b)(1)(B).
- *Service on and by parties not represented by an attorney.* Any party not represented by an attorney may serve a designation of a primary e-mail address and also may designate no more than two (2) secondary e-mail addresses to which service must be directed in that proceeding by the means provided in FL ST J ADMIN Rule 2.516(b)(1). If a party not represented by an attorney does not designate an e-mail address for service in a proceeding, service on and by that party must be by the means provided in FL ST J ADMIN Rule 2.516(b)(2). FL ST J ADMIN Rule 2.516(b)(1)(C).
- *Time of service.* Service by e-mail is complete when it is sent. FL ST J ADMIN Rule 2.516(b)(1)(D). An e-mail is deemed served on the date it is sent. FL ST J ADMIN Rule 2.516(b)(1)(D)(i). If the sender learns that the e-mail did not reach the address of the person to be served, the sender must immediately send another copy by e-mail, or by a means authorized by FL ST J ADMIN Rule 2.516(b)(2). FL ST J ADMIN Rule 2.516(b)(1)(D)(ii). E-mail service is treated as service by mail for the computation of time. FL ST J ADMIN Rule 2.516(b)(1)(D)(iii).

ii. *Format of e-mail for service.* Service of a document by e-mail is made by attaching a copy of the document in PDF format to an e-mail sent to all addresses designated by the attorney or party. FL ST J ADMIN Rule 2.516(b)(1)(E).

- All documents served by e-mail must be attached to an e-mail message containing a subject line beginning with the words "SERVICE OF COURT DOCUMENT" in all capital letters, followed by the case number of the proceeding in which the documents are being served. FL ST J ADMIN Rule 2.516(b)(1)(E)(i).
- The body of the e-mail must identify the court in which the proceeding is pending, the case number, the name of the initial party on each side, the title of each document served with that e-mail, and the sender's name and telephone number. FL ST J ADMIN Rule 2.516(b)(1)(E)(ii).
- Any document served by e-mail may be signed by the "/s/" format, as long as the filed original is signed in accordance with the applicable rule of procedure. FL ST J ADMIN Rule 2.516(b)(1)(E)(iii).
- Any e-mail which, together with its attached documents, exceeds five megabytes (5MB) in size, must be divided and sent as separate e-mails, no one of which may exceed five megabytes (5MB) in size and each of which must be sequentially numbered in the subject line. FL ST J ADMIN Rule 2.516(b)(1)(E)(iv).

iii. *Service by other means.* In addition to, and not in lieu of, service by e-mail, service may also be made upon attorneys by any of the means specified in FL ST J ADMIN Rule 2.516(b)(2). Service on and by all parties who are not represented by an attorney and who do not designate an e-mail address, and on and by all attorneys excused from e-mail service, must be made by delivering a copy of the document or by mailing it to the party or attorney at their last known address or, if no address is known, by leaving it with the clerk of the court. Service by mail is complete upon mailing. Delivery of a copy within FL ST J ADMIN Rule 2.516 is complete upon:

- Handing it to the attorney or to the party,

- Leaving it at the attorney's or party's office with a clerk or other person in charge thereof,
- If there is no one in charge, leaving it in a conspicuous place therein,
- If the office is closed or the person to be served has no office, leaving it at the person's usual place of abode with some person of his or her family above fifteen (15) years of age and informing such person of the contents, or
- Transmitting it by facsimile to the attorney's or party's office with a cover sheet containing the sender's name, firm, address, telephone number, and facsimile number, and the number of pages transmitted. When service is made by facsimile, a copy must also be served by any other method permitted by FL ST J ADMIN Rule 2.516. Facsimile service occurs when transmission is complete. FL ST J ADMIN Rule 2.516(b)(2)(A) through FL ST J ADMIN Rule 2.516(b)(2)(E).
- Service by delivery after 5:00 p.m. must be deemed to have been made by mailing on the date of delivery. FL ST J ADMIN Rule 2.516(b)(2)(F).

d. *Service; Numerous defendants.* In actions when the parties are unusually numerous, the court may regulate the service contemplated by the Florida Rules of Judicial Administration on motion or on its own initiative in such manner as may be found to be just and reasonable. FL ST J ADMIN Rule 2.516(c).

e. *Service by clerk.* Service of notices and other documents required to be made by the clerk must also be done as provided in FL ST J ADMIN Rule 2.516(b). FL ST J ADMIN Rule 2.516(g).

G. Hearings

1. There is no hearing required or contemplated with regard to notices of deposition in the Florida Rules of Civil Procedure.

H. Forms

1. Official Notice of Deposition Forms for Florida

a. Caption. FL ST RCP Form 1.901.

2. Notice of Deposition Forms for Florida

a. Form for motion by plaintiff for leave to take deposition within 20-day period. FL-RCPF R 1.310(6).

b. Form for order on motion for leave to take deposition within 20-day period. FL-RCPF R 1.310(8).

c. Notice of examination; Time and place. FL-RCPF R 1.310(9).

d. Nonparty witness, subpoena required. FL-RCPF R 1.310(10).

e. Form for notice to take deposition on oral examination. FL-RCPF R 1.310(11).

f. Form for notice of taking multiple depositions. FL-RCPF R 1.310(11.1).

g. Form for notice of taking deposition and examination of documents. FL-RCPF R 1.310(12).

h. Form for notice of taking video deposition duces tecum. FL-RCPF R 1.310(13).

i. Form for motion to modify time for taking deposition. FL-RCPF R 1.310(14).

j. Form for motion to take deposition by telephone. FL-RCPF R 1.310(16).

k. Form for order permitting deposition by telephone. FL-RCPF R 1.310(17).

l. Form for notice of taking deposition by telephone. FL-RCPF R 1.310(18).

m. Form for notice of deposition upon written questions. FL-RCPF R 1.320(2).

n. Form of questions. FL-RCPF R 1.320(3).

o. Form of cross-questions. FL-RCPF R 1.320(4).

p. Form for objection to form of written questions. FL-RCPF R 1.320(6).

I. Checklist

(I) ❑ Matters to be considered by deposing party (oral depositions)

- (a) ❑ Required documents
  - (1) ❑ Notice of deposition
  - (2) ❑ Certificate of service
- (b) ❑ Supplemental documents
  - (1) ❑ Motion for leave to request deposition
  - (2) ❑ Subpoena
  - (3) ❑ Request for production of documents
- (c) ❑ Time for service of notice of deposition
  - (1) ❑ After commencement of action
  - (2) ❑ Within thirty (30) days after service of initial pleadings by leave of court only
  - (3) ❑ As a general rule, notice should be provided (not including time for service) no less than five (5) business days for instate depositions, and ten (10) business days for out-of-state depositions

(II) ❑ Matters to be considered by deponent (oral depositions)

- (a) ❑ Required documents
  - (1) ❑ Production of documents (if subpoenaed)

(III) ❑ Matters to be considered by deposing party (depositions by written questions)

- (a) ❑ Required documents
  - (1) ❑ Notice of deposition
  - (2) ❑ Written questions
  - (3) ❑ Certificate of service
- (b) ❑ Supplemental documents
  - (1) ❑ Motion for leave to request deposition
  - (2) ❑ Subpoena
  - (3) ❑ Request for production of documents
- (c) ❑ Time for service of direct and redirect questions
  - (1) ❑ As a general rule, notice should be provided (not including time for service) no less than five (5) business days for instate depositions, and ten (10) business days for out-of-state depositions
  - (2) ❑ Within ten (10) days after being served with cross questions, a party may serve redirect questions upon all other parties
  - (3) ❑ Objections to the form of the question must be served within the time for service of redirect questions or ten (10) days after service of recross questions

(IV) ❑ Matters to be considered by deponent (depositions by written questions)

- (a) ❑ Required documents
  - (1) ❑ Cross questions, with certificate of service
  - (2) ❑ Recross questions with certificate of service
- (b) ❑ Time for service of cross and recross questions
  - (1) ❑ Within thirty (30) days after the notice and written questions are served, a party may serve cross questions upon all other parties

(2) ❑ Within ten (10) days after being served with redirect questions, a party may serve recross questions upon all other parties

(3) ❑ Objections to the form of the questions must be served within the time for serving succeeding questions

Appendix - Related Court Documents

Complaint

2013 WL 589796 (Fla.Cir.Ct.)

Westlaw Query>>

To find additional Complaint filings access the Florida Civil Trial Court Filings database (FL-FILING), choose Template search, select Search Pleadings, then select Complaints.

Circuit Court of Florida.

Eleventh Judicial Circuit

Miami-dade County

Raquel Lande - HAYES, as Personal Representative of the Estate of Saul Lande, Deceased, Plaintiff,

v.

PALM SPRINGS GENERAL HOSPITAL, INC., Defendant.

No. 2013-004320-CA-01.

January 24, 2013.

Complaint

Michael J. Brevda, Florida Bar No.: 84048, Domnick & Shevin Pl, 5100 Pga Boulevard, Suite 317, Palm Beach Gardens, FL 33418, Telephone: (561) 630-5363, Facsimile: (561) 630-5654, eservice: eservice@acallforjustice.com, Attorneys for Plaintiff.

Plaintiff, RAQUEL LANDE-HAYES, as Personal Representative of the Estate of SAUL LANDE, Deceased, hereby sues the Defendant, PALM SPRINGS GENERAL HOSPITAL, INC., and alleges:

1. This is an action for medical malpractice which resulted in severe injuries to SAUL LANDE.

2. The amount in controversy exceeds $15,000.00, exclusive of interest and costs.

3. Venue is proper in this Circuit because the Decedent resided in Miami-Dade County, Florida, and the events on which this claim is based occurred in Miami-Dade County, Florida.

4. SAUL LANDE, Decedent, was an adult resident of Miami-Dade County, Florida.

5. RAQUEL LANDE-HAYES is the natural daughter and Personal Representative of the Estate of SAUL LANDE, Deceased. Exhibit 1.

6. The Defendant, PALM SPRINGS GENERAL HOSPITAL, INC., is a business organized and existing under the laws of the State of Florida. Said Defendant was doing business in Miami-Dade County in the State of Florida, as Palm Springs General Hospital.

7. This case involves medical malpractice action, in which the reasonable basis for bringing the action was not known and should not have been known until sometime subsequent to July 29, 2010. The decedent and/or his heirs and/or the representatives were not in possession of the necessary records until said date. These records were obtained for purposes other than the instant matter.

8. A 90 day extension of the statute of limitations was filed on July 19, 2012, which was within the applicable statute of limitations. Copy attached as Exhibit 2.

9. The Notice of Intent was served upon the Defendants on October 12, 2012 by certified mail, which was within the 90 day extension period, and within the applicable statute of limitations.

10. The Pre-suit period concluded with all Defendants, when there was a written rejection served upon the Plaintiff on December 21, 2012.

11. This Complaint is being filed within 60 days of the conclusion of the pre-suit period, and thus is being filed within the applicable statute of limitations, pursuant to Fla. Stat. 766 et. al.

12. Plaintiff has satisfied all conditions precedent pursuant to Chapter 766, Florida Statutes and this action is being filed within the applicable statute of limitations period.

13. The Defendant, PALM SPRINGS GENERAL HOSPITAL, INC., was appropriately served with a pre-suit Notice of Intent, and the Plaintiff has complied with all pre-suit requirements.

14. On December 3, 2009, SAUL LANDE was admitted to Palm Springs General Hospital, and thereafter remained a patient until December 18, 2009.

15. Upon initial admission to Palm Springs General Hospital on December 3, 2009, SAUL LANDE's skin was intact.

16. While at Palm Springs General Hospital, SAUL LANDE was at a high risk for skin breakdowns.

17. While at Palm Springs General Hospital, SAUL LANDE endured negligent care that caused him to suffer pressure ulcers and skin breakdown that should have been prevented and/or limited by appropriate care.

18. The pressure ulcers developed on SAUL LANDE's buttocks area.

19. The pressure ulcers developed on SAUL LANDE's buttocks area because of the failures of the staff of Palm Springs General Hospital to provide appropriate care and pressure relief.

20. Following the initial development of the pressure ulcers, SAUL LANDE suffered further skin breakdown and a worsening of his pressure ulcers.

21. SAUL LANDE's continued skin breakdown occurred due to negligent care by staff at Palm Springs General Hospital.

22. PALM SPRINGS GENERAL HOSPITAL, INC., owed a duty to SAUL LANDE to administer health care to him in accord with the prevailing professional standards of care for like health care providers. In doing so, PALM SPRINGS GENERAL HOSPITAL, INC., administered care to SAUL LANDE, through various employees, nurses, agents and/or apparent agents for whom PALM SPRINGS GENERAL HOSPITAL, INC. has vicarious responsibility. These specifically include the nursing and administrative personnel assigned to SAUL LANDE's case. Each of these people acted in this case within the scope of their respective agency and employment, real or apparent with PALM SPRINGS GENERAL HOSPITAL, INC.

23. At all times material hereto, Defendant, PALM SPRINGS GENERAL HOSPITAL, INC., individually and by and through its employees, agents, apparent agents, and staff, had a non-delegable duty both by contract and law, to properly, competently, and adequately render to SAUL LANDE, the necessary care, support and treatment in accordance with the generally accepted standards of care.

24. PALM SPRINGS GENERAL HOSPITAL, INC. failed to administer health care in accord with the prevailing professional standard of care through its employees, agents and/or apparent agents at Palm Springs General Hospital, including but not limited to nurses, C.N.A.'s, therapists, doctors and others, all of whom were acting within the course and scope of their agency, real or apparent, such that they were negligent in the following respects:

a. Failing to identify SAUL LANDE's risk for skin compromise;

b. Failing to develop an appropriate plan for care to prevent the development of skin compromise;

c. Failing to implement appropriate measures to avoid the development of skin compromise;

d. Failing to modify the treatment plan to promote the healing of skin compromise;

e. Failing to act reasonably under the circumstances.

25. As a direct and proximate result of the negligence of PALM SPRINGS GENERAL HOSPITAL, INC., as described above, SAUL LANDE suffered bodily injury, resulting pain and suffering, aggravation of a pre-existing condition, disability, disfigurement, mental anguish, loss of capacity for the enjoyment of life, expensive hospitalization, medical and nursing care and treatment.

WHEREFORE, Plaintiff, RAQUEL LANDE-HAYES, as Personal Representative of the Estate of SAUL LANDE, Deceased, demands judgment against the Defendant, PALM SPRINGS GENERAL HOSPITAL, INC., and demands trial by jury.

DATED: January 24, 2013.

Amended Complaint

2012 WL 6067428 (Fla.Cir.Ct.)

Westlaw Query>>

To find additional Amended Complaint filings access the Florida Civil Trial Court Filings database (FL-FILING), choose Terms and Connectors search, then enter DT("amended complaint").

Circuit Court of Florida.

Fourth Judicial Circuit

Duval County

Arnika FRAZIER, Plaintiff,

v.

Gregory HARTLEY, DMD, North Florida Oral & Facial Surgery, P.A., Richard Stevenson, DDS, Defendants.

No. CA008016.

October 16, 2012.

Division: CV-E

First Amended Complaint

Law Offices of Steven R. Andrews, 822 North Monroe Street, Tallahassee, Florida 32303, (850) 681-6416 Fax: 681-6984, Steven R. Andrews, Fla. Bar No: 0263680, Stephen G. Webster, Fla. Bar No: 0014054, Brian O. Finnerty, Fla. Bar No: 0094647.

Plaintiff, ARNIKA FRAZIER, by and through her undersigned counsel, sues Defendants, GREGORY HARTLEY, DMD ("HARTLEY"), RICHARD STEVENSON, DDS ("RICHARDSON"), and NORTH FLORIDA ORAL & FACIAL SURGERY, P.A. ("NFOFS") and states:

GENERAL ALLEGATIONS

The Parties And Their Relationships

1. This is an action for damages in excess of $15,000.00 exclusive of costs and attorney's fees.

2. This action is brought under section 766.102, Florida Statutes, et seq. and section 768.18, Florida Statutes, *et seq.* All conditions precedent have been met prior to the filing of this Complaint.

3. This Complaint sounds in medical malpractice and vicarious liability. All conditions precedent have been met or have occurred, prior to the filing of this Complaint, including compliance with, and the filing of all pre-suit notice requirements set forth in Sections 766.102-212, Florida Statutes.

4. At all times relevant to this action the Plaintiff, ARNIKA FRAZIER, was a resident of Duval County, Florida.

5. The Defendant, GREGORY HARTLEY, DMD, at all material times hereto was a dentist licensed to practice dentistry in the State of Florida and who practiced dentistry in Duval County, Florida.

6. At all times relevant to this action, Defendant Hartley held himself out to be a competent doctor of dental medicine, Board Certified in oral and maxillofacial surgery.

7. Defendant Hartley, at all times material hereto, was employed by Defendant NORTH FLORIDA ORAL & FACIAL SURGERY, P.A., as a doctor of dental medicine. At all times material hereto, Defendant NFOFS held Defendant Hartley out to be a competent medical doctor, specializing in oral and maxillofacial surgery. At all times material hereto, Defendant Hartley acted within the course and scope of his employment with Defendant NFOFS. Defendant NFOFS is vicariously liable for the acts and omissions of Defendant Hartley.

8. The Defendant, RICHARD STEVENSON, DDS, at all material times hereto was a dentist licensed to practice dentistry in the State of Florida and who practiced dentistry in Duval County.

9. Pursuant to Florida Statute 47.021, venue is proper in Duval County, Florida.

10. At all material times hereto, Plaintiff was a patient of the Defendants.

COUNT I: MEDICAL MALPRACTICE CLAIM AGAINST GREGORY HARTLEY, DMD

11. Plaintiff, ARNIKA FRAZIER, re-alleges the allegations contained in paragraphs 1 through 10.

12. Defendant, GREGORY HARTLEY, DMD, owed a duty to Plaintiff, to provide adequate and competent dental care to Plaintiff while she was a patient of the Defendant.

13. Defendant, GREGORY HARTLEY, DMD, deviated from the standard of care provided by similar health care providers as detailed below. Such deviations caused negligent injury to the Plaintiff, ARNIKA FRAZIER.

14. Defendant, GREGORY HARTLEY, DMD, deviated from the standard of care by failing to diagnose and treat a large multilocular radiolucency which was located in Plaintiff's anterior mandible as seen on a panoramic radiograph dated December 29, 2008 and by failing to maintain adequate medical records.

15. The deviation from the standard of care was such that it could not be discovered by the Plaintiff until November 19, 2009 when Plaintiff was seen by a subsequent dentist who advised the Plaintiff that the large multilocular radiolucency was present as reflected in radiographic images taken by the Defendant on December 29, 2008. Defendant negligently failed to advise the Plaintiff of the multilocular radiolucency and further failed to maintain accurate and complete medical records concerning his care and treatment of the Plaintiff which acted to conceal the multilocular radiolucency.

16. As a direct and proximate cause of the deviations set forth above, the Plaintiff suffered negligent bodily injury and resulting pain and suffering, mental anguish, expense of medical treatment for which the Plaintiff is entitled to recover damages. These damages include the Plaintiff having to undergo fifteen (15) additional surgeries including plastic surgery to remove a benign odontogenic tumor which continued to grow aggressively and destructively after the Defendant negligently failed to diagnose the obvious tumor present in the Plaintiff's panoramic radiographic studies of December 29, 2008.

17. Plaintiff suffers from a slight speech impediment directly caused by the negligence of the Defendant, GREGORY HARTLEY, DMD. Plaintiff has a Master's of Science Degree in Integrated Marketing and Management Communications and seeks special damages related to this injury.

18. Attached hereto as **Exhibit "A"** is the Plaintiff's Petition to Extend the Statute of Limitations filed in the Circuit Court of the Fourth Judicial Circuit, in and for Duval County Florida on August 18, 2011.

WHEREFORE, Plaintiff ARNIKA FRAZIER demands judgment against Defendant GREGORY HARTLEY, DMD, for compensatory damages and reasonable costs, and other such relief as this Court deems appropriate.

COUNT II: MEDICAL MALPRACTICE CLAIM AGAINST RICHARD STEVENSON, DDS

19. Plaintiff, ARNIKA FRAZIER, re-alleges the allegations contained in paragraphs 1 through 10.

20. Defendant, RICHARD STEVENSON, DDS, owed a duty to Plaintiff, to provide adequate and competent dental care to Plaintiff while she was a patient of the Defendant.

21. Defendant, RICHARD STEVENSON, DDS, deviated from the standard of care provided by similar health care providers as detailed below. Such deviations caused negligent injury to the Plaintiff, ARNIKA FRAZIER.

22. Defendant, RICHARD STEVENSON, DDS, deviated from the standard of care by failing to diagnose and treat

a large multilocular radiolucency which was located in Plaintiff's anterior mandible as seen on a panoramic radiograph dated December 29, 2008.

23. The deviation from the standard of care was such that it could not be discovered by the Plaintiff until November 19, 2009 when Plaintiff was seen by a subsequent dentist who advised the Plaintiff that the large multilocular radiolucency was present as reflected in radiographic images taken by the Defendant on December 29, 2008. Defendant negligently failed to advise the Plaintiff of the multilocular radiolucency and further failed to maintain accurate and complete medical records concerning his care and treatment of the Plaintiff which acted to conceal the multilocular radiolucency.

24. As a direct and proximate cause of the deviations set forth above, the Plaintiff suffered negligent bodily injury and resulting pain and suffering, mental anguish, expense of medical treatment for which the Plaintiff is entitled to recover damages. These damages include the Plaintiff having to undergo fifteen (15) additional surgeries including plastic surgery to remove a benign odontogenic tumor which continued to grow aggressively and destructively after the Defendant negligently failed to diagnose the obvious tumor present in the Plaintiff's panoramic radiographic studies of December 29, 2008.

25. Plaintiff suffers from a slight speech impediment directly caused by the negligence of the Defendant, RICHARD STEVENSON, DDS. Plaintiff has a Master's of Science Degree in Integrated Marketing and Management Communications and seeks special damages related to this injury.

26. Attached hereto as **Exhibit "A"** is the Plaintiff's Petition to Extend the Statute of Limitations filed in the Circuit Court of the Fourth Judicial Circuit, in and for Duval County Florida on August 18, 2011.

WHEREFORE, Plaintiff ARNIKA FRAZIER demands judgment against Defendant GREGORY HARTLEY, DMD, for compensatory damages and reasonable costs, and other such relief as this Court deems appropriate.

COUNT III: MEDICAL MALPRACTICE CLAIM AGAINST NORTH FLORIDA ORAL & FACIAL SURGERY, P.A. (Vicarious Liability)

27. Plaintiff, ARNIKA FRAZIER, re-alleges the allegations contained in paragraphs 1 through 18.

28. At all material times hereto, Defendant Hartley was employed by Defendant, NORTH FLORIDA ORAL & FACIAL SURGERY, P.A., and at all material times hereto, Defendant Hartley acted within the course and scope of his employment with Defendant NORTH FLORIDA ORAL & FACIAL SURGERY, P.A.

29. Defendant, NORTH FLORIDA ORAL & FACIAL SURGERY, P.A. is vicariously liable for the negligent malpractice of Defendant Hartley.

30. As a direct and proximate cause of the deviations set forth in Count I above, the Plaintiff suffered negligent bodily injury and resulting pain and suffering, mental anguish, expense of medical treatment for which the Plaintiff is entitled to recover damages. These damages include the Plaintiff having to undergo fifteen (15) additional surgeries including plastic surgery to remove a benign odontogenic tumor which continued to grow aggressively and destructively after the Defendant negligently failed to diagnose the obvious tumor present in the Plaintiffs panoramic radiographic studies of December 29, 2008.

31. Plaintiff suffers from a slight speech impediment directly caused by the negligence of the Defendant, GREGORY HARTLEY, DMD. Plaintiff has a Master's of Science Degree in Integrated Marketing and Management Communications and seeks special damages related to this injury.

32. Attached hereto as **Exhibit "A"** is the Plaintiff's Petition to Extend the Statute of Limitations filed in the Circuit Court of the Fourth Judicial Circuit, in and for Duval County Florida on August 18, 2011.

WHEREFORE, Plaintiff ARNIKA FRAZIER demands judgment against Defendant NORTH FLORIDA ORAL & FACIAL SURGERY, P.A. for compensatory damages and reasonable costs, and other such relief as this Court deems appropriate.

DEMAND FOR JURY TRIAL

Plaintiff demands trial by jury of all said issues so triable.

DATED this 16th day of October, 2012

Answer

2012 WL 5342540 (Fla.Cir.Ct.)

Circuit Court of Florida.

Seventeenth Judicial Circuit

Broward County

US BANK, N.A., as Trustee for the Holders of the First Franklin Mortgage Loan Trust Mortgage Pass-Through Certificates Series 2006-Ff2, Plaintiff,

v.

Kevin J. KENNEY, et al., Defendants.

No. CACE12019601.

August 26, 2012.

Answer

The Strauss Law Firm, P.A., Bank of America Plaza, 401 E. Las Olas Blvd, Suite 1400, Fort Lauderdale, FL 33301, Ph.: (954) 522-2177, Fax: (954) 522-2176, E-mail:david@strausslaw.net, David A. Strauss, Esq., Florida Bar Number 721786.

Defendants, Kevin J. Kenney and Michelle R. Kenney, through undersigned counsel, hereby file this Answer and Affirmative Defenses, and allege:

1. Admitted for jurisdictional/venue purposes only.

2. Admitted that defendants executed a Note and Mortgage, but denied that the copies attached to the Complaint are true and correct copies. Defendants respectfully refer this honorable Court to the true, original documents to ascertain the true terms thereof.

3. Without knowledge, therefore, denied.

4. Denied.

5. Denied.

6. Denied.

7. Denied.

8. Admitted.

9. Denied. The Note requires 30-day's notice of plaintiff's intention to accelerate the full, principal balance of the loan. Plaintiff has failed to serve this notice and, therefore, has failed to satisfy a condition precedent to acceleration.

10. Without knowledge, therefore, denied.

11. Part a - Admitted Unknown Spouse of Michelle R. Kinney may claim some right, title or interest. Otherwise,

denied. Part b - Admitted Kevin Kinney may claim some right, title or interest. Otherwise, denied. Part c - without knowledge, therefore, denied.

12. Defendants repeat and re-allege the foregoing responses as if fully set forth herein.

13. Admitted that defendants executed a Note and Mortgage, but denied that the copies attached to the Complaint are true and correct copies. Defendants respectfully refer this honorable Court to the true, original documents to ascertain the true terms thereof.

14. Admitted that the legal description in the Mortgage is incorrect, but otherwise denied.

15. Without knowledge, therefore, denied.

16. Without knowledge, therefore, denied.

17. Without knowledge, therefore, denied.

18. Denied.

19. Denied.

20. Denied.

FIRST AFFIRMATIVE DEFENSE

Plaintiff has failed to satisfy a condition precedent. The Note requires 30 days' notice before lender may accelerate the full principal balance of the loan. Plaintiff failed to serve this notice and the action must, respectfully, be dismissed for failure to satisfy a condition precedent.

SECOND AFFIRMATIVE DEFENSE

The subject Mortgage does not constitute a valid lien against the property. The Mortgage does not include the correct legal description of the property sought to be foreclosed upon and it cannot, therefore, be foreclosed against the property.

THIRD AFFIRMATIVE DEFENSE

Plaintiff has failed to state a cause of action for reformation of the deed and/or mortgage. Specifically, plaintiff has failed to plead that the mortgage is vague, uncertain or indefinite such that parol evidence would be admissible to alter the clear language thereof. Furthermore, plaintiff has failed to plead whether the alleged error was caused by mistake of the parties, be it mutual or unilateral. As such, the subject Mortgage does not constitute a valid and effective lien against the subject property.

FOURTH AFFIRMATIVE DEFENSE

Plaintiff does not have standing to foreclose on the Mortgage, because the plaintiff is not the true owner and/or holder of the Note. The purported endorsements to the Note and purported Assignment of Mortgage are falsified and/or were executed by person(s) lacking proper authority and are, therefore, without legal effect. Plaintiff lacks standing.

FIFTH AFFIRMATIVE DEFENSE

The Mortgage was defectively executed and does not, therefore, constitute a valid lien. Specifically, Florida law requires that a mortgage have two witnesses. Mortgagor's signature was only witnessed by a single witness, and the mortgage is, therefore, not a valid lien against the subject property.

SIXTH AFFIRMATIVE DEFENSE

Plaintiff does not have standing to foreclose because plaintiff is not the true owner and holder of the Note and Mortgage. The Note incorporates the subject Mortgage by reference and, as such, the Note became non-negotiable. Consequently, the purported endorsement(s) to the Note and Assignment are without legal effect.

SEVENTH AFFIRMATIVE DEFENSE

The endorsements on the Note and the Assignment of Mortgage are falsified and/or were executed by persons lacking proper authority and are, therefore, without legal effect. Plaintiff lacks standing.

EIGHTH AFFIRMATIVE DEFENSE

Plaintiff is estopped from declaring a default. Authorized agents of the plaintiff instructed the defendant to stop making monthly mortgage payments when defendant was inquiring about a loan modification before this action was commenced. Having lulled the defendant into default, plaintiff should, respectfully, be estopped from declaring a default.

NINTH AFFIRMATIVE DEFENSE

In violation of Rule 1.13(a), plaintiff has failed to attach the complete agreement to the Complaint. Specifically, the Note contains two endorsements which are entirely illegible. in this respect, the defendants are prejudiced in that the defendants cannot properly respond to the Complaint.

TENTH AFFIRMATIVE DEFENSE

The undated, blank endorsements on the Note are falsified and/or were executed by persons lacking proper authority and are, therefore, without legal effect. Plaintiff lacks standing.

ELEVENTH AFFIRMATIVE DEFENSE

There has been a novation, the terms of which have been fully complied with by the defendants and there is, thus, no default. Specifically, plaintiff's predecessor and defendant(s) agreed to a loan modification, which was intended to resolve and satisfy the loan being sued upon. Plaintiff is apparently refusing to honor the agreement after defendants have tendered full performance and/or performed and/or relied upon the agreement to their detriment. Because plaintiff's predecessor accepted payments from the defendants after the end of the "trial" period, plaintiff is estopped from invoking the statute of frauds.

TWELFTH AFFIRMATIVE DEFENSE

Plaintiff is barred by promissory estoppel. Defendants entered into a modification of loan agreement with plaintiff's predecessor, which agreement was intended to resolve and satisfy defendants' obligations under the Note. Plaintiff has apparently reneged on the loan modification and should be equitably estopped from declaring a default and from recovering the relief plaintiff seeks. Defendants have tendered full performance and remain ready, willing and able to abide by the agreed-upon modification. Having accepted payments from the defendants after the end of the "trial" period, plaintiff is estopped from invoking the statute of frauds.

THIRTEENTH AFFIRMATIVE DEFENSE

The amounts sought by plaintiff are wrongfully and willfully exaggerated. Despite that the subject property was covered by qualified homeowners insurance and flood insurance at all times, plaintiff wrongfully and erroneously force-placed flood insurance against the property, which has artificially inflated the amounts that plaintiff is seeking in this action.

FOURTEENTH AFFIRMATIVE DEFENSE

Plaintiff failed to comply with the conditions and terms of the purported Note and Mortgage and/or the Real Estate Settlement Procedures Act with respect to the proper computation, collection and application of the borrowers' mortgage payments and the escrow accounts. In addition, plaintiff has collected payments and failed to properly credit the borrowers' account and escrow. Borrower(s) demand an accounting of all monies paid and other consideration offered and/or granted to plaintiff and/or its predecessor during the term of the loan; in addition, borrower(s) demand an accounting of all moneys and/or consideration collected by or on behalf of the lender.

FIFTEENTH AFFIRMATIVE DEFENSE

Plaintiff is in violation of the Federal Truth in Lending Act ("TILA") and the Real Estate Settlement Procedures Act ("RESPA"). In particular, plaintiff has:

(a) Failed to clearly and accurately disclose the amount financed;

(b) Failed to clearly and accurately disclose the finance charges;

(c) Failed to clearly and accurately disclose the annual percentage rate (including any variable feature disclosure);

(d) Failed to clearly and accurately disclose the number, amounts and timing of payments scheduled to repay the obligation;

(e) Failed to clearly and accurately disclose total number of payments;

(f) Failed to provide a Good Faith Estimate within 3 days of application for the loan;

(g) Failed to obtain and preserve a final Form 1003 Loan Application;

(h) Failed to provide notice of right to receive a copy of any appraisals;

(i) Failed to provide an initial escrow account disclosure;

(j) Failed to provide mortgage broker agreement disclosures; and

(k) Violated the finance charge tolerance error.

WHEREFORE, defendants, Kevin J. Kenney and Michelle R. Kenney, respectfully request that the Court enter an Order dismissing the Complaint and awarding attorneys' fees and costs pursuant to the Note (in conjunction with Section 57.105[7], Florida Statutes), and granting such other and further relief as the Court may deem appropriate.

CERTIFICATE OF SERVICE

I HEREBY CERTIFY that a true and correct copy of the foregoing was mailed on this 22th day of August 2012 to:

Aldridge Connors, LLP

7000 W. Palmetto Pk Rd, Ste 307

Boca Raton, FL 33433

T: (561) 392-6391

F: (561) 392-6965

Amended Answer

2010 WL 3180252 (Fla.Cir.Ct.)

Westlaw Query>>
To find additional Amended Answer filings access the Florida Civil Trial Court Filings database (FL-FILING), choose Terms and Connectors search, then enter DT("amended answer").

Circuit Court of Florida.

Seventeenth Judicial Circuit

St. Johns County

Doran D. YELTON II and Yelton Construction Company, Inc, a Florida corporation, Plaintiffs,

v.

Leslie H. ROTH and Bernice Y. Matalon, Trustee of the Bernice Y. Matalon Revocable Trust dated April 20, 2000, Defendant.

No. CA09-2747.

March 24, 2010.

Defendants' Amended Answer, Affirmative Defenses and Counterclaims

Attorneys for the Defendants/Counter Plaintiffs, Robert F. Cooke, Esq., Florida Bar Number 0590533, 8925 SW 148 Street, Suite 100, Palmetto Bay, FL 33176, Telephone (305) 259-8054, Fax (305) 259-7148.

DIVISION 55

COMES NOW, Defendants, LESLIE H. ROTH and BERNICE Y. MATALON, by and through undersigned counsel, and files this Amended Answer, Affirmative Defenses and Counterclaims and further states:

1. Admitted.
2. Admitted.
3. Admitted.
4. Admitted.
5. Denied; Voluntarily Dismissed with Prejudice.
6. Denied; Voluntarily Dismissed with Prejudice.
7. Denied; Voluntarily Dismissed with Prejudice.
8. Denied; Voluntarily Dismissed with Prejudice.
9. Denied; Voluntarily Dismissed with Prejudice.
10. Denied; Voluntarily Dismissed with Prejudice.
11. Denied; Voluntarily Dismissed with Prejudice.
12. Denied; Voluntarily Dismissed with Prejudice.

13. Denied; Voluntarily Dismissed with Prejudice.
14. Denied; Voluntarily Dismissed with Prejudice.
15. Denied; Voluntarily Dismissed with Prejudice.
16. Denied.
17. Admitted or Denied as stated in each paragraph.
18. Denied.
19. Denied, as stated.
20. Denied, as stated.
21. Denied.
22. Denied.
23. Denied.
24. Denied.
25. Denied.
26. Unknown therefore, Denied.
27. Unknown therefore, Denied.
28. Denied.
29. Admitted or Denied as stated in each paragraph.
30. Denied.
31. Denied.
32. Denied.
33. Denied.
34. Denied.
35. Denied.

AFFIRMATIVE DEFENSES

COMES NOW, the Defendants, LESLIE H. ROTH and BERNICE Y. MATALON Trustee of the Bernice Y. Matalon Revocable Trust dated April 20, 2000, and state the following Affirmative Defenses against Plaintiffs as follows:

36. *First affirmative defense* - Unclean Hands.
37. *Second affirmative defense* - Fraud or Collusion, pursuant to Section 713.31 of the Florida Statutes.
38. *Third affirmative defense* - Negligence.
39. *Fourth affirmative defense* - Statute of Frauds.

COUNTERCLAIMS

COMES NOW, Counter Plaintiffs LESLIE H. ROTH and BERNICE Y. MATALON, Trustee of the Bernice Y. Matalon Revocable Trust dated April 20, 2000, and asserts these Counterclaims against Counter Defendants DORAN D. YELTON II and YELTON CONSTRUCTION COMPANY, INC., a Florida corporation, (hereinafter Counter Defendants), and alleges as follows:

General Allegations Common to all Counts

40. Counter Defendants are licensed contractors, and as a normal course of business, develop land to include turn key construction of individual homes, and commercial buildings.
41. Counter Plaintiffs are the owners of real property subject to the allegations plead by Counter Defendants.

42. On or about August 31, 2006, Counter Plaintiffs accepted and agreed with Counter Defendants to purchase real property owned by Counter Defendants. Counter Defendants represented the sale of a specific lot with a verbal agreement to construct a single family residence on that lot. The verbal Agreement between the parties required Mr. YELTON and YELTON CONSTRUCTION INC., to provide land sale and construction services in an amount equal to an approximate value between $175.00 and $200.00 per square foot, and this amount included the price of the real property (lot) and all construction costs and pofit to build a 3000 square foot home as shown on architectural plans, on the property. The total dollar value for land and construction costs were represented to be between $525,000.00 and $600,000.00. There was no written contract, and the agreement could not be performed within one year, nor was it performed within one year.

43. Per the verbal agreement between these parties, Counter Plaintiffs were to pay $250,000.00 for the lot, and the remaining amount would be due and payable after construction was complete, passed final inspections, and the house was delivered to Counter Plaintiffs. Shortly before the closing on the real property (lot), Counter Defendants advised Counter Plaintiffs that the actual value for the lot had increased from $250,000.00, to $300,000.00, dollars due to value added to the land in preparation for construction. Counter Plaintiffs, believing these representations as true, and unable to secure financing in such a short period of time for the additional amount of $50,000.00, agreed to pay the originally represented amount of $250,000.00, as a down payment, and take a first mortgage in the amount of $50,000.00, from the Counter Defendants. The closing went forward, and a mortgage was recorded in O.R. Book 2777, at page 977 on September 6, 2006, in the amount of $50,000.00. Thereafter, Counter Defendants began the construction project, without a written contract, and after approximately two years and eight months, advised Counter Plaintiffs that construction was complete.

44. On or about August 31, 2007, Counter Plaintiffs paid interest in the amount of $3,500.00, check #3638, as agreed on the mortgaged property after the first year. See attached Exhibit "1".

45. On or about July 20, 2009, Counter Defendants made a demand in the amount of $857,088.86, represented as final payment for all services rendered as described herein. Counter Plaintiffs demanded to know how the originally agreed to total value of $175.00 to $200.00 per square foot or $525,000.00 to $600,000.00 dollar value had increased to $369.03 per, square foot or $1,107,088.86. Havin paid $250,000.00 as a down payment, Counter Plaintiffs could not accept the inflated numbers now being represented by Counter Defendants. Counter Plaintiffs demanded an accounting for these inflated numbers, and instead of receiving this accounting, received this current law suit.

46. On or about July 20, 2009, Counter Defendants filed a lien on the real property in the amount of $857,088.86, and instituted this action to recover under this inflated lien value.

47. On or about September 23, 2009, Counter Plaintiff Roth filed suit in Miami Dade County Florida to collect outstanding balances owed by Counter Defendants to Counter Plaintiff Roth for accounting services previously provided to Counter Defendants.

48. On or about February 22, 2010, these parties agreed to dismissal of Count One of this complaint, and the lawsuit in Miami, for an exchanged value of $50,000.00 which was the amount of the Note and Mortgage between these parties. This brings the total amount of consideration paid by Counter Plaintiffs for this property to $300,000.00.

49. Throughout this entire project, Counter Plaintiffs have contracted with several other providers, such as Architect, Appraiser, Tiling Supplier, Cabinetry Supplier, Appliance Supplier, Lighting Fixture Supplier, Electrical Contractor, two Granite Suppliers, Hand Railing Manufacturer/Supplier, House Indicia/Numbers Supplier Roofers and a Security Company. In total, Counter Plaintiffs have paid an additional amount to these vendors of $66,971.48, and owe an additional $60,069.82 to these vendors. Thus reducing the scope of Counter Defendants work, as Counter Defendants were not required to pay for these items as part of their construction costs.

COUNT 1

NEGLIGENT MISREPRESENTATION

50. The allegations in Paragraphs 40 - 49 are incorporated by reference herein as if set forth in their entirety.

51. Counter Defendants made (1) material misrepresentations of fact to Counter Plaintiffs, by offering to sell real property and build a single family home thereupon for a price materially less than the price Counter Defendants are now claiming as a lien value pursuant to an oral contract; (2) The representations made by Counter Defendants

were false, and Counter Defendants either knew or should have known that these representations were false, or made the representations without knowledge as to their truth or falsity, or made the representations under circumstances in which they ought to have known of their falsity at the time they were made; (3) Counter Defendants made these representations with the intent of inducing Counter Plaintiffs to act in reliance of the representations; and (4) in justifiable reliance upon Counter Defendants' representations, Counter Plaintiffs paid a $250,000.00, down payment, signed a Promissory Note for an additional $50,000.00 as consideration, and as a result have suffered and sustained injury in the form of actual and additional damages.

52. Counter Plaintiffs have suffered **and sustained damages** as a direct and proximate cause of Counter Defendants' negligent misrepresentations. **Counter Defendants demand trial by jury on all issues so triable.**

WHEREFORE, Counter Plaintiffs, demand judgment against Counter Defendants, in an amount in excess of $15,000.00, plus prejudgment interest, plus the costs of this action, plus any and all other relief this court deems necessary and proper.

COUNT II

VIOLATION OF SECTION 713.31 of the FLORIDA STATUS BY DEFENDANTS

53. The allegations in Paragraphs 40 -52 are incorporated by reference herein as if set forth in their entirety.

54. Counter Defendants are licensed contractors, who hire employees, subcontractors, and other service and material providers, and manage construction projects to completion. Counter Defendants have the skill and knowledge in the construction industry to properly cost out construction projects.

55. On or about July 20, 2009, Counter Defendants filed or caused to have filed a lien on the real property owned by Plaintiffs. The recorded amount of this lien was $857,088.86.

56. Counter Defendants have willfully exaggerated the amount of the claim of lien, or have willfully included in the claim of lien excessive amounts for work not performed upon or materials not furnished for the property upon which he, she or they seek to impress such lien. Alternatively, Counter Defendants have compiled their claim of lien with such willful and gross negligence as to amount to or constitute a willful exaggeration and thus have filed a fraudulent lien.

57. The amount exaggerated by Counter Defendants are not minor, but is large or excessive and constitutes an amount that can only be deemed as willful or gross negligence, as Counter Defendants, have the requisite knowledge to know how much it should have cost to build a home on land owned by Counter Plaintiffs as specified in architectural plans provided to Counter Defendants, by Counter Plaintiffs, without any construction change orders.

58. Counter Plaintiffs, in defending this action, and asserting these Counter Claims have been required to retain the services of an attorney, and are entitled to recover attorney's fees and costs pursuant to Section 713.31(c) of the Florida Statutes.

Counter Defendants demand trial by jury on all issues so triable.

WHEREFORE, Counter Plaintiffs, demand judgment against Counter Defendants, and request this Honorable Court to discharge this fraudulent lien, plus damages in an amount in excess of $15,000.00, plus prejudgment interest, plus legal fees and the costs of this action, plus any and all other relief this court deems necessary and proper.

Motion to Strike

2011 WL 3419536 (Fla.Cir.Ct.)

> **Westlaw Query>>**
> To find additional Motion to Strike filings access the Florida Civil Trial Court Filings database (FL-FILING), choose Template search, select Search Motions then select Motion to Strike.

Circuit Court of Florida.

Fourth Judicial Circuit

Duval County

Kim MEEKS,

v.

JACKSONVILLE AVENUES LIMITED PARTNERSHIP.

No. 162009CA018820.

January 19, 2011.

Division: CV-H

Third-Party Defendant Visionworks, Inc.'s Motion to Strike Parts of the Prayers for Relief in Jacksonville Avenues Limited Partnership's Third-Party Complaint

Boyd & Jenerette, P.A., Attorneys for Third-Party Defendant, 201 N. Hogan St., Suite 400, Jacksonville, FL 32202, Tel: (904) 353-6241, Fax: (904) 493-5657, Email: kvanderlinde@boyd-jenerette.com, aabramovich@boyd-jenerette.com, Kriten Van der Linde, Esquire, Florida Bar No.: 0964573, Andrew Abramovich, Esquire, Florida Bar No.: 43128.

COMES NOW Third-Party Defendant Visionworks, Inc. (hereinafter "Visionworks"), by and through its undersigned counsel, and pursuant to Rule 1.140(f), Florida Rules of Civil Procedure, and applicable Florida Statutes and case law, moves this Court to strike parts of the prayers for relief in Jacksonville Avenues Limited Partnership's (hereinafter "Avenues") Third-Party Plaintiff's Complaint (Dec. 28, 2010) (hereinafter "Third-Party Complaint") because they contain references to Section 57.105, Florida Statutes which are immaterial, impertinent or scandalous. In support of this motion, Visionworks states the following:

1. Florida law permits a court to award attorney's fees and other expenses as sanctions when a party knowingly presents unsupported claims or defenses or causes unreasonable delay. Fla. Stat. § 57.105.

2. Section 57.105, Florida Statutes requires that a party seeking sanctions pursuant to that section must serve a motion without filing or otherwise presenting that motion to the court "unless, within 21 days after service of the motion, the challenged paper, claim, defense, contention, allegation, or denial is not withdrawn or appropriately corrected."

3. The three prayers for relief in the Avenues' Third-Party Complaint seek, *inter alia,* "attorney's fees and costs pursuant to`57.105." Third-Party Complaint pp. 2, 4, 5.

4. In the case at bar, neither the Avenues nor its counsel has alleged any facts or circumstances that would support an award of attorneys fees or costs pursuant to Section 57.105, Florida Statutes.

5. Neither the Avenues nor its counsel have served a motion pursuant to Section 57.105, Florida Statutes prior to filing the Third-Party Complaint on or about December 28, 2010.

6. A "court may strike redundant, immaterial, impertinent, or scandalous matter from any pleading at any time." Fla. R. Civ. P. 1.140(f).

7. A prayer for attorney's fees and costs pursuant to Section 57.105, Florida Statutes is immaterial and impertinent to purported causes of action for contractual indemnification, common law indemnification and contribution.

8. A prayer for attorney's fees and costs pursuant to Section 57.105, Florida Statutes is immaterial and impertinent to a civil action for damages absent a basis for such an award and/or compliance with the statutorily-prescribed procedure by which a party may move for sanctions.

9. A prayer for attorney's fees and costs pursuant to Section 57.105, Florida Statutes is immaterial and impertinent to a civil action for damages absent a basis for such an award and/or compliance with the statutorily-prescribed procedure by which a party may move for sanctions.

10. To the extent that a prayer for attorney's fees and costs pursuant to Section 57.105, Florida Statutes constitutes an assertion of the entitlement to sanctions, such a prayer may be scandalous.

11. A court should strike a motion pursuant to Section 57.105, Florida Statutes if the party against which the motion is directed is not previously given an opportunity to retract the allegedly "frivolous paper, claim, defense, contention, allegation, or denial." O'Daniel v. Bd. of Comm'rs, 916 So.2d 40, 41 (Fla. 3d DCA 2005).

WHEREFORE, Third-Party Defendant Visionworks, Inc. respectfully moves this Court to strike those parts of the three prayers for relief in the Third-Party Complaint that read "attorney's fees and costs pursuant to `57.105," and grant any other relief this Court may deem just and proper.

CERTIFICATE OF SERVICE

I HEREBY CERTIFY that a copy hereof has been furnished by U.S. Mail this 18th day of January, 2011, to Jack D. Luks, Esquire and Todd T. Springer, Esquire, One Independent Drive, Suite 3232, Jacksonville, Florida 32202, Fred Stapp, Esquire, 7045 Blanding Boulevard, Jacksonville, Florida 32244, Craig M. Green, Esquire and Eric J. Stockel, Esquire, 4000 Hollywood Boulevard, Suite 485-S, Hollywood, Florida 33021.

Motion for Leave to Amend

2012 WL 6837976 (Fla.Cir.Ct.)

Westlaw Query>>

To find additional Motion for Leave to Amend filings access the Florida Civil Trial Court Filings database (FL-FILING), choose Terms and Connectors search, then enter DT("leave to amend").

Circuit Court of Florida,

11th Judicial Circuit.

Miami-dade County

Ralph BALLARD, and Maria Ballard, his wife, Plaintiffs,

v.

R. J. REYNOLDS TOBACCO COMPANY, a North Carolina (New Jersey) corporation, Philip Morris USA, Inc., a Virginia corporation, Lorillard Tobacco Company, a Delaware corporation, Liggett Group LLC, a Delaware corporation, and Vector Group LTD., Inc., a Delaware corporation, Defendants.

No. 07-30336 CA 23.

June 12, 2012.

Circuit Civil Division

Plaintiffs' Supplemental Motion for Leave to Amend Complaint to Clarify Comparative Fault Admission & Add Counts for Punitive Damages and Incorporated Memorandum of Law

The Alvarez Law Firm, Attorneys for the Plaintiff, 355 Palermo Avenue, Coral Gables, FL 33134, Telephone: (305) 444-7675, Facsimile: (305) 444-0075, Email: alex@integrityforjustice.com, Alex Alvarez, Florida Bar No. 94634.

Plaintiff, RALPH BALLARD, by and through the undersigned counsel, hereby files this Supplemental Motion for Leave to Amend Complaint to Clarify Plaintiff's Comparative Fault Admission and Add Counts for Punitive Damages and Incorporated Memorandum of Law, and in support thereof state as follows:

Punitive Damages for Negligence and Strict Liability

There should be no dispute over the general proposition that, so long as the substantive standard for an award of punitive damages is met, punitive damages may be awarded on claims of negligence or strict products liability. *Owens-Corning Fiberglas Corp. v. Ballard,* 749 So. 2d 483, 488-89 (Fla. 1999) (punitive damage appropriate where conduct showed apparent indifference to the health and safety of individuals); *Piper Aircraft Corp. v. Coulter,* 426 So. 2d 1108, 1110 (Fla. 4th DCA 1983) ("a finding of strict liability, if coupled with a finding that [a defendant's] conduct was sufficiently egregious, would be enough to support the punitive damages claim");

Johns-Manville Sales Corp. v. Janssens, 463 So. 2d 242, 247-52 (Fla. 1st DCA 1984) ("It is not necessary to prove actual malice or intent to cause the particular injury sustained; the requisite malice or evil intent may be inferred from the defendant's having willfully pursued a course of action in wanton disregard of the potential harm likely to result as a consequence of that wrongful conduct").

The Florida Supreme Court was clear that the only aspects of *Engle* that carry over to the individual cases are the extended deadline for filing claims and the *res judicata* effect of the very specific findings approved by the court. There was no suggestion that this created any limitation on the kinds of damages individual plaintiffs could recover on those claims. Indeed, *Engle* reversed all class treatment of the punitive damages issue and held that the issues of both entitlement and amount of punitive damages could only be resolved in individual cases after a finding of liability, which had not been made in *Engle*. *Engle v. Ligget Group, Inc.,* 945 So. 2d 1246, 1278 (Fla. 2006) (finding the Phase I verdict only determined a breach of duty, but not liability, and therefore could not support punitive damages under *Ault v. Lohr,* 538 So. 2d 454, 456 (Fla. 1989)).

Mr. Ballard has asserted the exact same claims as were asserted in *Engle,* and the only difference is the kind of damages he seeks. Punitive damages do not require an independent claim. Rather, punitive damages are a remedy and can be recovered pursuant to a substantive claim. *E.g., Country Club of Miami Corp. v. McDaniel,* 310 So. 2d 436, 437 (Fla. 3d DCA 1975). Mr. Ballard asserts the same substantive claims that were pursued in the *Engle* class action, and therefore should be allowed to seek punitive damages based on all of those claims, including negligence and strict liability.

Plaintiff's Comparative Fault

Plaintiffs also amend their allegations regarding the comparative fault of Plaintiff, RALPH BALLARD, as stated in the attached Second Amended Complaint.

WHEREFORE, Plaintiffs respectfully request this Honorable Court for leave to amend their complaint to add punitive damages for the reasons stated herein as well as those stated in Plaintiffs' Amended Motion for Leave to Amend Complaint. Plaintiffs' proposed Second Amended Complaint is attached hereto as Exhibit A.

THE ALVAREZ LAW FIRM

Attorneys for the Plaintiff

355 Palermo Avenue

Coral Gables, FL 33134

Telephone: (305) 444-7675

Facsimile: (305) 444-0075

Email: *alex@integrityforjustice.com*

BY: <<signature>>

ALEX ALVAREZ

Florida Bar No. 94634

SERVICE LIST BALLARD v. R.J. REYNOLDS, et al, etc.

COUNSEL FOR RJ REYNOLDS TOBACCO COMPANY:

Benjamin Reid, Esq.

Amy E Furness, Esq.

Olga M. Vieira, Esq.

CARLTON FIELDS, P.A.

4000 Bank of America Tower

100 SE Second Street

Miami, FL 33131

Stephanie E. Parker, Esquire

JONES DAY

1420 Peachtree Street, N.E., Suite 800
Atlanta, Georgia 30309
Telephone: (404) 521-3939
Facsimile: (404) 581-8330
COUNSEL FOR PHILIP MORRIS USA INC.:
Mark J. Heise, Esq.
Luis E. Suarez, Esq.
BOIES SCHILLER & FLEXNER LLP
100 S.E. Second Street, Suite 2800
Miami, FL 33131
COUNSEL FOR LIGGETT GROUP, INC. and VECTOR GROUP LTD:
Kelly Anne Luther, Esq.
Kasowitz, Benson, Torres & Friedman, LLP
1441 Brickell Avenue, Suite 1420
Miami, Florida 33131

Motion for Summary Judgment

2012 WL 6139076 (Fla.Cir.Ct.)

Westlaw Query>>

To find additional Motion for Summary Judgment filings access the Florida Civil Trial Court Filings database (FL-FILING), choose Template search, select Search Motions then select Motion for Summary Judgment.

Circuit Court of Florida,

17th Judicial Circuit.

Broward County

David RICCIARDI, as Personal Representative of the Estate of Robyn Mantilla Timmes, Plaintiff,

v.

Lise-Marie France LAMBERT, M.D.; Holy Cross Hospital, d/b/a/ Holy Cross Medical Group; and Holy Cross Hospital, Inc., Defendants.

No. CACE 10-20658 (25).

October 4, 2012.

Defendants' Motion for Partial Summary Judgment

Heath & Carcioppolo, Chartered Attorneys for Lise-Marie France Lambert, M.D., Holy Cross Hospital d/b/a Holy Cross Medical Group; and Holy Cross Hospital, Inc., The legal Center, Suite 202, 888 S.E Third Avenue, Fort Lauderdale, FL 33316, Telephone: (954) 635-4350, Facsimile: (954) 635-4499, Kathryn L. Shanley, Florida Bar No. 53936.

Defendants, LISE MARIE-FRANCE LAMBERT, M.D., HOLY CROSS HOSPITAL d/b/a/ HOLY CROSS MEDICAL GROUP and HOLY CROSS HOSPITAL, INC., by and through undersigned counsel, and pursuant to Fla R. Civ. P.1.510, respectfully move this Honorable Court to enter a Partial Summary Judgment in favor of the Defendants and against the Plaintiff, and as grounds therefore would state:

1. Plaintiff David Ricciardi, as Personal Representative of the Estate of Robyn Mantilla Timmes, has filed a five-count Complaint against Lise Marie-France Lambert, M.D., Holy Cross Hospital d/b/a Holy Cross Medical Group and Holy Cross Hospital, Inc., for medical negligence (See attached hereto as Exhibit "A").

2. Count One of Plaintiff's Complaint alleges a claim of medical negligence against Lise Marie-France Lambert, M.D.; Count two alleges a claim against Holy Cross Hospital d/b/a/ Holy Cross Medical Group for vicarious liability for the alleged actions and/or inactions of Lise Marie-France Lambert, M.D.; Count Three alleges a claim against Holy Cross Hospital, Inc., for vicarious liability for the alleged actions and/or inactions of Lise Marie-France Lambert, M.D.; Count Four alleges a claim of negligence against Holy Cross Hospital d/b/a Holy Medical Group; and Count Five alleges a claim of negligence against Holy Cross Hospital, Inc.

3. Specifically, Count Four alleges that Holy Cross Hospital d/b/a/ Holy Cross Medical Group, through its "agents, servants and/or employees, physicians, nurses, staff and other related medical personnel" failed to:

a. Timely arrange for a hematology consultation;

b. Coordinate all clinical data to arrive at a correct diagnosis and treatment plan;

c. Send the patient for appropriate consultation in a timely manner;

d. Timely hospitalize the patient; and

e. Timely treat and/or timely treat the patient's condition.

4. Count Five alleges the same failures on behalf of the agents, servants, employees and physicians, nurses and staff of Holy Cross Hospital, Inc.

5. Pursuant to this Court's Uniform Trial Order, Plaintiff recently filed his expert disclosures. (See attached hereto as Exhibit "B"). Pursuant to Plaintiff's disclosures, each of Plaintiff's expert witnesses will offer standard of care testimony against Dr. Lambert, Plaintiff has disclosed no witness who will provide opinions of direct negligence against either Holy Cross Hospital d/b/a Holy Cross Medical Group or Holy Cross Hospital, Inc. Accordingly, Defendants are entitled to partial Summary Judgment as to Counts Four and Five of Plaintiff's Complaint.

6. There is no genuine issue of material fact as to any pertinent matters which would allow the Plaintiff to maintain an action for negligence against Holy Cross Hospital d/b/a Holy Cross Medical Group or Holy Cross Hospital, Inc.

7. In order to prove an action for medical negligence, the Plaintiff has the burden of proving that there was a breach of the prevailing standard of care. In the instant case, the Plaintiff has failed to present or produce any competent evidence supporting this necessary element against either Holy Cross Hospital d/b/a Holy Cross Medical Group or Holy Cross Hospital, Inc. Defendants, Holy Cross Hospital d/b/a Holy Medical Group and Holy Cross Hospital, Inc., are therefore entitled to Partial Summary Judgment as to Counts Four and Five of Plaintiff's Complaint. See *Sims v. B. Helms,* 345 So.2d. 721 (Fla. 1977); *Hunt v. Gerber,* 166 So.2d. 720 (Fla.3d. DCA 1964); *Thomas v. Berrios,* 348 So.2d. 905 (Fla.3d. DCA 1977); see also. *Spinner v. Wainer,* 430 So.2d. 595 (Fla.4th DCA 1983).

8. Further, the Plaintiff is unable to prove proximate causation against Holy Cross Hospital d/b/a Holy Cross Medical Group or Holy Cross Hospital, Inc. Plaintiff cannot produce competent evidence establishing that any acts or omissions of Defendants, Holy Cross Hospital d/b/a Holy Cross Medical Group or Holy Cross Hospital, Inc., proximately caused the injuries allegedly sustained by the Plaintiff. In the absence of such evidence, there is insufficient basis to create a jury question as to causation in this medical malpractice action against Holy Cross Hospital d/b/a Holy Cross Medical Group or Holy Cross Hospital, Inc., *Beisel v. Lazenby,* 444 So.2d. 953 (Fla.1984); see also *Dawson v. Weems,* 352 So.2d. 1200 (Fla. 4th DCA 1978).

WHEREFORE, for the foregoing reasons, Defendants, Holy Cross Hospital d/b/a Holy Cross Medical Group and Holy Cross Hospital, Inc., respectfully request this Court enter an order granting Partial Summary Judgment as to Counts Four and Five of Plaintiff's Complaint.

HEATH & CARCIOPPOLO, CHARTERED

Attorneys for LISE-MARIE FRANCE LAMBERT, M.D., HOLY CROSS HOSPITAL d/b/a HOLY CROSS MEDICAL GROUP; and HOLY CROSS HOSPITAL, INC.

The legal Center, Suite 202

888 S.E Third Avenue

Fort Lauderdale, FL 33316

Telephone: (954) 635-4350

Facsimile: (954) 635-4499

By: <<signature>>

KATHRYN L. SHANLEY

Florida Bar No. 53936

Motion for Sanctions

2012 WL 6729841 (Fla.Cir.Ct.)

Westlaw Query>>

To find additional Motion for Sanctions filings access the Florida Civil Trial Court Filings database (FL-FILING), choose Terms and Connectors search, then enter DT(sanction!).

Circuit Court of Florida,

Eleventh Judicial Circuit.

Miami-dade County

WAYNE BLACK & ASSOCIATES, INC., a Florida corporation, Plaintiff,

v.

AL RUSHAID PETROLEUM INVESTMENT CO., a Foreign corporation, Defendant.

No. 11-08327 CA 11.

February 10, 2012.

Defendant's Motion for Sanctions Pursuant to Florida Statutes 57.105

Lyons & Lurvey, P.A., 175 Southwest 7th Street, Suite 2009, Miami, Florida 33130, Telephone: (305) 379-5554, Facsimile: (305) 379-4548, James J. Gangitano, Florida Bar No.: 74111.

Judge: Diane V. Ward.

COMES NOW Defendant, Al Rushaid Petroleum Investment Co. ("ARPIC" or "Defendant"), by and through undersigned counsel, and moves this Honorable Court for Sanctions pursuant to Florida Statutes 57.105, and as grounds thereof respectfully states:

I. *INTRODUCTION*

In the fall of 2009, Rasheed A.R. Al Rushaid ("Al Rushaid") retained the law firm of William L. Richey, P.A. ("Richey"), to provide certain legal services and to conduct the requisite investigations needed for those legal services. The Agreement attached to the Amended Complaint as Exhibit "1" (sometimes referred to as the "Agreement") demonstrates that ARPIC was not a party to that agreement. Neither was Black.

The Agreement further demonstrates that Black was to be retained by Richey (not by ARPIC or Al Rushaid); that Richey (not ARPIC or Al Rushaid) was obligated to pay Black; and that Al Rushaid (and not ARPIC) was then responsible for paying Richey for investigator's fees in accordance with the terms of the Agreement and the cap set forth therein.

The terms of this Agreement attached to the Amended Complaint rebut and negate each and every one of Black's claims against ARPIC. There is absolutely no good faith basis for the assertion that, somehow, someway, ARPIC is now obligated to pay Black. In fact, this assertion is wholly frivolous and without any factual and legal support. Furthermore, because Black has not sued Richey in this action, Plaintiff's Amended Complaint is deficient in that it fails to join an indispensable party.

For the foregoing reasons, this action is not supported by the material facts necessary to establish the claim or defense; and would not be supported by the application of then-existing law to those material facts.

II. *THE AMENDED COMPLAINT AND EXHIBITS*

Although Black alleges in purely conclusory terms that ARPIC is obligated to pay Black, the Agreement attached to the Amended Complaint as Exhibit "1" negates and refutes this allegation. The signature block at the bottom of page three clearly demonstrates that Al Rushaid signed the agreement individually, and not on behalf of ANY corporation. The Agreement further establishes that Al Rushaid (and not ARPIC) contracted with Richey (not Black). Neither Black nor ARPIC is a party to the Agreement.

The Agreement makes clear that, Al Rushaid, individually, retained Richey to perform certain services and agreed to reimburse Richey for costs, specifically including the costs of any necessary investigators. The key provision states:

> You [Rushaid] will be responsible for all costs and expenses, which include travel, private accounting or consulting fees, private investigator fees and the legal fees of all attorneys other than William L. Richey, P.A. Costs, such as filing fees, expedited mail, bulk copying costs, deposition costs, *expert and investigative fees,* and computerized legal research costs *will be itemized and billed on monthly invoices.* Prior to any large out-of-pocket expenditure, it is our policy and practice to consult with you in advance and obtain your approval. All travel is business class or equivalent accommodations.

See Agreement at p. 2. The contract also capped Al Rushaid's obligation to reimburse Richey at 60,000 British pounds. *Id.*

In fact, other than the false and conclusory allegations in the Amended Complaint that are negated and rebutted by the exhibits, there is absolutely no factual or legal support for the assertion that ARPIC ever had any obligation to pay Black for services Black provided to Richey and Al Rushaid, individually, in conjunction with the Agreement. None of the invoices (which are attached to the Amended Complaint as Exhibits "2", "3" and "4") were ever sent to ARPIC. None ever even mentioned ARPIC. The invoice attached as Exhibit "2" was sent to "Gerold Ibler, CFO/The Al Rushaid Companies." The invoices attached as Exhibits "3" and "4" were sent to "Gerold Ibler, CFO, The Al Rushaid Companies, c/o William L. Richey, Esq."

Furthermore, the e-mail dated October 8, 2009, from Gerold Ibler to Richey, not to Black, is attached as Exhibit "B" to the Motion to Dismiss Amended Complaint. This email demonstrates that payment of the 60,000 British pounds was to be made from Al Rushaid's personal account, and not from the account of ANY corporation. The exhibits to the Amended Complaint contradict the allegations set forth by Black in support of all of its claims against ARPIC. Under well-established legal principles, this action is not supported by the material facts necessary to establish the claim or defense; and would not be supported by the application of then-existing law to those material facts.

III. *LEGAL ARGUMENT*

A. *PLAINTIFF'S AMENDED COMPLAINT SHOULD BE DISMISSED FOR FAILURE TO STATE A CLAIM*

Because the exhibits attached to the Amended Complaint all demonstrate that either Richey, or Al Rushaid, individually, are the only parties that could possibly be responsible for paying the amounts claimed by Black in its Amended Complaint, these exhibits are fatal to ALL of the claims asserted against ARPIC. It is well-established that the court must consider exhibits attached to and incorporated in an amended complaint. *Harry Pepper & Assoc. v. Lasseter,* 247 So. 2d 736 (Fla. 3rd DCA 1971). An inconsistency between allegations of fact in the complaint and specific facts revealed by attached exhibit has the effect of neutralizing each allegation, "rendering the pleading objectable." *Id.*

If the attached exhibit negates the allegations of the complaint, "the plain language of the document will control and may be the basis for a motion to dismiss." *Warren v. Dairyland Ins. Co.,* 662 So. 2d 1387, 1388 (Fla. 4th DCA 1995); *see also Fladell v. Palm Beach Cnty. Canvassing Bd.,* 772 So. 2d 1240, 1243 (Fla. 2000) ("If an exhibit facially negates the cause of action asserted, the document attached as an exhibit controls and must be considered in determining a motion to dismiss."); *Health Care Systems, Inc. v. Hartford Life & Accident Ins. Co.,* 381 So. 2d 294 (Fla. 1st DCA 1980) ("Under Florida Rules of Civil Procedure, and case law interpreting the rule, exhibits attached to the pleading become a part for all purposes, and if an attached document negates pleader's cause of action. . . plain language of document will control and may be basis for motion to dismiss."). The exhibits attached to Black's Amended Complaint negate the claims filed by Black and this action is not supported by the material facts necessary to establish the claim or defense; and would not be supported by the application of then-existing law to those material facts.

1. Plaintiff's claim for breach of contract is not supported by the material facts necessary to establish the claim or defense; and would not be supported by the application of then-existing law to those material facts.

Black's breach of contract claim is purposefully vague. There is no real dispute that Black has no legitimate claim against ARPIC pursuant to the written Agreement attached to the Amended Complaint. ARPIC is not a party to that contract.

Black's attempt to assert a frivolous claim against ARPIC for breach of an oral agreement is likewise contradicted by the exhibits to the Amended Complaint; any imaginable agreement with Black, oral or otherwise, could only have been with Richey, or with Al Rushaid, individually. The exhibits to the Amended Complaint rebut the existence of any oral agreement with ARPIC.

Furthermore, any alleged oral agreement would be barred under the Statute of Frauds and is therefore unenforceable. The exhibits to the Amended Complaint make clear that either Black or Richey had the primary obligation to pay Black. Any alleged promise to pay by anyone else constitutes a promise to pay the debt of another under section 725.01 of the Florida Statutes, Florida's Statute of Frauds. Such a promise must be in writing and signed by the parties to be valid. No signed writing evidencing ARPIC's alleged promise to pay Black is attached to the Amended Complaint because none exists.

Specifically, section 725.01 of the Florida Statutes provides in pertinent part:

> Promise to pay another's debt, etc.
>
> "No action shall be brought whereby to charge any executor or administrator upon any special promise to answer or pay any debt or damages out of her or his own estate, or whereby to charge the defendant upon any special promise to answer for the debt, default or miscarriage of another person by the Statute of Frauds and should be dismissed unless the agreement or promise upon which such action shall be brought, or some note or memorandum thereof shall be in writing and signed by the party to be charged therewith or by some other person by her or him thereunto lawfully authorized."

Plaintiff's purported claim against ARPIC for breach of contract of an alleged oral agreement is barred by the Statute of Frauds and is not supported by the material facts necessary to establish the claim or defense; and would not be supported by the application of then-existing law to those material facts.

2. Plaintiff's claims for promissory estoppel are not supported by the material facts necessary to establish the claim or defense; and would not be supported by the application of then-existing law to those material facts.

The exhibits attached to the Amended Complaint also do not support Black's claim for promissory estoppel. First, the Statute of Frauds not only bars any claim based upon an oral agreement it also bars Plaintiff's claim for promissory estoppel. Promissory estoppel is never available to replace a writing required by the Statute. *See Tanenbaum v. Biscayne Osteopathic Hospital, Inc.,* 190 So. 2d 777 (Fla. 1966). As the court explained upon adopting this rule, "The question that emerges for resolution by us is whether or not we will adopt by judicial action the doctrine of promissory estoppel as a sort of counteraction to the legislatively created Statute of Frauds. This we decline to do." Under the court's reasoning, Black's only option was to meet the requirements of the Statute, if he truly expected payment from ARPIC. "The petitioner had but to follow the provisions of the Statute of Frauds to secure his rights under the arrangement with the respondent instead of taking the position, rather tardily, that [the Statute's provisions] did not apply to him." *Id.* (affirming directed verdict).

In *Shore Holdings, Inc. v. Seagate Beach Quarters, Inc.,* 842 So. 2d 1010 (Fla. 4th DCA 2003), plaintiff based a claim of promissory estoppel on oral assurances that defendant would modify a deal's written terms and convey property after the written contract had expired by its own terms. The court of appeals found error in the trial court's failure to direct a verdict. Where the subject of the transaction was within the Statute, neither a claim of promissory estoppel, nor an alleged oral modification of the written agreement, survived the Statute. Id., see also *Wharfside at Boca Pointe, Inc. v. Superior Bank,* 741 So. 2d 542, 545 (Fla. 4th DCA 1999) (explaining that "[a]n agreement that is required by the statute of frauds to be in writing cannot be orally modified"); *University Creek v. Boston*

American Financial, 100 F. Supp. 2d 1345 (S.D. Fla. 2000) (affirming summary judgment on claim for promissory estoppel where matter was within the statute of frauds).

Further, Black's promissory estoppel claim is also defective because the exhibits to the Amended Complaint demonstrate that ARPIC never made any promises to Black. How can Black in good faith allege reasonable reliance on a promise that ARPIC never made. Moreover, under well-established principles of law:

> Enforcement [of the alleged promise] must be necessary to avoid injustice. *Satisfaction of the latter requirement may depend on the reasonableness of the promisee's reliance,* on its definite and substantial character in relation to the remedy sought, on *the formality with which the promise is made,* on the extent to which the . . . functions of form are met by the commercial setting or otherwise, and on the extent to which such other policies as the enforcement of bargains and the prevention of unjust enrichment are relevant.

Restatement (Second) of Contracts, Section 90 (1979).

Since no representation or promise was made by ARPIC, Black never reasonably relied on any such promise. According to the Amended Complaint, Black knew the terms of the Al Rushaid/Richey contract and expected payment under *its* terms. Indeed, "the formality with which the [alleged oral promise] is made" pales in comparison to the formality of the agreement between Al Rushaid and Richey. Black's own actions, as described in the Amended Complaint, prove that he was not expecting payment directly from ARPIC.

3. Plaintiff's claim for quantum meruit is not supported by the material facts necessary to establish the claim or defense; and would not be supported by the application of then-existing law to those material facts.

As discussed in detail, the exhibits attached to the Amended Complaint establish that Al Rushaid individually contracted with Richey in connection with the investigative services ultimately provided by Black. Accordingly, any benefit that was conferred by Black could only have been conferred upon Al Rushaid, individually, or upon Richey. There is no good faith basis for the assertion that a benefit was conferred upon ARPIC, an entity that is not mentioned at all in the Agreement attached to the Amended Complaint or in any of the exhibits attached to the Amended Complaint. This assertion is negated and contradicted by the Amended Complaint's exhibits, and any claim based on this assertion is not supported by the material facts necessary to establish the claim or defense; and would not be supported by the application of then-existing law to those material facts.

In *W.R. Townsend Contracting, Inc. v. Jensen Civil Constr., Inc.,* the court stated that "[t]he law should place a tougher burden on a plaintiff who relies on an implied contract than it does on one `who uses reasonable care and foresight in protecting himself by means of an express contract.' " 728 So. 2d 297, 305 (Fla. 1st DCA 1999), *citing Hermanowski v. Naranja Lakes Condominium No. Five, Inc.,* 421 So. 2d 558, 560 (Fla. 3d DCA 1982); *Bromer v. Florida Power & Light Co.,* 45 So. 2d 658 (Fla.1949).

Black cannot meet this "tougher burden" here. If any benefit was conferred on anyone, the Agreement attached to the Amended Complaint establishes that it was conferred upon Richey or Al Rushaid, individually. The notion that ARPIC received a benefit in connection with Black's performance is not supported by the facts or the exhibits attached to the Amended Complaint. As in *Hermanowski,* "[t]he [defendant] should not be penalized for [plaintiff's] loose dealings." 421 So. 2d at 560.

Furthermore, it is well-established that the existence of an express contract precludes resort to equity and claims in quasi-contract. In *Ocean Communications, Inc. v. Bubeck,* 956 So.2d 1222, 1225 (Fla. 4th DCA 2007), the court stated a plaintiff cannot pursue an equitable theory such as unjust enrichment or quantum meruit if an express contract exists. Quantum meruit claims should be disallowed as a matter of law if there is an express contract on the same general subject matter. *Hagen v. Cobb,* 117 So. 853 (Fla. 1928); *Williams v. Stewart,* 424 So.2d 204 (Fla. 2d DCA 1983); *Poe v. Estate of Levy,* 411 So.2d 253 (Fla. 4th DCA 1982); *Tobin & Tobin Ins. Agency v. Zeskind,* 315 So.2d 518 (Fla. 3rd DCA 1975); *Solutec v. Young & Lawrence Assoc., Inc.,* 243 So.2d 605 (Fla. 4th DCA 1971).

Here, there is an express agreement on the same general subject matter -- the agreement attached to the Amended Complaint. This agreement bars Plaintiff's claim against ARPIC for quantum meruit.

4. Plaintiff's claim for account stated is not supported by the material facts necessary to establish the claim or defense; and would not be supported by the application of then-existing law to those material facts.

Plaintiff's claim for account stated is not supported by the material facts necessary to establish the claim or defense; and would not be supported by the application of then-existing law to those material facts. The exhibits to the

Amended Complaint reflect that no services were provided to ARPIC. Accordingly, there is simply no valid account between Black and ARPIC. "For an account stated to exist as a matter of law, there must be an agreement between the parties that a certain balance is correct and due and an express or implicit promise to pay this balance." *Merrill-Stevens Dry Dock Co. v. Corniche Exp.,* 400 So.2d 1286 (Fla. 3rd DCA 1981). No such agreement exists here.

Moreover, Plaintiff's claim for account stated is legally insufficient because the invoices attached to the Amended Complaint as Exhibits 2, 3 and 4 demonstrate that Black never sent a single statement of account to ARPIC. *See Myrick v. St. Catherine Laboure Manor, Inc.,* 529 So.2d 369 (Fla. 1st DCA 1988) (holding that an essential element of the cause of action is the defendant's failure to dispute an invoice issued *to the defendant).* Having issued no invoices to ARPIC, Black cannot "demonstrate that the parties had agreed `that a certain balance is correct and due' and that there was `an express or implicit promise to pay this balance,' " and the claim is properly dismissed as a matter of law. *See F.D.I.C. v. Brodie,* 602 So.2d 1358 (Fla. 3d DCA 1992). For this reason, Plaintiff's claim is not supported by the material facts necessary to establish the claim or defense; and would not be supported by the application of then-existing law to those material facts.

5. Plaintiff's claim as third party beneficiary is not supported by the material facts necessary to establish the claim or defense; and would not be supported by the application of then-existing law to those material facts.

Plaintiff finally contends that it is a third party beneficiary of the agreement between Al Rushaid and Richey. In making this allegation, Plaintiff still does not indicate why it is suing ARPIC rather than Rasheed A.R. Al Rushaid, who is the signatory to the underlying contract with Richey. For this reason, Plaintiff's claim is not supported by the material facts necessary to establish the claim or defense; and would not be supported by the application of then-existing law to those material facts.

Further, a "person who is not a party to a contract may not sue for breach of that contract where that person receives only an incidental or consequential benefit from the contract." *Caretta Trucking, Inc. v. Cheoy Lee Shipyards, Ltd.,* 647 So.2d 1028, 1030-31 (Fla. 4th DCA 1994 (*citing Metropolitan Life Ins. Co. v. McCarson,* 467 So.2d 277 (Fla. 1985). "The exception to this rule is where the entity that is not a party to the contract is an intended third party beneficiary of the contract." *Caretta,* 647 So.2d at 1031. The right of a third party beneficiary to sue under a contract is limited to those situations where the provisions of the contract clearly show an intention primarily and directly to benefit the individual bringing suit or to a class of persons to which he claims to belong as a third party beneficiary. *Security Mut. Cas. Co. v. Pacura,* 402 So.2d 1266 (Fla. 3rd DCA 1981); see also *Wright v. Terry,* 23 Fla. 160, 2 So. 6 (1887); *McCann Plumbing Co. v. Plumbing Industry Program,* 105 So.2d 26 (Fla. 3d DCA 1958); Bryant v. Cole, 282 So.2d 652 (Fla. 2d DCA 1973); *Mulligan v. Wallace,* 349 So.2d 745 (Fla. 3d DCA 1977).

"Additionally, in order to find the requisite intent, it must be shown that *both* contracting parties intended to benefit the third party. It is insufficient to show that only one party unilaterally intended to benefit the third party." *Caretta,* 647 So.2d at 1031; *see also Clark and Co. v. Department of Ins.*, 436 So.2d 1013, 1016 (Fla. 1st DCA 1983). The second page of the Agreement between Richey and Rasheed A. R. Al Rushaid provides a laundry list of examples of the types of expenses which would be reimbursable under the Agreement, including travel, private accounting or consulting fees, private investigator fees, legal fees to other attorneys, filing fees, expedited mail, bulk copying costs, deposition costs, and computerized legal research.

There is no indication that *both* parties intended to benefit Black, a third party. His services are placed in the same category under the Agreement as expedited mail, filing fees, and costs of bulk copying. *See* Agreement at 2. There is no indication that Black was an *intended* third-party beneficiary any more than FedEx or Westlaw. Black is an incidental beneficiary who has recourse against Richey, the entity who retained his services. Black inexplicably has not made Richey a party to this suit.

B. *PLAINTIFF'S AMENDED COMPLAINT FAILS TO JOIN AN INDISPENSABLE PARTY AND IS NOT SUPPORTED BY THE MATERIAL FACTS NECESSARY TO ESTABLISH THE CLAIM OR DEFENSE; AND WOULD NOT BE SUPPORTED BY THE APPLICATION OF THEN-EXISTING LAW TO THOSE MATERIAL FACTS.*

Plaintiff's failure to join Richey as a defendant in this action under Rule 1.140(b)(7) supports this motion as this action is not supported by the material facts necessary to establish the claim or defense; and would not be supported by the application of then-existing law to those material facts. "Indispensable parties" to a lawsuit are "[P]ersons who have not only an interest in the controversy, but an interest of such a nature that a final decree cannot be made without either affecting that interest or leaving the controversy in such a condition that its final termination may be wholly inconsistent with equity and good conscience." *Glancy v. First W. Bank,* 802 So.2d 498 (Fla. 4th DCA 2001); *see also Hertz Corp. v. Piccolo,* 453 So.2d 12, 14 n.3 (Fla. 1984) ("Indispensable parties are necessary parties so essential to a suit that no final decision can be rendered without their joinder."); *Kozich v. Shahady,* 702 So.2d 1289 (Fla. 4th DCA 1997) (holding that a law firm to which the client paid an initial retainer was an indispensable party in a legal malpractice action brought by a client against a separate law firm which included some of the same principals); *Lambert v. Dracos,* 403 So.2d 481 (Fla. 1st DCA 1981) (reversing order denying motion to dismiss for failure to join indispensable parties); *Aronovitz v. Stein Properties,* 322 So.2d 74 (Fla. 3d DCA 1975) (reversing order denying motion to dismiss for failure to join an indispensable party finding each partner of a partnership to be indispensable parties).

As discussed, Richey was the "centerpiece" of the relationship between Black and Al Rushaid. The exhibits to the Amended Complaint demonstrate that Richey had the obligation to pay Black and that Al Rushaid had the obligation to pay Richey. Richey is an indispensable party under Rule 1.140(b)(7).

C. *DEFENDANT HAS COMPLIED WITH THE NOTICE REQUIREMENT PURSUANT TO FLORIDA STATUTES 57.105.*

Pursuant to Florida Statutes 57.105(4), Defendant has previously provided statutory notice to its intent to file this motion pursuant to Florida Statutes 57.105(4). Demand was made to dismiss the Amended Complaint within twenty-one (21) days, and the twenty-one (21) days passed without Plaintiff voluntarily dismissing the Amended Complaint. Sanctions are appropriate pursuant to Florida Statutes 57.105 since this action is not supported by the material facts necessary to establish the claim or defense; and would not be supported by the application of then-existing law to those material facts.

Respectfully submitted,

LYONS & LURVEY, P.A.

175 Southwest 7th Street

Suite 2009

Miami, Florida 33130

Telephone: (305) 379-5554

Facsimile: (305) 379-4548

By: <<signature>>

James J. Gangitano

Florida Bar No.: 74111

Motion to Compel Discovery

2012 WL 6542690 (Fla.Cir.Ct.)

Westlaw Query>>
To find additional Motion to Compel Discovery filings access the Florida Civil Trial Court Filings database (FL-FILING), choose Template search, select Search Motions then select Motion to Compel Discovery.

Circuit Court of Florida,

11th Judicial Circuit.

Miami-dade County

Alberta HANKINS, Plaintiff,

v.

Yeseny SERRA, Defendant.

No. 11-10621 CA 09.

August 27, 2012.

General Jurisdiction Division

Florida Bar No.: 386110

Plaintiff's Emergency Motion to Compel Defendant to Sign Answers to Boecher Expert Witness Interrogatories and Motion to Compel Defendant to Produce Better/Complete Answers to Boecher Expert Interrogatories No. 2,3 and 4 Re: 2011 to Present Before the 8/28/12 3:00 P.M. Video/Trial Deposition of Dr. Michael Aptman

Jose Fernandez, Esq., Law Office of Jose C. Fernandez, 9725 N.W. 117th Avenue, Suite 410, Miami, Florida 33178.

Law Offices of Gregg R. Schwartz, P.A., 7700 N. Kendall Drive, Suite 503, Miami, Fl 33156, Tele: 305-595-4744 / Fax: 305-595-4739.

Plaintiff, ALBERTA HANKINS, by and through undersigned counsel, hereby files this Emergency Motion To Compel Defendant To Sign Answers to Boecher Expert Witness Interrogatories and Motion To Compel Defendant To Produce Better/Complete Answers To Boecher Expert Interrogatories No. 2, 3 and 4 Re: 2011 to Present Before The 8/28/12 3:00 p.m. Video/Trial Deposition of Dr. Michael Aptman, and as grounds therefore states:

1. This bodily injury two car accident case is scheduled for jury trial as the No. 1 case for the week commencing September 10, 2012.

2. Dr. Michael Aptman, a defense medical examiner (neurologist) is scheduled to be videotaped for trial by Progressive Ins. Co.'s in-house attorney at 3:00 p.m. on Tuesday, August 28, 2012.

3. Plaintiff served *Boecher* Expert Witness Interrogatories via facsimile on July 23, 2012 re: long-time defense medical examiner Dr. Michael Aptman, a neurologist. He has been a defense expert for decades and been retained by Defendants thousands of times. He has testified for the insurance carrier (Progressive Ins. Co.) for this defendant, on prior occasions.

4. The video/trial deposition of Dr. Aptman was originally scheduled by defense counsel for 10:00 a.m., on August 23, 2012. Defendant then changed the deposition to August 24, 2012. Now, the deposition is scheduled for tomorrow, August 28, 2012 at 3:00 p.m.

5. The answers to the interrogatories were due to be served by August 22, 2011.

6. Out of an abundance of caution, the undersigned filed a Motion To Shorten Time For Defendant to Respond to Plaintiff's Expert Witness Interrogatories. The undersigned was concerned that defendant might "serve" the answers in such a manner so that I might not physically receive them until after the August 23, 2012 deposition commenced. The Court Granted the Motion to the extent that the answers were required to be served at least 24 hours before Dr. Aptman's video/trial deposition of August 23, 2012.

7. In addition, the Order required Defendant to serve said Expert Interrogatories Answers *at least 24 hours before* Dr. Aptman's deposition, if the video/trial deposition was rescheduled by the parties.

8. The Defendant attempted to violate the letter and spirit of Judge Bagley's August 16, 2012 Order as Defendant failed to serve the answers to the *Boecher* interrogatories by 10:00 a.m. on August 23, 2012, for the August 24, 2012 10:00 a.m. deposition. The undersigned was in court before Judge Miller in the a.m. of August 23, 2012 and returned at approximately 11:30 a.m. The undersigned called defense counsel at about 11:45 a.m. and had to leave a voice mail asking why the answers to the Boecher Interrogatories were not in my possession, as 10:00 a.m. had passed. I had emailed Judge Bagley a letter and a Motion For Protective Order at 1:23 p.m. Thereafter, at approximately 1:35 p.m., I received a phone call from defense counsel on my cell while going to lunch and defense counsel said he was in a mediation in the a.m. and would have the answers to the *Boecher* interrogatories to me by 5:00 p.m. I advised defense counsel that such was not acceptable and a clear violation of Judge Bagley's order. *Defense counsel would not reschedule the deposition so* I could have 24 hours to review any Boecher *interrogatory answers/responses,* to check them for completeness and content. He claimed the August 24, 2012 was the only date Dr. Aptman could give the video/trial deposition. I told the in-house defense attorney I would not be attending the video/trial deposition and *defense counsel clearly stated he was going forward with the video/trial without me, despite being in violation of Judge Bagley's August 16, 2012 Order.* Per the generally accepted practice in this jurisdiction, I served a Motion For Protective Order and wasted much time doing so. Judge Bagley was on vacation. I had to call several Alternate Judges, until I found that only Judge Gayles was available. As soon as I sent the next letter to Judge Gayles, defense counsel somehow found a new deposition date of Tuesday, August 28, 2012 at 3:00 p.m.

9. We had a brief telephonic hearing before Judge Gayles, but no order was entered. Defense counsel for the FIRST TIME and as a surprise to me told Judge Gayles that the reason he could not timely provide the answers before the August 24, 2012 deposition was because his 85 year old father-in-law was seriously ill and hospitalized and that his house was turned "upside down" and that he and his wife were taking turns caring of his ill relative.

10. However, the defense attorney had time to attend an August 23, 2012 mediation and had time to prepare for Dr. Aptman's video/trial deposition. The undersigned firmly believes that defense counsel was simply trying to bully me into going to the video/trial deposition with late-answered and incomplete, significant expert discovery, in clear violation of Judge Bagley's Order. In other words, despite a very ill father-in-law, defense counsel was ready, willing, and able to attend the, morning mediation and was willing and able to attend the deposition of Dr. Aptman by himself, and without counsel for Ms. Hankins.

THE BOECHER EXPERT INTERROGATORY ANSWERS ARE UNSIGNED AND UNVERIFIED AND A NULLITY AND IMPROPER UNDER FLA. R. CIV. P. 1.340 (a) AND THE COURT SHOULD ORDER THEM SIGNED FORTHWITH

11. Defendant served incomplete answers to the *Boecher* Interrogatories with *no* signature and they are also unverified. Fla. R. Civ. P. 1.340 (a) requires interrogatories to be signed by the party. See *Parker v. James,* 997 So. 2d 1225 (Fla. 2d DCA 2008). These answers must be signed by the party and notarized forthwith for appropriate cross-examination at the video/trial deposition. I wrote Defense counsel a letter requesting same after orally being told by defense counsel last week that he does not have to serve signed expert interrogatory answers. The response was that he will try to get them signed. An Order is unfortunately required to get the defendant to act in accordance with the Florida Rules of Procedure and case law. I sent defense counsel the law as well. Attached is the August 27, 2012 correspondence sent to defense counsel.

THE LATE-FILED BOECHER INTERROGATORY ANSWERS/RESPONSES DO NOT CONTAIN ANSWERS RE: 2011-2012, AS REQUESTED

12. Interrogatories 2, 3 and 4 (attached) request financial and case information for the past 3 years with respect to Dr. Aptman.

13. *Allstate v. Boecher,* 733 So. 2d 993 (Fla. 1999) and its progeny, such as *Allstate Ins. Co. v. Hodges,* 855 So. 2d 636 (Fla. 2d DCA 2003) (attached) require complete answers to the subject interrogatories. Judge Bagley told defense counsel to try and get the answers re: 2011-12 before the originally scheduled deposition of August 23, 2012. Judge Bagley also stated that if the parties agree to reschedule the deposition later, that defense counsel should endeavor to get the 2011-12 answers. The undersigned is the one who requested and suggested a later deposition date so I could get the all important 2011-2012 answers. Sure enough, for reasons cited above, the deposition is now scheduled 35 days after the service of the *Boecher* interrgatories. Thus, Defendant should be providing the 2011-12 information re: cases Dr. Aptman worked on as a defense medical examiner for Progressive and amounts paid to Dr. Aptman. Progressive's in-house attorney represents the insured/defendant. Defense counsel had not even requested the 2011-12 financial information as of the August 16, 2012 hearing, despite that fact that the *Boecher* Interrogatories were served via facsimile on July 23, 2012. He now claims to have first asked for the discovery information on August 16, 2012.

14. Progressive must have possession of these answers and in this computer age, the answers/data can be obtained very quickly. It is inconceivable that Progressive Ins. Co. does not keep this information in the post *Boecher* era. See *Allstate Ins. Co. v. Hodges,* 855 So. 2d 636 (Fla. 2d DCA 2003) wherein the court agreed with the same argument and compelled the information. *Boecher* was decided in 1999 and *Hodges,* in 2003. In the nine (9) years since *Hodges,* Progressive has likely developed and probably perfected the computer system to maintain this often-requested and required financial and case information.

15. If this Court orders the 2011-12 information RIGHT NOW, in all likelihood it will and can be produced before the deposition of Dr. Aptman, scheduled at 3:00 p.m. on August 28, 2012. Otherwise, his deposition should be taken on another day before the possible trial of September 10, 2012. If Dr. Aptman cannot appear after August 28, 2012 due to his travel/vacation schedule, he should then be stricken or his cross-exam of the video deposition taken on another day. Defendant has an orthopedic defense medical examiner for this arthroscopic shoulder surgery (and neck injection) case. Plaintiff's all important cross exam should not be hindered and rendered significantly less effective due to Progressive Ins. Co. or Defendant's failure to provide timely, complete, and sworn *Boecher* interrogatory answers.

16. The Plaintiff understands that Dr. Aptman is semi-retired and probably does almost exclusively defense exams. Maybe this is the reason defendant is hesitating to answer the *Boecher* interrogatories re: 2011 and 2012 to date. The amount of money paid to Dr. Aptman is probably way more than it was from 2008-2010. A Court Order is necessary to enforce the Florida Rules of Procedure, *Boecher* and its progeny.

17. Failure to receive the 2011-12 information and sworn interrogatory answers is unduly prejudicial to Plaintiff and the Court should award sanctions in the form of reasonable attorney's fees under Fla. R. Civ. P. 1.380 (c) (4).

WHEREFORE, Plaintiff requests that the Court enter an order granting Plaintiff's Emergency Motion To Compel Defendant To Sign Answers to Boecher Expert Witness Interrogatories and Motion To Compel Defendant To Produce Better/Complete Answers To Boecher Expert Interrogatories No. 2, 3 and 4 Re: 2011 to Present Before The 8/28/12 3:00 p.m. Video/Trial Deposition of Dr. Michael Aptman, and for such other and further relief as the Court deems just and fair.

LAW OFFICES OF GREGG R. SCHWARTZ, P.A.

7700 N. Kendall Drive, Suite 503

Miami, Fl 33156

Tele: 305-595-4744 / Fax: 305-595-4739

BY: <<signature>>

GREGG R. SCHWARTZ

Motion for Directed Verdict

2012 WL 6542327 (Fla.Cir.Ct.)

Westlaw Query>>

To find additional Motion for Directed Verdict filings access the Florida Civil Trial Court Filings database (FL-FILING), choose Template search, select Search Motions then select Motion for Directed Verdict.

Circuit Court of Florida,

11th Judicial Circuit.

Miami-dade County

Dr. Katherine MURPHY, Plaintiff,

v.

CITY OF AVENTURA, a Municipality Governed Under the Laws of the State of Florida, Aventura City of Excellence School, an educational unit and public school, Charter Schools USA, Inc., a Florida Corporation, Charter Schools USA at Aventura, LLC, a Florida limited liability Company, Eric Soroka, in his official and individual capacities, Nicole Munroe, an individual, Teresa Soroka, an individual., Defendants.

No. 09-57209 CA (27).

October 31, 2012.

Defendant, Eric Soroka's, Motion for Directed Verdict on the Plaintiff's Claim for Tortious Interference with Business Relations with the Plaintiff's Business Relations with the City

Michael T. Burke, Fla. Bar No. 338771, Attorneys for Defendant Eric Soroka, Johnson, Anselmo, Murdoch, Burke, Piper & Hochman, PA, 2455 E. Sunrise Blvd., Suite 1000, Fort Lauderdale, FL 33304, Tel: 954-463-0100, Fax: 954-463-2444, Burke@jambg.com, Cardona@jambg.com.

Defendant, ERIC SOROKA, by and through his undersigned attorneys and pursuant to Florida Rule of Civil Procedure 1.480, requests entry of directed verdict on the claim for intentional interference with the Plaintiff's business relationship with the City and in support would state:

1. In Count III, Murphy alleges that Eric Soroka and others intentionally interfered with Murphy's business relationship with the City to serve as the principal of the Aventura City of Excellence School ("ACES"). *See* 5th Am. Compl.

2. The evidence presented by the Plaintiff in her case as to this claim is as follows:

a. Eric Soroka is the City of Aventura City Manager. As City Manager, he is responsible to the City Commission for the administration of all City affairs. His responsibilities include the hiring, supervision, and removal of all City employees.

b. The Aventura City of Excellence School ("ACES") is a municipal-sponsored charter school and is operated by the City.

c. The City Manager is responsible to the City Commission for the administration of the day-to-day operations of ACES.

d. The principal of ACES is an employee of the City, who, as a department head, reports directly to the City Manager. Among other duties, the principal of ACES is responsible for the admission of students.

e. The City hired the Plaintiff to be the principal at ACES on April 1, 2003.

f. The Plaintiff did not have a contract for employment with the City and served as an at-will employee.

g. Eric Soroka, as the City Manager, terminated the Plaintiff's employment on December 1, 2006.

h. Eric Soroka terminated the Plaintiff because he lost confidence in trustworthiness.

i. Eric Soroka's decision to terminate the Plaintiff was based on (1) the investigation in to Norman's admission, (2) the audit of the Sunshine Fund, and (3) his interviews with ACES teachers.

3. "A party moving for a directed verdict admits the truth of all facts in evidence and every reasonable conclusion or inference which can be drawn from such evidence favorable to the non-moving party." *Wald v. Grainger,* 64 So. 3d 1201, 1205 (Fla. 2011); *Williamson v. Superior Ins. Co.,* 746 So. 2d 483, 485 (Fla. 2d DCA 1999). A directed verdict is proper when the evidence and all inferences from the evidence, considered in the light most favorable to the non-moving party, support the movant's case as a matter of law and there is no evidence to rebut it. *State Farm Mut. Auto. Ins. Co. v. Orr,* 660 So. 2d 1061, 1062 (Fla. 4th DCA 1995).

4. The elements of a cause of action based on tortious interference with a business relationship are (1) the existence of a business relationship, (2) the defendant's knowledge of the relationship, (3) the defendant's intentional and unjustified interference with the relationship and (4) damage to the plaintiff as a result of the breach of the relationship. *Ethan Allen. Inc. v. Georgetown Manor, Inc.,* 647 So. 2d 812 (Fla. 1994); *Sobi v. Fairfield Resorts, Inc.,* 846 So. 2d 1204 (Fla. 5th DCA 2003).

5. Eric Soroka is entitled to a directed verdict on this claim for the following reasons:

a. Eric Soroka, as City Manager, is not a third party to the business relationship. *Salit v. Ruden, McClosky, Smith, Schuster, & Russell, P.A.,* 742 So.2d 381, 385 (Fla. 4th DCA 1999). *Abruzzo v. Haller,* 603 So.2d 1338, 1339-40 (Fla. 1st DCA 1992) ("An agent of a corporate party to a contract, acting within his capacity and scope as an agent, cannot be considered to be a separate entity outside of the contractual relationship which can interfere with that relationship."); *Sloan v. Sax,* 505 So.2d 526, 527-28 (Fla. 2d DCA 1987). Here, Eric Soroka as an agent of the City and the final decision-maker regarding Plaintiff's termination cannot be held liable for international interfering with the business relationship between Plaintiff and the City because he was not a third party to the relationship. The City acts through him and him alone in terminating the principal of ACES.

b. Eric Soroka has absolute immunity for the complained of conduct because it occurred within the scope of his employment as City Manager. *City of Stuart v. Monds,* 10 So. 3d 1134 (Fla. 4th DCA 2009).

c. Eric Soroka, as the City Manager, was the final-decision maker with respect to Murphy's employment with the City. *Buckner v. Lower Fla. Keys Hosp. Dist.,* 403 So.2d 1025, 1028-29 (Fla. 3d DCA 1981); *West v. Troelstrup,* 367 So. 2d 253 (Fla. 1st DCA 1979). Here, Eric Soroka, as the City Manager, was the Plaintiff's direct supervisor. He had the authority to terminate her employment. In this respect, Eric Soroka was the final decision-making authority. Further, the Plaintiff was an at-will employee of the City without a contract and, therefore, served at Eric Soroka's discretion. As such, Eric Soroka cannot be held liable for allegedly "interfering" with Plaintiff's employment.

d. Eric Soroka had a bona-fide reason to terminate Murphy's employment. *Salit v. Ruden, McClosky, Smith, Schuster, & Russell, P.A.,* 742 So.2d 381, 385 (Fla. 4th DCA 1999); *McCurdy v. Collis,* 508 So.2d 380, 383 (Fla. 1st DCA 1987). Eric Soroka terminated the Plaintiff because he lost confidence in trustworthiness. Eric Soroka's decision to terminate the Plaintiff was based on (1) the investigation in to Norman's admission, (2) the audit of the Sunshine Fund, and (3) his interviews with ACES teachers.

WHEREFORE, Defendant, ERIC SOROKA, respectfully requests entry of a directed verdict in his favor on the claim for intentional interfered with the Plaintiff's business relationship with the City asserted by the Plaintiff, KATHERINE MURPHY.

<<signature>>

MICHAEL T. BURKE

FLA. BAR NO. 338771
Attorneys for Defendant Eric Soroka
JOHNSON, ANSELMO, MURDOCH, BURKE, PIPER & HOCHMAN, PA
2455 E. Sunrise Blvd., Suite 1000
Fort Lauderdale, FL 33304
Tel: 954-463-0100
Fax: 954-463-2444
Burke@jambg.com
Cardona@jambg.com

Table of Laws and Rules

FLORIDA STATUTES

Sec.	Pg.
28.241	1, 8, 199, 206, 397, 405, 611, 618, 813, 820, 1038, 1244, 1464
34.041	1, 199, 397, 611, 813
48.19	1, 18, 199, 216, 397, 415, 611, 629, 813, 831, 1031, 1048, 1236, 1254, 1456, 1474
48.20	1, 14, 199, 212, 397, 410, 411, 611, 624, 813, 826, 1031, 1044, 1236, 1250, 1456, 1469
48.21	1, 15, 16, 199, 213, 214, 397, 412, 611, 626, 813, 828, 1031, 1045, 1046, 1236, 1251, 1252, 1456, 1471
48.25	1, 14, 199, 212, 397, 410, 611, 624, 813, 826, 1031, 1044, 1236, 1250, 1456, 1469
48.31	1, 14, 199, 212, 397, 410, 611, 624, 813, 826, 1031, 1044, 1236, 1250, 1456, 1469
48.101	1, 16, 199, 214, 397, 413, 611, 626, 813, 828, 1031, 1046, 1236, 1252, 1456, 1472
48.111	1, 18, 199, 216, 397, 415, 611, 628, 813, 830, 1031, 1048, 1236, 1254, 1456, 1474
48.121	1, 18, 199, 216, 397, 415, 611, 628, 813, 831, 1031, 1048, 1236, 1254, 1456, 1474
48.131	1, 18, 199, 216, 397, 415, 611, 628, 813, 830, 1031, 1048, 1236, 1254, 1456, 1474
48.141	1, 18, 199, 216, 397, 415, 611, 628, 813, 831, 1031, 1048, 1236, 1254, 1456, 1474
48.151	1, 17, 18, 199, 215, 216, 397, 413, 415, 611, 627, 629, 813, 829, 831, 1031, 1047, 1048, 1236, 1253, 1254, 1456, 1473, 1474
48.161	1, 17, 199, 215, 397, 413, 611, 627, 813, 829, 1031, 1047, 1236, 1253, 1456, 1473
48.171	1, 18, 199, 216, 397, 415, 611, 629, 813, 831, 1031, 1048, 1236, 1254, 1456, 1474
48.181	1, 15, 16, 199, 213, 214, 397, 412, 611, 626, 813, 828, 1031, 1045, 1046, 1236, 1251, 1252, 1456, 1471
48.183	1, 18, 199, 216, 397, 415, 611, 629, 813, 831, 1031, 1048, 1236, 1254, 1456, 1474
48.193	1, 3, 20, 23, 38, 55, 199, 201, 219, 221, 236, 253, 397, 399, 417, 420, 435, 453, 611, 613, 631, 633, 648, 666, 813, 815, 833, 835, 851, 868, 1031, 1033, 1051, 1053, 1068, 1085, 1236, 1238, 1256, 1259, 1276, 1295, 1456, 1458, 1476, 1479, 1495, 1513
48.194	1, 199, 397, 611, 813, 1031, 1236, 1456
48.011	1, 13, 199, 211, 397, 410, 611, 624, 813, 826, 1031, 1043, 1236, 1249, 1456, 1469
48.021	1, 14, 199, 212, 397, 410, 611, 624, 813, 826, 1031, 1044, 1236, 1250, 1456, 1469
48.031	1, 14, 16, 199, 212, 214, 397, 411, 412, 611, 624, 626, 813, 826, 828, 1031, 1044, 1046, 1236, 1250, 1252, 1456, 1470, 1472
48.041	1, 18, 199, 216, 397, 415, 611, 628, 813, 830, 1031, 1048, 1236, 1254, 1456, 1474
48.042	1, 18, 199, 216, 397, 415, 611, 628, 813, 830, 1031, 1048, 1236, 1254, 1456, 1474
48.051	1, 18, 199, 216, 397, 415, 611, 628, 813, 831, 1031, 1048, 1236, 1254, 1456, 1474
48.061	1, 199, 397, 611, 813, 1031, 1236, 1456
48.071	1, 15, 16, 17, 18, 199, 213, 214, 216, 397, 412, 414, 611, 626, 628, 813, 828, 830, 1031, 1045, 1046, 1048, 1236, 1251, 1252, 1253, 1254, 1456, 1471, 1473
48.081	1, 16, 199, 214, 397, 412, 413, 611, 626, 813, 828, 1031, 1046, 1236, 1252, 1456, 1472
48.091	1, 16, 199, 214, 397, 412, 611, 626, 813, 828, 1031, 1046, 1236, 1252, 1456, 1472
49.10	1, 17, 199, 215, 397, 414, 611, 628, 813, 830, 1031, 1047, 1236, 1253, 1456, 1473
49.11	1, 17, 199, 215, 397, 414, 611, 628, 813, 830, 1031, 1047, 1236, 1253, 1456, 1473
49.12	1, 17, 199, 215, 397, 414, 611, 628, 813, 830, 1031, 1047, 1236, 1253, 1456, 1473
49.08	1, 17, 199, 215, 397, 414, 611, 628, 813, 830, 1031, 1047, 1236, 1253, 1456, 1473
49.09	1, 17, 199, 215, 397, 414, 611, 628, 813, 830, 1031, 1047, 1236, 1253, 1456, 1473

FLORIDA STATUTES—Continued

Sec.	Pg.
49.011	1, 17, 199, 215, 397, 413, 611, 627, 813, 829, 1031, 1047, 1236, 1253, 1456, 1473
49.021	1, 17, 199, 215, 397, 413, 611, 627, 813, 829, 1031, 1047, 1236, 1253, 1456, 1473
49.031	1, 199, 397, 611, 813, 1031, 1236, 1456
49.041	1, 17, 199, 215, 397, 414, 611, 627, 813, 829, 1031, 1047, 1236, 1253, 1456, 1473
49.051	1, 17, 199, 215, 397, 414, 611, 627, 813, 829, 1031, 1047, 1236, 1253, 1456, 1473
49.061	1, 17, 199, 215, 397, 414, 611, 627, 813, 829, 1031, 1047, 1236, 1253, 1456, 1473
49.071	1, 17, 199, 215, 397, 414, 611, 627, 813, 829, 1031, 1047, 1236, 1253, 1456, 1473
50.011	1, 17, 199, 215, 397, 414, 611, 628, 813, 830, 1031, 1047, 1236, 1253, 1456, 1473
50.021	1, 17, 199, 215, 397, 414, 611, 628, 813, 830, 1031, 1047, 1236, 1253, 1456, 1473
50.031	1, 17, 199, 215, 397, 414, 611, 628, 813, 830, 1031, 1047, 1236, 1253, 1456, 1473
50.041	1, 17, 199, 215, 397, 414, 611, 628, 813, 830, 1031, 1047, 1236, 1253, 1456, 1473
50.051	1, 17, 199, 215, 397, 414, 611, 628, 813, 830, 1031, 1047, 1236, 1253, 1456, 1473
50.061	1, 17, 199, 215, 397, 414, 611, 628, 813, 830, 1031, 1047, 1236, 1253, 1456, 1473
57.105	110, 111, 113, 123, 308, 311, 320, 514, 515, 517, 529, 721, 722, 725, 735, 931, 932, 935, 946, 1143, 1144, 1146, 1157, 1357, 1358, 1360, 1372, 1578, 1579, 1581, 1594
57.081	1, 199, 397, 611, 813
57.085	1, 199, 397, 611, 813
90.616	187, 384, 598, 800, 1018, 1224, 1444, 1668
110.117	2, 22, 37, 54, 71, 84, 97, 112, 125, 139, 152, 167, 182, 200, 220, 236, 252, 268, 282, 295, 309, 322, 337, 350, 365, 379, 398, 419, 435, 452, 469, 484, 500, 516, 531, 547, 562, 578, 593, 612, 632, 648, 665, 681, 695, 709, 723, 737, 752, 765, 781, 795, 814, 834, 850, 867, 884, 900, 916, 933, 949, 965, 981, 997, 1012, 1032, 1052, 1068, 1084, 1101, 1115, 1130, 1145, 1159, 1175, 1189, 1204, 1219, 1238, 1258, 1275, 1294, 1312, 1327, 1343, 1359, 1375, 1391, 1406, 1423, 1438, 1457, 1478, 1494, 1512, 1529, 1546, 1563, 1580, 1597, 1614, 1630, 1647, 1662
120.50	110, 308, 514, 722, 931, 1143, 1358, 1578
120.52	110, 308, 514, 722, 931, 1143, 1358, 1578
120.68	110, 308, 514, 722, 931, 1143, 1358, 1578
120.81	110, 308, 514, 722, 931, 1143, 1358, 1578
768.28	36, 37, 234, 235, 434, 647, 849, 1066, 1067, 1273, 1274, 1493
768.79	110, 114, 308, 311, 514, 518, 722, 725, 931, 935, 1143, 1147, 1357, 1361, 1578, 1582

FLORIDA RULES OF CIVIL PROCEDURE

Rule	Pg.
1.010	7, 9, 27, 29, 44, 45, 61, 63, 69, 73, 74, 82, 86, 88, 96, 100, 102, 110, 114, 116, 124, 128, 130, 138, 141, 143, 157, 159, 172, 173, 189, 190, 205, 207, 225, 227, 242, 243, 259, 260, 267, 270, 271, 272, 280, 284, 285, 293, 298, 299, 308, 312, 313, 321, 325, 326, 327, 335, 339, 340, 355, 356, 369, 370, 386, 388, 404, 406, 424, 425, 426, 441, 443, 459, 461, 468, 472, 473, 482, 487, 489, 498, 502, 504, 514, 518, 519, 520, 529, 534, 536, 545, 549, 551, 567, 569, 582, 584, 601, 602, 618, 620, 638, 639, 654, 656, 671, 673, 680, 683, 685, 693, 697, 699, 707, 711, 713, 722, 726, 728, 735, 740, 742, 750, 754, 756, 770, 771, 772, 785, 786, 803, 804, 819, 821, 840, 841, 856, 858, 874, 876, 882, 887, 889, 898, 903, 905, 914, 919, 922, 931, 936, 939, 947, 952, 955, 964, 968, 970, 986, 988, 1001, 1003, 1020, 1022, 1037, 1038, 1039, 1058, 1059, 1074, 1075, 1091, 1093, 1099, 1103, 1105, 1113, 1117, 1119, 1128, 1132, 1134, 1143, 1148, 1149, 1158, 1163, 1165, 1173, 1177, 1179, 1194, 1196, 1209, 1210, 1226, 1227, 1243, 1245, 1264, 1265, 1281, 1283, 1301, 1302, 1309, 1314,

FLORIDA RULES OF CIVIL PROCEDURE—Continued

Rule	Pg.
	1316, 1325, 1329, 1331, 1340, 1345, 1347, 1357, 1362, 1364, 1373, 1378, 1380, 1389, 1393, 1395, 1412, 1413, 1427, 1429, 1446, 1447, 1462, 1465, 1483, 1485, 1500, 1502, 1518, 1520, 1527, 1532, 1534, 1544, 1548, 1551, 1561, 1565, 1568, 1578, 1583, 1585, 1595, 1600, 1603, 1612, 1616, 1619, 1636, 1637, 1651, 1653, 1670, 1671, 1672
1.030	1, 3, 9, 20, 23, 29, 36, 38, 45, 53, 55, 63, 69, 74, 82, 88, 96, 102, 110, 116, 124, 130, 138, 143, 151, 159, 166, 173, 180, 191, 199, 201, 207, 218, 221, 227, 234, 236, 243, 251, 253, 261, 267, 272, 280, 285, 293, 299, 308, 314, 321, 327, 335, 340, 348, 356, 363, 370, 377, 388, 397, 399, 406, 417, 420, 426, 433, 436, 443, 451, 454, 461, 468, 474, 483, 489, 498, 505, 514, 521, 529, 537, 545, 551, 560, 569, 576, 584, 591, 602, 611, 613, 620, 631, 633, 639, 646, 649, 656, 663, 666, 673, 680, 685, 693, 699, 707, 713, 722, 728, 735, 742, 750, 756, 764, 772, 779, 786, 793, 804, 813, 815, 821, 833, 835, 841, 848, 851, 858, 866, 869, 876, 883, 889, 898, 905, 914, 922, 931, 939, 947, 955, 964, 970, 979, 988, 995, 1003, 1011, 1022, 1031, 1033, 1039, 1050, 1053, 1059, 1066, 1068, 1076, 1083, 1086, 1093, 1099, 1105, 1113, 1119, 1128, 1134, 1143, 1150, 1158, 1165, 1173, 1179, 1187, 1196, 1203, 1210, 1217, 1228, 1236, 1239, 1245, 1256, 1260, 1266, 1273, 1276, 1283, 1292, 1295, 1303, 1310, 1316, 1325, 1332, 1341, 1348, 1357, 1364, 1373, 1380, 1389, 1395, 1404, 1413, 1421, 1429, 1436, 1447, 1456, 1458, 1465, 1476, 1479, 1485, 1492, 1495, 1502, 1510, 1513, 1521, 1528, 1534, 1544, 1551, 1561, 1568, 1578, 1585, 1595, 1603, 1612, 1619, 1628, 1637, 1645, 1653, 1660, 1672
1.050	1, 199, 200, 397, 398, 611, 612, 813, 1031, 1236, 1237, 1456, 1457
1.070	1, 18, 20, 36, 82, 199, 217, 219, 234, 280, 397, 415, 417, 433, 483, 611, 629, 631, 646, 693, 813, 831, 833, 848, 898, 1031, 1049, 1051, 1066, 1113, 1236, 1254, 1256, 1273, 1325, 1456, 1474, 1476, 1492, 1544
1.070(a)	8, 13, 206, 211, 404, 410, 618, 624, 820, 826, 1038, 1043, 1243, 1249, 1463, 1469
1.070(b)	14, 212, 410, 624, 826, 1044, 1250, 1469
1.070(c)	13, 211, 410, 624, 826, 1043, 1249, 1469
1.070(d)	17, 215, 413, 627, 829, 1047, 1253, 1473
1.070(e)	13, 211, 410, 623, 826, 1043, 1249, 1469
1.070(g)	18, 217, 415, 629, 831, 1049, 1254, 1474
1.070(h)	4, 24, 39, 56, 202, 222, 237, 254, 400, 420, 436, 454, 614, 634, 649, 667, 816, 836, 852, 869, 1034, 1054, 1069, 1086, 1239, 1260, 1276, 1296, 1459, 1479, 1496, 1514
1.070(i)	14, 212, 411, 625, 827, 1044, 1250, 1470
1.070(i)(1)	15, 213, 411, 625, 827, 1045, 1251, 1470
1.070(i)(2)	14, 15, 213, 411, 625, 827, 1045, 1250, 1251, 1470
1.070(i)(3)	15, 213, 411, 625, 827, 1045, 1251, 1471
1.070(i)(4)	15, 36, 213, 235, 411, 434, 625, 647, 827, 849, 1045, 1067, 1251, 1274, 1471, 1493
1.070(i)(5)	15, 213, 411, 625, 827, 1045, 1251, 1471
1.070(j)	2, 83, 200, 281, 398, 484, 612, 694, 814, 899, 1032, 1114, 1237, 1326, 1457, 1545
1.071	8, 28, 44, 62, 73, 87, 101, 115, 129, 142, 199, 206, 219, 226, 242, 251, 260, 271, 285, 298, 313, 326, 339, 405, 425, 442, 460, 473, 488, 504, 520, 536, 550, 611, 619, 631, 638, 646, 655, 663, 672, 684, 698, 712, 727, 741, 755, 821, 841, 857, 875, 888, 904, 921, 937, 953, 969, 1039, 1058, 1075, 1092, 1104, 1118, 1133, 1148, 1164, 1178, 1236, 1244, 1256, 1265, 1273, 1282, 1292, 1302, 1315, 1331, 1347, 1363, 1379, 1395, 1464, 1484, 1501, 1520, 1533, 1550, 1567, 1584, 1602, 1618
1.080	1, 6, 18, 20, 26, 36, 42, 53, 59, 69, 82, 96, 110, 124, 138, 151, 166, 180, 199, 204, 216, 219, 224, 234, 240, 251, 257, 267, 280, 293, 308, 321, 335, 348, 349, 363, 377, 397, 402, 415, 417, 422, 433, 439, 451, 457, 468, 483, 498, 514, 529, 545, 560, 561, 576, 591, 611, 616, 629, 631, 636, 646, 652, 663, 670, 680, 693, 707, 722, 735, 750, 764, 765, 779, 793, 813, 818, 831, 833, 838, 848, 855, 866, 872, 883, 898, 914, 931, 947, 964, 979, 980, 995, 996, 1011, 1031, 1036, 1048, 1051, 1056, 1066, 1072, 1083, 1089, 1099, 1113, 1128, 1143, 1158, 1173, 1187, 1188, 1202, 1203, 1217, 1236, 1241, 1254, 1256, 1262,

FLORIDA RULES OF CIVIL PROCEDURE—Continued

Rule **Pg.**

1273, 1280, 1292, 1299, 1310, 1325, 1341, 1357, 1373, 1389, 1404, 1405, 1421, 1436, 1456, 1461, 1474, 1476, 1481, 1492, 1499, 1510, 1517, 1528, 1544, 1561, 1578, 1595, 1612, 1628, 1629, 1645, 1660

1.080(a)............33, 49, 67, 78, 92, 106, 120, 134, 147, 163, 177, 195, 231, 247, 264, 276, 289, 303, 317, 331, 344, 360, 374, 392, 430, 447, 465, 477, 493, 508, 524, 540, 555, 573, 588, 607, 643, 660, 677, 689, 703, 717, 732, 746, 760, 776, 790, 809, 846, 862, 880, 894, 910, 926, 943, 959, 975, 992, 1008, 1027, 1063, 1079, 1097, 1109, 1123, 1138, 1153, 1169, 1183, 1200, 1214, 1232, 1270, 1287, 1307, 1320, 1336, 1352, 1368, 1385, 1400, 1418, 1433, 1452, 1489, 1506, 1525, 1538, 1555, 1572, 1589, 1607, 1623, 1642, 1657, 1677

1.080(b)......... ...31, 48, 65, 77, 90, 104, 118, 132, 145, 161, 175, 193, 229, 246, 263, 274, 288, 302, 316, 329, 343, 359, 373, 391, 428, 445, 463, 476, 491, 507, 523, 539, 554, 571, 586, 605, 642, 658, 675, 687, 701, 715, 730, 745, 758, 774, 789, 807, 844, 860, 878, 892, 908, 925, 941, 957, 973, 991, 1006, 1025, 1061, 1078, 1095, 1107, 1110, 1111, 1122, 1124, 1125, 1137, 1139, 1140, 1152, 1154, 1156, 1167, 1170, 1171, 1181, 1184, 1185, 1198, 1212, 1230, 1268, 1285, 1305, 1318, 1334, 1350, 1366, 1383, 1398, 1416, 1431, 1450, 1488, 1505, 1523, 1537, 1553, 1570, 1588, 1605, 1621, 1640, 1655, 1675

1.080(c)..........9, 29, 45, 62, 74, 88, 102, 116, 130, 143, 159, 173, 190, 207, 227, 243, 260, 272, 285, 299, 313, 327, 340, 356, 370, 388, 406, 426, 443, 461, 473, 489, 504, 520, 536, 551, 569, 584, 602, 620, 639, 656, 673, 685, 699, 713, 728, 742, 756, 772, 786, 804, 821, 841, 858, 876, 889, 905, 922, 939, 955, 970, 988, 1003, 1022, 1039, 1059, 1075, 1093, 1105, 1119, 1134, 1149, 1165, 1179, 1196, 1210, 1227, 1245, 1265, 1283, 1302, 1316, 1331, 1347, 1364, 1380, 1395, 1413, 1429, 1447, 1465, 1485, 1502, 1520, 1534, 1551, 1568, 1585, 1602, 1619, 1637, 1653, 1672

1.090......... ....1, 36, 53, 69, 82, 96, 110, 124, 138, 151, 166, 180, 199, 234, 251, 267, 280, 293, 308, 321, 335, 348, 363, 377, 397, 433, 451, 468, 483, 498, 514, 529, 546, 560, 577, 591, 611, 646, 663, 680, 693, 707, 722, 735, 750, 764, 779, 794, 813, 849, 866, 883, 898, 915, 931, 947, 964, 979, 996, 1011, 1031, 1066, 1083, 1099, 1113, 1128, 1144, 1158, 1173, 1187, 1203, 1217, 1236, 1273, 1292, 1310, 1325, 1341, 1357, 1373, 1389, 1404, 1421, 1436, 1456, 1492, 1510, 1528, 1544, 1561, 1578, 1595, 1612, 1628, 1645, 1660

1.090(a)..........2, 21, 37, 54, 70, 83, 97, 111, 125, 139, 152, 167, 181, 200, 219, 235, 252, 268, 281, 294, 309, 322, 336, 349, 364, 378, 398, 418, 434, 452, 469, 484, 499, 515, 530, 547, 561, 577, 592, 612, 631, 647, 664, 681, 694, 708, 723, 737, 751, 765, 780, 795, 814, 834, 850, 867, 884, 900, 916, 933, 948, 965, 980, 996, 1012, 1032, 1051, 1067, 1084, 1100, 1115, 1129, 1144, 1159, 1174, 1188, 1204, 1218, 1237, 1258, 1274, 1294, 1311, 1327, 1342, 1359, 1374, 1391, 1406, 1422, 1438, 1457, 1477, 1494, 1511, 1529, 1545, 1562, 1579, 1596, 1613, 1629, 1646, 1661

1.090(b)......... .2, 22, 38, 55, 71, 84, 97, 112, 125, 139, 152, 168, 182, 201, 220, 236, 253, 269, 282, 295, 310, 323, 337, 350, 365, 379, 399, 419, 435, 453, 470, 485, 500, 516, 531, 547, 562, 578, 593, 613, 632, 648, 665, 682, 695, 709, 724, 737, 752, 766, 781, 795, 814, 834, 850, 868, 885, 901, 917, 933, 949, 966, 981, 997, 1013, 1032, 1052, 1068, 1085, 1101, 1115, 1130, 1145, 1160, 1175, 1189, 1205, 1219, 1238, 1259, 1275, 1295, 1312, 1327, 1343, 1359, 1375, 1392, 1407, 1423, 1439, 1458, 1478, 1494, 1512, 1530, 1546, 1563, 1580, 1597, 1614, 1630, 1647, 1662

1.090(c)..........3, 22, 38, 55, 71, 84, 98, 112, 125, 139, 153, 168, 182, 201, 220, 236, 253, 269, 282, 295, 310, 323, 337, 350, 365, 379, 399, 419, 435, 453, 470, 485, 500, 516, 531, 547, 562, 578, 593, 613, 632, 648, 665, 682, 695, 709, 724, 738, 752, 766, 781, 796, 815, 834, 851, 868, 885, 901, 917, 934, 949, 966, 981, 997, 1013, 1033, 1052, 1068, 1085, 1101, 1116, 1130, 1145, 1160, 1175, 1189, 1205, 1219, 1238, 1259, 1275, 1295, 1312, 1328, 1343, 1360, 1375, 1392, 1407, 1423,

FLORIDA RULES OF CIVIL PROCEDURE—Continued

Rule	Pg.
	1439, 1458, 1478, 1495, 1512, 1530, 1546, 1563, 1580, 1597, 1614, 1630, 1647, 1662
1.090(d)	70, 83, 111, 124, 138, 268, 281, 309, 322, 336, 469, 484, 515, 530, 546, 681, 694, 722, 736, 751, 883, 899, 932, 948, 964, 1100, 1115, 1144, 1159, 1174, 1311, 1326, 1358, 1374, 1390, 1529, 1545, 1579, 1596, 1613
1.100	1, 20, 36, 53, 69, 82, 96, 110, 124, 138, 151, 166, 180, 199, 219, 234, 251, 267, 280, 293, 308, 321, 335, 348, 363, 377, 397, 417, 433, 451, 468, 483, 498, 514, 529, 546, 560, 577, 591, 611, 631, 646, 663, 680, 693, 707, 722, 735, 750, 764, 779, 793, 813, 833, 849, 866, 883, 898, 915, 931, 947, 964, 979, 996, 1011, 1031, 1051, 1066, 1083, 1099, 1113, 1128, 1144, 1158, 1173, 1187, 1203, 1217, 1236, 1256, 1273, 1292, 1310, 1325, 1341, 1357, 1373, 1389, 1404, 1421, 1436, 1456, 1476, 1492, 1510, 1528, 1544, 1561, 1578, 1595, 1612, 1628, 1645, 1660
1.100(b)	71, 73, 84, 86, 98, 100, 112, 115, 126, 129, 140, 142, 269, 271, 282, 284, 295, 298, 310, 312, 323, 326, 337, 339, 470, 472, 485, 487, 500, 503, 516, 519, 531, 535, 548, 550, 682, 684, 696, 698, 709, 712, 724, 726, 738, 741, 753, 754, 885, 887, 901, 903, 917, 920, 934, 936, 949, 952, 966, 968, 1101, 1103, 1116, 1118, 1130, 1133, 1145, 1148, 1160, 1163, 1175, 1177, 1312, 1314, 1328, 1330, 1343, 1346, 1360, 1362, 1375, 1378, 1392, 1394, 1530, 1532, 1546, 1549, 1563, 1566, 1580, 1584, 1597, 1601, 1614, 1617
1.100(c)(1)	9, 29, 45, 62, 74, 88, 102, 116, 130, 143, 159, 173, 190, 207, 227, 243, 260, 272, 285, 299, 313, 327, 340, 356, 370, 388, 406, 426, 443, 461, 473, 489, 504, 520, 536, 551, 569, 583, 602, 619, 639, 655, 673, 685, 699, 713, 728, 742, 756, 772, 786, 804, 821, 841, 858, 875, 889, 905, 922, 938, 955, 970, 988, 1003, 1022, 1039, 1059, 1075, 1093, 1105, 1119, 1134, 1149, 1165, 1179, 1196, 1210, 1227, 1245, 1265, 1283, 1302, 1316, 1331, 1347, 1364, 1380, 1395, 1413, 1429, 1447, 1465, 1485, 1502, 1520, 1534, 1551, 1568, 1585, 1602, 1619, 1637, 1653, 1672
1.100(c)(2)	8, 206, 404, 618, 820, 1038, 1243, 1463
1.110	1, 20, 36, 53, 199, 219, 234, 251, 397, 417, 433, 451, 611, 631, 646, 663, 813, 833, 849, 866, 1031, 1051, 1066, 1083, 1236, 1256, 1273, 1292, 1456, 1476, 1492, 1510
1.110(a)	4, 24, 39, 56, 202, 222, 237, 254, 400, 420, 436, 454, 614, 634, 649, 667, 816, 836, 852, 869, 1034, 1054, 1069, 1086, 1239, 1260, 1277, 1296, 1459, 1479, 1496, 1514
1.110(b)	3, 23, 38, 55, 56, 201, 221, 236, 253, 254, 399, 420, 436, 453, 454, 613, 633, 649, 666, 815, 835, 851, 868, 869, 1033, 1053, 1068, 1086, 1238, 1239, 1259, 1260, 1276, 1295, 1296, 1458, 1479, 1495, 1513
1.110(c)	39, 56, 237, 254, 437, 454, 650, 667, 852, 869, 1069, 1087, 1277, 1296, 1496, 1514
1.110(d)	40, 57, 238, 255, 438, 455, 651, 668, 853, 870, 1070, 1088, 1278, 1297, 1497, 1515
1.110(e)	40, 58, 238, 256, 438, 456, 651, 668, 853, 871, 1070, 1088, 1278, 1298, 1497, 1515
1.110(f)	3, 23, 38, 56, 201, 221, 236, 254, 399, 420, 436, 454, 613, 633, 649, 666, 815, 835, 851, 869, 1033, 1053, 1069, 1086, 1239, 1260, 1276, 1296, 1458, 1479, 1495, 1513
1.110(g)	3, 23, 39, 56, 201, 221, 237, 254, 399, 420, 436, 454, 614, 634, 649, 666, 815, 836, 851, 869, 1033, 1053, 1069, 1086, 1239, 1260, 1276, 1296, 1458, 1479, 1495, 1513
1.110(h)	3, 4, 23, 39, 56, 202, 222, 237, 254, 400, 420, 436, 454, 614, 634, 649, 667, 815, 816, 836, 851, 869, 1033, 1034, 1054, 1069, 1086, 1239, 1260, 1276, 1296, 1459, 1479, 1495, 1496, 1514
1.120	1, 20, 36, 53, 199, 219, 234, 251, 397, 417, 433, 451, 611, 631, 646, 663, 813, 833, 849, 866, 1031, 1051, 1066, 1083, 1236, 1256, 1273, 1292, 1456, 1476, 1492, 1510
1.120(a)	4, 24, 40, 58, 202, 222, 239, 256, 400, 421, 438, 456, 614, 634, 651, 668, 816, 837, 853, 871, 1034, 1054, 1071, 1088, 1240, 1261, 1278, 1298, 1459, 1480, 1497, 1515
1.120(b)	4, 24, 41, 58, 202, 222, 239, 256, 400, 421, 438, 456, 614, 635, 651, 668, 816, 837, 853, 871, 1034, 1054, 1071, 1088, 1240, 1261, 1278, 1298, 1459, 1480, 1497, 1515
1.120(c)	4, 24, 41, 58, 202, 203, 222, 239, 256,

FLORIDA RULES OF CIVIL PROCEDURE—Continued

Rule	Pg.
	400, 401, 421, 438, 456, 615, 635, 651, 668, 816, 837, 853, 871, 1034, 1054, 1071, 1088, 1240, 1261, 1278, 1298, 1459, 1460, 1480, 1497, 1515, 1516
1.120(e)	4, 24, 41, 58, 203, 223, 239, 256, 401, 421, 438, 456, 615, 635, 651, 669, 816, 837, 853, 871, 1034, 1055, 1071, 1088, 1240, 1261, 1278, 1298, 1460, 1480, 1498, 1516
1.120(f)	5, 24, 41, 58, 203, 223, 239, 256, 401, 421, 438, 456, 615, 635, 651, 669, 817, 837, 854, 871, 1035, 1055, 1071, 1088, 1240, 1261, 1278, 1298, 1460, 1480, 1498, 1516
1.120(g)	5, 25, 41, 58, 203, 223, 239, 256, 401, 421, 438, 456, 615, 635, 651, 669, 817, 837, 854, 871, 1035, 1055, 1071, 1088, 1240, 1261, 1279, 1298, 1460, 1480, 1498, 1516
1.130	1, 20, 36, 53, 199, 219, 234, 251, 397, 417, 433, 451, 611, 631, 646, 663, 813, 833, 849, 866, 1031, 1051, 1066, 1083, 1236, 1256, 1273, 1292, 1456, 1476, 1492, 1510
1.130(a)	8, 28, 44, 62, 206, 226, 242, 259, 405, 425, 442, 460, 619, 638, 655, 672, 820, 840, 857, 875, 1038, 1058, 1074, 1092, 1244, 1264, 1282, 1301, 1464, 1484, 1501, 1519
1.130(b)	3, 23, 38, 56, 201, 221, 237, 254, 399, 420, 436, 454, 613, 633, 649, 666, 815, 835, 851, 869, 1033, 1053, 1069, 1086, 1239, 1260, 1276, 1296, 1458, 1479, 1495, 1513
1.140	36, 37, 53, 69, 71, 82, 234, 235, 251, 267, 269, 280, 433, 434, 451, 468, 470, 483, 646, 647, 664, 680, 682, 693, 849, 866, 883, 885, 898, 1066, 1067, 1083, 1099, 1102, 1113, 1273, 1274, 1292, 1310, 1312, 1325, 1493, 1511, 1528, 1530, 1544
1.140(a)(1)	36, 234, 434, 647, 849, 1067, 1274, 1493
1.140(a)(2)	37, 235, 434, 647, 849, 1067, 1274, 1493
1.140(a)(3)	37, 235, 434, 647, 849, 1067, 1274, 1493
1.140(a)(4)	83, 281, 484, 694, 899, 1114, 1326, 1545
1.140(b)	37, 40, 57, 70, 235, 238, 255, 268, 434, 437, 455, 469, 647, 650, 667, 668, 680, 850, 852, 853, 870, 883, 1067, 1070, 1087, 1100, 1274, 1277, 1278, 1297, 1310, 1494, 1496, 1497, 1514, 1515, 1528
1.140(b)(1)	51, 249, 449, 662, 864, 1081, 1289
1.140(b)(7)	51, 249, 449, 662, 864, 1081, 1289
1.140(c)	51, 249, 449, 662, 864, 1081, 1289
1.140(d)	51, 249, 449, 662, 864, 912, 1081, 1289
1.140(e)	40, 57, 238, 255, 437, 455, 650, 668, 852, 870, 1070, 1087, 1277, 1297, 1497, 1515
1.140(f)	37, 40, 57, 70, 71, 235, 238, 255, 268, 269, 434, 437, 455, 468, 470, 647, 650, 668, 680, 682, 849, 852, 870, 883, 885, 1067, 1070, 1087, 1100, 1102, 1274, 1277, 1297, 1310, 1312, 1493, 1497, 1515, 1528, 1530
1.140(h)(1)	40, 57, 238, 255, 437, 455, 650, 668, 853, 870, 1070, 1087, 1277, 1297, 1497, 1515
1.140(h)(2)	40, 57, 238, 255, 437, 455, 650, 668, 853, 870, 1070, 1087, 1277, 1278, 1297, 1497, 1515
1.150	69, 267, 468, 680, 883, 1099, 1310, 1528
1.150(a)	70, 72, 98, 268, 270, 296, 469, 471, 501, 680, 683, 710, 883, 886, 918, 1100, 1102, 1131, 1310, 1313, 1344, 1528, 1531, 1564
1.150(b)	72, 270, 471, 683, 886, 1102, 1313, 1531
1.160	69, 82, 96, 110, 124, 138, 267, 280, 294, 308, 321, 335, 468, 483, 498, 514, 529, 546, 680, 693, 707, 722, 735, 750, 883, 898, 915, 931, 947, 964, 1099, 1114, 1128, 1144, 1158, 1173, 1310, 1325, 1341, 1357, 1373, 1389, 1528, 1544, 1561, 1578, 1595, 1612
1.170	1, 199, 397, 611, 813, 1031, 1236, 1456
1.170(a)	5, 25, 41, 59, 203, 223, 240, 257, 401, 422, 439, 457, 615, 635, 652, 669, 817, 837, 854, 872, 1035, 1055, 1072, 1089, 1241, 1262, 1279, 1299, 1460, 1481, 1498, 1516
1.170(b)	5, 25, 41, 59, 203, 223, 240, 257, 401, 422, 439, 457, 615, 635, 652, 669, 817, 838, 854, 872, 1035, 1055, 1072, 1089, 1241, 1262, 1279, 1299, 1460, 1481, 1498, 1516
1.170(c)	5, 25, 42, 59, 203, 223, 240, 257, 401, 422, 439, 457, 615, 636, 652, 669, 817, 838, 854, 872, 1035, 1055, 1072, 1089, 1241, 1262, 1279, 1299, 1460, 1481, 1498, 1516
1.170(d)	5, 25, 42, 59, 203, 223, 240, 257, 401, 422, 439, 457, 616, 636, 652, 669, 817, 838, 854, 872, 1035, 1055, 1072, 1089, 1241, 1262, 1279, 1299, 1460, 1481, 1498, 1516
1.170(e)	5, 25, 42, 59, 204, 223, 240, 257, 402, 422, 439, 457, 616, 636, 652, 669, 817, 838, 854, 872, 1035, 1055, 1072, 1089, 1241, 1262, 1279, 1299, 1461, 1481, 1498, 1517

FLORIDA RULES OF CIVIL PROCEDURE—Continued

Rule	Pg.
1.170(f)	5, 25, 42, 59, 204, 224, 240, 257, 402, 422, 439, 457, 616, 636, 652, 670, 817, 838, 854, 872, 1035, 1056, 1072, 1089, 1241, 1262, 1279, 1299, 1461, 1481, 1499, 1517
1.170(g)	6, 18, 26, 42, 59, 204, 216, 224, 240, 257, 402, 415, 422, 439, 457, 616, 629, 636, 652, 670, 818, 831, 838, 855, 872, 1036, 1048, 1056, 1072, 1089, 1241, 1254, 1262, 1280, 1299, 1461, 1474, 1481, 1499, 1517
1.170(h)	6, 26, 42, 59, 204, 224, 240, 257, 402, 423, 439, 457, 616, 636, 652, 670, 818, 838, 855, 872, 1036, 1056, 1072, 1089, 1241, 1262, 1280, 1299, 1461, 1482, 1499, 1517
1.170(i)	6, 26, 42, 59, 204, 224, 240, 257, 402, 423, 440, 457, 616, 636, 653, 670, 818, 838, 855, 872, 1036, 1056, 1072, 1090, 1241, 1262, 1280, 1299, 1461, 1482, 1499, 1517
1.170(j)	6, 26, 42, 60, 204, 224, 240, 258, 402, 423, 440, 458, 616, 636, 653, 670, 818, 838, 855, 873, 1036, 1056, 1073, 1090, 1242, 1263, 1280, 1300, 1461, 1482, 1499, 1517
1.190	20, 36, 40, 53, 57, 82, 219, 234, 238, 251, 255, 280, 417, 433, 438, 451, 455, 483, 631, 646, 651, 663, 668, 693, 833, 849, 853, 866, 870, 898, 1051, 1066, 1070, 1083, 1088, 1114, 1256, 1273, 1278, 1292, 1297, 1325, 1476, 1492, 1497, 1510, 1515, 1544
1.190(a)	6, 21, 22, 26, 28, 43, 53, 54, 55, 60, 61, 83, 87, 204, 219, 220, 224, 226, 241, 251, 252, 253, 258, 259, 281, 284, 402, 418, 419, 423, 425, 440, 452, 453, 458, 460, 483, 487, 617, 631, 633, 637, 638, 653, 664, 665, 670, 672, 694, 698, 818, 833, 835, 839, 840, 855, 867, 868, 873, 874, 899, 903, 1036, 1051, 1052, 1056, 1058, 1073, 1084, 1085, 1090, 1092, 1114, 1118, 1242, 1257, 1259, 1263, 1264, 1280, 1293, 1295, 1300, 1301, 1326, 1330, 1461, 1477, 1478, 1482, 1484, 1499, 1511, 1512, 1517, 1519, 1545, 1549
1.190(b)	85, 283, 486, 696, 902, 1116, 1328, 1547
1.190(c)	23, 55, 85, 221, 253, 283, 419, 453, 486, 633, 666, 696, 835, 868, 902, 1053, 1085, 1117, 1259, 1295, 1329, 1478, 1513, 1548
1.190(e)	21, 54, 85, 219, 252, 282, 418, 452, 485, 631, 664, 696, 833, 867, 901, 1051, 1084, 1116, 1257, 1293, 1328, 1477, 1511, 1547
1.190(f)	83, 85, 281, 283, 484, 486, 694, 696, 899, 902, 1114, 1117, 1326, 1329, 1545, 1548
1.200	21, 53, 151, 153, 166, 168, 171, 182, 219, 251, 348, 350, 363, 365, 368, 380, 417, 451, 560, 562, 577, 578, 581, 593, 631, 664, 764, 766, 779, 781, 784, 796, 833, 866, 979, 981, 996, 997, 1000, 1013, 1051, 1083, 1187, 1190, 1203, 1205, 1207, 1219, 1257, 1292, 1404, 1407, 1421, 1424, 1426, 1439, 1476, 1511, 1628, 1631, 1645, 1647, 1650, 1663
1.200(b)(2)	35, 68, 233, 266, 432, 467, 645, 679, 848, 882, 1065, 1099, 1272, 1309, 1491, 1527
1.210(a)	5, 25, 41, 58, 203, 223, 239, 256, 401, 422, 439, 456, 615, 635, 652, 669, 817, 837, 854, 871, 1035, 1055, 1071, 1089, 1240, 1261, 1279, 1298, 1460, 1481, 1498, 1516
1.210(b)	5, 25, 41, 58, 203, 223, 239, 256, 401, 422, 439, 457, 615, 635, 652, 669, 817, 837, 854, 872, 1035, 1055, 1071, 1089, 1241, 1261, 1279, 1298, 1460, 1481, 1498, 1516
1.250(a)	6, 26, 42, 60, 204, 224, 240, 258, 402, 423, 440, 458, 616, 636, 653, 670, 818, 838, 855, 873, 1036, 1056, 1073, 1090, 1242, 1263, 1280, 1300, 1461, 1482, 1499, 1517
1.250(b)	6, 26, 42, 43, 59, 60, 204, 224, 240, 241, 257, 258, 402, 423, 439, 440, 457, 458, 616, 636, 637, 652, 653, 670, 818, 838, 839, 855, 872, 873, 1036, 1056, 1072, 1073, 1089, 1090, 1241, 1242, 1262, 1263, 1280, 1299, 1300, 1461, 1482, 1499, 1517
1.250(c)	6, 26, 42, 43, 59, 60, 85, 204, 224, 240, 241, 257, 258, 283, 402, 423, 439, 440, 457, 458, 486, 616, 617, 636, 637, 652, 653, 670, 696, 818, 838, 839, 855, 872, 873, 902, 1036, 1056, 1072, 1073, 1089, 1090, 1116, 1241, 1242, 1262, 1263, 1280, 1299, 1300, 1328, 1461, 1482, 1499, 1517, 1547
1.260	5, 25, 41, 58, 203, 223, 239, 256, 401, 422, 439, 457, 615, 635, 652, 669, 817, 837, 854, 872, 1035, 1055, 1071, 1089, 1241, 1262, 1279, 1298, 1460, 1481, 1498, 1516
1.270(b)	6, 26, 42, 59, 204, 224, 240, 257, 402, 423, 440, 457, 616, 636, 653, 670, 818, 838, 855, 872, 1036, 1056, 1072, 1090, 1241, 1262, 1280, 1299, 1461, 1482, 1499, 1517
1.280	124, 151, 161, 166, 175, 180, 193, 321, 348,

FLORIDA RULES OF CIVIL PROCEDURE—Continued

Rule	Pg.
	358, 363, 373, 377, 390, 529, 560, 571, 577, 586, 591, 605, 735, 764, 774, 779, 789, 794, 807, 947, 979, 990, 996, 1006, 1011, 1025, 1158, 1187, 1198, 1203, 1212, 1217, 1230, 1373, 1405, 1416, 1421, 1431, 1436, 1450, 1595, 1628, 1640, 1645, 1655, 1660, 1675
1.280(a)	153, 168, 182, 350, 365, 380, 562, 578, 593, 766, 781, 796, 981, 997, 1013, 1190, 1205, 1219, 1407, 1424, 1439, 1631, 1647, 1663
1.280(b)	155, 170, 352, 353, 368, 565, 581, 768, 784, 983, 984, 1000, 1192, 1207, 1410, 1426, 1633, 1650
1.280(b)(1)	153, 154, 168, 169, 182, 183, 350, 351, 365, 366, 380, 563, 579, 593, 594, 766, 767, 781, 782, 796, 797, 981, 982, 998, 1013, 1014, 1190, 1205, 1206, 1219, 1220, 1407, 1408, 1424, 1439, 1440, 1631, 1647, 1648, 1663, 1664
1.280(b)(2)	153, 168, 183, 350, 366, 380, 563, 579, 593, 766, 782, 796, 981, 998, 1013, 1190, 1205, 1220, 1407, 1424, 1439, 1631, 1647, 1663
1.280(b)(3)	153, 168, 183, 350, 366, 380, 563, 579, 594, 766, 782, 796, 981, 998, 1013, 1190, 1205, 1220, 1407, 1424, 1439, 1631, 1647, 1663
1.280(b)(4)	153, 154, 168, 169, 183, 351, 366, 380, 563, 579, 594, 766, 767, 782, 796, 797, 982, 998, 1014, 1190, 1205, 1206, 1220, 1408, 1424, 1439, 1440, 1631, 1648, 1663
1.280(b)(5)	151, 153, 154, 167, 168, 169, 181, 183, 184, 349, 351, 364, 366, 367, 378, 380, 381, 561, 563, 564, 577, 579, 580, 592, 594, 595, 765, 766, 767, 780, 782, 783, 794, 796, 797, 980, 981, 982, 996, 998, 999, 1012, 1013, 1014, 1188, 1190, 1191, 1204, 1205, 1206, 1218, 1220, 1221, 1405, 1407, 1408, 1422, 1424, 1425, 1437, 1439, 1440, 1629, 1631, 1632, 1646, 1648, 1661, 1663, 1664
1.280(b)(5)(A)	154, 170, 184, 352, 367, 381, 564, 580, 595, 767, 783, 797, 983, 999, 1015, 1191, 1206, 1221, 1409, 1425, 1441, 1632, 1649, 1664
1.280(b)(5)(A)(i)	154, 169, 183, 351, 366, 381, 563, 579, 594, 767, 782, 797, 982, 998, 1014, 1190, 1206, 1220, 1408, 1425, 1440, 1632, 1648, 1664
1.280(b)(5)(A)(ii)	154, 169, 183, 351, 366, 381, 563, 579, 594, 767, 782, 797, 982, 998, 1014, 1191, 1206, 1220, 1408, 1425, 1440, 1632, 1648, 1664
1.280(b)(5)(A)(iii)(1)	154, 169, 183, 351, 366, 381, 563, 580, 594, 767, 782, 797, 982, 999, 1014, 1191, 1206, 1220, 1408, 1425, 1440, 1632, 1648, 1664
1.280(b)(5)(A)(iii)(2)	154, 169, 183, 351, 366, 381, 564, 580, 594, 767, 782, 797, 982, 999, 1014, 1191, 1206, 1220, 1408, 1425, 1440, 1632, 1648, 1664
1.280(b)(5)(A)(iii)(3)	154, 169, 183, 351, 366, 381, 564, 580, 594, 767, 782, 797, 982, 999, 1014, 1191, 1206, 1220, 1408, 1425, 1440, 1632, 1648, 1664
1.280(b)(5)(A)(iii)(4)	154, 169, 184, 351, 367, 381, 564, 580, 594, 767, 782, 797, 982, 999, 1014, 1191, 1206, 1220, 1408, 1425, 1440, 1632, 1648, 1664
1.280(b)(5)(B)	154, 169, 170, 184, 352, 367, 381, 564, 580, 595, 767, 783, 797, 983, 999, 1015, 1191, 1206, 1221, 1409, 1425, 1440, 1441, 1632, 1649, 1664
1.280(b)(5)(C)	154, 169, 170, 184, 351, 352, 367, 381, 564, 580, 595, 767, 768, 783, 797, 982, 983, 999, 1014, 1015, 1191, 1206, 1221, 1408, 1409, 1425, 1440, 1441, 1632, 1648, 1649, 1664
1.280(b)(5)(D)	154, 170, 184, 352, 367, 381, 564, 580, 595, 768, 783, 797, 983, 999, 1015, 1191, 1206, 1221, 1409, 1425, 1441, 1632, 1649, 1664
1.280(b)(6)	155, 170, 184, 352, 367, 381, 564, 580, 595, 768, 783, 798, 983, 999, 1015, 1191, 1207, 1221, 1409, 1425, 1441, 1632, 1649, 1664
1.280(c)	127, 153, 168, 182, 324, 350, 365, 380, 533, 562, 578, 593, 739, 766, 781, 796, 951, 981, 997, 1013, 1161, 1190, 1205, 1219, 1377, 1407, 1424, 1439, 1599, 1630, 1647, 1663
1.280(d)(1)	127, 155, 170, 184, 325, 352, 367, 382, 534, 564, 580, 595, 740, 768, 783, 798, 951, 983, 999, 1015, 1162, 1191, 1207, 1221, 1377, 1409, 1426, 1441, 1599, 1633, 1649, 1665
1.280(d)(2)	128, 155, 170, 184, 325, 352, 367, 382, 534, 565, 581, 595, 740, 768, 783, 798, 951, 983, 1000, 1015, 1162, 1192, 1207, 1221, 1377, 1409, 1426, 1441, 1599, 1633, 1649, 1665
1.280(e)	152, 167, 181, 349, 364, 378, 561, 577, 592, 765, 780, 794, 980, 996, 1012, 1188, 1204, 1218, 1405, 1422, 1437, 1629, 1646, 1661
1.280(f)	193, 390, 605, 807, 1025, 1230, 1450, 1675
1.280(g)	161, 175, 193, 358, 373, 390, 571, 586,

FLORIDA RULES OF CIVIL PROCEDURE—Continued

Rule	Pg.
	605, 774, 789, 807, 990, 1006, 1025, 1198, 1212, 1230, 1416, 1431, 1450, 1640, 1655, 1675
1.285	155, 170, 184, 352, 367, 382, 565, 581, 595, 768, 783, 798, 983, 1000, 1015, 1192, 1207, 1221, 1409, 1426, 1441, 1633, 1649, 1665
1.290	180, 377, 591, 793, 1011, 1217, 1436, 1660
1.290(a)(1)	186, 383, 597, 799, 1017, 1223, 1442, 1667
1.290(a)(2)	186, 383, 597, 799, 1017, 1223, 1443, 1667
1.290(a)(3)	186, 383, 597, 799, 1017, 1223, 1443, 1667
1.290(a)(4)	186, 383, 597, 799, 1017, 1223, 1443, 1667
1.300	180, 377, 591, 793, 1011, 1217, 1436, 1660
1.300(a)	185, 382, 596, 799, 1016, 1222, 1442, 1666
1.300(b)	185, 382, 596, 799, 1016, 1222, 1442, 1666
1.300(c)	185, 382, 596, 799, 1016, 1222, 1442, 1666
1.300(d)	185, 383, 597, 799, 1016, 1222, 1442, 1666
1.310	124, 126, 151, 156, 157, 180, 321, 324, 348, 353, 354, 377, 529, 532, 560, 566, 567, 591, 736, 739, 764, 769, 770, 793, 947, 950, 979, 984, 985, 1011, 1158, 1161, 1187, 1193, 1217, 1373, 1376, 1405, 1411, 1436, 1595, 1598, 1628, 1634, 1635, 1660
1.310(a)	181, 185, 378, 382, 592, 596, 794, 798, 1011, 1016, 1218, 1222, 1437, 1442, 1661, 1665
1.310(b)	185, 382, 596, 798, 1016, 1222, 1442, 1665
1.310(b)(1)	181, 185, 378, 382, 592, 596, 794, 798, 1011, 1016, 1218, 1222, 1437, 1441, 1661, 1665
1.310(b)(2)	181, 185, 378, 382, 592, 596, 794, 798, 1011, 1016, 1218, 1222, 1437, 1442, 1661, 1665
1.310(b)(3)	186, 383, 597, 800, 1017, 1223, 1443, 1667
1.310(b)(4)(A)	186, 383, 597, 800, 1017, 1223, 1443, 1667
1.310(b)(4)(B)	186, 383, 597, 800, 1017, 1223, 1443, 1667
1.310(b)(4)(C)	186, 384, 598, 800, 1017, 1223, 1443, 1667
1.310(b)(4)(D)	186, 384, 598, 800, 1017, 1223, 1443, 1667
1.310(b)(4)(E)	186, 384, 598, 800, 1017, 1223, 1443, 1667
1.310(b)(5)	187, 384, 598, 800, 1018, 1223, 1443, 1668
1.310(b)(6)	126, 187, 188, 324, 384, 385, 532, 598, 599, 739, 800, 802, 950, 1018, 1019, 1161, 1224, 1225, 1376, 1444, 1445, 1598, 1668, 1670
1.310(b)(7)	187, 384, 598, 800, 1018, 1224, 1444, 1668
1.310(b)(8)	187, 384, 598, 800, 1018, 1224, 1444, 1668
1.310(c)	187, 188, 384, 385, 386, 598, 599, 600, 800, 801, 802, 1018, 1019, 1224, 1225, 1444, 1445, 1668, 1669, 1670
1.310(d)	126, 187, 188, 323, 324, 384, 385, 532, 598, 599, 738, 801, 950, 1018, 1019, 1160, 1224, 1376, 1444, 1598, 1669
1.310(e)	188, 385, 386, 599, 600, 801, 802, 1019, 1225, 1445, 1669, 1670
1.310(f)	188, 386, 600, 802, 1019, 1225, 1445, 1670
1.310(f)(1)	188, 385, 599, 801, 1019, 1225, 1445, 1669
1.310(f)(2)	188, 385, 599, 802, 1019, 1225, 1445, 1670
1.310(f)(3)(A)	193, 390, 605, 807, 1025, 1230, 1450, 1675
1.310(f)(3)(B)	193, 390, 605, 807, 1025, 1230, 1450, 1675
1.310(g)	188, 385, 599, 802, 1019, 1225, 1445, 1670
1.320	124, 126, 180, 321, 324, 377, 529, 532, 591, 736, 739, 793, 947, 950, 1011, 1158, 1161, 1217, 1373, 1376, 1436, 1595, 1598, 1660
1.320(a)	126, 181, 185, 188, 324, 378, 382, 385, 386, 532, 592, 596, 599, 600, 739, 794, 798, 802, 950, 1012, 1016, 1019, 1161, 1218, 1222, 1225, 1376, 1437, 1442, 1445, 1598, 1661, 1665, 1670
1.320(b)	188, 386, 600, 802, 1019, 1225, 1445, 1670
1.330	180, 377, 591, 793, 1011, 1217, 1436, 1660
1.330(d)(4)	188, 385, 599, 801, 1019, 1225, 1445, 1669
1.340	124, 126, 151, 153, 166, 168, 182, 321, 324, 348, 350, 364, 365, 380, 529, 532, 560, 562, 577, 578, 593, 736, 739, 764, 766, 779, 781, 796, 947, 950, 979, 981, 996, 997, 1013, 1158, 1161, 1188, 1190, 1203, 1205, 1219, 1373, 1376, 1405, 1407, 1421, 1424, 1439, 1595, 1598, 1628, 1631, 1645, 1647, 1663
1.340(e)	158, 172, 189, 355, 369, 387, 568, 583, 601, 771, 785, 803, 986, 1002, 1021, 1195, 1209, 1226, 1412, 1428, 1446, 1636, 1652, 1671
1.350	124, 126, 151, 155, 156, 161, 186, 321, 324,

FLORIDA RULES OF CIVIL PROCEDURE—Continued

Rule	Pg.
	348, 349, 353, 358, 384, 529, 532, 560, 561, 565, 566, 571, 598, 736, 739, 764, 768, 769, 774, 800, 947, 950, 979, 980, 984, 990, 1017, 1158, 1161, 1188, 1192, 1193, 1198, 1223, 1373, 1376, 1405, 1410, 1416, 1443, 1595, 1598, 1628, 1629, 1633, 1634, 1640, 1667
1.351	151, 156, 157, 166, 186, 348, 349, 353, 354, 363, 384, 560, 561, 566, 567, 576, 598, 764, 765, 769, 770, 779, 800, 979, 980, 984, 985, 995, 1017, 1188, 1193, 1202, 1223, 1405, 1410, 1411, 1421, 1437, 1443, 1629, 1634, 1635, 1645, 1667
1.351(a)	156, 353, 566, 769, 984, 1193, 1411, 1634
1.351(b)	151, 156, 157, 349, 354, 561, 566, 567, 765, 769, 770, 980, 985, 1188, 1193, 1405, 1411, 1629, 1634, 1635
1.351(c)	156, 157, 354, 566, 567, 769, 770, 985, 1193, 1194, 1411, 1635
1.351(d)	156, 157, 354, 566, 567, 769, 770, 985, 1193, 1411, 1634, 1635
1.351(e)	157, 354, 567, 770, 985, 1194, 1411, 1635
1.351(f)	156, 353, 566, 769, 984, 1193, 1410, 1634
1.360	124, 151, 166, 321, 348, 364, 529, 560, 577, 736, 764, 779, 947, 979, 996, 1158, 1188, 1203, 1373, 1405, 1421, 1595, 1629, 1645
1.360(a)	127, 324, 532, 739, 950, 1161, 1376, 1598
1.360(b)	154, 169, 184, 352, 367, 381, 564, 580, 595, 767, 783, 797, 983, 999, 1015, 1191, 1206, 1221, 1409, 1425, 1440, 1632, 1649, 1664
1.370	151, 153, 166, 168, 171, 182, 348, 350, 364, 365, 368, 380, 561, 562, 577, 578, 581, 593, 764, 766, 779, 781, 784, 796, 979, 981, 996, 997, 1000, 1013, 1188, 1190, 1203, 1205, 1207, 1219, 1405, 1407, 1421, 1424, 1426, 1439, 1629, 1631, 1645, 1647, 1650, 1663
1.370(a)	167, 170, 171, 172, 364, 368, 369, 577, 581, 582, 583, 780, 784, 785, 996, 1000, 1001, 1002, 1204, 1207, 1208, 1209, 1422, 1426, 1427, 1428, 1646, 1650, 1652
1.370(b)	171, 368, 581, 784, 1000, 1208, 1426, 1650
1.380	124, 151, 155, 166, 180, 321, 348, 353, 364, 377, 529, 561, 565, 577, 591, 736, 764, 769, 779, 794, 947, 979, 984, 996, 1011, 1158, 1188, 1192, 1203, 1217, 1373, 1405, 1410, 1421, 1436, 1595, 1629, 1633, 1645, 1660
1.380(a)	124, 126, 127, 322, 324, 530, 532, 533, 736, 738, 739, 948, 950, 951, 1159, 1160, 1161, 1374, 1376, 1377, 1596, 1598, 1599
1.380(a)(1)	126, 324, 532, 738, 950, 1160, 1376, 1598
1.380(a)(2)	127, 129, 324, 326, 532, 533, 535, 739, 741, 950, 951, 953, 1161, 1162, 1163, 1376, 1377, 1378, 1598, 1599, 1601
1.380(a)(3)	127, 324, 533, 739, 951, 1161, 1377, 1599
1.380(a)(4)	127, 171, 324, 325, 368, 533, 581, 739, 784, 951, 1000, 1161, 1207, 1377, 1426, 1599, 1650
1.380(a)(5)	153, 169, 183, 351, 366, 380, 563, 579, 594, 767, 782, 796, 982, 998, 1014, 1190, 1205, 1220, 1408, 1424, 1440, 1631, 1648, 1663
1.380(b)	533
1.380(c)	171, 368, 582, 784, 1001, 1208, 1427, 1650
1.380(d)	156, 353, 565, 769, 984, 1192, 1410, 1633
1.380(e)	127, 325, 533, 739, 951, 1161, 1377, 1599
1.390	151, 154, 166, 169, 180, 183, 348, 351, 364, 366, 378, 381, 561, 563, 577, 579, 591, 594, 764, 767, 779, 782, 794, 797, 979, 982, 996, 998, 1011, 1014, 1188, 1191, 1203, 1206, 1217, 1220, 1405, 1408, 1421, 1425, 1436, 1440, 1629, 1632, 1645, 1648, 1660, 1664
1.390(a)	154, 170, 184, 352, 367, 381, 564, 580, 595, 768, 783, 797, 983, 999, 1015, 1191, 1206, 1221, 1409, 1425, 1441, 1632, 1649, 1664
1.410	181, 378, 592, 794, 1011, 1012, 1218, 1437, 1661
1.420	6, 26, 42, 60, 204, 224, 241, 258, 402, 423, 440, 458, 616, 636, 653, 670, 818, 839, 855, 873, 1036, 1056, 1073, 1090, 1242, 1263, 1280, 1300, 1461, 1482, 1499, 1517
1.420(a)(1)	6, 26, 42, 60, 204, 224, 241, 258, 402, 423, 440, 458, 616, 636, 653, 670, 818, 839, 855, 873, 1036, 1056, 1073, 1090, 1242, 1263, 1280, 1300, 1461, 1482, 1499, 1517
1.430	1, 7, 27, 36, 43, 60, 199, 205, 225, 234, 241, 258, 397, 403, 424, 433, 440, 458, 611, 617, 637, 646, 653, 671, 813, 819, 839, 849, 856, 873, 1031, 1037, 1057, 1066, 1073, 1090, 1236, 1242, 1263, 1273, 1281, 1300, 1456, 1462,

FLORIDA RULES OF CIVIL PROCEDURE—Continued

Rule	Pg.
	1482, 1492, 1500, 1518
1.430(a)	6, 26, 43, 60, 204, 224, 241, 258, 402, 423, 440, 458, 617, 637, 653, 670, 818, 839, 855, 873, 1036, 1056, 1073, 1090, 1242, 1263, 1280, 1300, 1461, 1482, 1499, 1517
1.430(b)	6, 26, 43, 60, 205, 225, 241, 258, 403, 423, 440, 458, 617, 637, 653, 671, 818, 839, 855, 873, 1036, 1057, 1073, 1090, 1242, 1263, 1280, 1300, 1462, 1482, 1500, 1518
1.430(c)	7, 27, 43, 60, 205, 225, 241, 258, 403, 423, 440, 458, 617, 637, 653, 671, 819, 839, 856, 873, 1037, 1057, 1073, 1090, 1242, 1263, 1281, 1300, 1462, 1482, 1500, 1518
1.430(d)	7, 27, 43, 60, 205, 225, 241, 258, 403, 424, 440, 458, 617, 637, 653, 671, 819, 839, 856, 873, 1037, 1057, 1073, 1090, 1242, 1263, 1281, 1300, 1462, 1482, 1483, 1500, 1518
1.442	110, 114, 308, 311, 514, 518, 722, 725, 931, 935, 1143, 1147, 1357, 1361, 1578, 1582
1.442(g)	111, 113, 309, 311, 515, 517, 722, 725, 932, 935, 1144, 1146, 1358, 1361, 1579, 1582
1.480	138, 335, 545, 750, 963, 1173, 1389, 1612
1.480(a)	138, 140, 336, 337, 546, 548, 751, 753, 964, 966, 1174, 1176, 1390, 1392, 1613, 1615
1.480(b)	138, 140, 336, 338, 546, 548, 751, 753, 964, 966, 1174, 1176, 1390, 1392, 1613, 1615
1.480(c)	140, 338, 548, 753, 967, 1176, 1392, 1615
1.510	96, 99, 294, 297, 498, 499, 501, 502, 707, 708, 710, 915, 918, 1128, 1129, 1131, 1341, 1344, 1561, 1562, 1564, 1565
1.510(a)	96, 98, 294, 296, 499, 500, 708, 709, 915, 917, 1129, 1130, 1341, 1343, 1562, 1563
1.510(b)	96, 98, 294, 296, 499, 500, 708, 709, 915, 917, 1129, 1130, 1341, 1343, 1562, 1563
1.510(c)	97, 98, 101, 294, 296, 298, 499, 501, 503, 708, 709, 710, 712, 915, 917, 918, 920, 1129, 1130, 1131, 1133, 1342, 1343, 1344, 1346, 1562, 1564, 1566
1.510(d)	99, 297, 502, 710, 711, 918, 919, 1131, 1132, 1345, 1565
1.510(e)	99, 101, 297, 298, 501, 503, 710, 712, 918, 920, 1131, 1133, 1344, 1346, 1564, 1566
1.510(f)	99, 297, 501, 710, 918, 1131, 1344, 1564
1.510(g)	99, 101, 297, 298, 502, 503, 710, 712, 918, 920, 1131, 1133, 1344, 1346, 1565, 1566
1.525	110, 111, 113, 308, 309, 311, 514, 515, 517, 722, 725, 931, 932, 935, 1143, 1144, 1146, 1147, 1357, 1358, 1361, 1578, 1579, 1582
1.540	1, 21, 36, 53, 69, 82, 96, 110, 124, 138, 151, 166, 180, 199, 219, 234, 251, 267, 280, 294, 308, 321, 335, 348, 364, 378, 397, 417, 433, 451, 468, 483, 498, 514, 529, 546, 561, 577, 591, 611, 631, 646, 664, 680, 693, 707, 722, 736, 751, 764, 779, 794, 813, 833, 849, 866, 883, 898, 915, 931, 947, 964, 979, 996, 1011, 1031, 1051, 1066, 1083, 1099, 1114, 1128, 1144, 1158, 1173, 1188, 1203, 1217, 1236, 1257, 1273, 1293, 1310, 1325, 1341, 1357, 1373, 1389, 1405, 1421, 1436, 1456, 1476, 1493, 1511, 1528, 1544, 1561, 1578, 1595, 1612, 1629, 1645, 1660
1.540(b)	2, 22, 38, 55, 71, 84, 97, 112, 125, 139, 152, 168, 182, 201, 220, 236, 253, 269, 282, 295, 310, 323, 337, 350, 365, 379, 399, 419, 435, 453, 470, 485, 500, 516, 531, 547, 562, 578, 593, 613, 632, 648, 665, 682, 695, 709, 724, 737, 752, 766, 781, 795, 814, 834, 850, 868, 885, 901, 917, 933, 949, 966, 981, 997, 1013, 1032, 1052, 1068, 1085, 1101, 1115, 1130, 1145, 1160, 1175, 1189, 1205, 1219, 1238, 1259, 1275, 1295, 1312, 1327, 1343, 1359, 1375, 1392, 1407, 1423, 1439, 1458, 1478, 1494, 1512, 1530, 1546, 1563, 1580, 1597, 1614, 1630, 1647, 1662
1.700	69, 82, 96, 110, 124, 138, 267, 280, 294, 308, 321, 335, 468, 483, 498, 514, 529, 546, 680, 693, 707, 722, 736, 751, 883, 898, 915, 931, 947, 964, 1099, 1114, 1128, 1144, 1158, 1173, 1310, 1325, 1341, 1357, 1373, 1389, 1528, 1544, 1561, 1578, 1595, 1612
1.700(a)	7, 27, 43, 60, 72, 86, 99, 114, 128, 141, 157, 171, 189, 205, 225, 241, 258, 270, 283, 297, 311, 325, 338, 354, 368, 386, 403, 424, 441, 459, 471, 486, 502, 518, 534, 549, 567, 582, 600, 617, 637, 654, 671, 683, 697, 711, 726, 740, 754, 770, 784, 802, 819, 839, 856, 873, 886, 902, 919, 935, 952, 967, 985, 1001, 1020, 1037, 1057, 1073, 1091, 1102, 1117, 1132, 1147, 1162, 1177, 1194, 1208,

FLORIDA RULES OF CIVIL PROCEDURE—Continued

Rule	Pg.
	1226, 1243, 1263, 1281, 1300, 1313, 1329, 1345, 1361, 1377, 1393, 1411, 1427, 1445, 1462, 1483, 1500, 1518, 1531, 1548, 1565, 1582, 1599, 1616, 1635, 1650, 1670
1.710	7, 27, 43, 61, 69, 72, 82, 86, 96, 100, 110, 114, 124, 128, 138, 141, 157, 171, 189, 205, 225, 241, 259, 267, 270, 280, 284, 294, 297, 308, 312, 321, 325, 335, 338, 355, 369, 386, 404, 424, 441, 459, 468, 471, 483, 487, 498, 502, 514, 518, 529, 534, 546, 549, 567, 582, 601, 617, 637, 654, 671, 680, 683, 693, 697, 707, 711, 722, 726, 736, 740, 751, 754, 770, 785, 802, 819, 839, 856, 874, 883, 886, 898, 903, 915, 919, 931, 936, 947, 952, 964, 968, 986, 1001, 1020, 1037, 1057, 1074, 1091, 1099, 1103, 1114, 1117, 1128, 1132, 1144, 1148, 1158, 1163, 1173, 1177, 1194, 1208, 1226, 1243, 1264, 1281, 1301, 1310, 1314, 1325, 1329, 1341, 1345, 1357, 1362, 1373, 1378, 1389, 1393, 1412, 1427, 1446, 1462, 1483, 1500, 1518, 1528, 1532, 1544, 1548, 1561, 1565, 1578, 1583, 1595, 1600, 1612, 1616, 1635, 1651, 1670
1.720	7, 27, 43, 61, 69, 72, 82, 86, 96, 100, 110, 114, 124, 128, 138, 141, 157, 171, 189, 205, 225, 241, 259, 267, 270, 280, 284, 294, 297, 308, 312, 321, 325, 335, 338, 355, 369, 386, 404, 424, 441, 459, 468, 471, 483, 487, 498, 502, 514, 518, 529, 534, 546, 549, 567, 582, 601, 617, 637, 654, 671, 680, 683, 693, 697, 707, 711, 722, 726, 736, 740, 751, 754, 770, 785, 802, 819, 839, 856, 874, 883, 886, 898, 903, 915, 919, 931, 936, 947, 952, 964, 968, 986, 1001, 1020, 1037, 1057, 1074, 1091, 1099, 1103, 1114, 1117, 1128, 1132, 1144, 1148, 1158, 1163, 1173, 1177, 1194, 1208, 1226, 1243, 1264, 1281, 1301, 1310, 1314, 1325, 1329, 1341, 1345, 1357, 1362, 1373, 1378, 1389, 1393, 1412, 1427, 1446, 1462, 1483, 1500, 1518, 1528, 1532, 1544, 1548, 1561, 1565, 1578, 1583, 1595, 1600, 1612, 1616, 1635, 1651, 1670
1.720(f)	1037, 1057, 1073, 1091, 1102, 1117, 1132, 1147, 1162, 1177, 1194, 1208, 1226
1.730	7, 27, 43, 61, 69, 72, 82, 86, 96, 100, 110, 114, 124, 128, 138, 141, 157, 171, 189, 205, 225, 241, 259, 267, 270, 280, 284, 294, 297, 308, 312, 321, 325, 335, 338, 355, 369, 386, 404, 424, 441, 459, 468, 471, 483, 487, 498, 502, 514, 518, 529, 534, 546, 549, 567, 582, 601, 618, 637, 654, 671, 680, 683, 693, 697, 707, 711, 722, 726, 736, 740, 751, 754, 770, 785, 802, 819, 839, 856, 874, 883, 886, 898, 903, 915, 919, 932, 936, 947, 952, 964, 968, 986, 1001, 1020, 1037, 1057, 1074, 1091, 1100, 1103, 1114, 1117, 1128, 1132, 1144, 1148, 1158, 1163, 1174, 1177, 1194, 1208, 1226, 1243, 1264, 1281, 1301, 1310, 1314, 1325, 1329, 1341, 1345, 1357, 1362, 1373, 1378, 1389, 1393, 1412, 1427, 1446, 1462, 1483, 1500, 1518, 1528, 1532, 1544, 1548, 1561, 1565, 1578, 1583, 1595, 1600, 1612, 1616, 1635, 1651, 1670
1.750	7, 27, 43, 61, 69, 72, 82, 86, 96, 100, 110, 114, 124, 128, 138, 141, 157, 171, 189, 205, 225, 241, 259, 267, 270, 280, 284, 294, 297, 308, 312, 321, 325, 335, 338, 355, 369, 386, 404, 424, 441, 459, 468, 471, 483, 487, 498, 502, 514, 518, 529, 534, 546, 549, 567, 582, 601, 618, 637, 654, 671, 680, 683, 693, 697, 707, 711, 722, 726, 736, 740, 751, 754, 770, 785, 802, 819, 839, 856, 874, 883, 886, 898, 903, 915, 919, 932, 936, 947, 952, 964, 968, 986, 1001, 1020, 1037, 1057, 1074, 1091, 1100, 1103, 1114, 1117, 1128, 1132, 1144, 1148, 1158, 1163, 1174, 1177, 1194, 1208, 1226, 1243, 1264, 1281, 1301, 1310, 1314, 1325, 1329, 1341, 1345, 1357, 1362, 1373, 1378, 1389, 1393, 1412, 1427, 1446, 1462, 1483, 1500, 1518, 1528, 1532, 1544, 1548, 1561, 1565, 1578, 1583, 1595, 1600, 1612, 1616, 1635, 1651, 1670
1.800	7, 27, 43, 61, 69, 72, 82, 86, 96, 100, 110, 114, 124, 128, 138, 141, 157, 171, 189, 205, 225, 241, 259, 267, 270, 280, 283, 284, 294, 297, 308, 312, 321, 325, 335, 338, 354, 355, 369, 386, 404, 424, 441, 459, 468, 471, 483, 486, 498, 502, 514, 518, 529, 534, 546, 549, 567, 582, 600, 617, 637, 654, 671, 680, 683, 693, 697, 707, 711, 722, 726, 736, 740, 751, 754, 770, 785, 802, 819, 839, 856, 874, 883, 886, 898, 902, 915, 919, 932, 936, 947, 952, 964, 967, 985, 1001, 1020, 1037, 1057, 1074, 1091,

FLORIDA RULES OF CIVIL PROCEDURE—Continued

Rule	Pg.
	1100, 1103, 1114, 1117, 1128, 1132, 1144, 1147, 1158, 1163, 1174, 1177, 1194, 1208, 1226, 1243, 1264, 1281, 1301, 1310, 1313, 1325, 1329, 1341, 1345, 1357, 1361, 1362, 1373, 1378, 1389, 1393, 1412, 1427, 1446, 1462, 1483, 1500, 1518, 1528, 1531, 1544, 1548, 1561, 1565, 1578, 1582, 1583, 1595, 1600, 1612, 1616, 1635, 1651, 1670
1.810	7, 27, 43, 61, 69, 72, 82, 86, 96, 100, 110, 114, 124, 128, 138, 141, 157, 171, 189, 205, 225, 241, 259, 267, 270, 280, 284, 294, 297, 308, 312, 321, 325, 335, 338, 355, 369, 386, 404, 424, 441, 459, 468, 471, 483, 486, 498, 502, 514, 518, 529, 534, 546, 549, 567, 582, 600, 617, 637, 654, 671, 680, 683, 693, 697, 707, 711, 722, 726, 736, 740, 751, 754, 770, 785, 802, 819, 839, 856, 874, 883, 886, 898, 902, 915, 919, 932, 936, 947, 952, 964, 967, 985, 1001, 1020, 1037, 1057, 1074, 1091, 1100, 1103, 1114, 1117, 1128, 1132, 1144, 1148, 1158, 1163, 1174, 1177, 1194, 1208, 1226, 1243, 1264, 1281, 1301, 1310, 1313, 1325, 1329, 1341, 1345, 1357, 1362, 1373, 1378, 1389, 1393, 1412, 1427, 1446, 1462, 1483, 1500, 1518, 1528, 1532, 1544, 1548, 1561, 1565, 1578, 1583, 1595, 1600, 1612, 1616, 1635, 1651, 1670
1.820	7, 27, 43, 61, 69, 72, 82, 86, 96, 100, 110, 114, 124, 128, 138, 141, 157, 171, 189, 205, 225, 241, 259, 267, 270, 280, 284, 294, 297, 308, 312, 321, 325, 335, 338, 355, 369, 386, 404, 424, 441, 459, 468, 471, 483, 486, 498, 502, 514, 518, 529, 534, 546, 549, 567, 582, 600, 617, 637, 654, 671, 680, 683, 693, 697, 707, 711, 722, 726, 736, 740, 751, 754, 770, 785, 802, 819, 839, 856, 874, 883, 886, 898, 902, 915, 919, 932, 936, 947, 952, 964, 967, 985, 1001, 1020, 1037, 1057, 1074, 1091, 1100, 1103, 1114, 1117, 1128, 1132, 1144, 1148, 1158, 1163, 1174, 1177, 1194, 1208, 1226, 1243, 1264, 1281, 1301, 1310, 1313, 1325, 1329, 1341, 1345, 1357, 1362, 1373, 1378, 1389, 1393, 1412, 1427, 1446, 1462, 1483, 1500, 1518, 1528, 1532, 1544, 1548, 1561, 1565, 1578, 1583, 1595, 1600, 1612, 1616, 1635, 1651, 1670
1.830	7, 27, 43, 61, 69, 72, 82, 86, 96, 100, 110, 114, 124, 128, 138, 141, 157, 171, 189, 205, 225, 241, 259, 267, 270, 280, 284, 294, 297, 308, 312, 321, 325, 335, 338, 355, 369, 386, 404, 424, 441, 459, 468, 471, 483, 486, 498, 502, 514, 518, 529, 534, 546, 549, 567, 582, 600, 617, 637, 654, 671, 680, 683, 693, 697, 707, 711, 722, 726, 736, 740, 751, 754, 770, 785, 802, 819, 839, 856, 874, 883, 886, 898, 902, 915, 919, 932, 936, 947, 952, 964, 967, 985, 1001, 1020, 1037, 1057, 1074, 1091, 1100, 1103, 1114, 1117, 1128, 1132, 1144, 1148, 1158, 1163, 1174, 1177, 1194, 1208, 1226, 1243, 1264, 1281, 1301, 1310, 1313, 1325, 1329, 1341, 1345, 1357, 1362, 1373, 1378, 1389, 1393, 1412, 1427, 1446, 1462, 1483, 1500, 1518, 1528, 1532, 1544, 1548, 1561, 1565, 1578, 1583, 1595, 1600, 1612, 1616, 1635, 1651, 1670
1.900	1, 21, 36, 53, 69, 83, 96, 110, 124, 138, 151, 166, 180, 199, 219, 234, 251, 267, 280, 294, 308, 321, 335, 348, 364, 378, 397, 417, 433, 451, 468, 483, 498, 514, 530, 546, 561, 577, 591, 611, 631, 646, 664, 680, 693, 707, 722, 736, 751, 764, 779, 794, 813, 833, 849, 866, 883, 899, 915, 932, 947, 964, 979, 996, 1011, 1031, 1051, 1066, 1083, 1100, 1114, 1128, 1144, 1158, 1174, 1188, 1203, 1217, 1236, 1257, 1273, 1293, 1310, 1325, 1341, 1357, 1373, 1389, 1405, 1421, 1436, 1456, 1476, 1493, 1511, 1528, 1544, 1561, 1578, 1595, 1612, 1629, 1645, 1660
1.900(a)	10, 30, 46, 63, 75, 89, 103, 117, 131, 144, 160, 174, 191, 208, 228, 244, 261, 273, 286, 300, 314, 328, 341, 357, 371, 389, 407, 427, 444, 462, 474, 490, 505, 521, 537, 552, 570, 585, 603, 621, 640, 657, 674, 686, 700, 714, 729, 743, 757, 773, 787, 805, 822, 842, 859, 877, 890, 906, 923, 940, 956, 971, 989, 1004, 1023, 1040, 1060, 1076, 1094, 1106, 1120, 1135, 1150, 1166, 1180, 1197, 1211, 1228, 1246, 1267, 1284, 1304, 1317, 1332, 1349, 1365, 1381, 1396, 1414, 1430, 1448, 1466, 1486, 1503, 1521, 1535, 1552, 1569, 1586, 1603, 1620, 1638, 1654, 1673
1.900(b)	10, 30, 46, 64, 75, 89, 103, 117, 131, 144, 160, 174, 191, 208, 228, 244, 261,

FLORIDA RULES OF CIVIL PROCEDURE—Continued

Rule	Pg.
	273, 286, 300, 314, 328, 341, 357, 371, 389, 407, 427, 444, 462, 474, 490, 505, 521, 537, 552, 570, 585, 603, 621, 640, 657, 674, 686, 700, 714, 729, 743, 757, 773, 787, 805, 823, 843, 859, 877, 890, 907, 923, 940, 956, 971, 989, 1004, 1023, 1040, 1060, 1076, 1094, 1106, 1120, 1135, 1150, 1166, 1180, 1197, 1211, 1228, 1246, 1267, 1284, 1304, 1317, 1333, 1349, 1365, 1381, 1397, 1414, 1430, 1448, 1466, 1486, 1503, 1521, 1535, 1552, 1569, 1586, 1604, 1620, 1638, 1654, 1673
1.900(c)	10, 30, 46, 64, 75, 89, 103, 117, 131, 144, 160, 174, 192, 208, 228, 244, 261, 273, 286, 300, 314, 328, 341, 357, 371, 389, 407, 427, 444, 462, 475, 490, 505, 521, 537, 552, 570, 585, 603, 621, 640, 657, 674, 686, 700, 714, 729, 743, 757, 773, 787, 805, 823, 843, 859, 877, 890, 907, 923, 940, 956, 971, 989, 1004, 1024, 1040, 1060, 1076, 1094, 1106, 1120, 1135, 1150, 1166, 1180, 1197, 1211, 1229, 1246, 1267, 1284, 1304, 1317, 1333, 1349, 1365, 1381, 1397, 1414, 1430, 1448, 1466, 1486, 1503, 1521, 1535, 1552, 1569, 1586, 1604, 1620, 1638, 1654, 1673
1.901	19, 35, 51, 68, 81, 94, 109, 123, 136, 149, 165, 179, 197, 217, 233, 249, 266, 279, 292, 306, 320, 334, 347, 362, 376, 394, 415, 432, 449, 467, 481, 497, 512, 528, 544, 559, 575, 590, 609, 629, 645, 662, 679, 692, 706, 720, 734, 749, 762, 778, 792, 811, 831, 848, 864, 882, 897, 913, 930, 946, 962, 978, 994, 1010, 1049, 1065, 1081, 1099, 1112, 1127, 1142, 1157, 1172, 1186, 1202, 1216, 1234, 1255, 1272, 1291, 1309, 1323, 1339, 1355, 1372, 1388, 1403, 1420, 1435, 1454, 1474, 1492, 1509, 1527, 1542, 1559, 1576, 1593, 1610, 1627, 1644, 1659, 1679
1.902	19, 217, 415, 629, 831, 1049, 1255, 1474
1.903	19, 51, 217, 249, 415, 449, 629, 662, 831, 864, 1049, 1081, 1255, 1291, 1474, 1509
1.904	19, 51, 217, 249, 415, 449, 629, 662, 831, 864, 1049, 1081, 1255, 1291, 1474, 1509
1.911	165, 362, 575, 778, 994, 1202, 1420, 1644
1.919	19, 217, 416, 629, 831, 1049, 1255, 1474
1.920	19, 217, 416, 629, 831, 1049, 1255, 1474
1.921	165, 362, 575, 778, 994, 1202, 1420, 1644
1.922	165, 362, 575, 778, 994, 1202, 1420, 1644
1.948	19, 217, 416, 629, 831, 1049, 1255, 1474
1.951	19, 217, 416, 629, 831, 1049, 1255, 1475
1.965	51, 249, 449, 662, 864, 1081, 1291, 1509
1.966	51, 249, 449, 662, 864, 1081, 1291, 1509
1.967	51, 249, 449, 662, 864, 1081, 1291, 1509
1.968	51, 249, 449, 662, 864, 1082, 1291, 1509
1.969	51, 249, 449, 662, 864, 1082, 1291, 1509
1.970	51, 249, 449, 662, 864, 1082, 1291, 1509
1.975	19, 35, 51, 68, 81, 94, 109, 123, 136, 149, 217, 233, 249, 266, 279, 292, 306, 320, 334, 347, 416, 449, 467, 481, 497, 512, 528, 544, 559, 629, 645, 662, 679, 692, 706, 720, 734, 749, 762, 831, 848, 865, 882, 897, 913, 930, 946, 962, 978, 1049, 1065, 1082, 1099, 1112, 1127, 1142, 1157, 1172, 1186, 1255, 1272, 1291, 1309, 1323, 1339, 1355, 1372, 1388, 1403, 1475, 1492, 1509, 1527, 1542, 1559, 1576, 1593, 1611, 1627
1.997	8, 19, 206, 217, 404, 416, 618, 629, 820, 831, 1038, 1049, 1243, 1255, 1463, 1474

FLORIDA FAMILY LAW RULES OF PROCEDURE

Rule	Pg.
12.310	124, 321, 529, 736, 947, 1158, 1373, 1595

FLORIDA RULES OF JUDICIAL ADMINISTRATION

Rule **Pg.**

2.071..........1542, 1559, 1576, 1593, 1610, 1626, 1627
2.071(c)................1542, 1559, 1576, 1593, 1610, 1627
2.110..........7, 9, 27, 29, 44, 45, 61, 63, 69, 73, 74, 82, 86, 88, 96, 100, 102, 110, 114, 116, 124, 128, 130, 138, 141, 143, 157, 159, 172, 173, 189, 191, 206, 207, 226, 227, 242, 243, 259, 260, 267, 271, 272, 280, 284, 285, 293, 298, 299, 308, 312, 313, 321, 326, 327, 335, 339, 340, 355, 356, 369, 370, 386, 388, 404, 406, 425, 426, 442, 443, 459, 461, 468, 472, 474, 482, 487, 489, 498, 503, 504, 514, 519, 520, 529, 535, 536, 545, 549, 551, 568, 569, 582, 584, 601, 602, 618, 620, 638, 639, 654, 656, 672, 673, 680, 684, 685, 693, 697, 699, 707, 711, 713, 722, 726, 728, 735, 740, 742, 750, 754, 756, 771, 772, 785, 786, 803, 804, 820, 821, 840, 841, 857, 858, 874, 876, 882, 887, 889, 898, 903, 905, 914, 919, 922, 931, 936, 939, 947, 952, 955, 964, 968, 970, 986, 988, 1001, 1003, 1020, 1022, 1038, 1039, 1058, 1059, 1074, 1075, 1091, 1093, 1099, 1103, 1105, 1113, 1118, 1119, 1128, 1132, 1134, 1143, 1148, 1149, 1158, 1163, 1165, 1173, 1177, 1179, 1194, 1196, 1209, 1210, 1226, 1228, 1243, 1245, 1264, 1265, 1281, 1283, 1301, 1302, 1309, 1314, 1316, 1325, 1329, 1331, 1340, 1345, 1347, 1357, 1362, 1364, 1373, 1378, 1380, 1389, 1393, 1395, 1412, 1413, 1428, 1429, 1446, 1447, 1463, 1465, 1483, 1485, 1501, 1502, 1519, 1520, 1527, 1532, 1534, 1544, 1549, 1551, 1561, 1565, 1568, 1578, 1583, 1585, 1595, 1600, 1603, 1612, 1616, 1619, 1636, 1637, 1651, 1653, 1671, 1672
2.205(a)(2)(B)(iv)..........2, 21, 37, 54, 70, 84, 97, 111, 125, 139, 152, 167, 181, 200, 219, 220, 235, 252, 268, 281, 295, 309, 322, 336, 349, 364, 379, 398, 418, 434, 435, 452, 469, 484, 499, 515, 530, 531, 547, 561, 562, 577, 578, 592, 612, 632, 647, 648, 664, 665, 681, 695, 708, 723, 737, 752, 765, 780, 795, 814, 834, 850, 867, 884, 900, 916, 933, 949, 965, 980, 996, 997, 1012, 1032, 1051, 1052, 1067, 1084, 1100, 1101, 1115, 1129, 1145, 1159, 1174, 1175, 1189, 1204, 1218, 1237, 1238, 1258, 1275, 1294, 1311, 1327, 1342, 1359, 1375, 1391, 1406, 1423, 1438, 1457, 1477, 1494, 1511, 1512, 1529, 1546, 1562, 1579, 1580, 1596, 1613, 1614, 1630, 1646, 1662
2.250..............9, 28, 45, 62, 74, 87, 101, 115, 129, 142, 158, 172, 190, 207, 226, 243, 260, 271, 285, 299, 313, 326, 340, 355, 370, 387, 405, 425, 442, 460, 473, 488, 504, 520, 536, 551, 568, 583, 602, 619, 639, 655, 672, 684, 698, 712, 727, 742, 755, 771, 786, 803, 821, 841, 857, 875, 888, 904, 921, 937, 954, 969, 987, 1002, 1021, 1039, 1058, 1075, 1092, 1104, 1118, 1133, 1149, 1164, 1178, 1195, 1209, 1227, 1244, 1265, 1282, 1302, 1315, 1331, 1347, 1363, 1379, 1395, 1413, 1428, 1447, 1464, 1484, 1502, 1520, 1534, 1550, 1567, 1585, 1602, 1618, 1637, 1652, 1672
2.425..........1, 11, 12, 21, 31, 36, 47, 53, 65, 69, 76, 83, 90, 96, 104, 110, 118, 124, 132, 138, 145, 151, 161, 166, 175, 180, 193, 199, 209, 210, 219, 229, 234, 245, 251, 263, 267, 274, 280, 288, 294, 301, 308, 316, 321, 329, 335, 342, 348, 358, 364, 372, 373, 378, 390, 397, 408, 417, 428, 433, 445, 451, 463, 468, 476, 483, 491, 498, 507, 514, 523, 530, 539, 546, 553, 561, 571, 577, 586, 591, 604, 605, 611, 622, 631, 641, 642, 646, 658, 664, 675, 680, 687, 693, 701, 707, 715, 722, 730, 736, 744, 745, 758, 764, 774, 779, 788, 789, 794, 806, 807, 813, 824, 833, 844, 849, 860, 866, 878, 883, 891, 892, 899, 908, 915, 924, 932, 941, 947, 957, 964, 973, 979, 990, 996, 1006, 1011, 1025, 1031, 1041, 1042, 1051, 1061, 1066, 1078, 1083, 1095, 1100, 1107, 1114, 1121, 1128, 1136, 1144, 1152, 1158, 1167, 1174, 1181, 1188, 1198, 1203, 1212, 1217, 1230, 1236, 1247, 1257, 1268, 1273, 1285, 1293, 1305, 1310, 1318, 1325, 1334, 1341, 1350, 1357, 1366, 1373, 1382, 1390, 1398, 1405, 1415, 1416, 1422, 1431, 1437, 1450, 1456, 1467, 1476, 1487, 1493, 1505, 1511, 1523, 1528, 1536, 1537, 1544, 1553, 1561, 1570, 1578, 1588, 1595, 1605, 1612, 1621, 1629, 1639, 1640, 1645, 1655, 1660, 1674, 1675
2.425(a)...........11, 31, 47, 64, 65, 76, 89, 90, 103, 104, 117, 118, 131, 132, 144, 145, 160, 161, 175, 192, 193, 209, 229, 245, 262, 274, 287, 301, 315, 329, 342, 358, 372, 389, 390, 407, 408, 428, 444, 445, 462, 463, 475, 476, 490,

FLORIDA RULES OF JUDICIAL ADMINISTRATION—Continued

Rule	Pg.
	491, 506, 522, 538, 553, 570, 571, 585, 586, 604, 621, 622, 641, 657, 658, 675, 687, 701, 715, 729, 730, 744, 757, 758, 773, 774, 788, 806, 823, 824, 843, 844, 860, 877, 878, 891, 907, 908, 924, 940, 941, 957, 972, 990, 1005, 1024, 1025, 1041, 1061, 1077, 1094, 1095, 1106, 1107, 1121, 1136, 1151, 1166, 1167, 1180, 1181, 1197, 1198, 1211, 1212, 1229, 1230, 1247, 1267, 1268, 1285, 1304, 1305, 1317, 1318, 1333, 1334, 1349, 1350, 1366, 1382, 1397, 1398, 1415, 1430, 1431, 1449, 1450, 1466, 1467, 1487, 1504, 1522, 1523, 1536, 1553, 1569, 1570, 1587, 1604, 1605, 1620, 1621, 1639, 1654, 1655, 1674
2.425(a)(3)	11, 30, 47, 64, 76, 89, 103, 117, 131, 144, 160, 174, 192, 209, 228, 245, 262, 274, 287, 301, 315, 329, 342, 358, 372, 389, 407, 428, 444, 462, 475, 490, 506, 522, 538, 553, 570, 585, 604, 621, 641, 657, 675, 687, 700, 715, 729, 744, 757, 773, 788, 806, 823, 843, 860, 877, 891, 907, 924, 940, 956, 972, 989, 1005, 1024, 1041, 1061, 1077, 1094, 1106, 1121, 1136, 1151, 1166, 1180, 1197, 1211, 1229, 1246, 1267, 1284, 1304, 1317, 1333, 1349, 1365, 1382, 1397, 1415, 1430, 1449, 1466, 1487, 1504, 1522, 1536, 1553, 1569, 1587, 1604, 1620, 1639, 1654, 1674
2.425(b)	11, 30, 31, 46, 47, 64, 65, 75, 76, 89, 90, 103, 104, 117, 118, 131, 132, 144, 145, 160, 161, 174, 175, 192, 209, 228, 229, 244, 245, 262, 273, 274, 287, 301, 315, 328, 329, 341, 342, 357, 358, 371, 372, 389, 390, 407, 408, 427, 428, 444, 445, 462, 463, 475, 490, 491, 506, 522, 538, 553, 570, 571, 585, 586, 604, 621, 622, 641, 657, 658, 674, 675, 686, 687, 700, 701, 714, 715, 729, 730, 744, 757, 758, 773, 774, 788, 805, 806, 823, 824, 843, 844, 859, 860, 877, 878, 891, 907, 908, 923, 924, 940, 941, 956, 957, 972, 989, 990, 1005, 1024, 1041, 1060, 1061, 1077, 1094, 1095, 1106, 1107, 1120, 1121, 1135, 1136, 1151, 1166, 1167, 1180, 1181, 1197, 1198, 1211, 1212, 1229, 1246, 1247, 1267, 1268, 1284, 1285, 1304, 1305, 1317, 1318, 1333, 1334, 1349, 1350, 1365, 1366, 1381, 1382, 1397, 1398, 1415, 1430, 1431, 1449, 1466, 1467, 1486, 1487, 1504, 1522, 1536, 1552, 1553, 1569, 1570, 1587, 1604, 1605, 1620, 1621, 1639, 1654, 1655, 1674
2.425(c)	11, 31, 47, 65, 76, 90, 104, 118, 132, 145, 161, 175, 193, 209, 229, 245, 263, 274, 287, 301, 316, 329, 342, 358, 372, 390, 408, 428, 445, 463, 476, 491, 507, 523, 539, 553, 571, 586, 604, 622, 641, 658, 675, 687, 701, 715, 730, 744, 758, 774, 788, 806, 824, 844, 860, 878, 891, 908, 924, 941, 957, 973, 990, 1005, 1025, 1041, 1061, 1078, 1095, 1107, 1121, 1136, 1152, 1167, 1181, 1198, 1212, 1230, 1247, 1268, 1285, 1305, 1318, 1334, 1350, 1366, 1382, 1398, 1415, 1431, 1450, 1467, 1487, 1504, 1523, 1536, 1553, 1570, 1587, 1605, 1621, 1639, 1655, 1674
2.425(d)	11, 31, 47, 65, 76, 90, 104, 118, 132, 145, 161, 175, 193, 210, 229, 245, 263, 274, 288, 301, 316, 329, 342, 358, 372, 390, 408, 428, 445, 463, 476, 491, 507, 523, 539, 553, 571, 586, 604, 622, 641, 658, 675, 687, 701, 715, 730, 744, 758, 774, 788, 806, 824, 844, 860, 878, 892, 908, 924, 941, 957, 973, 990, 1006, 1025, 1042, 1061, 1078, 1095, 1107, 1121, 1136, 1152, 1167, 1181, 1198, 1212, 1230, 1247, 1268, 1285, 1305, 1318, 1334, 1350, 1366, 1382, 1398, 1416, 1431, 1450, 1467, 1487, 1505, 1523, 1537, 1553, 1570, 1588, 1605, 1621, 1640, 1655, 1675
2.425(e)	12, 31, 47, 65, 76, 90, 104, 118, 132, 145, 161, 175, 193, 210, 229, 245, 263, 274, 288, 302, 316, 329, 342, 358, 372, 390, 408, 428, 445, 463, 476, 491, 507, 523, 539, 553, 571, 586, 605, 622, 642, 658, 675, 687, 701, 715, 730, 745, 758, 774, 789, 806, 824, 844, 860, 878, 892, 908, 924, 941, 957, 973, 990, 1006, 1025, 1042, 1061, 1078, 1095, 1107, 1121, 1136, 1152, 1167, 1181, 1198, 1212, 1230, 1247, 1268, 1285, 1305, 1318, 1334, 1350, 1366, 1382, 1398, 1416, 1431, 1450, 1467, 1487, 1505, 1523, 1537, 1553, 1570, 1588, 1605, 1621, 1640, 1655, 1675
2.430	1, 21, 36, 69, 83, 96, 111, 124, 138, 151, 166, 180, 199, 219, 234, 267, 280, 294, 308, 322, 335, 348, 364, 378, 397, 417, 433, 468, 483, 498, 514, 530, 546, 561, 577, 591, 611, 631,

FLORIDA RULES OF JUDICIAL ADMINISTRATION—Continued

Rule **Pg.**

646, 680, 693, 707, 722, 736, 751, 764, 780, 794, 813, 833, 849, 883, 899, 915, 932, 947, 964, 979, 996, 1011, 1031, 1051, 1066, 1100, 1114, 1128, 1144, 1158, 1174, 1188, 1203, 1217, 1236, 1257, 1273, 1310, 1325, 1341, 1357, 1373, 1389, 1405, 1421, 1436, 1456, 1476, 1493, 1528, 1544, 1561, 1578, 1595, 1612, 1629, 1645, 1660

2.430(a)(1)..........12, 31, 48, 65, 77, 90, 104, 118, 132, 145, 161, 176, 193, 210, 229, 246, 263, 275, 288, 302, 316, 330, 343, 359, 373, 391, 408, 429, 445, 463, 476, 491, 507, 523, 539, 554, 572, 586, 605, 622, 642, 658, 675, 688, 701, 715, 730, 745, 758, 774, 789, 807, 824, 844, 861, 878, 892, 908, 925, 941, 957, 973, 991, 1006, 1025, 1042, 1062, 1078, 1095, 1107, 1122, 1137, 1152, 1167, 1181, 1198, 1212, 1230, 1247, 1268, 1285, 1305, 1318, 1334, 1350, 1366, 1383, 1398, 1416, 1431, 1450, 1467, 1488, 1505, 1523, 1537, 1553, 1570, 1588, 1605, 1621, 1640, 1655, 1675

2.510..........1, 10, 21, 29, 36, 45, 53, 63, 69, 74, 83, 88, 96, 102, 111, 116, 124, 130, 138, 143, 151, 159, 166, 173, 180, 191, 199, 208, 219, 227, 234, 243, 251, 261, 267, 272, 280, 286, 294, 300, 308, 314, 322, 327, 335, 340, 349, 356, 364, 370, 378, 388, 397, 406, 417, 426, 433, 443, 461, 468, 474, 483, 489, 498, 505, 514, 521, 530, 537, 546, 552, 561, 569, 577, 584, 591, 603, 611, 620, 631, 640, 646, 656, 664, 673, 680, 685, 693, 699, 707, 713, 722, 728, 736, 743, 751, 756, 764, 772, 780, 787, 794, 804, 813, 822, 833, 842, 849, 858, 866, 876, 883, 890, 899, 906, 915, 922, 932, 939, 947, 955, 964, 971, 979, 988, 996, 1004, 1011, 1023, 1031, 1040, 1051, 1059, 1066, 1076, 1083, 1093, 1100, 1105, 1114, 1119, 1128, 1134, 1144, 1150, 1158, 1165, 1174, 1179, 1188, 1196, 1203, 1210, 1217, 1228, 1236, 1245, 1257, 1266, 1273, 1283, 1293, 1303, 1310, 1316, 1325, 1332, 1341, 1348, 1357, 1364, 1373, 1380, 1389, 1396, 1405, 1413, 1421, 1429, 1436, 1448, 1456, 1465, 1476, 1485, 1493, 1503, 1511, 1521, 1528, 1535, 1544, 1551, 1561, 1568, 1578, 1586, 1595, 1603, 1612, 1619, 1629, 1638, 1645, 1653, 1661, 1673

2.514..........2, 21, 37, 54, 70, 83, 97, 111, 125, 139, 152, 167, 181, 200, 219, 235, 252, 268, 281, 294, 309, 322, 336, 349, 364, 378, 398, 418, 434, 452, 469, 484, 499, 515, 530, 547, 561, 577, 592, 612, 631, 647, 664, 681, 694, 708, 723, 737, 751, 765, 780, 795, 814, 834, 850, 867, 884, 900, 916, 933, 948, 965, 980, 996, 1012, 1032, 1051, 1067, 1084, 1100, 1115, 1129, 1144, 1159, 1174, 1188, 1204, 1218, 1237, 1258, 1274, 1294, 1311, 1327, 1342, 1359, 1374, 1391, 1406, 1422, 1438, 1457, 1477, 1494, 1511, 1529, 1545, 1562, 1579, 1596, 1613, 1629, 1646, 1661

2.514(a)..........2, 21, 22, 37, 38, 54, 70, 71, 83, 84, 97, 111, 112, 125, 139, 152, 167, 168, 181, 182, 200, 219, 220, 235, 236, 252, 268, 269, 281, 282, 294, 295, 309, 322, 323, 336, 337, 349, 350, 364, 365, 378, 379, 398, 418, 419, 434, 435, 452, 469, 470, 484, 485, 499, 500, 515, 516, 530, 531, 547, 561, 562, 577, 578, 592, 593, 612, 632, 647, 648, 664, 665, 681, 695, 708, 709, 723, 737, 752, 765, 780, 781, 795, 814, 834, 850, 867, 884, 885, 900, 901, 916, 917, 933, 948, 949, 965, 966, 980, 981, 996, 997, 1012, 1013, 1032, 1051, 1052, 1067, 1068, 1084, 1085, 1100, 1101, 1115, 1129, 1130, 1144, 1145, 1159, 1174, 1175, 1188, 1189, 1204, 1218, 1219, 1237, 1238, 1258, 1275, 1294, 1311, 1312, 1327, 1342, 1343, 1359, 1374, 1375, 1391, 1406, 1407, 1422, 1423, 1438, 1439, 1457, 1477, 1478, 1494, 1511, 1512, 1529, 1530, 1545, 1546, 1562, 1563, 1579, 1580, 1596, 1597, 1613, 1614, 1629, 1630, 1646, 1647, 1662

2.514(a)(1)..........2, 21, 37, 54, 70, 84, 97, 111, 125, 139, 152, 167, 181, 200, 219, 235, 252, 268, 281, 295, 309, 322, 336, 349, 364, 379, 398, 418, 434, 452, 469, 484, 499, 515, 530, 547, 561, 577, 592, 612, 632, 647, 664, 681, 695, 708, 723, 737, 752, 765, 780, 795, 814, 834, 850, 867, 884, 900, 916, 933, 949, 965, 980, 997, 1012, 1032, 1051, 1067, 1084, 1100, 1115, 1129, 1145, 1159, 1174, 1189, 1204, 1218, 1237, 1258, 1275, 1294, 1311, 1327, 1342, 1359, 1375, 1391, 1406, 1423, 1438, 1457, 1477, 1494, 1512,

FLORIDA RULES OF JUDICIAL ADMINISTRATION—Continued

Rule **Pg.**

1529, 1546, 1562, 1579, 1596, 1614, 1630, 1646, 1662

2.514(a)(2)..............2, 22, 37, 54, 70, 84, 97, 111, 125, 139, 152, 167, 181, 200, 220, 235, 252, 268, 281, 295, 309, 322, 336, 349, 364, 379, 398, 418, 435, 452, 469, 484, 499, 515, 531, 547, 562, 578, 592, 612, 632, 648, 665, 681, 695, 708, 723, 737, 752, 765, 780, 795, 814, 834, 850, 867, 884, 900, 916, 933, 949, 965, 980, 997, 1012, 1032, 1052, 1067, 1084, 1101, 1115, 1129, 1145, 1159, 1175, 1189, 1204, 1218, 1238, 1258, 1275, 1294, 1311, 1327, 1342, 1359, 1375, 1391, 1406, 1423, 1438, 1457, 1477, 1494, 1512, 1529, 1546, 1562, 1580, 1596, 1614, 1630, 1646, 1662

2.514(a)(3)..............2, 22, 37, 54, 70, 84, 97, 111, 125, 139, 152, 167, 182, 200, 220, 235, 252, 268, 282, 295, 309, 322, 336, 349, 365, 379, 398, 418, 435, 452, 469, 484, 499, 516, 531, 547, 562, 578, 592, 612, 632, 648, 665, 681, 695, 708, 723, 737, 752, 765, 781, 795, 814, 834, 850, 867, 884, 900, 916, 933, 949, 965, 980, 997, 1012, 1032, 1052, 1067, 1084, 1101, 1115, 1129, 1145, 1159, 1175, 1189, 1204, 1219, 1238, 1258, 1275, 1294, 1312, 1327, 1342, 1359, 1375, 1391, 1406, 1423, 1438, 1457, 1477, 1494, 1512, 1529, 1546, 1562, 1580, 1596, 1614, 1630, 1646, 1662

2.514(a)(4)..............2, 22, 37, 54, 70, 84, 97, 112, 125, 139, 152, 167, 182, 200, 220, 235, 252, 268, 282, 295, 309, 322, 336, 349, 365, 379, 398, 419, 435, 452, 469, 484, 499, 516, 531, 547, 562, 578, 593, 612, 632, 648, 665, 681, 695, 708, 723, 737, 752, 765, 781, 795, 814, 834, 850, 867, 884, 900, 916, 933, 949, 965, 980, 997, 1012, 1032, 1052, 1067, 1084, 1101, 1115, 1129, 1145, 1159, 1175, 1189, 1204, 1219, 1238, 1258, 1275, 1294, 1312, 1327, 1343, 1359, 1375, 1391, 1406, 1423, 1438, 1457, 1477, 1494, 1512, 1529, 1546, 1562, 1580, 1596, 1614, 1630, 1646, 1662

2.514(a)(5)..............2, 22, 37, 54, 71, 84, 97, 112, 125, 139, 152, 167, 182, 200, 220, 235, 252, 268, 282, 295, 309, 322, 337, 350, 365, 379, 398, 419, 435, 452, 469, 484, 500, 516, 531, 547, 562, 578, 593, 612, 632, 648, 665, 681, 695, 708, 723, 737, 752, 765, 781, 795, 814, 834, 850, 867, 884, 900, 916, 933, 949, 965, 980, 997, 1012, 1032, 1052, 1068, 1084, 1101, 1115, 1129, 1145, 1159, 1175, 1189, 1204, 1219, 1238, 1258, 1275, 1294, 1312, 1327, 1343, 1359, 1375, 1391, 1406, 1423, 1438, 1457, 1478, 1494, 1512, 1529, 1546, 1563, 1580, 1596, 1614, 1630, 1646, 1662

2.514(a)(6)..............2, 22, 37, 54, 71, 84, 97, 112, 125, 139, 152, 167, 182, 200, 220, 236, 252, 269, 282, 295, 309, 323, 337, 350, 365, 379, 398, 419, 435, 452, 469, 485, 500, 516, 531, 547, 562, 578, 593, 612, 632, 648, 665, 681, 695, 709, 723, 737, 752, 765, 781, 795, 814, 834, 850, 867, 884, 900, 917, 933, 949, 965, 981, 997, 1013, 1032, 1052, 1068, 1085, 1101, 1115, 1130, 1145, 1159, 1175, 1189, 1204, 1219, 1238, 1258, 1275, 1294, 1312, 1327, 1343, 1359, 1375, 1391, 1407, 1423, 1438, 1457, 1478, 1494, 1512, 1529, 1546, 1563, 1580, 1597, 1614, 1630, 1647, 1662

2.514(b).........2, 22, 38, 54, 71, 84, 97, 112, 125, 139, 152, 168, 182, 200, 220, 236, 252, 269, 282, 295, 309, 323, 337, 350, 365, 379, 398, 419, 435, 452, 470, 485, 500, 516, 531, 547, 562, 578, 593, 612, 632, 648, 665, 681, 695, 709, 723, 737, 752, 765, 781, 795, 814, 834, 850, 867, 885, 901, 917, 933, 949, 966, 981, 997, 1013, 1032, 1052, 1068, 1085, 1101, 1115, 1130, 1145, 1159, 1175, 1189, 1204, 1219, 1238, 1258, 1275, 1294, 1312, 1327, 1343, 1359, 1375, 1391, 1407, 1423, 1439, 1457, 1478, 1494, 1512, 1530, 1546, 1563, 1580, 1597, 1614, 1630, 1647, 1662

2.515...........1, 8, 10, 21, 28, 29, 36, 44, 46, 53, 61, 63, 69, 73, 75, 83, 86, 88, 96, 100, 102, 111, 114, 116, 124, 128, 130, 138, 141, 143, 151, 158, 159, 166, 172, 173, 180, 189, 191, 199, 208, 219, 227, 234, 244, 251, 261, 267, 272, 280, 286, 294, 300, 308, 314, 322, 327, 335, 341, 349, 356, 364, 371, 378, 388, 397, 406, 418, 426, 433, 443, 451, 461, 468, 474, 483, 489, 498, 505, 514, 521, 530, 537, 546, 552, 561, 569, 577, 584, 591, 603, 611, 620, 631, 640, 646, 656, 664, 673, 680, 686, 693, 699, 707, 713, 722, 728, 736, 743, 751, 756, 764, 772, 780, 787, 794, 805, 813, 822,

FLORIDA RULES OF JUDICIAL ADMINISTRATION—Continued

Rule	Pg.
	833, 842, 849, 859, 866, 876, 883, 890, 899, 906, 915, 923, 932, 939, 947, 955, 964, 971, 979, 988, 996, 1004, 1011, 1023, 1031, 1040, 1051, 1059, 1066, 1076, 1083, 1093, 1100, 1105, 1114, 1120, 1128, 1135, 1144, 1150, 1158, 1165, 1174, 1179, 1188, 1196, 1203, 1210, 1217, 1228, 1236, 1245, 1257, 1266, 1273, 1283, 1293, 1303, 1310, 1316, 1325, 1332, 1341, 1348, 1357, 1364, 1373, 1380, 1389, 1396, 1405, 1414, 1421, 1429, 1437, 1448, 1456, 1465, 1476, 1486, 1493, 1503, 1511, 1521, 1528, 1535, 1544, 1551, 1561, 1568, 1578, 1586, 1595, 1603, 1612, 1619, 1629, 1638, 1645, 1653, 1661, 1673
2.515(a)	9, 10, 29, 30, 45, 46, 63, 74, 75, 88, 102, 116, 130, 143, 159, 173, 174, 191, 207, 208, 227, 228, 243, 244, 261, 272, 273, 285, 286, 299, 300, 314, 327, 328, 340, 341, 356, 357, 370, 371, 388, 406, 426, 427, 443, 461, 474, 489, 505, 521, 537, 551, 552, 569, 584, 602, 603, 620, 639, 640, 656, 673, 674, 685, 686, 699, 700, 713, 714, 728, 742, 743, 756, 772, 786, 787, 804, 805, 821, 822, 841, 842, 858, 859, 876, 889, 890, 905, 906, 922, 923, 939, 955, 956, 970, 971, 988, 989, 1003, 1004, 1022, 1023, 1039, 1040, 1059, 1060, 1076, 1093, 1105, 1119, 1120, 1134, 1135, 1150, 1165, 1179, 1196, 1210, 1228, 1245, 1266, 1283, 1303, 1316, 1332, 1348, 1364, 1380, 1381, 1395, 1396, 1413, 1414, 1429, 1447, 1448, 1465, 1485, 1486, 1502, 1503, 1521, 1534, 1535, 1551, 1552, 1568, 1585, 1586, 1603, 1619, 1637, 1638, 1653, 1672, 1673
2.515(b)	10, 29, 30, 46, 63, 75, 88, 102, 116, 130, 143, 159, 173, 174, 191, 208, 227, 228, 244, 261, 273, 286, 300, 314, 328, 341, 357, 371, 388, 406, 427, 443, 461, 474, 489, 505, 521, 537, 552, 569, 584, 603, 620, 640, 656, 674, 686, 699, 700, 714, 728, 743, 756, 772, 787, 805, 822, 842, 859, 876, 890, 906, 923, 939, 955, 956, 971, 989, 1004, 1023, 1040, 1060, 1076, 1093, 1105, 1120, 1135, 1150, 1165, 1179, 1196, 1210, 1228, 1245, 1266, 1283, 1303, 1316, 1332, 1348, 1364, 1381, 1396, 1414, 1429, 1448, 1465, 1486, 1503, 1521, 1535, 1552, 1568, 1586, 1603, 1619, 1638, 1653, 1673
2.515(c)(1)	10, 30, 46, 63, 75, 88, 102, 117, 131, 144, 159, 174, 191, 208, 228, 244, 261, 273, 286, 300, 314, 328, 341, 357, 371, 388, 407, 427, 444, 462, 474, 489, 505, 521, 537, 552, 570, 584, 603, 620, 640, 656, 674, 686, 700, 714, 728, 743, 757, 773, 787, 805, 822, 842, 859, 876, 890, 906, 923, 939, 956, 971, 989, 1004, 1023, 1040, 1060, 1076, 1094, 1105, 1120, 1135, 1150, 1165, 1180, 1196, 1211, 1228, 1246, 1266, 1284, 1303, 1316, 1332, 1348, 1365, 1381, 1396, 1414, 1429, 1448, 1465, 1486, 1503, 1521, 1535, 1552, 1569, 1586, 1603, 1620, 1638, 1653, 1673
2.515(c)(2)	10, 30, 46, 63, 75, 89, 103, 117, 131, 144, 160, 174, 191, 208, 228, 244, 261, 273, 286, 300, 314, 328, 341, 357, 371, 389, 407, 427, 444, 462, 474, 490, 505, 521, 537, 552, 570, 584, 603, 620, 640, 657, 674, 686, 700, 714, 729, 743, 757, 773, 787, 805, 822, 842, 859, 877, 890, 906, 923, 940, 956, 971, 989, 1004, 1023, 1040, 1060, 1076, 1094, 1106, 1120, 1135, 1150, 1166, 1180, 1196, 1211, 1228, 1246, 1266, 1284, 1303, 1317, 1332, 1348, 1365, 1381, 1396, 1414, 1429, 1448, 1466, 1486, 1503, 1521, 1535, 1552, 1569, 1586, 1603, 1620, 1638, 1654, 1673
2.516	28, 33, 34, 35, 44, 49, 51, 61, 67, 68, 73, 78, 80, 87, 92, 93, 100, 106, 107, 115, 120, 121, 129, 134, 135, 142, 147, 148, 158, 163, 164, 165, 172, 177, 178, 179, 190, 195, 196, 226, 231, 232, 233, 242, 247, 248, 249, 259, 264, 265, 266, 271, 276, 277, 278, 284, 289, 290, 291, 298, 303, 304, 305, 312, 317, 318, 319, 326, 331, 333, 339, 344, 345, 346, 355, 360, 361, 362, 369, 374, 375, 376, 387, 392, 394, 425, 430, 431, 432, 442, 447, 448, 449, 460, 465, 466, 472, 477, 478, 479, 487, 493, 494, 503, 508, 509, 510, 519, 524, 525, 526, 535, 540, 541, 542, 550, 555, 556, 557, 568, 573, 574, 575, 583, 588, 589, 601, 607, 608, 638, 643, 644, 645, 654, 660, 661, 672, 677, 678, 679, 684, 689, 690, 691, 698, 703, 704, 705, 712, 717, 718, 719, 727, 732, 733, 741, 746, 747, 748, 755, 760, 761, 771, 776, 777, 778, 785,

FLORIDA RULES OF JUDICIAL ADMINISTRATION—Continued

Rule	Pg.
	790, 791, 792, 803, 809, 810, 840, 846, 847, 857, 862, 863, 864, 874, 880, 881, 882, 887, 894, 895, 903, 910, 911, 920, 926, 927, 928, 937, 943, 944, 945, 953, 959, 961, 968, 975, 976, 986, 992, 993, 994, 1002, 1008, 1009, 1021, 1027, 1028, 1029, 1058, 1063, 1064, 1065, 1074, 1079, 1080, 1081, 1092, 1097, 1098, 1103, 1109, 1110, 1111, 1118, 1123, 1124, 1125, 1133, 1138, 1139, 1140, 1148, 1153, 1154, 1155, 1163, 1169, 1170, 1171, 1178, 1183, 1185, 1195, 1200, 1201, 1209, 1214, 1215, 1216, 1227, 1232, 1233, 1264, 1270, 1271, 1272, 1282, 1287, 1288, 1289, 1301, 1307, 1308, 1309, 1314, 1320, 1321, 1322, 1330, 1336, 1337, 1338, 1346, 1352, 1353, 1354, 1362, 1368, 1369, 1370, 1379, 1385, 1386, 1394, 1400, 1401, 1402, 1412, 1418, 1419, 1420, 1428, 1433, 1434, 1435, 1446, 1452, 1454, 1484, 1489, 1490, 1491, 1501, 1506, 1507, 1508, 1519, 1525, 1526, 1527, 1533, 1538, 1539, 1540, 1549, 1555, 1556, 1557, 1566, 1572, 1573, 1574, 1584, 1589, 1590, 1591, 1601, 1607, 1608, 1609, 1617, 1623, 1624, 1625, 1636, 1642, 1643, 1644, 1652, 1657, 1658, 1659, 1671, 1677, 1678, 1679
2.516(a)	33, 49, 67, 78, 92, 106, 120, 134, 147, 163, 177, 195, 231, 247, 265, 276, 290, 303, 318, 331, 344, 360, 375, 392, 430, 447, 465, 478, 493, 509, 525, 541, 555, 573, 588, 607, 643, 660, 677, 689, 703, 717, 732, 746, 760, 776, 791, 809, 846, 862, 880, 894, 910, 926, 943, 959, 975, 993, 1008, 1027, 1063, 1080, 1097, 1109, 1123, 1138, 1154, 1169, 1183, 1200, 1214, 1232, 1270, 1287, 1307, 1320, 1336, 1352, 1368, 1385, 1400, 1418, 1433, 1452, 1490, 1507, 1525, 1539, 1556, 1572, 1590, 1607, 1623, 1642, 1657, 1677
2.516(b)	12, 32, 33, 35, 48, 49, 51, 66, 67, 68, 77, 78, 80, 91, 92, 93, 105, 106, 107, 119, 120, 122, 133, 134, 136, 146, 147, 149, 162, 163, 165, 176, 177, 179, 194, 195, 197, 210, 230, 231, 233, 246, 247, 249, 264, 265, 266, 275, 276, 278, 289, 290, 291, 302, 304, 305, 317, 318, 319, 330, 331, 333, 343, 344, 346, 359, 360, 362, 373, 375, 376, 391, 392, 394, 409, 429, 430, 432, 446, 447, 449, 464, 465, 467, 477, 478, 479, 492, 493, 495, 508, 509, 510, 524, 525, 526, 540, 541, 542, 554, 555, 557, 572, 573, 575, 587, 588, 589, 606, 607, 608, 623, 642, 644, 645, 659, 660, 661, 676, 677, 679, 688, 689, 691, 702, 703, 705, 716, 717, 719, 731, 732, 734, 745, 747, 748, 759, 760, 762, 775, 776, 778, 790, 791, 792, 808, 809, 810, 824, 845, 846, 847, 861, 863, 864, 879, 880, 882, 892, 894, 895, 909, 910, 912, 925, 927, 928, 942, 943, 945, 958, 959, 961, 974, 975, 976, 991, 993, 994, 1007, 1008, 1009, 1026, 1027, 1029, 1042, 1062, 1063, 1065, 1079, 1080, 1081, 1096, 1097, 1099, 1108, 1109, 1111, 1122, 1123, 1125, 1137, 1138, 1140, 1153, 1154, 1156, 1168, 1169, 1171, 1182, 1183, 1185, 1199, 1200, 1202, 1213, 1214, 1216, 1231, 1232, 1234, 1248, 1269, 1270, 1272, 1286, 1288, 1289, 1306, 1307, 1309, 1319, 1320, 1322, 1335, 1336, 1338, 1351, 1352, 1354, 1367, 1369, 1370, 1383, 1385, 1386, 1399, 1400, 1402, 1417, 1418, 1420, 1432, 1433, 1435, 1451, 1452, 1454, 1468, 1488, 1490, 1491, 1505, 1507, 1509, 1524, 1525, 1527, 1537, 1539, 1541, 1554, 1556, 1557, 1571, 1573, 1574, 1588, 1590, 1592, 1606, 1607, 1609, 1622, 1624, 1625, 1641, 1642, 1644, 1656, 1657, 1659, 1676, 1677, 1679
2.516(b)(1)	33, 34, 50, 67, 79, 92, 106, 120, 121, 134, 147, 163, 164, 177, 178, 195, 231, 232, 248, 265, 276, 277, 290, 304, 318, 331, 332, 345, 361, 375, 393, 430, 431, 447, 448, 465, 478, 493, 509, 525, 541, 556, 573, 574, 588, 607, 644, 660, 677, 678, 689, 690, 703, 704, 717, 718, 732, 747, 760, 776, 777, 791, 809, 846, 863, 880, 881, 894, 910, 927, 943, 944, 960, 975, 993, 1008, 1027, 1028, 1063, 1064, 1080, 1097, 1109, 1124, 1139, 1154, 1169, 1183, 1184, 1200, 1214, 1215, 1232, 1270, 1271, 1288, 1307, 1308, 1321, 1336, 1337, 1352, 1353, 1369, 1385, 1400, 1401, 1418, 1419, 1434, 1452, 1453, 1490, 1507, 1525, 1526, 1539, 1556, 1573, 1590, 1607, 1608, 1624, 1642, 1643, 1658, 1677, 1678
2.516(b)(1)(A)	33, 50, 67, 79, 92, 106, 120, 134,

FLORIDA RULES OF JUDICIAL ADMINISTRATION—Continued

Rule **Pg.**

147, 163, 178, 195, 232, 248, 265, 277, 290, 304, 318, 332, 345, 361, 375, 393, 431, 447, 465, 478, 493, 509, 525, 541, 556, 574, 588, 607, 644, 660, 678, 690, 703, 718, 732, 747, 760, 777, 791, 809, 846, 863, 880, 894, 910, 927, 943, 960, 975, 993, 1008, 1027, 1064, 1080, 1097, 1109, 1124, 1139, 1154, 1169, 1183, 1200, 1214, 1232, 1270, 1288, 1307, 1321, 1336, 1352, 1369, 1385, 1400, 1418, 1434, 1453, 1490, 1507, 1525, 1539, 1556, 1573, 1590, 1607, 1624, 1642, 1658, 1678

2.516(b)(1)(B)..........34, 50, 67, 79, 92, 106, 120, 134, 147, 164, 178, 195, 232, 248, 265, 277, 290, 304, 318, 332, 345, 361, 375, 393, 431, 448, 465, 478, 493, 509, 525, 541, 556, 574, 588, 607, 644, 660, 678, 690, 704, 718, 732, 747, 760, 777, 791, 809, 846, 863, 881, 894, 910, 927, 944, 960, 975, 993, 1008, 1028, 1064, 1080, 1097, 1109, 1124, 1139, 1154, 1169, 1183, 1200, 1215, 1232, 1271, 1288, 1308, 1321, 1337, 1353, 1369, 1385, 1401, 1419, 1434, 1453, 1490, 1507, 1526, 1539, 1556, 1573, 1590, 1608, 1624, 1643, 1658, 1678

2.516(b)(1)(C)..........34, 50, 67, 79, 92, 106, 121, 134, 147, 164, 178, 195, 232, 248, 265, 277, 290, 304, 318, 332, 345, 361, 375, 393, 431, 448, 465, 478, 493, 509, 525, 541, 556, 574, 588, 607, 644, 660, 678, 690, 704, 718, 732, 747, 760, 777, 791, 809, 846, 863, 881, 894, 910, 927, 944, 960, 975, 993, 1008, 1028, 1064, 1080, 1097, 1109, 1124, 1139, 1154, 1169, 1184, 1200, 1215, 1232, 1271, 1288, 1308, 1321, 1337, 1353, 1369, 1385, 1401, 1419, 1434, 1453, 1490, 1508, 1526, 1540, 1556, 1573, 1591, 1608, 1624, 1643, 1658, 1678

2.516(b)(1)(D)..........34, 50, 67, 79, 92, 106, 121, 135, 148, 164, 178, 196, 232, 248, 265, 277, 290, 304, 318, 332, 345, 361, 375, 393, 431, 448, 466, 478, 494, 509, 525, 541, 556, 574, 588, 607, 644, 660, 678, 690, 704, 718, 733, 747, 761, 777, 791, 809, 846, 863, 881, 894, 911, 927, 944, 960, 975, 993, 1008, 1028, 1064, 1080, 1098, 1110, 1124, 1139, 1154, 1170, 1184, 1201, 1215, 1233, 1271, 1288, 1308, 1321, 1337, 1353, 1369, 1385, 1401, 1419, 1434, 1453, 1490, 1508, 1526, 1540, 1556, 1573, 1591, 1608, 1624, 1643, 1658, 1678

2.516(b)(1)(D)(i).........34, 50, 67, 79, 92, 106, 121, 135, 148, 164, 178, 196, 232, 248, 265, 277, 290, 304, 318, 332, 345, 361, 375, 393, 431, 448, 466, 478, 494, 509, 525, 541, 556, 574, 588, 607, 644, 660, 678, 690, 704, 718, 733, 747, 761, 777, 791, 809, 846, 863, 881, 894, 911, 927, 944, 960, 975, 993, 1008, 1028, 1064, 1080, 1098, 1110, 1124, 1139, 1154, 1170, 1184, 1201, 1215, 1233, 1271, 1288, 1308, 1321, 1337, 1353, 1369, 1385, 1401, 1419, 1434, 1453, 1490, 1508, 1526, 1540, 1556, 1573, 1591, 1608, 1624, 1643, 1658, 1678

2.516(b)(1)(D)(ii)..........34, 50, 67, 79, 93, 107, 121, 135, 148, 164, 178, 196, 232, 248, 265, 277, 290, 304, 318, 332, 345, 361, 375, 393, 431, 448, 466, 478, 494, 509, 525, 541, 556, 574, 589, 607, 644, 661, 678, 690, 704, 718, 733, 747, 761, 777, 791, 809, 847, 863, 881, 894, 911, 927, 944, 960, 976, 993, 1009, 1028, 1064, 1080, 1098, 1110, 1124, 1139, 1154, 1170, 1184, 1201, 1215, 1233, 1271, 1288, 1308, 1321, 1337, 1353, 1369, 1385, 1401, 1419, 1434, 1453, 1490, 1508, 1526, 1540, 1556, 1573, 1591, 1608, 1624, 1643, 1658, 1678

2.516(b)(1)(D)(iii).........34, 50, 67, 79, 93, 107, 121, 135, 148, 164, 178, 196, 232, 248, 265, 277, 290, 304, 318, 332, 345, 361, 375, 393, 431, 448, 466, 478, 494, 509, 525, 541, 556, 574, 589, 607, 644, 661, 678, 690, 704, 718, 733, 747, 761, 777, 791, 809, 847, 863, 881, 894, 911, 927, 944, 960, 976, 993, 1009, 1028, 1064, 1080, 1098, 1110, 1124, 1139, 1154, 1170, 1184, 1201, 1215, 1233, 1271, 1288, 1308, 1321, 1337, 1353, 1369, 1385, 1401, 1419, 1434, 1453, 1491, 1508, 1526, 1540, 1556, 1573, 1591, 1608, 1624, 1643, 1658, 1678

2.516(b)(1)(E)...........34, 50, 67, 79, 93, 107, 121, 135, 148, 164, 178, 196, 232, 248, 265, 277, 290, 304, 318, 332, 345, 361, 375, 393, 431, 448, 466, 478, 494, 509, 525, 541, 556, 574, 589, 608, 644, 661, 678, 690, 704, 718, 733, 747, 761, 777, 791, 810, 847, 863, 881, 895, 911, 927, 944, 960, 976, 993, 1009, 1028, 1064, 1080, 1098,

FLORIDA RULES OF JUDICIAL ADMINISTRATION—Continued

Rule Pg.

1110, 1124, 1139, 1155, 1170, 1184, 1201, 1215, 1233, 1271, 1288, 1308, 1321, 1337, 1353, 1369, 1385, 1401, 1419, 1434, 1453, 1491, 1508, 1526, 1540, 1556, 1573, 1591, 1608, 1624, 1643, 1658, 1678

2.516(b)(1)(E)(i)..............34, 50, 68, 79, 93, 107, 121, 135, 148, 164, 178, 196, 232, 248, 265, 277, 290, 304, 318, 332, 345, 361, 375, 393, 431, 448, 466, 478, 494, 509, 525, 541, 556, 574, 589, 608, 644, 661, 678, 690, 704, 718, 733, 747, 761, 777, 791, 810, 847, 863, 881, 895, 911, 927, 944, 960, 976, 993, 1009, 1028, 1064, 1080, 1098, 1110, 1125, 1140, 1155, 1170, 1184, 1201, 1215, 1233, 1271, 1288, 1308, 1321, 1337, 1353, 1369, 1386, 1401, 1419, 1434, 1453, 1491, 1508, 1526, 1540, 1556, 1573, 1591, 1608, 1624, 1643, 1658, 1678

2.516(b)(1)(E)(ii)..............34, 50, 68, 79, 93, 107, 121, 135, 148, 164, 178, 196, 232, 248, 266, 277, 290, 304, 319, 332, 345, 361, 375, 393, 431, 448, 466, 479, 494, 509, 525, 541, 556, 574, 589, 608, 644, 661, 678, 690, 704, 718, 733, 747, 761, 777, 791, 810, 847, 863, 881, 895, 911, 927, 944, 960, 976, 993, 1009, 1028, 1064, 1080, 1098, 1110, 1125, 1140, 1155, 1170, 1184, 1201, 1215, 1233, 1271, 1288, 1308, 1321, 1337, 1353, 1369, 1386, 1401, 1419, 1434, 1453, 1491, 1508, 1526, 1540, 1557, 1573, 1591, 1608, 1624, 1643, 1658, 1678

2.516(b)(1)(E)(iii).............34, 50, 68, 79, 93, 107, 121, 135, 148, 164, 178, 196, 232, 248, 266, 277, 291, 304, 319, 332, 345, 361, 376, 393, 431, 448, 466, 479, 494, 510, 526, 542, 556, 574, 589, 608, 644, 661, 678, 690, 704, 718, 733, 747, 761, 777, 792, 810, 847, 863, 881, 895, 911, 928, 944, 960, 976, 994, 1009, 1028, 1064, 1081, 1098, 1110, 1125, 1140, 1155, 1170, 1184, 1201, 1215, 1233, 1271, 1288, 1308, 1321, 1337, 1353, 1369, 1386, 1401, 1419, 1434, 1453, 1491, 1508, 1526, 1540, 1557, 1573, 1591, 1608, 1624, 1643, 1658, 1678

2.516(b)(1)(E)(iv)............34, 50, 68, 79, 93, 107, 121, 135, 148, 164, 178, 196, 232, 248, 266, 277, 291, 305, 319, 332, 345, 361, 376, 393, 431, 448, 466, 479, 494, 510, 526, 542, 556, 574, 589, 608, 645, 661, 678, 690, 704, 718, 733, 748, 761, 777, 792, 810, 847, 864, 881, 895, 911, 928, 944, 960, 976, 994, 1009, 1028, 1064, 1081, 1098, 1110, 1125, 1140, 1155, 1170, 1184, 1201, 1215, 1233, 1271, 1289, 1308, 1321, 1337, 1353, 1370, 1386, 1401, 1419, 1434, 1453, 1491, 1508, 1526, 1540, 1557, 1574, 1591, 1608, 1625, 1643, 1658, 1678

2.516(b)(2)..........33, 34, 50, 51, 67, 68, 79, 80, 92, 93, 106, 107, 120, 121, 134, 135, 147, 148, 163, 164, 177, 178, 195, 196, 231, 232, 248, 249, 265, 266, 276, 277, 290, 291, 304, 305, 318, 319, 331, 332, 345, 346, 361, 362, 375, 376, 393, 394, 430, 431, 447, 448, 465, 466, 478, 479, 493, 494, 509, 510, 525, 526, 541, 542, 556, 557, 573, 574, 588, 589, 607, 608, 644, 645, 660, 661, 677, 678, 689, 690, 703, 704, 717, 718, 732, 733, 747, 748, 760, 761, 776, 777, 791, 792, 809, 810, 846, 847, 863, 864, 880, 881, 894, 895, 910, 911, 927, 928, 943, 944, 960, 961, 975, 976, 993, 994, 1008, 1009, 1027, 1028, 1063, 1064, 1080, 1081, 1097, 1098, 1109, 1110, 1124, 1125, 1139, 1140, 1154, 1155, 1169, 1170, 1183, 1184, 1200, 1201, 1214, 1215, 1232, 1233, 1270, 1271, 1288, 1289, 1307, 1308, 1321, 1322, 1336, 1337, 1352, 1353, 1369, 1370, 1385, 1386, 1400, 1401, 1418, 1419, 1434, 1435, 1452, 1453, 1490, 1491, 1507, 1508, 1525, 1526, 1539, 1540, 1556, 1557, 1573, 1574, 1590, 1591, 1607, 1608, 1624, 1625, 1642, 1643, 1658, 1659, 1677, 1678

2.516(b)(2)(A)..........35, 51, 68, 80, 93, 107, 121, 135, 148, 165, 179, 196, 233, 249, 266, 278, 291, 305, 319, 333, 346, 362, 376, 394, 432, 449, 466, 479, 494, 510, 526, 542, 557, 575, 589, 608, 645, 661, 679, 691, 705, 719, 733, 748, 761, 778, 792, 810, 847, 864, 882, 895, 911, 928, 945, 961, 976, 994, 1009, 1029, 1065, 1081, 1098, 1111, 1125, 1140, 1155, 1171, 1185, 1201, 1216, 1233, 1272, 1289, 1309, 1322, 1338, 1354, 1370, 1386, 1402, 1420, 1435, 1454, 1491, 1508, 1527, 1540, 1557, 1574, 1591, 1609, 1625, 1644, 1659, 1679

2.516(b)(2)(E)...........35, 51, 68, 80, 93, 107, 121, 135, 148, 165, 179, 196, 233, 249, 266, 278, 291, 305, 319, 333, 346, 362, 376, 394, 432, 449, 466, 479, 494,

FLORIDA RULES OF JUDICIAL ADMINISTRATION—Continued

Rule	Pg.
	510, 526, 542, 557, 575, 589, 608, 645, 661, 679, 691, 705, 719, 733, 748, 761, 778, 792, 810, 847, 864, 882, 895, 911, 928, 945, 961, 976, 994, 1009, 1029, 1065, 1081, 1098, 1111, 1125, 1140, 1155, 1171, 1185, 1201, 1216, 1233, 1272, 1289, 1309, 1322, 1338, 1354, 1370, 1386, 1402, 1420, 1435, 1454, 1491, 1508, 1527, 1540, 1557, 1574, 1591, 1609, 1625, 1644, 1659, 1679
2.516(b)(2)(F)	35, 51, 68, 80, 93, 107, 122, 135, 148, 165, 179, 196, 233, 249, 266, 278, 291, 305, 319, 333, 346, 362, 376, 394, 432, 449, 466, 479, 494, 510, 526, 542, 557, 575, 589, 608, 645, 661, 679, 691, 705, 719, 733, 748, 761, 778, 792, 810, 847, 864, 882, 895, 911, 928, 945, 961, 976, 994, 1009, 1029, 1065, 1081, 1098, 1111, 1125, 1140, 1155, 1171, 1185, 1201, 1216, 1233, 1272, 1289, 1309, 1322, 1338, 1354, 1370, 1386, 1402, 1420, 1435, 1454, 1491, 1508, 1527, 1540, 1557, 1574, 1591, 1609, 1625, 1644, 1659, 1679
2.516(c)	35, 51, 68, 80, 93, 107, 122, 135, 148, 165, 179, 196, 233, 249, 266, 278, 291, 305, 319, 333, 346, 362, 376, 394, 432, 449, 466, 479, 494, 510, 526, 542, 557, 575, 589, 608, 645, 661, 679, 691, 705, 719, 733, 748, 761, 778, 792, 810, 847, 864, 882, 895, 911, 928, 945, 961, 976, 994, 1009, 1029, 1065, 1081, 1098, 1111, 1125, 1140, 1156, 1171, 1185, 1201, 1216, 1233, 1272, 1289, 1309, 1322, 1338, 1354, 1370, 1386, 1402, 1420, 1435, 1454, 1491, 1509, 1527, 1541, 1557, 1574, 1592, 1609, 1625, 1644, 1659, 1679
2.516(d)	31, 48, 65, 77, 90, 104, 118, 132, 145, 161, 175, 193, 229, 246, 263, 274, 288, 302, 316, 329, 343, 359, 373, 391, 428, 445, 463, 476, 491, 507, 523, 539, 554, 571, 586, 605, 642, 658, 675, 687, 701, 715, 730, 745, 758, 774, 789, 807, 844, 860, 878, 892, 908, 924, 941, 957, 973, 991, 1006, 1025, 1061, 1078, 1095, 1107, 1122, 1137, 1152, 1167, 1181, 1198, 1212, 1230, 1268, 1285, 1305, 1318, 1334, 1350, 1366, 1382, 1398, 1416, 1431, 1450, 1488, 1505, 1523, 1537, 1553, 1570, 1588, 1605, 1621, 1640, 1655, 1675
2.516(e)	32, 48, 65, 77, 90, 104, 119, 133, 146, 162, 176, 194, 230, 246, 263, 275, 288, 302, 316, 330, 343, 359, 373, 391, 429, 446, 464, 476, 492, 507, 523, 539, 554, 572, 586, 605, 642, 658, 676, 688, 702, 716, 731, 745, 759, 775, 789, 807, 844, 861, 879, 892, 908, 925, 942, 958, 973, 991, 1006, 1026, 1062, 1078, 1096, 1108, 1122, 1137, 1152, 1168, 1182, 1199, 1213, 1231, 1268, 1286, 1305, 1319, 1334, 1350, 1367, 1383, 1398, 1416, 1432, 1451, 1488, 1505, 1523, 1537, 1554, 1571, 1588, 1605, 1622, 1640, 1656, 1675
2.516(f)	28, 44, 61, 73, 87, 100, 115, 129, 142, 158, 172, 190, 226, 242, 259, 271, 284, 298, 312, 326, 339, 355, 369, 387, 425, 442, 460, 472, 487, 503, 519, 535, 550, 568, 583, 601, 638, 654, 672, 684, 698, 712, 727, 741, 755, 771, 785, 803, 840, 857, 874, 887, 903, 920, 937, 953, 968, 986, 1002, 1021, 1058, 1074, 1092, 1103, 1118, 1133, 1148, 1163, 1178, 1195, 1209, 1227, 1264, 1282, 1301, 1314, 1330, 1346, 1362, 1379, 1394, 1412, 1428, 1446, 1484, 1501, 1519, 1533, 1549, 1566, 1584, 1601, 1617, 1636, 1652, 1671
2.516(g)	35, 51, 68, 80, 93, 107, 122, 136, 149, 165, 179, 197, 233, 249, 266, 278, 291, 305, 319, 333, 346, 362, 376, 394, 432, 449, 467, 479, 495, 510, 526, 542, 557, 575, 589, 608, 645, 661, 679, 691, 705, 719, 734, 748, 762, 778, 792, 810, 847, 864, 882, 895, 912, 928, 945, 961, 976, 994, 1009, 1029, 1065, 1081, 1099, 1111, 1125, 1140, 1156, 1171, 1185, 1202, 1216, 1234, 1272, 1289, 1309, 1322, 1338, 1354, 1370, 1386, 1402, 1420, 1435, 1454, 1491, 1509, 1527, 1541, 1557, 1574, 1592, 1609, 1625, 1644, 1659, 1679
2.516(h)(1)	73, 87, 101, 115, 129, 142, 271, 284, 298, 312, 326, 339, 472, 488, 503, 519, 535, 550, 684, 698, 712, 727, 741, 755, 887, 904, 920, 937, 953, 968, 1104, 1118, 1133, 1148, 1164, 1178, 1314, 1330, 1346, 1362, 1379, 1394, 1533, 1550, 1566, 1584, 1601, 1617
2.520	1, 9, 21, 28, 29, 36, 44, 45, 53, 62, 70, 73, 74, 83, 87, 96, 101, 111, 115, 124, 129, 138, 142, 151, 158, 167, 172, 173, 180, 190, 199, 207, 219, 226,

FLORIDA RULES OF JUDICIAL ADMINISTRATION—Continued

Rule **Pg.**

227, 234, 242, 243, 251, 260, 267, 271, 272, 280, 285, 294, 299, 308, 313, 322, 326, 327, 335, 339, 340, 349, 355, 356, 364, 369, 370, 378, 387, 397, 405, 418, 425, 426, 433, 442, 443, 451, 460, 468, 473, 483, 488, 498, 504, 514, 520, 530, 536, 546, 551, 561, 568, 569, 577, 583, 591, 602, 611, 619, 631, 638, 639, 646, 655, 664, 672, 673, 680, 684, 685, 693, 698, 707, 712, 713, 722, 727, 736, 741, 742, 751, 755, 764, 771, 780, 785, 786, 794, 803, 804, 813, 821, 833, 841, 849, 857, 858, 866, 875, 883, 888, 899, 904, 915, 921, 932, 937, 938, 947, 953, 954, 964, 969, 979, 987, 996, 1002, 1011, 1021, 1031, 1039, 1051, 1058, 1059, 1066, 1075, 1083, 1092, 1100, 1104, 1114, 1118, 1119, 1128, 1133, 1134, 1144, 1149, 1158, 1164, 1174, 1178, 1188, 1195, 1203, 1209, 1217, 1227, 1236, 1244, 1257, 1265, 1273, 1282, 1293, 1302, 1310, 1315, 1325, 1331, 1341, 1347, 1357, 1363, 1373, 1379, 1380, 1389, 1395, 1405, 1412, 1413, 1421, 1428, 1437, 1447, 1456, 1464, 1476, 1484, 1485, 1493, 1502, 1511, 1520, 1528, 1533, 1534, 1544, 1550, 1551, 1561, 1567, 1568, 1578, 1585, 1595, 1602, 1612, 1618, 1619, 1629, 1637, 1645, 1652, 1661, 1672

2.520(a)..........12, 31, 48, 65, 77, 90, 104, 118, 132, 145, 161, 175, 193, 210, 229, 246, 263, 274, 288, 302, 316, 330, 343, 359, 373, 391, 408, 428, 445, 463, 476, 491, 507, 523, 539, 554, 571, 586, 605, 622, 642, 658, 675, 687, 701, 715, 730, 745, 758, 774, 789, 807, 824, 844, 860, 878, 892, 908, 925, 941, 957, 973, 991, 1006, 1025, 1042, 1061, 1078, 1095, 1107, 1122, 1137, 1152, 1167, 1181, 1198, 1212, 1230, 1247, 1268, 1285, 1305, 1318, 1334, 1350, 1366, 1383, 1398, 1416, 1431, 1450, 1467, 1488, 1505, 1523, 1537, 1553, 1570, 1588, 1605, 1621, 1640, 1655, 1675

2.520(b)..........9, 28, 45, 62, 74, 87, 101, 115, 129, 142, 158, 172, 190, 207, 226, 243, 260, 271, 285, 299, 313, 326, 340, 355, 370, 387, 405, 425, 442, 460, 473, 488, 504, 520, 536, 551, 568, 583, 602, 619, 639, 655, 672, 684, 698, 712, 727, 742, 755, 771, 786, 803, 821, 841, 857, 875, 888, 904, 921, 937, 954, 969, 987, 1002, 1021, 1039, 1058, 1075, 1092, 1104, 1118, 1133, 1149, 1164, 1178, 1195, 1209, 1227, 1244, 1265, 1282, 1302, 1315, 1331, 1347, 1363, 1379, 1395, 1413, 1428, 1447, 1464, 1484, 1502, 1520, 1534, 1550, 1567, 1585, 1602, 1618, 1637, 1652, 1672

2.520(c)..........9, 28, 45, 62, 74, 87, 101, 115, 129, 142, 158, 172, 190, 207, 226, 243, 260, 271, 285, 299, 313, 326, 340, 355, 370, 387, 405, 425, 442, 460, 473, 488, 504, 520, 536, 551, 568, 583, 602, 619, 639, 655, 672, 684, 698, 712, 727, 742, 755, 771, 786, 803, 821, 841, 857, 875, 888, 904, 921, 937, 954, 969, 987, 1002, 1021, 1039, 1058, 1075, 1092, 1104, 1118, 1133, 1149, 1164, 1178, 1195, 1209, 1227, 1244, 1265, 1282, 1302, 1315, 1331, 1347, 1363, 1379, 1395, 1413, 1428, 1447, 1464, 1484, 1502, 1520, 1534, 1550, 1567, 1585, 1602, 1618, 1637, 1652, 1672

2.520(d)..........9, 28, 45, 62, 74, 87, 101, 115, 129, 142, 158, 172, 190, 207, 226, 243, 260, 272, 285, 299, 313, 327, 340, 356, 370, 387, 405, 426, 442, 460, 473, 488, 504, 520, 536, 551, 568, 583, 602, 619, 639, 655, 672, 685, 698, 712, 727, 742, 755, 771, 786, 804, 821, 841, 857, 875, 888, 904, 921, 937, 954, 969, 987, 1002, 1021, 1039, 1059, 1075, 1092, 1104, 1119, 1134, 1149, 1164, 1178, 1195, 1209, 1227, 1244, 1265, 1282, 1302, 1315, 1331, 1347, 1363, 1380, 1395, 1413, 1428, 1447, 1464, 1485, 1502, 1520, 1534, 1550, 1567, 1585, 1602, 1618, 1637, 1652, 1672

2.520(e)..........9, 29, 45, 62, 74, 87, 101, 115, 129, 142, 158, 173, 190, 207, 227, 243, 260, 272, 285, 299, 313, 327, 340, 356, 370, 387, 405, 426, 443, 460, 473, 488, 504, 520, 536, 551, 569, 583, 602, 619, 639, 655, 673, 685, 698, 713, 727, 742, 755, 771, 786, 804, 821, 841, 858, 875, 888, 904, 921, 938, 954, 969, 987, 1002, 1021, 1039, 1059, 1075, 1092, 1104, 1119, 1134, 1149, 1164, 1178, 1195, 1209, 1227, 1244, 1265, 1282, 1302, 1315, 1331, 1347, 1363, 1380, 1395, 1413, 1428, 1447, 1464, 1485, 1502, 1520, 1534, 1551, 1567, 1585, 1602, 1618,

FLORIDA RULES OF JUDICIAL ADMINISTRATION—Continued

Rule	Pg.
	1637, 1652, 1672
2.520(f)	9, 29, 45, 62, 74, 87, 101, 116, 130, 142, 158, 173, 190, 207, 227, 243, 260, 272, 285, 299, 313, 327, 340, 356, 370, 387, 406, 426, 443, 461, 473, 488, 504, 520, 536, 551, 569, 583, 602, 619, 639, 655, 673, 685, 699, 713, 727, 742, 755, 771, 786, 804, 821, 841, 858, 875, 888, 904, 921, 938, 954, 969, 987, 1002, 1021, 1039, 1059, 1075, 1092, 1104, 1119, 1134, 1149, 1164, 1178, 1195, 1210, 1227, 1245, 1265, 1283, 1302, 1315, 1331, 1347, 1364, 1380, 1395, 1413, 1428, 1447, 1464, 1485, 1502, 1520, 1534, 1551, 1568, 1585, 1602, 1619, 1637, 1652, 1672
2.525	1, 12, 13, 21, 31, 32, 33, 36, 48, 49, 53, 65, 66, 70, 77, 78, 83, 90, 91, 92, 96, 104, 105, 106, 111, 118, 119, 120, 124, 132, 133, 134, 138, 145, 146, 147, 151, 161, 162, 163, 167, 175, 176, 177, 180, 193, 194, 195, 199, 210, 211, 219, 229, 230, 231, 234, 246, 247, 251, 263, 264, 267, 274, 275, 276, 280, 288, 289, 294, 302, 303, 308, 316, 317, 322, 329, 330, 331, 336, 343, 344, 349, 359, 360, 364, 373, 374, 378, 391, 392, 397, 408, 409, 410, 418, 428, 429, 430, 433, 445, 446, 447, 451, 463, 464, 465, 468, 476, 477, 483, 491, 492, 493, 498, 507, 508, 514, 523, 524, 530, 539, 540, 546, 554, 555, 561, 571, 572, 573, 577, 586, 587, 588, 591, 605, 606, 607, 611, 622, 623, 631, 642, 643, 646, 658, 659, 660, 664, 675, 676, 677, 680, 687, 688, 689, 694, 701, 702, 703, 707, 715, 716, 717, 722, 730, 731, 732, 736, 745, 746, 751, 758, 759, 760, 764, 774, 775, 776, 780, 789, 790, 794, 807, 808, 809, 813, 824, 825, 833, 844, 845, 846, 849, 860, 861, 862, 866, 878, 879, 880, 883, 892, 893, 899, 908, 909, 910, 915, 924, 925, 926, 932, 941, 942, 943, 948, 957, 958, 959, 964, 973, 974, 979, 991, 992, 996, 1006, 1007, 1008, 1011, 1025, 1026, 1027, 1031, 1042, 1043, 1051, 1061, 1062, 1063, 1066, 1078, 1079, 1083, 1095, 1096, 1097, 1100, 1107, 1108, 1109, 1114, 1122, 1123, 1128, 1137, 1138, 1144, 1152, 1153, 1158, 1167, 1168, 1169, 1174, 1181, 1182, 1183, 1188, 1198, 1199, 1200, 1203, 1212, 1213, 1214, 1217, 1230, 1231, 1232, 1236, 1247, 1248, 1249, 1257, 1268, 1269, 1270, 1273, 1285, 1286, 1287, 1293, 1305, 1306, 1307, 1310, 1318, 1319, 1320, 1325, 1334, 1335, 1341, 1350, 1351, 1352, 1357, 1366, 1367, 1368, 1373, 1382, 1383, 1384, 1389, 1398, 1399, 1405, 1416, 1417, 1421, 1431, 1432, 1433, 1437, 1450, 1451, 1452, 1456, 1467, 1468, 1476, 1488, 1489, 1493, 1505, 1506, 1511, 1523, 1524, 1528, 1537, 1538, 1544, 1553, 1554, 1555, 1561, 1570, 1571, 1572, 1578, 1588, 1589, 1595, 1605, 1606, 1612, 1621, 1622, 1623, 1629, 1640, 1641, 1645, 1655, 1656, 1657, 1661, 1675, 1676, 1677
2.525(a)	12, 32, 48, 65, 77, 90, 104, 119, 132, 145, 162, 176, 193, 210, 230, 246, 263, 275, 288, 302, 316, 330, 343, 359, 373, 391, 408, 429, 446, 463, 476, 491, 507, 523, 539, 554, 572, 586, 605, 622, 642, 658, 676, 688, 702, 716, 730, 745, 758, 775, 789, 807, 824, 844, 861, 878, 892, 908, 925, 941, 958, 973, 991, 1006, 1025, 1042, 1062, 1078, 1095, 1107, 1122, 1137, 1152, 1167, 1181, 1198, 1213, 1230, 1248, 1268, 1286, 1305, 1319, 1334, 1350, 1367, 1383, 1398, 1416, 1432, 1450, 1467, 1488, 1505, 1523, 1537, 1554, 1571, 1588, 1605, 1622, 1640, 1656, 1675
2.525(b)	12, 32, 48, 65, 77, 91, 105, 119, 133, 146, 162, 176, 194, 210, 230, 246, 263, 275, 288, 302, 316, 330, 343, 359, 373, 391, 409, 429, 446, 464, 476, 492, 507, 523, 539, 554, 572, 587, 605, 622, 642, 659, 676, 688, 702, 716, 731, 745, 759, 775, 789, 807, 824, 844, 861, 879, 892, 908, 925, 942, 958, 973, 991, 1006, 1026, 1042, 1062, 1078, 1096, 1108, 1122, 1137, 1152, 1168, 1182, 1199, 1213, 1231, 1248, 1268, 1286, 1305, 1319, 1334, 1350, 1367, 1383, 1398, 1416, 1432, 1451, 1467, 1488, 1505, 1523, 1537, 1554, 1571, 1588, 1605, 1622, 1640, 1656, 1676
2.525(c)(1)	12, 31, 48, 65, 77, 90, 104, 118, 132, 145, 161, 176, 193, 210, 230, 246, 263, 275, 288, 302, 316, 330, 343, 359, 373, 391, 408, 429, 445, 463, 476, 491, 507, 523, 539, 554, 572, 586, 605, 622, 642, 658, 676, 688, 701, 716, 730, 745, 758, 775, 789, 807, 824, 844, 861, 878, 892, 908, 925, 941, 957, 973, 991, 1006, 1025,

FLORIDA RULES OF JUDICIAL ADMINISTRATION—Continued

Rule	Pg.
	1042, 1062, 1078, 1095, 1107, 1122, 1137, 1152, 1167, 1181, 1198, 1212, 1230, 1247, 1268, 1285, 1305, 1318, 1334, 1350, 1366, 1383, 1398, 1416, 1431, 1450, 1467, 1488, 1505, 1523, 1537, 1554, 1570, 1588, 1605, 1621, 1640, 1655, 1675
2.525(c)(2)	13, 33, 49, 66, 78, 91, 105, 120, 133, 146, 163, 177, 194, 211, 231, 247, 264, 276, 289, 303, 317, 331, 344, 360, 374, 392, 409, 430, 447, 464, 477, 492, 508, 524, 540, 555, 573, 587, 606, 623, 643, 659, 677, 689, 703, 717, 731, 746, 759, 776, 790, 808, 825, 845, 862, 880, 893, 909, 926, 943, 959, 974, 992, 1007, 1027, 1043, 1063, 1079, 1096, 1108, 1123, 1138, 1153, 1168, 1183, 1199, 1214, 1231, 1248, 1269, 1287, 1306, 1320, 1335, 1351, 1368, 1384, 1399, 1417, 1433, 1451, 1468, 1489, 1506, 1524, 1538, 1555, 1572, 1589, 1606, 1623, 1641, 1657, 1676
2.525(c)(3)	13, 33, 49, 66, 78, 91, 105, 120, 133, 146, 163, 177, 194, 211, 231, 247, 264, 276, 289, 303, 317, 331, 344, 360, 374, 392, 409, 430, 447, 464, 477, 492, 508, 524, 540, 555, 573, 587, 606, 623, 643, 659, 677, 689, 703, 717, 731, 746, 759, 776, 790, 808, 825, 845, 862, 880, 893, 909, 926, 943, 959, 974, 992, 1007, 1027, 1043, 1063, 1079, 1096, 1108, 1123, 1138, 1153, 1168, 1183, 1199, 1214, 1231, 1248, 1269, 1287, 1306, 1320, 1335, 1351, 1368, 1384, 1399, 1417, 1433, 1451, 1468, 1489, 1506, 1524, 1538, 1555, 1572, 1589, 1606, 1623, 1641, 1657, 1676
2.525(c)(4)	13, 32, 49, 66, 78, 91, 105, 119, 133, 146, 162, 176, 194, 211, 230, 247, 264, 275, 289, 303, 317, 331, 344, 360, 374, 392, 409, 429, 446, 464, 477, 492, 508, 524, 540, 555, 572, 587, 606, 623, 643, 659, 676, 688, 702, 716, 731, 746, 759, 775, 790, 808, 825, 845, 861, 879, 893, 909, 926, 942, 958, 974, 992, 1007, 1026, 1043, 1062, 1079, 1096, 1108, 1123, 1138, 1153, 1168, 1182, 1199, 1213, 1231, 1248, 1269, 1286, 1306, 1319, 1335, 1351, 1367, 1384, 1399, 1417, 1432, 1451, 1468, 1489, 1506, 1524, 1538, 1554, 1571, 1589, 1606, 1622, 1641, 1656, 1676
2.525(c)(5)	13, 32, 49, 66, 78, 91, 105, 119, 133, 146, 162, 177, 194, 211, 230, 247, 264, 276, 289, 303, 317, 331, 344, 360, 374, 392, 409, 430, 446, 464, 477, 492, 508, 524, 540, 555, 573, 587, 606, 623, 643, 659, 677, 689, 702, 717, 731, 746, 759, 775, 790, 808, 825, 845, 862, 879, 893, 909, 926, 942, 958, 974, 992, 1007, 1026, 1043, 1063, 1079, 1096, 1108, 1123, 1138, 1153, 1168, 1182, 1199, 1213, 1231, 1248, 1269, 1286, 1306, 1319, 1335, 1351, 1367, 1384, 1399, 1417, 1432, 1451, 1468, 1489, 1506, 1524, 1538, 1555, 1571, 1589, 1606, 1622, 1641, 1656, 1676
2.525(c)(6)	13, 33, 49, 66, 78, 91, 105, 119, 133, 146, 162, 177, 194, 211, 231, 247, 264, 276, 289, 303, 317, 331, 344, 360, 374, 392, 409, 430, 446, 464, 477, 492, 508, 524, 540, 555, 573, 587, 606, 623, 643, 659, 677, 689, 703, 717, 731, 746, 759, 776, 790, 808, 825, 845, 862, 879, 893, 909, 926, 942, 959, 974, 992, 1007, 1026, 1043, 1063, 1079, 1096, 1108, 1123, 1138, 1153, 1168, 1182, 1199, 1214, 1231, 1248, 1269, 1287, 1306, 1319, 1335, 1351, 1368, 1384, 1399, 1417, 1432, 1451, 1468, 1489, 1506, 1524, 1538, 1555, 1571, 1589, 1606, 1622, 1641, 1656, 1676
2.525(c)(7)	13, 33, 49, 66, 78, 91, 105, 120, 133, 146, 163, 177, 194, 211, 231, 247, 264, 276, 289, 303, 317, 331, 344, 360, 374, 392, 409, 430, 447, 464, 477, 492, 508, 524, 540, 555, 573, 587, 606, 623, 643, 659, 677, 689, 703, 717, 731, 746, 759, 776, 790, 808, 825, 845, 862, 879, 893, 909, 926, 942, 959, 974, 992, 1007, 1026, 1043, 1063, 1079, 1096, 1108, 1123, 1138, 1153, 1168, 1183, 1199, 1214, 1231, 1248, 1269, 1287, 1306, 1320, 1335, 1351, 1368, 1384, 1399, 1417, 1433, 1451, 1468, 1489, 1506, 1524, 1538, 1555, 1572, 1589, 1606, 1623, 1641, 1657, 1676
2.525(d)	9, 12, 13, 28, 32, 44, 49, 62, 66, 73, 78, 87, 91, 101, 105, 115, 119, 129, 133, 142, 146, 158, 162, 172, 176, 177, 190, 194, 207, 210, 211, 226, 230, 231, 242, 247, 260, 264, 271, 275, 276, 285, 289, 298, 303, 313, 317, 326, 330, 331, 339, 344, 355, 360, 369, 374, 387, 392, 405, 409, 425, 429, 430, 442, 446, 460, 464, 473, 477, 488, 492, 504, 508, 520, 524, 536, 540, 550, 555, 568, 572, 573,

FLORIDA RULES OF JUDICIAL ADMINISTRATION—Continued

Rule **Pg.**

583, 587, 602, 606, 619, 623, 638, 643, 655, 659, 672, 676, 677, 684, 688, 689, 698, 702, 712, 716, 717, 727, 731, 741, 746, 755, 759, 771, 775, 776, 785, 790, 803, 808, 821, 825, 841, 845, 857, 861, 862, 875, 879, 888, 893, 904, 909, 921, 925, 926, 937, 942, 953, 958, 969, 974, 986, 992, 1002, 1007, 1021, 1026, 1039, 1042, 1043, 1058, 1062, 1063, 1075, 1079, 1092, 1096, 1104, 1108, 1118, 1123, 1133, 1138, 1148, 1153, 1164, 1168, 1178, 1182, 1195, 1199, 1209, 1213, 1227, 1231, 1244, 1248, 1265, 1269, 1282, 1286, 1302, 1306, 1315, 1319, 1331, 1335, 1347, 1351, 1363, 1367, 1379, 1383, 1384, 1395, 1399, 1412, 1417, 1428, 1432, 1446, 1451, 1464, 1468, 1484, 1489, 1502, 1506, 1520, 1524, 1533, 1538, 1550, 1554, 1555, 1567, 1571, 1585, 1589, 1602, 1606, 1618, 1622, 1636, 1641, 1652, 1656, 1671, 1676

2.525(d)(5)..........13, 32, 49, 66, 78, 91, 105, 119, 133, 146, 162, 177, 194, 211, 230, 247, 264, 276, 289, 303, 317, 331, 344, 360, 374, 392, 409, 430, 446, 464, 477, 492, 508, 524, 540, 555, 573, 587, 606, 623, 643, 659, 676, 689, 702, 716, 731, 746, 759, 775, 790, 808, 825, 845, 862, 879, 893, 909, 926, 942, 958, 974, 992, 1007, 1026, 1043, 1063, 1079, 1096, 1108, 1123, 1138, 1153, 1168, 1182, 1199, 1213, 1231, 1248, 1269, 1286, 1306, 1319, 1335, 1351, 1367, 1384, 1399, 1417, 1432, 1451, 1468, 1489, 1506, 1524, 1538, 1554, 1571, 1589, 1606, 1622, 1641, 1656, 1676

2.525(e)(2)..........33, 50, 67, 79, 92, 106, 120, 134, 147, 163, 177, 195, 231, 248, 265, 276, 290, 304, 318, 332, 345, 361, 375, 393, 430, 447, 465, 478, 493, 509, 525, 541, 556, 573, 588, 607, 644, 660, 677, 689, 703, 717, 732, 747, 760, 776, 791, 809, 846, 863, 880, 894, 910, 927, 943, 960, 975, 993, 1008, 1027, 1063, 1080, 1097, 1109, 1124, 1139, 1154, 1169, 1183, 1200, 1214, 1232, 1270, 1288, 1307, 1321, 1336, 1352, 1369, 1385, 1400, 1418, 1434, 1453, 1490, 1507, 1525, 1539, 1556, 1573, 1590, 1607, 1624, 1642, 1658, 1677

2.525(f)(2).........13, 33, 49, 66, 78, 91, 105, 120, 134, 147, 163, 177, 195, 211, 231, 247, 264, 276, 289, 303, 317, 331, 344, 360, 374, 392, 409, 430, 447, 465, 477, 493, 508, 524, 540, 555, 573, 587, 606, 623, 643, 659, 677, 689, 703, 717, 732, 746, 760, 776, 790, 808, 825, 845, 862, 880, 893, 909, 926, 943, 959, 974, 992, 1007, 1027, 1043, 1063, 1079, 1097, 1109, 1123, 1138, 1153, 1169, 1183, 1200, 1214, 1232, 1249, 1269, 1287, 1306, 1320, 1335, 1351, 1368, 1384, 1399, 1417, 1433, 1452, 1468, 1489, 1506, 1524, 1538, 1555, 1572, 1589, 1606, 1623, 1641, 1657, 1676

2.525(f)(3).........13, 33, 49, 66, 78, 92, 106, 120, 134, 147, 163, 177, 195, 211, 231, 247, 264, 276, 289, 303, 317, 331, 344, 360, 374, 392, 410, 430, 447, 465, 477, 493, 508, 524, 540, 555, 573, 588, 606, 623, 643, 660, 677, 689, 703, 717, 732, 746, 760, 776, 790, 808, 825, 846, 862, 880, 893, 910, 926, 943, 959, 974, 992, 1008, 1027, 1043, 1063, 1079, 1097, 1109, 1123, 1138, 1153, 1169, 1183, 1200, 1214, 1232, 1249, 1269, 1287, 1306, 1320, 1335, 1351, 1368, 1384, 1399, 1417, 1433, 1452, 1468, 1489, 1506, 1524, 1538, 1555, 1572, 1589, 1606, 1623, 1641, 1657, 1677

2.525(g)..........13, 33, 49, 66, 78, 92, 106, 120, 134, 147, 163, 177, 195, 211, 231, 247, 264, 276, 289, 303, 317, 331, 344, 360, 374, 392, 410, 430, 447, 465, 477, 493, 508, 524, 540, 555, 573, 588, 607, 623, 643, 660, 677, 689, 703, 717, 732, 746, 760, 776, 790, 809, 825, 846, 862, 880, 893, 910, 926, 943, 959, 975, 992, 1008, 1027, 1043, 1063, 1079, 1097, 1109, 1123, 1138, 1153, 1169, 1183, 1200, 1214, 1232, 1249, 1270, 1287, 1307, 1320, 1335, 1352, 1368, 1384, 1399, 1417, 1433, 1452, 1468, 1489, 1506, 1524, 1538, 1555, 1572, 1589, 1606, 1623, 1641, 1657, 1677

2.526..........1, 13, 21, 33, 36, 49, 53, 66, 70, 78, 83, 92, 96, 106, 111, 120, 124, 134, 138, 147, 151, 163, 167, 177, 180, 195, 199, 211, 219, 231, 234, 247, 251, 264, 267, 276, 280, 289, 294, 303, 308, 317, 322, 331, 336, 344, 349, 360, 364, 374, 378, 392, 397, 410, 418, 430, 433, 447, 451, 465, 468, 477, 483, 493, 498, 508, 514, 524, 530, 540, 546, 555, 561, 573, 577, 588,

FLORIDA RULES OF JUDICIAL ADMINISTRATION—Continued

Rule	Pg.
	591, 607, 611, 623, 631, 643, 646, 660, 664, 677, 680, 689, 694, 703, 707, 717, 722, 732, 736, 746, 760, 764, 776, 780, 790, 794, 809, 813, 825, 833, 846, 849, 862, 866, 880, 883, 893, 899, 910, 915, 926, 932, 943, 948, 959, 964, 975, 979, 992, 996, 1008, 1011, 1027, 1031, 1043, 1051, 1063, 1066, 1079, 1083, 1097, 1100, 1109, 1114, 1123, 1128, 1138, 1144, 1153, 1158, 1169, 1174, 1183, 1188, 1200, 1203, 1214, 1217, 1232, 1236, 1249, 1257, 1270, 1273, 1287, 1293, 1307, 1310, 1320, 1325, 1335, 1341, 1352, 1358, 1368, 1373, 1384, 1390, 1399, 1405, 1417, 1422, 1433, 1437, 1452, 1456, 1468, 1476, 1489, 1493, 1506, 1511, 1524, 1528, 1538, 1544, 1555, 1561, 1572, 1578, 1589, 1595, 1606, 1612, 1623, 1629, 1641, 1646, 1657, 1661, 1677
2.530	70, 81, 83, 94, 96, 108, 111, 122, 124, 136, 138, 149, 267, 279, 280, 292, 294, 306, 308, 320, 322, 334, 336, 347, 468, 480, 483, 496, 498, 511, 514, 527, 530, 543, 546, 558, 680, 692, 694, 706, 707, 720, 722, 734, 736, 749, 751, 762, 883, 897, 899, 913, 915, 929, 932, 946, 948, 962, 964, 978, 1100, 1112, 1114, 1126, 1128, 1141, 1144, 1156, 1158, 1172, 1174, 1186, 1290, 1310, 1323, 1325, 1339, 1341, 1355, 1357, 1371, 1373, 1387, 1389, 1403, 1528, 1542, 1544, 1558, 1559, 1561, 1575, 1576, 1578, 1593, 1595, 1610, 1612, 1626
2.530(a)	80, 94, 108, 122, 136, 149, 278, 291, 305, 319, 333, 346, 480, 495, 511, 527, 543, 557, 691, 705, 719, 734, 748, 762, 896, 912, 929, 945, 961, 977, 1111, 1126, 1141, 1156, 1171, 1185, 1289, 1322, 1338, 1354, 1370, 1386, 1402, 1541, 1558, 1575, 1592, 1609, 1626
2.530(b)	80, 94, 108, 122, 136, 149, 278, 291, 306, 319, 333, 346, 480, 495, 511, 527, 543, 558, 691, 705, 719, 734, 748, 762, 896, 912, 929, 945, 962, 977, 1111, 1126, 1141, 1156, 1171, 1185, 1289, 1322, 1338, 1354, 1370, 1387, 1402, 1541, 1558, 1575, 1592, 1609, 1626
2.530(c)	80, 94, 108, 122, 136, 149, 278, 292, 306, 320, 333, 346, 480, 495, 511, 527, 543, 558, 691, 705, 719, 734, 748, 762, 896, 913, 929, 945, 962, 977, 1111, 1126, 1141, 1156, 1171, 1185, 1290, 1322, 1338, 1354, 1370, 1387, 1402, 1541, 1542, 1558, 1559, 1575, 1576, 1592, 1593, 1609, 1610, 1626, 1627
2.530(d)(1)	80, 94, 108, 122, 136, 149, 278, 292, 306, 320, 333, 346, 480, 495, 511, 527, 543, 558, 691, 705, 720, 734, 749, 762, 897, 913, 929, 946, 962, 977, 1111, 1126, 1141, 1156, 1171, 1185, 1290, 1322, 1338, 1354, 1371, 1387, 1402, 1541, 1558, 1575, 1592, 1610, 1626
2.530(d)(2)	81, 94, 108, 122, 136, 149, 278, 292, 306, 320, 334, 347, 480, 495, 511, 527, 543, 558, 691, 705, 720, 734, 749, 762, 897, 913, 929, 946, 962, 977, 1111, 1126, 1141, 1156, 1171, 1186, 1290, 1323, 1338, 1355, 1371, 1387, 1402, 1542, 1558, 1575, 1593, 1610, 1626
2.530(d)(3)	81, 94, 108, 122, 136, 149, 279, 292, 306, 320, 334, 347, 480, 495, 511, 527, 543, 558, 692, 705, 720, 734, 749, 762, 897, 913, 929, 946, 962, 977, 1112, 1126, 1141, 1156, 1172, 1186, 1290, 1323, 1338, 1355, 1371, 1387, 1402, 1542, 1558, 1575, 1593, 1610, 1626
2.530(d)(4)	81, 94, 108, 122, 136, 149, 279, 292, 306, 320, 334, 347, 480, 496, 511, 527, 543, 558, 692, 705, 720, 734, 749, 762, 897, 913, 929, 946, 962, 978, 1112, 1126, 1141, 1156, 1172, 1186, 1290, 1323, 1338, 1355, 1371, 1387, 1402, 1542, 1558, 1575, 1593, 1610, 1626
2.530(d)(5)	81, 94, 108, 122, 136, 149, 279, 292, 306, 320, 334, 347, 480, 496, 511, 527, 543, 558, 692, 706, 720, 734, 749, 762, 897, 913, 929, 946, 962, 978, 1112, 1126, 1141, 1156, 1172, 1186, 1290, 1323, 1339, 1355, 1371, 1387, 1403, 1542, 1558, 1575, 1593, 1610, 1626
2.530(e)	81, 94, 108, 122, 136, 149, 279, 292, 306, 320, 334, 347, 480, 496, 511, 527, 543, 558, 692, 706, 720, 734, 749, 762, 897, 913, 930, 946, 962, 978, 1112, 1126, 1141, 1156, 1172, 1186, 1290, 1323, 1339, 1355, 1371, 1387, 1403, 1542, 1558, 1576, 1593, 1610, 1626
2.535	36, 53, 70, 83, 96, 111, 124, 138, 234, 251, 268, 281, 294, 308, 322, 336, 433, 451, 468, 483, 498, 514, 530, 546,

FLORIDA RULES OF JUDICIAL ADMINISTRATION—Continued

Rule	Pg.
	646, 664, 680, 694, 707, 722, 736, 751, 849, 866, 883, 899, 915, 932, 948, 964, 1066, 1083, 1100, 1114, 1128, 1144, 1158, 1174, 1273, 1293, 1310, 1325, 1341, 1357, 1373, 1389, 1493, 1511, 1528, 1544, 1561, 1578, 1595, 1612
2.540	1, 21, 36, 53, 70, 83, 96, 111, 124, 138, 151, 167, 181, 199, 219, 234, 251, 268, 281, 294, 308, 322, 336, 349, 364, 378, 397, 418, 433, 451, 468, 483, 498, 515, 530, 546, 561, 577, 591, 611, 631, 647, 664, 680, 694, 707, 722, 736, 751, 764, 780, 794, 813, 833, 849, 866, 883, 899, 915, 932, 948, 964, 979, 996, 1011, 1031, 1051, 1066, 1083, 1100, 1114, 1128, 1144, 1158, 1174, 1188, 1203, 1217, 1236, 1257, 1273, 1293, 1310, 1325, 1341, 1357, 1373, 1390, 1405, 1421, 1437, 1456, 1476, 1493, 1511, 1528, 1544, 1561, 1578, 1595, 1613, 1629, 1646, 1661
2.540(c)(1)	11, 30, 46, 64, 75, 89, 103, 117, 131, 144, 160, 174, 192, 209, 228, 244, 262, 273, 287, 300, 315, 328, 341, 357, 371, 389, 407, 427, 444, 462, 475, 490, 506, 522, 538, 552, 570, 585, 604, 621, 641, 657, 674, 686, 700, 714, 729, 744, 757, 773, 788, 805, 823, 843, 859, 877, 891, 907, 923, 940, 956, 972, 989, 1005, 1024, 1041, 1060, 1077, 1094, 1106, 1120, 1135, 1151, 1166, 1180, 1197, 1211, 1229, 1246, 1267, 1284, 1304, 1317, 1333, 1349, 1365, 1381, 1397, 1415, 1430, 1449, 1466, 1486, 1504, 1522, 1536, 1552, 1569, 1587, 1604, 1620, 1639, 1654, 1674
2.545	1456, 1463, 1476, 1484, 1493, 1501, 1511, 1519, 1528, 1532, 1544, 1549, 1561, 1566, 1578, 1583, 1595, 1600, 1613, 1617, 1629, 1636, 1646, 1651, 1661, 1671

FLORIDA—ADMINISTRATIVE ORDERS FOR THE SECOND JUDICIAL CIRCUIT

Order	Pg.
2007-05	1, 8, 19, 21, 28, 35, 36, 44, 52, 53, 61, 69, 70, 73, 81, 83, 86, 95, 96, 100, 109, 111, 114, 123, 124, 128, 137, 138, 141, 150, 151, 158, 165, 167, 172, 179, 181, 189, 197

FLORIDA—ADMINISTRATIVE ORDERS FOR THE FOURTH JUDICIAL CIRCUIT

Order	Pg.
95-5 (A1)	199, 206
2006-05	199, 210, 219, 229, 234, 245, 251, 263, 268, 274, 281, 288, 294, 301, 308, 316, 322, 329, 336, 342, 349, 358, 364, 372, 378, 390
2012-03	378, 390

FLORIDA—LOCAL RULES FOR THE SIXTH JUDICIAL CIRCUIT

Rule	Pg.
3	397, 403, 405, 418, 424, 425, 434, 441, 442, 451, 458, 459, 460
5	468, 472, 483, 487, 498, 503, 515, 519, 530, 533, 535, 546, 550, 561, 568, 577, 591, 601

FLORIDA—ADMINISTRATIVE ORDERS FOR THE SIXTH JUDICIAL CIRCUIT

Order **Pg.**

88-48................468, 481, 483, 496, 498, 512, 515, 528, 530, 544, 546, 559
96-63................397, 404, 418, 424, 434, 441, 451, 459, 468, 471, 483, 487, 498, 502, 515, 518, 530, 534, 546, 549, 561, 567, 577, 591, 601
98-30................468, 481, 483, 496, 498, 512, 515, 528, 530, 544, 546, 559
98-49................397, 403, 468, 469, 483, 484, 498, 499, 515, 530, 546
2009-066..........397, 403, 415, 418, 432, 434, 449, 451, 467, 468, 470, 472, 473, 479, 480, 481, 483, 485, 487, 488, 495, 496, 498, 500, 503, 510, 512, 515, 516, 519, 526, 527, 528, 530, 532, 533, 535, 542, 543, 544, 546, 548, 550, 557, 558, 559, 561, 565, 568, 575, 577, 581, 590, 591, 595, 596, 600, 601, 608, 609
2011-006..........397, 418, 434, 451, 468, 483, 498, 515, 530, 546, 561, 577, 591
2013-005..530, 533

FLORIDA—ADMINISTRATIVE ORDERS FOR THE SEVENTH JUDICIAL CIRCUIT

Order **Pg.**

CV-2000-007-SC.............................707, 712, 751, 755
CV-2000-011-VL.........611, 631, 639, 647, 656, 664, 673, 680, 685, 694, 699, 708, 713, 722, 728, 736, 742, 751, 756, 764, 772, 780, 786, 794, 804
CV-2003-002-SC............611, 617, 618, 631, 637, 647, 654, 664, 671, 680, 681, 683, 684, 694, 697, 698, 708, 711, 722, 723, 725, 726, 736, 737, 740, 741, 751, 754, 764, 765, 770, 780, 785, 794, 795, 802
CV-2003-009-SC............................794, 795, 803, 807
CV-2004-004-SC (A)......................736, 738, 741, 749
CV-2006-005-SC..611, 618
CV-2008-010-VL...612, 617
CV-2008-018-SC............611, 618, 631, 637, 647, 654, 664, 671, 680, 683, 694, 697, 708, 711, 722, 726, 736, 740, 751, 754, 764, 770, 780, 785, 794, 802
CV-2009-006-SC..611, 615
CV-2009-019-SC............611, 617, 631, 637, 647, 654, 664, 671, 680, 683, 694, 697, 708, 711, 722, 726, 736, 740, 751, 754, 764, 770, 780, 785, 794, 802
CV-2009-021-SJ..612, 624

FLORIDA—UNIFORM ADMIN. POLICIES AND PROCEDURES OF THE CIVIL DIVISION—CIRCUIT COURT ORANGE COUNTY

Sec. **Pg.**

7..............813, 822, 825, 833, 842, 845, 849, 858, 862, 866, 876, 879, 880, 889, 893, 906, 909, 922, 926, 939, 942, 943, 955, 959, 971, 974, 980, 988, 992, 996, 1003, 1007, 1023, 1027
10............883, 884, 887, 896, 899, 900, 904, 912, 915, 916, 920, 928, 929, 932, 937, 945, 948, 953, 961, 964, 965, 969, 977
11............862, 880, 883, 884, 885, 887, 888, 894, 896, 899, 900, 901, 903, 910, 912, 915, 916, 917, 920, 927, 929, 932, 933, 934, 936, 937, 943, 945, 948, 950, 953, 959, 961, 964, 965, 966, 968, 975, 977
12............883, 887, 888, 889, 899, 904, 905, 915, 920, 921, 922, 932, 937, 938, 948, 953, 954, 964, 969, 970, 987, 988, 1002, 1003, 1021, 1022
13............948, 980, 986, 996, 1001, 1011, 1020, 1025
14..1011, 1012, 1015
15............819, 840, 856, 874, 883, 886, 899, 902, 915, 919, 932, 936, 948, 952, 964, 967, 986, 1001, 1020

FLORIDA—BUSINESS COURT PROCEDURES FOR THE NINTH JUDICIAL CIRCUIT

Sec. **Pg.**

1..............813, 820, 833, 840, 849, 857, 866, 874, 883, 887, 899, 903, 915, 919, 932, 936, 948, 952, 964, 968, 986, 1001, 1020

FLORIDA—ADMINISTRATIVE ORDERS FOR THE ELEVENTH JUDICIAL CIRCUIT

Order **Pg.**

1-09-08...............1031, 1037, 1051, 1057, 1066, 1073, 1084, 1091, 1100, 1102, 1103, 1114, 1117, 1128, 1132, 1144, 1147, 1158, 1162, 1163, 1174, 1177, 1188, 1194, 1203, 1208, 1217, 1226

1-09-13-A1..........1100, 1104, 1105, 1108, 1110, 1111, 1112, 1114, 1118, 1119, 1122, 1124, 1125, 1126, 1127, 1129, 1133, 1134, 1137, 1139, 1140, 1142, 1144, 1148, 1149, 1152, 1155, 1156, 1157, 1159, 1164, 1165, 1168, 1170, 1171, 1172, 1174, 1178, 1179, 1182, 1184, 1185, 1186, 1188, 1203, 1218

FLORIDA—LOCAL RULES FOR THE SEVENTEENTH JUDICIAL CIRCUIT

Rule **Pg.**

8...............1310, 1315, 1325, 1330, 1341, 1346, 1358, 1363, 1373, 1379, 1390, 1394

10A...........1290, 1291, 1310, 1311, 1314, 1315, 1323, 1325, 1326, 1330, 1339, 1341, 1346, 1355, 1358, 1362, 1363, 1371, 1373, 1374, 1378, 1379, 1387, 1388, 1390, 1394, 1403

FLORIDA—ADMINISTRATIVE ORDERS FOR THE SEVENTEENTH JUDICIAL CIRCUIT

Order **Pg.**

2008-153-GEN.............1236, 1249, 1257, 1270, 1273, 1287, 1293, 1307, 1310, 1320, 1325, 1336, 1341, 1352, 1358, 1368, 1373, 1384, 1390, 1400, 1405, 1418, 1422, 1433, 1437, 1452

2010-49-GEN...............1236, 1246, 1257, 1267, 1273, 1284, 1293, 1304, 1310, 1317, 1325, 1333, 1341, 1349, 1358, 1365, 1373, 1381, 1390, 1397, 1405, 1415, 1422, 1430, 1437, 1449

2012-16-CIV.................1236, 1237, 1246, 1249, 1257, 1258, 1266, 1270, 1273, 1274, 1284, 1287, 1293, 1294, 1303, 1307, 1310, 1311, 1317, 1320, 1326, 1327, 1332, 1336, 1341, 1342, 1348, 1352, 1358, 1359, 1365, 1368, 1374, 1381, 1384, 1390, 1391, 1396, 1400, 1405, 1406, 1414, 1418, 1422, 1430, 1433, 1437, 1438, 1448, 1452

2012-21-GEN..1236, 1253

I-94-O-1..............1236, 1237, 1257, 1258, 1273, 1274, 1293, 1294, 1310, 1311, 1315, 1325, 1326, 1327, 1330, 1341, 1342, 1346, 1358, 1363, 1373, 1374, 1379, 1390, 1391, 1394, 1405, 1406, 1409, 1422, 1426, 1437, 1438, 1441

FLORIDA—LOCAL RULES FOR THE TWENTIETH JUDICIAL CIRCUIT

Rule **Pg.**

1.9..............1456, 1462, 1477, 1483, 1493, 1500, 1511, 1518, 1528, 1532, 1544, 1548, 1561, 1565, 1579, 1583, 1595, 1600, 1613, 1616, 1629, 1635, 1646, 1651, 1661, 1670

1.10...........1528, 1529, 1533, 1542, 1544, 1545, 1550, 1559, 1561, 1562, 1567, 1576, 1579, 1584, 1593, 1595, 1596, 1602, 1610, 1613, 1618, 1626, 1627

1.13...........1456, 1463, 1477, 1483, 1484, 1493, 1501, 1511, 1519, 1528, 1532, 1544, 1549, 1561, 1566, 1579, 1583, 1595, 1600, 1613, 1617, 1629, 1636, 1646, 1651, 1661, 1671

2.9..............1456, 1464, 1477, 1484, 1485, 1493, 1502, 1511, 1520, 1528, 1534, 1544, 1550, 1551, 1561, 1567, 1568, 1579, 1585,

FLORIDA—LOCAL RULES FOR THE TWENTIETH JUDICIAL CIRCUIT—Continued

Rule	Pg.
	1595, 1602, 1613, 1618, 1619, 1629, 1637, 1646, 1652, 1661, 1672
2.15	1456, 1466, 1477, 1486, 1493, 1504, 1511, 1522, 1528, 1536, 1545, 1552, 1561, 1569, 1579, 1587, 1595, 1604, 1613, 1620, 1629, 1639, 1646, 1654, 1661, 1674
2.20	1456, 1462, 1469, 1470, 1477, 1483, 1489, 1490, 1493, 1500, 1506, 1507, 1511, 1518, 1525, 1528, 1529, 1530, 1531, 1533, 1538, 1539, 1541, 1545, 1547, 1548, 1549, 1550, 1555, 1556, 1557, 1558, 1561, 1562, 1563, 1565, 1567, 1572, 1574, 1575, 1579, 1580, 1581, 1582, 1584, 1589, 1590, 1592, 1596, 1597, 1598, 1599, 1601, 1607, 1609, 1613, 1615, 1616, 1617, 1618, 1623, 1625, 1626, 1629, 1631, 1633, 1634, 1635, 1642, 1646, 1647, 1649, 1650, 1657, 1661, 1663, 1665, 1666, 1668, 1669, 1670, 1677

Table of Cases

B

Bowen v. G H C Properties, Limited, 251 So.2d 359 (Fla. 1st DCA 1971) — **4, 24, 202, 222, 400, 421, 614, 634, 816, 836, 1034, 1054, 1239, 1260, 1459, 1480**

Burns v. Equilease Corp., 357 So.2d 786, 24 U.C.C. Rep.Serv. 254 (Fla. 3d DCA 1978) — **72, 270, 471, 683, 886, 1102, 1313, 1531**

C

Cox v. Seaboard Coast Line R. Co., 360 So.2d 8 (Fla. 2d DCA 1978) — **85, 283, 486, 697, 902, 1117, 1329, 1548**

D

Dee v. Southern Brewing Company, 146 Fla. 588, 1 So.2d 562 (Fla. 1941) — **22, 55, 221, 253, 419, 453, 633, 666, 835, 868, 1053, 1085, 1259, 1295, 1478, 1513**

G

Gardner v. Sabal Point Properties, Inc., 616 So.2d 1111 (Fla. 5th DCA 1993) — **98, 296, 501, 710, 918, 1131, 1344, 1564**

H

Henderson v. CSX Transportation, Inc., 617 So.2d 770 (Fla. 1st DCA 1993) — **98, 296, 501, 710, 918, 1131, 1344, 1564**

Holl v. Talcott, 191 So.2d 40 (Fla. 1966) — **99, 296, 501, 710, 918, 1131, 1344, 1564**

Hughes v. Home Sav. of America, F.S.B., 675 So.2d 649 (Fla. 2d DCA 1996) — **22, 55, 221, 253, 419, 453, 633, 666, 835, 868, 1053, 1085, 1259, 1295, 1478, 1513**

J

Jones v. Directors Guild of America, Inc., 584 So.2d 1057 (Fla. 1st DCA 1991) — **99, 296, 501, 710, 918, 1131, 1344, 1564**

K

Kinetiks.Com, Inc. v. Sweeney, 789 So.2d 1221 (Fla. 1st DCA 2001) — **912**

Kozich v. Hartford Ins. Co. of Midwest, 609 So.2d 147 (Fla. 4th DCA 1992) — **108, 305, 511, 719, 928, 1141, 1354, 1574**

L

Landers v. Milton, 370 So.2d 368 (Fla. 1979) — **98, 99, 296, 501, 710, 918, 1131, 1344, 1564**

Lenhal Realty, Inc. v. Transamerica Commercial Finance Corp., 615 So.2d 207 (Fla. 4th DCA 1993) — **99, 296, 501, 710, 918, 1131, 1344, 1564**

M

McSwiggan v. Edson, 186 So.2d 13 (Fla. 1966) — **83, 281, 483, 694, 899, 1114, 1326, 1545**

Moore v. Morris, 475 So.2d 666 (Fla. 1985) — **98, 296, 501, 710, 918, 1131, 1344, 1564**

P

Pizzi v. Central Bank & Trust Co., 250 So.2d 895 (Fla. 1971) — **4, 24, 202, 222, 400, 421, 614, 634, 816, 836, 1034, 1054, 1239, 1260, 1459, 1480**

S

Shannon v. McBride, 105 So.2d 16 (Fla. 2d DCA 1958) — **22, 55, 221, 253, 419, 453, 633, 666, 835, 868, 1053, 1085, 1259, 1295, 1478, 1513**

Spradley v. Stick, 622 So.2d 610 (Fla. 1st DCA 1993) — **99, 296, 501, 710, 918, 1131, 1344, 1564**

Strickland v. Commerce Loan Co. of Jacksonville, 158 So.2d 814 (Fla. 1st DCA 1963) — **4, 24, 202, 222, 400, 421, 614, 634, 816, 836, 1034, 1054, 1239, 1260, 1459, 1480**

T

Turner v. Long, 225 So.2d 434 (Fla. 1st DCA 1969) — **85, 283, 486, 696, 902, 1116, 1328, 1547**

V

Versen v. Versen, 347 So.2d 1047 (Fla. 4th DCA 1977) — **83, 281, 483, 694, 899, 1114, 1326, 1545**

*

Index

References are to page number

ADMISSIONS, REQUEST FOR
Eleventh Judicial Circuit, **1203**
Fourth Judicial Circuit, **363**
Ninth Judicial Circuit, **995**
Second Judicial Circuit, **166**
Seventeenth Judicial Circuit, **1421**
Seventh Judicial Circuit, **779**
Sixth Judicial Circuit, **576**
Twentieth Judicial Circuit, **1645**

AMENDED ANSWER
Eleventh Judicial Circuit, **1083**
Fourth Judicial Circuit, **251**
Ninth Judicial Circuit, **866**
Second Judicial Circuit, **53**
Seventeenth Judicial Circuit, **1292**
Seventh Judicial Circuit, **663**
Sixth Judicial Circuit, **451**
Twentieth Judicial Circuit, **1510**

AMENDED COMPLAINT
Eleventh Judicial Circuit, **1050**
Fourth Judicial Circuit, **218**
Ninth Judicial Circuit, **833**
Second Judicial Circuit, **20**
Seventeenth Judicial Circuit, **1256**
Seventh Judicial Circuit, **631**
Sixth Judicial Circuit, **417**
Twentieth Judicial Circuit, **1476**

ANSWER
Amended Answer, this index
Eleventh Judicial Circuit, **1066, 1083**
Fourth Judicial Circuit, **234, 251**
Ninth Judicial Circuit, **848, 866**
Second Judicial Circuit, **36, 53**
Seventeenth Judicial Circuit, **1273, 1292**
Seventh Judicial Circuit, **646, 663**
Sixth Judicial Circuit, **433, 451**
Twentieth Judicial Circuit, **1492, 1510**

BROWARD COUNTY
Seventeenth Judicial Circuit, this index

CHARLOTTE COUNTY
Twentieth Judicial Circuit, this index

CLAY COUNTY
Fourth Judicial Circuit, this index

COLLIER COUNTY
Twentieth Judicial Circuit, this index

COMPEL DISCOVERY, MOTION TO
Eleventh Judicial Circuit, **1158**
Fourth Judicial Circuit, **321**
Ninth Judicial Circuit, **947**
Second Judicial Circuit, **124**
Seventeenth Judicial Circuit, **1373**
Seventh Judicial Circuit, **735**
Sixth Judicial Circuit, **529**
Twentieth Judicial Circuit, **1595**

COMPLAINT
Amended Complaint, this index
Eleventh Judicial Circuit, **1031, 1050**
Fourth Judicial Circuit, **199, 218**
Ninth Judicial Circuit, **813, 833**
Second Judicial Circuit, **1, 20**
Seventeenth Judicial Circuit, **1236, 1256**
Seventh Judicial Circuit, **611, 631**
Sixth Judicial Circuit, **397, 417**
Twentieth Judicial Circuit, **1456, 1476**

DEPOSITIONS
Eleventh Judicial Circuit, **1217**
Fourth Judicial Circuit, **377**
Ninth Judicial Circuit, **1011**
Second Judicial Circuit, **180**
Seventeenth Judicial Circuit, **1436**
Seventh Judicial Circuit, **793**
Sixth Judicial Circuit, **591**
Twentieth Judicial Circuit, **1660**

DIRECTED VERDICT
Eleventh Judicial Circuit, **1173**
Fourth Judicial Circuit, **335**
Ninth Judicial Circuit, **963**
Second Judicial Circuit, **138**
Seventeenth Judicial Circuit, **1389**
Seventh Judicial Circuit, **750**
Sixth Judicial Circuit, **545**
Twentieth Judicial Circuit, **1612**

DISCOVERY
Admissions, Request for, this index
Compel Discovery, Motion to, this index
Depositions, this index
Eleventh Judicial Circuit, this index
Fourth Judicial Circuit, this index
Ninth Judicial Circuit, this index
Production of Documents, this index
Second Judicial Circuit, this index
Seventeenth Judicial Circuit, this index
Seventh Judicial Circuit, this index
Sixth Judicial Circuit, this index
Twentieth Judicial Circuit, this index

DUVAL COUNTY
Fourth Judicial Circuit, this index

ELEVENTH JUDICIAL CIRCUIT
Admission requests, **1203**
Amended answer, **1083**
Amended complaint, **1050**
Answer, **1066, 1083**
Compel discovery, motion to, **1158**
Complaint, **1031, 1050**
Deposition, notice of, **1217**
Directed verdict, **1173**
Discovery
admission requests, **1203**
compel discovery, motion to, **1158**
deposition, notice of, **1217**
production of documents, **1187**
Judgments
summary judgment, **1128**
Leave to amend, motion for, **1113**
Motions, oppositions and replies
amend, motion for leave to amend, **1113**
directed verdict, **1173**
discovery motions. See "Discovery" under this index heading
sanctions, motion for, **1143**
strike, motion to, **1099**
summary judgment, **1128**
Oppositions. See "Motions, oppositions and replies" under this index heading
Pleadings
amended answer, **1083**
amended complaint, **1050**
answer, **1066, 1083**
complaint, **1031, 1050**
Production of documents, **1187**
Reply. See "Motions, oppositions and replies" under this index heading

ELEVENTH JUDICIAL CIRCUIT—Cont'd
Requests
admission requests, **1203**
deposition, notice of, **1217**
production of documents, **1187**
Sanctions, motion for, **1143**
Strike, motion to, **1099**
Summary judgment, **1128**
Verdict, motion for directed verdict, **1173**

FLAGLER COUNTY
Seventh Judicial Circuit, this index

FOURTH JUDICIAL CIRCUIT
Admission requests, **363**
Amended answer, **251**
Amended complaint, **218**
Answer, **234, 251**
Compel discovery, motion to, **321**
Complaint, **199, 218**
Deposition, notice of, **377**
Directed verdict, **335**
Discovery
admission requests, **363**
compel discovery, motion to, **321**
deposition, notice of, **377**
production of documents, **348**
Judgments
summary judgment, **293**
Leave to amend, motion for, **280**
Motions, oppositions and replies
amend, motion for leave to amend, **280**
directed verdict, **335**
discovery motions. See "Discovery" under this index heading
sanctions, motion for, **308**
strike, motion to, **267**
summary judgment, **293**
Oppositions. See "Motions, oppositions and replies" under this index heading
Pleadings
amended answer, **251**
amended complaint, **218**
answer, **234, 251**
complaint, **199, 218**
Production of documents, **348**
Reply. See "Motions, oppositions and replies" under this index heading
Requests
admission requests, **363**
deposition, notice of, **377**
production of documents, **348**

FOURTH JUDICIAL CIRCUIT—Cont'd
Sanctions, motion for, **308**
Strike, motion to, **267**
Summary judgment, **293**
Verdict, motion for directed verdict, **335**

FRANKLIN COUNTY
Second Judicial Circuit, this index

GADSDEN COUNTY
Second Judicial Circuit, this index

GLADES COUNTY
Twentieth Judicial Circuit, this index

HENDRY COUNTY
Twentieth Judicial Circuit, this index

JEFFERSON COUNTY
Second Judicial Circuit, this index

LEAVE TO AMEND
Eleventh Judicial Circuit, **1113**
Fourth Judicial Circuit, **280**
Ninth Judicial Circuit, **898**
Second Judicial Circuit, **82**
Seventeenth Judicial Circuit, **1325**
Seventh Judicial Circuit, **693**
Sixth Judicial Circuit, **482**
Twentieth Judicial Circuit, **1544**

LEE COUNTY
Twentieth Judicial Circuit, this index

LEON COUNTY
Second Judicial Circuit, this index

LIBERTY COUNTY
Second Judicial Circuit, this index

MIAMI-DADE COUNTY
Eleventh Judicial Circuit, this index

MOTIONS
Compel Discovery, Motion to, this index
Eleventh Judicial Circuit, this index
Fourth Judicial Circuit, this index
Ninth Judicial Circuit, this index
Second Judicial Circuit, this index
Seventeenth Judicial Circuit, this index
Seventh Judicial Circuit, this index
Sixth Judicial Circuit, this index
Strike, Motion to, this index
Twentieth Judicial Circuit, this index

NASSAU COUNTY
Fourth Judicial Circuit, this index

NINTH JUDICIAL CIRCUIT
Admission requests, **995**
Amended answer, **866**
Amended complaint, **833**
Answer, **848, 866**
Compel discovery, motion to, **947**
Complaint, **813, 833**
Deposition, notice of, **1011**
Directed verdict, **963**
Discovery
- admission requests, **995**
- compel discovery, motion to, **947**
- deposition, notice of, **1011**
- production of documents, **979**

Judgments, summary judgment, **914**
Leave to amend, motion for, **898**
Motions, oppositions and replies
- amend, motion for leave to amend, **898**
- directed verdict, **963**
- discovery motions. See "Discovery" under this index heading
- sanctions, motion for, **931**
- strike, motion to, **882**
- summary judgment, **914**

Oppositions. See "Motions, oppositions and replies" under this index heading
Pleadings
- amended answer, **866**
- amended complaint, **833**
- answer, **848, 866**
- complaint, **813, 833**

Production of documents, **979**
Reply. See "Motions, oppositions and replies" under this index heading
Requests
- admission requests, **995**
- deposition, notice of, **1011**
- production of documents, **979**

Sanctions, motion for, **931**
Strike, motion to, **882**
Summary judgment, **914**
Verdict, motion for directed verdict, **963**

ORANGE COUNTY
Ninth Judicial Circuit, this index

OSCEOLA COUNTY
Ninth Judicial Circuit, this index

PASCO COUNTY
Sixth Judicial Circuit, this index

PINELLAS COUNTY
Sixth Judicial Circuit, this index

PLEADINGS
Answer, this index
Complaint, this index
Eleventh Judicial Circuit, this index
Fourth Judicial Circuit, this index
Ninth Judicial Circuit, this index
Second Judicial Circuit, this index
Seventeenth Judicial Circuit, this index
Seventh Judicial Circuit, this index
Sixth Judicial Circuit, this index
Twentieth Judicial Circuit, this index

PRODUCTION OF DOCUMENTS
Eleventh Judicial Circuit, **1187**
Fourth Judicial Circuit, **348**
Ninth Judicial Circuit, **979**
Second Judicial Circuit, **151**
Seventeenth Judicial Circuit, **1404**
Seventh Judicial Circuit, **764**
Sixth Judicial Circuit, **560**
Twentieth Judicial Circuit, **1628**

PUTNAM COUNTY
Seventh Judicial Circuit, this index

REQUESTS
Eleventh Judicial Circuit, this index
Fourth Judicial Circuit, this index
Ninth Judicial Circuit, this index
Second Judicial Circuit, this index
Seventeenth Judicial Circuit, this index
Seventh Judicial Circuit, this index
Sixth Judicial Circuit, this index
Twentieth Judicial Circuit, this index

SANCTIONS
Eleventh Judicial Circuit, **1143**
Fourth Judicial Circuit, **308**
Ninth Judicial Circuit, **931**
Second Judicial Circuit, **110**
Seventeenth Judicial Circuit, **1357**
Seventh Judicial Circuit, **721**
Sixth Judicial Circuit, **514**
Twentieth Judicial Circuit, **1578**

SECOND JUDICIAL CIRCUIT
Admission requests, **166**
Amended answer, **53**
Amended complaint, **20**
Answer, **36, 53**
Compel discovery, motion to, **124**

SECOND JUDICIAL CIRCUIT—Cont'd
Complaint, **1, 20**
Deposition, notice of, **180**
Directed verdict, **138**
Discovery
admission requests, **166**
compel discovery, motion to, **124**
deposition, notice of, **180**
production of documents, **151**
Judgments, summary judgment, **96**
Leave to amend, motion for, **82**
Motions, oppositions and replies
amend, motion for leave to amend, **82**
directed verdict, **138**
discovery motions. See "Discovery" under this index heading
sanctions, motion for, **110**
strike, motion to, **69**
summary judgment, **96**
Oppositions. See "Motions, oppositions and replies" under this index heading
Pleadings
amended answer, **53**
amended complaint, **20**
answer, **36, 53**
complaint, **1, 20**
Production of documents, **151**
Reply. See "Motions, oppositions and replies" under this index heading
Requests
admission requests, **166**
deposition, notice of, **180**
production of documents, **151**
Sanctions, motion for, **110**
Strike, motion to, **69**
Summary judgment, **96**
Verdict, motion for directed verdict, **138**

SEVENTEENTH JUDICIAL CIRCUIT
Admission requests, **1421**
Amended answer, **1292**
Amended complaint, **1256**
Answer, **1273, 1292**
Compel discovery, motion to, **1373**
Complaint, **1236, 1256**
Deposition, notice of, **1436**
Directed verdict, **1389**
Discovery
admission requests, **1421**
compel discovery, motion to, **1373**
deposition, notice of, **1436**
production of documents, **1404**

SEVENTEENTH JUDICIAL CIRCUIT—Cont'd
Judgments, summary judgment, **1340**
Leave to amend, motion for, **1325**
Motions, oppositions and replies
amend, motion for leave to amend, **1325**
directed verdict, **1389**
discovery motions. See "Discovery" under this index heading
sanctions, motion for, **1357**
strike, motion to, **1309**
summary judgment, **1340**
Oppositions. See "Motions, oppositions and replies" under this index heading
Pleadings
amended answer, **1292**
amended complaint, **1256**
answer, **1273, 1292**
complaint, **1236, 1256**
Production of documents, **1404**
Reply. See "Motions, oppositions and replies" under this index heading
Requests
admission requests, **1421**
deposition, notice of, **1436**
production of documents, **1404**
Sanctions, motion for, **1357**
Strike, motion to, **1309**
Summary judgment, **1340**
Verdict, motion for directed verdict, **1389**

SEVENTH JUDICIAL CIRCUIT
Admission requests, **779**
Amended answer, **663**
Amended complaint, **631**
Answer, **646, 663**
Compel discovery, motion to, **735**
Complaint, **611, 631**
Deposition, notice of, **793**
Directed verdict, **750**
Discovery
admission requests, **779**
compel discovery, motion to, **735**
deposition, notice of, **793**
production of documents, **764**
Judgments, summary judgment, **707**
Leave to amend, motion for, **693**
Motions, oppositions and replies
amend, motion for leave to amend, **693**
directed verdict, **750**
discovery motions. See "Discovery" under this index heading
sanctions, motion for, **721**

SEVENTH JUDICIAL CIRCUIT—Cont'd
Motions, oppositions and replies—Cont'd
strike, motion to, **680**
summary judgment, **707**
Oppositions. See "Motions, oppositions and replies" under this index heading
Pleadings
amended answer, **663**
amended complaint, **631**
answer, **646, 663**
complaint, **611, 631**
Production of documents, **764**
Reply. See "Motions, oppositions and replies" under this index heading
Requests
admission requests, **779**
deposition, notice of, **793**
production of documents, **764**
Sanctions, motion for, **721**
Strike, motion to, **680**
Summary judgment, **707**
Verdict, motion for directed verdict, **750**

SIXTH JUDICIAL CIRCUIT
Admission requests, **576**
Amended answer, **451**
Amended complaint, **417**
Answer, **433, 451**
Compel discovery, motion to, **529**
Complaint, **397, 417**
Deposition, notice of, **591**
Directed verdict, **545**
Discovery
admission requests, **576**
compel discovery, motion to, **529**
deposition, notice of, **591**
production of documents, **560**
Judgments, summary judgment, **498**
Leave to amend, motion for, **482**
Motions, oppositions and replies
amend, motion for leave to amend, **482**
directed verdict, **545**
discovery motions. See "Discovery" under this index heading
sanctions, motion for, **514**
strike, motion to, **468**
summary judgment, **498**
Oppositions. See "Motions, oppositions and replies" under this index heading
Pleadings
amended answer, **451**
amended complaint, **417**

SIXTH JUDICIAL CIRCUIT—Cont'd
Pleadings—Cont'd
answer, **433, 451**
complaint, **397, 417**
Production of documents, **560**
Reply. See "Motions, oppositions and replies" under this index heading
Requests
admission requests, **576**
deposition, notice of, **591**
production of documents, **560**
Sanctions, motion for, **514**
Strike, motion to, **468**
Summary judgment, **498**
Verdict, motion for directed verdict, **545**

ST. JOHN'S COUNTY
Seventh Judicial Circuit, this index

STRIKE, MOTION TO
Eleventh Judicial Circuit, **1099**
Fourth Judicial Circuit, **267**
Ninth Judicial Circuit, **882**
Second Judicial Circuit, **69**
Seventeenth Judicial Circuit, **1309**
Seventh Judicial Circuit, **680**
Sixth Judicial Circuit, **468**
Twentieth Judicial Circuit, **1527**

SUMMARY JUDGMENT
Eleventh Judicial Circuit, **1128**
Fourth Judicial Circuit, **293**
Ninth Judicial Circuit, **914**
Second Judicial Circuit, **96**
Seventeenth Judicial Circuit, **1340**
Seventh Judicial Circuit, **707**
Sixth Judicial Circuit, **498**
Twentieth Judicial Circuit, **1561**

TWENTIETH JUDICIAL CIRCUIT
Admission requests, **1645**
Amended answer, **1510**
Amended complaint, **1476**
Answer, **1492, 1510**
Compel discovery, motion to, **1595**
Complaint, **1456, 1476**

TWENTIETH JUDICIAL CIRCUIT—Cont'd
Deposition, notice of, **1660**
Directed verdict, **1612**
Discovery
admission requests, **1645**
compel discovery, motion to, **1595**
deposition, notice of, **1660**
production of documents, **1628**
Judgments, summary judgment, **1561**
Leave to amend, motion for, **1544**
Motions, oppositions and replies
amend, motion for leave to amend, **1544**
directed verdict, **1612**
discovery motions. See "Discovery" under this index heading
sanctions, motion for, **1578**
strike, motion to, **1527**
summary judgment, **1561**
Oppositions. See "Motions, oppositions and replies" under this index heading
Pleadings
amended answer, **1510**
amended complaint, **1476**
answer, **1492, 1510**
complaint, **1456, 1476**
Production of documents, **1628**
Reply. See "Motions, oppositions and replies" under this index heading
Requests
admission requests, **1645**
deposition, notice of, **1660**
production of documents, **1628**
Sanctions, motion for, **1578**
Strike, motion to, **1527**
Summary judgment, **1561**
Verdict, motion for directed verdict, **1612**

VERDICT
Directed Verdict, this index

VOLUSIA COUNTY
Seventh Judicial Circuit, this index

WAKULLA COUNTY
Second Judicial Circuit, this index

†